Collins

CARIBBEAN
STUDENT'S
DICTIONARY

Published by Collins
An imprint of HarperCollins Publishers
Westerhill Road
Bishopbriggs
Glasgow G64 2QT

Second Edition 2017

10 9 8 7 6 5 4 3 2 1

© HarperCollins Publishers 2007, 2017

ISBN 978-0-00-821029-8

Collins® is a registered trademark of
HarperCollins Publishers Limited

collins.co.uk/dictionaries

Typeset by Davidson Publishing
Solutions, Glasgow

Printed and bound by Thompson Press
India Ltd

Acknowledgements
We would like to thank those authors
and publishers who kindly gave
permission for copyright material to be
used in the Collins Corpus. We would
also like to thank Times Newspapers Ltd
for providing valuable data.

Contents

Guide to the Dictionary

Main entry words

Main entry words are printed in blue bold type:

berry

Variant forms

Variant forms are printed in blue bold type after the main entry word:

bento *or* **bento box**

Pronunciations

Pronunciations are given in brackets for words that are difficult or confusing; the word is respelt as it is pronounced, with the stressed syllable in bold type:

beret (ber-ray)

Parts of speech

Parts of speech are shown in italics as an abbreviation. Where a word has several senses for one part of speech, the senses are numbered:

bereaved *adj* having recently lost a close relative or friend through death ▶ HISTORY Old English *bereafian* to deprive > **bereavement** *n*

When a word can be used as more than one part of speech, the change of part of speech is shown after an empty arrow:

besides *adv* **1** in addition ▷ *prep* **2** apart from; even considering ▷ *conj* **3** anyway; moreover

Irregular forms

Irregular forms of verbs, nouns, adjectives, and adverbs are shown in blue bold type:

bestride *vb* **-striding, -strode**

Definitions and examples

Definitions give the meaning of the word. Example sentences are in italics and show how the word is used:

better-off *adj* reasonably wealthy: *Catalonia aims to attract better-off tourists*

Guide to the Dictionary

Phrases

Phrases are given in blue bold type:

> **berserk** *adj* **go berserk** to become violent or
> destructive

Regional labels

Regional labels are given in italics:

> **bespoke** *adj chiefly Brit* **1** (esp. of a suit) made to
> the customer's specifications

Usage labels

Usage labels (showing register or context) are given in italics:

> **betrothed** *old-fashioned adj* **1** engaged to be
> married

Subject labels

Subject labels are given in italics:

> **bergschrund** (**berk**-shroont) *n geog* a crevasse at
> the head of a glacier ▶ HISTORY German: mountain
> crack

Related adjectives

Related adjectives are given in black bold type:

> **bird** *n* **1** a two-legged creature with feathers and
> wings, which lays eggs and can usually fly. *Related
> adjective:* **avian**

Related words

Related words are given at the end of an entry in blue bold type after a
chevron:

> **bereaved** *adj* having recently lost a close relative
> or friend through death ▶ HISTORY Old English
> *bereafian* to deprive > **bereavement** *n*

Guide to the Dictionary

Cross-references

Cross-references are given in black bold type:

> **beyond reasonable doubt** *n law* the standard
> of proof in a criminal case, meaning that, before
> someone can be found guilty, there must not be
> any reasonable doubt as to their guilt in the minds
> of the jury or magistrate. Compare **balance of
> probabilities**

Word histories

Word histories are given towards the end of an entry after a black filled arrow:

> **bête noire** (bet **nwahr**) *n*, *pl* **bêtes noires** a
> person or thing that one particularly dislikes or
> dreads ▶ HISTORY French, literally: black beast

Detailed word histories

Detailed word histories give more information about interesting words:

> **bonfire** *n* a large outdoor fire
> ■ WORD HISTORY
> ■ A 'bonfire' is literally a 'bone-fire'. Bones were
> ■ used as fuel in the Middle Ages.

Word Focus boxes

Word Focus boxes give alternatives for overused words. The sense numbers in the Word Focus box correspond to the sense numbers in the dictionary entry:

---

better · WORD FOCUS

Like **best**, the word **better** can be replaced with a number of alternatives to add variety and interest to your written and spoken English.

DEFINITION 2
- If you want to describe something as being more excellent than other things, you could try: the **greater** prize • **higher-quality** service • far **superior** to yours • **surpassing** quality

DEFINITION 3
- If you want to describe something as being more suitable or attractive than other things, you could try: no **finer** place • much **grander** house • much **nicer** room • **preferable** to • a **worthier** cause

DEFINITION 4
- If you want to describe someone as having improved health, you could say: now I'm **cured** • a lot **fitter** • **fully recovered** • much **healthier** • definitely **improving** • **on the mend** now • she's **recovering** • getting **stronger** • feeling **well** again

---

Abbreviations Used in the Dictionary

abbrev	abbreviation	*med*	medicine
adj	adjective	*meteorol*	meteorology
adv	adverb(ial)	*mil*	military
anat	anatomy	*myth*	mythology
anthropol	anthropology	*n*	noun
archaeol	archaeology	*N*	North(ern)
archit	architecture	*naut*	nautical
astrol	astrology	*NE*	Northeast(ern)
astron	astronomy	*NW*	Northwest(ern)
Austral	Australian	*NZ*	New Zealand
bacteriol	bacteriology	*ornithol*	ornithology
biochem	biochemistry	*pathol*	pathology
biol	biology	*pharmacol*	pharmacology
bot	botany	*photog*	photography
Brit	British	*physiol*	physiology
C	Celsius	*pl*	plural
Canad	Canadian	*pp*	past participle
cap	capital	*prep*	preposition
chem	chemistry	*pron*	pronoun
conj	conjuction	*psychoanal*	psychoanalysis
crystallog	crystallography	*psychol*	psychology
E	East(ern)	*pt*	past tense
econ	economics	*RC*	Roman Catholic
esp.	especially	*S*	South(ern)
etc.	et cetera	*Scot*	Scottish
F	Fahrenheit	*SE*	Southeast(ern)
fem	feminine	*sing*	singular
foll.	followed	*sociol*	sociology
geog	geography	*SW*	Southwest(ern)
geol	geology	*theol*	theology
geom	geometry	*US*	United States
interj	interjection	*vb*	verb
masc	masculine	*W*	West(ern)
maths	mathematics	*zool*	zoology

Aa

a¹ or **A** *n, pl* **a's, A's** or **As** **1** the first letter of the English alphabet **2 from A to B** from one place to another: *I just want a car that takes me from A to B* **3 from A to Z** from start to finish

a¹ *adj* (indefinite article) **1** used preceding a singular count noun that has not been mentioned before: *a book; a great shame* **2** used preceding a noun or adjective of quantity: *a litre of wine; a great amount has been written; I swim a lot and walk much more* **3** each or every; per: *I saw him once a week for six weeks*

A 1 *music* the sixth note of the scale of C major **2** ampere(s) **3** atomic: *an A-bomb*

Å angstrom unit

a- or before a vowel **an-** *prefix* not or without: *atonal; asocial; anaphrodisiac* ▸ HISTORY Greek

A1, A-1 or **A-one** *adj informal* first-class, excellent

A4 *n* a standard paper size, 297 × 210 mm

AA 1 Alcoholics Anonymous **2** (in Britain and S Africa) Automobile Association

AAA *Brit* (formerly) Amateur Athletic Association

A & R artists and repertoire

aardvark *n* a S African anteater with long ears and snout

■ **WORD HISTORY**

'Aardvark' is an obsolete Afrikaans word meaning 'earth pig', from *aarde*, meaning 'earth' and *vark*, meaning 'pig'. With its long ears and snout and its stout body, the aardvark does look rather like a pig, but pigs and aardvarks belong to totally separate animal families.

AB 1 able-bodied seaman **2** Alberta

ab- *prefix* away from or opposite to: *abnormal* ▸ HISTORY Latin

aback *adv* **taken aback** startled or disconcerted

abacus (**ab**-a-cuss) *n* a counting device consisting of a frame holding beads on metal rods ▸ HISTORY Latin

abaft *adv, adj naut* closer to the stern of a ship ▸ HISTORY Old English *be* by + *æftan* behind

abalone (ab-a-**lone**-ee) *n* an edible sea creature with a shell lined with mother-of-pearl ▸ HISTORY American Spanish *abulón*

abandon *vb* **1** to desert or leave: *he had already abandoned his first wife* **2** to give up completely: *did you abandon all attempts at contact with the boy?* **3** to give oneself over completely to an emotion ▷ *n* **4 with abandon** uninhibitedly and without restraint ▸ HISTORY Old French *a bandon* under one's control > **abandonment** *n*

abandoned *adj* **1** no longer used or occupied: *four people were found dead in an abandoned vehicle* **2** wild and uninhibited: *that fluffy abandoned laugh*

abase *vb* **abasing, abased · abase oneself** to make oneself humble ▸ HISTORY Old French *abaissier* > **abasement** *n*

abashed *adj written* embarrassed and ashamed ▸ HISTORY Old French *esbair* to be astonished

abate *vb* **abating, abated** to make or become less strong: *the tension has abated in recent months* ▸ HISTORY Old French *abatre* to beat down > **abatement** *n*

abattoir (**ab**-a-twahr) *n* a slaughterhouse ▸ HISTORY French *abattre* to fell

abbacy *n, pl* **-cies** the office or jurisdiction of an abbot or abbess ▸ HISTORY Church Latin *abbatia*

abbé (**ab**-bay) *n* a French abbot or other clergyman

abbess *n* the nun in charge of a convent ▸ HISTORY Church Latin *abbatissa*

abbey *n* **1** a church associated with a community of monks or nuns **2** a community of monks or nuns **3** a building inhabited by monks or nuns ▸ HISTORY Church Latin *abbatia* ABBACY

abbot *n* the head of an abbey of monks ▸ HISTORY Aramaic *abbā* father

abbreviate *vb* **-ating, -ated 1** to shorten a word by leaving out some letters **2** to cut short ▸ HISTORY Latin *brevis* brief > **abbreviation** *n*

ABC¹ *n* **1** the alphabet **2** an alphabetical guide **3** the basics of something

ABC² Australian Broadcasting Corporation

abdicate *vb* **-cating, -cated 1** to give up the throne formally **2** to give up one's responsibilities ▸ HISTORY Latin *abdicare* to disclaim > **abdication** *n*

abdomen *n* the part of the body that contains the stomach and intestines ▸ HISTORY Latin > **abdominal** *adj*

abduct *vb* to remove (a person) by force; kidnap ▸ HISTORY Latin *abducere* to lead away > **abduction** *n* > **abductor** *n*

abeam *adv, adj* at right angles to the length of a ship or aircraft

Aberdeen Angus *n* a black hornless breed of beef cattle originating in Scotland

aberrant *adj* not normal, accurate, or correct: *aberrant behaviour*

aberration *n* **1** a sudden change from what is normal, accurate, or correct **2** a brief lapse in control of one's thoughts or feelings: *he suddenly had a mental aberration* ▸ HISTORY Latin *aberrare* to wander away

abet *vb* **abetting, abetted** to help or encourage in wrongdoing ▸ HISTORY Old French *abeter* to lure on

abeyance *n* **in abeyance** put aside temporarily ▸ HISTORY Old French *abeance*, literally: a gaping after

abhor *vb* **-horring, -horred** to detest utterly ▸ HISTORY Latin *abhorrere* to shudder at

a

abhorrent *adj* hateful or disgusting
> **abhorrence** *n*

abide *vb* **1** to tolerate: *I can't abide stupid people* **2** to last or exist for a long time: *these instincts, while subdued in the individual, may abide in the race* **3 abide by** to act in accordance with: *he must abide by the findings of the report* **4** *archaic* to live ▸ **HISTORY** Old English *ābīdan*, from a- (intensive) + *bīdan* to wait

abiding *adj* lasting for ever: *an abiding interest in history*

ability *n*, *pl* **-ties 1** possession of the necessary skill or power to do something **2** great skill or competence: *his ability as a speaker was legendary* ▸ **HISTORY** Latin *habilitas*

abiotic (ay-bye-**ott**-ik) *adj* not living or not produced by living organisms. Compare **biotic**

abject *adj* **1** utterly miserable: *one Mexican in five lives in abject poverty* **2** lacking all self-respect ▸ **HISTORY** Latin *abjectus* thrown away > **abjectly** *adv*

abjure *vb* **-juring, -jured** to renounce or deny under oath ▸ **HISTORY** Latin *abjurare* > **abjuration** *n*

ablation *n* **1** the surgical removal of an organ or part **2** the wearing away of a rock or glacier **3** the melting of a part, such as the heat shield of a space re-entry vehicle ▸ **HISTORY** Latin *ablatus* carried away

ablaze *adj* **1** on fire **2** brightly illuminated: *the sky was ablaze with the stars shining bright* **3** emotionally aroused: *his eyes were ablaze with anger*

able *adj* **1** having the necessary power, skill, or opportunity to do something **2** capable or talented ▸ **HISTORY** Latin *habilis* easy to hold

-able *suffix forming adjectives* able to be acted upon as specified: *washable* ▸ **HISTORY** Latin *-abilis, -ibilis* > **-ably** *suffix forming adverbs* > **-ability** *suffix forming nouns*

able-bodied *adj* strong and healthy

able-bodied seaman *or* **able seaman** *n* a seaman who is trained in certain skills

ableism (**ay**-bel-iz-zum) *n* *Brit, Austral & S African* discrimination against disabled people

ablutions *pl n* the act of washing: *after the nightly ablutions, I settled down to read* ▸ **HISTORY** Latin *abluere* to wash away

ably *adv* competently or skilfully

ABM antiballistic missile

abnormal *adj* differing from the usual or typical > **abnormality** *n* > **abnormally** *adv*

aboard *adv, adj, prep* on, in, onto, or into (a ship, plane, or train)

abode *n* one's home ▸ **HISTORY** from ABIDE

abolish *vb* to do away with (laws, regulations, or customs) ▸ **HISTORY** Latin *abolere* to destroy

abolition *n* **1** the act of doing away with something: *the abolition of slavery* **2 Abolition** the ending of slavery > **abolitionist** *n, adj*

A-bomb *n* short for **atomic bomb**

abominable *adj* very bad or unpleasant: *I think that what is being done here is utterly abominable* > **abominably** *adv*

abominable snowman *n* a large creature, like a man or an ape, that is said to live in the Himalayas ▸ **HISTORY** translation of Tibetan *metohkangmi* foul snowman

abominate *vb* **-nating, -nated** to dislike intensely ▸ **HISTORY** Latin *abominari* to regard as an ill omen > **abomination** *n*

aboriginal *adj* existing in a place from the earliest known period

Aboriginal *adj* **1** of the Aborigines of Australia ▷ *n* **2** an Aborigine

aborigine (ab-or-**rij**-in-ee) *n* *Brit, Austral & NZ* an original inhabitant of a country or region, esp. (**A-**) Australia ▸ **HISTORY** from Latin *aborigines*, the name of the inhabitants of Latium in pre-Roman times

Aborigine *n* a member of a dark-skinned people who were already living in Australia when European settlers arrived

abort *vb* **1** (of a pregnancy) to end before the fetus is viable **2** to end a plan or process before completion ▸ **HISTORY** Latin *abortare*

abortion *n* **1** an operation to end pregnancy **2** the premature ending of a pregnancy when a fetus is expelled from the womb before it can live independently **3** the failure of a mission or project **4** *informal* something that is grotesque > **abortionist** *n*

abortion pill *n* a drug used to terminate a pregnancy in its earliest stage

abortive *adj* failing to achieve its purpose

abound *vb* **1** to exist in large numbers **2 abound in** to have a large number of ▸ **HISTORY** Latin *abundare* to overflow

about *prep* **1** relating to or concerning **2** near to **3** carried on: *I haven't any money about me* **4** on every side of ▷ *adv* **5** near in number, time, or degree; approximately **6** nearby **7** here and there: *there were some fifteen other people scattered about on the first floor* **8** all around; on every side **9** in or to the opposite direction **10** in rotation: *turn and turn about* **11** used to indicate understatement: *it's about time somebody told the truth on that subject* **12 about to** on the point of; intending to: *she was about to get in the car* **13 not about to** determined not to: *we're not about to help her out* ▷ *adj* **14** active: *he was off the premises well before anyone was up and about* ▸ **HISTORY** Old English *abūtan, onbūtan* on the outside of

about-turn *or US* **about-face** *n* **1** a complete change of opinion or direction **2** a reversal of the direction in which one is facing

above *prep* **1** higher than; over **2** greater than in quantity or degree: *above average* **3** superior to or higher than in quality, rank, or ability **4** too high-minded for: *he considered himself above the task of working* **5** too respected for; beyond: *his fleet was above suspicion* **6** too difficult to be understood by: *a discussion that was way above my head* **7** louder or higher than (other noise) **8** in preference to **9 above all** most of all; especially ▷ *adv* **10** in or to a higher place: *the hills above* **11** in a previous place (in something written or printed) **12** higher in rank or position ▷ *n* **13 the above** something previously mentioned ▷ *adj* **14** appearing in a previous place (in something written or printed): *for a copy of the free brochure write to the above address* ▶ HISTORY Old English *abufan*

above board *adj* completely honest and open

- **WORD HISTORY**
- The phrase 'above board' is in origin a gambling
- term. It is an allusion to the fact that it is
- difficult for a player to cheat at cards when his
- hands are above the 'board' or gambling table
- and therefore clearly visible to the other
- players.

abracadabra *n* a word used in magic spells, which is supposed to possess magic powers ▶ HISTORY Latin

abrasion *n* **1** a scraped area on the skin; graze **2** *geog* the erosion of rock by rock fragments scratching and scraping it ▶ HISTORY Latin *abradere* to scrape away

abrasive *adj* **1** rude and unpleasant in manner **2** tending to rub or scrape; rough ▷ *n* **3** a substance used for cleaning, smoothing, or polishing

abreast *adj* **1** alongside each other and facing in the same direction: *the two cars were abreast* **2 abreast of** up to date with

abridge *vb* **abridging, abridged** to shorten a written work by taking out parts ▶ HISTORY Late Latin *abbreviare* > **abridgment** or **abridgement** *n*

abroad *adv* **1** to or in a foreign country **2** generally known or felt: *there is a new spirit abroad*

abrogate *vb* **-gating, -gated** to cancel (a law or an agreement) formally ▶ HISTORY from Latin *ab-* away + *rogare* to propose a law > **abrogation** *n*

abrupt *adj* **1** sudden or unexpected: *an abrupt departure* **2** rather rude in speech or manner ▶ HISTORY Latin *abruptus* broken off > **abruptly** *adv* > **abruptness** *n*

abs *pl n informal* abdominal muscles

abscess (**ab**-sess) *n* **1** a swelling containing pus as a result of inflammation ▷ *vb* **2** to form a swelling containing pus ▶ HISTORY Latin *abscessus* literally: a throwing off > **abscessed** *adj*

abscissa *n*, *pl* **-scissas** or **-scissae** *maths* (in a two-dimensional system of Cartesian coordinates) the distance from the vertical axis measured parallel to the horizontal axis ▶ HISTORY New Latin *linea abscissa* a cut-off line

abscond *vb* to run away unexpectedly ▶ HISTORY Latin *abscondere* to conceal

abseil (**ab**-sale) *vb* **1** to go down a steep drop by a rope fastened at the top and tied around one's body ▷ *n* **2** an instance of abseiling ▶ HISTORY German *abseilen*

absence *n* **1** the state of being away **2** the time during which a person or thing is away **3** the fact of being without something

absent *adj* **1** not present in a place or situation **2** lacking **3** not paying attention ▷ *vb* **4 absent oneself** to stay away ▶ HISTORY Latin *absens* > **absently** *adv*

absentee *n* a person who should be present but is not

absenteeism *n* persistent absence from work or school

absent-minded *adj* inattentive or forgetful > **absent-mindedly** *adv*

absinthe *n* a strong, green, alcoholic drink, originally containing wormwood ▶ HISTORY Greek *apsinthion* wormwood

absolute *adj* **1** total and complete: *he ordered an immediate and absolute ceasefire* **2** with unrestricted power and authority: *she has absolute control with 50 per cent of the shares* **3** undoubted or certain: *I was telling the absolute truth* **4** not dependent on or relative to anything else **5** pure; unmixed: *absolute alcohol* ▷ *n* **6** a principle or rule believed to be unfailingly correct **7 the Absolute** *philosophy* that which is totally unconditioned, perfect, or complete ▶ HISTORY Latin *absolutus*

absolute error *n maths* the difference between the predicted value and the actual value of a quantity

absolutely *adv* **1** completely or perfectly ▷ *interj* **2** yes indeed, certainly

absolute majority *n* a number of votes totalling over 50 per cent, such as the total number of votes that beats the combined opposition

absolute pitch *n* the ability to identify the pitch of a note, or to sing a given note, without reference to one previously sounded

absolute zero *n physics* the lowest temperature theoretically possible, at which the particles that make up matter would be at rest: equivalent to $-273.15°C$ or $-459.67°F$

absolution *n Christianity* a formal forgiveness of sin pronounced by a priest

absolutism *n* a political system in which a monarch or dictator has unrestricted power

absolve *vb* **-solving, -solved** to declare to be free from blame or sin ▶ HISTORY Latin *absolvere*

absorb *vb* **1** to soak up a liquid **2** to engage the interest of someone **3** to receive the force of an impact **4** *physics* to take in radiant energy and retain it **5** to take in or incorporate: *this country has absorbed almost one million refugees* ▶ HISTORY Latin *absorbere* to suck > **absorbent** *adj* > **absorbing** *adj*

absorption *n* **1** the process of absorbing something or the state of being absorbed **2** *physiol* the process by which nutrients enter the tissues of an animal or a plant > **absorptive** *adj*

abstain *vb* **1** to choose not to do something: *you will be asked to abstain from food prior to your general anaesthetic* **2** to choose not to vote ▶ HISTORY Latin *abstinere* > **abstainer** *n*

abstemious (ab-**steem**-ee-uss) *adj* taking very little alcohol or food ▶ HISTORY Latin *abstemius* > **abstemiously** *adv* > **abstemiousness** *n*

abstention *n* **1** the formal act of not voting **2** the act of abstaining from something, such as drinking alcohol

abstinence *n* the practice of choosing not to do something one would like > **abstinent** *adj*

a

abstract *adj* **1** referring to ideas or qualities rather than material objects: *abstract words such as justice, equality and success* **2** not applied or practical; theoretical: *he was frustrated by the highly abstract mathematics being taught* **3** of art in which the subject is represented by shapes and patterns rather than by a realistic likeness ▷ *n* **4** a summary **5** an abstract painting or sculpture **6** an abstract word or idea **7 in the abstract** without referring to specific circumstances ▷ *vb* **8** to summarize **9** to remove or extract ▶ HISTORY Latin *abstractus* drawn off

abstracted *adj written* lost in thought; preoccupied > **abstractedly** *adv*

abstraction *n* **1** a general idea rather than a specific example: *these abstract philosophical abstractions continued to bother him* **2** *written* the quality of being abstract or abstracted

abstract noun *n grammar* a noun that refers to a quality, state, or concept, as for example *kindness, peace,* or *morality,* rather than to a physical object. Compare **concrete noun**

abstruse *adj* not easy to understand ▶ HISTORY Latin *abstrusus* concealed

absurd *adj* obviously senseless or illogical; ridiculous ▶ HISTORY Latin *absurdus* > **absurdity** *n* > **absurdly** *adv*

abundance *n* **1** a great amount **2** degree of plentifulness **3 in abundance** in great amounts: *they had fish and fruit in abundance* ▶ HISTORY Latin *abundare* to abound > **abundant** *adj*

abundantly *adv* **1** very: *he made his disagreement with the prime minister abundantly clear* **2** plentifully; in abundance

abuse *n* **1** prolonged ill-treatment of or violence towards someone: *child abuse* **2** insulting comments **3** improper use: *an abuse of power* ▷ *vb* **abusing, abused** **4** to take advantage of dishonestly: *these two ministers had abused their position for financial gain* **5** to ill-treat violently: *he had been abused as a child* **6** to speak insultingly or cruelly to ▶ HISTORY Latin *abuti* to misuse > **abuser** *n*

abusive *adj* rude or insulting: *he was alleged to have used abusive language towards spectators* > **abusively** *adv*

abut *vb* **abutting, abutted** to be next to or touching ▶ HISTORY Old French *abouter*

abysmal *adj informal* extremely bad ▶ HISTORY Medieval Latin *abysmus* abyss > **abysmally** *adv*

abyss *n* **1** a very deep hole in the ground **2** a frightening or threatening situation: *the abyss of revolution and war ahead* ▶ HISTORY Greek *abussos* bottomless

Ac *chem* actinium

AC 1 alternating current **2** athletic club

a/c 1 account **2** account current

acacia (a-**kay**-sha) *n* a shrub or tree with small yellow or white flowers ▶ HISTORY Greek *akakia*

academic *adj* **1** relating to a college or university **2** (of pupils) having an aptitude for study **3** relating to studies such as languages and pure science rather than technical or professional studies **4** of theoretical interest only: *the argument is academic* ▷ *n* **5** a member of the teaching or research staff of a college or university > **academically** *adv*

academy *n, pl* **-mies 1** a society for the advancement of literature, art, or science **2** a school for training in a particular skill: *sixteen hundred students would also spend their first year at the military academy* **3** (in Scotland) a secondary school

■ **WORD HISTORY**
■ The original Academy, in Greek *Akadēmeia,*
■ was an olive grove outside ancient Athens
■ where the philosopher Plato taught in the
■ 4th century BC. His school of philosophy
■ then became known as the Academy, and this
■ word came to be used for other bodies that
■ promoted learning.

acanthus *n* **1** a plant with large spiny leaves and spikes of white or purplish flowers **2** a carved ornament based on the leaves of the acanthus plant ▶ HISTORY Greek *akantha* thorn

a cappella *adj, adv music* without musical accompaniment: *an a cappella version; we decided to sing it a cappella* ▶ HISTORY Italian, literally: according to (the style of the) chapel

ACAS (in Britain) Advisory Conciliation and Arbitration Service

acc. 1 *grammar* accusative **2** account

ACC (in New Zealand) Accident Compensation Corporation

accede *vb* **-ceding, -ceded** • **accede to 1** to agree to **2** to take up (an office or position): *he acceded to the throne after his Irish exile* ▶ HISTORY Latin *accedere*

accelerando *adv music* with increasing speed ▶ HISTORY Italian

accelerate *vb* **-ating, -ated 1** to move or cause to move more quickly **2** to cause to happen sooner than expected ▶ HISTORY Latin *accelerare*

accelerated erosion *n geol* a wearing away of soil and rocks that is faster than normal

acceleration *n* **1** the act of increasing speed **2** the rate of increase of speed or the rate of change of velocity

accelerator *n* **1** a pedal in a motor vehicle that is pressed to increase speed **2** *physics* a machine for increasing the speed and energy of charged particles

accent *n* **1** the distinctive style of pronunciation of a person or group from a particular area, country, or social background **2** a mark used in writing to indicate the prominence of a syllable or the way a vowel is pronounced **3** particular emphasis: *there will be an accent on sport and many will enjoy rowing* **4** the stress on a syllable or musical note ▷ *vb* **5** to lay particular emphasis on ▶ HISTORY Latin *accentus*

accentuate *vb* **-ating, -ated** to stress or emphasize > **accentuation** *n*

accept *vb* **1** to take or receive something offered **2** to agree to **3** to consider something as true **4** to tolerate or resign oneself to **5** to take on the responsibilities of: *he asked if I would become his* assistant and I accepted that position **6** to receive someone into a community or group **7** to receive something as adequate or valid ▶ **HISTORY** Latin *acceptare*

acceptable adj **1** able to be endured; tolerable: *in war killing is acceptable* **2** good enough; adequate: *he found the article acceptable* > **acceptability** n > **acceptably** adv

acceptance n **1** the act of accepting something **2** favourable reception **3** belief or agreement

accepted adj commonly approved or recognized: *the accepted wisdom about old age*

access n **1** a means of approaching or entering a place **2** the condition of allowing entry, for example entry to a building by wheelchairs or prams **3** the right or opportunity to use something or enter a place: *the bourgeoisie gained access to political power* **4** the opportunity or right to see or approach someone: *my ex-wife sabotages my access to the children* ▷ vb **5** to obtain information from a computer ▶ **HISTORY** Latin *accedere* to accede

accessible adj **1** easy to approach, enter, or use **2** easy to understand: *the most accessible opera by Wagner* > **accessibility** n

accession n the act of taking up an office or position: *the 40th anniversary of her accession to the throne*

accessory n, pl **-ries 1** a supplementary part or object **2** a small item, such as a bag or belt, worn or carried by someone to complete his or her outfit **3** a person who is involved in a crime but who was not present when it took place ▶ **HISTORY** Late Latin *accessorius*

access road n a road providing a way to a particular place or on to a motorway

access time n the time required to retrieve a piece of stored information from a computer

accident n **1** an unpleasant event that causes damage, injury, or death **2** an unforeseen event or one without apparent cause: *they had met in town by accident* ▶ **HISTORY** Latin *accidere* to happen

accidental adj **1** occurring by chance or unintentionally ▷ n **2** music a symbol denoting a sharp, flat, or natural that is not a part of the key signature > **accidentally** adv

accident-prone adj (of a person) often involved in accidents

acclaim vb **1** to applaud or praise: *the highly acclaimed children's TV series* **2** to acknowledge publicly: *he was immediately acclaimed the new prime minister* ▷ n **3** an enthusiastic expression of approval ▶ **HISTORY** Latin *acclamare*

acclamation n **1** an enthusiastic reception or display of approval **2** Canad an instance of being elected without opposition **3 by acclamation** by a majority without a ballot

acclimatize or **-tise** vb **-tizing, -tized** or **-tising, -tised** to adapt to a new climate or environment > **acclimatization** or **-tisation** n

accolade n **1** an award, praise, or honour **2** a touch on the shoulder with a sword conferring knighthood ▶ **HISTORY** Latin *ad-* to + *collum* neck

accommodate vb **-dating, -dated 1** to provide with lodgings **2** to have room for **3** to do a favour for **4** to get used to (something) ▶ **HISTORY** Latin *accommodare*

accommodating adj willing to help; obliging

accommodation n a place in which to sleep, live, or work

accommodation address n Brit an address on letters to a person who cannot or does not wish to receive mail at a permanent address

accompaniment n **1** something that accompanies something else **2** music a supporting part for an instrument, a band, or an orchestra

accompanist n a person who plays a musical accompaniment

accompany vb **-nies, -nying, -nied 1** to go with (someone) **2** to happen or exist at the same time as **3** to provide a musical accompaniment for ▶ **HISTORY** Old French *accompaignier*

accomplice n a person who helps someone else commit a crime ▶ **HISTORY** Late Latin *complex* partner

accomplish vb **1** to manage to do; achieve: *most infants accomplish it immediately* **2** to complete ▶ **HISTORY** Latin *complere* to fill up

accomplished adj **1** expert or proficient: *an accomplished liar* **2** successfully completed

accomplishment n **1** the successful completion of something **2** something successfully completed **3 accomplishments** personal abilities or skills

accord n **1** agreement or harmony **2** a formal agreement between groups or nations: *the Paris peace accords* **3 of one's own accord** voluntarily or willingly **4 with one accord** unanimously ▷ vb **5** to grant: *she was at last accorded her true status* **6 accord with** to fit in with or be consistent with ▶ **HISTORY** Latin *ad-* to + *cor* heart

accordance n **in accordance with** conforming to or according to: *food is prepared in accordance with Jewish laws*

according adv **1 according to a** as stated by: *according to her, they were once engaged* **b** in conformity with: *work hours varied according to the tides* **2 according as** depending on whether

accordingly adv **1** in an appropriate manner **2** consequently

accordion n a box-shaped musical instrument played by moving the two sides apart and together, and pressing a keyboard or buttons to produce the notes ▶ **HISTORY** German *Akkordion* > **accordionist** n

accost vb to approach, stop, and speak to ▶ **HISTORY** Latin *ad-* to + *costa* side, rib

account n **1** a report or description **2** a person's money held in a bank **3** a statement of financial transactions with the resulting balance **4** part or behalf: *I am sorry that you suffered on my account* **5 call someone to account** to demand an explanation from someone **6 give a good** or **bad account of oneself** to perform well or fail to

a

perform well **7 of no account** of little importance or value **8 on account of** because of **9 take account of** *or* **take into account** to take into consideration; allow for ▷ *vb* **10** to consider as: *the evening was accounted a major step forward by all concerned* ▶ HISTORY Old French *acont*

accountable *adj* responsible to someone or for some action > **accountability** *n*

accountant *n* a person who maintains and audits business accounts > **accountancy** *n*

account for *vb* **1** to give reasons for **2** to explain or count up what has been spent

accounting *n* the skill or practice of maintaining and auditing business accounts

accoutrements (ak-**koo**-tra-ments) *or US* **accouterments** (ak-**koo**-ter-ments) *pl n* clothing and equipment for a particular activity ▶ HISTORY Old French *accoustrer* to equip

accredit *vb* **1** to give official recognition to **2** to send (a diplomat) with official credentials to a particular country **3** to certify as meeting required standards **4** to attribute (a quality or an action) to (a person) ▶ HISTORY French *accréditer* > **accreditation** *n*

accretion (ak-**kree**-shun) *n* **1** a gradual increase in size, through growth or addition **2** something added, such as an extra layer ▶ HISTORY Latin *accretio*

accrue *vb* **-cruing, -crued** **1** (of money or interest) to increase gradually over a period of time **2 accrue to** to fall naturally to: *some advantage must accrue to the weaker party* ▶ HISTORY Latin *accrescere*

accumulate *vb* **-lating, -lated** to gather together in an increasing quantity; collect ▶ HISTORY Latin *accumulare* to heap up > **accumulative** *adj*

accumulation *n* **1** something that has been collected **2** the collecting together of things

accumulator *n* **1** *Brit & Austral* a rechargeable device for storing electrical energy **2** *Brit horse racing* a collective bet on successive races, with both stake and winnings being carried forward to accumulate progressively

accuracy *n* faithful representation of the truth: *care is taken to ensure the accuracy of the content*

accurate *adj* faithfully representing the truth: *all the information was accurate* ▶ HISTORY Latin *accurare* to perform with care > **accurately** *adv*

accursed (a-**curse**-id) *adj* **1** under a curse **2** hateful or detestable

accusation *n* **1** an allegation that a person is guilty of some wrongdoing **2** a formal charge brought against a person > **accusatory** *adj*

accusative *or* **accusative case** *n grammar* a grammatical case in some languages that identifies the direct object of a verb

accuse *vb* **-cusing, -cused** to charge a person with wrongdoing ▶ HISTORY Latin *accūsāre* > **accuser** *n* > **accusing** *adj* > **accusingly** *adv*

accused *n* **the accused** *law* the defendant appearing on a criminal charge

accustom *vb* **accustom oneself to** to become familiar with or used to from habit or experience ▶ HISTORY Old French *acostumer*

accustomed *adj* **1** usual or customary: *he parked his motorcycle in its accustomed place* **2 accustomed to a** used to **b** in the habit of

ace *n* **1** a playing card with one symbol on it **2** *informal* an expert: *an American stock car ace* **3** *tennis* a winning serve that the opponent fails to reach **4** a fighter pilot who has destroyed several enemy aircraft ▷ *adj* **5** *informal* superb or excellent: *an ace tennis player* ▶ HISTORY Latin *as* a unit

acerbic (ass-**sir**-bik) *adj* harsh or bitter: *an acerbic critic* ▶ HISTORY Latin *acerbus* sharp, sour

acerbity *n, pl* **-ties** **1** bitter speech or temper **2** bitterness of taste

acetaldehyde (ass-it-**tal**-dee-hide) *n chem* a colourless volatile liquid, used as a solvent

acetate (**ass**-it-tate) *n* **1** *chem* any salt or ester of acetic acid **2** Also: **acetate rayon** a synthetic textile fibre made from cellulose acetate

acetic (ass-**see**-tik) *adj chem* of, containing, or producing acetic acid or vinegar ▶ HISTORY Latin *acetum* vinegar

acetic acid *n chem* a strong-smelling colourless liquid used to make vinegar

acetone (**ass**-it-tone) *n chem* a strong-smelling colourless liquid used as a solvent for paints and lacquers

acetylene (ass-**set**-ill-een) *n chem* a colourless soluble flammable gas used in welding metals

ache *vb* **aching, ached** **1** to feel or be the source of a continuous dull pain **2** *written* to suffer mental anguish ▷ *n* **3** a continuous dull pain ▶ HISTORY Old English *ācan*

achieve *vb* **achieving, achieved** to gain by hard work or effort ▶ HISTORY Old French *achever* to bring to an end > **achiever** *n*

achievement *n* **1** something that has been accomplished by hard work, ability, or heroism **2** the successful completion of something

Achilles heel (ak-**kill**-eez) *n* a small but fatal weakness ▶ HISTORY *Achilles* in Greek mythology was killed by an arrow in his unprotected heel

Achilles tendon *n* the fibrous cord that connects the muscles of the calf to the heel bone

achromatic *adj* **1** without colour **2** refracting light without breaking it up into its component colours **3** *music* involving no sharps or flats > **achromatically** *adv*

acid *n* **1** *chem* one of a class of compounds, corrosive and sour when dissolved in water, that combine with a base to form a salt **2** *slang* LSD **3** a sour-tasting substance ▷ *adj* **4** *chem* of, from, or containing acid **5** sharp or sour in taste **6** sharp in speech or manner ▶ HISTORY Latin *acidus* > **acidly** *adv*

acidic *adj* containing acid

acidify *vb* **-fies, -fying, -fied** to convert into acid > **acidification** *n*

acidity *n* **1** the quality of being acid **2** the amount of acid in a solution

acid rain *n* *environmental science* rain containing pollutants released into the atmosphere by the burning of coal or oil

acid rock *n* *geol* igneous rock with a silica content of more than two thirds and containing not less than ten per cent quartz

acid test *n* a rigorous and conclusive test of worth or value ▶ HISTORY from the testing of gold with nitric acid

ackee *n* **1** a tropical African tree cultivated in the Caribbean for its fruit which is edible when cooked **2** the fruit of this tree ▶ HISTORY of African origin

acknowledge *vb* **-edging, -edged 1** to recognize or admit the truth of a statement **2** to show recognition of a person by a greeting or glance **3** to make known that a letter or message has been received **4** to express gratitude for (a favour or compliment) ▶ HISTORY Old English *oncnāwan* to recognize

acknowledgment *or* **acknowledgement** *n* **1** the act of acknowledging something or someone **2** something done or given as an expression of gratitude

acme (**ak**-mee) *n* the highest point of achievement or excellence ▶ HISTORY Greek *akmē*

acne (**ak**-nee) *n* a skin disease in which pus-filled spots form on the face ▶ HISTORY New Latin

acolyte *n* **1** a follower or attendant **2** *Christianity* a person who assists a priest ▶ HISTORY Greek *akolouthos*

aconite *n* **1** a poisonous plant with hoodlike flowers **2** dried aconite root, used as a narcotic ▶ HISTORY Greek *akoniton*

acorn *n* the fruit of the oak tree, consisting of a smooth nut in a cuplike base ▶ HISTORY Old English *æcern*

acoustic *adj* **1** of sound, hearing, or acoustics **2** (of a musical instrument) without electronic amplification **3** designed to absorb sound: *acoustic tiles* ▶ HISTORY Greek *akouein* to hear > **acoustically** *adv*

acoustics *n* **1** the scientific study of sound ▷ *pl n* **2** the characteristics of a room or auditorium determining how well sound can be heard within it

acquaint *vb* **acquaint with** to make (someone) familiar with ▶ HISTORY Latin *accognoscere* to know well

acquaintance *n* **1** a person whom one knows slightly **2** slight knowledge of a person or subject **3** **make the acquaintance of** to come into social contact with **4** the people one knows: *an actress of my acquaintance*

acquainted *adj* **1** on terms of familiarity but not intimacy **2** **acquainted with** familiar with: *she became acquainted with the classics of Chinese literature*

acquiesce (ak-wee-**ess**) *vb* **-escing, -esced** to agree to what someone wants ▶ HISTORY Latin *acquiescere* > **acquiescence** *n* > **acquiescent** *adj*

acquire *vb* **-quiring, -quired** to get or develop (something such as an object, trait, or ability) ▶ HISTORY Latin *acquirere* > **acquirement** *n*

acquired taste *n* **1** a liking for something at first considered unpleasant **2** the thing liked

acquisition *n* **1** something acquired, often to add to a collection **2** the act of acquiring something

acquisitive *adj* eager to gain material possessions > **acquisitively** *adv* > **acquisitiveness** *n*

acquit *vb* **-quitting, -quitted 1** to pronounce someone not guilty: *he's been acquitted of negligence* **2** to behave in a particular way: *she acquitted herself well in the meeting* ▶ HISTORY Old French *aquiter*

acquittal *n* *law* (in a criminal case) the judgment by a court that the accused is not guilty

acre *n* **1** a unit of area equal to 4840 square yards (4046.86 square metres) **2** **acres** *informal* a large amount: *acres of skin* ▶ HISTORY Old English *æcer*

acreage (**ake**-er-rij) *n* land area in acres

acrid (**ak**-rid) *adj* **1** unpleasantly strong-smelling **2** sharp in speech or manner ▶ HISTORY Latin *acer* sharp, sour > **acridity** *n* > **acridly** *adv*

acrimony *n* bitterness and resentment felt about something ▶ HISTORY Latin *acrimonia* > **acrimonious** *adj*

acrobat *n* an entertainer who performs gymnastic feats requiring skill, agility, and balance ▶ HISTORY Greek *akrobatēs* one who walks on tiptoe > **acrobatic** *adj* > **acrobatically** *adv*

acrobatics *pl n* the skills or feats of an acrobat

acronym *n* a word made from the initial letters of other words, for example UNESCO for the *United Nations Educational, Scientific, and Cultural Organization* ▶ HISTORY Greek *akros* outermost + *onoma* name

acrophobia *n* abnormal fear of being at a great height ▶ HISTORY Greek *akron* summit + *phobos* fear

acropolis (a-**crop**-pol-liss) *n* the citadel of an ancient Greek city ▶ HISTORY Greek *akros* highest + *polis* city

acrosome *n* *biol* a structure that forms the tip of a sperm cell

across *prep* **1** from one side to the other side of **2** on or at the other side of ▷ *adv* **3** from one side to the other **4** on or to the other side ▶ HISTORY Old French *a croix* crosswise

acrostic *n* a number of lines of writing, such as a poem, in which the first or last letters form a word or proverb ▶ HISTORY Greek *akros* outermost + *stikhos* line of verse

acrylic *adj* **1** made of acrylic ▷ *n* **2** a man-made fibre used for clothes and blankets **3** a kind of paint made from acrylic acid ▶ HISTORY Latin *acer* sharp + *olere* to smell

acrylic acid *n* *chem* a strong-smelling colourless corrosive liquid

acrylic fibre *n* a man-made fibre used for clothes and blankets

acrylic resin *n* *chem* any of a group of polymers of acrylic acid, used as synthetic rubbers, in paints, and as plastics

act *n* **1** something done **2** a formal decision reached or law passed by a law-making body: *an act of parliament* **3** a major division of a play or opera

4 a short performance, such as a sketch or dance **5** a pretended attitude: *she appeared calm but it was just an act* **6 get in on the act** *informal* to become involved in something in order to share the benefit **7 get one's act together** *informal* to organize oneself ▷ *vb* **8** to do something **9** to perform (a part or role) in a play, film, or broadcast **10** to present (a play) on stage **11 act for** to be a substitute for: *Mr Lewis was acting for the head of the department* **12 act as** to serve the function of: *she is acting as my bodyguard* **13** to behave: *she acts as though she really hates you* **14** to behave in an unnatural way ▶ HISTORY Latin *actum* a thing done

ACT Australian Capital Territory

acting *n* **1** the art of an actor ▷ *adj* **2** temporarily performing the duties of: *the acting president has declared a state of emergency*

actinide series *n chem* a series of 15 radioactive elements with increasing atomic numbers from actinium to lawrencium

actinium *n chem* a radioactive element of the actinide series, occurring as a decay product of uranium. Symbol: Ac ▶ HISTORY Greek *aktis* ray

action *n* **1** doing something for a particular purpose **2** something done on a particular occasion **3** a lawsuit **4** movement during some physical activity **5** the operating mechanism in a gun or machine **6** the way in which something operates or works **7** *slang* the main activity in a place **8** the events that form the plot of a story or play **9** activity, force, or energy **10** a minor battle **11 actions** behaviour **12 out of action** not functioning

actionable *adj law* giving grounds for legal action

action painting *n* an art form in which paint is thrown, smeared, dripped, or spattered on the canvas

action plan *n* a detailed account of things that need to be done in order to achieve a goal

action replay *n* the rerunning of a small section of television footage, for example of a sporting event

action stations *pl n* the positions taken up by individuals in preparation for battle or for some other activity

activate *vb* **-vating, -vated 1** to make something active **2** *physics* to make something radioactive **3** *chem* to increase the rate of a reaction > **activation** *n*

activation energy *n chem* the smallest amount of energy required for the reacting species to undergo a specific reaction

active *adj* **1** busy and energetic **2** energetically involved in or working hard for: *active in the peace movement* **3** happening now and energetically: *the plan is under active discussion* **4** functioning or causing a reaction: *the active ingredient is held within the capsule* **5** (of a volcano) erupting periodically **6** *grammar* denoting a form of a verb used to indicate that it is the subject that is performing the

action, for example *kicked* in *The boy kicked the football* ▷ *n* **7** *grammar* the active form of a verb > **actively** *adv*

active list *n mil* a list of officers available for full duty

active service *n* military duty in an operational area

active voice *n grammar* a set of verb forms used to indicate that the subject of the verb is the performer of the action, for example *d iscovered* in *Fleming discovered penicillin*. Compare **passive voice**

activist *n* a person who works energetically to achieve political or social goals > **activism** *n*

activity *n* **1** the state of being active **2** lively movement **3** (*pl* **-ties**) any specific action or pursuit: *he was engaged in political activities abroad*

act of God *n law* a sudden occurrence caused by natural forces, such as a flood

Act of Parliament *n law* a bill that has become statute and law

actor *or fem* **actress** *n* a person who acts in a play, film, or broadcast

ACTU Australian Council of Trade Unions

actual *adj* existing in reality or as a matter of fact ▶ HISTORY Latin *actus* act

actuality *n, pl* **-ties** reality

actually *adv* as an actual fact; really

actuary *n, pl* **-aries** a person qualified to calculate commercial risks and probabilities involving uncertain future events, esp. in such contexts as life assurance ▶ HISTORY Latin *actuarius* one who keeps accounts > **actuarial** *adj*

actuate *vb* **-ating, -ated 1** to start up a mechanical device **2** to motivate someone ▶ HISTORY Medieval Latin *actuare*

actus reus *n law* the criminal act that must be proved if a defendant is to be found guilty. Compare **mens rea** ▶ HISTORY Latin: guilty act

acuity (ak-**kew**-it-ee) *n* keenness of vision or thought ▶ HISTORY Latin *acutus* acute

acumen (ak-**yew**-men) *n* the ability to make good decisions ▶ HISTORY Latin: sharpness

acupuncture *n* a medical treatment involving the insertion of needles at various parts of the body to stimulate the nerve impulses ▶ HISTORY Latin *acus* needle + PUNCTURE > **acupuncturist** *n*

acute *adj* **1** severe or intense: *acute staff shortages* **2** penetrating in perception or insight **3** sensitive or keen: *it was amazing how acute your hearing got in the bush* **4** (of a disease) sudden and severe **5** *maths* (of an angle) of less than 90° **6** (of a hospital or bed) intended to accommodate short-term patients ▷ *n* **7** an acute accent ▶ HISTORY Latin *acutus* > **acutely** *adv* > **acuteness** *n*

acute accent *n* the mark (´), used in some languages to indicate that the vowel over which it is placed is to be pronounced in a certain way

ad *n informal* an advertisement

AD (indicating years numbered from the supposed year of the birth of Christ) in the year of the Lord ▶ HISTORY Latin *anno Domini*

ad- *prefix* **1** to or towards: *adverb* **2** near or next to: *adrenal* ▶ **HISTORY** Latin

Ada *n* a high-level computer programming language, used esp. for military systems ▶ **HISTORY** after *Ada*, Countess of Lovelace, pioneer in computer programming

adage (**ad**-ij) *n* a traditional saying that is generally accepted as being true ▶ **HISTORY** Latin *adagium*

adagietto *music adv* **1** slowly, but more quickly than adagio ▷ *n, pl* **-tos** **2** a movement or piece to be performed fairly slowly

adagio (ad-**dahj**-yo) *music adv* **1** slowly ▷ *n, pl* **-gios** **2** a movement or piece to be performed slowly ▶ **HISTORY** Italian

Adam *n* **1** *Bible* the first man created by God **2 not know someone from Adam** to not know someone at all

adamant *adj* unshakable in determination or purpose ▶ **HISTORY** Greek *adamas* unconquerable > **adamantly** *adv*

Adam's apple *n* the projecting lump of thyroid cartilage at the front of a person's neck

adapt *vb* **1** to adjust (something or oneself) to different conditions **2** to change something to suit a new purpose ▶ **HISTORY** Latin *adaptare* > **adaptable** *adj* > **adaptability** *n*

adaptation *n* **1** something that is produced by adapting something else: *a TV adaptation of a Victorian novel* **2** the act of adapting

adapted feature *n biol* an inherited or acquired modification in an organism that makes it better suited to survive and reproduce in a particular environment

adaptor *or* **adapter** *n* **1** a device used to connect several electrical appliances to a single socket **2** any device for connecting two parts of different sizes or types

ADC aide-de-camp

add *vb* **1** to combine (numbers or quantities) so as to make a larger number or quantity **2** to join something to something else so as to increase its size, effect, or scope: *these new rules will add an extra burden on already overworked officials* **3** to say or write something further **4 add in** to include ▷ See also **add up** ▶ **HISTORY** Latin *addere*

addendum *n, pl* **-da** something added on, esp. an appendix to a book or magazine

adder *n* a small poisonous snake with a black zigzag pattern along the back ▶ **HISTORY** Old English *nædre*

addict *n* **1** a person who is unable to stop taking narcotic drugs **2** *informal* a person who is devoted to something: *he's a telly addict* ▶ **HISTORY** Latin *addictus* given over > **addictive** *adj*

addicted *adj* **1** dependent on a narcotic drug **2** *informal* devoted to something: *I'm a news freak and addicted to CNN* > **addiction** *n*

addition *n* **1** the act of adding **2** a person or thing that is added **3** a mathematical operation in which the total of two or more numbers or quantities is calculated **4 in addition (to)**

besides; as well (as) > **additional** *adj* > **additionally** *adv*

additive *n* any substance added to something, such as food, to improve it or prevent deterioration

addled *adj* **1** confused or unable to think clearly **2** (of eggs) rotten ▶ **HISTORY** Old English *adela* filth

add-on *n Brit, Austral & NZ* a feature that can be added to a standard model to give increased benefits

address *n* **1** the place at which someone lives **2** the conventional form by which the location of a building is described **3** a formal speech **4** *computers* a number giving the location of a piece of stored information ▷ *vb* **5** to mark (a letter or parcel) with an address **6** to speak to **7** to direct one's attention to (a problem or an issue) **8 address oneself to a** to speak or write to **b** to apply oneself to: *we have got to address ourselves properly to this problem* ▶ **HISTORY** Latin *ad-* to + *directus* direct

addressee *n* a person to whom a letter or parcel is addressed

adduce *vb* **-ducing, -duced** to mention something as evidence ▶ **HISTORY** Latin *adducere* to lead to

add up *vb* **1** to calculate the total of (two or more numbers or quantities) **2** *informal* to make sense: *there's something about it that doesn't add up* **3 add up to** to amount to

adenine *n anat* a purine base present in tissues of all living organisms

adenoidal *adj* having a nasal voice or impaired breathing because of enlarged adenoids

adenoids (**ad**-in-oidz) *pl n* a mass of tissue at the back of the throat ▶ **HISTORY** Greek *adenoeidēs* glandular

adept *adj* **1** proficient in something requiring skill ▷ *n* **2** a person skilled in something ▶ **HISTORY** Latin *adipisci* to attain > **adeptness** *n*

adequate *adj* just enough in amount or just good enough in quality ▶ **HISTORY** Latin *ad-* to + *aequus* equal > **adequacy** *n* > **adequately** *adv*

à deux (ah **duh**) *adj, adv* of or for two people ▶ **HISTORY** French

ADH *biochem* antidiuretic hormone

adhere *vb* **-hering, -hered** (foll. by *to*) **1** to stick to **2** to act according to (a rule or agreement) **3** to be a loyal supporter of (something) ▶ **HISTORY** Latin *adhaerere*

adherent *n* **1** a supporter or follower ▷ *adj* **2** sticking or attached > **adherence** *n*

adhesion *n* **1** the quality or condition of sticking together **2** *pathol* the joining together of two structures or parts of the body that are normally separate, for example after surgery

adhesive *n* **1** a substance used for sticking things together ▷ *adj* **2** able or designed to stick to things

ad hoc *adj, adv* for a particular purpose only ▶ **HISTORY** Latin: to this

adieu (a-**dew**) *interj, n, pl* **adieux** *or* **adieus** (a-**dewz**) goodbye ▶ **HISTORY** French

ad infinitum *adv* endlessly: *we would not be able to sustain the currency ad infinitum* ▶ **HISTORY** Latin

a

adipose *adj* of or containing fat; fatty: *adipose tissue* ▶ HISTORY Latin *adeps* fat

adj. adjective

adjacent *adj* **1** near or next: *the schools were adjacent but there were separate doors* **2** *geom* (of a side of a right-angled triangle) lying between a specified angle and the right angle ▶ HISTORY Latin *ad-* near + *jacere* to lie

adjacent angle *n geom* an angle which has the same vertex and one side in common with another

adjective *n* a word that adds information about a noun or pronoun ▶ HISTORY Latin *nomen adjectivum* attributive noun > **adjectival** *adj*

adjoin *vb* to be next to and joined onto > **adjoining** *adj*

adjourn *vb* **1** to close a court at the end of a session **2** to postpone or be postponed temporarily **3** *informal* to go elsewhere: *can we adjourn to the dining room?* ▶ HISTORY Old French *ajourner* to defer to an arranged day > **adjournment** *n*

adjudge *vb* **-judging, -judged** to declare someone to be something specified: *my wife was adjudged to be the guilty party*

adjudicate *vb* **-cating, -cated** **1** to give a formal decision on a dispute **2** to serve as a judge, for example in a competition ▶ HISTORY Latin *adjudicare* > **adjudication** *n* > **adjudicator** *n*

adjunct *n* **1** something added that is not essential **2** a person who is subordinate to another ▶ HISTORY Latin *adjunctus* adjoined

adjure *vb* **-juring, -jured** **1** to command someone to do something **2** to appeal earnestly to someone ▶ HISTORY Latin *adjurare* > **adjuration** *n*

adjust *vb* **1** to adapt to a new environment **2** to alter slightly, so as to be accurate or suitable **3** *insurance* to determine the amount payable in settlement of a claim ▶ HISTORY Old French *adjuster* > **adjustable** *adj* > **adjuster** *n*

adjustment *n* **1** a slight alteration **2** the act of adjusting

adjutant (**aj**-oo-tant) *n* an officer in an army who acts as administrative assistant to a superior ▶ HISTORY Latin *adjutare* to aid

ad-lib *vb* **-libbing, -libbed** **1** to improvise a speech or piece of music without preparation ▷ *adj* **2** improvised: *ad-lib studio chat* ▷ *n* **3** an improvised remark ▷ *adv* **ad lib** **4** spontaneously or freely ▶ HISTORY short for Latin *ad libitum*, literally: according to pleasure

Adm. *Brit* Admiral

adman *n*, *pl* **-men** *informal* a man who works in advertising

admin *n informal* administration

administer *vb* **1** to manage (an organization or estate) **2** to organize and put into practice: *anyone can learn to administer the test procedure* **3** to give medicine to someone **4** to supervise the taking of (an oath) ▶ HISTORY Latin *administrare*

administrate *vb* **-trating, -trated** to manage an organization

administration *n* **1** management of the affairs of an organization **2** the people who administer an organization **3** a government: *the first non-communist administration in the country's history* **4** the act of administering something, such as medicine or an oath > **administrative** *adj*

administrative law *n law* the branch of law concerned with the duties and powers of administrative authorities

administrative review *n law* an examination carried out by a competent body to ascertain whether correct procedures have been followed or appropriate measures taken. Compare **judicial review**

administrator *n* a person who administers an organization or estate

admirable (**ad**-mer-a-bl) *adj* deserving or inspiring admiration: *the boldness of the undertaking is admirable* > **admirably** *adv*

admiral *n* **1** Also called: **admiral of the fleet** a naval officer of the highest rank **2** any of various brightly coloured butterflies ▶ HISTORY Arabic *amīr-al* commander of

Admiralty *n Brit* the former government department in charge of the Royal Navy

admire *vb* **-miring, -mired** to respect and approve of (a person or thing) ▶ HISTORY Latin *admirari* to wonder at > **admiration** *n* > **admirer** *n* > **admiring** *adj* > **admiringly** *adv*

admissible *adj law* allowed to be brought as evidence in court

admission *n* **1** permission or the right to enter **2** permission to join an organization **3** the price charged for entrance **4** a confession: *she was, by her own admission, not educated*

admit *vb* **-mitting, -mitted** **1** to confess or acknowledge (a crime or mistake) **2** to concede (the truth of something) **3** to allow (someone) to enter **4** to take (someone) in to a hospital for treatment: *he was admitted for tests* **5** **admit someone to** to allow someone to participate in something **6** **admit of** to allow for: *these rules admit of no violation* ▶ HISTORY Latin *admittere*

admittance *n* **1** the right to enter **2** the act of entering a place

admittedly *adv* it must be agreed: *my research is admittedly incomplete*

admixture *n* **1** a mixture **2** an ingredient

admonish *vb* to reprimand sternly ▶ HISTORY Latin *admonere* > **admonition** *n* > **admonitory** *adj*

ad nauseam (ad **naw**-zee-am) *adv* to a boring or sickening extent: *she went on and on ad nauseam about her divorce* ▶ HISTORY Latin: to (the point of) nausea

ado *n* fuss: *without further ado* ▶ HISTORY Middle English *at do* a to-do

adobe (ad-**oh**-bee) *n* **1** a sun-dried brick **2** the claylike material from which such bricks are made **3** a building made of such bricks ▶ HISTORY Spanish

adolescence *n* the period between puberty and adulthood ▶ HISTORY Latin *adolescere* to grow up

adolescent *adj* **1** of or relating to adolescence **2** *informal* (of behaviour) immature ▷ *n* **3** an adolescent person

Adonis n a handsome young man ▶ HISTORY name of a handsome youth in Greek myth

adopt vb 1 law to make someone else's child legally one's own 2 to choose (a plan or method) 3 to choose (a country or name) to be one's own ▶ HISTORY Latin adoptare > **adoptee** n

adoption n 1 law the act of making (someone else's child) legally one's own 2 the choosing (of a plan or method) 3 the choosing (of a country or name)

adoptive adj 1 acquired or related by adoption: an adoptive father 2 of or relating to adoption

adorable adj very attractive; lovable

adore vb **adoring, adored** 1 to love intensely or deeply 2 informal to like very much: I adore being in the country 3 to worship a god with religious rites ▶ HISTORY Latin adorare > **adoration** n > **adoring** adj > **adoringly** adv

adorn vb to decorate; increase the beauty of ▶ HISTORY Latin adornare > **adornment** n

ADP automatic data processing

adrenal (ad-**reen**-al) adj anat 1 on or near the kidneys 2 of or relating to the adrenal glands ▶ HISTORY Latin ad- near + renes kidneys

adrenal glands pl n anat two endocrine glands covering the upper surface of the kidneys

adrenalin or **adrenaline** n biochem a hormone secreted by the adrenal gland in response to stress. It increases heart rate, pulse rate, and blood pressure

adrift adj, adv 1 drifting 2 without a clear purpose 3 informal off course, wrong: it was obvious that something had gone adrift

adroit adj quick and skilful in how one behaves or thinks ▶ HISTORY French à droit rightly > **adroitly** adv > **adroitness** n

adsorb vb (of a gas or vapour) to condense and form a thin film on a surface ▶ HISTORY Latin ad- to + sorbere to drink in > **adsorbent** adj > **adsorption** n

adulation n uncritical admiration ▶ HISTORY Latin adulari to flatter

adult n 1 a mature fully grown person, animal, or plant ▷ adj 2 having reached maturity; fully developed 3 suitable for or typical of adult people: she had very adult features ▶ HISTORY Latin adultus grown up > **adulthood** n

adulterate vb **-ating, -ated** to spoil something by adding inferior material ▶ HISTORY Latin adulterare > **adulteration** n

adulterer or fem **adulteress** n a person who has committed adultery

adultery n, pl **-teries** sexual unfaithfulness of a husband or wife ▶ HISTORY Latin adulterium > **adulterous** adj

adv. adverb

advance vb **-vancing, -vanced** 1 to go or bring forward 2 to make progress: this student has advanced in reading and writing 3 to further a cause: an association founded to advance the interests of ex-soldiers 4 **advance on** to move towards someone in a threatening manner 5 to present an idea for consideration 6 to lend a sum of money ▷ n 7 a forward movement 8 improvement or progress: the greatest advance in modern medicine 9 a loan of money 10 a payment made before it is legally due 11 an increase in price: any advance on fifty pounds? 12 **in advance** beforehand: you have to pay in advance 13 **in advance of** ahead of in time or development ▷ adj 14 done or happening before an event: advance warning ▷ See also **advances** ▶ HISTORY Latin abante from before

advanced adj 1 at a late stage in development 2 not elementary: he was taking the advanced class in economics

advance directive n chiefly Brit same as **living will**

Advanced level n Brit a formal name for **A level**

advancement n promotion in rank or status

advances pl n approaches made to a person with the hope of starting a romantic relationship

advantage n 1 a more favourable position or state 2 benefit or profit: they could make this work to their advantage 3 tennis the point scored after deuce 4 **take advantage of a** to use a person unfairly **b** to use an opportunity 5 **to advantage** to good effect: her hair was shaped to display to advantage her superb neck ▶ HISTORY Latin abante from before

advantaged adj in a superior social or financial position

advantageous adj likely to bring benefits > **advantageously** adv

advection n physics the transferring of heat in a horizontal stream of gas ▶ HISTORY Latin ad- to + vehere to carry

advent n an arrival: the advent of the personal computer ▶ HISTORY Latin ad- to + venire to come

Advent n the season that includes the four Sundays before Christmas

Adventist n a member of a Christian group that believes in the imminent return of Christ

adventitious adj 1 added or appearing accidentally 2 biol (of a plant or animal part) developing in an abnormal position ▶ HISTORY Latin adventicius coming from outside

adventure n 1 a risky undertaking, the ending of which is uncertain: our African adventure 2 exciting or unexpected events ▶ HISTORY Latin advenire to happen to (someone), arrive

adventure playground n Brit, Austral & NZ a playground for children that contains building materials and other equipment to build with or climb on

adventurer or fem **adventuress** n 1 a person who seeks money or power by unscrupulous means 2 a person who seeks adventure

adventurous adj daring or enterprising

adverb n a word that modifies a sentence, verb, adverb, or adjective, for example easily, very, and happily in They could easily envy the very happily married couple ▶ HISTORY Latin adverbium, literally: added word > **adverbial** adj

adversarial system or **adversary system** n law a legal system in which opposing advocates

adversary — aesthete

use their skills to present the case for the party they represent and a judge or magistrate acts as an impartial referee; usual in countries where the legal system is based on common law. Compare **inquisitorial system**

adversary (**ad**-verse-er-ree) *n, pl* **-saries** an opponent in a fight, disagreement, or sporting contest ▶ HISTORY Latin *adversus* against

adverse *adj* **1** unfavourable to one's interests: *adverse effects* **2** antagonistic or hostile ▶ HISTORY Latin *ad-* towards + *vertere* to turn > **adversely** *adv*

adversity *n, pl* **-ties** very difficult or hard circumstances

advert *n informal* an advertisement

advertise *vb* **-tising, -tised 1** to present or praise (goods or a service) to the public, in order to encourage sales **2** to make (a vacancy, an event, or an article for sale) publicly known ▶ HISTORY Latin *advertere* to turn one's attention to > **advertiser** *n* > **advertising** *n*

advertisement *n written* any public announcement designed to sell goods or publicize an event

advertising agency *n marketing* an organization that creates advertising material, finds space to advertise, and does market research for its clients

advertorial *n* advertising presented as if it is editorial material ▶ HISTORY ADVERT + (EDIT)ORIAL

advice *n* **1** recommendation as to an appropriate course of action **2** formal notification of facts ▶ HISTORY Latin *ad* to + *visum* view

advisable *adj* sensible and likely to achieve the desired result > **advisability** *n*

advise *vb* **-vising, -vised 1** to offer advice to **2** to inform or notify ▶ HISTORY Latin *ad-* to + *videre* to see > **adviser** or **advisor** *n*

advised *adj* thought-out: *ill-advised*

advisedly (ad-**vize**-id-lee) *adv* deliberately; after careful consideration: *I use the word advisedly*

advisory *adj* **1** able to offer advice ▷ *n, pl* **-ries 2** a statement giving advice or a warning **3** a person or organization that gives advice: *the Prime Minister's media advisory*

advocaat *n* a liqueur with a raw egg base ▶ HISTORY Dutch

advocacy *n* active support of a cause or course of action

advocate *vb* **-cating, -cated 1** to recommend a course of action publicly ▷ *n* **2** a person who upholds or defends a cause or course of action **3** a person who speaks on behalf of another in a court of law **4** *Scots Law* a barrister ▶ HISTORY Latin *advocare* to call, summon

adze or US **adz** *n* a tool with a blade at right angles to the handle, used for shaping timber ▶ HISTORY Old English *adesa*

AEEU (in Britain) Amalgamated Engineering and Electrical Union

aegis (**ee**-jiss) *n* **under the aegis of** with the sponsorship or protection of ▶ HISTORY Greek *aigis* shield of Zeus

aeolian (ee-oh-lee-an) *adj* of or relating to the wind; produced or carried by the wind ▶ HISTORY after *Aeolus*, god of winds in Greek myth

aeolian deposits *pl n geol* sediments that have been carried and left by the wind

aeolian erosion *n geol* erosion caused by the action of the wind

aeolian harp *n* a musical instrument that produces sounds when the wind passes over its strings ▶ HISTORY after *Aeolus*, god of winds in Greek myth

aeon or US **eon** (**ee**-on) *n* **1** an immeasurably long period of time **2** the longest division of geological time ▶ HISTORY Greek *aiōn*

aerate *vb* **-ating, -ated** to put gas into a liquid, for example when making a fizzy drink > **aeration** *n*

aerial *n* **1** the metal pole or wire on a television or radio which transmits or receives signals ▷ *adj* **2** in, from, or operating in the air **3** extending high into the air **4** of or relating to aircraft ▶ HISTORY Greek *aēr* air

aerial top dressing *n NZ* spreading of fertilizer from an aeroplane onto remote areas

aero-, aeri- or **aer-** *combining form* **1** relating to aircraft **2** relating to air, atmosphere, or gas ▶ HISTORY Greek *aēr* air

aerobatics *n* spectacular manoeuvres, such as loops or rolls, performed by aircraft ▶ HISTORY AERO- + (ACRO)BATICS

aerobe *n biol* an organism that requires oxygen to survive ▶ HISTORY Greek *aēr* air + *bios* life

aerobic *adj* designed for or relating to aerobics: *aerobic exercise*

aerobic respiration *n biol* the process by which cells convert glucose to carbon dioxide and water

aerobics *n* exercises to increase the amount of oxygen in the blood and strengthen the heart and lungs

aerodrome *n* a small airport

aerodynamics *n* the study of how air flows around moving objects > **aerodynamic** *adj* > **aerodynamicist** *n*

aero engine *n* an engine for an aircraft

aerofoil *n* a part of an aircraft, such as the wing, designed to give lift in flight

aerogram *n* an airmail letter on a single sheet of light paper that seals to form an envelope

aeronautics *n* the study or practice of flight through the air > **aeronautical** *adj*

aeroplane or US & Canad **airplane** *n* a heavier-than-air powered flying vehicle with fixed wings ▶ HISTORY AERO- + Greek *planos* wandering

aerosol *n* a small metal pressurized can from which a substance can be dispensed in a fine spray ▶ HISTORY AERO- + SOL(UTION)

aerospace *n* **1** the earth's atmosphere and space beyond ▷ *adj* **2** of rockets or space vehicles: *the aerospace industry*

aesthete or US **esthete** (**eess**-theet) *n* a person who has or who pretends to have a highly developed appreciation of beauty

12

aesthetic *or US* **esthetic** (iss-**thet**-ik) *adj*
1 relating to the appreciation of art and beauty
▷ *n* **2** a principle or set of principles relating to the appreciation of art and beauty ▸ **HISTORY** Greek *aisthanomai* to perceive, feel > **aesthetically** *or US* **esthetically** *adv* > **aestheticism** *or US* **estheticism** *n*

aesthetics *or US* **esthetics** *n* **1** the branch of philosophy concerned with the study of the concepts of beauty and taste **2** the study of the rules and principles of art

aestivate *or US* **estivate** *biol vb* **1** to pass the summer **2** to pass the summer or the dry season in a dormant condition > **aestivation** *or* **estivation** *n*

aether *n* same as **ether** (senses 2, 3)

aetiology (ee-tee-ol-a-jee) *n* same as **etiology**

a.f. audio frequency

afar *n* **from afar** from or at a great distance

affable *adj* showing warmth and friendliness
▸ **HISTORY** Latin *affabilis* > **affability** *n* > **affably** *adv*

affair *n* **1** an event or happening: *the Irangate affair* **2** a romantic relationship outside marriage **3** a thing to be done or attended to: *my wife's career is her own affair* **4** something previously specified: *lunch was a subdued affair* ▸ **HISTORY** Old French *à faire* to do

affairs *pl n* **1** personal or business interests **2** matters of public interest: *foreign affairs*

affect¹ *vb* **1** to influence (someone or something): *the very difficult conditions continued to affect our performance* **2** (of pain or disease) to attack: *the virus can spread to affect the heart muscle* **3** to move someone emotionally: *the experience has affected him deeply* ▸ **HISTORY** Latin *afficere*

affect² *vb* **1** to put on a show of: *he affects a certain disinterest* **2** to wear or use by preference: *he likes to be called Captain John and affects a nautical cap* ▸ **HISTORY** Latin *affectare* to strive after

affectation *n* an attitude or manner put on to impress others

affected *adj* **1** behaving or speaking in a manner put on to impress others **2** pretended: *an affected indifference*

affection *n* **1** fondness or tenderness for a person or thing **2** **affections** feelings of love; emotions: *I was angry with her for playing with their affections*

affectionate *adj* having or displaying tenderness, affection, or warmth > **affectionately** *adv*

affianced (af-**fie**-anst) *adj* old-fashioned engaged to be married ▸ **HISTORY** Medieval Latin *affidare* to trust (oneself) to

affidavit (af-fid-**dave**-it) *n law* a written statement made under oath ▸ **HISTORY** Medieval Latin, literally: he declares on oath

affiliate *vb* **-ating, -ated** **1** (of a group) to link up with a larger group ▷ *n* **2** a person or organization that is affiliated with another ▸ **HISTORY** Medieval Latin *affiliatus* adopted as a son > **affiliation** *n*

affiliation order *n Brit law* an order that the father of an illegitimate child must contribute towards the child's maintenance

affinity *n, pl* **-ties** **1** a feeling of closeness to and understanding of a person **2** a close similarity in appearance, structure, or quality **3** a chemical attraction ▸ **HISTORY** Latin *affinis* bordering on, related

affinity card *n Brit* a credit card linked to a charity or organization which receives a donation each time the card is used

affirm *vb* **1** to declare to be true **2** to state clearly one's support for (an idea or belief) ▸ **HISTORY** Latin *ad-* to + *firmare* to make firm > **affirmation** *n*

affirmative *adj* **1** indicating agreement: *an affirmative answer* ▷ *n* **2** a word or phrase indicating agreement, such as *yes*

affix *vb* **1** to attach or fasten ▷ *n* **2** a word or syllable added to a word to produce a derived or inflected form, such as *-ment* in *establishment* ▸ **HISTORY** Medieval Latin *affixare*

afflict *vb* to cause someone suffering or unhappiness ▸ **HISTORY** Latin *affligere* to knock against

affliction *n* **1** something that causes physical or mental suffering **2** a condition of great distress or suffering

affluent *adj* having plenty of money ▸ **HISTORY** Latin *ad-* to + *fluere* to flow > **affluence** *n*

affluent society *n* a society in which the material benefits of prosperity are widely available

afford *vb* **1 can afford** to be able to do or spare something without risking financial difficulties or undesirable consequences: *she can't afford to be choosy* **2** to give or supply: *afford me an opportunity to judge for myself* ▸ **HISTORY** Old English *geforthian* to further, promote > **affordable** *adj* > **affordability** *n*

afforest *vb* to plant trees on ▸ **HISTORY** Medieval Latin *afforestare*

afforestation *n geog* the creation of forests by planting trees

affray *n Brit, Austral & NZ* a noisy fight in a public place ▸ **HISTORY** Vulgar Latin *exfridare* (unattested) to break the peace

affront *n* **1** a deliberate insult ▷ *vb* **2** to hurt someone's pride or dignity ▸ **HISTORY** Old French *afronter* to strike in the face

afghan *n NZ* a type of biscuit

Afghan *adj* **1** of Afghanistan ▷ *n* **2** a person from Afghanistan **3** the language of Afghanistan

Afghan hound *n* a large slim dog with long silky hair

aficionado (af-fish-yo-**nah**-do) *n, pl* **-dos** an enthusiastic fan of a sport or interest ▸ **HISTORY** Spanish

afield *adv* **far afield** far away: *they used to travel as far afield as Hungary*

aflame *adv, adj* **1** in flames **2** deeply aroused: *his face was aflame with self-contempt and embarrassment*

afloat *adj, adv* **1** floating **2** free of debt: *his goal is to keep the company afloat* **3** aboard ship; at sea

afoot *adj, adv* happening; in operation: *I had no suspicion of what was afoot*

aforementioned *adj* mentioned before

aforesaid adj referred to previously

aforethought adj premeditated: malice aforethought

a fortiori (eh for-tee-or-rye) adv for similar but more convincing reasons ▶ HISTORY Latin

afraid adj 1 feeling fear or apprehension 2 spoken regretful: I'm afraid I lost my temper ▶ HISTORY Middle English affraied

afresh adv once more

African adj 1 of Africa ▷ n 2 a person from Africa

African-American n 1 an American of African descent ▷ adj 2 of African-Americans, their history, or their culture

Africander n a breed of humpbacked cattle originally from southern Africa ▶ HISTORY Afrikaans Afrikander

African time n S African, slang unpunctuality

African violet n a flowering house plant with pink or purple flowers and hairy leaves

Afrikaans n one of the official languages of South Africa, descended from Dutch ▶ HISTORY Dutch

Afrikaner n a White South African whose native language is Afrikaans

Afro- combining form indicating Africa or African: Afro-Caribbean

Afro-American n, adj same as **African-American**

aft adv, adj at or towards the rear of a ship or aircraft ▶ HISTORY shortened from ABAFT

after prep 1 following in time or place 2 in pursuit of: he was after my mother's jewellery 3 concerning: he asked after Laura 4 considering: you seem all right after what happened last night 5 next in excellence or importance to 6 in imitation of; in the manner of 7 in accordance with: a man after his own heart 8 with the same name as: the street is named after the designer of the church 9 US past (the hour of): fifteen after twelve 10 **after all** a in spite of everything: I was, after all, a suspect b in spite of expectations or efforts 11 **after you** please go before me ▷ adv 12 at a later time; afterwards ▷ conj 13 at a time later than the time when: she arrived after the reading had begun ▷ adj 14 naut further aft: the after cabin ▶ HISTORY Old English æfter

afterbirth n the placenta and fetal membranes expelled from the mother's womb after childbirth

aftercare n 1 the help and support given to a person discharged from a hospital or prison 2 the regular care required to keep something in good condition

afterdamp n a poisonous gas formed after the explosion of firedamp in a coal mine

aftereffect n any result occurring some time after its cause

afterglow n 1 the glow left after the source of a light has disappeared, for example after sunset 2 a pleasant feeling remaining after an enjoyable experience

afterlife n life after death

aftermath n effects or results of an event considered collectively: the aftermath of the weekend violence ▶ HISTORY after + Old English mæth a mowing

afternoon n the period between noon and evening

afterpains pl n pains caused by contraction of a woman's womb after childbirth

afters n informal the sweet course of a meal

aftershave n a scented lotion applied to a man's face after shaving

aftershock n one of a series of minor tremors occurring after the main shock of an earthquake

afterthought n 1 something thought of after the opportunity to use it has passed 2 an addition to something already completed

afterwards or **afterward** adv later ▶ HISTORY Old English æfterweard

Ag chem silver ▶ HISTORY Latin argentum

again adv 1 another or a second time: I want to look at that atlas again 2 once more in a previously experienced state or condition: he pictured her again as she used to be 3 in addition to the original amount: twice as much again 4 on the other hand 5 moreover or furthermore: she is beautiful and, again, intelligent 6 **again and again** continually or repeatedly ▶ HISTORY Old English ongegn opposite to

against prep 1 standing or leaning beside: he leaned against a tree 2 opposed to or in disagreement with 3 in contrast to: his complexion was a sickly white against the black stubble of his beard 4 coming in contact with: rain rattled against the window 5 having an unfavourable effect on: the system works against you when you don't have money 6 as a protection from: a safeguard against bacteria 7 in exchange for or in return for: the dollar has gained very slightly against the yen 8 **as against** as opposed to; as compared with ▶ HISTORY Middle English ageines

agape adj written 1 (of the mouth) wide open 2 (of a person) very surprised

agar (ayg-ar) or **agar-agar** n a jelly-like substance made from seaweed, used for growing cultures in biological experiments ▶ HISTORY Malay

agaric n any fungus with gills on the underside of the cap, such as a mushroom ▶ HISTORY Greek agarikon

agate (ag-git) n a hard semiprecious form of quartz with striped colouring ▶ HISTORY Greek akhatēs

agave (a-gave-vee) n a tropical American plant with tall flower stalks and thick leaves ▶ HISTORY Greek agauos illustrious

age n 1 the length of time that a person or thing has existed 2 a period or state of human life 3 the latter part of human life 4 a period of history marked by some feature 5 **ages** informal a long time 6 **come of age** to become legally responsible for one's actions (usually at 18 years) ▷ vb **ageing** or **aging, aged** 7 to become old: skin type changes *as one ages* **8** to appear or cause to appear older: *the years had not aged her in any way* ▶ **HISTORY** Latin *aetas*

aged *adj* **1** (**ay**-jid) advanced in years; old **2** (rhymes with **raged**) being at the age of: *a girl aged thirteen is missing*

ageing *or* **aging** *n* **1** the fact or process of growing old ▷ *adj* **2** becoming or appearing older

ageism *or* **agism** *n* discrimination against people on the grounds of age > **ageist** *or* **agist** *n*

ageless *adj* **1** apparently never growing old **2** seeming to have existed for ever; eternal: *an ageless profession*

agency *n, pl* **-cies** **1** an organization providing a specific service: *an advertising agency* **2** the business or functions of an agent **3** action or power by which something happens: *the intervention of a human agency in the sequence of events* ▶ **HISTORY** Latin *agere* to do

agenda *n* a schedule or list of items to be attended to, for example at a meeting ▶ **HISTORY** Latin: things to be done

agent *n* **1** a person who arranges business for other people, esp. for actors or singers **2** a spy **3** a substance which causes change in other substances: *an emulsifying agent* **4** someone or something which causes an effect: *the agent of change*

agent provocateur (azh-on prov-vok-at-**tur**) *n, pl* **agents provocateurs** (azh-on prov-vok-at-**tur**) a person employed by the authorities to tempt people to commit illegal acts and so be discredited or punished ▶ **HISTORY** French

age-old *adj written* very old; ancient

agglomerate *vb* **-ating, -ated** **1** to form or be formed into a mass ▷ *n* **2** a volcanic rock consisting of fused angular fragments of rock ▶ **HISTORY** Latin *agglomerare*

agglomeration *n* a confused mass or cluster

agglutinate *vb* **-nating, -nated** to stick as if with glue ▶ **HISTORY** Latin *agglutinare* > **agglutination** *n*

aggradation *n geol* the building up of the level of a land surface as a result of the deposition of sediment. Compare **degradation**

aggrandize *or* **-dise** *vb* **-dizing, -dized** *or* **-dising, -dised** to make greater in size, power, or rank ▶ **HISTORY** Old French *aggrandir* > **aggrandizement** *or* **-disement** *n*

aggravate *vb* **-vating, -vated** **1** to make (a disease, situation or problem) worse **2** *informal* to annoy ▶ **HISTORY** Latin *aggravare* to make heavier > **aggravating** *adj* > **aggravation** *n*

aggregate *n* **1** an amount or total formed from separate units **2** *geol* a rock, such as granite, consisting of a mixture of minerals **3** the sand and stone mixed with cement and water to make concrete ▷ *adj* **4** formed of separate units collected into a whole ▷ *vb* **-gating, -gated** **5** to combine or be combined into a whole **6** to amount to (a particular number) ▶ **HISTORY** Latin *aggregare* to add to a flock or herd > **aggregation** *n*

aggression *n* **1** violent and hostile behaviour **2** an unprovoked attack ▶ **HISTORY** Latin *aggredi* to attack > **aggressor** *n*

aggressive *adj* **1** full of anger or hostility **2** forceful or determined: *an aggressive salesman* > **aggressively** *adv* > **aggressiveness** *n*

aggrieved *adj* upset and angry ▶ **HISTORY** Latin *aggravare* to aggravate

aggro *n Brit, Austral & NZ, slang* aggressive behaviour ▶ **HISTORY** from *aggravation*

aghast *adj* overcome with amazement or horror ▶ **HISTORY** Old English *gæstan* to frighten

agile *adj* **1** quick in movement; nimble **2** mentally quick or acute ▶ **HISTORY** Latin *agilis* > **agility** *n*

agin *prep dialect* against or opposed to: *he gave the usual line of talk agin the government* ▶ **HISTORY** obsolete *again* against

agitate *vb* **-tating, -tated** **1** to excite, disturb, or trouble **2** to shake or stir (a liquid) **3** to attempt to stir up public opinion for or against something ▶ **HISTORY** Latin *agitare* > **agitated** *adj* > **agitatedly** *adv* > **agitation** *n* > **agitator** *n*

agitprop *n* political agitation and propaganda ▶ **HISTORY** Russian *Agitpropbyuro*

aglitter *adj* sparkling or glittering

aglow *adj* glowing

AGM annual general meeting

agnostic *n* **1** a person who believes that it is impossible to know whether God exists **2** a person who claims that the answer to some specific question cannot be known with certainty ▷ *adj* **3** of or relating to agnostics ▶ **HISTORY** A- + *gnostic* having knowledge > **agnosticism** *n*

ago *adv* in the past: *fifty years ago* ▶ **HISTORY** Old English *āgān* to pass away

agog *adj* eager or curious: *Marcia would be agog to hear his news* ▶ **HISTORY** Old French *en gogues* in merriments

agonic line *n geog* an imaginary line round the earth that passes through both magnetic north and true north, so that at any point along the line the compass points to both

agonize *or* **-nise** *vb* **-nizing, -nized** *or* **-nising, -nised** **1** to worry greatly **2** to suffer agony > **agonizing** *or* **-nising** *adj* > **agonizingly** *or* **-nisingly** *adv*

agony *n, pl* **-nies** acute physical or mental pain ▶ **HISTORY** Greek *agōnia* struggle

agony aunt *n* a person who replies to readers' letters in an agony column

agony column *n* a newspaper or magazine feature offering advice on readers' personal problems

agoraphobia *n* a pathological fear of being in public places ▶ **HISTORY** Greek *agora* marketplace + *phobos* fear > **agoraphobic** *adj, n*

AGR advanced gas-cooled reactor

agrarian *adj* of or relating to land or agriculture ▶ **HISTORY** Latin *ager* field > **agrarianism** *n*

Agrarian Reform Law *n history* a measure implemented by the Chinese People's Republic in 1950 to redistribute landed property

15

a

agree *vb* **agreeing, agreed 1** to be of the same opinion **2** to give assent; consent **3** to reach a joint decision: *the ministers agreed on a strategy* **4** to be consistent **5 agree with** to be agreeable or suitable to (one's health or appearance): *marriage and motherhood must agree with you* **6** to concede: *the unions have agreed that the results of appraisal are relevant* **7** *grammar* to be the same in number, gender, and case as a connected word ► HISTORY Old French *a gre* at will

agreeable *adj* **1** pleasant and enjoyable **2** prepared to consent: *I cannot say that she was agreeable to the project but she was resigned* > **agreeably** *adv*

agreement *n* **1** the act or state of agreeing **2** a legally enforceable contract

agribusiness *n* **1** the use of intensive methods to increase profits in agriculture **2** all of the businesses that process, distribute, and support farm products ► HISTORY *agri(culture)* + *business*

agriculture *n* the rearing of crops and livestock; farming ► HISTORY Latin *ager* field + *cultura* cultivation > **agricultural** *adj* > **agriculturalist** *n*

agrimony *n* a plant with small yellow flowers and bitter-tasting bristly fruits ► HISTORY Greek *argemōnē* poppy

agrochemical *n* a chemical used in agriculture

agronomy (ag-**ron**-om-mee) *n* the science of land cultivation, soil management, and crop production ► HISTORY Greek *agros* field + *nemein* to manage > **agronomist** *n*

agro-processing *n* the treatment of raw materials produced by agriculture

aground *adv* onto the bottom of shallow water: *they felt a jolt as the ship ran aground*

ague (**aig**-yew) *n* **1** *old-fashioned* malarial fever with shivering **2** a fit of shivering ► HISTORY Old French *(fievre) ague* acute fever

ah *interj* an exclamation expressing pleasure, pain, sympathy, etc.

aha *interj* an exclamation expressing triumph, surprise, etc.

ahead *adv* **1** at or in the front; before **2** forwards: *go straight ahead* **3 get ahead** to achieve success: *I was young and hungry to get ahead* ⊳ *adj* **4** in a leading position: *he is ahead in the polls*

ahem *interj* a clearing of the throat, used to attract attention or express doubt

ahoy *interj* *naut* a shout made to call a ship or to attract attention

AI 1 artificial insemination **2** artificial intelligence

aid *n* **1** money, equipment, or services provided for people in need; assistance **2** a person or device that helps or assists ⊳ *vb* **3** to help financially or in other ways ► HISTORY Latin *adjutare* to help

Aid *or* **-aid** *n combining form* denoting a charitable organization that raises money for a particular cause: *WaterAid*

AID (formerly) artificial insemination by donor

aide *n* an assistant: *a senior aide to the Prime Minister*

aide-de-camp (aid-de-kom) *n, pl* **aides-de-camp** (aid-de-kom) a military officer serving as personal assistant to a senior ► HISTORY French: camp assistant

AIDS acquired immunodeficiency syndrome: a viral disease that destroys the body's ability to fight infection

AIH artificial insemination by husband

ail *vb literary* **1** to trouble or afflict **2** to feel unwell ► HISTORY Old English *eglan*

aileron (**ale**-er-on) *n* a hinged flap on the back of an aircraft wing which controls rolling ► HISTORY French *aile* wing

ailing *adj* unwell or unsuccessful over a long period: *an ailing company*

ailment *n* a slight illness

aim *vb* **1** to point (a weapon or missile) or direct (a blow or remark) at a particular person or object **2** to propose or intend: *they aim to provide full and equal rights to all groups* ⊳ *n* **3** the action of directing something at an object **4** intention or purpose **5 take aim** to point a weapon or missile at a person or object ► HISTORY Latin *aestimare* to estimate

aimless *adj* having no purpose or direction > **aimlessly** *adv*

ain't *not standard, spoken* am not, is not, are not, have not, *or* has not: *it ain't fair*

air *n* **1** the mixture of gases that forms the earth's atmosphere. It consists chiefly of nitrogen, oxygen, argon, and carbon dioxide **2** the space above and around the earth; sky. *Related adjective:* **aerial 3** a distinctive quality, appearance, or manner: *I thought he had an air of elegance and celebrity about him* **4** a simple tune **5** transportation in aircraft: *I went off to Italy by air and train* **6 in the air** in circulation; current: *a sense of expectation is in the air* **7 into thin air** leaving no trace behind **8 on the air** in the act of broadcasting on radio or television **9 up in the air** uncertain ⊳ *vb* **10** to make known publicly: *these issues will be aired at a ministerial meeting* **11** to expose to air to dry or ventilate **12** (of a television or radio programme) to be broadcast ⊳ See also **airs** ► HISTORY Greek *aēr*

air bag *n* a safety device in a car, consisting of a bag that inflates automatically in an accident to protect the driver or passenger

air base *n* a centre from which military aircraft operate

airborne *adj* **1** carried by air **2** (of aircraft) flying; in the air

air brake *n* a brake in heavy vehicles that is operated by compressed air

airbrush *n* **1** an atomizer which sprays paint by means of compressed air ⊳ *vb* **2** to paint using an airbrush **3** to improve the image of (a person or thing) by hiding defects beneath a bland exterior

air chief marshal *n* a very senior officer in an air force

air commodore *n* a senior officer in an air force

air conditioning *n* a system for controlling the temperature and humidity of the air in a building > **air-conditioned** *adj* > **air conditioner** *n*

aircraft *n, pl* **-craft** any machine capable of flying, such as a glider or aeroplane

aircraft carrier *n* a warship with a long flat deck for the launching and landing of aircraft

aircraftman *n, pl* **-men** a serviceman of the most junior rank in an air force > **aircraftwoman** *fem n*

air cushion *n* **1** an inflatable cushion **2** the pocket of air that supports a hovercraft

Airedale *n* a large terrier with rough tan-coloured hair and a black patch covering most of the back

airfield *n* a place where aircraft can land and take off

air force *n* the branch of a nation's armed services that is responsible for air warfare

air gun *n* a gun fired by means of compressed air

airhead *n slang* a person who is stupid or incapable of serious thought

air hostess *n old-fashioned, chiefly Brit* a female flight attendant on an airline

airily *adv* in a light-hearted and casual manner

airing *n* **1** exposure to air or warmth for drying or ventilation **2** exposure to public debate: *both these notions got an airing during the campaign*

airless *adj* lacking fresh air; stuffy

airlift *n* **1** the transportation by air of troops or cargo when other routes are blocked ▷ *vb* **2** to transport by an airlift

airline *n* an organization that provides scheduled flights for passengers or cargo

airliner *n* a large passenger aircraft

airlock *n* **1** a bubble of air blocking the flow of liquid in a pipe **2** an airtight chamber between places that do not have the same air pressure, such as in a spacecraft or submarine

airmail *n* **1** the system of sending mail by aircraft **2** mail sent by aircraft

airman *or fem* **airwoman** *n, pl* **-men** *or* **-women** a person serving in an air force

air marshal *n* **1** a senior Royal Air Force officer of equivalent rank to a vice admiral in the Royal Navy **2** a Royal New Zealand Air Force officer of the highest rank when chief of defence forces

air mass *n meteorol* a large body of air whose temperature, pressure, and moisture content remain relatively uniform at the same altitude

Air Miles *pl n Brit* points awarded on buying flight tickets and certain other products which can be used to pay for other flights

airplane *n US & Canad* an aeroplane

airplay *n* the broadcast performances of a record on radio

air pocket *n* a small descending air current that causes an aircraft to lose height suddenly

air pollution *n environmental science* contamination of the air by poisonous or harmful substances

airport *n* a landing and taking-off area for civil aircraft, with facilities for aircraft maintenance and passenger arrival and departure

air pressure *n physics* the force exerted on the earth by the air

air pump *n* a device for pumping air into or out of something

air quality *n environmental science* a measurement of the amount of air pollution

air raid *n* an attack by enemy aircraft in which bombs are dropped

air resistance *n aeronautics* the force produced by the air when an object is moving through it. Also called: **drag**

airs *pl n* manners put on to impress people: *we're poor and we never put on airs*

airship *n* a lighter-than-air self-propelled aircraft

airsick *adj* nauseated from travelling in an aircraft

airside *n* the part of an airport nearest the aircraft

airspace *n* the atmosphere above a particular country, regarded as its territory

airspeed *n* the speed of an aircraft relative to the air in which it moves

airstrip *n* a cleared area for the landing and taking-off of aircraft

air terminal *n* a building in a city from which air passengers are transported to an airport

airtight *adj* **1** sealed so that air cannot enter **2** having no weak points: *your reasoning is airtight and your evidence sound*

airtime *n* the time allocated to a particular programme, topic, or type of material on radio or television

air vice-marshal *n* a senior officer in an air force

airwaves *pl n informal* radio waves used in radio and television broadcasting

airway *n* an air route used regularly by aircraft

airworthy *adj* (of an aircraft) safe to fly > **airworthiness** *n*

airy *adj* **airier, airiest** **1** spacious and well ventilated **2** light-hearted and casual **3** having little basis in reality; fanciful: *airy assurances*

aisle (rhymes with **mile**) *n* a passageway separating seating areas in a church, theatre, or cinema, or separating rows of shelves in a supermarket ▶ HISTORY Latin *ala* wing

aitchbone *n* a cut of beef from the rump bone ▶ HISTORY Middle English *nache-bone*

ajar *adj, adv* (of a door) slightly open ▶ HISTORY Old English *cierran* to turn

AK Alaska

akimbo *adv* **(with) arms akimbo** with hands on hips and elbows turned outwards ▶ HISTORY Middle English *in kenebowe* in keen (i.e. sharp) bow

akin *adj* **akin to** similar or very close to: *the technique is akin to impressionist painting*

Al *chem* aluminium

AL Alabama

à la *prep* in the manner or style of: *laced with Gothic allusion à la David Lynch* ▶ HISTORY French

alabaster *n* a kind of white stone used for making statues and vases ▶ HISTORY Greek *alabastros*

à la carte *adj, adv* (of a menu) having dishes individually priced ▶ HISTORY French

alacrity *n* speed or eagerness: *I accepted the invitation with alacrity* ▶ HISTORY Latin *alacer* lively

à la mode *adj* fashionable ▶ HISTORY French

alarm *n* **1** fear aroused by awareness of danger **2** a noise warning of danger: *there had been no time to put on life jackets or to sound the alarm* **3** a device that transmits a warning **4** short for **alarm clock** ▷ *vb* **5** to fill with fear **6** to fit or activate a burglar alarm on (a house, car, etc.) ▶ HISTORY Old Italian *all'arme* to arms > **alarming** *adj*

alarm clock *n* a clock that sounds at a set time to wake a person up

alarmist *n* **1** a person who alarms others needlessly ▷ *adj* **2** causing needless alarm

alas *adv* **1** unfortunately or regrettably: *the answer, alas, is that they cannot get any for the moment* ▷ *interj* **2** old-fashioned an exclamation of grief or alarm ▶ HISTORY Old French *ha las!*

alb *n* a long white linen robe worn by a Christian priest ▶ HISTORY Latin *albus* white

albacore *n* a tuna found in warm seas which is valued as a food fish ▶ HISTORY Arabic *al-bakrah*

Albanian *adj* **1** of Albania ▷ *n* **2** a person from Albania **3** the language of Albania

albatross *n* **1** a large sea bird with very long wings **2** *golf* a score of three strokes under par for a hole ▶ HISTORY Portuguese *alcatraz* pelican

albedo (al-**bee**-doe) *n* the ratio of the intensity of light reflected from an object, such as a planet, to that of the light it receives from the sun ▶ HISTORY Church Latin: whiteness, from Latin *albus* white

albeit *conj* even though: *these effects occur, albeit to a lesser degree* ▶ HISTORY Middle English *al be it* although it be (that)

albino *n, pl* **-nos** a person or animal with white or almost white hair and skin and pinkish eyes ▶ HISTORY Latin *albus* white > **albinism** *n*

Albion *n poetic* Britain or England ▶ HISTORY Latin

album *n* **1** a book with blank pages, for keeping photographs or stamps in **2** a long-playing CD or record ▶ HISTORY Latin: blank tablet

albumen *n* **1** egg white **2** *biochem* same as **albumin** ▶ HISTORY Latin *albus* white

albumin or **albumen** *n biochem* a water-soluble protein found in blood plasma, egg white, milk, and muscle

alchemy *n* a medieval form of chemistry concerned with trying to change base metals into gold and to find an elixir to prolong life indefinitely ▶ HISTORY Arabic *al* the + *kīmiyā'* transmutation > **alchemist** *n*

alcheringa (al-chi-**ring**-ga) *n* another name for **Dreamtime** ▶ HISTORY Aboriginal language

alcohol *n* **1** a colourless flammable liquid present in intoxicating drinks **2** intoxicating drinks generally ▶ HISTORY Arabic *al-kuhl* powdered antimony

alcoholic *n* **1** a person who is addicted to alcohol ▷ *adj* **2** of or relating to alcohol

alcoholism *n* a condition in which dependence on alcohol harms a person's health and everyday life

alcopop *n Brit, Austral & S African, informal* an alcoholic drink that tastes like a soft drink ▶ HISTORY ALCO(HOL) + POP[1] (sense 9)

alcove *n* a recess in the wall of a room ▶ HISTORY Arabic *al-qubbah* the vault

aldehyde *n chem* any organic compound containing the group –CHO, derived from alcohol by oxidation ▶ HISTORY New Latin *al(cohol) dehyd(rogenatum)* dehydrogenated alcohol

alder *n* a tree with toothed leaves and conelike fruits, often found in damp places ▶ HISTORY Old English *alor*

alderman *n, pl* **-men** **1** (formerly, in England and Wales) a senior member of a local council, elected by other councillors **2** (in the US, Canada & Australia) a member of the governing body of a city **3** (in some Caribbean countries) a person appointed to advise a council on a particular matter ▶ HISTORY Old English *ealdor* chief + *mann* man

ale *n* **1** a beer fermented in an open vessel using yeasts that rise to the top of the brew **2** (formerly) an alcoholic drink that is unflavoured by hops **3** *Brit* another word for **beer** ▶ HISTORY Old English *alu, ealu*

alembic *n* **1** an obsolete type of container used for distillation **2** anything that distils or purifies things ▶ HISTORY Arabic *al-anbīq* the still

alert *adj* **1** watchful and attentive **2 alert to** aware of ▷ *n* **3** a warning or the period during which a warning remains in effect **4 on the alert** watchful ▷ *vb* **5** to warn of danger **6** to make aware of a fact ▶ HISTORY Italian *all'erta* on the watch > **alertness** *n*

A level *n* **1** *Brit* the advanced level of a subject taken for the General Certificate of Education **2** a pass in a subject at A level

Alexander technique *n* a technique for improving posture by becoming more aware of it ▶ HISTORY after Frederick Matthias *Alexander*, Australian actor

alfalfa *n* a plant widely used for feeding farm animals ▶ HISTORY Arabic *al-fasfasah*

alfresco *adj, adv* in the open air ▶ HISTORY Italian: in the cool

algae (al-jee) *pl n, sing* **alga** (al-ga) plants which grow in water or moist ground, and which have no true stems, roots, or leaves ▶ HISTORY Latin *alga* seaweed

algal bloom *n environmental science* a sudden growth in the numbers of algae in the water

algebra *n* a branch of mathematics in which symbols are used to represent numbers > **algebraic** *adj*

■ **WORD HISTORY**
■ The term *al-jabr* is taken from the title of an
■ Arabic book on mathematics by the
■ 9th-century Persian mathematician
■ al-Khuwārizmī, *the Kitab al-jabr wa al-muqābulah*.
■ In Arabic *al-jabr* means 'reunion' or 'integration'.
■ When the book was later translated into Latin,
■ 'al-jabr' became 'algebra'.

algebraic expression *n maths* a mathematical expression in which symbols are used to represent numbers

ALGOL *n* an early computer programming language designed for mathematical and scientific purposes ▶ **HISTORY** alg(orithmic) o(riented) l(anguage)

algorism *n* the Arabic or decimal system of counting ▶ **HISTORY** from al-Khuwārizmi, 9th-century Persian mathematician

algorithm *n* a logical arithmetical or computational procedure for solving problems ▶ **HISTORY** changed from ALGORISM

alias *adv* **1** also known as: *Iris florentina, alias orris root* ▷ *n, pl* **-ases** **2** a false name ▶ **HISTORY** Latin: otherwise

alibi *n, pl* **-bis** **1** *law* a plea of being somewhere else when a crime was committed **2** *informal* an excuse ▷ *vb* **-biing, -bied** **3** to provide someone with an alibi ▶ **HISTORY** Latin: elsewhere

alien *adj* **1** foreign **2** from another world **3 alien to** repugnant or opposed to: *these methods are alien to the world of politics* ▷ *n* **4** a person who is a citizen of a country other than the one in which he or she lives **5** a being from another world **6** a person who does not seem to fit in with his or her environment ▶ **HISTORY** Latin *alienus*

alienable *adj law* able to be transferred to another owner

alienate *vb* **-ating, -ated** **1** to cause a friend to become unfriendly or hostile **2** *law* to transfer the ownership of property to another person > **alienation** *n*

alight[1] *vb* **alighting, alighted** *or* **alit 1** to step out of a vehicle or off a horse: *we alighted on Vladivostok station* **2** to land: *we saw thirty goldfinches alighting on the ledge* ▶ **HISTORY** Old English *ālīhtan*

alight[2] *adj, adv* **1** on fire **2** illuminated: *the lamp on the desk was alight*

align (a-**line**) *vb* **1** to bring (a person or group) into agreement with the policy of another **2** to place (two objects) in a particular position in relation to each other ▶ **HISTORY** Old French *à ligne* into line > **alignment** *n*

alike *adj* **1** similar: *they were thought to be very alike* ▷ *adv* **2** in the same way: *they even dressed alike* **3** considered together: *players and spectators alike* ▶ **HISTORY** Old English *gelīc*

alimentary *adj* of or relating to nutrition

alimentary canal *n* the tubular passage in the body through which food is passed and digested

alimony *n law* an allowance paid under a court order by one spouse to another after separation ▶ **HISTORY** Latin *alimonia* sustenance

A-line *adj* (of a skirt) slightly flared

aliphatic *adj chem* (of an organic compound) having an open chain structure ▶ **HISTORY** Greek *aleiphar* oil

aliquant *adj maths* denoting or belonging to a number that is not an exact divisor of a given number ▶ **HISTORY** Latin *aliquantus* somewhat

aliquot *adj maths* denoting or belonging to an exact divisor of a number ▶ **HISTORY** Latin: several

alive *adj* **1** living; having life **2** in existence: *he said that he would keep the company alive, no matter what* **3** lively **4 alive to** aware of **5 alive with** swarming with: *the rocky shoreline was alive with birds* ▶ **HISTORY** Old English *on līfe* in life

alkali (**alk**-a-lie) *n chem* a substance that combines with acid and neutralizes it to form a salt ▶ **HISTORY** Arabic *al-qili* the ashes (of saltwort)

alkali metal *n chem* a metal, such as sodium or potassium, that forms an alkaline solution in water

alkaline *adj chem* having the properties of or containing an alkali > **alkalinity** *n*

alkaloid *n chem* any of a group of organic compounds containing nitrogen. Many are poisonous and some are used as drugs

alkane *n chem* any saturated hydrocarbon with the general formula C_nH_{2n+2}

alkene *n chem* any unsaturated hydrocarbon with the general formula C_nH_{2n}

all *adj, adv* **1** the whole quantity or number (of): *all the banks agree; we're all to blame* **2** every one of a class: *almost all animals sneeze* **3** the greatest possible: *in all seriousness* **4** any whatever: *I'm leaving out all question of motive for the time being* **5 all along** since the beginning **6 all but** nearly **7 all in all** everything considered **8 all over a** finished **b** everywhere in or on: *we send them all over the world* **c** *informal* typically: *that's him all over* **9 all the** so much (more or less) than otherwise: *the need for new drugs is all the more important* **10 at all** used for emphasis: *my throat's no better at all* **11 be all for** *informal* to be strongly in favour of **12 for all** in spite of: *for all his cynicism, he's at heart a closet idealist* **13 in all** altogether: *there were five in all* ▷ *adv* **14** (in scores of games) each: *the score was two all* ▷ *n* **15 give one's all** to make the greatest possible effort ▶ **HISTORY** Old English *eall*

Allah *n* the name of God in Islam

allay *vb* to reduce (fear, doubt, or anger) ▶ **HISTORY** Old English *ālecgan* to put down

all clear *n* a signal indicating that danger is over

allegation *n* an unproved assertion or accusation

allege *vb* **-leging, -leged** to state without proof ▶ **HISTORY** Latin *allegare* to dispatch on a mission

alleged *adj* stated but not proved: *the spot where the alleged crime took place* > **allegedly** (al-**lej**-id-lee) *adv*

allegiance *n* loyalty or dedication to a person, cause, or belief ▶ **HISTORY** Old French *lige* liege

allegory *n, pl* **-ries** a story, poem, or picture with an underlying meaning as well as the literal one ▶ **HISTORY** Greek *allēgorein* to speak figuratively > **allegorical** *adj* > **allegorize** *or* **-rise** *vb*

allegretto *music adv* **1** fairly quickly or briskly ▷ *n, pl* **-tos 2** a piece or passage to be performed fairly quickly or briskly ▶ **HISTORY** Italian

allegro *music adv* **1** in a brisk lively manner ▷ *n, pl* **-gros 2** a piece or passage to be performed in a brisk lively manner ▶ **HISTORY** Italian

allele (al-**leel**) *n* any of two or more genes that are responsible for alternative characteristics, such as smooth or wrinkled seeds in peas

alleluia interj praise the Lord! ▶ HISTORY Hebrew halleluyah

allergen (**al**-ler-jen) n a substance capable of causing an allergic reaction > **allergenic** adj

allergic adj 1 having or caused by an allergy 2 **allergic to** informal having a strong dislike of: Father and son seemed to have been allergic to each other from the start

allergy n, pl -gies 1 extreme sensitivity to a substance such as a food or pollen, which causes the body to react to any contact with it 2 informal a strong dislike for something ▶ HISTORY Greek allos other + ergon activity

alleviate vb -ating, -ated to lessen (pain or suffering) ▶ HISTORY Latin levis light > **alleviation** n

alley n 1 a narrow passage between or behind buildings 2 a a building containing lanes for tenpin bowling b a long narrow wooden lane down which the ball is rolled in tenpin bowling 3 a path in a garden, often lined with trees ▶ HISTORY Old French alee

Allhallows n same as **All Saints' Day**

alliance n 1 the state of being allied 2 a formal relationship between two or more countries or political parties to work together 3 the countries or parties involved ▶ HISTORY Old French alier to ally

allied adj 1 united by a common aim or common characteristics: the allied areas of telepathy and clairvoyance 2 **Allied** history relating to the countries that fought against Germany and Austria-Hungary in World War I or against Germany and Japan in World War II: the Allied bombing of German cities

Allies pl n history **the Allies a** (in World War I) the countries of the Triple Entente (France, Russia, and Britain) together with the other nations allied with them against Germany and Austria-Hungary b (in World War II) the countries that fought against Germany and Japan (Britain and the Commonwealth countries, the US, the Soviet Union, France, China, and Poland)

alligator n a large reptile of the southern US, similar to the crocodile but with a shorter broader snout

■ WORD HISTORY

■ The word 'alligator' comes from Spanish el lagarto, meaning 'the lizard'.

all in adj 1 informal, spoken exhausted 2 (of wrestling) with no style forbidden ▷ adv 3 with all expenses included

alliteration n the use of the same sound at the start of words occurring together, as in round the rugged rock the ragged rascal ran ▶ HISTORY Latin litera letter > **alliterative** adj

allocate vb -cating, -cated to assign to someone or for a particular purpose ▶ HISTORY Latin locus a place > **allocation** n

allopathy (al-**lop**-ath-ee) n med an orthodox method of treating disease, by using drugs that produce an effect opposite to the effect of the

disease being treated, as contrasted with homeopathy ▶ HISTORY Greek allos other + pathos suffering > **allopathic** adj

allot vb -lotting, -lotted to assign as a share or for a particular purpose ▶ HISTORY Old French lot portion

allotment n 1 Brit a small piece of land rented by a person to grow vegetables on 2 a portion allotted 3 distribution

allotrope n chem any of two or more physical forms in which an element can exist

allotropy n chem the existence of an element in two or more physical forms ▶ HISTORY Greek allos other + tropos manner > **allotropic** adj

allow vb 1 to permit someone to do something 2 to set aside: I allowed plenty of time 3 to acknowledge (a point or claim) 4 **allow for** to take into account ▶ HISTORY Late Latin allaudare to extol > **allowable** adj

allowance n 1 an amount of money given at regular intervals 2 (in Britain) an amount of a person's income that is not subject to income tax 3 **make allowances for a** to treat or judge someone less severely because he or she has special problems b to take into account in one's plans

alloy n 1 a mixture of two or more metals ▷ vb 2 to mix metals in order to obtain a substance with a desired property ▶ HISTORY Latin alligare to bind

all right adj 1 acceptable or satisfactory: Is everything all right? 2 unharmed; safe: I'm going to check if he's all right ▷ interj 3 an expression of approval or agreement ▷ adv 4 satisfactorily 5 safely 6 without doubt: it was him all right

all-rounder n a person with many skills and abilities

All Saints' Day n a Christian festival celebrated on November 1 to honour all the saints

All Souls' Day n RC Church a day of prayer (November 2) for the dead in purgatory

allspice n a spice used in cooking, which comes from the berries of a tropical American tree

allude vb -luding, -luded • **allude to** to refer indirectly to ▶ HISTORY Latin alludere

allure n attractiveness or appeal ▶ HISTORY Old French alurer to lure

alluring adj extremely attractive

allusion n an indirect reference

alluvial adj 1 of or relating to alluvium ▷ n 2 same as **alluvium**

alluvial fan or **cone** n geol a fan-shaped accumulation of silt, sand, gravel, and boulders deposited by fast-flowing mountain rivers when they reach flatter land

alluvial soil n geol fertile soil containing mud, silt, and sand deposited by flowing water onto flood plains

alluvium n, pl -via a fertile soil consisting of mud, silt, and sand deposited by flowing water ▶ HISTORY Latin

ally n, pl -lies 1 a country, person, or group with an agreement to support another ▷ vb -lies, -lying,

-lied 2 ally oneself with to agree to support another country, person, or group ▶ HISTORY Latin *ligare* to bind

alma mater *n* the school, college, or university that one attended ▶ HISTORY Latin: bountiful mother

almanac *n* a yearly calendar with detailed information on matters like anniversaries and phases of the moon ▶ HISTORY Late Greek *almenikhiaka*

almighty *adj* **1** having power over everything **2** *informal* very great: *there was an almighty bang* ▷ *n* **3 the Almighty** God

almond *n* an edible oval nut with a yellowish-brown shell, which grows on a small tree ▶ HISTORY Greek *amugdalē*

almoner *n* *Brit* a former name for a hospital social worker ▶ HISTORY Old French *almosne* alms

almost *adv* very nearly

alms (**ahmz**) *pl n old-fashioned* donations of money or goods to poor people ▶ HISTORY Greek *eleēmosunē* pity

almshouse *n* *Brit* (formerly) a house, financed by charity, which offered accommodation to poor people

aloe *n* **1** a plant with fleshy spiny leaves **2 aloes** a bitter drug made from aloe leaves ▶ HISTORY Greek

aloe vera *n* a plant producing a juice which is used to treat skin and hair

aloft *adv* **1** in the air **2** *naut* in the rigging of a ship ▶ HISTORY Old Norse *ā lopt*

alone *adj, adv* **1** without anyone or anything else **2 leave someone** *or* **something alone** to refrain from annoying someone or interfering with something **3 let alone** not to mention: *it looked inconceivable that he could run again, let alone be elected* ▶ HISTORY Old English *al one* all (entirely) one

along *prep* **1** over part or all of the length of: *we were going along the railway tracks* ▷ *adv* **2** moving forward: *they were roaring along at 40mph* **3** in company with another or others: *let them go along for the ride* **4 along with** together with: *I'm including the good days along with the bad* ▶ HISTORY Old English *andlang*

alongside *prep* **1** close beside ▷ *adv* **2** near the side of something

aloof *adj* distant or haughty in manner ▶ HISTORY obsolete *a loof* to windward

alopecia (al-loh-**pee**-sha) *n* loss of hair, usually due to illness ▶ HISTORY Greek *alōpekia* mange in foxes

aloud *adv* in an audible voice

alp *n* **1** a high mountain **2 the Alps** a high mountain range in S central Europe ▶ HISTORY Latin *Alpes*

alpaca *n* **1** a South American mammal related to the llama, with dark shaggy hair **2** wool or cloth made from this hair ▶ HISTORY South American Indian *allpaca*

alpenstock *n* a strong stick with an iron tip used by hikers and mountain climbers ▶ HISTORY German

alpha *n* **1** the first letter in the Greek alphabet (A, α) **2** *Brit* the highest grade in an examination or for a piece of academic work **3 alpha and omega** the first and last

alphabet *n* a set of letters in fixed conventional order, used in a writing system ▶ HISTORY *alpha* + *beta*, the first two letters of the Greek alphabet

alphabetical *adj* in the conventional order of the letters of an alphabet > **alphabetically** *adv*

alphabetize *or* **-tise** *vb* **-tizing, -tized** *or* **-tising, -tised** to put in alphabetical order > **alphabetization** *or* **-tisation** *n*

alphanumeric *adj* consisting of alphabetical and numerical symbols

alpha particle *n* *physics* a positively charged particle, emitted during some radioactive transformations

alpha ray *n* *physics* a stream of alpha particles

alpine *adj* **1** of high mountains **2 Alpine** of the Alps ▷ *n* **3** a plant grown on or native to mountains

already *adv* **1** before the present time **2** before an implied or expected time

alright *adj, interj, adv* *not universally accepted* same as **all right**

Alsatian *n* a large wolflike dog

also *adv* in addition; too ▶ HISTORY Old English *alswā*

also-ran *n* a loser in a race, competition, or election

alt. *combining form informal* alternative: *alt. rock*

altar *n* **1** the table used for Communion in Christian churches **2** a raised structure on which sacrifices are offered and religious rites performed ▶ HISTORY Latin *altus* high

altarpiece *n* a painting or a decorated screen set above and behind the altar in a Christian church

alter *vb* to make or become different; change ▶ HISTORY Latin *alter* other

alteration *n* a change or modification

altercation *n* a noisy argument ▶ HISTORY Latin *altercari* to quarrel

alter ego *n* **1** a hidden side to one's personality **2** a very close friend ▶ HISTORY Latin: other self

alternate *vb* **-nating, -nated** **1** to occur by turns **2** to interchange regularly or in succession ▷ *adj* **3** occurring by turns **4** every second (one) of a series: *alternate days* **5** being a second choice ▶ HISTORY Latin *alternare* > **alternately** *adv* > **alternation** *n*

alternate angles *pl n geom* two angles at opposite ends and on opposite sides of a line intersecting two other lines

alternating current *n* an electric current that reverses direction at frequent regular intervals

alternative *n* **1** a possibility of choice between two or more things **2** either or any of such choices ▷ *adj* **3** presenting a choice between two or more possibilities **4** of a lifestyle etc. that is less conventional or materialistic than is usual > **alternatively** *adv*

alternative dispute resolution *n law* methods for resolving disputes outside the court system, such as mediation, conciliation, arbitration, etc.

alternative energy *n* a form of energy obtained from natural resources like waves and wind

alternative medicine *n* the treatment of disease by unconventional methods like homeopathy, and involving attention to the patient's emotional wellbeing

alternator *n* an electrical machine that generates an alternating current

although *conj* in spite of the fact that

altimeter (al-**tim**-it-er) *n* an instrument that measures altitude ▶ HISTORY Latin *altus* high +-METER

altitude *n* height, esp. above sea level ▶ HISTORY Latin *altus* high, deep

alto *n, pl* **-tos 1** short for **contralto 2** the highest adult male voice **3** a singer with an alto voice **4** a musical instrument, for instance a saxophone, that is the second or third highest in its family ▷ *adj* **5** denoting such an instrument, singer, or voice: *an alto flute* ▶ HISTORY Italian: high

altocumulus (alt-oh-**cue**-mew-luss) *n, pl* **-li** (-lie) *meteorol* a globular cloud at an intermediate height

altogether *adv* **1** completely: *an altogether different message* **2** on the whole: *this is not altogether a bad thing* **3** in total: *altogether, 25 aircraft took part* ▷ *n* **4 in the altogether** *informal* naked

altostratus (alt-oh-**stray**-tuss) *n, pl* **-ti** (-tie) *meteorol* a layer cloud at an intermediate height

altruism *n* unselfish concern for the welfare of others ▶ HISTORY Italian *altrui* others > **altruist** *n* > **altruistic** *adj*

ALU *abbrev computers* arithmetic logic unit: the part of a central processing unit that performs arithmetic and logical operations

alum *n chem* a double sulphate of aluminium and potassium, used in manufacturing and in medicine ▶ HISTORY Latin *alumen*

aluminium *or US & Canad* **aluminum** *n chem* a light malleable silvery-white metallic element that does not rust. Symbol: Al

aluminize *or* **-ise** *vb* **-nizing, -nized** *or* **-nising, -nised** to cover with aluminium

alumnus (al-**lumm**-nuss) *or fem* **alumna** (al-**lumm**-na) *n, pl* **-ni** (-nie) *or* **-nae** (-nee) *chiefly US & Canad* a graduate of a school or college ▶ HISTORY Latin: nursling, pupil

alveolus (al-**vee**-ol-luss) *n, pl* **-li** (-lie) any small pit, cavity, or saclike dilation, such as a honeycomb cell, a tooth socket, or the tiny air sacs in the lungs ▶ HISTORY Latin: a little hollow

always *adv* **1** without exception: *she was always at the top of her form in school work* **2** continually: *you're always shouting or whining* **3** in any case: *they're all adults, they can always say no* ▶ HISTORY Old English *ealne weg* all the way

alyssum *n* a garden plant with clusters of small white flowers ▶ HISTORY Greek *alussos* curing rabies

Alzheimer's disease (**alts**-hime-erz) *n* a disorder of the brain resulting in a progressive decline in intellectual and physical abilities and eventual dementia ▶ HISTORY after A. *Alzheimer,* German physician

am *vb* (with *I* as subject) a form of the present tense of **be** ▶ HISTORY Old English *eam*

Am *chem* americium

AM 1 amplitude modulation **2** (in Britain) Member of the National Assembly for Wales

Am. America(n)

a.m. before noon ▶ HISTORY Latin *ante meridiem*

amalgam *n* **1** a blend or combination **2** an alloy of mercury with another metal: *dental amalgam* ▶ HISTORY Medieval Latin *amalgama*

amalgamate *vb* **-ating, -mated 1** to combine or unite **2** to alloy (a metal) with mercury > **amalgamation** *n*

amandla (a-**mand**-la) *n S African* a political slogan calling for power to the Black population ▶ HISTORY Nguni (language group of southern Africa): power

amanuensis (am-man-yew-**en**-siss) *n, pl* **-ses** (-seez) a person who copies manuscripts or takes dictation ▶ HISTORY Latin *servus a manu* slave at hand

amaranth *n* **1** *poetic* an imaginary flower that never fades **2** a lily-like plant with small green, red, or purple flowers ▶ HISTORY Greek *a-* not + *marainein* to fade

amaryllis *n* a lily-like plant with large red or white flowers and a long stalk ▶ HISTORY *Amaryllis,* Greek name for a shepherdess

amass *vb* to accumulate or collect: *the desire to amass wealth* ▶ HISTORY Latin *ad-* to + *massa* mass

amateur *n* **1** a person who engages in a sport or other activity as a pastime rather than as a profession **2** a person unskilled in a subject or activity ▷ *adj* **3** doing something out of interest, not for money **4** amateurish ▶ HISTORY Latin *amator* lover > **amateurism** *n*

amateurish *adj* lacking skill

amatory *adj* of or relating to romantic love ▶ HISTORY Latin *amare* to love

amaze *vb* **amazing, amazed** to fill with surprise; astonish ▶ HISTORY Old English *āmasian* > **amazement** *n* > **amazing** *adj* > **amazingly** *adv*

Amazon *n* **1** a strong and powerful woman **2** *Greek myth* one of a race of women warriors of Scythia ▶ HISTORY Greek > **Amazonian** *adj*

ambassador *n* **1** a diplomat of the highest rank, sent to another country as permanent representative of his or her own country **2** a representative or messenger: *he saw himself as an ambassador for the game* ▶ HISTORY Old Provençal *ambaisador* > **ambassadorial** *adj*

amber *n* **1** a yellow translucent fossilized resin, used in jewellery ▷ *adj* **2** brownish-yellow ▶ HISTORY Arabic *'anbar* ambergris

ambergris (**am**-ber-greece) *n* a waxy substance secreted by the sperm whale, which is used in making perfumes ▸ **HISTORY** Old French *ambre gris* grey amber

ambidextrous *adj* able to use both hands with equal ease ▸ **HISTORY** Latin *ambi-* both + *dexter* right hand

ambience *or* **ambiance** *n* the atmosphere of a place

ambient *adj* **1** surrounding: *low ambient temperatures* **2** creating a relaxing atmosphere: *ambient music* ▸ **HISTORY** Latin *ambi-* round + *ire* to go

ambiguity *n, pl* **-ties 1** the possibility of interpreting an expression in more than one way **2** an ambiguous situation or expression: *the ambiguities of feminine identity*

ambiguous *adj* having more than one possible interpretation ▸ **HISTORY** Latin *ambigere* to go around > **ambiguously** *adv*

ambit *n* limits or boundary ▸ **HISTORY** Latin *ambire* to go round

ambition *n* **1** strong desire for success **2** something so desired; a goal ▸ **HISTORY** Latin *ambitio* a going round (of candidates)

ambitious *adj* **1** having a strong desire for success **2** requiring great effort or ability: *ambitious plans*

ambivalence (am-**biv**-a-lenss) *n* the state of feeling two conflicting emotions at the same time > **ambivalent** *adj*

amble *vb* **-bling, -bled 1** to walk at a leisurely pace ▷ *n* **2** a leisurely walk or pace ▸ **HISTORY** Latin *ambulare* to walk

ambrosia *n* **1** something delightful to taste or smell **2** *classical myth* the food of the gods ▸ **HISTORY** Greek: immortality

ambulance *n* a motor vehicle designed to carry sick or injured people ▸ **HISTORY** Latin *ambulare* to walk

ambulatory *adj* **1** of or relating to walking **2** able to walk ▷ *n, pl* **-ries 3** a place for walking in, such as a cloister

ambush *n* **1** the act of waiting in a concealed position to make a surprise attack **2** an attack from such a position ▷ *vb* **3** to attack suddenly from a concealed position ▸ **HISTORY** Old French *embuschier* to position in ambush

ameliorate (am-**meal**-yor-rate) *vb* **-rating, -rated** to make (something) better ▸ **HISTORY** Latin *melior* better > **amelioration** *n*

amen *interj* so be it: used at the end of a prayer ▸ **HISTORY** Hebrew: certainly

amenable (a-**mean**-a-bl) *adj* likely or willing to cooperate ▸ **HISTORY** Latin *minare* to drive (cattle)

amend *vb* to make small changes to something such as a piece of writing or a contract, in order to improve it: *he has amended the basic design* ▸ **HISTORY** Old French *amender*

amendment *n* an improvement or correction

amends *pl n* **make amends for** to compensate for some injury or insult

amenity *n, pl* **-ties** a useful or enjoyable feature: *all kinds of amenities including horse riding and golf* ▸ **HISTORY** Latin *amoenus* agreeable

amenorrhoea *or esp US* **amenorrhea** (aim-men-or-**ree**-a) *n* abnormal absence of menstruation ▸ **HISTORY** Greek *a-* not + *mēn* month + *rhein* to flow

American *adj* **1** of the United States of America or the American continent ▷ *n* **2** a person from the United States of America or the American continent

American football *n* a game similar to rugby, played by two teams of eleven players

American Indian *n* **1** a member of any of the original peoples of America ▷ *adj* **2** of any of these peoples

Americanism *n* an expression or custom that is characteristic of the people of the United States

Americanize *or* **-nise** *vb* **-nizing, -nized** *or* **-nising, -nised** to make American in outlook or form

americium *n chem* a white metallic element artificially produced from plutonium. Symbol: Am ▸ **HISTORY** from *America* (where it was first produced)

amethyst (**am**-myth-ist) *n* **1** a purple or violet variety of quartz used as a gemstone ▷ *adj* **2** purple or violet

■ **WORD HISTORY**
■ 'Amethyst' comes from Greek *amethustos*
■ meaning 'not drunk'. It was thought in ancient
■ times that anyone wearing or touching an
■ amethyst would not become drunk. Wine
■ goblets were sometimes carved from
■ amethyst.

Amex (**aah**-mex) **1** *trademark* American Express **2** American Stock Exchange

Amharic *n* the official language of Ethiopia

amiable *adj written* having a pleasant nature; friendly ▸ **HISTORY** Latin *amicus* friend > **amiability** *n* > **amiably** *adv*

amicable *adj* characterized by friendliness: *ideally the parting should be amicable* ▸ **HISTORY** Latin *amicus* friend > **amicability** *n* > **amicably** *adv*

amid *or* **amidst** *prep* in the middle of; among ▸ **HISTORY** Old English *on middan* in the middle

amide *n chem* **1** any organic compound containing the group –CONH2 **2** an inorganic compound having the general formula M(NH2)x, where M is a metal atom ▸ **HISTORY** from AMMONIA

amidships *adv naut* at, near, or towards the centre of a ship

amine (am-**mean**) *n chem* an organic base formed by replacing one or more of the hydrogen atoms of ammonia by organic groups ▸ **HISTORY** from AMMONIUM

amino acid (am-**mean**-oh) *n chem* any of a group of organic compounds containing the **amino** group, –NH2, and one or more carboxyl groups, –COOH, esp. one that is a component of protein

amir (am-**meer**) *n* same as **emir** ▸ **HISTORY** Arabic

amiss *adv* **1** wrongly or badly: *anxious not to tread amiss* **2 take something amiss** to be offended by something ▷ *adj* **3** wrong or faulty ▸ **HISTORY** Middle English *a mis*, from *mis* wrong

23

a

amity n formal friendship ▶ HISTORY from Latin amicus friend

ammeter n an instrument for measuring an electric current in amperes ▶ HISTORY am(pere) + -METER

ammo n informal ammunition

ammonia n 1 a colourless strong-smelling gas containing hydrogen and nitrogen 2 a solution of this in water ▶ HISTORY ultimately from a substance found near the shrine of the Roman-Egyptian god Jupiter Ammon

ammonite n the fossilized spiral shell of an extinct sea creature ▶ HISTORY Medieval Latin cornu Ammonis horn of Ammon

ammonium adj chem of or containing the chemical group NH4– or the ion NH4+

ammonium nitrate n chem a colourless highly soluble crystalline solid, used as a fertilizer and in explosives and fireworks

ammunition n 1 bullets, bombs, and shells that can be fired from or as a weapon 2 facts that can be used in an argument ▶ HISTORY Latin munitio fortification

amnesia n a partial or total loss of memory ▶ HISTORY Greek: forgetfulness > **amnesiac** adj, n

amnesty n, pl -ties 1 a general pardon for offences against a government 2 a period during which a law is suspended, to allow people to confess to crime or give up weapons without fear of prosecution ▶ HISTORY Greek a- not + mnasthai to remember

amniocentesis n, pl -ses removal of amniotic fluid from the womb of a pregnant woman in order to detect possible abnormalities in the fetus ▶ HISTORY amnion + Greek kentēsis a pricking

amnion n, pl -nia the innermost of two membranes enclosing an embryo ▶ HISTORY Greek: a little lamb > **amniotic** adj

amniotic fluid n the fluid surrounding the fetus in the womb

amniotic sac n anat the membranous bag that surrounds a fetus in the womb

amoeba or US **ameba** (am-**mee**-ba) n, pl -**bae** (-bee) or -**bas** a microscopic single-cell creature that is able to change its shape ▶ HISTORY Greek ameibein to change

amok or **amuck** adv **run amok** to run about in a violent frenzy

■ **WORD HISTORY**
■ 'Amok' comes from the Malay word amoq
■ meaning 'a furious assault'.

among or **amongst** prep 1 in the midst of: she decided to dwell among the Greeks 2 in the group, class, or number of: he is among the top trainers 3 to each of: the stakes should be divided among the players 4 with one another within a group: sort it out among yourselves ▶ HISTORY Old English amang

amoral (aim-**mor**-ral) adj without moral standards or principles > **amorality** n

amorous adj feeling, displaying, or relating to love or desire ▶ HISTORY Latin amor love

amorphous adj 1 lacking a definite shape 2 of no recognizable character or type ▶ HISTORY Greek a- not + morphē shape

amortize or **-tise** vb **-tizing, -tized** or **-tising, -tised** finance to pay off (a debt) gradually by periodic transfers to a sinking fund ▶ HISTORY Latin ad to + mors death

amount n 1 extent or quantity ▷ vb 2 **amount to** to be equal or add up to ▶ HISTORY Old French amonter to go up

amour n a secret love affair ▶ HISTORY Latin amor love

amour-propre (am-moor-**prop**-ra) n self-esteem

amp n 1 an ampere 2 informal an amplifier

amperage n the strength of an electric current measured in amperes

ampere (**am**-pair) n the basic unit of electric current ▶ HISTORY after A. M. Ampère, French physicist & mathematician

ampersand n the character &, meaning and ▶ HISTORY shortened from and per se and, that is, the symbol & by itself (represents) and

amphetamine (am-**fet**-am-mean) n a drug used as a stimulant ▶ HISTORY shortened from chemical name

amphibian n 1 an animal, such as a newt, frog, or toad, that lives on land but breeds in water 2 a vehicle that can travel on both water and land

amphibious adj 1 living or operating both on land and in or on water 2 relating to a military attack launched from the sea against a shore ▶ HISTORY Greek amphibios having a double life

amphitheatre or US **amphitheater** n a circular or oval building without a roof, in which tiers of seats rise from a central open arena ▶ HISTORY Greek amphitheatron

amphora (**am**-for-ra) n, pl -**phorae** (-for-ree) an ancient Greek or Roman jar with two handles and a narrow neck ▶ HISTORY Greek amphi- on both sides + phoreus bearer

ample adj 1 more than sufficient: there is already ample evidence 2 large: ample helpings of stewed pomegranates and pears ▶ HISTORY Latin amplus

amplifier n an electronic device used to increase the strength of a current or sound signal

amplify vb -fies, -fying, -fied 1 electronics to increase the strength of (a current or sound signal) 2 to explain in more detail 3 to increase the size, extent, or effect of ▶ HISTORY Latin amplificare > **amplification** n

amplitude n 1 greatness of extent 2 physics the maximum displacement of a wave or oscillation from the zero or mean position of a wave or oscillation ▶ HISTORY Latin amplus spacious

amplitude modulation n electronics a method of transmitting information using radio waves in which the amplitude of the carrier wave is varied in accordance with the amplitude of the input signal

amply adv fully or generously: she was amply rewarded for it

ampoule or US **ampule** n med a small glass container in which liquids for injection are sealed ▶ HISTORY French

ampulla *n*, *pl* **-pullae** **1** *anat* the dilated end part of certain tubes in the body **2** *Christianity* a container for the wine and water, or the oil, used in church ▶ HISTORY Latin

amputate *vb* **-tating, -tated** to cut off (a limb or part of a limb) for medical reasons ▶ HISTORY Latin *am-* around + *putare* to prune > **amputation** *n*

amputee *n* a person who has had a limb amputated

amuck *adv* same as **amok**

amulet *n* a trinket or jewel worn as a protection against evil ▶ HISTORY Latin *amuletum*

amuse *vb* **amusing, amused** **1** to cause to laugh or smile **2** to entertain or keep interested ▶ HISTORY Old French *amuser* to cause to be idle > **amusing** *adj* > **amusingly** *adv*

amusement *n* **1** the state of being amused **2** something that amuses or entertains someone

amylase *n* an enzyme present in saliva that helps to change starch into sugar

an *adj* (indefinite article) same as **a**: used before an initial vowel sound: *an old man; an hour* ▶ HISTORY Old English *ān* one

an- *prefix* See **a-**

Anabaptist *n* **1** a member of a 16th-century Protestant movement that believed in adult baptism ▷ *adj* **2** of this movement ▶ HISTORY Late Greek *anabaptizein* to baptize again

anabolic steroid *n* a synthetic steroid hormone used to stimulate muscle and bone growth

anabolism *n* *biol* a metabolic process in which body tissues are synthesized from food ▶ HISTORY Greek *anabolē* a rising up

anabranch *n* *geog* a branch of a river or stream which splits off from the main flow to rejoin it further on

anachronism (an-**nak**-kron-iz-zum) *n* **1** the representation of something in a historical context in which it could not have occurred or existed **2** a person or thing that seems to belong to another time ▶ HISTORY Greek *ana* against + *khronos* time > **anachronistic** *adj*

anaconda *n* a large S American snake which squeezes its prey to death ▶ HISTORY probably from Sinhalese *henakandayā* whip snake

anaemia *or US* **anemia** (an-**neem**-ee-a) *n* a deficiency of red blood cells or their haemoglobin content, resulting in paleness and lack of energy ▶ HISTORY Greek *an* without + *haima* blood

anaemic *or US* **anemic** *adj* **1** having anaemia **2** pale and sickly-looking **3** lacking vitality

anaerobe *n* *biol* an organism that does not require oxygen ▶ HISTORY Greek *an* not + *aēr* air + *bios* life > **anaerobic** *adj*

anaerobic respiration *n* *biol* the processing of glucose by cells in the absence of oxygen, producing a variety of end products such as ethanol or lactic acid

anaesthesia *or US* **anesthesia** (an-niss-**theez**-ee-a) *n* loss of bodily feeling caused by disease or accident or by drugs such as ether: called **general anaesthesia** when consciousness is lost and **local**

anaesthesia when only a specific area of the body is involved ▶ HISTORY Greek

anaesthetic *or US* **anesthetic** (an-niss-**thet**-ik) *n* **1** a substance that causes anaesthesia ▷ *adj* **2** causing anaesthesia

anaesthetist (an-**neess**-thet-ist) *n* *Brit* a doctor who administers anaesthetics

anaesthetize, anaesthetise *or US* **anesthetize** *vb* **-tizing, -tized** *or* **-tising, -tised** to cause to feel no pain by administering an anaesthetic

anagram *n* a word or phrase made by rearranging the letters of another word or phrase ▶ HISTORY Greek *anagrammatizein* to transpose letters

anal (**ain**-al) *adj* of or relating to the anus ▶ HISTORY New Latin *analis*

analgesia *n* the absence of pain ▶ HISTORY Greek

analgesic (an-nal-**jeez**-ik) *n* **1** a drug that relieves pain ▷ *adj* **2** pain-relieving: *an analgesic balm*

analog *n* *US & computers* same as **analogue**

analogize *or* **-gise** *vb* **-gizing, -gized** *or* **-gising, -gised** **1** to use analogy in argument **2** to reveal analogy between (one thing and another)

analogous *adj* similar in some respects ▶ HISTORY Greek *analogos* proportionate

analogue *or US* **analog** *n* **1** a physical object or quantity used to measure or represent another quantity **2** something that is analogous to something else ▷ *adj* **3** displaying information by means of a dial: *analogue speedometers*

analogue recording *n* a type of sound recording process

analogy *n*, *pl* **-gies** **1** a similarity, usually in a limited number of features **2** a comparison made to show such a similarity ▶ HISTORY Greek *analogia* > **analogical** *adj*

analyse *or US* **-lyze** (an-nal-**lize**) *vb* **-lysing, -lysed** *or* **-lyzing, -lyzed** **1** to examine (something) in detail in order to discover its meaning or essential features **2** to break (something) down into its components **3** to psychoanalyse (someone)

analysis (an-**nal**-liss-iss) *n*, *pl* **-ses** (-seez) **1** the separation of a whole into its parts for study or interpretation **2** a statement of the results of this **3** short for **psychoanalysis** ▶ HISTORY Greek *analusis* a dissolving

analyst *n* **1** a person who is skilled in analysis **2** a psychoanalyst

analytical *or* **analytic** *adj* relating to or using analysis > **analytically** *adv*

anarchism *n* a doctrine advocating the abolition of government and its replacement by a social system based on voluntary cooperation

anarchist *n* **1** a person who advocates anarchism **2** a person who causes disorder or upheaval > **anarchistic** *adj*

anarchy (**an**-ark-ee) *n* **1** general lawlessness and disorder **2** the absence of government ▶ HISTORY Greek *an* without + *arkh-* leader > **anarchic** *adj*

anastigmat *n* a lens corrected for astigmatism > **anastigmatic** *adj*

anathema (an-**nath**-im-a) *n* a detested person or thing: *the very colour was anathema to him* ▶ HISTORY Greek: something accursed

anathematize or **-tise** *vb* **-tizing, -tized** or **-tising, -tised** to curse: *he anathematized the world in general*

anatomist *n* an expert in anatomy

anatomy *n, pl* **-mies 1** the science of the physical structure of animals and plants **2** the structure of an animal or plant **3** *informal* a person's body: *the male anatomy* **4** a detailed analysis: *an anatomy of the massacre* ▶ HISTORY Greek *ana* up + *temnein* to cut > **anatomical** *adj*

ANC African National Congress: South African political movement instrumental in bringing an end to apartheid

ancestor *n* **1** a person in former times from whom one is descended **2** a forerunner: *the immediate ancestor of rock and roll is rhythm and blues* ▶ HISTORY Latin *antecedere* to go before

ancestral *adj* of or inherited from ancestors

ancestral worship *n* a form of religion in which one's ancestors are venerated and, sometimes, asked for favours and guidance

ancestry *n, pl* **-tries 1** family descent: *of Japanese ancestry* **2** origin or roots: *a vehicle whose ancestry dated back to the 1950s*

anchor *n* **1** a hooked device attached to a boat by a cable and dropped overboard to fasten the boat to the sea bottom **2** a source of stability or security: *a spiritual anchor* **3 anchors** *slang* the brakes of a motor vehicle: *he rammed on the anchors* ▷ *vb* **4** to use an anchor to hold (a boat) in one place **5** to fasten securely: *we anchored his wheelchair to a rock* ▶ HISTORY Greek *ankura*

anchorage *n* a place where boats can be anchored

anchoring *n* **1** (in the media) the use of captions, commentaries, and contexts to direct the viewer of a given image towards a particular interpretation of it **2** (in psychology) the deliberate setting up of an association of ideas or feelings with a specific stimulus; similar to conditioning

anchorite *n* a person who chooses to live in isolation for religious reasons ▶ HISTORY Greek *anakhōrein* to retire

anchorman or **anchorwoman** *n, pl* **-men** or **-women 1** a broadcaster in a central studio, who links up and presents items from outside camera units and reporters in other studios **2** the last person to compete in a relay team

anchovy (an-chov-ee) *n, pl* **-vies** a small marine food fish with a salty taste ▶ HISTORY Spanish *anchova*

ancien régime (on-syan ray-**zheem**) *n* **1** the political and social system of France before the 1789 Revolution **2** a former system ▶ HISTORY French: old regime

ancient *adj* **1** dating from very long ago **2** very old **3** of the far past, esp. before the collapse of the Western Roman Empire (476 AD) ▷ *n* **4 ancients** people who lived very long ago, such as the Romans and Greeks ▶ HISTORY Latin *ante* before

ancillary *adj* **1** supporting the main work of an organization: *hospital ancillary workers* **2** used as an extra or supplement: *I had a small ancillary sleeping tent* ▶ HISTORY Latin *ancilla* female servant

and *conj* **1** in addition to: *plants and birds* **2** as a consequence: *she fell downstairs and broke her neck* **3** afterwards: *she excused herself and left* **4** used for emphasis or to indicate repetition or continuity: *they called again and again* **5** used to express a contrast between instances of something: *there are jobs and jobs* **6** *informal* used in place of *to* in infinitives after verbs such as *try, go,* and *come*: *come and see us again* ▶ HISTORY Old English

andante (an-**dan**-tay) *music adv* **1** moderately slowly ▷ *n* **2** a passage or piece to be performed moderately slowly ▶ HISTORY Italian *andare* to walk

andantino (an-dan-**tee**-no) *music adv* **1** slightly faster than andante ▷ *n, pl* **-nos 2** a passage or piece to be performed in this way

andesite *n* a fine-grained grey or tan volcanic rock ▶ HISTORY after *Andes*, the mountain range in S America

andiron *n* either of a pair of metal stands for supporting logs in a fireplace ▶ HISTORY Old French *andier*

and/or *conj* *not universally accepted* either one or the other or both

androecium (an-**dree**-see-um) *n, pl* **-cia** (-see-a) *bot* the stamens of a flowering plant collectively

androgen *n* *biochem* any of the steroids that promote the development of male sexual organs and certain male sexual characteristics ▶ HISTORY Greek *anēr* man + *-gen* (suffix) producing

androgynous *adj* having both male and female characteristics ▶ HISTORY Greek *anēr* man + *gunē* woman

android *n* a robot resembling a human being ▶ HISTORY Late Greek *androeidēs* manlike

andrology (an-**drol**-la-jee) *n* the branch of medicine concerned with diseases and conditions specific to men ▶ HISTORY Greek *anēr* man + -LOGY > **andrologist** *n*

anecdote *n* a short amusing account of an incident ▶ HISTORY Greek *anekdotos* not published > **anecdotal** *adj*

anemia *n* *US* same as **anaemia**

anemometer *n* an instrument for recording wind speed

anemone (an-**nem**-on-ee) *n* a flowering plant with white, purple, or red flowers ▶ HISTORY Greek: windflower

aneroid barometer *n* a device for measuring air pressure, consisting of a partially evacuated chamber, in which variations in pressure cause a pointer on the lid to move ▶ HISTORY Greek *a* not + *nēros* wet

anesthesia *n* *US* same as **anaesthesia**

aneurysm *or* **aneurism** (an-new-riz-zum) *n*
med a permanent swelling of a blood vessel
▶ HISTORY Greek *aneurunein* to dilate

anew *adv written* **1** once more **2** in a different way

angel *n* **1** a spiritual being believed to be an
attendant or messenger of God **2** a conventional
representation of an angel as a human being with
wings **3** *informal* a person who is kind, pure, or
beautiful **4** *informal* an investor in a theatrical
production ▶ HISTORY Greek *angelos* messenger

angelfish *n, pl* **-fish** *or* **-fishes** a South American
aquarium fish with large fins

angelic *adj* **1** very kind, pure, or beautiful **2** of or
relating to angels > **angelically** *adv*

angelica (an-**jell**-ik-a) *n* a plant whose candied
stalks are used in cookery ▶ HISTORY Medieval
Latin *(herba) angelica* angelic herb

Angelus (an-jell-uss) *n* *RC Church* **1** prayers recited
in the morning, at midday, and in the evening **2** the
bell signalling the times of these prayers ▶ HISTORY
Latin *Angelus domini nuntiavit Mariae* the angel of
the Lord brought tidings to Mary

anger *n* **1** a feeling of extreme annoyance or
displeasure ▷ *vb* **2** to make (someone) angry
▶ HISTORY Old Norse *angr* grief

angina (an-**jine**-a) *or* **angina pectoris**
(**peck**-tor-riss) *n* a sudden intense pain in the chest
caused by a momentary lack of adequate blood
supply to the heart muscle ▶ HISTORY Greek
ankhonē a strangling

angle¹ *n* **1** the space between or shape formed by
two straight lines or surfaces that meet **2** the
divergence between two such lines or surfaces,
measured in degrees **3** a recess or corner **4** point of
view ▷ *vb* **-gling, -gled** **5** to move in or place at an
angle **6** to write (an article) from a particular point
of view ▶ HISTORY Latin *angulus* corner

angle² *vb* **-gling, -gled** **1** to fish with a hook and
line **2 angle for** to try to get by hinting: *he's just
angling for sympathy* ▶ HISTORY Old English *angul*
fish-hook

angle of depression *n* *maths* (in trigonometry)
a vertical angle measured below the horizontal

angle of elevation *n* *maths* (in trigonometry) a
vertical angle measured above the horizontal

angle of incidence *n* *physics* the angle that a
line or beam of radiation makes with a line
perpendicular to the surface at the point of
incidence

angle of refraction *n* *physics* the angle that a
refracted beam of radiation makes with the
normal to the surface between two media at the
point of refraction

angler *n* a person who fishes with a hook and line

Angles *pl n* a race from N Germany who settled in
E and N England in the 5th and 6th centuries AD
▶ HISTORY Latin *Anglus* a person from Angul,
Germany

Anglican *adj* **1** of or relating to the Church of
England ▷ *n* **2** a member of the Anglican Church
▶ HISTORY Latin *Anglicus* English, of the Angles
> **Anglicanism** *n*

Anglicism *n* an expression or custom that is
peculiar to the English

anglicize *or* **-cise** *vb* **-cizing, -cized** *or* **-cising,
-cised** to make or become English in outlook or
form

angling *n* the art or sport of fishing with a hook
and line

Anglo *n, pl* **-glos** **1** *US* a White inhabitant of the US
who is not of Latin extraction **2** *Canad* an
English-speaking Canadian

Anglo- *combining form* English or British: *the history
of Anglo-German relations* ▶ HISTORY Medieval Latin
Anglii the English

Anglo-French *adj* **1** of England and France
2 of the Anglo-French language ▷ *n* **3** the
Norman-French language of medieval England

Anglo-Indian *adj* **1** of England and India
2 denoting or relating to Anglo-Indians ▷ *n*
3 a person of mixed British and Indian descent
4 an English person who has lived for a long time
in India

Anglo-Norman *adj* **1** of or relating to the
Norman conquerors of England or their language
▷ *n* **2** a Norman inhabitant of England after 1066
3 the Anglo-French language

Anglophile *n* a person who admires England or
the English

Anglo-Saxon *n* **1** a member of any of the West
Germanic tribes that settled in Britain from the
5th century AD **2** any White person whose native
language is English **3** same as **Old English**
4 *informal* plain, blunt, and often rude English
▷ *adj* **5** of the Anglo-Saxons or the Old English
language **6** of the White Protestant culture of
Britain and the US

angora *n* **1** a variety of goat, cat, or rabbit
with long silky hair **2** the hair of the angora
goat or rabbit **3** cloth made from this hair
▶ HISTORY *Angora*, former name of Ankara, in
Turkey

Angostura Bitters *pl n* *trademark* a bitter tonic,
used as a flavouring in alcoholic drinks ▶ HISTORY
from *Angostura* in Venezuela

angry *adj* **-grier, -griest** **1** feeling or expressing
annoyance or rage **2** severely inflamed: *he had
angry welts on his forehead* **3** dark and stormy: *angry
waves* > **angrily** *adv*

angst *n* a feeling of anxiety ▶ HISTORY German

angstrom *n* a unit of length equal to 10^{-10} metre,
used to measure wavelengths ▶ HISTORY after
Anders J. *Ångström*, Swedish physicist

anguish *n* *written* great mental pain ▶ HISTORY
Latin *angustus* narrow

anguished *adj* *written* feeling or showing great
mental pain: *anguished cries*

angular *adj* **1** lean and bony: *his angular face*
2 having an angle or angles **3** measured by an
angle: *angular momentum* > **angularity** *n*

anhydride *n* *chem* a substance that combines
with water to form an acid

anhydrous *adj* *chem* containing no water
▶ HISTORY Greek *an* without + *hudōr* water

anil n a West Indian shrub which is a source of indigo ▶ HISTORY Arabic *an-nīl*, the indigo

aniline n *chem* a colourless oily poisonous liquid, obtained from coal tar and used for making dyes, plastics, and explosives

animal n **1** *zool* any living being that is capable of voluntary movement and possesses specialized sense organs **2** any living being other than a human being **3** any living being with four legs **4** a cruel or coarse person **5** *facetious* a person or thing: *there's no such animal* ▷ *adj* **6** of or from animals **7** of or relating to physical needs or desires ▶ HISTORY Latin *animalis* (adjective) living, breathing

animalcule n a microscopic animal

animal husbandry n the science of breeding, rearing, and caring for farm animals

animalism n **1** preoccupation with physical matters; sensuality **2** the doctrine that human beings lack a spiritual nature

animality n **1** the animal instincts of human beings **2** the state of being an animal

animal rights pl n the rights of animals to be protected from human abuse

animate vb **-mating, -mated 1** to give life to **2** to make lively **3** to produce (a story) as an animated cartoon ▷ *adj* **4** having life ▶ HISTORY Latin *anima* breath, spirit

animated adj **1** interesting and lively **2** (of a cartoon) made by using animation > **animatedly** adv

animated cartoon n a film produced by photographing a series of gradually changing drawings, which give the illusion of movement when the series is projected rapidly

animation n **1** the techniques used in the production of animated cartoons **2** liveliness and enthusiasm: *there's an animation in her that is new*

animator n a person who makes animated cartoons

animism n the belief that natural objects possess souls ▶ HISTORY Latin *anima* breath, spirit > **animist** n, adj > **animistic** adj

animosity n, pl **-ties** a powerful dislike or hostility ▶ HISTORY See ANIMUS

animus n intense dislike; hatred ▶ HISTORY Latin: mind, spirit

anion (an-eye-on) n an ion with negative charge ▶ HISTORY Greek *ana-* up + *ienai* to go > **anionic** adj

anise (an-niss) n a Mediterranean plant with liquorice-flavoured seeds ▶ HISTORY Greek *anison*

aniseed n the liquorice-flavoured seeds of the anise plant, used for flavouring

ankle n **1** the joint connecting the leg and the foot **2** the part of the leg just above the foot ▶ HISTORY Old Norse

anklet n an ornamental chain worn round the ankle

ankylosis (ang-kill-**loh**-siss) n abnormal immobility of a joint, caused by a fibrous growth within the joint ▶ HISTORY Greek *ankyloun* to crook

annals pl n **1** yearly records of events **2** regular reports of the work of a society or other organization ▶ HISTORY Latin *(libri) annales* yearly (books) > **annalist** n

anneal vb to toughen (glass or metal) by heat treatment ▶ HISTORY Old English *onǽlan*

annelid n a worm with a segmented body, such as the earthworm ▶ HISTORY Latin *anulus* ring

annex vb **1** to seize (territory) by conquest or occupation **2** to take without permission **3** to join or add (something) to something larger ▶ HISTORY Latin *annectere* to attach to > **annexation** n

annexe or esp US **annex** n **1** an extension to a main building **2** a building used as an addition to a main one nearby

annihilate vb **-lating, -lated 1** to destroy (a place or a group of people) completely **2** *informal* to defeat totally in an argument or a contest ▶ HISTORY Latin *nihil* nothing > **annihilation** n

anniversary n, pl **-ries 1** the date on which an event, such as a wedding, occurred in some previous year **2** the celebration of this ▶ HISTORY Latin *annus* year + *vertere* to turn

anno Domini adv in the year of our Lord

annotate vb **-tating, -tated** to add critical or explanatory notes to a written work ▶ HISTORY Latin *nota* mark > **annotation** n

announce vb **-nouncing, -nounced 1** to make known publicly **2** to proclaim **3** to declare the arrival of (a person) **4** to be a sign of: *snowdrops announced the arrival of spring* ▶ HISTORY Latin *annuntiare* > **announcement** n

announcer n a person who introduces programmes on radio or television

annoy vb to irritate or displease ▶ HISTORY Latin *in odio (esse)* (to be) hated > **annoyance** n > **annoying** adj

annual adj **1** occurring or done once a year: *the union's annual conference* **2** lasting for a year: *the annual subscription* ▷ n **3** a plant that completes its life cycle in one year **4** a book published once every year ▶ HISTORY Latin *annus* year > **annually** adv

annuity n, pl **-ties** a fixed sum payable at specified intervals over a period ▶ HISTORY Latin *annuus* annual

annul vb **-nulling, -nulled** to declare (a contract or marriage) invalid ▶ HISTORY Latin *nullus* not any

annular (an-new-lar) adj ring-shaped ▶ HISTORY Latin *anulus* ring

annular eclipse n an eclipse of the sun in which a ring of sunlight can be seen surrounding the shadow of the moon

annulate (an-new-lit) adj having, composed of, or marked with rings ▶ HISTORY Latin *anulus* ring

annulment n the formal declaration that a contract or marriage is invalid

Annunciation n **1 the Annunciation** the announcement by the angel Gabriel to the Virgin Mary of her conception of Christ **2** the festival commemorating this, on March 25 (Lady Day) ▶ HISTORY Latin *annuntiare* to announce

anode n *electronics* the positive electrode in an electrolytic cell or in an electronic valve ▶ HISTORY Greek *anodos* a way up

anodize or **-dise** vb **-dizing, -dized** or **-dising, -dised** chem to coat (a metal) with a protective oxide film by electrolysis

anodyne n **1** something that relieves pain or distress ▷ adj **2** neutral **3** capable of relieving pain or distress ▶ HISTORY Greek an- without + odunē pain

anoint vb to smear with oil as a sign of consecration ▶ HISTORY Latin inunguere

anointing of the sick n RC Church a sacrament in which a person who is dying is anointed by a priest

anomalous adj different from the normal or usual order or type ▶ HISTORY Greek an- not + homalos even

anomaly (an-**nom**-a-lee) n, pl **-lies** something that deviates from the normal; an irregularity

anomie or **anomy** (an-oh-mee) n sociol lack of social or moral standards ▶ HISTORY Greek a- without + nomos law

anon adv old-fashioned or informal soon: you shall see him anon ▶ HISTORY Old English on āne in one, that is, immediately

anon. anonymous

anonymous adj **1** by someone whose name is unknown or withheld: an anonymous letter **2** having no known name: an anonymous writer **3** lacking distinguishing characteristics: an anonymous little town **4 Anonymous** of an organization which helps applicants who remain anonymous: Alcoholics Anonymous ▶ HISTORY Greek an- without + onoma name > **anonymity** n

anorak n **1** Brit, Austral & S African a waterproof hip-length jacket with a hood **2** Brit, informal a socially inept person with a hobby considered to be boring

■ **WORD HISTORY**
■ The first people to wear anoraks were the Inuit.
■ In Inuktitut, ánorâq means 'a piece of clothing'
■ and denotes a long, hooded jacket made from
■ fur such as sealskin or caribou skin.

anorexia or **anorexia nervosa** n a psychological disorder characterized by fear of becoming fat and refusal to eat ▶ HISTORY Greek an- without + orexis appetite > **anorexic** adj, n

another adj **1** one more: they don't have the right to demand another chance **2** different: you'll have to find another excuse ▷ pron **3** one more: help yourself to another **4** a different one: one way or another ▶ HISTORY originally an other

Anschluss (an-shlooss) n history, politics a political or economic union, used esp. of the annexation of Austria by Nazi Germany (1938) ▶ HISTORY German anschliessen to join

answer vb **1** to reply or respond (to) by word or act **2** to be responsible (to a person) **3** to reply correctly to (a question) **4** to respond or react: a dog that answers to the name of Pugg **5** to meet the requirements of **6** to give a defence of (a charge) ▷ n **7** a reply to a question, request, letter, or article **8** a solution to a problem **9** a reaction or response ▶ HISTORY Old English andswaru

answerable adj **answerable for** or **to** responsible for or accountable to

answering machine n a device for answering a telephone automatically and recording messages

ant n a small often wingless insect, living in highly organized colonies ▶ HISTORY Old English ǣmette

antacid chem n **1** a substance used to treat acidity in the stomach ▷ adj **2** having the properties of this substance

antagonism n openly expressed hostility

antagonist n **1** an opponent or adversary **2** anat an antagonistic muscle > **antagonistic** adj

antagonistic muscle n anat a muscle that works with another, in the opposite direction

antagonize or **-nise** vb **-nizing, -nized** or **-nising, -nised** to arouse hostility in: it was not prudent to antagonize a hired killer ▶ HISTORY Greek anti- against + agōn contest

antalkali (ant-**alk**-a-lie) n chem a substance that neutralizes alkalis

Antarctic n **1 the Antarctic** the area around the South Pole ▷ adj **2** of this region ▶ HISTORY Greek antarktikos

Antarctic Circle n the imaginary circle around the earth at latitude 66° 32′ S

ante n **1** the stake put up before the deal in poker by the players **2** informal a sum of money representing a person's share **3 up the ante** informal to increase the costs or risks involved in an action ▷ vb **-teing, -ted** or **-teed 4** to place (one's stake) in poker **5 ante up** informal to pay ▶ HISTORY Latin: before

ante- prefix before in time or position: antediluvian; antechamber ▶ HISTORY Latin

anteater n a mammal with a long snout used for eating termites

antecedent n **1** an event or circumstance that happens or exists before another **2** grammar a word or phrase to which a relative pronoun, such as who, refers **3 antecedents** a person's ancestors and past history ▷ adj **4** preceding in time or order ▶ HISTORY Latin antecedere to go before

antechamber n an anteroom

antedate vb **-dating, -dated 1** to be or occur at an earlier date than **2** to give (something) a date that is earlier than the actual date

antediluvian adj **1** belonging to the ages before the biblical Flood **2** old-fashioned ▶ HISTORY Latin ante- before + diluvium flood

antelope n, pl **-lopes** or **-lope** any of a group of graceful deerlike mammals of Africa and Asia, which have long legs and horns ▶ HISTORY Late Greek antholops a legendary beast

antenatal adj before birth; during pregnancy: an antenatal clinic

antenna n **1** (pl **-nae**) one of a pair of mobile feelers on the heads of insects, lobsters, and certain other creatures **2** (pl **-nas**) an aerial: TV antennas ▶ HISTORY Latin: sail yard

antepenultimate adj **1** third from last ▷ n **2** anything that is third from last

ante-post adj Brit (of a bet) placed before the runners in a race are confirmed

29

anterior *adj* **1** at or towards the front **2** earlier ▶ HISTORY Latin

anteroom *n* a small room leading into a larger room, often used as a waiting room

anthem *n* **1** a song of loyalty or devotion: *a national anthem* **2** a piece of music for a choir, usually set to words from the Bible ▶ HISTORY Late Latin *antiphona* antiphon

anther *n* *bot* the part of the stamen of a flower which contains the pollen ▶ HISTORY Greek *anthos* flower

ant hill *n* a mound of soil built by ants around the entrance to their nest

anthology *n, pl* **-gies** a collection of poems or other literary pieces by various authors ▶ HISTORY Greek *anthos* flower + *legein* to collect > **anthologist** *n*

anthracite *n* a hard coal that burns slowly with little smoke or flame but intense heat ▶ HISTORY Greek *anthrax* coal

anthrax *n* a dangerous infectious disease of cattle and sheep, which can be passed to humans ▶ HISTORY Greek: carbuncle

anthropocentric *adj* regarding the human being as the most important factor in the universe ▶ HISTORY Greek *anthrōpos* human being + Latin *centrum* centre

anthropoid *adj* **1** resembling a human being ▷ *n* **2** an ape, such as the chimpanzee, that resembles a human being

anthropology *n* the study of human origins, institutions, and beliefs ▶ HISTORY Greek *anthrōpos* human being + *logos* word > **anthropological** *adj* > **anthropologist** *n*

anthropomorphism *n* the attribution of human form or personality to a god, animal, or object > **anthropomorphic** *adj*

anti *informal adj* **1** opposed to a party, policy, or attitude ▷ *n* **2** an opponent of a party, policy, or attitude

anti- *prefix* **1** against or opposed to: *antiwar* **2** opposite to: *anticlimax* **3** counteracting or neutralizing: *antifreeze* ▶ HISTORY Greek

anti-aircraft *adj* for defence against aircraft attack

antiballistic missile *n* a missile designed to destroy a ballistic missile in flight

antibiotic *n* **1** a chemical substance capable of destroying bacteria ▷ *adj* **2** of or relating to antibiotics

antibody *n, pl* **-bodies** a protein produced in the blood which destroys bacteria

Antichrist *n* **1** *New Testament* the chief enemy of Christ **2** an enemy of Christ or Christianity

anticipate *vb* **-pating, -pated** **1** to foresee and act in advance of: *he anticipated some probing questions* **2** to look forward to **3** to make use of (something, such as one's salary) before receiving it **4** to mention (part of a story) before its proper time ▶ HISTORY Latin *ante-* before + *capere* to take > **anticipatory** *adj*

anticipation *n* the act of anticipating; expectation, premonition, or foresight: *smiling in happy anticipation*

anticlerical *adj* opposed to the power and influence of the clergy in politics

anticlimax *n* a disappointing conclusion to a series of events > **anticlimactic** *adj*

anticline *n* *geol* a fold of rock raised up into a broad arch so that the strata slope down on both sides

anticlockwise *adv, adj* in the opposite direction to the rotation of the hands of a clock

anticoagulant (an-tee-koh-**ag**-yew-lant) *n* a substance that prevents the clotting of blood

antics *pl n* absurd acts or postures ▶ HISTORY Italian *antico* something grotesque (from fantastic carvings found in ruins of ancient Rome)

anticyclone *n* *meteorol* an area of moving air of high pressure in which the winds rotate outwards

antidepressant *n* **1** a drug used to treat depression ▷ *adj* **2** of or relating to such a drug

antidote *n* **1** *med* a substance that counteracts a poison **2** anything that counteracts a harmful condition: *exercise may be a good antidote to insomnia* ▶ HISTORY Greek *anti-* against + *didonai* to give

anti-Europeanism *n* opposition to or dislike of Europe or the European Union

antifreeze *n* a liquid added to water to lower its freezing point, used in the radiator of a motor vehicle to prevent freezing

antigen (**an**-tee-jen) *n* a substance, usually a toxin, that causes the body to produce antibodies ▶ HISTORY *anti(body)* + *-gen* (suffix) producing

antihero *n, pl* **-roes** a central character in a novel, play, or film, who lacks the traditional heroic virtues

antihistamine *n* a drug that neutralizes the effects of histamine, used in the treatment of allergies

antiknock *n* a substance added to motor fuel to reduce knocking in the engine caused by too rapid combustion

antilogarithm *n* *maths* a number corresponding to a given logarithm

antimacassar *n* a cloth put over the back of a chair to prevent it getting dirty ▶ HISTORY *anti-* + *Macassar (oil)*

antimatter *n* *physics* a hypothetical form of matter composed of antiparticles

anti-microbial *adj* *biochem* preventing the growth of disease-causing bacteria

antimony (**an**-tim-mon-ee) *n* *chem* a silvery-white metallic element that is added to alloys to increase their strength. Symbol: Sb ▶ HISTORY Medieval Latin *antimonium*

antinomy (**an**-tin-nom-ee) *n, pl* **-mies** contradiction between two laws or principles that are reasonable in themselves ▶ HISTORY Greek *anti-* against + *nomos* law

antinovel *n* a type of prose fiction in which conventional elements of the novel are rejected

antinuclear *adj* opposed to nuclear weapons or nuclear power

antioxidant *n* *chem* a substance that slows down the process of oxidation

antiparticle *n* *nuclear physics* an elementary particle that has the same mass as its corresponding particle, but opposite charge and opposite magnetism

antipasto *n, pl* **-tos** an appetizer in an Italian meal ▶ HISTORY Italian: before food

antipathy (an-**tip**-a-thee) *n* a feeling of strong dislike or hostility ▶ HISTORY Greek *anti*- against + *patheia* feeling > **antipathetic** *adj*

antipersonnel *adj* (of weapons or bombs) designed to be used against people rather than equipment

antiperspirant *n* a substance applied to the skin to reduce or prevent perspiration

antiphon *n* a hymn sung in alternate parts by two groups of singers ▶ HISTORY Greek *anti*- against + *phōnē* sound

antipodes (an-**tip**-pod-deez) *pl n* **1** any two places that are situated diametrically opposite one another on the earth's surface **2 the Antipodes** *Brit* Australia and New Zealand ▶ HISTORY Greek plural of *antipous* having the feet opposite > **antipodean** *adj*

antipope *n* a pope set up in opposition to the one chosen by church laws

antipyretic *adj* **1** reducing fever ▷ *n* **2** a drug that reduces fever

antiquarian *adj* **1** collecting or dealing with antiquities or rare books ▷ *n* **2** an antiquary

antiquary *n, pl* **-quaries** a person who collects, deals in, or studies antiques or ancient works of art

antiquated *adj* obsolete or old-fashioned ▶ HISTORY Latin *antiquus* ancient

antique *n* **1** a decorative object or piece of furniture, of an earlier period, that is valued for its beauty, workmanship, and age ▷ *adj* **2** made in an earlier period **3** *informal* old-fashioned ▶ HISTORY Latin *antiquus* ancient

antiquity *n, pl* **-ties** **1** great age **2** the far distant past **3 antiquities** objects dating from ancient times

antiracism *n* the policy of challenging racism or promoting racial tolerance > **antiracist** *n, adj*

antirrhinum *n* a two-lipped flower of various colours, such as the snapdragon ▶ HISTORY Greek *anti*- like, imitating + *rhis* nose

antiscorbutic *adj* preventing or curing scurvy

anti-Semitic *adj* discriminating against Jews > **anti-Semite** *n* > **anti-Semitism** *n*

antiseptic *adj* **1** preventing infection by killing germs ▷ *n* **2** an antiseptic substance

antiserum *n* blood serum containing antibodies used to treat or provide immunity to a disease

antishake *adj* (of photographic equipment) reducing the blurring caused by movement of the person taking a photograph

antisocial *adj* **1** avoiding the company of other people **2** (of behaviour) annoying or harmful to other people

antistatic *adj* reducing the effects of static electricity

antistrophe *n* **1** *drama* the movement of the chorus as it performs the second part of a choral ode in ancient Greek drama **2** *poetry* the second of two metrical systems used within a poem

antitank *adj* (of weapons) designed to destroy military tanks

antithesis (an-**tith**-iss-iss) *n, pl* **-ses** (-seez) **1** the exact opposite **2** *rhetoric* the placing together of contrasting ideas or words to produce an effect of balance, such as *where gods command, mere mortals must obey* ▶ HISTORY Greek *anti*- against + *tithenai* to place > **antithetical** *adj*

antitoxin *n* an antibody that acts against a toxin > **antitoxic** *adj*

antitrades *pl n* winds blowing in the opposite direction from and above the trade winds

antitrust *adj* *US, Austral & S African* (of laws) opposing business monopolies

antivirus *adj* designed to prevent viruses entering a computer system or network

antler *n* one of a pair of branched horns on the heads of male deer ▶ HISTORY Old French *antoillier*

antonym *n* a word that means the opposite of another ▶ HISTORY Greek *anti*- opposite + *onoma* name

antrum *n, pl* **-tra** *anat* a natural cavity, esp. in a bone ▶ HISTORY Latin: cave

Anubis *n* an Egyptian god with a jackal's head

anus (**ain**-uss) *n* the opening at the end of the alimentary canal, through which faeces are discharged ▶ HISTORY Latin

anvil *n* a heavy iron block on which metals are hammered into particular shapes ▶ HISTORY Old English *anfealt*

anxiety *n, pl* **-ties** **1** a state of uneasiness about what may happen **2** eagerness: *she was uneasy with his mixture of diffidence and anxiety to please*

anxious *adj* **1** worried and tense **2** causing anxiety: *Sharpe faces an anxious wait for a specialist's report* **3** intensely desiring: *both sides were anxious for a deal* ▶ HISTORY Latin *anxius* > **anxiously** *adv*

any *adj, pron* **1** one, some, or several, no matter how much or what kind: *the jar opener fits over the top of any bottle or jar; have you left me any?* **2** even the smallest amount or even one: *we can't answer any questions; don't give her any* **3** whatever or whichever: *police may board any bus or train* **4** an indefinite or unlimited amount or number: *he would sign cheques for any amount of money* ▷ *adv* **5** to even the smallest extent: *the outcome wouldn't have been any different* ▶ HISTORY Old English *ænig*

anybody *pron* same as **anyone**

anyhow *adv* same as **anyway**

anyone *pron* **1** any person: *is anyone there?* **2** a person of any importance: *is he anyone?*

anything *pron* **1** any object, event, or action whatever: *they'll do anything to please you* ▷ *adv* **2** in any way: *it is not a computer nor anything like a computer* **3 anything but** not at all: *the result is anything but simple*

anyway *adv* **1** at any rate; nevertheless **2** in any manner **3** carelessly

a

anywhere adv **1** in, at, or to any place **2 get anywhere** to be successful: *we will not get anywhere by being negative*

anzac n NZ a type of biscuit

Anzac n (in the First World War) a soldier serving with the Australian and New Zealand Army Corps

Anzac Day n 25th April, a public holiday in Australia and New Zealand commemorating the Anzac landing at Gallipoli in 1915

AOB (on the agenda for a meeting) any other business

aorta (eh-**or**-ta) n the main artery of the body, which carries oxygen-rich blood from the heart ▶ HISTORY Greek *aortē* something lifted

apace adv literary quickly: *repairs to the grid continued apace*

Apache n, pl **Apaches** or **Apache** a member of a Native American people of the southwestern US and N Mexico ▶ HISTORY Mexican Spanish

apart adj, adv **1** to or in pieces: *he took a couple of cars apart and rebuilt them* **2** separate in time, place, or position: *my father and myself stood slightly apart from them* **3** individual or distinct: *a nation apart* **4** not being taken into account: *early timing difficulties apart, they encountered few problems* **5 apart from** other than: *apart from searching the house there is little more we can do* ▶ HISTORY Old French *a part* at (the) side

apartheid n (formerly) the official government policy of racial segregation in South Africa ▶ HISTORY Afrikaans *apart* + *-heid* -hood

apartment n **1** any room in a building, usually one of several forming a suite, used as living accommodation **2** chiefly US & Canad a flat ▶ HISTORY French *appartement*

apathy n lack of interest or enthusiasm ▶ HISTORY Greek *a-* without + *pathos* feeling > **apathetic** adj

ape n **1** an animal, such as a chimpanzee or gorilla, which is closely related to human beings and the monkeys, and which has no tail **2** a stupid, clumsy, or ugly man ▷ vb **aping, aped 3** to imitate ▶ HISTORY Old English *apa* > **apelike** adj

apeman n, pl **-men** an extinct primate thought to have been the forerunner of true humans

aperient (ap-**peer**-ee-ent) med adj **1** having a mild laxative effect ▷ n **2** a mild laxative ▶ HISTORY Latin *aperire* to open

aperitif (ap-per-rit-**teef**) n an alcoholic drink taken before a meal ▶ HISTORY French

aperture n **1** a hole or opening **2** an opening in a camera or telescope that controls the amount of light entering it ▶ HISTORY Latin *aperire* to open

apex n the highest point ▶ HISTORY Latin: point

APEX Advance Purchase Excursion: a reduced fare for journeys booked a specified period in advance

aphasia n a disorder of the central nervous system that affects the ability to use and understand words ▶ HISTORY Greek *a-* not + *phanai* to speak

aphelion (ap-**heel**-lee-on) n, pl **-lia** (-lee-a) astron the point in the orbit of a planet or comet when it is farthest from the sun ▶ HISTORY Greek *apo-* from + *hēlios* sun

aphid (**eh**-fid) or **aphis** (**eh**-fiss) n, pl **aphids** or **aphides** (**eh**-fid-deez) a small insect which feeds by sucking the juices from plants ▶ HISTORY New Latin

aphorism n a short clever saying expressing a general truth ▶ HISTORY Greek *aphorizein* to define

aphrodisiac (af-roh-**diz**-zee-ak) n **1** a substance that arouses sexual desire ▷ adj **2** arousing sexual desire ▶ HISTORY Greek *aphrodisios* belonging to *Aphrodite*, goddess of love

Aphrodite n Greek myth the goddess of love

apiary (**ape**-yar-ee) n, pl **-aries** a place where bees are kept ▶ HISTORY Latin *apis* bee > **apiarist** n

apiculture n the breeding and care of bees ▶ HISTORY Latin *apis* bee + CULTURE > **apiculturist** n

apiece adv each: *they had another cocktail apiece and then went down to dinner*

aplomb (ap-**plom**) n calm self-possession ▶ HISTORY French: uprightness

apocalypse n **1** the end of the world **2** an event of great destructive violence > **apocalyptic** adj

■ **WORD HISTORY**
■ This word comes from Greek *apokaluptein*,
■ which means 'to reveal or disclose'. An
■ apocalypse is a prophetic disclosure of
■ something that is going to happen, such as
■ the description of the end of the world given
■ in the last book of the Bible, the 'Revelation of
■ St John the Divine', which is also known as
■ 'the Apocalypse'.

Apocalypse n **the Apocalypse** Bible the Book of Revelation, the last book of the New Testament

Apocrypha (ap-**pok**-rif-fa) pl n **the Apocrypha** the 14 books included as an appendix to the Old Testament, which are not accepted as part of the Hebrew scriptures ▶ HISTORY Late Latin *apocrypha (scripta)* hidden (writings), from Greek *apokruptein* to hide away

apocryphal adj of questionable authenticity: *the paranoid and clearly apocryphal story*

apogee (**ap**-oh-jee) n **1** astron the point in its orbit around the earth when the moon or a satellite is farthest from the earth **2** the highest point: *the concept found its apogee in Renaissance Italy* ▶ HISTORY Greek *apogaios* away from the earth

apolitical adj not concerned with political matters

Apollo n classical myth the god of the sun, music, and medicine

apologetic adj showing or expressing regret > **apologetically** adv

apologetics n the branch of theology concerned with the reasoned defence of Christianity

apologia n a formal written defence of a cause

apologist n a person who offers a formal defence of a cause

apologize or **-gise** vb **-gizing, -gized** or **-gising, -gised** to say that one is sorry for some wrongdoing

apology *n*, *pl* **-gies** **1** an expression of regret for some wrongdoing **2** same as **apologia** **3** **an apology for** a poor example of: *an apology for a man* ▶ HISTORY Greek *apologia* a verbal defence, speech

apoplectic *adj* **1** of apoplexy **2** *informal* furious

apoplexy *n* *med* a stroke ▶ HISTORY Greek *apoplēssein* to cripple by a stroke

apostasy (ap-**poss**-stass-ee) *n*, *pl* **-sies** abandonment of one's religious faith, political party, or cause ▶ HISTORY Greek *apostasis* desertion

apostate *n* **1** a person who has abandoned his or her religion, political party, or cause ▷ *adj* **2** guilty of apostasy

a posteriori (**eh** poss-steer-ee-**or**-rye) *adj* *logic* involving reasoning from effect to cause ▶ HISTORY Latin: from the latter

apostle *n* **1** one of the twelve disciples chosen by Christ to preach his gospel **2** an ardent supporter of a cause or movement ▶ HISTORY Greek *apostolos* a messenger

apostolic (ap-poss-**stoll**-ik) *adj* **1** of or relating to the Apostles or their teachings **2** of or relating to the pope

Apostolic See *n* the see of the pope, at Rome

apostrophe¹ (ap-**poss**-trof-fee) *n* the punctuation mark (') used to indicate the omission of a letter or letters, such as *he's* for *he has* or *he is*, and to form the possessive, as in *John's father* ▶ HISTORY Greek *apostrephein* to turn away

apostrophe² *n* *rhetoric* a digression from a speech to address an imaginary or absent person or thing ▶ HISTORY Greek: a turning away

apostrophize *or* **-phise** *vb* **-phizing, -phized** *or* **-phising, -phised** *rhetoric* to address an apostrophe to

apothecary *n*, *pl* **-caries** *old-fashioned* a chemist ▶ HISTORY Late Latin *apothecarius* warehouseman

apotheosis (ap-poth-ee-**oh**-siss) *n*, *pl* **-ses** (-seez) **1** a perfect example: *it was the apotheosis of elitism* **2** elevation to the rank of a god ▶ HISTORY Greek

app *n* *computers* a computer program that is written for a particular purpose, esp. one that can be downloaded to a mobile electronic device

appal *or US* **appall** *vb* **-palling, -palled** to fill with horror; terrify ▶ HISTORY Old French *appalir* to turn pale

appalling *adj* **1** causing dismay, horror, or revulsion **2** *very bad* > **appallingly** *adv*

apparatus *n* **1** a collection of equipment used for a particular purpose **2** any complicated device, system, or organization: *the whole apparatus of law enforcement* ▶ HISTORY Latin

apparel (ap-**par**-rel) *n* *old-fashioned* clothing ▶ HISTORY Latin *parare* to prepare

apparent *adj* **1** readily seen or understood; obvious **2** seeming as opposed to real: *he frowned in apparent bewilderment* **3** *physics* as observed but ignoring such factors as the motion of the observer and changes in the environment: *apparent depth* ▶ HISTORY Latin *apparere* to appear > **apparently** *adv*

apparition *n* a ghost or ghostlike figure ▶ HISTORY Latin *apparere* to appear

appeal *vb* **1** to make an earnest request **2** **appeal to** to attract, please, or interest **3** *law* to apply to a higher court to review (a case or issue decided by a lower court) **4** to resort to a higher authority to change a decision **5** to call on in support of an earnest request: *he appealed for volunteers to help in relief work* **6** *cricket* to request the umpire to declare a batsman out ▷ *n* **7** an earnest request for money or help **8** the power to attract, please, or interest people **9** *law* a request for a review of a lower court's decision by a higher court **10** an application to a higher authority to change a decision that has been made **11** *cricket* a request to the umpire to declare the batsman out ▶ HISTORY Latin *appellare* to entreat

appealing *adj* attractive or pleasing

appear *vb* **1** to come into sight **2** to seem: *it appears that no one survived the crash* **3** to come into existence: *a rash and small sores appeared around the shoulder and neck* **4** to perform: *she hadn't appeared in a film for almost fifty years* **5** to be present in court before a magistrate or judge: *two men have appeared in court in London charged with conspiracy* **6** to be published or become available: *both books appeared in 1934* ▶ HISTORY Latin *apparere*

appearance *n* **1** a sudden or unexpected arrival of someone or something at a place **2** the introduction or invention of something: *the appearance of credit cards* **3** an act or instance of appearing: *it will be his fiftieth appearance for his country* **4** the way a person or thing looks: *I spotted a man of extraordinary appearance* **5** **keep up appearances** to maintain the public impression of wellbeing or normality **6** **put in an appearance** to attend an event briefly **7** **to all appearances** apparently: *to all appearances they seemed enthralled by what he was saying*

appease *vb* **-peasing, -peased** **1** to pacify (someone) by yielding to his or her demands **2** to satisfy or relieve (a feeling) ▶ HISTORY Old French *apaisier*

appeasement *n* **1** the act of appeasing **2** *history* (in the 1930s) the policy adopted by Britain and France of giving in to Hitler's demands and accepting German political and military changes in the hope of maintaining peace with Germany

appellant *law* *n* **1** a person who appeals to a higher court to review the decision of a lower court ▷ *adj* **2** same as **appellate**

appellate (ap-**pell**-it) *adj* *law* **1** of appeals **2** (of a tribunal) having the power to review appeals

appellate jurisdiction *n* *law* the authority (of a court) to hear appeals

appellation *n* *formal* a name or title

append *vb* *formal* to add as a supplement: *a series of notes appended to his translation of the poems* ▶ HISTORY Latin *pendere* to hang

appendage *n* a secondary part attached to a main part

appendicectomy or esp US, Canad & Australia **appendectomy** n, pl **-mies** surgical removal of the appendix ▶ HISTORY *appendix* + Greek *tomē* a cutting

appendicitis n inflammation of the appendix, causing abdominal pain

appendix (ap-**pen**-dix) n, pl **-dices** (-diss-seez) or **-dixes** 1 separate additional material at the end of a book 2 anat a short thin tube, closed at one end and attached to the large intestine at the other end ▶ HISTORY Latin

appertain vb **appertain to** to belong to, relate to, or be connected with ▶ HISTORY Latin *ad-* to + *pertinere* to pertain

appetite n 1 a desire for food or drink 2 a liking or willingness: *he had an insatiable appetite for publicity* ▶ HISTORY Latin *appetere* to desire ardently

appetizer or **-iser** n a small amount of food or drink taken at the start of a meal to stimulate the appetite

appetizing or **-ising** adj stimulating the appetite; looking or smelling delicious

applaud vb 1 to show approval of by clapping one's hands 2 to express approval of: *we applaud her determination and ambition* ▶ HISTORY Latin *applaudere*

applause n appreciation shown by clapping one's hands

apple n 1 a round firm fruit, with red, yellow, or green skin and crisp whitish flesh, that grows on trees 2 **apple of one's eye** a person that one loves very much ▶ HISTORY Old English *æppel*

applet n computers a computing program that runs within a page on the World Wide Web ▶ HISTORY *app(lication program)* + *-let* small or lesser

appliance n a machine or device that has a specific function

applicable adj appropriate or relevant

applicant n a person who applies for something, such as a job or grant

application n 1 a formal request, for example for a job 2 the act of applying something to a particular use: *you can make practical application of this knowledge to everyday living* 3 concentrated effort: *success would depend on their talent and application* 4 the act of putting something, such as a lotion or paint, onto a surface 5 short for **application program**

application program n the full name for **app**

applicator n a device for applying cosmetics, medication, or some other substance

applied adj put to practical use: *applied mathematics*

appliqué (ap-**plee**-kay) n a kind of decoration in which one material is cut out and sewn or fixed onto another ▶ HISTORY French: applied

apply vb **-plies, -plying, -plied** 1 to make a formal request for something, such as a job or a loan 2 to put to practical use: *he applied his calligrapher's skill* 3 to put onto a surface: *the hand lotion should be applied whenever possible throughout the day* 4 to be relevant or appropriate: *he had been involved in research applied to flying wing aircraft* 5 **apply oneself** to concentrate one's efforts or faculties ▶ HISTORY Latin *applicare* to attach to

appoint vb 1 to assign officially to a job or position 2 to fix or decide (a time or place for an event) 3 to equip or furnish: *it was a beautifully appointed room with rows and rows of books* ▶ HISTORY Old French *apointer* to put into a good state > **appointee** n

appointment n 1 an arrangement to meet a person 2 the act of placing someone in a job or position 3 the person appointed 4 the job or position to which a person is appointed 5 **appointments** fixtures or fittings

apportion vb to divide out in shares

apposite adj suitable or appropriate: *an apposite saying* ▶ HISTORY Latin *ad-* near + *ponere* to put

apposition n a grammatical construction in which a noun or group of words is placed after another to modify its meaning, for example *my friend the mayor*

appraisal n an assessment of the worth or quality of a person or thing

appraise vb **-praising, -praised** to assess the worth, value, or quality of ▶ HISTORY Old French *aprisier*

appreciable adj enough to be noticed; significant > **appreciably** adv

appreciate vb **-ating, -ated** 1 to value highly: *we appreciate his music but can't afford £400 a seat* 2 to be aware of and understand: *I can fully appreciate how desperate you must feel* 3 to feel grateful for: *we do appreciate all you do for us* 4 to increase in value ▶ HISTORY Latin *pretium* price

appreciation n 1 gratitude 2 awareness and understanding of a problem or difficulty 3 recognition of a person's abilities, qualities, or efforts 4 sensitive recognition of the artistic qualities of something 5 an increase in value

appreciative adj feeling or expressing appreciation > **appreciatively** adv

apprehend vb 1 to arrest and take into custody 2 to grasp (something) mentally; understand ▶ HISTORY Latin *apprehendere* to lay hold of

apprehension n 1 anxiety or dread 2 the act of arresting 3 understanding

apprehensive adj fearful or anxious about the future

apprentice n 1 someone who works for a skilled person for a fixed period in order to learn his or her trade ▷ vb **-ticing, -ticed** 2 to take or place as an apprentice ▶ HISTORY Old French *aprendre* to learn > **apprenticeship** n

apprise or **-prize** vb **-prising, -prised** or **-prizing, -prized** to make aware: *I needed to apprise the students of the dangers that may be involved* ▶ HISTORY French *apprendre* to teach; learn

appro n **on appro** informal on approval

approach vb 1 to come close or closer to 2 to make a proposal or suggestion to 3 to begin to deal with (a matter) ▷ n 4 the act of coming close

a

or closer **5** a proposal or suggestion made to a person **6** the way or means of reaching a place; access **7** a way of dealing with a matter **8** an approximation **9** the course followed by an aircraft preparing for landing ▸ **HISTORY** Latin *ad-* to + *prope* near > **approachable** *adj*

approach road *n* NZ & S African a smaller road leading into a major road

approbation *n* approval

appropriate *adj* **1** right or suitable ▷ *vb* **-ating, -ated 2** to take for one's own use without permission **3** to put (money) aside for a particular purpose ▸ **HISTORY** Latin *ad-* to + *proprius* one's own > **appropriately** *adv*

appropriation *n* **1** the act of putting money aside for a particular purpose **2** money put aside for a particular purpose

approval *n* **1** consent **2** a favourable opinion **3 on approval** (of articles for sale) with an option to be returned without payment if unsatisfactory: *each volume in the collection will be sent to you on approval*

approve *vb* **-proving, -proved 1 approve of** to consider fair, good, or right **2** to authorize or agree to ▸ **HISTORY** Latin *approbare*

approx. approximate or approximately

approximate *adj* **1** almost but not quite exact ▷ *vb* **-mating, -mated 2 approximate to a** to come close to **b** to be almost the same as ▸ **HISTORY** Latin *ad-* to + *proximus* nearest > **approximately** *adv* > **approximation** *n*

appurtenances *pl n* minor or additional features or possessions ▸ **HISTORY** Old French *apartenance* secondary thing

APR annual percentage rate

Apr. April

après-ski (ap-ray-**skee**) *n* social activities after a day's skiing

apricot *n* **1** a yellowish-orange juicy fruit which resembles a small peach ▷ *adj* **2** yellowish-orange ▸ **HISTORY** Latin *praecox* early-ripening

■ **WORD HISTORY**
■ This word has a long and interesting history.
■ It comes originally from the Latin word *praecox*,
■ meaning 'early ripening'. From Latin it was
■ borrowed into Greek, and then into Arabic as
■ *al-birqūq*, denoting the apricot, which flowers
■ and ripens earlier than the peach. From Arabic,
■ it came back to Europe as Portuguese
■ *albricoque*, and from Portuguese into English
■ as the 'apricock', later altered to 'apricot'.

April *n* the fourth month of the year ▸ **HISTORY** Latin *Aprilis*

April fool *n* a victim of a practical joke played on the first of April (**April Fools' Day** or **All Fools' Day**)

a priori (eh pry-**or**-rye) *adj logic* involving reasoning from cause to effect ▸ **HISTORY** Latin: from the previous

apron *n* **1** a garment worn over the front of the body to protect one's clothes **2** a hard-surfaced area at an airport or hangar for manoeuvring and loading aircraft **3** the part of a stage extending in front of the curtain **4 tied to someone's apron strings** dependent on or dominated by someone ▸ **HISTORY** Old French *naperon* little cloth

apropos (ap-prop-**poh**) *adj* **1** appropriate ▷ *adv* **2** by the way; incidentally **3 apropos of** with regard to ▸ **HISTORY** French *à propos* to the purpose

apse *n* an arched or domed recess at the east end of a church ▸ **HISTORY** Greek *apsis* a fitting together

apsis (**ap**-siss) *n, pl* **apsides** (**ap**-sid-deez) *astron* either of two points lying at the extremities of the elliptical orbit of a planet or satellite ▸ **HISTORY** see APSE

apt *adj* **1** having a specified tendency: *they are apt to bend the rules* **2** suitable or appropriate **3** quick to learn: *she was turning out to be a more apt pupil than he had expected* ▸ **HISTORY** Latin *aptus* fitting > **aptly** *adv* > **aptness** *n*

apteryx *n* same as **kiwi** (sense 1) ▸ **HISTORY** Greek *a-* without + *pteron* wing

aptitude *n* natural tendency or ability

aptitude test *n* a test designed to assess a person's ability to do a particular type of work

aqua *adj* short for **aquamarine** ▸ **HISTORY** Latin: water

aquaculture or **aquiculture** *n agriculture* the cultivation of freshwater and marine organisms for human consumption or use ▸ **HISTORY** Latin *aqua* water + *cultura* cultivation

aqua fortis *n obsolete* nitric acid ▸ **HISTORY** Latin: strong water

aqualung *n* an apparatus for breathing underwater, consisting of a mouthpiece attached to air cylinders

aquamarine *n* **1** a clear greenish-blue gemstone ▷ *adj* **2** greenish-blue ▸ **HISTORY** Latin *aqua marina* sea water

aquaplane *n* **1** a board on which a person stands to be towed by a motorboat for sport ▷ *vb* **-planing, -planed 2** to ride on an aquaplane **3** (of a motor vehicle) to skim uncontrollably on a thin film of water

aqua regia (ak-wa **reej**-ya) *n* a mixture of nitric acid and hydrochloric acid ▸ **HISTORY** New Latin: royal water; referring to its use in dissolving gold, the royal metal

aquarium *n, pl* **aquariums** or **aquaria 1** a tank in which fish and other underwater creatures are kept **2** a building containing such tanks ▸ **HISTORY** Latin *aquarius* relating to water

Aquarius *n astrol* the eleventh sign of the zodiac: the Water Carrier ▸ **HISTORY** Latin

aquatic *adj* **1** growing or living in water **2** *sport* performed in or on water ▷ *n* **3** an aquatic animal or plant **4 aquatics** water sports ▸ **HISTORY** Latin *aqua* water

aquatint *n* a print like a watercolour, produced by etching copper with acid ▸ **HISTORY** Italian *acqua tinta* dyed water

aqua vitae (ak-wa **vee**-tie) *n old-fashioned* brandy ▸ **HISTORY** Medieval Latin: water of life

a

aqueduct *n* a structure, often a bridge, that carries water across a valley or river ▶ HISTORY Latin *aqua* water + *ducere* to convey

aqueous *adj* **1** of, like, or containing water **2** produced by the action of water ▶ HISTORY Latin *aqua* water

aqueous humour *n physiol* the watery fluid in the eyeball, between the cornea and the lens

aquifer *n geol* a water-bearing layer of rock that can be used to supply wells ▶ HISTORY Latin *aqua* water + *ferre* to carry

aquiline *adj* **1** (of a nose) curved like an eagle's beak **2** of or like an eagle ▶ HISTORY Latin *aquila* eagle

Ar *chem* argon

AR Arkansas

Arab *n* **1** a member of a Semitic people originally from Arabia ▷ *adj* **2** of the Arabs ▶ HISTORY Arabic *'Arab*

arabesque (ar-ab-**besk**) *n* **1** a ballet position in which one leg is raised behind and the arms are extended **2** *arts* an elaborate design of intertwined leaves, flowers, and scrolls **3** an ornate piece of music ▶ HISTORY Italian *arabesco* in the Arabic style

Arabian *adj* **1** of Arabia or the Arabs ▷ *n* **2** same as **Arab**

Arabic *n* **1** the language of the Arabs ▷ *adj* **2** of this language, the Arabs, or Arabia

Arabic numerals *pl n* the symbols 1, 2, 3, 4, 5, 6, 7, 8, 9, 0, used to represent numbers

arable *adj* (of land) suitable for growing crops on ▶ HISTORY Latin *arare* to plough

arable farming *n agriculture* the commercial growing of crops

arachnid (ar-**rak**-nid) *n* an eight-legged insect-like creature, such as a spider, scorpion, or tick ▶ HISTORY Greek *arakhnē* spider

arak *n* same as **arrack**

Aramaic *n* an ancient Semitic language spoken in parts of Syria and the Lebanon

Aran *adj* (of knitwear) knitted in a complicated pattern traditional to the Aran Islands off the west coast of Ireland

arbiter *n* **1** a person empowered to judge in a dispute **2** a person with influential opinions about something: *the customer must be the ultimate arbiter of quality*

arbitrary *adj* **1** not done according to any plan or for any particular reason **2** without consideration for the wishes of others: *the arbitrary power of the king* > **arbitrarily** *adv*

arbitrate *vb* **-trating, -trated** to settle (a dispute) by arbitration ▶ HISTORY Latin *arbitrari* to give judgment > **arbitrator** *n*

arbitration *n* the hearing and settlement of a dispute by an impartial referee chosen by both sides

arbor¹ *n US* same as **arbour**

arbor² *n* a revolving shaft or axle in a machine ▶ HISTORY Latin: tree

arboreal (ahr-**bore**-ee-al) *adj* **1** of or resembling a tree **2** living in or among trees

arboretum (ahr-bore-**ee**-tum) *n, pl* **-ta** (-ta) a botanical garden where rare trees or shrubs are cultivated ▶ HISTORY Latin *arbor* tree

arboriculture *n* the cultivation of trees or shrubs ▶ HISTORY Latin *arbor* tree + CULTURE

arbor vitae (**ahr**-bore **vee**-tie) *n* an evergreen tree ▶ HISTORY New Latin: tree of life

arbour *or US* **arbor** *n* a shelter in a garden shaded by trees or climbing plants ▶ HISTORY Latin *herba* grass

arbutus (ar-**byew**-tuss) *n* an evergreen shrub with berries like strawberries ▶ HISTORY Latin

arc *n* **1** something curved in shape **2** *maths* a section of a circle or other curve **3** *electricity* a stream of very bright light that forms when an electric current flows across a small gap between two electrodes ▷ *vb* **4** to form an arc ▶ HISTORY Latin *arcus* bow, arch

ARC AIDS-related complex: relatively mild symptoms suffered in the early stages of infection with the AIDS virus

arcade *n* **1** a covered passageway lined with shops **2** a set of arches and their supporting columns ▶ HISTORY Latin *arcus* bow, arch

Arcadian *literary adj* **1** rural, in an idealized way ▷ *n* **2** a person who leads a quiet simple country life ▶ HISTORY Arcadia, rural district of Ancient Greece

arcane *adj* very mysterious ▶ HISTORY Latin *arcanus* secret

arch¹ *n* **1** a curved structure that spans an opening or supports a bridge or roof **2** something curved **3** the curved lower part of the foot ▷ *vb* **4** to form an arch ▶ HISTORY Latin *arcus* bow, arc

arch² *adj* **1** knowing or superior **2** coyly playful: *he gave an arch smile to indicate his pride* ▶ HISTORY independent use of ARCH- > **archly** *adv*

arch- *or* **archi-** *combining form* chief or principal: *archbishop; archenemy* ▶ HISTORY Greek *arkhein* to rule

archaeobotany *n* the study of plant remains found at archaeological sites > **archaeobotanist** *n*

archaeology *or* **archeology** *n* the study of ancient cultures by the scientific analysis of physical remains ▶ HISTORY Greek *arkhaiologia* study of what is ancient > **archaeological** *or* **archeological** *adj* > **archaeologist** *or* **archeologist** *n*

archaeopteryx *n* an extinct primitive bird with teeth, a long tail, and well-developed wings ▶ HISTORY Greek *arkhaios* ancient + *pterux* winged creature

archaeozoology *n* the study of animal remains found at archaeological sites > **archaeozoologist** *n*

archaic (ark-**kay**-ik) *adj* **1** of a much earlier period **2** out of date or old-fashioned **3** (of a word or phrase) no longer in everyday use ▶ HISTORY Greek *arkhē* beginning > **archaically** *adv*

archaism (**ark**-kay-iz-zum) *n* an archaic word or style > **archaistic** *adj*

archangel (**ark**-ain-jell) *n* an angel of the highest rank

archbishop *n* a bishop of the highest rank

archbishopric *n* the rank, office, or diocese of an archbishop

archdeacon *n* a church official ranking just below a bishop > **archdeaconry** *n*

archdiocese *n* the diocese of an archbishop

archduchess *n* **1** a woman who holds the rank of archduke **2** the wife or widow of an archduke

archduchy *n*, *pl* **-duchies** the territory ruled by an archduke or archduchess

archduke *n* a duke of high rank, esp. one from Austria

archenemy *n*, *pl* **-mies** a chief enemy

archeology *n* same as **archaeology**

archer *n* a person who shoots with a bow and arrow ▶ HISTORY Latin *arcus* bow

archery *n* the art or sport of shooting with a bow and arrow

archetype (**ark**-ee-type) *n* **1** a perfect or typical specimen **2** an original model; prototype ▶ HISTORY Greek *arkhetupos* first-moulded > **archetypal** *adj*

archidiaconal (ark-ee-die-**ak**-on-al) *adj* of an archdeacon or his office

archiepiscopal (ark-ee-ip-**piss**-kop-al) *adj* of an archbishop or his office

Archimedes' principle (ark-ee-**mee**-deez) *n physics* the principle that the apparent loss in weight of an object immersed in a fluid is equal to the weight of the displaced fluid ▶ HISTORY after *Archimedes*, Greek mathematician & physicist

archipelago (ark-ee-**pel**-a-go) *n*, *pl* **-gos** *geog* **1** a group of islands **2** a sea full of small islands ▶ HISTORY Greek *arkhi-* chief + *pelagos* sea

architect *n* **1** a person qualified to design and supervise the construction of buildings **2** any planner or creator: *you will be the architect of your own future* ▶ HISTORY Greek *arkhi-* chief + *tektōn* workman

architecture *n* **1** the style in which a building is designed and built: *Gothic architecture* **2** the science of designing and constructing buildings **3** the structure or design of anything: *computer architecture* > **architectural** *adj*

architrave (**ark-ee**-trave) *n archit* **1** a beam that rests on top of columns **2** a moulding around a doorway or window opening ▶ HISTORY Italian, from *arch-* + *trave* beam

archive (**ark**-ive) *n* **1** a place where records or documents are kept **2 archives** a collection of records or documents **3** *computers* data put on tape or disk for long-term storage ▷ *vb* **4** to store in an archive

archivist (**ark**-iv-ist) *n* a person in charge of archives

archway *n* a passageway under an arch

Arctic *n* **1 the Arctic** the area around the North Pole ▷ *adj* **2** of this region

■ **WORD HISTORY**
■ The word 'arctic' comes from the Greek
■ adjective *arktikos*, meaning 'relating to a bear'
■ (Greek *arktos*). In Greek *arktikos* also meant
■ 'relating to the Great Bear', the constellation
■ which can be seen in the northern sky and
■ which points towards the Pole Star.

Arctic Circle *n* the imaginary circle around the earth at latitude 66° 32´ N

arctic hare *n* a large hare of the Canadian Arctic whose fur turns white in winter

arctic willow *n* a low-growing shrub of the Canadian Arctic

arcuate delta *n geog* a fan-shaped delta at the mouth of a river. Compare **bird's foot delta, cuspate delta**

arc welding *n* a technique in which metal is welded by heat generated by an electric arc

ardent *adj* **1** passionate **2** intensely enthusiastic ▶ HISTORY Latin *ardere* to burn > **ardently** *adv*

ardour *or US* **ardor** *n* **1** emotional warmth; passion **2** intense enthusiasm ▶ HISTORY Latin *ardere* to burn

arduous *adj* difficult to accomplish; strenuous ▶ HISTORY Latin *arduus* steep, difficult

are¹ *vb* the plural form of the present tense of **be**: used as the singular form with *you* ▶ HISTORY Old English *aron*

are² *n* a unit of measure equal to one hundred square metres ▶ HISTORY Latin *area* piece of ground

area *n* **1** a section, part, or region **2** a part having a specified function: *reception area* **3** the size of a two-dimensional surface **4** a subject field: *the area of literature* **5** *US & Canad* a sunken area giving access to a basement **6** any flat, curved, or irregular expanse of a surface **7** range or scope ▶ HISTORY Latin: level ground, threshing floor

area school *n NZ* a school in a rural area that includes primary and post-primary classes

arena *n* **1** a seated enclosure where sports events take place **2** the area of an ancient Roman amphitheatre where gladiators fought **3** a sphere of intense activity: *the political arena* ▶ HISTORY Latin *harena* sand

aren't are not

areola *n*, *pl* **-lae** *or* **-las** a small circular area, such as the coloured ring around the human nipple ▶ HISTORY Latin

Ares *n Greek myth* the god of war

arête *n* a sharp ridge separating valleys ▶ HISTORY French: fishbone

Argentine *or* **Argentinian** *adj* **1** of Argentina ▷ *n* **2** a person from Argentina

argon *n chem* an unreactive odourless element of the rare gas series, forming almost 1 per cent of the atmosphere. Symbol: Ar ▶ HISTORY Greek *argos* inactive

argosy *n*, *pl* **-sies** *old-fashioned or poetic* a large merchant ship, or a fleet of such ships ▶ HISTORY Italian *Ragusea (nave)* (ship) of Ragusa, a former name for Dubrovnik

argot (**ahr**-go) *n* slang or jargon peculiar to a particular group ▶ HISTORY French

argue *vb* **-guing, -gued 1** to try to prove by presenting reasons **2** to debate **3** to quarrel **4** to persuade: *we argued her out of going* **5** to suggest: *her looks argue despair* ▶ HISTORY Latin *arguere* to make clear, accuse ▶ **arguable** *adj* > **arguably** *adv*

argument *n* **1** a quarrel **2** a discussion **3** a point presented to support or oppose a proposition

argumentation *n* the process of reasoning methodically

argumentative *adj* likely to argue

argy-bargy *or* **argie-bargie** *n, pl* **-bargies** *Brit, informal* a squabbling argument ▶ HISTORY Scots

aria (**ah**-ree-a) *n* an elaborate song for solo voice in an opera or choral work ▶ HISTORY Italian

arid *adj* **1** having little or no rain **2** uninteresting ▶ HISTORY Latin *aridus* > **aridity** *n*

Aries *n* *astrol* the first sign of the zodiac: the Ram ▶ HISTORY Latin

aright *adv* correctly or properly

arise *vb* **arising, arose, arisen 1** to come into being: *the opportunity for action did not arise* **2** to come into notice: *people can seek answers to their problems as and when they arise* **3** **arise from** to happen as a result of **4** *old-fashioned* to get or stand up ▶ HISTORY Old English *ārīsan*

aristocracy *n, pl* **-cies 1** a class of people of high social rank **2** government by this class **3** a group of people considered to be outstanding in a particular sphere of activity ▶ HISTORY Greek *aristos* best + *kratein* to rule

aristocrat *n* a member of the aristocracy

aristocratic *adj* **1** of the aristocracy **2** grand or elegant

Aristotelian (ar-riss-tot-**eel**-ee-an) *adj* of Aristotle, 4th-century BC Greek philosopher, or his philosophy

arithmetic *n* **1** the branch of mathematics concerned with numerical calculations, such as addition, subtraction, multiplication, and division **2** calculations involving numerical operations **3** knowledge of or skill in arithmetic: *even simple arithmetic was beyond him* ▷ *adj also* **arithmetical 4** of or using arithmetic ▶ HISTORY Greek *arithmos* number > **arithmetically** *adv* > **arithmetician** *n*

arithmetic mean *n* the average value of a set of terms, expressed as their sum divided by their number: *the arithmetic mean of 3, 4, and 8 is 5*

arithmetic progression *n* a sequence, each term of which differs from the preceding term by a constant amount, such as 3, 6, 9, 12

ark *n* *Bible* the boat built by Noah, which survived the Flood ▶ HISTORY Latin *arca* box, chest

Ark *n* *Judaism* **1** Also called: **Holy Ark** the cupboard in a synagogue in which the Torah scrolls are kept **2** Also called: **Ark of the Covenant** a chest containing the laws of the Jewish religion, regarded as the most sacred symbol of God's presence among the Hebrew people

arm¹ *n* **1** (in humans, apes, and monkeys) either of the upper limbs from the shoulder to the wrist **2** the sleeve of a garment **3** the side of a chair on which one's arm can rest **4** a subdivision or section of an organization: *the London-based arm of a Swiss bank* **5** something resembling an arm in appearance or function: *the arm of a record player* **6** power or authority: *the long arm of the law* **7** **arm in arm** with arms linked **8** **at arm's length** at a distance **9** **with open arms** with warmth and hospitality ▶ HISTORY Old English

arm² *vb* **1** to supply with weapons **2** to prepare (an explosive device) for use **3** to provide (a person or thing) with something that strengthens, or protects: *you will be armed with all the information you will ever need* ▷ See also **arms** ▶ HISTORY Latin *arma* arms, equipment > **armed** *adj*

armada *n* **1** a large number of ships **2** **the Armada** the great fleet sent by Spain against England in 1588 ▶ HISTORY Medieval Latin *armata* fleet, armed forces

armadillo *n, pl* **-los** a small S American burrowing mammal covered in strong bony plates

■ **WORD HISTORY**
■ 'Armadillo' is a Spanish word meaning 'little
■ armed man'. The animal was given this name
■ because of its bony armour-like plates.

Armageddon *n* **1** *New Testament* the final battle between good and evil at the end of the world **2** a catastrophic and extremely destructive conflict

■ **WORD HISTORY**
■ 'Armageddon' comes from the Hebrew words
■ *har megiddōn*, 'the mountain district of
■ Megiddo'. Megiddo, which is in northern Israel,
■ was the site of several battles in Old Testament
■ times.

armament *n* **1** **armaments** the weapon equipment of a military vehicle, ship, or aircraft **2** preparation for war ▶ HISTORY Latin *armamenta* equipment

armature *n* **1** a revolving structure in an electric motor or generator, wound with the coils that carry the current **2** *sculpture* a framework to support the clay or other material used in modelling ▶ HISTORY Latin *armatura* armour, equipment

armchair *n* **1** an upholstered chair with side supports for the arms ▷ *adj* **2** taking no active part: *we are, on the whole, a nation of armchair athletes*

armed forces *pl n* all the military forces of a nation or nations

armful *n* as much as can be held in the arms: *armfuls of lovely flowers*

armhole *n* the opening in a piece of clothing through which the arm passes

armistice (**arm**-miss-stiss) *n* an agreement between opposing armies to stop fighting ▶ HISTORY Latin *arma* arms + *sistere* to stop

Armistice Day *n* the anniversary of the signing of the armistice that ended the First World War, on November 11, 1918

armlet *n* a band or bracelet worn around the arm

armour *or US* **armor** *n* **1** metal clothing worn by medieval warriors for protection in battle

2 *mil* armoured fighting vehicles in general **3** the protective metal plates on a tank or warship **4** protective covering, such as the shell of certain animals **5** a quality or attitude that gives protection ▷ *vb* **6** to equip or cover with armour ▶ HISTORY Latin *armātūra* armour, equipment

armoured *or US* **armored** *adj* **1** having a protective covering **2** consisting of armoured vehicles: *an armoured brigade*

armourer *or US* **armorer** *n* **1** a person who makes or mends arms and armour **2** a person in charge of small arms in a military unit

armoury *or US* **armory** *n, pl* **-mouries** *or* **-mories** **1** a secure storage place for weapons **2** military supplies **3** resources on which to draw: *modern medicine has a large armoury of drugs for the treatment of mental illness*

armpit *n* **1** the hollow beneath the arm where it joins the shoulder **2** *slang* an extremely unpleasant place: *the armpit of the Mediterranean*

arms *pl n* **1** weapons collectively **2** military exploits: *prowess in arms* **3** the heraldic symbols of a family or state **4** **take up arms** to prepare to fight **5** **under arms** armed and prepared for war **6** **up in arms** prepared to protest strongly

army *n, pl* **-mies** **1** the military land forces of a nation **2** a large number of people or animals ▶ HISTORY Medieval Latin *armata* armed forces

aroha *n NZ* love, compassion, or affection ▶ HISTORY Māori

aroma *n* **1** a distinctive pleasant smell **2** a subtle pervasive quality or atmosphere ▶ HISTORY Greek: spice

aromatherapy *n* the use of fragrant essential oils as a treatment in alternative medicine, often to relieve tension

aromatic *adj* **1** having a distinctive pleasant smell **2** *chem* (of an organic compound) having an unsaturated ring of atoms, usually six carbon atoms ▷ *n* **3** something, such as a plant or drug, that gives off a fragrant smell

arose *vb* the past tense of **arise**

around *prep* **1** situated at various points in: *cameramen were positioned around the auditorium* **2** from place to place in: *he had spent twenty-five minutes driving around Amsterdam* **3** somewhere in or near **4** approximately in: *around 1980* ▷ *adv* **5** in all directions from a point of reference: *there wasn't a house for miles around* **6** in the vicinity, esp. restlessly but idly: *I couldn't hang around too long* **7** in no particular place or direction: *a few tropical fish tanks dotted around* **8** *informal* present in some unknown or unspecified place **9** *informal* available: *cancer drugs have been around for years* **10** **have been around** *informal* to have gained considerable experience of a worldly or social nature

arouse *vb* **arousing, aroused** **1** to produce (a reaction, emotion, or response) **2** *written* to awaken from sleep > **arousal** *n*

arpeggio (arp-**pej**-ee-oh) *n, pl* **-gios** a chord whose notes are played or sung in rapid succession ▶ HISTORY Italian

arrack *or* **arak** *n* a coarse alcoholic drink distilled in Eastern countries from grain or rice ▶ HISTORY Arabic *'araq* sweat, sweet juice

arraign (ar-**rain**) *vb* **1** to bring (a prisoner) before a court to answer a charge **2** to accuse ▶ HISTORY Old French *araisnier* to accuse > **arraignment** *n*

arrange *vb* **-ranging, -ranged** **1** to plan in advance: *my parents had arranged a surprise party* **2** to arrive at an agreement: *they had arranged to go to the cinema* **3** to put into a proper or systematic order **4** to adapt (a musical composition) for performance in a certain way ▶ HISTORY Old French *a-* to + *rangier* to put in a row, range

arranged marriage *n* a marriage that has been agreed between the families of the bride and groom, rather than the bride and groom themselves

arrangement *n* **1** a preparation or plan made for an event: *travel arrangements* **2** an agreement or a plan to do something **3** a thing composed of various ordered parts: *a flower arrangement* **4** the form in which things are arranged **5** an adaptation of a piece of music for performance in a certain way

arrant *adj* utter or downright: *that's the most arrant nonsense I've ever heard* ▶ HISTORY Middle English variant of *errant* (wandering, vagabond)

arras *n* a tapestry wall-hanging ▶ HISTORY *Arras*, a town in N France

array *n* **1** an impressive display or collection **2** an orderly arrangement, such as of troops in battle order **3** *maths* a set of numbers or symbols arranged in rows and columns **4** *computers* a data structure in which elements may be located by index numbers **5** *poetic* rich clothing ▷ *vb* **6** to arrange in order **7** to dress in rich clothing ▶ HISTORY Old French *arayer* to arrange

arrears *pl n* **1** money owed **2** **in arrears** late in paying a debt ▶ HISTORY Latin *ad* to + *retro* backwards

arrest *vb* **1** to take (a person) into custody **2** to slow or stop the development of **3** to catch and hold (one's attention) ▷ *n* **4** the act of taking a person into custody **5** **under arrest** being held in custody by the police **6** the slowing or stopping of something: *a cardiac arrest* ▶ HISTORY Latin *ad* at, to + *restare* to stand firm, stop

arresting *adj* attracting attention; striking

arrival *n* **1** the act of arriving **2** a person or thing that has just arrived **3** *informal* a recently born baby

arrive *vb* **-riving, -rived** **1** to reach a place or destination **2** **arrive at** to come to (a conclusion, idea, or decision) **3** to occur: *the crisis he predicted then has now arrived* **4** *informal* to be born **5** *informal* to attain success ▶ HISTORY Latin *ad* to + *ripa* river bank

arrivederci (ar-reeve-a-**der**-chee) *interj* goodbye ▶ HISTORY Italian

arrogant *adj* having an exaggerated opinion of one's own importance or ability ▶ HISTORY Latin *arrogare* to claim as one's own > **arrogance** *n* > **arrogantly** *adv*

a

arrogate *vb* **-gating, -gated** to claim or seize without justification ▶ HISTORY Latin *arrogare* > **arrogation** *n*

arrow *n* **1** a long slender pointed weapon, with feathers at one end, that is shot from a bow **2** an arrow-shaped sign or symbol used to show the direction to a place ▶ HISTORY Old English *arwe*

arrowhead *n* the pointed tip of an arrow

arrowroot *n* an easily digestible starch obtained from the root of a West Indian plant

arsenal *n* **1** a building in which arms and ammunition are made or stored **2** a store of anything regarded as weapons: *this new weapon in the medical arsenal*

■ **WORD HISTORY**
■ The word 'arsenal' came into English from
■ Italian, but it has its origin in Arabic. In Arabic a
■ *dār as-sinā`a* is a workshop or factory. This word
■ was borrowed from Arabic into Italian as
■ *arsenale*, meaning 'dockyard'. And it was in the
■ sense of 'dockyard' that it came into English,
■ only later coming to have the meaning of an
■ arms and ammunition store.

arsenic *n* **1** a toxic metalloid element. Symbol: As **2** a nontechnical name for **arsenic trioxide**, a highly poisonous compound used as a rat poison and insecticide ▷ *adj also* **arsenical 3** of or containing arsenic ▶ HISTORY Syriac *zarnīg*

arson *n* the crime of intentionally setting fire to property ▶ HISTORY Latin *ardere* to burn > **arsonist** *n*

art *n* **1** the creation of works of beauty or other special significance **2** works of art collectively **3** human creativity as distinguished from nature **4** skill: *she was still new to the art of bargaining* **5** any branch of the visual arts, esp. painting **6** **get something down to a fine art** to become proficient at something through practice ▷ See also **arts, arts and crafts** ▶ HISTORY Latin *ars* craftsmanship

Art Deco (art **deck**-oh) *n* a style of design, at its height in the 1930s, characterized by geometrical shapes ▶ HISTORY French *art décoratif*

artefact or **artifact** *n* something made by human beings, such as a tool or a work of art ▶ HISTORY Latin *ars* skill + *facere* to make

Artemis *n* *Greek myth* the goddess of hunting

arterial *adj* **1** of or affecting an artery **2** being a major route: *an arterial road*

arteriole *n* *anat* a small subdivision of an artery

arteriosclerosis (art-ear-ee-oh-skler-**oh**-siss) *n* thickening and loss of elasticity of the walls of the arteries. Nontechnical name: **hardening of the arteries**

artery *n*, *pl* **-teries 1** any of the tubes that carry oxygenated blood from the heart to various parts of the body **2** a major road or means of communication ▶ HISTORY Latin *arteria*

artesian well (art-**teez**-ee-en) *n* *geog, engineering* a well tapping water that is under pressure in a confined aquifer with the result that the water rises naturally without the need for a pump

▶ HISTORY French *artésien*, from Old French *Arteis* Artois (in N France) where such wells were common

Artex *n* *trademark, Brit* a type of coating for walls and ceilings that gives a textured finish

art form *n* a recognized mode or medium of artistic expression

artful *adj* **1** cunning **2** skilful in achieving a desired end > **artfully** *adv*

artha *n* *Hinduism* the pursuit of activities that will provide a fulfilling life ▶ HISTORY Sanskrit

arthritis *n* inflammation of a joint or joints, causing pain and stiffness ▶ HISTORY Greek *arthron* joint > **arthritic** *adj*, *n*

arthropod *n* a creature, such as an insect or a spider, which has jointed legs and a hard case on its body ▶ HISTORY Greek *arthron* joint + *pous* foot

artic *n* *Brit, informal* an articulated lorry

artichoke *n* **1** Also called: **globe artichoke** the flower head of a thistle-like plant, cooked as a vegetable **2** same as **Jerusalem artichoke** ▶ HISTORY Arabic *al-kharshūf*

article *n* **1** a written composition in a magazine or newspaper **2** an item or object **3** a clause in a written document **4** *grammar* any of the words *a*, *an*, or *the* ▶ HISTORY Latin *articulus* small joint

articled *adj* bound by a written contract, such as one that governs a period of training: *an articled clerk*

articular *adj* of or relating to joints ▶ HISTORY Latin *articulus* small joint

articulate *adj* **1** able to express oneself fluently and coherently **2** distinct, clear, or definite: *his amiable and articulate campaign attracted support* **3** *zool* possessing joints ▷ *vb* **-lating, -lated 4** to speak clearly and distinctly **5** to express coherently in words ▶ HISTORY Latin *articulare* to divide into joints > **articulately** *adv*

articulation *n* **1** the expressing of an idea in words **2** the process of articulating a speech sound or the sound so produced **3** a being jointed together **4** *zool* a joint between bones or arthropod segments

artifact *n* same as **artefact**

artifice *n* **1** a clever trick **2** skill or cleverness ▶ HISTORY Latin *ars* skill + *facere* to make

artificer (art-**tiff**-iss-er) *n* a skilled craftsman

artificial *adj* **1** man-made; not occurring naturally **2** made in imitation of a natural product: *artificial flavourings* **3** not sincere ▶ HISTORY Latin *artificialis* belonging to art > **artificiality** *n* > **artificially** *adv*

artificial insemination *n* introduction of semen into the womb by means other than sexual intercourse

artificial intelligence *n* the branch of computer science aiming to produce machines which can imitate intelligent human behaviour

artificial respiration *n* any method of restarting a person's breathing after it has stopped

artillery *n* **1** large-calibre guns **2** military units specializing in the use of such guns ▶ HISTORY Old French *artillier* to equip with weapons

artisan *n* a skilled workman; craftsman
▶ **HISTORY** French > **artisanal** *adj*

artist *n* **1** a person who produces works of art such as paintings or sculpture **2** a person who is skilled at something **3** same as **artiste** > **artistic** *adj* > **artistically** *adv*

artiste *n* a professional entertainer such as a singer or dancer

artistic unity *n* the condition achieved when all the elements of a composition work together to achieve a satisfactory, integrated whole

artistry *n* **1** artistic ability **2** great skill

artless *adj* **1** free from deceit or cunning: *artless generosity* **2** natural or unpretentious > **artlessly** *adv*

Art Nouveau (ahr noo-**voh**) *n* a style of art and architecture of the 1890s, characterized by sinuous outlines and stylized natural forms ▶ **HISTORY** French: new art

arts *pl n* **1 the arts** the nonscientific branches of knowledge **2** See **fine art 3** cunning schemes

arts and crafts *pl n* decorative handicraft

artwork *n* all the photographs and illustrations in a publication

arty *adj* **artier, artiest** *informal* having an affected interest in art > **artiness** *n*

arum lily *n* a plant with a white funnel-shaped leaf surrounding a yellow spike of flowers

Aryan (**air**-ree-an) *n* **1** (in Nazi ideology) a non-Jewish person of the Nordic type **2** a person supposedly descended from the Indo-Europeans ▷ *adj* **3** of Aryans ▶ **HISTORY** Sanskrit *ārya* of noble birth

as *conj* **1** while or when: *he arrived just as the band finished the song* **2** in the way that: *they had talked and laughed as only the best of friends can* **3** that which; what: *George did as he was asked* **4** (of) which fact or event (referring to the previous statement): *to become wise, as we all know, is not easy* **5 as it were** in a way; in a manner of speaking: *he was, as it were, on probation* **6** since; seeing that **7** for instance ▷ *adv, conj* **8** used to indicate amount or extent in comparisons: *he was as fat as his mum and dad* ▷ *prep* **9** in the role of; being: *my task, as his physician, is to do the best that I can* **10 as for** or **to** with reference to **11 as if** or **though** as it would be if: *she felt as if she had been run over by a bulldozer* **12 as (it) is** in the existing state of affairs ▶ **HISTORY** Old English *alswā* likewise

As *chem* arsenic

ASA 1 (in Britain) Amateur Swimming Association **2** (in Britain) Advertising Standards Authority

asafoetida *n* a strong-smelling plant resin used as a spice in Eastern cookery ▶ **HISTORY** Medieval Latin *asa* gum + Latin *foetidus* evil-smelling

a.s.a.p. as soon as possible

asbestos *n* a fibrous mineral which does not burn, formerly widely used as a heat-resistant material ▶ **HISTORY** Greek: inextinguishable

asbestosis *n* inflammation of the lungs resulting from inhalation of asbestos fibre

ascend *vb* **1** *written* to go or move up **2** *written* to slope upwards **3 ascend the throne** *formal* to become king or queen ▶ **HISTORY** Latin *ascendere*

ascendancy *or* **ascendance** *n* the condition of being dominant: *when hardliners were in the ascendancy last winter*

ascendant *or* **ascendent** *adj* **1** dominant or influential ▷ *n* **2** *astrol* the sign of the zodiac that is rising on the eastern horizon at a particular moment **3 in the ascendant** increasing in power or influence

ascension *n* the act of ascending

Ascension Day *n* *Christianity* the 40th day after Easter, when the Ascension of Christ into Heaven is celebrated

ascent *n* **1** the act of ascending **2** an upward slope

ascertain *vb* to find out definitely ▶ **HISTORY** Old French *acertener* to make certain > **ascertainment** *n*

ascetic (ass-**set**-tik) *n* **1** a person who abstains from worldly comforts and pleasures ▷ *adj* **2** rigidly abstinent and self-denying ▶ **HISTORY** Greek *askētikos*

ASCII (**ass**-kee) *n* a code for transmitting data between computers ▶ **HISTORY** A(merican) S(tandard) C(ode for) I(nformation) I(nterchange)

ascorbic acid (ass-**core**-bik) *n* a vitamin that occurs in citrus fruits, tomatoes, and green vegetables, and which prevents and cures scurvy. Also called: **vitamin C** ▶ **HISTORY** A- + SCORBUTIC

ascribe *vb* **-cribing, -cribed 1** to attribute, as to a particular origin: *headaches which may be ascribed to stress* **2** to consider that (a particular quality) is possessed by something or someone: *specific human qualities are ascribed to each of the four elements* ▶ **HISTORY** Latin *ad* in addition + *scribere* to write > **ascription** *n*

aseptic (eh-**sep**-tik) *adj* free from harmful bacteria

asexual (eh-**sex**-yew-al) *adj* **1** having no apparent sex or sex organs **2** (of reproduction) not involving sexual activity > **asexually** *adv*

ash¹ *n* **1** the powdery substance formed when something is burnt **2** fine particles of lava thrown out by an erupting volcano ▶ **HISTORY** Old English *æsce*

ash² *n* a tree with grey bark and winged seeds ▶ **HISTORY** Old English *æsc*

ashamed *adj* **1** overcome with shame or remorse **2** unwilling through fear of humiliation or shame: *she'd be ashamed to admit to jealousy* ▶ **HISTORY** Old English *āscamod*

ashen *adj* grey with shock

ashes *pl n* **1** remains after burning **2** the remains of a human body after cremation

ashlar *or* **ashler** *n* **1** a square block of cut stone for use in building **2** a thin dressed stone used to face a wall ▶ **HISTORY** Old French *aisseler* crossbeam

ashore *adv* towards or on land

ashram *n* a religious retreat where a Hindu holy man lives ▶ **HISTORY** Sanskrit *āśrama*

ashtray *n* a dish for tobacco ash and cigarette ends   41

a

Ash Wednesday n the first day of Lent, named from the Christian custom of sprinkling ashes on penitents' heads

Asian adj 1 of Asia 2 Brit of the Indian subcontinent ▷ n 3 a person from Asia 4 Brit a person from the Indian subcontinent or a descendant of one

Asian pear n an apple-shaped pear with crisp juicy flesh

Asiatic adj Asian

aside adv 1 to one side 2 out of other people's hearing: her mother took her aside for a serious talk 3 out of mind: she pushed aside her fears of being beaten or killed 4 into reserve: a certain amount must also be put aside for defence and government ▷ n 5 a remark not meant to be heard by everyone present 6 a remark that is not connected with the subject being discussed

asinine (ass-in-nine) adj 1 obstinate or stupid 2 of or like an ass ▶ HISTORY Latin asinus ass

ask vb 1 to say or write (something) in a form that requires an answer: I asked him his name; 'Do you think we'll have trouble landing?' he asked 2 to make a request or demand: the chairman asked for a show of hands 3 to invite 4 to inquire about: I pretended to be lost and asked for directions 5 to expect: is that too much to ask? ▶ HISTORY Old English āscian

askance (ass-kanss) adv **look askance at a** to look at with an oblique glance **b** to regard with suspicion ▶ HISTORY origin unknown

askew adv, adj towards one side; crooked

asking price n the price suggested by a seller

aslant adv 1 at a slant ▷ prep 2 slanting across

asleep adj 1 in or into a state of sleep 2 (of limbs) numb 3 informal not listening or paying attention

ASM assistant stage manager

asp n a small viper of S Europe ▶ HISTORY Greek aspis

asparagus n the young shoots of a plant of the lily family, which can be cooked and eaten ▶ HISTORY Greek asparagos

aspartame n an artificial sweetener

aspect n 1 a distinct feature or element in a problem or situation 2 one part of the nature or character of a person or thing 3 a position facing a particular direction: the room's east-facing aspect 4 appearance or look: a room with a somewhat gloomy aspect ▶ HISTORY Latin ad- to, at + specere to look

aspen n a poplar tree whose leaves quiver in the wind ▶ HISTORY Old English æspe

asperity (ass-per-rit-ee) n, pl -ties roughness or sharpness of temper ▶ HISTORY Latin asper rough

aspersion n **cast aspersions on** to make disparaging or malicious remarks about ▶ HISTORY Latin aspergere to sprinkle

asphalt n 1 a black tarlike substance used in road-surfacing and roofing materials ▷ vb 2 to cover with asphalt ▶ HISTORY Greek asphaltos, probably from a- not + sphallein to cause to fall; referring to its use as a binding agent

asphodel n a plant with clusters of yellow or white flowers

asphyxia (ass-**fix**-ee-a) n unconsciousness or death caused by lack of oxygen ▶ HISTORY Greek a- without + sphuxis pulse

asphyxiate vb -ating, -ated to smother or suffocate > **asphyxiation** n

aspic n a savoury jelly based on meat or fish stock, used as a mould for meat or vegetables ▶ HISTORY French

aspidistra n a house plant with long tapered evergreen leaves ▶ HISTORY Greek aspis shield

aspirant n a person who aspires, such as to a powerful position

aspirate phonetics vb -rating, -rated 1 to pronounce (a word or syllable) with an initial h ▷ n 2 the sound represented in English and several other languages as h

aspiration n 1 a strong desire or aim 2 phonetics the pronunciation of an aspirated consonant > **aspirational** adj

aspirator n a device for removing fluids from a body cavity by suction

aspire vb -piring, -pired to yearn for something or hope to do or be something: it struck him as bizarre that somebody could aspire to be a dental technician ▶ HISTORY Latin aspirare to breathe upon > **aspiring** adj

aspirin n, pl -rin or -rins 1 a drug used to relieve pain and fever 2 a tablet of aspirin ▶ HISTORY German

ass n 1 a mammal resembling the horse but with longer ears 2 a foolish person ▶ HISTORY Old English assa

assagai n same as **assegai**

assail vb written 1 to attack violently 2 to criticize strongly 3 to disturb: he was assailed by a dizzy sensation ▶ HISTORY Latin assilire to leap on > **assailant** n

assassin n a murderer of a prominent person

■ **WORD HISTORY**

■ The source of this word is the Arabic word
■ hashshāshīn, meaning 'people who take
■ hashish'. The word comes from the name of a
■ feared medieval Muslim sect who allegedly ate
■ or smoked hashish before embarking on
■ missions to murder those they considered their
■ enemies, Crusaders and Muslim leaders alike.

assassinate vb -nating, -nated to murder (a prominent person) > **assassination** n

assault n 1 a violent attack, either physical or verbal ▷ vb 2 to attack violently ▶ HISTORY Old French asaut

assault and battery n criminal law a threat of attack to another person followed by actual attack

assault course n an obstacle course designed to give soldiers practice in negotiating hazards

assay vb 1 to analyse (a substance, such as gold) to find out how pure it is ▷ n 2 an analysis of the purity of an ore or precious metal ▶ HISTORY Old French assai

assegai or **assagai** n, pl -gais a sharp light spear used in southern Africa ▶ HISTORY Arabic az zaghayah

assemblage n 1 a collection or group of things 2 the act of assembling

assemble vb **-bling, -bled** 1 to collect or gather together 2 to put together the parts of (a machine) ▶ HISTORY Old French assembler

assembler n 1 a person or thing that assembles 2 a computer program that converts a set of low-level symbolic data into machine language

assembly n, pl **-blies** 1 a number of people gathered together for a meeting 2 the act of assembling

assembly line n a sequence of machines and workers in a factory assembling a product

assemblyman n, pl **-men** a member of a legislative assembly

assent n 1 agreement, consent ▷ vb 2 to agree ▶ HISTORY Latin assentiri

assert vb 1 to state or declare 2 to insist upon (one's rights, etc.) 3 **assert oneself** to speak and act forcefully ▶ HISTORY Latin asserere to join to oneself

assertion n 1 a positive statement, usually made without evidence 2 the act of asserting

assertive adj confident and direct in dealing with others > **assertively** adv > **assertiveness** n

assess vb 1 to judge the worth or importance of 2 to estimate the value of (income or property) for taxation purposes ▶ HISTORY Latin assidere to sit beside

assessment n 1 the act of assessing 2 the evaluation of a student's achievement on a course

assessor n 1 a person who values property for taxation or insurance purposes 2 a person with technical expertise called in to advise a court 3 a person who evaluates the merits of something

asset n 1 a thing or person that is valuable or useful 2 any property owned by a person or company ▶ HISTORY Latin ad- to + satis enough

asset-stripping n commerce the practice of taking over a failing company at a low price and then selling the assets piecemeal > **asset-stripper** n

asseverate vb **-ating, -ated** formal to declare solemnly ▶ HISTORY Latin asseverare to do (something) earnestly > **asseveration** n

assiduous adj 1 hard-working 2 done with care ▶ HISTORY Latin assidere to sit beside > **assiduity** n > **assiduously** adv

assign vb 1 to select (someone) for a post or task 2 to give a task or duty (to someone) 3 to attribute to a specified cause 4 to set apart (a place or time) for a particular function or event: to assign a day for the meeting 5 law to transfer (one's right, interest, or title to property) to someone else ▶ HISTORY Latin assignare

assignation (ass-sig-nay-shun) n a secret arrangement to meet ▶ HISTORY Latin assignatio a marking out

assignment n 1 something that has been assigned, such as a task 2 the act of assigning 3 law the transfer to another person of a right, interest, or title to property

assignment system n history a system whereby convicts arriving in Australia in the first part of the 19th century were assigned to settlers as cheap labour; in force until 1840

assimilate vb **-lating, -lated** 1 to learn (information) and understand it thoroughly 2 to adjust or become adjusted: they became assimilated to German culture 3 to absorb (food) ▶ HISTORY Latin ad- to + similis like > **assimilable** adj > **assimilation** n

assist vb 1 to give help or support ▷ n 2 sport a pass by a player which enables another player to score a goal ▶ HISTORY Latin assistere to stand by

assistance n help or support

assistant n 1 a helper or subordinate 2 same as **shop assistant** ▷ adj 3 junior or deputy: assistant manager

assistant referee n soccer the official name for **linesman** (sense 1)

assizes pl n Brit (formerly in England and Wales) the sessions of the principal court in each county ▶ HISTORY Latin assidere to sit beside

assoc. association

associate vb **-ating, -ated** 1 to connect in the mind 2 to mix socially: addicts are driven to associate with criminals 3 **be associated** or **associate oneself with** to be involved with (a group) because of shared views: she had long been associated with the far right ▷ n 4 a partner in business 5 a companion or friend ▷ adj 6 having partial rights or subordinate status: an associate member 7 joined with in business: an associate director ▶ HISTORY Latin ad- to + sociare to join

association n 1 a group of people with a common interest 2 the act of associating or the state of being associated 3 friendship: their association still had to remain a secret 4 a mental connection of ideas or feelings: the place contained associations for her

associative adj maths (of an operation such as multiplication or addition) producing the same answer regardless of the way the elements are grouped, for example $(2 \times 3) \times 4 = 2 \times (3 \times 4)$

assonance n the rhyming of vowel sounds but not consonants, as in time and light ▶ HISTORY Latin assonare to sound

assorted adj 1 consisting of various kinds mixed together 2 matched: an ill-assorted childless couple ▶ HISTORY Old French assorter

assortment n a collection of various things or sorts

asst assistant

assuage (ass-wage) vb **-suaging, -suaged** to relieve (grief, pain, or thirst) ▶ HISTORY Latin suavis pleasant

assume vb **-suming, -sumed** 1 to take to be true without proof 2 to undertake or take on: every general staff officer was able to assume control of the army 3 to make a pretence of: the man had assumed a debonair attitude 4 to take on: her eyes assumed a scared haunted look ▶ HISTORY Latin ad- to + sumere to take up

a

assumption n 1 something that is taken for granted 2 the act of assuming power or possession ▶ HISTORY Latin *assumptio* a taking up

Assumption n *Christianity* the taking up of the Virgin Mary into heaven when her earthly life was ended

assurance n 1 a statement or assertion intended to inspire confidence 2 feeling of confidence; certainty 3 insurance that provides for events that are certain to happen, such as death

assure vb **-suring, -sured** 1 to promise or guarantee 2 to convince: *they assured me that they had not seen the document* 3 to make (something) certain 4 *chiefly Brit* to insure against loss of life ▶ HISTORY Latin *ad-* to + *securus* secure

assured adj 1 confident or self-assured 2 certain to happen 3 *chiefly Brit* insured > **assuredly** (a-**sure**-id-lee) adv

Assyrian n an inhabitant of ancient Assyria, a kingdom of Mesopotamia

AST Atlantic Standard Time

astatine n *chem* a radioactive element occurring naturally in minute amounts or artificially produced by bombarding bismuth with alpha particles. Symbol: At ▶ HISTORY Greek *astatos* unstable

aster n a plant with white, blue, purple, or pink daisy-like flowers ▶ HISTORY Greek: star

asterisk n 1 a star-shaped character (*) used in printing or writing to indicate a footnote, etc. ▷ vb 2 to mark with an asterisk ▶ HISTORY Greek *asteriskos* a small star

astern adv, adj *naut* 1 at or towards the stern of a ship 2 backwards 3 behind a vessel

asteroid n any of the small planets that orbit the sun between Mars and Jupiter ▶ HISTORY Greek *asteroeidēs* starlike

asthenosphere n *geol* a thin semifluid layer of the earth below the outer lithosphere, forming part of the mantle and thought to be able to flow vertically and horizontally, enabling sections of lithosphere to move up, down, and sideways. Compare **lithosphere** ▶ HISTORY from *astheno-*, from Greek *asthenēs* weak + SPHERE

asthma (**ass**-ma) n an illness causing difficulty in breathing ▶ HISTORY Greek > **asthmatic** adj, n

astigmatic adj relating to or affected with astigmatism ▶ HISTORY Greek *a-* without + *stigma* spot, focus

astigmatism (ay-**stig**-mat-tiz-zum) n a defect of a lens, esp. of the eye, causing it not to focus properly

astir adj 1 out of bed 2 in motion

astonish vb to surprise greatly ▶ HISTORY Latin *ex-* out + *tonare* to thunder > **astonishing** adj > **astonishment** n

astound vb to overwhelm with amazement ▶ HISTORY Old French *estoner* > **astounding** adj

astrakhan n 1 a fur made of the dark curly fleece of lambs from Astrakhan in Russia 2 a cloth resembling this

astral adj 1 relating to or resembling the stars 2 of the spirit world ▶ HISTORY Greek *astron* star

astray adj, adv out of the right or expected way ▶ HISTORY Old French *estraier* to stray

astride adj 1 with a leg on either side 2 with legs far apart ▷ prep 3 with a leg on either side of

astringent adj 1 causing contraction of body tissue 2 checking the flow of blood from a cut 3 severe or harsh ▷ n 4 an astringent drug or lotion ▶ HISTORY Latin *astringens* drawing together > **astringency** n

astro- *combining form* indicating a star or stars: *astrology* ▶ HISTORY Greek

astrolabe n an instrument formerly used to measure the altitude of stars and planets ▶ HISTORY Greek *astron* star + *lambanein* to take

astrology n the study of the alleged influence of the stars, planets, sun, and moon on human affairs ▶ HISTORY Greek *astron* star + *logos* word, account > **astrologer** or **astrologist** n > **astrological** adj

astronaut n a person trained for travelling in space ▶ HISTORY Greek *astron* star + *nautēs* sailor

astronautics n the science and technology of space flight > **astronautical** adj

astronomical or **astronomic** adj 1 enormously large 2 of astronomy > **astronomically** adv

astronomical unit n a unit of distance equal to the average distance between the earth and the sun (1.495×10^{11}m)

astronomy n the scientific study of heavenly bodies ▶ HISTORY Greek *astron* star + *nomos* law > **astronomer** n

astrophysics n the study of the physical and chemical properties of celestial bodies > **astrophysical** adj > **astrophysicist** n

astute adj quick to notice or understand ▶ HISTORY Latin *astutus* > **astutely** adv > **astuteness** n

asunder adv, adj *literary* into parts or pieces; apart

asylum n 1 refuge granted to a political refugee from a foreign country 2 (formerly) a psychiatric hospital ▶ HISTORY Greek *asulon*

asymmetric bars (ass-sim-met-rik, ay-sim-met-rik) pl n *gymnastics* a pair of bars parallel to each other but at different heights, used for various exercises

asymmetry n lack of symmetry > **asymmetric** or **asymmetrical** adj

asymptote (**ass**-im-tote) n a straight line that is closely approached but never met by a curve ▶ HISTORY Greek *asumptōtos* not falling together > **asymptotic** adj

at prep 1 indicating location or position: *she had planted a vegetable garden at the back* 2 towards; in the direction of: *she was staring at the wall behind him* 3 indicating position in time: *we arrived at 12.30* 4 engaged in: *the innocent laughter of children at play* 5 during the passing of: *she works at night as a nurse's aide* 6 for; in exchange for: *crude oil is selling at its lowest price since September* 7 indicating the object of an emotion: *I'm angry at you because you were rude to me* ▶ HISTORY Old English *æt*

At *chem* astatine

at. 1 atmosphere **2** atomic

atavism (**at**-a-viz-zum) *n* **1** the recurrence of primitive characteristics that were present in distant ancestors but not in more recent ones **2** reversion to a former type ▶ HISTORY Latin *atavus* great-grandfather's grandfather, ancestor > **atavistic** *adj*

ataxia *n pathol* lack of muscular coordination ▶ HISTORY Greek > **ataxic** *adj*

ate *vb* the past tense of **eat**

-ate *suffix chem* indicating a chemical compound containing oxygen: *zinc sulphate*

atelier (**at**-tell-yay) *n* an artist's studio

atheism (**aith**-ee-iz-zum) *n* the belief that there is no God ▶ HISTORY Greek *a-* without + *theos* god > **atheist** *n*

Athena *or* **Athene** *n Greek myth* the goddess of wisdom

atheroma *n pathol* a fatty deposit on or in the inner lining of an artery

atherosclerosis *n, pl* **-ses** a disease in which deposits of fat cause the walls of the arteries to thicken ▶ HISTORY Greek *athērōma* tumour + SCLEROSIS > **atherosclerotic** *adj*

athlete *n* **1** a person trained to compete in sports or exercises **2** *chiefly Brit* a competitor in track-and-field events ▶ HISTORY Greek *athlos* a contest

athlete's foot *n* a fungal infection of the skin of the foot

athletic *adj* **1** physically fit or strong **2** of or for an athlete or athletics > **athletically** *adv* > **athleticism** *n*

athletics *pl n Brit & Austral* track-and-field events

at-home *n Brit & Austral* a social gathering in a person's home

athwart *prep* **1** across ▷ *adv* **2** transversely; from one side to another

Atlantic *adj* of the Atlantic Ocean, the world's second largest ocean, bounded by the Arctic, the Antarctic, America, and Europe and Africa ▶ HISTORY Greek *(pelagos) Atlantikos* (the sea) of Atlas (so called because it lay beyond the Atlas Mountains)

Atlanticism *n* belief in close economic and military cooperation between Europe and the United States > **Atlanticist** *n*

Atlantis *n* (in ancient legend) a continent said to have sunk beneath the Atlantic west of Gibraltar

atlas *n* a book of maps ▶ HISTORY because *Atlas*, a Titan in Greek mythology, was shown supporting the heavens in 16th-century books of maps

ATM automated teller machine: a computerized cash dispenser

atmosphere *n* **1** the mass of gases surrounding the earth or any other heavenly body **2** the air in a particular place **3** a pervasive feeling or mood: *the atmosphere was tense* **4** a unit of pressure equal to the normal pressure of the air at sea level ▶ HISTORY Greek *atmos* vapour + *sphaira* sphere > **atmospheric** *adj* > **atmospherically** *adv*

atmospheric circulation *n meteorol* the movement of air in the atmosphere

atmospheric depression *n meteorol* a body of moving air below normal atmospheric pressure, which often brings rain

atmospheric pressure *n physics* the pressure exerted by the atmosphere at the earth's surface. It has an average value of 1 atmosphere

atmospherics *pl n* radio interference caused by electrical disturbance in the atmosphere

atoll *n* a circular coral reef surrounding a lagoon ▶ HISTORY *atollon*, native name in the Maldive Islands

atom *n* **1 a** the smallest unit of matter which can take part in a chemical reaction **b** this entity as a source of nuclear energy **2** a very small amount ▶ HISTORY Greek *atomos* that cannot be divided

atom bomb *n* same as **atomic bomb**

atomic *adj* **1** of or using atomic bombs or atomic energy **2** of atoms > **atomically** *adv*

atomic bomb *or* **atom bomb** *n* a type of bomb in which the energy is provided by nuclear fission

atomic energy *n* same as **nuclear energy**

atomic mass unit *n* a unit of mass that is equal to one twelfth of the mass of an atom of carbon-12

atomic number *n* the number of protons in the nucleus of an atom of an element

atomic theory *n* any theory in which matter is regarded as consisting of atoms

atomic weight *n* the ratio of the average mass per atom of an element to one twelfth of the mass of an atom of carbon-12

atomize *or* **-mise** *vb* **-mizing, -mized** *or* **-mising, -mised 1** to separate into free atoms **2** to reduce to fine particles or spray **3** to destroy by nuclear weapons

atomizer *or* **-miser** *n* a device for reducing a liquid to a fine spray

atonal (ay-**tone**-al) *adj* (of music) not written in an established key > **atonality** *n*

atone *vb* **atoning, atoned** to make amends (for a sin, crime, or wrongdoing)

atonement *n* **1** something done to make amends for wrongdoing **2** *Christian theol* the reconciliation of humankind with God through the sacrificial death of Christ ▶ HISTORY Middle English *at onement* in harmony

atop *prep* on top of

atrium *n, pl* **atria 1** *anat* the upper chamber of each half of the heart **2** a central hall that extends through several storeys in a modern building **3** the open main court of an ancient Roman house ▶ HISTORY Latin > **atrial** *adj*

atrocious *adj* **1** extremely cruel or wicked **2** horrifying or shocking **3** *informal* very bad ▶ HISTORY Latin *atrox* dreadful > **atrociously** *adv*

atrocity *n* **1** behaviour that is wicked or cruel **2** (*pl* **-ties**) an act of extreme cruelty

atrophy (**at**-trof-fee) *n, pl* **-phies 1** a wasting away of a physical organ or part **2** a failure to grow ▷ *vb* **-phies, -phying, -phied 3** to waste away ▶ HISTORY Greek *atrophos* ill-fed

a

atropine *n* a poisonous alkaloid obtained from deadly nightshade ▸ HISTORY New Latin *atropa* deadly nightshade

attach *vb* **1** to join, fasten, or connect **2** to attribute or ascribe: *he attaches particular importance to the proposed sale* **3 attach oneself** or **be attached to** to become associated with or join ▸ HISTORY Old French *atachier*

attaché (at-**tash**-shay) *n* a specialist attached to a diplomatic mission ▸ HISTORY French

attaché case *n* a flat rectangular briefcase for carrying papers

attached *adj* **1** married, engaged, or in an exclusive relationship **2 attached to** fond of

attachment *n* **1** affection or regard for **2** an accessory that can be fitted to a device to change what it can do **3** a computer file sent with an email

attack *vb* **1** to launch a physical assault (against) **2** to criticize vehemently **3** to set about (a job or problem) with vigour **4** to affect adversely: *BSE attacks the animal's brain* **5** to take the initiative in a game or sport ▹ *n* **6** the act of attacking **7** any sudden appearance of a disease or symptoms: *a bad attack of mumps* ▸ HISTORY Old Italian *attaccare* > **attacker** *n*

attain *vb* **1** to manage to do or get (something): *the country attained economic growth* **2** to reach ▸ HISTORY Latin *attingere* > **attainable** *adj*

attainment *n* an achievement or the act of achieving something

attar *n* a perfume made from damask roses ▸ HISTORY Persian *'atir* perfumed

attempt *vb* **1** to make an effort (to do or achieve something); try ▹ *n* **2** an endeavour to achieve something; effort **3 attempt on someone's life** an attack on someone with the intention to kill ▸ HISTORY Latin *attemptare*

attempted *adj law* (of murder, rape, theft, etc.) incomplete, although the crime would have taken place had circumstances not prevented it. Attempted crimes are legally indictable

attend *vb* **1** to be present at (an event) **2** to go regularly to a school, college, etc. **3** to look after: *the actors lounged in their canvas chairs, attended by sycophants* **4** to pay attention **5 attend to** to apply oneself to: *I've a few things I must attend to* ▸ HISTORY Latin *attendere* to stretch towards

attendance *n* **1** the act of attending **2** the number of people present **3** regularity in attending

attendant *n* **1** a person who assists, guides, or provides a service ▹ *adj* **2** associated: *nuclear power and its attendant dangers* **3** being in attendance

attention *n* **1** concentrated direction of the mind **2** consideration, notice, or observation **3** detailed care or treatment **4** the alert position in military drill **5 attentions** acts of courtesy: *the attentions of men seemed to embarrass her*

attentive *adj* **1** paying close attention **2** considerately helpful: *at society parties he is attentive to his wife* > **attentively** *adv* > **attentiveness** *n*

attenuated *adj* **1** weakened **2** thin and extended ▸ HISTORY Latin *attenuare* to weaken > **attenuation** *n*

attest *vb* **1** to affirm or prove the truth of **2** to bear witness to (an act or event) ▸ HISTORY Latin *testari* to bear witness > **attestation** *n*

attested *adj Brit* (of cattle) certified to be free from a disease, such as tuberculosis

attic *n* a space or room within the roof of a house ▸ HISTORY from the *Attic* style of architecture

attire *n* clothes, esp. fine or formal ones ▸ HISTORY Old French *atirier* to put in order

attired *adj* dressed in a specified way

attitude *n* **1** the way a person thinks and behaves **2** a position of the body **3** *informal* a hostile manner **4** the orientation of an aircraft or spacecraft in relation to some plane or direction ▸ HISTORY Latin *aptus* apt

attorney *n* **1** a person legally appointed to act for another **2** *US* a lawyer ▸ HISTORY Old French *atourner* to direct to

attorney general *n*, *pl* **attorneys general** or **attorney generals** a chief law officer of some governments

attract *vb* **1** to arouse the interest or admiration of **2** (of a magnet) to draw (something) closer by exerting a force on it ▸ HISTORY Latin *attrahere* to draw towards

attraction *n* **1** the act or quality of attracting **2** an interesting or desirable feature: *the Scottishness of Scott is an attraction, but by no means his only merit* **3** an object or place that people visit for interest: *this carefully preserved tourist attraction* **4** (of a magnet) a force by which one object attracts another

attractive *adj* appealing to the senses or mind > **attractively** *adv* > **attractiveness** *n*

attribute *vb* **-uting, -uted** **1 attribute to** to regard as belonging to or produced by: *a play attributed to William Shakespeare* ▹ *n* **2** a quality or feature representative of a person or thing ▸ HISTORY Latin *attribuere* to associate with > **attributable** *adj* > **attribution** *n*

attributive *adj grammar* (of an adjective) coming before the noun modified

attrition *n* constant wearing down to weaken or destroy: *a war of attrition* ▸ HISTORY Latin *atterere* to weaken

attune *vb* **-tuning, -tuned** to adjust or accustom (a person or thing)

ATV all-terrain vehicle: a vehicle with wheels designed to travel on rough ground

atypical (eh-**tip**-ik-kl) *adj* not typical > **atypically** *adv*

Au *chem* gold ▸ HISTORY Latin *aurum*

aubergine (**oh**-bur-zheen) *n Brit* the dark purple fruit of a tropical plant, cooked and eaten as a vegetable ▸ HISTORY French, from Arabic *al-bādindjān*

aubrietia (aw-**bree**-sha) *n* a trailing purple-flowered rock plant ▸ HISTORY after Claude *Aubriet*, painter of flowers and animals

auburn *adj* (of hair) reddish-brown ▶ HISTORY (originally meaning: blond) Latin *albus* white

auction *n* **1** a public sale at which articles are sold to the highest bidder ▷ *vb* **2** to sell by auction ▶ HISTORY Latin *auctio* an increasing

auctioneer *n* a person who conducts an auction

audacious *adj* **1** recklessly bold or daring **2** impudent or presumptuous ▶ HISTORY Latin *audax* bold > **audacity** *n*

audible *adj* loud enough to be heard ▶ HISTORY Latin *audire* to hear > **audibility** *n* > **audibly** *adv*

audience *n* **1** a group of spectators or listeners at a concert or play **2** the people reached by a book, film, or radio or television programme **3** a formal interview ▶ HISTORY Latin *audire* to hear

audio *adj* **1** of or relating to sound or hearing **2** of or for the transmission or reproduction of sound ▶ HISTORY Latin *audire* to hear

audio frequency *n* a frequency in the range 20 hertz to 20 000 hertz, audible to the human ear

audiometer (aw-dee-**om**-it-er) *n* an instrument for testing hearing

audiovisual *adj* involving both hearing and sight: *audiovisual teaching aids*

audit *n* **1** an official inspection of business accounts, conducted by an independent qualified accountant **2** any thoroughgoing assessment or review: *an audit of their lifestyle* ▷ *vb* **auditing, audited 3** to examine (business accounts) officially ▶ HISTORY Latin *audire* to hear

audition *n* **1** a test of a performer's or musician's ability for a particular role or job ▷ *vb* **2** to test or be tested in an audition ▶ HISTORY Latin *audire* to hear

auditor *n* a person qualified to audit accounts ▶ HISTORY Latin *auditor* a hearer

auditorium *n, pl* **-toriums** *or* **-toria 1** the area of a concert hall or theatre in which the audience sits **2** *US & Canad* a building for public meetings ▶ HISTORY Latin

auditory *adj* of or relating to hearing ▶ HISTORY Latin *audire* to hear

au fait (oh **fay**) *adj* **1** fully informed **2** expert ▶ HISTORY French: to the point

auf Wiedersehen (owf **vee**-der-zay-en) *interj* goodbye ▶ HISTORY German

Aug. August

auger *n* a pointed tool for boring holes ▶ HISTORY Old English *nafugār* nave (i.e. hub of a wheel) spear

aught *pron* old-fashioned *or literary* anything whatever: *for aught I know* ▶ HISTORY Old English *āwiht*

augment *vb* to make or become greater in number or strength ▶ HISTORY Latin *augere* to increase > **augmentation** *n*

au gratin (oh **grat**-tan) *adj* cooked with a topping of breadcrumbs and sometimes cheese ▶ HISTORY French

augur *vb* to be a good or bad sign of future events: *a double fault on the opening point did not augur well* ▶ HISTORY Latin: diviner of omens

augury *n* **1** the foretelling of the future **2** (*pl* **-ries**) an omen

august *adj* dignified and imposing ▶ HISTORY Latin *augustus*

August *n* the eighth month of the year ▶ HISTORY Latin, after the emperor *Augustus*

Augustan *adj* **1** *history* of the Roman emperor Augustus Caesar or the poets writing during his reign **2** *literature* of any literary period noted for refinement and classicism, esp. the late 17th century in France (the period of dramatists Corneille, Racine, and Molière) or the 18th century in England (the period of Swift, Pope, and Johnson)

auk *n* a northern sea bird with a heavy body, short wings, and black-and-white plumage ▶ HISTORY Old Norse *ālka*

auld lang syne *n* times past ▶ HISTORY Scots, literally: old long since

Aum *n Hinduism* same as **Om**

aunt *n* **1** a sister of one's father or mother **2** the wife of one's uncle **3** a child's term of address for a female friend of the parents ▶ HISTORY Latin *amita* a father's sister

auntie *or* **aunty** *n, pl* **-ies** *informal* an aunt

Aunt Sally *n, pl* **-lies 1** a figure used in fairgrounds as a target **2** any target for insults or criticism

au pair *n* a young foreign woman who does housework in return for board and lodging ▶ HISTORY French

aura *n, pl* **auras** *or* **aurae 1** a distinctive air or quality associated with a person or thing **2** any invisible emanation ▶ HISTORY Greek: breeze

aural *adj* of or using the ears or hearing ▶ HISTORY Latin *auris* ear > **aurally** *adv*

aureate *adj literary* **1** covered with gold **2** (of a style of writing or speaking) excessively elaborate ▶ HISTORY Latin *aurum* gold

aureole *or* **aureola** *n* **1** a ring of light surrounding the head of a figure represented as holy; halo **2** the sun's corona, visible as a faint halo during eclipses ▶ HISTORY Latin *aurum* gold

au revoir (oh riv-**vwahr**) *interj* goodbye ▶ HISTORY French

auric *adj* of or containing gold in the trivalent state ▶ HISTORY Latin *aurum* gold

auricle *n* **1** the upper chamber of the heart **2** the outer part of the ear ▶ HISTORY Latin *auris* ear > **auricular** *adj*

auricula *n, pl* **-lae** *or* **-las** an alpine primrose with leaves shaped like a bear's ear ▶ HISTORY Latin *auris* ear

auriferous *adj* containing gold ▶ HISTORY Latin *aurum* gold + *ferre* to bear

aurochs *n, pl* **-rochs** a recently extinct European wild ox ▶ HISTORY German

aurora *n, pl* **-ras** *or* **-rae 1** an atmospheric phenomenon of bands of light sometimes seen in the polar regions **2** *poetic* the dawn ▶ HISTORY Latin: dawn

aurora australis *n* the aurora seen around the South Pole ▶ HISTORY New Latin: southern aurora

aurora borealis *n* the aurora seen around the North Pole ▶ HISTORY New Latin: northern aurora

auscultation *n* the listening to of the internal sounds of the body, usually with a stethoscope, to help with medical diagnosis ▶ HISTORY Latin *auscultare* to listen attentively

auspices (**aw**-spiss-siz) *pl n* **under the auspices of** with the support and approval of ▶ HISTORY Latin *auspicium* augury from birds

auspicious *adj* showing the signs of future success

Aussie *n, adj informal* Australian

austere *adj* **1** stern or severe: *his austere and serious attitude to events* **2** self-disciplined or ascetic: *an extraordinarily austere and puritanical organization* **3** severely simple or plain: *the austere backdrop of grey* ▶ HISTORY Greek *austēros* astringent

austerity *n, pl* -**ties 1** the state of being austere **2** reduced availability of luxuries and consumer goods

austral *adj* of or from the south ▶ HISTORY Latin *auster* the south wind

Austral. 1 Australasia **2** Australia(n)

Australasian *adj* of Australia, New Zealand, and neighbouring islands

Australia Day *n* a public holiday in Australia on 26th January

Australian *adj* **1** of Australia ▷ *n* **2** a person from Australia

Austrian *adj* **1** of Austria ▷ *n* **2** a person from Austria

autarchy (**aw**-tar-kee) *n, pl* -**chies** absolute power or autocracy ▶ HISTORY Greek *autarkhia*

autarky (**aw**-tar-kee) *n, pl* -**kies** a policy of economic self-sufficiency ▶ HISTORY Greek *autarkeia*

authentic *adj* **1** of undisputed origin or authorship; genuine **2** reliable or accurate **3** *music* using period instruments, scores, and playing techniques ▶ HISTORY Greek *authentikos*
> **authentically** *adv* > **authenticity** *n*

authenticate *vb* -**cating, -cated** to establish as genuine > **authentication** *n*

author *n* **1** a person who writes a book, article, or other written work **2** an originator or creator ▶ HISTORY Latin *auctor*

authoring *n* *computers* the creation of documents, esp. multimedia documents

authoritarian *adj* **1** insisting on strict obedience to authority ▷ *n* **2** a person who insists on strict obedience to authority
> **authoritarianism** *n*

authoritative *adj* **1** recognized as being reliable: *the authoritative book on Shakespeare* **2** possessing authority; official > **authoritatively** *adv*

authority *n, pl* -**ties 1** the power to command, control, or judge others **2** a person or group with this power: *a third escapee turned himself in to the authorities* **3** a decision-making organization or government department: *the local authority* **4** an expert in a particular field **5** official permission: *he had no authority to negotiate* **6** a position that has the power to command, control, or judge others: *people in authority* **7 on good authority** from

reliable evidence **8** confidence resulting from expertise ▶ HISTORY Latin *auctor* author

authorize *or* -**rise** *vb* -**rizing, -rized** *or* -**rising, -rised 1** to give authority to **2** to give official permission for > **authorization** *or* -**risation** *n*

Authorized Version *n* **the Authorized Version** an English translation of the Bible published in 1611

authorship *n* **1** the origin or originator of a written work or plan **2** the profession of writing

autism *n* *psychiatry* a developmental disorder characterized by difficulty responding normally to people and limited ability to communicate ▶ HISTORY Greek *autos* self > **autistic** *adj*

auto *n, pl* -**tos** *US & Canad, informal* short for **automobile**

auto- *or sometimes before a vowel* **aut-** *combining form* **1** self; of or by the same one: *autobiography* **2** self-propelling: *automobile* ▶ HISTORY Greek *autos* self

autobahn *n* a motorway in German-speaking countries ▶ HISTORY German, from *Auto* car + *Bahn* road

autobiography *n, pl* -**phies** an account of a person's life written by that person
> **autobiographer** *n* > **autobiographical** *adj*

autoclave *n* an apparatus for sterilizing objects by steam under pressure ▶ HISTORY AUTO- + Latin *clavis* key

autocracy *n, pl* -**cies** government by an individual with unrestricted authority

autocrat *n* **1** a ruler with absolute authority **2** a dictatorial person ▶ HISTORY AUTO- + Greek *kratos* power > **autocratic** *adj* > **autocratically** *adv*

autocross *n* a sport in which cars race over a circuit of rough grass

Autocue *n trademark* an electronic television prompting device displaying a speaker's script, unseen by the audience

auto-da-fé (aw-toe-da-**fay**) *n, pl* **autos-da-fé 1** *history* the ceremonial passing of sentence on heretics by the Spanish Inquisition **2** the burning to death of heretics ▶ HISTORY Portuguese, literally: act of the faith

autofocus *n* a camera system in which the lens is focused automatically

autogiro *or* **autogyro** *n, pl* -**ros** a self-propelled aircraft resembling a helicopter but with an unpowered rotor

autograph *n* **1** a handwritten signature of a famous person ▷ *vb* **2** to write one's signature on or in ▶ HISTORY AUTO- + Greek *graphein* to write

automat *n* *US* a vending machine

automate *vb* -**mating, -mated** to make (a manufacturing process) automatic

automatic *adj* **1** (of a device or mechanism) able to activate or regulate itself **2** (of a process) performed by automatic equipment **3** done without conscious thought **4** (of a firearm) utilizing some of the force of each explosion to reload and fire continuously **5** occurring as a necessary consequence: *the certificate itself carries no automatic legal benefits* ▷ *n* **6** an automatic firearm **7** a motor vehicle with automatic transmission ▶ HISTORY Greek *automatos* acting independently > **automatically** *adv*

automatic pilot *n* **1** a device that automatically maintains an aircraft on a preset course **2 on automatic pilot** repeating an action or process without thought

automatic transmission *n* a transmission system in a motor vehicle in which the gears change automatically

automation *n* the use of automatic, often electronic, methods to control industrial processes

automaton *n*, *pl* **-tons** *or* **-ta 1** a mechanical device operating under its own power **2** a person who acts mechanically ▶ HISTORY Greek *automatos* spontaneous

automobile *n* US a motorcar

automobilia *pl n* items connected with cars that are of interest to a collector

automotive *adj* **1** relating to motor vehicles **2** self-propelling

autonomous *adj* **1** having self-government **2** independent of others ▶ HISTORY AUTO- + Greek *nomos* law

autonomy *n*, *pl* **-mies 1** the right or state of self-government **2** freedom to determine one's own actions and behaviour ▶ HISTORY Greek *autonomia*

autopilot *n* an automatic pilot

autopsy *n*, *pl* **-sies** examination of a corpse to determine the cause of death ▶ HISTORY Greek *autopsia* seeing with one's own eyes

autoroute *n* a motorway in French-speaking countries ▶ HISTORY French, from *auto* car + *route* road

autostrada *n* a motorway in Italian-speaking countries ▶ HISTORY Italian, from *auto* car + *strada* road

autosuggestion *n* a process in which a person unconsciously supplies the means of influencing his or her own behaviour or beliefs

autotrophic *adj biochem* (of organisms such as green plants) able to manufacture complex organic nutritive compounds from simple inorganic sources such as carbon dioxide, water, and nitrates

autumn *n* **1** the season of the year between summer and winter **2** a period of late maturity followed by a decline ▶ HISTORY Latin *autumnus* > **autumnal** *adj*

auxiliaries *pl n* foreign troops serving another nation

auxiliary *adj* **1** secondary or supplementary **2** supporting ▷ *n*, *pl* **-ries 3** a person or thing that supports or supplements ▶ HISTORY Latin *auxilium* help

auxiliary verb *n* a verb used to indicate the tense, voice, or mood of another verb, such as *will* in *I will go*

auxin *n physiol* a plant hormone that promotes growth and controls fruit and flower development

AV (of the Bible) Authorized Version

av. 1 average **2** avoirdupois

avail *vb* **1** to be of use, advantage, or assistance (to) **2 avail oneself of** *formal* to make use of ▷ *n* **3** *written* use or advantage: *to no avail* ▶ HISTORY Latin *valere* to be strong

available *adj* **1** obtainable or accessible **2** able to be contacted and willing to talk: *a spokesman insisted she was not available for comment* > **availability** *n* > **availably** *adv*

avalanche *n* **1** a fall of large masses of snow and ice down a mountain **2** a sudden or overwhelming quantity of anything ▶ HISTORY French

avant- (**av**-ong) *prefix* belonging to the avant-garde of a field: *avant-jazz*

avant-garde (av-ong-**gard**) *n* **1** those artists, writers, or musicians, whose techniques and ideas are in advance of those generally accepted ▷ *adj* **2** using ideas or techniques in advance of those generally accepted ▶ HISTORY French: vanguard

avarice (**av**-a-riss) *n* extreme greed for wealth ▶ HISTORY Latin *avere* to crave > **avaricious** *adj*

avast *interj naut* stop! cease! ▶ HISTORY probably Dutch *hou'vast* hold fast

avatar *n* Hinduism the appearance of a god in human or animal form ▶ HISTORY Sanskrit *avatāra* a going down

Ave (**ah**-vay) *or* **Ave Maria** (ma-**ree**-a) *n* same as **Hail Mary** ▶ HISTORY Latin: hail, Mary!

Ave. avenue

avenge *vb* **avenging, avenged** to inflict a punishment in retaliation for (harm done) or on behalf of (the person harmed) ▶ HISTORY Latin *vindicare* > **avenger** *n*

avenue *n* **1** a wide street **2** a road bordered by two rows of trees **3** a line of approach: *the United States was exhausting every avenue to achieve a diplomatic solution* ▶ HISTORY French, from *avenir* to come to

aver (a-**vur**) *vb* **averring, averred** to state to be true ▶ HISTORY Latin *verus* true > **averment** *n*

average *n* **1** the typical or normal amount or quality **2** the result obtained by adding the numbers or quantities in a set and dividing the total by the number of members in the set **3 on average** usually or typically ▷ *adj* **4** usual or typical **5** calculated as an average **6** mediocre or inferior ▷ *vb* **-aging, -aged 7** to calculate or estimate the average of **8** to amount to or be on average ▶ HISTORY Middle English *averay* loss arising from damage to ships, ultimately from Arabic *awār* damage

averse *adj* opposed: *he's not averse to publicity, of the right kind* ▶ HISTORY Latin *avertere* to turn from

aversion *n* **1** extreme dislike or disinclination **2** a person or thing that arouses this

avert *vb* **1** to turn away: *he had to avert his eyes* **2** to ward off: *a final attempt to avert war* ▶ HISTORY Latin *avertere* to turn from

Avesta *n* a collection of sacred writings of Zoroastrianism

avian (**aiv**-ee-an) *adj* of or like a bird: *the treatment of avian diseases* ▶ HISTORY Latin *avis* bird

49

a

avian flu *n* same as **bird flu**

aviary *n, pl* **aviaries** a large enclosure in which birds are kept ▶ HISTORY Latin *avis* bird

aviation *n* the art or science of flying aircraft ▶ HISTORY Latin *avis* bird

aviator *n old-fashioned* the pilot of an aircraft > **aviatrix** *fem n*

avid *adj* **1** very keen or enthusiastic: *he is an avid football fan* **2** eager: *avid for economic development* ▶ HISTORY Latin *avere* to long for > **avidity** *n* > **avidly** *adv*

avocado *n, pl* **-dos** a pear-shaped tropical fruit with a leathery green skin and greenish-yellow flesh ▶ HISTORY Spanish *aguacate*

avocation *n* **1** *Brit, Austral & NZ, old-fashioned* a person's regular job **2** *formal* a hobby ▶ HISTORY Latin *avocare* to distract

avocet *n* a long-legged shore bird with a long slender upward-curving bill ▶ HISTORY Italian *avocetta*

avoid *vb* **1** to refrain from doing **2** to prevent f rom happening **3** to keep out of the way of ▶ HISTORY Old French *esvuidier* > **avoidable** *adj* > **avoidably** *adv* > **avoidance** *n*

avoirdupois *or* **avoirdupois weight** (av-er-de-**poise**) *n* a system of weights based on the pound, which contains 16 ounces ▶ HISTORY Old French *aver de peis* goods of weight

avow *vb* **1** to state or affirm **2** to admit openly ▶ HISTORY Latin *advocare* to call upon > **avowal** *n* > **avowed** *adj* > **avowedly** (a-**vow**-id-lee) *adv*

avuncular *adj* (of a man) friendly, helpful, and caring towards someone younger ▶ HISTORY Latin *avunculus* (maternal) uncle

await *vb* **1** to wait for **2** to be in store for

awake *adj* **1** not sleeping **2** alert or aware: *awake to the danger* ▷ *vb* **awaking, awoke** *or* **awaked, awoken** *or* **awaked** **3** to emerge or rouse from sleep **4** to become or cause to become alert ▶ HISTORY Old English *awacan*

awaken *vb* **1** to awake **2** to cause to be aware of: *anxieties awakened by reunification*

awakening *n* the start of a feeling or awareness in someone: *a picture of an emotional awakening*

award *vb* **1** to give (something) for merit **2** *law* to declare to be entitled, such as by decision of a court ▷ *n* **3** something awarded, such as a prize **4** *law* the decision of an arbitrator or court ▶ HISTORY Old French *eswarder* to decide after investigation

aware *adj* **1** **aware of** knowing about: *he's at least aware of the problem* **2** informed: *they are becoming more politically aware every day* ▶ HISTORY Old English *gewær* > **awareness** *n*

awash *adv, adj* washed over by water

away *adv* **1** from a particular place: *I saw them walk away and felt absolutely desolated* **2** in or to another, a usual, or a proper place: *he decided to put the car away in the garage* **3** at a distance: *keep away from the windows* **4** out of existence: *the pillars rotted away* **5** indicating motion or distance from a normal or proper place: *the child shook her head and looked away* **6** continuously: *he continued to scribble away* ▷ *adj* **7** not present: *he had been away from home for years* **8** distant: *the castle was farther away than he had thought* **9** *sport* played on an opponent's ground ▶ HISTORY Old English *on weg* on way

awe *n* **1** wonder and respect mixed with dread ▷ *vb* **awing, awed** **2** to inspire with reverence or dread ▶ HISTORY Old Norse *agi*

aweigh *adj* *naut* (of an anchor) no longer hooked into the bottom

awesome *adj* **1** inspiring or displaying awe **2** *slang* excellent or outstanding

awestruck *adj* *written* overcome or filled with awe

awful *adj* **1** very bad or unpleasant **2** *informal* considerable or great: *that's an awful lot of money, isn't it?* **3** *obsolete* inspiring reverence or dread ▷ *adv* **4** *not standard* very: *I'm working awful hard on my lines*

awfully *adv* **1** in an unpleasant way **2** *informal* very: *we were both awfully busy*

awhile *adv* for a brief period

awkward *adj* **1** clumsy or ungainly **2** embarrassed: *he was awkward and nervous around girls* **3** difficult to deal with: *the lawyer was in an awkward situation* **4** difficult to use or handle: *it was small but heavy enough to make it awkward to carry* **5** embarrassing: *there were several moments of awkward silence* ▶ HISTORY Old Norse *öfugr* turned the wrong way round > **awkwardly** *adv* > **awkwardness** *n*

awl *n* a pointed hand tool for piercing wood, leather, etc. ▶ HISTORY Old English *æl*

awn *n* any of the bristles growing from the flowering parts of certain grasses and cereals ▶ HISTORY Old English *agen* ear of grain

awning *n* a canvas roof supported by a frame to give protection against the weather ▶ HISTORY origin unknown

awoke *vb* a past tense and (now rare or dialectal) past participle of **awake**

awoken *vb* a past participle of **awake**

AWOL (**eh**-woll) *adj* *mil* absent without leave but without intending to desert

awry (a-**rye**) *adv, adj* **1** *written* not in its proper position; askew: *his dark hair was all awry* **2** amiss or faulty: *if a gear gets stuck, the whole system goes awry* ▶ HISTORY Middle English on *wry*

axe *or US* **ax** *n, pl* **axes** **1** a hand tool with one side of its head sharpened to a cutting edge, used for felling trees and splitting timber **2** **an axe to grind** a favourite topic one wishes to promote **3** *informal* a severe cut in spending or in the number of staff employed ▷ *vb* **axing, axed** **4** *informal* to dismiss (employees), restrict (expenditure), or terminate (a project) ▶ HISTORY Old English *æx*

axes¹ *n* the plural of **axis**

axes² *n* the plural of **axe**

axial *adj* **1** forming or of an axis **2** in, on, or along an axis > **axially** *adv*

axil *n* the angle where the stalk of a leaf joins a stem ▶ HISTORY Latin *axilla* armpit

axiom *n* **1** a generally accepted principle **2** a self-evident statement ▶ HISTORY Greek *axios* worthy

axiomatic *adj* **1** containing axioms **2** self-evident or obvious > **axiomatically** *adv*

axis (**ax**-iss) *n, pl* **axes** (**ax**-eez) **1** a real or imaginary line about which a body can rotate or about which an object or geometrical construction is symmetrical **2** one of two or three reference lines used in coordinate geometry to locate a point in a plane or in space ▶ **HISTORY** Latin

axis of symmetry *n geom* a line about which a geometric figure is symmetrical

axle *n* a shaft on which a wheel or pair of wheels revolves ▶ **HISTORY** Old Norse *öxull*

axolotl *n* an aquatic salamander of N America ▶ **HISTORY** Mexican Indian: water doll

ayatollah *n* one of a class of Islamic religious leaders in Iran ▶ **HISTORY** Arabic *aya* sign + *allah* God

aye *or* **ay** *interj* **1** *Brit, Austral & NZ* yes ▷ *n* **2** an affirmative vote or voter ▶ **HISTORY** probably from *I*, expressing assent

Ayrshire *n* one of a breed of brown-and-white dairy cattle ▶ **HISTORY** *Ayrshire*, district of Scotland

AZ Arizona

azalea (az-**zale**-ya) *n* a garden shrub grown for its showy flowers ▶ **HISTORY** Greek *azaleos* dry

azimuth *n* **1** the arc of the sky between the zenith and the horizon **2** *surveying* the horizontal angle of a bearing measured clockwise from the north ▶ **HISTORY** Arabic *as-samt* the path

Aztec *n* **1** a member of a Mexican Indian race who established a great empire, overthrown by the Spanish in the early 16th century **2** the language of the Aztecs ▷ *adj* **3** of the Aztecs or their language ▶ **HISTORY** *Aztlan*, their traditional place of origin, literally: near the cranes

azure *n* **1** the deep blue colour of a clear sky **2** *poetic* a clear blue sky ▷ *adj* **3** deep blue ▶ **HISTORY** Arabic *lāzaward* lapis lazuli

a

Bb

b¹ or **B** *n, pl* **b's, B's** or **Bs 1** the second letter of the English alphabet **2 from A to B** See **a** (sense 2)

b² *cricket* **a** bowled **b** bye

B 1 *music* the seventh note of the scale of C major **2** the second in a series, class, or rank **3** *chem* boron **4** *chess* bishop

Ba *chem* barium

BA 1 Bachelor of Arts **2** British Airways

baa *vb* **baaing, baaed 1** (of a sheep) to make a characteristic bleating sound ▷ *n* **2** the cry made by a sheep

baas *n S African* a boss ▶ HISTORY Afrikaans

baaskap *n* (in South Africa) control by White people of non-White people ▶ HISTORY Afrikaans

babaco *n* a greenish-yellow egg-shaped fruit

babble *vb* **-bling, -bled 1** to talk in a quick, foolish, or muddled way **2** to make meaningless sounds: *children first gurgle and babble at random* **3** to disclose secrets carelessly **4** *literary* (of streams) to make a low murmuring sound ▷ *n* **5** muddled or foolish speech **6** a murmuring sound ▶ HISTORY probably imitative > **babbler** *n* > **babbling** *n*

babe *n* **1** a baby **2 babe in arms** *informal* a naive or inexperienced person **3** *slang* a girl, esp. an attractive one

babel (**babe**-el) *n* **1** a confusion of noises or voices **2** a scene of noise and confusion ▶ HISTORY from the confusion of languages on the tower of *Babel* (Genesis 11:1–10)

baboon *n* a medium-sized monkey with a long face, large teeth, and a fairly long tail ▶ HISTORY Middle English *babewyn* gargoyle

baby *n, pl* **-bies 1** a newborn child **2** the youngest or smallest of a family or group **3** a recently born animal **4** an immature person **5** *slang* a sweetheart **6** a project of personal concern **7 be left holding the baby** to be left with a responsibility ▷ *adj* **8** comparatively small of its type: *baby carrots* ▷ *vb* **-bies, -bying, -bied 9** to treat like a baby ▶ HISTORY probably childish reduplication > **babyhood** *n* > **babyish** *adj*

baby bonus *n Canad, informal* Family Allowance

baby-sit *vb* **-sitting, -sat** to act or work as a baby-sitter > **baby-sitting** *n, adj*

baby-sitter *n* a person who takes care of a child while the parents are out

baccalaureate (back-a-**law**-ree-it) *n* the university degree of Bachelor of Arts ▶ HISTORY Medieval Latin *baccalarius* bachelor

baccarat (**back**-a-rah) *n* a card game in which two or more punters gamble against the banker ▶ HISTORY French *baccara*

bacchanalian (back-a-**nail**-ee-an) *adj literary* (of a party) unrestrained and involving a great deal of drinking ▶ HISTORY from *Bacchus*, Greek & Roman god of wine

Bacchus *n classical myth* the god of wine; Dionysus

bach (**batch**) *NZ n* **1** a small holiday cottage ▷ *vb* **2** to look after oneself when one's spouse is away

bachelor *n* **1** an unmarried man **2** a person who holds a first degree from a university or college ▶ HISTORY Old French *bacheler* youth, squire > **bachelorhood** *n*

Bachelor of Arts *n* a person with a first degree from a university or college, usually in the arts

Bach flower remedy *n* an alternative medicine consisting of a distillation from various flowers ▶ HISTORY after Dr E. *Bach*, homeopath

bacillary *adj* of or caused by bacilli

bacillus (bass-**ill**-luss) *n, pl* **-li** (-lie) a rod-shaped bacterium, esp. one causing disease ▶ HISTORY Latin *baculum* walking stick

back *n* **1** the rear part of the human body, from the neck to the pelvis **2** the spinal column **3** the part or side of an object opposite the front **4** the part of anything less often seen or used **5** *ball games* a defensive player or position **6 at the back of one's mind** not in one's conscious thoughts **7 behind someone's back** secretly or deceitfully **8 put** or **get someone's back up** to annoy someone **9 turn one's back on someone** to refuse to help someone ▷ *vb* **10** to move or cause to move backwards **11** to provide money for (a person or enterprise) **12** to bet on the success of: *to back a horse* **13** to provide (a pop singer) with a musical accompaniment **14** (foll. by *on* or *onto*) to have the back facing (towards): *his garden backs onto a school* **15** (of the wind) to change direction anticlockwise ▷ *adj* **16** situated behind: *back garden* **17** owing from an earlier date: *back rent* **18** remote: *a back road* ▷ *adv* **19** at, to, or towards the rear **20** to or towards the original starting point or condition: *I went back home* **21** in reply or retaliation: *to hit someone back* **22** in concealment or reserve: *to keep something back* **23 back and forth** to and fro **24 back to front a** in reverse **b** in disorder ▷ See also **back down** ▶ HISTORY Old English *bæc*

backbencher *n Brit, Austral, NZ, etc.* a Member of Parliament who does not hold office in the government or opposition

back boiler *n Brit* a tank at the back of a fireplace for heating water

backbone *n* **1** the spinal column **2** strength of character **3** *computers* a central section that connects segments of a network

backbreaking *adj* (of work) exhausting

backburn *Austral & NZ vb* **1** to clear (an area of bush) by creating a fire that burns in the opposite direction from the wind **2** to prevent a bush fire from spreading by clearing an area of land in front of it ▷ *n* **3** the act or result of backburning

b

backchat n informal impudent replies

backcloth n a painted curtain at the back of a stage set. Also called: **backdrop**

back country n Austral & NZ land far away from settled areas

backdate vb -dating, -dated to make (a document) effective from a date earlier than its completion

back door n a means of entry to a job or position that is secret or obtained through influence

back down vb to withdraw an earlier claim

back dune n geog a dune that is further away from the sea than the others. Compare **foredune**

backer n a person who gives financial or other support

backfire vb -firing, -fired 1 (of a plan or scheme) to fail to have the desired effect 2 (of an internal-combustion engine) to make a loud noise as a result of an explosion of unburnt gases in the exhaust system

backgammon n a game for two people played on a board with pieces moved according to throws of the dice ▶ HISTORY back + obsolete gammon game

background n 1 the events or circumstances that help to explain something 2 a person's social class, education, or experience 3 the part of a scene furthest from the viewer 4 an inconspicuous position: in the background 5 the space behind the chief figures or objects in a picture

background radiation n low-intensity radiation that is naturally present in the earth's surface and atmosphere

backhand n 1 tennis etc. a stroke made from across the body with the back of the hand facing the direction of the stroke 2 the side on which backhand strokes are made

backhanded adj 1 (of a blow or shot) performed with the arm moving from across the body 2 ambiguous or implying criticism: a backhanded compliment

backhander n 1 slang a bribe 2 a backhanded stroke or blow

backing n 1 support 2 something that forms or strengthens the back of something 3 musical accompaniment for a pop singer

backing dog n NZ a dog that moves a flock of sheep by jumping on their backs

backlash n 1 a sudden and adverse reaction 2 a recoil between interacting badly fitting parts in machinery

backlog n an accumulation of things to be dealt with

backlot n an area outside a film or television studio used for outdoor filming

back number n 1 an old issue of a newspaper or magazine 2 informal a person or thing considered to be old-fashioned

back out vb (often foll. by of) to withdraw from (an agreement)

backpack n 1 a rucksack ▷ vb 2 to go hiking with a backpack

back passage n the rectum

back-pedal vb -pedalling, -pedalled or US -pedaling, -pedaled to retract or modify a previous opinion or statement

back room n 1 a place where secret research or planning is done ▷ adj **back-room** 2 of or relating to secret research or planning: back-room boys

back-seat driver n informal a person who offers unwanted advice

backside n informal the buttocks

backslide vb -sliding, -slid to relapse into former bad habits or vices > **backslider** n

backspace vb -spacing, -spaced to move a typewriter carriage or computer cursor backwards

backspin n sport a backward spin given to a ball to reduce its speed at impact

backstage adv 1 behind the stage in a theatre ▷ adj 2 situated backstage

backstairs or **backstair** adj underhand: backstairs gossip

backstreet n 1 a street in a town far from the main roads ▷ adj 2 denoting secret or illegal activities: a backstreet abortion

backstroke n swimming a stroke performed on the back, using backward circular strokes of each arm

backswamp n geog the marshy part of a flood plain where silt settles following a flood

backtrack vb 1 to go back along the same route one has just travelled 2 to retract or reverse one's opinion or policy

back up vb 1 to support 2 computers to make a copy of (a data file), esp. as a security copy 3 (of traffic) to become jammed behind an obstruction ▷ n **backup** 4 a support or reinforcement 5 a reserve or substitute 6 computers a copy (of a data file), esp. made as a security copy ▷ adj **backup** 7 able to be substituted: a backup copy

backward adj 1 directed towards the rear 2 slow in physical, material, or intellectual development 3 reluctant or bashful ▷ adv 4 same as **backwards** > **backwardness** n

backwards or **backward** adv 1 towards the rear 2 with the back foremost 3 in the reverse of the usual direction 4 into a worse state: the Gothic novel's been going backwards since Radcliffe 5 **bend over backwards** informal to make a special effort to please someone

backwash n 1 water washed backwards by the motion of oars or a ship 2 water carried back from the shore following each break of the waves 3 an unpleasant aftereffect of an event or situation

backwater n 1 an isolated or backward place or condition 2 a body of stagnant water connected to a river

backwoods pl n 1 any remote sparsely populated place 2 partially cleared, sparsely populated forests > **backwoodsman** n

bacon n 1 meat from the back and sides of a pig, dried, salted, and often smoked 2 **bring home the bacon** informal **a** to achieve success **b** to provide material support ▶ HISTORY Old French

b

bad

WORD FOCUS

Bad is such a commonly used word that it has come to lose much of its effectiveness. Depending on the sense and context of what you are saying, there are many other much more expressive words that can be used instead.

DEFINITION 1
● If you would like to describe poor quality, you could try: **defective** products • **deficient** diet • **faulty** goods • **imperfect** work • **inadequate** work conditions • **inferior** quality • **poor** housing • **unsatisfactory** service

DEFINITION 2
● If you would like to describe something or someone that lacks skill, you could try: **incompetent** managers • **inept** performance • **poor** judge of character • **useless** at his job

DEFINITION 3
● If you would like to describe something as having a harmful effect, you could try: extremely **damaging** • **destructive** effect • **detrimental** impact • **harmful** effects • **unhealthy** lifestyle • **unpleasant** side-effects

DEFINITION 4
● If you would like to describe something or someone with an evil character, you could try: **criminal** actions • **depraved** criminals • **evil** tyrant • **immoral** conduct • **corrupt** institutions • **sinful** act • **villainous** thugs • **wicked** stepmother

DEFINITION 5
● If you would like to describe children who are behaving badly, you could try: **disobedient**

children • **mischievous** little scamp • **naughty** boy • **undisciplined** pupils • **unruly** kids

DEFINITION 6
● If you're talking or writing about food, you could try: **mouldy** cheese • **putrid** meat • **rancid** butter • **rotten** eggs • **sour** milk

DEFINITION 7
● If you would like to describe something that has or is causing physical pain, you could try: **acute** attack • **agonizing** death • **excruciating** pain • **intense** cramps • **painful** back • **serious** knee problems • **severe** stomach pains • **terrible** migraine

DEFINITION 8
● If you would like to describe something that is incorrect, you could try: **false** accusation • **flawed** logic • **inaccurate** description • **mistaken** belief • **untrue** statement • **wrong** decision

DEFINITION 9
● If you would like to talk about someone who feels sorry or guilty about something, you could try: look **apologetic** • look **ashamed** • feel **guilty** • sound **regretful** • feel **sorry** • feel **upset**

DEFINITION 10
● If you would like to describe something that has made someone feel upset or uneasy, you could try: **distressing** images • **disturbing** news • **grim** time • **painful** memories • **traumatic** period • **unsettling** atmosphere • **upsetting** experience

DEFINITION 11
● If you're talking about language, you could try: **obscene** lyrics • **offensive** language • **rude** words • **vulgar** expression

bacteria *pl n, sing* **-rium** a large group of microorganisms, many of which cause disease ▶ HISTORY Greek *baktron* rod > **bacterial** *adj*

bacteriology *n* the study of bacteria > **bacteriologist** *n*

Bactrian camel *n* a two-humped camel ▶ HISTORY *Bactria*, ancient country of Asia

bad *adj* **worse, worst** 1 not good; of poor quality 2 lacking skill or talent: *I'm so bad at that sort of thing* 3 harmful: *smoking is bad for you* 4 evil or immoral 5 naughty or mischievous 6 rotten or decayed: *a bad egg* 7 severe: *a bad headache* 8 incorrect or faulty: *bad grammar* 9 sorry or upset: *I feel bad about saying no* 10 unfavourable or distressing: *bad news* 11 offensive or unpleasant: *bad language* 12 not valid: *a bad cheque* 13 not recoverable: *a bad debt* 14 (**badder, baddest**) *slang* good; excellent 15 **not bad** *or* **not so bad** *informal* fairly good 16 **too bad** *informal* (often used dismissively) regrettable ▷ *n* 17 unfortunate or unpleasant events: *you've got to take the good with the bad* ▷ *adv* 18 not standard badly: *to want something bad* ▶ HISTORY Middle English > **badness** *n*
See WORD FOCUS **bad**

bad blood *n* a feeling of intense hatred or hostility between people

bad debt *n* a debt that is not able to be recovered

bade *or* **bad** *vb* a past tense of **bid**

badge *n* 1 a distinguishing emblem or mark worn to show membership or achievement 2 any revealing feature or mark ▶ HISTORY Old French *bage*

badger *n* 1 a stocky burrowing mammal with a black and white striped head ▷ *vb* 2 to pester or harass ▶ HISTORY probably from *badge*

badinage (**bad**-in-nahzh) *n* playful and witty conversation ▶ HISTORY French

badlands *pl n geog* areas of arid barren land with deep ridges and gullies caused by erosion

badly *adv* **worse, worst** 1 poorly; inadequately 2 unfavourably: *our plan worked out badly* 3 severely: *badly damaged* 4 very much: *he badly needed to improve his image* 5 **badly off** poor

badminton *n* a game played with rackets and a shuttlecock which is hit back and forth across a high net ▶ HISTORY *Badminton* House, Gloucestershire, England

Bafana Bafana (bah-**fan**-na) *pl n S African* the South African national soccer team ▶ HISTORY from Nguni (language group of southern Africa) *bafana* the boys

baffle *vb* **-fling, -fled 1** to perplex ▷ *n* **2** a mechanical device to limit or regulate the flow of fluid, light, or sound ▶ HISTORY origin unknown > **bafflement** *n* > **baffling** *adj*

bag *n* **1** a flexible container with an opening at one end **2** the contents of such a container **3** a piece of luggage **4** a handbag **5** a loose fold of skin under the eyes **6** any sac in the body of an animal **7** *offensive slang* an ugly or bad-tempered woman: *an old bag* **8** the amount of game taken by a hunter **9 in the bag** *slang* assured of succeeding ▷ *vb* **bagging, bagged 10** to put into a bag **11** to bulge or cause to bulge **12** to capture or kill, as in hunting **13** *Brit & NZ, informal* to secure the right to do or to have: *he bagged the best chair* ▷ See also **bags** ▶ HISTORY probably Old Norse *baggi*

bagatelle *n* **1** something of little value **2** a board game in which balls are struck into holes **3** a short piece of music ▶ HISTORY French

bagel (**bay**-gl) *n* a hard ring-shaped bread roll ▶ HISTORY Yiddish *beygel*

baggage *n* **1** suitcases packed for a journey **2** an army's portable equipment **3** *informal* previous knowledge or experience that may have an influence in new circumstances: *cultural baggage* ▶ HISTORY Old French *bagage*

baggy *adj* **-gier, -giest** (of clothes) hanging loosely > **bagginess** *n*

bagpipes *pl n* a musical wind instrument in which sounds are produced in reed pipes by air from an inflated bag

bags *pl n* **1** *informal* a lot ▷ *interj* **2** Also: **bags I** *children's slang, Brit & NZ* an indication of the desire to do, be, or have something

bah *interj* an expression of contempt or disgust

bahada *n* same as **bajada**

Bahamian *adj* **1** of the Bahamas ▷ *n* **2** a person from the Bahamas

bail¹ *law n* **1** a sum of money deposited with the court as security for a person's reappearance in court to **2** the person giving such security **3 jump bail** to fail to reappear in court after bail has been paid **4 stand** *or* **go bail** to act as surety for someone ▷ *vb* **5** (foll. by *out*) to obtain the release of (a person) from custody by depositing money with the court ▶ HISTORY Old French· custody

bail² *or* **bale** *vb* **bail out** to remove water from (a boat). See also **bail out** ▶ HISTORY Old French *baille* bucket

bail³ *n* **1** *cricket* either of two small wooden bars across the tops of the stumps **2** a partition between stalls in a stable or barn **3** *Austral & NZ* a framework in a cow shed used to secure the head of a cow during milking **4** a movable bar on a typewriter that holds the paper against the roller ▶ HISTORY Old French *baile* stake

bailey *n* the outermost wall or court of a castle ▶ HISTORY Old French *baille* enclosed court

Bailey bridge *n* a temporary bridge that can be rapidly assembled ▶ HISTORY after Sir Donald Coleman *Bailey*, its designer

bailiff *n* **1** *Brit* a sheriff's officer who serves writs and summonses **2** the agent of a landlord or landowner ▶ HISTORY Old French *baillif*

bailiwick *n* **1** *law* the area over which a bailiff has power **2** a person's special field of interest ▶ HISTORY *bailie* magistrate + obsolete *wick* district

bail out *or* **bale out** *vb* **1** *informal* to help (a person or organization) out of a predicament **2** to make an emergency parachute jump from an aircraft

bail up *vb* **1** *Austral & NZ, informal* to confine (a cow) or (of a cow) to be confined by the head in a bail. See **bail³ 2** *Austral history* (of a bushranger) to hold under guard in order to rob **3** *Austral* to submit to robbery without offering resistance **4** *Austral, informal* to accost or detain, esp. in conversation; buttonhole

bairn *n* *Scot & N English* a child ▶ HISTORY Old English *bearn*

bait *n* **1** something edible fixed to a hook or in a trap to attract fish or animals **2** an enticement ▷ *vb* **3** to put a piece of food on or in (a hook or trap) **4** to persecute or tease **5** to set dogs upon (a bear or badger) ▶ HISTORY Old Norse *beita* to hunt

baize *n* a feltlike woollen fabric, usually green, which is used for the tops of billiard and card tables ▶ HISTORY Old French *bai* reddish-brown

bajada *or* **bahada** (ba-**hah**-da) *n* *geog* a sloping area of sedimentary deposits at the foot of a desert mountain range formed by the overlapping of alluvial fans ▶ HISTORY Spanish

Bajan (**bay**-jun) *adj* **1** of Barbados ▷ *n* **2** a person from Barbados

bake *vb* **baking, baked 1** to cook by dry heat in an oven **2** to cook bread, pastry, or cakes **3** to make or become hardened by heat **4** *informal* to be extremely hot ▷ *n* **5** (in the Caribbean) a small flat fried cake ▶ HISTORY Old English *bacan*

baked beans *pl n* haricot beans, baked and tinned in tomato sauce

Bakelite (**bake**-a-lite) *n* *trademark* any of a class of resins used as electric insulators and for making plastics ▶ HISTORY after L. H. *Baekeland*, inventor

baker *n* a person who makes or sells bread, cakes, etc.

baker's dozen *n* thirteen

bakery *n, pl* **-eries** a place where bread, cakes, etc. are made or sold

baking powder *n* a powdered mixture that contains sodium bicarbonate and cream of tartar: used in baking as a raising agent

bakkie (**buck**-ee) *n* *S African* a small truck with an enclosed cab and an open goods area at the back ▶ HISTORY Afrikaans *bak* container

baksheesh *n* (in some Eastern countries) money given as a tip or present ▶ HISTORY Persian *bakhshīsh*

Balaclava *or* **Balaclava helmet** *n* a close-fitting woollen hood that covers the ears and neck ▶ HISTORY after *Balaklava*, in the Crimea

b

balalaika *n* a Russian musical instrument with a triangular body and three strings ▶ HISTORY Russian

balance *n* **1** stability of mind or body: *lose one's balance* **2** a state of being in balance **3** harmony in the parts of a whole **4** the power to influence or control: *the balance of power* **5** something that remains: *the balance of what you owe* **6** *accounting* **a** the matching of debit and credit totals in an account **b** a difference between such totals **7** a weighing device **8 in the balance** in an undecided condition **9 on balance** after weighing up all the factors ▷ *vb* **-ancing, -anced 10** to weigh in or as if in a balance **11** to be or come into equilibrium **12** to bring into or hold in equilibrium **13** to compare the relative weight or importance of **14** to arrange so as to create a state of harmony **15** *accounting* to compare or equalize the credit and debit totals of (an account) ▶ HISTORY Latin *bilanx* having two scales

balanced diet *n* a diet in which a wide variety of foods in the correct proportions are eaten, in order to maintain a healthy body weight

balanced forces *pl n physics* any number of forces acting on a single object and adding up to zero, so that if the object is not moving, then it will continue to stay still, and if the object is already moving, it will continue to move with a constant velocity

balance of payments *n* the difference in value between a nation's total payments to foreign countries and its total receipts from foreign countries

balance of power *n* the equal distribution of military and economic power among countries

balance of probabilities *n law* the standard of proof in a civil case, meaning that, to win a case, a claimant has only to prove that his or her version of events is the more or most likely one. Compare **beyond reasonable doubt**

balance of trade *n* the difference in value between exports and imports of goods

balance sheet *n* a statement that shows the financial position of a business

balcony *n, pl* **-nies 1** a platform projecting from a building with a balustrade along its outer edge, often with access from a door **2** an upper tier of seats in a theatre or cinema ▶ HISTORY Italian *balcone*

bald *adj* **1** having no hair or fur, esp. of a man having no hair on the scalp **2** lacking natural covering **3** plain or blunt: *the bald facts* **4** (of a tyre) having a worn tread ▶ HISTORY Middle English *ballede* > **baldly** *adv* > **baldness** *n*

balderdash *n* stupid or illogical talk ▶ HISTORY origin unknown

balding *adj* becoming bald

bale¹ *n* **1** a large bundle of hay or goods bound by ropes or wires for storage or transportation ▷ *vb* **baling, baled 2** to make (hay) or put (goods) into a bale or bales ▶ HISTORY Old High German *balla* ball

bale² *vb* **baling, baled** same as **bail²**

baleen *n* whalebone ▶ HISTORY Latin *balaena* whale

baleen whale *n* same as **whalebone whale**

baleful *adj* harmful, menacing, or vindictive > **balefully** *adv*

balk *or* **baulk** *vb* **1** to stop short: *the horse balked at the jump* **2** to recoil: *France balked at the parliament having a veto* **3** to thwart, check, or foil: *he was balked in his plans* ▶ HISTORY Old English *balca* ridge

Balkan *adj* of any of the countries of the Balkan Peninsula in SE Europe, between the Adriatic and Aegean Seas

ball¹ *n* **1** a spherical or nearly spherical mass: *a ball of wool* **2** a round or roundish object used in various games **3** a single delivery of the ball in a game **4** any more or less rounded part of the body: *the ball of the foot* **5 have the ball at one's feet** to have the chance of doing something **6 on the ball** *informal* alert; informed **7 play ball** *informal* to cooperate **8 set** *or* **keep the ball rolling** to initiate or maintain the progress of an action, discussion, or project ▷ *vb* **9** to form into a ball ▶ HISTORY Old Norse *böllr*

ball² *n* **1** a lavish or formal social function for dancing **2 have a ball** *informal* to have a very enjoyable time ▶ HISTORY Late Latin *ballare* to dance

ballad *n* **1** a narrative song or poem often with a chorus that is repeated **2** a slow sentimental song ▶ HISTORY Old Provençal *balada* song accompanying a dance

ballade *n* **1** *prosody* a verse form consisting of three stanzas and an envoy, all ending with the same line **2** *music* a romantic instrumental composition

ball-and-socket joint *n anat* a joint in which a rounded head fits into a rounded cavity, allowing a wide range of movement

ballast *n* **1** a substance, such as sand, used to stabilize a ship when it is not carrying cargo **2** crushed rock used for the foundation of a road or railway track ▷ *vb* **3** to give stability or weight to ▶ HISTORY probably Low German

ball bearing *n* **1** an arrangement of steel balls placed between moving parts of a machine in order to reduce friction **2** a metal ball used in such an arrangement

ball cock *n* a device consisting of a floating ball and valve for regulating the flow of liquid into a tank or cistern

ballerina *n* a female ballet dancer ▶ HISTORY Italian

ballet *n* **1** a classical style of expressive dancing based on precise conventional steps **2** a theatrical representation of a story performed by ballet dancers ▶ HISTORY Italian *balletto* a little dance > **balletic** *adj*

ballistic missile *n* a launched weapon which is guided automatically in flight but falls freely at its target

ballistics *n* the study of the flight of projectiles, often in relation to firearms ▶ HISTORY Greek *ballein* to throw > **ballistic** *adj*

balloon *n* **1** an inflatable rubber bag used as a plaything or party decoration **2** a large bag inflated with a lighter-than-air gas, designed to rise and float in the atmosphere with a basket for carrying passengers **3** an outline containing the words or thoughts of a character in a cartoon ▷ *vb* **4** to fly in a balloon **5** to swell or increase rapidly in size: *the cost of health care has ballooned* ▶ **HISTORY** Italian dialect *ballone* ball > **balloonist** *n*

ballot *n* **1** the practice of selecting a representative or course of action by voting **2** the number of votes cast in an election **3** the actual vote or paper indicating a person's choice ▷ *vb* **-loting, -loted** **4** to vote or ask for a vote from: *we balloted the members on this issue* **5** to vote for or decide on something by ballot

■ **WORD HISTORY**
■ 'Ballot' comes from Italian *ballotta* meaning
■ 'little ball'. In medieval Venice, votes were cast
■ by dropping black or white pebbles or balls into
■ a box.

ballot box *n* a box into which voting papers are dropped on completion

ballot paper *n* a paper used for voting

ballpoint *or* **ballpoint pen** *n* a pen which has a small ball bearing as a writing point

ballroom *n* a large hall for dancing

bally *adj, adv Brit, old-fashioned, slang* extreme or extremely: *a bally nuisance; he's too bally charming for his own good*

ballyhoo *n informal* unnecessary or exaggerated fuss ▶ **HISTORY** origin unknown

balm *n* **1** an aromatic substance obtained from certain tropical trees and used for healing and soothing **2** something comforting or soothing: *her calmness was like a balm to my troubled mind* **3** an aromatic herb, lemon balm ▶ **HISTORY** Latin *balsamum* balsam

balmy *adj* **balmier, balmiest** **1** (of weather) mild and pleasant **2** same as **barmy**

baloney *or* **boloney** *n informal* nonsense ▶ **HISTORY** *Bologna* (sausage)

balsa (**bawl**-sa) *n* **1** a tree of tropical America which yields light wood **2** Also: **balsawood** the light wood of this tree, used for making rafts, models, etc. ▶ **HISTORY** Spanish: raft

balsam *n* **1** an aromatic resin obtained from various trees and shrubs and used in medicines and perfumes **2** any plant yielding balsam **3** a flowering plant, such as busy Lizzie ▶ **HISTORY** Greek *balsamon*

Baltic (**bawl**-tik) *adj* of the Baltic Sea in N Europe or the states bordering it

baluster *n* a set of posts supporting a rail ▶ **HISTORY** French *balustre*

balustrade *n* an ornamental rail supported by a set of posts ▶ **HISTORY** French

bamboo *n* a tall treelike tropical grass with hollow stems which are used to make canes, furniture, etc. ▶ **HISTORY** probably from Malay *bambu*

bamboozle *vb* **-zling, -zled** *informal* **1** to cheat; mislead **2** to confuse ▶ **HISTORY** origin unknown > **bamboozlement** *n*

ban *vb* **banning, banned** **1** to prohibit or forbid officially ▷ *n* **2** an official prohibition ▶ **HISTORY** Old English *bannan* to proclaim

banal (ban-**nahl**) *adj* lacking originality > **banality** *n*

■ **WORD HISTORY**
■ In Old French, the adjective *banal* referred to
■ the mill, bakery, etc. that was owned by the
■ local lord and that all his tenants had to use.
■ The word 'banal' therefore came to mean
■ 'common to everyone' and from that,
■ 'commonplace' or 'ordinary'.

banana *n* a crescent-shaped fruit that grows on a tropical or subtropical treelike plant ▶ **HISTORY** Spanish or Portuguese, of African origin

bananaquit *n* any of a number of small birds of the West Indies, with a slim curved bill for getting nectar from flowers

banana republic *n informal, derogatory* a small politically unstable country whose economy is dominated by foreign interests

band[1] *n* **1** a group of musicians playing together, esp. on brass or percussion instruments **2** a group of people having a common purpose: *a band of revolutionaries* **3** *ethnography* (in Canada) a formally recognized group of Indians on a reserve ▷ *vb* **4** (foll. by *together*) to unite ▶ **HISTORY** French *bande*

band[2] *n* **1** a strip of some material, used to hold objects together: *a rubber band* **2** a strip of fabric used as an ornament or to reinforce clothing **3** a stripe of contrasting colour or texture **4** a driving belt in machinery **5** *physics* a range of frequencies or wavelengths between two limits ▷ *vb* **6** to fasten or mark with a band ▶ **HISTORY** Old French *bende*

bandage *n* **1** a piece of material to dress a wound or wrap an injured limb ▷ *vb* **-aging, -aged** **2** to cover or wrap with a bandage ▶ **HISTORY** French *bande* strip

bandanna *or* **bandana** *n* **1** a large brightly-coloured handkerchief or cloth for tying round the head or neck **2** a light cool fabric with a checked pattern, similar to tartan, often used in traditional Caribbean women's dress ▶ **HISTORY** Hindi *bāndhnū* tie-dyeing

B & B bed and breakfast

bandicoot *n* **1** an Australian marsupial with a long pointed muzzle and a long tail **2** **bandicoot rat** any of three burrowing rats of S and SE Asia ▶ **HISTORY** Telugu (language of SE India) *pandikokku*

bandit *n* a robber, esp. a member of an armed gang ▶ **HISTORY** Italian *bandito* > **banditry** *n*

bandmaster *n* the conductor of a band

bandolier *n* a shoulder belt with small pockets for cartridges ▶ **HISTORY** Old French *bandouliere*

band saw *n* a power-operated saw consisting of an endless toothed metal band running over two wheels

bandsman *n, pl* **-men** a player in a musical band

bandstand *n* a roofed outdoor platform for a band

b

57

b

bandwagon *n* **jump** or **climb on the bandwagon** to join a popular party or movement that seems assured of success

bandwidth *n* the range of frequencies used for transmitting electronic information

bandy *adj* **-dier, -diest 1** Also: **bandy-legged** having legs curved outwards at the knees **2** (of legs) curved outwards at the knees ▷ *vb* **-dies, -dying, -died 3** to exchange (words), sometimes in a heated manner **4 bandy about** to use (a name, term, etc.) frequently

■ **WORD HISTORY**
■ 'Bandy' comes from Old French *bander* meaning
■ 'to hit a ball backwards and forwards in tennis'.
■ The word 'bandy' also denotes an old form of
■ tennis that is no longer played.

bane *n* a person or thing that causes misery or distress: *the bane of my life* ▶ **HISTORY** Old English *bana* > **baneful** *adj*

bang *n* **1** a short loud explosive noise, such as the report of a gun **2** a hard blow or loud knock **3 with a bang** successfully: *the party went with a bang* ▷ *vb* **4** to hit or knock, esp. with a loud noise **5** to close (a door) noisily **6** to make or cause to make a loud noise, as of an explosion ▷ *adv* **7** with a sudden impact: *the car drove bang into a lamppost* **8** precisely: *bang in the middle* ▶ **HISTORY** Old Norse *bang, banga* hammer

banger *n* **1** *Brit & Austral, informal* an old decrepit car **2** *slang* a sausage **3** a firework that explodes loudly

Bangladeshi *adj* **1** of Bangladesh ▷ *n* **2** a person from Bangladesh

bangle *n* a bracelet worn round the arm or sometimes round the ankle ▶ **HISTORY** Hindi *bangrī*

banish *vb* **1** to send into exile **2** to drive away: *it's the only way to banish weeds from the garden* ▶ **HISTORY** Old French *banir* > **banishment** *n*

banisters or **bannisters** *pl n* the railing and supporting balusters on a staircase ▶ **HISTORY** altered from BALUSTER

banjo *n, pl* **-jos** or **-joes** a stringed musical instrument with a long neck and a circular drumlike body ▶ **HISTORY** US pronunciation of earlier *bandore* > **banjoist** *n*

bank¹ *n* **1** an institution offering services, such as the safekeeping and lending of money at interest **2** the building used by such an institution **3** the funds held by a banker or dealer in some gambling games **4** any supply, store, or reserve: *a data bank* ▷ *vb* **5** to deposit (cash or a cheque) in a bank **6** to transact business with a bank ▷ See also **bank on** ▶ **HISTORY** probably from Italian *banca* bench, moneychanger's table

bank² *n* **1** a long raised mass, esp. of earth **2** a slope, as of a hill **3** the sloping side and ground on either side of a river ▷ *vb* **4** to form into a bank or mound **5** to cover (a fire) with ashes and fuel so that it will burn slowly **6** (of an aircraft) to tip to one side in turning ▶ **HISTORY** Scandinavian

bank³ *n* **1** an arrangement of similar objects in a row or in tiers ▷ *vb* **2** to arrange in a bank ▶ **HISTORY** Old French *banc* bench

bankable *adj* likely to ensure financial success: *a bankable star* > **bankability** *n*

bank account *n* an arrangement whereby a customer deposits money at a bank and may withdraw it when it is needed

bank card *n* any plastic card issued by a bank, such as a cash card or a cheque card

banker¹ *n* **1** a person who owns or manages a bank **2** the keeper of the bank in various gambling games

banker² *n* *Austral & NZ, informal* a stream almost overflowing its banks: *the creek was running a banker*

banker's order *n* same as **standing order** (sense 1)

bankfull *n* *environmental science* the maximum height of water in a stream or river before it overflows its banks

bank holiday *n* (in Britain) a public holiday when banks are closed by law

banking *n* the business engaged in by a bank

banknote *n* a piece of paper money issued by a central bank

bank on *vb* to rely on

bankrupt *n* **1** a person, declared by a court to be unable to pay his or her debts, whose property is sold and the proceeds distributed among the creditors **2** a person no longer having a particular quality: *a spiritual bankrupt* ▷ *adj* **3** declared insolvent **4** financially ruined **5** no longer having a particular quality: *morally bankrupt* ▷ *vb* **6** to make bankrupt ▶ **HISTORY** Old Italian *banca* BANK¹ + *rotta* broken > **bankruptcy** *n*

banksia *n* an Australian evergreen tree or shrub

banner *n* **1** a long strip of material displaying a slogan, advertisement, etc. **2** a placard carried in a demonstration **3** Also called: **banner headline** a large headline in a newspaper extending across the page ▶ **HISTORY** Old French *baniere*

banns *pl n* the public announcement of an intended marriage ▶ **HISTORY** plural of obsolete *bann* proclamation

banquet *n* **1** an elaborate formal dinner often followed by speeches ▷ *vb* **-queting, -queted 2** to hold or take part in a banquet ▶ **HISTORY** Italian *banco* a table

banshee *n* (in Irish folklore) a female spirit whose wailing warns of a coming death ▶ **HISTORY** Irish Gaelic *bean sídhe* woman of the fairy mound

bantam *n* **1** a small breed of domestic fowl **2** a small but aggressive person ▶ **HISTORY** after *Bantam*, village in Java, said to be the original home of this fowl

bantamweight *n* a professional boxer weighing up to 118 pounds (53.5 kg) or an amateur weighing up to 54 kg

banter *vb* **1** to tease jokingly ▷ *n* **2** teasing or joking conversation ▶ **HISTORY** origin unknown

Bantu *n* **1** a group of languages of Africa **2** (*pl* **-tu** or **-tus**) *offensive* a Black speaker of a Bantu language ▷ *adj* **3** of the Bantu languages or the peoples who speak them ▶ **HISTORY** Bantu *Ba-ntu* people

Bantustan *n offensive* (formerly) an area reserved for occupation by a Black African people. Official name: **homeland** ▶ HISTORY *Bantu* + Hindi *-stan* country of

banyan *or* **banian** *n* an Indian tree whose branches grow down into the soil forming additional trunks ▶ HISTORY Hindi *baniyā*

baobab (bay-oh-bab) *n* an African tree with a massive grey trunk, short angular branches, and large pulpy fruit ▶ HISTORY probably from a native African word

bap *n Brit* a large soft bread roll ▶ HISTORY origin unknown

baptism *n* a Christian religious rite in which a person is immersed in or sprinkled with water as a sign of being cleansed from sin and accepted as a member of the Church > **baptismal** *adj*

baptism of fire *n* **1** any introductory ordeal **2** a soldier's first experience of battle

Baptist *n* **1** a member of a Protestant denomination that believes in the necessity of adult baptism by immersion **2 the Baptist** John the Baptist ▷ *adj* **3** of the Baptist Church

baptize *or* **-tise** *vb* **-tizing, -tized** *or* **-tising, -tised 1** *Christianity* to immerse (a person) in water or sprinkle water on (him or her) as part of the rite of baptism **2** to give a name to ▶ HISTORY Greek *baptein* to bathe, dip

bar¹ *n* **1** a rigid usually straight length of metal, wood, etc. used as a barrier or structural part **2** a solid usually rectangular block of any material: *a bar of soap* **3** anything that obstructs or prevents: *a bar to women's mobility* **4** a counter or room where alcoholic drinks are served **5** a narrow band or stripe, as of colour or light **6** a heating element in an electric fire **7** See **Bar 8** the place in a court of law where the accused stands during trial **9** *music* a group of beats that is repeated with a consistent rhythm throughout a piece of music **10** *football etc.* same as **crossbar 11** *heraldry* a narrow horizontal line across a shield **12 behind bars** in prison ▷ *vb* **barring, barred 13** to secure with a bar: *to bar the door* **14** to obstruct: *the fallen tree barred the road* **15** to exclude: *he was barred from membership of the club* **16** to mark with a bar or bars ▷ *prep* **17** except for ▶ HISTORY Old French *barre*

bar² *n* a unit of pressure equal to 10^5 newtons per square metre ▶ HISTORY Greek *baros* weight

Bar *n* **1 the Bar** barristers collectively **2 be called to the Bar** *Brit* to become a barrister

barb *n* **1** a cutting remark **2** a point facing in the opposite direction to the main point of a fish-hook, harpoon, etc. **3** a beardlike growth, hair, or projection ▷ *vb* **4** to provide with a barb or barbs ▶ HISTORY Latin *barba* beard > **barbed** *adj*

Barbadian *adj* **1** of Barbados ▷ *n* **2** a person from Barbados

barbarian *n* **1** a member of a primitive or uncivilized people **2** a coarse or vicious person ▷ *adj* **3** uncivilized or brutal

barbaric *adj* primitive or brutal

barbarism *n* **1** a brutal, coarse, or ignorant act **2** the condition of being backward, coarse, or ignorant **3** a substandard word or expression

barbarity *n, pl* **-ties 1** the state of being barbaric or barbarous **2** a vicious act

barbarous *adj* **1** uncivilized: *a barbarous and uninhabitable jungle* **2** brutal or cruel: *the barbarous tortures inflicted on them* ▶ HISTORY Greek *barbaros* barbarian, non-Greek

barbecue *n* **1** a grill on which food is cooked over hot charcoal, usually out of doors **2** food cooked over hot charcoal, usually out of doors **3** a party or picnic at which barbecued food is served ▷ *vb* **-cuing, -cued 4** to cook on a grill, usually over charcoal ▶ HISTORY American Spanish *barbacoa* frame made of sticks

barbed wire *n* strong wire with sharp points protruding at close intervals

barbel *n* **1** a long thin growth that hangs from the jaws of certain fishes, such as the carp **2** a freshwater fish with such a growth ▶ HISTORY Latin *barba* beard

barber *n* a person whose business is cutting men's hair and shaving beards ▶ HISTORY Latin *barba* beard

barberry *n, pl* **-ries** a shrub with orange or red berries ▶ HISTORY Arabic *barbāris*

barbican *n* a walled defence to protect a gate or drawbridge of a fortification ▶ HISTORY Old French *barbacane*

barbiturate *n* a derivative of barbituric acid used in medicine as a sedative

barbituric acid *n* a crystalline solid used in the preparation of barbiturate drugs ▶ HISTORY German *Barbitursäure*

barcarole *or* **barcarolle** *n* **1** a Venetian boat song **2** an instrumental composition resembling this ▶ HISTORY French

barchan *or* **barchan dune** *n geog* a crescent-shaped sand dune whose gently sloping convex side is towards the wind while the steeper concave side is sheltered from the wind

bar chart *or* **graph** *n* a diagram consisting of vertical or horizontal bars whose lengths are proportional to amounts or quantities

bar code *n* an arrangement of numbers and parallel lines on a package, which can be electronically scanned at a checkout to give the price of the goods

bard *n* **1** *archaic or literary* a poet **2 a** (formerly) an ancient Celtic poet **b** a poet who wins a verse competition at a Welsh eisteddfod **3 the Bard** William Shakespeare, English playwright and poet ▶ HISTORY Scottish Gaelic

bare *adj* **1** unclothed: used esp. of a part of the body **2** without the natural, conventional, or usual covering: *bare trees* **3** lacking appropriate furnishings, etc.: *a bare room* **4** simple: *the bare facts* **5** just sufficient: *the bare minimum* ▷ *vb* **baring, bared 6** *written* to uncover ▶ HISTORY Old English *bær* > **bareness** *n*

b

bareback *adj, adv* (of horse-riding) without a saddle

barefaced *adj* obvious or shameless: *a barefaced lie*

barefoot *or* **barefooted** *adj, adv* with the feet uncovered

bareheaded *adj, adv* with the head uncovered

barely *adv* **1** only just: *barely enough* **2** scantily: *barely furnished*

bargain *n* **1** an agreement establishing what each party will give, receive, or perform in a transaction **2** something acquired or received in such an agreement **3** something bought or offered at a low price **4 drive a hard bargain** to forcefully pursue one's own profit in a transaction **5 into the bargain** besides ▷ *vb* **6** to negotiate the terms of an agreement or transaction ▶ HISTORY Old French *bargaigne*

bargain for *vb* to anticipate

barge *n* **1** a flat-bottomed boat, used for transporting freight, esp. on canals **2** a boat, often decorated, used in pageants, etc. ▷ *vb* **barging, barged** *informal* **3** (foll. by *into*) to bump into **4** to push one's way violently **5** (foll. by *into* or *in*) to interrupt rudely: *he barged into our conversation* ▶ HISTORY Medieval Latin *barga*

bargee *n* *Brit* a person in charge of a barge

barista (bar-**ee**-sta) *n* a person who makes and sells coffee in a coffee bar

baritone *n* **1** the second lowest adult male voice **2** a singer with such a voice ▶ HISTORY Greek *barus* low + *tonos* tone

barium (**bare**-ee-um) *n* *chem* a soft silvery-white metallic chemical element. Symbol: Ba ▶ HISTORY Greek *barus* heavy

barium meal *n* a preparation of barium sulphate, which is opaque to X-rays, used in X-ray examination of the alimentary canal

bark¹ *n* **1** the loud harsh cry of a dog or certain other animals ▷ *vb* **2** (of a dog or other animal) to make its typical cry **3** to shout in an angry tone: *he barked an order* **4 bark up the wrong tree** *informal* to misdirect one's attention or efforts ▶ HISTORY Old English *beorcan*

bark² *n* **1** an outer protective layer of dead corklike cells on the trunks of trees ▷ *vb* **2** to scrape or rub off (skin), as in an injury **3** to remove the bark from (a tree) ▶ HISTORY Old Norse *börkr*

barker *n* a person at a fairground who loudly addresses passers-by to attract customers

barking *slang, chiefly Brit adj* **1** mad or crazy ▷ *adv* **2** extremely: *barking mad*

barley *n* **1** a tall grasslike plant with dense bristly flower spikes, widely cultivated for grain **2** the grain of this grass used in making beer and whisky and for soups ▶ HISTORY Old English *bere*

barleycorn *n* a grain of barley, or barley itself

barley sugar *n* a brittle clear amber-coloured sweet

barley water *n* a drink made from an infusion of barley

barmaid *n* a woman who serves in a pub

barman *n, pl* **-men** a man who serves in a pub

bar mitzvah *Judaism n* **1** a ceremony marking the 13th birthday of a boy and his assumption of religious obligations ▷ *adj* **2** (of a Jewish boy) having undergone this ceremony ▶ HISTORY Hebrew: son of the law

barmy *adj* **-mier, -miest** *slang* insane ▶ HISTORY originally, full of BARM, frothing, excited

barn *n* a large farm outbuilding, chiefly for storing grain, but also for livestock ▶ HISTORY Old English *bere* barley + *œrn* room

barnacle *n* a marine shellfish that lives attached to rocks, ship bottoms, etc. ▶ HISTORY Old French *bernac* > **barnacled** *adj*

barnacle goose *n* a goose with a black-and-white head and body ▶ HISTORY it was formerly believed that the goose developed from a shellfish

barn dance *n* **1** *US & Canad* a party with square-dancing **2** *Brit* a progressive round country dance

barney *n* *informal* a noisy fight or argument ▶ HISTORY origin unknown

barn owl *n* an owl with a pale brown-and-white plumage and a heart-shaped face

barnstorm *vb* **1** *chiefly US & Canad* to tour rural districts making speeches in a political campaign **2** to tour rural districts putting on shows > **barnstorming** *n, adj*

barnyard *n* a yard adjoining a barn

barograph *n* *meteorol* a barometer that automatically keeps a record of changes in atmospheric pressure ▶ HISTORY Greek *baros* weight + *graphein* to write

barometer *n* an instrument for measuring atmospheric pressure, used to determine weather or altitude changes ▶ HISTORY Greek *baros* weight + *metron* measure > **barometric** *adj*

baron *n* **1** a member of the lowest rank of nobility in the British Isles **2** a powerful businessman or financier: *a press baron* ▶ HISTORY Old French > **baronial** *adj*

baroness *n* **1** a woman holding the rank of baron **2** the wife or widow of a baron

baronet *n* a commoner who holds the lowest hereditary British title > **baronetcy** *n*

baroque (bar-**rock**) *n* **1** a highly ornate style of architecture and art, popular in Europe from the late 16th to the early 18th century **2** a highly ornamented 17th-century style of music ▷ *adj* **3** ornate in style ▶ HISTORY French from Portuguese *barroco* imperfectly shaped pearl

barque (**bark**) *n* **1** a sailing ship, esp. one with three masts **2** *poetic* any boat ▶ HISTORY Old Provençal *barca*

barrack¹ *vb* to house (soldiers) in barracks

barrack² *vb* **1** *Brit, Austral & NZ, informal* to criticize loudly or shout against (a team or speaker) **2** *Austral & NZ* (foll. by *for*) to shout encouragement for (a team) ▶ HISTORY Irish: to boast

barracks *pl n* **1** a building or group of buildings used to accommodate military personnel **2** a large and bleak building ▶ HISTORY French *baraque*

barracouta (bar-rack-**kew**-ta) *n* a large Pacific fish with a protruding lower jaw and strong teeth

barracuda (bar-rack-**kew**-da) *n, pl* **-da** *or* **-das** a tropical fish which feeds on other fishes ▶ HISTORY American Spanish

barrage (bar-**rahzh**) *n* **1** a continuous delivery of questions, complaints, etc. **2** *mil* the continuous firing of artillery over a wide area **3** a construction built across a river to control the water level ▶ HISTORY French *barrer* to obstruct

barrage balloon *n* a balloon tethered by cables, often with net suspended from it, used to deter low-flying air attack

barramundi *n* an edible Australian fish

barre (bar) *n* a rail at hip height used for ballet practice ▶ HISTORY French

barrel *n* **1** a cylindrical container usually with rounded sides and flat ends, and held together by metal hoops **2** a unit of capacity of varying amount in different industries **3** the tube through which the bullet of a firearm is fired **4 over a barrel** *informal* powerless ▷ *vb* **-relling, -relled** *or US* **-reling, -reled 5** to put into a barrel or barrels ▶ HISTORY Old French *baril*

barrel organ *n* a musical instrument played by turning a handle

barren *adj* **1** incapable of producing offspring **2** unable to support the growth of crops, fruit, etc.: *barren land* **3** *written* unprofitable or unsuccessful: *Real Madrid have had a barren two seasons* **4** dull ▶ HISTORY Old French *brahain* > **barrenness** *n*

barricade *n* **1** a barrier, esp. one erected hastily for defence ▷ *vb* **-cading, -caded 2** to erect a barricade across (an entrance) ▶ HISTORY Old French *barrique* a barrel

barrier *n* **1** anything that blocks a way or separates, such as a gate **2** anything that prevents progress: *a barrier of distrust* **3** anything that separates or hinders union: *a language barrier* ▶ HISTORY Old French *barre* bar

barrier cream *n* a cream used to protect the skin

barrier reef *n* a long narrow ridge of coral, separated from the shore by deep water

barrister *n* a lawyer who is qualified to plead in the higher courts ▶ HISTORY from BAR¹

barrow¹ *n* **1** same as **wheelbarrow 2** a handcart used by street traders ▶ HISTORY Old English *bearwe*

barrow² *n* a heap of earth placed over a prehistoric tomb ▶ HISTORY Old English *beorg*

barter *vb* **1** to trade goods or services in exchange for other goods or services, rather than for money ▷ *n* **2** trade by the exchange of goods ▶ HISTORY Old French *barater* to cheat

baryon (**bar**-ree-on) *n* an elementary particle that has a mass greater than or equal to that of the proton ▶ HISTORY Greek *barus* heavy

baryta (bar-**rite**-a) *n* a compound of barium, such as barium oxide ▶ HISTORY Greek *barus* heavy

barytes (bar-**rite**-eez) *n* a colourless or white mineral: a source of barium ▶ HISTORY Greek *barus* heavy

basal *adj* **1** at, of, or constituting a base **2** fundamental

basal metabolic rate *n* the amount of energy consumed by an animal's body at rest

basalt (**bass**-awlt) *n* a dark volcanic rock ▶ HISTORY Greek *basanitēs* touchstone > **basaltic** *adj*

bascule *n* a drawbridge that operates by a counterbalanced weight ▶ HISTORY French: seesaw

base¹ *n* **1** the bottom or supporting part of anything **2** the fundamental principle or part: *agriculture was the economic base of the city's growth* **3** a centre of operations, organization, or supply **4** a starting point: *the new discovery became the base for further research* **5** the main ingredient of a mixture: *to use rice as a base in cookery* **6** *chem* a compound that combines with an acid to form a salt **7** the lower side or face of a geometric construction **8** *maths* the number of units in a counting system that is equivalent to one in the next higher counting place: *10 is the base of the decimal system* **9** a starting or finishing point in any of various games ▷ *vb* **basing, based 10** (foll. by *on* or *upon*) to use as a basis for **11** (foll. by *at* or *in*) to station, post, or place ▶ HISTORY Latin *basis* pedestal

base² *adj* **1** dishonourable or immoral: *base motives* **2** of inferior quality or value: *a base coin* **3** debased; counterfeit: *base currency* ▶ HISTORY Late Latin *bassus* of low height

baseball *n* **1** a team game in which the object is to score runs by batting the ball and running round all four bases **2** the ball used in this game

baseless *adj* not based on fact

base level *n* *geog* the lowest level to which a river or stream bed can be eroded; equivalent to sea level in those rivers and streams that flow into the sea

baseline *n* **1** a value or starting point on an imaginary scale with which other things are compared **2** a line at each end of a tennis court that marks the limit of play

basement *n* a partly or wholly underground storey of a building

base metal *n* a common metal, such as copper or lead, that is not a precious metal

base number *n* *maths* of a logarithm or exponential, a number whose powers are expressed

base rate *n* **1** the rate of interest used by a bank as a basis for its lending rates **2** the rate at which the Bank of England lends to other financial organizations, which effectively controls interest rates throughout the UK

bases¹ *n* the plural of **basis**

bases² *n* the plural of **base¹**

bash *informal vb* **1** to strike violently or crushingly **2** (foll. by *into*) to crash into ▷ *n* **3** a heavy blow **4 have a bash** *informal* to make an attempt ▶ HISTORY origin unknown

bashful *adj* shy or modest ▶ HISTORY *bash*, short for ABASH > **bashfully** *adv*

b

-bashing *n and adj combining form informal*
a indicating a malicious attack on members of a group: *union-bashing* **b** indicating an activity undertaken energetically: *Bible-bashing*
> **-basher** *n combining form*

bashment *n* **1** (in Jamaica) a party **2** a type of reggae music

basic *adj* **1** of or forming a base or basis **2** elementary or simple: *a few basic facts* **3** excluding additions or extras: *basic pay* **4** *chem* of or containing a base ▷ *n* **5 basics** fundamental principles, facts, etc. > **basically** *adv*

BASIC *n* a computer programming language that uses common English terms ▶ HISTORY *b(eginner's) a(ll-purpose) s(ymbolic) i(nstruction) c(ode)*

basic rocks *pl n geol* igneous rocks, such as basalt, which have a low silica content (between 45 and 52 per cent)

basic slag *n* a slag produced in steel-making, containing calcium phosphate

basil *n* an aromatic herb used for seasoning food ▶ HISTORY Greek *basilikos* royal

basilica *n* **1** a Roman building, used for public administration, which is rectangular with two aisles and a rounded end **2** a Christian church of similar design ▶ HISTORY Greek *basilikē oikia* the king's house

basilisk *n* (in classical legend) a serpent that could kill by its breath or glance ▶ HISTORY Greek *basiliskos* royal child

basin *n* **1** a round wide container open at the top **2** the amount a basin will hold **3** a washbasin or sink **4** any partially enclosed area of water where ships or boats may be moored **5** *geog* the catchment area of a river and its tributaries or of a lake **6** a depression in the earth's surface ▶ HISTORY Old French *bacin*

basis *n, pl* **bases** **1** something that underlies, supports, or is essential to an idea, belief, etc. **2** a principle on which something depends ▶ HISTORY Greek: step

bask *vb* (foll. by *in*) **1** to lie in or be exposed (to pleasant warmth or sunshine) **2** to enjoy (approval or favourable conditions) ▶ HISTORY Old Norse *bathask* to bathe

basket *n* **1** a container made of interwoven strips of wood or cane **2** the amount a basket will hold **3** *basketball* **a** the high horizontal hoop through which a player must throw the ball to score points **b** a point scored in this way ▶ HISTORY Middle English

basketball *n* a team game in which points are scored by throwing the ball through a high horizontal hoop

basketwork *n* same as **wickerwork**

basking shark *n* a very large plankton-eating shark, which often floats at the sea surface

basque *n* a tight-fitting bodice for women ▶ HISTORY origin unknown

Basque *n* **1** a member of a people living in the W Pyrenees in France and Spain **2** the language of

the Basques ▷ *adj* **3** of the Basques ▶ HISTORY Latin *Vasco*

bas-relief *n* sculpture in which the figures project slightly from the background ▶ HISTORY Italian *basso rilievo*

bass¹ (**base**) *n* **1** the lowest adult male voice **2** a singer with such a voice **3** *informal* same as **bass guitar** or **double bass** ▷ *adj* **4** of the lowest range of musical notes: *the system is engineered to give good bass sound from very small speakers* **5** denoting a musical instrument that is lowest or second lowest in pitch in its family: *bass trombone* **6** of or relating to a bass guitar or double bass: *the band is unusual in that it has two bass players* **7** of or written for a singer with the lowest adult male voice: *the bass soloist in next week's performance of Handel's 'Messiah'* ▶ HISTORY Middle English *bas*

bass² (rhymes with **gas**) *n* **1** various Australian freshwater and sea fish **2** a European spiny-finned freshwater fish ▶ HISTORY Middle English

bass clef (**base**) *n* the clef that establishes F a fifth below middle C on the fourth line of the staff

bass drum (**base**) *n* a large drum of low pitch

basset hound *n* a smooth-haired dog with short legs and long ears ▶ HISTORY French *bas* low

bass guitar (**base**) *n* an electric guitar with the same pitch and tuning as a double bass

bassoon *n* a woodwind instrument that produces a range of low sounds ▶ HISTORY Italian *basso* deep > **bassoonist** *n*

bastard *n* **1** *taboo, offensive* an obnoxious or despicable person **2** *archaic or offensive* a person born of parents not married to each other ▷ *adj* **3** *archaic or offensive* illegitimate by birth **4** counterfeit; spurious ▶ HISTORY Old French *bastart* > **bastardy** *n*

bastardize *or* **-ise** *vb* **-izing, -ized** *or* **-ising, -ised** **1** to debase **2** to declare illegitimate

baste¹ *vb* **basting, basted** to sew with loose temporary stitches ▶ HISTORY Old French *bastir* to build

baste² *vb* **basting, basted** to moisten (meat) during cooking with hot fat ▶ HISTORY origin unknown

baste³ *vb* **basting, basted** to thrash ▶ HISTORY origin unknown

bastion *n* **1** a projecting part of a fortification **2** a thing or person regarded as defending a principle or way of life: *a bastion of anti-communism* ▶ HISTORY French *bastille* fortress

bat¹ *n* **1** any of various types of club used to hit the ball in certain sports **2** *cricket* a batsman **3 off one's own bat a** of one's own accord **b** by one's own unaided efforts ▷ *vb* **batting, batted** **4** to strike with or as if with a bat **5** *cricket etc.* to take a turn at batting ▶ HISTORY Old English *batt* club

bat² *n* **1** a nocturnal mouselike flying animal with leathery wings **2 blind as a bat** having extremely poor eyesight ▶ HISTORY Scandinavian

bat³ *vb* **batting, batted** **1** to flutter (one's eyelids) **2 not bat an eyelid** *informal* to show no surprise ▶ HISTORY probably from obsolete *bate* flutter, beat

batch *n* **1** a group of similar objects or people dispatched or dealt with at the same time **2** the bread, cakes, etc. produced at one baking ▷ *vb* **3** to group (items) for efficient processing ▶ HISTORY Middle English *bache*

batch processing *n* a system by which the computer programs of several users are submitted as a single batch

batch production *n business* the practice of manufacturing similar items in batches, resulting in a lower unit cost

bated *adj* **with bated breath** in suspense or fear

bath *n* **1** a large container in which to wash the body **2** the act of washing in such a container **3** the amount of water in a bath **4 baths** a public swimming pool **5 a** a liquid in which something is immersed as part of a chemical process, such as developing photographs **b** the vessel containing such a liquid ▷ *vb* **6** *Brit* to wash in a bath ▶ HISTORY Old English *bæth*

Bath chair *n* a wheelchair for invalids

bathe *vb* **bathing, bathed 1** to swim in open water for pleasure **2** to apply liquid to (the skin or a wound) in order to cleanse or soothe **3** *chiefly US & Canad* to wash in a bath **4** to spread over: *bathed in moonlight* ▷ *n* **5** *Brit* a swim in open water ▶ HISTORY Old English *bathian* > **bather** *n*

batholith *n geol* a very large irregular-shaped mass of igneous rock, esp. granite, formed from an intrusion of magma at great depth ▶ HISTORY Greek *bathus* deep + *lithos* stone

bathos (**bay**-thoss) *n* a sudden ludicrous descent from exalted to ordinary matters in speech or writing ▶ HISTORY Greek: depth > **bathetic** *adj*

bathroom *n* **1** a room with a bath or shower, washbasin, and toilet **2** *US & Canad* a toilet

bathyscaph *or* **bathyscaphe** *n* a deep-sea diving vessel for observation ▶ HISTORY Greek *bathus* deep + *skaphē* light boat

bathysphere *n* a strong steel deep-sea diving sphere, lowered by cable ▶ HISTORY Greek *bathus* deep + *sphere*

batik (bat-**teek**) *n* **a** a process of printing fabric in which areas not to be dyed are covered by wax **b** fabric printed in this way ▶ HISTORY Javanese: painted

batman *n, pl* -**men** an officer's servant in the armed forces ▶ HISTORY Old French *bat* packsaddle

baton *n* **1** a thin stick used by the conductor of an orchestra or choir **2** *athletics* a short bar transferred from one runner to another in a relay race **3** a police officer's truncheon ▶ HISTORY French

batsman *n, pl* -**men** *cricket etc.* a person who bats or specializes in batting

battalion *n* a military unit comprised of three or more companies ▶ HISTORY French *bataillon*

batten¹ *n* **1** a strip of wood used to strengthen something or make it secure **2** a strip of wood used for holding a tarpaulin in place over a hatch on a ship ▷ *vb* **3** to strengthen or fasten with battens ▶ HISTORY French *bâton* stick

batten² *vb* (foll. by *on*) to thrive at the expense of (someone else) ▶ HISTORY probably from Old Norse *batna* to improve

batter¹ *vb* **1** to hit repeatedly **2** to damage or injure, as by blows, heavy wear, etc. **3** to subject (someone, usually a close relative) to repeated physical violence ▶ HISTORY Middle English *bateren* > **battered** *adj* > **batterer** *n* > **battering** *n*

batter² *n* a mixture of flour, eggs, and milk, used in cooking ▶ HISTORY Middle English *bater*

batter³ *n baseball etc.* a player who bats

battering ram *n* (esp. formerly) a large beam used to break down fortifications

battery *n, pl* -**teries 1** two or more primary cells connected to provide a source of electric current **2** a number of similar things occurring together: *a battery of questions* **3** *criminal law* unlawful beating or wounding of a person **4** *chiefly Brit* a series of cages for intensive rearing of poultry **5** a fortified structure on which artillery is mounted ▷ *adj* **6** kept in a series of cages for intensive rearing: *battery hens* ▶ HISTORY Latin *battuere* to beat

battle *n* **1** a fight between large armed forces **2** conflict or struggle ▷ *vb* -**tling, -tled 3** to fight in or as if in military combat: *shop stewards battling to improve conditions at work* **4** to struggle: *she battled through the crowd* ▶ HISTORY Latin *battuere* to beat

battle-axe *n* **1** a domineering woman **2** (formerly) a large broad-headed axe

battle cruiser *n* a high-speed warship with lighter armour than a battleship, but of the same size

battle cry *n* **1** a slogan used to rally the supporters of a campaign, movement, etc. **2** a shout uttered by soldiers going into battle

battledore *n* **1** Also called: **battledore and shuttlecock** an ancient racket game **2** a light racket used in this game ▶ HISTORY Middle English *batyldoure*

battledress *n* the ordinary uniform of a soldier

battlefield *or* **battleground** *n* the place where a battle is fought

battlement *n* a wall with gaps, originally for firing through ▶ HISTORY Old French *bataille* battle

battleship *n* a large heavily armoured warship

batty *adj* -**tier, -tiest** *slang* **1** crazy **2** eccentric: *a batty OAP* ▶ HISTORY from BAT²

bauble *n* a trinket of little value ▶ HISTORY Old French *baubel* plaything

baud *n computers* a unit used to measure the speed of transmission of electronic data ▶ HISTORY after J. M. E. *Baudot*, inventor

bauera *n* a small evergreen Australian shrub

Bauhaus (**bow**-house) *adj* of a school of architecture and applied arts in Germany in the 1920s and 30s characterized by a functionalist approach to design ▶ HISTORY German: building house

baulk *vb, n* same as **balk**

bauxite *n* a claylike substance that is the chief source of aluminium ▶ HISTORY (Les) *Baux* in southern France, where originally found

bawdy *adj* **bawdier, bawdiest** (of language, writing, etc.) containing humorous references to sex ▶ HISTORY Old French *baud* merry > **bawdily** *adv* > **bawdiness** *n*

bawl *vb* **1** to cry noisily **2** to shout loudly ▷ *n* **3** a loud shout or cry ▶ HISTORY imitative > **bawling** *n*

bay¹ *n* a stretch of shoreline that curves inwards ▶ HISTORY Old French *baie*

bay² *n* **1** a recess in a wall **2** an area set aside for a particular purpose: *a sick bay; a loading bay* **3** same as **bay window 4** an area off a road in which vehicles may park or unload **5** a compartment in an aircraft: *the bomb bay* ▶ HISTORY Old French *baee* gap

bay³ *n* **1** a deep howl of a hound or wolf **2 at bay a** forced to turn and face attackers: *the stag at bay* **b** at a safe distance: *to keep his mind blank and his despair at bay* ▷ *vb* **3** to howl in deep prolonged tones ▶ HISTORY Old French *abaiier* to bark

bay⁴ *n* **1** a Mediterranean laurel tree with glossy aromatic leaves **2 bays** a wreath of bay leaves ▶ HISTORY Latin *baca* berry

bay⁵ *adj* **1** reddish-brown ▷ *n* **2** a reddish-brown horse ▶ HISTORY Latin *badius*

bayberry *n, pl* **-ries** a tropical American tree that yields an oil used in making bay rum. Also: **bay**

bay leaf *n* the dried leaf of a laurel, used for flavouring in cooking

bayonet *n* **1** a blade that can be attached to the end of a rifle and used as a weapon ▷ *vb* **-neting, -neted** *or* **-netting, -netted 2** to stab or kill with a bayonet

■ **WORD HISTORY**
■ Bayonets were first made in the 16th century in
■ the town of *Bayonne* in southwestern France,
■ and it is from the name of the town that they
■ take their name.

bay rum *n* an aromatic liquid, used in medicines and cosmetics, which was originally obtained by distilling bayberry leaves with rum

bay window *n* a window projecting from a wall

bazaar *n* **1** a sale in aid of charity **2** (esp. in the Orient) a market area, esp. a street of small stalls ▶ HISTORY Persian *bāzār*

bazooka *n* a portable rocket launcher that fires a projectile capable of piercing armour ▶ HISTORY after a pipe instrument devised by an American comedian

BB *Brit* Boys' Brigade

BBC British Broadcasting Corporation

BC 1 (indicating years numbered back from the supposed year of the birth of Christ) before Christ **2** British Columbia

BCE Before Common Era (used, esp. by non-Christians, in numbering years BC)

BCG Bacillus Calmette-Guérin (antituberculosis vaccine)

BD Bachelor of Divinity

BDS Bachelor of Dental Surgery

be *vb, present sing 1st person* **am;** *2nd person* **are;** *3rd person* **is.** *present pl* **are.** *past sing 1st person* **was;** *2nd person* **were;** *3rd person* **was.** *past pl* **were.**

present participle **being.** *past participle* **been. 1** to exist; live: *I think, therefore I am* **2** to pay a visit; go: *have you been to Spain?* **3** to take place: *my birthday was last Thursday* **4** used as a linking verb between the subject of a sentence and its complement: *John is a musician; honey is sweet; the dance is on Saturday* **5** forms the progressive present tense: *the man is running* **6** forms the passive voice of all transitive verbs: *a good film is being shown on television tomorrow* **7** expresses intention, expectation, or obligation: *the president is to arrive at 9.30* ▶ HISTORY Old English *bēon*

Be *chem* beryllium

BE Bachelor of Engineering

be- *prefix forming verbs mainly from nouns* **1** to surround or cover: *befog* **2** to affect completely: *bedazzle* **3** to consider as or cause to be: *befriend* **4** to provide or cover with: *bejewel* **5** (from verbs) at, for, against, on, or over: *bewail* ▶ HISTORY Old English *be-, bi-* by

beach *n* **1** an area of sand or pebbles sloping down to the sea or a lake ▷ *vb* **2** to run or haul (a boat) onto a beach ▶ HISTORY origin unknown

beachcomber *n* a person who searches shore debris for anything of worth

beachhead *n mil* an area of shore captured by an attacking army, on which troops and equipment are landed

beach nourishment *n building* the process of building or restoring a beach by artificial methods such as pumping sand from another location

beacon *n* **1** a signal fire or light on a hill or tower, used formerly as a warning of invasion **2** a lighthouse **3** a radio or other signal marking a flight course in air navigation **4** same as **Belisha beacon** ▶ HISTORY Old English *beacen* sign

bead *n* **1** a small pierced piece of glass, wood, or plastic that may be strung with others to form a necklace, rosary, etc. **2** a small drop of moisture **3** a small metal knob acting as the sight of a firearm ▷ *vb* **4** to decorate with beads ▶ HISTORY Old English *bed* prayer > **beaded** *adj*

beading *n* a narrow rounded strip of moulding used for edging furniture

beadle *n* **1** *Brit* (formerly) a minor parish official who acted as an usher **2** *Scot* a church official who attends the minister ▶ HISTORY Old English *bydel*

beady *adj* **beadier, beadiest** small, round, and glittering: *beady eyes*

beagle *n* a small hound with a smooth coat, short legs, and drooping ears ▶ HISTORY origin unknown

beak¹ *n* **1** the projecting horny jaws of a bird **2** *slang* a person's nose ▶ HISTORY Latin *beccus* > **beaky** *adj*

beak² *n* in *Brit, Austral & NZ, slang* a judge, magistrate, or headmaster ▶ HISTORY originally thieves' jargon

beaker *n* **1** a tall drinking cup **2** a lipped glass container used in laboratories ▶ HISTORY Old Norse *bikarr*

beam *n* **1** a broad smile **2** a ray of light **3** a narrow flow of electromagnetic radiation or particles: *an electron beam* **4** a long thick piece of wood, metal, etc. used in building **5** the central shaft of a plough to which all the main parts are attached **6** the breadth of a ship at its widest part **7 off (the) beam** *informal* mistaken or irrelevant ▷ *vb* **8** *written* to smile broadly **9** to send out or radiate **10** to divert or aim (a radio signal, light, etc.) in a certain direction: *the concert was beamed live from Geneva* ▶ HISTORY Old English

bean *n* **1** the seed or pod of various climbing plants, eaten as a vegetable **2** any of various beanlike seeds, such as coffee **3 full of beans** *informal* full of energy and vitality **4 not have a bean** *slang* to be without money ▶ HISTORY Old English *bēan*

beanie *n* *Brit, Austral & NZ* a close-fitting woollen hat

beano *n, pl* **beanos** *Brit, old-fashioned, slang* a celebration or party

beanpole *n* *slang* a tall thin person

beansprout *n* a small edible shoot grown from a bean seed, often used in Chinese dishes

bear[1] *vb* **bearing, bore, borne 1** to support or hold up **2** to bring: *to bear gifts* **3** to accept the responsibility of: *to bear a heavier burden of taxation* **4** to give birth to **5** to produce by natural growth: *to bear fruit* **6** to tolerate or endure **7** to stand up to; sustain: *his story does not bear scrutiny* **8** to hold in the mind: *to bear a grudge* **9** to show or be marked with: *he still bears the scars* **10** to have, be, or stand in (relation or comparison): *her account bears no relation to the facts* **11** to move in a specified direction: *bear left* **12 bring to bear** to bring into effect ▷ See also **bear down on** ▶ HISTORY Old English *beran*

bear[2] *n, pl* **bears** or **bear 1** a large heavily-built mammal with a long shaggy coat **2** a bearlike animal, such as the koala **3** an ill-mannered person **4** *Stock Exchange* a person who sells shares in anticipation of falling prices to make a profit on repurchase **5 like a bear with a sore head** *informal* bad-tempered, irritable ▶ HISTORY Old English *bera*

bearable *adj* endurable; tolerable

bear-baiting *n* *history* an entertainment in which dogs attacked a chained bear

beard *n* **1** the hair growing on the lower parts of a man's face **2** any similar growth in animals ▷ *vb* **3** to oppose boldly: *I bearded my formidable employer in her den* ▶ HISTORY Old English > **bearded** *adj*

bear down on *vb* **1** to press down on **2** to approach (someone) in a determined manner

bearer *n* **1** a person or thing that carries, presents, or upholds something **2** a person who presents a note or bill for payment

bear hug *n* a rough tight embrace

bearing *n* **1** (foll. by *on* or *upon*) relevance: *it has no bearing on this problem* **2** a part of a machine supporting another part, and usually reducing friction **3** the act of producing fruit or young **4** a person's general social conduct **5** the angular direction of a point measured from a known position **6** the position, as of a ship, fixed with reference to two or more known points **7 bearings**

a sense of one's relative position: *I lost my bearings in the dark* **8** *heraldry* a device on a heraldic shield

bear out *vb* to show to be truthful: *the witness will bear me out*

bearskin *n* **1** the pelt of a bear **2** a tall fur helmet worn by certain British Army regiments

beast *n* **1** a large wild animal **2** a brutal or uncivilized person **3** savage nature or characteristics: *the beast in man* ▶ HISTORY Latin *bestia*

beastly *adj* *informal* **-lier, -liest** unpleasant; disagreeable

beat *vb* **beating, beat; beaten** or **beat 1** to strike with a series of violent blows **2** to move (wings) up and down **3** to throb rhythmically **4** *cookery* to stir or whisk vigorously **5** to shape (metal) by repeated blows **6** *music* to indicate (time) by one's hand or a baton **7** to produce (a sound) by striking a drum **8** to overcome or defeat: *he was determined to beat his illness* **9** to form (a path or track) by repeated use **10** to arrive, achieve, or finish before (someone or something): *she beat her team-mate fair and square* **11** (foll. by *back, down, off* etc.) to drive, push, or thrust **12** to scour (woodlands or undergrowth) to rouse game for shooting **13** *informal, spoken* to puzzle or baffle: *it beats me* ▷ *n* **14** a stroke or blow **15** the sound made by a stroke or blow **16** a regular throb **17** an assigned route, as of a policeman **18** the basic rhythmic unit in a piece of music **19** pop or rock music characterized by a heavy rhythmic beat ▷ *adj* **20** *slang* totally exhausted ▷ See also **beat down, beat up** ▶ HISTORY Old English *bēatan* > **beating** *n*

beatbox *n* **1** a drum machine ▷ *vb* **2** to simulate percussion instruments with the voice, especially in hip-hop music

beatboxing *n* a form of hip-hop music in which the voice is used to simulate percussion instruments

beat down *vb* **1** (of the sun) to shine intensely **2** *informal* to force or persuade (a seller) to accept a lower price

beater *n* **1** a device used for beating: *a carpet beater* **2** a person who rouses wild game

beatific *adj* *literary* **1** displaying great happiness **2** having a divine aura ▶ HISTORY Latin *beatus*

beatify (bee-**at**-if-fie) *vb* **-fies, -fying, -fied 1** *RC Church* to declare (a deceased person) to be among the blessed in heaven: the first step towards canonization **2** to make extremely happy > **beatification** *n*

beatitude *n* supreme blessedness or happiness ▶ HISTORY Latin *beatitudo*

Beatitude *n* *Christianity* any of the blessings on the poor, meek, etc. in the Sermon on the Mount

Beat movement *n* *literature* a group of US writers who emerged in the 1950s, noted for their rejection of the social and political systems of the West and their espousal of alternative lifestyles

beatnik *n* a young person in the late 1950s who rebelled against conventional attitudes and styles of dress ▶ HISTORY BEAT (noun) + -NIK

b

beat up *informal vb* **1** to inflict severe physical damage on (someone) by striking or kicking repeatedly ▷ *n* **2** *Austral & NZ* a small matter deliberately exaggerated ▷ *adj* **beat-up** **3** dilapidated

beau (boh) *n, pl* **beaux** *or* **beaus** (bohz) **1** *chiefly US* a boyfriend **2** a man who is greatly concerned with his appearance ▶ **HISTORY** French

Beaufort scale *n meteorol* a scale for measuring wind speeds, ranging from 0 (calm) to 12 (hurricane) ▶ **HISTORY** after Sir Francis *Beaufort*, who devised it

Beaujolais *n* a red or white wine from southern Burgundy in France

beauteous *adj poetic* beautiful

beautician *n* a person who works in a beauty salon

beautiful *adj* **1** being very attractive to look at **2** highly enjoyable; very pleasant > **beautifully** *adv*

beautify *vb* **-fies, -fying, -fied** to make beautiful > **beautification** *n*

beauty *n, pl* **-ties** **1** the combination of all the qualities of a person or thing that delight the senses and mind **2** a very attractive woman **3** *informal* an outstanding example of its kind **4** *informal* an advantageous feature: *the beauty of this job is the short hours* ▶ **HISTORY** Latin *bellus* handsome

beauty queen *n* a woman who has been judged the most beautiful in a contest

beauty spot *n* **1** a place of outstanding beauty **2** a small dark-coloured spot formerly worn on a lady's face as decoration

beaver *n* **1** a large amphibious rodent with soft brown fur, a broad flat tail, and webbed hind feet **2** its fur **3** a tall hat made of this fur ▷ *vb* **4 beaver away** to work very hard and steadily ▶ **HISTORY** Old English *beofor*

becalmed *adj* (of a sailing ship) motionless through lack of wind

became *vb* the past tense of **become**

because *conj* **1** on account of the fact that: *because it's so cold we'll go home* **2 because of** on account of: *I lost my job because of her* ▶ **HISTORY** Middle English *bi cause*

beck[1] *n* **at someone's beck and call** having to be constantly available to do as someone asks ▶ **HISTORY** Middle English *becnen* to beckon

beck[2] *n* (in N England) a stream ▶ **HISTORY** Old English *becc*

beckon *vb* **1** to summon with a gesture **2** to lure: *fame beckoned* ▶ **HISTORY** Old English *bīecnan*

become *vb* **-coming, -came, -come 1** to come to be: *he became Prime Minister last year* **2** (foll. by *of*) to happen to: *what became of him?* **3** to suit: *that dress becomes you* ▶ **HISTORY** Old English *becuman* happen

becoming *adj* suitable or appropriate: *his conduct was not becoming to the rank of officer*

becquerel (beck-a-**rell**) *n* the SI unit of activity of a radioactive source ▶ **HISTORY** after A. H. *Becquerel*, physicist

bed *n* **1** a piece of furniture on which to sleep **2** a plot of ground in which plants are grown **3** the bottom of a river, lake, or sea **4** any underlying structure or part **5** a layer of rock **6 get out of bed on the wrong side** *informal* to begin the day in a bad mood **7 go to bed with** to have sexual intercourse with ▷ *vb* **bedding, bedded 8** (foll. by *down*) to go to or put into a place to sleep or rest **9** to place firmly into position; embed: *the poles were bedded in concrete* **10** *geol* to form or be arranged in a distinct layer **11** to plant in a bed of soil ▶ **HISTORY** Old English *bedd*

BEd Bachelor of Education

bed and breakfast *n chiefly Brit* overnight accommodation and breakfast

bedaub *vb* to smear over with something sticky or dirty

bedbug *n* a small blood-sucking wingless insect that infests dirty houses

bedclothes *pl n* coverings for a bed

bedding *n* **1** bedclothes, sometimes with a mattress **2** litter, such as straw, for animals **3** the distinct layered deposits of rocks

bedeck *vb* to cover with decorations

bedevil (bid-**dev**-ill) *vb* **-illing, -illed** *or US* **-iling, -iled 1** to harass or torment **2** to throw into confusion > **bedevilment** *n*

bedlam *n* a noisy confused situation

■ **WORD HISTORY**
■ The Hospital of St Mary of Bethlehem in
■ London was an institution where insane
■ people were cared for. Its name was
■ colloquially shortened to *Bethlem* or *Bedlam*,
■ from which the word 'bedlam' comes.

bedload *n geol* the sediment carried along by a river in the form of heavy particles

Bedouin *n* **1** (*pl* **-ins** *or* **-in**) a nomadic Arab tribesman of the deserts of Arabia, Jordan, and Syria **2** a wanderer ▶ **HISTORY** Arabic *badw* desert

bedpan *n* a shallow container used as a toilet by people who are not well enough to leave bed

bedraggled *adj* with hair or clothing that is untidy, wet, or dirty

bedridden *adj* unable to leave bed because of illness

bedrock *n* **1** the solid rock beneath the surface soil **2** basic principles or facts

bedroom *n* a room used for sleeping

bedsit *or* **bedsitter** *n* a furnished sitting room with a bed

bedsore *n* an ulcer on the skin, caused by a lengthy period of lying in bed due to illness

bedspread *n* a top cover on a bed

bedstead *n* the framework of a bed

bedstraw *n* a plant with small white or yellow flowers

bed-wetting *n* involuntary urination in bed

bee[1] *n* **1** a four-winged insect that collects nectar and pollen to make honey and wax **2 have a bee in one's bonnet** to be obsessed with an idea ▶ **HISTORY** Old English *bīo*

bee² n a social gathering to carry out a communal task: *quilting bee* ▶ HISTORY probably from Old English *bēn* boon

Beeb n **the Beeb** *Brit, informal* the BBC

beech n **1** a tree with smooth greyish bark **2** the hard wood of this tree **3** See **copper beech** ▶ HISTORY Old English *bēce*

beechnut n the small brown triangular edible nut of the beech tree

beef n **1** the flesh of a cow, bull, or ox **2** *slang* a complaint ▷ vb **3** *slang* to complain ▷ See also **beef up** ▶ HISTORY Old French *boef*, from Latin *bos* ox

beefburger n a flat fried or grilled cake of minced beef; hamburger

beefeater n a yeoman warder of the Tower of London

beef tomato or **beefsteak tomato** n a type of large fleshy tomato

beef up vb *informal* to strengthen

beefy adj **beefier, beefiest 1** *informal* muscular **2** like beef > **beefiness** n

beehive n a structure in which bees are housed

Beelzebub (bee-**ell**-zib-bub) n Satan or any devil ▶ HISTORY Hebrew *bá'al zebūb*, literally: lord of flies

been vb the past participle of **be**

beep n **1** a high-pitched sound, like that of a car horn ▷ vb **2** to make or cause to make such a noise ▶ HISTORY imitative

beer n **1** an alcoholic drink brewed from malt, sugar, hops, and water **2** a glass, can, or bottle containing this drink ▶ HISTORY Old English *beor*

beer parlour n *Canad* a licensed place in which beer is sold and drunk

beery adj **beerier, beeriest** smelling or tasting of beer

beeswax n **1** a wax produced by honeybees for making honeycombs **2** this wax after refining, used in polishes, etc.

beet n a plant with an edible root and leaves, such as the sugar beet and beetroot ▶ HISTORY Old English *bēte*

beetle¹ n **1** an insect with a hard wing-case closed over its back for protection ▷ vb **-tling, -tled 2** (foll. by *along, off* etc.) *informal* to scuttle or scurry ▶ HISTORY Old English *bitela*

beetle² vb **-tling, -tled** to overhang; jut: *the eaves of the roof beetled out over the windows* ▶ HISTORY origin unknown > **beetling** adj

beetle-browed adj having bushy or overhanging eyebrows

beetroot n a variety of the beet plant with a dark red root that may be eaten as a vegetable, in salads, or pickled

beet sugar n the sucrose obtained from sugar beet

befall vb **-falling, -fell, -fallen** *archaic or literary* to happen to ▶ HISTORY Old English *befeallan*

befit vb **-fitting, -fitted** to be appropriate to or suitable for > **befitting** adj

before conj **1** earlier than the time when **2** rather than: *she'll resign before she agrees to it* ▷ prep **3** preceding in space or time; in front of; ahead of: *they stood before the altar* **4** in the presence of: *to be brought before a judge* **5** in preference to: *to put friendship before money* ▷ adv **6** previously **7** in front ▶ HISTORY Old English *beforan*

beforehand adj, adv early; in advance

befriend vb to become a friend to

befuddled adj stupefied or confused, as through alcoholic drink

beg vb **begging, begged 1** to ask for money or food in the street **2** to ask formally, humbly, or earnestly: *I beg forgiveness; I beg to differ* **3 beg the question** *written* to put forward an argument that assumes the very point it is supposed to establish, or that depends on some other questionable assumption **4 go begging** to be unwanted or unused ▶ HISTORY probably from Old English *bedecian*

began vb the past tense of **begin**

beget vb **-getting, -got** or **-gat, -gotten** or **-got** *old-fashioned* **1** to cause or create: *repetition begets boredom* **2** to father ▶ HISTORY Old English *begietan*

beggar n **1** a person who lives by begging **2** *chiefly Brit* a fellow: *lucky beggar!* ▷ vb **3 beggar description** to be impossible to describe > **beggarly** adj

begin vb **-ginning, -gan, -gun 1** to start (something) **2** to bring or come into being **3** to start to say or speak **4** to have the least capacity to do something: *it doesn't even begin to address the problem* ▶ HISTORY Old English *beginnan* > **beginner** n

beginning n **1** a start **2 beginnings** an early part or stage **3** the place where or time when something starts **4** an origin; source

begone interj go away!

begonia n a tropical plant with ornamental leaves and waxy flowers ▶ HISTORY after Michel *Bégon*, patron of science

begot vb a past tense and past participle of **beget**

begotten vb a past participle of **beget**

begrudge vb **-grudging, -grudged 1** to envy (someone) the possession of something **2** to give or allow unwillingly: *he begrudged her an apology*

beguile (big-**gile**) vb **-guiling, -guiled** to charm (someone) into doing something he or she would not normally do

beguiling adj *written* charming, often in a deceptive way

beguine (big-**geen**) n **1** a dance of South American origin **2** music for this dance ▶ HISTORY French *béguin* flirtation

begum (bay-**gum**) n (in certain Muslim countries) a woman of high rank ▶ HISTORY Turkish *begim*

begun vb the past participle of **begin**

behalf n **on** or *US & Canad* **in behalf of** in the interest of or for the benefit of ▶ HISTORY Old English *be* by + *halfe* side

behave vb **-having, -haved 1** to act or function in a particular way **2** to conduct oneself in a particular way: *the baby behaved very well* **3** to conduct oneself properly ▶ HISTORY Middle English

b

behaviour or US **behavior** n **1** manner of behaving **2** psychol the response of an organism to a stimulus > **behavioural** or US **behavioral** adj

behavioural science n the scientific study of the behaviour of organisms

behaviourism or US **behaviorism** n a school of psychology that regards objective observation of the behaviour of organisms as the only valid subject for study > **behaviourist** or US **behaviorist** adj, n

behead vb to remove the head from ▶ HISTORY Old English behēafdian

beheld vb the past of **behold**

behemoth (bee-**hee**-moth) n a huge person or thing ▶ HISTORY Hebrew bĕhēmāh beast, name given to a huge beast in the Bible (Job 40:15)

behest n an order or earnest request: I came at her behest ▶ HISTORY Old English behǣs

behind prep **1** in or to a position further back than **2** in the past in relation to: I want to leave the past behind me **3** late according to: running behind schedule **4** concerning the circumstances surrounding: the reasons behind his departure **5** supporting: I'm right behind you in your application ▷ adv **6** in or to a position further back **7** remaining after someone's departure: she left her books behind **8** in arrears: to fall behind with payments ▷ adj **9** in a position further back ▷ n **10** informal the buttocks ▶ HISTORY Old English behindan

behold vb **-holding, -held** archaic or literary to look (at); observe ▶ HISTORY Old English bihealdan > **beholder** n

beholden adj indebted; obliged: I am beholden to you

behove vb **-hoving, -hoved** archaic to be necessary or fitting for: it behoves me to warn you ▶ HISTORY Old English behōfian

beige adj pale creamy-brown ▶ HISTORY Old French

being n **1** the state or fact of existing **2** essential nature; self **3** something that exists or is thought to exist: a being from outer space **4** a human being

bel n a unit for comparing two power levels or measuring the intensity of a sound, equal to 10 decibels ▶ HISTORY after A. G. Bell, scientist

belabour or US **belabor** vb to attack verbally or physically

belated adj late or too late: belated greetings > **belatedly** adv

belay vb **-laying, -layed 1** naut to secure a line to a pin or cleat **2** naut to stop **3** mountaineering to secure (a climber) by fixing a rope round a rock or piton ▶ HISTORY Old English belecgan

belch vb **1** to expel wind from the stomach noisily through the mouth **2** to expel or be expelled forcefully: smoke belching from factory chimneys ▷ n **3** an act of belching ▶ HISTORY Old English bialcan

beleaguered adj **1** struggling against difficulties or criticism: the country's beleaguered health system **2** besieged by an enemy: a ship bringing food to the beleaguered capital of Monrovia ▶ HISTORY BE- + obsolete leaguer a siege

belfry n, pl **-fries 1** the part of a tower or steeple in which bells are hung **2** a tower or steeple ▶ HISTORY Germanic

Belgian adj **1** of Belgium ▷ n **2** a person from Belgium

belgium sausage n NZ large smooth bland sausage

Belial (**bee**-lee-al) n the devil or Satan ▶ HISTORY Hebrew balīyya'al worthless

belie vb **-lying, -lied 1** to show to be untrue: the facts belied the theory **2** to misrepresent: the score belied the closeness of the match **3** to fail to justify: the promises were soon belied ▶ HISTORY Old English belēogan

belief n **1** trust or confidence: belief in the free market **2** opinion; conviction: it's my firm belief **3** a principle, etc. accepted as true, often without proof **4** religious faith

belief system n any set of beliefs regarding religion, philosophy, politics, etc. held by a person or group

believe vb **-lieving, -lieved 1** to accept as true or real: I believe God exists **2** to think, assume, or suppose: I believe you know my father **3** to accept the statement or opinion of (a person) as true **4** to have religious faith **5** **believe in** to be convinced of the truth or existence of: I don't believe in ghosts ▶ HISTORY Old English belīefan > **believable** adj > **believer** n

Belisha beacon (bill-**lee**-sha) n Brit a flashing orange globe mounted on a striped post, indicating a pedestrian crossing ▶ HISTORY after L. Hore-Belisha, politician

belittle vb **-tling, -tled** to treat (something or someone) as having little value or importance

bell n **1** a hollow, usually metal, cup-shaped instrument that emits a ringing sound when struck **2** the sound made by such an instrument **3** an electrical device that rings or buzzes as a signal **4** something shaped like a bell **5** Brit, slang a telephone call **6** **ring a bell** to sound familiar; recall something previously experienced ▶ HISTORY Old English belle

belladonna n **1** a drug obtained from deadly nightshade **2** same as **deadly nightshade** ▶ HISTORY Italian, literally: beautiful lady; supposed to refer to its use as a cosmetic

bell-bottoms pl n trousers that flare from the knee > **bell-bottomed** adj

belle n a beautiful woman, esp. the most attractive woman at a function: the belle of the ball ▶ HISTORY French

belles-lettres (bell-**let**-tra) n literary works, particularly essays and poetry ▶ HISTORY French

bellicose adj warlike; aggressive ▶ HISTORY Latin bellum war

belligerence n the act or quality of being belligerent or warlike

belligerent adj **1** marked by readiness to fight **2** relating to or engaged in a war ▷ n **3** a person or country engaged in war ▶ HISTORY Latin bellum war + gerere to wage

bell jar n a bell-shaped glass cover used to protect flower arrangements or cover apparatus to confine gases in experiments

bellow vb 1 to make a loud deep cry like that of a bull 2 to shout in anger ▷ n 3 the characteristic noise of a bull 4 a loud deep roar ▶ **HISTORY** probably from Old English bylgan

bellows n 1 a device consisting of an air chamber with flexible sides that is used to create and direct a stream of air 2 a flexible corrugated part, such as that connecting the lens system of some cameras to the body ▶ **HISTORY** plural of Old English belig belly

bells and whistles pl n attractive but nonessential additional features ▶ **HISTORY** from the bells and whistles which used to decorate fairground organs

belly n, pl **-lies** 1 the part of the body of a vertebrate containing the intestines and other organs 2 the stomach 3 the front, lower, or inner part of something 4 **go belly up** informal to die, fail, or end ▷ vb **-lies, -lying, -lied** 5 to swell out; bulge ▶ **HISTORY** Old English belig

bellyache n 1 informal a pain in the abdomen ▷ vb **-aching, -ached** 2 slang to complain repeatedly

bellybutton n informal the navel

belly flop n 1 a dive into water in which the body lands horizontally ▷ vb **belly-flop, -flopping, -flopped** 2 to perform a belly flop

bellyful n 1 slang more than one can tolerate 2 as much as one wants or can eat

belly laugh n a loud deep hearty laugh

belong vb 1 (foll. by to) to be the property of 2 (foll. by to) to be bound to (a person, organization, etc.) by ties of affection, association, membership, etc.: the nations concerned belonged to NATO 3 (foll. by to, under, with etc.) to be classified with: it belongs to a different class of comets 4 (foll. by to) to be a part of: this lid belongs to that tin 5 to have a proper or usual place 6 informal to be acceptable, esp. socially ▶ **HISTORY** Middle English belongen

belonger n a native-born Caribbean person

belongings pl n the things that a person owns or has with him or her

beloved adj 1 dearly loved ▷ n 2 a person who is dearly loved

below prep 1 at or to a position lower than; under 2 less than 3 unworthy of; beneath ▷ adv 4 at or to a lower position 5 at a later place in something written 6 archaic on earth or in hell ▶ **HISTORY** Middle English bilooghe

belt n 1 a band of leather or cloth worn around the waist 2 an area where a specific thing is found; zone: a belt of high pressure 3 same as **seat belt** 4 a band of flexible material between rotating shafts or pulleys to transfer motion or transmit goods: a fan belt; a conveyer belt 5 informal a sharp blow 6 **below the belt** informal unscrupulous or cowardly 7 **tighten one's belt** to reduce expenditure 8 **under one's belt** as part of one's experience: he had a string of successes under his belt ▷ vb 9 to fasten with or as if with a belt 10 to hit with a belt 11 slang to give (someone) a sharp blow 12 (foll. by along) slang to move very fast ▶ **HISTORY** Old English

belt out vb informal to sing (a song) loudly

beluga (bill-**loo**-ga) n a large white sturgeon of the Black and Caspian Seas, from which caviar and isinglass are obtained ▶ **HISTORY** Russian byeluga

bemoan vb to lament: he's always bemoaning his fate

bemused adj puzzled or confused

ben n Scot, Irish a mountain peak: Ben Lomond ▶ **HISTORY** Gaelic beinn

bench n 1 a long seat for more than one person 2 **the bench a** a judge or magistrate sitting in court **b** judges or magistrates collectively 3 a long and strong worktable ▶ **HISTORY** Old English benc

benchmark n 1 a mark on a fixed object, used as a reference point in surveying 2 a criterion by which to measure something: the speech was a benchmark of his commitment

bend[1] vb bending, bent 1 to form a curve 2 to turn from a particular direction: the road bends right 3 (often foll. by down etc.) to incline the body 4 to submit: to bend before public opinion 5 to turn or direct (one's eyes, steps, or attention) 6 **bend someone's ear** informal to complain (to someone) for a long time 7 **bend the rules** informal to ignore or change rules to suit oneself ▷ n 8 a curved part 9 the act of bending 10 **round the bend** Brit, slang mad ▶ **HISTORY** Old English bendan > **bendy** adj

bend[2] n heraldry a diagonal line across a shield ▶ **HISTORY** Old English: a band, strip

bends pl n **the bends** informal decompression sickness

bend sinister n heraldry a diagonal line across a shield, indicating a bastard line

beneath prep 1 below; under 2 too trivial for: beneath his dignity ▷ adv 3 below; underneath ▶ **HISTORY** Old English beneothan

Benedictine n 1 a monk or nun of the Christian order of Saint Benedict 2 a liqueur first made by Benedictine monks ▷ adj 3 of Saint Benedict or his order

benediction n 1 a prayer for divine blessing 2 a Roman Catholic service in which the congregation is blessed with the sacrament ▶ **HISTORY** Latin benedictio > **benedictory** adj

benefaction n 1 the act of doing good, particularly donating to charity 2 the donation or help given ▶ **HISTORY** Latin bene well + facere to do

benefactor n a person who supports a person or institution by giving money > **benefactress** fem n

benefice n Christianity a Church office that provides its holder with an income ▶ **HISTORY** Latin beneficium benefit

beneficent (bin-**eff**-iss-ent) adj charitable; generous ▶ **HISTORY** Latin beneficus > **beneficence** n

beneficial adj helpful or advantageous ▶ **HISTORY** Latin beneficium kindness

b

beneficiary *n, pl* **-ciaries 1** a person who gains or benefits **2** *law* a person entitled to receive funds or property under a trust, will, etc.

benefit *n* **1** something that improves or promotes **2** advantage or sake: *I'm doing this for your benefit* **3** a payment made by an institution or government to a person who is ill, unemployed, etc. **4** a theatrical performance or sports event to raise money for a charity ▷ *vb* **-fiting, -fited** *or US* **-fitting, -fitted 5** to do or receive good; profit ▶ HISTORY Latin *bene facere* to do well

benevolence *n* **1** inclination to do good **2** an act of kindness > **benevolent** *adj*

Bengali *n* **1** a member of a people living chiefly in Bangladesh and West Bengal **2** the language of this people ▷ *adj* **3** of Bengal or the Bengalis

benighted *adj* lacking cultural, moral, or intellectual enlightenment

benign (bin-**nine**) *adj* **1** showing kindliness **2** favourable: *a stroke of benign fate* **3** *pathol* (of a tumour, etc.) able to be controlled ▶ HISTORY Latin *benignus* > **benignly** *adv*

benioff zone *n* *geol* a narrow downward-sloping earthquake zone which is usually externally indicated by the presence of deep-sea trenches

bent *adj* **1** not straight; curved **2** *slang* dishonest; corrupt: *bent officials* **3** **bent on** determined to pursue (a course of action) ▷ *n* **4** personal inclination or aptitude: *he had a strong practical bent in his nature*

Benthamism *n* the utilitarian philosophy of Jeremy Bentham, which holds that the ultimate goal of society should be to promote the greatest happiness of the greatest number > **Benthamite** *n, adj*

bento *or* **bento box** *n* a thin box, made of plastic or lacquered wood, divided into compartments, which contain small separate dishes comprising a Japanese meal, esp. lunch ▶ HISTORY Japanese *bento* box lunch

benumb *vb* **1** to make numb or powerless **2** to stupefy (the mind, senses, will, etc.): *the work benumbed their minds and crushed their spirits*

benzene *n* a flammable poisonous liquid used as a solvent, insecticide, etc. ▶ HISTORY from *benzoin*, a fragrant resin from certain Asiatic trees

benzine *n* a volatile liquid obtained from coal tar and used as a solvent

bequeath *vb* **1** *law* to dispose of (property) as in a will **2** to hand down: *the author bequeaths no solutions* ▶ HISTORY Old English *becwethan*

bequest *n* **1** the act of gifting money or property in a will **2** money or property that has been gifted in a will

berate *vb* **-rating, -rated** to scold harshly

Berber *n* **1** a member of a Muslim people of N Africa **2** the language of this people ▷ *adj* **3** of the Berbers

berberis *n* a shrub with red berries ▶ HISTORY Medieval Latin

berceuse (bare-**suhz**) *n* **1** a lullaby **2** an instrumental piece suggestive of this ▶ HISTORY French

bereaved *adj* having recently lost a close relative or friend through death ▶ HISTORY Old English *bereafian* to deprive > **bereavement** *n*

bereft *adj* (foll. by *of*) deprived: *a government bereft of ideas*

beret (**ber**-ray) *n* a round flat close-fitting brimless cap ▶ HISTORY French

berg¹ *n* short for **iceberg**

berg² *n* *S African* a mountain

bergamot *n* **1** a small Asian tree with sour pear-shaped fruit **2** **essence of bergamot** a fragrant essential oil from the fruit rind of this plant, used in perfumery ▶ HISTORY French *bergamote*

bergschrund (**berk**-shroont) *n* *geog* a crevasse at the head of a glacier ▶ HISTORY German: mountain crack

beri-beri *n* a disease caused by a dietary deficiency of thiamine (vitamin B1) ▶ HISTORY Sinhalese

berk *or* **burk** *n* *Brit, Austral & NZ, slang* a stupid person; fool

berkelium *n* *chem* an artificial radioactive element. Symbol: Bk ▶ HISTORY after *Berkeley*, California, where it was discovered

Berlin Wall *n* *history* a wall that divided Berlin into the eastern sector and the western sector, built in 1961 to stop the flow of refugees from East Germany to West Germany, and demolished in 1989-90, when the city was reunited

berm *n* *NZ* narrow grass strip between the road and the footpath in a residential area

Bermuda shorts *pl n* shorts that come down to the knees ▶ HISTORY after *Bermudas*, islands in NW Atlantic

Bernoulli principle *n* *physics* the principle that the pressure in a moving fluid becomes less as the speed rises ▶ HISTORY after Daniel *Bernoulli*, mathematician & physicist

berry *n, pl* **-ries** a small round fruit that grows on bushes or trees and is often edible ▶ HISTORY Old English *berie*

berserk *adj* **go berserk** to become violent or destructive

- **WORD HISTORY**
- 'Berserk' comes from the Old Norse word
- *berserkr*, denoting a Viking warrior who wore a
- shirt (*serkr*) made from the skin of a bear (*björn*).
- Berserkrs worked themselves into a frenzy
- before going into battle, from which comes the
- notion of someone 'going berserk'.

berth *n* **1** a bunk in a ship or train **2** *naut* a place assigned to a ship at a mooring **3** *naut* sufficient room for a ship to manoeuvre **4** **give a wide berth to** to keep clear of ▷ *vb* **5** *naut* to dock (a ship) **6** to provide with a sleeping place **7** *naut* to pick up a mooring in an anchorage ▶ HISTORY probably from BEAR¹

beryl *n* a transparent hard mineral, used as a source of beryllium and as a gemstone ▶ HISTORY Greek *bērullos*

beryllium *n* a toxic silvery-white metallic element. Symbol: Be ▶ HISTORY Greek *bērullos*

best

There are a number of alternatives for the word **best** which will make your writing more interesting.

DEFINITION 2
• If you would like to call someone or something 'most excellent', you could try: **first-rate** performance • **foremost** painter • **greatest** film • Britain's **leading** actors • the West Indies' **outstanding** cricketers • **superlative** products • **supreme** achievement • **top** athletes

DEFINITION 3
• If you would like to describe something as the most suitable or desirable thing, you could try: **correct** thing • **most desirable** outcome • **most fitting** location • **right** person

DEFINITION 6
• If you would like to describe someone or something as the most outstanding of its kind, you could try: the **cream** of Trinidadian artists • the **elite** of the sporting world • the **finest** of ingredients • the **pick** of the crop

b

beseech vb -seeching, -sought or -seeched to ask earnestly; beg ▸ HISTORY Middle English; see BE-, SEEK

beset vb -setting, -set 1 to trouble or harass constantly 2 to surround or attack from all sides

beside prep 1 next to; at, by, or to the side of 2 as compared with 3 away from: beside the point 4 **beside oneself** overwhelmed; overwrought: beside oneself with grief ▷ adv 5 at, by, to, or along the side of something or someone ▸ HISTORY Old English be sīdan

besides adv 1 in addition ▷ prep 2 apart from; even considering ▷ conj 3 anyway; moreover

besiege vb -sieging, -sieged 1 to surround with military forces to bring about surrender 2 to hem in 3 to overwhelm, as with requests

besmirch vb to tarnish (someone's name or reputation)

besom n a broom made of a bundle of twigs tied to a handle ▸ HISTORY Old English besma

besotted adj 1 having an irrational passion for a person or thing 2 stupefied with alcohol

besought vb a past of **beseech**

bespatter vb 1 to splash with dirty water 2 to dishonour or slander

bespeak vb -speaking, -spoke; -spoken or -spoke 1 to indicate or suggest: imitation bespeaks admiration 2 to engage or ask for in advance: she was bespoke to a family in the town

bespoke adj chiefly Brit 1 (esp. of a suit) made to the customer's specifications 2 making or selling such suits: a bespoke tailor

best adj 1 the superlative of **good** 2 most excellent of a particular group, category, etc. 3 most suitable, desirable, etc. ▷ adv 4 the superlative of **well** 5 in a manner surpassing all others; most attractively, etc. ▷ n 6 **the best** the most outstanding or excellent person, thing, or group in a category 7 the utmost effort: I did my best 8 a person's finest clothes 9 **at best** a in the most favourable interpretation b under the most favourable conditions 10 **for the best** a for an ultimately good outcome b with good intentions 11 **get the best of** to defeat or outwit 12 **make the best of** to cope as well as possible with ▷ vb 13 to defeat ▸ HISTORY Old English betst See WORD FOCUS **best**

bestial adj 1 brutal or savage 2 of or relating to a beast ▸ HISTORY Latin bestia beast

bestiality n, pl -ties brutal behaviour, character, or action

bestiary n, pl -aries a medieval collection of descriptions of animals

bestir vb -stirring, -stirred to cause (oneself) to become active

best man n the male attendant of the bridegroom at a wedding

bestow vb to present (a gift) or confer (an honour) > **bestowal** n

bestride vb -striding, -strode to have or put a leg on either side of

bestseller n a book or other product that has sold in great numbers > **bestselling** adj

bet n 1 the act of staking a sum of money or other stake on the outcome of an event 2 the stake risked 3 a course of action: your best bet is to go by train 4 informal an opinion: my bet is that you've been up to no good ▷ vb **betting, bet** or **betted** 5 to make or place a bet with (someone) 6 to stake (money, etc.) in a bet 7 informal, spoken to predict (a certain outcome): I bet she doesn't turn up 8 **you bet** informal, spoken of course ▸ HISTORY probably short for abet

beta n 1 the second letter in the Greek alphabet (Β, β) 2 the second in a group or series

beta-blocker n a drug that decreases the activity of the heart: used in the treatment of high blood pressure and angina pectoris

beta-carotene n biochem the most important form of the plant pigment carotene, which occurs in milk, vegetables, and other foods and, when eaten by man and animals, is converted in the body to vitamin A

betake vb -taking, -took, -taken • **betake oneself** formal to go or move: he betook himself to the public house

beta particle n a high-speed electron or positron emitted by a nucleus during radioactive decay or nuclear fission

betatron n a type of particle accelerator for producing high-energy beams of electrons

betel (bee-tl) n an Asian climbing plant, the leaves and nuts of which can be chewed ▸ HISTORY Malayalam (language of SW India) vettila

b

better

WORD FOCUS

Like **best**, the word **better** can be replaced with a number of alternatives to add variety and interest to your written and spoken English.

DEFINITION 2
• If you want to describe something as being more excellent than other things, you could try: the **greater** prize • **higher-quality** service • far **superior** to yours • **surpassing** quality

DEFINITION 3
• If you want to describe something as being more

suitable or attractive than other things, you could try: no **finer** place • much **grander** house • much **nicer** room • **preferable** to • a **worthier** cause

DEFINITION 4
• If you want to describe someone as having improved health, you could say: now I'm **cured** • a lot **fitter** • **fully recovered** • much **healthier** • definitely **improving** • **on the mend** now • she's **recovering** • getting **stronger** • feeling **well** again

---

bête noire (bet **nwahr**) *n*, *pl* **bêtes noires** a person or thing that one particularly dislikes or dreads ▶ HISTORY French, literally: black beast

betide *vb* **-tiding, -tided** to happen or happen to: *woe betide us if we're not ready on time* ▶ HISTORY BE- + obsolete *tide* to happen

betoken *vb* to indicate; signify

betray *vb* **1** to hand over or expose (one's nation, friend, etc.) treacherously to an enemy **2** to disclose (a secret or confidence) treacherously **3** to reveal unintentionally: *his singing voice betrays his origins* ▶ HISTORY Latin *tradere* to hand over > **betrayal** *n* > **betrayer** *n*

betrothed *old-fashioned adj* **1** engaged to be married ▷ *n* **2** the person to whom one is engaged

better *adj* **1** the comparative of **good 2** more excellent than others **3** more suitable, attractive, etc. **4** improved or fully recovered in health **5 the better part of** a large part of ▷ *adv* **6** the comparative of **well 7** in a more excellent manner **8** in or to a greater degree **9 better off** in more favourable circumstances, esp. financially **10 had better** would be sensible, etc. to: *I had better be off* ▷ *n* **11 the better** something that is the more excellent, useful, etc. of two such things **12 betters** people who are one's superiors, esp. in social standing **13 get the better of** to defeat or outwit ▷ *vb* **14** to improve upon ▶ HISTORY Old English *betera*
See WORD FOCUS **better**

betterment *n* improvement

better-off *adj* reasonably wealthy: *Catalonia aims to attract better-off tourists*

between *prep* **1** at a point intermediate to two other points in space, time, etc. **2** in combination; together: *between them, they saved enough money to buy a car* **3** confined to: *between you and me* **4** indicating a linking relation or comparison **5** indicating alternatives, strictly only two alternatives ▷ *adv also* **in between 6** between one specified thing and another ▶ HISTORY Old English *betwēonum*

betwixt *prep, adv* **1** archaic between **2 betwixt and between** in an intermediate or indecisive position

bevel *n* **1** a slanting edge ▷ *vb* **-elling, -elled** *or US* **-eling, -eled 2** to be inclined; slope **3** to cut a bevel on (a piece of timber, etc.) ▶ HISTORY Old French *baer* to gape

bevel gear *n* a toothed gear meshed with another at an angle to it

beverage *n* any drink other than water ▶ HISTORY Old French *bevrage*

beverage room *n Canad* same as **beer parlour**

bevy *n*, *pl* **bevies** a flock; group ▶ HISTORY origin unknown

bewail *vb* to express great sorrow over; lament

beware *vb* **-waring, -wared** (often foll. by *of*) to be wary (of); be on one's guard (against) ▶ HISTORY *be* (imperative) + obsolete *ware* to be cautious

bewilder *vb* to confuse utterly; puzzle ▶ HISTORY BE- + obsolete *wilder* to lose one's way > **bewildering** *adj* > **bewilderment** *n*

bewitch *vb* **1** to attract and fascinate **2** to cast a spell over ▶ HISTORY Middle English *bewicchen* > **bewitching** *adj*

bey *n* **1** (in modern Turkey) a title of address, corresponding to *Mr* **2** (in the Ottoman Empire) a title given to provincial governors ▶ HISTORY Turkish: lord

beyond *prep* **1** at or to a point on the other side of: *beyond those hills* **2** outside the limits or scope of ▷ *adv* **3** at or to the other or far side of something **4** outside the limits of something ▷ *n* **5 the beyond** the unknown, esp. life after death ▶ HISTORY Old English *begeondan*

beyond reasonable doubt *n law* the standard of proof in a criminal case, meaning that, before someone can be found guilty, there must not be any reasonable doubt as to their guilt in the minds of the jury or magistrate. Compare **balance of probabilities**

bezel *n* **1** the sloping edge of a cutting tool **2** the slanting face of a cut gem **3** a groove holding a gem, watch crystal, etc. ▶ HISTORY French *biseau*

bezique *n* a card game for two or more players ▶ HISTORY French *bésigue*

B/F *or* **b/f** *book-keeping* brought forward

BFPO British Forces Post Office

Bh *chem* bohrium

Bhagavad-Gita (**bug**-a-vad-**geet**-a) *n* a sacred Hindu text composed about 200 BC ▶ HISTORY Sanskrit: song of the Blessed One

bhaji *n*, *pl* **bhaji** *or* **bhajis** an Indian savoury made of chopped vegetables mixed in a spiced batter and deep-fried ▶ HISTORY Hindi

bhang *n* a preparation of Indian hemp used as a narcotic and intoxicant

bhangra *n* a type of traditional Punjabi folk music combined with elements of Western pop music ▶ HISTORY Hindi

bhp brake horsepower

Bi *chem* bismuth

bi- *combining form* **1** having two: *bifocal* **2** occurring or lasting for two: *biennial* **3** on both sides, directions, etc.: *bilateral* **4** occurring twice during: *biweekly* **5** *chem* **a** denoting a compound containing two identical cyclical hydrocarbon systems: *biphenyl* **b** indicating an acid salt of a dibasic acid: *sodium bicarbonate* ▶ HISTORY Latin *bis* twice

biannual *adj* occurring twice a year > **biannually** *adv*

bias *n* **1** mental tendency, esp. prejudice **2** a diagonal cut across the weave of a fabric **3** *bowls* a bulge or weight inside one side of a bowl that causes it to roll in a curve ▷ *vb* **-asing, -ased** *or* **-assing, -assed** **4** to cause to have a bias; prejudice ▶ HISTORY Old French *biais* > **biased** *or* **biassed** *adj*

bias binding *n* a strip of material used for binding hems

bib *n* **1** a piece of cloth or plastic worn to protect a very young child's clothes while eating **2** the upper front part of some aprons, dungarees, etc. ▶ HISTORY Middle English *bibben* to drink

Bible *n* **1 the Bible** the sacred writings of the Christian religion, comprising the Old and New Testaments **2 bible** a book regarded as authoritative: *this guide has long been regarded as the hill walkers' bible* ▶ HISTORY Greek *biblion* book > **biblical** *adj*

bibliography *n*, *pl* **-phies 1** a list of books on a subject or by a particular author **2** a list of sources used in a book, etc. **3** the study of the history, etc. of literary material ▶ HISTORY Greek *biblion* book + *graphein* to write > **bibliographer** *n*

bibliophile *n* a person who collects or is fond of books ▶ HISTORY Greek *biblion* book + *philos* loving

bibulous *adj literary* addicted to alcohol ▶ HISTORY Latin *bibere* to drink

bicameral *adj* (of a legislature) consisting of two chambers ▶ HISTORY BI- + Latin *camera* chamber

bicarb *n* short for **bicarbonate of soda**

bicarbonate *n* a salt of carbonic acid

bicarbonate of soda *n* sodium bicarbonate used as medicine or a raising agent in baking

bicentenary *or US* **bicentennial** *adj* **1** marking a 200th anniversary ▷ *n*, *pl* **-naries 2** a 200th anniversary

biceps *n*, *pl* **-ceps** *anat* a muscle with two origins, esp. the muscle that flexes the forearm ▶ HISTORY BI- + Latin *caput* head

bicker *vb* to argue over petty matters; squabble ▶ HISTORY origin unknown

bicuspid *adj* **1** having two points ▷ *n* **2** a bicuspid tooth

bicuspid valve *n anat* the valve between the left atrium and the left ventricle of the heart

bicycle *n* **1** a vehicle with a metal frame and two wheels, one behind the other, pedalled by the rider ▷ *vb* **-cling, -cled 2** to ride a bicycle ▶ HISTORY BI- + Greek *kuklos* wheel

bid *vb* **bidding; bad, bade** *or* **bid; bidden** *or* **bid 1** to offer (an amount) in an attempt to buy something **2** to say (a greeting): *to bid farewell* **3** to order: *do as you are bid!* **4** *Bridge etc.* to declare how many tricks one expects to make ▷ *n* **5 a** an offer of a specified amount **b** the price offered **6 a** the quoting by a seller of a price **b** the price quoted **7** an attempt, esp. to attain power **8** *Bridge etc.* the number of tricks a player undertakes to make ▶ HISTORY Old English *biddan* > **bidder** *n*

biddable *adj* obedient

bidding *n* **1** an order or command: *she had done his bidding* **2** an invitation; summons: *he knew to knock and wait for bidding before he entered* **3** the bids in an auction, card game, etc.

biddy-bid, biddy-biddy *n*, *pl* **-bids, -biddies** NZ a low-growing plant with hooked burrs

bide *vb* **biding, bided** *or* **bode, bided 1** *archaic or dialect* to remain **2 bide one's time** to wait patiently for an opportunity ▶ HISTORY Old English *bidan*

bidet (**bee**-day) *n* a small low basin for washing the genital area ▶ HISTORY French: small horse

biennial *adj* **1** occurring every two years ▷ *n* **2** a plant that completes its life cycle in two years

bier *n* a stand on which a corpse or a coffin rests before burial ▶ HISTORY Old English *bǣr*

biff *slang n* **1** a blow with the fist ▷ *vb* **2** to give (someone) such a blow ▶ HISTORY probably imitative

bifocal *adj* having two different focuses, esp. (of a lens) permitting near and distant vision

bifocals *pl n* a pair of spectacles with bifocal lenses

bifurcate *vb* **-cating, -cated 1** to fork into two branches ▷ *adj* **2** forked into two branches ▶ HISTORY BI- + Latin *furca* fork > **bifurcation** *n*

bifurcation ratio *n geog* in a system in which streams are ordered according to whether they have tributaries or not, the ratio of the number of streams without tributaries to the streams they flow into, or the ratio of small streams with tributaries to the next biggest streams, and so on. See also **stream order**

big *adj* **bigger, biggest 1** of great or considerable size, weight, number, or capacity **2** having great significance; important **3** important through having power, wealth, etc. **4 a** elder: *my big brother* **b** grown-up **5** generous: *that's very big of you* **6** extravagant; boastful: *big talk* **7 too big for one's boots** conceited; unduly self-confident **8** in an advanced stage of pregnancy: *big with child* **9 in a big way** in a very grand or enthusiastic way ▷ *adv informal* **10** boastfully; pretentiously:

big

When you are writing or talking and you are going to use the word **big**, try to think of a more descriptive and interesting word instead. Here are some ideas for words that you might use to describe different aspects of people and things.

DEFINITION 1
- If you would like to describe something that is large in size or scale, you could try: **colossal** statue • **enormous** building • **gigantic** creature • **great** commotion • **hefty** fine • **huge** cake • **immense** task • **large** map • **massive** display • **significant** difference • **vast** stadium

DEFINITION 2
- If you would like to describe something that is very significant, you could try: **grave** crisis • **momentous** decision • **serious** disadvantage • **urgent** need • **weighty** problem

DEFINITION 3
- If you would like to emphasize someone's importance, you could try: **eminent** politician • **important** influence • **influential** figure • **leading** screenwriters • **major** role • **powerful** businessman • **principal** guest • **prominent** jazz musician • **significant** investor

DEFINITION 4
- If you would like to describe someone or something that is grown-up, you could try: **elder** sibling • **full-grown** animal • **grown** woman • **mature** tree

DEFINITION 5
- If you would like to describe someone or their actions as generous, you could try: **benevolent** ruler • **gracious** host • **heroic** deed • **kind-hearted** stranger • **noble** gesture • **unselfish** act

DEFINITION 6
- If you would like to describe something that someone has said as extravagant or big-headed, you could try: **arrogant** comment • **boastful** words • **extravagant** claims • **inflated** rhetoric

---

he talks big **11** on a grand scale: *think big* ▶ HISTORY origin unknown
See WORD FOCUS **big**

bigamy *n* the crime of marrying a person while still legally married to someone else ▶ HISTORY BI- + Greek *gamos* marriage > **bigamist** *n* > **bigamous** *adj*

big-bang theory *n* a cosmological theory that suggests that the universe was created as the result of a massive explosion

Big Brother *n* a person or organization that exercises total dictatorial control ▶ HISTORY from the novel *1984* by George Orwell

big business *n* large commercial organizations collectively

big end *n* the larger end of a connecting rod in an internal-combustion engine

bighead *n informal* a conceited person > **big-headed** *adj*

bight *n* **1** a long curved shoreline **2** the slack part or a loop in a rope ▶ HISTORY Old English *byht*

bigot *n* a person who is intolerant, esp. regarding religion, politics, or race ▶ HISTORY Old French > **bigoted** *adj* > **bigotry** *n*

big shot *n informal* an important person

big top *n informal* the main tent of a circus

bigwig *n informal* an important person

bijou (bee-zhoo) *n, pl* **-joux** (-zhooz) **1** something small and delicately worked ▷ *adj* **2** small but tasteful: *a bijou residence* ▶ HISTORY French: a jewel

bike *n informal* a bicycle or motorcycle

biker *n* a person who rides a motorcycle

bikini *n* a woman's brief two-piece swimming costume

> ■ **WORD HISTORY**
> ■ The bikini takes its name from the *Bikini* Atoll in
> ■ the Marshall Islands in the Pacific Ocean,
> ■ where an atom-bomb was exploded in 1946.

> ■ The bikini was given its name because it was
> ■ said that the effect on men caused by women
> ■ wearing bikinis was as explosive and
> ■ devastating as the effect of the atom-bomb.

bilateral *adj* affecting or undertaken by two parties; mutual

bilberry *n, pl* **-ries** a blue or blackish edible berry that grows on a shrub ▶ HISTORY probably Scandinavian

bilby *n, pl* **-bies** an Australian marsupial with long pointed ears and grey fur

Bildungsroman (bil-doong-sro-marn) *n literature* a novel concerned with a person's formative years and development ▶ HISTORY German, literally: education novel

bile *n* **1** a greenish fluid secreted by the liver to aid digestion of fats **2** irritability or peevishness ▶ HISTORY Latin *bilis*

bilge *n* **1** *informal* nonsense **2** *naut* the bottom of a ship's hull **3** the dirty water that collects in a ship's bilge ▶ HISTORY probably variant of *bulge*

bilharzia (bill-hart-see-a) *n* a disease caused by infestation of the body with blood flukes ▶ HISTORY after T. *Bilharz*, who discovered the blood fluke

biliary *adj* of bile, the ducts that convey bile, or the gall bladder

bilingual *adj* **1** able to speak two languages **2** expressed in two languages > **bilingualism** *n*

bilious *adj* **1** nauseous; sick: *a bilious attack* **2** *written* bad-tempered; irritable: *the regime's most persistent and bilious critic* **3** *written* (of a colour) harsh and offensive ▶ HISTORY Latin *biliosus* full of bile

bilk *vb* to cheat or deceive, esp. to avoid making payment to ▶ HISTORY perhaps variant of *balk* > **bilker** *n*

bill¹ *n* **1** a statement of money owed for goods or services supplied **2** a draft of a proposed new law presented to a law-making body **3** a printed notice or advertisement **4** *US & Canad* a piece of paper money; note **5** any list of items, events, etc. such as a theatre programme ▷ *vb* **6** to send or present an account for payment to (a person) **7** to advertise by posters **8** to schedule as a future programme: *next week they will discuss what are billed as new ideas for economic reform* **9 fit** or **fill the bill** *informal* to be suitable or adequate ▶ **HISTORY** Late Latin *bulla* document

bill² *n* **1** the projecting jaws of a bird; beak ▷ *vb* **2 bill and coo** (of lovers) to kiss and whisper amorously ▶ **HISTORY** Old English *bile*

billabong *n Austral* a pool in the bed of a stream with an interrupted water flow ▶ **HISTORY** Aboriginal

billboard *n* a hoarding

billet¹ *vb* **-leting, -leted 1** to assign a lodging to (a soldier) ▷ *n* **2** accommodation, esp. for a soldier, in civilian lodgings **3** *Austral & NZ* a person who is billeted ▶ **HISTORY** Old French *billette*, from *bulle* a document

billet² *n* **1** a chunk of wood, esp. for fuel **2** a small bar of iron or steel ▶ **HISTORY** Old French *billette* a little log

billet-doux (**bill**-ee-**doo**) *n*, *pl* **billets-doux** (**bill**-ee-**dooz**) *old-fashioned or jocular* a love letter ▶ **HISTORY** French: a sweet letter

billhook *n* a tool with a hooked blade, used for chopping, etc.

billiards *n* a game in which a long cue is used to propel balls on a table ▶ **HISTORY** Old French *billard* curved stick

billion *n*, *pl* **-lions** or **-lion 1** one thousand million: 1 000 000 000 or 10⁹ **2** (in Britain, originally) one million million: 1 000 000 000 000 or 10¹² **3** (often *pl*) *informal* an extremely large but unspecified number: *billions of dollars* ▶ **HISTORY** French > **billionth** *adj, n*

billionaire *n* a person who has money or property worth at least a billion pounds, dollars, etc.

bill of exchange *n* a document instructing a third party to pay a stated sum at a designated date or on demand

bill of fare *n* a menu

bill of lading *n* a document containing full particulars of goods shipped

Bill of Rights *n law* **1** an English statute of 1689 guaranteeing the rights and liberty of the individual subject **2** the first ten amendments to the US Constitution which guarantee the liberty of the individual **3** (*usually not caps.*) any charter of basic human rights

billow *n* **1** a large sea wave **2** a swelling or surging mass, as of smoke or sound ▷ *vb* **3** to rise up or swell out ▶ **HISTORY** Old Norse *bylgja* > **billowing** *adj, n* > **billowy** *adj*

billy or **billycan** *n*, *pl* **-lies** or **-lycans** a metal can or pot for boiling water, etc. over a campfire ▶ **HISTORY** Scots *billypot*

billy goat *n* a male goat

biltong *n S African* strips of meat dried and cured in the sun ▶ **HISTORY** Afrikaans

Bim *n informal* a native or inhabitant of Barbados ▶ **HISTORY** origin unknown

bimbo *n*, *pl* **-bos** *slang* an attractive but empty-headed young woman ▶ **HISTORY** Italian: little child

bimetallic *adj* consisting of two metals

bimetallism *n* the use of two metals, esp. gold and silver, in fixed relative values as the standard of value and currency > **bimetallist** *n*

bimodal *adj maths* having two modes

bin *n* **1** a container for rubbish, etc. **2** a large container for storing something in bulk, such as coal, grain, or bottled wine ▷ *vb* **binning, binned 3** to put in a rubbish bin: *I bin my junk mail without reading it* ▶ **HISTORY** Old English *binne* basket

binary (**bine**-a-ree) *adj* **1** composed of two parts **2** *maths, computers* of or expressed in a system with two as its base **3** *chem* containing atoms of two different elements ▷ *n*, *pl* **-ries 4** something composed of two parts ▶ **HISTORY** Late Latin *binarius*

binary fission *n biol* reproduction in single-celled organisms by division into two similar daughter cells

binary star *n* a system of two stars revolving around a common centre of gravity

bind *vb* **binding, bound 1** to make secure, such as with a rope **2** to unite with emotional ties or commitment **3** to place (someone) under legal or moral obligation **4** to place under certain constraints: *bound by the rules* **5** to stick together or cause to stick: *egg binds fat and flour* **6** to enclose and fasten (the pages of a book) between covers **7** to provide (a garment) with an edging **8** (foll. by *up*) to bandage ▷ *n* **9** *informal* a difficult or annoying situation ▶ **HISTORY** Old English *bindan*

binder *n* **1** a firm cover for holding loose sheets of paper together **2** a person who binds books **3** something used to fasten or tie, such as rope or twine **4** *obsolete* a machine for cutting and binding grain into sheaves

binding *n* **1** anything that binds or fastens **2** the covering of a book ▷ *adj* **3** imposing an obligation or duty

bind over *vb* to place (a person) under a legal obligation, esp. to keep the peace

bindweed *n* a plant that twines around a support

binge *n informal* **1** a bout of excessive drinking **2** excessive indulgence in anything ▶ **HISTORY** probably dialect: to soak

bingo *n* a gambling game in which numbers called out are covered by players on their individual cards. The first to cover a given arrangement is the winner ▶ **HISTORY** origin unknown

binnacle *n* a housing for a ship's compass ▶ **HISTORY** Late Latin *habitaculum* dwelling-place

binocular *adj* involving or intended for both eyes: *binocular vision* ▶ **HISTORY** BI- + Latin *oculus* eye

binoculars *pl n* an optical instrument for use with both eyes, consisting of two small telescopes joined together

75

binomial *n* **1** a mathematical expression consisting of two terms, such as 3x + 2y ▷ *adj* **2** referring to two names or terms ▶ HISTORY BI- + Latin *nomen* name

binomial theorem *n* a general mathematical formula that expresses any power of a binomial without multiplying out, as in (a+b)² = a²+2ab+b²

bio- *combining form* **1** indicating life or living organisms: *biogenesis* **2** indicating a human life or career: *biography* ▶ HISTORY Greek *bios* life

bioastronautics *n* the study of the effects of space flight on living organisms

biochemistry *n* the study of the chemical compounds, reactions, etc. occurring in living organisms > **biochemical** *adj* > **biochemist** *n*

biocide *n* a substance used to destroy living things ▶ HISTORY BIO- + Latin *caedere* to kill

biocoenosis *or US* **biocenosis** (bye-oh-see-**no**-siss) *n* the relationships between animals and plants subsisting together ▶ HISTORY BIO- + Greek *koinōsis* sharing

biodegradable *adj* (of sewage and packaging) capable of being decomposed by natural means > **biodegradability** *n*

biodiesel *n* a biofuel intended for use in diesel engines

biodiversity *n* the existence of a wide variety of plant and animal species in their natural environments

bioengineering *n* the design and manufacture of aids, such as artificial limbs, to help people with disabilities

biofuel *n* a substance of biological origin that is used as a fuel

biogas *n* gaseous fuel produced by the fermentation of organic waste

biogenesis *n* the principle that a living organism must originate from a similar parent organism

biogenic (bye-oh-**jen**-ik) *adj* originating from a living organism

biogeochemical *adj biol* of the study of relationships between chemical elements and the environment

biogeography *n biol, geog* the branch of biology concerned with the geographical distribution of plants and animals > **biogeographical** *adj* > **biogeographically** *adv*

biography *n, pl* **-phies 1** an account of someone's life by another person **2** such accounts collectively ▶ HISTORY BIO- + Greek *graphein* to write > **biographer** *n* > **biographical** *adj*

biol. **1** biological **2** biology

biological *adj* **1** of or relating to biology **2** (of a detergent) containing enzymes that remove natural stains, such as blood or grass > **biologically** *adv*

biological clock *n* an inherent timing mechanism that controls the rhythmic repetition of processes in living organisms, such as sleeping

biological control *n* the control of destructive organisms, esp. insects, by nonchemical means, such as introducing a natural predator of the pest

biological magnification *n biol* the phenomenon whereby the higher up the food chain an animal is, the higher the concentrations of certain toxins in its body; caused by the tendency of each animal in the chain to store rather than to eliminate these toxins so that those eating other animals ingest multiple concentrations

biological warfare *n* the use of living organisms or their toxic products to induce death or incapacity in humans

biological weapon *n* a weapon used in biological warfare

biological weathering *n geol* changes to rocks caused by living organisms such as algae, lichen, or tree roots

biology *n* the study of living organisms > **biologist** *n*

biomass *n biol, geog* the total number of living organisms in a given area

biome *n biol, geog* a major ecological community, extending over a large area and usually characterized by a dominant vegetation

biomechanics *n* the study of the mechanics of the movement of living organisms

biomedicine *n* **1** the medical and biological study of the effects of unusual environmental stress **2** the study of herbal remedies

biometric *adj* using physiological or behavioural traits as a means of identification

bionic *adj* **1** of or relating to bionics **2** (in science fiction) having physical functions augmented by electronic equipment ▶ HISTORY BIO- + (*electro*)*nic*

bionics *n* **1** the study of biological functions in order to develop electronic equipment that operates similarly **2** the replacement of limbs or body parts by artificial electronically powered parts

biophysics *n* the physics of biological processes and the application of methods used in physics to biology > **biophysical** *adj* > **biophysicist** *n*

biopic (**bye**-oh-pick) *n informal* a film based on the life of a famous person ▶ HISTORY *bio*(*graphical*) + *pic*(*ture*)

biopsy *n, pl* **-sies** examination of tissue from a living body to determine the cause or extent of a disease ▶ HISTORY BIO- + Greek *opsis* sight

biorhythm *n* a complex recurring pattern of physiological states, believed to affect physical, emotional, and mental states

bioscope *n* **1** a kind of early film projector **2** *S African* a cinema

biosphere *n* the part of the earth's surface and atmosphere inhabited by living things

biosynthesis *n* the formation of complex compounds in living organisms > **biosynthetic** *adj*

biotech *n* short for **biotechnology**

biotechnology *n* the use of microorganisms, such as cells or bacteria, in industry and technology

bioterrorism *n* the use of viruses, bacteria, etc. by terrorists > **bioterrorist** *n*

biotic *adj biol* of or relating to living organisms or produced by living organisms ▶ HISTORY Greek *biotikos*, from *bios* life Compare **abiotic**

biotin *n* a vitamin of the B complex, abundant in egg yolk and liver ▶ HISTORY Greek *biotē* life

bipartisan *adj* consisting of or supported by two political parties

bipartite *adj* 1 consisting of or having two parts 2 affecting or made by two parties: *a bipartite agreement*

biped (**bye**-ped) *n* 1 any animal with two feet ▷ *adj also* **bipedal** 2 having two feet ▶ HISTORY BI- + Latin *pes* foot

biplane *n* an aeroplane with two sets of wings, one above the other

bipolar *adj* 1 having two poles 2 having two extremes > **bipolarity** *n*

birch *n* 1 a tree with thin peeling bark and hard close-grained wood 2 **the birch** a bundle of birch twigs or a birch rod used, esp. formerly, for flogging offenders ▷ *vb* 3 to flog with the birch ▶ HISTORY Old English *bierce*

bird *n* 1 a two-legged creature with feathers and wings, which lays eggs and can usually fly. *Related adjective: avian* 2 *slang, chiefly Brit* a girl or young woman 3 *informal* a person: *he's a rare bird* 4 **a bird in the hand** something definite or certain 5 **birds of a feather** people with the same ideas or interests 6 **kill two birds with one stone** to accomplish two things with one action ▶ HISTORY Old English *bridd*

bird flu *n* a form of influenza occurring in poultry caused by a virus capable of spreading to humans

birdie *n* 1 *informal* a bird 2 *golf* a score of one stroke under par for a hole

bird of paradise *n* a songbird of New Guinea, the male of which has brilliantly coloured plumage

bird of prey *n* a bird, such as a hawk or owl, that hunts other animals for food

bird's-eye view *n* 1 a view seen from above 2 a general or overall impression of something

bird's foot delta *n geog* a delta at the mouth of a river characterized by strips of land projecting beyond the main land mass like the claws of a bird. Compare **arcuate delta, cuspate delta**

biretta *n RC Church* a stiff square clerical cap ▶ HISTORY Italian *berretta*

Biro *n, pl* **-ros** *trademark* a kind of ballpoint pen

birth *n* 1 the process of bearing young; childbirth 2 the act of being born 3 the beginning of something; origin 4 ancestry: *of noble birth* 5 **give birth to a** to bear (offspring) **b** to produce or originate (an idea, plan, etc.) ▶ HISTORY Old Norse *byrth*

birth control *n* limitation of child-bearing by means of contraception

birthday *n* 1 an anniversary of the day of one's birth 2 the day on which a person was born

birthmark *n* a blemish on the skin formed before birth

birth mother *n* the woman who gives birth to a child, regardless of whether she is the genetic mother or subsequently brings up the child

birth rate *n sociol* the ratio of live births to population, usually expressed per 1000 population per year

birthright *n* privileges or possessions that a person has or is believed to be entitled to as soon as he or she is born

biscuit *n* 1 a small flat dry sweet or plain cake 2 porcelain that has been fired but not glazed ▷ *adj* 3 pale brown or yellowish-grey ▶ HISTORY Old French (*pain*) *bescuit* twice-cooked (bread)

bisect *vb* 1 *maths* to divide into two equal parts 2 to cut or split into two ▶ HISTORY BI- + Latin *secare* to cut > **bisection** *n*

bisector *n geom* a straight line or plane that bisects an angle or another line

bisexual *adj* 1 sexually attracted to both men and women 2 showing characteristics of both sexes ▷ *n* 3 a bisexual person > **bisexuality** *n*

bishop *n* 1 a member of the clergy having spiritual and administrative powers over a diocese 2 a chessman capable of moving diagonally ▶ HISTORY Greek *episkopos* overseer

bishopric *n* the see, diocese, or office of a bishop

bismuth *n chem* a brittle pinkish-white metallic element. Some compounds are used in alloys and in medicine. Symbol: Bi ▶ HISTORY German *Wismut*

bison *n, pl* **-son** an animal of the cattle family with a massive head, shaggy forequarters, and a humped back ▶ HISTORY Germanic

bisque[1] *n* a thick rich soup made from shellfish ▶ HISTORY French

bisque[2] *adj* 1 pink-to-yellowish-tan ▷ *n* 2 *ceramics* same as **biscuit** (sense 2) ▶ HISTORY shortened from *biscuit*

bistable *adj* (of an electronic system) having two stable states

bistro *n, pl* **-tros** a small restaurant ▶ HISTORY French

bit[1] *n* 1 a small piece, portion, or quantity 2 a short time or distance 3 **a bit** rather; somewhat: *a bit stupid* 4 **a bit of** rather: *a bit of a fool* 5 **bit by bit** gradually 6 **do one's bit** to make one's expected contribution ▶ HISTORY Old English *bite* action of biting

bit[2] *n* 1 a metal mouthpiece on a bridle for controlling a horse 2 a cutting or drilling tool, part, or head in a brace, drill, etc. ▶ HISTORY Old English *bita*

bit[3] *vb* the past tense of **bite**

bit[4] *n maths, computers* 1 a single digit of binary notation, represented either by 0 or by 1 2 the smallest unit of information, indicating the presence or absence of a single feature ▶ HISTORY b(*inary*) + *dig*)it

bitch *n* 1 a female dog, fox, or wolf 2 *slang, offensive* a malicious or spiteful woman 3 *informal* a difficult situation or problem ▷ *vb* 4 *informal* to complain; grumble ▶ HISTORY Old English *bicce*

bitchy *adj* **bitchier, bitchiest** *informal* spiteful or malicious > **bitchiness** *n*

bite *vb* **biting, bit, bitten** 1 to grip, cut off, or tear with the teeth or jaws 2 (of animals or insects) to

77

injure by puncturing (the skin) with the teeth or fangs **3** (of corrosive material) to eat away or into **4** to smart or cause to smart; sting **5** *angling* (of a fish) to take the bait or lure **6** to take firm hold of or act effectively upon: *turn the screw till it bites the wood* **7** *slang* to annoy or worry: *what's biting her?* ▷ *n* **8** the act of biting **9** a thing or amount bitten off **10** a wound or sting inflicted by biting **11** *angling* an attempt by a fish to take the bait or lure **12** a snack **13** a stinging or smarting sensation ▸ HISTORY Old English *bītan* > **biter** *n*

biting *adj* **1** piercing; keen: *a biting wind* **2** sarcastic; incisive

bitmap *n computers* a picture created by colour or shading on a visual display unit

bit part *n* a very small acting role with few lines to speak

bitter *adj* **1** having an unpalatable harsh taste, as the peel of an orange **2** showing or caused by hostility or resentment **3** difficult to accept: *a bitter blow* **4** sarcastic: *bitter words* **5** bitingly cold: *a bitter night* ▷ *n* **6** *Brit* beer with a slightly bitter taste ▸ HISTORY Old English *biter* > **bitterly** *adv* > **bitterness** *n*

bittern *n* a large wading marsh bird with a booming call ▸ HISTORY Old French *butor*

bitters *pl n* bitter-tasting spirits flavoured with plant extracts

bittersweet *adj* **1** tasting of or being a mixture of bitterness and sweetness **2** pleasant but tinged with sadness

bitty *adj* **-tier, -tiest** lacking unity; disjointed > **bittiness** *n*

bitumen *n* a sticky or solid substance that occurs naturally in asphalt and tar and is used in road surfacing ▸ HISTORY Latin > **bituminous** *adj*

bituminous coal *n* a soft black coal that burns with a smoky yellow flame

bivalve *n* **1** a sea creature, such as an oyster or mussel, that has a shell consisting of two hinged valves and breathes through gills ▷ *adj* **2** of these molluscs

bivouac *n* **1** a temporary camp, as used by soldiers or mountaineers ▷ *vb* **-acking, -acked** **2** to make a temporary camp ▸ HISTORY French

biz *n informal* business

bizarre *adj* odd or unusual, esp. in an interesting or amusing way ▸ HISTORY Italian *bizzarro* capricious

Bk *chem* berkelium

BL **1** *chiefly Brit* Bachelor of Law **2** Bachelor of Letters **3** Barrister-at-Law

blab *vb* **blabbing, blabbed** to divulge (secrets) indiscreetly ▸ HISTORY Germanic

blabber *n* **1** a person who blabs ▷ *vb* **2** to talk without thinking ▸ HISTORY Middle English *blabberen*

black *adj* **1** having no hue, owing to the absorption of all or almost all light; of the colour of coal **2** without light **3** without hope; gloomy: *the future looked black* **4** dirty or soiled **5** angry or resentful: *black looks* **6** unpleasant in a cynical or macabre manner: *black comedy* **7** (of coffee or tea) without

milk or cream **8** wicked or harmful: *a black lie* ▷ *n* **9** the darkest colour; the colour of coal **10** a dye or pigment producing this colour **11** black clothing, worn esp. in mourning: *she was in black, as though in mourning* **12** complete darkness: *the black of the night* **13** **in the black** in credit or without debt ▷ *vb* **14** same as **blacken** **15** to polish (shoes or boots) with blacking **16** *Brit, Austral & NZ* (of trade unionists) to organize a boycott of (specified goods, work, etc.) ▸ See also **blackout** ▸ HISTORY Old English *blæc* > **blackness** *n* > **blackish** *adj*

Black *adj* **1** of or relating to a race of people with dark skin **2** of or relating to a Black person or Black people ▷ *n* **3** a member of a dark-skinned race

black-and-blue *adj* (of the skin) bruised, as from a beating

black-and-white *adj* **1** a photograph, film, etc. in black, white, and shades of grey, rather than in colour **2** **in black and white a** in print or writing **b** in extremes: *he always sees things in black and white*

black-backed gull *n* a large common black-and-white European gull

blackball¹ *vb* **1** to vote against **2** to exclude (someone) from a group, etc. ▸ HISTORY from *black ball*, used formerly to veto

blackball² *n NZ* hard boiled sweet with black-and-white stripes

black bear *n* **1** a bear inhabiting forests of North America **2** a bear of central and E Asia

black belt *n judo, karate, etc.* **a** a black belt that signifies that the wearer has reached a high standard in martial art **b** a person entitled to wear this

blackberry *n, pl* **-ries** a small blackish edible fruit that grows on a woody bush with thorny stems. Also called: **bramble**

blackbird *n* a common European thrush, the male of which has black plumage and a yellow bill

blackboard *n* a hard or rigid surface made of a smooth usually dark substance, used for writing or drawing on with chalk, esp. in teaching

black box *n informal* a flight recorder

black cake *n* a rich, dark cake containing fruit and rum, traditionally eaten in the Caribbean at Christmas

blackcap *n* a brownish-grey warbler, the male of which has a black crown

blackcock *n* the male of the black grouse

blackcurrant *n* a very small blackish edible fruit that grows in bunches on a bush

blackdamp *n* air that is low in oxygen content and high in carbon dioxide as a result of an explosion in a mine

Black Death *n history* **the Black Death** a form of bubonic plague in Europe and Asia during the 14th century

black economy *n Brit, Austral & NZ* that portion of the income of a nation that remains illegally undeclared

blacken *vb* **1** to make or become black or dirty **2** to damage (someone's reputation); discredit: *they planned to blacken my father's name*

black eye *n* bruising round the eye

Black Friar *n* a Dominican friar

blackguard (**blag**-gard) *n* an unprincipled contemptible person ▶ HISTORY originally, lowest group at court

blackhead *n* **1** a black-tipped plug of fatty matter clogging a pore of the skin **2** a bird with black plumage on the head

black hole *n* *astron* a hypothetical region of space resulting from the collapse of a star and surrounded by a gravitational field from which neither matter nor radiation can escape

black ice *n* a thin transparent layer of new ice on a road

blacking *n* any preparation for giving a black finish to shoes, metals, etc.

blackjack¹ *n* pontoon or a similar card game ▶ HISTORY *black* + *jack* (the knave)

blackjack² *n* *chiefly US & Canad* a truncheon of leather-covered lead with a flexible shaft ▶ HISTORY *black* + *jack* (implement)

black lead *n* same as **graphite**

blackleg *n* *Brit* **1** a person who continues to work or does another's job during a strike ▷ *vb* **-legging, -legged** **2** to refuse to join a strike

blacklist *n* **1** a list of people or organizations considered untrustworthy or disloyal ▷ *vb* **2** to put (someone) on a blacklist

black magic *n* magic used for evil purposes

blackmail *n* **1** the act of attempting to obtain money by threatening to reveal shameful information **2** the use of unfair pressure in an attempt to influence someone ▷ *vb* **3** to obtain or attempt to obtain money by intimidation **4** to attempt to influence (a person) by unfair pressure ▶ HISTORY *black* + Old English *māl* terms > **blackmailer** *n*

Black Maria (mar-**rye**-a) *n* a police van for transporting prisoners

black market *n* a place or a system for buying or selling goods or currencies illegally, esp. in violation of controls or rationing > **black marketeer** *n*

blackout *n* **1** (in wartime) the putting out or hiding of all lights as a precaution against a night air attack **2** a momentary loss of consciousness, vision, or memory **3** a temporary electrical power failure **4** the prevention of information broadcasts: *a news blackout* ▷ *vb* **black out** **5** to put out (lights) **6** to lose vision, consciousness, or memory temporarily **7** to stop (news, a television programme, etc.) from being broadcast

Black Power *n* *hist* (esp. in the US) a movement of Black people to obtain equality with White people

black pudding *n* *Brit* a black sausage made from pig's blood, suet, etc.

Black Rod *n* (in Britain) the chief usher of the House of Lords and of the Order of the Garter

black sheep *n* a person who is regarded as a disgrace or failure by his or her family or peer group

Blackshirt *n* a member of the Italian Fascist party before and during the Second World War

blacksmith *n* a person who works iron with a furnace, anvil, and hammer

black spot *n* **1** a place on a road where accidents frequently occur **2** an area where a particular situation is exceptionally bad: *an unemployment black spot*

Black Stone *n* **the Black Stone** *Islam* a stone in the Kaaba in Mecca, believed by Muslims to have been sent to Earth by God

blackthorn *n* a thorny shrub with black twigs, white flowers, and small sour plumlike fruits

Black Thursday *n* *history* 24 October, 1929, the date that the American stock market crashed, marking the beginning of the Great Depression

Black Watch *n* **the Black Watch** the Royal Highland Regiment in the British Army

black widow *n* an American spider, the female of which is highly venomous and commonly eats its mate

bladder *n* **1** *anat* a membranous sac, usually containing liquid, esp. the urinary bladder **2** a hollow bag made of leather, etc. which becomes round when filled with air or liquid **3** a hollow saclike part in certain plants, such as seaweed ▶ HISTORY Old English *blædre* > **bladdery** *adj*

blade *n* **1** the part of a sharp weapon, tool, or knife that forms the cutting edge **2** the thin flattish part of a propeller, oar, or fan **3** the flattened part of a leaf, sepal, or petal **4** the long narrow leaf of a grass or related plant ▶ HISTORY Old English *blæd*

blain *n* a blister, blotch, or sore on the skin ▶ HISTORY Old English *blegen*

blame *vb* **blaming, blamed** **1** to consider (someone) responsible for: *I blame her for the failure* **2** (foll. by *on*) to put responsibility for (something) on (someone): *she blames the failure on me* **3 be to blame** to be at fault ▷ *n* **4** responsibility for something that is wrong: *they must take the blame for the failure* **5** an expression of condemnation: *analysts lay the blame on party activists* ▶ HISTORY Late Latin *blasphemare* to blaspheme > **blamable** *or* **blameable** *adj* > **blameless** *adj*

blameworthy *adj* deserving blame > **blameworthiness** *n*

blanch *vb* **1** to whiten **2** to become pale, as with sickness or fear **3** to prepare (meat or vegetables) by plunging them in boiling water **4** to cause (celery, chicory, etc.) to grow white from lack of light ▶ HISTORY Old French *blanc* white

blancmange (blam-**monzh**) *n* a jelly-like dessert of milk, stiffened usually with cornflour ▶ HISTORY Old French *blanc manger* white food

bland *adj* **1** dull and uninteresting: *the bland predictability of the film* **2** smooth in manner: *he looked at his visitor with a bland smile* ▶ HISTORY Latin *blandus* flattering > **blandly** *adv*

blandishments *pl n* flattery intended to coax or cajole

blank *adj* **1** (of a writing surface) not written on **2** (of a form, etc.) with spaces left for details to be filled in **3** without ornament or break: *a blank wall* **4** empty or void: *a blank space* **5** showing no interest or expression: *a blank look* **6** lacking ideas or inspiration: *his mind went blank* ▷ *n* **7** an empty space **8** an empty space for writing in **9** the condition of not understanding: *my mind went a complete blank* **10** a mark, often a dash, in place of a word **11 draw a blank** to get no results from something ▷ *vb* **12** (foll. by *out*) to cross out, blot, or obscure **13** *slang* to ignore: *the crowd blanked her for the first four numbers* ▶ **HISTORY** Old French *blanc* white ▷ **blankly** *adv*

blank cheque *n* **1** a signed cheque on which the amount payable has not been specified **2** complete freedom of action

blanket *n* **1** a large piece of thick cloth for use as a bed covering **2** a concealing cover, as of smoke, leaves, or snow ▷ *adj* **3** applying to or covering a wide group or variety of people, conditions, situations, etc.: *a blanket ban on all supporters travelling to away matches* ▷ *vb* **-keting, -keted** **4** to cover as if with a blanket **5** to cover a wide area; give blanket coverage to ▶ **HISTORY** Old French *blancquete*

blank verse *n* *prosody* unrhymed verse, esp. in iambic pentameters

blare *vb* **blaring, blared** **1** to sound loudly and harshly **2** to proclaim loudly: *the newspaper headlines blared the news* ▷ *n* **3** a loud harsh noise ▶ **HISTORY** Middle Dutch *bleren*

blarney *n* flattering talk ▶ **HISTORY** after the *Blarney* Stone in SW Ireland, said to endow whoever kisses it with skill in flattery

blasé (blah-**zay**) *adj* indifferent or bored, esp. through familiarity ▶ **HISTORY** French

blaspheme *vb* **-pheming, -phemed** **1** to speak disrespectfully of (God or sacred things) **2** to utter curses ▶ **HISTORY** Greek *blasphēmos* evil-speaking > **blasphemer** *n*

blasphemy *n*, *pl* **-mies** behaviour or language that shows disrespect for God or sacred things > **blasphemous** *adj*

blast *n* **1** an explosion, such as that caused by dynamite **2** the charge used in a single explosion **3** a sudden strong gust of wind or air **4** a sudden loud sound, such as that made by a trumpet **5** a violent verbal outburst, esp. critical **6** *US & Austral. slang* a very enjoyable or thrilling experience: *the party was a blast* **7 at full blast** at maximum speed, volume, etc. ▷ *interj* **8** an exclamation of annoyance ▷ *vb* **9** to blow up (a rock, tunnel, etc.) with explosives **10** to make or cause to make a loud harsh noise **11** to criticize severely ▶ **HISTORY** Old English *blæst*

blasted *adj*, *adv* *slang* extreme or extremely: *a blasted idiot*

blast furnace *n* a furnace for smelting using a blast of preheated air

blastoff *n* **1** the launching of a rocket under its own power ▷ *vb* **blast off** **2** (of a rocket) to be launched

blastula *n* *biol* an early form of an animal embryo, consisting of a sphere of cells with a central cavity

blatant (**blay**-tant) *adj* **1** glaringly obvious: *a blatant lie* **2** offensively noticeable: *their blatant*

disregard for my feelings ▶ **HISTORY** coined by Edmund Spenser, poet > **blatantly** *adv*

blather *vb*, *n* same as **blether**

blaze¹ *n* **1** a strong fire or flame **2** a very bright light or glare **3** an outburst (of passion, patriotism, etc.) ▷ *vb* **blazing, blazed** **4** to burn fiercely **5** to shine brightly **6** to become stirred, as with anger or excitement **7 blaze away** to shoot continuously ▶ **HISTORY** Old English *blæse*

blaze² *n* **1** a mark, usually indicating a path, made on a tree **2** a light-coloured marking on the face of an animal ▷ *vb* **blazing, blazed** **3** to mark (a tree, path, etc.) with a blaze **4 blaze a trail** to explore new territories, areas of knowledge, etc. ▶ **HISTORY** probably from Middle Low German *bles* white marking

blaze³ *vb* **blazing, blazed** • **blaze something abroad** to make something widely known ▶ **HISTORY** Middle Dutch *blāsen*

blazer *n* a fairly lightweight jacket, often in the colours of a sports club, school, etc.

blazon *vb* **1** to proclaim publicly: *the newspaper photographs were blazoned on the front pages* **2** *heraldry* to describe or colour (heraldic arms) conventionally ▷ *n* **3** *heraldry* a coat of arms ▶ **HISTORY** Old French *blason* coat of arms

bleach *vb* **1** to make or become white or colourless by exposure to sunlight, or by the action of chemical agents ▷ *n* **2** a bleaching agent ▶ **HISTORY** Old English *blǣcan*

bleaching powder *n* a white powder consisting of chlorinated calcium hydroxide

bleak *adj* **1** exposed and barren **2** cold and raw **3** offering little hope; dismal: *a bleak future* ▶ **HISTORY** Old English *blāc* pale > **bleakly** *adv* > **bleakness** *n*

bleary *adj* **blearier, bleariest** **1** with eyes dimmed, by tears or tiredness: *a few bleary hacks* **2** indistinct or unclear > **blearily** *adv*

bleat *vb* **1** (of a sheep, goat, or calf) to utter its plaintive cry **2** to whine ▷ *n* **3** the characteristic cry of sheep, goats, and calves **4** a weak complaint or whine ▶ **HISTORY** Old English *blǣtan*

bleed *vb* **bleeding, bled** **1** to lose or emit blood **2** to remove or draw blood from (a person or animal) **3** (of plants) to exude (sap or resin), esp. from a cut **4** *informal* to obtain money, etc. from (someone), esp. by extortion **5** to draw liquid or gas from (a container or enclosed system) **6 my heart bleeds for you** I am sorry for you: often used ironically ▶ **HISTORY** Old English *blēdan*

bleep *n* **1** a short high-pitched signal made by an electrical device **2** same as **bleeper** ▷ *vb* **3** to make a bleeping signal **4** to call (someone) by means of a bleeper ▶ **HISTORY** imitative

bleeper *n* a small portable radio receiver that makes a bleeping signal

blemish *n* **1** a defect; flaw; stain ▷ *vb* **2** to spoil or tarnish ▶ **HISTORY** Old French *blemir* to make pale

blench *vb* to shy away, as in fear ▶ **HISTORY** Old English *blencan* to deceive

blend *vb* **1** to mix or mingle (components) **2** to mix (different varieties of tea, whisky, etc.) **3** to look good together; harmonize **4** (esp. of colours) to shade gradually into each other ▷ *n* **5** a mixture produced by blending **6** a word formed by joining the beginning and end of two other words: *'brunch' is a blend of 'breakfast' and 'lunch'* ▶ HISTORY Old English *blandan*

blende *n* a mineral consisting mainly of zinc sulphide: the chief source of zinc

blender *n* an electrical kitchen appliance for pureeing vegetables, etc.

blenny *n, pl* **-nies** a small fish of coastal waters with a tapering scaleless body and long fins ▶ HISTORY Greek *blennos* slime

bless *vb* **blessing, blessed** *or* **blest** **1** to make holy by means of a religious rite **2** to give honour or glory to (a person or thing) as holy **3** to call upon God to protect **4** to worship or adore (God) **5 be blessed with** to be endowed with: *she is blessed with immense energy* **6 bless me!** an exclamation of surprise **7 bless you!** *spoken* said to a person who has just sneezed ▶ HISTORY Old English *blædsian* to sprinkle with sacrificial blood

blessed *adj* **1** made holy **2** RC Church (of a person) beatified by the pope **3** bringing great happiness or good fortune: *he was blessed with good looks* **4** *euphemistic* damned: *I'm blessed if I know*

blessing *n* **1** the act of invoking divine protection or aid **2** approval; good wishes **3** a happy event

blether *Scot vb* **1** to speak foolishly at length ▷ *n* **2** foolish talk **3** a person who blethers ▶ HISTORY Old Norse *blathr* nonsense

blew *vb* the past tense of **blow**

blight *n* **1** a person or thing that spoils or prevents growth **2** any plant disease characterized by withering and shrivelling without rotting **3** a fungus or insect that causes blight in plants **4** an ugly urban district ▷ *vb* **5** to cause to suffer a blight **6** to frustrate or disappoint: *blighted love* **7** to destroy: *the event blighted her life* ▶ HISTORY origin unknown

blighter *n Brit, Austral & NZ, informal* a despicable or irritating person or thing

Blighty *n Brit, Austral & NZ, slang* (used esp. by troops serving abroad) **1** Britain; home **2** (*pl* **Blighties**) (esp. in the First World War) a wound that causes the recipient to be sent home to Britain ▶ HISTORY Hindi *bilāyatī* foreign land

blimey *interj Brit & NZ, slang* an exclamation of surprise or annoyance ▶ HISTORY short for *gorblimey* God blind me

blimp[1] *n* **1** a small nonrigid airship **2** *films* a soundproof cover fixed over a camera during shooting ▶ HISTORY probably from (*type*) B-limp

blimp[2] *n chiefly Brit* a person who is stupidly complacent and reactionary. Also called: **Colonel Blimp** ▶ HISTORY a cartoon character

blind *adj* **1** unable to see **2** unable or unwilling to understand: *she is blind to his faults* **3** not determined by reason: *blind hatred* **4** acting or performed without control or preparation **5** done without being able to see, relying on instruments

for information **6** hidden from sight: *a blind corner* **7** closed at one end: *a blind alley* **8** completely lacking awareness or consciousness: *a blind stupor* **9** having no openings: *a blind wall* ▷ *adv* **10** without being able to see ahead or using only instruments: *flying blind* **11** without adequate information: *we bought the house blind* **12 blind drunk** *informal* very drunk ▷ *vb* **13** to deprive of sight permanently or temporarily **14** to deprive of good sense, reason, or judgment **15** to darken; conceal **16** to overwhelm by showing detailed knowledge: *he tried to blind us with science* ▷ *n* **17** a shade for a window **18** any obstruction or hindrance to sight, light, or air **19** a person, action, or thing that serves to deceive or conceal the truth ▶ HISTORY Old English > **blinding** *adj* > **blindly** *adv* > **blindness** *n*

blind alley *n* **1** an alley open at one end only **2** *informal* a situation in which no further progress can be made

blind date *n informal* a prearranged social meeting between two people who have not met before

blindfold *vb* **1** to prevent (a person or animal) from seeing by covering the eyes ▷ *n* **2** a piece of cloth used to cover the eyes ▷ *adj, adv* **3** having the eyes covered with a cloth ▶ HISTORY Old English *blindfellian* to strike blind

blind man's buff *n* a game in which a blindfolded person tries to catch and identify the other players ▶ HISTORY obsolete *buff* a blow

blind spot *n* **1** a small oval-shaped area of the retina which is unable to see **2** a place where vision is obscured **3** a subject about which a person is ignorant or prejudiced

blindworm *n* same as **slowworm**

blink *vb* **1** to close and immediately reopen (the eyes), usually involuntarily **2** to shine intermittently or unsteadily ▷ *n* **3** the act or an instance of blinking **4** a glance; glimpse **5 on the blink** *slang* not working properly ▶ HISTORY variant of BLENCH

blinker *vb* **1** to provide (a horse) with blinkers **2** to obscure or be obscured with or as with blinkers

blinkered *adj* **1** considering only a narrow point of view **2** (of a horse) wearing blinkers

blinkers *pl n Brit & Austral* leather side pieces attached to a horse's bridle to prevent sideways vision

blip *n* **1** a repetitive sound, such as the kind produced by an electronic device **2** the spot of light on a radar screen indicating the position of an object **3** a temporary irregularity in the performance of something ▶ HISTORY imitative

bliss *n* **1** perfect happiness; serene joy **2** the joy of heaven ▶ HISTORY Old English *blīths* > **blissful** *adj* > **blissfully** *adv*

blister *n* **1** a small bubble on the skin filled with a watery fluid **2** a swelling containing air or liquid, such as on a painted surface ▷ *vb* **3** to have or cause to have blisters **4** to attack verbally with great scorn ▶ HISTORY Old French *blestre* > **blistering** *adj*

blithe *adj* **1** heedless; casual and indifferent **2** very happy or cheerful ▸ HISTORY Old English *blīthe* > **blithely** *adv*

blithering *adj* *informal* stupid; foolish: *you blithering idiot* ▸ HISTORY variant of *blethering*

BLitt Bachelor of Letters ▸ HISTORY Latin *Baccalaureus Litterarum*

blitz *n* **1** a violent and sustained attack by enemy aircraft **2** any intensive attack or concerted effort ▷ *vb* **3** to attack suddenly and intensively ▸ HISTORY see BLITZKRIEG

Blitz *n* **the Blitz** the systematic bombing of Britain in 1940–41 by the German Air Force

blitzkrieg *n* a swift intensive military attack designed to defeat the opposition quickly ▸ HISTORY German: lightning war

blizzard *n* a blinding storm of wind and snow ▸ HISTORY origin unknown

bloat *vb* **1** to cause to swell, as with a liquid or air **2** to cause to be puffed up, as with conceit **3** to cure (fish, esp. herring) by half drying in smoke ▸ HISTORY Old Norse *blautr* soaked > **bloated** *adj*

bloater *n Brit* a herring that has been salted in brine, smoked, and cured

blob *n* **1** a soft mass or drop **2** a spot of colour, ink, etc. **3** an indistinct or shapeless form or object ▸ HISTORY imitative

bloc *n* a group of people or countries combined by a common interest ▸ HISTORY French

block *n* **1** a large solid piece of wood, stone, etc. **2** such a piece on which particular tasks may be done, as chopping, cutting, etc. **3** a large building of offices, flats, etc. **4** a group of buildings in a city bounded by intersecting streets on each side **5** an obstruction or hindrance: *a writer with a block* **6** one of a set of wooden or plastic cubes as a child's toy **7** *slang* a person's head **8** a piece of wood, metal, etc. engraved for printing **9** a casing housing one or more freely rotating pulleys. See also **block and tackle** **10** a quantity considered as a single unit ▷ *vb* **11** to obstruct or impede by introducing an obstacle: *lorry drivers had blocked the routes to Paris* **12** to impede, retard, or prevent (an action or procedure) **13** to stamp (a title or design) on (a book cover, etc.) **14** *cricket* to play (a ball) defensively ▷ See also **block out** ▸ HISTORY Dutch *blok* > **blockage** *n*

blockade *n* **1** *mil* the closing off of a port or region to prevent the passage of goods ▷ *vb* **-ading, -aded** **2** to impose a blockade on

block and tackle *n* a hoisting device in which a rope or chain is passed around a pair of blocks containing one or more pulleys

blockbuster *n informal* **1** a film, novel, etc. that has been or is expected to be highly successful **2** a large bomb used to demolish extensive areas

block disintegration *n geol* breaking up of rocks caused by repeated expansion and contraction due to changes in temperature

block fault *n geol* the structure formed when faults divide the crust into blocks of different heights

blockhead *n* a stupid person > **blockheaded** *adj*

block letter *n* a plain capital letter. Also called: **block capital**

block mountain *n* See **fault-block mountain**

block out *vb* **1** to plan or describe (something) in a general fashion **2** to prevent the entry or consideration of (something)

blog *n* **1** Short for: **weblog** a person's online journal ▷ *vb* **-gging, -gged** **2** to write a blog **3** to write about (a subject) in a blog > **blogger** *n* > **blogging** *n*

bloke *n Brit, Austral & NZ, informal* a man ▸ HISTORY Shelta > **blokeish** or **blokey** *adj*

blonde *or masc* **blond** *adj* **1** (of hair) fair **2** (of a person) having fair hair and a light complexion ▷ *n* **3** a person having light-coloured hair and skin ▸ HISTORY Old French > **blondeness** *or masc* **blondness** *n*

blood *n* **1** a reddish fluid in vertebrates that is pumped by the heart through the arteries and veins. *Related adjective:* **haemal** **2** bloodshed, esp. when resulting in murder: *they were responsible for the spilling of blood throughout the country* **3** life itself; lifeblood **4** relationship through being of the same family, race, or kind; kinship **5 the blood** royal or noble descent: *a prince of the blood* **6 flesh and blood** **a** near kindred or kinship, esp. that between a parent and child **b** human nature: *it's more than flesh and blood can stand* **7 in one's blood** as a natural or inherited characteristic or talent **8** newcomers viewed as an invigorating force: *new blood* **9 in cold blood** showing no passion; ruthlessly **10 make one's blood boil** to cause to be angry or indignant **11 make one's blood run cold** to fill with horror ▷ *vb* **12** *hunting* to cause (young hounds) to taste the blood of a freshly killed quarry **13** to initiate (a person) to war or hunting ▸ HISTORY Old English *blōd*

blood-and-thunder *adj* denoting melodramatic behaviour

blood bank *n* a place where blood is stored until required for transfusion

blood bath *n* a massacre

blood brother *n* a man or boy who has sworn to treat another as his brother, often in a ceremony in which their blood is mingled

blood count *n* determination of the number of red and white blood corpuscles in a specific sample of blood

bloodcurdling *adj* terrifying

blood donor *n* a person who gives blood to be used for transfusion

blood group *n* any one of the various groups into which human blood is classified

blood heat *n* the normal temperature of the human body, 98.4°F or 37°C

bloodhound *n* a large hound, formerly used in tracking and police work

bloodless *adj* **1** without blood: *bloodless surgery* **2** conducted without violence: *a bloodless coup* **3** anaemic-looking; pale **4** lacking vitality; lifeless: *the bloodless ambience of supermarkets*

blood-letting n **1** bloodshed, esp. in a feud **2** the former medical practice of removing blood

blood money n **1** money obtained by ruthlessly sacrificing others **2** money paid to a hired murderer **3** compensation paid to the relatives of a murdered person

blood orange n a variety of orange the pulp of which is dark red when ripe

blood poisoning n same as **septicaemia**

blood pressure n the pressure exerted by the blood on the inner walls of the blood vessels

blood relation or **relative** n a person related by birth

bloodshed n slaughter; killing

bloodshot adj (of an eye) inflamed

blood sport n any sport involving the killing of an animal

bloodstained adj discoloured with blood

bloodstock n thoroughbred horses

bloodstream n the flow of blood through the vessels of a living body

bloodsucker n **1** an animal that sucks blood, esp. a leech **2** informal a person who preys upon another person, esp. by extorting money

bloodthirsty adj **-thirstier, -thirstiest** taking pleasure in bloodshed or violence

blood ties pl n connections between people who are related by birth

blood vessel n a tube through which blood travels in the body

bloody adj **bloodier, bloodiest 1** covered with blood **2** marked by much killing and bloodshed: a bloody war **3** cruel or murderous: a bloody tyrant ▷ adj, adv **4** slang extreme or extremely: a bloody fool; a bloody good idea ▷ vb **bloodies, bloodying, bloodied 5** to stain with blood

Bloody Mary n a drink consisting of tomato juice and vodka

bloody-minded adj Brit & NZ, informal deliberately obstructive and unhelpful

bloom n **1** a blossom on a flowering plant **2** the state or period when flowers open **3** a healthy or flourishing condition; prime **4** a youthful or healthy glow **5** a fine whitish coating on the surface of fruits or leaves ▷ vb **6** (of flowers) to open **7** to bear flowers **8** to flourish or grow **9** to be in a healthy, glowing condition ▶ HISTORY Germanic

bloomer n Brit, informal a stupid mistake; blunder ▶ HISTORY from BLOOMING

bloomers pl n **1** informal women's baggy knickers **2** (formerly) loose trousers gathered at the knee worn by women ▶ HISTORY after Mrs A. Bloomer, social reformer

blooming adv, adj Brit, informal extreme or extremely: blooming painful ▶ HISTORY euphemistic for bloody

blossom n **1** the flower or flowers of a plant, esp. producing edible fruit **2** the period of flowering ▷ vb **3** (of plants) to flower **4** to come to a promising stage ▶ HISTORY Old English blōstm

blot n **1** a stain or spot, esp. of ink **2** something that spoils **3** a stain on one's character ▷ vb **blotting,**

blotted 4 to stain or spot **5** to cause a blemish in or on: he blotted his copybook by missing a penalty **6** to soak up (excess ink, etc.) by using blotting paper **7 blot out a** to darken or hide completely: the mist blotted out the sea **b** to block from one's mind: to blot out the memories ▶ HISTORY Germanic

blotch n **1** an irregular spot or discoloration ▷ vb **2** to become or cause to become marked by such discoloration ▶ HISTORY probably from botch, influenced by blot > **blotchy** adj

blotter n a sheet of blotting paper

blotting paper n a soft absorbent paper, used for soaking up surplus ink

blotto adj Brit, Austral & NZ, slang extremely drunk ▶ HISTORY from blot (verb)

blouse n **1** a woman's shirtlike garment **2** a waist-length belted jacket worn by soldiers ▷ vb **blousing, bloused 3** to hang or cause to hang in full loose folds ▶ HISTORY French

blouson (**blew**-zon) n a short loose jacket with a tight-fitting waist ▶ HISTORY French

blow¹ vb **blowing, blew, blown 1** (of a current of air, the wind, etc.) to be or cause to be in motion **2** to move or be carried by or as if by wind **3** to expel (air, etc.) through the mouth or nose **4** to breathe hard; pant **5** to inflate with air or the breath **6** (of wind, etc.) to make a roaring sound **7** to cause (a musical instrument) to sound by forcing air into it **8** (often foll. by up, down, in) to explode, break, or disintegrate completely **9** electronics (of a fuse or valve) to burn out because of excessive current **10** to shape (glass, etc.) by forcing air or gas through the material when molten **11** slang to spend (money) freely **12** slang to use (an opportunity) ineffectively **13** slang to expose or betray (a secret) **14** (past participle **blowed**) informal same as **damn 15 blow hot and cold** informal to keep changing one's attitude towards someone or something **16 blow one's top** informal to lose one's temper ▷ n **17** the act or an instance of blowing **18** the sound produced by blowing **19** a blast of air or wind **20** Brit, slang cannabis ▷ See also **blow away, blow out**, etc. ▶ HISTORY Old English blāwan

blow² n **1** a powerful or heavy stroke with the fist, a weapon, etc. **2** a sudden setback: the scheme was dealt a blow by the introduction of martial law **3** an attacking action: a blow for freedom **4 come to blows a** to fight **b** to result in a fight ▶ HISTORY probably Germanic

blow away vb US, slang **1** to kill by shooting **2** to defeat utterly

blow-by-blow adj explained in great detail: a blow-by-blow account

blow-dry vb **-dries, -drying, -dried 1** to style (the hair) while drying it with a hand-held hair dryer ▷ n **2** this method of styling hair

blower n **1** a mechanical device, such as a fan, that blows **2** informal a telephone

blowfly n, pl **-flies** a fly that lays its eggs in meat

blowhole n **1** the nostril of a whale **2** a hole in ice through which seals, etc. breathe **3** a vent for air or gas **4** geol a hole in a cliff top leading to a sea cave

blowie *n* *Austral, informal* a bluebottle

blown *vb* a past participle of **blow**

blow out *vb* **1** (of a flame) to extinguish or be extinguished **2** (of a tyre) to puncture suddenly **3** (of an oil or gas well) to lose oil or gas in an uncontrolled manner ▷ *n* **blowout 4** a sudden burst in a tyre **5** the uncontrolled escape of oil or gas from a well **6** *slang* a large filling meal **7** *geol* a wind-eroded depression in a land surface or sand dune

blow over *vb* **1** to be forgotten **2** to cease or be finished: *the crisis blew over*

blowpipe *n* **1** a long tube from which poisoned darts, etc. are shot by blowing **2** a tube for blowing air into a flame to intensify its heat **3** an iron pipe used to blow glass into shape

blowsy *adj* **blowsier, blowsiest** (of a woman) **1** slovenly or sluttish **2** ruddy in complexion ▸ HISTORY dialect *blowze* beggar girl

blowtorch *or* **blowlamp** *n* a small burner that produces a very hot flame, used to remove old paint, soften metal, etc.

blow up *vb* **1** to explode or cause to explode **2** to inflate with air **3** to increase the importance of (something): *an affair blown up out of all proportion* **4** *informal* to lose one's temper **5** *informal* to reprimand (someone) **6** *informal* to enlarge (a photograph) **7** to come into existence with sudden force: *a crisis had blown up* ▷ *n* **blow-up 8** *informal* an enlarged photograph

blowy *adj* **blowier, blowiest** windy

blubber *n* **1** the fatty tissue of aquatic mammals such as the whale **2** *informal* flabby body fat ▷ *vb* **3** to sob without restraint ▸ HISTORY probably imitative

bludge *Austral & NZ, informal vb* **bludging, bludged 1** (foll. by *on*) to scrounge from **2** to evade work ▷ *n* **3** a very easy task

bludgeon *n* **1** a stout heavy club, typically thicker at one end ▷ *vb* **2** to hit as if with a bludgeon **3** to force; bully; coerce ▸ HISTORY origin unknown

blue *n* **1** the colour of a clear unclouded sky **2** anything blue, such as blue clothing or blue paint: *she is clothed in blue* **3** a sportsman who represents or has represented Oxford or Cambridge University **4** *Brit, informal* a Tory **5** *Austral & NZ, slang* an argument or fight **6** Also: **bluey** *Austral & NZ, slang* a court summons **7** *Austral & NZ, informal* a mistake **8 out of the blue** unexpectedly ▷ *adj* **bluer, bluest 9** of the colour blue; of the colour of a clear unclouded sky **10** (of the flesh) having a purple tinge from cold **11** depressed or unhappy **12** pornographic: *blue movies* ▷ *vb* **blueing** *or* **bluing, blued 13** to make or become blue or bluer **14** *old-fashioned, informal* to spend extravagantly or wastefully: *I consoled myself by blueing my royalty cheque* ▷ See also **blues** ▸ HISTORY Old French *bleu* > **blueness** *n*

blue baby *n* a baby born with a bluish tinge to the skin because of lack of oxygen in the blood

bluebell *n* a woodland plant with blue bell-shaped flowers

blueberry *n, pl* **-ries** a very small blackish edible fruit that grows on a North American shrub

bluebird *n* a North American songbird with a blue plumage

blue blood *n* royal or aristocratic descent

bluebook *n* **1** (in Britain) a government publication, usually the report of a commission **2** (in Canada) an annual statement of government accounts

bluebottle *n* **1** a large fly with a dark-blue body; blowfly **2** *Austral & NZ, informal* a Portuguese man-of-war

blue cheese *n* cheese containing a blue mould, such as Stilton or Danish blue

blue chip *n* **1** *finance* a stock considered reliable ▷ *adj* **blue-chip 2** denoting something considered to be a valuable asset

blue-collar *adj* denoting manual industrial workers

blue-eyed boy *n* *Brit, Austral & NZ, informal* a favourite

blue funk *n* *slang* a state of great terror

blue heeler *n* *Austral & NZ, informal* a dog that controls cattle by biting their heels

blue pencil *n* **1** deletion or alteration of the contents of a book or other work ▷ *vb* **blue-pencil, -cilling, -cilled** *or* US **-ciling, -ciled 2** to alter or delete parts of (a book, film, etc.)

blue peter *n* a signal flag of blue with a white square at the centre, displayed by a vessel about to leave port

blueprint *n* **1** an original description of a plan or idea that explains how it is expected to work **2** a photographic print of plans, technical drawings, etc. consisting of white lines on a blue background

blue ribbon *n* **1** a badge awarded as the first prize in a competition **2** (in Britain) a badge of blue silk worn by members of the Order of the Garter

blues *pl n* **the blues 1** a feeling of depression or deep unhappiness **2** a type of folk song originating among Black Americans

bluestocking *n* *usually disparaging* a scholarly or intellectual woman ▸ HISTORY from the blue worsted stockings worn by members of an 18th-century literary society

bluetit *n* a small European bird with a blue crown, wings, and tail and yellow underparts

bluetongue *n* an Australian lizard with a blue tongue

blue whale *n* a very large bluish-grey whale: the largest mammal

bluff¹ *vb* **1** to pretend to be confident in order to influence (someone) ▷ *n* **2** deliberate deception to create the impression of a strong position **3 call someone's bluff** to challenge someone to give proof of his or her claims ▸ HISTORY Dutch *bluffen* to boast

bluff² *n* **1** a steep promontory, bank, or cliff **2** *Canad* a clump of trees on the prairie; copse ▷ *adj* **3** good-naturedly frank and hearty ▸ HISTORY probably from Middle Dutch *blaf* broad

bluish *or* **blueish** *adj* slightly blue

blunder *n* **1** a stupid or clumsy mistake ▷ *vb*
2 to make stupid or clumsy mistakes **3** to act
clumsily; stumble ▶ HISTORY Scandinavian
> **blundering** *n, adj*

blunderbuss *n* an obsolete gun with wide barrel
and flared muzzle ▶ HISTORY Dutch *donderbus*
thunder gun

blunt *adj* **1** (esp. of a knife) lacking sharpness
2 not having a sharp edge or point: *a blunt
instrument* **3** (of people, manner of speaking, etc.)
straightforward and uncomplicated ▷ *vb* **4** to
make less sharp **5** to diminish the sensitivity or
perception of: *prison life has blunted his mind*
▶ HISTORY Scandinavian > **bluntly** *adv*

blur *vb* **blurring, blurred** **1** to make or become
vague or less distinct **2** to smear or smudge **3** to
make (the judgment, memory, or perception) less
clear; dim ▷ *n* **4** something vague, hazy, or
indistinct **5** a smear or smudge ▶ HISTORY perhaps
variant of *blear* > **blurred** *adj* > **blurry** *adj*

blurb *n* a promotional description, such as on the
jackets of books ▶ HISTORY coined by G. Burgess,
humorist & illustrator

blurt *vb* (foll. by *out*) to utter suddenly and
involuntarily ▶ HISTORY probably imitative

blush *vb* **1** to become suddenly red in the face, esp.
from embarrassment or shame ▷ *n* **2** a sudden
reddening of the face, esp. from embarrassment or
shame **3** a rosy glow **4** same as **rosé** ▶ HISTORY
Old English *blўscan*

blusher *n* a cosmetic applied to the cheeks to give
a rosy colour

bluster *vb* **1** to speak loudly or in a bullying way
2 (of the wind) to be gusty ▷ *n* **3** empty threats or
protests ▶ HISTORY probably from Middle Low
German *blüsteren* to blow violently > **blustery** *adj*

BM **1** Bachelor of Medicine **2** British Museum

BMA British Medical Association

BMI body mass index: an index used to define
whether a person is overweight or underweight,
calculated by height and weight

B-movie *n* a film originally made as a supporting
film, now considered a genre in its own right

BMR basal metabolic rate

BMus Bachelor of Music

BO **1** *informal* body odour **2** box office

boa *n* **1** a large nonvenomous snake of Central and
South America that kills its prey by constriction
2 a woman's long thin scarf of feathers or fur
▶ HISTORY Latin

boab (boh-ab) *n Austral, informal* short for **baobab**

boa constrictor *n* a very large snake of tropical
America and the West Indies that kills its prey by
constriction

boar *n* **1** an uncastrated male pig **2** a wild pig
▶ HISTORY Old English *bār*

board *n* **1** a long wide flat piece of sawn timber
2 a smaller flat piece of rigid material for a specific
purpose: *ironing board* **3 a** a group of people who
officially administer a company, trust, etc.
b any other official group, such as examiners or
interviewers **4** a person's meals, provided regularly
for money **5** stiff cardboard or similar material,
used for the outside covers of a book **6** a flat thin
rectangular sheet of composite material, such as
chipboard **7** *naut* the side of a ship **8** a portable
surface for indoor games such as chess or
backgammon **9 go by the board** *informal* to be in
disuse, neglected, or lost **10 on board** on or in a
ship, aeroplane, etc. **11 the boards** the stage ▷ *vb*
12 to go aboard (a train or other vehicle) **13** to
attack (a ship) by forcing one's way aboard **14** (foll.
by *up, in*) to cover with boards **15** to receive meals
and lodging in return for money **16 board out** to
arrange for (someone, esp. a child) to receive food
and lodging away from home **17** (in ice hockey and
box lacrosse) to bodycheck an opponent against
the boards ▶ HISTORY Old English *bord*

boarder *n Brit* a pupil who lives at school during
term time

boarding house *n* a private house that provides
accommodation and meals for paying guests

boarding school *n* a school providing living
accommodation for pupils

boardroom *n* a room where the board of directors
of a company meets

boast *vb* **1** to speak in excessively proud terms of
one's possessions, talents, etc. **2** to possess
(something to be proud of): *a team which boasts
five current world record holders* ▷ *n* **3** a bragging
statement **4** something that is bragged about:
this proved to be a false boast ▶ HISTORY origin
unknown

boastful *adj* tending to boast

boat *n* **1** a small vessel propelled by oars, paddle,
sails, or motor **2** *informal* a ship **3 in the same
boat** sharing the same problems **4 miss the boat**
to lose an opportunity **5 rock the boat** *informal* to
cause a disturbance in the existing situation ▷ *vb*
6 to travel or go in a boat, esp. as recreation
▶ HISTORY Old English *bāt*

boater *n* a stiff straw hat with a straight brim and
flat crown

boating *n* rowing, sailing, or cruising in boats as a
form of recreation

boatman *n, pl* **-men** a man who works on, hires
out, or repairs boats

boatswain (boh-sn) *n naut* same as **bosun**

boat train *n* a train scheduled to take passengers
to or from a particular ship

bob¹ *vb* **bobbing, bobbed** **1** to move or cause to
move up and down repeatedly, such as while
floating in water **2** to move or cause to move with
a short abrupt movement, esp. of the head **3 bob
up** to appear or emerge suddenly ▷ *n* **4** a short
abrupt movement, as of the head ▶ HISTORY origin
unknown

bob² *n* **1** a hairstyle in which the hair is cut short
evenly all round the head **2** a dangling weight on a
pendulum or plumb line ▷ *vb* **bobbing, bobbed**
3 to cut (the hair) in a bob ▶ HISTORY Middle
English *bobbe* bunch of flowers

bob³ *n, pl* **bob** *Brit, Austral & NZ, informal* (formerly)
a shilling: *two bob* ▶ HISTORY origin unknown

b

bobbejaan *n S African* **1** a baboon **2** a large black spider **3** a monkey wrench ▸ HISTORY Afrikaans

bobbin *n* a reel on which thread or yarn is wound ▸ HISTORY Old French *bobine*

bobble *n* **1** a tufted ball, usually woollen, that is used for decoration ▷ *vb* **-bling, -bled 2** (of a ball) to bounce erratically because of an uneven playing surface ▸ HISTORY from BOB¹

bobby *n, pl* **-bies** *Brit, informal* a British policeman ▸ HISTORY after *Robert* Peel, who set up the Metropolitan Police Force

bobby pin *n US, Canad, Austral & NZ* a metal hairpin

bobotie (ba-**boot**-ee) *n S African* a traditional Cape dish of curried minced meat ▸ HISTORY probably from Malay

bobsleigh *n* **1** a sledge for racing down a steeply banked ice-covered run ▷ *vb* **2** to ride on a bobsleigh

bobtail *n* **1** a docked tail **2** an animal with such a tail ▷ *adj also* **bobtailed 3** having the tail cut short

Boche (bosh) *n offensive slang* a German, esp. a German soldier ▸ HISTORY French

bod *n informal* **1** a person: *he's a queer bod* **2** short for **body** (sense 1) ▸ HISTORY short for *body*

bode¹ *vb* **boding, boded** to be an omen of (good or ill); portend ▸ HISTORY Old English *bodian*

bode² *vb* a past tense of **bide**

bodega *n* a shop in a Spanish-speaking country that sells wine ▸ HISTORY Spanish

bodge *vb* **bodging, bodged** *Brit, Austral & NZ, informal* to make a mess of; botch

bodice *n* **1** the upper part of a woman's dress, from the shoulder to the waist **2** a tight-fitting corset worn laced over a blouse, or (formerly) as a woman's undergarment ▸ HISTORY originally Scots *bodies*, plural of *body*

bodily *adj* **1** relating to the human body ▷ *adv* **2** by taking hold of the body: *he threw him bodily from the platform* **3** in person; in the flesh

bodkin *n* a blunt large-eyed needle ▸ HISTORY origin unknown

body *n, pl* **bodies 1** the entire physical structure of an animal or human. *Related adjective:* **corporal 2** the trunk or torso **3** a corpse **4** a group regarded as a single entity: *a local voluntary body* **5** the main part of anything: *the body of a car* **6** a separate mass of water or land **7** the flesh as opposed to the spirit **8** fullness in the appearance of the hair **9** the characteristic full quality of certain wines **10** *informal* a person: *all the important bodies from the council were present* **11** a woman's one-piece undergarment **12 keep body and soul together** to manage to survive ▸ HISTORY Old English *bodig*

body-board *n Austral, NZ & S African* a small polystyrene surfboard > **body-boarder** *n*

bodycheck *ice hockey etc. n* **1** obstruction of another player ▷ *vb* **2** to deliver a bodycheck to (an opponent)

body corporate *n, pl* **bodies corporate** *law* **1** a group of persons incorporated to carry out a specific enterprise and legally recognized as a single entity **2** *Austral* the association of apartment owners in a building in which there is common property

body double *n* a person who substitutes for a star in the filming of a scene showing the body rather than the face

bodyguard *n* a person or group of people employed to protect someone

body language *n* the communication of one's thoughts or feelings by the position or movements of one's body rather than by words

body politic *n* **the body politic** the people of a nation or the nation itself considered as a political entity

body search *n* **1** a search by police, customs officials, etc. that involves examination of a prisoner's or suspect's bodily orifices ▷ *vb* **body-search 2** to search (a prisoner or suspect) in this manner

body shop *n* a repair yard for vehicle bodywork

body snatcher *n* (formerly) a person who robbed graves and sold the corpses for dissection

body stocking *n* **1** a one-piece undergarment for women, covering the torso **2** a tightly fitting garment covering the whole of the body, worn esp. for dancing or exercising

bodywork *n* the external shell of a motor vehicle

Boer *n* a descendant of any of the Dutch or Huguenot colonists who settled in South Africa ▸ HISTORY Dutch

boere- *combining form S African* rustic or country-style ▸ HISTORY from Afrikaans *boer* a farmer

boeremeisie (**boor**-a-may-see) *n S African* a country girl of Afrikaans stock

boereseun (**boor**-a-see-oon) *n S African* a country boy of Afrikaans stock

boerewors (**boor**-a-vorss) *n S African* a traditional home-made farmer's sausage

boffin *n Brit & S African, informal* a scientist or expert ▸ HISTORY origin unknown

bog *n* **1** a wet spongy area of land **2** *slang* a toilet ▸ HISTORY Gaelic *bogach* swamp > **boggy** *adj* > **bogginess** *n*

bog down *vb* **bogging, bogged** to impede physically or mentally

bogey *or* **bogy** *n* **1** an evil or mischievous spirit **2** something that worries or annoys **3** *golf* a score of one stroke over par on a hole **4** *slang* a piece of dried mucus from the nose ▸ HISTORY probably obsolete *bug* an evil spirit

boggle *vb* **-gling, -gled 1** to be surprised, confused, or alarmed: *the mind boggles at the idea* **2** to hesitate or be evasive when confronted with a problem ▸ HISTORY probably Scots

bogie *or* **bogy** *n* an assembly of wheels forming a pivoted support at either end of a railway coach ▸ HISTORY origin unknown

bogle (**boh**-gul) *n* a rhythmic dance performed to ragga music ▸ HISTORY origin unknown

bog-standard *adj Brit & Irish, slang* completely ordinary; run-of-the-mill

bogus (boh-guss) *adj* not genuine ▶ HISTORY origin unknown

bogy *n, pl* **-gies** same as **bogey, bogie**

bohemian *n* **1** a person, esp. an artist or writer, who lives an unconventional life ▷ *adj* **2** unconventional in appearance, behaviour, etc. > **Bohemianism** *n*

bohrium *n chem* an element artificially produced in minute quantities. Symbol: Bh ▶ HISTORY after N. *Bohr*, physicist

boil¹ *vb* **1** to change or cause to change from a liquid to a vapour so rapidly that bubbles of vapour are formed in the liquid **2** to reach or cause to reach boiling point **3** to cook or be cooked by the process of boiling **4** to bubble and be agitated like something boiling: *the sea was boiling* **5** to be extremely angry ▷ *n* **6** the state or action of boiling ▷ See also **boil away, boil down** ▶ HISTORY Latin *bullire* to bubble

boil² *n* a red painful swelling with a hard pus-filled core caused by infection of the skin ▶ HISTORY Old English *bȳle*

boil away *vb* to cause (liquid) to evaporate completely by boiling or (of liquid) to evaporate completely

boil down *vb* **1** to reduce or be reduced in quantity by boiling **2 boil down to** to be the essential element in

boiler *n* **1** a closed vessel in which water is heated to provide steam to drive machinery **2** a domestic device to provide hot water, esp. for central heating

boiler suit *n Brit* a one-piece overall

boiling point *n* **1** the temperature at which a liquid boils **2** *informal* the condition of being angered or highly excited

boisterous *adj* **1** noisy and lively; unruly **2** (of the sea, etc.) turbulent or stormy ▶ HISTORY Middle English *boistuous*

bold *adj* **1** courageous, confident, and fearless **2** immodest or impudent: *she gave him a bold look* **3** standing out distinctly; conspicuous: *a figure carved in bold relief* **4** *typography* in bold face ▶ HISTORY Old English *beald* > **boldly** *adv* > **boldness** *n*

bold face *n typography* type which is characterized by thick heavy lines, as the entry words in this dictionary

bole *n* the trunk of a tree ▶ HISTORY Old Norse *bolr*

bolero *n, pl* **-ros** **1** a Spanish dance, usually in triple time **2** music for this dance **3** a short open jacket not reaching the waist ▶ HISTORY Spanish

boll *n* the rounded seed capsule of flax, cotton, etc. ▶ HISTORY Dutch *bolle*

bollard *n* **1** *Brit & Austral* a small post marking a kerb or traffic island or barring cars from entering **2** a strong wooden or metal post on a wharf, quay, etc., used for securing mooring lines ▶ HISTORY perhaps from *bole*

Bolshevik *n* **1** (formerly) a Russian Communist, especially one of the more radical members of the Russian Social Democratic Party. Compare **Menshevik 2** any Communist **3** *informal, offensive* any political radical, esp. a revolutionary ▶ HISTORY Russian *Bol'shevik* majority > **Bolshevism** *n* > **Bolshevist** *adj, n*

bolshie *or* **bolshy** *Brit & NZ, informal adj* **1** difficult to manage; rebellious **2** politically radical or left-wing ▷ *n, pl* **-shies** **3** any political radical ▶ HISTORY from BOLSHEVIK

bolson (bowl-**sown**) *n US geog* a desert valley surrounded by mountains, with a shallow lake at the centre ▶ HISTORY American Spanish *bolsón*, from Spanish *bolsa* purse, from Late Latin *bursa* bag

bolster *vb* **1** to support or strengthen: *the government were unwilling to bolster sterling* ▷ *n* **2** a long narrow pillow **3** any pad or support ▶ HISTORY Old English

bolt¹ *n* **1** a bar that can be slid into a socket to lock a door, gate, etc. **2** a metal rod or pin that has a head and a screw thread to take a nut **3** a flash (of lightning) **4** a sudden movement, esp. in order to escape **5** an arrow, esp. for a crossbow **6 a bolt from the blue** a sudden, unexpected, and usually unwelcome event **7 shoot one's bolt** to exhaust one's efforts ▷ *vb* **8** to run away suddenly **9** to secure or lock with or as if with a bolt **10** to attach firmly one thing to another by means of a nut and bolt **11** to eat hurriedly: *bolting your food may lead to indigestion* **12** (of a horse) to run away without control **13** (of vegetables) to produce flowers and seeds too soon ▷ *adv* **14 bolt upright** stiff and rigid ▶ HISTORY Old English: arrow

bolt² *or* **boult** *vb* **1** to pass (flour, a powder, etc.) through a sieve **2** to examine and separate ▶ HISTORY Old French *bulter*

bolt hole *n* a place of escape

bomb *n* **1** a hollow projectile containing explosive, incendiary, or other destructive substance **2** an object in which an explosive device has been planted: *a car bomb* **3** *Brit, slang* a large sum of money: *it cost a bomb* **4** *US & Canad, slang* a disastrous failure: *the new play was a total bomb* **5 like a bomb** *Brit & NZ, informal* with great speed or success **6 the bomb** a hydrogen or an atom bomb considered as the ultimate destructive weapon ▷ *vb* **7** to attack with a bomb or bombs; drop bombs (on) **8** (foll. by *along*) *informal* to move or drive very quickly **9** *chiefly US & Canad, slang* to fail disastrously **10** (foll. by *out*) *NZ, informal* to fail disastrously ▶ HISTORY Greek *bombos* booming noise > **bombing** *n*

bombard *vb* **1** to attack with concentrated artillery fire or bombs **2** to attack persistently **3** to attack verbally, esp. with questions **4** *physics* to direct high-energy particles or photons against (atoms, nuclei, etc.) ▶ HISTORY Old French *bombarde* stone-throwing cannon > **bombardment** *n*

bombardier *n* **1** *Brit* a noncommissioned rank in the Royal Artillery **2** *US* the member of a bomber aircrew responsible for releasing the bombs

b

Bombardier n *Canad trademark* a snow tractor, usually having caterpillar tracks at the rear and skis at the front

bombast n pompous and flowery language ▶ HISTORY Medieval Latin *bombax* cotton > **bombastic** adj

Bombay duck n a fish that is eaten dried with curry dishes as a savoury ▶ HISTORY through association with *Bombay*, port in India

bomber n **1** a military aircraft designed to carry out bombing missions **2** a person who plants bombs

bomb out vb *informal* to fail disastrously

bombshell n a shocking or unwelcome surprise

bona fide (bone-a **fide**-ee) adj **1** genuine: *a bona fide manuscript* **2** undertaken in good faith: *a bona fide agreement* ▶ HISTORY Latin

bonanza n **1** sudden and unexpected luck or wealth **2** *US & Canad* a mine or vein rich in ore ▶ HISTORY Spanish: calm sea, hence, good luck

bonbon n a sweet ▶ HISTORY French

bond n **1** something that binds, fastens, or holds together **2** something that brings or holds people together; tie: *a bond of friendship* **3 bonds** something that restrains or imprisons **4** a written or spoken agreement, esp. a promise: *a marriage bond* **5** *chem* a means by which atoms are combined in a molecule **6** *finance* a certificate of debt issued in order to raise funds **7** *S African* the conditional pledging of property, esp. a house, as security for the repayment of a loan **8** *law* a written acknowledgment of an obligation to pay a sum or to perform a contract **9 in bond** *commerce* securely stored until duty is paid ▷ vb **10** to hold or be held together; bind **11** to put or hold (goods) in bond ▶ HISTORY Old Norse *band*

bondage n **1** slavery **2** subjection to some influence or duty

bonded adj **1** *finance* consisting of, secured by, or operating under a bond or bonds **2** *commerce* in bond

bondservant n a serf or slave

bone n **1** any of the various structures that make up the skeleton in most vertebrates **2** the porous rigid tissue of which these parts are made **3** something consisting of bone or a bonelike substance **4 bones** the human skeleton **5** a thin strip of plastic, etc. used to stiffen corsets and brassieres **6 close to** or **near the bone** risqué or indecent **7 have a bone to pick** to have grounds for a quarrel **8 make no bones about a** to be direct and candid about **b** to have no scruples about **9 the bare bones** the essentials ▷ vb **boning, boned 10** to remove the bones from (meat for cooking, etc.) **11** to stiffen (a corset, etc.) by inserting bones ▶ HISTORY Old English *bān* > **boneless** adj

bone china n a type of fine porcelain containing powdered bone

bone-dry adj *informal* completely dry

bone-idle adj extremely lazy

bone meal n dried and ground animal bones, used as a fertilizer or in stock feeds

bonfire n a large outdoor fire

■ **WORD HISTORY**
■ A 'bonfire' is literally a 'bone-fire'. Bones were
■ used as fuel in the Middle Ages.

bongo n, pl **-gos** or **-goes** a small bucket-shaped drum, usually one of a pair, played by beating with the fingers ▶ HISTORY American Spanish

bonhomie (bon-om-**mee**) n exuberant friendliness ▶ HISTORY French

bonito (ba-**nee**-toh) n, pl **-os 1** a small tunny-like marine food fish **2** a related fish, whose flesh is dried and flaked and used in Japanese cookery

bonk vb *informal* to hit ▶ HISTORY probably imitative > **bonking** n

bonkers adj *Brit, Austral & NZ, slang* mad; crazy ▶ HISTORY origin unknown

bon mot (bon **moh**) n, pl **bons mots** *written* a clever and fitting remark ▶ HISTORY French, literally: good word

bonnet n **1** the hinged metal cover over a motor vehicle's engine **2** any of various hats tied with ribbons under the chin **3** (in Scotland) a soft cloth cap ▶ HISTORY Old French *bonet*

bonny adj **-nier, -niest 1** *Scot & N English, dialect* beautiful: *a bonny lass* **2** good or fine ▶ HISTORY Latin *bonus*

bonsai n, pl **-sai** an ornamental tree or shrub grown in a small shallow pot in order to stunt its growth ▶ HISTORY Japanese *bon* bowl + *sai* to plant

bonsela (bon-**sell**-a) n *S African, informal* a small gift of money ▶ HISTORY Zulu *ibanselo* gift

bonus n something given, paid, or received above what is due or expected ▶ HISTORY Latin: good

bon voyage interj a phrase used to wish a traveller a pleasant journey ▶ HISTORY French

bony adj **bonier, boniest 1** resembling or consisting of bone **2** thin **3** having many bones

boo interj **1** a shout uttered to express dissatisfaction or contempt **2** an exclamation uttered to startle someone ▷ vb **booing, booed 3** to shout 'boo' at (someone or something) as an expression of disapproval

boob *slang* n **1** *Brit, Austral & NZ* an embarrassing mistake; blunder **2** a female breast ▷ vb **3** *Brit, Austral & NZ* to make a blunder ▶ HISTORY from *booby*

boobook (**boo**-book) n a small spotted Australian brown owl

booby n, pl **-bies 1** *Brit, Austral & NZ* an ignorant or foolish person **2** a tropical marine bird related to the gannet ▶ HISTORY Latin *balbus* stammering

booby prize n a mock prize given to the person with the lowest score in a competition

booby trap n **1** a hidden explosive device primed so as to be set off by an unsuspecting victim **2** a trap for an unsuspecting person, esp. one intended as a practical joke

boogie vb **-gieing, -gied** *slang* to dance to fast pop music ▶ HISTORY origin unknown

boohai n **up the boohai** *NZ, informal* **1** a very remote area ▷ adj **2** very mistaken or astray ▶ HISTORY from the remote township of *Puhoi*

b

book n **1** a number of printed pages bound together along one edge and protected by covers **2** a written work or composition, such as a novel **3** a number of sheets of paper bound together: an account book **4** books a record of the transactions of a business or society **5** the libretto of an opera or musical **6** a major division of a written composition, such as of a long novel or of the Bible **7** a number of tickets, stamps, etc. fastened together along one edge **8** a record of betting transactions **9 a closed book** a subject that is beyond comprehension: art remains a closed book to him **10 bring to book** to reprimand or require (someone) to give an explanation of his or her conduct **11 by the book** according to the rules **12 in someone's good** or **bad books** regarded by someone with favour (or disfavour) **13 throw the book at someone a** to charge someone with every relevant offence **b** to inflict the most severe punishment on someone ▷ vb **14** to reserve (a place, passage, etc.) or engage the services of (someone) in advance **15** (of a police officer) to take the name and address of (a person) for an alleged offence with a view to prosecution **16** (of a football referee) to take the name of (a player) who has broken the rules seriously ▷ See also **book in** ▶ HISTORY Old English bōc

bookcase n a piece of furniture containing shelves for books

book club n a club that sells books at low prices to members, usually by mail order

bookie n informal short for **bookmaker**

book in vb chiefly Brit & NZ to register one's arrival at a hotel

booking n **1** Brit, Austral & NZ a reservation, as of a table or seat **2** theatre an engagement of a performer

bookish adj **1** fond of reading; studious **2** forming opinions through reading rather than experience

book-keeping n the skill or occupation of systematically recording business transactions > **book-keeper** n

booklet n a thin book with paper covers

bookmaker n a person who as an occupation accepts bets, esp. on horse racing > **bookmaking** n

bookmark n **1** a strip of some material put between the pages of a book to mark a place **2** computers an identifier put on a website that enables the user to return to it quickly and easily ▷ vb **3** computers to identify and store a website so that one can return to it quickly and easily

bookstall n a stall or stand where periodicals, newspapers, or books are sold

bookworm n **1** a person devoted to reading **2** a small insect that feeds on the binding paste of books

Boolean algebra (boo-lee-an) n a system of symbolic logic devised to codify nonmathematical logical operations: used in computers ▶ HISTORY after George Boole, mathematician

boom¹ vb **1** to make a loud deep echoing sound **2** to prosper vigorously and rapidly: business boomed ▷ n **3** a loud deep echoing sound **4** a period of high economic growth ▶ HISTORY imitative

boom² n **1** naut a spar to which the foot of a sail is fastened to control its position **2** a pole carrying an overhead microphone and projected over a film or television set **3** a barrier across a waterway ▶ HISTORY Dutch: tree

boomer n Austral a large male kangaroo

boomerang n **1** a curved wooden missile of Australian Aborigines which can be made to return to the thrower **2** an action or statement that recoils on its originator ▷ vb **3** (of a plan) to recoil unexpectedly, harming its originator ▶ HISTORY Aboriginal

boomslang n a large greenish venomous tree-living snake of southern Africa ▶ HISTORY Afrikaans

boon¹ n something extremely useful, helpful, or beneficial ▶ HISTORY Old Norse bōn request

boon² adj close or intimate: boon companion ▶ HISTORY Latin bonus good

boongary (boong-gar-ree) n, pl **-garies** a tree kangaroo of NE Queensland, Australia

boor n an ill-mannered, clumsy, or insensitive person ▶ HISTORY Old English gebūr dweller, farmer > **boorish** adj

boost n **1** encouragement or help: a boost to morale **2** an upward thrust or push **3** an increase or rise ▷ vb **4** to encourage or improve: to boost morale **5** to cause to rise; increase: we significantly boosted our market share **6** to advertise on a big scale ▶ HISTORY origin unknown

booster n **1** a supplementary injection of a vaccine given to ensure that the first injection will remain effective **2** a radio-frequency amplifier to strengthen signals **3** the first stage of a multistage rocket

boot¹ n **1** an outer covering for the foot that extends above the ankle **2** Brit an enclosed compartment of a car for holding luggage **3** informal a kick: he gave the door a boot **4 lick someone's boots** to behave flatteringly towards someone **5 put the boot in** slang **a** to kick a person when already down **b** to finish something off with unnecessary brutality **6 the boot** slang dismissal from employment ▷ vb **7** to kick **8** to start up (computer) **9 boot out** informal **a** to eject forcibly **b** to dismiss from employment ▶ HISTORY Middle English bote

boot² n **to boot** as well; in addition ▶ HISTORY Old English bōt compensation

boot camp n a centre for juvenile offenders, with strict discipline and hard physical exercise

bootee n a soft boot for a baby, esp. a knitted one

booth n, pl **booths 1** a small partially enclosed cubicle **2** a stall, esp. a temporary one at a fair or market ▶ HISTORY Scandinavian

bootleg vb **-legging, -legged 1** to make, carry, or sell (illicit goods, esp. alcohol) ▷ adj **2** produced, distributed, or sold illicitly ▶ HISTORY smugglers carried bottles of liquor concealed in their boots > **bootlegger** n

booty n, pl **-ties** any valuable article or articles obtained as plunder ▶ HISTORY Old French *butin*

booze informal n **1** alcoholic drink ▷ vb **boozing, boozed 2** to drink alcohol, esp. to excess ▶ HISTORY Middle Dutch *būsen* > **boozy** adj

boozer n informal **1** a person who is fond of drinking **2** Brit, Austral & NZ a bar or pub

booze-up n Brit, Austral & NZ, slang a drinking spree

bop n **1** a form of jazz with complex rhythms and harmonies ▷ vb **bopping, bopped 2** informal to dance to pop music ▶ HISTORY from BEBOP > **bopper** n

bora n Austral an Aboriginal ceremony ▶ HISTORY from a native Australian language

boracic adj same as **boric**

borage n a Mediterranean plant with star-shaped blue flowers ▶ HISTORY Arabic *abū 'āraq* literally: father of sweat

borax n a white mineral in crystalline form used in making glass, soap, etc. ▶ HISTORY Persian *būrah*

Bordeaux n a red or white wine produced around Bordeaux in SW France ·

border n **1** the dividing line between political or geographic regions **2** a band or margin around or along the edge of something **3** a design around the edge of something **4** a narrow strip of ground planted with flowers or shrubs: *a herbaceous border* ▷ vb **5** to provide with a border **6 a** to be adjacent to; lie along the boundary of **b** to be nearly the same as; verge on: *a story that borders on the unbelievable* ▶ HISTORY Old French *bort* side of a ship

borderland n **1** land located on or near a boundary **2** an indeterminate state or condition

bore¹ vb **boring, bored 1** to produce (a hole) with a drill, etc. **2** to produce (a tunnel, mine shaft, etc.) by drilling ▷ n **3** a hole or tunnel in the ground drilled in search of minerals, oil, etc. **4 a** the hollow of a gun barrel **b** the diameter of this hollow; calibre ▶ HISTORY Old English *borian*

bore² vb **boring, bored 1** to tire or make weary by being dull, repetitious, or uninteresting ▷ n **2** a dull or repetitious person, activity, or state ▶ HISTORY origin unknown > **bored** adj > **boring** adj

bore³ n a high wave moving up a narrow estuary, caused by the tide ▶ HISTORY Old Norse *bāra*

bore⁴ vb the past tense of **bear¹**

boreal (**bore**-ee-al) adj of or relating to the north or the north wind ▶ HISTORY from Latin *boreās* the north wind

boreal forest (**bore**-ee-al) n the forest of northern latitudes, esp. in Scandinavia, Canada, and Siberia, consisting mainly of spruce and pine ▶ HISTORY Latin *boreas* the north wind

boredom n the state of being bored

boree (**baw**-ree) n Austral same as **myall**

boric adj of or containing boron

boric acid n a white soluble crystalline solid used as a mild antiseptic

born vb **1** a past participle of **bear¹** (sense 4) **2 not to have been born yesterday** not to be gullible or foolish ▷ adj **3** possessing certain qualities from birth: *a born musician* **4** being in a particular social status at birth: *ignobly born*

born-again adj **1** having experienced conversion, esp. to evangelical Christianity **2** showing the enthusiasm of someone newly converted to any cause: *a born-again romantic* ▷ n **3** a person with fervent enthusiasm for a newfound cause

borne vb a past participle of **bear¹**

boron n chem a hard almost colourless crystalline metalloid element that is used in hardening steel. Symbol: B ▶ HISTORY *bor(ax)* + *(carb)on*

boronia n an Australian aromatic flowering shrub

borough n **1** a town, esp. (in Britain) one that forms the constituency of an MP or that was originally incorporated by royal charter **2** any of the constituent divisions of Greater London or New York City **3** (in some Caribbean countries) a town or district with certain local powers and responsibilities ▶ HISTORY Old English *burg*

borrow vb **1** to obtain (something, such as money) on the understanding that it will be returned to the lender **2** to adopt (ideas, words, etc.) from another source ▶ HISTORY Old English *borgian* > **borrower** n > **borrowing** n

borscht or **borsch** n a Russian soup based on beetroot ▶ HISTORY Russian *borshch*

borstal n (formerly in Britain) a prison for offenders aged 15 to 21 ▶ HISTORY after *Borstal*, village in Kent where the first institution was founded

borzoi n a tall dog with a narrow head and a long coat ▶ HISTORY Russian: swift

bosh n Brit, Austral & NZ, informal meaningless talk or opinions; nonsense ▶ HISTORY Turkish *boş* empty

Bosnian adj **1** from Bosnia ▷ n **2** a person from Bosnia

bosom n **1** the chest or breast of a person, esp. the female breasts **2** a protective centre or part: *the bosom of the family* **3** the breast considered as the seat of emotions ▷ adj **4** very dear: *a bosom friend* ▶ HISTORY Old English *bōsm*

boss¹ informal n **1** a person in charge of or employing others ▷ vb **2** to employ, supervise, or be in charge of **3 boss around** or **about** to be domineering or overbearing towards ▶ HISTORY Dutch *baas* master

boss² n a raised knob or stud, esp. an ornamental one on a vault, shield, etc. ▶ HISTORY Old French *boce*

bossy adj **bossier, bossiest** informal domineering, overbearing, or authoritarian > **bossiness** n

bosun or **boatswain** (**boh**-sn) n an officer who is responsible for the maintenance of a ship and its equipment

bot. **1** botanical **2** botany

botany n, pl **-nies** the study of plants, including their classification, structure, etc. ▶ HISTORY Greek *botanē* plant > **botanical** or **botanic** adj > **botanist** n

botch vb **1** to spoil through clumsiness or ineptitude **2** to repair badly or clumsily ▷ n also **botch-up 3** a badly done piece of work or repair ▶ HISTORY origin unknown

both *adj* **1** two considered together: *both parents were killed during the war* ▷ *pron* **2** two considered together: *both are to blame* ▷ *conj* **3** not just one but also the other of two (people or things): *both Darren and Keith enjoyed the match* ▶ HISTORY Old Norse *bāthir*

bother *vb* **1** to take the time or trouble: *don't bother to come with me* **2** to give annoyance, pain, or trouble to **3** to trouble (a person) by repeatedly disturbing; pester ▷ *n* **4** a state of worry, trouble, or confusion **5** a person or thing that causes fuss, trouble, or annoyance **6** *informal* a disturbance or fight: *a spot of bother* ▷ *interj* **7** *Brit, Austral & NZ* an exclamation of slight annoyance ▶ HISTORY origin unknown

bothersome *adj* causing bother

bothy *n, pl* **bothies** *chiefly Scot* **1** a hut used for temporary shelter **2** (formerly) a farm worker's quarters ▶ HISTORY perhaps from *booth*

bottle *n* **1** a container, often of glass and usually cylindrical with a narrow neck, for holding liquids **2** the amount such a container will hold **3** *Brit, slang* courage; nerve: *you don't have the bottle* **4 the bottle** *informal* drinking of alcohol, esp. to excess ▷ *vb* **-tling, -tled** **5** to put or place in a bottle or bottles ▷ See also **bottle up** ▶ HISTORY Late Latin *buttis* cask

bottle bank *n* a large container into which members of the public can throw glass bottles and jars for recycling

bottle-green *adj* dark green

bottleneck *n* **1** a narrow stretch of road or a junction at which traffic is or may be held up **2** something that holds up progress

bottlenose dolphin *n* a grey or greenish dolphin with a bottle-shaped snout

bottler *n* *Austral & NZ, old-fashioned, informal* an exceptional person or thing

bottle shop *n* *Austral & NZ* a shop licensed to sell alcohol for drinking elsewhere

bottle store *n* *S African* a shop licensed to sell alcohol for drinking elsewhere

bottle tree *n* an Australian tree with a bottle-shaped swollen trunk

bottle up *vb* to restrain (powerful emotion)

bottom *n* **1** the lowest, deepest, or farthest part of a thing: *the bottom of a hill* **2** the least important or successful position: *the bottom of a class* **3** the ground underneath a sea, lake, or river **4** the underneath part of a thing **5** the buttocks **6 at bottom** in reality; basically **7 be at the bottom of** to be the ultimate cause of **8 get to the bottom of** to discover the real truth about ▷ *adj* **9** lowest or last ▶ HISTORY Old English *botm*

bottomless *adj* **1** unlimited; inexhaustible: *bottomless resources* **2** very deep: *bottomless valleys*

bottom line *n* **1** the conclusion or main point of a process, discussion, etc. **2** the last line of a financial statement that shows the net profit or loss of a company or organization

bottom out *vb* to reach the lowest point and level out: *consumer spending has bottomed out*

bottom-up reading *n* a text-based approach to reading and understanding based on in-depth analyses of the choice, function, and interrelationship of words. Compare **top-down reading**

botulism *n* severe food poisoning resulting from the toxin **botulin**, produced in imperfectly preserved food ▶ HISTORY Latin *botulus* sausage

bouclé *n* a curled or looped yarn or fabric giving a thick knobbly effect ▶ HISTORY French: curly

boudoir (boo-dwahr) *n* a woman's bedroom or private sitting room ▶ HISTORY French, literally: room for sulking in

bouffant (boof-fong) *adj* (of a hairstyle) having extra height and width through backcombing ▶ HISTORY French *bouffer* to puff up

bougainvillea *n* a tropical climbing plant with flowers surrounded by showy red or purple bracts ▶ HISTORY after L. A. de *Bougainville*, navigator

bough *n* any of the main branches of a tree ▶ HISTORY Old English *bōg* arm, twig

bought *vb* the past of **buy**

bouillon (boo-yon) *n* a thin clear broth or stock ▶ HISTORY French *bouillir* to boil

boulder *n* a smooth rounded mass of rock shaped by erosion ▶ HISTORY Scandinavian

boulder clay *n* an unstratified glacial deposit of fine clay, boulders, and pebbles

boule (boo-ley) *n* **1** *politics* the parliament in modern Greece **2** *ancient history* the senate of an ancient Greek city-state

boulevard *n* a wide usually tree-lined road in a city ▶ HISTORY Middle Dutch *bolwerc* bulwark; because originally often built on the ruins of an old rampart

bounce *vb* **bouncing, bounced** **1** (of a ball, etc.) to rebound from an impact **2** to cause (a ball, etc.) to hit a solid surface and spring back **3** to move or cause to move suddenly; spring: *I bounced down the stairs* **4** *slang* (of a bank) to send (a cheque) back or (of a cheque) to be sent back unredeemed because of lack of funds in the account ▷ *n* **5** the action of rebounding from an impact **6** a leap or jump **7** springiness **8** *informal* vitality; vigour ▶ HISTORY probably imitative > **bouncy** *adj*

bouncer *n* **1** *slang* a person employed at a club, disco, etc. to prevent unwanted people from entering and to eject drunks or troublemakers **2** *cricket* a ball bowled so that it bounces high on pitching

bouncing *adj* vigorous and robust: *a bouncing baby*

bound¹ *vb* **1** the past of **bind** ▷ *adj* **2** tied as if with a rope **3** restricted or confined: *housebound* **4** *spoken* certain: *it's bound to happen* **5** compelled or obliged: *they agreed to be bound by the board's recommendations* **6** (of a book) secured within a cover or binding **7 bound up with** closely or inextricably linked with

bound² *vb* **1** to move forwards by leaps or jumps **2** to bounce; spring away from an impact ▷ *n* **3** a jump upwards or forwards **4** a bounce, as of a ball ▶ HISTORY Old French *bondir*

b

bound³ *vb* **1** to place restrictions on; limit: *ancient art is bound by tradition* **2** to form a boundary of ▷ *n* **3** See **bounds** ▸ HISTORY Old French *bonde* > **boundless** *adj*

bound⁴ *adj* going or intending to go towards: *homeward bound* ▸ HISTORY Old Norse *buinn*, past participle of *búa* prepare

boundary *n, pl* **-ries 1** something that indicates the farthest limit, such as of an area **2** *cricket* **a** the marked limit of the playing area **b** a stroke that hits the ball beyond this limit, scoring four or six runs

bounder *n Brit, old-fashioned, slang* a morally reprehensible person; cad

bounds *pl n* **1** a limit; boundary: *their jealousy knows no bounds* **2** something that restricts or controls, esp. the standards of a society: *within the bounds of good taste*

bountiful *or* **bounteous** *adj literary* **1** plentiful; ample: *a bountiful harvest* **2** giving freely; generous

bounty *n, pl* **-ties 1** *literary* generosity; liberality **2** something provided in generous amounts: *nature's bounty* **3** a reward or premium by a government ▸ HISTORY Latin *bonus* good

bounty system *n history* in 19th century Australia, a system whereby settlers received grants for helping skilled immigrants come into the country

bouquet *n* **1** a bunch of flowers, esp. a large carefully arranged one **2** the aroma of wine ▸ HISTORY French: thicket

bouquet garni *n, pl* **bouquets garnis** a bunch of herbs tied together and used for flavouring soups, stews, or stocks ▸ HISTORY French

bourbon (**bur**-bn) *n* a whiskey distilled, chiefly in the US, from maize ▸ HISTORY after *Bourbon* county, Kentucky, where it was first made

bourgeois (**boor**-zhwah) *often disparaging adj* **1** characteristic of or comprising the middle class **2** conservative or materialistic in outlook **3** (in Marxist thought) dominated by capitalism ▷ *n, pl* **-geois 4** a member of the middle class, esp. one regarded as being conservative and materialistic ▸ HISTORY Old French *borjois* citizen

bourgeoisie (boor-zhwah-**zee**) *n* **the bourgeoisie 1** the middle classes **2** (in Marxist thought) the capitalist ruling class

bourn *n chiefly S Brit* a stream ▸ HISTORY Old French *bodne* limit

bourrée (**boor**-ray) *n* **1** a traditional French dance in fast duple time **2** music for this dance ▸ HISTORY French

Bourse (**boorss**) *n* a stock exchange, esp. of Paris ▸ HISTORY French: purse

bout *n* **1 a** a period of time spent doing something, such as drinking **b** a period of illness: *a bad bout of flu* **2** a boxing, wrestling or fencing match ▸ HISTORY obsolete *bought* turn

boutique *n* a small shop, esp. one that sells fashionable clothes ▸ HISTORY French

bouzouki *n* a Greek long-necked stringed musical instrument related to the mandolin ▸ HISTORY Modern Greek

bovine *adj* **1** of or relating to cattle **2** dull, sluggish, or ugly ▸ HISTORY Latin *bos* ox

bow¹ (rhymes with **cow**) *vb* **1** to lower (one's head) or bend (one's knee or body) as a sign of respect, greeting, agreement, or shame **2** to comply or accept: *bow to the inevitable* **3 bow and scrape** to behave in a slavish manner ▷ *n* **4** a lowering or bending of the head or body as a mark of respect, etc. **5 take a bow** to acknowledge applause ▸ HISTORY Old English *būgan*

bow² (rhymes with **know**) *n* **1** a decorative knot usually having two loops and two loose ends **2** a long stick across which are stretched strands of horsehair, used for playing a violin, viola, cello, etc. **3** a weapon for shooting arrows, consisting of an arch of flexible wood, plastic, etc. bent by a string fastened at each end **4** something that is curved, bent, or arched ▷ *vb* **5** to form or cause to form a curve or curves ▸ HISTORY Old English *boga* arch, bow

bow³ (rhymes with **cow**) *n* **1** *chiefly naut* the front end or part of a vessel **2** *rowing* the oarsman at the bow ▸ HISTORY probably Low German *boog*

bowdlerize *or* **-ise** *vb* **-izing, -ized** *or* **-ising, -ised** to remove passages or words regarded as indecent from (a play, novel, etc.) ▸ HISTORY after Thomas *Bowdler*, editor who expurgated Shakespeare > **bowdlerization** *or* **-isation** *n*

bowel *n* **1** an intestine, esp. the large intestine in humans **2 bowels** entrails **3 bowels** the innermost part: *the bowels of the earth* ▸ HISTORY Latin *botellus* a little sausage

bower *n* a shady leafy shelter in a wood or garden ▸ HISTORY Old English *būr* dwelling

bowerbird *n* a brightly coloured songbird of Australia and New Guinea

bowie knife *n* a stout hunting knife ▸ HISTORY after Jim *Bowie*, Texan adventurer

bowl¹ *n* **1** a round container open at the top, used for holding liquid or serving food **2** the amount a bowl will hold **3** the hollow part of an object, esp. of a spoon or tobacco pipe ▸ HISTORY Old English *bolla*

bowl² *n* **1 a** a wooden ball used in the game of bowls **b** a large heavy ball with holes for gripping used in the game of bowling ▷ *vb* **2** to roll smoothly or cause to roll smoothly along the ground **3** *cricket* **a** to send (a ball) from one's hand towards the batsman **b** Also: **bowl out** to dismiss (a batsman) by delivering a ball that breaks his wicket **4** to play bowls **5 bowl along** to move easily and rapidly, as in a car ▷ See also **bowls** ▸ HISTORY French *boule*

bow-legged *adj* having legs that curve outwards at the knees

bowler¹ *n* **1** a person who bowls in cricket **2** a player at the game of bowls

bowler² *n* a stiff felt hat with a rounded crown and narrow curved brim ▸ HISTORY after John *Bowler*, hatter

bowline *n naut* **1** a line used to keep the sail taut against the wind **2** a knot used for securing a loop that will not slip at the end of a piece of rope ▶ HISTORY probably from Middle Low German *bōlīne*

bowling *n* **1** a game in which a heavy ball is rolled down a long narrow alley at a group of wooden pins **2** *cricket* the act of delivering the ball to the batsman

bowls *n* a game played on a very smooth area of grass in which opponents roll biased wooden bowls as near a small bowl (the jack) as possible

bowsprit *n naut* a spar projecting from the bow of a sailing ship ▶ HISTORY Middle Low German *bōch* BOW[3] + *sprēt* pole

bow window *n* a curved bay window

box[1] *n* **1** a container with a firm base and sides and sometimes a removable or hinged lid **2** the contents of such a container **3** a separate compartment for a small group of people, as in a theatre **4** a compartment for a horse in a stable or a vehicle **5** a section of printed matter on a page, enclosed by lines or a border **6** a central agency to which mail is addressed and from which it is collected or redistributed: *a post-office box* **7** same as **penalty box 8 the box** *Brit, informal* television ▷ *vb* **9** to put into a box ▷ See also **box in** ▶ HISTORY Greek *puxos* BOX[3] > **boxlike** *adj*

box[2] *vb* **1** to fight (an opponent) in a boxing match **2** to engage in boxing **3** to hit (esp. a person's ears) with the fist ▷ *n* **4** a punch with the fist, esp. on the ear ▶ HISTORY origin unknown

box[3] *n* **1** a slow-growing evergreen tree or shrub with small shiny leaves **2** a eucalyptus with similar timber and foliage, and with rough bark ▶ HISTORY Greek *puxos*

box-and-whisker plot *n statistics* a method for depicting statistical information in which the results are divided into four quartiles, with a box representing the second and third quartiles, and lines (whiskers) representing the figures in the first and fourth quartiles

boxer *n* **1** a person who boxes **2** a medium-sized dog with smooth hair and a short nose

Boxer Rebellion *n history* an unsuccessful rebellion by a Chinese secret society in 1900 against foreign interests in China ▶ HISTORY rough translation of Chinese *I Ho Ch'üan*, literally: virtuous harmonious fist

boxer shorts *or* **boxers** *pl n* men's underpants shaped like shorts but with a front opening

box in *vb* to prevent from moving freely; confine

boxing *n* the act, art, or profession of fighting with the fists

Boxing Day *n* the first day after Christmas (in Britain, traditionally and strictly, the first weekday), observed as a holiday ▶ HISTORY from the former custom of giving Christmas boxes to tradesmen on this day

box jellyfish *n* a highly venomous jellyfish with a cuboidal body that lives in Australian tropical waters

box junction *n* (in Britain) a road junction marked with yellow crisscross lines which vehicles may only enter when their exit is clear

box lacrosse *n Canad* lacrosse played indoors

box number *n* a number used as an address for mail, esp. one used by a newspaper for replies to an advertisement

box office *n* **1** an office at a theatre, cinema, etc. where tickets are sold **2** the public appeal of an actor or production ▷ *adj* **box-office 3** relating to the sales at the box office: *a box-office success*

box pleat *n* a flat double pleat made by folding under the fabric on either side of it

boxwood *n* the hard yellow wood of the box tree, used to make tool handles, etc. See **box**[3]

boy *n* **1** a male child **2** a man regarded as immature or inexperienced **3** *S African, offensive* a Black male servant ▶ HISTORY origin unknown > **boyhood** *n* > **boyish** *adj*

boycott *vb* **1** to refuse to deal with (an organization or country) as a protest against its actions or policy ▷ *n* **2** an instance or the use of boycotting

■ **WORD HISTORY**
■ Captain Charles Boycott (1832–1897) was a
■ retired British army officer who became an
■ estate manager in Ireland. When in 1880
■ he was asked to reduce his tenants' rents
■ after a bad harvest, he refused and tried to
■ have some of the tenants evicted. For this,
■ the tenants refused to have anything further
■ to do with him, and he left Ireland shortly
■ afterwards.

boyfriend *n* a male friend with whom a person is romantically involved

Boyle's law *n* the principle that the pressure of a gas varies inversely with its volume at constant temperature ▶ HISTORY after Robert *Boyle*, scientist

BP 1 blood pressure **2** British Pharmacopoeia

bpi bits per inch (used of a computer tape)

Bq *physics* becquerel

Br *chem* bromine

bra *n* a woman's undergarment for covering and supporting the breasts ▶ HISTORY from *brassiere*

braaivleis (**brye**-flayss) *n S African* ▷ *n* **1** a grill on which food is cooked over hot charcoal, usually outdoors **2** an outdoor party at which food like this is served ▷ *vb* **3** cook (food) in this way. Also: **braai** ▶ HISTORY Afrikaans

brace *n* **1** something that steadies, binds, or holds up another thing **2** a beam or prop, used to stiffen a framework **3** a hand tool for drilling holes **4** a pair, esp. of game birds **5** either of a pair of characters, { }, used for connecting lines of printing or writing **6** See **braces** ▷ *vb* **bracing, braced 7** to steady or prepare (oneself) before an impact **8** to provide, strengthen, or fit with a brace ▶ HISTORY Latin *bracchia* arms

brace and bit *n* a hand tool for boring holes, consisting of a cranked handle into which a drilling bit is inserted

bracelet *n* an ornamental chain or band worn around the arm or wrist ▶ HISTORY Latin *bracchium* arm

braces *pl n* **1** *Brit & NZ* a pair of straps worn over the shoulders for holding up the trousers **2** an appliance of metal bands and wires for correcting unevenness of teeth

brachiopod (**brake**-ee-oh-pod) *n* an invertebrate sea animal with a shell consisting of two valves ▶ HISTORY Greek *brakhiōn* arm + *pous* foot

brachium (**brake**-ee-um) *n, pl* **brachia** (**brake**-ee-a) *anat* the arm, esp. the upper part ▶ HISTORY Latin *bracchium* arm

bracing *adj* refreshing: *the bracing climate*

bracken *n* **1** a fern with large fronds **2** a clump of these ferns ▶ HISTORY Scandinavian

bracket *n* **1** a pair of characters, [ ], ( ), or { }, used to enclose a section of writing or printing **2** a group or category falling within certain defined limits: *the lower income bracket* **3** an L-shaped or other support fixed to a wall to hold a shelf, etc. ▷ *vb* **-eting, -eted 4** to put (written or printed matter) in brackets **5** to group or class together ▶ HISTORY Latin *braca* breeches

brackish *adj* (of water) slightly salty ▶ HISTORY Middle Dutch *brac*

bract *n* a leaf, usually small and scaly, growing at the base of a flower ▶ HISTORY Latin *bractea* thin metal plate

brad *n* a small tapered nail with a small head ▶ HISTORY Old English *brord* point

brae *n* *Scot* a hill or slope ▶ HISTORY Middle English *bra*

brag *vb* **bragging, bragged 1** to speak arrogantly and boastfully ▷ *n* **2** boastful talk or behaviour **3** a card game similar to poker ▶ HISTORY origin unknown

braggart *n* a person who boasts loudly or exaggeratedly

Brahma *n* **1** a Hindu god, the Creator **2** same as **Brahman** (sense 2)

Brahman *n, pl* **-mans 1** Also: **Brahmin** a member of the highest or priestly caste in the Hindu caste system **2** *Hinduism* the ultimate and impersonal divine reality of the universe ▶ HISTORY Sanskrit: prayer > **Brahmanic** *adj*

braid *vb* **1** to interweave (hair, thread, etc.) **2** to decorate with an ornamental trim or border ▷ *n* **3** a length of hair that has been braided **4** narrow ornamental tape of woven silk, wool, etc. ▶ HISTORY Old English *bregdan* > **braiding** *n*

braided stream *n* *geog* a stream that flows in several shallow interconnected channels separated by banks of deposited material

Braille *n* a system of writing for blind people, consisting of raised dots interpreted by touch ▶ HISTORY after Louis *Braille*, its inventor

brain *n* **1** the soft mass of nervous tissue within the skull of vertebrates that controls and coordinates the nervous system **2** (often *pl*) *informal* intellectual ability: *he's got brains* **3** *informal* an intelligent person **4 on the brain** *informal* constantly in mind: *I had that song on the brain* **5 the brains** *informal* a person who plans and organizes something: *the brains behind the bid* ▷ *vb* **6** *slang* to hit (someone) hard on the head ▶ HISTORY Old English *brægen*

brainchild *n* *informal* an idea or plan produced by creative thought

braindead *adj* **1** having suffered brain death **2** *informal* stupid

brain death *n* complete stoppage of breathing due to irreparable brain damage

brain drain *n* *informal* the emigration of scientists, technologists, academics, etc.

brainfood *n* any foodstuff containing nutrients thought to promote brain function

brainless *adj* stupid or foolish

brainstorm *n* **1** *Brit, informal* a sudden mental aberration **2** a sudden and violent attack of insanity **3** *informal* same as **brainwave**

brainstorming *n* a thorough discussion to solve problems or create ideas

brains trust *n* a group of knowledgeable people who discuss topics in public or on radio or television

brain up *vb* *Brit* to make (something) more intellectually demanding or sophisticated: *we need to brain up the curriculum*

brainwash *vb* to cause (a person) to alter his or her beliefs, by methods based on isolation, sleeplessness, etc. > **brainwashing** *n*

brainwave *n* *informal* a sudden idea or inspiration

brain wave *n* a fluctuation of electrical potential in the brain

brainy *adj* **brainier, brainiest** *informal* clever; intelligent

braise *vb* **braising, braised** to cook (food) slowly in a closed pan with a small amount of liquid ▶ HISTORY Old French *brese* live coals

brak¹ (**bruck**) *n* *S African* a crossbred dog; mongrel ▶ HISTORY Dutch

brak² (**bruck**) *adj* *S African* (of water) slightly salty; brackish ▶ HISTORY Afrikaans

brake¹ *n* **1** a device for slowing or stopping a vehicle **2** something that slows down or stops progress: *he put a brake on my enthusiasm* ▷ *vb* **braking, braked 3** to slow down or cause to slow down, by or as if by using a brake ▶ HISTORY Middle English *braeke*

brake² *n* *Brit* an area of dense undergrowth; thicket ▶ HISTORY Old English *bracu*

brake horsepower *n* the rate at which an engine does work, measured by the resistance of an applied brake

brake light *n* a red light at the rear of a motor vehicle that lights up when the brakes are applied

brake lining *n* a renewable strip of asbestos riveted to a brake shoe to increase friction

brake shoe *n* a curved metal casting that acts as a brake on a wheel

bramble *n* **1** a prickly plant or shrub such as the blackberry **2** *Scot, N English & NZ* a blackberry ▶ HISTORY Old English *bræmbel* > **brambly** *adj*

bran *n* husks of cereal grain separated from the flour ▶ HISTORY Old French

branch *n* **1** a secondary woody stem extending from the trunk or main branch of a tree **2** one of a number of shops, offices, or groups that belongs to a central organisation: *he was transferred to their*

Japanese branch **3** a subdivision or subsidiary section of something larger or more complex: *branches of learning* ▷ *vb* **4** to divide, then develop in different directions ▶ HISTORY Late Latin *branca* paw > **branchlike** *adj*

branch out *vb* to expand or extend one's interests

brand *n* **1** a particular product or a characteristic that identifies a particular producer **2** a particular kind or variety **3** an identifying mark made, usually by burning, on the skin of animals as a proof of ownership **4** an iron used for branding animals **5** a mark of disgrace **6** *archaic or poetic* a flaming torch ▷ *vb* **7** to label, burn, or mark with or as if with a brand **8** to label (someone): *he was branded a war criminal* ▶ HISTORY Old English: fire

brand image *n marketing* the attributes of a brand as perceived by potential and actual customers

brandish *vb* to wave (a weapon, etc.) in a triumphant or threatening way ▶ HISTORY Old French *brandir*

brand name *n marketing* a trade name or trademark

brand-new *adj* absolutely new

brandy *n, pl* **-dies** an alcoholic spirit distilled from wine

■ **WORD HISTORY**
■ 'Brandy' is short for 'brandywine', which comes
■ from Dutch *brandewijn* meaning 'burnt wine' or
■ 'distilled wine'.

brandy snap *n* a crisp sweet biscuit, rolled into a cylinder

brash *adj* **1** tastelessly or offensively loud, or showy: *brash modernization* **2** impudent or bold: *I thought it was very brash of her to ask me* ▶ HISTORY origin unknown > **brashness** *n*

brass *n* **1** an alloy of copper and zinc **2** an object, ornament, or utensil made of brass **3 a** the large family of wind instruments including the trumpet, trombone, etc. made of brass **b** instruments of this family forming a section in an orchestra **4** same as **top brass 5** *N English, dialect* money **6** *Brit* an engraved brass memorial tablet in a church **7** *informal* bold self-confidence; nerve ▶ HISTORY Old English *bræs*

brass band *n* a group of musicians playing brass and percussion instruments

brasserie *n* a bar or restaurant serving drinks and cheap meals ▶ HISTORY French *brasser* to stir

brass hat *n Brit, informal* a top-ranking official, esp. a military officer

brassica *n* any plant of the cabbage and turnip family ▶ HISTORY Latin: cabbage

brassiere *n* same as **bra** ▶ HISTORY French

brass rubbing *n* an impression of an engraved brass tablet made by rubbing a paper placed over it with graphite or chalk

brassy *adj* **brassier, brassiest 1** brazen or flashy **2** like brass, esp. in colour **3** (of sound) harsh and strident

brat *n* a child, esp. one who is unruly ▶ HISTORY origin unknown

bravado *n* an outward display of self-confidence ▶ HISTORY Spanish *bravada*

brave *adj* **1** having or displaying courage, resolution, or daring **2** fine; splendid: *a brave sight* ▷ *n* **3** a warrior of a Native American tribe of N America ▷ *vb* **braving, braved** *written* **4** to confront with resolution or courage: *she braved the 21 miles of Lake Tahoe* ▶ HISTORY Italian *bravo* > **bravery** *n*

bravo *interj* **1** well done! ▷ *n* **2** (*pl* **-vos**) a cry of 'bravo' **3** (*pl* **-voes** *or* **-vos**) a hired killer or assassin ▶ HISTORY Italian

bravura *n* **1** a display of boldness or daring **2** *music* brilliance of execution ▶ HISTORY Italian

brawl *n* **1** a loud disagreement or fight ▷ *vb* **2** to quarrel or fight noisily ▶ HISTORY probably from Dutch *brallen* to boast

brawn *n* **1** strong well-developed muscles **2** physical strength **3** *Brit & NZ* a seasoned jellied loaf made from the head of a pig ▶ HISTORY Old French *braon* meat > **brawny** *adj*

bray *vb* **1** (of a donkey) to utter its characteristic loud harsh sound **2** *written* to utter something with a loud harsh sound ▷ *n* **3** the loud harsh sound uttered by a donkey **4** a similar loud sound ▶ HISTORY Old French *braire*

braze *vb* **brazing, brazed** to join (two metal surfaces) by fusing brass between them ▶ HISTORY Old French: to burn

brazen *adj* **1** shameless and bold **2** made of or resembling brass **3** having a ringing metallic sound ▷ *vb* **4 brazen it out** to face and overcome a difficult or embarrassing situation boldly or shamelessly > **brazenly** *adv*

brazier¹ (**bray**-zee-er) *n* a portable metal container for burning charcoal or coal ▶ HISTORY French *braise* live coals

brazier² *n* a worker in brass

brazil *n* **1** the red wood of various tropical trees of America **2** same as **brazil nut** ▶ HISTORY Old Spanish *brasa* glowing coals; referring to the redness of the wood

Brazilian *adj* **1** of Brazil ▷ *n* **2** a person from Brazil

brazil nut *n* a large three-sided nut of a tropical American tree

breach *n* **1** a breaking of a promise, obligation, etc. **2** any serious disagreement or separation **3** a crack, break, or gap ▷ *vb* **4** to break (a promise, law, etc.) **5** to break through or make an opening or hole in ▶ HISTORY Old English *bræc*

breach of contract *n law* failure by a party to carry out obligations required under a contract

breach of promise *n law* (formerly) failure to carry out one's promise to marry

breach of the peace *n law* an offence against public order causing an unnecessary disturbance of the peace

bread *n* **1** a food made from a dough of flour or meal mixed with water or milk, usually raised with yeast and then baked **2** necessary food **3** *slang* money ▷ *vb* **4** to cover (food) with breadcrumbs before cooking ▶ HISTORY Old English *brēad*

b

break

WORD FOCUS

The word **break** is often overused. There are lots of more descriptive words which you can use to give additional information about how something **breaks**, so try to choose one of them instead.

DEFINITION 1

- If something hard **cracks**, or you **crack** it, it becomes slightly damaged, with lines appearing on its surface: A gas main had **cracked** under my garden. • To get at the coconut flesh, **crack** the shell with a hammer.
- If something **fractures**, or you **fracture** it, it gets a slight crack in it: One strut had **fractured** and had to be repaired. • You've **fractured** a rib.
- If something **snaps**, or you **snap** it, it breaks suddenly, with a sharp cracking noise: A twig **snapped** under his foot. • She gripped the pipe in both hands, trying to **snap** it in half.
- If something **splits**, or you **split** it, it breaks into two or more parts: In the **severe** gale, the ship **split** in two. • We **split** the boards down the middle.
- If something **splinters**, or you **splinter** it, it breaks into thin, sharp pieces: The ruler **splintered** into pieces. • The stone hit the glass, **splintering** it.
- If something **fragments**, or is **fragmented**, it breaks or separates into small parts: The rock began to **fragment** and crumble.
- If something **crumbles**, or you **crumble** it, it breaks into many small pieces: Under the pressure, the flint **crumbled** into fragments. • **Crumble** the cheese into a bowl.
- If something **shatters**, it breaks into many small pieces: safety glass that won't **shatter** if it's hit
- If something **disintegrates**, it breaks into many pieces and is destroyed: The car's windscreen **disintegrated** with the impact of the crash.
- If you **smash** something, or it **smashes**, it breaks into many small pieces, often because it has been hit or dropped: Someone had **smashed** a bottle. • Two glasses fell off the table and **smashed** into pieces.
- If you **wreck** or **demolish** something, you completely destroy it: The bridge was **wrecked** by the storms. • The hurricane **demolished** houses across the area.

breadboard n **1** a wooden board on which bread is sliced **2** an experimental arrangement of electronic circuits

breadfruit n, pl **-fruits** or **-fruit** a tree of the Pacific Islands, whose edible round fruit has a texture like bread when baked

breadline n **on the breadline** impoverished; living at subsistence level

breadth n **1** the extent or measurement of something from side to side **2** openness and lack of restriction, esp. of viewpoint or interest; liberality ▶ HISTORY Old English brād broad

breadwinner n a person supporting a family with his or her earnings

break vb **breaking, broke, broken 1** to separate or become separated into two or more pieces **2** to damage or become damaged so as not to work **3** to burst or cut the surface of (skin) **4** to fracture (a bone) in (a limb, etc.) **5** to fail to observe (an agreement, promise, or law): they broke their promise **6** to reveal or be revealed: she broke the news gently **7** (foll. by with) to separate oneself from **8** to discontinue or become discontinued: to break a journey **9** to bring or come to an end: the winter weather broke at last **10** to weaken or overwhelm or be weakened or overwhelmed, as in spirit: he felt his life was broken by his illness **11** to cut through or penetrate: silence broken by shouts **12** to improve on or surpass: she broke three world records **13** (often foll. by in) to accustom (a horse) to the bridle and saddle, to being ridden, etc. **14** (foll. by of) to cause (a person) to give up (a habit): this cure will break you of smoking **15** to weaken the impact or force of: this net will break his fall **16** to decipher: to break a code **17** to lose the order of: to break ranks **18** to reduce to poverty or the state of bankruptcy **19** to come into being: light broke over the mountains **20** (foll. by into) **a** to burst into (song, laughter, etc.) **b** to change to (a faster pace) **21** to open with explosives: to break a safe **22** (of waves) **a** to strike violently against **b** to collapse into foam or surf **23** snooker to scatter the balls at the start of a game **24** boxing, wrestling (of two fighters) to separate from a clinch **25** (of the male voice) to undergo a change in register, quality, and range at puberty **26** to interrupt the flow of current in (an electrical circuit) **27 break camp** to pack up and leave a camp **28 break even** to make neither a profit nor a loss **29 break the mould** to make a change that breaks an established habit or pattern ▷ n **30** the act or result of breaking; fracture **31** a brief rest **32** a sudden rush, esp. to escape: they made a sudden break for freedom **33** any sudden interruption in a continuous action **34** Brit & NZ a short period between classes at school **35** informal a fortunate opportunity, esp. to prove oneself **36** informal a piece of good or bad luck **37** billiards, snooker a series of successful shots during one turn **38** snooker the opening shot that scatters the placed balls **39** a discontinuity in an electrical circuit **40 break of day** the dawn ▷ See also **breakaway, break down**, etc. ▶ HISTORY Old English brecan > **breakable** adj
See WORD FOCUS **break**

b

breakage *n* **1** the act or result of breaking **2** compensation or allowance for goods damaged while in use, transit, etc.

breakaway *n* **1** loss or withdrawal of a group of members from an association, club, etc. **2** *Austral* a stampede of cattle, esp. at the smell of water ▷ *adj* **3** dissenting: *a breakaway faction* ▷ *vb* **break away 4** to leave hastily or escape **5** to withdraw or quit

break-bulk *adj commerce* denoting a system of transporting goods as separate pieces rather than altogether in a container

break down *vb* **1** to cease to function; become ineffective **2** to give way to strong emotion or tears **3** to crush or destroy **4** to have a nervous breakdown **5** to separate into component parts: *with exercise the body breaks down fat to use as fuel* **6** to separate or cause to separate into simpler chemical elements; decompose **7** to analyse or be subjected to analysis ▷ *n* **breakdown 8** an act or instance of breaking down; collapse **9** same as **nervous breakdown 10** an analysis of something into its parts

breaker *n* **1** a large sea wave with a white crest or one that breaks into foam on the shore **2** a citizens' band radio operator

breakfast *n* **1** the first meal of the day ▷ *vb* **2** to eat breakfast ▶ HISTORY BREAK + FAST²

break in *vb* **1** to enter a building, illegally, esp. by force **2** to interrupt **3** to accustom (a person or animal) to normal duties or practice **4** to use or wear (new shoes or new equipment) until comfortable or running smoothly ▷ *n* **break-in 5** the act of illegally entering a building, esp. by thieves

breakneck *adj* (of speed or pace) excessively fast and dangerous

break off *vb* **1** to sever or detach **2** to end (a relationship or association) **3** to stop abruptly

break out *vb* **1** to begin or arise suddenly: *fighting broke out between the two factions* **2** to make an escape, esp. from prison **3** **break out in** to erupt in (a rash or spots) ▷ *n* **break-out 4** an escape, esp. from prison

break through *vb* **1** to penetrate **2** to achieve success after lengthy efforts ▷ *n* **breakthrough 3** a significant development or discovery

break up *vb* **1** to separate or cause to separate **2** to put an end to (a relationship) or (of a relationship) to come to an end **3** to dissolve or cause to dissolve: *the meeting broke up at noon* **4** *Brit* (of a school) to close for the holidays ▷ *n* **break-up 5** a separation or disintegration

breakwater *n* a massive wall built out into the sea to protect a shore or harbour from the force of waves

bream *n*, *pl* **bream 1** a freshwater fish covered with silvery scales **2** a food fish of European seas **3** a food fish of Australasian seas ▶ HISTORY Old French *bresme*

breast *n* **1** either of the two soft fleshy milk-secreting glands on a woman's chest **2** the front part of the body from the neck to the abdomen; chest **3** the corresponding part in certain other mammals **4** the source of human emotions **5** the part of a garment that covers the breast **6 make a clean breast of something** to divulge truths about oneself ▷ *vb literary* **7** to reach the summit of: *breasting the mountain top* **8** to confront boldly; face: *breast the storm* ▶ HISTORY Old English *brēost*

breastbone *n* same as **sternum**

breast-feed *vb* **-feeding, -fed** to feed (a baby) with milk from the breast; suckle

breastplate *n* a piece of armour covering the chest

breaststroke *n* a swimming stroke in which the arms are extended in front of the head and swept back on either side

breastwork *n fortifications* a temporary defensive work, usually breast-high

breath *n* **1** the taking in and letting out of air during breathing **2** a single instance of this **3** the air taken in or let out during breathing **4** the vapour, heat, or odour of air breathed out **5** a slight gust of air **6** a short pause or rest **7** *written* a suggestion or slight evidence; suspicion: *trembling at the least breath of scandal* **8** a whisper or soft sound **9 catch one's breath a** to rest until breathing is normal **b** to stop breathing momentarily from excitement, fear, etc. **10 out of breath** gasping for air after exertion **11 save one's breath** to avoid useless talk **12 take someone's breath away** to overwhelm someone with surprise, etc. **13 under one's breath** in a quiet voice or whisper ▶ HISTORY Old English *brǣth*

breathable *adj* **1** (of air) fit to be breathed **2** *textiles* (of a material) allowing air to pass through so that perspiration can evaporate

Breathalyser or **-lyzer** *n Brit trademark* a device for estimating the amount of alcohol in the breath ▶ HISTORY breath + (an)alyser > **breathalyse** or **-lyze** *vb*

breathe *vb* **breathing, breathed 1** to take in oxygen and give out carbon dioxide; respire **2** to exist; be alive **3** to rest to regain breath or composure **4** (esp. of air) to blow lightly **5** to exhale or emit: *the dragon breathed fire* **6** to impart; instil: *a change that breathed new life into Polish industry* **7** to speak softly; whisper **8 breathe again** or **freely** or **easily** to feel relief **9 breathe one's last** to die

breather *n informal* a short pause for rest

breathing *n* **1** the passage of air into and out of the lungs to supply the body with oxygen **2** the sound this makes

breathless *adj* **1** out of breath; gasping, etc. **2** holding one's breath or having it taken away by excitement, etc. **3** (esp. of the atmosphere) motionless and stifling > **breathlessness** *n*

breathtaking *adj* causing awe or excitement

breath test *n* a chemical test of a driver's breath to determine the amount of alcohol consumed

bred *vb* the past of **breed**

bredie (**breed**-ee) *n S African* a meat and vegetable stew ▶ HISTORY Portuguese *bredo* ragout

b

breech _n_ **1** the buttocks **2** the part of a firearm behind the barrel ▶ HISTORY Old English _brēc_, plural of _brōc_ leg covering

breech delivery _n_ birth of a baby with the feet or buttocks appearing first

breeches _pl n_ trousers extending to the knee or just below, worn for riding, etc.

breed _vb_ **breeding, bred 1** to produce new or improved strains of (domestic animals and plants) **2** to produce or cause to produce by mating **3** to bear (offspring) **4** to bring up; raise: _she was city bred_ **5** to produce or be produced: _the agreement bred confidence between the two_ ▷ _n_ **6** a group of animals, esp. domestic animals, within a species, that have certain clearly defined characteristics **7** a kind, sort, or group: _he was a gentleman, a breed not greatly admired_ **8** a lineage or race ▶ HISTORY Old English _brēdan_ > **breeder** _n_

breeder reactor _n_ a nuclear reactor that produces more fissionable material than it uses

breeding _n_ **1** the process of producing plants or animals by controlled methods of reproduction **2** the process of bearing offspring **3** the result of good upbringing or training

breeze¹ _n_ **1** a gentle or light wind **2** _informal_ an easy task ▷ _vb_ **breezing, breezed 3** to move quickly or casually: _he breezed into the room_ ▶ HISTORY probably from Old Spanish _briza_

breeze² _n_ ashes of coal, coke, or charcoal ▶ HISTORY French _braise_ live coals

breeze block _n_ a light building brick made from the ashes of coal, coke, etc. bonded together by cement

breezy _adj_ **breezier, breeziest 1** fresh; windy **2** casual or carefree

Bren gun _n_ an air-cooled gas-operated light machine gun ▶ HISTORY after _Br(no)_, Czech Republic, and _En(field)_, England, where it was made

brent _or esp US_ **brant** _n_ a small goose with dark grey plumage and a short neck

brethren _pl n archaic_ a plural of **brother**

Breton _adj_ **1** of Brittany ▷ _n_ **2** a person from Brittany **3** the Celtic language of Brittany

breve _n_ an accent (˘), placed over a vowel to indicate that it is short or is pronounced in a specified way ▶ HISTORY Latin _brevis_ short

breviary _n, pl_ **-ries** _RC Church_ a book of psalms, hymns, prayers, etc. to be recited daily ▶ HISTORY Latin _brevis_ short

brevity _n_ **1** a short duration; brief time **2** lack of verbosity ▶ HISTORY Latin _brevitas_

brew _vb_ **1** to make (beer, ale, etc.) from malt and other ingredients by steeping, boiling, and fermentation **2** to prepare (a drink, such as tea) by infusing **3** to devise or plan: _to brew a plot_ **4** to be in the process of being brewed **5** to be about to happen or forming: _a rebellion was brewing_ ▷ _n_ **6** a beverage produced by brewing, esp. tea or beer **7** an instance of brewing: _last year's brew_ ▶ HISTORY Old English _brēowan_ > **brewer** _n_

brewery _n, pl_ **-eries** a place where beer, ale, etc. is brewed

briar¹ _or_ **brier** _n_ **1** a shrub of S Europe, with a hard woody root (briarroot) **2** a tobacco pipe made from this root ▶ HISTORY French _bruyère_

briar² _n_ same as **brier**¹

bribe _vb_ **bribing, bribed 1** to promise, offer, or give something, often illegally, to (a person) to receive services or gain influence ▷ _n_ **2** a reward, such as money or favour, given or offered for this purpose ▶ HISTORY Old French _briber_ to beg > **bribery** _n_

bric-a-brac _n_ miscellaneous small ornamental objects

■ **WORD HISTORY**
■ This word came into English from French. The
■ French word itself comes from an obsolete
■ phrase _à bric et à brac_ meaning 'at random'.

brick _n_ **1** a rectangular block of baked or dried clay, used in building construction **2** the material used to make such blocks **3** any rectangular block: _a brick of ice cream_ **4** bricks collectively **5** _informal_ a reliable, trustworthy, or helpful person **6 drop a brick** _Brit & NZ, informal_ to make a tactless or indiscreet remark ▷ _vb_ **7** (foll. by _in, up_ or _over_) to construct, line, pave, fill, or wall up with bricks: _they bricked up access to the historic pillar_ ▶ HISTORY Middle Dutch _bricke_

brickbat _n_ **1** blunt criticism **2** a piece of brick used as a weapon ▶ HISTORY BRICK + BAT¹

bricklayer _n_ a person who builds with bricks

bridal _adj_ of a bride or a wedding ▶ HISTORY Old English _brȳdealu_ bride ale

bride _n_ a woman who has just been or is about to be married ▶ HISTORY Old English _brȳd_

bridegroom _n_ a man who has just been or is about to be married ▶ HISTORY Old English _brȳdguma_

bridesmaid _n_ a girl or young woman who attends a bride at her wedding

bridge¹ _n_ **1** a structure that provides a way over a railway, river, etc. **2** a platform from which a ship is piloted and navigated **3** the hard ridge at the upper part of the nose **4** a dental plate containing artificial teeth that is secured to natural teeth **5** a piece of wood supporting the strings of a violin, guitar, etc. ▷ _vb_ **bridging, bridged 6** to build or provide a bridge over (something) **7** to connect or reduce the distance between: _talks aimed at bridging the gap between the two sides_ ▶ HISTORY Old English _brycg_

bridge² _n_ a card game for four players, based on whist, in which the trump suit is decided by bidding between the players ▶ HISTORY origin unknown

bridgehead _n mil_ a fortified or defensive position at the end of a bridge nearest to the enemy

bridgework _n_ a partial denture attached to the surrounding teeth

bridging loan _n_ a loan made to cover the period between two transactions, such as the buying of another house before the sale of the first is completed

bridle _n_ **1** headgear for controlling a horse, consisting of straps and a bit and reins **2** something that curbs or restrains ▷ _vb_ **-dling,**

-dled 3 to show anger or indignation: *he bridled at the shortness of her tone* **4** to put a bridle on (a horse) **5** to restrain; curb ▶ **HISTORY** Old English *brigdels*

bridle path *n* a path suitable for riding or leading horses

Brie (**bree**) *n* a soft creamy white cheese ▶ **HISTORY** *Brie*, region in N France

brief *adj* **1** short in duration **2** short in length or extent; scanty: *a brief bikini* **3** terse or concise ▷ *n* **4** a condensed statement or written synopsis **5** *law* a document containing all the facts and points of law of a case by which a solicitor instructs a barrister to represent a client **6** *RC Church* a papal letter that is less formal than a bull **7** Also called: **briefing** instructions **8 hold a brief for** to argue for; champion **9 in brief** in short; to sum up ▷ *vb* **10** to prepare or instruct (someone) by giving a summary of relevant facts **11** *English law* **a** to instruct (a barrister) by brief **b** to retain (a barrister) as counsel ▶ **HISTORY** Latin *brevis* > **briefly** *adv*

briefcase *n* a flat portable case for carrying papers, books, etc.

briefs *pl n* men's or women's underpants without legs

brier¹ or **briar** *n* any of various thorny shrubs or other plants, such as the sweetbrier ▶ **HISTORY** Old English *brēr, brǣr*

brier² *n* same as **briar¹**

brig¹ *n* *naut* a two-masted square-rigged ship ▶ **HISTORY** from BRIGANTINE

brig² *n* *Scot & N English* a bridge

Brig. Brigadier

brigade *n* **1** a military formation smaller than a division and usually commanded by a brigadier **2** a group of people organized for a certain task: *a rescue brigade* ▶ **HISTORY** Old French

brigadier *n* a senior officer in an army, usually commanding a brigade

brigalow *n* *Austral* a type of acacia tree ▶ **HISTORY** from a native Australian language

brigand *n* a bandit, esp. a member of a gang operating in mountainous areas ▶ **HISTORY** Old French

brigantine *n* a two-masted sailing ship ▶ **HISTORY** Old Italian *brigantino* pirate ship

bright *adj* **1** emitting or reflecting much light; shining **2** (of colours) intense or vivid **3** full of promise: *a bright future* **4** lively or cheerful **5** quick-witted or clever ▷ *adv* **6** brightly: *the light burned bright in his office* ▶ **HISTORY** Old English *beorht* > **brightly** *adv* > **brightness** *n*

brighten *vb* **1** to make or become bright or brighter **2** to make or become cheerful

brill *n*, *pl* **brill** or **brills** a European flatfish similar to the turbot ▶ **HISTORY** probably Cornish *brýthel* mackerel

brilliance or **brilliancy** *n* **1** great brightness **2** excellence in physical or mental ability **3** splendour

brilliant *adj* **1** shining with light; sparkling **2** (of a colour) vivid **3** *informal, spoken* splendid; magnificent: *a brilliant show* **4** of outstanding

intelligence or intellect ▷ *n* **5** a diamond cut with many facets to increase its sparkle ▶ **HISTORY** French *brillant* shining

brilliantine *n* a perfumed oil used to make the hair smooth and shiny ▶ **HISTORY** French

brim *n* **1** the upper rim of a cup, bowl, etc. **2** a projecting edge of a hat ▷ *vb* **brimming, brimmed 3** to be full to the brim: *he saw the tears that brimmed in her eyes* ▶ **HISTORY** Middle High German *brem* > **brimless** *adj*

brimstone *n* *obsolete* sulphur ▶ **HISTORY** Old English *brynstān*

brindled *adj* brown or grey streaked with a darker colour: *a brindled dog* ▶ **HISTORY** Middle English *brended*

brine *n* **1** a strong solution of salt and water, used for pickling **2** *literary* the sea or its water ▶ **HISTORY** Old English *brīne*

bring *vb* **bringing, brought 1** to carry, convey, or take (something or someone) to a designated place or person **2** to cause to happen: *responsibility brings maturity* **3** to cause to come to mind: *it brought back memories* **4** to cause to be in a certain state, position, etc.: *the punch brought him to his knees* **5** to make (oneself): *she couldn't bring herself to do it* **6** to sell for: *the painting brought a large sum* **7** *law* **a** to institute (proceedings, charges, etc.) **b** to put (evidence, etc.) before a tribunal ▷ See also **bring about** ▶ **HISTORY** Old English *bringan*

bring about *vb* to cause to happen: *a late harvest brought about by bad weather*

bring-and-buy sale *n* *Brit & NZ* an informal sale, often for charity, to which people bring items for sale and buy those that others have brought

bring forward *vb* **1** to move (a meeting or event) to an earlier date or time **2** to present or introduce (a subject) for discussion **3** *book-keeping* to transfer (a sum) to the top of the next page or column

bring in *vb* **1** to yield (income, profit, or cash) **2** to introduce (a legislative bill, etc.) **3** to return (a verdict)

bring off *vb* to succeed in achieving (something difficult)

bring out *vb* **1** to produce, publish, or have (a book) published **2** to expose, reveal, or cause to be seen: *he brought out the best in me* **3** (foll. by *in*) to cause (a person) to become covered with (a rash, spots, etc.)

bring round *vb* **1** to restore (a person) to consciousness after a faint **2** to convince (another person) of an opinion or point of view

bring to *vb* to restore (a person) to consciousness: *the smelling salts brought her to*

bring up *vb* **1** to care for and train (a child); rear **2** to raise (a subject) for discussion; mention **3** to vomit (food)

brinjal *n* *S African & Indian* a dark purple tropical fruit, cooked and eaten as a vegetable ▶ **HISTORY** Portuguese *berinjela*

brink *n* **1** the edge or border of a steep place **2** the land at the edge of a body of water **3 on the brink of** very near, on the point of: *on the brink of disaster* ▶ **HISTORY** Middle Dutch *brinc*

b

brinkmanship *n* the practice of pressing a dangerous situation to the limit of safety in order to win an advantage

briny *adj* **brinier, briniest** **1** of or like brine; salty ▷ *n* **2 the briny** *informal* the sea

brio (bree-oh) *n* liveliness or spirit ▶ HISTORY Italian

briquette *n* a small brick made of compressed coal dust, used for fuel ▶ HISTORY French

brisk *adj* **1** lively and quick; vigorous: *brisk trade* **2** invigorating or sharp: *brisk weather* **3** practical and businesslike: *his manner was brisk* ▶ HISTORY probably variant of BRUSQUE > **briskly** *adv*

brisket *n* beef from the breast of a cow ▶ HISTORY probably Scandinavian

brisling *n* same as **sprat** ▶ HISTORY Norwegian

bristle *n* **1** any short stiff hair, such as on a pig's back **2** something resembling these hairs: *toothbrush bristle* ▷ *vb* **-tling, -tled** **3** to stand up or cause to stand up like bristles **4** to show anger or indignation: *she bristled at the suggestion* **5** to be thickly covered or set: *the hedges bristled with blossom* ▶ HISTORY Old English *byrst* > **bristly** *adj*

Brit *n informal* a British person

Brit. **1** Britain **2** British

Britannia *n* a female warrior carrying a trident and wearing a helmet, personifying Great Britain

Britannia metal *n* an alloy of tin with antimony and copper

Britannic *adj* of Britain; British: *Her Britannic Majesty*

British *adj* **1** of Britain or the British Commonwealth **2** denoting the English language as spoken and written in Britain ▷ *pl n* **3 the British** the people of Britain

British Summer Time *n* a time set one hour ahead of Greenwich Mean Time: used in Britain from the end of March to the end of October, providing an extra hour of daylight in the evening. Abbrev: **BST**

Briton *n* **1** a native or inhabitant of Britain **2** *history* any of the early Celtic inhabitants of S Britain ▶ HISTORY of Celtic origin

brittle *adj* **1** easily cracked or broken; fragile **2** curt or irritable: *a brittle reply* **3** hard or sharp in quality: *a brittle laugh* ▶ HISTORY Old English *brēotan* to break > **brittly** *adv*

broach *vb* **1** to initiate or introduce (a topic) for discussion **2** to tap or pierce (a container) to draw off (a liquid) **3** to open in order to begin to use ▷ *n* **4** a spit for roasting meat ▶ HISTORY Latin *brochus* projecting

broad *adj* **1** having great breadth or width **2** of vast extent: *broad plains* **3** not detailed; general **4** clear and open: *broad daylight* **5** obvious: *broad hints* **6** tolerant: *a broad view* **7** extensive: *broad support* **8** vulgar or coarse **9** strongly marked: *he spoke broad Australian English* ▷ *n* **10** *slang, chiefly US & Canad* a woman **11 the Broads** in East Anglia, a group of shallow lakes connected by a network of rivers ▶ HISTORY Old English *brād* > **broadly** *adv*

B-road *n* a secondary road in Britain

broadband *n* a telecommunications technique that uses a wide range of frequencies to allow messages to be sent simultaneously, used in fast internet connections

broad bean *n* the large edible flattened seed of a Eurasian bean plant

broadcast *n* **1** a transmission or programme on radio or television ▷ *vb* **-casting, -cast** *or* **-casted** **2** to transmit (announcements or programmes) on radio or television **3** to take part in a radio or television programme **4** to make widely known throughout an area: *to broadcast news* **5** to scatter (seed, etc.) > **broadcaster** *n* > **broadcasting** *n*

broaden *vb* to make or become broad or broader; widen

broad-leaved *adj* denoting trees other than conifers; having broad rather than needle-shaped leaves

broad-minded *adj* **1** tolerant of opposing viewpoints; liberal **2** not easily shocked

broadsheet *n* a newspaper in a large format

broadside *n* **1** a strong or abusive verbal or written attack **2** *naval* the simultaneous firing of all the guns on one side of a ship **3** *naut* the entire side of a ship ▷ *adv* **4** with a broader side facing an object

brocade *n* **1** a rich fabric woven with a raised design ▷ *vb* **-cading, -caded** **2** to weave with such a design ▶ HISTORY Spanish *brocado*

broccoli *n* a variety of cabbage with greenish flower heads ▶ HISTORY Italian

brochure *n* a pamphlet or booklet, esp. one containing introductory information or advertising ▶ HISTORY French

broderie anglaise *n* open embroidery on white cotton, fine linen, etc. ▶ HISTORY French: English embroidery

broekies (brook-eez) *pl n* S African, informal underpants ▶ HISTORY Afrikaans

brogue¹ *n* a sturdy walking shoe, often with ornamental perforations ▶ HISTORY Irish Gaelic *bróg*

brogue² *n* a broad gentle-sounding dialectal accent, esp. that used by the Irish in speaking English ▶ HISTORY origin unknown

broil *vb* *Austral, NZ, US & Canad* same as **grill** (sense 1) ▶ HISTORY Old French *bruillir*

broiler *n* a young tender chicken suitable for roasting

broke *vb* **1** the past tense of **break** ▷ *adj* **2** *informal* having no money

broken *vb* **1** the past participle of **break** ▷ *adj* **2** fractured, smashed, or splintered **3** interrupted; disturbed: *broken sleep* **4** not functioning **5** (of a promise or contract) violated; infringed **6** (of the speech of a foreigner) imperfectly spoken: *broken English* **7** Also: **broken-in** made tame by training **8** exhausted or weakened, as through ill-health or misfortune

broken chord *n* same as **arpeggio**

broken-down *adj* **1** worn out, as by age or long use; dilapidated **2** not in working order

brokenhearted *adj* overwhelmed by grief or disappointment

broken home *n* a family which does not live together because the parents are separated or divorced

broker *n* **1** an agent who buys or sells goods, securities, etc.: *insurance broker* **2** a person who deals in second-hand goods ▶ HISTORY Anglo-French *brocour* broacher

brokerage *n* commission charged by a broker

broker-dealer *n* same as **stockbroker**

brolga *n* a large grey Australian crane with a trumpeting call. Also: **native companion**

brolly *n*, *pl* **-lies** *Brit, Austral & NZ, informal* an umbrella

bromide *n* **1** *chem* any compound of bromine with another element or radical **2** a dose of sodium or potassium bromide given as a sedative **3** a boring, meaningless, or obvious remark

bromide paper *n* a type of photographic paper coated with an emulsion of silver bromide

bromine *n* *chem* a dark red liquid chemical element that gives off a pungent vapour. Symbol: Br ▶ HISTORY Greek *brōmos* bad smell

bromothymol blue *n* *chem* an indicator with pH range of 6.0–7.6 that turns from yellow to blue in acid-alkali tartrations

bronchial *adj* of or relating to both of the bronchi or the smaller tubes into which they divide

bronchiole *n* any of the smallest bronchial tubes

bronchitis *n* inflammation of the bronchial tubes, causing coughing and difficulty in breathing

bronchus (**bronk**-uss) *n*, *pl* **bronchi** (**bronk**-eye) either of the two main branches of the windpipe ▶ HISTORY Greek *bronkhos*

bronco *n*, *pl* **-cos** (in the US and Canada) a wild or partially tamed horse ▶ HISTORY Mexican Spanish

brontosaurus *n* a very large plant-eating four-footed dinosaur that had a long neck and long tail ▶ HISTORY Greek *brontē* thunder + *sauros* lizard

bronze *n* **1** an alloy of copper and smaller proportions of tin **2** a statue, medal, or other object made of bronze ▷ *adj* **3** made of or resembling bronze **4** yellowish-brown ▷ *vb* **bronzing, bronzed** **5** (esp. of the skin) to make or become brown; tan ▶ HISTORY Italian *bronzo*

Bronze Age *n* a phase of human culture, lasting in Britain from about 2000 to 500 BC during which weapons and tools were made of bronze

bronze medal *n* a medal awarded as third prize

brooch *n* an ornament with a hinged pin and catch, worn fastened to clothing ▶ HISTORY Old French *broche*

brood *n* **1** a number of young animals, esp. birds, produced at one hatching **2** all the children in a family: often used jokingly ▷ *vb* **3** (of a bird) to sit on or hatch eggs **4** to think long and unhappily about something: *he brooded on his failure to avert the confrontation* ▶ HISTORY Old English *brōd* > **brooding** *n, adj*

broody *adj* **broodier, broodiest** **1** moody; introspective **2** (of poultry) wishing to sit on or hatch eggs **3** *informal* (of a woman) wishing to have a baby

brook¹ *n* a natural freshwater stream ▶ HISTORY Old English *brōc*

brook² *vb* to bear; tolerate: *she would brook no opposition* ▶ HISTORY Old English *brūcan*

broom *n* **1** a type of long-handled sweeping brush **2** a yellow-flowered shrub **3 a new broom** a newly appointed official, etc. eager to make radical changes ▶ HISTORY Old English *brōm*

broomstick *n* the long handle of a broom

bros. *or* **Bros.** brothers

broth *n* a soup made by boiling meat, vegetables, etc. in water ▶ HISTORY Old English

brothel *n* a house where prostitutes work ▶ HISTORY short for *brothel-house*, from Middle English *brothel* useless person

brother *n* **1** a man or boy with the same parents as another person. *Related adjective:* **fraternal** **2** a man belonging to the same group, trade union, etc. as another or others; fellow member **3** comrade; friend **4** *Christianity* a member of a male religious order ▶ HISTORY Old English *brōthor*

brotherhood *n* **1** fellowship **2** an association, such as a trade union **3** the state of being a brother

brother-in-law *n*, *pl* **brothers-in-law** **1** the brother of one's wife or husband **2** the husband of one's sister

brotherly *adj* of or like a brother, esp. in showing loyalty and affection

brougham (**brew**-am) *n* a horse-drawn closed carriage with a raised open driver's seat in front ▶ HISTORY after Lord *Brougham*

brought *vb* the past of **bring**

brouhaha *n* loud confused noise ▶ HISTORY French

brow *n* **1** the part of the face from the eyes to the hairline; forehead **2** same as **eyebrow** **3** the jutting top of a hill ▶ HISTORY Old English *brū*

browbeat *vb* **-beating, -beat, -beaten** to frighten (someone) with threats

brown *adj* **1** of the colour of wood or the earth **2** (of bread) made from wheatmeal or wholemeal flour **3** deeply tanned ▷ *n* **4** the colour of wood or the earth **5** anything brown, such as brown paint or brown clothing: *clad in brown* ▷ *vb* **6** to make or become brown or browner, for example as a result of cooking ▶ HISTORY Old English *brūn* > **brownish** *adj*

brown bear *n* a large ferocious brownish bear of N America, Europe, and Asia

brown coal *n* same as **lignite**

browned-off *adj* *informal, chiefly Brit* thoroughly bored and depressed

brownfield *adj* relating to an urban area which has previously been built on: *brownfield sites*

Brownian motion *n* *physics* the random movement of particles in a fluid, caused by continuous bombardment from molecules of the fluid ▶ HISTORY after Robert *Brown*, physicist

brownie n 1 (in folklore) an elf said to do helpful work, esp. household chores, at night 2 a small square nutty chocolate cake

Brownie Guide or **Brownie** n a member of the junior branch of the Guides

Brownie point n a notional mark to one's credit for being seen to do the right thing

brown rice n unpolished rice, in which the grains retain the outer yellowish-brown layer (bran)

Brown Shirt n 1 (in Nazi Germany) a storm trooper 2 a member of any fascist party or group

brown trout n a common brownish trout

browse vb **browsing, browsed** 1 to look through (a book or articles for sale) in a casual leisurely manner 2 computers to read hypertext, esp. on the World Wide Web 3 (of deer, goats, etc.) to feed upon vegetation by continual nibbling ▷ n 4 an instance of browsing ▶ HISTORY French broust bud

browser n computers a software package that enables a user to read hypertext, esp. on the World Wide Web

brucellosis n an infectious disease of cattle, goats, and pigs, caused by bacteria and transmittable to humans ▶ HISTORY after Sir David Bruce, bacteriologist

bruise vb **bruising, bruised** 1 to injure (body tissue) without breaking the skin, usually with discoloration, or (of body tissue) to be injured in this way 2 to hurt (someone's feelings) 3 to damage (fruit) ▷ n 4 a bodily injury without a break in the skin, usually with discoloration ▶ HISTORY Old English brȳsan

bruiser n informal a strong tough person, esp. a boxer or a bully

brumby n, pl **-bies** Austral 1 a wild horse 2 an unruly person ▶ HISTORY origin unknown

brunch n a meal eaten late in the morning, combining breakfast with lunch ▶ HISTORY BR(EAKFAST) + (L)UNCH

brunette n a girl or woman with dark brown hair ▶ HISTORY French

brunt n the main force or shock of a blow, attack, etc.: the town bore the brunt of the earthquake

brush¹ n 1 a device of bristles, hairs, wires, etc. set into a firm back or handle: used to apply paint, groom the hair, etc. 2 the act of brushing 3 a brief encounter, esp. an unfriendly one 4 the bushy tail of a fox 5 an electric conductor, esp. one made of carbon, that conveys current between stationary and rotating parts of a generator, motor, etc. ▷ vb 6 to clean, scrub, or paint with a brush 7 to apply or remove with a brush or brushing movement 8 to touch lightly and briefly ▷ See also **brush off, brush up** ▶ HISTORY Old French broisse

brush² n a thick growth of shrubs and small trees; scrub ▶ HISTORY Old French broce

brushed adj textiles treated with a brushing process to raise the nap and give a softer and warmer finish: brushed nylon

brush off slang vb 1 to dismiss and ignore (a person), esp. curtly ▷ n **brushoff** 2 **give someone the brushoff** to reject someone

brush turkey n a bird of New Guinea and Australia resembling the domestic fowl, with black plumage

brush up vb 1 (often foll. by on) to refresh one's knowledge or memory of (a subject) ▷ n **brush-up** 2 Brit the act of tidying one's appearance: have a wash and brush-up

brushwood n 1 cut or broken-off tree branches, twigs, etc. 2 same as **brush²**

brushwork n a characteristic manner of applying paint with a brush: Rembrandt's brushwork

brusque adj blunt or curt in manner or speech ▶ HISTORY Italian brusco sour > **brusquely** adv > **brusqueness** n

Brussels sprout n a vegetable like a tiny cabbage

brutal adj 1 cruel; vicious; savage 2 extremely honest or frank in speech or manner > **brutality** n > **brutally** adv

brutalism n an austere architectural style of the 1950s on, characterized by the use of exposed concrete and angular shapes

brutalize or **-ise** vb **-izing, -ized** or **-ising, -ised** 1 to make or become brutal 2 to treat (someone) brutally > **brutalization** or **-isation** n

brute n 1 a brutal person 2 any animal except man; beast ▷ adj 3 wholly instinctive or physical, like that of an animal: cricket is not a game of brute force 4 without reason or intelligence 5 coarse and grossly sensual ▶ HISTORY Latin brutus irrational

brutish adj 1 of or resembling a brute; animal 2 coarse; cruel; stupid

bryony n, pl **-nies** a herbaceous climbing plant with greenish flowers and red or black berries ▶ HISTORY Greek bruōnia

Brythonic (brith-**on**-ik) n 1 the S group of Celtic languages, consisting of Welsh, Cornish, and Breton ▷ adj 2 of this group of languages ▶ HISTORY Welsh Brython Celt

BS 1 Bachelor of Surgery 2 British Standard(s)

BSc Bachelor of Science

BSE bovine spongiform encephalopathy: a fatal virus disease of cattle

BSI British Standards Institution

BST British Summer Time

Bt Baronet

BT British Telecom

btu or **BThU** British thermal unit

bubble n 1 a small globule of air or a gas in a liquid or a solid 2 a thin film of liquid forming a ball around air or a gas: a soap bubble 3 a dome, esp. a transparent glass or plastic one 4 an unreliable scheme or enterprise ▷ vb **-bling, -bled** 5 to form bubbles 6 to move or flow with a gurgling sound 7 **bubble over** written to express an emotion freely: she was bubbling over with excitement ▶ HISTORY probably Scandinavian

bubble and squeak n Brit, Austral & NZ a dish of boiled cabbage and potatoes fried together

bubble car n Brit a small car of the 1950s with a transparent bubble-shaped top

b

bubbly *adj* **-blier, -bliest** **1** lively; animated; excited **2** full of or resembling bubbles ▷ *n* **3** *informal* champagne

bubo (**byew**-boh) *n*, *pl* **-boes** *pathol* inflammation and swelling of a lymph node, esp. in the armpit or groin ▶ HISTORY Greek *boubōn* groin > **bubonic** (bew-**bonn**-ik) *adj*

bubonic plague *n* an acute infectious disease characterized by the formation of buboes

buccaneer *n* a pirate, esp. in the Caribbean in the 17th and 18th centuries ▶ HISTORY French *boucanier*

buck¹ *n* **1** the male of the goat, hare, kangaroo, rabbit, and reindeer **2** *archaic* a spirited young man **3** the act of bucking ▷ *vb* **4** (of a horse or other animal) to jump vertically, with legs stiff and back arched **5** (of a horse, etc.) to throw (its rider) by bucking **6** *informal* to resist or oppose obstinately: *bucking the system* ▷ See also **buck up** ▶ HISTORY Old English *bucca* he-goat

buck² *n* *US, Canad, Austral & NZ, informal* a dollar ▶ HISTORY origin unknown

buck³ *n* **pass the buck** *informal* to shift blame or responsibility onto another ▶ HISTORY probably from *buckhorn knife*, placed before a player in poker to indicate that he was the next dealer

bucket *n* **1** an open-topped cylindrical container with a handle **2** the amount a bucket will hold **3** a bucket-like part of a machine, such as the scoop on a mechanical shovel **4** *slang* to die ▷ *vb* **-eting, -eted** **5** (often foll. by *down*) (of rain) to fall very heavily ▶ HISTORY Old English *būc*

bucket shop *n* **1** *chiefly Brit* a travel agency specializing in cheap airline tickets **2** an unregistered firm of stockbrokers that engages in fraudulent speculation

buckle *n* **1** a clasp for fastening together two loose ends, esp. of a belt or strap ▷ *vb* **-ling, -led** **2** to fasten or be fastened with a buckle **3** to bend or cause to bend out of shape, esp. as a result of pressure or heat ▶ HISTORY Latin *buccula* cheek strap

buckle down *vb* *informal* to apply oneself with determination

buckshee *adj* *Brit, slang* without charge; free ▶ HISTORY from BAKSHEESH

buckshot *n* large lead pellets used for hunting game

buckteeth *pl n* projecting upper front teeth > **buck-toothed** *adj*

buckthorn *n* a thorny shrub whose berries were formerly used as a purgative

buck up *vb* *informal* **1** to make or become more cheerful or confident **2** to make haste

buckwheat *n* **1** a type of small black seed used as animal fodder and in making flour **2** the flour obtained from such seeds ▶ HISTORY Middle Dutch *boecweite*

bucolic (byew-**koll**-ik) *adj* **1** of the countryside or country life; rustic **2** of or relating to shepherds; pastoral ▷ *n* **3** a pastoral poem ▶ HISTORY Greek *boukolos* cowherd

bud *n* **1** a swelling on the stem of a plant that develops into a flower or leaf **2** a partially opened flower: *rosebud* **3** any small budlike outgrowth: *taste buds* **4** **nip something in the bud** to put an end to something in its initial stages ▷ *vb* **budding, budded** **5** (of plants and some animals) to produce buds **6** *horticulture* to graft (a bud) from one plant onto another ▶ HISTORY Middle English *budde*

Buddha *n* a title of Gautama Siddhartha (6th century BC), the Indian religious teacher who founded Buddhism ▶ HISTORY Sanskrit, literally: the enlightened one

Buddhism *n* a religion founded by the Buddha that teaches that all suffering can be brought to an end by overcoming greed, hatred, and delusion > **Buddhist** *n*, *adj*

budding *adj* beginning to develop or grow: *a budding actor*

buddleia *n* a shrub which has long spikes of purple flowers ▶ HISTORY after A. Buddle, botanist

buddy *n*, *pl* **-dies** **1** *chiefly US & Canad, informal* a friend **2** a volunteer who helps and supports a person suffering from AIDS ▷ *vb* **-dies, -dying, -died** **3** to act as a buddy to (a person suffering from AIDS) ▶ HISTORY probably variant of BROTHER

budge *vb* **budging, budged** **1** to move slightly: *he refuses to budge off that chair* **2** to change or cause to change opinions: *nothing would budge him from this idea* ▶ HISTORY Old French *bouger*

budgerigar *n* a small cage bird bred in many different-coloured varieties ▶ HISTORY Aboriginal

budget *n* **1** a plan of expected income and expenditure over a specified period **2** the total amount of money allocated for a specific purpose during a specified period ▷ *adj* **3** inexpensive: *a budget hotel* ▷ *vb* **-eting, -eted** **4** to enter or provide for in a budget **5** to plan the expenditure of (money or time) ▶ HISTORY Latin *bulga* leather pouch > **budgetary** *adj*

Budget *n* **the Budget** an annual estimate of British government expenditures and revenues and the financial plans for the following financial year

budget deficit *n* the amount by which government spending exceeds income from taxation, etc.

budgie *n* *informal* same as **budgerigar**

buff¹ *n* **1** a soft thick flexible undyed leather **2** a cloth or pad of material used for polishing **3** **in the buff** *informal* completely naked ▷ *adj* **4** dull yellowish-brown ▷ *vb* **5** to clean or polish (a metal, floor, shoes, etc.) with a buff ▶ HISTORY Late Latin *bufalus* buffalo

buff² *n* *informal* an expert on or devotee of a given subject: *an opera buff* ▶ HISTORY from the buff-coloured uniforms worn by volunteer firemen in New York City

buffalo *n*, *pl* **-loes** *or* **-lo** **1** a type of cattle with upward-curving horns **2** same as **water buffalo** **3** *US & Canad* a bison ▶ HISTORY Greek *bous* ox

b

buffer[1] *n* **1** one of a pair of spring-loaded steel pads at the ends of railway vehicles and railway tracks that reduces shock on impact **2** a person or thing that lessens shock or protects from damaging impact, circumstances, etc. **3** *chem* **a** a substance added to a solution to resist changes in its acidity or alkalinity **b** Also called: **buffer solution** a solution containing such a substance **4** *computers* a device for temporarily storing data ▶ HISTORY from BUFFET[2]

buffer[2] *n Brit, informal* a stupid or bumbling person, esp. a man: *an old buffer* ▶ HISTORY origin unknown

buffer state *n* a small and usually neutral state between two rival powers

buffer zone *n* a strip of land acting as a separator between two other areas of land dedicated to incompatible uses

buffet[1] (boof-fay, buff-ay) *n* **1** a counter where light refreshments are served **2** a meal at which guests help themselves from a number of dishes ▶ HISTORY French

buffet[2] (buff-it) *vb* **-feting, -feted 1** to knock against or about; batter: *the ship was buffeted by strong winds* **2** to hit, esp. with the fist ▷ *n* **3** a blow, esp. with a hand ▶ HISTORY Old French *buffeter*

buffoon *n* a person who amuses others by silly behaviour ▶ HISTORY Latin *bufo* toad
> **buffoonery** *n*

bug *n* **1** any of various insects having piercing and sucking mouthparts **2** *chiefly US & Canad* any insect **3** *informal* a minor illness caused by a germ or virus **4** *informal* an obsessive idea or hobby **5** *informal* a concealed microphone used for recording conversations in spying **6** *Austral* a flattish edible shellfish ▷ *vb* **bugging, bugged** *informal* **7** to irritate or upset (someone) **8** to conceal a microphone in (a room or telephone) ▶ HISTORY origin unknown

bugbear *n* a thing that causes obsessive anxiety ▶ HISTORY obsolete *bug* an evil spirit + BEAR[2]

bugger *n* **1** *taboo slang* a person or thing considered to be unpleasant or difficult **2** *slang* a humorous or affectionate term for someone: *a friendly little bugger* ▷ *vb* **3** *slang* to tire; weary ▷ *interj* **4** *taboo slang* an exclamation of annoyance or disappointment ▶ HISTORY Medieval Latin *Bulgarus* Bulgarian heretic

bugger off *vb taboo slang* to go away; depart

buggy *n, pl* **-gies 1** a light horse-drawn carriage having two or four wheels **2** a lightweight folding pram for babies or young children ▶ HISTORY origin unknown

bugle *music n* **1** a brass instrument used chiefly for military calls ▷ *vb* **-gling, -gled 2** to play or sound (on) a bugle ▶ HISTORY short for *bugle horn* ox horn, from Latin *buculus* bullock > **bugler** *n*

build *vb* **building, built 1** to make or construct by joining parts or materials: *more than 100 bypasses have been built in the past decade* **2** to establish and develop: *it took ten years to build the business* **3** to make in a particular way or for a particular

purpose: *she's built for speed, not stamina* **4** (often foll. by *up*) to increase in intensity ▷ *n* **5** physical form, figure, or proportions: *he has an athletic build* ▶ HISTORY Old English *byldan*

builder *n* a person who constructs houses and other buildings

building *n* **1** a structure, such as a house, with a roof and walls **2** the business of building houses, etc.

building society *n* a cooperative banking enterprise where money can be invested and mortgage loans made available

build up *vb* **1** to construct (something) gradually, systematically, and in stages **2** to increase by degrees: *he steadily built up a power base* **3** to prepare for or gradually approach a climax ▷ *n* **build-up 4** a progressive increase in number or size: *the build-up of industry* **5** a gradual approach to a climax **6** extravagant publicity or praise, esp. as a campaign

built *vb* the past of **build**

built environment *n civil engineering* an environment that includes elements created or altered by man, such as streets, buildings, and electricity

built-in *adj* **1** included as an essential part: *a built-in cupboard* **2** essential: *a built-in instinct*

built-up *adj* **1** having many buildings: *the area has become more built-up* **2** increased by the addition of parts: *built-up heels*

built-up area *n* an area in which there are many buildings

bulb *n* **1** same as **light bulb 2** the onion-shaped base of the stem of some plants, which sends down roots **3** a plant, such as a daffodil, which grows from a bulb **4** any bulb-shaped thing ▶ HISTORY Greek *bolbos* onion > **bulbous** *adj*

Bulgarian *adj* **1** of Bulgaria ▷ *n* **2** a person from Bulgaria **3** the language of Bulgaria

bulge *n* **1** a swelling or an outward curve on a normally flat surface **2** a sudden increase in number, esp. of population ▷ *vb* **bulging, bulged 3** to swell outwards ▶ HISTORY Latin *bulga* bag > **bulging** *adj*

bulimia *n* a disorder characterized by compulsive overeating followed by vomiting ▶ HISTORY Greek *bous* ox + *limos* hunger > **bulimic** *adj, n*

bulk *n* **1** volume or size, esp. when great **2** the main part: *he spends the bulk of his time abroad* **3** *written* a large body, esp. of a person **4** the part of food which passes unabsorbed through the digestive system **5** **in bulk** in large quantities: *how frequently do you buy food in bulk for your family?* ▷ *vb* **6** **bulk large** to be or seem important or prominent ▶ HISTORY Old Norse *bulki* cargo

bulk buying *n* the purchase of goods in large amounts, often at reduced prices

bulkhead *n* any upright partition in a ship or aeroplane ▶ HISTORY probably from Old Norse *bálkr* partition + HEAD

bulky *adj* **bulkier, bulkiest** very large and massive, esp. so as to be unwieldy > **bulkiness** *n*

bull¹ *n* **1** a male of domestic cattle **2** the male of various other animals including the elephant and whale **3** a very large, strong, or aggressive person **4** *Stock Exchange* a speculator who buys in anticipation of rising prices in order to make a profit on resale **5** *chiefly Brit* same as **bull's-eye** (senses 1, 2) **6 like a bull in a china shop** clumsy **7 take the bull by the horns** to face and tackle a difficulty without shirking ▶ HISTORY Old English *bula*

bull² *n* a ludicrously self-contradictory or nonsensical statement ▶ HISTORY origin unknown

bull³ *n* a formal document issued by the pope ▶ HISTORY Latin *bulla* round object

bull bars *pl n* a large protective metal grille on the front of some vehicles, esp. four-wheel-drive vehicles

bulldog *n* a thickset dog with a broad head and a muscular body

bulldog clip *n* a clip for holding papers together, consisting of two metal clamps and a spring

bulldoze *vb* **-dozing, -dozed 1** to move, demolish, or flatten with a bulldozer **2** *informal* to coerce (someone) into doing something by intimidation ▶ HISTORY origin unknown

bulldozer *n* a powerful tractor fitted with caterpillar tracks and a blade at the front, used for moving earth

bullet *n* a small metallic missile used as the projectile of a gun or rifle ▶ HISTORY French *boulette* little ball

bulletin *n* **1** a broadcast summary of the news **2** an official statement on a matter of public interest **3** a periodical published by an organization for its members

- ■ **WORD HISTORY**
- ■ A 'bull' is an edict issued by the pope, so called
- ■ from the official seal (Latin *bulla*) attached to it.
- ■ *Bullettino* in Italian originally meant a 'small
- ■ papal bull', and came to be applied to other
- ■ official announcements.

bulletin board *n* **1** *US* same as **notice board** **2** *computers* a type of data-exchange system by which messages can be sent and read

bullfight *n* a public show, popular in Spain, in which a matador baits and usually kills a bull in an arena > **bullfighter** *n* > **bullfighting** *n*

bullfinch *n* a common European songbird with a black head and, in the male, a pinkish breast

bullfrog *n* any of various large frogs having a loud deep croak

bullion *n* gold or silver in the form of bars and ingots ▶ HISTORY Anglo-French: mint

bull-necked *adj* having a short thick neck

bullock *n* a gelded bull; steer ▶ HISTORY Old English *bulluc*

bull's-eye *n* **1** the small central disc of a target or a dartboard **2** a shot hitting this **3** *informal* something that exactly achieves its aim **4** a peppermint-flavoured boiled sweet **5** a small circular window **6** a thick disc of glass set into a ship's deck, etc. to admit light **7** the glass boss at the centre of a sheet of blown glass **8 a** a convex lens used as a condenser **b** a lamp or lantern containing such a lens

bull terrier *n* a terrier with a muscular body and a short smooth coat

bully *n, pl* **-lies 1** a person who hurts, persecutes, or intimidates weaker people ▷ *vb* **-lies, -lying, -lied 2** to hurt, intimidate, or persecute (a weaker or smaller person) ▷ *interj* **3 bully for you** or **him,** etc. *informal* well done! bravo!: now usually used sarcastically ▶ HISTORY originally, sweetheart, fine fellow, swaggering coward, probably from Middle Dutch *boele* lover

bully beef *n* canned corned beef ▶ HISTORY French *bœuf bouilli* boiled beef

bully-off *hockey n* **1** the method of restarting play in which two opposing players stand with the ball between them and strike their sticks together three times before trying to hit the ball ▷ *vb* **bully off 2** to restart play with a bully-off ▶ HISTORY origin unknown

bulrush *n* **1** a tall reedlike marsh plant with brown spiky flowers **2** *Bible* same as **papyrus** (sense 1) ▶ HISTORY Middle English *bulrish*

bulwark *n* **1** a wall or similar structure used as a fortification; rampart **2** a person or thing acting as a defence ▶ HISTORY Middle High German *bolwerk*

bum¹ *n* *Brit, Austral & NZ, slang* the buttocks or anus ▶ HISTORY origin unknown

bum² *informal n* **1** a disreputable loafer or idler **2** a tramp; hobo ▷ *vb* **bumming, bummed 3** to get by begging; cadge: *to bum a lift* **4 bum around** to spend time to no good purpose; loaf ▷ *adj* **5** of poor quality; useless: *he hit a bum note* ▶ HISTORY probably from German *bummeln* to loaf

bumbag *n* a small bag worn on a belt around the waist

bumble *vb* **-bling, -bled 1** to speak or do in a clumsy, muddled, or inefficient way **2** to move in a clumsy or unsteady way ▶ HISTORY origin unknown > **bumbling** *adj, n*

bumblebee *n* a large hairy bee ▶ HISTORY obsolete *bumble* to buzz

bumf or **bumph** *n* *Brit, Austral & NZ* **1** *informal* official documents or forms **2** *slang* toilet paper ▶ HISTORY short for *bumfodder*

bump *vb* **1** to knock or strike (someone or something) with a jolt **2** to travel or proceed in jerks and jolts **3** to hurt by knocking ▷ *n* **4** an impact; knock; jolt; collision **5** a dull thud from an impact or collision **6** a lump on the body caused by a blow **7** a raised uneven part, such as on a road surface ▷ See also **bump into, bump off** ▶ HISTORY probably imitative > **bumpy** *adj*

bumper¹ *n* a horizontal bar attached to the front and rear of a vehicle to protect against damage from impact

bumper² *n* **1** a glass or tankard, filled to the brim, esp. as a toast **2** an unusually large or fine example of something ▷ *adj* **3** unusually large, fine, or abundant: *a bumper crop* ▶ HISTORY probably obsolete *bump* to bulge

bumph *n* same as **bumf**

bump into *vb informal* to meet (someone) by chance

bumpkin *n* an awkward simple rustic person: *a country bumpkin* ▶ HISTORY probably from Dutch

bump off *vb slang* to murder (someone)

bumptious *adj* offensively self-assertive or conceited ▶ HISTORY probably *bump + fractious*

bun *n* **1** a small sweetened bread roll, often containing currants or spices **2** a small round cake **3** a hairstyle in which long hair is gathered into a bun shape at the back of the head ▶ HISTORY origin unknown

bunch *n* **1** a number of things growing, fastened, or grouped together: *a bunch of grapes; a bunch of keys* **2** a collection; group: *a bunch of queries* **3** a group or company: *a bunch of cowards* ▷ *vb* **4** to group or be grouped into a bunch ▶ HISTORY origin unknown

bundle *n* **1** a number of things or a quantity of material gathered or loosely bound together: *a bundle of sticks* **2** something wrapped or tied for carrying; package **3** *biol* a collection of strands of specialized tissue such as nerve fibres **4** *bot* a strand of conducting tissue within plants ▷ *vb* **-dling, -dled** **5** (foll. by *out, off, into*) to cause (someone) to go, esp. roughly or unceremoniously: *she bundled them unceremoniously out into the garden* **6** to push or throw (something), esp. in a quick untidy way: *the soiled items were bundled into a black plastic bag* ▶ HISTORY probably from Middle Dutch *bundel*

bundle up *vb* to make (something) into a bundle or bundles

bundu *n S African & Zimbabwean, slang* a largely uninhabited wild region far from towns ▶ HISTORY from a Bantu language

bun fight *n Brit, Austral & NZ, slang* a tea party

bung *n* **1** a stopper, esp. of cork or rubber, used to close something such as a cask or flask ▷ *vb* **2** (foll. by *up*) *informal* to close or seal (something) with or as if with a bung **3** *Brit, Austral & NZ, slang* to throw (something) somewhere in a careless manner; sling ▶ HISTORY Middle Dutch *bonghe*

bungalow *n* a one-storey house

- ■ **WORD HISTORY**
- ■ 'Bungalow' comes from Hindi *banglā* meaning
- ■ 'of Bengal'. A bungalow was originally a house
- ■ of the style generally occupied by Europeans in
- ■ Bengal, a one-storey house with a verandah
- ■ round it and a thatched roof.

bungee jumping *or* **bungy jumping** *n* a sport in which a person jumps from a high bridge, tower, etc. to which he or she is connected by a rubber rope ▶ HISTORY from *bungie*, slang word for India rubber

bungle *vb* **-gling, -gled** **1** to spoil (an operation) through clumsiness or incompetence; botch ▷ *n* **2** a clumsy or unsuccessful performance; blunder ▶ HISTORY origin unknown > **bungler** *n* > **bungling** *adj, n*

bunion *n* an inflamed swelling of the first joint of the big toe ▶ HISTORY origin unknown

bunk¹ *n* **1** a narrow shelflike bed fixed along a wall, esp. in a caravan or ship **2** same as **bunk bed** ▶ HISTORY probably from *bunker*

bunk² *n informal* same as **bunkum**

bunk³ *n* **do a bunk** *Brit, Austral & NZ, slang* to make a hurried and secret departure ▷ *vb Brit, NZ & S African* to be absent without permission ▶ HISTORY origin unknown

bunk bed *n* one of a pair of beds constructed one above the other to save space

bunker *n* **1** an obstacle on a golf course, usually a sand-filled hollow bordered by a ridge **2** an underground shelter **3** a large storage container for coal, etc. ▶ HISTORY Scots *bonkar*

bunkum *n* empty talk; nonsense ▶ HISTORY after *Buncombe*, North Carolina, alluded to in an inane speech by its Congressional representative

bunny *n, pl* **-nies** a child's word for **rabbit** ▶ HISTORY Scottish Gaelic *bun* rabbit's tail

Bunsen burner *n* a gas burner consisting of a metal tube with an adjustable air valve at the base ▶ HISTORY after R. W. *Bunsen*, chemist

bunting¹ *n* decorative flags, pennants, and streamers ▶ HISTORY origin unknown

bunting² *n* a songbird with a short stout bill ▶ HISTORY origin unknown

bunya *n* a tall dome-shaped Australian coniferous tree. Also called: **bunya-bunya**

bunyip *n Austral* a legendary monster said to live in swamps and lakes ▶ HISTORY from a native Australian language

buoy *n* **1** a brightly coloured floating object anchored to the sea bed for marking moorings, navigable channels, or obstructions in the water ▷ *vb* **2** (foll. by *up*) to prevent from sinking: *the life belt buoyed him up* **3** to raise the spirits of; hearten: *exports are on the increase, buoyed by a weak dollar* **4** *naut* to mark (a channel or obstruction) with a buoy or buoys ▶ HISTORY probably Germanic

buoyant *adj* **1** able to float in or rise to the surface of a liquid **2** (of a liquid or gas) able to keep a body afloat **3** cheerful or resilient > **buoyancy** *n*

bur *or* **burr** *n* **1** a seed case or flower head with hooks or prickles **2** any plant that produces burs ▶ HISTORY probably from Old Norse

burble *vb* **-bling, -bled** **1** to make or utter with a bubbling sound; gurgle **2** to talk quickly and excitedly ▶ HISTORY probably imitative

burbot *n, pl* **-bots** *or* **-bot** a freshwater fish of the cod family that has barbels around its mouth ▶ HISTORY Old French *bourbotte*

burden¹ *n* **1** something that is carried; load **2** something that is difficult to bear. *Related adjective:* **onerous** *vb* **3** to put or impose a burden on; load **4** to weigh down; oppress ▶ HISTORY Old English *byrthen* > **burdensome** *adj*

burden² *n* **1** a line of words recurring at the end of each verse of a song **2** the theme of a speech, book, etc. ▶ HISTORY Old French *bourdon* droning sound

burden of proof *n law* the obligation to provide evidence that will convince the court or jury of the truth of one's contention if the case is to succeed; in criminal cases, the *burden of proof* lies with the prosecution and in civil cases, it lies with the plaintiff

burdock *n* a weed with large heart-shaped leaves, and burlike fruits ▶ **HISTORY** BUR + DOCK⁴

bureau (**byew**-roe) *n*, *pl* **-reaus** *or* **-reaux** (-rose) **1** an office or agency, esp. one providing services for the public **2** *US* a government department **3** *chiefly Brit* a writing desk with pigeonholes and drawers against which the writing surface can be closed when not in use **4** *US* a chest of drawers ▶ **HISTORY** French

bureaucracy *n*, *pl* **-cies 1** a rigid system of administration based upon organization into bureaus, division of labour, a hierarchy of authority, etc. **2** government by such a system **3** government officials collectively **4** any administration in which action is impeded by unnecessary official procedures

bureaucrat *n* **1** an official in a bureaucracy **2** an official who adheres rigidly to bureaucracy > **bureaucratic** *adj*

burette *or US* **buret** *n* a graduated glass tube with a stopcock on one end for dispensing known volumes of fluids ▶ **HISTORY** Old French *buire* ewer

burgeon *vb* to develop or grow rapidly; flourish ▶ **HISTORY** Old French *burjon*

burger *n informal* same as **hamburger**

burgh *n* (in Scotland until 1975) a town with a degree of self-government ▶ **HISTORY** Scots form of *borough*

burgher *n archaic* a citizen, esp. one from the Continent ▶ **HISTORY** German *Bürger* or Dutch *burger*

burglar *n* a person who illegally enters a property to commit a crime ▶ **HISTORY** Medieval Latin *burglator*

burglary *n*, *pl* **-ries** the crime of entering a building as a trespasser to commit theft or another offence

burgle *vb* **-gling, -gled** to break into (a house, shop, etc.)

burgomaster *n* the chief magistrate of a town in Austria, Belgium, Germany, or the Netherlands ▶ **HISTORY** Dutch *burgemeester*

Burgundy *n* **1** a red or white wine produced in the Burgundy region, around Dijon in France ▷ *adj* **2 burgundy** dark purplish-red

burial *n* the burying of a dead body

burin (**byoor**-in) *n* a steel chisel used for engraving metal, wood, or marble ▶ **HISTORY** French

burl *or* **birl** *n informal* **1** *Scot, Austral & NZ* an attempt; try: *give it a burl* **2** *Austral & NZ* a ride in a car ▶ **HISTORY** from Scots *birl* to spin or turn

burlesque *n* **1** an artistic work, esp. literary or dramatic, satirizing a subject by caricaturing it **2** *US & Canad theatre* a bawdy comedy show of the late 19th and early 20th centuries ▷ *adj* **3** of or characteristic of a burlesque ▶ **HISTORY** Italian *burla* a jest

burly *adj* **-lier, -liest** large and thick of build; sturdy ▶ **HISTORY** Germanic

burn¹ *vb* **burning, burnt** *or* **burned 1** to be or set on fire **2** to destroy or be destroyed by fire **3** to damage, injure, or mark by heat: *he burnt his hand* **4** to die or put to death by fire **5** to be or feel hot: *my forehead is burning* **6** to smart or cause to smart: *brandy burns your throat* **7** to feel strong emotion, esp. anger or passion **8** to use for the purposes of light, heat, or power: *to burn coal* **9** to form by or as if by fire: *to burn a hole* **10** to char or become charred: *the toast is burning* **11** to record data on (a compact disc) **12 burn one's bridges** *or* **boats** to commit oneself to a particular course of action with no possibility of turning back **13 burn one's fingers** to suffer from having meddled or interfered ▷ *n* **14** an injury caused by exposure to heat, electrical, chemical, or radioactive agents **15** a mark caused by burning ▷ See also **burn out** ▶ **HISTORY** Old English *beornan*

burn² *n Scot & N English* a small stream ▶ **HISTORY** Old English *burna*

burner *n* the part of a stove or lamp that produces flame or heat

burning *adj* **1** intense; passionate **2** urgent; crucial: *a burning problem*

burning glass *n* a convex lens for concentrating the sun's rays to produce fire

burnish *vb* to make or become shiny or smooth by friction; polish ▶ **HISTORY** Old French *brunir* to make brown

burnous *n* a long circular cloak with a hood, worn esp. by Arabs ▶ **HISTORY** Arabic *burnus*

burn out *vb* **1** to become or cause to become inoperative as a result of heat or friction: *the clutch burnt out* ▷ *n* **burnout 2** total exhaustion and inability to work effectively as a result of excessive demands or overwork

burnt *vb* **1** a past of **burn¹** ▷ *adj* **2** affected by or as if by burning; charred

burp *n* **1** *informal* a belch ▷ *vb* **2** *informal* to belch **3** to cause (a baby) to belch ▶ **HISTORY** imitative

burr *n* **1** the soft trilling sound given to the letter (r) in some English dialects **2** a whirring or humming sound **3** a rough edge left on metal or paper after cutting **4** a small hand-operated drill ▶ **HISTORY** origin unknown

burrawang *n* an Australian plant with fernlike leaves and an edible nut

burrow *n* **1** a hole dug in the ground by a rabbit or other small animal ▷ *vb* **2** to dig (a tunnel or hole) in, through, or under ground **3** to move through a place by or as if by digging **4** to delve deeply: *he burrowed into his coat pocket* **5** to live in or as if in a burrow ▶ **HISTORY** probably variant of *borough*

bursar *n* a treasurer of a school, college, or university ▶ **HISTORY** Medieval Latin *bursarius* keeper of the purse

bursary *n*, *pl* **-ries 1** a scholarship or grant awarded esp. in Scottish and New Zealand schools and universities **2** *NZ* a state examination for senior pupils at secondary school

b

burst *vb* **bursting, burst 1** to break or cause to break open or apart suddenly and noisily; explode **2** to come or go suddenly and forcibly: *he burst into the room* **3** to be full to the point of breaking open: *bursting at the seams* **4** (foll. by *into*) to give vent to (something) suddenly or loudly: *she burst into song* ▷ *n* **5** an instance of breaking open suddenly; explosion **6** a break; breach: *there was a burst in the pipe* **7** a sudden increase of effort; spurt: *a burst of speed* **8** a sudden and violent occurrence or outbreak: *a burst of applause* ▶ HISTORY Old English *berstan*

burton *n* **go for a burton** *Brit & NZ, slang* **a** to be broken, useless, or lost **b** to die ▶ HISTORY origin unknown

bury *vb* **buries, burying, buried 1** to place (a corpse) in a grave **2** to place (something) in the earth and cover it with soil **3** to cover (something) from sight; hide **4** to occupy (oneself) with deep concentration: *he buried himself in his work* **5** written to dismiss (a feeling) from the mind: *they decided to bury any hard feelings* ▶ HISTORY Old English *byrgan*

bus *n* **1** a large motor vehicle designed to carry passengers between stopping places along a regular route **2** *informal* a car or aircraft that is old and shaky **3** *electronics, computers* an electrical conductor used to make a common connection between several circuits ▷ *vb* **bussing, bussed** or **busing, bused 4** to travel or transport by bus **5** *chiefly US & Canad* to transport (children) by bus from one area to another in order to create racially integrated schools ▶ HISTORY short for OMNIBUS

busby *n, pl* **-bies** a tall fur helmet worn by certain British soldiers ▶ HISTORY origin unknown

bush¹ *n* **1** a dense woody plant, smaller than a tree, with many branches; shrub **2** a dense cluster of such shrubs; thicket **3** something resembling a bush, esp. in density: *a bush of hair* **4** **the bush** an uncultivated area covered with trees or shrubs in Australia, Africa, New Zealand, and Canada **5** *Canad* an area on a farm on which timber is grown and cut **6** **beat about the bush** to avoid the point at issue ▶ HISTORY Germanic

bush² *n* **1** a thin metal sleeve or tubular lining serving as a bearing ▷ *vb* **2** to fit a bush to (a casing or bearing) ▶ HISTORY Middle Dutch *busse* box

bushbaby *n, pl* **-babies** a small agile tree-living mammal with large eyes and a long tail

bushed *adj informal* extremely tired; exhausted

bushel *n* *Brit* an obsolete unit of dry or liquid measure equal to 8 gallons (36.4 litres) ▶ HISTORY Old French *boissel*

bushman *n, pl* **-men** *Austral & NZ* a person who lives or travels in the bush

Bushman *n, pl* **-men** a member of a hunting and gathering people of southern Africa ▶ HISTORY Afrikaans *boschjesman*

bush sickness *n NZ* a disease of animals caused by mineral deficiency in old bush country > **bush-sick** *adj*

bush telegraph *n* a means of spreading rumour or gossip

bushveld *n S African* bushy countryside ▶ HISTORY Afrikaans

bushwalking *n Austral* the leisure activity of walking in the bush > **bushwalker** *n*

bushy *adj* **bushier, bushiest 1** (of hair) thick and shaggy **2** covered or overgrown with bushes

business *n* **1** the purchase and sale of goods and services **2** a commercial or industrial establishment **3** a trade or profession **4** commercial activity; dealings: *the two countries should do business with each other* **5** proper or rightful concern or responsibility: *mind your own business* **6** an affair; matter: *it's a dreadful business* **7** serious work or activity: *get down to business* **8** a difficult or complicated matter: *it's a business trying to see him* **9** **mean business** to be in earnest ▶ HISTORY Old English *bisignis* care, attentiveness

businesslike *adj* efficient and methodical

businessman *or fem* **businesswoman** *n, pl* **-men** *or* **-women** a person engaged in commercial or industrial business, usually an owner or executive

business park *n* an area specially designated to accommodate business offices, light industry, etc.

business rate *n* a tax levied on businesses, based on the value of their premises

busker *n* a person who entertains for money in streets or stations ▶ HISTORY perhaps from Spanish *buscar* to look for > **busk** *vb*

bust¹ *n* **1** a woman's bosom **2** a sculpture of the head, shoulders, and upper chest of a person ▶ HISTORY Italian *busto* a sculpture

bust² *informal vb* **busting, busted** *or* **bust 1** to burst or break **2** (of the police) to raid or search (a place) or arrest (someone) **3** *US & Canad* to demote in military rank ▷ *adj* **4** broken **5** **go bust** to become bankrupt ▶ HISTORY from *burst*

bustard *n* a bird with long strong legs, a heavy body, a long neck, and speckled plumage

bustle¹ *vb* **-tling, -tled 1** (often foll. by *about*) to hurry with a great show of energy or activity ▷ *n* **2** energetic and noisy activity ▶ HISTORY probably obsolete *buskle* to prepare > **bustling** *adj*

bustle² *n* a cushion or framework worn by women in the late 19th century at the back in order to expand the skirt ▶ HISTORY origin unknown

bust-up *informal n* **1** a serious quarrel, esp. one ending a relationship **2** *Brit, Austral & NZ* a disturbance or brawl ▷ *vb* **bust up 3** to quarrel and part **4** to disrupt (a meeting), esp. violently

busy *adj* **busier, busiest 1** actively or fully engaged; occupied **2** crowded with or characterized by activity **3** (of a telephone line) in use; engaged ▷ *vb* **busies, busying, busied 4** to make or keep (someone, esp. oneself) busy; occupy ▶ HISTORY Old English *bisig* > **busily** *adv*

busybody *n, pl* **-bodies** a meddlesome, prying, or officious person

but *conj* **1** contrary to expectation: *he cut his hand but didn't cry* **2** in contrast; on the contrary: *I like seafood but my husband doesn't* **3** other than: *we can't* do anything but wait **4** without it happening: *we never go out but it rains* ▷ *prep* **5** except: *they saved all but one* **6 but for** were it not for: *but for you, we couldn't have managed* ▷ *adv* **7** only: *I can but try; he was but a child* ▷ *n* **8** an objection: *ifs and buts* ▶ HISTORY Old English *būtan* without, except

butane (**byew**-tane) *n* a colourless gas used in the manufacture of rubber and fuels ▶ HISTORY from *butyl*

butch *adj slang* (of a woman or man) markedly or aggressively masculine ▶ HISTORY from *butcher*

butcher *n* **1** a person who sells meat **2** a person who kills animals for meat **3** a brutal murderer ▷ *vb* **4** to kill and prepare (animals) for meat **5** to kill (people) at random or brutally **6** to make a mess of; botch ▶ HISTORY Old French *bouchier*

butcherbird *n* an Australian magpie that impales its prey on thorns

butchery *n, pl* **-eries 1** senseless slaughter **2** the business of a butcher

butler *n* the head manservant of a household, in charge of the wines, table, etc. ▶ HISTORY Old French *bouteille* bottle

butt¹ *n* **1** the thicker or blunt end of something, such as the stock of a rifle **2** the unused end of a cigarette or cigar; stub **3** *chiefly US & Canad, slang* the buttocks ▶ HISTORY Middle English

butt² *n* **1** a person or thing that is the target of ridicule or teasing **2** *shooting, archery* **a** a mound of earth behind the target **b butts** the target range ▶ HISTORY Old French *but*

butt³ *vb* **1** to strike (something or someone) with the head or horns **2** (foll. by *in* or *into*) to intrude, esp. into a conversation; interfere ▷ *n* **3** a blow with the head or horns ▶ HISTORY Old French *boter*

butt⁴ *n* a large cask for collecting or storing liquids ▶ HISTORY Late Latin *buttis* cask

butte (**byewt**) *n* *US & Canad* an isolated steep flat-topped hill ▶ HISTORY Old French *bute* mound behind a target

butter *n* **1** an edible fatty yellow solid made from cream by churning **2** any substance with a butter-like consistency, such as peanut butter ▷ *vb* **3** to put butter on or in (something) ▷ See also **butter up** ▶ HISTORY Greek *bous* cow + *turos* cheese > **buttery** *adj*

butter bean *n* a large pale flat edible bean

buttercup *n* a small bright yellow flower

butterfingers *n informal* a person who drops things by mistake or fails to catch things

butterflies *pl n informal* a nervous feeling in the stomach

butterfly *n, pl* **-flies 1** an insect with a slender body and brightly coloured wings **2** a swimming stroke in which the arms are plunged forward together in large circular movements **3** a person who never settles with one interest or occupation for long ▶ HISTORY Old English *buttorflēoge*

butterfly nut *n* same as **wing nut**

buttermilk *n* the sourish liquid remaining after the butter has been separated from milk

butterscotch *n* a hard brittle toffee made with butter, brown sugar, etc.

butter up *vb* to flatter

buttery *n, pl* **-teries** *Brit* (in some universities) a room in which food and drink are sold to students ▶ HISTORY Latin *butta* cask

buttock *n* **1** either of the two large fleshy masses that form the human rump **2** the corresponding part in some mammals ▶ HISTORY perhaps from Old English *buttuc* round slope

button *n* **1** a disc or knob of plastic, wood, etc. attached to a garment, which fastens two surfaces together by passing through a buttonhole **2** a small disc that operates a door bell or machine when pressed **3** a small round object, such as a sweet or badge **4 not worth a button** *Brit* of no value; useless ▷ *vb* **5** to fasten (a garment) with a button or buttons ▶ HISTORY Old French *boton*

buttonhole *n* **1** a slit in a garment through which a button is passed to fasten two surfaces together **2** a flower worn pinned to the lapel or in the buttonhole ▷ *vb* **-holing, -holed 3** to detain (a person) in conversation

buttress *n* **1** a construction, usually of brick or stone, built to support a wall **2** any support or prop ▷ *vb* **3** to support (a wall) with a buttress **4** *written* to support or sustain: *his observations are buttressed by the most recent scholarly research* ▶ HISTORY Old French *bouter* to thrust

buttress root *n bot* a tree root that extends above ground as a platelike outgrowth of the trunk supporting the tree. Buttress roots are mainly found in trees of tropical rain forests

butyl (**byew**-tile) *adj* of or containing any of four isomeric forms of the group C_4H_9-: *butyl rubber* ▶ HISTORY Latin *butyrum* butter

buxom *adj* (of a woman) healthily plump, attractive, and full-bosomed ▶ HISTORY Middle English *buhsum* compliant

buy *vb* **buying, bought 1** to acquire (something) by paying a sum of money for it; purchase **2** to be capable of purchasing: *money can't buy love* **3** to acquire by any exchange or sacrifice: *the rise in interest rates was just to buy time until the weekend* **4** to bribe (someone) **5** *slang* to accept (something) as true **6** (foll. by *into*) to purchase shares of (a company) ▷ *n* **7** a purchase: *a good buy*. See also **buy in** ▶ HISTORY Old English *bycgan*

buyer *n* **1** a person who buys; customer **2** a person employed to buy merchandise for a shop or factory

buy in *vb* to purchase (goods) in large quantities

buy-out *n* **1** the purchase of a company, often by its former employees ▷ *vb* **buy out 2** to purchase the ownership of a company or property from (someone)

buy up *vb* **1** to purchase all that is available of (something) **2** to purchase a controlling interest in (a company)

buzz *n* **1** a rapidly vibrating humming sound, such as of a bee **2** a low sound, such as of many voices in conversation **3** *informal* a telephone call **4** *informal* a sense of excitement ▷ *vb* **5** to make a vibrating sound like that of a prolonged *z* **6** (of a place) to be filled with an air of excitement: *the city buzzed with the news* **7** to summon (someone) with a buzzer **8** *informal* to fly an aircraft very low over (people, buildings, or another aircraft) **9 buzz about** or **around** *written* to move around quickly and busily ▶ HISTORY imitative

buzzard *n* a bird of prey with broad wings and tail and a soaring flight ▶ HISTORY Latin *buteo* hawk

buzzer *n* an electronic device that produces a buzzing sound as a signal

buzzkill *n* *informal* someone or something that stops people from enjoying themselves

buzz off *vb* *Brit & Austral, informal* to go away; depart

buzz word *n* *informal* a word, originally from a particular jargon, which becomes a popular vogue word

by *prep* **1** used to indicate the performer of the action of a passive verb: *seeds eaten by the birds* **2** used to indicate the person responsible for a creative work: *three songs by Britten* **3** via; through: *enter by the back door* **4** used to indicate a means used: *he frightened her by hiding behind the door* **5** beside; next to; near: *a tree by the stream* **6** passing the position of; past: *I drove by the place she works* **7** not later than; before: *return the books by Tuesday* **8** used to indicate extent: *it is hotter by five degrees* **9** multiplied by: *four by three equals twelve* **10** during the passing of: *by night* **11** placed between measurements of the various dimensions of something: *a plank fourteen inches by seven* ▷ *adv* **12** near: *the house is close by* **13** away; aside: *he put some money by each week* **14** passing a point near something; past: *he drove by* ▷ *n, pl* **byes 15** same as **bye¹** ▶ HISTORY Old English *bī*

by and by *adv* presently or eventually

by and large *adv* in general; on the whole

bye¹ *n* **1** *sport* status of a player or team who wins a preliminary round by virtue of having no opponent **2** *cricket* a run scored off a ball not struck by the batsman **3 by the bye** incidentally; by the way ▶ HISTORY variant of *by*

bye² *or* **bye-bye** *interj* *informal* goodbye

by-election *or* **bye-election** *n* an election held during the life of a parliament to fill a vacant seat

bygone *adj* past; former: *a bygone age*

bygones *pl n* **let bygones be bygones** to agree to forget past quarrels

bylaw *or* **bye-law** *n* *law* a rule made by a local authority ▶ HISTORY probably Scandinavian

by-line *n* **1** *journalism* a line under the title of a newspaper or magazine article giving the author's name **2** same as **touchline**

BYO(G) *n* *Austral & NZ* an unlicensed restaurant at which diners may bring their own alcoholic drink ▶ HISTORY *bring your own (grog)*

bypass *n* **1** a main road built to avoid a city **2** a secondary pipe, channel, or appliance through which the flow of a substance, such as gas or electricity, is redirected **3** a surgical operation in which the blood flow is redirected away from a diseased or blocked part of the heart ▷ *vb* **4** to go around or avoid (a city, obstruction, problem, etc.) **5** to proceed without reference to (regulations or a superior); get round; avoid

by-play *n* secondary action in a play, carried on apart while the main action proceeds

by-product *n* **1** a secondary or incidental product of a manufacturing process **2** a side effect

byre *n* *Brit* a shelter for cows ▶ HISTORY Old English *bȳre*

bystander *n* a person present but not involved; onlooker; spectator

byte *n* *computers* a group of bits processed as one unit of data ▶ HISTORY origin unknown

byway *n* a secondary or side road, esp. in the country

byword *n* **1** a person or thing regarded as a perfect example of something: *their name is a byword for quality* **2** a common saying; proverb

Byzantine *adj* **1** of Byzantium, an ancient Greek city on the Bosphorus **2** of the Byzantine Empire, the continuation of the Roman Empire in the East **3** of the style of architecture developed in the Byzantine Empire, with massive domes, rounded arches, and mosaics **4** (of attitudes, methods, etc.) inflexible or complicated ▷ *n* **5** an inhabitant of Byzantium

Cc

C 1 centi- **2** *cricket* caught **3** cubic **4** the speed of light in free space

C 1 *music* the first note of a major scale containing no sharps or flats (**C major**) **2** *chem* carbon **3** Celsius **4** centigrade **5** century: C20 **6** coulomb **7** the Roman numeral for 100 **8** a high-level computer programming language

c. (used preceding a date) about: *c. 1800* ▶ **HISTORY** Latin *circa*

Ca *chem* calcium

CA 1 California **2** Central America **3** Chartered Accountant

ca. (used preceding a date) about: *ca. 1930* ▶ **HISTORY** Latin *circa*

cab *n* **1** a taxi **2** the enclosed driver's compartment of a lorry, bus, or train ▶ **HISTORY** from *cabriolet*

cabal (kab-**bal**) *n* **1** a small group of political plotters **2** a secret plot or conspiracy ▶ **HISTORY** French *cabale*

cabaret (**kab**-a-ray) *n* **1** a floor show of dancing and singing at a nightclub or restaurant **2** a place providing such entertainment ▶ **HISTORY** French: tavern

cabbage *n* **1** a vegetable with a large head of green or reddish-purple leaves **2** *offensive* a person who is unable to move or think, as a result of brain damage ▶ **HISTORY** Norman French *caboche* head

cabbage tree *n* NZ a palm-like tree with a bare trunk and spiky leaves

cabbage white *n* a large white butterfly whose larvae feed on cabbage leaves

cabbie *or* **cabby** *n*, *pl* **-bies** *informal* a taxi driver

caber *n* Scot a heavy section of trimmed tree trunk tossed in competition at Highland games ▶ **HISTORY** Gaelic *cabar* pole

cabin *n* **1** a room used as living quarters in a ship or boat **2** a small simple dwelling: *a log cabin* **3** the enclosed part of an aircraft in which the passengers or crew sit ▶ **HISTORY** Late Latin *capanna* hut

cabin boy *n* a boy who waits on the officers and passengers of a ship

cabin cruiser *n* a motorboat with a cabin

cabinet *n* a piece of furniture containing shelves, cupboards, or drawers for storage or display: *a filing cabinet; a cocktail cabinet* ▶ **HISTORY** Old French *cabine* cabin

Cabinet *n* a committee of senior government ministers or advisers to a president

cabinet-maker *n* a person who makes fine furniture > **cabinet-making** *n*

cable *n* **1** a strong thick rope of twisted hemp or wire **2** a bundle of wires covered with plastic or rubber that conducts electricity **3** a telegram sent abroad by submarine cable or telephone line **4** Also called: **cable stitch** a knitted design which resembles a twisted rope ▷ *vb* **-bling, -bled 5** to send (someone) a message by cable ▶ **HISTORY** Late Latin *capulum* halter

cable car *n* a vehicle that is pulled up a steep slope by a moving cable

cablegram *n* a more formal name for **cable** (sense 3)

cable television *n* a television service in which the subscriber's television is connected to a central receiver by cable

caboodle *n* **the whole caboodle** *informal* the whole lot ▶ **HISTORY** origin unknown

caboose *n* **1** US & Canad a railway car at the rear of a train, used as quarters for the crew **2** Canad a mobile building used as a cookhouse or bunkhouse for a work crew ▶ **HISTORY** Dutch *cabūse*

cabriolet (kab-ree-oh-**lay**) *n* a small two-wheeled horse-drawn carriage with a folding hood ▶ **HISTORY** French: a little skip; referring to the lightness of movement

cacao (kak-**kah**-oh) *n* a tropical American tree with seed pods (**cacao beans**) from which cocoa and chocolate are prepared ▶ **HISTORY** Mexican Indian *cacauatl* cacao beans

cachalot *n* the sperm whale ▶ **HISTORY** Portuguese *cachalote*

cache (kash) *n* a hidden store of weapons, provisions, or treasure ▶ **HISTORY** French *cacher* to hide

cachet (**kash**-shay) *n written* prestige or distinction: *a Mercedes carries a certain cachet* ▶ **HISTORY** French

cachou *n* a lozenge eaten to sweeten the breath ▶ **HISTORY** Malay *kāchu*

cack-handed *adj informal* clumsy: *I open cans in a very cack-handed way* ▶ **HISTORY** dialect *cack* excrement

cackle *vb* **-ling, -led 1** to laugh shrilly **2** (of a hen) to squawk with shrill broken notes ▷ *n* **3** the sound of cackling ▶ **HISTORY** probably imitative > **cackling** *adj*

cacophony (kak-**koff**-on-ee) *n* harsh discordant sound: *a cacophony of barking* ▶ **HISTORY** Greek *kakos* bad + *phōnē* sound > **cacophonous** *adj*

cactoblastis (kak-toe-blah-stiss) *n* a type of moth; introduced into Australia to act as a biological control on the prickly pear

cactus *n*, *pl* **-tuses** *or* **-ti** a thick fleshy desert plant with spines but no leaves ▶ **HISTORY** Greek *kaktos* type of thistle

cad *n old-fashioned, informal* a man who behaves dishonourably ▶ **HISTORY** from *caddie* > **caddish** *adj*

CAD *computing* computer-aided design

cadastral map *n law, geog* an official large-scale map showing details of properties, boundaries, and ownership

cadaver (kad-**dav**-ver) *n med* a corpse ▶ HISTORY Latin

cadaverous *adj written* pale, thin, and haggard

caddie *n* **1** a person who carries a golfer's clubs ▷ *vb* **-dying, -died 2** to act as a caddie ▶ HISTORY from *cadet*

caddis fly *n* an insect whose larva (the **caddis worm**) lives underwater in a protective case of silk, sand, and stones

caddy¹ *n, pl* **-dies** *chiefly Brit* a small container for tea ▶ HISTORY Malay *kati*

caddy² *n, pl* **-dies** *vb* **-dies, -dying, -died** same as **caddie**

cadence (kade-enss) *n* **1** the rise and fall in the pitch of the voice **2** the close of a musical phrase ▶ HISTORY Latin *cadere* to fall

cadenza *n* a complex solo passage in a piece of music ▶ HISTORY Italian

cadet *n* a young person training for the armed forces or the police ▶ HISTORY French

cadge *vb* **cadging, cadged** *informal* to get (something) from someone by taking advantage of his or her generosity ▶ HISTORY origin unknown > **cadger** *n*

cadi *n* a judge in a Muslim community ▶ HISTORY Arabic *qādī* judge

cadmium *n chem* a bluish-white metallic element found in zinc ores and used in electroplating and alloys. Symbol: Cd ▶ HISTORY Latin *cadmia* zinc ore

cadre (**kah**-der) *n* a small group of people selected and trained to form the core of a political organization or military unit ▶ HISTORY Latin *quadrum* square

caecum *or US* **cecum** (**seek**-um) *n, pl* **-ca** (-ka) the pouch at the beginning of the large intestine ▶ HISTORY short for Latin *intestinum caecum* blind intestine

Caenozoic *adj* same as **Cenozoic**

Caerphilly *n* a creamy white mild-flavoured cheese

Caesar (**seez**-ar) *n* **1** a Roman emperor **2** any emperor or dictator ▶ HISTORY after Gaius Julius *Caesar*, Roman general & statesman

Caesarean, Caesarian *or US* **Cesarean** (siz-**zair**-ee-an) *n* short for **Caesarean section**

Caesarean section *n* surgical incision into the womb in order to deliver a baby ▶ HISTORY from the belief that Julius Caesar was delivered in this way

caesium *or US* **cesium** *n chem* a silvery-white metallic element used in photocells. Symbol: Cs ▶ HISTORY Latin *caesius* bluish-grey

caesura (siz-**your**-ra) *n, pl* **-ras** *or* **-rae** (-ree) a pause in a line of verse ▶ HISTORY Latin: a cutting

café *n* **1** a small or inexpensive restaurant that serves drinks and snacks or light meals **2** *S African* a corner shop ▶ HISTORY French

cafeteria *n* a self-service restaurant ▶ HISTORY American Spanish: coffee shop

caffeine *n* a stimulant found in tea, coffee, and cocoa ▶ HISTORY German *Kaffee* coffee

caftan *n* same as **kaftan**

cage *n* **1** an enclosure made of bars or wires, for keeping birds or animals in **2** the enclosed platform of a lift in a mine ▷ *vb* **caging, caged 3** to confine in a cage ▶ HISTORY Latin *cavea* enclosure > **caged** *adj*

cagey *adj* **cagier, cagiest** *informal* reluctant to go into details; wary: *he is cagey about what he paid for the business* ▶ HISTORY origin unknown > **cagily** *adv*

cagoule (kag-**gool**) *n Brit* a lightweight hooded waterproof jacket ▶ HISTORY French

cahoots *pl n* **in cahoots** *informal* conspiring together: *the loan sharks were in cahoots with the home-improvement companies* ▶ HISTORY origin unknown

caiman *n, pl* **-mans** same as **cayman**

cairn *n* a mound of stones erected as a memorial or marker ▶ HISTORY Gaelic *carn*

cairngorm *n* a smoky yellow or brown quartz gemstone ▶ HISTORY *Cairn Gorm* (blue cairn), mountain in Scotland

caisson (**kayss**-on) *n* a watertight chamber used to carry out construction work under water ▶ HISTORY French

cajole *vb* **-joling, -joled** to persuade by flattery; coax: *he allowed himself to be cajoled into staying on* ▶ HISTORY French *cajoler* > **cajolery** *n*

cake *n* **1** a sweet food baked from a mixture of flour, sugar, eggs, etc. **2** a flat compact mass of something: *a cake of soap* **3 have one's cake and eat it** to enjoy both of two incompatible alternatives **4 piece of cake** *informal* something that is easy to do **5 sell like hot cakes** *informal* to be sold very quickly: *commercial novels sell like hot cakes* ▷ *vb* **caking, caked 6** to form into a hardened mass or crust: *there was blood caked an inch thick on the walls* ▶ HISTORY Old Norse *kaka*

cal. calorie (small)

Cal. 1 Calorie (large) **2** California

calabash *n* **1** a large round gourd that grows on a tropical American tree **2** a bowl made from the dried hollow shell of a calabash ▶ HISTORY obsolete French *calabasse*

calabrese (kal-lab-**bray**-zee) *n* a kind of green sprouting broccoli ▶ HISTORY Italian: from Calabria (region of SW Italy)

calamine *n* a pink powder consisting chiefly of zinc oxide, used to make soothing skin lotions and ointments ▶ HISTORY Medieval Latin *calamina*

calamitous *adj* resulting in or from disaster: *the country's calamitous economic decline*

calamity *n, pl* **-ties** a disaster or misfortune ▶ HISTORY Latin *calamitas*

calcareous (kal-**care**-ee-uss) *adj* of or containing calcium carbonate ▶ HISTORY Latin *calx* lime

calciferol *n* a substance found in fish oils and used in the treatment of rickets. Also called: **vitamin D₂** ▶ HISTORY *calcif(erous* + *ergost)erol*, a substance in plants that is a source of vitamin D

calciferous *adj* producing salts of calcium, esp. calcium carbonate

C

calcify *vb* **-fies, -fying, -fied** to harden by the depositing of calcium salts ▶ HISTORY Latin *calx* lime > **calcification** *n*

calcine *vb* **-cining, -cined** to oxidize (a substance) by heating ▶ HISTORY Medieval Latin *calcinare* to heat > **calcination** *n*

calcite *n* a colourless or white form of calcium carbonate

calcium *n chem* a soft silvery-white metallic element found in bones, teeth, limestone, and chalk. Symbol: Ca ▶ HISTORY Latin *calx* lime

calcium carbonate *n* a white crystalline salt found in limestone, chalk, and pearl, used to make cement

calcium chloride *n chem* a white deliquescent salt which occurs naturally in seawater and is used in de-icing roads and as a drying agent

calcium hydroxide *n* a white crystalline alkali used to make mortar and soften water

calcium oxide *n* same as **quicklime**

calculable *adj* able to be computed or estimated

calculate *vb* **-lating, -lated 1** to solve or find out by a mathematical procedure or by reasoning **2** to aim to have a particular effect: *this ad campaign is calculated to offend*

■ **WORD HISTORY**
■ 'Calculate' comes from the Latin word *calculare*
■ meaning 'to count using small stones', from
■ *calculus*, meaning a 'stone' or 'pebble'. The
■ Romans used pebbles to count with.

calculated *adj* **1** undertaken after considering the likelihood of success: *a calculated gamble* **2** carefully planned: *a calculated and callous murder*

calculating *adj* selfishly scheming

calculation *n* **1** the act or result of calculating **2** selfish scheming: *there was an element of calculation in her insistence on arriving after dark*

calculator *n* a small electronic device for doing mathematical calculations

calculus *n* **1** the branch of mathematics dealing with infinitesimal changes to a variable number or quantity **2** (*pl* **-li**) *pathol* same as **stone** (sense 7) ▶ HISTORY Latin: pebble

caldera (kal-**dare**-ruh) *n geol* a large basin-shaped crater at the top of a volcano, formed by the collapse of the cone ▶ HISTORY Spanish *caldera*, literally: CAULDRON

Caledonian *adj* Scottish ▶ HISTORY from *Caledonia*, the Roman name for Scotland

calendar *n* **1** a chart showing a year divided up into months, weeks, and days **2** a system for determining the beginning, length, and divisions of years: *the Jewish calendar* **3** a schedule of events or appointments: *concerts were an important part of the social calendar of the Venetian nobility*

■ **WORD HISTORY**
■ This word comes from medieval Latin
■ *kalendārium*, meaning 'account book'. The word
■ 'kalendarium' itself comes from Latin *kalendae*,
■ the 'calends', the first day of the month in the
■ Roman calendar and the day on which interest
■ on debts was due.

calender *n* **1** a machine in which paper or cloth is smoothed by passing it between rollers ▷ *vb* **2** to smooth in such a machine ▶ HISTORY French *calandre*

calends *or* **kalends** *pl n* (in the ancient Roman calendar) the first day of each month ▶ HISTORY Latin *kalendae*

calendula *n* a plant with orange-and-yellow rayed flowers ▶ HISTORY Medieval Latin

calf¹ *n, pl* **calves** a young cow, bull, elephant, whale, or seal ▶ HISTORY Old English *cealf*

calf² *n, pl* **calves** the back of the leg between the ankle and the knee ▶ HISTORY Old Norse *kálfi*

calf love *n* adolescent infatuation

calibrate *vb* **-brating, -brated** to mark the scale or check the accuracy of (a measuring instrument) > **calibration** *n*

calibre *or US* **caliber** (**kal**-lib-ber) *n* **1** a person's ability or worth: *a poet of Wordsworth's calibre* **2** the diameter of the bore of a gun or of a shell or bullet ▶ HISTORY Arabic *qālib* shoemaker's last, mould

calico *n* a white or unbleached cotton fabric ▶ HISTORY *Calicut*, town in India

californium *n chem* a radioactive metallic element produced artificially. Symbol: Cf ▶ HISTORY after the University of *California*, where it was discovered

caliper *n US* same as **calliper**

caliph *n Islam* the title of the successors of Mohammed as rulers of the Islamic world ▶ HISTORY Arabic *khalīfa* successor

caliphate *n* the office, jurisdiction, or reign of a caliph

call *vb* **1** to name: *a town called Eyemouth* **2** to describe (someone or something) as being: *they called him a Hitler* **3** to speak loudly so as to attract attention **4** to telephone: *he left a message for Lynch to call him* **5** to summon: *a doctor must be called immediately* **6** to pay someone a visit: *the social worker called and she didn't answer the door* **7** to arrange: *the meeting was called for the lunch hour* **8 call someone's bluff** See **bluff¹** (sense 3) ▷ *n* **9** a cry or shout **10** the cry made by a bird or animal **11** a communication by telephone **12** a short visit: *I paid a call on an old friend* **13** a summons or invitation: *the police and fire brigade continued to respond to calls* **14** need, demand, or desire: *a call for economic sanctions* **15** allure or fascination: *the call of the open road* **16 on call** available when summoned: *there's a doctor on call in town* ▷ See also **call for, call in**, etc. ▶ HISTORY Old English *ceallian* > **caller** *n*

See WORD FOCUS **call** on page 114

callaloo *n* (in the Caribbean) the edible leaves of various plants, used as greens or in making soup ▶ HISTORY probably of African origin

call box *n* a soundproof enclosure for a public telephone

call centre *n Brit, Austral & NZ* an office where staff carry out an organization's telephone transactions

call for *vb* **1** to require: *appendicitis calls for removal of the appendix* **2** to come and fetch

C

call

WORD FOCUS

Depending on which sense of **call** you are thinking of, there are a number of words which you can substitute for it to make your language more interesting.

DEFINITION 1
• If you are talking about giving someone or something a name, you could try: **christen** his first-born son Arthur • **designated** an "area of natural beauty" • the man **dubbed** "the world's greatest living explorer" • They **named** their child Anna.

DEFINITION 2
• If you are describing something as being a particular way, you could try: I **consider** myself • I'm not what you'd **describe** as • do you **judge** this • he **referred** to her as • widely **regarded** as • **termed** as political • people will **think** us

DEFINITION 3
• If you are talking about someone saying

something loudly, you could try: he **announced** • she **cried** • she **cried out** • he **shouted** to me • he **yelled** over to us

DEFINITION 4
• If you are talking about using the telephone, you could try: **contact** us immediately • **phone** me • I'll **ring** you • please **telephone**

DEFINITION 5
• If you are talking about sending for someone, you could try: please **fetch** • **sent** for • I was **summoned**

DEFINITION 6
• If you are talking about paying someone a visit, you could try: **drop in** (informal) • **pop in** (informal) • **stop by** (informal)

DEFINITION 7
• If you are talking about bringing a group of things or people together, you could try: **assembled** the group • **convened** a council • **gathered** together • **muster** an army • **summoned** to a meeting

---

call forth vb to cause (something) to come into action or existence

calligraphy n beautiful handwriting ▶ HISTORY Greek kallos beauty + -GRAPHY > **calligrapher** n > **calligraphic** adj

call in vb 1 to summon to one's assistance: she called in a contractor to make the necessary repairs 2 to pay a brief visit 3 to demand payment of (a loan): if the share price continues to drop, some banks may call in their loans

calling n 1 a strong urge to follow a particular profession or occupation, esp. a caring one 2 a profession or occupation, esp. a caring one

Calliope n Greek myth the Muse of epic poetry

calliper or US **caliper** n 1 a metal splint for supporting the leg 2 a measuring instrument consisting of two steel legs hinged together ▶ HISTORY variant of calibre

callisthenics or **calisthenics** n light exercises designed to promote general fitness ▶ HISTORY Greek kalli- beautiful + sthenos strength > **callisthenic** or **calisthenic** adj

call off vb 1 to cancel or abandon: the strike has now been called off 2 to order (a dog or a person) to stop attacking someone

callous adj showing no concern for other people's feelings ▶ HISTORY Latin callosus > **callously** adv > **callousness** n

calloused adj covered in calluses

callow adj young and inexperienced: a callow youth ▶ HISTORY Old English calu

call up vb 1 to summon for active military service 2 to cause one to remember ▷ n **call-up** 3 a general order to report for military service

callus n, pl **-luses** an area of hard or thickened skin on the hand or foot ▶ HISTORY Latin callum hardened skin

calm adj 1 not showing or not feeling agitation or excitement 2 not ruffled by the wind: a flat calm sea 3 (of weather) windless ▷ n 4 a peaceful state ▷ vb 5 (often foll. by down) to make or become calm ▶ HISTORY Late Latin cauma heat, hence a rest during the heat of the day > **calmly** adv > **calmness** n

Calor Gas n trademark, Brit butane gas liquefied under pressure in portable containers for domestic use

caloric (kal-**or**-ik) adj of heat or calories

calorie n 1 a unit of measure for the energy value of food 2 Also: **small calorie** the quantity of heat required to raise the temperature of 1 gram of water by 1°C ▶ HISTORY Latin calor heat

Calorie n 1 Also: **large calorie** a unit of heat, equal to one thousand calories 2 the amount of a food capable of producing one calorie of energy

calorific adj of calories or heat

calumniate vb -ating, -ated to make false or malicious statements about (someone)

calumny n, pl **-nies** a false or malicious statement; slander ▶ HISTORY Latin calumnia slander

Calvary n Christianity the place just outside the walls of Jerusalem where Jesus Christ was crucified ▶ HISTORY Latin calvaria skull

calve vb **calving, calved** to give birth to a calf

calves n the plural of **calf**

Calvinism n the theological system of Calvin, the 16th-century French theologian, stressing predestination and salvation solely by God's grace > **Calvinist** n, adj > **Calvinistic** adj

calypso n, pl **-sos** a West Indian song with improvised topical lyrics ▶ HISTORY probably from Calypso, sea nymph in Greek mythology

calyx (**kale**-ix) n, pl **calyxes** or **calyces** (**kal**-iss-seez) the outer leaves that protect the developing bud of a flower ▶ HISTORY Latin: shell, husk

cam n a part of an engine that converts a circular motion into a to-and-fro motion ▶ HISTORY Dutch *kam* comb

camaraderie n familiarity and trust between friends ▶ HISTORY French

camber n a slight upward curve to the centre of a road surface ▶ HISTORY Latin *camurus* curved

Cambodian adj 1 of Cambodia ▷ n 2 a person from Cambodia

Cambrian adj geol of the period of geological time about 600 million years ago

cambric n a fine white linen fabric ▶ HISTORY Flemish *Kamerijk* Cambrai

camcorder n a combined portable video camera and recorder

came vb the past tense of **come**

camel n either of two humped mammals, the dromedary and Bactrian camel, that can survive long periods without food or water in desert regions ▶ HISTORY Greek *kamēlos*

camellia (kam-**meel**-ya) n an ornamental shrub with glossy leaves and white, pink, or red flowers ▶ HISTORY after G. J. Kamel, Jesuit missionary

Camembert (**kam**-mem-bare) n a soft creamy cheese ▶ HISTORY *Camembert*, village in Normandy

cameo n, pl **cameos** 1 a brooch or ring with a profile head carved in relief 2 a small but important part in a film or play played by a well-known actor or actress ▶ HISTORY Italian *cammeo*

camera n 1 a piece of equipment used for taking photographs, videos, or film 2 **in camera** in private ▶ HISTORY Greek *kamara* vault

camera angle n films, photog the position of the camera in relation to the subject being filmed or photographed

camera distance n films, photog the distance of the camera from the subject being filmed or photographed

cameraman n, pl **-men** a man who operates a camera for television or cinema

camera obscura n a darkened room with an opening through which images of outside objects are projected onto a flat surface ▶ HISTORY New Latin

camera phone n a mobile phone incorporating a camera

camiknickers pl n Brit a woman's undergarment consisting of knickers attached to a camisole top

camisole n a woman's bodice-like garment with shoulder straps ▶ HISTORY French

camomile or **chamomile** (**kam**-mo-mile) n a sweet-smelling plant used to make herbal tea ▶ HISTORY Greek *khamaimēlon* earth-apple (referring to the scent of the flowers)

camouflage (**kam**-moo-flahzh) n 1 the use of natural surroundings or artificial aids to conceal or disguise something ▷ vb **-flaging, -flaged** 2 to conceal by camouflage ▶ HISTORY French

camp¹ n 1 a place where people stay in tents 2 a collection of huts and other buildings used as temporary lodgings for military troops or for prisoners of war 3 a group that supports a particular doctrine: *the socialist camp* ▷ vb 4 to stay in a camp ▶ HISTORY Latin *campus* field > **camper** n > **camping** n

camp² informal adj 1 consciously artificial, vulgar, or affected 2 effeminate ▷ vb 3 **camp it up** to behave in a camp manner ▶ HISTORY origin unknown

campaign n 1 a series of coordinated activities designed to achieve a goal 2 mil a number of operations aimed at achieving a single objective ▷ vb 3 to take part in a campaign: *he paid tribute to all those who'd campaigned for his release* ▶ HISTORY Latin *campus* field > **campaigner** n

campanile (camp-an-**neel**-lee) n a bell tower, usually one not attached to another building ▶ HISTORY Italian

campanology n the art of ringing bells ▶ HISTORY Late Latin *campana* bell > **campanologist** n

campanula n a plant with blue or white bell-shaped flowers ▶ HISTORY New Latin: a little bell

camp follower n 1 a person who supports a particular group or organization without being a member of it 2 a civilian who unofficially provides services to military personnel

camphor n a sweet-smelling crystalline substance obtained from the wood of the **camphor tree**, which is used medicinally and in mothballs ▶ HISTORY Arabic *kāfūr*

camphorated adj impregnated with camphor

campion n a red, pink, or white European wild flower ▶ HISTORY origin unknown

camp oven n Austral & NZ a heavy metal pot or box with a lid, used for baking over an open fire

campus n, pl **-puses** the grounds and buildings of a university or college ▶ HISTORY Latin: field

camshaft n a part of an engine consisting of a rod to which cams are attached

can¹ vb, past **could** 1 be able to: *make sure he can breathe easily* 2 be allowed to: *you can swim in the large pool* ▶ HISTORY Old English *cunnan*

can² n 1 a metal container, usually sealed, for food or liquids ▷ vb **canning, canned** 2 to put (something) into a can ▶ HISTORY Old English *canne*

Canada goose n a greyish-brown North American goose with a black neck and head

Canada jay n a grey jay of northern N America, notorious for stealing

Canadian adj 1 of Canada ▷ n 2 a person from Canada

Canadian Shield n the wide area of Precambrian rock extending over most of central and E Canada: rich in minerals

canal n 1 an artificial waterway constructed for navigation or irrigation 2 a passage or duct in a person's body: *the alimentary canal* ▶ HISTORY Latin *canna* reed

canalize or **-lise** vb **-lizing, -lized** or **-lising, -lised** 1 to give direction to (a feeling or activity) 2 to convert into a canal > **canalization** or **-lisation** n

canapé (kan-nap-pay) *n* a small piece of bread or toast spread with a savoury topping ▶ HISTORY French: sofa

canard *n* a false report ▶ HISTORY French: a duck

canary *n, pl* **-naries** a small yellow songbird often kept as a pet

canasta *n* a card game like rummy, played with two packs of cards ▶ HISTORY Spanish: basket (because two packs, or a basketful, of cards are required)

cancan *n* a lively high-kicking dance performed by a female group ▶ HISTORY French

cancel *vb* **-celling, -celled** *or US* **-celing, -celed** **1** to stop (something that has been arranged) from taking place **2** to mark (a cheque or stamp) with an official stamp to prevent further use **3** *maths* to eliminate numbers, quantities, or terms because they occur in both the numerator and denominator of a fraction or on opposite sides of an equation **4 cancel out** to make ineffective by having the opposite effect: *economic vulnerability cancels out any possible political gain* ▶ HISTORY Late Latin *cancellare* to strike out, make iike a lattice > **cancellation** *n*

cancer *n* **1** a serious disease resulting from a malignant growth or tumour, caused by abnormal and uncontrolled cell division **2** a malignant growth or tumour **3** an evil influence that spreads dangerously: *their country would remain a cancer of instability* ▶ HISTORY Latin: crab, creeping tumour > **cancerous** *adj*

Cancer *n* **1** *astrol* the fourth sign of the zodiac; the Crab **2 tropic of Cancer** See **tropic** (sense 1) ▶ HISTORY Latin

candela (kan-dee-la) *n* the SI unit of luminous intensity (the amount of light a source gives off in a given direction) ▶ HISTORY Latin: candle

candelabrum *or* **candelabra** *n, pl* **-bra, -brums** *or* **-bras** a large branched holder for candles or overhead lights ▶ HISTORY Latin *candela* candle

candid *adj* honest and straightforward in speech or behaviour ▶ HISTORY Latin *candere* to be white > **candidly** *adv*

candidate *n* **1** a person seeking a job or position **2** a person standing for election **3** a person taking an examination **4** a person or thing regarded as suitable or likely for a particular fate or position: *someone who smokes, drinks, or eats too much is a candidate for heart disease* > **candidacy** *or* **candidature** *n*

- ■ **WORD HISTORY**
- ■ *Candidatus* in Latin means 'white-robed'. In
- ■ ancient Rome, candidates for public office
- ■ wore white togas.

candied *adj* coated with or cooked in sugar: *candied peel*

candle *n* **1** a stick or block of wax or tallow surrounding a wick, which is burned to produce light **2 burn the candle at both ends** to exhaust oneself by doing too much ▶ HISTORY Latin *candela*

Candlemas *n Christianity* February 2, the Feast of the Purification of the Virgin Mary

candlepower *n* the luminous intensity of a source of light: now expressed in candelas

candlestick *or* **candleholder** *n* a holder for a candle

candlewick *n* cotton with a tufted pattern, used to make bedspreads and dressing gowns

candour *or US* **candor** *n* honesty and straightforwardness of speech or behaviour ▶ HISTORY Latin *candor*

candy *n, pl* **-dies** *chiefly US & Canad* a sweet or sweets ▶ HISTORY Arabic *qand* cane sugar

candyfloss *n Brit* a light fluffy mass of spun sugar, held on a stick

candy-striped *adj* having narrow coloured stripes on a white background

candytuft *n* a garden plant with clusters of white, pink, or purple flowers

cane *n* **1** the long flexible stems of the bamboo or any similar plant **2** strips of such stems, woven to make wickerwork **3** a bamboo stem tied to a garden plant to support it **4** short for **sugar cane** **5** a flexible rod used to beat someone **6** a slender walking stick ▷ *vb* **caning, caned 7** to beat with a cane ▶ HISTORY Greek *kanna*

cane sugar *n* the sugar that is obtained from sugar cane

cane toad *n biol* a large toad native to Central and South America but introduced into other countries to control pests in sugar-cane plantations

canine (kay-nine) *adj* **1** of or like a dog ▷ *n* **2** a sharp-pointed tooth between the incisors and the molars ▶ HISTORY Latin *canis* dog

canister *n* a metal container for dry food ▶ HISTORY Latin *canistrum* basket woven from reeds

canker *n* **1** an ulceration or ulcerous disease **2** something evil that spreads and corrupts ▶ HISTORY Latin *cancer* cancerous sore

cannabis *n* a drug obtained from the dried leaves and flowers of the hemp plant ▶ HISTORY Greek *kannabis*

canned *adj* **1** preserved in a can **2** *informal* recorded in advance: *canned carols*

cannelloni *or* **canneloni** *pl n* tubular pieces of pasta filled with meat or cheese ▶ HISTORY Italian

cannery *n, pl* **-neries** a place where foods are canned

cannibal *n* **1** a person who eats human flesh **2** an animal that eats the flesh of other animals of its kind ▶ HISTORY Spanish *Canibales* natives of Cuba and Haiti > **cannibalism** *n*

cannibalize *or* **-ise** *vb* **-izing, -ized** *or* **-ising, -ised** to use parts from (one machine or vehicle) to repair another

cannon *n, pl* **-nons** *or* **-non 1** a large gun consisting of a metal tube mounted on a carriage, formerly used in battles **2** an automatic aircraft gun **3** *billiards* a shot in which the cue ball strikes two balls successively ▷ *vb* **4 cannon into** to collide with ▶ HISTORY Italian *canna* tube

cannonade *n* continuous heavy gunfire

cannonball *n* a heavy metal ball fired from a cannon

cannon fodder *n* men regarded as expendable in war

cannot *vb* can not

canny *adj* **-nier, -niest** shrewd or cautious ▶ HISTORY from *can* (in the sense: to know how) > **cannily** *adv*

canoe *n* a light narrow open boat, propelled by one or more paddles ▶ HISTORY Carib > **canoeist** *n*

canoeing *n* the sport of rowing or racing in a canoe

canon¹ *n* a priest serving in a cathedral ▶ HISTORY Late Latin *canonicus* person living under a rule

canon² *n* **1** *Christianity* a Church decree regulating morals or religious practices **2** a general rule or standard: *the Marx-Engels canon* **3** a list of the works of an author that are accepted as authentic: *the Yeats canon* **4** a piece of music in which a melody in one part is taken up in one or more other parts successively ▶ HISTORY Greek *kanōn* rule

canonical *adj* **1** conforming with canon law **2** included in a canon of writings

canonical hour *n* *RC Church* one of the seven prayer times appointed for each day

canonicals *pl n* the official clothes worn by clergy when taking services

canonize *or* **-ise** *vb* **-izing, -ized** *or* **-ising, -ised** *RC Church* to declare (a dead person) to be a saint > **canonization** *or* **-isation** *n*

canon law *n* the body of laws of a Christian Church

canoodle *vb* **-dling, -dled** *slang* to kiss and cuddle ▶ HISTORY origin unknown

canopied *adj* covered with a canopy: *canopied niches*

canopy *n, pl* **-pies 1** an ornamental awning above a bed or throne **2** a rooflike covering over an altar, niche, or door **3** any large or wide covering: *the thick forest canopy* **4** the part of a parachute that opens out **5** the transparent hood of an aircraft cockpit ▶ HISTORY Greek *kōnōpeion* bed with a mosquito net

cant¹ *n* **1** insincere talk concerning religion or morals **2** specialized vocabulary of a particular group, such as thieves or lawyers ▷ *vb* **3** to use cant: *canting hypocrites* ▶ HISTORY probably from Latin *cantare* to sing

cant² *n* **1** a tilted position ▷ *vb* **2** to tilt or overturn: *the engine was canted to one side* ▶ HISTORY perhaps from Latin *canthus* iron hoop round a wheel

can't can not

cantabile (kan-**tah**-bill-lay) *adv music* flowingly and melodiously ▶ HISTORY Italian

cantaloupe *or* **cantaloup** *n* *Brit* a kind of melon with sweet-tasting orange flesh ▶ HISTORY *Cantaluppi*, near Rome, where first cultivated in Europe

cantankerous *adj written* quarrelsome or bad-tempered ▶ HISTORY origin unknown

cantata (kan-**tah**-ta) *n* a musical setting of a text, consisting of arias, duets, and choruses ▶ HISTORY Italian

canteen *n* **1** a restaurant attached to a workplace or school **2** a box containing a set of cutlery ▶ HISTORY Italian *cantina* wine cellar

canter *n* **1** a gait of horses that is faster than a trot but slower than a gallop ▷ *vb* **2** (of a horse) to move at a canter ▶ HISTORY short for *Canterbury trot*, the pace at which pilgrims rode to Canterbury

canticle *n* a short hymn with words from the Bible ▶ HISTORY Latin *canticulum*

cantilever *n* a beam or girder fixed at one end only ▶ HISTORY origin unknown

cantilever bridge *n* a bridge made of two cantilevers which meet in the middle

canto (**kan**-toe) *n, pl* **-tos** a main division of a long poem ▶ HISTORY Italian: song

canton *n* a political division of a country, such as Switzerland ▶ HISTORY Old French: corner

Cantonese *adj* **1** of Canton, a port in SE China ▷ *n* **2** (*pl* **-nese**) a person from Canton **3** the Chinese dialect of Canton

cantonment (kan-**toon**-ment) *n* a permanent military camp in British India ▶ HISTORY Old French *canton* corner

cantor *n* *Judaism* a man employed to lead synagogue services ▶ HISTORY Latin: singer

canvas *n* **1** a heavy cloth of cotton, hemp, or jute, used to make tents and sails and for painting on in oils **2** an oil painting done on canvas **3 under canvas** in a tent: *sleeping under canvas* ▶ HISTORY Latin *cannabis* hemp

canvass *vb* **1** to try to persuade (people) to vote for a particular candidate or party in an election **2** to find out the opinions of (people) by conducting a survey ▷ *n* **3** the activity of canvassing ▶ HISTORY probably from obsolete sense of *canvas* (to toss someone in a canvas sheet, hence, to criticize) > **canvasser** *n* > **canvassing** *n*

canyon *n* a deep narrow steep-sided valley ▶ HISTORY Spanish *cañon*

caoutchouc (**cow**-chook) *n* same as **rubber¹** (sense 1) ▶ HISTORY from S American Indian

cap *n* **1** a soft close-fitting covering for the head **2** *sport* a cap given to someone selected for a national team **3** a small flat lid: *petrol cap* **4** a small amount of explosive enclosed in paper and used in a toy gun **5** a contraceptive device placed over the mouth of the womb **6** an upper financial limit **7 cap in hand** humbly ▷ *vb* **capping, capped 8** to cover or top with something: *a thick cover of snow capped the cars* **9** *sport* to select (a player) for a national team: *Australia's most capped player* **10** to impose an upper level on (a tax): *charge capping* **11** *informal* to outdo or excel: *capping anecdote with anecdote* ▶ HISTORY Late Latin *cappa* hood

CAP (in the EU) Common Agricultural Policy

cap. capital

capability *n, pl* **-ties** the ability or skill to do something.

C

capable adj 1 having the ability or skill to do something: *a side capable of winning the championship* 2 competent and efficient: *capable high achievers* ▶ HISTORY Latin *capere* to take
> **capably** adv

capacious adj having a large capacity or area ▶ HISTORY Latin *capere* to take

capacitance n physics 1 the ability of a capacitor to store electrical charge 2 a measure of this

capacitor n physics a device for storing a charge of electricity

capacity n, pl **-ties** 1 the ability to contain, absorb, or hold something 2 the maximum amount something can contain or absorb: *filled to capacity* 3 the ability to do something: *his capacity to elicit great loyalty* 4 written a position or function: *acting in an official capacity* 5 the maximum output of which an industry or factory is capable: *the refinery had a capacity of three hundred thousand barrels a day* 6 physics same as **capacitance** ▷ adj 7 of the maximum amount or number possible: *a capacity crowd* ▶ HISTORY Latin *capere* to take

caparisoned (kap-**par**-riss-sond) adj (esp. of a horse) magnificently decorated or dressed ▶ HISTORY Old Spanish *caparazón* saddlecloth

cape¹ n a short sleeveless cloak ▶ HISTORY Late Latin *cappa*

cape² n a large piece of land that juts out into the sea ▶ HISTORY Latin *caput* head

Cape n **the Cape** 1 the Cape of Good Hope 2 the SW region of South Africa's Cape Province

CAPE trademark Caribbean Advanced Proficiency Examination

caper n 1 a high-spirited escapade ▷ vb 2 to skip about light-heartedly ▶ HISTORY probably from CAPRIOLE

capercaillie or **capercailzie** (kap-per-**kale**-yee) n a large black European woodland grouse ▶ HISTORY Scottish Gaelic *capull coille* horse of the woods

capers pl n the pickled flower buds of a Mediterranean shrub, used in making sauces ▶ HISTORY Greek *kapparis* caper plant

capillarity n physics a phenomenon caused by surface tension that results in the surface of a liquid rising or falling in contact with a solid

capillary (kap-**pill**-a-ree) n, pl **-laries** 1 anat one of the very fine blood vessels linking the arteries and the veins ▷ adj 2 (of a tube) having a fine bore 3 anat of the capillaries ▶ HISTORY Latin *capillus* hair

capital¹ n 1 the chief city of a country, where the government meets 2 the total wealth owned or used in business by an individual or group 3 wealth used to produce more wealth by investment 4 **make capital out of** to gain advantage from: *to make political capital out of the hostage situation* 5 a capital letter ▷ adj 6 law involving or punishable by death: *a capital offence* 7 denoting the large letter used as the initial letter in a sentence, personal name, or place name 8 Brit, Austral & NZ, old-fashioned excellent or first-rate: *a capital dinner* ▶ HISTORY Latin *caput* head

capital² n the top part of a column or pillar ▶ HISTORY Old French *capitel*, from Latin *caput* head

capital gain n profit from the sale of an asset

capital goods pl n econ goods that are themselves utilized in the production of other goods

capital-intensive adj econ, business requiring large capital investments as opposed to involving a large labour force. Compare **labour-intensive**

capitalism n an economic system based on the private ownership of industry

capitalist adj 1 based on or supporting capitalism: *capitalist countries* ▷ n 2 a supporter of capitalism 3 a person who owns a business
> **capitalistic** adj

capitalize or **-ise** vb **-izing, -ized** or **-ising, -ised** 1 **capitalize on** to take advantage of: *to capitalize on the available opportunities* 2 to write or print (words) in capital letters 3 to convert (debt or earnings) into capital stock > **capitalization** or **-isation** n

capital levy n a tax on capital or property as contrasted with a tax on income

capital punishment n law the punishment of death for committing certain crimes; the death penalty

capital stock n 1 the value of the total shares that a company can issue 2 the total capital existing in an economy at a particular time

capitation n a tax of a fixed amount per person ▶ HISTORY Latin *caput* head

capitulate vb **-lating, -lated** to surrender under agreed conditions ▶ HISTORY Medieval Latin *capitulare* to draw up under headings
> **capitulation** n

capo n, pl **-pos** a device fitted across the strings of a guitar or similar instrument so as to raise the pitch ▶ HISTORY Italian *capo tasto* head stop

capon (**kay**-pon) n a castrated cock fowl fattened for eating ▶ HISTORY Latin *capo*

cappuccino (kap-poo-**cheen**-oh) n, pl **-nos** coffee with steamed milk, usually sprinkled with powdered chocolate ▶ HISTORY Italian

caprice (kap-**reess**) n 1 a sudden change of attitude or behaviour 2 a tendency to have such changes ▶ HISTORY Italian *capriccio* a shiver, caprice

capricious adj having a tendency to sudden unpredictable changes of attitude or behaviour
> **capriciously** adv

Capricorn n 1 astrol the tenth sign of the zodiac; the Goat 2 **tropic of Capricorn** See **tropic** (sense 1) ▶ HISTORY Latin *caper* goat + *cornu* horn

caps. capital letters

capsicum n a kind of pepper used as a vegetable or ground to produce a spice ▶ HISTORY Latin *capsa* box

capsize vb **-sizing, -sized** (of a boat) to overturn accidentally ▶ HISTORY origin unknown

capstan n a vertical rotating cylinder round which a ship's rope or cable is wound ▶ HISTORY Old Provençal *cabestan*

capsule *n* **1** a soluble gelatine case containing a dose of medicine **2** *bot* a plant's seed case that opens when ripe **3** *anat* a membrane or sac surrounding an organ or part **4** See **space capsule** ▷ *adj* **5** very concise: *capsule courses* ▶ HISTORY Latin *capsa* box

Capt. Captain

captain *n* **1** the person in charge of a ship, boat, or civil aircraft **2** a middle-ranking naval officer **3** a junior officer in the army **4** the leader of a team or group ▷ *vb* **5** to be captain of ▶ HISTORY Latin *caput* head > **captaincy** *n*

caption *n* **1** a title, brief explanation, or comment accompanying a picture ▷ *vb* **2** to provide with a caption ▶ HISTORY Latin *captio* a seizing

captious *adj* tending to make trivial criticisms ▶ HISTORY Latin *captio* a seizing

captivate *vb* **-vating, -vated** to attract and hold the attention of; enchant ▶ HISTORY Latin *captivus* captive > **captivating** *adj*

captive *n* **1** a person who is kept in confinement ▷ *adj* **2** kept in confinement **3** (of an audience) unable to leave ▶ HISTORY Latin *captivus*

captivity *n* the state of being kept in confinement

captor *n* a person who captures a person or animal

capture *vb* **-turing, -tured** **1** to take by force **2** to succeed in representing (something elusive) in words, pictures, or music: *today's newspapers capture the mood of the nation* **3** *physics* (of an atomic nucleus) to acquire (an additional particle) ▷ *n* **4** the act of capturing or the state of being captured ▶ HISTORY Latin *capere* to take

capuchin (**kap**-yew-chin) *n* a S American monkey with a cowl of thick hair on the top of its head ▶ HISTORY Italian *cappuccio* hood

Capuchin *n* **1** a friar belonging to a branch of the Franciscan Order founded in 1525 ▷ *adj* **2** of this order ▶ HISTORY Italian *cappuccio* hood

capybara *n* the largest living rodent, found in S America

car *n* **1** a motorized road vehicle designed to carry a small number of people **2** the passenger compartment of a cable car, airship, lift, or balloon **3** *US & Canad* a railway carriage ▶ HISTORY Latin *carra, carrum* two-wheeled wagon

caracal *n* a lynx with reddish fur, which inhabits deserts of N Africa and S Asia ▶ HISTORY Turkish *kara kūlāk* black ear

carafe (kar-**raff**) *n* a wide-mouthed bottle for water or wine ▶ HISTORY Arabic *gharrāfah* vessel

carambola *n* a yellow edible star-shaped fruit that grows on a Brazilian tree ▶ HISTORY Spanish

caramel *n* **1** a chewy sweet made from sugar and milk **2** burnt sugar, used for colouring and flavouring food ▶ HISTORY French

caramelize *or* **-ise** *vb* **-izing, -ized** *or* **-ising, -ised** to turn into caramel

carapace *n* the thick hard upper shell of tortoises and crustaceans ▶ HISTORY Spanish *carapacho*

carat *n* **1** a unit of weight of precious stones, equal to 0.20 grams **2** a measure of the purity of gold in

an alloy, expressed as the number of parts of gold in 24 parts of the alloy ▶ HISTORY Arabic *qīrāt* weight of four grains

caravan *n* **1** a large enclosed vehicle designed to be pulled by a car or horse and equipped to be lived in **2** (in some Eastern countries) a company of traders or other travellers journeying together ▶ HISTORY Persian *kārwān*

caravanserai *n* (in some Eastern countries, esp. formerly) a large inn enclosing a courtyard, providing accommodation for caravans ▶ HISTORY Persian *kārwānsarāī* caravan inn

caraway *n* a Eurasian plant with seeds that are used as a spice in cooking ▶ HISTORY Arabic *karawyā*

carb *n* *informal* short for **carbohydrate**

carbide *n* *chem* a compound of carbon with a metal

carbine *n* a type of light rifle ▶ HISTORY French *carabine*

carbohydrate *n* any of a large group of energy-producing compounds, including sugars and starches, that contain carbon, hydrogen, and oxygen

carbolic acid *n* a disinfectant derived from coal tar

carbon *n* **1** a nonmetallic element occurring in three forms, charcoal, graphite, and diamond, and present in all organic compounds. Symbol: C **2** short for **carbon paper, carbon copy** ▶ HISTORY Latin *carbo* charcoal

carbonaceous *adj* of, resembling, or containing carbon

carbonate *n* a salt or ester of carbonic acid

carbonated *adj* (of a drink) containing carbon dioxide; fizzy

carbon black *n* powdered carbon produced by partial burning of natural gas or petroleum, used in pigments and ink

carbon copy *n* **1** a duplicate obtained by using carbon paper **2** *informal* a person or thing that is identical or very similar to another

carbon cycle *n* **1** *biol, environmental science* the circulation of carbon between living organisms and their surroundings. Carbon dioxide from the atmosphere is synthesized by plants into plant tissue, which is ingested and metabolized by animals and converted back to carbon dioxide during respiration and decay **2** *physics* four thermonuclear reactions believed to be the source of energy in many stars. Carbon nuclei function as catalysts in the fusion of protons to form helium nuclei

carbon dating *n* a technique for finding the age of organic materials, such as wood, based on their content of radioactive carbon

carbon dioxide *n* a colourless odourless incombustible gas formed during breathing, and used in fire extinguishers and in making fizzy drinks

carbon footprint *n* the amount of carbon dioxide produced by an individual or organization

carbonic adj containing carbon

carbonic acid n a weak acid formed when carbon dioxide combines with water

carboniferous adj yielding coal or carbon

Carboniferous adj geol of the period of geological time about 330 million years ago, during which coal seams were formed

carbonize or **-ise** vb **-izing, -ized** or **-ising, -ised** **1** to turn into carbon as a result of partial burning **2** to coat (a substance) with carbon > **carbonization** or **-isation** n

carbon monoxide n a colourless odourless poisonous gas formed by the incomplete burning of carbon compounds; part of the gases that come from a vehicle's exhaust

carbon-neutral adj neither adding to nor reducing the amount of carbon dioxide in the Earth's atmosphere

carbon offset n a compensatory measure, such as tree planting, taken by an individual or organization producing carbon emissions

carbon paper n a thin sheet of paper coated on one side with a dark waxy pigment, containing carbon, used to make a duplicate of something as it is typed or written

carbon tax n a tax on the emissions caused by the burning of coal, gas, and oil, aimed at reducing the production of greenhouse gases

carbon tetrachloride n a colourless nonflammable liquid used as a solvent, cleaning fluid, and insecticide

Carborundum n trademark an abrasive material consisting of silicon carbide

carboxyl group or **radical** n chem the chemical group —COOH: the functional group in organic acids

carboy n a large bottle protected by a basket or box ▶ HISTORY Persian qarāba

carbuncle n a large painful swelling under the skin like a boil ▶ HISTORY Latin carbo coal

carburettor or US & Canad **carburetor** n a device in an internal-combustion engine that mixes petrol with air and regulates the intake of the mixture into the engine

carcass or **carcase** n **1** the dead body of an animal **2** informal a person's body: ask that person to move his carcass ▶ HISTORY Old French carcasse

carcinogen n a substance that produces cancer ▶ HISTORY Greek karkinos cancer > **carcinogenic** adj

carcinoma n, pl **-mas** or **-mata** a malignant tumour ▶ HISTORY Greek karkinos cancer

card¹ n **1** a piece of stiff paper or thin cardboard used for identification, reference, proof of membership, or sending greetings or messages: a Christmas card **2** one of a set of small pieces of cardboard, marked with figures or symbols, used for playing games or for fortune-telling **3** a small rectangle of stiff plastic with identifying numbers for use as a credit card, cheque card, or charge card **4** old-fashioned informal a witty or eccentric person

▷ See also **cards** ▶ HISTORY Greek khartēs leaf of papyrus

card² n **1** a machine or tool for combing fibres of cotton or wool to disentangle them before spinning ▷ vb **2** to process with such a machine or tool ▶ HISTORY Latin carduus thistle

cardamom n a spice that is obtained from the seeds of a tropical plant ▶ HISTORY Greek kardamon cress + amōmon an Indian spice

cardboard n a thin stiff board made from paper pulp

card-carrying adj being an official member of an organization: a card-carrying Conservative

cardholder n a person who owns a credit or debit card

cardiac adj of or relating to the heart ▶ HISTORY Greek kardia heart

cardigan n a knitted jacket ▶ HISTORY after 7th Earl of Cardigan

cardinal n **1** any of the high-ranking clergymen of the Roman Catholic Church who elect the pope and act as his chief counsellors ▷ adj **2** fundamentally important; principal

■ **WORD HISTORY**
■ The word 'cardinal' comes from Latin cardo,
■ meaning 'hinge'. When something is
■ important, other things can be said to hinge
■ on it.

cardinal number n a number denoting quantity but not order in a group, for example one, two, or three

cardinal points pl n the four main points of the compass: north, south, east, and west

cardinal virtues pl n the most important moral qualities, traditionally justice, prudence, temperance, and fortitude

cardiogram n an electrocardiogram. See **electrocardiograph**

cardiograph n an electrocardiograph > **cardiographer** n > **cardiography** n

cardiology n the branch of medicine dealing with the heart and its diseases > **cardiologist** n

cardiovascular adj of or relating to the heart and the blood vessels

cards n **1** any game played with cards, or card games generally **2 lay one's cards on the table** to declare one's intentions openly **3 on the cards** likely to take place: a military coup was on the cards **4 play one's cards right** to handle a situation cleverly

cardsharp or **cardsharper** n a professional card player who cheats

card vote n Brit & NZ a vote by delegates in which each delegate's vote counts as a vote by all his or her constituents

care vb **caring, cared** **1** to be worried or concerned: he does not care what people think about him **2** to like (to do something): anybody care to go out? **3 care for a** to look after or provide for: it is still largely women who care for dependent family members **b** to like or be fond of: he did not care for his concentration to be disturbed; I don't suppose you could ever care for me seriously **4 I couldn't care less** I am completely indifferent ▷ *n* **5** careful or serious attention; caution: *treat all raw meat with extreme care to avoid food poisoning* **6** protection or charge: *the children are now in the care of a state orphanage* **7** trouble or worry: *his mind turned towards money cares* **8 care of** (written on envelopes) at the address of **9 in** or **into care** Brit & NZ (of a child) made the legal responsibility of a local authority or the state by order of a court **10 take care** to be careful **11 take care of** to look after: *women have to take greater care of themselves during pregnancy* ▶ **HISTORY** Old English *cearian*

careen *vb* to tilt over to one side ▶ **HISTORY** Latin *carina* keel

career *n* **1** the series of jobs in a profession or occupation that a person has through his or her life: *a career in child psychology* **2** the part of a person's life spent in a particular occupation or type of work: *a school career punctuated with exams* ▷ *vb* **3** to rush in an uncontrolled way ▷ *adj* **4** having chosen to dedicate his or her life to a particular occupation: *a career soldier* ▶ **HISTORY** Latin *carrus* two-wheeled wagon

careerist *n* a person who seeks to advance his or her career by any means possible > **careerism** *n*

carefree *adj* without worry or responsibility

careful *adj* **1** cautious in attitude or action **2** very exact and thorough > **carefully** *adv* > **carefulness** *n*

caregiver *n* same as **carer**

careless *adj* **1** done or acting with insufficient attention **2** unconcerned in attitude or action > **carelessly** *adv* > **carelessness** *n*

carer *n* a person who looks after someone who is ill or old, often a relative: *the group offers support for the carers of those with dementia*

caress *n* written **1** a gentle affectionate touch or embrace ▷ *vb* **2** to touch gently and affectionately ▶ **HISTORY** Latin *carus* dear

caret (**kar**-ret) *n* a symbol (ʌ) indicating a place in written or printed matter where something is to be inserted ▶ **HISTORY** Latin: there is missing

caretaker *n* **1** a person employed to look after a place or thing ▷ *adj* **2** performing the duties of an office temporarily: *a caretaker administration*

careworn *adj* showing signs of stress or worry

cargo *n*, *pl* **-goes** or *esp US* **-gos** goods carried by a ship, aircraft, or other vehicle ▶ **HISTORY** Spanish *cargar* to load

cargo pants or **trousers** *pl n* loose trousers with a large external pocket on the side of each leg

cargo port *n* a port where cargo is loaded and unloaded

Carib *n* **1** (*pl* **-ibs** or **-ib**) a member of a group of Native American peoples of NE South America and the S West Indies **2** any of the languages of these peoples ▶ **HISTORY** Spanish *Caribe*

Caribbean *adj* of the Caribbean Sea, bounded by Central America, South America, and the West Indies, or the surrounding countries and islands

Caribbean Community and Common Market *n* the former name of **Caricom**

Caribbean Court of Justice *n* the judicial branch of Caricom

caribou *n*, *pl* **-bou** or **-bous** a large North American reindeer ▶ **HISTORY** from a Native American language

caricature *n* **1** a drawing or description of a person which exaggerates characteristic features for comic effect **2** a description or explanation of something that is so exaggerated or over-simplified that it is difficult to take seriously: *the classic caricature of the henpecked husband* ▷ *vb* **-turing, -tured 3** to make a caricature of ▶ **HISTORY** Italian *caricatura* a distortion

Caricom Caribbean Community: an organization founded (in 1973) to promote economic integration and diplomatic coordination between certain Caribbean countries (Antigua and Barbuda, Bahamas, Barbados, Belize, Dominica, Guyana, Grenada, Haiti, Jamaica, Montserrat, St Kitts and Nevis, St Lucia, St Vincent and the Grenadines, Suriname, and Trinidad and Tobago)

caries (**care**-reez) *n* tooth decay ▶ **HISTORY** Latin: decay

Carifesta Caribbean Festival of Arts: an international festival (founded in 1972) held periodically by Caribbean countries to celebrate the creative arts of the Caribbean and Latin America

Carifta Caribbean Free Trade Area: an organization (1965–72) that promoted economic links between various English-speaking Caribbean countries

carillon (kar-**rill**-yon) *n* **1** a set of bells hung in a tower and played either from a keyboard or mechanically **2** a tune played on such bells ▶ **HISTORY** French

caring *adj* **1** feeling or showing care and compassion for other people **2** of or relating to professional social or medical care: *the caring professions*

carjack *vb* to attack (a driver in a car) in order to rob the driver or to steal the car for another crime ▶ **HISTORY** CAR + (HI)JACK

cark *vb* **cark it** Austral & NZ, slang to die

Carmelite *n* **1** a Christian friar or nun belonging to the order of Our Lady of Carmel ▷ *adj* **2** of this order ▶ **HISTORY** after Mount *Carmel*, in Palestine, where the order was founded

carminative *adj* **1** able to relieve flatulence ▷ *n* **2** a carminative drug ▶ **HISTORY** Latin *carminare* to card wool, comb out

carmine *adj* vivid red ▶ **HISTORY** Arabic *qirmiz* kermes

carnage *n* extensive slaughter of people ▶ **HISTORY** Latin *caro* flesh

carnal *adj* of a sensual nature ▶ **HISTORY** Latin *caro* flesh > **carnality** *n*

carnation *n* a cultivated plant with clove-scented white, pink, or red flowers ▶ **HISTORY** Latin *caro* flesh

carnelian n a reddish-yellow variety of chalcedony, used as a gemstone ▶ HISTORY Old French *corneline*

carnet (kar-nay) n a customs licence permitting motorists to take their cars across certain frontiers ▶ HISTORY French: notebook

carnival n **1** a festive period with processions, music, and dancing in the street **2** a travelling funfair ▶ HISTORY Old Italian *carnelevare* a removing of meat (referring to the Lenten fast)

carnivore (car-niv-vore) n **1** a meat-eating animal **2** informal an aggressively ambitious person ▶ HISTORY Latin *caro* flesh + *vorare* to consume > **carnivorous** (car-niv-or-uss) adj

carob n the pod of a Mediterranean tree, used as a chocolate substitute ▶ HISTORY Arabic al *kharrūbah*

carol n **1** a joyful religious song sung at Christmas ▷ vb **-olling, -olled** or US **-oling, -oled** **2** to sing carols **3** to sing joyfully ▶ HISTORY Old French

carotene n biochem any of four orange-red hydrocarbons, found in many plants, converted to vitamin A in the liver ▶ HISTORY from Latin *carota* carrot

carotid (kar-rot-id) n **1** either of the two arteries that supply blood to the head and neck ▷ adj **2** of either of these arteries ▶ HISTORY Greek *karoun* to stupefy; so named because pressure on them produced unconsciousness

carousal n a merry drinking party

carouse vb **-rousing, -roused** to have a merry drinking party: *carousing with friends* ▶ HISTORY German *(trinken) gar aus* (to drink) right out

carousel (kar-roo-sell) n **1** a revolving conveyor for luggage at an airport or for slides for a projector **2** US & Canad a merry-go-round ▶ HISTORY Italian *carosello*

carp[1] n, pl **carp** or **carps** a large freshwater food fish ▶ HISTORY Old French *carpe*

carp[2] vb to complain or find fault ▶ HISTORY Old Norse *karpa* to boast > **carping** adj, n

carpal n a wrist bone ▶ HISTORY Greek *karpos* wrist

car park n an area or building reserved for parking cars

carpel n the female reproductive organ of a flowering plant ▶ HISTORY Greek *karpos* fruit

carpenter n a person who makes or repairs wooden structures ▶ HISTORY Latin *carpentarius* wagon-maker

carpentry n the skill or work of a carpenter

carpet n **1** a heavy fabric for covering floors **2** a covering like a carpet: *a carpet of leaves* **3 on the carpet** informal being or about to be reprimanded **4 sweep something under the carpet** to conceal or keep silent about something that one does not want to be discovered ▷ vb **-peting, -peted** **5** to cover with a carpet or a covering like a carpet ▶ HISTORY Latin *carpere* to pluck, card

carpetbagger n **1** a politician who seeks office in a place where he or she has no connections **2** Brit a person who makes a short-term investment in a mutual savings or life-assurance organization in order to benefit from free shares issued following the organization's conversion to a public limited company

carpet snake or **python** n a large nonvenomous Australian snake with a carpet-like pattern on its back

car phone n a telephone that operates by cellular radio for use in a car

carpus n, pl **-pi** the set of eight bones of the human wrist ▶ HISTORY Greek *karpos*

carrageen n an edible red seaweed of North America and N Europe ▶ HISTORY *Carragheen*, near Waterford, Ireland

carriage n **1** Brit, Austral & NZ one of the sections of a train for passengers **2** the way a person holds and moves his or her head and body **3** a four-wheeled horse-drawn passenger vehicle **4** the moving part of a machine, such as a typewriter, that supports and shifts another part **5** the charge made for conveying goods ▶ HISTORY Old French *cariage*

carriageway n **1** Brit the part of a road along which traffic passes in one direction: *the westbound carriageway of the M4* **2** NZ the part of a road used by vehicles

carrier n **1** a person, vehicle, or organization that carries something: *armoured personnel carriers* **2** a person or animal that, without suffering from a disease, is capable of transmitting it to others **3** short for **aircraft carrier**

carrier bag n Brit a large plastic or paper bag for carrying shopping

carrier pigeon n a homing pigeon used for carrying messages

carrion n dead and rotting flesh ▶ HISTORY Latin *caro* flesh

carrion crow n a scavenging European crow with a completely black plumage and bill

carrot n **1** a long tapering orange root vegetable **2** something offered as an incentive ▶ HISTORY Greek *karōton*

carroty adj (of hair) reddish-orange

carry vb **-ries, -rying, -ried** **1** to take from one place to another **2** to have with one habitually, for example in one's pocket or handbag: *to carry a donor card* **3** to transmit or be transmitted: *to carry disease* **4** to have as a factor or result: *the charge of desertion carries a maximum penalty of twenty years* **5** to be pregnant with: *women carrying Down's Syndrome babies* **6** to hold (one's head or body) in a specified manner: *she always wears a sari and carries herself like an Indian* **7** to secure the adoption of (a bill or motion): *the resolution was carried by fewer than twenty votes* **8** (of a newspaper or television or radio station) to include in the contents: *several papers carried front-page pictures of the Russian president* **9** maths to transfer (a number) from one column of figures to the next **10** to travel a certain distance or reach a specified point: *his faint voice carried no farther than the front few rows* **11 carry the can** informal to take all the blame for something ▷ See also **carry forward** ▶ HISTORY Latin *carrum* transport wagon

carrycot n a light portable bed for a baby, with handles and a hood, which usually also serves as the body of a pram

carry forward vb to transfer (an amount) to the next column, page, or accounting period

carrying capacity n ecology the maximum number of individuals that an area of land can support

carry on vb 1 to continue: we'll carry on exactly where we left off 2 to do, run, or take part in: the vast trade carried on in the city 3 informal to cause a fuss: I don't want to carry on and make a big scene ▷ n **carry-on** 4 informal, chiefly Brit a fuss

carry out vb 1 to follow (an order or instruction) 2 to accomplish (a task): to carry out repairs

carry over vb to extend from one period or situation into another: major debts carried over from last year

carry through vb to bring to completion: these are difficult policies to carry through

cart n 1 an open horse-drawn vehicle, usually with two wheels, used to carry goods or passengers 2 any small vehicle that is pulled or pushed by hand ▷ vb 3 to carry, usually with some effort: men carted bricks and tiles and wooden boards ▶ HISTORY Old Norse kartr

carte blanche n complete authority: she's got carte blanche to redecorate ▶ HISTORY French: blank paper

cartel n an association of competing firms formed in order to fix prices ▶ HISTORY German Kartell

Cartesian adj of René Descartes, 17th-century French philosopher and mathematician, or his works ▶ HISTORY Cartesius, Latin form of Descartes

Cartesian coordinates pl n a set of numbers that determine the location of a point in a plane or in space by its distance from two fixed intersecting lines

Cartesian plane n maths the two-dimensional set of axes used for plotting points and sketching graphs

carthorse n a large heavily built horse kept for pulling carts or for farm work

Carthusian n 1 a Christian monk or nun belonging to a strict monastic order founded in 1084 ▷ adj 2 of this order ▶ HISTORY Latin Carthusia Chartreuse, near Grenoble

cartilage (**kar**-till-ij) n a strong flexible tissue forming part of the skeleton ▶ HISTORY Latin cartilago > **cartilaginous** adj

cartography n the art of making maps or charts ▶ HISTORY French carte map, chart > **cartographer** n > **cartographic** adj

carton n 1 a cardboard box or container 2 a container of waxed paper in which drinks are sold ▶ HISTORY Italian carta card

cartoon n 1 a humorous or satirical drawing in a newspaper or magazine 2 same as **comic strip** 3 same as **animated cartoon** ▶ HISTORY Italian cartone pasteboard > **cartoonist** n

cartouche n 1 an ornamental tablet or panel in the form of a scroll 2 (in ancient Egypt) an oblong or oval figure containing royal or divine names ▶ HISTORY French: scroll, cartridge

cartridge n 1 a metal casing containing an explosive charge and bullet for a gun 2 the part of the pick-up of a record player that converts the movements of the stylus into electrical signals 3 a sealed container of film or tape, or ink for a special kind of pen ▶ HISTORY from French cartouche

cartridge paper n a type of heavy rough drawing paper

cartwheel n 1 a sideways somersault supported by the hands with legs outstretched 2 the large spoked wheel of a cart

carve vb **carving, carved** 1 to cut in order to form something: carving wood 2 to form (something) by cutting: the statue which was carved by Michelangelo 3 to slice (cooked meat) ▷ See also **carve out** ▶ HISTORY Old English ceorfan > **carver** n

carve out vb informal to make or create: to carve out a political career

carving n a figure or design produced by carving stone or wood

caryatid (kar-ree-**at**-id) n a supporting column in the shape of a female figure ▶ HISTORY Greek Karuatides priestesses of Artemis at Karuai (Caryae), in Laconia

Casanova n a promiscuous man ▶ HISTORY after Giovanni Casanova, Italian adventurer

casbah n the citadel of a North African city ▶ HISTORY Arabic kasba citadel

cascade n 1 a waterfall or series of waterfalls over rocks 2 something flowing or falling like a waterfall: a cascade of luxuriant hair ▷ vb **-cading, -caded** 3 to flow or fall in a cascade: rays of sunshine cascaded down ▶ HISTORY Italian cascare to fall

cascara n the bark of a N American shrub, used as a laxative ▶ HISTORY Spanish: bark

case¹ n 1 a single instance or example of something: cases of teenage pregnancies 2 a matter for discussion: the case before the Ethics Committee 3 a specific condition or state of affairs: a sudden-death play-off in the case of a draw 4 a set of arguments supporting an action or cause: I put my case before them 5 a person or problem dealt with by a doctor, social worker, or solicitor 6 a an action or lawsuit: a rape case b the evidence offered in court to support a claim: he will try to show that the case against his client is largely circumstantial 7 grammar a form of a noun, pronoun, or adjective showing its relation to other words in the sentence: the accusative case 8 informal an amusingly eccentric person 9 **in any case** no matter what 10 **in case** so as to allow for the possibility that: the President has ordered a medical team to stand by in case hostages are released 11 **in case of** in the event of: in case of a future conflict ▶ HISTORY Old English casus (grammatical) case, associated with Old French cas a happening; both from Latin cadere to fall

case² n 1 a container, such as a box or chest 2 a suitcase 3 a protective outer covering ▷ vb **casing, cased** 4 slang to inspect carefully (a place one plans to rob) ▶ HISTORY Latin capsa box

123

case-hardened *adj* having been made callous by experience: *a case-hardened senior policewoman*

case history *n* a record of a person's background or medical history

casein *n* a protein found in milk, which forms the basis of cheese ▶ **HISTORY** Latin *caseus* cheese

case law *n* law established by following judicial decisions made in earlier cases

caseload *n* the number of cases that someone like a doctor or social worker deals with at any one time

casement *n written* a window that is hinged on one side ▶ **HISTORY** probably from Old French *encassement* frame

case study *n* an analysis of a group or person in order to make generalizations about a larger group or society as a whole

casework *n* social work based on close study of the personal histories and circumstances of individuals and families > **caseworker** *n*

cash *n* **1** banknotes and coins, rather than cheques **2** *informal* money: *strapped for cash* ▷ *adj* **3** of, for, or paid in cash: *cash hand-outs* ▷ *vb* **4** to obtain or pay banknotes or coins for (a cheque or postal order) ▷ See also **cash in on** ▶ **HISTORY** Old Italian *cassa* money box

cash-and-carry *adj* operating on a basis of cash payment for goods that are taken away by the purchaser: *the cash-and-carry wholesalers*

cashback *n* **1** a discount offered in return for immediate payment **2** a service by which a customer in a shop can draw out cash on a debit card

cash-book *n book-keeping* a journal in which all money transactions are recorded

cash card *n* a card issued by a bank or building society which can be inserted into a cash dispenser in order to obtain money

cash crop *n agriculture* a crop produced for sale rather than for subsistence

cash desk *n* a counter or till in a shop where purchases are paid for

cash discount *n* a discount granted to a purchaser who pays within a specified period

cash dispenser *n* a computerized device outside a bank which supplies cash when a special card is inserted and the user's code number keyed in

cashew *n* an edible kidney-shaped nut ▶ **HISTORY** S American Indian *acajú*

cash flow *n* the movement of money into and out of a business

cashier¹ *n* a person responsible for handling cash in a bank, shop, or other business ▶ **HISTORY** French *casse* money chest

cashier² *vb* to dismiss with dishonour from the armed forces ▶ **HISTORY** Latin *quassare* to QUASH

cash in on *vb informal* to gain profit or advantage from: *trying to cash in on the dispute*

cashmere *n* a very fine soft wool obtained from goats ▶ **HISTORY** from *Kashmir*, in SW central Asia

cash on delivery *n* a system involving cash payment to the carrier on delivery of merchandise. Abbrev: **COD**

cash register *n* a till that has a mechanism for displaying and adding the prices of the goods sold

casing *n* a protective case or covering

casino *n*, *pl* **-nos** a public building or room where gambling games are played ▶ **HISTORY** Italian

cask *n* **1** a strong barrel used to hold alcoholic drink **2** *Austral* a cubic carton containing wine, with a tap for dispensing ▶ **HISTORY** Spanish *casco* helmet

casket *n* **1** a small box for valuables **2** *US* a coffin ▶ **HISTORY** probably from Old French *cassette* little box

Cassandra *n* someone whose prophecies of doom are unheeded ▶ **HISTORY** Trojan prophetess in Greek mythology

cassava *n* a starch obtained from the root of a tropical American plant, used to make tapioca ▶ **HISTORY** West Indian *caçábi*

casserole *n* **1** a covered dish in which food is cooked slowly, usually in an oven, and served **2** a dish cooked and served in this way: *beef casserole* ▷ *vb* **-roling, -roled** **3** to cook in a casserole ▶ **HISTORY** French

cassette *n* a plastic case containing a reel of film or magnetic tape ▶ **HISTORY** French: little box

cassia *n* **1** a tropical plant whose pods yield a mild laxative **2 cassia bark** a cinnamon-like spice obtained from the bark of a tropical Asian tree ▶ **HISTORY** Greek *kasia*

cassock *n* an ankle-length garment, usually black, worn by some Christian priests ▶ **HISTORY** Italian *casacca* a long coat

cassowary *n*, *pl* **-waries** a large flightless bird of Australia and New Guinea ▶ **HISTORY** Malay *kěsuari*

cast *n* **1** the actors in a play collectively **2 a** an object made of material that has been shaped, while molten, by a mould **b** the mould used to shape such an object **3** *surgery* a rigid casing made of plaster of Paris for immobilizing broken bones while they heal **4** a sort, kind, or style: *people of an academic cast of mind* **5** a slight squint in the eye ▷ *vb* **casting, cast** **6** to select (an actor) to play a part in a play or film **7** to give or deposit (a vote) **8** to express (doubts or aspersions) **9** *written* to cause to appear: *a shadow cast by the grandstand; the gloom cast by the recession* **10 a** to shape (molten material) by pouring it into a mould **b** to make (an object) by such a process **11** to throw (a fishing line) into the water **12** to throw with force: *cast into a bonfire* **13** *written* to direct (a glance): *he cast his eye over the horse-chestnut trees* **14** to roll or throw (a dice) **15 cast aside** to abandon or reject: *cast aside by her lover* **16 cast a spell a** to perform magic **b** to have an irresistible influence ▶ **HISTORY** Old Norse *kasta*

castanets *pl n* a musical instrument, used by Spanish dancers, consisting of curved pieces of hollow wood, held between the fingers and thumb and clicked together ▶ **HISTORY** Spanish *castañeta*, from *castaña* chestnut

C

castaway *n* a person who has been shipwrecked

caste *n* **1** any of the four major hereditary classes into which Hindu society is divided **2** social rank ▶ HISTORY Latin *castus* pure, not polluted

castellated *adj* having turrets and battlements, like a castle ▶ HISTORY Medieval Latin *castellare* to fortify as a castle

caster *n* same as **castor**

caster sugar *n* finely ground white sugar

castigate *vb* **-gating, -gated** to find fault with or reprimand (a person) harshly ▶ HISTORY Latin *castigare* to correct > **castigation** *n*

casting *n* an object that has been cast in metal from a mould

casting vote *n* the deciding vote used by the chairperson of a meeting when an equal number of votes are cast on each side

cast iron *n* **1** iron containing so much carbon that it is brittle and must be cast into shape rather than wrought ▷ *adj* **cast-iron 2** made of cast iron **3** definite or unchallengeable: *cast-iron guarantees*

castle *n* **1** a large fortified building or set of buildings, often built as a residence for a ruler or nobleman in medieval Europe **2** same as **rook²** ▶ HISTORY Latin: *castellum*

castle in the air *or* **in Spain** *n* a hope or desire unlikely to be realized

cast-off *adj* **1** discarded because no longer wanted or needed: *cast-off clothing* ▷ *n* **castoff 2** a person or thing that has been discarded because no longer wanted or needed ▷ *vb* **cast off 3** to discard (something no longer wanted or needed) **4** to untie a ship from a dock **5** to knot and remove (a row of stitches, esp. the final row) from the needle in knitting

cast on *vb* to make (a row of stitches) on the needle in knitting

castor *n* a small swivelling wheel fixed to a piece of furniture to enable it to be moved easily in any direction

castor oil *n* an oil obtained from the seeds of an Indian plant, used as a lubricant and purgative

castrate *vb* **-trating, -trated 1** to remove the testicles of **2** to deprive of vigour or masculinity ▶ HISTORY Latin *castrare* > **castration** *n*

castrato *n, pl* **-ti** *or* **-tos** (in 17th- and 18th-century opera) a male singer whose testicles were removed before puberty, allowing the retention of a soprano or alto voice ▶ HISTORY Italian

casual *adj* **1** being or seeming careless or nonchalant: *he was casual about security* **2** occasional or irregular: *casual workers* **3** shallow or superficial: *casual relationships* **4** for informal wear: *a casual jacket* **5** happening by chance or without planning: *a casual comment* ▷ *n* **6** an occasional worker ▶ HISTORY Latin *casus* event, chance > **casually** *adv*

casualty *n, pl* **-ties 1** a person who is killed or injured in an accident or war **2** the hospital department where victims of accidents are given emergency treatment **3** a person or thing that has suffered as the result of a particular event or circumstance: *583 job losses with significant casualties among public-sector employees*

casuarina (kass-yew-a-**reen**-a) *n bot* an Australian tree with jointed green branches ▶ HISTORY Malay *kĕsuari*, referring to the resemblance of the branches to the feathers of the cassowary

casuistry *n* reasoning that is misleading or oversubtle ▶ HISTORY Latin *casus* case > **casuist** *n*

cat *n* **1 a** a small domesticated mammal with thick soft fur and whiskers **2** a wild animal related to the cat, such as the lynx, lion, or tiger. *Related adjective*: **feline 3 let the cat out of the bag** to disclose a secret **4 raining cats and dogs** raining very heavily **5 set the cat among the pigeons** to stir up trouble ▶ HISTORY Latin *cattus* > **catlike** *adj*

catabolism *n biol* a metabolic process in which complex molecules are broken down into simple ones with the release of energy ▶ HISTORY Greek *kata-* down + *ballein* to throw > **catabolic** *adj*

cataclysm (**kat**-a-kliz-zum) *n* **1** a violent upheaval of a social, political, or military nature: *the cataclysm of the Second World War* **2** a disaster such as an earthquake or a flood ▶ HISTORY Greek *katakluzein* to flood > **cataclysmic** *adj*

catacombs (**kat**-a-koomz) *pl n* an underground burial place consisting of tunnels with side recesses for tombs

- ■ **WORD HISTORY**
- ■ *Catacumbas* was the name given to the
- ■ underground cemetery built below the Basilica
- ■ of St Sebastian near Rome. In the course of
- ■ time, the name was applied to similar
- ■ cemeteries elsewhere.

catafalque (**kat**-a-falk) *n* a raised platform on which a body lies in state before or during a funeral ▶ HISTORY Italian *catafalco*

Catalan *adj* **1** of Catalonia ▷ *n* **2** a language of Catalonia in NE Spain **3** a person from Catalonia

catalepsy *n* a trancelike state in which the body is rigid ▶ HISTORY Greek *katalēpsis* a seizing > **cataleptic** *adj*

catalogue *or US* **catalog** *n* **1** a book containing details of items for sale **2** a list of all the books of a library **3** a list of events, qualities, or things considered as a group: *a catalogue of killings* ▷ *vb* **-loguing, -logued** *or* **-loging, -loged 4** to enter (an item) in a catalogue **5** to list a series of (events, qualities, or things): *the report catalogues two decades of human-rights violations* ▶ HISTORY Greek *katalegein* to list > **cataloguer** *n*

catalpa *n* a tree of N America and Asia with bell-shaped whitish flowers ▶ HISTORY Carolina Creek (a Native American language) *kutuhlpa* winged head

catalyse *or US* **-lyze** *vb* **-lysing, -lysed** *or* **-lyzing, -lyzed** to influence (a chemical reaction) by catalysis

catalysis *n* acceleration of a chemical reaction by the action of a catalyst ▶ HISTORY Greek *kataluein* to dissolve > **catalytic** *adj*

catalyst *n* **1** a substance that speeds up a chemical reaction without itself undergoing any permanent chemical change **2** a person or thing that causes an important change to take place: *a catalyst for peace*

catalytic converter *n* a device which uses catalysts to reduce the quantity of poisonous substances emitted by the exhaust of a motor vehicle

catalytic cracker *n* a unit in an oil refinery in which mineral oils are converted into fuels by a catalytic process

catamaran *n* a boat with twin parallel hulls
- **WORD HISTORY**
- A catamaran was originally a type of raft found
- in India, made by tying three logs together. The
- word 'catamaran' comes from Tamil
- *kattumaram*, which means 'tied logs'.

catapult *n* **1** a Y-shaped device with a loop of elastic fastened to the ends of the prongs, used by children for firing stones **2** a device used to launch aircraft from a warship ▷ *vb* **3** to shoot forwards or upwards violently: *traffic catapulted forward with a roar* **4** to cause (someone) suddenly to be in a particular situation: *catapulted to stardom* ▶ HISTORY Greek *kata-* down + *pallein* to hurl

cataract *n* **1** *pathol* **a** a condition in which the lens of the eye becomes partially or totally opaque **b** the opaque area **2** a large waterfall ▶ HISTORY Greek *katarassein* to dash down

catarrh (kat-**tar**) *n* excessive mucus in the nose and throat, often experienced during or following a cold ▶ HISTORY Greek *katarrhein* to flow down > **catarrhal** *adj*

catastrophe (kat-**ass**-trof-fee) *n* a great and sudden disaster or misfortune ▶ HISTORY Greek *katastrephein* to overturn > **catastrophic** *adj*

catatonia *n* a form of schizophrenia in which the sufferer experiences stupor, with outbreaks of excitement ▶ HISTORY Greek *kata-* down + *tonos* tension > **catatonic** *adj*

catcall *n* a shrill whistle or cry of disapproval or derision

catch *vb* **catching, caught** **1** to seize and hold **2** to capture (a person or a fish or animal) **3** to surprise in an act: *two boys were caught stealing* **4** to reach (a bus, train, or plane) in time to board it **5** to see or hear: *you'll have to be quick if you want to catch her dj-ing* **6** to be infected with (an illness) **7** to entangle or become entangled **8** to attract (someone's attention, imagination, or interest) **9** to comprehend or make out: *you have to work hard to catch his tone and meaning* **10** to reproduce (a quality) accurately in a work of art **11** (of a fire) to start burning **12** *cricket* to dismiss (a batsman) by catching a ball struck by him before it touches the ground **13 catch at a** to attempt to grasp **b** to take advantage of (an opportunity) **14 catch it** *informal* to be punished ▷ *n* **15** a device such as a hook, for fastening a door, window, or box **16** the total number of fish caught **17** *informal* a concealed or unforeseen drawback **18** an emotional break in the voice **19** *informal* a person considered worth having as a husband or wife **20** *cricket* the act of catching a ball struck by a batsman before it touches the ground, resulting in him being out ▷ See also **catch on, catch out** ▶ HISTORY Latin *capere* to seize

catch-22 *n* a situation in which a person is frustrated by a set of circumstances that prevent any attempt to escape from them ▶ HISTORY from the title of a novel by J. Heller

catch crop *n* *agriculture* a quick-growing crop planted between two regular crops grown in consecutive seasons, or between two rows of regular crops in the same season; such crops increase productivity or help make up for failed crops

catching *adj* infectious

catchment *n* **1** a structure in which water is collected **2** all the people served by a school or hospital in a particular catchment area

catchment area *n* **1** the area of land draining into a river, basin, or reservoir **2** the area served by a particular school or hospital

catch on *vb* *informal* **1** to become popular or fashionable **2** to understand: *I was slow to catch on to what she was trying to tell me*

catch out *vb* *informal, chiefly Brit* to trap (someone) in an error or a lie

catchpenny *adj* *Brit* designed to have instant appeal without regard for quality

catch phrase *n* a well-known phrase or slogan associated with a particular entertainer or other celebrity

catchword *n* a well-known and frequently used phrase or slogan

catchy *adj* **catchier, catchiest** (of a tune) pleasant and easily remembered

catechism (**kat**-tik-kiz-zum) *n* instruction on the doctrine of a Christian Church by a series of questions and answers ▶ HISTORY Greek *katēkhizein* to catechize

catechize *or* **-echise** *vb* **-echizing, -echized** *or* **-echising, -echised** **1** to instruct in Christianity using a catechism **2** to question (someone) thoroughly ▶ HISTORY Greek *katēkhizein* > **catechist** *n*

categorical *or* **categoric** *adj* absolutely clear and certain: *he was categorical in his denial* > **categorically** *adv*

categorize *or* **-rise** *vb* **-rizing, -rized** *or* **-rising, -rised** to put in a category > **categorization** *or* **-risation** *n*

category *n, pl* **-ries** a class or group of things or people with some quality or qualities in common ▶ HISTORY Greek *katēgoria* assertion

cater *vb* **1** to provide what is needed or wanted: *operating theatres that can cater for open-heart surgery* **2** to provide food or services: *chef is pleased to cater for vegetarians and vegans* ▶ HISTORY Anglo-Norman *acater* to buy

caterer *n* a person whose job is to provide food for social events such as parties and weddings

causeway *n* a raised path or road across water or marshland ▶ **HISTORY** Middle English *cauciwey* paved way

caustic *adj* **1** capable of burning or corroding by chemical action: *caustic soda* **2** bitter and sarcastic: *caustic critics* ▷ *n* **3** *chem* a caustic substance ▶ **HISTORY** Greek *kaiein* to burn > **caustically** *adv*

caustic soda *n* same as **sodium hydroxide**

cauterize *or* **-ise** *vb* **-izing, -ized** *or* **-ising, -ised** to burn (a wound) with heat or a caustic agent to prevent infection ▶ **HISTORY** Greek *kaiein* to burn > **cauterization** *or* **-isation** *n*

cautery *n, pl* **-teries** **1** the coagulation of blood or destruction of body tissue by cauterizing **2** an instrument or chemical agent for cauterizing

caution *n* **1** care or prudence, esp. in the face of danger **2** warning: *a word of caution* **3** *law, chiefly Brit* a formal warning given to a person suspected of an offence ▷ *vb* **4** to warn or advise: *he cautioned against an abrupt turnaround* ▶ **HISTORY** Latin *cautio* > **cautionary** *adj*

cautious *adj* showing or having caution > **cautiously** *adv*

cavalcade *n* a procession of people on horseback or in cars ▶ **HISTORY** Italian *cavalcare* to ride on horseback

cavalier *adj* **1** showing haughty disregard; offhand ▷ *n* **2** *old-fashioned* a gallant or courtly gentleman ▶ **HISTORY** Late Latin *caballarius* rider

Cavalier *n* a supporter of Charles I during the English Civil War

cavalry *n* the part of an army originally mounted on horseback, but now often using fast armoured vehicles ▶ **HISTORY** Italian *cavaliere* horseman > **cavalryman** *n*

cave *n* a hollow in the side of a hill or cliff, or underground ▶ **HISTORY** Latin *cavus* hollow

caveat (**kav**-vee-at) *n* **1** *law* a formal notice requesting the court not to take a certain action without warning the person lodging the caveat **2** a caution ▶ **HISTORY** Latin: let him beware

caveat emptor (**kav**-vee-at-**emp**-tor) *n law, formal, written* the principle that it is the buyer rather than the seller who must bear responsibility for checking the quality of goods purchased ▶ **HISTORY** Latin: let the buyer beware

cave in *vb* **1** to collapse inwards **2** *informal* to yield completely under pressure: *the government caved in to the revolutionaries' demands* ▷ *n* **cave-in 3** the sudden collapse of a roof or piece of ground

caveman *n, pl* **-men 1** a prehistoric cave dweller **2** *informal* a man who is primitive or brutal in behaviour

cavern *n* a large cave ▶ **HISTORY** Latin *cavus* hollow

cavernous *adj* like a cavern in vastness, depth, or hollowness: *the cavernous building*

caviar *or* **caviare** *n* the salted roe of the sturgeon, regarded as a delicacy and usually served as an appetizer ▶ **HISTORY** Turkish *havyār*

cavil *vb* **-illing, -illed** *or US* **-iling, -iled 1** to raise annoying petty objections ▷ *n* **2** a petty objection ▶ **HISTORY** Latin *cavillari* to jeer

caving *n* the sport of climbing in and exploring caves > **caver** *n*

cavity *n, pl* **-ties 1** a hollow space **2** *dentistry* a decayed area on a tooth ▶ **HISTORY** Latin *cavus* hollow

cavort *vb* to skip about; caper ▶ **HISTORY** origin unknown

caw *n* **1** the cry of a crow, rook, or raven ▷ *vb* **2** to make this cry ▶ **HISTORY** imitative

cay *n* a small low island or bank of sand and coral fragments ▶ **HISTORY** Spanish *cayo*

cayenne pepper *or* **cayenne** *n* a very hot red spice made from the dried seeds of capsicums ▶ **HISTORY** S American Indian *quiynha*

cayman *or* **caiman** *n, pl* **-mans** a tropical American reptile similar to an alligator ▶ **HISTORY** Carib

CB 1 Citizens' Band **2** Commander of the Order of the Bath

CBD central business district

CBE Commander of the Order of the British Empire (a Brit. title)

CBI Confederation of British Industry

cc *or* **c.c. 1** carbon copy: indicates that a copy of a message or document has been sent to another person **2** cubic centimetre

CC 1 County Council **2** Cricket Club

CCSLC *trademark* Caribbean Certificate of Secondary Level Competence

CCTV closed-circuit television

cd candela

Cd *chem* cadmium

CD compact disc

CDEMA Caribbean Disaster Emergency Management Agency: a network of emergency response units throughout the Caribbean who cooperate with each other when required

CDI compact disc interactive: a system for storing a mix of software, data, audio, and compressed video for interactive use under processor control

CD player *n* a device for playing compact discs

Cdr Commander

CD-R compact disk recordable

CD-ROM compact disc read-only memory: a compact disc used with a computer system as a read-only optical disc

CD-RW compact disk read-write

CDT Central Daylight Time

CD-video *n* a compact-disc player that, when connected to a television and a hi-fi, produces high-quality stereo sound and synchronized pictures from a compact disc

Ce *chem* cerium

cease *vb* **ceasing, ceased 1** to bring or come to an end ▷ *n* **2 without cease** without stopping ▶ **HISTORY** Latin *cessare*

ceasefire *n* a temporary period of truce

ceaseless *adj* without stopping > **ceaselessly** *adv*

cedar *n* **1** a coniferous tree with needle-like evergreen leaves and barrel-shaped cones

2 the sweet-smelling wood of this tree ▶ HISTORY Greek *kedros*

cede *vb* **ceding, ceded** to transfer or surrender (territory or legal rights) ▶ HISTORY Latin *cedere* to yield

cedilla *n* a character (˛) placed underneath a *c*, esp. in French or Portuguese, indicating that it is to be pronounced (s), not (k) ▶ HISTORY Spanish: little *z*

ceilidh (**kay**-lee) *n* an informal social gathering in Scotland or Ireland with folk music and country dancing ▶ HISTORY Gaelic

ceiling *n* **1** the inner upper surface of a room **2** an upper limit set on something such as a payment or salary **3** the upper altitude to which an aircraft can climb ▶ HISTORY origin unknown

celandine *n* a wild plant with yellow flowers ▶ HISTORY Greek *khelidōn* swallow; the plant's season was believed to parallel the migration of swallows

celebrant *n* a person who performs or takes part in a religious ceremony

celebrate *vb* **-brating, -brated 1** to hold festivities to mark (a happy event, birthday, or anniversary) **2** to perform (a solemn or religious ceremony) **3** to praise publicly: *the novel is justly celebrated as a masterpiece* ▶ HISTORY Latin *celeber* numerous, renowned > **celebration** *n* > **celebratory** *adj*

celebrated *adj* well known: *the celebrated musician*

celebrity *n, pl* **-ties 1** a famous person **2** the state of being famous

celeriac (sill-**ler**-ree-ak) *n* a variety of celery with a large turnip-like root

celerity (sill-**ler**-rit-tee) *n* formal swiftness ▶ HISTORY Latin *celeritas*

celery *n* a vegetable with long green crisp edible stalks ▶ HISTORY Greek *selinon* parsley

celestial *adj* **1** heavenly or divine: *celestial music* **2** of or relating to the sky or space: *celestial objects such as pulsars and quasars* ▶ HISTORY Latin *caelum* heaven

celestial equator *n* an imaginary circle lying on the celestial sphere in a plane perpendicular to the earth's axis

celestial sphere *n* an imaginary sphere of infinitely large radius enclosing the universe

celibate *adj* **1** unmarried or abstaining from sex, esp. because of a religious vow of chastity ▷ *n* **2** a celibate person ▶ HISTORY Latin *caelebs* unmarried > **celibacy** *n*

cell *n* **1** *biol* the smallest unit of an organism that is able to function independently **2** a small simple room in a prison, convent, or monastery **3** any small compartment, such as a cell of a honeycomb **4** a small group operating as the core of a larger organization: *Communist cells* **5** a device that produces electrical energy by chemical action ▶ HISTORY Latin *cella* room, storeroom

cellar *n* **1** an underground room, usually used for storage **2** a place where wine is stored **3** a stock of bottled wines ▶ HISTORY Latin *cellarium* food store

cell membrane *n* anat a very thin membrane that surrounds the cytoplasm of a cell

cello (**chell**-oh) *n, pl* **-los** a large low-pitched musical instrument of the violin family, held between the knees and played with a bow ▶ HISTORY short for *violoncello* > **cellist** *n*

Cellophane *n* trademark a thin transparent material made from cellulose that is used as a protective wrapping, esp. for food ▶ HISTORY *cellulose* + Greek *phainein* to shine, appear

cellular *adj* **1** of, consisting of, or resembling a cell or cells: *cellular changes* **2** woven with an open texture: *cellular blankets* **3** designed for or using cellular radio: *cellular phones*

cellular radio *n* radio communication, used esp. in car phones, based on a network of transmitters each serving a small area known as a cell

cellular respiration *n* biochem the chemical breakdown of complex organic substances, such as carbohydrates and fats, that takes place in the cells and tissues of animals and plants, during which energy is released and carbon dioxide is produced

cellulite *n* fat deposits under the skin alleged to resist dieting

celluloid *n* **1** a kind of plastic made from cellulose nitrate and camphor, used to make toys and, formerly, photographic film **2** the cinema or films generally: *a Shakespeare play committed to celluloid*

cellulose *n* the main constituent of plant cell walls, used in making paper, rayon, and plastics

cellulose acetate *n* a nonflammable material used to make film, lacquers, and artificial fibres

cellulose nitrate *n* a compound used in plastics, lacquers, and explosives

cell wall *n* anat the outer layer of a cell

Celsius *adj* denoting a measurement on the Celsius scale ▶ HISTORY after Anders *Celsius*, astronomer who invented it

Celsius scale *n* a scale of temperature in which 0° represents the melting point of ice and 100° represents the boiling point of water

Celt (**kelt**) *n* **1** a person from Scotland, Ireland, Wales, Cornwall, or Brittany **2** a member of a people who inhabited Britain, Gaul, and Spain in pre-Roman times ▶ HISTORY Latin *Celtae* the Celts

Celtic (**kel**-tik, **sel**-tik) *n* **1** a group of languages that includes Gaelic, Welsh, and Breton ▷ *adj* **2** of the Celts or the Celtic languages

cement *n* **1 a** a fine grey powder made of limestone and clay, mixed with water and sand to make mortar or concrete **b** mortar or concrete **2** something that unites, binds, or joins things or people: *bone cement; the cement of fear and hatred of the Left* **3** dentistry a material used for filling teeth ▷ *vb* **4** to join, bind, or cover with cement **5** to make (a relationship) stronger: *this would cement a firm alliance between the army and rebels* ▶ HISTORY Latin *caementum* stone from the quarry

cemetery *n, pl* **-teries** a place where dead people are buried: *a military cemetery* ▶ HISTORY Greek *koimētērion* room for sleeping

cenotaph *n* a monument honouring soldiers who died in a war ▶ HISTORY Greek *kenos* empty + *taphos* tomb

Cenozoic *or* **Caenozoic** (see-no-**zoh**-ik) *adj geol* of the most recent geological era, beginning 65 million years ago, characterized by the development and increase of the mammals ▶ HISTORY Greek *kainos* recent + *zōion* animal

censer *n* a container for burning incense

censor *n* **1** a person authorized to examine films, letters, or publications, in order to ban or cut anything considered obscene or objectionable ▷ *vb* **2** to ban or cut portions of (a film, letter, or publication) ▶ HISTORY Latin *censere* to consider

censorious *adj* harshly critical

censorship *n* the practice or policy of censoring films, letters, or publications

censure *n* **1** severe disapproval ▷ *vb* **-suring, -sured 2** to criticize (someone or something) severely ▶ HISTORY Latin *censere* to assess

censure motion *n* *Parliament* a motion expressing severe criticism (of the government, a minister, etc.)

census *n*, *pl* **-suses** an official periodic count of a population including such information as sex, age, and occupation ▶ HISTORY Latin *censere* to assess

cent *n* a monetary unit worth one hundredth of the main unit of currency in many countries ▶ HISTORY Latin *centum* hundred

cent. 1 central **2** century

centaur *n* *Greek myth* a creature with the head, arms, and torso of a man, and the lower body and legs of a horse ▶ HISTORY Greek *kentauros*

centenarian *n* a person who is at least 100 years old

centenary (sen-**teen**-a-ree) *n*, *pl* **-naries** chiefly Brit a 100th anniversary or the celebration of one. US equivalent: **centennial** ▶ HISTORY Latin *centum* hundred

centesimal *n* **1** one hundredth ▷ *adj* **2** of or divided into hundredths ▶ HISTORY Latin *centum* hundred

centi- *prefix* **1** denoting one hundredth: *centimetre* **2** a hundred: *centipede* ▶ HISTORY Latin *centum* hundred

centigrade *adj* same as **Celsius**

centigram *or* **centigramme** *n* one hundredth of a gram

centilitre *or* US **centiliter** *n* a measure of volume equivalent to one hundredth of a litre

centime (**son**-teem) *n* a monetary unit worth one hundredth of the main unit of currency in a number of countries ▶ HISTORY Latin *centum* hundred

centimetre *or* US **centimeter** *n* a unit of length equal to one hundredth of a metre

centipede *n* a small wormlike creature with many legs

central *adj* **1** of, at, or forming the centre of something: *eastern and central parts of the country* **2** main or principal: *a central issue* > **centrally** *adv* > **centrality** *n*

central bank *n* a national bank that acts as the government's banker, controls credit, and issues currency

central business district *n* the main centre of a town, containing shops, businesses, and places of entertainment

Central European Time *n* the standard time adopted by Western European countries one hour ahead of Greenwich Mean Time, corresponding to British Summer Time. Abbrev: **CET**

central government *n* the government of a whole country, as opposed to the smaller organizations that govern counties, towns, and districts

central heating *n* a system for heating a building by means of radiators or air vents connected to a central source of heat > **centrally heated** *adj*

centralism *n* the principle of bringing a country or an organization under central control > **centralist** *adj*

centralize *or* **-ise** *vb* **-izing, -ized** *or* **-ising, -ised** to bring (a country or an organization) under central control > **centralization** *or* **-isation** *n*

central locking *n* a system by which all the doors of a motor vehicle are locked automatically when the driver's door is locked manually

central nervous system *n* the part of the nervous system of vertebrates that consists of the brain and spinal cord

central processing unit *n* the part of a computer that performs logical and arithmetical operations on the data

central reservation *n* Brit & NZ the strip that separates the two sides of a motorway or dual carriageway

centre *or* US **center** *n* **1** the middle point or part of something **2** a place where a specified activity takes place: *a shopping centre* **3** a person or thing that is a focus of interest: *the centre of a long-running dispute* **4** a place of activity or influence: *the parliament building was the centre of resistance* **5** a political party or group that favours moderation **6** *sport* a player who plays in the middle of the field rather than on a wing ▷ *vb* **-tring, -tred** *or* US **-tering, -tered 7** to put in the centre of something **8 centre on** to have as a centre or main theme: *the summit is expected to centre on expanding the role of the UN* ▶ HISTORY Greek *kentron* needle, sharp point

centre forward *n* *sport* the middle player in the forward line of a team

centre half *or* **centre back** *n* *soccer* a defender who plays in the middle of the defence

centre of gravity *n* the point in an object around which its mass is evenly distributed

centre pass *n* *hockey* a push or hit made in any direction to start the game

centre stage *n* **1** *theatre* the centre point on a stage **2** the main focus of attention

centrifugal (sent-**riff**-few-gl) *adj* **1** moving or tending to move away from a centre **2** of or

operated by centrifugal force: *centrifugal extractors*
▶ HISTORY Greek *kentron* centre + Latin *fugere* to flee

centrifugal force *n* a force that acts outwards on any body that rotates or moves along a curved path ·

centrifuge *n* a machine that separates substances by the action of centrifugal force

centripetal (sent-**rip**-it-al) *adj* moving or tending to move towards a centre ▶ HISTORY Greek *kentron* centre + Latin *petere* to seek

centripetal force *n* a force that acts inwards on any body that rotates or moves along a curved path

centrist *n* a person who holds moderate political views

centromere *n biol* the dense nonstaining region of a chromosome that attaches it to the spindle during mitosis

centrosome *n biol* a small protoplasmic body found near the cell nucleus

centrosphere *n* **1** *geol* the central part of the earth. Also called: **core 2** *biol* another name for **centrosome**

centurion *n* (in ancient Rome) the officer in command of a century ▶ HISTORY Latin *centurio*

century *n*, *pl* **-ries 1** a period of 100 years **2** a score of 100 runs in cricket **3** (in ancient Rome) a unit of foot soldiers, originally consisting of 100 men ▶ HISTORY Latin *centuria*

CEO chief executive officer

cephalopod (**seff**-a-loh-pod) *n* a sea mollusc with a head and tentacles, such as the octopus ▶ HISTORY Greek *kephalē* head + *pous* foot

ceramic *n* **1** a hard brittle material made by heating clay to a very high temperature **2** an object made of this material ▷ *adj* **3** made of ceramic: *ceramic tiles* ▶ HISTORY Greek *keramos* potter's clay

Cerberus (**sir**-ber-uss) *n Greek myth* a three-headed dog who guarded the entrance to Hades

cere *n* a soft waxy swelling, containing the nostrils, at the base of the upper beak of a parrot ▶ HISTORY Latin *cera* wax

cereal *n* **1** any grass that produces an edible grain, such as oat, wheat, or rice **2** the grain produced by such a plant **3** a breakfast food made from this grain, usually eaten mixed with milk ▶ HISTORY Latin *cerealis* concerning agriculture

cerebellum (serr-rib-**bell**-lum) *n*, *pl* **-lums** *or* **-la** (-la) the back part of the brain, which controls balance and muscular coordination ▶ HISTORY Latin

cerebral (**serr**-rib-ral) *adj* **1** of the brain: *a cerebral haemorrhage* **2** involving intelligence rather than emotions or instinct: *the cerebral joys of the literary world*

cerebral palsy *n* a condition in which the limbs and muscles are permanently weak, caused by damage to the brain

cerebrospinal *adj* of the brain and spinal cord: *a sample of cerebrospinal fluid*

cerebrovascular (serr-rib-roh-**vass**-kew-lar) *adj* of the blood vessels and blood supply of the brain

cerebrum (**serr**-rib-rum) *n*, *pl* **-brums** *or* **-bra** (-bra) the main part of the human brain, associated with thought, emotion, and personality ▶ HISTORY Latin: the brain

ceremonial *adj* **1** of ceremony or ritual **2** (of a position) not having any influence or authority: *a ceremonial post* ▷ *n* **3** a system of formal rites; ritual > **ceremonially** *adv*

ceremonious *adj* excessively polite or formal > **ceremoniously** *adv*

ceremony *n*, *pl* **-nies 1** a formal act or ritual performed for a special occasion: *a wedding ceremony* **2** formally polite behaviour **3 stand on ceremony** to insist on or act with excessive formality ▶ HISTORY Latin *caerimonia* what is sacred

Ceres *n* the Roman goddess of agriculture

cerise (ser-**reess**) *adj* cherry-red ▶ HISTORY French: cherry

cerium *n chem* a steel-grey metallic element found only in combination with other elements. Symbol: Ce ▶ HISTORY from *Ceres* (an asteroid)

CERN Conseil Européen pour la Recherche Nucléaire: a European organization for research in high-energy particle physics

cert *n* **a dead cert** *informal* something that is certain to happen or to be successful

certain *adj* **1** positive and confident about something: *he was certain they would agree* **2** definitely known: *it is by no means certain the tomb still exists* **3** sure or bound: *the cuts are certain to go ahead* **4** some but not much: *a certain amount* **5** particular: *certain aspects* **6** named but not known: *a running commentary by a certain Mr Fox* **7 for certain** without doubt ▶ HISTORY Latin *certus* sure

certain chance *n maths* the point at one of the furthest ends of a likelihood scale

certainly *adv* without doubt: *he will certainly be back*

certainty *n* **1** the condition of being certain **2** (*pl* **-ties**) something established as inevitable

certifiable *adj* considered to be legally insane

certificate *n* an official document stating the details of something such as birth, death, or completion of an academic course ▶ HISTORY Old French *certifier* to certify

certificate of incorporation *n company law* a signed statement that a company is duly incorporated

certified *adj* **1** holding or guaranteed by a certificate: *a certified acupuncturist* **2** declared legally insane

certify *vb* **-fies, -fying, -fied 1** to confirm or attest to **2** to guarantee (that certain required standards have been met) **3** to declare legally insane ▶ HISTORY Latin *certus* certain + *facere* to make > **certification** *n*

certitude *n formal* confidence or certainty

cervical smear *n med* a smear taken from the neck (cervix) of the womb for detection of cancer

C

cervix *n, pl* **cervixes** *or* **cervices** **1** the lower part of the womb **2** *anat* the neck ▶ HISTORY Latin > **cervical** *adj*

cesium *n US* same as **caesium**

cessation *n* an ending or pause: *a cessation of hostilities* ▶ HISTORY Latin *cessare* to be idle

cession *n* the act of ceding territory or legal rights ▶ HISTORY Latin *cedere* to yield

cesspool *or* **cesspit** *n* a covered tank or pit for collecting and storing sewage or waste water ▶ HISTORY Old French *souspirail* air vent

CET Central European Time

cetacean (sit-**tay**-shun) *n* a sea creature such as a whale or dolphin, which belongs to a family of fish-shaped mammals and breathes through a blowhole ▶ HISTORY Greek *kētos* whale

cetane (**see**-tane) *n* a colourless liquid hydrocarbon, used as a solvent ▶ HISTORY Latin *cetus* whale

cetane number *n* a measure of the quality of a diesel fuel expressed as the percentage of cetane in it

cf compare ▶ HISTORY Latin *confer*

Cf *chem* californium

CF Canadian Forces

CFC chlorofluorocarbon

CFS chronic fatigue syndrome

cg centigram

CGI computer-generated image(s)

cgs units *pl n* a metric system of units based on the centimetre, gram, and second: for scientific and technical purposes, replaced by SI units

ch. **1** chapter **2** church

cha-cha *or* **cha-cha-cha** *n* **1** a modern ballroom dance from Latin America **2** music for this dance ▶ HISTORY American (Cuban) Spanish

chaconne *n* a musical form consisting of a set of variations on a repeated melodic bass line

chad *n* the small pieces removed during the punching of holes in punch cards, printer paper, etc.

chafe *vb* **chafing, chafed** **1** to make sore or worn by rubbing **2** to be annoyed or impatient: *the lower castes are chafing against 20 years of servitude* ▶ HISTORY Old French *chaufer* to warm

chafer *n* a large slow-moving beetle ▶ HISTORY Old English *ceafor*

chaff¹ *n* **1** grain husks separated from the seeds during threshing **2** something of little worth; rubbish: *you had to be a very perceptive listener to sort the wheat from the chaff of his discourse* ▶ HISTORY Old English *ceaf*

chaff² *vb* to tease good-naturedly ▶ HISTORY probably slang variant of *chafe*

chaffinch *n* a small European songbird with black-and-white wings and, in the male, a reddish body and blue-grey head ▶ HISTORY Old English *ceaf* CHAFF¹ + *finc* finch

chagrin (shag-**grin**) *n written* a feeling of annoyance and disappointment ▶ HISTORY French

chagrined *adj written* annoyed and disappointed

chain *n* **1** a flexible length of metal links, used for fastening, binding, or connecting, or in jewellery **2** **chains** anything that restricts or restrains someone: *bound by the chains of duty* **3** a series of connected facts or events **4** a number of establishments, such as hotels or shops, that have the same owner or management **5** *chem* a number of atoms or groups bonded together so that the resulting molecule, ion, or radical resembles a chain **6** a row of mountains or islands ▷ *vb* **7** to restrict, fasten or bind with or as if with a chain: *the demonstrators chained themselves to railings* ▶ HISTORY Latin *catena*

chain gang *n US* a group of convicted prisoners chained together

chain letter *n* a letter, often with a request for or promise of money, that is sent to many people who are asked to send copies to other people

chain mail *n* same as **mail**²

chain of command *n business* a hierarchy of officials in an organization, each person reporting to the person above him or her in the hierarchy

chain of distribution *n marketing* the network of organizations, including manufacturers, wholesalers, and retailers, that distributes goods or services to consumers

chain reaction *n* **1** a series of events, each of which causes the next **2** a chemical or nuclear reaction in which the product of one step triggers the following step

chain saw *n* a motor-driven saw in which the cutting teeth form links in a continuous chain

chain-smoke *vb* **-smoking, -smoked** to smoke continuously, lighting one cigarette from the preceding one > **chain smoker** *n*

chair *n* **1** a seat with a back and four legs, for one person to sit on **2** an official position of authority or the person holding it: *the chair of the Security Council* **3** a professorship **4** **in the chair** presiding over a meeting **5** **the chair** *informal* the electric chair ▷ *vb* **6** to preside over (a meeting) ▶ HISTORY Greek *kathedra*

chairlift *n* a series of chairs suspended from a moving cable for carrying people up a slope

chairman *n, pl* **-men** a person who is in charge of a company's board of directors or a meeting > **chairwoman** *fem n* > **chairmanship** *n*

chaise (shaze) *n* a light horse-drawn carriage with two wheels ▶ HISTORY French

chaise longue (long) *n, pl* **chaise longues** *or* **chaises longues** a couch with a back and a single armrest ▶ HISTORY French

chalcedony (kal-**sed**-don-ee) *n, pl* **-nies** a form of quartz composed of very fine crystals, often greyish or blue in colour ▶ HISTORY Greek *khalkēdōn* a precious stone

chalet *n* **1** a type of Swiss wooden house with a steeply sloping roof **2** a similar house used as a ski lodge or holiday home ▶ HISTORY French

chalice (**chal**-liss) *n* **1** *poetic* a drinking cup or goblet **2** *Christianity* a gold or silver goblet containing the wine at communion ▶ HISTORY Latin *calix* cup

chalk *n* **1** a soft white rock consisting of calcium carbonate **2** a piece of chalk, either white or coloured, used for writing and drawing on blackboards **3 as different as chalk and cheese** *informal* totally different **4 not by a long chalk** *informal* by no means: *you haven't finished by a long chalk* ▷ *vb* **5** to draw or mark with chalk ▶ HISTORY Latin *calx* limestone > **chalky** *adj*

chalk up *vb informal* **1** to score or register: *the home side chalked up a 9–1 victory* **2** to charge or credit (money) to an account

challenge *n* **1** a demanding or stimulating situation **2** a call to engage in a contest, fight, or argument **3** a questioning of a statement or fact **4** a demand by a sentry for identification or a password **5** *law* a formal objection to a juror ▷ *vb* **-lenging, -lenged 6** to invite or call (someone) to take part in a contest, fight, or argument **7** to call (a decision or action) into question **8** to order (a person) to stop and be identified **9** *law* to make formal objection to (a juror) ▶ HISTORY Latin *calumnia* calumny > **challenger** *n* > **challenging** *adj*

challenged *adj* disabled as specified: *physically challenged; mentally challenged*

chalybeate (kal-**lib**-bee-it) *adj* containing or impregnated with iron salts: *a natural chalybeate spring rises at the edge of the lake* ▶ HISTORY Greek *khalups* iron

chamber *n* **1** a meeting hall, usually one used for a legislative or judicial assembly **2** a room equipped for a particular purpose: *a decompression chamber* **3** a legislative or judicial assembly: *the Senate, the upper chamber of Canada's parliament* **4** old-fashioned *or poetic* a room in a house, esp. a bedroom **5** a compartment or cavity: *the heart chambers* **6** a compartment for a cartridge or shell in a gun ▷ See also **chambers** ▶ HISTORY Greek *kamara* vault

chamberlain *n history* an officer who managed the household of a king or nobleman ▶ HISTORY Old French *chamberlayn*

chamber magistrate *n Austral law* a solicitor employed to provide free legal advice at a local court

chambermaid *n* a woman employed to clean bedrooms in a hotel

chamber music *n* classical music to be performed by a small group of musicians

chamber pot *n* a bowl for urine, formerly used in bedrooms

chambers *pl n* **1** a judge's room for hearing private cases not taken in open court **2** (in England) the set of rooms used as offices by a barrister

chameleon (kam-**meal**-yon) *n* a small lizard with long legs that is able to change colour to blend in with its surroundings

- ■ **WORD HISTORY**
- ■ Although it may not much look like one, a
- ■ chameleon is, in terms of its word origins, a
- ■ type of lion, a 'ground lion'. The word comes
- ■ from two Greek words, *khamai*, meaning 'on
- ■ the ground', and *leōn*, meaning 'lion'.

chamfer (**cham**-fer) *n* **1** a bevelled surface at an edge or corner ▷ *vb* **2** to cut a chamfer on or in ▶ HISTORY Old French *chant* edge + *fraindre* to break

chamois *n, pl* **-ois 1** (**sham**-wah) a small mountain antelope of Europe and SW Asia **2** (**sham**-ee) a soft suede leather made from the skin of this animal or from sheep or goats **3** (**sham**-ee) Also: **chamois leather, shammy, chammy** a piece of such leather or similar material, used for cleaning and polishing ▶ HISTORY Old French

chamomile (**kam**-mo-mile) *n* same as **camomile**

champ¹ *vb* **1** to chew noisily **2 champ at the bit** *informal* to be restless or impatient to do something ▶ HISTORY probably imitative

champ² *n informal* short for **champion** (sense 1)

champagne *n* **1** a white sparkling wine produced around Reims and Épernay, France ▷ *adj* **2** denoting a luxurious lifestyle: *a champagne capitalist* ▶ HISTORY *Champagne*, region of France

champion *n* **1** a person, plant, or animal that has defeated all others in a competition: *the Olympic 100 metres champion* **2** someone who defends a person or cause: *a champion of the downtrodden* ▷ *vb* **3** to support: *he unceasingly championed equal rights and opportunities* ▷ *adj* **4** N English dialect excellent ▶ HISTORY Latin *campus* field > **championship** *n*

chance *n* **1** the extent to which something is likely to happen; probability **2** an opportunity or occasion to do something: *a chance to escape rural poverty* **3** a risk or gamble: *the government is not in the mood to take any more chances* **4** the unknown and unpredictable element that causes something to happen in one way rather than another: *in Buddhism there is no such thing as chance or coincidence* **5 by chance** by accident: *by chance she met an old school friend* **6 on the off chance** acting on the slight possibility: *he had called on the agents on the off chance that he might learn something of value* ▷ *vb* **chancing, chanced 7** to risk or hazard: *a few picnickers chanced the perilous footpath* **8** to do something without planning to: *I chanced to look down* **9 chance on** or **upon** to discover by accident: *I chanced upon a copy of this book* ▶ HISTORY Latin *cadere* to occur

chancel *n* the part of a church containing the altar and choir ▶ HISTORY Latin *cancelli* lattice

chancellery *or* **chancellory** *n, pl* **-leries** *or* **-lories 1** *Brit & Austral* the residence or office of a chancellor **2** *US* the office of an embassy or consulate ▶ HISTORY Anglo-French *chancellerie*

chancellor *n* **1** the head of government in several European countries **2** *US* the president of a university **3** *Brit, Austral & Canad* the honorary head of a university ▶ HISTORY Late Latin *cancellarius* porter > **chancellorship** *n*

Chancellor of the Exchequer *n Brit* the cabinet minister responsible for finance

Chancery *n* (in England) the Lord Chancellor's court, a division of the High Court of Justice ▶ HISTORY shortened from CHANCELLERY

133

chancre (shang-ker) *n pathol* a painless ulcer that develops as a primary symptom of syphilis ▸ HISTORY French

chancy *adj* **chancier, chanciest** *informal* uncertain or risky

chandelier (shan-dill-**eer**) *n* an ornamental hanging light with branches and holders for several candles or bulbs ▸ HISTORY French

chandler *n* a dealer in a specified trade or merchandise: *a ship's chandler* ▸ HISTORY Old French *chandelier* dealer in candles > **chandlery** *n*

change *n* **1** the fact of becoming different **2** variety or novelty: *they wanted to print some good news for a change* **3** a different set, esp. of clothes **4** money exchanged for its equivalent in a larger denomination or in a different currency **5** the balance of money when the amount paid is larger than the amount due **6** coins of a small denomination ▷ *vb* **changing, changed 7** to make or become different **8** to replace with or exchange for another: *the Swedish Communist Party changed its name to the Left Party* **9** to give and receive (something) in return: *slaves and masters changed places* **10** to give or receive (money) in exchange for its equivalent sum in a smaller denomination or different currency **11** to put on other clothes **12** to get off one bus, train or airliner and on to another: *there's no direct train, so you'll need to change at York* ▷ See also **change down, change up** ▸ HISTORY Latin *cambire* to exchange, barter > **changeless** *adj*

changeable *adj* changing often > **changeability** *n*

change down *vb* to select a lower gear when driving

changeling *n* a child believed to have been exchanged by fairies for the parents' real child

change of life *n* the menopause

change up *vb* to select a higher gear when driving

channel *n* **1** a band of radio frequencies assigned for the broadcasting of a radio or television signal **2** a path for an electrical signal or computer data **3** a means of access or communication: *reports coming through diplomatic channels* **4** a broad strait connecting two areas of sea **5** the bed or course of a river, stream, or canal **6** a navigable course through an area of water **7** a groove ▷ *vb* **-nelling, -nelled** or US **-neling, -neled 8** to direct or convey through a channel or channels: *tunnels that channel the pilgrims into the area; to channel funds abroad* ▸ HISTORY Latin *canalis* pipe, conduit

Channel *n* **the Channel** the English Channel

channel-hop *vb* **-hopping, -hopped** to change television channels repeatedly using a remote control device

channel of distribution *n marketing* same as **chain of distribution**

chant *vb* **1** to repeat (a slogan) over and over **2** to sing or recite (a psalm) ▷ *n* **3** a rhythmic or repetitious slogan repeated over and over, usually by more than one person **4** a religious song with a short simple melody in which several words or

syllables are sung on one note ▸ HISTORY Latin *canere* to sing

chanter *n* the pipe on a set of bagpipes on which the melody is played

chanticleer *n* a name for a cock, used in fables ▸ HISTORY Old French *chanter cler* to sing clearly

chanty *n, pl* **-ties** same as **shanty²**

Chanukah or **Hanukkah** (hah-na-ka) *n* an eight-day Jewish festival, held in December, commemorating the rededication of the temple by Judas Maccabaeus ▸ HISTORY Hebrew

chaos *n* complete disorder or confusion ▸ HISTORY Greek *khaos* > **chaotic** *adj* > **chaotically** *adv*

chap *n informal* a man or boy ▸ HISTORY from Old English *cēapman* pedlar

chapati or **chapatti** *n* (in Indian cookery) a kind of flat thin unleavened bread ▸ HISTORY Hindi

chapel *n* **1** a place of worship with its own altar, in a church or cathedral **2** a similar place of worship in a large house or institution **3** (in England and Wales) a Nonconformist place of worship **4** (in Scotland) a Roman Catholic church **5** the members of a trade union in a newspaper office, printing house, or printing firm

■ **WORD HISTORY**
■ According to legend, St Martin of Tours once
■ gave half his cloak to a beggar. This cloak (Latin
■ *cappella*) was kept as a relic and the place where
■ it was kept also became known as the 'cappella'
■ or, in Old French, *chapelle*. The use of this word
■ then spread to other places of worship.

chaperone (**shap**-per-rone) *n* **1** an older person who accompanies and supervises a young person or young people on social occasions ▷ *vb* **-oning, -oned 2** to act as a chaperone to ▸ HISTORY Old French *chape* hood

chaplain *n* a member of the clergy attached to a chapel, military body, or institution ▸ HISTORY Late Latin *cappella* chapel > **chaplaincy** *n*

chaplet *n* a garland worn on the head ▸ HISTORY Old French *chapelet*

chapman *n, pl* **-men** *old-fashioned* a travelling pedlar ▸ HISTORY Old English *cēapman*

chapped *adj* (of the skin) raw and cracked, through exposure to cold ▸ HISTORY probably Germanic

chaps *pl n* leather leggings without a seat, worn by cowboys ▸ HISTORY shortened from Spanish *chaparejos*

chapter *n* **1** a division of a book **2** *written* a period in a life or history: *the latest chapter in the long and complex tale of British brewing* **3** a sequence of events: *a chapter of accidents* **4** a branch of some societies or clubs **5** a group of the canons of a cathedral **6** **chapter and verse** exact authority for an action or statement ▸ HISTORY Latin *caput* head

char¹ *vb* **charring, charred** to blacken by partial burning ▸ HISTORY short for *charcoal*

char² *Brit, informal n* **1** short for **charwoman** ▷ *vb* **charring, charred 2** to clean other people's houses as a job ▸ HISTORY Old English *cerr* turn of work

char[3] *n Brit, old-fashioned slang* tea ▶ HISTORY Chinese *ch'a*

char[4] *n, pl* **char** *or* **chars** a troutlike fish of cold lakes and northern seas ▶ HISTORY origin unknown

charabanc (**shar**-rab-bang) *n Brit, old-fashioned* a coach for sightseeing ▶ HISTORY French: wagon with seats

character *n* **1** the combination of qualities distinguishing an individual person, group of people, or place: *the unique charm and character of this historic town* **2** a distinguishing quality or characteristic: *bodily movements of a deliberate character* **3** reputation, esp. good reputation: *a man of my Dad's character and standing in the community* **4** an attractively unusual or interesting quality: *the little town was full of life and character* **5** a person represented in a play, film, or story **6** an unusual or amusing person: *quite a character* **7** *informal* a person: *a flamboyant character* **8** a single letter, numeral, or symbol used in writing or printing **9** **in** *or* **out of character** typical *or* not typical of the apparent character of a person ▶ HISTORY Greek *kharaktēr* engraver's tool > **characterless** *adj*

characteristic *n* **1** a distinguishing feature or quality **2** *maths* the integral part of a logarithm: *the characteristic of 2.4771 is 2* ▷ *adj* **3** typical or representative of someone or something: *the prime minister fought with characteristic passion* > **characteristically** *adv*

characterization *or*-**isation** *n* **1** the description or portrayal of a person by an actor or writer: *a novel full of rich characterization and complex plotting* **2** the act or an instance of characterizing

characterize *or*-**ise** *vb* -**izing,** -**ized** *or*-**ising,** -**ised** **1** to be a characteristic of: *the violence that characterized the demonstrations* **2** to describe: *we have made what I would characterize as outstanding progress*

characterology *n literature* the study of the development and differences of character

charade (shar-**rahd**) *n* an absurd pretence ▶ HISTORY French

charcoal *n* **1** a black form of carbon made by partially burning wood or other organic matter **2** a stick of this used for drawing **3** a drawing done in charcoal ▷ *adj* **4** Also: **charcoal-grey** very dark grey ▶ HISTORY origin unknown

charge *vb* **charging, charged** **1** to ask (an amount of money) as a price **2** to enter a debit against a person's account for (a purchase) **3** *written* to accuse (someone) formally of a crime in a court of law **4** to make a rush at or sudden attack upon **5** to fill (a glass) **6** to cause (an accumulator or capacitor) to take and store electricity **7** to fill or saturate with liquid or gas: *old mine workings charged with foul gas* **8** to fill with a feeling or mood: *the emotionally charged atmosphere* **9** *formal* to command or assign: *the president has charged his foreign minister with trying to open talks* ▷ *n* **10** a price charged for something; cost **11** a formal accusation of a crime in a court of law **12** an onrush or attack **13** custody or guardianship: *in the charge of the police* **14** a person or thing committed to someone's care: *a nanny reported the cruel father of one of her charges to social workers* **15 a** a cartridge or shell **b** the explosive required to fire a gun **16** *physics* **a** the attribute of matter responsible for all electrical phenomena, existing in two forms, positive and negative **b** the total amount of electricity stored in a capacitor or an accumulator **17 in charge of** in control of and responsible for: *in charge of defence and foreign affairs* ▶ HISTORY Old French *chargier* to load

chargeable *adj* **1** liable to be taxed or charged **2** liable to result in a legal charge

charge card *n* a card issued by a chain store, shop, or organization, that enables customers to obtain goods and services for which they pay later

chargé d'affaires (**shar**-zhay daf-**fair**) *n, pl* **chargés d'affaires** (**shar**-zhay daf-**fair**) **1** the temporary head of a diplomatic mission in the absence of the ambassador or minister **2** the head of a small or unimportant diplomatic mission ▶ HISTORY French

charger *n* **1** a device for charging a battery **2** (in the Middle Ages) a warhorse

chariot *n* a two-wheeled horse-drawn vehicle used in ancient times for wars and races ▶ HISTORY Old French *char* car

charioteer *n* a chariot driver

charisma (kar-**rizz**-ma) *n* the quality or power of an individual to attract, influence, or inspire people ▶ HISTORY Greek *kharis* grace, favour > **charismatic** (kar-rizz-**mat**-ik) *adj*

charismatic movement *n Christianity* a group that believes in divine gifts such as instantaneous healing and uttering unintelligible sounds while in a religious ecstasy

charitable *adj* **1** kind or lenient in one's attitude towards others **2** of or for charity: *a charitable organization* > **charitably** *adv*

charity *n* **1** (*pl* -**ties**) an organization set up to provide help to those in need **2** the giving of help, such as money or food, to those in need **3** help given to those in need; alms **4** a kindly attitude towards people ▶ HISTORY Latin *caritas* affection

charlady *n, pl* -**ladies** *Brit* same as **charwoman**

charlatan (**shar**-lat-tan) *n* a person who claims expertise that he or she does not have ▶ HISTORY Italian *ciarlare* to chatter

Charles' law *n physics* the principle that the volume of a gas varies in proportion to its temperature at constant pressure ▶ HISTORY after Jacques *Charles*, physicist

charleston *n* a lively dance of the 1920s ▶ HISTORY after *Charleston*, South Carolina

charlock *n* a weed with hairy leaves and yellow flowers ▶ HISTORY Old English *cerlic*

charlotte *n* a dessert made with fruit and bread or cake crumbs: *apple charlotte* ▶ HISTORY French

charm *n* **1** the quality of attracting, fascinating, or delighting people **2** a trinket worn on a bracelet **3** a small object worn for supposed magical powers

4 a magic spell ▷ *vb* **5** to attract, fascinate, or delight **6** to influence or obtain by personal charm: *you can easily be charmed into changing your mind* **7** to protect as if by magic: *a charmed life* ▶ HISTORY Latin *carmen* song > **charmer** *n* > **charmless** *adj*

charming *adj* delightful or attractive > **charmingly** *adv*

charnel house *n* (formerly) a building or vault for the bones of the dead ▶ HISTORY Latin *carnalis* fleshly

chart *n* **1** a graph, table, or sheet of information in the form of a diagram **2** a map of the sea or the stars **3 the charts** *informal* the weekly lists of the bestselling pop records or the most popular videos ▷ *vb* **4** to plot the course of **5** to make a chart of **6** to appear in the pop charts ▶ HISTORY Greek *khartēs* papyrus

charter *n* **1** a formal document granting or demanding certain rights or liberties: *a children's charter* **2** the fundamental principles of an organization: *the UN Charter* **3** the hire or lease of transportation for private use ▷ *vb* **4** to lease or hire by charter **5** to grant a charter to ▶ HISTORY Latin *charta* leaf of papyrus

chartered accountant *n* (in Britain and Australia) an accountant who has passed the examinations of the Institute of Chartered Accountants

Chartism *n* *English history* a movement (1838–48) for social and political reforms, demand for which was presented to Parliament in charters > **Chartist** *n, adj*

chartreuse (shar-**truhz**) *n* a green or yellow liqueur made from herbs ▶ HISTORY after *La Grande Chartreuse*, monastery near Grenoble, where the liqueur is produced

charwoman *n, pl* **-women** *Brit* a woman whose job is to clean other people's houses

chary (**chair**-ee) *adj* **charier, chariest** wary or careful: *chary of interfering* ▶ HISTORY Old English *cearig*

chase[1] *vb* **chasing, chased 1** to pursue (a person or animal) persistently or quickly **2** to force (a person or animal) to leave a place **3** *informal* to court (someone) in an unsubtle manner **4** *informal* to rush or run: *chasing around the world* **5** *informal* to pursue (something or someone) energetically in order to obtain results or information ▷ *n* **6** the act or an instance of chasing a person or animal ▶ HISTORY Latin *capere* to take

chase[2] *vb* **chasing, chased** to engrave or emboss (metal) ▶ HISTORY Old French *enchasser*

chaser *n* a drink drunk after another of a different kind, for example beer after whisky

chasm (**kaz**-zum) *n* **1** a very deep crack in the ground **2** a wide difference in interests or feelings: *a deep chasm separating science from politics* ▶ HISTORY Greek *khasma*

chassis (**shass**-ee) *n, pl* **chassis** (**shass**-eez) the steel frame, wheels, and mechanical parts of a vehicle ▶ HISTORY French

chaste *adj* **1** abstaining from sex outside marriage or from all sexual intercourse **2** (of conduct or speech) pure, decent, or modest: *a chaste kiss on the forehead* **3** simple in style: *chaste furniture* ▶ HISTORY Latin *castus* pure > **chastely** *adv* > **chastity** *n*

chasten (**chase**-en) *vb* to subdue (someone) by criticism ▶ HISTORY Latin *castigare*

chastise *vb* **-tising, -tised 1** to scold severely **2** *old-fashioned* to punish by beating ▶ HISTORY Middle English *chastisen* > **chastisement** *n*

chasuble (**chazz**-yew-bl) *n Christianity* a long sleeveless robe worn by a priest when celebrating Mass ▶ HISTORY Late Latin *casubla* garment with a hood

chat *n* **1** an informal conversation ▷ *vb* **chatting, chatted 2** to have an informal conversation ▷ See also **chat up** ▶ HISTORY short for *chatter*

chateau (**shat**-toe) *n, pl* **-teaux** (-toe) *or* **-teaus** a French country house or castle ▶ HISTORY French

chatelaine (**shat**-tell-lane) *n* (formerly) the mistress of a large house or castle ▶ HISTORY French

chatline *n* a telephone service enabling callers to join in general conversation with each other

chatroom *n* a site on the internet where users have group discussions by electronic mail

chattels *pl n old-fashioned* possessions ▶ HISTORY Old French *chatel* personal property

chatter *vb* **1** to speak quickly and continuously about unimportant things **2** (of birds or monkeys) to make rapid repetitive high-pitched noises **3** (of the teeth) to click together rapidly through cold or fear ▷ *n* **4** idle talk or gossip **5** the high-pitched repetitive noise made by a bird or monkey ▶ HISTORY imitative

chatterbox *n informal* a person who talks a great deal, usually about unimportant things

chattering classes *n* **the chattering classes** *informal, often derogatory* the members of the educated sections of society who enjoy discussion of political, social, and cultural issues

chatty *adj* **-tier, -tiest 1** (of a person) fond of friendly, informal conversation; talkative **2** (of a letter) informal and friendly; gossipy

chat up *vb Brit & Austral, informal* to talk flirtatiously to (someone) with a view to starting a romantic relationship

chauffeur *n* **1** a person employed to drive a car for someone ▷ *vb* **2** to act as driver for (someone) ▶ HISTORY French: stoker > **chauffeuse** *fem n*

chauvinism (**show**-vin-iz-zum) *n* an irrational belief that one's own nation, race, group, or sex is superior: *male chauvinism* ▶ HISTORY after Nicolas Chauvin, French soldier under Napoleon > **chauvinist** *n, adj* > **chauvinistic** *adj*

cheap *adj* **1** costing relatively little; inexpensive **2** of poor quality; shoddy: *planks of cheap, splintery pine* **3** not valued highly; not worth much: *promises are cheap* **4** *informal* mean or despicable: *a cheap jibe* ▷ *n* **5 on the cheap** *Brit, informal* at a low cost ▷ *adv* **6** at a low cost ▶ HISTORY Old English *ceap* barter, price > **cheaply** *adv* > **cheapness** *n*

cheapen vb 1 to lower the reputation of; degrade 2 to reduce the price of

cheap-jack n informal a person who sells cheap and shoddy goods

cheapskate n informal a miserly person

cheat vb 1 to act dishonestly in order to gain some advantage or profit 2 **cheat on** informal to be unfaithful to (one's spouse or lover) ▷ n 3 a person who cheats 4 a fraud or deception ▶ HISTORY short for escheat

check vb 1 to examine, investigate, or make an inquiry into 2 to slow the growth or progress of 3 to stop abruptly 4 to correspond or agree: that all checks with our data here ▷ n 5 a test to ensure accuracy or progress 6 a means to ensure against fraud or error 7 a break in progress; stoppage 8 US same as **cheque** 9 chiefly US & Canad the bill in a restaurant 10 a pattern of squares or crossed lines 11 a single square in such a pattern 12 chess the state or position of a king under direct attack 13 **in check** under control or restraint ▷ interj 14 chiefly US & Canad an expression of agreement ▷ See also **check in, check out**, etc. ▶ HISTORY Old French eschec a check at chess

checked adj having a pattern of squares

checkers n US & Canad same as **draughts**

check in vb 1 a to register one's arrival at a hotel or airport b to register the arrival of (guests or passengers) at a hotel or airport ▷ n **check-in** 2 a the formal registration of arrival at a hotel or airport b the place where one registers one's arrival at a hotel or airport

checkmate n 1 chess the winning position in which an opponent's king is under attack and unable to escape 2 utter defeat ▷ vb **-mating, -mated** 3 chess to place the king of (one's opponent) in checkmate 4 to thwart or defeat

■ **WORD HISTORY**
- The purpose of the game of chess may be to
- capture your opponent's king, but in terms of
- word origins, a player's aim is really to kill the
- king: 'checkmate' comes from the Arabic phrase
- shāh māt, meaning 'the king is dead'.

check out vb 1 to pay the bill and leave a hotel 2 to investigate, examine, or look at: he asked if he could check out the old man's theory; start the evening off by checking out one of the bars in the city ▷ n **checkout** 3 a counter in a supermarket, where customers pay

checks and balances pl n a means of regulating a system by ensuring that no individual parts can become too powerful and overrule the other parts

checkup n a thorough examination to see if a person or thing is in good condition

Cheddar n a firm orange or yellowy-white cheese ▶ HISTORY Cheddar, village in Somerset, where it was originally made

cheek n 1 either side of the face below the eye 2 informal impudence, boldness, or lack of respect 3 informal a buttock 4 **cheek by jowl** close together 5 **turn the other cheek** to refuse to retaliate ▷ vb 6 Brit, Austral & NZ, informal to speak or behave disrespectfully to someone ▶ HISTORY Old English ceace

cheekbone n the bone at the top of the cheek, just below the eye

cheeky adj **cheekier, cheekiest** disrespectful; impudent > **cheekily** adv > **cheekiness** n

cheep n 1 the short weak high-pitched cry of a young bird ▷ vb 2 to utter a cheep ▶ HISTORY imitative

cheer vb 1 to applaud or encourage with shouts 2 **cheer up** to make or become happy or hopeful; comfort or be comforted ▷ n 3 a shout of applause or encouragement 4 a feeling of cheerfulness: the news brought little cheer ▶ HISTORY Middle English (in the sense: face, welcoming aspect), from Greek kara head

cheerful adj 1 having a happy disposition 2 pleasantly bright: a cheerful colour 3 ungrudging: a cheerful giver > **cheerfully** adv > **cheerfulness** n

cheerio interj 1 informal a farewell greeting ▷ n 2 Austral & NZ a small red cocktail sausage

cheerless adj dreary or gloomy

cheers interj informal, chiefly Brit 1 a drinking toast 2 a farewell greeting 3 an expression of gratitude

cheery adj **cheerier, cheeriest** cheerful > **cheerily** adv

cheese¹ n 1 a food made from coagulated milk curd 2 a block of this ▶ HISTORY Latin caseus

cheese² n **big cheese** slang an important person ▶ HISTORY perhaps from Hindi chiz thing

cheeseburger n a hamburger with a slice of cheese melted on top of it

cheesecake n 1 a dessert with a biscuit-crumb base covered with a sweet cream-cheese mixture and sometimes with a fruit topping 2 slang magazine photographs of naked or scantily dressed women

cheesecloth n a light, loosely woven cotton cloth

cheesed off adj Brit, Austral & NZ, slang bored, disgusted, or angry ▶ HISTORY origin unknown

cheeseparing adj 1 mean or miserly ▷ n 2 meanness or miserliness

cheesy adj **cheesier, cheesiest** 1 like cheese 2 informal (of a smile) broad but possibly insincere 3 informal in poor taste: a cheesy game show

cheetah n a large fast-running wild cat of Africa and SW Asia, which has a light brown coat with black spots

■ **WORD HISTORY**
- 'Cheetah' comes from Hindi cītā, which is
- derived from Sanskrit citrakāya, meaning
- 'leopard', from citra, meaning 'bright' or
- 'speckled', and kāya, meaning 'body'.

chef n a cook, usually the head cook, in a restaurant or hotel ▶ HISTORY French

chef-d'oeuvre (shay-**durv**) n, pl **chefs-d'oeuvre** (shay-**durv**) a masterpiece ▶ HISTORY French

Cheka (**check**-a) n Russian hist the secret police set up in 1917 by the Bolshevik government ▶ HISTORY from Russian, acronym of Chrezvychainaya Komissiya Extraordinary Commission (to combat Counter-Revolution)

137

chem. 1 chemical 2 chemist 3 chemistry

chemical *n* 1 any substance used in or resulting from a reaction involving changes to atoms or molecules ▷ *adj* 2 of or used in chemistry 3 of, made from, or using chemicals: *a chemical additive found in many foods* > **chemically** *adv*

chemical energy *n chem* the energy released by a chemical reaction

chemical engineering *n* the applications of chemistry in industrial processes > **chemical engineer** *n*

chemical equilibrium *n chem* a state in which a chemical reaction and its reverse reaction take place at equal rates

chemical fertilizer *n agriculture* a chemical substance, not derived from animal or plant matter, used as a fertilizer

chemical reaction *n chem* a process that involves changes in the structure and energy content of atoms, molecules, or ions, but not their nuclei. Compare **nuclear reaction**

chemical warfare *n* warfare using weapons such as gases and poisons

chemical weathering *n geol* the breakdown of rocks as a result of chemical reactions which occur when they are exposed to water in the environment

chemise (shem-**meez**) *n* a woman's old-fashioned loose-fitting slip or dress ▶ HISTORY Late Latin *camisa*

chemist *n* 1 *Brit, Austral & NZ* a shop selling medicines and cosmetics 2 *Brit, Austral & NZ* a qualified dispenser of prescribed medicines 3 a specialist in chemistry ▶ HISTORY Medieval Latin *alchimista* alchemist

chemistry *n* the branch of science concerned with the composition, properties, and reactions of substances

chemotherapy *n* the treatment of disease, often cancer, by means of chemicals

chenille (shen-**neel**) *n* 1 a thick soft tufty yarn 2 a fabric made of this ▶ HISTORY French

cheque *or US* **check** *n* a written order to someone's bank to pay money from his or her account to the person to whom the cheque is made out ▶ HISTORY from *check* (in the sense: means of verification)

cheque book *n* a book of detachable blank cheques issued by a bank

cheque card *n Brit* a plastic card issued by a bank guaranteeing payment of a customer's cheques

chequer *or US* **checker** *n* a piece used in Chinese chequers ▶ HISTORY Middle English: chessboard

chequered *or US* **checkered** *adj* 1 marked by varied fortunes: *a chequered career* 2 marked with alternating squares of colour

cherish *vb* 1 to cling to (an idea or feeling): *cherished notions* 2 to care for ▶ HISTORY Latin *carus* dear

Cherokee *n* 1 a member of a Native American people, formerly of the Appalachian mountains, now living chiefly in Oklahoma 2 the language of this people

cheroot (sher-**root**) *n* a cigar with both ends cut off squarely ▶ HISTORY Tamil *curuttu* curl, roll

cherry *n, pl* -**ries** 1 a small round soft fruit with red or blackish skin and a hard stone 2 the tree on which this fruit grows ▷ *adj* 3 deep red: *cherry lips* ▶ HISTORY Greek *kerasios*

cherry tomato *n* a miniature tomato, slightly bigger than a cherry

cherub *n, pl* **cherubs** *or (for sense 1)* **cherubim** 1 *Christianity* an angel, often represented as a winged child 2 an innocent or sweet child ▶ HISTORY Hebrew *kĕrūbh* > **cherubic** (chair-**roo**-bik) *adj*

chervil *n* an aniseed-flavoured herb ▶ HISTORY Old English *cerfelle*

chess *n* a game of skill for two players using a chessboard on which chessmen are moved, with the object of checkmating the opponent's king ▶ HISTORY Old French *esches*, plural of *eschec* check

chessman *n, pl* -**men** a piece used in chess ▶ HISTORY Middle English *chessemeyne* chess company

chest *n* 1 the front of the body, from the neck to the waist 2 **get something off one's chest** *informal* to unburden oneself of worries or secrets by talking about them 3 a heavy box for storage or shipping: *a tea chest* ▶ HISTORY Greek *kistē* box

chesterfield *n* a large couch with high padded sides and back ▶ HISTORY after a 19th-century Earl of *Chesterfield*

chestnut *n* 1 a reddish-brown edible nut 2 the tree that this nut grows on 3 a horse of a reddish-brown colour 4 *informal* an old or stale joke ▷ *adj* 5 dark reddish-brown: *chestnut hair* ▶ HISTORY Greek *kastanea*

chest of drawers *n* a piece of furniture consisting of a set of drawers in a frame

chesty *adj* **chestier, chestiest** *Brit, informal* suffering from or symptomatic of chest disease: *chesty colds* > **chestiness** *n*

cheval glass (shev-**val**) *n* a full-length mirror mounted so as to swivel within a frame ▶ HISTORY French *cheval* support (literally: horse)

chevalier (shev-a-**leer**) *n* 1 a member of the French Legion of Honour 2 a chivalrous man ▶ HISTORY Medieval Latin *caballarius* horseman

Cheviot *n* a large British sheep with a heavy medium-length fleece ▶ HISTORY *Cheviot* Hills on borders of England & Scotland

chevron (**shev**-ron) *n* a V-shaped pattern, such as those worn on the sleeve of a military uniform to indicate rank ▶ HISTORY Old French

chew *vb* 1 to work the jaws and teeth in order to grind (food) ▷ *n* 2 the act of chewing 3 something that is chewed, such as a sweet or a piece of tobacco ▶ HISTORY Old English *ceowan*

chewing gum *n* a flavoured gum which is chewed but not swallowed

chew over *vb* to consider carefully

chewy *adj* **chewier, chewiest** of a consistency requiring a lot of chewing

chianti (kee-**ant**-ee) *n* a dry red wine produced in Tuscany, Italy

chiaroscuro (kee-ah-roh-**skew**-roh) *n, pl* **-ros** the distribution of light and shade in a picture ▶ HISTORY Italian *chiaro* clear + *oscuro* obscure

chic (**sheek**) *adj* **1** stylish or elegant ▷ *n* **2** stylishness or elegance ▶ HISTORY French

chicane (shik-**kane**) *n* an obstacle placed on a motor-racing circuit to slow the cars down ▶ HISTORY French *chicaner* to quibble

chicanery *n* trickery or deception

chick *n* **1** a baby bird, esp. a domestic fowl **2** *slang* a young woman ▶ HISTORY short for *chicken*

chicken *n* **1** a domestic fowl bred for its flesh or eggs **2** the flesh of this bird used for food **3** *slang* a coward ▷ *adj* **4** *slang* cowardly ▶ HISTORY Old English *ciecen*

chicken feed *n slang* a trifling amount of money

chicken out *vb informal* to fail to do something through cowardice

chickenpox *n* an infectious viral disease, usually affecting children, which produces an itchy rash

chickpea *n* an edible hard yellow pealike seed ▶ HISTORY Latin *cicer*

chickweed *n* a common garden weed with small white flowers

chicory *n* **1** a plant grown for its leaves, which are used in salads, and for its roots **2** the root of this plant, roasted, dried, and used as a coffee substitute ▶ HISTORY Greek *kikhōrion*

chide *vb* **chiding, chided** *old-fashioned* to rebuke or scold ▶ HISTORY Old English *cīdan*

chief *n* **1** the head of a group or body of people **2** the head of a tribe ▷ *adj* **3** most important: *the chief suspects* **4** highest in rank: *the Chief Constable* ▶ HISTORY Latin *caput* head

chief justice *n* the judge presiding over a supreme court

chiefly *adv* **1** especially or essentially **2** mainly or mostly

chief petty officer *n* a senior noncommissioned officer in a navy

chief secretary *n* (in certain Caribbean countries) the leader of the parliament

chieftain *n* the leader of a tribe or clan ▶ HISTORY Late Latin *capitaneus* commander

chief technician *n* a noncommissioned officer in the Royal Air Force

chiffchaff *n* a European warbler with a yellowish-brown plumage ▶ HISTORY imitative

chiffon (**shif**-fon) *n* a fine see-through fabric of silk or nylon ▶ HISTORY French *chiffe* rag

chignon (**sheen**-yon) *n* a roll or knot of long hair pinned up at the back of the head ▶ HISTORY French

chigoe (**chig**-go) *n* a tropical flea that burrows into the skin. Also: **chigger** ▶ HISTORY Carib *chigo*

chihuahua (chee-**wah**-wah) *n* a tiny short-haired dog, originally from Mexico ▶ HISTORY after *Chihuahua*, state in Mexico

chilblain *n* an inflammation of the fingers or toes, caused by exposure to cold ▶ HISTORY CHILL (noun) + BLAIN

child *n, pl* **children 1** a young human being; boy or girl **2** a son or daughter. *Related adjective:* **filial 3** a childish or immature person **4** the product of an influence or environment: *a child of the Army* **5 with child** *old-fashioned* pregnant ▶ HISTORY Old English *cild* > **childless** *adj* > **childlessness** *n*

child benefit *n Brit* a regular government payment to parents of children up to a certain age

childbirth *n* the act of giving birth to a child. *Related adjective:* **natal**

childhood *n* the time or condition of being a child

childish *adj* **1** immature or silly: *childish fighting over who did what* **2** of or like a child: *childish illnesses*

childlike *adj* like a child, for example in being innocent or trustful

child minder *n* a person who looks after children whose parents are working

children *n* the plural of **child**

child's play *n informal* something that is easy to do

chill *n* **1** a feverish cold **2** a moderate coldness **3** a feeling of coldness resulting from a cold or damp environment or from sudden fear ▷ *vb* **4** to make (something) cool or cold: *chilled white wine* **5** *written* to cause (someone) to feel cold or frightened **6** *informal* to calm oneself ▷ *adj* **7** unpleasantly cold: *chill winds* ▶ HISTORY Old English *ciele* > **chilling** *adj* > **chillingly** *adv*

chiller *n* **1** short for **spine-chiller 2** a cooling or refrigerating device

chilli or **chili** *n* (*pl* **chillies** or **chilies**) the small red or green hot-tasting pod of a type of capsicum, used in cookery, often in powdered form ▶ HISTORY Mexican Indian

chilly *adj* **-lier, -liest 1** causing or feeling moderately cold **2** without warmth; unfriendly: *a chilly reception*

chilly bin *n NZ, informal* a portable insulated container for packing food and drink in ice

Chiltern Hundreds *pl n* (in Britain) a nominal office that an MP applies for in order to resign his or her seat

chime *n* **1** the musical ringing sound made by a bell or clock ▷ *vb* **chiming, chimed 2** (of a bell) to make a clear musical ringing sound **3** (of a clock) to indicate (the time) by chiming ▶ HISTORY Latin *cymbalum* cymbal

chimera (kime-**meer**-a) *n* **1** a wild and unrealistic dream or idea **2** *Greek myth* a fire-breathing monster with the head of a lion, body of a goat, and tail of a serpent ▶ HISTORY Greek *khimaira* she-goat

chimerical *adj* wildly fanciful or imaginary

chimney *n* a hollow vertical structure that carries smoke or steam away from a fire or engine ▶ HISTORY Greek *kaminos* oven

chimney breast *n* the walls surrounding the base of a chimney or fireplace

chimney sweep n a person who cleans soot from chimneys

chimp n informal short for **chimpanzee**

chimpanzee n an intelligent small black ape of central W Africa ▶ HISTORY African dialect

chin n the front part of the face below the mouth ▶ HISTORY Old English cinn

china¹ n 1 ceramic ware of a type originally from China 2 dishes or ornamental objects made of china ▶ HISTORY Persian chīnī

china² n Brit & S African, informal a friend or companion ▶ HISTORY from cockney rhyming slang china plate mate

china clay n same as **kaolin**

Chinatown n a section of a town or city outside China with a mainly Chinese population

chinchilla n 1 a small S American rodent bred in captivity for its soft silvery-grey fur 2 the fur of this animal ▶ HISTORY Spanish

chine n 1 a cut of meat including part of the backbone ▷ vb chining, chined 2 to cut (meat) along the backbone ▶ HISTORY Old French eschine

Chinese adj 1 of China ▷ n 2 (pl -nese) a person from China or a descendant of one 3 any of the languages of China

Chinese chequers n a game played with marbles or pegs on a six-pointed star-shaped board

Chinese lantern n a collapsible lantern made of thin paper

chink¹ n a small narrow opening: a chink of light ▶ HISTORY Old English cine crack

chink² vb 1 to make a light ringing sound ▷ n 2 a light ringing sound ▶ HISTORY imitative

chinoiserie (sheen-**wahz**-a-ree) n 1 a style of decorative art based on imitations of Chinese motifs 2 objects in this style ▶ HISTORY French chinois Chinese

Chinook n 1 (pl -nook or -nooks) a member of a Native American people of the Pacific coast of N America 2 the language of this people

Chinook salmon n a Pacific salmon valued as a food fish

chintz n a printed patterned cotton fabric with a glazed finish, used for curtains and chair coverings ▶ HISTORY Hindi chīnt

chinwag n Brit, Austral & NZ, informal a chat

chip n 1 a thin strip of potato fried in deep fat 2 US, Canad, Austral & NZ a potato crisp 3 electronics a tiny wafer of semiconductor material, such as silicon, processed to form an integrated circuit 4 a counter used to represent money in gambling games 5 a small piece removed by chopping, cutting, or breaking 6 a mark left where a small piece has been broken off something 7 **chip off the old block** informal a person who resembles one of his or her parents in personality 8 **have a chip on one's shoulder** informal to be resentful or bear a grudge 9 **when the chips are down** informal at a time of crisis ▷ vb chipping, chipped 10 to break small pieces from ▶ HISTORY Old English cipp

chipboard n thin rigid board made of compressed wood particles

chip in vb informal 1 to contribute to a common fund 2 to interrupt with a remark

chipmunk n a squirrel-like striped burrowing rodent of North America and Asia ▶ HISTORY from a Native American language

chipolata n chiefly Brit a small sausage ▶ HISTORY Italian cipolla onion

chiropodist (kir-**rop**-pod-ist) n a person who treats minor foot complaints like corns > **chiropody** n

chiropractic (kire-oh-**prak**-tik) n a system of treating bodily disorders by manipulation of the spine ▶ HISTORY Greek kheir hand + praktikos practical > **chiropractor** n

chirp vb 1 (of some birds and insects) to make a short high-pitched sound 2 Brit, Austral & NZ, written to speak in a lively fashion ▷ n 3 a chirping sound ▶ HISTORY imitative

chirpy adj chirpier, chirpiest informal lively and cheerful > **chirpiness** n

chirrup vb 1 (of some birds) to chirp repeatedly ▷ n 2 a chirruping sound ▶ HISTORY variant of chirp

chisel n 1 a metal tool with a sharp end for shaping wood or stone ▷ vb -elling, -elled or US -eling, -eled 2 to carve or form with a chisel ▶ HISTORY Latin caesus cut

chit¹ n a short official note, such as a memorandum, requisition, or receipt. Also: **chitty** ▶ HISTORY Hindi cittha note

chit² n Brit, Austral & NZ, old-fashioned a pert or impudent girl ▶ HISTORY Middle English: young animal, kitten

chitchat n chat or gossip

chitin (**kite**-in) n the tough substance forming the outer layer of the bodies of arthropods ▶ HISTORY Greek khitōn tunic

chitterlings pl n the intestines of a pig or other animal prepared as food ▶ HISTORY origin unknown

chivalrous adj gallant or courteous > **chivalrously** adv

chivalry n 1 courteous behaviour, esp. by men towards women 2 the medieval system and principles of knighthood ▶ HISTORY Old French chevalier knight > **chivalric** adj

chives pl n the long slender hollow leaves of a small Eurasian plant, used in cooking for their onion-like flavour ▶ HISTORY Latin caepa onion

chivvy vb -vies, -vying, -vied Brit to harass or nag ▶ HISTORY probably from Chevy Chase, a Scottish ballad

chloral hydrate n a colourless crystalline solid used as a sedative

chlorate n chem any salt containing the ion ClO₃⁻

chloride n chem 1 any compound of chlorine and another element and radical 2 any salt or ester of hydrochloric acid

chlorinate vb -ating, -ated 1 to disinfect (water) with chlorine 2 chem to combine or treat (a substance) with chlorine: chlorinated hydrocarbons > **chlorination** n

chlorine _n_ a poisonous strong-smelling greenish-yellow gaseous element, used in water purification and as a disinfectant, and, combined with sodium, to make common salt. Symbol: Cl

chloro- _combining form_ green ▶ **HISTORY** Greek _khlōros_

chlorofluorocarbon _n chem_ any of various gaseous compounds of carbon, hydrogen, chlorine, and fluorine, used as refrigerants and aerosol propellants, some of which break down the ozone in the atmosphere

chloroform _n_ a sweet-smelling liquid, used as a solvent and cleansing agent, and formerly as an anaesthetic ▶ **HISTORY** CHLORO- + _formyl_: see FORMIC ACID

chlorophyll _or US_ **chlorophyl** _n_ the green colouring matter of plants, which enables them to convert sunlight into energy ▶ **HISTORY** CHLORO- + Greek _phullon_ leaf

chloroplast _n biol_ one of the parts of a plant cell that contains chlorophyll ▶ **HISTORY** CHLORO- + Greek _plastos_ formed

chlorosis _n pathol_ a disorder marked by pale greenish-yellow skin, weakness, and palpitation, caused by insufficient iron in the body

chock _n_ **1** a block or wedge of wood used to prevent the sliding or rolling of a heavy object ▷ _vb_ **2** to fit with or secure by a chock ▶ **HISTORY** origin unknown

chock-a-block _adj_ filled to capacity

chock-full _adj_ completely full

chocolate _n_ **1** a food made from roasted ground cacao seeds, usually sweetened and flavoured **2** a sweet or drink made from this ▷ _adj_ **3** deep brown > **chocolaty** _adj_

■ **WORD HISTORY**
■ Europeans were first introduced to chocolate
■ at the court of the Aztec king Montezuma in
■ the 16th century. 'Chocolate' or _xocolatl_ was a
■ bitter Aztec drink made from cocoa beans. The
■ name _xocolatl_ means 'bitter water', from Aztec
■ _xococ_, meaning 'bitter', and _atl_, meaning 'water'.

choice _n_ **1** the act of choosing or selecting **2** the opportunity or power of choosing: _parental choice_ **3** a person or thing chosen or that may be chosen: _the president's choice as the new head of the CIA_ **4** an alternative action or possibility: _they had no choice but to accept_ **5** a range from which to select: _a choice of weapons_ ▷ _adj_ **6** of high quality: _choice government jobs_ **7** carefully chosen: _a few choice words_ **8** vulgar: _choice language_ ▶ **HISTORY** Old French _choisir_ to choose

choir _n_ **1** an organized group of singers, usually for singing in church **2** the part of a church, in front of the altar, occupied by the choir ▶ **HISTORY** Latin _chorus_

choke _vb_ **choking, choked** **1** to hinder or stop the breathing of (a person or animal) by strangling or smothering **2** to have trouble in breathing, swallowing, or speaking **3** to block or clog up: _the old narrow streets become choked to a standstill_ **4** to hinder the growth of: _weeds would outgrow and_ choke the rice crop ▷ _n_ **5** a device in a vehicle's engine that enriches the petrol-air mixture by reducing the air supply ▶ **HISTORY** Old English _ācēocian_

choke back _vb_ to suppress (tears or anger)

choker _n_ a tight-fitting necklace

choko _n, pl_ **-kos** the pear-shaped fruit of a tropical American vine, eaten as a vegetable ▶ **HISTORY** Brazilian Indian

choler (kol-ler) _n archaic_ anger or bad temper ▶ **HISTORY** Greek _kholē_ bile

cholera (kol-ler-a) _n_ a serious infectious disease causing severe diarrhoea and stomach cramps, caught from contaminated water or food ▶ **HISTORY** Greek _kholē_ bile

choleric _adj_ bad-tempered

cholesterol (kol-**lest**-er-oll) _n_ a fatty alcohol found in all animal fats, tissues, and fluids, an excess of which is thought to contribute to heart and artery disease ▶ **HISTORY** Greek _kholē_ bile + _stereos_ solid

chomp _vb_ to chew (food) noisily

chook _n informal, chiefly Austral & NZ_ a hen or chicken

choose _vb_ **choosing, chose, chosen** **1** to select (a person, thing, or course of action) from a number of alternatives **2** to like or please: _when she did choose to reveal her secret, the group were initially hushed_ **3** to consider it desirable or proper: _I don't choose to read that sort of book_ ▶ **HISTORY** Old English _ceosan_

choosy _adj_ **choosier, choosiest** _informal_ fussy; hard to please

chop¹ _vb_ **chopping, chopped** **1** (often foll. by _down_ or _off_) to cut (something) with a blow from an axe or other sharp tool **2** to cut into pieces **3** _boxing, karate_ to hit (an opponent) with a short sharp blow **4** _Brit, Austral & NZ, informal_ to dispense with or reduce **5** _sport_ to hit (a ball) sharply downwards ▷ _n_ **6** a cutting blow **7** a slice of mutton, lamb, or pork, usually including a rib **8** _sport_ a sharp downward blow or stroke **9** **the chop** _slang_ dismissal from employment ▶ **HISTORY** variant of _chap_: see CHAPPED

chop² _vb_ **chopping, chopped** **1** **chop and change** to change one's mind repeatedly **2** **chop logic** to use excessively subtle or involved argument ▶ **HISTORY** Old English _ceapian_ to barter

chopper _n_ **1** _informal_ a helicopter **2** _chiefly Brit_ a small hand axe **3** a butcher's cleaver **4** a type of bicycle or motorcycle with very high handlebars **5** _NZ_ a child's bicycle

choppy _adj_ **-pier, -piest** (of the sea) fairly rough > **choppiness** _n_

chops _pl n Brit, Austral & NZ, informal_ **1** the jaws or cheeks **2** **lick one's chops** to anticipate something with pleasure ▶ **HISTORY** origin unknown

chopsticks _pl n_ a pair of thin sticks of ivory, wood, or plastic, used for eating Chinese or other East Asian food ▶ **HISTORY** pidgin English, from Chinese

chop suey _n_ a Chinese-style dish of chopped meat, bean sprouts, and other vegetables in a sauce ▶ **HISTORY** Chinese _tsap sui_ odds and ends

141

choral *adj* of or for a choir

chorale (kor-**rahl**) *n* **1** a slow stately hymn tune **2** *chiefly US* a choir or chorus ▶ HISTORY German *Choralgesang* choral song

chord¹ *n* **1** *maths* a straight line connecting two points on a curve **2** *anat* same as **cord 3 strike** or **touch a chord** to bring about an emotional response, usually of sympathy ▶ HISTORY Greek *khordē* string

chord² *n* the simultaneous sounding of three or more musical notes ▶ HISTORY short for *accord*

chordate *n* any animal that has a long fibrous rod just above the gut to support the body, such as the vertebrates

chore *n* **1** a small routine task **2** an unpleasant task ▶ HISTORY Old English *cerr* a turn of work

chorea (kor-**ree**-a) *n* a disorder of the nervous system characterized by uncontrollable brief jerky movements ▶ HISTORY Greek *khoreia* dance

choreograph *vb* to compose the dance steps for a piece of music

choreography *n* **1** the composition of steps and movements for ballet and other dancing **2** the steps and movements of a ballet or dance ▶ HISTORY Greek *khoreia* dance + -GRAPHY > **choreographer** *n* > **choreographic** *adj*

chorister *n* a singer in a church choir

choroid *n* *physiol* a brownish membrane in the eye, between the retina and the sclera

choropleth map (**core**-uh-pleth) *n* *geog* a map which presents statistical data relating to given areas using proportionally darker or lighter shading or colour to represent proportionally different numerical values

chortle *written vb* **-tling, -tled 1** to chuckle with amusement ▷ *n* **2** an amused chuckle ▶ HISTORY coined by Lewis Carroll

chorus *n, pl* **-ruses 1** a large choir **2** a piece of music to be sung by a large choir **3** a part of a song repeated after each verse **4** something expressed by many people at once: *a chorus of boos* **5** the noise made by a group of birds or small animals: *the dawn chorus* **6** a group of singers or dancers who perform together in a show **7** (in ancient Greece) a group of actors who commented on the action of a play **8** (in Elizabethan drama) the actor who spoke the prologue and epilogue **9 in chorus** in unison ▷ *vb* **10** *written* to sing or say together ▶ HISTORY Greek *khoros*

chorus girl *n* a young woman who dances or sings in the chorus of a show or film

chose *vb* the past tense of **choose**

chosen *vb* **1** the past participle of **choose** ▷ *adj* **2** selected for some special quality: *the chosen one*

chough (chuff) *n* a large black bird of the crow family ▶ HISTORY origin unknown

choux pastry (shoo) *n* a very light pastry made with eggs ▶ HISTORY French *pâte choux* cabbage dough

chow *n* **1** a thick-coated dog with a curled tail, originally from China **2** *informal* food ▶ HISTORY pidgin English

chowder *n* a thick soup containing clams or fish ▶ HISTORY French *chaudière* kettle

chow mein *n* a Chinese-American dish consisting of chopped meat or vegetables fried with noodles ▶ HISTORY from Chinese

chrism *n* consecrated oil used for anointing in some churches ▶ HISTORY Greek *khriein* to anoint

Christ *n* **1** Jesus of Nazareth (Jesus Christ), regarded by Christians as the Messiah of Old Testament prophecies **2** the Messiah of Old Testament prophecies **3** an image or picture of Christ ▶ HISTORY Greek *khristos* anointed one

christen *vb* **1** same as **baptize 2** to give a name to (a person or thing) **3** *informal* to use for the first time ▶ HISTORY Old English *cristnian* > **christening** *n*

Christendom *n* all Christian people or countries

Christian *n* **1** a person who believes in and follows Jesus Christ **2** *informal* a person who displays the virtues of kindness and mercy encouraged in the teachings of Jesus Christ ▷ *adj* **3** of Jesus Christ, Christians, or Christianity **4** kind or good

Christian Democrat *n* a member or supporter of political parties in Europe and Latin America that combine moderate conservatism with historic links to the church > **Christian Democratic** *adj*

Christian Era *n* the period beginning with the year of Christ's birth

Christianity *n* **1** the religion based on the life and teachings of Christ **2** Christian beliefs or practices **3** same as **Christendom**

Christianize or **-ise** *vb* **-izing, -ized** or **-ising, -ised 1** to convert to Christianity **2** to fill with Christian principles, spirit, or outlook > **Christianization** or **-isation** *n*

Christian name *n* a personal name formally given to Christians at baptism: loosely used to mean a person's first name

Christian Science *n* the religious system founded by Mary Baker Eddy (1866), which emphasizes spiritual regeneration and healing through prayer > **Christian Scientist** *n*

Christmas *n* **1 a** *Christianity* a festival commemorating the birth of Christ, held by most Churches to have occurred on Dec. 25 **b** Also: **Christmas Day** Dec. 25, as a day of secular celebrations when gifts and greetings are exchanged ▷ *adj* **2** connected with or taking place at the time of year when this festival is celebrated: *the Christmas holidays* ▶ HISTORY Old English *Crīstes mæsse* Mass of Christ > **Christmassy** *adj*

Christmas box *n* a tip or present given at Christmas, esp. to postmen or tradesmen

Christmas Eve *n* the evening or the whole day before Christmas Day

Christmas pudding *n* *Brit & Austral* a rich steamed pudding containing suet, dried fruit, and spices

Christmas rose *n* an evergreen plant with white or pink winter-blooming flowers

Christmas tree *n* an evergreen tree or an imitation of one, decorated as part of Christmas celebrations

chromate *n chem* any salt or ester of chromic acid

chromatic *adj* **1** of or in colour or colours **2** *music* **a** involving the sharpening or flattening of notes or the use of such notes **b** of the chromatic scale ▶ HISTORY Greek *khrōma* colour

> **chromatically** *adv*

chromatics *n* the science of colour

chromatic scale *n* a twelve-note scale including all the semitones of the octave

chromatid *n biol* either of the two strands into which a chromosome divides during mitosis

chromatin *n biochem* the part of the nucleus of a cell that forms the chromosomes and can easily be dyed ▶ HISTORY from *chrome*

chromatogram *n chem* a column or strip of material showing the different constituents of a mixture separated by chromatography

chromatography *n* the technique of separating and analysing the components of a mixture of liquids or gases by slowly passing it through an adsorbing material ▶ HISTORY Greek *khrōma* colour + -GRAPHY

chrome *n* **1** same as **chromium** **2** anything plated with chromium ▷ *vb* **chroming, chromed** **3** to plate or be plated with chromium ▶ HISTORY Greek *khrōma* colour

chromite *n* a brownish-black mineral which is the only commercial source of chromium

chromium *n chem* a hard grey metallic element, used in steel alloys and electroplating to increase hardness and corrosion resistance. Symbol: Cr ▶ HISTORY from *chrome*

chromosome *n* any of the microscopic rod-shaped structures that appear in a cell nucleus during cell division, consisting of units (genes) that are responsible for the transmission of hereditary characteristics ▶ HISTORY Greek *khrōma* colour + *sōma* body

chromosphere *n* a gaseous layer of the sun's atmosphere extending from the photosphere to the corona

chronic *adj* **1** (of a disease) developing slowly or lasting for a long time **2** (of a bad habit or bad behaviour) having continued for a long time; habitual: *chronic drug addiction* **3** very serious or severe: *chronic food shortages* **4** *Brit, Austral & NZ, informal* very bad: *the play was chronic* ▶ HISTORY Greek *khronos* time > **chronically** *adv*

chronic fatigue syndrome *n* a condition characterized by painful muscles and general weakness sometimes persisting long after a viral illness

chronicle *n* **1** a record of events in chronological order ▷ *vb* **-cling, -cled** **2** to record in or as if in a chronicle ▶ HISTORY Greek *khronika* annals > **chronicler** *n*

chronological *adj* **1** (of a sequence of events) arranged in order of occurrence **2** relating to chronology > **chronologically** *adv*

chronology *n, pl* **-gies** **1** the arrangement of dates or events in order of occurrence **2** the determining of the proper sequence of past events **3** a table of events arranged in order of occurrence ▶ HISTORY Greek *khronos* time + -LOGY > **chronologist** *n*

chronometer *n* a timepiece designed to be accurate in all conditions ▶ HISTORY Greek *khronos* time + -METER

chrysalis (**kriss**-a-liss) *n* an insect in the stage between larva and adult, when it is in a cocoon ▶ HISTORY Greek *khrusos* gold

chrysanthemum *n* a garden plant with large round flowers made up of many petals ▶ HISTORY Greek *khrusos* gold + *anthemon* flower

chub *n, pl* **chub** or **chubs** a common freshwater game fish of the carp family with a dark greenish body ▶ HISTORY origin unknown

chubby *adj* **-bier, -biest** plump and round ▶ HISTORY perhaps from *chub* > **chubbiness** *n*

chuck¹ *vb* **1** *informal* to throw carelessly **2** *informal* (sometimes foll. by *in* or *up*) to give up; reject: *he chucked in his job* **3** to pat (someone) affectionately under the chin **4** *Austral & NZ, informal* to vomit ▷ *n* **5** a throw or toss **6** a pat under the chin ▷ See also **chuck off** ▶ HISTORY origin unknown

chuck² *n* **1** Also: **chuck steak** a cut of beef from the neck to the shoulder blade **2** a device that holds a workpiece in a lathe or a tool in a drill ▶ HISTORY variant of *chock*

chuck³ *n W Canada* **1** a large body of water **2** Also: **saltchuck** the sea ▶ HISTORY Chinook

chuckle *vb* **-ling, -led** **1** to laugh softly or to oneself ▷ *n* **2** a partly suppressed laugh ▶ HISTORY probably from *chuck* cluck

chuck off *vb* (often foll. by *at*) *Austral & NZ, informal* to abuse or make fun of

chuff *vb* to move while making a puffing sound, as a steam engine ▶ HISTORY imitative

chuffed *adj informal* pleased or delighted: *I suppose you're feeling pretty chuffed* ▶ HISTORY origin unknown

chug *n* **1** a short dull sound like the noise of an engine ▷ *vb* **chugging, chugged** **2** (esp. of an engine) to operate or move with this sound: *lorries chug past* ▶ HISTORY imitative

chukka or **chukker** *n polo* a period of continuous play, usually 7½ minutes ▶ HISTORY Hindi *cakkar*

chum *n* **1** *informal* a close friend ▷ *vb* **chumming, chummed** **2 chum up with** to form a close friendship with ▶ HISTORY probably from *chamber fellow*

chummy *adj* **-mier, -miest** *informal* friendly > **chummily** *adv* > **chumminess** *n*

chump *n* **1** *informal* a stupid person **2** a thick piece of meat **3** a thick block of wood **4 off one's chump** *Brit, slang* crazy ▶ HISTORY origin unknown

chunk *n* **1** a thick solid piece of something **2** a considerable amount ▶ HISTORY variant of CHUCK²

chunky *adj* **chunkier, chunkiest** **1** thick and short **2** containing thick pieces **3** *chiefly Brit* (of clothes, esp. knitwear) made of thick bulky material > **chunkiness** *n*

church *n* **1** a building for public Christian worship **2** religious services held in a church **3** a particular Christian denomination **4** Christians collectively **5** the clergy as distinguished from the laity **6** **Church** institutional religion as a political or social force: *conflict between Church and State* ▶ **HISTORY** Greek *kuriakon* (*dōma*) the Lord's (house)

churchgoer *n* a person who attends church regularly

churchman *n*, *pl* -**men** a clergyman

Church of England *n* the reformed established state Church in England, with the sovereign as its temporal head

Church of Scotland *n* the established Presbyterian church in Scotland

churchwarden *n* **1** *Church of England, Episcopal Church* a lay assistant of a parish priest **2** an old-fashioned long-stemmed tobacco pipe made of clay

churchyard *n* the grounds round a church, used as a graveyard

churl *n* **1** a surly ill-bred person **2** *archaic* a farm labourer ▶ **HISTORY** Old English *ceorl*

churlish *adj* surly and rude

churn *n* **1** a machine in which cream is shaken to make butter **2** a large container for milk ▷ *vb* **3** to stir (milk or cream) vigorously in order to make butter **4** to move about violently: *a hot tub of churning water* ▶ **HISTORY** Old English *ciern*

churn out *vb informal* to produce (something) rapidly and in large numbers

chute¹ (**shoot**) *n* a steep sloping channel or passage down which things may be dropped ▶ **HISTORY** Old French *cheoite* fallen

chute² *n informal* short for **parachute**

chutney *n* a pickle of Indian origin, made from fruit, vinegar, spices, and sugar: *mango chutney* ▶ **HISTORY** Hindi *catni*

chyle *n* a milky fluid formed in the small intestine during digestion ▶ **HISTORY** Greek *khulos* juice

chyme *n* the thick fluid mass of partially digested food that leaves the stomach ▶ **HISTORY** Greek *khumos* juice

Ci curie

CIA Central Intelligence Agency; a US bureau responsible for espionage and intelligence activities

cicada (sik-**kah**-da) *n* a large broad insect, found in hot countries, that makes a high-pitched drone ▶ **HISTORY** Latin

cicatrix (**sik**-a-trix) *n*, *pl* **cicatrices** (sik-a-**trice-**eez) the tissue that forms in a wound during healing; scar ▶ **HISTORY** Latin: scar

CID (in Britain) Criminal Investigation Department; the detective division of a police force

cider *n* an alcoholic drink made from fermented apple juice ▶ **HISTORY** Hebrew *shēkhār* strong drink

cigar *n* a tube-like roll of cured tobacco leaves for smoking

■ **WORD HISTORY**
■ 'Cigar' came into English from Spanish, but it
■ probably originally comes from Mayan (a
■ Central American language) *sicar*, meaning 'to
■ smoke'.

cigarette *n* a thin roll of shredded tobacco in thin paper, for smoking ▶ **HISTORY** French: a little cigar

cilium *n*, *pl* **cilia** *biol* **1** any of the short threads projecting from a cell or organism, whose rhythmic beating causes movement **2** an eyelash ▶ **HISTORY** Latin > **ciliary** *adj*

C in C *mil* Commander in Chief

cinch (**sinch**) *n* **1** *informal* an easy task **2** *slang* a certainty ▶ **HISTORY** Spanish *cincha* saddle girth

cinchona (sing-**kone**-a) *n* **1** a South American tree or shrub with medicinal bark **2** its dried bark which yields quinine **3** a drug made from cinchona bark ▶ **HISTORY** after the Countess of *Chinchón*

cinder *n* **1** a piece of material that will not burn, left after burning coal or wood **2** **cinders** ashes ▶ **HISTORY** Old English *sinder*

cinder cone *n geol* a volcano whose sides are made entirely of loose fragments, ash, and pumice

Cinderella *n* a poor, neglected, or unsuccessful person or thing ▶ **HISTORY** after *Cinderella*, the heroine of a fairy tale

cine camera *n* a camera for taking moving pictures

cinema *n* **1** a place designed for showing films **2** **the cinema a** the art or business of making films **b** films collectively ▶ **HISTORY** shortened from *cinematograph* > **cinematic** *adj*

cinematograph *n chiefly Brit* a combined camera, printer, and projector ▶ **HISTORY** Greek *kinēma* motion + -**GRAPH** > **cinematographer** *n* > **cinematographic** *adj*

cinematography *n* the technique of making films: *he won an Oscar for his stunning cinematography*

cineraria *n* a garden plant with daisy-like flowers ▶ **HISTORY** Latin *cinis* ashes

cinerarium *n*, *pl* -**raria** a place for keeping the ashes of the dead after cremation ▶ **HISTORY** Latin *cinerarius* relating to ashes > **cinerary** *adj*

cinnabar *n* **1** a heavy red mineral containing mercury **2** a large red-and-black European moth ▶ **HISTORY** Greek *kinnabari*

cinnamon *n* the spice obtained from the aromatic bark of a tropical Asian tree ▶ **HISTORY** Hebrew *qinnamown*

cinquefoil *n* **1** a plant with five-lobed compound leaves **2** an ornamental carving in the form of five arcs arranged in a circle ▶ **HISTORY** Latin *quinquefolium* plant with five leaves

Cinque Ports *pl n* an association of ports on the SE coast of England, with certain ancient duties and privileges

cipher or **cypher** (**sife**-er) *n* **1** a method of secret writing using substitution of letters according to a key **2** a secret message **3** the key to a secret message **4** a person or thing of no importance **5** *obsolete* the numeral zero ▷ *vb* **6** to put (a message) into secret writing ▶ HISTORY Arabic *sifr* zero

circa (**sir**-ka) *prep* (used with a date) approximately; about: *circa 1788* ▶ HISTORY Latin

circadian *adj* of biological processes that occur regularly at 24-hour intervals ▶ HISTORY Latin *circa* about + *dies* day

circle *n* **1** a curved line surrounding a central point, every point of the line being the same distance from the centre **2** the figure enclosed by such a curve **3** something formed or arranged in the shape of a circle: *they ran round in little circles* **4** a group of people sharing an interest, activity, or upbringing: *his judgment is well respected in diplomatic circles* **5** *theatre* the section of seats above the main level of the auditorium **6** a process or chain of events or parts that forms a connected whole; cycle **7 come full circle** to arrive back at one's starting point ▷ *vb* **-cling, -cled 8** to move in a circle (around) **9** to enclose in a circle ▶ HISTORY Latin *circus*

circlet *n* a small circle or ring, esp. a circular ornament worn on the head ▶ HISTORY Old French *cerclet* little circle

circuit *n* **1** a complete route or course, esp. one that is circular or that lies around an object **2** a complete path through which an electric current can flow **3 a** a periodical journey around an area, as made by judges or salesmen **b** the places visited on such a journey **4** a motor-racing track **5** *sport* a series of tournaments in which the same players regularly take part: *the professional golf circuit* **6** a number of theatres or cinemas under one management ▶ HISTORY Latin *circum* around + *ire* to go

circuit breaker *n* a device that stops the flow of current in an electrical circuit if there is a fault

circuitous (sir-**kew**-it-uss) *adj* indirect and lengthy: *a circuitous route*

circuitry (**sir**-kit-tree) *n* **1** the design of an electrical circuit **2** the system of circuits used in an electronic device

circular *adj* **1** of or in the shape of a circle **2** travelling in a circle **3** (of an arguments) not valid because a statement is used to prove the conclusion and the conclusion to prove the statement **4** (of letters or announcements) intended for general distribution ▷ *n* **5** a letter or advertisement sent to a large number of people at the same time **> circularity** *n*

circular saw *n* a power-driven saw in which a circular disc with a toothed edge is rotated at high speed

circulate *vb* **-lating, -lated 1** to send, go, or pass from place to place or person to person: *rumours were circulating that he was about to resign* **2** to move through a circuit or system, returning to the starting point: *regular exercise keeps the blood circulating around the body* **3** to move around the guests at a party, talking to different people: *it wasn't like her not to circulate among all the guests* ▶ HISTORY Latin *circulari* **> circulatory** *adj*

circulation *n* **1** the flow of blood from the heart through the arteries, and then back through the veins to the heart, where the cycle is renewed **2** the number of copies of a newspaper or magazine that are sold **3** the distribution of newspapers or magazines **4** sending or moving around: *the circulation of air* **5 in circulation a** (of currency) being used by the public **b** (of people) active in a social or business context

circum- *prefix* around; on all sides: *circumlocution* ▶ HISTORY Latin

circumcise *vb* **-cising, -cised 1** to remove the foreskin of (a male) **2** to cut or remove the clitoris of (a female) **3** to perform such an operation as a religious rite on (someone) ▶ HISTORY Latin CIRCUM- + *caedere* to cut **> circumcision** *n*

circumference *n* **1** the boundary of a specific area or figure, esp. of a circle **2** the distance round this ▶ HISTORY Latin CIRCUM- + *ferre* to bear **> circumferential** *adj*

circumflex *n* a mark (^) placed over a vowel to show that it is pronounced in a particular way, for instance as a long vowel in French ▶ HISTORY Latin CIRCUM- + *flectere* to bend

circumlocution *n* **1** an indirect way of saying something **2** an indirect expression **> circumlocutory** *adj*

circumnavigate *vb* **-gating, -gated** to sail, fly, or walk right around **> circumnavigation** *n*

circumscribe *vb* **-scribing, -scribed 1** *formal* to limit or restrict within certain boundaries: *the President's powers are circumscribed by the Constitution* **2** *geom* to draw a geometric figure around (another figure) so that the two are in contact but do not intersect ▶ HISTORY Latin CIRCUM- + *scribere* to write **> circumscription** *n*

circumspect *adj* cautious and careful not to take risks ▶ HISTORY Latin CIRCUM- + *specere* to look **> circumspection** *n* **> circumspectly** *adv*

circumstance *n* **1** an occurrence or condition that accompanies or influences a person or event **2** unplanned events and situations which cannot be controlled: *a victim of circumstance* **3 pomp and circumstance** formal display or ceremony **4 under** or **in no circumstances** in no case; never **5 under the circumstances** because of conditions ▶ HISTORY Latin CIRCUM- + *stare* to stand

circumstantial *adj* **1** of or dependent on circumstances **2** fully detailed

circumstantial evidence *n* *law* indirect evidence that suggests a conclusion but does not prove it

circumstantiate *vb* **-ating, -ated** to prove by giving details

circumvent *vb* *formal* **1** to avoid or get round (a rule, restriction, etc.) **2** to outwit (a person) ▶ HISTORY Latin CIRCUM- + *venire* to come **> circumvention** *n*

circus *n, pl* **-cuses 1** a travelling company of entertainers such as acrobats, clowns, trapeze artists, and trained animals **2** a public performance given by such a company **3** *Brit* an open place in a town where several streets meet **4** *informal* a hectic or well-published situation: *her second marriage turned into a media circus* **5** (in ancient Rome) an open-air stadium for chariot races or public games **6** a travelling group of professional sportsmen: *the Formula One circus* ▶ **HISTORY** Greek *kirkos* ring

cirque (**sirk**) *n* a steep-sided semicircular hollow found in mountainous areas

cirrhosis (sir-**roh**-siss) *n* a chronic progressive disease of the liver, often caused by drinking too much alcohol ▶ **HISTORY** Greek *kirrhos* orange-coloured

cirrocumulus (sirr-oh-**kew**-myew-luss) *n, pl* **-li** (-lie) a high cloud of ice crystals grouped into small separate globular masses

cirrostratus (sirr-oh-**strah**-tuss) *n, pl* **-ti** (-tie) a uniform layer of cloud above about 6000 metres

cirrus *n, pl* **-ri** **1** a thin wispy cloud found at high altitudes **2** a plant tendril **3** a slender tentacle in certain sea creatures ▶ **HISTORY** Latin: curl

CIS Commonwealth of Independent States

cisalpine *adj* on this (the southern) side of the Alps, as viewed from Rome

cisco *n, pl* **-coes** *or* **-cos** a whitefish, esp. the lake herring of cold deep lakes of North America ▶ **HISTORY** from a Native American language

Cistercian *n* **1** a Christian monk or nun belonging to an especially strict Benedictine order ▷ *adj* **2** of or relating to this order ▶ **HISTORY** *Cîteaux*, original home of the order

cistern *n* **1** a water tank, esp. one which holds water for flushing a toilet **2** an underground reservoir ▶ **HISTORY** Latin *cista* box

citadel *n* a fortress in a city ▶ **HISTORY** Latin *civitas*

citation *n* **1** an official commendation or award, esp. for bravery **2** the quoting of a book or author **3** a quotation

cite *vb* **citing, cited 1** to quote or refer to (a passage, book, or author) **2** to bring forward as proof **3** to summon to appear before a court of law **4** to mention or commend (someone) for outstanding bravery **5** to enumerate: *the president cited the wonders of the American family* ▶ **HISTORY** Old French *citer* to summon

citizen *n* **1** a native or naturalized member of a state or nation **2** an inhabitant of a city or town

Citizens' Band *n* a range of radio frequencies for use by the public for private communication

citizenship *n* the condition or status of a citizen, with its rights and duties

citrate *n* any salt or ester of citric acid

citric *adj* of or derived from citrus fruits or citric acid

citric acid *n* a weak acid found especially in citrus fruits and used as a flavouring (**E330**)

citron *n* **1** a lemon-like fruit of a small Asian tree **2** the candied rind of this fruit, for decorating foods ▶ **HISTORY** Latin *citrus* citrus tree

citronella *n* **1** a tropical Asian grass with lemon-scented leaves **2** the aromatic oil obtained from this grass

citrus fruit *n* juicy, sharp-tasting fruit such as oranges, lemons, or limes ▶ **HISTORY** Latin *citrus* citrus tree

city *n, pl* **cities 1** any large town **2** (in Britain) a town that has received this title from the Crown **3** the people of a city collectively **4** (in the US and Canada) a large town with its own government established by charter from the state or provincial government ▶ **HISTORY** Latin *civis* citizen

City *n* **the City** *Brit* **1** the area in central London in which the United Kingdom's major financial business is transacted **2** the various financial institutions in this area

city editor *n* (on a newspaper) **1** *Brit* the editor in charge of business news **2** *US & Canad* the editor in charge of local news

city-state *n* *ancient history* a state consisting of a sovereign city and its dependencies

civet (**siv**-vit) *n* **1** a spotted catlike mammal of Africa and S Asia **2** the musky fluid produced by this animal, used in perfumes ▶ **HISTORY** Arabic *zabād* civet perfume

civic *adj* of a city or citizens: *civic responsibility* > **civically** *adv*

civic centre *n* *Brit & NZ* a complex of public buildings, including recreational facilities and offices of local government

civics *n* the study of the rights and responsibilities of citizenship

civil *adj* **1** of or occurring within the state or between citizens: *civil unrest* **2** of or relating to the citizen as an individual: *civil rights* **3** not part of the military, legal, or religious structures of a country: *civil aviation* **4** polite or courteous: *he seemed very civil and listened politely* ▶ **HISTORY** Latin *civis* citizen > **civilly** *adv*

civil defence *n* the organizing of civilians to deal with enemy attacks and natural disasters

civil disobedience *n* a nonviolent protest, such as a refusal to obey laws or pay taxes

civil engineer *n* a person qualified to design and construct public works, such as roads or bridges > **civil engineering** *n*

civilian *n* **1** a person who is not a member of the armed forces or police ▷ *adj* **2** not relating to the armed forces or police: *civilian clothes*

civility *n, pl* **-ties 1** polite or courteous behaviour **2** **civilities** polite words or actions

civilization *or* **-lisation** *n* **1** the total culture and way of life of a particular people, nation, region, or period **2** a human society that has a complex cultural, political, and legal organization **3** the races collectively who have achieved such a state **4** cities or populated areas, as contrasted with sparsely inhabited areas **5** intellectual, cultural, and moral refinement

civilize *or* **-lise** *vb* **-lizing, -lized** *or* **-lising, -lised** **1** to bring out of barbarism into a state of civilization **2** to refine, educate, or enlighten > **civilized** *or* **-lised** *adj*

civil law *n* *law* **1** the law of a state, relating to private and civilian affairs and rights rather than

C

criminal offences. Compare **criminal law 2** the body of law in ancient Rome, esp. as applicable to private citizens **3** a system of law based on the Roman system as distinguished from common law and canon law

civil liberties *pl n* a person's rights to freedom of speech and action

civil list *n* (in Britain) the annual amount given by Parliament to the royal household and the royal family

civil marriage *n law* a marriage performed by an official other than a member of the clergy

civil offence *n law* an act that contravenes civil law. Compare **criminal offence**

civil rights *pl n* the personal rights of the individual citizen to have equal treatment and equal opportunities

civil servant *n* a member of the civil service

civil service *n* the service responsible for the public administration of the government of a country

civil war *n* a war between people of the same country, such as the **English Civil War**, between the supporters of Charles I and those of Parliament (1642–51), the **American Civil War**, between the North and the South (1861–65), and the **Spanish Civil War**, between the nationalists and the republicans (1936–39)

civvies *pl n Brit, Austral & NZ, slang* civilian clothes as opposed to uniform

CJD Creutzfeldt-Jakob disease: a fatal virus disease that affects the central nervous system

cl centilitre

Cl *chem* chlorine

clack *n* **1** the sound made by two hard objects striking each other ▷ *vb* **2** to make this sound ▶ HISTORY imitative

clad *vb* a past of **clothe**

cladding *n* **1** the material used to cover the outside of a building **2** a protective metal coating attached to another metal ▶ HISTORY special use of CLAD

cladistics *n* a method of grouping animals by measurable likenesses ▶ HISTORY Greek *klados* branch

claim *vb* **1** to assert as a fact: *he had claimed to be too ill to return* **2** to demand as a right or as one's property: *you can claim housing benefit to help pay your rent* **3** to call for or need: *this problem claims our attention* **4** to cause the death of: *violence which has claimed at least fifty lives* **5** to succeed in obtaining; win: *she claimed her fifth European tour victory with a closing round of 64* ▷ *n* **6** an assertion of something as true or real **7** an assertion of a right; a demand for something as due **8** a right or just title to something: *a claim to fame* **9** anything that is claimed, such as a piece of land staked out by a miner **10 a** a demand for payment in connection with an insurance policy **b** the sum of money demanded ▶ HISTORY Latin *clamare* to shout
> **claimant** *n*

clairvoyance *n* the alleged power of perceiving things beyond the natural range of the senses ▶ HISTORY French: clear-seeing

clairvoyant *n* **1** a person claiming to have the power to foretell future events ▷ *adj* **2** of or possessing clairvoyance

clam *n* an edible shellfish with a hinged shell ▶ HISTORY earlier *clamshell* shell that clamps

clamber *vb* **1** to climb awkwardly, using hands and feet ▷ *n* **2** a climb performed in this manner ▶ HISTORY probably variant of *climb*

clammy *adj* -**mier**, -**miest** unpleasantly moist and sticky ▶ HISTORY Old English *clæman* to smear
> **clammily** *adv* > **clamminess** *n*

clamour *or US* **clamor** *n* **1** a loud protest **2** a loud and persistent noise or outcry ▷ *vb* **3 clamour for** to demand noisily **4** to make a loud noise or outcry ▶ HISTORY Latin *clamare* to cry out
> **clamorous** *adj*

clamp[1] *n* **1** a mechanical device with movable jaws for holding things together tightly **2** See **wheel clamp** ▷ *vb* **3** to fix or fasten with a clamp **4** to immobilize (a car) by means of a wheel clamp ▶ HISTORY Dutch or Low German *klamp*

clamp[2] *n* a mound of a harvested root crop, covered with straw and earth to protect it from winter weather ▶ HISTORY Middle Dutch *klamp* heap

clan *n* **1** a group of families with a common surname and a common ancestor, esp. among Scottish Highlanders **2** an extended family related by ancestry or marriage: *America's leading political clan, the Kennedys* **3** a group of people with common characteristics, aims, or interests ▶ HISTORY Scottish Gaelic *clann* > **clansman** *n*

clandestine *adj formal* secret and concealed: *a base for clandestine activities* ▶ HISTORY Latin *clam* secretly > **clandestinely** *adv*

clang *vb* **1** to make a loud ringing noise, as metal does when it is struck ▷ *n* **2** a ringing metallic noise ▶ HISTORY Latin *clangere*

clanger *n* **drop a clanger** *informal* to make a very noticeable mistake

clangour *or US* **clangor** *n* a loud continuous clanging sound ▶ HISTORY Latin *clangor*
> **clangorous** *adj*

clank *n* **1** an abrupt harsh metallic sound ▷ *vb* **2** to make such a sound ▶ HISTORY imitative

clannish *adj* (of a group) tending to exclude outsiders: *the villagers can be very clannish*

clap *vb* **clapping, clapped 1** to applaud by striking the palms of one's hands sharply together **2** to place or put quickly or forcibly: *in former times he would have been clapped in irons or shot* **3** to strike (a person) lightly with an open hand as in greeting **4** to make a sharp abrupt sound like two objects being struck together **5 clap eyes on** *informal* to catch sight of ▷ *n* **6** the act or sound of clapping **7** a sharp abrupt sound, esp. of thunder **8** a light blow ▶ HISTORY Old English *clæppan*

clapped out *adj informal* worn out; dilapidated

clapper n **1** a small piece of metal hanging inside a bell, which causes it to sound when struck against the side **2 like the clappers** Brit, informal extremely quickly: he left, pedalling like the clappers

clapperboard n a pair of hinged boards clapped together during film shooting to help in synchronizing sound and picture

claptrap n informal foolish or pretentious talk: pseudo-intellectual claptrap

claque n formal **1** a group of people hired to applaud **2** a group of fawning admirers ▶ HISTORY French claquer to clap

claret (**klar**-rit) n **1** a dry red wine, esp. one from Bordeaux ▷ adj **2** purplish-red ▶ HISTORY Latin clarus clear

clarify vb **-fies, -fying, -fied 1** to make or become clear or easy to understand **2** to make or become free of impurities, esp. by heating: clarified butter ▶ HISTORY Latin clarus clear + facere to make > **clarification** n

clarinet n a keyed woodwind instrument with a single reed ▶ HISTORY French clarinette > **clarinettist** n

clarion n **1** an obsolete high-pitched trumpet **2** its sound ▶ HISTORY Latin clarus clear

clarion call n strong encouragement to do something

clarity n clearness ▶ HISTORY Latin claritas

clash vb **1** to come into conflict **2** to be incompatible **3** (of dates or events) to coincide **4** (of colours or styles) to look ugly or incompatible together: patterned fabrics which combine seemingly clashing shades to great effect **5** to make a loud harsh sound, esp. by striking together ▷ n **6** a collision or conflict **7** a loud harsh noise ▶ HISTORY imitative

clasp n **1** a fastening, such as a catch or hook, for holding things together **2** a firm grasp or embrace ▷ vb **3** to grasp or embrace tightly **4** to fasten together with a clasp ▶ HISTORY origin unknown

clasp knife n a large knife with blades which fold into the handle

class n **1** a group of people sharing a similar social and economic position **2** the system of dividing society into such groups **3** a group of people or things sharing a common characteristic **4 a** a group of pupils or students who are taught together **b** a meeting of a group of students for tuition **5** a standard of quality or attainment: second class **6** informal excellence or elegance, esp. in dress, design, or behaviour: a full-bodied red wine with real class **7** biol one of the groups into which a phylum is divided, containing one or more orders **8 in a class of its own** or **in a class by oneself** without an equal for ability, talent, etc. ▷ adj **9** informal excellent, skilful, or stylish: a class act ▷ vb **10** to place in a class ▶ HISTORY Latin classis class, rank

class action n law a legal action undertaken by one or more people representing the interests of a large group of people with the same grievance

class boundary n maths the higher or lower limit of a class interval on a graph

class-conscious adj aware of belonging to a particular social rank

classic adj **1** serving as a standard or model of its kind; typical: it is a classic symptom of iron deficiency **2** of lasting interest or significance because of excellence: the classic work on Central America **3** characterized by simplicity and purity of form: a classic suit ▷ n **4** an author, artist, or work of art of the highest excellence **5** a creation or work considered as definitive ▶ HISTORY Latin classicus of the first rank

classical adj **1** of or in a restrained conservative style: it had been built in the eighteenth century in a severely classical style **2** music **a** in a style or from a period marked by stability of form, intellectualism, and restraint **b** denoting serious art music in general **3** of or influenced by ancient Greek and Roman culture **4** of the form of a language historically used for formal and literary purposes: classical Chinese **5** (of an education) based on the humanities and the study of Latin and Greek > **classically** adv

classic car n chiefly Brit a car that is more than twenty five years old

classicism n **1** an artistic style based on Greek and Roman models, showing emotional restraint and regularity of form **2** knowledge of the culture of ancient Greece and Rome > **classicist** n

classics pl n **1** the study of ancient Greek and Roman literature and culture **2 the classics a** those works of literature regarded as great or lasting **b** the ancient Greek and Latin languages

classification n **1** placing things systematically in categories **2** a division or category in a classifying system ▶ HISTORY French > **classificatory** adj

classified adj **1** arranged according to some system of classification **2** Government (of information) not available to people outside a restricted group, esp. for reasons of national security

classified advertisement n journalism (in an advertisement column in a newspaper) a small advertisement grouped according to type, usually selling or trying to buy something

classifier n grammar a noun or adjective that categorizes a person or thing mentioned or described as being of a particular kind

classify vb **-fies, -fying, -fied 1** to arrange or order by classes **2** Government to declare (information) to be officially secret > **classifiable** adj

class interval n maths one of the divisions of the base line of a bar chart or histogram

classless adj **1** not belonging to a class **2** distinguished by the absence of economic or social distinctions: a classless society

classmate n a friend or contemporary in the same class of a school

classroom n a room in a school where lessons take place

classy adj **classier, classiest** informal stylish and sophisticated > **classiness** n

clatter vb 1 to make a rattling noise, as when hard objects hit each other ▷ n 2 a rattling sound or noise ▶ HISTORY Old English clatrung clattering

clause n 1 a section of a legal document such as a will or contract 2 grammar a group of words, consisting of a subject and a predicate including a finite verb, that does not necessarily constitute a sentence ▶ HISTORY Latin clausula conclusion > **clausal** adj

claustrophobia n an abnormal fear of being in a confined space ▶ HISTORY Latin claustrum cloister + -PHOBIA > **claustrophobic** adj

claves pl n a pair of hardwood sticks hit together to make a hollow sound, used esp. in Latin-American music

clavichord n an early keyboard instrument with a very soft tone ▶ HISTORY Latin clavis key + chorda string

clavicle n either of the two bones connecting the shoulder blades with the upper part of the breastbone; the collarbone ▶ HISTORY Latin clavis key

claw n 1 a curved pointed nail on the foot of birds, some reptiles, and certain mammals 2 a similar part in some invertebrates, such as a crab's pincer ▷ vb 3 to scrape, tear, or dig with claws or nails: she clawed his face with her fingernails 4 to achieve (something) only after overcoming great difficulties: he clawed his way to power and wealth; settlers attempting to claw a living from the desert ▶ HISTORY Old English clawu

claw back vb 1 to get back (something) with difficulty 2 to recover (a part of a grant or allowance) in the form of a tax or financial penalty

clay n 1 a very fine-grained earth, soft when moist and hardening when baked, used to make bricks and pottery 2 earth or mud 3 poetic the material of the human body ▶ HISTORY Old English clǣg > **clayey, clayish** or **claylike** adj

claymore n a large two-edged broadsword used formerly by Scottish Highlanders ▶ HISTORY Gaelic claidheamh mōr great sword

clay pigeon n a disc of baked clay hurled into the air from a machine as a target for shooting

Clayton's adj Austral & NZ acting as an imitation or substitute: this latest ploy is simply a Clayton's resignation ▶ HISTORY from the trademark of a non-alcoholic drink marketed as 'the drink you have when you're not having a drink'

clean adj 1 free from dirt or impurities: clean water 2 habitually hygienic and neat 3 morally sound: clean living 4 without objectionable language or obscenity: good clean fun 5 without anything in it or on it: a clean sheet of paper 6 causing little contamination or pollution: rape seed oil may provide a clean alternative to petrol 7 recently washed; fresh 8 thorough or complete: a clean break with the past 9 skilful and done without fumbling; dexterous: a clean catch 10 sport played fairly and without fouls 11 free from dishonesty or corruption: clean government 12 simple and streamlined in design: the clean lines and colourful simplicity of these ceramics

13 (esp. of a driving licence) showing or having no record of offences 14 slang a innocent b not carrying illegal drugs, weapons, etc. ▷ vb 15 to make or become free of dirt: he wanted to help me clean the room ▷ adv 16 in a clean way 17 not standard completely: she clean forgot to face the camera 18 **come clean** informal to make a revelation or confession ▷ n 19 the act or an instance of cleaning: the fridge could do with a clean ▶ HISTORY Old English clǣne

clean-cut adj 1 clearly outlined 2 wholesome in appearance

cleaner n 1 a person, device, or substance that removes dirt 2 a shop or firm that provides a dry-cleaning service 3 **take someone to the cleaners** informal to rob or defraud someone

cleanly adv 1 easily or smoothly 2 in a fair manner ▷ adj **-lier, -liest** 3 habitually clean or neat > **cleanliness** n

cleanse vb **cleansing, cleansed** 1 to remove dirt from 2 to remove evil or guilt from > **cleanser** n

clean sheet n sport an instance of conceding no goals or points in a match

clean-tech informal adj 1 using clean technology ▷ n 2 same as **clean technology**

clean technology n techniques that minimize the damage caused to the environment as a result of manufacturing processes

clear adj 1 free from doubt or confusion: clear evidence of police thuggery 2 certain in the mind; sure: I am still not clear about what they can and cannot do 3 easy to see or hear; distinct 4 perceptive, alert: clear thinking 5 evident or obvious: it is not clear how he died 6 transparent: clear glass doors 7 free from darkness or obscurity; bright 8 (of sounds or the voice) not harsh or hoarse 9 even and pure in tone or colour 10 free of obstruction; open: a clear path runs under the trees 11 (of weather) free from dullness or clouds 12 without blemish or defect: a clear skin 13 free of suspicion, guilt, or blame: a clear conscience 14 (of money) without deduction; net 15 free from debt or obligation 16 without qualification or limitation; complete: a clear lead ▷ adv 17 in a clear or distinct manner 18 completely 19 **clear of** out of the way of: once we were clear of the harbour we headed east ▷ n 20 **in the clear** free of suspicion, guilt, or blame ▷ vb 21 to free from doubt or confusion 22 to rid of objects or obstructions 23 to make or form (a path) by removing obstructions 24 to move or pass by or over without contact: he cleared the fence easily 25 to make or become free from darkness or obscurity 26 to rid (one's throat) of phlegm 27 a (of the weather) to become free from dullness, fog, or rain b (of mist or fog) to disappear 28 (of a cheque) to pass through one's bank and be charged against one's account 29 to free from impurity or blemish 30 to obtain or give (clearance) 31 to prove (someone) innocent of a crime or mistake 32 to permit (someone) to see or handle classified information 33 to make or gain (money) as profit 34 to discharge or settle (a debt)

C

35 clear the air to sort out a misunderstanding ▷ See also **clear off** ▸ HISTORY Latin *clarus* > **clearly** *adv*

clearance *n* **1** the act of clearing: *slum clearance* **2** permission for a vehicle or passengers to proceed **3** official permission to have access to secret information or areas **4** space between two parts in motion

clear-cut *adj* **1** easy to distinguish or understand: *there is no clear-cut distinction between safe and unsafe areas of the city* **2** clearly outlined

clearing *n* an area with few or no trees or shrubs in wooded or overgrown land

clearing bank *n* (in Britain) any bank that makes use of the central clearing house in London

clearing house *n* **1** *banking* an institution where cheques and other commercial papers drawn on member banks are cancelled against each other so that only net balances are payable **2** a central agency for the collection and distribution of information or materials

clear off *vb informal* to go away: often used as a command

clear out *vb* **1** to remove and sort the contents of (a room or container) **2** *informal* to go away: often used as a command

clearway *n Brit & Austral* a stretch of road on which motorists may stop only in an emergency

cleat *n* **1** a wedge-shaped block attached to a structure to act as a support **2** a piece of wood or iron with two projecting ends round which ropes are fastened ▸ HISTORY Germanic

cleavage *n* **1** the space between a woman's breasts **2** a division or split **3** (of crystals) the act of splitting or the tendency to split along definite planes so as to make smooth surfaces

cleave¹ *vb* **cleaving; cleft, cleaved** *or* **clove; cleft, cleaved** *or* **cloven** **1** to split apart: *cleave the stone along the fissures* **2** to make by or as if by cutting: *a two-lane highway that cleaved its way through the northern extremities of the Everglades* ▸ HISTORY Old English *cléofan*

cleave² *vb* **cleaving, cleaved** to cling or stick: *a farmhouse cleaved to the hill* ▸ HISTORY Old English *cleofian*

cleaver *n* a heavy knife with a square blade, used for chopping meat

cleavers *n* a plant with small white flowers and sticky fruits ▸ HISTORY Old English *clífe*

clef *n music* a symbol placed at the beginning of each stave indicating the pitch of the music written after it ▸ HISTORY French

cleft *n* **1** a narrow opening in a rock **2** an indentation or split ▷ *adj* **3 in a cleft stick** in a very difficult position ▷ *vb* **4** a past of **cleave¹**

cleft palate *n* a congenital crack in the mid line of the hard palate

clematis *n* a climbing plant grown for its large colourful flowers ▸ HISTORY Greek *klēma* vine twig

clemency *n* mercy

clement *adj* **1** (of the weather) mild **2** merciful ▸ HISTORY Latin *clemens* mild

clementine *n* a citrus fruit resembling a tangerine ▸ HISTORY French

clench *vb* **1** to close or squeeze together (the teeth or a fist) tightly **2** to grasp or grip firmly ▷ *n* **3** a firm grasp or grip ▸ HISTORY Old English *beclencan*

clerestory (**clear**-store-ee) *n, pl* **-ries** a row of windows in the upper part of the wall of the nave of a church above the roof of the aisle ▸ HISTORY *clear* + *storey* > **clerestoried** *adj*

clergy *n, pl* **-gies** priests and ministers as a group ▸ HISTORY see CLERK

clergyman *n, pl* **-men** a male member of the clergy

clergywoman *n, pl* **-women** a female member of the clergy

cleric *n* a member of the clergy

clerical *adj* **1** of clerks or office work: *a clerical job* **2** of or associated with the clergy: *a Lebanese clerical leader*

clerihew *n* a form of comic or satiric verse, consisting of two couplets and containing the name of a well-known person ▸ HISTORY after E. *Clerihew* Bentley, who invented it

clerk *n* **1** an employee in an office, bank, or court who keeps records, files, and accounts **2** *US & Canad* a hotel receptionist **3** *archaic* a scholar ▷ *vb* **4** to work as a clerk ▸ HISTORY Greek *klērikos* cleric, from *klēros* heritage > **clerkship** *n*

clever *adj* **1** displaying sharp intelligence or mental alertness **2** skilful with one's hands **3** smart in a superficial way **4** *Brit, informal* sly or cunning ▸ HISTORY Middle English *cliver* > **cleverly** *adv* > **cleverness** *n*

clianthus *n* a plant of Australia and New Zealand with clusters of ornamental scarlet flowers ▸ HISTORY probably from Greek *kleos* glory + *anthos* flower

cliché (**klee**-shay) *n* an expression or idea that is no longer effective because of overuse ▸ HISTORY French > **clichéd** *or* **cliché'd** *adj*

click *n* **1** a short light often metallic sound ▷ *vb* **2** to make a clicking sound: *cameras clicked and whirred* **3** Also: **click on** *computers* to press and release (a button on a mouse) or select (a particular function) by pressing and releasing a button on a mouse **4** *informal* to become suddenly clear: *it wasn't until I saw the photograph that everything clicked into place* **5** *slang* (of two people) to get on well together: *I met him at a dinner party and we clicked straight away* **6** *slang* to be a great success: *the film cost so much that if it hadn't clicked at the box office we'd have been totally wiped out* ▸ HISTORY imitative

client *n* **1** someone who uses the services of a professional person or organization **2** a customer **3** *computers* a program or work station that requests data from a server ▸ HISTORY Latin *cliens* retainer

clientele (klee-on-**tell**) *n* customers or clients collectively

cliff *n* a steep rock face, esp. along the seashore ▸ HISTORY Old English *clif*

cliffhanger n a film, game, etc. which is exciting and full of suspense because its outcome is uncertain > **cliffhanging** adj

climacteric n 1 same as **menopause** 2 the period in the life of a man corresponding to the menopause, during which sexual drive and fertility diminish ▶ HISTORY Greek klimakter rung of a ladder

climate n 1 the typical weather conditions of an area 2 an area with a particular kind of climate 3 a prevailing trend: the current economic climate ▶ HISTORY Greek klima inclination, region > **climatic** adj > **climatically** adv

climate change n change in the Earth's overall climate and in particular climates, resulting in global warming

climatic stress n biol damage to living organisms caused by changes in weather conditions

climatology n meteorol the study of climates > **climatologist** n

climax n 1 the most intense or highest point of an experience or of a series of events: a striking climax to the year's efforts to promote tourism 2 a decisive moment in a dramatic or other work: the film has a climax set atop a gale-swept lighthouse ▷ vb 3 not universally accepted to reach or bring to a climax ▶ HISTORY Greek klimax ladder > **climactic** adj

climax vegetation n biol, geog the balanced plant community that will develop if a given environment is left undisturbed for long enough for the species best-equipped to flourish in it to take over

climb vb 1 to go up or ascend (stairs, a mountain, etc.) 2 to move or go with difficulty: she climbed through a window 3 to rise to a higher point or intensity: I grew increasingly delirious as my temperature climbed 4 to increase in value or amount: the number could eventually climb to half-a-million 5 to ascend in social position: he climbed the ranks of the organization 6 (of plants) to grow upwards by twining, using tendrils or suckers 7 to incline or slope upwards: the road climbed up through the foothills 8 **climb into** informal to put on or get into: I climbed into the van ▷ n 9 the act or an instance of climbing 10 a place or thing to be climbed, esp. a route in mountaineering ▶ HISTORY Old English climban > **climbable** adj > **climber** n > **climbing** n, adj

climb down vb 1 to retreat (from an opinion or position) ▷ n **climb-down** 2 a retreat from an opinion or position

clime n poetic a region or its climate

clinch vb 1 to settle (an argument or agreement) decisively 2 to secure (a nail) by bending the protruding point over 3 to engage in a clinch, as in boxing or wrestling ▷ n 4 the act of clinching 5 boxing, wrestling a movement in which one or both competitors hold on to the other to avoid punches or regain wind 6 slang a lovers' embrace ▶ HISTORY variant of clench

clincher n informal something decisive, such as fact, argument, or point scored

cling vb **clinging, clung** 1 to hold fast or stick closely 2 to be emotionally overdependent on 3 to continue to do or believe in: he clings to the belief that people are capable of change ▶ HISTORY Old English clingan > **clinging** or **clingy** adj

clingfilm n Brit a thin polythene material used for wrapping food

clinic n 1 a place in which outpatients are given medical treatment or advice 2 a similar place staffed by specialist physicians or surgeons: I have an antenatal clinic on Friday afternoon 3 Brit & NZ a private hospital or nursing home 4 the teaching of medicine to students at the bedside ▶ HISTORY Greek klinē bed

clinical adj 1 of or relating to the observation and treatment of patients directly: clinical trials of a new drug 2 of or relating to a clinic 3 logical and unemotional: they have a somewhat clinical attitude to their children's upbringing 4 (of a room or buildings) plain, simple, and usually unattractive > **clinically** adv

clinical thermometer n a thermometer for measuring the temperature of the body

clink¹ vb 1 to make a light sharp metallic sound ▷ n 2 such a sound ▶ HISTORY perhaps from Middle Dutch klinken

clink² n slang prison ▶ HISTORY after Clink, a former prison in London

clinker n the fused coal left over in a fire or furnace ▶ HISTORY Dutch klinker a type of brick

clinker-built adj (of a boat or ship) with a hull made from overlapping planks ▶ HISTORY obsolete clinker a nailing together, probably from clinch

clint n physical geog a section of a limestone pavement separated from adjacent sections by solution fissures

Clio n Greek myth the Muse of history

clip¹ vb **clipping, clipped** 1 to cut or trim with scissors or shears 2 to remove a short section from (a film or newspaper) 3 Brit & Austral to punch a hole in (something, esp. a ticket) 4 informal to strike with a sharp, often slanting, blow 5 to shorten (a word) 6 slang to obtain (money) by cheating ▷ n 7 the act of clipping 8 a short extract from a film 9 something that has been clipped 10 informal a sharp, often slanting, blow: a clip on the ear 11 informal speed: proceeding at a smart clip 12 Austral & NZ the total quantity of wool shorn, as in one place or season ▶ HISTORY Old Norse klippa to cut

clip² n 1 a device for attaching or holding things together 2 an article of jewellery that can be clipped onto a dress or hat ▷ vb **clipping, clipped** 3 to attach or hold together with a clip ▶ HISTORY Old English clyppan to embrace

clipboard n 1 a portable writing board with a clip at the top for holding paper 2 computers a temporary storage area where text or graphics are held after the cut command or the copy command

clipped adj (of speech) abrupt, clearly pronounced, and using as few words as possible

clipper n a fast commercial sailing ship

C

C

clippers *pl n* a tool used for clipping and cutting

clipping *n* something cut out, esp. an article from a newspaper

clique (**kleek**) *n* a small exclusive group of friends or associates ▶ HISTORY French > **cliquey, cliquy** or **cliquish** *adj*

clitoris (**klit**-or-riss) *n* a small organ at the front of the vulva ▶ HISTORY Greek *kleitoris* > **clitoral** *adj*

Cllr councillor

cloaca (kloh-**ake**-a) *n, pl* **-cae** a cavity in most animals, except higher mammals, into which the alimentary canal and the genital and urinary ducts open ▶ HISTORY Latin: sewer

cloak *n* **1** a loose sleeveless outer garment, fastened at the throat and falling straight from the shoulders **2** something that covers or conceals ▷ *vb written* **3** to hide or disguise **4** to cover with or as if with a cloak ▶ HISTORY Medieval Latin *clocca* cloak, bell

cloakroom *n* **1** a room in which coats may be left temporarily **2** *Brit, euphemistic* a toilet

clobber[1] *vb informal* **1** to batter **2** to defeat utterly **3** to criticize severely ▶ HISTORY origin unknown

clobber[2] *n Brit, Austral & NZ, informal* personal belongings, such as clothes ▶ HISTORY origin unknown

cloche (**klosh**) *n* **1** *Brit, Austral & NZ* a small glass or plastic cover for protecting young plants **2** a woman's close-fitting hat ▶ HISTORY French: bell

clock[1] *n* **1** a device for showing the time, either through pointers that revolve over a numbered dial, or through a display of figures **2** a device with a dial for recording or measuring **3** the downy head of a dandelion that has gone to seed **4** *informal* same as **speedometer, mileometer 5** *Brit, slang* the face **6 round the clock** all day and all night ▷ *vb* **7** to record (time) with a stopwatch, esp. in the calculation of speed **8** *Brit, Austral & NZ, slang* to strike, esp. on the face or head **9** *informal* to turn back the mileometer on (a car) illegally so that its mileage appears less **10** *Brit, slang* to see or notice ▶ HISTORY Medieval Latin *clocca* bell

clock[2] *n* an ornamental design on the side of a sock ▶ HISTORY origin unknown

clock in *or* **on** *vb* to register one's arrival at work on an automatic time recorder

clock out *or* **off** *vb* to register one's departure from work on an automatic time recorder

clock up *vb* to record or reach (a total): *he has now clocked up over 500 games for the club*

clockwise *adv, adj* in the direction in which the hands of a clock rotate

clockwork *n* **1** a mechanism similar to that of a spring-driven clock, as in a wind-up toy **2 like clockwork** with complete regularity and precision

clod *n* **1** a lump of earth or clay **2** *Brit, Austral & NZ* a dull or stupid person ▶ HISTORY Old English > **cloddish** *adj*

clodhopper *n informal* **1** a clumsy person **2 clodhoppers** large heavy shoes

clog *vb* **clogging, clogged 1** to obstruct or become obstructed with thick or sticky matter **2** to

encumber **3** to stick in a mass ▷ *n* **4** a wooden or wooden-soled shoe ▶ HISTORY origin unknown

cloisonné (klwah-**zon**-nay) *n* a design made by filling in a wire outline with coloured enamel ▶ HISTORY French

cloister *n* **1** a covered pillared walkway within a religious building **2** a place of religious seclusion, such as a monastery ▷ *vb* **3** to confine or seclude in or as if in a monastery ▶ HISTORY Medieval Latin *claustrum* monastic cell, from Latin *claudere* to close

cloistered *adj* sheltered or protected

clone *n* **1** a group of organisms or cells of the same genetic constitution that have been reproduced asexually from a single plant or animal **2** *informal* a person who closely resembles another **3** *slang* a mobile phone that has been given the electronic identity of an existing mobile phone, so that calls made on it are charged to that owner ▷ *vb* **cloning, cloned 4** to produce as a clone **5** *informal* to produce near copies of (a person) **6** *slang* to give (a mobile phone) the electronic identity of an existing mobile phone so that calls made on it are charged to that owner ▶ HISTORY Greek *klôn* twig, shoot > **cloning** *n*

close[1] *vb* **closing, closed 1** to shut: *he lay back and closed his eyes* **2** to bar, obstruct, or fill up (an entrance, a hole, etc.): *the blockades had closed major roads, railways and border crossings* **3** to cease or cause to cease giving service: *both stores closed at 9 p.m.; the Shipping Company closed its offices in Bangkok* **4** to end; terminate: *'Never,' she said, so firmly that it closed the subject* **5** (of agreements or deals) to complete or be completed successfully **6** to come closer (to): *he was still in second place but closing fast on the leader* **7** to take hold: *his small fingers closed around the coin* **8** *Stock Exchange* to have a value at the end of a day's trading, as specified: *the pound closed four-and-a-half cents higher* **9** to join the ends or edges of something: *to close a circuit* ▷ *n* **10** the act of closing **11** the end or conclusion: *the close of play* **12** (rhymes with **dose**) *Brit* a courtyard or quadrangle enclosed by buildings **13** *Scot* the entry from the street to a tenement building ▷ See also **close down** ▶ HISTORY Latin *claudere*

close[2] *adj* **1** near in space or time **2** intimate: *we were such close friends in those days* **3** near in relationship: *the dead man seems to have had no close relatives* **4** careful, strict, or searching: *their research will not stand up to close scrutiny* **5** having the parts near together: *a close formation* **6** near to the surface; short: *an NCO's haircut, cropped close on top, shaved clean at sides and back* **7** almost equal: *a close game* **8** not deviating or varying greatly from something: *a close resemblance* **9** confined or enclosed **10** oppressive, heavy, or airless: *damp, close weather* **11** strictly guarded: *he had been placed in close arrest* **12** secretive or reticent **13** miserly; not generous **14** restricted as to public admission or membership ▷ *adv* **15** closely; tightly **16** near or in proximity ▶ HISTORY Old French *clos* > **closely** *adv* > **closeness** *n*

See WORD FOCUS **close**

close

WORD FOCUS

Close is an overused word. Depending on whether you are talking about people or things which are close in distance or in time, the closeness of personal relationships, a closeness in resemblance between two things, or you are referring to a description or translation, you can use various other words as substitutes.

DEFINITION 1
- If you would like to describe something that is close in space, you could try: **adjacent** buildings • **adjoining** stall • **at hand** • keep something **handy** • quite **near** • **nearby** shop • **neighbouring** table
- If you would like to describe something which is close in time, you could try: My birthday is **approaching**. • The time is **at hand**. • Winter is **coming**. • A deal is **imminent**. • **impending** disaster • The day is **near**.

DEFINITION 2
- If you would like to describe people who have a close relationship, you could try: **attached** to one another • **dear** companion • deeply **devoted** couple • too **familiar** • very **friendly** • **intimate** friends • **loving** relationship

DEFINITION 3
- If you are talking about close relatives, you could try: **direct** descendant • **immediate** family • **near** relative

DEFINITION 4
- If you are talking about a strict description or translation, you could try: **accurate** description • **exact** translation • **faithful** rendition • **literal** interpretation • **precise** detail • **strict** account
- If you are talking about careful examination or scrutiny, you could try: **careful** monitoring • **detailed** analysis • **intense** scrutiny • **keen** observation • **rigorous** examination • **thorough** investigation

DEFINITION 5
- If you are talking about something in which the parts are near together, you might use: **compact**

cluster of stars • **concentrated** groups of people • **dense** traffic • in **tight** formation

DEFINITION 6
- If you are talking about something near to the surface, you might use: **cropped** hairstyle • grass cut **short**

DEFINITION 7
- If you are talking about a situation where things are almost equal, you might use: **balanced** game • **even** contest • two **evenly matched** teams • **fifty-fifty** chance (*informal*) • **level** score • **neck and neck** with the competition • **tight** finish

DEFINITION 8
- If you would like to describe people or things that have a resemblance, you could try: **distinct** resemblance • **marked** similarity • **pronounced** similarities to • **strong** resemblance

DEFINITION 9
- If you want to describe something that is enclosed, you might use: **confined** space • **limited** boundaries • **restricted** area

DEFINITION 10
- If you want to describe a heavy, airless atmosphere, you could try: **humid** weather • **muggy** air • **oppressive** atmosphere • **stifling** heat • **stuffy** room

DEFINITION 11
- If you are talking about something that is closely guarded, you might use: **guarded** cell • **strict** supervision • **tight** security

DEFINITION 12
- If you are describing someone secretive or their actions, you could try: **evasive** answer • **guarded** reply • **private** about his personal life • **reticent** about her plans • **uncommunicative** with his ideas • **unforthcoming** about her next project

DEFINITION 13
- If you are describing someone who is careful with money, you could try: **mean** with money • a **miserly** streak • **niggardly** way with money • a **parsimonious** nature • **stingy** employer • **tight** with his cash

---

closed *adj* **1** blocked against entry **2** only admitting a selected group of people; exclusive: *he had a fairly closed circle of friends* **3** not open to question or debate **4** *maths* **a** (of a curve or surface) completely enclosing an area or volume **b** (of a set) made up of members on which a specific operation, such as addition, gives as its result another existing member of the set

closed circuit *n* a complete electrical circuit through which current can flow

closed-circuit television *n* a television system used within a limited area such as a building

close down *vb* **1** to stop operating or working: *the factory closed down many years ago* ▷ *n* **close-down** **2** *Brit & NZ radio, television* the end of a period of broadcasting

closed shop *n* *Brit, Austral & NZ* (formerly) a place of work in which all workers had to belong to a particular trade union

close season *n* **1** the period of the year when it is illegal to kill certain game or fish **2** *sport* the period of the year when there is no domestic competition

close shave *n* *informal* a narrow escape

closet *n* **1** *US & Austral* a small cupboard **2** a small private room **3** short for **water closet** ▷ *adj* **4** private or secret: *a closet homosexual* ▷ *vb* **-eting, -eted** **5** to shut away in private, esp. in order to talk: *he was closeted with the President* ▶ HISTORY Old French *clos* enclosure

close-up *n* **1 a** photograph or film or television shot taken at close range **2** a detailed or intimate

153

view or examination ▷ *vb* **close up 3** to shut entirely: *every other shop front seemed to be closed up* **4** to draw together: *the ranks closed up and marched on* **5** (of wounds) to heal completely

close with *vb* to engage in battle with (an enemy)

closure *n* **1** the act of closing or the state of being closed **2** something that closes or shuts **3** a procedure by which a debate may be stopped and an immediate vote taken **4** *chiefly US* **a** a resolution of a significant event or relationship in a person's life **b** the sense of contentment experienced after such a resolution

clot *n* **1** a soft thick lump formed from liquid **2** *informal* a stupid person ▷ *vb* **clotting, clotted 3** to form soft thick lumps ▶ HISTORY Old English *clott*

cloth *n, pl* **cloths 1** a fabric formed by weaving, felting, or knitting fibres **2** a piece of such fabric used for a particular purpose **3 the cloth** the clergy ▶ HISTORY Old English *clāth*

clothe *vb* **clothing, clothed** *or* **clad 1** to put clothes on **2** to provide with clothes **3** to cover or envelop (something) so as to change its appearance: *a small valley clothed in thick woodland* ▶ HISTORY Old English *clāthian*

clothes *pl n* **1** articles of dress **2** *chiefly Brit* short for **bedclothes** ▶ HISTORY Old English *clāthas*, plural of *clāth* cloth

clothier *n* a person who makes or sells clothes or cloth

clothing *n* **1** garments collectively **2** something that covers or clothes

cloud *n* **1** a mass of water or ice particles visible in the sky **2** a floating mass of smoke, dust, etc. **3** a large number of insects or other small animals in flight **4** something that darkens, threatens, or carries gloom **5 the cloud** a network of servers on the internet used to store data and services **6 in the clouds** not in contact with reality **7 on cloud nine** *informal* elated; very happy **8 under a cloud a** under reproach or suspicion **b** in a state of gloom or bad temper ▷ *vb* **9** to make or become more difficult to see through: *my glasses kept clouding up; mud clouded the water* **10** to confuse or impair: *his judgment was no longer clouded by alcohol* **11** to make or become gloomy or depressed: *insanity clouded the last years of his life* ▶ HISTORY Old English *clūd* rock, hill > **cloudless** *adj*

cloudburst *n* a heavy fall of rain

cloud chamber *n physics* an apparatus for detecting high-energy particles by observing their tracks through a chamber containing a supersaturated vapour

cloudy *adj* **cloudier, cloudiest 1** covered with cloud or clouds **2** (of liquids) opaque or muddy **3** confused or unclear > **cloudily** *adv* > **cloudiness** *n*

clout *n* **1** *informal* a fairly hard blow **2** power or influence ▷ *vb* **3** *informal* to hit hard ▶ HISTORY Old English *clūt* piece of cloth

clove¹ *n* a dried closed flower bud of a tropical tree, used as a spice ▶ HISTORY Latin *clavus* nail

clove² *n* a segment of a bulb of garlic ▶ HISTORY Old English *clufu* bulb

clove³ *vb* a past tense of **cleave¹**

clove hitch *n* a knot used to fasten a rope to a spar or a larger rope

cloven *vb* **1** a past participle of **cleave¹** ▷ *adj* **2** split or divided

cloven hoof *or* **foot** *n* the divided hoof of a pig, goat, cow, or deer

clover *n* **1** a plant with three-lobed leaves and dense flower heads **2 in clover** *informal* in ease or luxury ▶ HISTORY Old English *clāfre*

clown *n* **1** a comic entertainer, usually bizarrely dressed and made up, appearing in the circus **2** an amusing person **3** a clumsy rude person ▷ *vb* **4** to behave foolishly **5** to perform as a clown ▶ HISTORY origin unknown > **clownish** *adj*

cloying *adj* so sweet or pleasurable that it ultimately becomes sickly: *cloying sentimentality* ▶ HISTORY Middle English *cloy* originally to nail, hence, to obstruct > **cloyingly** *adv*

club *n* **1** a group or association of people with common aims or interests **2** the building used by such a group **3** a stout stick used as a weapon **4** a stick or bat used to strike the ball in various sports, esp. golf **5** an establishment or regular event at which people dance to records; disco: *a new weekly club with resident DJ* **6** a building in which members go to meet, dine, read, etc. **7** *chiefly Brit* an organization, esp. in a shop, set up as a means of saving **8** a playing card marked with one or more black trefoil symbols ▷ *vb* **clubbing, clubbed 9** to beat with a club **10 club together** to combine resources or efforts for a common purpose ▶ HISTORY Old Norse *klubba*

club class *n* **1** a class of air travel which is less luxurious than first class but more luxurious than economy class ▷ *adj* **club-class 2** of this class of air travel

club foot *n* a congenital deformity of the foot

club root *n* a fungal disease of cabbages and related plants, in which the roots become thickened and distorted

cluck *n* **1** the low clicking noise made by a hen ▷ *vb* **2** (of a hen) to make a clicking sound **3** to express (a feeling) by making a similar sound: *the landlady was clucking feverishly behind them* ▶ HISTORY imitative

clue *n* **1** something that helps to solve a problem or unravel a mystery **2 not have a clue a** to be completely baffled **b** to be ignorant or incompetent ▷ *adj* **3 clued-up** shrewd and well-informed ▶ HISTORY variant of *clew* ball of thread

clueless *adj slang* helpless or stupid

clump *n* **1** a small group of things or people together **2** a dull heavy tread ▷ *vb* **3** to walk or tread heavily **4** to form into clumps ▶ HISTORY Old English *clympe* > **clumpy** *adj*

clumsy *adj* **-sier, -siest 1** lacking in skill or physical coordination: *an extraordinarily clumsy player* **2** badly made or done **3** said or done without thought or tact: *I took the clumsy hint and left* ▶ HISTORY Middle English *clumse* to benumb > **clumsily** *adv* > **clumsiness** *n*

clung *vb* the past of **cling**

clunk *n* **1** a dull metallic sound ▷ *vb* **2** to make such a sound ▶ HISTORY imitative

cluster *n* **1** a number of things growing, fastened, or occurring close together **2** a number of people or things grouped together **3** a group of two or more consecutive vowels or consonants ▷ *vb* **4** to gather or be gathered in clusters ▶ HISTORY Old English *clyster*

clutch¹ *vb* **1** to seize with or as if with hands or claws **2** to grasp or hold firmly **3** **clutch at** to attempt to get hold or possession of ▷ *n* **4** a device that enables two revolving shafts to be joined or disconnected, esp. one that transmits the drive from the engine to the gearbox in a vehicle **5** the pedal which operates the clutch in a car **6** a firm grasp **7** **clutches a** hands or claws in the act of clutching: *his free kick escaped the clutches of the rival goalkeeper* **b** power or control: *rescued from the clutches of the Gestapo* ▶ HISTORY Old English *clyccan*

clutch² *n* **1** a set of eggs laid at the same time **2** a group, bunch, or cluster: *a clutch of gloomy economic reports* ▶ HISTORY Old Norse *klekja* to hatch

clutter *vb* **1** to scatter objects about (a place) in an untidy manner ▷ *n* **2** an untidy heap or mass of objects **3** a state of untidiness ▶ HISTORY Middle English *clotter*

Clydesdale *n* a heavy powerful carthorse, originally from Scotland

cm centimetre

Cm *chem* curium

Cmdr Commander

CND Campaign for Nuclear Disarmament

CNS *biol* central nervous system

Co *chem* cobalt

CO **1** Colorado **2** Commanding Officer

Co.¹ or **co.** **1** Company **2** **and co** *informal* and the rest of them: *Harold and co*

Co.² County

co- *prefix* **1** together; joint or jointly: *coproduction* **2** indicating partnership or equality: *co-star; copilot* **3** to the same or a similar degree: *coextend* **4** (in mathematics and astronomy) of the complement of an angle: *cosecant* ▶ HISTORY Latin; see COM-

c/o **1** care of **2** *book-keeping* carried over

coach *n* **1** a large comfortable single-decker bus used for sightseeing or long-distance travel **2** a railway carriage **3** a large four-wheeled enclosed carriage, usually horse-drawn **4** a trainer or instructor: *the coach of the Mexican national team* **5** a tutor who prepares students for examinations ▷ *vb* **6** to train or teach ▶ HISTORY from *Kocs*, village in Hungary where horse-drawn coaches were first made > **coaching** *n*

coachman *n, pl* **-men** the driver of a horse-drawn coach or carriage

coachwork *n* the body of a car

coagulate (koh-**ag**-yew-late) *vb* **-lating, -lated** to change from a liquid into a soft semisolid mass; clot ▶ HISTORY Latin *coagulare* > **coagulant** *n* > **coagulation** *n*

coal *n* **1** a compact black or dark brown rock consisting largely of carbon formed from partially decomposed vegetation: a fuel and a source of coke, coal gas, and coal tar **2** one or more lumps of coal **3** **coals to Newcastle** something supplied to a place where it is already plentiful ▶ HISTORY Old English *col*

coalesce (koh-a-**less**) *vb* **-lescing, -lesced** to unite or come together in one body or mass ▶ HISTORY Latin *co-* together + *alescere* to increase > **coalescence** *n* > **coalescent** *adj*

coalface *n* the exposed seam of coal in a mine

coalfield *n* an area rich in deposits of coal

coal gas *n* a mixture of gases produced by the distillation of bituminous coal and used for heating and lighting

coalition (koh-a-**lish**-un) *n* a temporary alliance, esp. between political parties ▶ HISTORY Latin *coalescere* to coalesce

coal scuttle *n* a container for holding coal for a domestic fire

coal tar *n* a black tar, produced by the distillation of bituminous coal, used for making drugs and chemical products

coal tit *n* a small songbird with a black head with a white patch on the nape

coaming *n* a raised frame round a ship's hatchway for keeping out water ▶ HISTORY origin unknown

coarse *adj* **1** rough in texture or structure **2** unrefined or indecent: *coarse humour* **3** of inferior quality ▶ HISTORY origin unknown > **coarsely** *adv* > **coarseness** *n*

coarse fish *n* *Brit* a freshwater fish that is not of the salmon family > **coarse fishing** *n*

coarsen *vb* to make or become coarse

coast *n* **1** the place where the land meets the sea **2** **the coast is clear** *informal* the obstacles or dangers are gone ▷ *vb* **3** to move by momentum or force of gravity, without the use of power **4** to proceed without great effort: *they coasted to a 31–9 win in the pairs* ▶ HISTORY Latin *costa* side, rib > **coastal** *adj*

coastal flooding *n* *geog* a raising of the level of the sea along the coastline caused by unusual tidal action or winds from tropical storms and hurricanes

coastal plain *n* *geog* a low-lying area sloping gently down to the sea, often formed as a result of sedimentary deposition

coaster *n* **1** a small mat placed under a bottle or glass to protect a table **2** *Brit* a small ship used for coastal trade

coastguard *n* **1** an organization which aids shipping, saves lives at sea, and prevents smuggling **2** a member of this

coastline *n* the outline of a coast

coat *n* **1** an outer garment with sleeves, covering the body from the shoulders to below the waist **2** the hair, wool, or fur of an animal **3** any layer that covers a surface ▷ *vb* **4** to cover with a layer ▶ HISTORY Old French *cote*

coat hanger n a curved piece of wood, wire or plastic, fitted with a hook and used to hang up clothes

coating n a layer or film spread over a surface: *a thick coating of breadcrumbs*

coat of arms n the heraldic emblem of a family or organization

coat of mail n *history* a protective garment made of linked metal rings or plates

coax vb 1 to persuade (someone) gently 2 to obtain (something) by persistent coaxing 3 to work on (something) carefully and patiently so as to make it function as desired: *I watched him coax the last few drops of beer out of his glass* ▶ HISTORY obsolete *cokes* a fool

coaxial (koh-**ax**-ee-al) adj 1 *electronics* (of a cable) transmitting by means of two concentric conductors separated by an insulator 2 having a common axis

cob n 1 a male swan 2 a thickset type of horse 3 the stalk of an ear of maize 4 *Brit & Austral* a round loaf of bread 5 *Brit* a hazel tree or hazelnut ▶ HISTORY origin unknown

cobalt n *chem* a brittle hard silvery-white metallic element used in alloys. Symbol: Co ▶ HISTORY Middle High German *kobolt* goblin; from the miners' belief that goblins placed it in the silver ore

cobber n *Austral, NZ, informal* a friend ▶ HISTORY dialect *cob* to take a liking to someone

cobble n a cobblestone

cobbler n a person who makes or mends shoes ▶ HISTORY origin unknown

cobblers pl n *Brit, Austral & NZ, slang* nonsense ▶ HISTORY rhyming slang *cobblers' awls* balls

cobblestone n a rounded stone used for paving ▶ HISTORY from *cob*

cobble together vb **-bling, -bled** to put together clumsily: *a coalition cobbled together from parties with widely differing aims*

cobia (koh-bee-a) n a large dark-striped game fish of tropical and subtropical seas

COBOL n a high-level computer programming language designed for general commercial use ▶ HISTORY *co(mmon) b(usiness) o(riented) l(anguage)*

cobra n a highly venomous hooded snake of tropical Africa and Asia ▶ HISTORY Latin *colubra* snake

cobweb n 1 a web spun by certain spiders 2 a single thread of such a web ▶ HISTORY Old English (*ātor*)*coppe* spider > **cobwebbed** adj > **cobwebby** adj

coca n the dried leaves of a S American shrub which contain cocaine ▶ HISTORY S American Indian *kúka*

Coca-Cola n *trademark* a carbonated soft drink

cocaine n an addictive drug derived from coca leaves, used as a narcotic and local anaesthetic

coccus n, pl **cocci** (**kok**-sigh) *biol* a spherical or nearly spherical bacterium

coccyx (**kok**-six) n, pl **coccyges** (kok-**sije**-eez) *anat* a small triangular bone at the base of the spine in human beings and some apes ▶ HISTORY Greek

kokkux cuckoo, from its likeness to a cuckoo's beak > **coccygeal** adj

cochineal n a scarlet dye obtained from a Mexican insect, used for colouring food ▶ HISTORY Greek *kokkos* kermes berry

cochlea (**kok**-lee-a) n, pl **-leae** (-lee-ee) *anat* the spiral tube in the internal ear, which converts sound vibrations into nerve impulses ▶ HISTORY Greek *kokhlias* snail > **cochlear** adj

cochlear implant n a device that stimulates the acoustic nerve in the inner ear in order to produce some form of hearing in people who are deaf from inner ear disease

cock n 1 a male bird, esp. of domestic fowl 2 a stopcock 3 the hammer of a gun 4 *Brit, informal* friend: used as a term of address ▷ vb 5 to draw back the hammer of (a gun) so that it is ready to fire 6 to lift and turn (part of the body) in a particular direction ▷ See also **cockup** ▶ HISTORY Old English *cocc*

cockabully n a small fresh-water fish of New Zealand ▶ HISTORY Māori *kokopu*

cockade n a feather or rosette worn on the hat as a badge ▶ HISTORY French *coq* cock

cock-a-hoop adj *Brit, Austral & NZ* in very high spirits ▶ HISTORY origin unknown

cock-and-bull story n *informal* an obviously improbable story, esp. one used as an excuse

cockatiel, cockateel n a crested Australian parrot with a greyish-brown and yellow plumage

cockatoo n, pl **-toos** a light-coloured crested parrot of Australia and the East Indies ▶ HISTORY Malay *kakatua*

cockchafer n a large flying beetle ▶ HISTORY COCK + *chafer* beetle

cockerel n a young domestic cock, less than a year old

cocker spaniel n a small spaniel ▶ HISTORY from *cocking* hunting woodcocks

cockeyed adj *informal* 1 crooked or askew 2 foolish or absurd 3 cross-eyed

cockie, cocky n, pl **-kies** *Austral & NZ, informal* a cockatoo

cockle n 1 an edible bivalve shellfish 2 its shell 3 **warm the cockles of one's heart** to make one feel happy ▶ HISTORY Greek *konkhule* mussel

cockleshell n 1 the rounded shell of the cockle 2 a small light boat

cockney n 1 a native of London, esp. of its East End 2 the urban dialect of London or its East End ▷ adj 3 characteristic of cockneys or their dialect ▶ HISTORY Middle English *cokeney* cock's egg, later applied contemptuously to townsmen

cockpit n 1 the compartment in an aircraft for the pilot and crew 2 the driver's compartment in a racing car 3 *naut* a space in a small vessel containing the wheel and tiller 4 the site of many battles or conflicts: *the south of the country is a cockpit of conflicting interests* 5 an enclosure used for cockfights

cockroach n a beetle-like insect which is a household pest ▶ HISTORY Spanish *cucaracha*

cockscomb *n* same as **coxcomb**

cocksure *adj* overconfident or arrogant ▶ HISTORY origin unknown

cocktail *n* **1** a mixed alcoholic drink **2** an appetizer of seafood or mixed fruits **3** any combination of diverse elements: *Central America was a cocktail of death, poverty, and destruction* ▶ HISTORY origin unknown

cockup *Brit & Austral, slang n* **1** something done badly ▷ *vb* **cock up 2** to ruin or spoil

cocky *adj* **cockier, cockiest** excessively proud of oneself > **cockily** *adv* > **cockiness** *n*

coco *n, pl* **-cos** the coconut palm ▶ HISTORY Portuguese: grimace

cocoa *or* **cacao** *n* **1** a powder made by roasting and grinding cocoa beans **2** a hot or cold drink made from cocoa powder ▶ HISTORY from CACAO

coconut *n* **1** the fruit of a type of palm tree (**coconut palm**), which has a thick fibrous oval husk and a thin hard shell enclosing edible white flesh. The hollow centre is filled with a milky fluid (**coconut milk**) **2** the flesh of the coconut

cocoon *n* **1** a silky protective covering produced by a silkworm or other insect larva, in which the pupa develops **2** a protective covering ▷ *vb* **3** to wrap in or protect as if in a cocoon ▶ HISTORY Provençal *coucoun* eggshell

cocotte *n* a small fireproof dish in which individual portions of food are cooked and served ▶ HISTORY French

co-curricular *adj* same as **extracurricular**

cod¹ *n, pl* **cod** *or* **cods 1** a large N Atlantic food fish **2** any of various unrelated Australian fish, such as the Murray cod ▶ HISTORY probably Germanic

cod² *adj Brit, slang* having the character of an imitation or parody: *the chorus were dressed in exuberant cod-medieval costumes* ▶ HISTORY origin unknown

COD cash (in the US collect) on delivery

coda (**kode**-a) *n music* the final part of a musical movement or work ▶ HISTORY Italian: tail

coddle *vb* **-dling, -dled 1** to pamper or overprotect **2** to cook (eggs) in water just below boiling point ▶ HISTORY origin unknown

code *n* **1** a system of letters, symbols, or prearranged signals, by which information can be communicated secretly or briefly: *binary code; morse code* **2** a set of principles or rules: *a code of practice* **3** a system of letters or digits used for identification purposes: *area code; tax code* **4** *law* a body of written law ▷ *vb* **coding, coded 5** to translate or arrange into a code ▶ HISTORY Latin *codex* book, wooden block

codeine (**kode**-een) *n* a drug made mainly from morphine, used as a painkiller and sedative ▶ HISTORY Greek *kōdeia* head of a poppy

codependence *or* **codependency** *n* dependence between two people, groups, or things > **codependent** *adj*

codex (**koh**-dex) *n, pl* **-dices** (-diss-seez) a volume of manuscripts of an ancient text ▶ HISTORY Latin: wooden block, book

codfish *n, pl* **-fish** *or* **-fishes** a cod

codger *n Brit, Austral & NZ, informal* an old man ▶ HISTORY probably variant of *cadger*

codicil (**cod**-iss-ill) *n law* an addition to a will ▶ HISTORY from CODEX

codify (**kode**-if-fie) *vb* **-fies, -fying, -fied** to organize or collect together (rules or procedures) systematically > **codification** *n*

codling *n* a young cod

cod-liver oil *n* an oil extracted from fish, rich in vitamins A and D

codpiece *n history* a bag covering the male genitals, attached to breeches ▶ HISTORY obsolete *cod* scrotum

codswallop *n Brit, Austral & NZ, slang* nonsense ▶ HISTORY origin unknown

coeducation *n* the education of boys and girls together > **coeducational** *adj*

coefficient *n* **1** *maths* a number or constant placed before and multiplying another quantity: *the coefficient of the term 3xyz is 3* **2** *physics* a number or constant used to calculate the behaviour of a given substance under specified conditions

coelacanth (**seel**-a-kanth) *n* a primitive marine fish, thought to be extinct until a living specimen was discovered in 1938 ▶ HISTORY Greek *koilos* hollow + *akanthos* spine

coelenterate (seel-**lent**-a-rate) *n* any invertebrate that has a saclike body with a single opening, such as a jellyfish or coral ▶ HISTORY Greek *koilos* hollow + *enteron* intestine

coeliac disease (**seel**-ee-ak) *n* a disease which makes the digestion of food difficult ▶ HISTORY Greek *koilia* belly

coenobite (**seen**-oh-bite) *n* a member of a religious order in a monastic community ▶ HISTORY Greek *koinos* common + *bios* life

coequal *adj, n* equal

coerce (koh-**urss**) *vb* **-ercing, -erced** to compel or force ▶ HISTORY Latin *co-* together + *arcere* to enclose > **coercion** *n*

coercive *adj* using force or authority to make a person do something against his or her will

coeval (koh-**eev**-al) *adj, n* contemporary ▶ HISTORY Latin *co-* together + *aevum* age > **coevally** *adv*

coexist *vb* **1** to exist together at the same time or in the same place **2** to exist together in peace despite differences > **coexistence** *n* > **coexistent** *adj*

coextensive *adj* covering the same area, either literally or figuratively: *the concepts of 'the nation' and 'the people' are not coextensive*

C of E Church of England

coffee *n* **1** a drink made from the roasted and ground seeds of a tall tropical shrub **2** Also called: **coffee beans** the beanlike seeds of this shrub **3** the shrub yielding these seeds ▷ *adj* **4** medium-brown

■ **WORD HISTORY**

■ 'Coffee' comes, via Italian, from Turkish *kahve*,
■ from Arabic *qahwah*, meaning 'wine' or 'coffee'. 157

coffee bar — coir

coffee bar *n* a café; snack bar

coffee house *n* a place where coffee is served, esp. one that was a fashionable meeting place in 18th-century London

coffee table *n* a small low table

coffee-table book *n* a large expensive illustrated book

coffer *n* **1** a chest for storing valuables **2 coffers** a store of money **3** an ornamental sunken panel in a ceiling or dome ▶ HISTORY Greek *kophinos* basket

cofferdam *n* a watertight enclosure pumped dry to enable construction work or ship repairs to be done

coffin *n* a box in which a corpse is buried or cremated ▶ HISTORY Latin *cophinus* basket

cog *n* **1** one of the teeth on the rim of a gearwheel **2** a gearwheel, esp. a small one **3** an unimportant person in a large organization or process ▶ HISTORY Scandinavian

cogent (koh-jent) *adj* forcefully convincing ▶ HISTORY Latin *co-* together + *agere* to drive > **cogency** *n*

cogitate (koj-it-tate) *vb* **-tating, -tated** to think deeply about (something) ▶ HISTORY Latin *cogitare* > **cogitation** *n* > **cogitative** *adj*

cognac (kon-yak) *n* high-quality French brandy

cognate *adj* **1** derived from a common original form: *cognate languages* **2** related to or descended from a common ancestor ▷ *n* **3** a cognate word or language **4** a relative ▶ HISTORY Latin *co-* same + *gnatus* born > **cognation** *n*

cognition *n formal* **1** the processes of getting knowledge, including perception, intuition and reasoning **2** the results of such a process ▶ HISTORY Latin *cognoscere* to learn > **cognitive** *adj*

cognizance *or* **cognisance** *n formal* **1** knowledge or understanding **2 take cognizance of** to take notice of **3** the range or scope of knowledge or understanding ▶ HISTORY Latin *cognoscere* to learn > **cognizant** *or* **cognisant** *adj*

cognomen (kog-**noh**-men) *n, pl* **-nomens** *or* **-nomina** (-**nom**-min-a) *formal* **1** a nickname **2** a surname **3** an ancient Roman's third name or nickname ▶ HISTORY Latin: additional name

cognoscenti (kon-yo-**shen**-tee) *pl n, sing* **-te** (-tee) connoisseurs ▶ HISTORY obsolete Italian

cogwheel *n* same as **gearwheel**

cohabit *vb* to live together as husband and wife without being married ▶ HISTORY Latin *co-* together + *habitare* to live > **cohabitation** *n*

cohabitation agreement *n law* a legal agreement drawn up between some couples living together to regulate matters such as the conditions of their cohabitation as well as the division of property and any financial arrangements in the event of their splitting up

cohere *vb* **-hering, -hered** **1** to be logically connected and consistent **2** to hold or stick firmly together ▶ HISTORY Latin *co-* together + *haerere* to cling

coherent *adj* **1** logical and consistent **2** capable of intelligible speech **3** cohering or sticking together

4 *physics* (of two or more waves) having the same frequency and a constant fixed phase difference > **coherence** *n*

cohesion *n* **1** the quality of sticking together, being united and working well together **2** *physics* the force that holds together the atoms or molecules in a solid or liquid

cohesive *adj* **1** characterized by sticking together, being united and working well together: *a cohesive society* **2** causing cohesion: *they lacked a cohesive strategy*

cohesiveness *n* **1** the quality of sticking together, being united and working well together **2** *grammar* the clear and logical linking of references in a text that ensures clarity and lack of ambiguity

cohesive tie *n grammar* a word or expression that refers back to or provides a link to a previous reference and helps ensure cohesiveness

cohort *n* **1** a band of associates **2** a tenth part of an ancient Roman Legion ▶ HISTORY Latin *cohors* yard, company of soldiers

coif *n* **1** a close-fitting cap worn in the Middle Ages **2** a hairstyle ▷ *vb* **coiffing, coiffed** **3** to arrange (the hair) ▶ HISTORY Late Latin *cofea* helmet, cap

coiffeur *n* a hairdresser ▶ HISTORY French > **coiffeuse** *fem n*

coiffure *n* a hairstyle ▶ HISTORY French

coil¹ *vb* **1** to wind or be wound into loops **2** to move in a winding course ▷ *n* **3** something wound in a connected series of loops **4** a single loop of such a series **5** a contraceptive device in the shape of a coil, inserted in the womb **6** an electrical conductor wound into a spiral, to provide inductance ▶ HISTORY Old French *coillir* to collect together

coil² *n* **mortal coil** the troubles of the world ▶ HISTORY coined by William Shakespeare

coin *n* **1** a metal disc used as money **2** metal currency collectively ▷ *vb* **3** to invent (a new word or phrase) **4** to make or stamp (coins) **5 coin it in** *or* **coin money** *informal* to make money rapidly ▶ HISTORY Latin *cuneus* wedge

coinage *n* **1** coins collectively **2** the currency of a country **3** a newly invented word or phrase **4** the act of coining

coincide *vb* **-ciding, -cided** **1** to happen at the same time **2** to agree or correspond exactly: *what she had said coincided exactly with his own thinking* **3** to occupy the same place in space ▶ HISTORY Latin *co-* together + *incidere* to occur

coincidence *n* **1** a chance occurrence of simultaneous or apparently connected events **2** a coinciding

coincident *adj* **1** having the same position in space or time **2 coincident with** in exact agreement with

coincidental *adj* resulting from coincidence; not intentional > **coincidentally** *adv*

coir *n* coconut fibre, used in making rope and matting ▶ HISTORY Malayalam (a language of SW India) *kāyar* rope

coitus (koh-it-uss) *or* **coition** (koh-ish-un) *n* sexual intercourse ▶ HISTORY Latin *coire* to meet > **coital** *adj*

coke¹ *n* **1** a solid fuel left after gas has been distilled from coal ▷ *vb* **coking, coked 2** to become or convert into coke ▶ HISTORY probably dialect *colk* core

coke² *n slang* cocaine

Coke *n trademark* short for **Coca-Cola**

col *n* the lowest point of a ridge connecting two mountain peaks ▶ HISTORY French: neck

Col. Colonel

cola *n* **1** a soft drink flavoured with an extract from the nuts of a tropical tree **2** the W African tree whose nuts contain this extract ▶ HISTORY probably variant of W African *kolo* nut

colander *n* a bowl with a perforated bottom for straining or rinsing foods ▶ HISTORY Latin *colum* sieve

cold *adj* **1** low in temperature: *the cold March wind; cans of cold beer* **2** not hot enough: *eat your food before it gets cold!* **3** lacking in affection or enthusiasm **4** not affected by emotion: *the cold truth* **5** dead **6** (of a trail or scent in hunting) faint **7** (of a colour) giving the impression of coldness **8** *slang* unconscious **9** *informal* (of a seeker) far from the object of a search **10** denoting the contacting of potential customers without previously approaching them to establish their interest: *cold mailing* **11 cold comfort** little or no comfort **12 have** *or* **get cold feet** to be or become fearful or reluctant **13 in cold blood** deliberately and without mercy **14 leave someone cold** *informal* to fail to excite or impress someone **15 throw cold water on** *informal* to discourage ▷ *n* **16** the absence of heat **17** a viral infection of the nose and throat characterized by catarrh and sneezing **18** the sensation caused by loss or lack of heat **19 (out) in the cold** *informal* neglected or ignored ▷ *adv* **20** *informal* unrehearsed or unprepared: *he played his part cold* ▶ HISTORY Old English *ceald* > **coldly** *adv* > **coldness** *n*

cold-blooded *adj* **1** callous or cruel **2** *zool* (of all animals except birds and mammals) having a body temperature that varies according to the temperature of the surroundings

cold chisel *n* a toughened steel chisel

cold cream *n* a creamy preparation used for softening and cleansing the skin

cold frame *n* an unheated wooden frame with a glass top, used to protect young plants

cold front *n meteorol* the boundary line between a warm air mass and the cold air pushing it from beneath and behind

cold snap *n* a short period of cold and frosty weather

cold sore *n* a cluster of blisters near the lips, caused by a virus

cold sweat *n informal* coldness and sweating as a bodily reaction to fear or nervousness

cold war *n* **1** *politics* a state of political hostility between two countries without actual warfare **2** *history* **the Cold War** the state of hostility between the American and Soviet blocs after World War II

cole *n* any of various plants such as the cabbage and rape ▶ HISTORY Latin *caulis* cabbage

coleslaw *n* a salad dish of shredded raw cabbage in a dressing ▶ HISTORY Dutch *koolsalade* cabbage salad

coley *n Brit* an edible fish with white or grey flesh ▶ HISTORY perhaps from *coalfish*

colic *n* severe pains in the stomach and bowels ▶ HISTORY Greek *kolon* COLON² > **colicky** *adj*

colitis (koh-lie-tiss) *n* inflammation of the colon, usually causing diarrhoea and lower abdominal pain

collaborate *vb* **-rating, -rated 1** to work with another or others on a joint project **2** to cooperate with an enemy invader ▶ HISTORY Latin *com-* together + *laborare* to work > **collaboration** *n* > **collaborative** *adj* > **collaborator** *n*

collage (kol-lahzh) *n* **1** an art form in which various materials or objects are glued onto a surface to make a picture **2** a picture made in this way **3** a work, such as a piece of music, created by combining unrelated styles ▶ HISTORY French > **collagist** *n*

collagen *n* a protein found in cartilage and bone that yields gelatine when boiled ▶ HISTORY Greek *kolla* glue

collapse *vb* **-lapsing, -lapsed 1** to fall down or cave in suddenly **2** to fail completely: *a package holiday company which collapsed last year* **3** to fall down from lack of strength, exhaustion, or illness: *he collapsed with an asthma attack* **4** to sit down and rest because of tiredness or lack of energy: *she collapsed in front of the telly when she got home* **5** to fold compactly, esp. for storage ▷ *n* **6** the act of falling down or falling to pieces **7** a sudden failure or breakdown ▶ HISTORY Latin *collabi* to fall in ruins

collapsible *adj* able to be folded up for storage

collar *n* **1** the part of a garment round the neck **2** a band of leather, rope, or metal placed around an animal's neck **3** *biol* a ringlike marking around the neck of a bird or animal **4** a cut of meat, esp. bacon, from the neck of an animal **5** a ring or band around a pipe, rod, or shaft ▷ *vb Brit, Austral & NZ, informal* **6** to seize; arrest **7** to catch in order to speak to **8** to take for oneself ▶ HISTORY Latin *collum* neck

collarbone *n* same as **clavicle**

collate *vb* **-lating, -lated 1** to examine and compare carefully **2** to gather together and put in order ▶ HISTORY Latin *com-* together + *latus* brought > **collator** *n*

collateral *n* **1** security pledged for the repayment of a loan **2** a person, animal, or plant descended from the same ancestor as another but through a different line ▷ *adj* **3** descended from a common ancestor but through different lines **4** additional but subordinate: *a spokeswoman said that there was no collateral information to dispute the assurances the government had been given* **5** situated or running side 159 by side: *collateral ridges of mountains* ▶ HISTORY Latin *com-* together + *lateralis* of the side

collateral damage *n mil* unintentional civilian casualties or damage to civilian property caused by military action: *to minimize collateral damage maximum precision in bombing is required*

collation *n* **1** the act or result of collating **2** *formal* a light meal

colleague *n* a fellow worker, esp. in a profession ▶ HISTORY Latin *collega*

collect[1] *vb* **1** to gather together or be gathered together **2** to gather (objects, such as stamps) as a hobby or for study **3** to go to a place to fetch (a person or thing) **4** to receive payments of (taxes, dues, or contributions) **5** to regain control of (oneself or one's emotions) ▶ HISTORY Latin *com-* together + *legere* to gather

collect[2] *n Christianity* a short prayer said during certain church services ▶ HISTORY Medieval Latin *oratio ad collectam* prayer at the assembly

collected *adj* **1** calm and self-controlled **2** brought together into one book or set of books: *the collected works of Dickens*

collection *n* **1** things collected or accumulated **2** the act or process of collecting **3** *art* a number of works of art such as paintings, sculptures, etc. owned by a person, organization, or museum: *the Peggy Guggenheim Collection* **4** a selection of clothes usually presented by a particular designer **5** a sum of money collected, as in church **6** a regular removal of letters from a postbox

collective *adj* **1** done by or characteristic of individuals acting as a group: *the army's collective wisdom regarding peacekeeping* ▷ *n* **2** a group of people working together on an enterprise and sharing the benefits from it > **collectively** *adv*

collective bargaining *n* negotiation between a trade union and an employer on the wages and working conditions of the employees

collective noun *n grammar* a noun that is singular in form but that refers to a group of people or things, as *crowd* or *army*

collective security *n politics* a system of maintaining world peace and security by concerted action on the part of the nations of the world

collectivism *n* the theory that the state should own all means of production > **collectivist** *adj*

collectivize *or* **-vise** *vb* **-vizing, -vized** *or* **-vising, -vised** to organize according to the theory of collectivism > **collectivization** *or* **-visation** *n*

collector *n* **1** a person who collects objects as a hobby **2** a person employed to collect debts, rents, or tickets

colleen *n Irish* a girl ▶ HISTORY Irish Gaelic *cailín*

college *n* **1** an institution of higher or further education that is not a university **2** a self-governing section of certain universities **3** *Brit & NZ* a name given to some secondary schools **4** an organized body of people with specific rights and duties: *the president is elected by an electoral college* **5** a body organized within a particular profession,

concerned with regulating standards **6** the staff and students of a college ▶ HISTORY Latin *collega* colleague

collegian *n* a member of a college

collegiate *adj* **1** of a college or college students **2** (of a university) composed of various colleges

collide *vb* **-liding, -lided** **1** to crash together violently **2** to conflict or disagree ▶ HISTORY Latin *com-* together + *laedere* to strike

collie *n* a silky-haired dog used for herding sheep and cattle ▶ HISTORY Scots, probably from earlier *colie* black

collier *n chiefly Brit* **1** a coal miner **2** a ship designed to carry coal

colliery *n, pl* **-lieries** *chiefly Brit* a coal mine and its buildings

collision *n* **1** a violent crash between moving objects **2** the conflict of opposed ideas or wishes ▶ HISTORY Latin *collidere* to collide

collocate *vb* **-cating, -cated** (of words) to occur together regularly

collocation *n grammar* **1** the way words combine **2** a common combination of words

colloid *n* a mixture of particles of one substance suspended in a different substance ▶ HISTORY Greek *kolla* glue > **colloidal** *adj*

colloquial *adj* suitable for informal speech or writing > **colloquially** *adv*

colloquialism *n* **1** a colloquial word or phrase **2** the use of colloquial words and phrases

colloquium *n, pl* **-quiums** *or* **-quia** an academic conference or seminar ▶ HISTORY Latin; see COLLOQUY

colloquy *n, pl* **-quies** *formal* a conversation or conference ▶ HISTORY Latin *com-* together + *loqui* to speak > **colloquist** *n*

collude *vb* **-luding, -luded** to cooperate secretly or dishonestly with someone ▶ HISTORY Latin *colludere* to conspire

collusion *n* secret or illegal agreement or cooperation > **collusive** *adj*

collywobbles *pl n slang* **1** an intense feeling of nervousness **2** an upset stomach ▶ HISTORY probably from *colic* + *wobble*

cologne *n* a perfumed toilet water ▶ HISTORY *Cologne*, Germany, where it was first manufactured

colon[1] *n, pl* **-lons** the punctuation mark (:) used before an explanation or an example, a list, or an extended quotation ▶ HISTORY Greek *kōlon* limb, clause

colon[2] *n, pl* **-lons** *or* **-la** the part of the large intestine connected to the rectum ▶ HISTORY Greek *kolon* large intestine > **colonic** *adj*

colonel *n* a senior commissioned officer in the army or air force ▶ HISTORY Old Italian *colonnello* column of soldiers > **colonelcy** *n*

colonial *adj* **1** of or inhabiting a colony or colonies **2** of a style of architecture popular in North America in the 17th and 18th centuries: *a colonial mansion* **3** *Austral* of a style of architecture popular during Australia's colonial period ▷ *n* **4** an inhabitant of a colony

colonial goose n NZ, old-fashioned stuffed roast mutton

colonialism n the policy of acquiring and maintaining colonies, esp. for exploitation > **colonialist** n, adj

colonist n a settler in or inhabitant of a colony

colonize or **-nise** vb **-nizing, -nized** or **-nising, -nised 1** to establish a colony in (an area) **2** to settle in (an area) as colonists > **colonization** or **-nisation** n

colonnade n a row of evenly spaced columns, usually supporting a roof ▶ HISTORY French colonne column > **colonnaded** adj

colony n, pl **-nies 1** a group of people who settle in a new country but remain under the rule of their homeland **2** the territory occupied by such a settlement **3** a group of people with the same nationality or interests, forming a community in a particular place: an artists' colony **4** zool a group of the same type of animal or plant living or growing together **5** bacteriol a group of microorganisms when grown on a culture medium ▶ HISTORY Latin colere to cultivate, inhabit

colophon n a publisher's symbol on a book ▶ HISTORY Greek kolophōn a finishing stroke

Colorado beetle n a black-and-yellow beetle that is a serious pest of potatoes ▶ HISTORY Colorado, state of central US

coloration or **colouration** n arrangement of colours: a red coloration of the eyes

coloratura n music **1** a part for a solo singer which has much complicated ornamentation of the basic melody **2** a soprano who specializes in such music ▶ HISTORY obsolete Italian, literally: colouring

colossal adj **1** very large in size: the turbulent rivers and colossal mountains of New Zealand **2** very serious or significant: a colossal legal blunder

colossus n, pl **-si** or **-suses 1** a very large statue **2** a huge or important person or thing ▶ HISTORY Greek kolossos

colostomy n, pl **-mies** an operation to form an opening from the colon onto the surface of the body, for emptying the bowel ▶ HISTORY COLON² + Greek stoma mouth

colour or US **color** n **1** a property of things that results from the particular wavelengths of light which they reflect or give out, producing a sensation in the eye **2** a colour, such as a red or green, that possesses hue, as opposed to black, white, or grey **3** a substance, such as a dye, that gives colour **4** the skin complexion of a person **5** the use of all the colours in painting, drawing, or photography **6** the distinctive tone of a musical sound **7** details which give vividness or authenticity: I walked the streets and absorbed the local colour **8** semblance or pretext: under colour of ▷ vb **9** to apply colour to (something) **10** to influence or distort: anger coloured her judgment **11** to become red in the face, esp. when embarrassed or annoyed **12** to give a convincing appearance to: he coloured his account of what had happened ▷ See also **colours** ▶ HISTORY Latin color

colour bar n racial discrimination by White people against non-White people

colour-blind adj **1** unable to distinguish between certain colours, esp. red and green **2** not discriminating on grounds of skin colour: colour-blind policies > **colour blindness** n

coloured or US **colored** adj having a colour or colours other than black or white: coloured glass bottles; a peach-coloured outfit with matching hat

Coloured or US **Colored** n **1** offensive a person who is not White **2** in South Africa, a person of racially mixed parentage or descent ▷ adj **3** S African of mixed White and non-White parentage

colourful or US **colorful** adj **1** with bright or richly varied colours **2** vivid or distinctive in character

colouring or US **coloring** n **1** the application of colour **2** something added to give colour **3** appearance with regard to shade and colour **4** the colour of a person's complexion

colourless or US **colorless** adj **1** without colour: a colourless gas **2** dull and uninteresting: a colourless personality **3** grey or pallid in tone or hue: a watery sun hung low in the colourless sky

colours or US **colors** pl n **1** the flag of a country, regiment, or ship **2** Brit sport a badge or other symbol showing membership of a team, esp. at a school or college **3 nail one's colours to the mast** to commit oneself publicly to a course of action **4 show one's true colours** to display one's true nature or character

colour sergeant n a sergeant who carries the regimental, battalion, or national colours

colour supplement n Brit an illustrated magazine accompanying a newspaper

colt n **1** a young male horse or pony **2** sport a young and inexperienced player ▶ HISTORY Old English: young ass

coltsfoot n, pl **-foots** a weed with yellow flowers and heart-shaped leaves

columbine n a plant that has brightly coloured flowers with five spurred petals ▶ HISTORY Medieval Latin columbina herba dovelike plant

column n **1** an upright pillar usually having a cylindrical shaft, a base, and a capital **2** a form or structure in the shape of a column: a column of smoke **3** a vertical division of a newspaper page **4** a regular feature in a paper: a cookery column **5** a vertical arrangement of numbers **6** mil a narrow formation in which individuals or units follow one behind the other ▶ HISTORY Latin columna > **columnar** adj

columnist n a journalist who writes a regular feature in a newspaper

com- or **con-** prefix used with a main word to mean together; with; jointly: commingle ▶ HISTORY Latin, from cum with

coma n a state of unconsciousness from which a person cannot be aroused, caused by injury, disease, or drugs ▶ HISTORY Greek kōma heavy sleep

C

Comanche (kom-**man**-chee) *n, pl* **-ches** *or* **-che** a member of a N American Indian people, formerly living in the plains to the east of the Rockies, now chiefly in Oklahoma

comatose *adj* **1** in a coma **2** sound asleep

comb *n* **1** a toothed instrument for disentangling or arranging hair **2** a tool or machine that cleans and straightens wool or cotton **3** a fleshy serrated crest on the head of a domestic fowl **4** a honeycomb ▷ *vb* **5** to use a comb on **6** to search with great care: *police combed the streets for the missing girl* ▶ HISTORY Old English *camb*

combat *n* **1** a fight or struggle ▷ *vb* **-bating, -bated 2** to fight: *a coordinated approach to combating the growing drugs problem* ▶ HISTORY Latin *com-* with + *battuere* to beat > **combative** *adj*

combatant *n* **1** a person taking part in a combat ▷ *adj* **2** engaged in or ready for combat

combat trousers, combats *pl n* loose casual trousers with large pockets on the legs

combe *n* same as **coomb**

comber *n* a long curling wave

combination *n* **1** the act of combining or state of being combined **2** people or things combined **3** the set of numbers or letters that opens a combination lock **4** a motorcycle with a sidecar **5** maths an arrangement of the members of a set into specified groups without regard to order in the group

combine *vb* **-bining, -bined 1** to join together **2** to form a chemical compound ▷ *n* **3** an association of people or firms for a common purpose **4** short for **combine harvester** ▶ HISTORY Latin *com-* together + *bini* two by two

combine harvester *n* a machine used to reap and thresh grain in one process

combining form *n* a part of a word that occurs only as part of a compound word, such as *anthropo-* in *anthropology*

combo *n, pl* **-bos** a small group of jazz musicians

combustible *adj* capable of igniting and burning easily

combustion *n* **1** the process of burning **2** a chemical reaction in which a substance combines with oxygen to produce heat and light ▶ HISTORY Latin *comburere* to burn up

come *vb* **coming, came, come 1** to move towards a place considered near to the speaker or hearer: *come and see me as soon as you can* **2** to arrive or reach: *turn left and continue until you come to a cattle-grid; he came to Britain in the 1920s* **3** to occur: *Christmas comes but once a year* **4** to happen as a result: *no good will come of this* **5** to occur to the mind: *the truth suddenly came to me* **6** to reach a specified point, state, or situation: *a dull brown dress that came down to my ankles; he'd come to a decision* **7** to be produced: *it also comes in other colours* **8 come from** to be or have been a resident or native (of): *my mother comes from Greenock* **9** to become: *it was like a dream come true* **10** Brit & NZ, *informal* to play the part of: *don't come the innocent with me* **11** (subjunctive use) when a specified time arrives: *come next August* **12 as ... as they come**

the most characteristic example of a type: *he's an arrogant swine and as devious as they come* **13 come again?** *informal, spoken* what did you say? **14 come to light** to be revealed ▷ *interj* **15** *spoken* an exclamation expressing annoyance or impatience: *come now!* ▷ See also **come across** ▶ HISTORY Old English *cuman*

come across *vb* **1** to meet or find by accident **2** to communicate the intended meaning or impression **3 come across as** to give a certain impression

comeback *n informal* **1** a return to a former position or status **2** a response or retaliation ▷ *vb* **come back 3** to return, esp. to the memory **4** to become fashionable again

come by *vb* to find or obtain, esp. accidentally: *Graham filled him in on how he came by the envelope*

Comecon (**kom**-meek-on) *n* (formerly) an economic league of Soviet-oriented Communist nations ▶ HISTORY *Co(uncil for) M(utual) Econ(omic Aid)*

comedian *or fem* **comedienne** *n* **1** an entertainer who tells jokes **2** a person who performs in comedy

comedown *n* **1** a decline in status or prosperity **2** *informal* a disappointment ▷ *vb* **come down 3** (of prices) to become lower **4** to reach a decision: *a 1989 court ruling came down in favour of three councils who wanted Sunday trading banned* **5** to be handed down by tradition or inheritance **6 come down with** to begin to suffer from (illness) **7 come down on** to reprimand sharply **8 come down to** to amount to: *at the end the case came down to the one simple issue* **9 come down in the world** to lose status or prosperity

comedy *n, pl* **-dies 1** a humorous film, play, or broadcast **2** such works as a genre **3** the humorous aspect of life or of events **4** (in classical literature) a play which ends happily ▶ HISTORY Greek *kōmos* village festival + *aeidein* to sing

come in *vb* **1** to prove to be: *it came in useful* **2** to become fashionable or seasonable **3** to finish a race (in a certain position) **4** to be received: *reports of more deaths came in today* **5** (of money) to be received as income **6** to be involved in a situation: *where do I come in?* **7 come in for** to be the object of: *she came in for a lot of criticism*

come into *vb* **1** to enter **2** to inherit

comely *adj* **-lier, -liest** *old-fashioned* good-looking ▶ HISTORY Old English *cȳmlīc* beautiful > **comeliness** *n*

come of *vb* to result from: *nothing came of it*

come out *vb* **1** to be made public or revealed: *it was only then that the truth came out* **2** to be published or put on sale: *their latest album which came out last month* **3** Also: **come out of the closet** to reveal something formerly concealed, esp. that one is a homosexual **4** *chiefly Brit* to go on strike **5** to declare oneself: *the report has come out in favour of maintaining child benefit* **6** to end up or turn out: *this wine consistently came out top in our tastings; the figures came out exactly right* **7 come out in** to become covered with (a rash or spots) **8 come out with** to say or disclose: *she came out with a remark that left me speechless* **9** to enter society formally

comestibles *pl n* food ▶ **HISTORY** Latin *comedere* to eat up

comet *n* a heavenly body that travels round the sun, leaving a long bright trail behind it ▶ **HISTORY** Greek *komētēs* long-haired

come to *vb* **1** to regain consciousness **2** to amount to (a total figure)

come up *vb* **1** to be mentioned or arise: *we hope that the difficulties that have arisen in the past will not keep coming up* **2** to be about to happen: *the club has important games coming up* **3 come up against** to come into conflict with **4 come up in the world** to rise in status **5 come up to** to meet a standard **6 come up with** to produce or propose: *he has a knack for coming up with great ideas*

comeuppance *n informal* deserved punishment ▶ **HISTORY** from *come up* (in the sense: to appear before a court)

comfit *n* a sugar-coated sweet ▶ **HISTORY** Latin *confectum* something prepared

comfort *n* **1** a state of physical ease or well-being **2** relief from suffering or grief **3** a person or thing that brings ease **4 comforts** things that make life easier or more pleasant: *the comforts of home* ▷ *vb* **5** to soothe or console **6** to bring physical ease to ▶ **HISTORY** Latin *con-* (intensive) + *fortis* strong > **comforting** *adj*

comfortable *adj* **1** giving comfort; relaxing **2** free from trouble or pain **3** *informal* well-off financially **4** not afraid or embarrassed: *he was not comfortable expressing sympathy* > **comfortably** *adv*

comforter *n* **1** a person or thing that comforts **2** *Brit* a baby's dummy **3** *Brit* a woollen scarf

comfrey *n* a tall plant with bell-shaped blue, purple, or white flowers ▶ **HISTORY** Latin *conferva* water plant

comfy *adj* **-fier, -fiest** *informal* comfortable

comic *adj* **1** humorous; funny **2** of or relating to comedy ▷ *n* **3** a comedian **4** a magazine containing comic strips ▶ **HISTORY** Greek *kōmikos*

comical *adj* causing amusement, often because of being ludicrous or ridiculous: *an enthusiasm comical to behold* > **comically** *adv*

comic opera *n* an opera with speech and singing that tells an amusing story

comic strip *n* a sequence of drawings in a newspaper or magazine, telling a humorous story or an adventure

coming *adj* **1** (of time or events) approaching or next: *in the coming weeks* **2** likely to be important in the future: *he was regarded as a coming man at the Foreign Office* **3 have it coming to one** *informal* to deserve what one is about to suffer ▷ *n* **4** arrival or approach

comity *n, pl* **-ties** *formal* friendly politeness, esp. between different countries ▶ **HISTORY** Latin *comis* affable

comma *n* the punctuation mark (,) indicating a slight pause and used where there is a list of items or to separate the parts of a sentence ▶ **HISTORY** Greek *komma* clause

command *vb* **1** *written* to order or compel **2** to have authority over **3** to deserve and get: *a public figure who commands almost universal respect* **4** to look down over: *the house commands a magnificent view of the sea and the islands* ▷ *n* **5** an authoritative instruction that something must be done **6** the authority to command **7** knowledge; control: *a fluent command of French* **8** a military or naval unit with a specific function **9** a part of a program consisting of a coded instruction to the computer to perform a specified function ▶ **HISTORY** Latin *com-* (intensive) + *mandare* to order

commandant *n* an officer in charge of a place or group of people

commandeer *vb* **1** to seize for military use **2** to take as if by right: *he commandeered the one waiting taxi outside the station* ▶ **HISTORY** Afrikaans *kommandeer*

commander *n* **1** an officer in command of a military group or operation **2** a middle-ranking naval officer **3** a high-ranking member of some orders of knights

commander-in-chief *n, pl* **commanders-in-chief** the supreme commander of a nation's armed forces

commanding *adj* **1** being in charge: *the commanding officer* **2** in a position or situation where success looks certain: *a commanding lead* **3** having the air of authority: *a commanding voice* **4** having a wide view

commandment *n* a divine command, esp. one of the Ten Commandments in the Old Testament

commando *n, pl* **-dos** or **-does a** a military unit trained to make swift raids in enemy territory **b** a member of such a unit ▶ **HISTORY** Dutch *commando* command

commedia dell'arte (kom-**made**-ee-a dell-**art**-tay) *n* a form of improvised comedy popular in Italy in the 16th century, with stock characters and a stereotyped plot ▶ **HISTORY** Italian

commemorate *vb* **-rating, -rated** to honour or keep alive the memory of: *a series of events to commemorate the end of the Second World War* ▶ **HISTORY** Latin *com-* (intensive) + *memorare* to remind > **commemoration** *n* > **commemorative** *adj*

commence *vb* **-mencing, -menced** to begin ▶ **HISTORY** Latin *com-* (intensive) + *initiare* to begin

commencement *n* **1** the beginning; start **2** *US & Canad* a graduation ceremony

commend *vb* **1** to praise in a formal manner: *the judge commended her bravery* **2** to recommend: *he commended the scheme warmly* **3** to entrust: *I commend my child to your care* ▶ **HISTORY** Latin *com-* (intensive) + *mandare* to entrust > **commendable** *adj* > **commendation** *n*

commensurable *adj* **1** measurable by the same standards **2** *maths* **a** having a common factor **b** having units of the same dimensions and being related by whole numbers > **commensurability** *n*

commensurate adj **1** corresponding in degree, size, or value **2** commensurable ▸ HISTORY Latin com- same + mensurare to measure

comment n **1** a remark, criticism, or observation **2** a situation or event that expresses some feeling: a sad comment on the nature of many relationships **3** talk or gossip **4** a note explaining or criticizing a passage in a text **5 no comment** I decline to say anything about the matter ▷ vb **6** to remark or express an opinion ▸ HISTORY Latin commentum invention

commentary n, pl **-taries 1** a spoken accompaniment to an event, broadcast, or film **2** a series of explanatory notes on a subject

commentate vb **-tating, -tated** to act as a commentator

commentator n **1** a person who provides a spoken commentary for a broadcast, esp. of a sporting event **2** an expert who reports on and analyses a particular subject

commerce n **1** the buying and selling of goods and services **2** literary social relations ▸ HISTORY Latin commercium

commercial adj **1** of or engaged in commerce: commercial exploitation of sport **2** sponsored or paid for by an advertiser: commercial radio **3** having profit as the main aim: this is a more commercial, accessible album than its predecessor ▷ n **4** a radio or television advertisement

commercial bank n a bank that is mainly engaged in making short-term loans from funds deposited in current accounts

commercial farming n agriculture the cultivation of crops and rearing of livestock for the purpose of making money

commercialism n **1** the principles and practices of commerce **2** exclusive or inappropriate emphasis on profit

commercialize or **-ise** vb **-izing, -ized** or **-ising, -ised 1** to make commercial **2** to exploit for profit, esp. at the expense of quality ▸ **commercialization** or **-isation** n

commercial traveller n a travelling salesman

commie n, pl **-mies** adj informal, offensive Communist

commingle vb **-gling, -gled** to mix or be mixed

commis adj Brit (of a waiter or chef) apprentice: the commis chef ▸ HISTORY French

commiserate vb **-ating, -ated** (usually foll. by with) to express sympathy or pity (for) ▸ HISTORY Latin com- together + miserari to bewail ▸ **commiseration** n

commissar n (formerly) an official responsible for political education in Communist countries

commissariat n a military department in charge of food supplies ▸ HISTORY Medieval Latin commissarius commissary

commissary n, pl **-saries 1** US a shop supplying food or equipment, as in a military camp **2** a representative or deputy ▸ HISTORY Medieval Latin commissarius official in charge

commission n **1** an order for a piece of work, esp. a work of art or a piece of writing **2** a duty given to a person or group to perform **3** the fee or percentage paid to a salesperson for each sale made **4** a group of people appointed to perform certain duties: a new parliamentary commission on defence **5** the act of committing a sin or crime **6** mil the rank or authority officially given to an officer **7** authority to perform certain duties **8 in** or **out of commission** in or not in working order ▷ vb **9** to place an order for: a report commissioned by the United Nations; a new work commissioned by the BBC Symphony Orchestra **10** mil to give a commission to **11** to prepare (a ship) for active service **12** to grant authority to ▸ HISTORY Latin committere to commit

commissionaire n chiefly Brit a uniformed doorman at a hotel, theatre, or cinema ▸ HISTORY French

commissioned officer n a military officer holding a rank by a commission

commissioner n **1** an appointed official in a government department or other organization **2** a member of a commission

commission of inquiry n an official body set up to investigate an issue and make recommendations as a result

commit vb **-mitting, -mitted 1** to perform (a crime or error) **2** to hand over or allocate: a marked reluctance to commit new money to business **3** to pledge to a cause or a course of action **4** to send (someone) to prison or hospital **5 commit to memory** to memorize **6 commit to paper** to write down ▸ HISTORY Latin committere to join

commitment n **1** dedication to a cause or principle **2** an obligation, responsibility, or promise that restricts freedom of action **3** the act of committing or state of being committed

committal n the official consignment of a person to a prison or psychiatric hospital

committal hearing n law (in criminal cases) a preliminary hearing at a magistrates' court to decide whether there is enough evidence to proceed to a full trial in a higher court

committee n a group of people appointed to perform a specified service or function ▸ HISTORY Middle English committen to entrust

commode n **1** a chair with a hinged flap concealing a chamber pot **2** a chest of drawers ▸ HISTORY French

commodious adj written with plenty of space ▸ HISTORY Latin commodus convenient

commodity n, pl **-ties** something that can be bought or sold ▸ HISTORY Latin commoditas suitability

commodore n **1** Brit a senior commissioned officer in the navy **2** the president of a yacht club ▸ HISTORY probably from Dutch commandeur

common adj **1** frequently encountered: a fairly common plant; this disease is most common in kittens and young cats **2** widespread among people in general: common practice **3** belonging to two or more people: we share common interests **4** belonging

to the whole community: *common property*
5 low-class, vulgar, or coarse **6** *maths* belonging
to two or more: *the lowest common denominator*
7 not belonging to the upper classes: *the common
people* **8 common or garden** *informal* ordinary
▷ *n* **9** a piece of open land belonging to all the
members of a community **10 in common** shared,
in joint use ▷ See also **Commons** ▶ **HISTORY** Latin
communis general **> commonly** *adv*

commonality *n, pl* **-ties 1** the sharing of common
attributes **2** the ordinary people

commonalty *n, pl* **-ties 1** the ordinary people
2 the members of an incorporated society

common cold *n* same as **cold** (sense 17)

commoner *n* a person who does not belong to
the nobility

common fraction *n* same as **simple fraction**

common law *n* **1** the body of law based on
judicial decisions and custom, as distinct from
statute law ▷ *adj* **common-law 2** (of a
relationship) regarded as a marriage through being
long-standing

Common Market *n* a former name for
European Union

common noun *n* *grammar* a noun that refers to
any member of a class of things sharing features in
common, as for example *bird*, *cup*, and *tree*.
Compare **proper noun**

commonplace *adj* **1** so common or frequent as
not to be worth commenting on: *foreign holidays
have now become commonplace* **2** dull or unoriginal:
a commonplace observation ▷ *n* **3** a cliché **4** an
ordinary thing ▶ **HISTORY** translation of Latin *locus
communis* argument of wide application

common room *n* *chiefly Brit & Austral* a sitting
room for students or staff in schools or colleges

commons *pl n* **1** *Brit* shared food or rations
2 short commons reduced rations

Commons *n* **the Commons** same as **House of
Commons**

common sense *n* **1** good practical
understanding ▷ *adj* **common-sense 2** inspired by
or displaying this

common time *n* *music* a time signature with four
crotchet beats to the bar; four-four time: *a dance in
common time*

commonwealth *n* the people of a state or
nation viewed politically

Commonwealth *n* **the Commonwealth a**
Official name: **the Commonwealth of Nations**
an association of sovereign states that are or at
some time have been ruled by Britain **b** the official
title of the federated states of Australia

Commonwealth Caribbean *n* the
English-speaking countries of the Caribbean that
were previously under the control of the United
Kingdom

commotion *n* noisy disturbance ▶ **HISTORY** Latin
com- (intensive) + *movere* to move

communal *adj* **1** belonging to or used by a
community as a whole **2** of a commune
> communally *adv*

communautaire (kom-**myune**-aw-ter) *adj*
supporting the principles of the European Union
▶ **HISTORY** French: community

commune[1] *n* **1** a group of people living together
and sharing possessions and responsibilities **2** the
smallest district of local government in Belgium,
France, Italy, and Switzerland ▶ **HISTORY** Latin
communia things held in common

commune[2] *vb* **-muning, -muned • commune
with a** to experience strong emotion for:
communing with nature **b** to talk intimately with
▶ **HISTORY** Old French *comuner* to hold in common

communicable *adj* **1** capable of being
communicated **2** (of a disease) capable of being
passed on easily

communicant *n* *Christianity* a person who
receives Communion

communicate *vb* **-cating, -cated 1** to exchange
(thoughts) or make known (information or
feelings) by speech, writing, or other means
2 (usually foll. by *to*) to transmit (to): *the reaction of
the rapturous audience communicated itself to the
performers* **3** to have a sympathetic mutual
understanding **4** *Christianity* to receive
Communion ▶ **HISTORY** Latin *communicare* to share
> communicator *n* **> communicative** *adj*

communicating *adj* making or having a direct
connection from one room to another: *the suite is
made up of three communicating rooms; the
communicating door*

communication *n* **1** the exchange of
information, ideas, or feelings **2** something
communicated, such as a message
3 communications means of travelling or
sending messages

communion *n* **1** a sharing of thoughts, emotions,
or beliefs **2 communion with** strong feelings for:
private communion with nature **3** a religious group
with shared beliefs and practices: *the Anglican
communion* ▶ **HISTORY** Latin *communis* common

Communion *n* *Christianity* **1** a ritual
commemorating Christ's Last Supper by the
consecration of bread and wine **2** the consecrated
bread and wine. Also called: **Holy Communion**

communiqué (kom-**mune**-ik-kay) *n* an official
announcement ▶ **HISTORY** French

communism *n* the belief that private ownership
should be abolished and all work and property
should be shared by the community ▶ **HISTORY**
French *communisme* **> communist** *n, adj*

Communism *n* **1** a political movement based
upon the writings of Karl Marx that advocates
communism **2** the political and social system
established in countries with a ruling Communist
Party **> Communist** *n, adj*

community *n, pl* **-ties 1** all the people living in
one district **2** a group of people with shared origins
or interests: *the local Jewish community* **3** a group of
countries with certain interests in common **4** the
public; society **5** a group of interdependent plants
and animals inhabiting the same region ▶ **HISTORY**
Latin *communis* common

community centre *n* a building used by a community for social gatherings or activities

community charge *n* (in Britain) the formal name for **poll tax**

community college *n US & Canad* a nonresidential college offering two-year courses of study

community service *n* organized unpaid work intended for the good of the community: often used as a punishment for minor criminals

commutative *adj maths* giving the same result irrespective of the order of the numbers or symbols

commutator *n* a device used to change alternating electric current into direct current

commute *vb* **-muting, -muted 1** to travel some distance regularly between one's home and one's place of work **2** *law* to reduce (a sentence) to one less severe **3** to substitute **4** to pay (an annuity or pension) at one time, instead of in instalments ▷ *n* **5** a journey made by commuting ▶ HISTORY Latin *com-* mutually + *mutare* to change > **commutable** *adj* > **commutation** *n*

commuter *n* a person who regularly travels a considerable distance to work

compact¹ *adj* **1** closely packed together **2** neatly fitted into a restricted space **3** concise; brief ▷ *vb* **4** to pack closely together ▷ *n* **5** a small flat case containing a mirror and face powder ▶ HISTORY Latin *com-* together + *pangere* to fasten > **compactly** *adv* > **compactness** *n*

compact² *n* a contract or agreement ▶ HISTORY Latin *com-* together + *pacisci* to contract

compact disc *n* a small digital audio disc on which the sound is read by an optical laser system

companion *n* **1** a person who associates with or accompanies someone: *a travelling companion* **2** a woman paid to live or travel with another woman **3** a guidebook or handbook **4** one of a pair > **companionship** *n*

■ **WORD HISTORY**

■ A companion was originally someone you liked
■ enough to share a meal with. The Latin word
■ *companio* consists of the roots *com-*, meaning
■ 'with' or 'together', and *panis*, meaning 'bread'.

companionable *adj written* friendly and pleasant to be with > **companionably** *adv*

companionway *n* a ladder from one deck to another in a ship

company *n, pl* **-nies 1** a business organization **2** a group of actors **3** a small unit of troops **4** the officers and crew of a ship **5** the fact of being with someone: *I enjoy her company* **6** a number of people gathered together **7** a guest or guests **8** a person's associates **9 keep someone company** to accompany someone **10** *written* **part company** to disagree or separate ▶ HISTORY see COMPANION

company sergeant-major *n mil* the senior noncommissioned officer in a company

comparable *adj* **1** worthy of comparison **2** able to be compared (with) > **comparability** *n*

comparative *adj* **1** relative: *despite the importance of his discoveries, he died in comparative poverty*

2 involving comparison: *comparative religion* **3** *grammar* the form of an adjective or adverb that indicates that the quality denoted is possessed to a greater extent. In English the comparative is marked by the suffix *-er* or the word *more* ▷ *vb* **4** the comparative form of an adjective or adverb > **comparatively** *adv*

comparator *n electronics* an electric circuit that compares two signals and gives an indication of the extent of their dissimilarity

compare *vb* **-paring, -pared 1** to examine in order to observe resemblances or differences: *the survey compared the health of three groups of children* **2 compare to** to declare to be like: *one ambulance driver compared the carnage to an air crash* **3** (usually foll. by *with*) to resemble: *his storytelling compares with the likes of Le Carré* **4** to bear a specified relation when examined: *this full-flavoured white wine compares favourably with more expensive French wines* **5 compare notes** to exchange opinions ▷ *n* **6 beyond compare** without equal ▶ HISTORY Latin *com-* together + *par* equal

comparison *n* **1** a comparing or being compared **2** likeness or similarity: *there is no comparison at all between her and Catherine* **3** *grammar* the positive, comparative, and superlative forms of an adjective or adverb **4 in comparison to** or **with** compared to **5 bear** or **stand comparison with** to be able to be compared with (something else), esp. favourably: *his half-dozen best novels can stand comparison with anyone's*

compartment *n* **1** one of the sections into which a railway carriage is sometimes divided **2** a separate section: *filing the information away in some compartment of his mind* **3** a small storage space: *the ice-making compartment of the fridge* ▶ HISTORY French *compartiment*

compass *n* **1** an instrument for finding direction, with a magnetized needle which points to magnetic north **2** limits or range: *within the compass of a normal sized book such a comprehensive survey is not possible* **3 compasses** an instrument, used for drawing circles or measuring distances, consisting of two arms joined at one end ▶ HISTORY Latin *com-* together + *passus* step

compassion *n* a feeling of distress and pity for the suffering or misfortune of another ▶ HISTORY Latin *com-* with + *pati* to suffer

compassionate *adj* showing or having compassion > **compassionately** *adv*

compass rose *n geog* an illustration on a map showing directions as on a compass

compatible *adj* **1** able to exist together harmoniously **2** consistent: *his evidence is fully compatible with the other data* **3** (of pieces of equipment) capable of being used together ▶ HISTORY Late Latin *compati* to suffer with > **compatibility** *n*

compatriot *n* a fellow countryman or countrywoman ▶ HISTORY French *compatriote*

compel *vb* **-pelling, -pelled 1** to force (to be or do something) **2** to obtain by force: *his performance* *compelled attention* ▶ HISTORY Latin *com-* together + *pellere* to drive

compelling *adj* **1** arousing strong interest: *a compelling new novel* **2** convincing: *compelling evidence*

compendious *adj* brief but comprehensive

compendium *n, pl* **-diums** *or* **-dia 1** *Brit* a selection of different table games in one container **2** a concise but comprehensive summary ▶ HISTORY Latin: a saving, literally: something weighed

compensate *vb* **-sating, -sated 1** to make amends to (someone), esp. for loss or injury **2** to cancel out the effects of (something): *the car's nifty handling fails to compensate for its many flaws* **3** to serve as compensation for (injury or loss) ▶ HISTORY Latin *compensare* > **compensatory** *adj*

compensation *n* **1** payment made as reparation for loss or injury **2** the act of making amends for something

compere *Brit, Austral & NZ n* **1** a person who introduces a stage, radio, or television show ▷ *vb* **-pering, -pered 2** to be the compere of ▶ HISTORY French: godfather

compete *vb* **-peting, -peted 1** to take part in (a contest or competition) **2** to strive (to achieve something or to be successful): *able to compete on the international market* ▶ HISTORY Latin *com-* together + *petere* to seek

competence *or* **competency** *n* **1** the ability to do something well or effectively **2** a sufficient income to live on **3** the state of being legally competent or qualified

competent *adj* **1** having sufficient skill or knowledge: *he was a very competent engineer* **2** suitable or sufficient for the purpose: *it was a competent performance, but hardly a remarkable one* **3** having valid legal authority: *lawful detention after conviction by a competent court* ▶ HISTORY Latin *competens*

competition *n* **1** the act of competing; rivalry: *competition for places was keen* **2** an event in which people compete **3** the opposition offered by competitors **4** people against whom one competes

competitive *adj* **1** involving rivalry: *the increasingly competitive computer industry* **2** characterized by an urge to compete: *her naturally competitive spirit* **3** of good enough value to be successful against commercial rivals: *we offer worldwide flights at competitive prices* > **competitiveness** *n*

competitor *n* a person, team, or firm that competes

compile *vb* **-piling, -piled 1** to collect and arrange (information) from various sources **2** *computers* to convert (commands for a computer) from the language used by the person using it into machine code suitable for the computer, using a compiler ▶ HISTORY Latin *com-* together + *pilare* to thrust down, pack > **compilation** *n*

compiler *n* **1** a person who compiles information **2** a computer program which converts a high-level

programming language into the machine language used by a computer

complacency *n* extreme self-satisfaction > **complacent** *adj* > **complacently** *adv*

complain *vb* **1** to express resentment or displeasure **2 complain of** to state that one is suffering from a pain or illness: *he complained of breathing trouble and chest pains* **3** to make a formal protest: *he complained to the police about his rowdy neighbours* ▶ HISTORY Latin *com-* (intensive) + *plangere* to bewail

complainant *n law* a plaintiff

complaint *n* **1** the act of complaining **2** a reason for complaining **3** a mild illness **4** a formal protest

complaisant (kom-**play**-zant) *adj* willing to please or oblige ▶ HISTORY Latin *complacere* to please greatly > **complaisance** *n*

complement *n* **1** a person or thing that completes something **2** a complete amount or number: *a full complement of staff nurses and care assistants* **3** the officers and crew needed to man a ship **4** *grammar* a word or words added to the verb to complete the meaning of the predicate in a sentence, as *a fool* in *He is a fool* or *that he would come* in *I hoped that he would come* **5** *maths* the angle that when added to a specified angle produces a right angle ▷ *vb* **6** to complete or form a complement to ▶ HISTORY Latin *com-* (intensive) + *plere* to fill

complementary *adj* **1** forming a complete or balanced whole **2** forming a complement

complementary angle *n geom* an angle that is the difference between a given angle and a right angle: *the acute angles of a right-angled triangle are complementary angles*

complementary medicine *n* same as **alternative medicine**

complete *adj* **1** thorough; absolute: *it was a complete shambles* **2** perfect in quality or kind: *he is the complete modern footballer* **3** finished **4** having all the necessary parts **5 complete with** having as an extra feature or part: *a mansion complete with swimming pool* ▷ *vb* **-pleting, -pleted 6** to finish **7** to make whole or perfect **8 complete the square** *maths* to write a quadratic expression in a form in which the variable appears in a squared term ▶ HISTORY Latin *complere* to fill up > **completely** *adv* > **completion** *n*

complete flower *n biol* a flower with sepals, petals, stamens, and carpels

complex *adj* **1** made up of interconnected parts **2** intricate or complicated **3** *maths* of or involving complex numbers ▷ *n* **4** a whole made up of related parts: *a leisure complex including a gymnasium, squash courts, and a 20-metre swimming pool* **5** *psychoanal* a group of unconscious feelings that influences a person's behaviour **6** *informal* an obsession or phobia: *I have never had a complex about my height* ▶ HISTORY Latin *com-* together + *plectere* to braid

complex fraction *n maths* a fraction in which the numerator or denominator or both contain fractions

complexion n 1 the colour and general appearance of the skin of a person's face 2 character or nature: *the political complexion of the government* ▸ HISTORY Latin *complexio* a combination

complexity n, pl **-ties** 1 the state or quality of being intricate or complex 2 something complicated

complex number n any number of the form $a + bi$, where a and b are real numbers and $i = \sqrt{-1}$

complex sentence n grammar a sentence containing at least one main clause and one subordinate clause, as in *call me when you get back*

compliance n 1 complying 2 a tendency to do what others want > **compliant** adj

complicate vb **-cating, -cated** to make or become complex or difficult to deal with ▸ HISTORY Latin *complicare* to fold together

complication n 1 something which makes a situation more difficult to deal with: *an added complication is the growing concern for the environment* 2 a medical condition arising as a consequence of another

complicity n, pl **-ties** the fact of being an accomplice in a crime

compliment n 1 an expression of praise 2 **compliments** formal greetings ▷ vb 3 to express admiration for ▸ HISTORY Italian *complimento*

complimentary adj 1 expressing praise 2 free of charge: *a complimentary drink*

comply vb **-plies, -plying, -plied** to act in accordance (with a rule, order, or request) ▸ HISTORY Spanish *cumplir* to complete

component n 1 a constituent part or feature of a whole 2 *maths* one of a set of two or more vectors whose resultant is a given vector ▷ adj 3 forming or functioning as a part or feature: *over 60 component parts* ▸ HISTORY Latin *componere* to put together

comport vb formal 1 to behave (oneself) in a specified way 2 **comport with** to suit or be appropriate to ▸ HISTORY Latin *comportare* to collect > **comportment** n

compose vb **-posing, -posed** 1 to put together or make up 2 to be the component elements of 3 to create (a musical or literary work) 4 to calm (oneself) 5 to arrange artistically 6 *printing* to set up (type) ▸ HISTORY Latin *componere* to put in place

composed adj (of people) in control of their feelings

composer n a person who writes music

composite adj 1 made up of separate parts 2 (of a plant) with flower heads made up of many small flowers, such as the dandelion 3 *maths* capable of being factorized: *a composite function* ▷ n 4 something composed of separate parts 5 a composite plant ▸ HISTORY Latin *compositus* well arranged

Composite adj of a style of classical architecture which combines elements of the Ionic and Corinthian styles

composite cone n geol a steep cone-shaped volcano composed of alternate layers of viscous lava and pyroclastic material. Also called: **strato-volcano**

composite school n Canad a secondary school which offers both academic courses and vocational training

composite volcano n geol a cone-shaped volcano with sloping sides built by successive eruptions from a long central pipe system through which magma from a reservoir deep in the Earth's crust rises to the surface

composition n 1 the act of putting together or composing 2 something composed 3 the things or parts which make up a whole 4 a work of music, art, or literature 5 the harmonious arrangement of the parts of a work of art 6 a written exercise; an essay 7 *printing* the act or technique of setting up type

compositor n a person who arranges type for printing

compos mentis adj sane ▸ HISTORY Latin

compost n 1 a mixture of decaying plants and manure, used as a fertilizer 2 soil mixed with fertilizer, used for growing plants ▷ vb 3 to make (vegetable matter) into compost ▸ HISTORY Latin *compositus* put together

composure n the state of being calm or unworried

compote n fruit stewed with sugar or in a syrup ▸ HISTORY French

compound[1] n 1 *chem* a substance that contains atoms of two or more chemical elements held together by chemical bonds 2 any combination of two or more parts, features, or qualities 3 a word formed from two existing words or combining forms ▷ vb 4 to combine so as to create a compound 5 to make by combining parts or features: *the film's score is compounded from surging strings, a heavenly chorus and jazzy saxophones* 6 to intensify by an added element: *the problems of undertaking relief work are compounded by continuing civil war* 7 *law* to agree not to prosecute in return for payment: *to compound a crime* ▷ adj 8 composed of two or more parts or elements 9 *music* with a time in which the number of beats per bar is a multiple of three: *such tunes are usually in a form of compound time, for example six-four* ▸ HISTORY Latin *componere* to put in order > **compoundable** adj

compound[2] n a fenced enclosure containing buildings, such as a camp for prisoners of war ▸ HISTORY Malay *kampong* village

compound events pl n *maths* (in probability) an event in which two or more items are used to generate outcome

compound fracture n a fracture in which the broken bone pierces the skin

compound interest n interest paid on a sum and its accumulated interest

compound sentence n grammar a sentence containing at least two independent clauses usually joined by a coordinating conjunction, as in *I love them and they love me*

comprehend *vb* 1 to understand 2 to include
▶ HISTORY Latin *comprehendere*
> **comprehensible** *adj*

comprehension *n* 1 understanding 2 inclusion

comprehensive *adj* 1 of broad scope or content 2 (of car insurance) providing protection against most risks, including third-party liability, fire, theft, and damage 3 *Brit* of the comprehensive school system ▷ *n* 4 *Brit* a comprehensive school

comprehensive school *n Brit* a secondary school for children of all abilities

compress *vb* 1 to squeeze together 2 to condense ▷ *n* 3 a cloth or pad applied firmly to some part of the body to cool inflammation or relieve pain
▶ HISTORY Latin *comprimere*

compression *n* 1 the act of compressing 2 the reduction in volume and increase in pressure of the fuel mixture in an internal-combustion engine before ignition

compressional plate boundary *n geol* a place where the edge of part of the earth's crust passes over the edge of another part. See also **destructive plate boundary**

compressor *n* a device that compresses a gas

comprise *vb* -prising, -prised 1 to be made up of: *the group comprised six French diplomats, five Italians and three Bulgarians* 2 to form or make up: *women comprised 57 per cent of all employees, but less than 10 per cent of managers* ▶ HISTORY French *compris* included

compromise (kom-prom-mize) *n* 1 settlement of a dispute by concessions on each side: *everyone pleaded for compromise; the compromise was only reached after hours of hard bargaining* 2 the terms of such a settlement 3 something midway between different things ▷ *vb* -mising, -mised 4 to settle (a dispute) by making concessions 5 to put (oneself or another person) in a dishonourable position ▷ *adj* 6 being, or having the nature of, a compromise: *a compromise solution* ▶ HISTORY Latin *compromittere* to promise at the same time
> **compromising** *adj*

comptroller *n* a financial controller

compulsion *n* 1 an irresistible urge to perform some action 2 compelling or being compelled
▶ HISTORY Latin *compellere* to compel

compulsive *adj* 1 resulting from or acting from a compulsion 2 irresistible or absorbing
> **compulsively** *adv*

compulsory *adj* required by regulations or laws

compulsory purchase *n* the enforced purchase of a property by a local authority or government department

compunction *n* a feeling of guilt or regret
▶ HISTORY Latin *compungere* to sting

computation *n* a calculation involving numbers or quantities > **computational** *adj*

compute *vb* -puting, -puted to calculate (an answer or result), often by using a computer
▶ HISTORY Latin *computare*

computer *n* an electronic device that processes data according to a set of instructions

computer-aided manufacture *n computing* the use of computers to automate manufacturing processes

computer game *n* a game played on a home computer by manipulating a controller in response to the graphics on the screen

computerize *or* -ise *vb* -izing, -ized *or* -ising, -ised 1 to equip with a computer 2 to control or perform (operations) by means of a computer
> **computerization** *or* -isation *n*

computing *n* 1 the activity of using computers and writing programs for them 2 the study of computers and their application

comrade *n* 1 a fellow member of a union or a socialist political party 2 a companion ▶ HISTORY French *camarade* > **comradely** *adj*
> **comradeship** *n*

con¹ *informal n* 1 same as **confidence trick** ▷ *vb* **conning, conned** 2 to swindle or defraud

con² *n* See **pros and cons** ▶ HISTORY Latin *contra* against

con³ *n slang* a convict

Con *politics* Conservative

con- *prefix* See **com-**

concatenation *n formal* a series of linked events ▶ HISTORY Latin *com-* together + *catena* chain

concave *adj* curving inwards like the inside surface of a ball ▶ HISTORY Latin *concavus* arched
> **concavity** *n*

conceal *vb* 1 to cover and hide 2 to keep secret
▶ HISTORY Latin *com-* (intensive) + *celare* to hide
> **concealment** *n*

concede *vb* -ceding, -ceded 1 to admit (something) as true or correct 2 to give up or grant (something, such as a right) 3 to acknowledge defeat in (a contest or argument) ▶ HISTORY Latin *concedere*

conceit *n* 1 an excessively high opinion of oneself 2 *literary* a far-fetched and clever comparison
▶ HISTORY See CONCEIVE

conceited *adj* having an excessively high opinion of oneself > **conceitedness** *n*

conceivable *adj* capable of being understood, believed, or imagined > **conceivably** *adv*

conceive *vb* -ceiving, -ceived 1 to imagine or think 2 to consider in a certain way: *we must do what we conceive to be right* 3 to form in the mind 4 to become pregnant ▶ HISTORY Latin *concipere* to take in

concentrate *vb* -trating, -trated 1 to focus all one's attention, thoughts, or efforts on something: *she tried hard to concentrate, but her mind kept flashing back to the previous night* 2 to bring or come together in large numbers or amounts in one place: *a flawed system that concentrates power in the hands of the few* 3 to make (a liquid) stronger by removing water from it ▷ *n* 4 a concentrated substance ▶ HISTORY Latin *com-* same + *centrum* centre > **concentrated** *adj*

concentrated acid *n chem* an acid with a large number of acid molecules and few water molecules

concentration *n* **1** intense mental application **2** the act of concentrating **3** something that is concentrated **4** the amount or proportion of a substance in a mixture or solution

concentration camp *n* a prison camp for civilian prisoners, as in Nazi Germany

concentric *adj* having the same centre: *concentric circles* ▶ HISTORY Latin *com-* same + *centrum* centre

concept *n* an abstract or general idea: *one of the basic concepts of quantum theory* ▶ HISTORY Latin *concipere* to conceive

conception *n* **1** a notion, idea, or plan **2** the fertilization of an egg by a sperm in the Fallopian tube followed by implantation in the womb **3** origin or beginning: *the gap between the conception of an invention and its production* ▶ HISTORY Latin *concipere* to conceive

conceptual *adj* of or based on concepts

conceptualize *or* **-ise** *vb* **-izing, -ized** *or* **-ising, -ised** to form a concept or idea of
> **conceptualization** *or* **-isation** *n*

concern *n* **1** anxiety or worry: *the current concern over teenage pregnancies* **2** something that is of interest or importance to a person **3** regard or interest: *a scrupulous concern for client confidentiality* **4** a business or firm ▷ *vb* **5** to worry or make anxious **6** to involve or interest: *he had converted the building into flats without concerning himself with the niceties of planning permission* **7** to be relevant or important to ▶ HISTORY Latin *com-* together + *cernere* to sift

concerned *adj* **1** interested or involved: *I have spoken to the person concerned and he has no recollection of saying such a thing* **2** worried or anxious: *we are increasingly concerned for her safety*

concerning *prep* about; regarding

concert *n* **1** a performance of music by players or singers in front of an audience **2** **in concert a** working together **b** (of musicians or singers) performing live ▶ HISTORY Latin *com-* together + *certare* strive

concerted *adj* decided or planned by mutual agreement: *a concerted effort*

concertina *n* **1** a small musical instrument similar to an accordion ▷ *vb* **-naing, -naed** **2** to collapse or fold up like a concertina ▶ HISTORY from *concert*

concerto (kon-**chair**-toe) *n*, *pl* **-tos** *or* **-ti** (-tee) a large-scale composition for an orchestra and one or more soloists ▶ HISTORY Italian

concert pitch *n* the internationally agreed pitch to which concert instruments are tuned for performance

concession *n* **1** any grant of rights, land, or property by a government, local authority, or company **2** a reduction in price for a certain category of person: *fare concessions for senior citizens* **3** the act of yielding or conceding **4** something conceded **5** *Canad* **a** a land subdivision in a township survey **b** same as **concession road**

▶ HISTORY Latin *concedere* to concede
> **concessionary** *adj*

concessionaire *n* someone who holds a concession

concession road *n Canad* one of a series of roads separating concessions in a township

conch *n*, *pl* **conchs** *or* **conches** **1** a marine mollusc with a large brightly coloured spiral shell **2** its shell ▶ HISTORY Greek *konkhē* shellfish

concierge (kon-see-**airzh**) *n* (esp. in France) a caretaker in a block of flats ▶ HISTORY French

conciliate *vb* **-ating, -ated** to try to end a disagreement with or pacify (someone) ▶ HISTORY Latin *conciliare* to bring together > **conciliator** *n*

conciliation *n* **1** the act of conciliating **2** a method of helping the parties in a dispute to reach agreement, esp. divorcing or separating couples to part amicably

conciliatory *adj* intended to end a disagreement

concise *adj* brief and to the point ▶ HISTORY Latin *concidere* to cut short > **concisely** *adv*
> **conciseness** *or* **concision** *n*

conclave *n* **1** a secret meeting **2** *RC Church* a private meeting of cardinals to elect a new pope ▶ HISTORY Latin *clavis* key

conclude *vb* **-cluding, -cluded** **1** to decide by reasoning: *the investigation concluded that key data for the paper were faked* **2** to come or bring to an end: *the festival concludes on December 19th* **3** to arrange or settle finally: *officials have refused to comment on the failure to conclude an agreement* ▶ HISTORY Latin *concludere*

conclusion *n* **1** a final decision, opinion, or judgment based on reasoning: *the obvious conclusion is that something is being covered up* **2** end or ending **3** outcome or result: *if you take that strategy to its logical conclusion you end up with communism* **4** **in conclusion** finally **5** **jump to conclusions** to come to a conclusion too quickly, without sufficient thought or evidence

conclusive *adj* putting an end to doubt: *there is no conclusive proof of this* > **conclusively** *adv*

concoct *vb* **1** to make by combining different ingredients **2** to invent or make up (a story or plan) ▶ HISTORY Latin *coquere* to cook > **concoction** *n*

concomitant *adj* **1** existing or along with (something else): *the concomitant health gains* ▷ *n* **2** something which is concomitant ▶ HISTORY Latin *com-* with + *comes* companion

concord *n* **1** agreement or harmony **2** peaceful relations between nations **3** *music* a harmonious combination of musical notes ▶ HISTORY Latin *com-* same + *cor* heart > **concordant** *adj*

concordance *n* **1** a state of harmony or agreement **2** an alphabetical list of words in a literary work, with the context and often the meaning

concordat *n formal* a treaty or agreement, such as one between the Vatican and another state ▶ HISTORY Latin *concordatum* something agreed

concourse *n* **1** a large open space in a public place, where people can meet: *a crowded concourse at*

Heathrow airport **2** a crowd ▶ **HISTORY** Latin *concurrere* to run together

concrete *n* **1** a building material made of cement, sand, stone, and water that hardens to a stonelike mass ▷ *vb* **-creting, -creted 2** to cover with concrete ▷ *adj* **3** made of concrete **4** specific as opposed to general **5** relating to things that can be perceived by the senses, as opposed to abstractions ▶ **HISTORY** Latin *concrescere* to grow together

concrete noun *n grammar* a noun that refers to a physical object, substance, or being, as for example *shoe*, *water*, or *horse*, rather than to a quality, state, or concept. Compare **abstract noun**

concretion *n* **1** a solidified mass **2** the act of solidifying

concubine (**kon**-kew-bine) *n* **1** *old-fashioned* a woman living with a man as his wife, but not married to him **2** a secondary wife in polygamous societies ▶ **HISTORY** Latin *concumbere* to lie together > **concubinage** *n*

concupiscence (kon-**kew**-piss-enss) *n formal* strong sexual desire ▶ **HISTORY** Latin *concupiscere* to covet > **concupiscent** *adj*

concur *vb* **-curring, -curred** to agree; be in accord ▶ **HISTORY** Latin *concurrere* to run together

concurrence *n* **1** agreement **2** simultaneous occurrence

concurrent *adj* **1** taking place at the same time or place **2** meeting at, approaching, or having a common point: *concurrent lines* **3** in agreement > **concurrently** *adv*

concurrent power *n* **1** a power shared by two authorities **2** (in Australia) a power that may be exercised by both the Commonwealth and the States under the Constitution

concuss *vb* to injure (the brain) by a fall or blow ▶ **HISTORY** Latin *concutere* to disturb greatly

concussion *n* **1** a brain injury caused by a blow or fall, usually resulting in loss of consciousness **2** violent shaking

concyclic *adj geom* (of points) lying on the same circle

condemn *vb* **1** to express strong disapproval of **2** to pronounce sentence on in a court of law **3** to force into a particular state: *a system that condemns most of our youngsters to failure* **4** to judge or declare (something) unfit for use **5** to indicate the guilt of: *everything the man had said condemned him, morally if not technically* ▶ **HISTORY** Latin *condemnare* > **condemnation** *n* > **condemnatory** *adj*

condensation *n* **1** anything that has condensed from a vapour, esp. on a window **2** the act of condensing, or the state of being condensed

condense *vb* **-densing, -densed 1** to express in fewer words **2** to increase the density of; concentrate **3** to change from a gas to a liquid or solid ▶ **HISTORY** Latin *condensare*

condenser *n* **1** an apparatus for reducing gases to their liquid or solid form by the removal of heat **2** same as **capacitor 3** a lens that concentrates light

condescend *vb* **1** to behave patronizingly towards one's supposed inferiors **2** to do something as if it were beneath one's dignity ▶ **HISTORY** Church Latin *condescendere* > **condescending** *adj* > **condescension** *n*

condiment *n* any seasoning for food, such as salt, pepper, or sauces ▶ **HISTORY** Latin *condire* to pickle

condition *n* **1** a particular state of being: *the human condition; the van is in very poor condition* **2 conditions** circumstances: *worsening weather conditions; the government pledged to improve living and working conditions* **3** a necessary requirement for something else to happen: *food is a necessary condition for survival* **4** a restriction or a qualification **5** a term of an agreement: *the conditions of the lease are set out* **6** state of physical fitness, esp. good health: *she is in a serious condition in hospital; out of condition* **7** an ailment: *a heart condition* **8 on condition that** provided that ▷ *vb* **9** to accustom or alter the reaction of (a person or animal) to a particular stimulus or situation **10** to treat with a conditioner **11** to make fit or healthy **12** to influence or determine the form that something takes: *he argued that the failure of Latin American industry was conditioned by international economic structures* ▶ **HISTORY** Latin *con-* together + *dicere* to say *adj*

conditional *adj* **1** depending on other factors **2** *grammar* expressing a condition on which something else depends, for example 'If he comes' is a conditional clause in the sentence 'If he comes I shall go'

conditioner *n* a thick liquid used when washing to make hair or clothes feel softer

conditioning *n psychol* the process by which the behaviour of an animal or person becomes dependent on an event occurring in the immediate environment

condolence *n* sympathy expressed for someone in grief or pain ▶ **HISTORY** Latin *com-* together + *dolere* to grieve > **condole** *vb*

condom *n* a rubber sheath worn on the penis or in the vagina during sexual intercourse to prevent conception or infection ▶ **HISTORY** origin unknown

condominium *n, pl* **-ums 1** *Austral, US & Canad* **a** an apartment building in which each apartment is individually owned **b** an apartment in such a building **2** joint rule of a state by two or more other states ▶ **HISTORY** Latin *com-* together + *dominium* ownership

condone *vb* **-doning, -doned** to overlook or forgive (an offence or wrongdoing) ▶ **HISTORY** Latin *com-* (intensive) + *donare* to donate

condor *n* a very large rare S American vulture ▶ **HISTORY** S American Indian *kuntur*

conducive *adj* (often foll. by *to*) likely to lead to or produce (a result) ▶ **HISTORY** Latin *com-* together + *ducere* to lead

conduct *n* **1** behaviour **2** the management or handling of an activity or business ▷ *vb* **3** to carry out: *the police are conducting an investigation into the affair* **4** to behave (oneself) **5** to control (an orchestra or choir) by the movements of the hands or a baton **6** to accompany and guide (people or a party): *a conducted tour* **7** to transmit (heat or electricity) ▶ HISTORY Latin *com-* together + *ducere* to lead

conductance *n* the ability of a specified body to conduct electricity

conduction *n* the transmission of heat or electricity

conductivity *n* the property of transmitting heat, electricity, or sound

conductor *n* **1** a person who conducts an orchestra or choir **2** an official on a bus who collects fares **3** *US, Canad & NZ* a railway official in charge of a train **4** something that conducts electricity or heat > **conductress** *fem n*

conduit (**kon-dew-it**) *n* **1** a route or system for transferring things from one place to another: *a conduit for smuggling cocaine into the United States* **2** a channel or tube for carrying a fluid or electrical cables **3** a means of access or communication ▶ HISTORY Latin *conducere* to lead

cone *n* **1** a geometric solid consisting of a circular or oval base, tapering to a point **2** a cone-shaped wafer shell used to contain ice cream **3** the scaly fruit of a conifer tree **4** *Brit, Austral & NZ* a plastic cone used as a temporary traffic marker on roads **5** a type of cell in the retina, sensitive to colour and bright light ▶ HISTORY Greek *kōnus* pine cone, geometrical cone

coney *n* same as **cony**

confab *n* *informal* a conversation

confection *n* *written* **1** any sweet food, such as a cake or a sweet **2** *old-fashioned* an elaborate piece of clothing ▶ HISTORY Latin *confectio* a preparing

confectioner *n* a person who makes or sells confectionery

confectionery *n, pl* **-eries** **1** *written* sweets and chocolates collectively: *a drop in confectionery sales* **2** the art or business of a confectioner

confederacy *n, pl* **-cies** a union of states or people joined for a common purpose ▶ HISTORY Late Latin *confoederatio* agreement > **confederal** *adj*

confederate *n* **1** a state or individual that is part of a confederacy **2** an accomplice or conspirator ▷ *adj* **3** united; allied ▷ *vb* **-ating, -ated** **4** to unite in a confederacy ▶ HISTORY Late Latin *confoederare* to unite by a league

Confederate *adj* of or supporting those American states which withdrew from the USA in 1860–61, leading to the US Civil War

confederation *n* **1** a union or alliance of states or groups **2** confederating or being confederated **3** a federation

confer *vb* **-ferring, -ferred** **1** to discuss together **2** to grant or give: *the power conferred by wealth* ▶ HISTORY Latin *com-* together + *ferre* to bring > **conferment** *n* > **conferrable** *adj*

conference *n* a meeting for formal consultation or discussion ▶ HISTORY Medieval Latin *conferentia*

confess *vb* **1** to admit (a fault or crime) **2** to admit to be true, esp. reluctantly **3** *Christianity* to declare (one's sins) to God or to a priest, so as to obtain forgiveness ▶ HISTORY Latin *confiteri* to admit

confession *n* **1** something confessed **2** an admission of one's faults, sins, or crimes **3 confession of faith** a formal public statement of religious beliefs

confessional *n* **1** *Christianity* a small room or enclosed stall in a church where a priest hears confessions ▷ *adj* **2** of or suited to a confession

confessor *n* **1** *Christianity* a priest who hears confessions and gives spiritual advice **2** *history* a person who demonstrates his or her Christian religious faith by the holiness of his or her life: *Edward the Confessor*

confetti *n* small pieces of coloured paper thrown at weddings ▶ HISTORY Italian

confidant *or fem* **confidante** *n* a person to whom private matters are confided ▶ HISTORY French *confident*

confide *vb* **-fiding, -fided** **1 confide in** to tell (something) in confidence to **2** *formal* to entrust into another's keeping ▶ HISTORY Latin *confidere*

confidence *n* **1** trust in a person or thing **2** a belief in one's own abilities **3** trust or a trustful relationship: *she won first the confidence, then the admiration, of her bosses* **4** something confided, such as a secret **5 in confidence** as a secret

confidence trick *n* a swindle in which the swindler gains the victim's trust in order to cheat him or her

confident *adj* **1** having or showing certainty: *we are now confident that this technique works* **2** sure of oneself ▶ HISTORY Latin *confidere* to have complete trust in > **confidently** *adv*

confidential *adj* **1** spoken or given in confidence **2** entrusted with another's secret affairs: *a confidential secretary* **3** suggestive of intimacy: *a halting, confidential manner* > **confidentiality** *n* > **confidentially** *adv*

configuration *n* **1** the arrangement of the parts of something **2** the form or outline of such an arrangement ▶ HISTORY Late Latin *configurare* to model on something

confine *vb* **-fining, -fined** **1** to keep within bounds **2** to restrict the free movement of: *a nasty dose of flu which confined her to bed for days* ▷ *n* **3 confines** boundaries or limits ▶ HISTORY Latin *finis* boundary

confinement *n* **1** being confined **2** the period of childbirth

confirm *vb* **1** to prove to be true or valid **2** to reaffirm (something), so as to make (it) more definite: *she confirmed that she is about to resign as leader of the council* **3** to strengthen: *this cruise confirmed my first impressions of the boat's performance* **4** to formally make valid **5** to administer the rite of confirmation to ▶ HISTORY Latin *confirmare*

confirmation *n* **1** the act of confirming **2** something that confirms **3** a rite in several Christian churches that admits a baptized person to full church membership

confirmed *adj* long-established in a habit or condition: *a confirmed bachelor*

confiscate *vb* **-cating, -cated** to seize (property) by authority ▶ HISTORY Latin *confiscare* to seize for the public treasury > **confiscation** *n*

conflagration *n* a large destructive fire ▶ HISTORY Latin *com-* (intensive) + *flagrare* to burn

conflate *vb* **-flating, -flated** to combine or blend into a whole ▶ HISTORY Latin *conflare* to blow together > **conflation** *n*

conflict *n* **1** opposition between ideas or interests **2** *written* a struggle or battle ▷ *vb* **3** to be incompatible ▶ HISTORY Latin *confligere* to combat > **conflicting** *adj*

conflict resolution *n* a way of resolving a disagreement that is satisfactory to all the parties involved

confluence *n* **1** a place where rivers flow into one another **2** a gathering ▶ HISTORY Latin *confluere* to flow together > **confluent** *adj*

conform *vb* **1** to comply with accepted standards, rules, or customs **2** to be like or in accordance with: *people tend to absorb ideas that conform with their existing beliefs, and reject those that do not* ▶ HISTORY Latin *confirmare* to strengthen

conformation *n* **1** the general shape of an object **2** the arrangement of the parts of an object

conformist *adj* **1 a** (of a person) behaving or thinking like most other people rather than in an original or unconventional way: *a shy and conformist type of boy* **b** (of an organization or society) expecting everyone to behave in the same way: *the school was a dull, conformist place for staff and students alike* ▷ *n* **2** a person who behaves or thinks like most other people rather than in an original or unconventional way

conformity *n*, *pl* **-ities** **1** compliance in actions or behaviour with certain accepted rules, customs, or standards **2** likeness

confound *vb* **1** to astound or bewilder **2** to fail to distinguish between **3 confound it!** damn it! ▶ HISTORY Latin *confundere* to mingle, pour together

confounded *adj* **1** *informal* damned: *what a confounded nuisance!* **2** bewildered; confused: *her silent, utterly confounded daughter*

confront *vb* **1** (of a problem or task) to present itself to **2** to meet face to face in hostility or defiance **3** to present (someone) with something, esp. in order to accuse or criticize: *she finally confronted him with her suspicions* ▶ HISTORY Latin *com-* together + *frons* forehead

confrontation *n* a serious argument or fight

Confucianism *n* the teachings of Confucius (551–479 BC), the ancient Chinese philosopher, which emphasize moral order > **Confucian** *n*, *adj* > **Confucianist** *n*

confuse *vb* **-fusing, -fused** **1** to fail to distinguish between one thing and another **2** to perplex or disconcert **3** to make unclear: *he confused his talk with irrelevant detail* **4** to throw into disorder

▶ HISTORY Latin *confundere* to pour together > **confusing** *adj* > **confusingly** *adv*

confused *adj* **1** lacking a clear understanding of something **2** disordered and difficult to understand or make sense of: *a confused dream*

confusion *n* **1** mistaking one person or thing for another **2** bewilderment **3** lack of clarity **4** disorder

confute *vb* **-futing, -futed** to prove to be wrong ▶ HISTORY Latin *confutare* to check, silence > **confutation** *n*

conga *n* **1** a Latin American dance performed by a number of people in single file **2** a large single-headed drum played with the hands ▷ *vb* **-gaing, -gaed** **3** to dance the conga ▶ HISTORY from American Spanish

congeal *vb* to change from a liquid to a semisolid state ▶ HISTORY Latin *com-* together + *gelare* to freeze

congenial *adj* **1** friendly, pleasant, or agreeable: *he found the Botanic Gardens a most congenial place for strolling* **2** having a similar disposition or tastes ▶ HISTORY *con-* (same) + *genial* > **congeniality** *n*

congenital *adj* (of an abnormal condition) existing at birth but not inherited: *congenital heart disease* ▶ HISTORY Latin *con-* together + *genitus* born > **congenitally** *adv*

conger *n* a large sea eel ▶ HISTORY Greek *gongros*

congested *adj* **1** crowded to excess **2** clogged or blocked ▶ HISTORY Latin *congerere* to pile up > **congestion** *n*

conglomerate *n* **1** a large corporation made up of many different companies **2** a thing composed of several different elements **3** a type of rock consisting of rounded pebbles or fragments held together by silica or clay ▷ *vb* **-ating, -ated** **4** to form into a mass ▷ *adj* **5** made up of several different elements **6** (of rock) consisting of rounded pebbles or fragments held together by silica or clay ▶ HISTORY Latin *conglomerare* to roll up > **conglomeration** *n*

congratulate *vb* **-lating, -lated** **1** to express one's pleasure to (a person) at his or her success or good fortune **2 congratulate oneself** to consider oneself clever or fortunate (as a result of): *she congratulated herself on her own business acumen* ▶ HISTORY Latin *congratulari* > **congratulatory** *adj*

congratulations *pl n*, *interj* expressions of pleasure or joy on another's success or good fortune

congregate *vb* **-gating, -gated** to collect together in or as a crowd ▶ HISTORY Latin *congregare* to collect into a flock

congregation *n* a group of worshippers > **congregational** *adj*

Congregationalism *n* a system of Protestant church government in which each church is self-governing > **Congregationalist** *adj*, *n*

congress *n* a formal meeting of representatives for discussion ▶ HISTORY Latin *com-* together + *gradi* to walk > **congressional** *adj*

Congress *n* the federal legislature of the US, consisting of the House of Representatives and the

Senate > **Congressional** adj > **Congressman** n > **Congresswoman** fem n

congruent adj **1** agreeing or corresponding **2** geom identical in shape and size: congruent triangles ▶ HISTORY Latin congruere to agree > **congruence** n

conical adj in the shape of a cone

conic section n a figure, either a circle, ellipse, parabola, or hyperbola, formed by the intersection of a plane and a cone

conifer n a tree or shrub bearing cones and evergreen leaves, such as the fir or larch ▶ HISTORY Latin conus cone + ferre to bear > **coniferous** adj

coniferous forest n a forest of trees bearing cones and evergreen leaves, such as the fir or larch ▶ HISTORY Latin conus cone + ferre to bear

conjecture n **1** the formation of conclusions from incomplete evidence **2** a guess ▷ vb **-turing, -tured 3** to form (an opinion or conclusion) from incomplete evidence ▶ HISTORY Latin conjicere to throw together > **conjectural** adj

conjoined twins pl n the technical name for **Siamese twins**

conjugal (kon-jew-gal) adj of marriage: conjugal rights ▶ HISTORY Latin conjunx wife or husband

conjugate vb (kon-jew-gate) **-gating, -gated 1** grammar to give the inflections of (a verb) **2** (of a verb) to undergo inflection according to a specific set of rules **3** formal to combine: a country in which conjugating Marxism with Christianity has actually been tried ▷ n (kon-jew-git) **4** formal something formed by conjugation: haemoglobin is a conjugate of a protein with an iron-containing pigment ▶ HISTORY Latin com- together + jugare to connect

conjugation n **1** grammar **a** inflection of a verb for person, number, tense, voice, and mood **b** the complete set of the inflections of a given verb **2** a joining

conjunction n **1** joining together **2** simultaneous occurrence of events **3** a word or group of words that connects words, phrases, or clauses; for example and, if, and but **4** astron the apparent nearness of two heavenly bodies to each other > **conjunctional** adj

conjunctiva n, pl **-vas** or **-vae** the delicate mucous membrane that covers the eyeball and inner eyelid ▶ HISTORY New Latin membrana conjunctiva the conjunctive membrane > **conjunctival** adj

conjunctive adj **1** joining or joined **2** used as a conjunction: a conjunctive adverb ▷ n **3** a word or words used as a conjunction ▶ HISTORY Latin conjungere to join

conjunctivitis n inflammation of the conjunctiva

conjuncture n a combination of events, esp. one that leads to a crisis

conjure vb **-juring, -jured 1** to perform tricks that appear to be magic **2** to summon (a spirit or demon) by magic **3** formal or literary to appeal earnestly to: I conjure you by all which you profess: answer me! ▶ HISTORY Latin conjurare to swear together > **conjuring** n

conjure up vb **1** to create an image in the mind: the name Versailles conjures up a past of sumptuous grandeur **2** to produce as if from nowhere: he conjured up a fabulous opening goal

conjuror or **conjurer** n a person who performs magic tricks for people's entertainment

conk Brit, Austral & NZ, slang n **1** the head or nose ▷ vb **2** to strike (someone) on the head or nose ▶ HISTORY probably changed from conch

conker n same as **horse chestnut** (sense 2)

conkers n Brit a game in which a player swings a horse chestnut (conker), threaded onto a string, against that of another player to try to break it ▶ HISTORY dialect conker snail shell, originally used in the game

conk out vb informal **1** (of a machine or car) to break down **2** to become tired or fall asleep suddenly ▶ HISTORY origin unknown

connect vb **1** to link or be linked: high blood pressure is closely connected to heart disease **2** to put into telephone communication with **3** computing to join pieces of equipment so that they work together: connect the printer to the computer **4** computing to put into internet communication with **5** (of two public vehicles) to have the arrival of one timed to occur just before the departure of the other, for the convenience of passengers **6** to associate in the mind: he had always connected sex with violence and attacks rather than loving and concern **7** to relate by birth or marriage: she was distantly connected with the Wedgwood family ▶ HISTORY Latin connectere to bind together

connection or **connexion** n **1** a relationship or association **2** a link or bond **3** a link between two components in an electric circuit **4 a** an opportunity to transfer from one public vehicle to another **b** the vehicle scheduled to provide such an opportunity **5** an influential acquaintance **6** a relative **7** logical sequence in thought or expression **8** a telephone link **9** computing access to the internet **10** slang a supplier of illegal drugs, such as heroin **11 in connection with** with reference to: a number of people have been arrested in connection with the explosion

connective adj **1** connecting ▷ n **2** grammar a conjunction; any word that connects phrases, clauses, or individual words, for example and, if, and but

connective tissue n body tissue that supports organs, fills the spaces between them, and forms tendons and ligaments

connectivity n **1** the state of being connected **2** computing the state of being connected to the internet

conning tower n the raised observation tower containing the periscope on a submarine ▶ HISTORY con to steer a ship

connivance n encouragement or permission of wrongdoing

connive *vb* **-niving, -nived 1 connive at** to allow or encourage (wrongdoing) by ignoring it **2** to conspire ▶ HISTORY Latin *connivere* to blink, hence, leave uncensured

connoisseur (kon-noss-**sir**) *n* a person with special knowledge of the arts, food, or drink ▶ HISTORY French

connotation *n* an additional meaning or association implied by a word: *the German term carries a connotation of elitism* ▶ HISTORY Latin *con-* + together *notare* to mark, note > **connote** *vb*

connubial (kon-**new**-bee-al) *adj formal* of marriage: *connubial bliss* ▶ HISTORY Latin *conubium* marriage

conquer *vb* **1** to defeat (an opponent or opponents) **2** to overcome (a difficulty or feeling) **3** to gain possession of (a place) by force or war ▶ HISTORY Latin *conquirere* to search for > **conquering** *adj* > **conqueror** *n*

conquest *n* **1** the act of conquering **2** a person or thing that has been conquered **3** a person whose affections have been won

conquistador *n, pl* **-dors** or **-dores** one of the Spanish conquerors of Mexico and Peru in the 16th century ▶ HISTORY Spanish: conqueror

Cons. Conservative

conscience *n* **1** the sense of right and wrong that governs a person's thoughts and actions **2** a feeling of guilt: *he showed no hint of conscience over the suffering he had inflicted* **3 in (all) conscience** in fairness **4 on one's conscience** causing feelings of guilt ▶ HISTORY Latin *conscire* to know

conscience-stricken *adj* feeling guilty because of having done something wrong

conscientious *adj* **1** painstaking or thorough in one's work **2** governed by conscience > **conscientiously** *adv* > **conscientiousness** *n*

conscientious objector *n* a person who refuses to serve in the armed forces on moral or religious grounds

conscious *adj* **1** alert and awake **2** aware of one's surroundings and of oneself **3** aware of (something): *he was conscious of a need to urinate* **4** deliberate or intentional: *a conscious attempt* **5** of the part of the mind that is aware of a person's self, surroundings, and thoughts, and that to a certain extent determines choices of action ▷ *n* **6** the conscious part of the mind ▶ HISTORY Latin *com-* with + *scire* to know > **consciously** *adv* > **consciousness** *n*

conscript *n* **1** a person who is enrolled for compulsory military service ▷ *vb* **2** to enrol (someone) for compulsory military service ▶ HISTORY Latin *conscriptus* enrolled

conscription *n* compulsory military service

consecrate *vb* **-crating, -crated 1** to make or declare sacred or for religious use **2** to devote or dedicate (something) to a specific purpose **3** *Christianity* to sanctify (bread and wine) to be received as the body and blood of Christ ▶ HISTORY Latin *consecrare* > **consecration** *n*

consecutive *adj* following in order without interruption: *three consecutive nights of rioting* ▶ HISTORY Latin *consequi* to pursue > **consecutively** *adv*

consensus *n* general or widespread agreement ▶ HISTORY Latin *consentire* to agree

consent *n* **1** agreement, permission, or approval **2 age of consent** the age at which sexual intercourse is permitted by law ▷ *vb* **3** to permit or agree (to) ▶ HISTORY Latin *consentire* to agree > **consenting** *adj*

consequence *n* **1** a logical result or effect **2** significance or importance: *we said little of consequence to each other; a woman of little consequence* **3 in consequence** as a result **4 take the consequences** to accept whatever results from one's action

consequent *adj* **1** following as an effect **2** following as a logical conclusion ▶ HISTORY Latin *consequens* following closely

consequential *adj* **1** important or significant **2** following as a result

consequently *adv* as a result; therefore

conservancy *n* environmental conservation

conservation *n* **1** protection and careful management of the environment and natural resources **2** protection from change, loss, or injury **3** *physics* the principle that the quantity of a specified aspect of a system, such as momentum or charge, remains constant > **conservationist** *n*

conservative *adj* **1** favouring the preservation of established customs and values, and opposing change **2** moderate or cautious: *a conservative estimate* **3** conventional in style: *people in this area are conservative in their tastes* ▷ *n* **4** a conservative person > **conservatism** *n*

Conservative *adj* **1** of or supporting the Conservative Party, the major right-wing political party in Britain, which believes in private enterprise and capitalism **2** of or supporting a similar right-wing party in other countries ▷ *n* **3** a supporter or member of the Conservative Party

conservatoire (kon-**serv**-a-twahr) *n* a school of music ▶ HISTORY French

conservatory *n, pl* **-tories 1** a greenhouse attached to a house **2** a conservatoire

conserve *vb* **-serving, -served 1** to protect from harm, decay, or loss **2** to preserve (fruit or other food) with sugar ▷ *n* **3** fruit preserved by cooking in sugar ▶ HISTORY Latin *conservare* to keep safe

consider *vb* **1** to be of the opinion that **2** to think carefully about (a problem or decision) **3** to bear in mind: *Corsica is well worth considering for those seeking a peaceful holiday in beautiful surroundings* **4** to have regard for or care about: *you must try to consider other people's feelings more* **5** to discuss (something) in order to make a decision **6** to look at: *he considered her and she forced herself to sit calmly under his gaze* ▶ HISTORY Latin *considerare* to inspect closely

considerable *adj* **1** large enough to reckon with: *a considerable number of people* **2** a lot of: *he was in considerable pain* > **considerably** *adv*

considerate *adj* thoughtful towards other people

consideration *n* **1** careful thought **2** a fact to be taken into account when making a decision **3** thoughtfulness for other people **4** payment for a service **5 take into consideration** to bear in mind **6 under consideration** being currently discussed

considered *adj* **1** presented or thought out with care: *a considered opinion* **2** thought of in a specified way: *highly considered*

considering *conj, prep* **1** taking (a specified fact) into account: *considering the mileage the car had done, it was lasting well* ▷ *adv* **2** *informal, spoken* taking into account the circumstances: *it's not bad considering*

consign *vb* **1** to give into the care or charge of **2** to put irrevocably: *those events have been consigned to history* **3** to put (in a specified place or situation): *only a few months ago such demands would have consigned the student leaders to prisons and labour camps* **4** to address or deliver (goods): *a cargo of oil drilling equipment consigned to Saudi Arabia* ▶ HISTORY Latin *consignare* to put one's seal to, sign > **consignee** *n* > **consignor** *n*

consignment *n* **1** a shipment of goods **2** the act or an instance of consigning: *the goods are sent to Hong Kong for onward consignment to customers in the area*

consignment note *n commerce* a document that records details about a consignment of goods and acts as a receipt for the sender

consist *vb* **1 consist of** to be made up of: *a match consists of seven games* **2 consist in** to have as its main or only part: *his madness, if he is mad, consists in believing that he is a sundial* ▶ HISTORY Latin *consistere* to stand firm

consistency *n, pl* **-encies 1** degree of thickness or smoothness **2** being consistent

consistent *adj* **1** holding to the same principles **2** in agreement > **consistently** *adv*

consolation *n* **1** a person or thing that is a comfort in a time of sadness or distress **2** a consoling or being consoled

console¹ *vb* **-soling, -soled** to comfort (someone) in sadness or distress ▶ HISTORY Latin *consolari* > **consolable** *adj*

console² *n* **1** a panel of controls for electronic equipment **2** a cabinet for a television or audio equipment **3** an ornamental bracket used to support a wall fixture **4** the desklike case of an organ, containing the pedals, stops, and keys ▶ HISTORY Old French *consolateur* one that provides support

consolidate *vb* **-dating, -dated 1** to make or become stronger or more stable **2** to combine into a whole ▶ HISTORY Latin *consolidare* to make firm > **consolidation** *n* > **consolidator** *n*

consommé (kon-**som**-may) *n* a thin clear meat soup ▶ HISTORY French

consonance *n formal* agreement or harmony

consonant *n* **1 a** a speech sound made by partially or completely blocking the breath streams, for example *b* or *f* **b** a letter representing this ▷ *adj*

2 consonant with in keeping or agreement with: *an individualistic style of religion, more consonant with liberal society* **3** harmonious: *this highly-dissonant chord is followed by a more consonant one* ▶ HISTORY Latin *consonare* to sound at the same time

consort *vb* **1 consort with** to keep company with ▷ *n* **2** a husband or wife of a reigning monarch **3** a small group of voices or instruments ▶ HISTORY Latin *consors* partner

consortium *n, pl* **-tia** an association of business firms ▶ HISTORY Latin: partnership

conspectus *n formal* a survey or summary ▶ HISTORY Latin: a viewing

conspicuous *adj* **1** clearly visible **2** noteworthy or striking: *conspicuous bravery* ▶ HISTORY Latin *conspicuus* > **conspicuously** *adv*

conspiracy *n, pl* **-cies 1** a secret plan to carry out an illegal or harmful act **2** the act of making such plans

conspire *vb* **-spiring, -spired 1** to plan a crime together in secret **2** to act together as if by design: *the weather and the recession conspired to hit wine production and sales* ▶ HISTORY Latin *conspirare* to plot together > **conspirator** *n* > **conspiratorial** *adj*

constable *n* a police officer of the lowest rank ▶ HISTORY Late Latin *comes stabuli* officer in charge of the stable

constabulary *n, pl* **-laries** *chiefly Brit* the police force of an area

constant *adj* **1** continuous: *she has endured constant criticism, mockery and humiliation* **2** unchanging: *the average speed of the winds remained constant over this period* **3** faithful ▷ *n* **4** *maths, physics* a quantity or number which remains invariable: *the velocity of light is a constant* **5** something that is unchanging ▶ HISTORY Latin *constare* to be steadfast > **constancy** *n* > **constantly** *adv*

constellation *n* **1** a group of stars which form a pattern and are given a name **2** a group of people or things: *the constellation of favourable circumstances* ▶ HISTORY Latin *com-* together + *stella* star

consternation *n* a feeling of anxiety or dismay

constipated *adj* unable to empty one's bowels ▶ HISTORY Latin *constipare* to press closely together

constipation *n* a condition in which emptying one's bowels is difficult

constituency *n, pl* **-cies 1** the area represented by a person who has been elected to a legislature **2** the voters in such an area

constituent *n* **1** a resident of a constituency, esp. one who is entitled to vote **2** a component part ▷ *adj* forming part of a whole: *the constituent parts of the universe* ▶ HISTORY Latin *constituere* to constitute

constituent assembly *n politics* a body of representatives that is elected to create or change their country's constitution

constitute *vb* **-tuting, -tuted 1** to form or make up: *the amazing range of crags that constitute the Eglwyseg Mountains* **2** to set up (an institution) formally ▶ HISTORY Latin *com-* (intensive) + *statuere* to place

constitution *n* 1 the principles on which a state is governed 2 **the Constitution** (in certain countries) the statute embodying such principles 3 a person's state of health 4 the make-up or structure of something: *changes in the very constitution of society*

constitutional *adj* 1 of a constitution: *constitutional reform* 2 authorized by or in accordance with the Constitution of a nation: *constitutional monarchy* 3 inherent in the nature of a person or thing: *a constitutional sensitivity to cold* ▷ *n* 4 a regular walk taken for the good of one's health > **constitutionally** *adv*

constitutive *adj* 1 forming a part of something 2 with the power to appoint or establish

constrain *vb* 1 to compel or force: *he felt constrained to apologize* 2 to limit, restrict, or inhibit: *the mobility of workers is constrained by the serious housing shortage* ▶ HISTORY Latin *constringere* to bind together

constrained *adj* embarrassed or unnatural: *his constrained expression*

constraint *n* 1 something that limits a person's freedom of action 2 repression of natural feelings 3 a forced unnatural manner

constrict *vb* 1 to make smaller or narrower by squeezing 2 to limit or restrict ▶ HISTORY Latin *constringere* to tie up together > **constrictive** *adj*

constriction *n* 1 a feeling of tightness in some part of the body, such as the chest 2 a narrowing 3 something that constricts

constrictor *n* 1 a snake that coils around and squeezes its prey to kill it 2 a muscle that contracts an opening

construct *vb* 1 to build or put together 2 *geom* to draw (a figure) to specified requirements 3 to compose (an argument or sentence) ▷ *n* 4 a complex idea resulting from the combination of simpler ideas 5 something formulated or built systematically ▶ HISTORY Latin *construere* to build > **constructor** *n*

construction *n* 1 the act of constructing or manner in which a thing is constructed 2 something that has been constructed 3 the business or work of building houses or other structures 4 *formal* an interpretation: *the financial markets will put the worst possible construction on any piece of news which might affect them* 5 *grammar* the way in which words are arranged in a sentence, clause, or phrase 6 *geom* **a** the drawing of a line, angle, or figure so that certain requirements are satisfied in order to solve a problem or prove a theorem **b** the line or figure drawn > **constructional** *adj*

constructive *adj* 1 useful and helpful: *constructive criticism* 2 *law* deduced by inference; not openly expressed > **constructively** *adv*

constructive interference *n physics* the effect that occurs when the crests or troughs of two waves coincide

constructive wave *n geog* a wave in which there is a circular motion and no friction with the seabed

constructive waves *pl n geog* long low waves that wash material onto the shore and build up beaches. Compare **destructive waves**

construe *vb* **-struing, -strued** 1 to interpret the meaning of (something): *her indifference was construed as rudeness* 2 to analyse the grammatical structure of (a sentence) 3 to combine (words) grammatically 4 *old-fashioned* to translate literally ▶ HISTORY Latin *construere* to build

consul *n* 1 an official representing a state in a foreign country 2 one of the two chief magistrates in ancient Rome ▶ HISTORY Latin > **consular** *adj* > **consulship** *n*

consulate *n* 1 the workplace and official home of a consul 2 the position or period of office of a consul

consult *vb* 1 to ask advice from or discuss matters with (someone): *he never consults his wife about what he's about to do* 2 to refer to for information: *he consulted his watch* ▶ HISTORY Latin *consultare*

consultant *n* 1 a specialist doctor with a senior position in a hospital 2 a specialist who gives expert professional advice > **consultancy** *n*

consultation *n* 1 the act of consulting 2 a meeting for discussion or the seeking of advice > **consultative** *adj*

consulting room *n* a room in which a doctor sees patients

consume *vb* **-suming, -sumed** 1 to eat or drink 2 to use up 3 to destroy: *the ship blew up and was consumed by flames* 4 to obsess: *he was consumed with jealousy over the ending of their affair* ▶ HISTORY Latin *com-* (intensive) + *sumere* to take up > **consumable** *adj* > **consuming** *adj*

consumer *n* 1 a person who buys goods or uses services 2 *biol* an organism within a community that feeds upon other plants or animals

consumer durables *pl n* manufactured products that have a relatively long life, such as cars or televisions

consumer goods *pl n* goods bought for personal needs rather than those required for the production of other goods or services

consumerism *n* 1 the belief that a high level of consumer spending is desirable and beneficial to the economy 2 protection of the rights of consumers

consumer society *n* a society in which people are encouraged to buy goods, often unnecessarily, as a means of stimulating the economy

consummate *vb* (**kon**-sum-mate) **-mating, -mated** 1 to make (a marriage) legal by sexual intercourse 2 to complete or fulfil ▷ *adj* (kon-**sum**-mit) 3 supremely skilled: *a consummate craftsman* 4 complete or extreme: *consummate skill; consummate ignorance* ▶ HISTORY Latin *consummare* to complete > **consummation** *n*

consumption *n* 1 the quantity of something consumed or used: *for such a powerful car, fuel*

C

consumption is modest **2** the act of eating or drinking something: *this meat is unfit for human consumption* **3** *econ* purchase of goods and services for personal use **4** *old-fashioned* tuberculosis of the lungs

consumptive *adj* **1** wasteful or destructive **2** of tuberculosis of the lungs ▷ *n* **3** a person with tuberculosis of the lungs

cont. continued

contact *n* **1** the state or act of communication: *the airport lost contact with the plane shortly before the crash* **2** the state or act of touching: *rugby is a game of hard physical contact* **3** an acquaintance who might be useful in business **4** a connection between two electrical conductors in a circuit **5** a person who has been exposed to a contagious disease ▷ *vb* **6** to come or be in communication or touch with ▶ HISTORY Latin *contingere* to touch on all sides

contact lens *n* a small lens placed on the eyeball to correct defective vision

contact order *n law* a court order specifying in detail the contact a child is to have with a named person or people and requiring the parent or guardian with whom he or she lives to make provision for this

contact process *n chem* a method of making sulphuric acid by oxidizing sulphur dioxide under the influence of a catalyst

contagion *n* **1** the passing on of disease by contact **2** a contagious disease **3** a corrupting influence that tends to spread ▶ HISTORY Latin *contagio* infection

contagious *adj* **1** (of a disease) capable of being passed on by contact **2** (of a person) capable of passing on a transmissible disease **3** spreading from person to person: *contagious enthusiasm*

contain *vb* **1** to hold or be capable of holding: *the bag contained a selection of men's clothing* **2** to have as one of its ingredients or constituents: *tea and coffee both contain appreciable amounts of caffeine* **3** to consist of: *the book contains 13 very different and largely separate chapters* **4** to check or restrain (feelings or behaviour) **5** to prevent from spreading or going beyond fixed limits: *the blockade was too weak to contain the French fleet* ▶ HISTORY Latin *continere* > **containable** *adj*

container *n* **1** an object used to hold or store things in **2** a large standard-sized box for transporting cargo by lorry or ship ▷ *adj* relating to cargo containers: *container ship; container terminal*

containerize *or* **-ise** *vb* **-izing, -ized** *or* **-ising, -ised** **1** to pack (cargo) in large standard-sized containers **2** to fit (a port, ship, or lorry) to carry goods in standard-sized containers > **containerization** *or* **-isation** *n*

containment *n* the prevention of the spread of something harmful

contaminate *vb* **-nating, -nated** **1** to make impure; pollute **2** to make radioactive ▶ HISTORY Latin *contaminare* to defile > **contaminant** *n* > **contamination** *n*

contemn *vb formal* to regard with contempt ▶ HISTORY Latin *contemnere*

contemplate *vb* **-plating, -plated** **1** to think deeply about **2** to consider as a possibility **3** to look at thoughtfully **4** to meditate ▶ HISTORY Latin *contemplare* > **contemplation** *n*

contemplative *adj* **1** of or given to contemplation ▷ *n* **2** a person dedicated to religious contemplation

contemporaneous *adj* happening at the same time > **contemporaneity** *n*

contemporary *adj* **1** existing or occurring at the present time **2** living or occurring in the same period **3** modern in style or fashion **4** of approximately the same age ▷ *n, pl* **-raries** **5** a person or thing living at the same time or of approximately the same age as another ▶ HISTORY Latin *com-* together + *temporarius* relating to time

contempt *n* **1** scorn **2** **hold in contempt** to scorn or despise **3** same as **contempt of court** ▶ HISTORY Latin *contemnere* to scorn

contemptible *adj* deserving to be despised or hated: *a contemptible lack of courage*

contempt of court *n law* an action that interferes with the normal delivery of justice in court or that shows deliberate disrespect for the authority of a court of law ▶ HISTORY Latin *contemnere* to scorn

contemptuous *adj* showing or feeling strong dislike or disrespect > **contemptuously** *adv*

contend *vb* **1** **contend with** to deal with **2** to assert **3** to compete or fight **4** to argue earnestly ▶ HISTORY Latin *contendere* to strive > **contender** *n*

content¹ *n* **1** **contents** everything inside a container **2** **contents** a list of chapters at the front of a book **3** the meaning or substance of a piece of writing, often as distinguished from its style or form **4** the information, material, etc. presented on a website or other digital medium **5** the amount of a substance contained in a mixture: *the water vapour content of the atmosphere* ▶ HISTORY Latin *contentus* contained

content² *adj* **1** satisfied with things as they are **2** willing to accept a situation or a proposed course of action ▷ *vb* **3** to satisfy (oneself or another person) ▷ *n* **4** peace of mind ▶ HISTORY Latin *contentus* contented, having restrained desires > **contentment** *n*

contented *adj* satisfied with one's situation or life > **contentedly** *adv* > **contentedness** *n*

contention *n* **1** disagreement or dispute **2** a point asserted in argument **3** **bone of contention** a point of dispute ▶ HISTORY Latin *contentio*

contentious *adj* **1** causing disagreement **2** tending to quarrel > **contentiousness** *n*

contest *n* **1** a game or match in which people or teams compete **2** a struggle for power or control ▷ *vb* **3** to dispute: *he has said he will not contest the verdict* **4** to take part in (a contest or struggle for power): *all parties which meet the legal requirements will be allowed to contest the election* ▶ HISTORY Latin *contestari* to introduce a lawsuit > **contestable** *adj*

contestant *n* a person who takes part in a contest

context *n* **1** the circumstances relevant to an event or fact **2** the words before and after a word or passage in a piece of writing that contribute to its meaning: *taken out of context, lines like these sound ridiculous, but, as part of a scrupulously written play, they are just right* ▶ **HISTORY** Latin *com-* together + *texere* to weave > **contextual** *adj*

contiguous *adj formal* very near or touching ▶ **HISTORY** Latin *contiguus*

continent¹ *n* one of the earth's large landmasses (Asia, Australia, Africa, Europe, North and South America, and Antarctica) ▶ **HISTORY** Latin *terra continens* continuous land > **continental** *adj*

continent² *adj* **1** able to control one's bladder and bowels **2** sexually restrained ▶ **HISTORY** Latin *continere* to contain, retain > **continence** *n*

Continent *n* **the Continent** the mainland of Europe as distinct from the British Isles > **Continental** *adj*

continental breakfast *n* a light breakfast of coffee and rolls

continental climate *n* a climate with hot summers, cold winters, and little rainfall, typical of the interior of a continent

continental divide *n geog* a watershed that divides adjacent river systems on a continent and determines in which direction they will flow and into which ocean they will empty

continental drift *n geol* the theory that the earth's continents drift gradually over the surface of the planet, due to currents in its mantle

continental quilt *n Brit* a large quilt used as a bed cover in place of the top sheet and blankets

continental shelf *n* the gently sloping shallow sea bed surrounding a continent

contingency *n, pl* **-cies** **1** an unknown or unforeseen future event or condition **2** something dependent on a possible future event

contingent *n* **1** a group of people with a common interest that represents a larger group: *a contingent of European scientists* **2** a military group that is part of a larger force: *the force includes a contingent of the Foreign Legion* ▷ *adj* **3** (foll. by *on* or *upon*) dependent on (something uncertain) **4** happening by chance ▶ **HISTORY** Latin *contingere* to touch, befall

continual *adj* **1** occurring without interruption **2** recurring frequently ▶ **HISTORY** Latin *continuus* uninterrupted > **continually** *adv*

continuance *n* **1** the act of continuing **2** duration

continuation *n* **1** the act of continuing **2** a part or thing added, such as a sequel **3** a renewal of an interrupted action or process

continue *vb* **-tinuing, -tinued** **1** to remain or cause to remain in a particular condition or place **2** to carry on (doing something): *we continued kissing; heavy fighting continued until Thursday afternoon* **3** to resume after an interruption: *we'll continue after lunch* **4** to go on to a further place: *the*

road continues on up the hill ▶ **HISTORY** Latin *continuare* to join together

continuity *n, pl* **-ties** **1** a smooth development or sequence **2** the arrangement of scenes in a film so that they follow each other logically and without breaks

continuity person *n films, television* a person whose job it is to ensure that film or TV sequences follow on logically as regards sets, props, lighting, clothing, etc.

continuo *n, pl* **-tinuos** *music* a continuous bass accompaniment played usually on a keyboard instrument ▶ **HISTORY** Italian

continuous *adj* **1** without end: *a continuous process* **2** not having any breaks or gaps in it: *a continuous line of boats; continuous rain* ▶ **HISTORY** Latin *continuus* > **continuously** *adv*

continuous data *n statistics* data which consists of a continuum of possible values, having certain limits but not being divided into fixed class intervals. Compare **discrete data**

continuum *n, pl* **-tinua** or **-tinuums** a continuous series or whole, no part of which is noticeably different from the parts immediately next to it, although the ends or extremes of it are very different from each other: *the continuum from minor misbehaviour to major crime* ▶ **HISTORY** Latin

contort *vb* to twist or bend out of shape ▶ **HISTORY** Latin *contortus* intricate > **contortion** *n*

contortionist *n* a performer who contorts his or her body to entertain others

contour *n* **1** an outline **2** same as **contour line** ▷ *vb* **3** to shape so as to form or follow the contour of something ▶ **HISTORY** Italian *contornare* to sketch

contour line *n geog* a line on a map or chart joining points of equal height or depth

contour map *n geog* a map showing topography by means of contour lines

contour ploughing *n agriculture* ploughing following the contours of the land, to minimize the effects of erosion

contra- *prefix* **1** against or contrasting: *contraceptive* **2** (in music) lower in pitch: *contrabass* ▶ **HISTORY** Latin *contra* against

contraband *n* **1** smuggled goods ▷ *adj* **2** (of goods) smuggled ▶ **HISTORY** Spanish *contrabanda*

contraception *n* the deliberate use of artificial or natural means to prevent pregnancy ▶ **HISTORY** CONTRA- + CONCEPTION

contraceptive *n* **1** a device, such as a condom, that is used to prevent pregnancy ▷ *adj* **2** providing or relating to contraception: *the contraceptive pill*

contract *n* **1** a formal agreement between two or more parties **2** a document setting out a formal agreement ▷ *vb* **3** to make a formal agreement with (a person or company) to do or deliver (something) **4** to enter into (a relationship or marriage) formally: *she had contracted an alliance with a wealthy man* **5** to make or become smaller, narrower, or shorter **6** to become affected by (an illness) **7** to draw (muscles) together or (of muscles) to be drawn together **8** to shorten (a word or phrase) by omitting letters or syllables, usually indicated in writing by an apostrophe ▶ **HISTORY** Latin *contractus* agreement > **contractible** *adj*

contraction *n* **1** a contracting or being contracted **2** a shortening of a word or group of words, often marked by an apostrophe, for example *I've come* for *I have come* **3 contractions** *med* temporary shortening and tensing of the uterus during pregnancy and labour

contract of employment *n law* a written agreement between an employer and an employee that determines the employment relations between them

contractor *n* a person or firm that supplies materials or labour for other companies

contractual *adj* of or in the nature of a contract

contradict *vb* **1** to declare the opposite of (a statement) to be true **2** (of a fact or statement) to suggest that (another fact or statement) is wrong ▶ **HISTORY** Latin *contra-* against + *dicere* to speak > **contradiction** *n*

contradictory *adj* (of facts or statements) inconsistent

contradistinction *n* a distinction made by contrasting different qualities > **contradistinctive** *adj*

contraflow *n* a flow of road traffic going alongside but in an opposite direction to the usual flow

contralto *n*, *pl* **-tos** *or* **-ti** **1** the lowest female voice **2** a singer with such a voice ▶ **HISTORY** Italian

contraption *n informal* a strange-looking device or gadget ▶ **HISTORY** origin unknown

contrapuntal *adj music* of or in counterpoint ▶ **HISTORY** Italian *contrappunto* counterpoint

contrariwise *adv* **1** from a contrasting point of view **2** in the opposite way

contrary *n*, *pl* **-ries 1 on** *or* **to the contrary** in opposition to what has just been said or implied ▷ *adj* **2** opposed; completely different: *a contrary view, based on equally good information* **3** perverse; obstinate **4** (of the wind) unfavourable ▷ *adv* **contrary to 5** in opposition or contrast to: *contrary to popular belief* **6** in conflict with: *contrary to nature* ▶ **HISTORY** Latin *contrarius* opposite > **contrariness** *n*

contrast *n* **1** a difference which is clearly seen when two things are compared **2** a person or thing showing differences when compared with another **3** the degree of difference between the colours in a photograph or television picture ▷ *vb* **4** to compare or be compared in order to show the differences between (things): *he contrasts that society with contemporary America* **5 contrast with** to be very different from: *her speed of reaction contrasted with her husband's vagueness* ▶ **HISTORY** Latin *contra-* against + *stare* to stand > **contrasting** *adj*

contravene *vb* **-vening, -vened** *formal* to break (a rule or law) ▶ **HISTORY** Latin *contra-* against + *venire* to come > **contravention** *n*

contretemps (**kon**-tra-tahn) *n*, *pl* **-temps** an embarrassing minor disagreement ▶ **HISTORY** French

contribute *vb* **-uting, -uted** (often foll. by *to*) **1** to give (support or money) for a common purpose or fund **2** to supply (ideas or opinions) **3 contribute to** to be partly responsible for: *his own unconvincing play contributed to his defeat* **4** to write (an article) for a publication ▶ **HISTORY** Latin *contribuere* to collect > **contribution** *n* > **contributory** *adj* > **contributor** *n*

contrite *adj* full of guilt or regret ▶ **HISTORY** Latin *contritus* worn out > **contritely** *adv* > **contrition** *n*

contrivance *n* **1** an ingenious device **2** an elaborate or deceitful plan **3** the act or power of contriving

contrive *vb* **-triving, -trived 1** to make happen: *he had already contrived the murder of King Alexander* **2** to devise or construct ingeniously: *he contrived a plausible reason to fly back to London; he contrived a hook from a bent nail* ▶ **HISTORY** Old French *controver*

control *n* **1** power to direct something: *the province is mostly under guerrilla control* **2** a curb or check: *import controls* **3 controls** instruments used to operate a machine **4** a standard of comparison used in an experiment **5** an experiment used to verify another by having all aspects identical except for the one that is being tested ▷ *vb* **-trolling, -trolled 6** to have power over: *the gland which controls the body's metabolic rate* **7** to limit or restrain: *he could not control his jealousy* **8** to regulate or operate (a machine) **9** to restrict the authorized supply of (certain drugs) ▶ **HISTORY** Old French *conteroller* to regulate > **controllable** *adj*

controller *n* **1** a person who is in charge **2** a person in charge of the financial aspects of a business

controlling variables *n science* the process of deciding which variables or factors will influence the outcome of an experiment, situation, or event, and deliberately controlling all recognized variables in a systematic manner

control tower *n* a tall building at an airport from which air traffic is controlled

control variable *n science* a factor that remains the same in several experiments or tests

controversy *n*, *pl* **-sies** argument or debate concerning a matter about which there is strong disagreement ▶ **HISTORY** Latin *contra-* against + *vertere* to turn > **controversial** *adj*

contumacy (**kon**-tume-mass-ee) *n*, *pl* **-cies** *literary* obstinate disobedience ▶ **HISTORY** Latin *contumax* obstinate > **contumacious** (kon-tume-may-shuss) *adj*

contumely (**kon**-tume-mill-ee) *n*, *pl* **-lies** *literary* **1** scornful or insulting treatment **2** a humiliating insult ▶ **HISTORY** Latin *contumelia*

contusion *n formal* a bruise ▶ **HISTORY** Latin *contusus* bruised > **contuse** *vb*

conundrum *n* **1** a puzzling question or problem **2** a riddle whose answer contains a pun ▶ **HISTORY** origin unknown

conurbation n a large heavily populated urban area formed by the growth and merging of towns ▶ HISTORY Latin con- together + urbs city

convalesce vb **-lescing, -lesced** to recover health after an illness or operation ▶ HISTORY Latin com- (intensive) + valescere to grow strong

convalescence n **1** gradual return to health after illness or an operation **2** the period during which such recovery occurs > **convalescent** n, adj

convection n **1** the transmission of heat caused by movement of molecules from cool regions to warmer regions of lower density **2** meteorol the process by which masses of warm air are raised into the atmosphere, often cooling and forming clouds as cooler air moves downwards > **convectional** adj ▶ HISTORY Latin convehere to bring together

convectional rainfall n meteorol rain that occurs when hot air rises, cools, and condenses; common in equatorial regions

convector n a heating device which gives out hot air

convene vb **-vening, -vened** to gather or summon for a formal meeting ▶ HISTORY Latin convenire to assemble

convener or **convenor** n a person who calls or chairs a meeting: the shop stewards' convener at the factory > **convenership** or **convenorship** n

convenience n **1** the quality of being suitable or convenient **2 at your convenience** at a time suitable to you **3** an object that is useful: a house with every modern convenience **4** euphemistic, chiefly Brit a public toilet

convenient adj **1** suitable or opportune **2** easy to use **3** nearby ▶ HISTORY Latin convenire to be in accord with

convent n **1** a building where nuns live **2** a school in which the teachers are nuns **3** a community of nuns ▶ HISTORY Latin conventus meeting

conventicle n Brit & US history a secret or unauthorized religious meeting ▶ HISTORY Latin conventiculum

convention n **1** the established view of what is thought to be proper behaviour **2** an accepted rule or method: a convention used by printers **3** a formal agreement or contract between people and nations **4** a large formal assembly of a group with common interests ▶ HISTORY Latin conventio an assembling

conventional adj **1** following the accepted customs and lacking originality **2** established by accepted usage or general agreement **3** (of weapons or warfare) not nuclear > **conventionally** adv

conventional current n electronics a current that flows from the positive terminal to the negative terminal of a cell or battery

conventionality n, pl **-ties 1** the quality of being conventional **2** something conventional

conventionalize or **-ise** vb **-izing, -ized** or **-ising, -ised** to make conventional

converge vb **-verging, -verged 1** to move towards or meet at the same point **2** (of opinions or effects) to move towards a shared conclusion or result ▶ HISTORY Latin com- together + vergere to incline > **convergence** n > **convergent** adj

convergence zone n geol a zone where tectonic plates collide, typified by earthquakes, mountain formation, and volcanic activity. Compare **divergence zone**

conversant adj **conversant with** having knowledge or experience of ▶ HISTORY Latin conversari to keep company with

conversation n informal talk between two or more people

conversational adj **1** of or used in conversation: conversational French **2** resembling informal spoken language: the author's easy, conversational style

conversationalist n a person with a specified ability at conversation: a brilliant conversationalist

conversation piece n something, such as an unusual object, that provokes conversation

converse[1] vb **-versing, -versed** to have a conversation ▶ HISTORY Latin conversari to keep company with

converse[2] adj **1** reversed or opposite ▷ n **2** a statement or idea that is the opposite of another ▶ HISTORY Latin conversus turned around > **conversely** adv

conversion n **1** a change or adaptation **2** maths a calculation in which a weight, volume, or distance is worked out in a different system of measurement: the conversion from Fahrenheit to Celsius **3** a change to another belief or religion **4** rugby a score made after a try by kicking the ball over the crossbar from a place kick ▶ HISTORY Latin conversio a turning around

convert vb **1** to change or adapt **2** to cause (someone) to change in opinion or belief **3** to change (a measurement) from one system of units to another **4** to change (money) into a different currency **5** rugby to make a conversion after (a try) ▷ n **6** a person who has been converted to another belief or religion ▶ HISTORY Latin convertere to turn around, alter > **converter** or **convertor** n

convertible adj **1** capable of being converted **2** finance (of a currency) freely exchangeable into other currencies ▷ n **3** a car with a folding or removable roof

convex adj curving outwards like the outside surface of a ball ▶ HISTORY Latin convexus vaulted, rounded > **convexity** n

convey vb **1** to communicate (information) **2** to carry or transport from one place to another **3** (of a channel or path) to transfer or transmit **4** law to transfer (the title to property) ▶ HISTORY Old French conveier > **conveyable** adj > **conveyor** n

conveyance n **1** old-fashioned a vehicle **2** law **a** a transfer of the legal title to property **b** the document effecting such a transfer **3** the act of conveying: the conveyance of cycles on peak hour trains > **conveyancer** n

C

conveyancing *n* the branch of law dealing with the transfer of ownership of property

conveyor belt *n* an endless moving belt driven by rollers and used to transport objects, esp. in a factory

convict *vb* **1** to declare (someone) guilty of an offence ▷ *n* **2** a person serving a prison sentence ▶ HISTORY Latin *convictus* convicted

conviction *n* **1** a firmly held belief or opinion **2** an instance of being found guilty of a crime: *he had several convictions for petty theft* **3** a convincing or being convinced **4 carry conviction** to be convincing

convictism *n* *history* the practice of sending convicts to a penal colony, esp. Australia, to carry out forced labour

convince *vb* **-vincing, -vinced** to persuade by argument or evidence ▶ HISTORY Latin *convincere* to demonstrate incontrovertibly > **convinced** *adj* > **convincible** *adj* > **convincing** *adj*

convivial *adj* sociable or lively: *a convivial atmosphere; convivial company* ▶ HISTORY Late Latin *convivialis* > **conviviality** *n*

convocation *n* *formal* a large formal meeting

convoke *vb* **-voking, -voked** *formal* to call together ▶ HISTORY Latin *convocare*

convoluted *adj* **1** coiled or twisted **2** (of an argument or sentence) complex and difficult to understand

convolution *n* **1** a coil or twist **2** an intricate or confused matter or condition **3** a convex fold in the surface of the brain

convolvulus *n, pl* **-luses** *or* **-li** a twining plant with funnel-shaped flowers and triangular leaves ▶ HISTORY Latin: bindweed

convoy *n* a group of vehicles or ships travelling together ▶ HISTORY Old French *convoier* to convey

convulse *vb* **-vulsing, -vulsed** **1** to shake or agitate violently **2** (of muscles) to undergo violent spasms **3** *informal* to be overcome (with laughter or rage) **4** to disrupt the normal running of: *student riots have convulsed India* ▶ HISTORY Latin *con-* together + *vellere* to pluck, pull > **convulsive** *adj*

convulsion *n* **1** a violent muscular spasm **2** a violent upheaval **3 convulsions** *informal* uncontrollable laughter: *I was in convulsions*

cony *or* **coney** *n, pl* **-nies** *or* **-neys** *Brit* **1** a rabbit **2** rabbit fur ▶ HISTORY Latin *cuniculus* rabbit

coo *vb* **cooing, cooed** **1** (of a dove or pigeon) to make a soft murmuring sound **2 bill and coo** to murmur softly or lovingly ▷ *n* **3** a cooing sound ▷ *interj* **4** *Brit, slang* an exclamation of surprise or amazement ▶ HISTORY imitative > **cooing** *adj, n*

cooee *interj* **1** *Brit, Austral & NZ* a call used to attract attention **2** *Austral & NZ* **within cooee** within calling distance: *the school was within cooee of our house* ▶ HISTORY Aboriginal

cook *vb* **1** to prepare (food) by heating or (of food) to be prepared in this way **2** *slang* to alter or falsify (figures or accounts): *she had cooked the books* ▷ *n*

3 a person who prepares food for eating ▷ See also **cook up** ▶ HISTORY Latin *coquere*

cooker *n* **1** *chiefly Brit* an apparatus for cooking heated by gas or electricity **2** *Brit* an apple suitable for cooking but not for eating raw

cookery *n* the art or practice of cooking. *Related adjective:* **culinary**

cookie *n, pl* **cookies** **1** *US & Canad* a biscuit **2** *computers* a piece of data downloaded from a website to a user's computer, allowing the user to be identified on future visits to the website **3 that's the way the cookie crumbles** *informal* that is how things inevitably are **4** *informal* a person: *a real tough cookie* ▶ HISTORY Dutch *koekje* little cake

cook up *vb* *informal* to invent (a story or scheme)

cool *adj* **1** moderately cold: *it should be served cool, even chilled* **2** comfortably free of heat: *it was one of the few cool days that summer* **3** calm and unemotional: *a cool head* **4** indifferent or unfriendly: *the idea met with a cool response* **5** calmly impudent **6** *informal* (of a large sum of money) without exaggeration: *a cool million* **7** *informal* sophisticated or elegant **8** (of a colour) having violet, blue, or green predominating **9** *informal* marvellous ▷ *vb* **10** to make or become cooler **11** to calm down ▷ *n* **12** coolness: *in the cool of the evening* **13** *slang* calmness; composure: *he lost his cool and wantonly kicked the ball away* ▶ HISTORY Old English *cōl* > **coolly** *adv* > **coolness** *n*

coolant *n* a fluid used to cool machinery while it is working

cool drink *n* *S African* a soft drink

cooler *n* a container for making or keeping things cool

coolibah *n* an Australian eucalypt that grows beside rivers ▶ HISTORY Aboriginal

coolie *n* *old-fashioned, offensive* an unskilled Oriental labourer ▶ HISTORY Hindi *kulī*

cooling tower *n* a tall hollow structure in a factory or power station, inside which hot water cools as it trickles down

coomb *or* **coombe** *n* a short valley or deep hollow ▶ HISTORY Old English *cumb*

coon *n* *informal* short for **raccoon**

coop¹ *n* **1** a cage or pen for poultry or small animals ▷ *vb* **2 coop up** to confine in a restricted place ▶ HISTORY Latin *cupa* basket, cask

coop² *or* **co-op** (**koh**-op) *n* *Brit, Austral & NZ* a cooperative society or a shop run by a cooperative society

cooper *n* a person who makes or repairs barrels or casks ▶ HISTORY see COOP¹

cooperate *or* **co-operate** *vb* **1** to work or act together **2** to assist or be willing to assist ▶ HISTORY Latin *co-* with + *operari* to work > **cooperation** *or* **co-operation** *n*

cooperative *or* **co-operative** *adj* **1** willing to cooperate **2** (of an enterprise or farm) owned and managed collectively ▷ *n* **3** a cooperative organization > **cooperatively** *or* **co-operatively** *adv*

cooperative society n a commercial enterprise owned and run by customers or workers, in which the profits are shared among the members

coopt or **co-opt** (koh-**opt**) vb to add (someone) to a group by the agreement of the existing members ▶ HISTORY Latin *cooptare* to choose, elect

coordinate or **co-ordinate** vb **-nating, -nated 1** to bring together and cause to work together efficiently ▷ n **2** maths any of a set of numbers defining the location of a point with reference to a system of axes ▷ adj **3** of or involving coordination **4** of or involving the use of coordinates: *coordinate geometry* ▶ HISTORY Latin *co-* together + *ordinatio* arranging > **coordination** or **co-ordination** n > **coordinator** or **co-ordinator** n

coordinate clause n grammar one of two or more clauses in a sentence having the same status and joined by a coordinating conjunction such as *and, but*, or *or*

coordinating conjunction n grammar a conjunction that joins coordinate clauses, such as *and, but*, or *or*

coot n **1** a small black water bird **2** Brit, Austral & NZ a foolish person ▶ HISTORY probably Low German

cop slang n **1** a policeman **2 not much cop** of little value or worth ▷ vb **copping, copped 3** to take or seize **4 cop it** to get into trouble or be punished: *he copped it after he was spotted driving a car without a seat belt* ▷ See also **cop out** ▶ HISTORY perhaps from Old French *caper* to seize

copal n a resin used in varnishes

copartner n a partner or associate > **copartnership** n

cope¹ vb **coping, coped 1** to deal successfully (with): *well-nourished people cope better with stress* **2** to tolerate or endure: *the ability to cope with his pain* ▶ HISTORY Old French *coper* to strike, cut

cope² n a large ceremonial cloak worn by some Christian priests ▶ HISTORY Late Latin *cappa* hooded cloak

cope³ vb **coping, coped** to provide (a wall) with a coping ▶ HISTORY probably from French *couper* to cut

Copernican (kop-**per**-nik-an) adj of the theory that the earth and the planets rotate round the sun ▶ HISTORY after *Copernicus*, astronomer

copier n a person or machine that copies

copilot n the second pilot of an aircraft

coping n a layer of rounded or sloping bricks on the top of a wall

coping saw n a handsaw with a U-shaped frame, used for cutting curves in wood

copious (**kope**-ee-uss) adj existing or produced in large quantities ▶ HISTORY Latin *copiosus* > **copiously** adv

cop out slang vb **1** to avoid taking responsibility or committing oneself ▷ n **cop-out 2** a way or an instance of avoiding responsibility or commitment ▶ HISTORY probably from COP

copper¹ n **1** a soft reddish metallic element, used in such alloys as brass and bronze. Symbol: Cu **2** informal any copper or bronze coin **3** chiefly Brit a large metal container used to boil water ▷ adj **4** reddish-brown ▶ HISTORY Latin *Cyprium aes* Cyprian metal, from Greek *Kupris* Cyprus

copper² n Brit, slang a policeman ▶ HISTORY from COP (verb)

copper beech n a European beech with reddish leaves

copper-bottomed adj financially reliable ▶ HISTORY from the practice of coating the bottom of ships with copper to prevent the timbers rotting

copperhead n a poisonous snake with a reddish-brown head

copperplate n **1** an elegant handwriting style **2** a polished copper plate engraved for printing **3** a print taken from such a plate

copper sulphate n a blue crystalline copper salt used in electroplating and in plant sprays

coppice n a small group of trees or bushes growing close together ▶ HISTORY Old French *copeiz*

copra n the dried oil-yielding kernel of the coconut ▶ HISTORY Malayalam (a language of SW India) *koppara* coconut

copse n same as **coppice** ▶ HISTORY from COPPICE

Copt n **1** a member of the Coptic Church, a part of the Christian Church which was founded in Egypt **2** an Egyptian descended from the ancient Egyptians ▶ HISTORY Coptic *kyptios* Egyptian

Coptic n **1** the language of the Copts, descended from Ancient Egyptian and surviving only in the Coptic Church ▷ adj **2** of the Copts or the Coptic Church

copula n, pl **-las** or **-lae** a verb, such as *be*, that is used to link the subject with the complement of a sentence, as in *he became king* ▶ HISTORY Latin: bond

copulate vb **-lating, -lated** to have sexual intercourse ▶ HISTORY Latin *copulare* to join together > **copulation** n

copy n, pl **copies 1** a thing made to look exactly like another **2** a single specimen of a book, magazine, or record of which there are many others exactly the same: *my copy of 'Death on the Nile'* **3** written material for printing **4** the text of an advertisement **5** journalism, informal suitable material for an article: *disasters are always good copy* ▷ vb **copies, copying, copied 6** to make a copy (of) **7** to act or try to be like another **8** computers to make a copy of (information in a document) in order to reproduce it elsewhere ▶ HISTORY Latin *copia* abundance

copybook n **1** a book of specimens of handwriting for imitation **2 blot one's copybook** informal to spoil one's reputation by a mistake or indiscretion ▷ adj **3** done exactly according to the rules **4** trite or unoriginal

copyright n **1** the exclusive legal right to reproduce and control an original literary, musical, or artistic work ▷ vb **2** to take out a copyright on ▷ adj **3** protected by copyright

copywriter n a person employed to write advertising copy

coquette n a woman who flirts ▸ HISTORY French > **coquetry** n > **coquettish** adj

coracle n a small round boat made of wicker covered with skins ▸ HISTORY Welsh *corwgl*

coral n 1 the stony substance formed by the skeletons of marine animals called polyps, often forming an island or reef 2 any of the polyps whose skeletons form coral ▷ adj 3 orange-pink ▸ HISTORY Greek *korallion*

coral island n geog an island formed from coral and other substances

coral reef n geog a marine ridge or reef consisting of coral and other organic material consolidated into limestone, lying just beneath the surface of the sea

cor anglais n, pl **cors anglais** music an alto woodwind instrument of the oboe family ▸ HISTORY French: English horn

corbel n archit a stone or timber support sticking out of a wall ▸ HISTORY Old French: a little raven

corbie n Scot a raven or crow ▸ HISTORY Latin *corvus*

cord n 1 string or thin rope made of twisted strands 2 anat a structure in the body resembling a rope: *the vocal cords* 3 a ribbed fabric like corduroy 4 US, Canad, Austral & NZ an electrical flex 5 a unit for measuring cut wood, equal to 128 cubic feet ▷ adj 6 (of fabric) ribbed ▷ See also **cords** ▸ HISTORY Greek *khordē*

cordate adj heart-shaped

corded adj 1 tied or fastened with cord 2 (of a fabric) ribbed: *white corded silk* 3 (of muscles) standing out like cords

cordial adj 1 warm and friendly: *a cordial atmosphere* 2 heartfelt or sincere: *I developed a cordial dislike for the place* ▷ n 3 a drink with a fruit base: *lime cordial* ▸ HISTORY Latin *cor* heart > **cordially** adv

cordiality n warmth of feeling

cordite n a smokeless explosive used in guns and bombs ▸ HISTORY from *cord*, because of its stringy appearance

cordless adj (of an electrical appliance such as a kettle or telephone) powered by an internal battery or kept in a holder which is connected to the mains, so that there is no cable connecting the appliance itself to the electrical mains

cordon n 1 a chain of police, soldiers, or vehicles guarding an area 2 an ornamental braid or ribbon 3 horticulture a fruit tree trained to grow as a single stem bearing fruit ▷ vb 4 **cordon off** to put or form a cordon round ▸ HISTORY Old French: a little cord

cordon bleu (**bluh**) adj (of cookery or cooks) of the highest standard: *a cordon bleu chef* ▸ HISTORY French: blue ribbon

cords pl n trousers made of corduroy

corduroy n a heavy cotton fabric with a velvety ribbed surface ▸ HISTORY origin unknown

core n 1 the central part of certain fleshy fruits, containing the seeds 2 the central or essential part of something: *the historic core of the city* 3 a piece of magnetic soft iron inside an electromagnet or transformer 4 geol the central part of the earth 5 a cylindrical sample of rock or soil, obtained by the use of a hollow drill 6 physics the region of a nuclear reactor containing the fissionable material 7 computers the main internal memory of a computer ▷ vb **coring, cored** 8 to remove the core from (fruit) ▸ HISTORY origin unknown

corella n a white Australian cockatoo

co-respondent n a person with whom someone being sued for divorce is claimed to have committed adultery

corgi n a short-legged sturdy dog ▸ HISTORY Welsh *cor* dwarf + *ci* dog

coriander n a European plant, cultivated for its aromatic seeds and leaves, used in flavouring foods ▸ HISTORY Greek *koriannon*

Corinthian adj 1 of Corinth, a port in S Greece 2 of a style of classical architecture characterized by a bell-shaped capital with carved leaf-shaped ornaments ▷ n 3 a person from Corinth

Coriolis effect n geog the horizontal deflection of air, water, or moving objects to the right or to the left depending on whether they are in the northern or the southern hemisphere; caused by the earth's rotation ▸ HISTORY after Gaspard G. *Coriolis* (1792--1843), French civil engineer

Coriolis force n a hypothetical force postulated to explain the deflection in the path of a body moving relative to the earth ▸ HISTORY after Gaspard G. *Coriolis* (1792--1843), French civil engineer

cork n 1 the thick light porous outer bark of a Mediterranean oak 2 a piece of cork used as a stopper 3 bot the outer bark of a woody plant ▷ vb 4 to stop up (a bottle) with a cork ▸ HISTORY probably from Arabic *qurq*

corkage n a charge made at a restaurant for serving wine bought elsewhere

corked adj (of wine) spoiled through being stored in a bottle with a decayed cork

corkscrew n 1 a device for pulling corks from bottles, usually consisting of a pointed metal spiral attached to a handle ▷ adj 2 like a corkscrew in shape ▷ vb 3 to move in a spiral or zigzag course

corm n the scaly bulblike underground stem of certain plants ▸ HISTORY Greek *kormos* tree trunk

cormorant n a large dark-coloured long-necked sea bird ▸ HISTORY Old French *corp* raven + *mareng* of the sea

corn¹ n 1 a cereal plant such as wheat, oats, or barley 2 the grain of such plants 3 US, Canad, Austral & NZ maize 4 slang something unoriginal or oversentimental ▸ HISTORY Old English

corn² n a painful hardening of the skin around a central point in the foot, caused by pressure ▸ HISTORY Latin *cornu* horn

corn circle n same as **crop circle**

corncob n the core of an ear of maize, to which the kernels are attached

corncrake n a brown bird with a harsh grating cry

cornea (**korn-ee-a**) n the transparent membrane covering the eyeball ▸ HISTORY Latin *cornu* horn > **corneal** adj

corned beef *n* cooked beef preserved in salt

cornelian *n* same as **carnelian**

corner *n* **1** the place or angle formed by the meeting of two converging lines or surfaces **2** the space within the angle formed, as in a room **3** the place where two streets meet **4** a sharp bend in a road **5** *written* a remote place: *far-flung corners of the world* **6** any secluded or private place **7** *sport* a free kick or shot taken from the corner of the field **8 cut corners** to take the shortest or easiest way at the expense of high standards **9 turn the corner** to pass the critical point of an illness or a difficult time ▷ *adj* **10** on or in a corner: *a corner seat* ▷ *vb* **11** to force (a person or animal) into a difficult or inescapable position **12** (of a vehicle or its driver) to turn a corner **13** to obtain a monopoly of ▶ HISTORY Latin *cornu* point, horn

cornerstone *n* **1** an indispensable part or basis: *the food we eat is one of the cornerstones of good health* **2** a stone at the corner of a wall

cornet *n* **1** a brass instrument of the trumpet family **2** *Brit* a cone-shaped ice-cream wafer ▶ HISTORY Latin *cornu* horn > **cornetist** *n*

corn exchange *n* a building where corn is bought and sold

cornflakes *pl n* a breakfast cereal made from toasted maize

cornflour *n* **1** a fine maize flour, used for thickening sauces **2** *NZ* fine wheat flour

cornflower *n* a small plant with blue flowers

cornice (**korn**-iss) *n* **1** a decorative moulding round the top of a wall or building **2** *archit* the projecting mouldings at the top of a column ▶ HISTORY Old French

Cornish *adj* **1** of Cornwall ▷ *n* **2** a Celtic language of Cornwall, extinct by 1800 ▷ *pl n* **3 the Cornish** the people of Cornwall

Cornish pasty *n* a pastry case with a filling of meat and vegetables

cornucopia (korn-yew-**kope**-ee-a) *n* **1** a great abundance: *a cornucopia of rewards* **2** a symbol of plenty, consisting of a horn overflowing with fruit and flowers ▶ HISTORY Latin *cornu copiae* horn of plenty

corny *adj* **cornier, corniest** *slang* unoriginal or oversentimental

corolla *n* the petals of a flower collectively ▶ HISTORY Latin: garland

corollary (kor-**oll**-a-ree) *n*, *pl* -laries **1** a proposition that follows directly from another that has been proved **2** a natural consequence ▶ HISTORY Latin *corollarium* money paid for a garland

corona (kor-**rone**-a) *n*, *pl* -nas *or* -nae (-nee) **1** a circle of light around a luminous body, usually the moon **2** the outermost part of the sun's atmosphere, visible as a faint halo during a total eclipse **3** a long cigar with blunt ends **4** *bot* a crownlike part of some flowers on top of the seed or on the inner side of the corolla **5** *physics* an electrical glow appearing around the surface of a charged conductor ▶ HISTORY Latin: crown

coronary (**kor**-ron-a-ree) *adj* **1** *anat* of the arteries that supply blood to the heart ▷ *n*, *pl* -naries **2** a coronary thrombosis ▶ HISTORY Latin *coronarius* belonging to a wreath or crown

coronary heart disease *n* *pathol* any heart disorder caused by disease of the coronary arteries

coronary thrombosis *n* a condition where the blood flow to the heart is blocked by a clot in a coronary artery

coronation *n* the ceremony of crowning a monarch ▶ HISTORY Latin *coronare* to crown

coroner *n* a public official responsible for the investigation of violent, sudden, or suspicious deaths ▶ HISTORY Anglo-French *corouner*

coronet *n* **1** a small crown worn by princes or peers **2** a band of jewels worn as a headdress ▶ HISTORY Old French *coronete*

corpora *pl n* the plural of **corpus**

corporal[1] *n* a noncommissioned officer in an army ▶ HISTORY Old French *caporal*, from Latin *caput* head

corporal[2] *adj* of the body ▶ HISTORY Latin *corpus* body

corporal punishment *n* physical punishment, such as caning

corporate *adj* **1** relating to business corporations: *corporate finance* **2** shared by a group **3** forming a corporation; incorporated ▶ HISTORY Latin *corpus* body

corporation *n* **1** a large business or company **2** a city or town council **3** *informal* a large paunch > **corporative** *adj*

corporation tax *n* *econ* a British tax on the profits of a company

corporatism *n* organization of a state on the lines of a business enterprise, with substantial government management of the economy

corporeal (kore-**pore**-ee-al) *adj* of the physical world rather than the spiritual ▶ HISTORY Latin *corpus* body

corps (**kore**) *n*, *pl* **corps** **1** a military unit with a specific function: *medical corps* **2** an organized body of people: *the diplomatic corps* ▶ HISTORY French

corpse *n* a dead body, esp. of a human being ▶ HISTORY Latin *corpus*

corpulent *adj* fat or plump ▶ HISTORY Latin *corpulentus* > **corpulence** *n*

corpus *n*, *pl* -pora a collection of writings, such as one by a single author or on a specific topic: *the corpus of Marxist theory* ▶ HISTORY Latin: body

corpuscle *n* a red blood cell (see **erythrocyte**) or white blood cell (see **leucocyte**) ▶ HISTORY Latin *corpusculum* a little body > **corpuscular** *adj*

corral *US & Canad n* **1** an enclosure for cattle or horses ▷ *vb* -ralling, -ralled **2** to put in a corral ▶ HISTORY Spanish

corrasion *n* *geol* erosion of rocks caused by fragments transported over them by water, wind, or ice ▶ HISTORY Latin *corradere* to scrape together

correct *adj* **1** free from error; true: *the correct answer* **2** in conformity with accepted standards: *in most cultures there is a strong sense of correct conduct*

▷ vb **3** to make free from or put right errors **4** to indicate the errors in (something) **5** to rebuke or punish in order to improve: *I stand corrected* **6** to make conform to a standard ▶ HISTORY Latin *corrigere* to make straight > **correctly** *adv* > **correctness** *n*

correction *n* **1** an act or instance of correcting **2** an alteration correcting something: *corrections to the second proofs* **3** a reproof or punishment > **correctional** *adj*

corrective *adj* intended to put right something that is wrong: *corrective action*

correlate *vb* **-lating, -lated** **1** to place or be placed in a mutual relationship: *water consumption is closely correlated to the number of people living in a house* ▷ *n* **2** either of two things mutually related > **correlation** *n*

correlative *adj* **1** having a mutual relationship **2** *grammar* (of words, usually conjunctions) corresponding to each other and occurring regularly together, for example *neither* and *nor*

correspond *vb* **1** to be consistent or compatible (with) **2** to be similar (to) **3** to communicate (with) by letter ▶ HISTORY Latin *com-* together + *respondere* to respond > **corresponding** *adj* > **correspondingly** *adv*

correspondence *n* **1** communication by letters **2** the letters exchanged in this way **3** relationship or similarity

correspondence course *n* a course of study conducted by post

correspondent *n* **1** a person who communicates by letter **2** a person employed by a newspaper or news service to report on a special subject or from a foreign country

corresponding angle *n* *geom* in a diagram where two straight lines are crossed by a transversal, either of the two angles on the same side of the transversal above each straight line, or the ones below them. The corresponding angles are equal when the two straight lines are parallel

corridor *n* **1** a passage in a building or a train **2** a strip of land or airspace that provides access through the territory of a foreign country **3** **corridors of power** the higher levels of government or the Civil Service ▶ HISTORY Old Italian *corridore*, literally: place for running

corrie *n* (in Scotland) a circular hollow on the side of a hill ▶ HISTORY Gaelic *coire* cauldron

corrigendum (kor-rij-**end**-um) *n, pl* **-da** (-da) **1** an error to be corrected **2** a slip of paper inserted into a book after printing, listing corrections ▶ HISTORY Latin: that which is to be corrected

corroborate *vb* **-rating, -rated** to support (a fact or opinion) by giving proof ▶ HISTORY Latin *com-* (intensive) + *roborare* to make strong > **corroboration** *n* > **corroborative** *adj*

corroborating evidence *n* *law* evidence by another witness that supports or confirms the accuracy of evidence already given

corroboree *n* *Austral* **1** an Aboriginal gathering or dance of festive or warlike character **2** *informal* any noisy gathering ▶ HISTORY Aboriginal

corrode *vb* **-roding, -roded** **1** to eat away or be eaten away by chemical action or rusting **2** to destroy gradually: *rumours corroding the public's affection for the royal family* ▶ HISTORY Latin *corrodere* to gnaw to pieces

corrosion *n* **1** the process by which something, esp. a metal, is corroded **2** the result of corrosion > **corrosive** *adj*

corrugate *vb* **-gating, -gated** to fold into alternate grooves and ridges ▶ HISTORY Latin *corrugare* > **corrugation** *n*

corrugated iron *n* a thin sheet of iron or steel, formed with alternating ridges and troughs

corrupt *adj* **1** open to or involving bribery or other dishonest practices: *corrupt practices* **2** morally depraved **3** (of a text or data) made unreliable by errors or alterations ▷ *vb* **4** to make corrupt ▶ HISTORY Latin *corruptus* spoiled > **corruptive** *adj*

corruptible *adj* capable of being corrupted

corruption *n* **1** dishonesty and illegal behaviour **2** the act of corrupting morally **3** the process of rotting or decaying **4** an unintentional or unauthorized alteration in a text or data **5** an altered form of a word

corsage (kore-**sahzh**) *n* a small bouquet worn on the bodice of a dress ▶ HISTORY Old French *cors* body

corsair *n* **1** a pirate **2** a pirate ship **3** a privateer ▶ HISTORY Old French *corsaire*

corselet *n* **1** a woman's one-piece undergarment, combining corset and bra **2** a piece of armour to cover the trunk ▶ HISTORY Old French *cors* bodice

corset *n* **1** a close-fitting undergarment worn by women to shape the torso **2** a similar garment worn by either sex to support and protect the back ▶ HISTORY Old French: a little bodice > **corsetry** *n*

cortege (kore-**tayzh**) *n* a funeral procession ▶ HISTORY Italian *corteggio*

cortex (**kore**-tex) *n, pl* **-tices** (-tiss-seez) *anat* the outer layer of the brain or some other internal organ ▶ HISTORY Latin: bark, outer layer > **cortical** *adj*

cortisone *n* a steroid hormone used in treating rheumatoid arthritis, allergies, and skin diseases ▶ HISTORY *corticosterone*, a hormone

corundum *n* a hard mineral used as an abrasive, and of which the ruby and white sapphire are precious forms ▶ HISTORY Tamil *kuruntam*

coruscate *vb* **-cating, -cated** *formal* to emit flashes of light; sparkle ▶ HISTORY Latin *coruscare* to flash > **coruscating** *adj* > **coruscation** *n*

corvette *n* a lightly armed escort warship ▶ HISTORY perhaps from Middle Dutch *corf*

corymb *n* *bot* a flat-topped flower cluster with the stems growing progressively shorter towards the centre ▶ HISTORY Greek *korumbos* cluster

cos^1 *or* **cos lettuce** *n* a lettuce with a long slender head and crisp leaves ▶ HISTORY after *Kos*, the Aegean island of its origin

cos^2 cosine

cosec (**koh**-sek) cosecant

cosecant (koh-**seek**-ant) *n* (in trigonometry) the ratio of the length of the hypotenuse to that of the opposite side in a right-angled triangle

cosh *chiefly Brit n* **1** a heavy blunt weapon, often made of hard rubber ▷ *vb* **2** to hit on the head with a cosh ▶ **HISTORY** Romany *kosh*

cosignatory *n, pl* **-ries** a person or country that signs a document jointly with others

cosine (koh-sine) *n* (in trigonometry) the ratio of the length of the adjacent side to that of the hypotenuse in a right-angled triangle ▶ **HISTORY** see CO-, SINE

cosmetic *n* **1** anything applied to the face or body in order to improve the appearance ▷ *adj* **2** done or used to improve the appearance of the face or body **3** improving in appearance only: *glossy brochures are part of a cosmetic exercise* ▶ **HISTORY** Greek *kosmētikos*, from *kosmein* to arrange

cosmetic surgery *n* surgery performed to improve the appearance, rather than for medical reasons

cosmic *adj* **1** of or relating to the whole universe: *the cosmic order* **2** occurring in or coming from outer space: *cosmic dust*

cosmogony *n, pl* **-nies** the study of the origin of the universe ▶ **HISTORY** Greek *kosmos* world + *gonos* creation

cosmology *n* the study of the origin and nature of the universe ▶ **HISTORY** Greek *kosmos* world + -LOGY > **cosmological** *adj*
> **cosmologist** *n*

cosmonaut *n* the Russian name for an astronaut ▶ **HISTORY** Russian *kosmonavt*, from Greek *kosmos* universe + *nautēs* sailor

cosmopolitan *adj* **1** composed of people or elements from many different countries or cultures **2** having lived and travelled in many countries ▷ *n* **3** a cosmopolitan person ▶ **HISTORY** Greek *kosmos* world + *politēs* citizen > **cosmopolitanism** *n*

cosmos *n* the universe considered as an ordered system ▶ **HISTORY** Greek *kosmos* order

Cossack *n* **1** a member of a S Russian people, famous as horsemen and dancers ▷ *adj* **2** of the Cossacks: *a Cossack dance* ▶ **HISTORY** Russian *kazak* vagabond

cosset *vb* **-seting, -seted** to pamper or pet ▶ **HISTORY** origin unknown

cost *n* **1** the amount of money, time, or energy required to obtain or produce something **2** suffering or sacrifice: *these were crucial truths which rugby never grasped, to its cost* **3** the amount paid for a commodity by its seller: *to sell at cost* **4 costs** *law* the expenses of a lawsuit **5 at all costs** regardless of any cost or effort involved **6 at the cost of** at the expense of losing: *a boat costs about a thousand dollars* ▷ *vb* **costing, cost** **7** to be obtained or obtainable in exchange for: *calls cost 36p a minute cheap rate, 48p at other times* **8** to involve the loss or sacrifice of: *a fall which almost cost him his life* **9** to estimate the cost of producing something ▶ **HISTORY** Latin *constare* to stand at, cost

cost accounting *n* the recording and controlling of all the costs involved in running a business
> **cost accountant** *n*

costal *adj* of the ribs

cost-effective *adj* providing adequate financial return in relation to outlay

costermonger *n* Brit a person who sells fruit and vegetables from a barrow in the street
▶ **HISTORY** *costard* a kind of apple + *monger* trader

costive *adj* old-fashioned having or causing constipation ▶ **HISTORY** Old French *costivé*

costly *adj* **-lier, -liest** **1** expensive **2** involving great loss or sacrifice: *a bitter and costly war*
> **costliness** *n*

cost of living *n* the average cost of the basic necessities of life, such as food, housing, and clothing

costume *n* **1** a style of dressing, including all the clothes and accessories, typical of a particular country or period **2** the clothes worn by an actor or performer: *a jester's costume* **3** short for **swimming costume** ▷ *vb* **-tuming, -tumed** **4** to provide with a costume: *she was costumed by many of the great Hollywood designers* ▶ **HISTORY** Italian: dress, custom > **costumed** *adj*

costume jewellery *n* inexpensive but attractive jewellery

costumier *n* a make or supplier of theatrical or fancy dress costumes

cosy *or US* **cozy** *adj* **-sier, -siest** *or US* **-zier, -ziest** **1** warm and snug **2** intimate and friendly: *a cosy chat* ▷ *n, pl* **-sies** *or US* **-zies** **3** a cover for keeping things warm: *a tea cosy* ▶ **HISTORY** Scots
> **cosiness** *or US* **coziness** *n*

cot¹ *n* **1** a bed with high sides for a baby or very young child **2** a small portable bed ▶ **HISTORY** Hindi *khāt* bedstead

cot² *n* **1** *literary or archaic* a small cottage **2** a cote ▶ **HISTORY** Old English

cot³ cotangent

cotangent *n* (in trigonometry) the ratio of the length of the adjacent side to that of the opposite side in a right-angled triangle

cot death *n* the unexplained sudden death of a baby while asleep

cote *or* **cot** *n* a small shelter for birds or animals ▶ **HISTORY** Old English

coterie (**kote**-er-ee) *n* a small exclusive group of friends or people with common interests
▶ **HISTORY** French

cotoneaster (kot-tone-ee-**ass**-ter) *n* a garden shrub with red berries

cottage *n* a small simple house, usually in the country ▶ **HISTORY** from COT² > **cottager** *n*

cottage cheese *n* a mild soft white cheese made from skimmed milk curds

cottage industry *n* a craft industry in which employees work at home

cottage pie *n* a dish of minced meat topped with mashed potato

cotter¹ *n* *machinery* a bolt or wedge that is used to secure parts of machinery ▶ **HISTORY** Middle English *cotterel*

cotter² *n Scot & history* a farm labourer occupying a cottage and land rent-free ▶ **HISTORY** see COT²

cotter pin *n machinery* a split pin used to hold parts together and fastened by having the ends spread apart after it is inserted

cotton *n* **1** the soft white downy fibre surrounding the seeds of a plant grown in warm climates, used to make cloth and thread **2** cloth or thread made from cotton fibres ▶ **HISTORY** Arabic *qutn* > **cottony** *adj*

cotton wool *n* absorbent fluffy cotton, used for surgical dressings and to apply creams to the skin

cotyledon (kot-ill-**ee**-don) *n* the first leaf produced by a plant embryo ▶ **HISTORY** Greek *kotulē* cup

couch *n* **1** a piece of upholstered furniture for seating more than one person **2** a bed on which patients of a doctor or a psychoanalyst lie during examination or treatment ▷ *vb* **3** *written* to express in a particular style of language: *a proclamation couched in splendidly archaic phraseology* **4** *archaic* (of an animal) to crouch, as when preparing to leap ▶ **HISTORY** Old French *coucher* to lay down

couchette (koo-**shett**) *n* a bed converted from seats on a train or ship ▶ **HISTORY** French

couch grass *n* a grassy weed which spreads quickly

couch potato *n slang* a lazy person whose main hobby is watching television

cougar (**koo**-gar) *n* same as **puma** ▶ **HISTORY** from S American Indian

cough *vb* **1** to expel air abruptly and noisily from the lungs **2** (of an engine or other machine) to make a sound similar to this ▷ *n* **3** an act or sound of coughing **4** an illness which causes frequent coughing ▶ **HISTORY** Old English *cohhetten*

cough up *vb* **1** *informal* to give up (money or information) **2** to bring up into the mouth by coughing: *to cough up blood*

could *vb* **1** used to make the past tense of **can¹** **2** *spoken* used to make the subjunctive mood of **can¹**, esp. in polite requests or conditional sentences: *could I have a word with you, please?* **3** used to indicate the suggestion of a course of action: *we could make a fortune from selling players, but that would not be in the long-term interests of the club* **4** used to indicate a possibility: *it could simply be a spelling mistake* ▶ **HISTORY** Old English *cūthe*

couldn't could not

coulomb (**koo**-lom) *n* the SI unit of electric charge ▶ **HISTORY** after C. A. de *Coulomb*, physicist

coulter (**kole**-ter) *n* a vertical blade on a plough in front of the ploughshare ▶ **HISTORY** Latin *culter* ploughshare, knife

council *n* **1** a group meeting for discussion or consultation **2** a legislative or advisory body: *the United Nations Security Council* **3** the local governing authority of a town or county **4** *Austral* the local governing authority of a district or shire ▷ *adj* **5** of or provided by a local council: *a council house* ▶ **HISTORY** Latin *concilium* assembly

councillor *or US* **councilor** *n* a member of a council

council tax *n* (in Britain) a tax based on the relative value of property levied to fund local council services

counsel *n* **1** advice or guidance **2** discussion or consultation: *when it was over they took counsel of their consciences* **3** a barrister or group of barristers who conduct cases in court and advise on legal matters ▷ *vb* **-selling, -selled** *or US* **-seling, -seled** **4** to give advice or guidance to **5** to recommend or urge ▶ **HISTORY** Latin *consilium* deliberating body > **counselling** *or US* **counseling** *n*

counsellor *or US* **counselor** *n* **1** an adviser **2** *US* a lawyer who conducts cases in court

count¹ *vb* **1** to say numbers in ascending order up to and including: *count from one to ten* **2** to add up or check (each thing in a group) in order to find the total: *he counted the money he had left* **3** to be important: *it's the thought that counts* **4** to consider: *he can count himself lucky* **5** to take into account or include: *the time he'd spent in prison on remand counted towards his sentence* **6** **not counting** excluding **7** *music* to keep time by counting beats ▷ *n* **8** the act of counting **9** the number reached by counting: *a high pollen count* **10** *law* one of a number of charges **11** **keep** or **lose count** to keep or fail to keep an accurate record of items or events **12** **out for the count** unconscious ▷ See also **countdown** ▶ **HISTORY** Latin *computare* to calculate > **countable** *adj*

count² *n* a middle-ranking European nobleman ▶ **HISTORY** Latin *comes* associate

countdown *n* the act of counting backwards to zero to time exactly an operation such as the launching of a rocket

countenance *n* **1** *literary* the face or facial expression ▷ *vb* **-nancing, -nanced** **2** to support or tolerate ▶ **HISTORY** Latin *continentia* restraint, control

counter¹ *n* **1** a long flat surface in a bank or shop, on which business is transacted **2** a small flat disc used in board games **3** a disc or token used as an imitation coin **4** **under the counter** (of the sale of goods) illegal ▶ **HISTORY** Latin *computare* to compute

counter² *n* an apparatus for counting things

counter³ *vb* **1** to say or do (something) in retaliation or response **2** to oppose or act against **3** to return the attack of (an opponent) ▷ *adv* **4** in an opposite or opposing direction or manner **5** **run counter to** to be in direct contrast with ▷ *adj* **6** opposing or opposite ▷ *n* **7** something that is contrary or opposite to something else **8** an opposing action **9** a return attack, such as a blow in boxing ▶ **HISTORY** Latin *contra* against

counter- *prefix* **1** against or opposite: *counterattack* **2** complementary or corresponding: *counterpart* ▶ **HISTORY** Latin *contra*

counteract *vb* to act against or neutralize > **counteraction** *n* > **counteractive** *adj*

counterattack *n* **1** an attack in response to an attack ▷ *vb* **2** to make a counterattack (against)

counterbalance *n* **1** a weight or influence that balances or neutralizes another ▷ *vb* **-ancing, -anced** **2** to act as a counterbalance to

counterblast *n* an aggressive response to a verbal attack

counterclockwise *adv, adj US & Canad* same as **anticlockwise**

counterespionage *n* activities to counteract enemy espionage

counterfeit *adj* **1** made in imitation of something genuine with the intent to deceive or defraud: *counterfeit currency* **2** pretended: *counterfeit friendship* ▷ *n* **3** an imitation designed to deceive or defraud ▷ *vb* **4** to make a fraudulent imitation of **5** to feign: *surprise is an easy emotion to counterfeit* ▶ HISTORY Old French *contrefait*

counterfoil *n* Brit the part of a cheque or receipt kept as a record

counterintelligence *n* activities designed to frustrate enemy espionage

countermand *vb* to cancel (a previous order) ▶ HISTORY Old French *contremander*

counterpane *n* a bed covering ▶ HISTORY Medieval Latin *culcita puncta* quilted mattress

counterpart *n* **1** a person or thing complementary to or corresponding to another **2** a duplicate of a legal document

counterpoint *n* **1** the harmonious combining of two or more parts or melodies **2** a melody or part combined in this way ▷ *vb* **3** to set in contrast ▶ HISTORY Old French *contrepoint* an accompaniment set against the notes of a melody

counterpoise *vb* **-poising, -poised** to oppose with something of equal weight or effect: *counterpoising humour and horror*

counterproductive *adj* having an effect opposite to the one intended

countersign *vb* **1** to sign (a document already signed by another) as confirmation ▷ *n* **2** the signature so written

countersink *vb* **-sinking, -sank, -sunk** to drive (a screw) into a shaped hole so that its head is below the surface

countertenor *n* **1** an adult male voice with an alto range **2** a singer with such a voice

counterterrorism *n* activities intended to prevent terrorist acts or to eradicate terrorist groups > **counterterrorist** *adj*

counter urbanization *or* **urbanisation** *n* *sociol* the settlement of an increasing proportion of city dwellers in rural areas

countess *n* **1** a woman holding the rank of count or earl **2** the wife or widow of a count or earl

countless *adj* too many to count

count noun *n* a noun that may be preceded by an indefinite article and can be used in the plural, such as *telephone* or *thing*

count on *vb* to rely or depend on

count out *vb* **1** *informal* to exclude **2** to declare (a boxer) defeated when he has not risen from the floor within ten seconds

countrified *adj* having an appearance or manner associated with the countryside rather than a town

country *n, pl* **-tries 1** an area distinguished by its people, culture, language, or government **2** the territory of a nation or state **3** the people of a nation or state **4** the part of the land that is away from cities or industrial areas **5** a person's native land **6** same as **country and western 7 across country** not keeping to roads **8 go to the country** Brit & NZ to dissolve Parliament and hold a general election ▶ HISTORY Medieval Latin *contrata (terra)* (land) lying opposite

country and western *or* **country music** *n* popular music based on American White folk music

countryman *n, pl* **-men 1** a person from one's own country **2** Brit, Austral & NZ a person who lives in the country > **countrywoman** *fem n*

countryside *n* land away from the cities

county *n, pl* **-ties 1** (in some countries) a division of a country, esp as a unit for local administration ▷ *adj* **2** Brit, informal upper-class ▶ HISTORY Old French *conté* land belonging to a count

county court *n* law (in England) a local court exercising limited jurisdiction in civil matters

coup (**koo**) *n* **1** a brilliant and successful action **2** a coup d'état ▶ HISTORY French

coup de grâce (**koo** de **grahss**) *n, pl* **coups de grâce** (**koo** de **grahss**) a final or decisive action ▶ HISTORY French

coup d'état (**koo** day-**tah**) *n, pl* **coups d'état** (**kooz** day-**tah**) a sudden violent or illegal overthrow of a government ▶ HISTORY French

coupé (**koo**-pay) *n* a sports car with two doors and a sloping fixed roof ▶ HISTORY French *carrosse coupé* cut-off carriage

couple *n* **1** two people who are married or romantically involved **2** two partners in a dance or game **3 a couple of a** a pair of: *a couple of guys* **b** informal a few: *a couple of weeks* ▷ *pron* **4 a couple a** two **b** informal a few: *give him a couple* ▷ *vb* **-pling, -pled 5** to connect or link: *an ingrained sense of shame, coupled with a fear of ridicule* ▶ HISTORY Latin *copula* a bond

couplet *n* two successive lines of verse, usually rhyming and of the same metre

coupling *n* a device for connecting things, such as railway carriages

coupon *n* **1** a piece of paper entitling the holder to a discount or free gift **2** a detachable slip that can be used as a commercial order form **3** Brit a football pools entry form ▶ HISTORY Old French *colpon* piece cut off

courage *n* **1** the ability to face danger or pain without fear **2 the courage of one's convictions** the confidence to act according to one's beliefs ▶ HISTORY Latin *cor* heart

courageous *adj* showing courage > **courageously** *adv*

courgette n a type of small vegetable marrow ▶ **HISTORY** French

courier n **1** a person who looks after and guides travellers **2** a person paid to deliver urgent messages ▶ **HISTORY** Latin *currere* to run

course n **1** a complete series of lessons or lectures: *a training course* **2** a sequence of medical treatment prescribed for a period of time: *a course of antibiotics* **3** an onward movement in time or space: *during the course of his career he worked with many leading actors* **4** a route or direction taken: *the ships were blown off course by a gale* **5** the path or channel along which a river moves **6** an area on which a sport is played or a race is held: *a golf course* **7** any of the successive parts of a meal **8** a continuous, usually horizontal layer of building material, such as bricks or tiles, at one level in a building **9** a mode of conduct or action: *the safest course of action was to do nothing* **10** the natural development of a sequence of events: *allow the fever to run its course* **11** a period of time: *over the course of the last two years* **12 as a matter of course** as a natural or normal consequence or event **13 in the course of** in the process of **14 in due course** at the natural or appropriate time **15 of course a** (adv) as expected; naturally **b** (interj) certainly; definitely ▷ vb **coursing, coursed 16** (of a liquid) to run swiftly **17** to hunt with hounds that follow the quarry by sight and not scent ▶ **HISTORY** Latin *cursus* a running

coursebook n a book that is used as part of an educational course

courser[1] n **1** a person who courses hounds **2** a hound trained for coursing

courser[2] n *literary* a swift horse; steed ▶ **HISTORY** Old French *coursier*

coursework n work done by a student and assessed as part of an educational course

court n **1** *law* **a** a judicial body which hears and makes decisions on legal cases **b** the room or building in which such a body meets **2** a marked area used for playing a racket game **3** an area of ground wholly or partly surrounded by walls or buildings **4** a name given to some short street, blocks of flats, or large country houses as a part of their address: *Carlton Court* **5** the residence or retinue of a sovereign **6** any formal assembly held by a sovereign **7 go to court** to take legal action **8 hold court** to preside over a group of admirers **9 out of court** without a trial or legal case **10 pay court to** to give flattering attention to ▷ vb **11** to attempt to gain the love of **12** to pay attention to (someone) in order to gain favour **13** to try to obtain (something): *he has not courted controversy, but he has certainly attracted it* **14** to make oneself open or vulnerable to: *courting disaster* ▶ **HISTORY** Latin *cohors* cohort

courteous adj polite and considerate in manner ▶ **HISTORY** Middle English *corteis* with courtly manners > **courteously** adv > **courteousness** n

courtesan (kore-tiz-**zan**) n *history* a mistress or high-class prostitute ▶ **HISTORY** Old French *courtisane*

courtesy n, pl **-sies 1** politeness; good manners **2** a courteous act or remark **3 by courtesy of** with the consent of ▶ **HISTORY** Old French *corteis* courteous

courthouse n a public building in which courts of law are held

courtier n an attendant at a royal court

courtly adj **-lier, -liest 1** ceremoniously polite **2** of or suitable for a royal court > **courtliness** n

court martial n, pl **court martials** or **courts martial 1** the trial of a member of the armed forces charged with breaking military law ▷ vb **court-martial, -tialling, -tialled** or US **-tialing, -tialed 2** to try by court martial

court of appeal n a court that hears appeals from other lower courts

courtship n the courting of an intended spouse or mate

court shoe n a low-cut shoe for women, without laces or straps

courtyard n an open area of ground surrounded by walls or buildings

cousin n the child of one's aunt or uncle. Also called: **first cousin** ▶ **HISTORY** Latin *consobrinus*

couture (koo-**toor**) n **1** high-fashion designing and dressmaking ▷ adj **2** relating to high fashion design and dressmaking: *couture clothes* ▶ **HISTORY** French: sewing

couturier n a person who designs fashion clothes for women ▶ **HISTORY** French

covalency or US **covalence** n *chem* **1** the ability to form a bond in which two atoms share a pair of electrons **2** the number of covalent bonds which a particular atom can make with others > **covalent** adj

covalent bonding n *chem* the process of forming a bond in which two atoms share a pair of electrons

cove[1] n a small bay or inlet ▶ **HISTORY** Old English *cofa*

cove[2] n *old-fashioned, slang* a fellow; chap ▶ **HISTORY** probably from Romany *kova*

coven (**kuv**-ven) n a meeting of witches ▶ **HISTORY** Latin *convenire* to come together

covenant (**kuv**-ven-ant) n **1** *chiefly Brit* a formal agreement to make an annual payment to charity **2** *law* a formal sealed agreement **3** *Bible* God's promise to the Israelites and their commitment to worship him alone ▷ vb **4** to agree by a legal covenant ▶ **HISTORY** Latin *convenire* to come together, agree > **covenanter** n

Covenanter n *Scot history* a person upholding either of two 17th-century covenants to establish and defend Presbyterianism

Coventry n **send someone to Coventry** to punish someone by refusing to speak to him or her ▶ **HISTORY** after *Coventry*, England

cover vb **1** to place something over so as to protect or conceal **2** to put a garment on; clothe **3** to extend over or lie thickly on the surface of: *the ground was covered with dry leaves* **4** (sometimes foll. by up) to screen or conceal; hide from view

5 to travel over **6** to protect (an individual or group) by taking up a position from which fire may be returned if those being protected are fired upon **7** to keep a gun aimed at **8 a** to insure against loss or risk **b** to provide for (loss or risk) by insurance **9** to include or deal with: *the course covers accounting, economics, statistics, law and computer applications* **10** to act as reporter or photographer on (a news event) for a newspaper or magazine **11** (of a sum of money) to be enough to pay for (something) **12** *music* to record a cover version of **13** *sport* to guard or obstruct (an opponent, team-mate, or area) **14 cover for** to deputize for (a person) **15** (foll. by *for* or *up for*) to provide an alibi (for): *can my men count on your friends at City Hall to cover for us?* ▷ *n* **16** anything which covers **17** a blanket or bedspread **18** the outside of a book or magazine **19** a pretext or disguise: *he claimed UN resolutions were being used as a cover for planned American aggression* **20** an envelope or other postal wrapping: *under plain cover* **21** an individual table setting **22** insurance **23** a cover version **24 the covers** *cricket* the area roughly at right angles to the pitch on the off side and about halfway to the boundary **25 break cover** to come out from a shelter or hiding place **26 take cover** to make for a place of safety or shelter **27 under cover** protected or in secret ▶ HISTORY Latin *cooperire* to cover completely > **covering** *adj, n*

coverage *n journalism* the amount of reporting given to a subject or event

cover charge *n* a fixed service charge added to the bill in a restaurant

cover girl *n* an attractive woman whose picture appears on the cover of a magazine

covering letter *n* an accompanying letter sent as an explanation

coverlet *n* same as **bedspread**

cover note *n Brit & Austral* a temporary certificate from an insurance company giving proof of a current policy

covert *adj* **1** concealed or secret ▷ *n* **2** a thicket or woodland providing shelter for game **3** *ornithol* any of the small feathers on the wings and tail of a bird that surround the bases of the larger feathers ▶ HISTORY Old French: covered > **covertly** *adv*

covet *vb* **-eting, -eted** to long to possess (something belonging to another person) ▶ HISTORY Latin *cupiditas* cupidity

covetous *adj* jealously longing to possess something > **covetously** *adv* > **covetousness** *n*

covey (**kuv**-vee) *n* **1** a small flock of grouse or partridge **2** a small group of people ▶ HISTORY Old French *cover* to sit on, hatch

cow¹ *n* **1** the mature female of cattle **2** the mature female of various other mammals, such as the elephant or whale **3** *not in technical use* any domestic species of cattle **4** *informal, offensive* a disagreeable woman ▶ HISTORY Old English *cū*

cow² *vb* to frighten or subdue with threats ▶ HISTORY Old Norse *kūga* to oppress

coward *n* a person who is easily frightened and avoids dangerous or difficult situations ▶ HISTORY Latin *cauda* tail > **cowardly** *adj*

cowardice *n* lack of courage

cowbell *n* a bell hung around a cow's neck

cowboy *n* **1** (in the US and Canada) a ranch worker who herds and tends cattle, usually on horseback **2** a conventional character of Wild West folklore or films **3** *informal* an irresponsible or unscrupulous worker or businessman > **cowgirl** *fem n*

cow cocky *n Austral & NZ* a one-man dairy farmer

cower *vb* to cringe or shrink in fear ▶ HISTORY Middle Low German *kūren* to lie in wait

cowl *n* **1** a loose hood **2** a monk's hooded robe **3** a cover fitted to a chimney to increase ventilation and prevent draughts ▶ HISTORY Latin *cucullus* hood > **cowled** *adj*

cowling *n* a streamlined detachable metal covering around an engine

cow parsley *n* a hedgerow plant with umbrella-shaped clusters of white flowers

cowpat *n* a pool of cow dung

cowpox *n* a contagious disease of cows, the virus of which is used to make smallpox vaccine

cowrie *n, pl* **-ries** the glossy brightly-marked shell of a marine mollusc ▶ HISTORY Hindi *kaurī*

cowslip *n* a European wild plant with yellow flowers ▶ HISTORY Old English *cūslyppe*, from *cū* cow + *slyppe* slime, dung

cox *n* **1** a coxswain ▷ *vb* **2** to act as coxswain of (a boat)

coxcomb *or* **cockscomb** *n* **1** the comb of a domestic cock **2** *informal* a conceited dandy

coxswain (**kok**-sn) *n* the person who steers a lifeboat or rowing boat ▶ HISTORY *cock* a ship's boat + SWAIN

coy *adj* **1** affectedly shy and modest **2** unwilling to give information ▶ HISTORY Latin *quietus* quiet > **coyly** *adv* > **coyness** *n*

coyote (koy-**ote**-ee) *n, pl* **-otes** *or* **-ote** a small wolf of the deserts and prairies of North America ▶ HISTORY Mexican Indian *coyotl*

coypu *n, pl* **-pus** *or* **-pu** a beaver-like amphibious rodent, bred for its fur ▶ HISTORY From a Native American language, *kóypu*

cozen *vb literary* to cheat or trick ▶ HISTORY originally a cant term > **cozenage** *n*

Cpl Corporal

CPU *computers* central processing unit

Cr *chem* chromium

crab *n* **1** an edible shellfish with five pairs of legs, the first pair modified into pincers **2** short for **crab louse 3 catch a crab** *rowing* to make a stroke in which the oar misses the water or digs too deeply, causing the rower to fall backwards ▶ HISTORY Old English *crabba*

crab apple *n* a kind of small sour apple

crabbed *adj* **1** (of handwriting) cramped and hard to read **2** bad-tempered ▶ HISTORY probably from *crab*, because of its sideways movement, influenced by *crab apple*, because of its sourness

191

crab louse *n* a parasitic louse living in the pubic area of humans

crack *vb* **1** to break or split without complete separation of the parts **2** to break with a sudden sharp sound **3** to make or cause to make a sudden sharp sound: *the coachman cracked his whip* **4** (of the voice) to become harsh or change pitch suddenly **5** *informal* to fail or break down: *he had cracked under the strain of losing his job* **6** to yield or cease to resist: *he had cracked under torture* **7** to hit with a forceful or resounding blow **8** to break into or force open: *it'll take me longer if I have to crack the safe myself* **9** to solve or decipher (a code or problem) **10** *informal* to tell (a joke) **11** to break (a molecule) into smaller molecules or radicals by heat or catalysis as in the distillation of petroleum **12** to open (a bottle) for drinking **13 crack it** *informal* to achieve something ▷ *n* **14** a sudden sharp noise **15** a break or fracture without complete separation of the two parts **16** a narrow opening or fissure **17** *informal* a sharp blow **18 crack of dawn** daybreak **19** a broken or cracked tone of voice **20** *informal* an attempt **21** *informal* a gibe or joke **22** *slang* a highly addictive form of cocaine **23 a fair crack of the whip** *informal* a fair chance or opportunity ▷ *adj* **24** *slang* first-class or excellent: *crack troops* ▷ See also **crack up** ▶ HISTORY Old English *cracian*

cracker *n* **1** a thin crisp unsweetened biscuit **2** a decorated cardboard tube, pulled apart with a bang, containing a paper hat and a joke or a toy **3** a small explosive firework **4** *slang* an excellent or notable thing or person

crackers *adj Brit & NZ, slang* insane

cracking *adj* **1 get cracking** *informal* to start doing something immediately **2 a cracking pace** *informal* a high speed ▷ *adv, adj* **3** *Brit, informal* first-class: *five cracking good saves* ▷ *n* **4** the oil-refining process in which heavy oils are broken down into smaller molecules by heat or catalysis

crackle *vb* **-ling, -led 1** to make small sharp popping noises ▷ *n* **2** a crackling sound > **crackly** *adj*

crackling *n* **1** a series of small sharp popping noises **2** the crisp browned skin of roast pork

crackpot *informal* ▷ *n* **1** an eccentric person ▷ *adj* **2** eccentric: *crackpot philosophies*

crack up *vb* **1** *informal* to have a physical or mental breakdown **2** to begin to break into pieces: *there are worrying reports of buildings cracking up as the earth dries out and foundations move* **3 not all it is cracked up to be** *informal* not as good as people have claimed it to be ▷ *n* **crackup 4** *informal* a physical or mental breakdown

-cracy *n combining form* indicating a type of government or rule: *plutocracy; mobocracy*. See also **-crat** ▶ HISTORY Greek *kratos* power

cradle *n* **1** a baby's bed on rockers **2** a place where something originates: *the cradle of civilization* **3** a supporting framework or structure **4** a platform or trolley in which workmen are suspended on the side of a building or ship ▷ *vb* **-dling, -dled 5** to hold gently as if in a cradle ▶ HISTORY Old English *cradol*

craft *n* **1** an occupation requiring skill or manual dexterity **2** skill or ability **3** cunning or guile **4** (*pl* **craft**) a boat, ship, aircraft, or spacecraft ▷ *vb* **5** to make skilfully ▶ HISTORY Old English *cræft* skill, strength

craftsman *or fem* **craftswoman** *n, pl* **-men** *or* **-women 1** a skilled worker **2** a skilled artist > **craftsmanship** *n*

craftwork *n* **1** the act of making things skilfully by hand **2** a piece of work made in this way

crafty *adj* **-tier, -tiest** skilled in deception > **craftily** *adv* > **craftiness** *n*

crag *n* a steep rugged rock or peak ▶ HISTORY Celtic > **craggy** *adj*

crake *n zool* a bird of the rail family, such as the corncrake ▶ HISTORY Old Norse *krāka* crow or *krākr* raven

cram *vb* **cramming, crammed 1** to force (more people or things) into (a place) than it can hold **2** to eat or feed to excess **3** *chiefly Brit* to study hard just before an examination ▶ HISTORY Old English *crammian*

crammer *n* a person or school that prepares pupils for an examination

cramp¹ *n* **1** a sudden painful contraction of a muscle **2** temporary stiffness of a muscle group from overexertion: *writer's cramp* **3** severe stomach pain **4** a clamp for holding masonry or timber together ▷ *vb* **5** to affect with a cramp ▶ HISTORY Old French *crampe*

cramp² *vb* **1** to confine or restrict **2 cramp someone's style** *informal* to prevent someone from impressing another person or from behaving naturally: *shyness will cramp their style* ▶ HISTORY Middle Dutch *crampe* hook

cramped *adj* **1** closed in **2** (of handwriting) small and irregular

crampon *n* a spiked iron plate strapped to a boot for climbing on ice ▶ HISTORY French

cranberry *n, pl* **-ries** a sour edible red berry ▶ HISTORY Low German *kraanbere* crane berry

crane *n* **1** a machine for lifting and moving heavy objects, usually by suspending them from a movable projecting arm **2** a large wading bird with a long neck and legs ▷ *vb* **craning, craned 3** to stretch out (the neck) in order to see something ▶ HISTORY Old English *cran*

crane fly *n* a fly with long legs, slender wings, and a narrow body

cranesbill *n* a plant with pink or purple flowers

crane shot *n films, television* a shot taken from a camera mounted on a crane

cranial *adj* of or relating to the skull

craniology *n* the scientific study of the human skull ▶ HISTORY Greek *kranion* skull + -LOGY

cranium *n, pl* **-niums** *or* **-nia** *anat* **1** the skull **2** the part of the skull that encloses the brain ▶ HISTORY Greek *kranion*

crank *n* **1** a device for transmitting or converting motion, consisting of an arm projecting at right angles from a shaft **2** a handle incorporating a crank, used to start an engine or motor **3** *informal* an eccentric or odd person ▷ *vb* **4** to turn with a crank **5** to start (an engine) with a crank ▶ **HISTORY** Old English *cranc*

crankcase *n* the metal case that encloses the crankshaft in an internal-combustion engine

crankpin *n* a short cylindrical pin in a crankshaft, to which the connecting rod is attached

crankshaft *n* a shaft with one or more cranks, to which the connecting rods are attached

cranky *adj* **crankier, crankiest** *informal* **1** eccentric **2** bad-tempered > **crankiness** *n*

cranny *n, pl* **-nies** a narrow opening ▶ **HISTORY** Old French *cran*

crap¹ *slang n* **1** nonsense **2** junk **3** *taboo* faeces ▷ *vb* **crapping, crapped** **4** *taboo* to defecate ▶ **HISTORY** Middle English *crappe* chaff > **crappy** *adj*

crap² *n* same as **craps**

crape *n* same as **crepe**

craps *n* **1** a gambling game played with two dice **2 shoot craps** to play this game ▶ **HISTORY** probably from *crabs* lowest throw at dice

crash *n* **1** a collision involving a vehicle or vehicles **2** a sudden descent of an aircraft as a result of which it crashes **3** a sudden loud noise **4** a breaking and falling to pieces **5** the sudden collapse of a business or stock exchange ▷ *vb* **6** to cause (a vehicle or aircraft) to collide with another vehicle, the ground, or some other object or (of vehicles or aircraft) to be involved in a collision **7** to make or cause to make a loud smashing noise **8** to drop with force and break into pieces with a loud noise **9** to break or smash into pieces with a loud noise **10** (of a business or stock exchange) to collapse or fail suddenly **11** to move violently or noisily **12** (of a computer system or program) to fail suddenly because of a malfunction **13** *Brit & Austral, informal* to gate-crash ▷ *adj* **14** requiring or using great effort in order to achieve results quickly: *a crash course* ▶ **HISTORY** probably Middle English *crasen* to smash + *dasshen* to strike

crash barrier *n* a safety barrier along the centre of a motorway, around a racetrack, or at the side of a dangerous road

crash dive *n* **1** a sudden steep emergency dive by a submarine ▷ *vb* **crash-dive, -diving, -dived** **2** to perform a crash dive

crash helmet *n* a helmet worn by motorcyclists to protect the head in case of a crash

crash-land *vb* (of an aircraft) to land in an emergency, causing damage > **crash-landing** *n*

crash out *vb informal* **1** to go to sleep or become unconscious **2** to be eliminated from a competition in a way that brings disgrace or embarrassment

crash team *n* a medical team with special equipment who can arrive quickly to treat a patient having a heart attack

crass *adj* stupid and insensitive: *the enquiry is crass and naive* ▶ **HISTORY** Latin *crassus* thick > **crassly** *adv* > **crassness** *n*

-crat *n combining form* indicating a supporter or member of a particular form of government:

autocrat; democrat ▶ **HISTORY** Greek *-kratēs* > **-cratic** *or* **-cratical** *adj combining form*

crate *n* **1 a** large container made of wooden slats, used for packing goods **2** *slang* an old car or aeroplane ▷ *vb* **crating, crated** **3** to put in a crate ▶ **HISTORY** Latin *cratis* wickerwork > **crateful** *n*

crater *n* **1** the bowl-shaped opening in a volcano or a geyser **2** a cavity made by the impact of a meteorite or an explosion **3** a roughly circular cavity on the surface of the moon and some planets ▷ *vb* **4** to make or form craters in (a surface, such as the ground) ▶ **HISTORY** Greek *kratēr* mixing bowl > **cratered** *adj*

cravat *n* a scarf worn round the neck instead of a tie

■ **WORD HISTORY**

■ 'Cravat' came into English from French *cravate*,
■ but ultimately comes from Serbo-Croat *Hrvat*,
■ meaning 'Croat'. Croat mercenaries in the
■ French army during the Thirty Years War were
■ noted for the linen scarves they wore.

crave *vb* **craving, craved** **1** to desire intensely: *a vulnerable, unhappy girl who craved affection* **2** *formal* to beg or plead for: *may I crave your lordship's indulgence?* ▶ **HISTORY** Old English *crafian* > **craving** *n*

craven *adj written* **1** cowardly ▷ *n* **2** a coward ▶ **HISTORY** Middle English *cravant*

craw *n* **1** the crop of a bird **2** the stomach of an animal **3 stick in one's craw** *informal* to be difficult for one to agree with or accept ▶ **HISTORY** Middle English

crawfish *n, pl* **-fish** *or* **-fishes** same as **crayfish**

crawl *vb* **1** to move on one's hands and knees **2** (of insects, worms, or snakes) to creep slowly **3** to move very slowly **4** to act in a servile manner **5** to be or feel as if covered with crawling creatures: *the kind of smile that made your hair stand on end and your flesh crawl* ▷ *n* **6** a slow creeping pace or motion **7** *swimming* a stroke in which the feet are kicked like paddles while each arm in turn reaches forward and pulls back through the water ▶ **HISTORY** probably from Old Norse *krafla*

crayfish *or esp US* **crawfish** *n, pl* **-fish** *or* **-fishes** **1** an edible shellfish like a lobster **2** an Australian freshwater crustacean ▶ **HISTORY** Old French *crevice* crab

crayon *n* **1** a small stick or pencil of coloured wax or clay ▷ *vb* **2** to draw or colour with a crayon ▶ **HISTORY** Latin *creta* chalk

craze *n* **1 a** short-lived fashion or enthusiasm ▷ *vb* **crazing, crazed** **2** to make mad **3** *ceramics, metallurgy* to develop or cause to develop fine cracks: *you must prevent the drill crazing the glazed surface of the tile* ▶ **HISTORY** probably from Old Norse

crazed *adj* **1** *written* wild and uncontrolled in behaviour **2** (of porcelain) having fine cracks

crazy *adj* **-zier, -ziest** *informal* **1** ridiculous **2 crazy about** extremely fond of: *he was crazy about me* **3** extremely annoyed or upset **4** insane > **crazily** *adv* > **craziness** *n*

193

crazy paving *n Brit, Austral & NZ* a form of paving on a path, made of irregular slabs of stone

creak *vb* **1** to make or move with a harsh squeaking sound ▷ *n* **2** a harsh squeaking sound ▶ HISTORY imitative > **creaky** *adj* > **creakiness** *n*

cream *n* **1** the fatty part of milk, which rises to the top **2** a cosmetic or medication that resembles cream in consistency **3** any of various foods resembling or containing cream **4** the best part of something **5 cream sherry** a full-bodied sweet sherry ▷ *adj* **6** yellowish-white ▷ *vb* **7** to beat (foodstuffs) to a light creamy consistency **8** to remove the cream from (milk) **9** to prepare or cook (foodstuffs) with cream or milk **10 cream off** to take away the best part of ▶ HISTORY Late Latin *cramum* > **creamy** *adj*

cream cheese *n* a type of very rich soft white cheese

creamer *n chiefly Brit* a powdered milk substitute for coffee

creamery *n, pl* **-eries** a place where dairy products are made or sold

cream of tartar *n* a purified form of the tartar produced in wine-making, an ingredient in baking powder

crease *n* **1** a line made by folding or pressing **2** a wrinkle or furrow, esp. on the face **3** *cricket* any of four lines near each wicket marking positions for the bowler or batsman ▷ *vb* **creasing, creased 4** to make or become wrinkled or furrowed ▶ HISTORY Middle English *crēst* > **creasy** *adj*

create *vb* **-ating, -ated 1** to cause to come into existence **2** to be the cause of **3** to appoint to a new rank or position **4** *Brit, slang* to make an angry fuss ▶ HISTORY Latin *creare*

creation *n* **1** a creating or being created **2** something brought into existence or created

Creation *n Christianity* **1** God's act of bringing the universe into being **2** the universe as thus brought into being by God

creationism *n theol* the doctrine that ascribes the origins of all things to God's acts of creation rather than to evolution > **creationist** *n, adj*

creative *adj* **1** having the ability to create **2** imaginative or inventive ▷ *n* **3** a creative person, esp. one who devises advertising campaigns > **creativity** *n*

creator *n* a person who creates

Creator *n* **the Creator** God

creature *n* **1** an animal, bird, or fish **2** a person **3** a person or thing controlled by another

crèche *n* **1** a day nursery for very young children **2** a supervised play area provided for young children for short periods ▶ HISTORY French

credence (**kreed**-enss) *n* belief in the truth or accuracy of a statement: *the question is, how much credence to give to their accounts?* ▶ HISTORY Latin *credere* to believe

credentials *pl n* **1** something that entitles a person to credit or confidence **2** a document giving evidence of the bearer's identity or qualifications

credible *adj* **1** capable of being believed; convincing: *there is no credible evidence* **2** trustworthy or reliable: *the latest claim is the only one to involve a credible witness* ▶ HISTORY Latin *credere* to believe > **credibility** *n*

credit *n* **1 a** the system of allowing customers to receive goods or services before payment **b** the time allowed for paying for such goods or services **2** reputation for trustworthiness in paying debts **3 a** the positive balance in a person's bank account **b** the sum of money that a bank makes available to a client in excess of any deposit **4** a sum of money or equivalent purchasing power, available for a person's use **5** *accounting* **a** acknowledgment of a sum of money by entry on the right-hand side of an account **b** an entry or total of entries on this side **6** praise or approval, as for an achievement or quality: *you must give him credit for his perseverance* **7** a person or thing who is a source of praise or approval: *he is a credit to his family* **8** influence or reputation based on the good opinion of others: *he acquired credit within the community* **9** belief or confidence in someone or something: *this theory is now gaining credit among the scientific community* **10** *education* **a** a distinction awarded to an examination candidate obtaining good marks **b** certification that a section of an examination syllabus has been satisfactorily completed **11 on credit** with payment to be made at a future date ▷ *vb* **-iting, -ited 12** *accounting* **a** to enter (an item) as a credit in an account **b** to acknowledge (a payer) by making such an entry **13 credit with** to attribute to: *credit us with some intelligence* **14** to believe ▷ See also **credits** ▶ HISTORY Latin *credere* to believe

creditable *adj* deserving praise or honour > **creditably** *adv*

credit account *n Brit* a credit system in which shops allow customers to obtain goods and services before payment

credit card *n* a card issued by banks or shops, allowing the holder to buy on credit

credit crunch *n* a sudden reduction in the availability of credit from banks, mortgage lenders, etc.

creditor *n* a person or company to whom money is owed

credit rating *n* an evaluation of the ability of a person or business to repay money lent

credits *pl n* a list of people responsible for the production of a film, programme, or record

credit union *n* a cooperative association whose members can obtain low-interest loans out of their combined savings

creditworthy *adj* (of a person or a business) regarded as deserving credit on the basis of earning power and previous record of debt repayment > **creditworthiness** *n*

credo *n, pl* **-dos** a creed

credulity *n written* willingness to believe something on little evidence

credulous *adj* **1** too willing to believe: *he has convinced only a few credulous American intellectuals*

2 arising from or showing credulity: *credulous optimism* ▸ HISTORY Latin *credere* to believe

creed *n* **1** a system of beliefs or principles **2** a formal statement of the essential parts of Christian belief ▸ HISTORY Latin *credo* I believe

creek *n* **1** a narrow inlet or bay **2** *US, Canad, Austral & NZ* a small stream or tributary **3 up the creek** *slang* in a difficult position ▸ HISTORY Old Norse *kriki* nook

creel *n* a wickerwork basket used by fishermen ▸ HISTORY Scots

creep *vb* **creeping, crept** **1** to move quietly and cautiously **2** to crawl with the body near to or touching the ground **3** to have the sensation of something crawling over the skin, from fear or disgust: *she makes my flesh creep* **4** (of plants) to grow along the ground or over rocks ▷ *n* **5** a creeping movement **6** *slang* an obnoxious or servile person ▸ HISTORY Old English *crēopan*

creeper *n* **1** a plant, such as ivy, that grows by creeping **2** *US & Canad* same as **tree creeper**

creeps *pl n* **give someone the creeps** *informal* to give someone a feeling of fear or disgust

creepy *adj* **creepier, creepiest** *informal* causing a feeling of fear or disgust > **creepiness** *n*

creepy-crawly *n, pl* **-crawlies** *Brit, informal* a small crawling creature

cremate *vb* **-mating, -mated** to burn (a corpse) to ash ▸ HISTORY Latin *cremare* > **cremation** *n*

crematorium *n, pl* **-riums** or **-ria** a building where corpses are cremated

crème de menthe *n* a liqueur flavoured with peppermint ▸ HISTORY French

crenellated or *US* **crenelated** *adj* having battlements ▸ HISTORY Late Latin *crena* a notch > **crenellation** or *US* **crenelation** *n*

creole *n* **1** a language developed from a mixture of different languages which has become the main language of a place ▷ *adj* **2** of or relating to a creole ▸ HISTORY Spanish

Creole *n* **1** (in the West Indies and Latin America) a native-born person of mixed European and African descent **2** (in the Gulf States of the US) a native-born person of French descent **3** the French creole spoken in the Gulf States ▷ *adj* **4** of or relating to any of these peoples: *Creole cooking*

creosote *n* **1** a thick dark liquid made from coal tar and used for preserving wood **2** a colourless liquid made from wood tar and used as an antiseptic ▷ *vb* **-soting, -soted** **3** to treat with creosote ▸ HISTORY Greek *kreas* flesh + *sōtēr* preserver

crepe (**krayp**) *n* **1** a thin light fabric with a crinkled texture **2** a very thin pancake, often folded around a filling **3** a type of rubber with a wrinkled surface, used for the soles of shoes ▸ HISTORY French

crepe paper *n* paper with a crinkled texture, used for decorations

crept *vb* the past of **creep**

crepuscular *adj* **1** of or like twilight **2** (of animals) active at twilight ▸ HISTORY Latin *crepusculum* dusk

Cres. Crescent

crescendo (krish-**end**-oh) *n, pl* **-dos** **1** a gradual increase in loudness **2** a musical passage that gradually gets louder ▷ *adv* **3** gradually getting louder ▸ HISTORY Italian

crescent *n* **1** the curved shape of the moon when in its first or last quarter **2** *chiefly Brit & NZ* a crescent-shaped street ▷ *adj* **3** crescent-shaped ▸ HISTORY Latin *crescere* to grow

cress *n* a plant with strong-tasting leaves, used in salads and as a garnish ▸ HISTORY Old English *cressa*

crest *n* **1** the top of a mountain, hill, or wave **2** a tuft or growth of feathers or skin on the top of a bird's or animal's head **3** a heraldic design or figure used on a coat of arms and elsewhere **4** an ornamental plume or emblem on top of a helmet ▷ *vb* **5** to come or rise to a high point **6** to lie at the top of **7** *written* to reach the top of (a hill or wave) ▸ HISTORY Latin *crista* > **crested** *adj*

crestfallen *adj* disappointed or disheartened

Cretaceous *adj geol* of the period of geological time about 135 million years ago, at the end of which the dinosaurs died out ▸ HISTORY Latin *creta* chalk

cretin *offensive n* **1** a very stupid person **2** *no longer in technical use* a person who is mentally and physically disabled because of a thyroid deficiency ▸ HISTORY French from Latin *Christianus* Christian, alluding to the humanity of such people despite their disabilities > **cretins** *n* > **cretinous** *adj*

cretonne *n* a heavy printed cotton or linen fabric, used in furnishings ▸ HISTORY French

crevasse *n* a deep open crack in a glacier ▸ HISTORY French

crevice *n* a narrow crack or gap in rock ▸ HISTORY Latin *crepare* to crack

crew¹ *n* **1** the people who man a ship or aircraft **2** a group of people working together: *a film crew* **3** *informal* any group of people ▷ *vb* **4** to serve as a crew member on a ship or boat ▸ HISTORY Middle English *crue* reinforcement, from Latin *crescere* to increase

crew² *vb archaic* a past of **crow²**

crew cut *n* a closely cut haircut for men

crewel *n* a loosely twisted worsted yarn, used in embroidery ▸ HISTORY origin unknown > **crewelwork** *n*

crib *n* **1** a piece of writing stolen from elsewhere **2** a translation or list of answers used by students, often dishonestly **3** a baby's cradle **4** a rack or manger for fodder **5** a model of the manger scene at Bethlehem **6** short for **cribbage 7** *NZ* a small holiday house ▷ *vb* **cribbing, cribbed** **8** to copy (someone's work) dishonestly **9** to confine in a small space ▸ HISTORY Old English *cribb*

cribbage *n* a card game for two to four players, who each try to win a set number of points before the others ▸ HISTORY origin unknown

crib-wall *n NZ* a retaining wall built against an earth bank

crick *informal n* **1** a painful muscle spasm or cramp in the neck or back ▷ *vb* **2** to cause a crick in ▸ HISTORY origin unknown

cricket¹ n **1** a game played by two teams of eleven players using a ball, bats, and wickets **2 not cricket** informal not fair play ▶ HISTORY Old French criquet wicket > **cricketer** n

cricket² n a jumping insect like a grasshopper, which produces a chirping sound by rubbing together its forewings ▶ HISTORY Old French criquer to creak, imitative

cried vb the past of **cry**

crier n an official who makes public announcements

crime n **1** an act prohibited and punished by law **2** unlawful acts collectively **3** informal a disgraceful act: to be a woman writing music is neither a crime against nature nor a freakish rarity ▶ HISTORY Latin crimen

criminal n **1** a person guilty of a crime ▷ adj **2** of or relating to crime or its punishment **3** informal senseless or disgraceful > **criminally** adv > **criminality** n

criminalize or **-ise** vb **-izing, -ized** or **-ising, -ised 1** to make (an action or activity) criminal **2** to treat (a person) as a criminal

criminal law n law the body of law dealing with criminal offences and offenders. Compare **civil law**

criminal offence n law an act that contravenes criminal law. Compare **civil offence**

criminology n the scientific study of crime ▶ HISTORY Latin crimen crime + -LOGY > **criminologist** n

crimp vb **1** to fold or press into ridges **2** to curl (hair) tightly with curling tongs **3** chiefly US, informal to restrict or hinder: a slowdown in the US economy could crimp some big Swedish concerns' profits ▷ n **4** the act or result of crimping ▶ HISTORY Old English crympan

crimson adj deep purplish-red ▶ HISTORY Arabic qirmizi kermes (dried bodies of insects used to make a red dye)

cringe vb **cringing, cringed 1** to shrink or flinch in fear: he cringed and shrank against the wall **2** to behave in a submissive or timid way: women who cringe before abusive husbands **3** informal to be very embarrassed: I cringe every time I see that old photo of me ▷ n **4** the act of cringing

■ **WORD HISTORY**
■ To 'cringe' comes from Old English cringan
■ meaning 'to yield in battle'.

crinkle vb **-kling, -kled 1** to become slightly creased or folded ▷ n **2** a crease or fold ▶ HISTORY Old English crincan to bend > **crinkly** adj

crinoline n a petticoat stiffened with hoops to make the skirt stand out ▶ HISTORY Latin crinis hair + lino flax

cripple n offensive **1** a person who is lame or disabled **2** a person with a mental or social problem: an emotional cripple ▷ vb **-pling, -pled 3** to make a cripple of **4** to damage (something) ▶ HISTORY Old English crypel > **crippled** adj > **crippling** adj

crisis n, pl **-ses 1** a crucial stage or turning point in the course of anything **2** a time of extreme trouble or danger ▶ HISTORY Greek krisis decision

crisp adj **1** fresh and firm: a crisp green salad **2** dry and brittle: bake until crisp and golden brown **3** clean and neat: crisp white cotton **4** (of weather) cold but invigorating: a crisp autumn day **5** clear and sharp: the telescope is designed to provide the first crisp images of distant galaxies **6** lively or brisk: the service is crisp and efficient ▷ n **7** Brit a very thin slice of potato fried till crunchy ▷ vb **8** to make or become crisp ▶ HISTORY Latin crispus curled > **crisply** adv > **crispness** n

crispbread n a thin dry biscuit made of wheat or rye

crispy adj **crispier, crispiest** hard and crunchy > **crispiness** n

crisscross vb **1** to move in or mark with a crosswise pattern ▷ adj **2** (of lines) crossing one another in different directions

criterion n, pl **-ria** or **-rions** a standard by which something can be judged or decided ▶ HISTORY Greek kritērion

critic n **1** a professional judge of art, music, or literature **2** a person who finds fault and criticizes ▶ HISTORY Greek kritēs judge

critical adj **1** very important or dangerous: this was a critical moment in her career **2** so seriously ill or injured as to be in danger of dying: he is in a critical condition in hospital **3** fault-finding or disparaging: the article is highly critical of the government **4** examining and judging analytically and without bias: he submitted the plans to critical examination **5** of a critic or criticism **6** physics denoting a constant value at which the properties of a s ystem undergo an abrupt change: the critical temperature above which the material loses its superconductivity **7** (of a nuclear power station or reactor) having reached a state in which a nuclear chain reaction becomes self-sustaining > **critically** adv

critical angle n physics the smallest possible angle of incidence for which light rays are totally reflected at an interface between substances of different refractive index

criticism n **1** fault-finding or censure **2** an analysis of a work of art or literature **3** the occupation of a critic **4** a work that sets out to analyse

criticize or **-cise** vb **-cizing, -cized** or **-cising, -cised 1** to find fault with **2** to analyse (something)

critique n **1** a critical essay or commentary **2** the act or art of criticizing ▶ HISTORY French

croak vb **1** (of a frog or crow) to make a low hoarse cry **2** to utter or speak with a croak **3** slang to die ▷ n **4** a low hoarse sound ▶ HISTORY Old English crācettan > **croaky** adj

Croatian (kroh-**ay**-shun) adj **1** of Croatia ▷ n **2** a person from Croatia **3** the dialect of Serbo-Croat spoken in Croatia

crochet (**kroh**-shay) vb **-cheting, -cheted 1** to make (a piece of needlework) by looping and intertwining thread with a hooked needle ▷ n **2** work made by crocheting ▶ HISTORY French: small hook

crock¹ n an earthenware pot or jar ▸ HISTORY Old English *crocc* pot

crock² n **old crock** Brit, Austral & NZ, slang a person or thing that is old or broken-down ▸ HISTORY Scots

crockery n china dishes or earthenware vessels collectively

crocodile n **1** a large amphibious tropical reptile **2** Brit, Austral & NZ, informal a line of people, esp. schoolchildren, walking two by two ▸ HISTORY Greek *krokodeilos* lizard

crocodile tears pl n an insincere show of grief ▸ HISTORY from the belief that crocodiles wept over their prey to lure further victims

crocus n, pl **-cuses** a plant with white, yellow, or purple flowers in spring ▸ HISTORY Greek *krokos* saffron

croft n a small farm worked by one family in Scotland ▸ HISTORY Old English > **crofter** n > **crofting** adj, n

croissant (krwah-son) n a flaky crescent-shaped bread roll ▸ HISTORY French

cromlech n Brit **1** a circle of prehistoric standing stones **2** no longer in technical use a dolmen ▸ HISTORY Welsh

crone n a witchlike old woman ▸ HISTORY Old French *carogne* carrion

crony n, pl **-nies** a close friend ▸ HISTORY Greek *khronios* long-lasting

crook n **1** informal a dishonest person **2** a bent or curved place or thing: *she held the puppy in the crook of her arm* **3** a bishop's or shepherd's staff with a hooked end ▸ vb **4** to bend or curve ▸ adj **5** Austral & NZ, informal **a** ill **b** of poor quality **c** unpleasant; bad **6** **go (off) crook** Austral & NZ, informal to lose one's temper ▸ HISTORY Old Norse *krokr* hook

crooked adj **1** bent or twisted **2** set at an angle **3** informal dishonest or illegal > **crookedly** adv > **crookedness** n

croon vb to sing, hum, or speak in a soft low tone ▸ HISTORY Middle Dutch *crōnen* to groan > **crooner** n

crop n **1** a cultivated plant, such as a cereal, vegetable, or fruit plant **2** the season's total yield of farm produce **3** any group of things appearing at one time: *a remarkable crop of new Scottish plays* **4** the handle of a whip **5** a pouchlike part of the gullet of a bird, in which food is stored or prepared for digestion **6** a short cropped hairstyle ▸ vb **cropping, cropped 7** to cut (something) very short **8** to cut off or hide unwanted edges or areas of an image **9** to produce or harvest as a crop **10** (of animals) to feed on (grass) **11** to clip part of (the ear or ears) of (an animal), esp. for identification ▸ See also **crop up** ▸ HISTORY Old English *cropp*

crop circle n a pattern made up of ring shapes formed by the unexplained flattening of cereals growing in a field

crop-dusting n agriculture the spreading of fungicides, pesticides, etc. on crops in the form of dust, often from an aircraft

Crop Over n (in Barbados) a summer festival originally celebrating the end of the sugar-cane harvest

cropper n **come a cropper** informal **a** to fail completely **b** to fall heavily

crop rotation n agriculture the system of growing a sequence of different crops on the same ground so as to maintain or increase its fertility

crop-top n a short T-shirt or vest that reveals the wearer's midriff

crop up vb informal to occur or appear unexpectedly

croquet (kroh-kay) n a game played on a lawn in which balls are hit through hoops ▸ HISTORY French

croquette (kroh-kett) n a fried cake of mashed potato, meat, or fish ▸ HISTORY French

crosier n same as **crozier**

cross vb **1** to move or go across (something): *she crossed the street to the gallery* **2** to meet and pass: *further south, the way is crossed by Brewer Street* **3** Brit & NZ to draw two parallel lines across (a cheque) and so make it payable only into a bank account **4** to mark with a cross or crosses **5** (usually foll. by out, off, or through) to cancel or delete with a cross or with lines: *she crossed out the first three words* **6** to place across or crosswise: *he sat down and crossed his legs* **7** to make the sign of the cross upon as a blessing **8** to annoy or anger someone by challenging or opposing their wishes and plans **9** to interbreed or cross-fertilize **10** soccer to pass (the ball) from a wing to the middle of the field **11** (of each of two letters in the post) to be sent before the other is received **12** (of telephone lines) to interfere with each other so that several callers are connected together at one time **13** **cross one's fingers** to fold one finger across another in the hope of bringing good luck **14** **cross one's heart** to promise by making the sign of a cross over one's heart **15** **cross one's mind** to occur to one briefly or suddenly ▸ n **16** a structure, symbol, or mark consisting of two intersecting lines **17** an upright post with a bar across it, used in ancient times as a means of execution **18** a representation of the Cross on which Jesus Christ was executed as an emblem of Christianity **19** a symbol (×) used as a signature or error mark **20** **the sign of the cross** a sign made with the hand by some Christians to represent the Cross **21** a medal or monument in the shape of a cross **22** the place in a town or village where a cross has been set up **23** biol **a** the process of crossing; hybridization **b** a hybrid **24** a mixture of two things **25** a hindrance or misfortune: *we've all got our own cross to bear* **26** soccer a pass of the ball from a wing to the middle of the field ▸ adj **27** angry **28** lying or placed across: *a cross beam* ▸ HISTORY Latin *crux* > **crossly** adv > **crossness** n

Cross n **the Cross a** the cross on which Jesus Christ was crucified **b** Christianity

cross- combining form **1** indicating action from one individual or group to another: *cross-cultural;*

197

cross-refer **2** indicating movement or position across something: *crosscurrent; crosstalk* **3** indicating a crosslike figure or intersection: *crossbones*

crossbar *n* **1** a horizontal beam across a pair of goalposts **2** the horizontal bar on a man's bicycle

cross-bench *n Brit* a seat in Parliament for a member belonging to neither the government nor the opposition > **cross-bencher** *n*

crossbill *n* a finch that has a bill with crossed tips

crossbow *n* a weapon consisting of a bow fixed across a wooden stock, which releases an arrow when the trigger is pulled

crossbreed *vb* **-breeding, -bred** **1** to produce (a hybrid animal or plant) by crossing two different species ▷ *n* **2** a hybrid animal or plant

cross-country *adj, adv* **1** by way of open country or fields ▷ *n* **2** a long race held over open ground

crosscut *vb* **-cutting, -cut** **1** to cut across ▷ *adj* **2** cut across ▷ *n* **3** a transverse cut or course

cross-examine *vb* **-examining, -examined** **1** *law* to question (a witness for the opposing side) in order to check his or her testimony **2** to question closely or relentlessly > **cross-examination** *n* > **cross-examiner** *n*

cross-eyed *adj* with one or both eyes turning inwards towards the nose

cross-fertilize *or* **-lise** *vb* **-lizing, -lized** *or* **-lising, -lised** to fertilize (an animal or plant) by fusion of male and female reproductive cells from different individuals of the same species > **cross-fertilization** *or* **-lisation** *n*

crossfire *n* **1** *mil* gunfire crossing another line of fire **2** a lively exchange of ideas or opinions

crosshatch *vb drawing* to shade with two or more sets of parallel lines that cross one another

crossing *n* **1** a place where a street, railway, or river may be crossed **2** the place where one thing crosses another **3** a journey across water

cross-ply *adj* (of a tyre) having the fabric cords in the outer casing running diagonally to stiffen the sidewalls

cross-pollination *n bot* the transfer of pollen from the anthers of one flower to the stigma of another flower, e.g. by wind or insects

cross-purposes *pl n* **at cross-purposes** misunderstanding each other in a discussion

cross-reference *n* **1** a reference within a text to another part of the text ▷ *vb* **-referencing, -referenced** **2** to cross-refer

crossroad *n US & Canad* **1** a road that crosses another road **2** a road that connects one main road to another

crossroads *n* **1** the point at which roads cross one another **2** **at the crossroads** at the point at which an important choice has to be made

cross section *n* **1** *maths* a surface formed by cutting across a solid, usually at right angles to its longest axis **2** a diagram showing what would be visible if something were split vertically and the cut section exposed to view **3** a random sample regarded as representative: *a cross section of society* > **cross-sectional** *adj*

crosstalk *n* **1** *Brit* rapid or witty talk **2** unwanted signals transferred between communication channels

crosswise *or* **crossways** *adj, adv* **1** across: *slice the celery crosswise* **2** in the shape of a cross

crossword puzzle *or* **crossword** *n* a puzzle in which vertically and horizontally crossing words suggested by clues are written into a grid of squares

crotch *n* **1** the forked part of the human body between the legs **2** the corresponding part of a pair of trousers or pants **3** any forked part formed by the joining of two things: *the crotch of the tree* ▶ HISTORY probably variant of CRUTCH > **crotched** *adj*

crotchet *n music* a note having the time value of a quarter of a semibreve ▶ HISTORY Old French *crochet* little hook

crotchety *adj informal* bad-tempered

crouch *vb* **1** to bend low with the legs and body pulled close together ▷ *n* **2** this position ▶ HISTORY Old French *crochir* to become bent like a hook

croup¹ (**kroop**) *n* a throat disease of children, with a hoarse cough and laboured breathing ▶ HISTORY Middle English: to cry hoarsely, probably imitative

croup² (**kroop**) *n* the hindquarters of a horse ▶ HISTORY Old French *croupe*

croupier (**kroop-ee-ay**) *n* a person who collects bets and pays out winnings at a gambling table ▶ HISTORY French

crouton *n* a small piece of fried or toasted bread served in soup ▶ HISTORY French

crow¹ *n* **1** a large black bird with a harsh call **2** **as the crow flies** in a straight line ▶ HISTORY Old English *crāwa*

crow² *vb* **1** (*past* **crowed** *or* **crew**) (of a cock) to utter a shrill squawking sound **2** to boast about one's superiority **3** (of a baby) to utter cries of pleasure ▷ *n* **4** a crowing sound ▶ HISTORY Old English *crāwan*

crowbar *n* a heavy iron bar used as a lever

crowd *n* **1** a large number of things or people gathered together **2** a particular group of people: *we got to know a French crowd from Lyons* **3** **the crowd** the masses ▷ *vb* **4** to gather together in large numbers **5** to press together into a confined space **6** to fill or occupy fully **7** *informal* to make (someone) uncomfortable by coming too close ▶ HISTORY Old English *crūdan* > **crowded** *adj*

crown *n* **1** a monarch's ornamental headdress, usually made of gold and jewels **2** a wreath for the head, given as an honour **3** the highest or central point of something arched or curved: *the crown of the head* **4 a** the enamel-covered part of a tooth projecting beyond the gum **b** a substitute crown, usually of gold or porcelain, fitted over a decayed or broken tooth **5** a former British coin worth 25 pence **6** the outstanding quality or achievement: *the last piece is the crown of the evening* ▷ *vb* **7** to put a crown on the head of (someone) to proclaim him or her monarch **8** to put on the top of **9** to reward

10 to form the topmost part of **11** to put the finishing touch to (a series of events): *he crowned a superb display with three goals* **12** to attach a crown to (a tooth) **13** *Brit, Austral & NZ, slang* to hit over the head **14** *draughts* to promote (a draught) to a king by placing another draught on top of it ► **HISTORY** Greek *korōnē*

Crown *n* **the Crown** the power or institution of the monarchy

crown colony *n* a British colony controlled by the Crown

crown court *n* a local criminal court in England and Wales

crown jewels *pl n* the jewellery used by a sovereign on ceremonial occasions

crown land *n* *law* **1** (in the United Kingdom) land belonging to the Crown **2** (in some dominions of the Commonwealth) public land

crown-of-thorns *n* a starfish with a spiny outer covering that feeds on living coral

crown prince *n* the male heir to a sovereign throne > **crown princess** *n*

crow's feet *pl n* wrinkles at the outer corners of the eye

crow's nest *n* a lookout platform fixed at the top of a ship's mast

crozier *or* **crosier** *n* a hooked staff carried by bishops as a symbol of office ► **HISTORY** Old French *crossier* staff-bearer

crucial *adj* **1** of exceptional importance **2** *Brit, slang* very good ► **HISTORY** Latin *crux* cross > **crucially** *adv*

crucible *n* a pot in which metals or other substances are melted ► **HISTORY** Medieval Latin *crucibulum* night lamp

crucifix *n* a model cross with a figure of Christ upon it ► **HISTORY** Church Latin *crucifixus* the crucified Christ

crucifixion *n* a method of execution by fastening to a cross, normally by the hands and feet

Crucifixion *n* **1 the Crucifixion** the crucifying of Christ **2** a representation of this

cruciform *adj* shaped like a cross

crucify *vb* **-fies, -fying, -fied 1** to put to death by crucifixion **2** to treat cruelly **3** *slang* to defeat or ridicule totally ► **HISTORY** Latin *crux* cross + *figere* to fasten

crude *adj* **1** rough and simple: *crude farm implements* **2** tasteless or vulgar **3** in a natural or unrefined state ▷ *n* **4** short for **crude oil** ► **HISTORY** Latin *crudus* bloody, raw > **crudely** *adv* > **crudity** *or* **crudeness** *n*

crude oil *n* unrefined petroleum

cruel *adj* **1** deliberately causing pain without pity **2** causing pain or suffering ► **HISTORY** Latin *crudelis* > **cruelly** *adv* > **cruelty** *n*

cruet *n* **1** a small container for pepper, salt, etc. at table **2** a set of such containers on a stand ► **HISTORY** Old French *crue* flask

cruise *n* **1** a sail taken for pleasure, stopping at various places ▷ *adj* **2** of or relating to a cruise: *cruise ship; cruise port* ▷ *vb* **cruising, cruised**

3 to sail about from place to place for pleasure **4** (of a vehicle, aircraft, or ship) to travel at a moderate and efficient speed **5** to proceed steadily or easily: *they cruised into the final of the qualifying competition* ► **HISTORY** Dutch *kruisen* to cross

cruise missile *n* a low-flying subsonic missile that is guided throughout its flight

cruiser *n* **1** a large fast warship armed with medium-calibre weapons **2** Also called: **cabin cruiser** a motorboat with a cabin

cruiserweight *n* a professional boxer weighing up to 195 pounds (88.5 kg)

crumb *n* **1** a small fragment of bread or other dry food **2** a small bit or scrap: *a crumb of comfort* ► **HISTORY** Old English *cruma*

crumble *vb* **-bling, -bled 1** to break into crumbs or fragments **2** to fall apart or decay ▷ *n* **3** a baked pudding consisting of stewed fruit with a crumbly topping: *rhubarb crumble* > **crumbly** *adj* > **crumbliness** *n*

crumby *adj* **crumbier, crumbiest 1** full of crumbs **2** same as **crummy**

crummy *adj* **-mier, -miest** *slang* **1** of very bad quality: *a crummy hotel* **2** unwell: *I felt really crummy* ► **HISTORY** variant spelling of *crumby*

crumpet *n* a light soft yeast cake, eaten buttered ► **HISTORY** origin unknown

crumple *vb* **-pling, -pled 1** to crush or become crushed into untidy wrinkles or creases **2** *written* to collapse in an untidy heap: *her father lay crumpled on the floor* ▷ *n* **3** an untidy crease or wrinkle ► **HISTORY** obsolete *crump* to bend > **crumply** *adj*

crunch *vb* **1** to bite or chew with a noisy crushing sound **2** to make a crisp or brittle sound ▷ *n* **3** a crunching sound **4 the crunch** *informal* the critical moment or situation ► **HISTORY** imitative > **crunchy** *adj* > **crunchiness** *n*

crupper *n* **1** a strap that passes from the back of a saddle under a horse's tail **2** the horse's rump ► **HISTORY** Old French *crupiere*

crusade *n* **1** any of the medieval military expeditions undertaken by European Christians to recapture the Holy Land from the Muslims **2** a vigorous campaign in favour of a cause ▷ *vb* **-sading, -saded 3** to take part in a crusade ► **HISTORY** Latin *crux* cross > **crusader** *n*

cruse *n* a small earthenware container for liquids ► **HISTORY** Old English *crūse*

crush *vb* **1** to press or squeeze so as to injure, break, or put out of shape **2** to break or grind into small pieces **3** to control or subdue by force **4** to extract (liquid) by pressing: *crush a clove of garlic* **5** to defeat or humiliate utterly **6** to crowd together ▷ *n* **7** a dense crowd **8** the act of crushing **9** *informal* an infatuation: *I had a teenage crush on my French teacher* **10** a drink made by crushing fruit: *orange crush* ► **HISTORY** Old French *croissir*

crust *n* **1** the hard outer part of bread **2** the baked shell of a pie or tart **3** any hard outer layer: *a thin crust of snow* **4** the solid outer shell of the earth ▷ *vb* **5** to cover with or form a crust ► **HISTORY** Latin *crusta* hard surface, rind

crustacean n **1** an animal with a hard outer shell and several pairs of legs, which usually lives in water, such as a crab or lobster ▷ adj **2** of crustaceans ▶ HISTORY Latin *crusta* shell

crusty adj **crustier, crustiest** **1** having a crust **2** rude or irritable > **crustiness** n

crutch n **1** a long staff with a rest for the armpit, used by a lame person to support the weight of the body **2** something that supports **3** Brit same as **crotch** (sense 1) ▶ HISTORY Old English *crycc*

crutchings pl n Austral & NZ the wool clipped from a sheep's hindquarters

crux n, pl **cruxes** or **cruces** a crucial or decisive point ▶ HISTORY Latin: cross

cry vb **cries, crying, cried** **1** to shed tears **2** to make a loud vocal sound, usually to express pain or fear or to appeal for help **3** to utter loudly or shout **4** (of an animal or bird) to utter loud characteristic sounds **5 cry for** to appeal urgently for ▷ n, pl **cries** **6** a fit of weeping **7** the act or sound of crying **8** the characteristic utterance of an animal or bird **9** an urgent appeal: *a cry for help* **10** a public demand: *a cry for more law and order on the streets* **11 a far cry from** something very different from **12 in full cry a** in eager pursuit **b** in the middle of talking or doing something ▷ See also **cry off** ▶ HISTORY Old French *crier*

crying adj **a crying shame** a great shame

cry off vb informal to withdraw from an arrangement

cryogenics n the branch of physics concerned with very low temperatures and their effects ▶ HISTORY Greek *kruos* cold + *-genēs* born > **cryogenic** adj

crypt n a vault or underground chamber, such as one beneath a church, used as a burial place ▶ HISTORY Greek *kruptē*

cryptic adj having a hidden or secret meaning; puzzling: *no-one knew what he meant by that cryptic remark* ▶ HISTORY Greek *kruptos* concealed > **cryptically** adv

cryptogam n bot a plant that reproduces by spores not seeds ▶ HISTORY Greek *kruptos* hidden + *gamos* marriage

cryptography n the art of writing in and deciphering codes ▶ HISTORY Greek *kruptos* hidden + -GRAPHY > **cryptographer** n > **cryptographic** adj

crystal n **1** a solid with a regular internal structure and symmetrical arrangement of faces **2** a single grain of a crystalline substance **3** a very clear and brilliant glass **4** something made of crystal **5** crystal glass articles collectively **6** electronics a crystalline element used in certain electronic devices, such as a detector or oscillator ▷ adj **7** bright and clear: *the crystal waters of the pool* ▶ HISTORY Greek *krustallos* ice, crystal

crystal healing n in alternative medicine, the use of the supposed power of crystals to affect the human energy field

crystalline adj **1** of or like crystal or crystals **2** clear

crystallize, crystalize or **-ise** vb **-izing, -ized** or **-ising, -ised** **1** to make or become definite **2** to form into crystals **3** to preserve (fruit) in sugar > **crystallization, crystalization** or **-isation** n

crystallography n the science of crystal structure

crystalloid n a substance that in solution can pass through a membrane

Cs chem caesium

CSA (in Britain) Child Support Agency

CSE (in Britain) (formerly) Certificate of Secondary Education: an examination the first grade pass of which was an equivalent to a GCE O level

CSEC trademark Caribbean Secondary Education Certificate

CS gas n a gas causing tears and painful breathing, used to control civil disturbances ▶ HISTORY initials of its US inventors, Ben Carson and Roger Staughton

CSME Caricom Single Market and Economy: a proposed single economic unit within the Caricom nations, allowing free trade and movement of people

CST Central Standard Time

CT Connecticut

CT scanner n an X-ray machine that can produce cross-sectional images of the soft tissues ▶ HISTORY c(omputerized) t(omography) scanner

Cu chem copper ▶ HISTORY Late Latin *cuprum*

cu. cubic

cub n **1** the young of certain mammals, such as the lion or bear **2** a young or inexperienced person ▷ vb **cubbing, cubbed** **3** to give birth to (cubs) ▶ HISTORY origin unknown

Cuban adj **1** from Cuba ▷ n **2** a person from Cuba

cubbyhole n a small enclosed space or room ▶ HISTORY dialect *cub* cattle pen

cube n **1** an object with six equal square faces **2** the product obtained by multiplying a number by itself twice: *the cube of 2 is 8* ▷ vb **cubing, cubed** **3** to find the cube of (a number) **4** to cut into cubes ▶ HISTORY Greek *kubos*

cube root n the number or quantity whose cube is a given number or quantity: *2 is the cube root of 8*

cubic adj **1 a** having three dimensions **b** having the same volume as a cube with length, width, and depth each measuring the given unit: *a cubic metre* **2** having the shape of a cube **3** maths involving the cubes of numbers

cubicle n an enclosed part of a large room, screened for privacy ▶ HISTORY Latin *cubiculum*

cubic measure n a system of units for the measurement of volumes

cubic proportion n maths a relationship between two variables in which one is proportional to the cube of the other

cubism n a style of art, begun in the early 20th century, in which objects are represented by geometrical shapes > **cubist** adj, n

cubit n an ancient measure of length based on the length of the forearm ▶ HISTORY Latin *cubitum* elbow, cubit

cuboid *adj* **1** shaped like a cube ▷ *n* **2** *maths* a geometric solid whose six faces are rectangles

Cub Scout *or* **Cub** *n* a member of a junior branch of the Scout Association

cuckold *literary or old-fashioned n* **1** a man whose wife has been unfaithful to him ▷ *vb* **2** to make a cuckold of ▶ HISTORY Middle English *cukeweld*

cuckoo *n, pl* **cuckoos 1** a migratory bird with a characteristic two-note call, noted for laying its eggs in the nests of other birds ▷ *adj* **2** *informal* insane or foolish ▶ HISTORY Old French *cucu*, imitative

cuckoopint *n* a plant with arrow-shaped leaves, purple flowers, and red berries

cuckoo spit *n* a white frothy mass produced on plants by the larvae of some insects

cucumber *n* **1** a long fruit with thin green rind and crisp white flesh, used in salads **2 as cool as a cucumber** calm and self-possessed ▶ HISTORY Latin *cucumis*

cud *n* **1** partially digested food which a ruminant brings back into its mouth to chew again **2 chew the cud** to think deeply ▶ HISTORY Old English *cudu*

cuddle *vb* **-dling, -dled 1** to hug or embrace fondly **2 cuddle up** to lie close and snug ▷ *n* **3** a fond hug ▶ HISTORY origin unknown > **cuddly** *adj*

cudgel *n* a short thick stick used as a weapon ▶ HISTORY Old English *cycgel*

cue[1] *n* **1** a signal to an actor or musician to begin speaking or playing **2** a signal or reminder **3 on cue** at the right moment ▷ *vb* **cueing, cued 4** to give a cue to ▶ HISTORY perhaps from the letter *q*, used in an actor's script to represent Latin *quando* when

cue[2] *n* **1** a long tapering stick used to hit the balls in billiards, snooker, or pool ▷ *vb* **cueing, cued 2** to hit (a ball) with a cue ▶ HISTORY variant of QUEUE

cuesta (**quest**-uh) *n* a long low ridge with a steep scarp slope and a gentle back slope ▶ HISTORY Spanish: shoulder, from Latin *costa* side, rib

cuff[1] *n* **1** the end of a sleeve **2** *US, Canad, Austral & NZ* a turn-up on trousers **3 off the cuff** *informal* impromptu: *he delivers many speeches off the cuff* ▶ HISTORY Middle English *cuffe* glove

cuff[2] *Brit, Austral & NZ vb* **1** to strike with an open hand ▷ *n* **2** a blow with an open hand ▶ HISTORY origin unknown

cuff link *n* one of a pair of decorative fastenings for shirt cuffs

cuisine (quiz-**zeen**) *n* **1** a style of cooking: *Italian cuisine* **2** the range of food served in a restaurant ▶ HISTORY French

cul-de-sac *n, pl* **culs-de-sac** *or* **cul-de-sacs** a road with one end blocked off ▶ HISTORY French: bottom of the bag

culinary *adj* of the kitchen or cookery ▶ HISTORY Latin *culina* kitchen

cull *vb* **1** to choose or gather **2** to remove or kill (the inferior or surplus) animals from a herd ▷ *n* **3** the act of culling ▶ HISTORY Latin *colligere* to gather together

culminate *vb* **-nating, -nated** to reach the highest point or climax: *the parade culminated in a memorial service* ▶ HISTORY Latin *culmen* top > **culmination** *n*

culottes *pl n* women's flared trousers cut to look like a skirt ▶ HISTORY French

culpable *adj* deserving blame ▶ HISTORY Latin *culpa* fault > **culpability** *n*

culprit *n* the person guilty of an offence or misdeed ▶ HISTORY Anglo-French *culpable* guilty + *prit* ready

cult *n* **1** a specific system of religious worship **2** a sect devoted to the beliefs of a cult **3** devoted attachment to a person, idea, or activity **4** a popular fashion: *the bungee-jumping cult* ▷ *adj* **5** very popular among a limited group of people: *a cult TV series* ▶ HISTORY Latin *cultus* cultivation, refinement

cultic *adj* of a religious cult

cultivate *vb* **-vating, -vated 1** to prepare (land) to grow crops **2** to grow (plants) **3** to develop or improve (something) by giving special attention to it: *he tried to cultivate a reputation for fairness* **4** to try to develop a friendship with (a person) ▶ HISTORY Latin *colere* to till

cultivated *adj* well-educated: *a civilized and cultivated man*

cultivation *n* **1** the act of cultivating **2** culture or refinement

cultivator *n* a farm implement used to break up soil and remove weeds

cultural *adj* **1** of or relating to artistic pursuits: *cultural festival* **2** of or relating to a culture or civilization: *cultural diversity; cultural tradition*

cultural heritage *n* the complete culture of a place or people, including works of art, literature, physical monuments, archaeological relics, performing arts, oral traditions, and rituals

cultural retention *n* the act of preserving the culture of a group or place, esp. when it is considered to be at risk of disappearing

Cultural Revolution *n history* (in China) an idealistic mass movement (1965-68) intended by Mao Zedong to destroy the power of the bureaucrats but which resulted in anarchy, terror, and a huge fall in industrial and agricultural production

culture *n* **1** the ideas, customs, and art of a particular society **2** a particular civilization at a particular period **3** a developed understanding of the arts **4** development or improvement by special attention or training: *physical culture* **5** the cultivation and rearing of plants or animals **6** a growth of bacteria for study ▷ *vb* **-turing, -tured 7** to grow (bacteria) in a special medium ▶ HISTORY Latin *colere* to till

cultured *adj* **1** showing good taste or manners **2** artificially grown or synthesized

cultured pearl *n* a pearl artificially grown in an oyster shell

culture shock *n sociol* the feelings of isolation and anxiety experienced by a person on first

201

coming into contact with a culture very different from his or her own

culvert n a drain or pipe that crosses under a road or railway ▶ HISTORY origin unknown

cum prep with: *a small living-cum-dining room* ▶ HISTORY Latin

cumbersome or **cumbrous** adj **1** awkward because of size or shape **2** difficult because of complexity: *the cumbersome appeals procedure*

cumin or **cummin** n **1** the spicy-smelling seeds of a Mediterranean herb, used in cooking **2** the plant from which these seeds are obtained ▶ HISTORY Greek *kuminon*

cummerbund n a wide sash worn round the waist, esp. with a dinner jacket ▶ HISTORY Hindi *kamarband*, from Persian *kamar* loins + *band* band

cumquat n same as **kumquat**

cumulative (**kew**-myew-la-tiv) adj growing in amount, strength, or effect by small steps: *the cumulative effect of twelve years of war*

cumulative frequency n *statistics* the frequency of occurrence of all values of a variable either below or above a specified value

cumulative frequency graph n *statistics* a graph which shows the frequency of occurrence of a set of values as a cumulative total

cumulative graph n *statistics* a graph which shows the cumulative totals of a set of values up to each of the points on the graph

cumulative preference shares pl n *finance* preference shares that entitle the holder to receive any arrears of dividend before any dividend is distributed to ordinary shareholders

cumulonimbus (kew-mew-low-**nim**-bes) n, pl **cumulonimbi** or **cumulonimbuses** *meteorol* a towering cumulus cloud, dark-coloured at the bottom and often anvil-shaped at the top, indicating rain or hail; associated with thunderstorms

cumulus (**kew**-myew-luss) n, pl **-li** (-lie) a thick or billowing white or dark grey cloud ▶ HISTORY Latin: mass

cuneiform (**kew**-nif-form) n **1** an ancient system of writing using wedge-shaped characters ▷ adj **2** written in cuneiform ▶ HISTORY Latin *cuneus* wedge

cunjevoi (**kun**-ji-voy) n *Austral* **1** a plant of tropical Asia and Australia, cultivated for its edible rhizome **2** a sea squirt

cunning adj **1** clever at deceiving **2** made with skill ▷ n **3** cleverness at deceiving **4** skill or ingenuity ▶ HISTORY Old English *cunnende*

cup n **1** a small bowl-shaped drinking container with a handle **2** the contents of a cup **3** something shaped like a cup: *a bra with padded cups* **4** a cup-shaped trophy awarded as a prize **5** a sporting contest in which a cup is awarded to the winner **6** a mixed drink with fruit juice or wine as a base: *claret cup* **7** one's lot in life: *his cup of bitterness was full to overflowing* **8 someone's cup of tea** *informal* someone's chosen or preferred thing ▷ vb **cupping, cupped 9** to form (the hands) into the

shape of a cup **10** to hold in cupped hands ▶ HISTORY Old English *cuppe*

cupboard n a piece of furniture or a recess with a door, used for storage

Cupid n **1** the Roman god of love, represented as a winged boy with a bow and arrow **2** a picture or statue of Cupid ▶ HISTORY Latin *cupido* desire

cupidity (kew-**pid**-it-ee) n *formal* strong desire for wealth or possessions ▶ HISTORY Latin *cupere* to long for

cupola (**kew**-pol-la) n **1** a domed roof or ceiling **2** a small dome on the top of a roof **3** an armoured revolving gun turret on a warship ▶ HISTORY Latin *cupa* tub

cupreous (**kew**-pree-uss) adj of or containing copper ▶ HISTORY Latin *cuprum* copper

cupric (**kew**-prick) adj of or containing copper in the divalent state

cupronickel (kew-proh-**nik**-el) n a copper alloy containing up to 40 per cent nickel

cup tie n *Brit sport* an eliminating match between two teams in a cup competition

cur n **1** a vicious mongrel dog **2** a contemptible person ▶ HISTORY Middle English *kurdogge*

curable adj capable of being cured > **curability** n

curaçao (**kew**-rah-so) n an orange-flavoured liqueur

curacy (**kew**-rah-see) n, pl **-cies** the work or position of a curate

curare (kew-**rah**-ree) n a poisonous resin obtained from a South American tree, used as a muscle relaxant in medicine ▶ HISTORY Carib *kurari*

curate n a member of the clergy who assists a vicar or parish priest ▶ HISTORY Medieval Latin *cura* spiritual oversight

curative adj **1** able to cure ▷ n **2** something able to cure

curator n the person in charge of a museum or art gallery ▶ HISTORY Latin: one who cares > **curatorial** adj > **curatorship** n

curb n **1** something that restrains or holds back **2** a horse's bit with an attached chain or strap, used to check the horse **3** a raised edge that strengthens or encloses ▷ vb **4** to control or restrain ▷ See also **kerb** ▶ HISTORY Latin *curvus* curved

curd n **1** coagulated milk, used in making cheese or as a food **2** any similar substance: *bean curd* ▶ HISTORY origin unknown

curdle vb **-dling, -dled 1** to turn into curd; coagulate **2 make someone's blood curdle** to fill someone with horror

cure vb **curing, cured 1** to get rid of (an ailment or problem) **2** to restore (someone) to health **3** to preserve (meat or fish) by salting or smoking **4** to preserve (leather or tobacco) by drying **5** to vulcanize (rubber) ▷ n **6** a restoration to health **7** medical treatment that restores health **8** a means of restoring health or improving a situation **9** a curacy ▶ HISTORY Latin *cura* care

cure-all n something supposed to cure all ailments or problems

curette or **curet** n 1 a surgical instrument for scraping tissue from body cavities ▷ vb **-retting, -retted** 2 to scrape with a curette ▶ HISTORY French > **curettage** n

curfew n 1 a law which states that people must stay inside their houses after a specific time at night 2 the time set as a deadline by such a law 3 history the ringing of a bell at a fixed time, as a signal for putting out fires and lights ▶ HISTORY Old French *cuevrefeu* cover the fire

Curia n, pl **-riae** the court and government of the Roman Catholic Church ▶ HISTORY Latin > **curial** adj

curie n the standard unit of radioactivity ▶ HISTORY after Pierre *Curie*, French physicist

curio (kew-ree-oh) n, pl **-rios** a rare or unusual thing valued as a collector's item ▶ HISTORY from *curiosity*

curiosity n, pl **-ties** 1 eagerness to know or find out 2 a rare or unusual thing

curious adj 1 eager to learn or know 2 eager to find out private details 3 unusual or peculiar ▶ HISTORY Latin *curiosus* taking pains over something > **curiously** adv

curium (kew-ree-um) n chem a silvery-white metallic radioactive element artificially produced from plutonium. Symbol: Cm ▶ HISTORY after Pierre & Marie *Curie*, French physicists

curl vb 1 to twist (hair) or (of hair) to grow in coils or ringlets 2 to twist into a spiral or curve 3 to play the game of curling 4 **curl one's lip** to show contempt by raising a corner of the lip ▷ n 5 a coil of hair 6 a curved or spiral shape ▶ HISTORY probably from Middle Dutch *crullen* > **curly** adj

curler n 1 a pin or small tube for curling hair 2 a person who plays curling

curlew n a large wading bird with a long downward-curving bill ▶ HISTORY Old French *corlieu*

curlicue n an intricate ornamental curl or twist ▶ HISTORY *curly* + CUE[2]

curling n a game played on ice, in which heavy stones with handles are slid towards a target circle

curmudgeon n a bad-tempered or mean person ▶ HISTORY origin unknown > **curmudgeonly** adj

currajong n same as **kurrajong**

currant n 1 a small dried seedless raisin 2 a small round acid berry, such as the redcurrant

- ■ **WORD HISTORY**
- ■ Currants originally came from Corinth in
- ■ Greece. The word 'currant' is from early English
- ■ *rayson of Corannte*, which translates Norman
- ■ French *raisin de Corauntz*, meaning 'grape from
- ■ Corinth'.

currawong n an Australian songbird ▶ HISTORY Aboriginal

currency n, pl **-cies** 1 the system of money or the actual coins and banknotes in use in a particular country 2 general acceptance or use: *ideas that had gained currency during the early 1960s* ▶ HISTORY Latin *currere* to run, flow

current adj 1 of the immediate present: *current affairs; the current economic climate* 2 most recent or up-to-date: *the current edition* 3 commonly accepted: *current thinking on this issue* 4 circulating and valid at present: *current coins* ▷ n 5 a flow of water or air in a particular direction 6 physics a flow or rate of flow of electric charge through a conductor 7 a general trend or drift: *two opposing currents of thought* ▶ HISTORY Latin *currere* to run, flow > **currently** adv

current account n a bank account from which money may be drawn at any time using a chequebook or computerized card

current liabilities pl n business business liabilities maturing within a year

curriculum n, pl **-la** or **-lums** 1 all the courses of study offered by a school or college 2 a course of study in one subject at a school or college: *the history curriculum* ▶ HISTORY Latin: course > **curricular** adj

curriculum vitae (vee-tie) n, pl **curricula vitae** an outline of someone's educational and professional history, prepared for job applications ▶ HISTORY Latin: the course of one's life

curry[1] n, pl **-ries** 1 a dish of Indian origin consisting of meat or vegetables in a hot spicy sauce 2 curry seasoning or sauce 3 **curry powder** a mixture of spices for making curry ▷ vb **-ries, -rying, -ried** 4 to prepare (food) with curry powder ▶ HISTORY Tamil *kari* sauce, relish

curry[2] vb **-ries, -rying, -ried** 1 to groom (a horse) 2 to dress (leather) after it has been tanned 3 **curry favour** to ingratiate oneself with an important person ▶ HISTORY Old French *correer* to make ready

curse vb **cursing, cursed** 1 written to swear or swear at (someone) 2 to call on supernatural powers to bring harm to (someone or something) ▷ n 3 a profane or obscene expression, usually of anger 4 an appeal to a supernatural power for harm to come to a person 5 harm resulting from a curse 6 something that causes great trouble or harm 7 **the curse** informal menstruation or a menstrual period ▶ HISTORY Old English *cursian*

cursed adj 1 under a curse 2 **cursed with** having (something unfortunate or unwanted): *I've been cursed with a bad memory for names*

cursive adj 1 of handwriting or print in which letters are joined in a flowing style ▷ n 2 a cursive letter or printing type ▶ HISTORY Medieval Latin *cursivus* running

cursor n 1 a movable point of light that shows a specific position on a visual display unit 2 the sliding part of a slide rule or other measuring instrument

cursory adj hasty and usually superficial ▶ HISTORY Late Latin *cursorius* of running > **cursorily** adv

curt adj so blunt and brief as to be rude ▶ HISTORY Latin *curtus* cut short > **curtly** adv > **curtness** n

curtail vb 1 to cut short: *the opening round was curtailed by heavy rain* 2 to restrict: *a plan to curtail drinks advertising* ▶ HISTORY obsolete *curtal* to dock > **curtailment** n

203

curtain n **1** a piece of material hung at an opening or window to shut out light or to provide privacy **2** a hanging cloth that conceals all or part of a theatre stage from the audience **3** the end of a scene or a performance in the theatre, marked by the fall or closing of the curtain **4** the rise or opening of the curtain at the start of a performance **5** something forming a barrier or screen: *a curtain of rain* ▷ vb **6** to shut off or conceal with a curtain **7** to provide with curtains ▶ HISTORY Late Latin *cortina*

curtain call n *theatre* a return to the stage by performers to receive applause

curtain-raiser n **1** *theatre* a short play performed before the main play **2** a minor event happening before a major one

curtains pl n *informal* death or ruin; the end

curtsy or **curtsey** n, pl **-sies** or **-seys 1** a woman's formal gesture of respect made by bending the knees and bowing the head ▷ vb **-sies, -sying, -sied** or **-seys, -seying, -seyed 2** to make a curtsy ▶ HISTORY variant of *courtesy*

curvaceous adj *informal* having a curved shapely body

curvature n the state or degree of being curved

curve n **1** a continuously bending line with no straight parts **2** something that curves or is curved **3** curvature **4** *maths* a system of points whose coordinates satisfy a given equation **5** a line representing data on a graph ▷ vb **curving, curved 6** to form into or move in a curve ▶ HISTORY Latin *curvare* to bend > **curvy** adj

curvilinear adj consisting of or bounded by a curved line

cuscus n, pl **-cuses** a large nocturnal possum of N Australia and New Guinea ▶ HISTORY probably from a native word in New Guinea

cushion n **1** a bag filled with a soft material, used to make a seat more comfortable **2** something that provides comfort or absorbs shock **3** the resilient felt-covered rim of a billiard table ▷ vb **4** to protect from injury or shock **5** to lessen the effects of **6** to provide with cushions ▶ HISTORY Latin *culcita* mattress > **cushiony** adj

cushy adj **cushier, cushiest** *informal* easy: *a cushy job* ▶ HISTORY Hindi *khush* pleasant

cusp n **1** a small point on the grinding or chewing surface of a tooth **2** a point where two curves meet **3** *astrol* any division between houses or signs of the zodiac **4** *astron* either of the points of a crescent moon ▶ HISTORY Latin *cuspis* pointed end

cuspate delta n *geog* a type of delta whose distinguishing feature is the presence of horn-shaped pieces of land formed from sedimentary deposits at the river mouth. Compare **arcuate delta, bird's foot delta**

cuss *informal* n **1** a curse or oath **2** an annoying person ▷ vb **3** to swear or swear at

cussed (**kuss**-id) adj *informal* **1** obstinate: *the older she got the more cussed she became* **2** same as **cursed** > **cussedness** n

custard n **1** a sauce made of milk and sugar thickened with cornflour **2** a baked sweetened mixture of eggs and milk ▶ HISTORY Middle English *crustade* kind of pie

custodian n the person in charge of a public building > **custodianship** n

custody n, pl **-dies 1** the act of keeping safe **2** imprisonment prior to being tried ▶ HISTORY Latin *custos* guard, defender > **custodial** adj

custom n **1** a long-established activity, action, or festivity: *the custom of serving port after dinner* **2** the long-established habits or traditions of a society **3** a usual practice or habit: *she held his hand more tightly than was her custom in public* **4** regular use of a shop or business **5** *law* a practice which by long-established usage has come to have the force of law ▷ adj **6** made to the specifications of an individual customer: *a custom car; custom-tailored suits* ▷ See also **customs** ▶ HISTORY Latin *consuetudo*

customary adj **1** usual **2** established by custom > **customarily** adv > **customariness** n

customary law n *law* law which is founded upon long-continued practices and usage rather than upon written rules

custom-built or **-made** adj made according to the specifications of an individual customer

customer n **1** a person who buys goods or services **2** *informal* a person with whom one has to deal: *a tricky customer*

custom house n a government office where customs are collected

customize or **-mise** vb **-mizing, -mized** or **-mising, -mised** to modify (something) according to a customer's individual requirements > **customization** or **-misation** n

customs n **1** duty charged on imports or exports **2** the government department responsible for collecting this **3** the area at a port, airport, or border where baggage and freight are examined for dutiable goods

custos rotulorum (**kust**-os rote-you-**lore**-um) n, pl **custodes rotulorum** (kuh-**stow**-deez) (in Jamaica) a public official within a parish, with various civic duties including the role of chief magistrate and the representative of the governor general ▶ HISTORY Latin: keeper of the rolls

cut vb **cutting, cut 1** to open up or penetrate (a person or thing) with a sharp instrument **2** (of a sharp instrument) to penetrate or open up (a person or thing) **3** to divide or be divided with or as if with a sharp instrument **4** to trim **5** to abridge or shorten **6** to reduce or restrict: *cut your intake of fried foods* **7** to form or shape by cutting **8** to reap or mow **9** *sport* to hit (the ball) so that it spins and swerves **10** to hurt the feelings of (a person): *her rudeness cut me to the core* **11** *informal* to pretend not to recognize **12** *informal* to absent oneself from without permission: *he found the course boring, and was soon cutting classes* **13** to stop (doing something): *cut the nonsense* **14** to dilute or adulterate: *heroin cut with talcum powder*

cut

There are many useful alternatives for the word **cut**. Different words can be used instead, depending on what it is that is being cut, what is being used to do the cutting, and how deep or extensive the cutting is.

DEFINITIONS 1 AND 2

- If you **nick** something, you make a small cut on its surface: He **nicked** his chin while he was shaving.
- If you **score** something, you cut a line or lines on its surface: Lightly **score** the surface of the steaks with a cook's knife.
- If you **pierce** something with a sharp object, or a sharp object **pierces** it, the object goes through it and makes a hole in it: **Pierce** the skin of the potato with a fork. • One bullet had **pierced** his lung.
- If something **penetrates** an object, it goes inside it or passes through it: a spider with fangs big enough to **penetrate** the skin
- If you **slit** something, you make a long narrow cut in it: He began to **slit** open each envelope.
- If you **gash** or **slash** something, you make a long, deep cut in it: He **gashed** his leg on the barbed wire. • She **slashed** the tyres.
- If you **hack** something, you cut it using rough strokes: Matthew desperately **hacked** through the straps.

DEFINITION 3

- If you **split** or **divide** something, you cut it into two or more parts: **Split** the planks down the middle. • **Divide** the pastry into four equal parts.
- If you **sever** something, you cut it off or cut right through it: He **severed** the tendon of his thumb in an industrial accident.
- If you **saw** something, you cut it with a saw: Your father is **sawing** wood in the garden.
- If you **slice** something, you cut it into thin pieces: I **sliced** the beef into thin strips.
- If you **chop** something, you cut it into pieces with strong downward movements of a knife or axe: You will need to **chop** the onions very finely.

- If you **carve** meat, you cut slices from it: Jane began to **carve** the roast.
- If you **hew** stone or wood, you cut it, perhaps with an axe: He felled, peeled, and **hewed** his own timber.
- If you **lop** something off, you cut it off with one quick stroke: Somebody has **lopped** the heads off our tulips.

DEFINITION 4

- If you **trim** something, you cut off small amounts of it to make it look neater: I have my hair **trimmed** every eight weeks.
- If you **clip** something, you cut small pieces from it in order to shape it: I saw an old man out **clipping** his hedge.
- If you **prune** a tree or bush, you cut off some of its branches: Apple trees can be **pruned** once they've lost their leaves.
- If you **mow** grass, you cut it with a lawnmower: I **mowed** the lawn and did various other chores.
- If you **snip** something, you cut it with scissors or shears: The hairdresser **snipped** off my split ends.
- If you **pare** something, you cut off its skin or outer layer: She was sitting **paring** her nails with a pair of clippers.
- If you **dock** an animal's tail, you cut it off: I think it is cruel to **dock** the tail of any animal.

DEFINITION 5

- If you are talking about shortening something such as a text, you might try: She **abbreviates** her name. • had to **abridge** the story • **condense** this into something simple • He **edited** it all down.

DEFINITION 6

- If you are talking about reducing something, you might try: **cut down on** bread • **decrease** expenditure • **lowered** the inflation rate • **restrict** your calorie intake • **slash** prices

DEFINITION 7

- If you are talking about forming an object, you might use: He **carves** figures from pine. • medieval monasteries **hewn** out of the rockface • men chipping and **shaping** boomerangs

15 to make a sharp or sudden change in direction: *the path cuts to the right just after you pass the quarry* **16** to grow (teeth) through the gums **17** *films* **a** to call a halt to a shooting sequence **b** **cut to** to move quickly to (another scene) **18** *films* to edit (film) **19** to switch off (a light or engine) **20** to make (a commercial recording): *he cut his first solo album in 1971* **21** *cards* **a** to divide (the pack) at random into two parts after shuffling **b** to pick cards from a spread pack to decide the dealer or who plays first **22** **cut a dash** to make a stylish impression **23** **cut a person dead** *informal* to ignore a person completely **24** **cut and run** *informal* to escape quickly from a difficult situation **25** **cut both ways**

a to have both good and bad effects **b** to serve both sides of an argument **26** **cut it fine** *informal* to allow little margin of time or space **27** **cut no ice** *informal* to fail to make an impression **28** **cut one's teeth on** *informal* to get experience from ▷ *n* **29** the act of cutting **30** a stroke or incision made by cutting **31** a piece cut off **32** a channel or path cut or hollowed out **33** a reduction: *a pay cut* **34** a deletion in a text, film, or play **35** *informal* a portion or share **36** the style in which hair or a garment is cut **37** a direct route; short cut **38** *sport* a stroke which makes the ball spin and swerve **39** *films* an immediate transition from one shot to the next **40** *Brit* a canal **41** **a cut above** *informal* superior to;

better than ▷ *adj* **42** made or shaped by cutting **43** reduced by cutting: *the shop has hundreds of suits, all at cut prices* **44** adulterated or diluted **45 cut and dried** *informal* settled in advance ▷ See also **cutback** ▶ HISTORY probably from Old Norse See WORD FOCUS **cut** on page 205

cutaneous (kew-**tane**-ee-uss) *adj* of the skin ▶ HISTORY Latin *cutis* skin

cutaway *adj* (of a drawing or model) having part of the outside omitted to reveal the inside

cutback *n* **1** a decrease or reduction ▷ *vb* **cut back 2** to shorten by cutting **3** to make a reduction: *we may cut back on other expenditure*

cute *adj* **1** appealing or attractive **2** *informal* clever or shrewd ▶ HISTORY from ACUTE > **cuteness** *n*

cuticle (**kew**-tik-kl) *n* **1** hardened skin round the base of a fingernail or toenail **2** same as **epidermis** ▶ HISTORY Latin *cuticula* skin

cut in *vb* **1** to interrupt **2** to move in front of another vehicle, leaving too little space

cutlass *n* a curved one-edged sword formerly used by sailors ▶ HISTORY French *coutelas*

cutler *n* a person who makes or sells cutlery ▶ HISTORY Latin *culter* knife

cutlery *n* knives, forks, and spoons, used for eating

cutlet *n* **1** a small piece of meat taken from the neck or ribs **2** a flat croquette of chopped meat or fish ▶ HISTORY Old French *costelette* a little rib

cut off *vb* **1** to remove or separate by cutting **2** to stop the supply of **3** to interrupt (a person who is speaking), esp. during a telephone conversation **4** to bring to an end **5** to disinherit: *cut off without a penny* **6** to intercept so as to prevent retreat or escape ▷ *n* **cutoff 7** the point at which something is cut off; limit **8** *chiefly US* a short cut **9** a device to stop the flow of a fluid in a pipe

cut-off meander *n geog* a former bend of a river now by-passed by the water owing to the river having cut out a more direct course through erosion

cut out *vb* **1** to shape by cutting **2** to delete or remove **3** *informal* to stop doing (something) **4** (of an engine) to cease to operate suddenly **5** (of an electrical device) to switch off, usually automatically **6 be cut out for** to be suited or equipped for: *you're not cut out for this job* **7 have one's work cut out** to have as much work as one can manage ▷ *n* **cutout 8** a device that automatically switches off a circuit or engine as a safety device **9** something that has been cut out from something else

cut-price *or esp US* **cut-rate** *adj* **1** at a reduced price **2** offering goods or services at prices below the standard price

cutter *n* **1** a person or tool that cuts **2** a small fast boat

cut-throat *adj* **1** fierce or ruthless in competition: *the cut-throat world of international finance* **2** (of a card game) played by three people: *cut-throat poker* ▷ *n* **3** a murderer **4** *Brit & NZ* a razor with a long blade that folds into its handle

cutting *n* **1** an article cut from a newspaper or magazine **2** a piece cut from a plant for rooting or grafting **3** a passage cut through high ground for a road or railway **4** the editing process of a film ▷ *adj* **5** (of a remark) likely to hurt the feelings **6** keen; piercing: *a cutting wind* **7** designed for cutting: *the hatchet's blade is largely stone, but its cutting edge is made of copper*

cutting edge *n* **1** the leading position in any field ▷ *adj* **cutting-edge 2** at the forefront of a field of activity: *cutting-edge technology*

cuttlefish *n, pl* **-fish** *or* **-fishes** a flat squidlike mollusc which squirts an inky fluid when in danger ▶ HISTORY Old English *cudele*

cut up *vb* **1** to cut into pieces **2** *informal* (of a driver) to overtake or pull in front of (another driver) in a dangerous manner **3 be cut up** *informal* to be very upset **4 cut up rough** *Brit, informal* to become angry or violent

CV curriculum vitae

cwm (**koom**) *n* (in Wales) a valley ▶ HISTORY Welsh

cwt hundredweight

CXC *trademark* Caribbean Examinations Council

cyanic acid *n* a colourless poisonous volatile liquid acid

cyanide *n* any of a number of highly poisonous substances containing a carbon-nitrogen group of atoms

cyanogen *n* a poisonous colourless flammable gas ▶ HISTORY Greek *kuanos* dark blue

cyanosis *n pathol* a blue discoloration of the skin, caused by a deficiency of oxygen in the blood ▶ HISTORY Greek *kuanos* dark blue

cyber- *combining form* indicating computers: *cyberspace* ▶ HISTORY from CYBERNETICS

cyberbullying *n* the act of threatening or intimidating a person by means of electronic communication

cybercafé *n* a café equipped with computer terminals which customers can use to access the internet ▶ HISTORY CYBER- + CAFÉ

cybernetics *n* the branch of science in which electronic and mechanical systems are studied and compared to biological systems ▶ HISTORY Greek *kubernētēs* steersman > **cybernetic** *adj*

cyberpet *n* an electronic toy that mimics the actions of a pet

cyberspace *n* the hypothetical environment which contains all the data stored in computers ▶ HISTORY CYBER- + SPACE

cybersquatting *n* the practice of registering an internet domain name that is likely to be wanted by another person or organization in the hope that it can be sold to them for a profit > **cybersquatter** *n*

cyclamen (**sik**-la-men) *n* a plant with white, pink, or red flowers, with turned-back petals ▶ HISTORY Greek *kuklaminos*

cycle *vb* **-cling, -cled 1** to ride a bicycle **2** to occur in cycles ▷ *n* **3** *Brit, Austral & NZ* a bicycle **4** *US* a motorcycle **5** a complete series of recurring events **6** the time taken or needed for one such series **7** a single complete movement in an electrical, electronic, or mechanical process **8** a set of plays, songs, or poems about a figure or event ▶ HISTORY Greek *kuklos* > **cycling** *n*

cyclical *or* **cyclic** *adj* **1** occurring in cycles **2** *chem* (of an organic compound) containing a closed ring of atoms **3** *geom* (of a polygon) having vertices that lie on a circle

cyclic quadrilateral *n geom* a quadrilateral with all its vertices lying on the circumference of a circle

cyclist *n* a person who rides a bicycle

cyclo- *or before a vowel* **cycl-** *combining form* **1** indicating a circle or ring: *cyclotron* **2** *chem* denoting a cyclical compound: *cyclopropane* ▶ HISTORY Greek *kuklos* cycle

cyclometer (sike-**lom**-it-er) *n* a device that records the number of revolutions made by a wheel and the distance travelled

cyclone *n* **1** a body of moving air below normal atmospheric pressure, which often brings rain **2** a violent tropical storm ▶ HISTORY Greek *kuklōn* a turning around > **cyclonic** *adj*

cyclopedia *or* **cyclopaedia** *n* same as **encyclopedia**

Cyclops *n*, *pl* **Cyclopes** *or* **Cyclopses** *classical myth* one of a race of giants having a single eye in the middle of the forehead ▶ HISTORY Greek *Kuklōps* round eye

cyclotron *n* an apparatus, used in atomic research, which accelerates charged particles by means of a strong vertical magnetic field

cygnet *n* a young swan ▶ HISTORY Latin *cygnus* swan

cylinder *n* **1** a solid or hollow body with circular equal ends and straight parallel sides **2** a container or other object shaped like a cylinder **3** the chamber in an internal-combustion engine within which the piston moves **4** the rotating mechanism of a revolver, containing cartridge chambers ▶ HISTORY Greek *kulindein* to roll > **cylindrical** *adj*

cymbal *n* a percussion instrument consisting of a round brass plate which is struck against another or hit with a stick ▶ HISTORY Greek *kumbē* something hollow > **cymbalist** *n*

cyme *n bot* a flower cluster which has a single flower on the end of each stem and of which the central flower blooms first ▶ HISTORY Greek *kuma* anything swollen > **cymose** *adj*

Cymric (**kim**-rik) *adj* **1** of Wales ▷ *n* **2** the Celtic language of Wales

cynic (**sin**-ik) *n* a person who believes that people always act selfishly ▶ HISTORY Greek *kuōn* dog

Cynic *n* a member of an ancient Greek philosophical school that had contempt for worldly things > **Cynicism** *n*

cynical *adj* **1** believing that people always act selfishly **2** sarcastic or sneering > **cynically** *adv*

cynicism *n* the attitude or beliefs of a cynic

cynosure (**sin**-oh-zyure) *n literary* a centre of interest or attention ▶ HISTORY Greek *Kunosoura* dog's tail (name of the constellation of Ursa Minor)

cypher (**sife**-er) *n*, *vb* same as **cipher**

cypress *n* **1** an evergreen tree with dark green leaves **2** the wood of this tree ▶ HISTORY Greek *kuparissos*

Cypriot *adj* **1** of Cyprus ▷ *n* **2** a person from Cyprus **3** the dialect of Greek spoken in Cyprus

Cyrillic *adj* of the Slavic alphabet devised supposedly by Saint Cyril, now used primarily for Russian and Bulgarian

cyst (**sist**) *n* **1** *pathol* an abnormal membranous sac containing fluid or diseased matter **2** *anat* any normal sac in the body ▶ HISTORY Greek *kustis* pouch, bag

cystic fibrosis *n* a congenital disease, usually affecting young children, which causes breathing disorders and malfunctioning of the pancreas

cystitis (siss-**tite**-iss) *n* inflammation of the bladder, causing a desire to urinate frequently, accompanied by a burning sensation

-cyte *n combining form* indicating a cell: *leucocyte* ▶ HISTORY Greek *kutos* vessel

cytokinesis *n biol* division of the cytoplasm of a cell contained within the cell membrane but excluding the nucleus

cytology (site-**ol**-a-jee) *n* the study of plant and animal cells > **cytological** *adj* > **cytologically** *adv* > **cytologist** *n*

cytoplasm *n* the protoplasm of a cell excluding the nucleus > **cytoplasmic** *adj*

cytosine *n biol* a white crystalline pyrimidine occurring in nucleic acids

czar (**zahr**) *n* same as **tsar**

Czech *adj* **1** of the Czech Republic ▷ *n* **2** a person from the Czech Republic **3** the language of the Czech Republic

Czechoslovak *or* **Czechoslovakian** *adj* **1** of the former Czechoslovakia ▷ *n* **2** a person from the former Czechoslovakia

Dd

d

d 1 *physics* density **2** deci-

D 1 *music* the second note of the scale of C major **2** *chem* deuterium **3** the Roman numeral for 500

d. 1 *Brit & NZ* (before decimalization) penny *or* pennies ▸ HISTORY Latin *denarius* **2** died **3** daughter

dab¹ *vb* **dabbing, dabbed 1** to pat lightly and quickly **2** to apply with short tapping strokes: *dabbing antiseptic on cuts* ▷ *n* **3** a small amount of something soft or moist **4** a light stroke or tap **5 dabs** *slang, chiefly Brit* fingerprints ▸ HISTORY imitative

dab² *n* a small European flatfish covered with rough toothed scales ▸ HISTORY Anglo-French *dabbe*

dabble *vb* **-bling, -bled 1** to be involved in an activity in a superficial way: *she dabbles in right-wing politics* **2** to splash (one's toes or fingers) in water ▸ HISTORY probably from Dutch *dabbelen* > **dabbler** *n*

dab hand *n informal* a person who is particularly skilled at something: *a dab hand with a needle and thread* ▸ HISTORY origin unknown

dace *n, pl* **dace** *or* **daces** a European freshwater fish of the carp family ▸ HISTORY Old French *dars* dart

dachshund *n* a small dog with short legs and a long body

- ■ **WORD HISTORY**
- ■ 'Dachshund' is a German word meaning
- ■ 'badger-dog', from *Dachs*, meaning 'badger',
- ■ and *Hund*, meaning 'dog'. (*Hund* is related to
- ■ the English word 'hound'.) Dachshunds were
- ■ originally bred to hunt badgers.

dactyl *n prosody* a metrical foot of three syllables, one long followed by two short ▸ HISTORY Greek *daktulos* finger, comparing the finger's three joints to the three syllables > **dactylic** *adj*

dad *or* **daddy** *n informal* father ▸ HISTORY from child's *da da*

Dada *or* **Dadaism** *n* an art movement of the early 20th century that systematically used arbitrary and absurd concepts ▸ HISTORY French: hobbyhorse > **Dadaist** *n, adj*

daddy-longlegs *n informal* **1** *Brit* crane fly **2** a small web-spinning spider with long legs

dado (**day**-doe) *n, pl* **-does** *or* **-dos 1** the lower part of an interior wall, often separated by a rail, that is decorated differently from the upper part **2** *archit* the part of a pedestal between the base and the

cornice ▸ HISTORY Italian: die, die-shaped pedestal

daffodil *n* **1** a spring plant with yellow trumpet-shaped flowers ▷ *adj* **2** brilliant yellow ▸ HISTORY variant of Latin *asphodelus* asphodel

daft *adj informal, chiefly Brit* **1** foolish or crazy **2 daft about** very enthusiastic about: *he's daft about football*

- ■ **WORD HISTORY**
- ■ 'Daft' and 'deft' both come from Old English
- ■ *gedæfte*, meaning 'gentle'.

dag *Austral & NZ n* **1** the dried dung on a sheep's rear **2** *informal* an amusing person ▷ *pl n* **3 rattle one's dags** *informal* hurry up ▷ *vb* **4** to remove the dags from a sheep ▸ HISTORY origin unknown

dagga (**duhh**-a) *n S African* a local name for marijuana ▸ HISTORY probably from Khoikhoi *daxa*

dagger *n* **1** a short knifelike weapon with a double-edged pointed blade **2** a character (†) used to indicate a cross-reference **3 at daggers drawn** in a state of open hostility **4 look daggers** to glare with hostility ▸ HISTORY origin unknown

daggy *adj NZ, informal* amusing

daguerreotype (dag-**gair**-oh-type) *n* a type of early photograph produced on chemically treated silver ▸ HISTORY after L. *Daguerre*, its inventor

dahlia (**day**-lya) *n* a garden plant with showy flowers ▸ HISTORY after Anders *Dahl*, botanist

Dáil Éireann (doil **air**-in) *or* **Dáil** *n* (in the Republic of Ireland) the lower chamber of parliament ▸ HISTORY Irish *dáil* assembly + *Éireann* of Eire

daily *adj* **1** occurring every day or every weekday: *there have been daily airdrops of food, blankets, and water* **2** of or relating to a single day or to one day at a time: *her home help comes in on a daily basis; exercise has become part of our daily lives* ▷ *adv* **3** every day ▷ *n, pl* **-lies 4** *Brit & Austral* a daily newspaper **5** *Brit, informal* a woman employed to clean someone's house ▸ HISTORY Old English *dæglīc*

dainty *adj* **-tier, -tiest 1** delicate, pretty, or elegant: *dainty little pink shoes* ▷ *n, pl* **-ties 2** *Brit* a small choice cake or sweet ▸ HISTORY Old French *deintié* > **daintily** *adv*

daiquiri (**dak**-eer-ee) *n, pl* **-ris** an iced drink containing rum, lime juice, and sugar ▸ HISTORY after *Daiquiri*, town in Cuba

dairy *n, pl* **dairies 1** a company or shop that sells milk and milk products **2** a place where milk and cream are stored or made into butter and cheese **3** *NZ* small shop selling groceries and milk often outside normal trading hours **4** food containing milk or milk products: *I can't eat dairy* ▷ *adj* **5** of milk or milk products: *dairy produce* ▸ HISTORY Old English *dæge* servant girl

dairy cattle *n* cows reared mainly for their milk

dairy farm *n* a farm where cows are kept mainly for their milk

dairymaid *n Brit, Austral & NZ* (formerly) a woman employed to milk cows

dairyman *n Brit, Austral & S African* a man employed to look after cows

dais (**day**-iss) *n* a raised platform in a hall or

meeting place used by a speaker ▸ HISTORY Old French *deis*

daisy *n, pl* **-sies** a small low-growing flower with a yellow centre and pinkish-white petals

■ **WORD HISTORY**
■ 'Daisy' comes from Old English *dæges êage*,
■ meaning 'day's eye'. The flower was given this
■ name because it opens in the daytime and
■ closes at night.

daisy chain *n* a string of daisies joined together by their stems to make a necklace

daisywheel *n* a flat disc in a word processor with radiating spokes for printing characters

dal¹ *n* same as **dhal**

dal² decalitre(s)

Dalai Lama *n* the chief lama and (until 1959) ruler of Tibet

dale *n* an open valley ▸ HISTORY Old English *dæl*

dalliance *n* old-fashioned flirtation

dally *vb* **-lies, -lying, -lied** **1** *old-fashioned* to waste time or dawdle **2** **dally with** to deal frivolously with: *to dally with someone's affections* ▸ HISTORY Anglo-French *dalier* to gossip

Dalmatian *n* a large dog with a smooth white coat and black spots

dam¹ *n* **1** a barrier built across a river to create a lake **2** a lake created by such a barrier ▷ *vb* **damming, dammed** **3** to block up (a river) by a dam ▸ HISTORY probably from Middle Low German

dam² *n* the female parent of an animal such as a sheep or horse ▸ HISTORY variant of *dame*

dam³ decametre(s)

damage *vb* **-aging, -aged** **1** to harm or injure ▷ *n* **2** injury or harm caused to a person or thing **3** *informal* cost: *what's the damage?* ▸ HISTORY Latin *damnum* injury, loss ▸ **damaging** *adj*

damages *pl n law* money awarded as compensation for injury or loss

damask *n* a heavy fabric with a pattern woven into it, used for tablecloths, curtains, etc. ▸ HISTORY *Damascus*, where fabric originally made

dame *n slang* a woman ▸ HISTORY Latin *domina* lady

Dame *n* (in Britain) the title of a woman who has been awarded the Order of the British Empire or another order of chivalry

damn *interj* **1** *slang* an exclamation of annoyance ▷ *adv, adj also* **damned** **2** *slang* extreme or extremely: *a damn good idea* ▷ *vb* **3** to condemn as bad or worthless **4** to curse **5** (of God) to condemn to hell or eternal punishment **6** to prove (someone) guilty **7** **damn with faint praise** to praise so unenthusiastically that the effect is condemnation ▷ *n* **8** **not give a damn** *informal* not care ▸ HISTORY Latin *damnum* loss, injury ▸ **damning** *adj*

damnable *adj* very unpleasant or annoying ▸ **damnably** *adv*

damnation *interj* **1** an exclamation of anger ▷ *n* **2** *theol* eternal punishment

damned *adj* **1** condemned to hell ▷ *adv, adj slang* **2** extreme or extremely: *a damned good try* **3** used to

indicate amazement or refusal: *I'm damned if I'll do it!*

damp *adj* **1** slightly wet ▷ *n* **2** slight wetness; moisture ▷ *vb* **3** to make slightly wet **4** **damp down a** to reduce the intensity of (someone's emotions or reactions): *they attempted to damp down protests* **b** to reduce the flow of air to (a fire) to make it burn more slowly ▸ HISTORY Middle Low German: steam ▸ **damply** *adv* ▸ **dampness** *n*

damper *n* **1** **put a damper on** to produce a depressing or inhibiting effect on **2** a movable plate to regulate the draught in a stove or furnace **3** the pad in a piano or harpsichord that deadens the vibration of each string as its key is released **4** *chiefly Austral & NZ* any of various unleavened loaves and scones, typically cooked on an open fire

damsel *n* *archaic or poetic* a young woman ▸ HISTORY Old French *damoisele*

damson *n* a small blue-black edible plumlike fruit that grows on a tree ▸ HISTORY Latin *prunum damascenum* Damascus plum

dan *n judo, karate* **1** any of the 10 black-belt grades of proficiency **2** a competitor entitled to dan grading ▸ HISTORY Japanese

dance *vb* **dancing, danced** **1** to move the feet and body rhythmically in time to music **2** to perform (a particular dance): *to dance a tango* **3** to skip or leap **4** to move in a rhythmic way: *their reflection danced in the black waters* **5** **dance attendance on someone** to carry out someone's slightest wish in an overeager manner ▷ *n* **6** a social meeting arranged for dancing **7** a series of rhythmic steps and movements in time to music **8** a piece of music in the rhythm of a particular dance ▸ HISTORY Old French *dancier* ▸ **dancer** *n* ▸ **dancing** *n, adj*

D and C *n med* dilatation of the cervix and curettage of the uterus: a minor operation to clear the womb or remove tissue for diagnosis

dandelion *n* a wild plant with yellow rayed flowers and deeply notched leaves ▸ HISTORY Old French *dent de lion* tooth of a lion, referring to its leaves

dander *n* **get one's dander up** *Brit, Austral & NZ, slang* to become angry ▸ HISTORY from *dandruff*

dandified *adj* dressed like or resembling a dandy

dandle *vb* **-dling, -dled** to move (a young child) up and down on one's knee ▸ HISTORY origin unknown

dandruff *n* loose scales of dry dead skin shed from the scalp ▸ HISTORY origin unknown

dandy *n, pl* **-dies** **1** a man who is greatly concerned with the elegance of his appearance ▷ *adj* **-dier, -diest** **2** *informal* very good or fine ▸ HISTORY origin unknown

Dane *n* a person from Denmark

danger *n* **1** the possibility that someone may be injured or killed **2** someone or something that may cause injury or harm **3** a likelihood that something unpleasant will happen: *the danger of flooding* ▸ HISTORY Middle English *daunger* power, hence power to inflict injury

209

danger money *n* extra money paid to compensate for the risks involved in dangerous work

dangerous *adj* likely or able to cause injury or harm > **dangerously** *adv*

dangle *vb* **-gling, -gled** **1** to hang loosely **2** to display (something attractive) as an enticement ▶ HISTORY probably imitative

Danish *adj* **1** of Denmark ▷ *n* **2** the language of Denmark

Danish blue *n* a white cheese with blue veins and a strong flavour

Danish pastry *n* a rich puff pastry filled with apple, almond paste, etc. and topped with icing

dank *adj* (esp. of cellars or caves) unpleasantly damp and chilly ▶ HISTORY probably from Old Norse

dapper *adj* (of a man) neat in appearance and slight in build ▶ HISTORY Middle Dutch

dappled *adj* **1** marked with spots of a different colour; mottled **2** covered in patches of light and shadow ▶ HISTORY origin unknown

dapple-grey *n* a horse with a grey coat and darker coloured spots

Darby and Joan *n* *chiefly Brit* a happily married elderly couple ▶ HISTORY couple in 18th-century ballad

Darby and Joan Club *n* *chiefly Brit* a club for elderly people

dare *vb* **daring, dared** **1** to be courageous enough to try (to do something) **2** to challenge (someone) to do something risky **3 I dare say a** it is quite possible **b** probably ▷ *n* **4** a challenge to do something risky ▶ HISTORY Old English *durran*

daredevil *n* **1** a recklessly bold person ▷ *adj* **2** recklessly bold or daring

daring *adj* **1** willing to do things that may be dangerous ▷ *n* **2** the courage to do things that may be dangerous > **daringly** *adv*

dark *adj* **1** having little or no light **2** (of a colour) reflecting little light: *dark brown* **3** (of hair or skin) brown or black **4** (of thoughts or ideas) gloomy or sad **5** sinister or evil: *a dark deed* **6** sullen or angry: *a dark scowl* **7** secret or mysterious: *keep it dark* ▷ *n* **8** absence of light; darkness **9** night or nightfall **10 in the dark** in ignorance ▶ HISTORY Old English *deorc* > **darkly** *adv* > **darkness** *n*

dark age *n written* a period of ignorance or barbarism

Dark Ages *n* the period of European history between 500 and 1000 AD

darken *vb* **1** to make or become dark or darker **2** to make gloomy, angry, or sad

dark horse *n* a person who reveals little about himself or herself, esp. someone who has unexpected talents

darkroom *n* a darkened room in which photographs are developed

darling *n* **1** a person very much loved: used as a term of address **2** a favourite: *the darling of the gossip columns* ▷ *adj* **3** beloved **4** pleasing: *a darling film* ▶ HISTORY Old English *dēorling*

darn¹ *vb* **1** to mend a hole in (a knitted garment) with a series of interwoven stitches ▷ *n* **2** a patch of darned work on a garment ▶ HISTORY origin unknown

darn² *interj, adj, adv, vb, n* euphemistic same as **damn**

darnel *n* a weed that grows in grain fields ▶ HISTORY origin unknown

dart *n* **1** a small narrow pointed missile that is thrown or shot, as in the game of darts **2** a sudden quick movement **3** a tapered tuck made in dressmaking ▷ *vb* **4** *written* to move or throw swiftly and suddenly ▶ HISTORY Germanic > **darting** *adj*

Darwinism *or* **Darwinian theory** *n* the theory of the origin of animal and plant species by evolution ▶ HISTORY after Charles *Darwin*, English naturalist > **Darwinian** *adj, n* > **Darwinist** *n, adj*

dash *vb* **1** to move hastily; rush **2** to hurl; crash: *deep-sea rollers dashing spray over jagged rocks* **3** to frustrate: *prospects for peace have been dashed* ▷ *n* **4** a sudden quick movement **5** a small amount: *a dash of milk* **6** a mixture of style and courage: *the commander's dash did not impress him* **7** the punctuation mark (—), used to indicate a change of subject **8** the symbol (–), used in combination with the symbol *dot* (.) in Morse code ▷ See also **dash off** ▶ HISTORY Middle English *daschen, dassen*

dashboard *n* the instrument panel in a car, boat, or aircraft

dasheen *n* another name for **taro**

dasher *n* *Canad* one of the boards surrounding an ice hockey rink

dashiki (dah-**shee**-ki) *n, pl* **dashikis** a large loose-fitting buttonless upper garment worn in Africa and the Caribbean ▶ HISTORY of W African origin

dashing *adj* stylish and attractive: *a splendidly dashing character*

dash off *vb* to write down or finish off hastily

dassie *n* *S African* a hyrax, esp. a rock hyrax ▶ HISTORY Afrikaans

dastardly *adj* *old-fashioned* mean and cowardly ▶ HISTORY Middle English *dastard* dullard

dasyure (**dass**-ee-your) *n* a small marsupial of Australia, New Guinea, and adjacent islands

dat. dative

data *n* **1** a series of observations, measurements, or facts; information **2** *computers* the numbers, digits, characters, and symbols operated on by a computer ▶ HISTORY Latin: (things) given

database *n* **1** a store of information in a form that can be easily handled by a computer **2** a large store of information: *a database of knowledge*

data capture *n* a process for converting information into a form that can be handled by a computer

data processing *n* a sequence of operations performed on data, esp. by a computer, in order to extract or interpret information

data search *n* *computing* an attempt to find information, especially by using a search engine on the internet

data set *n science* information collected and organized for research purposes

date¹ *n* **1** a specified day of the month **2** the particular day or year when an event happened **3 a** an appointment, esp. with a person to whom one is romantically attached **b** the person with whom the appointment is made **4 to date** up to now ▷ *vb* **dating, dated 5** to mark (a letter or cheque) with the date **6** to assign a date of occurrence or creation to **7** to reveal the age of: *that dress dates her* **8** to make or become old-fashioned: *it's the freshest look this year but may date quickly* **9** *informal, chiefly US & Canad* to be a boyfriend or girlfriend of **10 date from** *or* **date back to** to have originated at (a specified time) ▶ HISTORY Latin *dare* to give, as in the Latin way of specifying a time and place in letters, for example *epistula data Romae* letter handed over at Rome

date² *n* the dark-brown, sweet-tasting fruit of the date palm ▶ HISTORY Greek *daktulos* finger

dated *adj* unfashionable; outmoded

dateline *n journalism* information placed at the top of an article stating the time and place the article was written

Date Line *n* short for **International Date Line**

date palm *n* a tall palm grown in tropical regions for its fruit

date rape *n* the act of a man raping a woman or pressuring her into having sex while they are on a date together

dative *or* **dative case** *n grammar* the grammatical case in certain languages that expresses the indirect object ▶ HISTORY Latin *dativus*

datum *n, pl* **-ta** a single piece of information usually in the form of a fact or statistic ▶ HISTORY Latin: something given

daub *vb* **1** to smear (paint or mud) quickly or carelessly over a surface **2** to paint (a picture) clumsily or badly ▷ *n* **3** a crude or badly done painting: *a typical child's daub* ▶ HISTORY Old French *dauber* to paint

daughter *n* **1** a female child **2** a girl or woman who comes from a certain place or is connected with a certain thing: *a daughter of the church* ▷ *adj* **3** *biol* denoting a cell, chromosome, etc. produced by the division of one of its own kind **4** *physics* (of a nuclide) formed from another nuclide by radioactive decay ▶ HISTORY Old English *dohtor* > **daughterly** *adj*

daughter-in-law *n, pl* **daughters-in-law** the wife of one's son

daunting *adj* intimidating or worrying: *this project grows more daunting every day* ▶ HISTORY Latin *domitare* to tame

dauntless *adj* fearless; not discouraged

dauphin (**daw**-fin) *n* formerly, the eldest son of the king of France ▶ HISTORY Old French: originally a family name

davenport *n* **1** *chiefly Brit* a writing desk with drawers at the side **2** *Austral, US & Canad* a large sofa ▶ HISTORY sense 1 supposedly after Captain Davenport, who commissioned the first ones

davit (**dav**-vit) *n* a crane, usually one of a pair, on the side of a ship for lowering or hoisting a lifeboat ▶ HISTORY Anglo-French *daviot*, from *Davi* David

Davy Jones's locker *n* the ocean's bottom, regarded as the grave of those lost or buried at sea ▶ HISTORY origin unknown

Davy lamp *n* same as **safety lamp** ▶ HISTORY after Sir Humphrey *Davy*, chemist

dawdle *vb* **-dling, -dled** to walk slowly or lag behind ▶ HISTORY origin unknown

dawn *n* **1** daybreak **2** the beginning of something ▷ *vb* **3** to begin to grow light after the night **4** *written* to begin to develop or appear **5 dawn on** *or* **upon** to become apparent (to someone) ▶ HISTORY Old English *dagian* to dawn

dawn chorus *n* the singing of birds at dawn

day *n* **1** the period of 24 hours from one midnight to the next **2** the period of light between sunrise and sunset **3** the part of a day occupied with regular activity, esp. work **4** a period or point in time: *in days gone by; in Shakespeare's day* **5** a day of special observance: *Christmas Day* **6** a time of success or recognition: *his day will come* **7 all in a day's work** part of one's normal activity **8 at the end of the day** in the final reckoning **9 call it a day** to stop work or other activity **10 day in, day out** every day without changing **11 that'll be the day a** that is most unlikely to happen **b** I look forward to that. *Related adjective:* **diurnal** ▶ HISTORY Old English *dæg*

daybreak *n* the time in the morning when light first appears

day centre *n* a place that provides care where elderly or disabled people can spend the day

daydream *n* **1** a pleasant fantasy indulged in while awake ▷ *vb* **2** to indulge in idle fantasy > **daydreamer** *n*

daylight *n* **1** light from the sun **2** daytime **3** daybreak **4 see daylight** to realize that the end of a difficult task is approaching

daylight robbery *n informal* blatant overcharging

daylight-saving time *n* time set one hour ahead of the local standard time, to provide extra daylight in the evening in summer

Day of Atonement *n* same as **Yom Kippur**

day release *n Brit* a system whereby workers go to college one day a week for vocational training

day return *n* a reduced fare for a train or bus journey travelling both ways in one day

day room *n* a communal living room in a hospital or similar institution

day-to-day *adj* routine; everyday

daze *vb* **dazing, dazed 1** to cause to be in a state of confusion or shock ▷ *n* **2** a state of confusion or shock: *in a daze* ▶ HISTORY Old Norse *dasa* > **dazed** *adj*

dazzle *vb* **-zling, -zled 1** to impress greatly: *she was dazzled by his wit* **2** to blind for a short time by sudden excessive light: *he passed two cars and they dazzled him with their headlights* ▷ *n* **3** bright light that dazzles ▸ HISTORY from *daze* > **dazzling** *adj* > **dazzlingly** *adv*

dB *or* **db** decibel(s)

Db *chem* dubnium

DC 1 direct current **2** District of Columbia

D.C. District of Columbia

DD Doctor of Divinity

D-day *n* the day selected for the start of some operation ▸ HISTORY after *D(ay)-day*, the day of the Allied invasion of Europe on June 6, 1944

DDT *n* dichlorodiphenyltrichloroethane; an insecticide, now banned in many countries

DE Delaware

de- *prefix* **1** indicating removal: *dethrone* **2** indicating reversal: *declassify* **3** indicating departure from: *decamp* ▸ HISTORY Latin

deacon *n Christianity* **1** (in Episcopal churches) an ordained minister ranking immediately below a priest **2** (in some Protestant churches) a lay official who assists the minister ▸ HISTORY Greek *diakonos* servant

deactivate *vb* **-vating, -vated** to make (a bomb or other explosive device) harmless

dead *adj* **1** no longer alive **2** no longer in use or finished: *a dead language; a dead match* **3** unresponsive **4** (of a limb) numb **5** complete or absolute: *there was dead silence* **6** *informal, spoken* very tired **7** (of a place) lacking activity **8** *electronics* **a** drained of electric charge **b** not connected to a source of electric charge **9** *sport* (of a ball) out of play **10 dead from the neck up** *informal* stupid **11 dead to the world** *informal* fast asleep ▷ *n* **12** a period during which coldness or darkness is most intense: *the dead of winter* ▷ *adv* **13** *spoken, informal* extremely: *dead easy* **14** suddenly and abruptly: *stop dead* **15 dead on** exactly right ▸ HISTORY Old English *dēad*

deadbeat *n informal* a lazy or socially undesirable person

dead beat *adj informal* exhausted

deaden *vb* to make (something) less intense: *drugs deaden the pain; heavy curtains deadened the echo* > **deadening** *adj*

dead end *n* **1** a cul-de-sac **2** a situation in which further progress is impossible: *efforts to free the hostages had reached a dead end*

deadhead *n US & Canad* **1** *informal* a person who does not pay on a bus, at a game, etc. **2** *informal* a commercial vehicle travelling empty **3** *slang* a dull person **4** *US & Canad* a totally or partially submerged log floating in a lake

dead heat *n* a tie for first place between two or more participants in a race or contest

dead letter *n* **1** a letter that cannot be delivered or returned due to lack of information **2** a law or rule that is no longer enforced

deadline *n* a time or date by which a job or task must be completed

deadlock *n* a point in a dispute at which no agreement can be reached

deadlocked *adj* having reached a deadlock

dead loss *n informal* a useless person or thing

deadly *adj* **-lier, -liest 1** likely to cause death: *deadly poison* **2** *informal* extremely boring ▷ *adv, adj* **3** like or suggestive of death: *deadly pale* **4** extremely: *she was being deadly serious*

deadly nightshade *n* a poisonous plant with purple bell-shaped flowers and black berries

dead man's handle *or* **pedal** *n* a safety device which only allows equipment to operate when a handle or pedal is being pressed

dead-nettle *n* a plant with leaves like nettles but without stinging hairs

deadpan *adj, adv* with a deliberately emotionless face or manner

dead reckoning *n* a method of establishing one's position using the distance and direction travelled

dead set *adv* firmly decided: *he is dead set on leaving*

dead weight *n* **1** a heavy weight or load **2** the difference between the loaded and the unloaded weights of a ship

dead wood *n informal* people or things that are no longer useful

deaf *adj* **1** unable to hear **2 deaf to** refusing to listen or take notice of ▸ HISTORY Old English *dēaf* > **deafness** *n*

deaf-and-dumb *adj offensive* unable to hear or speak

deafblind *adj* unable to hear or see

deafen *vb* to make deaf, esp. momentarily by a loud noise > **deafening** *adj*

deaf-mute *n offensive* a person who is unable to hear or speak

deal¹ *n* **1** an agreement or transaction **2** a particular type of treatment received: *a fair deal* **3** a large amount: *the land alone is worth a good deal* **4** *cards* a player's turn to distribute the cards **5 big deal** *slang* an important matter: often used sarcastically ▷ *vb* **dealing, dealt** (delt) **6** to inflict (a blow) on **7** *slang* to sell any illegal drug **8 deal in** to engage in commercially **9 deal out** *written* to apportion or distribute ▷ See also **deal with** ▸ HISTORY Old English *dǣlan*

deal² *n* **1** a plank of softwood timber **2** the sawn wood of various coniferous trees ▸ HISTORY Middle Low German *dele* plank

dealer *n* **1** a person or organization whose business involves buying and selling things **2** *slang* a person who sells illegal drugs **3** *cards* the person who distributes the cards

dealings *pl n* business relations with a person or organization

deal with *vb* **1** to take action on: *he was not competent to deal with the legal aspects* **2** to be concerned with: *I do not wish to deal with specifics* **3** to do business with

dean *n* **1** the chief administrative official of a college or university faculty **2** *chiefly Church of England* the chief administrator of a cathedral or collegiate church

■ **WORD HISTORY**
■ 'Dean' comes, via Old French, from Latin
■ *decanus*, meaning 'someone in charge of ten
■ people', from Latin *decem*, meaning 'ten'. The
■ chapter of a cathedral or collegiate church
■ consisted of ten canons.

deanery *n, pl* **-eries 1** a place where a dean lives
2 the parishes presided over by a rural dean

dear *n* **1** (often used in direct address) someone
regarded with affection ▷ *adj* **2** beloved; precious
3 a highly priced **b** charging high prices **4** *written* a
form of address used at the beginning of a letter
before the name of the recipient: *Dear Mr Anderson*
5 dear to important or close to ▷ *interj* **6** an
exclamation of surprise or dismay: *oh dear, I've
broken it* ▷ *adv* **7** dearly: *her errors have cost her dear*
▶ HISTORY Old English *dēore* > **dearly** *adv*

dearth (**dirth**) *n* an inadequate amount; scarcity
▶ HISTORY Middle English *derthe*

death *n* **1** the permanent end of life in a person or
animal **2** an instance of this: *his sudden death*
3 ending or destruction **4 at death's door** likely to
die soon **5 catch one's death (of cold)** *informal* to
contract a severe cold **6 like death warmed up**
informal looking or feeling very ill or very tired
7 put to death to execute **8 to death a** until dead
b very much: *I had probably scared him to death*
▶ HISTORY Old English *dēath*

deathbed *n* the bed in which a person dies or is
about to die

death certificate *n* a document signed by a
doctor certifying the death of a person and stating
the cause of death if known

death duty *n* (in Britain) the former name for
inheritance tax

death knell *n* something that heralds death or
destruction

deathless *adj literary or humorous* everlasting
because of fine qualities: *highbrow, deathless, and
often endless prose*

deathly *adj* **1** resembling death: *a deathly pallor*
2 deadly

death mask *n* a cast taken from the face of a
person who has recently died

death rate *n* the ratio of deaths in an area or
group to the population of that area or group

death row *n US* part of a prison where convicts
awaiting execution are imprisoned

death's-head *n* a human skull or a picture of one
used to represent death or danger

death trap *n* a place or vehicle considered very
unsafe

death warrant *n* **1** the official authorization for
carrying out a sentence of death **2 sign one's
(own) death warrant** to cause one's own
destruction

deathwatch beetle *n* a beetle that bores into
wood and produces a tapping sound

deb *n informal* a debutante

debacle (day-**bah**-kl) *n* something that ends in a
disastrous failure, esp. because it has not been
properly planned ▶ HISTORY French

debar *vb* **-barring, -barred** to prevent (someone)
from doing something

debase *vb* **-basing, -based** to lower in quality,
character, or value ▶ HISTORY see DE-, BASE²
> **debasement** *n*

debatable *adj* not absolutely certain: *her motives
are highly debatable*

debate *n* **1** a discussion **2** a formal discussion, as in
a parliament, in which opposing arguments are
put forward ▷ *vb* **-bating, -bated 3** to discuss
(something) formally **4** to consider (possible
courses of action) ▶ HISTORY Old French *debatre*

debauch (dib-**bawch**) *vb* to make someone bad or
corrupt ▶ HISTORY Old French *desbaucher* to
corrupt

debauched *adj* immoral; corrupt

debauchery *n* excessive drunkenness or sexual
activity

debenture *n* a long-term bond, bearing fixed
interest and usually unsecured, issued by a
company or governmental agency ▶ HISTORY Latin
debentur mihi there are owed to me > **debentured** *adj*

debenture stock *n* shares issued by a company,
guaranteeing a fixed return at regular intervals

debilitate *vb* **-tating, -tated** to make gradually
weaker ▶ HISTORY Latin *debilis* weak
> **debilitation** *n* > **debilitating** *adj*

debility *n, pl* **-ties** a state of weakness, esp. caused
by illness

debit *n* **1** the money, or a record of the money,
withdrawn from a person's bank account
2 *accounting* **a** acknowledgment of a sum owing by
entry on the left side of an account **b** an entry or
the total of entries on this side ▷ *vb* **-iting, -ited**
3 to charge (an account) with a debit: *they had
debited our account* **4** *accounting* to record (an item)
as a debit in an account ▶ HISTORY Latin *debitum*
debt

debit card *n Brit, Austral & S African* a card issued by
a bank or building society enabling customers to
pay for goods by inserting it into a computer-
controlled device at the place of sale, which is
connected through the telephone network to the
bank or building society

debonair *or* **debonnaire** *adj* (of a man)
confident, charming, and well-dressed ▶ HISTORY
Old French

debouch *vb* **1** (esp. of troops) to move into a more
open space **2** (of a river, glacier, etc.) to flow into a
larger area or body ▶ HISTORY Old French *dé-* from
+ *bouche* mouth > **debouchment** *n*

debrief *vb* to interrogate (a soldier, diplomat,
astronaut, etc.) on the completion of a mission
> **debriefing** *n*

debris (**deb**-ree) *n* **1** fragments of something
destroyed; rubble **2** a mass of loose stones and
earth ▶ HISTORY French

debt *n* **1** a sum of money owed **2 bad debt** a debt
that is unlikely to be paid **3 in debt** owing money
4 in someone's debt grateful to someone for his
or her help: *I couldn't have managed without you – I'm
in your debt* ▶ HISTORY Latin *debitum*

d

213

debt of honour n a debt that is morally but not legally binding

debtor n a person who owes money

debug vb **-bugging, -bugged** informal **1** to locate and remove defects in (a computer program) **2** to remove concealed microphones from (a room or telephone)

debunk vb informal to expose the falseness of: *many commonly held myths are debunked by the book* ▶ HISTORY DE- + BUNK² > **debunker** n

debut (**day**-byoo) n the first public appearance of a performer ▶ HISTORY French

debutante (**day**-byoo-tont) n a young upper-class woman who is formally presented to society ▶ HISTORY French

Dec. December

decade n a period of ten years ▶ HISTORY Greek *deka* ten

decadence (**deck**-a-denss) n a decline in morality or culture ▶ HISTORY Medieval Latin *decadentia* a falling away > **decadent** adj

decaffeinated (dee-**kaf**-fin-ate-id) adj with the caffeine removed: *decaffeinated tea*

decagon n geom a figure with ten sides ▶ HISTORY Greek *deka* ten + *gōnia* angle > **decagonal** adj

decahedron (deck-a-**heed**-ron) n a solid figure with ten plane faces ▶ HISTORY Greek *deka* ten + *hedra* base > **decahedral** adj

decalitre or US **decaliter** n a measure of volume equivalent to 10 litres

Decalogue n same as **Ten Commandments** ▶ HISTORY Greek *deka* ten + *logos* word

decametre or US **decameter** n a unit of length equal to ten metres

decamp vb to leave secretly or suddenly

decant vb **1** to pour (a liquid, esp. wine) from one container to another **2** chiefly Brit to rehouse (people) while their homes are being renovated ▶ HISTORY Medieval Latin *de-* from + *canthus* spout, rim

decanter n a stoppered bottle into which a drink is poured for serving

decapitate vb **-tating, -tated** to behead ▶ HISTORY Latin *de-* from + *caput* head > **decapitation** n

decapod n **1** a creature, such as a crab, with five pairs of walking limbs **2** a creature, such as a squid, with eight short tentacles and two longer ones ▶ HISTORY Greek *deka* ten + *pous* foot

decarbonize or **-ise** vb **-izing, -ized** or **-ising, -ised** to remove carbon from (an internal-combustion engine) > **decarbonization** or **-isation** n

decathlon n an athletic contest in which each athlete competes in ten different events ▶ HISTORY Greek *deka* ten + *athlon* contest > **decathlete** n

decay vb **1** to decline gradually in health, prosperity, or power **2** to rot or cause to rot **3** physics (of an atomic nucleus) to undergo radioactive disintegration ▷ n **4** the process of something rotting: *too much sugar can cause tooth decay* **5** the state brought about by this process

6 physics disintegration of a nucleus, occurring spontaneously or as a result of electron capture ▶ HISTORY Latin *de-* from + *cadere* to fall

decease n formal death ▶ HISTORY Latin *decedere* to depart

deceased adj formal **1** dead ▷ n **2** a dead person: *the deceased*

deceit n behaviour intended to deceive

deceitful adj full of deceit

deceive vb **-ceiving, -ceived 1** to mislead by lying **2 deceive oneself** to refuse to acknowledge something one knows to be true **3** to be unfaithful to (one's partner) ▶ HISTORY Latin *decipere* to ensnare, cheat

decelerate vb **-ating, -ated** to slow down ▶ HISTORY DE- + (AC)CELERATE > **deceleration** n

December n the twelfth month of the year ▶ HISTORY Latin: the tenth month (the Roman year originally began with March)

decency n conformity to the prevailing standards of what is right

decennial adj **1** lasting for ten years **2** occurring every ten years

decent adj **1** conforming to an acceptable standard or quality: *a decent living wage; he's made a few decent films* **2** polite or respectable: *he's a decent man* **3** fitting or proper: *that's the decent thing to do* **4** conforming to conventions of acceptable behaviour **5** informal kind; generous: *she was pretty decent to me* ▶ HISTORY Latin *decens* suitable > **decently** adv

decentralize or **-ise** vb **-izing, -ized** or **-ising, -ised** to reorganize into smaller local units > **decentralization** or **-isation** n

deception n **1** the act of deceiving someone or the state of being deceived **2** something that deceives; trick

deceptive adj likely or designed to deceive > **deceptively** adv > **deceptiveness** n

deci- combining form denoting one tenth: *decimetre* ▶ HISTORY Latin *decimus* tenth

decibel n a unit for comparing two power levels or measuring the intensity of a sound ▶ HISTORY DECI- + BEL

decide vb **-ciding, -cided 1** to reach a decision: *we must decide on suitable action; he decided to stay on* **2** to cause to reach a decision **3** to settle (a question): *possible profits decided the issue* **4** to influence the outcome of (a contest) decisively: *the goal that decided the match came just before half-time* ▶ HISTORY Latin *decidere* to cut off

decided adj **1** definite or noticeable: *a decided improvement* **2** strong and definite: *he has decided views on the matter* > **decidedly** adv

deciduous adj **1** (of a tree) shedding all leaves annually **2** (of antlers or teeth) being shed at the end of a period of growth ▶ HISTORY Latin *deciduus* falling off

decilitre or US **deciliter** n a measure of volume equivalent to one tenth of a litre

decimal n **1** a fraction written in the form of a dot followed by one or more numbers, for example

·2=²⁄₁₀ ▷ *adj* **2** relating to or using powers of ten **3** expressed as a decimal ▶ HISTORY Latin *decima* a tenth

decimal currency *n* a system of currency in which the units are parts or powers of ten

decimal fraction *n* *maths* same as **fraction** (sense 1)

decimalize or **-ise** *vb* **-izing, -ized** or **-ising, -ised** to change (a system or number) to the decimal system > **decimalization** or **-isation** *n*

decimal place *n* the position of a digit after a decimal point, each successive position having a denominator with an increased power of ten. For example, in 0.025, 5 is in the third decimal place

decimal point *n* the dot between the unit and the fraction of a number in the decimal system

decimal system *n* a number system with a base of ten, in which numbers are expressed by combinations of the digits 0 to 9

decimate *vb* **-mating, -mated** to destroy or kill a large proportion of ▶ HISTORY Latin *decimare* > **decimation** *n*

decimetre or US **decimeter** *n* a unit of length equal to one tenth of a metre

decipher *vb* **1** to make out the meaning of (something obscure or illegible) **2** to convert from code into plain text > **decipherable** *adj*

decision *n* **1** a choice or judgment made about something **2** the act of making up one's mind **3** the ability to make quick and definite decisions ▶ HISTORY Latin *decisio* a cutting off

decisive *adj* **1** having great influence on the result of something: *the decisive goal was scored in the closing minutes* **2** having the ability to make quick decisions > **decisively** *adv* > **decisiveness** *n*

deck *n* **1** an area of a ship that forms a floor, at any level **2** a similar area in a bus **3** US & Austral a pack of playing cards **4** **clear the decks** *informal* to prepare for action, as by removing obstacles ▷ *vb* **5** *slang* to knock (a person) to the ground ▶ HISTORY Middle Dutch *dec* a covering

deck chair *n* a folding chair with a wooden frame and a canvas seat

decking *n* a wooden platform in a garden, esp. for deckchairs, etc.

deck out *vb* to make more attractive by decorating: *the village was decked out in the blue-and-white flags*

declaim *vb* **1** *written* to speak loudly and dramatically **2** **declaim against** to protest against loudly and publicly ▶ HISTORY Latin *declamare* > **declamation** *n* > **declamatory** *adj*

declaration *n* **1** a firm, emphatic statement **2** an official announcement or statement > **declaratory** *adj*

declarative sentence *n* *grammar* a sentence which states a fact, as in *Glasgow is in Scotland*

declare *vb* **-claring, -clared** **1** *written* to state firmly and forcefully **2** to announce publicly or officially: *a state of emergency has been declared* **3** to state officially that (someone or something) is as specified: *he was declared fit to play* **4** to

acknowledge (dutiable goods or income) for tax purposes **5** *cards* to decide (the trump suit) by making the winning bid **6** *cricket* to bring an innings to an end before the last batsman is out **7** **declare for** or **against** to state one's support or opposition for something ▶ HISTORY Latin *declarare* to make clear

declassify *vb* **-fies, -fying, -fied** to state officially that (information or a document) is no longer secret > **declassification** *n*

declension *n* *grammar* changes in the form of nouns, pronouns, or adjectives to show case, number, and gender ▶ HISTORY Latin *declinatio* a bending aside, hence variation

declination *n* **1** *astron* the angular distance of a star or planet north or south from the celestial equator **2** the angle made by a compass needle with the direction of the geographical north pole

decline *vb* **-clining, -clined** **1** to become smaller, weaker, or less important **2** to politely refuse to accept or do (something) **3** *grammar* to list the inflections of (a noun, pronoun, or adjective) ▷ *n* **4** a gradual weakening or loss ▶ HISTORY Latin *declinare* to bend away

declivity *n*, *pl* **-ties** a downward slope ▶ HISTORY Latin *declivitas* > **declivitous** *adj*

declutch *vb* to disengage the clutch of a motor vehicle

decoct *vb* to extract the essence from (a substance) by boiling ▶ HISTORY Latin *decoquere* to boil down > **decoction** *n*

decode *vb* **-coding, -coded** to convert from code into ordinary language > **decoder** *n*

decoke *vb* **-coking, -coked** same as **decarbonize**

décolletage (day-kol-**tahzh**) *n* a low-cut dress or neckline ▶ HISTORY French

décolleté (day-**kol**-tay) *adj* **1** (of a woman's garment) low-cut ▷ *n* **2** a low-cut neckline ▶ HISTORY French

decommission *vb* to dismantle or remove from service (a nuclear reactor, weapon, ship, etc. which is no longer required)

decompose *vb* **-posing, -posed** **1** to rot **2** *chem* to break down or cause to break down into simpler chemical compounds **3** to separate into constituent parts > **decomposition** *n*

decomposer *n* *biol* any organism in a community, such as a bacterium or fungus, that breaks down dead tissue into its constituent parts. See also **consumer** (sense 2), **producer** (sense 5)

decompress *vb* **1** to free from pressure **2** to return (a diver) to normal atmospheric pressure > **decompression** *n*

decompression sickness *n* a disorder characterized by severe pain and difficulty in breathing caused by a sudden and sustained change in atmospheric pressure

decongestant *n* a drug that relieves nasal congestion

deconstruction *n* *literature* a technique of literary analysis, developed by French philosopher Jacques Derrida, that regards meaning as resulting

d

from the differences between words rather than their reference to the things they stand for

decontaminate *vb* **-nating, -nated** to make (a place or object) safe by removing poisons, radioactivity, etc. > **decontamination** *n*

decor (**day**-core) *n* a style or scheme of interior decoration and furnishings in a room or house ▶ **HISTORY** French

decorate *vb* **-rating, -rated** 1 to make more attractive by adding some ornament or colour 2 to paint or wallpaper 3 to confer a mark of distinction, esp. a medal, upon ▶ **HISTORY** Latin *decorare* > **decorative** *adj* > **decorator** *n*

Decorated style *or* **architecture** *n* a 14th-century style of English architecture characterized by the ogee arch, geometrical tracery, and floral decoration

decoration *n* 1 an addition that makes something more attractive or ornate 2 the way in which a room or building is decorated 3 something, esp. a medal, conferred as a mark of honour

decorous (**deck**-or-uss) *adj* polite, calm, and sensible in behaviour ▶ **HISTORY** Latin *decorus* > **decorously** *adv* > **decorousness** *n*

decorum (dik-**core**-um) *n* polite and socially correct behaviour

decoy *n* 1 a person or thing used to lure someone into danger 2 an image of a bird or animal, used to lure game into a trap or within shooting range ▷ *vb* 3 to lure into danger by means of a decoy ▶ **HISTORY** probably from Dutch *de kooi* the cage

decrease *vb* **-creasing, -creased** 1 to make or become less in size, strength, or quantity ▷ *n* 2 a lessening; reduction 3 the amount by which something has been diminished ▶ **HISTORY** Latin *decrescere* to grow less > **decreasing** *adj* > **decreasingly** *adv*

decree *n* 1 a law made by someone in authority 2 a judgment of a court ▷ *vb* **decreeing, decreed** 3 to order by decree ▶ **HISTORY** Latin *decretum* ordinance

decree absolute *n* the final decree in divorce proceedings, which leaves the parties free to remarry

decree nisi *n* a provisional decree in divorce proceedings, which will later be made absolute unless cause is shown why it should not ▶ **HISTORY** Latin *nisi* unless

decrepit *adj* weakened or worn out by age or long use ▶ **HISTORY** Latin *crepare* to creak > **decrepitude** *n*

decrescendo *n, adv* same as **diminuendo**

decretal *n* RC Church a papal decree ▶ **HISTORY** Late Latin *decretalis*

decriminalize *or* **-lise** *vb* **-lizing, -lized** *or* **-lising, -lised** to change the law so that something that was illegal is no longer illegal

decry *vb* **-cries, -crying, -cried** to express open disapproval of ▶ **HISTORY** Old French *descrier*

decrypt *vb* 1 to decode (a message) with or without previous knowledge of its key 2 to make intelligible (a television or other signal) that has

been deliberately distorted for transmission. Compare **encrypt** ▶ **HISTORY** DE- + (EN)CRYPT > **decryption** *n*

dedicate *vb* **-cating, -cated** 1 to devote (oneself or one's time) wholly to a special purpose or cause 2 to inscribe or address (a book, piece of music, etc.) to someone as a token of affection or respect 3 to play (a recording) on radio for someone as a greeting 4 to set apart for sacred uses ▶ **HISTORY** Latin *dedicare* to announce

dedicated *adj* 1 devoted to a particular purpose or cause 2 *computers* designed to fulfil one function

dedication *n* 1 wholehearted devotion 2 an inscription in a book dedicating it to a person

deduce *vb* **-ducing, -duced** to reach (a conclusion) by reasoning from evidence; work out ▶ **HISTORY** Latin *de-* away + *ducere* to lead > **deducible** *adj*

deduct *vb* to subtract (a number, quantity, or part) ▶ **HISTORY** Latin *deducere* to deduce

deductible *adj* 1 capable of being deducted 2 *US* tax-deductible

deduction *n* 1 the act or process of subtracting 2 something that is deducted 3 *logic* **a** a process of reasoning by which a conclusion necessarily follows from a set of general premises **b** a conclusion reached by this process > **deductive** *adj*

deed *n* 1 something that is done 2 a notable achievement 3 action as opposed to words 4 *law* a legal document, esp. one concerning the ownership of property ▶ **HISTORY** Old English *dēd*

deed box *n* a strong box in which deeds and other documents are kept

deed of partnership *n* *business* a formal agreement between business partners covering points of mutual interest, such as the amount of capital that each should provide

deed poll *n* *law* a deed made by one party only, esp. to change one's name

deejay *n* *informal* a disc jockey ▶ **HISTORY** from the initials DJ

deem *vb* to judge or consider: *common sense is deemed to be a virtue* ▶ **HISTORY** Old English *dēman*

deep *adj* 1 extending or situated far down from a surface: *a deep ditch* 2 extending or situated far inwards, backwards, or sideways 3 of a specified dimension downwards, inwards, or backwards: *six metres deep* 4 coming from or penetrating to a great depth 5 difficult to understand 6 of great intensity: *deep doubts* 7 **deep in** totally absorbed in: *deep in conversation* 8 (of a colour) intense or dark 9 low in pitch: *a deep laugh* 10 **go off the deep end** *informal* to lose one's temper 11 **in deep water** *informal* in a tricky position or in trouble ▷ *n* 12 any deep place on land or under water 13 **the deep a** *poetic* the ocean **b** *cricket* the area of the field relatively far from the pitch 14 the most profound, intense, or central part: *the deep of winter* ▷ *adv* 15 late: *deep into the night* 16 profoundly or intensely: *deep down I was afraid it was all my fault* ▶ **HISTORY** Old English *dēop* > **deeply** *adv*

deepen *vb* to make or become deeper or more intense

deep-freeze *n* **1** same as **freezer** ▷ *vb* **-freezing, -froze, -frozen 2** to freeze or keep in a deep-freeze

deep-fry *vb* **-fries, -frying, -fried** to cook in hot oil deep enough to completely cover the food

deep-rooted *or* **deep-seated** *adj* (of ideas, beliefs, etc.) firmly fixed or held

deep-sea trench *n* same as **ocean trench**

Deep South *n* the SE part of the US, esp. South Carolina, Georgia, Alabama, Mississippi, and Louisiana

deep-vein thrombosis *n* a blood clot in one of the major veins, usually in the legs or pelvis

deer *n, pl* **deer** *or* **deers** a large hoofed mammal ▶ **HISTORY** Old English *dēor* beast

deerstalker *n* a cloth hat with peaks at the front and back and earflaps

deface *vb* **-facing, -faced** to deliberately spoil the surface or appearance of > **defacement** *n*

de facto *adv* **1** in fact ▷ *adj* **2** existing in fact, whether legally recognized or not ▶ **HISTORY** Latin

defalcate *vb* **-cating, -cated** *law* to make wrong use of funds entrusted to one ▶ **HISTORY** Medieval Latin *defalcare* to cut off > **defalcation** *n*

defamation *n law* **1** the injuring of a person's good name or reputation. Compare **libel, slander 2** the act of defaming or state of being defamed

defame *vb* **-faming, -famed** to attack the good reputation of ▶ **HISTORY** Latin *diffamare* to spread by unfavourable report > **defamatory** (dif-**fam**-a-tree) *adj*

default *n* **1** a failure to do something, esp. to meet a financial obligation or to appear in court **2** *computers* an instruction to a computer to select a particular option unless the user specifies otherwise **3 by default** happening because something else has not happened: *they gained a colony by default because no other European power wanted it* **4 in default of** in the absence of ▷ *vb* **5** to fail to fulfil an obligation, esp. to make payment when due ▶ **HISTORY** Old French *defaillir* to fail > **defaulter** *n*

default judgment *n law* a judgment in favour of the plaintiff when the defendant has failed to appear or put in a defence

defeat *vb* **1** to win a victory over **2** to thwart or frustrate: *this accident has defeated all his hopes of winning* ▷ *n* **3** the act of defeating or state of being defeated ▶ **HISTORY** Old French *desfaire* to undo, ruin

defeatism *n* a ready acceptance or expectation of defeat > **defeatist** *n, adj*

defecate *vb* **-cating, -cated** to discharge waste from the body through the anus ▶ **HISTORY** Latin *defaecare* > **defecation** *n*

defect *n* **1** an imperfection or blemish ▷ *vb* **2** to desert one's country or cause to join the opposing forces ▶ **HISTORY** Latin *deficere* to forsake, fail > **defection** *n* > **defector** *n*

defective *adj* imperfect or faulty: *defective hearing*

defence *or US* **defense** *n* **1** resistance against attack **2** something that provides such resistance **3** an argument or piece of writing in support of something that has been criticized or questioned **4** a country's military resources **5** *law* a defendant's denial of the truth of a charge **6** *law* the defendant and his or her legal advisers collectively **7** *sport* the players in a team whose function is to prevent the opposing team from scoring **8 defences** fortifications ▶ **HISTORY** Latin *defendere* to defend > **defenceless** *or US* **defenseless** *adj*

defend *vb* **1** to protect from harm or danger **2** to support in the face of criticism: *I spoke up to defend her* **3** to represent (a defendant) in court **4** to protect (a title or championship) against a challenge ▶ **HISTORY** Latin *defendere* to ward off > **defender** *n*

defendant *n* a person accused of a crime

defensible *adj* capable of being defended because believed to be right > **defensibility** *n*

defensive *adj* **1** intended for defence **2** guarding against criticism or exposure of one's failings: *he can be highly defensive and wary* ▷ *n* **3 on the defensive** in a position of defence, as in being ready to reject criticism > **defensively** *adv*

defer¹ *vb* **-ferring, -ferred** to delay until a future time; postpone: *payment was deferred indefinitely* ▶ **HISTORY** Old French *differer* to be different, postpone > **deferment** *or* **deferral** *n*

defer² *vb* **-ferring, -ferred · defer to** to comply with the wishes (of) ▶ **HISTORY** Latin *deferre* to bear down

deference *n* polite and respectful behaviour

deferential *adj* showing respect > **deferentially** *adv*

defiance *n* open resistance to authority or opposition > **defiant** *adj*

defibrillator *n med* an apparatus for stopping fibrillation of the heart by application of an electric current

deficiency *n, pl* **-cies 1** the state of being deficient **2** a lack or shortage

deficiency disease *n* any condition, such as scurvy, caused by a lack of vitamins or other essential substances

deficient *adj* **1** lacking something essential **2** inadequate in quantity or quality ▶ **HISTORY** Latin *deficere* to fall short

deficit *n* the amount by which a sum is lower than that expected or required ▶ **HISTORY** Latin: there is lacking

defile¹ *vb* **-filing, -filed 1** to make foul or dirty **2** to make unfit for ceremonial use ▶ **HISTORY** Old French *defouler* to trample underfoot, abuse > **defilement** *n*

defile² *n* a narrow pass or gorge: *the sandy defile of Wadi Rum* ▶ **HISTORY** French *défiler* to file off

define *vb* **-fining, -fined 1** to describe the nature of **2** to state precisely the meaning of **3** to show clearly the outline of: *the picture was sharp and cleanly defined* **4** to fix with precision; specify: *define one's duties* ▶ **HISTORY** Latin *definire* to set bounds to > **definable** *adj*

definite *adj* **1** firm, clear, and precise: *I have very definite views on this subject* **2** having precise limits or boundaries **3** known for certain: *it's definite that they have won* ▶ **HISTORY** Latin *definitus* limited, distinct > **definitely** *adv*

definite article *n grammar* the word 'the'

definition *n* **1** a statement of the meaning of a word or phrase **2** a description of the essential qualities of something **3** the quality of being clear and distinct **4** sharpness of outline

definitive *adj* **1** final and unable to be questioned or altered: *a definitive verdict* **2** most complete, or the best of its kind: *the book was hailed as the definitive Dickens biography* > **definitively** *adv*

deflate *vb* **-flating, -flated** **1** to collapse or cause to collapse through the release of gas **2** to take away the self-esteem or conceit from **3** to cause deflation of (an economy) ▶ **HISTORY** DE- + (IN)FLATE

deflation *n* **1** *econ* a reduction in economic activity resulting in lower levels of output and investment **2** a feeling of sadness following excitement > **deflationary** *adj*

deflect *vb* to turn or cause to turn aside from a course ▶ **HISTORY** Latin *deflectere* > **deflection** *n* > **deflector** *n*

deflower *vb literary* to deprive (a woman) of her virginity

defoliate *vb* **-ating, -ated** to deprive (a plant) of its leaves ▶ **HISTORY** Latin *de-* from + *folium* leaf > **defoliant** *n* > **defoliation** *n*

deforestation *n geog* the cutting down or destruction of forests

deform *vb* to put (something) out of shape or spoil its appearance ▶ **HISTORY** Latin *de-* from + *forma* shape beauty

deformed *adj* disfigured or misshapen

deformity *n, pl* **-ties** **1** *pathol* a distortion of an organ or part **2** the state of being deformed

defraud *vb* to cheat out of money, property, or a right to do something

defray *vb* to provide money to cover costs or expenses ▶ **HISTORY** Old French *deffroier* to pay expenses > **defrayal** *n*

defrock *vb* to deprive (a priest) of ecclesiastical status

defrost *vb* **1** to make or become free of frost or ice **2** to thaw (frozen food) by removing from a deep-freeze

deft *adj written* quick and skilful in movement; dexterous ▶ **HISTORY** Middle English variant of *daft* (in the sense: gentle) > **deftly** *adv* > **deftness** *n*

defunct *adj* no longer existing or working properly ▶ **HISTORY** Latin *defungi* to discharge (one's obligations), die

defuse *or US sometimes* **defuze** *vb* **-fusing, -fused** *or* **-fuzing, -fuzed** **1** to remove the fuse of (an explosive device) **2** to reduce the tension in (a difficult situation): *I said it in a bid to defuse the situation*

defy *vb* **-fies, -fying, -fied** **1** to resist openly and boldly **2** to elude in a baffling way: *his actions defy* explanation **3** *formal* to challenge (someone to do something) ▶ **HISTORY** Old French *desfier*

degenerate *adj* **1** having deteriorated to a lower mental, moral, or physical level ▷ *n* **2** a degenerate person ▷ *vb* **-ating, -ated** **3** to become degenerate ▶ **HISTORY** Latin *degener* departing from its kind, ignoble > **degeneracy** *n*

degeneration *n* **1** the process of degenerating **2** *biol* the loss of specialization or function by organisms

degenerative *adj* (of a disease or condition) getting steadily worse

degradation *n* **1** a degrading or being degraded **2** a state of degeneration or squalor **3** some act, constraint, etc. that is degrading **4** *geol* the wearing down of the surface of rocks, cliffs, etc. by erosion. Compare **aggradation**

degrade *vb* **-grading, -graded** **1** to reduce to dishonour or disgrace **2** to reduce in status or quality **3** *chem* to decompose into atoms or smaller molecules ▶ **HISTORY** Latin *de-* from + *gradus* rank, degree > **degrading** *adj*

degree *n* **1** a stage in a scale of relative amount or intensity: *this task involved a greater degree of responsibility* **2** an academic award given by a university or college on successful completion of a course **3** *grammar* any of the forms of an adjective used to indicate relative amount or intensity **4** a unit of temperature. Symbol: ° **5** a measure of angle equal to one three-hundred-and-sixtieth of the circumference of a circle. Symbol: ° **6** a unit of latitude or longitude. Symbol: ° **7 by degrees** little by little; gradually ▶ **HISTORY** Latin *de-* down + *gradus* step

dehisce *vb* **-hiscing, -hisced** (of the seed capsules of some plants) to burst open spontaneously ▶ **HISTORY** Latin *dehiscere* to split open > **dehiscence** *n* > **dehiscent** *adj*

dehumanize *or* **-ise** *vb* **-izing, -ized** *or* **-ising, -ised** **1** to deprive of the qualities thought of as being best in human beings, such as kindness **2** to make (an activity) mechanical or routine > **dehumanization** *or* **-isation** *n*

dehydrate *vb* **-drating, -drated** **1** to remove water from (food) in order to preserve it **2 be dehydrated** (of a person) to become weak or ill through losing too much water from the body > **dehydration** *n*

de-ice *vb* **de-icing, de-iced** to free of ice > **de-icer** *n*

deictic *n grammar* a term whose reference depends on the context of the utterance, such as *I, you, here, now,* or *tomorrow*

deify (**day**-if-fie) *vb* **-fies, -fying, -fied** to treat or worship (someone or something) as a god ▶ **HISTORY** Latin *deus* god + *facere* to make > **deification** *n*

deign (**dane**) *vb* to do something that one considers beneath one's dignity: *she did not deign to reply* ▶ **HISTORY** Latin *dignari* to consider worthy

deindustrialization *or* **-sation** *n* a decline in

the importance of a country's manufacturing industry

deism (**day**-iz-zum) *n* belief in the existence of God based only on natural reason, without reference to revelation > **deist** *n*, *adj* > **deistic** *adj*

deity (**day**-it-ee) *n*, *pl* **-ties** **1** a god or goddess **2** the state of being divine ▸ **HISTORY** Latin *deus* god

Deity *n* **the Deity** God

déjà vu (**day**-zhah **voo**) *n* a feeling of having experienced before something that is happening at the present moment ▸ **HISTORY** French: already seen

dejected *adj* in low spirits; downhearted ▸ **HISTORY** Latin *deicere* to cast down > **dejectedly** *adv* > **dejection** *n*

de jure *adv* according to law ▸ **HISTORY** Latin

dekko *n* *Brit, Austral & NZ, slang* **have a dekko** have a look ▸ **HISTORY** Hindi *dekhnā* to see

delay *vb* **1** to put (something) off to a later time **2** to slow up or cause to be late **3 a** to hesitate in doing something **b** to deliberately take longer than necessary to do something ▹ *n* **4** the act of delaying **5** a period of inactivity or waiting before something happens or continues ▸ **HISTORY** Old French *des-* off + *laier* to leave

delectable *adj* delightful or very attractive ▸ **HISTORY** Latin *delectare* to delight

delectation *n* *formal* great pleasure and enjoyment

delegate *n* **1** a person chosen to represent others at a conference or meeting ▹ *vb* **-gating, -gated** **2** to entrust (duties or powers) to another person **3** to appoint as a representative ▸ **HISTORY** Latin *delegare* to send on a mission

delegated legislation *n* *law* laws made under powers delegated to ministers and bodies by Parliament

delegation *n* **1** a group chosen to represent others **2** the act of delegating

delete *vb* **-leting, -leted** to remove or cross out (something printed or written) ▸ **HISTORY** Latin *delere* > **deletion** *n*

deleterious (del-lit-**eer**-ee-uss) *adj* *formal* harmful or injurious ▸ **HISTORY** Greek *dēlētērios*

Delft *n* tin-glazed earthenware which originated in Delft in the Netherlands, typically with blue decoration on a white ground. Also: **delftware**

deliberate *adj* **1** carefully thought out in advance; intentional **2** careful and unhurried: *a deliberate gait* ▹ *vb* **-ating, -ated** **3** to consider (something) deeply; think over ▸ **HISTORY** Latin *deliberare* to consider well > **deliberately** *adv* > **deliberative** *adj*

deliberation *n* **1** careful consideration **2** calmness and absence of hurry **3 deliberations** formal discussions

delicacy *n*, *pl* **-cies** **1** fine or subtle quality, construction, etc.: *delicacy of craftsmanship* **2** fragile or graceful beauty **3** something that is considered particularly nice to eat **4** frail health **5** refinement of feeling, manner, or appreciation: *the delicacy of the orchestra's playing* **6** requiring careful or tactful treatment

delicate *adj* **1** fine or subtle in quality or workmanship **2** having a fragile beauty **3** (of colour, smell, or taste) pleasantly subtle **4** easily damaged; fragile **5** precise or sensitive in action: *the delicate digestive system* **6** requiring tact: *a delicate matter* **7** showing consideration for the feelings of other people ▸ **HISTORY** Latin *delicatus* affording pleasure > **delicately** *adv*

delicatessen *n* a shop selling unusual or imported foods, often already cooked or prepared ▸ **HISTORY** German *Delikatessen* delicacies

delicious *adj* **1** very appealing to taste or smell **2** extremely enjoyable ▸ **HISTORY** Latin *deliciae* delights > **deliciously** *adv*

delight *n* **1** extreme pleasure **2** something or someone that causes this ▹ *vb* **3** to please greatly **4 delight in** to take great pleasure in ▸ **HISTORY** Latin *delectare* to please > **delightful** *adj* > **delightfully** *adv*

delighted *adj* greatly pleased

delimit *vb* **-iting, -ited** to mark or lay down the limits of > **delimitation** *n*

delineate (dill-**lin**-ee-ate) *vb* **-ating, -ated** **1** to show by drawing **2** to describe in words ▸ **HISTORY** Latin *delineare* to sketch out > **delineation** *n*

delinquent *n* **1** someone, esp. a young person, who breaks the law ▹ *adj* **2** repeatedly breaking the law ▸ **HISTORY** Latin *delinquens* offending > **delinquency** *n*

deliquesce *vb* **-quescing, -quesced** (esp. of certain salts) to dissolve in water absorbed from the air ▸ **HISTORY** Latin *deliquescere* to melt away > **deliquescence** *n* > **deliquescent** *adj*

delirious *adj* **1** suffering from delirium **2** wildly excited and happy > **deliriously** *adv*

delirium *n* **1** a state of excitement and mental confusion, often with hallucinations **2** violent excitement ▸ **HISTORY** Latin: madness

delirium tremens (**trem**-enz) *n* a severe condition characterized by delirium and trembling, caused by chronic alcoholism ▸ **HISTORY** New Latin: trembling delirium

deliver *vb* **1** to carry (goods or mail) to a destination **2** to hand over: *the tenants were asked to deliver up their keys* **3** to aid in the birth of (offspring) **4** to present (a lecture or speech) **5** to release or rescue (from captivity or danger) **6** *written* to strike (a blow) suddenly **7** *informal* Also: **deliver the goods** to produce something promised ▸ **HISTORY** Latin *de-* from + *liberare* to free > **deliverance** *n*

delivery *n*, *pl* **-eries** **1 a** the act of delivering goods or mail **b** something that is delivered **2** the act of giving birth to a baby **3** manner or style in public speaking: *her delivery was clear and humorous* **4** *cricket* the act or manner of bowling a ball **5** *S African* a semi-official slogan for the provision of services to previously disadvantaged communities

dell *n* *chiefly Brit* a small wooded hollow ▸ **HISTORY** Old English

Delphic *adj* obscure or ambiguous, like the ancient Greek oracle at Delphi

delphinium *n*, *pl* **-iums** *or* **-ia** a large garden plant

d

with spikes of blue flowers ▶ HISTORY Greek *delphis* dolphin

delta *n* **1** the fourth letter in the Greek alphabet (Δ, δ) **2** the flat area at the mouth of some rivers where the main stream splits up into several branches

delude *vb* **-luding, -luded** to make someone believe something that is not true ▶ HISTORY Latin *deludere*

deluge (**del**-lyooj) *n* **1** a great flood of water **2** torrential rain **3** an overwhelming number ▷ *vb* **-uging, -uged 4** *written* to flood **5** to overwhelm ▶ HISTORY Latin *diluere* to wash away

Deluge *n* **the Deluge** same as the **Flood**

delusion *n* **1** a mistaken idea or belief **2** the state of being deluded > **delusive** *adj* > **delusory** *adj*

de luxe *adj* rich or sumptuous; superior in quality: *a de luxe hotel* ▶ HISTORY French

delve *vb* **delving, delved 1** to research deeply or intensively (for information) **2** *old-fashioned, written* to dig ▶ HISTORY Old English *delfan*

demagnetize *or* **-ise** *vb* **-izing, -ized** *or* **-ising, -ised** to remove magnetic properties > **demagnetization** *or* **-isation** *n*

demagogue *or US sometimes* **demagog** *n* a political agitator who attempts to win support by appealing to the prejudice and passions of the mob ▶ HISTORY Greek *dēmagōgos* people's leader > **demagogic** *adj* > **demagogy** *n*

demand *vb* **1** to request forcefully **2** to require as just, urgent, etc.: *the situation demands intervention* **3** to claim as a right ▷ *n* **4** a forceful request **5** something that requires special effort or sacrifice: *demands upon one's time* **6** *econ* the amount of a commodity that consumers are willing and able to buy at a specified price **7 in demand** sought after; popular **8 on demand** as soon as requested: *the funds will be available on demand* ▶ HISTORY Latin *demandare* to commit to

demanding *adj* requiring a lot of skill, time, or effort: *a demanding relationship*

demarcation *n* **1** the act of establishing limits or boundaries between areas or groups **2** the act of establishing boundaries between the work performed by members of different trade unions ▶ HISTORY Spanish *demarcar* to appoint the boundaries of

demean *vb* to do something unworthy of one's status or character: *there is no doubt that he will lose face with the boss by having to demean himself in this way* ▶ HISTORY DE- + MEAN²

demeanour *or US* **demeanor** *n* the way a person behaves ▶ HISTORY Old French *de-* (intensive) + *mener* to lead

demented *adj* mad; insane ▶ HISTORY Late Latin *dementare* to drive mad > **dementedly** *adv*

dementia (dim-**men**-sha) *n* a state of serious mental deterioration ▶ HISTORY Latin: madness

demerara sugar *n* brown crystallized cane sugar from the West Indies ▶ HISTORY after *Demerara*, a region of Guyana

demerit *n* **1** a fault or disadvantage **2** *US & Canad* a

mark given against a student for failure or misconduct

demesne (dim-**mane**) *n* **1** land surrounding a house or manor **2** *property law* the possession of one's own property or land **3** a region or district; domain ▶ HISTORY Old French *demeine*

Demeter *n Greek myth* the goddess of agriculture

demi- *combining form* **1** half: *demirelief* **2** of less than full size, status, or rank: *demigod* ▶ HISTORY Latin *dimidius* half

demigod *n* **1 a** a being who is part mortal, part god **b** a lesser deity **2** a godlike person

demijohn *n* a large bottle with a short narrow neck, often encased in wickerwork ▶ HISTORY probably from French *dame-jeanne*

demilitarize *or* **-rise** *vb* **-rizing, -rized** *or* **-rising, -rised** to remove all military forces from (an area): *demilitarized zone* > **demilitarization** *or* **-risation** *n*

demimonde *n* **1** (esp. in the 19th century) a class of women considered to be outside respectable society because of promiscuity **2** any group considered not wholly respectable ▶ HISTORY French: half-world

demise *n* **1** the eventual failure of something originally successful **2** *euphemistic, formal* death **3** *property law* a transfer of an estate by lease ▷ *vb* **-mising, -mised 4** *property law* to transfer for a limited period; lease ▶ HISTORY Old French *demis* dismissed

demisemiquaver *n music* a note with the time value of one thirty-second of a semibreve

demist *vb* to make or become free of condensation > **demister** *n*

demo *n, pl* **-os** *informal* **1** short for **demonstration** (sense 1) **2** a demonstration record ing, used for auditioning

demob *vb* **-mobbing, -mobbed** *Brit, Austral & NZ, informal* to demobilize

demobilize *or* **-lise** *vb* **-lizing, -lized** *or* **-lising, -lised** to release from the armed forces > **demobilization** *or* **-lisation** *n*

democracy *n, pl* **-cies 1** a system of government or organization in which the citizens or members choose leaders or make other important decisions by voting **2** a country in which the citizens choose their government by voting ▶ HISTORY Greek *dēmokratia*

democrat *n* a person who believes in democracy

Democrat *n US politics* a member or supporter of the Democratic Party, the more liberal of the two main political parties in the US > **Democratic** *adj*

democratic *adj* of or relating to a country, organization, or system in which leaders are chosen or decisions are made by voting > **democratically** *adv*

demodulation *n electronics* the process by which an output wave or signal is obtained having the characteristics of the original modulating wave or signal

demography *n* the study of population statistics, such as births and deaths ▶ HISTORY Greek *dēmos* the populace + -GRAPHY > **demographic** *adj*

demolish *vb* **1** to tear down or break up (buildings) **2** to put an end to; destroy: *I demolished her argument in seconds* **3** *facetious* to eat up: *he demolished the whole cake* ▶ HISTORY Latin *demoliri* to throw down > **demolisher** *n* > **demolition** *n*

demon *n* **1** an evil spirit **2** a person, obsession, etc. thought of as evil or persistently tormenting **3** a person extremely skilful in or devoted to a given activity: *a demon at cricket* ▶ HISTORY Greek *daimōn* spirit, fate > **demonic** *adj*

demonetize or **-tise** *vb* **-tizing, -tized** or **-tising, -tised** to withdraw from use or devoted to a given currency > **demonetization** or **-tisation** *n*

demoniac or **demoniacal** *adj* **1** appearing to be possessed by a devil **2** suggesting inner possession or inspiration: *the demoniac fire of genius* **3** frantic or frenzied: *demoniac activity* > **demoniacally** *adv*

demonolatry *n* the worship of demons ▶ HISTORY *demon* + Greek *latreia* worship

demonology *n* the study of demons or demonic beliefs ▶ HISTORY *demon* + -LOGY

demonstrable *adj* able to be proved > **demonstrably** *adv*

demonstrate *vb* **-strating, -strated** **1** to show or prove by reasoning or evidence **2** to display and explain the workings of (a machine, product, etc.) **3** to reveal the existence of: *the adult literacy campaign demonstrated the scale of educational deprivation* **4** to show support or opposition by public parades or rallies ▶ HISTORY Latin *demonstrare* to point out

demonstration *n* **1** a march or public meeting to demonstrate opposition to something or support for something **2** an explanation or display showing how something works **3** proof or evidence leading to proof

demonstrative *adj* **1** tending to show one's feelings freely and openly **2** *grammar* denoting a word used to point out the person or thing referred to, such as *this* and *those* **3** **demonstrative of** giving proof of > **demonstratively** *adv*

demonstrator *n* **1** a person who demonstrates how a device or machine works **2** a person who takes part in a public demonstration

demoralize or **-ise** *vb* **-izing, -ized** or **-ising, -ised** to deprive (someone) of confidence or enthusiasm: *she had been demoralized and had just given up* > **demoralization** or **-isation** *n*

demote *vb* **-moting, -moted** to lower in rank or position ▶ HISTORY DE- + (PRO)MOTE > **demotion** *n*

demotic *adj* of or relating to the common people ▶ HISTORY Greek *dēmotikos*

demur *vb* **-murring, -murred** **1** to show reluctance; object ▷ *n* **2** **without demur** without objecting ▶ HISTORY Latin *demorari* to linger

demure *adj* quiet, reserved, and rather shy ▶ HISTORY perhaps from Old French *demorer* to delay, linger > **demurely** *adv* > **demureness** *n*

demutualize or **-ise** *vb* **-izing, -ized** or **-ising, -ised** (of a mutual savings or life-assurance organization) to convert to a public limited company > **demutualization** or **-isation** *n*

demystify *vb* **-fies, -fying, -fied** to remove the mystery from: *he attempted to demystify the contemporary jargon of psychology* > **demystification** *n*

den *n* **1** the home of a wild animal; lair **2** *chiefly US* a small secluded room in a home, often used for a hobby **3** a place where people indulge in criminal or immoral activities: *a den of iniquity* ▶ HISTORY Old English *denn*

denarius (din-**air**-ee-uss) *n, pl* **-narii** (-**nair**-ee-eye) a silver coin of ancient Rome, often called a penny in translation ▶ HISTORY Latin

denary (**dean**-a-ree) *adj* calculated by tens; decimal ▶ HISTORY Latin *denarius*

denationalize or **-lise** *vb* **-lizing, -lized** or **-lising, -lised** to transfer (an industry or a service) from public to private ownership > **denationalization** or **-lisation** *n*

denature *vb* **-turing, -tured** **1** to change the nature of **2** to make (alcohol) unfit to drink by adding another substance

dendrology *n* the study of trees ▶ HISTORY Greek *dendron* tree + -LOGY

dene or **dean** *n* *chiefly Brit* a narrow wooded valley

dengue (**deng**-gee) *n* a viral disease transmitted by mosquitoes, characterized by headache, fever, pains in the joints, and a rash ▶ HISTORY probably of African origin

denial *n* **1** a statement that something is not true **2** a rejection of a request **3** *psychol* a process by which painful thoughts are not permitted into the consciousness

denier (**den**-yer) *n* a unit of weight used to measure the fineness of silk and man-made fibres ▶ HISTORY Old French: coin

denigrate *vb* **-grating, -grated** to criticize (someone or something) unfairly ▶ HISTORY Latin *denigrare* to make very black > **denigration** *n* > **denigrator** *n*

denim *n* **1** a hard-wearing cotton fabric used for jeans, skirts, etc. **2** **denims** jeans made of denim ▶ HISTORY French *(serge) de Nîmes* (serge) of Nîmes, in S France

denizen *n* **1** a person, animal, or plant that lives or grows in a particular place **2** an animal or plant established in a place to which it is not native ▶ HISTORY Old French *denzein*

denominate *vb* **-nating, -nated** to give a specific name to; designate ▶ HISTORY Latin *denominare*

denomination *n* **1** a group which has slightly different beliefs from other groups within the same faith **2** a unit in a system of weights, values, or measures: *coins of small denomination have been withdrawn* **3** a name given to a class or group; classification > **denominational** *adj*

denominator *n* the number below the line in a fraction, as 8 in ⅞

denotation *n* the strict meaning of something. Compare **connotation**

denote *vb* **-noting, -noted** **1** to be a sign or indication of: *these contracts denote movement on the* 221 *widest possible scale* **2** (of a word or phrase) to have as a literal or obvious meaning ▶ **HISTORY** Latin *denotare* to mark

denouement (day-**noo**-mon) *n* the final outcome or solution in a play or other work ▶ **HISTORY** French

denounce *vb* **-nouncing, -nounced 1** to condemn openly or vehemently **2** to give information against ▶ **HISTORY** Latin *denuntiare* to make an official proclamation, threaten

dense *adj* **1** thickly crowded or closely packed **2** difficult to see through: *dense clouds of smoke* **3** *informal* stupid or dull **4** (of a film, book, etc.) difficult to follow or understand: *the content should be neither too dense nor too abstract* ▶ **HISTORY** Latin *densus* thick > **densely** *adv*

density *n, pl* **-ties 1** the degree to which something is filled or occupied: *an average population density* **2** *physics* a measure of the compactness of a substance, expressed as its mass per unit volume **3** a measure of a physical quantity per unit of length, area, or volume

dent *n* **1** a hollow in the surface of something ▷ *vb* **2** to make a dent in ▶ **HISTORY** variant of *dint*

dental *adj* of or relating to the teeth or dentistry ▶ **HISTORY** Latin *dens* tooth

dental floss *n* a waxed thread used to remove particles of food from between the teeth

dental surgeon *n* same as **dentist**

dentate *adj* having teeth or toothlike notches ▶ **HISTORY** Latin *dentatus*

dentifrice (**den**-tif-riss) *n* paste or powder for cleaning the teeth ▶ **HISTORY** Latin *dens* tooth + *fricare* to rub

dentine (**den**-teen) *n* the hard dense tissue that forms the bulk of a tooth ▶ **HISTORY** Latin *dens* tooth

dentist *n* a person qualified to practise dentistry ▶ **HISTORY** French *dentiste*

dentistry *n* the branch of medicine concerned with the teeth and gums

dentition *n* the typical arrangement, type, and number of teeth in a species ▶ **HISTORY** Latin *dentitio* a teething

denture *n* (often pl) a partial or full set of artificial teeth ▶ **HISTORY** French *dent* tooth

denudation *n* **1** the process of making something bare **2** *geog* the processes of erosion and weathering that wear away land and vegetation and expose rock

denude *vb* **-nuding, -nuded 1** to make bare; strip: *the atrocious weather denuded the trees* **2** *geol* to expose (rock) by the erosion of the layers above

denumerable *adj maths* countable

denunciation *n* open condemnation; denouncing ▶ **HISTORY** Latin *denuntiare* to proclaim

deny *vb* **-nies, -nying, -nied 1** to declare (a statement) to be untrue **2** to refuse to give or allow: *we have been denied permission* **3** to refuse to acknowledge: *the baron denied his wicked son* ▶ **HISTORY** Latin *denegare*

deodar *n* a Himalayan cedar with drooping branches ▶ **HISTORY** Hindi

deodorant *n* a substance applied to the body to prevent or disguise the odour of perspiration

deodorize *or* **-ise** *vb* **-izing, -ized** *or* **-ising, -ised** to remove or disguise the odour of > **deodorization** *or* **-isation** *n*

deoxygenate *vb chem* to remove the oxygen from a substance such as water or air

deoxyribonucleic acid *n* same as **DNA**

depart *vb* **1** to leave **2** to differ or deviate: *to depart from the original concept* ▶ **HISTORY** Old French *departir*

departed *adj euphemistic* dead

department *n* **1** a specialized division of a large business organization, hospital, university, etc. **2** a major subdivision of the administration of a government **3** an administrative division in several countries, such as France **4** *informal* a specialized sphere of activity: *wine-making is my wife's department* ▶ **HISTORY** French *département* > **departmental** *adj*

department store *n* a large shop divided into departments selling many kinds of goods

departure *n* **1** the act of departing **2** a divergence from previous custom, rule, etc. **3** a course of action or venture: *the album represents a new departure for them*

depend *vb* **depend on a** to put trust (in); rely (on) **b** to be influenced or determined (by): *the answer depends on four main issues* **c** to rely (on) for income or support ▶ **HISTORY** Latin *dependere* to hang from

dependable *adj* reliable and trustworthy > **dependability** *n* > **dependably** *adv*

dependant *n* a person who depends on another for financial support

dependence *n* **1** the state of relying on something in order to be able to survive or operate properly **2** reliance or trust: *they had a bond between them of mutual dependence and trust*

dependency *n, pl* **-cies 1** a territory subject to a state on which it does not border **2** *psychol* overreliance on another person or on a drug

dependent *adj* **1** depending on a person or thing for aid or support **2** *maths* (of a variable) dependent for its value on another variable **3** **dependent on** *or* **upon** influenced or conditioned by

dependent clause *n* another term for **subordinate clause**

dependent territory *n* same as **dependency** (sense 1)

dependent variable *n maths* a variable in an equation or statement whose value depends on the value of the independent variable

depict *vb* **1** to represent by drawing, painting, etc. **2** to describe in words ▶ **HISTORY** Latin *depingere* > **depiction** *n*

depilatory (dip-**pill**-a-tree) *adj* **1** able or serving to remove hair ▷ *n, pl* **-ries 2** a chemical used to remove hair ▶ **HISTORY** Latin *depilare* to pull out the hair

deplete *vb* **-pleting, -pleted 1** to use up (supplies or money) **2** to reduce in number ▶ HISTORY Latin *deplere* to empty out > **depletion** *n*

deplorable *adj* very bad or unpleasant
> **deplorably** *adv*

deplore *vb* **-ploring, -plored** to express or feel strong disapproval of ▶ HISTORY Latin *deplorare* to weep bitterly

deploy *vb* to organize (troops or resources) into a position ready for immediate and effective action ▶ HISTORY Latin *displicare* to unfold
> **deployment** *n*

deponent *n law* a person who makes a statement on oath ▶ HISTORY Latin *deponens* putting down

depopulate *vb* **-lating, -lated** to cause to be reduced in population > **depopulation** *n*

deport *vb* **1** to remove forcibly from a country **2 deport oneself** to behave in a specified manner ▶ HISTORY Latin *deportare* to carry away, banish

deportation *n* the act of expelling someone from a country

deportee *n* a person deported or awaiting deportation

deportment *n* the way in which a person moves and stands: *she had the manners and deportment of a great lady* ▶ HISTORY Old French *deporter* to conduct (oneself)

depose *vb* **-posing, -posed 1** to remove from an office or position of power **2** *law* to testify on oath ▶ HISTORY Latin *deponere* to put aside

deposit *vb* **-iting, -ited 1** to put down **2** to entrust (money or valuables) for safekeeping **3** to place (money) in a bank account or other savings account **4** to lay down naturally: *the river deposits silt* ▷ *n* **5** a sum of money placed in a bank account or other savings account **6** money given in part payment for goods or services **7** an amount of a substance left on a surface as a result of chemical or geological process **8** an underground accumulation of ores, coal, etc.: *gold deposits* ▶ HISTORY Latin *depositus* put down

deposit account *n Brit* a bank account that earns interest

depositary *n, pl* **-taries** a person or group to whom something is entrusted for safety

deposition *n* **1** *law* the sworn statement of a witness used in court in his or her absence **2** the act of deposing **3** the act of depositing **4** something deposited ▶ HISTORY Late Latin *depositio* a laying down, testimony

depositor *n* a person who places or has money on deposit in a bank or similar organization: *panic-stricken depositors*

depository *n, pl* **-ries 1** a store where furniture, valuables, etc. can be kept for safety **2** same as **depositary**

depot (**dep**-oh) *n* **1** a place where goods and vehicles are kept when not in use **2** *US, Canad & NZ* a bus or railway station ▶ HISTORY French

depraved *adj* morally bad; corrupt ▶ HISTORY Latin *depravare* to distort, corrupt

depravity *n, pl* **-ties** moral corruption

deprecate *vb* **-cating, -cated** *written* to express

disapproval of ▶ HISTORY Latin *deprecari* to avert, ward off > **deprecation** *n* > **deprecatory** *adj*

depreciate *vb* **-ating, -ated 1** to decline in value or price **2** to deride or criticize ▶ HISTORY Latin *de-* down + *pretium* price > **depreciatory** *adj*

depreciation *n* **1** *accounting* the reduction in value of a fixed asset through use, obsolescence, etc. **2** a decrease in the exchange value of a currency **3** the act or an instance of belittling

depredation *n* plundering; pillage ▶ HISTORY Latin *depraedare* to pillage

depress *vb* **1** to make sad and gloomy **2** to lower (prices) **3** to push down ▶ HISTORY Old French *depresser* > **depressing** *adj* > **depressingly** *adv*

depressant *adj* **1** *med* able to reduce nervous or functional activity; sedative ▷ *n* **2** a depressant drug

depressed *adj* **1** low in spirits; downcast **2** suffering from economic hardship, such as unemployment: *the current depressed conditions* **3** pressed down or flattened

depression *n* **1** a mental state in which a person has feelings of gloom and inadequacy **2** an economic condition in which there is substantial unemployment, low output and investment; slump **3** *meteorol* a mass of air below normal atmospheric pressure, which often causes rain **4** a sunken place

Depression *n* **the Depression** the worldwide economic depression of the early 1930s

depressive *adj* causing sadness and lack of energy

deprive *vb* **-priving, -prived • deprive of** to prevent from having or enjoying ▶ HISTORY Latin *de-* from + *privare* to deprive of > **deprivation** *n*

deprived *adj* lacking adequate living conditions, education, etc.: *deprived ghettos*

dept department

depth *n* **1** the distance downwards, backwards, or inwards **2** intensity of emotion or feeling **3** the quality of having a high degree of knowledge, insight, and understanding **4** intensity of colour **5** lowness of pitch **6 depths a** a remote inaccessible region: *the depths of the forest* **b** the most severe part: *the depths of depression* **c** a low moral state **7 out of one's depth a** in water deeper than one is tall **b** beyond the range of one's competence or understanding ▶ HISTORY Middle English *dep* deep

depth charge *n* a bomb used to attack submarines that explodes at a preset depth of water

deputation *n* a body of people appointed to represent others

depute *vb* **-puting, -puted** to appoint (someone) to act on one's behalf ▶ HISTORY Late Latin *deputare* to assign, allot

deputize *or* **-tise** *vb* **-tizing, -tized** *or* **-tising, -tised** to act as deputy

deputy *n, pl* **-ties** a person appointed to act on behalf of another ▶ HISTORY Old French *deputer* to appoint

d

derail *vb* to cause (a train) to go off the rails
> **derailment** *n*

derailleur (dee-**rail**-yer) *n* a type of gear-change mechanism for bicycles

deranged *adj* **1** mad, or behaving in a wild and uncontrolled way **2** in a state of disorder
▶ HISTORY from Old French *desrengier* to disorder, disturb > **derangement** *n*

derby *n, pl* **-bies** *US & Canad* a bowler hat

Derby *n, pl* **-bies** **1 the Derby** an annual horse race for three-year-olds, run at Epsom Downs, Surrey **2 local derby** a sporting event between teams from the same area ▶ HISTORY after the Earl of *Derby*, who founded the race in 1780

deregulate *vb* **-lating, -lated** to remove regulations or controls from > **deregulation** *n*

derelict *adj* **1** abandoned or unused and falling into ruins ▷ *n* **2** a social outcast or vagrant ▶ HISTORY Latin *derelinquere* to abandon

dereliction *n* **1** the state of being abandoned **2 dereliction of duty** wilful neglect of one's duty

derestrict *vb* **Brit, Austral & NZ** to make (a road) free from speed limits > **derestriction** *n*

deride *vb* **-riding, -rided** to speak of or treat with contempt or ridicule ▶ HISTORY Latin *deridere* to laugh to scorn > **derision** *n*

de rigueur (de rig-**gur**) *adj* required by fashion ▶ HISTORY French, literally: of strictness

derisive *adj* mocking or scornful > **derisively** *adv*

derisory *adj* too small or inadequate to be considered seriously: *the shareholders have dismissed the offer as derisory*

derivation *n* the origin or descent of something, such as a word

derivative *adj* **1** based on other sources; not original ▷ *n* **2** a word, idea, etc. that is derived from another **3** *maths* the rate of change of one quantity with respect to another

derive *vb* **-riving, -rived** to draw or be drawn (from) in source or origin ▶ HISTORY Old French *deriver* to spring from

dermatitis *n* inflammation of the skin ▶ HISTORY Greek *derma* skin

dermatology *n* the branch of medicine concerned with the skin ▶ HISTORY Greek *derma* skin + -LOGY > **dermatologist** *n*

derogate *vb* **-gating, -gated** • **derogate from** to cause to seem inferior; detract from ▶ HISTORY Latin *derogare* to diminish > **derogation** *n*

derogatory (dir-**rog**-a-tree) *adj* expressing or showing a low opinion of someone or something

derrick *n* **1** a simple crane that has lifting tackle slung from a boom **2** the framework erected over an oil well to enable drill tubes to be raised and lowered ▶ HISTORY after *Derrick*, famous hangman

derring-do *n* *archaic or literary* a daring spirit or deed ▶ HISTORY Middle English *durring don* daring to do

derv *n* **Brit** diesel oil, when used for road transport ▶ HISTORY d(*iesel*) e(*ngine*) r(*oad*) v(*ehicle*)

dervish *n* a member of a Muslim religious order noted for a frenzied, ecstatic, whirling dance
▶ HISTORY Persian *darvīsh* mendicant monk

desalination *n* the process of removing salt, esp. from sea water

descale *vb* to remove the hard coating which sometimes forms inside kettles, pipes, etc.

descant *n* **1** a tune played or sung above a basic melody ▷ *adj* **2** of the highest member in a family of musical instruments: *a descant clarinet*
▶ HISTORY Latin *dis-* apart + *cantus* song

descend *vb* **1** to move down (a slope, staircase, etc.) **2** to move or fall to a lower level, pitch, etc. **3 be descended from** to be connected by a blood relationship to **4 descend on** to visit unexpectedly **5** to stoop to (unworthy behaviour) ▶ HISTORY Latin *descendere*

descendant *n* a person or animal descended from an individual, race, or species

descendent *adj* descending

descent *n* **1** the act of descending **2** a downward slope **3** a path or way leading downwards **4** derivation from an ancestor; family origin **5** a decline or degeneration

describe *vb* **-scribing, -scribed** **1** to give an account of (something or someone) in words **2** to trace the outline of (a circle, etc.) ▶ HISTORY Latin *describere* to copy off, write out

description *n* **1** a statement or account that describes someone or something **2** the act of describing **3** sort, kind, or variety: *antiques of every description*

descriptive *adj* describing something: *it was a very descriptive account of the play* > **descriptively** *adv*

descry *vb* **-scries, -scrying, -scried** **1** to catch sight of **2** to discover by looking carefully
▶ HISTORY Old French *descrier* to proclaim

desecrate *vb* **-crating, -crated** to violate the sacred character of (an object or place) ▶ HISTORY DE- + (CON)SECRATE > **desecration** *n*

desegregate *vb* **-gating, -gated** to end racial segregation in (a school or other public institution) > **desegregation** *n*

deselect *vb* **Brit** *politics* (of a constituency organization) to refuse to select (an MP) for re-election > **deselection** *n*

desensitize *or* **-tise** *vb* **-tizing, -tized** *or* **-tising, -tised** to make insensitive or less sensitive: *the patient was desensitized to the allergen; to desensitize photographic film*

desert¹ (**dez**-ert) *n* a region that has little or no vegetation because of low rainfall ▶ HISTORY Church Latin *desertum*

desert² (di-**zert**) *vb* **1** to abandon (a person or place) without intending to return **2** *chiefly mil* to leave (a post or duty) with no intention of returning ▶ HISTORY Latin *deserere* > **deserted** *adj* > **deserter** *n* > **desertion** *n*

desertification *n* a process by which fertile land turns into desert

desert island *n* a small uninhabited island in the tropics

desert rat *n* **1** a jerboa, inhabiting the deserts of

N Africa **2** *history, informal* an Allied soldier who took part in the desert campaigns of World War II in 1941-42 ▶ HISTORY from the jerboa symbol of the British 7th Armoured division

deserts (di-**zerts**) *pl n* **get one's just deserts** get the punishment one deserves ▶ HISTORY Old French *deserte* something deserved

deserve *vb* **-serving, -served** to be entitled to or worthy of ▶ HISTORY Latin *deservire* to serve devotedly

deserved *adj* rightfully earned > **deservedly** (diz-**zerv**-id-lee) *adv*

deserving *adj* worthy of a reward, help, or praise

deshabille (day-zab-**beel**) or **dishabille** *n* the state of being partly dressed ▶ HISTORY French *déshabillé*

desiccate *vb* **-cating, -cated** to remove most of the water from; dry ▶ HISTORY Latin *desiccare* to dry up > **desiccated** *adj* > **desiccation** *n*

design *vb* **1** to work out the structure or form of (something), by making a sketch or plans **2** to plan and make (something) artistically **3** to intend (something) for a specific purpose: *the move is designed to reduce travelling costs* ▷ *n* **4** a sketch, plan, or preliminary drawing **5** the arrangement or features of an artistic or decorative work: *he built it to his own design* **6** a finished artistic or decorative creation **7** the art of designing **8** an intention; purpose **9** **have designs on** to plot to gain possession of ▶ HISTORY Latin *designare* to mark out, describe

designate (**dez**-zig-nate) *vb* **-nating, -nated** **1** to give a name to or describe as: *vessels sunk during battle are designated as war graves* **2** to select (someone) for an office or duty; appoint ▷ *adj* **3** appointed, but not yet in office: *a Prime Minister designate* ▶ HISTORY Latin *designatus* marked out

designation *n* **1** something that designates, such as a name **2** the act of designating

designedly (dee-**zine**-id-lee) *adv* by intention

designer *n* **1** a person who draws up original sketches or plans from which things are made ▷ *adj* **2** designed by a well-known fashion designer: *a wardrobe full of designer clothes* **3** having an appearance of fashionable trendiness: *designer stubble*

designing *adj* cunning and scheming

desirable *adj* **1** worth having or doing: *a desirable lifestyle* **2** arousing desire > **desirability** *n* > **desirably** *adv*

desire *vb* **-siring, -sired** **1** to want very much **2** *formal* to request: *we desire your company at the wedding of our daughter* ▷ *n* **3** a wish or longing **4** a person or thing that is desired ▶ HISTORY Latin *desiderare*

desist *vb* to stop doing: *please desist from talking* ▶ HISTORY Latin *desistere*

desk *n* **1** a piece of furniture with a writing surface and usually drawers **2** a service counter in a public building, such as a hotel **3** the section of a newspaper or television station responsible for a particular subject: *the picture desk*

▶ HISTORY Medieval Latin *desca* table

desk research *n* research conducted by studying existing data. Compare **field research**

desktop *n* **1** the main screen display on a personal computer ▷ *adj* **2** (esp. of a computer system) small enough to use at a desk

desktop publishing *n* a computer system which combines text and graphics and presents them in a professional-looking printed format

desolate *adj* **1** uninhabited and bleak **2** made uninhabitable; devastated **3** without friends, hope, or encouragement **4** gloomy or dismal; depressing ▷ *vb* **-lating, -lated** **5** to deprive of inhabitants **6** to make barren; devastate **7** to make wretched or forlorn ▶ HISTORY Latin *desolare* to leave alone > **desolately** *adv* > **desolateness** *n*

desolation *n* **1** ruin or devastation **2** solitary misery; wretchedness

despair *n* **1** total loss of hope ▷ *vb* **2** to lose or give up hope: *we must not despair of finding a peaceful solution* ▶ HISTORY Old French *despoir* hopelessness

despatch *vb, n* same as **dispatch**

desperado *n, pl* **-does** *or* **-dos** a reckless person ready to commit any violent illegal act ▶ HISTORY probably pseudo-Spanish

desperate *adj* **1** willing to do anything to improve one's situation **2** (of an action) undertaken as a last resort **3** very grave: *in desperate agony* **4** having a great need or desire: *I was desperate for a child* ▶ HISTORY Latin *desperare* to have no hope > **desperately** *adv*

desperation *n* **1** desperate recklessness **2** the state of being desperate

despicable *adj* deserving contempt > **despicably** *adv*

despise *vb* **-pising, -pised** to look down on with contempt ▶ HISTORY Latin *despicere* to look down

despite *prep* in spite of ▶ HISTORY Old French *despit*

despoil *vb formal* to plunder ▶ HISTORY Latin *despoliare* > **despoliation** *n*

despondent *adj* dejected or depressed ▶ HISTORY Latin *despondere* to lose heart > **despondency** *n* > **despondently** *adv*

despot *n* any person in power who acts tyrannically ▶ HISTORY Greek *despotēs* lord, master > **despotic** *adj* > **despotically** *adv*

despotism *n* **1** absolute or tyrannical government **2** tyrannical behaviour

dessert *n* the sweet course served at the end of a meal ▶ HISTORY French

dessertspoon *n* a spoon between a tablespoon and a teaspoon in size

destination *n* the place to which someone or something is going

destined (**dess**-tinnd) *adj* **1** certain to be or do something: *the school is destined to close this summer* **2** heading towards a specific destination: *some of the oil was destined for Eastern Europe* ▶ HISTORY Latin *destinare* to appoint

destiny *n, pl* **-nies** **1** the future destined for a person or thing **2** the predetermined course of events **3** the power that predetermines the course of events ▶ HISTORY Old French *destinee*

destitute *adj* lacking the means to live; totally impoverished ▶ HISTORY Latin *destituere* to leave alone > **destitution** *n*

destroy *vb* **1** to ruin; demolish **2** to put an end to **3** to kill (an animal) **4** to crush or defeat ▶ HISTORY Latin *destruere* to pull down

destroyer *n* **1** a small heavily armed warship **2** a person or thing that destroys

destructible *adj* capable of being destroyed

destruction *n* **1** the act of destroying something or state of being destroyed **2** a cause of ruin ▶ HISTORY Latin *destructio* a pulling down

destructive *adj* **1** causing or capable of causing harm, damage, or injury **2** intended to discredit, esp. without positive suggestions or help: *destructive speeches against the platform* > **destructively** *adv*

destructive interference *n physics* the effect that occurs when the crest of one wave coincides with the trough of another wave

destructive plate boundary *n geol* a tectonic plate boundary where an oceanic plate is forced under a continental plate

destructive wave *n geog* a wave in which the water moves forward and there is friction with the seabed

destructive waves *pl n geog* strong steep waves that drag sand and pebbles away from the shore causing erosion and destroying beaches. Compare **constructive waves**

desuetude (diss-**syoo**-it-tude) *n formal* the condition of not being in use ▶ HISTORY Latin *desuescere* to lay aside a habit

desultory (**dez**-zl-tree) *adj* **1** passing or jumping from one thing to another; disconnected: *desultory conversation* **2** occurring in a random way: *a desultory thought* ▶ HISTORY Latin *de-* from + *salire* to jump > **desultorily** *adv*

detach *vb* **1** to disengage and separate **2** *mil* to send (a regiment, officer, etc.) on a special assignment ▶ HISTORY Old French *destachier* > **detachable** *adj*

detached *adj* **1** *Brit, Austral & S African* separate or standing apart: *a detached farmhouse* **2** showing no emotional involvement: *she continued to watch him in her grave and detached manner*

detachment *n* **1** the state of not being personally involved in something **2** *mil* a small group of soldiers separated from the main group

detail *n* **1** an item that is considered separately **2** an item considered to be unimportant: *a mere detail* **3** treatment of individual parts: *the census provides a considerable amount of detail* **4** a small section of a work of art often enlarged to make the smaller features more distinct **5** *chiefly mil* **a** personnel assigned a specific duty **b** the duty **6 in detail** including all the important particulars ▷ *vb* **7** to list fully **8** *chiefly mil* to select (personnel) for a specific duty ▶ HISTORY Old French *detailler* to cut in pieces

detain *vb* **1** to delay (someone) **2** to force (someone) to stay: *the police detained him for questioning* ▶ HISTORY Latin *detinere* > **detainee** *n* > **detainment** *n*

detect *vb* **1** to perceive or notice: *to detect a note of sarcasm* **2** to discover the existence or presence of: *to detect alcohol in the blood* ▶ HISTORY Latin *detegere* to uncover > **detectable** *adj* > **detector** *n*

detection *n* **1** the act of noticing, discovering, or sensing something **2** the act or process of extracting information

detective *n* **a** a police officer who investigates crimes **b** same as **private detective**

detente (day-**tont**) *n* the easing of tension between nations ▶ HISTORY French

detention *n* **1** imprisonment, esp. of a suspect awaiting trial **2** a form of punishment in which a pupil is detained after school

detention centre *n* a place where young people may be detained for short periods of time by order of a court

deter *vb* **-terring, -terred** to discourage or prevent (someone) from doing something by instilling fear or doubt in them ▶ HISTORY Latin *deterrere*

detergent *n* **1** a chemical substance used for washing clothes, dishes, etc. ▷ *adj* **2** having cleansing power ▶ HISTORY Latin *detergens* wiping off

deteriorate *vb* **-rating, -rated** to become worse ▶ HISTORY Latin *deterior* worse > **deterioration** *n*

determinant *adj* **1** serving to determine or affect ▷ *n* **2** a factor that controls or influences what will happen **3** *maths* a square array of elements that represents the sum of certain products of these elements

determinate *adj* definitely limited or fixed

determination *n* **1** the condition of being determined; resoluteness **2** the act of making a decision

determine *vb* **-mining, -mined** **1** to settle (an argument or a question) conclusively **2** to find out the facts about (something): *the tests determined it was in fact cancer* **3** to fix in scope, extent, etc.: *to determine the degree of the problem* **4** to make a decision ▶ HISTORY Latin *determinare* to set boundaries to

determined *adj* firmly decided > **determinedly** *adv*

determiner *n grammar* a word, such as a number, article, or personal pronoun, that determines the meaning of a noun phrase

determinism *n* the theory that human choice is not free, but is decided by past events > **determinist** *n, adj*

deterrent *n* **1** something that deters **2** a weapon or set of weapons held by one country to deter another country attacking ▷ *adj* **3** tending to deter ▶ HISTORY Latin *deterrens* hindering > **deterrence** *n*

detest *vb* to dislike intensely ▶ HISTORY Latin *detestari* > **detestable** *adj*

detestation *n* intense hatred

dethrone *vb* **-throning, -throned** to remove from a throne or deprive of any high position > **dethronement** *n*

detonate *vb* **-nating, -nated** to make (an explosive device) explode or (of an explosive device) to explode ▶ HISTORY Latin *detonare* to thunder down > **detonation** *n*

detonator *n* a small amount of explosive or a device used to set off an explosion

detour *n* a deviation from a direct route or course of action ▶ HISTORY French

detoxify *vb* **-fies, -fying, -fied** to remove poison from > **detoxification** *n*

detract *vb* **detract from** to make (something) seem less good, valuable, or impressive: *I wouldn't want to detract from your triumph* ▶ HISTORY Latin *detrahere* to pull away, disparage > **detractor** *n* > **detraction** *n*

detriment *n* disadvantage or damage ▶ HISTORY Latin *detrimentum* a rubbing off > **detrimental** *adj* > **detrimentally** *adv*

detritus (dit-**trite**-uss) *n* **1** a loose mass of stones and silt worn away from rocks **2** debris ▶ HISTORY Latin: a rubbing away > **detrital** *adj*

de trop (de **troh**) *adj* unwanted or unwelcome: *I know when I'm de trop, so I'll leave you two together* ▶ HISTORY French

detumescence *n* the subsidence of a swelling ▶ HISTORY Latin *detumescere* to cease swelling

deuce (**dyewss**) *n* **1** *tennis* a tied score that requires one player to gain two successive points to win the game **2** a playing card or dice with two spots ▶ HISTORY Latin *duo* two

deus ex machina *n* an unlikely development introduced into a play or film to resolve the plot

deuterium *n* a stable isotope of hydrogen. Symbol: D or ²H ▶ HISTORY Greek *deuteros* second

deuterium oxide *n* same as **heavy water**

Deutschmark (**doytch**-mark) *or* **Deutsche Mark** (**doytch**-a) *n* a former monetary unit of Germany ▶ HISTORY German: German mark

deutzia (**dyewt**-see-a) *n* a shrub with clusters of pink or white flowers

devalue *vb* **-valuing, -valued** **1** to reduce the exchange value of (a currency) **2** to reduce the value of (something or someone) > **devaluation** *n*

devastate *vb* **-tating, -tated** to damage (a place) severely or destroy it ▶ HISTORY Latin *devastare* > **devastation** *n*

devastated *adj* shocked and extremely upset > **devastating** *adj* > **devastatingly** *adv*

develop *vb* **1** to grow or bring to a later, more elaborate, or more advanced stage **2** to come or bring into existence: *the country has developed a consumer society* **3** to make or become gradually clearer or more widely known **4** to follow as a result of something: *Cubism developed from attempts to give painting a more intellectual concept of form* **5** to contract (an illness) **6** to improve the value or change the use of (land) **7** to exploit the natural resources of (a country or region) **8** *photog* to treat (a photographic plate or film) to produce a visible image ▶ HISTORY Old French *desveloper* to unwrap

developed country *n* a country with a high level of industrialization

developer *n* **1** a person who develops property **2** *photog* a chemical used to develop photographs or films

developing country *n* a poor or nonindustrial country that is seeking to develop its resources by industrialization

development *n* **1** the process of growing or developing **2** the product of developing **3** an event or incident that changes a situation **4** an area of land that has been developed > **developmental** *adj*

development area *n* (in Britain) an area which has experienced economic depression and which is given government assistance to establish new industry

deviant *adj* **1** deviating from what is considered acceptable behaviour ▷ *n* **2** a person whose behaviour deviates from what is considered to be acceptable > **deviance** *n*

deviate *vb* **-ating, -ated** **1** to differ from others in belief or thought **2** to depart from one's usual or previous behaviour ▶ HISTORY Late Latin *deviare* to turn aside from the direct road > **deviation** *n*

device *n* **1** a machine or tool used for a particular purpose **2** *euphemistic* a bomb **3** a scheme or plan **4** a design or emblem **5 leave someone to his** *or* **her own devices** to leave someone alone to do as he or she wishes ▶ HISTORY Old French *devis* contrivance + *devise* intention

devil *n* **1** *theol* **the Devil** the chief spirit of evil and enemy of God **2** any evil spirit **3** a person regarded as wicked **4** a person: *lucky devil* **5** a person regarded as daring: *be a devil!* **6** *informal* something difficult or annoying **7 between the devil and the deep blue sea** between equally undesirable alternatives **8 give the devil his due** to acknowledge the talent or success of an unpleasant person **9 talk of the devil!** used when an absent person who has been the subject of conversation arrives unexpectedly **10 the devil** used as an exclamation to show surprise or annoyance: *what the devil is she doing here?* ▷ *vb* **-illing, -illed** *or US* **-iling, -iled** **11** to prepare (food) by coating with a highly flavoured spiced mixture **12** *chiefly Brit* to do routine literary work for a lawyer or author ▶ HISTORY Greek *diabolos* enemy, accuser

devilish *adj* **1** of or like a devil; fiendish ▷ *adv, adj* **2** *informal* extreme or extremely: *devilish good food* > **devilishly** *adv*

devil-may-care *adj* happy-go-lucky; reckless

devilment *n* mischievous conduct

devilry *n* **1** reckless fun or mischief **2** wickedness

devil's advocate *n* a person who takes an opposing or unpopular point of view for the sake of argument

devious *adj* **1** insincere and dishonest **2** (of a route or course of action) indirect ▶ HISTORY Latin *devius* lying to one side of the road > **deviously** *adv*

d

227

devise *vb* **-vising, -vised** to work out (something) in one's mind ▶ HISTORY Old French *deviser* to divide

devoid *adj* **devoid of** completely lacking in a particular quality: *she was a woman totally devoid of humour* ▶ HISTORY Old French *devoider* to remove

devolution *n* a transfer of authority from a central government to regional governments ▶ HISTORY Medieval Latin *devolutio* a rolling down > **devolutionist** *n, adj*

devolve *vb* **-volving, -volved** to pass or cause to pass to a successor or substitute, as duties or power ▶ HISTORY Latin *devolvere* to roll down

Devon *n* a breed of large red cattle originally from Devon

Devonian *adj* **1** *geol* of the period of geological time about 405 million years ago **2** of or relating to Devon

devote *vb* **-voting, -voted** to apply or dedicate (one's time, money, or effort) to a particular purpose ▶ HISTORY Latin *devovere* to vow

devoted *adj* feeling or demonstrating loyalty or devotion: *he was clearly devoted to his family* > **devotedly** *adv*

devotee (dev-vote-**tee**) *n* **1** a person fanatically enthusiastic about a subject or activity **2** a zealous follower of a religion

devotion *n* **1** strong attachment to or affection for someone or something **2** religious zeal; piety **3 devotions** religious observance or prayers > **devotional** *adj*

devour *vb* **1** to eat up greedily **2** to engulf and destroy **3** to read avidly ▶ HISTORY Latin *devorare* to gulp down > **devouring** *adj*

devout *adj* **1** deeply religious **2** sincere; heartfelt: *a devout confession* ▶ HISTORY Latin *devotus* faithful > **devoutly** *adv*

dew *n* drops of water that form on the ground or on a cool surface at night from vapour in the air ▶ HISTORY Old English *dēaw* > **dewy** *adj*

dewberry *n, pl* **-berries** a type of bramble with blue-black fruits

dewclaw *n* a nonfunctional claw on a dog's leg

Dewey Decimal System *n* a system of library book classification with ten main subject classes ▶ HISTORY after Melvil *Dewey*, educator

dewlap *n* a loose fold of skin hanging under the throat in cattle, dogs, etc. ▶ HISTORY Middle English *dew* + *lap* hanging flap

dew point *n* the temperature at which water droplets begin to form in the air

dew-worm *n* US & Canad a large earthworm used as fishing bait

dewy-eyed *adj* innocent and inexperienced

dexter *adj* of or on the right side of a shield, etc., from the bearer's point of view ▶ HISTORY Latin

dexterity *n* **1** skill in using one's hands **2** mental quickness ▶ HISTORY Latin *dexteritas* aptness, readiness

dexterous *adj* possessing or done with dexterity > **dexterously** *adv*

dextrin *or* **dextrine** *n* a sticky substance obtained from starch: used as a thickening agent in food ▶ HISTORY French *dextrine*

dextrose *n* a glucose occurring in fruit, honey, and in the blood of animals

deya *n* same as **diya**

DFC (in Britain) Distinguished Flying Cross

dg decigram

dhal *or* **dal** *n* **1** the nutritious pealike seed of a tropical shrub **2** a curry made from lentils or other pulses ▶ HISTORY Hindi *dāl*

dharma *n* **1** *Hinduism* moral law or behaviour **2** *Buddhism* ideal truth ▶ HISTORY Sanskrit

dhoti *n, pl* **-tis** a long loincloth worn by men in India ▶ HISTORY Hindi

DI Detective Inspector

di- *prefix* **1** twice; two; double: *dicotyledon* **2** containing two specified atoms or groups of atoms: *carbon dioxide* ▶ HISTORY Greek

diabetes (die-a-**beet**-eez) *n* a medical condition in which the body is unable to control the level of sugar in the blood ▶ HISTORY Greek: a passing through

diabetic *n* **1** a person who has diabetes ▷ *adj* **2** of or having diabetes **3** suitable for people suffering from diabetes: *diabetic chocolate*

diabolic *adj* of the Devil; satanic ▶ HISTORY Greek *diabolos* devil

diabolical *adj* *informal* **1** unpleasant or annoying: *the weather was diabolical* **2** extreme: *diabolical cheek* **3** same as **diabolic** > **diabolically** *adv*

diabolism *n* **a** witchcraft or sorcery **b** worship of devils > **diabolist** *n*

diaconate *n* the position or period of office of a deacon ▶ HISTORY Late Latin *diaconatus* > **diaconal** *adj*

diacritic *n* a sign placed above or below a character or letter to indicate phonetic value or stress ▶ HISTORY Greek *diakritikos* serving to distinguish

diadem *n* old-fashioned a small jewelled crown or headband, usually worn by royalty: *a gold diadem* ▶ HISTORY Greek: royal headdress

diaeresis *or esp US* **dieresis** (die-**air**-iss-iss) *n, pl* **-ses** (-seez) the mark (¨) placed over the second of two adjacent vowels to indicate that it is to be pronounced separately, as in naïve ▶ HISTORY Greek: a division

diagnose *vb* **-nosing, -nosed** to determine by diagnosis

diagnosis (die-ag-**no**-siss) *n, pl* **-ses** (-seez) the discovery and identification of diseases from the examination of symptoms ▶ HISTORY Greek: a distinguishing > **diagnostic** *adj*

diagonal *adj* **1** *maths* connecting any two vertices in a polygon that are not adjacent **2** slanting ▷ *n* **3** a diagonal line, plane, or pattern ▶ HISTORY Greek *dia-* through + *gōnia* angle > **diagonally** *adv*

diagram *n* a sketch or plan showing the form or workings of something ▶ HISTORY Greek *diagraphein* to mark out > **diagrammatic** *adj*

dial *n* **1** the face of a clock or watch, marked with divisions representing units of time

2 the graduated disc on a measuring instrument **3** the control on a radio or television set used to change the station **4** a numbered disc on the front of some telephones ▷ *vb* **dialling, dialled** *or US* **dialing, dialed 5** to try to establish a telephone connection with (someone) by operating the dial or buttons on a telephone ▶ HISTORY Latin *dies* day

dialect *n* a form of a language spoken in a particular geographical area ▶ HISTORY Greek *dialektos* speech, dialect > **dialectal** *adj*

dialectic *n* **1** logical debate by question and answer to resolve differences between two views **2** the art of logical argument ▶ HISTORY Greek *dialektikē (tekhnē)* (the art) of argument > **dialectical** *adj*

dialling tone *or US, Canad, Austral & NZ* **dial tone** *n* a continuous sound heard on picking up a telephone receiver, indicating that a number can be dialled

dialogue *or US sometimes* **dialog** *n* **1** conversation between two people **2** a conversation in a literary or dramatic work **3** a discussion between representatives of two nations or groups ▶ HISTORY Greek *dia-* between + *legein* to speak

dialysis (die-**al**-iss-iss) *n*, *pl* **-ses** (-seez) **1** *med* the filtering of blood through a semipermeable membrane to remove waste products **2** the separation of the particles in a solution by filtering through a semipermeable membrane ▶ HISTORY Greek *dialuein* to tear apart, dissolve > **dialyser** *or US* **-lyzer** *n* > **dialytic** *adj*

diamagnetism *n* the phenomenon exhibited by substances that are repelled by both poles of a magnet

diamanté (die-a-**man**-tee) *adj* decorated with glittering bits of material, such as sequins ▶ HISTORY French

diameter *n* **a** a straight line through the centre of a circle or sphere **b** the length of such a line ▶ HISTORY Greek *dia-* through + *metron* measure

diametric *or* **diametrical** *adj* **1** of or relating to a diameter **2** completely opposed: *the diametric opposition of the two camps* > **diametrically** *adv*

diamond *n* **1** a usually colourless exceptionally hard precious stone of crystallized carbon **2** *geom* a figure with four sides of equal length forming two acute and two obtuse angles **3** a playing card marked with one or more red diamond-shaped symbols **4** *baseball* the playing field ▷ *adj* **5** (of an anniversary) the sixtieth: *diamond wedding* ▶ HISTORY Latin *adamas* the hardest iron or steel, diamond

diapason (die-a-**pay**-zon) *n music* **1** either of two stops found throughout the range of a pipe organ **2** the range of an instrument or voice ▶ HISTORY Greek *dia pasōn* through all (the notes)

diaper *n US & Canad* a nappy ▶ HISTORY Medieval Greek *diaspros* pure white

diaphanous (die-**af**-fan-uss) *adj* (of fabrics) fine and translucent ▶ HISTORY Greek *diaphanēs* transparent

diaphoretic *n* **1** a drug that causes perspiration or sweat ▷ *adj* **2** relating to or causing perspiration or sweat

diaphragm (**die**-a-fram) *n* **1** *anat* the muscular partition that separates the abdominal cavity and chest cavity **2** same as **cap** (sense 5) **3** a device to control the amount of light entering an optical instrument **4** a thin vibrating disc which converts sound to electricity or vice versa, as in a microphone or loudspeaker ▶ HISTORY Greek *dia-* across + *phragma* fence

diapositive *n* a positive transparency; slide

diarist *n* a person who writes a diary that is subsequently published

diarrhoea *or esp US* **diarrhea** (die-a-**ree**-a) *n* frequent discharge of abnormally liquid faeces ▶ HISTORY Greek *dia-* through + *rhein* to flow

diary *n*, *pl* **-ries 1** a book containing a record of daily events, appointments, or observations **2** a written record of daily events, appointments, or observations ▶ HISTORY Latin *dies* day

Diaspora (die-**ass**-spore-a) *n* **1** the dispersion of the Jews after the Babylonian conquest of Palestine **2** a dispersion of people originally belonging to one nation ▶ HISTORY Greek: a scattering

diastase (**die**-ass-stayss) *n* an enzyme that converts starch into sugar ▶ HISTORY Greek *diastasis* a separation > **diastasic** *adj*

diastole (die-**ass**-stoh-lee) *n* dilation of the chambers of the heart > **diastolic** *adj*

diatom *n* a microscopic unicellular alga ▶ HISTORY Greek *diatomos* cut in two

diatomic *adj* containing two atoms

diatonic *adj* of or relating to any scale of five tones and two semitones produced by playing the white keys of a keyboard instrument ▶ HISTORY Greek *diatonos* extending

diatribe *n* a bitter critical attack ▶ HISTORY Greek *dia-* through + *tribein* to rub

dibble *n* a small hand tool used to make holes in the ground for bulbs, seeds, or roots ▶ HISTORY origin unknown

dice *n*, *pl* **dice 1** a small cube, each of whose sides has a different number of spots (1 to 6), used in games of chance ▷ *vb* **dicing, diced 2** to cut (food) into small cubes **3 dice with death** to take a risk ▶ HISTORY originally plural of DIE²

dicey *adj* **dicier, diciest** *informal, chiefly Brit & NZ* dangerous or tricky

dichotomy (die-**kot**-a-mee) *n*, *pl* **-mies 1** division into two opposed groups or parts **2** *bot* a method of branching by repeated division into two equal parts ▶ HISTORY Greek *dicha* in two + *temnein* to cut > **dichotomous** *adj*

dichromatic *adj* having two colours ▶ HISTORY Greek *di-* double + *khrōma* colour

dick *n slang* **clever dick** an opinionated person ▶ HISTORY *Dick* familiar form of *Richard*

Dickensian *adj* **1** of Charles Dickens (1812–70), British novelist **2** denoting poverty, distress, and exploitation, as depicted in the novels of Dickens

d

dicky[1] *n, pl* **dickies** a false shirt front ▶ HISTORY from *Dick*, name

dicky[2] *adj* **dickier, dickiest** *Brit & NZ, informal* shaky or weak: *a dicky heart* ▶ HISTORY origin unknown

dicky-bird *n* a child's word for a bird

dicotyledon (die-kot-ill-**leed**-on) *n* a flowering plant with two seed leaves

dictate *vb* **-tating, -tated** 1 to say (words) aloud for another person to transcribe 2 to seek to impose one's will on others ▷ *n* 3 an authoritative command 4 a guiding principle: *the dictates of reason* ▶ HISTORY Latin *dictare* to say repeatedly

dictation *n* 1 the act of dictating words to be taken down in writing 2 the words dictated

dictator *n* 1 a ruler who has complete power 2 a person who behaves in a tyrannical manner > **dictatorship** *n*

dictatorial *adj* 1 of or pertaining to a dictator 2 tyrannical; overbearing > **dictatorially** *adv*

diction *n* the manner of pronouncing words and sounds ▶ HISTORY Latin *dicere* to speak

dictionary *n, pl* **-aries** 1 **a** a book that consists of an alphabetical list of words with their meanings **b** a similar book giving equivalent words in two languages 2 a reference book listing terms and giving information about a particular subject ▶ HISTORY Late Latin *dictio* word

dictum *n, pl* **-tums** *or* **-ta** 1 a formal statement; pronouncement 2 a popular saying or maxim ▶ HISTORY Latin

did *vb* the past tense of **do**[1]

didactic *adj* intended to teach or instruct people: *an Impressionist work can be as didactic in its way as a sermon* ▶ HISTORY Greek *didaktikos* skilled in teaching > **didactically** *adv* > **didacticism** *n*

diddle *vb* **-dling, -dled** *informal* to swindle ▶ HISTORY Jeremy *Diddler*, a scrounger in a 19th-century play > **diddler** *n*

didgeridoo *n* an Australian Aboriginal deep-toned wind instrument ▶ HISTORY imitative

didn't did not

die[1] *vb* **dying, died** 1 (of a person, animal, or plant) to cease all biological activity permanently 2 (of something inanimate) to cease to exist 3 to lose strength, power, or energy by degrees 4 *written to* stop working: *the engine died* 5 **be dying** to be eager (for something or to do something) 6 **be dying of** *informal* to be nearly overcome with (laughter, boredom, etc.) 7 **die hard** to change or disappear only slowly: *old loyalties die hard* 8 **to die for** *informal* highly desirable: *a salary to die for* ▷ See also **die down, die out** ▶ HISTORY Old English *dīegan*

die[2] *n* 1 a shaped block used to cut or form metal 2 a casting mould 3 same as **dice** (sense 1) 4 **the die is cast** an irrevocable decision has been taken ▶ HISTORY Latin *dare* to give, play

die down *vb* 1 to lose strength or power by degrees 2 to become calm: *the storm has died down now*

die-hard *or* **diehard** *n* a person who resists change

dieldrin *n* a highly toxic crystalline insecticide

dielectric *n* 1 a substance of very low electrical conductivity; insulator ▷ *adj* 2 having the properties of a dielectric ▶ HISTORY Greek *dia-* through + ELECTRIC

die out *or* **off** *vb* to become extinct or disappear after a gradual decline

dieresis (die-**air**-iss-iss) *n, pl* **-ses** (-seez) same as **diaeresis**

diesel *n* 1 same as **diesel engine** 2 a vehicle driven by a diesel engine 3 *informal* diesel oil ▶ HISTORY after R. *Diesel*, engineer

diesel engine *n* an internal-combustion engine in which oil is ignited by compression

diesel oil *or* **fuel** *n* a fuel obtained from petroleum distillation, used in diesel engines

diet[1] *n* 1 the food that a person or animal regularly eats 2 a specific allowance or selection of food, to control weight or for health reasons: *a high-fibre diet* ▷ *vb* 3 to follow a special diet so as to lose weight ▷ *adj* 4 suitable for eating with a weight-reduction diet: *diet soft drinks* ▶ HISTORY Greek *diaita* mode of living > **dietary** *adj* > **dieter** *n*

diet[2] *n* a legislative assembly in some countries ▶ HISTORY Medieval Latin *dieta* public meeting

dietary fibre *n* the roughage in fruits and vegetables that aid digestion

dietetic *adj* prepared for special dietary requirements

dietetics *n* the study of diet, nutrition, and the preparation of food

dietician *n* a person qualified to advise people about healthy eating

differ *vb* 1 to be dissimilar in quality, nature, or degree 2 to disagree ▶ HISTORY Latin *differre* to scatter, be different

difference *n* 1 the state or quality of being unlike 2 a disagreement or argument 3 the result of the subtraction of one number or quantity from another 4 **make a difference** to have an effect 5 **split the difference a** to compromise **b** to divide a remainder equally

different *adj* 1 partly or completely unlike 2 new or unusual 3 not identical or the same; other: *he wears a different tie every day* > **differently** *adv*

differential *adj* 1 of, relating to, or using a difference 2 *maths* involving differentials ▷ *n* 3 a factor that differentiates between two comparable things 4 *maths* a minute difference between values in a scale 5 *chiefly Brit* the difference between rates of pay for different types of labour, esp. within a company or industry

differential calculus *n* the branch of mathematics concerned with derivatives and differentials

differential gear *n* the gear in the driving axle of a road vehicle that permits one driving wheel to rotate faster than the other when cornering

differentiate *vb* **-ating, -ated** 1 to perceive or show the difference (between) 2 to make (one thing) distinct from other such things **3** *maths* to determine the derivative of a function or variable **> differentiation** *n*

difficult *adj* **1** not easy to do, understand, or solve **2** not easily pleased or satisfied: *a difficult patient* **3** full of hardships or trials: *he had recently had a difficult time with his job as a self-employed builder*

difficulty *n, pl* **-ties** **1** the state or quality of being difficult **2** a task or problem that is hard to deal with **3** a troublesome or embarrassing situation: *in financial difficulties* **4** an objection or obstacle: *you're just making difficulties* **5** lack of ease; awkwardness: *he could run only with difficulty* ▶ HISTORY Latin *difficultas*

diffident *adj* lacking self-confidence; shy ▶ HISTORY Latin *dis-* not + *fidere* to trust **> diffidence** *n* **> diffidently** *adv*

diffract *vb* to cause to undergo diffraction **> diffractive** *adj*

diffraction *n* **1** *physics* a deviation in the direction of a wave at the edge of an obstacle in its path **2** the formation of light and dark fringes by the passage of light through a small aperture ▶ HISTORY Latin *diffringere* to shatter

diffuse *written vb* **-fusing, -fused** **1** to spread over a wide area **2** *physics* to cause to undergo diffusion ▷ *adj* **3** spread out over a wide area **4** lacking conciseness ▶ HISTORY Latin *diffusus* spread abroad **> diffusible** *adj* **> diffuser** *n*

diffusion *n* **1** the act of diffusing or the fact of being diffused; dispersion **2** *physics* the random thermal motion of atoms and molecules in gases, liquids, and some solids **3** *physics* the transmission or reflection of light, in which the radiation is scattered in many directions

dig *vb* **digging, dug** **1** to cut into, break up, and turn over or remove (earth), esp. with a spade **2** to excavate (a hole or tunnel) by digging, usually with an implement or (of animals) with claws **3** to obtain by digging: *dig out potatoes* **4** to find by effort or searching: *he dug out a mini cassette from his pocket* **5** *informal* to like or understand **6** (foll. by *in* or *into*) to thrust or jab ▷ *n* **7** the act of digging **8** an archaeological excavation **9** a thrust or poke **10** a cutting remark ▷ See also **dig in** ▶ HISTORY Middle English *diggen*

digest *vb* **1** to subject (food) to a process of digestion **2** to absorb mentally ▷ *n* **3** a shortened version of a book, report, or article ▶ HISTORY Latin *digerere* to divide **> digestible** *adj*

digestion *n* **1** the process of breaking down food into easily absorbed substances **2** the body's system for doing this

digestive *adj* relating to digestion

digger *n* a machine used for excavation

dig in *vb* **1** to mix (compost or fertilizer) into the soil by digging **2** *informal* to begin to eat vigorously **3** *informal* (of soldiers) to dig a trench and prepare for an enemy attack **4** **dig one's heels in** *informal* to refuse to move or be persuaded

digit (**dij**-it) *n* **1** a finger or toe **2** any numeral from 0 to 9 ▶ HISTORY Latin *digitus* toe, finger

digital *adj* **1** displaying information as numbers rather than with a dial **2** representing data as a series of numerical values **3** of or possessing digits **> digitally** *adv*

digital computer *n* a computer in which the input consists of numbers, letters, and other characters that are represented internally in binary notation

digitalis *n* a drug made from foxglove leaves: used as a heart stimulant ▶ HISTORY Latin: relating to a finger (from the shape of the foxglove flowers)

digital recording *n* a sound recording process that converts audio or analogue signals into a series of pulses

digital switchover *n* the process of changing the method of transmitting television from analogue to digital format

digital television *n* television in which the picture information is transmitted in digital form and decoded at the television receiver

digitate *adj* **1** (of leaves) having leaflets in the form of a spread hand **2** (of animals) having digits

digitize *or* **-ise** *vb* **-izing, -ized** *or* **-ising, -ised** to transcribe (data) into a digital form for processing by a computer **> digitizer** *or* **-iser** *n*

dignify *vb* **-fies, -fying, -fied** **1** to add distinction to: *the meeting was dignified by the minister* **2** to add a semblance of dignity to by the use of a pretentious name or title: *she dignifies every plant with its Latin name* ▶ HISTORY Latin *dignus* worthy + *facere* to make

dignitary *n, pl* **-taries** a person of high official position or rank

dignity *n, pl* **-ties** **1** serious, calm, and controlled behaviour or manner **2** the quality of being worthy of honour **3** sense of self-importance: *he considered the job beneath his dignity* ▶ HISTORY Latin *dignus* worthy

digraph *n* two letters used to represent a single sound, such as *gh* in *tough*

digress *vb* to depart from the main subject in speech or writing ▶ HISTORY Latin *digressus* turned aside **> digression** *n*

digs *pl n* *Brit, Austral & S African, informal* lodgings ▶ HISTORY from *diggings*, perhaps referring to where one digs or works

dihedral *adj* having or formed by two intersecting planes

dilapidated *adj* (of a building) having fallen into ruin ▶ HISTORY Latin *dilapidare* to waste **> dilapidation** *n*

dilate *vb* **-lating, -lated** to make or become wider or larger: *her eyes dilated in the dark* ▶ HISTORY Latin *dilatare* to spread out **> dilation** *or* **dilatation** *n*

dilatory (**dill**-a-tree) *adj* tending or intended to waste time ▶ HISTORY Late Latin *dilatorius* **> dilatorily** *adv* **> dilatoriness** *n*

dilemma *n* a situation offering a choice between two equally undesirable alternatives ▶ HISTORY Greek *di-* double + *lēmma* proposition

dilettante (dill-it-**tan**-tee) *n, pl* **-tantes** *or* **-tanti** a person whose interest in a subject is superficial 231

rather than serious ▶ HISTORY Italian
> **dilettantism** n

diligent adj **1** careful and persevering in carrying out tasks or duties **2** carried out with care and perseverance: *a diligent approach to work* ▶ HISTORY Latin *diligere* to value > **diligence** n > **diligently** adv

dill n a sweet-smelling herb used for flavouring ▶ HISTORY Old English *dile*

dilly-dally vb **-lies, -lying, -lied** *Brit, Austral & NZ, informal* to dawdle or waste time ▶ HISTORY reduplication of *dally*

dilute vb **-luting, -luted 1** to make (a liquid) less concentrated by adding water or another liquid **2** to make (someone's power, idea, or role) weaker or less effective: *socialists used their majority in parliament to dilute legislation crucial to developing a market economy* ▷ adj **3** *chem* (of a solution) having a low concentration ▶ HISTORY Latin *diluere* > **dilution** n

dilute acid n *chem* an acid with a large number of water molecules and few acid molecules

diluvian or **diluvial** adj of a flood, esp. the great Flood described in the Old Testament ▶ HISTORY Latin *diluere* to wash away

dim adj **dimmer, dimmest 1** badly lit **2** not clearly seen; faint: *a dim figure in the doorway* **3** not seeing clearly: *eyes dim with tears* **4** *informal* mentally dull **5** not clear in the mind; obscure: *a dim awareness* **6** lacking in brightness or lustre: *a dim colour* **7 take a dim view of** to disapprove of ▷ vb **dimming, dimmed 8** to become or cause to become dim **9** to cause to seem less bright **10** *US & Canad* same as **dip** (sense 4) ▶ HISTORY Old English *dimm* > **dimly** adv > **dimness** n

dime n a coin of the US and Canada worth ten cents ▶ HISTORY Latin *decem* ten

dimension n **1** an aspect or factor: *the attack brought a whole new dimension to the bombing campaign* **2 dimensions** scope or extent **3** (often pl) a measurement of the size of something in a particular direction ▶ HISTORY Latin *dimensio* an extent > **dimensional** adj

dimer n *chem* a molecule made up of two identical molecules bonded together

dimeter n *poetry* a line of verse consisting of two metrical feet

diminish vb **1** to make or become smaller, fewer, or less **2** *music* to decrease (a minor interval) by a semitone **3** to reduce in authority or status ▶ HISTORY Latin *deminuere* to make smaller + archaic *minish* to lessen

diminished responsibility n *law* a plea under which evidence of an abnormal state of mind is submitted to demonstrate lack of criminal responsibility at the time of an offence

diminuendo *music* n, pl **-dos 1 a** a gradual decrease in loudness **b** a passage which gradually decreases in loudness ▷ adv **2** gradually decreasing in loudness ▶ HISTORY Italian

diminution n reduction in size, volume, intensity, or importance ▶ HISTORY Latin *deminutio*

diminutive adj **1** very small; tiny **2** *grammar* **a** denoting an affix added to a word to convey the meaning *small* or *unimportant* or to express affection, as for example, the suffix *-ette* in French **b** denoting a word formed by the addition of a diminutive affix ▷ n **3** *grammar* a diminutive word or affix > **diminutiveness** n

dimmer n **1** a device for dimming an electric light **2** *US* **a** a dipped headlight on a road vehicle **b** a parking light on a car

dimple n **1** a small natural dent on the cheeks or chin ▷ vb **-pling, -pled 2** to produce dimples by smiling ▶ HISTORY Middle English *dympull*

dimwit n *informal* a stupid person > **dim-witted** adj

din n **1** a loud unpleasant confused noise ▷ vb **dinning, dinned 2 din something into someone** to instil something into someone by constant repetition ▶ HISTORY Old English *dynn*

dinar (dee-nahr) n a monetary unit of various Balkan, Middle Eastern, and North African countries ▶ HISTORY Latin *denarius* a Roman coin

dine vb **dining, dined 1** to eat dinner **2** *written* **dine on** or **off** to make one's meal of: *the guests dined on roast beef* ▶ HISTORY Old French *disner*

diner n **1** a person eating a meal in a restaurant **2** *chiefly US & Canad* a small cheap restaurant **3** short for **dining car**

ding n *Austral, dated, NZ, informal* a small dent in a vehicle

ding-dong n **1** the sound of a bell **2** a violent exchange of blows or words ▶ HISTORY imitative

dinges (ding-uss) n *S African, informal* a jocular word for something whose name is unknown or forgotten; thingumabob ▶ HISTORY Dutch *ding* thing

dinghy (ding-ee, ding-gee) n, pl **-ghies** a small boat, powered by sail, oars, or outboard motor ▶ HISTORY Hindi or Bengali *dingi*

dingle n a small wooded hollow or valley ▶ HISTORY origin unknown

dingo n, pl **-goes** an Australian native wild dog ▶ HISTORY Aboriginal

dingy (din-jee) adj **-gier, -giest 1** *Brit, Austral & NZ* dull, neglected, and drab: *he waited in this dingy little outer office* **2** shabby and discoloured: *she was wearing dingy white overalls* ▶ HISTORY origin unknown > **dinginess** n

dining car n a railway coach in which meals are served

dining room n a room where meals are eaten

dinkum adj *Austral & NZ, informal* genuine or right: *a fair dinkum offer* ▶ HISTORY English dialect: work

dinky adj **dinkier, dinkiest** *chiefly Brit, informal* small and neat; dainty ▶ HISTORY dialect *dink* neat

dinky-di adj *Austral, informal* typical ▶ HISTORY variant of DINKUM

dinner n **1** the main meal of the day, eaten either in the evening or at midday **2** a formal social occasion at which an evening meal is served ▶ HISTORY Old French *disner* to dine

d

dinner jacket n a man's semiformal black evening jacket without tails

dinosaur n any of a large order of extinct prehistoric reptiles many of which were gigantic ▶ HISTORY Greek *deinos* fearful + *sauros* lizard

dint n written **by dint of** by means of: *by dint of their own efforts* ▶ HISTORY Old English *dynt* a blow

diocesan adj of or relating to a diocese

diocese (**die**-a-siss) n the district over which a bishop has control ▶ HISTORY Greek *dioikēsis* administration

diode n **1** a semiconductor device for converting alternating current to direct current **2** an electronic valve with two electrodes between which a current can flow only in one direction ▶ HISTORY Greek *di-* double + *hodos* a way, road

dioecious (die-**eesh**-uss) adj (of plants) having the male and female reproductive organs on separate plants ▶ HISTORY Greek *di-* twice + *oikia* house

Dionysian (die-on-**niz**-zee-an) adj wild or orgiastic ▶ HISTORY from *Dionysus*, Greek god of wine

Dionysus n Greek myth the god of wine

dioptre or US **diopter** (die-**op**-ter) n a unit for measuring the refractive power of a lens ▶ HISTORY Greek *dia-* through + *opsesthai* to see

diorama n **1** a miniature three-dimensional scene, in which models of figures are seen against a background **2** a picture made up of illuminated translucent curtains, viewed through an aperture ▶ HISTORY Greek *dia-* through + *horama* view

dioxide n an oxide containing two oxygen atoms per molecule

dip vb **dipping, dipped 1** to plunge or be plunged quickly or briefly into a liquid **2** to put one's hands into something, esp. to obtain an object: *she dipped into her handbag looking for change* **3** to slope downwards **4** to switch (car headlights) from the main to the lower beam **5** to undergo a slight decline, esp. temporarily: *sales dipped in November* **6** to immerse (farm animals) briefly in a chemical to rid them of insects **7** to lower or be lowered briefly: *she dipped her knee in a curtsy* ▷ n **8** the act of dipping **9** a brief swim **10** a liquid chemical in which farm animals are dipped **11** a depression, esp. in a landscape **12** a momentary sinking down **13** a creamy mixture into which pieces of food are dipped before being eaten ▷ See also **dip into** ▶ HISTORY Old English *dyppan*

Dip Ed (in Britain) Diploma in Education

dipeptide n biochem a compound consisting of two linked amino acids

diphtheria (dif-**theer**-ree-a) n a contagious disease producing fever and difficulty in breathing and swallowing ▶ HISTORY Greek *diphthera* leather; from the membrane that forms in the throat

diphthong n a vowel sound, occupying a single syllable, in which the speaker's tongue moves continuously from one position to another, as in the pronunciation of *a* in *late* ▶ HISTORY Greek *di-* double + *phthongos* sound

dip into vb **1** to draw upon: *he dipped into his savings* **2** to read passages at random from (a book or journal)

diploid adj biol denoting a cell or organism with pairs of homologous chromosomes ▶ HISTORY Greek *di-* double + *-ploos* -fold

diploma n a document conferring a qualification or recording successful completion of a course of study ▶ HISTORY Latin: official document, literally: letter folded double

diplomacy n **1** the conduct of the relations between nations by peaceful means **2** skill in the management of international relations **3** tact or skill in dealing with people

diplomat n an official, such as an ambassador, engaged in diplomacy

diplomatic adj **1** of or relating to diplomacy **2** skilled in negotiating between nations **3** tactful in dealing with people ▶ HISTORY French *diplomatique* concerning the documents of diplomacy; see DIPLOMA > **diplomatically** adv

diplomatic immunity n the freedom from legal action and exemption from taxation which diplomats have in the country where they are working

dipole n **1** two equal but opposite electric charges or magnetic poles separated by a small distance **2** a molecule that has two such charges or poles > **dipolar** adj

dipper n **1** a ladle used for dipping **2** a songbird that inhabits fast-flowing streams

diprotodont (die-**pro**-toe-dont) n a marsupial with fewer than three upper incisor teeth on each side of the jaw

dipsomania n a compulsive desire to drink alcoholic beverages ▶ HISTORY Greek *dipsa* thirst + *mania* madness > **dipsomaniac** n, adj

dipstick n a rod with notches on it dipped into a container to indicate the fluid level

dip switch n a device for dipping headlights on a vehicle

dipterous adj having two wings or winglike parts ▶ HISTORY Greek *dipteros* two-winged

diptych (**dip**-tik) n a painting on two hinged panels ▶ HISTORY Greek *di-* double + *ptuchē* a panel

dire adj disastrous, urgent, or terrible: *he was now in dire financial straits* ▶ HISTORY Latin *dirus* ominous

direct adj **1** shortest; straight: *a direct route* **2** without intervening people: *they secretly arranged direct links to their commanders* **3** honest; frank: *he was polite but very direct* **4** diametric: *the direct opposite* **5** in an unbroken line of descent: *a direct descendant* ▷ adv **6** directly; straight ▷ vb **7** to conduct or control the affairs of **8** to give orders with authority to (a person or group) **9** to tell (someone) the way to a place **10** to address (a letter, parcel, etc.) **11** to address (a look or remark) at someone: *the look she directed at him was one of unconcealed hatred* **12 a** to provide guidance to (actors, cameramen, etc.) in (a play or film) **b** to supervise the making or staging of (a film or play) ▶ HISTORY Latin *dirigere* to guide > **directness** n

233

direct access *n* a method of reading data from a computer file without reading through the file from the beginning

direct current *n* an electric current that flows in one direction only

direct debit *n* an order given to a bank or other financial institution by an account holder to pay an amount of money from the account to a specified person or company at regular intervals

direct democracy *n* a political system in which the people have a vote on all policy decisions. Compare **representative democracy**

direction *n* **1** the course or line along which a person or thing moves, points, or lies **2** management or guidance: *the campaign was successful under his direction* **3** the work of a stage or film director

directional *adj* **1** of or showing direction **2** *electronics* (of an aerial) transmitting or receiving radio waves more effectively in some directions than in others

directions *pl n* instructions for doing something or for reaching a place

directive *n* an instruction; order

directly *adv* **1** in a direct manner **2** at once; without delay **3** immediately or very soon: *I'll go that directly* ▷ *conj* **4** as soon as: *we left directly the money arrived*

direct marketing *n* *marketing* selling goods directly to consumers rather than through retailers, for example by mail order or telephone selling

direct object *n* *grammar* a noun, pronoun, or other noun group denoting the person or thing receiving the direct action of a verb. For example, *a book* in *they bought Anne a book*

director *n* **1** a person or thing that directs or controls **2** a member of the governing board of a business, trust, etc. **3** the person responsible for the artistic and technical aspects of the making of a film or television programme > **directorial** *adj* > **directorship** *n*

directorate *n* **1** a board of directors **2** the position of director

director-general *n*, *pl* **directors-general** a person in overall charge of certain large organizations

directory *n*, *pl* **-ries 1** a book listing names, addresses, and telephone numbers of individuals or business companies **2** *computers* an area of a disk containing the names and locations of the files it currently holds

direct speech *n* *grammar* the reporting of what someone has said by quoting the exact words

direct tax *n* a tax paid by the person or organization on which it is levied

dirge *n* **1** a chant of lamentation for the dead **2** any mournful song ▶ **HISTORY** Latin *dirige* direct (imperative), opening word of antiphon used in the office of the dead

dirigible (dir-rij-jib-bl) *adj* **1** able to be steered ▷ *n* **2** same as **airship** ▶ **HISTORY** Latin *dirigere* to direct

dirk *n* a dagger, formerly worn by Scottish Highlanders ▶ **HISTORY** Scots *durk*

dirndl *n* **1** a woman's dress with a full gathered skirt and fitted bodice **2** a gathered skirt of this kind ▶ **HISTORY** from German

dirt *n* **1** any unclean substance, such as mud; filth **2** loose earth; soil **3** packed earth, cinders, etc. used to make a racetrack **4** obscene speech or writing **5** *informal* harmful gossip ▶ **HISTORY** Old Norse *drit* excrement

dirt-cheap *adj*, *adv* at an extremely low price

dirt track *n* a racetrack made of packed earth or cinders

dirty *adj* **dirtier, dirtiest 1** covered or marked with dirt; filthy **2** causing one to become grimy: *a dirty job* **3** (of a colour) not clear and bright **4** unfair, dishonest, or unkind: *dirty tricks* **5** obscene: *dirty jokes* **6** revealing dislike or anger: *a dirty look* **7** (of weather) rainy or stormy **8** (of an explosive device) modified to cause radioactive contamination **9 dirty work** unpleasant or illicit activity ▷ *n* **10 do the dirty on** *informal* to behave meanly towards ▷ *vb* **dirties, dirtying, dirtied 11** to make dirty; soil > **dirtiness** *n*

dis- *prefix* **1** indicating reversal: *disconnect* **2** indicating negation or lack: *dissimilar; disgrace* **3** indicating removal or release: *disembowel*

disability *n*, *pl* **-ties 1** a severe physical or mental condition that restricts the way a person lives his or her life **2** something that disables someone

disable *vb* **-abling, -abled** to make ineffective, unfit, or incapable > **disablement** *n*

disabled *adj* lacking one or more physical powers, such as the ability to walk or to coordinate one's movements

disabuse *vb* **-abusing, -abused** to rid (someone) of a mistaken idea: *Arnold felt unable to disabuse her of her prejudices*

disaccharide (die-**sack**-a-ride) *n* a sugar, such as sucrose, whose molecules consist of two linked monosaccharides

disadvantage *n* **1** an unfavourable or harmful circumstance **2 at a disadvantage** in a less favourable position than other people: *he continued to insist that he was at a disadvantage at the hearings* > **disadvantageous** *adj*

disadvantaged *adj* socially or economically deprived

disaffected *adj* having lost loyalty to or affection for someone or something; alienated: *three million disaffected voters* > **disaffection** *n*

disagree *vb* **-greeing, -greed 1** to have differing opinions or argue about (something) **2** to fail to correspond; conflict **3** to cause physical discomfort to: *curry disagrees with me*

disagreeable *adj* **1** (of an incident or situation) unpleasant **2** (of a person) bad-tempered or disobliging > **disagreeably** *adv*

disagreement *n* **1** refusal or failure to agree **2** a difference between results, totals, etc. which shows that they cannot all be true **3** an argument

disallow *vb* to reject as untrue or invalid; cancel

d

disappear *vb* **1** to cease to be visible; vanish **2** to go away or become lost, esp. without explanation **3** to cease to exist: *the pain has disappeared* > **disappearance** *n*

disappoint *vb* **1** to fail to meet the expectations or hopes of; let down **2** to prevent the fulfilment of (a plan, etc.); frustrate ▶ **HISTORY** Old French *desapointier* > **disappointed** *adj* > **disappointing** *adj*

disappointment *n* **1** the feeling of being disappointed **2** a person or thing that disappoints

disapprobation *n* disapproval

disapprove *vb* **-proving, -proved** to consider wrong or bad > **disapproval** *n* > **disapproving** *adj*

disarm *vb* **1** to deprive of weapons **2** to win the confidence or affection of **3** (of a country) to decrease the size and capability of one's armed forces

disarmament *n* the reduction of fighting capability by a country

disarming *adj* removing hostility or suspicion > **disarmingly** *adv*

disarrange *vb* **-ranging, -ranged** to throw into disorder > **disarrangement** *n*

disarray *n* **1** confusion and lack of discipline **2** extreme untidiness ▷ *vb* **3** to throw into confusion

disassemble *vb* *technology* to take apart piece by piece

disassociate *vb* **-ating, -ated** same as **dissociate** > **disassociation** *n*

disaster *n* **1** an accident that causes great distress or destruction **2** something, such as a project, that fails or has been ruined ▶ **HISTORY** Italian *disastro* > **disastrous** *adj* > **disastrously** *adv*

disavow *vb* to deny connection with or responsibility for (something) > **disavowal** *n*

disband *vb* to stop or cause to stop functioning as a unit or group > **disbandment** *n*

disbar *vb* **-barring, -barred** to deprive (a barrister) of the right to practise

disbelieve *vb* **-lieving, -lieved** **1** to reject (a person or statement) as being untruthful **2 disbelieve in** to have no faith or belief in: *to disbelieve in the supernatural* > **disbelief** *n*

disburse *vb* **-bursing, -bursed** to pay out ▶ **HISTORY** Old French *desborser* > **disbursement** *n*

disc *n* **1** a flat circular object **2** a gramophone record **3** *anat* a circular flat structure in the body, esp. between the vertebrae **4** *computers* same as **disk** ▶ **HISTORY** Latin *discus* discus

discard *vb* to get rid of (something or someone) as useless or undesirable ▶ **HISTORY** DIS- + *card* (the playing card)

disc brake *n* a brake in which two pads rub against a flat disc

discern *vb* to see or be aware of (something) clearly ▶ **HISTORY** Latin *discernere* to divide > **discernible** *adj*

discerning *adj* having or showing good judgment > **discernment** *n*

discharge *vb* **-charging, -charged** **1** to release or allow to go **2** to dismiss (someone) from duty or employment **3** to fire (a gun) **4** to cause to pour forth: *the scar was red and swollen and began to discharge pus* **5** to remove (the cargo) from a boat, etc.; unload **6** to meet the demands of (a duty or responsibility) **7** to relieve oneself of (a debt) **8** *physics* to take or supply electrical current from (a cell or battery) ▷ *n* **9** something that is discharged **10** dismissal or release from an office, job, etc. **11** a pouring out of a fluid; emission **12** *physics* a conduction of electricity through a gas **13** *geog* the volume of water passing through an aquifer or stream at a given point during a given interval of time

disciple (diss-**sipe**-pl) *n* **1** a follower of the doctrines of a teacher **2** one of the personal followers of Christ during his earthly life ▶ **HISTORY** Latin *discipulus* pupil

disciplinarian *n* a person who practises strict discipline

disciplinary *adj* of or imposing discipline; corrective

discipline *n* **1** the practice of imposing strict rules of behaviour on other people **2** the ability to behave and work in a controlled manner **3** a particular area of academic study ▷ *vb* **-plining, -plined** **4** to improve or attempt to improve the behaviour of (oneself or someone else) by training or rules **5** to punish ▶ **HISTORY** Latin *disciplina* teaching

disciplined *adj* able to behave and work in a controlled way

disc jockey *n* a person who announces and plays pop recordings on a radio programme or at a club

disclaim *vb* **1** to deny (responsibility for or knowledge of something) **2** to give up (any claim to)

disclaimer *n* a statement denying responsibility for or knowledge of something

disclose *vb* **-closing, -closed** **1** to make (information) known **2** to allow to be seen: *she agreed to disclose the contents of the box* > **disclosure** *n*

disco *n, pl* **-cos** **1** a nightclub for dancing to amplified pop recordings **2** an occasion at which people dance to amplified pop recordings **3** mobile equipment for providing music for a disco ▶ **HISTORY** from DISCOTHEQUE

discography *n, pl* **-phies** a classified list of music recordings

discolour *or US* **discolor** *vb* to change in colour; fade or stain > **discoloration** *n*

discomfit *vb* **-fiting, -fited** *written* to make uneasy or confused ▶ **HISTORY** Old French *desconfire* to destroy > **discomfiture** *n*

discomfort *n* **1** a mild pain **2** a feeling of worry or embarrassment **3 discomforts** conditions that cause physical uncomfortableness: *the physical discomforts of pregnancy*

discommode *vb* **-moding, -moded** to cause inconvenience ▶ **HISTORY** DIS- + obsolete *commode* to suit > **discommodious** *adj*

d

discompose *vb* **-posing, -posed** to disturb or upset someone > **discomposure** *n*

disconcert *vb* to disturb the confidence or self-possession of; upset, embarrass, or take aback > **disconcerting** *adj*

disconnect *vb* **1** to undo or break the connection between (two things) **2** to stop the supply of (gas or electricity to a building) > **disconnection** *n*

disconnected *adj* (of speech or ideas) not logically connected

disconsolate *adj written* sad beyond comfort ▶ **HISTORY** Medieval Latin *disconsolatus* > **disconsolately** *adv*

discontent *n* lack of contentment, as with one's condition or lot in life > **discontented** *adj* > **discontentedly** *adv*

discontinue *vb* **-uing, -ued** to come or bring to an end; stop

discontinuous *adj* characterized by interruptions; intermittent > **discontinuity** *n*

discord *n* **1** lack of agreement or harmony between people **2** harsh confused sounds **3** a combination of musical notes that lacks harmony ▶ **HISTORY** Latin *discors* at variance

discordant *adj* **1** at variance; disagreeing **2** harsh in sound; inharmonious > **discordance** *n*

discotheque *n* same as **disco** ▶ **HISTORY** French

discount *vb* **1** to leave (something) out of account as being unreliable, prejudiced, or irrelevant **2** to deduct (an amount or percentage) from the price of something ▷ *n* **3** a deduction from the full amount of a price **4 at a discount** below the regular price

discountenance *vb* **-nancing, -nanced** to make (someone) ashamed or confused

discourage *vb* **-aging, -aged** **1** to deprive of the will or enthusiasm to persist in something **2** to oppose by expressing disapproval > **discouragement** *n* > **discouraging** *adj*

discourse *n* **1** conversation **2** a formal treatment of a subject in speech or writing ▷ *vb* **-coursing, -coursed** **3** to speak or write (about) at length ▶ **HISTORY** Medieval Latin *discursus* argument

discourse analysis *n linguistics* the study of how language is used by members of a particular speech community

discourteous *adj* showing bad manners; rude > **discourteously** *adv* > **discourtesy** *n*

discover *vb* **1** to be the first to find or find out about **2** to learn about for the first time **3** to find after study or search > **discoverer** *n*

discovery *n, pl* **-eries** **1** the act of discovering **2** a person, place, or thing that has been discovered

discredit *vb* **-iting, -ited** **1** to damage the reputation of (someone) **2** to cause (an idea) to be disbelieved or distrusted ▷ *n* **3** something that causes disgrace > **discreditable** *adj*

discreet *adj* **1** careful to avoid embarrassment when dealing with secret or private matters **2** unobtrusive: *there was a discreet entrance down a side alley* ▶ **HISTORY** Old French *discret* > **discreetly** *adv*

discrepancy *n, pl* **-cies** a conflict or variation between facts, figures, or claims ▶ **HISTORY** Latin *discrepare* to differ in sound > **discrepant** *adj*

discrete *adj* separate or distinct ▶ **HISTORY** Latin *discretus* separated > **discreteness** *n*

discrete data *n statistics* data which has a succession of distinct values. Compare **continuous data**

discretion (diss-**kresh**-on) *n* **1** the quality of behaving so as to avoid social embarrassment or distress **2** freedom or authority to make judgments and to act as one sees fit: *at his discretion* > **discretionary** *adj*

discriminate *vb* **-nating, -nated** **1** to make a distinction against or in favour of a particular person or group **2** to recognize or understand a difference: *to discriminate between right and wrong* ▶ **HISTORY** Latin *discriminare* to divide > **discriminating** *adj*

discrimination *n* **1** unfair treatment of a person, racial group, or minority **2** subtle appreciation in matters of taste **3** the ability to see fine distinctions

discriminatory *adj* based on prejudice

discursive *adj* passing from one topic to another ▶ **HISTORY** Latin *discursus* a running to and fro

discus *n field sports* a disc-shaped object with a heavy middle, thrown by athletes ▶ **HISTORY** Greek *diskos*

discuss *vb* **1** to consider (something) by talking it over **2** to treat (a subject) in speech or writing ▶ **HISTORY** Latin *discutere* to dash to pieces > **discussion** *n*

discussion genre *n* a form of writing or speech in which the writer or speaker sets out facts and possible interpretations in an objective manner before offering an opinion based on the evidence

disdain *n* **1** a feeling of superiority and dislike; contempt ▷ *vb* **2** to refuse or reject with disdain: *he disdained domestic conventions* ▶ **HISTORY** Old French *desdeign* > **disdainful** *adj* > **disdainfully** *adv*

disease *n* an unhealthy condition in a person, animal, or plant which is caused by bacteria or infection ▶ **HISTORY** Old French *desaise* > **diseased** *adj*

diseconomy *n econ* a disadvantage, such as higher costs, resulting from the scale on which a business operates

disembark *vb* to land or cause to land from a ship, aircraft, or other vehicle > **disembarkation** *n*

disembodied *adj* **1** lacking a body **2** seeming not to be attached to or come from anyone > **disembodiment** *n*

disembowel *vb* **-elling, -elled** *or US* **-eling, -eled** to remove the entrails of > **disembowelment** *n*

disenchanted *adj* disappointed and disillusioned (with something) > **disenchantment** *n*

disenfranchise *vb* **-chising, -chised** to deprive (someone) of the right to vote or of other rights of citizenship

disengage *vb* **-gaging, -gaged** **1** to release from a connection **2** *mil* to withdraw from close action > **disengagement** *n*

disentangle *vb* **-gling, -gled 1** to release from entanglement or confusion **2** to unravel or work out > **disentanglement** *n*

disequilibrium *n* a loss or absence of stability or balance

disestablish *vb* to deprive (a church or religion) of established status > **disestablishment** *n*

disfavour *or US* **disfavor** *n* **1** disapproval or dislike **2** the state of being disapproved of or disliked

disfigure *vb* **-uring, -ured** to spoil the appearance or shape of > **disfigurement** *n*

disfranchise *vb* **-chising, -chised** same as **disenfranchise**

disgorge *vb* **-gorging, -gorged 1** to vomit **2** *written* to discharge (contents)

disgrace *n* **1** a condition of shame, loss of reputation, or dishonour **2** a shameful person or thing **3** exclusion from confidence or trust: *he was sent home in disgrace* ▷ *vb* **-gracing, -graced 4** to bring shame upon (oneself or others) > **disgraceful** *adj* > **disgracefully** *adv*

disgruntled *adj* sulky or discontented: *the disgruntled home supporters* ▶ HISTORY DIS- + obsolete *gruntle* to complain > **disgruntlement** *n*

disguise *vb* **-guising, -guised 1** to change the appearance or manner in order to conceal the identity of (someone or something) **2** to misrepresent (something) in order to obscure its actual nature or meaning ▷ *n* **3** a mask, costume, or manner that disguises **4** the state of being disguised ▶ HISTORY Old French *desguisier* > **disguised** *adj*

disgust *n* **1** a great loathing or distaste ▷ *vb* **2** to sicken or fill with loathing ▶ HISTORY Old French *desgouster* to sicken > **disgusted** *adj* > **disgusting** *adj*

dish *n* **1** a container used for holding or serving food, esp. an open shallow container **2** the food in a dish **3** a particular kind of food **4** short for **dish aerial 5** *informal* an attractive person ▷ See also **dish out, dish up** ▶ HISTORY Old English *disc*

dishabille (diss-a-**beel**) *n* same as **deshabille**

dish aerial *n* a large disc-shaped aerial with a concave reflector, used to receive signals in radar, radio telescopes, and satellite broadcasting

disharmony *n* lack of agreement or harmony > **disharmonious** *adj*

dishcloth *n* a cloth for washing dishes

dishearten *vb* to weaken or destroy the hope, courage, or enthusiasm of > **disheartened** *adj* > **disheartening** *adj*

dishevelled *or US* **disheveled** *adj* (of a person's hair, clothes, or general appearance) disordered and untidy ▶ HISTORY Old French *deschevelé*

dishonest *adj* not honest or fair > **dishonestly** *adv* > **dishonesty** *n*

dishonour *or US* **dishonor** *vb* **1** to treat with disrespect **2** to refuse to pay (a cheque) ▷ *n* **3** a lack of honour or respect **4** a state of shame or disgrace

5 something that causes a loss of honour > **dishonourable** *adj* > **dishonourably** *adv*

dish out *vb* **1** *informal* to distribute **2** **dish it out** to inflict punishment

dish up *vb* to serve (food)

dishwasher *n* a machine for washing and drying dishes, cutlery, etc.

disillusion *vb* **1** to destroy the illusions or false ideas of (someone) ▷ *n also* **disillusionment 2** the state of being disillusioned

disincentive *n* something that discourages someone from behaving or acting in a particular way

disinclined *adj* unwilling or reluctant > **disinclination** *n*

disinfect *vb* to rid of harmful germs by cleaning with a chemical substance > **disinfection** *n*

disinfectant *n* a substance that destroys harmful germs

disinformation *n* false information intended to mislead

disingenuous *adj* dishonest and insincere > **disingenuously** *adv*

disinherit *vb* **-iting, -ited** *law* to deprive (an heir) of inheritance > **disinheritance** *n*

disintegrate *vb* **-grating, -grated 1** to lose cohesion; break up: *the business disintegrated* **2** (of an object) to break into fragments; shatter **3** *physics* **a** to undergo nuclear fission or include nuclear fission in **b** same as **decay** (sense 3) > **disintegration** *n*

disinter *vb* **-terring, -terred 1** to dig up **2** to bring to light; expose

disinterested *adj* **1** free from bias; objective **2** *not universally accepted* feeling or showing a lack of interest; uninterested > **disinterest** *n*

disjointed *adj* having no coherence; disconnected: *a disjointed conversation*

disjunctive *adj* serving to disconnect or separate

disk *n* **1** *chiefly US & Canad* same as **disc 2** *computers* a storage device, consisting of a stack of plates coated with a magnetic layer, which rotates rapidly as a single unit ▶ HISTORY see DISC

disk drive *n computers* the controller and mechanism for reading and writing data on computer disks

dislike *vb* **-liking, -liked 1** to consider unpleasant or disagreeable ▷ *n* **2** a feeling of not liking something or someone

dislocate *vb* **-cating, -cated 1** to displace (a bone or joint) from its normal position **2** to disrupt or shift out of place > **dislocation** *n*

dislodge *vb* **-lodging, -lodged** to remove (something) from a previously fixed position

disloyal *adj* not loyal; deserting one's allegiance or duty > **disloyalty** *n*

dismal *adj* **1** gloomy and depressing **2** *informal* of poor quality > **dismally** *adv*

■ **WORD HISTORY**
■ In medieval times, 'dismal' (from Latin *dies mali*,
■ meaning 'evil days') was the name given to the
■ 24 days of the year (two in each month) that
■ were believed to be unlucky.

dismantle vb **-tling, -tled 1** to take apart piece by piece **2** to cause (an organization or political system) to stop functioning by gradually reducing its power or purpose ▶ HISTORY Old French *desmanteler*

dismay vb **1** to fill with alarm or depression ▷ n **2** a feeling of alarm or depression ▶ HISTORY Old French *des-* (intensive) + *esmayer* to frighten

dismember vb **1** to remove the limbs of **2** to cut to pieces > **dismemberment** n

dismiss vb **1** to remove (an employee) from a job **2** to allow (someone) to leave **3** to put out of one's mind; no longer think about **4** (of a judge) to state that (a case) will not be brought to trial **5** *cricket* to bowl out (a side) for a particular number of runs ▶ HISTORY Latin *dis-* from + *mittere* to send > **dismissal** n > **dismissive** adj

dismount vb to get off a horse or bicycle

disobedient adj refusing to obey > **disobedience** n

disobey vb to neglect or refuse to obey (a person or an order)

disobliging adj unwilling to help

disorder n **1** a state of untidiness and disorganization **2** public violence or rioting **3** an illness > **disordered** adj

disorderly adj **1** untidy and disorganized **2** uncontrolled; unruly **3** *law* violating public peace

disorganize or **-ise** vb **-izing, -ized** or **-ising, -ised** to disrupt the arrangement or system of > **disorganization** or **-isation** n

disorientate or **disorient** vb **-tating, -tated** or **-enting, -ented** to cause (someone) to lose his or her bearings > **disorientation** n

disown vb to deny any connection with (someone)

disparage vb **-aging, -aged** to speak contemptuously of ▶ HISTORY Old French *desparagier* > **disparagement** n > **disparaging** adj

disparate adj utterly different in kind ▶ HISTORY Latin *disparare* to divide > **disparity** n

dispassionate adj not influenced by emotion; objective > **dispassionately** adv

dispatch or **despatch** vb **1** to send off to a destination or to perform a task **2** to carry out (a duty or task) promptly **3** to murder ▷ n **4** an official communication or report, sent in haste **5** a report sent to a newspaper by a correspondent **6** murder **7** **with dispatch** quickly ▶ HISTORY Italian *dispacciare*

dispatch rider n *Brit, Austral & NZ* a motorcyclist who carries dispatches

dispel vb **-pelling, -pelled** to disperse or drive away ▶ HISTORY Latin *dispellere*

dispensable adj not essential; expendable

dispensary n, pl **-ries** a place where medicine is prepared and given out

dispensation n **1** the act of distributing or dispensing **2** *chiefly RC Church* permission to dispense with an obligation of church law **3** any exemption from an obligation **4** the ordering of life and events by God

dispense vb **-pensing, -pensed 1** to distribute in portions **2** to prepare and distribute (medicine) **3** to administer (the law, etc.) **4** **dispense with** to do away with or manage without ▶ HISTORY Latin *dispendere* to weigh out > **dispenser** n

dispensing optician n See **optician** (sense 2)

disperse vb **-persing, -persed 1** to scatter over a wide area **2** to leave or cause to leave a gathering: *police dispersed rioters* **3** to separate (light) into its different wavelengths **4** to separate (particles) throughout a solid, liquid, or gas ▶ HISTORY Latin *dispergere* to scatter widely > **dispersal** or **dispersion** n

dispersed settlement n *geog* a pattern of settlement found in rural areas in which dwellings are scattered rather than clustered together. Compare **nucleated settlement**

dispirit vb to make downhearted > **dispirited** adj > **dispiriting** adj

displace vb **-placing, -placed 1** to move (something) from its usual place **2** to remove (someone) from a post or position of authority

displaced person n a person forced from his or her home or country, esp. by war or revolution

displacement n **1** the act of displacing **2** *physics* the weight or volume of liquid displaced by an object submerged or floating in it **3** *maths* the distance measured in a particular direction from a reference point. Symbol: *s*

displacement reaction n *chem* a chemical reaction where one element displaces another in a compound

display vb **1** to show **2** to reveal or make evident: *to display anger* ▷ n **3** the act of exhibiting or displaying **4** something displayed **5** an exhibition **6** *electronics* a device capable of representing information visually, as on a screen **7** *zool* a pattern of behaviour by which an animal attracts attention while courting, defending its territory, etc. ▶ HISTORY Anglo-French *despleier* to unfold

display advertisement n (in a magazine or newspaper) an eye-catching, often full-page, advertisement

displease vb **-pleasing, -pleased** to annoy or offend (someone) > **displeasure** n

disport vb **disport oneself** to indulge oneself in pleasure ▶ HISTORY Anglo-French *desporter*

disposable adj **1** designed for disposal after use: *disposable cigarette lighters* **2** available for use if needed: *disposable capital*

disposal n **1** the act or means of getting rid of something **2** **at one's disposal** available for use

dispose vb **-posing, -posed 1** **dispose of a** to throw away **b** to give, sell, or transfer to another **c** to deal with or settle: *I disposed of that problem right away* **d** to kill **2** to arrange or place in a particular way: *around them are disposed the moulded masks of witch doctors* ▶ HISTORY Latin *disponere* to set in different places

disposed adj **1** willing or eager (to do something): *few would feel disposed to fault his judgment* **2** having an inclination as specified (towards someone or something): *my people aren't too well disposed towards defectors*

disposition *n* **1** a person's usual temperament **2** a tendency or habit **3** arrangement; layout

dispossess *vb* to deprive (someone) of (a possession) > **dispossessed** *adj* > **dispossession** *n*

disproportion *n* lack of proportion or equality

disproportionate *adj* out of proportion > **disproportionately** *adv*

disprove *vb* **-proving, -proved** to show (an assertion or claim) to be incorrect

dispute *n* **1** a disagreement between workers and their employer **2** an argument between two or more people ▷ *vb* **-puting, -puted 3** to argue or quarrel about (something) **4** to doubt the validity of **5** to fight over possession of **6 beyond dispute** unable to be questioned or denied: *it's beyond dispute that tensions already existed between them* ▶ HISTORY Latin *disputare* to discuss > **disputation** *n* > **disputatious** *adj*

disqualify *vb* **-fies, -fying, -fied 1** to officially ban (someone) from doing something: *he was disqualified from driving for ten years* **2** to make ineligible, as for entry to an examination > **disqualification** *n*

disquiet *n* **1** a feeling of anxiety or uneasiness ▷ *vb* **2** to make (someone) anxious > **disquieting** *adj* > **disquietude** *n*

disquisition *n* a formal written or oral examination of a subject

disregard *vb* **1** to give little or no attention to; ignore ▷ *n* **2** lack of attention or respect

disrepair *n* the condition of being worn out or in poor working order

disreputable *adj* having or causing a bad reputation > **disreputably** *adv*

disrepute *n* a loss or lack of good reputation

disrespect *n* contempt or lack of respect > **disrespectful** *adj*

disrobe *vb* **-robing, -robed** *literary* to undress

disrupt *vb* to interrupt the progress of ▶ HISTORY Latin *disruptus* burst asunder > **disruption** *n* > **disruptive** *adj*

dissatisfied *adj* displeased or discontented > **dissatisfaction** *n*

dissect *vb* **1** to cut open (a corpse) to examine it **2** to examine critically and minutely: *the above conclusion causes one to dissect that policy more closely* ▶ HISTORY Latin *dissecare* > **dissection** *n*

dissemble *vb* **-bling, -bled** to conceal one's real motives or emotions by pretence ▶ HISTORY Latin *dissimulare* > **dissembler** *n*

disseminate *vb* **-nating, -nated** to spread (information, ideas, etc.) widely ▶ HISTORY Latin *disseminare* > **dissemination** *n*

dissension *n* disagreement and argument ▶ HISTORY Latin *dissentire* to dissent

dissent *vb* **1** to disagree **2** *Christianity* to reject the doctrines of an established church ▷ *n* **3** a disagreement **4** *Christianity* separation from an established church ▶ HISTORY Latin *dissentire* to

disagree > **dissenter** *n* > **dissenting** *adj*

Dissenter *n* *Christianity, chiefly Brit* a Protestant who refuses to conform to the established church

dissentient *adj* dissenting from the opinion of the majority

dissertation *n* **1** a written thesis, usually required for a higher degree **2** a long formal speech ▶ HISTORY Latin *dissertare* to debate

disservice *n* a harmful action

dissident *n* **1** a person who disagrees with a government or a powerful organization ▷ *adj* **2** disagreeing or dissenting ▶ HISTORY Latin *dissidere* to be remote from > **dissidence** *n*

dissimilar *adj* not alike; different > **dissimilarity** *n*

dissimulate *vb* **-lating, -lated** to conceal one's real feelings by pretence > **dissimulation** *n*

dissipate *vb* **-pating, -pated 1** to waste or squander **2** to scatter or break up ▶ HISTORY Latin *dissipare* to disperse

dissipated *adj* showing signs of overindulgence in alcohol or other physical pleasures

dissipation *n* **1** the process of dissipating **2** unrestrained indulgence in physical pleasures **3** *physics* an undesirable loss or lessening of power, which is converted into heat

dissociate *vb* **-ating, -ated 1 dissociate oneself from** to deny or break an association with (a person or organization) **2** to regard or treat as separate > **dissociation** *n*

dissoluble *adj* same as **soluble** ▶ HISTORY Latin *dissolubilis* > **dissolubility** *n*

dissolute *adj* leading an immoral life ▶ HISTORY Latin *dissolutus* loose

dissolution *n* **1** the act of officially breaking up an organization or institution **2** the act of officially ending a formal agreement, such as a marriage **3** the formal ending of a meeting or assembly, such as a Parliament

dissolve *vb* **-solving, -solved 1** to become or cause to become liquid; melt **2** to officially break up (an organization or institution) **3** to formally end: *the campaign started as soon as Parliament was dissolved last month* **4** to collapse emotionally: *she dissolved in loud tears* **5** *films, television* to fade out one scene and replace with another to make two scenes merge imperceptibly ▶ HISTORY Latin *dissolvere* to make loose

dissonance *n* a lack of agreement or harmony between things: *this dissonance of colours* > **dissonant** *adj*

dissuade *vb* **-suading, -suaded** to deter (someone) by persuasion from doing something or believing in something ▶ HISTORY Latin *dissuadere* > **dissuasion** *n*

dissyllable *or* **disyllable** *n* a word of two syllables > **dissyllabic** *or* **disyllabic** *adj*

distaff *n* the rod on which flax is wound for spinning ▶ HISTORY Old English *distæf*

distaff side *n* the female side of a family

distance *n* **1** the space between two points or places **2** the state of being apart **3** a distant place **4** remoteness in manner **5 the distance** the most

239

distant part of the visible scene **6 go the distance** *boxing* to complete a bout without being knocked out **7 keep one's distance** to maintain a reserved attitude to another person ▷ *vb* **-tancing, -tanced 8 distance oneself** *or* **be distanced from** to separate oneself or be separated mentally from

distance learning *n* a teaching system involving video and written material for studying at home

distant *adj* **1** far apart **2** separated by a specified distance: *five kilometres distant* **3** apart in relationship: *a distant cousin* **4** going to a faraway place **5** remote in manner; aloof **6** abstracted: *a distant look entered her eyes* ▶ HISTORY Latin *dis-* apart + *stare* to stand > **distantly** *adv*

distaste *n* a dislike of something offensive

distasteful *adj* unpleasant or offensive > **distastefulness** *n*

distemper¹ *n* a highly contagious viral disease that can affect young dogs ▶ HISTORY Latin *dis-* apart + *temperare* to regulate

distemper² *n* **1** paint mixed with water, glue, etc. which is used for painting walls ▷ *vb* **2** to paint with distemper ▶ HISTORY Latin *dis-* (intensive) + *temperare* to mingle

distend *vb* to expand by pressure from within; swell ▶ HISTORY Latin *distendere* > **distensible** *adj* > **distension** *n*

distich (**diss**-stick) *n prosody* a unit of two verse lines ▶ HISTORY Greek *di-* two + *stikhos* row, line

distil *or US* **distill** *vb* **-tilling, -tilled 1** to subject to or obtain by distillation **2** to give off (a substance) in drops **3** to extract the essence of ▶ HISTORY Latin *de-* down + *stillare* to drip

distillation *n* **1** the process of evaporating a liquid and condensing its vapour **2** Also: **distillate** a concentrated essence

distiller *n* a person or company that makes spirits

distillery *n, pl* **-eries** a place where alcoholic drinks are made by distillation

distinct *adj* **1** not the same; different: *these two areas produce wines with distinct characteristics* **2** clearly seen, heard, or recognized: *it is not possible to draw a distinct line between the two categories; there's a distinct smell of burning* **3** clear and definite: *there is a distinct possibility of rain* **4** obvious: *a distinct improvement* ▶ HISTORY Latin *distinctus* > **distinctly** *adv*

distinction *n* **1** the act of distinguishing or differentiating **2** a distinguishing feature **3** the state of being different or distinguishable **4** special honour, recognition, or fame **5** excellence of character **6** a symbol of honour or rank

distinctive *adj* easily recognizable; characteristic > **distinctively** *adv* > **distinctiveness** *n*

distinguish *vb* **1** to make, show, or recognize a difference: *I have tried to distinguish between fact and theory* **2** to be a distinctive feature of: *what distinguishes the good teenage reader from the less competent one?* **3** to make out by hearing, seeing, or tasting: *she listened but could distinguish nothing*

except the urgency of their discussion **4 distinguish oneself** to make oneself noteworthy ▶ HISTORY Latin *distinguere* to separate > **distinguishable** *adj* > **distinguishing** *adj*

distinguished *adj* **1** dignified in appearance or behaviour **2** highly respected: *a distinguished historian*

distort *vb* **1** to alter or misrepresent (facts) **2** to twist out of shape; deform **3** *electronics* to reproduce or amplify (a signal) inaccurately ▶ HISTORY Latin *distorquere* to turn different ways > **distorted** *adj* > **distortion** *n*

distract *vb* **1** to draw (a person or his or her attention) away from something **2** to amuse or entertain ▶ HISTORY Latin *distrahere* to pull in different directions

distracted *adj* unable to concentrate because one's mind is on other things

distraction *n* **1** something that diverts the attention **2** something that serves as an entertainment **3** mental turmoil

distrain *vb law* to seize (personal property) to enforce payment of a debt ▶ HISTORY Latin *di-* apart + *stringere* to draw tight > **distraint** *n*

distrait (diss-**tray**) *adj* absent-minded or abstracted ▶ HISTORY French

distraught (diss-**trawt**) *adj* upset or agitated ▶ HISTORY obsolete *distract*

distress *n* **1** extreme unhappiness or worry **2** great physical pain **3** financial trouble ▷ *vb* **4** to upset badly **5 in distress** in dire need of help ▶ HISTORY Latin *districtus* divided in mind > **distressing** *adj* > **distressingly** *adv*

distressed *adj* **1** much troubled; upset **2** in great physical pain **3** in financial difficulties **4** (of furniture or fabric) having signs of ageing artificially applied

distributary *n, pl* **-taries** one of several outlet streams draining a river, esp. on a delta

distribute *vb* **-uting, -uted 1** to hand out or deliver (leaflets, mail, etc.) **2** to share (something) among the members of a particular group ▶ HISTORY Latin *distribuere*

distribution *n* **1** the delivering of leaflets, mail, etc. to individual people or organizations **2** the sharing out of something among a particular group **3** the arrangement or spread of anything over an area, space, or period of time: *the unequal distribution of wealth* **4** *commerce* the process of satisfying the demand for goods and services

distribution chain *n commerce* a system of businesses through which goods are moved until they reach the consumer

distributive *adj* **1** of or relating to distribution **2** *maths* of the rule that the same result is produced when multiplication is performed on a set of numbers as when performed on the members of the set individually

distributor *n* **1** a wholesaler who distributes goods to retailers in a specific area **2** the device in a petrol engine that sends the electric current to the sparking plugs

district n **1** an area of land regarded as an administrative or geographical unit **2** an area which has recognizable or special features: an upper-class residential district ▶ HISTORY Medieval Latin districtus area of jurisdiction

district court judge n Austral & NZ a judge presiding over a lower court

district nurse n (in Britain) a nurse who attends to patients in their homes within a particular district

distrust vb **1** to regard as untrustworthy ▷ n **2** a feeling of suspicion or doubt > **distrustful** adj

disturb vb **1** to intrude on; interrupt **2** to upset or worry **3** to disarrange; muddle **4** to inconvenience ▶ HISTORY Latin disturbare > **disturbing** adj > **disturbingly** adv

disturbance n **1** an interruption or intrusion **2** an unruly outburst in public

disturbed adj psychiatry emotionally upset, troubled, or maladjusted

disunite vb **-niting, -nited** to cause disagreement among > **disunion** n > **disunity** n

disuse n the state of being neglected or no longer used; neglect

disused adj no longer used

disyllable n same as **dissyllable**

ditch n **1** a narrow channel dug in the earth for drainage or irrigation ▷ vb **2** slang to abandon or discard: she ditched her boyfriend last month ▶ HISTORY Old English díc

dither vb **1** chiefly Brit & NZ to be uncertain or indecisive ▷ n **2** chiefly Brit a state of indecision or agitation ▶ HISTORY Middle English didder > **ditherer** n > **dithery** adj

dithyramb n (in ancient Greece) a passionate choral hymn in honour of Dionysus ▶ HISTORY Greek dithurambos > **dithyrambic** adj

ditto n, pl **-tos 1** the above; the same: used in lists to avoid repetition, and represented by the mark (,,) placed under the thing repeated ▷ adv **2** in the same way ▶ HISTORY Italian (dialect) detto said

ditty n, pl **-ties** written a short simple song or poem ▶ HISTORY Latin dictare to say repeatedly

diuretic (die-yoor-**et**-ik) n a drug that increases the flow of urine ▶ HISTORY Greek dia- through + ourein to urinate

diurnal (die-**urn**-al) adj **1** happening during the day or daily **2** (of animals) active during the day ▶ HISTORY Latin diurnus

diurnal range n meteorol the difference between the highest and lowest temperatures over a 24-hour period

diva n, pl **-vas** or **-ve** a distinguished female singer; prima donna ▶ HISTORY Latin: a goddess

divalent adj chem having two valencies or a valency of two > **divalency** n

divan n **a** a low bed with a thick base under the mattress **b** a couch with no back or arms ▶ HISTORY Turkish dīvān

dive vb **diving, dived** or US **dove, dived 1** to plunge headfirst into water **2** (of a submarine or diver) to submerge under water **3** (of a bird or aircraft) to fly in a steep nose-down descending path **4** to move quickly in a specified direction: he dived for the door **5 dive in** or **into a** to put (one's hand) quickly or forcefully (into) **b** to start doing (something) enthusiastically ▷ n **6** a headlong plunge into water **7** the act of diving **8** a steep nose-down descent of a bird or aircraft **9** slang a disreputable bar or club ▶ HISTORY Old English dýfan

dive bomber n a military aircraft designed to release bombs on a target during a dive > **dive-bomb** vb

diver n **1** a person who works or explores underwater **2** a person who dives for sport **3** a large diving bird of northern oceans with a straight pointed bill and webbed feet

diverge vb **-verging, -verged 1** to separate and go in different directions **2** to be at variance; differ: the two books diverge in setting and in style **3** to deviate (from a prescribed course) ▶ HISTORY Latin dis- apart + vergere to turn > **divergence** n > **divergent** adj

divergence zone n geol a zone where tectonic plates move apart and new crust and lithosphere are formed; characterized by earthquakes and volcanic activity. Compare **convergence zone**

diverse adj **1** having variety; assorted **2** different in kind ▶ HISTORY Latin diversus turned in different directions

diversify vb **-fies, -fying, -fied 1** to create different forms of; vary **2** econ (of a business) to vary the products or services offered in order to increase profits or reduce risk **3** econ to distribute investments among several securities in order to spread risk ▶ HISTORY Latin diversus different + facere to make > **diversification** n

diversion n **1** chiefly Brit an official detour used by traffic when a main route is closed **2** something that distracts someone's attention or concentration **3** the act of diverting from a specified course **4** a pleasant or amusing pastime or activity > **diversionary** adj

diversity n **1** the quality of being different or varied **2** a point of difference

divert vb **1** to change the course or direction of (traffic) **2** to distract the attention of **3** to entertain or amuse ▶ HISTORY Latin divertere to turn aside

diverticulitis n inflammation of pouches in the wall of the colon, causing lower abdominal pain ▶ HISTORY Latin deverticulum path, track

divertimento n, pl **-ti** a piece of entertaining music in several movements ▶ HISTORY Italian

divest vb **1** to strip (of clothes) **2** to deprive of a role, function, or quality: the chairman felt duty-bound to stay with the company after it was divested of all its aviation interests ▶ HISTORY earlier devest

divide vb **-viding, -vided 1** to separate into parts **2** to share or be shared out in parts **3** to disagree or cause to disagree: experts are divided over the plan **4** to keep apart or be a boundary between

241

d

5 to categorize or classify **6** to calculate how many times one number can be contained in another ▷ *n* **7** a division or split **8** *chiefly US & Canad* an area of high ground separating drainage basins ▶ HISTORY Latin *dividere* to force apart

dividend *n* **1** a portion of a company's profits paid to its shareholders **2** an extra benefit: *Saudi progressives saw a dividend to the crisis* **3** a number to be divided by another number ▶ HISTORY Latin *dividendum* what is to be divided

divider *n* a screen placed so as to divide a room into separate areas

dividers *pl n* compasses with two pointed arms, used for measuring or dividing lines

divination *n* the art of discovering future events as though by supernatural powers

divine *adj* **1** of God or a god **2** godlike **3** *informal* splendid or perfect ▷ *n* **4** a priest who is learned in theology ▷ *vb* **-vining, -vined** **5** to discover (something) by intuition or guessing ▶ HISTORY Latin *divus* a god > **divinely** *adv* > **diviner** *n*

diving bell *n* a diving apparatus with an open bottom, supplied with compressed air from above

diving board *n* a platform from which swimmers may dive

diving suit *n* a waterproof suit used for diving with a detachable helmet and an air supply

divining rod *n* a forked twig said to move when held over ground in which water or metal is to be found

divinity *n*, *pl* **-ties** **1** the study of religion **2** a god or goddess **3** the state of being divine

divisible *adj* capable of being divided > **divisibility** *n*

division *n* **1** the separation of something into two or more distinct parts **2** the act of dividing or sharing out **3** one of the parts into which something is divided **4** the mathematical operation of dividing **5** a difference of opinion **6** a part of an organization that has been made into a unit for administrative or other reasons **7** a formal vote in Parliament **8** one of the groups of teams that make up a football or other sports league **9** *Army* a major formation containing the necessary arms to sustain independent combat **10** *biol* one of the major groups into which the plant kingdom is divided, corresponding to a phylum ▶ HISTORY Latin *dividere* to divide > **divisional** *adj*

division sign *n* the symbol ÷, placed between two numbers to indicate that the first number should be divided by the second, as in $12 \div 6 = 2$

divisive (div-**vice**-iv) *adj* tending to cause disagreement: *he played an important role in defusing potentially divisive issues*

divisor *n* a number to be divided into another number

divorce *n* **1** the legal ending of a marriage **2** a separation, esp. one that is permanent ▷ *vb* **-vorcing, -vorced** **3** to separate or be separated by divorce **4** to remove or separate ▶ HISTORY Latin *divertere* to separate

divot *n* a small piece of turf

divulge *vb* **-vulging, -vulged** to make known: *I am not permitted to divulge his name* ▶ HISTORY Latin *divulgare* > **divulgence** *n*

divvy¹ *vb* **-vies, -vying, -vied** • **divvy up** *informal* to divide and share

divvy² *n*, *pl* **-vies** *Brit, informal* a stupid person

Diwali (duh-**wah**-lee) *n* an annual Hindu festival honouring Lakshmi, the goddess of wealth

Dixie *n* the southern states of the US. Also called: **Dixieland** ▶ HISTORY origin unknown

DIY or **d.i.y.** *Brit, Austral & NZ* do-it-yourself

diya or **deya** (**dee**-ya) *n* a small oil lamp, often made of clay, used in some Hindu and Sikh religious festivals ▶ HISTORY Sanskrit

dizzy *adj* **-zier, -ziest** **1** feeling giddy **2** unable to think clearly; confused **3** tending to cause giddiness or confusion ▷ *vb* **-zies, -zying, -zied** **4** to cause to feel giddy or confused ▶ HISTORY Old English *dysig* silly > **dizzily** *adv* > **dizziness** *n*

DJ or **dj** **1** disc jockey **2** *Brit* dinner jacket

djinni or **djinny** *n*, *pl* **djinn** same as **jinni**

dl decilitre(s)

DLitt or **DLit** **1** Doctor of Letters **2** Doctor of Literature ▶ HISTORY Latin *Doctor Litterarum*

dm decimetre(s)

DM Deutschmark

DMus Doctor of Music

DNA deoxyribonucleic acid, the main constituent of the chromosomes of all organisms

DNA fingerprinting or **profiling** *n* same as **genetic fingerprinting**

D-notice *n* *Brit & Austral* an official notice sent to newspapers prohibiting the publication of certain security information ▶ HISTORY from their administrative classification letter

do¹ *vb* **does, doing, did, done** **1** to perform or complete (a deed or action): *we do a fair amount of entertaining* **2** to be adequate: *it's not what I wanted but it will have to do* **3** to provide: *this hotel only does bed and breakfast* **4** to make tidy or elegant: *he watched her do her hair* **5** to improve: *that style does nothing for you* **6** to find an answer to (a problem or puzzle) **7** to conduct oneself: *do as you want* **8** to cause or produce: *herbal teas have active ingredients that can do good* **9** to give or grant: *do me a favour* **10** *spoken* to work at as a course of study or a job **11** to mimic **12** to achieve a particular speed, amount, or rate: *this computer system can do 40 different cross checks; this car can do sixty miles to the gallon* **13 a** used to form questions: *do you like it?* **b** used to intensify positive statements and commands: *tensions do exist* **c** used to form negative statements or commands: *do not talk while I'm talking!* **d** used to replace an earlier verb: *he drinks much more than I do* **14** *informal* to visit (a place) as a tourist: *we plan to do the States this year* **15** *slang* to serve (a period of time) as a prison sentence **16** *informal* to cheat or rob: *I was done out of ten pounds* **17** *slang* **a** to arrest **b** to convict of a crime: *he was done for 3 years for housebreaking* **18** *slang, chiefly Brit* to assault **19** *slang* to take or use (drugs) **20 make do** to manage with whatever is available ▷ *n, pl* **dos** or **do's 21** *informal, chiefly Brit & NZ* a party or other social event **22 do's and don'ts** *informal* rules ▷ See also **do away with** ▶ HISTORY Old English *dōn*

do² *n, pl* **dos** *music* same as **doh**

do away with *vb* to get rid of (someone or something)

Doberman pinscher *or* **Doberman** *n* a large dog with a glossy black-and-tan coat ▶ HISTORY after L. *Dobermann*, dog breeder

dob in *vb* **dobbing, dobbed** *Austral & NZ, informal* **1** to inform against **2** to contribute to a fund

doc *n informal* same as **doctor**

DOC (in New Zealand) Department of Conservation

docile *adj* (of a person or animal) easily controlled ▶ HISTORY Latin *docilis* easily taught > **docilely** *adv* > **docility** *n*

dock¹ *n* **1** an enclosed area of water where ships are loaded, unloaded, or repaired **2** a wharf or pier ▷ *vb* **3** to moor or be moored at a dock **4** to link (two spacecraft) or (of two spacecraft) to be linked together in space ▶ HISTORY Middle Dutch *docke*

dock² *vb* **1** to deduct (an amount) from (a person's wages) **2** to remove part of (an animal's tail) by cutting through the bone ▶ HISTORY Middle English *dok*

dock³ *n* an enclosed space in a court of law where the accused person sits or stands ▶ HISTORY Flemish *dok* sty

dock⁴ *n* a weed with broad leaves ▶ HISTORY Old English *docce*

docker *n Brit* a person employed to load and unload ships

docket *n* **1** *chiefly Brit* a label on a package or other delivery, stating contents, delivery instructions, etc. ▷ *vb* **-eting, -eted 2** to fix a docket to (a package or other delivery) ▶ HISTORY origin unknown

dockyard *n* a place where ships are built or repaired

doctor *n* **1** a person licensed to practise medicine **2** a person who has been awarded a doctorate **3** *chiefly US & Canad* a person licensed to practise dentistry or veterinary medicine ▷ *vb* **4** to change in order to deceive: *she confessed to having doctored the figures* **5** *written* to poison or drug (food or drink) **6** to castrate (an animal) ▶ HISTORY Latin: teacher > **doctoral** *adj*

doctorate *n* the highest academic degree in any field of knowledge

doctrinaire *adj* stubbornly insistent on the application of a theory without regard to practicality

doctrine (**dock**-trin) *n* **1** a body of teachings of a religious, political, or philosophical group **2** a principle or body of principles that is taught or advocated ▶ HISTORY Latin *doctrina* teaching > **doctrinal** *adj*

document *n* **1** a piece of paper that provides an official record of something **2** *computing* a

computer file with text or graphics that can be altered using the appropriate software ▷ *vb* **3** to record or report (something) in detail **4** to support (a claim) with evidence ▶ HISTORY Latin *documentum* a lesson

documentary *n, pl* **-ries 1** a film or television programme presenting the facts about a particular subject ▷ *adj* **2** of or based on documents: *vital documentary evidence has been found*

documentation *n* documents supplied as proof or evidence of something

docu-soap *n* a television documentary series presenting the lives of the people filmed as entertainment

dodder *vb* to move unsteadily ▶ HISTORY variant of earlier *dadder* > **dodderer** *n* > **doddery** *adj*

doddle *n Brit, Austral & NZ, informal* something easily accomplished: *the test turned out to be a doddle* ▶ HISTORY origin unknown

dodecagon (doe-**deck**-a-gon) *n* a polygon with twelve sides ▶ HISTORY Greek *dōdeka* twelve + *gōnia* angle

dodecahedron (doe-deck-a-**heed**-ron) *n* a solid figure with twelve plane faces

dodge *vb* **dodging, dodged 1** to avoid being hit, caught, or seen by moving suddenly **2** to evade by cleverness or trickery: *the Government will not be able to dodge the issue* ▷ *n* **3** a cunning and deceitful trick ▶ HISTORY origin unknown

Dodgem *n trademark* a small electric car driven and bumped against similar cars in a rink at a funfair

dodger *n* a person who evades a duty or obligation

dodgy *adj* **dodgier, dodgiest** *Brit, Austral & NZ, informal* **1** dangerous, risky, or unreliable: *he's in a very dodgy political position* **2** untrustworthy: *they considered him a very dodgy character*

dodo *n, pl* **dodos** or **dodoes 1** a large extinct bird that could not fly **2 as dead as a dodo** no longer existing ▶ HISTORY Portuguese *duodo* stupid

do down *vb* to belittle or humiliate: *the moderate constructionist does not wish to do science down*

doe *n, pl* **does** or **doe** the female of the deer, hare, or rabbit ▶ HISTORY Old English *dā*

doek (rhymes with **book**) *n S African, informal* a square of cloth worn on the head by women ▶ HISTORY Afrikaans

does *vb* third person singular of the present tense of **do¹**

doff *vb* to take off or lift (one's hat) in salutation ▶ HISTORY Old English *dōn of*

do for *vb informal* **1** to cause the ruin, death, or defeat of: *I'm done for if this error comes to light* **2** to do housework for **3 do well for oneself** to thrive or succeed

dog *n* **1** a domesticated canine mammal occurring in many different breeds **2** any other member of the dog family, such as the dingo or coyote. *Related adjective:* **canine 3** the male of animals of the dog family **4** *informal* a person: *you lucky dog!* **5** *US & Canad, informal* something unsatisfactory or inferior **6 a dog's life** a wretched existence **7 dog eat dog** ruthless competition **8 like a dog's**

dinner dressed smartly and ostentatiously ▷ *vb* **dogging, dogged 9** to follow (someone) closely **10** to trouble: *dogged by ill health* ▷ See also **dogs** ► HISTORY Old English *docga*

dog box *n Austral & NZ, informal* same as **doghouse**

dogcart *n* a light horse-drawn two-wheeled cart

dog collar *n* **1** a collar for a dog **2** *informal* a clerical collar

dog days *pl n Brit, Austral & NZ* the hottest period of the summer ► HISTORY in ancient times reckoned from the heliacal rising of the Dog Star

doge (doje) *n* (formerly) the chief magistrate of Venice or Genoa ► HISTORY Latin *dux* leader

dog-eared *adj* **1** (of a book) having pages folded down at the corner **2** shabby or worn

dog-end *n Brit, Austral & NZ, informal* a cigarette end

dogfight *n* **1** close-quarters combat between fighter aircraft **2** any rough fight

dogfish *n, pl* **-fish** or **-fishes** a small shark

dogged (**dog**-gid) *adj* obstinately determined > **doggedly** *adv* > **doggedness** *n*

doggerel *n* poorly written, usually comic, verse ► HISTORY Middle English *dogerel* worthless

doggo *adv* **lie doggo** *informal* to hide and keep quiet ► HISTORY probably from *dog*

doggy or **doggie** *n, pl* **-gies 1** a child's word for a **dog** ▷ *adj* **-gier, -giest 2** of or like a dog **3** fond of dogs: *I suppose dogs are all right but doggy folk can be real bores*

doggy bag *n* a bag in which leftovers from a meal may be taken away, supposedly for the diner's dog

doghouse *n* **1** *US & Canad* a kennel **2 in the doghouse** *informal* in disfavour

dogie, dogy or **dogey** (**dohg**-ee) *n, pl* **-gies** or **-geys** *US & Canad* a motherless calf ► HISTORY from *dough-guts*, because they were fed on flour-and-water paste

dogleg *n* a sharp bend

dogma *n* a doctrine or system of doctrines proclaimed by authority as true ► HISTORY Greek: opinion

dogmatic *adj* habitually stating one's opinions in a forceful or arrogant manner > **dogmatically** *adv* > **dogmatism** *n*

do-gooder *n informal* a well-intentioned but naive or impractical person

dog paddle *n* a swimming stroke in which the hands are paddled in imitation of a swimming dog. Also called: **doggy paddle**

dogs *pl n* **1 the dogs** *Brit & Austral, informal* greyhound racing **2 go to the dogs** *informal* to go to ruin physically or morally **3 let sleeping dogs lie** to leave things undisturbed

dogsbody *n, pl* **-bodies** *informal* a person who carries out boring or unimportant tasks for others

dog-tired *adj informal* exhausted

doh or **do** *n music* (in tonic sol-fa) the first note of any ascending major scale

doily or **doyley** *n, pl* **-lies** or **-leys** a decorative lacelike paper mat laid on a plate ► HISTORY after *Doily*, a London draper

do in *vb slang* **1** to kill **2** to exhaust

do-it-yourself *n* the practice of constructing and repairing things oneself

dolce (**dol**-chay) *adv music* sweetly ► HISTORY Italian

doldrums *n* **the doldrums 1 a** a feeling of depression **b** a state of inactivity **2** a belt of sea along the equator noted for absence of winds ► HISTORY probably from Old English *dol* dull

dole *n* **1 the dole** *Brit, Austral & NZ, informal* money received from the state while unemployed **2 on the dole** *Brit, Austral & NZ, informal* receiving benefit while unemployed ▷ *vb* **doling, doled 3 dole out** to distribute in small quantities ► HISTORY Old English *dāl* share

dole bludger *n Austral & NZ, informal* a person who chooses to live off unemployment benefit

doleful *adj* dreary or mournful ► HISTORY from Latin *dolere* to lament > **dolefully** *adv* > **dolefulness** *n*

doll *n* **1** a small model of a human being, used as a toy **2** *slang* a pretty girl or young woman ► HISTORY probably from *Doll*, pet name for *Dorothy*

dollar *n* the standard monetary unit of various countries ► HISTORY Low German *daler*

dollop *n informal* an amount of food served in a lump: *he shook the bottle and added a large dollop of ketchup* ► HISTORY origin unknown

doll up *vb slang* **get dolled up** to dress (oneself) in a stylish or showy manner

dolly *n, pl* **-lies 1** a child's word for a **doll** (sense 1) **2** *films, television* a wheeled support on which a camera may be mounted **3** Also called: **dolly bird** *slang, chiefly Brit* an attractive and fashionable girl

dolman sleeve *n* a sleeve that is very wide at the armhole and tapers to a tight wrist ► HISTORY Turkish *dolaman* a winding round

dolmen *n* a prehistoric monument consisting of a horizontal stone supported by vertical stones, thought to be a tomb ► HISTORY French

dolomite *n* a mineral consisting of calcium magnesium carbonate ► HISTORY after Déodat de *Dolomieu*, mineralogist

dolphin *n* a sea mammal of the whale family, with a long pointed snout ► HISTORY Greek *delphis*

dolphinarium *n* an aquarium for dolphins, esp. one in which they give public displays

dolphinfish *n, pl* **-fish** or **-fishes** any of a number of marine fish caught for food

dolt *n* a stupid person ► HISTORY probably related to Old English *dol* stupid > **doltish** *adj*

domain *n* **1** a particular area of activity or interest **2** land under one ruler or government **3** *computers* a group of computers that have the same suffix in their names on the internet, specifying the country, type of institution, etc. where they are located **4** *NZ* public park ► HISTORY French *domaine*

dome *n* **1** a rounded roof built on a circular base **2** something shaped like this ► HISTORY Latin *domus* house

domed *adj* shaped like a dome

domestic *adj* **1** of one's own country or a specific

country: *the domestic economy was generally better* **2** of the home or family **3** enjoying home or family life: *she was never a very domestic sort of person* **4** intended for use in the home: *the kitchen was equipped with all the latest domestic appliances* **5** (of an animal) bred or kept as a pet or for the supply of food ▷ *n* **6** a household servant ▶ **HISTORY** Latin *domesticus* belonging to the house > **domestically** *adv*

domesticate *vb* **-cating, -cated 1** to bring or keep (wild animals or plants) under control or cultivation **2** to accustom (someone) to home life > **domestication** *n*

domesticity *n*, *pl* **-ties 1** home life **2** devotion to home life

domestic science *n* the study of cooking, needlework, and other household skills

domicile (**dom**-miss-ile) *n formal* a person's regular dwelling place ▶ **HISTORY** Latin *domus* house > **domiciliary** *adj*

dominant *adj* **1** having control, authority, or influence: *a dominant leader* **2** main or chief: *coal is still, worldwide, the dominant fuel* **3** *genetics* (in a pair of genes) designating the gene that produces a particular character in an organism > **dominance** *n*

dominate *vb* **-nating, -nated 1** to control or govern **2** to tower above (surroundings): *the building had been designed to dominate the city skyscape* **3** to predominate in ▶ **HISTORY** Latin *dominari* to be lord over > **dominating** *adj* > **domination** *n*

dominee (**doom**-in-nee) *n S African* a minister of the Dutch Reformed Church ▶ **HISTORY** Dutch, from Latin *dominus* master

domineering *adj* acting arrogantly or tyrannically ▶ **HISTORY** Dutch *domineren*

Dominican *n* **1** a friar or nun of the Christian order founded by Saint Dominic ▷ *adj* **2** of the Dominican order

dominion *n* **1** control or authority **2** the land governed by one ruler or government **3** (formerly) a self-governing division of the British Empire ▶ **HISTORY** Latin *dominium* ownership

domino¹ *n*, *pl* **-noes** a small rectangular block marked with dots, used in dominoes ▶ **HISTORY** Italian, perhaps from *domino!* master!, said by the winner

domino² *n*, *pl* **noes** or **nos** a large hooded cloak worn with an eye mask at a masquerade ▶ **HISTORY** Latin *dominus* lord, master

dominoes *n* a game in which dominoes with matching halves are laid together

domino theory *n politics* the theory first advanced by President Eisenhower in 1954 that if one Southeast Asian country became communist, the other countries in the region would follow

don¹ *vb written* **donning, donned** to put on (clothing) ▶ **HISTORY** Middle English

don² *n* **1** *Brit* a member of the teaching staff at a university or college **2** a Spanish gentleman or nobleman **3** (in the Mafia) the head of a family

▶ **HISTORY** Latin *dominus* lord

donate *vb* **-nating, -nated** to give (something) to a charity or other organization

donation *n* **1** the act of donating **2** a contribution to a charity or other organization ▶ **HISTORY** Latin *donum* gift

donder *S African, slang vb* **1** to beat (someone) up ▷ *n* **2** a wretch; swine ▶ **HISTORY** Dutch *donderen* to swear, bully

done *vb* **1** the past participle of **do¹** ▷ *interj* **2** *spoken* an expression of agreement: *sixty pounds seems reasonable, done!* ▷ *adj* **3** (of a task) completed **4** (of food) cooked enough **5** used up: *the milk is done* **6** *Brit, Austral & NZ* socially acceptable: *the done thing* **7** *informal* cheated or tricked **8 done in** or **up** *informal* exhausted

doner kebab *n* a dish of grilled minced lamb, served in a split slice of unleavened bread ▶ **HISTORY** Turkish *döner* rotating

dongle *n computers* an electronic device that accompanies software to prevent the unauthorized copying of programs

donjon *n* the heavily fortified central tower of a castle ▶ **HISTORY** archaic variant of *dungeon*

Don Juan *n* a successful seducer of women ▶ **HISTORY** after the legendary Spanish philanderer

donkey *n* **1** a long-eared member of the horse family **2** a person who is considered to be stupid or stubborn ▶ **HISTORY** origin unknown

donkey jacket *n Brit, Austral & NZ* a man's thick hip-length jacket with a waterproof panel across the shoulders

donkey's years *pl n informal* a long time

donkey vote *n Austral politics* a vote in which the voter's order of preference follows the order in which the candidates are listed

donkey-work *n* uninteresting groundwork

donnish *adj* resembling a university don; pedantic or fussy

donor *n* **1** *med* a person who gives blood or organs for use in the treatment of another person **2** a person who makes a donation ▶ **HISTORY** Latin *donare* to give

donor card *n* a card carried by someone to show that the body parts specified may be used for transplants after the person's death

Don Quixote (**don** kee-**hoe**-tee) *n* an impractical idealist ▶ **HISTORY** after the hero of Miguel de Cervantes' novel *Don Quixote de la Mancha*

don't do not

doodle *vb* **-dling, -dled 1** to scribble or draw aimlessly ▷ *n* **2** a shape or picture drawn aimlessly ▶ **HISTORY** originally, a foolish person

doom *n* **1** death or a terrible fate ▷ *vb* **2** to destine or condemn to death or a terrible fate ▶ **HISTORY** Old English *dōm*

doomsday or **domesday** *n* **1** the day on which the Last Judgment will occur **2** any dreaded day ▶ **HISTORY** Old English *dæg* Judgment Day

doona *n Austral* a large quilt used as a bed cover in place of the top sheet and blankets

door *n* **1** a hinged or sliding panel for closing the

entrance to a building, room, or cupboard
2 a doorway or entrance **3** a means of access or escape: *the door to happiness* **4 lay something at someone's door** to blame someone for something **5 out of doors** in the open air ▶ **HISTORY** Old English *duru*

doorjamb *n* one of the two vertical posts that form the sides of a door frame. Also called: **doorpost**

doorman *n, pl* **-men** a man employed to be on duty at the main entrance of a large building

doormat *n* **1** a mat, placed at an entrance, for wiping dirt from shoes **2** *informal* a person who offers little resistance to being treated badly

door-to-door *adj* **1** (of selling) from one house to the next **2** (of a journey) direct

doorway *n* an opening into a building or room

dop *n* S African, informal a tot or small drink, usually alcoholic ▶ **HISTORY** Afrikaans

dope *n* **1** *slang* an illegal drug, such as cannabis **2** a drug administered to a person or animal to affect performance in a race or other sporting competition **3** *informal* a slow-witted person **4** confidential information **5** a thick liquid, such as a lubricant ▷ *vb* **doping, doped 6** to administer a drug to

■ **WORD HISTORY**
■ 'Dope' comes from Dutch *doop*, meaning 'a thick
■ sauce'.

dopey *or* **dopy** *adj* **dopier, dopiest 1** *informal* half-asleep, as when under the influence of a drug **2** *slang* silly

doppelgänger (**dop**-pl-geng-er) *n legend* a ghostly duplicate of a living person ▶ **HISTORY** German *Doppelgänger* double-goer

Doppler effect *n* a change in the apparent frequency of a sound or light wave as a result of relative motion between the observer and the source ▶ **HISTORY** after C. J. *Doppler*, physicist

DORA English law Defence of the Realm Act: a law passed in 1914 giving the state more powers

Doric *adj* **1** of a style of classical architecture characterized by a heavy fluted column and a simple capital ▷ *n* **2** a rustic dialect, esp. a Scots one ▶ **HISTORY** *Doris*, in ancient Greece

dormant *adj* **1** temporarily quiet, inactive, or not being used **2** *biol* alive but in a resting condition **3** *geol* (of a volcano) not extinct but not recently active ▶ **HISTORY** Latin *dormire* to sleep > **dormancy** *n*

dormer *or* **dormer window** *n* a window that is built upright in a sloping roof ▶ **HISTORY** Latin *dormitorium* dormitory

dormitory *n, pl* **-ries 1** a large room, esp. at a school, containing several beds **2** a building, esp. at a college, providing living accommodation ▷ *adj* **3** Brit & Austral denoting an area from which most of the residents commute to work: *the swelling suburban dormitory areas* ▶ **HISTORY** Latin *dormitorium*, from *dormire* to sleep

Dormobile *n trademark* a vanlike vehicle specially equipped for living in while travelling

dormouse *n, pl* **-mice** a small rodent resembling a mouse with a furry tail ▶ **HISTORY** origin unknown

dorothy dixer *n* Austral Parliament, informal a prearranged question put to a minister which gives him or her the opportunity to praise the government or criticize the opposition

dorp *n* S African a small town or village ▶ **HISTORY** Dutch

dorsal *adj* anat, zool of or on the back ▶ **HISTORY** Latin *dorsum* back

dory *n, pl* **-ries** a spiny-finned food fish. Also called: **John Dory** ▶ **HISTORY** French *dorée* gilded

DOS *computers* disk operating system

dose *n* **1** a specific quantity of a medicine taken at one time **2** *informal* something unpleasant to experience: *a dose of the cold* **3** the total energy of radiation absorbed ▷ *vb* **dosing, dosed 4** to administer a quantity of medicine to (someone) ▶ **HISTORY** Greek *dosis* a giving > **dosage** *n*

dosh *n slang* money

dosing strip *n* (in New Zealand) an area for treating dogs suspected of having hydatid disease

doss *vb slang* **1 doss down** to sleep on a makeshift bed **2** to pass time aimlessly: *I doss around a lot* ▷ *n* **3** a task requiring little effort ▶ **HISTORY** origin unknown

dosshouse *n slang* a cheap lodging house for homeless people

dossier (**doss**-ee-ay) *n* a collection of papers about a subject or person ▶ **HISTORY** French

dot *n* **1** a small round mark **2** the small round mark used to represent the short sound in Morse code **3 on the dot** at exactly the arranged time ▷ *vb* **dotting, dotted 4** to mark with a dot **5** to scatter or intersperse: *there are numerous churches dotted around Rome* **6 dot one's i's and cross one's t's** *informal* to pay meticulous attention to detail ▶ **HISTORY** Old English *dott* head of a boil

dotage *n* feebleness of mind as a result of old age ▶ **HISTORY** Middle English *doten* to dote

dotcom *or* **dot.com** *n* a company that conducts most of its business on the internet ▶ **HISTORY** from *.com*, the domain name suffix of businesses trading on the internet

dote *vb* **doting, doted** • **dote on** *or* **upon** to love (someone or something) to an excessive degree ▶ **HISTORY** Middle English *doten* > **doting** *adj*

dot map *n geog* a map using dots representing a particular numerical value to show the distribution of something such as population or rainfall

dotterel *n* a shore bird with reddish-brown underparts and white bands around the head and neck ▶ **HISTORY** Middle English *dotrelle*

dottle *n* the tobacco left in a pipe after smoking ▶ **HISTORY** obsolete *dot* lump

dotty *adj* **-tier, -tiest** *slang* slightly crazy ▶ **HISTORY** from *dot* > **dottiness** *n*

double *adj* **1** as much again in size, strength, number, etc.: *a double scotch* **2** composed of two equal or similar parts **3** designed for two users: *a double bed* **4** folded in half: *the blanket had been folded double* **5** stooping: *she was bent double over the flower* *bed* **6** ambiguous: *a double meaning* **7** false, deceitful, or hypocritical: *double standards* **8** *music* (of an instrument) sounding an octave lower: *a double bass* ▷ *adv* **9** twice over: *that's double the amount requested* ▷ *n* **10** twice the size, strength, number, etc. **11** a double measure of spirits **12** a person who closely resembles another person **13** a bet on two horses in different races in which any winnings from the first race are placed on the horse in the later race. **14 at** *or* **on the double** quickly or immediately ▷ *vb* **-bling, -bled** **15** to make or become twice as much **16** to bend or fold so that one part covers another **17** to play two parts or serve two roles **18** to turn sharply **19** *Bridge* to make a call that will double certain scoring points if the preceding bid becomes the contract **20 double for** to act as substitute ▷ See also **doubles** ▶ HISTORY Latin *duplus* twofold > **doubler** *n*

double agent *n* a spy employed by two enemy countries at the same time

double-barrelled *or US* **-barreled** *adj* **1** (of a gun) having two barrels **2** *Brit* (of a surname) having hyphenated parts

double bass *n* a stringed instrument, the largest and lowest member of the violin family

double-breasted *adj* (of a garment) having overlapping fronts

double-check *vb* to make certain by checking again

double chin *n* a fold of fat under the chin

double cream *n* *Brit & Austral* thick cream with a high fat content

double-cross *vb* **1** to cheat or betray ▷ *n* **2** an instance of double-crossing

double-dealing *n* treacherous or deceitful behaviour

double-decker *n* **1** *chiefly Brit* a bus with two passenger decks one on top of the other ▷ *adj* **2** *informal* having two layers: *a double-decker sandwich*

double dissolution *n* *Austral Parliament* the simultaneous dissolution of both houses of the federal parliament, allowed for in the Australian Constitution in cases of deadlock over the approval of a law

double Dutch *n* *informal* speech or writing that is difficult to understand: *it was double Dutch to me*

double-edged *adj* **1** (of a remark) malicious in intent though apparently complimentary **2** (of a knife) having a cutting edge on either side of the blade

double entendre (doob-bl on-**tond**-ra) *n* a word or phrase with two interpretations, esp. with one meaning that is rude ▶ HISTORY obsolete French

double entry *n* a book-keeping system in which a transaction is entered as a debit in one account and as a credit in another

double glazing *n* a window consisting of two layers of glass separated by a space, fitted to reduce heat loss

double helix *n* *biochem* the form of the molecular structure of DNA, consisting of two helical chains linked by hydrogen bonds and coiled around the same axis

double jeopardy rule *n* *law* the principle that a defendant cannot be prosecuted a second time for an offence for which he or she has already been tried

double-jointed *adj* (of a person) having unusually flexible joints

double negative *n* a grammatical construction, considered incorrect, in which two negatives are used where one is needed, for example *I wouldn't never have believed it*

double-page spread *n* *journalism* (in a newspaper or magazine) two facing pages devoted to a single article, picture, or series of related images

double-park *vb* to park (a vehicle) alongside another vehicle, causing an obstruction

double pneumonia *n* pneumonia affecting both lungs

doubles *n* **1** a game between two pairs of players **2** (in Trinidad and Tobago) a street food comprising two fried thin pancakes with a filling of spicy chickpeas

double standard *n* a set of principles that allows greater freedom to one person or group than to another

doublet (**dub**-lit) *n* *history* a man's close-fitting jacket, with or without sleeves ▶ HISTORY Old French

double take *n* a delayed reaction by a person to a remark or situation: *she did a double take when he said he was leaving*

double talk *n* deceptive or ambiguous talk

double time *n* **1** *Brit, Austral & NZ* a doubled wage rate sometimes paid for overtime work **2** *music* two beats per bar

double whammy *n* *informal, chiefly US* a devastating setback made up of two elements

doubloon *n* a former Spanish gold coin ▶ HISTORY Spanish *doblón*

doubly *adv* **1** to or in a greater degree, quantity, or measure: *I have to be doubly careful* **2** in two ways: *the defence debate was doubly complicated*

doubt *n* **1** uncertainty about the truth, facts, or existence of something **2** an unresolved difficulty or point **3 give someone the benefit of the doubt** accept that someone is speaking the truth **4 no doubt** almost certainly ▷ *vb* **5** to be inclined to disbelieve: *I doubt that we are late* **6** to distrust or be suspicious of: *he doubted their motives* ▶ HISTORY Latin *dubitare* to hesitate > **doubter** *n*

doubtful *adj* **1** unlikely or improbable: *it's doubtful that I will marry again* **2** unsure or uncertain: *I was doubtful about some of his ideas* > **doubtfully** *adv* > **doubtfulness** *n*

doubtless *adv* probably or almost certainly: *somebody will know and doubtless somebody will ring us*

douche (**doosh**) *n* **1** a stream of water directed onto or into the body for cleansing or medical

d

purposes **2** an instrument for applying a douche ▷ vb **douching, douched 3** to cleanse or treat by means of a douche ▶ HISTORY French

douen (doo-wen) n (in the folklore of Trinidad and Tobago) the soul of a child who died before baptism, condemned to walk the earth for eternity, and feared because it can lure living children to join it ▶ HISTORY from Spanish *duende* ghost

dough n **1** a thick mixture of flour and water or milk, used for making bread, pastry, or biscuits **2** *slang* money ▶ HISTORY Old English *dāg*

doughnut n a small cake of sweetened dough cooked in hot fat

doughty (dowt-ee) adj **-tier, -tiest** *old-fashioned* brave and determined ▶ HISTORY Old English *dohtig*

do up vb **1** to wrap and make into a bundle: *he did up the parcel* **2** to fasten: *to do up one's blouse* **3** to renovate or redecorate

dour (doo-er, dow-er) adj sullen and unfriendly ▶ HISTORY probably from Latin *durus* hard > **dourness** n

douse or **dowse** (rhymes with **mouse**) vb **dousing, doused** or **dowsing, dowsed 1** to drench with water or other liquid **2** to put out (a light) ▶ HISTORY origin unknown

dove n **1** a bird with a heavy body, small head, and short legs **2** *politics* a person opposed to war ▶ HISTORY Old English *dūfe*

dovecote or **dovecot** n a box, shelter, or part of a house built for doves or pigeons to live in

dovetail n **1** Also called: **dovetail joint** a wedge-shaped joint used to fit two pieces of wood tightly together ▷ vb **2** to fit together closely or neatly: *her resignation dovetails well with the new structure*

dowager n a woman possessing property or a title obtained from her dead husband ▶ HISTORY Old French *douagiere*

dowdy adj **-dier, -diest** wearing dull and unfashionable clothes ▶ HISTORY Middle English *dowd* slut > **dowdily** adv > **dowdiness** n

dowel n a wooden or metal peg that fits into two corresponding holes to join larger pieces of wood or metal together ▶ HISTORY Middle Low German *dövel* plug

dower n **1** the life interest in a part of her husband's estate allotted to a widow by law **2** *archaic* a dowry ▶ HISTORY Latin *dos* gift

do with vb **1 could do with** need or would benefit from: *I could do with some royal treatment* **2 have to do with** to be associated with: *his illness has a lot to do with his failing the exam* **3 to do with** concerning; related to: *this book has to do with the occult*

do without vb to manage without

down¹ prep **1** from a higher to a lower position in or on **2** at a lower or further level or position on, in, or along: *I wandered down the corridor* ▷ adv **3** at or to a lower level or position: *he bent down* **4** indicating lowering or destruction: *to bring down an aircraft* **5** indicating intensity or completion: *calm down and*

mind your manners **6** immediately: *cash down* **7** on paper: *she copied it down* **8** *spoken* away from a more important place: *he came down from head office* **9** reduced to a state of lack: *he was down to his last pound* **10** lacking a specified amount: *down several pounds* **11** lower in price **12** from an earlier to a later time: *the ring was handed down from my grandmother* **13** to a finer state: *to grind down* **14** *sport* being a specified number of points or goals behind an opponent **15** (of a person) being inactive, owing to illness: *down with the cold* ▷ adj **16** depressed or unhappy: *he seems very down today* **17** made in cash: *a down payment* ▷ vb **18** *informal* to eat or drink quickly ▷ n **19 have a down on** *spoken, informal* to feel hostile towards: *you seem to have a down on the family tonight* ▶ HISTORY Old English *dūne* from the hill

down² n soft fine feathers ▶ HISTORY Old Norse *dūnn* > **downy** adj

down-and-out n **1** a person who is homeless and destitute ▷ adj **2** without any means of support; destitute

downbeat adj *informal* **1** depressed or gloomy: *she was in one of her downbeat moods* **2** casual and restrained: *the chairman's statement was decidedly downbeat* ▷ n **3** *music* the first beat of a bar

downcast adj **1** sad and dejected **2** (of the eyes) directed downwards

downer n *slang* **1** a barbiturate, tranquillizer, or narcotic **2 on a downer** in a state of depression

downfall n **1** a sudden loss of position or reputation **2** the cause of this

downgrade vb **-grading, -graded** to reduce in importance or value

downhearted adj sad and discouraged

downhill adj **1** going or sloping down ▷ adv **2** towards the bottom of a hill **3 go downhill** *informal* to deteriorate

Downing Street n the British prime minister or the British government ▶ HISTORY after the street in London which contains the official residence of the prime minister and the chancellor of the exchequer

download vb **1** to transfer (data) from the memory of one computer to that of another ▷ n **2** a file transferred in this way

down-market adj cheap, popular, and of poor quality

down payment n the deposit paid on an item purchased on hire-purchase, mortgage, etc.: *an initial down payment is usually required*

downpour n a heavy continuous fall of rain

downright adv, adj extreme or extremely: *it's just downright cruel*

downs pl n an area of low grassy hills, esp. in S England

downshifting n the practice of simplifying one's lifestyle and becoming less materialistic

downside n the disadvantageous aspect of a situation: *the downside of capitalism*

downsize vb **1** to reduce the number of people employed by (a company) **2** to reduce the size of or produce a smaller version of (something)

Down's syndrome n pathol a genetic disorder characterized by a flat face, slanting eyes, and learning difficulties ▶ HISTORY after John Langdon-Down, physician

downstage theatre adv **1** at or towards the front of the stage ▷ adj **2** of or relating to the front of the stage

downstairs adv **1** down the stairs; to or on a lower floor ▷ n **2** a lower or ground floor

downstream adv, adj in or towards the lower part of a stream; with the current

downtime n commerce time during which a computer or other machine is not working

down-to-earth adj sensible or practical

downtown chiefly US, Canad & NZ n **1** the central or lower part of a city, esp. the main commercial area ▷ adv **2** towards, to, or into this area

downtrodden adj oppressed and lacking the will to resist

downturn n a drop in the success of an economy or a business

down under informal n **1** Australia or New Zealand ▷ adv **2** in or to Australia or New Zealand

downward adj **1** descending from a higher to a lower level, condition, or position ▷ adv **2** same as **downwards** > **downwardly** adv

downwards or **downward** adv **1** from a higher to a lower level, condition, or position **2** from an earlier time or source to a later one

downwind adv, adj in the same direction towards which the wind is blowing; with the wind from behind

dowry n, pl **-ries** the property brought by a woman to her husband at marriage ▶ HISTORY Latin dos

dowse (rhymes with **cows**) vb **dowsing, dowsed** to search for underground water or minerals using a divining rod ▶ HISTORY origin unknown > **dowser** n

doxology n, pl **-gies** a hymn or verse of praise to God ▶ HISTORY Greek doxologos uttering praise

doyen (**doy**-en) n the senior member of a group, profession, or society ▶ HISTORY French > **doyenne** (doy-**en**) fem n

doze vb **dozing, dozed 1** to sleep lightly or for a short period **2 doze off** to fall into a light sleep ▷ n **3** a short sleep ▶ HISTORY probably from Old Norse dūs lull

dozen adj, n twelve ▶ HISTORY Latin duodecim > **dozenth** adj

dozy adj **dozier, doziest 1** feeling sleepy **2** Brit, informal stupid and slow-witted

DP displaced person

DPB (in New Zealand) Domestic Purposes Benefit

dpi computers dots per inch

DPP (in Britain) Director of Public Prosecutions

Dr 1 Doctor **2** Drive

drab adj **drabber, drabbest 1** dull and dreary **2** light olive-brown ▶ HISTORY Old French drap cloth > **drabness** n

drachm (**dram**) n Brit a unit of liquid measure equal to one eighth of a fluid ounce (3.55 ml)

▶ HISTORY variant of DRAM

drachma n, pl **-mas** or **-mae** a former monetary unit of Greece ▶ HISTORY Greek drakhmē a handful

draconian adj severe or harsh: draconian measures were taken by the government ▶ HISTORY after Draco, Athenian statesman

draft n **1** a preliminary outline of a letter, book, or speech **2** a written order for payment of money by a bank **3** US & Austral selection for compulsory military service ▷ vb **4** to write a preliminary outline of a letter, book, or speech **5** to send (personnel) from one place to another to carry out a specific job **6** chiefly US to select for compulsory military service ▷ n, vb **7** US same as **draught** ▶ HISTORY variant of DRAUGHT

drag vb **dragging, dragged 1** to pull with force along the ground **2** to trail on the ground **3** to persuade (someone) to go somewhere: he didn't want to come so I had to drag him along **4** to move (oneself) slowly and with difficulty: I had to drag myself out of bed this morning **5** to linger behind: she dragged along behind her mother **6** to search (a river) with a dragnet or hook **7** to draw (on a cigarette) **8** computers to move (a graphics image) from one place to another on the screen by manipulating a mouse with its button held down **9 drag away** or **from** to force (oneself) to come away from something interesting: I was completely spellbound and couldn't drag myself away from the film **10 drag on** or **out** to last or be prolonged tediously: winter dragged on **11 drag one's feet** informal to act with deliberate slowness ▷ n **12** a person or thing that slows up progress **13** informal a tedious or boring thing: it was a drag having to walk 2 miles to the station every day **14** informal a draw on a cigarette **15** an implement, such as a dragnet, used for dragging **16** aeronautics the resistance to the motion of a body passing through air **17 in drag** (of a man) wearing women's clothes, usually as a form of entertainment ▶ HISTORY Old English dragan to draw

dragnet n a net used to scour the bottom of a pond or river when searching for something

dragoman n, pl **-mans** or **-men** (in some Middle Eastern countries) a professional interpreter or guide ▶ HISTORY Arabic targumān

dragon n **1** a mythical monster that resembles a large fire-breathing lizard **2** informal a fierce woman **3 chase the dragon** slang to smoke opium or heroin ▶ HISTORY Greek drakōn

dragonfly n, pl **-flies** a brightly coloured insect with a long slender body and two pairs of wings

dragoon n **1** a heavily armed cavalryman ▷ vb **2** to coerce or force: we were dragooned into participating ▶ HISTORY French dragon

drag race n a race in which specially built or modified cars or motorcycles are timed over a measured course > **drag racing** n

drain n **1** a pipe that carries off water or sewage **2** a cause of a continuous reduction in energy or resources: the expansion will be a drain on resources **3** a metal grid on a road or pavement through

d

which rainwater flows **4 down the drain** wasted ▷ *vb* **5** to draw off or remove (liquid) from **6** to flow (away) or filter (off) **7** to dry or be emptied as a result of liquid running off or flowing away **8** to drink the entire contents of (a glass or cup) **9** to make constant demands on (energy or resources); exhaust **10** (of a river) to carry off the surface water from (an area) ▶ HISTORY Old English *drēahnian*

drainage *n* **1** a system of pipes, drains, or ditches used to drain water or other liquids **2** the process or a method of draining

drainage basin *n geog* the area of land that drains into a river, basin, or reservoir. Also called: **catchment area**

drainage density *n geog* the combined length of streams per square kilometre or mile, etc. in a given area

drainage network *n geog* the system of interconnected streams draining a drainage basin

drainage pattern *n geog* the pattern of branching of streams, such as dendritic (branching like a tree), deranged (random-looking), and trellised (characterized by having branches at right angles, many with their own right-angle branches)

draining board *n* a grooved surface at the side of a sink, used for draining washed dishes

drainpipe *n* a pipe for carrying off rainwater or sewage

drake *n* the male of a duck ▶ HISTORY origin unknown

dram *n* **1** a small amount of spirits, such as whisky **2** a unit of weight equal to one sixteenth of an ounce (avoirdupois) ▶ HISTORY Greek *drakhmē*; see DRACHMA

drama *n* **1** a serious play for theatre, television, or radio **2** plays in general, as a form of literature **3** the art of writing, producing, or acting in a play **4** a situation that is exciting or highly emotional ▶ HISTORY Greek: something performed

dramatic *adj* **1** of or relating to drama **2** like a drama in suddenness or effectiveness: *the government's plan has had a dramatic effect on employment in television* **3** acting or performed in a flamboyant way: *he spread his hands in a dramatic gesture of helplessness* > **dramatically** *adv*

dramatic irony *n theatre* the irony occurring when the implications of a situation or speech are understood by the audience but not by the characters in the play

dramatic monologue *n theatre, prosody* an address, especially in poetry, by a single character in which he or she reveals to the audience, seemingly unintentionally, aspects of his or her character or situation

dramatics *n* **1** the art of acting or producing plays ▷ *pl n* **2** exaggerated, theatrical behaviour

dramatis personae (drah-mat-tiss per-**soh**-nigh) *pl n* the characters in a play ▶ HISTORY New Latin

dramatist *n* a playwright: *Austria's greatest living dramatist*

dramatize *or* **-tise** *vb* **-tizing, -tized** *or* **-tising,**

-tised 1 to rewrite (a book or story) in a form suitable for performing on stage **2** to express (something) in a dramatic or exaggerated way: *he dramatizes his illness* > **dramatization** *or* **-tisation** *n*

drank *vb* the past tense of **drink**

drape *vb* **draping, draped 1** to cover with material or fabric **2** to hang or arrange in folds **3** to place casually: *he draped his arms across the back of the seat* ▷ See also **drapes** ▶ HISTORY Old French *draper*

draper *n Brit* a person who sells fabrics and sewing materials

drapery *n, pl* **-peries 1** fabric or clothing arranged and draped **2** fabrics and cloth collectively

drapes *pl n Austral, NZ, US & Canad* material hung at an opening or window to shut out light or to provide privacy

drastic *adj* strong and severe: *the police are taking drastic measures against car thieves* ▶ HISTORY Greek *drastikos* > **drastically** *adv*

draught *or US* **draft** *n* **1** a current of cold air, usually one coming into a room or vehicle **2** a portion of liquid to be drunk, esp. a dose of medicine **3** a gulp or swallow: *she took a deep draught then a sip* **4 on draught** (of beer) drawn from a cask **5** one of the flat discs used in the game of draughts. US and Canad. equivalent: **checker 6 feel the draught** to be short of money ▷ *adj* **7** (of an animal) used for pulling heavy loads: *horses are specialized draught animals* ▶ HISTORY probably Old Norse *drahtr*

draught beer *n* beer stored in a cask

draughts *n* a game for two players using a draughtboard and 12 draughtsmen each ▶ HISTORY plural of *draught* (in obsolete sense: a chess move)

draughtsman *or US* **draftsman** *n, pl* **-men 1** a person employed to prepare detailed scale drawings of equipment, machinery, or buildings **2** a person skilled in drawing **3** US and Canad. equivalent: **checker** *Brit* a flat disc used in the game of draughts > **draughtsmanship** *n*

draughty *or US* **drafty** *adj* **draughtier, draughtiest** *or US* **draftier, draftiest** exposed to draughts of air > **draughtily** *adv* > **draughtiness** *n*

draw *vb* **drawing, drew, drawn 1** to sketch (a picture, pattern, or diagram) with a pen or pencil **2** *written* to cause (a person or thing) to move closer or further away from a place by pulling **3** to bring, take, or pull (something) out of a container: *he drew a gun and laid it on the table* **4** to take (something) from a particular source: *the inhabitants drew water from the well two miles away* **5** *written* to move in a specified direction: *he drew alongside me* **6** to attract: *she drew enthusiastic audiences from all over the country* **7** to formulate or decide: *he drew similar conclusions* **8** to cause to flow: *the barman nodded and drew two pints* **9** to choose or be given by lottery: *Brazil have drawn Spain in the semi-final of the Cup* **10** (of two teams or contestants) to finish a game with an equal number of points **11** *archery* to bend (a bow) by pulling the string **12** to cause (pus) to discharge from an abscess or wound ▷ *n* **13** a raffle or lottery **14** *informal* a person, place, show, or event that attracts a large audience **15** a contest or game ending in a tie ▷ See also **drawback** ▶ HISTORY Old English *dragan*

drawback *n* **1** a disadvantage or hindrance ▷ *vb* **draw back 2** to move backwards: *the girl drew back as though in pain* **3** to turn aside from an undertaking: *the prime minister drew back from his original intention*

drawbridge *n* a bridge that may be raised to prevent access or to enable vessels to pass

drawer *n* **1** a sliding box-shaped part of a piece of furniture used for storage **2** a person or thing that draws

drawers *pl n old-fashioned* an undergarment worn on the lower part of the body

drawing *n* **1** a picture or plan made by means of lines on a surface **2** the art of making drawings

drawing pin *n Brit & NZ* a short tack with a broad smooth head used for fastening papers to a drawing board or other surface

drawing room *n* a room where visitors are received and entertained

drawl *vb* **1** to speak slowly with long vowel sounds ▷ *n* **2** the way of speech of someone who drawls ▶ HISTORY probably frequentative of *draw* > **drawling** *adj*

drawn *vb* **1** the past participle of **draw** ▷ *adj* **2** haggard, tired, or tense in appearance

draw off *vb* to cause (a liquid) to flow from something

draw on *vb* **1** to make use of from a source or fund: *they are able to draw on a repertoire of around 400 songs* **2** (of a period of time) to come near or pass by: *summer draws on; time draws on*

draw out *vb* **1** (of a train) to leave a station **2** to encourage (someone) to talk freely: *therapy groups will continue to draw her out* **3 draw out of** to find out (information) from

drawstring *n* a cord run through a hem around an opening, so that when it is pulled tighter, the opening closes

draw up *vb* **1** to prepare and write out: *the signatories drew up a draft agreement* **2** (of a vehicle) to come to a halt

dray *n* a low cart used for carrying heavy loads ▶ HISTORY Old English *dræge* dragnet

dread *vb* **1** to anticipate with apprehension or terror ▷ *n* **2** great fear ▶ HISTORY Old English *ondrædan*

dreadful *adj* **1** extremely disagreeable or shocking **2** extreme: *there were dreadful delays* > **dreadfully** *adv*

dreadlocks *pl n* hair worn in the Rastafarian style of tightly curled strands. Sometimes shortened to: **dreads**

dreadnought *n* a battleship armed with heavy guns

dream *n* **1** an imagined series of events experienced in the mind while asleep **2** a daydream: *the dream of success turning into a nightmare* **3** a goal or aim:

Unity has been their constant dream **4** a wonderful person or thing: *her house is a dream* ▷ *vb* **dreaming, dreamed** *or* **dreamt 5** to experience (a dream) **6** to indulge in daydreams **7** to be unrealistic: *you're dreaming if you think we can win* **8 dream of** to consider the possibility of: *she would not dream of taking his advice* **9 dream of** *or* **about** to have an image of or fantasy about: *they often dream about what life will be like for them on the outside* ▷ *adj* **10** beautiful or pleasing: *a dream kitchen* ▶ HISTORY Old English *drēam* song > **dreamer** *n*

dream team *n informal* a group of people regarded as having the perfect combination of talents

Dreamtime *n* **1** (in the mythology of Australian Aboriginal peoples) a mythical golden age of the past, when the first men were created **2** *Austral, informal* any remote period, out of touch with the realities of the present

dream up *vb* to formulate in the imagination: *a character dreamed up by a scriptwriter*

dreamy *adj* **dreamier, dreamiest 1** vague or impractical: *she was wild-eyed and dreamy* **2** relaxing or gentle: *I felt this dreamy contentment* **3** *informal* wonderful or impressive: *he drives a dreamy Jaguar* > **dreamily** *adv* > **dreaminess** *n*

dreary *adj* **drearier, dreariest** dull or uninteresting: *there are long streets of dreary red houses spreading everywhere* ▶ HISTORY Old English *drēorig* gory > **drearily** *adv* > **dreariness** *n*

dredge[1] *n* **1** a machine used to scoop or suck up silt or mud from a river bed or harbour ▷ *vb* **dredging, dredged 2** to remove silt or mud from (a river bed or harbour) by means of a dredge **3** to search for (a submerged object) with or as if with a dredge ▶ HISTORY origin unknown > **dredger** *n*

dredge[2] *vb* **dredging, dredged** to sprinkle (food) with a substance, such as flour ▶ HISTORY Old French *dragie* > **dredger** *n*

dredge up *vb informal* to remember (something obscure or half-forgotten): *I didn't retain you to dredge up unfortunate incidents from my past*

dregs *pl n* **1** solid particles that settle at the bottom of some liquids **2 the dregs** the worst or most despised elements: *the dregs of colonial society* ▶ HISTORY Old Norse *dregg*

drench *vb* **1** to make completely wet **2** to give medicine to (an animal) ▶ HISTORY Old English *drencan* to cause to drink > **drenching** *n, adj*

Dresden *or* **Dresden china** *n* delicate and decorative porcelain made near Dresden, Germany

dress *n* **1** a one-piece garment worn by a woman or girl, with a skirt and bodice and sometimes sleeves **2** complete style of clothing: *contemporary dress* ▷ *adj* **3** suitable for a formal occasion: *he was wearing a dress shirt* ▷ *vb* **4** to put clothes on **5** to put on formal clothes **6** to apply protective covering to (a wound) **7** to cover (a salad) with dressing **8** to prepare (meat, poultry, or fish) for selling or cooking by cleaning or gutting **9** to put a

d

d

finish on (the surface of stone, metal, or other building material) ▷ See also **dress up** ▶ HISTORY Old French *drecier* to arrange

dressage (**dress**-ahzh) *n* **a** the method of training horses to perform manoeuvres as a display of obedience **b** the manoeuvres performed ▶ HISTORY French

dress circle *n* the first gallery in a theatre

dress code *n* a set of rules or guidelines regarding the manner of dress acceptable in a religion, school, workplace, etc.

dresser¹ *n* **1** a piece of furniture with shelves and cupboards, used for storing or displaying dishes **2** *US* a chest of drawers ▶ HISTORY Old French *drecier* to arrange

dresser² *n* **1** a person who dresses in a specified way: *Lars was a meticulous, elegant dresser* **2** *theatre* a person employed to assist performers with their costumes

dressing *n* **1** a sauce for food: *salad dressing* **2** *US & Canad* same as **stuffing** (sense 1) **3** a covering for a wound **4** manure or fertilizer spread on land **5** a gluey material used for stiffening paper, textiles, etc.

dressing-down *n* *informal* a severe reprimand

dressing gown *n* a loose-fitting garment worn over one's pyjamas or nightdress

dressing room *n* a room used for changing clothes and applying make-up, esp. a backstage room in a theatre

dressing table *n* a piece of bedroom furniture with a mirror and a set of drawers

dressmaker *n* a person who makes clothes for women > **dressmaking** *n*

dress rehearsal *n* **1** the last rehearsal of a play, opera, or show using costumes, lighting, and other effects **2** any full-scale practice: *astronauts are in the midst of a two day dress rehearsal of their launch countdown*

dress up *vb* **1** to put on glamorous or stylish clothes **2** to put fancy dress on: *the guests dressed up like cowboys* **3** to disguise (something) to make it more attractive or acceptable: *the offer was simply an old one dressed up in new terms*

dressy *adj* **dressier, dressiest 1** (of clothes or occasions) elegant **2** (of people) dressing stylishly > **dressiness** *n*

drew *vb* the past tense of **draw**

drey or **dray** *n* *Brit & Austral* a squirrel's nest ▶ HISTORY origin unknown

dribble *vb* **-bling, -bled 1** to flow or allow to flow in a thin stream or drops **2** to allow saliva to trickle from the mouth **3** (in soccer, hockey, etc.) to propel (the ball) by kicking or tapping in quick succession ▷ *n* **4** a small quantity of liquid falling in drops or flowing in a thin stream **5** a small supply: *there's only a dribble of milk left* **6** an act or instance of dribbling ▶ HISTORY obsolete *drib*, variant of *drip* > **dribbler** *n*

dribs and drabs *pl n* *informal* small occasional amounts

dried *vb* the past of **dry**

drier¹ *adj* a comparative of **dry**

drier² *n* same as **dryer¹**

driest *adj* a superlative of **dry**

drift *vb* **1** to be carried along by currents of air or water **2** to move aimlessly from one place or activity to another **3** to wander away from a fixed course or point **4** (of snow) to pile up in heaps ▷ *n* **5** something piled up by the wind or current, as a snowdrift **6** a general movement or development: *there has been a drift away from family control* **7** the main point of an argument or speech: *I was beginning to get his drift* **8** the extent to which a vessel or aircraft is driven off course by winds, etc. **9** a current of water created by the wind ▶ HISTORY Old Norse

drifter *n* **1** a person who moves aimlessly from place to place **2** a boat used for drift-net fishing

drift net *n* a fishing net that is allowed to drift with the tide

driftwood *n* wood floating on or washed ashore by the sea

drill¹ *n* **1** a machine or tool for boring holes **2** *mil* training in procedures or movements, as for parades **3** strict and often repetitious training **4** *informal* correct procedure: *he knows the drill as well as anybody* ▷ *vb* **5** to bore a hole in (something) with or as if with a drill **6** to instruct or be instructed in military procedures or movements **7** to teach by rigorous exercises or training ▶ HISTORY Middle Dutch *drillen*

drill² *n* **1** a machine for planting seeds in rows **2** a furrow in which seeds are sown **3** a row of seeds planted by means of a drill ▷ *vb* **4** to plant (seeds) by means of a drill ▶ HISTORY origin unknown

drill³ *n* a hard-wearing cotton cloth, used for uniforms ▶ HISTORY German *Drillich*

drill⁴ *n* a W African monkey, related to the mandrill ▶ HISTORY from a West African word

drily or **dryly** *adv* in a dry manner

drink *vb* **drinking, drank, drunk 1** to swallow (a liquid) **2** to consume alcohol, esp. to excess **3** to bring (oneself) into a specified condition by consuming alcohol: *he drank himself senseless every night* **4 drink someone's health** to wish someone health or happiness with a toast **5 drink in** to pay close attention to: *I drank in what the speaker said* **6 drink to** to drink a toast: *I drank to their engagement* ▷ *n* **7** liquid suitable for drinking **8** a portion of liquid for drinking **9** alcohol, or the habit of drinking too much of it ▶ HISTORY Old English *drincan* > **drinkable** *adj* > **drinker** *n*

drink-driving *adj* *Brit, Austral & NZ* of or relating to driving a car after drinking alcohol: *a drink-driving offence*

drip *vb* **dripping, dripped 1** to fall or let fall in drops ▷ *n* **2** the falling of drops of liquid **3** the sound made by falling drops **4** *informal* a weak or foolish person **5** *med* a device that administers a liquid drop by drop into a vein ▶ HISTORY Old English *dryppan*

drip-dry *adj* **1** (of clothes or fabrics) designed to dry without creases if hung up when wet ▷ *vb*

-dries, -drying, -dried 2 to dry or become dry thus

drip-feed vb **-feeding, -fed 1** to feed (someone) a liquid drop by drop, usually through a vein ▷ n **drip feed 2** same as **drip** (sense 5)

dripping n the fat that comes from meat while it is being roasted

drive vb **driving, drove, driven 1** to guide the movement of (a vehicle) **2** to transport or be transported in a vehicle **3** to goad into a specified state: *the black despair that finally drove her to suicide* **4** to push or propel: *he drove the nail into the wall with a hammer* **5** *sport* to hit (a ball) very hard and straight **6** *golf* to strike (the ball) with a driver **7** to chase (game) from cover **8 drive home** to make (a point) clearly understood by emphasis ▷ n **9** a journey in a driven vehicle **10** a road for vehicles, esp. a private road leading to a house **11** a special effort made by a group of people for a particular purpose: *a charity drive* **12** energy, ambition, or initiative **13** *psychol* a motive or interest: *sex drive* **14** a sustained and powerful military offensive **15** the means by which power is transmitted in a machine **16** *sport* a hard straight shot or stroke ▶ HISTORY Old English *drīfan*

drive at vb *informal* to intend or mean: *he had no idea what she was driving at*

drive-by shooting n an incident in which a person is shot at by a person in a moving vehicle. Sometimes shortened to: **drive-by**

drive-in n **1** a cinema, restaurant, etc. offering a service where people remain in their cars while using the service provided ▷ adj **2** denoting a cinema, etc. of this kind

drivel n **1** foolish talk ▷ vb **-elling, -elled** or US **-eling, -eled 2** to speak foolishly **3** to allow (saliva) to flow from the mouth ▶ HISTORY Old English *dreflian* to slaver

driver n **1** a person who drives a vehicle **2** *golf* a long-shafted club with a large head and steep face, used for tee shots

drive-thru n **1** a takeaway restaurant, bank, etc., designed so that customers can use it without leaving their cars ▷ adj **2** denoting a restaurant etc. of this kind

drive-time n **1** the time of day when many people are driving to or from work, considered as a broadcasting slot ▷ adj **2** of this time of day: *the daily drive-time show*

driveway n a path for vehicles connecting a building to a public road

driving licence n an official document authorizing a person to drive a motor vehicle

drizzle n **1** very light rain ▷ vb **-zling, -zled 2** to rain lightly ▶ HISTORY Old English *drēosan* to fall > **drizzly** adj

droll adj *written* quaintly amusing ▶ HISTORY French *drôle* scamp > **drollery** n > **drolly** adv

dromedary (drom-mid-er-ee) n, pl **-daries** a camel with a single hump ▶ HISTORY Greek *dromas* running

drone[1] n **1** a male honeybee **2** a person who lives off the work of others **3** a pilotless radio-controlled aircraft ▶ HISTORY Old English *drān*

drone[2] vb **droning, droned 1** to make a monotonous low dull sound **2 drone on** to talk in a monotonous tone without stopping ▷ n **3** a monotonous low dull sound **4** a single-reed pipe in a set of bagpipes ▶ HISTORY related to DRONE[1]

drongo n, pl **-gos** a tropical songbird with a glossy black plumage, a forked tail, and a stout bill

drool vb **1 drool over** to show excessive enthusiasm for or pleasure in **2** same as **drivel** (senses 2, 3) ▶ HISTORY probably alteration of DRIVEL

droop vb **1** to sag, as from weakness or lack of support **2** to be overcome by weariness: *her eyelids drooped as if she were falling asleep* ▶ HISTORY Old Norse *drūpa* > **drooping** adj

droopy adj hanging or sagging downwards: *a droopy moustache*

drop vb **dropping, dropped 1** to fall or allow (something) to fall vertically **2** to decrease in amount, strength, or value **3** to fall to the ground, as from exhaustion **4** to sink to a lower position, as on a scale **5** to mention casually: *he dropped a hint* **6** to set down (passengers or goods): *can you drop me at the hotel?* **7** *informal* to send: *drop me a letter* **8** to discontinue: *can we drop the subject?* **9** *informal* to be no longer friendly with: *I dropped him when I discovered his political views* **10** to leave out in speaking: *he has a tendency to drop his h's* **11** (of animals) to give birth to (offspring) **12** *sport* to omit (a player) from a team **13** to lose (a game or point) **14 drop back** to progress more slowly than other people going in the same direction **15 drop in** or **by** *informal* to pay someone a casual visit ▷ n **16** a small quantity of liquid forming a round shape **17** a small quantity of liquid **18** a small round sweet: *a lemon drop* **19** a decrease in amount, strength, or value **20** the vertical distance that anything may fall **21** the act of unloading troops or supplies by parachute ▷ See also **drop off, dropout, drops** ▶ HISTORY Old English *dropian*

drop curtain n *theatre* a curtain that can be raised and lowered onto the stage

droplet n a very small drop of liquid

drop off vb **1** to set down (passengers or goods) **2** *informal* to fall asleep **3** to decrease or decline: *sales dropped off during our period of transition*

dropout n **1** a person who rejects conventional society **2** a student who does not complete a course of study ▷ vb **drop out 3** to abandon or withdraw (from an institution or group)

dropper n a small tube with a rubber part at one end for drawing up and dispensing drops of liquid

droppings pl n the dung of certain animals, such as rabbits or birds

drops pl n any liquid medication applied by means of a dropper

dropsy n an illness in which watery fluid collects in the body ▶ HISTORY Middle English *ydropesie*, from Greek *hudōr* water > **dropsical** adj

dross n **1** the scum formed on the surfaces of

drought – DT's

molten metals **2** anything of inferior quality ▶ HISTORY Old English *drōs* dregs

drought (rhymes with **out**) *n* a prolonged period of time during which no rain falls ▶ HISTORY Old English *drūgoth*

drove¹ *vb* the past tense of **drive**

drove² *n* **1** a herd of livestock being driven together **2** a moving crowd of people ▶ HISTORY Old English *drāf* herd

drover *n* a person who drives sheep or cattle

drown *vb* **1** to die or kill by immersion in liquid **2** to drench thoroughly **3** to make (a sound) impossible to hear by making a loud noise ▶ HISTORY probably from Old English *druncnian*

drowse *vb* **drowsing, drowsed** to be sleepy, dull, or sluggish ▶ HISTORY probably from Old English *drūsian* to sink

drowsy *adj* **drowsier, drowsiest** **1** feeling sleepy **2** peaceful and quiet: *row upon row of windows looked out over drowsy parkland* > **drowsily** *adv* > **drowsiness** *n*

drubbing *n* an utter defeat, as in a contest: *the Communists received a drubbing* ▶ HISTORY probably from Arabic *dáraba* to beat

drudge *n* **1** a person who works hard at an uninteresting task ▷ *vb* **drudging, drudged** **2** to work at such tasks ▶ HISTORY origin unknown

drudgery *n* uninteresting work that must be done

drug *n* **1** any substance used in the treatment, prevention, or diagnosis of disease **2** a chemical substance, such as a narcotic, taken for the effects it produces ▷ *vb* **drugging, drugged** **3** to administer a drug to (a person or animal) in order to induce sleepiness or unconsciousness **4** to mix a drug with (food or drink): *who drugged my wine?* ▶ HISTORY Old French *drogue*

druggist *n* US & Canad a pharmacist

drugstore *n* US & Canad a pharmacy where a wide variety of goods is available

Druid *n* a member of an ancient order of Celtic priests ▶ HISTORY Latin *druides* > **Druidic** *adj*

drum *n* **1** a percussion instrument sounded by striking a skin stretched across the opening of a hollow cylinder **2** the sound produced by a drum **3** an object shaped like a drum: *an oil drum* **4** same as **eardrum** ▷ *vb* **drumming, drummed** **5** to play (music) on a drum **6** to tap rhythmically or regularly: *he drummed his fingers on the desk* **7** to fix in someone's mind by constant repetition: *my father always drummed into us how privileged we were* ▷ See also **drum up** ▶ HISTORY Middle Dutch *tromme* > **drummer** *n*

drumhead *n* the part of a drum that is struck

drum machine *n* a synthesizer programmed to reproduce the sound of percussion instruments

drum major *n* the noncommissioned officer in the army who is in command of the drums and the band when paraded together

drumstick *n* **1** a stick used for playing a drum **2** the lower joint of the leg of a cooked fowl

drum up *vb* to obtain (support or business) by making requests or canvassing

drunk *vb* **1** the past participle of **drink** ▷ *adj* **2** intoxicated with alcohol to the extent of losing control over normal functions **3** overwhelmed by strong influence or emotion: *he was half drunk with satisfaction at his victory over the intruder* ▷ *n* **4** a person who is drunk or drinks habitually to excess ▶ HISTORY Old English *druncen*, past participle of *drincan* to drink

drunkard *n* a person who is frequently or habitually drunk

drunken *adj* **1** intoxicated with alcohol **2** habitually drunk **3** caused by or relating to alcoholic intoxication: *a drunken argument* > **drunkenly** *adv* > **drunkenness** *n*

drupe *n* a fleshy fruit with a stone, such as the peach or cherry ▶ HISTORY Greek *druppa* olive

dry *adj* **drier, driest** or **dryer, dryest** **1** lacking moisture **2** having little or no rainfall **3** having the water drained away or evaporated: *a dry gully for the most part of the year* **4** not providing milk: *a dry cow* **5** (of the eyes) free from tears **6** Brit, Austral & NZ, informal thirsty **7** eaten without butter or jam: *a dry cracker* **8** (of wine) not sweet **9** dull and uninteresting: *a dry subject* **10** (of humour) subtle and sarcastic **11** prohibiting the sale of alcoholic liquor: *a dry district* ▷ *vb* **dries, drying, dried** **12** to make or become dry **13** to preserve (food) by removing the moisture ▷ See also **dry out, dry up** ▶ HISTORY Old English *drȳge* > **dryness** *n*

dryad *n, pl* **dryads** or **dryades** (dry-ad-deez) Greek *myth* a wood nymph ▶ HISTORY Greek *druas*

dry battery *n* an electric battery composed of dry cells

dry cell *n* an electric cell in which the electrolyte is in the form of a paste to prevent it from spilling

dry-clean *vb* to clean (clothes, etc.) with a solvent other than water > **dry-cleaner** *n* > **dry-cleaning** *n*

dry dock *n* a dock that can be pumped dry to permit work on a ship's bottom

dryer¹ *n* any device that removes moisture by heating or by hot air

dryer² *adj* same as **drier**¹

dry ice *n* solid carbon dioxide used as a refrigerant

dryly *adv* same as **drily**

dry out *vb* **1** to make or become dry **2** to undergo or cause to undergo treatment for alcoholism or drug addiction

dry rot *n* **1** crumbling and drying of timber, caused by certain fungi **2** a fungus causing this decay

dry run *n* informal a rehearsal

dry stock *n* NZ cattle raised for meat

dry-stone *adj* (of a wall) made without mortar

dry up *vb* **1** to make or become dry **2** to dry (dishes, cutlery, etc.) with a tea towel after they have been washed **3** (of a resource) to come to an end **4** informal to stop speaking: *she suddenly dried up in the middle of her speech*

DSC (in Britain) Distinguished Service Cross

DSO (in Britain) Distinguished Service Order

DTP *computers* desktop publishing

DT's *informal* delirium tremens

254

dual *adj* having two parts, functions, or aspects: *dual controls; dual nationality* ▶ **HISTORY** Latin *duo* two > **duality** *n*

dual carriageway *n Brit, Austral & NZ* a road with a central strip of grass or concrete to separate traffic travelling in opposite directions

dual-intercept *n maths* a method of sketching a straight line on a graph by joining the x- and y- intercepts on the x- and y-axes

dub¹ *vb* **dubbing, dubbed** to give (a person or place) a name or nickname ▶ **HISTORY** Old English *dubbian*

dub² *vb* **dubbing, dubbed 1** to provide (a film) with a new soundtrack in a different language **2** to provide (a film or tape) with a soundtrack ▷ *n* **3** *music* a style of reggae record production involving exaggeration of instrumental parts, echo, etc. ▶ **HISTORY** shortened from DOUBLE

dubbin *n* a kind of thick grease applied to leather to soften it and make it waterproof ▶ **HISTORY** *dub* to dress leather

dubious (**dew**-bee-uss) *adj* **1** not entirely honest, safe, or reliable: *this allegation was at best dubious and at worst an outright fabrication* **2** unsure or undecided: *she felt dubious about the entire proposition* **3** of doubtful quality or worth: *she had the dubious honour of being taken for his mother* ▶ **HISTORY** Latin *dubius* wavering > **dubiety** (dew-**by**-it-ee) *n* > **dubiously** *adv*

dubnium *n chem* an element produced in minute quantities by bombarding plutonium with high-energy neon ions. Symbol: Db ▶ **HISTORY** after *Dubna* in Russia, where it was first reported

ducal (**duke**-al) *adj* of a duke

ducat (**duck**-it) *n* a former European gold or silver coin ▶ **HISTORY** Old Italian *ducato*

duchess *n* **1** a woman who holds the rank of duke **2** the wife or widow of a duke ▶ **HISTORY** Old French *duchesse*

duchy *n, pl* **duchies** the area of land owned or ruled by a duke or duchess ▶ **HISTORY** Old French *duche*

duck¹ *n, pl* **ducks** or **duck 1** a water bird with short legs, webbed feet, and a broad blunt bill **2** the flesh of this bird used for food **3** the female of such a bird **4** *cricket* a score of nothing **5 like water off a duck's back** without effect: *I reprimanded him but it was like water off a duck's back* ▶ **HISTORY** Old English *dūce*

duck² *vb* **1** to move (the head or body) quickly downwards, to escape being seen or avoid a blow **2** to plunge suddenly under water **3** *informal* to dodge (a duty or responsibility) ▶ **HISTORY** Middle English

duck-billed platypus *n* See **platypus**

duckboard *n building* a board or boards laid so as to form a floor or path over muddy ground

duckling *n* a young duck

duct *n* **1** a tube, pipe, or channel through which liquid or gas is sent **2** a tube in the body through which liquid such as tears or bile can pass ▶ **HISTORY** Latin *ducere* to lead

ductile *adj* (of a metal) able to be shaped into sheets or drawn out into threads ▶ **HISTORY** Latin *ductilis* > **ductility** *n*

dud *informal n* **1** an ineffectual person or thing: *they had the foresight to pick on someone who was not a total dud* ▷ *adj* **2** bad or useless: *a dud cheque* ▶ **HISTORY** origin unknown

dude *n informal* **1** *US & Canad* a man: *he was a black dude in his late twenties* **2** *chiefly US & Canad, old-fashioned* a dandy **3** *Western US & Canad* a city dweller who spends his or her holiday on a ranch ▶ **HISTORY** origin unknown

dudgeon *n* **in high dudgeon** angry or resentful: *the scientist departed in high dudgeon* ▶ **HISTORY** origin unknown

due *adj* **1** expected to happen, be done, or arrive at a particular time: *he is due to return on Thursday* **2** immediately payable: *the balance is now due* **3** owed as a debt: *they finally agreed to pay her the money she was due* **4** fitting or proper **5 due to** happening or existing as a direct result of someone or something else: *chronic kidney failure due to diabetes* ▷ *n* **6** something that is owed or required **7 give someone his** or **her due** to acknowledge someone's good points: *I'll give him his due, he's resourceful* ▷ *adv* **8** directly or exactly: *due west* ▶ **HISTORY** Latin *debere* to owe

duel *n* **1** a formal fight between two people using guns, swords, or other weapons to settle a quarrel ▷ *vb* **duelling, duelled** or US **dueling, dueled 2** to fight in a duel ▶ **HISTORY** Latin *duellum*, poetical variant of *bellum* war > **duellist** *n*

duenna *n* (esp. in Spain) an elderly woman acting as chaperone to girls ▶ **HISTORY** Spanish *dueña*

due process of law *n law* the administration of justice in accordance with established rules and principles

dues *pl n* membership fees paid to a club or organization: *union dues*

duet *n* a piece of music sung or played by two people ▶ **HISTORY** Latin *duo* two > **duettist** *n*

duff *adj* **1** *chiefly Brit, informal* broken or useless: *my car had a duff clutch* ▷ *vb* **2** *golf, informal* to bungle (a shot) **3 duff up** *Brit, slang* to beat (someone) severely ▶ **HISTORY** probably from *duffer*

duffel or **duffle** *n* same as **duffel coat** ▶ **HISTORY** after *Duffel*, Belgian town

duffel bag *n* a cylinder-shaped canvas bag fastened with a drawstring

duffel coat *n* a wool coat usually with a hood and fastened with toggles

duffer *n informal* a dull or incompetent person ▶ **HISTORY** origin unknown

dug¹ *vb* the past of **dig**

dug² *n* a teat or udder of a female animal ▶ **HISTORY** Scandinavian

dugite (**doo**-gyte) *n* a medium-sized Australian venomous snake

dugong *n* a whalelike mammal found in tropical waters ▶ **HISTORY** Malay *duyong*

dugout *n* **1** a canoe made by hollowing out a log **2** *Brit* (at a sports ground) the covered bench where managers and substitutes sit **3** *mil* a covered shelter 255 dug in the ground to provide protection

duiker or **duyker** (dike-er) n, pl -**kers** or -**ker** a small African antelope ▶ HISTORY Dutch: diver

duke n 1 a nobleman of the highest rank 2 the prince or ruler of a small principality or duchy ▶ HISTORY Latin *dux* leader > **dukedom** n

dulcet (dull-sit) adj (of a sound) soothing or pleasant: *she smiled and, in dulcet tones, told me I would be next* ▶ HISTORY Latin *dulcis* sweet

dulcimer n a tuned percussion instrument consisting of a set of strings stretched over a sounding board and struck with hammers ▶ HISTORY Old French *doulcemer*

dull adj 1 not interesting: *the finished article would make dull reading* 2 slow to learn or understand 3 (of an ache) not intense: *I have a dull ache in the middle of my back* 4 (of weather) not bright or clear 5 not lively or energetic: *she appeared, looking dull and apathetic* 6 (of colour) lacking brilliance 7 (of the blade of a knife) not sharp 8 (of a sound) not loud or clear: *his head fell back to the carpet with a dull thud* ▷ vb 9 to make or become dull ▶ HISTORY Old English *dol* > **dullness** n > **dully** adv

dullard n old-fashioned a dull or stupid person

dulse n a seaweed with large red edible fronds ▶ HISTORY Irish *duilesc* seaweed

duly adv 1 in a proper manner: *my permit was duly stamped* 2 at the proper time: *the photographer duly arrived*

duma n 1 *Russian hist* the legislative assembly established by Tsar Nicholas II in 1905 and overthrown by the Bolsheviks in 1917. 2 *politics* the lower house of the post-Soviet Russian parliament ▶ HISTORY from Russian: thought

dumb adj 1 *offensive* (of a person) lacking the power to speak 2 lacking the power of human speech: *dumb animals* 3 temporarily unable to speak: *I was struck dumb when I heard the news* 4 done or performed without speech: *I looked at her in dumb puzzlement* 5 *informal* stupid or slow to understand ▷ See also **dumb down** ▶ HISTORY Old English > **dumbly** adv

dumbbell n 1 a short bar with a heavy ball or disc at either end, used for physical exercise 2 *slang, chiefly US & Canad* a stupid person

dumb down vb to make (something) less intellectually demanding or sophisticated: *a move to dumb down its news coverage*

dumbfounded adj speechless with amazement ▶ HISTORY *dumb* + (con)*found*

dumb show n meaningful gestures without speech

dumbwaiter n 1 a lift for carrying food, etc. from one floor of a building to another 2 *Brit* a stand placed near a dining table to hold food b a revolving tray placed on a table to hold food

dumdum or **dumdum bullet** n a soft-nosed bullet that expands on impact and causes large and serious wounds ▶ HISTORY after *Dum-Dum*, town near Calcutta where originally made

dummy n, pl -**mies** 1 a large model that looks like a human being, used for displaying clothes in a shop,

as a target, etc. 2 a copy of an object, often lacking some essential feature of the original 3 *slang* a stupid person 4 *Bridge* a the hand exposed on the table by the declarer's partner and played by the declarer b the declarer's partner 5 a rubber teat for babies to suck ▷ adj 6 imitation or substitute: *dummy bombs* ▶ HISTORY from *dumb*

dummy run n a practice or test carried out to test if any problems remain: *we'll do a dummy run on the file to see if the program works*

dump vb 1 to drop or let fall in a careless manner: *he dumped the books on the bed* 2 *informal* to abandon (someone or something) without proper care: *the unwanted babies were dumped in orphanages* 3 to dispose of (nuclear waste) 4 *commerce* to sell (goods) in bulk and at low prices, usually in another country, in order to keep prices high in the home market 5 *computers* to record (the contents of the memory) on a storage device at a series of points during a computer run ▷ n 6 a place where rubbish is left 7 *informal* a dirty, unattractive place 8 *mil* a place where weapons or supplies are stored ▶ HISTORY probably from Old Norse

dumpling n 1 a small ball of dough cooked and served with stew 2 a round pastry case filled with fruit ▶ HISTORY obsolete *dump* lump

dumps pl n **down in the dumps** *informal* feeling depressed and miserable ▶ HISTORY probably from Middle Dutch *domp* haze

dumpy adj **dumpier, dumpiest** short and plump ▶ HISTORY perhaps related to DUMPLING

dun¹ vb **dunning, dunned** 1 to press (a debtor) for payment ▷ n 2 a demand for payment ▶ HISTORY origin unknown

dun² adj brownish-grey ▶ HISTORY Old English *dunn*

dunce n *Brit, Austral & NZ* a person who is stupid

■ **WORD HISTORY**
■ In medieval times, the followers of the
■ 13th-century theologian John Duns Scotus were
■ called 'Dunses'. They were ridiculed by later
■ philosophers as opponents of learning, and so
■ the term came to be applied to those incapable
■ of learning.

dunderhead n *Brit, Austral & NZ* a slow-witted person ▶ HISTORY probably from Dutch *donder* thunder + HEAD

dune n a mound or ridge of drifted sand ▶ HISTORY Middle Dutch

dung n the faeces from large animals ▶ HISTORY Old English: prison

dungarees pl n trousers with a bib attached ▶ HISTORY *Dungrī*, district of Bombay, where the fabric used originated

dungeon n a prison cell, often underground ▶ HISTORY Old French *donjon*

dunghill n a heap of dung

dunk vb 1 to dip (a biscuit or piece of bread) in a drink or soup before eating it 2 to put (something) in liquid: *dunk the garment in the dye for fifteen minutes* ▶ HISTORY Old High German *dunkōn*

dunlin n a small sandpiper, of northern and arctic

regions, with a brown back and a black breast
▶ HISTORY from DUN²

dunnock n same as **hedge sparrow** ▶ HISTORY
from DUN²

dunny n, pl **-nies** Austral & NZ, informal a toilet
▶ HISTORY of obscure origin

duo n, pl **duos** 1 two singers or musicians who sing
or play music together as a pair 2 informal two
people who have something in common or do
something together ▶ HISTORY Latin: two

duodecimal adj relating to twelve or twelfths
▶ HISTORY Latin duodecim twelve

duodenum (dew-oh-**deen**-um) n the first part of
the small intestine, just below the stomach
▶ HISTORY Medieval Latin intestinum duodenum
digitorum intestine of twelve fingers' length
> **duodenal** adj

duologue or US sometimes **duolog** n a part or all
of a play in which the speaking roles are limited to
two actors ▶ HISTORY DUO + (MONO)LOGUE

DUP (in Northern Ireland) Democratic Unionist
Party

dupe vb **duping, duped** 1 to deceive or cheat:
you duped me into doing exactly what you wanted ▷ n
2 a person who is easily deceived ▶ HISTORY French

duple adj 1 same as **double** 2 music having two
beats in a bar ▶ HISTORY Latin duplus double

duplex n 1 US & Canad **a** an apartment on two
floors **b** US & Austral a semidetached house ▷ adj
2 having two parts ▶ HISTORY Latin: twofold

duplicate adj 1 copied exactly from an original: he
had a duplicate key to the front door ▷ n 2 an exact
copy 3 **in duplicate** in two exact copies: submit the
draft in duplicate, please ▷ vb **-cating, -cated** 4 to
make an exact copy of 5 to do again (something
that has already been done) ▶ HISTORY Latin
duplicare to double > **duplication** n
> **duplicator** n

duplicity n deceitful behaviour ▶ HISTORY Old
French duplicite

durable adj strong and long-lasting: the car's body
was made of a light but durable plastic ▶ HISTORY
Latin durare to last > **durability** n

durable goods pl n goods that do not require
frequent replacement. Also called: **durables**

duration n the length of time that something
lasts ▶ HISTORY Latin durare to last

durbar n (formerly) **a** the court of a native ruler or
a governor in India **b** a reception at such a court
▶ HISTORY HIndl darbār

duress n physical or moral pressure used to force
someone to do something: confessions obtained
under duress ▶ HISTORY Latin durus hard

duricrust n geol a hard crust found on or in soils in
arid regions

during prep throughout or within the limit of (a
period of time) ▶ HISTORY Latin durare to last

dusk n the time just before nightfall when it is
almost dark ▶ HISTORY Old English dox

dusky adj **duskier, duskiest** 1 dark in colour: her
gold earrings gleamed against her dusky cheeks 2 dim
or shadowy: the dusky room was crowded with absurd

objects > **duskily** adv > **duskiness** n

dust n 1 small dry particles of earth, sand, or dirt
2 **bite the dust a** to stop functioning: my television
has finally bitten the dust **b** to fall down dead
3 **shake the dust off one's feet** to depart angrily
4 **throw dust in someone's eyes** to confuse or
mislead someone ▷ vb 5 to remove dust from
(furniture) by wiping 6 to sprinkle (something)
with a powdery substance: serve dusted with brown
sugar and cinnamon ▶ HISTORY Old English dūst

dustbin n a large, usually cylindrical, container for
household rubbish

dust bowl n a dry area in which the surface soil is
exposed to wind erosion

dustcart n chiefly Brit & NZ a lorry for collecting
household rubbish

duster n a cloth used for dusting

dust jacket or **cover** n a removable paper cover
used to protect a book

dustman n, pl **-men** Brit a man whose job is to
collect household rubbish

dust mite n one of two mites that feed on shed
human skin cells

dustpan n a short-handled shovel into which dust
is swept from floors

dustsheet n a large cloth cover used to protect
furniture from dust

dust-up n informal a fight or argument

dusty adj **dustier, dustiest** 1 covered with dust
2 (of a colour) tinged with grey

Dutch adj 1 of the Netherlands ▷ n 2 the language
of the Netherlands ▷ pl n 3 **the Dutch** the people
of the Netherlands ▷ adv 4 **go Dutch** informal to go
on an outing where each person pays his or her
own expenses

Dutch auction n an auction in which the price is
lowered by stages until a buyer is found

Dutch barn n Brit a farm building with a steel
frame and a curved roof

Dutch courage n false courage gained from
drinking alcohol

Dutch elm disease n a fungal disease of elm
trees

dutiable adj (of goods) requiring payment of duty

dutiful adj doing what is expected: she is a
responsible and dutiful mother > **dutifully** adv

duty n, pl **-ties** 1 the work performed as part of
one's job: it is his duty to supervise the memorial
services 2 an obligation to fulfil one's
responsibilities: it's my duty as a doctor to keep it
confidential 3 a government tax on imports 4 **on** or
off duty at or not at work ▶ HISTORY Anglo-French
dueté

duty-bound adj morally obliged to do something:
we are duty-bound to help

duty-free adj, adv with exemption from customs
or excise duties

duty-free shop n a shop, esp. at an airport, that
sells duty-free goods

duty of care n law the legal obligation to take
measures to avoid causing foreseeable damage to
other people or their property through negligence

duvet (doo-vay) *n* same as **continental quilt** ▶ HISTORY French

DVD Digital Versatile *or* Video Disk: a type of compact disc that can store large amounts of video and audio information

DVLA (Brit) Driver and Vehicle Licensing Agency

dwaal *n* S African a state of absent-mindedness; a daze ▶ HISTORY Afrikaans

dwang *n* NZ & S African a short piece of wood inserted in a timber-framed wall

dwarf *vb* **1** to cause (someone or something) to seem small by being much larger ▷ *adj* **2** (of an animal or plant) much below the average size for the species ▷ *n, pl* **dwarfs** *or* **dwarves** **3** a person who is smaller than average size as a result of a medical condition **4** (in folklore) a small ugly manlike creature, often possessing magical powers ▶ HISTORY Old English *dweorg*

dwell *vb* **dwelling, dwelt** *or* **dwelled** *formal, literary* to live as a permanent resident ▶ HISTORY Old English *dwellan* to seduce, get lost > **dweller** *n*

dwelling *n* *formal, literary* a place of residence

dwell on *or* **upon** *vb* to think, speak, or write at length about (something)

dwindle *vb* **-dling, -dled** to grow less in size, strength, or number ▶ HISTORY Old English *dwīnan*

Dy *chem* dysprosium

dyad *n* a group of two ▶ HISTORY Late Latin *dyas*

dye *n* **1** a colouring substance **2** the colour produced by dyeing ▷ *vb* **dyeing, dyed** **3** to colour (hair or fabric) by applying a dye ▶ HISTORY Old English *dēag* > **dyer** *n*

dyed-in-the-wool *adj* having strong and unchanging attitudes or opinions: *he's a dyed-in-the-wool communist*

dying *vb* **1** the present participle of **die¹** ▷ *adj* **2** occurring at the moment of death: *in accordance with his dying wish* **3** (of a person or animal) very ill and likely to die soon **4** becoming less important or less current: *coal mining is a dying industry*

dyke *or esp US* **dike** *n* **1** a wall built to prevent flooding **2** a ditch **3** Scot a dry-stone wall ▶ HISTORY Old English *dic* ditch

dynamic *adj* **1** (of a person) full of energy, ambition, or new ideas **2** relating to a force of society, history, or the mind that produces a change: *the government needs a more dynamic policy towards poverty* **3** *physics* relating to energy or forces that produce motion ▶ HISTORY Greek *dunamis* power > **dynamically** *adv*

dynamic equilibrium *n* **1** *geog* a state of ever-changing balance in a system **2** *chem* a state of balance between ongoing processes

dynamics *n* **1** the branch of mechanics concerned with the forces that change or produce the motions of bodies ▷ *pl n* **2** those forces that produce change in any field or system **3** *music* the various degrees of loudness in a performance

dynamism *n* great energy or enthusiasm

dynamite *n* **1** an explosive made of nitroglycerine **2** *informal* a dangerous or exciting person or thing: *she's still dynamite* ▷ *vb* **-miting, -mited** **3** to mine or blow (something) up with dynamite ▶ HISTORY Greek *dunamis* power

dynamo *n, pl* **-mos** a device for converting mechanical energy into electricity ▶ HISTORY short for *dynamoelectric machine*

dynamoelectric *adj* of the conversion of mechanical energy into electricity or vice versa

dynamometer (dine-a-**mom**-it-er) *n* an instrument for measuring mechanical power

dynast *n* a hereditary ruler ▶ HISTORY Greek *dunasthai* to be powerful

dynasty *n, pl* **-ties** **1** a series of rulers of a country from the same family **2** a period of time during which a country is ruled by the same family ▶ HISTORY Greek *dunastēs* dynast > **dynastic** *adj*

dysentery *n* infection of the intestine which causes severe diarrhoea ▶ HISTORY Greek *dusentera* bad bowels

dysfunction *n* **1** *med* any disturbance or abnormality in the function of an organ or part **2** (esp. of a family) failure to show the characteristics or fulfil the purposes accepted as normal or beneficial > **dysfunctional** *adj*

dyslexia *n* a developmental disorder that causes learning difficulty with reading, writing, and numeracy ▶ HISTORY Greek *dus*- not + *lexis* word > **dyslexic** *adj, n*

dysmenorrhoea *or esp US* **dysmenorrhea** *n* painful or difficult menstruation ▶ HISTORY Greek *dus*- bad + *rhoia* a flowing

dyspepsia *n* indigestion ▶ HISTORY Greek *dus*- bad + *pepsis* digestion > **dyspeptic** *adj, n*

dysprosium *n* *chem* a metallic element of the lanthanide series. Symbol: Dy ▶ HISTORY Greek *dusprositos* difficult to get near

dystopia *n* *literature* an imaginary place where everything is as bad as it can be ▶ HISTORY (coined by John Stuart Mill (1806–73), English philosopher and economist): from Latin *dys*- bad + UTOPIA > **dystopian** *adj, n*

dystrophy (**diss**-trof-fee) *n* See **muscular dystrophy** ▶ HISTORY Greek *dus*- not + *trophē* food

d

Ee

e *maths* a number used as the base of natural logarithms. Approximate value: 2.718 282

E **1** *music* the third note of the scale of C major **2** East(ern) **3** English **4** *physics* **a** energy **b** electromotive force **5** *slang* the drug ecstasy

e- *prefix* electronic: *e-mail; e-tailer*

E- *prefix* used with a number following it to indicate that something, such as a food additive, conforms to an EU standard

each *adj* **1** every one of two or more people or things considered individually: *each year* ▷ *pron* **2** every one of two or more people or things: *each had been given one room to design* ▷ *adv* **3** for, to, or from each person or thing: *twenty pounds each* **4 each other** (of two or more people) each one to or at the other or others; one another: *they stared at each other* ▶ HISTORY Old English *ǣlc*

eager *adj* very keen to have or do something ▶ HISTORY Latin *acer* sharp, keen > **eagerly** *adv* > **eagerness** *n*

eagle *n* **1** a large bird of prey with broad wings and strong soaring flight **2** *golf* a score of two strokes under par for a hole ▶ HISTORY Latin *aquila*

eaglet *n* a young eagle

ear¹ *n* **1** the part of the body with which a person or animal hears **2** the external, visible part of the ear **3** the ability to hear musical and other sounds and interpret them accurately: *a good ear for languages* **4** willingness to listen: *they are always willing to lend an ear* **5 be all ears** to be prepared to listen attentively to something **6 fall on deaf ears** to be ignored: *his words fell on deaf ears* **7 in one ear and out the other** heard but quickly forgotten or ignored **8 out on one's ear** *informal* dismissed suddenly and unpleasantly **9 play by ear** to play without written music **10 play it by ear** *informal* to make up one's plan of action as one goes along **11 turn a deaf ear to** to be deliberately unresponsive to: *many countries have turned a deaf ear to their cries for help* **12 up to one's ears in** *informal* deeply involved in ▶ HISTORY Old English *ēare*

ear² *n* the part of a cereal plant, such as wheat or barley, that contains the seeds ▶ HISTORY Old English *ēar*

earache *n* pain in the ear

earbash *vb* *Brit, Austral & NZ, informal* to talk incessantly > **earbashing** *n*

eardrum *n* the thin membrane separating the external ear from the middle ear

earl *n* (in Britain) a nobleman ranking below a marquess and above a viscount ▶ HISTORY Old English *eorl* > **earldom** *n*

ear lobe *n* the soft hanging lowest part of the human ear

early *adj, adv* **-lier, -liest 1** occurring or arriving before the correct or expected time **2** in the first part of a period of time: *early April; early in the war* **3** near the beginning of the development or history of something: *early Britain was very primitive; early models of this car rust easily* ▶ HISTORY Old English *ǣrlīce*

Early English *n* a style of architecture used in England in the 12th and 13th centuries, characterized by narrow pointed arches and ornamental intersecting stonework in windows

earmark *vb* **1** to set (something) aside for a specific purpose ▷ *n* **2** a feature that enables the nature of something to be identified: *it had all the earmarks of a disaster*

■ **WORD HISTORY**

■ The notion of 'earmarking' something comes
■ from the practice of putting identification
■ marks on the ears of domestic or farm animals.

earn *vb* **1** to gain or be paid (money) in return for work **2** to acquire or deserve through one's behaviour or action: *you've earned a good night's sleep* **3** to make (money) as interest or profit: *her savings earned 8% interest* ▶ HISTORY Old English *earnian* > **earner** *n*

earnest¹ *adj* **1** serious and sincere, often excessively so ▷ *n* **2 in earnest** with serious or sincere intentions ▶ HISTORY Old English *eornost* > **earnestly** *adv* > **earnestness** *n*

earnest² *n* *Brit, Austral & NZ, old-fashioned* a part payment given in advance as a guarantee of the remainder, esp. to confirm a contract ▶ HISTORY Old French *erres* pledges

earnings *pl n* money earned

earphone *n* a small device connected to a digital audio player and worn over the ear, so that a person can listen to an audio file without anyone else hearing it

ear-piercing *adj* extremely loud or shrill

earplug *n* a piece of soft material placed in the ear to keep out noise or water

earring *n* a piece of jewellery worn in or hanging from the ear lobe

earshot *n* the range within which a sound can be heard: *out of earshot*

earth *n* **1** (sometimes cap) the planet that we live on, the third planet from the sun, the only one on which life is known to exist. *Related adjective:* **terrestrial 2** the part of the surface of this planet that is not water **3** the soil in which plants grow **4** the hole in which a fox lives **5** a wire in a piece of electrical equipment through which electricity can escape into the ground if a fault develops **6 come down to earth** to return to reality from a daydream or fantasy **7 on earth** used for emphasis: *what on earth happened?* ▷ *vb* **8** to fit (a piece of electrical equipment) with an earth ▶ HISTORY Old English *eorthe*

earthen *adj* made of earth or baked clay: *an earthen floor*

earthenware *n* dishes and other objects made of baked clay: *an earthenware flowerpot*

earthly *adj* **-lier, -liest 1** of life on earth as opposed to any heavenly or spiritual state **2** *informal* conceivable or possible: *what earthly reason would they have for lying?*

earthquake *n* a series of vibrations at the earth's surface caused by movement of the earth's crust

earth science *n* any science, such as geology, concerned with the structure, age, etc. of the earth

earthwork *n* **1** excavation of earth, as in engineering construction **2** a fortification made of earth

earthworm *n* a common worm that burrows in the soil

earthy *adj* **earthier, earthiest 1** open and direct in the treatment of sex, excretion, etc. **2** of or like earth: *earthy colours* > **earthiness** *n*

earwig *n* a thin brown insect with pincers at the tip of its abdomen

- ■ **WORD HISTORY**
- ■ 'Earwig' comes from Old English *ēarwicga*,
- ■ meaning 'ear insect'. It was once believed that
- ■ earwigs would creep into people's ears.

ease *n* **1** lack of difficulty **2** freedom from discomfort or worry **3** rest, leisure, or relaxation **4** freedom from poverty: *a life of leisure and ease* **5 at ease a** *mil* (of a soldier) standing in a relaxed position with the feet apart **b** in a relaxed attitude or frame of mind ▷ *vb* **easing, eased 6** to make or become less difficult or severe: *the pain gradually eased* **7** to move into or out of a place or situation slowly and carefully **8 ease off** or **up** to lessen or cause to lessen in severity, pressure, tension, or strain: *the rain eased off* ▶ HISTORY Old French *aise*

easel *n* a frame on legs, used for supporting an artist's canvas, a display, or a blackboard ▶ HISTORY Dutch *ass*

easement *n* **1** *law* the right enjoyed by a landowner of making limited use of his neighbour's land, as by crossing it to reach his own property **2** the act of easing or something that brings ease

easily *adv* **1** without difficulty **2** without doubt; by far: *easily the most senior Chinese minister to visit the West*

east *n* **1** one of the four cardinal points of the compass, at 90° clockwise from north **2** the direction along a line of latitude towards the sunrise **3 the east** any area lying in or towards the east ▷ *adj* **4** situated in, moving towards, or facing the east **5** (esp. of the wind) from the east ▷ *adv* **6** in, to, or towards the east ▶ HISTORY Old English *ēast*

East *n* **1 the East a** the southern and eastern parts of Asia **b** (esp. formerly) the countries in Eastern Europe and Asia which are or have been under Communist rule ▷ *adj* **2** of or denoting the eastern part of a country or region

eastbound *adj* going towards the east

Easter *n* **1** *Christianity* a festival commemorating the Resurrection of Christ ▷ *adj* **2** taking place at the time of the year when this festival is celebrated: *the Easter holidays*

- ■ **WORD HISTORY**
- ■ Although Easter is a Christian festival, its name
- ■ comes from Old English *Eostre*, the name of a
- ■ pre-Christian Germanic goddess whose festival
- ■ was celebrated at the spring equinox.

Easter egg *n* a chocolate egg given at Easter

easterly *adj* **1** of or in the east ▷ *adv, adj* **2** towards the east **3** from the east: *an easterly breeze*

eastern *adj* **1** situated in or towards the east **2** facing or moving towards the east **3** (sometimes cap) of or characteristic of the east or East > **easternmost** *adj*

Easterner *n* a person from the east of a country or region

eastern hemisphere *n* the half of the globe that contains Europe, Asia, Africa, and Australia

easting *n* *geog* a longitudinal grid line. Compare **northing**

eastward *adj, adv* also **eastwards 1** towards the east ▷ *n* **2** the eastward part or direction

easy *adj* **easier, easiest 1** not difficult; simple: *the house is easy to keep clean* **2** free from pain, care, or anxiety: *an easy life* **3** tolerant and undemanding; easy-going **4** defenceless or readily fooled: *easy prey* **5** moderate and not involving any great effort: *an easy ride* **6** *informal* ready to fall in with any suggestion made: *he wanted to do something and I was easy about it* **7** *informal* pleasant and not involving any great effort to enjoy: *easy on the eye* ▷ *adv* **8 go easy on a** to avoid using too much of: *he'd tried to go easy on the engines* **b** to treat less severely than is deserved: *go easy on him, he's just a kid* **9 take it easy** to relax and avoid stress or undue hurry ▶ HISTORY Old French *aisié* > **easiness** *n*

easy chair *n* a comfortable upholstered armchair

easy-going *adj* relaxed in manner or attitude; very tolerant

eat *vb* **eating, ate, eaten 1** to take (food) into the mouth and swallow it **2** to have a meal: *sometimes we eat out of doors* **3** *informal* to make anxious or worried: *what's eating you?* **4 eat away** or **into** or **up** to destroy or use up partly or wholly: *inflation ate into the firm's profits* ▶ HISTORY Old English *etan* > **eater** *n*

See WORD FOCUS **eat**

eatable *adj* fit or suitable for eating

eau de Cologne (oh de kol-**lone**) *n* full form of **cologne** ▶ HISTORY French: water of Cologne

eaves *pl n* the edge of a sloping roof that overhangs the walls ▶ HISTORY Old English *efes*

eavesdrop *vb* **-dropping, -dropped** to listen secretly to a private conversation > **eavesdropper** *n*

eat

There are a number of more descriptive words which you can use instead of the basic **eat** to say something about the way in which a person eats.

DEFINITION 1

- If you **consume** something, you eat it. This is a formal word: Andrew would **consume** nearly a pound of cheese a day.
- When an animal **feeds**, or **feeds on** something, it eats: After a few days the caterpillars stopped **feeding**. • Slugs **feed on** decaying plant material.
- If you **swallow** something, you make it go from your mouth into your stomach: Snakes **swallow** their prey whole.
- If you **snack**, you eat things between meals: Instead of **snacking** on crisps and chocolate, eat fruit.
- If you **chew** something, you break it up with your teeth so that it is easier to swallow: I pulled out a filling while I was **chewing** a toffee.

- If you **nibble** food, you eat it by biting very small pieces of it, perhaps because you are not very hungry: She **nibbled** at a piece of dry toast.
- If you **munch** food, you eat it by chewing it slowly, thoroughly, and rather noisily: Luke **munched** his sandwiches appreciatively.
- If you **stuff** yourself, you eat a lot of food: They'd **stuffed** themselves with sweets before dinner.
- If you **gobble**, **guzzle**, **wolf (down)**, or **scoff** food, you eat it quickly and greedily. **Wolf (down)** and **scoff** are informal words: Pete **gobbled** all the stew before anyone else arrived. • I **guzzled** the chocolate biscuits which she had left out. • I was back in the changing room, **wolfing** sandwiches. • She bought a hot dog from a stand and **wolfed** it **down**. • You're so greedy! You've **scoffed** the lot!
- If you **devour** something, you eat it quickly and eagerly: She **devoured** half an apple pie.

e

The word 'eavesdrop' comes from Old English *yfesdrype*, meaning 'water dripping from the eaves'. The 'eavesdrop' was the ground around a house where the water dripped down from the eaves, and an 'eavesdropper' was someone who would stand outside in the rain to eavesdrop to hear what was being said inside the house.

ebb *vb* **1** (of the sea or the tide) to flow back from its highest point **2** to fall away or decline: *her anger ebbed away* ▷ *n* **3** the flowing back of the tide from high to low water **4 at a low ebb** in a weak state: *her creativity was at a low ebb* ▶ **HISTORY** Old English *ebba* ebb-tide

ebony *n* **1** a very hard dark-coloured wood used to make furniture, etc. ▷ *adj* **2** very deep black ▶ **HISTORY** Greek *ebenos*

e-book *n* Also: **electronic book** a book that can be read on a computer or other electronic device ▷ *vb* to book (appointments, tickets, etc.) through the internet

ebullient *adj* full of enthusiasm or excitement ▶ **HISTORY** Latin *ebullire* to bubble forth, be boisterous > **ebullience** *n*

EC 1 Eastern Caribbean **2** European Commission **3** European Community: a former name for the European Union

e-card *n* a greetings card that can be read on a computer or other electronic device

eccentric *adj* **1** unconventional or odd **2** (of circles) not having the same centre ▷ *n* **3** a person who behaves unconventionally or oddly ▶ **HISTORY** Greek *ek-* away from + *kentron* centre > **eccentrically** *adv*

eccentricity *n* **1** unconventional or odd behaviour **2** (*pl* **-ties**) an unconventional or odd habit or act

ecclesiastic *n* **1** a member of the clergy ▷ *adj* **2** of or relating to the Christian Church or its clergy ▶ **HISTORY** Greek *ekklēsia* assembly

ecclesiastical *adj* of or relating to the Christian Church or its clergy

ECG electrocardiogram

echelon (**esh**-a-lon) *n* **1** a level of power or responsibility: *the upper echelons of society* **2** *mil* a formation in which units follow one another but are spaced out sideways to allow each a line of fire ahead ▶ **HISTORY** French *échelon* rung of a ladder

echidna (ik-**kid**-na) *n, pl* **-nas, -nae** (-nee) an Australian spiny egg-laying mammal. Also called: **spiny anteater**

echinoderm (ik-**kine**-oh-durm) *n* a sea creature with a five-part symmetrical body, such as a starfish or sea urchin ▶ **HISTORY** Greek *ekhinos* sea urchin + *derma* skin

echo *n, pl* **-oes 1 a** the reflection of sound by a solid object **b** a sound reflected by a solid object **2** a repetition or imitation of someone else's opinions **3** something that brings back memories: *an echo of the past* **4** the signal reflected back to a radar transmitter by an object ▷ *vb* **-oing, -oed 5** (of a sound) to be reflected off an object in such a way that it can be heard again **6** (of a place) to be filled with a sound and its echoes: *the church echoed with singing* **7** (of people) to repeat or imitate (what someone else has said): *his conclusion echoed that of Jung* ▶ **HISTORY** Greek *ēkhō* > **echoing** *adj*

echo chamber *n* a room with walls that reflect sound, used to create an echo effect in recording and broadcasting

echolocation *n* the discovery of an object's position by measuring the time taken for an echo to return from it

echo sounder *n* a navigation device that

determines depth by measuring the time taken for a pulse of sound to reach the sea bed and for the echo to return

e-cigarette n an electronic vaporizer that simulates the effect of smoking

éclair n a finger-shaped cake of choux pastry, filled with cream and coated with chocolate ▶ HISTORY French: lightning (probably because it does not last long)

eclampsia n pathol a serious condition that can develop towards the end of a pregnancy, causing high blood pressure, swelling, and convulsions

eclectic adj **1** composed of elements selected from a wide range of styles, ideas, or sources: the eclectic wine list includes bottles from all round the world **2** selecting elements from a wide range of styles, ideas, or sources: an eclectic approach that takes the best from all schools of psychology ▷ n **3** a person who takes an eclectic approach ▶ HISTORY Greek eklegein to select > **eclecticism** n

eclipse n **1** the obscuring of one star or planet by another. A **solar eclipse** occurs when the moon passes between the sun and the earth; a **lunar eclipse** when the earth passes between the sun and the moon **2** a loss of importance, power, or fame: communism eventually went into eclipse ▷ vb **eclipsing, eclipsed 3** to overshadow or surpass **4** (of a star or planet) to hide (another planet or star) from view ▶ HISTORY Greek ekleipsis a forsaking

ecliptic n astron the great circle on the celestial sphere representing the apparent annual path of the sun relative to the stars

eco- combining form denoting ecology or ecological: ecotourism

eco-friendly adj not causing damage to the environment: eco-friendly washing powder

E.coli (ee-**koal**-eye) n a common bacterium often found in the intestines ▶ HISTORY shortened from Escherichia coli, after Theodor Escherich, paediatrician

ecological adj **1** of or relating to ecology **2** tending or intended to benefit or protect the environment: an ecological approach to agriculture > **ecologically** adv

ecological pyramid n ecology a hierarchy of organisms shown in a diagram where the base is the producer level, and then green plants, herbivores and carnivores form the remaining tiers

ecology n the study of the relationships between people, animals, and plants, and their environment ▶ HISTORY Greek oikos house > **ecologist** n

e-commerce or **ecommerce** n business transactions conducted on the internet

econ. economy

economic adj **1** of or relating to an economy or economics **2** Brit & Austral capable of being produced or operated for profit **3** informal inexpensive or cheap

economical adj **1** not requiring a lot of money to use: low fuel consumption makes this car very

economical **2** (of a person) spending money carefully and sensibly **3** using no more time, effort, or resources than is necessary **4** **economical with the truth** euphemistic deliberately withholding information > **economically** adv

economics n **1** the study of the production and consumption of goods and services and the commercial activities of a society ▷ pl n **2** financial aspects: the economics of health care

economist n a person who specializes in economics

economize or **-mise** vb **-mizing, -mized** or **-mising, -mised** to reduce expense or waste: people are being advised to economize on fuel use

economy n, pl **-mies 1** the system by which the production, distribution, and consumption of goods and services is organized in a country or community: the rural economy **2** the ability of a country to generate wealth through business and industry: unless the economy improves, more jobs will be lost **3** careful use of money or resources to save expense, time, or energy **4** an instance of this: we can make economies by reusing envelopes ▷ adj **5** denoting a class of air travel that is cheaper than first-class **6** offering a larger quantity for a lower price: an economy pack ▶ HISTORY Greek oikos house + nemein to manage

economy of scale n econ a fall in average costs resulting from an increase in the scale of production

ecosphere n biol the parts of the universe, esp. on earth, where life can exist

ecosystem n ecology the system of relationships between animals and plants and their environment

ecoterrorist n a person who uses violence in order to achieve environmentalist aims > **ecoterrorism** n

ecotone n environmental science a transition zone between two major ecological communities

ecotourism n tourism designed to contribute to the protection of the environment or at least minimize damage to it > **ecotourist** n

ecotype n biol a group of organisms within a species that is adapted to particular environmental conditions and therefore exhibits behavioural, structural, or physiological differences from other members of the species

ecru adj pale creamy-brown ▶ HISTORY French

ecstasy n, pl **-sies 1** a state of extreme delight or joy **2** slang a strong drug that acts as a stimulant and can cause hallucinations ▶ HISTORY Greek ekstasis displacement, trance > **ecstatic** adj > **ecstatically** adv

ECT electroconvulsive therapy: the treatment of depression and some other mental disorders by passing a current of electricity through the brain, producing a convulsion

ectomorph n physiol a person with a thin body build. Compare **endomorph, mesomorph** ▶ HISTORY Greek ektos outside + morphē shape > **ectomorphic** adj

ectopic pregnancy (eck-**top**-ick) *n* the abnormal development of a fertilized egg outside the uterus, usually in a Fallopian tube

ectoplasm *n* (in spiritualism) the substance that supposedly is emitted from the body of a medium during a trance ▶ HISTORY Greek *ektos* outside + *plasma* something moulded

ecumenical *adj* **1** of or relating to the Christian Church throughout the world **2** tending to promote unity among Christian churches ▶ HISTORY Greek *oikoumenikos* of the inhabited world

ecumenism *or* **ecumenicism** *n* the aim of unity among Christian churches throughout the world

eczema (**ek**-sim-a, ig-**zeem**-a) *n* *pathol* a condition in which the skin becomes inflamed and itchy ▶ HISTORY Greek *ek*- out + *zein* to boil

ed. 1 edition **2** editor

Edam *n* a round yellow Dutch cheese with a red waxy covering ▶ HISTORY after *Edam*, in Holland

edaphic (ee-**dah**-fic) *adj* of or relating to the physical and chemical conditions of the soil, in relation to the plant and animal life it supports ▶ HISTORY Greek *edaphos* bottom, soil

eddo (**ed**-doh) *n, pl* **eddoes** same as **taro**

eddy *n, pl* **-dies 1** a circular movement of air, water, or smoke ▷ *vb* **-dies, -dying, -died 2** to move with a gentle circular motion; swirl gently ▶ HISTORY probably from Old Norse

edelweiss (**ade**-el-vice) *n* a small white alpine flower ▶ HISTORY German: noble white

edema (id-**deem**-a) *n, pl* **-mata** same as **oedema**

Eden *n* **1** Also called: **Garden of Eden** *Bible* the garden in which Adam and Eve were placed at the Creation **2** a place of great delight or contentment ▶ HISTORY Hebrew *'ēdhen* place of pleasure

edentate *n* **1** a mammal with few or no teeth, such as an armadillo or a sloth ▷ *adj* **2** denoting such a mammal ▶ HISTORY Latin *edentatus* lacking teeth

edge *n* **1** a border or line where something ends or begins: *the edge of the city* **2** a line along which two faces or surfaces of a solid meet **3** the sharp cutting side of a blade **4** keenness, sharpness, or urgency: *there was a nervous edge to his voice* **5 have the edge on** to have a slight advantage over **6 on edge** nervous and irritable **7 set someone's teeth on edge** to make someone acutely irritated ▷ *vb* **edging, edged 8** to make, form, or be an edge or border for: *a pillow edged with lace* **9** to move very gradually in a particular direction: *I edged through to the front of the crowd* ▶ HISTORY Old English *ecg*

edgeways *or esp US & Canad* **edgewise** *adv* **1** with the edge forwards or uppermost **2 get a word in edgeways** to interrupt a conversation in which someone else is talking continuously

edging *n* anything placed along an edge for decoration

edgy *adj* **edgier, edgiest** nervous, irritable, or anxious > **edginess** *n*

edible *adj* fit to be eaten; eatable ▶ HISTORY Latin *edere* to eat > **edibility** *n*

edict (**ee**-dikt) *n* a decree or order given by any authority ▶ HISTORY Latin *edicere* to declare

edifice (**ed**-if-iss) *n* **1** a large or impressive building **2** an elaborate system of beliefs and institutions: *the crumbling edifice of Communist rule* ▶ HISTORY Latin *aedificare* to build

edify (**ed**-if-fie) *vb* **-fies, -fying, -fied** to inform or instruct (someone) with a view to improving his or her morals or understanding ▶ HISTORY Latin *aedificare* to build > **edification** *n* > **edifying** *adj*

edit *vb* **editing, edited 1** to prepare (text) for publication by checking and improving its accuracy or clarity **2** to be in charge of (a newspaper or magazine) **3** to prepare (a film, tape, etc.) by rearranging or selecting material **4 edit out** to remove (a section) from a text, film, etc.

edition *n* **1** a particular version of a book, newspaper, or magazine produced at one time: *the revised paperback edition* **2** a single television or radio programme which forms part of a series: *the first edition goes on the air in thirty minutes*

editor *n* **1** a person who edits **2** a person in overall charge of a newspaper or magazine **3** a person in charge of one section of a newspaper or magazine: *the Political Editor* **4** a person in overall control of a television or radio programme ▶ HISTORY Latin *edere* to publish > **editorship** *n*

editorial *n* **1** an article in a newspaper expressing the opinion of the editor or publishers ▷ *adj* **2** of editing or editors: *an editorial meeting* **3** relating to the contents and opinions of a magazine or newspaper: *the paper's editorial policy* > **editorially** *adv*

EDP electronic data processing

educate *vb* **-cating, -cated 1** to teach (someone) over a long period of time so that he or she acquires knowledge and understanding of a range of subjects **2** to send (someone) to a particular educational establishment: *he was educated at mission schools* **3** to teach (someone) about a particular matter: *a campaign to educate people to the dangers of smoking* ▶ HISTORY Latin *educare* to rear, educate > **educative** *adj*

education *n* **1** the process of acquiring knowledge and understanding **2** knowledge and understanding acquired through study and training: *education is the key to a good job* **3** the process of teaching, esp. at a school, college, or university **4** the theory of teaching and learning > **educational** *adj* > **educationally** *adv* > **educationalist** *or* **educationist** *n*

Edwardian *adj* of or in the reign of King Edward VII of Great Britain and Ireland (1901–10)

EEC European Economic Community: a former name for the European Union

EEG electroencephalogram

eel *n* a slimy snakelike fish ▶ HISTORY Old English *ǣl*

eerie *adj* **eerier, eeriest** strange and frightening ▶ HISTORY probably from Old English *earg* cowardly > **eerily** *adv*

e

efface vb **-facing, -faced 1** to obliterate or make dim: *nothing effaced the memory* **2** to rub out or erase **3 efface oneself** to make oneself inconspicuous ▸ **HISTORY** French *effacer* to obliterate the face > **effacement** n

effect n **1** a change or state of affairs caused by something or someone: *the gales have had a serious effect on the crops* **2** power to influence or produce a result: *the wine had little effect on him* **3** the condition of being operative: *a new law has come into effect* **4** the overall impression: *the whole effect is one of luxury* **5** basic meaning or purpose: *words to that effect* **6** an impression, usually a contrived one: *he paused for effect* **7** a physical phenomenon: *the greenhouse effect* **8 in effect** for all practical purposes: *in effect he has no choice* **9 take effect** to begin to produce results ▸ vb **10** to cause (something) to take place: *a peace treaty was effected* ▸ **HISTORY** Latin *efficere* to accomplish

effective adj **1** producing a desired result: *an effective vaccine against HIV* **2** officially coming into operation: *the new rates become effective at the end of May* **3** impressive: *a highly effective speech* **4** in reality, although not officially or in theory: *he is in effective control of the company* > **effectively** adv > **effectiveness** n

effector n physiol a nerve ending that ends in a muscle or gland and provides stimulation causing contraction or secretion

effects pl n **1** personal belongings **2** lighting, sounds, etc. to accompany a stage, film, or broadcast production

effectual adj **1** producing the intended result **2** (of a document, etc.) having legal force > **effectually** adv

effeminate adj (of a man) displaying characteristics regarded as typical of a woman ▸ **HISTORY** Latin *femina* woman > **effeminacy** n

effervescent adj **1** (of a liquid) giving off bubbles of gas **2** (of a person) lively and enthusiastic ▸ **HISTORY** Latin *effervescere* to foam up > **effervescence** n

effete (if-**feet**) adj weak, powerless, and decadent ▸ **HISTORY** Latin *effetus* exhausted by bearing young

efficacious adj producing the intended result ▸ **HISTORY** Latin *efficere* to achieve > **efficacy** n

efficient adj working or producing effectively without wasting effort, energy, or money ▸ **HISTORY** Latin *efficiens* effecting > **efficiency** n > **efficiently** adv

effigy (**ef**-fij-ee) n, pl **-gies 1** a statue or carving of someone, often as a memorial: *a 14th-century wooden effigy of a knight* **2** a crude representation of someone, used as a focus for contempt: *an effigy of the president was set on fire* ▸ **HISTORY** Latin *effingere* to portray

efflorescence n **1** the blooming of flowers on a plant **2** a brief period of high-quality artistic activity ▸ **HISTORY** Latin *efflorescere* to blossom

effluent n liquid discharged as waste, for instance from a factory or sewage works ▸ **HISTORY** Latin *effluere* to flow out

effluvium n, pl **-via** an unpleasant smell, such as the smell of decaying matter ▸ **HISTORY** Latin: a flowing out

efflux n **1** the process of flowing out **2** something that flows out

effort n **1** physical or mental energy needed to do something **2** a determined attempt to do something **3** achievement or creation: *his earliest literary efforts* **4** physics an applied force acting against inertia ▸ **HISTORY** Latin *fortis* strong > **effortless** adj > **effortlessly** adv

effrontery n insolence or boldness ▸ **HISTORY** Late Latin *effrons* putting forth one's forehead

effusion n **1** an unrestrained verbal expression of emotions or ideas **2** a sudden pouring out: *small effusions of blood* ▸ **HISTORY** Latin *effundere* to shed

effusive adj enthusiastically showing pleasure, gratitude, or approval > **effusively** adv > **effusiveness** n

E-FIT n trademark an image generated by a computer to create the likeness of a face, used by police to trace people from witnesses' descriptions ▸ **HISTORY** from Electronic *F*acial *I*dentification *T*echnique

EFL English as a Foreign Language

EFTA European Free Trade Association

EFTPOS electronic funds transfer at point of sale

e.g. for example ▸ **HISTORY** Latin *exempli gratia*

egalitarian adj **1** expressing or supporting the idea that all people should be equal ▸ n **2** a person who believes that all people should be equal ▸ **HISTORY** French *égal* equal > **egalitarianism** n

egest (ee-**jest**) vb physiol to discharge waste material from the body > **egestion** n

egg n **1** the oval or round object laid by the females of birds, reptiles, and other creatures, containing a developing embryo **2** a hen's egg used for food **3** a type of cell produced in the body of a female animal which can develop into a baby if fertilized by a male reproductive cell **4 have egg on one's face** informal to have been made to look ridiculous **5 put all one's eggs in one basket** to rely entirely on one action or decision, with no alternative in case of failure ▸ **HISTORY** Old Norse

egghead n informal an intellectual person

eggplant n US, Canad, Austral & NZ a dark purple tropical fruit, cooked and eaten as a vegetable

eggshell n **1** the hard porous outer layer of a bird's egg ▸ adj **2** (of paint) having a very slight sheen

ego n, pl **egos 1** the part of a person's self that is able to recognize that person as being distinct from other people and things **2** a person's opinion of his or her own worth: *men with fragile egos* ▸ **HISTORY** Latin: I

egocentric adj thinking only of one's own interests and feelings > **egocentricity** n

egomania n an obsessive concern with fulfilling one's own needs and desires, regardless of the effect on other people > **egomaniac** n

egotism or **egoism** n concern only for one's own interests and feelings > **egotist** or **egoist** n > **egotistical, egoistical, egotistic** or **egoistic** adj

e

egregious (ig-**greej**-uss) *adj* shockingly bad: *egregious government waste* ▶ HISTORY Latin *egregius* outstanding (literally: standing out from the herd)

egress (**ee**-gress) *n formal* **1** the act of going out **2** a way out or exit ▶ HISTORY Latin *egredi* to come out

egret (**ee**-grit) *n* a wading bird like a heron, with long white feathery plumes ▶ HISTORY Old French *aigrette*

Egyptian *adj* **1** of Egypt **2** of the ancient Egyptians ▷ *n* **3** a person from Egypt **4** a member of an ancient people who established an advanced civilization in Egypt **5** the language of the ancient Egyptians

Egyptology *n* the study of the culture of ancient Egypt > **Egyptologist** *n*

eh *interj* an exclamation used to ask for repetition or confirmation

eider *or* **eider duck** *n* a large sea duck of the N hemisphere ▶ HISTORY Old Norse *æthr*

eiderdown *n* a thick warm cover for a bed, filled with soft feathers, originally the breast feathers of the female eider duck

Eid-ul-Adha (**eed**-ool-**ah**-da) *n* an annual Muslim festival, marking the end of the pilgrimage to Mecca ▶ HISTORY from Arabic *id ul adha* festival of sacrifice

Eid-ul-Fitr (**eed**-ool-**feet**-er) *n* an annual Muslim festival, marking the end of Ramadan ▶ HISTORY from Arabic *id ul fitr* festival of fast-breaking

eight *n* **1** the cardinal number that is the sum of one and seven **2** a numeral, 8 or VIII, representing this number **3** something representing or consisting of eight units **4** *rowing* **a** a light narrow boat rowed by eight people **b** the crew of such a boat ▷ *adj* **5** amounting to eight: *eight apples* ▶ HISTORY Old English *eahta* > **eighth** *adj, n*

eighteen *n* **1** the cardinal number that is the sum of ten and eight **2** a numeral, 18 or XVIII, representing this number **3** something representing or consisting of 18 units ▷ *adj* **4** amounting to eighteen: *eighteen months* > **eighteenth** *adj, n*

eightfold *adj* **1** having eight times as many or as much **2** composed of eight parts ▷ *adv* **3** by eight times as many or as much

eighty *n, pl* **eighties 1** the cardinal number that is the product of ten and eight **2** a numeral, 80 or LXXX, representing this number **3** something representing or consisting of 80 units ▷ *adj* **4** amounting to eighty: *eighty miles* > **eightieth** *adj, n*

eina (**ay**-na) *interj S African* an exclamation of pain ▶ HISTORY Khoikhoi

einsteinium *n chem* a radioactive metallic element artificially produced from plutonium. Symbol: Es ▶ HISTORY after Albert *Einstein*, physicist

Eire *n* Ireland or the Republic of Ireland ▶ HISTORY Irish Gaelic

EIS Educational Institute of Scotland

eisteddfod (ice-**sted**-fod) *n* a Welsh festival with competitions in music, poetry, drama, and art ▶ HISTORY Welsh: session

either *adj, pron* **1** one or the other (of two): *we were offered either fish or beef* **2** both one and the other: *we sat at either end of a long settee* ▷ *conj* **3** used preceding two or more possibilities joined by *or*: *it must be stored either in the fridge or in a cool place* ▷ *adv* **4** likewise: *I don't eat meat and my husband doesn't either* **5** used to qualify or modify a previous statement: *he wasn't exactly ugly, he wasn't an oil painting either* ▶ HISTORY Old English *ægther*

ejaculate *vb* **-lating, -lated 1** to discharge semen from the penis while having an orgasm **2** *literary* to say or shout suddenly ▶ HISTORY Latin *ejaculari* to hurl out > **ejaculation** *n* > **ejaculatory** *adj*

eject *vb* **1** to push or send out forcefully **2** to compel (someone) to leave a place or position **3** to leave an aircraft rapidly in mid-flight, using an ejector seat ▶ HISTORY Latin *ejicere* > **ejection** *n* > **ejector** *n*

ejector seat *or* **ejection seat** *n* a seat in a military aircraft that throws the pilot out in an emergency

eke out *vb* **eking, eked 1** to make (a supply) last for a long time by using as little as possible **2** to manage to sustain (a living) despite having barely enough food or money ▶ HISTORY obsolete *eke* to enlarge

elaborate *adj* **1** very complex because of having many different parts: *elaborate equipment* **2** having a very complicated design: *elaborate embroidery* ▷ *vb* **-rating, -rated 3 elaborate on** to describe in more detail: *he did not elaborate on his plans* **4** to develop (a plan or theory) in detail ▶ HISTORY Latin *elaborare* to take pains > **elaborately** *adv* > **elaboration** *n*

élan (ale-**an**) *n* style and liveliness ▶ HISTORY French

eland (**eel**-and) *n* a large spiral-horned antelope of southern Africa ▶ HISTORY Dutch: elk

elapse *vb* **elapsing, elapsed** (of time) to pass by ▶ HISTORY Latin *elabi* to slip away

elastic *adj* **1** capable of returning to its original shape after stretching, compression, or other distortion **2** capable of being adapted to meet the demands of a particular situation: *an elastic interpretation of the law* **3** made of elastic ▷ *n* **4** tape, cord, or fabric containing flexible rubber ▶ HISTORY Greek *elastikos* propellent > **elastically** *adv* > **elasticated** *adj* > **elasticity** *n*

elastic energy *n physics* the energy contained in an object that is capable of returning to its original shape after stretching, compression, or other distortion

elated *adj* extremely happy and excited ▶ HISTORY Latin *elatus* carried away > **elatedly** *adv*

elation *n* a feeling of great happiness and excitement

elbow *n* **1** the joint between the upper arm and the forearm **2** the part of a garment that covers the elbow ▷ *vb* **3** to push with one's elbow or elbows: *she elbowed him aside; he elbowed his way to the bar* ▶ HISTORY Old English *elnboga*

elbow grease *n facetious* vigorous physical labour, esp. hard rubbing

elbow room *n* sufficient scope to move or to function

elder[1] *adj* **1** (of one of two people) born earlier ▷ *n* **2** an older person: *have some respect for your elders* **3** a senior member of a tribe, who has authority **4** (in certain Protestant Churches) a member of the church who has certain administrative, teaching, or preaching powers ▶ HISTORY Old English *eldra*

elder[2] *n* a shrub or small tree with clusters of small white flowers and dark purple berries ▶ HISTORY Old English *ellern*

elderberry *n*, *pl* -ries **1** the fruit of the elder **2** same as **elder**[2]

elderly *adj* **1** rather old ▷ *pl n* **2 the elderly** old people

eldest *adj* (of a person, esp. a child) oldest ▶ HISTORY Old English *eldesta*

El Dorado (el dor-**rah**-doe) *n* **1** a fabled city in South America, supposedly rich in treasure **2** Also: **eldorado** any place of great riches or fabulous opportunity ▶ HISTORY Spanish: the golden (place)

eldritch *adj poetic*, *Scot* unearthly or weird ▶ HISTORY origin unknown

elect *vb* **1** to choose (someone) to fill a position by voting for him or her: *she was elected President in* 1990 **2** to choose or decide: *those who elected to stay* ▷ *adj* **3** voted into office but not yet having taken over from the current office-bearer: *the President elect* ▷ *pl n* **4 the elect** any group of people specially chosen for some privilege ▶ HISTORY Latin *eligere* to select > **electable** *adj*

election *n* **1 a** a process whereby people vote for a person or party to fill a position: *last month's presidential election* **b** short for **general election** **2** the gaining of political power or taking up of a position in an organization as a result of being voted for: *he will be seeking election as the President of Romania*

electioneering *n* the act of taking an active part in a political campaign, for example by canvassing

elective *adj* **1** of or based on selection by vote: *an elective office* **2** not compulsory or necessary: *an elective hysterectomy*

elector *n* **1** someone who is eligible to vote in an election **2** (in the Holy Roman Empire) any of the German princes who were entitled to elect a new emperor: *the Elector of Hanover*

electoral *adj* of or relating to elections: *the electoral system* > **electorally** *adv*

electoral college *n* a body of electors who are chosen by a larger group of voters to vote on their behalf

electoral register *n* the official list of all the people in an area who are eligible to vote in elections

electorate *n* **1** all the people in an area or country who have the right to vote in an election **2** the rank or territory of an elector of the Holy Roman Empire

electric *adj* **1** produced by, transmitting, or powered by electricity: *an electric fire* **2** very tense or exciting: *the atmosphere was electric* ▷ *n* **3 electrics** *Brit* an electric circuit or electric appliances ▶ HISTORY Greek *ēlektron* amber (because friction causes amber to become electrically charged)

electrical *adj* of or relating to electricity > **electrically** *adv*

electrical conductivity *n physics* a measure of the ability of a substance to conduct electricity

electrical energy *n physics* electricity generated by electrons, ions, or other charged particles

electrical engineering *n* the branch of engineering concerned with practical applications of electricity and electronics > **electrical engineer** *n*

electric blanket *n* a blanket fitted with an electric heating element, used to warm a bed

electric chair *n* (in the US) a chair for executing criminals by passing a strong electric current through them

electric current *n electronics* a flow or rate of flow of electric charge through a conductor

electric eel *n* an eel-like South American freshwater fish, which can stun or kill its prey with a powerful electric shock

electric field *n physics* a region of space surrounding a charged particle within which another charged particle experiences a force

electric generator *n physics* a device for converting mechanical energy into electricity

electrician *n* a person trained to install and repair electrical equipment

electricity *n* **1** a form of energy associated with stationary or moving electrons, ions, or other charged particles **2** the supply of electricity to houses, factories, etc. for heating, lighting, etc.

- ■ **WORD HISTORY**
- ■ 'Electricity' comes from the Greek word *ēlektron*,
- ■ meaning 'amber'. The ancient Greeks had found
- ■ out that if you rub a piece of amber, it will
- ■ attract small particles by the force that we now
- ■ understand to be electricity.

electric shock *n* pain and muscular spasms caused by an electric current passing through the body

electrify *vb* -fies, -fying, -fied **1** to adapt or equip (a system or device) to work by electricity: *the whole track has now been electrified* **2** to provide (an area) with electricity **3** to startle or excite intensely > **electrification** *n*

electro- *combining form* electric or electrically: *electroconvulsive* ▶ HISTORY Greek *ēlektron* amber; see ELECTRIC

electrocardiograph *n* an instrument for making tracings (**electrocardiograms**) recording the electrical activity of the heart

electrocute *vb* -cuting, -cuted to kill or injure by an electric shock ▶ HISTORY ELECTRO- + (EXE)CUTE > **electrocution** *n*

electrode *n* a small piece of metal used to take an electric current to or from a power source, piece of equipment, or living body

electrodynamics *n* the branch of physics

concerned with the interactions between electrical and mechanical forces

electroencephalograph (ill-lek-tro-en-**sef**-a-loh-graf) *n* an instrument for making tracings (**electroencephalograms**) recording the electrical activity of the brain

electrolysis (ill-lek-**troll**-iss-iss) *n* **1** the process of passing an electric current through a liquid in order to produce a chemical reaction in the liquid **2** the destruction of living tissue, such as hair roots, by an electric current

electrolyte *n* a solution or molten substance that conducts electricity > **electrolytic** *adj*

electromagnet *n* a magnet consisting of a coil of wire wound round an iron core through which a current is passed

electromagnetic *adj* **1** of or operated by an electromagnet **2** of or relating to electromagnetism > **electromagnetically** *adv*

electromagnetic induction *n physics* the process by which a conductor moving through an electric field creates an electric current

electromagnetic spectrum *n physics* the complete range of electromagnetic radiation from the longest radio waves to the shortest gamma radiation

electromagnetic wave *n physics* a wave of energy produced in an electromagnetic field

electromagnetism *n* magnetism produced by an electric current

electromotive *adj physics* of or producing an electric current

electromotive force *n physics* **1** a source of energy that can cause current to flow in an electrical circuit **2** the rate at which energy is drawn from such a source when a unit of current flows through the circuit, measured in volts

electron *n physics* an elementary particle in all atoms that has a negative electrical charge

electronegative *adj physics* **1** having a negative electric charge **2** tending to gain or attract electrons

electron flow *n electronics* a continuous stream of electrons from the negative terminal to the positive terminal of a battery or cell

electronic *adj* **1** (of a device, circuit, or system) containing transistors, silicon chips, etc. which control the current passing through it **2** making use of electronic systems: *electronic surveillance devices* > **electronically** *adv*

electronic mail *n* See **e-mail**

electronic publishing *n* Also: **e-publishing** the publication of information on discs, magnetic tape, etc., so that it can be accessed by computer

electronics *n* the technology concerned with the development, behaviour, and applications of devices and circuits, for example televisions and computers, which make use of electronic components such as transistors or silicon chips

electron microscope *n* a powerful microscope that uses electrons, rather than light, to produce a magnified image

electronvolt *n physics* a unit of energy equal to the work done on an electron accelerated through a potential difference of 1 volt

electroplate *vb* **-plating, -plated 1** to coat (an object) with metal by dipping it in a special liquid through which an electric current is passed ▷ *n* **2** electroplated articles collectively

electropositive *adj physics* **1** having a positive electric charge **2** tending to release electrons

electroscope *n physics* an apparatus for detecting an electric charge, typically consisting of a rod holding two gold foils that separate when a charge is applied

electrostatics *n* the branch of physics concerned with static electricity > **electrostatic** *adj*

elegant *adj* **1** attractive and graceful or stylish **2** cleverly simple and clear: *an elegant summary* ▶ HISTORY Latin *elegans* tasteful > **elegance** *n* > **elegantly** *adv*

elegiac *adj literary* sad, mournful, or plaintive

elegy (**el**-lij-ee) *n, pl* **-gies** a mournful poem or song, esp. a lament for the dead ▶ HISTORY Greek *elegos* lament

element *n* **1** one of the fundamental components making up a whole **2** *chem* any of the known substances that cannot be separated into simpler substances by chemical means **3** a distinguishable section of a social group: *liberal elements in Polish society* **4** a metal part in an electrical device, such as a kettle, that changes the electric current into heat **5** one of the four substances (earth, air, water, and fire) formerly believed to make up the universe **6** *maths* any of the members of a set **7 in one's element** in a situation in which one is happy and at ease: *she was in her element behind the wheel* **8 elements a** the basic principles of something **b** weather conditions, esp. wind, rain, and cold: *only 200 braved the elements* ▶ HISTORY Latin *elementum*

elemental *adj* of or like basic and powerful natural forces or passions

elementary *adj* **1** simple, basic, and straightforward: *elementary precautions* **2** involving only the most basic principles of a subject: *elementary mathematics*

elementary particle *n physics* any of several entities, such as electrons, neutrons, or protons, that are less complex than atoms

elementary school *n* **1** *Brit* same as **primary school 2** *US & Canad* a state school for the first six to eight years of a child's education

elephant *n* a very large four-legged animal that has a very long flexible nose called a trunk, large ears, and two ivory tusks, and lives in Africa or India ▶ HISTORY Greek *elephas*

elephantiasis (el-lee-fan-**tie**-a-siss) *n pathol* a skin disease, caused by parasitic worms, in which the affected parts of the body become extremely enlarged

elephantine *adj* like an elephant, esp. in being huge, clumsy, or ponderous

elevate *vb* **-vating, -vated 1** to raise in rank or

status: *she had elevated flirting to an art form* **2** to lift to a higher place: *this action elevates the upper back* ▸ **HISTORY** Latin *elevare*

elevated *adj* **1** higher than normal: *elevated cholesterol levels* **2** (of ideas or pursuits) on a high intellectual or moral level: *elevated discussions about postmodernism* **3** (of land or part of a building) higher than the surrounding area

elevation *n* **1** the act of elevating someone or something: *his elevation to the peerage* **2** height above sea level **3** a raised area **4** a scale drawing of one side of a building

elevator *n* **1** *Austral, US & Canad* a lift for carrying people **2** a mechanical hoist

eleven *n* **1** the cardinal number that is the sum of ten and one **2** a numeral, 11 or XI, representing this number **3** something representing or consisting of 11 units **4** a team of 11 players in football, cricket, etc. ▷ *adj* **5** amounting to eleven: *eleven years* ▸ **HISTORY** Old English *endleofan* > **eleventh** *adj, n*

eleven-plus *n* (in Britain, esp. formerly) an examination taken by children aged 10 or 11 that determines the type of secondary education they will be given

elevenses *pl n Brit & S African, informal* a mid-morning snack

eleventh hour *n* **1** the latest possible time ▷ *adj* **eleventh-hour 2** done at the latest possible time: *an eleventh-hour rescue*

elf *n, pl* **elves** (in folklore) a small mischievous fairy ▸ **HISTORY** Old English *ælf*

elfin *adj* **1** small and delicate: *her elfin features* **2** of or relating to elves

elicit *vb* **1** to bring about (a response or reaction): *her remarks elicited a sharp retort* **2** to draw out (information) from someone: *a phone call elicited the fact that she had just awakened* ▸ **HISTORY** Latin *elicere*

elide *vb* **eliding, elided** to omit (a syllable or vowel) from a spoken word ▸ **HISTORY** Latin *elidere* to knock

eligible *adj* **1** meeting the requirements or qualifications needed: *he may be eligible for free legal services* **2** *old-fashioned* desirable as a spouse ▸ **HISTORY** Latin *eligere* to elect > **eligibility** *n*

eliminate *vb* **-nating, -nated 1** to get rid of (something or someone unwanted, unnecessary, or not meeting the requirements needed): *he can be eliminated from the list of suspects* **2** to remove (a competitor or team) from a contest, esp. following a defeat: *they were eliminated in the third round* **3** *slang* to murder in cold blood: *Stalin had thousands of his former comrades eliminated* ▸ **HISTORY** Latin *eliminare* to turn out of the house > **elimination** *n*

elision *n* omission of a syllable or vowel from a spoken word ▸ **HISTORY** Latin *elidere* to elide

elite (ill-**eet**) *n* the most powerful, rich, or gifted members of a group or community ▸ **HISTORY** French

elitism *n* **1** the belief that society should be governed by a small group of people who are superior to everyone else **2** pride in being part of an elite > **elitist** *n, adj*

elixir (ill-**ix**-er) *n* **1** an imaginary substance that is supposed to be capable of prolonging life and changing base metals into gold **2** a liquid medicine mixed with syrup ▸ **HISTORY** Arabic *al iksīr*

Elizabethan *adj* **1** of or in the reign of Queen Elizabeth I of England (1558–1603) **2** a person who lived during the reign of Queen Elizabeth I

elk *n* a very large deer of N Europe and Asia with broad flat antlers ▸ **HISTORY** Old English *eolh*

ellipse *n* an oval shape resembling a flattened circle

ellipsis (ill-**lip**-siss) *n, pl* **-ses** (-seez) **1** the omission of a word or words from a sentence **2** *printing* three dots (…) indicating an omission ▸ **HISTORY** Greek *elleipein* to leave out

ellipsoid *n geom* a surface whose plane sections are ellipses or circles

elliptical *or* **elliptic** *adj* **1** oval-shaped **2** (of speech or writing) obscure or ambiguous

elm *n* **1** a tall tree with broad leaves **2** the hard heavy wood of this tree ▸ **HISTORY** Old English

El Niño (el-**nee**-nyo) *n meteorol* a warming of the eastern tropical Pacific that occurs every few years and disrupts weather in the region ▸ **HISTORY** Spanish: The Child, i.e. Christ, referring to the original occurrence at Christmas time

El Niño effect *n meteorol* unusual and often severe weather conditions set in motion by the occurrence of El Niño

elocution *n* the art of speaking clearly in public ▸ **HISTORY** Latin *e-* out + *loqui* to speak > **elocutionist** *n*

elongate (**eel**-long-gate) *vb* **-gating, -gated** to make or become longer ▸ **HISTORY** Latin *e-* away + *longe* (adverb) far > **elongation** *n*

elope *vb* **eloping, eloped** (of two people) to run away secretly to get married ▸ **HISTORY** Anglo-French *aloper* > **elopement** *n*

eloquence *n* the ability to speak or write in a skilful and convincing way

eloquent *adj* **1** (of speech or writing) fluent and persuasive **2** (of a person) able to speak in a fluent and persuasive manner **3** visibly or vividly expressive: *he raised an eloquent eyebrow* ▸ **HISTORY** Latin *e-* out + *loqui* to speak > **eloquently** *adv*

else *adv* **1** in addition or more: *what else do you want to know?* **2** other or different: *it was unlike anything else that had happened* **3 or else a** if not, then: *tell us soon or else we shall go mad* **b** *informal, spoken* or something terrible will result: used as a threat: *do it our way or else* ▸ **HISTORY** Old English *elles*

elsewhere *adv* in or to another place

ELT English Language Teaching

elucidate *vb* **-dating, -dated** to make (something obscure or difficult) clear ▸ **HISTORY** Late Latin *elucidare* to enlighten > **elucidation** *n*

elude *vb* **eluding, eluded 1** to avoid or escape from (someone or something) **2** to fail to be understood or remembered by: *the mysteries of commerce elude me* ▸ **HISTORY** Latin *eludere* to deceive

elusive *adj* **1** difficult to find or catch **2** difficult to remember or describe > **elusiveness** n

elver n a young eel ▶ **HISTORY** variant of *eelfare* eel-journey

elves n the plural of **elf**

Elysium (ill-**liz**-zee-um) n 1 *Greek myth* the dwelling place of the blessed after death 2 a state or place of perfect bliss ▶ **HISTORY** Greek *Ēlusion pedion* blessed fields > **Elysian** adj

emaciated (im-**mace**-ee-ate-id) adj extremely thin through illness or lack of food ▶ **HISTORY** Latin *macer* thin > **emaciation** n

e-mail or **email** (ee-mail) n 1 the transmission of messages from one computer terminal to another ▷ vb 2 to contact (a person) by e-mail 3 to send (a message) by e-mail

emanate (em-a-nate) vb -**nating, -nated** to come or seem to come from someone or something: *an aura of power emanated from him* ▶ **HISTORY** Latin *emanare* to flow out > **emanation** n

emancipate vb -**pating, -pated** 1 to free from social, political, or legal restrictions 2 to free (a person) from slavery ▶ **HISTORY** Latin *emancipare* to give independence (to a son) > **emancipation** n

emasculate vb -**lating, -lated** to deprive of power or strength ▶ **HISTORY** Latin *emasculare* to remove the testicles of > **emasculation** n

embalm vb to preserve (a corpse) by the use of chemicals and oils ▶ **HISTORY** Old French *embaumer*

embankment n a man-made ridge of earth or stone that carries a road or railway or prevents a river or lake from overflowing

embargo n, pl -**goes** 1 an order by a government or international body prohibiting trade with a country: *the world trade embargo against Iraq* ▷ vb -**going, -goed** 2 to place an official prohibition on ▶ **HISTORY** Spanish

embark vb 1 to go on board (a ship or aircraft) 2 **embark on** to begin (a new project or venture) ▶ **HISTORY** Old Provençal *embarcar* > **embarkation** n

embarrass vb 1 to make (someone) feel shy, ashamed, or guilty about something 2 to cause political problems for (a government or party) 3 to cause to have financial difficulties ▶ **HISTORY** Italian *imbarrare* to confine within bars > **embarrassed** adj > **embarrassing** adj > **embarrassingly** adv > **embarrassment** n

embassy n, pl -**sies** 1 the residence or place of business of an ambassador 2 an ambassador and his or her assistants and staff ▶ **HISTORY** Old Provençal *ambaisada*

embattled adj 1 (of a country) involved in fighting a war, esp. when surrounded by enemies 2 facing many problems and difficulties: *the embattled Mayor*

embed vb -**bedding, -bedded** 1 to fix firmly in a surrounding solid mass: *the boy has shrapnel embedded in his spine* 2 to fix (an attitude or idea) in a society or in someone's mind: *corruption was deeply embedded in the ruling party*

embedded clause n *grammar* a clause that defines or clarifies another element in the sentence

embedded phrase n *grammar* a group of words, especially a prepositional phrase, that functions as a single unit and defines or clarifies another element in the sentence

embellish vb 1 to make (something) more attractive by adding decorations 2 to make (a story) more interesting by adding details which may not be true ▶ **HISTORY** Old French *embelir* > **embellishment** n

ember n a smouldering piece of coal or wood remaining after a fire has died ▶ **HISTORY** Old English *æmyrge*

embezzle vb -**zling, -zled** to steal (money) that belongs to the company or organization that one works for ▶ **HISTORY** Anglo-French *embeseiller* to destroy > **embezzler** n

embezzlement n *law* the crime of stealing money from the company or organization that one works for

embittered adj feeling anger and despair as a result of misfortune: *embittered by poverty* > **embitterment** n

emblazon (im-**blaze**-on) vb 1 to decorate with a coat of arms, slogan, etc.: *a jacket emblazoned with his band's name* 2 to proclaim or publicize: *I am not sure he would want his name emblazoned in my column*

emblem n an object or design chosen to symbolize an organization or idea ▶ **HISTORY** Greek *emblēma* insertion > **emblematic** adj

embody vb -**bodies, -bodying, -bodied** 1 to be an example of or express (an idea or other abstract concept) 2 to include as part of a whole: *the proposal has been embodied in a draft resolution* > **embodiment** n

embolden vb to make bold

embolism n *pathol* the blocking of a blood vessel by a blood clot, air bubble, etc.

embolus n, pl -**li** *pathol* a blood clot, air bubble, or other stoppage that blocks a small blood vessel ▶ **HISTORY** Greek *embolos* stopper

emboss vb to mould or carve a decoration on (a surface) so that it stands out from the surface ▶ **HISTORY** Old French *embocer*

embrace vb -**bracing, -braced** 1 to clasp (someone) with one's arms as an expression of affection or a greeting 2 to accept eagerly: *he has embraced the Islamic faith* 3 to include or be made up of: *a church that embraces two cultures* ▷ n 4 an act of embracing ▶ **HISTORY** Latin *im-* in + *bracchia* arms

embrasure n 1 an opening for a door or window which is wider on the inside of the wall than on the outside 2 an opening in a battlement or wall, for shooting through ▶ **HISTORY** French

embrocation n a lotion rubbed into the skin to ease sore muscles ▶ **HISTORY** Greek *brokhē* a moistening

embroider vb 1 to do decorative needlework on (a piece of cloth or a garment) 2 to add imaginary details to (a story) ▶ **HISTORY** Old French *embroder* > **embroiderer** n

embroidery n 1 decorative needlework, usually

on cloth or canvas **2** the act of adding imaginary details to a story

embroil *vb* to involve (oneself or another person) in problems or difficulties ▶ HISTORY French *embrouiller* > **embroilment** *n*

embryo (**em**-bree-oh) *n, pl* -**bryos 1** an unborn animal or human being in the early stages of development, in humans up to approximately the end of the second month of pregnancy **2** something in an early stage of development: *the embryo of a serious comic novel* ▶ HISTORY Greek *embruon*

embryology *n* the scientific study of embryos
embryonic *adj* **1** of or relating to an embryo **2** in an early stage

emend *vb* to make corrections or improvements to (a text) ▶ HISTORY Latin *e-* out + *mendum* a mistake > **emendation** *n*

emerald *n* **1** a green transparent variety of beryl highly valued as a gem ▷ *adj* **2** bright green ▶ HISTORY Greek *smaragdos*

emerge *vb* **emerging, emerged 1** to come into view out of something: *two men emerged from the pub* **2** to come out of a particular state of mind or way of existence: *she emerged from the trance* **3** to come to the end of a particular event or situation: *no party emerged from the election with a clear majority* **4** to become apparent, esp. as the result of a discussion or investigation: *it emerged that he had been drinking* **5** to come into existence over a long period of time: *a new style of dance music emerged in the late 1980s* ▶ HISTORY Latin *emergere* to rise up from > **emergence** *n* > **emergent** *adj*

emergency *n, pl* -**cies 1** an unforeseen or sudden occurrence, esp. of danger demanding immediate action **2 state of emergency** a time of crisis, declared by a government, during which normal laws and civil rights can be suspended ▷ *adj* **3** for use in an emergency: *the emergency exit* **4** made necessary because of an emergency: *emergency surgery*

emeritus (im-**mer**-rit-uss) *adj* retired, but retaining one's title on an honorary basis: *a professor emeritus* ▶ HISTORY Latin *merere* to deserve

emery *n* a hard greyish-black mineral used for smoothing and polishing ▶ HISTORY Greek *smuris* powder for rubbing

emery board *n* a strip of cardboard coated with crushed emery, for filing one's fingernails

emetic (im-**met**-ik) *n* **1** a substance that causes vomiting ▷ *adj* **2** causing vomiting ▶ HISTORY Greek *emetikos*

EMF electromotive force

emigrate *vb* -**grating, -grated** to leave one's native country to settle in another country ▶ HISTORY Latin *emigrare* > **emigrant** *n, adj* > **emigration** *n*

émigré (**em**-mig-gray) *n* someone who has left his or her native country for political reasons ▶ HISTORY French

eminence *n* **1** the state of being well-known and well-respected **2** a piece of high ground

Eminence *n* **Your** or **His Eminence** a title used to address or refer to a cardinal

eminent *adj* well-known and well-respected ▶ HISTORY Latin *eminere* to stand out

eminently *adv* extremely: *eminently sensible*

emir (em-**meer**) *n* an independent ruler in the Islamic world ▶ HISTORY Arabic *'amīr* commander > **emirate** *n*

emissary *n, pl* -**saries** an agent sent on a mission by a government or head of state ▶ HISTORY Latin *emissarius*

emission *n* **1** the act of giving out heat, light, a smell, etc. **2** energy or a substance given out by something: *exhaust emissions from motor vehicles*

emit *vb* **emitting, emitted 1** to give or send forth (heat, light, a smell, etc.) **2** to produce (a sound) ▶ HISTORY Latin *emittere* to send out

emoji (i-**moh**-jee) *n* a small image used in electronic messages to express an idea or emotion ▶ HISTORY Japanese *e* picture + MOJI letter

emollient *adj* **1** (of skin cream or lotion) having a softening effect **2** helping to avoid confrontation; calming: *his emollient political style* ▷ *n* **3** a cream or lotion that softens the skin ▶ HISTORY Latin *emollire* to soften

emolument *n* fees or wages from employment ▶ HISTORY Latin *emolumentum* benefit; originally fee paid to a miller

emoticon (i-**mote**-i-kon) *n* computers a group of symbols depicting a facial expression, used in electronic messages ▶ HISTORY EMOT(ION) + ICON

emotion *n* **1** any strong feeling, such as joy or fear **2** the part of a person's character based on feelings rather than thought: *the conflict between emotion and logic* ▶ HISTORY Latin *emovere* to disturb

emotional *adj* **1** of or relating to the emotions: *emotional abuse* **2** influenced by feelings rather than rational thinking: *he was too emotional to be a good doctor* **3** appealing to the emotions: *emotional appeals for public support* **4** showing one's feelings openly, esp. when upset: *he became very emotional and burst into tears* > **emotionalism** *n* > **emotionally** *adv*

emotive *adj* tending or designed to arouse emotion

empathize or -**thise** *vb* -**thizing, -thized** or -**thising, -thised** to sense and understand someone else's feelings as if they were one's own

empathy *n* the ability to sense and understand someone else's feelings as if they were one's own ▶ HISTORY Greek *empatheia* affection, passion > **empathic** *adj*

emperor *n* a man who rules an empire ▶ HISTORY Latin *imperare* to command

emperor penguin *n* a very large Antarctic penguin with orange-yellow patches on its neck

emphasis *n, pl* -**ses 1** special importance or significance given to something, such as an object or idea **2** stress on a particular syllable, word, or phrase in speaking ▶ HISTORY Greek

emphasize or -**sise** *vb* -**sizing, -sized** or -**sising, -sised** to give emphasis or prominence to: *to emphasize her loyalty*

emphatic *adj* **1** expressed, spoken, or done forcefully: *an emphatic denial of the allegations* **2** forceful and positive: *he was emphatic about his desire for peace talks* ▶ HISTORY Greek *emphainein* to display > **emphatically** *adv*

emphysema (em-fiss-**see**-ma) *n pathol* a condition in which the air sacs of the lungs are grossly enlarged, causing breathlessness ▶ HISTORY Greek *emphusēma* a swelling up

empire *n* **1** a group of countries under the rule of a single person or sovereign state **2** a large industrial organization that is controlled by one person: *the heiress to a jewellery empire* ▶ HISTORY Latin *imperare* to command

empirical *adj* derived from experiment, experience, and observation rather than from theory or logic: *there is no empirical data to support this claim* ▶ HISTORY Greek *empeirikos* practised > **empirically** *adv*

empiricism *n philosophy* the doctrine that all knowledge derives from experience > **empiricist** *n*

emplacement *n* a prepared position for an artillery gun

employ *vb* **1** to hire (someone) to do work in return for money **2** to keep busy or occupy: *she was busily employed cutting the grass* **3** to use as a means: *you can employ various methods to cut your heating bills* ▷ *n* **4** **in the employ of** doing regular paid work for: *he is in the employ of The Sunday Times* ▶ HISTORY Old French *emploier* > **employable** *adj*

employee *or US* **employe** *n* a person who is hired to work for someone in return for payment

employer *n* a person or company that employs workers

employment *n* **1** the act of employing or state of being employed **2** a person's work or occupation **3** the availability of jobs for the population of a town, country, etc.: *the party's commitment to full employment*

employment tribunal *n econ* a tribunal that rules on disputes between employees and employers regarding unfair dismissal, redundancy, etc.

emporium *n*, *pl* **-riums** *or* **-ria** *old-fashioned* a large retail shop with a wide variety of merchandise ▶ HISTORY Latin, from Greek *emporos* merchant

empower *vb* to give (someone) the power or authority to do something

empowerment *n S African* a semi-official slogan for the empowering of previously disadvantaged populations

empress *n* **1** a woman who rules an empire **2** the wife or widow of an emperor ▶ HISTORY Latin *imperatrix*

empty *adj* **-tier, -tiest** **1** containing nothing **2** without inhabitants; unoccupied **3** without purpose, substance, or value: *he contemplated yet another empty weekend* **4** insincere or trivial: *empty words* **5** *informal* drained of energy or emotion **6** *maths, logic* (of a set or class) containing no members ▷ *vb* **-ties, -tying, -tied** **7** to make or become empty **8** to remove from something: *they emptied out the remains of the tin of paint* ▷ *n*, *pl* **-ties** **9** an empty container, esp. a bottle ▶ HISTORY Old English *ǣmtig* > **emptiness** *n*

empty set *n maths* a set that contains no members

empyrean (em-pie-**ree**-an) *n poetic* the sky or the heavens ▶ HISTORY Greek *empuros* fiery

EMS European Monetary System: the system enabling some EU members to coordinate their exchange rates

emu *n* a large Australian long-legged bird that cannot fly

■ **WORD HISTORY**
■ 'Emu' is from Portuguese *ema*, meaning
■ 'ostrich'. The name was also applied to the birds
■ we now know as the cassowary, and the rhea,
■ since emus, cassowaries, and rheas all bear
■ some resemblance to ostriches.

EMU European Monetary Union

emulate *vb* **-lating, -lated** to imitate (someone) in an attempt to do as well as or better than him or her ▶ HISTORY Latin *aemulus* competing with > **emulation** *n* > **emulator** *n*

emulsifier *n* a substance that helps to combine two liquids, esp. a water-based liquid and an oil

emulsify *vb* **-fies, -fying, -fied** to make or form into an emulsion

emulsion *n* **1** a mixture of two liquids in which particles of one are suspended evenly throughout the other **2** *photog* a light-sensitive coating for paper or film **3** a type of water-based paint ▶ HISTORY Latin *emulgere* to milk out

enable *vb* **-abling, -abled** **1** to provide (someone) with the means or opportunity to do something **2** to make possible: *to enable the best possible chance of cure*

enabling act *n law* a legislative act giving certain powers to a person or organization

enact *vb* **1** to establish by law: *plans to enact a bill of rights* **2** to perform (a story or play) by acting > **enactment** *n*

enamel *n* **1** a coloured glassy coating on the surface of articles made of metal, glass, or pottery **2** an enamel-like paint or varnish **3** the hard white substance that covers teeth ▷ *vb* **-elling, -elled** *or US* **-eling, -eled** **4** to decorate or cover with enamel ▶ HISTORY Old French *esmail*

enamoured *or US* **enamored** *adj* **enamoured of a** in love with **b** very fond of and impressed by: *he is not enamoured of Moscow* ▶ HISTORY Latin *amor* love

en bloc *adv* as a whole; all together ▶ HISTORY French

encamp *vb formal* to set up a camp > **encampment** *n*

encapsulate *vb* **-lating, -lated** **1** to put in a concise form; summarize **2** to enclose in, or as if in, a capsule > **encapsulation** *n*

encase *vb* **-casing, -cased** to enclose or cover completely: *her arms were encased in plaster* > **encasement** *n*

encephalitis (en-sef-a-**lite**-iss) *n* inflammation of the brain ▶ HISTORY Greek *en-* in + *kephalē* head > **encephalitic** *adj*

encephalogram *n* an electroencephalogram ▶ HISTORY Greek *en-* in + *kephalē* head + *gramma* drawing

enchant *vb* **1** to delight and fascinate **2** to cast a spell on ▶ HISTORY Latin *incantare* to chant a spell > **enchanted** *adj* > **enchantment** *n* > **enchanter** *n* > **enchantress** *fem n*

enchilada (en-chill-**lah**-da) *n* a Mexican dish consisting of a tortilla filled with meat, served with chilli sauce

encircle *vb* **-cling, -cled** to form a circle round > **encirclement** *n*

enclave *n* a part of a country entirely surrounded by foreign territory: *a Spanish enclave* ▶ HISTORY Latin *in-* in + *clavis* key

enclose *vb* **-closing, -closed** **1** to surround completely: *the house enclosed a courtyard* **2** to include along with something else: *he enclosed a letter with the parcel*

enclosure *n* **1** an area of land enclosed by a fence, wall, or hedge **2** something, such as a cheque, enclosed with a letter

encode *vb* **-coding, -coded** to convert (a message) into code

encomium *n* a formal expression of praise ▶ HISTORY Latin

encompass *vb* **1** to enclose within a circle; surround **2** to include all of: *the programme encompasses the visual arts, music, literature, and drama*

encore *interj* **1** again: used by an audience to demand a short extra performance ▷ *n* **2** an extra song or piece performed at a concert in response to enthusiastic demand from the audience ▶ HISTORY French

encounter *vb* **1** to meet (someone) unexpectedly **2** to be faced with: *he had rarely encountered such suffering* **3** to meet (an opponent or enemy) in a competition or battle ▷ *n* **4** a casual or unexpected meeting **5** a game or battle: *a fierce encounter between the army and armed rebels* ▶ HISTORY Latin *in-* in + *contra* against, opposite

encourage *vb* **-aging, -aged** **1** to give (someone) the confidence to do something **2** to stimulate (something or someone) by approval or help ▶ HISTORY French *encourager* > **encouragement** *n* > **encouraging** *adj*

encroach *vb* to intrude gradually on someone's rights or on a piece of land ▶ HISTORY Old French *encrochier* to seize > **encroachment** *n*

encrust *vb* to cover (a surface) with a layer of something, such as jewels or ice > **encrustation** *n*

encrypt *vb* **1** to put (a message or data) into a coded form **2** to distort (a television or other signal) so that it cannot be received without the use of specific equipment. Compare **decrypt** ▶ HISTORY Greek *en-* in + *kruptos* hidden > **encryption** *n*

encumber *vb* **1** to hinder or impede: *neither was greatly encumbered with social engagements* **2** to burden with a load or with debts ▶ HISTORY Old French *en-* into + *combre* a barrier

encumbrance *n* something that impedes or is burdensome

encyclical (en-**sik**-lik-kl) *n* a letter sent by the pope to all Roman Catholic bishops ▶ HISTORY Greek *kuklos* circle

encyclopedia *or* **encyclopaedia** *n* a book or set of books, often in alphabetical order, containing facts about many different subjects or about one particular subject ▶ HISTORY Greek *enkuklios* general + *paideia* education

encyclopedic *or* **encyclopaedic** *adj* (of knowledge or information) very full and thorough; comprehensive

end *n* **1** one of the two extreme points of something such as a road **2** the surface at one of the two extreme points of an object: *a pencil with a rubber at one end* **3** the extreme extent or limit of something: *the end of the runway* **4** the most distant place or time that can be imagined: *the ends of the earth* **5** the act or an instance of stopping doing something or stopping something from continuing: *I want to put an end to all the gossip* **6** the last part of something: *at the end of the story* **7** a remnant or fragment: *cigarette ends* **8** death or destruction **9** the purpose of an action: *he will only use you to achieve his own ends* **10** sport either of the two defended areas of a playing field **11 in the end** finally **12 make ends meet** to have just enough money to meet one's needs **13 no end** used for emphasis: *these moments give me no end of trouble* **14 on end** *informal* without pause or interruption: *for months on end* **15 the end** *slang* the worst, esp. beyond the limits of endurance ▷ *vb* **16** to bring or come to a finish **17 end it all** *informal* to commit suicide ▶ HISTORY Old English *ende* See WORD FOCUS **end**

endanger *vb* to put in danger

endangered *adj* (of a species of animal) in danger of becoming extinct

endear *vb* to cause to be liked: *his wit endeared him to a great many people* > **endearing** *adj*

endearment *n* an affectionate word or phrase

endeavour *or US* **endeavor** *formal vb* **1** to try (to do something) ▷ *n* **2** an effort to do something ▶ HISTORY Middle English *endeveren*

endemic *adj* present within a localized area or only found in a particular group of people: *he found 100 species of plant endemic to that ridge* ▶ HISTORY Greek *en-* in + *dēmos* the people

ending *n* **1** the last part or conclusion of something: *the film has a happy ending* **2** the tip or end of something: *nerve endings*

endive *n* a plant with crisp curly leaves, used in salads ▶ HISTORY Old French

endless *adj* **1** having no end; eternal or infinite **2** continuing too long or continually recurring: *an endless stream of visitors* > **endlessly** *adv*

endnote *n* a note printed at the end of an article, chapter or book

end

End is a commonly overused word. Depending on your context, you can use the following substitutes to add variety and interest to your writing.

DEFINITION 1
● If you are talking about one of the two extreme points of something, you might use: the southernmost **point** • the western **extremity**

DEFINITION 2
● If you are talking about the surface at either end of the points of an object, you might use: **tips** of his fingers

DEFINITION 3
● If you would like to describe the furthest-away part of something, you could try: the **boundaries** of the paths • beyond the **bounds** • the **edge** of the cliff • the farthest **extremity** • official city **limits** • beyond the forest **margin**

DEFINITION 4
● If you would like to describe the most distant place you can imagine, you could try: the **edge** of the earth • the absolute **limit**

DEFINITION 5
● If you would like to describe something stopping, you could try: by the **close** of last year • **conclusion** of hostilities • **ending** of a great era

• the **expiry** of his passport • nearing its **finish**
• put a **stop** to

DEFINITION 6
● If you would like to describe the last part of something, you could try: the dramatic **climax** • the **close** • the **conclusion** of • the remarkable **culmination** • tragic **ending** • grand **finale** • a disappointing **finish**

DEFINITION 7
● If you would like to describe a leftover piece of something, you could try: a cigarette **butt** • trimmings and **leftovers** • **remnants** of fabric • **scraps** of spare material • a ticket **stub** • the **stump** of his left arm

DEFINITION 8
● If you are talking about death or the destruction of something, you could try: the band's **demise** • **destruction** of the earth • foretold his own **doom** • the **extinction** of a species • plotted her **ruin**

DEFINITION 9
● If you would like to describe the purpose of doing something, you could try: united by a common **aim** • working towards the same **goal** • real **intentions** • the stated **object** • the **objective** of • the true **purpose** • business **reasons**

---

endocrine *adj* of or denoting a gland that secretes hormones directly into the blood stream, or a hormone secreted by such a gland ▶ HISTORY Greek *endon* within + *krinein* to separate

endogenous (en-**dodge**-in-uss) *adj biol* developing or originating from within

endolymph *n physiol* the fluid that fills the membranous labyrinth of the internal ear

endometrium (end-oh-**meet**-tree-um) *n* the mucous membrane lining the womb ▶ HISTORY Greek *endon* within + *mētra* womb > **endometrial** *adj*

endomorph *n physiol* a person with a fat and heavy body build. Compare **ectomorph**, **mesomorph** ▶ HISTORY Greek *endon* within + *morphē* shape > **endomorphic** *adj*

endoneurium *n anat* the delicate connective tissue surrounding nerve fibres within a bundle

endorphin *n* any of a group of chemicals found in the brain, which have an effect similar to morphine

endorse *vb* -**dorsing, -dorsed** 1 to give approval or support to 2 to sign the back of (a cheque) to specify the payee 3 *chiefly Brit* to record a conviction on (a driving licence) ▶ HISTORY Old French *endosser* to put on the back > **endorsement** *n*

endoscope *n med* a long slender medical instrument used for examining the interior of hollow organs > **endoscopy** *n*

endoskeleton *n zool* an internal skeleton,

such as the bony skeleton of vertebrates

endothermic *adj* (of a chemical reaction) involving or requiring the absorption of heat

endow *vb* 1 to provide with a source of permanent income, esp. by leaving money in a will 2 **endowed with** provided with or possessing (a quality or talent) ▶ HISTORY Old French *endouer*

endowment *n* 1 the money given to an institution, such as a hospital 2 a natural talent or quality

endowment assurance *or* **insurance** *n* a kind of life insurance that pays a specified sum directly to the policyholder at a designated date or to his or her beneficiary should he or she die before this date

end product *n* the final result of a process

endurance *n* the ability to withstand prolonged hardship

endure *vb* -**during, -dured** 1 to bear (hardship) patiently: *they endured a lot of pain* 2 to tolerate or put up with: *I cannot endure your disloyalty any longer* 3 to last for a long time ▶ HISTORY Latin *indurare* to harden > **endurable** *adj*

enduring *adj* long-lasting

endways *or esp US & Canad* **endwise** *adv* having the end forwards or upwards

enema (en-**im**-a) *n med* a quantity of fluid inserted into the rectum to empty the bowels, for example before an operation ▶ HISTORY Greek: injection

enemy *n, pl* -**mies** 1 a person who is hostile or

opposed to a person, group, or idea **2** a hostile nation or people **3** something that harms or opposes something: *oil is an enemy of the environment*. *Related adjective:* **inimical** *adj* **4** of or belonging to an enemy: *enemy troops* ▶ **HISTORY** Latin *inimicus* hostile

energetic *adj* **1** having or showing energy and enthusiasm: *an energetic campaigner for democracy* **2** involving a lot of movement and physical effort: *energetic exercise* > **energetically** *adv*

energize *or* **-ise** *vb* **-gizing, -gized** *or* **-gising, -gised** to stimulate or enliven

energy *n, pl* **-gies 1** capacity for intense activity; vigour **2** intensity or vitality of action or expression; forcefulness **3** *physics* the capacity to do work and overcome resistance **4** a source of power, such as electricity ▶ **HISTORY** Greek *energeia* activity

energy drink *n* a soft drink supposed to boost the drinker's energy levels

energy transfer *n physics* the displacement of energy from one object or substance to another

enervate *vb* **-vating, -vated** to deprive of strength or vitality ▶ **HISTORY** Latin *enervare* to remove the nerves from > **enervating** *adj* > **enervation** *n*

enfant terrible (on-fon ter-**reeb**-la) *n, pl* **enfants terribles** a talented but unconventional or indiscreet person ▶ **HISTORY** French, literally: terrible child

enfeeble *vb* **-bling, -bled** to make (someone or something) weak

enfilade *mil n* **1** a burst of gunfire sweeping from end to end along a line of troops ▷ *vb* **-lading, -laded 2** to attack with an enfilade ▶ **HISTORY** French *enfiler* to thread on string

enfold *vb* **1** to cover (something) by, or as if by, wrapping something round it: *darkness enfolded the city* **2** to embrace or hug

enforce *vb* **-forcing, -forced 1** to ensure that (a law or decision) is obeyed **2** to impose (obedience) by, or as if by, force > **enforceable** *adj* > **enforcement** *n*

enfranchise *vb* **-chising, -chised** to grant (a person or group of people) the right to vote > **enfranchisement** *n*

engage *vb* **-gaging, -gaged 1** Also: **be engaged** to take part or participate: *he engaged in criminal and illegal acts; they were engaged in espionage* **2** to involve (a person or his or her attention) intensely: *there's nothing to engage the intellect in this film* **3** to employ (someone) to do something **4** to promise to do something **5** *mil* to begin a battle with **6** to bring (part of a machine or other mechanism) into operation, esp. by causing components to interlock **7 engage in conversation** to start a conversation with ▶ **HISTORY** Old French *en-* in + *gage* a pledge

engaged *adj* **1** having made a promise to get married **2** (of a telephone line or a toilet) already being used

engagement *n* **1** a business or social appointment

2 the period when a couple has agreed to get married but the wedding has not yet taken place **3** a limited period of employment, esp. in the performing arts **4** a battle

engaging *adj* pleasant and charming > **engagingly** *adv*

engender *vb* to produce (a particular feeling, atmosphere, or situation) ▶ **HISTORY** Latin *ingenerare*

engine *n* **1** any machine designed to convert energy into mechanical work, esp. one used to power a vehicle **2** a railway locomotive ▶ **HISTORY** Latin *ingenium* nature, talent

engineer *n* **1** a person trained in any branch of engineering **2** a person who repairs and maintains mechanical or electrical devices **3** a soldier trained in engineering and construction work **4** an officer responsible for a ship's engines **5** *US & Canad* a train driver ▷ *vb* **6** to cause or plan (an event or situation) in a clever or devious manner **7** to design or construct as a professional engineer

engineering *n* the profession of applying scientific principles to the design and construction of engines, cars, buildings, bridges, roads, and electrical machines

English *adj* **1** of England or the English language ▷ *n* **2** the principal language of Britain, Ireland, Australia, New Zealand, the US, Canada, and several other countries ▷ *pl n* **3 the English** the people of England

Englishman *or fem* **Englishwoman** *n, pl* **-men** *or* **-women** a person from England

engorge *vb* **-gorging, -gorged** *pathol* to clog or become clogged with blood > **engorgement** *n*

engrave *vb* **-graving, -graved 1** to carve or etch a design or inscription into (a surface) **2** to print (designs or characters) from a plate into which they have been cut or etched **3** to fix deeply or permanently in the mind ▶ **HISTORY** *en-* in + obsolete *grave* to carve > **engraver** *n*

engraving *n* **1** a printing surface that has been engraved **2** a print made from this

engross (en-**groce**) *vb* to occupy the attention of (someone) completely ▶ **HISTORY** *en-* in + Latin *grossus* thick > **engrossing** *adj*

engulf *vb* **1** to immerse, plunge, or swallow up: *engulfed by flames* **2** to overwhelm: *a terrible fear engulfed her*

enhance *vb* **-hancing, -hanced** to improve or increase in quality, value, or power: *grilling on the barbecue enhances the flavour* ▶ **HISTORY** Old French *enhaucier* > **enhancement** *n* > **enhancer** *n*

enigma *n* something or someone that is mysterious or puzzling ▶ **HISTORY** Greek *ainissesthai* to speak in riddles > **enigmatic** *adj* > **enigmatically** *adv*

enjambment *or* **enjambement** (in-**jam**-ment) *n prosody* the running over of a sentence from one line of verse into the next ▶ **HISTORY** French: a straddling

enjoin *vb* **1** to order (someone) to do something **2** to impose (a particular kind of behaviour) on

someone: *the sect enjoins poverty on its members*
3 *law* to prohibit (someone) from doing something
by an injunction ▶ HISTORY Old French *enjoindre*

enjoy *vb* **1** to receive pleasure from **2** to have or
experience (something, esp. something good):
many fat people enjoy excellent health **3 enjoy
oneself** to have a good time ▶ HISTORY Old French
enjoir > **enjoyable** *adj* > **enjoyably** *adv*
> **enjoyment** *n*

enlarge *vb* **-larging, -larged** **1** to make or grow
larger **2 enlarge on** to speak or write about in
greater detail > **enlargement** *n* > **enlarger** *n*

enlighten *vb* to give information or
understanding to > **enlightening** *adj*

enlightened *adj* **1** rational and having beneficial
effects: *an enlightened approach to social welfare*
2 (of a person) tolerant and unprejudiced

enlightenment *n* **1** the act of enlightening or the
state of being enlightened **2** (in Buddhism) the
final spiritual state in which perfect understanding
has been achieved

enlist *vb* **1** to enter the armed forces **2** to obtain
(someone's help or support) > **enlistment** *n*

enliven *vb* to make lively, cheerful, or bright
> **enlivening** *adj*

en masse *adv* all together; as a group ▶ HISTORY
French

enmeshed *adj* deeply involved: *enmeshed in turmoil*

enmity *n* a feeling of hostility or ill will ▶ HISTORY
Latin *inimicus* hostile

ennoble *vb* **-bling, -bled** **1** to make (someone) a
member of the nobility **2** to make (someone or his
or her life) noble or dignified: *poverty does not
ennoble people*

ennui (on-**nwee**) *n* *literary* boredom and
dissatisfaction resulting from lack of activity or
excitement ▶ HISTORY French

enormity *n* **1** extreme wickedness **2** (*pl* **-ties**) an
act of great wickedness **3** the vastness or extent of
a problem or difficulty

enormous *adj* unusually large in size, extent,
or degree ▶ HISTORY Latin *e-* out of, away from
+ *norma* rule, pattern > **enormously** *adv*

enough *adj* **1** as much or as many as necessary
2 that's enough! used to stop someone behaving
in a particular way ▷ *pron* **3** an adequate amount
or number: *I don't know enough about the subject to be
able to speak about it* ▷ *adv* **4** as much as necessary
5 fairly or quite: *that's a common enough experience*
6 very: used to give emphasis to the preceding
word: *funnily enough, I wasn't alarmed* **7** just
adequately: *he sang well enough* ▶ HISTORY Old
English *genōh*

en passant (on pass-**on**) *adv* in passing: *references
made en passant* ▶ HISTORY French

enquire *vb* **-quiring, -quired** same as **inquire**
> **enquiry** *n*

enraptured *adj* filled with delight and fascination

enrich *vb* **1** to improve or increase the quality or
value of: *his poetry has vastly enriched the English
language* **2** to improve in nutritional value, colour,
or flavour: *a sauce enriched with beer* **3** to make

wealthy or wealthier > **enriched** *adj*
> **enrichment** *n*

enrol *or US* **enroll** *vb* **-rolling, -rolled** to become
or cause to become a member > **enrolment** *or US*
enrollment *n*

en route *adv* on or along the way ▶ HISTORY
French

ensconce *vb* **-sconcing, -sconced** to settle firmly
or comfortably ▶ HISTORY Middle English *en-* in +
sconce fortification

ensemble (on-**som**-bl) *n* **1** all the parts of
something considered as a whole **2** the complete
outfit of clothes a person is wearing **3** a group of
musicians or actors performing together **4** *music* a
passage in which all or most of the performers are
playing or singing at once ▶ HISTORY French:
together

enshrine *vb* **-shrining, -shrined** to contain and
protect (an idea or right) in a society, legal system,
etc.: *the university's independence is enshrined in its
charter*

enshroud *vb* to cover or hide (an object)
completely, as if by draping something over it:
fog enshrouded the forest

ensign *n* **1** a flag flown by a ship to indicate its
nationality **2** any flag or banner **3** (in the US Navy)
a commissioned officer of the lowest rank
4 (formerly, in the British infantry) a commissioned
officer of the lowest rank ▶ HISTORY Latin *insignia*
badges

enslave *vb* **-slaving, -slaved** to make a slave of
(someone) > **enslavement** *n*

ensnare *vb* **-snaring, -snared** **1** to trap or gain
power over (someone) by dishonest or underhand
means **2** to catch (an animal) in a snare

ensue *vb* **-suing, -sued** **1** to happen next **2** to
occur as a consequence: *if glaucoma is not treated,
blindness can ensue* ▶ HISTORY Latin *in-* in + *sequi* to
follow > **ensuing** *adj*

en suite *adv* (of a bathroom) connected to a
bedroom and entered directly from it ▶ HISTORY
French, literally: in sequence

ensure *or esp US* **insure** *vb* **-suring, -sured**
1 to make certain: *we must ensure that similar
accidents do not happen again* **2** to make safe or
protect: *female athletes should take extra iron to
ensure against anaemia*

ENT *med* ear, nose, and throat

entablature *n* *archit* the part of a classical
building supported by the columns, consisting of
an architrave, a frieze, and a cornice ▶ HISTORY
Italian *intavolatura* something put on a table,
hence, something laid flat

entail *vb* **1** to bring about or impose inevitably: *few
women enter marriage knowing what it really entails*
2 *Brit, Austral & NZ property law* to restrict the ability
to inherit (a piece of property) to designated heirs
▶ HISTORY Middle English *en-* in + *taille* limitation

entangle *vb* **-gling, -gled** **1** to catch very firmly in
something, such as a net or wire: *a fishing line had
entangled his legs* **2** to involve in a complicated
series of problems or difficulties: *he entangles*

275

himself in contradictions **3** to involve in a troublesome relationship: *she kept getting entangled with unsuitable boyfriends* > **entanglement** *n*

entente (on-**tont**) *n* short for **entente cordiale**
▶ **HISTORY** French: understanding

entente cordiale (cord-ee-**ahl**) *n* a friendly understanding between two or more countries
▶ **HISTORY** French: cordial understanding

enter *vb* **1** to come or go into (a particular place): *he entered the room* **2** to join (a party or organization) **3** to become involved in or take part in: *1500 schools entered the competition* **4** to become suddenly present or noticeable in: *a note of anxiety entered his voice* **5** to record (an item) in a journal or list **6** *theatre* to come on stage: used as a stage direction: *enter Joseph* **7** to begin (a new process or period of time): *the occupation of the square has entered its eleventh day* ▶ **HISTORY** Latin *intrare*

enteric (en-**ter**-ik) *adj* of the intestines
▶ **HISTORY** Greek *enteron* intestine

enteritis (en-ter-**rite**-iss) *n* inflammation of the small intestine

enterprise *n* **1** a business firm **2** a project or undertaking, esp. one that requires boldness or effort **3** boldness and energy ▶ **HISTORY** Old French *entreprendre* to undertake

enterprise zone *n* an inner-city area where businesses are given incentives to create jobs

enterprising *adj* full of boldness and initiative
> **enterprisingly** *adv*

entertain *vb* **1** to provide amusement for (a person or audience) **2** to show hospitality to (guests) **3** to consider (an idea or suggestion)
▶ **HISTORY** Old French *entre-* mutually + *tenir* to hold

entertainer *n* a person who entertains, esp. professionally

entertaining *adj* **1** interesting, amusing, and enjoyable ▷ *n* **2** the provision of hospitality to guests: *the smart kitchen is perfect for entertaining*

entertainment *n* **1** enjoyment and interest: *a match of top-quality entertainment and goals* **2** an act or show that entertains, or such acts and shows collectively

enthral *or US* **enthrall** (en-**thrawl**) *vb* **-thralling, -thralled** to hold the attention or interest of > **enthralling** *adj* > **enthralment** *or US* **enthrallment** *n*

enthrone *vb* **-throning, -throned 1** to place (a person) on a throne in a ceremony to mark the beginning of his or her new role as a monarch or bishop **2** to give an important or prominent position to (something): *the religious fundamentalism now enthroned in American life*
> **enthronement** *n*

enthuse *vb* **-thusing, -thused** to feel or cause to feel enthusiasm

enthusiasm *n* ardent and lively interest or eagerness: *your enthusiasm for literature* ▶ **HISTORY** Greek *enthousiazein* to be possessed by a god

enthusiast *n* a person who is very interested in and keen on something > **enthusiastic** *adj*
> **enthusiastically** *adv*

entice *vb* **-ticing, -ticed** to attract (someone) away from one place or activity to another
▶ **HISTORY** Old French *enticier* > **enticement** *n*
> **enticing** *adj*

entire *adj* made up of or involving all of something, including every detail, part, or aspect ▶ **HISTORY** Latin *integer* whole > **entirely** *adv*

entirety *n, pl* **-ties 1** all of a person or thing: *you must follow this diet for the entirety of your life* **2 in its entirety** as a whole

entitle *vb* **-tling, -tled 1** to give (someone) the right to do or have something **2** to give a name or title to (a book or film) > **entitlement** *n*

entity *n, pl* **-ties** something that exists in its own right and not merely as part of a bigger thing
▶ **HISTORY** Latin *esse* to be

entomb *vb* **1** to place (a corpse) in a tomb **2** to bury or trap: *a circulatory system entombed in fat*
> **entombment** *n*

entomology *n* the study of insects ▶ **HISTORY** Greek *entomon* insect > **entomological** *adj*
> **entomologist** *n*

entourage (on-toor-ahzh) *n* a group of people who assist or travel with an important or well-known person ▶ **HISTORY** French *entourer* to surround

entozoon (en-toe-**zoe**-on) *n, pl* **-zoa** (-**zoe**-a) a parasite, such as a tapeworm, that lives inside another animal

entrails *pl n* **1** the internal organs of a person or animal; intestines **2** the innermost parts of anything ▶ **HISTORY** Latin *interanea* intestines

entrance[1] (en-trunss) *n* **1** something, such as a door or gate, through which it is possible to enter a place **2** the act of coming into a place, esp. with reference to the way in which it is done: *she made a sudden startling entrance* **3** *theatre* the act of appearing on stage **4** the right to enter a place: *he refused her entrance because she was carrying her Scottie dog* **5** ability or permission to join or become involved with a group or organization: *entrance to the profession should be open to men and women alike* ▷ *adj* **6** necessary in order to enter something: *they have paid entrance fees for English-language courses*

entrance[2] (en-**transs**) *vb* **-trancing, -tranced** to fill with delight > **entrancement** *n*
> **entrancing** *adj*

entrant *n* a person who enters a university, competition, etc.

entrap *vb* **-trapping, -trapped 1** to trick (someone) into danger or difficulty **2** to catch in a trap > **entrapment** *n*

entreat *vb* to ask (someone) earnestly to do something ▶ **HISTORY** Old French *entraiter*

entreaty *n, pl* **-treaties** an earnest request or plea

entrée (on-tray) *n* **1** the right to enter a place **2** a dish served before a main course **3** *chiefly US* the main course ▶ **HISTORY** French

entrench *vb* **1** to fix or establish firmly: *the habit had become entrenched* **2** *mil* to fortify (a position) by digging trenches around it > **entrenchment** *n*

entrepreneur *n* the owner of a business who

attempts to make money by risk and initiative ▶ HISTORY French > **entrepreneurial** adj

entropy (**en**-trop-ee) n 1 formal lack of pattern or organization 2 physics a thermodynamic quantity that represents the amount of energy present in a system that cannot be converted into work because it is tied up in the atomic structure of the system ▶ HISTORY Greek entropē a turning towards

entrust vb 1 to give (someone) a duty or responsibility: Miss Conway, who was entrusted with the child's education 2 to put (something) into the care of someone: he stole all the money we had entrusted to him

entry n, pl -**tries** 1 something, such as a door or gate, through which it is possible to enter a place 2 the act of coming in to a place, esp. with reference to the way in which it is done 3 the right to enter a place: he was refused entry to Britain 4 the act of joining an organization or group: Britain's entry into the EU 5 a brief note, article, or group of figures in a diary, book, or computer file 6 a quiz form, painting, etc. submitted in an attempt to win a competition 7 a person, horse, car, etc. entering a competition ▷ adj 8 necessary in order to enter something: entry fee

entry-level adj 1 (of a job or worker) at the most elementary level in a career structure 2 (of a product) most appropriate for use by a beginner: an entry-level software

entwine vb -**twining, -twined** to twist together or round something else

E number n any of a series of numbers with the prefix E- indicating a specific food additive recognized by the EU

enumerate vb -**ating, -ated** 1 to name or list one by one 2 to count 3 Canad to compile the voting list for an area ▶ HISTORY Latin e- out + numerare to count > **enumeration** n > **enumerator** n

enunciate vb -**ating, -ated** 1 to pronounce (words) clearly 2 to state precisely or formally ▶ HISTORY Latin enuntiare to declare > **enunciation** n

enuresis (en-yoo-**reece**-iss) n involuntary urination, esp. during sleep ▶ HISTORY Greek en- in + ouron urine

envelop vb to cover, surround, or enclose ▶ HISTORY Old French envoluper > **envelopment** n

envelope n 1 a flat covering of paper, that can be sealed, used to enclose a letter, etc. 2 any covering, wrapper, or enclosing structure: an envelope of filo pastry 3 geom a curve that is tangential to each one of a group of curves ▶ HISTORY French envelopper to wrap round

enviable adj so desirable or fortunate that it is likely to cause envy > **enviably** adv

envious adj feeling, showing, or resulting from envy > **enviously** adv

environment (en-**vire**-on-ment) n 1 the external conditions or surroundings in which people live: working in a multicultural environment 2 ecology the natural world of land, sea, air, plants, and animals: nuclear waste must be prevented from leaking into the environment ▶ HISTORY French environs surroundings > **environmental** adj

environmentalist n a person concerned with the protection and preservation of the natural environment

environs pl n a surrounding area, esp. the outskirts of a city

envisage or US **envision** vb -**aging, -aged** or -**ioning, -ioned** to believe to be possible or likely in the future: the commission envisages a mix of government and private funding ▶ HISTORY French en- in + visage face

envoy n 1 a messenger or representative 2 a diplomat ranking next below an ambassador ▶ HISTORY French envoyer to send

envy n, pl -**vies** 1 a feeling of discontent aroused by someone else's possessions, achievements, or qualities 2 something that causes envy: their standards are the envy of the world ▷ vb -**vies, -vying, -vied** 3 to wish that one had the possessions, achievements, or qualities of (someone else) ▶ HISTORY Latin invidia > **envyingly** adv

enzyme n any of a group of complex proteins that act as catalysts in specific biochemical reactions ▶ HISTORY Greek en- in + zumē leaven > **enzymatic** adj

Eocene (**ee**-oh-seen) adj of the epoch of geological time about 55 million years ago ▶ HISTORY Greek ēōs dawn + kainos new

Eolithic adj of the early period of the Stone Age, when crude stone tools were used

EP n an extended-play record or CD

epaulette n a piece of ornamental material on the shoulder of a garment, esp. a military uniform ▶ HISTORY French

epeirogeny (eh-pye-**ro**-dgi-nee) or **epeirogenesis** (ee-pye-ro-**ge**-ne-sis) n geol the formation of continents by relatively slow displacements of the earth's crust ▶ HISTORY Greek ēpeiros continent + -geny, from -genēs born > **epeirogenic** or **epeirogenetic** adj

ephedrine (**eff**-fid-dreen) n an alkaloid used for the treatment of asthma and hay fever ▶ HISTORY Ephedra, genus of plants which produce it

ephemera (if-**fem**-a-ra) pl n items designed to last only for a short time, such as programmes or posters

ephemeral adj lasting only for a short time ▶ HISTORY Greek hēmera day

epic n 1 a long exciting book, poem, or film, usually telling of heroic deeds 2 a long narrative poem telling of the deeds of a legendary hero ▷ adj 3 very large or grand: a professional feud of epic proportions ▶ HISTORY Greek epos word, song

epicene adj (esp. of a man) having characteristics or features which are not definitely male or female ▶ HISTORY Greek epikoinos common to many

epicentre or US **epicenter** n the point on the earth's surface immediately above the origin of an earthquake ▶ HISTORY Greek epi above + kentron point

epic theatre n theatre drama that creates alienation by the use of distancing devices such as narration, masks, and placards

epicure n a person who enjoys good food and drink ▶ HISTORY after Epicurus, Greek philosopher, who held that pleasure is the highest good > **epicurism** n

epicurean adj **1** devoted to sensual pleasures, esp. food and drink ▷ n **2** same as **epicure** > **epicureanism** n

epidemic n **1** a widespread occurrence of a disease **2** a rapid development or spread of something: an epidemic of rape ▷ adj **3** (esp. of a disease) affecting many people in an area: stress has now reached epidemic proportions ▶ HISTORY Greek epi among + dēmos people

epidemiology (ep-pid-deem-ee-**ol**-a-jee) n the branch of medical science concerned with the occurrence and control of diseases in populations > **epidemiologist** n

epidermis n the thin protective outer layer of the skin ▶ HISTORY Greek epi upon + derma skin > **epidermal** adj

epidural (ep-pid-**dure**-al) adj **1** on or over the outermost membrane covering the brain and spinal cord (**dura mater**) ▷ n **2 a** an injection of anaesthetic into the space outside the outermost membrane enveloping the spinal cord **b** anaesthesia produced by this method ▶ HISTORY from dura mater

epiglottis n a thin flap of cartilage at the back of the mouth that covers the entrance to the larynx during swallowing ▶ HISTORY Greek epi upon + glōtta tongue

epigram n **1** a witty remark **2** a short poem with a witty ending ▶ HISTORY Greek epi upon + graphein to write > **epigrammatic** adj

epigraph n **1** a quotation at the beginning of a book **2** an inscription on a monument or building ▶ HISTORY Greek epi upon + graphein to write

epilepsy n a disorder of the central nervous system which causes periodic loss of consciousness and sometimes convulsions ▶ HISTORY Greek epi upon + lambanein to take

epileptic adj **1** of or having epilepsy

epilogue n a short concluding passage or speech at the end of a book or play ▶ HISTORY Greek epi upon + logos word, speech

epineurium n anat a sheath of connective tissue around two or more bundles of nerve fibres

Epiphany (ip-**piff**-a-nee) n, pl **-nies** a Christian festival held on the 6th of January commemorating, in the Western church, the manifestation of Christ to the Magi and, in the Eastern church, the baptism of Christ ▶ HISTORY Greek epiphaneia an appearing

epiphyte n a plant that grows on another plant but is not parasitic on it ▶ HISTORY Greek, from epi upon + phusis growth > **epiphytic, epiphytal** or **epiphytical** adj

episcopacy (ip-**piss**-kop-a-see) n **1** government of a Church by bishops **2** (pl **-cies**) same as **episcopate**

episcopal (ip-**piss**-kop-al) adj of or relating to bishops ▶ HISTORY Greek episkopos overseer

Episcopal Church n (in Scotland and the US) a self-governing branch of the Anglican Church

episcopalian adj also **episcopal 1** practising or advocating Church government by bishops ▷ n **2** an advocate of such Church government

Episcopalian (ip-piss-kop-**pale**-ee-an) adj **1** of or relating to the Episcopal Church ▷ n **2** a member of this Church > **Episcopalianism** n

episcopate (ip-**piss**-kop-it) n **1** the office, status, or term of office of a bishop **2** bishops collectively

episiotomy (ip-peez-ee-**ot**-tom-ee) n, pl **-tomies** an operation involving cutting into the area between the genitals and the anus sometimes performed during childbirth to make the birth easier

episode n **1** an event or series of events **2** any of the sections into which a novel or a television or radio serial is divided ▶ HISTORY Greek epi in addition + eisodios coming in

episodic adj **1** resembling or relating to an episode **2** occurring at irregular and infrequent intervals

epistemology (ip-iss-stem-**ol**-a-jee) n the theory of knowledge, esp. the critical study of its validity, methods, and scope ▶ HISTORY Greek epistēmē knowledge > **epistemological** adj > **epistemologist** n

epistle n **1** formal or humorous a letter **2** a literary work in letter form, esp. a poem ▶ HISTORY Greek epistolē

Epistle n New Testament any of the letters written by the apostles

epistolary adj **1** of or relating to letters **2** (of a novel) presented in the form of a series of letters

epitaph n **1** a commemorative inscription on a tombstone **2** a commemorative speech or written passage ▶ HISTORY Greek epi upon + taphos tomb

epithelium n, pl **-lia** anat a cellular tissue covering the external and internal surfaces of the body ▶ HISTORY Greek epi upon + thēlē nipple > **epithelial** adj

epithet n a word or short phrase used to describe someone or something: these tracks truly deserve that overworked epithet 'classic' ▶ HISTORY Greek epitithenai to add

epitome (ip-**pit**-a-mee) n **1** a person or thing that is a typical example of a characteristic or class: the epitome of rural tranquillity **2** a summary, esp. of a written work ▶ HISTORY Greek epitemnein to abridge

epitomize or **-mise** vb **-mizing, -mized** or **-mising, -mised** to be or make a perfect or typical example of

EPNS electroplated nickel silver

epoch (**ee**-pok) n **1** a long period of time marked by some predominant characteristic: the cold-war epoch **2** the beginning of a new or distinctive period: the invention of nuclear weapons marked an epoch in the history of warfare **3** geol a unit of time within a period during which a series of rocks is formed ▶ HISTORY Greek epokhē cessation > **epochal** adj

e

epoch-making *adj* very important or significant

epode *poetry n* **1** the part of a Greek lyric ode that follows the strophe and the antistrophe **2** a type of poem composed of couplets in which a long line is followed by a shorter one

eponymous (ip-**pon**-im-uss) *adj* **1** (of a person) being the person after whom a literary work, film, etc. is named: *the eponymous heroine in the film of Jane Eyre* **2** (of a literary work, film, etc.) named after its central character or creator: *The Stooges' eponymous debut album* ▶ **HISTORY** Greek *epōnumos* giving a significant name

EPOS *Brit* electronic point of sale

epoxy *chem adj* **1** of or containing an oxygen atom joined to two different groups that are themselves joined to other groups **2** of or consisting of an epoxy resin ▷ *n, pl* **epoxies** **3** an epoxy resin ▶ **HISTORY** Greek *epi* upon + oxy(GEN)

epoxy resin *n* a tough resistant thermosetting synthetic resin, used in laminates and adhesives

EPROM *n computers* erasable programmable read-only memory: a storage device that can be reprogrammed to hold different data

Epsom salts *pl n* a medicinal preparation of hydrated magnesium sulphate, used to empty the bowels ▶ **HISTORY** after *Epsom*, a town in England

equable (**ek**-wab-bl) *adj* **1** even-tempered and reasonable **2** (of a climate) not varying much throughout the year, and neither very hot nor very cold ▶ **HISTORY** Latin *aequabilis* > **equably** *adv*

equal *adj* **1** identical in size, quantity, degree, or intensity **2** having identical privileges, rights, or status **3** applying in the same way to all people or in all circumstances: *equal rights* **4** **equal to** having the necessary strength, ability, or means for: *she was equal to any test the corporation put to her* ▷ *n* **5** a person or thing equal to another ▷ *vb* **equalling, equalled** *or US* **equaling, equaled** **6** to be equal to; match **7** to make or do something equal to: *he has equalled his world record in the men's 100 metres* ▶ **HISTORY** Latin *aequalis* > **equally** *adv*

equality *n, pl* **-ties** the state of being equal

equalize *or* **-ise** *vb* **-izing, -ized** *or* **-ising, -ised** **1** to make equal or uniform **2** (in a sport) to reach the same score as one's opponent or opponents > **equalization** *or* **-isation** *n* > **equalizer** *or* **-iser** *n*

equally likely *adj, adv maths* appearing midway along a likelihood scale

equal opportunity *n law* the offering of employment or promotion equally to all, without discrimination as to sex, race, colour, etc.

equal set *n maths* a set that has the same members as another set

equanimity *n* calmness of mind or temper; composure ▶ **HISTORY** Latin *aequus* even + *animus* mind, spirit

equate *vb* **equating, equated** **1** to make or regard as equivalent **2** *maths* to form an equation from > **equatable** *adj*

equation *n* **1** a mathematical statement that two expressions are equal **2** a situation or problem in which a number of different factors need to be considered: *this plan leaves human nature out of the equation* **3** the act of equating **4** *chem* a representation of a chemical reaction using symbols of the elements

equator *n* an imaginary circle around the earth at an equal distance from the North Pole and the South Pole ▶ **HISTORY** Medieval Latin *(circulus) aequator (diei et noctis)* (circle) that equalizes (the day and night)

equatorial *adj* of, like, or existing at or near the equator

equatorial region *n geog* a large area of land at or near the equator

equerry (**ek**-kwer-ee) *n, pl* **-ries** *Brit* an officer of the royal household who acts as a personal attendant to a member of the royal family ▶ **HISTORY** Old French *escuirie* group of squires

equestrian *adj* **1** of or relating to horses and riding **2** on horseback: *an equestrian statue of the Queen* ▶ **HISTORY** Latin *equus* horse > **equestrianism** *n*

equidistant *adj* equally distant > **equidistance** *n*

equilateral *adj* **1** having all sides of equal length ▷ *n* **2** a geometric figure having all sides of equal length

equilibrium *n, pl* **-ria** **1** a stable condition in which forces cancel one another **2** a state of mental and emotional balance; composure **3** *econ* the economic condition in which there is neither excess demand nor excess supply in a market ▶ **HISTORY** Latin *aequi-* equal + *libra* balance

equine *adj* of or like a horse ▶ **HISTORY** Latin *equus* horse

equinoctial *adj* **1** relating to or occurring at an equinox ▷ *n* **2** a storm at or near an equinox

equinox *n* either of the two occasions when day and night are of equal length, around March 21 and September 23 ▶ **HISTORY** Latin *aequi-* equal + *nox* night

equip *vb* **equipping, equipped** **1** to provide with supplies, components, etc.: *the car comes equipped with a catalytic converter* **2** to provide with abilities, understanding, etc.: *stress is something we are all equipped to cope with* ▶ **HISTORY** Old French *eschiper* to fit out (a ship)

equipment *n* **1** a set of tools or devices used for a particular purpose: *communications equipment* **2** an act of equipping

equipoise *n* the state of being perfectly balanced; equilibrium

equitable *adj* fair and reasonable > **equitably** *adv*

equitation *n* the study of riding and horsemanship ▶ **HISTORY** Latin *equitare* to ride

equities *pl n* same as **ordinary shares**

equity *n, pl* **-ties** **1** the quality of being impartial; fairness **2** *law* a system of using principles of natural justice and fair conduct to reach a judgment when common law is inadequate or inappropriate **3** the difference in value between a person's debts and the value of the property on which they are secured: *negative equity* ▶ **HISTORY** Latin *aequus* level, equal

Equity *n Brit, Austral & NZ* the actors' trade union

equivalent *n* **1** something that has the same use or function as something else: *Denmark's equivalent to Silicon Valley* ▷ *adj* **2** equal in value, quantity, significance, etc. **3** having the same or a similar effect or meaning ▶ **HISTORY** Latin *aequi-* equal + *valere* to be worth > **equivalence** *n*

equivalent fraction *n* maths a fraction which can be reduced to the same proper fraction as another: ¾ and ⅜ are equivalent fractions that can be reduced to ½

equivalent ratio *n* maths a ratio that has the same comparison as another ratio: 12:8 and 3:2 are equivalent ratios

equivalent set *n* maths a set that has the same number of members as another set

equivocal *adj* **1** capable of varying interpretations; ambiguous **2** deliberately misleading or vague **3** of doubtful character or sincerity: *the party's commitment to genuine reform is equivocal* ▶ **HISTORY** Latin *aequi-* equal + *vox* voice > **equivocally** *adv*

equivocate *vb* **-cating, -cated** to use vague or ambiguous language in order to deceive someone or to avoid telling the truth > **equivocation** *n* > **equivocator** *n*

er *interj* a sound made when hesitating in speech

Er *chem* erbium

ER Queen Elizabeth ▶ **HISTORY** Latin *Elizabeth Regina*

era *n* **1** a period of time considered as distinctive; epoch **2** an extended period of time measured from a fixed point: *the Communist era* **3** geol a major division of time

■ **WORD HISTORY**

■ In Latin *aera* means 'copper counters'. The word

■ came to mean 'a number', and hence 'a number

■ of years reckoned from a particular point in

■ time'.

eradicate *vb* **-cating, -cated** to destroy or get rid of completely: *measures to eradicate racism* ▶ **HISTORY** Latin *e-* out + *radix* root > **eradicable** *adj* > **eradication** *n* > **eradicator** *n*

erase *vb* **erasing, erased** **1** to destroy all traces of: *he could not erase the memory of his earlier defeat* **2** to rub or wipe out (something written) **3** to remove sound or information from (a magnetic tape or disk) ▶ **HISTORY** Latin *e-* out + *radere* to scrape > **erasable** *adj*

eraser *n* an object, such as a piece of rubber, for erasing something written

erasure *n* **1** an erasing **2** the place or mark where something has been erased

Erato *n* Greek myth the Muse of love poetry

erbium *n* chem a soft silvery-white element of the lanthanide series of metals. Symbol: Er ▶ **HISTORY** after Ytterby, Sweden

ere *conj, prep poetic* before ▶ **HISTORY** Old English *ǣr*

e-reader *n* a portable device that allows readers to download and read texts in electronic form

erect *vb* **1** to build **2** to raise to an upright position **3** to found or form: *the caricature of socialism erected by Lenin* ▷ *adj* **4** upright in posture or position **5** physiol (of the penis, clitoris, or nipples) firm or rigid after swelling with blood ▶ **HISTORY** Latin *erigere* to set up > **erection** *n*

erectile *adj* physiol (of an organ, such as the penis) capable of becoming erect

eremite (**air**-rim-mite) *n* a Christian hermit ▶ **HISTORY** Greek *erēmos* lonely

erg *n* geog an area of shifting sand dunes, esp. in the Sahara Desert in N Africa ▶ **HISTORY** Arabic *irj*

ergo *conj* therefore ▶ **HISTORY** Latin

ergonomic *adj* **1** designed to minimize effort and discomfort **2** of or relating to ergonomics

ergonomics *n* the study of the relationship between workers and their environment ▶ **HISTORY** Greek *ergon* work + (ECO)NOMICS

ergot *n* **1** a disease of a cereal, such as rye, caused by a fungus **2** the dried fungus used in medicine ▶ **HISTORY** French: spur (of a cock)

ermine *n, pl* **-mines** *or* **-mine** **1** the stoat in northern regions, where it has a white winter coat **2** the fur of this animal, used to trim state robes of judges, nobles, etc. ▶ **HISTORY** Medieval Latin *Armenius (mus)* Armenian (mouse)

erne *or* **ern** *n* a fish-eating sea eagle ▶ **HISTORY** Old English *earn*

Ernie *n* (in Britain) a machine that randomly selects winning numbers of Premium Bonds ▶ **HISTORY** acronym of Electronic Random Number Indicator Equipment

erode *vb* **eroding, eroded** **1** to wear down or away **2** to deteriorate or cause to deteriorate ▶ **HISTORY** Latin *e-* away + *rodere* to gnaw

erogenous (ir-**roj**-in-uss) *adj* sensitive to sexual stimulation: *an erogenous zone* ▶ **HISTORY** Greek *erōs* love + *-genēs* born

erosion *n* **1** the wearing away of rocks or soil by the action of water, ice, or wind **2** a gradual lessening or reduction: *an erosion of national sovereignty* > **erosive** *or* **erosional** *adj*

erotic *adj* of, concerning, or arousing sexual desire or giving sexual pleasure ▶ **HISTORY** Greek *erōs* love > **erotically** *adv*

err *vb* **1** to make a mistake **2** to sin ▶ **HISTORY** Latin *errare*

errand *n* **1** a short trip to get or do something for someone **2** **run an errand** to make such a trip ▶ **HISTORY** Old English *ǣrende*

errant *adj* **1** behaving in a way considered to be unacceptable: *an errant schoolboy* **2** old-fashioned or literary wandering in search of adventure: *a knight errant* ▶ **HISTORY** Latin *iter* journey > **errantry** *n*

erratic *adj* **1** irregular or unpredictable: *his increasingly erratic behaviour* ▷ *n* **2** geol a rock that has been transported by glacial action ▶ **HISTORY** Latin *errare* to wander > **erratically** *adv*

erratum *n, pl* **-ta** an error in writing or printing ▶ **HISTORY** Latin

erroneous *adj* based on or containing an error or errors; incorrect > **erroneously** *adv*

error *n* **1** a mistake, inaccuracy, or misjudgment **2** the act or state of being wrong or making a misjudgment: *the plane was shot down in error* **3** the amount by which the actual value of a quantity

e

might differ from an estimate: *a 3% margin of error* ▶ HISTORY Latin

ersatz (**air**-zats) *adj written* made in imitation of something more expensive: *ersatz coffee* ▶ HISTORY German *ersetzen* to substitute

Erse *n, adj* Irish Gaelic ▶ HISTORY Lowland Scots *Erisch* Irish

erstwhile *adj* **1** former ▷ *adv* **2** *archaic* formerly

eruct *or* **eructate** *vb formal* to belch ▶ HISTORY Latin *e-* out + *ructare* to belch > **eructation** *n*

erudite (**air**-rude-ite) *adj* having or showing great academic knowledge ▶ HISTORY Latin *erudire* to polish > **erudition** *n*

erupt *vb* **1** (of a volcano) to throw out molten lava, ash, and steam in a sudden and violent way **2** to burst forth suddenly and violently: *riots erupted across the country* **3** (of a group of people) to suddenly become angry and aggressive: *the meeting erupted in fury* **4** (of a blemish) to appear on the skin ▶ HISTORY Latin *e-* out + *rumpere* to burst > **eruptive** *adj*

eruption *n* **1** an instance of erupting: *a volcanic eruption* **2** an outbreak: *a recent eruption of violence in the capital* **3** the flaring up of a rash or spots; also the rash itself: *acne or other skin eruptions*

erysipelas (air-riss-**sip**-ill-ass) *n* an acute disease of the skin, with fever and raised purplish patches ▶ HISTORY Greek *erusi-* red + *-pelas* skin

erythrocyte (ir-**rith**-roe-site) *n* a red blood cell that transports oxygen through the body ▶ HISTORY Greek *eruthros* red + *kutos* hollow vessel

Es *chem* einsteinium

escalate *vb* **-lating, -lated** to increase or be increased in size, seriousness, or intensity ▶ HISTORY from *escalator* > **escalation** *n*

escalator *n* a moving staircase consisting of stair treads fixed to a conveyor belt ▶ HISTORY Latin *scala* ladder

escalope (**ess**-kal-lop) *n* a thin slice of meat, usually veal ▶ HISTORY Old French: shell

escapade *n* a mischievous act or adventure ▶ HISTORY French

escape *vb* **-caping, -caped** **1** to get away or break free from (confinement) **2** to manage to avoid (something dangerous, unpleasant, or difficult) **3** (of gases, liquids, etc.) to leak gradually **4** to elude; be forgotten by: *those little round cakes whose name escapes me* ▷ *n* **5** the act of escaping or state of having escaped **6** a way of avoiding something difficult, dangerous, or unpleasant: *his frequent illnesses provided an escape from intolerable stress* **7** a means of relaxation or relief: *he found temporary escape through the local cinema* **8** a leakage of gas or liquid ▶ HISTORY Late Latin *e-* out + *cappa* cloak

escapee *n* a person who has escaped from prison

escapement *n* the mechanism in a clock or watch which connects the hands to the pendulum or balance

escape road *n* a small road leading off a steep hill, into which a car can be driven if the brakes fail

escape velocity *n* the minimum velocity necessary for a particle, space vehicle, etc. to

escape from the gravitational field of the earth or other celestial body

escapism *n* an inclination to retreat from unpleasant reality, for example through fantasy > **escapist** *n, adj*

escapologist *n* an entertainer who specializes in freeing himself or herself from chains, ropes, etc. > **escapology** *n*

escarpment *n* the long continuous steep face of a ridge or mountain ▶ HISTORY French *escarpement*

eschatology (ess-cat-**tol**-a-jee) *n* the branch of theology concerned with the end of the world ▶ HISTORY Greek *eskhatos* last > **eschatological** *adj*

escheat (iss-**cheat**) *law n* **1** formerly, the return of property to the state in the absence of legal heirs **2** the property so reverting ▷ *vb* **3** to obtain (land) by escheat ▶ HISTORY Old French *escheoir* to fall to the lot of

eschew (iss-**chew**) *vb* to avoid doing or being involved in (something disliked or harmful) ▶ HISTORY Old French *eschiver* > **eschewal** *n*

escort *n* **1** people or vehicles accompanying another to protect or guard them **2** a person who accompanies someone of the opposite sex on a social occasion ▷ *vb* **3** to act as an escort to ▶ HISTORY French *escorte*

escritoire (ess-kree-**twahr**) *n* a writing desk with compartments and drawers ▶ HISTORY Medieval Latin *scriptorium* writing room in a monastery

escudo (ess-**kew**-doe) *n, pl* **-dos** a former monetary unit of Portugal ▶ HISTORY Spanish: shield

escutcheon *n* **1** a shield displaying a coat of arms **2 blot on one's escutcheon** a stain on one's honour ▶ HISTORY Latin *scutum* shield

esker *or* **eskar** *n geol* a long winding ridge of gravel, sand, etc., originally deposited by a stream of melted snow or ice running under a glacier ▶ HISTORY Irish *escir* ridge

Eskimo *n* **1** (*pl* **-mos** *or* **-mo**) a member of a group of peoples who live in N Canada, Greenland, Alaska, and E Siberia **2** the language of these peoples ▷ *adj* **3** of the Eskimos ▶ HISTORY probably from Native American *Esquimawes*

ESN *Brit* educationally subnormal; formerly used to designate a child who needs special schooling

esoteric (ee-so-**ter**-rik) *adj* understood by only a small number of people, esp. because they have special knowledge ▶ HISTORY Greek *esōterō* inner > **esoterically** *adv*

ESP extrasensory perception

esp. especially

espadrille (**ess**-pad-drill) *n* a light canvas shoe with a braided cord sole ▶ HISTORY French

espalier (ess-**pal**-yer) *n* **1** a shrub or fruit tree trained to grow flat **2** the trellis on which such plants are grown ▶ HISTORY French

esparto *or* **esparto grass** *n, pl* **-tos** any of various grasses of S Europe and N Africa, used to make ropes, mats, etc. ▶ HISTORY Greek *spartos* a kind of rush

especial *adj formal* same as **special** ▶ HISTORY Latin *specialis* individual

especially *adv* 1 particularly: *people are dying, especially children and babies* 2 more than usually: *an especially virulent disease*

Esperanto *n* an international artificial language ▶ HISTORY literally: the one who hopes, pseudonym of Dr L. L. Zamenhof, its Polish inventor > **Esperantist** *n, adj*

espionage (**ess**-pyon-ahzh) *n* 1 the use of spies to obtain secret information, esp. by governments 2 the act of spying ▶ HISTORY French *espionnage*

esplanade *n* a long open level stretch of ground, esp. beside the seashore or in front of a fortified place ▶ HISTORY French

espousal *n* 1 adoption or support: *his espousal of the free market* 2 *old-fashioned* a marriage or engagement ceremony

espouse *vb* **-pousing, -poused** 1 to adopt or give support to (a cause, ideal, etc.) 2 *old-fashioned* (esp. of a man) to marry ▶ HISTORY Latin *sponsare*

espresso *n, pl* **-sos** coffee made by forcing steam or boiling water through ground coffee ▶ HISTORY Italian: pressed

esprit (ess-**pree**) *n* spirit, liveliness, or wit ▶ HISTORY French

esprit de corps (de **kore**) *n* consciousness of and pride in belonging to a particular group ▶ HISTORY French

espy *vb* **espies, espying, espied** to catch sight of ▶ HISTORY Old French *espier*

Esq. esquire

esquire *n* 1 *chiefly Brit* a title of respect placed after a man's name and usually shortened to *Esq.*: *J Davies, Esquire* 2 (in medieval times) the attendant of a knight ▶ HISTORY Late Latin *scutarius* shield bearer

essay *n* 1 a short literary composition on a single subject 2 a short piece of writing on a subject done as an exercise by a student 3 an attempt ▷ *vb* 4 *formal* to attempt: *he essayed a faint smile* ▶ HISTORY Old French *essai* an attempt

essayist *n* a person who writes essays

essence *n* 1 the most important and distinctive feature of something, which determines its identity 2 a concentrated liquid used to flavour food 3 **in essence** essentially 4 **of the essence** vitally important ▶ HISTORY Latin *esse* to be

essential *adj* 1 vitally important; absolutely necessary: *it is essential to get this finished on time* 2 basic or fundamental: *she translated the essential points of the lecture into English* ▷ *n* 3 something fundamental or indispensable > **essentially** *adv*

essential oil *n* any of various volatile oils in plants, which have the odour or flavour of the plant from which they are extracted

EST 1 Eastern Standard Time 2 electric-shock treatment

est. 1 established 2 estimate(d)

establish *vb* 1 to create or set up (an organization, link, etc.): *the regime wants to establish better relations with neighbouring countries* 2 to make

become firmly associated with a particular activity or reputation: *the play that established him as a major dramatist* 3 to prove: *a test to establish if your baby has any chromosomal disorder* 4 to cause (a principle) to be accepted: *our study establishes the case for further research* ▶ HISTORY Latin *stabilis* firm, stable

Established Church *n* a church, such as the Church of England, that is recognized as the official church of a country

establishment *n* 1 the act of establishing or state of being established 2 **a** a business organization or other institution **b** a place of business 3 the people employed by an organization

Establishment *n* **the Establishment** a group of people having authority within a society: usually seen as conservative

estate *n* 1 a large piece of landed property, esp. in the country 2 *Brit & Austral* a large area of land with houses or factories built on it: *an industrial estate* 3 *law* property or possessions, esp. of a deceased person 4 *history* any of the orders or classes making up a society ▶ HISTORY Latin *status* condition

estate agent *n Brit & Austral* a person whose job is to help people buy and sell houses and other property

estate car *n Brit* a car which has a long body with a door at the back end and luggage space behind the rear seats

estate duty *n* a former name for **inheritance tax**

esteem *n* 1 admiration and respect ▷ *vb* 2 to have great respect or high regard for (someone) 3 *formal* to judge or consider: *I should esteem it a kindness* ▶ HISTORY Latin *aestimare* to assess the worth of > **esteemed** *adj*

ester *n chem* a compound produced by the reaction between an acid and an alcohol ▶ HISTORY German

estimable *adj* worthy of respect

estimate *vb* **-mating, -mated** 1 to form an approximate idea of (size, cost, etc.); calculate roughly 2 to form an opinion about; judge 3 to submit an approximate price for a job to a prospective client ▷ *n* 4 an approximate calculation 5 a statement of the likely charge for certain work 6 an opinion ▶ HISTORY Latin *aestimare* to assess the worth of > **estimator** *n*

estimation *n* 1 a considered opinion; judgment: *overall, he went up in my estimation* 2 the act of estimating

Estonian *adj* 1 from Estonia ▷ *n* 2 a person from Estonia

estranged *adj* 1 no longer living with one's husband or wife: *his estranged wife* 2 having quarrelled and lost touch with one's family or friends: *I am estranged from my son* ▶ HISTORY from Latin *extraneus* foreign > **estrangement** *n*

estuary *n, pl* **-aries** the widening channel of a river where it nears the sea ▶ HISTORY Latin *aestus* tide > **estuarine** *adj*

ETA estimated time of arrival

e-tail (**ee**-tail) *n* retail conducted via the internet

et al. 1 and elsewhere ▶ HISTORY Latin *et alibi*

2 and others ▶ HISTORY Latin *et alii*

etc. et cetera

et cetera *or* **etcetera** (et **set**-ra) *adv* **1** and the rest; and others; or the like **2** and so forth
▶ HISTORY Latin *et* and + *cetera* the other (things)

etceteras *pl n* miscellaneous extra things or people

etch *vb* **1** to wear away the surface of a metal, glass, etc. by the action of an acid **2** to cut a design or pattern into a printing plate with acid **3** to imprint vividly: *the scene is etched on my mind*
▶ HISTORY Dutch *etsen* > **etcher** *n*

etching *n* **1** the art or process of preparing or printing etched designs **2** a print made from an etched plate

eternal *adj* **1** without beginning or end; lasting for ever **2** unchanged by time: *eternal truths* **3** seemingly unceasing: *his eternal whingeing* **4** of or like God or a god: *the Eternal Buddha*
▶ HISTORY Latin *aeternus* > **eternally** *adv*

eternity *n*, *pl* **-ties** **1** endless or infinite time **2** a seemingly endless period of time: *it seemed an eternity before he could feel his heart beating again* **3** the timeless existence after death **4** the state of being eternal

eternity ring *n* a ring given as a token of lasting affection, esp. one set all around with stones to symbolize continuity

ethane *n* a flammable gaseous alkane obtained from natural gas and petroleum: used as a fuel
▶ HISTORY from *ethyl*

ethanoic acid *n* same as **acetic acid**

ethanol *n* same as **alcohol** (sense 1)

ethene *n* same as **ethylene**

ether *n* **1** a colourless sweet-smelling liquid used as a solvent and anaesthetic **2** the substance formerly believed to fill all space and to transmit electromagnetic waves **3** the upper regions of the atmosphere; clear sky. Also (for senses 2 and 3): **aether** ▶ HISTORY Greek *aithein* to burn

ethereal (eth-**eer**-ee-al) *adj* **1** extremely delicate or refined **2** heavenly or spiritual ▶ HISTORY Greek *aithēr* ether > **ethereally** *adv*

ethic *n* a moral principle or set of moral values held by an individual or group ▶ HISTORY Greek *ēthos* custom

ethical *adj* **1** of or based on a system of moral beliefs about right and wrong **2** in accordance with principles of professional conduct **3** of or relating to ethics > **ethically** *adv*

ethics *pl n* **1** a code of behaviour, esp. of a particular group, profession, or individual: *business ethics* **2** the moral fitness of a decision, course of action, etc. ▷ *n* **3** the study of the moral value of human conduct

Ethiopian *adj* **1** of Ethiopia ▷ *n* **2** a person from Ethiopia

ethnic *or* **ethnical** *adj* **1** of or relating to a human group with racial, religious, and linguistic characteristics in common **2** characteristic of another culture, esp. a peasant one: *ethnic foodstuffs*
▶ HISTORY Greek *ethnos* race > **ethnically** *adv*

ethnic cleansing *n* the practice, by the dominant ethnic group in an area, of removing other ethnic groups by expulsion or extermination

ethnicity *n* the condition or fact of belonging to a particular ethnic group: *harassment based on gender, race, religion, or ethnicity*

ethnography *n* the branch of anthropology that deals with the scientific description of individual human societies > **ethnographer** *n*
> **ethnographic** *or* **ethnographical** *adj*

ethnology *n* the branch of anthropology that deals with races and peoples and their relations to one another > **ethnological** *adj* > **ethnologist** *n*

ethos (**eeth**-oss) *n* the distinctive spirit and attitudes of a people, culture, etc. ▶ HISTORY Greek

ethyl (**eth**-ill) *adj* of, consisting of, or containing the monovalent group C_2H_5- ▶ HISTORY from *ether*

ethyl alcohol *n* same as **alcohol** (sense 1)

ethylene *or* **ethene** *n* a colourless flammable gaseous alkene used to make polythene and other chemicals

etiolate (**ee**-tee-oh-late) *vb* **-lating, -lated** **1** *formal* to become or cause to become weak **2** *bot* to make a green plant paler through lack of sunlight ▶ HISTORY French *étioler* to make pale > **etiolation** *n*

etiology *n*, *pl* **-gies** **1** the study of causation **2** the study of the cause of diseases ▶ HISTORY Greek *aitia* cause + -LOGY > **etiological** *adj*

etiquette *n* **1** the customs or rules of behaviour regarded as correct in social life **2** a conventional code of practice in certain professions ▶ HISTORY French

étude (**ay**-tewd) *n* *music* a short composition for a solo instrument, esp. intended to be played as an exercise or to demonstrate virtuosity ▶ HISTORY French: study

etymology *n*, *pl* **-gies** **1** the study of the sources and development of words **2** an account of the source and development of a word ▶ HISTORY Greek *etumon* basic meaning + -LOGY
> **etymological** *adj* > **etymologist** *n*

Eu *chem* europium

EU European Union

eucalyptus *or* **eucalypt** *n*, *pl* **-lyptuses, -lyptus** *or* **-lypts** any of a mostly Australian genus of trees, widely cultivated for timber and gum, and for the medicinal oil in their leaves (**eucalyptus oil**)
▶ HISTORY Greek *eu-* well + *kaluptos* covered

Eucharist (**yew**-kar-ist) *n* **1** the Christian sacrament commemorating Christ's Last Supper by the consecration of bread and wine **2** the consecrated elements of bread and wine
▶ HISTORY Greek *eukharistos* thankful
> **Eucharistic** *adj*

Euclidean *or* **Euclidian** (yew-**klid**-ee-an) *adj* denoting a system of geometry based on the rules of Euclid, 3rd-century BC Greek mathematician

eugenics (yew-**jen**-iks) *n* the study of methods of improving the human race, esp. by selective breeding ▶ HISTORY Greek *eugenēs* well-born
> **eugenic** *adj* > **eugenically** *adv* > **eugenicist** *n*

283

euglena n biol a freshwater single-celled organism that moves by means of flagella

eukaryotic adj biol denoting cells that each have a distinct nucleus containing the genetic material

eulogize or **-gise** vb **-gizing, -gized** or **-gising, -gised** to praise (a person or thing) highly in speech or writing > **eulogistic** adj

eulogy n, pl **-gies 1** a speech or piece of writing praising a person or thing, esp. a person who has recently died **2** high praise ▶ HISTORY Greek eulogia praise

eunuch n a man who has been castrated, esp. (formerly) a guard in a harem ▶ HISTORY Greek eunoukhos bedchamber attendant

euphemism n an inoffensive word or phrase substituted for one considered offensive or upsetting, such as departed for dead ▶ HISTORY Greek eu- well + phēmē speech > **euphemistic** adj > **euphemistically** adv

euphonious adj pleasing to the ear

euphonium n a brass musical instrument with four valves, resembling a small tuba ▶ HISTORY euph(ony + harm)onium

euphony n, pl **-nies** a pleasing sound, esp. in speech ▶ HISTORY Greek eu- well + phōnē voice

euphoria n a feeling of great but often unjustified or exaggerated happiness ▶ HISTORY Greek eu- well + pherein to bear > **euphoric** adj

Eurasian adj **1** of Europe and Asia **2** of mixed European and Asian descent ▷ n **3** a person of mixed European and Asian descent

eureka (yew-**reek**-a) interj an exclamation of triumph on discovering or solving something ▶ HISTORY Greek heurēka I have found (it)

euro n, pl **euros** the unit of the European Union's single currency

Euro- combining form Europe or European

Eurocentric adj chiefly concerned with Europe and European culture: a Eurocentric view of British history

Euroland or **Eurozone** n the geographical area containing the countries that have joined the European single currency

European adj **1** of Europe ▷ n **2** a person from Europe **3** a person of European descent **4** an advocate of closer links between the countries of Europe, esp. those in the European Union > **Europeanism** n

European Community or **European Economic Community** n former names for **European Union**

European Union n an economic organization of European states, which have some shared monetary, social, and political goals

Europhile (**you**-roh-file) n **1** a person who admires Europe or the European Union ▷ adj **2** marked by admiration of Europe or the European Union

europium n chem a silvery-white element of the lanthanide series. Symbol: Eu ▶ HISTORY after Europe

Euro-sceptic (in Britain) n **1** a person who is opposed to closer links with the European Union

▷ adj **2** opposing closer links with the European Union: three Euro-sceptic MPs

Eurozone n same as **Euroland**

Eustachian tube n a tube that connects the middle ear with the pharynx and equalizes the pressure between the two sides of the eardrum ▶ HISTORY after Bartolomeo Eustachio, anatomist

Euterpe n Greek myth the Muse of lyric poetry

euthanasia n the act of killing someone painlessly, esp. to relieve suffering from an incurable illness ▶ HISTORY Greek: easy death

eutrophic adj biol (of lakes, etc.) rich in organic and mineral nutrients and supporting an abundant plant life ▶ HISTORY probably from Greek eutrophos well-fed

eutrophication n biol the process by which the number of organic and mineral nutrients builds up excessively in a body of water, favouring abundant growth of algae and consequent oxygen depletion ▶ HISTORY probably from Greek eutrophos well-fed

eV electronvolt

evacuate vb **-ating, -ated 1** to send away from a dangerous place to a safe place: 200 people were evacuated from their homes because of the floods **2** to empty (a place) of people because it has become dangerous: the entire street was evacuated until the fire was put out **3** physiol to discharge waste from the body ▶ HISTORY Latin evacuare to empty > **evacuation** n > **evacuee** n

evade vb **evading, evaded 1** to get away from or avoid (imprisonment, captors, etc.) **2** to get around, shirk, or dodge (the law, a duty, etc.) **3** to avoid answering (a question) ▶ HISTORY Latin evadere to go forth

evaluate vb **-ating, -ated** to find or judge the quality or value of something ▶ HISTORY French évaluer > **evaluation** n

evanescent adj formal quickly fading away; ephemeral or transitory > **evanescence** n

evangelical Christianity adj **1** of or following from the Gospels **2** of certain Protestant sects which emphasize salvation through faith alone and a belief in the absolute authority of the Bible ▷ n **3** a member of an evangelical sect ▶ HISTORY Greek evangelion good news > **evangelicalism** n > **evangelically** adv

evangelism n the practice of spreading the Christian gospel

evangelist n a preacher, sometimes itinerant > **evangelistic** adj

Evangelist n any of the writers of the Gospels: Matthew, Mark, Luke, or John

evangelize or **-lise** vb **-lizing, -lized** or **-lising, -lised** to preach the Christian gospel (to) > **evangelization** or **-lisation** n

evaporate vb **-rating, -rated 1** to change from a liquid or solid to a vapour **2** to become less and less and finally disappear: faith in the government evaporated rapidly after the election ▶ HISTORY Latin e- out + vapor steam > **evaporable** adj > **evaporation** n

evaporated milk n thick unsweetened tinned

e

milk from which some of the water has been removed

evapotranspiration n *environmental science* the return of water vapour to the atmosphere by evaporation from land and water surfaces and by the transpiration of vegetation

evasion n **1** the act of evading something, esp. a duty or responsibility, by cunning or illegal means: *tax evasion* **2** cunning or deception used to dodge a question, duty, etc.

evasive adj **1** seeking to evade; not straightforward: *an evasive answer* **2** avoiding or seeking to avoid trouble or difficulties: *evasive action* > **evasively** adv

eve n **1** the evening or day before some special event **2** the period immediately before an event: *on the eve of the Second World War* **3** *poetic or old-fashioned* evening ▸ **HISTORY** variant of EVEN²

Eve n *Bible* the first woman, created by God from Adam's rib

even¹ adj **1** level and regular; flat **2** on the same level: *make sure the surfaces are even with one another* **3** regular and unvarying: *an even pace* **4** equally balanced between two sides **5** equal in number, quantity, etc. **6** (of a number) divisible by two **7** denoting alternatives, events, etc. that have an equal probability: *they have a more than even chance of winning the next election* **8** having scored the same number of points **9** **even money** or **evens** a bet in which the winnings are exactly the same as the amount staked **10** **get even with** *informal* to exact revenge on; settle accounts with ▷ adv **11** used to suggest that the content of a statement is unexpected or paradoxical: *it's chilly in Nova Scotia, even in August* **12** used to intensify a comparative adjective or adverb: *an even greater demand* **13** used to introduce a word that is stronger and more accurate than one already used: *a normal, even inevitable aspect of ageing* **14** used preceding a hypothesis to emphasize that whether or not the condition is fulfilled, the statement remains valid: *the remark didn't call for an answer even if he could have thought of one* **15** *spoken* **even so** in spite of any assertion to the contrary; nevertheless **16** **even though** despite the fact that ▸ **HISTORY** Old English *efen* > **evenly** adv > **evenness** n

even² n *poetic or old-fashioned* **1** eve **2** evening ▸ **HISTORY** Old English *æfen*

evening n **1** the latter part of the day, esp. from late afternoon until nightfall ▷ adj **2** of or in the evening: *the evening meal* ▸ **HISTORY** Old English *æfnung*

evening class n *Brit, Austral & NZ* an educational class for adults, held during the evening

evening dress n clothes for a formal occasion during the evening

evening primrose n a plant with yellow flowers that open in the evening

evening star n a planet, usually Venus, seen shining brightly just after sunset

evensong n *Church of England* the daily evening service. Also called: **Evening Prayer**

event n **1** anything that takes place, esp. something important **2** a planned and organized occasion: *the wedding was one of the social events of the year* **3** any one contest in a sporting programme **4** **in any event** or **at all events** whatever happens **5** **in the event** when it came to the actual or final outcome: *in the event, neither of them turned up* **6** **in the event of** if (such a thing) happens **7** **in the event that** if it should happen that ▸ **HISTORY** Latin *evenire* to happen

eventful adj full of exciting or important incidents

eventing n *Brit, Austral & NZ* riding competitions (esp. **three-day events**), usually involving cross-country riding, jumping, and dressage

eventual adj happening or being achieved at the end of a situation or process: *the Fascists' eventual victory in the Spanish Civil War* > **eventually** adv

eventuality n, pl **-ties** a possible occurrence or result: *I was utterly unprepared for such an eventuality*

ever adv **1** at any time: *it was the fourth fastest time ever* **2** always: *ever present* **3** used to give emphasis: *tell him to put to sea as soon as ever he can* **4** **ever so** or **ever such** *informal, chiefly Brit* used to give emphasis: *I'm ever so sorry* ▸ **HISTORY** Old English *æfre*

evergreen adj **1** (of certain trees and shrubs) bearing foliage throughout the year ▷ n **2** an evergreen tree or shrub

everlasting adj **1** never coming to an end; eternal **2** lasting so long or occurring so often as to become tedious > **everlastingly** adv

evermore adv all time to come

every adj **1** each without exception: *they were winning every battle* **2** the greatest or best possible: *there is every reason to believe in the sincerity of their commitment* **3** each: *every 20 years* **4** **every bit as** *informal* just as: *she's every bit as clever as you* **5** **every other** each alternate: *every other month* ▸ **HISTORY** Old English *æfre* ever + *ælc* each

everybody pron every person; everyone

everyday adj **1** commonplace or usual **2** happening each day **3** suitable for or used on ordinary days

Everyman n the ordinary person; common man ▸ **HISTORY** after the central figure in a medieval morality play

everyone pron every person; everybody

everything pron **1** the whole; all things: *everything had been carefully packed* **2** the thing that is most important: *work was everything to her*

everywhere adv to or in all parts or places

evict vb to expel (someone) legally from his or her home or land ▸ **HISTORY** Latin *evincere* to vanquish utterly > **eviction** n

evidence n **1** something which provides ground for belief or disbelief: *there is no evidence that depression is inherited* **2** *law* matter produced before a court of law in an attempt to prove or disprove a point in issue **3** **in evidence** on display; apparent ▷ vb **-dencing, -denced** **4** to show clearly; demonstrate: *you evidenced no talent for music*

evident adj easy to see or understand ▸ **HISTORY** Latin *videre* to see > **evidently** adv

285

evidential *adj* of, serving as, or based on evidence > **evidentially** *adv*

evil *n* **1** a force or power that brings about wickedness and harm: *the battle between good and evil* **2** a wicked or morally wrong act or thing: *the evil of racism* ▷ *adj* **3** (of a person) deliberately causing great harm and misery; wicked: *an evil dictator* **4** (of an act, idea, etc.) causing great harm and misery; morally wrong: *what you did was deeply evil* **5** very unpleasant: *it was fascinating to see people vanish as if we had some very evil smell* ▶ HISTORY Old English *yfel* > **evilly** *adv*

evildoer *n* a person who does evil > **evildoing** *n*

evil eye *n* **the evil eye** a look superstitiously supposed to have the power of inflicting harm

evince *vb* **evincing, evinced** *formal* to show or display (a quality or feeling) clearly: *a humility which he had never evinced in earlier days* ▶ HISTORY Latin *evincere* to overcome

eviscerate *vb* **-ating, -ated** to remove the internal organs of; disembowel ▶ HISTORY Latin *e-* out + *viscera* entrails > **evisceration** *n*

evocation *n* the act of evoking > **evocative** *adj*

evoke *vb* **evoking, evoked 1** to call or summon up (a memory or feeling) from the past **2** to provoke or bring about: *his sacking evoked a huge public protest* ▶ HISTORY Latin *evocare* to call forth

evolution *n* **1** *biol* a gradual change in the characteristics of a population of animals or plants over successive generations **2** a gradual development, esp. to a more complex form ▶ HISTORY Latin *evolutio* an unrolling > **evolutionary** *adj*

evolve *vb* **evolving, evolved 1** to develop gradually **2** (of animal or plant species) to undergo evolution ▶ HISTORY Latin *evolvere* to unfold

ewe *n* a female sheep ▶ HISTORY Old English *ēowu*

ewer *n* a large jug with a wide mouth ▶ HISTORY Latin *aqua* water

ex¹ *prep finance* excluding or without: *ex dividend* ▶ HISTORY Latin: out of, from

ex² *n, pl* **exes** *informal* one's former wife or husband

ex- *prefix* **1** out of, outside, or from: *exit* **2** former: *his glamorous ex-wife* ▶ HISTORY Latin

exacerbate (ig-**zass**-er-bate) *vb* **-bating, -bated** to make (pain, emotion, or a situation) worse ▶ HISTORY Latin *acerbus* bitter > **exacerbation** *n*

exact *adj* **1** correct in every detail; strictly accurate **2** precise, as opposed to approximate **3** based on measurement and the formulation of laws: *forecasting floods is not an exact science* ▷ *vb* **4** to obtain or demand as a right, esp. through force or strength: *the rebels called for revenge to be exacted for the killings* ▶ HISTORY Latin *exigere* to demand

exacting *adj* making rigorous or excessive demands

exaction *n formal* **1** the act of obtaining or demanding money as a right **2** a sum or payment exacted

exactitude *n* the quality of being exact; precision

exactly *adv* **1** with complete accuracy and precision: *I don't know exactly where they live* **2** in every respect: *he looks exactly like his father* ▷ *interj* **3** just so! precisely!

exaggerate *vb* **-ating, -ated 1** to regard or represent as greater than is true **2** to make greater or more noticeable ▶ HISTORY Latin *exaggerare* to heap up > **exaggerated** *adj* > **exaggeratedly** *adv* > **exaggeration** *n*

exalt *vb* **1** to praise highly **2** to raise to a higher rank ▶ HISTORY Latin *exaltare* to raise > **exalted** *adj* > **exaltation** *n*

exam *n* short for **examination**

examination *n* **1** the act of examining **2** *education* exercises, questions, or tasks set to test a person's knowledge and skill **3** *med* physical inspection of a patient **4** *law* the formal questioning of a person on oath

examination in chief *n law* the questioning (of a witness) by the side that called the witness

examine *vb* **-ining, -ined 1** to inspect carefully or in detail; investigate **2** *education* to test a person's knowledge of a subject by written or oral questions **3** *med* to investigate a patient's state of health **4** *law* to formally question someone on oath ▶ HISTORY Latin *examinare* to weigh > **examinee** *n* > **examiner** *n*

example *n* **1** a specimen that is typical of its group; sample: *a fine example of Georgian architecture* **2** a particular event, object, or person that demonstrates a point or supports an argument, theory, etc.: *Germany is a good example of how federalism works in practice* **3** a person, action, or thing that is worthy of imitation **4** a punishment or the person punished regarded as a warning to others **5 for example** as an illustration ▶ HISTORY Latin *exemplum*

exasperate *vb* **-ating, -ated** to cause great irritation to ▶ HISTORY Latin *exasperare* to make rough > **exasperated** *adj* > **exasperating** *adj* > **exasperation** *n*

ex cathedra *adj, adv* **1** with the authority of one's official position **2** *RC Church* (of doctrines of faith or morals) defined by the pope as infallibly true ▶ HISTORY Latin: from the chair

excavate *vb* **-vating, -vated 1** to unearth (buried objects) methodically to discover information about the past **2** to make a hole in something by digging into it or hollowing it out: *one kind of shrimp excavates a hole for itself* ▶ HISTORY Latin *excavare* to make hollow > **excavation** *n* > **excavator** *n*

exceed *vb* **1** to be greater in degree or quantity **2** to go beyond the limit of (a restriction) ▶ HISTORY Latin *excedere* to go beyond

exceedingly *adv* very; extremely

excel *vb* **-celling, -celled 1** to be better than; surpass **2 excel in** *or* **at** to be outstandingly good at ▶ HISTORY Latin *excellere* to rise up

excellence *n* the quality of being exceptionally good

Excellency *or* **Excellence** *n, pl* **-lencies** *or* **-lences • Your** *or* **His** *or* **Her Excellency** a title used to address a high-ranking official, such as an ambassador

excellent *adj* exceptionally good; outstanding

except *prep* **1** Also: **except for** not including; apart from: *everyone except Jill laughed* **2 except that** but for the fact that ▷ *vb* **3** to leave out or exclude ▶ HISTORY Latin *excipere* to take out

excepting *prep* except

exception *n* **1** anything excluded from or not conforming to a general rule or classification **2 take exception to** to make objections to

exceptionable *adj* open to objection

exceptional *adj* **1** forming an exception **2** having much more than average intelligence, ability, or skill > **exceptionally** *adv*

excerpt *n* **1** a passage taken from a book, speech, etc.; extract ▷ *vb* **2** to take a passage from a book, speech, etc. ▶ HISTORY Latin *excerptum* (something) picked out

excess *n* **1** the state or act of going beyond normal or permitted limits **2** an immoderate or abnormal amount **3** the amount, number, etc. by which one thing exceeds another **4** behaviour regarded as too extreme or immoral to be acceptable: *a life of drunken excess* **5 excesses** acts or actions that are unacceptably cruel or immoral: *one of the bloodiest excesses of a dictatorial regime* **6 in excess of** more than **7 to excess** to an extreme or unhealthy extent: *he had started to drink to excess* ▷ *adj* **8** more than normal, necessary, or permitted: *excess fat* ▶ HISTORY Latin *excedere* to go beyond > **excessive** *adj* > **excessively** *adv*

excess luggage *or* **baggage** *n* luggage that is more in weight or number of pieces than an airline etc. will carry free .

exchange *vb* **-changing, -changed** **1** (of two or more people, governments, etc.) to give each other (something similar) at the same time: *they nervously exchanged smiles* **2** to replace (one thing) with another, esp. to replace unsatisfactory goods: *could I exchange this for a larger size, please?* ▷ *n* **3** the act of exchanging **4** anything given or received as an equivalent or substitute for something else **5** an argument **6** Also called: **telephone exchange** a centre in which telephone lines are interconnected **7** a place where securities or commodities are traded, esp. by brokers or merchants **8** a transfer of sums of money of equivalent value, as between different currencies **9** the system by which commercial debts are settled, esp. by bills of exchange, without direct payment of money ▶ HISTORY Latin *cambire* to barter > **exchangeable** *adj*

exchange rate *n* the rate at which the currency unit of one country may be exchanged for that of another

Exchequer *n Government* (in Britain and certain other countries) the accounting department of the Treasury ▶ HISTORY Old French *eschequier* counting table

excise¹ *n* **1** a tax on goods, such as spirits, produced for the home market **2** (formerly in Britain) the section of the government service responsible for the collection of excise ▶ HISTORY Latin *assidere* to sit beside, assist in judging

excise² *vb* **-cising, -cised** **1** to delete a passage from a book **2** to remove an organ or part surgically ▶ HISTORY Latin *excidere* to cut down > **excision** *n*

excitable *adj* nervous and easily excited > **excitability** *n*

excite *vb* **-citing, -cited** **1** to make (a person) feel so happy that he or she is unable to relax because he or she is looking forward eagerly to something: *he was excited at the long-awaited arrival of a son* **2** to cause or arouse (an emotion, response, etc.): *the idea strongly excited his interest* **3** *physiol* to cause a response in (an organ, tissue, or part) **4** *physics* to raise (an atom, molecule, etc.) to a higher energy level ▶ HISTORY Latin *exciere* to stimulate > **excited** *adj* > **excitedly** *adv*

excitement *n* **1** the state of being excited **2** a person or thing that excites

exciting *adj* causing excitement; stirring; stimulating > **excitingly** *adv*

exclaim *vb* to cry out or speak suddenly or excitedly, as from surprise, delight, horror, etc. ▶ HISTORY Latin *exclamare*

exclamation *n* **1** an abrupt or excited cry or utterance **2** the act of exclaiming > **exclamatory** *adj*

exclamation mark *or US* **point** *n* the punctuation mark (!) used after exclamations and forceful commands

exclude *vb* **-cluding, -cluded** **1** to keep out; prevent from entering **2** to leave out of consideration ▶ HISTORY Latin *excludere* > **exclusion** *n*

exclusive *adj* **1** excluding or incompatible with anything else: *these two theories are mutually exclusive* **2** not shared: *exclusive rights* **3** used or lived in by a privileged minority, esp. a fashionable clique: *an exclusive skiing resort* **4** not including the numbers, dates, etc. mentioned **5 exclusive of** except for; not taking account of **6 exclusive to** limited to; found only in ▷ *n* **7** a story reported in only one newspaper > **exclusively** *adv* > **exclusivity** *or* **exclusiveness** *n*

exclusive power *n Austral law* the exclusive right of the federal parliament, as opposed to the state parliaments, to legislate on certain matters

excommunicate *vb* **-cating, -cated** to expel (someone) from membership of a church and ban him or her from taking part in its services ▶ HISTORY Late Latin *excommunicare* to exclude from the community > **excommunication** *n*

excoriate *vb* **-ating, -ated** **1** *literary* to censure severely **2** to strip skin from a person or animal ▶ HISTORY Late Latin *excoriare* to strip, flay > **excoriation** *n*

excrement *n* waste matter discharged from the body; faeces ▶ HISTORY Latin *excernere* to sift, excrete > **excremental** *adj*

excrescence *n* something that protrudes, esp. an outgrowth from a part of the body ▶ HISTORY Latin *excrescrere* to grow out > **excrescent** *adj*

excreta (ik-**skree**-ta) *pl n* urine and faeces discharged from the body

287

excrete *vb* **-creting, -creted** to discharge waste matter, such as urine, sweat, or faeces, from the body ▶ HISTORY Latin *excernere* to discharge > **excretion** *n* > **excretory** *adj*

excruciating *adj* **1** unbearably painful; agonizing **2** hard to bear: *never had an afternoon passed with such excruciating slowness* ▶ HISTORY Latin *excruciare* to torture > **excruciatingly** *adv*

exculpate *vb* **-pating, -pated** to free from blame or guilt ▶ HISTORY Latin *ex* from + *culpa* fault

excursion *n* a short outward and return journey, esp. for sightseeing, etc.; outing ▶ HISTORY Latin *excurrere* to run out

excuse *n* **1** an explanation offered to justify an action which has been criticized or as a reason for not fulfilling an obligation, etc. ▷ *vb* **-cusing, -cused 2** to put forward a reason or justification for (an action, fault, or offending person) **3** to pardon (a person) or overlook (a fault) **4** to free (someone) from having to carry out a task, obligation, etc.: *a doctor's letter excusing him from games at school* **5** to allow to leave **6 be excused** *euphemistic* to go to the toilet **7 excuse me!** an expression used to catch someone's attention or to apologize for an interruption, disagreement, etc. ▶ HISTORY Latin *ex* out + *causa* cause, accusation > **excusable** *adj*

ex-directory *adj* Brit & NZ not listed in a telephone directory by request

execrable (eks-sik-rab-bl) *adj* of very poor quality ▶ HISTORY See EXECRATE > **execrably** *adv*

execute *vb* **-cuting, -cuted 1** to put a condemned person to death **2** to carry out or accomplish **3** to produce or create (a work of art) **4** *law* to render (a deed) effective, for example by signing it **5** to carry out the terms of (a contract, will, etc.) ▶ HISTORY Old French *executer* > **executer** *n*

execution *n* **1** the act of executing **2** the carrying out or undergoing of a sentence of death **3** the manner in which something is performed; technique

executioner *n* a person whose job is to kill people who have been sentenced to death

executive *n* **1** a person or group responsible for the administration of a project or business **2** the branch of government responsible for carrying out laws, decrees, etc. ▷ *adj* **3** having the function of carrying plans, orders, laws, etc. into effect: *the executive producer* **4** of or for executives: *the executive car park* **5** *informal* very expensive or exclusive: *executive cars*

Executive Council *n* (in Australia and New Zealand) a body of ministers of the Crown, presided over by the governor or governor-general, that formally approves cabinet decisions, etc.

executor *n* *law* a person appointed by someone to ensure that the conditions set out in his or her will are carried out > **executorial** *adj* > **executrix** *fem n*

exegesis (eks-sij-**jee**-siss) *n*, *pl* **-ses** (-seez) explanation of a text, esp. of the Bible ▶ HISTORY Greek *exēgeisthai* to interpret

exemplar *n* **1** a person or thing to be copied; model **2** a typical specimen; example ▶ HISTORY Latin *exemplum* example

exemplary *adj* **1** so good as to be an example worthy of imitation **2** (of a punishment) extremely harsh, so as to discourage others from committing a similar crime

exemplify *vb* **-fies, -fying, -fied 1** to show by example **2** to serve as an example of ▶ HISTORY Latin *exemplum* example + *facere* to make > **exemplification** *n*

exempt *adj* **1** not subject to an obligation, tax, etc. ▷ *vb* **2** to release (someone) from an obligation, tax, etc. ▶ HISTORY Latin *exemptus* removed > **exemption** *n*

exequies (eks-sik-weez) *pl n*, *sing* **-quy** funeral rites ▶ HISTORY Latin *exequiae*

exercise *n* **1** physical exertion, esp. for training or keeping fit **2** an activity planned to achieve a particular purpose: *the group's meeting was mainly an exercise in mutual reassurance* **3** a set of movements, tasks, etc. designed to improve or test one's ability or fitness **4** the use or practice of (a right, power, or authority) **5** *mil* a manoeuvre or simulated combat operation ▷ *vb* **-cising, -cised 6** to put into use; make use of: *we urge all governments involved to exercise restraint* **7** to take exercise or perform exercises **8** to practise using in order to develop or train: *to exercise one's voice* **9** to worry or vex: *Western governments have been exercised by the need to combat international terrorism* **10** *mil* to carry out simulated combat, manoeuvres, etc. ▶ HISTORY Latin *exercere* to drill > **exerciser** *n*

exert *vb* **1** to use influence, authority, etc. forcefully or effectively **2 exert oneself** to make a special effort ▶ HISTORY Latin *exserere* to thrust out

exertion *n* **1** effort or exercise, esp. physical effort: *the sudden exertion of running for a bus* **2** the act or an instance of using one's influence, powers, or authority: *the exertion of parental authority*

exeunt (eks-see-unt) they go out: used as a stage direction ▶ HISTORY Latin

exfoliate *vb* **-ating, -ated** to peel off in scales or layers > **exfoliation** *n*

exhale *vb* **-haling, -haled 1** to expel breath or smoke from the lungs; breathe out **2** to give off or to be given off as gas, fumes, etc.: *the crater exhaled smoke* ▶ HISTORY Latin *exhalare* > **exhalation** *n*

exhaust *vb* **1** to tire out **2** to use up totally **3** to discuss a topic so thoroughly that no more remains to be said ▷ *n* **4** gases ejected from an engine as waste products **5** the parts of an engine through which waste gases pass ▶ HISTORY Latin *exhaurire* to draw out > **exhausted** *adj* > **exhaustible** *adj*

exhaustible resources *pl n* Same as **non-renewable resources**

exhaustion *n* **1** extreme tiredness **2** the act of exhausting or state of being exhausted

exhaustive *adj* very thorough; comprehensive > **exhaustively** *adv*

exhibit *vb* **1** to display (a work of art) to the public **2** to show (a quality or feeling): *they exhibited* extraordinary courage ▷ n **3** an object exhibited to the public **4** law a document or object produced in court as evidence ▶ HISTORY Latin exhibere to hold forth > **exhibitor** n

exhibition n **1** a public display of art, skills, etc. **2** the act of exhibiting or the state of being exhibited: an exhibition of bad temper **3 make an exhibition of oneself** to behave so foolishly that one attracts public attention

exhibitionism n a compulsive desire to attract attention to oneself > **exhibitionist** n

exhilarate vb **-rating, -rated** to make (someone) feel lively and cheerful ▶ HISTORY Latin exhilarare > **exhilaration** n

exhort vb formal to urge (someone) earnestly ▶ HISTORY Latin exhortari > **exhortation** n

exhume (ig-**zyume**) vb **-huming, -humed** formal to dig up something buried, esp. a corpse ▶ HISTORY Latin ex out + humus the ground > **exhumation** n

exigency n, pl **-gencies** formal **1** an urgent demand or need **2** an emergency ▶ HISTORY Latin exigere to require > **exigent** adj

exiguous adj formal scanty or meagre ▶ HISTORY Latin exiguus > **exiguity** n

exile n **1** a prolonged, usually enforced absence from one's country **2** a person banished or living away from his or her country ▷ vb **-iling, -iled 3** to expel (someone) from his or her country; banish ▶ HISTORY Latin exsilium

exist vb **1** to have being or reality; be: does God exist? **2** to only just be able to keep oneself alive, esp. because of poverty or hunger **3** to be living; live **4** to be present under specified conditions or in a specified place ▶ HISTORY Latin exsistere to step forth > **existing** adj

existence n **1** the fact or state of being real, live, or actual **2** a way of life, esp. a poor or hungry one **3** everything that exists > **existent** adj

existential adj **1** of or relating to existence, esp. human existence **2** of or relating to existentialism

existentialism n a philosophical movement stressing personal experience and responsibility of the individual, who is seen as a free agent > **existentialist** adj, n

exit n **1** a way out **2** the act of going out **3** theatre the act of going offstage **4** Brit & Austral a point at which vehicles may leave or join a motorway ▷ vb **exiting, exited 5** to go away or out; depart **6** theatre to go offstage: used as a stage direction: exit bleeding from the room ▶ HISTORY Latin exire to go out

exnuptial adj law (of children) born to parents unmarried at the time of their birth

exocrine adj of or denoting a gland, such as the sweat gland, that discharges its product through a duct ▶ HISTORY Greek exō outside + krinein to separate

exodus (**eks**-so-duss) n the departure of a large number of people ▶ HISTORY Greek ex out + hodos way

Exodus n Bible the second book of the Old

Testament, containing a description of the departure of the Israelites from Egypt

ex officio (eks off-**fish**-ee-oh) adv, adj by right of position or office ▶ HISTORY Latin

exonerate vb **-ating, -ated** to clear (someone) of blame or a criminal charge ▶ HISTORY Latin exonerare to free from a burden > **exoneration** n

exorbitant adj (of prices, demands, etc.) excessively great or high: an exorbitant rent ▶ HISTORY Latin ex out, away + orbita track > **exorbitantly** adv

exorcize or **-cise** vb **-cizing, -cized** or **-cising, -cised** to expel (evil spirits) by prayers and religious rites ▶ HISTORY Greek ex out + horkos oath > **exorcism** n > **exorcist** n

exoskeleton n zool the protective or supporting structure covering the outside of the body of many animals, for example insects or crabs

exosmosis n biol osmosis in which the water flows from a cell or organism into the surrounding solution

exosphere n the outermost layer of the earth's atmosphere

exothermic adj (of a chemical reaction) involving or leading to the giving off of heat

exotic adj **1** having a strange allure or beauty **2** originating in a foreign country; not native ▷ n **3** a non-native plant ▶ HISTORY Greek exō outside > **exotically** adv

exotica pl n exotic objects, esp. as a collection

expand vb **1** to make or become greater in extent, size, or scope **2** to spread out; unfold **3 expand on** to go into more detail about (a story or subject) **4** to become increasingly relaxed, friendly, and talkative **5** maths to express a function or expression as the sum or product of terms ▶ HISTORY Latin expandere to spread out > **expandable** adj

expanse n an uninterrupted wide area; stretch: a large expanse of water

expansion n **1** the act of expanding **2** an increase or development, esp. in the activities of a company

expansionism n the practice of expanding the economy or territory of a country > **expansionist** n, adj

expansive adj **1** wide or extensive **2** friendly, open, and talkative > **expansiveness** n

expat adj, n short for **expatriate**

expatiate (iks-**pay**-shee-ate) vb **-ating, -ated** • **expatiate on** formal to speak or write at length on (a subject) ▶ HISTORY Latin exspatiari to digress > **expatiation** n

expatriate (eks-**pat**-ree-it) adj **1** living away from one's native country: an expatriate American **2** exiled ▷ n **3** a person living away from his or her native country **4** an exile ▶ HISTORY Latin ex out, away + patria native land > **expatriation** n

expect vb **1** to regard as likely **2** to look forward to or be waiting for **3** to require (something) as an obligation: he expects an answer by January **4 be expecting** informal to be pregnant ▶ HISTORY Latin exspectare to watch for

e

expectancy *n* **1** something expected, esp. on the basis of a norm: *a life expectancy of 78* **2** anticipation or expectation

expectant *adj* **1** expecting or hopeful **2 a** pregnant **b** married to or living with a woman who is pregnant: *an expectant father* > **expectantly** *adv*

expectation *n* **1** the state of expecting or of being expected **2** something looked forward to, whether feared or hoped for **3** belief that someone should behave in a particular way: *women with expectations of old-fashioned gallantry*

expectorant *med adj* **1** helping to bring up phlegm from the respiratory passages ▷ *n* **2** an expectorant medicine

expectorate *vb* **-rating, -rated** *formal* to cough up and spit out (phlegm from the respiratory passages) ▶ **HISTORY** Latin *expectorare* to drive from the breast, expel > **expectoration** *n*

expediency *or* **expedience** *n, pl* **-encies** *or* **-ences** **1** the use of methods that are advantageous rather than fair or just **2** appropriateness or suitability

expedient (iks-**pee**-dee-ent) *n* **1** something that achieves a particular purpose: *income controls were used only as a short-term expedient* ▷ *adj* **2** useful or advantageous in a given situation: *they only talk about human rights when it is politically expedient* ▶ **HISTORY** Latin *expediens* setting free; see EXPEDITE

expedite *vb* **-diting, -dited** *formal* **1** to hasten the progress of **2** to do quickly ▶ **HISTORY** Latin *expedire* to free the feet

expedition *n* **1** an organized journey or voyage, esp. for exploration **2** the people and equipment comprising an expedition **3** a pleasure trip or excursion: *an expedition to the seaside* ▶ **HISTORY** Latin *expedire* to prepare, expedite > **expeditionary** *adj*

expeditious *adj* done quickly and efficiently

expel *vb* **-pelling, -pelled** **1** to drive out with force **2** to dismiss from a school, club, etc. permanently ▶ **HISTORY** Latin *expellere*

expend *vb formal* to spend or use up (time, energy, or money) ▶ **HISTORY** Latin *expendere* to weigh out, pay

expendable *adj* **1** not worth preserving **2** able to be sacrificed to achieve an objective, esp. a military one

expenditure *n* **1** something expended, esp. money **2** the amount expended

expense *n* **1** a particular payment of money; expenditure **2** the amount of money needed to buy or do something; cost **3 expenses** money spent in the performance of a job, etc. **4** something requiring money for its purchase or upkeep **5 at the expense of** to the detriment of ▶ **HISTORY** Latin *expensus* weighed out

expense account *n* **1** an arrangement by which an employee's expenses are refunded by his or her employer **2** a record of such expenses

expensive *adj* costing a great deal of money > **expensiveness** *n*

experience *n* **1** direct personal participation or observation of something: *his experience of prison life* **2** a particular incident, feeling, etc. that a person has undergone **3** accumulated knowledge, esp. of practical matters ▷ *vb* **-encing, -enced** **4** to participate in or undergo **5** to be moved by; feel ▶ **HISTORY** Latin *experiri* to prove

experienced *adj* skilful or knowledgeable as a result of having done something many times before

experiential *adj philosophy* relating to or derived from experience

experiment *n* **1** a test or investigation to provide evidence for or against a theory: *a scientific experiment* **2** the trying out of a new idea or method ▷ *vb* **3** to carry out an experiment or experiments ▶ **HISTORY** Latin *experiri* to test > **experimentation** *n* > **experimenter** *n*

experimental *adj* **1** relating to, based on, or having the nature of an experiment **2** trying out new ideas or methods > **experimentally** *adv*

expert *n* **1** a person who has extensive skill or knowledge in a particular field ▷ *adj* **2** skilful or knowledgeable **3** of, involving, or done by an expert ▶ **HISTORY** Latin *expertus* known by experience > **expertly** *adv*

expertise (eks-per-**teez**) *n* special skill, knowledge, or judgment ▶ **HISTORY** French

expiate *vb* **-ating, -ated** *formal* to make amends for a sin or wrongdoing ▶ **HISTORY** Latin *expiare* > **expiation** *n*

expiration *n* **1** the finish of something; expiry **2** the act, process, or sound of breathing out > **expiratory** *adj*

expire *vb* **-piring, -pired** **1** to finish or run out; come to an end **2** to breathe out air **3** to die ▶ **HISTORY** Latin *exspirare* to breathe out

expiry *n, pl* **-ries** a coming to an end, esp. of the period of a contract

explain *vb* **1** to make something easily understandable, esp. by giving a clear and detailed account of it **2 explain oneself** to justify or attempt to justify oneself by giving reasons for one's actions **3 explain away** to offer excuses or reasons for (mistakes) ▶ **HISTORY** Latin *explanare* to flatten, make clear

explanation *n* **1** the reason or reasons why a particular event or situation happened: *there is no reasonable explanation for her behaviour* **2** a detailed account or description: *a 90-minute explanation of his love of jazz*

explanation genre *n* a form of writing or speech in which the writer or speaker explains how something works or happens and the sequence of processes involved

explanatory *adj* serving or intended to serve as an explanation

expletive (iks-**plee**-tiv) *n* an exclamation or swearword expressing emotion rather than meaning ▶ **HISTORY** Latin *explere* to fill up

explicable *adj* capable of being explained

explicate *vb* **-cating, -cated** *formal* to make clear;

explain ▶ HISTORY Latin *explicare* to unfold
> **explication** *n*

explicit *adj* **1** precisely and clearly expressed, leaving nothing to implication: *an explicit commitment to democracy* **2** leaving little to the imagination; graphically detailed **3** (of a person) expressing something in a precise and clear way, so as to leave no doubt about what is meant ▶ HISTORY Latin *explicitus* unfolded
> **explicitly** *adv*

explode *vb* **-ploding, -ploded 1** to burst with great violence; blow up **2** (of a gas) to undergo a sudden violent expansion as a result of a fast chemical or nuclear reaction **3** to react suddenly or violently with emotion **4** (esp. of a population) to increase rapidly **5** to show (a theory, etc.) to be baseless ▶ HISTORY Latin *explodere* to drive off by clapping

exploit *vb* **1** to take advantage of a person or situation for one's own ends **2** to make the best use of ▷ *n* **3** a notable deed or feat ▶ HISTORY Old French: accomplishment > **exploitation** *n*
> **exploiter** *n*

explore *vb* **-ploring, -plored 1** to examine or investigate, esp. systematically **2** to travel into an unfamiliar region, esp. for scientific purposes ▶ HISTORY Latin *ex* out + *plorare* to cry aloud
> **exploration** *n* > **exploratory** or **explorative** *adj*
> **explorer** *n*

explosion *n* **1** an exploding **2** a violent release of energy resulting from a rapid chemical or nuclear reaction **3** a sudden or violent outburst of activity, noise, emotion, etc. **4** a rapid increase

explosive *adj* **1** able or likely to explode **2** potentially violent: *an explosive situation* ▷ *n* **3** a substance capable of exploding
> **explosiveness** *n*

expo *n, pl* **-pos** short for **exposition** (sense 3)

exponent *n* **1** a person who advocates an idea, cause, etc.: *an exponent of free speech* **2** a person who is a skilful performer of some activity: *one of the greatest modern exponents of the blues* **3** maths a number placed as a superscript to another number indicating how many times the number is to be used as a factor ▶ HISTORY Latin *exponere* to expound

exponential *n* **1** maths a function, curve, series, or equation containing or involving one or more numbers or quantities raised to an exponent ▷ *adj* **2** maths of or involving numbers raised to an exponent **3** *informal* very rapid
> **exponentially** *adv*

exponential function *n* maths a function involving numbers raised to exponents

export *n* **1** the sale of goods and services to a foreign country: *a ban on the export of arms* **2** **exports** goods or services sold to a foreign country ▷ *vb* **3** to sell goods or services or transport goods to a foreign country **4** *computers* to transfer (data) into a different format ▶ HISTORY Latin *exportare* to carry away > **exporter** *n*

expose *vb* **-posing, -posed 1** to uncover (something previously covered) **2** to reveal the truth about (someone or something), esp. when it is shocking or scandalous: *an MP whose private life was recently exposed in the press* **3** to leave (a person or thing) unprotected in a potentially harmful situation: *workers were exposed to relatively low doses of radiation* **4** **expose someone to** to give someone an introduction to or experience of (something new) **5** *photog* to subject (a film) to light ▶ HISTORY Latin *exponere* to set out

exposé (iks-**pose**-ay) *n* the bringing of a scandal, crime, etc. to public notice ▶ HISTORY French

exposition *n* **1** a systematic explanation of a subject **2** the act of expounding or setting out a viewpoint **3** a large public exhibition **4** *music* the first statement of the themes of a movement ▶ HISTORY Latin *exponere* to display

exposition genre *n* a form of writing or speech in which the writer or speaker puts forward an argument and backs it up with analysis and background information before summing up

expostulate *vb* **-lating, -lated** • **expostulate with** to reason or argue with, esp. in order to dissuade or as a protest ▶ HISTORY Latin *expostulare* to require > **expostulation** *n*
> **expostulatory** *adj*

exposure *n* **1** the state of being exposed to, or lacking protection from, something: *the body cannot cope with sudden exposure to stress* **2** the revealing of the truth about someone or something, esp. when it is shocking or scandalous: *the exposure of a loophole in the tax laws* **3** the harmful effect on a person's body caused by lack of shelter from the weather, esp. the cold **4** appearance before the public, as on television **5** *photog* **a** the act of exposing a film to light **b** an area on a film that has been exposed **6** *photog* **a** the intensity of light falling on a film multiplied by the time for which it is exposed **b** a combination of lens aperture and shutter speed used in taking a photograph

exposure meter *n* *photog* an instrument for measuring the intensity of light so that suitable camera settings can be chosen

expound *vb* to explain a theory, belief, etc. in detail ▶ HISTORY Latin *exponere* to set forth

express *vb* **1** to state (an idea or feeling) in words; utter: *two record labels have expressed an interest in signing the band* **2** to show (an idea or feeling): *his body and demeanour expressed distrust* **3** to indicate through a symbol or formula **4** to squeeze out (juice, etc.) **5** **express oneself** to communicate one's thoughts or ideas ▷ *adj* **6** explicitly stated **7** deliberate and specific: *she came with the express purpose of causing a row* **8** of or for rapid transportation of people, mail, etc. ▷ *n* **9** a fast train stopping at only a few stations **10** *chiefly US & Canad* a system for sending mail rapidly ▷ *adv* **11** using a system for rapid transportation of people, mail, etc.: *please send this letter express: it's very urgent!* ▶ HISTORY Latin *exprimere* to force out
> **expressible** *adj*

e

expression n 1 the transforming of ideas into words 2 a showing of emotion without words 3 communication of emotion through music, painting, etc. 4 a look on the face that indicates mood or emotion 5 a particular phrase used conventionally to express something 6 maths a variable, function, or some combination of these > **expressionless** adj

expressionism n an early 20th-century artistic and literary movement which sought to express emotions rather than to represent the physical world > **expressionist** n, adj

expression mark n music one of a set of symbols indicating how a piece or passage is to be performed

expressive adj 1 of or full of expression 2 **expressive of** written showing or suggesting: looks expressive of hatred and revenge

expressway n chiefly US a motorway

expropriate vb -ating, -ated (of a government or other official body) formal to take (money or property) away from its owners ▶ HISTORY Medieval Latin expropriare to deprive of possessions > **expropriation** n > **expropriator** n

expulsion n the act of expelling or the fact of being expelled ▶ HISTORY Latin expellere to expel > **expulsive** adj

expunge (iks-**sponge**) vb -punging, -punged formal to remove all traces of: he had tried to expunge his failure from his mind ▶ HISTORY Latin expungere to blot out

expurgate (**eks**-per-gate) vb -gating, -gated to amend a piece of writing by removing sections thought to be offensive ▶ HISTORY Latin expurgare to clean out > **expurgation** n > **expurgator** n

exquisite adj 1 extremely beautiful or attractive 2 showing unusual delicacy and craftsmanship 3 sensitive or discriminating: exquisite manners 4 intensely felt: exquisite joy ▶ HISTORY Latin exquisitus excellent > **exquisitely** adv

ex-serviceman or fem **ex-servicewoman** n, pl -**men** or -**women** a person who has served in the armed forces

extant adj still in existence; surviving ▶ HISTORY Latin exstans standing out

extemporaneous adj spoken or performed without preparation > **extemporaneously** adv

extemporize or -**rise** vb -rizing, -rized or -rising, -rised to perform or speak without preparation > **extemporization** or -**risation** n > **extemporizer** or -**riser** n

extend vb 1 to make bigger or longer than before: they extended the house by building a conservatory 2 to reach to a certain distance or in a certain direction: the suburbs extend for many miles 3 to last for a certain time: in Norway maternity leave extends to 52 weeks 4 to include or affect more people or things than before: the law was extended to ban all guns 5 to make something exist or be valid for longer than before: her visa was extended for three months 6 to present or offer: a tradition of extending asylum to refugees 7 to straighten or stretch out

(part of the body): she extended a hand in welcome 8 **extend oneself** to make use of all one's ability or strength, often because forced to: she'll have to really extend herself if she wants to win ▶ HISTORY Latin extendere to stretch out > **extendable** adj

extended family n a social unit in which parents, children, grandparents, and other relatives live as a family unit

extension n 1 a room or rooms added to an existing building 2 a development that includes or affects more people or things than before: an extension of democracy within the EU 3 an additional telephone connected to the same line as another 4 an extra period of time in which something continues to exist or be valid: an extension of the contract for another 2 years ▷ adj 5 denoting something that can be extended or that extends another object: an extension ladder 6 of or relating to the provision of teaching and other facilities by a school or college to people who cannot attend full-time courses

extensive adj 1 covering a large area: extensive moorland 2 very great in effect: the bomb caused extensive damage 3 containing many details, ideas, or items on a particular subject: an extensive collection of modern art > **extensively** adv

extensive agriculture n farming of crops and animals that involves minimum expenditure of capital and labour but requires large areas of land. Compare **intensive agriculture**

extensor n any muscle that stretches or extends an arm, leg, or other part of the body

extent n 1 the length, area, or size of something 2 the scale or seriousness of a situation or difficulty: the extent of the damage 3 the degree or amount to which something applies: to a certain extent that's true

extenuate vb formal -ating, -ated to make an offence or fault less blameworthy, by giving reasons that partly excuse it ▶ HISTORY Latin extenuare to make thin > **extenuating** adj > **extenuation** n

exterior n 1 a part or surface that is on the outside 2 the outward appearance of a person: Jim's grumpy exterior concealed a warm heart 3 a film scene shot outside ▷ adj 4 of, situated on, or suitable for the outside 5 coming or acting from outside or abroad ▶ HISTORY Latin comparative of exterus on the outside

exterior angle n an angle of a polygon contained between one side extended and the adjacent side

exterminate vb -nating, -nated to destroy a group or type of people, animals, or plants completely ▶ HISTORY Latin exterminare to drive away > **extermination** n > **exterminator** n

external adj 1 of, situated on, or suitable for the outside: there was damage to the house's external walls 2 coming or acting from outside: most ill health is caused by external influences 3 of or involving foreign nations: Hong Kong's external trade 4 anat situated on or near the outside of the body: the external ear 5 brought into an organization to do a task which must be done impartially, esp. one involving testing or checking: *external examiners* **6** of or relating to someone taking a university course, but not attending a university: *an external degree* ▷ *n* **7 externals** obvious circumstances or aspects, esp. superficial ones: *despite the war, the externals of life in the city remain normal* ▶ HISTORY Latin *externus* > **externality** *n* > **externally** *adv*

external conflict *n literature* the struggle between a character and forces, situations, or people beyond his or her control. Compare **internal conflict**

externalize *or* **-ise** *vb* **-izing, -ized** *or* **-ising, -ised** to express (thoughts or feelings) in words or actions > **externalization** *or* **-isation** *n*

extinct *adj* **1** (of an animal or plant species) having died out **2** no longer in existence, esp. because of social changes: *shipbuilding is virtually extinct in Scotland* **3** (of a volcano) no longer liable to erupt ▶ HISTORY Latin *exstinguere* to extinguish

extinction *n* **1** the dying out of a plant or animal species **2** the end of a particular way of life or type of activity

extinguish *vb* **1** to put out (a fire or light) **2** to remove or destroy entirely ▶ HISTORY Latin *exstinguere* > **extinguishable** *adj* > **extinguisher** *n*

extirpate (**eks**-ter-pate) *vb* **-pating, -pated** to remove or destroy completely: *the Romans attempted to extirpate the Celtic religion* ▶ HISTORY Latin *exstirpare* to root out > **extirpation** *n*

extol *or US* **extoll** *vb* **-tolling, -tolled** to praise lavishly ▶ HISTORY Latin *extollere* to elevate

extort *vb* to obtain money or favours by intimidation, violence, or the misuse of authority ▶ HISTORY Latin *extorquere* to wrest away > **extortion** *n*

extortionate *adj* (of prices, profits, etc.) much higher than is fair > **extortionately** *adv*

extra *adj* **1** more than is usual, expected, or needed; additional ▷ *n* **2** a person or thing that is additional **3** something for which an additional charge is made **4** *films* a person temporarily engaged, usually for crowd scenes **5** *cricket* a run not scored from the bat **6** an additional edition of a newspaper ▷ *adv* **7** unusually; exceptionally ▶ HISTORY probably from *extraordinary*

extra- *prefix* outside or beyond an area or scope: *extracellular; extraterrestrial* ▶ HISTORY Latin

extract *vb* **1** to pull out or uproot by force **2** to remove or separate **3** to derive (pleasure, information, etc.) from some source **4** *informal* to obtain (money, information, etc.) from someone who is not willing to provide it: *a confession extracted by force* **5** to obtain (a substance) from a material or the ground by mining, distillation, digestion, etc.: *oil extracted from shale* **6** to copy out (an article, passage, etc.) from a publication ▷ *n* **7** something extracted, such as a passage from a book, etc. **8** a preparation containing the concentrated essence of a substance ▶ HISTORY Latin *extrahere* to draw out > **extractive** *adj* > **extractor** *n*

extraction *n* **1** the act or an instance of extracting **2** the removal of a tooth by a dentist: *few patients need an extraction* **3** the origin or ancestry of a person: *he is of German extraction*

extractive industries *pl n* industries that involve mining or drilling to extract resources such as coal, gold, oil, or gas; sometimes extended to include any industries that harvest natural resources, such as logging and fishing

extractive production *n econ* same as **primary production**

extractor fan *n* a fan used to remove stale air from a room

extracurricular *adj* not part of the normal courses taken by students: *her free time is devoted to extracurricular duties*

extradite *vb* **-diting, -dited** to hand over an alleged offender to the country where the crime took place for trial: *an agreement to extradite him to Hong Kong* ▶ HISTORY Latin *ex* away + *traditio* a handing over > **extraditable** *adj* > **extradition** *n*

extramural *adj* connected with but outside the normal courses of a university or college ▶ HISTORY Latin *extra* beyond + *murus* wall

extraneous (iks-**train**-ee-uss) *adj* not essential or relevant to the situation or subject being considered ▶ HISTORY Latin *extraneus* external

extranet *n computers* an intranet that is modified to allow outside users access to it

extraordinary *adj* **1** very unusual or surprising: *the extraordinary sight of my grandfather wearing a dress* **2** having some special or extreme quality: *an extraordinary first novel* **3** (of a meeting, ambassador, etc.) specially called or appointed to deal with one particular topic ▶ HISTORY Latin *extraordinarius* beyond what is usual > **extraordinarily** *adv*

extraordinary rendition *n* the process by which a person is transported to a country where due process of law is unlikely to be respected, usually for the purposes of interrogation

extrapolate (iks-**trap**-a-late) *vb* **-lating, -lated** **1** to infer something not known from the known facts, using logic and reason **2** *maths* to estimate the value of a function or measurement beyond the known values, by the extension of a curve ▶ HISTORY EXTRA- + -*polate*, as in *interpolate* > **extrapolation** *n*

extrasensory *adj* of or relating to extrasensory perception

extrasensory perception *n* the supposed ability to obtain information without the use of normal senses of sight, hearing, etc.

extraterrestrial *adj* happening or existing beyond the earth's atmosphere ▶ HISTORY Latin *extra* outside + *terra* earth

extravagant *adj* **1** spending more than is reasonable or affordable **2** costing more than is reasonable or affordable: *an extravagant gift* **3** going beyond usual or reasonable limits: *extravagant expectations* **4** (of behaviour or gestures) extreme,

293

esp. in order to make a particular impression: *an extravagant display of affection* **5** very elaborate and impressive: *extravagant costumes* ▶ HISTORY Latin *extra* beyond + *vagari* to wander
> **extravagance** *n*

extravaganza *n* **1** an elaborate and lavish entertainment **2** any fanciful display, literary composition, etc. ▶ HISTORY Italian: extravagance

extravert *adj, n* same as **extrovert**

extreme *adj* **1** of a high or the highest degree or intensity **2** exceptionally severe or unusual: *people can survive extreme conditions* **3** (of an opinion, political group, etc.) beyond the limits regarded as acceptable; fanatical **4** farthest or outermost ▷ *n* **5** either of the two limits of a scale or range **6 go to extremes** to be unreasonable in speech or action **7 in the extreme** to the highest or further degree: *the effect was dramatic in the extreme* ▶ HISTORY Latin *extremus* outermost
> **extremely** *adv*

extreme sport *n* any of various sports with a high risk of injury or death

extreme unction *n* RC *Church* a former name for **anointing of the sick**

extremist *n* **1** a person who favours or uses extreme or violent methods, esp. to bring about political change ▷ *adj* **2** holding extreme opinions or using extreme methods > **extremism** *n*

extremity *n, pl* **-ties** **1** the farthest point **2** an unacceptable or extreme nature or degree: *the extremity of his views alienated other nationalists* **3** an extreme condition, such as misfortune **4 extremities** hands and feet

extricate *vb* **-cating, -cated** to free from a difficult or complicated situation or place ▶ HISTORY Latin *extricare* > **extricable** *adj* > **extrication** *n*

extrinsic *adj* **1** not an integral or essential part **2** originating or acting from outside ▶ HISTORY Latin *exter* outward + *secus* alongside > **extrinsically** *adv*

extroversion *n* *psychol* the directing of one's interests outwards, esp. towards making social contacts

extrovert *adj* **1** lively and outgoing **2** *psychol* concerned more with external reality than inner feelings ▷ *n* **3** a person who has these characteristics ▶ HISTORY *extro-* (variant of EXTRA-, contrasting with *intro-*) + Latin *vertere* to turn > **extroverted** *adj*

extrude *vb* **-truding, -truded** **1** to squeeze or force out **2** to produce moulded sections of plastic, metal, etc. by forcing through a shaped die ▶ HISTORY Latin *extrudere* to thrust out > **extruded** *adj* > **extrusion** *n*

extrusive *adj* *geol* (of igneous rocks) formed from magma issuing from volcanoes or cracks in the earth's crust; volcanic

exuberant *adj* **1** full of vigour and high spirits **2** (of vegetation) growing thickly; flourishing ▶ HISTORY Latin *exuberans* abounding > **exuberance** *n*

exude *vb* **-uding, -uded** **1** (of a liquid or smell) to seep or flow out slowly and steadily **2** to seem to have (a quality or feeling) to a great degree: *the Chancellor exuded confidence* ▶ HISTORY Latin *exsudare* > **exudation** *n*

exult *vb written* to be joyful or jubilant ▶ HISTORY Latin *exsultare* to jump for joy > **exultation** *n* > **exultant** *adj*

eye *n* **1** the organ of sight in humans and animals **2** the external part of an eye, often including the area around it **3** (often pl) the ability to see or record what is happening: *the eyes of an entire nation were upon us* **4** a look, glance, or gaze **5** attention or observation: *his new shirt caught my eye* **6** the ability to judge or appreciate something: *his shrewd eye for talent* **7** (often pl) opinion, judgment, or authority: *in the eyes of the law* **8** a dark spot on a potato from which new shoots can grow **9** a small hole, such as the one at the blunt end of a sewing needle **10** a small area of calm in the centre of a storm, hurricane, or tornado **11 all eyes** *informal* acutely vigilant **12 an eye for an eye** justice consisting of an equivalent action to the original wrong or harm **13 have eyes for** to be interested in **14 in one's mind's eye** imagined or remembered vividly **15 in the public eye** exposed to public curiosity **16 keep an eye on** to take care of **17 keep an eye open** *or* **out for** to watch with special attention for **18 keep one's eyes peeled** *or* **skinned** to watch vigilantly **19 look someone in the eye** to look openly and without embarrassment at someone **20 make eyes at someone** to look at someone in an obviously attracted manner **21 more than meets the eye** hidden motives, meanings, or facts **22 my eye!** *old-fashioned informal* nonsense! **23 see eye to eye with** to agree with **24 set** *or* **lay** *or* **clap eyes on** to see: *I never laid eyes on him again* **25 turn a blind eye to** *or* **close one's eyes to** to pretend not to notice **26 up to one's eyes in** extremely busy with **27 with an eye to** with the intention of **28 with one's eyes open** in full knowledge of all the facts ▷ *vb* **eyeing** *or* **eying, eyed 29** to look at carefully or warily ▶ HISTORY Old English *ēage* > **eyeless** *adj* > **eyelike** *adj*

eyeball *n* **1** the entire ball-shaped part of the eye **2 eyeball to eyeball** in close confrontation ▷ *vb* **3** *slang* to stare at

eyebrow *n* **1** the bony ridge over each eye **2** the arch of hair on this ridge **3 raise an eyebrow** to show doubt or disapproval

eye-catching *adj* very striking and tending to catch people's attention > **eye-catcher** *n*

eye dog *n* NZ a dog trained to control sheep by staring at them

eyeful *n* **1** *slang* a good look at or view of something **2** *slang* an attractive sight, esp. a woman **3** an amount of liquid, dust, etc. that has got into someone's eye

eyeglass *n* a lens for aiding defective vision

eyelash *n* any of the short hairs that grow from the edge of the eyelids

eyelet *n* **1** a small hole for a lace or cord to be passed through **2** a small metal ring reinforcing such a hole

eyelid *n* either of the two folds of skin that cover an eye when it is closed

eyeliner *n* a cosmetic used to outline the eyes

eye-opener *n* *informal* something startling or revealing

eyepiece *n* the lens in a microscope, telescope, etc. into which the person using it looks

eye shadow *n* a coloured cosmetic worn on the upper eyelids

eyesight *n* the ability to see: *poor eyesight*

eyesore *n* something very ugly

eyestrain *n* fatigue or irritation of the eyes, caused by tiredness or a failure to wear glasses

eyewash *n* **1** a lotion for the eyes **2** *informal* nonsense; rubbish

eyewitness *n* a person present at an event who can describe what happened

eyrie *n* **1** the nest of an eagle, built in a high inaccessible place **2** any high isolated place
▶ **HISTORY** Latin *area* open field, hence, nest

e

Ff

f¹ *physics* frequency

f², **f/** *or* **f:** f-number

F 1 *music* the fourth note of the scale of C major **2** Fahrenheit **3** farad(s) **4** *chem* fluorine **5** *physics* force **6** franc(s)

f. *or* **F. 1** fathom(s) **2** female **3** *grammar* feminine **4** (*pl* **ff.**) following (page)

fa *n music* same as **fah**

FA (in Britain) Football Association

Fabian (**fay**-bee-an) *adj* **1** of the Fabian Society, which aims to establish socialism gradually and democratically ▷ *n* **2** a member of the Fabian Society ▶ HISTORY after *Fabius*, Roman general, who wore out Hannibal's strength while avoiding a pitched battle > **Fabianism** *n*

fable *n* **1** a short story, often one with animals as characters, that illustrates a moral **2** an unlikely story which is usually untrue **3** a story about mythical characters or events ▶ HISTORY Latin *fabula* story

fabled *adj* well-known from anecdotes and stories rather than experience: *the fabled Timbuktu*

fabric *n* **1** any cloth made from yarn or fibres by weaving or knitting **2** the structure that holds a system together: *the fabric of society* **3** the walls, floor, and roof of a building ▶ HISTORY Latin *faber* craftsman

fabricate *vb* **-cating, -cated 1** to invent a story or lie: *fabricated reports about the opposition* **2** to make or build ▶ HISTORY Latin *fabrica* workshop > **fabrication** *n*

fabulous *adj* **1** *informal* extremely good **2** almost unbelievable: *a city of fabulous wealth* **3** told of in fables and legends: *a fabulous horned creature* ▶ HISTORY Latin *fabulosus* celebrated in fable > **fabulously** *adv*

facade (fass-**sahd**) *n* **1** the front of a building **2** a front or deceptive outer appearance ▶ HISTORY French

face *n* **1** the front of the head from the forehead to the lower jaw **2 a** one's expression: *as his eyes met hers his face sobered* **b** a distorted expression to show disgust or defiance: *she was pulling a face at him* **3** the front or main side of an object, building, etc. **4** the surface of a clock or watch that has the numbers or hands on it **5** the functional side of an object, such as a tool or playing card **6** the exposed area of a mine from which coal or metal can be mined **7** *Brit, slang* a well-known or important person **8 face to face** opposite one another **9 in the face of** in spite of: *a determined character in the face of adversity* **10 lose face** to lose one's credibility **11 on the face of it** to all appearances **12 put a good face** *or* **brave face on** to maintain a cheerful appearance despite misfortune **13 save face** to keep one's good reputation **14 set one's face against** to oppose with determination **15 to someone's face** directly and openly ▷ *vb* **facing, faced 16** to look towards **17** to be opposite **18** to be confronted by: *they were faced with the prospect of high inflation* **19** to provide with a surface of a different material ▷ See also **face up to** ▶ HISTORY Latin *facies* form

faceless *adj* without individual identity or character: *faceless government officials*

face-lift *n* **1** cosmetic surgery for tightening sagging skin and smoothing wrinkles on the face **2** an outward improvement designed to give a more modern appearance: *the stadium was given a face-lift*

facer *n Brit, old-fashioned informal* a difficulty or problem

face-saving *adj* preventing damage to one's reputation > **face-saver** *n*

facet *n* **1** an aspect of something, such as a personality **2** any of the surfaces of a cut gemstone ▶ HISTORY French *facette* little face

facetious (fass-**see**-shuss) *adj* joking, or trying to be amusing, esp. at inappropriate times ▶ HISTORY Old French *facetie* witticism > **facetiously** *adv*

face up to *vb* to accept an unpleasant fact or reality

face value *n* apparent worth or meaning: *only a fool would take it at face value*

facia (**fay**-shee-a) *n, pl* **-ciae** (-shee-ee) same as **fascia**

facial *adj* **1** of the face ▷ *n* **2** a beauty treatment for the face > **facially** *adv*

facile (**fass**-ile) *adj* **1** (of a remark, argument, etc.) overly simple and showing lack of real thought **2** easily performed or achieved: *a facile winner of his only race this year* ▶ HISTORY Latin *facilis* easy

facilitate *vb* **-tating, -tated** to make easier the progress of: *the agreement helped facilitate trade between the countries* > **facilitation** *n*

facility *n, pl* **-ties 1 facilities** the means or equipment needed for an activity: *leisure and shopping facilities* **2** the ability to do things easily and well **3** skill or ease: *grown human beings can forget with remarkable facility* ▶ HISTORY Latin *facilis* easy

facing *n* **1** a piece of material used esp. to conceal the seam of a garment **2 facings** contrasting collar and cuffs on a jacket **3** an outer layer of material applied to the surface of a wall

facsimile (fak-**sim**-ill-ee) *n* **1** an exact copy **2** same as **fax** (senses 1, 2) ▶ HISTORY Latin *fac simile!* make something like it!

fact *n* **1** an event or thing known to have happened or existed **2** a truth that can be proved from experience or observation **3** a piece of information

4 after or **before the fact** criminal law after or before the commission of the offence **5 as a matter of fact** or **in fact** in reality or actuality **6 fact of life** an inescapable truth, esp. an unpleasant one. See also **facts of life** ▶ HISTORY Latin *factum* something done

faction¹ n **1** a small group of people within a larger body, but differing from it in certain aims and ideas **2** strife within a group ▶ HISTORY Latin *factio* a making > **factional** adj

faction² n a dramatized presentation of actual events ▶ HISTORY blend of FACT + FICTION

factious adj inclined to quarrel and cause divisions: *A factious political party is unelectable*

factitious adj artificial rather than natural ▶ HISTORY Latin *facticius*

factor n **1** an element that contributes to a result: *reliability was an important factor in the success of the car* **2** maths any whole number that will divide exactly into a given number, for example 2 and 3 are factors of 6 **3** a quantity by which an amount is multiplied or divided to become that number of times bigger or smaller: *production increased by a factor of 3* **4** med any of several substances that participate in the clotting of blood: *factor VIII* **5** a level on a scale of measurement: *suntan oil with a factor of 5* **6** (in Scotland) the manager of an estate ▶ HISTORY Latin: one who acts

factorial maths n **1** the product of all the whole numbers from one to a given whole number ▷ adj **2** of factorials or factors

factorize or **-rise** vb **-izing, -ized** or **-ising, -ised** maths to resolve a whole number or an algebraic expression into factors > **factorization** or **-risation** n

factor of production n econ a resource or input entering the production of wealth, such as land or labour

factory n, pl **-ries** a building where goods are manufactured in large quantities ▶ HISTORY Late Latin *factorium*, from *facere* to make

factory farm n Brit, Austral & NZ a farm in which animals are given foods that increase the amount of meat, eggs, or milk they yield > **factory farming** n

factory ship n a vessel that processes fish supplied by a fleet

factotum n a person employed to do all kinds of work ▶ HISTORY Latin *fac!* do! + *totum* all

facts of life pl n the details of sexual behaviour and reproduction

factual adj concerning facts rather than opinions or theories: *a factual report* > **factually** adv

faculty n, pl **-ties 1** one of the powers of the mind or body, such as memory, sight, or hearing **2** any ability or power, either inborn or acquired: *his faculties of reasoning were considerable* **3 a** a department within a university or college **b** its staff **c** chiefly US & Canad all the teaching staff of a university, school, or college ▶ HISTORY Latin *facultas* capability

fad n informal **1** an intense but short-lived fashion: *the skateboard fad* **2** a personal whim ▶ HISTORY origin unknown > **faddish** adj

faddy adj **-dier, -diest** unreasonably fussy, particularly about food

fade vb **fading, faded 1** to lose brightness, colour, or strength **2 fade away** or **out** to vanish slowly ▶ HISTORY Middle English *fade* dull

faeces or esp US **feces** (fee-seez) pl n bodily waste matter discharged through the anus ▶ HISTORY Latin: dregs > **faecal** or esp US **fecal** (fee-kl) adj

Faeroese or **Faroese** (fair-oh-**eez**) adj **1** of the Faeroes, islands in the N Atlantic ▷ n **2** (pl **-ese**) a person from the Faeroes **3** the language of the Faeroes

faff about vb Brit & S African, informal to dither or fuss ▶ HISTORY origin unknown

fag¹ n **1** informal a boring or tiring task: *weeding was a fag* **2** Brit (esp. formerly) a young public school boy who performs menial chores for an older boy ▷ vb **fagging, fagged 3** Brit to do menial chores in a public school ▶ HISTORY origin unknown

fag² n slang a cigarette ▶ HISTORY origin unknown

fag end n **1** the last and worst part: *another dull game at the fag end of the football season* **2** Brit & NZ, informal the stub of a cigarette

faggot or esp US **fagot** n **1** Brit, Austral & NZ a ball of chopped liver bound with herbs and bread **2** a bundle of sticks ▶ HISTORY from Old French

fah n music (in tonic sol-fa) the fourth note of any ascending major scale

Fahrenheit (far-ren-hite) adj of or measured according to the scale of temperature in which 32° represents the melting point of ice and 212° the boiling point of water ▶ HISTORY after Gabriel Fahrenheit, physicist

faïence (fie-ence) n tin-glazed earthenware ▶ HISTORY *Faenza*, N Italy, where made

fail vb **1** to be unsuccessful in an attempt **2** to stop operating **3** to judge or be judged as being below the officially accepted standard required in a course or examination **4** to prove disappointing or useless to someone: *the government has failed homeless people* **5** to neglect or be unable to do something: *he failed to repair the car* **6** to go bankrupt ▷ n **7** a failure to attain the required standard **8 without fail a** regularly or without exception: *use this shampoo once a week without fail* **b** definitely: *they agreed to enforce the embargo without fail* ▶ HISTORY Latin *fallere* to disappoint

failing n **1** a weak point ▷ prep **2 failing that** alternatively: *your doctor will normally be able to advise you or, failing that, one of the self-help agencies*

fail-safe adj **1** designed to return to a safe condition in the event of a failure or malfunction **2** safe from failure

failure n **1** the act or an instance of failing **2** someone or something that is unsuccessful: *he couldn't help but regard his own son as a failure* **3** the fact of something required or expected not being done or not happening: *his failure to appear at the meeting* **4** a halt in normal operation: *heart failure* **5** a decline or loss of something: *crop failure* **6** the

f

fact of not reaching the required standard in an examination or test

fain *adv* old-fashioned gladly or willingly ▶ **HISTORY** Old English *fægen*

faint *adj* **1** lacking clarity, brightness, or volume: *her voice was very faint* **2** feeling dizzy or weak **3** lacking conviction or force: *a faint attempt to smile* ▷ *vb* **4** to lose consciousness ▷ *n* **5** a sudden loss of consciousness ▶ **HISTORY** Old French *faindre* to be idle > **faintly** *adv*

faint-hearted *adj* lacking courage and confidence

fair[1] *adj* **1** reasonable and just: *a move towards fair trade* **2** free from discrimination **3** in agreement with rules **4** light in colour: *her fair skin* **5** old-fashioned young and beautiful: *a fair maiden* **6** quite good: *a fair attempt at making a soufflé* **7** quite large: *they made a fair amount of money* **8** (of the tide or wind) favourable to the passage of a ship or plane **9** fine or cloudless **10 fair and square** in a correct or just way ▷ *adv* **11** in a fair way **12** absolutely or squarely: *he was caught fair off his guard* ▶ **HISTORY** Old English *fæger* > **fairness** *n*

fair[2] *n* **1** a travelling entertainment with sideshows, rides, and amusements **2** an exhibition of goods produced by a particular industry to promote business: *the Frankfurt book fair* ▶ **HISTORY** Latin *feriae* holidays

fair copy *n* a neat copy, without mistakes or alterations, of a piece of writing

fair game *n* a person regarded as a justifiable target for criticism or ridicule

fairground *n* an open space used for a fair

fairing *n* a metal structure fitted around parts of an aircraft, car, etc. to reduce drag ▶ **HISTORY** *fair* to streamline

Fair Isle *n* an intricate multicoloured knitted pattern ▶ **HISTORY** after one of the Shetland Islands where this type of pattern originated

fairly *adv* **1** to a moderate degree or extent: *in the Philippines labour is fairly cheap* **2** to a great degree or extent: *the folder fairly bulged with documents* **3** as deserved: *the pound was fairly valued against the dollar*

fair play *n* a conventional standard of honourable behaviour

fair test *n science* a test in which only one variable is changed

fair trade *n* the practice of buying goods from producers in the developing world at a guaranteed price

fairway *n* **1** (on a golf course) the mown areas between tees and greens **2** *naut* a part of a river or sea on which ships may sail

fair-weather *adj* not reliable in difficult situations: *a fair-weather friend*

fairy *n*, *pl* **fairies** an imaginary supernatural being with magical powers ▶ **HISTORY** Old French *faerie* fairyland, from *feie* fairy

fairy floss *n Austral* a light fluffy mass of spun sugar, held on a stick

fairy godmother *n* a generous friend who

appears unexpectedly and offers help in time of trouble

fairyland *n* **1** an imaginary place where fairies live **2** an enchanted or wonderful place

fairy lights *pl n* small coloured electric bulbs used as decoration, esp. on a Christmas tree

fairy penguin *n* a small penguin with a bluish head and back, found on the Australian coast

fairy ring *n* a ring of dark grass caused by fungi

fairy tale *or* **story** *n* **1** a story about fairies or magical events **2** a highly improbable account: *his report was little more than a fairy tale* ▷ *adj* **fairy-tale 3** of or like a fairy tale: *a fairy-tale wedding* **4** highly improbable: *a fairy-tale account of his achievements*

fait accompli (fate ak-**kom**-plee) *n* something already done and beyond alteration: *they had to accept the invasion as a fait accompli* ▶ **HISTORY** French

faith *n* **1** strong belief in something, esp. without proof **2** a specific system of religious beliefs **3** complete confidence or trust, such as in a person or remedy **4** allegiance to a person or cause **5 bad faith** dishonesty **6 good faith** honesty ▶ **HISTORY** Latin *fides* trust, confidence

faithful *adj* **1** remaining true or loyal **2** consistently reliable: *my old, but faithful, four cylinder car* **3** accurate in detail: *a faithful translation of the book* ▷ *pl n* **4 a** the believers in a religious faith **b** loyal followers > **faithfully** *adv* > **faithfulness** *n*

faithless *adj* treacherous or disloyal

faith school *n Brit* a school that provides a general education within a framework of a specific religious belief

fake *vb* **faking, faked 1** to cause something not genuine to appear real or more valuable by fraud **2** to pretend to have (an illness, emotion, etc.) ▷ *n* **3** an object, person, or act that is not genuine ▷ *adj* **4** not genuine: *fake fur* ▶ **HISTORY** probably from Italian *facciare* to make or do

fakir (**fay**-keer) *n* **1** a Muslim religious ascetic who spurns worldly possessions **2** a Hindu holy man ▶ **HISTORY** Arabic *faqīr* poor

falcon *n* a type of bird of prey that can be trained to hunt other birds and small animals ▶ **HISTORY** Late Latin *falco* hawk

falconry *n* **1** the art of training falcons to hunt **2** the sport of hunting with falcons > **falconer** *n*

fall *vb* **falling, fell, fallen 1** to descend by the force of gravity from a higher to a lower place **2** to drop suddenly from an upright position **3** to collapse to the ground **4** to become less or lower in number or quality: *inflation fell by one percentage point* **5** to slope downwards **6** to be badly wounded or killed **7** to give in to attack: *in 1939 Barcelona fell to the Nationalists* **8** to lose power or status **9** to pass into a specified condition: *I fell asleep* **10** to adopt a downhearted expression: *his face fell and he pouted like a child* **11** (of night or darkness) to begin **12** to occur at a specified time: *Christmas falls on a Sunday* **13** to give in to temptation or sin **14 fall apart a** to break owing to long use or poor construction: *the* *chassis is falling apart* **b** to become disorganized and ineffective: *since you resigned, the office has fallen apart* **15 fall short** to prove inadequate **16 fall short of** to fail to reach (a standard) ▷ *n* **17** an instance of falling **18** an amount of something, such as snow or soot, that has fallen **19** a decrease in value or number **20** a decline in status or importance: *the town's fall from prosperity* **21** a capture or overthrow: *the fall of Budapest in February 1945* **22** *wrestling* a scoring move, pinning both shoulders of one's opponent to the floor for a specified period **23** *chiefly US* autumn ▷ See also **falls** ▶ HISTORY Old English *feallan*

Fall *n* **the Fall** *theol* the state of mankind's innate sinfulness following Adam's sin of disobeying God

fallacy *n, pl* **-cies** **1** an incorrect or misleading notion based on inaccurate facts or faulty reasoning: *the fallacy underlying the government's industrial policy* **2** reasoning that is unsound ▶ HISTORY Latin *fallere* to deceive > **fallacious** *adj*

fall behind *vb* **1** to fail to keep up **2** to be in arrears, such as with a payment

fallen *vb* **1** the past participle of **fall** ▷ *adj* **2** *old-fashioned* (of a woman) having had sex outside marriage **3** killed in battle

fall for *vb* **1** to become strongly attracted to (someone) **2** to be deceived by (a lie or trick)

fall guy *n informal* **1** the victim of a confidence trick **2** a person who is publicly blamed for something, though it may not be his or her fault

fallible *adj* **1** (of a person) liable to make mistakes **2** capable of error: *our all-too-fallible economic indicators* ▶ HISTORY Latin *fallere* to deceive > **fallibility** *n*

fall in *vb* **1** to collapse **2** to get into line or formation in a display, march, or procession **3 fall in with a** to meet and join **b** to agree with or support (a person or a suggestion)

falling star *n informal* a meteor

fall on *vb* **1** to attack (an enemy) **2** to meet with (something unpleasant): *his family had fallen on hard times* **3** to affect: *a horrified hush fell on the company* **4 fall on one's feet** to emerge unexpectedly well from a difficult situation

Fallopian tube *n* either of a pair of slender tubes through which eggs pass from the ovaries to the uterus in female mammals ▶ HISTORY after Gabriello *Fallopio*, anatomist

fallout *n* **1** radioactive material in the atmosphere following a nuclear explosion **2** unpleasant circumstances following an event: *the political fallout of the riots* ▷ *vb* **fall out 3** *informal* to disagree and quarrel: *I hope we don't fall out over this issue* **4** to leave a military formation

fallow¹ *adj* (of land) left unseeded after being ploughed to regain fertility for a future crop ▶ HISTORY Old English *fealga*

fallow² *adj* light yellowish-brown ▶ HISTORY Old English *fealu*

fallow deer *n* a deer that has a reddish coat with white spots in summer

falls *pl n* a waterfall

fall through *vb* to fail before completion: *his transfer deal fell through*

fall to *vb written* **1** to become the responsibility of: *it fell to the Prime Minister to announce the plans* **2** to begin (some activity, such as eating, working, or fighting)

false *adj* **1** not in accordance with the truth or facts: *false allegations* **2** not real or genuine but intended to seem so: *false teeth* **3** misleading or deceptive: *their false promises* **4** forced or insincere: *false cheer* **5** based on mistaken ideas ▶ HISTORY Latin *falsus* > **falsely** *adv* > **falseness** *n*

falsehood *n* **1** the quality of being untrue **2** a lie

false pretences *pl n* **under false pretences** so as to mislead people about one's true intentions

false start *n athletics & swimming* an occasion when one competitor starts a race before the starter's signal has been given, which means that all competitors have to be recalled and the race restarted

falsetto *n, pl* **-tos** a voice pitch higher than one's normal range ▶ HISTORY Italian

falsify *vb* **-fies, -fying, -fied** to make a report or evidence false by alteration in order to deceive ▶ HISTORY Latin *falsus* false + *facere* to make > **falsification** *n*

falsity *n, pl* **-ties** **1** the state of being false **2** a lie

falter *vb* **1** to be hesitant, weak, or unsure **2** (of a machine) to lose power or strength in an uneven way: *the engine began to falter and the plane lost height* **3** to speak nervously and without confidence **4** to stop moving smoothly and start moving unsteadily: *as he neared the house his steps faltered* ▶ HISTORY origin unknown > **faltering** *adj*

fame *n* the state of being widely known or recognized ▶ HISTORY Latin *fama* report

famed *adj* extremely well-known: *a nation famed for its efficiency*

familial *adj formal* of or relating to the family

familiar *adj* **1** well-known **2** frequent or common: *it was a familiar argument* **3 familiar with** well acquainted with **4** friendly and informal **5** more intimate than is acceptable ▷ *n* **6** an animal or bird believed to share with a witch her supernatural powers **7** a friend ▶ HISTORY Latin *familia* family > **familiarly** *adv* > **familiarity** *n*

familiarize *or* **-rise** *vb* **-izing, -ized** *or* **-ising, -ised** to make (oneself or someone else) fully aware of a particular subject > **familiarization** *or* **-risation** *n*

family *n, pl* **-lies** **1** a social group consisting of parents and their offspring. *Related adjective:* **familial 2** one's wife or husband and one's children **3** one's children **4** a group descended from a common ancestor **5** all the people living together in one household **6** any group of related objects or beings: *a family of chemicals* **7** *biol* one of the groups into which an order is divided, containing one or more genera: *the cat family* ▷ *adj* **8** of or suitable for a family or any of its members: *films for a family audience* **9 in the family way** *informal* pregnant ▶ HISTORY Latin *familia*

f

family assistance n (in New Zealand) a tax credit given to families on the basis of their income and family size

family court n law (in some countries) a court established to deal with cases relating to family law

family doctor n Brit, Austral & NZ, informal same as **general practitioner**

family law n law the law as it relates to matters such as marriage, divorce, custody of children, maintenance, and adoption

family name n a surname, esp. when regarded as representing a family's good reputation

family planning n the control of the number of children in a family by the use of contraceptives

family tree n a chart showing the relationships between individuals in a family over many generations

famine n a severe shortage of food ▶ HISTORY Latin fames hunger

famous adj known to or recognized by many people ▶ HISTORY Latin famosus

famously adv 1 well-known: her famously relaxed manner 2 very well: the two got on famously

fan¹ n 1 any device for creating a current of air, esp. a rotating machine of blades attached to a central hub 2 a hand-held object, usually made of paper, which creates a draught of cool air when waved 3 something shaped like such a fan, such as the tail of certain birds ▷ vb **fanning, fanned** 4 to create a draught of air in the direction of someone or something 5 **fan out** to spread out in the shape of a fan: the troops fanned out along the beach ▶ HISTORY Latin vannus

fan² n a person who admires or is enthusiastic about a pop star, actor, sport, or hobby: he was a big fan of Woody Allen ▶ HISTORY from fanatic

fanatic n 1 a person whose enthusiasm for something, esp. a political or religious cause, is extreme 2 informal a person devoted to a particular hobby or pastime ▷ adj also **fanatical** 3 excessively enthusiastic ▶ HISTORY Latin fanaticus belonging to a temple, hence, inspired by a god, frenzied > **fanatically** adv > **fanaticism** n

fanbase n the body of admirers of a particular pop singer, sports team, etc.

fan belt n the belt that drives a cooling fan in a car engine

fancier n a person with a keen interest in the thing specified: a pigeon fancier

fanciful adj 1 not based on fact 2 made in a curious or imaginative way: fanciful architecture 3 guided by unrestrained imagination: fanciful tales of fairy folk > **fancifully** adv

fancy adj **-cier, -ciest** 1 special, unusual, and elaborate 2 (often used ironically) superior in quality 3 (of a price) higher than expected ▷ n, pl **-cies** 4 a sudden idea 5 a sudden or irrational liking for a person or thing 6 old-fashioned or literary a person's imagination ▷ vb **-cies, -cying, -cied** 7 Brit, informal to be physically attracted to (another person) 8 informal to have a wish for 9 to picture in the imagination 10 to think or

suppose: I fancy I am redundant here 11 **fancy oneself** to have a high opinion of oneself ▷ interj 12 Also: **fancy that!** an exclamation of surprise ▶ HISTORY Middle English fantsy > **fancily** adv

fancy dress n clothing worn for a party at which people dress up to look like a particular animal or character

fancy-free adj free from commitments, esp. marriage

fancy goods pl n small decorative gifts

fandango n, pl **-gos** 1 a lively Spanish dance 2 music for this dance ▶ HISTORY Spanish

fanfare n a short rousing tune played on brass instruments ▶ HISTORY French

fang n 1 the long pointed tooth of a poisonous snake through which poison is injected 2 the canine tooth of a meat-eating mammal ▶ HISTORY Old English: what is caught, prey

fanjet n same as **turbofan**

fanlight n a semicircular window over a door or another window

fanny n, pl **-nies** slang, chiefly US & Canad the buttocks ▶ HISTORY origin unknown

fantail n 1 a breed of domestic pigeon with a large tail like a fan 2 a fly-catching bird of Australia, New Zealand, and SE Asia with a broad fan-shaped tail

fantasia n 1 any musical work not composed in a strict form 2 a mixture of popular tunes arranged as a continuous whole ▶ HISTORY Italian: fancy

fantasize or **-sise** vb **-sizing, -sized** or **-sising, -sised** to imagine pleasant but unlikely events

fantastic adj 1 informal excellent 2 informal very large in degree or amount: a fantastic amount of money 3 strange or exotic in appearance: fantastic costumes 4 difficult to believe or unlikely to happen > **fantastically** adv

fantasy n, pl **-sies** 1 a far-fetched idea 2 imagination unrestricted by reality 3 a daydream 4 fiction with a large fantasy content 5 music same as **fantasia** ▷ adj 6 of a competition in which a participant selects players for an imaginary, ideal team and points are awarded according to the actual performances of the chosen players: fantasy football ▶ HISTORY Greek phantazein to make visible

fan vaulting n archit vaulting with ribs that radiate like those of a fan from the top part of a pillar

fanzine (fan-zeen) n a magazine produced by fans of a specific interest, football club, etc. for fellow fans

FAQ n computers frequently asked question or questions: a text file containing basic information on a particular subject

far adv **farther, farthest** or **further, furthest** 1 at, to, or from a great distance 2 at or to a remote time: as far back as 1984 3 by a considerable degree: far greater 4 **as far as a** to the degree or extent that **b** to the distance or place of **c** informal with reference to 5 **by far** by a considerable margin 6 **far and away** by a very great margin: far and away the ugliest building in the city 7 written **far and**

wide in a great many places over a large area
8 go far a to be successful **b** to be sufficient or last long: *her wages didn't go far* **9 go too far** to go beyond reasonable limits: *the press have gone too far this time* **10 so far a** up to the present moment **b** up to a certain point, extent, or degree ▷ *adj* **11** distant in space or time: *the far south* **12** extending a great distance **13** more distant: *over in the far corner* **14 far from** by no means: *the battle is far from over* ▶ HISTORY Old English *feorr*

farad *n physics* the SI unit of electric capacitance ▶ HISTORY after Michael *Faraday*, physicist

Faraday's law *n physics* a law that states that the current induced in a circuit is directly proportional to the rate of change of the magnetic flux linked with the circuit ▶ HISTORY after Michael *Faraday*, English physicist and chemist

faraway *adj* **1** very distant **2** dreamy or absent-minded: *a faraway look in his eyes*

farce *n* **1** a humorous play involving characters in unlikely and ridiculous situations **2** the style of comedy of this kind **3** a ludicrous situation: *the game degenerated into farce* ▶ HISTORY Latin *farcire* to stuff, interpolate passages (in plays) > **farcical** *adj* > **farcically** *adv*

fare *n* **1** the amount charged or paid for a journey in a bus, train, or plane **2** a paying passenger **3** *written* a range of food and drink: *marvellous picnic fare* ▷ *vb* **faring, fared 4** to get on (in a specified way): *he fared well in the exam* ▶ HISTORY Old English *faran*

Far East *n* the countries of E Asia > **Far Eastern** *adj*

fare stage *n* **1** a section of a bus journey for which a set charge is made **2** the bus stop marking the end of such a section

farewell *interj* **1** *old-fashioned* goodbye ▷ *n* **2** the act of saying goodbye and leaving ▷ *vb* **3** *NZ* to say goodbye ▷ *adj* **4** parting or closing: *the President's farewell speech*

far-fetched *adj* unlikely to be true

far-flung *adj* **1** distributed over a wide area **2** far distant or remote

farinaceous *adj* containing starch or having a starchy texture ▶ HISTORY Latin *far* coarse meal

farm *n* **1** a tract of land, usually with a house and buildings, cultivated as a unit or used to rear livestock **2** a unit of land or water devoted to the growing or rearing of some particular type of fruit, animal, or fish: *a salmon farm; an ostrich farm* ▷ *vb* **3 a** to cultivate land **b** to rear animals or fish on a farm **4** to do agricultural work as a way of life **5** to collect and keep the profits from a tax district or business ▷ See also **farm out** ▶ HISTORY Old French *ferme* rented land

farmed *adj* (of fish or game) reared on a farm rather than caught in the wild

farmer *n* a person who owns or manages a farm

farmers' market *n* a market at which farm produce is sold directly to the public by the producer

farm hand *n* a person who is hired to work on a farm

farmhouse *n* a house attached to a farm

farming *n* the business or skill of agriculture

farming subsidy *n agriculture* financial aid for farmers supplied by a government

farmland *n* land that is used for or suitable for farming

farm out *vb* **1** to send (work) to be done by another person or firm **2** (of the state) to put a child into the care of a private individual

farmstead *n* a farm and its main buildings

farmyard *n* the small area of land enclosed by or around the farm buildings

farrago (far-**rah**-go) *n, pl* **-gos** or **-goes** a hotchpotch or mixture, esp. a ridiculous or unbelievable one: *a farrago of patriotic nonsense*

far-reaching *adj* extensive in influence, effect, or range

farrier *n chiefly Brit* a person who shoes horses ▶ HISTORY Latin *ferrarius* smith

farrow *n* **1** a litter of piglets ▷ *vb* **2** (of a sow) to give birth to a litter ▶ HISTORY Old English *fearh*

far-sighted *adj* **1** able to look forward and plan ahead **2** *US* long-sighted

fart *slang n* **1** an emission of intestinal gas from the anus ▷ *vb* **2** to break wind ▶ HISTORY Middle English *farten*

farther *adv* **1** to or at a greater distance in space or time **2** in addition ▷ *adj* **3** more distant or remote in space or time ▶ HISTORY Middle English

farthest *adv* **1** to or at the greatest distance in space or time ▷ *adj* **2** most distant or remote in space or time ▶ HISTORY Middle English *ferthest*

farthing *n* a former British coin worth a quarter of an old penny ▶ HISTORY Old English *fēorthing*

farthingale *n* a hoop worn under skirts in the Elizabethan period ▶ HISTORY Old Spanish *verdugo* rod

fasces (**fass**-eez) *pl n, sing* **-cis** (-siss) (in ancient Rome) a bundle of rods containing an axe with its blade pointing out; a symbol of a magistrate's power ▶ HISTORY Latin

fascia or **facia** (**fay**-shee-a) *n, pl* **-ciae** (-shee-ee) **1** the flat surface above a shop window **2** *archit* a flat band or surface **3** *Brit* the outer panel which surrounds the instruments and dials of a motor vehicle ▶ HISTORY Latin: band

fascinate *vb* **-nating, -nated** to attract and delight by arousing interest ▶ HISTORY Latin *fascinum* a bewitching > **fascinating** *adj* > **fascinatingly** *adv* > **fascination** *n*

Fascism (**fash**-iz-zum) *n* **1** the authoritarian and nationalistic political movement in Italy (1922–43) **2** any ideology or movement like this ▶ HISTORY Italian *fascio* political group > **Fascist** *n, adj*

fashion *n* **1** style in clothes, hairstyles, behaviour, etc. that is popular at a particular time **2** the way that something happens or is done: *conversing in a very animated fashion* **3 after a fashion** in some way, but not very well: *he apologized, after a fashion, for his haste* ▷ *vb* **4** to form, make, or shape: *he had fashioned a crude musical instrument* ▶ HISTORY Latin *facere* to make

f

fat

WORD FOCUS

Some words used to describe a person who is overweight can be more hurtful or insulting than others. There are also words to describe varying degrees of being overweight.

DEFINITION 1

- Someone who is **overweight** weighs more than is considered healthy. However, you can be just a little **overweight** as well as very **overweight**: Since having my baby, I feel slightly **overweight**.
- If you say someone is **podgy**, you mean that they are slightly fat: Eddie's getting a little **podgy** round the middle.
- If you describe someone as **fleshy**, you mean that they are slightly too fat: He was well-built, but too **fleshy** to be an imposing figure.
- A **chubby**, **tubby**, or **stout** person is rather fat: I was greeted by a small, **chubby** man. • He had been a short, **tubby** child who was taunted about his weight. • a tall, **stout** man with grey hair
- A **portly** person is rather fat. This word is mostly used to describe men: a **portly**, middle-aged man
- You can use the word **plump** to describe someone whose body is rather full or rounded, usually when you think this is a good quality: Maria was a pretty little girl, small and **plump** with a mass of dark curls.
- If you describe a woman's figure as **curvy**, you mean that it is attractive because it is not too thin: She's very **curvy**.
- A **roly-poly** person is pleasantly fat and round. This is an informal word: a short, **roly-poly** little woman with laughing eyes
- If you describe someone as **obese**, you mean that they are extremely overweight, perhaps to the point of being unhealthy: **Obese** people tend to have higher blood pressure than lean people.

fashionable adj 1 popular with a lot of people at a particular time 2 popular among well-off or famous people: the fashionable Côte d'Azur > **fashionably** adv

fast¹ adj 1 acting or moving quickly 2 accomplished in or lasting a short time 3 adapted to or allowing for rapid movement: the fast lane 4 (of a clock or watch) indicating a time in advance of the correct time 5 given to a life of expensive and exciting activities: the desire for a fast life 6 firmly fixed, fastened, or shut 7 (of colours and dyes) not likely to fade 8 photog very sensitive and able to be used in low-light conditions 9 **fast friends** devoted and loyal friends 10 **pull a fast one** informal play an unscrupulous trick ▷ adv 11 quickly 12 **fast asleep** in a deep sleep 13 firmly and tightly: stuck fast 14 **play fast and loose** to behave in an insincere or unreliable manner ▶ HISTORY Old English fæst strong, tight

fast² vb 1 to go without food for a period of time, esp. for religious reasons ▷ n 2 a period of fasting ▶ HISTORY Old English fæstan

fast-breeder reactor n a nuclear reactor that produces more fissionable material (plutonium) than it consumes for the purposes of generating electricity

fasten vb 1 to make or become secure or joined 2 to close by fixing firmly in place or locking 3 **fasten on** to direct one's attention in a concentrated way towards: the mind needs such imagery to fasten on to **b** to take a firm hold on ▶ HISTORY Old English fæstnian > **fastener** n

fastening n something that fastens something, such as a clasp or lock

fast food n food, such as hamburgers, that is prepared and served very quickly

fastidious adj 1 paying great attention to neatness, detail, and order: a fastidious dresser 2 excessively concerned with cleanliness ▶ HISTORY Latin fastidiosus scornful > **fastidiously** adv > **fastidiousness** n

fast lane n 1 the outside lane on a motorway for overtaking or travelling fast 2 informal the quickest but most competitive route to success: the hectic pace of life in the corporate fast lane

fastness n Brit & Austral, literary a stronghold or safe place that is hard to get to

fast-track adj 1 taking the quickest but most competitive route to success or personal advancement: a fast-track marketer's dream ▷ vb 2 to speed up the progress of (a project or person)

fat adj **fatter, fattest** 1 having more flesh on the body than is thought necessary or desirable; overweight 2 (of meat) containing a lot of fat 3 thick or wide: his obligatory fat cigar 4 profitable or productive: fat years for the farmers are few and far between 5 **a fat chance** slang unlikely to happen 6 **a fat lot of good** slang not at all good or useful ▷ n 7 extra or unwanted flesh on the body 8 a greasy or oily substance obtained from animals or plants and used in cooking 9 **the fat is in the fire** an action has been taken from which disastrous consequences are expected 10 **the fat of the land** the best that is obtainable ▶ HISTORY Old English fætt crammed > **fatless** adj > **fatness** n See WORD FOCUS **fat**

fatal adj 1 resulting in death: a fatal accident 2 resulting in unfortunate consequences: the president's second fatal mistake ▶ HISTORY Latin fatum fate > **fatally** adv

fatalism n the belief that all events are decided in advance by God or Fate so that human beings are powerless to alter their destiny > **fatalist** n > **fatalistic** adj > **fatalistically** adv

fatality n, pl **-ties** a death caused by an accident or disaster

fate n **1** the ultimate force that supposedly predetermines the course of events **2** the inevitable fortune that happens to a person or thing **3** death or downfall: *Custer met his fate at Little Bighorn* ▶ **HISTORY** Latin *fatum*

fated adj **1** certain to be or do something: *he was always fated to be a musician* **2** doomed to death or destruction

fateful adj having important, and usually disastrous, consequences > **fatefully** adv

Fates pl n *classical myth* the goddesses who control human destiny

fathead n *informal* a stupid person > **fatheaded** adj

father n **1 a** a male parent **2** a person who founds a line or family; forefather **3** a man who starts, creates, or invents something: *the father of democracy in Costa Rica* **4** a leader of an association or council: *the city fathers* ▷ vb **5** (of a man) to be the biological cause of the conception and birth of (a child) ▶ **HISTORY** Old English *fæder* > **fatherhood** n

Father n **1** God **2** a title used for Christian priests **3** any of the early writers on Christian doctrine

father-in-law n, pl **fathers-in-law** the father of one's wife or husband

fatherland n a person's native country

fatherly adj kind or protective, like a father

fathom n **1** a unit of length, used in navigation, equal to six feet (1.83 metres) ▷ vb **2** to understand by thinking carefully about: *I couldn't fathom his intentions* ▶ **HISTORY** Old English *fæthm* > **fathomable** adj

fathomless adj too deep or difficult to fathom

fatigue (fat-**eeg**) n **1** extreme physical or mental tiredness **2** the weakening of a material caused by repeated stress or movement **3** the duties of a soldier that are not military **4 fatigues** a soldier's clothing for nonmilitary or battlefield duties ▷ vb **-tiguing, -tigued 5** to make or become weary or exhausted ▶ **HISTORY** Latin *fatigare* to tire

fat stock n livestock fattened and ready for market

fatten vb to grow or cause to grow fat or fatter > **fattening** adj

fatty adj **-tier, -tiest 1** containing or derived from fat **2** greasy or oily ▷ n, pl **-ties 3** *informal* a fat person

fatty acid n any of a class of organic acids some of which, such as stearic acid, are found in animal or vegetable fats

fatuity n, pl **-ties 1** foolish thoughtlessness **2** a fatuous remark

fatuous adj foolish, inappropriate, and showing no thought ▶ **HISTORY** Latin *fatuus* > **fatuously** adv

faucet (**faw**-set) n **1** a tap fitted to a barrel **2** *US & Canad* a tap ▶ **HISTORY** Old French *fausset*

fault n **1** responsibility for something wrong **2** a defect or failing: *they shut the production line to remedy a fault* **3** a weakness in a person's character **4** *geol* a fracture in the earth's crust with displacement of the rocks on either side **5** *tennis, squash, etc.* a serve that bounces outside the proper service court or fails to get over the net **6** (in showjumping) a penalty mark for failing to clear, or refusing, a fence **7 at fault** to blame for something wrong **8 find fault with** to seek out minor imperfections in **9 to a fault** more than is usual or necessary: *generous to a fault* ▷ vb **10** to criticize or blame **11** *geol* to undergo or cause to undergo a fault ▶ **HISTORY** Latin *fallere* to fail > **faultless** adj > **faultlessly** adv

fault block n *geol* a rock mass bounded by faults on at least two opposite sides

fault-block mountain n *geol* a mountain formed by the displacement of rock between faults

fault-finding n continual criticism

fault plane n *geol* the plane along the fracture surface of a fault

fault scarp n *geol* a cliff formed as a result of vertical displacement along a fault

faulty adj **faultier, faultiest** badly designed or not working properly: *a faulty toaster*

faun n (in Roman legend) a creature with the head and torso of a man and the legs, ears, and horns of a goat ▶ **HISTORY** Latin *Faunus*, god of forests

fauna n, pl **-nas** or **-nae** all the animal life of a given place or time: *the fauna of the Arctic* ▶ **HISTORY** Late Latin *Fauna*, a goddess of living things

Fauvism n a French expressionist movement at the beginning of the 20th century, characterized by the use of bright colours and simplified forms > **Fauvist** n

faux pas (foe **pah**) n, pl **faux pas** (foe **pahz**) a socially embarrassing action or mistake ▶ **HISTORY** French

favour or US **favor** n **1** an approving attitude: *the company looked with favour on his plan* **2** an act done out of goodwill or generosity **3** bias at the expense of others: *his fellow customs officers, showing no favour, demanded to see his luggage* **4 in** or **out of favour** regarded with approval or disapproval **5 in favour of a** approving **b** to the benefit of ▷ vb **6** to prefer **7** to show bias towards (someone) at the expense of others: *parents sometimes favour the youngest child in the family* **8** to support or agree with (something): *he favours the abolition of capital punishment* ▶ **HISTORY** Latin *favere* to protect > **favoured** or US **favored** adj

favourable or US **favorable** adj **1** advantageous, encouraging, or promising: *a favourable climate for business expansion* **2** giving consent or approval > **favourably** or US **favorably** adv

favourite or US **favorite** adj **1** most liked ▷ n **2** a person or thing regarded with especial preference or liking **3** *sport* a competitor thought likely to win ▶ **HISTORY** Latin *favere* to protect

favouritism or US **favoritism** n the practice of giving special treatment to a person or group: *favouritism in the allocation of government posts*

fawn¹ n **1** a young deer aged under one year ▷ adj **2** pale greyish-brown ▶ **HISTORY** Latin *fetus* offspring

fawn² *vb* **fawn on 1** to seek attention from (someone) by insincere flattery: *it makes me sick to see the way you fawn on that awful woman* **2** (of a dog) to try to please (someone) by a show of extreme friendliness ▶ **HISTORY** Old English *fægnian* to be glad **> fawning** *adj*

fax *n* **1** an electronic system for transmitting an exact copy of a document **2** a document sent by this system **3** Also called: **fax machine, facsimile machine** a machine which transmits and receives exact copies of documents ▷ *vb* **4** to send (a document) by this system ▶ **HISTORY** short for *facsimile*

FBI (in the US) Federal Bureau of Investigation

FC (in Britain) Football Club

FD Defender of the Faith: the title of the British sovereign as head of the Church of England ▶ **HISTORY** Latin *Fidei Defensor*

Fe *chem* iron ▶ **HISTORY** Latin *ferrum*

fealty *n, pl* **-ties** (in feudal society) the loyalty sworn to a lord by his tenant or servant ▶ **HISTORY** Latin *fidelitas* fidelity

fear *n* **1** a feeling of distress or alarm caused by danger or pain that is about to happen **2** something that causes fear **3** possibility or likelihood: *there is no fear of her agreeing to that* **4 no fear** *informal* certainly not ▷ *vb* **5** to be afraid of (someone or something) **6** *formal* to be sorry: *I fear the children were not very good yesterday* **7 fear for** to feel anxiety about something ▶ **HISTORY** Old English *fǣr* **> fearless** *adj* **> fearlessly** *adv*

fearful *adj* **1** afraid and full of fear **2** frightening or causing fear: *the ship hit a fearful storm* **3** *informal* very bad: *they were making a fearful noise* **> fearfully** *adv*

fearsome *adj* terrible or frightening

feasible *adj* able to be done: *a manned journey to Mars is now feasible* ▶ **HISTORY** Anglo-French *faisable* **> feasibility** *n* **> feasibly** *adv*

feast *n* **1** a large and special meal for many people **2** something extremely pleasing: *a feast of colour* **3** an annual religious celebration ▷ *vb* **4** to take part in a feast **5** to give a feast to **6 feast on** to eat a large amount of: *down come hundreds of vultures to feast on the remains* **7 feast one's eyes on** to look at (someone or something) with a great deal of attention and pleasure ▶ **HISTORY** Latin *festus* joyful

Feast of Tabernacles *n* same as **Sukkoth**

feat *n* a remarkable, skilful, or daring action: *an extraordinary feat of engineering* ▶ **HISTORY** Anglo-French *fait*

feather *n* **1** any of the flat light structures that form the plumage of birds, each consisting of a shaft with soft thin hairs on either side **2 feather in one's cap** a cause for pleasure at one's achievements ▷ *vb* **3** to fit, cover, or supply with feathers **4** *rowing* to turn an oar parallel to the water between strokes, in order to lessen wind resistance **5 feather one's nest** to collect possessions and money to make one's life comfortable, often dishonestly ▶ **HISTORY** Old English *fether* **> feathered** *adj* **> feathery** *adj*

featherbedding *n* the practice of working in a factory or office deliberately slowly and inefficiently so that more workers are employed than are necessary

featherweight *n* **1** a professional or an amateur boxer weighing up to 126 pounds (57 kg) **2** something very light or of little importance: *a featherweight politician*

feature *n* **1 features** any one of the parts of the face, such as the nose, chin, or mouth **2** a prominent or distinctive part of something or somewhere **3** the main film in a cinema programme **4** an item appearing regularly in a newspaper or magazine **5** a prominent story in a newspaper ▷ *vb* **-turing, -tured 6** to have as a feature or make a feature of: *this cooker features a fan-assisted oven* **7** to give special prominence to: *the film features James Mason as Rommel* ▶ **HISTORY** Anglo-French *feture* **> featureless** *adj*

feature article *n* *journalism* a prominent article (in a newspaper or magazine) involving in-depth research and analysis

Feb. February

febrile (**fee**-brile) *adj* *formal* **1** very active and nervous: *increasingly febrile activity at the Stock Exchange* **2** of or relating to fever ▶ **HISTORY** Latin *febris* fever

February *n, pl* **-aries** the second month of the year ▶ **HISTORY** Latin *Februarius mensis* month of expiation

feckless *adj* irresponsible and lacking character and determination: *her feckless brother was always in debt* ▶ **HISTORY** obsolete *feck* value, effect

fecund *adj* *literary* **1** fertile or capable of producing many offspring **2** intellectually productive or creative: *an extraordinarily fecund year even by Mozart's standards* ▶ **HISTORY** Latin *fecundus* **> fecundity** *n*

fed *vb* the past of **feed**

federal *adj* **1** of a form of government in which power is divided between one central and several regional governments **2** of the central government of a federation **3** *Austral* of a style of house built around the time of Federation ▶ **HISTORY** Latin *foedus* league **> federalism** *n* **> federalist** *n, adj*

Federal *adj* of or supporting the Union government during the American Civil War

Federal Government *n* the national government of a federated state, such as that of Canada located in Ottawa or of Australia in Canberra

federalism *n* *Government & politics* **1** the principle or a system of federal union **2** advocacy of federal union **> federalist** *n, adj* **> federalistic** *adj*

federalize *or* **-ise** *vb* **-izing, -ized** *or* **-ising, -ised 1** to unite in a federal union **2** to subject to federal control **> federalization** *or* **-isation** *n*

federate *vb* **-ating, -ated** to unite in a federal union **> federative** *adj*

federation *n* **1** the union of several provinces, states, etc. **2** any alliance or association of organizations which have freely joined together for a common purpose: *a federation of twenty regional unions*

fed up *adj informal* annoyed or bored

fee *n* **1** a charge paid to be allowed to do something: *many people resent the licence fee* **2** a payment asked by professional people for their services **3** *property law* an interest in land that can be inherited. The interest can be with unrestricted rights (**fee simple**) or restricted (**fee tail**) ▶ HISTORY Old French *fie*

feeble *adj* **1** lacking in physical or mental strength **2** not effective or convincing: *feeble excuses for Aberdeen's latest defeat* ▶ HISTORY Old French *feble* > **feebly** *adv*

feeble-minded *adj* unable to think or understand effectively

feed *vb* **feeding, fed** **1** to give food to (a person or an animal) **2** to give (something) as food: *people feeding bread to their cattle* **3** to eat food: *red squirrel feed in the pines* **4** to supply or prepare food for **5** to provide what is needed for the continued existence, operation, or growth of: *illustrations which will feed an older child's imagination; pools fed by waterfalls* ▷ *n* **6** the act of feeding **7** food, esp. that given to animals or babies **8** *Brit, Austral & NZ, informal* a meal ▶ HISTORY Old English *fēdan*

feedback *n* **1** information in response to an inquiry or experiment: *considerable feedback from the customers* **2** the return of part of the output of an electronic circuit to its input **3** the return of part of the sound output of a loudspeaker to the microphone, so that a high-pitched whine is produced

feeder *n* **1** a device used to feed an animal, child, or sick person **2** an animal or a person who feeds: *these larvae are voracious feeders* **3** a road, rail, or air service that links outlying areas to the main network **4** a tributary or channel of a river

feel *vb* **feeling, felt** **1** to have a physical or emotional sensation of: *he felt a combination of shame and relief* **2** to become aware of or examine by touching **3** Also: **feel in one's bones** to sense by intuition **4** to believe or think: *I felt I got off pretty lightly* **5 feel for** to show compassion (towards) **6 feel like** to have an inclination (for something or doing something): *I feel like going to the cinema* **7 feel up to** to be fit enough for (something or doing something) ▷ *n* **8** the act of feeling **9** an impression: *all this mixing and matching has a French feel to it* **10** the sense of touch **11** an instinctive ability: *a feel for art* ▶ HISTORY Old English *fēlan*

feeler *n* **1** an organ on an insect's head that is sensitive to touch **2 put out feelers** to make informal suggestions or remarks designed to probe the reactions of others

feeling *n* **1** an emotional reaction: *a feeling of discontent* **2 feelings** emotional sensitivity: *I don't want to hurt your feelings* **3** instinctive appreciation and understanding: *your feeling for language* **4** an intuitive understanding that cannot be explained: *I began to have a sinking feeling that I was not going to*

get rid of her **5** opinion or view: *it was his feeling that the report was a misinterpretation of what had been said* **6** capacity for sympathy or affection: *moved by feeling for his fellow citizens* **7 a** the ability to experience physical sensations: *he has no feeling in his left arm* **b** the sensation so experienced **8** the impression or mood created by something: *a feeling of excitement in the air* **9 bad feeling** resentment or anger between people, for example after an argument or an injustice: *his refusal may have triggered bad feeling between the two men* > **feelingly** *adv*

feet *n* **1** the plural of **foot 2 be run** or **rushed off one's feet** to be very busy **3 feet of clay** a weakness that is not widely known **4 have** or **keep one's feet on the ground** to be practical and reliable **5 put one's feet up** to take a rest **6 stand on one's own feet** to be independent **7 sweep off one's feet** to fill with enthusiasm

feign (**fane**) *vb* to pretend to experience (a particular feeling): *he didn't have to feign surprise* ▶ HISTORY Old French *feindre* > **feigned** *adj*

feint[1] (**faint**) *n* **1** a misleading movement designed to distract an opponent, such as in boxing or fencing ▷ *vb* **2** to make a feint ▶ HISTORY Old French *feindre* to feign

feint[2] (**faint**) *n printing* paper that has pale lines across it for writing on ▶ HISTORY variant of *faint*

feldspar or **felspar** *n* a hard mineral that is the main constituent of igneous rocks ▶ HISTORY German *feldspath* > **feldspathic** or **felspathic** *adj*

felicitations *pl n, interj* expressions of pleasure at someone's success or good fortune; congratulations

felicitous *adj* appropriate and well-chosen: *a felicitous combination of architectural styles*

felicity *n* **1** great happiness and pleasure **2** the quality of being pleasant or desirable: *small moments of architectural felicity amidst acres of monotony* **3** (*pl* **-ties**) an appropriate and well-chosen remark: *Nietzsche's verbal felicities are not lost in translation* ▶ HISTORY Latin *felicitas* happiness

feline *adj* **1** of or belonging to the cat family **2** like a cat, esp. in stealth or grace ▷ *n* **3** any member of the cat family ▶ HISTORY Latin *feles* cat > **felinity** *n*

fell[1] *vb* the past tense of **fall**

fell[2] *vb* **1** to cut down (a tree) **2** to knock down (a person), esp. in a fight ▶ HISTORY Old English *fellan*

fell[3] *adj* **in one fell swoop** in one single action or on one single occasion: *they arrested all the hooligans in one fell swoop* ▶ HISTORY Middle English *fel*

fell[4] *n Scot & N English* a mountain, hill, or moor ▶ HISTORY Old Norse *fjall*

fell[5] *n* an animal's skin or hide with its hair ▶ HISTORY Old High German *fel* skin

felloe or **felly** *n, pl* **-loes** or **-lies** a segment or the whole rim of a wooden wheel ▶ HISTORY Old English *felge*

fellow *n* **1** a man or boy **2** comrade or associate **3** a person in the same group or condition: *he earned the respect of his fellows at Dunkirk* **4** a member of

f

305

the governing body at any of various universities or colleges **5** (in Britain) a postgraduate research student ▷ *adj* **6** in the same group or condition: *a conversation with a fellow passenger* ► HISTORY Old English *fēolaga*

Fellow *n* a senior member of an academic institution

fellow feeling *n* sympathy existing between people who have shared similar experiences

fellowship *n* **1** the state of sharing mutual interests or activities **2** a society of people sharing mutual interests or activities **3** companionship or friendship **4** *education* a financed research post providing study facilities

fellow traveller *n* *history* a person who sympathized with the Communist Party but was not a member of it

felon *n* *criminal law* (formerly) a person who committed a serious crime ► HISTORY Old French: villain

felony *n*, *pl* **-nies** *criminal law* (formerly) a serious crime, such as murder or arson > **felonious** *adj*

felspar *n* same as **feldspar**

felt[1] *vb* the past of **feel**

felt[2] *n* a matted fabric of wool, made by working the fibres together under pressure ► HISTORY Old English

felt-tip pen *n* a pen with a writing point made from pressed fibres

fem. 1 female **2** feminine

female *adj* **1** of the sex producing offspring **2** of or characteristic of a woman **3** (of reproductive organs such as the ovary and carpel) capable of producing reproductive cells (**gametes**) that are female **4** (of flowers) not having parts in which pollen is produced (**stamens**) **5** (of a mechanical component) having an opening into which a projecting male component can be fitted ▷ *n* **6** a female animal or plant ► HISTORY Latin *femina* a woman

feminine *adj* **1** possessing qualities considered typical of or appropriate to a woman **2** of women **3** *grammar* denoting a gender of nouns that includes some female animate things ► HISTORY Latin *femina* a woman > **femininity** *n*

feminism *n* a doctrine or movement that advocates equal rights for women > **feminist** *n*, *adj*

femme fatale (fam fat-**tahl**) *n*, *pl* **femmes fatales** (fam fat-**tahlz**) an alluring or seductive woman who leads men into dangerous or difficult situations by her charm ► HISTORY French

femto- *combining form* denoting 10^{-15}: *femtometer* ► HISTORY Danish *femten* fifteen

femur (fee-mer) *n*, *pl* **femurs** or **femora** (fee-mer-ra) the thighbone ► HISTORY Latin: thigh > **femoral** *adj*

fen *n* *Brit* low-lying flat marshy land ► HISTORY Old English *fenn*

fence *n* **1** a barrier that encloses an area such as a garden or field, usually made of posts connected by wire rails or boards **2** an obstacle for a horse to jump in steeplechasing or showjumping **3** *slang* a

dealer in stolen property **4** *machinery* a guard or guide, esp. in a circular saw or plane **5** (**sit) on the fence** (to be) unwilling to commit oneself ▷ *vb* **fencing**, **fenced 6** to construct a fence on or around (a piece of land) **7** **fence in** *or* **off** to close in or separate off with or as if with a fence **8** to fight using swords or foils **9** to argue cleverly but evasively: *they fenced for a while, weighing each other up* ► HISTORY Middle English *fens*, from *defens* defence

fencing *n* **1** the sport of fighting with swords or foils **2** materials used for making fences

fend *vb* **1** **fend for oneself** to look after oneself; be independent **2** **fend off** to defend oneself against (verbal or physical attack) ► HISTORY Middle English *fenden*

fender *n* **1** a low metal barrier that stops coals from falling out of a fireplace **2** a soft but solid object, such as a coil of rope, hung over the side of a vessel to prevent damage when docking **3** *US & Canad* the wing of a car

fenestration *n* the arrangement of windows in a building ► HISTORY Latin *fenestra* window

feng shui (fung shway) *n* the Chinese art of deciding the best design or position of a grave, building, etc., in order to bring good luck ► HISTORY Chinese *feng* wind + *shui* water

Fenian (feen-yan) *n* (formerly) a member of an Irish revolutionary organization founded to fight for an independent Ireland ► HISTORY after *Fianna*, legendary band of Irish warriors > **Fenianism** *n*

fenland *n* *Brit* an area of low-lying flat marshy land

fennel *n* a fragrant plant whose seeds, leaves, and root are used in cookery ► HISTORY Old English *fenol*

fenugreek *n* a Mediterranean plant grown for its heavily scented seeds ► HISTORY Old English *fēnogrēcum*

feoff (feef) *n* same as **fief** ► HISTORY Anglo-French

feral *adj* **1** (of animals and plants) existing in a wild state, esp. after being domestic or cultivated **2** savage ► HISTORY Latin *ferus* savage

ferment *n* **1** excitement and unrest caused by change or uncertainty **2** any substance, such as yeast, that causes fermentation ▷ *vb* **3** to undergo or cause to undergo fermentation ► HISTORY Latin *fermentum* yeast

fermentation *n* a chemical reaction in which an organic molecule splits into simpler substances, esp. the conversion of sugar to ethyl alcohol by yeast

fermium *n* *chem* an element artificially produced by neutron bombardment of plutonium. Symbol: Fm ► HISTORY after Enrico *Fermi*, physicist

fern *n* a flowerless plant with roots, stems, and long feathery leaves that reproduces by releasing spores ► HISTORY Old English *fearn* > **ferny** *adj*

ferocious *adj* savagely fierce or cruel ► HISTORY Latin *ferox* > **ferocity** *n*

ferret *n* **1** a small yellowish-white animal related to the weasel and bred for hunting rats and rabbits

▷ *vb* **-reting, -reted 2** to hunt rabbits or rats with ferrets **3** to search around **4 ferret out a** to drive from hiding **b** to find by determined investigation: *she could ferret out little knowledge of his background*

- **WORD HISTORY**
- 'Ferret' comes from Old French *furet* meaning
- 'little thief', from Latin *fur*, meaning 'thief', a
- Latin root also found in 'furtive'.

ferric *adj* of or containing iron in the trivalent state ▶ HISTORY Latin *ferrum* iron

Ferris wheel *n* a large vertical fairground wheel with hanging seats for riding on ▶ HISTORY after G. W. G. Ferris, American engineer

ferrous *adj* of or containing iron in the divalent state ▶ HISTORY Latin *ferrum* iron

ferruginous (fur-**rooj**-in-uss) *adj* (of a mineral or rock) containing iron ▶ HISTORY Latin *ferrum* iron

ferrule *n* a metal ring or cap placed over the end of a stick for added strength ▶ HISTORY Latin *viria* bracelet

ferry *n, pl* **-ries 1** a boat for transporting passengers and vehicles across a body of water, esp. as a regular service **2** such a service ▷ *vb* **-ries, -rying, -ried 3** to transport or go by ferry **4** to transport (passengers or goods) on a regular basis ▶ HISTORY Old English *ferian* to carry > **ferryman** *n*

fertile *adj* **1** capable of producing offspring, crops, or vegetation **2** *biol* capable of growth and development: *fertile seeds* **3** highly productive: *a fertile imagination* **4** *physics* (of a substance) able to be transformed into fissile or fissionable material ▶ HISTORY Latin *fertilis* > **fertility** *n*

fertilize *or* **-lise** *vb* **-lizing, -lized** *or* **-lising, -lised 1** to provide (an animal or plant) with sperm or pollen to bring about fertilization **2** to supply (soil) with nutrients > **fertilization** *or* **-lisation** *n*

fertilizer *or* **-liser** *n* any substance, such as manure, added to soil to increase its productivity

fervent *or* **fervid** *adj* intensely sincere and passionate ▶ HISTORY Latin *fervere* to boil > **fervently** *adv*

fervour *or US* **fervor** *n* great intensity of feeling or belief ▶ HISTORY Latin *fervere* to boil

fescue *n* a pasture and lawn grass with stiff narrow leaves ▶ HISTORY Old French *festu*

fester *vb* **1** to grow worse and increasingly hostile: *the bitterness which had been festering beneath the surface* **2** (of a wound) to form pus **3** to rot and decay: *rubbish festered in the heat* ▶ HISTORY Old French *festre* suppurating sore

festival *n* **1** an organized series of special events and performances: *the Edinburgh Festival* **2** a day or period set aside for celebration ▶ HISTORY Latin *festivus* joyful

festive *adj* of or like a celebration ▶ HISTORY Latin *festivus* joyful

festivity *n, pl* **-ties 1** happy celebration: *a spirit of joy and festivity* **2** **festivities** celebrations

festoon *vb* **1** to drape with decorations: *Christmas trees festooned with fairy lights* ▷ *n* **2** a decorative chain of flowers or ribbons suspended in loops ▶ HISTORY Italian *festone* ornament for a feast

feta *n* a white Greek cheese made from sheep's or goat's milk ▶ HISTORY Modern Greek

fetal alcohol syndrome *n* a condition in newborn babies caused by excessive alcohol intake by the mother during pregnancy: characterized by retarded growth and mental disability

fetch[1] *vb* **1** to go after and bring back **2** to be sold for (a certain price): *Impressionist pictures fetch very high prices* **3** *informal* to give someone (a blow or slap) **4 fetch and carry** to perform menial tasks ▶ HISTORY Old English *feccan*

fetch[2] *n* the ghost or apparition of a living person ▶ HISTORY origin unknown

fetching *adj informal* attractive: *a fetching dress*

fetch up *vb* **1** *US & NZ, informal* to arrive or end up **2** *slang* to vomit food

fete (fate) *n* **1** an event, usually outdoors, with stalls, competitions, etc., held to raise money for charity **2** *informal* (in the Caribbean) an organized group entertainment, esp. a party or dance ▷ *vb* **feting, feted 3** to honour and entertain (someone) publicly: *the President was feted with an evening of music and dancing* ▶ HISTORY French

fetid *or* **foetid** *adj* having a stale and unpleasant smell ▶ HISTORY Latin *fetere* to stink

fetish *n* **1 a** a form of behaviour in which a person derives satisfaction from handling an object **b** any object that is involved in such behaviour **2** any object, activity, etc. to which one is excessively devoted: *cleanliness is almost a fetish with her* **3** an object that is believed to have magical powers ▶ HISTORY Portuguese *feitiço* sorcery > **fetishism** *n* > **fetishist** *n*

fetlock *n* **1** the back part of a horse's leg, just behind the hoof **2** the tuft of hair growing from this part ▶ HISTORY Middle English *fetlak*

fetter *n* **1 fetters** checks or restraints: *free from the fetters of religion* **2** a chain fixed around a prisoner's ankle ▷ *vb* **3** to prevent from behaving freely and naturally: *fettered by bureaucracy* **4** to tie up in fetters ▶ HISTORY Old English *fetor*

fettle *n* **in fine fettle** in good spirits or health ▶ HISTORY Old English *fetel* belt

fetus *or* **foetus** (**fee**-tuss) *n, pl* **-tuses** the embryo of a mammal in the later stages of development ▶ HISTORY Latin: offspring > **fetal** *or* **foetal** *adj*

feu *n Scots Law* a right to the use of land in return for a fixed annual payment (**feu duty**) ▶ HISTORY Old French

feud *n* **1** long and bitter hostility between two families, clans, or individuals ▷ *vb* **2** to carry on a feud ▶ HISTORY Old French *feide*

feudal *adj* of or characteristic of feudalism ▶ HISTORY Medieval Latin *feudum* fief

feudalism *n history* the legal and social system in medieval Europe, in which people were given land and protection by a lord in return for which they worked and fought for him. Also called: **feudal system**

fever *n* **1** an abnormally high body temperature, accompanied by a fast pulse rate, shivering, and nausea. *Related adjective:* **febrile 2** any disease characterized by a high temperature **3** intense nervous excitement: *she waited in a fever of anxiety* ▶ HISTORY Latin *febris*

feverish *or* **fevered** *adj* **1** suffering from fever **2** *written* in a state of nervous excitement: *a feverish scramble to buy shares* > **feverishly** *adv*

fever pitch *n* a state of intense excitement

few *adj* **1** hardly any: *few homes had telephones in Paris in the 1930s* **2 a few** a small number of: *a few days ago* **3 a good few** *informal* several **4 few and far between** scarce **5 quite a few** *informal* several ▶ HISTORY Old English *fēawa*

fey *adj* **1** vague and whimsically strange **2** having the ability to look into the future ▶ HISTORY Old English *fǣge* marked out for death

fez *n, pl* **fezzes** a round red brimless hat with a flat top and a tassel hanging from it. Formerly worn by men in Turkey and some Arab countries ▶ HISTORY Turkish

ff. and the following (pages, lines, etc.)

fiancé *or fem* **fiancée** (fee-**on**-say) *n* a person who is engaged to be married ▶ HISTORY Old French *fiancier* to promise, betroth

fiasco *n, pl* **-cos** *or* **-coes** an action or attempt that fails completely in a ridiculous or disorganized way: *the invasion of Cuba ended in a fiasco* ▶ HISTORY Italian: flask; sense development obscure

fiat (**fie**-at) *n* **1** an official order issued without the consultation of those expected to obey it: *the junta ruled by fiat* **2** official permission ▶ HISTORY Latin: let it be done

fib *n* **1** a trivial and harmless lie ▷ *vb* **fibbing, fibbed 2** to tell such a lie ▶ HISTORY origin unknown > **fibber** *n*

fibre *or US* **fiber** *n* **1** a natural or synthetic thread that may be spun into yarn **2** a threadlike animal or plant tissue: *a simple network of nerve fibres* **3** a fibrous substance that helps the body digest food: *fruits, vegetables, grains, lentils, and beans are high in fibre* **4** strength of character: *moral fibre* **5** essential substance or nature: *my every fibre sang out in sudden relief* ▶ HISTORY Latin *fibra* filament, entrails > **fibrous** *adj*

fibreboard *n* a building material made of compressed wood

fibreglass *n* **1** material consisting of matted fine glass fibres, used as insulation **2** a light strong material made by bonding fibreglass with a synthetic resin, used for boats and car bodies

fibre optics *n* the transmission of information by light along very thin flexible fibres of glass > **fibre optic** *adj*

fibril (**fibe**-rill) *n* a small fibre

fibrillation *n* uncontrollable twitching of muscle fibres, esp. those of the heart

fibrin *n* a white insoluble elastic protein formed when blood clots

fibrinogen (fib-**rin**-no-jen) *n biol* a soluble plasma protein involved in blood clotting

fibro *n Austral* a mixture of cement and asbestos fibre, used in sheets for building. Also: **fibrocement**

fibroid (**fibe**-royd) *adj* **1** *anat* (of structures or tissues) containing or resembling fibres ▷ *n* **2** a harmless tumour composed of fibrous connective tissue

fibrosis (fibe-**roh**-siss) *n* the formation of an abnormal amount of fibrous tissue

fibrositis (fibe-roh-**site**-iss) *n* inflammation of fibrous tissue, esp. of the back muscles, causing pain and stiffness

fibula (**fib**-yew-la) *n, pl* **-lae** (-lee) *or* **-las** the outer and thinner of the two bones between the knee and ankle of the human leg ▶ HISTORY Latin: a clasp > **fibular** *adj*

fiche (**feesh**) *n* a sheet of film for storing publications in miniature form

fickle *adj* **1** changeable in purpose, affections, etc.: *notoriously fickle voters* **2** (of the weather) changing often and suddenly ▶ HISTORY Old English *ficol* deceitful > **fickleness** *n*

fiction *n* **1** literary works invented by the imagination, such as novels **2** an invented story or explanation: *the fiction that the Baltic states freely joined the USSR* **3** *law* something assumed to be true for the sake of convenience, though probably false ▶ HISTORY Latin *fictio* a fashioning > **fictional** *adj*

fictionalize *or* **-ise** *vb* **-izing, -ized** *or* **-ising, -ised** to make into fiction

fictitious *adj* **1** not genuine: *rumours of false accounting and fictitious loans had surrounded the bank for years* **2** of or in fiction

fiddle *n* **1** *informal or disparaging* the violin **2** a violin played as a folk instrument **3** *Brit & NZ, informal* a dishonest action or scheme **4 on the fiddle** *informal* engaged in an illegal or fraudulent undertaking **5 fit as a fiddle** *informal* in very good health **6 play second fiddle** *informal* to undertake a role that is less important or powerful than someone else's ▷ *vb* **-dling, -dled 7** to play (a tune) on the fiddle **8** *informal* to do (something) by illegal or dishonest means **9** *informal* to falsify (accounts) **10 fiddle with** to move or touch (something) restlessly or nervously **11 fiddle about** *or* **around** *informal* to waste time ▶ HISTORY Old English *fithele*

fiddler *n* **1** a person who plays the fiddle **2** a small burrowing crab **3** *informal* a person who dishonestly alters something or lies in order to get money

fiddlesticks *interj* an expression of annoyance or disagreement

fiddling *adj* small or unimportant

fiddly *adj* **-dlier, -dliest** small and awkward to do or handle

fidelity *n, pl* **-ties 1** faithfulness to one's spouse or lover **2** loyalty to a person, belief, or cause **3** accuracy in reporting detail: *an account of the invasion written with objectivity and fidelity* **4** *electronics* the degree to which an amplifier or radio accurately reproduces the input signal ▶ HISTORY Latin *fides* faith

fidget *vb* **-eting, -eted 1** to move about restlessly **2 fidget with** to make restless or uneasy movements with (something): *he broke off, fidgeting*

f

with the papers, unable to meet their gaze ▷ *n*
3 a person who fidgets **4 the fidgets** a state of restlessness: *these youngsters are very highly strung and tend to get the fidgets* ▶ **HISTORY** earlier *fidge* > **fidgety** *adj*

fiduciary (fid-**yewsh**-ya-ree) *law n* **1** a person bound to act for someone else's benefit, as a trustee ▷ *adj* **2** of or relating to a trust or trustee ▶ **HISTORY** Latin *fiducia* trust

fie *interj obsolete or facetious* an exclamation of disapproval ▶ **HISTORY** Old French *fi*

fief (feef) *n* (in feudal Europe) land granted by a lord in return for military service ▶ **HISTORY** Old French *fie*

fiefdom *n* **1** (in Feudal Europe) the property owned by a lord **2** an area over which a person has influence or authority

field *n* **1** an area of uncultivated grassland; meadow **2** a piece of cleared land used for pasture or growing crops **3** a marked off area on which sports or athletic competitions are held **4** an area that is rich in minerals or other natural resources: *an oil field* **5 a** all the competitors in a competition **b** the competitors in a competition excluding the favourite **6** a battlefield **7** *cricket* the fielders collectively **8** a wide expanse of land covered by some substance such as snow or lava **9** an area of human activity or knowledge: *the most distinguished physicist in the field of quantum physics* **10** a place away from the laboratory or classroom where practical work is done **11** the surface or background of something, such as a flag **12** *physics* In full: **field of force** the region surrounding a body, such as a magnet, within which it can exert a force on another similar body not in contact with it **13 play the field** *informal* to have many romantic relationships before getting married ▷ *adj* **14** *mil* of equipment or personnel for operations in the field: *field guns* ▷ *vb* **15** *sport* to catch or return (the ball) as a fielder **16** *sport* to send (a player or team) onto the field to play **17** *sport* (of a player or team) to act or take turn as a fielder or fielders **18** *informal* to deal successfully with (a question or remark) ▶ **HISTORY** Old English *feld*

field day *n* **1** *informal* an opportunity or occasion for unrestrained action, esp. if previously denied or restricted: *the revelations gave the press a field day* **2** *mil* a day devoted to manoeuvres or exercises

fielder *n cricket etc.* a member of the fielding side

field event *n* an athletic competition, such as the discus, pole vault, or long jump, that takes place on a field rather than a running track. Compare **track event**

fieldfare *n* a type of large thrush ▶ **HISTORY** Old English *feldefare*

field glasses *pl n* binoculars

field hockey *n US & Canad* hockey played on a field, as distinguished from ice hockey

field marshal *n* an officer holding the highest rank in certain armies

fieldmouse *n*, *pl* **-mice** a nocturnal mouse that lives in woods and fields

field officer *n* an officer holding the rank of major, lieutenant colonel, or colonel

field research *n* research conducted by acquiring new data about a subject. Compare **desk research**

fieldsman *n*, *pl* **-men** *cricket* a fielder

field sports *pl n* sports carried on in the countryside, such as hunting or fishing

field trip *n* an expedition, esp. by students, to study something at first hand

fieldwork *n mil* a temporary structure used in defending a place or position

field work *n* an investigation made in the field as opposed to the classroom or laboratory > **field worker** *n*

fiend (feend) *n* **1** an evil spirit **2** *written* a cruel or wicked person **3** *informal* a person who is extremely interested in or fond of something: *a fitness fiend* ▶ **HISTORY** Old English *fēond* > **fiendish** *adj* > **fiendishly** *adv*

Fiend *n* **the Fiend** the devil

fierce *adj* **1** very aggressive or angry: *a fierce dog* **2** intense or strong: *a fierce wind* ▶ **HISTORY** Latin *ferus* > **fiercely** *adv*

fiery (**fire**-ee) *adj* **fierier, fieriest** **1** consisting of or like fire: *a fiery explosion* **2** *written* displaying strong passion, esp. anger: *a fiery speech* **3** *written* (of food) very spicy > **fierily** *adv* > **fieriness** *n*

fiesta *n* (esp. in Spain and Latin America) a religious festival or carnival ▶ **HISTORY** Spanish

FIFA (**fee**-fa) International Association Football Federation ▶ **HISTORY** French *Fédération Internationale de Football Association*

fife *n* a small high-pitched flute, often used in military bands ▶ **HISTORY** Old High German *pfifa*

fifteen *n* **1** the cardinal number that is the sum of ten and five **2** a numeral, 15 or XV, representing this number **3** something representing or consisting of 15 units **4** a Rugby Union team ▷ *adj* **5** amounting to fifteen: *fifteen trees* > **fifteenth** *adj*, *n*

fifth *adj* **1** of or being number five in a series ▷ *n* **2** one of five equal parts of something **3** *music* the interval between one note and the note three-and-a-half tones higher or lower than it **4** an additional high gear fitted to some vehicles, esp. certain sports cars

fifth column *n* any group that secretly helps the enemies of its own country or organization > **fifth columnist** *n*

fifty *n*, *pl* **-ties** **1** the cardinal number that is the product of ten and five **2** a numeral, 50 or L, representing this number **3** something representing or consisting of 50 units ▷ *adj* **4** amounting to fifty: *fifty bodies* > **fiftieth** *adj*, *n*

fifty-fifty *adj*, *adv informal* **1** in equal parts **2** just as likely to happen as not to happen: *a fifty-fifty chance of survival*

fig *n* **1** a soft sweet fruit full of tiny seeds, which grows on a tree **2 not care** or **give a fig** not to care at all: *he did not give a fig for his enemies* ▶ **HISTORY** Latin *ficus* fig tree

fig. **1** figurative(ly) **2** figure

fight *vb* **fighting, fought** **1** to struggle against (an enemy) in battle or physical combat **2** to struggle to overcome or destroy: *to fight drug trafficking* **3** to carry on (a battle or contest) **4** to make (one's way) somewhere with difficulty: *they fought their way upstream* **5 fight for** to uphold (a cause) by struggling: *fight for your rights* **6 fight it out** to struggle or compete until a decisive result is obtained **7 fight shy of** to avoid: *they fought shy of direct involvement in the conflict* ▷ *n* **8** a battle **9** a quarrel or contest **10** a boxing match **11 put up a fight** to offer resistance ▶ HISTORY Old English *feohtan* > **fighting** *n*

fighter *n* **1** a professional boxer **2** a person who has determination **3** *mil* an armed aircraft for destroying other aircraft

fight off *vb* **1** to drive away (an attacker) **2** to struggle to avoid: *to fight off infection*

fig leaf *n* **1** a representation of a leaf of the fig tree used in sculpture to cover the genitals of nude figures **2** anything used to conceal something thought to be shameful: *the agreement was a fig leaf for Hitler's violation of the treaty*

figment *n* **a figment of one's imagination** something nonexistent and only imagined by someone ▶ HISTORY Latin *fingere* to shape

figuration *n* ornamentation

figurative *adj* **1** (of language) abstract, imaginative, or symbolic; not literal **2** (of art) involving realistic representation of people and things > **figuratively** *adv*

figure *n* **1** a written symbol for a number **2** an amount expressed in numbers **3 figures** calculations with numbers **4** visible shape or form; outline **5** a slim bodily shape: *it's not good for your figure* **6** a well-known person: *a public figure* **7** a representation in painting or sculpture, esp. of the human body **8** an illustration or diagram in a text **9** a decorative pattern **10** a fixed set of movements in dancing or skating **11** *geom* any combination of points, lines, curves, or planes **12** *music* a characteristic short pattern of notes **13 figure of fun** a person who is often laughed at by other people ▷ *vb* **-uring, -ured** **14** to calculate (sums or amounts) **15** *US, Canad, Austral & NZ, informal* to consider **16** to be included or play a part: *a house which figures in several of White's novels* **17** *informal* to be consistent with expectation: *Small-time crook, earns most of his cash as an informer. – That figures* ▶ HISTORY Latin *figura* a shape

figured *adj* **1** decorated with a design: *a chair upholstered in figured velvet* **2** *music* ornamental

figurehead *n* **1** a person who is formally the head of a movement or an organization, but has no real authority **2** a carved bust on the bow of some sailing vessels

figure of speech *n* an expression, such as a simile, in which words do not have their literal meaning

figure out *vb informal* to work out, solve, or understand: *I can't figure him out*

figurine *n* a small carved or moulded figure

▶ HISTORY French

filament *n* **1** the thin wire inside a light bulb that emits light **2** *electronics* a high-resistance wire forming the cathode in some valves **3** a single strand of fibre **4** *bot* the stalk of a stamen ▶ HISTORY Latin *filum* thread > **filamentary** *adj*

filbert *n* the brown edible nuts of the hazel ▶ HISTORY after St *Philbert*, because the nuts are ripe around his feast day, August 22

filch *vb* to steal in small amounts ▶ HISTORY Middle English *filchen* to steal, attack

file¹ *n* **1** a folder or box used to keep documents in order **2** the documents, etc. kept in this way **3** documents or information about a specific subject or person: *the doctor handed him his file* **4** a line of people in marching formation, one behind another **5** *computers* an organized collection of related records **6 on file** recorded for reference, as in a file ▷ *vb* **filing, filed** **7** to place (a document) in a file **8** to place (a legal document) on public or official record **9** to bring a lawsuit, esp. for divorce **10** to submit (a report or story) to a newspaper **11** to march or walk in a line ▶ HISTORY Latin *filum* a thread

file² *n* **1** a hand tool consisting of a steel blade with small cutting teeth on its faces, used for shaping or smoothing ▷ *vb* **filing, filed** **2** to shape or smooth (a surface) with a file ▶ HISTORY Old English *fil*

file photograph *n journalism, publishing* a photograph kept on file in a photograph collection for use as and when needed

file sharing *n* the practice of sharing computer data or space on a network

filial *adj* of or suitable to a son or daughter: *filial duty* ▶ HISTORY Latin *filius* son

filibuster *n* **1** the process of obstructing legislation by means of long speeches so that time runs out and a vote cannot be taken **2** a legislator who engages in such obstruction ▷ *vb* **3** to obstruct (legislation) with such delaying tactics ▶ HISTORY probably from Dutch *vrijbuiter* pirate

filigree *n* **1** delicate ornamental work of gold or silver wire ▷ *adj* **2** made of filigree ▶ HISTORY Latin *filum* thread + *granum* grain

filings *pl n* shavings or particles removed by a file: *iron filings*

Filipino (fill-lip-**pee**-no) *adj* **1** of the Philippines ▷ *n, pl* **-nos 2** Also (fem): **Filipina** a person from the Philippines

fill *vb* (often foll. by *up*) **1** to make or become full **2** to occupy the whole of: *their supporters filled the entire stand* **3** to plug (a gap or crevice) **4** to meet (a requirement or need) satisfactorily: *this book fills a major gap* **5** to cover (a page or blank space) with writing or drawing **6** to hold and perform the duties of (an office or position) **7** to appoint or elect an occupant to (an office or position) ▷ *n* **8 one's fill** sufficient for one's needs or wants ▷ See also **fill in** ▶ HISTORY Old English *fyllan*

filler *n* **1** a paste used for filling in cracks or holes in a surface before painting **2** *journalism* an item to fill space between more important articles

fillet *n* **1** a piece of boneless meat or fish **2** a thin strip of ribbon or lace worn in the hair or around the neck **3** *archit* a narrow flat moulding ▷ *vb* **-leting, -leted 4** to cut or prepare (meat or fish) as a fillet ▶ **HISTORY** Latin *filum* thread

fill in *vb* **1** to complete (a form) **2** to act as a substitute **3** to put material into (a hole) so as to make it level with a surface **4** *informal* to give (a person) fuller details

filling *n* **1 a** a substance or thing used to fill something: *a sandwich filling* **2** *dentistry* a substance that fills a gap or cavity of a tooth ▷ *adj* **3** (of food or a meal) substantial and satisfying

filling station *n chiefly Brit* a place where petrol and other supplies for motorists are sold

fillip *n* **1** *written* something that adds stimulation or enjoyment **2** the action of holding a finger towards the palm with the thumb and suddenly releasing it with a snapping sound ▶ **HISTORY** imitative

filly *n, pl* **-lies** a young female horse ▶ **HISTORY** Old Norse *fylja*

film *n* **1 a** a sequence of images projected onto a screen, creating the illusion of movement **b** a form of entertainment in such a sequence of images. *Related adjective:* **cinematic 2** a thin flexible strip of cellulose coated with a photographic emulsion, used to make negatives and slides **3** a thin coating, covering, or layer: *a fine film of dust covered the floor* **4** a thin sheet of any material, as of plastic for packaging ▷ *vb* **5 a** to photograph with a movie or video camera **b** to make a film of (a screenplay or event) **6 film over** to cover or become covered with a thin layer ▷ *adj* **7** of or relating to films or the cinema ▶ **HISTORY** Old English *filmen* membrane

filmic *adj* of or suggestive of films or the cinema > **filmically** *adv*

film star *n* a popular film actor or actress

film strip *n* a strip of film composed of different images projected separately as slides

filmy *adj* **filmier, filmiest** very thin and almost transparent: *a shirt of filmy black chiffon* > **filmily** *adv* > **filminess** *n*

filter *n* **1** a substance, such as paper or sand, that allows fluid to pass but retains solid particles **2** any device containing such a substance, esp. a tip on the mouth end of a cigarette **3** any electronic or acoustic device that blocks signals of certain frequencies while allowing others to pass **4** any transparent disc of gelatine or glass used to reduce the intensity of given frequencies from the light leaving a lamp or entering a camera **5** *Brit* a traffic signal which permits vehicles to turn either left or right when the main signals are red ▷ *vb* **6** Also: **filter out** to remove or separate (particles from (a liquid or gas) by a filter **7** Also: **filter through** to pass through a filter or something like a filter ▶ **HISTORY** Medieval Latin *filtrum* piece of felt used as a filter

filter paper *n* a porous paper used for filtering liquids

filter tip *n* **1** an attachment to the mouth end of a cigarette for trapping impurities **2** a cigarette with such an attachment > **filter-tipped** *adj*

filth *n* **1** disgusting dirt and muck **2** offensive material or language ▶ **HISTORY** Old English *fylth* > **filthiness** *n* > **filthy** *adj*

filtrate *n* **1** a liquid or gas that has been filtered ▷ *vb* **-trating, -trated 2** to filter ▶ **HISTORY** Medieval Latin *filtrare* to filter > **filtration** *n*

fin *n* **1** any of the winglike projections from a fish's body enabling it to balance and swim **2** *Brit* a vertical surface to which the rudder is attached at the rear of an aeroplane **3** a swimmer's flipper ▶ **HISTORY** Old English *finn* > **finned** *adj*

finagle (fin-**nay**-gl) *vb* **-gling, -gled** *informal* to use or achieve by craftiness or trickery ▶ **HISTORY** origin unknown

final *adj* **1** of or occurring at the end; last **2** having no possibility of further discussion, action, or change: *a final decision* ▷ *n* **3** a deciding contest between the winners of previous rounds in a competition ▷ See also **finals** ▶ **HISTORY** Latin *finis* limit, boundary > **finality** *n* > **finally** *adv*

finale (fin-**nah**-lee) *n* the concluding part of a dramatic performance or musical composition ▶ **HISTORY** Italian

finalist *n* a contestant who has reached the last stage of a competition

finalize *or* **-ise** *vb* **-izing, -ized** *or* **-ising, -ised** to put into final form; settle: *plans have yet to be finalized* > **finalization** *or* **-isation** *n*

finals *pl n* **1** the deciding part of a competition **2** *education, Brit & S African* the last examinations in an academic course

finance *vb* **-nancing, -nanced 1** to provide or obtain funds for (a project or large purchase) ▷ *n* **2** the system of money, credit, and investment **3** management of money, loans, or credits: *the dangerous political arena of public-sector finance* **4** funds or the provision of funds **5 finances** money resources: *the company's crumbling finances* ▶ **HISTORY** Old French *finer* to end, settle by payment

financial *adj* **1** of or relating to finance, finances, or people who manage money **2** *Austral & NZ, informal* having ready money > **financially** *adv*

financial market *n econ* the buying and selling of stocks, shares, currencies, and commodities, and the results of this trade expressed in prices

financial year *n* any annual accounting period

financier *n* a person who is engaged in large-scale financial operations

finch *n* a small songbird with a short strong beak ▶ **HISTORY** Old English *finc*

find *vb* **finding, found 1** to discover by chance **2** to discover by search or effort **3** to realize or become aware: *I have found that if you make the effort then people will be more willing to help you* **4** to consider (someone or something) to have a particular quality: *his business partner had found that odd* **5** to experience (a particular feeling): *she found comfort in his words* **6** *law* to pronounce (the defendant) guilty or not guilty **7** to reach (a target) **8** to provide, esp. with difficulty: *we'll find room for you too* **9 find one's feet** to become capable or

311

confident ▷ *n* **10** a person or thing that is found, esp. a valuable discovery: *the archaeological find of the century* ▶ HISTORY Old English *findan*

finder *n* **1** a small telescope fitted to a larger one **2** a person or thing that finds **3** *photog* short for **viewfinder**

finding *n* the conclusion reached after an inquiry or investigation

find out *vb* **1** to learn something that one did not already know **2 find someone out** to discover that someone has been dishonest or deceitful

fine¹ *adj* **1** very good **2** superior in skill: *a fine doctor* **3** (of weather) clear and dry **4** *informal* quite well: *I felt fine* **5** satisfactory: *as far as we can tell, everything is fine* **6** of delicate or careful workmanship: *fine porcelain* **7** subtle: *too fine a distinction* **8** very thin or slender: *fine soft hair* **9** very small: *fine print* **10** (of edges or blades) sharp **11** fancy, showy, or smart **12** good-looking **13** *ironic* disappointing or terrible: *a fine mess!* ▷ *adv* **14** *informal* very well: *that's what we've always done, and it suits us just fine* ▷ *vb* **fining, fined 15** to make (something) finer or thinner **16 fine down** to make (a theory or criticism) more precise or exact ▶ HISTORY Latin *finis* end, boundary, as in *finis honorum* the highest degree of honour > **finely** *adv*

fine² *n* **1** a payment imposed as a penalty ▷ *vb* **fining, fined 2** to impose a fine on ▶ HISTORY Old French *fin*

fine art *n* **1** art produced chiefly to appeal to the sense of beauty **2** any of the fields in which such art is produced, such as painting, sculpture, and engraving

fine-drawn *adj* **1** (of arguments or distinctions) subtle **2** (of wire) drawn out until very fine

finery *n* elaborate or showy decoration, esp. clothing and jewellery: *the actress dressed up in her finery*

finesse (fin-**ness**) *n* **1** elegant and delicate skill **2** subtlety and tact in handling difficult situations: *a lack of diplomatic finesse* **3** *Bridge, whist* an attempt to win a trick when opponents hold a high card in the suit led by playing a lower card ▷ *vb* **-nessing, -nessed 4** to bring about with finesse **5** *Bridge, whist* to play (a card) as a finesse ▶ HISTORY Old French

fine-tune *vb* **-tuning, -tuned** to make fine adjustments to (something) so that it works really well

finger *n* **1** one of the four long jointed parts of the hand **2** the part of a glove made to cover a finger **3** something that resembles a finger in shape or function **4** a quantity of liquid in a glass as deep as a finger is wide **5 get** or **pull one's finger out** *Brit & NZ, informal* to begin or speed up activity, esp. after initial delay **6 put one's finger on** to identify precisely **7 put the finger on** *informal* to inform on or identify, esp. for the police **8 twist around one's little finger** to have easy and complete influence over ▷ *vb* **9** to touch or manipulate with the fingers; handle **10** to use one's fingers in playing (a musical instrument) **11** *informal,*

chiefly US to identify as a criminal or suspect ▶ HISTORY Old English > **fingerless** *adj*

fingerboard *n* the long strip of hard wood on a violin, guitar, etc. upon which the strings are stopped by the fingers

finger bowl *n* a small bowl of water for rinsing the fingers at table during a meal, esp. at a formal dinner

fingering *n* **1** the technique of using one's fingers in playing a musical instrument **2** the numerals in a musical part indicating this

fingernail *n* a thin hard clear plate covering part of the upper surface of the end of each finger

fingerprint *n* **1** an impression of the pattern of ridges on the inner surface of the end of each finger and thumb ▷ *vb* **2** to take an inked impression of the fingerprints of (a person) **3** to take a sample of the DNA of (a person)

fingerstall *n* a protective covering for a finger

fingertip *n* **1** the end of a finger **2 have at one's fingertips** to know thoroughly

finicky *or* **finicking** *adj* **1** extremely fussy **2** overelaborate or ornate: *finicky designer patterns* ▶ HISTORY earlier *finical*, from FINE¹

finis *n* the end: used at the end of books ▶ HISTORY Latin

finish *vb* **1** to bring to an end; conclude or stop **2** to be at or come to the end; use up **3** to bring to a desired or complete condition **4** to put a particular surface texture on (wood, cloth, or metal) **5 finish off a** to complete by doing the last part of: *he finished off his thesis last week* **b** to destroy or defeat completely: *he finished off McIlroy at the 16th hole* **6 finish with** to end a relationship with (someone) ▷ *n* **7** the final stage or part; end **8** death or absolute defeat **9** the surface texture of wood, cloth, or metal **10** a thing or event that completes ▶ HISTORY Latin *finire*

finishing school *n* a private school for girls that teaches social skills and polite behaviour

finite (**fine**-ite) *adj* **1** having limits in size, space, or time: *finite supplies of fossil fuels* **2** *maths, logic* having a countable number of elements **3** *grammar* denoting any form of a verb inflected for person, number, and tense ▶ HISTORY Latin *finitus* limited

finite verb *n* *grammar* a verb in an inflected form, reflecting the subject, number, and tense, as opposed to an infinitive or participle

Finn *n* a person from Finland

Finnish *adj* **1** of Finland ▷ *n* **2** the language of Finland

fiord (fee-**ord**) *n* same as **fjord**

fipple flute *n* an end-blown flute with a plug (**fipple**) at the mouthpiece, such as the recorder or flageolet

fir *n* a pyramid-shaped tree with needle-like leaves and erect cones ▶ HISTORY Old English *furh*

fire *n* **1** the state of combustion producing heat, flames, and often smoke **2** *Brit* burning coal or wood, esp. in a hearth to heat a room **3** a destructive uncontrolled burning that destroys building, crops, etc. **4** an electric or gas device for heating a room **5** the act of shooting weapons **6** passion and enthusiasm: *her questions brought new fire to the debate* **7 catch fire** to start burning **8 on fire a** burning **b** ardent or eager **9 open fire** to start firing a gun, artillery, etc. **10 play with fire** to be involved in something risky **11 set fire to** or **set on fire a** to ignite **b** to arouse or excite **12 under fire** being attacked, such as by weapons or by harsh criticism ▷ *vb* **firing, fired 13** to discharge (a firearm) **14** to detonate (an explosive device) **15** *informal* to dismiss from employment **16** to ask a lot of questions quickly in succession **17** *ceramics* to bake in a kiln to harden the clay **18** to kindle or be kindled **19** (of an internal-combustion engine) to produce an electrical spark which causes the fuel to burn and the engine to start **20** to provide with fuel **21** to arouse to strong emotion: *he fired his team mates with enthusiasm* ▶ **HISTORY** Old English *fȳr*

fire alarm *n* a device to give warning of fire

firearm *n* a weapon, such as a pistol, that fires bullets

fireball *n* **1** ball-shaped lightning **2** the hot ionized gas at the centre of a nuclear explosion **3** a large bright meteor **4** *slang* an energetic person

firebrand *n* a person who arouses passionate political feelings, often causing trouble

firebreak *n* a strip of open land in a forest to stop the advance of a fire

firebrick *n* a heat-resistant brick, used for lining furnaces, flues, and fireplaces

fire brigade *n* *Brit & Austral* an organized body of firefighters

firecracker *n* a firework which produces a loud bang

firedamp *n* *Brit, Austral & NZ* an explosive mixture of hydrocarbons, chiefly methane, formed in coal mines

fire drill *n* a rehearsal of procedures for escape from a fire

fire-eater *n* **1** a performer who pretends to swallow flaming rods **2** a very quarrelsome person

fire engine *n* a vehicle that carries firefighters and firefighting equipment to a fire

fire escape *n* a metal staircase or ladder on the outside of a building for escape in the event of fire

fire-extinguisher *n* a portable device for spraying water, foam, or powder to extinguish a fire

firefighter *n* a person whose job is to put out fires and rescue people endangered by them > **firefighting** *adj, n*

firefly *n, pl* **-flies** a beetle that glows in the dark

fireguard *n* a screen made of wire mesh put before an open fire to protect against sparks

fire hydrant *n* an outlet from a water main in the street, from which firefighters can draw water in an emergency

fire irons *pl n* a shovel, poker, and tongs for tending a domestic fire

fireman *n, pl* **-men 1** a man whose job is to put out fires and rescue people endangered by them

2 (on steam trains) the man who stokes the fire

fireplace *n* an open recess at the base of a chimney for a fire; hearth

fireplug *n* *chiefly US & NZ* same as **fire hydrant**

fire power *n* *mil* the amount of fire that can be delivered by a unit or weapon

fire raiser *n* *Brit* a person who deliberately sets fire to property > **fire raising** *n*

fire ship *n* *history* a ship loaded with explosives, set on fire and left to drift among an enemy's warships

fire station *n* a building where firefighting vehicles and equipment are stationed

firewall *n* *computers* a computer that prevents unauthorized access to a computer network from the internet

firework *n* a device containing chemicals that is ignited to produce coloured sparks and sometimes bangs

firing *n* **1** a discharge of a firearm **2** the process of baking ceramics in a kiln **3** something used as fuel

firing line *n* **1** *mil* the positions from which fire is delivered **2** the leading or most vulnerable position in an activity: *the manager is in the firing line after a string of bad results*

firing squad *n* a group of soldiers appointed to shoot a condemned criminal dead

firm¹ *adj* **1** not soft or yielding to a touch or pressure **2** securely in position **3** definitely established: *a firm agreement* **4** having determination or strength: *if you are firm and consistent she will come to see things your way* ▷ *adv* **5 stand firm** to refuse to give in ▷ *vb* **6** to make or become firm: *to firm up flabby thighs* ▶ **HISTORY** Latin *firmus* > **firmly** *adv* > **firmness** *n*

firm² *n* **1** a business company **2** *Brit, slang* a gang of criminals or football hooligans ▶ **HISTORY** Spanish *firma* signature

firmament *n* *literary* the sky or the heavens ▶ **HISTORY** Late Latin *firmamentum*

first *adj* **1** earliest in time or order **2** rated, graded, or ranked above all other levels: *the First Lord of the Admiralty* **3** denoting the lowest forward gear in a motor vehicle **4** *music* denoting the highest voice part in a chorus or one of the sections of an orchestra: *the first violin* ▷ *n* **5** the person or thing coming before all others **6** the beginning or outset **7** *education, chiefly Brit* an honours degree of the highest class **8** the lowest forward gear in a motor vehicle ▷ *adv* **9** before anything else: *I would advise you to try surgery first* **10** for the first time: *this story first came to public attention in January 1984* ▶ **HISTORY** Old English *fyrest*

first aid *n* immediate medical assistance given in an emergency

first class *n* **1** the class or grade of the best or highest value, rank, or quality ▷ *adj* **first-class 2** of the best or highest class or grade **3** excellent **4** denoting the most comfortable class of accommodation in a hotel, aircraft, or train **5** denoting mail that is handled faster than second-class mail ▷ *adv* **first-class 6** by first-class mail, transport, etc.

first-day cover *n philately* an envelope postmarked on the first day of the issue of its stamps

first-degree burn *n* a burn in which the skin surface is red and painful

first-foot *Scot & NZ n* **1** the first person to enter a household in the New Year ▷ *vb* **2** to visit (someone) as first-foot > **first-footing** *n*

first-hand *adj, adv* **1** (obtained) directly from the original source **2 at first hand** directly

firstly *adv* same as **first** (sense 9)

first mate *n* an officer second in command to the captain of a merchant ship

First Minister *n* **1** the chief minister of the Scottish Parliament **2** the chief minister of the Northern Ireland Assembly

first night *n* the first public performance of a play or other production

first offender *n* a person convicted of a criminal offence for the first time

first officer *n* same as **first mate**

first-past-the-post *adj politics* of a voting system in which the candidate with the most votes wins

first peoples *pl n* the indigenous population of a place

first person *n grammar* the form of the pronoun or verb used by the speaker to refer to himself or herself or to a group including himself or herself, as in *I see* or *we hope*

first-person narration *n literature* a type of storytelling in which the fictional or non-fictional narrator tells his or her own story in the first person

first-rate *adj* of the best quality; excellent

first reading *n Parliament* the introduction of a bill in a legislative assembly

First Secretary *n* the chief minister of the National Assembly for Wales

firth *n* a narrow inlet of the sea, esp. in Scotland ▶ HISTORY Old Norse *fjörthr* fjord

fiscal *adj* **1** of or relating to government finances, esp. tax revenues ▷ *n* **2** (in Scotland) same as **procurator fiscal** ▶ HISTORY Latin *fiscalis* concerning the state treasury

fish *n, pl* **fish** or **fishes 1** a cold-blooded animal with a backbone, gills, and usually fins and a skin covered in scales, that lives in water. *Related adjective:* **piscine 2** the flesh of fish used as food **3 cold fish** a person who shows little emotion **4 drink like a fish** to drink alcohol to excess **5 have other fish to fry** to have other more important concerns **6 like a fish out of water** ill at ease in an unfamiliar situation ▷ *vb* **7** to attempt to catch fish **8** to fish in (a particular area of water): *the first trawler to fish these waters* **9** to grope for and find with some difficulty: *he fished a cigarette from his pocket* **10 fish for** to seek (something) indirectly: *he was fishing for compliments* ▶ HISTORY Old English *fisc*

fisherman *n, pl* **-men** a person who fishes as a profession or for sport

fishery *n, pl* **-eries 1 a** the industry of catching, processing, and selling fish **b** a place where this is carried on **2** a place where fish are reared

fish-eye lens *n photog* a lens with a highly curved front that covers almost 180°

fishfinger *n* an oblong piece of fish coated in breadcrumbs

fishing *n* the occupation of catching fish

fishmeal *n* ground dried fish used as feed for farm animals or as a fertilizer

fishmonger *n chiefly Brit* a seller of fish

fishnet *n* an open mesh fabric resembling netting, sometimes used for tights or stockings

fishplate *n* a flat piece of metal joining one rail or beam to the next, esp. on railway tracks

fishtail *n* a nozzle having a long narrow slot at the top, placed over a Bunsen burner to produce a thin fanlike flame

fishwife *n, pl* **-wives** a coarse or bad-tempered woman with a loud voice

fishy *adj* **fishier, fishiest 1** of or suggestive of fish **2** *informal* suspicious or questionable: *something a bit fishy about his explanation* > **fishily** *adv*

fissile *adj* **1** capable of undergoing nuclear fission **2** tending to split

fission *n* **1** the act or process of splitting into parts **2** *biol* a form of asexual reproduction involving a division into two or more equal parts **3** the splitting of atomic nuclei with the release of a large amount of energy ▶ HISTORY Latin *fissio* a splitting > **fissionable** *adj*

fissure (fish-er) *n* any long narrow cleft or crack, esp. in a rock ▶ HISTORY Latin *fissus* split

fissure eruption *n geol* a volcanic eruption in which the lava comes out through a linear crack

fist *n* a hand with the fingers clenched into the palm ▶ HISTORY Old English *fȳst*

fisticuffs *pl n* fighting with the fists ▶ HISTORY probably from obsolete *fisty* with the fist + CUFF²

fistula (fist-yew-la) *n pathol* a long narrow ulcer ▶ HISTORY Latin: tube, ulcer

fit¹ *vb* **fitting, fitted 1** to be appropriate or suitable for **2** to be of the correct size or shape (for) **3** to adjust in order to make appropriate **4** to try clothes on and note any adjustments needed **5** to make competent or ready: *the experience helped to fit him for the task* **6** to correspond with the facts or circumstances: *this part doesn't fit in with the rest of his theory* ▷ *adj* **fitter, fittest 7** appropriate **8** in good health **9** worthy or suitable: *houses fit for human habitation* ▷ *n* **10** the manner in which something fits: *the suit was an excellent fit* ▷ See also **fit in, fit out** ▶ HISTORY probably from Middle Dutch *vitten* > **fitly** *adv* > **fitness** *n*

fit² *n* **1** a sudden attack or convulsion, such as an epileptic seizure **2** a sudden short burst or spell: *fits of laughter; a fit of pique* **3 in fits and starts** in spasmodic spells **4 have a fit** *informal* to become very angry ▶ HISTORY Old English *fitt* conflict

fitful *adj* occurring in irregular spells > **fitfully** *adv*

fit in *vb* **1** to give a place or time to (someone or something) **2** to belong or conform, esp. after adjustment

fitment *n* **1** an accessory attached to a machine **2** *chiefly Brit* a detachable part of the furnishings of a room

fit out *vb* to equip: *he started to fit out a ship in secret*

fitted *adj* **1** designed for excellent fit: *a fitted suit* **2** (of a carpet) covering a floor completely **3 a** (of furniture) built to fit a particular space **b** (of a kitchen, bathroom, etc.) having equipment and furniture built or selected to suit the measurements of the room **4** (of sheets) having ends that are elasticated to fit tightly over a mattress

fitter *n* **1** a person who is skilled in the installation and adjustment of machinery **2** a person who fits garments

fitting *adj* **1** appropriate or proper ▷ *n* **2** an accessory or part **3** the trying-on of clothes so that they can be adjusted to fit **4 fittings** furnishings or accessories in a building ▷ **fittingly** *adv*

five *n* **1** the cardinal number that is the sum of one and four **2** a numeral, 5 or V, representing this number **3** something representing or consisting of five units ▷ *adj* **4** amounting to five: *five years* ▷ See also **fives** ▶ HISTORY Old English *fīf*

five-eighth *n Austral & NZ* a rugby player positioned between the halfbacks and three-quarters

fivefold *adj* **1** having five times as many or as much **2** composed of five parts ▷ *adv* **3** by five times as many or as much

fiver *n Brit, Austral & NZ, informal* a five-pound or five-dollar note

fives *n* a ball game similar to squash but played with bats or the hands

fix *vb* **1** to make or become firm, stable, or secure **2** to repair **3** to attach or place permanently: *fix the mirror to the wall* **4** to settle definitely or decide upon: *the meeting is fixed for the 12th* **5** to direct (the eyes, etc.) steadily: *she fixed her eyes upon the jewels* **6** *informal* to unfairly influence the outcome of: *the fight was fixed by the promoter* **7** *informal* to put a stop to the activities of (someone): *the Party was determined to fix him* **8** *informal* to prepare: *let me fix you a drink* **9** *photog* to treat (a film, plate, or paper) with fixer to make the image permanent **10** to convert (atmospheric nitrogen) into nitrogen compounds **11** *slang* to inject a narcotic drug ▷ *n* **12** *informal* a difficult situation **13** the reckoning of a navigational position of a ship by radar, etc. **14** *slang* an injection of a narcotic ▷ See also **fix up** ▶ HISTORY Latin *fixus* fixed

fixation *n* **1** an obsessive interest in something **2** *psychol* a strong attachment of a person to another person or an object in early life **3** *chem* the conversion of nitrogen in the air into a compound, esp. a fertilizer ▷ **fixated** *adj*

fixative *n* **1** a fluid sprayed over drawings to prevent smudging **2** a liquid used to hold objects, esp. dentures, in place **3** a substance added to a perfume to make it less volatile

fixed *adj* **1** attached or placed so as to be immovable **2** stable: *fixed rates* **3** unchanging and appearing artificial: *a fixed smile* **4** established as to relative position: *a fixed point* **5** always at the same time **6** (of ideas) firmly maintained **7** *informal* equipped or provided for, esp. with money or possessions **8** *informal* illegally arranged: *a fixed trial* ▷ **fixedly** (**fix**-id-lee) *adv*

fixed cost *n econ* a cost of production that does not vary with output. Compare **variable cost**

fixed star *n* an extremely distant star that appears to be almost stationary

fixer *n* **1** *photog* a solution used to make an image permanent **2** *slang* a person who makes arrangements, esp. illegally

fixture *n* **1** an object firmly fixed in place, esp. a household appliance **2** something or someone regarded as fixed in a particular place or position: *the diplomatic wife seems a fixture of international politics* **3 a** a sports match **b** the date of it

fix up *vb* **1** to arrange **2 fix up with** to provide with: *can you fix me up with tickets?*

fizz *vb* **1** to make a hissing or bubbling sound **2** (of a drink) to produce bubbles of carbon dioxide ▷ *n* **3** a hissing or bubbling sound **4** releasing of small bubbles of gas by a liquid **5** any effervescent drink ▶ HISTORY imitative ▷ **fizzy** *adj* ▷ **fizziness** *n*

fizzle *vb* **-zling, -zled** **1** to make a hissing or bubbling sound **2 fizzle out** *informal* to fail or die out, esp. after a promising start ▶ HISTORY probably from obsolete *fist* to break wind

fjord (fee-**ord**) *n* a long narrow inlet of the sea between high cliffs, esp. in Norway ▶ HISTORY Norwegian, from Old Norse *fjörthr*

FL Florida

flab *n* unsightly or unwanted fat on the body ▶ HISTORY from *flabby*

flabbergasted *adj informal* completely astonished ▶ HISTORY origin unknown

flabby *adj* **-bier, -biest** **1** having flabby flesh **2** loose or limp **3** weak and lacking purpose: *flabby hesitant leaders* ▶ HISTORY alteration of *flappy*, from *flap* ▷ **flabbiness** *n*

flaccid (**fla**-sid) *adj* soft and limp ▶ HISTORY Latin *flaccidus* ▷ **flaccidity** *n*

flag¹ *n* **1** a piece of cloth often attached to a pole, used as an emblem or for signalling **2** a code inserted into a computer file to distinguish certain information ▷ *vb* **flagging, flagged** **3** to mark with a tag or sticker **4** *NZ* to give up an activity **5 flag down** to signal (a vehicle) to stop ▶ HISTORY origin unknown

flag² *n* same as **iris** (sense 2) ▶ HISTORY origin unknown

flag³ *vb* **flagging, flagged** **1** to lose enthusiasm or energy **2** to become limp ▶ HISTORY origin unknown ▷ **flagging** *adj*

flag⁴ *n* short for **flagstone**

flag day *n Brit* a day on which money is collected by a charity and small stickers are given to contributors

315

flagellate vb (**flaj**-a-late) **-lating, -lated 1** to whip, esp. in religious penance ▷ adj (**flaj**-a-lit) **2** possessing one or more flagella **3** like a whip ▶ HISTORY Latin *flagellare* to whip > **flagellation** n

flagellum (flaj-**jell**-lum) n, pl **-la** (-la) or **-lums 1** biol a long whiplike outgrowth that acts as an organ of movement **2** bot a long thin shoot or runner ▶ HISTORY Latin: a little whip

flageolet (flaj-a-**let**) n a high-pitched musical instrument of the recorder family ▶ HISTORY French

flag fall n Austral the minimum charge for hiring a taxi, to which the rate per kilometre is added

flagged adj paved with flagstones

flag of convenience n a foreign flag flown by a ship registered in that country to gain financial or legal advantage

flag of truce n a white flag indicating an invitation to an enemy to negotiate

flagon n **1** a large bottle of wine, cider, etc. **2** a narrow-necked jug for containing liquids ▶ HISTORY Late Latin *flasco* flask

flagpole or **flagstaff** n a pole on which a flag is flown

flagrant (**flay**-grant) adj openly outrageous: *flagrant violation of international law* ▶ HISTORY Latin *flagrare* to blaze, burn > **flagrancy** n

flagship n **1** a ship aboard which the commander of a fleet is quartered **2** the most important ship belonging to a shipping company **3** the most modern or impressive product or asset of an organization: *the company has opened its own flagship store*

flagstone n a flat slab of hard stone for paving ▶ HISTORY Old Norse *flaga* slab

flag up vb to bring (something) to someone's attention

flail n **1** a tool formerly used for threshing grain by hand ▷ vb **2** to wave about wildly: *arms flailing, they staggered about* **3** to beat with or as if with a flail ▶ HISTORY Latin *flagellum* whip

flair n **1** natural ability **2** originality and stylishness ▶ HISTORY French

flak n **1** anti-aircraft fire **2** severe criticism: *most of the flak was directed at the umpire*

- **WORD HISTORY**
- 'Flak' is formed from the first letters 'fl-a-k' of
- the component parts of the German word for
- an anti-aircraft gun, *Fliegerabwehrkanone*,
- literally an 'aircraft defence gun'.

flake¹ n **1** a small thin piece chipped off an object or substance **2** a small piece: *flakes of snow* **3** slang an eccentric or unreliable person ▷ vb **flaking, flaked 4** to peel or cause to peel off in flakes **5** to break into small thin pieces: *bake for 30 minutes, or until the fish is firm and flakes easily* ▶ HISTORY from Old Norse > **flaky** adj

flake² n (in Australia) the commercial name for the meat of the gummy shark

flake out vb informal to collapse or fall asleep from exhaustion

flak jacket n a reinforced sleeveless jacket for protection against gunfire or shrapnel

flambé (**flahm**-bay) vb **flambéeing, flambéed** to cook or serve (food) in flaming brandy ▶ HISTORY French

flamboyant adj **1** behaving in a very noticeable, extravagant way: *a flamboyant jazz pianist* **2** very bright and showy ▶ HISTORY French: flaming > **flamboyance** n

flame n **1** a hot luminous body of burning gas coming in flickering streams from burning material **2 flames** the state of burning: *half the building was in flames* **3** literary intense passion: *the flame of love* **4** informal an abusive message sent by e-mail ▷ vb **flaming, flamed 5** to burn brightly **6** written to become red or fiery: *colour flamed in Sally's cheeks* **7** to become angry or excited **8** informal to send an abusive message by e-mail ▶ HISTORY Latin *flamma*

flamenco n, pl **-cos 1** a rhythmic Spanish dance accompanied by a guitar and vocalist **2** music for this dance ▶ HISTORY Spanish

flame-thrower n a weapon that ejects a stream or spray of burning fluid

flamingo n, pl **-gos** or **-goes** a large pink wading bird with a long neck and legs ▶ HISTORY Portuguese *flamengo*

flammable adj easily set on fire; inflammable > **flammability** n

flan n an open sweet or savoury tart ▶ HISTORY French

flange n a projecting collar or rim on an object for strengthening it or for attaching it to another object ▶ HISTORY origin unknown

flank n **1** the side of a man or animal between the ribs and the hip **2** a cut of beef from the flank **3** the side of a naval or military formation ▷ vb **4** to be positioned at the side of (a person or thing) ▶ HISTORY Old French *flanc*

flannel n **1** Brit a small piece of towelling cloth used to wash the face **2** a soft light woollen fabric used for clothing **3 flannels** trousers made of flannel **4** Brit, informal evasive talk that avoids giving any commitment or direct answer ▷ vb **-nelling, -nelled** or US **-neling, -neled 5** Brit, informal to flatter or talk evasively ▶ HISTORY Welsh *gwlân* wool

flannelette n a cotton imitation of flannel, used to make sheets and nightdresses

flap vb **flapping, flapped 1** to move backwards and forwards or up and down, like a bird's wings in flight ▷ n **2** the action of or noise made by flapping **3** a piece of material attached at one edge and usually used to cover an opening, such as on a pocket **4** a hinged section of an aircraft wing that is raised or lowered to control the aircraft's speed **5** informal a state of panic or agitation ▶ HISTORY probably imitative

flapjack n **1** Brit a chewy biscuit made with rolled oats **2** NZ a small thick pancake

flapper n (in the 1920s) a lively young woman who dressed and behaved unconventionally

flare vb **flaring, flared 1** to burn with an unsteady or sudden bright flame **2** (of temper, violence, or trouble) to break out suddenly **3** to spread outwards from a narrow to a wider shape ▷ *n* **4** an unsteady flame **5** a sudden burst of flame **6 a** a blaze of light used to illuminate, signal distress, alert, etc. **b** the device producing such a blaze **7 flares** trousers with legs that flare out at the bottom ▶ HISTORY origin unknown > **flared** *adj*

flash *n* **1** a sudden short blaze of intense light or flame **2** a sudden occurrence of a particular emotion or experience: *a flash of anger* **3** a very brief time: *in a flash he was inside and locked the door behind him* **4** a short unscheduled news announcement **5** *Brit & Austral* an emblem on a uniform or vehicle to identify its military formation **6** *photog* short for **flashlight 7 flash in the pan** a project, person, etc. that enjoys only short-lived success ▷ *adj* **8** *informal* ostentatious or vulgar **9** brief and rapid: *a flash fire* ▷ *vb* **10** to burst or cause to burst suddenly into flame **11** to shine with a bright light suddenly or repeatedly **12** to move very fast **13** *written* to come rapidly (into the mind or vision) **14 a** to signal very fast: *a warning was flashed onto a computer screen in the cockpit* **b** to signal by use of a light, such as car headlights **15** *informal* to display in a boastful and extravagant way: *flashing banknotes around* **16** *informal* to show briefly **17** *Brit, slang* to expose oneself indecently ▶ HISTORY origin unknown > **flasher** *n*

flashback *n* a scene in a book, play, or film that shows earlier events

flashbulb *n* *photog* a small light bulb that produces a bright flash of light

flash drive *n* a portable computer hard drive and data storage device. Also: **memory stick**

flash flood *n* a sudden short-lived flood

flashing *n* a weatherproof material used to cover the joins in a roof

flashlight *n* **1** *photog* the brief bright light emitted by a flashbulb **2** *chiefly US & Canad* a torch

flash point *n* **1** a critical time beyond which a situation will inevitably erupt into violence **2** the lowest temperature at which the vapour above a liquid can be ignited

flask *n* **1** same as **vacuum flask 2** a small flat container for alcoholic drink designed to be carried in a pocket **3** a bottle with a narrow neck, esp. used in a laboratory ▶ HISTORY Medieval Latin *flasca*, *flasco*

flat¹ *adj* **flatter, flattest 1** horizontal or level: *roofs are now flat instead of slanted* **2** even or smooth: *a flat surface* **3** lying stretched out at full length **4** (of a tyre) deflated **5** (of shoes) having an unraised heel **6** without qualification; total: *a flat rejection* **7** fixed: *a flat rate* **8** unexciting: *a picture curiously flat in tone* **9** without variation or emotion: *a flat voice* **10** (of drinks) no longer fizzy **11** (of a battery) fully discharged **12** (of paint) without gloss **13** *music* **a** denoting a note that has been lowered in pitch by one chromatic semitone: *B flat* **b** (of an instrument, voice, etc.) out of tune by being too low in pitch ▷ *adv* **14** in or into a level or

flat position: *the boat was knocked almost flat* **15** completely: *flat broke* **16** exactly: *in three months flat* **17** *music* **a** lower than a standard pitch **b** too low in pitch: *singing flat* **18 fall flat (on one's face)** to fail to achieve a desired effect **19 flat out** *informal* with maximum speed and effort ▷ *n* **20** a flat object or part **21** low-lying land, esp. a marsh **22** a mud bank exposed at low tide **23** *music* **a** an accidental that lowers the pitch of a note by one semitone. Symbol: ♭ **b** a note affected by this accidental **24** *theatre* a wooden frame covered with painted canvas, used to form part of a stage setting **25** a punctured car tyre **26 the flat** *chiefly Brit* the season of flat racing ▶ HISTORY Old Norse *flatr* > **flatly** *adv*

flat² *n* **1** a set of rooms forming a home entirely on one floor of a building ▷ *vb* **flatting, flatted 2** *Austral & NZ* to share a flat **3 go flatting** *Austral & NZ* to leave home to share a flat ▶ HISTORY Old English *flett* floor, hall, house

flat character *n* *literature* a character in a story who lacks psychological depth, often representing a single quality such as honesty or deceit, without changing or developing as the story progresses

flatfish *n, pl* **-fish** or **-fishes** a sea fish, such as the sole, which has a flat body with both eyes on the uppermost side

flat-footed *adj* **1** having less than the usual degree of arching in the insteps of the feet **2** *informal* clumsy or insensitive

flathead *n* a common Australian flatfish

flatlet *n* *Brit, Austral & S African* a small flat

flatmate *n* a person with whom one shares a flat

flat-pack *adj* (of furniture, etc.) supplied in pieces in a flat box for assembly by the buyer

flat racing *n* the racing of horses on racecourses without jumps

flatscreen *n* a television set or computer monitor with a flat screen

flat spin *n* **1** an aircraft spin in which the longitudinal axis is more nearly horizontal than vertical **2** *informal* a state of confusion

flatten *vb* **1** to make or become flat or flatter **2** *informal* **a** to knock down or injure **b** to crush or subdue

flatter *vb* **1** to praise insincerely, esp. in order to win favour **2** to show to advantage: *she wore a simple green cotton dress which she knew flattered her* **3** to make (a person) appear more attractive than in reality: *a portrait that flattered him* **4** to cater to the vanity of (a person): *I was flattered by her praise* **5 flatter oneself** to believe, perhaps mistakenly, something good about oneself ▶ HISTORY Old French *flater* to lick, fawn upon > **flatterer** *n*

flattery *n, pl* **-teries** excessive or insincere praise

flattie *n* *NZ & S African, informal* flat tyre

flatulent *adj* suffering from or caused by too much gas in the stomach or intestines ▶ HISTORY Latin *flatus* blowing > **flatulence** *n*

flatworm *n* a worm, such as a tapeworm, with a flattened body

flaunt *vb* to display (oneself or one's possessions)

arrogantly: *flaunting his new car* ▶ HISTORY origin unknown

flautist (**flaw**-tist) *n* a flute player ▶ HISTORY Italian *flautista*

flavour *or US* **flavor** *n* **1** taste perceived in food or liquid in the mouth **2** a distinctive quality or atmosphere: *Rome has its own particular flavour* ▷ *vb* **3** to give flavour to: *salmon flavoured with dill* ▶ HISTORY Old French *flaour* > **flavourless** *or US* **flavorless** *adj*

flavouring *or US* **flavoring** *n* a substance used to flavour food

flaw *n* **1** an imperfection or blemish **2** a mistake in something that makes it invalid: *a flaw in the system* ▶ HISTORY probably from Old Norse *flaga* stone slab > **flawed** *adj* > **flawless** *adj*

flax *n* **1** a plant that has blue flowers and is cultivated for its seeds and the fibres of its stems **2** its fibres, made into linen fabrics **3** *NZ* a perennial plant producing a fibre that is used by Māoris for decorative work and weaving baskets ▶ HISTORY Old English *fleax*

flaxen *adj* **1** of flax **2** (of hair) pale yellow

flay *vb* **1** to strip off the skin of, esp. by whipping **2** to criticize severely ▶ HISTORY Old English *flēan*

flea *n* **1** a small wingless jumping insect feeding on the blood of mammals and birds **2** **flea in one's ear** *informal* a sharp rebuke ▶ HISTORY Old English *flēah*

fleabite *n* **1** the bite of a flea **2** a slight annoyance or discomfort

flea-bitten *adj* **1** bitten by or infested with fleas **2** *informal* shabby or decrepit: *a flea-bitten hotel*

flea market *n* an open-air market selling cheap second-hand goods

fleapit *n* *informal* a shabby cinema or theatre

fleck *n* **1** a small marking or streak **2** a small or tiny piece of something: *a fleck of grit* ▷ *vb* **3** to speckle: *a grey suit flecked with white* ▶ HISTORY probably from Old Norse *flekkr* stain, spot

fled *vb* the past of **flee**

fledged *adj* **1** (of young birds) able to fly **2** qualified and competent: *a fully fledged doctor* ▶ HISTORY Old English *-flycge*, as in *unflycge* unfledged

fledgling *or* **fledgeling** *n* **1** a young bird that has grown feathers ▷ *adj* **2** new or inexperienced: *Poland's fledgling market economy*

flee *vb* *written* **fleeing**, **fled** **1** to run away from (a place, danger, etc.) **2** to run or move quickly ▶ HISTORY Old English *flēon*

fleece *n* **1** the coat of wool that covers a sheep **2** the wool removed from a sheep at one shearing **3** sheepskin or a fabric with soft pile, used as a lining for coats, etc. **4** a warm outdoor jacket or top made from a polyester fabric with a brushed nap **5** *Brit* a jacket or top made of this fabric ▷ *vb* **fleecing, fleeced** **6** to defraud or overcharge **7** same as **shear** (sense 1) ▶ HISTORY Old English *flēos*

fleecy *adj* **1** of or resembling fleece ▷ *n, pl* **-ies** **2** *NZ, informal* a person who collects fleeces after shearing and prepares them for baling

fleet¹ *n* **1** a number of warships organized as a tactical unit **2** all the ships of a nation or company: *the British merchant fleet* **3** a number of vehicles under the same ownership ▶ HISTORY Old English *flēot* ship, flowing water

fleet² *adj* rapid in movement ▶ HISTORY probably from Old English *flēotan* to float

fleet chief petty officer *n* a noncommissioned officer in a navy

fleeting *adj* rapid and soon passing: *a fleeting moment* > **fleetingly** *adv*

Fleet Street *n* **1** the street in London where many newspaper offices were formerly situated **2** British national newspapers collectively: *Fleet Street's obsession with the Royal Family*

Fleming *n* a person from Flanders or Flemish-speaking Belgium

Fleming's rules *pl n* *physics* two rules, assigning significance to the thumb and first and second fingers of each hand, used as mnemonics for the relationship between the directions of current flow, motion, and magnetic field in electromagnetic induction ▶ HISTORY named after Sir John Ambrose *Fleming*, English electrical engineer who devised them

Flemish *adj* **1** of Flanders, in Belgium ▷ *n* **2** one of the two official languages of Belgium ▷ *pl n* **3** **the Flemish** people from Flanders or Flemish-speaking Belgium

flesh *n* **1** the soft part of the body of an animal or human, esp. muscular tissue **2** *informal* excess weight; fat **3** the meat of animals as opposed to that of fish or, sometimes, fowl **4** the thick soft part of a fruit or vegetable **5** **the flesh** sensuality: *pleasures of the flesh*. Related adjective: **carnal** **6** **flesh and blood** human beings or human nature: *it is almost more than flesh and blood can bear* **7** **in the flesh** in person; actually present **8** **one's own flesh and blood** one's own family **9** **press the flesh** *informal* to shake hands with large numbers of people, esp. in political campaigning ▶ HISTORY Old English *flǣsc*

flesh-coloured *adj* yellowish-pink

fleshly *adj* **-lier, -liest** **1** relating to sensuality **2** worldly as opposed to spiritual

flesh wound *n* a wound affecting superficial tissues

fleshy *adj* **fleshier, fleshiest** **1** plump **2** resembling flesh **3** *bot* (of some fruits) thick and pulpy > **fleshiness** *n*

fleur-de-lys *or* **fleur-de-lis** (**flur**-de-**lee**) *n, pl* **fleurs-de-lys** *or* **fleurs-de-lis** (**flur**-de-**leez**) a representation of a lily with three distinct petals ▶ HISTORY Old French *flor de lis* lily flower

flew *vb* the past tense of **fly¹**

flews *pl n* the fleshy hanging upper lip of a bloodhound or similar dog ▶ HISTORY origin unknown

flex *n* **1** *Brit & Austral* a flexible insulated electric cable: *a coiled kettle flex* ▷ *vb* **2** to bend **3** to bend and stretch (a muscle) ▶ HISTORY Latin *flexus* bent, winding

flexible *adj* **1** able to be bent easily without breaking **2** adaptable to changing circumstances: *flexible working arrangements* > **flexibility** *n* > **flexibly** *adv*

flexion *n physiol* the act of bending a joint or limb

flexitime *n* a system permitting flexibility of working hours at the beginning or end of the day, provided an agreed total is worked

flick *vb* **1** to touch or move with the finger or hand in a quick jerky movement **2** to move with a short sudden movement, often repeatedly: *the windscreen wipers flicked back and forth* **3 flick through** to look at (a book or magazine) quickly or idly ▷ *n* **4** a tap or quick stroke ▶ **HISTORY** imitative

flicker *vb* **1** to give out an unsteady or irregular light **2** to move quickly to and fro ▷ *n* **3** an unsteady or brief light **4** a brief or faint indication of emotion: *a flicker of fear in his voice* ▶ **HISTORY** Old English *flicorian*

flick knife *n* a knife with a retractable blade that springs out when a button is pressed

flier *n* same as **flyer**

flight[1] *n* **1** a journey by aircraft **2** the act or manner of flying **3** a group of flying birds or aircraft **4** an aircraft flying on a scheduled journey **5** a set of stairs between one landing and the next **6 flight of fancy** an idea that is imaginative but not practical **7** small plastic or feather fins at the rear of an arrow or dart which make it stable in flight ▶ **HISTORY** Old English *flyht*

flight[2] *n* **1** the act of running away, esp. from danger **2 put to flight** to cause to run away **3 take (to) flight** to run away ▶ **HISTORY** Old English *flyht* (unattested)

flight attendant *n* a person who attends to the needs of passengers on a commercial flight

flight deck *n* **1** the crew compartment in an airliner **2** the upper deck of an aircraft carrier from which aircraft take off

flightless *adj* (of certain birds and insects) unable to fly

flight lieutenant *n* a junior commissioned officer in an air force

flight recorder *n* an electronic device in an aircraft for storing information concerning its performance in flight. It is often used to determine the cause of a crash. Also called: **black box**

flight sergeant *n* a noncommissioned officer in an air force

flighty *adj* **flightier, flightiest** frivolous and not very reliable or serious > **flightiness** *n*

flimsy *adj* **-sier, -siest** **1** not strong or substantial **2** light and thin: *a flimsy gauze mask* **3** not very convincing: *flimsy evidence* ▶ **HISTORY** origin unknown > **flimsily** *adv* > **flimsiness** *n*

flinch *vb* **1** to draw back suddenly from pain or something unpleasant **2 flinch from** to avoid: *I wouldn't flinch from saying that to his face* ▶ **HISTORY** Old French *flenchir*

fling *vb* **flinging, flung** **1** to throw with force **2** to move or go hurriedly or violently: *she flung her arms open wide* **3** to put or send without warning: *they used to fling me in jail* **4** to put (something) somewhere hurriedly or carelessly **5 fling oneself into** to apply oneself with enthusiasm to ▷ *n* **6** a short spell of self-indulgent enjoyment **7** a brief romantic relationship **8** a vigorous Scottish country dance: *a Highland fling* ▶ **HISTORY** from Old Norse

flint *n* **1** a very hard stone that produces sparks when struck with steel **2** any piece of flint, esp. one used as a primitive tool **3** a small piece of an iron alloy, used in cigarette lighters ▶ **HISTORY** Old English > **flinty** *adj*

flintlock *n* an obsolete gun in which the powder was lit by a spark produced by a flint

flip *vb* **flipping, flipped** **1** to throw (something light or small) carelessly **2** to turn (something) over: *flip the fish on its back* **3** to turn (a device or machine) on or off by quickly pressing a switch **4** to throw (an object such as a coin) so that it turns in the air **5 flip through** to look at (a book or magazine) idly Also: **flip one's lid** *slang* to fly into an emotional outburst ▷ *n* **7** a snap or tap, usually with the fingers ▷ *adj* **8** *informal* flippant or pert ▶ **HISTORY** probably imitative

flipchart *n* a large pad of paper mounted on a stand, used in giving lectures, etc.

flip-flop *n Brit & S African* a rubber-soled sandal attached to the foot by a thong between the big toe and the next toe ▶ **HISTORY** reduplication of *flip*

flippant *adj* treating serious matters with inappropriate light-heartedness or lack of respect ▶ **HISTORY** probably from *flip* > **flippancy** *n*

flipper *n* **1** the flat broad limb of seals, whales, and other aquatic animals specialized for swimming **2** either of a pair of rubber paddle-like devices worn on the feet as an aid in swimming

flirt *vb* **1** to behave as if attracted to someone **2 flirt with** to consider lightly; toy with: *he had often flirted with the idea of emigrating* ▷ *n* **3** a person who flirts ▶ **HISTORY** origin unknown > **flirtation** *n* > **flirtatious** *adj*

flit *vb* **flitting, flitted** **1** to fly or move along rapidly and lightly **2** to pass quickly: *a shadow flitted across his face* **3** *Scot & N English dialect* to move house **4** *Brit, informal* to leave hurriedly and stealthily in order to avoid debts ▷ *n* **5** the act of flitting **6 do a flit** *NZ, informal* to abandon rented accommodation ▶ **HISTORY** Old Norse *flytja* to carry

float *vb* **1** to rest on the surface of a fluid without sinking **2** to move lightly or freely across a surface or through air or water **3** to move about aimlessly, esp. in the mind: *a pleasant image floated into his mind* **4 a** to launch (a commercial enterprise, etc.) **b** to offer for sale on the stock market **5** *finance* to allow (a currency) to fluctuate against other currencies ▷ *n* **6** an inflatable object that helps people learning to swim stay afloat **7** *angling* an indicator attached to a baited line that moves when a fish bites **8** a long rigid boatlike structure, of which there are usually two, attached to an aircraft instead of wheels so that it can land on and take off from water **9** a decorated lorry that is part of a procession **10** a small delivery vehicle: *milk floats* **11** *Austral & NZ* a vehicle for transporting horses **12** a sum of money used to cover small expenses or provide change **13** the hollow floating ball of a ball cock ▶ **HISTORY** Old English *flotian*

floatation *n* same as **flotation**

floating *adj* **1** (of a population) moving about; not settled **2** (of an organ or part) displaced or abnormally movable: *a floating kidney* **3** (of a voter) not committed to one party **4** *finance* **a** (of capital) available for current use **b** (of a currency) free to fluctuate against other currencies

floating rib *n* a lower rib not attached to the breastbone

floats *pl n theatre* footlights

flocculent *adj* like tufts of wool ▶ **HISTORY** Latin *floccus* tuft of wool > **flocculence** *n*

flock¹ *n* **1** a group of animals of one kind, esp. sheep or birds **2** a large number of people **3** a congregation of Christians regarded as the responsibility of a member of the clergy ▷ *vb* **4** to gather together or move in large numbers ▶ **HISTORY** Old English *flocc*

flock² *n* **1** waste from fabrics such as cotton or wool, used for stuffing mattresses ▷ *adj* **2** (of wallpaper) having a velvety raised pattern ▶ **HISTORY** Latin *floccus* tuft of wool

floe *n* a sheet of floating ice ▶ **HISTORY** probably from Norwegian *flo* slab, layer

flog *vb* **flogging, flogged 1** to beat harshly, esp. with a whip or stick **2** (sometimes foll. by *off*) *informal* to sell **3** *Austral & NZ, informal* to steal **4 flog a dead horse** *chiefly Brit* to waste one's energy ▶ **HISTORY** probably from Latin *flagellare* > **flogging** *n*

flood *n* **1** an overflowing of water on an area that is normally dry **2** a large amount of water **3** the rising of the tide from low to high water. *Related adjectives:* **diluvial, diluvian 4** a large amount: *a flood of letters* **5** *theatre* short for **floodlight** ▷ *vb* **6** to cover or become covered with water **7** to fill to overflowing **8** to put a large number of goods on sale on (a market) at the same time, often at a cheap price: *the US was flooded with cheap televisions* **9** to flow or surge: *the memories flooded back* **10** to supply excess petrol to (a petrol engine) so that it cannot work properly **11** to bleed profusely from the womb ▶ **HISTORY** Old English *flōd* > **flooding** *n*

Flood *n* **the Flood** *Old Testament* the flood from which Noah and his family and livestock were saved in the ark (Genesis 7–8)

flood bank *n civil engineering* an embankment built beside a river to prevent flooding

floodgate *n* **1** a gate used to control the flow of water **2 floodgates** controls against an outpouring of emotion: *it had opened the floodgates of her anxiety*

flood irrigation *n agriculture* a method of irrigation in which the entire soil surface of a given area is flooded with water following the opening of channels or pipes

floodlight *n* **1** a lamp that casts a broad intense light, used in the theatre or to illuminate sports grounds or the exterior of buildings ▷ *vb* **-lighting, -lit 2** to illuminate by floodlight

flood plain *n geog* a flat area beside a river that becomes flooded when the river overflows its banks

floodwall *n* a wall built as a defence against floods

floor *n* **1** the lower surface of a room **2** a storey of a building **3** a flat bottom surface: *the ocean floor* **4** that part of a legislative hall in which debate is conducted **5** a minimum limit: *a wages floor for low-paid employees* **6 have the floor** to have the right to speak in a debate or discussion ▷ *vb* **7** to knock to the ground **8** *informal* to disconcert or defeat ▶ **HISTORY** Old English *flōr*

floorboard *n* one of the boards forming a floor

floored *adj* covered with a floor: *an attic floored with pine planks*

flooring *n* **1** the material used in making a floor: *pine flooring* **2** a floor

floor plan *n* a scale drawing of the arrangement of rooms on one floor of a building

floor show *n* a series of entertainments, such as singing and dancing, in a nightclub

floozy, floozie *or* **floosie** *n, pl* **-zies** *or* **-sies** *slang, old-fashioned* a woman considered to be disreputable or immoral ▶ **HISTORY** origin unknown

flop *vb* **flopping, flopped 1** to bend, fall, or collapse loosely or carelessly **2** *informal* to fail: *his first big film flopped* **3** to fall or move with a sudden noise ▷ *n* **4** *informal* a complete failure **5** the act of flopping ▶ **HISTORY** variant of *flap* > **floppy** *adj*

flora *n* all the plant life of a given place or time ▶ **HISTORY** *Flora*, Roman goddess of flowers

floral *adj* decorated with or consisting of flowers or patterns of flowers

Florentine *adj* **1** of Florence, a city in central Italy ▷ *n* **2** a person from Florence

floret (**flaw**-ret) *n* a small flower forming part of a composite flower head ▶ **HISTORY** Old French *florete*

floribunda *n* a type of rose whose flowers grow in large clusters ▶ **HISTORY** New Latin *floribundus* flowering freely

florid *adj* **1** having a red or flushed complexion **2** very ornate and extravagant: *florid prose* ▶ **HISTORY** Latin *floridus* blooming

florin *n* a former British, Australian, and New Zealand coin, equivalent to ten pence or twenty cents ▶ **HISTORY** Old Italian *fiorino* Florentine coin

florist *n* a person or shop selling flowers

floss *n* **1** fine silky fibres, such as those obtained from silkworm cocoons **2** See **dental floss** ▷ *vb* **3** to clean (between the teeth) with dental floss ▶ **HISTORY** probably from Old French *flosche* down > **flossy** *adj*

flotation *or* **floatation** *n* the launching or financing of a commercial enterprise by bond or share issues

flotilla n a small fleet or a fleet of small ships ▶ HISTORY Spanish *flota* fleet

flotsam n **1** floating wreckage from a ship **2 flotsam and jetsam a** odds and ends **b** Brit homeless or vagrant people ▶ HISTORY Anglo-French *floteson*

flounce¹ vb **flouncing, flounced 1** to move or go with emphatic movements ▷ n **2** the act of flouncing ▶ HISTORY Scandinavian

flounce² n an ornamental frill on a garment or tablecloth ▶ HISTORY Old French *froncir* to wrinkle

flounder¹ vb **1** to struggle to move or stay upright, esp. in water or mud **2** to behave or speak in an awkward, confused way ▶ HISTORY probably a blend of FOUNDER + BLUNDER

flounder² n, pl **-der** or **-ders** an edible flatfish ▶ HISTORY Scandinavian

flour n **1** a powder prepared by grinding grain, esp. wheat ▷ vb **2** to sprinkle (food or utensils) with flour ▶ HISTORY Middle English *flur* 'flower', i.e. best part > **floury** adj

flourish vb **1** to be active, successful, or widespread; prosper **2** to be at the peak of development **3** to wave (something) dramatically ▷ n **4** a dramatic waving or sweeping movement: *he created a flourish with an imaginary wand* **5** an ornamental curly line in writing **6** a fancy or extravagant action or part of something: *he took his tie off with a flourish* ▶ HISTORY Latin *florere* to flower > **flourishing** adj

flout (rhymes with **out**) vb to deliberately disobey (a rule, law, etc.) ▶ HISTORY probably from Middle English *flouten* to play the flute

flow vb **1** (of liquids) to move in a stream **2** (of blood, electricity, etc.) to circulate **3** to move steadily and smoothly: *a golf club with rich-looking cars flowing into it* **4** to be produced effortlessly: *words flowed from him in a steady stream* **5** to hang freely: *her hair loose and flowing down her back* **6** to be abundant: *at the buffet lunch, wine flowed like water* **7** (of tide water) to rise ▷ n **8** the act, rate, or manner of flowing: *the abundant flow of water through domestic sprinklers* **9** a continuous stream or discharge **10** the advancing of the tide ▶ HISTORY Old English *flōwan*

flow chart or **sheet** n a diagram showing a sequence of operations in an industrial process, computer program, etc.

flower n **1** the part of a plant that is, usually, brightly coloured, and quickly fades, producing seeds **2** a plant grown for its colourful flowers. *Related adjective:* **floral 3** the best or finest part: *in the flower of her youth* **4 in flower** with flowers open ▷ vb **5** to produce flowers; bloom **6** to reach full growth or maturity: *liberty only flowers in times of peace* ▶ HISTORY Latin *flos*

flowered adj decorated with flowers or a floral design

flowerpot n a pot in which plants are grown

flowery adj **1** decorated with flowers or floral patterns **2** (of language or style) containing elaborate literary expressions > **floweriness** n

flown vb the past participle of **fly¹**

fl. oz. fluid ounce(s)

flu n informal short for **influenza**

fluctuate vb **-ating, -ated** to change frequently and erratically: *share prices fluctuated wildly throughout the day* ▶ HISTORY Latin *fluctus* a wave > **fluctuation** n

flue n a passage or pipe in a chimney, used to carry off smoke, gas, or hot air ▶ HISTORY origin unknown

fluent adj **1** able to speak or write with ease: *they spoke fluent English; fluent in French* **2** spoken or written with ease ▶ HISTORY Latin *fluere* to flow > **fluency** n > **fluently** adv

fluff n **1** soft light particles, such as the down of cotton or wool **2** informal a mistake, esp. in speaking or reading lines ▷ vb **3** to make or become soft and puffy **4** informal to make a mistake in performing ▶ HISTORY probably from earlier *flue* downy matter > **fluffy** adj > **fluffiness** n

fluid n **1 a** a substance, such as a liquid or gas, that can flow and has no fixed shape ▷ adj **2** capable of flowing and easily changing shape **3** constantly changing or apt to change ▶ HISTORY Latin *fluere* to flow > **fluidity** n

fluid ounce n **1** Brit a unit of liquid measure equal to one twentieth of an Imperial pint (28.4 ml) **2** US a unit of liquid measure equal to one sixteenth of a US pint (29.6 ml)

fluke¹ n an accidental stroke of luck ▶ HISTORY origin unknown > **fluky** adj

fluke² n **1** the flat triangular point of an anchor **2** either of the two lobes of the tail of a whale ▶ HISTORY perhaps a special use of FLUKE³ (in the sense: a flounder, flatfish)

fluke³ n any parasitic flatworm, such as the liver fluke ▶ HISTORY Old English *flōc*

flume n **1** a narrow sloping channel for water **2** an enclosed water slide at a swimming pool

flummox vb to puzzle or confuse ▶ HISTORY origin unknown

flung vb the past of **fling**

flunk vb US, Canad, Austral, NZ & S African, informal to fail (an examination, course, etc.) ▶ HISTORY origin unknown

flunky or **flunkey** n, pl **flunkies** or **flunkeys 1** a manservant who wears ceremonial dress **2** a person who performs small unimportant tasks for a powerful or important person in the hope of being rewarded ▶ HISTORY origin unknown

fluor (**flew**-or) n same as **fluorspar** ▶ HISTORY Latin: a flowing; so called from its use as a metallurgical flux

fluoresce vb **-rescing, -resced** to exhibit fluorescence ▶ HISTORY back formation from FLUORESCENCE

fluorescence n **1** physics the emission of light from atoms or molecules that are bombarded by particles, such as electrons, or by radiation from a separate source **2** the radiation emitted as a result of fluorescence ▶ HISTORY from *fluor* > **fluorescent** adj

321

fluorescent lamp *n* a lamp in which ultraviolet radiation from an electrical gas discharge causes a thin layer of phosphor on a tube's inside surface to fluoresce

fluoridate *vb* **-dating, -dated** to add fluoride to (water) as protection against tooth decay > **fluoridation** *n*

fluoride *n chem* any compound containing fluorine and another element or radical

fluorinate *vb* **-nating, -nated** to treat or combine with fluorine > **fluorination** *n*

fluorine *n chem* a poisonous strong-smelling pale yellow gas that is the most reactive of all the elements. Symbol: F

fluoroscopy (floor-**oss**-kop-ee) *n* same as **radioscopy**

fluorspar, fluor *or US & Canad* **fluorite** *n* a white or colourless mineral, consisting of calcium fluoride in crystalline form: the chief ore of fluorine

flurry *n, pl* **-ries 1** a short rush of vigorous activity or movement **2** a light gust of wind or rain or fall of snow > *vb* **-ries, -rying, -ried 3** to confuse or bewilder ▶ HISTORY obsolete *flurr* to scatter

flush¹ *vb* **1** to blush or cause to blush **2** to send water quickly through (a pipe or a toilet) so as to clean it **3** to elate: *she was flushed with excitement* > *n* **4** a rosy colour, esp. in the cheeks **5** a sudden flow, such as of water **6** a feeling of elation: *in the flush of victory* **7** freshness: *in the first flush of youth* ▶ HISTORY perhaps from FLUSH³ > **flushed** *adj*

flush² *adj* **1** level with another surface **2** *informal* having plenty of money > *adv* **3** so as to be level ▶ HISTORY probably from FLUSH¹ (in the sense: spring out)

flush³ *vb* to drive out of a hiding place ▶ HISTORY Middle English *flusshen*

flush⁴ *n* (in poker and similar games) a hand containing only one suit ▶ HISTORY Latin *fluxus* flux

fluster *vb* **1** to make or become nervous or upset > *n* **2** a nervous or upset state ▶ HISTORY from Old Norse

flute *n* **1** a wind instrument consisting of a tube of wood or metal with holes in the side stopped either by the fingers or keys. The breath is directed across a mouth hole in the side **2** a tall narrow wineglass, used esp. for champagne > *vb* **fluting, fluted 3** to utter in a high-pitched tone ▶ HISTORY Old French *flahute* > **fluty** *adj*

fluted *adj* having decorated grooves

fluting *n* a design or decoration of flutes on a column

flutter *vb* **1** to wave rapidly **2** (of birds or butterflies) to flap the wings **3** to move with an irregular motion **4** *pathol* (of the heart) to beat abnormally rapidly **5** to move about restlessly > *n* **6** a quick flapping or vibrating motion **7** a state of nervous excitement or confusion **8** excited interest **9** *Brit, informal* a modest bet **10** *pathol* an abnormally rapid beating of the heart **11** *electronics* a slow variation in pitch in a sound-reproducing system ▶ HISTORY Old English *floterian* to float to and fro

fluvial (**flew**-vee-al) *adj* of or relating to a river ▶ HISTORY Latin *fluvius* river

fluvioglacial *adj geog* relating to streams flowing from melted glaciers or to deposits left by them

flux *n* **1** continuous change or instability **2** a flow or discharge **3** a substance mixed with a metal oxide to assist in fusion **4** *physics* **a** the rate of flow of particles, energy, or a fluid **b** the strength of a field in a given area: *magnetic flux* ▶ HISTORY Latin *fluxus* a flow

fly¹ *vb* **flies, flying, flew, flown 1** to move through the air on wings or in an aircraft **2** to control the flight of (an aircraft) **3** to float, flutter, display, or be displayed in the air: *the Red Cross flag flew at each corner of the compound* **4** to transport or be transported through the air by aircraft, wind, etc. **5** to move very quickly or suddenly: *the front door flew open* **6** to pass quickly: *how time flies* **7** to escape from (an enemy or a place) **8 fly a kite** to release information or take a step in order to test public opinion **9 fly at** to attack (someone) **10 fly high** *informal* to have a high aim **11 let fly** *informal* to lose one's temper: *a young child letting fly at you in a sudden moment of temper* > *n, pl* **flies 12** Also: **flies** a closure that conceals a zip, buttons, or other fastening, as on trousers **13** a flap forming the entrance to a tent **14 flies** *theatre* the space above the stage, used for storing scenery ▶ HISTORY Old English *flēogan*

fly² *n, pl* **flies 1** a small insect with two pairs of wings **2** any of various similar but unrelated insects, such as the dragonfly **3** *angling* a lure made from a fish-hook attached with feathers to resemble a fly **4 fly in the ointment** *informal* a slight flaw that detracts from value or enjoyment **5 fly on the wall** a person who watches others, while not being noticed himself or herself **6 there are no flies on him or her** *informal* he or she is no fool ▶ HISTORY Old English *flēoge*

fly³ *adj slang, chiefly Brit* sharp and cunning ▶ HISTORY origin unknown

flyblown *adj* **1** covered with blowfly eggs **2** in a dirty and bad condition

fly-by-night *informal adj* **1** unreliable or untrustworthy, esp. in money matters > *n* **2** an untrustworthy person

flycatcher *n* a small insect-eating songbird

flyer *or* **flier** *n* **1** a small advertising leaflet **2** a person or thing that flies or moves very fast **3** *old-fashioned* an aircraft pilot

fly-fishing *n angling* fishing using artificial flies as lures

flying *n* **1** the act of piloting, navigating, or travelling in an aircraft > *adj* **2** hurried and brief: *a flying visit* **3** fast or built for speed: *Australia's flying fullback* **4** hanging, waving, or floating freely: *flags flying proudly*

flying boat *n* a seaplane in which the fuselage consists of a hull that provides buoyancy

flying buttress *n* an arch and vertical column that supports a wall from the outside

flying colours *pl n* conspicuous success;

triumph: *they passed with flying colours*

flying fish *n* a fish of warm and tropical seas, with winglike fins used for gliding above the water

flying fox *n* **1** a large fruit bat of tropical Africa and Asia **2** *Austral & NZ* a platform suspended from an overhead cable, used for transporting people or materials

flying officer *n* a junior commissioned officer in an air force

flying phalanger *n* a phalanger with black-striped greyish fur, which moves with gliding leaps

flying saucer *n* an unidentified disc-shaped flying object alleged to come from outer space

flying squad *n* a small group of police or soldiers ready to move into action quickly

flying start *n* **1** any promising beginning: *a flying start to the new financial year* **2** a start to a race in which the competitor is already travelling at speed as he or she passes the starting line

flyleaf *n, pl* **-leaves** the inner leaf of the endpaper of a book

flyover *n* an intersection of two roads at which one is carried over the other by a bridge

flypaper *n* paper with a sticky and poisonous coating, hung up to trap flies

fly-past *n* a ceremonial flight of aircraft over a given area

flyweight *n* a professional or an amateur boxer weighing up to 112 pounds (51 kg)

flywheel *n* a heavy wheel that regulates the speed of a machine

Fm *chem* fermium

FM frequency modulation

f-number *n* *photog* the ratio of the effective diameter of a lens to its focal length

foal *n* **1** the young of a horse or related animal ▷ *vb* **2** to give birth to (a foal) ▶ **HISTORY** Old English *fola*

foam *n* **1** a mass of small bubbles of gas formed on the surface of a liquid **2** frothy saliva **3** a light spongelike solid used for insulation, packing, etc. ▷ *vb* **4** to produce or cause to produce foam **5 foam at the mouth** to be very angry ▶ **HISTORY** Old English *fām* > **foamy** *adj*

fob *n* **1** a chain by which a pocket watch is attached to a waistcoat **2** a small pocket in a man's waistcoat, for holding a watch ▶ **HISTORY** Germanic

f.o.b. *or* **FOB** *commerce* free on board

fob off *vb* **fobbing, fobbed 1** to pretend to satisfy (a person) with lies or excuses **2** to sell or pass off (inferior goods) as valuable ▶ **HISTORY** probably from German *foppen* to trick

focal *adj* **1** of or relating to a focus **2** situated at or measured from the focus

focalization *or* **-isation** *n* *literature* the viewpoint from which the events of a story are presented

focal length *n* the distance from the focal point of a lens or mirror to the surface of the mirror or the centre of the lens

focal point *n* **1** the point where the rays of light from a lens or mirror meet **2** the centre of attention or interest: *a focal point for the new high-technology industries*

focus (**foe**-kuss) *vb* **-cusing, -cused** *or* **-cussing, -cussed 1** to adjust one's eyes or an instrument on an object so that its image is clear **2** to concentrate ▷ *n, pl* **-cuses** *or* **-ci** (-sigh, -kye, -kee) **3** a point of convergence of light or sound waves, or a point from which they appear to diverge **4 in focus** (of an object or image being viewed) clear and sharp **5 out of focus** (of an object or image being viewed) blurred and fuzzy **6** same as **focal point** (sense 1), **focal length 7** *optics* the state of an optical image when it is distinct or the state of an instrument producing this image **8** a point upon which attention or activity is concentrated: *the focus was on health and education* **9** *geom* a fixed reference point on the concave side of a conic section, used when defining its eccentricity ▶ **HISTORY** Latin: hearth, fireplace

focus group *n* a group of people gathered by a market research company to discuss and assess a product or service

fodder *n* bulk feed for livestock, esp. hay or straw ▶ **HISTORY** Old English *fōdor*

foe *n* *formal or literary* an enemy ▶ **HISTORY** Old English *fāh* hostile

FoE *or* **FOE** Friends of the Earth

foetid *adj* same as **fetid**

foetus *n, pl* **-tuses** same as **fetus**

fog *n* **1** a mass of droplets of condensed water vapour suspended in the air, often greatly reducing visibility **2** *photog* a blurred area on a developed negative, print, or transparency ▷ *vb* **fogging, fogged 3** to envelop or become enveloped with or as if with fog ▶ **HISTORY** probably from Old Norse > **foggy** *adj*

fog bank *n* a distinct mass of fog, esp. at sea

fogbound *adj* prevented from operating by fog

fogey *or* **fogy** *n, pl* **-geys** *or* **-gies** an extremely old-fashioned person: *a stick-in-the-mud old fogey* ▶ **HISTORY** origin unknown > **fogeyish** *or* **fogyish** *adj*

foghorn *n* a large horn sounded at intervals as a warning to ships in fog

foible *n* a slight peculiarity or minor weakness: *he was intolerant of other people's foibles* ▶ **HISTORY** obsolete French form of *faible* feeble

foil[1] *vb* to baffle or frustrate (a person or an attempt) ▶ **HISTORY** Middle English *foilen* to trample

foil[2] *n* **1** metal in the form of very thin sheets **2** a person or thing setting off another thing to advantage: *mint sauce is an excellent foil to lamb* ▶ **HISTORY** Latin *folia* leaves

foil[3] *n* a light slender flexible sword tipped by a button, used in fencing ▶ **HISTORY** origin unknown

foist *vb* **foist on** to force (someone) to have or experience (something): *the tough economic policies which have been foisted on the developing world* ▶ **HISTORY** probably from obsolete Dutch *vuisten* to enclose in one's hand fold — food

fold¹ *vb* **1** to bend double so that one part covers another **2** to bring together and intertwine (the arms or legs) **3 fold up** to enclose in a surrounding material **4** *literary* to clasp (a person) in one's arms **5** Also: **fold in** to mix (ingredients) by gently turning one over the other with a spoon **6** *informal* (of a business, organization, or project) to fail or go bankrupt ▷ *n* **7** a piece or section that has been folded **8** a mark, crease, or hollow made by folding **9** a bend in stratified rocks that results from movements within the earth's crust ▶ **HISTORY** Old English *fealdan*

fold² *n* **1** *Brit, Austral and S African* a small enclosure for sheep **2** a church or the members of it ▶ **HISTORY** Old English *falod*

folder *n* a binder or file for holding loose papers

foliaceous *adj* **1** like a leaf **2** *geol* consisting of thin layers ▶ **HISTORY** Latin *foliaceus*

foliage *n* **1** the green leaves of a plant **2** leaves together with the stems, twigs, and branches they are attached to, esp. when used for decoration ▶ **HISTORY** Old French *fueillage*

foliation *n* **1** *bot* **a** the process of producing leaves **b** the state of being in leaf **2** a leaflike decoration

folio *n, pl* **-lios 1** a sheet of paper folded in half to make two leaves for a book **2** a book of the largest common size made up of such sheets **3 a** a leaf of paper numbered on the front side only **b** the page number of a book **4** *NZ* a collection of related material ▷ *adj* **5** of or made in the largest book size, common esp. in early centuries of European printing: *the entire series is being reissued, several in the original folio format* ▶ **HISTORY** Latin *in folio* in a leaf

folk *pl n* **1** people in general, esp. those of a particular group or class: *ordinary folk* **2** Also: **folks** *informal* members of one's family; relatives ▷ *n* **3** *informal* short for **folk music 4** a people or tribe ▷ *adj* **5** originating from or traditional to the common people of a country: *folk art* ▶ **HISTORY** Old English *folc*

folk dance *n* **1** a traditional country dance **2** music for such a dance

folk etymology *n* the gradual change in the form of a word through the influence of a more familiar word, as for example *crayfish* from its Middle English form *crevis*

folklore *n* the traditional beliefs of a people as expressed in stories and songs

folk music *n* **1** music that is passed on from generation to generation **2** a piece written in the style of this music

folk song *n* **1** a song handed down among the common people **2** a modern song like this > **folk singer** *n*

folksy *adj* **-sier, -siest** simple and unpretentious, sometimes in an artificial way

folk tale *n* a story originating among a people and typically becoming part of an oral tradition

follicle *n* any small sac or cavity in the body, esp. one from which a hair grows ▶ **HISTORY** Latin *folliculus* small bag > **follicular** *adj*

follow *vb* **1** to go or come after **2** to accompany: *he followed Isabel everywhere* **3** to be a logical or natural consequence of **4** to keep to the course or track of **5** to act in accordance with: *follow the rules below and it will help you a great deal* **6** to accept the ideas or beliefs of **7** to understand (an explanation) **8** to have a keen interest in: *he's followed the singer's career for more than 25 years* ▷ See also **follow-on, follow through, follow up** ▶ **HISTORY** Old English *folgian*

follower *n* **1** a person who accepts the teachings of another: *a follower of Nietzsche* **2** a supporter, such as of a sport or team

following *adj* **1** about to be mentioned **2** next in time **3** (of winds or currents) moving in the same direction as a vessel ▷ *prep* **4** as a result of: *uncertainty following the collapse of communism* ▷ *n* **5** a group of supporters or enthusiasts

follow-on *cricket n* **1** an immediate second innings forced on a team scoring a prescribed number of runs fewer than its opponents in the first innings ▷ *vb* **follow on 2** to play a follow-on: *England had to follow on*

follow through *vb* **1** to continue an action or series of actions until finished **2** *sport* to continue a stroke, kick, etc. after striking the ball ▷ *n* **follow-through 3** *sport* continuation of a kick, stroke, etc. after striking the ball: *McIlroy's controlled follow-through*

follow up *vb* **1** to investigate (a person, evidence, etc.) closely **2** to continue (action) after a beginning, esp. to increase its effect ▷ *n* **follow-up 3** something done to reinforce an initial action: *a routine follow-up to his operation*

folly *n, pl* **-lies 1** the quality of being foolish **2** a foolish action, idea, etc. **3** an imitation castle, temple, etc., built as a decoration in a large garden or park ▶ **HISTORY** Old French *folie* madness

foment (foam-**ent**) *vb* to encourage or stir up (trouble) ▶ **HISTORY** Latin *fomentum* a poultice > **fomentation** *n*

fond *adj* **1 fond of** having a liking for **2** loving and affectionate: *his fond parents* **3** (of hopes or wishes) cherished but unlikely to be realized ▶ **HISTORY** Middle English *fonnen* to be foolish > **fondly** *adv* > **fondness** *n*

fondant *n* (a sweet made from) a thick flavoured paste of sugar and water ▶ **HISTORY** French

fondle *vb* **-dling, -dled** to touch or stroke tenderly ▶ **HISTORY** obsolete *fond* to fondle

fondue *n* a Swiss dish, consisting of melted cheese into which small pieces of bread are dipped ▶ **HISTORY** French: melted

font¹ *n* a large bowl in a church for baptismal water ▶ **HISTORY** Latin *fons* fountain

font² *n* *printing* same as **fount²**

fontanelle *or esp US* **fontanel** *n* *anat* a soft membranous gap between the bones of a baby's skull ▶ **HISTORY** Old French *fontenele* a little spring

food *n* any substance that can be taken into the body by a living organism and changed into energy and body tissue. *Related adjective:* **gastronomical**

324

▶ HISTORY Old English *fōda*

food chain *n biol* a series of organisms in a community, each member of which is connected to another in the chain by eating or being eaten by it. Compare **food web**

food group *n* any of the categories into which different foods may be placed according to the type of nourishment they supply

foodie *n informal* a person with a keen interest in food and cookery

food poisoning *n* an acute illness caused by food that is contaminated by bacteria

food processor *n* a machine for chopping, mixing, or liquidizing food

foodstuff *n* any substance that can be used as food

food web *n biol* the plants in a community together with all the primary, secondary, and tertiary consumers of any organisms in this interrelated system. Compare **food chain**

fool[1] *n* **1** a person who lacks sense or judgment **2** a person who is made to appear ridiculous **3** (formerly) a professional jester living in a royal or noble household **4 play** or **act the fool** to deliberately act foolishly ▷ *vb* **5** to deceive (someone), esp. in order to make them look ridiculous **6 fool around** or **about with** *informal* to act or play with irresponsibly or aimlessly **7** to speak or act in a playful or jesting manner ▶ HISTORY Latin *follis* bellows

fool[2] *n chiefly Brit* a dessert made from a puree of fruit with cream ▶ HISTORY perhaps from FOOL[1]

foolery *n* foolish behaviour

foolhardy *adj* **-hardier, -hardiest** recklessly adventurous ▶ HISTORY Old French *fol* foolish + *hardi* bold > **foolhardily** *adv* > **foolhardiness** *n*

foolish *adj* very silly, unwise, or absurd > **foolishly** *adv* > **foolishness** *n*

foolproof *adj informal* **1** incapable of going wrong; infallible: *a foolproof identification system* **2** (of machines etc.) guaranteed to function as intended despite human misuse or error

foolscap *n chiefly Brit* a standard paper size, 34.3 × 43.2 CM ▶ HISTORY from the watermark of a *fool's* (i.e. dunce's) *cap*, formerly used on it

fool's gold *n* a yellow-coloured mineral, such as pyrite, that is sometimes mistaken for gold

fool's paradise *n* a state of happiness based on false hopes or beliefs

foosball *n US & Canad* same as **table football**

foot *n, pl* **feet 1** the part of the leg below the ankle joint that is in contact with the ground during standing and walking **2** the part of a garment covering a foot **3** a unit of length equal to 12 inches (0.3048 metre) **4** the bottom, base, or lower end of something: *at the foot of the hill; the foot of the page* **5** *old-fashioned* infantry **6** *prosody* a group of two or more syllables in which one syllable has the major stress, forming the basic unit of poetic rhythm **7 one foot in the grave** *informal* near to death **8 on foot** walking **9 put one's best foot forward** to try to do one's best **10 put one's foot down**

informal to act firmly **11 put one's foot in it** *informal* to make an embarrassing and tactless mistake **12 under foot** on the ground ▷ *vb* **13 foot it** *informal* to travel on foot **14 foot the bill** to pay the entire cost of something ▷ See also **feet** ▶ HISTORY Old English *fōt* > **footless** *adj*

footage *n* **1** a length of film **2** the sequences of filmed material: *footage of refugees leaving the city*

foot-and-mouth disease *n* a highly infectious viral disease of cattle, pigs, sheep, and goats, in which blisters form in the mouth and on the feet

football *n* **1** any of various games played with a ball in which two teams compete to kick, head, or propel the ball into each other's goal **2** the ball used in any of these games > **footballer** *n*

football pools *pl n* same as **pools**

footbridge *n* a narrow bridge for the use of pedestrians

footfall *n* the sound of a footstep

foothills *pl n geog* relatively low hills at the foot of a mountain

foothold *n* **1** a secure position from which further progress may be made: *a firm foothold in Europe's telecommunications market* **2** a ledge or other place where a foot can be securely positioned, as during climbing

footing *n* **1** basis or foundation: *on a sound financial footing* **2** the relationship between two people or groups: *on an equal footing* **3** a secure grip by or for the feet

footle *vb* **-ling, -led** *chiefly Brit, informal* to loiter aimlessly ▶ HISTORY probably from French *foutre* to copulate with > **footling** *adj*

footlights *pl n theatre* lights set in a row along the front of the stage floor

footloose *adj* free to go or do as one wishes

footloose industry *n econ* an industry that is not tied to any particular area either by its raw materials or its market and is therefore free to relocate to take advantage of more favourable economic conditions

footman *n, pl* **-men** a male servant in uniform

footnote *n* a note printed at the bottom of a page

footpad *n old-fashioned* a highwayman, on foot rather than horseback

footpath *n* **1** a narrow path for walkers only **2** *Austral* a raised space alongside a road, for pedestrians

footplate *n chiefly Brit* a platform in the cab of a locomotive on which the crew stand to operate the controls

footprint *n* **1** an indentation or outline of the foot on a surface **2** short for **carbon footprint**

footsie *n informal* flirtation involving the touching together of feet

footstep *n* **1** a step in walking **2** the sound made by walking **3** a footmark **4 follow in someone's footsteps** to continue the example of another

footstool *n* a low stool used for supporting the feet of a seated person

footwear *n* anything worn to cover the feet

footwork *n* the way in which the feet are used, for example in sports or dancing: *nimble footwork*

fop *n* a man who is excessively concerned with fashion ▶ HISTORY perhaps from Middle English *foppe* fool > **foppery** *n* > **foppish** *adj*

for *prep* **1** directed or belonging to: *a bottle of beer for himself* **2** to the advantage of: *he spelt it out for her* **3** in the direction of: *he headed for the door* **4** over a span of (time or distance): *she considered him coolly for a moment* **5** in favour of: *support for the war* **6** in order to get: *for a bit of company* **7** designed to meet the needs of: *the instructions are for right-handed players* **8** at a cost of: *two dishes for one* **9** in place of: *she had to substitute for her mother because they woke late* **10** because of: *dancing for joy* **11** regarding the usual characteristics of: *unusually warm for the time of year* **12** concerning: *our idea for the last scene* **13** as being: *do you take me for an idiot?* **14** at (a specified time): *multiparty elections are planned for next year* **15** doing or taking part in: *two guests for dinner* **16** in the duty or task of: *that's for you to decide* **17** in relation to; as it affects: *it's too hard for me* **18** in order to preserve or retain: *fighting for survival* **19** as a direct equivalent to: *word for word* **20** in order to become or enter: *training for the priesthood* **21** in exchange for: *the cash was used to pay for medical supplies* **22 for all** See **all** (sense 12) **23 for it** Brit & Austral, informal liable for punishment or blame: *you'll be for it if you get caught* ▷ *conj* **24** formal because or seeing that: *implausibility cries aloud, and this is a pity, for much of the narrative is entertaining* ▶ HISTORY Old English

forage (**for**-ridge) *vb* **-aging, -aged 1** to search for food **2** to obtain by searching about: *she foraged for her shoes* ▷ *n* **3** food for horses or cattle, esp. hay or straw **4** the act of searching for food or provisions ▶ HISTORY Old French *fourrage*

forage cap *n* a cap with a flat round crown and a visor, worn by soldiers when not in battle or on parade

foramen (for-**ray**-men) *n, pl* -**ramina** (-**ram**-in-a) *or* -**ramens** *anat* a natural hole, esp. one in a bone through which nerves pass ▶ HISTORY Latin

foray *n* **1** a short raid or incursion **2** a first attempt or new undertaking: *his first foray into films* ▶ HISTORY Middle English *forrayen* to pillage

forbear¹ *vb* **-bearing, -bore, -borne** to cease or refrain (from doing something) ▶ HISTORY Old English *forberan* > **forbearance** *n*

forbear² *n* same as **forebear**

forbid *vb* **-bidding, -bade** *or* **-bad, -bidden** *or* **-bid** to prohibit or refuse to allow ▶ HISTORY Old English *forbēodan*

forbidding *adj* severe and threatening in appearance or manner: *a forbidding grey sky*

force¹ *n* **1** strength or power: *the force of the impact had thrown him into the fireplace* **2** exertion or the use of exertion against a person or thing that resists: *they used force and repression against those who opposed their policies* **3** physics an influence that changes a body from a state of rest to one of motion or changes its rate of motion. Symbol: F

4 a intellectual or moral influence: *the Superintendent acknowledged the force of the Chief Constable's argument* **b** a person or thing with such influence: *Hitler quickly became the decisive force behind German foreign policy* **5** drive or intensity **6** a group of people organized for particular duties or tasks: *a UN peacekeeping force* **7 in force a** (of a law) having legal validity **b** in great strength or numbers ▷ *vb* **forcing, forced 8** to compel (a person, group, etc.) to do something through effort, superior strength, etc.: *forced into an arranged marriage* **9** to acquire or produce through effort, superior strength, etc.: *he forced a smile* **10** to propel or drive despite resistance **11** to break down or open (a lock, door, etc.) **12** to impose or inflict **13** to cause (plants or farm animals) to grow at an increased rate ▶ HISTORY Latin *fortis* strong

force² *n* (in N England) a waterfall ▶ HISTORY Old Norse *fors*

forced *adj* **1** done because of force: *forced labour* **2** false or unnatural: *forced jollity* **3** due to an emergency: *a forced landing*

forced migration *n* sociol the fact of being forced to leave one's home, for example because of war, famine, or religious persecution

force-feed *vb* **-feeding, -fed** to force (a person or animal) to swallow food

forceful *adj* **1** strong, emphatic, and confident: *a forceful speech* **2** effective > **forcefully** *adv*

forcemeat *n* a mixture of chopped ingredients used for stuffing ▶ HISTORY from *force* (see FARCE) + *meat*

forceps *n, pl* -**ceps** a surgical instrument in the form of a pair of pincers ▶ HISTORY Latin *formus* hot + *capere* to seize

forcible *adj* **1** involving physical force **2** convincing or effective > **forcibly** *adv*

ford *n* **1** a shallow area in a river that can be crossed by car, on horseback, etc. ▷ *vb* **2** to cross (a river) over a shallow area ▶ HISTORY Old English > **fordable** *adj*

fore *adj* **1** at, in, or towards the front: *the fore foot* ▷ *n* **2** the front part **3 fore and aft** located at both ends of a vessel: *two double cabins fore and aft* **4 to the fore** to the front or prominent position ▷ *interj* **5** a golfer's shouted warning to a person in the path of a flying ball ▶ HISTORY Old English

fore- *prefix* **1** before in time or rank: *foregoing* **2** at or near the front: *foreground* ▶ HISTORY Old English

forearm¹ *n* the part of the arm from the elbow to the wrist

forearm² *vb* to prepare or arm beforehand

forebear *or* **forbear** *n* an ancestor

foreboding *n* a strong feeling that something bad is about to happen

forecast *vb* **-casting, -cast** *or* **-casted 1** to predict or calculate (weather, events, etc.), in advance ▷ *n* **2** a statement predicting the weather **3** a prediction > **forecaster** *n*

forecastle, fo'c's'le *or* **fo'c'sle** (foke-sl) *n* the raised front part of a ship

foreclose *vb* **-closing, -closed** law to take

possession of property bought with borrowed money because repayment has not been made ▶ **HISTORY** Old French *for-* out + *clore* to close > **foreclosure** *n*

forecourt *n* a courtyard in front of a building, such as one in a filling station

foredune *n geog* a dune that is further forward and nearer the sea than the others. Compare **back dune**

forefather *n* an ancestor

forefinger *n* the finger next to the thumb. Also called: **index finger**

forefoot *n, pl* **-feet** either of the front feet of an animal

forefront *n* **1** the most active or prominent position: *at the forefront of medical research* **2** the very front

foregather *or* **forgather** *vb* to gather together or assemble

forego¹ *vb* **-going, -went, -gone** to precede in time, place, etc. ▶ **HISTORY** Old English *foregān*

forego² *vb* **-going, -went, -gone** same as **forgo**

foregoing *adj* (esp. of writing or speech) going before; preceding

foregone conclusion *n* an inevitable result

foreground *n* **1** the part of a view, esp. in a picture, nearest the viewer **2** an important or prominent position

foregrounding *n literature* a literary device whereby particular details or passages are made to stand out thanks to the use of unexpected language, arresting images, or unusual word order

forehand *tennis, squash, etc. adj* **1** (of a stroke) made so that the racket is held with the wrist facing the direction of play ▷ *n* **2** a forehand stroke

forehead *n* the part of the face between the natural hairline and the eyes ▶ **HISTORY** Old English *forhēafod*

foreign *adj* **1** of, located in, or coming from another country, area, or people **2** dealing or concerned with another country, area, or people: *the Foreign Minister* **3** not familiar; strange **4** in an abnormal place or position: *a foreign body in the food* ▶ **HISTORY** Latin *foris* outside

foreigner *n* **1** a person from a foreign country **2** an outsider

foreign exchange *n econ* the system by which one currency is converted into another

foreign minister *or* **secretary** *n* (in Britain) a cabinet minister who is responsible for a country's dealings with other countries

foreign office *n* (in Britain) the ministry of a country that is concerned with dealings with other states

foreknowledge *n* knowledge of something before it actually happens

foreleg *n* either of the front legs of an animal

forelock *n* a lock of hair growing or falling over the forehead

foreman *n, pl* **-men** **1** a person who supervises other workmen **2** *law* the leader of a jury

foremast *n* the mast nearest the bow of a ship

foremost *adj, adv* first in time, place, or importance: *Germany's foremost conductor* ▶ **HISTORY** Old English *formest*, from *forma* first

forename *n* first name

forenoon *n* the daylight hours before noon

forensic (for-**ren**-sik) *adj* used in or connected with a court of law ▶ **HISTORY** Latin *forensis* public > **forensically** *adv*

forensic medicine *n* the application of medical knowledge for the purposes of the law, such as in determining the cause of death

foreordain *vb* to determine (events, etc.) in the future

forepaw *n* either of the front feet of a land mammal that does not have hooves

foreplay *n* sexual stimulation before intercourse

forerunner *n* **1** a person or thing that existed or happened before another and is similar in some way: *a forerunner of the surrealist painters* **2** a person or thing that is a sign of what will happen in the future

foresail *n* the main sail on the foremast of a ship

foresee *vb* **-seeing, -saw, -seen** to see or know beforehand > **foreseeable** *adj*

foreshadow *vb* to show, indicate, or suggest in advance

foreshore *n* the part of the shore between high- and low-tide marks

foreshorten *vb* to see or draw (an object) from such an angle that it appears to be shorter than it really is

foresight *n* **1** the ability to anticipate and provide for future needs **2** the front sight on a firearm

foreskin *n anat* the fold of skin covering the tip of the penis

forest *n* **1** a large wooded area with a thick growth of trees and plants **2** a group of narrow or tall objects standing upright: *a forest of waving arms* **3** NZ an area planted with pines or other trees that are not native to the country ▶ **HISTORY** Medieval Latin *forestis* unfenced woodland, from Latin *foris* outside > **forested** *adj*

forestall *vb* to delay, stop, or guard against beforehand: *an action forestalling any further talks* ▶ **HISTORY** Middle English *forestallen* to waylay

forestation *n* the planting of trees over a wide area

forester *n* a person skilled in forestry or in charge of a forest

forestry *n* the science or skill of growing and maintaining trees in a forest, esp. to obtain wood

foretaste *n* an early but limited experience of something to come

foretell *vb* **-telling, -told** *literary* to correctly predict (an event, a result, etc.) beforehand

forethought *n* thoughtful planning for future events: *a little forethought can avoid a lot of problems later*

for ever *or* **forever** *adv* **1** without end **2** at all times **3** *informal* for a long time: *I could go on for ever about similar incidents*

forewarn *vb* to warn beforehand

foreword *n* an introductory statement to a book

forfeit (**for**-fit) *n* 1 something lost or given up as a penalty for a fault, mistake, etc. ▷ *vb* 2 to lose as a forfeit ▷ *adj* 3 lost as a forfeit ▶ HISTORY Old French *forfet* offence > **forfeiture** *n*

forgather *vb* same as **foregather**

forgave *vb* the past tense of **forgive**

forge¹ *n* 1 a place in which metal is worked by heating and hammering; smithy 2 a furnace used for heating metal ▷ *vb* 3 to shape (metal) by heating and hammering 4 to make a fraudulent imitation of (a signature, money, a painting, etc.) 5 to create (an alliance, relationship, etc.) ▶ HISTORY Old French *forgier* to construct > **forger** *n*

forge² *vb* **forging, forged** 1 to move at a steady pace 2 **forge ahead** to increase speed or progress; take the lead ▶ HISTORY origin unknown

forgery *n, pl* **-geries** 1 an illegal copy of a painting, banknote, antique, etc. 2 the crime of making a fraudulent imitation

forget *vb* **-getting, -got, -gotten** 1 to fail to remember (someone or something once known) 2 to neglect, either by mistake or on purpose 3 to leave behind by mistake 4 **forget oneself** to act in an uncharacteristically unrestrained or unacceptable manner ▶ HISTORY Old English *forgietan* > **forgettable** *adj*

forgetful *adj* 1 tending to forget 2 **forgetful of** inattentive to or neglectful of: *Fiona, forgetful of the time, was still in bed* > **forgetfully** *adv*

forget-me-not *n* a low-growing plant with clusters of small blue flowers

forgive *vb* **-giving, -gave, -given** 1 to stop feeling anger and resentment towards (a person) or at (an action that has caused upset or harm) 2 to pardon (a mistake) 3 to free from (a debt) ▶ HISTORY Old English *forgiefan*

forgiveness *n* the act of forgiving or the state of being forgiven

forgiving *adj* willing to forgive

forgo *or* **forego** *vb* **-going, -went, -gone** to give up or do without ▶ HISTORY Old English *forgān*

forgot *vb* 1 the past tense of **forget** 2 *old-fashioned or dialect* a past participle of **forget**

forgotten *vb* a past participle of **forget**

fork *n* 1 a small tool with long thin prongs on the end of a handle, used for lifting food to the mouth 2 a larger similar-shaped gardening tool, used for lifting or digging 3 **forks** the part of a bicycle that links the handlebars to the front wheel 4 (of a road, river, etc.) **a** a division into two or more branches **b** the point where the division begins **c** such a branch ▷ *vb* 5 to pick up, dig, etc. with a fork 6 to be divided into two or more branches 7 to take one or other branch at a fork in a road, etc. ▶ HISTORY Latin *furca*

forked *adj* 1 having a fork or forklike parts 2 zigzag: *forked lightning*

fork-lift truck *n* a vehicle with two moveable arms at the front that can be raised and lowered for transporting and unloading goods

fork out *vb slang* to pay, esp. with reluctance

forlorn *adj* 1 lonely, unhappy, and uncared-for 2 (of a place) having a deserted appearance 3 desperate and without any expectation of success ▶ HISTORY Old English *forloren* lost > **forlornly** *adv*

forlorn hope *n* 1 a hopeless enterprise 2 a faint hope ▶ HISTORY changed (by folk etymology) from Dutch *verloren hoop* lost troop

form *n* 1 the shape or appearance of something 2 a visible person or animal 3 the particular mode in which a thing or person appears: *wood in the form of paper* 4 a type or kind: *abortion was widely used as a form of birth control* 5 physical or mental condition 6 a printed document, esp. one with spaces in which to fill details or answers 7 the previous record of a horse, athlete, etc. 8 *Brit, slang* a criminal record 9 *education, chiefly Brit & NZ* a group of children who are taught together 10 manners and etiquette: *it is considered bad form not to wear a tie* 11 the structure and arrangement of a work of art or piece of writing as distinguished from its content 12 a bench 13 a hare's nest 14 any of the various ways in which a word may be spelt or inflected ▷ *vb* 15 to give shape to or take shape, esp. a particular shape 16 to come or bring into existence: *glaciers dammed the valley bottoms with debris behind which lakes have formed* 17 to make or construct or be made or constructed 18 to train or mould by instruction or example 19 to acquire or develop: *they've formed this impression; we formed a bond* 20 to be an element of ▶ HISTORY Latin *forma* shape, model

formal *adj* 1 of or following established conventions: *formal talks; a formal announcement* 2 characterized by conventional forms of ceremony and behaviour: *a small formal dinner party* 3 suitable for occasions organized according to conventional ceremony: *formal cocktail frocks* 4 methodical and organized: *a formal approach* 5 (of education and training) given officially at a school, college, etc.: *he had no formal training in maths* 6 symmetrical in form: *a formal garden* 7 relating to the form or structure of something as distinguished from its substance or content: *they addressed the formal elements of the structure of police work* 8 *philosophy* logically deductive rather than based on facts and observation ▶ HISTORY Latin *formalis* > **formally** *adv*

formaldehyde (for-**mal**-de-hide) *n* a colourless poisonous strong-smelling gas, used as formalin and in synthetic resins. Also: **methanal** ▶ HISTORY *form(ic) + aldehyde*

formalin *n* a solution of formaldehyde in water, used as a disinfectant and as a preservative for biological specimens

formalism *n* concerned with outward appearances and structure at the expense of content > **formalist** *n*

formality *n, pl* **-ties** 1 something done as a requirement of custom or good manners: *he dealt with the formalities regarding the cremation* 2 a necessary procedure without real effect: *trials* *were often a mere formality with the verdict decided beforehand* **3** strict observance of ceremony

formalize *or* **-ise** *vb* **-izing, -ized** *or* **-ising, -ised** **1** to make official or valid **2** to give a definite form to > **formalization** *or* **-isation** *n*

format *n* **1** the shape, size, and general appearance of a publication **2** style or arrangement, such as of a television programme: *a chat-show format* **3** *computers* the arrangement of data on disk or magnetic tape to comply with a computer's input device ▷ *vb* **-matting, -matted 4** to arrange in a specified format ▶ **HISTORY** Latin *formatus* formed

formation *n* **1** the act of having or taking form or existence **2** something that is formed **3** the manner in which something is arranged **4** an arrangement of people or things acting as a unit, such as a troop of soldiers **5** a series of rocks or clouds of a particular structure or shape

formative *adj* **1** of or relating to formation, development, or growth: *formative years at school* **2** shaping or moulding: *the formative influence on his life*

former *adj* **1** belonging to or occurring in an earlier time: *a grotesque parody of a former greatness* **2** having been at a previous time: *the former prime minister* ▷ *n* **3 the former** the first or first mentioned of two

formerly *adv* in the past

Formica *n trademark* a hard laminated plastic used esp. for heat-resistant surfaces

formic acid *n* an acid derived from ants ▶ **HISTORY** Latin *formica* ant

formidable *adj* **1** frightening because very difficult to deal with or overcome: *the Finnish winter presents formidable problems to drivers* **2** extremely impressive: *a formidable Juventus squad* ▶ **HISTORY** Latin *formido* fear > **formidably** *adv*

formless *adj* without a definite shape or form

formula (**form**-yew-la) *n, pl* **-las** *or* **-lae** (-lee) **1** a group of letters, numbers, or other symbols which represents a mathematical or scientific rule **2** a plan or set of rules for doing or producing something **3** an established form of words, as used in religious ceremonies, legal proceedings, etc. **4** a powder used to make a milky drink for babies **5** *motor racing* the category in which a car competes, judged according to engine size ▶ **HISTORY** Latin *forma* form > **formulaic** *adj*

formulary *n, pl* **-laries** a book of prescribed formulas

formulate *vb* **-lating, -lated 1** to express in a formula **2** to plan or describe precisely and clearly > **formulation** *n*

fornicate *vb* **-cating, -cated** to have sexual intercourse without being married ▶ **HISTORY** Latin *fornix* vault, brothel situated therein > **fornication** *n* > **fornicator** *n*

forsake *vb* **-saking, -sook, -saken 1** to withdraw support or friendship from **2** to give up (something valued or enjoyed) ▶ **HISTORY** Old English *forsacan*

forsooth *adv old-fashioned* in truth or indeed ▶ **HISTORY** Old English *forsōth*

forswear *vb* **-swearing, -swore, -sworn 1** to reject or renounce with determination **2** to testify falsely in a court of law ▶ **HISTORY** Old English *forswearian*

forsythia (for-**syth**-ee-a) *n* a shrub with yellow flowers which appear in spring before the leaves ▶ **HISTORY** after William *Forsyth*, botanist

fort *n* **1** a fortified building or position **2 hold the fort** *informal* to keep things in operation during someone's absence ▶ **HISTORY** Latin *fortis* strong

forte¹ (**for**-tay) *n* something at which a person excels: *cooking is his forte* ▶ **HISTORY** Latin *fortis* strong

forte² *adv music* loudly ▶ **HISTORY** Italian

forth *adv* **1** *formal or old-fashioned* forward, out, or away **2 and so forth** and so on ▶ **HISTORY** Old English

forthcoming *adj* **1** about to appear or happen: *the forthcoming elections* **2** made available **3** (of a person) willing to give information

forthright *adj* direct and outspoken

forthwith *adv* at once

fortification *n* **1** the act of fortifying **2 fortifications** walls, mounds, etc. used to strengthen the defences of a place

fortify *vb* **-fies, -fying, -fied 1** to make (a place) defensible, such as by building walls **2** to strengthen physically, mentally, or morally **3** to increase the nutritious value of (a food), such as by adding vitamins ▶ **HISTORY** Latin *fortis* strong + *facere* to make

fortissimo *adv music* very loudly ▶ **HISTORY** Italian

fortitude *n* calm and patient courage in trouble or pain ▶ **HISTORY** Latin *fortitudo* courage

fortnight *n* a period of 14 consecutive days ▶ **HISTORY** Old English *fēowertīene niht* fourteen nights

fortnightly *chiefly Brit adj* **1** occurring or appearing once each fortnight ▷ *adv* **2** once a fortnight

FORTRAN *n* a high-level computer programming language designed for mathematical and scientific purposes ▶ **HISTORY** *for(mula) tran(slation)*

fortress *n* a large fort or fortified town ▶ **HISTORY** Latin *fortis* strong

fortuitous (for-**tyew**-it-uss) *adj* happening by chance, esp. by a lucky chance ▶ **HISTORY** Latin *fortuitus* > **fortuitously** *adv*

fortunate *adj* **1** having good luck **2** occurring by good luck > **fortunately** *adv*

fortune *n* **1** luck, esp. when favourable **2** a person's destiny **3** a power regarded as being responsible for human affairs **4** wealth or material prosperity ▶ **HISTORY** Latin *fors* chance

fortune-teller *n* a person who claims to predict events in other people's lives

forty *n, pl* **-ties 1** the cardinal number that is the product of ten and four **2** a numeral, 40 or XL, representing this number **3** something representing or consisting of 40 units ▷ *adj* **4** amounting to forty: *forty pages* > **fortieth** *adj, n*

forty winks *n informal* a short light sleep   329

forum *n* **1** a meeting or medium for the open discussion of subjects of public interest **2** (in ancient Roman cities) an open space serving as a marketplace and centre of public business **3** (in S Africa) a pressure group of leaders and representatives ▶ HISTORY Latin

forward *adj* **1** directed or moving ahead **2** at, in, or near the front **3** overfamiliar or disrespectful **4** well developed or advanced **5** of or relating to the future or favouring change ▷ *n* **6** an attacking player in any of various sports, such as soccer ▷ *adv* **7** same as **forwards** ▷ *vb* **8** to send (a letter, etc.) on to an ultimate destination **9** *written* to advance or promote ▶ HISTORY Old English *foreweard*

forward purchasing *n commerce* the practice of buying in materials in greater quantities than current requirements demand

forwards *or* **forward** *adv* **1** towards or at a place ahead or in advance, esp. in space but also in time **2** towards the front

fosse *or* **foss** *n* a ditch or moat, esp. one dug as a fortification ▶ HISTORY Latin *fossa*

fossick *vb Austral & NZ* **1** to search for gold or precious stones in abandoned workings, rivers, etc. **2** to search for (something) ▶ HISTORY probably from English dialect *fussock* to bustle about

fossil *n* **1** remains of a plant or animal that existed in a past geological age, occurring in the form of mineralized bones, shells, etc. ▷ *adj* **2** of, like, or being a fossil ▶ HISTORY Latin *fossilis* dug up

fossil fuel *n* fuel, such as coal or oil, formed from the decayed remains of prehistoric animals and plants

fossilize *or* **-ise** *vb* **-izing, -ized** *or* **-ising, -ised 1** to convert or be converted into a fossil **2** to become out-of-date or inflexible

foster *adj* **1** of or involved in the bringing up of a child not one's own: *foster care* ▷ *vb* **2** to bring up (a child not one's own) **3** to promote the growth or development of ▶ HISTORY Old English *fōstrian* to feed > **fostering** *n*

fought *vb* the past of **fight**

foul *adj* **1** offensive or loathsome: *a foul deed* **2** stinking or dirty **3** full of dirt or offensive matter **4** (of language) obscene or vulgar **5** unfair: *by fair or foul means* **6** (of weather) unpleasant **7** very bad-tempered and irritable: *he was in a foul mood* **8** *informal* disgustingly bad ▷ *n* **9** *sport* a violation of the rules ▷ *vb* **10** to make dirty or polluted **11** to make or become entangled **12** to make or become clogged **13** *sport* to commit a foul against (an opponent) ▷ *adv* **14** **fall foul of** to come into conflict with ▶ HISTORY Old English *fūl*

foul-mouthed *adj* habitually using swearwords and bad language

foul play *n* **1** violent activity esp. murder **2** a violation of the rules in a game

found¹ *vb* the past of **find**

found² *vb* **1** to bring into being or establish (something, such as an institution) **2** to lay the foundation of **3 founded on** to have a basis in:

a political system founded on fear ▶ HISTORY Latin *fundus* bottom > **founder** *n* > **founding** *adj*

found³ *vb* **1** to cast (metal or glass) by melting and pouring into a mould **2** to make (articles) in this way ▶ HISTORY Latin *fundere* to melt

foundation *n* **1** the basic experience, idea, or attitude on which a way of life or belief is based: *respect for the law is the foundation of commercial society* **2** a construction below the ground that distributes the load of a building, wall, etc. **3** the base on which something stands **4** the act of founding **5** an endowment for the support of an institution, such as a college **6** an institution supported by an endowment **7** a cosmetic used as a base for make-up

founder *vb* **1** to break down or fail: *his negotiations have foundered on economic grounds* **2** (of a ship) to sink **3** to sink into or become stuck in soft ground **4** (of a horse) to stumble or go lame ▶ HISTORY Old French *fondrer* to submerge

foundling *n chiefly Brit* an abandoned baby whose parents are not known ▶ HISTORY Middle English *foundeling*

foundry *n, pl* **-ries** a place where metal is melted and cast

fount¹ *n* **1** *poetic* a spring or fountain **2** a source or supply: *a fount of knowledge* ▶ HISTORY from *fountain*

fount² *n printing, chiefly Brit* a complete set of type of one style and size ▶ HISTORY Old French *fonte* a founding, casting

fountain *n* **1** an ornamental feature in a pool or lake consisting of a jet of water forced into the air by a pump **2** a jet or spray of water **3** a natural spring of water **4** a source or supply: *a fountain of many new ideas* **5** a cascade of sparks, lava, etc. ▶ HISTORY Latin *fons* spring

fountainhead *n* a principal or original source

fountain pen *n* a pen supplied with ink from a container inside it

four *n* **1** the cardinal number that is the sum of one and three **2** a numeral, 4 or IV, representing this number **3** something representing or consisting of four units **4** *cricket* a score of four runs, obtained by hitting the ball so that it crosses the boundary after hitting the ground **5** *rowing* **a** a rowing boat propelled by four oarsmen **b** the crew of such a rowing boat ▷ *adj* **6** amounting to four: *four zones* ▶ HISTORY Old English *fēower*

four-by-four *n* a vehicle with four-wheel drive

fourfold *adj* **1** having four times as many or as much **2** composed of four parts ▷ *adv* **3** by four times as many or as much

four-in-hand *n* a carriage drawn by four horses and driven by one driver

four-letter word *n* any of several short English words referring to sex or excrement: regarded generally as offensive or obscene

four-poster *n* a bed with posts at each corner supporting a canopy and curtains

foursome *n* **1** a group of four people **2** *golf* a game between two pairs of players

foursquare *adv* **1** squarely or firmly ▷ *adj* **2** solid and strong **3** forthright and uncompromising

four-stroke *adj* designating an internal-combustion engine in which the piston makes four strokes for every explosion

fourteen *n* **1** the cardinal number that is the sum of ten and four **2** a numeral, 14 or XIV, representing this number **3** something representing or consisting of 14 units ▷ *adj* **4** amounting to fourteen: *fourteen points* > **fourteenth** *adj, n*

fourth *adj* **1** of or being number four in a series **2** denoting the highest forward gear in a motor vehicle ▷ *n* **3** the highest forward gear in a motor vehicle

fourth dimension *n* **1** the dimension of time, which in addition to three spatial dimensions specifies the position of a point or particle **2** the concept in science fiction of an extra dimension

fourth estate *n* the press

four-wheel drive *n* a system in a vehicle in which all four wheels are connected to the source of power

fowl *n* **1** a domesticated bird such as a hen **2** any other bird that is used as food or hunted as game **3** the meat of fowl **4** *old-fashioned* a bird ▷ *vb* **5** to hunt wild birds ▶ **HISTORY** Old English *fugol*

fox *n, pl* **foxes** *or* **fox** **1** a doglike wild animal with a pointed muzzle and a bushy tail **2** its reddish-brown or grey fur **3** a person who is cunning and sly ▷ *vb* **4** *informal* to confuse ▶ **HISTORY** Old English

foxglove *n* a tall plant with purple or white flowers

foxhole *n* *mil* a small pit dug to provide shelter against enemy fire

foxhound *n* a breed of short-haired terrier, originally kept for hunting foxes

foxtrot *n* **1** a ballroom dance with slow and quick steps **2** music for this ▷ *vb* **-trotting, -trotted** **3** to perform this dance

foxy *adj* **foxier, foxiest** **1** of or resembling a fox, esp. in craftiness **2** reddish-brown > **foxily** *adv* > **foxiness** *n*

foyer (**foy**-ay) *n* an entrance hall in a hotel, theatre, or cinema ▶ **HISTORY** French: fireplace

FP **1** fire plug **2** freezing point

Fr **1** *Christianity* **a** Father **b** Frater ▶ **HISTORY** Latin *brother* **2** *chem* francium

fracas (**frak**-ah) *n* a noisy quarrel or fight ▶ **HISTORY** French

fracking *n* a method of extracting oil or gas from rock by forcing liquid at high pressure into the rock. Also called: **hydraulic fracturing** ▶ **HISTORY** shortened from *fracking*

fraction *n* **1** *maths* a numerical quantity that is not a whole number **2** any part or subdivision **3** a very small proportion or amount of something **4** *chem* a component of a mixture separated by distillation ▶ **HISTORY** Latin *fractus* broken > **fractional** *adj* > **fractionally** *adv*

fractional distillation *or* **fractionation** *n* *chem* the process of separating the constituents of

a liquid mixture by heating it and condensing the components separately according to their different boiling points

fractious *adj* (esp. of children) easily upset and angered, often due to tiredness ▶ **HISTORY** obsolete *fraction* discord

fracture *n* **1** breaking, esp. the breaking or cracking of a bone **2** a division, split, or breach **3** *geol* **a** the characteristic appearance of the surface of a freshly broken mineral or rock **b** the way in which a mineral or rock naturally breaks ▷ *vb* **-turing, -tured** **4** to break ▶ **HISTORY** Latin *frangere* to break > **fractural** *adj*

fracture zone *n* *geol* an area where there are fractures in the rock

fragile *adj* **1** able to be broken or damaged easily **2** in a weakened physical state: *you're looking a bit fragile this morning* ▶ **HISTORY** Latin *fragilis* > **fragility** *n*

fragment *n* **1** a piece broken off **2** an incomplete piece: *fragments of information* ▷ *vb* **3** to break into small pieces or different parts ▶ **HISTORY** Latin *fragmentum* > **fragmentation** *n*

fragmentary *adj* made up of small or unconnected pieces: *fragmentary evidence to support his theory*

fragrance *n* **1** a pleasant smell **2** a perfume or scent

fragrant *adj* having a pleasant smell ▶ **HISTORY** Latin *fragrare* to emit a smell

frail *adj* **1** physically weak and delicate **2** easily damaged: *the frail aircraft* **3** easily tempted ▶ **HISTORY** Old French *frele*

frailty *n* **1** physical or moral weakness **2** (*pl* **-ties**) an inadequacy or fault resulting from moral weakness

frame *n* **1** an open structure that gives shape and support to something, such as a building **2** an enclosing case or border into which something is fitted: *the window frame* **3** the system around which something is built up: *caught up in the frame of the revolution* **4** the structure of the human body **5** one of a series of exposures on film used in making motion pictures **6** a television picture scanned by electron beams at a particular frequency **7** *snooker* **a** a single game in a match **b** a wooden triangle used to arrange the red balls in formation before the start of a game **8** short for **cold frame** **9** *slang* a frame-up **10** **frame of mind** a state of mind: *in a complacent frame of mind* ▷ *vb* **framing, framed** **11** to construct by fitting parts together **12** *written* to create and develop (plans or a policy) **13** to construct (a statement) in a particular kind of language **14** to provide or enclose with a frame **15** *slang* to conspire to incriminate (someone) on a false charge ▶ **HISTORY** Old English *framian* to avail

frame of reference *n* **1** a set of standards that determines behaviour **2** any set of planes or curves, such as the three coordinate axes, used to locate a point in space

frame-up *n* *slang* a conspiracy to incriminate someone on a false charge

framework n **1** a particular set of beliefs, ideas, or rules referred to in order to solve a problem: *a moral framework* **2** a structure supporting something

franc n the standard monetary unit of Switzerland, various African countries, and formerly of France and Belgium ▶ HISTORY Latin *Rex Francorum* King of the Franks, inscribed on 14th-century francs

franchise n **1** the right to vote, esp. for a member of parliament **2** any exemption, privilege, or right granted by a public authority **3** *commerce* authorization granted to a distributor to sell a company's goods ▷ vb **-chising, -chised** **4** *commerce* to grant (a person, etc.) a franchise ▶ HISTORY Old French *franchir* to set free

franchisee n *commerce* a person or a firm that has been granted a franchise

franchisor n *commerce* a person or a firm that grants franchises

Franciscan n **1** a member of a Christian religious order of friars or nuns founded by Saint Francis of Assisi ▷ adj **2** of this order

francium n *chem* an unstable radioactive element of the alkali-metal group. Symbol: Fr ▶ HISTORY from *France*, because first found there

Franco- *combining form* indicating France or French: *the Franco-Prussian war* ▶ HISTORY Medieval Latin *Francus*

frangipani (fran-jee-**pah**-nee) n **1** an Australian evergreen tree with large yellow fragrant flowers **2** a tropical shrub with fragrant flowers

frank adj **1** honest and straightforward in speech or attitude ▷ vb **2** to put a mark on (a letter), ensuring free delivery ▷ n **3** an official mark stamped on a letter ensuring free delivery ▶ HISTORY Medieval Latin *francus* free > **frankly** adv > **frankness** n

Frank n a member of the West Germanic peoples who in the late 4th century AD gradually conquered most of Gaul ▶ HISTORY Old English *Franca*

frankfurter n a smoked sausage of pork or beef ▶ HISTORY short for German *Frankfurter Wurst* sausage from Frankfurt

frankincense n an aromatic gum resin burnt as incense ▶ HISTORY Old French *franc* free, pure + *encens* incense

Frankish n **1** the ancient West Germanic language of the Franks ▷ adj **2** of the Franks or their language

frantic adj **1** distracted with fear, pain, joy, etc. **2** hurried and disorganized: *frantic activity* ▶ HISTORY Latin *phreneticus* mad > **frantically** adv

frappé adj (of drinks) chilled ▶ HISTORY French

fraternal adj **1** of a brother; brotherly **2** designating twins that developed from two separate fertilized ova ▶ HISTORY Latin *frater* brother > **fraternally** adv

fraternity n, pl **-ties 1** a body of people united in interests, aims, etc. **2** friendship between groups of people **3** *US & Canad* a society of male students

fraternize or **-nise** vb **-nizing, -nized** or **-nising, -nised** to associate on friendly terms > **fraternization** or **-nisation** n

fratricide n **1** the act of killing one's brother

2 a person who kills his or her brother ▶ HISTORY Latin *frater* brother + *caedere* to kill > **fratricidal** adj

Frau (rhymes with **how**) n, pl **Frauen** or **Fraus** a German form of address equivalent to *Mrs* or *Ms* ▶ HISTORY German

fraud n **1** deliberate deception or cheating intended to gain an advantage **2** an act of such deception **3** *informal* a person who acts in a false or deceitful way ▶ HISTORY Latin *fraus*

fraudulent adj **1** acting with intent to deceive **2** proceeding from fraud ▶ HISTORY Latin *fraudulentus* > **fraudulence** n

fraught (**frawt**) adj **1 fraught with** involving or filled with: *we expected the trip to be fraught with difficulties* **2** tense or anxious ▶ HISTORY Middle Dutch *vrachten*

Fräulein (**froy**-line) n, pl **-lein** or **-leins** a German form of address equivalent to *Miss* ▶ HISTORY German

fray¹ n **1** *Brit, Austral & NZ* a noisy quarrel or brawl **2** **the fray** any challenging conflict: *after an hour Warne entered the fray* ▶ HISTORY short for *affray*

fray² vb **1** to wear away into loose threads, esp. at an edge **2** to make or become strained or irritated ▶ HISTORY French *frayer* to rub

frazil (**fray**-zil) n small pieces of ice that form in water moving turbulently enough to prevent the formation of a sheet of ice ▶ HISTORY French *fraisil* cinders

frazzle n *informal* the state of being exhausted: *worn to a frazzle* ▶ HISTORY probably from Middle English *faselen* to fray

freak n **1** a person, animal, or plant that is abnormal or deformed **2** an object, event, etc. that is abnormal: *a statistical freak* **3** *informal* a person whose appearance or behaviour is very unusual **4** *informal* a person who is very enthusiastic about something specified: *a health freak* ▷ adj **5** abnormal or unusual: *a freak accident* ▶ HISTORY origin unknown > **freakish** adj > **freaky** adj

freak out vb *informal* to be or cause to be in a heightened emotional state

freckle n a small brownish spot on the skin ▶ HISTORY Old Norse *freknur* freckles > **freckled** adj

free adj **freer, freest 1** able to act at will; not under compulsion or restraint **2** not enslaved or confined **3** (of a country) independent **4** (of a translation) not exact or literal **5** provided without charge: *free school meals* **6** not occupied or in use; available: *is this seat free?* **7** (of a person) not busy **8** open or available to all **9** not fixed or joined; loose: *the free end* **10** without obstruction or blockage: *the free flow of capital* **11** *chem* chemically uncombined: *free nitrogen* **12 free and easy** casual or tolerant **13 free from** not subject to: *free from surveillance* **14 free with** using or giving (something) a lot: *he was free with his tongue* **15 make free with** to behave too familiarly towards ▷ adv **16** in a free manner **17** without charge or cost ▷ vb **freeing, freed 18** to release or liberate **19** to remove obstructions or impediments from **20** to make available or usable: *capital freed by the local authority* **21 free of** or **from** to relieve or rid of (obstacles, pain, etc.) ▶ **HISTORY** Old English *frēo* > **freely** *adv*

-free *adj combining form* free from: *duty-free*

freebooter *n* a pirate ▶ **HISTORY** Dutch *vrijbuit* booty

freeborn *adj history* not born in slavery

Free Church *n chiefly Brit* any Protestant Church other than the Established Church

Freecycle *vb* (sometimes not cap) *trademark* to recycle (an unwanted item) by offering it free of charge

freedman *n, pl* **-men** *history* a man freed from slavery

freedom *n* **1** the state of being free, esp. to enjoy political and civil liberties **2** exemption or immunity: *freedom from government control* **3** liberation, such as from slavery **4** the right or privilege of unrestricted access: *freedom of the skies* **5** self-government or independence **6** the power to order one's own actions **7** ease of manner

freedom fighter *n* a person who is involved in a revolution to overthrow a government or system

freedom of contract *n law* the principle that adults of full capacity are free to set up and enter into contracts and should expect to abide by the terms of the small print

free enterprise *n* an economic system in which commercial organizations compete for profit with little state control

free fall *n* **1** the part of a parachute descent before the parachute opens **2** free descent of a body in which gravity is the only force acting on it

free-for-all *n informal* a disorganized brawl or argument involving all those present

freehand *adj, adv* (done) by hand without the use of guiding instruments: *a freehand drawing*

freehold *property law n* **1** tenure of property for life without restrictions ▷ *adj* **2** of or held by freehold > **freeholder** *n*

free house *n Brit* a public house not bound to sell only one brewer's products

free kick *n soccer* an unopposed kick of the ball awarded for a foul or infringement

freelance *n* **1** a self-employed person doing specific pieces of work for various employers ▷ *vb* **-lancing, -lanced** **2** to work as a freelance ▷ *adj, adv* **3** of or as a freelance ▶ **HISTORY** originally applied to a mercenary soldier

freeloader *n slang* a person who habitually depends on others for food, accommodation, etc.

freeman *n, pl* **-men** a person who has been given the freedom of a city as an honour in return for public service

free-market *adj* denoting an economic system which allows supply and demand to regulate prices and wages

Freemason *n* Also called: **Mason** a member of a widespread secret order whose members are pledged to help each other > **Freemasonry** *n*

free-range *adj* kept or produced in natural conditions: *free-range eggs*

freesia *n* a plant with fragrant tubular flowers ▶ **HISTORY** after F. H. T. *Freese*, physician

free space *n* a region that has no gravitational and electromagnetic fields

freestanding *adj* not attached to or supported by another object

freethinker *n* a person who forms his or her ideas independently of authority

free trade *n* international trade that is free of such government interference as protective tariffs and import quotas

free verse *n prosody* unrhymed verse without a fixed rhythm

Freeview *n trademark* (in Britain) a free service providing digital terrestrial television

free village *n* (in the Caribbean) a village established for freedmen

free vote *n Parliament* a parliamentary division in which members are free to vote according to their consciences rather than as directed by their party

freeware *n computers* software that may be distributed and used without payment

freeway *n US & Austral* a motorway

freewheel *vb* **1** to travel downhill on a bicycle without pedalling ▷ *n* **2** a device in the rear hub of a bicycle wheel that permits it to rotate freely while the pedals are stationary

freewheeling *adj* behaving in a relaxed spontaneous manner, without any long-term plans or commitments

free will *n* **1** the ability to make a choice without outside coercion or pressure **2** *philosophy* the belief that human behaviour is an expression of personal choice and is not determined by physical forces, Fate, or God

Free World *n* the non-Communist countries collectively

freeze *vb* **freezing, froze, frozen** **1** to change from a liquid to a solid by the reduction of temperature, such as water to ice **2** to preserve (food) by subjection to extreme cold **3** to cover or become covered with ice **4** to fix fast or become fixed (to something) because of frost **5** to feel or cause to feel the effects of extreme cold **6** to die of extreme cold **7** *written* to become motionless through fear, shock, etc. **8** to cause (moving film) to stop at a particular frame **9** to fix (prices, incomes, etc.) at a particular level **10** to forbid by law the exchange or collection of (loans, assets, etc.) ▷ *n* **11** the act of freezing or state of being frozen **12** *meteorol* a spell of temperatures below freezing point **13** the fixing of incomes, prices, etc. by legislation ▶ **HISTORY** Old English *frēosan*

freeze-dry *vb* **-dries, -drying, -dried** to preserve (food) by rapid freezing and drying in a vacuum

freezer *n* an insulated cabinet for cold-storage of perishable foods

freeze-thaw weathering *n geol* damage suffered by rocks as a result of surface moisture repeatedly freezing and thawing

freezing *adj informal* very cold

333

freezing point *n* the temperature below which a liquid turns into a solid

freezing works *n* *Austral & NZ* a slaughterhouse at which animals are slaughtered and carcasses frozen especially for export

freight (**frate**) *n* **1 a** commercial transport of goods **b** the cargo transported **c** the cost of this **2** *chiefly Brit* a ship's cargo or part of it ▷ *vb* **3** to transport (goods) by freight **4** to load with goods for transport ▶ HISTORY Middle Dutch *vrecht*

freighter *n* a ship or aircraft designed for transporting cargo

French *adj* **1** of France ▷ *n* **2** the official language of France and an official language of Switzerland, Belgium, Canada, and certain other countries ▷ *pl n* **3 the French** the people of France ▶ HISTORY Old English *Frencisc* French, Frankish

French bread *n* white bread in a long, thin, crusty loaf

French chalk *n* a variety of talc used to mark cloth or remove grease stains

French dressing *n* a salad dressing made from oil and vinegar with seasonings

French fries *pl n* *chiefly US & Canad* potato chips

French horn *n* *music* a valved brass wind instrument with a coiled tube

French letter *n* *Brit & NZ, slang* a condom

Frenchman *or fem* **Frenchwoman** *n*, *pl* **-men** *or* **-women** a person from France

French polish *n* a shellac varnish for wood, giving a high gloss

frenetic (frin-**net**-ik) *adj* wild, excited, and uncontrolled ▶ HISTORY Greek *phrenitis* insanity > **frenetically** *adv*

frenzy *n*, *pl* **-zies 1** violent or wild and uncontrollable behaviour **2** excited or agitated activity: *a frenzy of speculation* ▶ HISTORY Late Latin *phrenesis* madness, from Greek *phrēn* mind > **frenzied** *adj*

Freon *n* *trademark* any of a group of gas or liquid chemical compounds of methane with chlorine and fluorine: used in propellants, aerosols, and solvents

frequency *n*, *pl* **-cies 1** the number of times that an event occurs within a given period **2** the state of being frequent **3** *physics* the number of times a wave repeats itself in a given time

frequency distribution *n* statistical data arranged to show the frequency with which the possible values of a variable occur

frequency modulation *n* a method of transmitting information by varying the frequency of the carrier wave in accordance with the amplitude of the input signal

frequency polygon *n* *maths* a graph or a frequency table where the intervals are shown on the x-axis and the number of scores in each interval is represented by the height of a point above the middle of the interval. The points are connected so that together with the x-axis they form a polygon

frequent *adj* **1** happening often **2** habitual ▷ *vb* **3** to visit often ▶ HISTORY Latin *frequens* numerous > **frequently** *adv*

frequentative *grammar adj* **1** denoting a verb or an affix meaning repeated action ▷ *n* **2** a frequentative verb or affix

fresco *n*, *pl* **-coes** *or* **-cos 1** a method of wall-painting using watercolours on wet plaster **2** a painting done in this way ▶ HISTORY Italian: fresh plaster

fresh *adj* **1** newly made, acquired, etc. **2** not thought of before; novel: *fresh ideas* **3** most recent: *fresh allegations* **4** further or additional: *a fresh supply* **5** (of food) not canned or frozen **6** (of water) not salty **7** bright and clear: *a fresh morning* **8** (of a wind) cold and fairly strong **9** not tired; alert **10** not worn or faded: *the fresh colours of spring* **11** having a healthy or ruddy appearance **12** having recently come (from somewhere): *cakes fresh from the oven* **13** youthful or inexperienced **14** *informal* overfamiliar or disrespectful ▷ *adv* **15** recently ▶ HISTORY Old English *fersc* > **freshly** *adv* > **freshness** *n*

freshen *vb* **1** to make or become fresh or fresher **2** (of the wind) to become stronger **3 freshen up** to wash and tidy up one's appearance

fresher *or* **freshman** *n*, *pl* **-ers** *or* **-men** *Brit & US* a first-year student at college or university

freshet *n* **1** the sudden overflowing of a river **2** a stream of fresh water emptying into the sea

freshwater *adj* of or living in fresh water

fret¹ *vb* **fretting, fretted 1** to worry: *he would fret about the smallest of problems* **2** to rub or wear away **3** to feel or give annoyance ▷ *n* **4** a state of irritation or anxiety ▶ HISTORY Old English *fretan* to eat

fret² *n* **1** a repetitive geometrical figure used for ornamentation ▷ *vb* **fretting, fretted 2** to ornament with fret or fretwork ▶ HISTORY Old French *frete* interlaced design used on a shield

fret³ *n* a small metal bar set across the fingerboard of a musical instrument, such as a guitar, as a guide to fingering ▶ HISTORY origin unknown

fretful *adj* irritable or upset > **fretfully** *adv*

fret saw *n* a fine-toothed saw with a long thin narrow blade, used for cutting designs in thin wood or metal

fretwork *n* decorative geometrical carving in wood

Freudian (**froy**-dee-an) *adj* of or relating to Sigmund Freud (1856–1939), Austrian psychiatrist, or his ideas > **Freudianism** *n*

Freudian slip *n* a slip of the tongue that may reveal an unconscious wish

Fri. Friday

friable (**fry**-a-bl) *adj* easily broken up ▶ HISTORY Latin *friare* to crumble > **friability** *n*

friar *n* a member of a male Roman Catholic religious order ▶ HISTORY Latin *frater* brother

friar's balsam *n* a compound with a camphor-like smell, used as an inhalant to relieve bronchitis

friary *n*, *pl* **-aries** a house of friars

fricassee *n* stewed meat, esp. chicken or veal, served in a thick white sauce ▶ HISTORY Old French

fricative *n* **1** a consonant produced by friction of breath through a partly closed mouth, such as (f) or (z) ▷ *adj* **2** relating to or being a fricative
▶ **HISTORY** Latin *fricare* to rub

friction *n* **1** a resistance encountered when one body moves relative to another body with which it is in contact **2** the act of rubbing one object against another **3** disagreement or conflict
▶ **HISTORY** Latin *fricare* to rub > **frictional** *adj*

frictional force *n physics* same as **friction** (sense 1)

Friday *n* the sixth day of the week

■ **WORD HISTORY**

■ Friday, in Old English *Frīgedæg*, is 'Freya's day'.
■ Freya was the Norse goddess of love.

fridge *n* a cabinet for keeping food and drink cool. In full: **refrigerator**

fried *vb* the past of **fry¹**

friend *n* **1** a person known well to another and regarded with liking, affection, and loyalty **2** an ally in a fight or cause **3** a patron or supporter **4 make friends (with)** to become friendly (with)
▶ **HISTORY** Old English *frēond* > **friendless** *adj* > **friendship** *n*

Friend *n* a member of the Society of Friends; Quaker

friendly *adj* **-lier, -liest** **1** showing or expressing liking, goodwill, or trust **2** on the same side; not hostile **3** tending to help or support ▷ *n, pl* **-lies** **4** *sport* a match played for its own sake and not as part of a competition > **friendliness** *n*

-friendly *adj combining form* helpful, easy, or good for the person or thing specified: *a user-friendly computer system*

friendly society *n Brit* an association of people who pay regular dues in return for old-age pensions, sickness benefits, etc.

fries *pl n* short for **French fries**

Friesian (**free**-zhan) *n* any of several breeds of black-and-white dairy cattle

frieze (**freeze**) *n* **1** a sculptured or decorated band on a wall **2** *archit* the horizontal band between the architrave and cornice of a classical temple
▶ **HISTORY** French *frise*

frigate (**frig**-it) *n* **1** a fast warship, smaller than a destroyer **2** a medium-sized warship of the 18th and 19th centuries ▶ **HISTORY** French *frégate*

fright *n* **1** sudden fear or alarm **2** a sudden alarming shock **3** *informal* a very strange or unattractive person or thing ▶ **HISTORY** Old English *fryhto*

frighten *vb* **1** to terrify or scare **2** to force (someone) to do something from fear > **frightening** *adj*

frightful *adj* **1** very alarming or horrifying **2** annoying or disagreeable **3** *informal* extreme: *a frightful mess* > **frightfully** *adv*

frigid (**frij**-id) *adj* **1** very cold: *the frigid air* **2** formal or stiff in behaviour or temperament ▶ **HISTORY** Latin *frigidus* cold > **frigidity** *n*

Frigid Zone *n geog* the cold regions inside the Arctic and Antarctic Circles where the sun's rays

are very oblique. Compare **Temperate Zone, Torrid Zone**

frill *n* **1** a long narrow strip of fabric with many folds in it attached at one edge of something as a decoration **2** an unnecessary part of something added to make it more attractive or interesting
▶ **HISTORY** origin unknown > **frilly** *or* **frilled** *adj*

frilled lizard *n* a large tree-living Australian lizard with an erectile fold of skin round the neck

fringe *n* **1** hair cut short and hanging over the forehead **2** an ornamental edge of hanging threads, tassels, etc. **3** an outer edge: *London's southern fringe* **4** the minor and less important parts of an activity or organization: *two agents on the fringes of espionage activity* **5** a small group of people within a larger body, but differing from it in certain aims and ideas: *the radical fringe of the Green Party* ▷ *adj* **6** (of theatre) unofficial or unconventional ▷ *vb* **fringing, fringed** **7** to form a border for: *sandy paths fringing the water's edge* **8** to decorate with a fringe: *tinsel fringed the desk*
▶ **HISTORY** Latin *fimbria* fringe, border

fringe benefit *n* a benefit given in addition to a regular salary or wage

fringed *adj* **1** (of clothes, curtains, etc.) decorated with a fringe **2 fringed with** *or* **by** bordered with or by: *a field fringed with trees*

fringing reef *n geog* a coral reef close to the shore to which it is attached, having a steep seaward edge

frippery *n, pl* **-peries** **1** showy but useless ornamentation **2** unimportant or trivial matters
▶ **HISTORY** Old French *frepe* frill, rag

Frisian (**free**-zhan) *n* **1** a language spoken in the NW Netherlands **2** a speaker of this language ▷ *adj* **3** of this language or its speakers ▶ **HISTORY** Latin *Frisii* people of northern Germany

frisk *vb* **1** to leap, move about, or act in a playful manner **2** *informal* to search (someone) by feeling for concealed weapons, etc. ▷ *n* **3** a playful movement **4** *informal* an instance of frisking a person ▶ **HISTORY** Old French *frisque*

frisky *adj* **friskier, friskiest** lively, high-spirited, or playful > **friskily** *adv*

frisson (**freess**-on) *n* a short sudden feeling of fear or excitement ▶ **HISTORY** French

fritter *n* a piece of food, such as apple, that is dipped in batter and fried in deep fat ▶ **HISTORY** Latin *frigere* to fry

fritter away *vb* to waste ▶ **HISTORY** obsolete *fitter* to break into small pieces

frivolous *adj* **1** not serious or sensible in content, attitude, or behaviour **2** unworthy of serious or sensible treatment: *frivolous distractions* ▶ **HISTORY** Latin *frivolus* > **frivolity** *n*

frizz *vb* **1** (of hair) to form or cause (hair) to form tight curls ▷ *n* **2** hair that has been frizzed
▶ **HISTORY** French *friser* to curl > **frizzy** *adj*

frock *n old-fashioned* **1** a girl's or woman's dress **2** a loose garment, formerly worn by peasants
▶ **HISTORY** Old French *froc*

frock coat *n* a man's skirted coat, as worn in the 19th century

335

frog[1] *n* **1** a smooth-skinned tailless amphibian with long back legs used for jumping **2 a frog in one's throat** phlegm on the vocal cords, hindering speech ▶ HISTORY Old English *frogga*

frog[2] *n* a military style fastening on a coat consisting of a button and a loop ▶ HISTORY origin unknown > **frogging** *n*

frog[3] *n* horny material in the centre of the sole of a horse's foot ▶ HISTORY origin unknown

frogman *n, pl* **-men** a swimmer equipped with a rubber suit, flippers, and breathing equipment for working underwater

frogmarch *n* **1** a method of carrying a resisting person in which each limb is held and the victim is face downwards ▷ *vb* **2** to carry in a frogmarch or cause to move forward unwillingly

frogspawn *n* a jelly-like substance containing a frog's eggs

frolic *vb* **-icking, -icked** **1** to run and play in a lively way ▷ *n* **2** lively and merry behaviour **3** a light-hearted occasion ▶ HISTORY Dutch *vrolijk*

frolicsome *adj* merry and playful

from *prep* **1** indicating the original location, situation, etc.: *from America* **2** in a period of time starting at: *from 1950 to the current year* **3** indicating the distance between two things or places: *60 miles from the Iraqi border* **4** indicating a lower amount: *from 5 to 6* **5** showing the model of: *drawn from life* **6** used with a verbal noun to denote prohibition, etc.: *she was banned from smoking at meetings* **7** because of: *five hundred horses collapsed from exhaustion* ▶ HISTORY Old English *fram*

frond *n* **1** the compound leaf of a fern **2** the leaf of a palm ▶ HISTORY Latin *frons*

front *n* **1** that part or side that is forward, or most often seen or used **2** a position or place directly before or ahead **3** the beginning, opening, or first part **4** the position of leadership **5** a promenade at a seaside resort **6** *mil* **a** the total area in which opposing armies face each other **b** the space in which a military unit is operating **7** *meteorol* the dividing line between two different air masses **8** an outward appearance: *he put on a bold front* **9** *informal* a business or other activity serving as a respectable cover for another, usually criminal, organization **10** Also called: **front man** a nominal leader of an organization **11** a particular field of activity: *on the economic front* **12** a group of people with a common goal: *the National Liberation Front* ▷ *adj* **13** of, at, or in the front ▷ *vb* **14** to face (onto) **15** to be a front of or for **16** to appear as a presenter in (a television show) **17** to be the leader of (a band) on stage ▶ HISTORY Latin *frons* forehead, foremost part

frontage *n* **1** the facade of a building or the front of a plot of ground **2** the extent of the front of a shop, plot of land, etc.

frontal *adj* **1** of, at, or in the front **2** of or relating to the forehead ▶ HISTORY Latin *frons* forehead

frontal rainfall *n meteorol* rain that occurs when a warm air mass meets a cooler air mass and, being lighter, is forced upwards where it cools, causing the water vapour in it to condense

front bench *n* (in Britain) the leadership of either the Government or Opposition in the House of Commons or in various other legislative assemblies > **front-bencher** *n*

frontier *n* **1** the region of a country bordering on another or a line marking such a boundary **2** the edge of the settled area of a country **3 frontiers** the limit of knowledge in a particular field: *twenty years ago, laser spectroscopy was on the frontiers of chemical research* ▶ HISTORY Old French *front* part which is opposite

frontispiece *n* an illustration facing the title page of a book ▶ HISTORY Late Latin *frontispicium* facade

frontrunner *n informal* the leader or a favoured contestant in a race or election

frost *n* **1** a white deposit of ice particles **2** an atmospheric temperature of below freezing point, producing this deposit ▷ *vb* **3** to cover with frost **4** to kill or damage (plants) with frost ▶ HISTORY Old English

frostbite *n* destruction of tissues, esp. of the fingers, ears, toes, and nose, by freezing > **frostbitten** *adj*

frosted *adj* (of glass) having the surface roughened so that it cannot be seen through clearly

frosting *n chiefly US & Canad* icing

frosty *adj* **frostier, frostiest** **1** characterized by frost: *the frosty air* **2** covered by frost **3** unfriendly or disapproving: *a frosty reception from the bank manager* > **frostily** *adv* > **frostiness** *n*

froth *n* **1** a mass of small bubbles of air or a gas in a liquid **2** a mixture of saliva and air bubbles formed at the lips in certain diseases, such as rabies **3** trivial but superficially attractive ideas or entertainment ▷ *vb* **4** to produce or cause to produce froth ▶ HISTORY Old Norse *frotha* > **frothy** *adj*

frown *vb* **1** to wrinkle one's brows in worry, anger, or concentration **2 frown on** to disapprove of: *smoking at work is frowned on* ▷ *n* **3** the act of frowning **4** a look of disapproval or displeasure ▶ HISTORY Old French *froigner*

frowsty *adj* **frowstier, frowstiest** *Brit* stale or musty ▶ HISTORY from *frowzy*

frowzy or **frowsy** *adj* **-zier, -ziest** or **-sier, -siest** **1** slovenly or unkempt in appearance **2** musty and stale ▶ HISTORY origin unknown

froze *vb* the past tense of **freeze**

frozen *vb* **1** the past participle of **freeze** ▷ *adj* **2** turned into or covered with ice **3** killed or stiffened by extreme cold **4** (of food) preserved by a freezing process **5 a** (of prices or wages) officially fixed at a certain level **b** (of business assets) not convertible into cash **6** motionless: *she was frozen in horror*

FRS (in Britain) Fellow of the Royal Society

fructify *vb* **-fies, -fying, -fied** to bear or cause to bear fruit ▶ HISTORY Latin *fructus* fruit + *facere* to produce

fructose *n* a crystalline sugar occurring in honey and many fruits ▶ HISTORY Latin *fructus* fruit

frugal (**froo**-gl) adj 1 economical in the use of money or resources; thrifty 2 meagre and inexpensive: a frugal meal ▶ HISTORY Latin frugi useful, temperate > **frugality** n > **frugally** adv

fruit n 1 any fleshy part of a plant that supports the seeds and is edible, such as the strawberry 2 bot the ripened ovary of a flowering plant, containing one or more seeds 3 any plant product useful to man, including grain and vegetables 4 **fruits** the results of an action or effort, esp. if pleasant: they have enjoyed the fruits of a complete victory ▷ vb 5 to bear fruit ▶ HISTORY Latin fructus enjoyment, fruit

fruiterer n chiefly Brit & Austral a person who sells fruit

fruit fly n 1 a small fly that feeds on and lays its eggs in plant tissues 2 a similar fly that feeds on plant sap, decaying fruit, etc., and is widely used in genetics experiments

fruitful adj 1 producing good and useful results: a fruitful relationship 2 bearing much fruit > **fruitfully** adv

fruition (froo-**ish**-on) n 1 the fulfilment of something worked for or desired 2 the act of bearing fruit ▶ HISTORY Latin frui to enjoy

fruitless adj 1 producing nothing of value: a fruitless debate 2 without fruit > **fruitlessly** adv

fruit machine n Brit & NZ a coin-operated gambling machine that pays out money when a particular combination of diagrams, usually of fruit, appear on a screen

fruit sugar n same as **fructose**

fruity adj **fruitier, fruitiest** 1 of or like fruit 2 (of a voice) mellow or rich > **fruitiness** n

frump n a woman who dresses in a dull and old-fashioned way ▶ HISTORY Middle Dutch verrompelen to wrinkle > **frumpy** or **frumpish** adj

frustrate vb -**trating, -trated** 1 to upset or anger (a person) by presenting difficulties that cannot be overcome: his lack of ambition frustrated me 2 to hinder or prevent (the efforts, plans, or desires) of ▶ HISTORY Latin frustrare to cheat > **frustrating** adj > **frustration** n

frustrated adj dissatisfied or unfulfilled

frustum n, pl -**tums** or -**ta** geom the part of a solid, such as a cone or pyramid, contained between the base and a plane parallel to the base that intersects the solid ▶ HISTORY Latin: piece

fry¹ vb **fries, frying, fried** 1 to cook or be cooked in fat or oil, usually over direct heat ▷ n, pl **fries** 2 Also: **fry-up** informal a dish of mixed fried food ▷ See also **fries** ▶ HISTORY Latin frigere > **fryer** or **frier** n

fry² pl n 1 the young of various species of fish 2 See **small fry** ▶ HISTORY Old French freier to spawn

frying pan n 1 a long-handled shallow pan used for frying 2 **out of the frying pan into the fire** from a bad situation to a worse one

FSH biol follicle-stimulating hormone: a hormone secreted by the pituitary gland

f-stop n photog any of the lens aperture settings of a camera

ft. foot or feet

FTP file transfer protocol: the standard protocol used to transfer files across the internet between computer systems

fuchsia (**fyew**-sha) n an ornamental shrub with hanging purple, red, or white flowers ▶ HISTORY after Leonhard Fuchs, botanist

fuddle vb -**dling, -dled** 1 to cause to be confused or intoxicated ▷ n 2 a confused state ▶ HISTORY origin unknown > **fuddled** adj

fuddy-duddy n, pl -**dies** informal a person, esp. an elderly one, who is extremely conservative or dull ▶ HISTORY origin unknown

fudge¹ n a soft sweet made from sugar, butter, and milk ▶ HISTORY origin unknown

fudge² vb **fudging, fudged** 1 to make (an issue or problem) less clear deliberately 2 to avoid making a firm statement or decision ▶ HISTORY origin unknown

fuel n 1 any substance burned for heat or power, such as coal or petrol 2 the material that produces energy by fission in a nuclear reactor 3 **add fuel to** to make (a difficult situation) worse ▷ vb **fuelling, fuelled** or US **fueling, fueled** 4 to supply with or receive fuel 5 to intensify or make worse (a feeling or situation): the move is bound to fuel speculation ▶ HISTORY Old French feu fire

fuel cell n a cell in which chemical energy is converted directly into electrical energy

fug n chiefly Brit & NZ a hot stale atmosphere ▶ HISTORY origin unknown > **fuggy** adj

fugitive (**fyew**-jit-iv) n 1 a person who flees, esp. from arrest or pursuit ▷ adj 2 fleeing 3 not permanent; fleeting ▶ HISTORY Latin fugere to flee

fugue (**fyewg**) n a musical form consisting of a theme repeated above or below the continuing first statement ▶ HISTORY French > **fugal** adj

Führer n a leader: the title used by Hitler as Nazi dictator ▶ HISTORY German

-ful adj suffix 1 full of or characterized by: painful; restful 2 able or tending to: useful ▷ n suffix 3 as much as will fill the thing specified: mouthful

fulcrum n, pl -**crums** or -**cra** the pivot about which a lever turns ▶ HISTORY Latin: foot of a couch

fulfil or US **fulfill** vb -**filling, -filled** 1 to bring about the achievement of (a desire or promise) 2 to carry out (a request or order) 3 to satisfy (demands or conditions) 4 **fulfil oneself** to achieve one's potential ▶ HISTORY Old English fulfyllan > **fulfilment** or US **fulfillment** n

full¹ adj 1 holding as much or as many as possible 2 abundant in supply: full of enthusiasm 3 having consumed enough food or drink 4 (of the face or figure) rounded or plump 5 complete: the full amount 6 with all privileges or rights: full membership 7 music powerful or rich in volume and sound 8 (of a garment) containing a large amount of fabric 9 **full of** engrossed with: she had been full of her own plans 10 **full of oneself** full of pride or conceit 11 **full up** filled to capacity ▷ adv 12 completely or entirely 13 directly or right: she hit him full in the face 14 **full well** very or extremely well: we knew full well that she was watching

▷ *n* **15 in full** without omitting or shortening **16 to the full** thoroughly or fully ▶ HISTORY Old English > **fullness** *or esp US* **fulness** *n*

full² *vb* to make (cloth) more compact during manufacture through shrinking and beating ▶ HISTORY Old French *fouler*

fullback *n soccer, hockey & rugby* a defensive player

full-blooded *adj* **1** vigorous or enthusiastic **2** (esp. of horses) having ancestors of a single race

full-blown *adj* fully developed

full board *n* the daily provision by a hotel of bed, breakfast, and midday and evening meals

full-bodied *adj* having a full rich flavour or quality: *a full-bodied vintage port*

fuller's earth *n* a natural absorbent clay used for fulling cloth

full house *n* **1** a theatre filled to capacity **2** (in bingo) the set of numbers needed to win

full-length *adj* **1** (of a mirror, etc.) showing the complete human figure **2** not abridged

full moon *n* the phase of the moon when it is visible as a fully illuminated disc

full-scale *adj* **1** (of a plan) of actual size **2** using all resources; all-out

full stop *n* the punctuation mark (.) used at the end of a sentence and after abbreviations. Also called (esp. US and Canad.): **period**

full-time *adj* **1** for all of the normal working week: *a full-time job* ▷ *adv* **full time 2** on a full-time basis: *she worked full time until she was 72* ▷ *n* **full time 3** *soccer, rugby & hockey* the end of the game

full toss *or* **pitch** *n cricket* a bowled ball that reaches the batsman without bouncing

fully *adv* **1** to the greatest degree or extent **2** amply or adequately **3** *written* at least: *fully a hundred people*

fulmar *n* a heavily-built Arctic sea bird with a short tail ▶ HISTORY Scandinavian

fulminate *vb* **-nating, -nated** • **fulminate against** to criticize or denounce angrily ▶ HISTORY Latin *fulmen* lightning that strikes > **fulmination** *n*

fulsome *adj* **1** exaggerated and elaborate, and often sounding insincere: *fulsome praise* **2** *not standard* extremely complimentary

fumarole *n geol* a vent in or near a volcano from which hot gases, esp. steam, are emitted ▶ HISTORY late Latin *fūmāriolum* smoke hole, from Latin *fūmus* smoke

fumble *vb* **-bling, -bled 1** to use the hands clumsily or grope about blindly: *fumbling for a cigarette* **2** to say or do awkwardly ▷ *n* **3** the act of fumbling ▶ HISTORY probably Scandinavian

fume *vb* **fuming, fumed 1** to be overcome with anger or fury **2** to give off (fumes) or (of fumes) to be given off, esp. during a chemical reaction **3** to treat with fumes ▷ *n* **4** a pungent or toxic vapour, gas, or smoke ▶ HISTORY Latin *fumus* smoke

fumigate (**fyew**-mig-gate) *vb* **-gating, -gated** to treat (something contaminated) with fumes ▶ HISTORY Latin *fumus* smoke + *agere* to drive > **fumigation** *n*

fun *n* **1** pleasant, enjoyable, and light-hearted activity or amusement **2 for** *or* **in fun** for amusement or as a joke **3 make fun of** *or* **poke fun at** to ridicule or tease ▷ *adj* **4** (of a person) amusing and likeable **5** (of a place or activity) amusing and enjoyable ▶ HISTORY obsolete *fon* to make a fool of

function *n* **1** the intended role or purpose of a person or thing **2** an official or formal social gathering **3** a factor, the precise nature of which depends upon another thing in some way **4** *maths* a quantity, the value of which depends on the varying value of another quantity **5** a sequence of operations that a computer or calculator performs when a specified key is pressed ▷ *vb* **6** to operate or work **7 function as** to perform the action or role of (something or someone else) ▶ HISTORY Latin *functio*

functional *adj* **1** of or performing a function **2** practical rather than decorative **3** in working order **4** *med* affecting a function of an organ without structural change > **functionally** *adv*

functional food *n* a food containing additives which provide extra nutritional value. Also called: **nutraceutical**

functional grammar *n grammar* a method of analysing and understanding language that examines the function of groups of words in each sentence. Compare **traditional grammar**

functionalism *n* the theory that the form of a thing should be determined by its use > **functionalist** *n, adj*

functionary *n, pl* **-aries** a person acting in an official capacity, such as for a government; official

function notation *n maths* the representation of a mathematical function using a series of symbols

fund *n* **1** a reserve of money set aside for a certain purpose **2** a supply or store of something ▷ *vb* **3** to provide money to **4** *finance* to convert (short-term debt) into long-term debt bearing fixed interest ▷ See also **funds** ▶ HISTORY Latin *fundus* bottom, piece of land > **funder** *n*

fundamental *adj* **1** essential or primary: *fundamental mathematical concepts* **2** basic: *a fundamental error* ▷ *n* **3 fundamentals** the most important and basic parts of a subject or activity **4** the lowest note of a harmonic series > **fundamentally** *adv*

fundamentalism *n* **1** *Christianity* the view that the Bible is literally true **2** *Islam* a movement favouring strict observance of Islamic law > **fundamentalist** *n, adj*

fundamental particle *n physics* same as **elementary particle**

fundholding *n* the system in which general practitioners may choose to receive a fixed budget from which they pay for non-urgent hospital treatment and drug costs for patients

fundi (**foon**-dee) *n S African* an expert ▶ HISTORY Nguni (language group of southern Africa) *umfindisi*

funding *n* **1** the provision of money for a project or organization **2** the amount of money provided

funds *pl n* money that is readily available

fundus *n, pl* **-di** *anat* the base of an organ

funeral *n* **1** a ceremony at which a dead person is buried or cremated **2 it's your funeral** *informal* a mistake has been made and you alone will be responsible for its consequences ▷ *adj* **3** of or for a funeral ▶ **HISTORY** Latin *funus* > **funerary** *adj*

funeral director *n* an undertaker

funeral parlour *n* a place where the dead are prepared for burial or cremation

funereal (fyew-**neer**-ee-al) *adj* suggestive of a funeral; gloomy or sombre > **funereally** *adv*

funfair *n Brit* an amusement park with machines to ride on and stalls

fungicide *n* a substance used to destroy fungi ▶ **HISTORY** FUNGUS + Latin *caedere* to kill

fungoid *adj* resembling a fungus

fungous *adj* appearing suddenly and spreading quickly like a fungus

fungus *n, pl* **fungi** or **funguses** an organism without leaves, flowers, or roots that reproduces by spores, such as a mould, yeast, or mushroom ▶ **HISTORY** Latin > **fungal** *adj*

funicular (fyew-**nik**-yew-lar) *n* a railway up the side of a mountain, consisting of two cars at either end of a cable passing round a driving wheel at the summit ▶ **HISTORY** Latin *funis* rope

funk¹ *old-fashioned, Brit n* **1** a state of nervousness, fear, or depression **2** a coward ▷ *vb* **3** to avoid doing (something) through fear ▶ **HISTORY** origin unknown

funk² *n* a type of Black dance music with a strong beat ▶ **HISTORY** from *funky*

funky *adj* **-kier, -kiest** (of jazz or pop) having a strong beat ▶ **HISTORY** from obsolete *funk* to smoke tobacco, perhaps referring to music that is smelly, i.e. earthy

funnel *n* **1** a tube with a wide mouth tapering to a small hole, used for pouring liquids into narrow openings **2** a chimney of a ship or steam train ▷ *vb* **-nelling, -nelled** or US **-neling, -neled** **3** to move or cause to move through or as if through a funnel ▶ **HISTORY** Old Provençal *fonilh*

funnel-web *n Austral* a large poisonous black spider that builds funnel-shaped webs

funny *adj* **-nier, -niest** **1** causing amusement or laughter; humorous **2** peculiar or odd **3** *informal* faint or ill: *this smell is making me feel a bit funny* **4 funny business** *informal* suspicious or dubious behaviour > **funnily** *adv* > **funniness** *n*

funny bone *n* a sensitive area near the elbow where the nerve is close to the surface of the skin

fur *n* **1** the dense coat of fine silky hairs on many mammals **2** the skin of certain animals, with the hair left on **3** a garment made of fur **4 make the fur fly** to cause a scene or disturbance **5** *informal* a whitish coating on the tongue, caused by illness **6** *Brit* a deposit on the insides of water pipes or kettles, caused by hard water ▷ *vb* **furring, furred** **7** Also: **fur up** to cover or become covered with a furlike deposit ▶ **HISTORY** Old French *fuerre* sheath

furbish *vb formal* to brighten up or renovate ▶ **HISTORY** Old French *fourbir* to polish

furcate *vb* **-cating, -cated** **1** to divide into two parts ▷ *adj* **2** forked: *furcate branches* ▶ **HISTORY** Latin *furca* a fork > **furcation** *n*

Furies *pl n, sing* **Fury** *classical myth* the goddesses of vengeance, who pursued unpunished criminals

furious *adj* **1** extremely angry or annoyed **2** violent or unrestrained, such as in speed or energy > **furiously** *adv*

furl *vb* to roll up (an umbrella, flag, or sail) neatly and securely ▶ **HISTORY** Old French *ferm* tight + *lier* to bind

furlong *n* a unit of length equal to 220 yards (201.168 metres) ▶ **HISTORY** Old English *furlang*, from *furh* furrow + *lang* long

furlough (fur-loh) *n* leave of absence from military or other duty ▶ **HISTORY** Dutch *verlof*

furnace *n* **1** an enclosed chamber in which heat is produced to destroy refuse or smelt ores **2** *informal* a very hot place ▶ **HISTORY** Latin *fornax*

furnish *vb* **1** to provide (a house or room) with furniture, etc. **2** to supply or provide ▶ **HISTORY** Old French *fournir* > **furnished** *adj*

furnishings *pl n* furniture, carpets, and fittings with which a room or house is furnished

furniture *n* the large movable articles, such as chairs and tables, that equip a room or house ▶ **HISTORY** Old French *fournir* to equip

furore (fyew-**ror**-ee) *n* a very angry or excited reaction by people to something: *the furore over 'The Satanic Verses'* ▶ **HISTORY** Latin *furor* frenzy

furrier *n* a person who makes or sells fur garments ▶ **HISTORY** Middle English *furour*

furrow *n* **1** a long narrow trench made in the ground by a plough **2** any long deep groove, esp. a deep wrinkle on the forehead ▷ *vb* **3** to become wrinkled **4** to make furrows in (land) ▶ **HISTORY** Old English *furh*

furry *adj* **-rier, -riest** like or covered with fur or something furlike

further *adv* **1** in addition **2** to a greater degree or extent **3** to or at a more advanced point **4** to or at a greater distance in time or space ▷ *adj* **5** additional **6** more distant or remote in time or space ▷ *vb* **7** to assist the progress of (something) ▶ **HISTORY** Old English *furthor* > **furtherance** *n*

further education *n* (in Britain and Australia) formal education beyond school other than at a university

furthermore *adv* in addition

furthest *adv* **1** to the greatest degree or extent **2** to or at the greatest distance in time or space; farthest ▷ *adj* **3** most distant in time or space; farthest

furtive *adj* sly, cautious, and secretive ▶ **HISTORY** Latin *furtivus* stolen > **furtively** *adv*

fury *n, pl* **-ries** **1** violent anger **2** uncontrolled violence: *the fury of the sea* **3** an outburst of violent anger **4** a person with a violent temper ▶ **HISTORY** Latin *furere* to be furious

furze *n* gorse ▶ **HISTORY** Old English *fyrs*

339

fuse¹ *or US* **fuze** *n* **1** a lead containing an explosive for detonating a bomb ▷ *vb* **fusing, fused** *or US* **fuzing, fuzed** **2** to equip with such a fuse ▶ HISTORY Latin *fusus* spindle

fuse² *n* **1** a protective device for safeguarding electric circuits, containing a wire that melts and breaks the circuit when the current exceeds a certain value ▷ *vb* **fusing, fused** **2** *Brit* to fail or cause to fail as a result of a fuse blowing **3** to equip (a plug or circuit) with a fuse **4** to join or become combined: *the two ideas fused in his mind* **5** to unite or become united by melting **6** to become or cause to become liquid, esp. by the action of heat ▶ HISTORY Latin *fusus* melted, cast

fuselage (**fyew**-zill-lahzh) *n* the main body of an aircraft ▶ HISTORY French

fusible *adj* capable of being melted

fusilier (fyew-zill-**leer**) *n* (formerly) an infantryman armed with a light musket: a term still used in the names of certain British regiments ▶ HISTORY French

fusillade (fyew-zill-**lade**) *n* **1** a rapid continual discharge of firearms **2** a sudden outburst of criticism, questions, etc. ▶ HISTORY French *fusiller* to shoot

fusion *n* **1** the act or process of melting together **2** something produced by fusing **3** a kind of popular music that is a blend of two or more styles, such as jazz and funk **4** something new created by a mixture of qualities, ideas, or things **5** See **nuclear fusion** ▷ *adj* **6** relating to a style of cooking that combines traditional Western techniques and ingredients with those used in Eastern cuisine ▶ HISTORY Latin *fusio* a melting

fuss *n* **1** needless activity and worry **2** complaint or objection: *it was silly to make a fuss over seating arrangements* **3** an exhibition of affection or admiration ▷ *vb* **4** to worry unnecessarily **5** to be excessively concerned over trivial matters **6** to bother (a person) **7** **fuss over** to show great or excessive concern or affection for ▶ HISTORY origin unknown

fussy *adj* **fussier, fussiest** **1** inclined to fuss` **2** very particular about detail **3** overelaborate: *a fussy, overdecorated palace* > **fussily** *adv*

fusty *adj* **-tier, -tiest** **1** smelling of damp or mould **2** old-fashioned ▶ HISTORY Middle English *fust* wine cask > **fustiness** *n*

futile (**fyew**-tile) *adj* **1** useless or having no chance of success **2** foolish and of no value: *her futile remarks began to annoy me* ▶ HISTORY Latin *futtilis* pouring out easily > **futility** *n*

futon (**foo**-tonn) *n* a Japanese padded quilt, laid on the floor as a bed

future *n* **1** the time yet to come **2** undetermined events that will occur in that time **3** the condition of a person or thing at a later date **4** prospects: *he had faith in its future* **5** *grammar* same as **future tense** **6** **in future** from now on ▷ *adj* **7** that is yet to come or be **8** of or expressing time yet to come **9** destined to become **10** *grammar* in or denoting the future as a tense of verbs ▷ See also **futures** ▶ HISTORY Latin *futurus* about to be

future perfect *or* **future perfect tense** *n* *grammar* a compound tense formed in English using *will* have or *shall* have plus a past participle to describe an action that will have been performed by a certain time

futures *pl n* commodities bought or sold at an agreed price for delivery at a specified future date

future tense *n* *grammar* a tense of verbs used when the action specified has not yet taken place; in the sentence, *I'll see you later, I'll see* is the future tense

futurism *n* an early 20th-century artistic movement making use of the characteristics of the machine age > **futurist** *n, adj*

futuristic *adj* **1** of design or technology that appears to belong to some future time **2** of futurism

fuzz¹ *n* a mass or covering of fine or curly hairs, fibres, etc. ▶ HISTORY probably from Low German *fussig* loose

fuzz² *n* *Brit, Austral & NZ, slang* the police or a policeman ▶ HISTORY origin unknown

fuzzy *adj* **fuzzier, fuzziest** **1** of, like, or covered with fuzz **2** unclear, blurred, or distorted: *fuzzy pictures* **3** (of hair) tightly curled > **fuzzily** *adv* > **fuzziness** *n*

fwd forward

FX *films, informal* special effects ▶ HISTORY a phonetic respelling of *effects*

Gg

g **1** gallon(s) **2** gram(s) **3** acceleration due to gravity

G **1** *music* the fifth note of the scale of C major **2** gravity **3** good **4** giga- **5** *slang* grand (a thousand pounds or dollars)

G8 Group of Eight: a group of eight countries whose heads of government meet to discuss economic matters and international relations

G20 Group of Twenty: an international organization established to promote global economic stability

Ga *chem* gallium

GA Georgia

Ga. Georgia

gab *informal vb* **gabbing, gabbed 1** to talk a lot, esp. about unimportant things ▷ *n* **2** idle talk **3 gift of the gab** the ability to talk easily and persuasively ▶ **HISTORY** probably from Irish Gaelic *gob* mouth

gabardine *or* **gaberdine** *n* **1** a strong twill cloth used esp. for raincoats **2** a coat made of this cloth ▶ **HISTORY** Old French *gauvardine* pilgrim's garment

gabble *vb* **-bling, -bled 1** to speak rapidly and indistinctly: *the interviewee started to gabble furiously* ▷ *n* **2** rapid and indistinct speech ▶ **HISTORY** Middle Dutch *gabbelen*

gabbro *n, pl* **gabbros** *geol* a dark coarse-grained igneous rock ▶ **HISTORY** Italian, probably from Latin *glaber* smooth, bald

gable *n* the triangular upper part of a wall between the sloping ends of a ridged roof ▶ **HISTORY** probably from Old Norse *gafl* > **gabled** *adj*

gad *vb* **gadding, gadded** (often foll. by *about* or *around*) to go about in search of pleasure ▶ **HISTORY** obsolete *gadling* companion

gadabout *n informal* a person who restlessly seeks amusement

gadfly *n, pl* **-flies 1** a large fly that bites livestock **2** a constantly irritating person ▶ **HISTORY** obsolete *gad* sting

gadget *n* a small mechanical device or appliance ▶ **HISTORY** perhaps from French *gâchette* trigger > **gadgetry** *n*

gadoid (**gay**-doid) *adj* **1** of or belonging to the cod family of marine fishes ▷ *n* **2** any gadoid fish ▶ **HISTORY** New Latin *gadus* cod

gadolinium *n chem* a silvery-white metallic element of the rare-earth group. Symbol: Gd ▶ **HISTORY** after Johan *Gadolin*, mineralogist

Gael (**gayl**) *n* a Gaelic-speaker of Scotland, Ireland,

---

or the Isle of Man ▶ **HISTORY** Gaelic *Gaidheal* > **Gaeldom** *n*

Gaelic (**gal**-lik, **gay**-lik) *n* **1** any of the closely related Celtic languages of Scotland, Ireland, or the Isle of Man ▷ *adj* **2** of the Celtic people of Scotland, Ireland, or the Isle of Man, or their language

gaff¹ *n* **1** *angling* a pole with a hook attached for landing large fish **2** *naut* a spar hoisted to support a fore-and-aft sail ▶ **HISTORY** Provençal *gaf* boat hook

gaff² *n* **blow the gaff** *Brit, slang* to give away a secret ▶ **HISTORY** origin unknown

gaffe *n* something said or done that is socially upsetting or incorrect ▶ **HISTORY** French

gaffer *n* **1** *informal, chiefly Brit* a boss or foreman **2** *informal* an old man: often used affectionately **3** the senior electrician on a television or film set ▶ **HISTORY** from *godfather*

gag¹ *vb* **gagging, gagged 1** to choke as if about to vomit or as if struggling for breath **2** to stop up (a person's mouth), usually with a piece of cloth, to prevent them from speaking or crying out **3** to deprive of free speech ▷ *n* **4** something, usually a piece of cloth, stuffed into or tied across the mouth **5** any restraint on free speech **6** a device for keeping the jaws apart: *a dentist's gag* ▶ **HISTORY** Middle English *gaggen*

gag² *informal n* **1** a joke, usually one told by a professional comedian ▷ *vb* **gagging, gagged 2** to tell jokes ▶ **HISTORY** origin unknown

gaga (**gah**-gah) *adj informal* **1** confused and suffering some memory loss as a result of old age **2** foolishly doting: *she's gaga over him* ▶ **HISTORY** French

gage¹ *n* (formerly) a glove or other object thrown down to indicate a challenge to fight ▶ **HISTORY** Old French

gage² *n, vb* **gaging, gaged** *US* same as **gauge**

gaggle *n* **1** *informal* a group of people gathered together **2** a flock of geese ▶ **HISTORY** Germanic

Gaia hypothesis *or* **theory** *n* the theory that the earth and everything on it constitutes a single self-regulating living entity ▶ **HISTORY** *Gaia*, variant of *Gaea*, Greek goddess of the earth

gaiety *n, pl* **-ties 1** a state of lively good spirits **2** festivity; merrymaking

gaily *adv* **1** in a lively manner; cheerfully **2** with bright colours

gain *vb* **1** to acquire (something desirable) **2** to increase, improve, or advance: *wholesale prices gained 5.6 percent* **3 gain on** to get nearer to or catch up on **4** to get to; reach: *gaining the top the hill* **5** (of a watch or clock) to become or be too fast ▷ *n* **6** something won or acquired; profit; advantage: *a clear gain would result* **7** an increase in size or amount **8** *electronics* the ratio of the output signal of an amplifier to the input signal, usually measured in decibels ▶ **HISTORY** Old French *gaignier*

gainful *adj* useful or profitable > **gainfully** *adv*

gainsay *vb* **-saying, -said** *archaic or literary* to deny or contradict ▶ HISTORY Middle English *gainsaien*, from *gain-* against + *saien* to say

gait *n* **1** *written* manner of walking **2** (of horses and dogs) the pattern of footsteps at a particular speed, such as a trot ▶ HISTORY variant of *gate*

gal *n* *slang* a girl

gala (**gah**-la) *n* **1** a special social occasion, esp. a special performance **2** *chiefly Brit* a sporting occasion with competitions in several events: *next week's sports gala* ▶ HISTORY Old French *galer* to make merry

galactic *adj* of the Galaxy or other galaxies

galactose *n chem* a white water-soluble monosaccharide found in lactose

galaxy *n, pl* **-axies 1** a star system held together by gravitational attraction **2** a collection of brilliant people or things: *a galaxy of legal talent* ▶ HISTORY Middle English (in the sense: the Milky Way); from Greek *gala* milk

Galaxy *n* **the Galaxy** the spiral galaxy that contains the solar system. Also called: **Milky Way**

gale *n* **1** a strong wind, specifically one of force 8 on the Beaufort scale **2** *written* **gales** a loud outburst: *gales of laughter* ▶ HISTORY origin unknown

galena *or* **galenite** *n* a soft bluish-grey mineral consisting of lead sulphide: the chief source of lead ▶ HISTORY Latin: lead ore

gall¹ (**gawl**) *n* **1** *informal* bold impudence: *she was stunned I had the gall to ask* **2** a feeling of great bitterness **3** *physiol, obsolete* same as **bile** ▶ HISTORY Old Norse

gall² (**gawl**) *vb* **1** to annoy or irritate **2** to make the skin sore by rubbing ▷ *n* **3** something that causes annoyance **4** a sore on the skin caused by rubbing ▶ HISTORY Germanic

gall³ (**gawl**) *n* an abnormal outgrowth on a tree or plant caused by parasites ▶ HISTORY Latin *galla*

gallant *adj* **1** *written* persistent and courageous in the face of overwhelming odds: *a gallant fight* **2** (of a man) making a show of polite attentiveness to women **3** having a reputation for bravery: *Police Medal for gallant and meritorious services* ▷ *n* **4** *history* a young man who tried to impress women with his fashionable clothes or daring acts ▶ HISTORY Old French *galer* to make merry ▶ **gallantly** *adv*

gallantry *n* **1** showy, attentive treatment of women **2** great bravery in war or danger

gall bladder *n* a muscular sac, attached to the liver, that stores bile

galleon *n* a large, three-masted sailing ship used from the 15th to the 18th centuries ▶ HISTORY Spanish *galeón*

gallery *n, pl* **-leries 1** a room or building for displaying works of art **2** a balcony running along or around the inside wall of a church, hall, or other building **3** *theatre* **a** an upper floor that projects from the rear and contains the cheapest seats **b** the audience seated there **4** an underground passage in a mine or cave **5** a group of spectators, for instance at a golf match **6 play to the gallery**

to try to gain approval by appealing to popular taste ▶ HISTORY Old French *galerie*

gallery forest *n geog* a stretch of forest along a river in an area of otherwise open country

galley *n* **1** the kitchen of a ship, boat, or aircraft **2** a ship propelled by oars or sails, used in ancient or medieval times ▶ HISTORY Old French *galie*

galley slave *n* **1** a criminal or slave forced to row in a galley **2** *informal* a drudge

Gallic *adj* **1** French **2** of ancient Gaul or the Gauls

Gallicism *n* a word or idiom borrowed from French

gallinaceous *adj* of an order of birds, including poultry, pheasants, and grouse, that have a heavy rounded body ▶ HISTORY Latin *gallina* hen

galling (**gawl**-ing) *adj* annoying or bitterly humiliating

gallium *n chem* a silvery metallic element used in high-temperature thermometers and low-melting alloys. Symbol: Ga ▶ HISTORY Latin *gallus* cock, translation of French *coq* in the name of its discoverer, *Lecoq* de Boisbaudran

gallivant *vb* to go about in search of pleasure ▶ HISTORY perhaps from *gallant*

gallon *n* **1** *Brit* a unit of liquid measure equal to 4.55 litres **2** *US* a unit of liquid measure equal to 3.79 litres ▶ HISTORY Old Northern French *galon*

gallop *vb* **1** (of a horse) to run fast with a two-beat stride in which all four legs are off the ground at once **2** to ride (a horse) at a gallop **3** to move or progress rapidly ▷ *n* **4** the fast two-beat gait of horses **5** an instance of galloping ▶ HISTORY Old French *galoper*

Galloway *n* a breed of black cattle originally bred in Galloway ▶ HISTORY after *Galloway*, district of SW Scotland

gallows *n, pl* **-lowses** *or* **-lows 1** a wooden structure consisting of two upright posts with a crossbeam, used for hanging criminals **2 the gallows** execution by hanging ▶ HISTORY Old Norse *galgi*

gallstone *n* a small hard mass formed in the gall bladder or its ducts

Gallup Poll *n* a sampling of the views of a representative cross section of the population, usually used to forecast voting ▶ HISTORY after G. H. *Gallup*, statistician

galop *n* **1** a 19th-century dance in quick duple time **2** music for this dance ▶ HISTORY French

galore *adj* *written* in abundance: *there were bargains galore* ▶ HISTORY Irish Gaelic *go leór* to sufficiency

galoshes *pl n* *Brit, Austral & NZ* a pair of waterproof overshoes ▶ HISTORY Old French *galoche* wooden shoe

galumph *vb* *Brit, Austral & NZ, informal* to leap or move about clumsily or joyfully ▶ HISTORY probably a blend of GALLOP + TRIUMPH

galvanic *adj* **1** of or producing an electric current by chemical means, such as in a battery **2** *informal* stimulating, startling, or energetic

galvanize *or* **-nise** *vb* **-nizing, -nized** *or* **-nising,**

g

-nised 1 to stimulate into action **2** to cover (metal) with a protective zinc coating **3** to stimulate by an electric current ▶ HISTORY after *Galvani,* physiologist > **galvanization** or **-nisation** *n*

galvanometer *n* a sensitive instrument for detecting or measuring small electric currents

gambit *n* **1** an opening remark or action intended to gain an advantage **2** *chess* an opening move in which a piece, usually a pawn, is sacrificed to gain an advantageous position ▶ HISTORY Italian *gambetto* a tripping up

gamble *vb* **-bling, -bled 1** to play games of chance to win money or prizes **2** to risk or bet (something) on the outcome of an event or sport **3 gamble on** to act with the expectation of: *she has gambled on proving everyone wrong* **4 gamble away** to lose by gambling ▷ *n* **5** a risky act or venture **6** a bet or wager ▶ HISTORY probably variant of GAME¹ > **gambler** *n* > **gambling** *n*

gamboge (gam-**boje**) *n* a gum resin obtained from a tropical Asian tree, used as a yellow pigment and as a purgative ▶ HISTORY from *Cambodia,* where first found

gambol *vb* **-bolling, -bolled** or US **-boling, -boled 1** to jump about playfully; frolic ▷ *n* **2** a playful jumping about; frolicking ▶ HISTORY French *gambade*

game¹ *n* **1** an amusement for children **2** a competitive activity with rules **3** a single period of play in such an activity **4** (in some sports) the score needed to win **5** a single contest in a series; match **6** short for **computer game 7** style or ability in playing a game: *in the second set his overall game improved markedly* **8** an activity that seems to operate according to unwritten rules: *the political game of power* **9** an activity undertaken in a spirit of playfulness: *marriage is just a game to him* **10** wild animals, birds, or fish, hunted for sport or food **11** the flesh of such animals, used as food **12** an object of pursuit: *fair game* **13** *informal* a trick or scheme: *what's his game?* **14 games** an event consisting of various sporting contests, usually in athletics: *Commonwealth Games* **15 on the game** *slang* working as a prostitute **16 give the game away** to reveal one's intentions or a secret **17 play the game** to behave fairly **18 the game is up** the scheme or trick has been found out and so cannot succeed ▷ *adj* **19** *informal* full of fighting spirit; plucky **20** *informal* prepared or willing: *I'm always game for a new sensation* ▷ *vb* **gaming, gamed 21** to play games of chance for money; gamble ▶ HISTORY Old English *gamen* > **gamely** *adv* > **gameness** *n*

game² *adj Brit, Austral & NZ* lame: *he had a game leg* ▶ HISTORY probably from Irish *cam* crooked

gamekeeper *n Brit* a person employed to take care of game on an estate

gamer *n* a person who plays computer games

gamesmanship *n informal* the art of winning by cunning practices without actually cheating

gamete (gam-**eet**) *n* a cell that can fuse with another in reproduction ▶ HISTORY Greek *gametē*

wife > **gametic** or **gametal** *adj*

gamey or **gamy** *adj* **gamier, gamiest** having the smell or flavour of game

gamin *n* a street urchin ▶ HISTORY French

gamine (gam-**een**) *n* a slim and boyish girl or young woman ▶ HISTORY French

gaming *n* gambling

gamma *n* the third letter in the Greek alphabet (Γ, γ)

gamma radiation *n* electromagnetic radiation of shorter wavelength and higher energy than X-rays

gamma rays *pl n* streams of gamma radiation

gammon *n* **1** cured or smoked ham **2** the hindquarter of a side of bacon ▶ HISTORY Old French *gambe* leg

gammy *adj* **-mier, -miest** *Brit & NZ, slang* (of the leg) lame ▶ HISTORY dialect variant of GAME²

gamut *n* **1** entire range or scale: *a rich gamut of facial expressions* **2** *music* **a** a scale **b** the whole range of notes ▶ HISTORY Medieval Latin, from *gamma,* the lowest note of the hexachord as established by Guido d'Arezzo + *ut* (now, *doh*), the first of the notes of the scale *ut, re, mi, fa, sol, la, si*

gander *n* **1** a male goose **2** *informal* a quick look: *have a gander* ▶ HISTORY Old English *gandra, ganra*

gang¹ *n* **1** a group of people who go around together, often to commit crime **2** an organized group of workmen ▷ *vb* **3** to become or act as a gang ▶ HISTORY Old English: journey

gang² *vb Scot* to go or walk ▶ HISTORY Old English *gangan*

gangland *n* the criminal underworld

gangling or **gangly** *adj* lanky and awkward in movement ▶ HISTORY see GANG²

ganglion *n, pl* **-glia** or **-glions** a collection of nerve cells outside the brain and spinal cord ▶ HISTORY Greek: cystic tumour > **ganglionic** *adj*

gangplank *n naut* a portable bridge for boarding and leaving a ship

gangrene *n* decay of body tissue caused by the blood supply being interrupted by disease or injury ▶ HISTORY Greek *gangraina* an eating sore > **gangrenous** *adj*

gangsta rap *n* a style of rap music portraying life in Black ghettos in the US and featuring lyrics that are anti-authority and derogatory to women ▶ HISTORY phonetic rendering of GANGSTER

gangster *n* a member of an organized gang of criminals > **gangsterism**

gangue *n* valueless material in an ore ▶ HISTORY German *Gang* vein of metal, course

gangway *n* **1** *Brit* an aisle between rows of seats **2** same as **gangplank 3** an opening in a ship's side to take a gangplank

gannet *n* **1** a heavily built white sea bird **2** *Brit, slang* a greedy person ▶ HISTORY Old English *ganot*

ganoid *adj* **1** (of the scales of certain fishes) consisting of an inner bony layer covered with an enamel-like substance **2** (of a fish) having such scales ▷ *n* **3** a ganoid fish ▶ HISTORY Greek *ganos* brightness

g

343

gantry *n, pl* **-tries** a large metal framework used to support something, such as a travelling crane, or to position a rocket on its launch pad ▶ HISTORY Latin *cantherius* supporting frame, pack ass

gaol (**jayl**) *n, vb* *Brit & Austral* same as **jail**
> **gaoler** *n*

gap *n* **1** a break or opening in something **2** an interruption or interval **3** a difference in ideas or viewpoint: *the generation gap* ▶ HISTORY Old Norse: chasm > **gappy** *adj*

gape *vb* **gaping, gaped 1** to stare in wonder with the mouth open **2** to open the mouth wide, as in yawning **3** to be or become wide open: *a hole gaped in the roof* ▶ HISTORY Old Norse *gapa* > **gaping** *adj*

gap year *n* a year's break between leaving school and starting further education

garage *n* **1** a building used to keep cars **2** a place where cars are repaired and petrol is sold ▷ *vb* **-aging, -aged 3** to put or keep a car in a garage ▶ HISTORY French

garb *n* **1** *written* clothes, usually the distinctive dress of an occupation or group: *modern military garb* ▷ *vb* **2** to clothe ▶ HISTORY Old French *garbe* graceful contour

garbage *n* **1** *US, Austral & NZ* household waste **2** worthless rubbish or nonsense ▶ HISTORY probably from Anglo-French

garbled *adj* (of a story, message, etc.) jumbled and confused ▶ HISTORY Old Italian *garbellare* to strain, sift

garden *n* **1** an area of land usually next to a house, for growing flowers, fruit, or vegetables. *Related adjective:* **horticultural 2** Also: **gardens** a cultivated area of land open to the public: *Kensington Gardens* **3 lead someone up the garden path** *informal* to mislead or deceive someone ▷ *vb* **4** to work in or take care of a garden ▶ HISTORY Old French *gardin* > **gardener** *n*
> **gardening** *n*

garden centre *n* a place where plants and gardening tools and equipment are sold

garden city *n* *Brit* a planned town of limited size surrounded by countryside

gardenia (gar-**deen**-ya) *n* **1** a large fragrant waxy white flower **2** the evergreen shrub on which it grows ▶ HISTORY after Dr Alexander *Garden*, botanist

garfish *n* **1** a freshwater fish with a long body and very long toothed jaws **2** a sea fish with similar characteristics

gargantuan *adj* *written* huge or enormous ▶ HISTORY after *Gargantua*, a giant in Rabelais' *Gargantua and Pantagruel*

gargle *vb* **-gling, -gled 1** to rinse the mouth and throat with (a liquid) by slowly breathing out through the liquid ▷ *n* **2** the liquid used for gargling **3** the act or sound of gargling ▶ HISTORY Old French *gargouille* throat

gargoyle *n* (on ancient buildings) a waterspout below the roof carved in the form of a grotesque face or figure ▶ HISTORY Old French *gargouille* gargoyle, throat

garish *adj* crudely bright or colourful ▶ HISTORY obsolete *gaure* to stare > **garishly** *adv*
> **garishness** *n*

garland *n* **1** a wreath of flowers and leaves worn round the head or neck or hung up ▷ *vb* **2** to decorate with a garland or garlands ▶ HISTORY Old French *garlande*

garlic *n* the bulb of a plant of the onion family, with a strong taste and smell, made up of small segments which are used in cooking ▶ HISTORY Old English *gārlēac* > **garlicky** *adj*

garment *n* an article of clothing ▶ HISTORY Old French *garniment*

garner *vb* to collect or gather: *the financial rewards garnered by his book* ▶ HISTORY Latin *granum* grain

garnet *n* a red semiprecious gemstone ▶ HISTORY Old French *grenat* red, from *pome grenate* pomegranate

garnish *vb* **1** to decorate (food) with something to add to its appearance or flavour ▷ *n* **2** a decoration for food ▶ HISTORY Old French *garnir* to adorn, equip

garnishee *law n* **1** a person upon whom a garnishment has been served ▷ *vb* **garnishees, garnisheeing, garnisheed 2** to seize (a debt or other property) by garnishment **3** to serve (a person) with a garnishment

garnishment *n* **1** decoration or embellishment **2** *law* **a** a notice or warning **b** a notice warning a person holding money, pay, or property belonging to a debtor to hold it until directed otherwise by the court

garret *n* an attic in a house ▶ HISTORY Old French *garite* watchtower

garrison *n* **1** soldiers who guard a base or fort **2** the place itself ▷ *vb* **3** to station (soldiers) in (a fort or base) ▶ HISTORY Old French *garir* to defend

garrotte or **garotte** *n* **1** a Spanish method of execution by strangling **2** a cord, wire, or iron collar, used to strangle someone ▷ *vb* **-rotting, -rotted 3** to execute with a garrotte ▶ HISTORY Spanish *garrote*

garrulous *adj* constantly chattering; talkative ▶ HISTORY Latin *garrire* to chatter
> **garrulousness** *n*

garter *n* **1** a band, usually of elastic, worn round the leg to hold up a sock or stocking **2** *US & Canad* a suspender ▶ HISTORY Old French *gartier*

gas *n, pl* **gases** or **gasses 1** an airlike substance that is neither liquid nor solid at room temperature and atmospheric pressure **2** a fossil fuel in the form of a gas, used as a source of heat **3** an anaesthetic in the form of a gas **4** *mining* firedamp or the explosive mixture of firedamp and air **5** *US, Canad, Austral, NZ* petrol **6** a poisonous gas used in war **7** *informal* idle talk or boasting **8** *slang* an entertaining person or thing: *Monterey was a gas for musicians and fans alike* **9** *US, informal* gas generated in the alimentary canal ▷ *vb* **gases** or **gasses, gassing, gassed 10** to subject to gas fumes so as to make unconscious or to suffocate **11** *informal* to talk a lot; chatter ▶ **HISTORY** coined from Greek *khaos* atmosphere

gasbag *n informal* a person who talks too much

gas chamber *n* an airtight room which is filled with poison gas to kill people

gaseous *adj* of or like a gas

gash *n* **1** a long deep cut ▷ *vb* **2** to make a long deep cut in ▶ **HISTORY** Old French *garser* to scratch, wound

gasholder *n* a large tank for storing gas before distributing it to users

gasify *vb* **-fies, -fying, -fied** to change into a gas > **gasification** *n*

gasket *n* a piece of paper, rubber, or metal sandwiched between the faces of a metal joint to provide a seal ▶ **HISTORY** probably from French *garcette* rope's end

gaslight *n* **1** a lamp in which light is produced by burning gas **2** the light produced by such a lamp

gas mask *n* a mask fitted with a chemical filter to protect the wearer from breathing in harmful gases

gas meter *n* a device for measuring and recording the amount of gas passed through it

gasoline *or* **gasolene** *n US & Canad* petrol

gasometer (gas-**som**-it-er) *n* same as **gasholder**

gasp *vb* **1** to draw in the breath sharply or with difficulty **2** to utter breathlessly ▷ *n* **3** a short convulsive intake of breath ▶ **HISTORY** Old Norse *geispa* to yawn

gas pressure *n physics* the pressure a gas exerts on the side of its container

gassy *adj* **-sier, -siest** filled with, containing, or like gas > **gassiness** *n*

gastric *adj* of the stomach

gastric juice *n* a digestive fluid secreted by the stomach

gastric ulcer *n* an ulcer on the lining of the stomach

gastritis *n* inflammation of the lining of the stomach, causing vomiting or gastric ulcers

gastroenteritis *n* inflammation of the stomach and intestine, causing vomiting and diarrhoea

gastronomy *n* the art of good eating ▶ **HISTORY** Greek *gastēr* stomach + *nomos* law > **gastronomic** *adj*

gastropod *n* a mollusc, such as a snail or whelk that has a single flat muscular foot, eyes on stalks, and usually a spiral shell ▶ **HISTORY** Greek *gastēr* stomach + *-podos* -footed

gasworks *n* a factory in which coal gas is made

gate *n* **1** a movable barrier, usually hinged, for closing an opening in a wall or fence **2 a** the number of people admitted to a sporting event or entertainment **b** the total entrance money received from them **3** an exit at an airport by which passengers get to an aircraft **4** *electronics* a circuit with one or more input terminals and one output terminal, the output being determined by the combination of input signals **5** a slotted metal frame that controls the positions of the gear lever in a motor vehicle ▶ **HISTORY** Old English *geat*

gate-crash *vb informal* to gain entry to (a party) without invitation > **gate-crasher** *n*

gatehouse *n* a building at or above a gateway

gateway *n* **1** an entrance that may be closed by a gate **2** a means of entry or access: *his only gateway to the outside world*

gather *vb* **1** to come or bring together **2** to increase gradually in (pace, speed, or momentum) **3** to prepare oneself for a task or challenge by collecting one's thoughts, strength, or courage **4** to learn from information given; conclude: *this is pretty important, I gather* **5** to draw (fabric) into small folds or tucks **6** to pick or harvest (crops) ▷ *n* **7 gathers** small folds or tucks in fabric ▶ **HISTORY** Old English *gadrian*

gathering *n* a group of people, usually meeting for some particular purpose: *the Braemar Highland Gathering*

GATT General Agreement on Tariffs and Trade: a former name for the World Trade Organization

gauche (**gohsh**) *adj* socially awkward ▶ **HISTORY** French

gaucho (**gow**-choh) *n, pl* **-chos** a cowboy of the South American pampas ▶ **HISTORY** American Spanish

gaudy *adj* **gaudier, gaudiest** vulgarly bright or colourful ▶ **HISTORY** from *gaud* trinket > **gaudily** *adv* > **gaudiness** *n*

gauge (**gayj**) *vb* **gauging, gauged 1** to estimate or judge (people's feelings or reactions) **2** to measure using a gauge ▷ *n* **3** an instrument for measuring quantities: *a petrol gauge* **4** a scale or standard of measurement **5** a standard for estimating people's feelings or reactions: *a gauge of public opinion* **6** the diameter of the barrel of a gun **7** the distance between the rails of a railway track ▶ **HISTORY** from Old French

Gaul *n* a native of ancient Gaul

gaunt *adj* **1** bony and emaciated in appearance **2** (of a place) bleak or desolate: *the gaunt disused flour mill* ▶ **HISTORY** origin unknown > **gauntness** *n*

gauntlet¹ *n* **1** a long heavy protective glove **2** a medieval armoured glove **3 take up the gauntlet** to accept a challenge ▶ **HISTORY** Old French *gantelet*

gauntlet² *n* **run the gauntlet** to be exposed to criticism or harsh treatment ▶ **HISTORY** Swedish *gatlopp* passageway

gauss (rhymes with **mouse**) *n, pl* **gauss** the cgs unit of magnetic flux density ▶ **HISTORY** after K. F. *Gauss*, mathematician

gauze *n* a transparent, loosely woven cloth, often used for surgical dressings ▶ **HISTORY** French *gaze* > **gauzy** *adj*

gave *vb* the past tense of **give**

gavel (**gav**-vl) *n* a small hammer used by a judge, auctioneer, or chairman to call for order or attention ▶ **HISTORY** origin unknown

g

gavotte n **1** an old formal dance in quadruple time **2** music for this dance ▶ HISTORY French

gawk vb **1** to stare stupidly ▷ n **2** a clumsy stupid person ▶ HISTORY Old Danish gaukr

gawky adj **gawkier, gawkiest** clumsy and awkward

gawp vb slang to stare stupidly ▶ HISTORY Middle English galpen > **gawper** n

gay adj **1** homosexual **2** carefree and merry: with gay abandon **3** bright and cheerful: smartly dressed in gay colours ▷ n **4** a homosexual, esp. a homosexual man: solidarity amongst lesbians and gays ▶ HISTORY Old French gai

gayness n homosexuality

gaze vb **gazing, gazed 1** to look long and steadily at someone or something ▷ n **2** written a long steady look ▶ HISTORY Swedish dialect gasa to gape at

gazebo (gaz-**zee**-boh) n, pl **-bos** a summerhouse or pavilion with a good view ▶ HISTORY perhaps a pseudo-Latin coinage based on gaze

gazelle n a small graceful fawn-coloured antelope of Africa and Asia ▶ HISTORY Arabic ghazāl

gazette n an official newspaper that gives lists of announcements, for instance in legal or military affairs ▶ HISTORY French

gazetteer n a book or section of a book that lists and describes places

gazump vb Brit & Austral, informal to raise the price of a house after agreeing a price verbally with (an intending buyer) ▶ HISTORY origin unknown

gazunder vb Brit, informal to reduce an offer on a house immediately before exchanging contracts, having earlier agreed a higher price with (the seller) > **gazunderer** n

GB Great Britain

GBH (in Britain) grievous bodily harm

GC George Cross (a Brit. award for bravery)

GCE (in Britain) **1** General Certificate of Education **2** informal a pass in a GCE examination

GCSE (in Britain) **1** General Certificate of Secondary Education; an examination in specified subjects which replaced the GCE O level and CSE **2** informal a pass in a GCSE examination

Gd chem gadolinium

g'day interj Austral & NZ same as **gidday**

GDP gross domestic product

Ge chem germanium

geanticline n geol a gently sloping anticline covering a large area ▶ HISTORY Greek gē earth, land + ANTICLINE

gear n **1** a set of toothed wheels that engages with another or with a rack in order to change the speed or direction of transmitted motion **2** a mechanism for transmitting motion by gears **3** the setting of a gear to suit engine speed or direction: a higher gear; reverse gear **4** clothing or personal belongings **5** equipment for a particular task: police in riot gear **6** **in** or **out of gear** with the gear mechanism engaged or disengaged ▷ vb **7** to prepare or organize for something: to gear for war ▷ See also **gear up** ▶ HISTORY Old Norse gervi

gearbox n the metal casing enclosing a set of gears in a motor vehicle

gearing n a system of gears designed to transmit motion

gear lever or US & Canad **gearshift** n a lever used to engage or change gears in a motor vehicle

gear up vb to prepare for an activity: to gear up for a massive relief operation

gearwheel n one of the toothed wheels in the gears of a motor vehicle

gecko n, pl **geckos** a small tropical lizard ▶ HISTORY Malay ge'kok

gee interj US & Canad, informal a mild exclamation of surprise, admiration, etc. Also: **gee whizz** ▶ HISTORY euphemism for Jesus

geebung (**gee**-bung) n **1** an Australian tree or shrub with an edible but tasteless fruit **2** the fruit of this tree

geek n informal a boring and unattractive person ▶ HISTORY perhaps from Scottish geck fool > **geeky** adj

geelbek (**heel**-bek) n S African an edible marine fish with yellow jaws ▶ HISTORY Afrikaans geel yellow + bek mouth

geese n the plural of **goose**[1]

geezer n Brit, Austral & NZ, informal a man ▶ HISTORY probably dialect pronunciation of guiser, a mummer

Geiger counter (**guy**-ger) or **Geiger-Müller counter** n an instrument for detecting and measuring radiation ▶ HISTORY after Hans Geiger, physicist

geisha (**gay**-sha) n a professional female companion for men in Japan, trained in music, dancing, and conversation ▶ HISTORY Japanese

gel (**jell**) n **1** a thick jelly-like substance, esp. one used to keep a hairstyle in shape ▷ vb **gelling, gelled 2** to become a gel **3** same as **jell 4** to apply gel to (one's hair) ▶ HISTORY from gelatine

gelatine (**jell**-a-teen) or **gelatin** n a clear water-soluble protein made by boiling animal hides and bones, used in cooking, photography, etc. ▶ HISTORY Latin gelare to freeze

gelatinous (jill-**at**-in-uss) adj with a thick, semi-liquid consistency

geld vb **gelding, gelded** or **gelt** to castrate (a horse or other animal) ▶ HISTORY Old Norse gelda

gelding n a castrated male horse ▶ HISTORY Old Norse geldingr

gelignite n a type of dynamite used for blasting ▶ HISTORY GELATINE + Latin ignis fire

gem n **1** a precious stone used for decoration. Related adjective: **lapidary 2** a person or thing regarded as precious or special: a perfect gem of a hotel ▶ HISTORY Latin gemma bud, precious stone

gemfish n an Australian food fish with a delicate flavour

Gemini n astrol the third sign of the zodiac; the Twins ▶ HISTORY Latin

gemsbok (**hemss**-bok) n S African same as **oryx** ▶ HISTORY Afrikaans

gen n Brit, Austral & NZ, informal information: I want

to get as much gen as I can about the American market
▷ See also **gen up on** ▶ HISTORY from gen(eral information)

Gen. General

gendarme (**zhahn**-darm) n a member of the French police force ▶ HISTORY French

gender n **1** the state of being male, female, or neuter **2** the classification of nouns in certain languages as masculine, feminine, or neuter ▶ HISTORY Latin genus kind

gene (**jean**) n a unit composed of DNA forming part of a chromosome, by which inherited characteristics are transmitted from parent to offspring ▶ HISTORY German Gen

genealogy (jean-ee-**al**-a-jee) n **1** the direct descent of an individual or group from an ancestor **2** (pl-**gies**) a chart showing the descent of an individual or group ▶ HISTORY Greek genea race
> **genealogical** adj > **genealogist** n

genera (**jen**-er-a) n a plural of **genus**

general adj **1** common or widespread: general goodwill **2** of, affecting, or including all or most of the members of a group **3** not specialized or specializing: a general hospital **4** including various or miscellaneous items: general knowledge **5** not definite; vague: the examples used will give a general idea **6** highest in authority or rank: the club's general manager ▷ n **7** a very senior military officer **8 in general** generally; mostly or usually ▶ HISTORY Latin generalis

general anaesthetic n a substance that causes general anaesthesia. See **anaesthesia**

general election n an election in which representatives are chosen in all constituencies of a state

generalissimo n, pl-**mos** a supreme commander of combined armed forces ▶ HISTORY Italian

generality n **1** (pl-**ties**) a general principle or observation: speaking in generalities **2** old-fashioned the majority: the generality of mankind

generalization or-**isation** n a principle or statement based on specific instances but applied generally: the argument sinks to generalizations and name-calling

generalize or-**ise** vb -**izing**, -**ized** or-**ising**, -**ised** **1** to form general principles or conclusions from specific instances **2** to speak in generalities **3** to make widely used or known: generalized violence

generally adv **1** usually; as a rule: these protests have generally been peaceful **2** commonly or widely: it's generally agreed he has performed well **3** not specifically; broadly: what are your thoughts generally about the war?

general practitioner n a doctor who does not specialize but has a general medical practice in which he or she treats all illnesses

general staff n officers who assist commanders in the planning and execution of military operations

general strike n a strike by all or most of the workers of a country

generate vb -**ating**, -**ated** to produce or create

▶ HISTORY Latin generare to beget

generation n **1** all the people of approximately the same age: the younger generation **2** a successive stage in descent of people or animals: passed on from generation to generation **3** the average time between two generations of a species, about 35 years for humans: an alliance which has lasted a generation **4** a specified stage of development: the next generation of fighter aircraft **5** production, esp. of electricity or heat

generative adj capable of producing or originating something

generator n a device for converting mechanical energy into electrical energy

generic (jin-**ner**-ik) adj of a whole class, or group, or genus ▶ HISTORY Latin genus kind, race
> **generically** adv

generous adj **1** ready to give freely; unselfish **2** free from pettiness in character and mind **3** large or plentiful: a generous donation ▶ HISTORY Latin generosus nobly born > **generosity** n
> **generously** adv

genesis (**jen**-iss-iss) n, pl-**ses** (-seez) the beginning or origin of anything ▶ HISTORY Greek

Genesis n Bible the first book of the Old Testament, containing a description of the creation the world

gene therapy n genetics the replacement or alteration of defective genes in order to prevent the occurrence of inherited diseases

genetic (jin-**net**-ik) adj of genetics, genes, or the origin of something ▶ HISTORY from genesis
> **genetically** adv

genetically modified adj (of an organism) having DNA which has been altered for the purpose of improvement or correction of defects

genetic code n biochem the order in which the four nucleic acid bases of DNA are arranged in the molecule for transmitting genetic information to the cells

genetic engineering n alteration of the genetic structure of an organism in order to produce more desirable traits

genetic fingerprinting n the use of a person's unique pattern of DNA, which can be obtained from blood, saliva, or tissue, as a means of identification > **genetic fingerprint** n

genetic information n biol information about an individual that is carried in the genes and can be transferred to subsequent generations

genetics n the study of heredity and variation in organisms > **geneticist** n

genial (**jean**-ee-al) adj cheerful, easy-going, and friendly ▶ HISTORY Latin genius guardian deity
> **geniality** n > **genially** adv

genie (**jean**-ee) n (in fairy tales) a servant who appears by magic and fulfils a person's wishes ▶ HISTORY Arabic jinni demon

genital adj of the sexual organs or reproduction ▶ HISTORY Latin genitalis concerning birth

genitals or **genitalia** (jen-it-**ail**-ya) pl n the external sexual organs

<del>347</del>

genitive or **genitive case** n grammar a grammatical case in some languages used to indicate a relation of ownership or association ▶ HISTORY Latin genetivus relating to birth

genius (jean-yuss) n, pl **-uses** 1 a person with exceptional ability in a particular subject or activity 2 such ability 3 a person considered as exerting influence of a certain sort: the evil genius behind the drug-smuggling empire ▶ HISTORY Latin

genocide (jen-no-side) n the deliberate killing of a people or nation ▶ HISTORY Greek genos race + Latin caedere to kill > **genocidal** adj

genome (jee-nome) n biol 1 the full complement of genetic material within an organism 2 all the genes comprising a haploid set of chromosomes ▶ HISTORY German Genom, from Gen gene + (CHROMOS)OME > **genomic** (jee-**nom**-ik) adj

genotype (jen-oh-type) n biol the genetic constitution of an organism

genre (zhahn-ra) n 1 a kind or type of literary, musical, or artistic work: the mystery and supernatural genres 2 a kind of painting depicting incidents from everyday life ▶ HISTORY French

gent n Brit, Austral & NZ, informal short for **gentleman**

genteel adj 1 overly concerned with being polite 2 respectable, polite, and well-bred ▶ HISTORY French gentil well-born > **genteelly** adv

gentian (jen-shun) n a mountain plant with blue or purple flowers ▶ HISTORY Latin gentiana

gentian violet n a violet-coloured solution used as an antiseptic and in the treatment of burns

Gentile n 1 a person who is not a Jew ▷ adj 2 not Jewish ▶ HISTORY Latin gentilis belonging to the same tribe

gentility n, pl **-ties** 1 noble birth or ancestry 2 respectability and good manners ▶ HISTORY Old French gentilite

gentle adj 1 kind and calm in character 2 temperate or moderate: gentle autumn rain 3 soft; not sharp or harsh: gentle curves ▶ HISTORY Latin gentilis belonging to the same family > **gentleness** n > **gently** adv

gentlefolk pl n old-fashioned people regarded as being of good breeding

gentleman n, pl **-men** 1 a cultured, courteous, and well-bred man 2 a man who comes from a family of high social position 3 a polite name for a man > **gentlemanly** adj

gentrification n a process by which the character of a traditionally working-class area is made fashionable by middle-class people > **gentrify** vb

gentry n Brit, old-fashioned people just below the nobility in social rank ▶ HISTORY Old French genterie

gents n Brit & Austral, informal a men's public toilet

genuflect vb to bend the knee as a sign of reverence or deference, esp. in church ▶ HISTORY Latin genu knee + flectere to bend > **genuflection** n

genuine adj 1 real and exactly what it appears to be: a genuine antique 2 sincerely felt: genuine concern 3 (of a person) honest and without pretence ▶ HISTORY Latin genuinus inborn > **genuinely** adv > **genuineness** n

gen up on vb **genning, genned** Brit & Austral, informal to become, or make someone else, fully informed about

genus (jean-uss) n, pl **genera** or **genuses** 1 biol one of the groups into which a family is divided, containing one or more species 2 a class or group ▶ HISTORY Latin: race

geocentric adj 1 having the earth as a centre 2 measured as from the centre of the earth

geochemistry n geol the geology and chemistry concerned with the chemical composition of, and chemical reactions taking place within, the earth's crust > **geochemical** adj > **geochemist** n

geodesic adj 1 relating to the geometry of curved surfaces ▷ n 2 the shortest line between two points on a curved surface

geodesy n the study of the shape and size of the earth ▶ HISTORY Greek gē earth + daiein to divide

geographic information system n geog a computer system for storing, updating, accessing, analysing, and manipulating geographical data indexed by map coordinates. Abbrev: **GIS**

geography n 1 the study of the earth's surface, including physical features, climate, and population 2 the physical features of a region ▶ HISTORY Greek gē earth + -GRAPHY > **geographer** n > **geographical** or **geographic** adj > **geographically** adv

geoisotherm n same as **isogeotherm**

geological timescale n geol the system used by geologists to measure time, based on time units called aeons, eras, periods, and ages

geology n 1 the study of the origin, structure, and composition of the earth 2 the geological features of an area ▶ HISTORY Greek gē earth + -LOGY > **geological** adj > **geologically** adv > **geologist** n

geometric or **geometrical** adj 1 of geometry 2 consisting of shapes used in geometry, such as circles, triangles, and straight lines: geometric design > **geometrically** adv

geometric progression n a sequence of numbers, each of which differs from the succeeding one by a constant ratio, for example 1, 2, 4, 8

geometry n the branch of mathematics concerned with points, lines, curves, and surfaces ▶ HISTORY Greek geōmetrein to measure the land > **geometrician** n

geomorphic adj geol of, relating to, or resembling the earth's surface

geomorphology n geol the branch of geology that is concerned with the structure, origin, and development of the features of the earth's crust > **geomorphological** adj

geophysics *n* the study of the earth's physical properties and the physical forces which affect it > **geophysical** *adj* > **geophysicist** *n*

Geordie *Brit n* **1** a person from Tyneside **2** the Tyneside dialect ▷ *adj* **3** of Tyneside: *a Geordie accent*

George Cross *n* a British award for bravery, usually awarded to civilians

georgette (jor-**jet**) *n* a thin crepe dress material ▶ HISTORY after Mme *Georgette*, a French dressmaker

Georgian *adj* **1** of or in the reigns of any of the kings of Great Britain and Ireland called George **2** denoting a style of architecture or furniture prevalent in Britain in the 18th century: *an elegant Georgian terrace in Edinburgh*

geostationary *adj* (of a satellite) orbiting so as to remain over the same point on the earth's surface

geosyncline *n geol* a broad elongated depression in the earth's crust containing great thicknesses of sediment > **geosynclinal** *adj*

geotectonic *adj geol* of or relating to the formation, arrangement, and structure of the rocks of the earth's crust

geothermal *or* **geothermic** *adj* of or using the heat in the earth's interior

geothermal energy *n geol* power generated using steam produced by heat from the molten core of the earth

geotropism *n bot* the response of a plant part to the stimulus of gravity

geranium *n* a cultivated plant with scarlet, pink, or white flowers ▶ HISTORY Latin: cranesbill

gerbil (**jur**-bill) *n* a small rodent with long back legs, often kept as a pet ▶ HISTORY French *gerbille*

geriatric *adj* **1** of geriatrics or old people ▷ *n* **2** *old-fashioned, offensive* an old person, esp. as a patient

geriatrics *n* the branch of medicine concerned with illnesses affecting old people

germ *n* **1** a tiny living thing, esp. one that causes disease: *a diphtheria germ* **2** the beginning from which something may develop: *the germ of a book* ▶ HISTORY Latin *germen* sprout, seed

German *adj* **1** of Germany ▷ *n* **2** a person from Germany **3** the official language of Germany, Austria, and parts of Switzerland

germane *adj* relevant: *the studies provided some evidence germane to these questions* ▶ HISTORY Latin *germanus* of the same race

Germanic *n* **1** the ancient language from which English, German, and the Scandinavian languages developed ▷ *adj* **2** of this ancient language or the languages that developed from it **3** characteristic of German people or things: *Germanic-looking individuals*

germanium *n chem* a brittle grey metalloid element that is a semiconductor and is used in transistors. Symbol: Ge ▶ HISTORY after *Germany*

German measles *n* same as **rubella**

German shepherd dog *n* same as **Alsatian**

germ cell *n* a sexual reproductive cell

germicide *n* a substance used to destroy germs ▶ HISTORY *germ* + Latin *caedere* to kill

germinal *adj* **1** of or in the earliest stage of development: *the germinal phases of the case* **2** of germ cells

germinate *vb* **-nating, -nated** to grow or cause to grow ▶ HISTORY Latin *germinare* to sprout > **germination** *n*

germ warfare *n* the military use of disease-spreading bacteria against an enemy

gerontology *n* the scientific study of ageing and the problems of old people ▶ HISTORY Greek *gerōn* old man + -LOGY > **gerontologist** *n*

gerrymandering *n* the practice of dividing the constituencies of a voting area so as to give one party an unfair advantage ▶ HISTORY from Elbridge *Gerry*, US politician + (*sala*)*mander*, from the salamander-like outline of a reshaped electoral district

gerund (**jer**-rund) *n* a noun formed from a verb, ending in *-ing*, denoting an action or state, for example *running* ▶ HISTORY Latin *gerundum* something to be carried on

gesso (**jess**-oh) *n* plaster used for painting or in sculpture ▶ HISTORY Italian: chalk

Gestapo *n* the secret state police of Nazi Germany ▶ HISTORY German *Ge(heime) Sta(ats)po(lizei)* secret state police

gestation *n* **1** the process of carrying and developing babies in the womb during pregnancy, or the time during which this process takes place **2** the process of developing a plan or idea in the mind ▶ HISTORY Latin *gestare* to bear

gesticulate *vb* **-lating, -lated** *mainly Written* to make expressive movements with the hands and arms, usually while talking ▶ HISTORY Latin *gesticulari* > **gesticulation** *n*

gesture *n* **1** a movement of the hands, head, or body to express or emphasize an idea or emotion **2** something said or done to indicate intention, or as a formality: *a gesture of goodwill* ▷ *vb* **-turing, -tured** **3** to make expressive movements with the hands and arms ▶ HISTORY Latin *gestus*

get *vb* **getting, got** **1** to come into possession of **2** to bring or fetch **3** to catch (an illness) **4** to become: *they get frustrated and angry* **5** to cause to be done or to happen: *he got a wart removed; to get steamed up* **6** to hear or understand: *did you get that joke?* **7** to reach (a place or point): *we could not get to the airport in time* **8** to catch (a bus or train) **9** to persuade: *she trying to get him to give secrets away* **10** *informal* to annoy: *you know what really gets me?* **11** *informal* to baffle: *now you've got me* **12** *informal* to hit: *a bit of grenade got me on the left hip* **13** *informal* to be revenged on **14** *informal* to start: *we got talking about it; it got me thinking* ▶ HISTORY Old English *gietan*

get across *vb* to make (something) understood

get at *vb* **1** to gain access to: *to get at the information on these disks* **2** to imply or mean: *it is hard to see quite what he is getting at* **3** to annoy or criticize persistently: *people who know they're being got at*

349

get by *vb informal* to manage in spite of difficulties: *he saw for himself what people did to get by*

Gethsemane (geth-**sem**-a-nee) *n Christianity* the garden in Jerusalem where Jesus Christ was betrayed by Judas Iscariot before his crucifixion

get in *vb* **1** to arrive **2** to be elected **3** *spoken*
get in on to join in (an activity)

get off *vb* **1** to leave (a bus or train or a place) **2** to escape the consequences of or punishment for an action: *the real culprits have got off scot-free*

get on *vb* **1** to enter (a bus or train) **2** to have a friendly relationship: *he had a flair for getting on with people* **3** to grow old: *he was getting on in years* **4** (of time) to elapse: *the time was getting on* **5** to make progress: *how are the children getting on?* **6 get on with** to continue to do: *you can get on with whatever you were doing before* **7 getting on for** approaching (a time, age, or amount): *getting on for half a century ago*

get out *vb* **1** to leave or escape **2** to become known **3** to gain something of significance or value: *that's all I got out of it* **4 get out of** to avoid: *to get out of doing the dishes*

get over *vb* **1** to recover from (an illness or unhappy experience) **2** to overcome (a problem) **3 get over with** to bring (something necessary but unpleasant) to an end: *better to get it over with*

get through *vb* **1** to complete (a task or process) **2** to use up (money or supplies) **3** to succeed in (an examination or test) **4 get through to a** to succeed in making (someone) understand **b** to contact (someone) by telephone

geyser (**geez**-er) *n* **1** a spring that discharges steam and hot water **2** *Brit & S African* a domestic gas water heater ▶ HISTORY Icelandic *Geysir*

ghastly *adj* **-lier, -liest 1** *informal* very unpleasant **2** deathly pale **3** horrible: *a ghastly accident* ▶ HISTORY Old English *gāstlīc* spiritual

ghat *n* (in India) **1** stairs leading down to a river **2** a place of cremation **3** a mountain pass ▶ HISTORY Hindi

ghee (**gee**) *n* clarified butter, used in Indian cookery ▶ HISTORY Hindi *ghī*

gherkin *n* a small pickled cucumber ▶ HISTORY Dutch *agurkkijn*

ghetto *n, pl* **-tos** or **-toes** an area that is inhabited by people of a particular race, religion, nationality, or class ▶ HISTORY Italian

ghetto blaster *n informal* a large portable CD player or cassette recorder with built-in speakers

ghillie *n* same as **gillie**

ghost *n* **1** the disembodied spirit of a dead person, supposed to haunt the living **2** a faint trace: *the ghost of a smile on his face* **3** a faint secondary image in an optical instrument or on a television screen ▷ *vb* **4** short for **ghostwrite** ▶ HISTORY Old English *gāst*

ghost gum *n Austral* a eucalyptus with white trunk and branches

ghostly *adj* **-lier, -liest** frightening in appearance or effect: *ghostly noises*

ghost town *n* a town that used to be busy but is now deserted

ghostwrite *vb* **-writing, -wrote, -written** to write (an article or book) on behalf of a person who is then credited as author > **ghostwriter** *n*

ghoul (**gool**) *n* **1** a person who is interested in morbid or disgusting things **2** a demon that eats corpses ▶ HISTORY Arabic *ghūl* > **ghoulish** *adj* > **ghoulishly** *adv*

GHQ *mil* General Headquarters

GI[1] *n, pl* **GIs** or **GI's** *US, informal* a soldier in the US Army ▶ HISTORY abbreviation of *government issue*

GI[2] glycaemic index

giant *n* **1** a mythical figure of superhuman size and strength **2** a person or thing of exceptional size, ability, or importance: *industrial giants* ▷ *adj* **3** remarkably large **4** (of an atom or ion or its structure) having large numbers of particles present in a crystal lattice, with each particle exerting a strong force of attraction on those near to it ▶ HISTORY Greek *gigas*

giant panda *n* See **panda**

gibber[1] (**jib**-ber) *vb* to talk in a fast and unintelligible manner ▶ HISTORY imitative

gibber[2] (**gib**-ber) *n Austral* a boulder ▶ HISTORY Aboriginal

gibberish *n* rapid incomprehensible talk; nonsense

gibber plain *n Austral geog* barren land covered with stones ▶ HISTORY Aboriginal

gibbet (**jib**-bit) *n* a gallows ▶ HISTORY Old French *gibet*

gibbon (**gib**-bon) *n* a small agile ape of the forests of S Asia ▶ HISTORY French

gibbous (**gib**-bus) *adj* (of the moon) more than half but less than fully illuminated ▶ HISTORY Latin *gibba* hump

gibe (**jibe**) *n, vb* **gibing, gibed** same as **jibe**[1] ▶ HISTORY perhaps from Old French *giber* to treat roughly

giblets (**jib**-lits) *pl n* the gizzard, liver, heart, and neck of a fowl ▶ HISTORY Old French *gibelet* stew of game birds

gidday, g'day *interj Austral & NZ* an expression of greeting

giddy *adj* **-dier, -diest 1** feeling weak and unsteady on one's feet, as if about to faint **2** happy and excited: *a state of giddy expectation* ▶ HISTORY Old English *gydig* mad, frenzied, possessed by God > **giddiness** *n*

gift *n* **1** something given to someone: *a birthday gift* **2** a special ability or power: *a gift for caricature* ▶ HISTORY Old English: payment for a wife, dowry

gifted *adj* having natural talent or aptitude: *that era's most gifted director*

gig[1] *n* **1** a single performance by jazz or pop musicians ▷ *vb* **gigging, gigged 2** to play gigs ▶ HISTORY origin unknown

gig[2] *n* a light open two-wheeled one-horse carriage ▶ HISTORY origin unknown

gig[3] *n informal* short for **gigabyte**

giga- *prefix* **1** denoting 10⁹: *gigavolt* **2** *computers* denoting 2³⁰: *gigabyte* ▶ **HISTORY** Greek *gigas* giant

gigabyte *n computers* 1024 megabytes

gigantic *adj* extremely large: *the most gigantic gold paperweight ever* ▶ **HISTORY** Greek *gigantikos*

giggle *vb* **-gling, -gled 1** to laugh nervously or foolishly ▷ *n* **2** a nervous or foolish laugh **3** *informal* an amusing person or thing ▶ **HISTORY** imitative > **giggly** *adj*

gigolo (**jig**-a-lo) *n, pl* **-los** a man who is paid by an older woman to be her escort or lover ▶ **HISTORY** French

gigot *n chiefly Brit* a leg of lamb or mutton ▶ **HISTORY** French

gild *vb* **gilding, gilded** *or* **gilt 1** to cover with a thin layer of gold **2** to make (something) appear golden: *the morning sun gilded the hills* **3 gild the lily a** to adorn unnecessarily something already beautiful **b** to praise someone excessively ▶ **HISTORY** Old English *gyldan*

gill¹ (jill) *n* a unit of liquid measure equal to one quarter of a pint (0.14 litres) ▶ **HISTORY** Old French *gille* vat, tub

gillie *or* **ghillie** *n Scot* a sportsman's attendant or guide for hunting or fishing ▶ **HISTORY** Scottish Gaelic *gille* boy, servant

gills (gillz) *pl n* the breathing organs of fish and other water creatures ▶ **HISTORY** from Old Norse

gilt *vb* **1** a past of **gild** ▷ *adj* **2** covered with a thin layer of gold ▷ *n* **3** a thin layer of gold, used as decoration

gilt-edged *adj* denoting government securities on which interest payments and final repayments are guaranteed

gimcrack (**jim**-krak) *adj* showy but cheap; shoddy ▶ **HISTORY** origin unknown

gimlet (**gim**-let) *n* **1** a small hand tool with a pointed spiral tip, used for boring holes in wood ▷ *adj* **2** *written* penetrating or piercing: *gimlet eyes* ▶ **HISTORY** Old French *guimbelet*

gimmick *n informal* something designed to attract attention or publicity ▶ **HISTORY** origin unknown > **gimmickry** *n* > **gimmicky** *adj*

gin¹ *n* an alcoholic drink distilled from malted grain and flavoured with juniper berries ▶ **HISTORY** Dutch *genever* juniper

gin² *n* a noose of thin strong wire for catching small mammals ▶ **HISTORY** Middle English *gyn*

ginger *n* **1** the root of a tropical plant, powdered and used as a spice or sugared and eaten as a sweet ▷ *adj* **2** light reddish-brown: *ginger hair* ▶ **HISTORY** Old French *gingivre* > **gingery** *adj*

ginger ale *n* a nonalcoholic fizzy drink flavoured with ginger extract

gingerbread *n* a moist brown cake flavoured with ginger

ginger group *n Brit, Austral & NZ* a group within a larger group that agitates for a more active policy

gingerly *adv written* carefully or cautiously: *she sat gingerly on the edge of the chair* ▶ **HISTORY** perhaps from Old French *gensor* dainty

ginger nut *or* **snap** *n* a hard biscuit flavoured with ginger

gingham *n* a cotton fabric with a checked or striped design ▶ **HISTORY** Malay *ginggang* striped cloth

gingivitis (jin-jiv-**vite**-iss) *n* inflammation of the gums ▶ **HISTORY** Latin *gingiva* gum

ginseng (**jin**-seng) *n* the root of a plant of China and North America, believed to have tonic and energy-giving properties ▶ **HISTORY** Mandarin Chinese *jen shen*

Gipsy *n, pl* **-sies** same as **Gypsy**

giraffe *n* a cud-chewing African mammal with a very long neck and long legs and a spotted yellowy skin ▶ **HISTORY** Arabic *zarāfah*

gird *vb* **girding, girded** *or* **girt 1** to put a belt or girdle around **2 gird (up) one's loins** to prepare oneself for action ▶ **HISTORY** Old English *gyrdan*

girder *n* a large steel or iron beam used in the construction of bridges and buildings

girdle *n* **1** a woman's elastic corset that covers the stomach and hips **2** anything that surrounds something or someone: *his girdle of supporters* **3** *anat* an encircling arrangement of bones: *the shoulder girdle* ▷ *vb* **-dling, -dled 4** to surround: *a ring of volcanic ash girdling the earth* ▶ **HISTORY** Old English *gyrdel*

girl *n* **1** a female child **2** a young woman ▶ **HISTORY** Middle English *girle* > **girlhood** *n* > **girlish** *adj*

girlfriend *n* **1** a female friend with whom a person is romantically involved **2** any female friend

Girl Guide *n* a former name for **Guide**

girlie *adj informal* **1** featuring naked or scantily dressed women: *girlie magazines* **2** suited to or designed to appeal to young women: *a real girlie night out*

giro (**jire**-oh) *n, pl* **-ros 1** (in some countries) a system of transferring money within a bank or post office, directly from one account into another **2** *Brit, informal* a social-security payment by giro cheque ▶ **HISTORY** Greek *guros* circuit

girt *vb* a past of **gird**

girth *n* **1** the measurement around something **2** a band fastened round a horse's middle to keep the saddle in position ▶ **HISTORY** Old Norse *gjörth* belt

GIS 1 geographic information system **2** global information system

gist (jist) *n* the main point or meaning of something: *the gist of the letter* ▶ **HISTORY** Anglo-French, as in *cest action gist en* this action consists in

give *vb* **giving, gave, given 1** to present (something) to someone **2** to pay (an amount of money) for a purchase **3** to grant or provide: *to give an answer* **4** to utter (a shout or cry) **5** to perform, make, or do: *the prime minister gave a speech* **6** to host (a party) **7** to sacrifice or devote: *comrades who gave their lives for their country* **8** to concede: *he was very efficient, I have to give him that* **9** to yield or break under pressure: *something has got to give* **10 give or take** plus or minus: *about one hundred metres, give or take five* ▷ *n* **11** a tendency to yield under pressure; elasticity ▷ See also **give away, give in**, etc. ▶ **HISTORY** Old English *giefan* > **giver** *n*

give away *vb* **1** to donate as a gift **2** to reveal (a secret) **3** to present (a bride) formally to her husband in a marriage ceremony **4** *NZ* to give (something) up ▷ *n* **giveaway 5** something that reveals hidden feelings or intentions ▷ *adj* **giveaway 6** very cheap or free: *a giveaway rent*

give in *vb* to admit defeat

given *vb* **1** the past participle of **give** ▷ *adj* **2** specific or previously stated: *priorities within the given department* **3** to be assumed: *any given place on the earth* **4 given to** inclined to: *a man not given to undue optimism*

give off *vb* to send out (heat, light, or a smell)

give out *vb* **1** to hand out: *the bloke that was giving out those tickets* **2** to send out (heat, light, or a smell) **3** to make known: *the man who gave out the news* **4** to fail: *the engine gave out*

give over *vb* **1** to set aside for a specific purpose: *the amount of space given over to advertisements* **2** *informal* to stop doing something annoying: *tell him to give over*

give up *vb* **1** to stop (doing something): *I did give up smoking* **2** to resign from (a job or position) **3** to admit defeat or failure **4** to abandon (hope) **5 give oneself up a** to surrender to the police or other authorities **b** to devote oneself completely: *she gave herself up to her work*

gizzard *n* the part of a bird's stomach in which hard food is broken up ▶ **HISTORY** Old French *guisier* fowl's liver

glacé (**glass**-say) *adj* preserved in a thick sugary syrup: *glacé cherries* ▶ **HISTORY** French: iced

glacial *adj* **1** of glaciers or ice **2** extremely cold **3** cold and unfriendly: *a glacial stare*

glacial period *or* **epoch** *n geol* **1** any period of time during which a large part of the earth's surface was covered with ice, caused by the advance of glaciers **2** the Pleistocene epoch ▷ Also called: **ice age**

glaciation *n* the process of covering part of the earth's surface with glaciers or masses of ice > **glaciated** *adj*

glacier *n* a slowly moving mass of ice formed by an accumulation of snow ▶ **HISTORY** Latin *glacies* ice

glad *adj* **gladder, gladdest 1** happy and pleased **2** very willing: *he was only too glad to help* **3** *archaic* causing happiness: *glad tidings* ▶ **HISTORY** Old English *glæd* > **gladden** *vb* > **gladly** *adv* > **gladness** *n*

glade *n* an open space in a forest: *a peaceful and sheltered glade* ▶ **HISTORY** origin unknown

gladiator *n* (in ancient Rome) a man trained to fight in arenas to provide entertainment ▶ **HISTORY** Latin: swordsman > **gladiatorial** *adj*

gladiolus (glad-ee-**oh**-luss) *n, pl* **-li** (-lie) a garden plant with brightly coloured funnel-shaped flowers ▶ **HISTORY** Latin: a small sword

glad rags *pl n informal* one's best clothes

gladwrap *Austral, NZ & S African n* **1** *trademark* thin polythene material for wrapping ▷ *vb* **2** to wrap in gladwrap

glamorous *adj* attractive or fascinating

glamour *or US* **glamor** *n* exciting or alluring charm or beauty ▶ **HISTORY** Scots variant of *grammar* (hence a spell, because occult practices were popularly associated with learning) > **glamorize** *or* **-ise** *vb*

glance *n* **1** a quick look ▷ *vb* **glancing, glanced 2** to look quickly at something **3** to be deflected off an object at an oblique angle: *the ball glanced off a spectator* ▶ **HISTORY** Middle English *glacen* to strike obliquely > **glancing** *adj*

gland *n* **1** an organ that synthesizes and secretes chemical substances for the body to use or eliminate **2** a similar organ in plants ▶ **HISTORY** Latin *glans* acorn

glandular *adj* of or affecting a gland or glands

glandular fever *n* an acute infectious viral disease that causes fever, sore throat, and painful swollen lymph nodes

glare *vb* **glaring, glared 1** to stare angrily **2** (of light or colour) to be too bright ▷ *n* **3** an angry stare **4** a dazzling light or brilliance **5 in the glare of publicity** receiving a lot of attention from the media or the public ▶ **HISTORY** Middle English

glaring *adj* conspicuous or obvious: *glaring inconsistencies* > **glaringly** *adv*

glasnost *n hist* a policy of public frankness and accountability, developed in the USSR in the 1980s under Mikhail Gorbachev ▶ **HISTORY** Russian: publicity, openness

glass *n* **1** a hard brittle transparent solid, consisting of metal silicates or similar compounds **2** a drinking vessel made of glass **3** the amount contained in a drinking glass: *a glass of wine* **4** objects made of glass, such as drinking glasses and bowls ▶ **HISTORY** Old English *glæs*

glass ceiling *n* a situation in which progress, esp. promotion, appears to be possible, but restrictions or discrimination create a barrier that prevents it

glasses *pl n* a pair of lenses for correcting faulty vision, in a frame that rests on the nose and hooks behind the ears

glasshouse *n Brit & NZ* same as **greenhouse**

glassy *adj* **glassier, glassiest** *written* **1** smooth, clear, and shiny, like glass: *the glassy sea* **2** expressionless: *that glassy look*

Glaswegian (glaz-**weej**-an) *adj* **1** of Glasgow, a city in W Scotland ▷ *n* **2** a person from Glasgow **3** the Glasgow dialect

glaucoma *n* an eye disease in which increased pressure in the eyeball causes gradual loss of sight ▶ **HISTORY** Greek *glaukos* silvery, bluish-green

glaze *vb* **glazing, glazed 1** to fit or cover with glass **2** to cover (a piece of pottery) with a protective shiny coating **3** to cover (food) with beaten egg or milk before cooking, in order to produce a shiny coating ▷ *n* **4** a protective shiny coating applied to a piece of pottery **5** a shiny coating of beaten egg or milk applied to food ▶ **HISTORY** Middle English *glasen* > **glazed** *adj* > **glazing** *n*

glazier *n* a person who fits windows or doors with glass

GLB *maths* greatest lower bound

gleam *written n* **1** a small beam or glow of light **2** a brief or dim indication: *a gleam of anticipation in his eye* ▷ *vb* **3** to shine ▶ HISTORY Old English *glǣm* > **gleaming** *adj*

glean *vb* **1** to gather (information) bit by bit **2** to gather the useful remnants of (a crop) after harvesting ▶ HISTORY Old French *glener* > **gleaner** *n*

gleanings *pl n* pieces of information that have been gleaned

glebe *n Brit & Austral* land granted to a member of the clergy as part of his or her benefice ▶ HISTORY Latin *glaeba*

glee *n* great merriment or joy, esp. caused by the misfortune of another person ▶ HISTORY Old English *glēo*

gleeful *adj written* merry or joyful, esp. over someone else's mistake or misfortune > **gleefully** *adv*

glen *n* a deep narrow mountain valley ▶ HISTORY Scottish Gaelic *gleann*

glengarry *n, pl* **-ries** a brimless Scottish cap with a crease down the crown ▶ HISTORY after *Glengarry*, Scotland

glib *adj* **glibber, glibbest** fluent and easy, often in an insincere or deceptive way: *there were no glib or easy answers* ▶ HISTORY probably from Middle Low German *glibberich* slippery > **glibly** *adv* > **glibness** *n*

glide *vb* **gliding, glided** **1** to move easily and smoothly **2** (of an aircraft) to land without engine power **3** to fly a glider **4** to float on currents of air ▶ HISTORY Old English *glīdan*

glider *n* **1** an aircraft that does not use an engine, but flies by floating on air currents **2** *Austral* another name for **flying phalanger**

glide time *n NZ* same as **flexitime**

gliding *n* the sport of flying in a glider

glimmer *vb* **1** (of a light) to glow faintly or flickeringly ▷ *n* **2** a faint indication: *a glimmer of hope* **3** a glow or twinkle ▶ HISTORY Middle English

glimpse *n* **1** a brief view: *a glimpse of a rare snow leopard* **2** a vague indication: *glimpses of insecurity* ▷ *vb* **glimpsing, glimpsed** **3** to catch sight of momentarily ▶ HISTORY Germanic

glint *written vb* **1** to gleam brightly ▷ *n* **2** a bright gleam ▶ HISTORY probably from Old Norse

glissade *n* **1** a gliding step in ballet **2** a controlled slide down a snow slope ▷ *vb* **-sading, -saded** **3** to perform a glissade ▶ HISTORY French

glissando *n, pl* **-dos** *music* a slide between two notes in which all intermediate notes are played ▶ HISTORY mock Italian, from French *glisser* to slide

glisten *vb* (of a wet or glossy surface) to gleam by reflecting light: *sweat glistened above his eyes* ▶ HISTORY Old English *glisnian*

glitch *n* a small problem that stops something from working properly ▶ HISTORY Yiddish *glitsh* a slip

glitter *vb* **1** (of a surface) to reflect light in bright flashes **2** (of light) to be reflected in bright flashes

3 to be brilliant in a showy way: *she glitters socially* ▷ *n* **4** a sparkling light **5** superficial glamour: *the trappings and glitter of the European aristocracy* **6** tiny pieces of shiny decorative material **7** *Canad* ice formed from freezing rain ▶ HISTORY Old Norse *glitra* > **glittering** *adj* > **glittery** *adj*

glitzy *adj* **glitzier, glitziest** *slang* showily attractive ▶ HISTORY probably from German *glitzern* to glitter

gloaming *n Scot, poetic* twilight; dusk ▶ HISTORY Old English *glōmung*

gloat *vb* to regard one's own good fortune or the misfortune of others with smug or malicious pleasure ▶ HISTORY probably Scandinavian

glob *n informal* a rounded mass of thick fluid ▶ HISTORY probably from *globe*, influenced by *blob*

global *adj* **1** of or applying to the whole earth: *global environmental problems* **2** of or applying to the whole of something: *a global total for local-authority revenue* > **globally** *adv*

global circulation *n meteorol* the circulation of winds round the earth, which results in global weather patterns

global information system *n* a computer system used for storing and analysing geographical data. Abbrev: **GIS**

globalization *or* **-isation** *n* **1** the presence of a single world market dominated by multinational companies, leading to a diminishing capacity for national governments to control their economies **2** the process by which a company, etc. expands to operate internationally

global warming *n* an increase in the overall temperature worldwide believed to be caused by the greenhouse effect

globe *n* **1** a sphere on which a map of the world is drawn **2** **the globe** the earth **3** a spherical object, such as a glass lampshade or fishbowl **4** *S African* an electric light bulb ▶ HISTORY Latin *globus*

globetrotter *n* a habitual worldwide traveller > **globetrotting** *n, adj*

globular *adj* shaped like a globe or globule

globule *n* a small round drop of liquid ▶ HISTORY Latin *globulus*

globulin *n* a simple protein found in living tissue

glockenspiel *n* a percussion instrument consisting of tuned metal plates played with a pair of small hammers ▶ HISTORY German *Glocken* bells + *Spiel* play

glomerulus (glom-**err**-oo-luss) *n, pl* **-li** (-lye) *anat* a knot of blood vessels in the kidney projecting into the end of a urine-secreting tubule

gloom *n* **1** depression or melancholy: *all doom and gloom* **2** partial or total darkness ▶ HISTORY Middle English *gloumben* to look sullen

gloomy *adj* **gloomier, gloomiest** **1** despairing or sad **2** causing depression or gloom: *gloomy economic forecasts* **3** dark or dismal > **gloomily** *adv*

glorify *vb* **-fies, -fying, -fied** **1** to make (something) seem more important than it really is: *computers are just glorified adding machines* **2** to praise: *few countries have glorified success in business*

more than the United States **3** to worship (God)
> **glorification** n

glorious adj **1** brilliantly beautiful: in glorious colour
2 delightful or enjoyable: the glorious summer
weather **3** having or full of glory: glorious successes
> **gloriously** adv

glory n, pl **-ries 1** fame, praise, or honour: tales of
glory **2** splendour: the glory of the tropical day
3 something worthy of praise: the Lady Chapel is
the great glory of Lichfield **4** adoration or worship:
the greater glory of God ▷ vb **-ries, -rying, -ried**
5 **glory in** to take great pleasure in: the workers
were glorying in their new-found freedom ▶ HISTORY
Latin gloria

glory box n Austral & NZ, old-fashioned, informal a
box in which a young woman stores her trousseau

glory hole n an untidy cupboard or storeroom

gloss[1] n **1** a bright shine on a surface **2** a superficially
attractive appearance **3** a paint with a shiny finish
4 a cosmetic used to give a shiny appearance: lip
gloss ▷ vb **5** to paint with gloss **6** **gloss over** to
conceal (an error, failing, or awkward moment) by
minimizing it: don't try to gloss over bad news
▶ HISTORY probably Scandinavian

gloss[2] n **1** an explanatory comment added to the
text of a book ▷ vb **2** to add a gloss or glosses to
▶ HISTORY Latin glossa unusual word requiring
explanatory note

glossary n, pl **-ries** an alphabetical list of technical
or specialist words in a book, with explanations
▶ HISTORY Late Latin glossarium; see GLOSS[2]

glossy adj **glossier, glossiest 1** smooth and shiny:
glossy black hair **2** superficially attractive or
sophisticated: his glossy Manhattan flat **3** (of a
magazine) produced on expensive shiny paper

glottal stop n phonetics a speech sound produced
by tightly closing and then opening the glottis

glottis n the opening at the top of the windpipe,
between the vocal cords ▶ HISTORY Greek glōtta
tongue

glove n **1** a shaped covering for the hand with
individual sheaths for each finger and the thumb
2 a protective hand covering worn in sports such as
boxing ▶ HISTORY Old English glōfe

glove compartment n a small storage area in
the dashboard of a car

gloved adj written covered by a glove or gloves: a
gloved hand

glow n **1** light produced as a result of great heat **2** a
steady light without flames **3** brightness of
complexion **4** a feeling of wellbeing or satisfaction
▷ vb **5** to produce a steady light without flames
6 to shine intensely **7** to experience a feeling of
wellbeing or satisfaction: she glowed with pleasure
8 (of the complexion) to have a strong bright
colour: his pale face glowing at the recollection
▶ HISTORY Old English glōwan

glower (rhymes with **power**) vb **1** to stare angrily
▷ n **2** an angry stare ▶ HISTORY origin unknown

glow-worm n a European beetle, the females and
larvae of which have organs producing a soft
greenish light

gloxinia n a plant with white, red, or purple
bell-shaped flowers ▶ HISTORY after Benjamin P.
Gloxin, botanist

glucagon n biochem a hormone that stimulates
the release of glucose into the blood

glucose n a white crystalline sugar found in plant
and animal tissues ▶ HISTORY Greek gleukos sweet
wine

glue n **1** a substance used for sticking things
together ▷ vb **gluing** or **glueing, glued 2** to join or
stick together with glue **3** **glued to** paying full
attention to: golf fans will be glued to their televisions
today for the Open Championship ▶ HISTORY Late
Latin glus > **gluey** adj

glue ear n an accumulation of fluid in the middle
ear of children, caused by infection and causing
deafness

glue-sniffing n the practice of inhaling glue
fumes to produce intoxicating or hallucinatory
effects > **glue-sniffer** n

glum adj **glummer, glummest** gloomy and quiet,
usually because of a disappointment ▶ HISTORY
variant of gloom > **glumly** adv

glut n **1** an excessive supply ▷ vb **glutting, glutted**
2 to supply (a market) with a commodity in excess
of the demand for it **3** **glut oneself** to eat or drink
more than one really needs ▶ HISTORY probably
from Old French gloutir to swallow

gluten (**gloo**-ten) n a sticky protein found in
cereal grains, such as wheat ▶ HISTORY Latin:
glue

glutinous (**gloo**-tin-uss) adj gluelike in texture

glutton n **1** someone who eats and drinks too
much **2** a person who has a great capacity for
something: a glutton for work ▶ HISTORY Latin
gluttire to swallow > **gluttonous** adj

gluttony n the practice of eating too much

glycaemic index or US **glycemic index**
(glie-**seem**-ik) n an indication of the effects of
various foods on blood sugar. Abbrev: **GI** ▶ HISTORY
Greek glukus sweet + haima blood

glycerine (**gliss**-ser-reen) or **glycerin** n a
nontechnical name for **glycerol** ▶ HISTORY Greek
glukeros sweet

glycerol (**gliss**-ser-ol) n a colourless, odourless
syrupy liquid obtained from animal and vegetable
fats, used as a solvent, antifreeze, and sweetener,
and in explosives

glycogen (**glike**-oh-jen) n a starchlike
carbohydrate stored in the liver and muscles of
humans and animals

glycolysis (glike-**kol**-iss-iss) n biochem the
breakdown of glucose by enzymes, with the
release of energy

glycoside n biochem a substance derived from
monosaccharides by replacing the hydroxyl group
by another group > **glycosidic** adj

gm gram

GM 1 genetically modified **2** Brit grant-maintained

G-man n, pl **G-men** US, slang an FBI agent

GMO genetically modified organism

GMT Greenwich Mean Time

gnarled *adj* rough, twisted, and knobbly, usually through age

gnash *vb* to grind (the teeth) together in pain or anger ▸ HISTORY probably from Old Norse

gnat *n* a small biting two-winged insect ▸ HISTORY Old English *gnætt*

gnaw *vb* **1** to bite or chew constantly so as to wear away bit by bit **2** *gnaw at* *written* to cause constant distress or anxiety to: *uneasiness gnawed at his mind* ▸ HISTORY Old English *gnagan* > **gnawing** *adj*

gneiss *n* a coarse-grained layered metamorphic rock ▸ HISTORY German *Gneis*

gnome *n* **1** an imaginary creature in fairy tales that looks like a little old man **2** a small statue of a gnome in a garden ▸ HISTORY French

gnomic (**no**-mik) *adj literary, written* of or containing short clever sayings: *gnomic pronouncements*

Gnosticism (**noss**-tiss-siz-zum) *n* a religious movement involving belief in intuitive spiritual knowledge > **Gnostic** *n, adj*

GNP gross national product

gnu (noo) *n, pl* **gnus** *or* **gnu** a sturdy African antelope with an oxlike head ▸ HISTORY Xhosa *nqu*

go *vb* **going, went, gone 1** to move or proceed to or from a place: *go forward* **2** to be in regular attendance at (work, church, or a place of learning) **3** to lead to a particular place: *the path that goes right along the bank* **4** to be kept in a particular place: *where does this go?* **5** to do or become as specified: *he went white; the gun went bang* **6** to be or continue to be in a specified state: *to go to sleep* **7** to operate or function: *the car wouldn't go* **8** to follow a specified course; fare: *I'd hate the meeting to go badly* **9** to be allotted to a particular purpose or expenditure: *a third of the total budget goes on the army* **10** to be sold: *the portrait went for a fortune to a telephone bidder* **11** (of words or music) to be expressed or sung: *the song goes like this* **12** to fail or break down: *my eyesight is going; he was on lap nineteen when the engine went* **13** to die: *he went quickly at the end* **14** to be spent or finished: *all hope had gone* **15** to proceed up to or beyond certain limits: *I think this is going too far* **16** to carry authority: *what Daddy says goes* **17** to endure or last out: *they go for eight or ten hours without resting* **18** *not standard* to say: *then she goes, 'shut up'* **19** *anything goes* anything is acceptable **20** *be going to* to intend or be about to: *she was afraid of what was going to happen next* **21** *let go* to relax one's hold on; release **22** *let oneself go* **a** to act in an uninhibited manner **b** to lose interest in one's appearance **23** *to go* remaining: *two days to go till the holidays* ▷ *n, pl* **goes 24** an attempt: *he had a go at the furniture business* **25** a verbal or physical attack: *he couldn't resist having another go at me* **26** a turn to do something in a game: *'Your go now!' I shouted* **27** *informal* the quality of being active and energetic: *a grand old man, full of go and determination* **28** *from the word go* *informal* from the very beginning **29** *make a go of* *informal* to be

successful in (a business venture or a relationship) **30** *on the go* *informal* active and energetic ▷ See also **go back on**, **go for**, etc. ▸ HISTORY Old English *gān*

goad *vb* **1** to provoke (someone) to take some kind of action, usually in anger ▷ *n* **2** something that provokes someone to take some kind of action **3** a sharp pointed stick for driving cattle ▸ HISTORY Old English *gād*

go-ahead *n* **1** *give the go-ahead* *informal* to give permission to proceed ▷ *adj* **2** enterprising or ambitious: *prosperous and go-ahead republics*

goal *n* **1** *sport* the space into which players try to propel the ball or puck to score **2** *sport* **a** a successful attempt at scoring **b** the score so made **3** an aim or purpose: *the goal is to get homeless people on their feet* ▸ HISTORY origin unknown > **goalless** *adj*

goalie *n informal* a goalkeeper

goalkeeper *n sport* a player whose duty is to prevent the ball or puck from entering the goal

goal line *n sport* the line marking each end of the pitch, on which the goals stand

goalpost *n* **1** either of two uprights supporting the crossbar of a goal **2** *move the goalposts* to change the aims of an activity to ensure the desired results

goanna *n* a large Australian lizard ▸ HISTORY from IGUANA

goat *n* **1** an agile cud-chewing mammal with hollow horns **2** *act the goat* *informal* to behave in a silly manner **3** *get someone's goat* *slang* to annoy someone ▸ HISTORY Old English *gāt*

goatee *n* a small pointed beard that does not cover the cheeks

goatherd *n* a person who looks after a herd of goats

goatsucker *n US & Canad* same as **nightjar**

go-away bird *n S African* a grey lourie ▸ HISTORY imitative

gob¹ *n* a thick mass of a soft substance ▸ HISTORY Old French *gobe* lump

gob² *n Brit, Austral & NZ, slang* the mouth ▸ HISTORY origin unknown

go back on *vb* to fail to fulfil (a promise): *he went back on his promise not to raise taxes*

gobbet *n* a chunk or lump ▸ HISTORY Old French *gobet*

gobble¹ *vb* **-bling, -bled** to eat quickly and greedily ▸ HISTORY probably from GOB¹

gobble² *n* **1** the loud rapid gurgling sound made by a turkey ▷ *vb* **-bling, -bled 2** to make this sound ▸ HISTORY probably imitative

gobbledegook *or* **gobbledygook** *n* pretentious or unintelligible language ▸ HISTORY whimsical formation from GOBBLE²

gobbler *n informal* a turkey

go-between *n* a person who acts as a messenger between two people or groups

goblet *n* a drinking vessel with a base and stem but without handles ▸ HISTORY Old French *gobelet* a little cup

355

goblin n a small grotesque creature in fairy tales that causes trouble for people ▶ HISTORY Old French

gobsmacked adj Brit, Austral & NZ, slang astonished

goby n, pl **-by** or **-bies** a small spiny-finned fish ▶ HISTORY Latin gobius gudgeon

go-cart n same as **go-kart**

god n **1** a supernatural being, worshipped as the controller of the universe or some aspect of life or as the personification of some force **2** an image of such a being **3** a person or thing to which excessive attention is given: the All Blacks are gods in New Zealand **4 the gods** the top balcony in a theatre ▶ HISTORY Old English > **goddess** fem n

God n **1** the sole Supreme Being, Creator, and ruler of all, in religions such as Christianity, Judaism, and Islam ▷ interj **2** an oath or exclamation of surprise or annoyance

godchild n, pl **-children** a person who is sponsored by godparents at baptism

goddaughter n a female godchild

godetia n a garden plant with showy flowers ▶ HISTORY after C. H. Godet, botanist

godfather n **1** a male godparent **2** the head of a Mafia family or other criminal ring

godforsaken adj desolate or dreary: some godforsaken village in the Himalayas

Godhead n the nature and condition of being God

godly adj **-lier, -liest** deeply religious > **godliness** n

godmother n a female godparent

godparent n a person who promises at a person's baptism to look after his or her religious upbringing

godsend n a person or thing that comes unexpectedly but is very welcome

godson n a male godchild

goer n a person who attends something regularly: a church goer

go-faster stripe n informal a decorative line suggestive of high speed on the side of a car

go for vb **1** to choose: any politician will go for the soft option **2** informal to like very much **3** to attack **4** to apply equally to: the same might go for the other woman

go-getter n informal an ambitious enterprising person > **go-getting** adj

gogga (hohh-a) n S African, informal an insect ▶ HISTORY Nama (language of southern Africa) xo xo

goggle vb **-gling, -gled** to stare with wide-open eyes ▷ See also **goggles** ▶ HISTORY Middle English gogelen to look aside > **goggle-eyed** adj

goggles pl n close-fitting protective spectacles

Goidelic n **1** the group of Celtic languages, consisting of Irish Gaelic, Scottish Gaelic, and Manx ▷ adj **2** of this group of languages ▶ HISTORY Old Irish Goidel Celt

going n **1** the condition of the ground with regard to walking or riding: the going for the cross-country is perfect **2** informal speed or progress: not bad going for a lad of 58 ▷ adj **3** thriving: the racecourse was a going concern **4** current or accepted: this is the going rate for graduates

going-over n, pl **goings-over** informal **1** a thorough examination or investigation **2** a physical beating

goings-on pl n informal mysterious or shady activities

goitre or US **goiter** (goy-ter) n pathol a swelling of the thyroid gland in the neck ▶ HISTORY French

go-kart n a small four-wheeled motor vehicle, used for racing

gold n **1** a bright yellow precious metal, used as a monetary standard and in jewellery and plating. Symbol: Au **2** jewellery or coins made of this metal **3** short for **gold medal** ▷ adj **4** deep yellow ▶ HISTORY Old English

goldcrest n a small bird with a bright yellow-and-black crown

gold-digger n informal a woman who marries or has a relationship with a man for his money

golden adj **1** made of gold: golden bangles **2** of the colour of gold: golden corn **3** informal very successful or destined for success: the golden girl of British athletics **4** excellent or valuable: a golden opportunity for peace **5** (of an anniversary) the fiftieth: golden wedding; Golden Jubilee

golden age n the most flourishing and outstanding period in the history of an art or nation: the golden age of Dixieland jazz

golden eagle n a large mountain eagle of the N hemisphere with golden-brown feathers

golden handshake n informal money given to an employee either on retirement or to compensate for loss of employment

golden hour n the first hour after a serious accident, when medical treatment for the victim is crucial

golden mean n the middle course between extremes

golden retriever n a retriever with silky wavy gold-coloured hair

goldenrod n a tall plant with spikes of small yellow flowers

golden rule n an important principle: the golden rule is to start with the least difficult problems

golden wattle n an Australian plant with yellow flowers that yields a useful gum and bark

goldfinch n a European finch, the adult of which has yellow-and-black wings

goldfish n, pl **-fish** or **-fishes** a gold or orange-red freshwater fish, often kept as a pet

gold foil n thin gold sheet that is thicker than gold leaf

gold leaf n very thin gold sheet made by rolling or hammering gold and used for gilding

gold medal n a medal made of gold, awarded to the winner of a race or competition

gold rush n a large-scale migration of people to a territory where gold has been found

goldsmith n a person who makes gold jewellery and other articles

g

good

WORD FOCUS

Like bad, the word good is used in so many ways to describe so many things that it has lost a great deal of its effectiveness. A wide range of alternatives is available to you for every context in which you might be tempted to use good; try to vary your language and vocabulary by choosing these instead.

DEFINITION 1
- If you would like to describe something that is of good quality, you could try: **acceptable** standard • **excellent** meal • **fine** food • **first-class** game • **first-rate** service • **great** book • **satisfactory** quality • **splendid** hotel • **super** recipe (*informal*) • **superb** selection

DEFINITION 2
- If you would like to describe someone or something that is morally virtuous, you could try: **commendable** character • **decent** person • **ethical** stance • **honest** citizens • **honourable** person • **righteous** people • morally **upright** • **virtuous** life • **worthy** causes

DEFINITION 3
- If you would like to describe something that has a beneficial effect, you could try: **advantageous** changes • **beneficial** effects • **favourable** conditions • **positive** results

DEFINITION 4
- If you would like to describe a kind and thoughtful person or action, you could try: kindly and **benevolent** • too **charitable** • He's **considerate** to his sisters. • **generous** and selfless nature • a **gracious** and genial host • a **humane** and caring woman • It's very **kind** of you. • **kind-hearted** colleagues • a **kindly** soul • an **obliging** fellow • **thoughtful** of him to offer

DEFINITION 5
- If you would like to describe someone who is skilled at something, you could try: **able** student • an **accomplished** pianist • **adept** at.

manipulating the press • very **capable** nanny • very **clever** at raising money • careful and **competent** worker • **efficient** manager • **expert** cyclists • **first-rate** teacher • **proficient** driver • **skilled** carpenter • most **talented** musicians

DEFINITION 6
- If you would like to describe someone's behaviour, you could try: **disciplined** behaviour • meek and **docile** child • three **obedient** children • **orderly** behaviour • polite and **well-behaved**

DEFINITION 7
- If you would like to describe something reliable, you could try: **reputable** company • **sound** source of information

DEFINITION 8
- If you would like to describe something thorough, you could try: **complete** overhaul • **full** scan • **thorough** clean

DEFINITION 9
- If you would like to describe a good opportunity, you could try: **appropriate** occasion • **convenient** time • **opportune** moment • **sensible** timing • a **wise** plan

DEFINITION 10
- If you would like to describe a good experience, you could try: **agreeable** evening • **delightful** few hours • **enjoyable** trip • **lovely** vacation • **pleasant** stay

DEFINITION 11
- If you would like to describe something you have that is the newest or best quality, you could try: **best** cutlery • **finest** clothes • **most valuable** jewellery • **nicest** dress • **special** dishes

DEFINITION 12
- If you would like to describe a good price, sum of money, amount, or quantity, you could try: **ample** supply • a **considerable** income • **fair** bit over the asking price • a **large** profit • **reasonable** number • **substantial** amount

g

gold standard *n* a monetary system in which the basic currency unit equals a specified weight of gold

golf *n* **1** a game in which a ball is struck with clubs into a series of eighteen holes in a grassy course ▷ *vb* **2** to play golf ▶ HISTORY origin unknown > **golfer** *n*

Golgi body (**goll**-jee) *n biol* a membranous complex of vesicles, vacuoles, and flattened sacs in the cytoplasm of most cells ▶ HISTORY named after Camillo *Golgi*, Italian neurologist

golliwog *n* a soft doll with a black face, usually made of cloth ▶ HISTORY from a doll in a series of American children's books

golly *interj* an exclamation of mild surprise ▶ HISTORY originally a euphemism for *God*

gonad *n* an organ in which reproductive cells are produced, such as a testis or ovary ▶ HISTORY Greek *gonos* seed

gondola *n* **1** a long narrow flat-bottomed boat with a high ornamented stem, traditionally used on the canals of Venice **2** a moving cabin suspended from a cable, used as a ski lift ▶ HISTORY Italian

gondolier *n* a person who propels a gondola

Gondwanaland *or* **Gondwana** *n geol* one of the two ancient supercontinents comprising chiefly what is now Africa, South America, Australia, Antarctica, and the Indian subcontinent ▶ HISTORY from *Gondwana*, region in central north India, where the rock series was originally found

gone *vb* **1** the past participle of **go** ▷ *adj* **2** no longer present or no longer in existence

goner *n slang* a person who is about to die or who is beyond help

gong *n* **1** a flat circular metal disc that is hit with a hammer to give out a loud sound **2** *Brit, slang* a medal ▶ HISTORY Malay

gonorrhoea *or esp US* **gonorrhea** (gon-or-**ree**-a) *n* a sexually transmitted disease that causes inflammation and a discharge from the genital organs ▶ HISTORY Greek *gonos* semen + *rhoia* flux

good *adj* **better, best** **1** having admirable, pleasing, or superior qualities: *a good listener* **2** morally excellent; virtuous: *a good person* **3** beneficial: *exercise is good for the heart* **4** kindly or generous: *he is so good to us* **5** competent or talented: *she's good at physics* **6** obedient or well-behaved: *a good boy* **7** reliable or recommended: *a good make* **8** complete or thorough: *she went to have a good look round* **9** appropriate or opportune: *a good time to clear the air* **10** satisfying or enjoyable: *a good holiday* **11** newest or of the best quality: *keep the good dishes for guests* **12** fairly large, extensive, or long: *they contain a good amount of protein* **13 as good as** virtually or practically: *the war was as good as over* ▷ *n* **14** advantage or benefit: *what is the good of it all?* **15** positive moral qualities; virtue **16 for good** for ever; permanently: *his political career was over for good* ▷ See also **goods** ▶ HISTORY Old English *gōd* See WORD FOCUS **good** on page 357

goodbye *interj* **1** an expression used on parting ▷ *n* **2** the act of saying goodbye: *he said his goodbyes* ▶ HISTORY from *God be with ye*

good day *interj* an expression of greeting or farewell used during the day

good-for-nothing *n* **1** an irresponsible or worthless person ▷ *adj* **2** irresponsible or worthless

Good Friday *n Christianity* the Friday before Easter, observed as a commemoration of the Crucifixion of Jesus Christ

goodies *pl n* any things considered particularly desirable

goodly *adj* **-lier, -liest** fairly large: *a goodly number of children*

good-natured *adj* tolerant and kindly

goodness *n* **1** the quality of being good ▷ *interj* **2** an exclamation of surprise

goods *pl n* **1** articles produced to be sold: *consumer goods* **2** movable personal property: *houses and goods are insured from fire* **3 deliver the goods** *informal* to do what is expected or required **4 have the goods on someone** *US & Canad, slang* to know something incriminating about someone

Good Samaritan *n* a person who helps someone in difficulty or distress ▶ HISTORY from a parable in Luke 10: 30–37

goodwill *n* **1** kindly feelings towards other people **2** the popularity and good reputation of a well-established business, considered as a valuable asset

goody *interj* **1** a child's exclamation of pleasure ▷ *n*, *pl* **goodies** **2** *informal* the hero in a film or book **3** See **goodies**

goody-goody *informal* *n, pl* **-goodies** **1** a person who behaves well in order to please people in authority ▷ *adj* **2** behaving well in order to please people in authority

gooey *adj* **gooier, gooiest** *informal* **1** sticky, soft, and often sweet **2** sentimental: *one knows the whole gooey performance is an act*

goof *vb informal* **1** to bungle or botch **2 goof off** *US & Canad* to spend time in a lazy or foolish way: *he's goofing off on the Costa del Sol* ▶ HISTORY probably from dialect *goff* simpleton

go off *vb* **1** to stop functioning: *the heating went off* **2** to make a sudden loud noise: *a bomb went off* **3** to occur as specified: *the actual launch went off perfectly* **4** *informal* (of food) to become stale or rotten **5** *Brit, informal* to stop liking

goofy *adj* **goofier, goofiest** *informal* silly or ridiculous

Google *n trademark* **1** a popular internet search engine ▷ *vb* **google** **2** to search for (something on the internet) using a search engine

googly *n, pl* **-lies** *cricket* a ball bowled like a leg break but spinning from off to leg on pitching ▶ HISTORY Australian English

goon *n* **1** a stupid person **2** *US, informal* a hired thug ▶ HISTORY dialect *gooney* fool; influenced by US cartoon character Alice the *goon*

go on *vb* **1** to continue or proceed **2** to take place: *there's a war going on* **3** to talk at length and annoyingly

goosander *n* a duck of Europe and North America with a dark head and white body ▶ HISTORY probably from GOOSE[1] + Old Norse *önd* (genitive *andar*) duck

goose[1] *n, pl* **geese** **1** a fairly large web-footed long-necked migratory bird **2** the female of such a bird **3** the flesh of the goose used for food **4** *informal* a silly person ▶ HISTORY Old English *gōs*

goose[2] *vb* **goosing, goosed** *slang* to prod (someone) playfully in the bottom ▶ HISTORY from the jabbing of a goose's bill

gooseberry *n, pl* **-ries** **1** a small edible green berry with tiny hairs on the skin **2 play gooseberry** *Brit & NZ, informal* to be an unwanted single person accompanying a couple

goose flesh *n* the bumpy condition of the skin due to cold or fear, in which the muscles at the base of the hair follicles contract, making the hair bristle. Also: **goose pimples**

go out *vb* **1** to go to entertainments or social functions **2 go out with** to have a romantic relationship with **3** to be extinguished or cease to function: *the lights went out* **4** (of information) to be released publicly **5** (of a broadcast) to be transmitted

go over *vb* **1** to examine very carefully **2 go over to** to change to: *he went over to the Free Orthodox Church*

gopher (**go**-fer) *n* an American burrowing rodent

with wide cheek pouches ▸ HISTORY origin unknown

gore¹ n blood shed from a wound ▸ HISTORY Old English gor dirt

gore² vb **goring, gored** (of an animal) to pierce or stab (a person or another animal) with a horn or tusk ▸ HISTORY probably from Old English gār spear

gore³ n a tapering piece of material in a garment, sail, or umbrella ▸ HISTORY Old English gāra

gorge n 1 a deep narrow steep-sided valley 2 **one's gorge rises** one feels disgusted or nauseated ▹ vb **gorging, gorged** 3 Also: **gorge oneself** to eat greedily ▸ HISTORY Latin gurges whirlpool

gorgeous adj 1 strikingly beautiful or attractive 2 informal warm, sunny, and very pleasant: a gorgeous day ▸ HISTORY Old French gorgias elegant > **gorgeously** adv

Gorgon n 1 Greek myth one of three monstrous sisters who had live snakes for hair, and were so horrifying that anyone who looked at them was turned to stone 2 informal a terrifying or repulsive woman ▸ HISTORY Greek gorgos terrible

Gorgonzola n a sharp-flavoured blue-veined Italian cheese ▸ HISTORY after Gorgonzola, Italian town where it originated

gorilla n a very large W African ape with coarse black hair

■ **WORD HISTORY**
■ 'Gorilla' comes from Greek Gorillai, the name the
■ ancient Greeks gave to a supposed African tribe
■ with hairy bodies.

gormless adj Brit & NZ, informal stupid or dull-witted ▸ HISTORY obsolete gaumless

gorse n an evergreen shrub with small yellow flowers and prickles, which grows wild in the countryside ▸ HISTORY Old English gors

gory adj **gorier, goriest** 1 horrific or bloodthirsty: the gory details 2 bloody: gory remains

gosh interj an exclamation of mild surprise or wonder ▸ HISTORY euphemistic for God

goshawk n a large swift short-winged hawk ▸ HISTORY Old English gōshafoc

gosling n a young goose ▸ HISTORY Old Norse gæslingr

go-slow n Brit & NZ a deliberate slowing of the rate of production by workers as a tactic in industrial conflict

gospel n 1 a the teachings of Jesus Christ b the story of Christ's life and teachings 2 a doctrine held to be of great importance: the gospel of self-help 3 Also called: **gospel truth** unquestionable truth: gross inaccuracies which are sometimes taken as gospel ▹ adj 4 denoting a kind of religious music originating in the churches of the Black people in the Southern US ▸ HISTORY Old English gōdspell, from gōd good + spell message

Gospel n Christianity any of the first four books of the New Testament, namely Matthew, Mark, Luke, and John, which tell the story of Jesus Christ

gossamer n 1 a very fine fabric 2 a filmy cobweb often seen on foliage or floating in the air

▸ HISTORY probably Middle English gos goose + somer summer; referring to St Martin's summer, a period in November when goose was eaten and cobwebs abound

gossip n 1 idle talk, usually about other people's private lives, esp. of a disapproving or malicious nature: office gossip 2 an informal conversation, esp. about other people's private lives: to have a gossip and a giggle 3 a person who habitually talks about other people, usually maliciously ▹ vb 4 to talk idly or maliciously, esp. about other people's private lives ▸ HISTORY Old English godsibb godparent, applied to a woman's female friends at the birth of a child > **gossipy** adj

got vb 1 the past of **get** 2 **have got** spoken to possess 3 **have got to** spoken must: you have got to be prepared to work hard

Gothic adj 1 of a style of architecture used in W Europe from the 12th to the 16th centuries, characterized by pointed arches, ribbed vaults, and flying buttresses 2 of a literary style featuring stories of gloom, horror, and the supernatural, popular in the late 18th century 3 of or in a heavy ornate script typeface ▹ n 4 Gothic architecture or art ▸ HISTORY Greek Gothoi

go through vb 1 to experience (a difficult time or process) 2 to name or describe: the president went through a list of government ministers 3 to qualify for the next stage of a competition: Belgium, Spain, and Uruguay all went through from Group E 4 to be approved: the bill went through parliament 5 **go through with** to bring to a conclusion, often by persistence

gotten vb chiefly US a past participle of **get**

gouache (goo-ash) n opaque watercolour paint bound with glue ▸ HISTORY French

Gouda n a round mild-flavoured Dutch cheese

gouge (gowj) vb **gouging, gouged** 1 to scoop or force (something) out of its position 2 to cut (a hole or groove) in something with a pointed object ▹ n 3 a mark or groove made by gouging ▸ HISTORY French

goulash (goo-lash) n a rich stew seasoned with paprika, originating in Hungary ▸ HISTORY Hungarian gulyás hus herdsman's meat

gourd (goord) n 1 a large hard-shelled fruit similar to a cucumber or marrow 2 a container made from a dried gourd shell ▸ HISTORY Old French gourde

gourmand (goor-mand) n a person devoted to eating and drinking, usually to excess ▸ HISTORY Old French gourmant

gourmet (goor-may) n an expert on good food and drink ▸ HISTORY French

gout (gowt) n a disease that causes painful inflammation of certain joints, for example of the big toe ▸ HISTORY Latin gutta a drop > **gouty** adj

govern vb 1 to direct and control the policy and affairs of (a country or an organization) 2 to control or determine: the international organizations governing athletics and rugby ▸ HISTORY Latin gubernare to steer > **governable** adj

governance n government, control, or authority 359

g

governess *n* a woman employed in a private household to teach the children

government *n* **1** the executive policy-making body of a country or state **2** the state and its administration: *the assembled heads of state and government* **3** the system by which a country or state is ruled: *the old hard-line government* > **governmental** *adj*

government school *n* (in certain Caribbean countries) any school that is funded by the state, in which education is free

governor *n* **1** the chief political administrator of a region, such as a US state or a colony. *Related adjective:* **gubernatorial 2** *Brit* the senior administrator of a school, prison, or other institution **3** *Brit, informal* one's employer or father > **governorship** *n*

governor general *n, pl* **governors general** *or* **governor generals** *law* the chief representative of the British government in a Commonwealth country

gown *n* **1** a woman's long formal dress **2** a surgeon's overall **3** a loose wide official robe worn by members of the clergy, judges, lawyers, and academics ▶ **HISTORY** Late Latin *gunna* garment made of fur

goy *n, pl* **goyim** *or* **goys** a Jewish word for a **Gentile** ▶ **HISTORY** Yiddish

GP general practitioner

GPO (in Britain) general post office

GPS Global Positioning System: a satellite-based navigation system

Graafian follicle *n* *anat* a cavity in the ovary that contains a developing egg cell ▶ **HISTORY** after R. de *Graaf*, anatomist

grab *vb* **grabbing, grabbed 1** to seize hold of **2** to take (food, drink, or rest) hurriedly **3** to take (an opportunity) eagerly **4** to seize illegally or unscrupulously: *grabbing land* **5** *informal* to interest or impress ▷ *n* **6** the act of grabbing ▶ **HISTORY** probably from Middle Dutch *grabben*

grab bag *n* **1** a collection of miscellaneous things **2** *US, Canad & Austral* a bag from which gifts are drawn at random

grace *n* **1** elegance and beauty of movement, form, or expression **2** a pleasing or charming quality: *architecture with few redeeming graces* **3** courtesy or decency: *at least she had the grace to laugh* **4** a delay granted for the completion of a task or payment of a debt: *another year's grace* **5** *Christian theol* the free and unmerited favour of God shown towards humankind **6** a short prayer of thanks for a meal **7 airs and graces** an affected manner **8 with bad grace** unwillingly or grudgingly: *independence was granted with bad grace* **9 with good grace** willingly or ungrudgingly: *to accept with good grace* ▷ *vb* **gracing, graced 10** to honour or favour: *graced by the presence of the prime minister* **11** to decorate or make more attractive: *bedroom walls graced by Lady Gaga and Taylor Swift* ▶ **HISTORY** Latin *gratia*

Grace *n* **Your** *or* **His** *or* **Her Grace** a title used to address or refer to a duke, duchess, or archbishop

graceful *adj* having beauty of movement, style, or form > **gracefully** *adv* > **gracefulness** *n*

graceless *adj* **1** lacking elegance **2** lacking manners

grace note *n* *music* a note that ornaments a melody

Graces *pl n* *Greek myth* the three sister goddesses of charm and beauty

gracious *adj* **1** showing kindness and courtesy **2** characterized by elegance, ease, and indulgence: *gracious living* ▷ *interj* **3** an expression of mild surprise or wonder > **graciously** *adv* > **graciousness** *n*

gradation *n* **1** a series of systematic stages; gradual progression **2** a stage in such a series or progression

grade *n* **1** a place on a scale of quality, rank, or size **2** a mark or rating indicating a student's level of achievement **3** a rank or level of importance in a company or organization **4** *US, Canad, Austral & S African* a class or year in a school **5 make the grade** *informal* to be successful by reaching a required standard ▷ *vb* **grading, graded 6** to arrange according to quality or rank: *passes are graded from A down to E* **7** to give a grade to: *senior secretaries will need shorthand and be graded accordingly* ▶ **HISTORY** Latin *gradus* step

gradient *n* **1** Also (esp. US): **grade** a sloping part of a railway, road, or path **2** Also (esp. US): **grade** a measure of the steepness of such a slope **3** a measure of the change in something, such as the angle of a curve, over a specified distance ▶ **HISTORY** Latin *gradiens* stepping

gradual *adj* occurring, developing, or moving in small stages: *a gradual handover of power* ▶ **HISTORY** Latin *gradus* a step > **gradually** *adv*

gradualism *n* the policy of changing something gradually > **gradualist** *adj*

graduate *n* **1** a person who holds a university or college degree **2** *US & Canad* a student who has completed a course of studies at a high school and received a diploma **3** same as **postgraduate** ▷ *vb* **-ating, -ated 4** to receive a degree or diploma **5** to change by degrees: *the winds graduate from tropical storms to cyclones* **6** to mark (a measuring flask or instrument) with units of measurement ▶ **HISTORY** Latin *gradus* a step

graduation *n* **1** the act of graduating from university or college **2** *US & Canad* the act of graduating from high school **3** the ceremony at which degrees and diplomas are given to graduating students **4** a mark indicating measure on an instrument or container

Graeco-Roman *or esp US* **Greco-Roman** (greek-oh-**rome**-an) *adj* of, or showing the influence of, both Greek and Roman cultures

graffiti (graf-**fee**-tee) *n* drawings or words scribbled or sprayed on walls or posters ▶ **HISTORY** Italian: little scratches

graft¹ *n* **1** *surgery* a piece of tissue transplanted to an area of the body in need of the tissue **2** a small piece of tissue from one plant that is joined to another plant so that they grow together as one ▷ *vb* **3** to transplant (tissue) to an area of the body in need of the tissue **4** to join (part of one plant) onto another plant so that they grow together as one **5** to attach or incorporate: *to graft Japanese production methods onto the American talent for innovation* ▶ HISTORY Greek *graphein* to write

graft² *n* **1** *Brit, informal* hard work **2** the practice of obtaining money by taking advantage of one's position ▷ *vb* **3** *informal* to work hard ▶ HISTORY origin unknown

grain *n* **1** the small hard seedlike fruit of a cereal plant **2** a mass of such fruits gathered for food **3** cereal plants in general **4** a small hard particle: *a grain of salt* **5** a very small amount: *a grain of compassion* **6 a** the arrangement of the fibres, layers, or particles in wood, leather, or stone **b** the pattern or texture resulting from this **7 go against the grain** to be contrary to one's natural inclinations ▶ HISTORY Latin *granum* > **grainy** *adj*

gram *or* **gramme** *n* a metric unit of weight equal to one thousandth of a kilogram ▶ HISTORY Greek *gramma* small weight

graminivorous *adj* (of an animal) grass-eating ▶ HISTORY Latin *gramen* grass + *vorare* to swallow

grammar *n* **1** the rules of a language that show how sentences are formed, or how words are inflected **2** the way in which grammar is used: *the teacher found errors of spelling and grammar* **3** a book on the rules of grammar ▶ HISTORY Greek *gramma* letter

grammarian *n* a person who studies or writes about grammar for a living

grammar school *n* **1** *Brit* (esp. formerly) a secondary school for children of high academic ability **2** *US* same as **elementary school 3** *Austral* a private school, usually one controlled by a church

grammatical *adj* **1** of grammar **2** (of a sentence) following the rules of grammar > **grammatically** *adv*

gramme *n* same as **gram**

gramophone *n* an old-fashioned type of record player ▶ HISTORY inversion of *phonogram*

grampus *n, pl* **-puses** a dolphin-like mammal with a blunt snout ▶ HISTORY Old French *gras* fat + *pois* fish

gran *n* *Brit, Austral & NZ, informal* a grandmother

grana *n* *biol* plural of **granum**

granary *n, pl* **-ries 1** a building for storing threshed grain **2** a region that produces a large amount of grain ▶ HISTORY Latin *granarium*

grand *adj* **1** large or impressive in size or appearance; magnificent: *the grand hall* **2** ambitious or important: *grand themes* **3** dignified or haughty **4** *informal, spoken* excellent or wonderful **5** comprehensive or complete: *the grand total* ▷ *n* **6** (*pl* **grand**) *slang* a thousand pounds or dollars **7** short for **grand piano** ▶ HISTORY Latin *grandis* > **grandly** *adv*

grand apartheid *n* *history* (formerly, in South Africa) a form of apartheid that involved wide-ranging racial segregation and the creation of black homelands

grandchild *n, pl* **-children** a son or daughter of one's son or daughter

granddaughter *n* a daughter of one's son or daughter

grand duke *n* a prince or nobleman who rules a territory, state, or principality > **grand duchess** *fem n* > **grand duchy** *n*

grandee *n* **1** a high-ranking Spanish nobleman **2** a person who has a high rank or position: *the Party's grandees* ▶ HISTORY Spanish *grande*

grandeur *n* **1** personal greatness, dignity, or nobility: *delusions of grandeur* **2** magnificence or splendour: *cathedral-like grandeur*

grandfather *n* the father of one's father or mother

grandfather clock *n* an old-fashioned clock in a tall wooden case that stands on the floor

grandiloquent *adj* using pompous or unnecessarily complicated language ▶ HISTORY Latin *grandiloquus* > **grandiloquence** *n*

grandiose *adj* impressive, or meant to impress: *grandiose plans for constructing a new stadium* ▶ HISTORY French

grand jury *n* *law, chiefly US* a jury that investigates accusations of crime to decide whether the evidence is adequate to bring a prosecution

grand mal *n* a form of epilepsy in which there is loss of consciousness and violent convulsions ▶ HISTORY French: great illness

grandmother *n* the mother of one's father or mother

grand opera *n* an opera that has a serious plot and no spoken dialogue

grandparent *n* the father or mother of one's father or mother

grand piano *n* a large piano in which the strings are arranged horizontally

Grand Prix (gron **pree**) *n* **1** an international formula motor race **2** a very important international competitive event in other sports, such as athletics ▶ HISTORY French: great prize

grand slam *n* **1** the achievement of winning all the games or major tournaments in a sport in one season **2** See **slam²**

grandson *n* a son of one's son or daughter

grandstand *n* the main block of seats giving the best view at a sports ground

grand tour *n* **1** (formerly) an extended tour of continental Europe **2** *informal* a tour of inspection: *a grand tour of the house*

grange *n* *Brit* a farmhouse or country house with its farm buildings ▶ HISTORY Anglo-French *graunge*

granite (**gran**-nit) *n* a very hard rock consisting of quartz and feldspars that is widely used for building ▶ HISTORY Italian *granito* grained

granivorous *adj* (of an animal) grain-eating ▶ HISTORY Latin *granum* grain + *vorare* to swallow

granny *or* **grannie** *n, pl* **-nies** *informal* a grandmother

g

granny flat *n* a flat in or joined onto a house, suitable for an elderly relative to live in

grant *vb* **1** to give (a sum of money or a right) formally: *to grant an eight per cent pay rise; only the President can grant a pardon* **2** to consent to perform or fulfil: *granting the men's request for sanctuary* **3** to admit that (something) is true: *I grant that her claims must be true* **4 take for granted a** to accept that something is true without requiring proof **b** to take advantage of (someone or something) without showing appreciation ▷ *n* **5** a sum of money provided by a government or public fund to a person or organization for a specific purpose: *student grants* ▶ HISTORY Old French *graunter*

Granth (**grunt**) *n* the sacred scripture of the Sikhs ▶ HISTORY Hindi

granular *adj* of, like, or containing granules: *granular materials such as powders*

granulated *adj* (of sugar) in the form of coarse grains

granule *n* a small grain of something: *gravy granules* ▶ HISTORY Late Latin *granulum* a small grain

granum *n, pl* **grana** *biol* a stack of thin layers in a chloroplast that contains chlorophyll

grape *n* a small round sweet juicy fruit with a purple or green skin, which can be eaten raw, dried to make raisins, currants, or sultanas, or used to make wine ▶ HISTORY Old French *grape* bunch of grapes

grapefruit *n, pl* **-fruit** or **-fruits** a large round yellow juicy citrus fruit with a slightly bitter taste

grapeshot *n* ammunition for cannons consisting of a cluster of iron balls that scatter after firing

grapevine *n* **1** a vine grown for its grapes **2** *informal* an unofficial means of passing on information from person to person: *he'd doubtless heard rumours on the grapevine*

graph *n* a diagram showing the relation between certain sets of numbers or quantities by means of a series of dots or lines plotted with reference to a set of axes ▶ HISTORY short for *graphic formula*

-graph *n combining form* **1** an instrument that writes or records: *tachograph* **2** a writing or record: *autograph* ▶ HISTORY Greek *graphein* to write
> **-graphic** or **-graphical** *adj combining form*
> **-graphically** *adv combining form*

graphic *adj* **1** vividly described: *a graphic account of her three days in captivity* **2** of the graphic arts: *graphic design* **3** Also: **graphical** *maths* of or using a graph: *a graphic presentation* ▷ *n* **4** *computing* a diagram or picture produced on a computer screen ▶ HISTORY Greek *graphikos* > **graphically** *adv*

graphic arts *pl n* the visual arts based on drawing or the use of line

graphics *n* **1** the art of drawing in accordance with mathematical rules ▷ *pl n* **2** the illustrations in a magazine or book, or in a television or film production **3** *computers* information displayed in the form of diagrams or graphs

graphite *n* a soft black form of carbon used in pencils, as a lubricant, and in some nuclear reactors ▶ HISTORY German *Graphit*

graphology *n* the study of handwriting, usually to analyse the writer's character > **graphologist** *n*

graph paper *n* paper printed with a design of small squares for drawing graphs or diagrams on

-graphy *n combining form* **1** indicating a form of writing or representing things: *calligraphy; photography* **2** indicating an art or descriptive science: *choreography; topography* ▶ HISTORY Greek *graphein* to write

grapnel *n* a device with several hooks at one end, which is used to grasp or secure an object, esp. in sailing ▶ HISTORY Old French *grapin* a little hook

grapple *vb* **-pling, -pled** • **grapple with a** to try to cope with: *a difficult concept to grapple with* **b** to come to grips with (someone) in hand-to-hand combat ▶ HISTORY Old French *grappelle* a little hook

grappling iron *n* same as **grapnel**

grasp *vb* **1** to grip firmly **2** to understand: *his failure to grasp the gravity of the crisis* ▷ *n* **3** a very firm grip **4** understanding or comprehension: *a good grasp of detail* **5 within someone's grasp** almost certain to be accomplished or won: *he now has that prize within his grasp* ▶ HISTORY Low German *grapsen*

grasping *adj* greedy for money

grass *n* **1** a very common green plant with jointed stems and long narrow leaves, eaten by animals such as sheep and cows, and used for lawns and sports fields **2** a particular kind of grass, such as bamboo **3** a lawn **4** *slang* marijuana **5** *Brit & Austral, slang* a person who informs, usually on criminals ▷ *vb* **6 grass on** or **up** *Brit, slang* to inform on (someone) to the police or some other authority **7 grass over** to cover with grass ▶ HISTORY Old English *græs* > **grassy** *adj*

grasshopper *n* an insect with long hind legs which it uses for leaping

grassland *n* **1** land covered with grass **2** pasture land

grass roots *pl n* **1** ordinary members of a group or organization, as distinct from its leaders ▷ *adj* **grassroots** **2** of the ordinary members of a group or organization: *the focus of a virulent grassroots campaign*

grass snake *n* a harmless snake with a brownish-green body

grass tree *n* an Australian plant with stiff grasslike leaves and small white flowers

grass widow *n* a woman whose husband is regularly absent for a time ▶ HISTORY perhaps an allusion to a grass bed as representing an illicit relationship

grate¹ *vb* **grating, grated** **1** to reduce to shreds by rubbing against a rough surface: *grated cheese* **2** to produce a harsh rasping sound by scraping against an object or surface: *the clutch plates grated* **3 grate on** to annoy: *his manner always grated on me* ▶ HISTORY Old French *grater*

grate² *n* **1** a framework of metal bars for holding coal or wood in a fireplace **2** same as **grating¹** ▶ HISTORY Latin *cratis* hurdle

grateful *adj* feeling or showing thanks ▶ HISTORY Latin *gratus* > **gratefully** *adv*

grater *n* a tool with a sharp surface for grating food

gratify *vb* **-fies, -fying, -fied** **1** to satisfy or please (someone) **2** to yield to (a desire or whim): *all his wishes were to be gratified* ▶ HISTORY Latin *gratus* grateful + *facere* to make > **gratification** *n*

grating¹ *n* a framework of metal bars covering an opening in a wall or in the ground

grating² *adj* **1** (of a sound) rough or unpleasant **2** annoying or irritating: *his cringing obsequiousness was grating*

gratis *adv, adj* without payment; free: *the first lesson is gratis* ▶ HISTORY Latin

gratitude *n* a feeling of being grateful for gifts or favours ▶ HISTORY Latin *gratus* grateful

gratuitous (grat-**tyoo**-it-uss) *adj* **1** unjustified or unreasonable: *gratuitous violence* **2** given or received without charge or obligation: *his gratuitous voluntary services* ▶ HISTORY Latin *gratuitus* > **gratuitously** *adv*

gratuity (grat-**tyoo**-it-ee) *n, pl* **-ties** money given for services rendered; tip

grave¹ *adj* **1** (rhymes with **save**) serious and worrying: *grave concern* **2** (rhymes with **save**) serious and solemn in appearance or behaviour: *the man looked grave and respectful* **3** (rhymes with **halve**) denoting an accent (ˋ) over a vowel in some languages, such as French, which indicates that the vowel is pronounced in a particular way ▷ *n* (rhymes with **halve**) **4** a grave accent ▶ HISTORY Latin *gravis* > **gravely** *adv*

grave² (rhymes with **save**) *n* **1** a place where a dead person is buried. *Related adjective:* **sepulchral** **2** death: *people are smoking themselves into an early grave* **3 make someone turn in his** *or* **her grave** to do something that would have shocked a person who is now dead ▶ HISTORY Old English *græf*

gravel *n* **1** a mixture of rock fragments and pebbles that is coarser than sand **2** *pathol* small rough stones in the kidneys or bladder ▷ *vb* **-elling, -elled** *or US* **-eling, -eled** **3** to cover with gravel ▶ HISTORY Old French *gravele*

gravelly *adj* **1** covered with gravel **2** (of a voice or sound) harsh and grating

graven image *n* *chiefly Bible* a carved image used as an idol

gravestone *n* a stone marking a grave

graveyard *n* a place where dead people are buried, esp. one by a church

graveyard slot *n* *television* the hours from late night until early morning when relatively few people are watching television

gravid (**grav**-id) *adj* *med* pregnant ▶ HISTORY Latin *gravis* heavy

gravimeter (grav-**vim**-it-er) *n* **1** an instrument for measuring the force of gravity **2** an instrument for measuring relative density ▶ HISTORY French *gravimètre*

gravitate *vb* **-tating, -tated** **1 gravitate towards** to be attracted or influenced by: *the mathematically inclined often gravitate towards computers* **2** *physics* to move under the influence of gravity

gravitation *n* *physics* **1** the force of attraction that bodies exert on one another as a result of their mass **2** the process or result of this interaction > **gravitational** *adj*

gravitational attraction *n* *physics* a mutual attraction between particles or bodies resulting from their mass

gravitational force *n* *physics* an interaction between particles or bodies resulting from their mass

gravity *n, pl* **-ties** **1** *physics* **a** the force that attracts bodies towards the centre of the earth, a moon, or any planet **b** same as **gravitation** **2** seriousness or importance: *the gravity of the situation* **3** seriousness or solemnity of appearance or behaviour: *his priestly gravity* ▶ HISTORY Latin *gravitas* weight

gravy *n, pl* **-vies** **a** the juices that come from meat during cooking **b** the sauce made by thickening and flavouring these juices ▶ HISTORY Old French *gravé*

gray *adj, n, vb chiefly US* grey

graze¹ *vb* **grazing, grazed** **a** (of an animal) to eat (grass or other growing plants) **b** to feed (animals) on grass or other growing plants ▶ HISTORY Old English *grasian*

graze² *vb* **grazing, grazed** **1** to break the skin of (a part of the body) by scraping **2** to brush against someone gently in passing ▷ *n* **3** an injury on the skin caused by scraping ▶ HISTORY probably special use of GRAZE¹

grazier *n* a rancher or farmer who keeps cattle or sheep on grazing land

grazing *n* land where grass is grown for farm animals to feed upon

grease *n* **1** soft melted animal fat **2** a thick oily substance, such as the kind put on machine parts to make them work smoothly ▷ *vb* **greasing, greased** **3** to apply grease to: *lightly grease a baking tin* **4 grease someone's palm** *slang* to bribe someone ▶ HISTORY Latin *crassus* thick

greasepaint *n* theatrical make-up

greasy *adj* **greasier, greasiest** **1** covered with or containing grease **2** excessively pleasant or flattering in an insincere manner > **greasiness** *n*

great *adj* **1** large in size **2** large in number or amount: *the great majority* **3** larger than others of its kind: *the great white whale* **4** extreme or more than usual: *great difficulty* **5** of importance or consequence: *a great discovery* **6** of exceptional talents or achievements: *a great artist* **7** skilful: *he's a great storyteller; they are great at problem solving* **8** *informal* excellent ▷ *n* **9 the greats** the most successful people in a particular field: *the all-time greats of golf* ▷ See also **Greats** ▶ HISTORY Old English *grēat* > **greatly** *adv* > **greatness** *n* See WORD FOCUS **great** on page 364

great- *prefix* (in expressing relationship) one generation older or younger than: *great-grandmother* 363

great

There are a number of ways in which the word **great** can be used, depending on what you are referring to. But why not make your language more interesting and use one of the following instead?

DEFINITION 1
- If you would like to describe something that is great in size, you could try: a **colossal** palace • an **enormous** hall • **gigantic** theme park • a **huge** marquee • an **immense** building • **large** pile of logs • a **massive** crowd • a **vast** area

DEFINITION 2
- If you would like to describe something that is great in amount, you could try: **considerable** interest • **huge** majority • **significant** proportion • **stupendous** sum of money • **substantial** payments • **vast** numbers of refugees

DEFINITION 3
- If you are talking about something that is larger in size than others of its kind, you could try: **largest** of its kind

DEFINITION 4
- If you would like to describe something that is great in degree, you could try: **excessive** speeds • **extravagant** claims • **extreme** violence • a **high** degree of risk • **tremendous** strength

DEFINITION 5
- If you would like to describe something that is great in importance, you could try: one of our **chief** problems • an **important** question

- our **main** competitor • a **major** issue in the next election • a **momentous** occasion • our **principal** aim • a **serious** deficiency in the system • a **significant** step towards peace

DEFINITION 6
- If you would like to describe someone or something that is famous for their achievements, you could try: the **celebrated** author • a **distinguished** professor • **eminent** scientists • the **famed** actor • a **famous** artist • the world's most **illustrious** ballerinas • a **notable** chess player • Jamaica's most **prominent** historian • the **renowned** heart surgeon

DEFINITION 7
- If you would like to describe someone's skill, you could try: an **excellent** maths teacher • suitable only for **expert** skiers • a **masterly** display • an **outstanding** cricketer • the most **skilful** snooker player • a **skilled** boxer • a **superb** goalkeeper • a **superlative** thriller writer • a **talented** management team

DEFINITION 8
- If you would like to describe the quality of something or someone, you could try: **excellent** pasta sauce • **fantastic** firework display (*informal*) • good food and **fine** wines • their **first-rate** service • **marvellous** rooftop restaurant • **outstanding** works of art • **superb** staircase made from oak • a **terrific** party • a **tremendous** job • a **wonderful** time

---

great auk *n* an extinct large auk that could not fly

Great Britain *n* the mainland part of the British Isles; England, Scotland, and Wales

great circle *n maths* a circular section of a sphere that has a radius equal to the sphere's radius

greatcoat *n* a heavy overcoat

Great Dane *n* a very large dog with short smooth hair

greatest common factor *n maths* the largest number that divides equally into each member of a group of numbers

Greats *pl n* (at Oxford University) **1** the Honours course in classics and philosophy **2** the final examinations at the end of this course

Great War *n* same as **World War I**

greave *n* a piece of armour for the shin ▸ HISTORY Old French *greve*

grebe *n* a diving water bird ▸ HISTORY French

Grecian (**gree**-shan) *adj* of ancient Greece

greed *n* excessive desire for something, such as food or money

greedy *adj* **greedier, greediest** having an excessive desire for something, such as food or money: *greedy for personal possessions* ▸ HISTORY Old English *grǣdig* > **greedily** *adv*

Greek *adj* **1** of Greece ▷ *n* **2** a person from Greece **3** the language of Greece

green *adj* **1** of a colour between yellow and blue; of the colour of grass **2** covered with grass, plants, or trees: *green fields* **3** of or concerned with conservation and improvement of the environment: used in a political context: *green issues* **4** (of fruit) fresh, raw, or unripe **5** pale and sick-looking **6** inexperienced or gullible **7 green with envy** very envious ▷ *n* **8** a colour between yellow and blue **9** anything green, such as green clothing or green ink: *printed in green* **10** a small area of grassy land: *the village green* **11** an area of smooth turf kept for a special purpose: *putting greens* **12 greens** the leaves and stems of certain plants, eaten as a vegetable: *turnip greens* **13 Green** a person who supports environmentalist issues ▸ HISTORY Old English *grēne* > **greenish** *or* **greeny** *adj* > **greenness** *n*

green belt *n* a protected zone of parkland or open country surrounding a town or city

green card *n* an official permit allowing the holder permanent residence and employment, issued to foreign nationals in the US

Green Cross Code *n Brit* a code for children giving rules on road safety

g

greenery *n* green leaves or growing plants: *lush greenery*

greenfield *adj* relating to a rural area which has not previously been built on: *greenfield factory sites*

greenfinch *n* a European finch, the male of which has olive-green feathers

green fingers *pl n Brit* skill in growing plants

greenfly *n, pl* **-flies** a green aphid commonly occurring as a pest on plants

greengage *n* a green sweet variety of plum ▶ HISTORY after Sir W. *Gage*, botanist

greengrocer *n Brit & Austral* a shopkeeper who sells fruit and vegetables

greenhorn *n* an inexperienced person; novice ▶ HISTORY originally an animal with *green* (that is, young) horns

greenhouse *n* a building with glass walls and roof where plants are grown under controlled conditions

greenhouse effect *n* the gradual rise in temperature in the earth's atmosphere due to heat being absorbed from the sun and being trapped by gases such as carbon dioxide in the air around the earth

greenhouse gas *n* any gas that contributes to the greenhouse effect: *greenhouse gases such as carbon dioxide*

green light *n* **1** a signal to go **2** permission to proceed with a project ▷ *vb* **greenlight, -lighting, -lighted** **3** to permit (a project) to proceed

green paper *n* a government document containing policy proposals to be discussed

green pepper *n* the green unripe fruit of the sweet pepper, eaten as a vegetable

greenroom *n* (esp. formerly) a backstage room in a theatre where performers rest or receive visitors

greenstick fracture *n* a fracture in which the bone is partly bent and splinters only on the outer side of the bend

greenstone *n NZ* a type of green jade used for Māori carvings and ornaments

green tax *n* a tax imposed with the aim of regulating behaviour in a way that benefits the environment

Greenwich Mean Time (gren-itch) *n* the local time of the 0° meridian passing through Greenwich, England: a basis for calculating times throughout most of the world. Abbrev: **GMT**

greet¹ *vb* **1** to address or meet with expressions of friendliness or welcome **2** to receive in a specified manner: *a direct request would be greeted coolly* **3** *written* to be immediately noticeable to: *the scene of devastation which greeted him* ▶ HISTORY Old English *grētan*

greet² *vb Scot* to weep ▶ HISTORY Old English *grǣtan*

greeting *n* the act or words of welcoming on meeting

greetings *interj* an expression of friendly salutation

gregarious *adj* **1** enjoying the company of others

2 (of animals) living together in herds or in flocks ▶ HISTORY Latin *grex* flock

Gregorian calendar *n* the revision of the calendar introduced in 1582 by Pope Gregory XIII and still widely used

Gregorian chant *n* same as **plainsong**

gremlin *n* an imaginary imp jokingly blamed for malfunctions in machinery ▶ HISTORY origin unknown

grenade *n* a small bomb filled with explosive or gas, thrown by hand or fired from a rifle ▶ HISTORY Spanish *granada* pomegranate

grenadier *n mil* **1** (in the British Army) a member of the senior regiment of infantry in the Household Brigade (the **Grenadier Guards**) **2** (formerly) a soldier trained to throw grenades ▶ HISTORY French

grenadine (gren-a-**deen**) *n* a syrup made from pomegranate juice, often used as an ingredient in cocktails

grevillea *n* any of various Australian evergreen trees and shrubs ▶ HISTORY after C.F. *Greville*, botanist

grew *vb* the past tense of **grow**

grey *or US* **gray** *adj* **1** of a colour between black and white; of the colour of ashes **2 a** (of hair) having partly turned white **b** (of a person) having grey hair **3** dismal, dark, or gloomy: *a grey and misty morning* **4** dull or boring: *in 1948 life generally was grey* ▷ *n* **5** a colour between black and white **6** anything grey, such as grey paint or grey clothing: *available in grey or brown* **7** a grey or whitish horse ▶ HISTORY Old English *grǣg* > **greyish** *adj* > **greyness** *n*

grey area *n* a situation or area that has no clearly defined characteristics or that falls somewhere between two categories

Grey Friar *n* a Franciscan friar

greyhound *n* a tall slender dog that can run very fast and is used for racing

greying *adj* becoming grey: *greying hair*

greylag *or* **greylag goose** *n* a large grey Eurasian goose ▶ HISTORY GREY + LAG, because it migrates later than other species

grey matter *n informal* intellect or brains: *those who don't have lots of grey matter*

grey squirrel *n* a grey-furred squirrel, native to E North America but now common in Britain

grid *n* **1** a network of crossing parallel lines on a map, plan, or graph paper for locating points **2 the grid** the national network of cables or pipes by which electricity, gas, or water is distributed **3** *electronics* an electrode that controls the flow of electrons between the cathode and anode of a valve ▶ HISTORY from *gridiron*

griddle *n* a thick round iron plate placed on top of a cooker and used to cook food ▶ HISTORY Old French *gridil*

gridiron *n* **1** a utensil of parallel metal bars, used to grill food **2 a** the field of play in American football **b** *informal* same as **American football** ▶ HISTORY Middle English *gredire*

365

grid line *n* a horizontal or vertical line that divides a map into squares that are used to locate a point

gridlock *n* **1** obstruction of traffic caused by queues of vehicles forming across junctions and so causing queues in intersecting streets **2** a point in a dispute at which no agreement can be reached: *political gridlock* ▷ *vb* **3** (of traffic) to obstruct (an area)

grid reference *n* a series of numbers indicating the location of a point on a map

grief *n* **1** deep or intense sorrow **2 come to grief** to have an unfortunate or unsuccessful end or outcome **3** *informal* trouble or annoyance: *people were giving me grief for leaving ten minutes early*

grievance *n* **1** a real or imaginary cause for complaint **2** a feeling of resentment at having been unfairly treated

grieve *vb* **grieving, grieved** to feel or cause to feel great sorrow or distress ▶ HISTORY Old French *grever* > **grieved** *adj* > **grieving** *adj*

grievous *adj* **1** very severe or painful: *grievous injuries* **2** very serious or worrying: *a grievous loss* > **grievously** *adv*

grievous bodily harm *n* *criminal law* serious injury caused by one person to another

griffin, griffon *or* **gryphon** *n* a mythical winged monster with an eagle's head and a lion's body ▶ HISTORY Old French *grifon*

griffon *n* **1** a large vulture with pale feathers and black wings **2** a small wire-haired breed of dog ▶ HISTORY French

grike *n geol* a solution fissure that divides an exposed limestone surface into sections

grill *vb* **1** to cook by direct heat under a grill or over a hot fire **2** *informal* to subject to relentless questioning: *the jury pool was grilled for signs of prejudice* ▷ *n* **3** a device on a cooker that radiates heat downwards for grilling food **4** a gridiron for cooking food **5** a dish of grilled food **6** See **grillroom** ▶ HISTORY Latin *craticula* fine wickerwork > **grilled** *adj* > **grilling** *n*

grille *or* **grill** *n* a metal or wooden grating, used as a screen or partition ▶ HISTORY Latin *craticula* fine hurdlework

grillroom *n* a restaurant specializing in grilled foods

grilse (**grillss**) *n, pl* **grilses** *or* **grilse** a salmon on its first return from the sea to fresh water ▶ HISTORY origin unknown

grim *adj* **grimmer, grimmest 1** unfavourable and worrying: *grim figures on unemployment* **2** harsh and unpleasant: *grim conditions in the detention centres* **3** stern or resolute: *a grim determination to fight on* **4** unpleasant or disagreeable ▶ HISTORY Old English *grimm* > **grimly** *adv* > **grimness** *n*

grimace *n written* **1** an ugly or distorted facial expression of disgust, pain, or displeasure ▷ *vb* **-macing, -maced 2** to make a grimace ▶ HISTORY French

grime *n* **1** ingrained dirt ▷ *vb* **griming, grimed 2** to make very dirty: *sweat-grimed faces* ▶ HISTORY Middle Dutch > **grimy** *adj*

grin *vb* **grinning, grinned 1** to smile broadly, showing one's teeth **2 grin and bear it** *informal* to suffer hardship without complaint ▷ *n* **3** a broad smile ▶ HISTORY Old English *grennian* > **grinning** *adj*

grind *vb* **grinding, ground 1** to reduce to small particles by pounding or rubbing: *grinding coffee* **2** to smooth, sharpen, or polish by friction **3** (of two objects) to scrape together with a harsh rasping sound **4 an axe to grind** See **axe** (sense 2) **5 grind one's teeth** to rub one's upper and lower teeth against each other, as if chewing **6 grind to a halt** to come to an end or a standstill: *without enzymes life would grind to a halt* ▷ *n* **7** *informal* hard or tedious work: *the grind of everyday life* ▶ HISTORY Old English *grindan*

grinder *n* a device for grinding substances: *an electric coffee grinder*

grindstone *n* **1** a revolving stone disc used for sharpening, grinding, or polishing things **2 keep one's nose to the grindstone** to work hard and steadily

grip *n* **1** a very tight hold: *he felt a grip at his throat* **2** the style or manner of holding something, such as a golf club or tennis racket **3** power or control over a situation, person, or activity: *rebel forces tighten their grip around the capital* **4 get** *or* **come to grips with** to face up to and deal with (a problem or subject) **5** a travelling bag or holdall **6** a small bent clasp used to fasten the hair **7** a handle **8** a person who manoeuvres the cameras in a film or television studio ▷ *vb* **gripping, gripped 9** to take a tight hold of **10** to affect strongly: *sudden panic gripped her* **11** to hold the interest or attention of: *gripped by the intensity of the film; the story gripped him* ▶ HISTORY Old English *gripe* grasp

gripe *vb* **griping, griped 1** *informal* to complain persistently **2** to cause sudden intense pain in the bowels ▷ *n* **3** *informal* a complaint **4 the gripes** a sudden intense pain in the bowels ▶ HISTORY Old English *grīpan*

grippe *n* a former name for **influenza** ▶ HISTORY French

gripping *adj* very interesting and exciting: *a gripping story*

grisly *adj* **-lier, -liest** causing horror or dread: *grisly murders* ▶ HISTORY Old English *grislic*

grist *n* **1** grain that is to be or that has been ground **2 grist to the mill** anything that can be turned to profit or advantage ▶ HISTORY Old English *grīst*

gristle *n* tough stringy animal tissue found in meat ▶ HISTORY Old English > **gristly** *adj*

grit *n* **1** small hard particles of sand, earth, or stone **2** courage and determination ▷ *vb* **gritting, gritted 3** to cover (an icy road) with grit **4 grit one's teeth a** to rub one's upper and lower teeth against each other, as if chewing **b** to decide to carry on in a difficult situation: *he urged the Cabinet to grit its teeth and continue cutting public spending* ▶ HISTORY Old English *grēot*

gritter *n* a vehicle that spreads grit on the roads in icy weather

gritty *adj* **-tier, -tiest** **1** courageous and tough **2** covered with grit

grizzle *vb* **-zling, -zled** *Brit, Austral & NZ, informal* to whine or complain ▶ **HISTORY** Germanic

grizzled *adj* **1** (of hair) streaked or mixed with grey **2** (of a person) having grey hair

grizzly *n, pl* **-zlies** a large fierce greyish-brown bear of North America. In full: **grizzly bear**

groan *n* **1** a long deep cry of pain, grief, or disapproval **2** *informal* a grumble or complaint ▷ *vb* **3** to give a long deep cry of pain, grief, or disapproval **4** *informal* to complain or grumble **5 groan under** to be weighed down by: *chemists' shelves groan under the weight of slimming aids* ▶ **HISTORY** Old English *grānian* > **groaning** *adj, n*

groat *n* a former British coin worth four old pennies ▶ **HISTORY** Middle Dutch *groot*

groats *pl n* the crushed grain of various cereals ▶ **HISTORY** Old English *grot* particle

grocer *n* a shopkeeper who sells food and other household supplies ▶ **HISTORY** Old French *grossier*

groceries *pl n* food and other household supplies

grocery *n, pl* **-ceries** the business or premises of a grocer

grog *n* **1** an alcoholic drink, usually rum, diluted with water **2** *Brit, Austral & NZ, informal* any alcoholic drink ▶ **HISTORY** Old *Grog*, nickname of Edward Vernon, British admiral, who in 1740 issued naval rum diluted with water

groggy *adj* **-gier, -giest** *informal* faint, weak, or dizzy

groin *n* **1** the part of the body where the abdomen joins the legs **2** *archit* a curved edge formed where two intersecting vaults meet ▶ **HISTORY** origin unknown

grommet *n* **1** a rubber, plastic, or metal ring or eyelet **2** *med* a small tube inserted into the eardrum to drain fluid from the middle ear ▶ **HISTORY** obsolete French *gourmer* bridle

groom *n* **1** a person employed to clean and look after horses **2** short for **bridegroom** ▷ *vb* **3** to clean and smarten (a horse or other animal) **4** to keep (oneself or one's appearance) clean and tidy: *carefully groomed hair* **5** to train (someone) for a particular task or occupation: *groomed for future leadership* ▶ **HISTORY** Middle English *grom* manservant > **grooming** *n*

groove *n* **1** a long narrow furrow cut into a surface **2** the spiral channel in a gramophone record ▶ **HISTORY** obsolete Dutch *groeve* > **grooved** *adj*

groovy *adj* **groovier, grooviest** *old-fashioned, slang* attractive, fashionable, or exciting

grope *vb* **groping, groped** **1** to feel about uncertainly for something **2** to find (one's way) by groping **3** to search uncertainly for a solution or expression: *the new democracies are groping for stability* **4** *slang* to fondle (someone) in a rough way ▷ *n* **5** an instance of groping ▶ **HISTORY** Old English *grāpian*

gross *adj* **1** outrageously wrong: *gross violations of human rights* **2** very coarse or vulgar: *gross bad taste* **3** *slang* disgusting or repulsive: *I think beards are gross* **4** repulsively fat **5** with no deductions for tax or the weight of the container; total: *gross income; a gross weight of 20 000 lbs* ▷ *n* **6** (*pl* **gross**) twelve dozen (144) **7** the entire amount or weight ▷ *vb* **8** to earn as total revenue, before deductions ▶ **HISTORY** Old French *gros* large > **grossly** *adv*

gross domestic product *n* the total value of all goods and services produced domestically by a nation during a year

gross national product *n* the total value of all final goods and services produced annually by a nation: equivalent to gross domestic product plus net investment income from abroad

gross profit *n* *accounting* the difference between total revenue from sales and the total cost of purchases or materials

grotesque (groh-**tesk**) *adj* **1** strangely distorted or bizarre: *a grotesque and pervasive personality cult* **2** ugly or repulsive ▷ *n* **3** a grotesque person or thing **4** an artistic style in which parts of human, animal, and plant forms are distorted and mixed, or a work of art in this style ▶ **HISTORY** Old Italian (*pittura*) *grottesca* cave (painting) > **grotesquely** *adv*

grotto *n, pl* **-toes** *or* **-tos** a small picturesque cave ▶ **HISTORY** Old Italian *grotta*

grotty *adj* **-tier, -tiest** *Brit & NZ, slang* **1** nasty or unattractive **2** in bad condition ▶ **HISTORY** from *grotesque*

grouch *informal* *vb* **1** to complain or grumble ▷ *n* **2** a person who is always complaining **3** a persistent complaint ▶ **HISTORY** Old French *grouchier*

grouchy *adj* **grouchier, grouchiest** bad-tempered

ground[1] *n* **1** the land surface **2** earth or soil **3** an area used for a particular purpose: *a cricket ground* **4** a matter for consideration or discussion: *there is no need to cover the same ground* **5** an advantage in an argument or competition: *neither side seems willing to give ground in this trial of strength* **6** the background colour of a painting **7** *US & Canad* an electrical earth **8 grounds a** the land around a building **b** reason or justification: *the hostages should be freed on humanitarian grounds* **c** sediment or dregs: *coffee grounds* **9 break new ground** to do something that has not been done before **10 common ground** an agreed basis for identifying issues in an argument **11 get something off the ground** to get something started: *to get the peace conference off the ground* **12 into the ground** to exhaustion or excess: *he was running himself into the ground* **13 suit someone down to the ground** *Brit, informal* to be totally suitable or appropriate for someone ▷ *adj* **14** on the ground: *ground troops* ▷ *vb* **15** to confine (an aircraft or pilot) to the ground **16** *naut* to move (a ship) onto the bottom of shallow water, so that it cannot move **17** to instruct in the basics of a subject: *the student who is not grounded in the elements cannot understand the advanced teaching* **18** to provide a basis for; establish: *a scientifically* grounded documentation **19** to forbid (a child) to go out and enjoy himself or herself as a punishment **20** *US & Canad* to connect (a circuit or electrical device) to an earth ▶ HISTORY Old English *grund*

ground² *vb* **1** the past of **grind** ▷ *adj* **2** reduced to fine particles by grinding: *ground glass*

ground bass *n music* a short melodic bass line that is repeated over and over again

ground beef *n US* finely chopped beef, sometimes used to make hamburgers

ground-breaking *adj* innovative

ground control *n* the people and equipment on the ground that monitor the progress of aircraft or spacecraft

ground cover *n* dense low plants that spread over the surface of the ground

ground floor *n* the floor of a building that is level, or almost level, with the ground

grounding *n* a foundation, esp. the basic general knowledge of a subject

groundless *adj* without reason or justification: *the scare turned out to be groundless*

groundnut *n Brit* a peanut

ground provisions *pl n* starchy vegetables, esp. root crops and plantains

groundsel (**grounce**-el) *n* a yellow-flowered weed ▶ HISTORY Old English *grundeswelge*

groundsheet *n* a waterproof sheet placed on the ground in a tent to keep out damp

groundsman *n, pl* **-men** a person employed to maintain a sports ground or park

groundswell *n* a rapidly developing general feeling or opinion

ground water *n* water that has seeped through from the surface and is held underground

groundwork *n* preliminary work as a foundation or basis

group *n* **1** a number of people or things considered as a unit **2** a small band of players or singers, esp. of popular music **3** an association of business firms that have the same owner **4** *chem* two or more atoms that are bound together in a molecule and behave as a single unit: *a methyl group –CH3* **5** *chem* a vertical column of elements in the periodic table that all have similar properties: *the halogen group* ▷ *vb* **6** to put into or form into a group ▶ HISTORY French *groupe*

group captain *n* a middle-ranking officer in some air forces

grouped data *n maths* data which is grouped into classes ▷ Compare **discrete data**

group therapy *n psychol* the treatment of people by bringing them together to share their problems in group discussion

grouse¹ *n, pl* **grouse 1** a game bird with a stocky body and feathered legs and feet **2** the flesh of this bird used for food ▶ HISTORY origin unknown

grouse² *vb* **grousing, groused 1** to complain or grumble ▷ *n* **2** a persistent complaint ▶ HISTORY origin unknown

grouse³ *adj Austral & NZ, slang* fine or excellent ▶ HISTORY origin unknown

grout *n* **1** a thin mortar for filling joints between tiles or masonry ▷ *vb* **2** to fill with grout ▶ HISTORY Old English *grūt*

grove *n* a small wood or group of trees: *orange groves* ▶ HISTORY Old English *grāf*

grovel (**grov**-el) *vb* **-elling, -elled** or US **-eling, -eled 1** to behave excessively humbly towards someone, esp. a superior, in an attempt to win his or her favour **2** to crawl on the floor, often in search of something: *grovelling on the floor for missing cards* ▶ HISTORY Middle English *on grufe* on the face > **grovelling** or US **groveling** *adj, n*

grow *vb* **growing, grew, grown 1** (of a person or animal) to increase in size and develop physically **2** (of a plant) to exist and increase in size: *an ancient meadow where wild flowers grow* **3** to produce (a plant) by planting seeds, bulbs, or cuttings, and looking after it: *many farmers have expressed a wish to grow more cotton* **4** to let (one's hair or nails) develop: *to grow a beard* **5** to increase in size or degree: *the gulf between rich and poor is growing* **6** to originate or develop: *Melbourne grew from a sheep-farming outstation and occasional port to a city* **7** to become increasingly as specified: *as the night wore on the audience grew more intolerant* ▷ See also **grow on, grow up** ▶ HISTORY Old English *grōwan* > **grower** *n* > **growing** *adj*

growing pains *pl n* **1** pains in muscles or joints sometimes experienced by growing children **2** difficulties experienced in the early stages of a new enterprise

growl *vb* **1** (of a dog or other animal) to make a low rumbling sound, usually in anger **2** *written* to say in a gruff or angry manner: *'You're late,' he growled* **3** to make a deep rumbling sound: *his stomach growled* ▷ *n* **4** the act or sound of growling ▶ HISTORY Old French *grouller* to grumble

grown *adj* developed or advanced: *fully grown; a grown man*

grown-up *adj* **1** having reached maturity; adult **2** of or suitable for an adult ▷ *n* **3** an adult

grow on *vb* to become progressively more acceptable or pleasant to: *I didn't like that programme at first but it has grown on me*

growth *n* **1** the process of growing **2** an increase in size, number, or significance: *the growth of drug trafficking* **3** something grown or growing: *a thick growth of ivy* **4** any abnormal tissue, such as a tumour ▷ *adj* **5** of or relating to growth: *growth hormone*

growth pole *n econ* an area in which many businesses and industries are located

grow up *vb* to reach maturity; become adult

groyne *n* a wall or breakwater built out from a shore to curb erosion ▶ HISTORY Old French *groign* snout

grub *n* **1** *slang* food **2** the short legless larva of certain insects, such as beetles ▷ *vb* **grubbing, grubbed 3** to search carefully for something by digging or by moving things about **4 grub up** to dig (roots or plants) out of the ground ▶ HISTORY Germanic

grubby *adj* **-bier, -biest 1** rather dirty **2** unsavoury or morally unacceptable: *grubby activities*
> **grubbiness** *n*

grudge *n* **1** a persistent feeling of resentment against a person who has caused harm or upset ▷ *vb* **grudging, grudged 2** to give unwillingly: *rich men who grudged pennies for poor people* **3** to resent or envy the success or possessions of: *none of their guests grudged them this celebration* ▷ *adj* **4** planned or carried out in order to settle a grudge: *a grudge match* ▶ HISTORY Old French *grouchier* to grumble

grudging *adj* felt or done unwillingly: *grudging admiration for his opponent* > **grudgingly** *adv*

gruel *n* thin porridge made by boiling oatmeal in water or milk ▶ HISTORY Old French

gruelling *or US* **grueling** *adj* extremely severe or tiring: *a gruelling journey* ▶ HISTORY obsolete *gruel* to punish

gruesome *adj* inspiring horror and disgust ▶ HISTORY Scandinavian

gruff *adj* **1** rough or surly in manner or speech **2** (of a voice) low and throaty ▶ HISTORY Germanic > **gruffly** *adv* > **gruffness** *n*

grumble *vb* **-bling, -bled 1** to complain in a nagging way: *his neighbour grumbled about the long wait* **2** to make low rumbling sounds: *the storm grumbled in the distance* ▷ *n* **3** a complaint **4** a low rumbling sound: *a distant grumble of artillery fire* ▶ HISTORY Middle Low German *grommelen*
> **grumbling** *adj, n*

grumpy *adj* **grumpier, grumpiest** sulky and bad-tempered ▶ HISTORY imitative > **grumpily** *adv*

grunge *n* **1** a style of rock music with a fuzzy guitar sound **2** a deliberately untidy and uncoordinated fashion style ▶ HISTORY from US slang: dirt, rubbish

grunt *vb* **1** to make a low short gruff noise, such as the sound made by a pig, or by a person to express annoyance **2** to express (something) gruffly: *he grunted his thanks* ▷ *n* **3** a low short gruff noise, such as the sound made by a pig, or by a person to express annoyance ▶ HISTORY Old English *grunnettan*

gryphon *n* same as **griffin**

GSAT (in Jamaica) Grade Six Achievement Test

GST (in Australia, New Zealand, and Canada) Goods and Services Tax

G-string *n* a strip of cloth worn between the legs and attached to a waistband

G-suit *n* a close-fitting pressurized garment that is worn by the crew of high-speed aircraft ▶ HISTORY from *g(ravity) suit*

GT gran turismo: a touring car, usually a fast sports car with a hard fixed roof

guanine (**gwah**-neen) *n biochem* a white, almost insoluble compound

guano (**gwah**-no) *n* the dried manure of seabirds, used as a fertilizer ▶ HISTORY S American Indian *huano* dung

guarantee *n* **1** a formal assurance in writing that a product or service will meet certain standards or specifications **2** something that makes a specified condition or outcome certain: *there was no guarantee that there would not be another military coup* **3** same as **guaranty** ▷ *vb* **-teeing, -teed 4** to promise or make certain: *to guarantee absolute loyalty* **5** (of a company) to provide a guarantee in writing for (a product or service) **6** to take responsibility for the debts or obligations of (another person) ▶ HISTORY Germanic

guarantor *n* a person who gives or is bound by a guarantee or guaranty

guaranty *n, pl* **-ties 1** a pledge of responsibility for fulfilling another person's obligations in case of that person's default **2** a thing given or taken as security for a guaranty

guard *vb* **1** to watch over or shield from danger or harm; protect: *US marines who guard the American embassy* **2** to keep watch over (a prisoner) to prevent escape **3** to protect (a right or privilege) **4** to take precautions: *to guard against a possible coup attempt* ▷ *n* **5** a person or group of people who protect or watch over people or things **6** *Brit, Austral & NZ* the official in charge of a train **7** a device or part of a machine designed to protect the user against injury **8** anything that provides protection: *a guard against future shocks* **9 off guard** having one's defences down; unprepared: *England were caught off guard as the Dutch struck two telling blows* **10 on guard** on duty to protect or watch over people or things **11 on one's guard** prepared to face danger or difficulties: *parents have been warned to be on their guard against kidnappers* **12 stand guard** (of a sentry) to keep watch ▶ HISTORY Old French *garder* to protect

guarded *adj* cautious and avoiding any commitment: *a guarded welcome*
> **guardedly** *adv*

guardhouse *or* **guardroom** *n mil* a military police office in which prisoners can be detained

guardian *n* **1** one who looks after, protects, or defends someone or something: *the nation's moral guardians* **2** someone legally appointed to manage the affairs of another person, such as a child or vulnerable adult > **guardianship** *n*

guardsman *n, pl* **-men** *mil* a member of a regiment responsible for ceremonial duties

guard's van *n Brit, Austral & NZ* a small railway carriage in which the guard travels

guava (**gwah**-va) *n* a round tropical fruit with yellow skin and pink pulp ▶ HISTORY from S American Indian

gubernatorial *adj chiefly US* of or relating to a governor ▶ HISTORY Latin *gubernator* governor

gudgeon¹ *n* a small slender European freshwater fish, used as bait by anglers ▶ HISTORY Old French *gougon*

gudgeon² *n* the socket of a hinge, which fits round the pin ▶ HISTORY Old French *goujon*

Guernsey (**gurn**-zee) *n* a breed of dairy cattle that produces rich creamy milk, originating from Guernsey, in the Channel Islands

369

guerrilla *or* **guerilla** *n* a member of an irregular, politically motivated, armed force that fights regular forces ▸ **HISTORY** Spanish

guess *vb* **1** to form an estimate or conclusion about (something), without proper knowledge: *a competition to guess the weight of the cake* **2** to arrive at a correct estimate of (something) by guessing: *I had a notion that he guessed my thoughts* **3** *informal* to think or suppose: *I guess he must have been a great athlete* ▷ *n* **4** an estimate or conclusion arrived at by guessing: *we can hazard a guess at the answer* ▸ **HISTORY** probably from Old Norse

guesswork *n* the process of arriving at conclusions or estimates by guessing

guest *n* **1** a person who receives hospitality at someone else's home **2** a person who is taken out socially by someone else who pays all the expenses **3** a performer or speaker taking part in an event, show, or film by special invitation **4** a person who is staying in a hotel ▷ *vb* **5** to be a guest in an event, show, or film: *he guested in concert with Eric Clapton* ▸ **HISTORY** Old English *giest* guest, stranger, enemy

guesthouse *n* a private home or boarding house offering accommodation

guff *n* *Brit, Austral & NZ, slang* ridiculous talk; nonsense ▸ **HISTORY** imitative

guffaw *vb* **1** to laugh loudly and raucously ▷ *n* **2** a loud raucous laugh ▸ **HISTORY** imitative

guidance *n* help, advice, or instruction, usually from someone more experienced or more qualified: *marriage guidance*

guide *n* **1** a person who conducts parties of tourists around places of interest, such as museums **2** a person who leads travellers to a place, usually in a dangerous area: *a mountain guide* **3** something that can be used to gauge something or to help in planning one's actions: *starting salary was not an accurate guide to future earnings* **4** same as **guidebook** **5** a book that explains the basics of a subject or skill: *a guide to higher education* ▷ *vb* **guiding, guided** **6** to lead the way for (tourists or travellers) **7** to control the movement or course of; steer **8** to direct the affairs of (a person, team, or country): *he will stay with the club he guided to promotion to the First Division* **9** to influence (a person) in his or her actions or opinions: *to be guided by the law* ▸ **HISTORY** Germanic > **guiding** *adj*

Guide *n* a member of an organization for girls that encourages discipline and practical skills

guidebook *n* a book which gives tourist information on a place

guided missile *n* a missile whose course is controlled electronically

guide dog *n* a dog that has been trained to lead a blind person

guideline *n* a principle put forward to set standards or determine a course of action: *guidelines for arms exporting*

guild *n* **1** an organization or club for people with shared interests **2** (in Medieval Europe) an association of men in the same trade or craft ▸ **HISTORY** Old Norse *gildi*

guilder *n*, *pl* **-ders** *or* **-der** a former monetary unit of the Netherlands ▸ **HISTORY** Middle Dutch *gulden*

guildhall *n* *Brit* a hall where members of a guild meet

guile (gile) *n* craftiness or deviousness ▸ **HISTORY** Old French > **guileless** *adj*

guillemot (gil-lee-mot) *n* a northern oceanic black-and-white diving sea bird ▸ **HISTORY** French

guillotine *n* **1** a device formerly used, esp. in France, for beheading people, consisting of a weighted blade between two upright posts, which was dropped on the neck **2** a device with a blade for cutting paper ▷ *vb* **-tining, -tined** **3** to behead with a guillotine ▸ **HISTORY** after J. I. *Guillotin*, who advocated its use

guilt *n* **1** the fact or state of having done wrong: *the court was unable to establish guilt* **2** remorse or self-reproach caused by feeling that one has done something wrong: *he feels no guilt about the planned cutbacks* ▸ **HISTORY** Old English *gylt*

guiltless *adj* free of all responsibility for wrongdoing or crime; innocent

guilty *adj* **guiltier, guiltiest** **1** *law* judged to have committed a crime: *she has been found guilty of drug trafficking* **2** responsible for doing something wrong: *students who are guilty of cheating* **3** showing, feeling, or indicating guilt: *guilty conscience* > **guiltily** *adv*

guinea *n* a former British unit of currency worth £1.05 (21 shillings), sometimes still used in quoting professional fees ▸ **HISTORY** the coin was originally made of gold from Guinea

guinea fowl *n* a domestic bird with a heavy rounded body and speckled feathers

guinea pig *n* **1** a tailless S American rodent, commonly kept as a pet or used in scientific experiments **2** a person used in an experiment ▸ **HISTORY** origin unknown

guise (rhymes with **size**) *n* **1** a false appearance: *in the guise of a wood-cutter* **2** general appearance or form: *haricot beans are best known in Britain in their popular guise of baked beans* ▸ **HISTORY** Old French

guitar *n* a stringed instrument with a flat back and a long neck with a fretted fingerboard, which is played by plucking or strumming ▸ **HISTORY** Spanish *guitarra* > **guitarist** *n*

Gulag *n* a system or department that silences dissidents, esp. in the former Soviet Union ▸ **HISTORY** Russian G(lavnoye) U(pravleniye Ispravitelno-Trudovykh) Lag(erei) Main Administration for Corrective Labour Camps

gulch *n* *US & Canad* a narrow ravine with a stream running through it ▸ **HISTORY** origin unknown

gulf *n* **1** a large deep bay **2** something that divides or separates people, such as a lack of understanding: *gradually the gulf between father and son has lessened* ▸ **HISTORY** Greek *kolpos*

Gulf War syndrome *n* a group of various debilitating symptoms experienced by many soldiers who served in the Gulf War of 1991, claimed to be associated with damage to the central nervous system

gull *n* a large seabird with white feathers tipped with black or grey ▶ **HISTORY** Celtic

gullet *n* the muscular tube through which food passes from the throat to the stomach ▶ **HISTORY** Latin *gula* throat

gullible *adj* easily tricked; too trusting > **gullibility** *n*

gully *or* **gulley** *n, pl* **-lies** *or* **-leys** **1** a channel or small valley originally worn away by running water **2** *cricket* a fielding position on the off side, between the slips and point ▶ **HISTORY** French *goulet* neck of a bottle

gully erosion *n* *geog* the process whereby water run-off flows in the same narrow channels, wearing away soil and rock

gulp *vb* **1** to swallow (a drink or food) rapidly in large mouthfuls **2** to gasp or breathe in violently, for example when nervous or when swimming **3 gulp back** to stifle or suppress: *he gulped back the tears as he said his goodbyes* ▷ *n* **4** the act of gulping **5** the quantity taken in a gulp ▶ **HISTORY** imitative

gum¹ *n* **1** a sticky substance obtained from certain plants, which hardens on exposure to air and dissolves in water **2** a substance used for sticking things together **3** short for **chewing gum** or **bubble gum** **4** *chiefly Brit* a gumdrop ▷ *vb* **gumming, gummed 5** to stick with gum ▶ **HISTORY** Old French *gomme*

gum² *n* the fleshy tissue that covers the bases of the teeth ▶ **HISTORY** Old English *gōma* jaw

gum arabic *n* a gum obtained from certain acacia trees, used to make ink, food thickeners, and pills

gumboil *n* an abscess on the gum

gumboots *pl n* *Brit & NZ* long rubber boots, worn in wet or muddy conditions

gumdrop *n* a small hard fruit-flavoured jelly-like sweet

gummy¹ *adj* **-mier, -miest 1** sticky or tacky **2** producing gum

gummy² *adj* **-mier, -miest** toothless

gumption *n* *Brit & NZ, informal* common sense or initiative ▶ **HISTORY** origin unknown

gumtree *n* **1** any of various trees that yield gum, such as the eucalyptus **2 up a gumtree** *Brit & NZ, informal* in an awkward position; in difficulties

gun *n* **1** a weapon with a metallic tube or barrel from which a missile is fired, usually by force of an explosion **2** a device used to force out (a substance, such as grease or paint) under pressure: *a spray gun* **3 jump the gun** *informal* to act prematurely **4 stick to one's guns** *informal* to stand by one's opinions or intentions in spite of opposition ▷ *vb* **gunning, gunned 5 gun down** to shoot (someone) with a gun **6** to press hard on the accelerator of (a vehicle's engine) ▷ See also **gun for** ▷ *adj* **7** *NZ, slang* expert: *a gun surfer* ▶ **HISTORY** Middle English *gonne*

gunboat *n* a small ship carrying mounted guns

gunboat diplomacy *n* diplomacy conducted by threats of military intervention

guncotton *n* a form of cellulose nitrate used as an explosive

gun dog *n* **1** a dog trained to locate or retrieve birds or animals that have been shot in a hunt **2** a dog belonging to any breed traditionally used for these activities

gunfire *n* the repeated firing of guns

gun for *vb* *informal* to search for (someone) in order to harm him or her in some way

gunge *n* *informal* a sticky or congealed substance ▶ **HISTORY** imitative > **gungy** *adj*

gunk *n* *informal* a slimy, oily, or dirty substance ▶ **HISTORY** perhaps imitative

gunman *n, pl* **-men** a man who uses a gun to commit a crime

gunmetal *n* **1** a type of bronze containing copper, tin, and zinc ▷ *adj* **2** dark grey

gunnel *n* same as **gunwale**

gunner *n* a member of the armed forces who works with, uses, or specializes in guns

gunnery *n* the art and science of the efficient design and use of large guns

gunny *n* *chiefly US* a coarse hard-wearing fabric, made from jute and used for sacks ▶ **HISTORY** Hindi *gōnī*

gunpowder *n* an explosive mixture of potassium nitrate, charcoal, and sulphur, used to make fireworks

gunrunning *n* the practice of smuggling guns and ammunition into a country > **gunrunner** *n*

gunshot *n* **1** bullets fired from a gun **2** the sound of a gun being fired **3** the firing range of a gun: *within gunshot*

gunwale (**gun**-nel) *n* *naut* the top of the side of a ship ▶ **HISTORY** *wale*, ridge of planking originally supporting guns

gunyah *n* *Austral* a hut or shelter in the bush ▶ **HISTORY** Aboriginal

guppy *n, pl* **-pies** a small brightly coloured tropical fish, often kept in aquariums in people's homes ▶ **HISTORY** after R. J. L. *Guppy*, who gave specimens to the British Museum

gurdwara (gur-**dwah**-ra) *n* a Sikh place of worship ▶ **HISTORY** from Sanskrit *guru* teacher + *dvārā* door

gurgle *vb* **-gling, -gled 1** (of water) to make low bubbling noises when flowing **2** to make low throaty bubbling noises: *the baby gurgled in delight* ▷ *n* **3** the sound of gurgling ▶ **HISTORY** origin unknown

Gurkha *n* **1** a member of a Hindu people living mainly in Nepal **2** a member of a Gurkha regiment in the Indian or British Army ▶ **HISTORY** Sanskrit

gurnard *n, pl* **-nard** *or* **-nards** a sea fish with a spiny head and long finger-like pectoral fins ▶ **HISTORY** Old French *gornard* grunter

guru *n* **1** a Hindu or Sikh religious teacher or leader **2** a leader or adviser of a person or group of people: *inside a team of advertising gurus are at work* ▶ **HISTORY** Hindi

Guru Granth *or* **Guru Granth Sahib** *n* same as **Granth**

gush *vb* **1** to pour out suddenly and profusely **2** to speak or behave in an overenthusiastic manner: *I'm not about to start gushing about raspberry coulis* ▷ *n* **3** a sudden large flow of liquid **4** a sudden surge of strong feeling: *she felt a gush of pure affection for her mother* ▶ HISTORY probably imitative

gusher *n* **1** a person who gushes **2** a spurting oil well

gushing *adj* behaving in an overenthusiastic manner: *gushing television commentators*

gusset *n* a piece of material sewn into a garment to strengthen it ▶ HISTORY Old French *gousset*

gust *n* **1** a sudden blast of wind **2** a sudden surge of strong feeling: *a gust of joviality* ▷ *vb* **3** to blow in gusts ▶ HISTORY Old Norse *gustr* > **gusty** *adj*

gusto *n* vigorous enjoyment: *he downed a pint with gusto* ▶ HISTORY Spanish: taste

gut *n* **1** same as **intestine 2** *slang* a stomach, esp. a fat one **3** short for **catgut 4** a silky fibrous substance extracted from silkworms and used in the manufacture of fishing tackle ▷ *vb* **gutting, gutted 5** to remove the internal organs from (a dead animal or fish) **6** (of a fire) to destroy the inside of (a building): *a local pub was gutted* ▷ *adj* **7** *informal* basic, essential, or natural: *I have a gut feeling she's after something* ▷ See also **guts** ▶ HISTORY Old English *gutt*

gutless *adj informal* lacking courage or determination

guts *pl n* **1** the internal organs of a person or an animal **2** *informal* courage, willpower, or daring **3** *informal* the inner or essential part: *the new roads have torn apart the guts of the city*

gutsy *adj* **gutsier, gutsiest** *slang* **1** bold or courageous: *the gutsy kid who lost a leg to cancer* **2** robust or vigorous: *a gutsy rendering of 'Bobby Shaftoe'*

gutta-percha *n* a whitish rubber substance, obtained from a tropical Asian tree and used in electrical insulation and dentistry ▶ HISTORY Malay *getah* gum + *percha* gumtree

gutted *adj* Brit, Austral & NZ, *informal* disappointed and upset: *the supporters will be absolutely gutted if the manager leaves the club*

gutter *n* **1** a channel on the roof of a building or alongside a kerb, used to collect and carry away rainwater **2** *tenpin bowling* one of the channels on either side of an alley **3** **the gutter** a poverty-stricken, degraded, or criminal environment: *he dragged himself up from the gutter* ▷ *vb* **4** (of a candle) to flicker and be about to go out ▶ HISTORY Latin *gutta* a drop > **guttering** *n*

gutter press *n informal* the section of the popular press that concentrates on the sensational aspects of the news

guttersnipe *n* Brit a child who spends most of his or her time in the streets, usually in a slum area

guttural (**gut**-ter-al) *adj* **1** *phonetics* pronounced at the back of the throat **2** harsh-sounding ▶ HISTORY Latin *guttur* gullet

guy¹ *n* **1** *informal* a man or boy **2** *informal* a person of either sex: *it's been very nice talking to you guys again* **3** Brit a crude model of Guy Fawkes that is burnt on top of a bonfire on Guy Fawkes Day (November 5) ▶ HISTORY short for *Guy Fawkes*, who plotted to blow up the Houses of Parliament

guy² *n* a rope or chain for steadying or securing something such as a tent. Also: **guyrope** ▶ HISTORY probably Low German

guzzle *vb* **-zling, -zled** to eat or drink quickly or greedily: *the guests guzzled their way through squid with mushrooms* ▶ HISTORY origin unknown

gybe *or* **jibe** (**jibe**) *naut vb* **gybing, gybed** *or* **jibing, jibed 1** (of a fore-and-aft sail) to swing suddenly from one side of a ship to the other **2** to change the course of (a ship) by letting the sail gybe ▷ *n* **3** an instance of gybing ▶ HISTORY obsolete Dutch *gijben*

gym *n* short for **gymnasium, gymnastics**

gymkhana (jim-**kah**-na) *n* Brit, Austral & NZ an event in which horses and riders take part in various races and contests

■ **WORD HISTORY**

■ Originally the word 'gymkhana' did not apply to
■ horse-riding but to other sporting and athletic
■ activities. Hindi *gend-khānā* literally means a
■ 'ball house' or 'racket court', and that is where
■ sports activities were held. *Gend* was altered to
■ 'gym' under the influence of words like
■ 'gymnastics'.

gymnasium *n* a large room containing equipment such as bars, weights, and ropes, for physical exercise ▶ HISTORY Greek *gumnazein* to exercise naked

gymnast *n* a person who is skilled or trained in gymnastics

gymnastics *n* **1** practice or training in exercises that develop physical strength and agility ▷ *pl n* **2** such exercises > **gymnastic** *adj*

gym shoes *pl n* same as **plimsolls**

gymslip *n* a tunic formerly worn by schoolgirls as part of school uniform

gynaecology *or* US **gynecology** (guy-nee-**kol**-la-jee) *n* the branch of medicine concerned with diseases and conditions specific to women ▶ HISTORY Greek *gunē* woman + -LOGY > **gynaecological** *or* US **gynecological** *adj* > **gynaecologist** *or* US **gynecologist** *n*

gynoecium (guy-**nee**-see-um) *n, pl* -**cia** (-see-a) *bot* the carpels of a flowering plant collectively

gyp *or* **gip** *n* **give someone gyp** Brit, Austral & NZ, *slang* to cause someone severe pain: *her back's still giving her gyp* ▶ HISTORY probably a contraction of *gee up!*

gypsophila *n* a garden plant with small white flowers

gypsum *n* a mineral used in making plaster of Paris ▶ HISTORY Greek *gupsos*

Gypsy *or* **Gipsy** *n, pl* -**sies** a member of a travelling people scattered throughout Europe and North America ▶ HISTORY from *Egyptian*, since they were thought to have come originally from Egypt

gyrate (jire-rate) *vb* **-rating, -rated** to turn round and round in a circle ▶ **HISTORY** Greek *guros* circle > **gyration** *n*

gyre *n* **1** a circular or spiral movement or path **2** a ring, circle, or spiral **3** *geog* a circular current that goes clockwise (N Hemisphere) or anticlockwise (S Hemisphere) round an ocean basin due to the rotation of the earth and the Coriolis effect ▷ *vb* **gyres, gyring, gyred 4** to whirl ▶ **HISTORY** Latin *gȳrus* circle, from Greek *guros*

gyrfalcon (jur-fawl-kon) *n* a very large rare falcon of northern regions ▶ **HISTORY** Old French *gerfaucon*

gyro *n, pl* **-ros** short for **gyroscope**

gyrocompass *n* a nonmagnetic compass that uses a motor-driven gyroscope to indicate true north ▶ **HISTORY** Greek *guros* circle + COMPASS

gyroscope (jire-oh-skope) *n* a device containing a disc rotating on an axis that can turn freely in any direction, so that the disc maintains the same position regardless of the movement of the surrounding structure ▶ **HISTORY** Greek *guros* circle + *skopein* to watch > **gyroscopic** *adj*

g

Hh

H 1 *chem* hydrogen **2** *physics* henry

ha¹ or **hah** *interj spoken* an exclamation expressing triumph, surprise, or scorn

ha² *chem* hectare

Ha *chem* hahnium

habeas corpus (hay-bee-ass **kor**-puss) *n law* a writ ordering a person to be brought before a judge, so as to decide whether his or her detention is lawful ▶ HISTORY Latin: you may have the body

haberdasher *n Brit, Austral & NZ* a dealer in small articles used for sewing ▶ HISTORY Anglo-French *hapertas* small items of merchandise
> **haberdashery** *n*

Haber process (**hah**-ber) *n chem* a method of making ammonia by reacting nitrogen with hydrogen at high pressure in the presence of a catalyst ▶ HISTORY after Fritz Haber, German chemist

habit *n* **1** a tendency to act in a particular way **2** established custom or use: *the English habit of taking tea in the afternoon* **3** an addiction to a drug **4** mental disposition or attitude: *deference was a deeply ingrained habit of mind* **5** the costume of a nun or monk **6** a woman's riding costume ▶ HISTORY Latin *habitus* custom

habitable *adj* fit to be lived in > **habitability** *n*

habitant *n* an early French settler in Canada or Louisiana or a descendant of one, esp. a farmer

habitat *n* the natural home of an animal or plant ▶ HISTORY Latin: it inhabits

habitation *n* **1** occupation of a dwelling place: *unfit for human habitation* **2** *formal* a dwelling place

habitual *adj* **1** done regularly and repeatedly: *habitual behaviour patterns* **2** by habit: *a habitual criminal* > **habitually** *adv*

habituate *vb* **-ating, -ated** to accustom; get used to: *habituated to failure* > **habituation** *n*

habitué (hab-**it**-yew-ay) *n* a frequent visitor to a place ▶ HISTORY French

hachure (**hash**-yoor) *n* shading of short lines drawn on a map to indicate the degree of steepness of a hill ▶ HISTORY French

hacienda (hass-ee-**end**-a) *n* (in Spanish-speaking countries) a ranch or large estate with a house on it ▶ HISTORY Spanish

hack¹ *vb* **1** to chop roughly or violently **2** to cut and clear (a way) through undergrowth **3** (in sport) to foul (an opposing player) by kicking his or her shins **4** *Brit & NZ, informal* to tolerate **5** to manipulate a computer program skilfully, esp., to gain unauthorized access to another computer system ▷ *n* **6** a cut or gash **7** a tool, such as a pick **8** a chopping blow **9** a kick on the shins, such as in rugby ▶ HISTORY Old English *haccian*

hack² *n* **1** a writer or journalist who produces work fast and on a regular basis **2** a horse kept for riding, often one for hire **3** *Brit* a country ride on horseback ▷ *vb* **4** *Brit* to ride (a horse) cross-country for pleasure ▷ *adj* **5** unoriginal or of a low standard: *clumsily contrived hack verse* ▶ HISTORY short for *hackney*

hacker *n slang* a computer enthusiast, esp. one who through a personal computer breaks into the computer system of a company or government
> **hacking** or **hackery** *n*

hacking *adj* (of a cough) dry, painful, and harsh-sounding

hackles *pl n* **1 make one's hackles rise** make one feel angry or hostile **2** the hairs or feathers on the back of the neck of certain animals or birds, which rise when they are angry ▶ HISTORY Middle English *hakell*

hackney *n* **1** *Brit* a taxi **2** same as **hack²** (sense 2) ▶ HISTORY probably after *Hackney*, London, where horses were formerly raised

hackneyed (**hak**-need) *adj* (of a word or phrase) unoriginal and overused

hacksaw *n* a small saw for cutting metal

had *vb* the past of **have**

haddock *n, pl* **-dock** a North Atlantic food fish ▶ HISTORY origin unknown

hadedah or **hadeda** (**hah**-dee-dah) *n* a large grey-green S African ibis ▶ HISTORY imitative

Hades (**hay**-deez) *n Greek myth* **1** the underworld home of the souls of the dead **2** the god of the underworld

Hadith (**had**-dith, hah-**deeth**) *n Islam* the body of tradition and legend about Mohammed and his followers, used as a basis of Islamic law ▶ HISTORY Arabic

hadj *n* same as **hajj**

hadji *n, pl* **hadjis** same as **hajji**

Hadley cell *n meteorol* the pattern of air circulation in which warm air rises near the Equator to sink around 30° latitude in each hemisphere; first suggested by George Hadley in 1735 to explain trade winds

haemal or *US* **hemal** (**heem**-al) *adj* of the blood ▶ HISTORY Greek *haima* blood

haematic or *US* **hematic** (hee-**mat**-ik) *adj* relating to or containing blood

haematite or **hematite** *n geol* a red, grey, or black mineral, found as massive beds and in veins and igneous rocks. It is the chief source of iron ▶ HISTORY via Latin from Greek *haimatitēs* resembling blood, from *haima* blood > **haematitic** or **hematitic** *adj*

haematology or *US* **hematology** *n* the branch of medical science concerned with the blood ▶ HISTORY Greek *haima* blood + -LOGY > **haematologist** or *US* **hematologist** *n*

haemoglobin *or US* **hemoglobin** (hee-moh-**globe**-in) *n* a protein in red blood cells that carries oxygen from the lungs to the tissues ▸ HISTORY Greek *haima* blood + Latin *globus* ball

haemophilia *or US* **hemophilia** (hee-moh-**fill**-lee-a) *n* a hereditary disorder, usually affecting males, in which the blood does not clot properly ▸ HISTORY Greek *haima* blood + *philos* loving > **haemophiliac** *n*

haemorrhage *or US* **hemorrhage** (**hem**-or-ij) *n* **1** heavy bleeding from ruptured blood vessels ▹ *vb* **-rhaging, -rhaged 2** to bleed heavily ▸ HISTORY Greek *haima* blood + *rhêgnunai* to burst

haemorrhoids *or US* **hemorrhoids** (**hem**-or-oydz) *pl n pathol* swollen veins in the wall of the anus ▸ HISTORY Greek *haimorrhoos* discharging blood

haere mai (hire-a-my) *interj NZ* an expression of greeting or welcome ▸ HISTORY Māori

hafnium *n chem* a metallic element found in zirconium ores. Symbol: Hf ▸ HISTORY after *Hafnia*, Latin name of Copenhagen

haft *n* the handle of an axe, knife, or dagger ▸ HISTORY Old English *hæft*

hag *n* **1** an unpleasant or ugly old woman **2** a witch ▸ HISTORY Old English *hægtesse* witch > **haggish** *adj*

haggard *adj* looking tired and ill ▸ HISTORY Old French *hagard* wild

haggis *n* a Scottish dish made from sheep's or calf's offal, oatmeal, suet, and seasonings boiled in a skin made from the animal's stomach ▸ HISTORY origin unknown

haggle *vb* **-gling, -gled** to bargain or wrangle (over a price) ▸ HISTORY Scandinavian

hagiography *n, pl* **-phies** the writing of lives of the saints ▸ HISTORY Greek *hagios* holy + *graphein* to write > **hagiographer** *n*

hagiology *n, pl* **-gies** literature about the lives and legends of saints ▸ HISTORY Greek *hagios* holy + -LOGY

hag-ridden *adj* distressed or worried

ha-ha¹ *or* **haw-haw** *interj* a written representation of the sound of laughter

ha-ha² *n* a wall set in a ditch so as not to interrupt a view of the landscape ▸ HISTORY French

hahnium *n chem* a transuranic element artificially produced from californium. Symbol: Ha

haiku (hie-koo) *n, pl* **-ku** a Japanese verse form in 17 syllables ▸ HISTORY Japanese

hail¹ *n* **1** small pellets of ice falling from thunderclouds **2** words, ideas, missiles, etc., directed with force and in great quantity: *a hail of abuse* ▹ *vb* **3** to fall as hail: *it's hailing* **4** to fall like hail: *blows hailed down on him* ▸ HISTORY Old English *hægl*

hail² *vb* **1** to call out to; greet: *a voice from behind hailed him* **2** to praise, acclaim, or acknowledge: *his crew had been hailed as heroes* **3** to stop (a taxi) by shouting or gesturing **4** **hail from** to come originally from: *she hails from Nova Scotia*

▹ *n* **5** **within hailing distance** within hearing range ▹ *interj* **6** *poetic* an exclamation of greeting ▸ HISTORY Old Norse *heill* healthy

Hail Mary *n RC Church* a prayer to the Virgin Mary

hailstone *n* a pellet of hail

hailstorm *n* a storm during which hail falls

hair *n* **1** any of the threadlike outgrowths on the skin of mammals **2** a mass of such outgrowths, such as on a person's head or an animal's body **3** *bot* a threadlike growth from the outer layer of a plant **4** a very small distance or margin: *he missed death by a hair* **5** **get in someone's hair** *informal* to annoy someone **6** **hair of the dog** an alcoholic drink taken as a cure for a hangover **7** **let one's hair down** to enjoy oneself without restraint **8** **not turn a hair** to show no reaction **9** **split hairs** to make petty and unnecessary distinctions ▸ HISTORY Old English *hær* > **hairless** *adj*

hairclip *n NZ & S African* a small bent metal hairpin

hairdo *n, pl* **-dos** *informal* the style of a person's hair

hairdresser *n* **1** a person who cuts and styles hair. Related adjective: **tonsorial 2** a hairdresser's premises > **hairdressing** *n*

hairgrip *n chiefly Brit* a small bent clasp used to fasten the hair

hairline *n* **1** the edge of hair at the top of the forehead ▹ *adj* **2** very fine or narrow: *a hairline crack*

hairpiece *n* a section of false hair added to a person's real hair

hairpin *n* a thin U-shaped pin used to fasten the hair

hairpin bend *n* a bend in the road that curves very sharply

hair-raising *adj* very frightening or exciting

hair's-breadth *n* an extremely small margin or distance

hair shirt *n* a shirt made of horsehair cloth worn against the skin as a penance

hairstyle *n* the cut and arrangement of a person's hair > **hairstylist** *n*

hairy *adj* **hairier, hairiest 1** covered with hair **2** *slang* dangerous, exciting, and difficult > **hairiness** *n*

hajj *or* **hadj** *n* the pilgrimage a Muslim makes to Mecca ▸ HISTORY Arabic

hajji *or* **hadji** *n, pl* **hajjis** *or* **hadjis** a Muslim who has made a pilgrimage to Mecca

haka *n NZ* **1** a Māori war chant accompanied by actions **2** a similar chant by a sports team

hake *n, pl* **hake** *or* **hakes 1** a northern hemisphere edible fish of the cod family **2** *Austral* same as **barracouta** ▸ HISTORY origin unknown

hakea (hah-kee-a) *n* an Australian tree or shrub with hard woody fruit

halal *or* **hallal** *n* meat from animals that have been slaughtered according to Muslim law ▸ HISTORY Arabic: lawful

halberd *n history* a tall spear that includes an axe blade and a pick ▸ HISTORY Middle High German *helm* handle + *barde* axe

halcyon (**hal**-see-on) *adj* **1** peaceful, gentle, and calm **2** **halcyon days** a time, usually in the past, of greatest happiness or success ▶ HISTORY Greek *alkuōn* kingfisher

hale *adj* healthy and robust: *hale and hearty* ▶ HISTORY Old English *hæl* whole

half *n*, *pl* **halves** **1** either of two equal or corresponding parts that together make up a whole **2** the fraction equal to one divided by two **3** half a pint, esp. of beer **4** *sport* one of two equal periods of play in a game **5** a half-price ticket **6 by half** to an excessive degree: *too clever by half* **7 by halves** without being thorough: *in Italy they rarely do things by halves* **8 go halves** to share expenses ▷ *adj* **9** denoting one of two equal parts: *a half chicken* ▷ *adv* **10** half in degree or quantity: *half as much* **11** partially; to an extent: *half hidden in the trees* **12 not half** *informal* **a** *Brit* very; indeed: *it isn't half hard to look at these charts* **b** yes, indeed ▶ HISTORY Old English *healf*

half-and-half *adj* half one thing and half another thing

halfback *n* *rugby* a player positioned immediately behind the forwards

half-baked *adj* *informal* poorly planned: *half-baked policies*

half board *n* *Brit* the daily provision by a hotel of bed, breakfast, and evening meal

half-breed *n* *offensive* a person whose parents are of different races

half-brother *n* the son of either one's mother or father by another partner

half-caste *n* *offensive* a person whose parents are of different races

half-crown *or* **half-a-crown** *n* a former British coin worth two shillings and sixpence (12½p)

half-day *n* a day when one works only in the morning or only in the afternoon

half-hearted *adj* without enthusiasm or determination ▶ **half-heartedly** *adv*

half-hour *n* **1** a period of 30 minutes **2** the point of time 30 minutes after the beginning of an hour > **half-hourly** *adv*, *adj*

half-life *n* the time taken for radioactive material to lose half its radioactivity

half-mast *n* the halfway position of a flag on a mast as a sign of mourning

half-moon *n* **1** the moon when half its face is illuminated **2** the time at which a half-moon occurs **3** something shaped like a half-moon

half-nelson *n* a wrestling hold in which a wrestler places an arm under his opponent's arm from behind and exerts pressure with his palm on the back of his opponent's neck

halfpenny *or* **ha'penny** (**hayp**-nee) *n*, *pl* **-pennies** a former British coin worth half a penny

half-pie *adj* *NZ*, *informal* badly planned; not properly thought out: *a half-pie scheme* ▶ HISTORY Māori *pai* good

half-sister *n* the daughter of either one's mother or father by another partner

half term *n* *Brit education* a short holiday midway through a term

half-timbered *adj* (of a building) having an exposed timber framework filled with brick or plaster

half-time *n* *sport* an interval between the two halves of a game

halftone *n* a photographic illustration in which the image is composed of a large number of black and white dots

half-track *n* a vehicle with moving tracks on the rear wheels

half volley *n* *sport* **1** a stroke or shot in which the ball is hit immediately after it bounces ▷ *vb* **half-volley** **2** to hit or kick (a ball) immediately after it bounces

halfway *adv*, *adj* **1** at or to half the distance **2** at or towards the middle of a period of time or of an event or process: *he only managed to get halfway up the hill* **3 meet someone halfway** to compromise with someone

halfway house *n* **1** a place to rest midway on a journey **2** the halfway stage in any process: *a halfway house between the theatre and cinema is possible*

halfwit *n* a foolish or feeble-minded person > **halfwitted** *adj*

halibut *n* a large edible flatfish ▶ HISTORY Middle English *hali* holy (because it was eaten on holy days) + *butte* flatfish

halitosis *n* bad-smelling breath ▶ HISTORY Latin *halitus* breath

hall *n* **1** an entry area to other rooms in a house **2** a building or room for public meetings, dances, etc. **3** a residential building in a college or university **4** *Brit* a great house of an estate; manor **5** a large dining room in a college or university **6** the large room of a castle or stately home ▶ HISTORY Old English *heall*

hallelujah, halleluiah (hal-ee-**loo**-ya) *or* **alleluia** *interj* an exclamation of praise to God ▶ HISTORY Hebrew *hellēl* to praise + *yāh* the Lord

hallmark *n* **1** a typical feature: *secrecy became the hallmark of government* **2** *Brit* an official seal stamped on gold, silver, or platinum articles to guarantee purity and date of manufacture **3** a mark of authenticity or excellence ▷ *vb* **4** to stamp with a hallmark ▶ HISTORY after Goldsmiths' *Hall* in London, where items were stamped

hallo *interj*, *n* same as **hello**

hallowed *adj* **1** regarded as holy: *hallowed ground* **2** respected and revered because of age, importance, or reputation: *the hallowed pitch at Lord's* ▶ HISTORY Old English *hālgian* to consecrate

Halloween *or* **Hallowe'en** *n* October 31, celebrated by children by dressing up as ghosts, witches, etc.

- **WORD HISTORY**
- 'Halloween' means 'holy evening', from Old
- English *halig*, meaning 'holy', and *æfen*,
- meaning 'evening'. Halloween is the evening
- before All Saints' Day, November 1.

hallucinate *vb* **-nating, -nated** to seem to see something that is not really there ▶ HISTORY Latin *alucinari*

hallucination *n* the experience of seeming to see something that is not really there > **hallucinatory** *adj*

hallucinogen *n* any drug that causes hallucinations > **hallucinogenic** *adj*

halo (**hay**-loh) *n, pl* **-loes** *or* **-los** 1 a ring of light around the head of a sacred figure 2 a circle of refracted light around the sun or moon ▷ *vb* **-loes** *or* **-los, -loing, -loed** 3 to surround with a halo ▶ **HISTORY** Greek *halōs* circular threshing floor

halogen (**hal**-oh-jen) *n chem* any of the nonmetallic chemical elements fluorine, chlorine, bromine, iodine, and astatine which form salts when combined with metal ▶ **HISTORY** Greek *hals* salt + *-genēs* born

halt *vb* 1 to come to a stop or bring (someone or something) to a stop ▷ *n* 2 a temporary standstill 3 a military command to stop 4 *chiefly Brit* a minor railway station without a building: *Deeside Halt* 5 **call a halt to** to put an end to ▶ **HISTORY** German *halten* to stop

halter *n* 1 a strap around a horse's head with a rope to lead it with ▷ *vb* 2 to put a halter on (a horse) ▶ **HISTORY** Old English *hælfter*

halterneck *n* a woman's top or dress which fastens behind the neck, leaving the back and arms bare

halting *adj* hesitant or uncertain: *she spoke halting Italian*

halve *vb* **halving, halved** 1 to divide (something) into two equal parts 2 to reduce (the size or amount of something) by half 3 *golf* to draw with one's opponent (a hole or round)

halyard *n naut* a line for hoisting or lowering a ship's sail or flag ▶ **HISTORY** Middle English *halier*

ham[1] *n* smoked or salted meat from a pig's thigh ▶ **HISTORY** Old English *hamm*

ham[2] *informal n* 1 an amateur radio operator 2 *theatre* an actor who overacts and exaggerates the emotions and gestures of a part ▷ *adj* 3 (of actors or their performances) exaggerated and overstated ▷ *vb* **hamming, hammed** 4 **ham it up** to overact ▶ **HISTORY** special use of HAM[1]

hamada *n geog* an area of desert where bedrock is exposed as a consequence of erosion

hamba *interj S African, usually offensive* go away ▶ **HISTORY** Nguni (language group of southern Africa): to go

hamburger *n* a flat round of minced beef, often served in a bread roll

- **WORD HISTORY**
- Hamburgers are named after their city of
- origin, *Hamburg* in Germany. Similarly
- Frankfurters are sausages from the town of
- Frankfurt. The word 'hamburger' has nothing
- to do with 'ham', but the 'burger' part has now
- been taken as a noun in its own right, on the
- basis of which we now have 'beefburgers',
- 'cheeseburgers', and so on.

ham-fisted *or* **ham-handed** *adj informal* very clumsy or awkward

hamlet *n* a small village ▶ **HISTORY** Old French *hamelet*

hammer *n* 1 a hand tool consisting of a heavy metal head on the end of a handle, used for driving in nails, beating metal, etc. 2 the part of a gun that causes the bullet to shoot when the trigger is pulled 3 *athletics* **a** a heavy metal ball attached to a flexible wire: thrown in competitions **b** the sport of throwing the hammer 4 an auctioneer's mallet 5 the part of a piano that hits a string when a key is pressed 6 **come** *or* **go under the hammer** to be on sale at auction 7 **hammer and tongs** with great effort or energy ▷ *vb* 8 to hit with or as if with a hammer 9 **hammer in** *or* **into** to force (facts or ideas) into someone through repetition 10 **hammer away at** to work at (something) constantly: *the paper hammered away at the same theme all the way through the campaign* 11 *Brit* to criticize severely 12 *informal* to defeat heavily 13 to feel or sound like hammering: *his heart was hammering* ▶ **HISTORY** Old English *hamor*

hammer and sickle *n* the emblem on the flag of the former Soviet Union, representing the industrial workers and the peasants

hammerhead *n* a shark with a wide flattened head

hammer out *vb* to produce (an agreement) with great effort

hammertoe *n* a condition in which the toe is permanently bent at the joint

hammock *n* a hanging bed made of canvas or net ▶ **HISTORY** Spanish *hamaca*

hamper[1] *vb* to make it difficult for (someone or something) to move or progress ▶ **HISTORY** origin unknown

hamper[2] *n* 1 a large basket with a lid 2 *Brit* a selection of food and drink packed as a gift ▶ **HISTORY** Middle English *hanaper* a small basket

hamster *n* a small rodent with a stocky body, short tail, and cheek pouches ▶ **HISTORY** German

hamstring *n* 1 one of the tendons at the back of the knee ▷ *vb* **-stringing, -strung** 2 to make it difficult for someone to take any action ▶ **HISTORY** *ham* (in the sense: leg)

hand *n* 1 the part of the body at the end of the arm, consisting of a thumb, four fingers, and a palm. *Related adjective:* **manual** 2 a person's style of writing: *scrolls written in her own hand* 3 the influence a person or thing has over a particular situation: *the hand of the military in shaping policy was obvious* 4 a part in some activity: *I remember with gratitude Fortune's hand in starting my collection* 5 assistance: *give me a hand with the rice* 6 a round of applause: *give a big hand to the most exciting duo in the game* 7 consent to marry someone: *he asked for her hand in marriage* 8 a manual worker 9 a member of a ship's crew 10 a pointer on a dial or gauge, esp. on a clock 11 **a** the cards dealt in one round of a card game **b** one round of a card game 12 a position indicated by its location to the side of an object or the observer: *on the right hand* 13 a contrasting aspect or condition: *on the other*

hand 14 source: *I had experienced at first hand many management styles* **15** a person who creates something: *a good hand at baking* **16** a unit of length equalling four inches, used for measuring the height of horses **17 by hand a** by manual rather than mechanical means **b** by messenger: *the letter was delivered by hand* **18 from hand to mouth** with no food or money in reserve: *living from hand to mouth* **19 hand in glove** in close association **20 hand over fist** steadily and quickly: *losing money hand over fist* **21 in hand a** under control **b** receiving attention: *the business in hand* **c** available in reserve: *Pakistan have a game in hand* **22 keep one's hand in** to continue to practise something **23 (near) at hand** very close **24 on hand** close by; available **25 out of hand a** beyond control **b** decisively, without possible reconsideration: *he dismissed the competition out of hand* **26 show one's hand** to reveal one's plans **27 to hand** accessible ▷ *vb* **28** to pass or give by the hand or hands **29 hand it to someone** to give credit to someone ▷ See also **hand down, hands,** etc. ▸ HISTORY Old English > **handless** *adj*

handbag *n* a woman's small bag carried to contain personal articles

handbill *n* a small printed notice for distribution by hand

handbook *n* a reference manual giving practical information on a subject

handbrake *n* a brake in a motor vehicle operated by a hand lever

handbrake turn *n* a turn sharply reversing the direction of a vehicle by applying the handbrake while turning the steering wheel

h & c hot and cold (water)

handcart *n* a simple cart pushed or pulled by hand, used for transporting goods

handcuff *n* **1 handcuffs** a linked pair of locking metal rings used for securing prisoners ▷ *vb* **2** to put handcuffs on (a person)

hand down *vb* **1** to pass on (knowledge, possessions, or skills) to a younger generation **2** to pass (outgrown clothes) on from one member of a family to a younger one **3** *US & Canad law* to announce (a verdict)

handful *n, pl* **-fuls 1** the amount that can be held in the hand **2** a small number: *a handful of parents* **3** *informal* a person or animal that is difficult to control: *as a child she was a real handful*

hand-held *adj* **1** held in position by the hand ▷ *n* **2** a device, such as a computer, that can be held in the hand

handicap *n* **1** *old-fashioned, often offensive* a physical or mental disability **2** something that makes progress difficult **3 a** a contest in which competitors are given advantages or disadvantages in an attempt to equalize their chances **b** the advantage or disadvantage given **4** *golf* the number of strokes by which a player's averaged score exceeds par for the course ▷ *vb* **-capping, -capped 5** to make it difficult for (someone) to do something ▸ HISTORY probably

hand in cap, a lottery game in which players drew forfeits from a cap

handicapped *adj* *old-fashioned, often offensive* physically or mentally disabled

handicraft *n* **1** a skill performed with the hands, such as weaving **2** the objects produced by people with such skills

handiwork *n* **1** the result of someone's work or activity **2** work produced by hand

handkerchief *n* a small square of fabric used to wipe the nose

handle *n* **1** the part of an object that is held or operated in order that it may be used **2** a small lever used to open and close a door or window **3** *slang* a person's name **4** a reason for doing something: *trying to get a handle on why companies borrow money* **5 fly off the handle** *informal* to become suddenly extremely angry ▷ *vb* **-dling, -dled 6** to hold, move, operate, or touch with the hands **7** to have responsibility for: *she handles all their affairs personally* **8** to manage successfully: *I can handle this challenge* **9** to discuss (a subject) **10** to deal with in a specified way: *the affair was neatly handled* **11** to trade or deal in (specified merchandise): *we handle 1800 properties in Normandy* **12** to react or respond in a specified way to operation or control: *it's light and handles well* ▸ HISTORY Old English > **handling** *n*

handlebars *pl n* a metal tube with handles at each end, used for steering a bicycle or motorcycle

handler *n* **1** a person who trains and controls an animal **2** a person who handles something: *a baggage handler*

hand-out *n, pl* **hand-outs 1** clothing, food, or money given to a needy person **2** a leaflet, free sample, etc., given out to publicize something **3** a piece of written information given out to the audience at a talk, lecture, etc. ▷ *vb* **hand out 4** to distribute

hand-pick *vb* to select (a person) with great care, such as for a special job > **hand-picked** *adj*

handrail *n* a rail alongside a stairway, to provide support

hands *pl n* **1 in someone's hands** in someone's control or power: *that's in the hands of the courts* **2 change hands** to pass from the possession of one person to another **3 have one's hands full** to be completely occupied **4 off one's hands** no longer one's responsibility **5 on one's hands** for which one is responsible: *what a problem case I've got on my hands* **6 wash one's hands of** to have nothing more to do with **7 win hands down** to win easily

handset *n* a telephone mouthpiece and earpiece in a single unit

hands-free *adj* **1** able to be operated without using the hands ▷ *n* **2** a device, such as a telephone, that can be operated without using the hands

handsome *adj* **1** (esp. of a man) good-looking **2** (of a building, garden, etc.) large, well-made, and with an attractive appearance: *a handsome building*

3 (of an amount of money) generous or large: *a handsome dividend* ▸ HISTORY obsolete *handsom* easily handled > **handsomely** *adv*

hands-on *adj* involving practical experience of equipment: *Navy personnel joined the 1986 expedition for hands-on operating experience*

handstand *n* the act of supporting the body on the hands in an upside-down position

hand-to-hand *adj, adv* (of combat) at close quarters, with fists or knives

hand-to-mouth *adj, adv* with barely enough money or food to live on

handwriting *n* **1** writing by hand rather than by typing or printing **2** a person's characteristic writing style > **handwritten** *adj*

handy *adj* **handier, handiest** **1** conveniently within reach **2** easy to handle or use **3** good at manual work > **handily** *adv*

handyman *n, pl* **-men** a man skilled at odd jobs

hang *vb* **hanging, hung** **1** to fasten or be fastened from above **2** to place (something) in position, for instance by a hinge, so as to allow free movement: *to hang a door* **3** to be suspended so as to allow movement from the place where it is attached: *her long hair hung over her face* **4** to decorate with something suspended, such as pictures **5** (of cloth or clothing) to fall or flow in a particular way: *the fine gauge knit hangs loosely with graceful femininity* **6** (*pt & pp* **hanged**) to suspend or be suspended by the neck until dead **7** to hover: *clouds hung over the mountains* **8** to fasten to a wall: *to hang wallpaper* **9** to exhibit or be exhibited in an art gallery **10 hang over** to threaten or overshadow: *the threat of war hung over the Middle East* **11** (*pt & pp* **hanged**) *slang* to damn: used in mild curses or interjections **12 hang fire** to put off doing something ▷ *n* **13** the way in which something hangs **14 get the hang of something** *informal* to understand the technique of doing something ▷ See also **hang about, hang back**, etc. ▸ HISTORY Old English *hangian*

hang about *or* **around** *vb* **1** to stand about idly somewhere **2** (foll. by *with*) to spend a lot of time in the company (of someone)

hangar *n* a large building for storing aircraft ▸ HISTORY French: shed

hang back *vb* to be reluctant to do something

hangdog *adj* dejected, ashamed, or guilty in appearance or manner

hanger *n* same as **coat hanger**

hanger-on *n, pl* **hangers-on** an unwanted follower, esp. of a rich or famous person

hang-glider *n* an unpowered aircraft consisting of a large cloth wing stretched over a light framework from which the pilot hangs in a harness > **hang-gliding** *n*

hangi (**hung**-ee) *n NZ* **1** an open-air cooking pit **2** the food cooked in it **3** the social gathering at the resultant meal ▸ HISTORY Māori

hanging *n* **1** the act or practice of putting a person to death by suspending the body by the neck **2** a large piece of cloth hung on a wall as a decoration

hanging valley *n geog* a tributary valley that enters a main valley high up because the main valley has been deepened through erosion by a glacier

hangman *n, pl* **-men** an official who carries out a sentence of hanging

hangover *n* a feeling of sickness and headache after drinking too much alcohol

hang up *vb* **1** to replace (a telephone receiver) at the end of a conversation **2** to put on a hook or hanger ▷ *n* **hang-up** *n* **3** *informal* an emotional or psychological problem

hank *n* a loop or coil, esp. of yarn ▸ HISTORY from Old Norse

hanker *vb* (foll. by *for* or *after*) to have a great desire for ▸ HISTORY probably from Dutch dialect *hankeren* > **hankering** *n*

hanky *or* **hankie** *n, pl* **hankies** *informal* short for **handkerchief**

Hanoverian (han-no-**veer**-ee-an) *adj* of or relating to the British royal house ruling from 1714 to 1901 ▸ HISTORY after *Hanover*, Germany

Hansard *n* the official report of the proceedings of the British or Canadian parliament ▸ HISTORY after L. *Hansard*, its original compiler

Hanseatic League (han-see-**at**-ik) *n history* a commercial organization of towns in N Germany formed in the 14th century to protect and control trade

hansom *n* formerly, a two-wheeled one-horse carriage with a fixed hood. Also called: **hansom cab** ▸ HISTORY after its designer J. A. *Hansom*

Hanukkah *n* same as **Chanukah**

haphazard *adj* not organized or planned ▸ HISTORY Old Norse *happ* chance, good luck + HAZARD > **haphazardly** *adv*

hapless *adj* unlucky: *the hapless victim of a misplaced murder attempt* ▸ HISTORY Old Norse *happ* chance, good luck

haploid *adj biol* denoting a cell or organism with unpaired chromosomes ▸ HISTORY Greek *haplous* single

haplotype *n genetics* a set of alleles inherited by an individual from a single parent

happen *vb* **1** to take place; occur **2** to chance (to be or do something): *I happen to know him* **3** to be the case, esp. by chance: *it happens that I know him* **4 happen to** (of some unforeseen event, such as death) to be the experience or fate of: *if anything happens to me you will know* ▸ HISTORY obsolete *hap*

happening *n* an event that often occurs in a way that is unexpected or hard to explain: *some strange happenings in the village recently*

happy *adj* **-pier, -piest** **1** feeling or expressing joy **2** causing joy or gladness: *the happiest day of my life* **3** fortunate or lucky: *it was a happy coincidence* **4** satisfied or content: *he seems happy to let things go on as they are* **5** willing: *I'll be happy to arrange a loan for you* ▸ HISTORY Old Norse *happ* chance, good luck > **happily** *adv* > **happiness** *n*
See WORD FOCUS **happy** on page 380

happy-go-lucky *adj* carefree or easy-going

happy

WORD FOCUS

Happy is an overused word. You can vary your language by choosing one of the alternatives shown here.

DEFINITION 1

- If you would like to describe someone or something as expressing or feeling joy, you could try: a **cheerful** disposition • a **cheery** face • You're very **chirpy** today. (informal) • I was **ecstatic** to see Marianne again. • **elated** that she had won • He is **euphoric** at the news. • **glad** to be back • a **jolly** fellow • a **joyful** pride in his work • They were **jubilant** over their election victory. • a **merry** laugh • **overjoyed** to be reunited • The team are **over the moon** with this result. (informal) • We're very **pleased** to meet you. • her unfailingly **sunny** nature • **thrilled** to meet his hero

DEFINITION 2

- If you would like to describe something that causes joy, you could try: the **agreeable** task • **blissful** marriage • truly **festive** occasion

- a **gratifying** relationship • a **joyful** event • the **joyous** news • a **pleasurable** memory

DEFINITION 3

- If you would like to describe something as lucky, you could try: an **auspicious** start • a **convenient** outcome • a **favourable** result • a very **fortunate** situation • a **lucky** chance • hardly an **opportune** moment • his **timely** arrival

DEFINITION 4

- If you would like to describe someone who is content with or to do something, you could try: **content** just to sit quietly • **delighted** with their new home • **glad** just to be there • **pleased** with the way things are going • **satisfied** with the conclusion

DEFINITION 5

- If you would like to describe someone who is willing to do something, you could try: always **glad** to be of service • **pleased** to take you there myself • I'd be **prepared** to talk. • He's **ready** to help anyone. • I'm **willing** to wait.

---

hara-kiri n (formerly, in Japan) ritual suicide by disembowelment when disgraced or under sentence of death ▶ HISTORY Japanese *hara* belly + *kiri* cut

harangue vb **-ranguing, -rangued 1** to address (a person or group) in an angry or forcefully persuasive way ▷ n **2** a forceful or angry speech ▶ HISTORY Old Italian *aringa* public speech

harass vb to trouble or annoy (someone) by repeated attacks, questions, or problems ▶ HISTORY French *harasser* > **harassed** adj > **harassment** n

harbinger (**har**-binge-er) n literary a person or thing that announces or indicates the approach of something: *a harbinger of death* ▶ HISTORY Old French *herbergere*

harbour or US **harbor** n **1** a sheltered port **2** a place of refuge or safety ▷ vb **3** to maintain secretly in the mind: *he might be harbouring a death wish* **4** to give shelter or protection to: *the government accused her of harbouring criminals* ▶ HISTORY Old English *hereboerg*, from *here* army + *beorg* shelter

hard adj **1** firm, solid, or rigid **2** difficult to do or understand: *a hard sum* **3** showing or requiring a lot of effort or application: *hard work* **4** unkind or unfeeling: *she's very hard, no pity for anyone* **5** causing pain, sorrow, or hardship: *the hard life of a northern settler* **6** tough or violent: *a hard man* **7** forceful: *a hard knock* **8** cool or uncompromising: *we took a long hard look at our profit factor* **9** indisputable and proven to be true: *hard facts* **10** (of water) containing calcium salts which stop soap lathering freely **11** practical, shrewd, or calculating: *he is a hard man in business* **12** harsh: *hard light* **13** (of currency) high and stable in exchange value **14** (of alcoholic drink) being a spirit rather than a wine or beer **15** (of a drug) highly addictive **16** hard-core **17** phonetics denoting the consonants *c* and *g* when they are pronounced as in *cat* and *got* **18** politically extreme: *the hard left* **19** **hard of hearing** slightly deaf **20** **hard up** informal in need of money ▷ adv **21** with great energy or force: *they fought so hard and well in Spain* **22** with great intensity: *thinking hard about the conversation* **23** **hard by** very close to: *Cleveland Place, hard by Bruntsfield Square* **24** **hard put (to it)** scarcely having the capacity (to do something) ▶ HISTORY Old English *heard* > **hardness** n

hard-and-fast adj (of rules) fixed and not able to be changed

hardback n **1** a book with stiff covers ▷ adj **2** of or denoting a hardback

hard-bitten adj informal tough and determined

hardboard n stiff board made in thin sheets of compressed sawdust and wood glue

hard-boiled adj **1** (of an egg) boiled until solid **2** informal tough, realistic, and unemotional

hard cash n money or payment in money, as opposed to payment by cheque, credit, etc.

hard copy n computer output printed on paper

hard core n **1** the members of a group who most resist change **2** broken stones used to form a foundation for a road ▷ adj **hard-core 3** extremely committed or fanatical: *a hard-core Communist*

hard disk n computers an inflexible disk in a sealed container

hard drive n computers a mechanism that handles the reading, writing, and storage of data on the hard disk

harden vb **1** to make or become hard; freeze, stiffen, or set **2** to make or become tough or unfeeling: *life in the camp had hardened her* considerably **3** to make or become stronger or firmer: *they hardened defences* **4** to make or become more determined or resolute: *the government has hardened its attitude to the crisis* **5** *commerce* (of prices or a market) to cease to fluctuate

hardened *adj* toughened by experience: *a hardened criminal*

hardfill *n* *NZ & S African* a stone waste material used for landscaping

hard-headed *adj* tough, realistic, or shrewd, esp. in business

hardhearted *adj* unsympathetic and uncaring

hard labour *n* difficult and tiring physical work: used as a punishment for a crime in some countries

hard line *n* **1** an uncompromising policy: *a hard line on drugs* ▷ *adj* **hard-line 2** tough and uncompromising: *a hard-line attitude to the refugee problem* > **hardliner** *n*

hardly *adv* **1** scarcely; barely: *he'd hardly sipped his whisky* **2** ironic not at all: *it was hardly in the Great Train Robbery league* **3** with difficulty: *their own families would hardly recognize them*

hard news *n* news stories based on important real events rather than analysis, interpretation, or gossip. Compare **soft news**

hard pad *n* (in dogs) an abnormal increase in the thickness of the foot pads: a sign of distemper

hard palate *n* the bony front part of the roof of the mouth

hard sell *n* an aggressive insistent technique of selling

hardship *n* **1** conditions of life that are difficult to endure **2** something that causes suffering

hard shoulder *n* *Brit & NZ* a surfaced verge running along the edge of a motorway and other roads for emergency stops

hardware *n* **1** metal tools or implements, esp. cutlery or cooking utensils **2** *computers* the physical equipment used in a computer system **3** heavy military equipment, such as tanks and missiles

hard-wired *adj* (of a circuit or instruction) permanently wired into a computer

hardwood *n* the wood of a deciduous tree such as oak, beech, or ash

hardy *adj* **-dier, -diest 1** able to stand difficult conditions **2** (of plants) able to live out of doors throughout the winter ▶ **HISTORY** Old French *hardi* emboldened > **hardiness** *n*

hare *n, pl* **hares** *or* **hare 1** a mammal like a large rabbit, with longer ears and legs ▷ *vb* **haring, hared 2** (foll. by *off or after*) *Brit & Austral, informal* to run fast or wildly ▶ **HISTORY** Old English *hara*

harebell *n* a blue bell-shaped flower

harebrained *adj* foolish or impractical: *harebrained schemes*

harelip *n* a slight split in the mid line of the upper lip

harem *n* **1** a Muslim man's wives and concubines collectively **2** the part of an Oriental house reserved for wives and concubines ▶ **HISTORY** Arabic *harīm* forbidden (place)

haricot bean *or* **haricot** (har-rik-oh) *n* a white edible bean, which can be dried ▶ **HISTORY** French *haricot*

hark *vb* *old-fashioned* to listen; pay attention: *hark, the cocks are crowing* ▶ **HISTORY** Old English *heorcnian*

hark back *vb* to return (to an earlier subject in speech or thought): *he keeps harking back to his music-hall days*

harlequin *n* **1** *theatre* a stock comic character, usually wearing a diamond-patterned multicoloured costume and a black mask ▷ *adj* **2** written in varied colours ▶ **HISTORY** Old French *Herlequin* leader of a band of demon horsemen

harlequinade *n* *theatre* a play in which harlequin has a leading role

harlot *n* *literary* a prostitute ▶ **HISTORY** Old French *herlot* rascal > **harlotry** *n*

harm *vb* **1** to injure physically, morally, or mentally ▷ *n* **2** physical, moral, or mental injury ▶ **HISTORY** Old English *hearm*

harmful *adj* causing or tending to cause harm, esp. to a person's health

harmless *adj* **1** safe to use, touch, or be near **2** unlikely to annoy or worry people: *a harmless habit*

harmonic *adj* **1** of, producing, or characterized by harmony; harmonious ▷ *n* **2** *music* an overtone of a musical note produced when that note is played, but not usually heard as a separate note ▷ See also **harmonics** ▶ **HISTORY** Latin *harmonicus* relating to harmony > **harmonically** *adv*

harmonica *n* a small wind instrument in which reeds enclosed in a narrow oblong box are made to vibrate by blowing and sucking

harmonics *n* the science of musical sounds

harmonious *adj* **1** (esp. of colours or sounds) consisting of parts which blend together well **2** showing agreement, peacefulness, and friendship: *a harmonious relationship* **3** tuneful or melodious

harmonium *n* a musical keyboard instrument in which air from pedal-operated bellows causes the reeds to vibrate

harmonize *or* **-nise** *vb* **-nizing, -nized** *or* **-nising, -nised 1** to sing or play in harmony, such as with another singer or player **2** to make or become harmonious

harmony *n, pl* **-nies 1** a state of peaceful agreement and cooperation **2** *music* a pleasant combination of two or more notes sounded at the same time **3** the way parts combine well together or into a whole ▶ **HISTORY** Greek *harmonia*

harness *n* **1** an arrangement of straps for attaching a horse to a cart or plough **2** something resembling this, for attaching something to a person's body: *a parachute harness* **3 in harness** at one's routine work ▷ *vb* **4** to put a harness on (a horse or other animal) **5** to control something in order to make use of it: *learning to harness the power of your own mind* ▶ **HISTORY** Old French *harneis* baggage

harp *n* **1** a large upright triangular stringed instrument played by plucking the strings with the fingers ▷ *vb* **2 harp on** to speak in a persistent and tedious manner (about a subject) ▶ HISTORY Old English *hearpe* > **harpist** *n*

harpoon *n* **1** a barbed spear attached to a long rope and thrown or fired when hunting whales, etc. ▷ *vb* **2** to spear with a harpoon ▶ HISTORY probably from Dutch *harpoen*

harpsichord *n* a keyboard instrument, resembling a small piano, with strings that are plucked mechanically ▶ HISTORY Late Latin *harpa* harp + Latin *chorda* string > **harpsichordist** *n*

harpy *n*, *pl* **-pies** a violent, unpleasant, or greedy woman ▶ HISTORY Greek *Harpuiai* the Harpies, literally: snatchers (mythical birdlike female monsters)

harridan *n* a scolding old woman; nag ▶ HISTORY origin unknown

harrier² *n* a cross-country runner ▶ HISTORY from *hare*

harrier² *n* a bird of prey with broad wings and long legs and tail

harrow *n* **1** an implement used to break up clods of soil ▷ *vb* **2** to draw a harrow over (land) ▶ HISTORY from Old Norse

harrowing *adj* very upsetting or disturbing

harry *vb* **-ries, -rying, -ried** to keep asking (someone) to do something; pester ▶ HISTORY Old English *hergian*

harsh *adj* **1** severe and difficult to cope with: *harsh winters* **2** unkind and showing no understanding: *the judge was very harsh on the demonstrators* **3** excessively hard, bright, or rough: *harsh sunlight* **4** (of sounds) unpleasant and grating ▶ HISTORY probably Scandinavian > **harshly** *adv* > **harshness** *n*

hart *n*, *pl* **harts** or **hart** the male of the deer, esp. the red deer ▶ HISTORY Old English *heorot*

hartebeest *n* a large African antelope with curved horns and a fawn-coloured coat ▶ HISTORY Dutch

harum-scarum *adj* **1** reckless ▷ *adv* **2** recklessly ▷ *n* **3** an impetuous person ▶ HISTORY origin unknown

harvest *n* **1** the gathering of a ripened crop **2** the crop itself **3** the season for gathering crops **4** the product of an effort or action ▷ *vb* **5** to gather (a ripened crop) **6** *chiefly US* to remove (an organ) from the body for transplantation ▶ HISTORY Old English *hærfest*

harvester *n* **1** a harvesting machine, esp. a combine harvester **2** a person who harvests

harvest moon *n* the full moon occurring nearest to the autumn equinox

harvest mouse *n* a very small reddish-brown mouse that lives in cornfields or hedgerows

has *vb* third person singular of the present tense of **have**

has-been *n informal* a person who is no longer popular or successful

hash¹ *n* **1** a dish of diced cooked meat, vegetables, etc., reheated: *corned-beef hash* **2** a reworking of old

material **3 make a hash of** *informal* to mess up or destroy ▶ HISTORY Old French *hacher* to chop up

hash² *n slang* short for **hashish**

hashish (**hash**-eesh) *n* a drug made from the hemp plant, smoked for its intoxicating effects ▶ HISTORY Arabic

hasp *n* a clasp which fits over a staple and is secured by a pin, bolt, or padlock, used as a fastening ▶ HISTORY Old English *hæpse*

hassium *n chem* an element synthetically produced in small quantities by high-energy ion bombardment. Symbol: Hs ▶ HISTORY Latin, from *Hesse*, the German state where it was discovered

hassle *informal n* **1** a great deal of trouble **2** a prolonged argument ▷ *vb* **-sling, -sled** **3** to cause annoyance or trouble to (someone): *stop hassling me!* ▶ HISTORY origin unknown

hassock *n* a cushion for kneeling on in church ▶ HISTORY Old English *hassuc* matted grass

haste *n* **1** speed, esp. in an action **2** the act of hurrying in a careless manner **3 make haste** to hurry or rush ▷ *vb* **hasting, hasted 4** *poetic* to hasten ▶ HISTORY Old French

hasten *vb* **1** to hurry or cause to hurry **2** to be anxious (to say something)

hasty *adj* **-tier, -tiest 1** done or happening suddenly or quickly **2** done too quickly and without thought; rash > **hastily** *adv*

hat *n* **1** a head covering, often with a brim, usually worn to give protection from the weather **2** *informal* a role or capacity: *I'm wearing my honorary consul's hat* **3 keep something under one's hat** to keep something secret **4 pass the hat round** to collect money for a cause **5 take off one's hat to someone** to admire or congratulate someone ▶ HISTORY Old English *hætt*

hatch¹ *vb* **1** to cause (the young of various animals, esp. birds) to emerge from the egg or (of young birds, etc.) to emerge from the egg **2** (of eggs) to break and release the young animal within **3** to devise (a plot or plan) ▶ HISTORY Germanic

hatch² *n* **1** a hinged door covering an opening in a floor or wall **2 a** short for **hatchway b** a door in an aircraft or spacecraft **3** Also called: **serving hatch** an opening in a wall between a kitchen and a dining room **4** *informal* short for **hatchback** ▶ HISTORY Old English *hæcc*

hatch³ *vb drawing, engraving, etc.* to mark (a figure, etc.) with fine parallel or crossed lines to indicate shading ▶ HISTORY Old French *hacher* to chop > **hatching** *n*

hatchback *n* a car with a single lifting door in the rear

hatchet *n* **1** a short axe used for chopping wood, etc. **2 bury the hatchet** to make peace or resolve a disagreement ▷ *adj* **3** narrow and sharp: *a hatchet face* ▶ HISTORY Old French *hachette*

hatchet job *n informal* a malicious verbal or written attack

hatchet man *n informal* a person who carries out unpleasant tasks on behalf of an employer

hatchling *n* a young animal that has newly hatched from an egg

hatchway *n* an opening in the deck of a vessel to provide access below

hate *vb* **hating, hated 1** to dislike (someone or something) intensely **2** to be unwilling (to do something): *I hate to trouble you* ▷ *n* **3** intense dislike **4** *informal* a person or thing that is hated: *my own pet hate is restaurants* ▶ HISTORY Old English *hatian* > **hater** *n*

hateful *adj* causing or deserving hate

hatred *n* intense dislike

hat trick *n* **1** *cricket* the achievement of a bowler in taking three wickets with three successive balls **2** any achievement of three successive goals, victories, etc.

hauberk *n* *history* a long sleeveless coat of mail ▶ HISTORY Old French *hauberc*

haughty *adj* **-tier, -tiest** having or showing excessive pride or arrogance ▶ HISTORY Latin *altus* high > **haughtily** *adv* > **haughtiness** *n*

haul *vb* **1** to drag or pull (something) with effort **2** to transport, such as in a lorry **3** *naut* to alter the course of (a vessel) ▷ *n* **4** the act of dragging with effort **5** a quantity of something obtained: *a good haul of fish; a huge haul of stolen goods* **6** long haul **a** a long journey **b** a long difficult process ▶ HISTORY Old French *haler*

haulage *n* **1** the business of transporting goods **2** a charge for transporting goods

haulier *n* *Brit & Austral* a person or firm that transports goods by road

haulm (**hawm**) *n* the stalks of beans, peas, or potatoes collectively ▶ HISTORY Old English *healm*

haunch *n* **1** the human hip or fleshy hindquarter of an animal **2** the leg and loin of an animal, used for food ▶ HISTORY Old French *hanche*

haunt *vb* **1** to visit (a person or place) in the form of a ghost **2** to remain in the memory or thoughts of: *it was a belief which haunted her* **3** to visit (a place) frequently ▷ *n* **4** a place visited frequently ▶ HISTORY Old French *hanter*

haunted *adj* **1** (of a place) frequented or visited by ghosts **2** (of a person) obsessed or worried

haunting *adj* having a quality of great beauty or sadness so as to be memorable: *a haunting melody*

hautboy (**oh**-boy) *n* *old-fashioned* an oboe ▶ HISTORY French *haut* high + *bois* wood

haute couture (**oat** koo-**ture**) *n* high fashion ▶ HISTORY French

hauteur (oat-**ur**) *n* haughtiness ▶ HISTORY French *haut* high

Havana *n* a hand-rolled cigar from Cuba

have *vb* **has, having, had 1** to possess: *he has a massive collection of old movies; I have an iron constitution* **2** to receive, take, or obtain: *I had a long letter* **3** to hold in the mind: *she always had a yearning to be a schoolteacher* **4** to possess a knowledge of: *I have no German* **5** to experience or be affected by: *a good way to have a change* **6** to suffer from: *to have a blood pressure problem* **7** to gain control of or advantage over: *you have me on that point* **8** *slang* to cheat or outwit: *I've been had* **9** to show: *have mercy on me* **10** to take part in; hold: *I had a telephone conversation* **11** to cause to be done: *have my shoes mended by Friday* **12** have to used to express compulsion or necessity: *you'd have to wait six months* **13** to eat or drink **14** to tolerate or allow: *I won't have all this noise* **15** to receive as a guest: *we have visitors* **16** to be pregnant with or give birth to (offspring) **17** used to form past tenses: *I have gone; I had gone* **18** have had it *informal* **a** to be exhausted or killed **b** to have lost one's last chance ▷ *n* **19** haves *informal* people who have wealth, security, etc.: *the haves and the have-nots* ▷ See also **have on** ▶ HISTORY Old English *habban*

haven *n* **1** a place of safety **2** a harbour for shipping ▶ HISTORY Old English *hæfen*

have on *vb* **1** to wear: *he had a long pair of trousers on* **2** to have a commitment: *what do you have on this afternoon?* **3** *informal* to trick or tease: *he's having you on* **4** to have (information, esp. when incriminating) about (a person): *she has something on him*

haver *vb* **1** *Scot & N English dialect* to talk nonsense **2** to be unsure and hesitant; dither ▶ HISTORY origin unknown

haversack *n* a canvas bag carried on the back or shoulder ▶ HISTORY French *havresac*

have up *vb* to bring to trial: *what, and get me had up for kidnapping?*

havoc *n* **1** *informal* chaos, disorder, and confusion **2** play havoc with to cause a great deal of damage or confusion to ▶ HISTORY Old French *havot* pillage

haw¹ *n* the fruit of the hawthorn ▶ HISTORY Old English *haga*

haw² *vb* hum *or* hem and haw to hesitate in speaking ▶ HISTORY imitative

hawk¹ *n* **1** a bird of prey with short rounded wings and a long tail **2** a supporter or advocate of warlike policies ▷ *vb* **3** to hunt with falcons or hawks ▶ HISTORY Old English *hafoc* > **hawkish** *adj* > **hawklike** *adj*

hawk² *vb* to offer (goods) for sale in the street or door-to-door ▶ HISTORY from *hawker* pedlar

hawk³ *vb* **1** to clear the throat noisily **2** to force (phlegm) up from the throat ▶ HISTORY imitative

hawker *n* a person who travels from place to place selling goods ▶ HISTORY probably from Middle Low German *hōken* to peddle

hawk-eyed *adj* having extremely keen eyesight

hawser *n* *naut* a large heavy rope ▶ HISTORY Anglo-French *hauceour*

hawthorn *n* a thorny tree or shrub with white or pink flowers and reddish fruits ▶ HISTORY Old English *haguthorn*

hay *n* **1** grass cut and dried as fodder **2** hit the hay *slang* to go to bed **3** make hay while the sun shines to take full advantage of an opportunity ▶ HISTORY Old English *hieg*

hay fever *n* an allergic reaction to pollen, which causes sneezing, runny nose, and watery eyes

haystack *or* **hayrick** *n* a large pile of hay built in the open and covered with thatch

haywire *adj* **go haywire** *informal* to stop functioning properly

hazard *n* **1** a thing likely to cause injury, loss, etc. **2 at hazard** at risk **3** risk or likelihood of injury, loss, etc.: *evaluate the level of hazard in a situation* **4** *golf* an obstacle such as a bunker ▷ *vb* **5** *written to* risk: *hazarding the health of his crew* **6 hazard a guess** to make a guess ▶ HISTORY Arabic *az-zahr* the die

hazard lights *or* **hazard warning lights** *n* the indicator lights on a motor vehicle which flashing simultaneously to indicate that the vehicle is stationary

hazardous *adj* involving great risk

haze *n* **1** *meteorol* reduced visibility as a result of condensed water vapour, dust, etc. in the air **2** confused or unclear understanding or feeling ▶ HISTORY from *hazy*

hazel *n* **1** a shrub with edible rounded nuts ▷ *adj* **2** greenish-brown: *hazel eyes* ▶ HISTORY Old English *hæsel*

hazelnut *n* the nut of a hazel shrub, which has a smooth shiny hard shell

hazy *adj* **-zier, -ziest 1** (of the sky or a view) unable to be seen clearly because of dust or heat **2** dim or vague: *my memory is a little hazy on this* ▶ HISTORY origin unknown > **hazily** *adv* > **haziness** *n*

Hb haemoglobin

HB *Brit & Austral* (of pencil lead) hard-black: denoting a medium-hard lead

H-bomb *n* short for **hydrogen bomb**

he *pron* **1** (refers to) a male person or animal **2** (refers to) a person or animal of unknown or unspecified sex: *a member may vote as he sees fit* ▷ *n* **3** (refers to) a male person or animal: *a he-goat* ▶ HISTORY Old English *hē*

He *chem* helium

HE His *or* Her Excellency

head *n* **1** the upper or front part of the body that contains the brain, eyes, mouth, nose, and ears **2** a person's mind and mental abilities: *I haven't any head for figures* **3** the most forward part of a thing: *the head of a queue* **4** the highest part of a thing; upper end: *the head of the pass* **5** something resembling a head in form or function, such as the top of a tool **6** the position of leadership or command: *head of government* **7** the person commanding most authority within a group or an organization **8** *bot* the top part of a plant, where the leaves or flowers grow in a cluster **9** a culmination or crisis: *the matter came to a head in December 1928* **10** the froth on the top of a glass of beer **11** the pus-filled tip of a pimple or boil **12** part of a computer or tape recorder that can read, write, or erase information **13** the source of a river or stream **14** the side of a coin that usually bears a portrait of the head of a monarch, etc. **15** a headland or promontory: *Beachy Head* **16** pressure of water or steam in an enclosed space **17** (*pl* **head**) a person or animal considered as a unit: *the cost per head of Paris's refuse collection; six hundred head of cattle* **18** a headline or heading **19** *informal* short for

headmaster, headmistress, head teacher 20 *informal* short for **headache 21 give someone his head** to allow someone greater freedom or responsibility **22 go to one's head a** (of an alcoholic drink) to make one slightly drunk **b** to make one conceited: *success has gone to his head* **23 head over heels (in love)** very much (in love) **24 keep one's head** to remain calm **25 not make head nor tail of** not to understand (a problem, etc.) **26 off one's head** *slang* very foolish or insane **27 on one's own head** at one's own risk **28 over someone's head a** to a higher authority: *the taboo of going over the head of their immediate boss* **b** beyond a person's understanding **29 put our** *or* **your** *or* **their heads together** *informal* to consult together **30 turn someone's head** to make someone conceited ▷ *vb* **31** to be at the front or top of: *Barnes headed the list* **32** to be in charge of **33** (often foll. by *for*) to go or cause to go (towards): *to head for the Channel ports* **34** *soccer* to propel (the ball) by striking it with the head **35** to provide with a heading ▷ See also **heads** ▶ HISTORY Old English *hēafod*

headache *n* **1** a continuous pain in the head **2** *informal* any cause of worry, difficulty, or annoyance: *financial headaches*

head-banger *n* *Brit, Austral & NZ, slang* **1** a person who shakes his head violently to the beat of heavy-metal music **2** a crazy or stupid person

headboard *n* a vertical board at the head of a bed

headdress *n* any decorative head covering

header *n* **1** *soccer* the action of striking a ball with the head **2** *informal* a headlong fall or dive

head-hunting *n* **1** (of companies) the practice of actively searching for new high-level personnel, often from rival companies **2** the practice among certain peoples of removing the heads of enemies they have killed and preserving them as trophies > **head-hunter** *n*

heading *n* **1** a title for a page, chapter, etc. **2** a main division, such as of a speech **3** *mining* a horizontal tunnel

headland *n* a narrow area of land jutting out into a sea

headlight *or* **headlamp** *n* a powerful light on the front of a vehicle

headline *n* **1** a phrase in heavy large type at the top of a newspaper or magazine article indicating the subject **2 headlines** the main points of a television or radio news broadcast

headlong *adv, adj* **1** with the head foremost; headfirst **2** with great haste and without much thought: *they rushed headlong into buying a house*

headmaster *or fem* **headmistress** *n* the principal of a school

head of state *n* the highest-ranking person in a country, such as the president or monarch

head-on *adv, adj* **1** front foremost: *a head-on collision* **2** with directness or without compromise: *a head-on confrontation with the unions*

headphones *pl n* two small loudspeakers held against the ears, worn to listen to the radio or recorded music without other people hearing it

headquarters *pl n* any centre from which operations are directed

headroom *n* the space below a roof or bridge which allows an object to pass or stay underneath it without touching it

heads *adv* with the side of a coin uppermost which has a portrait of a head on it

headship *n* the position or state of being a leader, esp. the head teacher of a school

headshrinker *n* slang a psychiatrist

head start *n* an initial advantage in a competitive situation

headstone *n* a memorial stone at the head of a grave

headstrong *adj* determined to do something in one's own way and ignoring the advice of others

head teacher *n* the principal of a school

headwaters *pl n* the tributary streams of a river in the area in which it rises

headway *n* **1** progress towards achieving something: *have the police made any headway?* **2** motion forward: *we felt our way out to the open sea, barely making headway* **3** same as **headroom**

headwind *n* a wind blowing directly against the course of an aircraft or ship

heady *adj* **headier, headiest 1** (of an experience or period of time) extremely exciting **2** (of alcoholic drink, atmosphere, etc.) strongly affecting the physical senses: *a powerful, heady scent of cologne* **3** rash and impetuous

heal *vb* **1** (of a wound) to repair by natural processes, such as by scar formation **2** to restore (someone) to health **3** to repair (a rift in a personal relationship or an emotional wound) ▶ HISTORY Old English *hǣlan* > **healer** *n* > **healing** *n, adj*

health *n* **1** the general condition of body and mind: *better health* **2** the state of being bodily and mentally vigorous and free from disease **3** the condition of an organization, society, etc.: *the economic health of the republics*

- ■ **WORD HISTORY**
- ■ In origin, 'health' (Old English *hǣlth*) is the noun
- ■ related to the adjective 'hale' (as in the phrase
- ■ 'hale and hearty'), in the same way as 'warmth'
- ■ is related to 'warm' and 'depth' is related to
- ■ 'deep'. 'Health' is 'haleness' or 'wholeness'.
- ■ To drink to someone's health is to drink a toast
- ■ to their wellbeing.

health camp *n NZ* a camp for children with health or behavioural problems

health care *n* **1** the provision of medical services ▷ *adj* **healthcare 2** of or relating to health care: *the healthcare sector*

health centre *n Brit* the surgery and offices of the doctors in a district

health farm *n* a residential establishment for people wishing to improve their health by losing weight, exercising, etc.

health food *n* natural food, organically grown and free from additives

health stamp *n NZ* a postage stamp with a small surcharge used to support health camps

health visitor *n* (in Britain) a nurse employed to visit mothers, their preschool children, and older people in their homes

healthy *adj* **healthier, healthiest 1** having or showing good health **2** likely to produce good health: *healthy seaside air* **3** functioning well or being sound: *this is a very healthy business to be in* **4** *informal* considerable: *healthy profits* **5** sensible: *a healthy scepticism about his promises* > **healthily** *adv* > **healthiness** *n*

heap *n* **1** a pile of things lying one on top of another **2** (often *pl*) *informal* a large number or quantity ▷ *adv* **3 heaps** much: *he was heaps better* ▷ *vb* **4** to collect into a pile **5** to give freely (to): *film roles were heaped on her* ▶ HISTORY Old English *hēap*

hear *vb* **hearing, heard 1** to perceive (a sound) with the sense of hearing **2** to listen to: *I didn't want to hear what he had to say* **3** to be informed (of something); receive information (about something): *I hear you mean to join the crusade* **4** *law* to give a hearing to (a case) **5 hear of** to allow: *she wouldn't hear of it* **6 hear from** to receive a letter or telephone call from **7 hear! hear!** an exclamation of approval ▶ HISTORY Old English *hieran* > **hearer** *n*

hearing *n* **1** the sense by which sound is perceived **2** an opportunity for someone to be listened to **3** the range within which sound can be heard; earshot **4** the investigation of a matter by a court of law

hearing aid *n* a small amplifier worn by a partially deaf person in or behind the ear to improve his or her hearing

hearing dog *n* a dog that has been trained to help a deaf person by alerting him or her to various sounds

hearsay *n* gossip or rumour

hearse *n* a large car used to carry a coffin at a funeral ▶ HISTORY Latin *hirpex* harrow

heart *n* **1** a hollow muscular organ whose contractions pump the blood throughout the body **2** this organ considered as the centre of emotions, esp. love **3** tenderness or pity: *my heart went out to her* **4** courage or spirit **5** the most central part or important part: *at the heart of Italian motor racing* **6** (of vegetables, such as cabbage) the inner compact part **7** the breast: *she held him to her heart* **8** a shape representing the heart, with two rounded lobes at the top meeting in a point at the bottom **9 a** a red heart-shaped symbol on a playing card **b** a card with one or more of these symbols or (*when pl*) the suit of cards so marked **10 break someone's heart** to cause someone to grieve very deeply, esp. by ending a love affair **11 by heart** by memorizing **12 have a change of heart** to experience a profound change of outlook or attitude **13 have one's heart in one's mouth** to be full of apprehension, excitement, or fear **14 have the heart** to have the necessary will or callousness (to do something): *I didn't have the heart to tell him* **15 set one's heart on something** to have something as one's ambition **16 take heart**

h

to become encouraged **17 take something to heart** to take something seriously or be upset about something **18 wear one's heart on one's sleeve** to show one's feelings openly **19 with all one's heart** deeply and sincerely ▶ **HISTORY** Old English *heorte*

heartache *n* very great sadness and emotional suffering

heart attack *n* a sudden severe malfunction of the heart

heartbeat *n* one complete pulsation of the heart

heartbreak *n* intense and overwhelming grief, esp. after the end of a love affair > **heartbreaking** *adj* > **heartbroken** *adj*

heartburn *n* a burning sensation in the chest caused by indigestion

hearten *vb* to encourage or make cheerful > **heartening** *adj*

heart failure *n* **1** a condition in which the heart is unable to pump an adequate amount of blood to the tissues **2** sudden stopping of the heartbeat, resulting in death

heartfelt *adj* sincerely and strongly felt: *heartfelt thanks*

hearth *n* **1** the floor of a fireplace **2** this as a symbol of the home ▶ **HISTORY** Old English *heorth*

heartland *n written* **1** the central region of a country or continent: *we headed west towards the heartland of Tibet* **2** the area where the thing specified is most common or strongest: *Germany's industrial heartland*

heartless *adj* unkind or cruel > **heartlessly** *adv*

heart-rending *adj* causing great sadness and pity: *a heart-rending story*

heart-throb *n* a man, esp. a film or pop star, who is attractive to a lot of women or girls

heart-to-heart *adj* **1** (of a talk) concerned with personal problems or intimate feelings ▷ *n* **2** an intimate conversation

heartwood *n* the central core of dark hard wood in tree trunks

hearty *adj* **heartier, heartiest 1** warm, friendly, and enthusiastic **2** strongly felt: *a hearty dislike* **3** (of a meal) substantial and nourishing > **heartily** *adv*

heat *vb* **1** to make or become hot or warm ▷ *n* **2** the state of being hot **3** the energy transferred as a result of a difference in temperature. *Related adjectives:* **thermal, calorific 4** hot weather: *he loves the heat of Africa* **5** intensity of feeling: *the heat of their argument* **6** the most intense part: *in the heat of an election campaign* **7** pressure: *political heat on the government* **8** *sport* a preliminary eliminating contest in a competition **9 on** or **in heat** (of some female mammals) ready for mating ▶ **HISTORY** Old English *hǣtu* > **heating** *n*

heat budget *n* the balance or imbalance of heat gain from solar radiation against heat loss through evaporation, reflection, etc.

heated *adj* impassioned or highly emotional: *a heated debate* > **heatedly** *adv*

heater *n* a device for supplying heat

heath *n* **1** *Brit* a large open area, usually with sandy soil, low shrubs, and heather **2** an evergreen shrub with small bell-shaped flowers ▶ **HISTORY** Old English *hǣth*

heathen *n, pl* **-thens** or **-then** *old-fashioned* **1** a person who does not believe in an established religion; pagan ▷ *adj* **2** of or relating to heathen peoples ▶ **HISTORY** Old English *hǣthen*

heather *n* a shrub with small bell-shaped flowers growing on heaths and mountains ▶ **HISTORY** origin unknown

Heath Robinson *adj* (of a mechanical device) absurdly complicated in design for a simple function ▶ **HISTORY** after William *Heath Robinson*, cartoonist

heat island *n meteorol* the characteristically higher average temperatures to be found in a large city than in the surrounding area

heatstroke *n* same as **sunstroke**

heat wave *n* **1** a spell of unusually hot weather **2** an extensive slow-moving air mass at a relatively high temperature

heave *vb* **heaving, heaved** or **hove 1** to lift or move (something) with a great effort **2** to throw (something heavy) with effort **3** to utter (a sigh) noisily or unhappily **4** to rise and fall heavily **5** (*pt & pp* **hove**) *naut* **a** to move in a specified direction: *heave her bows around and head north* **b** (of a vessel) to pitch or roll **6** to vomit or retch ▷ *n* **7** the act of heaving ▶ **HISTORY** Old English *hebban*

heaven *n* **1** the place where God is believed to live and where those leading good lives are believed to go when they die **2** a place or state of happiness **3 heavens** the sky **4** Also: **heavens** *spoken* God or the gods, used in exclamatory phrases: *for heaven's sake!* ▶ **HISTORY** Old English *heofon*

heavenly *adj* **1** *informal* wonderful or very enjoyable: *a heavenly meal* **2** of or occurring in space: *a heavenly body* **3** of or relating to heaven

heave to *vb* to stop (a ship) or (of a ship) to stop

heavy *adj* **heavier, heaviest 1** of comparatively great weight **2** with a relatively high density: *lead is a heavy metal* **3** great in degree or amount: *heavy traffic* **4** considerable: *heavy emphasis* **5** hard to fulfil: *an exceptionally heavy demand for this issue* **6** using or consuming a lot of something quickly: *a heavy drinker* **7** deep and loud: *heavy breathing* **8** clumsy and slow: *a heavy lumbering trot* **9** (of a movement or action) with great downward force or pressure: *a heavy blow with a club* **10** solid or fat: *mountain animals acquire a heavy layer of fat* **11** not easily digestible: *a heavy meal* **12** (of cakes or bread) insufficiently raised **13** (of soil) with a high clay content **14** sad or dejected: *you feel heavy or sad afterwards* **15** (of facial features) looking sad and tired **16** (of a situation) serious and causing anxiety or sadness **17** cloudy or overcast: *heavy clouds obscured the sun* **18** (of an industry) engaged in the large-scale manufacture of large objects or extraction of raw materials **19** *mil* (of guns, etc.) large and powerful **20** dull and uninteresting **21** (of music, literature, etc.) difficult to understand or not immediately appealing **22** *slang* (of rock music) loud and having a powerful beat **23** *slang* using, or prepared to use, violence or brutality ▷ *n, pl* **heavies 24** *slang* a large strong man hired to threaten violence or deter others by his presence **25 a** a villainous role **b** an actor who plays such a part ▷ *adv* **26** heavily: *time hung heavy* ▶ **HISTORY** Old English *hefig* > **heavily** *adv* > **heaviness** *n*

heavy-duty *adj* made to withstand hard wear, bad weather, etc.

heavy hydrogen *n* same as **deuterium**

heavy industry *n econ* the manufacturing of large products or the extraction of raw materials

heavy metal *n* **1** a type of very loud rock music featuring guitar riffs **2** a metal with a high specific gravity

heavy water *n* water formed of oxygen and deuterium

heavyweight *n* **1** a professional boxer weighing over 195 pounds (88.5 kg) or an amateur weighing over 91 kg **2** a person who is heavier than average **3** *informal* an important person

Heb. *or* **Hebr.** Hebrew (language)

Hebraic (hib-**ray**-ik) *adj* of the Hebrews or their language or culture

Hebrew *n* **1** the ancient language of the Hebrews, revived as the official language of Israel **2** a member of an ancient Semitic people; an Israelite ▷ *adj* **3** of the Hebrews or their language ▶ **HISTORY** Hebrew *'ibhrī* one from beyond (the river)

heckle *vb* **-ling, -led** to interrupt (a public speaker) with comments, questions, or taunts ▶ **HISTORY** form of *hackle* > **heckler** *n*

hectare *n* a unit of measure equal to one hundred ares (10 000 square metres or 2.471 acres) ▶ **HISTORY** French

hectic *adj* involving a lot of rushed activity ▶ **HISTORY** Greek *hektikos* hectic, consumptive

hector *vb* **1** to bully or torment ▷ *n* **2** a blustering bully ▶ **HISTORY** after *Hector*, legendary Trojan warrior

hedge *n* **1** a row of shrubs or bushes forming a boundary **2** a barrier or protection against something, esp. against the risk of loss on an investment ▷ *vb* **hedging, hedged 3** to avoid making a decision by making noncommittal statements **4 hedge against** to guard against the risk of loss in (a bet or disagreement), by supporting the opposition as well ▶ **HISTORY** Old English *hecg*

hedgehog *n* a small mammal with a protective covering of spines

hedgehop *vb* **-hopping, -hopped** (of an aircraft) to fly close to the ground, such as in crop spraying

hedgerow *n* a hedge of shrubs or low trees bordering a field

hedge sparrow *n* a small brownish songbird

hedonism *n* the doctrine that the pursuit of pleasure is the most important thing in life ▶ **HISTORY** Greek *hēdonē* pleasure > **hedonist** *n* > **hedonistic** *adj*

heed *formal n* **1** careful attention: *he must have taken heed of her warning* ▷ *vb* **2** to pay close attention to (a warning or piece of advice) ▶ **HISTORY** Old English *hēdan*

heedless *adj* taking no notice; careless or thoughtless > **heedlessly** *adv*

heel[1] *n* **1** the back part of the foot **2** the part of a stocking or sock designed to fit the heel **3** the part of a shoe supporting the heel **4** *slang* a contemptible person **5 at one's heels** following closely behind one **6 kick** *or* **cool one's heels** to be kept waiting **7 down at heel** untidy and in poor condition **8 take to one's heels** to run off **9 to heel** under control, such as a dog walking by a person's heel ▷ *vb* **10** to repair or replace the heel of (a shoe or boot) ▶ **HISTORY** Old English *hēla*

heel[2] *vb* to lean to one side ▶ **HISTORY** Old English *hieldan*

heeler *n Austral & NZ* a dog that herds cattle by biting at their heels

hefty *adj* **heftier, heftiest** *informal* **1** large in size, weight, or amount **2** forceful and vigorous: *a hefty slap on the back* **3** involving a large amount of money: *a hefty fine*

hegemony (hig-**em**-on-ee) *n, pl* **-nies** domination of one state, country, or class within a group of others ▶ **HISTORY** Greek *hēgemonia*

Hegira *n* the starting point of the Muslim era; the flight of Mohammed from Mecca to Medina in 622 AD, regarded as being the starting point of the Muslim era ▶ **HISTORY** Arabic *hijrah* flight

heifer (**hef**-fer) *n* a young cow ▶ **HISTORY** Old English *heahfore*

height *n* **1** the vertical distance from the bottom of something to the top **2** the vertical distance of a place above sea level **3** relatively great distance from bottom to top **4** the topmost point; summit **5** the period of greatest intensity: *the height of the shelling* **6** an extreme example: *the height of luxury* **7 heights** extremes: *dizzy heights of success* ▶ **HISTORY** Old English *hīehthu*

heighten *vb* to make or become higher or more intense > **heightened** *adj*

height of land *n US & Canad* a ridge of high ground dividing two river basins

heinous *adj* evil and shocking ▶ **HISTORY** Old French *haineus*

heir *n* the person legally succeeding to the property of a deceased person ▶ **HISTORY** Latin *heres* > **heiress** *fem n*

heir apparent *n, pl* **heirs apparent 1** *law* a person whose right to succeed to certain property cannot be defeated **2** a person whose succession to a role or position is extremely likely: *heir apparent to the England captaincy*

heirloom *n* an object that has been in a family for generations ▶ **HISTORY** HEIR + *lome* tool

heir presumptive *n property law* a person who expects to succeed to an estate but whose right may be defeated by the birth of an heir nearer in blood to the ancestor

held *vb* the past of **hold**[1]

helical *adj* of or like a helix

helicopter *n* an aircraft, powered by rotating overhead blades, that is capable of hovering, vertical flight, and horizontal flight in any direction ▶ HISTORY Greek *helix* spiral + *pteron* wing

heliograph *n* an instrument with mirrors and a shutter used for sending messages in Morse code by reflecting the sun's rays ▶ HISTORY Greek *hēlios* sun + -GRAPHY

heliophyte *n* *bot* any plant that grows best in direct sunlight

heliotrope *n* a plant with small fragrant purple flowers ▶ HISTORY Greek *hēlios* sun + *trepein* to turn

heliport *n* an airport for helicopters ▶ HISTORY *heli(copter)* + *port*

helium (**heel**-ee-um) *n* *chem* a very light colourless odourless inert gas. Symbol: He ▶ HISTORY Greek *hēlios* sun, because first detected in the solar spectrum

helix (**heel**-iks) *n*, *pl* **helices** (**hell**-iss-seez) *or* **helixes** a spiral ▶ HISTORY Greek: spiral

hell *n* **1** (in Christianity and some other religions) the place or state of eternal punishment of the wicked after death **2** (in various religions and cultures) the abode of the spirits of the dead **3** *informal* a situation that causes suffering or extreme difficulty: *war is hell* **4 come hell or high water** *informal* whatever difficulties may arise **5 for the hell of it** *informal* for the fun of it **6 from hell** *informal* denoting a person or thing that is particularly bad or alarming: *the boss from hell* **7 give someone hell** *informal* **a** to give someone a severe reprimand or punishment **b** to be a torment to someone **8 hell for leather** at great speed **9 the hell** *informal* **a** used for emphasis: *what the hell* **b** an expression of strong disagreement: *the hell you do!* ▷ *interj* **10** *informal* an exclamation of anger or surprise ▶ HISTORY Old English

hellbent *adj* *informal* rashly intent: *hellbent on revenge*

hellebore *n* a plant with white flowers that bloom in winter ▶ HISTORY Greek *helleboros*

Hellenic *adj* **1** of the Greeks or their language **2** of or relating to ancient Greece during the classical period (776–323 BC)

Hellenism *n* **1** the principles and ideals of classical Greek civilization **2** the spirit or national character of the Greeks > **Hellenist** *n*

Hellenistic *adj* of Greek civilization during the period 323–30 BC

hellfire *n* the torment of hell, imagined as eternal fire

hellish *adj* *informal* very unpleasant

hello, hallo *or* **hullo** *interj* **1** an expression of greeting or surprise **2** a call used to attract attention ▷ *n*, *pl* -**los 3** the act of saying 'hello' ▶ HISTORY French *holà*

helm *n* **1** *naut* the tiller or wheel for steering a ship **2 at the helm** in a position of leadership or control ▶ HISTORY Old English *helma*

helmet *n* a piece of protective headgear worn by motorcyclists, soldiers, policemen, divers, etc. ▶ HISTORY Old French

help *vb* **1** to assist (someone to do something) **2** to contribute to: *to help Latin America's economies* **3** to improve a situation: *a felt or rubber underlay will help* **4 a** to refrain from: *I couldn't help feeling foolish* **b** to be responsible for: *you must not blame him, he simply can't help it* **5** to serve (a customer) **6 help oneself** to take something, esp. food or drink, for oneself, without being served ▷ *n* **7** the act of helping **8** a person or thing that helps **9** a remedy: *there's no help for it* ▷ *interj* **10** used to call for assistance ▶ HISTORY Old English *helpan* > **helper** *n*

helpful *adj* giving help > **helpfully** *adv* > **helpfulness** *n*

helping *n* a single portion of food

helpless *adj* **1** unable to manage independently **2** made weak: *it reduced her to helpless laughter* > **helplessly** *adv* > **helplessness** *n*

helpline *n* a telephone line set aside for callers to contact an organization for help with a problem

helpmate *or* **helpmeet** *n* a companion and helper, esp. a husband or wife

helter-skelter *adj* **1** hurried or disorganized ▷ *adv* **2** in a hurried or disorganized manner ▷ *n* **3** *Brit* a high spiral slide at a fairground ▶ HISTORY probably imitative

hem[1] *n* **1** the bottom edge of a garment, folded under and stitched down ▷ *vb* **hemming, hemmed 2** to provide (a garment) with a hem ▷ See also **hem in** ▶ HISTORY Old English *hemm*

hem[2] *n* **1** a representation of the sound of clearing the throat, used to gain attention ▷ *vb* **hemming, hemmed 2** to make this sound **3 hem and haw** See **haw**[2]

he-man *n*, *pl* -**men** *informal* a strong man, esp. one who shows off his strength

hematite *or* **haematite** *n* *geol* a red, grey, or black mineral, found as massive beds and in veins and igneous rocks. It is the chief source of iron ▶ HISTORY via Latin from Greek *haimatitēs* resembling blood, from *haima* blood > **hematitic** *or* **haematitic** *adj*

hemi- *prefix* half: *hemisphere* ▶ HISTORY Greek

hem in *vb* to surround and prevent from moving

hemipterous *or* **hemipteran** *adj* of an order of insects with sucking or piercing mouthparts ▶ HISTORY Greek *hēmi* half + *pteron* wing

hemisphere *n* one half of a sphere, esp. of the earth (**northern** and **southern hemisphere**) or of the brain > **hemispherical** *adj*

hemline *n* the level to which the hem of a skirt or dress hangs: *the hemline debate*

hemlock *n* a poisonous drug derived from a plant with spotted stems and small white flowers ▶ HISTORY Old English *hymlic*

hemp *n* **1** an Asian plant with tough fibres **2** the fibre of this plant, used to make canvas and rope **3** a narcotic drug obtained from this plant ▶ HISTORY Old English *hænep* > **hempen** *adj*

hen *n* the female of any bird, esp. the domestic fowl ▶ HISTORY Old English *henn*

henbane *n* a poisonous plant with sticky hairy leaves

h

hence *adv* **1** for this reason; therefore **2** from this time: *two weeks hence* **3** *archaic* from here ▶ **HISTORY** Old English *hionane*

henceforth *or* **henceforward** *adv* from now on

henchman *n, pl* **-men** a person employed by someone powerful to carry out orders ▶ **HISTORY** Middle English *hengestman*

henge *n* a circular monument, often containing a circle of stones, dating from the Neolithic and Bronze Ages ▶ **HISTORY** from *Stonehenge*

henna *n* **1** a reddish dye, obtained from a shrub or tree of Asia and N Africa which is used to colour hair ▷ *vb* **2** to dye (the hair) with henna ▶ **HISTORY** Arabic *hinnā'*

henpecked *adj* (of a man) harassed by the persistent nagging of his wife

henry *n, pl* **-ry, -ries** *or* **-rys** the SI unit of electric inductance ▶ **HISTORY** after Joseph *Henry*, physicist

hepatic *adj* of the liver ▶ **HISTORY** Greek *hēpar* liver

hepatic portal vein *n anat* a vein connecting two capillary networks in the liver

hepatitis *n* inflammation of the liver, causing fever, jaundice, and weakness

Hephaestus *n Greek myth* the god of fire

hepta- *combining form* seven: *heptameter*

heptagon *n geom* a figure with seven sides ▶ **HISTORY** Greek *heptagōnos* having seven angles > **heptagonal** *adj*

heptathlon *n* an athletic contest for women in which athletes compete in seven different events

her *pron* **1** (refers to) a female person or animal: *he loves her* **2** *formal, written* (refers to) things personified as feminine, such as ships and nations ▷ *adj* **3** of, belonging to, or associated with her: *her hair* ▶ **HISTORY** Old English *hire*

Hera *or* **Here** *n Greek myth* the queen of the gods

herald *n* **1** a person who announces important news **2** *often literary* a forerunner ▷ *vb* **3** to announce or signal the approach of: *his arrival was heralded by excited barking* ▶ **HISTORY** Germanic > **heraldic** *adj*

heraldry *n, pl* **-ries** the study of coats of arms and family trees

herb *n* **1** an aromatic plant that is used for flavouring in cookery, and in medicine **2** *bot* a seed-bearing plant whose parts above ground die back at the end of the growing season ▶ **HISTORY** Latin *herba* grass, green plants > **herbal** *adj* > **herby** *adj*

herbaceous *adj* designating plants that are soft-stemmed rather than woody

herbaceous border *n* a flower bed that contains perennials rather than annuals

herbage *n* herbaceous plants collectively, esp. those on which animals graze

herbalist *n* a person who grows or specializes in the use of medicinal herbs

herbicide *n* a substance used to destroy plants, esp. weeds ▶ **HISTORY** Latin *herba* plant + *caedere* to kill

herbivore (**her**-biv-vore) *n* **1** an animal that feeds only on plants **2** *informal* a liberal or idealistic person ▶ **HISTORY** Latin *herba* plant + *vorare* to swallow > **herbivorous** (her-**biv**-or-uss) *adj*

herculean (her-kew-**lee**-an) *adj* **1** (of a task) requiring tremendous effort or strength **2** resembling Hercules, hero of classical myth, in strength or courage

herd *n* **1** a large group of mammals, esp. cattle living and feeding together **2** *often disparaging* a large group of people ▷ *vb* **3** to collect or be collected into or as if into a herd ▶ **HISTORY** Old English *heord*

herd instinct *n psychol* the inborn tendency to associate with others and follow the group's behaviour

herdsman *n, pl* **-men** *chiefly Brit* a man who looks after a herd of animals

here *adv* **1** in, at, or to this place, point, case, or respect: *I am pleased to be back here* **2 here and there** at several places in or throughout an area **3 here's to** a convention used in proposing a toast **4 neither here nor there** of no relevance ▷ *n* **5** this place: *they leave here tonight* ▶ **HISTORY** Old English *hēr*

hereabouts *or* **hereabout** *adv* in this region

hereafter *formal adv* **1** *legal* in a subsequent part of this document, matter, or case **2** at some time in the future ▷ *n* **3 the hereafter a** life after death **b** the future

hereby *adv* (used in official statements and documents) by means of or as a result of this

hereditable *adj* same as **heritable**

hereditary *adj* **1** passed on genetically from one generation to another **2** *law* passed on to succeeding generations by inheritance

heredity (hir-**red**-it-ee) *n, pl* **-ties** the passing on from one generation to another of genetic factors that determine individual characteristics ▶ **HISTORY** Latin *hereditas* inheritance

Hereford *n* a hardy breed of beef cattle which has a reddish body with white markings ▶ **HISTORY** after *Hereford*, English city

herein *adv formal or legal* in this place, matter, or document

hereinafter *adv formal or legal* from this point on in this document, matter, or case

hereof *adv formal or legal* of or concerning this

heresy (**herr**-iss-ee) *n, pl* **-sies** **1** an opinion contrary to the principles of a religion **2** any belief thought to be contrary to official or established theory ▶ **HISTORY** Greek *hairein* to choose

heretic (**herr**-it-ik) *n* **1** *chiefly RC Church* a person who maintains beliefs contrary to the established teachings of the Church **2** a person who holds unorthodox opinions in any field > **heretical** (hir-**ret**-ik-kl) *adj*

hereto *adv formal or legal* to this place, matter, or document

heretofore *adv formal or legal* until now

hereupon *adv* following immediately after this; at this stage

389

herewith *adv formal, written* together with this: *a schedule of the event is appended herewith*

heritable *adj* capable of being inherited

heritage *n* **1** something inherited at birth **2** anything that has been carried over from the past or handed down by tradition **3** the evidence of the past, such as historical sites, considered as the inheritance of present-day society

hermaphrodite (her-**maf**-roe-dite) *n* an animal, flower, or person that has both male and female reproductive organs ▶ **HISTORY** after *Hermaphroditus*, son of Hermes and Aphrodite, who merged with the nymph Salmacis to form one body > **hermaphroditic** *adj*

Hermes *n Greek myth* the messenger of the gods

hermetic *adj* sealed so as to be airtight ▶ **HISTORY** after the Greek god *Hermes Trismegistus*, traditionally the inventor of a magic seal > **hermetically** *adv*

hermit *n* a person living in solitude, esp. for religious reasons ▶ **HISTORY** Greek *erēmos* lonely

hermitage *n* **1** the home of a hermit **2** any retreat

hermit crab *n* a small crab that lives in the empty shells of other shellfish

hernia *n* protrusion of an organ or part through the lining of the body cavity in which it is normally situated ▶ **HISTORY** Latin

hero *n, pl* **-roes 1** the principal male character in a novel, play, etc. **2** a man of exceptional courage, nobility, etc. **3** a man who is idealized for having superior qualities in any field ▶ **HISTORY** Greek *hērōs*

heroic *adj* **1** brave and courageous: *heroic work by the army engineers* **2** of, like, or befitting a hero > **heroically** *adv*

heroic couplet *n prosody* a verse form consisting of two rhyming lines in iambic pentameter

heroics *pl n spoken* behaviour or language considered too melodramatic or extravagant for the particular situation in which they are used

heroic verse *n prosody* a type of verse suitable for epic or heroic subjects, such as the classical hexameter, the French Alexandrine, or the English iambic pentameter

heroin *n* a highly addictive drug derived from morphine ▶ **HISTORY** probably from *hero*, referring to its aggrandizing effect on the personality

heroine *n* **1** the principal female character in a novel, play, etc. **2** a woman of exceptional courage, nobility, etc. **3** a woman who is idealized for having superior qualities in any field

heroism (**herr**-oh-izz-um) *n* great courage and bravery

heron *n* a wading bird with a long neck, long legs, and grey or white feathers ▶ **HISTORY** Old French *hairon*

heronry *n, pl* **-ries** a colony of breeding herons

hero worship *n* admiration for heroes or idealized people

herpes (**her**-peez) *n* any of several inflammatory skin diseases, including shingles and cold sores ▶ **HISTORY** Greek *herpein* to creep

herpes simplex *n* an acute viral disease causing clusters of watery blisters ▶ **HISTORY** New Latin: simple herpes

herpes zoster *n* same as **shingles** ▶ **HISTORY** New Latin: girdle herpes

Herr (**hair**) *n, pl* **Herren** a German form of address equivalent to *Mr* ▶ **HISTORY** German

herring *n, pl* **-rings** or **-ring** a food fish of northern seas, with a long silver-coloured body ▶ **HISTORY** Old English *hæring*

herringbone *n* a zigzag pattern consisting of short lines of V shapes, used esp. in fabrics

herring gull *n* a common gull that has white feathers with black-tipped wings

hers *pron* **1** something belonging to her: *hers is the highest paid part-time job; the money which is rightfully hers* **2 of hers** belonging to her

herself *pron* **1 a** the reflexive form of *she* or *her*: *she busied herself at the stove* **b** used for emphasis: *none other than The Great Mother herself* **2** her normal self: *she hasn't been herself all week*

hertz *n, pl* **hertz** the SI unit of frequency, equal to one cycle per second ▶ **HISTORY** after H. R. Hertz, physicist

hesitant *adj* doubtful and unsure in speech or action > **hesitancy** *n* > **hesitantly** *adv*

hesitate *vb* **-tating, -tated 1** to be slow and uncertain in acting **2** to be reluctant (to do something): *I hesitate to use the word 'squandered'* **3** to pause during speech because of uncertainty ▶ **HISTORY** Latin *haesitare* > **hesitation** *n*

hessian *n* a coarse jute fabric similar to sacking ▶ **HISTORY** after *Hesse*, Germany

hetero- *combining form* other, another, or different: *heterosexual* ▶ **HISTORY** Greek *heteros* other

heterodox *adj* different from established or accepted doctrines or beliefs ▶ **HISTORY** HETERO- + Greek *doxa* opinion > **heterodoxy** *n*

heterodyne *electronics vb* **-dyning, -dyned 1** to combine (two alternating signals) so as to produce two signals with frequencies corresponding to the sum and the difference of the original frequencies ▷ *adj* **2** produced or operating by heterodyning two signals ▶ **HISTORY** HETERO- + Greek *dunamis* power

heterogeneous (het-er-oh-**jean**-ee-uss) *adj* varied in content; composed of different parts: *a heterogeneous collection of art* ▶ **HISTORY** HETERO- + Greek *genos* sort > **heterogeneity** *n*

heteromorphic *adj biol* **1** differing from the normal form **2** (esp. of insects) having different forms at different stages of the life cycle ▶ **HISTORY** HETERO- + Greek *morphē* form > **heteromorphism** *n*

heterosexual *n* **1** a person who is sexually attracted to members of the opposite sex ▷ *adj* **2** (of a person) sexually attracted to members of the opposite sex **3** (of a sexual relationship) between a man and a woman > **heterosexuality** *n*

heterotrophic *adj biochem* (of animals and some plants) using complex organic compounds to manufacture their own organic constituents

heterozygous *adj biol* having two different alleles of the same gene ▶ HISTORY HETERO- + Greek *zugōtos* yoked

het up *adj informal* agitated or excited: *he was very het up about the traffic* ▶ HISTORY dialect for *heated*

heuristic (hew-**rist**-ik) *adj* (of a method of teaching) allowing students to learn things for themselves by trial and error ▶ HISTORY Greek *heuriskein* to discover

hew *vb* **hewing, hewed, hewed** *or* **hewn** 1 to chop or cut with an axe 2 to carve (something) from a substance: *a tunnel hewn out of the living rock* ▶ HISTORY Old English *hēawan*

hex *n* 1 short for **hexadecimal notation** ▷ *adj* 2 of or relating to hexadecimal notation: *hex code*

hexa- *combining form* six: *hexameter* ▶ HISTORY Greek *hex* six

hexadecimal notation *n* a number system with a base of 16, the numbers 10–15 being represented by the letters A–F

hexagon *n geom* a figure with six sides > **hexagonal** *adj*

hexagram *n geom* a star formed by extending the sides of a regular hexagon to meet at six points

hexameter (hek-**sam**-it-er) *n prosody* a verse line consisting of six metrical feet

hexose *n chem* a monosaccharide that contains six carbon atoms per molecule

hey *interj* 1 an expression of surprise or for catching attention 2 **hey presto!** an exclamation used by conjurors at the climax of a trick ▶ HISTORY imitative

heyday *n* the time of most power, popularity, or success: *the heyday of classical composition* ▶ HISTORY probably based on *hey*

Hf *chem* hafnium

Hg *chem* mercury

HGV (in Britain, formerly) heavy goods vehicle

HH 1 His (*or* Her) Highness 2 His Holiness (title of the pope)

hi *interj informal* hello ▶ HISTORY probably from *how are you?*

HI Hawaii

hiatus (hie-**ay**-tuss) *n, pl* **-tuses** *or* **-tus** a pause or an interruption in continuity ▶ HISTORY Latin: gap, cleft

hiatus hernia *n* protrusion of the stomach through the diaphragm at the hole for the gullet

Hib Haemophilus influenzae type b: a vaccine against a specific type of bacterial meningitis, administered to children under four years of age

hibernate *vb* **-nating, -nated** (of some animals) to pass the winter in a resting state in which heartbeat, temperature, and breathing rate are very low ▶ HISTORY Latin *hibernare* to spend the winter > **hibernation** *n*

Hibernia *n poetic* Ireland > **Hibernian** *adj, n*

hibiscus *n, pl* **-cuses** a tropical plant with large brightly coloured flowers ▶ HISTORY Greek *hibiskos* marsh mallow

hiccup *n* 1 a spasm of the breathing organs with a sharp coughlike sound 2 **hiccups** the state of having such spasms 3 *informal* a minor difficulty ▷ *vb* **-cuping, -cuped** *or* **-cupping, -cupped** 4 to make a hiccup or hiccups. Also: **hiccough** ▶ HISTORY imitative

hick *n US, Austral & NZ, informal* an unsophisticated country person ▶ HISTORY after *Hick*, familiar form of *Richard*

hickory *n, pl* **-ries** 1 a North American tree with edible nuts 2 the hard wood of this tree ▶ HISTORY Native American *pawcohiccora*

hidden agenda *n* a set of motives or intentions concealed from others who might object to them

hide¹ *vb* **hiding, hid, hidden** *or* **hid** 1 to conceal (oneself or an object) from view or discovery 2 to keep (information or one's feelings) secret 3 to obscure or cover (something) from view ▷ *n* 4 *Brit* a place of concealment, disguised to appear as part of its surrounding, used by hunters, bird-watchers, etc. ▶ HISTORY Old English *hȳdan*

hide² *n* the skin of an animal, either tanned or raw ▶ HISTORY Old English *hȳd*

hideaway *n* a hiding place or secluded spot

hidebound *adj* restricted by petty rules and unwilling to accept new ideas

hideous (**hid**-ee-uss) *adj* extremely ugly and unpleasant ▶ HISTORY Old French *hisdos*

hide-out *n* a hiding place

hiding¹ *n* 1 a state of concealment: *in hiding* 2 **hiding place** a place of concealment

hiding² *n informal* a severe beating

hierarchy (**hire**-ark-ee) *n, pl* **-chies** 1 a system of people or things arranged in a graded order 2 **the hierarchy** the people in power in any organization ▶ HISTORY Late Greek *hierarkhēs* high priest > **hierarchical** *adj*

hieroglyphic (hire-oh-**gliff**-ik) *adj* 1 of or relating to a form of writing using picture symbols, as used in ancient Egypt ▷ *n also* **hieroglyph** 2 a symbol that is difficult to decipher 3 a picture or symbol representing an object, idea, or sound ▶ HISTORY Greek *hieros* holy + *gluphein* to carve

hieroglyphics *n* 1 a form of writing, as used in ancient Egypt, in which pictures or symbols are used to represent objects, ideas, or sounds 2 writing that is difficult to decipher

hi-fi *n informal* 1 a set of high-quality sound-reproducing equipment 2 short for **high fidelity** ▷ *adj* 3 producing high-quality sound

higgledy-piggledy *adj, adv informal* in a muddle ▶ HISTORY origin unknown

high *adj* 1 being a relatively great distance from top to bottom: *a high stone wall* 2 being at a relatively great distance above sea level: *a high village* 3 being a specified distance from top to bottom: *three feet high* 4 coming up to a specified level: *waist-high* 5 being at its peak: *high summer* 6 of greater than average height: *a high ceiling* 7 greater than usual in intensity or amount: *high blood pressure; high fees* 8 (of a sound) acute in pitch 9 (of food) slightly decomposed, regarded as enhancing the flavour of game 10 towards the top of a scale of importance

h

391

high

High is a word which has a number of meanings. Depending on just what you are describing as high, you have a whole range of substitutes to choose from to give your writing some added variety and expressiveness.

DEFINITION 1
- If you are describing a building, ceiling, or mountain, you could try: **lofty** towers and spires • a **soaring** spire • the **steep** hill • **tall** walls • **towering** red sandstone cliffs

DEFINITION 2
- If you are describing something at a distance above sea level, you could try: a village in an **elevated** position

DEFINITION 3
- If you are talking about something with a specified distance from top to bottom, you could try: 3cm **from top to bottom** • two metres **in height**

DEFINITION 4
- If you are talking about something coming up to a certain level, you could try: **at** shoulder **height** • eye-**level**

DEFINITION 5
- If you are talking about something at its peak, you could try: **the height of** stupidity • summer's **peak**

DEFINITION 6
- If you are describing something of greater than average height, you could try: **tall** windows

DEFINITION 7
- If you are describing a high amount or high degree of something, you could try: state of **acute** anxiety • driving at **excessive** speed • drinking **extraordinary** quantities • under **extreme** pressure • a **great** level of interest • **severe** penalties

- If you are describing the cost or price of something, you could try: **costly** premiums • too **dear** • **expensive** prices • Charges are very **steep**. (informal)
- If you are describing the wind, you could try: **blustery** breezes • **extreme** wind and cold • thunder and **squally** winds • **strong** gusts • **violent** gales

DEFINITION 8
- If you are describing a voice or a sound, you could try: **high-pitched** cry • a **penetrating** whistle • a **piercing** note • **shrill** scream • **soprano** voice

DEFINITION 9
- If you are describing food that smells slightly off, you could try: **gamey** pheasant • The milk's a bit **off**. • **strong-smelling** meat • **tainted** fruit

DEFINITION 10
- If you are describing someone or something important, you could try: **chief** position in the company • most **eminent** scientists • in **exalted** circles • an **important** post • an **influential** place • a **leading** figure • the **most powerful** • her **pre-eminent** position • **prominent** political figures • their **superior** status

DEFINITION 11
- If you are describing drama, you could try: **emotional** events • **heated** scenes • **impassioned** rhetoric • **intense** drama

DEFINITION 12
- If you are describing a person's spirits, you could try: in **buoyant** spirits • in such **cheerful** spirits • that **elated** feeling • an **exhilarated** frame of mind • his **exuberant** moods • I felt **joyful**. • in a very **merry** mood

---

or quality: high fashion **11** intensely emotional: high drama **12** very cheerful: high spirits **13** informal under the influence of alcohol or drugs **14** luxurious or extravagant: high life **15** advanced in complexity: high finance **16** formal and elaborate: High Mass **17 high and dry** abandoned in a difficult situation **18 high and mighty** informal too confident and full of self-importance **19 high opinion** a favourable opinion ▷ adv **20** at or to a height: flying high ▷ n **21** a high level **22** same as **anticyclone 23 on a high** informal **a** in a state of intoxication by alcohol or drugs **b** in a state of great excitement and happiness ▶ HISTORY Old English hēah See WORD FOCUS **high**

High Arctic n the regions of Canada, esp. the northern islands, within the Arctic Circle
highball n chiefly US a long iced drink consisting of whisky with soda water or ginger ale
highbrow adj **1** concerned with serious, intellectual subjects ▷ n **2** a person with such tastes

highchair n a long-legged chair with a table-like tray, used for a child at meal times
High Church n **1** the movement within the Church of England stressing the importance of ceremony and ritual ▷ adj **High-Church 2** of or relating to this movement
High Commission n the embassy of one Commonwealth country in another
high commissioner n the senior diplomatic representative sent by one Commonwealth country to another
high country n **the high country** NZ sheep pastures in the foothills of the Southern Alps
High Court n (in England, Wales, Australia, and New Zealand) the supreme court dealing with civil and criminal law cases
Higher n (in Scotland) **1** the advanced level of the Scottish Certificate of Education **2** a pass in a subject at this level: she has got four Highers
higher education n education and training at colleges and universities

highest common factor *n maths* the largest number that divides equally into each member of a group of numbers

high explosive *n* an extremely powerful chemical explosive, such as TNT or gelignite

highfalutin (hie-fa-**loot**-in) *adj informal* (of behaviour) excessively grand or pompous ▶ HISTORY *-falutin* perhaps variant of *fluting*

high fidelity *n* **1** the electronic reproduction of sound with little or no distortion ▷ *adj* **high-fidelity 2** able to produce sound with little or no distortion: *high-fidelity stereo earphones*

high-flown *adj* extravagant or pretentious: *high-flown language*

high frequency *n* a radio frequency between 30 and 3 megahertz

High German *n* the standard German language

high-handed *adj* using authority in an unnecessarily forceful way **> high-handedness** *n*

high jump *n* **the high jump a** an athletic event in which competitors have to jump over a high bar **b** *Brit & Austral, informal* a severe reprimand or punishment: *I was for the high jump again*

Highland *adj* of or denoting the Highlands, a mountainous region of NW Scotland **> Highlander** *n*

Highland cattle *n* a breed of cattle with shaggy reddish-brown hair and long horns

highlands *pl n* relatively high ground

high-level language *n* a computer programming language that is close to human language

highlight *n* **1** Also called: **high spot** the most exciting or memorable part of something **2** an area of the lightest tone in a painting or photograph **3** a lightened streak in the hair produced by bleaching ▷ *vb* **4** to give emphasis to: *the prime minister repeatedly highlighted the need for lower pay*

highly *adv* **1** extremely: *highly desirable* **2** towards the top of a scale of importance, admiration, or respect: *highly paid doctors*

highly strung *or US & Canad* **high-strung** *adj* tense and easily upset

High Mass *n* a solemn and elaborate Mass

high-minded *adj* having high moral principles

Highness *n* (preceded by *Your, His* or *Her*) a title used to address or refer to a royal person

high-octane *adj* **1** (of petrol) having a high octane number **2** *informal* dynamic or intense: *a high-octane lifestyle*

high-powered *adj* **1** (of machinery or equipment) powerful, advanced, and sophisticated **2** important, successful, or influential: *a high-powered business contact*

high-pressure *adj informal* (of selling) persuasive in an aggressive and persistent manner

high priest *n* the head of a cult or movement **> high priestess** *fem n*

high-rise *adj* of or relating to a building that has many storeys: *a high-rise block*

highroad *n* a main road

high school *n* a secondary school

high-spirited *adj* lively and wishing to have fun and excitement

high tea *n Brit* an early evening meal consisting of a cooked dish, bread, cakes, and tea

high technology *n* any type of sophisticated industrial process, esp. one involving electronics

high-tension *adj* (of electrical cable) carrying a powerful current

high tide *n* the sea at its highest level on the coast

high time *adv informal* the latest possible time: *it was high time she got married*

high treason *n* a serious crime directly affecting a sovereign or state

high-water mark *n* **1** the level reached by sea water at high tide or a river in flood **2** the highest or most successful stage: *the premature high-water mark of his career*

highway *n* **1** a public road that everyone may use **2** *US, Canad, Austral & NZ* a main road, esp. one that connects towns

Highway Code *n* (in Britain) a booklet of regulations and recommendations for all road users

highwayman *n, pl* **-men** (formerly) a robber, usually on horseback, who held up travellers on public roads

hijab *or* **hejab** (hi-**jab**) *n* a covering for the head worn by some Muslim women

hijack *vb* **1** to seize control of or divert (a vehicle or aircraft) while travelling ▷ *n* **2** an instance of hijacking ▶ HISTORY origin unknown **> hijacker** *n*

hike *vb* **hiking, hiked 1** to walk a long way in the country, usually for pleasure **2** to raise (prices) **3** to pull up with a quick movement: *he hiked up his trouser legs* ▷ *n* **4** a long walk **5** a rise in price ▶ HISTORY origin unknown **> hiker** *n*

hilarious *adj* very funny ▶ HISTORY Greek *hilaros* cheerful **> hilariously** *adv* **> hilarity** *n*

hill *n* **1** a natural elevation of the earth's surface, less high than a mountain **2** a heap or mound **3** an incline or slope ▶ HISTORY Old English *hyll* **> hilly** *adj*

hillbilly *n, pl* **-lies 1** *usually disparaging* an unsophisticated person from the mountainous areas in the southeastern US **2** same as **country and western** ▶ HISTORY *hill* + *Billy* (the nickname)

hillock *n* a small hill or mound

hilt *n* **1** the handle or shaft of a sword, dagger, or knife **2 to the hilt** to the full: *he plays the role to the hilt* ▶ HISTORY Old English

hilum *n, pl* **-la** *bot* a scar on a seed marking its point of attachment to the seed vessel ▶ HISTORY Latin: trifle

him *pron* refers to a male person or animal: *I greeted him at the hotel; I must send him a note of congratulation* ▶ HISTORY Old English

himself *pron* **1 a** the reflexive form of *he* or *him*: *he secretly asked himself* **b** used for emphasis: *approved of by the Creator himself* **2** his normal self: *he was almost himself again*

hind¹ *adj* **hinder, hindmost** situated at the back: *a hind leg* ▶ HISTORY Old English *hindan* at the back

393

hind² *n, pl* **hinds** *or* **hind** the female of the deer, esp. the red deer ▶ HISTORY Old English

Hindenburg Line *n history* a line of strong fortifications built by the German army near the Franco-Belgian border in 1916–17 and breached by the Allies in August 1918

hinder¹ *vb* to get in the way of (someone or something) ▶ HISTORY Old English *hindrian*

hinder² *adj* situated at the back ▶ HISTORY Old English

Hindi *n* **1** a language or group of dialects of N central India **2** a formal literary dialect of this language, the official language of India ▶ HISTORY Old Persian *Hindu* the river Indus

hindquarters *pl n* the rear of a four-legged animal

hindrance *n* **1** an obstruction or snag **2** the act of hindering

hindsight *n* the ability to understand, after something has happened, what should have been done or what caused the event

Hindu *n, pl* **-dus 1** a person who practises Hinduism ▷ *adj* **2** of Hinduism

Hindu-Arabic numeral system *n* the most common system for numerical representation in the world today, using the characters 0, 1, 2, 3, 4, 5, 6, 7, 8, and 9

Hinduism *n* the dominant religion of India, which involves the worship of many gods and belief in reincarnation

Hindustani *n* a group of northern Indian languages that includes Hindi and Urdu

hinge *n* **1** a device for holding together two parts, such as a door and its frame, so that one can swing freely ▷ *vb* **hinging, hinged 2 hinge on** to depend on **3** to join or open (something) by means of a hinge ▶ HISTORY probably Germanic > **hinged** *adj*

hinny *n, pl* **-nies** the offspring of a male horse and a female donkey ▶ HISTORY Greek *hinnos*

hint *n* **1** a suggestion given in an indirect or subtle manner **2** a helpful piece of advice **3** a small amount: *a hint of irony* ▷ *vb* **4** (sometimes foll. by *at*) to suggest indirectly ▶ HISTORY origin unknown

hinterland *n* **1** land lying behind a coast or the shore of a river **2** an area near and dependent on a large city, esp. a port ▶ HISTORY German *hinter* behind + LAND

hip¹ *n* either side of the body below the waist and above the thigh ▶ HISTORY Old English *hype*

hip² *n* the berry-like brightly coloured fruit of a rose bush. Also called: **rosehip** ▶ HISTORY Old English *hēope*

hip³ *interj* an exclamation used to introduce cheers: *hip, hip, hurrah* ▶ HISTORY origin unknown

hip⁴ *adj* **hipper, hippest** *slang* aware of or following the latest trends ▶ HISTORY variant of earlier *hep*

hipbone *n* either of the two bones that form the sides of the pelvis

hip-hop *n* a US pop-culture movement originating in the 1980s, comprising rap music, graffiti, and break dancing

hippie *n* same as **hippy²**

hippo *n, pl* **-pos** *informal* short for **hippopotamus**

Hippocratic oath *n* an oath taken by a doctor to observe a code of medical ethics ▶ HISTORY after *Hippocrates*, Greek physician

hippodrome *n* **1** a music hall, variety theatre, or circus **2** (in ancient Greece or Rome) an open-air course for horse and chariot races ▶ HISTORY Greek *hippos* horse + *dromos* race

hippopotamus *n, pl* **-muses** *or* **-mi** a very large mammal with thick wrinkled skin and short legs, which lives around the rivers of tropical Africa

■ **WORD HISTORY**

■ A hippopotamus is literally a 'water horse'.
■ The word comes from Greek *hippos*, meaning
■ 'horse', and *potamos*, meaning 'river'.

hippy¹ *adj* **-pier, -piest** *informal* having large hips

hippy² *or* **hippie** *n, pl* **-pies** (esp. during the 1960s) a person whose behaviour and dress imply a rejection of conventional values ▶ HISTORY from HIP⁴

hire *vb* **hiring, hired 1** to acquire the temporary use of (a thing) or the services of (a person) in exchange for payment **2** to employ (a person) for wages **3** to provide (something) or the services of (oneself or others) for payment **4 hire out** *chiefly Brit* to pay independent contractors for (work to be done) ▷ *n* **5** the act of hiring **6 for hire** available to be hired ▶ HISTORY Old English *hȳrian*

hireling *n disparaging* a person who works only for money

hire-purchase *n* a system in which a buyer takes possession of merchandise on payment of a deposit and completes the purchase by paying a series of instalments while the seller retains ownership until the final instalment is paid

hirsute (**her**-suit) *adj* hairy ▶ HISTORY Latin *hirsutus* shaggy

his *adj* **1** of, belonging to, or associated with him: *his birthday* ▷ *pron* **2** something belonging to him: *his is on the left; that book is his* **3 of his** belonging to him ▶ HISTORY Old English

Hispanic *adj* **1** of or derived from Spain or the Spanish ▷ *n* **2** *US* a US citizen of Spanish or Latin-American descent ▶ HISTORY Latin *Hispania* Spain

hiss *n* **1** a sound like that of a prolonged *s* **2** such a sound as an expression of dislike ▷ *vb* **3** to utter a hiss **4** to express with a hiss: *she hissed the name* **5** to show dislike towards (a speaker or performer) by hissing ▶ HISTORY imitative

histamine (**hiss**-ta-meen) *n* a chemical compound released by the body tissues in allergic reactions ▶ HISTORY Greek *histos* tissue + *amine*

histogram *n* a statistical graph that represents the frequency of values of a quantity by vertical bars of varying heights and widths ▶ HISTORY probably *histo(ry)* + Greek *grammē* line

histology *n* the study of the tissues of an animal or plant ▶ HISTORY Greek *histos* tissue + -LOGY

historian *n* a person who writes or studies history

historic *adj* important in history, or likely to be seen as important in the future

hit

The word **hit** is often overused. There are a number of more descriptive words which you can use to give additional information about the way in which something is **hit**, or how hard it is **hit**.

DEFINITION 1

- If you **strike** someone or something, you hit them deliberately. This is rather a formal word: She stepped forward and **struck** him across the mouth.
- If you **tap** something, you hit it with a quick light blow or series of blows: **Tap** the egg gently with a teaspoon to crack the shell.
- If you **rap** something, or **rap on** it, you hit it with a series of quick blows: **rapping** the glass with the knuckles of his right hand • He **rapped on** the door with his cane.
- If you **slap** or **smack** someone, you hit them with the palm of your hand: I **slapped** him hard across the face. • She **smacked** the child on the back of the leg.
- If you **swat** something such as an insect, you hit it with a quick, swinging movement using your hand or a flat object: Every time a fly came near, I **swatted** it with a newspaper.
- If you **knock** something, you hit it roughly, especially so that it falls or moves: She accidentally **knocked** the tin off the shelf.

- If you **beat** something, you hit it hard, usually several times or continuously for a period of time: a circle of men **beating** drums
- If you **hammer** something, you hit it hard several times to make a noise: We had to **hammer** the door and shout to attract their attention.
- If you **pound** something, you hit it with great force, usually loudly and repeatedly: He **pounded** the table with both fists.
- If you **batter** someone or something, you hit them very hard, using your fists or a heavy object: He **battered** the oil drum with a club.
- If you **bang** something, you hit it hard, making a loud noise: We **banged** on the door and shouted to be let out.
- If you **belt** someone, you hit them very hard. This is a slang word: She drew back her fist and **belted** the other boxer in the stomach.
- If you **bash** someone or something, you hit them hard. This is an informal word: The chef was **bashed** over the head with a bottle.
- If you **whack** someone or something, you hit them hard: He **whacked** the ball with the bat.
- If you **wallop** someone or something, you hit them very hard, often causing a dull sound. This is an informal word: Jerry **walloped** Tom over the head with a frying pan.
- If you **thump** someone or something, you hit them hard, usually with your fist: I'm warning you, if you don't shut up, I'll **thump** you.

h

historical *adj* **1** occurring in the past **2** describing or representing situations or people that existed in the past: *a historical novel* **3** belonging to or typical of the study of history: *historical perspective* ▷ **historically** *adv*

historicism *n* **1** the belief that natural laws govern historical events **2** excessive respect for historical institutions, such as traditions or laws

historicity *n* historical authenticity

historiographer *n* a historian employed to write the history of a group or public institution

history *n, pl* **-ries** **1** a record or account of past events and developments **2** all that is preserved of the past, esp. in written form **3** the study of interpreting past events **4** the past events or previous experiences of a place, thing, or person **5** a play that depicts historical events ▶ **HISTORY** Greek *historia* inquiry

histrionic *adj* **1** very dramatic and full of exaggerated emotion: *histrionic bursts of invective* ▷ *n* **2 histrionics** behaviour of this kind ▶ **HISTORY** Latin *histrio* actor ▷ **histrionically** *adv*

hit *vb* **hitting, hit 1** to strike or touch (a person or thing) forcefully **2** to come into violent contact with: *a helicopter hit a Volvo* **3** to propel (a ball) by striking **4** *cricket* to score (runs) **5** to affect (a person, place, or thing) badly: *the airline says that*

its revenue will be hit **6** to reach (a point or place): *the city's crime level hit new heights* **7 hit the bottle** *slang* to start drinking excessive amounts of alcohol **8 hit the road** *informal* to set out on a journey ▷ *n* **9** an impact or collision **10** a shot or blow that reaches its target **11** *informal* a person or thing that gains wide appeal **12** *computers, slang* a single visit to a website: *over 500 000 hits a day to its site* ▷ See also **hit on** ▶ **HISTORY** Old English *hittan*
See **WORD FOCUS hit**

hit-and-miss *adj informal* happening in an unplanned way

hit-and-run *adj* denoting a motor-vehicle accident in which the driver does not stop to give assistance or inform the police

hitch *n* **1** a temporary or minor problem or difficulty **2** a knot that can be undone by pulling against the direction of the strain that holds it ▷ *vb* **3** *informal* to obtain (a ride) by hitchhiking **4** to fasten with a knot or tie **5 get hitched** *slang* to get married **6 hitch up** to pull up (one's trousers, etc.) with a quick jerk ▶ **HISTORY** origin unknown

hitchhike *vb* **-hiking, -hiked** to travel by getting free lifts in motor vehicles ▷ **hitchhiker** *n*

hi-tech *adj* using sophisticated, esp. electronic, technology

hither *adv old-fashioned* to or towards this place: *come hither* ▶ HISTORY Old English *hider*

hitherto *adv formal* until this time: *fundamental questions which have hitherto been ignored*

hit man *n* a person hired to murder someone

hit on *or* **upon** *vb* to think of (an idea)

hit-or-miss *adj informal* unplanned or unpredictable: *hit-or-miss service*. Also: **hit-and-miss**

hit wicket *n cricket* a batsman breaking the wicket while playing a stroke and so being out

HIV human immunodeficiency virus, the cause of AIDS

hive *n* **1** a structure in which bees live **2 hive of activity** a busy place with many people working hard ▶ HISTORY Old English *hȳf*

hive off *vb* to transfer (part of a business, esp. the profitable part of a nationalized industry) to new ownership

hives *n pathol* an allergic reaction in which itchy red or whitish raised patches develop on the skin ▶ HISTORY origin unknown

HM (in Britain) Her (*or* His) Majesty

H.M.A.S. *or* **HMAS** Her (*or* His) Majesty's Australian Ship

HMI (in Britain) Her (*or* His) Majesty's Inspector; a government official who examines and supervises schools

HMRC (in Britain) Her (*or* His) Majesty's Revenue and Customs: a government department responsible for collecting taxes

H.M.S. *or* **HMS** (in Britain) Her (*or* His) Majesty's Ship

HMSO (in Britain) Her (*or* His) Majesty's Stationery Office

HNC (in Britain) Higher National Certificate; a qualification recognized by many national technical and professional institutions

HND (in Britain) Higher National Diploma; a qualification in a technical subject equivalent to an ordinary degree

Ho *chem* holmium

hoar *n* short for **hoarfrost** ▶ HISTORY Old English *hār*

hoard *n* **1** a store of money, food, etc., hidden away for future use ▷ *vb* **2** to save or store (money, food, etc.) ▶ HISTORY Old English *hord* > **hoarder** *n*

hoarding *n* a large board at the side of a road, used for displaying advertising posters ▶ HISTORY Old English *hourd* palisade

hoarfrost *n* a white layer of ice crystals formed on the ground by condensation at temperatures below freezing point

hoarse *adj* **1** (of a voice) rough and unclear through illness or too much shouting **2** having a rough and unclear voice ▶ HISTORY from Old Norse > **hoarsely** *adv* > **hoarseness** *n*

hoary *adj* **hoarier, hoariest 1** having grey or white hair **2** very old: *a hoary old problem*

hoax *n* **1** a deception, esp. a practical joke ▷ *vb* **2** to deceive or play a joke on (someone) ▶ HISTORY probably from *hocus* to trick

hob *n Brit* the flat top part of a cooker, or a separate flat surface, containing hotplates or burners ▶ HISTORY perhaps from *hub*

hobble *vb* **-bling, -bled 1** to walk with a lame awkward movement **2** to tie the legs of (a horse) together in order to restrict its movement ▶ HISTORY probably from Low German

hobby *n, pl* **-bies** an activity pursued in one's spare time for pleasure or relaxation ▶ HISTORY probably variant of name *Robin*

hobby farm *n* a farm run as a hobby rather than as a means of making a living

hobbyhorse *n* **1** a favourite topic about which a person likes to talk at every opportunity **2** a toy consisting of a stick with a figure of a horse's head at one end

hobgoblin *n* a small, mischievous creature in fairy stories ▶ HISTORY *hob*, variant of the name *Rob* + GOBLIN

hobnail boots *n old-fashioned* heavy boots with short nails in the soles to lessen wear and tear ▶ HISTORY *hob* (in archaic sense: peg)

hobnob *vb* **-nobbing, -nobbed** to socialize or talk informally: *hobnobbing with the rich* ▶ HISTORY *hob or nob* to drink to one another in turns

hobo *n, pl* **-bos** *or* **-boes** *US, Canad, Austral & NZ* a tramp or vagrant ▶ HISTORY origin unknown

Hobson's choice *n* the choice of taking what is offered or nothing at all ▶ HISTORY after Thomas Hobson, liveryman who gave his customers no choice

hock¹ *n* the joint in the leg of a horse or similar animal that corresponds to the human ankle ▶ HISTORY Old English *hōhsinu* heel sinew

hock² *n* a white wine from the German Rhine ▶ HISTORY German *Hochheimer*

hock³ *informal vb* **1** to pawn or pledge ▷ *n* **2 in hock a** in debt **b** in pawn ▶ HISTORY Dutch *hok* prison, debt

hockey *n* **1** a game played on a field by two teams of 11 players who try to hit a ball into their opponents' goal using long sticks curved at the end **2** *US* ice hockey ▶ HISTORY origin unknown

hocus-pocus *n informal* something said or done in order to confuse or trick someone ▶ HISTORY an exclamation used by conjurors

hod *n* an open metal or plastic box attached to a pole, for carrying bricks or mortar ▶ HISTORY Old French *hotte* pannier

Hodgkin's disease *n* a malignant disease that causes enlargement of the lymph nodes, spleen, and liver ▶ HISTORY after Thomas *Hodgkin*, physician

hoe *n* **1** a long-handled implement used to loosen the soil or to weed ▷ *vb* **hoeing, hoed 2** to scrape or weed with a hoe ▶ HISTORY Germanic

hog *n* **1** a castrated male pig **2** *US & Canad* any mammal of the pig family **3** *informal* a greedy person **4 go the whole hog** *slang* to do something in the most complete way possible ▷ *vb* **hogging, hogged 5** *slang* to take more than one's share of (something) ▶ HISTORY Old English *hogg*

hogback *n geog* a narrow ridge with steep sides

Hogmanay *n* New Year's Eve in Scotland
▶ HISTORY probably from Old French *aguillanneuf* a New Year's Eve gift

hogshead *n* a large cask for storing alcoholic drinks ▶ HISTORY origin unknown

hogwash *n informal* nonsense

ho-ho *interj* a written representation of the sound of a deep laugh

hoick *vb* **1** to raise abruptly and sharply **2** *NZ* to clear the throat and spit ▶ HISTORY origin unknown

hoi polloi *pl n* the ordinary people when compared to the rich or well-educated ▶ HISTORY Greek: the many

hoist *vb* **1** to raise or lift up, esp. by mechanical means ▷ *n* **2** any apparatus or device for lifting things ▶ HISTORY probably from Low German

hoity-toity *adj informal* arrogant or haughty ▶ HISTORY obsolete *hoit* to romp

hokey-pokey *n NZ* a brittle toffee sold in lumps

hokum *n slang, chiefly US & Canad* **1** nonsense; bunk **2** obvious sentimental material in a play or film ▶ HISTORY probably a blend of *hocus-pocus + bunkum*

hold¹ *vb* **holding, held 1** to keep (an object or a person) with or within the hands or arms **2** to support: *a rope made from 1000 hairs would hold a large adult* **3** to maintain in a specified state or position: *his reputation continued to hold secure* **4** to have the capacity for: *trains designed to hold more than 400* **5** to set aside or reserve: *they will hold our tickets until tomorrow* **6** to restrain or keep back: *designed to hold dangerous criminals* **7** to remain unbroken: *if the elastic holds* **8** (of the weather) to remain dry and bright **9** to keep (the attention of): *a writer holds a reader by his temperament* **10** to arrange and cause to take place: *we must hold an inquiry* **11** to have the ownership or possession of: *she holds a degree in Egyptology* **12** to have responsibility for: *she cannot hold an elective office* **13** to be able to control the outward effects of drinking (alcohol): *he can't hold his liquor* **14** to (cause to) remain committed to (a promise, etc.) **15** to claim or believe: *some Sufis hold that all religious leaders were prophets* **16** to remain valid or true: *the categories are not the same and equivalency does not hold* **17** to consider in a specified manner: *philosophies which we hold so dear* **18** to defend successfully: *the Russians were holding the Volga front* **19** *music* to sustain the sound of (a note) ▷ *n* **20** a way of holding something or the act of holding it **21** something to hold onto for support **22** controlling influence: *drugs will take a hold* **23 with no holds barred** with all limitations removed ▶ HISTORY Old English *healdan* > **holder** *n*

hold² *n* the space in a ship or aircraft for storing cargo ▶ HISTORY variant of *hole*

holdall *n Brit* a large strong travelling bag

hold forth *vb* to speak for a long time

holding *n* **1** land held under a lease **2** property to which the holder has legal title, such as land, stocks, or shares

holding company *n* a company that holds the controlling shares in one or more other companies

holding paddock *n Austral & NZ* a paddock in which cattle or sheep are kept temporarily

hold on *vb* **1** to maintain a firm grasp (of something or someone) **2 hold on to** to keep **3** *informal, spoken* to wait, esp. on the telephone

hold over *vb* to postpone: *several cases had to be held over pending further investigation*

hold-up *n* **1** an armed robbery **2** a delay: *a traffic hold-up* ▷ *vb* **hold up 3** to delay **4** to support (an object) **5** to stop and rob (someone), using a weapon **6** to exhibit or present (something) as an example: *he was held up as a model professional*

hold with *vb* approve of: *I don't hold with divorce*

hole *n* **1** an area hollowed out in a solid **2** an opening in or through something **3** an animal's burrow **4** *informal* a fault or error: *this points to a very big hole in parliamentary security* **5 pick holes in** to point out faults in **6** *informal* an unattractive town or other place **7 in a hole** *slang* in a difficult and embarrassing situation **8** (on a golf course) any one of the divisions of a course (usually 18) represented by the distance between the tee and the sunken cup on the green into which the ball is to be played **9 make a hole in** *informal* to use a great amount of (one's money or food supply) ▷ *vb* **holing, holed 10** to make a hole or holes in (something) **11** to hit (a golf ball) into a hole ▶ HISTORY Old English *hol* > **holey** *adj*

hole in the heart *n* a congenital defect of the heart, in which there is an abnormal opening in the partition between the left and right halves

hole up *vb informal* to go into hiding

Holi (**holl**-lee) *n* an annual Hindu spring festival, honouring Krishna

holiday *n* **1** a period of time spent away from home for enjoyment and relaxation **2** (often *pl*) *chiefly Brit & NZ* a period in which a break is taken from work or studies for rest or recreation **3** a day on which work is suspended by law or custom, such as a bank holiday ▷ *vb* **4** *chiefly Brit* to spend a holiday ▶ HISTORY Old English *hāligdæg* holy day

holiday-maker *n* a person who goes on holiday

holier-than-thou *adj* offensively self-righteous

Holiness *n* (preceded by *His* or *Your*) a title reserved for the pope

holism *n* **1** the view that a whole is greater than the sum of its parts **2** (in medicine) consideration of the complete person in the treatment of disease ▶ HISTORY Greek *holos* whole > **holistic** *adj*

holler *informal vb* **1** to shout or yell ▷ *n* **2** a shout or yell ▶ HISTORY French *holà* stop!

hollow *adj* **1** having a hole or space within; not solid: *a hollow tree* **2** curving inwards: *hollow cheeks* **3** (of sounds) as if echoing in a hollow place **4** without any real value or worth: *a hollow enterprise, lacking purpose, and lacking soul* ▷ *adv* **5 beat someone hollow** *Brit & NZ, informal* to defeat someone thoroughly ▷ *n* **6** a cavity or space in something **7** a dip in the land ▷ *vb* **8** (often foll. by *out*) to form a hole or cavity in ▶ HISTORY Old English *holh* cave > **hollowly** *adv*

397

holly *n* an evergreen tree with prickly leaves and bright red berries, used for Christmas decorations ▶ HISTORY Old English *holegn*

hollyhock *n* a tall garden plant with spikes of colourful flowers ▶ HISTORY *holy* + obsolete *hock* mallow

holmium *n chem* a silver-white metallic element, the compounds of which are highly magnetic. Symbol: Ho ▶ HISTORY after *Holmia*, Latin name of Stockholm

holm oak *n* an evergreen oak tree with prickly leaves like holly

holocaust *n* 1 destruction or loss of life on a massive scale 2 **the Holocaust** mass murder of the Jews in Europe by the Nazis (1940–45) ▶ HISTORY Greek *holos* whole + *kaiein* to burn

Holocene *adj* of the current geological epoch, which began about 10 000 years ago

hologram *n* a three-dimensional photographic image produced by means of a split laser beam ▶ HISTORY Greek *holos* whole + *grammē* line

holograph *n* a book or document handwritten by its author ▶ HISTORY Greek *holos* whole + *graphein* to write

holography *n* the science of using lasers to produce holograms ▶ HISTORY Greek *holos* whole + -GRAPHY > **holographic** *adj*

hols *pl n Brit & S African school, slang* holidays

holster *n* a sheathlike leather case for a pistol, worn attached to a belt ▶ HISTORY Germanic

holt *n* the lair of an otter ▶ HISTORY from HOLD²

holy *adj* **-lier, -liest** 1 of or associated with God or a deity 2 (of a person) religious and leading a virtuous life ▶ HISTORY Old English *hālig, hǣlig* > **holiness** *n*

Holy Communion *n Christianity* a church service in which people take bread and wine in remembrance of Christ's Last Supper and His atonement for the sins of the world

Holy Ghost *n* **the Holy Ghost** same as **Holy Spirit**

Holy Grail *n* **1 the Holy Grail** (in medieval legend) the bowl used by Jesus at the Last Supper 2 *informal* any ambition or goal ▶ HISTORY *grail* from Medieval Latin *gradalis* bowl

Holy Land *n* **the Holy Land** Palestine

holy of holies *n* 1 any sacred place or a place considered as if it were sacred: *the holy of holies they called the Captain's Cabin* 2 the innermost chamber of a Jewish temple

holy orders *pl n* the status of an ordained Christian minister

Holy See *n* **the Holy See** *RC Church* the see of the pope as bishop of Rome

Holy Spirit *n* **the Holy Spirit** *Christianity* one of the three aspects of God

Holy Week *n Christianity* the week before Easter Sunday

homage *n* a public show of respect or honour towards someone or something ▶ HISTORY Latin *homo* man

homburg *n* a man's soft felt hat with a dented crown and a stiff upturned brim

home *n* 1 the place where one lives 2 the country or area of one's birth 3 a building or organization set up to care for people in a certain category, such as orphans or the aged 4 the place where something is invented or started: *the home of the first aircraft* 5 *sport* a team's own ground: *the match is at home* 6 *baseball, rounders, etc.* the objective towards which a player runs after striking the ball 7 **at home a** in one's own home or country **b** at ease: *he felt more at home with the Russians* **c** receiving visitors ▷ *adj* 8 of one's home, birthplace, or native country 9 (of an activity) done in one's house: *home movies* 10 *sport* played on one's own ground: *a home game* 11 **home and dry** *Brit, slang* definitely safe or successful ▷ *adv* 12 to or at home: *I came home* 13 to or on the point: *the message struck home* 14 to the fullest extent: *they drove their spears home* 15 **bring something home to someone** to make something clear to someone ▷ *vb* **homing, homed** 16 **home in on** to be directed towards (a goal or target) 17 (of birds) to return home accurately from a distance ▶ HISTORY Old English *hām*

home-brew *n* beer or other alcoholic drink brewed at home

homecoming *n* a return home, esp. after a long absence

home economics *n* the study of diet, budgeting, child care, and other subjects concerned with running a home

home farm *n Brit* a farm that belonged to and provided food for a large country house

Home Guard *n* a part-time military force of volunteers recruited for the defence of the United Kingdom in the Second World War

home help *n Brit, Austral & NZ* a person employed by a local authority to do housework in an elderly or disabled person's home

homeland *n* 1 *written* the country from which the ancestors of a person or group came 2 the official name in S Africa for a **Bantustan**

homeless *adj* 1 having nowhere to live ▷ *pl n* 2 people who have nowhere to live: *night shelters for the homeless* > **homelessness** *n*

homely *adj* **-lier, -liest** 1 simple, ordinary, and comfortable 2 (of a person) **a** *Brit* warm and friendly **b** *chiefly US & Canad* plain or unattractive > **homeliness** *n*

home-made *adj* (esp. of foods) made at home or on the premises

Home Office *n Brit government* the department responsible for law and order, immigration, and other domestic affairs

homeopathy *or* **homoeopathy** (home-ee-**op**-ath-ee) *n* a method of treating disease by the use of small amounts of a drug that produces symptoms of the disease in healthy people ▶ HISTORY Greek *homoios* similar + *patheia* suffering > **homeopath** *or* **homoeopath** (home-ee-oh-path) *n* > **homeopathic** *or* **homoeopathic** *adj*

homeostasis *or* **homoeostasis** (hom-ee-oh-**stass**-iss) *n* the tendency of an organism to achieve a stable metabolic state by compensating automatically for violent changes in the environment and other disruptions ▶ HISTORY Greek *homoios* similar + *stasis* a standing

homeowner *n* a person who owns the home in which he or she lives

home page *n internet* the introductory information about a website with links to the information or services provided

Homeric (home-**mer**-rik) *adj* of or relating to Homer, Greek epic poet (circa 800 BC)

home rule *n* self-government in domestic affairs

Home Secretary *n Brit government* the head of the Home Office

homesick *adj* depressed by being away from home and family > **homesickness** *n*

homestead *n* **1** a farmhouse and the adjoining land **2** (in the western US & Canada) a house and adjoining tract of land (originally often 160 acres) that was granted by the government for development as a farm

homesteader *n* (in the western US & Canada) a person who lives on and farms a homestead

homestead law *n* (in the western US & Canada) any of various laws granting certain privileges to owners of homesteads

home truths *pl n* unpleasant facts told to a person about himself or herself

home unit *n Austral & NZ* a self-contained residence which is part of a block of such residences

homeward *adj* **1** going home ▷ *adv also* **homewards 2** towards home

homework *n* **1** school work done at home **2** research or preparation

homicide *n* **1** the act of killing someone **2** a person who kills someone ▶ HISTORY Latin *homo* man + *caedere* to kill > **homicidal** *adj*

homily *n, pl* -**lies** a moralizing talk or piece of writing ▶ HISTORY Greek *homilia* discourse

homing *adj* **1** *zool* denoting the ability to return home after travelling great distances **2** (of a missile) capable of guiding itself onto a target

homing pigeon *n* a pigeon developed for its homing instinct, used for racing

hominid *n* **1** any member of the family of primates that includes modern man and the extinct forerunners of man ▷ *adj* **2** of or belonging to this family ▶ HISTORY Latin *homo* man

hominoid *adj* **1** of or like man; manlike ▷ *n* **2** a manlike animal ▶ HISTORY Latin *homo* man

homo- *combining form* same or like: *homologous* ▶ HISTORY Greek *homos* same

Homo erectus *n* an extinct species of primitive man, able to walk upright ▶ HISTORY Latin *homo* man + *erectus* erect

homogeneous (home-oh-**jean**-ee-uss) *adj* having parts or members which are all the same or which consist of only one substance: *the Arabs are not a single, homogeneous nation* ▶ HISTORY Greek *homos* same + *genos* kind > **homogeneity** *n*

homogenize *or* -**nise** *vb* -**nizing, -nized** *or* -**nising, -nised** **1** to break up the fat globules in (milk or cream) so that they are evenly distributed **2** to make different elements the same or similar: *homogenized products for a mass market*

homogenous (hom-**oj**-in-uss) *adj* having a similar structure because of common ancestry

homograph *n* a word spelt the same as another, but having a different meaning, such as *bear* (to carry) and *bear* (the animal) ▶ HISTORY Greek *homos* same + *graphein* to write

Homo habilis *n* an extinct species of primitive man, the first to use stone tools ▶ HISTORY Latin *homo* man + *habilis* skilled

homologous (hom-**ol**-log-uss) *adj* **1** having a related or similar position or structure **2** *biol* (of organs and parts) having the same origin but different functions: *the wing of a bat and the arm of a monkey are homologous* ▶ HISTORY Greek *homos* same + *logos* ratio

homologous series *n chem* a series of organic compounds with similar characteristics and structure but differing by a number of CH_2 groups

homology (hom-**ol**-a-jee) *n* the condition of being homologous

homonym *n* a word pronounced and spelt the same as another, but having a different meaning, such as *novel* (a book) and *novel* (new)

homophobia *n* intense hatred or fear of homosexuals ▶ HISTORY *homo(sexual)* + *phobia* > **homophobic** *adj*

homophone *n* a word pronounced the same as another, but having a different meaning or spelling or both, such as *bear* and *bare* ▶ HISTORY Greek *homos* same + *phōnē* sound > **homophonic** *adj*

Homo sapiens (**home**-oh **sap**-ee-enz) *n* the name for modern man as a species ▶ HISTORY Latin *homo* man + *sapiens* wise

homosexual *n* **1** a person who is sexually attracted to members of the same sex ▷ *adj* **2** (of a person) sexually attracted to members of the same sex **3** (of a sexual relationship) between members of the same sex ▶ HISTORY Greek *homos* same > **homosexuality** *n*

homozygous *adj biol* having two identical alleles of the same gene ▶ HISTORY Greek *homos* same + *zugōtos* yoked

Hon. Honourable (title)

hone *vb* **honing, honed 1** to develop and improve (a quality or ability) **2** to sharpen (a tool) ▷ *n* **3** a fine whetstone used for sharpening edged tools and knives ▶ HISTORY Old English *hān* stone

honest *adj* **1** truthful and moral in behaviour; trustworthy **2** open and sincere in relationships and attitudes; without pretensions **3** gained or earned fairly ▶ HISTORY Latin *honos* esteem

honestly *adv* **1** in an honest manner **2** truly

honesty *n, pl* -**ties 1** the quality of being truthful and trustworthy **2** a plant with flattened silvery pods which are used for indoor decoration

honey *n* **1** a sweet edible sticky substance made by bees from nectar **2** *chiefly US & Canad* a term

399

of affection **3** *informal, chiefly US & Canad* something very good of its kind ▶ HISTORY Old English *huneg*

honeybee *n* a bee widely domesticated as a source of honey and beeswax

honeycomb *n* a waxy structure, constructed by bees in a hive, that consists of many six-sided cells in which honey is stored

honeydew *n* a sugary substance excreted by aphids and similar insects

honeydew melon *n* a melon with yellow skin and sweet pale flesh

honeyed *adj poetic* flattering or soothing

honeymoon *n* **1** a holiday taken by a newly married couple **2** the early period of an undertaking or activity, such as the start of new government's term of office, when an attitude of goodwill prevails ▷ *vb* **3** to take a honeymoon ▶ HISTORY traditionally, referring to the feelings of married couples as changing with the phases of the moon > **honeymooner** *n*

honeysuckle *n* **1** a climbing shrub with sweet-smelling white, yellow, or pink flowers **2** an Australian tree or shrub with nectar-rich flowers ▶ HISTORY Old English *hunigsūce*

hongi (hong-jee) *n NZ* a Māori greeting in which people touch noses

honk *n* **1** the sound made by a motor horn **2** the sound made by a goose ▷ *vb* **3** to make or cause (something) to make a honking sound

honorarium *n, pl* **-iums** *or* **-ia** a voluntary fee paid for a service which is usually free ▶ HISTORY Latin *honorarium (donum)* honorary gift

honorary *adj* **a** held or given as a mark of respect, without the usual qualifications, payment, or work: *an honorary degree* **b** (of a secretary, treasurer, etc.) unpaid

honorific *adj* showing respect: *an honorific title*

honour *or US* **honor** *n* **1** a person's good reputation and the respect they are given by other people **2** a fame or glory **b** a person who wins fame or glory for his or her country, school, etc.: *he was an honour to his nation* **3** great respect or esteem, or an outward sign of this **4** a privilege or pleasure: *it was an honour to meet him* **5** *old-fashioned* a woman's virginity **6** *Bridge, whist* any of the top four or five cards in a suit **7** *golf* the right to tee off first **8** **in honour of** out of respect for **9** **on one's honour** under a moral obligation ▷ *vb* **10** to hold someone in respect **11** to give (someone) special praise, attention, or an award **12** to accept and then pay (a cheque or bill) **13** to keep (one's promise); fulfil (a previous agreement) ▶ HISTORY Latin *honor* esteem

Honour *n* (preceded by *Your, His* or *Her*) a title used to address or refer to certain judges

honourable *or US* **honorable** *adj* worthy of respect or esteem > **honourably** *adv*

Honourable *adj* **the Honourable** a title of respect placed before a name: used of various officials, of the children of certain peers, and in Parliament by one member speaking of another

honours *or US* **honors** *pl n* **1** (in a university degree course) a rank or mark of the highest academic standard: *an honours degree* **2** observances of respect, esp. at a funeral **3** **do the honours** to serve as host or hostess by serving food or pouring drinks

hooch (rhymes with **smooch**) *n informal* alcoholic drink, esp. illegally distilled spirits ▶ HISTORY from a Native American language

hood¹ *n* **1** a loose head covering either attached to a coat or made as a separate garment **2** *US, Canad & Austral* the bonnet of a car **3** the folding roof of a convertible car or a pram ▷ *vb* **4** to cover with or as if with a hood ▶ HISTORY Old English *hōd* > **hoodlike** *adj*

hood² *n slang* short for **hoodlum**

hooded *adj* **1** (of a garment) having a hood **2** (of eyes) having heavy eyelids that appear to be half-closed

hooded crow *n* a crow that has a grey body and black head, wings, and tail

hoodlum *n* a violent criminal, esp. one who is a member of a gang ▶ HISTORY origin unknown

hoodoo *n, pl* **-doos** **1** *informal* bad luck **2** *informal* a person or thing that brings bad luck **3** *chiefly US* same as **voodoo**

hoodwink *vb* to trick or deceive ▶ HISTORY originally, to cover the eyes with a hood

hooey *n slang* nonsense ▶ HISTORY origin unknown

hoof *n, pl* **hooves** *or* **hoofs** **1** the horny covering of the end of the foot in the horse, deer, and certain other mammals **2** **on the hoof a** (of livestock) alive **b** in an impromptu way: *thinking on the hoof* ▷ *vb* **3** **hoof it** *slang* to walk ▶ HISTORY Old English *hōf* > **hoofed** *adj*

hoo-ha *n* a noisy commotion or fuss ▶ HISTORY origin unknown

hook *n* **1** a curved piece of metal or plastic used to hang, hold, or pull something **2** something resembling a hook, such as a sharp bend in a river or a sharply curved strip of land **3** *boxing* a short swinging blow with the elbow bent **4** *cricket, golf* a shot that causes the ball to go to the player's left **5** **by hook or by crook** by any means: *get into the charts by hook or by crook* **6** **hook, line, and sinker** *informal* completely: *we fell for it hook, line, and sinker* **7** **let someone off the hook** *slang* to free someone from an obligation or a difficult situation **8** **sling one's hook** *Brit & Austral, slang* to leave ▷ *vb* **9** to fasten with or as if with a hook **10** to catch (a fish) on a hook **11** *cricket, golf* to play (a ball) with a hook **12** *rugby* to obtain and pass (the ball) backwards from a scrum, using the feet ▶ HISTORY Old English *hōc*

hookah *n* an oriental pipe for smoking marijuana or tobacco, with a long flexible stem connected to a container of water through which smoke is drawn and cooled ▶ HISTORY Arabic *huqqah*

hooked *adj* **1** bent like a hook **2** **hooked on a** *slang* addicted to: *hooked on drugs* **b** obsessed with: *hooked on football*

hooker n 1 slang a prostitute 2 rugby a player who uses his feet to get the ball in a scrum

Hooke's law n physics the principle that a solid stretches or contracts in proportion to the force placed on it, within the limits of its elasticity ▶ HISTORY after Robert Hooke, physicist

hook-up n the linking of broadcasting equipment or stations to transmit a special programme

hookworm n a blood-sucking worm with hooked mouthparts

hooligan n slang a young person who behaves in a noisy and violent way in public ▶ HISTORY origin unknown > **hooliganism** n

hoon n Austral & NZ, slang 1 a loutish youth who drives irresponsibly ▷ vb 2 to drive irresponsibly

hoop n 1 a rigid circular band of metal, plastic, or wood 2 a child's toy shaped like a hoop and rolled on the ground or whirled around the body 3 croquet any of the iron arches through which the ball is driven 4 a large ring through which performers or animals jump 5 **go** or **be put through the hoops** to go through an ordeal or test ▷ vb 6 to surround (something) with a hoop ▶ HISTORY Old English hōp > **hooped** adj

hoopla n Brit & Austral a fairground game in which hoops are thrown over objects in an attempt to win them

hoopoe (**hoop-**oo) n a bird with pinkish-brown plumage with black-and-white wings and a fanlike crest ▶ HISTORY imitative

hoop pine n an Australian tree or shrub with flowers in dense spikes

hooray interj, n same as **hurrah**

hoot n 1 the sound of a car horn 2 the cry of an owl 3 a high-pitched noise showing disapproval 4 informal an amusing person or thing ▷ vb 5 Brit to blow (a car horn) 6 to make a hoot 7 to jeer or yell contemptuously at someone 8 to drive (speakers or performers on stage) off by hooting ▶ HISTORY imitative

hooter n chiefly Brit 1 a device that hoots, such as a car horn 2 slang a nose

Hoover n 1 trademark a vacuum cleaner ▷ vb **hoover** 2 to vacuum-clean (a carpet) 3 (often foll. by up) to devour (something) quickly and completely

hooves n a plural of **hoof**

hop¹ vb **hopping, hopped** 1 to jump forwards or upwards on one foot 2 (of frogs, birds, etc.) to move forwards in short jumps 3 to jump over something 4 informal to move quickly (in, on, out of, etc.): hop into bed 5 **hop it** Brit & Austral, slang to go away ▷ n 6 an instance of hopping 7 informal an informal dance 8 informal a short journey, usually in an aircraft 9 **on the hop** informal a active or busy: he keeps me on the hop b unawares or unprepared: you caught me on the hop ▶ HISTORY Old English hoppian

hop² n a climbing plant with green conelike flowers. See also **hops** ▶ HISTORY Middle Dutch hoppe

hope vb **hoping, hoped** 1 to desire (something), usually with some possibility of fulfilment: you would hope for their cooperation 2 to trust or believe: I hope I've arranged that ▷ n 3 a feeling of desire for something, usually with confidence in the possibility of its fulfilment: the news was greeted by some as hope for further interest rate cuts 4 a reasonable ground for this feeling: there is hope for you yet 5 the person, thing, situation, or event that gives cause for hope or is desired: the young are a symbol of hope for the future ▶ HISTORY Old English hopa

hopeful adj 1 having, inspiring, or expressing hope ▷ n 2 a person considered to be on the brink of success: a young hopeful

hopefully adv 1 in a hopeful manner 2 informal it is hoped: hopefully I've got a long career ahead of me

hopeless adj 1 having or offering no hope 2 impossible to solve 3 informal without skill or ability: I'm hopeless at maths > **hopelessly** adv > **hopelessness** n

hopper n a funnel-shaped device from which solid materials can be discharged into a receptacle below

hops pl n the dried flowers of the hop plant, used to give a bitter taste to beer

hopscotch n a children's game in which a player throws a stone to land in one of a pattern of squares marked on the ground and then hops over to it to pick it up ▶ HISTORY hop + obsolete scotch a line, scratch

horde n a very large crowd, often frightening or unpleasant ▶ HISTORY Turkish ordū camp

horehound n a plant that produces a bitter juice formerly used as a cough medicine ▶ HISTORY Old English hārhūne

horizon n 1 the apparent line that divides the earth and the sky 2 **horizons** the limits of a person's interests and activities 3 **on the horizon** almost certainly going to happen or be done in the future ▶ HISTORY Greek horizein to limit

horizontal adj 1 flat and level with the ground or with a line considered as a base 2 affecting or happening at one level in a system or organization: a horizontal division of labour ▷ n 3 a horizontal plane, position, or line > **horizontally** adv

hormone n 1 a chemical substance produced in an endocrine gland and transported in the blood to a certain tissue, on which it has a specific effect 2 a similar substance produced by a plant that is essential for growth 3 a synthetic substance having the same effects ▶ HISTORY Greek hormōn > **hormonal** adj

horn n 1 either of a pair of permanent bony outgrowths on the heads of animals such as cattle and antelopes 2 any hornlike projection, such as the eyestalk of a snail 3 the antler of a deer 4 the hard substance of which horns are made 5 a musical wind instrument made from horn 6 any musical instrument consisting of a pipe or tube of brass fitted with a mouthpiece 7 a device, such as on a vehicle, for producing a warning or signalling noise ▶ HISTORY Old English > **horned** adj

hornbeam *n* a tree with smooth grey bark

hornbill *n* a tropical bird with a bony growth on its large beak

hornblende *n* a green-to-black mineral containing aluminium, calcium, sodium, magnesium, and iron

hornet *n* **1** a large wasp that can inflict a severe sting **2 hornet's nest** a very unpleasant situation that is difficult to deal with: *you'll stir up a hornet's nest* ▶ HISTORY Old English *hyrnetu*

horn of plenty *n* same as **cornucopia**

hornpipe *n* **1** a solo dance, traditionally performed by sailors **2** music for this dance

horny *adj* **hornier, horniest** of, like, or hard as horn

horoscope *n* **1** the prediction of a person's future based on the positions of the planets, sun, and moon at the time of birth **2** a diagram showing the positions of the planets, sun, and moon at a particular time and place

- ■ WORD HISTORY
- ■ 'Horoscope' comes via Latin from Greek
- ■ *hōroskopos*, meaning 'hour observer' or 'time
- ■ observer', referring to the time of a person's
- ■ birth. The word derives from *hōra*, meaning
- ■ 'hour' or 'time' and *skopos*, meaning 'observer'
- ■ (the same word as is seen in 'microscope',
- ■ 'telescope', etc.).

horrendous *adj* very unpleasant or shocking ▶ HISTORY Latin *horrendus* fearful

horrible *adj* **1** disagreeable and unpleasant: *a horrible hotel room* **2** causing fear, shock, or disgust: *he died a horrible death* ▶ HISTORY Latin *horribilis* > **horribly** *adv*

horrid *adj* **1** disagreeable or unpleasant: *it had been a horrid day at school* **2** *informal* (of a person) unkind and nasty: *her horrid parents* ▶ HISTORY Latin *horridus* prickly

horrific *adj* provoking horror: *horrific injuries* > **horrifically** *adv*

horrify *vb* **-fies, -fying, -fied** to cause feelings of horror in (someone); shock (someone) greatly

horror *n* **1** extreme fear or terror **2** intense hatred: *she had a horror of violence* **3** a thing or person causing fear, loathing, or distaste ▷ *adj* **4** having a frightening subject, usually concerned with the supernatural: *a horror film* ▶ HISTORY Latin: a trembling with fear

horrors *pl n* **the horrors** *slang* a fit of nervousness or anxiety

hors d'oeuvre (or **durv**) *n*, *pl* **hors d'oeuvre** or **hors d'oeuvres** (or **durv**) an appetizer, usually served before the main meal ▶ HISTORY French

horse *n* **1** a four-footed mammal with hooves, a mane, and a tail, used for riding and pulling carts, etc. *Related adjectives:* **equestrian, equine 2** the adult male of this species; stallion **3 the horses** *informal* horse races on which bets may be placed: *an occasional flutter on the horses* **4** gymnastics a padded apparatus on legs, used for vaulting **5 be** or **get on one's high horse** *informal* to act in a haughty manner **6 the horse's mouth** the most reliable source: *I'll tell you straight from the horse's mouth* ▶ HISTORY Old English *hors*

horse around or **about** *vb informal* to play roughly or boisterously

horsebox *n Brit & Austral* a van or trailer used for transporting horses

horse chestnut *n* **1** a tree with broad leaves and brown shiny inedible nuts enclosed in a spiky case **2** the nut of this tree

horseflesh *n* **1** horses collectively **2** the flesh of a horse as food

horsefly *n*, *pl* **-flies** a large fly which sucks the blood of horses, cattle, and people

horsehair *n* hair from the tail or mane of a horse, used in upholstery

horse latitudes *pl n geog* the latitudes near 30°N or 30°S at sea, characterized by baffling winds, calms, and high barometric pressure ▶ HISTORY referring either to the high mortality of horses on board ship in these latitudes or to *dead horse* (nautical slang: advance pay), which sailors expected to work off by this stage of a voyage

horse laugh *n* a loud and coarse laugh

horseman *n*, *pl* **-men 1** a man who is skilled in riding **2** a man riding a horse > **horsemanship** *n* > **horsewoman** *fem n*

horseplay *n* rough or rowdy play

horsepower *n* a unit of power (equivalent to 745.7 watts), used to measure the power of an engine

horseradish *n* a plant with a white strong-tasting root, which is used to make a sauce

horse sense *n* same as **common sense**

horseshoe *n* **1** a piece of iron shaped like a U, nailed to the bottom of a horse's hoof to protect the foot **2** an object of similar shape: often regarded as a symbol of good luck

horsetail *n* a plant with small dark toothlike leaves

horsey or **horsy** *adj* **horsier, horsiest 1** of or relating to horses: *a horsey smell* **2** devoted to horses: *the horsey set* **3** like a horse: *a horsey face*

horst *n geog* a ridge of land that has been forced upwards between two parallel faults ▶ HISTORY German *Horst* thicket

horticulture *n* the art or science of cultivating gardens ▶ HISTORY Latin *hortus* garden + CULTURE > **horticultural** *adj* > **horticulturalist** or **horticulturist** *n*

hosanna *interj* an exclamation of praise to God ▶ HISTORY Hebrew *hōshī'āh nnā* save now, we pray

hose¹ *n* **1** a flexible pipe for conveying a liquid or gas ▷ *vb* **hosing, hosed 2** to wash or water (a person or thing) with a hose ▶ HISTORY later use of HOSE²

hose² *n* **1** *old-fashioned* stockings, socks, and tights collectively **2** *history* a man's garment covering the legs and reaching up to the waist ▶ HISTORY Old English *hosa*

hosiery *n* stockings, socks, and knitted underclothing collectively

hospice (**hoss**-piss) *n* **1** a nursing home that specializes in caring for the terminally ill **2** *archaic* a place of shelter for travellers, esp. one kept by a religious order ▶ HISTORY Latin *hospes* guest

hospitable *adj* generous, friendly, and welcoming to guests or strangers: *charming and hospitable lodgings* ▶ HISTORY Medieval Latin *hospitare* to receive as a guest > **hospitably** *adv*

hospital *n* an institution for the medical or psychiatric care and treatment of patients ▶ HISTORY Latin *hospes* guest

hospitality *n, pl* **-ties** kindness in welcoming strangers or guests

hospitalize *or* **-ise** *vb* **-izing, -ized** *or* **-ising, -ised** to admit or send (a person) into a hospital > **hospitalization** *or* **-isation** *n*

hospitaller *or US* **hospitaler** *n* a member of a religious order dedicated to hospital work, ambulance services, etc.

host[1] *n* **1** a person who receives or entertains guests, esp. in his or her own home **2** the organization or country providing the facilities for a function or event: *Barcelona, host of the 1992 Olympic Games* **3** the compere of a radio or television programme **4** *biol* an animal or plant in or on which a parasite lives **5** *computers* a computer connected to a network and providing facilities to other computers and their users **6** *old-fashioned* the owner or manager of an inn ▷ *vb* **7** to be the host of (a party, programme, or event): *he's hosting a radio show* ▶ HISTORY Latin *hospes* guest, host

host[2] *n* a great number; multitude ▶ HISTORY Latin *hostis* stranger

Host *n* *Christianity* the bread used in Holy Communion ▶ HISTORY Latin *hostia* victim

hostage *n* a person who is illegally held prisoner until certain demands are met by other people ▶ HISTORY Old French *hoste* guest

hostel *n* **1** a building providing overnight accommodation for homeless people **2** a building providing cheap accommodation and meals for tourists, hikers, etc. **3** same as **youth hostel** **4** *Brit & NZ* a supervised lodging house for nurses, students, etc. ▶ HISTORY Medieval Latin *hospitale* hospice > **hosteller** *or US* **hosteler** *n*

hostelry *n, pl* **-ries** *archaic or facetious* an inn

hostel school *n* *Canad* same as **residential school**

hostess *n* **1** a woman who receives and entertains guests, esp. in her own house **2** a woman who receives and entertains patrons of a club, restaurant, or dance hall

hostile *adj* **1** unfriendly and aggressive **2** opposed (to): *hostile to the referendum* **3** relating to or involving the enemies of a country ▶ HISTORY Latin *hostis* enemy

hostility *n, pl* **-ties 1** unfriendly and aggressive feelings or behaviour **2 hostilities** acts of warfare

hot *adj* **hotter, hottest 1** having a relatively high temperature **2** having a temperature higher than desirable **3** spicy or causing a burning sensation on the tongue: *hot chillies* **4** (of a temper) quick to flare up **5** (of a contest or conflict) intense **6** recent or new: *hot from the press* **7** much favoured: *a hot favourite* **8** *informal* having a dangerously high level of radioactivity **9** *slang* stolen or otherwise illegally

obtained **10** (of a colour) intense; striking: *hot pink* **11** following closely: *this LP appeared hot on the heels of the debut smash* **12** *informal* dangerous or unpleasant: *they're making it hot for me here* **13** (in various games) very near the answer **14 hot on** *informal* **a** strict about: *they are extremely hot on sloppy language* **b** particularly knowledgeable about **15 hot under the collar** *informal* aroused with anger, annoyance, or resentment **16 in hot water** *informal* in trouble ▷ See also **hot up** ▶ HISTORY Old English *hāt* > **hotly** *adv*

hot air *n informal* empty and usually boastful talk

hotbed *n* a place offering ideal conditions for the growth of an idea or activity: *a hotbed of resistance*

hot-blooded *adj* passionate or excitable

hotchpotch *or esp US & Canad* **hodgepodge** *n* a jumbled mixture ▶ HISTORY Old French *hochepot* shake pot

hot-desking *n Brit, Austral & NZ* the practice of not assigning permanent desks in a workplace, so that employees may work at any available desk

hot dog *n* a long roll split lengthways with a hot sausage inside

hotel *n* a commercially run establishment providing lodging and meals for guests ▶ HISTORY French

hotelier *n* an owner or manager of a hotel

hotfoot *adv* with all possible speed: *hotfoot to the accident*

hot-headed *adj* impetuous or rash

hothouse *n* a greenhouse in which the temperature is maintained at a fixed level

hot key *n computers* a single key on a computer keyboard which carries out a series of commands

hotline *n* a direct telephone link between heads of government for emergency use

hotlink *n computers* an instant connection from one computer file to another

hot money *n* capital that is transferred from one financial centre to another seeking the best opportunity for short-term gain

hotplate *n* **1** a heated metal surface on an electric cooker **2** a portable device on which food can be kept warm

hot pool *n NZ* a geothermally heated pool

hotpot *n* a casserole of meat and vegetables covered with a layer of potatoes

hot rod *n* a car with an engine that has been modified to produce increased power

hot spot *n* **1** a place where there is a lot of exciting activity or entertainment **2** an area where there is fighting or political unrest **3** a small area of abnormally high temperature or radioactivity **4** a place from which the internet can be accessed by a wireless signal

Hottentot *n offensive* same as **Khoikhoi**

hotting *n Brit, informal* the performing of high-speed stunts in a stolen car > **hotter** *n*

hot up *vb* **hotting, hotted** *informal* to make or become more active and exciting

hot-water bottle *n* a rubber container, designed to be filled with hot water and used for warming a bed

hound *n* **1** a dog used for hunting: *to ride with the hounds* **2** a despicable person ▷ *vb* **3** to pursue, disturb, or criticize relentlessly: *hounded by the press* ▶ HISTORY Old English *hund*

hour *n* **1** a period of time equal to 60 minutes; ¹⁄₂₄ of a day **2** any of the points on the face of a clock or watch that indicate intervals of 60 minutes: *in my hurry I mistook the hour* **3** the time of day **4** the time allowed for or used for something: *a three and a half hour test* **5** the distance covered in an hour: *an hour from the heart of Tokyo* **6** a special moment: *the decisive hour* ▷ See also **hours** ▶ HISTORY Latin *hora*

hourglass *n* a device consisting of two transparent sections linked by a narrow channel, containing a quantity of sand that takes an hour to trickle from one section to the other

houri *n, pl* **-ris** (in Muslim belief) any of the nymphs of Paradise ▶ HISTORY Arabic *haurā'* woman with dark eyes

hourly *adj* **1** of, occurring, or done once every hour **2** measured by the hour: *hourly charges* **3** frequent ▷ *adv* **4** once every hour **5** by the hour: *hourly paid* **6** frequently **7** at any moment: *the arrival of the men was hourly expected*

hours *pl n* **1** an indefinite time: *they play on their bikes for hours* **2** a period regularly appointed for work or business **3** one's times of rising and going to bed: *you keep very late hours* **4** RC Church prayers recited at seven specified times of the day

Hours *pl n* classical myth the goddesses of the seasons

house *n, pl* **houses** **1** a building used as a home; dwelling **2** the people in a house **3** a building for some specific purpose: *beach house* **4** a family or dynasty: *the House of Windsor* **5** a commercial company: *auction house* **6** a law-making body or the place where it meets **7** a division of a large school: *he was captain of the house rugby team* **8** the audience in a theatre or cinema **9** *astrol* any of the 12 divisions of the zodiac **10** *informal* a brothel **11** **get on like a house on fire** *informal* (of people) to get on very well together **12** **on the house** (usually of drinks) paid for by the management **13** **put one's house in order** to settle or organize one's affairs ▷ *adj* **14** (of wine) sold unnamed by a restaurant, at a lower price than wines specified on the wine list: *house red* ▷ *vb* **housing, housed** **15** to give accommodation to **16** to contain or cover (something) ▶ HISTORY Old English *hūs*

house arrest *n* confinement to one's own home rather than in prison

houseboat *n* a stationary boat used as a home

housebound *adj* unable to leave one's house, usually because of illness

housebreaking *n* criminal law the act of entering a building as a trespasser for an unlawful purpose > **housebreaker** *n*

housecoat *n* a woman's loose robelike garment for casual wear

housefly *n, pl* **-flies** a common fly often found in houses

household *n* **1** all the people living together in one house ▷ *adj* **2** relating to the running of a household: *household budget*

householder *n* a person who owns or rents a house

household name *or* **word** *n* a person or thing that is very well known

housekeeper *n* a person employed to run someone else's household

housekeeping *n* **1** the running of a household **2** money allotted for this

house lights *pl n* the lights in the auditorium of a theatre or cinema

housemaid *n* (esp. formerly) a female servant employed to do housework

housemaid's knee *n* a fluid-filled swelling of the kneecap

houseman *n, pl* **-men** med a junior doctor in a hospital

house martin *n* a swallow with a slightly forked tail

House music *or* **House** *n* a type of disco music of the late 1980s, based on funk, with fragments of other recordings edited in electronically

House of Assembly *n* a legislative assembly or the lower chamber of such an assembly

House of Commons *n* (in Britain and Canada) the lower chamber of Parliament

House of Keys *n* the lower chamber of the law-making body of the Isle of Man

House of Lords *n* (in Britain) the upper chamber of Parliament, composed of the peers of the realm

House of Representatives *n* **1** (in the US) the lower chamber of Congress, or of many state legislatures **2** (in many countries) the lower chamber of Parliament **3** the sole chamber of New Zealand's Parliament

house-proud *adj* excessively concerned with the appearance, cleanliness, and tidiness of one's house

house-train *vb* to train (a pet) to urinate and defecate outside

house-warming *n* a party given after moving into a new home

housewife *n, pl* **-wives** a woman who runs her own household and does not have a paid job

housework *n* the work of running a home, such as cleaning, cooking, and shopping

housing *n* **1** houses collectively **2** the job of providing people with accommodation **3** a part designed to contain and support a component or mechanism: *the inspection panel set within the concrete housing*

hove *vb* chiefly naut a past of **heave**

hovea *n* an Australian plant with purple flowers

hovel *n* a small house or hut that is dirty or badly in need of repair ▶ HISTORY origin unknown

hover *vb* **1** (of a bird, insect, or helicopter) to remain suspended in one place in the air **2** to linger uncertainly in a place **3** to be in an unsettled or uncertain situation or frame of mind: *hovering between two options* ▶ HISTORY Middle English *hoveren*

h

hovercraft *n* a vehicle that is able to travel across both land and water on a cushion of air

how *adv* **1** in what way, by what means: *how did you spend the evening?*; observing *how elderly people coped* **2** to what extent: *they don't know how tough I am* **3** how good, how well, what … like: *how good are the copies?*; so *that's how things are* **4 how about?** used to suggest something: *how about some tea?* **5 how are you?** what is your state of health? **6 how's that? a** what is your opinion?: *we'll go out for a late-night supper – how's that?* **b** *cricket* Also written: **howzat** (an appeal to the umpire) is the batsman out? ▶ **HISTORY** Old English *hu*

howdah *n* a seat for riding on an elephant's back ▶ **HISTORY** Hindi *haudah*

however *adv* **1** still; nevertheless: *the book does, however, almost get funny* **2** by whatever means: *get there however you can* **3** (with an adjective or adverb) no matter how: *however low we plunge, there is always hope*

howitzer *n* a large gun that fires shells at a steep angle ▶ **HISTORY** Czech *houfnice* stone-sling

howl *n* **1** the long, loud wailing noise made by a wolf or a dog **2** a similar cry of pain or sorrow **3** a loud burst of laughter ▷ *vb* **4** to express (something) in a howl or utter such cries **5** (of the wind, etc.) to make a wailing noise ▶ **HISTORY** Middle English *houlen*

howler *n informal* a glaring mistake

how-to *adj* (of a book or guide) giving basic instructions to the lay person

howzit *sentence substitute* S African an informal word for hello ▶ **HISTORY** from the phrase *how is it?*

hoyden *n old-fashioned* a wild boisterous girl; tomboy ▶ **HISTORY** perhaps from Middle Dutch *heidijn* heathen > **hoydenish** *adj*

HP *or* **h.p.** **1** *Brit* hire-purchase **2** horsepower

HQ *or* **h.q.** headquarters

hr hour

HRH Her (or His) Royal Highness

HRT **1** hormone replacement therapy **2** *Austral & NZ* high rising terminal

Hs *chem* hassium

HTML *n computers* a text description language that is used on the World Wide Web ▶ **HISTORY** *hypertext markup language*

hub *n* **1** the central portion of a wheel, through which the axle passes **2** the central, most important, or active part of a place or organization ▶ **HISTORY** probably variant of *hob*

hubble-bubble *n* **1** same as **hookah 2** *archaic* turmoil or confusion ▶ **HISTORY** imitative

hubbub *n* **1** *written* a confused noise of many voices **2** great confusion or excitement ▶ **HISTORY** probably from Irish *hooboobbes*

hubby *n, pl* **-bies** *informal* a husband

hubcap *n* a metal disc that fits on to and protects the hub of a wheel, esp. on a car

hubris (**hew**-briss) *n formal* pride or arrogance ▶ **HISTORY** Greek > **hubristic** *adj*

huckster *n* **1** a person who uses aggressive methods of selling **2** *now rare* a person who sells

small articles or fruit in the street ▶ **HISTORY** probably from Middle Dutch *hoekster*

huddle *n* **1** a small group of people or things standing or lying close together **2 go into a huddle** *informal* to have a private conference ▷ *vb* **-dling, -dled 3** (of a group of people) to crowd or nestle closely together **4** to curl up one's arms and legs close to one's body through cold or fear ▶ **HISTORY** origin unknown

hue *n* **1** the feature of colour that enables an observer to classify it as red, blue, etc. **2** a shade of a colour ▶ **HISTORY** Old English *hīw* beauty

hue and cry *n written* a loud public outcry ▶ **HISTORY** Old French *hue* outcry

huff *n* **1** a passing mood of anger or resentment: *in a huff* ▷ *vb* **2** to blow or puff heavily **3** *draughts* to remove (an opponent's draught) from the board for failure to make a capture **4 huffing and puffing** empty threats or objections ▶ **HISTORY** imitative > **huffy** *adj* > **huffily** *adv*

hug *vb* **hugging, hugged 1** to clasp (someone or something) tightly, usually with affection **2** *written* to keep close to (a shore or the kerb) ▷ *n* **3** a tight or fond embrace ▶ **HISTORY** probably Scandinavian

huge *adj* extremely large ▶ **HISTORY** Old French *ahuge* > **hugely** *adv*

Huguenot (**hew**-gan-oh) *n* a French Calvinist of the 16th or 17th centuries ▶ **HISTORY** French

huh *interj* an exclamation of derision, bewilderment, or inquiry

hui (**hoo**-ee) *n NZ* **1** a Māori social gathering **2** a meeting to discuss Māori matters **3** any party ▶ **HISTORY** Māori

hula *n* a Hawaiian dance performed by a woman ▶ **HISTORY** Hawaiian

Hula Hoop *n trademark* a plastic hoop swung round the body by wiggling the hips

hulk *n* **1** the body of an abandoned ship **2** *disparaging* a large ungainly person or thing ▶ **HISTORY** Old English *hulc*

hulking *adj* big and ungainly

hull *n* **1** the main body of a boat **2** the outer covering of a fruit or seed such as a pea or bean **3** the leaves round the stem of a strawberry, raspberry, or similar fruit ▷ *vb* **4** to remove the hulls from (fruit or seeds) ▶ **HISTORY** Old English *hulu*

hullabaloo *n, pl* **-loos** a loud confused noise or commotion ▶ **HISTORY** *hallo* + Scots *baloo* lullaby

hullo *interj, n* same as **hello**

hum *vb* **humming, hummed 1** to make a low continuous vibrating sound **2** (of a person) to sing with the lips closed **3** to utter an indistinct sound when hesitating **4** *informal* to be in a state of feverish activity: *the town hums with activity and life* **5** *slang* to smell unpleasant **6 hum and haw** See **haw²** ▷ *n* **7** a low continuous murmuring sound **8** an unpleasant smell ▷ *interj, n* **9** an indistinct sound of hesitation ▶ **HISTORY** imitative

human *adj* **1** of or relating to people: *human occupants* **2** having the qualities of people as opposed to animals, divine beings, or machines:

h

human nature **3** kind or considerate ▷ *n* **4** a human being ▶ HISTORY Latin *humanus*

human being *n* a man, woman, or child

human capital *n econ* the abilities and skills of a person that enhance the potential for earning

Human Development Index *n* a way of measuring the development of a country by using comparative data concerning life expectancy, adult literacy, the standard of living, etc.

humane *adj* **1** showing kindness and sympathy **2** inflicting as little pain as possible: *a humane method of killing minke whales* **3** considered to have a civilizing effect on people: *the humane tradition of a literary education* ▶ HISTORY variant of *human*

human geography *n* the branch of geography that deals with the impact that people have on the earth's surface

humanism *n* the rejection of religion in favour of a belief in the advancement of humanity by its own efforts > **humanist** *n, adj* > **humanistic** *adj*

humanitarian *adj* **1** having the interests of mankind at heart: *humanitarian aid* ▷ *n* **2** a person who has the interests of mankind at heart > **humanitarianism** *n*

humanity *n, pl* **-ties 1** the human race **2** the quality of being human **3** kindness or mercy **4 humanities** the study of literature, philosophy, and the arts

humanize *or* **-ise** *vb* **-izing, -ized** *or* **-ising, -ised** to make human or humane

humankind *n* the human race; humanity

humanly *adv* by human powers or means: *as fast as is humanly possible*

humanoid *adj* **1** like a human being in appearance ▷ *n* **2** (in science fiction) a robot or creature resembling a human being

human race *n* all men, women, and children collectively

human resources *pl n* **1** the people employed in an organization or for a service **2** (functioning as sing) the department in an organization that appoints or keeps records of employees

human rights *pl n* the basic rights of individuals to liberty, justice, etc.

humble *adj* **1** conscious of one's failings **2** modest and unpretentious: *humble domestic objects* **3** ordinary or not very important: *humble beginnings* ▷ *vb* **-bling, -bled 4** to cause to become humble; humiliate ▶ HISTORY Latin *humilis* low > **humbly** *adv*

humbug *n* **1** *Brit* a hard peppermint sweet with a striped pattern **2** a speech or piece of writing that is obviously untrue, dishonest, or nonsense **3** a dishonest person ▶ HISTORY origin unknown

humdinger *n slang* **1** something unusually large **2** an excellent person or thing ▶ HISTORY origin unknown

humdrum *adj* ordinary, dull, and uninteresting ▶ HISTORY probably based on *hum*

humerus (hew-mer-uss) *n, pl* **-meri** (-mer-rye) the bone from the shoulder to the elbow ▶ HISTORY Latin *umerus* > **humeral** *adj*

humid *adj* (of the weather) damp and warm ▶ HISTORY Latin *umidus*

humidex (hew-mid-ex) *n Canad* a system of measuring discomfort showing the combined effect of humidity and temperature

humidify *vb* **-fies, -fying, -fied** to make the air in (a room) more humid or damp > **humidifier** *n*

humidity *n* **1** dampness **2** a measure of the amount of moisture in the air

humiliate *vb* **-ating, -ated** to hurt the dignity or pride of: *the English cricket team was humiliated by Australia* ▶ HISTORY Latin *humilis* humble > **humiliating** *adj* > **humiliation** *n*

humility *n* the quality of being humble and modest

hummingbird *n* a very small brightly-coloured American bird with a long slender bill, and powerful wings that hum as they vibrate

hummock *n* a very small hill or a mound ▶ HISTORY origin unknown

humongous *or* **humungous** *adj informal* exceptionally large ▶ HISTORY origin unknown

humorist *n* a person who speaks or writes in a humorous way

humorous *adj* amusing, esp. in a witty or clever way > **humorously** *adv*

humour *or US* **humor** *n* **1** the quality of being funny **2** the ability to appreciate or express things that are humorous: *a sense of humour* **3** situations, speech, or writings that are humorous **4** a state of mind; mood: *in astoundingly good humour* **5** *archaic* any of various fluids in the body: *aqueous humour* ▷ *vb* **6** to be kind and indulgent to: *he decided the patient needed to be humoured* ▶ HISTORY Latin *humor* liquid > **humourless** *adj*

hump *n* **1** a rounded lump on the ground **2** a rounded deformity of the back **3** a rounded lump on the back of a camel or related animal **4 the hump** *Brit, informal* a fit of sulking ▷ *vb* **5** *slang* to carry or heave: *they were injured humping heavy gear around* ▶ HISTORY probably from *humpbacked*

humpback *n* **1** same as **hunchback 2** Also called: **humpback whale** a large whalebone whale with a hump on its back **3** Also called: **humpback bridge** *Brit* a road bridge with a sharp slope on either side > **humpbacked** *adj*

humus (hew-muss) *n* a dark brown or black mass of partially decomposed plant and animal matter in the soil ▶ HISTORY Latin: soil

Hun *n, pl* **Huns** *or* **Hun 1** a member of any of several Asiatic peoples who invaded the Roman Empire in the 4th and 5th centuries AD **2** *offensive, informal* (esp. in World War I) a German ▶ HISTORY Old English *Hūnas*

hunch *n* **1** a feeling or suspicion not based on facts: *she said that she had had a hunch that the coup would not succeed* **2** same as **hump** ▷ *vb* **3** to draw (oneself or one's shoulders) up or together ▶ HISTORY origin unknown

hunchback *n* a person who has an abnormal curvature of the spine > **hunchbacked** *adj*

h

hundred *n, pl* **-dreds** *or* **-dred 1** the cardinal number that is the product of ten and ten **2** a numeral, 100 or C, representing this number **3** (often pl) a large but unspecified number ▷ *adj* **4** amounting to a hundred: *a hundred yards* ▶ **HISTORY** Old English > **hundredth** *adj, n*

Hundred Flowers Campaign *n history* a period of debate in China in 1956–57, when people were encouraged to express their opinions of the government ▶ **HISTORY** from the slogan 'Let a hundred flowers bloom and a hundred schools of thought contend'

hundredweight *n, pl* **-weights** *or* **-weight 1** *Brit* a unit of weight equal to 112 pounds or 50.802kg **2** *US & Canad* a unit of weight equal to 100 pounds or 45.359kg **3** a metric unit of weight equal to 50 kilograms

hung *vb* **1** the past of **hang** ▷ *adj* **2** (of a parliament or jury) with no side having a clear majority **3 hung over** *informal* suffering the effects of a hangover

Hungarian *adj* **1** of Hungary ▷ *n* **2** a person from Hungary **3** the language of Hungary

hunger *n* **1** a feeling of emptiness or weakness caused by lack of food **2** a lack of food that causes suffering or death **3** desire or craving ▷ *vb* **4 hunger for** *written* to have a great desire for ▶ **HISTORY** Old English *hungor*

hunger strike *n* a refusal of all food, usually by a prisoner, as a means of protest

hungry *adj* **-grier, -griest 1** desiring food **2** (foll. by *for*) having a craving, desire, or need for: *hungry for revenge* **3** expressing greed, craving, or desire: *the media's hungry search for news* > **hungrily** *adv*

hunk *n* **1** a large piece: *a hunk of bread* **2** *slang* a well-built, attractive man ▶ **HISTORY** probably related to Flemish *hunke*

hunt *vb* **1** to seek out and kill (animals) for food or sport **2 hunt for** to search for **3 hunt down** to track in an attempt to capture (someone): *hunting down villains* ▷ *n* **4** the act or an instance of hunting **5** a party organized for the pursuit of wild animals for sport **6** the members of such a party ▶ **HISTORY** Old English *huntian* > **hunting** *n*

huntaway *n* *NZ* a sheepdog trained to drive sheep by barking

hunter *n* **1** a person or animal that seeks out and kills or captures game **2** a person who looks carefully for something: *a house hunter* **3** a horse or dog bred for hunting **4** a watch with a hinged metal lid or case to protect the glass

hunter-gatherer *n* a member of a society that lives by hunting and gathering naturally occurring resources

huntsman *n, pl* **-men 1** a person who hunts **2** a person who trains hounds and manages them during a hunt

hurdle *n* **1** *athletics* one of a number of light barriers over which runners leap in certain events **2** a difficulty or problem: *the main technical hurdle is the environment* **3 hurdles** a race involving hurdles ▷ *vb* **-dling, -dled 4** to jump over (a hurdle or other obstacle) ▶ **HISTORY** Old English *hyrdel* > **hurdler** *n*

hurdy-gurdy *n, pl* **hurdy-gurdies** a mechanical musical instrument, such as a barrel organ ▶ **HISTORY** probably imitative

hurl *vb* **1** to throw (something) with great force **2** to utter (something) with force; yell: *onlookers hurled abuse at them* ▶ **HISTORY** probably imitative

hurling *or* **hurley** *n* a traditional Irish game resembling hockey

hurly-burly *n* great noise and activity; commotion ▶ **HISTORY** obsolete *hurling* uproar

hurrah *or* **hooray** *interj, n* a cheer of joy or victory ▶ **HISTORY** probably from German *hurra*

hurricane *n* a severe, often destructive storm, esp. a tropical cyclone ▶ **HISTORY** Spanish *huracán*

hurricane lamp *n* a paraffin lamp with a glass covering

hurried *adj* done quickly or too quickly > **hurriedly** *adv* > **hurriedness** *n*

hurry *vb* **-ries, -rying, -ried 1** to move or act or cause to move or act in great haste: *the umpires hurried the players off the ground* **2** to speed up the completion or progress of: *eat a small snack rather than hurry a main meal* ▷ *n* **3** haste **4** urgency or eagerness **5 in a hurry** *informal* **a** easily: *striking old guy, not the sort you'd forget in a hurry* **b** willingly: *he would not ease interest rates again in a hurry* ▶ **HISTORY** probably imitative

hurt *vb* **hurting, hurt 1** to cause physical or mental injury to: *is she badly hurt?* **2** to cause someone to feel pain: *my head hurt* **3** *informal* to feel pain: *she was hurting* ▷ *n* **4** physical or mental pain or suffering ▷ *adj* **5** injured or pained: *his hurt head; a hurt expression* ▶ **HISTORY** Old French *hurter* to knock against > **hurtful** *adj*

hurtle *vb* **-ling, -led** to move very quickly or violently ▶ **HISTORY** Middle English *hurtlen*

husband *n* **1** a woman's partner in marriage ▷ *vb* **2** to use (resources, finances, etc.) economically ▶ **HISTORY** Old English *hūsbonda*

husbandry *n* **1** the art or skill of farming **2** management of resources

hush *vb* **1** to make or be silent ▷ *n* **2** stillness or silence ▷ *interj* **3** a plea or demand for silence ▶ **HISTORY** earlier *husht* quiet! > **hushed** *adj*

hush-hush *adj* *informal* (esp. of official work) secret and confidential

hush money *n* *slang* money given to a person to ensure that something is kept secret

hush up *vb* to suppress information or rumours about (something)

husk *n* **1** the outer covering of certain fruits and seeds ▷ *vb* **2** to remove the husk from ▶ **HISTORY** probably from Middle Dutch *hūs* house

husky[1] *adj* **huskier, huskiest 1** (of a voice) slightly hoarse **2** *informal* (of a man) big and strong ▶ **HISTORY** probably from *husk*, from the toughness of a corn husk > **huskily** *adv*

husky[2] *n, pl* **huskies** an Arctic sledge dog with thick hair and a curled tail ▶ **HISTORY** probably based on *Eskimo*

hussar (hoo-**zar**) *n history* a member of a light cavalry regiment ▶ **HISTORY** Hungarian *huszár*

407

hussy n, pl **-sies** old-fashioned a woman considered immoral or improper ▶ HISTORY from hussif housewife

hustings pl n the campaigns and speeches at a parliamentary election ▶ HISTORY Old Norse hūsthing, from hūs house + thing assembly

hustle vb **-tling, -tled** 1 to make (someone) move by pushing or jostling them: he hustled her away 2 to deal with (something) hurriedly: they did not heedlessly hustle the tempo 3 US & Canad, slang (of a prostitute) to solicit clients ▷ n 4 lively activity and excitement ▶ HISTORY Dutch husselen to shake

hut n a small house or shelter ▶ HISTORY French hutte

hutch n a cage for small animals ▶ HISTORY Old French huche

hyacinth n a plant with bell-shaped sweet-smelling flowers ▶ HISTORY Greek huakinthos

hyaena n same as **hyena**

hybrid n 1 an animal or plant resulting from a cross between two different types of animal or plant 2 anything that is a mixture of two different things 3 a vehicle powered by an internal-combustion engine and another source of power, especially an electric motor ▷ adj 4 of mixed origin 5 (of a vehicle) powered by more than one source ▶ HISTORY Latin hibrida

hybridize or **-ise** vb **-izing, -ized** or **-ising, -ised** to produce or cause (species) to produce hybrids; crossbreed > **hybridization** or **-isation** n

hydra n 1 a mythical many-headed serpent 2 a persistent problem 3 a microscopic freshwater creature with a slender tubular body and tentacles around the mouth ▶ HISTORY Greek hudra water serpent

hydrangea n an ornamental shrub with large clusters of white, pink, or blue flowers ▶ HISTORY Greek hudōr water + angeion vessel

hydrant n an outlet from a water main, from which water can be tapped for fighting fires

hydrate chem n 1 a compound containing water chemically combined with a substance: chloral hydrate ▷ vb **-drating, -drated** 2 to treat (a substance) with water > **hydration** n

hydraulic adj operated by pressure transmitted through a pipe by a liquid, such as water or oil ▶ HISTORY Greek hudōr water + aulos pipe > **hydraulically** adv

hydraulic erosion n geog erosion caused by moving water

hydraulic fracturing n same as **fracking**

hydraulics n the study of the mechanical properties of fluids as they apply to practical engineering

hydride n chem a compound of hydrogen with another element

hydro¹ n, pl **-dros** Brit a hotel offering facilities for hydropathic treatment

hydro² adj short for **hydroelectric**

hydro- or before a vowel **hydr-** combining form 1 indicating water or fluid: hydrodynamics 2 chem indicating hydrogen in a chemical compound: hydrochloric acid ▶ HISTORY Greek hudōr water

hydrocarbon n chem a compound containing only carbon and hydrogen

hydrocephalus n accumulation of fluid in the cavities of the brain, causing enlargement of the head in children ▶ HISTORY Greek hudōr water + kephalē head > **hydrocephalic** adj

hydrochloric acid n chem a solution of hydrogen chloride in water: a strong acid used in many industrial and laboratory processes

hydrodynamics n the branch of science concerned with the mechanical properties of fluids

hydroelectric adj 1 generated by the pressure of falling water: hydroelectric power 2 of the generation of electricity by water pressure: a hydroelectric scheme > **hydroelectricity** n

hydrofoil n 1 a fast light vessel the hull of which is raised out of the water on one or more pairs of fins 2 any of these fins

hydrogen n chem a colourless gas that burns easily and is the lightest element in the universe. It occurs in water and in most organic compounds. Symbol: H ▶ HISTORY HYDRO- + -gen (producing); because its combustion produces water > **hydrogenous** adj

hydrogenate (hide-**roj**-in-nate) vb **-ating, -ated** chem to combine (a substance) with hydrogen: hydrogenated vegetable oil > **hydrogenation** n

hydrogen bomb n an extremely powerful bomb in which energy is released by fusion of hydrogen nuclei to give helium nuclei

hydrogen peroxide n a colourless oily unstable liquid chemical used as a hair bleach and as an antiseptic

hydrogen sulphide n a colourless poisonous gas with an odour of rotten eggs

hydrograph n geog a graph showing variations in the amount of water in a river over a period of time

hydrography (hide-**rog**-ra-fee) n the study of the oceans, seas, and rivers > **hydrographic** adj

hydrolase n biochem an enzyme that controls hydrolysis

hydrologic cycle n geog same as **water cycle**

hydrology n the study of the distribution, conservation, and use of the water of the earth and its atmosphere

hydrolysis (hide-**rol**-iss-iss) n chem a process of decomposition in which a compound reacts with water to produce other compounds ▶ HISTORY Greek hudōr water + lusis a loosening

hydrometer (hide-**rom**-it-er) n an instrument for measuring the density of a liquid

hydropathy n a method of treating disease by the use of large quantities of water both internally and externally ▶ HISTORY Greek hudōr water + patheia suffering > **hydropathic** adj

hydrophilic adj chem tending to dissolve in or mix with water: a hydrophilic layer

hydrophobia n 1 same as **rabies** 2 a fear of drinking fluids > **hydrophobic** adj

hydrophyte *n* *bot* a plant that grows only in water or very moist soil > **hydrophytic** *adj*

hydroplane *n* **1** a motorboat that raises its hull out of the water at high speeds **2** a fin on the hull of a submarine for controlling its vertical motion

hydroponics *n* *agriculture* a method of growing plants in gravel, etc. through which water containing the necessary nutrients is pumped ▶ HISTORY HYDRO- + (*geo*)*ponics* science of agriculture

hydrosphere *n* the watery part of the earth's surface

hydrostatics *n* the branch of science concerned with the properties and behaviour of fluids that are not in motion > **hydrostatic** *adj*

hydrotherapy *n* *med* the treatment of certain diseases by exercise in water

hydrotropism *n* *bot* the growth of plants in response to the stimulus of water

hydrous *adj* containing water

hydroxide *n* *chem* a compound containing a hydroxyl group or ion

hydroxyl *adj* *chem* of or containing the monovalent group –OH or the ion OH⁻: *forming a hydroxyl radical*

hyena *or* **hyaena** *n* a meat-eating doglike mammal of Africa and S Asia ▶ HISTORY Greek *hus* hog

hygiene *n* **1** the principles and practices of health and cleanliness: *personal hygiene* **2** Also called: **hygienics** the science concerned with the maintenance of health ▶ HISTORY Greek *hugieinē* > **hygienic** *adj* > **hygienically** *adv* > **hygienist** *n*

hygrometer (hie-**grom**-it-er) *n* an instrument for measuring humidity ▶ HISTORY Greek *hugros* wet

hygroscope *n* any device that indicates the humidity of the air without necessarily measuring it, such as an animal or vegetable fibre which contracts with moisture ▶ HISTORY Greek *hugros* wet + *skopein* to observe

hygroscopic *adj* (of a substance) tending to absorb water from the air

hymen *n* *anat* a membrane that partly covers the entrance to the vagina and is usually ruptured when sexual intercourse takes place for the first time ▶ HISTORY Greek: membrane

hymenopterous *adj* of or belonging to an order of insects with two pairs of membranous wings ▶ HISTORY Greek *humen* membrane + *pteron* wing

hymn *n* a Christian song of praise sung to God or a saint ▶ HISTORY Greek *humnos*

hymnal *n* a book of hymns. Also: **hymn book**

hype *slang n* **1** intensive or exaggerated publicity or sales promotion ▷ *vb* **hyping, hyped 2** to market or promote (a commodity) using intensive or exaggerated publicity ▶ HISTORY origin unknown

hyper *adj* *informal* overactive or overexcited

hyper- *prefix* above, over, or in excess: *hypercritical* ▶ HISTORY Greek *huper* over

hyperactive *adj* (of a person) unable to relax and always in a state of restless activity

hyperbola (hie-**per**-bol-a) *n* *geom* a curve produced when a cone is cut by a plane at a steeper angle to its base than its side ▶ HISTORY Greek *huperbolē*

hyperbole (hie-**per**-bol-ee) *n* a deliberate exaggeration of speech or writing used for effect, such as *he embraced her a thousand times* ▶ HISTORY Greek *huper* over + *ballein* to throw

hyperbolic *or* **hyperbolical** *adj* of a hyperbola or a hyperbole

hyperglycaemia *or US* **hyperglycemia** (hie-per-glice-**seem**-ee-a) *n* *pathol* an abnormally large amount of sugar in the blood ▶ HISTORY Greek *huper* over + *glukus* sweet

hyperinflation *n* *econ* extremely high inflation, usually over 50% per month

hyperlink *computers n* **1** a link from a hypertext file that gives users instant access to related material in another file ▷ *vb* **2** to link (files) in this way

hypermarket *n* a huge self-service store ▶ HISTORY translation of French *hypermarché*

hypersensitive *adj* **1** unduly emotionally vulnerable **2** abnormally sensitive to an allergen, a drug, or high or low temperatures

hypersonic *adj* having a speed of at least five times the speed of sound

hypertension *n* *pathol* abnormally high blood pressure

hypertext *n* computer software and hardware that allows users to store and view text and move between related items easily

hypertonic *adj* (of a solution) having a higher osmotic pressure than a specified solution

hypertrophy (hie-**per**-trof-fee) *n*, *pl* **-phies** enlargement of an organ or part resulting from an increase in the size of the cells ▶ HISTORY Greek *huper* over + *trophē* nourishment

hyperventilation *n* an increase in the rate of breathing at rest, sometimes resulting in cramp and dizziness > **hyperventilate** *vb*

hyphen *n* the punctuation mark (-), used to separate parts of compound words and between syllables of a word split between two consecutive lines ▶ HISTORY Greek *huphen* together

hyphenate *vb* **-ating, -ated** to separate (words) with a hyphen > **hyphenation** *n*

hyphenated *adj* having two words or syllables connected by a hyphen

hypnosis *n* an artificially induced state of relaxation in which the mind is more than usually receptive to suggestion

hypnotherapy *n* the use of hypnosis in the treatment of emotional and mental problems > **hypnotherapist** *n*

hypnotic *adj* **1** of or producing hypnosis or sleep **2** having an effect resembling hypnosis: *the film makes for hypnotic viewing* ▷ *n* **3** a drug that induces sleep ▶ HISTORY Greek *hupnos* sleep > **hypnotically** *adv*

hypnotism *n* the practice of or process of inducing hypnosis > **hypnotist** *n*

h

hypnotize or **-tise** vb **-tizing, -tized** or **-tising, -tised 1** to induce hypnosis in (a person) **2** to hold the attention of (someone) completely; fascinate; mesmerize: *hypnotized by her beauty*

hypo- or before a vowel **hyp-** prefix beneath; less than: *hypodermic* ▸ HISTORY Greek *hupo* under

hypoallergenic adj not likely to cause an allergic reaction

hypocaust n an ancient Roman heating system in which hot air circulated under the floor and between double walls ▸ HISTORY Latin *hypocaustum*

hypochondria n abnormal anxiety concerning one's health ▸ HISTORY Late Latin: abdomen, supposedly the seat of melancholy

hypochondriac n a person abnormally concerned about his or her health

hypocrisy (hip-**ok**-rass-ee) n, pl **-sies 1** the practice of claiming to have standards or beliefs that are contrary to one's real character or actual behaviour **2** an act or instance of this

hypocrite (hip-oh-krit) n a person who pretends to be what he or she is not ▸ HISTORY Greek *hupokrinein* to pretend > **hypocritical** adj

hypodermic adj **1** used for injecting ▷ n **2** a hypodermic syringe or needle

hypodermic syringe n med a syringe consisting of a hollow cylinder, a piston, and a hollow needle, used for withdrawing blood samples or injecting drugs under the skin

hypotension n pathol abnormally low blood pressure

hypotenuse (hie-**pot**-a-news) n the side in a right-angled triangle that is opposite the right angle ▸ HISTORY Greek *hupoteinousa grammē* subtending line

hypothalamus n, pl **-mi** an area at the base of the brain, which controls hunger, thirst, and other functions

hypothermia n pathol an abnormally low body temperature, as a result of exposure to cold

hypothesis (hie-**poth**-iss-iss) n, pl **-ses** (-seez) a suggested explanation for a group of facts, accepted either as a basis for further verification or as likely to be true ▸ HISTORY Greek *hupotithenai* to propose, literally: put under > **hypothesize** or **-ise** vb

hypothetical adj based on assumption rather than fact or reality > **hypothetically** adv

hypotonic adj (of a solution) having a lower osmotic pressure than a specified solution

hyrax (**hire**-ax) n, pl **hyraxes** or **hyraces** (**hire**-a-seez) a genus of hoofed rodent-like animals

hyssop n **1** an aromatic plant used in herbal medicine **2** a Biblical plant, used for sprinkling in the ritual practices of the Hebrews ▸ HISTORY Greek *hussōpos*

hysterectomy n, pl **-mies** surgical removal of the womb ▸ HISTORY Greek *hustera* womb + *tomē* a cutting

hysteria n **1** a mental disorder marked by emotional outbursts and, often, symptoms such as paralysis **2** any uncontrolled emotional state, such as panic, anger, or excitement ▸ HISTORY Greek *hustera* womb, from the belief that hysteria in women originated in disorders of the womb

hysteric n a hysterical person

hysterical adj **1** in a state of uncontrolled panic, anger, or excitement: *a crazy hysterical adolescent* **2** informal wildly funny > **hysterically** adv

hysterics n **1** an attack of hysteria **2** informal wild uncontrollable bursts of laughter

Hz hertz

Ii

i the imaginary number √−1

I[1] *pron* used by a speaker or writer to refer to himself or herself as the subject of a verb ▶ HISTORY Old English *ic*

I[2] **1** *chem* iodine **2** the Roman numeral for one

I. **1** Independent **2** Institute **3** International **4** Island **5** Isle

IA Iowa

iamb (**eye**-am) or **iambus** *n, pl* **iambs** or **iambuses** *prosody* a metrical foot of two syllables, a short one followed by a long one ▶ HISTORY Greek *iambos*

iambic (eye-**am**-bik) *prosody adj* **1** written in metrical units of one short and one long syllable ▷ *n* **2** an iambic foot, line, or stanza

iambic pentameter *n prosody* (in poetry) a pattern consisting of five iambs commonly used in blank verse

IBA (in Britain) Independent Broadcasting Authority

Iberian *adj* **1** of Iberia, the peninsula made up of Spain and Portugal ▷ *n* **2** a person from Iberia

ibex (**ibe**-eks) *n, pl* **ibexes** or **ibex** a wild mountain goat with large backward-curving horns ▶ HISTORY Latin: chamois

ibid. in the same place: used to refer to a book, page, or passage previously cited ▶ HISTORY Latin *ibidem*

ibis (**ibe**-iss) *n, pl* **ibises** or **ibis** a large wading bird with a long thin curved bill ▶ HISTORY Egyptian *hby*

Ibo (**ee**-boh) *n* **1** (*pl* **Ibos** or **Ibo**) a member of an African people of S Nigeria **2** their language

ICBM intercontinental ballistic missile

ice *n* **1** water that has frozen and become solid **2** *chiefly Brit* a portion of ice cream **3 break the ice** to relax the atmosphere, esp. between strangers **4 on ice** in readiness or reserve **5 on thin ice** in an dangerous situation: *he knew he was on thin ice* **6 the Ice** *NZ, informal* Antarctica ▷ *vb* **icing, iced** **7** (foll. by *up* or *over*) to become covered with ice **8** to cover with icing **9** to cool or chill with ice ▶ HISTORY Old English *īs*

ice age *n* **1** any period of time during which a large part of the earth's surface was covered with ice, caused by the advance of glaciers **2** the Pleistocene epoch

iceberg *n* **1** a large mass of ice floating in the sea **2 tip of the iceberg** the small visible part of a problem that is much larger

■ **WORD HISTORY**
■ An iceberg is an 'ice mountain'. The word is a
■ partial translation of the Dutch word *ijsberg*,
■ from *ijs*, meaning 'ice', and *berg*, meaning
■ 'mountain'.

icebox *n* **1** *US & Canad* a refrigerator **2** a compartment in a refrigerator for making or storing ice **3** a container packed with ice for keeping food and drink cold

icebreaker *n* **1** a ship designed to break a channel through ice **2** something intended to relieve mutual shyness at a social gathering

icebreaker question *n* a question designed to get people talking in a relaxed way at a social or business gathering

icecap *n* a thick mass of glacial ice that permanently covers an area

ice cream *n* a sweet frozen food, made from cream, milk, or a custard base, flavoured in various ways

iced *adj* **1** served very cold **2** covered with icing

ice field *n* a large expanse of floating sea ice

ice floe *n* a sheet of ice floating in the sea

ice hockey *n* a game like hockey played on ice by two teams wearing skates

Icelander *adj* a person from Iceland

Icelandic *adj* **1** of Iceland ▷ *n* **2** the official language of Iceland

ice lolly *n* *Brit, informal* a water ice or an ice cream on a stick

ice pack *n* **1** a bag or folded cloth containing crushed ice, applied to a part of the body to reduce swelling **2** *geog* same as **pack ice**

ice skate *n* **1** a boot with a steel blade fitted to the sole which enables the wearer to glide over ice ▷ *vb* **ice-skate, -skating, -skated** **2** to glide over ice on ice skates > **ice-skater** *n*

I Ching *n* an ancient Chinese book of divination and a source of Confucian and Taoist philosophy

ichneumon (ik-**new**-mon) *n* a greyish-brown mongoose

ichthyology (ik-thi-**ol**-a-jee) *n* the study of fishes ▶ HISTORY Greek *ikhthus* fish + -LOGY > **ichthyological** *adj* > **ichthyologist** *n*

icicle *n* a tapering spike of ice hanging where water has dripped ▶ HISTORY from ICE + Old English *gicel* icicle

icing *n* **1** Also (esp. US and Canad.): **frosting** a mixture of sugar and water or egg whites used to cover and decorate cakes **2 icing on the cake** any unexpected extra or bonus **3** the formation of ice on a ship or aircraft

icing sugar *n* *Brit & Austral* a very finely ground sugar used for making icing or sweets

icon or **ikon** *n* **1** a picture of Christ, the Virgin Mary, or a saint, venerated in the Orthodox Church **2** a picture on a computer screen representing a computer function that can be activated by moving the cursor over it **3** a person or thing regarded as a symbol of a belief or cultural movement: *a feminist icon* ▶ HISTORY Greek *eikōn* image

iconoclast n **1** a person who attacks established or traditional ideas or principles **2** a destroyer of religious images or objects ▶ HISTORY Late Greek *eikōn* icon + *klastēs* breaker > **iconoclastic** adj > **iconoclasm** n

icosahedron (ike-oh-sa-**heed**-ron) n, pl **-drons** or **-dra** (-dra) a solid figure with 20 faces ▶ HISTORY Greek *eikosi* twenty + *-edron* -sided

ICT Information and Communications Technology

icy adj **icier, iciest 1** freezing or very cold **2** covered with ice: *an icy runway* **3** cold or reserved in manner > **icily** adv > **iciness** n

id n *psychoanal* the primitive instincts and energies in the unconscious mind that underlie all psychological impulses ▶ HISTORY Latin: it

ID 1 Idaho **2** identification

idea n **1** any product of mental activity; thought **2** a scheme, intention, or plan **3** the thought of something: *the idea excites me* **4** a belief or opinion **5** a vague notion; inkling: *they had no idea of the severity of my injuries* **6** a person's conception of something: *his idea of integrity is not the same as mine* **7** aim or purpose: *the idea is to economize on transport* **8** *philosophy* (in Plato) a universal model of which all things in the same class are only imperfect imitations ▶ HISTORY Greek: model, outward appearance

ideal n **1** a conception of something that is perfect **2** a person or thing considered to represent perfection **3** something existing only as an idea ▷ adj **4** most suitable: *they seem to have adopted an ideal man as their candidate* **5** of, involving, or existing only as an idea; imaginary: *an ideal world* > **ideally** adv

idealism n **1** belief in or striving towards ideals **2** the tendency to represent things in their ideal forms, rather than as they are **3** *philosophy* the doctrine that material objects and the external world do not exist in reality, but are creations of the mind > **idealist** n > **idealistic** adj

idealize or **-ise** vb **-izing, -ized** or **-ising, -ised** to consider or represent (something) as ideal or more nearly perfect than is true > **idealization** or **-isation** n

idem pron, adj the same: used to refer to an article, chapter, or book already quoted ▶ HISTORY Latin

identical adj **1** that is the same: *they got the identical motel room as last year* **2** exactly alike or equal **3** (of twins) developed from a single fertilized ovum that has split into two, and thus of the same sex and very much alike ▶ HISTORY Latin *idem* the same > **identically** adv

identification parade n a group of people, including one suspected of a crime, assembled to discover whether a witness can identify the suspect

identify vb **-fies, -fying, -fied 1** to prove or recognize as being a certain person or thing; determine the identity of **2** (often foll. by *with*) to understand and sympathize with a person or group because one regards oneself as being similar or similarly situated **3** to consider or treat as the same **4** to connect or associate closely: *he was closely identified with the community charge* > **identifiable** adj > **identification** n

Identikit n *trademark* (formerly) a composite picture, assembled from descriptions given, of a person wanted by the police

identity n, pl **-ties 1** the state of being a specified person or thing: *the identity of his murderers was not immediately established* **2** the individual characteristics by which a person or thing is recognized **3** the state of being the same **4** *maths* Also called: **identity element** a member of a set that when combined with any other member of the set, leaves it unchanged: *the identity for multiplication of numbers is* 1 ▶ HISTORY Latin *idem* the same

identity theft n the crime of fraudulently setting up and using bank accounts, credit facilities, etc. in another person's name

identity transformation n *maths* (in transformational geometry) the process of changing the form of an identity without changing its value

ideo- *combining form* of or indicating ideas. *ideology* ▶ HISTORY from French *idéo-*, from Greek *idea* idea

ideogram or **ideograph** n a character or symbol that directly represents a concept or thing, rather than the sounds that form its name ▶ HISTORY Greek *idea* idea + *gramma* a drawing

ideology n, pl **-gies** the body of ideas and beliefs of a person, group, or nation ▶ HISTORY from IDEO- + -LOGY > **ideological** adj > **ideologically** adv > **ideologist** n

ides n (in the ancient Roman calendar) the 15th day in March, May, July, and October and the 13th of the other months ▶ HISTORY Latin *idus*

idiocy n, pl **-cies 1** utter stupidity **2** a foolish act or remark

idiolect n *linguistics* the personal variety of language unique to an individual

idiom n **1** a group of words which, when used together, have a different meaning from the one suggested by the individual words, e.g. *it was raining cats and dogs* **2** linguistic usage that is grammatical and natural to native speakers **3** the characteristic vocabulary or usage of a person or group **4** the characteristic artistic style of an individual or school ▶ HISTORY Greek *idios* private, separate > **idiomatic** adj

idiosyncrasy n, pl **-sies** a personal peculiarity of mind, habit, or behaviour; quirk ▶ HISTORY Greek *idios* private, separate + *sunkrasis* mixture > **idiosyncratic** adj

idiot n **1** a foolish or senseless person ▶ HISTORY Greek *idiōtēs* private person, ignoramus > **idiotic** adj > **idiotically** adv

idle adj **1** not doing anything **2** not operating or being used **3** not wanting to work; lazy **4** ineffective or useless: *it would be idle to look for a solution at this stage* **5** frivolous or trivial: *idle pleasures* **6** without basis; unfounded: *idle rumours*

▷ *vb* **idling, idled 7** (often foll. by *away*) to waste or pass (time) in idleness **8** (of an engine) to run at low speed without transmitting any power ▶ HISTORY Old English *īdel* > **idleness** *n* > **idler** *n* > **idly** *adv*

idol (**eye**-dl) *n* **1** an object of excessive devotion or admiration **2** an image of a god used as an object of worship ▶ HISTORY Greek *eidōlon* image

idolatry (ide-**ol**-a-tree) *n* **1** the worship of idols **2** excessive devotion or reverence > **idolater** *n* > **idolatrous** *adj*

idolize *or* **-ise** *vb* **-izing, -ized** *or* **-ising, -ised 1** to love or admire excessively **2** to worship as an idol > **idolization** *or* **-isation** *n*

idyll *or US sometimes* **idyl** (**id**-ill) *n* **1** a scene or time of peace and happiness **2** a poem or prose work describing a charming rural scene or episode ▶ HISTORY Greek *eidullion* > **idyllic** *adj*

i.e. that is to say ▶ HISTORY Latin *id est*

if *conj* **1** in the event that, or on condition that: *if you work hard you'll succeed* **2** used to introduce an indirect question to which the answer is either *yes* or *no*; whether: *it doesn't matter if the play is any good or not* **3** even though: *a splendid if slightly decaying house* **4** used to introduce an unfulfilled wish, with *only*: *if only you had told her* ▷ *n* **5** a condition or stipulation: *there are no hidden ifs or buts* ▶ HISTORY Old English *gif*

iffy *adj informal* full of uncertainty

igloo *n, pl* **-loos** a dome-shaped Inuit house, built of blocks of solid snow ▶ HISTORY Inuit *igdlu*

igneous (**ig**-nee-uss) *adj* **1** (of rocks) formed as molten rock cools and hardens **2** of or like fire ▶ HISTORY Latin *ignis* fire

ignite *vb* **-niting, -nited** to catch fire or set fire to ▶ HISTORY Latin *ignis* fire > **ignitable** *adj*

ignition *n* **1** the system used to ignite the fuel in an internal-combustion engine **2** an igniting or the process of igniting

ignoble *adj* **1** dishonourable **2** of low birth or origins ▶ HISTORY Latin *in-* not + *nobilis* noble > **ignobly** *adv*

ignominy (**ig**-nom-in-ee) *n, pl* **-minies** disgrace or public shame: *the ignominy of being replaced* ▶ HISTORY Latin *ignominia* disgrace > **ignominious** *adj*

ignoramus *n, pl* **-muses** an ignorant person

- **WORD HISTORY**
- The word 'ignoramus' comes from *Ignoramus*,
- the name of an uneducated lawyer in a
- 17th-century play of the same name written
- by George Ruggle. In Latin *ignoramus* means
- 'we do not know'.

ignorance *n* lack of knowledge or education

ignorant *adj* **1** lacking in knowledge or education **2** rude through lack of knowledge of good manners: *an ignorant remark* **3 ignorant of** lacking in awareness or knowledge of: *ignorant of Asian culture*

ignore *vb* **-noring, -nored** to refuse to notice; disregard deliberately ▶ HISTORY Latin *ignorare* not to know

iguana *n* a large tropical tree lizard of the W Indies and S America with a spiny back ▶ HISTORY S American Indian *iwana*

ikebana (eek-a-**bah**-na) *n* the Japanese art of flower arrangement ▶ HISTORY Japanese

ikon *n* same as **icon**

IL Illinois

il- *prefix* same as **in-¹ in-²**

ileum *n* the third and lowest part of the small intestine ▶ HISTORY Latin: flank, groin

ilex *n* **1** a genus of trees or shrubs that includes holly **2** same as **holm oak** ▶ HISTORY Latin

ilium *n, pl* **-ia** the uppermost and widest of the three sections of the hipbone

ilk *n* a type or class: *three or four others of the same ilk* ▶ HISTORY Old English *ilca* the same family

ill *adj* **worse, worst 1** not in good health **2** bad, harmful, or hostile: *ill effects* **3** promising an unfavourable outcome: *ill omen* **4 ill at ease** unable to relax ▷ *n* **5** evil or harm ▷ *adv* **6** badly, wrongly: *the title ill befits him* **7** with difficulty; hardly: *we can ill afford another scandal* ▶ HISTORY Old Norse *illr* bad

ill-advised *adj* **1** (of a plan or action) badly thought out **2** (of a person) acting without reasonable care or thought

ill-bred *adj* lacking good manners > **ill-breeding** *n*

ill-disposed *adj* unfriendly or unsympathetic

illegal *adj* against the law > **illegally** *adv* > **illegality** *n*

illegible *adj* unable to be read or deciphered > **illegibility** *n*

illegitimate *adj* **1** born of parents who were not married to each other at the time **2** illegal; unlawful > **illegitimacy** *n*

ill-fated *adj* doomed or unlucky

ill-favoured *adj* ugly or unattractive

ill-gotten *adj* obtained dishonestly or illegally: *ill-gotten gains*

ill-health *n* the condition of being unwell

illiberal *adj* **1** narrow-minded or intolerant **2** not generous; mean **3** lacking in culture or refinement > **illiberality** *n*

illicit *adj* **1** same as **illegal 2** forbidden or disapproved of by society: *an illicit kiss*

illiterate *adj* **1** unable to read and write **2** uneducated or ignorant: *linguistically illiterate* ▷ *n* **3** an illiterate person > **illiteracy** *n*

ill-mannered *adj* having bad manners

illness *n* **1** a disease or indisposition **2** a state of ill health

illogical *adj* **1** senseless or unreasonable **2** not following logical principles > **illogicality** *n* > **illogically** *adv*

ill-starred *adj* very unlucky or unfortunate

ill-tempered *adj* having a bad temper

ill-timed *adj* done or happening at an unsuitable time

ill-treat *vb* to treat cruelly or harshly > **ill-treatment** *n*

illuminate *vb* **-nating, -nated 1** to light up **2** to make easily understood; explain: *the report obscures* *rather than illuminates the most relevant facts* **3** to decorate with lights **4** to decorate (an initial letter or manuscript) with designs of gold, silver, or bright colours ▸ HISTORY Latin *illuminare* to light up > **illuminating** *adj* > **illuminative** *adj*

illumination *n* **1** an illuminating or being illuminated **2** a source of light **3 illuminations** *chiefly Brit* lights used as decorations in streets or towns **4** the decoration in colours, gold, or silver used on some manuscripts

illusion *n* **1** a false appearance or deceptive impression of reality: *her upswept hair gave the illusion of above average height* **2** a false or misleading idea or belief: *we may suffer from the illusion that we are special* ▸ HISTORY Latin *illusio* deceit

illusionist *n* a conjuror

illusory *or* **illusive** *adj* seeming to be true, but actually false: *the economic benefits of such reforms were largely illusory*

illustrate *vb* **-trating, -trated** **1** to clarify or explain by use of examples or comparisons **2** to provide (a book or text) with pictures **3** to be an example of ▸ HISTORY Latin *illustrare* to make light, explain > **illustrative** *adj* > **illustrator** *n*

illustration *n* **1** a picture or diagram used to explain or decorate a text **2** an example: *an illustration of the brutality of the regime* **3** the art of illustrating

illustrious *adj* famous and distinguished ▸ HISTORY Latin *illustris* bright, famous

ill will *n* unkind feeling; hostility

IM **1** instant message **2** instant messaging

im- *prefix* same as **in-¹ in-²**

image *n* **1** a mental picture of someone or something produced by the imagination or memory **2** the appearance or impression given to the public by a person or organization **3** a simile or metaphor **4** a representation of a person or thing in a work of art or literature **5** an optical reproduction of an object, formed by the lens of an eye or camera or by a mirror **6** a person or thing that resembles another closely **7** a personification of a specified quality; epitome: *the image of good breeding* ▷ *vb* **-aging, -aged** **8** to picture in the mind **9** to mirror or reflect an image of **10** to portray or describe ▸ HISTORY Latin *imago*

image printer *n computers* a printer which uses optical technology to produce an image of a complete page from digital input

imagery *n*, *pl* **-ries** **1** figurative or descriptive language in a literary work **2** mental images **3** images collectively, esp. statues or carvings

imaginary *adj* **1** existing only in the imagination **2** *maths* relating to the square root of a negative number

imagination *n* **1** the faculty or action of producing mental images of what is not present or in one's experience **2** creative mental ability

imaginative *adj* **1** produced by or showing a creative imagination **2** having a vivid imagination

imagine *vb* **-ining, -ined** **1** to form a mental image of **2** to think, believe, or guess: *I would imagine they'll be here soon* ▸ HISTORY Latin *imaginari* > **imaginable** *adj*

imago (im-**may**-go) *n*, *pl* **imagoes** *or* **imagines** (im-**maj**-in-eez) a sexually mature adult insect ▸ HISTORY Latin: likeness

imam *n Islam* **1** a leader of congregational prayer in a mosque **2** the title of some Muslim leaders ▸ HISTORY Arabic

IMAX (**eye**-max) *n trademark* a film projection process that produces an image ten times larger than standard

imbalance *n* a lack of balance, for instance in emphasis or proportion: *a chemical imbalance in the brain*

imbecile (**im**-biss-eel) *n* **1** *informal* an extremely stupid person **2** *old-fashioned* a person of abnormally low intelligence ▷ *adj* **3** stupid or senseless: *imbecile fanaticism* ▸ HISTORY Latin *imbecillus* feeble > **imbecility** *n*

imbed *vb* **-bedding, -bedded** same as **embed**

imbibe *vb* **-bibing, -bibed** *formal* **1** to drink (alcoholic drinks) **2** to take in or assimilate (ideas): *values she had imbibed as a child* ▸ HISTORY Latin *imbibere*

imbroglio (imb-**role**-ee-oh) *n*, *pl* **-glios** a confusing and complicated situation ▸ HISTORY Italian

imbue *vb* **-buing, -bued** to fill or inspire (with ideals or principles) ▸ HISTORY Latin *imbuere* to stain

IMF International Monetary Fund

imitate *vb* **-tating, -tated** **1** to copy the manner or style of or take as a model: *he remains rock's most imitated guitarist* **2** to mimic or impersonate, esp. for amusement **3** to make a copy or reproduction of; duplicate ▸ HISTORY Latin *imitari* > **imitable** *adj* > **imitator** *n*

imitation *n* **1** a copy of an original or genuine article **2** an instance of imitating someone: *her Beyoncé imitations were not the best thing she did* **3** behaviour modelled on the behaviour of someone else: *to learn by imitation* ▷ *adj* **4** made to resemble something which is usually superior or more expensive: *imitation leather*

imitative *adj* **1** imitating or tending to copy **2** copying or reproducing an original, esp. in an inferior manner: *imitative painting* **3** onomatopoeic

immaculate *adj* **1** completely clean or tidy: *an immaculate pinstripe suit* **2** completely flawless: *his equestrian pedigree is immaculate* ▸ HISTORY Latin *in-* not + *macula* blemish > **immaculately** *adv*

immanent *adj* **1** present within and throughout something **2** (of God) present throughout the universe ▸ HISTORY Latin *immanere* to remain in > **immanence** *n*

immaterial *adj* **1** of no real importance or relevance **2** not formed of matter

immature *adj* **1** not fully grown or developed **2** lacking wisdom, insight, or stability because of youth > **immaturity** *n*

immeasurable *adj* too great to be measured
> **immeasurably** *adv*

immediate *adj* **1** taking place without delay: *an immediate cut in interest rates* **2** next or nearest in space, time, or relationship: *our immediate neighbour* **3** present; current: *they had no immediate plans to close it* ▶ **HISTORY** Latin *in-* not + *mediare* to be in the middle > **immediacy** *n* > **immediately** *adv*

immemorial *adj* having existed or happened for longer than anyone can remember: *this has been the custom since time immemorial*

immense *adj* **1** huge or vast **2** *informal* very great ▶ **HISTORY** Latin *immensus* unmeasured
> **immensely** *adv* > **immensity** *n*

immerse *vb* **-mersing, -mersed** **1** to plunge or dip into liquid **2** to involve deeply: *he immersed himself in the history of Rome* **3** to baptize by dipping the whole body into water ▶ **HISTORY** Latin *immergere*
> **immersion** *n*

immersion heater *n* an electrical device in a domestic hot-water tank for heating water

immigrant *n* a person who comes to a foreign country in order to settle there

immigration *n* the act of coming to a foreign country in order to settle there ▶ **HISTORY** Latin *immigrare* to go into > **immigrate** *vb*

imminent *adj* likely to happen soon ▶ **HISTORY** Latin *imminere* to project over > **imminence** *n*

immiscible (i-**miss**-sib-bl) *adj* not able to be mixed: *oil and water are immiscible* ▶ **HISTORY** Latin *miscere* to mix > **immiscibility** *n*

immobile *adj* **1** not moving **2** not able to move or be moved > **immobility** *n*

immobilize *or* **-lise** *vb* **-lizing, -lized** *or* **-lising, -lised** to make unable to move or work: *a device for immobilizing steering wheels* > **immobilization** *or* **-lisation** *n*

immoderate *adj* excessive or unreasonable: *immoderate consumption of alcohol*
> **immoderately** *adv*

immodest *adj* **1** behaving in an indecent or improper manner **2** behaving in a boastful or conceited manner > **immodesty** *n*

immolate *vb* **-lating, -lated** *literary* to kill or offer as a sacrifice, esp. by fire ▶ **HISTORY** Latin *immolare*
> **immolation** *n*

immoral *adj* morally wrong; corrupt
> **immorality** *n*

immortal *adj* **1** not subject to death or decay **2** famous for all time **3** everlasting ▷ *n* **4** a person whose fame will last for all time **5** an immortal being > **immortality** *n*

immortalize *or* **-ise** *vb* **-izing, -ized** *or* **-ising, -ised** **1** *written* to give everlasting fame to: *a name immortalized by countless writers* **2** to give immortality to

immovable *or* **immoveable** *adj* **1** unable to be moved **2** unwilling to change one's opinions or beliefs **3** not affected by feeling; emotionless **4** unchanging **5** *law* (of property) consisting of land or houses > **immovability** *or* **immoveability** *n* > **immovably** *or* **immoveably** *adv*

immune *adj* **1** protected against a specific disease by inoculation or as the result of natural resistance **2** **immune to** secure against: *football is not immune to economic recession* **3** exempt from obligation or penalty ▶ **HISTORY** Latin *immunis* exempt from a public service

immune system *n* *biol* the mechanism by which a body reacts to foreign materials, involving the production of antibodies

immunity *n*, *pl* **-ties** **1** the ability of an organism to resist disease **2** freedom from prosecution, tax, etc.

immunize *or* **-nise** *vb* **-nizing, -nized** *or* **-nising, -nised** to make (someone) immune to a disease, esp. by inoculation > **immunization** *or* **-nisation** *n*

immunodeficiency *n* a deficiency in or breakdown of a person's ability to fight diseases

immunology *n* the branch of medicine concerned with the study of immunity
> **immunological** *adj* > **immunologist** *n*

immure *vb* **-muring, -mured** **1** *archaic or literary* to imprison **2** to shut (oneself) away from society ▶ **HISTORY** Latin *im-* in + *murus* wall

immutable (im-**mute**-a-bl) *adj* unchangeable or unchanging: *the immutable sequence of night and day* > **immutability** *n*

imp *n* **1** a small demon **2** a mischievous child ▶ **HISTORY** Old English *impa* bud, hence offspring, child

imp. **1** imperative **2** imperfect

impact *n* **1** the effect or impression made by something **2** the act of one object striking another; collision **3** the force of a collision ▷ *vb* **4** to press firmly against or into ▶ **HISTORY** Latin *impactus* pushed against > **impaction** *n*

impacted *adj* (of a tooth) unable to grow out because of being wedged against another tooth below the gum

impair *vb* to damage or weaken in strength or quality ▶ **HISTORY** Old French *empeirer* to make worse > **impairment** *n*

impala (imp-**ah**-la) *n*, *pl* **-las** *or* **-la** an African antelope with lyre-shaped horns ▶ **HISTORY** Zulu

impale *vb* **-paling, -paled** to pierce through or fix with a sharp object: *they impaled his severed head on a spear* ▶ **HISTORY** Latin *im-* on + *palus* pole > **impalement** *n*

impalpable *adj* *formal* **1** not able to be felt by touching: *impalpable shadows* **2** difficult to understand > **impalpability** *n*

impart *vb* **1** to communicate (information or knowledge) **2** to give (a specified quality): *flavouring to impart a sweet taste* ▶ **HISTORY** Latin *im-* in + *partire* to share

impartial *adj* not favouring one side or the other > **impartiality** *n* > **impartially** *adv*

impassable *adj* (of terrain or roads) not able to be travelled through or over > **impassability** *n*

impasse (**am**-pass) *n* a situation in which progress or escape is impossible ▶ **HISTORY** French

impassible *adj* **1** *rare* not susceptible to pain or injury **2** impassive; unmoved > **impassibility** or **impassibleness** *n*

impassioned *adj* *written* full of emotion: *an impassioned plea to the United Nations*

impassive *adj* *written* not showing or feeling emotion > **impassively** *adv* > **impassivity** *n*

impasto *n* the technique of applying paint thickly, so that brush marks are evident ▶ HISTORY Italian

impatient *adj* **1** irritable at any delay or difficulty **2** restless to have or do something > **impatience** *n* > **impatiently** *adv*

impeach *vb* **1** *chiefly US* to charge (a public official) with an offence committed in office **2** *Brit & Austral criminal law* to accuse of treason or serious crime **3** to challenge or question (a person's honesty or honour) ▶ HISTORY Late Latin *impedicare* to entangle > **impeachable** *adj* > **impeachment** *n*

impeccable *adj* without flaw or error: *impeccable manners* ▶ HISTORY Latin *in-* not + *peccare* to sin > **impeccably** *adv*

impecunious *adj* *formal* without money; penniless ▶ HISTORY Latin *in-* not + *pecuniosus* wealthy

impedance (imp-**eed**-anss) *n* *electricity* the total effective resistance in an electric circuit to the flow of an alternating current

impede *vb* **-peding, -peded** to block or make progress or action difficult ▶ HISTORY Latin *impedire*

impediment *n* **1** a hindrance or obstruction **2** a physical disability that makes speech or walking difficult

impedimenta *pl n* any objects that impede progress, esp. the baggage and equipment carried by an army

impel *vb* **-pelling, -pelled** **1** to urge or force (a person) to do something **2** to push, drive, or force into motion ▶ HISTORY Latin *impellere* to drive forward

impending *adj* (esp. of something bad) about to happen ▶ HISTORY Latin *impendere* to overhang

impenetrable *adj* **1** impossible to get through: *an impenetrable barrier* **2** impossible to understand **3** not receptive to ideas or influence: *impenetrable ignorance* > **impenetrability** *n* > **impenetrably** *adv*

imperative *adj* **1** extremely urgent; essential **2** commanding or authoritative: *an imperative tone of voice* **3** *grammar* denoting a mood of verbs used in commands ▷ *n* **4** *grammar* the imperative mood ▶ HISTORY Latin *imperare* to command

imperceptible *adj* too slight, subtle, or gradual to be noticed > **imperceptibly** *adv*

imperfect *adj* **1** having faults or errors **2** not complete **3** *grammar* denoting a tense of verbs describing continuous, incomplete, or repeated past actions ▷ *n* **4** *grammar* same as **imperfect tense** > **imperfectly** *adv*

imperfection *n* **1** the state of being imperfect **2** a fault or defect

imperfect tense *n* *grammar* a verb tense describing continuous, incomplete, or repeated past actions; in *he was having a bath when I phoned*, *was having* is the imperfect tense

imperial *adj* **1** of an empire, emperor, or empress **2** majestic; commanding **3** exercising supreme authority; imperious **4** (of weights or measures) conforming to the standards of a system formerly official in Great Britain ▷ *n* **5** a wine bottle holding the equivalent of eight normal bottles ▶ HISTORY Latin *imperium* authority

imperialism *n* **1** the policy or practice of extending a country's influence over other territories by conquest, colonization, or economic domination **2** an imperial system, authority, or government > **imperialist** *adj, n* > **imperialistic** *adj*

imperil *vb* **-illing, -illed** or *US* **-iling, -iled** *formal* to put in danger

imperious *adj* *written* used to being obeyed; domineering ▶ HISTORY Latin *imperium* power > **imperiously** *adv*

impermeable *adj* (of a substance) not allowing fluid to pass through: *an impermeable layer* > **impermeability** *n*

impersonal *adj* **1** without reference to any individual person; objective: *Buddhism began as a very impersonal doctrine* **2** without human warmth or sympathy: *an impersonal manner* **3** *grammar* **a** (of a verb) having no subject, as in *it is raining* **b** (of a pronoun) not referring to a person > **impersonality** *n* > **impersonally** *adv*

impersonal narrator *n* *literature* an objective storyteller who is not evident as a personality but simply gives information

impersonate *vb* **-ating, -ated** **1** to pretend to be (another person) **2** to imitate the character or mannerisms of (another person) for entertainment > **impersonation** *n* > **impersonator** *n*

impertinent *adj* disrespectful or rude ▶ HISTORY Latin *impertinens* not belonging > **impertinence** *n*

imperturbable *adj* *written* not easily upset; calm > **imperturbability** *n* > **imperturbably** *adv*

impervious *adj* **1** not letting water, etc. through **2** *written* not influenced by a feeling, argument, etc.

impetigo (imp-it-**tie**-go) *n* a contagious skin disease causing spots or pimples ▶ HISTORY Latin: scabby eruption

impetuous *adj* **1** acting without consideration **2** done rashly or hastily ▶ HISTORY Late Latin *impetuosus* violent > **impetuosity** *n*

impetus (**imp**-it-uss) *n, pl* **-tuses** **1** an incentive or impulse **2** *physics* the force that starts a body moving or that tends to resist changes in its speed or direction once it is moving ▶ HISTORY Latin: attack

impi *n, pl* **-pi** or **-pies** a group of Zulu warriors ▶ HISTORY Nguni (language group of southern Africa) *impi* regiment, army

impinge *vb* **-pinging, -pinged** to encroach, affect, or restrict: *international economic forces impinging on the local economy* ▶ HISTORY Latin *impingere* to dash against > **impingement** *n*

impious (**imp**-euss, im-**pie**-uss) *adj* showing a lack of respect or religious reverence

impish *adj* mischievous > **impishness** *n*

implacable *adj* **1** incapable of being appeased or pacified **2** unyielding > **implacability** *n* > **implacably** *adv*

implant *vb* **1** to fix firmly in the mind: *to implant sound moral principles* **2** to plant or embed **3** *surgery* to graft or insert (a tissue or hormone) into the body ▷ *n* **4** anything implanted in the body, such as a tissue graft > **implantation** *n*

implement *vb* **1** to carry out (instructions, etc.): *she refused to implement the agreed plan* ▷ *n* **2** a tool or other piece of equipment ▶ HISTORY Late Latin *implementum*, literally: a filling up > **implementation** *n*

implicate *vb* **-cating, -cated** **1** to show (someone) to be involved, esp. in a crime **2** to imply ▶ HISTORY Latin *implicare* to involve

implication *n* **1** something that is suggested or implied **2** an act or instance of suggesting or implying or being implied

implicit *adj* **1** expressed indirectly: *an implicit agreement* **2** absolute and unquestioning: *implicit trust* **3** contained in, although not stated openly: *this view of the mind was implicit in all his work* ▶ HISTORY Latin *implicitus* > **implicitly** *adv*

implied term *n law* a condition that will be assumed by the courts to be part of a contract even though it is not specified in the agreement

implode *vb* **-ploding, -ploded** to collapse inwards ▶ HISTORY im- in + (ex)plode

implore *vb* **-ploring, -plored** to beg desperately ▶ HISTORY Latin *implorare*

imply *vb* **-plies, -plying, -plied** **1** to express or indicate by a hint; suggest **2** to suggest or involve as a necessary consequence: *a spending commitment implies a corresponding tax imposition* ▶ HISTORY Old French *emplier*

impolite *adj* discourteous; rude > **impoliteness** *n*

impolitic *adj* ill-advised; unwise

imponderable *adj* **1** unable to be weighed or assessed ▷ *n* **2** something difficult or impossible to assess

import *vb* **1** to bring in (goods) from another country **2** *computers* to transfer (data) into a file in a different format **3** *formal* to signify; mean: *to import doom* ▷ *n* **4** something imported **5** *formal* Importance: *his new work is of great import* **6** meaning **7** *Canad, slang* a sportsman who is not native to the area where he plays ▶ HISTORY Latin *importare* to carry in > **importer** *n* > **importation** *n*

important *adj* **1** of great significance, value, or consequence **2** of social significance: *an important man in the company hierarchy* **3** of great concern: *it was important to me to know* ▶ HISTORY Medieval Latin *importare* to signify, from Latin: to carry in > **importance** *n* > **importantly** *adv*

importunate *adj* *formal* persistent or demanding

importune *vb* **-tuning, -tuned** *formal* to harass with persistent requests ▶ HISTORY Latin *importunus* tiresome > **importunity** *n*

impose *vb* **-posing, -posed** **1** to establish (a rule, condition, etc.) as something to be obeyed or complied with **2** to take advantage of (a person or quality): *she imposed on her kindness* **3** to force (oneself) on others **4** *printing* to arrange (pages) in the correct order for printing **5** to pass off (something) deceptively on someone ▶ HISTORY Latin *imponere* to place upon

imposing *adj* grand or impressive: *an imposing building*

imposition *n* **1** the act of imposing **2** something imposed, esp. unfairly, on someone **3** the arrangement of pages for printing **4** *old-fashioned* a task set as a school punishment

impossibility *n, pl* **-ties** **1** the state or quality of being impossible **2** something that is impossible

impossible *adj* **1** not able to be done or to happen **2** absurd or unreasonable **3** *informal* intolerable or outrageous: *those children are impossible* > **impossibly** *adv*

imposter *or* **impostor** *n* a person who cheats or swindles by pretending to be someone else ▶ HISTORY Late Latin *impostor* deceiver

imposture *n* *formal* deception, esp. by pretending to be someone else

impotent (**imp**-a-tent) *adj* **1** not having the power to influence people or events **2** (of a man) incapable of sexual intercourse > **impotence** *n*

impound *vb* **1** to take legal possession of; confiscate **2** to confine (an animal) in a pound

impoverish *vb* to make (someone) poor or weaken the quality of (something) ▶ HISTORY Old French *empovrir* > **impoverished** *adj* > **impoverishment** *n*

impracticable *adj* **1** not able to be put into practice **2** unsuitable for a desired use > **impracticability** *n*

impractical *adj* **1** not sensible or workable: *the use of force was viewed as impractical* **2** not having practical skills > **impracticality** *n*

imprecation *n* *formal* a curse ▶ HISTORY Latin *imprecari* to invoke > **imprecate** *vb*

impregnable *adj* **1** unable to be broken into or taken by force: *an impregnable fortress* **2** unable to be affected or overcome: *a confident, impregnable person* ▶ HISTORY Old French *imprenable* > **impregnability** *n*

impregnate *vb* **-nating, -nated** **1** to saturate, soak, or fill throughout **2** to make pregnant **3** to imbue or permeate: *the party has been impregnated with an enthusiasm for reform* ▶ HISTORY Latin in- in + *praegnans* pregnant > **impregnation** *n*

impresario *n, pl* **-sarios** a person who runs theatre performances, concerts, etc. ▶ HISTORY Italian

impress *vb* **1** to make a strong, lasting, or favourable impression on: *he was impressed by the standard of play* **2** to stress or emphasize **3** to imprint or stamp by pressure: *a pattern impressed in* paint on the rock ▷ n **4** an impressing **5** a mark produced by impressing ▶ **HISTORY** Latin *imprimere* to press into > **impressible** *adj*

impression n **1** an effect produced in the mind by a person or thing: *she was keen to create a relaxed impression* **2** a vague idea or belief: *he only had a vague impression of how it worked* **3** a strong, favourable, or remarkable effect **4** an impersonation for entertainment **5** an imprint or mark produced by pressing **6** *printing* the number of copies of a publication printed at one time

impressionable *adj* easily impressed or influenced: *the promotion of smoking to the impressionable young* > **impressionability** *n*

Impressionism n a style of painting developed in 19th-century France, with the aim of reproducing the immediate impression or mood of things, especially the effects of light and atmosphere, rather than form or structure

impressionist n **1** **Impressionist** an artist who painted in the style of Impressionism **2** a person who imitates the character or mannerisms of another person for entertainment

impressive *adj* capable of impressing, esp. by size, magnificence, or importance > **impressively** *adv*

imprimatur (imp-rim-**ah**-ter) n official approval for something to be printed, usually given by the Roman Catholic Church ▶ **HISTORY** New Latin: let it be printed

imprint n **1** a mark or impression produced by pressing, printing, or stamping **2** the publisher's name and address, often with the date of publication, printed on the title page of a book ▷ *vb* **3** to produce (a mark) by pressing, printing, or stamping: *T-shirts imprinted with slogans* **4** to establish firmly; impress: *he couldn't dislodge the images imprinted on his brain*

imprison *vb* to confine in or as if in prison > **imprisonment** n

improbable *adj* not likely or probable > **improbability** n > **improbably** *adv*

improbity n, pl **-ties** *formal* dishonesty or wickedness

impromptu *adj* **1** without planning or preparation; improvised ▷ *adv* **2** in a spontaneous or improvised way: *he spoke impromptu* ▷ n **3** a short piece of instrumental music resembling improvisation **4** something that is impromptu ▶ **HISTORY** Latin *in promptu* in readiness

improper *adj* **1** indecent **2** irregular or incorrect > **improperly** *adv*

improper fraction n a fraction in which the numerator is greater than the denominator, as ⅞

impropriety (imp-roe-**pry**-a-tee) n, pl **-ties** *formal* unsuitable or slightly improper behaviour

improve *vb* **-proving, -proved** **1** to make or become better in quality **2** **improve on** to achieve a better standard or quality in comparison with: *both had improved on their previous performance* ▶ **HISTORY** Anglo-French *emprouer* to turn to profit > **improvable** *adj*

improved pasture n *agriculture* **1** grazing land that has been sown with a mixture of introduced plant species to improve productivity **2** such plants used for grazing

improvement n **1** the act of improving or the state of being improved **2** a change that makes something better or adds to its value: *home improvements* **3** *Austral & NZ* a building on a piece of land, adding to its value

improvident *adj* **1** not providing for the future **2** incautious or rash > **improvidence** n

improvisation n the process of making up (a piece of music, speech, etc.) as one goes along; used especially of actors working without a script ▶ **HISTORY** Latin *improvisus* unforeseen

improvise *vb* **-vising, -vised** **1** to do or make quickly from whatever is available, without previous planning **2** to make up (a piece of music, speech, etc.) as one goes along ▶ **HISTORY** Latin *improvisus* unforeseen

imprudent *adj* not carefully thought out; rash > **imprudence** n

impudent *adj* impertinent or insolent ▶ **HISTORY** Latin *impudens* shameless > **impudence** n > **impudently** *adv*

impugn (imp-**yoon**) *vb* *formal* to challenge or attack as false ▶ **HISTORY** Latin *impugnare* to fight against > **impugnment** n

impulse n **1** a sudden desire or whim **2** an instinctive drive; urge: *the mothering impulse* **3** *physics* **a** the product of a force acting on a body and the time for which it acts **b** the change in the momentum of a body as a result of a force acting upon it **4** *physiol* a stimulus transmitted in a nerve or muscle ▶ **HISTORY** Latin *impulsus* incitement

impulsive *adj* **1** tending to act without thinking first: *an impulsive man* **2** done without thinking first **3** forceful or impelling

impunity (imp-**yoon**-it-ee) n **with impunity** without punishment or unpleasant consequences ▶ **HISTORY** Latin *impunis* unpunished

impure *adj* **1** having unwanted substances mixed in **2** immoral or obscene: *impure thoughts* **3** dirty or unclean

impurity n, pl **-ties** **1** an impure element or thing: *impurities in the water* **2** the quality of being impure

impute *vb* **-puting, -puted** **1** to attribute (blame or a crime) to a person **2** to attribute to a source or cause: *I impute your success to nepotism* ▶ **HISTORY** Latin *in-* in + *putare* to think > **imputation** n

IMR infant mortality rate

in *prep* **1** inside; within: *in the room* **2** at a place where there is: *in the shade* **3** indicating a state, situation, or condition: *in silence* **4** when (a period of time) has elapsed: *come back in one year* **5** using: *written in code* **6** wearing: *the man in the blue suit* **7** with regard to (a specified activity or occupation): *in journalism* **8** while performing the action of: *in crossing the street he was run over* **9** having as purpose: *in honour of the president* **10** (of certain animals) pregnant with: *in calf* **11** into: *he fell in the* *water* **12 have it in one** to have the ability (to do something) **13 in that** *or* **in so far as** because or to the extent that: *it was of great help in that it gave me more confidence* ▷ *adv* **14** in or into a particular place; indoors: *come in* **15** at one's home or place of work: *he's not in at the moment* **16** fashionable or popular: *long skirts are in this year* **17** in office or power: *the Conservatives got in at the last election* **18** so as to enclose: *block in* **19** (in certain games) so as to take one's turn of the play: *you have to get the other side out before you go in* **20** *Brit* (of a fire) alight **21** indicating prolonged activity, esp. by a large number: *teach-in; sit-in* **22 in for** about to experience (something, esp. something unpleasant): *they're in for a shock* **23 in on** acquainted with or sharing in: *I was in on all his plans* **24 in with** friendly with **25 have got it in for** *informal* to wish or intend harm towards ▷ *adj* **26** fashionable; modish: *the in thing to do* ▷ *n* **27 ins and outs** the detailed points or facts (of a situation) ▶ **HISTORY** Old English

In *chem* indium

IN Indiana

in. inch(es)

in-¹, il-, im- *or* **ir-** *prefix* **a** not; non: *incredible; illegal; imperfect; irregular* **b** lack of: *inexperience* ▶ **HISTORY** Latin

in-², il-, im- *or* **ir-** *prefix* in; into; towards; within; on: *infiltrate* ▶ **HISTORY** from *in*

inability *n* the fact of not being able to do something

inaccessible *adj* **1** impossible or very difficult to reach **2** unable to be used or seen: *his works are inaccessible to English-speaking readers* **3** difficult to understand or appreciate: *Webern's music is still considered inaccessible* > **inaccessibility** *n*

inaccuracy *n, pl* **-cies 1** lack of accuracy; imprecision **2** an error or mistake > **inaccurate** *adj*

inaction *n* lack of action; inertia

inactive *adj* **1** idle; not active **2** *chem* (of a substance) having little or no reactivity > **inactivity** *n*

inadequacy *n, pl* **-cies 1** lack or shortage **2** the state of being or feeling inferior **3** a weakness or failing: *their own failures or inadequacies*

inadequate *adj* **1** not enough; insufficient **2** not good enough > **inadequately** *adv*

inadmissible *adj* not allowable or acceptable

inadvertent *adj* done unintentionally > **inadvertence** *n* > **inadvertently** *adv*

inalienable *adj* not able to be taken away or transferred to another: *the inalienable rights of the citizen*

inamorata *or masc* **inamorato** *n, pl* **-tas** *or masc* **-tos** *literary* a sweetheart or lover ▶ **HISTORY** Italian *innamorata, innamorato*

inane *adj* senseless or silly: *inane remarks* ▶ **HISTORY** Latin *inanis* empty > **inanity** *n*

inanimate *adj* lacking the qualities of living beings: *inanimate objects*

inanition *n formal* exhaustion or weakness, as

from lack of food ▶ **HISTORY** Latin *inanis* empty

inapplicable *adj* not suitable or relevant

inappropriate *adj* not suitable or proper > **inappropriately** *adv*

inapt *adj* **1** not apt or fitting **2** lacking skill > **inaptitude** *n*

inarticulate *adj* unable to express oneself clearly or well

inasmuch as *conj* **1** since; because **2** in so far as

inattentive *adj* not paying attention > **inattention** *n*

inaudible *adj* not loud enough to be heard > **inaudibly** *adv*

inaugural *adj* **1** of or for an inauguration ▷ *n* **2** *US* a speech made at an inauguration

inaugurate *vb* **-rating, -rated 1** to open or celebrate the first public use of ceremonially: *the newest electrified line was inaugurated today* **2** to formally establish (a new leader) in office **3** to begin officially or formally ▶ **HISTORY** Latin *inaugurare* to take omens, hence to install in office after taking auguries > **inauguration** *n* > **inaugurator** *n*

inauspicious *adj* unlucky; suggesting an unfavourable outcome

inboard *adj* **1** (of a boat's motor or engine) situated within the hull **2** situated close to the fuselage of an aircraft ▷ *adv* **3** within the sides of or towards the centre of a vessel or aircraft

inborn *adj* existing from birth: *an inborn sense of optimism*

inbox *n computers* a folder in which incoming messages are stored and displayed

inbred *adj* **1** produced as a result of inbreeding **2** inborn or ingrained: *inbred good manners*

inbreeding *n* breeding from closely related individuals

inbuilt *adj* (of a quality or feeling) present from the beginning: *an inbuilt prejudice*

Inc. *US & Austral* (of a company) incorporated

Inca *n* **1** (*pl* **Inca** *or* **Incas**) a member of a S American indigenous people whose empire, centred on Peru, lasted until the early 1530s **2** the language of this people

incalculable *adj* impossible to estimate or predict > **incalculability** *n*

in camera *adv* in private session: *the proceedings were held in camera* ▶ **HISTORY** Latin

incandescent *adj* **1** glowing with heat **2** (of artificial light) produced by a glowing filament ▶ **HISTORY** Latin *incandescere* to glow > **incandescence** *n*

incandescent lamp *n* a lamp that contains a filament which is electrically heated to incandescence

incantation *n* **1** ritual chanting of magic words or sounds **2** a magic spell ▶ **HISTORY** Latin *incantare* to repeat magic formulas > **incantatory** *adj*

incapable *adj* **1** **incapable of** lacking the ability to **2** helpless: *drunk and incapable*

incapacitate *vb* **-tating, -tated** to deprive (a person) of strength, power, or ability; disable

incapacity *n, pl* **-ties 1** lack of power, strength, or ability **2** *law* legal disqualification or ineligibility

incarcerate *vb* **-ating, -ated** *formal* to confine or imprison ▶ HISTORY Latin *in-* in + *carcer* prison > **incarceration** *n*

incarnate *adj* **1** possessing human form: *a devil incarnate* **2** personified or typified: *stupidity incarnate* ▷ *vb* **-nating, -nated 3** to give a bodily or concrete form to **4** to be representative or typical of ▶ HISTORY Late Latin *incarnare* to make flesh

incarnation *n* **1** the act of embodying or state of being embodied in human form **2** a person or thing that typifies some quality or idea

Incarnation *n* *Christian theol* God's coming to earth in human form as Jesus Christ

incendiary (in-**send**-ya-ree) *adj* **1** (of bombs, etc.) designed to cause fires **2** tending to create strife or violence **3** relating to the illegal burning of property or goods ▷ *n, pl* **-aries 4** a bomb that is designed to start fires **5** a person who illegally sets fire to property or goods ▶ HISTORY Latin *incendere* to kindle > **incendiarism** *n*

incense¹ *n* **1** an aromatic substance burnt for its fragrant odour, esp. in religious ceremonies **2** the odour or smoke so produced ▷ *vb* **-censing, -censed 3** to burn incense to (a deity) **4** to perfume or fumigate with incense ▶ HISTORY Church Latin *incensum*

incense² *vb* **-censing, -censed** to make very angry ▶ HISTORY Latin *incensus* set on fire > **incensed** *adj*

incentive *n* **1** something that encourages effort or action **2** an additional payment made to employees to increase production ▷ *adj* **3** encouraging greater effort: *an incentive scheme for workers* ▶ HISTORY Latin *incentivus* setting the tune

inception *n* the beginning of a project ▶ HISTORY Latin *incipere* to begin

incessant *adj* never stopping ▶ HISTORY Latin *in-* not + *cessare* to cease > **incessantly** *adv*

incest *n* sexual intercourse between two people who are too closely related to marry ▶ HISTORY Latin *in-* not + *castus* chaste > **incestuous** *adj*

inch *n* **1** a unit of length equal to one twelfth of a foot (2.54cm) **2** *meteorol* the amount of rain or snow that would cover a surface to a depth of one inch **3** a very small distance, degree, or amount: *neither side was prepared to give an inch* **4 every inch** in every way: *she arrived looking every inch a star* **5 inch by inch** gradually **6 within an inch of one's life** almost to death ▷ *vb* **7** to move very slowly or gradually: *I inched my way to the bar* ▶ HISTORY Old English *ynce*

inchoate (in-**koe**-ate) *adj* *formal* just begun and not yet properly developed ▶ HISTORY Latin *incohare* to make a beginning

incidence *n* **1** extent or frequency of occurrence: *the rising incidence of car fires* **2** *physics* the arrival of a beam of light or particles at a surface **3** *geom* the partial overlapping of two figures or a figure and a line

incident *n* **1** an occurrence or event, esp. a minor one **2** a relatively insignificant event that might have serious consequences **3** a public disturbance ▷ *adj* **4** *physics* (of a beam of light or particles) arriving at or striking a surface **5 incident to** *formal* likely to occur in connection with: *the dangers are incident to a policeman's job* ▶ HISTORY Latin *incidere* to happen

incidental *adj* **1** happening in connection with or resulting from something more important **2** secondary or minor: *incidental expenses* > **incidentally** *adv*

incidental music *n* background music for a film or play

incident ray *n* *physics* a ray of light striking a surface

incinerate *vb* **-ating, -ated** to burn up completely ▶ HISTORY Latin *in-* to + *cinis* ashes > **incineration** *n*

incinerator *n* a furnace for burning rubbish

incipient *adj* *formal* just starting to be or happen ▶ HISTORY Latin *incipere* to begin

incise *vb* **-cising, -cised** to cut into with a sharp tool ▶ HISTORY Latin *incidere* to cut into

incised meander *n* *geog* a bend in a river where the water has carved a deep steep-sided channel in the bedrock

incision *n* a cut, esp. one made during a surgical operation

incisive *adj* direct and forceful: *witty and incisive comments*

incisor *n* a sharp cutting tooth at the front of the mouth

incite *vb* **-citing, -cited** to stir up or provoke to action ▶ HISTORY Latin *in-* in, on + *citare* to excite > **incitement** *n*

incivility *n, pl* **-ties 1** rudeness **2** an impolite act or remark

inclement *adj* *formal* (of weather) stormy or severe > **inclemency** *n*

inclination *n* **1** a liking, tendency, or preference: *he showed no inclination to change his routine* **2** the degree of slope from a horizontal or vertical plane **3** a slope or slant **4** *surveying* the angular distance of the horizon below the plane of observation

incline *vb* **-clining, -clined 1** to veer from a vertical or horizontal plane; slope or slant **2** to have or cause to have a certain tendency or disposition: *that does not incline me to think that you are right* **3** *written* to bend or lower (part of the body, esp. the head) **4 incline one's ear** to listen favourably ▷ *n* **5** *written* an inclined surface or slope ▶ HISTORY Latin *inclinare* to cause to lean > **inclined** *adj*

include *vb* **-cluding, -cluded 1** to have as part of the whole **2** to put in as part of a set, group, or category ▶ HISTORY Latin *in-* in + *claudere* to close

inclusion *n* **1** an including or being included **2** something included

inclusive *adj* **1** including everything: *capital inclusive of profit* **2** including the limits specified: *Monday to Friday inclusive* **3** comprehensive

inclusive language n language that avoids male pronouns and the use of words such as *mankind*, on the grounds that they exclude women

incognito (in-kog-**nee**-toe) *adv, adj* **1** under an assumed name or appearance ▷ n, pl **-tos** **2** a false identity **3** a person who is incognito ▶ HISTORY Latin *incognitus* unknown

incoherent *adj* **1** unable to express oneself clearly **2** not logically connected or ordered: *an incoherent argument* > **incoherence** n

income n the total amount of money earned from work or obtained from other sources over a given period of time

income support n (in Britain) an allowance paid by the government to people with a very low income

income tax n a personal tax levied on annual income

incoming *adj* **1** about to arrive **2** about to come into office

incommensurable *adj* **1** not able to be judged, measured, or compared **2** *maths* not having a common divisor other than 1, such as 2 and √–5 > **incommensurability** n

incommode *vb* **-moding, -moded** *formal* to bother, disturb, or inconvenience ▶ HISTORY Latin *incommodus* inconvenient

incommunicado *adv, adj* not allowed to communicate with other people, for instance while in solitary confinement ▶ HISTORY Spanish *incomunicado*

incomparable *adj* so excellent as to be beyond or above comparison > **incomparably** *adv*

incompatible *adj* not able to exist together in harmony; conflicting or inconsistent > **incompatibility** n

incompetent *adj* **1** not having the necessary ability or skill to do something **2** *law* not legally qualified: *an incompetent witness* ▷ n **3** an incompetent person > **incompetence** n

incomplete *adj* not finished or whole

incomplete flower n *bot* a flower which lacks either the calyx or corolla, or both

inconceivable *adj* so unlikely to be true as to be unthinkable > **inconceivability** n

inconclusive *adj* not giving a final decision or result

incongruous *adj* out of place; inappropriate: *an incongruous figure among the tourists* > **incongruously** *adv* > **incongruity** n

inconnu (**In**-kon-new) n *Canad* a whitefish of arctic waters ▶ HISTORY French, literally: unknown

inconsequential *or* **inconsequent** *adj* **1** unimportant or insignificant **2** not following logically as a consequence > **inconsequentially** *adv*

inconsiderable *adj* **1** **not inconsiderable** fairly large: *he gets not inconsiderable royalties from his musicals* **2** not worth considering; insignificant > **inconsiderably** *adv*

inconsiderate *adj* lacking in care or thought for others; thoughtless > **inconsiderateness** n

inconsistent *adj* **1** unstable or changeable in behaviour or mood **2** containing contradictory elements: *an inconsistent argument* **3** not in accordance: *actions inconsistent with high office* > **inconsistency** n

inconsolable *adj* very distressed > **inconsolably** *adv*

inconspicuous *adj* not easily noticed or seen

inconstant *adj* **1** liable to change one's loyalties or opinions **2** variable: *their household income is inconstant* > **inconstancy** n

incontestable *adj* impossible to deny or argue with

incontinent *adj* **1** unable to control the bladder and bowels **2** lacking self-restraint ▶ HISTORY Latin *in-* not + *continere* to restrain > **incontinence** n

incontrovertible *adj* absolutely certain; undeniable > **incontrovertibly** *adv*

inconvenience n **1** a state or instance of trouble or difficulty ▷ vb **-iencing, -ienced** **2** to cause trouble or difficulty to (someone) > **inconvenient** *adj*

incorporate *vb* **-rating, -rated** **1** to include or be included as part of a larger unit **2** to form a united whole or mass **3** to form into a corporation ▷ *adj* **4** incorporated ▶ HISTORY Latin *in-* in + *corpus* body > **incorporated** *adj* > **incorporation** n

incorporated *adj* **1** united or combined into a whole **2** *US & Austral* organized as a legal corporation, esp. in commerce. Abbrev: **Inc.**

incorporeal *adj* without material form, substance, or existence

incorrigible *adj* (of a person or behaviour) beyond correction or reform; incurably bad > **incorrigibility** n > **incorrigibly** *adv*

incorruptible *adj* **1** too honest to be bribed or corrupted **2** not prone to decay or disintegration > **incorruptibility** n

increase *vb* **-creasing, -creased** **1** to make or become greater in size, degree, or frequency ▷ n **2** a rise in size, degree, or frequency **3** the amount by which something increases **4 on the increase** becoming more common ▶ HISTORY Latin *in-* in + *crescere* to grow > **increasingly** *adv*

incredible *adj* **1** unbelievable **2** *informal* marvellous; amazing > **incredibility** n > **incredibly** *adv*

incredulity n unwillingness to believe

incredulous *adj* not prepared or willing to believe something

increment n **1** the amount by which something increases **2** a regular salary increase **3** *maths* a small positive or negative change in a variable or function ▶ HISTORY Latin *incrementum* increase > **incremental** *adj*

incriminate *vb* **-nating, -nated** **1** to make (someone) seem guilty of a crime **2** to charge (someone) with a crime ▶ HISTORY Late Latin *incriminare* to accuse > **incrimination** n > **incriminatory** *adj*

incubate (in-cube-ate) *vb* **-bating, -bated** **1** (of birds) to hatch (eggs) by sitting on them **2** to cause (bacteria) to develop, esp. in an incubator or culture medium **3** (of disease germs) to remain inactive in an animal or human before causing disease **4** to develop gradually ▶ HISTORY Latin *incubare* > **incubation** *n*

incubator *n* **1** *med* a heated enclosed apparatus for rearing premature babies **2** an apparatus for hatching birds' eggs or growing bacterial cultures

inculcate *vb* **-cating, -cated** to fix in someone's mind by constant repetition ▶ HISTORY Latin *inculcare* to tread upon > **inculcation** *n*

inculpate *vb* **-pating, -pated** *formal* to incriminate ▶ HISTORY Latin *in-* on + *culpare* to blame

incumbency *n, pl* **-cies** the office, duty, or tenure of an incumbent

incumbent *formal n* **1** a person who holds a particular office or position ▷ *adj* **2** morally binding as a duty: *it is incumbent on cricketers to respect the umpire's impartiality* ▶ HISTORY Latin *incumbere* to lie upon

incur *vb* **-curring, -curred** *written* to bring (something undesirable) upon oneself ▶ HISTORY Latin *incurrere* to run into

incurable *adj* **1** not able to be cured: *an incurable tumour* **2** not able to be changed: *he is an incurable romantic* ▷ *n* **3** a person with an incurable disease > **incurability** *n* > **incurably** *adv*

incurious *adj* showing no curiosity or interest > **incuriously** *adv*

incursion *n* **1** a sudden or brief invasion **2** an inroad or encroachment: *a successful incursion into the American book-shop market* ▶ HISTORY Latin *incursio* attack > **incursive** *adj*

ind. 1 independent **2** index **3** indicative **4** indirect **5** industrial

Ind. 1 Independent **2** India **3** Indian **4** Indiana **5** Indies

indaba (in-**dah**-ba) *n* **1** (among native peoples of southern Africa) a meeting to discuss a serious topic **2** S African, informal a matter of concern or for discussion ▶ HISTORY Zulu

indebted *adj* **1** owing gratitude for help or favours **2** owing money > **indebtedness** *n*

indecent *adj* **1** morally offensive **2** unseemly or improper: *indecent haste* > **indecency** *n* > **indecently** *adv*

indecipherable *adj* impossible to read

indecisive *adj* **1** unable to make decisions **2** not decisive or conclusive: *an indecisive argument* > **indecision** or **indecisiveness** *n*

indeed *adv* **1** certainly; actually: *indeed, the sea featured heavily in his poems* **2** truly, very: *it has become a dangerous place indeed* **3** in fact; what is more: *it is necessary, indeed indispensable* ▷ *interj* **4** *spoken* an expression of doubt or surprise

indefatigable *adj* never getting tired or giving up: *Mitterrand was an indefatigable organizer* ▶ HISTORY Latin *in-* not + *fatigare* to tire > **indefatigably** *adv*

indefensible *adj* **1** (of behaviour or statements) unable to be justified or supported **2** (of places or buildings) impossible to defend against attack > **indefensibility** *n*

indefinable *adj* *written* difficult to describe or explain completely

indefinite *adj* **1** without exact limits: *an indefinite number* **2** vague or unclear > **indefinitely** *adv*

indefinite article *n* *grammar* either of the words 'a' or 'an'

indelible *adj* **1** impossible to erase or remove **2** making indelible marks: *indelible ink* ▶ HISTORY Latin *in-* not + *delere* to destroy > **indelibly** *adv*

indelicate *adj* **1** offensive, embarrassing, or tasteless **2** coarse, crude, or rough > **indelicacy** *n*

indemnify *vb* **-fies, -fying, -fied** **1** to secure against loss, damage, or liability **2** to compensate for loss or damage > **indemnification** *n*

indemnity *n, pl* **-ties** **1** insurance against loss or damage **2** compensation for loss or damage **3** legal exemption from penalties incurred ▶ HISTORY Latin *in-* not + *damnum* damage

indent *vb* **1** to start (a line of writing) further from the margin than the other lines **2** to order (goods) using a special order form **3** to notch (an edge or border) **4** to write out (a document) in duplicate **5** to bind (an apprentice) by indenture ▷ *n* **6** *chiefly Brit* an official order for goods, esp. foreign merchandise ▶ HISTORY Latin *in-* in + *dens* tooth

indentation *n* **1** a hollow, notch, or cut, as on an edge or on a coastline **2** an indenting or being indented **3** Also: **indention** the leaving of space or the amount of space left between a margin and the start of an indented line

indenture *n* **1** a contract, esp. one binding an apprentice to his or her employer ▷ *vb* **-turing, -tured** **2** to bind (an apprentice) by indenture **3** to enter into an agreement by indenture > **indentureship** *n*

independent *adj* **1** free from the influence or control of others **2** (of a country) ruling itself **3** not dependent on anything else for function or validity **4** not relying on others, esp. financial support, of others **5** capable of acting for oneself or on one's own **6** of or having a private income large enough to enable one to live without working: *independent means* **7** not representing any political party: *an independent candidate* **8** *maths* (of a variable) not dependent on another variable ▷ *n* **9** an independent person or thing **10** a politician who does not represent any political party > **independence** *n* > **independently** *adv*

independent clause *n* *grammar* another term for **main clause**

independent school *n* (in Britain and Australia) a school that is neither financed nor controlled by the government or local authorities

independent variable *n* *maths* a variable in an equation or statement whose value determines that of the dependent variable

in-depth *adj* detailed or thorough: *an in-depth analysis*

indescribable *adj* too intense or extreme for words > **indescribably** *adv*

indestructible *adj* not able to be destroyed

indeterminate *adj* **1** uncertain in extent, amount, or nature **2** left doubtful; inconclusive: *an indeterminate reply* **3** *maths* **a** having no numerical meaning, as % **b** (of an equation) having more than one variable and an unlimited number of solutions > **indeterminable** *adj* > **indeterminacy** *n*

index (in-dex) *n, pl* **-dexes** *or* **-dices** **1** an alphabetical list of names or subjects dealt with in a book, indicating where they are referred to **2** a file or catalogue in a library which enables a book or reference to be found **3** a number indicating the level of wages or prices as compared with some standard value **4** an indication or sign: *national birth rate was once an index of military power* **5** *maths* **a** same as **exponent** **b** a superscript number placed to the left of a radical sign indicating the root to be extracted: *the index of $^3\sqrt{8}$ is* 3 **6** a number or ratio indicating a specific characteristic or property: *refractive index* ▷ *vb* **7** to put an index in (a book) **8** to enter (a word or item) in an index **9** to make index-linked ▶ HISTORY Latin: pointer

indexation *or* **index-linking** *n* the act of making wages, pensions, or interest rates index-linked

index finger *n* the finger next to the thumb. Also called: **forefinger**

index-linked *adj* (of pensions, wages, or interest rates) rising and falling in line with the cost of living

index notation *n maths* the system of writing a small number above and to the right of a number or term to indicate how many times that number or term has to be multiplied by itself. See also **exponent**

Indiaman *n, pl* **-men** (formerly) a merchant ship engaged in trade with India

Indian *adj* **1** of India **2** of the original inhabitants of the American continent ▷ *n* **3** a person from India **4** a person descended from the original inhabitants of the American continent

Indian corn *n* same as **maize**

Indian hemp *n* same as **hemp**

Indian summer *n* **1** a period of warm sunny weather in autumn **2** a period of tranquillity or of renewed productivity towards the end of a person's life or career

Indic *adj* **1** of a branch of Indo-European consisting of many of the languages of India, including Sanskrit, Hindi, and Urdu ▷ *n* **2** this group of languages

indicate *vb* **-cating, -cated** **1** to be or give a sign or symptom of: *to concede 18 goals in 7 games indicates a serious malaise* **2** to point out or show **3** to state briefly **4** to switch on the indicators in a motor vehicle to show that one is changing direction **5** (of measuring instruments) to show a reading of **6** (usually passive) to recommend or require: *surgery seems to be indicated for this patient* ▶ HISTORY Latin *indicare* > **indication** *n*

indicative (in-**dik**-a-tiv) *adj* **1** **indicative of** suggesting: *the symptoms aren't indicative of anything serious* **2** *grammar* denoting a mood of verbs used to make a statement ▷ *n* **3** *grammar* the indicative mood

indicator *n* **1** something that acts as a sign or indication: *an indicator of the moral decline of our society* **2** a device for indicating that a motor vehicle is about to turn left or right, esp. two pairs of lights that flash **3** an instrument, such as a gauge, that registers or measures something **4** *chem* a substance used to indicate the completion of a chemical reaction, usually by a change of colour

indices (in-diss-seez) *n* a plural of **index**

indict (in-**dite**) *vb* to charge (a person) formally with a crime, esp. in writing ▶ HISTORY Latin *in-* against + *dictare* to declare > **indictable** *adj*

indictable offence *n law* a serious criminal offence for which the defendant has the right to be tried by jury. Compare **summary offence**

indictment *n* **1** *criminal law* a formal charge of crime, esp. in writing: *the indictment contained three similar charges against each of the defendants* **2** a serious criticism: *a scathing indictment of faith healing*

indie *n informal* an independent record company

indifference *n* **1** lack of concern or interest: *elite indifference to mass opinion* **2** lack of importance: *a matter of indifference to me*

indifferent *adj* **1** showing no concern or interest: *he was indifferent to politics* **2** of only average standard or quality **3** not at all good: *she had starred in several very indifferent movies* **4** unimportant **5** showing or having no preferences ▶ HISTORY Latin *indifferens* making no distinction

indigenous (in-**dij**-in-uss) *adj* originating or occurring naturally in a country or area: *the indigenous population is under threat* ▶ HISTORY Latin *indigenus*

indigent *adj formal* so poor as to lack even necessities: *the indigent widow of a fellow writer* ▶ HISTORY Latin *indigere* to need > **indigence** *n*

indigestible *adj* difficult or impossible to digest > **indigestibility** *n*

indigestion *n* difficulty in digesting food, accompanied by stomach pain, heartburn, and belching

indignant *adj* feeling or showing indignation ▶ HISTORY Latin *indignari* to be displeased with > **indignantly** *adv*

indignation *n* anger aroused by something felt to be unfair or wrong

indignity *n, pl* **-ties** embarrassing or humiliating treatment

indigo *adj* **1** deep violet-blue ▷ *n, pl* **-gos** *or* **-goes** **2** a dye of this colour originally obtained from plants ▶ HISTORY Spanish *indico*, from Greek *Indikos* of India

indirect *adj* **1** done or caused by someone or something else: *indirect benefits* **2** not going in a direct course or line: *he took the indirect route home*

423

3 not coming straight to the point: *an indirect question* > **indirectly** *adv*

indirect object *n grammar* the person or thing indirectly affected by the action of a verb and its direct object, as *John* in the sentence *I bought John a newspaper*

indirect speech *n grammar* same as **reported speech**

indirect tax *n* a tax levied on goods or services which is paid indirectly by being added to the price

indiscernible *adj* not able or scarcely able to be seen

indiscreet *adj* incautious or tactless in revealing secrets

indiscretion *n* **1** the lack of discretion **2** an indiscreet act or remark

indiscriminate *adj* lacking discrimination or careful choice: *an indiscriminate bombing campaign* > **indiscriminately** *adv* > **indiscrimination** *n*

indispensable *adj* absolutely necessary: *an indispensable guide for any traveller* > **indispensability** *n*

indisposed *adj* **1** sick or ill **2** unwilling ▶ **HISTORY** Latin *indispositus* disordered > **indisposition** *n*

indisputable *adj* beyond doubt

indissoluble *adj* permanent: *joining a political party is not an indissoluble marriage*

indistinct *adj* unable to be seen or heard clearly > **indistinctly** *adv*

indium *n chem* a rare soft silvery metallic element. Symbol: In ▶ **HISTORY** Latin *indicum* indigo

individual *adj* **1** of, relating to, or meant for a single person or thing: *small sums from individual donors* **2** separate or distinct from others of its kind: *please mark the individual pages* **3** characterized by unusual and striking qualities ▷ *n* **4** a single person, esp. when regarded as distinct from others: *respect for the individual* **5** *informal* a person: *a most annoying individual* **6** *biol* a single animal or plant, esp. as distinct from a species ▶ **HISTORY** Latin *individuus* indivisible > **individually** *adv*

individualism *n* **1** the principle of leading one's life in one's own way **2** same as **laissez faire** **3** egotism > **individualist** *n* > **individualistic** *adj*

individuality *n*, *pl* **-ties** **1** distinctive or unique character or personality: *a house of great individuality* **2** the qualities that distinguish one person or thing from another **3** a separate existence

indivisible *adj* **1** unable to be divided **2** *maths* leaving a remainder when divided by a given number

indoctrinate *vb* **-nating, -nated** to teach (someone) systematically to accept a doctrine or opinion uncritically > **indoctrination** *n*

Indo-European *adj* **1** of a family of languages spoken in most of Europe and much of Asia, including English, Russian, and Hindi ▷ *n* **2** the Indo-European family of languages

indolent *adj* lazy; idle ▶ **HISTORY** Latin *indolens* not feeling pain > **indolence** *n*

indomitable *adj* too strong to be defeated or discouraged: *an indomitable work ethic* ▶ **HISTORY** Latin *indomitus* untamable

Indonesian *adj* **1** of Indonesia ▷ *n* **2** a person from Indonesia

indoor *adj* situated, happening, or used inside a building: *an indoor pool*

indoors *adv, adj* inside or into a building

indubitable (in-**dew**-bit-a-bl) *adj* beyond doubt; definite ▶ **HISTORY** Latin *in-* not + *dubitare* to doubt > **indubitably** *adv*

induce *vb* **-ducing, -duced** **1** to persuade or use influence on **2** to cause or bring about **3** *med* to cause (labour) to begin by the use of drugs or other means **4** *logic, obsolete* to draw (a general conclusion) from particular instances **5** to produce (an electromotive force or electrical current) by induction **6** to transmit (magnetism) by induction ▶ **HISTORY** Latin *inducere* to lead in > **inducible** *adj*

inducement *n* **1** something that encourages someone to do something **2** the act of inducing

induct *vb* **1** to bring in formally or install in a job, rank, or position **2** to initiate in knowledge of (a group or profession): *boys are inducted into the world of men* ▶ **HISTORY** Latin *inductus* led in

inductance *n* the property of an electric circuit as a result of which an electromotive force is created by a change of current in the same or in a neighbouring circuit

induction *n* **1** *logic* a process of reasoning by which a general conclusion is drawn from particular instances **2** *med* the process of inducing labour **3** the process by which electrical or magnetic properties are transferred, without physical contact, from one circuit or body to another **4** a formal introduction or entry into an office or position **5** (in an internal-combustion engine) the drawing in of mixed air and fuel from the carburettor to the cylinder > **inductional** *adj*

induction coil *n* a transformer for producing a high voltage from a low voltage. It consists of a soft-iron core, a primary coil of few turns, and a concentric secondary coil of many turns

induction course *n* a training course to help familiarize someone with a new job

inductive *adj* **1** *logic* of or using induction: *inductive reasoning* **2** of or operated by electrical or magnetic induction

inductor *n* a device designed to create inductance in an electrical circuit

indulge *vb* **-dulging, -dulged** **1** (often foll. by *in*) to yield to or gratify (a whim or desire for): *to indulge in new clothes* **2** to allow (someone) to have or do everything he or she wants: *he had given her too much, indulged her in everything* **3** to allow (oneself) the pleasure of something: *he indulged himself* **4** *informal* to take alcoholic drink ▶ **HISTORY** Latin *indulgere* to concede

indulgence *n* **1** something that is allowed because it gives pleasure; extravagance **2** the act of indulging oneself or someone else **3** liberal or tolerant treatment **4** something granted as a favour or privilege **5** *RC Church* a remission of the temporal punishment for sin after its guilt has been forgiven

indulgent *adj* kind or lenient, often to excess > **indulgently** *adv*

industrial *adj* **1** of, used in, or employed in industry **2** with an economy relying heavily on industry: *northern industrial cities*

industrial action *n Brit & Austral* action, such as a strike or work-to-rule, by which workers complain about their conditions

industrial estate *n* **1** *Brit & Austral* an area of land set aside for factories and warehouses **2** (in some Caribbean countries) an area set up with government money in order to encourage manufacturing and processing industries

industrialism *n* an organization of society characterized by large-scale manufacturing industry rather than trade or farming

industrialist *n* a person who owns or controls large amounts of money or property in industry

industrialize or **-ise** *vb* **-izing, -ized** or **-ising, -ised** to develop industry on a large scale in (a country or region) > **industrialization** or **-isation** *n*

industrial relations *pl n* the relations between management and workers

Industrial Revolution *n history* **the Industrial Revolution** the transformation in the 18th and 19th centuries of Britain and other countries into industrial nations

industrious *adj* hard-working

industry *n, pl* **-tries 1** the work and process involved in manufacture: *Japanese industry increased output considerably last year* **2** a branch of commercial enterprise concerned with the manufacture of a specified product: *the steel industry* **3** the quality of working hard ▶ **HISTORY** Latin *industrius* active

inebriate *n* **1** a person who is habitually drunk ▷ *adj* **2** drunk, esp. habitually ▶ **HISTORY** Latin *ebrius* drunk > **inebriation** *n*

inebriated *adj* drunk

inedible *adj* not fit to be eaten

ineducable (in-**ed**-yuke-a-bl) *adj* incapable of being educated

ineffable *adj* too great or intense to be expressed in words ▶ **HISTORY** Latin *in-* not + *effabilis* utterable > **ineffably** *adv*

ineffectual *adj* having no effect or an inadequate effect: *the raids were costly and ineffectual*

inefficient *adj* not performing a task or function to the best advantage > **inefficiency** *n*

inelegant *adj* lacking elegance or refinement

ineligible *adj* not qualified for or entitled to something

ineluctable *adj formal* impossible to avoid: *the ineluctable collapse of the coalition* ▶ **HISTORY** Latin *in-* not + *eluctari* to escape

inept *adj* **1** awkward, clumsy, or incompetent **2** not suitable or fitting; out of place ▶ **HISTORY** Latin *in-* not + *aptus* fitting > **ineptitude** *n*

inequality *n, pl* **-ties 1** the state or quality of being unequal **2** an instance of this **3** lack of smoothness or regularity of a surface **4** *maths* a statement indicating that the value of one quantity or expression is not equal to another

inequation *n maths* a mathematical statement showing that two values are not equal, but greater or less than each other

inequitable *adj* unjust or unfair

inequity *n, pl* **-ties 1** injustice or unfairness **2** something which is unjust or unfair

ineradicable *adj* impossible to remove or root out: *an ineradicable distrust of foreigners*

inert *adj* **1** without the power to move or to resist motion **2** inactive or lifeless **3** having only a limited ability to react chemically ▶ **HISTORY** Latin *iners* unskilled

inertia *n* **1** a feeling of unwillingness to do anything **2** *physics* the tendency of a body to remain still or continue moving unless a force is applied to it > **inertial** *adj*

inertia selling *n Brit* the illegal practice of sending unrequested goods to householders, followed by a bill for the goods if they do not return them

inescapable *adj* not able to be avoided

inestimable *adj* too great to be calculated

inevitable *adj* **1** unavoidable; sure to happen **2** *informal* so regular as to be predictable: *the inevitable guitar solo* ▷ *n* **3** (often preceded by *the*) something that is unavoidable ▶ **HISTORY** Latin *in-* not + *evitare* to avoid > **inevitability** *n* > **inevitably** *adv*

inexorable *adj* unable to be prevented from continuing or progressing: *an inexorable trend* ▶ **HISTORY** Latin *in-* not + *exorare* to prevail upon > **inexorably** *adv*

inexperienced *adj* having no knowledge or experience of a particular situation, activity, etc. > **inexperience** *n*

inexpert *adj* lacking skill

inexplicable *adj* impossible to explain

in extremis *adv* **1** in dire straits **2** at the point of death

inextricable *adj* **1** impossible to escape from: *an inextricable dilemma* **2** impossible to disentangle or separate: *an inextricable mass of twisted metal* > **inextricably** *adv*

inf. 1 infantry **2** infinitive **3** informal **4** information

infallible *adj* **1** incapable of error **2** always successful: *an infallible cure* **3** (of the Pope) incapable of error in setting forth matters of doctrine on faith and morals > **infallibility** *n* > **infallibly** *adv*

infamous (**in**-fam-uss) *adj* well-known for something bad

infamy *n, pl* **-mies 1** the state of being infamous **2** an infamous act or event ▶ **HISTORY** Latin *infamis* of evil repute

infancy *n, pl* **-cies 1** the state or period of being an infant **2** an early stage of growth or development: *virtual reality is in its infancy* **3** *law* the state or period of being a minor

infant *n* **1** a very young child; baby **2** *law* same as **minor** (sense 4) **3** *Brit* a young school child ▷ *adj* **4** of, relating to, or designed for young children: *infant school* **5** in an early stage of development: *an infant democracy*

- ■ **WORD HISTORY**
- ■ An infant is literally a child who is too young
- ■ to have learned to talk. The word comes from
- ■ Latin *infans*, meaning 'unable to speak', from
- ■ *in-*, meaning 'not', and *fārī*, meaning 'to speak'.

infanta *n* (formerly) **1** a daughter of a king of Spain or Portugal **2** the wife of an infante ▶ HISTORY Spanish and Portuguese

infante *n* (formerly) any son of a king of Spain or Portugal, except the heir to the throne ▶ HISTORY Spanish and Portuguese

infanticide *n* **1** the act of killing an infant **2** a person who kills an infant ▶ HISTORY INFANT + Latin *caedere* to kill

infantile *adj* **1** childishly immature **2** of infants or infancy

infantile paralysis *n* same as **poliomyelitis**

infant mortality rate *n* the number of deaths of infants under the age of one per 1000 live births. Abbrev: **IMR**

infantry *n, pl* **-tries** soldiers who fight on foot ▶ HISTORY Italian *infanteria*

infant school *n* (in England and Wales) a school for children aged between 5 and 7

infatuate *vb* **-ating, -ated** to inspire or fill with an intense and unreasoning passion ▶ HISTORY Latin *infatuare* > **infatuation** *n*

infatuated *adj* (often foll. by *with*) carried away by an intense and unreasoning passion for someone

infect *vb* **1** to contaminate (a person or thing) with a germ or virus or its consequent disease **2** to taint or contaminate **3** to affect with an opinion or feeling as if by contagion: *even she was infected by the excitement* ▶ HISTORY Latin *inficere* to stain

infection *n* **1** an infectious disease **2** contamination of a person or thing by a germ or virus or its consequent disease

infectious *adj* **1** (of a disease) capable of being transmitted without actual contact **2** causing or transmitting infection **3** spreading from one person to another: *infectious laughter*

infectious mononucleosis *n* same as **glandular fever**

infer *vb* **-ferring, -ferred** **1** to conclude by reasoning from evidence; deduce **2** *not universally accepted* to imply or suggest ▶ HISTORY Latin *inferre* to bring into

inference *n* **1** the act or process of reaching a conclusion by reasoning from evidence **2** an inferred conclusion or deduction

inferior *adj* **1** lower in quality, quantity, or usefulness **2** lower in rank, position, or status **3** of poor quality **4** lower in position **5** *printing* (of a character) printed at the foot of an ordinary character ▷ *n* **6** a person inferior to another, esp. in rank ▶ HISTORY Latin: lower > **inferiority** *n*

inferior court *n* *law* a court of limited jurisdiction. Compare **superior court**

inferiority complex *n* *psychiatry* a disorder arising from a feeling of inferiority to others, characterized by aggressiveness or extreme shyness

infernal *adj* **1** of or relating to hell **2** *informal* irritating: *stop that infernal noise* ▶ HISTORY Latin *infernus* lower

inferno *n, pl* **-nos** **1** an intense raging fire **2** a place or situation resembling hell, because it is crowded and noisy **3 the inferno** hell ▶ HISTORY Late Latin *infernus* hell

infertile *adj* **1** not capable of producing offspring **2** (of soil) not productive; barren > **infertility** *n*

infest *vb* to inhabit or overrun (a place, plant, etc.) in unpleasantly large numbers: *the area was infested with moles* ▶ HISTORY Latin *infestare* to molest > **infestation** *n*

infidel *n* **1** a person who has no religious belief **2** a person who rejects a specific religion, esp. Christianity or Islam ▷ *adj* **3** of unbelievers or unbelief ▶ HISTORY Latin *infidelis* unfaithful

infidelity *n, pl* **-ties** **1** unfaithfulness to one's partner **2** an act or instance of unfaithfulness

infield *n* **1** *cricket* the area of the field near the pitch **2** *baseball* the area of the playing field enclosed by the base lines > **infielder** *n*

infighting *n* **1** rivalry or quarrelling between members of the same group or organization **2** *boxing* combat at close quarters

infiltrate *vb* **-trating, -trated** **1** to enter (an organization, area, etc.) gradually and in secret, so as to gain influence or control: *they infiltrated the party structure* **2** to pass (a liquid or gas) through (a substance) by filtering or (of a liquid or gas) to pass through (a substance) by filtering > **infiltrator** *n*

infiltration *n* **1** the act of entering (an organization, area, etc.) gradually and in secret, so as to gain influence or control **2** the passing (of a liquid or gas) through (a substance) by filtering **3** *geog* the seeping of surface water into the soil

infinite (**in**-fin-it) *adj* **1** having no limits or boundaries in time, space, extent, or size **2** extremely or immeasurably great or numerous: *infinite wealth* **3** *maths* having an unlimited or uncountable number of digits, factors, or terms > **infinitely** *adv*

infinitesimal *adj* **1** extremely small: *an infinitesimal risk* **2** *maths* of or involving a small change in the value of a variable that approaches zero as a limit ▷ *n* **3** *maths* an infinitesimal quantity

infinitive (in-**fin**-it-iv) *n* *grammar* a form of the verb which in most languages is not inflected for tense or person and is used without a particular subject: in English, the infinitive usually consists of the word *to* followed by the verb

infinity *n, pl* **-ties** **1** an infinitely great number or amount **2** endless time, space, or quantity **3** *maths* the concept of a value greater than any finite numerical value

infirm *adj* physically or mentally weak, esp. from old age

infirmary *n, pl* **-ries** a place for the treatment of sick or injured people; hospital

infirmity *n, pl* **-ties** 1 the state of being infirm 2 physical weakness or frailty

infix *vb* 1 to fix firmly in 2 to instil or impress on the mind by repetition **> infixation** *or* **infixion** *n*

in flagrante delicto (in flag-**grant**-ee dee-**lick**-toe) *adv chiefly law* while committing the offence ▶ HISTORY Latin

inflame *vb* **-flaming, -flamed** 1 to make angry or excited 2 to increase or intensify; aggravate 3 to produce inflammation in or become inflamed 4 to set or be set on fire

inflammable *adj* 1 liable to catch fire 2 easily aroused to anger or passion **> inflammability** *n*

inflammation *n* 1 the reaction of living tissue to injury or infection, characterized by heat, redness, swelling, and pain 2 an inflaming or being inflamed

inflammatory *adj* 1 likely to provoke anger 2 characterized by or caused by inflammation

inflatable *adj* 1 capable of being inflated ▷ *n* 2 a plastic or rubber object which can be inflated

inflate *vb* **-flating, -flated** 1 to expand or cause to expand by filling with gas or air 2 to give an impression of greater importance than is justified: *something to inflate their self-esteem* 3 to cause or undergo economic inflation ▶ HISTORY Latin *inflare* to blow into

inflation *n* 1 an inflating or being inflated 2 *econ* a progressive increase in the general level of prices brought about by an increase in the amount of money in circulation or by increases in costs 3 *informal* the rate of increase of prices **> inflationary** *adj*

inflect *vb* 1 to change (the voice) in tone or pitch 2 *grammar* to change (the form of a word) by inflection 3 to bend or curve ▶ HISTORY Latin *inflectere* to curve, alter **> inflective** *adj*

inflection *or* **inflexion** *n* 1 *written* a change in the pitch of the voice 2 *grammar* a change in the form of a word, signalling change in such grammatical functions as tense or number 3 an angle or bend 4 an inflecting or being inflected 5 *maths* a change in curvature from concave to convex or vice versa **> inflectional** *or* **inflexional** *adj*

inflexible *adj* 1 unwilling to be persuaded; obstinate 2 (of a rule, etc.) firmly fixed: *inflexible schedules* 3 incapable of being bent: *inflexible joints* **> inflexibility** *n*

inflict *vb* 1 to impose (something unpleasant) on 2 to deliver (a blow or wound) ▶ HISTORY Latin *infligere* to strike (something) against **> infliction** *n* **> inflictor** *n*

inflorescence *n bot* 1 the arrangement of the flowers on the stalks 2 the part of a plant that consists of the flower-bearing stalks 3 the process of flowering; blossoming ▶ HISTORY Latin *in-* into + *florescere* to bloom

inflow *n* 1 something, such as a liquid or gas, that flows in 2 the act of flowing in; influx

influence *n* 1 an effect of one person or thing on another 2 the power of a person or thing to have such an effect 3 power resulting from ability, wealth, or position 4 a person or thing with influence 5 **under the influence** *informal* drunk ▷ *vb* **-encing, -enced** 6 to have an effect upon (actions or events) 7 to persuade or induce ▶ HISTORY Latin *influere* to flow into

influential *adj* having or exerting influence

influenza *n* a highly contagious viral disease characterized by fever, muscular pains, and catarrh ▶ HISTORY Italian: influence, hence incursion, epidemic

influx *n* 1 the arrival or entry of many people or things 2 the act of flowing in ▶ HISTORY Latin *influere* to flow into

info *n informal* short for **information**

inform *vb* 1 to give information to; tell: *he informed me that he would be free after lunch* 2 to make knowledgeable (about) or familiar (with): *he'll be informed of his rights* 3 to give incriminating information to the police 4 to impart some essential or formative characteristic to 5 to animate or inspire ▶ HISTORY Latin *informare* to describe **> informed** *adj*

informal *adj* 1 relaxed and friendly: *an informal interview* 2 appropriate to everyday life or use rather than formal occasions: *informal clothes* 3 (of speech or writing) appropriate to ordinary conversation rather than to formal written language **> informality** *n* **> informally** *adv*

informant *n* a person who gives information

information *n* 1 knowledge acquired in any manner; facts 2 *computers* **a** the meaning given to data by the way it is interpreted **b** same as **data** (sense 2)

information age *n* a time when large amounts of information are available to people through computer technology

information superhighway *n* the concept of a worldwide network of computers transferring information at high speed

information technology *n* the production, storage, and communication of information using computers and electronic technology

information theory *n* the study of the processes of communication and the transmission of information

informative *adj* giving useful information

informer *n* a person who informs to the police

infra dig *adj informal* beneath one's dignity ▶ HISTORY Latin *infra dignitatem*

infrared *adj* 1 of or using rays with a wavelength just beyond the red end of the visible spectrum ▷ *n* 2 the infrared part of the spectrum ▶ HISTORY Latin *infra* beneath

infrasonic *adj* having a frequency below the range audible to the human ear ▶ HISTORY Latin *infra* beneath

infrasound *n* infrasonic waves

427

infrastructure *n* **1** the basic structure of an organization or system **2** the stock of facilities, services, and equipment in a country, including factories, roads, and schools, that are needed for it to function properly ▶ HISTORY Latin *infra* beneath

infrequent *adj* not happening often > **infrequently** *adv*

infringe *vb* **-fringing, -fringed 1** to violate or break (a law or agreement) **2 infringe on** *or* **upon** to encroach or trespass on: *the press infringed on their privacy* ▶ HISTORY Latin *infringere* to break off > **infringement** *n*

infuriate *vb* **-ating, -ated** to make very angry ▶ HISTORY Medieval Latin *infuriare* > **infuriating** *adj* > **infuriatingly** *adv*

infuse *vb* **-fusing, -fused 1** to fill with (an emotion or quality) **2** to soak or be soaked in order to extract flavour ▶ HISTORY Latin *infundere* to pour into

infusion *n* **1** the act of infusing **2** a liquid obtained by infusing

ingenious (in-**jean**-ee-uss) *adj* showing cleverness and originality: *a truly ingenious invention* ▶ HISTORY Latin *ingenium* natural ability

ingenuity (in-jen-**new**-it-ee) *n* cleverness at inventing things ▶ HISTORY Latin *ingenuitas* a freeborn condition; meaning influenced by INGENIOUS

ingenuous (in-**jen**-new-uss) *adj* **1** unsophisticated and trusting **2** frank and straightforward ▶ HISTORY Latin *ingenuus* freeborn, virtuous

ingest *vb* to take (food or liquid) into the body ▶ HISTORY Latin *ingerere* to put into > **ingestion** *n*

inglenook *n Brit* a corner by a fireplace

inglorious *adj* dishonourable or shameful

ingoing *adj* going in; entering

ingot *n* a piece of metal cast in a form suitable for storage, usually a bar ▶ HISTORY origin unknown

ingrained *or* **engrained** *adj* **1** (of a habit, feeling, or belief) deeply impressed or instilled **2** (of dirt) worked into or through the fibre or pores ▶ HISTORY *dyed in grain* dyed with kermes through the fibre

ingratiate *vb* **-ating, -ated** to act in order to bring (oneself) into favour (with someone) ▶ HISTORY Latin *in-* in + *gratia* favour > **ingratiating** *adj*

ingratitude *n* lack of gratitude or thanks

ingredient *n* a component of a mixture or compound, esp. in cooking ▶ HISTORY Latin *ingrediens* going into

ingress *n formal* **1** the act of going or coming in **2** the right or permission to enter ▶ HISTORY Latin *ingressus*

ingrowing *adj* (esp. of a toenail) growing abnormally into the flesh > **ingrown** *adj*

inhabit *vb* to live or dwell in ▶ HISTORY Latin *inhabitare* > **inhabitable** *adj*

inhabitant *n* a person or animal that is a permanent resident of a particular place or region

inhalant (in-**hale**-ant) *n* a medicinal preparation inhaled to help breathing problems

inhale *vb* **-haling, -haled** to breathe in (air, smoke, or vapour) ▶ HISTORY Latin *in-* in + *halare* to breathe > **inhalation** *n*

inhaler *n* a container used to administer an inhalant

inherent *adj* existing as an inseparable part > **inherently** *adv*

inherit *vb* **1** to receive money, property, or a title from someone who has died **2** to receive (a characteristic) from an earlier generation by heredity **3** to receive (a position or situation) from a predecessor: *he inherited a mess* ▶ HISTORY Old French *enheriter* > **inheritor** *n*

inheritable *adj* **1** capable of being transmitted by heredity from one generation to a later one **2** capable of being inherited

inheritance *n* **1** *law* **a** hereditary succession to an estate or title **b** the right of an heir to succeed on the death of an ancestor **2** something inherited or to be inherited **3** the act of inheriting **4** the fact of receiving characteristics from an earlier generation by heredity

inheritance tax *n* (in Britain) a tax consisting of a percentage levied on the part of an inheritance that exceeds a specified allowance

inhibit *vb* **1** to restrain or hinder (an impulse or desire) **2** to prohibit or prevent: *an attempt to inhibit nuclear proliferation* **3** *chem* to stop, prevent, or decrease the rate of (a chemical reaction) ▶ HISTORY Latin *inhibere* > **inhibited** *adj* > **inhibitor** *n*

inhibition *n* **1** *psychol* a feeling of fear or embarrassment that stops one from behaving naturally **2** an inhibiting or being inhibited **3** the process of stopping or retarding a chemical reaction

inhospitable *adj* **1** not welcoming; unfriendly **2** (of a place or climate) not easy to live in; harsh

inhuman *adj* **1** cruel or brutal **2** not human

inhumane *adj* extremely cruel or brutal

inhumanity *n, pl* **-ties 1** lack of kindness or compassion **2** an inhumane act

inimical *adj* **1** adverse or unfavourable: *inimical to change* **2** unfriendly or hostile ▶ HISTORY Latin *in-* not + *amicus* friendly

inimitable *adj* impossible to imitate > **inimitably** *adv*

iniquity *n, pl* **-ties 1** injustice or wickedness **2** a wicked act ▶ HISTORY Latin *iniquus* unfair > **iniquitous** *adj*

initial *adj* **1** of or at the beginning ▷ *n* **2** the first letter of a word, esp. a person's name **3** *printing* a large letter set at the beginning of a chapter or work ▷ *vb* **-tialling, -tialled** *or US* **-tialing, -tialed 4** to sign with one's initials, esp. to indicate approval ▶ HISTORY Latin *initium* beginning > **initially** *adv*

initiate *vb* **-ating, -ated 1** to begin or set going: *more women initiate divorce today* **2** to accept (new members) into a group, often through secret

ceremonies **3** to teach the fundamentals of a skill or knowledge to (someone) ▷ *n* **4** a person who has been initiated, esp. recently **5** a beginner
▶ **HISTORY** Latin *initiare* > **initiation** *n* > **initiator** *n*

initiative *n* **1** a first step; commencing move: *a peace initiative* **2** the right or power to initiate something: *it forced local people to take the initiative* **3** enterprise: *the drive and initiative to create new products* **4** **on one's own initiative** without being prompted

inject *vb* **1** *med* to put (a fluid) into the body with a syringe **2** to introduce (a new element): *to inject a dose of realism into the assessment* ▶ **HISTORY** Latin *injicere* to throw in > **injection** *n*

injudicious *adj* showing poor judgment; unwise

injunction *n* **1** *law* a court order not to do something **2** an authoritative command
▶ **HISTORY** Latin *injungere* to enjoin
> **injunctive** *adj*

injure *vb* **-juring, -jured** **1** to hurt physically or mentally **2** to do wrong to (a person), esp. by an injustice: *the injured party* **3** to damage: *an opportunity to injure your reputation* > **injured** *adj*

injurious *adj* **1** causing harm **2** abusive, slanderous, or libellous

injury *n, pl* **-ries** **1** physical hurt **2** a specific instance of this: *a leg injury* **3** harm done to the feelings **4** damage: *inflict no injury on the wealth of the nation* ▶ **HISTORY** Latin *injuria* injustice

injury time *n* *sport* playing time added at the end of a match to compensate for time spent treating injured players. Also called: **stoppage time**

injustice *n* **1** unfairness **2** an unfair action

ink *n* **1** a black or coloured liquid used for printing, writing, and drawing **2** a dark brown fluid squirted for self-concealment by an octopus or cuttlefish ▷ *vb* **3** to mark or cover with ink **4** **ink in** to arrange or confirm definitely ▶ **HISTORY** Old French *enque*

inkling *n* a vague idea or suspicion ▶ **HISTORY** Middle English *inclen* to hint at

inky *adj* **inkier, inkiest** **1** dark or black, like ink **2** stained with ink > **inkiness** *n*

inlaid *adj* **1** set in another material so that the surface is smooth, such as a design in wood **2** made in this way: *an inlaid table-top*

inland *adj* **1** of or in the interior of a country or region, away from a sea or border **2** *chiefly Brit* operating within a country or region; domestic: *inland trade* ▷ *adv* **4** towards or into the interior of a country or region

Inland Revenue *n* (in New Zealand and formerly in Britain) a government department that collects major direct taxes

inlay *vb* **-laying, -laid** **1** to decorate (an article, esp. of furniture) by inserting pieces of wood, ivory, or metal so that the surfaces are smooth and flat ▷ *n* **2** decoration made by inlaying **3** an inlaid article **4** *dentistry* a filling shaped to fit a cavity

inlet *n* **1** a narrow strip of water extending from the sea into the land **2** a passage or valve through which a liquid or gas enters a machine

in loco parentis (par-**rent**-iss) in place of a parent: said of a person acting for a parent
▶ **HISTORY** Latin

inmate *n* a person who is confined to an institution such as a prison or hospital

in media res *adv* *literature* in or into the middle of events or a narrative; used of books which start in the middle of events and then make use of flashback ▶ **HISTORY** literally: into the midst of things, taken from a passage in Horace's *Ars Poetica*

inmost *adj* same as **innermost**

inn *n* a pub or small hotel providing food and accommodation ▶ **HISTORY** Old English

innards *pl n* *informal* **1** the internal organs of the body, esp. the entrails **2** the working parts of a machine ▶ **HISTORY** variant of *inwards*

innate *adj* existing from birth, rather than acquired; inborn: *his innate decency* ▶ **HISTORY** Latin *innasci* to be born in > **innately** *adv*

inner *adj* **1** happening or located inside or further inside: *the door to the inner office* **2** of the mind or spirit: *her inner self* **3** exclusive or private: *the inner sanctum of the party secretariat* **4** more profound; less apparent: *the inner meaning* ▷ *n* **5** *archery* **a** the red innermost ring on a target **b** a shot which hits this ring

inner child *n* *psychol* the part of the psyche that retains the feelings as they were experienced in childhood

inner city *n* the parts of a city in or near its centre, where there are often social and economic problems

inner ear *n* the innermost part of the ear, responsible for the detection of sound

innermost *adj* **1** most intimate or private: *innermost secrets* **2** furthest within

inner tube *n* an inflatable rubber tube inside a pneumatic tyre casing

inning *n* *baseball* a division of the game consisting of a turn at batting and a turn in the field for each side ▶ **HISTORY** Old English *innung* a going in

innings *n* **1** *cricket* **a** the batting turn of a player or team **b** the runs scored during such a turn **2** a period of opportunity or action

innkeeper *n* an owner or manager of an inn

innocence *n* the quality or state of being innocent ▶ **HISTORY** Latin *innocentia* harmlessness

innocent *adj* **1** not guilty of a particular crime **2** without experience of evil **3** harmless or innocuous **4** **innocent of** without or lacking: *innocent of prejudice* ▷ *n* **5** an innocent person, esp. a young child or a naive adult > **innocently** *adv*

innocuous *adj* having no adverse or harmful effect ▶ **HISTORY** Latin *innocuus*

innovate *vb* **-vating, -vated** to introduce new ideas or methods ▶ **HISTORY** Latin *innovare* to renew > **innovative** or **innovatory** *adj* > **innovator** *n*

innovation *n* **1** something newly introduced, such as a new method or device **2** the act of innovating

innuendo *n, pl* **-dos** *or* **-does** an indirect or subtle reference to something rude or unpleasant
▶ HISTORY Latin: by hinting

Innuit (in-new-it) *n* same as **Inuit**

innumerable *adj* too many to be counted
> **innumerably** *adv*

innumerate *adj* having no understanding of mathematics or science > **innumeracy** *n*

inoculate *vb* **-lating, -lated** **1** to protect against disease by injecting with a vaccine **2** to introduce (microorganisms, esp. bacteria) into (a culture medium) ▶ HISTORY Latin *inoculare* to implant
> **inoculation** *n*

inoffensive *adj* causing no harm or annoyance

inoperable *adj* *surgery* unable to be safely operated on: *an inoperable tumour*

inoperative *adj* not working or functioning: *continued shelling has rendered the ceasefire inoperative*

inopportune *adj* badly timed or inappropriate

inordinate *adj* **1** excessive: *an inordinate amount of time spent arguing* **2** unrestrained, as in behaviour or emotion: *inordinate anger* ▶ HISTORY Latin *inordinatus* disordered > **inordinately** *adv*

inorganic *adj* **1** not having the structure or characteristics of living organisms **2** *chem* of or denoting chemical compounds that do not contain carbon **3** not resulting from or produced by growth; artificial: *inorganic fertilizers*

inorganic chemistry *n* the branch of chemistry concerned with the elements and compounds which do not contain carbon

inpatient *n* a patient who stays in a hospital for treatment

input *n* **1** resources, such as money, labour, or power, put into a project **2** *computers* the data fed into a computer ▷ *vb* **-putting, -put** **3** to enter (data) in a computer

inquest *n* **1** an official inquiry into an unexplained, sudden, or violent death, held by a coroner **2** *informal* an investigation or discussion ▶ HISTORY Latin *in-* into + *quaesitus* investigation

inquietude *n* *formal* restlessness or anxiety

inquire *or* **enquire** *vb* **-quiring, -quired** **1** to seek information (about) **2** **inquire into** to make an investigation **3** **inquire after** to ask about the health or progress of (a person) **4** **inquire of** to ask (a person) for information: *I'll inquire of my aunt when she is coming* ▶ HISTORY Latin *inquirere*
> **inquirer** *or* **enquirer** *n*

inquiry *or* **enquiry** *n, pl* **-ries** **1** a question **2** an investigation

inquisition *n* **1** a thorough investigation **2** an official inquiry, esp. one held by a jury before an officer of the Crown > **inquisitional** *adj*

Inquisition *n* *history* an organization within the Catholic Church (1232–1820) for suppressing heresy

inquisitive *adj* **1** excessively curious about other people's business **2** eager to learn > **inquisitively** *adv* > **inquisitiveness** *n*

inquisitor *n* **1** a person who inquires, esp. deeply or ruthlessly **2** **Inquisitor** an officer of the Inquisition

inquisitorial *adj* **1** of or like an inquisition or an inquisitor **2** offensively curious
> **inquisitorially** *adv*

inquisitorial system *n* *law* a legal system in which it is the duty of judges to investigate cases and to try to ascertain the truth; usual in countries where the legal system is based on civil law. Compare **adversarial system**

inquorate *adj* without enough people present to make a quorum

in re (in *ray*) *prep* in the matter of; concerning
▶ HISTORY Latin

INRI Jesus of Nazareth, king of the Jews (the inscription placed over Christ's head during the Crucifixion) ▶ HISTORY Latin *Iesus Nazarenus Rex Iudaeorum*

inroads *pl n* **make inroads into** to start affecting or reducing: *my gambling has made great inroads into my savings*

ins. **1** inches **2** insurance

insane *adj* **1** mentally deranged **2** stupidly irresponsible: *acting on an insane impulse*
> **insanely** *adv*

insanitary *adj* dirty or unhealthy

insanity *n, pl* **-ties** **1** the state of being insane **2** stupidity

insatiable (in-*saysh*-a-bl) *adj* impossible to satisfy > **insatiability** *n* > **insatiably** *adv*

inscribe *vb* **-scribing, -scribed** **1** to mark or engrave with (words, symbols, or letters) **2** to write one's name, and sometimes a brief dedication, on (a book) before giving to someone **3** to enter (a name) on a list **4** *geom* to draw (a geometric construction) inside another construction so that the two are in contact at as many points as possible but do not intersect
▶ HISTORY Latin *inscribere*

inscription *n* **1** something inscribed, esp. words carved or engraved on a coin, tomb, or ring **2** a signature or brief dedication in a book or on a work of art

inscrutable *adj* mysterious or enigmatic
▶ HISTORY Latin *in-* not + *scrutari* to examine
> **inscrutability** *n*

insect *n* **1** a small animal that has six legs and usually has wings, such as an ant, fly, or butterfly **2** (loosely) any similar invertebrate, such as a spider, tick, or centipede ▶ HISTORY Latin *insectum* (animal that has been) cut into

insecticide *n* a substance used to destroy insects
▶ HISTORY *insect* + Latin *caedere* to kill

insectivore *n* **1** a small mammal, such as a hedgehog or a shrew, that eats invertebrates **2** a plant or animal that eats insects ▶ HISTORY *insect* + Latin *vorare* to swallow
> **insectivorous** *adj*

insecure *adj* **1** anxious or uncertain **2** not adequately protected: *low-paid or insecure employment* **3** unstable or shaky > **insecurity** *n*

inselberg *n* *geog* an isolated rocky hill rising abruptly from a flat plain ▶ HISTORY German *Insel* island + *Berg* mountain

inseminate *vb* **-nating, -nated** to impregnate (a female) with semen ▶ HISTORY Latin *in-* in + *semen* seed > **insemination** *n*

insensate *adj* **1** lacking sensation or consciousness **2** insensitive or unfeeling **3** foolish

insensible *adj* **1** unconscious **2** without feeling **3** insensible of *or* to unaware of or indifferent to: *insensible to suffering* **4** imperceptible > **insensibility** *n*

insensitive *adj* unaware of or ignoring other people's feelings > **insensitivity** *n*

inseparable *adj* **1** constantly together because of mutual liking: *they became inseparable companions* **2** too closely connected to be separated > **inseparably** *adv*

insert *vb* **1** to place or fit (something) inside something else **2** to introduce (a clause or comment) into text or a speech ▷ *n* **3** something inserted, esp. an advertisement in between the pages of a magazine ▶ HISTORY Latin *inserere* to plant in

insertion *n* **1** the act of inserting **2** something inserted, such as an advertisement in a newspaper

inset *vb* **-setting, -set** **1** to place in or within; insert ▷ *n* **2** something inserted **3** *printing* a small map or diagram set within the borders of a larger one ▷ *adj* **4** decorated with something inserted

inshore *adj* **1** in or on the water, but close to the shore: *inshore fishermen* ▷ *adv, adj* **2** towards the shore from the water: *the boat was forced inshore; an inshore wind dashes the boats*

inside *prep* **1** in or to the interior of: *a bomb had gone off inside the parliament building* **2** in a period of time less than: *they took the lead inside seven minutes* ▷ *adj* **3** on or of the inside: *an article on the paper's inside pages* **4** by or from someone within an organization, esp. illicitly: *inside information* **5** of or being the lane in a road which is nearer the side than other lanes going in the same direction: *all the lorries were in the inside lane* ▷ *adv* **6** on, in, or to the inside; indoors: *when the rain started we took our drinks inside* **7** *Brit, Austral & NZ, slang* in or into prison ▷ *n* **8** the inner side, surface, or part of something **9** inside out with the inside facing outwards **10** know inside out to know thoroughly ▷ See also **insides**

insider *n* a member of a group or organization who therefore has exclusive information about it

insider dealing *n* the illegal practice of a person on the stock exchange or in the civil service taking advantage of early confidential information in order to deal in shares for personal profit

insides *pl n informal* the stomach and bowels

insidious *adj* working in a subtle or apparently harmless way, but nevertheless dangerous or deadly: *an insidious virus* ▶ HISTORY Latin *insidiae* an ambush > **insidiously** *adv* > **insidiousness** *n*

insight *n* **1** a penetrating understanding, as of a complex situation or problem **2** the ability to perceive clearly or deeply the inner nature of things

insignia (in-**sig**-nee-a) *n, pl* **-nias** *or* **-nia** a badge or emblem of membership, office, or honour ▶ HISTORY Latin: badges

insignificant *adj* having little or no importance > **insignificance** *n*

insincere *adj* pretending what one does not feel > **insincerely** *adv* > **insincerity** *n*

insinuate *vb* **-ating, -ated** **1** to suggest indirectly by allusion, hints, or innuendo **2** to get (someone, esp. oneself) into a position by gradual manoeuvres: *she insinuated herself into the conversation* ▶ HISTORY Latin *insinuare* to wind one's way into

insinuation *n* **1** an indirect or devious hint or suggestion **2** an act or the practice of insinuating

insipid *adj* **1** dull and boring **2** lacking flavour ▶ HISTORY Latin *in-* not + *sapidus* full of flavour > **insipidity** *n*

insist *vb* (often foll. by *on* or *upon*) **1** to make a determined demand (for): *he insisted on his rights* **2** to express a convinced belief (in) or assertion (of): *she insisted that she had been given permission* ▶ HISTORY Latin *insistere* to stand upon, urge

insistent *adj* **1** making continual and persistent demands **2** demanding attention: *the chirruping of an insistent bird* > **insistence** *n* > **insistently** *adv*

in situ *adv, adj* in the original position ▶ HISTORY Latin

in so far as *or* **insofar as** *prep* to the degree or extent that

insolation *n* **1** *geog* the quantity of solar radiation falling upon a body or planet, esp. per unit area **2** exposure to the sun's rays **3** another name for **sunstroke**

insole *n* **1** the inner sole of a shoe or boot **2** a loose inner sole used to give extra warmth or to make a shoe fit

insolent *adj* rude and disrespectful ▶ HISTORY Latin *in-* not + *solere* to be accustomed > **insolence** *n* > **insolently** *adv*

insoluble *adj* **1** impossible to solve **2** not able to be dissolved > **insolubility** *n*

insolvent *adj* **1** unable to pay one's debts ▷ *n* **2** a person who is insolvent > **insolvency** *n*

insomnia *n* inability to sleep ▶ HISTORY Latin *in-* not + *somnus* sleep > **insomniac** *n, adj*

insomuch *adv* **1** (foll. by *as* or *that*) to such an extent or degree **2** (foll. by *as*) because of the fact (that)

insouciant *adj* carefree or unconcerned ▶ HISTORY French > **insouciance** *n*

inspan *vb* **-spanning, -spanned** *chiefly S African* **1** to harness (animals) to (a vehicle); yoke **2** to press (people) into service ▶ HISTORY Middle Dutch *inspannen*

inspect *vb* **1** to examine closely, esp. for faults or errors **2** to examine officially ▶ HISTORY Latin *inspicere* > **inspection** *n*

inspector *n* **1** an official who checks that things or places meet certain regulations and standards **2** a police officer ranking below a superintendent and above a sergeant

inspectorate *n* **1** a group of inspectors **2** the position or duties of an inspector

inspiration *n* **1** stimulation of the mind or feelings to activity or creativity **2** a person or thing that causes this state **3** an inspired idea or action **4** *biol* the action of drawing air or gas into the lungs > **inspirational** *adj*

inspire *vb* **-spiring, -spired 1** to stimulate (a person) to activity or creativity **2** to arouse (an emotion or a reaction): *he inspires confidence* **3** *biol* to draw air or gas into the lungs ▷ **HISTORY** Latin *in-* into + *spirare* to breathe

inst. *old-fashioned* instant (this month)

instability *n* lack of steadiness or reliability

install *vb* **1** to put in and prepare (equipment) for use **2** to place (a person) formally in a position or rank **3** to settle (a person, esp. oneself) in a position or state: *Tony installed himself in an armchair* ▷ **HISTORY** Medieval Latin *installare*

installation *n* **1** installing **2** equipment that has been installed **3** a place containing equipment for a particular purpose: *radar installation*

installment plan *n* US same as **hire-purchase**. Also (Canad): **instalment plan**

instalment *or US* **installment** *n* **1** one of the portions into which a debt is divided for payment at regular intervals **2** a portion of something that is issued, broadcast, or published in parts ▷ **HISTORY** probably from Old French *estal* something fixed

instance *n* **1** a case or particular example **2 for instance** as an example **3 in the first instance** in the first place; initially **4** urgent request or order: *at the instance of* ▷ *vb* **-stancing, -stanced 5** to mention as an example ▷ **HISTORY** Latin *instantia* a being close upon

instant *n* **1** a very brief time; moment **2** a particular moment: *at the same instant* ▷ *adj* **3** immediate **4** (of foods) able to be prepared very quickly and easily: *instant coffee* **5** urgent or pressing **6** of the present month: *a letter of the 7th instant* ▷ **HISTORY** Latin *instans* present, pressing closely

instantaneous *adj* happening at once: *the applause was instantaneous* > **instantaneously** *adv*

instantly *adv* immediately

instant message *n* **1** an electronic message sent in real time over a computer network ▷ *vb* **instant-message 2** to communicate with (another person) using such messages > **instant messaging** *n*

instead *adv* **1** as a replacement or substitute for the person or thing mentioned **2 instead of** in place of or as an alternative to ▷ **HISTORY** *in stead* in place

instep *n* **1** the middle part of the foot forming the arch between the ankle and toes **2** the part of a shoe or stocking covering this

instigate *vb* **-gating, -gated 1** to cause to happen: *to instigate rebellion* **2** to urge on to some action ▷ **HISTORY** Latin *instigare* > **instigation** *n* > **instigator** *n*

instil *or US* **instill** *vb* **-stilling, -stilled 1** to introduce (an idea or feeling) gradually in someone's mind **2** *rare* to pour in or inject drop by drop ▷ **HISTORY** Latin *instillare* to pour in a drop at a time > **instillation** *n* > **instiller** *n*

instinct *n* **1** the inborn tendency to behave in a particular way without the need for thought: *maternal instinct* **2** natural reaction: *my first instinct was to get out of the car* **3** intuition: *Mr Barr's mother said she knew by instinct that her son was safe* ▷ **HISTORY** Latin *instinctus* roused

instinctive *or* **instinctual** *adj* written done or happening without any logical thought: *an instinctive understanding of people* > **instinctively** *or* **instinctually** *adv*

institute *n* **1** an organization set up for a specific purpose, especially research or teaching **2** the building where such an organization is situated **3** a rule, custom, or precedent ▷ *vb* **-tuting, -tuted 4** to start or establish **5** to install in a position or office ▷ **HISTORY** Latin *instituere*, from *statuere* to place

institution *n* **1** a large important organization such as a university or bank **2** a hospital, etc. for people with special needs **3** an established custom, law, or principle: *the institution of marriage* **4** *informal* a well-established person or feature: *the programme has become an institution* **5** an instituting or being instituted

institutional *adj* **1** of or relating to an institution: *institutional care* **2** dull, routine, and uniform: *institutional meals* > **institutionalism** *n*

institutionalize *or* **-ise** *vb* **-izing, -ized** *or* **-ising, -ised 1** (often passive) to subject (a person) to institutional life, often causing apathy and dependence on routine **2** to make or become an institution: *institutionalized religion* **3** to place in an institution

instruct *vb* **1** to order to do something **2** to teach (someone) how to do something **3** to brief (a solicitor or barrister) ▷ **HISTORY** Latin *instruere*

instruction *n* **1** a direction or order **2** the process or act of teaching > **instructional** *adj*

instructions *pl n* information on how to do or use something: *the plane had ignored instructions from air traffic controllers*

instructive *adj* informative or helpful

instructor *n* **1** a person who teaches something **2** *US & Canad* a college teacher ranking below assistant professor

instrument *n* **1** a tool or implement, esp. one used for precision work **2** *music* any of various devices that can be played to produce musical sounds **3** a measuring device to show height, speed, etc.: *the pilot's eyes never left his instruments* **4** *informal* a person used by another to gain an end **5** an important factor in something: *her evidence was an instrument in his arrest* **6** a formal legal document ▷ **HISTORY** Latin *instrumentum*

instrumental *adj* **1** helping to cause **2** played by or composed for musical instruments **3** of or done with an instrument: *instrumental error*

instrumentalist *n* a person who plays a musical instrument

instrumentation *n* **1** a set of instruments in a vehicle, etc. **2** the arrangement of music for instruments **3** the list of instruments needed for a piece of music

instrument panel *n* a panel holding the instruments in a vehicle or on a machine

insubordinate *adj* not submissive to authority > **insubordination** *n*

insubstantial *adj* **1** flimsy, fine, or slight **2** imaginary or unreal

insufferable *adj* unbearable > **insufferably** *adv*

insular *adj* **1** not open to change or new ideas: *theatre tradition become rather insular* **2** of or like an island ▶ **HISTORY** Latin *insula* island > **insularity** *n*

insulate *vb* **-lating, -lated** **1** to prevent or reduce the transfer of electricity, heat, or sound by surrounding or lining with a nonconducting material **2** to isolate or set apart ▶ **HISTORY** Late Latin *insulatus* made into an island > **insulator** *n*

insulation *n* **1** material used to insulate something **2** the act of insulating

insulin (in-syoo-lin) *n* a hormone produced in the pancreas which controls the amount of sugar in the blood ▶ **HISTORY** Latin *insula* islet (of tissue in the pancreas)

insult *vb* **1** to treat or speak to rudely: *they insulted us and even threatened to kill us* ▷ *n* **2** an offensive remark or action **3** a person or thing producing the effect of an insult: *their explanation is an insult to our intelligence* ▶ **HISTORY** Latin *insultare* to jump upon

insuperable *adj* impossible to overcome; insurmountable > **insuperability** *n*

insupportable *adj* **1** impossible to tolerate **2** incapable of being upheld or justified: *an insupportable accusation*

insurable interest *n* *law* a financial or other interest in the life or property covered by an insurance contract, without which the contract cannot be enforced

insurance *n* **1** the agreement by which one makes regular payments to a company who pay an agreed sum if damage, loss, or death occurs **2** the money paid for insurance or by an insurance company **3** a means of protection: *sensible insurance against heart attacks*

insurance policy *n* a contract of insurance

insure *vb* **-suring, -sured** **1** to guarantee or protect (against risk or loss) **2** (often foll. by *against*) to issue (a person) with an insurance policy or take out an insurance policy (on): *the players were insured against accidents* **3** *chiefly US* same as **ensure** > **insurable** *adj* > **insurability** *n*

insurgent *adj* **1** rebellious or in revolt against an established authority ▷ *n* **2** a person who takes part in a rebellion ▶ **HISTORY** Latin *insurgens* rising > **insurgency** *n*

insurmountable *adj* impossible to overcome: *insurmountable problems*

insurrection *n* the act of rebelling against an established authority ▶ **HISTORY** Latin *insurgere* to rise up > **insurrectionist** *n, adj*

int. **1** internal **2** Also: **Int** international

intact *adj* not changed or damaged in any way ▶ **HISTORY** Latin *intactus*

intaglio (in-**tah**-lee-oh) *n, pl* **-lios** or **-li** **1** a seal or gem decorated with an engraved design **2** an engraved design ▶ **HISTORY** Italian > **intagliated** *adj*

intake *n* **1** a thing or a quantity taken in: *an intake of students* **2** the act of taking in **3** the opening through which fluid or gas enters a pipe or engine

intangible *adj* **1** difficult for the mind to grasp: *intangible ideas* **2** incapable of being felt by touch > **intangibility** *n*

integer *n* any positive or negative whole number or zero, as opposed to a number with fractions or decimals ▶ **HISTORY** Latin: untouched

integral *adj* **1** being an essential part of a whole **2** whole or complete **3** *maths* **a** of or involving an integral **b** involving or being an integer ▷ *n* **4** *maths* the sum of a large number of minute quantities, summed either between stated limits (**definite integral**) or in the absence of limits (**indefinite integral**)

integral calculus *n* *maths* the branch of calculus concerned with the determination of integrals and their use in solving differential equations

integrand *n* *maths* a mathematical function to be integrated

integrate *vb* **-grating, -grated** **1** to make or be made into a whole **2** to amalgamate (a racial or religious group) with an existing community **3** to designate (an institution) for use by all races or groups **4** *maths* to determine the integral of a function or variable ▶ **HISTORY** Latin *integrare* > **integration** *n*

integrated circuit *n* a tiny electronic circuit

integrity *n* **1** honesty **2** the quality of being whole or united: *respect for a state's territorial integrity* **3** the quality of being unharmed or sound: *the integrity of the cell membrane* ▶ **HISTORY** Latin *integritas*

integument *n* any natural protective covering, such as a skin, rind, or shell ▶ **HISTORY** Latin *integumentum*

intellect *n* **1** the ability to understand, think, and reason **2** a particular person's mind or intelligence, esp. a brilliant one: *his intellect is wasted on that job* **3** *informal* a person who has a brilliant mind ▶ **HISTORY** Latin *intellectus* comprehension

intellectual *adj* **1** of, involving, or appealing to the intellect: *intellectual literature* **2** clever or intelligent ▷ *n* **3** a person who has a highly developed intellect > **intellectualism** *n* > **intellectually** *adv*

intellectual property *n* something such as an invention or copyright that is officially owned by someone

intelligence *n* **1** the ability to understand, learn, and think things out quickly **2** the collection of secret information, esp. for military purposes **3** a group or department collecting military

433

information **4** *old-fashioned* news or information ▶ HISTORY Latin *intellegere* to understand, literally: to choose between

intelligence quotient *n* a measure of the intelligence of a person calculated by dividing the person's mental age by his or her actual age and multiplying the result by 100

intelligent *adj* **1** having or showing intelligence: *an intelligent child; an intelligent guess* **2** (of a computerized device) able to initiate or modify action in the light of ongoing events ▷ **intelligently** *adv*

intelligent design *n* the theory that the universe was created and develops according to the plan of an intelligent creator

intelligentsia *n* **the intelligentsia** the educated or intellectual people in a society ▶ HISTORY Russian *intelligentsiya*

intelligible *adj* able to be understood ▷ **intelligibility** *n*

intemperate *adj* **1** unrestrained or uncontrolled: *intemperate remarks* **2** drinking alcohol too much or too often **3** extreme or severe: *an intemperate climate* ▷ **intemperance** *n*

intend *vb* **1** to propose or plan (something or to do something) **2** to have as one's purpose **3** to mean to express or indicate: *no criticism was intended* **4** (often foll. by *for*) to design or destine (for a certain purpose or person): *the plane was never intended for combat* ▶ HISTORY Latin *intendere* to stretch forth

intended *adj* **1** planned or future ▷ *n* **2** *informal* a person whom one is to marry

intense *adj* **1** of very great force, strength, degree, or amount: *intense heat* **2** characterized by deep or forceful feelings: *an intense person* ▶ HISTORY Latin *intensus* stretched ▷ **intensely** *adv* ▷ **intenseness** *n*

intensifier *n* a word, esp. an adjective or adverb, that intensifies the meaning of the word or phrase that it modifies, for example, *very* or *extremely*

intensify *vb* **-fies, -fying, -fied** to make or become intense or more intense ▷ **intensification** *n*

intensity *n, pl* **-ties** **1** the state or quality of being intense **2** extreme force, degree, or amount **3** *physics* the amount or degree of strength of electricity, heat, light, or sound per unit area of volume

intensive *adj* **1** of or needing concentrated effort or resources: *intensive training* **2** using one specified factor more than others: *labour-intensive* **3** *agriculture* designed to increase production from a particular area: *intensive farming* **4** *grammar* of a word giving emphasis, for example, *very* in *the very same* ▷ **intensively** *adv* ▷ **intensiveness** *n*

intensive agriculture *or* **farming** *n agriculture* farming that aims for maximum output from the land and involves relatively high capital or labour costs. Compare **extensive agriculture**

intensive care *n* thorough, continuously supervised treatment of an acutely ill patient in a hospital

intent *n* **1** something that is intended **2** *law* the will or purpose to commit a crime: *loitering with intent* **3 to all intents and purposes** in almost every respect; virtually ▷ *adj* **4** *written* having one's attention firmly fixed: *an intent look* **5 intent on** or **upon** strongly resolved on: *intent on winning the election* ▶ HISTORY Late Latin *intentus* aim ▷ **intently** *adv* ▷ **intentness** *n*

intention *n* something intended; a plan, idea, or purpose: *he had no intention of resigning*

intentional *adj* done on purpose ▷ **intentionally** *adv*

inter (in-**ter**) *vb* **-terring, -terred** to bury (a corpse) ▶ HISTORY Latin *in-* into + *terra* earth

inter- *prefix* **1** between or among: *international* **2** together, mutually, or reciprocally: *interdependent* ▶ HISTORY Latin

interact *vb* to act on or in close relation with each other ▷ **interaction** *n*

interactive *adj technology* allowing two-way communication between a user and a system such as a computer or television

interbreed *vb* **-breeding, -bred** **1** to breed within a related group so as to produce particular characteristics in the offspring **2** same as **crossbreed** (sense 1)

intercede *vb* **-ceding, -ceded** **1** to plead in favour of **2** to act as a mediator in order to end a disagreement: *a policeman was watching the beatings without interceding* ▶ HISTORY Latin *inter-* between + *cedere* to move

intercept *vb* **1** to stop or seize on the way from one place to another **2** *maths* to mark off or include (part of a line, curve, plane, or surface) between two points or lines ▷ *n* **3** *maths* **a** a point at which two figures intersect **b** the distance from the origin to the point at which a line, curve, or surface cuts a coordinate axis ▶ HISTORY Latin *intercipere* to seize before arrival ▷ **interception** *n* ▷ **interceptor** *n*

intercession *n* **1** the act of interceding **2** a prayer offered to God on behalf of others ▷ **intercessor** *n*

interchange *vb* **-changing, -changed** **1** to change places or cause to change places ▷ *n* **2** the act of interchanging **3** a motorway junction of interconnecting roads and bridges designed to prevent streams of traffic crossing one another ▷ **interchangeable** *adj* ▷ **interchangeably** *adv*

Intercity *adj trademark* (in Britain) denoting a fast train (service) travelling between cities

intercom *n* an internal communication system with loudspeakers ▶ HISTORY short for *intercommunication*

intercommunion *n* association between Churches, involving mutual reception of Holy Communion

intercontinental *adj* travelling between or linking continents

intercostal *adj anat* between the ribs: *an intercostal nerve*

intercourse *n* **1** the act of having sex **2** communication or dealings between individuals or groups ▶ HISTORY Latin *intercurrere* to run between

interdenominational *adj* among or involving more than one denomination of the Christian Church

interdependence *n* dependence between two or more people, groups, or things
> **interdependent** *adj*

interdict *n* **1** *law* an official prohibition or restraint **2** *RC Church* the exclusion of a person or place from certain sacraments, although not from communion ▷ *vb* to prohibit or forbid ▶ **HISTORY** Latin *interdicere* to forbid > **interdiction** *n* > **interdictory** *adj*

interdisciplinary *adj* involving more than one branch of learning

interest *n* **1** curiosity or concern about something or someone **2** the power of causing this: *to have great interest* **3** something in which one is interested; a hobby or pursuit **4** (often *pl*) advantage: *in one's own interests* **5** money paid for the use of credit or borrowed money: *she borrowed money at 25 per cent interest* **6** (often *pl*) a right, share, or claim, esp. in a business or property **7** (often *pl*) a group of people with common aims: *foreign interests* ▷ *vb* **8** to arouse the curiosity or concern of **9** to cause to become interested or involved in something ▶ **HISTORY** Latin: it concerns

interested *adj* **1** showing or having interest **2** involved in or affected by: *a consultation paper sent to interested parties*

interest group *n* a group of people who attempt to influence legislators on behalf of a particular interest

interesting *adj* causing interest
> **interestingly** *adv*

interface *n* **1** an area where two things interact or link: *the interface between Islamic culture and Western modernity* **2** an electrical circuit linking one device, esp. a computer, with another **3** *physics, chem* a surface that forms the boundary between two liquids or chemical phases that cannot be mixed ▷ *vb* **-facing, -faced** **4** to connect or be connected with by interface > **interfacial** *adj*

interfaith *adj* relating to or involving different religions

interfere *vb* **-fering, -fered** **1** to try to influence other people's affairs where one is not involved or wanted **2 interfere with a** to clash with or hinder: *child-bearing may interfere with your career* **b** *Brit, Austral & NZ, euphemistic* to abuse sexually *and* **3** *physics* to produce or cause to produce interference ▶ **HISTORY** Old French *s'entreferir* to collide > **interfering** *adj*

interference *n* **1** the act of interfering **2** any undesired signal that interferes with the reception of radio waves **3** *physics* the meeting of two waves which reinforce or neutralize each other depending on whether they are in or out of phase

interferon *n* *biochem* a protein made by cells that stops the development of an invading virus

interfluve *n* *geog* a ridge or area of land dividing two river valleys ▶ **HISTORY** back formation from *interfluvial*, from INTER- + Latin *fluvius* river
> **interfluvial** *adj*

interim *adj* **1** temporary or provisional: *an interim government* ▷ *n* **2 in the interim** during the intervening time ▶ **HISTORY** Latin: meanwhile

interior *n* **1** a part or region that is on the inside: *the interior of the earth* **2** the inside of a building or room, with respect to design and decoration **3** the central area of a country or continent, furthest from the sea **4** a picture of the inside of a room or building ▷ *adj* **5** of, situated on, or suitable for the inside **6** mental or spiritual: *interior development* **7** coming or acting from within **8** of a nation's domestic affairs ▶ **HISTORY** Latin

interior angle *n* an angle of a polygon contained between two adjacent sides

interj. interjection

interject *vb* to make (a remark) suddenly or as an interruption ▶ **HISTORY** Latin *interjicere* to place between

interjection *n* a word or phrase that is used on its own and which expresses sudden emotion

interlace *vb* **-lacing, -laced** *written* to join by lacing or weaving together: *interlaced fingers*

interleave *vb* **-leaving, -leaved** to insert (blank leaves in a book) between other leaves

interleukin (in-ter-**loo**-kin) *n* *biochem* a substance obtained from white blood cells that stimulates their activity against infection and may by used to fight some forms of cancer

interlink *vb* to connect together

interlock *vb* **1** to join or be joined firmly together ▷ *n* **2** a device used to prevent a mechanism from operating independently or unsafely

interlocking spur *n* *geog* one of a series of ridges of land that slant towards each other from alternate sides of a river valley and appear to overlap at their nearest point by the river

interlocutor (in-ter-**lock**-yew-ter) *n* *formal* a person who takes part in a conversation ▶ **HISTORY** Latin *inter-* between + *loqui* to talk

interlocutory (in-ter-**lock**-yew-tree) *adj* **1** *law* pronounced during the course of legal proceedings; provisional: *an interlocutory injunction* **2** *formal* of dialogue; conversational

interloper (in-ter-**lope**-er) *n* a person in a place or situation where he or she has no right to be

interlude *n* **1** a period of time or different activity between longer periods or events **2 a** a pause between the acts of a play **b** a brief piece of music or other entertainment performed during this pause ▶ **HISTORY** Latin *inter-* between + *ludus* play

intermarry *vb* **-ries, -rying, -ried** **1** (of different races, religions, or social groups) to become connected by marriage **2** to marry within one's own family or tribe > **intermarriage** *n*

intermediary *n, pl* **-aries** **1** a person who tries to bring about agreement between others **2** a messenger ▷ *adj* **3** acting as an intermediary **4** intermediate

intermediate *adj* **1** occurring between two points or extremes **2** (of a class, course, etc.)

435

suitable for learners with some level of skill or competence ▷ *n* **3** something intermediate **4** *chem* a substance formed between the first and final stages of a chemical process ▶ HISTORY Latin *inter-* between + *medius* middle
> **intermediation** *n*

interment *n* a burial

intermezzo (in-ter-**met**-so) *n, pl* **-zos** *or* **-zi**
1 a short piece of instrumental music performed between the acts of a play or opera **2 a** a short composition between two longer movements in an extended musical work **b** a similar composition intended for independent performance ▶ HISTORY Italian

interminable *adj* seemingly endless because boring: *an interminable, rambling anecdote*
> **interminably** *adv*

intermingle *vb* **-gling, -gled** to mix together

intermission *n* an interval between parts of a play, film, etc. ▶ HISTORY Latin *intermittere* to leave off, cease

intermittent *adj* **1** occurring at intervals **2** *geol* (of an active volcano) erupting periodically
> **intermittently** *adv*

intern *vb* **1** to imprison, esp. during wartime ▷ *n* **2** *chiefly US* a trainee doctor in a hospital ▶ HISTORY Latin *internus* internal
> **internment** *n*

internal *adj* **1** of, situated on, or suitable for the inside **2** *anat* affecting or relating to the inside of the body: *internal bleeding* **3** of a nation's domestic affairs: *internal politics* **4** coming or acting from within an organization: *an internal reorganization* **5** spiritual or mental: *internal conflict* ▶ HISTORY Latin *internus* > **internally** *adv*

internal-combustion engine *n* an engine in which power is produced by the explosion of a fuel-and-air mixture within the cylinders

internal conflict *n* *literature* the struggle between a character and his or her own emotions, beliefs, personal dilemmas, or nature. Compare **external conflict**

internal market *n* a system in which goods and services are sold to a range of purchasers within the same organization, who compete to establish the price

internal migration *n* *sociol* the movement of people settling in another region of the same country or state

internal rhyme *n* *prosody* rhyme that occurs between words within a verse line

international *adj* **1** of or involving two or more nations **2** controlling or legislating for several nations: *an international court* **3** available for use by all nations: *international waters* ▷ *n* **4** *sport* **a** a game or match between the national teams of different countries **b** a member of a national team
> **internationally** *adv*

International *n* any of several international socialist organizations

International Date Line *n* the line approximately following the 180° meridian from Greenwich on the east side of which the date is one day earlier than on the west

internationalism *n* the ideal or practice of cooperation and understanding for the good of all nations > **internationalist** *n*

international law *n* *law* the body of rules generally recognized by civilized nations as governing their conduct towards each other and towards each other's subjects

international migration *n* *sociol* the movement of people settling in another country

International Phonetic Alphabet *n* a series of signs and letters for the representation of human speech sounds

International Style *or* **Modernism** *n* a 20th-century architectural style characterized by undecorated straight forms and the use of glass, steel, and reinforced concrete

internecine *adj* *formal* destructive to both sides: *internecine war* ▶ HISTORY Latin *internecare* to destroy

internee *n* a person who is interned

internet *n* (sometimes cap) a large public-access computer network linked to others worldwide

internist *n* a physician who specializes in internal medicine

internode *n* *biol* the part of a plant stem between two nodes

interphase *n* *biol* the period between two divisions of a cell

interplanetary *adj* of or linking planets

interplay *n* the action and reaction of things upon each other

Interpol International Criminal Police Organization: an association of over 100 national police forces, devoted chiefly to fighting international crime

interpolate (in-**ter**-pole-ate) *vb* **-lating, -lated**
1 to insert (a comment or passage) into (a conversation or text) **2** *maths* to estimate (a value of a function) between the values already known ▶ HISTORY Latin *interpolare* to give a new appearance to > **interpolation** *n*

interpose *vb* **-posing, -posed 1** to place (something) between or among other things **2** to interrupt (with comments or questions) **3** to put forward so as to interrupt: *he ended the discussion by interposing a veto* ▶ HISTORY Latin *inter-* between + *ponere* to put > **interposition** *n*

interpret *vb* **1** to explain the meaning of **2** to work out the significance of: *his remarks were widely interpreted as a promise not to raise taxes* **3** to convey the meaning of (a poem, song, etc.) in performance **4** to act as an interpreter ▶ HISTORY Latin *interpretari* > **interpretive** *adj*

interpretation *n* **1** the act or result of interpreting or explaining **2** the particular way in which a performer expresses his or her view of a composition: *an interpretation of Mahler's fourth symphony* **3** explanation, as of a historical site, provided by the use of original objects, visual display material, etc.

interpreter n **1** a person who translates orally from one language into another **2** computers a program that translates a statement in a source program to machine language and executes it before translating and executing the next statement

interpretive centre n a building situated at a place of interest, such as a country park or historical site, that provides information about the site by showing videos, exhibiting objects, etc.

interquartile range n statistics the difference between the value of two variables, one below which lie 25% of the population and the other below which lie 75% of the population

interracial adj between or among people of different races

interregnum n, pl **-nums** or **-na** a period between the end of one ruler's reign and the beginning of the next ▶ HISTORY Latin inter- between + regnum reign ▶ **interregnal** adj

interrelate vb **-lating, -lated** to connect (two or more things) or (of two or more things) to become connected to each other > **interrelation** n > **interrelationship** n

interrogate vb **-gating, -gated** to question (someone) closely ▶ HISTORY Latin interrogare > **interrogation** n > **interrogator** n

interrogative (in-ter-**rog**-a-tiv) adj **1** used in asking a question: an interrogative pronoun **2** written of or like a question: an interrogative look ▷ n **3** an interrogative word, phrase, sentence, or construction

interrogative clause n grammar a type of clause used to ask a question, e.g. What's this? or Have you met my sister?

interrupt vb **1** to break into (a conversation or discussion) by questions or comment **2** to stop (a process or activity) temporarily ▶ HISTORY Latin inter- between + rumpere to break > **interrupted** adj > **interruptive** adj

interrupter or **interruptor** n a device for opening and closing an electric circuit

interruption n **1** something that interrupts, such as a comment or question **2** an interval or intermission **3** the act of interrupting or the state of being interrupted

interscholastic adj occurring between two or more schools: an interscholastic competition

intersect vb **1** (of roads or lines) to cross (each other) **2** to divide or mark off (a place, area, or surface) by passing through or across ▶ HISTORY Latin intersecare to divide

intersection n **1** a point at which things intersect, esp. a road junction **2** the act of intersecting or the state of being intersected **3** maths **a** a point or set of points common to two or more geometric figures **b** the set of elements that are common to two sets > **intersectional** adj

intersex n **1** the condition of having characteristics in between those of a male and a female **2** a person with such characteristics

interstellar adj between or among stars

interstice (in-ter-stiss) n (usually pl) **1** a small gap or crack between things **2** physics the space between adjacent atoms in a crystal lattice ▶ HISTORY Latin interstitium interval

intertextuality n literature the connections between one text and others as a result of imitation, allusion, quotation, and adaptation

intertwine vb **-twining, -twined** to twist together

interval n **1** the period of time between two events **2** Brit & Austral a short period between parts of a play, concert, etc. **3** music the difference of pitch between two notes **4 at intervals a** now and then: turn the chicken at intervals **b** with a certain amount of space between: the poles were placed at intervals of twenty metres ▶ HISTORY Latin intervallum, literally: space between two palisades

intervene vb **-vening, -vened 1** (often foll. by in) to involve oneself in a situation, esp. to prevent conflict **2** to interrupt a conversation **3** to happen so as to stop something: he hoped to play but a serious injury intervened **4** to come or be among or between: ten years had intervened since he had seen Joe ▶ HISTORY Latin intervenire to come between

intervention n the act of intervening, esp. to influence or alter a situation in some way > **interventionist** n, adj

interview n **1** a formal discussion, esp. one in which an employer assesses a job applicant **2** a conversation in which a well-known person is asked about his or her views, career, etc. by a reporter ▷ vb **3** to question (someone) ▶ HISTORY Old French entrevue > **interviewee** n > **interviewer** n

interwar adj of or happening in the period between World War I and World War II

interweave vb **-weaving, -wove** or **-weaved, -woven** or **-weaved** to weave together

intestate adj **1** (of a person) not having made a will ▷ n **2** a person who dies without having made a will ▶ HISTORY Latin intestatus > **intestacy** n

intestine n the part of the alimentary canal between the stomach and the anus. See **large intestine, small intestine** ▶ HISTORY Latin intestinus internal > **intestinal** adj

intifada (in-tiff-**ah**-da) n the Palestinian uprising against Israel in the West Bank and Gaza Strip ▶ HISTORY Arabic

intimacy n, pl **-cies 1** close or warm friendship **2** (often pl) intimate words or acts within a close relationship

intimate[1] adj **1** characterized by a close or warm personal relationship: an intimate friend **2** deeply personal, private, or secret **3** (of knowledge) extensive and detailed **4** euphemistic having sexual relations **5** having a friendly quiet atmosphere: an intimate nightclub ▷ n **6** a close friend ▶ HISTORY Latin intimus innermost > **intimately** adv

intimate[2] vb **-mating, -mated** formal **1** to make (something) known in an indirect way: he has

437

intimated his intention to retire **2** to announce ▶ HISTORY Late Latin *intimare* to proclaim > **intimation** *n*

intimidate *vb* **-dating, -dated** to subdue or influence (someone) through fear ▶ HISTORY Latin *in-* in + *timidus* fearful > **intimidating** *adj* > **intimidation** *n*

into *prep* **1** to the inner part of: *they went into the house* **2** to the middle of so as to be surrounded by: *into the bushes* **3** against; up against: *he drove into a wall* **4** used to indicate the result of a change: *they turned the theatre into a garage* **5** maths used to indicate division: *three into six is two* **6** informal interested in: *I'm really into healthy food*

intolerable *adj* more than can be endured > **intolerably** *adv*

intolerant *adj* refusing to accept practices and beliefs that differ from one's own > **intolerance** *n*

intonation *n* **1** the sound pattern produced by variations in the voice **2** the act of intoning **3** music the ability to play or sing in tune > **intonational** *adj*

intone *vb* **-toning, -toned** written **1** to speak or recite in a monotonous tone **2** to speak with a particular tone ▶ HISTORY Medieval Latin *intonare*

in toto *adv* totally or entirely ▶ HISTORY Latin

intoxicant *n* **1** something, such as an alcoholic drink, that causes intoxication ▷ *adj* **2** causing intoxication

intoxicate *vb* **-cating, -cated** **1** (of an alcoholic drink) to make (a person) drunk **2** to stimulate or excite to a point beyond self-control ▶ HISTORY Latin *in-* in + *toxicum* poison > **intoxicated** *adj* > **intoxicating** *adj*

intoxication *n* **1** the state of being drunk **2** great excitement and exhilaration

intractable *adj* **1** (of a person) difficult to influence or direct **2** (of a problem or illness) difficult to solve or cure > **intractability** *n* > **intractably** *adv*

intramural *adj* chiefly US & Canad operating within or involving those within a school or college: *intramural sports* ▶ HISTORY Latin *intra-* inside + *murus* wall

intranet *n* computers an internal network that makes use of internet technology ▶ HISTORY *intra-* + INTERNET

intransigent *adj* **1** refusing to change one's attitude ▷ *n* **2** an intransigent person, esp. in politics ▶ HISTORY Latin *in-* not + *transigere* to settle > **intransigence** *n*

intransitive *adj* (of a verb) not taking a direct object: *'to faint' is an intransitive verb* > **intransitively** *adv*

intransitive verb *n* grammar a verb that does not take a direct object: *'to rise' is an intransitive verb*. Compare **transitive verb**

intrapreneur *n* Brit and US a person who while remaining within a larger organization uses entrepreneurial skills to develop new services or systems as a subsidiary of the organization

▶ HISTORY *intra-* inside + *(entre)preneur*

intrauterine *adj* situated within the womb ▶ HISTORY Latin *intra-* inside + *uterus* womb

intrauterine device *n* a contraceptive device in the shape of a coil, inserted into the womb

intravenous (in-tra-**vee**-nuss) *adj* anat into a vein: *intravenous drug users* ▶ HISTORY Latin *intra-* inside + *vena* vein > **intravenously** *adv*

intrepid *adj* fearless or bold ▶ HISTORY Latin *in-* not + *trepidus* fearful > **intrepidity** *n* > **intrepidly** *adv*

intricate *adj* **1** difficult to sort out: *an intricate problem* **2** full of complicated detail: *intricate Arab mosaics* ▶ HISTORY Latin *intricare* to entangle > **intricacy** *n* > **intricately** *adv*

intrigue *vb* **-triguing, -trigued** **1** to make interested or curious: *a question which has intrigued him for years* **2** to plot secretly or dishonestly ▷ *n* **3** secret plotting **4** a secret love affair ▶ HISTORY French *intriguer* > **intriguing** *adj* > **intriguingly** *adv*

intrinsic *adj* **1** essential to the real nature of a thing: *hedgerows are an intrinsic part of the countryside* **2** anat situated within or peculiar to a part: *intrinsic muscles* ▶ HISTORY Latin *intrinsecus* inwardly > **intrinsically** *adv*

introduce *vb* **-ducing, -duced** **1** to present (someone) by name (to another person) **2** to present (a radio or television programme) **3** to present for consideration or approval: *he introduced the bill to Parliament in 1967* **4** to bring into use: *Latvia has introduced its own currency into circulation* **5 introduce to** to cause to experience for the first time: *his father introduced him to golf* **6** to start **7 introduce with** to start: *he introduced his talk with some music* ▶ HISTORY Latin *introducere* to bring inside > **introducible** *adj*

introduction *n* **1** the act of introducing something or someone **2** a preliminary part, as of a book or musical composition **3** a book that explains the basic facts about a particular subject to a beginner **4** a presentation of one person to another or others

introductory *adj* serving as an introduction

introit *n* **1** RC Church a short prayer said or sung as the celebrant is entering the sanctuary to celebrate Mass **2** Church of England a hymn or psalm sung at the beginning of a service ▶ HISTORY Latin *introitus* entrance

introspection *n* the examining of one's own thoughts, impressions, and feelings ▶ HISTORY Latin *introspicere* to look within > **introspective** *adj*

introversion *n* psychol the directing of interest inwards towards one's own thoughts and feelings rather than towards the external world or making social contacts

introvert *adj* **1** shy and quiet **2** psychol concerned more with inner feelings than with external reality ▷ *n* **3** such a person ▶ HISTORY Latin *intro-* inward + *vertere* to turn > **introverted** *adj*

intrude *vb* **-truding, -truded** **1** to come in or join in without being invited **2** geol to force rock material, esp. molten magma, between solid rocks ▶ HISTORY Latin *intrudere* to thrust in

intruder *n* a person who enters a place without permission

intrusion *n* **1** the act of intruding; an unwelcome visit, etc.: *an intrusion into her private life* **2** *geol* **a** the forcing of molten rock into spaces in the overlying strata **b** molten rock formed in this way

intrusive *adj* **1** characterized by intrusion or tending to intrude **2** *geog* (of igneous rocks) formed by intrusion **3** *phonetics* relating to or denoting a speech sound that is introduced into a word or piece of connected speech for a phonetic reason > **intrusively** *adv* > **intrusiveness** *n*

intrusive narrator *n* *literature* a storyteller whose thoughts or opinions are evident and an intentional part of the narrative style

intuition *n* instinctive knowledge of or belief about something without conscious reasoning: *intuition told her something was wrong* ▶ HISTORY Latin *intueri* to gaze upon > **intuitional** *adj*

intuitive *adj* of, possessing, or resulting from intuition: *an intuitive understanding* > **intuitively** *adv*

Inuit *n, pl* **-it** or **-its** an indigenous inhabitant of North America or Greenland ▶ HISTORY plural of *inuk* person

Inuktitut *n* the language of the Inuit

inundate *vb* **-dating, -dated** **1** to cover completely with water **2** to overwhelm, as if with a flood: *the police were inundated with calls* ▶ HISTORY Latin *inundare* > **inundation** *n*

inured *adj* able to tolerate something unpleasant because one has become accustomed to it: *he became inured to the casual brutality of his captors* ▶ HISTORY Middle English *enuren* to accustom > **inurement** *n*

invade *vb* **-vading, -vaded** **1** to enter (a country or territory) by military force **2** to enter in large numbers: *the town was invaded by rugby supporters* **3** to disturb (privacy, etc.) ▶ HISTORY Latin *invadere* > **invader** *n*

invalid[1] *n* **1** a person who is disabled or chronically ill ▷ *adj* **2** sick or disabled ▷ *vb* **3** *chiefly Brit* to dismiss (a soldier, etc.) from active service because of illness ▶ HISTORY Latin *in-* not + *validus* strong > **invalidism** *n*

invalid[2] *adj* **1** having no legal force: *an invalid cheque* **2** (of an argument, result, etc.) not valid because it has been based on a mistake > **invalidity** *n* > **invalidly** *adv*

invalidate *vb* **-dating, -dated** **1** to make or show (an argument) to be invalid **2** to take away the legal force of (a contract) > **invalidation** *n*

invaluable *adj* having great value that is impossible to calculate

invariable *adj* unchanging > **invariably** *adv*

invasion *n* **1** the act of invading with armed forces **2** any intrusion: *an invasion of privacy* **3** *biol* the movement of plants to a new area or to an area to which they are not native > **invasive** *adj*

invective *n* abusive speech or writing ▶ HISTORY Late Latin *invectivus* scolding

inveigh (in-**vay**) *vb* *formal* **inveigh against** to make harsh criticisms against ▶ HISTORY Latin *invehi*, literally: to be carried in, hence assail

inveigle *vb* **-gling, -gled** to coax or manipulate (someone) into an action or situation ▶ HISTORY Old French *avogler* to blind, deceive > **inveiglement** *n*

invent *vb* **1** to think up or create (something new) **2** to make up (a story, excuse, etc.) ▶ HISTORY Latin *invenire* to find > **inventor** *n*

invention *n* **1** something that is invented **2** the act of inventing **3** creative power; inventive skill **4** *euphemistic* a lie: *his story is a malicious invention*

inventive *adj* creative and resourceful: *her inventive use of colour*

inventory (**in**-ven-tree) *n, pl* **-tories** **1** a detailed list of the objects in a particular place ▷ *vb* **-tories, -torying, -toried** **2** to make a list of ▶ HISTORY Medieval Latin *inventorium*

inverse *adj* **1** opposite in effect, sequence, direction, etc. **2** *maths* linking two variables in such a way that one increases as the other decreases ▷ *n* **3** the exact opposite: *the inverse of this image* **4** *maths* an inverse element

inverse operation *n* *maths* an operation that undoes another: *addition and subtraction are inverse operations*

inverse proportion *n* *maths* a relationship between two variables in which one increases as the other decreases

inversion *n* **1** the act of inverting or state of being inverted **2** something inverted, esp. a reversal of order, functions, etc.: *an inversion of their previous relationship* > **inversive** *adj*

invert *vb* **1** to turn upside down or inside out **2** to reverse in effect, sequence, or direction ▶ HISTORY Latin *in-* in + *vertere* to turn > **invertible** *adj*

invertebrate *n* **1** any animal without a backbone, such as an insect, worm, or octopus ▷ *adj* **2** of or designating invertebrates

inverted commas *pl n* same as **quotation marks**

invest *vb* **1** (often foll. by *in*) to put (money) into an enterprise with the expectation of profit **2** (often foll. by *in*) to devote (time or effort to a project) **3** **invest in** to buy: *she invested in some barbecue equipment* **4** to give power or authority to: *invested with the powers of government* **5** (often foll. by *in*) to install someone (in an official position) **6** (foll. by *with* or *in*) to credit or provide (a person with qualities): *he was invested with great common sense* **7** **invest with** *usually poetic* to cover, as if with a coat: *when spring invests the trees with leaves* ▶ HISTORY Medieval Latin *investire* to clothe > **investor** *n*

investigate *vb* **-gating, -gated** to inquire into (a situation or problem) thoroughly in order to discover the truth: *the police are currently investigating the case* ▶ HISTORY Latin *investigare* to search after > **investigative** *adj* > **investigator** *n*

investigation *n* a careful search or examination in order to discover facts

investiture *n* the formal installation of a person in an office or rank

investment *n* **1** the act of investing **2** money invested **3** something in which money is invested

investment trust *n* a financial enterprise that invests its subscribed capital in a wide range of securities for its investors' benefit

inveterate *adj* **1** deep-rooted or ingrained: *an inveterate enemy of Marxism* **2** confirmed in a habit or practice: *an inveterate gambler* ▶ HISTORY Latin *inveteratus* of long standing > **inveteracy** *n*

invidious *adj* likely to cause resentment or unpopularity ▶ HISTORY Latin *invidia* envy

invigilate (in-**vij**-il-late) *vb* -**lating, -lated** *Brit* to supervise people who are sitting an examination ▶ HISTORY Latin *invigilare* to watch over > **invigilation** *n* > **invigilator** *n*

invigorate *vb* -**ating, -ated** to give energy to or refresh ▶ HISTORY Latin *in-* + *vigor* vigour > **invigorating** *adj*

invincible *adj* incapable of being defeated: *an army of invincible strength* ▶ HISTORY Latin *in-* not + *vincere* to conquer > **invincibility** *n* > **invincibly** *adv*

inviolable *adj* that must not be broken or violated: *an inviolable oath* > **inviolability** *n*

inviolate *adj* free from harm or injury > **inviolacy** *n*

invisible *adj* **1** not able to be seen by the eye: *invisible radiation* **2** concealed from sight **3** *econ* relating to services, such as insurance and freight, rather than goods: *invisible earnings* > **invisibility** *n* > **invisibly** *adv*

invitation *n* **1** a request to attend a dance, meal, etc. **2** the card or paper on which an invitation is written

invite *vb* -**viting, -vited** **1** to ask (a person) in a friendly or polite way (to do something, attend an event, etc.) **2** to make a request for, esp. publicly or formally: *we invite applications for six scholarships* **3** to bring on or provoke: *his theory invites disaster* **4** to tempt ▷ *n* **5** *informal* an invitation ▶ HISTORY Latin *invitare*

inviting *adj* tempting or attractive

in vitro *adv, adj* (of biological processes or reactions) happening outside the body of the organism in an artificial environment ▶ HISTORY New Latin, literally: in glass

invocation *n* **1** the act of invoking **2** a prayer to God or another deity asking for help, forgiveness, etc. > **invocatory** *adj*

invoice *n* **1** a bill for goods and services supplied ▷ *vb* -**voicing, -voiced** **2** to present (a customer) with an invoice ▶ HISTORY Old French *envois*, plural of *envoi* message

invoke *vb* -**voking, -voked** **1** to put (a law or penalty) into use: *chapter 8 of the UN charter was invoked* **2** to bring about: *the hills invoked a feeling of serenity* **3** to call on (God or another deity) for help, inspiration, etc. **4** to summon (a spirit) by uttering magic words ▶ HISTORY Latin *invocare* to appeal to

involuntary *adj* **1** carried out without one's conscious wishes; unintentional **2** *physiol* (esp. of a movement or muscle) performed or acting without conscious control > **involuntarily** *adv*

involute *adj* also **involuted 1** complex, intricate, or involved **2** rolled inwards or curled in a spiral ▷ *n* **3** *geom* the curve described by the free end of a thread as it is wound around another curve on the same plane ▶ HISTORY Latin *involutus*

involve *vb* -**volving, -volved** **1** to include as a necessary part **2** to have an effect on: *around fifty riders were involved and some were hurt* **3** to implicate: *several people were involved in the crime* **4** to make complicated: *the situation was further involved by her disappearance* ▶ HISTORY Latin *in-* in + *volvere* to roll > **involvement** *n*

involved *adj* **1** complicated **2 involved in** concerned in

invulnerable *adj* not able to be wounded or damaged > **invulnerability** *n*

inward *adj* **1** directed towards the middle of something **2** situated within **3** of the mind or spirit: *inward meditation* **4** of one's own country or a specific country: *inward investment* ▷ *adv* **5** same as **inwards**

inwardly *adv* **1** within the private thoughts or feelings: *inwardly troubled, he kept smiling* **2** not aloud: *to laugh inwardly* **3** in or on the inside

inwards *or* **inward** *adv* towards the inside or middle of something

Io *chem* ionium

iodide *n chem* a compound containing an iodine atom, such as methyl iodide

iodine *n chem* a bluish-black element found in seaweed and used in medicine, photography, and dyeing. Symbol: I ▶ HISTORY Greek *iōdēs* rust-coloured, but mistakenly derived from *ion* violet

iodine solution *n* a liquid containing iodine, used as a disinfectant

iodize *or* -**dise** *vb* -**dizing, -dized** *or* -**dising, -dised** to treat with iodine > **iodization** *or* -**disation** *n*

ion *n* an electrically charged atom or group of atoms formed by the loss or gain of one or more electrons ▶ HISTORY Greek, literally: going

ion exchange *n* the process in which ions are exchanged between a solution and an insoluble solid. It is used to soften water

ionic *adj* of or in the form of ions

Ionic *adj* of a style of classical architecture characterized by fluted columns with scroll-like ornaments on the capital

ionic bond *n chem* a chemical bond in which one atom loses an electron to form a positive ion, the other atom gains the electron to form a negative ion, and the ions are held together by electrostatic attraction

ionize *or* -**ise** *vb* -**izing, -ized** *or* -**ising, -ised** to change or become changed into ions > **ionization** *or* -**isation** *n*

ionosphere *n* a region of ionized layers of air in the earth's upper atmosphere, which reflects radio waves > **ionospheric** *adj*

iota (eye-**oh**-ta) *n* **1** the ninth letter in the Greek alphabet (Ι, ι) **2** a very small amount: *I don't feel one iota of guilt*

IOU *n* a written promise or reminder to pay a debt ▶ HISTORY representing *I owe you*

IOW Isle of Wight

IP Internet Protocol: a code used to label packets of data sent across the internet, identifying both the sending and receiving computers

IPA International Phonetic Alphabet

ipecacuanha (ip-pee-kak-yew-**ann**-a) *or* **ipecac** (**ip**-pee-kak) *n* a drug made from the dried roots of a S American plant, used to cause vomiting ▶ HISTORY S American Indian *ipekaaguéne*

iPhone *n* *trademark* a type of mobile phone which includes a music player and internet browser

i-Player *n* *trademark* a service provided by the BBC, allowing its recently broadcast television programmes to be viewed over the internet

iPod *n* *trademark* a pocket-sized device used to play digital music files

ipso facto *adv* by that very fact or act ▶ HISTORY Latin

IQ intelligence quotient

Ir *chem* iridium

IRA Irish Republican Army

Iranian *adj* **1** of Iran ▷ *n* **2** a person from Iran **3** a branch of the Indo-European family of languages, including Persian

Iraqi *adj* **1** of Iraq ▷ *n* **2** a person from Iraq

irascible *adj* *written* easily angered ▶ HISTORY Latin *ira* anger > **irascibility** *n* > **irascibly** *adv*

irate *adj* very angry ▶ HISTORY Latin *iratus* enraged

ire *n* *literary* anger ▶ HISTORY Latin *ira*

iridaceous (ir-rid-**day**-shuss) *adj* of or belonging to the iris family

iridescent *adj* having shimmering changing colours like a rainbow ▶ HISTORY Latin *irid-* iris > **iridescence** *n*

iridium *n* *chem* a hard yellowish-white chemical element that occurs in platinum ores and is used as an alloy with platinum. Symbol: Ir ▶ HISTORY Latin *irid-* iris

iris *n* **1** the coloured muscular membrane in the eye that surrounds and controls the size of the pupil **2** a tall plant with long pointed leaves and large flowers ▶ HISTORY Greek: rainbow

Irish *adj* **1** of Ireland ▷ *n* **2** same as **Irish Gaelic 3** the dialect of English spoken in Ireland ▷ *pl n* **4 the Irish** the people of Ireland

Irish coffee *n* hot coffee mixed with Irish whiskey and topped with double cream

Irish Gaelic *n* the Celtic language of Ireland

Irishman *or fem* **Irishwoman** *n, pl* **-men** *or* **-women** a person from Ireland

Irish moss *n* same as **carrageen**

irk *vb* to irritate or vex ▶ HISTORY Middle English *irken* to grow weary

irksome *adj* annoying or tiresome

iron *n* **1** a strong silvery-white metallic element, widely used for structural and engineering purposes. Symbol: Fe **2** a tool made of iron **3** a small electrically heated device with a weighted flat bottom for pressing clothes **4** *golf* a club with an angled metal head **5** a splintlike support for a malformed leg **6** great strength or resolve: *a will of iron* **7 strike while the iron is hot** to act at a suitable moment ▷ *adj* **8** made of iron **9** very hard or merciless: *iron determination* **10** very strong: *an iron constitution* ▷ *vb* **11** to smooth (clothes or fabric) by removing (creases) with an iron. See also **iron out, irons** ▶ HISTORY Old English *irēn*

Iron Age *n* a phase of human culture that began in the Middle East about 1100 BC during which iron tools and weapons were used

ironbark *n* an Australian eucalyptus with hard rough bark

ironclad *adj* **1** covered or protected with iron: *an ironclad warship* **2** unable to be contradicted: *ironclad proof* ▷ *n* **3** *history* a large wooden 19th-century warship with armoured plating

Iron Curtain *n* *history* **the Iron Curtain** (formerly) the guarded border between the countries of the Soviet bloc and the rest of Europe

ironic *or* **ironical** *adj* of, characterized by, or using irony > **ironically** *adv*

ironing *n* clothes to be ironed

ironing board *n* a narrow cloth-covered board, usually with folding legs, on which to iron clothes

iron lung *n* an airtight metal cylinder enclosing the entire body up to the neck and providing artificial respiration

iron maiden *n* a medieval instrument of torture, consisting of a hinged case (often shaped in the form of a woman) lined with iron spikes

ironmaster *n* *Brit history* a manufacturer of iron

ironmonger *n* *Brit* a shopkeeper or shop dealing in hardware > **ironmongery** *n*

iron out *vb* to settle (a problem or difficulty) through negotiation or discussion

iron pyrites *n* same as **pyrite**

iron rations *pl n* emergency food supplies, esp. for military personnel in action

irons *pl n* **1** fetters or chains **2 have several irons in the fire** to have several projects or plans at once

ironstone *n* **1** any rock consisting mainly of iron ore **2** a tough durable earthenware

ironwood *n* **1** any of various trees, such as hornbeam, with exceptionally hard wood **2** the wood of any of these trees

ironworks *n* a building in which iron is smelted, cast, or wrought

irony *n, pl* **-nies 1** the mildly sarcastic use of words to imply the opposite of what they normally mean **2** a situation or result that is the direct opposite of what was expected or intended ▶ HISTORY Greek *eirōneia*

irradiate *vb* **-ating, -ated 1** *physics* to subject to or treat with light or other electromagnetic radiation **2** to make clear or bright intellectually or spiritually **3** to light up; illuminate > **irradiation** *n*

441

irrational *adj* **1** not based on logical reasoning **2** incapable of reasoning **3** *maths* (of an equation or expression) involving radicals or fractional exponents > **irrationality** *n* > **irrationally** *adv*

irrational number *n maths* any real number that cannot be expressed as the ratio of two integers, such as π

irreconcilable *adj* not able to be resolved or settled: *irreconcilable differences* > **irreconcilability** *n*

irredeemable *adj* **1** not able to be reformed, improved, or corrected **2** (of bonds or shares) not able to be bought back directly or paid off **3** (of paper money) not able to be converted into coin > **irredeemably** *adv*

irredentist *n* a person in favour of seizing territory that was once part of his or her country ▶ HISTORY Italian *irredenta* unredeemed > **irredentism** *n*

irreducible *adj* impossible to put in a reduced or simpler form > **irreducibility** *n*

irrefutable *adj* impossible to deny or disprove

irregular *adj* **1** uneven in shape, position, arrangement, etc. **2** not conforming to accepted practice or routine **3** (of a word) not following the usual pattern of formation in a language **4** not occurring at expected or equal intervals: *an irregular pulse* **5** (of troops) not belonging to regular forces ▷ *n* **6** a soldier not in a regular army > **irregularity** *n* > **irregularly** *adv*

irrelevant *adj* not connected with the matter in hand > **irrelevance** *or* **irrelevancy** *n*

irreligious *adj* **1** lacking religious faith **2** indifferent or opposed to religion

irreparable *adj* not able to be repaired or put right: *irreparable damage to his reputation* > **irreparably** *adv*

irreplaceable *adj* impossible to replace: *acres of irreplaceable moorland were devastated*

irrepressible *adj* not capable of being repressed, controlled, or restrained > **irrepressibility** *n* > **irrepressibly** *adv*

irreproachable *adj* blameless or faultless > **irreproachability** *n*

irresistible *adj* **1** not able to be resisted or refused: *irresistible pressure from the financial markets* **2** extremely attractive: *an irresistible woman* > **irresistibility** *n* > **irresistibly** *adv*

irresolute *adj* unable to make decisions > **irresolution** *n*

irresponsible *adj* **1** not showing or done with due care for the consequences of one's actions or attitudes; reckless **2** not capable of accepting responsibility > **irresponsibility** *n* > **irresponsibly** *adv*

irretrievable *adj* impossible to put right or make good > **irretrievability** *n* > **irretrievably** *adv*

irreverence *n* **1** lack of due respect **2** a disrespectful remark or act > **irreverent** *adj*

irreversible *adj* not able to be reversed or put right again: *irreversible loss of memory* > **irreversibly** *adv*

irrevocable *adj* not possible to change or undo > **irrevocably** *adv*

irrigate *vb* **-gating, -gated** **1** to supply (land) with water through ditches or pipes in order to encourage the growth of crops **2** *med* to bathe (a wound or part of the body) ▶ HISTORY Latin *irrigare* > **irrigation** *n* > **irrigator** *n*

irritable *adj* **1** easily annoyed or angered **2** *pathol* abnormally sensitive **3** *biol* (of all living organisms) capable of responding to such stimuli as heat, light, and touch > **irritability** *n*

irritant *n* **1** something that annoys or irritates **2** a substance that causes a part of the body to become tender or inflamed ▷ *adj* **3** causing irritation

irritate *vb* **-tating, -tated** **1** to annoy or anger (someone) **2** *pathol* to cause (an organ or part of the body) to become inflamed or tender **3** *biol* to stimulate (an organ) to respond in a characteristic manner ▶ HISTORY Latin *irritare* to provoke > **irritation** *n*

irrupt *vb* to enter forcibly or suddenly ▶ HISTORY Latin *irrumpere* > **irruption** *n* > **irruptive** *adj*

is *vb* third person singular of the present tense of **be** ▶ HISTORY Old English

ISA (**eye**-sa) (in Britain) individual savings account

isallobar (ice-**sal**-oh-bar) *n* a line on a map connecting places with equal pressure changes ▶ HISTORY Greek *isos* equal + *allos* other + *baros* weight

ISBN International Standard Book Number

isect (**eye**-sect) *n maths* a calculator key that is used to locate points of intersection of two graphs

isinglass (**ize**-ing-glass) *n* **1** a gelatine made from the air bladders of freshwater fish **2** same as **mica** ▶ HISTORY Middle Dutch *huysenblase* sturgeon bladder

Isl. **1** Island **2** Isle

Islam *n* **1** the Muslim religion teaching that there is only one God and that Mohammed is his prophet **2** Muslim countries and civilization > **Islamic** *adj* > **Islamist** *adj*, *n*

■ **WORD HISTORY**
■ In Arabic, *'islām* means 'surrender (to God)',
■ from the verb *'aslama*, meaning 'to surrender'.
■ The same verb also underlies the word
■ 'Muslim', which means 'someone who
■ surrenders (to God)'.

island *n* **1** a piece of land that is completely surrounded by water **2** something isolated, detached, or surrounded **3** See **traffic island** *Related adjective:* **insular** ▶ HISTORY Old English *īgland*

islander *n* a person who lives on an island

Islander *n NZ* a Pacific Islander

isle *n* **1** *poetic* an island **2** (*as part of place names*): *the Isle of Skye*

islet *n* a small island

islets of Langerhans *pl n anat* small groups of endocrine cells in the pancreas that secrete insulin and glucagon ▶ HISTORY C19: named after Paul Langerhans, German physician

-ism *n suffix* **1** indicating a political or religious belief: *socialism; Judaism* **2** indicating a characteristic quality: *heroism* **3** indicating an action: *exorcism* **4** indicating prejudice on the basis specified: *sexism*

isn't is not

iso- *or before a vowel* **is-** *combining form* equal or identical: *isomagnetic* ▶ HISTORY Greek *isos* equal

isobar (**ice**-oh-bar) *n* **1** a line on a map connecting places of equal atmospheric pressure **2** *physics* any of two or more atoms that have the same mass number but different atomic numbers ▶ HISTORY Greek *isobarēs* of equal weight > **isobaric** *adj* > **isobarism** *n*

isobath *n geog* a line on a map connecting points of equal underwater depth ▶ HISTORY Greek *isobathēs* of equal depth, from ISO- + *bathos* depth

isochronal *or* **isochronous** *adj* **1** equal in length of time **2** occurring at equal time intervals ▶ HISTORY Greek *isos* equal + *khronos* time > **isochronism** *n*

isoclinal *or* **isoclinic** *adj* **1** sloping in the same direction and at the same angle **2** *geol* (of folds) having sides that are parallel to each other ▷ *n* **3** *geog* Also: **isocline, isoclinal line** an imaginary line connecting points on the earth's surface having equal angles of magnetic dip

isocline *n* **1** *geol* a series of rock strata with isoclinal folds **2** *geog* same as **isoclinal** (sense 3)

isogeotherm *n geog* an imaginary line below the surface of the earth connecting points of equal temperature > **isogeothermal** *or* **isogeothermic** *adj*

isohel *n* a line on a map connecting places with an equal period of sunshine ▶ HISTORY Greek *isos* equal + *hēlios* sun

isohyet (ice-oh-**hie**-it) *n* a line on a map connecting places having equal rainfall ▶ HISTORY Greek *isos* equal + *huetos* rain

isolate *vb* **-lating, -lated** **1** to place apart or alone **2** *chem* to obtain (a substance) in an uncombined form **3** *med* to quarantine (a person or animal) with a contagious disease **4** to obtain a pure culture of (bacteria causing a particular disease) ▶ HISTORY Latin *insulatus*, literally: made into an island > **isolation** *n*

isolationism *n politics* **1** a policy of nonparticipation in international affairs; used especially of the US in the periods prior to its entry in the two world wars **2** an attitude favouring such a policy > **isolationist** *n, adj*

isomer (**ice**-oh-mer) *n chem* a substance whose molecules contain the same atoms as another but in a different arrangement > **isomeric** *adj*

isometric *adj* **1** having equal dimensions or measurements **2** *physiol* relating to muscular contraction that does not produce shortening of the muscle **3** (of a three-dimensional drawing) having the three axes equally inclined and all lines drawn to scale ▶ HISTORY Greek *isometria* equal measurement > **isometrically** *adv*

isometrics *n* a system of isometric exercises

isomorphism *n* **1** *biol* similarity of form, as in different generations of the same life cycle **2** *chem* the existence of two or more substances of different composition in a similar crystalline form **3** *maths* a one-to-one correspondence between the elements of two or more sets > **isomorph** *n* > **isomorphic** *or* **isomorphous** *adj*

isosceles triangle (ice-**soss**-ill-eez) *n* a triangle with two sides of equal length

- ■ **WORD HISTORY**
- ■ 'Isosceles' comes from Greek *isos*, meaning
- ■ 'equal', and *skelos*, meaning 'leg'.

isostasy *n* the state of balance which sections of the earth's lithosphere are thought to achieve when the vertical forces upon them remain unchanged. If a section is loaded as by ice, it slowly subsides. If a section is reduced in mass, as by erosion, it slowly rises ▶ HISTORY ISO- +*stasy*, from Greek *stasis* a STANDING > **isostatic** *adj*

isotherm (**ice**-oh-therm) *n* a line on a map linking places of equal temperature ▶ HISTORY Greek *isos* equal + *thermē* heat

isotonic *adj* **1** *physiol* (of two or more muscles) having equal tension **2** (of a drink) designed to replace the fluid and salts lost from the body during exercise

isotope (**ice**-oh-tope) *n* one of two or more atoms with the same number of protons in the nucleus but a different number of neutrons ▶ HISTORY Greek *isos* equal + *topos* place > **isotopic** *adj* > **isotopy** *n*

isotropic *or* **isotropous** *adj* having uniform physical properties, such as elasticity or conduction in all directions > **isotropy** *n*

ISP internet service provider: a business providing its customers with connection to the internet

Israeli *adj* **1** of Israel ▷ *n, pl* **-lis** *or* **-li** **2** a person from Israel

Israelite *n Bible* a member of the ethnic group claiming descent from Jacob; a Hebrew

issue *n* **1** a topic of interest or discussion **2** an important subject requiring a decision **3** a particular edition of a magazine or newspaper **4** a consequence or result **5** *law* the descendants of a person **6** the act of sending or giving out something **7** the act of emerging; outflow **8** something flowing out, such as a river **9 at issue a** under discussion **b** in disagreement **10 force the issue** to compel decision on some matter **11 join issue** to join in controversy **12 take issue** to disagree ▷ *vb* **-suing, -sued** **13** to make (a statement, etc.) publicly **14** to supply officially (with) **15** to send out or distribute **16** to publish **17** to come forth or emerge ▶ HISTORY Old French *eissue* way out > **issuable** *adj*

isthmus (**iss**-muss) *n* a narrow strip of land connecting two relatively large land areas ▶ HISTORY Greek *isthmos*

it *pron* **1** refers to a nonhuman, animal, plant, or inanimate thing, or sometimes to a small baby **2** refers to something unspecified or implied or to a 443 previous or understood clause, phrase, or word: *I knew it* **3** used to represent human life or experience in respect of the present situation: *how's it going?* **4** used as the subject of impersonal verbs: *it is snowing; it's Friday* **5** *informal* the crucial or ultimate point: *the steering failed and I thought that was it* ▷ *n* **6** a desirable quality or ability ▶ HISTORY Old English *hit*

IT information technology

ITA initial teaching alphabet: a partly phonetic alphabet used to teach reading

Italian *adj* **1** of Italy ▷ *n* **2** a person from Italy **3** the official language of Italy and one of the official languages of Switzerland

italic *adj* **1** of a style of printing type in which the characters slant to the right ▷ *pl n* **2** **italics** italic type or print, used for emphasis ▶ HISTORY Latin *Italicus* of Italy (where it was first used)

italicize *or* **-cise** *vb* **-cizing, -cized** *or* **-cising, -cised** to print (text) in italic type > **italicization** *or* **-cisation** *n*

itch *n* **1** a skin irritation causing a desire to scratch **2** a restless desire **3** any skin disorder, such as scabies, characterized by intense itching ▷ *vb* **4** to feel an irritating or tickling sensation **5** to have a restless desire (to do something): *they were itching to join the fight* ▶ HISTORY Old English *gīccean* to itch

itchy *adj* **itchier, itchiest** **1** having an itch **2** **have itchy feet** to have a desire to travel > **itchiness** *n*

item *n* **1** a single thing in a list or collection **2** a piece of information: *a news item* **3** *book-keeping* an entry in an account **4** *informal* a couple ▶ HISTORY Latin: in like manner

itemize *or* **-ise** *vb* **-izing, -ized** *or* **-ising, -ised** to put on a list or make a list of > **itemization** *or* **-isation** *n*

iterate *vb* **-ating, -ated** to say or do again ▶ HISTORY Latin *iterum* again > **iteration** *n* > **iterative** *adj*

itinerant *adj* **1** working for a short time in various places ▷ *n* **2** an itinerant worker or other person ▶ HISTORY Latin *iter* a journey

itinerary *n, pl* **-aries** **1** a detailed plan of a journey **2** a record of a journey **3** a guidebook for travellers

-itis *suffix forming nouns* indicating inflammation of a specified part: *tonsillitis* ▶ HISTORY Greek *-itēs* belonging to

it'll it will *or* it shall

its *adj* **1** of or belonging to it: *its left rear wheel; I can see its logical consequence* ▷ *pron* **2** something belonging to it: *its is over there*

it's it is *or* it has

itself *pron* **1 a** the reflexive form of it: *the cat scratched itself* **b** used for emphasis: *even the money itself won't convince me* **2** its normal or usual self: *my parrot doesn't seem itself these days*

ITV (in Britain) Independent Television

IUD intrauterine device: a coil-shaped contraceptive fitted into the womb

I've I have

IVF in vitro fertilization

ivory *n, pl* **-ries** **1** a hard smooth creamy white type of bone that makes up a major part of the tusks of elephants ▷ *adj* **2** yellowish-white ▶ HISTORY Latin *ebur* > **ivory-like** *adj*

ivory tower *n* remoteness from the realities of everyday life > **ivory-towered** *adj*

IVR International Vehicle Registration

ivy *n, pl* **ivies** **1** a woody climbing or trailing plant with evergreen leaves and black berry-like fruits **2** any of various other climbing or creeping plants, such as the poison ivy ▶ HISTORY Old English *īfig*

iwi (ee-wee) *n* *NZ* a Māori tribe ▶ HISTORY Māori

ixia *n* a southern African plant of the iris family with showy ornamental funnel-shaped flowers ▶ HISTORY Greek *ixos* mistletoe

Jj

J joule(s)

jab *vb* **jabbing, jabbed 1** to poke sharply ▷ *n* **2** a quick short punch **3** *informal* an injection: *a flu jab* **4** a sharp poke ▶ HISTORY variant of *job*

jabber *vb* **1** to speak very quickly and excitedly; chatter ▷ *n* **2** quick excited chatter ▶ HISTORY imitative

jabiru *n* a large white-and-black Australian stork

jacaranda *n* a tropical American tree with sweet-smelling wood and pale purple flowers ▶ HISTORY from a Native American language

jack *n* **1** a mechanical device used to raise a motor vehicle or other heavy object **2** a playing card with a picture of a pageboy on it **3** *bowls* a small white bowl at which the players aim their bowls **4** *electrical engineering* a socket into which a plug can be inserted **5** a flag flown at the bow of a ship, showing nationality **6 every man jack** everyone without exception ▷ See also **jack in, jack up** ▶ HISTORY from short form of *John*

jackal *n* a doglike wild animal of Africa and Asia, which feeds on the decaying flesh of dead animals ▶ HISTORY Persian *shagāl*

jackanapes *n* *Brit* a mischievous child ▶ HISTORY literally: Jack of the ape, nickname of first Duke of Suffolk, whose badge showed an ape's ball and chain

jackaroo, jackeroo *n*, *pl* **-roos** *Austral* a trainee on a sheep station ▶ HISTORY from *jack* man + *(kang)aroo*

jackass *n* **1** a fool **2** a male donkey **3 laughing jackass** same as **kookaburra** ▶ HISTORY *jack* (male) + *ass*

jackboot *n* **1** a leather military boot reaching up to the knee **2** brutal and authoritarian rule

jackdaw *n* a large black-and-grey crowlike bird of Europe and Asia ▶ HISTORY *jack* + *daw*, obsolete name for jackdaw

jacket *n* **1** a short coat with a front opening and long sleeves **2** the skin of a potato **3** same as **dust jacket** ▶ HISTORY Old French *jaquet*

jacket potato *n* a potato baked in its skin

jack in *vb* *Brit, slang* to abandon (an attempt or enterprise)

jack-in-the-box *n* a toy consisting of a box containing a figure on a compressed spring, which jumps out when the lid is opened

jackknife *vb* **-knifing, -knifed 1** (of an articulated lorry) to go out of control in such a way that the trailer swings round at a sharp angle to the cab ▷ *n, pl* **-knives 2** a knife with a blade that can be folded into the handle **3** a dive in which the diver bends at the waist in midair

jack of all trades *n*, *pl* **jacks of all trades** a person who can do many different kinds of work

jackpot *n* **1** the most valuable prize that can be won in a gambling game **2 hit the jackpot** *informal* to be very fortunate or very successful ▶ HISTORY probably from *jack* (playing card)

jack rabbit *n* a hare of W North America with very long hind legs and large ears ▶ HISTORY *jackass-rabbit*, referring to its long ears

jack-up *n* *NZ, informal* something achieved dishonestly

jack up *vb* **1** to raise (a motor vehicle) with a jack **2** to increase (prices or salaries) **3** *NZ, informal* to organize something through unorthodox channels

Jacobean (jak-a-**bee**-an) *adj* of or in the reign of James I of England and Ireland (1603–25) ▶ HISTORY Latin *Jacobus* James

Jacobite *n* *history* a supporter of James II and his descendants ▶ HISTORY Latin *Jacobus* James

Jacquard (**jak**-ard) *n* a fabric with an intricate design incorporated into the weave ▶ HISTORY after J. M. *Jacquard*, its inventor

Jacuzzi (jak-**oo**-zee) *n* *trademark* a large circular bath with a mechanism that swirls the water

jade *n* **1** an ornamental semiprecious stone, usually green in colour ▷ *adj* **2** bluish-green ▶ HISTORY obsolete Spanish *piedra de ijada* colic stone, because it was believed to cure colic

jaded *adj* tired or bored from overindulgence or overwork

Jaffa *n* *Brit* a large thick-skinned orange ▶ HISTORY after *Jaffa*, port in W Israel

jagged (**jag**-gid) *adj* having an uneven edge with sharp points ▶ HISTORY from *jag* a sharp point

jaguar *n* a large wild cat of Central and South America, with a spotted coat ▶ HISTORY from S American Indian

Jah *n* the Rastafarian name for God ▶ HISTORY shortened from *Jahveh*, the Hebrew name for God

jail *or* **gaol** *n* **1** a prison ▷ *vb* **2** to confine in prison ▶ HISTORY Old French *jaiole* cage

jailbird *n* *informal* a person who is or has often been in jail

jailer *or* **gaoler** *n* a person in charge of a jail

jake *adj* **she's jake** *Austral & NZ, slang* it is all right ▶ HISTORY probably from the name *Jake*

jalopy (jal-**lop**-ee) *n*, *pl* **-lopies** *informal* a dilapidated old car ▶ HISTORY origin unknown

jam¹ *vb* **jamming, jammed 1** to wedge (an object) into a tight space or against another object **2** to fill (a place) with people or vehicles: *the surrounding roads were jammed for miles* **3** to make or become stuck or locked **4** *radio* to prevent the clear reception of (radio communications) by transmitting other signals on the same wavelength **5** *slang* to play in a jam session

6 jam on the brakes to apply the brakes of a vehicle very suddenly ▷ *n* **7** a situation where a large number of people or vehicles are crowded into a place: *a traffic jam* **8** *informal* a difficult situation **9** same as **jam session** ▶ HISTORY probably imitative

jam² *n* a food made from fruit boiled with sugar until the mixture sets, used for spreading on bread ▶ HISTORY perhaps from JAM¹ (the act of squeezing)

Jamaican *adj* **1** of Jamaica ▷ *n* **2** a person from Jamaica

jamb *n* a side post of a doorframe or window frame ▶ HISTORY Old French *jambe* leg, jamb

jamboree *n* a large gathering or celebration ▶ HISTORY origin unknown

jammy *adj* **-mier, -miest 1** covered with or tasting like jam **2** *Brit, slang* lucky

jam-packed *adj* filled to capacity

jam session *n slang* an improvised performance by jazz or rock musicians ▶ HISTORY probably from JAM¹

Jan. January

jandal *n NZ* a rubber-soled sandal attached to the foot by a thong between the big toe and the next toe

jangle *vb* **-gling, -gled 1** to make a harsh unpleasant ringing noise **2** to produce an irritating or unpleasant effect on: *the caffeine in coffee can jangle the nerves* ▶ HISTORY Old French *jangler*

janitor *n chiefly Scot, US & Canad* the caretaker of a school or other building ▶ HISTORY Latin: doorkeeper

January *n* the first month of the year ▶ HISTORY Latin *Januarius*

japan *n* **1** a glossy black lacquer, originally from the Orient, which is used on wood or metal ▷ *vb* **-panning, -panned 2** to varnish with japan

Japanese *adj* **1** of Japan ▷ *n* **2** (*pl* **-nese**) a person from Japan **3** the language of Japan

jape *n old-fashioned* a joke or prank ▶ HISTORY origin unknown

japonica *n* **1** a Japanese shrub with red flowers and yellowish fruit **2** same as **camellia** ▶ HISTORY New Latin *Japonia* Japan

jar¹ *n* **1** a wide-mouthed cylindrical glass container, used for storing food **2** *Brit, informal* a glass of beer ▶ HISTORY Arabic *jarrah* large earthen vessel

jar² *vb* **jarring, jarred 1** to have an irritating or unpleasant effect: *sometimes a light remark jarred on her father* **2** to be in disagreement or conflict: *their very different temperaments jarred* **3** to jolt or bump ▷ *n* **4** a jolt or shock ▶ HISTORY probably imitative > **jarring** *adj*

jardiniere *n* an ornamental pot or stand for plants ▶ HISTORY French

jargon *n* **1** specialized language relating to a particular subject, profession, or group **2** pretentious or unintelligible language ▶ HISTORY Old French

jarrah *n* an Australian eucalyptus yielding valuable timber

jasmine *n* a shrub or climbing plant with sweet-smelling flowers ▶ HISTORY Persian *yāsmīn*

jasper *n* a kind of quartz, usually red in colour, which is used as a gemstone and for ornamental decoration ▶ HISTORY Greek *iaspis*

jaundice *n* yellowing of the skin and the whites of the eyes, caused by an excess of bile pigments in the blood ▶ HISTORY French *jaune* yellow

jaundiced *adj* **1** bitter or cynical: *a jaundiced view* **2** having jaundice

jaunt *n* **1** a pleasure trip or outing ▷ *vb* **2** to go on a jaunt ▶ HISTORY origin unknown

jaunty *adj* **-tier, -tiest 1** cheerful and energetic **2** smart and attractive: *a jaunty little hat* ▶ HISTORY French *gentil* noble > **jauntily** *adv*

Java *n trademark* a computer programming language that is widely used on the internet ▶ HISTORY after *Java* coffee from the Indonesian island, allegedly drunk by its creators

Javanese *adj* **1** of the island of Java, in Indonesia ▷ *n* **2** (*pl* **-nese**) a person from Java **3** the language of Java

javelin *n* a light spear thrown in a sports competition ▶ HISTORY Old French *javeline*

jaw *n* **1** either of the bones that hold the teeth and frame the mouth **2** the lower part of the face below the mouth **3** *slang* a long chat ▷ *vb* **4** *slang* to have a long chat ▶ HISTORY probably Old French *joue* cheek

jawbone *n* the bone in the lower jaw of a person or animal

jaws *pl n* **1** the mouth of a person or animal **2** the parts of a machine or tool that grip an object **3** the narrow opening of a gorge or valley **4** a dangerous or threatening position: *the jaws of death*

jay *n* a bird of Europe and Asia with a pinkish-brown body and blue-and-black wings ▶ HISTORY Old French *jai*

jaywalking *n* crossing the road in a dangerous or careless manner ▶ HISTORY *jay* (in sense: a foolish person) > **jaywalker** *n*

jazz *n* **1** a kind of popular music of African-American origin that has an exciting rhythm and often involves improvisation **2 and all that jazz** *slang* and other related things ▶ HISTORY origin unknown

jazz up *vb informal* **1** to play (a piece of music) in a jazzy style **2** to make (something) appear more interesting or lively

jazzy *adj* **-zier, -ziest 1** colourful and modern: *jazzy shop fronts* **2** of or like jazz

JCB *n trademark, Brit* a large machine used in building that has a shovel on the front and a digger arm on the back ▶ HISTORY initials of *Joseph Cyril Bamford*, its manufacturer

jealous *adj* **1** suspicious or fearful of being displaced by a rival **2** envious: *I was jealous of the girls who had boyfriends* **3** resulting from jealousy: *my jealous tears* ▶ HISTORY Late Latin *zelus* emulation > **jealously** *adv*

jealousy *n, pl* **-ousies** the state of or an instance of feeling jealous

jeans *pl n* casual denim trousers ▶ HISTORY from *jean fustian* fabric from Genoa

Jeep n trademark a small road vehicle with four-wheel drive ▶ HISTORY perhaps *general-purpose (vehicle)*, influenced by Eugene the *Jeep*, creature in a comic strip

jeer vb **1** to be derisive towards (someone) ▷ n **2** a cry of derision ▶ HISTORY origin unknown > **jeering** adj, n

Jehovah n God ▶ HISTORY Hebrew *Yahweh*

Jehovah's Witness n a member of a Christian Church whose followers believe that the end of the world is near

jejune adj **1** simple and unsophisticated **2** dull and uninteresting ▶ HISTORY Latin *jejunus* empty

jejunum (jij-**june**-um) n anat the part of the small intestine between the duodenum and the ileum ▶ HISTORY Latin > **jejunal** adj

Jekyll and Hyde n a person with two distinct personalities, one good and the other evil ▶ HISTORY after the character in a novel by R. L. Stevenson

jell vb **1** to take on a definite form **2** same as **gel** (sense 2) ▶ HISTORY from *jelly*

jellaba n a loose robe with a hood, worn by some Arab men ▶ HISTORY Arabic *jallabah*

jellied adj prepared in a jelly: *jellied eels*

jelly n, pl -**lies 1** a fruit-flavoured dessert set with gelatine **2** a food made from fruit juice boiled with sugar until the mixture sets, used for spreading on bread **3** a savoury food preparation set with gelatine ▶ HISTORY Latin *gelare* to freeze

jellyfish n, pl -**fish** a small sea creature with a jelly-like body and trailing tentacles

jemmy or US **jimmy** n, pl -**mies** a short steel crowbar, used by burglars to prise open doors and windows ▶ HISTORY from short form of *James*

jenny n, pl -**nies** a female donkey, ass, or wren ▶ HISTORY from the name *Jenny*

jeopardize or -**ise** vb -**izing, -ized** or -**ising, -ised** to put (something) at risk

jeopardy n danger of harm, loss, or death: *the survival of public hospitals is in jeopardy* ▶ HISTORY Old French *jeu parti*, literally: divided game, hence uncertain issue

jerboa n a small rodent of Asia and N Africa with long hind legs used for jumping ▶ HISTORY Arabic *yarbū'*

jerepigo (jer-ree-**pee**-go) n S African a sweet fortified wine similar to port ▶ HISTORY Portuguese *jeropiga*

Jerk[1] vb **1** to move with an irregular or spasmodic motion **2** to pull or push (something) abruptly or spasmodically ▷ n **3** an abrupt or spasmodic movement **4** an irregular jolting motion **5** slang, chiefly US & Canad a stupid or ignorant person ▶ HISTORY probably variant of *yerk* to pull stitches tight

jerk[2] vb **1** to preserve (meat) by cutting into thin strips and drying in the sun ▷ n **2** meat preserved in this way ▷ adj **3** preserved by the process of jerking: *jerk beef* **4** rubbed or marinated with jerk seasoning: *jerk chicken*

jerkin n a short jacket ▶ HISTORY origin unknown

jerk seasoning n a mixture of hot spices which are either used as a marinade or rubbed into meat before cooking

jerky[1] adj **jerkier, jerkiest** having an irregular jolting motion > **jerkily** adv > **jerkiness** n

jerky[2] n same as **jerk**[2]

Jerry n old-fashioned, Brit, slang **1** (pl -**ries**) a German, esp. a German soldier **2** Germans collectively

jerry-built adj (of houses) built badly with cheap materials

jerry can n a flat-sided can used for carrying petrol or water ▶ HISTORY from *Jerry* German soldier

jersey n **1** a knitted garment covering the upper part of the body **2** a soft, slightly stretchy, machine-knitted fabric ▶ HISTORY originally referring to a type of woollen fabric made in *Jersey*, in the Channel Islands

Jersey n a breed of reddish-brown dairy cattle that produces milk with a high butterfat content ▶ HISTORY after *Jersey*, island in the English Channel

Jerusalem artichoke n a small yellowish-white vegetable that grows underground ▶ HISTORY altered from Italian *girasole* sunflower

jest n **1** something done or said to amuse people **2 in jest** as a joke ▷ vb **3** to do or say something to amuse people ▶ HISTORY variant of *gest* exploit

jester n a professional clown employed by a king or nobleman during the Middle Ages

Jesuit (**jezz**-yew-it) n a member of the Society of Jesus, a Roman Catholic religious order ▶ HISTORY New Latin *Jesuita* > **Jesuitical** adj

Jesus n the founder of Christianity, believed by Christians to be the Son of God

jet[1] n **1** an aircraft driven by jet propulsion **2** a thin stream of liquid or gas forced out of a small hole **3** an outlet or nozzle through which a stream of liquid or gas is forced ▷ vb **jetting, jetted 4** to travel by jet aircraft ▶ HISTORY Old French *jeter* to throw

jet[2] n a hard black mineral that is polished and used in jewellery ▶ HISTORY Old French *jaiet*

jet-black adj deep black

jetboat n NZ a motorboat propelled by a jet of water

jet engine n an aircraft engine that uses jet propulsion for forward motion

jet lag n a feeling of fatigue and disorientation often experienced by air passengers who have crossed several time zones in a short space of time

jet-propelled adj driven by jet propulsion

jet propulsion n a method of propulsion by which an aircraft is moved forward by the force of the exhaust gases ejected from the rear

jetsam n **1** goods thrown overboard to lighten a ship during a storm **2 flotsam and jetsam** See **flotsam** (sense 2) ▶ HISTORY from *jettison*

jet set n rich and fashionable people who travel widely for pleasure > **jet-setter** n > **jet-setting** adj

jet stream n meteorol a narrow belt of high-altitude winds moving east at high speeds

jettison — jockstrap

jettison *vb* **1** to abandon or give up **2** to throw overboard ▶ HISTORY Latin *jactatio* a tossing about

jetty *n, pl* **-ties** **1** a landing pier or dock **2** a structure built from a shore out into the water to protect a harbour ▶ HISTORY Old French *jetee* projecting part

Jew *n* **1** a person whose religion is Judaism **2** a descendant of the ancient Hebrews ▶ HISTORY Hebrew *yehūdāh* Judah

jewel *n* **1** a precious or semiprecious stone **2** a person or thing regarded as precious or special: *a fantastic little car, a real little jewel* **3** a gemstone used as part of the machinery of a watch ▶ HISTORY Old French *jouel*

jeweller *or US* **jeweler** *n* a person who buys, sells, and repairs jewellery

jewellery *or US* **jewelry** *n* objects such as rings, necklaces, and bracelets, worn for decoration

Jewess *n often offensive* a woman whose religion is Judaism

jewfish *n Austral* a freshwater catfish

Jewish *adj* of Jews or Judaism

Jewry *n* Jews collectively

jew's-harp *n* a small musical instrument held between the teeth and played by plucking a metal strip with the finger

Jezebel *n* a wicked or shameless woman ▶ HISTORY after the wife of Ahab, in the Bible

jib¹ *n* **1** *naut* a triangular sail set in front of the foremast **2 the cut of someone's jib** a person's manner or style ▶ HISTORY origin unknown

jib² *vb* **jibbing, jibbed** *chiefly Brit* **1** (of an animal) to stop short and refuse to go forwards: *my animal jibbed three times* **2 jib at** to object to: *he jibs at any suggestion that his side are the underdogs* ▶ HISTORY origin unknown

jib³ *n* the projecting arm of a crane ▶ HISTORY probably from *gibbet*

jibe¹ *n* **1** an insulting or taunting remark ▷ *vb* **jibing, jibed** **2** *written* to make insulting or taunting remarks

jibe² *vb* **jibing, jibed** *informal* to be in accord or be consistent: *their apparent devotion hardly jibed with what he had heard about them*

jibe³ *vb* **jibing, jibed** *n naut* same as **gybe**

jiffy *n, pl* **jiffies** *informal* a very short time: *won't be a jiffy!* ▶ HISTORY origin unknown

jig *n* **1** a lively folk dance **2** music for this dance **3** a mechanical device that holds and locates a part during machining ▷ *vb* **jigging, jigged** **4** to dance a jig **5** to move with quick jerky movements ▶ HISTORY origin unknown

jigger *n* a small whisky glass

jiggery-pokery *n informal, chiefly Brit* dishonest behaviour; cheating ▶ HISTORY Scots dialect *joukery-pawkery*

jiggle *vb* **-gling, -gled** to move with quick jerky movements ▶ HISTORY frequentative of *jig*

jigsaw *n* **1** Also called: **jigsaw puzzle** a puzzle in which the player has to put together a picture that has been cut into irregularly shaped interlocking pieces **2** a mechanical saw with a fine steel blade for cutting along curved or irregular lines in sheets

of material ▶ HISTORY *jig* (to jerk up and down) + SAW¹

jihad *n* Islamic holy war against unbelievers

jilt *vb* to leave or reject (a lover) abruptly or callously ▶ HISTORY dialect *jillet* flighty girl

jingle *n* **1** a short catchy song used to advertise a product on radio or television **2** a light ringing sound ▷ *vb* **-gling, -gled** **3** to make a light ringing sound ▶ HISTORY probably imitative

jingoism *n* excessive and aggressive patriotism ▶ HISTORY after the use of *by Jingo!* in a 19th-century song > **jingoistic** *or* **jingoist** *adj*

jinks *pl n* **high jinks** boisterous or mischievous behaviour ▶ HISTORY origin unknown

jinni *or* **djinni** *n, pl* **jinn** *or* **djinn** a being or spirit in Muslim belief that could take on human or animal form ▶ HISTORY Arabic

jinx *n* **1** someone or something believed to bring bad luck ▷ *vb* **2** to bring bad luck to ▶ HISTORY perhaps from Greek *iunx* wryneck, a bird used in magic

jitters *pl n* **the jitters** *informal* a feeling of extreme nervousness experienced before an important event ▶ HISTORY origin unknown

jittery *adj* nervous

jive *n* **1** a lively jerky dance that was popular in the 1940s and 1950s ▷ *vb* **jiving, jived** **2** to dance the jive ▶ HISTORY origin unknown > **jiver** *n*

Jnr Junior

job *n* **1** a person's occupation or paid employment **2** a piece of work; task **3** the performance of a task: *he made a good job of the repair* **4** *informal* a difficult task: *they are having a job to fill his shoes* **5** *Brit, Austral & NZ, informal* a crime, esp. a robbery **6 just the job** *informal* exactly what is required **7 make the best of a bad job** to cope as well as possible in unsatisfactory circumstances ▶ HISTORY origin unknown

jobbing *adj* doing individual jobs for payment: *a jobbing gardener*

Jobcentre *or* **job centre** *n* (in Britain) a government office where advertisements of available jobs are displayed

jobless *adj* **1** unemployed ▷ *pl n* **2** people who are unemployed: *the young jobless*

job lot *n* a miscellaneous collection of articles sold together

Job's comforter *n* a person who adds to someone else's distress while pretending to be sympathetic ▶ HISTORY after Job in the Bible

jobseeker's allowance *n* (in Britain) a social-security payment for unemployed people

job sharing *n* an arrangement by which a job is shared by two part-time workers

jockey *n* **1** a person who rides horses in races as a profession ▷ *vb* **2 jockey for position** to try to obtain an advantage by skilful manoeuvring ▶ HISTORY from the name *Jock*

jockstrap *n* an elasticated belt with a pouch to support the genitals, worn by male athletes. Also called: **athletic support** ▶ HISTORY slang *jock* penis

jocose (joke-**kohss**) *adj old-fashioned* playful or humorous ▶ HISTORY Latin *jocus* joke > **jocosely** *adv*

jocular *adj* **1** (of a person) often joking; good-humoured **2** (of a remark) meant lightly or humorously ▶ HISTORY Latin *joculus* little joke > **jocularity** *n* > **jocularly** *adv*

jocund (jok-kund) *adj literary* cheerful or merry ▶ HISTORY Latin *jucundus* pleasant

jodhpurs *pl n* trousers worn for riding, which are loose-fitting around the thighs and tight-fitting below the knees

■ **WORD HISTORY**
■ 'Jodhpurs' are named after the town of Jodhpur
■ in Northwestern India.

joey *n Austral* a young kangaroo

jog *vb* **jogging, jogged** **1** to run at a gentle pace for exercise **2** to nudge slightly **3 jog along** to continue in a plodding way **4 jog someone's memory** to remind someone of something ▷ *n* **5** a slow run as a form of exercise ▶ HISTORY probably variant of *shog* to shake > **jogger** *n* > **jogging** *n*

joggle *vb* **-gling, -gled** to shake or move with a slightly jolting motion ▶ HISTORY frequentative of *jog*

john *n slang, chiefly US & Canad* a toilet ▶ HISTORY special use of the name

joie de vivre (zhwah de **veev**-ra) *n* enjoyment of life ▶ HISTORY French, literally: joy of living

join *vb* **1** to become a member of (a club or organization) **2** to become part of (a queue or list) **3** to meet (someone) as a companion: *join me for a beer* **4** to take part in (an activity): *join the war effort* **5** (of two roads or rivers) to meet and come together **6** to bring into contact: *join hands* **7 join forces** to combine efforts with someone ▷ *n* **8** a place where two things are joined together ▷ See also **join in, join up** ▶ HISTORY Latin *jungere* to yoke

joined-up *adj* integrated by an overall strategy: *joined-up government*

joiner *n* a person whose job is making finished woodwork, such as window frames and stairs

joinery *n* the skill or work of a joiner

join in *vb* to take part in (an activity)

joint *adj* **1** shared by or belonging to two or more parties: *a joint statement* ▷ *n* **2** *anat* the junction between two or more bones: *a hip joint* **3** a junction of two or more parts or objects: *a mortar joint* **4** a piece of meat suitable for roasting **5** *slang* a building or place of entertainment: *strip joints* **6** *slang* a cannabis cigarette **7 out of joint a** *informal* out of order or out of keeping **b** (of a bone) knocked out of its normal position **8 put someone's nose out of joint** See **nose** (sense 10) ▷ *vb* **9** to provide a joint or joints **10** to cut or divide (meat) into joints > **jointed** *adj* > **jointly** *adv*

joint committee *n* a committee composed of members of both chambers of parliament

joint-stock company *n Brit* a business firm whose capital is owned jointly by shareholders

joint tenancy *n law* ownership of land or property by two or more parties, each with an equal interest; upon the death of a joint tenant, the property so owned is automatically inherited by the surviving party or parties

join up *vb* to become a member of a military organization

joist *n* a beam made of timber, steel, or concrete, used as a support in the construction of floors and roofs ▶ HISTORY Old French *giste*

jojoba (hoe-**hoe**-ba) *n* a shrub whose seeds contain an oil used in cosmetics ▶ HISTORY Mexican Spanish

joke *n* **1** something that is said or done to amuse people **2** someone or something that is ridiculous: *the country's inexperienced leaders are regarded as something of a joke* **3 no joke** *informal* a serious or difficult matter: *getting over mountain passes at ten thousand feet is no joke* ▷ *vb* **joking, joked** **4** to say or do something to amuse people ▶ HISTORY Latin *jocus* > **jokey** *adj* > **jokingly** *adv*

joker *n* **1** a person who jokes a lot **2** *slang* a person regarded without respect: *waiting for the next jokers to sign up* **3** an extra playing card in a pack, which can replace any other card in some games **4** *Austral & NZ, informal* a chap

jol (joll) *S African, slang n* **1** a party ▷ *vb* **jolling, jolled** **2** to have a good time ▶ HISTORY Dutch

jollification *n* a merry festivity

jollity *n* the condition of being jolly

jolly *adj* **-lier, -liest** **1** full of good humour **2** involving a lot of fun: *big jolly birthday parties* ▷ *adv* **3** *Brit, informal* very: *I'm going to have a jolly good try* ▷ *vb* **-lies, -lying, -lied** **4 jolly along** *informal* to try to keep (someone) cheerful by flattery or cheerful chat ▶ HISTORY Old French *jolif*

jolt *n* **1** a severe shock **2** a sudden violent movement ▷ *vb* **3** to surprise or shock: *he was momentarily jolted by the news* **4** to bump against (someone or something) with a sudden violent movement **5** to move in a jerking manner ▶ HISTORY origin unknown

Jonah *n* a person believed to bring bad luck to those around him or her ▶ HISTORY after Jonah in the Bible

jonquil *n* a narcissus with sweet-smelling yellow or white flowers ▶ HISTORY French *jonquille*

Jordanian *adj* **1** of Jordan ▷ *n* **2** a person from Jordan

josh *vb slang* to joke or tease ▶ HISTORY origin unknown

joss stick *n* a stick of incense, giving off a sweet smell when burnt ▶ HISTORY *joss* (a Chinese idol) from Portuguese *deos* god

jostle *vb* **-tling, -tled** **1** to bump or push roughly **2** to compete with someone: *jostling for power* ▶ HISTORY Old French *jouster* to joust

jot *vb* **jotting, jotted** **1 jot down** to write a brief note of: *quickly jot down the answers to these questions* ▷ *n* **2** the least bit: *it makes not one jot of difference* ▶ HISTORY Greek *iōta* iota, smallest letter

jotter *n* a small notebook

jottings *pl n* notes jotted down

joule (**jool**) *n physics* the SI unit of work or energy ▶ HISTORY after J. P. *Joule*, physicist

journal *n* **1** a newspaper or magazine **2** a daily record of events ▶ HISTORY Latin *diurnalis* daily

journalese *n* a superficial style of writing regarded as typical of newspapers and magazines

journalism *n* the profession of collecting, writing, and publishing news through newspapers and magazines or by radio and television

journalist *n* a person who writes or edits news items for a newspaper or magazine or for radio or television > **journalistic** *adj*

journey *n* **1** the process of travelling from one place to another **2** the time taken or distance travelled on a journey ▷ *vb* **3** to make a journey ▶ HISTORY Old French *journee* a day, a day's travelling

journeyman *n*, *pl* **-men** a qualified craftsman who works for an employer ▶ HISTORY *journey* (in obsolete sense: a day's work)

joust *history n* **1** a combat with lances between two mounted knights ▷ *vb* **2** to take part in such a tournament ▶ HISTORY Old French *j ouster*

J'ouvert (**zhoo-vay**) *n* a street festival celebrated in some Caribbean countries on the eve of Mardi Gras ▶ HISTORY from French *jour ouvert* the day having been opened

Jove *n* **1** Jupiter (the god) **2 by Jove** old-fashioned an exclamation of surprise or for emphasis

jovial *adj written* happy and cheerful ▶ HISTORY Latin *jovialis* of (the planet) Jupiter > **joviality** *n* > **jovially** *adv*

jowl[1] *n* **1** the lower jaw **2 cheek by jowl** See **cheek 3 jowls** cheeks ▶ HISTORY Old English *ceafl* jaw > **jowled** *adj*

jowl[2] *n* fatty flesh hanging from the lower jaw ▶ HISTORY Old English *ceole* throat

joy *n* **1** deep happiness and contentment **2** something that brings deep happiness: *a thing of beauty is a joy for ever* **3** *informal* success or satisfaction: *we checked ports and airports without any joy* ▶ HISTORY Latin *gaudium*

joyful *adj* feeling or bringing great joy: *joyful crowds; a joyful event* > **joyfully** *adv*

joyless *adj* feeling or bringing no joy

joyous *adj* extremely happy and enthusiastic > **joyously** *adv*

joyride *n* a drive in a car one has stolen > **joyriding** *n* > **joyrider** *n*

joystick *n* the control lever of an aircraft or a computer

JP (in Britain) Justice of the Peace

JPEG *n computing* **a** a standard compressed file format used for pictures **b** a picture held in this file format

Jr Junior

JSA jobseeker's allowance: in Britain, a payment made to unemployed people

jube *n Austral & NZ, informal* same as **jujube**

jubilant *adj* feeling great joy ▶ HISTORY Latin *jubilare* to give a joyful cry > **jubilantly** *adv*

jubilation *n* a feeling of great joy and celebration

jubilee *n* a special anniversary, esp. a 25th (**silver jubilee**) or 50th one (**golden jubilee**)

- ■ **WORD HISTORY**
- ■ 'Jubilee' comes from the Hebrew word *yōbhēl*
- ■ meaning a 'ram's horn'. In Old Testament times
- ■ a 'jubilee' year among the Jews occurred every
- ■ fifty years. In a jubilee year, fields and vineyards
- ■ were left uncultivated, property that had been
- ■ sold was returned to its original owner or his
- ■ descendants, and people who had been sold
- ■ as slaves were released from their bondage.
- ■ The beginning of the jubilee was marked by
- ■ the blowing of a ram's horn trumpet.

Judaic *adj* of Jews or Judaism

Judaism *n* the religion of the Jews, based on the Old Testament and the Talmud

Judas *n* a person who betrays a friend ▶ HISTORY after *Judas* Iscariot in the Bible

judder *vb informal, chiefly Brit* to shake or vibrate violently: *the van juddered before it moved away* ▶ HISTORY probably blend of *jar* (jolt) + *shudder*

judder bar *n NZ* a raised strip across a road designed to slow down vehicles

judge *n* **1** a public official with authority to hear cases and pass sentences in a court of law **2** a person appointed to determine the result of a competition **3** a person whose opinion on a particular subject is usually reliable: *a fine judge of men* ▷ *vb* **judging, judged 4** to determine the result of (a competition) **5** to appraise critically: *she hopes people judge her on her work rather than her appearance* **6** to decide (something) after inquiry: *we use a means test to judge the most needy cases* **7** to believe or consider: *doctors judged that the benefits of such treatment outweighed the risk* ▶ HISTORY Latin *judex*

judgment *or* **judgement** *n* **1** a decision formed after careful consideration **2** the verdict pronounced by a court of law **3** the ability to make critical distinctions and achieve a balanced viewpoint **4** the formal decision of the judge of a competition **5 against one's better judgment** contrary to what one thinks is sensible **6 pass judgment** to give one's opinion, usually a critical one, on a matter

judgmental *or* **judgemental** *adj* making judgments, esp. critical ones, about other people's conduct

Judgment Day *n Christianity* the occasion of the Last Judgment by God at the end of the world

judicial *adj* **1** of judges or the administration of justice **2** showing or using good judgment ▶ HISTORY Latin *judicium* judgment > **judicially** *adv*

judicial review *n law* the process by which the courts decide whether a government or other authority had the right to act as it did or whether it exceeded its power, acting illegally, irrationally, or improperly. Compare **administrative review**

judiciary *n* the branch of the central authority in a country that administers justice

judicious *adj* having or showing good judgment: *the judicious use of charge cards* > **judiciously** *adv*

judo *n* a sport derived from jujitsu, in which the two opponents try to throw or force each other on to the ground ▶ **HISTORY** Japanese *jū* gentleness + *dō* way

jug *n* a container with a handle and a small spout, used for holding and pouring liquids ▶ **HISTORY** origin unknown

jugged hare *n* hare stewed in an earthenware pot

juggernaut *n* **1** *Brit* a very large heavy lorry **2** any terrible force that demands complete self-sacrifice

■ **WORD HISTORY**
■ Hindi *Jagannath* comes from Sanskrit
■ *Jagannātha*, meaning 'Lord of the World', the
■ title given to a huge idol of the god Krishna,
■ wheeled every year on a chariot through the
■ streets of Puri in India. It was said that
■ devotees of Krishna would throw themselves
■ under the chariot and be crushed to death in
■ the hope of going to heaven, but this story is
■ without foundation.

juggle *vb* **-gling, -gled 1** to throw and catch several objects continuously so that most are in the air at the same time **2** to keep (several activities) in progress at the same time **3** to manipulate (facts or figures) to suit one's purpose ▶ **HISTORY** Old French *jogler* to perform as a jester > **juggler** *n*

jugular *n* a large vein in the neck that carries blood to the heart from the head. Also called: **jugular vein** ▶ **HISTORY** Latin *jugulum* throat

juice *n* **1 a** a drink made from the liquid part of a fruit or vegetable **2** *informal* **a** petrol **b** electricity **3 juices a** the fluids in a person's or animal's body: *digestive juices* **b** the liquid that comes out of meat when it is cooked ▶ **HISTORY** Old French *jus*

juicy *adj* **juicier, juiciest 1** full of juice **2** *informal* interesting and exciting: *juicy details*

jujitsu *n* the traditional Japanese system of unarmed self-defence ▶ **HISTORY** Japanese *jū* gentleness + *jutsu* art

juju *n* **1** a magic charm or fetish used by some tribes in W Africa **2** the power associated with a juju ▶ **HISTORY** probably from W African *djudju* evil spirit, fetish

jujube *n* a chewy sweet made of flavoured gelatine ▶ **HISTORY** Medieval Latin *jujuba*

jukebox *n* an automatic coin-operated record player ▶ **HISTORY** *juke* (from a Black American language) bawdy

jukskei *n* *S African* a game in which a peg is thrown over a fixed distance at a stake fixed into the ground ▶ **HISTORY** Afrikaans *juk* yoke + *skei* pin

Jul. July

julep *n* a sweet alcoholic drink, usually garnished with sprigs of mint

Julian calendar *n* the calendar introduced by Julius Caesar, in which leap years occur every fourth year and in every centenary year

julienne *adj* **1** (of vegetables or meat) cut into thin shreds ▷ *n* **2** a clear soup containing thinly shredded vegetables ▶ **HISTORY** French

July *n, pl* **-lies** the seventh month of the year ▶ **HISTORY** after *Julius* Caesar

jumble *n* **1** a disordered mass or state **2** articles donated for a jumble sale ▷ *vb* **-bling, -bled 3** to mix up ▶ **HISTORY** origin unknown

jumble sale *n* a sale, usually of second-hand articles, often in aid of charity

jumbo *adj* **1** *Brit, Austral & NZ, informal* very large: *jumbo prawns* ▷ *n, pl* **-bos 2** short for **jumbo jet**

■ **WORD HISTORY**
■ *Jumbo* was the name of a famous and very
■ large 19th-century African elephant that was
■ used to give rides to children at London Zoo,
■ before being sold in 1882 to Barnum and
■ Bailey's circus.

jumbo jet *n* *informal* a very large jet-propelled airliner

jumbuck *n* *Austral, old-fashioned slang* sheep ▶ **HISTORY** from a native Australian language

jump *vb* **1** to move suddenly up into the air by using the muscles in the legs and feet **2** to move quickly: *he jumps on a No. 6 bus* **3** to jerk with astonishment or shock: *he jumped when he heard a loud noise* **4** (of prices) to rise suddenly or abruptly **5** to change quickly from one subject to another: *any other comments before I jump on to the next section?* **6** *informal* to attack without warning: *the officer was jumped by three prisoners who broke his jaw* **7 jump down someone's throat** *informal* to speak sharply to someone **8 jump the gun** See **gun** (sense 3) **9 jump the queue a** to take a place in a queue ahead of people who are already queuing **b** to have an unfair advantage over other people **10 jump to it** *informal* to begin doing something immediately ▷ *n* **11** the act or an instance of jumping **12** *sport* any of several contests that involve jumping: *the long jump* **13** a sudden rise: *a 78% jump in taxable profits* **14** a sudden change from one subject to another: *stunning jumps from thought to thought* **15** a step or degree: *one jump ahead of the competition* **16 take a running jump** *informal* a contemptuous expression of dismissal ▷ See also **jump at, jump on** ▶ **HISTORY** probably imitative

jump at *vb* to accept eagerly

jumped-up *adj* *informal* having suddenly risen in significance and appearing arrogant

jumper¹ *n* **1** *Brit & Austral* a knitted garment covering the upper part of the body **2** *US & Canad* a pinafore dress ▶ **HISTORY** obsolete *jump* man's loose jacket

jumper² *n* a person or animal that jumps

jump jet *n* *informal* a fixed-wing jet aircraft that can land and take off vertically

jump leads *pl n* two heavy cables used to start a motor vehicle with a flat battery by connecting the flat battery to the battery of another vehicle

451

jump on *vb informal* to make a sudden physical or verbal attack on: *the press really jumped on him*

jump-start *vb* **1** to start the engine of (a motor vehicle) by pushing or rolling it and then engaging the gears ▷ *n* **2** the act of starting a motor vehicle in this way

jump suit *n* a one-piece garment combining trousers and top

jump-up *n* (in the Caribbean) an occasion of mass dancing and merrymaking, as in a carnival

jumpy *adj* **jumpier, jumpiest** nervous

Jun. 1 June **2** Junior

junction *n* a place where roads or railway lines meet, link, or cross each other ▶ HISTORY Latin *junctio* a joining

juncture *n* a point in time, esp. a critical one: *trade has been halted at a crucial juncture*

June *n* the sixth month of the year ▶ HISTORY probably from Latin *Junius* of the goddess Juno

jungle *n* **1** a forest area in a hot country with luxuriant vegetation **2** a confused or confusing situation: *the administrative jungle* **3** a situation where there is an intense struggle for survival: *the economic jungle* **4** a type of fast electronic dance music ▶ HISTORY Hindi *jangal*

junior *adj* **1** lower in rank or position: *junior officers* **2** younger: *world junior champion* **3** (in England and Wales) of school children between the ages of 7 and 11 approximately **4** US of the third year of a four-year course at college or high school ▷ *n* **5** a person holding a low rank or position **6** a person who is younger than another person **7** (in England and Wales) a junior school child **8** US a junior student ▶ HISTORY Latin: younger

juniper *n* an evergreen shrub with purple berries which are used to make gin ▶ HISTORY Latin *juniperus*

junk¹ *n* **1** old or unwanted objects **2** *informal* rubbish **3** *slang* narcotic drugs, esp. heroin ▶ HISTORY Middle English *jonke* old useless rope

junk² *n* a Chinese sailing boat with a flat bottom and square sails ▶ HISTORY Portuguese *junco*, from Javanese *jon*

Junkanoo *n* (in Jamaica) **1** a Caribbean Christmas ceremony or dance **2** a dancer or prop in such a performance

junket *n* **1** an excursion made by a public official and paid for out of public funds **2** a sweet dessert made of flavoured milk set with rennet **3** a feast ▶ HISTORY Middle English: rush basket, hence custard served on rushes > **junketing** *n*

junk food *n* food with a low nutritional value

junkie *n informal* a drug addict

junk mail *n* unsolicited mail advertising goods or services

Juno *n* the queen of the Roman gods

junta *n* a group of military officers holding the power in a country after a revolution ▶ HISTORY Spanish: council

Jupiter *n* **1** the king of the Roman gods **2** the largest planet

Jurassic *adj geol* of the geological period about 180 million years ago, during which dinosaurs flourished ▶ HISTORY after the *Jura* (Mountains) in W central Europe

juridical *adj* of law or the administration of justice ▶ HISTORY Latin *jus* law + *dicere* to say

jurisdiction *n* **1** the right or power to administer justice and to apply laws **2** the exercise or extent of such right or power **3** authority in general ▶ HISTORY Latin *jurisdictio*

jurisprudence *n* the science or philosophy of law ▶ HISTORY Latin *juris prudentia*

jurist *n* a person who is an expert on law ▶ HISTORY French *juriste*

juror *n* a member of a jury ▶ HISTORY Old French *jurer* to take an oath

jury *n, pl* **-ries 1** a group of, usually, twelve people, sworn to deliver a true verdict according to the evidence upon a case presented in a court of law **2** a group of people appointed to judge a competition ▶ HISTORY Old French *jurer* to swear

jury box *n* an enclosure where the jury sits in a court of law

jury-rigged *adj chiefly naut* set up in a makeshift manner ▶ HISTORY origin unknown

just *adv* **1** very recently: *the results have just been published* **2** at this very instant or in the very near future: *news is just coming in of a nuclear explosion* **3** no more than; only: *nothing fancy, just solid German fare* **4** exactly: *just the opposite* **5** barely: *the swimmers arrived just in time for the opening ceremony* **6** just about practically or virtually: *just about everyone* **7** just about to very soon going to: *it was just about to explode* **8** *spoken* just a moment *or* second *or* minute an expression requesting someone to wait for a short time **9** just now a a short time ago: *as you said just now* b at the present time: *all the support he can get just now* c S African, *informal* in a little while **10** just so arranged with precision: *a cottage with the gardens all just so* ▷ *adj* **11** fair and right: *a just war* ▶ HISTORY Latin *jus* justice > **justly** *adv*

justice *n* **1** the quality of being just **2** the administration of law according to prescribed and accepted principles **3** a judge **4** bring to justice to capture, try, and punish (a criminal) **5** do justice to to show to full advantage: *white slacks that did full justice to her figure* ▶ HISTORY Latin *justitia*

justice of the peace *n* **1** (in Britain) a magistrate who is authorized to act as a judge in a local court of law **2** (in New Zealand) a person authorised to act in a limited judicial capacity

justifiable *adj* having a good cause or reason: *justifiable indignation* > **justifiably** *adv*

justify *vb* **-fies, -fying, -fied 1** to prove (something) to be just or valid: *the idea of the ends justifying the means* **2** to defend (an action) as being warranted **3** to arrange (text) when typing or printing so that both margins are straight ▶ HISTORY Latin *justificare* > **justification** *n*

jute *n* a fibre that comes from the bark of an East Indian plant, used in making rope, sacks, and mats ▶ HISTORY Bengali *jhuto*

juvenile *adj* **1** young; not fully adult: *juvenile offenders* **2** of or for young people: *juvenile court* **3** immature in behaviour ▷ *n* **4** a young person ▶ HISTORY Latin *juvenilis*

juvenile delinquent *n* a young person who is guilty of a crime > **juvenile delinquency** *n*

juvenile water *n geol* water occurring at the earth's surface for the first time as a result of volcanic activity

juvenilia *pl n* works produced in an artist's youth

juxtapose *vb* **-posing, -posed** to place (two objects or ideas) close together or side by side

juxtaposition *n* close positioning; often used to describe the placing together of contrasting elements for effect ▶ HISTORY Latin *juxta* next to + POSITION

Kk

K 1 kelvin(s) **2** *chess* king **3** *chem* potassium ▶ HISTORY New Latin *kalium* **4** one thousand ▶ HISTORY from KILO- **5** *computers* a unit of 1024 words, bits, or bytes

Kaaba *n Islam* a cube-shaped building inside the mosque at Mecca, which contains the Black Stone, and in the direction of which Muslims turn to pray ▶ HISTORY from Arabic *ka'b* cube

Kaddish *n, pl* **Kaddishim** *Judaism* an ancient Jewish liturgical prayer, recited esp. by mourners ▶ HISTORY Aramaic *qaddîsh* holy

Kaffir (**kaf**-fer) *n S African, offensive, obsolete* a Black African ▶ HISTORY Arabic *kāfir* infidel

kaftan *or* **caftan** *n* **1** a long loose garment worn by men in eastern countries **2** a woman's dress resembling this ▶ HISTORY Turkish *qaftān*

kahawai *n* a food and game fish of New Zealand ▶ HISTORY Māori

kai *n NZ, informal* food ▶ HISTORY Māori

kail *n* same as **kale**

kaiser (**kize**-er) *n history* a German or Austro-Hungarian emperor ▶ HISTORY German, from Latin *Caesar* emperor

kaka *n* a parrot of New Zealand ▶ HISTORY Māori

kakapo *n, pl* **-pos** a ground-living nocturnal New Zealand parrot that resembles an owl ▶ HISTORY Māori

Kalashnikov *n* a Russian-made automatic rifle ▶ HISTORY after M. *Kalashnikov*, its designer

kale *n* a type of cabbage with crinkled leaves ▶ HISTORY Old English *cāl*

kaleidoscope *n* **1** a tube-shaped toy lined with angled mirrors and containing loose pieces of coloured paper that form intricate patterns when viewed through a hole in the end **2** any complicated or rapidly changing set of colours, circumstances, etc.: *a kaleidoscope of shifting political groups and alliances* ▶ HISTORY Greek *kalos* beautiful + *eidos* form + *skopein* to look at > **kaleidoscopic** *adj*

kalends *pl n* same as **calends**

kamikaze (kam-mee-**kah**-zee) *n* **1** (in World War II) a Japanese pilot who performed a suicidal mission ▷ *adj* **2** (of an action) undertaken in the knowledge that it will result in the death or injury of the person performing it: *a kamikaze attack*

- ■ **WORD HISTORY**
- ■ 'Kamikaze' comes from Japanese *kami*,
- ■ meaning 'divine', and *kaze*, meaning 'wind'.

Kamloops trout *n* a bright silvery rainbow trout common in British Columbia, Canada

kangaroo *n, pl* **-roos** a large Australian marsupial with powerful hind legs used for leaping ▶ HISTORY probably Aboriginal

kangaroo court *n* an unofficial court set up by a group to discipline its members

kangaroo paw *n* an Australian plant with green-and-red flowers

kaolin *n* a fine white clay used in making porcelain and in some medicines ▶ HISTORY *Kaoling*, Chinese mountain where supplies for Europe were first obtained

kapok *n* a fluffy fibre from a tropical tree, used for stuffing pillows and padding sleeping bags ▶ HISTORY Malay

kaput (kap-**poot**) *adj informal* ruined or broken: *the chronometer, incidentally, is kaput* ▶ HISTORY German *kaputt*

karakul *n* **1** a sheep of central Asia, the lambs of which have soft curled dark hair **2** the fur prepared from these lambs ▶ HISTORY Russian

karaoke *n* a form of entertainment in which members of the public sing well-known songs over a prerecorded backing tape ▶ HISTORY Japanese *kara* empty + *ōkesutora* orchestra

karate *n* a Japanese system of unarmed combat, in which punches, chops, and kicks are made with the hands, feet, elbows, and legs ▶ HISTORY Japanese: empty hand

karma *n Hinduism, Buddhism* a person's actions affecting his or her fate in the next reincarnation ▶ HISTORY Sanskrit: action, effect

karoo *or* **karroo** *n, pl* **-roos** *S African* an arid semidesert plateau of Southern Africa ▶ HISTORY Khoikhoi *karo* dry

kaross (ka-**ross**) *n S African* a blanket made of animal skins sewn together ▶ HISTORY Khoikhoi *caro-s* animal-skin blanket

karri *n, pl* **-ris** **1** an Australian eucalypt **2** its wood, used for building

karst *n geol* (*modifier*) denoting the characteristic scenery of a limestone region, including underground streams, gorges, etc.: *karst landscapes and cave systems* ▶ HISTORY C19: German, from *Karst*, limestone plateau near Trieste

kart *n* same as **go-kart**

karyokinesis *n biol* same as **mitosis**

kasbah *n* same as **casbah**

katabatic *adj meteorol* (of winds) blowing downhill through having become denser with cooling

katipo *n, pl* **-pos** a small poisonous black spider of New Zealand

katydid *n* a large green grasshopper of North America ▶ HISTORY imitative

kauri *n* a large New Zealand conifer grown for its valuable wood and resin ▶ HISTORY Māori

kayak *n* **1** an Inuit canoe-like boat consisting of a frame covered with animal skins **2** a fibreglass or canvas-covered canoe of similar design ▶ HISTORY Inuit

k

kazoo *n, pl* **-zoos** a cigar-shaped metal musical instrument that produces a buzzing sound when the player hums into it ▶ HISTORY probably imitative

KBE (in Britain) Knight (Commander of the Order) of the British Empire

kbyte *computers* kilobyte

kcal kilocalorie

kea *n* a large brown-green parrot of New Zealand ▶ HISTORY Māori

kebab *n* a dish consisting of small pieces of meat and vegetables, usually threaded onto skewers and grilled ▶ HISTORY Arabic *kabāb* roast meat

kedge *naut vb* **kedging, kedged** 1 to move (a ship) along by hauling in on the cable of a light anchor ▷ *n* 2 a light anchor used for kedging ▶ HISTORY Middle English *caggen* to fasten

kedgeree *n chiefly Brit* a dish consisting of rice, fish, and eggs ▶ HISTORY Hindi *khicarī*

keel *n* 1 one of the main lengthways steel or timber pieces along the base of a ship, to which the frames are fastened 2 **on an even keel** working or progressing smoothly without any sudden changes ▶ HISTORY Old Norse *kjölr*

keelhaul *vb* 1 to reprimand (someone) harshly 2 *history* to drag (someone) under the keel of a ship as a punishment

keel over *vb* 1 (of an object) to turn upside down 2 *informal* (of a person) to collapse suddenly

keen¹ *adj* 1 eager or enthusiastic: *a keen gardener* 2 **keen on** fond of; devoted to: *he is very keen on sport* 3 intense or strong: *a keen interest in environmental issues* 4 intelligent, quick, and perceptive: *a keen sense of humour* 5 (of sight, smell, or hearing) capable of recognizing fine distinctions 6 (of a knife or blade) having a sharp cutting edge 7 very strong and cold: *a keen wind* 8 very competitive: *keen prices* ▶ HISTORY Old English *cēne* > **keenly** *adv* > **keenness** *n*

keen² *vb* 1 to lament the dead ▷ *n* 2 a lament for the dead ▶ HISTORY Irish Gaelic *caoine*

keep *vb* **keeping, kept** 1 to have or retain possession of (something) 2 to have temporary charge of: *he'd kept my broken beads in his pocket for me all evening* 3 to store in a customary place: *I keep it at the back of the drawer with my journal* 4 to remain or cause (someone or something) to remain in a specified state or condition: *keep still* 5 to continue or cause (someone) to continue: *keep going straight on* 6 to stay (in, on, or at a place or position): *keep to the paths* 7 to have as part of normal stock: *they keep a small stock of first-class German wines* 8 to support (someone) financially 9 to detain (someone) 10 to be faithful to (something): *to keep a promise* 11 (of food) to stay in good condition for a certain time: *fish doesn't keep very well* 12 to observe (a religious festival) with rites or ceremonies 13 to maintain by writing regular records in: *he keeps a nature diary in his spare time* 14 to look after or maintain for use, pleasure, or profit: *an old man who kept goats and cows* 15 to associate with: *she has started keeping bad company* 16 **keep in with** to stay friendly with someone as they may be useful to you 17 **how are you keeping?** are you well? ▷ *n* 18 the cost of food and other everyday expenses: *I have to earn my keep* 19 the main tower within the walls of a medieval castle or fortress 20 **for keeps** *informal* permanently ▶ HISTORY Old English *cēpan* to observe

keeper *n* 1 a person in charge of animals in a zoo 2 a person in charge of a museum, collection, or section of a museum 3 a person who supervises a person or thing: *the self-appointed keeper of the village conscience* 4 short for **gamekeeper, goalkeeper, wicketkeeper**

keep fit *n* exercises designed to promote physical fitness if performed regularly

keeping *n* 1 **in keeping with** suitable or appropriate to or for 2 **out of keeping with** unsuitable or inappropriate to or for

keepsake *n* a gift kept in memory of the giver

keep up *vb* 1 to maintain (prices, standards, or one's morale) at the present level 2 to maintain in good condition 3 **keep up with a** to maintain a pace set by (someone) **b** to remain informed about: *he liked to think he kept up with current musical trends* **c** to remain in contact with (someone) 4 **keep up with the Joneses** *informal* to compete with one's friends or neighbours in material possessions

keg *n* a small barrel in which beer is transported and stored ▶ HISTORY Scandinavian

Kellogg-Briand Pact *n history* a treaty for the renunciation of war, signed in Paris in 1928 by representatives of 15 nations ▶ HISTORY after French Prime Minister Aristide *Briand* and US Secretary of State Frank B *Kellogg*

kelp *n* a large brown seaweed rich in iodine and potash ▶ HISTORY origin unknown

kelpie *n* 1 (in Scottish folklore) a water spirit in the form of a horse ▷ *n* 2 an Australian sheepdog with a smooth coat and upright ears ▶ HISTORY origin unknown

kelt *n* a salmon that has recently spawned ▶ HISTORY origin unknown

kelvin *n physics* the basic SI unit of thermodynamic temperature ▶ HISTORY after W. T. *Kelvin*, physicist

Kelvin scale *n physics* a thermodynamic temperature scale starting at absolute zero

ken *n* 1 **beyond one's ken** beyond one's range of knowledge ▷ *vb* **kenning, kenned** *or* **kent** 2 *Scot & N English dialect* to know ▶ HISTORY Old English *cennan*

kendo *n* the Japanese sport of fencing using wooden staves ▶ HISTORY Japanese

kennel *n* 1 a hutlike shelter for a dog 2 **kennels** a place where dogs are bred, trained, or boarded ▷ *vb* **-nelling, -nelled** *or US* **-neling, -neled** 3 to keep (a dog) in a kennel ▶ HISTORY Latin *canis* dog

Kenyan *adj* 1 from Kenya ▷ *n* 2 a person from Kenya

kept *vb* 1 the past of **keep** 2 **kept woman** *or* **man** a person financially supported by someone in return for sexual favours

keratin n a fibrous protein found in the hair and nails

kerb or US & Canad **curb** n a line of stone or concrete forming an edge between a pavement and a roadway ▸ HISTORY Old French *courbe* bent

kerb crawling n Brit the act of driving slowly beside a kerb to pick up a prostitute > **kerb crawler** n

kerchief n a piece of cloth worn over the head or round the neck ▸ HISTORY Old French *cuevrechef*

kerfuffle n Brit & NZ, informal a noisy and disorderly incident ▸ HISTORY Scots *curfuffle, carfuffle*

kermes (kur-meez) n the dried bodies of female scale insects, used as a red dyestuff ▸ HISTORY Arabic *qirmiz*

kernel n 1 the edible seed of a nut or fruit within the shell or stone 2 the grain of a cereal, such as wheat, consisting of the seed in a hard husk 3 the central or essential part of something: *there is a kernel of truth in these remarks* ▸ HISTORY Old English *cyrnel* a little seed

kerosene n US, Canad, Austral & NZ same as **paraffin** (sense 1) ▸ HISTORY Greek *kēros* wax

Kerry n, pl **-ries** a small black breed of dairy cattle, originally from Ireland ▸ HISTORY after *Kerry*, county in SW Ireland

kestrel n a small falcon that feeds on small animals such as mice ▸ HISTORY Old French *cresserele*

ketch n a two-masted sailing ship ▸ HISTORY Middle English *cache*

ketchup n a thick cold sauce, usually made of tomatoes ▸ HISTORY Chinese *kôetsiap* brine of pickled fish

ketone (kee-tone) n chem any of a class of compounds with the general formula $R'COR$, where R and R' are alkyl or aryl groups ▸ HISTORY German *Keton*, from *Aketon* acetone

kettle n 1 a metal container with a handle and spout, for boiling water 2 any of various metal containers for heating liquid, cooking, etc. 3 **a different kettle of fish** a different matter entirely 4 **a fine kettle of fish** a difficult or awkward situation ▸ HISTORY Old Norse *ketill*

kettledrum n a large bowl-shaped metal drum that can be tuned to play specific notes

key[1] n 1 a specially shaped metal instrument, for moving the bolt of a lock so as to lock or unlock a door, suitcase, etc. 2 an instrument that is turned to operate a valve, clock winding mechanism, etc. 3 any of a set of levers pressed to operate a typewriter, computer, or musical keyboard instrument 4 a scale of musical notes that starts at one specific note 5 something that is crucial in providing an explanation or interpretation 6 a means of achieving a desired end: *education is the key to success in most walks of life today* 7 a list of explanations of symbols, codes, or abbreviations 8 pitch: *he spoke in a low key* ▷ adj 9 of great importance: *key prosecution witnesses have been giving evidence* ▷ vb 10 to harmonize with: *training and educational programmes uniquely keyed for local needs* 11 to adjust or fasten (something) with a key

or some similar device 12 same as **keyboard** ▷ See also **key in** ▸ HISTORY Old English *cæg*

key[2] n same as **cay**

keyboard n 1 a set of keys on a typewriter, computer, or piano 2 a musical instrument played using a keyboard ▷ vb 3 to enter (text) in type using a keyboard ▸ **keyboarder** n

keyed up adj very excited or nervous

key grip n the person in charge of moving and setting up camera tracks and scenery in a film or television studio

keyhole n an opening for inserting a key into a lock

keyhole surgery n surgery carried out using very small instruments, performed through a narrow hole cut in the body rather than through a major incision

key in vb to enter (information or instructions) into a computer by means of a keyboard

keylogging n computers the practice of covertly recording and monitoring keystrokes made on a remote computer

key money n Brit a sum of money required from a new tenant of a house or flat before he or she moves in

Keynesian (cane-zee-an) adj of the economic theories of J.M. Keynes, who argued that governments should fund public works to maintain full employment, accepting if necessary the consequence of inflation

keynote n 1 a central or dominant idea in a speech or literary work 2 the note on which a scale or key is based ▷ adj 3 central or dominating: *his keynote speech to the party conference*

keypad n a small panel with a set of buttons for operating a Teletext system, electronic calculator, etc.

keyring n a metal ring, often decorative, for keeping keys on

key signature n music a group of sharps or flats at the beginning of each stave line to indicate the key

keystone n 1 the most important part of a process, organization, etc.: *the keystone of the government's economic policy* 2 the central stone at the top of an arch

keyword n computers a word or phrase that a computer will search for in order to locate the information or file that the computer user has requested

key worker n chiefly Brit 1 a social worker, mental health worker, or nursery nurse assigned to an individual case, patient, or child 2 a worker in a public-sector profession considered to be essential to society

kg kilogram

KG (in Britain) Knight of the Order of the Garter

KGB (formerly) the Soviet secret police ▸ HISTORY Russian *Komitet Gosudarstvennoi Bezopasnosti* State Security Committee

khaki adj 1 dull yellowish-brown ▷ n 2 a hard-wearing fabric of this colour, used for military uniforms ▸ HISTORY Urdu, from Persian: dusty

k

khan *n* a title of respect in Afghanistan and central Asia ▶ HISTORY Turkish

Khoikhoi *or* **Khoi** *n* 1 a race of indigenous people of South Africa which is now almost extinct 2 a member of this race 3 the language of this race ▶ HISTORY origin unknown

kHz kilohertz

kia ora *interj* NZ Māori greeting ▶ HISTORY Māori

kibbutz *n, pl* **kibbutzim** a farm, factory, or other workplace in Israel, owned and run communally by its members ▶ HISTORY Modern Hebrew *qibbūs* gathering

kibosh *n* **put the kibosh on** *slang* to put a stop to ▶ HISTORY origin unknown

kick *vb* 1 to drive, push, or hit with the foot or feet 2 to strike out with the feet, as in swimming 3 to raise a leg high, as in dancing 4 *rugby* to score (a conversion, drop kick, or penalty) with a kick: *he kicked his third penalty* 5 (of a firearm) to recoil when fired 6 *informal* to object or resist: *school uniforms give children something to kick against* 7 *informal* to free oneself of (an addiction): *smokers who want to kick the habit* 8 **alive and kicking** *informal* active and in good health 9 **kick someone upstairs** to promote someone to a higher but effectively powerless position ▷ *n* 10 a thrust or blow with the foot 11 any of certain rhythmic leg movements used in swimming 12 the recoil of a firearm 13 *informal* an exciting effect: *we get a kick out of attacking opposing fans and overturning their buses; a few small bets just for kicks* 14 *informal* the intoxicating effect of an alcoholic drink: *a cocktail with a kick in it* 15 **kick in the teeth** *slang* a humiliating rebuff ▷ See also **kick off** ▶ HISTORY Middle English *kiken*

kickback *n* 1 part of an income paid to a person in return for an opportunity to make a profit, often by some illegal arrangement 2 a strong reaction

kick off *vb* 1 to start play in a game of football by kicking the ball from the centre of the field 2 *informal* to commence (a discussion, event, etc.) ▷ *n* **kickoff** 3 **a** the kick that officially starts a game of football **b** the time when the first kick is due to take place 4 *informal* the time when an event is due to begin

kick out *vb informal* to dismiss (someone) or throw (someone) out forcefully

kick-start *n* 1 Also: **kick-starter** a pedal on a motorcycle that is kicked downwards to start the engine 2 an action or event that reactivates something ▷ *vb* 3 to start (a motorcycle) with a kick-start 4 to do something bold or drastic in order to begin or improve the performance of something: *to kick-start the economy*

kick up *vb informal* to cause (trouble)

kid[1] *n* 1 *informal* a young person; child 2 a young goat 3 soft smooth leather made from the hide of a kid ▷ *adj* 4 younger: *my kid sister* ▷ *vb* **kidding, kidded** 5 (of a goat) to give birth to (young) ▶ HISTORY from Old Norse

kid[2] *vb* **kidding, kidded** *informal* 1 to tease or deceive (someone) for fun 2 to fool (oneself) into believing something: *don't kid yourself that no-one else knows* ▶ HISTORY probably from KID[1] > **kidder** *n*

kidnap *vb* **-napping, -napped** *or US* **-naping, -naped** to capture and hold (a person), usually for ransom ▶ HISTORY KID[1] + obsolete *nap* to steal > **kidnapper** *or US* **-naper** *n* > **kidnapping** *or US* **-naping** *n*

kidney *n* 1 either of two bean-shaped organs at the back of the abdominal cavity. They filter waste products from the blood, which are excreted as urine 2 the kidneys of certain animals used as food ▶ HISTORY origin unknown

kidney bean *n* a reddish-brown kidney-shaped bean, edible when cooked

kidney machine *n* a machine carrying out the functions of damaged human kidneys

kill *vb* 1 to cause the death of (a person or animal) 2 *informal* to cause (someone) pain or discomfort: *my feet are killing me* 3 to put an end to: *his infidelity had killed his marriage* 4 *informal* to quash or veto: *the main opposition party tried to kill the bill* 5 to overwhelm (someone) completely with laughter, attraction, or surprise: *her jokes really kill me* 6 **kill oneself** *informal* to overexert oneself 7 **kill time** to spend time on something unimportant or trivial while waiting for something: *I'm just killing time until I can talk to the other witnesses* 8 **kill two birds with one stone** to achieve two results with one action ▷ *n* 9 the act of causing death at the end of a hunt or bullfight 10 the animal or animals killed during a hunt 11 **in at the kill** present when something comes to a dramatic end with unpleasant results for someone else ▶ HISTORY Middle English *cullen* > **killer** *n*

killer whale *n* a black-and-white toothed whale, most common in cold seas

killing *adj* 1 *informal* very tiring: *a killing pace* 2 *informal* extremely funny 3 causing death; fatal ▷ *n* 4 the act of causing death; slaying 5 **make a killing** *informal* to have a sudden financial success

killjoy *n* a person who spoils other people's pleasure

kiln *n* a large oven for burning, drying, or processing pottery, bricks, etc. ▶ HISTORY Latin *culina* kitchen

kilo *n, pl* **kilos** short for **kilogram, kilometre**

kilo- *combining form* 1 denoting one thousand (10³): *kilometre* 2 (in computers) denoting 2¹⁰ (1024): *kilobyte*. In computer usage, *kilo-* is restricted to sizes of storage (e.g. *kilobit*) when it means 1024: in other computer contexts it retains its usual meaning of 1000 ▶ HISTORY Greek *khilioi* thousand

kilobyte *n computers* 1024 bytes

kilocalorie *n* one thousand calories

kilocycle *n* an old word for kilohertz

kilogram *or* **kilogramme** *n* 1 one thousand grams 2 the basic SI unit of mass

kilohertz *n, pl* **kilohertz** one thousand hertz; one thousand cycles per second

kilojoule *n* one thousand joules

kilolitre *or US* **kiloliter** *n* a measure of volume equivalent to one thousand litres

457

kilometre *or US* **kilometer** *n* a unit of length equal to one thousand metres

kiloton *n* **1** one thousand tons **2** an explosive power, esp. of a nuclear weapon, equal to the power of 1000 tons of TNT

kilovolt *n* one thousand volts

kilowatt *n* one thousand watts

kilowatt-hour *n* a unit of energy equal to the work done by a power of 1000 watts in one hour

kilt *n* **1** a knee-length pleated tartan skirt, worn by men in Highland dress and by women and girls ▷ *vb* **2** to put pleats in (cloth) ▶ HISTORY Scandinavian > **kilted** *adj*

kimono (kim-**moan**-no) *n, pl* -**nos 1** a loose wide-sleeved Japanese robe, fastened with a sash **2** a European dressing gown resembling this ▶ HISTORY Japanese: clothing

kin *n* a person's relatives collectively ▶ HISTORY Old English *cyn*

kind¹ *adj* **1** considerate, friendly, and helpful: *a good, kind man; a few kind words* **2** cordial; courteous: *reprinted by kind permission* ▶ HISTORY Old English *gecynde* natural, native

kind² *n* **1** a class or group having characteristics in common: *what kind of music do you like?* **2** essential nature or character: *differences of degree rather than of kind* **3 in kind a** (of payment) in goods or services rather than in money **b** with something of the same sort: *the government threatened to retaliate in kind to any use of nuclear weapons* **4 kind of** spoken to a certain extent; loosely: *kind of hard; a kind of socialist* **5 of a kind** of poorer quality or standard than is wanted or expected: *a few farmers wrest subsistence of a kind from the thin topsoil* ▶ HISTORY Old English *gecynd* nature

kindergarten *n* a class or school for children under six years old ▶ HISTORY from German, literally: children's garden

kind-hearted *adj* considerate and sympathetic

kindle *vb* -**dling**, -**dled 1** to set (a fire) alight or (of a fire) to start to burn **2** to arouse or be aroused: *his passions were kindled as quickly as her own* ▶ HISTORY Old Norse *kynda*

kindling *n* material for starting a fire, such as dry wood or straw

kindly *adj* -**lier**, -**liest 1** having a warm-hearted and caring nature **2** pleasant or agreeable: *a kindly climate* ▷ *adv* **3** in a considerate or humane way **4** please: *will you kindly stop prattling on about it!* **5 not take kindly to** to react unfavourably towards > **kindliness** *n*

kindness *n* **1** the quality of being kind **2** a kind or helpful act

kindred *adj* **1** having similar qualities: *cholera, and other kindred diseases* **2** related by blood or marriage **3 kindred spirit** a person with whom one has something in common ▷ *n* **4** relationship by blood or marriage **5** similarity in character **6** a person's relatives collectively ▶ HISTORY Middle English *kinred*

kindy *or* **kindie** *n, pl* -**dies** *Austral & NZ, informal* a kindergarten

kine *pl n archaic* cows or cattle ▶ HISTORY Old English *cȳna* of cows

kinematics (kin-nim-**mat**-iks) *n physics* the study of the motion of bodies without reference to mass or force ▶ HISTORY Greek *kinēma* movement > **kinematic** *adj*

kinetic (kin-**net**-ik) *adj* relating to or caused by motion ▶ HISTORY Greek *kinein* to move > **kinetically** *adv*

kinetic art *n* art, such as sculpture, that moves or has moving parts

kinetic energy *n physics* the energy of motion of a body equal to the work it would do if it were brought to rest

kinetics *n physics* the branch of mechanics concerned with the study of bodies in motion

king *n* **1** a male ruler of a country who has inherited the throne from his parents **2** a ruler or chief: *the king of the fairies* **3** a person, animal, or thing considered as the best or most important of its kind: *the king of rock and roll* **4** a playing card with a picture of a king on it **5** a chessman, able to move one square in any direction: the object of the game is to checkmate one's opponent's king **6** *draughts* a piece which has moved entirely across the board and been crowned and which may therefore move backwards as well as forwards ▶ HISTORY Old English *cyning* > **kingship** *n*

kingcup *n Brit* a yellow-flowered plant; marsh marigold

kingdom *n* **1** a territory or state ruled by a king or queen **2** any of the three groups into which natural objects may be divided: the animal, plant, and mineral kingdoms **3** a place or area considered to be under the total power and control of a person, organization, or thing: *the kingdom of God*

kingfisher *n* a fish-eating bird with a greenish-blue and orange plumage ▶ HISTORY originally *king's fisher*

kingklip *n* an edible eel-like marine fish of S Africa ▶ HISTORY Afrikaans

kingpin *n* **1** the most important person in an organization: *a Mexican narcotics kingpin* **2** a pivot pin that provides a steering joint in a motor vehicle

king post *n building* a vertical post connecting the apex of a triangular roof truss to the tie beam

king prawn *n* a large prawn, fished commercially in Australian waters

king-size *or* **king-sized** *adj* larger than a standard size

kink *n* **1** a twist or bend in something such as a rope or hair **2** *informal* a flaw or quirk in someone's personality ▷ *vb* **3** to form or cause to form a kink ▶ HISTORY Dutch

kinky *adj* **kinkier**, **kinkiest 1** *slang* given to unusual sexual practices **2** tightly looped or curled

kinsfolk *pl n* one's family or relatives

kinship *n* **1** blood relationship **2** the state of having common characteristics

kinsman *n, pl* -**men** *written* a relation by blood or marriage > **kinswoman** *fem n*

kiosk *n* **1** a small booth from which cigarettes, newspapers, and sweets are sold **2** *chiefly Brit* a

k

public telephone box ▶ HISTORY French *kiosque* bandstand, from Persian *kūshk* pavilion

kip *Brit, slang n* **1** sleep: *a couple of hours' kip* **2** a bed ▷ *vb* **kipping, kipped 3** to sleep or take a nap **4 kip down** to sleep in a makeshift bed ▶ HISTORY origin unknown

kipper *n* **1** a herring that has been cleaned, salted, and smoked ▷ *vb* **2** to cure (a herring) by salting and smoking it ▶ HISTORY Old English *cypera*

kirk *n Scot* a church ▶ HISTORY Old Norse *kirkja*

Kirsch *or* **Kirschwasser** *n* a brandy distilled from black cherries ▶ HISTORY German *Kirschwasser* cherry water

kiskadee *n* either of two types of tropical flycatcher with a yellow breast and black-and-white striped head ▶ HISTORY imitative of its call

kismet *n* fate or destiny ▶ HISTORY Persian *qismat*

kiss *vb* **1** to touch with the lips as an expression of love, greeting, or respect **2** to join lips with another person as an act of love or desire **3** *literary* to touch lightly: *a long, high free kick that kissed the top of the crossbar* ▷ *n* **4** a caress with the lips **5** a light touch ▶ HISTORY Old English *cyssan* > **kissable** *adj*

kissagram *n Brit, Austral & NZ* a greetings service in which a person is employed to present greetings by kissing the person celebrating

kisser *n slang* the mouth or face

kissing crust *n NZ* the soft end of a loaf of bread where two loaves have been separated

kiss of life *n* **the kiss of life** mouth-to-mouth resuscitation in which a person blows gently into the mouth of an unconscious person

kist *n S African* a large wooden chest

kit[1] *n* **1** a set of tools or supplies for use together or for a purpose: *a first-aid kit* **2** the container for such a set **3** a set of parts sold ready to be assembled: *a model aircraft kit* **4** a basket or box for holding fish **5** clothing and other personal effects, such as those of a soldier: *a complete set of school team kit* ▷ See also **kit out** ▶ HISTORY Middle Dutch *kitte* tankard

kit[2] *n NZ* a flax basket ▶ HISTORY Māori *kete*

kitbag *n* a canvas or other bag for a serviceman's kit

kitchen *n* a room equipped for preparing and cooking food ▶ HISTORY Late Latin *coquina*

kitchenette *n* a small kitchen or part of a room equipped for use as a kitchen

kitchen garden *n* a garden for growing vegetables, herbs, etc.

kitchen-sink drama *n theatre* a type of drama of the 1950s depicting the sordid aspects of domestic reality

kitchen tea *n Austral & NZ* a party held before a wedding to which guests bring kitchen equipment as presents

kite *n* **1** a light frame covered with a thin material flown in the wind at the end of a length of string **2** a bird of prey with a long forked tail and large wings **3** a four-sided geometrical shape in which each side is equal in length to one of the sides joining it ▶ HISTORY Old English *cȳta*

Kite mark *n Brit* the official mark in the form of a kite on articles approved by the British Standards Institution

kith *n* **kith and kin** *old-fashioned* one's friends and relations ▶ HISTORY Old English *cȳthth*

kit out *or* **up** *vb* **kitting, kitted** *chiefly Brit* to provide with clothes or equipment needed for a particular activity

kitsch *n* tawdry or sentimental art or literature ▶ HISTORY from German > **kitschy** *adj*

kitten *n* **1** a young cat **2 have kittens** *informal* to react with disapproval or anxiety: *she had kittens when she discovered the price* ▶ HISTORY Old French *caton*

kittenish *adj* lively and flirtatious

kittiwake *n* a type of seagull with pale grey black-tipped wings and a square-cut tail ▶ HISTORY imitative

kitty[1] *n, pl* **-ties** a diminutive or affectionate name for a **kitten** or **cat**

kitty[2] *n, pl* **-ties 1** any shared fund of money **2** the pool in certain gambling games ▶ HISTORY probably from KIT[1]

kiwi *n, pl* **kiwis 1** a flightless bird of New Zealand with a long beak, stout legs, and no tail **2** a New Zealander ▶ HISTORY Māori

kiwi fruit *n* an edible fruit with a fuzzy brown skin and green flesh

kJ kilojoule(s)

kl kilolitre(s)

klaxon *n* a type of loud horn used on fire engines and ambulances as a warning signal ▶ HISTORY former trademark

kleinhuisie (**klayn**-hay-see) *n S African* an outside toilet ▶ HISTORY Afrikaans, literally: little house

kleptomania *n psychol* a strong impulse to steal ▶ HISTORY Greek *kleptein* to steal + *mania* madness > **kleptomaniac** *n*

klipspringer *n* a small agile antelope of rocky regions of Africa south of the Sahara ▶ HISTORY Afrikaans: rock jumper

kloof *n S African* a mountain pass or gorge ▶ HISTORY Afrikaans

km kilometre(s)

knack *n* **1** a skilful way of doing something **2** an ability to do something difficult with apparent ease ▶ HISTORY probably from Middle English *knak* sharp knock

knacker *n Brit* a person who buys up old horses for slaughter ▶ HISTORY origin unknown

knackered *adj slang* **1** extremely tired: *they'd been marching for three hours and were absolutely knackered* **2** broken or no longer functioning: *a knackered TV set*

knapsack *n* a canvas or leather bag carried strapped on the back or shoulder ▶ HISTORY Low German *knappen* to eat + *sack* bag

knapweed *n* a plant with purplish thistle-like flowers ▶ HISTORY Middle English *knopwed*

knave *n* **1** *cards* the jack **2** *archaic* a dishonest man ▶ HISTORY Old English *cnafa* > **knavish** *adj*

knead *vb* **1** to work and press (a soft substance, such as dough) into a smooth mixture with the

459

hands **2** to squeeze or press with the hands ▸ **HISTORY** Old English *cnedan* > **kneader** *n*

knee *n* **1** the joint of the leg between the thigh and the lower leg **2** the area around this joint **3** the upper surface of a sitting person's thigh: *a little girl being cuddled on her father's knee* **4** the part of a garment that covers the knee **5 bring someone to his knees** to force someone into submission ▷ *vb* **kneeing, kneed** **6** to strike, nudge, or push with the knee ▸ **HISTORY** Old English *cnēow*

kneecap *n* **1** *anat* a small flat triangular bone in front of and protecting the knee ▷ *vb* **-capping, -capped** **2** (of terrorists) to shoot (a person) in the kneecap

knee-jerk *n* **1** *physiol* a sudden involuntary kick of the lower leg caused by a sharp tap on the tendon just below the kneecap ▷ *adj* **kneejerk** **2** made or occurring as a predictable and automatic response: *a kneejerk reaction*

kneel *vb* **kneeling, knelt** *or* **kneeled 1** to rest, fall, or support oneself on one's knees ▷ *n* **2** the act or position of kneeling ▸ **HISTORY** Old English *cnēowlian*

knees-up *n Brit, informal* a party

knell *n* **1** the sound of a bell rung to announce a death or a funeral **2** something that indicates death or destruction ▷ *vb* **3** to ring a knell **4** to proclaim by a tolling bell ▸ **HISTORY** Old English *cnyll*

knew *vb* the past tense of **know**

knickerbockers *pl n* loose-fitting short trousers gathered in at the knee or calf ▸ **HISTORY** after Diedrich *Knickerbocker*, fictitious author of Washington Irving's *History of New York*

knickers *pl n* a woman's or girl's undergarment covering the lower trunk and having separate legs or leg-holes ▸ **HISTORY** contraction of *knickerbockers*

knick-knack *n* a small ornament or trinket ▸ **HISTORY** reduplication of obsolete *knack* a toy

knickpoint *or esp US* **nickpoint** *n geog* a break in the slope of a river profile caused by renewed erosion by a rejuvenated river ▸ **HISTORY** partial translation of German *Knickpunkt*, from *knicken* to bend + *Punkt* POINT

knife *n, pl* **knives 1** a cutting instrument or weapon consisting of a sharp-edged blade of metal fitted into a handle ▷ *vb* **knifing, knifed** **2** to stab or kill with a knife ▸ **HISTORY** Old English *cnīf* > **knifelike** *adj*

knife edge *n* **1** the sharp cutting edge of a knife **2** a critical point in the development of a situation: *and at this point the election result is still poised on a knife edge*

knight *n* **1** a man who has been given a knighthood in recognition of his achievements **2** (in medieval Europe) **a** a person who served his lord as a mounted and heavily armed soldier **b** a devoted male admirer of a noblewoman, esp. her champion in a jousting tournament **3** a chessman shaped like a horse's head, able to move either two squares horizontally and one square vertically or two

squares vertically and one square horizontally ▷ *vb* **4** to make (a man) a knight ▸ **HISTORY** Old English *cniht* servant

knight errant *n, pl* **knights errant** (esp. in medieval romance) a knight who wanders in search of deeds of courage, chivalry, etc. > **knight errantry** *n*

knighthood *n* an honorary title given to a man by the British sovereign in recognition of his achievements

knightly *adj* of, resembling, or appropriate for a knight > **knightliness** *n*

knit *vb* **knitting, knitted** *or* **knit 1** to make (a garment) by looping (wool) using long eyeless needles or a knitting machine **2** to join together closely **3** to draw (one's eyebrows) together ▷ *n* **4** a fabric made by knitting ▸ **HISTORY** Old English *cnyttan* to tie in > **knitter** *n*

knitting *n* knitted work or the process of producing it

knitwear *n* knitted clothes, such as sweaters

knives *n* the plural of **knife**

knob *n* **1** a rounded projection from a surface, such as a rotating switch on a radio **2** a rounded handle of a door or drawer **3** a small amount of butter or margarine ▸ **HISTORY** Middle Low German *knobbe* knot in wood > **knoblike** *adj*

knobbly *adj* having or covered with small bumps: *a curious knobbly root vegetable*

knobkerrie *n S African* a club or a stick with a rounded end ▸ **HISTORY** Khoikhoi *kirri* stick

knock *vb* **1** to give a blow or push to **2** to rap sharply with the knuckles: *he knocked on the door of the guest room* **3** to make by striking: *he knocked a hole in the wall* **4** to collide (with) **5** to bring into a certain condition by hitting: *he was knocked unconscious in a collision* **6** *informal* to criticize adversely **7** to emit a regular banging sound as a result of a fault: *the engine was knocking badly* **8 knock on the head** to prevent the further development of (a plan) ▷ *n* **9 a** a blow, push, or rap: *he gave the table a knock* **b** the sound so caused **10** the sound of knocking in an engine or bearing **11** *informal* a misfortune, rejection, or setback **12** *informal* criticism ▷ *See also* **knock about, knock back,** etc. ▸ **HISTORY** Old English *cnocian*

knock about *or* **around** *vb* **1** to wander or travel about: *I have knocked about the world through three continents* **2** (foll. by *with*) to associate **3** to treat brutally: *she looked knocked about, with bruises and cuts to her head* **4** to consider or discuss informally ▷ *adj* **knockabout 5** (of comedy) lively, boisterous, and physical

knock back *vb informal* **1** to drink quickly: *he fell over after knocking back eight pints of lager* **2** to cost: *lunch for two here will knock you back fifty pounds* **3** to reject or refuse: *I don't know any man who'd knock back an offer like that* ▷ *n* **knockback 4** *slang* a refusal or rejection

knock down *vb* **1** to strike to the ground with a blow, such as in boxing **2** (in auctions) to declare an article sold **3** to demolish **4** *informal* to reduce (a price) ▷ *adj* **knockdown 5** powerful: *a knockdown argument* **6** *chiefly Brit* (of a price) very cheap **7** easily dismantled: *knockdown furniture*

knocker *n* a metal object attached to a door by a hinge and used for knocking

knock-knees *pl n* legs that are bent inwards at the knees > **knock-kneed** *adj*

knock off *vb* **1** *informal* to finish work: *around ten, the day shift knocked off* **2** *informal* to make or do hastily or easily: *she knocked off 600 books in all during her long life* **3** *informal* to take (an amount) off the price of (an article): *I'll knock off 10% if you pay cash* **4** *Brit, Austral & NZ, informal* to steal **5** *slang* to kill **6** *slang* to stop doing something; used as a command: *knock it off!*

knock-on *rugby n* **1** the foul of playing the ball forward with the hand or arm ▷ *vb* **knock on 2** to play (the ball) forward with the hand or arm

knock-on effect *n* the indirect result of an action or decision

knockout *n* **1** the act of rendering someone unconscious **2** *boxing* a blow that renders an opponent unable to continue after the referee has counted to ten **3** a competition in which competitors are eliminated progressively **4** *informal* a person or thing that is very impressive or attractive: *at my youngest sister's wedding she was a knockout in navy and scarlet* ▷ *vb* **knock out 5** to render (someone) unconscious **6** *boxing* to defeat (an opponent) by a knockout **7** to destroy: *communications in many areas were knocked out by the earthquake* **8** to eliminate from a knockout competition **9** *informal* to amaze: *the fantastic audience reaction knocked me out*

knock up *vb* **1** Also: **knock together** *informal* to make or assemble quickly: *my boyfriend can knock up a wonderful lasagne* **2** *Brit, informal* to waken: *to knock someone up early* **3** *slang* to make pregnant **4** to practise before a game of tennis, squash, or badminton ▷ *n* **knock-up 5** a practice session at tennis, squash, or badminton

knoll *n* a small rounded hill ▶ **HISTORY** Old English *cnoll*

knot *n* **1** a fastening formed by looping and tying pieces of rope, cord, or string **2** a tangle, such as in hair **3** a decorative bow, such as of ribbon **4** *written* a small cluster or huddled group: *a knot of passengers gathered on the platform* **5** a bond: *to tie the knot of friendship* **6 a** a hard mass of wood where a branch joins the trunk of a tree **b** a cross section of this visible in timber **7** a feeling of tightness, caused by tension or nervousness: *a dull knot of anxiety that sat in the pit of her stomach* **8** a unit of speed used by ships and aircraft, equal to one nautical mile per hour **9 at a rate of knots** very fast **10 tie someone in knots** to confuse someone completely ▷ *vb* **knotting, knotted 11** to tie or fasten in a knot **12** to form into a knot **13** to entangle or become entangled ▶ **HISTORY** Old English *cnotta* > **knotted** *adj* > **knotless** *adj*

knotty *adj* **-tier, -tiest 1** full of knots **2** extremely difficult or puzzling: *a knotty problem*

know *vb* **knowing, knew, known 1** to be or feel certain of the truth or accuracy of (a fact, answer, or piece of information) **2** to be acquainted with: *I'd known him for many years, since I was seventeen* **3** to have a grasp of or understand (a skill or language) **4** to understand or be aware of (something, or how to do or be something): *she knew how to get on with people* **5** to experience: *you had to have known poverty before you could give money its true value, he claimed* **6** to be intelligent, informed, or sensible enough (to do something): *how did he know to send the letter in the first place?* **7** to be able to distinguish: *I don't know one flower from another* **8 know what's what** to know how one thing or things in general work **9 you never know** things are uncertain ▷ *n* **10 in the know** *informal* aware or informed ▶ **HISTORY** Old English *gecnāwan* > **knowable** *adj*

know-all *n informal, disparaging* a person who pretends or appears to know a lot more than other people

know-how *n informal* the ability to do something that is difficult or technical

knowing *adj* **1** suggesting secret knowledge: *Paul saw the knowing look that passed between them* **2** cunning or shrewd **3** deliberate > **knowingly** *adv* > **knowingness** *n*

knowledge *n* **1** the facts or experiences known by a person or group of people **2** the state of knowing **3** specific information about a subject **4 to my knowledge** as I understand it

knowledgeable *or* **knowledgable** *adj* intelligent or well-informed > **knowledgeably** *or* **knowledgably** *adv*

known *vb* **1** the past participle of **know** ▷ *adj* **2** identified: *consorting with known criminals*

knuckle *n* **1** a joint of a finger **2** the knee joint of a calf or pig **3 near the knuckle** *informal* likely to offend people because of frankness or rudeness ▷ See also **knuckle under** ▶ **HISTORY** Middle English

knuckle-duster *n* a metal appliance worn over the knuckles to add force to a blow

knuckle under *vb* **-ling, -led** to give way under pressure or authority

knurl *n* a small ridge, often one of a series ▶ **HISTORY** probably from *knur* a knot in wood

KO *or* **k.o.** *vb* **KO'ing, KO'd** *or* **k.o.'ing, k.o.'d 1** to knock out ▷ *n, pl* **KO's** *or* **k.o.'s 2** a knockout

koala *n* a tree-dwelling Australian marsupial with dense grey fur ▶ **HISTORY** Aboriginal

koeksister (kook-sist-er) *n S African* a plaited doughnut deep-fried and soaked in syrup ▶ **HISTORY** Afrikaans

kohanga reo *or* **kohanga** *n NZ* an infant class where children are taught in Māori ▶ **HISTORY** Māori: language nest

kohl *n* a cosmetic powder used to darken the area around the eyes ▶ **HISTORY** Arabic

kohlrabi (kole-rah-bee) *n, pl* **-bies** a type of cabbage with an edible stem ▶ **HISTORY** Italian *cavolo* cabbage + *rapa* turnip

k

kokanee (coke-**can**-ee) *n* a freshwater salmon of lakes and rivers in W North America ▶ HISTORY after *Kokanee Creek*, in British Columbia

kola *n* same as **cola**

kolkhoz (kol-**hawz**) *n* (formerly) a collective farm in the Soviet Union ▶ HISTORY Russian

komatik (koh-ma-tik) *n Canad* a sledge with wooden runners and crossbars bound with animal hides ▶ HISTORY Inuit

kook *n US & Canad, informal* an eccentric or foolish person ▶ HISTORY probably from *cuckoo* > **kooky** or **kookie** *adj*

kookaburra *n* a large Australian kingfisher with a cackling cry ▶ HISTORY Aboriginal

koori *n, pl* -**ris** an Australian Aborigine

kopeck *n* a former Russian monetary unit worth one hundredth of a rouble ▶ HISTORY Russian *kopeika*

kopje or **koppie** (kop-ee) *n S African* a small isolated hill ▶ HISTORY Afrikaans

Köppen's climate classification system *n meteorol* a system recognizing five, and later six, main climate types from tropical humid to polar, and charted on a map co-authored by German climatologist Wladimir Köppen (1846—1940) and Rudolph Geiger

Koran *n* the sacred book of Islam, believed by Muslims to be the infallible word of God dictated to Mohammed ▶ HISTORY Arabic *qur'ān* reading, book > **Koranic** *adj*

Korean *adj* **1** of Korea ▷ *n* **2** a person from Korea **3** the official language of North and South Korea

kosher (koh-sher) *adj* **1** *Judaism* **a** conforming to religious law **b** (of food) prepared in accordance with the dietary laws **2** *informal* legitimate, genuine, or proper ▷ *n* **3** kosher food ▶ HISTORY Yiddish

kowhai (koh-wye, koh-fye) *n* a small tree of New Zealand and Chile with clusters of yellow flowers ▶ HISTORY Māori

kowtow *vb* **1** to be humble and very respectful (towards): *the senior editors accused each other of kowtowing to his demands* **2** to touch the forehead to the ground in deference ▷ *n* **3** the act of kowtowing ▶ HISTORY Chinese *k'o* to strike, knock + *t'ou* head

kph kilometres per hour

Kr *chem* krypton

kraal *n* **1** a Southern African hut village surrounded by a strong fence **2** *S African* an enclosure for livestock ▶ HISTORY Afrikaans, from Portuguese *curral* enclosure

krans *n S African* a sheer rock face ▶ HISTORY Afrikaans

Kremlin *n* the central government of Russia and, formerly, the Soviet Union

krill *n, pl* **krill** a small shrimplike crustacean ▶ HISTORY Norwegian *kril* young fish

Krishna *n* a Hindu god, the incarnation of Vishnu

krona *n, pl* -**nor** the standard monetary unit of Sweden ▶ HISTORY Swedish, from Latin *corona* crown

krone (kroh-na) *n, pl* -**ner** (-ner) the standard monetary unit of Norway and Denmark ▶ HISTORY Danish or Norwegian, from Latin *corona* crown

krugerrand *n* a one-ounce gold coin minted in South Africa ▶ HISTORY Paul *Kruger*, Boer statesman + *rand*

krypton *n chem* an inert gaseous element occurring in trace amounts in air and used in fluorescent lights and lasers. Symbol: Kr ▶ HISTORY Greek *kruptos* hidden

KS Kansas

kt. kiloton

kudos (kew-doss) *n* personal fame or glory ▶ HISTORY Greek

kudu or **koodoo** *n* a spiral-horned African antelope ▶ HISTORY Afrikaans, from Khoikhoi

kugel (koog-el) *n S African* a rich, fashion-conscious, materialistic young Jewish woman ▶ HISTORY from Yiddish *kugel*, a type of savoury pudding popular in Jewish cookery

Ku Klux Klan *n* a secret organization of White Protestant Americans who use violence against Black people and Jews ▶ HISTORY probably based on Greek *kuklos* circle + CLAN > **Ku Klux Klanner** *n*

kulak *n* (formerly) a property-owning Russian peasant ▶ HISTORY Russian

kumera or **kumara** *n NZ* a tropical root vegetable with yellow flesh ▶ HISTORY Māori

Kumina (koo-min-uh) *n* a Jamaican religion of African origin, in which dance and ritual are used to invoke ancestral spirits

kumquat (kumm-kwott) *n* a citrus fruit resembling a tiny orange ▶ HISTORY Cantonese Chinese *kam kwat* golden orange

kung fu *n* a Chinese martial art combining techniques of karate and judo ▶ HISTORY Chinese: martial art

Kuomintang (kwoh-min-**tang**) *n history* a political party dominant in China from 1928 until 1949 under the leadership of Chiang Kai-shek

kura kaupapa Māori *n NZ* a primary school where the teaching is done in Māori

kurrajong *n* an Australian tree or shrub with tough fibrous bark ▶ HISTORY from a native Australian language

kV kilovolt

kW kilowatt

Kwanzaa *n* an African-American festival held from December 26 through January 1 ▶ HISTORY from Swahili (*matunda ya*) *kwanza* first (fruits)

kwashiorkor *n* severe malnutrition of young children, caused by not eating enough protein ▶ HISTORY native word in Ghana

kWh kilowatt-hour

KWIC *computers* keyword in context

KWOC *computers* keyword out of context

KY Kentucky

kyle *n Scot* a narrow strait or channel: *Kyle of Lochalsh* ▶ HISTORY Gaelic *caol* narrow

Kyoto protocol *n politics* a commitment to reducing emissions of carbon dioxide, agreed by participating countries at a conference in Kyoto, Japan, in 1997

l litre(s)

L **1** large **2** Latin **3** learner driver **4** Usually written: **£** pound ▶ HISTORY Latin *libra* **5** the Roman numeral for 50

L. *or* **l.** **1** lake **2** left **3** length **4** (*pl* **LL** *or* **ll**) line

la *n music* same as **lah**

La *chem* lanthanum

LA **1** Los Angeles **2** Louisiana

laager *n* (in Africa) a camp defended by a circular formation of wagons ▶ HISTORY Afrikaans *lager*

lab *n informal* short for **laboratory**

Lab *politics* Labour

label *n* **1** a piece of card or other material attached to an object to show its contents, ownership, use, or destination **2** a brief descriptive term given to a person, group, or school of thought: *we would need a handy label to explain the new company* ▷ *vb* **-belling, -belled** *or US* **-beling, -beled** **3** to attach a label to **4** to describe or classify in a word or phrase ▶ HISTORY Old French: ribbon

labial (lay-bee-al) *adj* **1** of or near the lips **2** *phonetics* relating to a speech sound made using the lips ▷ *n* **3** *phonetics* a speech sound, such as English *p* or *m*, that involves the lips ▶ HISTORY Latin *labium* lip

labiate (lay-bee-ate) *n* **1** any of a family of plants with square stems, aromatic leaves, and a two-lipped flower, such as mint or thyme ▷ *adj* **2** of this family ▶ HISTORY Latin *labium* lip

labium (lay-bee-um) *n, pl* **-bia** (-bee-a) **1** a lip or liplike structure **2** any one of the four lip-shaped folds of the vulva ▶ HISTORY Latin: lip

labor *n US, Austral & sometimes Canad* same as **labour**

laboratory *n, pl* **-ries** a building or room equipped for conducting scientific research or for teaching practical science ▶ HISTORY Latin *laborare* to work

Labor Day *n* **1** (in the US and Canada) a public holiday in honour of labour, held on the first Monday in September **2** (in Australia) a public holiday observed on different days in different states

laborious *adj* involving great exertion or prolonged effort > **laboriously** *adv*

Labor Party *n* the main left-wing political party in Australia

labour *or US, Austral & sometimes Canad* **labor** *n* **1** productive work, esp. physical work done for wages **2** the people involved in this, as opposed to management **3** the final stage of pregnancy, leading to childbirth **4** difficult work or a difficult job ▷ *vb* **5** to do physical work: *the girls were labouring madly on it* **6** to work hard (for something) **7** to make one's way with difficulty: *she was now labouring down the return length* **8** to emphasize too persistently: *I have laboured the point* **9** (usually foll. by *under*) to be at a disadvantage because of a mistake or false belief: *she laboured under the illusion that I understood her* ▶ HISTORY Latin *labor*

Labour Day *n* **1** a public holiday in honour of work, held in Britain on May 1 **2** (in New Zealand) a public holiday commemorating the introduction of the eight-hour day, held on the 4th Monday in October

laboured *or US, Austral & sometimes Canad* **labored** *adj* undertaken with difficulty: *laboured breathing*

labourer *or US, Austral & sometimes Canad* **laborer** *n* a person engaged in physical work

labour-intensive *adj econ, business* requiring a large labour force as opposed to involving large capital investments. Compare **capital-intensive**

Labour Party *n* **1** the main left-wing political party in a number of countries including Britain and New Zealand **2** any similar party in various other countries

Labrador *or* **Labrador retriever** *n* a powerfully built dog with short dense usually black or golden hair

laburnum *n* a small ornamental tree that has clusters of yellow drooping flowers. It is highly poisonous ▶ HISTORY Latin

labyrinth (lab-er-inth) *n* **1** a mazelike network of tunnels or paths, either natural or man-made **2** any complex or confusing system **3** the interconnecting cavities of the internal ear ▶ HISTORY Greek *laburinthos* > **labyrinthine** *adj*

lac *n* a resinous substance secreted by certain insects (**lac insects**), used in the manufacture of shellac ▶ HISTORY Hindi *lākh* resin

lace *n* **1** a delicate decorative fabric made from threads woven in an open web of patterns **2** a cord or string drawn through eyelets to fasten a shoe or garment ▷ *vb* **lacing, laced** **3** to fasten (shoes) with a lace **4** to draw (a cord or thread) through holes as when tying shoes **5** to add a small amount of alcohol, a drug, or poison to (food or drink) **6** to intertwine; interlace ▶ HISTORY Latin *laqueus* noose

lacerate (lass-er-rate) *vb* **-ating, -ated** **1** to tear (the flesh) jaggedly **2** to hurt (the feelings): *it would only lacerate an overburdened conscience* ▶ HISTORY Latin *lacerare* to tear > **laceration** *n*

lachrymal *adj* same as **lacrimal**

lachrymose *adj* **1** given to weeping; tearful **2** mournful; sad ▶ HISTORY Latin *lacrima* a tear

lack *n* **1** shortage or absence of something required or desired: *a lack of confidence* ▷ *vb* **2** (often foll. by *in*) to be short (of) or have need (of): *lacking in sparkle* ▶ HISTORY related to Middle Dutch *laken* to be wanting

lackadaisical *adj* **1** lacking vitality and purpose **2** lazy and careless in a dreamy way ▸ HISTORY earlier *lackadaisy*

lackey *n* **1** a servile follower; hanger-on **2** a liveried male servant or valet ▸ HISTORY Catalan *lacayo, alacayo*

lacklustre *or US* **lackluster** *adj* lacking brilliance, force, or vitality

laconic *adj* (of a person's speech) using few words
- ■ **WORD HISTORY**
- ■ 'Laconic' comes from the Greek word
- ■ *Lakōnikos*, meaning 'Laconian' or 'Spartan'.
- ■ Sparta was the capital city of the region of
- ■ ancient Greece known as Laconia, and the
- ■ Spartans were famous for using few words.

lacquer *n* **1** a hard glossy coating made by dissolving natural or synthetic resins in a solvent that evaporates quickly **2** a black resin, obtained from certain trees, used to give a hard glossy finish to wooden furniture **3** a clear sticky substance for spraying onto the hair to hold a style in place ▸ HISTORY Portuguese *laca* lac

lacquered *adj* coated with lacquer

lacrimal *or* **lachrymal** (**lack**-rim-al) *adj* of tears or the glands that secrete tears ▸ HISTORY Latin *lacrima* a tear

lacrosse *n* a sport in which two teams try to propel a ball into each other's goal using long-handled sticks with a pouched net at the end ▸ HISTORY Canadian French: the hooked stick

lactate¹ *vb* **-tating, -tated** (of mammals) to secrete milk

lactate² *n* an ester or salt of lactic acid

lactation *n* **1** the secretion of milk from the mammary glands **2** the period during which milk is secreted

lacteal *adj* **1** of or like milk **2** (of lymphatic vessels) conveying or containing chyle ▹ *n* **3** any of the lymphatic vessels that convey chyle from the small intestine to the blood ▸ HISTORY Latin *lacteus* of milk

lactic *adj* relating to or derived from milk ▸ HISTORY Latin *lac* milk

lactic acid *n* a colourless syrupy acid found in sour milk and used as a preservative (**E270**) for foodstuffs

lactose *n* a white crystalline sugar occurring in milk

lacuna (lak-**kew**-na) *n, pl* **-nae** (-nee) a gap or space in a book or manuscript ▸ HISTORY Latin: pool, cavity

lacy *adj* **lacier, laciest** of or like lace

lad *n* **1** a boy or young man **2** *informal* any male **3 the lads** *informal* a group of males ▸ HISTORY perhaps from Old Norse

ladder *n* **1** a portable frame consisting of two long parallel supports connected by steps, for climbing up or down **2** any system thought of as having a series of ascending stages: *the career ladder* **3** *chiefly Brit* a line of connected stitches that have come undone in tights or stockings ▹ *vb* **4** *chiefly Brit* to have or cause to have a line of undone stitches ▸ HISTORY Old English *hlædder*

laddish *adj* *Brit, Austral & NZ, informal, often derogatory* characteristic of young men, esp. by being rowdy or immature

lade *vb* **lading, laded, laden** *or* **laded 1** to put cargo on board (a ship) or (of a ship) to take on cargo **2** (foll. by *with*) to burden or load ▸ HISTORY Old English *hladen* to load

laden *adj* **1** loaded **2** burdened

La Diablesse *n* (in the folklore of Trinidad and Tobago) a beautiful enchantress with one cloven hoof who leads men to their deaths ▸ HISTORY French, literally: devil woman

la-di-da *or* **lah-di-dah** *adj informal* affected or pretentious in speech or manners ▸ HISTORY mockingly imitative of affected speech

ladies *or* **ladies' room** *n informal* a women's public toilet

ladle *n* **1** a long-handled spoon with a deep bowl for serving soup, stew, etc. ▹ *vb* **-dling, -dled 2** to serve out as with a ladle ▸ HISTORY Old English *hlædel*

lady *n, pl* **-dies 1** a woman regarded as having the characteristics of a good family, such as dignified manners **2** a polite name for a woman ▹ *adj* **3** female: *a lady chef* ▸ HISTORY Old English *hlǣfdige*

Lady *n, pl* **-dies 1** (in Britain) a title borne by various classes of women of the peerage **2 Our Lady** a title of the Virgin Mary

ladybird *n* a small red beetle with black spots ▸ HISTORY after Our *Lady*, the Virgin Mary

Lady Day *n* March 25, the feast of the Annunciation of the Virgin Mary: a quarter day in England, Wales, and Ireland

lady-in-waiting *n, pl* **ladies-in-waiting** a lady who attends a queen or princess

ladylike *adj* refined and fastidious

Ladyship *n* (preceded by *Your* or *Her*) a title used to address or refer to any peeress except a duchess

lady's-slipper *n* an orchid with reddish or purple flowers

lag¹ *vb* **lagging, lagged 1** (often foll. by *behind*) to hang (back) or fall (behind) in movement, progress, or development **2** to fall away in strength or intensity ▹ *n* **3** a slowing down or falling behind **4** the interval of time between two events, esp. between an action and its effect: *the time lag between mobilization and combat* ▸ HISTORY origin unknown

lag² *vb* **lagging, lagged 1** to wrap (a pipe, cylinder, or boiler) with insulating material to prevent heat loss ▹ *n* **2** the insulating casing of a steam cylinder or boiler ▸ HISTORY Scandinavian

lag³ *n* **old lag** *Brit, Austral & NZ, slang* a convict or ex-convict ▸ HISTORY origin unknown

lager *n* a light-bodied effervescent beer, fermented in a closed vessel using yeasts that sink to the bottom of the brew ▸ HISTORY German *Lagerbier* beer for storing

laggard *n* a person who lags behind

lagging *n* insulating material wrapped around pipes, boilers, or tanks to prevent loss of heat

lagoon *n* a body of water cut off from the open sea by coral reefs or sand bars ▶ HISTORY Latin *lacuna* pool

lah *n* *music* (in tonic sol-fa) the sixth note of any ascending major scale

lahar (**lah**-hah) *n* a landslide of volcanic debris mixed with water down the sides of a volcano, usually precipitated by heavy rainfall ▶ HISTORY Javanese: lava

laid *vb* the past of **lay¹**

laid-back *adj* relaxed in style or character

lain *vb* the past participle of **lie²**

lair *n* **1** the resting place of a wild animal **2** *informal* a place of seclusion or hiding ▶ HISTORY Old English *leger*

laird *n* *Scot* a landowner, esp. of a large estate ▶ HISTORY Scots variant of *lord*

laissez faire *or* **laisser faire** (**less**-ay **fair**) *n* the policy of nonintervention, esp. by a government in commerce ▶ HISTORY French, literally: let (them) act

laity (**lay**-it-ee) *n* **1** people who are not members of the clergy **2** all the people who do not belong to a specific profession ▶ HISTORY from LAY³

lake¹ *n* an expanse of water entirely surrounded by land ▶ HISTORY Latin *lacus*

lake² *n* **1** a bright pigment produced by combining organic colouring matter with an inorganic compound **2** a red dye obtained by combining a metallic compound with cochineal ▶ HISTORY variant of *lac*

lama *n* a Buddhist priest or monk in Mongolia or Tibet ▶ HISTORY Tibetan *blama*

lamb *n* **1** the young of a sheep **2** the meat of a young sheep eaten as food **3** someone who is innocent, gentle, and good ▷ *vb* **4** (of a ewe) to give birth ▶ HISTORY Old English

Lamb *n* **the Lamb** a title given to Christ

lambast *or* **lambaste** *vb* **1** to beat severely **2** to reprimand severely ▶ HISTORY LAM¹ + BASTE³

lambent *adj* **1** (of a flame or light) flickering softly over a surface **2** (of wit or humour) light or brilliant ▶ HISTORY Latin *lambere* to lick > **lambency** *n*

lambing *n* **1** the birth of lambs at the end of winter **2** the shepherd's work of tending the ewes and newborn lambs at this time

lamb's fry *n* *Austral & NZ* lamb's liver for cooking

lambskin *n* the skin of a lamb, usually with the wool still on, used to make coats, slippers, etc.

lame *adj* **1** disabled or crippled in the legs or feet **2** weak; unconvincing: *lame arguments* ▷ *vb* **laming, lamed** **3** to make lame ▶ HISTORY Old English *lama* > **lamely** *adv* > **lameness** *n*

lamé (**lah**-may) *n* a fabric interwoven with gold or silver threads ▶ HISTORY Old French *lame* gold or silver thread

lame duck *n* a person who is unable to cope without the help of other people

lamella *n*, *pl* **-lae** (-lee) *biol* a calcified layer of which bone is formed

lament *vb* **1** *written* to feel or express sorrow or regret (for or over) ▷ *n* **2** *written* an expression of sorrow **3** a poem or song in which a death is lamented ▶ HISTORY Latin *lamentum* > **lamentation** *n*

lamentable *adj* very unfortunate or disappointing > **lamentably** *adv*

lamented *adj* grieved for: usually said of someone dead

lamina *n*, *pl* **-nae** a thin plate, esp. of bone or mineral ▶ HISTORY Latin: thin plate > **laminar** *adj*

laminate *vb* **-nating, -nated** **1** to make (material in sheet form) by sticking together thin sheets **2** to cover with a thin sheet of material **3** to split or be split into thin sheets ▷ *n* **4** a material made by sticking sheets together ▷ *adj* **5** composed of lamina; laminated > **lamination** *n*

laminated *adj* **1** composed of many layers stuck together **2** covered with a thin protective layer of plastic

lamington *n* *Austral & NZ* a sponge cake coated with a sweet coating

Lammas *n* August 1, formerly observed in England as a harvest festival: a quarter day in Scotland ▶ HISTORY Old English *hlāfmæsse* loaf mass

lamp *n* **1** a device that produces light: *an electric lamp; a gas lamp; an oil lamp* **2** a device that produces radiation, esp. for therapeutic purposes: *an ultraviolet lamp* ▶ HISTORY Greek *lampein* to shine

lampblack *n* a fine black soot used as a pigment in paint and ink

lampoon *n* **1** a piece of writing ridiculing a person ▷ *vb* **2** to ridicule and criticize (someone) in a lampoon ▶ HISTORY French *lampon* > **lampooner** *or* **lampoonist** *n*

lamppost *n* a metal or concrete pole supporting a lamp in a street

lamprey *n* an eel-like fish with a round sucking mouth ▶ HISTORY Late Latin *lampreda*

LAN *computers* local area network

Lancastrian *n* **1** a person from Lancashire or Lancaster **2** a supporter of the house of Lancaster in the Wars of the Roses (1455–85) ▷ *adj* **3** of Lancashire or Lancaster **4** of the house of Lancaster

lance *n* **1** a long weapon with a pointed head used by horsemen ▷ *vb* **lancing, lanced** **2** to pierce (an abscess or boil) with a lancet **3** to pierce with or as with a lance ▶ HISTORY Latin *lancea*

lance corporal *n* a noncommissioned officer of the lowest rank

lanceolate *adj* narrow and tapering to a point at each end, like some leaves ▶ HISTORY Latin *lanceola* small lance

lancer *n* (formerly) a cavalryman armed with a lance

lancet *n* a pointed surgical knife with two sharp edges ▶ HISTORY Old French *lancette* small lance

lancewood *n* a New Zealand tree with slender leaves

land *n* **1** the solid part of the surface of the earth as distinct from seas and lake. *Related adjective:* **terrestrial 2** ground, esp. with reference to its use or quality: *agricultural land* **3** rural or agricultural areas: *he couldn't leave the land* **4** *law* ground owned as property **5** a country, region, or area: *to bring peace and riches to your land* ▷ *vb* **6** to come down or bring (something) down to earth after a flight or jump **7** to transfer (something) or go from a ship to the shore: *sacks of malt were landed from barges* **8** to come to or touch shore **9** *informal* to obtain: *he landed a handsomely paid job at Lloyd's* **10** *angling* to retrieve (a hooked fish) from the water **11** *informal* to deliver (a blow or punch) ▷ See also **land up** ▶ HISTORY Old English > **landless** *adj*

land army *n history* a body of women recruited to do farm work in Britain during World Wars I and II

landau (**lan**-daw) *n* a four-wheeled horse-drawn carriage with two folding hoods ▶ HISTORY after *Landau*, a town in Germany, where first made

land breeze *n meteorol* a breeze that blows from land to sea, usually at night, caused by the land cooling faster than the sea and cooler air from the land flowing to replace rising warmer air from the sea. Compare **sea breeze**

land degradation *n geog* a decline in the condition of soil, plant life, and water, often caused by human activities and soil erosion

landed *adj* **1** owning land: *landed gentry* **2** consisting of land: *landed property*

landfall *n* the act of sighting or nearing land, esp. from the sea

landfill *n* **1** disposing of rubbish by covering it with earth **2** an area where rubbish is disposed of in this way

landform *n geol* any natural feature of the earth's surface

land girl *n* a girl or woman who does farm work, esp. in wartime

landing *n* **1** the floor area at the top of a flight of stairs **2** the act of coming to land, esp. after a flight or sea voyage **3** a place of disembarkation

landing field *n* an area of land on which aircraft land and from which they take off

landing gear *n* the undercarriage of an aircraft

landlady *n, pl* -**dies 1** a woman who owns and leases property **2** a woman who owns or runs a lodging house or pub

landline *n* **1** a telephone attached to a network by a socket, as opposed to a mobile phone **2** a telecommunications wire or cable laid over land

landlocked *adj* (of a country) completely surrounded by land

landlord *n* **1** a man who owns and leases property **2** a man who owns or runs a lodging house or pub

landlubber *n naut* any person without experience at sea

landmark *n* **1** a prominent object in or feature of a particular landscape **2** an important or unique event or development: *a landmark in scientific progress*

landmass *n* a large continuous area of land

land mine *n mil* an explosive device placed in the ground, usually detonated when someone steps on it or drives over it

landowner *n* a person who owns land

landscape *n* **1** an extensive area of land regarded as being visually distinct **2** a painting, drawing, or photograph depicting natural scenery ▷ *vb* **-scaping, -scaped 3** to improve the natural features of (an area of land) ▶ HISTORY Middle Dutch *lantscap* region

landscape gardening *n* the art of laying out grounds in imitation of natural scenery > **landscape gardener** *n*

landside *n* the part of an airport farthest from the aircraft

landslide *n* **1** Also called: **landslip a** the sliding of a large mass of rocks and soil down the side of a mountain or cliff **b** the material dislodged in this way **2** an overwhelming electoral victory

land tenure *n law* the system of property rights under which land is held, occupied, and used

land up *vb* to arrive at a final point or condition

landward *adj* **1** lying, facing, or moving towards land **2** in the direction of the land ▷ *adv also* **landwards 3** towards land

lane *n* **1** a narrow road, esp. in the country **2** one of the parallel strips into which the carriageway of a major road or motorway is divided **3** any well-defined route or course, such as for ships or aircraft **4** one of the parallel strips into which a running track or swimming bath is divided for races ▶ HISTORY Old English *lane, lanu*

lang. language

language *n* **1** a system of spoken sounds or conventional symbols for communicating thought **2** the language of a particular nation or people **3** the ability to use words to communicate **4** any other means of communicating: *body language* **5** the specialized vocabulary used by a particular group: *legal language* **6** a particular style of verbal expression: *rough language* **7** *computers* See **programming language** ▶ HISTORY Latin *lingua* tongue

languid *adj* lacking energy; dreamy and inactive ▶ HISTORY Latin *languere* to languish > **languidly** *adv*

languish *vb literary* **1** to suffer deprivation, hardship, or neglect: *she won't languish in jail for it* **2** to lose or diminish in strength or energy: *the design languished into oblivion* **3** (often foll. by *for*) to be listless with desire; pine ▶ HISTORY Latin *languere* > **languishing** *adj*

languor (**lang**-ger) *n literary* a pleasant state of dreamy relaxation ▶ HISTORY Latin *languere* to languish > **languorous** *adj*

La Niña (la-**nee**-nya) *n meteorol* a cooling of the central and eastern Pacific Ocean associated with a strengthening of tropical Pacific trade winds and wetter weather conditions in Australia ▶ HISTORY Spanish: the girl child Compare **El Niño**

lank *adj* **1** (of hair) straight and limp **2** thin or gaunt: *a lank bespectacled boy* ▶ HISTORY Old English *hlanc* loose

lanky *adj* **lankier, lankiest** ungracefully tall and thin > **lankiness** *n*

lanolin *n* a yellowish sticky substance extracted from wool: used in some ointments ▶ HISTORY Latin *lana* wool + *oleum* oil

lantana (lan-**tay**-na) *n* a shrub with orange or yellow flowers, considered a weed in Australia

lantern *n* **1** a light with a transparent protective case **2** a raised part on top of a dome or roof which lets in light or air **3** the upper part of a lighthouse that houses the light ▶ HISTORY Greek *lampein* to shine

lantern jaw *n* a long hollow jaw that gives the face a drawn appearance > **lantern-jawed** *adj*

lanthanide series *n* *chem* a class of 15 chemically related elements (**lanthanides**) with atomic numbers from 57 (lanthanum) to 71 (lutetium)

lanthanum *n* *chem* a silvery-white metallic element of the lanthanide series: used in electronic devices and glass manufacture. Symbol: La ▶ HISTORY Greek *lanthanein* to lie unseen

lanyard *n* **1** a cord worn round the neck to hold a whistle or knife **2** *naut* a line for extending or tightening rigging ▶ HISTORY Old French *lasne* strap

lap¹ *n* **1** the area formed by the upper surface of the thighs of a seated person **2** a protected place or environment: *in the lap of luxury* **3** the part of a person's clothing that covers the lap **4** **drop in someone's lap** to give someone the responsibility of ▶ HISTORY Old English *læppa* flap

lap² *n* **1** one circuit of a racecourse or track **2** a stage or part of a journey **3 a** an overlapping part **b** the extent of overlap ▷ *vb* **lapping, lapped** **4** to overtake (an opponent) in a race so as to be one or more circuits ahead **5** to enfold or wrap around **6** to place or lie partly or completely over or project beyond: *deep-pile carpet that lapped against his ankles* **7** to envelop or surround with comfort, love, or peace: *she was lapped by the luxury of Seymour House* ▶ HISTORY probably same as LAP¹

lap³ *vb* **lapping, lapped** **1** (of small waves) to wash against (the shore or a boat) with light splashing sounds **2** (often foll. by *up*) (esp. of animals) to scoop (a liquid) into the mouth with the tongue ▷ *n* **3** the act or sound of lapping ▷ See also **lap up** ▶ HISTORY Old English *lapian*

lapdog *n* a small pet dog

lapel (lap-**pel**) *n* the part on the front of a jacket or coat that folds back towards the shoulders ▶ HISTORY from LAP¹

lapidary *n*, *pl* **-daries** **1** a person who cuts, polishes, sets, or deals in gemstones ▷ *adj* **2** of or relating to gemstones or the work of a lapidary ▶ HISTORY Latin *lapidarius*, from *lapis* stone

lapis lazuli (**lap**-iss **lazz**-yew-lie) *n* a brilliant blue mineral used as a gemstone ▶ HISTORY Latin *lapis* stone + Medieval Latin *lazulum* azure

Lapp *n* **1** Also: **Laplander** a member of a nomadic people living chiefly in N Scandinavia **2** the language of this people ▷ *adj* **3** of this people or their language

lappet *n* **1** a small hanging flap or piece of lace **2** *zool* a flap of flesh or membrane, such as the ear lobe or a bird's wattle ▶ HISTORY LAP¹ + *-et* (diminutive suffix)

lapse *n* **1** a temporary drop in standard as a result of forgetfulness or lack of concentration **2** a moment or instance of bad behaviour, esp. by someone who is usually well-behaved **3** a period of time sufficient for a change to take place: *the lapse between phone call and now* **4** a gradual decline to a lower degree, condition, or state: *its lapse from the tradition of Disraeli* **5** *law* the loss of some right by neglecting to exercise or renew it ▷ *vb* **lapsing, lapsed** **6** to drop in standard or fail to maintain a standard **7** to decline gradually in status, condition, or degree **8** to allow to end or become no longer valid, esp. through negligence: *a bid that lapsed last July* **9** (usually foll. by *into*) to drift (into a condition): *she appeared to lapse into a brief reverie* **10** (often foll. by *from*) to turn away (from beliefs or standards) **11** (of time) to slip away ▶ HISTORY Latin *lapsus* error > **lapsed** *adj*

laptop *adj* (of a computer) small and light enough to be held on the user's lap

lap up *vb* **1** to eat or drink **2** to accept (information or attention) eagerly: *the public are lapping up the scandal*

lapwing *n* a bird of the plover family with a crested head. Also called: **peewit** ▶ HISTORY Old English *hlēapewince* plover

larboard *n* *naut* an old word for **port²** (sense 1) ▶ HISTORY Middle English *laddeborde*

larceny *n*, *pl* **-nies** *law* theft ▶ HISTORY Old French *larcin* > **larcenist** *n*

larch *n* **1** a coniferous tree with deciduous needle-like leaves and egg-shaped cones **2** the wood of this tree ▶ HISTORY Latin *larix*

lard *n* **1** the soft white fat obtained from pigs and prepared for use in cooking ▷ *vb* **2** to prepare (lean meat or poultry) by inserting small strips of bacon or fat before cooking **3** to add unnecessary material to (speech or writing) ▶ HISTORY Latin *laridum* bacon fat

larder *n* a room or cupboard used for storing food ▶ HISTORY Old French *lardier*

large *adj* **1** having a relatively great size, quantity, or extent; big **2** of wide or broad scope, capacity, or range; comprehensive: *a large effect* ▷ *n* **3 at large a** as a whole; in general: *both the Navy and the country at large* **b** (of a dangerous criminal or wild animal) out of captivity; free **c** in full detail ▶ HISTORY Latin *largus* ample > **largeness** *n*

large intestine *n* the part of the alimentary canal consisting of the caecum, colon, and rectum

467

largely *adv* principally; to a great extent

large-scale *adj* **1** wide-ranging or extensive **2** (of maps and models) constructed or drawn to a big scale

largesse *or* **largess** (lar-**jess**) *n* the generous giving of gifts, favours, or money ▶ HISTORY Old French

largish *adj* fairly large

largo *music adv* **1** in a slow and stately manner ▷ *n*, *pl* **-gos 2** a piece or passage to be performed in a slow and stately manner ▶ HISTORY Italian

lariat *n US & Canad* **1** a lasso **2** a rope for tethering animals ▶ HISTORY Spanish *la reata* the lasso

lark[1] *n* a small brown songbird, esp. the skylark ▶ HISTORY Old English *lāwerce, lǣwerce*

lark[2] *informal n* **1** a carefree adventure or frolic **2** a harmless piece of mischief **3** an activity or job viewed with disrespect ▷ *vb* **4 lark about** to have a good time frolicking or playing pranks ▶ HISTORY origin unknown > **larky** *adj*

larkspur *n* a plant with blue, pink, or white flowers with slender spikes at the base ▶ HISTORY LARK[1] + SPUR

larrikin *n Austral & NZ, old-fashioned slang* a mischievous or unruly person

larva *n, pl* **-vae** the immature form of many insects before it develops into its adult form ▶ HISTORY New Latin > **larval** *adj*

laryngeal *adj* of or relating to the larynx

laryngitis *n* inflammation of the larynx, causing huskiness or loss of voice

larynx (**lar**-rinks) *n, pl* **larynges** (lar-**rin**-jeez) *or* **larynxes** a hollow organ forming part of the air passage to the lungs: it contains the vocal cords ▶ HISTORY Greek *larunx*

lasagne *or* **lasagna** (laz-**zan**-ya) *n* **1** a form of pasta in wide flat sheets **2** a dish made from layers of lasagne, meat, and cheese ▶ HISTORY Italian, from Latin *lasanum* cooking pot

lascivious (lass-**iv**-ee-uss) *adj* showing or producing sexual desire; lustful ▶ HISTORY Latin *lascivia* wantonness > **lasciviously** *adv*

laser (**lay**-zer) *n* a device that produces a very narrow intense beam of light, which is used for cutting very hard materials and in surgery, etc. ▶ HISTORY from *light amplification by stimulated emission of radiation*

laser printer *n* a computer printer that uses a laser beam to produce characters which are then transferred to paper

lash[1] *n* **1** an eyelash **2** a sharp cutting blow from a whip **3** the flexible end of a whip ▷ *vb* **4** to hit (a person or thing) sharply with a whip, esp. formerly as punishment **5** *written* (of rain or waves) to beat forcefully against **6** to attack (someone) with words of ridicule or scolding **7** to flick or wave sharply to and fro: *his tail lashing in irritation* **8** to urge as with a whip: *to lash the audience into a violent mood* ▷ See also **lash out** ▶ HISTORY perhaps imitative

lash[2] *vb* to bind or secure with rope, string, or cord ▶ HISTORY Latin *laqueus* noose

lashings *pl n Brit & NZ, old-fashioned, informal* large amounts; lots: *lashings of cream*

lash out *vb* **1** to make a sudden verbal or physical attack **2** *informal* to spend extravagantly

lass *n* a girl or young woman ▶ HISTORY origin unknown

Lassa fever *n* a serious viral disease of Central West Africa, characterized by high fever and muscular pains ▶ HISTORY after *Lassa*, the Nigerian village where it was first identified

lassie *n Scot & N English, informal* a little lass; girl

lassitude *n* physical or mental weariness ▶ HISTORY Latin *lassus* tired

lasso (lass-**oo**) *n, pl* **-sos** *or* **-soes 1** a long rope with a noose at one end used for catching horses and cattle ▷ *vb* **-soing, -soed 2** to catch as with a lasso ▶ HISTORY Spanish, from Latin *laqueus* noose > **lassoer** *n*

last[1] *adj* **1** being, happening, or coming at the end or after all others **2** most recent: *last April* **3** only remaining: *that's the last one* **4** most extreme; utmost **5** least suitable or likely: *China was the last place on earth he intended to go* ▷ *adv* **6** after all others **7** most recently: *we last saw him on Thursday night* **8** as the last or latest item ▷ *n* **9 the last a** a person or thing that is last **b** the final moment; end **10** the final appearance, mention, or occurrence: *the last of this season's visitors* **11 at last** in the end; finally **12 at long last** finally, after difficulty or delay ▶ HISTORY variant of Old English *latest, lætest*

last[2] *vb* **1** to continue to exist for a length of time: *the soccer war lasted 100 hours* **2** to be sufficient for the needs of (a person) for a length of time: *I shall make a couple of bottles to last me until next summer* **3** to remain fresh, uninjured, or unaltered for a certain time: *the flowers haven't lasted well* ▶ HISTORY Old English *lǣstan*

last[3] *n* the wooden or metal form on which a shoe or boot is made or repaired ▶ HISTORY Old English *lǣst* footprint

last-ditch *adj* done as a final resort: *a last-ditch attempt*

lasting *adj* existing or remaining effective for a long time

Last Judgment *n* **the Last Judgment** *theol* God's verdict on the destinies of all human beings at the end of the world

lastly *adv* **1** at the end or at the last point **2** finally

last post *n mil* **1** a bugle call used to signal the time to retire at night **2** a similar call sounded at military funerals

last rites *pl n Christianity* religious rites for those close to death

last straw *n* a small incident, irritation, or setback that coming after others is too much to cope with

Last Supper *n* **the Last Supper** the meal eaten by Christ with his disciples on the night before his Crucifixion

lat. latitude

latch *n* **1** a fastening for a gate or door that consists of a bar that may be slid or lowered into a groove, hole, or notch **2** a spring-loaded door lock that can only be opened by a key from outside ▷ *vb* **3** to fasten, fit, or be fitted with a latch ▶ HISTORY Old English *læccan* to seize

latchkey child *n* Brit, Austral & NZ a child who has to let himself or herself in at home after school, as both parents are out at work

late *adj* **1** occurring or arriving after the correct or expected time: *the plane will be late* **2** towards or near the end: *the late afternoon* **3** occurring or being at a relatively advanced time: *a late starter, his first novel was effectively his last* **4** at an advanced time in the evening or at night: *it's late, I have to get back* **5** having died recently: *her late father* **6** recent: *recollect the late defeats which your enemies have experienced* **7** former: *the late manager of the team* **8 of late** recently ▷ *adv* **9** after the correct or expected time: *Mark Wright arrived late* **10** at a relatively advanced age: *coming late to motherhood* **11** recently: *as late as in 1983, only 9 per cent of that labour force was unionized* **12 late in the day a** at a late or advanced stage **b** too late ▶ HISTORY Old English *læt* > **lateness** *n*

lateen *adj naut* denoting a rig with a triangular sail bent to a yard hoisted to the head of a low mast ▶ HISTORY French *voile latine* Latin sail

Late Greek *n* the Greek language from about the 3rd to the 8th centuries AD

Late Latin *n* the form of written Latin used from the 3rd to the 7th centuries AD

lately *adv* in recent times; of late

latent *adj* lying hidden and not yet developed within a person or thing ▶ HISTORY Latin *latere* to lie hidden > **latency** *n*

latent heat *n physics* the heat needed to turn a solid into a liquid or a liquid into a gas and released if the process is reversed

lateral (**lat**-ter-al) *adj* of or relating to the side or sides ▶ HISTORY Latin *latus* side > **laterally** *adv*

lateral erosion *n geol* erosion occurring at the sides of a stream or river that widens or changes its course

lateral thinking *n* a way of solving problems by apparently illogical methods

latex *n* a milky fluid produced by many plants: latex from the rubber plant is used in the manufacture of rubber ▶ HISTORY Latin: liquid

lath *n* one of several thin narrow strips of wood used as a supporting framework for plaster or tiles ▶ HISTORY Old English *lætt*

lathe *n* a machine for shaping metal or wood by turning it against a fixed tool ▶ HISTORY perhaps from Old Norse

lather *n* **1** foam formed by soap or detergent in water **2** foamy sweat, as produced by a horse **3** *informal* a state of agitation ▷ *vb* **4** to coat or become coated with lather **5** to form a lather **6** *informal* to beat; flog ▶ HISTORY Old English *léathor* soap > **lathery** *adj*

Latin *n* **1** the language of ancient Rome and the Roman Empire **2** a member of any of those peoples whose languages are derived from Latin ▷ *adj* **3** of

the Latin language **4** of those peoples whose languages are derived from Latin **5** of the Roman Catholic Church ▶ HISTORY Latin *Latinus* of Latium

Latin America *n* those areas of South and Central America whose official languages are Spanish and Portuguese > **Latin American** *adj, n*

latish *adj, adv* rather late

latitude *n* **1 a** an angular distance measured in degrees north or south of the equator (often pl) a region considered with regard to its distance from the equator **2** scope for freedom of action and thought ▶ HISTORY Latin *latus* broad > **latitudinal** *adj*

latitudinarian *adj* **1** liberal, esp. in religious matters ▷ *n* **2** a person with latitudinarian views

latrine *n* a toilet in a barracks or camp ▶ HISTORY Latin *lavatrina* bath

latter *n* **1 the latter** the second or second mentioned of two ▷ *adj* **2** near or nearer the end: *the latter half of the season* **3** more advanced in time or sequence; later ▶ HISTORY Old English *lætra*

latter-day *adj* present-day; modern

latterly *adv written* recently; lately

lattice (**lat**-iss) *n* **1** Also called: **latticework** a framework of strips of wood or metal interlaced in a diagonal pattern **2** a gate, screen, or fence formed of such a framework **3** an array of atoms, ions, or molecules in a crystal or an array of points indicating their positions in space ▷ *vb* **-ticing, -ticed 4** to make, adorn, or supply with a lattice ▶ HISTORY Old French *latte* lath > **latticed** *adj*

Latvian *adj* **1** from Latvia ▷ *n* **2** a person from Latvia **3** the language of Latvia

laud *literary vb* **1** to praise or glorify ▷ *n* **2** praise or glorification ▶ HISTORY Latin *laudare* to praise

laudable *adj* deserving praise; commendable > **laudability** *n* > **laudably** *adv*

laudanum (**lawd**-a-num) *n* a sedative extracted from opium ▶ HISTORY New Latin

laudatory *adj* (of speech or writing) expressing praise

laugh *vb* **1** to express amusement or happiness by producing a series of inarticulate sounds **2** to utter or express with laughter: *'Where do you think you are going?' he laughed* **3** to bring or force (oneself) into a certain condition by laughter: *laughing herself silly* **4 laugh at** to make fun of; jeer at **5 laugh up one's sleeve** to laugh secretly ▷ *n* **6** the act or an instance of laughing **7** *informal* a person or thing that causes laughter: *he's a laugh, that one* **8 the last laugh** final success after previous defeat ▷ See also **laugh off** ▶ HISTORY Old English *læhan, hliehhen* > **laughingly** *adv*

laughable *adj* ridiculous because so obviously inadequate or unsuccessful

laughing gas *n* nitrous oxide used as an anaesthetic: it may cause laughter and exhilaration when inhaled

laughing stock *n* a person or thing that is treated with ridicule

laugh off *vb* to treat (something serious or difficult) lightly

469

laughter *n* the action or noise of laughing
▶ HISTORY Old English *hleahtor*

launch¹ *vb* **1** to move (a vessel) into the water, esp. for the first time **2 a** to start off or set in motion: *to launch an appeal* **b** to put (a new product) on the market **3** to set (a rocket, missile, or spacecraft) into motion **4** to involve (oneself) totally and enthusiastically: *Francis launched himself into the transfer market with gusto* **5 launch into** to start talking or writing about **6** (usually foll. by *out*) to start (out) on a new enterprise ▷ *n* **7** an act or instance of launching ▶ HISTORY Late Latin *lanceare* to use a lance, hence to set in motion
> **launcher** *n*

launch² *n* an open motorboat ▶ HISTORY Malay *lancharan* boat, from *lanchar* speed

launch pad *or* **launching pad** *n* a platform from which a spacecraft, rocket, or missile is launched

launder *vb* **1** to wash and iron (clothes and linen) **2** to make (money illegally obtained) appear to be legally gained by passing it through foreign banks or legitimate enterprises ▶ HISTORY Latin *lavare* to wash

Launderette *n Brit, Austral & NZ trademark* an establishment where clothes can be washed and dried, using coin-operated machines. Also called (US, Canad, Austral and NZ): **Laundromat**

laundry *n, pl* **-dries 1** the clothes or linen to be laundered or that have been laundered **2** a place where clothes and linen are washed and ironed

laureate (**lor**-ee-at) *adj* **1** *literary* crowned with laurel leaves as a sign of honour ▷ *n* **2** short for **poet laureate** ▶ HISTORY Latin *laurea* laurel
> **laureateship** *n*

laurel *n* **1** a small Mediterranean evergreen tree with glossy leaves **2 laurels** a wreath of laurel, worn on the head as an emblem of victory or honour in classical times **3 laurels** honour, distinction, or fame **4 rest on one's laurels** to be satisfied with what one has already achieved and stop striving for further success **5 look to one's laurels** to be on guard against one's rivals
▶ HISTORY Latin *laurus*

lava *n* **1** molten rock discharged by volcanoes **2** any rock formed by the solidification of lava ▶ HISTORY Latin *lavare* to wash

lavatory *n, pl* **-ries** same as **toilet** ▶ HISTORY Latin *lavare* to wash

lavender *n* **1** a plant grown for its bluish-purple flowers and as the source of a sweet-smelling oil **2** its dried flowers, used to perfume clothes ▷ *adj* **3** pale bluish-purple ▶ HISTORY Medieval Latin *lavendula*

lavender water *n* a light perfume made from lavender

lavish *adj* **1** great in quantity or richness: *lavish banquets* **2** very generous in giving **3** extravagant; wasteful: *lavish spending habits* ▷ *vb* **4** to give or to spend very generously or in great quantities ▶ HISTORY Old French *lavasse* torrent > **lavishly** *adv*

law *n* **1** a rule or set of rules regulating what may or may not be done by members of a society or community **2** a rule or body of rules made by the legislature or other authority. *Related adjectives:* **legal, judicial, juridical 3** the control enforced by such rules: *scant respect for the rule of law* **4 the law a** the legal or judicial system **b** the profession or practice of law **c** *informal* the police or a policeman **5 law and order** the policy of strict enforcement of the law, esp. against crime and violence **6** a rule of behaviour: *an unwritten law that Nanny knows best* **7** Also called: **law of nature** a generalization based on a recurring fact or event **8** the science or knowledge of law; jurisprudence **9** a general principle, formula, or rule in mathematics, science, or philosophy: *the law of gravity* **10 the Law** the laws contained in the first five books of the Old Testament **11 go to law** to resort to legal proceedings on some matter **12 lay down the law** to speak in an authoritative manner ▶ HISTORY Old English *lagu*

law-abiding *adj* obeying the laws: *a law-abiding citizen*

lawbreaker *n* a person who breaks the law
> **lawbreaking** *n, adj*

lawful *adj* allowed, recognized, or sanctioned by law; legal > **lawfully** *adv*

lawgiver *n* **1** the giver of a code of laws **2** Also called: **lawmaker** a maker of laws
> **lawgiving** *n, adj*

lawless *adj* **1** breaking the law, esp. in a wild or violent way: *lawless butchery* **2** not having laws
> **lawlessness** *n*

Law Lords *pl n* (in Britain) members of the House of Lords who sit as the highest court of appeal

lawn¹ *n* an area of cultivated and mown grass ▶ HISTORY Old French *lande*

lawn² *n* a fine linen or cotton fabric ▶ HISTORY probably from *Laon*, town in France where made

lawn mower *n* a hand-operated or power-operated machine for cutting grass

lawn tennis *n* **1** tennis played on a grass court **2** same as **tennis**

lawrencium *n chem* an element artificially produced from californium. Symbol: Lr ▶ HISTORY after E. O. *Lawrence*, physicist

lawsuit *n* a case in a court of law brought by one person or group against another

lawyer *n* a member of the legal profession who can advise clients about the law and represent them in court

lax *adj* lacking firmness; not strict ▶ HISTORY Latin *laxus* loose > **laxity** *n*

laxative *n* **1** a medicine that induces the emptying of the bowels ▷ *adj* **2** easing the emptying of the bowels ▶ HISTORY Latin *laxare* to loosen

lay¹ *vb* **lays, laying, laid 1** to put in a low or horizontal position; cause to lie: *Mary laid a clean square of white towelling carefully on the grass* **2** to establish as a basis: *settlers had laid their plans for rebellion* **3** to place or be in a particular state or position: *underneath lay a key* **4** to regard as the responsibility of: *ridiculous attempts to lay the loss at the door of the Admiralty* **5** to put forward: *ruses by which we lay claim on one another* **6** to arrange or prepare: *she would lay her plans* **7** to place in position: *he laid a wreath* **8** (of birds, esp. the domestic hen) to produce (eggs) **9** to make (a bet) with (someone): *I'll lay money he's already gone home* **10** to arrange (a table) for a meal **11** to prepare (a fire) by arranging fuel in the grate **12 lay bare** to reveal or explain: *a century of neurophysiology has now laid bare the structures of the brain* **13 lay hold of** to seize or grasp **14 lay oneself open** to make oneself vulnerable (to criticism or attack) **15 lay open** to reveal or disclose **16 lay waste** to destroy completely ▷ *n* **17** the manner or position in which something lies or is placed ▷ See also **lay down** ▶ **HISTORY** Old English *lecgan*

lay² *vb* the past tense of **lie²**

lay³ *adj* **1** of or involving people who are not members of the clergy **2** nonprofessional or nonspecialist ▶ **HISTORY** Greek *laos* people

lay⁴ *n* a short narrative poem intended to be sung ▶ **HISTORY** Old French *lai*

layabout *n* a lazy person

lay-by *n* **1** *Brit* a place where drivers can stop by the side of a main road **2** *Austral & NZ* a system of payment whereby a buyer pays a deposit on an article, which is reserved for him or her until he or she has paid the full price

lay down *vb* **1** to place on the ground or a surface **2** to sacrifice: *willing to lay down their lives for the truth* **3** to formulate (a rule or principle) **4** to record (plans) on paper **5** to store or stock: *the speed with which we lay down extra, unwanted fat*

layer *n* **1** a single thickness of something, such as a cover or a coating on a surface **2** a laying hen **3** *horticulture* a shoot that forms its own root while still attached to the parent plant ▷ *vb* **4** to form or make a layer or layers ▶ **HISTORY** from LAY¹

layette *n* a complete set of clothing, bedclothes, and other accessories for a newborn baby ▶ **HISTORY** Middle Dutch *laege* box

lay figure *n* **1** an artist's jointed dummy, used esp. for studying effects of drapery **2** a person considered to be subservient or unimportant ▶ **HISTORY** Dutch *leeman*, literally: joint-man

lay in *vb* to accumulate and store: *they've already laid in five hundred bottles of great vintages*

lay into *vb* *informal* to attack or scold severely

layman *or fem* **laywoman** *n, pl* **-men** *or* **-women** **1** a person who is not a member of the clergy **2** a person who does not have specialized knowledge of a subject: *the layman's guide to nuclear power*

lay off *vb* **1** to suspend (staff) during a slack period at work **2** *informal* to leave (a person, thing, or activity) alone: *'lay off the defence counsel bit!' he snapped* ▷ *n* **lay-off 3** a period of imposed unemployment

lay on *vb* **1** to provide or supply: *they laid on a treat for the entourage* **2 lay it on thick** *slang* to exaggerate, esp. when flattering

lay out *vb* **1** to arrange or spread out **2** to plan or design: *the main streets were laid out on a grid system* **3** to prepare (a corpse) for burial or cremation **4** *informal* to spend (money), esp. lavishly **5** *informal* to knock (someone) unconscious ▷ *n* **layout 6** the arrangement or plan of something, such as a building **7** the arrangement of printed material

lay reader *n* **1** *Church of England* a person licensed to conduct religious services other than the Eucharist **2** *RC Church* a layman chosen to read the epistle at Mass

lay up *vb* **1** *informal* to confine through illness: *laid up with a bad cold* **2** to store for future use

laze *vb* **lazing, lazed 1** to be idle or lazy **2** (often foll. by *away*) to spend (time) in idleness ▷ *n* **3** time spent lazing ▶ **HISTORY** from *lazy*

lazy *adj* **lazier, laziest 1** not inclined to work or exert oneself **2** done in a relaxed manner with little effort **3** moving in a sluggish manner: *the lazy drift of the bubbles* ▶ **HISTORY** origin unknown > **lazily** *adv* > **laziness** *n*

lazybones *n* *informal* a lazy person

lb 1 pound (weight) ▶ **HISTORY** Latin *libra* **2** *cricket* leg bye

lbw *cricket* leg before wicket

lc 1 in the place cited ▶ **HISTORY** Latin *loco citato* **2** *printing* lower case

LCD 1 liquid crystal display **2** Also: **lcd** lowest common denominator

lcm *or* **LCM** lowest common multiple

LDC less developed country

lea *n* **1** *poetic* a meadow or field **2** grassland ▶ **HISTORY** Old English *lēah*

LEA (in Britain) Local Education Authority

leach *vb* **1** to remove or be removed from a substance by a liquid passing through it **2** to lose soluble substances by the action of a liquid passing through ▶ **HISTORY** perhaps Old English *leccan* to water

lead¹ *vb* **leading, led 1** to show the way to (an individual or a group) by going with or ahead: *he led her into the house* **2** to guide, control, or direct: *he dismounted and led his horse back* **3** to influence someone to act, think, or behave in a certain way: *researching our family history has led her to correspond with relatives abroad* **4** to have the principal part in (something): *planners led the development of policy* **5** to go at the head of or have the top position in (something): *the pair led the field by almost two minutes* **6** (of a road or way) to be the means of reaching a place: *the footbridge leads on to a fine promenade* **7** to pass or spend: *I've led a happy life* **8** to guide or be guided by physical means: *he took her firmly by the arm and led her home* **9** to direct the course of (water, a rope, or wire) along or as if along a channel **10** (foll. by *with*) to have as the most important item: *the Review leads with a critique of A Place of Greater Safety* **11** *Brit music* to play first violin in (an orchestra) **12** to begin a round of cards by putting down the first card ▷ *n* **13** the first or most prominent place **14** example or leadership:

some of his children followed his lead **15** an advantage over others: *Essex have a lead of 24 points* **16** an indication; clue: *we've got a lead on how the body got into the water* **17** a length of leather, nylon, or chain used to walk or control a dog **18** the principal role in a play, film, or other production, or the person playing such a role **19** the most important news story in a newspaper: *the shooting makes the lead in the Times* **20** the act of playing the first card in a round of cards or the card so played **21** a wire, cable, or other conductor for making an electrical connection ▷ *adj* **22** acting as a leader or lead: *lead singer* ▷ See also **lead on** ▶ HISTORY Old English *lǽdan*

lead² *n* **1** a heavy toxic bluish-white metallic element: used in alloys, cable sheaths, and paints, and as a radiation shield. Symbol: Pb **2 a** graphite used for drawing **b** a thin stick of this as the core of a pencil **3** a lead weight suspended on a line, used to take soundings of the depth of water **4** lead weights or shot, as used in cartridges or fishing lines **5** a thin strip of lead for holding small panes of glass or pieces of stained glass **6 leads a** thin sheets or strips of lead used as a roof covering **b** a roof covered with such sheets **7** Also called: **leading** *printing* a thin strip of metal, formerly used for spacing between lines of type ▷ *adj* **8** of, relating to, or containing lead ▷ *vb* **9** to surround, cover, or secure with lead or leads ▶ HISTORY Old English *lēad*

leaded *adj* (of windows) made from many small panes of glass held together by lead strips

leaden *adj* **1** heavy or sluggish: *my limbs felt leaden* **2** of a dull greyish colour: *leaden November sky* **3** made of lead **4** gloomy, spiritless, or lifeless: *hollow characters and leaden dialogue*

leader *n* **1** a person who rules, guides, or inspires others; head **2** *Brit & Austral* Also: **leading article** the leading editorial in a newspaper **3** *music* the principal first violinist of an orchestra who acts as the conductor's deputy **4** the person or animal who is leading in a race **5** the best or the most successful of its kind: *the company is a world leader in its field* **6** the leading horse or dog in a team **7** a strip of blank film or tape at the beginning of a reel **8** *bot* any of the long slender shoots that grow from the stem or branch of a tree > **leadership** *n*

lead-in *n* an introduction to a subject

leading *adj* **1** principal or primary: *the leading designers* **2** in the first position: *the leading driver*

leading aircraftman *n* the rank above aircraftman in the British air force > **leading aircraftwoman** *fem n*

leading light *n* an important and influential person in an organization or campaign

leading question *n* a question worded to suggest the desired answer, such as *What do you think of the horrible effects of pollution?*

leading rating *n* a rank in the Royal Navy comparable to a corporal in the army

lead on *vb* to trick (someone) into believing or doing something wrong

lead poisoning *n* acute or chronic poisoning by lead

lead story *n journalism, television, etc.* the story given most prominence in a newspaper or on a news programme

lead time *n manufacturing* the time between the design of a product and its production

lead up to *vb* **1** to act as a preliminary or introduction to **2** to approach (a topic) gradually or cautiously

leaf *n, pl* **leaves 1** one of the flat usually green blades attached to the stem of a plant **2** the foliage of a tree or plant: *shrubs have been planted for their leaf interest* **3 in leaf** (of shrubs or trees) with all its leaves fully opened **4** a very thin sheet of metal **5** one of the sheets of paper in a book **6** a hinged, sliding, or detachable part, such as an extension to a table **7 take a leaf out of someone's book** to imitate someone in a particular course of action **8 turn over a new leaf** to begin a new and improved course of behaviour ▷ *vb* **9** (usually foll. by *through*) to turn pages casually or hurriedly without reading them **10** (of plants) to produce leaves ▶ HISTORY Old English *lēaf* > **leafless** *adj*

leafage *n* the leaves of plants

leaflet *n* **1** a sheet of printed matter distributed, usually free, for advertising or information **2** any small leaf **3** one of the divisions of a compound leaf ▷ *vb* **-leting, -leted 4** to distribute leaflets (to)

leaf mould *n* a rich soil consisting of decayed leaves

leafy *adj* **leafier, leafiest 1** covered with leaves **2** having many trees or shrubs: *a leafy suburb*

league¹ *n* **1** an association of people or nations formed to promote the interests of its members **2** an association of sporting clubs that organizes matches between member teams **3** *informal* a class or level: *the guy is not even in the same league* **4 in league (with)** working or planning together (with) ▷ *vb* **leaguing, leagued 5** to form or be formed into a league ▶ HISTORY Latin *ligare* to bind

league² *n* an obsolete unit of distance of varying length: commonly equal to 3 miles (4.8 kilometres) ▶ HISTORY Late Latin *leuga, leuca*

League of Nations *n history* an international association of states, founded in 1920 with the aim of preserving world peace, and dissolved in 1946

leak *n* **1 a** a crack or hole that allows the accidental escape or entrance of liquid, gas, radiation, etc. **b** such escaping or entering liquid, etc. **2 a** disclosure of secret information **3** the loss of current from an electrical conductor because of faulty insulation **4** the act or an instance of leaking **5** *slang* urination ▷ *vb* **6** to enter or escape or allow to enter or escape through a crack or hole **7** to make (secret information) public, esp. deliberately ▶ HISTORY from Old Norse > **leaky** *adj*

leakage *n* the act or an instance or the result of leaking: *the leakage of 60 tonnes of oil*

lean¹ *vb* **leaning; leaned** *or* **leant 1** (foll. by *against, on* or *upon*) to rest or put (something) so that it rests against a support **2** to bend or make (something) bend from an upright position **3** (foll. by *to* or *towards*) to have or express a tendency or preference ▷ *n* **4** the condition of bending from an upright position ▷ See also **lean on** ▶ HISTORY Old English *hleonian, hlinian*

lean² *adj* **1** (esp. of a person) having a trim body with no surplus flesh **2** (of meat) having little or no fat **3** (of a period) sparse, difficult, or causing hardship: *these are lean days in Baghdad* ▷ *n* **4** the part of meat that contains little or no fat ▶ HISTORY Old English *hlǣne* > **leanness** *n*

leaning *n* a tendency or inclination

lean on *vb* **1** *informal* to try to influence (someone) by using threats **2** to depend on (someone) for help and advice

lean-to *n, pl* **-tos** a building with a sloping roof attached to another building or a wall

leap *vb* **leaping; leapt** *or* **leaped** **1** to jump suddenly from one place to another **2** (often foll. by *at*) to move or react quickly **3** to jump over ▷ *n* **4** the act of jumping **5** an abrupt or important change or increase: *a leap to full European union* **6 a leap in the dark** an action performed without knowledge of the consequences **7 by leaps and bounds** with unexpectedly rapid progress ▶ HISTORY Old English *hlēapan*

leapfrog *n* **1** a children's game in which each player in turn leaps over the others' bent backs ▷ *vb* **-frogging, -frogged** **2 a** to play leapfrog **b** to leap over (something) **3** to advance by jumps or stages

leap year *n* a calendar year of 366 days, February 29 (**leap day**) being the additional day, that occurs every four years

learn *vb* **learning; learned** *or* **learnt** **1** to gain knowledge (of something) or acquire skill in (some art or practice) **2** to memorize (something) **3** to gain by experience, example, or practice: *I learned everything the hard way* **4** (often foll. by *of* or *about*) to become informed; find out: *Captain Nelson learned of the disaster from his wireless* ▶ HISTORY Old English *leornian* > **learnable** *adj* > **learner** *n*

learned (lurn-id) *adj* **1** having great knowledge **2** involving or characterized by scholarship: *your learned paper on the subject*

learning *n* knowledge gained by studying

lease *n* **1** a contract by which an owner rents buildings or land to another person for a specified period **2 a new lease of life** a prospect of renewed energy, health, or happiness ▷ *vb* **leasing, leased** **3** to let or rent (land or buildings) by lease ▶ HISTORY Old French *laissier* to let go

leasehold *n* **1** land or property held under a lease **2** the holding of such property under lease > **leaseholder** *n*

leash *n* **1** a dog's lead **2 straining at the leash** eagerly impatient to begin something ▷ *vb* **3** to put a leash on ▶ HISTORY Old French *laissier* to loose (hence to let a dog run on a leash)

least *adj, adv* **1 the least** the superlative of **little**: *without encountering the least sign of civilization; he is the least well-educated prime minister* ▷ *adj* **2** of very little importance **3** smallest ▷ *adv* **4 at least** if

nothing else: *at least I wrote* **5 at the least** at the minimum: *at the very least you should have some self-respect* **6 not in the least** not at all: *you're not detaining me, not in the least* ▶ HISTORY Old English *lǣst*, superlative of *lǣssa* less

leather *n* **1** the skin of an animal made smooth and flexible by tanning and removing the hair **2 leathers** leather clothes, esp. as worn by motorcyclists ▷ *adj* **3** made of leather ▷ *vb* **4** to whip as if with a leather strap **5** to dress in leather ▶ HISTORY Old English *lether-* (in compound words)

leatherjacket *n* **1** any of various tropical fishes having a leathery skin **2** the tough-skinned larva of certain crane flies, which destroy the roots of grasses

leathery *adj* looking or feeling like leather, esp. in toughness

leave¹ *vb* **leaving, left** **1** to go away (from a person or place) **2** to cause to remain behind, often by mistake, in a place: *I left the paper under the table* **3** to cause to be or remain in a specified state: *the poll leaves the parties neck-and-neck* **4** to stop attending or belonging to a particular organization or institution: *at seventeen she left the convent* **5** to not eat something or not deal with something: *he left a half-eaten lunch* **6** to result in; cause: *I have been terribly hurt by women, it leaves indelible marks* **7** to allow (someone) to do something without interfering: *the governor left them to it for a further few hours* **8** to be survived by (members of one's family): *he leaves a widow and one daughter* **9** to bequeath: *her adored son left his millions to an unknown half-sister* **10** to have as a remainder: *37 – 14 leaves 23* **11 leave (someone) alone a** to stop annoying (someone) **b** to permit (someone) to stay or be alone ▷ See also **leave out** ▶ HISTORY Old English *lǣfan*

leave² *n* **1** permission to be absent, for instance from work: *so I asked for leave* **2** the length of such absence: *weekend leave* **3** permission to do something: *they were refused leave to appeal* **4 on leave** officially excused from work or duty **5 take (one's) leave of** to say farewell to ▶ HISTORY Old English *lēaf*

leaven (lev-ven) *n also* **leavening** **1** any substance, such as yeast, that produces fermentation in dough and makes it rise **2** an influence that produces a gradual change ▷ *vb* **3** to cause fermentation in (dough) **4** to spread through, causing a gradual change ▶ HISTORY Latin *levare* to raise

leave out *vb* to omit or exclude: *leave out everything not necessary to living*

leaves *n* the plural of **leaf**

leavings *pl n* things left behind unwanted, such as food on a plate

Lebanese *adj* **1** from the Lebanon ▷ *n, pl* **-nese** **2** a person from the Lebanon

Lebensraum (lay-benz-rowm) *n* territory claimed by a nation or state because it is necessary for survival or growth ▶ HISTORY German: living space

473

lecherous (**letch**-er-uss) *adj* (of a man) having or showing strong and uncontrolled sexual desire ▶ **HISTORY** Old French *lechier* to lick > **lecher** *n* > **lechery** *n*

lecithin (**less**-sith-in) *n biochem* a yellow-brown compound found in plant and animal tissues, esp. egg yolk: used in making cosmetics and inks, and as an emulsifier and stabilizer (**E322**) in foods ▶ **HISTORY** Greek *lekithos* egg yolk

lectern *n* a sloping reading desk, esp. in a church ▶ **HISTORY** Latin *legere* to read

lecture *n* **1** a talk on a particular subject delivered to an audience **2** a lengthy scolding ▷ *vb* **-turing, -tured 3** to deliver a lecture (to an audience or class) **4** to scold (someone) at length ▶ **HISTORY** Latin *legere* to read > **lecturer** *n* > **lectureship** *n*

led *vb* the past of **lead**[1]

LED *electronics* light-emitting diode: a semiconductor that gives out light when an electric current is applied to it

LEDC less economically developed country

ledge *n* **1** a narrow horizontal surface that projects from a wall or window **2** a narrow shelflike projection on a cliff or mountain ▶ **HISTORY** perhaps Middle English *leggen* to lay

ledger *n book-keeping* the principal book in which the commercial transactions of a company are recorded ▶ **HISTORY** perhaps Middle English *leggen* to lay (because kept in a specific place)

ledger line *n music* a short line above or below the staff used to indicate the pitch of notes higher or lower than the range of the staff

lee *n* **1** a sheltered part or side; the side away from the direction from which the wind is blowing ▷ *adj* **2** *naut* on, at, or towards the side away from the wind: *her lee rail was awash* ▶ **HISTORY** Old English *hlēow* shelter

leech *n* **1** a worm which has a sucker at each end of the body and feeds on the blood or tissues of other animals **2** a person who lives off another person; parasite ▶ **HISTORY** Old English *lǣce*

leek *n* a vegetable of the onion family with a slender white bulb and broad flat green overlapping leaves: the national emblem of Wales ▶ **HISTORY** Old English *lēac*

leer *vb* **1** to give a sneering or suggestive look or grin ▷ *n* **2** such a look ▶ **HISTORY** Old English *hlēor* cheek

leery *adj* **leerier, leeriest 1** *slang* (foll. by *of*) suspicious or wary **2** *chiefly dialect* knowing or sly ▶ **HISTORY** perhaps obsolete sense (to look askance) of *leer*

lees *pl n* the sediment from an alcoholic drink ▶ **HISTORY** plural of obsolete *lee*, from Old French

leet *n Scot* a list of candidates for an office ▶ **HISTORY** perhaps Anglo-French *litte*, variant of LIST[1]

leeward *chiefly naut adj* **1** of, in, or moving in the direction towards which the wind blows ▷ *n* **2** the side towards the lee ▷ *adv* **3** towards the lee

leeway *n* **1** flexibility of action or expenditure: *he gave me a lot of leeway in the work I did* **2** sideways drift of a boat or aircraft

left[1] *adj* **1** denoting the side of something or someone that faces west when the front is turned towards the north **2** on the left side of the body: *I grabbed it with my left hand* **3** liberal, radical, or socialist ▷ *adv* **4** on or in the direction of the left ▷ *n* **5** a left side, direction, position, area, or part **6** **the left** the people in a political party or society who have more socialist or liberal views: *the biggest party of the French Left* **7** *boxing* **a** a blow with the left hand **b** the left hand ▶ **HISTORY** Old English: idle, weak

left[2] *vb* the past of **leave**[1]

left-branching sentence *n grammar* a sentence in which much of the information precedes the main verb in the main clause, owing to a long initial noun phrase. Compare **right-branching sentence**

left-handed *adj* **1** better at using the left hand than the right **2** done with the left hand **3** designed for use by the left hand **4** awkward or clumsy **5** ambiguous or insincere: *a left-handed compliment* **6** turning from right to left; anticlockwise ▷ *adv* **7** with the left hand: *I write left-handed* > **left-hander** *n*

leftist *adj* **1** of or relating to the political left or its principles ▷ *n* **2** a person who supports the political left > **leftism** *n*

leftover *n* **1** (often *pl*) an unused portion, esp. of cooked food ▷ *adj* **2** left as an unused portion

left-wing *adj* **1** socialist or radical: *the party ditched many of its more left-wing policies* **2** belonging to the more radical part of a political party: *a group of left-wing Conservatives* ▷ *n* **left wing 3** (often *cap*) the more radical or progressive section, esp. of a political party: *the Left Wing of the Labour Party* **4** *sport* **a** the left-hand side of the field of play **b** a player positioned in this area in certain games > **left-winger** *n*

lefty *n, pl* **lefties** *Brit, Austral & NZ, informal* **1** a left-winger **2** *chiefly US & Canad* a left-handed person

leg *n* **1** either of the two lower limbs in humans, or any similar structure in animals that is used for movement or support **2** the part of a garment that covers the leg **3** a lower limb of an animal, esp. the thigh, used for food: *leg of lamb* **4** something similar to a leg in appearance or function, such as one of the supports of a chair **5** a section of a journey **6** a single stage, lap, or length in a relay race **7** one of a series of games, matches, or parts of games **8** *cricket* the side of the field to the left of a right-handed batsman as he faces the bowler **9** **not have a leg to stand on** *informal* to have no reasonable basis for an opinion or argument **10** **on one's last legs** worn out or exhausted **11** **to pull someone's leg** *informal* to tease or make fun of someone **12** **shake a leg** *informal* to hurry up **13** **stretch one's legs** to stand up or walk around, esp. after

sitting for some time ▷ *vb* **legging, legged**
14 leg it *informal* to walk, run, or hurry ▶ HISTORY
Old Norse *leggr*

legacy *n, pl* **-cies 1** money or personal property left
to someone by a will **2** something handed down to
a successor ▶ HISTORY Medieval Latin *legatia*
commission

legal *adj* **1** established by or permitted by law;
lawful **2** of or relating to law **3** relating to or
characteristic of lawyers ▶ HISTORY Latin *legalis*
> **legally** *adv*

legal aid *n* financial assistance available to people
who are unable to meet the full cost of legal
proceedings

legal capacity *n* *law* a person's ability, dependent
on age and mental competence, to exercise legal
rights and responsibilities

legalese *n* the conventional language in which
legal documents are written

legalism *n* strict adherence to the letter of the law
> **legalist** *n, adj* > **legalistic** *adj*

legality *n, pl* **-ties** the state or quality of being legal
or lawful

legalize *or* **-ise** *vb* **-izing, -ized** *or* **-ising, -ised**
to make lawful or legal > **legalization** *or*
-isation *n*

legal tender *n* currency that a creditor must by
law accept to pay a debt

legate *n* a messenger, esp. one representing the
Pope ▶ HISTORY Latin *legare* to delegate

legatee *n* the recipient of a legacy

legation *n* **1** a diplomatic mission headed by a
minister **2** the official residence and office of a
diplomatic minister

legato (leg-**ah**-toe) *music adv* **1** smoothly and
evenly ▷ *n, pl* **-tos 2** a style of playing with no gaps
between notes ▶ HISTORY Italian

leg before wicket *n* *cricket* a dismissal on the
grounds that a batsman has been struck on the leg
by a bowled ball that otherwise would have hit the
wicket. Abbrev: **lbw**

leg break *n* *cricket* a bowled ball that spins from
leg to off on pitching

leg bye *n* *cricket* a run scored after the ball has hit
the batsman's leg or some other part of his body,
except his hand, without touching the bat.
Abbrev: **lb**

legend *n* **1** a popular story handed down from
earlier times that may or may not be true **2** such
stories collectively **3** a person whose fame makes
him or her seem exceptional: *he is a living legend*
4 modern stories about a famous person which
may or may not be true: *no Garland fan could
complain about sordid revelations tarnishing the legend*
5 words written on something to explain it: *a pub
mirror spelling out the legend 'Saloon Bar'* **6** an
explanation on a table, map, or chart, of the
symbols used ▶ HISTORY Medieval Latin *legenda*
passages to be read

legendary *adj* **1** very famous: *the legendary beauty
of the Alps* **2** of or relating to legend **3** described in
legend: *the legendary birthplace of Aphrodite*

legerdemain (lej-er-de-**main**) *n* **1** same as
sleight of hand 2 cunning deception ▶ HISTORY
Old French: light of hand

leggings *pl n* **1** an extra outer covering for the
lower legs **2** close-fitting trousers for women or
children

leggy *adj* **1** having unusually long legs **2** (of a plant)
having a long weak stem

leghorn *n* **1** a type of Italian wheat straw that is
woven into hats **2** any hat made from this straw
▶ HISTORY English name for *Livorno*, in Italy

Leghorn (leg-**gorn**) *n* a breed of domestic fowl

legible *adj* (of handwriting) able to be read
▶ HISTORY Latin *legere* to read > **legibility** *n*
> **legibly** *adv*

legion *n* **1** any large military force: *the French
Foreign Legion* **2** (often *pl*) *written* any very large
number **3** an infantry unit in the ancient Roman
army of three to six thousand men **4** an
association of veterans ▶ HISTORY Latin *legio*
> **legionary** *adj, n*

legionnaire *n* (often *cap*) a member of a legion

legislate *vb* **-lating, -lated 1** to make or pass laws
2 to bring into effect by legislation ▶ HISTORY Latin
lex, legis law + *latus*, past participle of *ferre* to bring
> **legislator** *n*

legislation *n* **1** the act or process of making laws
2 the laws so made

legislative *adj* **1** of or relating to the process of
making laws **2** having the power or function of
making laws: *the election to Singapore's new
legislative assembly*

legislative assembly *n* (often *caps*) **1** the
bicameral legislature in 28 states of the US **2** the
lower chamber of the bicameral state legislatures
in several Commonwealth countries, such as
Australia **3** the unicameral legislature in most
Canadian provinces **4** any assembly with
legislative powers

legislative council *n* (often *caps*) **1** the upper
chamber of certain bicameral legislatures,
such as those of the Indian and Australian
states (except Queensland) **2** the unicameral
legislature of certain colonies or dependent
territories **3** (in the US) a committee of members
of both chambers of a state legislature that
discusses problems, constructs a legislative
programme, etc.

legislature *n* a body of people authorized to
make, amend, and repeal laws

legitimate *adj* **1** authorized by or in
accordance with law: *legitimate accounting
practices* **2** based on correct or acceptable
principles of reasoning: *a legitimate argument*
3 (of a child) born of parents legally married to
each other **4** of, relating to, or ruling by hereditary
right: *under their legitimate ruling house* **5** of or
relating to serious drama as distinct from films,
television, or vaudeville ▷ *vb* **-mating, -mated**
6 to make, pronounce, or show to be legitimate
▶ HISTORY Medieval Latin *legitimatus* made legal
> **legitimacy** *n* > **legitimately** *adv*

475

legitimize or **-mise** vb **-mizing, -mized** or **-mising, -mised** to make legitimate; legalize > **legitimization** or **-misation** n

legless adj **1** without legs **2** slang very drunk

Lego n trademark a construction toy consisting of plastic bricks and other components that fit together ▶ HISTORY Danish leg godt play well

leguaan n a large amphibious S African lizard ▶ HISTORY Dutch, from French l'iguane the iguana

legume n **1** the pod of a plant of the pea or bean family **2** the seed from such pods, esp. beans or peas ▶ HISTORY Latin legere to pick (a crop)

leguminous adj of or relating to any family of flowering plants having pods (or legumes) as fruits

lei n (in Hawaii) a garland of flowers, worn around the neck ▶ HISTORY Hawaiian

leisure n **1** time or opportunity for relaxation or hobbies **2** at leisure **a** having free time **b** not occupied **3** at one's leisure when one has free time ▶ HISTORY Old French leisir > **leisured** adj

leisure centre n a building providing facilities, such as a swimming pool, gym, and café, for a range of leisure pursuits

leisurely adj **1** unhurried; relaxed ▷ adv **2** in a relaxed way > **leisureliness** n

leitmotif or **leitmotiv** (**lite**-mote-eef) n **1** music a recurring melodic phrase used to suggest a character, thing, or idea **2** literature an often repeated image in a literary work ▶ HISTORY German: leading motif

lekker adj S African, slang pleasing, enjoyable, or tasty ▶ HISTORY Afrikaans, from Dutch

lemming n **1** a small rodent of northern and arctic regions, reputed to rush into the sea in large groups and drown **2** a member of any group following an unthinking course towards destruction ▶ HISTORY Norwegian

lemon n **1** a yellow oval edible fruit with juicy acidic flesh that grows on an evergreen tree in warm and tropical regions **2** slang a person or thing considered to be useless or defective ▷ adj **3** light yellow ▶ HISTORY Arabic laymūn > **lemony** adj

lemonade n a drink made from lemon juice, sugar, and water or from carbonated water, citric acid, and sweetener

lemon sole n an edible European flatfish

lemur n a nocturnal animal, related to the monkey, with a foxy face and long tail, found on Madagascar ▶ HISTORY Latin lemures ghosts

lend vb **lending, lent** **1** to permit the temporary use of **2** to provide (money) temporarily, often at interest **3** to contribute (some abstract quality): a painted trellis lends a classical air to any garden **4** lend an ear to listen **5** lend oneself or itself to be appropriate for: the building lends itself to loft conversion ▶ HISTORY Old English lǣnan > **lender** n

length n **1** the extent or measurement of something from end to end **2** a specified distance, esp. between two positions: the length of a cricket pitch **3** a period of time, as between specified limits or moments **4** the quality, state, or fact of being long rather than short **5** a piece of something,

usually longer than it is wide: a length of twine **6** (usually pl) the amount of trouble taken in doing something: to go to great lengths **7** prosody, phonetics the duration of a vowel or syllable **8** at length **a** after a long interval or period of time **b** in great detail ▶ HISTORY Old English lengthu

lengthen vb to make or become longer

lengthways or **lengthwise** adv, adj in, according to, or along the direction of length

lengthy adj **lengthier, lengthiest** very long or tiresome > **lengthily** adv > **lengthiness** n

lenient (**lee**-nee-ent) adj tolerant, not strict or severe ▶ HISTORY Latin lenis soft > **leniency** n > **leniently** adv

lens n **1** a piece of glass or other transparent material with a curved surface or surfaces, used to bring together or spread rays of light passing through it: used in cameras, telescopes, and spectacles **2** anat a transparent structure in the eye, behind the iris, that focuses images on the retina ▶ HISTORY Latin: lentil

lent vb the past of **lend**

Lent n Christianity the period from Ash Wednesday to Easter Saturday, during which some Christians give up doing something they enjoy ▶ HISTORY Old English lencten, lengten spring, literally: lengthening (of hours of daylight) > **Lenten** adj

lentil n any of the small edible seeds of a leguminous Asian plant ▶ HISTORY Latin lens

lento music adv **1** slowly ▷ n, pl **-tos** **2** a movement or passage performed slowly ▶ HISTORY Italian

Lenz's law (**lents**-iz) n physics the principle that the direction of an induced current is such that the magnetic field produced by this current will oppose the current field ▶ HISTORY after H Lenz, German physicist

Leo n astrol the fifth sign of the zodiac; the Lion ▶ HISTORY Latin

leonine adj of or like a lion ▶ HISTORY Latin leo lion

leopard or fem **leopardess** n a large African and Asian mammal of the cat family, which has a tawny yellow coat with black spots. Also called: **panther** ▶ HISTORY Greek leōn lion + pardos panther

leotard n a tight-fitting garment covering the body from the shoulders to the thighs and worn by acrobats, ballet dancers, and people doing exercises ▶ HISTORY after Jules Léotard, acrobat

leper n **1** offensive a person who has leprosy **2** a person who is avoided ▶ HISTORY Greek lepros scaly

lepidopteran n, pl **-terans** or **-tera** **1** an insect that has two pairs of fragile wings and develops from a caterpillar: a butterfly or moth ▷ adj also **lepidopterous** **2** denoting such an insect ▶ HISTORY Greek lepis scale + pteron wing

lepidopterist n a person who studies or collects moths and butterflies

leprechaun n (in Irish folklore) a mischievous elf ▶ HISTORY Irish Gaelic leipreachān

leprosy n pathol a chronic infectious disease, characterized by painful inflamed lumps beneath the skin and disfigurement and wasting away of affected parts ▷ **leprous** adj

lepton n physics any of a group of elementary particles with weak interactions ▶ HISTORY Greek leptos thin

lesbian n **1** a female homosexual ▷ adj **2** of or characteristic of lesbians ▶ HISTORY Lesbos, Greek Aegean island ▷ **lesbianism** n

lese-majesty (lezz-maj-ist-ee) n **1** an offence against the sovereign power in a state; treason **2** an act of disrespect towards authority ▶ HISTORY from Latin laesa majestas wounded majesty

lesion n **1** any structural change in an organ or tissue resulting from injury or disease **2** an injury or wound ▶ HISTORY Late Latin laesio injury

less adj, adv **1** the comparative of **little**: less fibre; his sharpness will be blunted by playing less ▷ adj **2** not universally accepted fewer ▷ adv **3** **less of** to a smaller extent or degree: it would become less of a problem **4** **no less** sometimes ironic used to indicate admiration or surprise: sculpted by a famous Frenchman, Rodin no less ▷ prep **5** minus: a £2-a-week rise (less tax) ▶ HISTORY Old English lǣssa, lǣs

lessee n a person to whom a lease is granted ▶ HISTORY Old French lesser to lease

lessen vb to make or become less

lesser adj not as great in quantity, size, or worth

lesson n **1 a** a single period of instruction in a subject **b** the content of such a period **2** material assigned for individual study **3** something from which useful knowledge or principles can be learned: one could still learn an important lesson from these masters **4** an experience that serves as a warning or example: the experience will prove a sobering lesson for the military **5** a passage of Scripture read during a church service ▶ HISTORY Old French leçon

lessor n a person who grants a lease of property

lest conj **1** so as to prevent any possibility that: one grabbed it lest a neighbour got there first **2** for fear that: his anxiety lest anything mar the family event ▶ HISTORY Old English thȳ lǣs the, literally: whereby less that

let¹ vb **letting, let 1** to allow: a child lets a friend play with his favourite toy **2 a** an auxiliary expressing a request, proposal, or command, or to convey a warning or threat: well, let's try it; just let me catch you here again! **b** an auxiliary expressing an assumption or hypothesis: let 'a' equal 'b' **c** an auxiliary expressing resigned acceptance of the inevitable: let the worst happen **3** to allow someone to rent (property or accommodation) **4** to cause the movement of (something) in a specified direction: this lets aluminium creep into the brain **5 let alone** not to mention: I could hardly think, let alone find words to say **6 let alone** or **be** stop annoying or interfering with: let the poor cat alone **7 let go** to relax one's hold (on) **8 let loose a** to allow (a person or animal) to leave or escape **b** informal to make (a sound) suddenly: he let loose a laugh **c** informal to fire (ammunition) from a gun ▷ n **9** Brit & Austral the act of letting property or accommodation ▷ See also **let down, let off**, etc. ▶ HISTORY Old English lǣtan to permit

let² n **1** tennis, squash etc. a minor infringement or obstruction of the ball, requiring a point to be replayed **2 without let or hindrance** without obstruction ▶ HISTORY Old English lettan to hinder

let down vb **1** to fail to satisfy the expectations of (someone); disappoint **2** to lower **3** to lengthen a garment by decreasing the hem **4** to deflate: to let down a tyre ▷ n **letdown 5** a disappointment

lethal adj capable of causing death ▶ HISTORY Latin letum death ▷ **lethally** adv

lethargy n, pl **-gies 1** sluggishness or dullness **2** an abnormal lack of energy ▶ HISTORY Greek lēthargos drowsy ▷ **lethargic** adj ▷ **lethargically** adv

let off vb **1** to excuse from (work or duties): I'll let you off homework for a week **2** informal to spare (someone) the expected punishment: lots were let off because they couldn't be bothered to prosecute anybody **3** to explode or fire (a bomb, gun, or firework) **4** to release (liquid, air, or steam)

let on vb informal **1** to reveal (a secret) **2** to pretend: he let on that he was a pilgrim

let out vb written **1** to emit: he let out a scream **2** to allow to leave; release **3** to make (property) available for people to rent **4** to make (a garment) wider by reducing the seams **5** to reveal (a secret) ▷ n **let-out 6** a chance to escape

letter n **1 a** a written or printed message, usually enclosed in an envelope and sent by post **2** any of a set of conventional symbols used in writing or printing a language: character of the alphabet **3** the strict meaning of an agreement or document; exact wording: the letter of the law **4 to the letter** precisely: you have to follow treatment to the letter for it to be effective ▷ vb **5** to write or mark letters on (a sign) ▶ HISTORY Latin littera letter of the alphabet ▷ **lettering** n

letter bomb n an explosive device in an envelope or parcel that explodes when the envelope or parcel is opened

letter box n chiefly Brit **1** a slot in a door through which letters are delivered **2** Also called: **pillar box, postbox** a public box into which letters and postcards are put for collection

lettered adj **1** well educated **2** printed or marked with letters

letterhead n a printed heading on stationery giving the name and address of the sender

letter of credit n a letter issued by a bank entitling the bearer to draw money from other banks

letters pl n **1** literary knowledge or ability: a man of letters **2** literary culture in general

letters patent pl n See **patent** (senses 1, 3)

lettuce n a plant cultivated for its large edible leaves, which are used in salads ▶ HISTORY Latin lactuca, from lac milk, because of its milky juice

let up vb **1** to diminish or stop **2** (foll. by on) informal to be less harsh (towards someone) ▷ n **let-up 3** informal a lessening: there has been no let-up in the war

477

leucocyte (**loo**-koh-site) *n* any of the various large white cells in the blood of vertebrates ▶ HISTORY Greek *leukos* white + *kutos* vessel

leukaemia *or esp US* **leukemia** (loo-**kee**-mee-a) *n* an acute or chronic disease characterized by extreme overproduction of white blood cells ▶ HISTORY Greek *leukos* white + *haima* blood

levee¹ *n* US **1** *geog* a natural or artificial river embankment **2** a quay ▶ HISTORY French, from Latin *levare* to raise

levee² *n* a formal reception held by a sovereign just after rising from bed ▶ HISTORY French, from Latin *levare* to raise

level *adj* **1** on a horizontal plane **2** having an even surface **3** being of the same height as something else: *the floor of the lean-to was level with the patio* **4** equal to or even with (something or someone else): *Johnson was level with the overnight leader* **5** not exceeding the upper edge of (a spoon, etc.) **6** consistent or regular: *a level pulse* **7 one's level best** the best one can do ▷ *vb* **-elling, -elled** *or US* **-eling, -eled** **8** (sometimes foll. by *off*) to make horizontal or even **9** to make equal in position or status **10** to direct (an accusation or criticism) emphatically at someone **11** to focus (a look) directly at someone **12** to aim (a weapon) horizontally **13** to demolish completely ▷ *n* **14** a horizontal line or plane **15** a device, such as a spirit level, for determining whether a surface is horizontal **16** position or status in a scale of values: *a high-level delegation* **17** stage or degree of progress: *primary school level* **18** a specified vertical position: *floor level* **19** the topmost horizontal line or plane from which the height of something is calculated: *sea level* **20** a flat even surface or area of land **21** a degree or intensity reached on a measurable or notional scale: *noise level* **22 on the level** *informal* sincere or genuine ▶ HISTORY Latin *libella*, diminutive of *libra* scales

level crossing *n* *Brit, Austral & NZ* a point at which a railway line and a road cross

level-headed *adj* calm and sensible

lever *n* **1** a handle used to operate machinery **2** a bar used to move a heavy object or to prise something open **3** a rigid bar that turns on a fixed support (fulcrum) to transfer effort and motion, for instance to move a load **4** a means of exerting pressure in order to achieve an aim: *using the hostages as a lever to gain concessions from the west* ▷ *vb* **5** to open or move with a lever ▶ HISTORY Latin *levare* to raise

leverage *n* **1** the mechanical advantage gained by using a lever **2** the ability to influence people or events: *information gives leverage*

leveraged buyout *n* a takeover bid in which a small company uses its assets, and those of the target company, to raise the loans required to finance the takeover

leveret (**lev**-ver-it) *n* a young hare ▶ HISTORY Latin *lepuş* hare

leviathan (lev-**vie**-ath-an) *n* any huge or powerful thing ▶ HISTORY Hebrew *liwyāthān*, a Biblical sea monster

Levis *pl n trademark* denim jeans

levitate *vb* **-tating, -tated** to rise or cause to rise, suspended, in the air ▶ HISTORY Latin *levis* light > **levitation** *n*

levity *n, pl* **-ties** a frivolous or too light-hearted attitude to serious matters ▶ HISTORY Latin *levis* light

levy (**lev**-vee) *vb* **levies, levying, levied 1** to impose and collect (a tax, tariff, or fine) **2** to conscript troops for service ▷ *n, pl* **levies 3 a** the imposition and collection of taxes, tariffs, or fines **b** the money so raised **4** troops conscripted for service ▶ HISTORY Latin *levare* to raise

lewd *adj* indecently vulgar; obscene ▶ HISTORY Old English *lǣwde* lay, ignorant > **lewdly** *adv* > **lewdness** *n*

lexical *adj* **1** relating to the vocabulary of a language **2** relating to a lexicon > **lexically** *adv*

lexical chain *n grammar* a series of semantically related words in a text

lexicography *n* the process or profession of compiling dictionaries > **lexicographer** *n*

lexicon *n* **1** a dictionary, esp. one of an ancient language such as Greek **2** the vocabulary of a language or of an individual ▶ HISTORY Greek *lexis* word

lexis *n* the set of all the morphemes of a language ▶ HISTORY Greek *lexis* word

ley *n* land temporarily under grass ▶ HISTORY variant of *lea*

Leyden jar (**lide**-en) *n physics* an early type of capacitor consisting of a glass jar with the lower part of the inside and outside coated with tinfoil ▶ HISTORY from *Leiden*, city in the Netherlands

LGBT lesbian, gay, bisexual, and transgender

LGV (in Britain) large goods vehicle

Li *chem* lithium

liability *n, pl* **-ties 1** someone or something that is a problem or embarrassment **2** the state of being legally responsible **3** (often pl) sums of money owed by an organization

liable *adj* **1** probable or likely: *weak and liable to give way* **2** commonly suffering a condition: *he's liable to get colds in his chest* **3** legally obliged or responsible; answerable ▶ HISTORY Old French *lier* to bind

liaise *vb* **liaising, liaised** (usually foll. by *with*) to communicate and maintain contact (with)

liaison *n* **1** communication and cooperative contact between groups **2** a secretive relationship ▶ HISTORY Old French *lier* to bind

liana *n* a woody climbing and twining plant of tropical forests ▶ HISTORY French

liar *n* a person who tells lies

lib *n informal* liberation: used in the name of certain movements: *women's lib; gay lib*

Lib *Brit, Austral & S African politics* Liberal

libation (lie-**bay**-shun) *n* **a** the pouring out of wine in honour of a deity **b** the wine so poured out ▶ HISTORY Latin *libare* to pour an offering of drink

libel *n* **1** *law* the publication of something false which damages a person's reputation **2** any damaging or unflattering representation or statement ▷ *vb* **-belling, -belled** or US **-beling, -beled 3** *law* to make or publish a false damaging statement or representation about (a person) ▶ HISTORY Latin *libellus* a little book > **libellous** or **libelous** *adj*

liberal *adj* **1** having social and political views that favour progress and reform **2** generous in temperament or behaviour **3** tolerant of other people **4** using or existing in large quantities; lavish: *the world's finest gadgetry, in liberal quantities* **5** not rigid; free: *a more liberal interpretation* **6** (of an education) designed to develop general cultural interests and intellectual ability **7 Liberal** of or relating to a Liberal Party ▷ *n* **8** a person who has liberal ideas or opinions ▶ HISTORY Latin *liber* free > **liberalism** *n* > **liberally** *adv*

Liberal Democrat *n* a member or supporter of the Liberal Democrats, a British centrist political party that advocates proportional representation

liberality *n*, *pl* **-ties 1** generosity **2** the quality of being broad-minded

liberalize or **-ise** *vb* **-izing, -ized** or **-ising, -ised** to make (a law) less strict > **liberalization** or **-isation** *n*

Liberal Party *n* **1** *history* a British non-Socialist political party which advocated progress and reform **2** any similar party in various other countries **3** the main right-wing political party in Australia

liberate *vb* **-ating, -ated 1** to free (someone) from social prejudices or injustices **2** to give liberty to; make free **3** to release (a country) from enemy occupation > **liberation** *n* > **liberator** *n*

liberated *adj* **1** not bound by traditional sexual and social roles: *a liberated woman* **2** given liberty **3** released from enemy occupation

libertarian *n* **1** a person who believes in freedom of thought and action ▷ *adj* **2** believing in freedom of thought and action

libertine (**lib**-er-teen) *n* **1** a person who is promiscuous and unscrupulous ▷ *adj* **2** promiscuous and unscrupulous ▶ HISTORY Latin *libertus* freed

liberty *n*, *pl* **-ties 1** the freedom to choose, think, and act for oneself **2** the right of unrestricted movement and access; freedom **3** (often *pl*) a social action regarded as being forward or improper **4 at liberty** free or unconfined **5 at liberty to** unrestricted or authorized: *I am not at liberty to divulge his name* **6 take liberties (with)** to be overfamiliar (towards someone) ▶ HISTORY Latin *libertas*

libidinous *adj* characterized by excessive sexual desire > **libidinously** *adv*

libido (**lib**-ee-doe) *n*, *pl* **-dos 1** *psychoanal* psychic energy from the id **2** sexual urge or desire ▶ HISTORY Latin: desire > **libidinal** *adj*

Libra *n* *astrol* the seventh sign of the zodiac; the Scales ▶ HISTORY Latin

librarian *n* a person in charge of or assisting in a library > **librarianship** *n*

library *n*, *pl* **-braries 1** a room or building where books and other literary materials are kept **2** a collection of literary materials, films, or recordings, kept for borrowing or reference **3** the building or institution that houses such a collection **4** a set of books published as a series, often in a similar format **5** *computers* a collection of standard programs, usually stored on disk ▶ HISTORY Latin *liber* book

libretto *n*, *pl* **-tos** or **-ti** a text written for an opera ▶ HISTORY Italian: little book > **librettist** *n*

Libyan *adj* **1** from Libya ▷ *n* **2** a person from Libya

lice *n* the plural of **louse**

licence or US **license** *n* **1** a document giving official permission to do, use, or own something **2** formal permission or exemption **3** intentional disregard of conventional rules to achieve a certain effect: *poetic licence* **4** excessive freedom ▶ HISTORY Latin *licet* it is allowed

license *vb* **-censing, -censed 1** to grant a licence to or for **2** to give permission to or for > **licensable** *adj*

licensee *n* a person who holds a licence, esp. one to sell alcoholic drink

licentiate *n* a person who holds a certificate of competence to practise a certain profession

licentious *adj* sexually unrestrained or promiscuous ▶ HISTORY Latin *licentia* licence > **licentiousness** *n*

lichee *n* same as **lychee**

lichen *n* any of various small mossy plants that grow in patches on tree trunks, bare ground, rocks, and stone walls ▶ HISTORY Greek *leikhein* to lick

licit *adj* *formal* lawful; permitted ▶ HISTORY Latin *licere* to be permitted

lick *vb* **1** to pass the tongue over in order to taste, wet, or clean **2** to flicker over or round (something): *flames licked the gutters* **3** *informal* **a** to defeat **b** to thrash **4 lick into shape** to put into a satisfactory condition **5 lick one's wounds** to retire after a defeat ▷ *n* **6** an instance of passing the tongue over something **7** a small amount: *a lick of paint* **8** *informal* a blow **9** *informal* a fast pace: *a pulsating rhythm taken at a lick* **10 a lick and a promise** something hastily done, esp. a hurried wash ▶ HISTORY Old English *liccian*

licorice *n* US & Canad same as **liquorice**

lid *n* **1** a removable or hinged cover: *a saucepan lid* **2** short for **eyelid 3 put the (tin) lid on** *informal* to put an end to ▶ HISTORY Old English *hlid* > **lidded** *adj*

lido (**lee**-doe) *n*, *pl* **-dos** Brit an open-air swimming pool or a part of a beach used by the public for swimming and sunbathing ▶ HISTORY *Lido*, island bathing beach near Venice

lie¹ *vb* **lying, lied 1** to speak untruthfully with the intention of deceiving **2** to convey a false impression: *the camera cannot lie* ▷ *n* **3** an untrue statement deliberately used to mislead **4** something that is deliberately intended to deceive

479

lie — lift

5 give the lie to a to disprove **b** to accuse of lying ▸ HISTORY Old English *lyge, lēogan*

lie² *vb* **lying, lay, lain 1** (often foll. by *down*) to place oneself or be in a horizontal position **2** to be situated: *I left the money lying on the table; Nepal became the only country lying between China and India* **3** to be and remain (in a particular state or condition): *others of their species lie asleep* **4** to stretch or extend: *an enormous task lies ahead* **5** (usually foll. by *in*) to exist or comprise: *her charm lies in her inner beauty* **6** (foll. by *with*) to rest (with): *the fault lies with them* ▸ *n* **7** the manner, place, or style in which something is situated **8** an animal's lair **9 lie of the land** the way in which a situation is developing ▸ See also **lie in** ▸ HISTORY Old English *licgan*

lied (leed) *n, pl* **lieder** *music* a musical setting for solo voice and piano of a romantic or lyrical poem ▸ HISTORY German: song

liege (leej) *adj* **1** (of a lord) owed feudal allegiance: *their liege lord* **2** (of a vassal or subject) owing feudal allegiance: *a liege subject* **3** faithful; loyal ▸ *n* **4** a liege lord **5** a subject ▸ HISTORY Old French *lige*

lie in *vb* **1** to remain in bed late into the morning ▸ *n* **lie-in 2** a long stay in bed in the morning

lien *n law* a right to retain possession of someone else's property until a debt is paid ▸ HISTORY Latin *ligamen* bond

lieu (lyew) *n* **in lieu of** instead of ▸ HISTORY Old French

lieutenant (lef-**ten**-ant, loo-**ten**-ant) *n* **1** a junior officer in the army, navy, or the US police force **2** a person who acts as principal assistant ▸ HISTORY Old French, literally: place-holding ▸ **lieutenancy** *n*

lieutenant colonel *n* an officer in an army, air force, or marine corps immediately junior to a colonel

lieutenant general *n* a senior officer in an army, air force, or marine corps

lieutenant governor *n* **1** a deputy governor **2** (in Canada) the representative of the Crown in a province

life *n, pl* **lives 1** the state or quality that identifies living beings, characterized chiefly by growth, reproduction, and response to stimuli **2** the period between birth and death or between birth and the present time **3** a living person or being: *riots which claimed 22 lives* **4** the remainder or extent of one's life: *with that lady for the rest of her life* **5** the process of living: *rituals gave his life stability* **6** *informal* a sentence of life imprisonment, usually approximating to 15 years **7** a characteristic state or mode of existence: *country life is best* **8** the length of time that something is active or functioning: *the life of a battery* **9** a present condition or mode of existence: *they are leading a joyous life* **10** a biography **11** the sum or course of human events and activities **12** liveliness or high spirits: *full of life* **13** a source of strength, animation, or vitality: *he was the life of the show* **14** all living things collectively: *there is no life on Mars; marine life*

15 a matter of life and death a matter of extreme urgency **16 as large as life** *informal* real and living **17 not on your life** *informal* certainly not **18 true to life** faithful to reality **19 to the life** (of a copy of a painting or drawing) resembling the original exactly ▸ HISTORY Old English *līf*

life assurance *n* insurance that provides for a sum of money to be paid to the insured person at a certain age or to the spouse or children on the death of the insured. Also called: **life insurance**

lifeblood *n* **1** the blood vital to life **2** something that is essential for existence, development, or success

lifeboat *n* a boat used for rescuing people at sea

life cycle *n* the series of changes occurring in each generation of an animal or plant

life expectancy *n statistics* according to statistics, the number of years a person can expect to live

lifeguard *n* a person at a beach or pool whose job is to rescue people in danger of drowning

lifeless *adj* **1** inanimate; dead **2** lacking liveliness or animation **3** unconscious

lifelike *adj* closely resembling or representing life

lifeline *n* **1** a single means of contact or support on which a person or an area relies **2** a rope used for life-saving

lifelong *adj* lasting for a lifetime

lifelong learning *n* the provision or use of learning opportunities throughout people's lives

life peer *n Brit* a peer whose title ceases at his or her death

lifer *n informal* a prisoner sentenced to life imprisonment

life science *n* any of the sciences concerned with the structure and behaviour of living organisms, such as biology, botany, or zoology

life-size *or* **life-sized** *adj* representing actual size

life span *n* the period of time during which a human being, animal, machine, etc. may be expected to live or function under normal conditions

lifestyle *n* a set of attitudes, habits, and possessions regarded as typical of a particular group or an individual

lifestyle disease *n* a disease that can be prevented by changes in diet, environment, and exercise, such as obesity and stroke

life-support *adj* (of equipment or treatment) necessary to sustain life

lifetime *n* **1** the length of time a person is alive **2 of a lifetime** (of an opportunity or experience) the most important or memorable

lift *vb* **1** to rise or raise upwards to a higher place: *the breakdown truck was lifting the lorry* **2** to move upwards: *he slowly lifted his hand* **3** to raise in status or estimation: *lifted from poverty* **4** to revoke or cancel: *the government lifted its restrictions on imported beef* **5** to remove (plants or underground crops) from the ground for harvesting **6** to disappear or disperse: *the tension lifted* **7** *informal* to plagiarize (music or writing) ▸ *n* **8 a** a compartment raised or lowered in a vertical shaft to transport people or goods to another floor in a building **b** See **chairlift** **9** a ride in a car or other vehicle as a passenger **10** a rise in morale or feeling of cheerfulness **11** the act of lifting **12** the force that lifts airborne objects ▸ HISTORY from Old Norse

liftoff *n* the initial movement of a rocket as it leaves its launch pad

ligament *n anat* a band of tough tissue that connects various bones or cartilage ▸ HISTORY Latin *ligare* to bind

ligature *n* **1** a link, bond, or tie **2** *printing* a character of two or more joined letters, such as ff **3** *music* a slur or the group of notes connected by it ▸ *vb* **-turing, -tured** **4** to bind with a ligature ▸ HISTORY Latin *ligare* to bind

light¹ *n* **1** the natural medium, electromagnetic radiation, that makes sight possible **2** anything that illuminates, such as a lamp or candle **3** a particular type of light: *dim yellow light* **4 a** daylight **b** daybreak; dawn **5** anything that lets in light, such as a window **6** an aspect or view: *we have seen the world in a new light* **7** mental understanding or spiritual insight: *suddenly he saw the light* **8** an outstanding person: *a leading light of the movement* **9** brightness of countenance, esp. a sparkle in the eyes **10 a** something that ignites, such as a spark or flame **b** something used for igniting, such as a match **11** See **lighthouse** **12 come to light** to become known or visible **13 in (the) light of** taking into account **14 see the light** to understand **15 see the light (of day) a** to come into being **b** to come to public notice ▸ *adj* **16** full of light **17** (of a colour) pale: *light blue* ▸ *vb* **lighting, lighted** *or* **lit** **18** to ignite **19** (often foll. by *up*) to illuminate or cause to illuminate **20** to guide by light ▸ See also **light up** ▸ HISTORY Old English *lēoht* > **lightish** *adj*

light² *adj* **1** not heavy; weighing relatively little **2** relatively low in density, strength, amount, degree, etc.: *light oil; light alloy* **3** lacking sufficient weight **4** not bulky or clumsy: *light bedclothes* **5** not serious or difficult to understand; entertaining: *light music* **6** graceful or agile: *light movements* **7** without strong emphasis or serious meaning: *he gazed about with a light inattentive smile* **8** easily digested: *a light lunch* **9** relatively low in alcohol: *a light wine* **10** without burdens, difficulties, or problems: *a light heart lives longest* **11** dizzy or unclear: *a light head* **12** (of bread or cake) spongy or well risen **13** (of a vessel, lorry, or other transport) **a** designed to carry light loads **b** not loaded **14** carrying light arms or equipment: *light infantry* **15** (of an industry) producing small consumer goods using light machinery **16 make light of** to treat as insignificant or unimportant ▸ *adv* **17** with little equipment or luggage: *travelling light* ▸ *vb* **lighting, lighted** *or* **lit** **18** (esp. of birds) to settle or land after flight **19** (foll. by *on* or *upon*) to discover by chance ▸ See also **lights** ▸ HISTORY Old English *lēoht* > **lightish** *adj* > **lightly** *adv* > **lightness** *n*

light bulb *n* a hollow rounded glass fitting containing a gas and a thin metal filament that gives out light when an electric current is passed through it

lighten¹ *vb* **1** to make less dark **2** to shine; glow **3** (of lightning) to flash

lighten² *vb* **1** to make or become less heavy **2** to make or become less burdensome **3** to make or become more cheerful or lively

lighter¹ *n* a small portable device for lighting cigarettes, etc.

lighter² *n* a flat-bottomed barge used in loading or unloading a ship ▸ HISTORY probably from Middle Dutch

light-fingered *adj* skilful at thieving, esp. by picking pockets

light-headed *adj* giddy; feeling faint

light-hearted *adj* cheerful or carefree in mood or disposition > **light-heartedly** *adv*

light heavyweight *n* a professional boxer weighing up to 175 pounds (79.5 kg) or an amateur weighing up to 81 kg

lighthouse *n* a tower with a light to guide ships and warn of obstructions

light industry *n econ* the manufacturing of small products such as clothing and household goods

lighting *n* **1** the apparatus for and design of artificial light effects to a stage, film, or television set **2** the act or quality of illumination

lightning *n* **1** a flash of light in the sky caused by a discharge of electricity ▸ *adj* **2** fast and sudden: *a lightning attack* ▸ HISTORY variant of *lightening*

lightning conductor *or* **rod** *n* a metal rod attached to the highest part of a building to divert lightning safely to earth

light pen *n* a penlike photoelectric device that in conjunction with a computer can be used to draw lines or identify symbols on a VDU screen

lights *pl n* the lungs of sheep, bullocks, and pigs, used for feeding pets ▸ HISTORY because of the light weight of the lungs

lightship *n* a moored ship equipped as a lighthouse

light up *vb* **1** to illuminate **2** to make or become cheerful or animated: *their faces lit up and one dug the other in the ribs* **3** to light a cigarette or pipe

lightweight *adj* **1** not serious **2** of relatively light weight ▸ *n* **3** *informal* a person of little importance or influence **4** a person or animal of relatively light weight **5** a professional boxer weighing up to 135 pounds (61 kg) or an amateur weighing up to 60 kg

light year *n astron* the distance travelled by light in one mean solar year, i.e. 9.4607×10^{15} metres

ligneous *adj* of or like wood ▸ HISTORY Latin *lignum* wood

lignite (lig-nite) *n* a brown sedimentary rock with a woody texture: used as a fuel

lignum vitae (lig-num vite-ee) *n* a tropical American tree with heavy resinous wood ▸ HISTORY Late Latin, literally: wood of life

like¹ *adj* **1** resembling ▸ *prep* **2** in the manner of; similar to: *she was like a child; it looks like a traffic cone*

3 such as: *a modern material, like carbon fibre*
4 characteristic of ▷ *adv* **5** in the manner of: *cheering like mad* **6** *dialect* likely ▷ *conj* **7** not universally accepted as though; as if: *I don't want to make it seem like I had this bad childhood* **8** in the same way that: *she doesn't dance like you do* ▷ *n* **9** the equal or counterpart of a person or thing **10 the like** similar things: *magic, supernormal powers and the like* **11 the likes** or **like of** people or things similar to (someone or something specified): *the theatre was not meant for the likes of him* ▶ HISTORY Old English *gelīc*

like² *vb* **liking, liked 1** to find enjoyable **2** to be fond of **3** to prefer or choose: *I'd like to go home* **4** to feel disposed or inclined; choose; wish: *do as you like* ▷ *n* **5** (usually pl) a favourable feeling, desire, or preference: *tell me your likes and dislikes* ▶ HISTORY Old English *līcian* > **likeable** or **likable** *adj*

likelihood *n* chance; probability

likelihood scale *n statistics* a scale giving an indication of how often an outcome is likely to happen

likely *adj* **1** tending or inclined: *likely to win* **2** probable: *the likely effects of the tunnel* **3** appropriate for a purpose or activity: *a likely candidate* ▷ *adv* **4** probably or presumably **5 not likely** *informal* definitely not ▶ HISTORY Old Norse *līkligr*

liken *vb* to compare

likeness *n* **1** resemblance **2** portrait **3** an imitative appearance; semblance: *in the likeness of a dragon*

likewise *adv* **1** in addition; also **2** similarly

liking *n* **1** fondness **2** what one likes or prefers: *if it's not to your liking, do let me know*

lilac *n* **1** a small tree with large sprays of purple or white sweet-smelling flowers ▷ *adj* **2** pale purple ▶ HISTORY Persian *nīlak* bluish

Lilliputian (lil-lip-**pew**-shun) *n* **1** a tiny person or being ▷ *adj* **2** tiny; very small ▶ HISTORY *Lilliput*, an imaginary country of tiny people in Swift's *Gulliver's Travels*

Lilo *n, pl* -**los** *trademark* a type of inflatable plastic mattress

lilt *n* **1** a pleasing musical quality in a speaking voice **2** (in music) a jaunty rhythm **3** a graceful rhythmic motion ▷ *vb* **4** (of a voice, tune, or song) to rise and fall in a pleasant way **5** to move gracefully and rhythmically ▶ HISTORY origin unknown > **lilting** *adj*

lily *n, pl* **lilies 1** a perennial plant, such as the tiger lily, with scaly bulbs and showy white or coloured flowers **2** a water lily ▶ HISTORY Latin *lilium*

lily of the valley *n, pl* **lilies of the valley** a small plant with spikes of sweet-smelling white bell-shaped flowers

limb¹ *n* **1** an arm, leg, or wing **2** any of the main branches of a tree **3 out on a limb a** in a precarious or questionable position **b** *Brit & NZ* isolated, esp. because of unpopular opinions ▶ HISTORY Old English *lim* > **limbless** *adj*

limb² *n* the apparent outer edge of the sun, a moon, or a planet ▶ HISTORY Latin *limbus* edge

limber¹ *adj* **1** pliant; supple **2** able to move or bend the body freely; agile ▶ HISTORY origin unknown

limber² *n* **1** part of a gun carriage, consisting of an axle, pole, and two wheels ▷ *vb* **2** to attach the limber (to a gun) ▶ HISTORY Middle English *lymour* shaft of a gun carriage

limbo¹ *n, pl* -**bos 1** (often cap) *RC Church* (formerly) the supposed region intermediate between heaven and hell for the unbaptized **2 in limbo** not knowing the result or next stage of something and powerless to influence it

- **■ WORD HISTORY**
- ■ The word 'limbo' comes from the Latin phrase
- ■ *in limbo*, meaning 'on the border' (i.e. on the
- ■ border of hell).

limbo² *n, pl* -**bos** a West Indian dance in which dancers lean backwards and pass under a horizontal bar which is gradually lowered ▶ HISTORY origin unknown

lime¹ *n* **1** *agriculture* calcium hydroxide spread as a dressing on acidic land ▷ *vb* **liming, limed 2** to spread a calcium compound upon (land) ▶ HISTORY Old English *līm*

lime² *n* the green oval fruit of a small Asian citrus tree with acid fleshy pulp rich in vitamin C ▶ HISTORY Arabic *līmah*

lime³ *n* a European linden tree planted for ornament ▶ HISTORY Old English *lind* linden

lime-green *adj* light yellowish-green

limelight *n* **1 the limelight** glare of publicity: *this issue will remain in the limelight* **2 a** a type of lamp, formerly used in stage lighting, in which lime is heated to white heat **b** brilliant white light produced in this way

limerick (**lim**-mer-ik) *n* a form of comic verse consisting of five lines ▶ HISTORY allegedly from *will you come up to Limerick?*, a refrain sung between nonsense verses at a party

limestone *n* rock consisting mainly of calcium carbonate: used as a building stone and in making cement

lime water *n chem* a clear colourless solution of calcium hydroxide in water

limey *n US, Canad & Austral, slang* **1** a British person **2** a British sailor or ship ▶ HISTORY from *lime-juicer*, because British sailors drank lime juice as a protection against scurvy

limit *n* **1** (sometimes pl) the ultimate extent or amount of something: *each soloist was stretched to his or her limit by the demands of the vocal writing* **2** (often pl) the boundary of a specific area: *beyond the city limits* **3** the largest quantity or amount allowed **4 the limit** *informal* a person or thing that is intolerably exasperating ▷ *vb* **5** -**iting, -ited 5** to restrict ▶ HISTORY Latin *limes* boundary > **limitable** *adj*

limitation *n* **1** a restriction or controlling of quantity, quality, or achievement **2 limitations** the limit or extent of an ability to achieve something: *learn your own limitations*

limited *adj* **1** having a limit; restricted **2** without fullness or scope; narrow **3** (of governing powers or sovereignty) restricted by a constitution, laws, or an assembly: *limited government* **4** (of a business enterprise) owned by shareholders whose liability for the enterprise's debts is restricted

limited edition *n* an edition of something, such as a book, which has been restricted to a particular number of copies

limited liability *n Brit business* liability for the debts of an enterprise that is restricted to the unpaid portion of the value of the company's shares

limited point of view *n literature* a narrative style which is presented from a particular point of view, usually that of one of the characters involved in the story

limn *vb old-fashioned* to represent in drawing or painting ▶ HISTORY Latin *inluminare* to brighten

limousine *n* any large luxurious car ▶ HISTORY French, literally: cloak

limp¹ *vb* **1** to walk with an uneven step, esp. with a weak or injured leg **2** to advance in a labouring or faltering manner ▷ *n* **3** an uneven walk or progress ▶ HISTORY Old English *lemphealt* lame **> limping** *adj, n*

limp² *adj* **1** lacking firmness or stiffness **2** not energetic or vital **3** (of the binding of a book) paperback ▶ HISTORY probably Scandinavian **> limply** *adv*

limpet *n* **1** a conical shellfish that clings tightly to rocks with its muscular foot ▷ *adj* **2** denoting certain weapons that are magnetically attached to their targets and resist removal: *limpet mines* ▶ HISTORY Old English

limpid *adj* **1** clear or transparent **2** (of speech or writing) clear and easy to understand ▶ HISTORY Latin *limpidus* clear **> limpidity** *n*

linage *n* **1** the number of lines in written or printed matter **2** payment according to the number of lines

linchpin *or* **lynchpin** *n* **1** a pin inserted through an axle to keep a wheel in position **2** an essential person or thing: *she was the linchpin of the experiment* ▶ HISTORY Old English *lynis*

linctus *n, pl* **-tuses** a soothing syrupy cough mixture ▶ HISTORY Latin *lingere* to lick

linden *n* a large tree with heart-shaped leaves and fragrant yellowish flowers. See also **lime³** ▶ HISTORY Old English *linde* lime tree

line¹ *n* **1** a narrow continuous mark, such as one made by a pencil or brush **2** a thin indented mark or wrinkle on skin **3** a continuous length without breadth **4** a boundary: *the United Nations established a provisional demarcation line* **5** *sport* **a** a white band indicating a division on a field or track **b** a mark or imaginary mark at which a race begins or ends **6** a point of change or limit: *the dividing line between success and failure* **7** the edge or contour of a shape: *the shoulder line* **8** a wire or string with a particular function: *a long washing line* **9** a telephone connection: *it was a very bad line* **10** a conducting wire, cable, or circuit for electric-power transmission or telecommunications

11 a system of travel or transportation: *a shipping line* **12** a route between two points on a railway **13** a railway track **14** a course or direction of movement: *the birds' line of flight* **15** a course of action or behaviour: *to adopt a more aggressive line* **16** a policy or prescribed way of thinking: *city commentators supported the CBI line* **17** a field of interest or activity: *heroin – that was their line* **18** straight or orderly alignment: *stand in line* **19** one kind of product or article: *a line of smart suits* **20** a row of people or things **21** a row of printed or written words **22** a unit of verse consisting of words in a single row **23** one of a number of narrow horizontal bands forming a television picture **24** *music* any of the five horizontal marks that make up the stave **25** the most forward defensive position: *the front line* **26** a formation of ships or soldiers abreast of each other **27** the combatant forces of certain armies and navies **28** *US & Canad* a queue **29 all along the line** at every stage in a series **30 draw the line (at)** to object (to) or set a limit (on): *I'm not a killer, I draw the line at that* **31 drop someone a line** to send someone a short note **32 get a line on** *informal* to obtain information about **33 in line for** likely to receive: *high achievers are in line for cash bonuses* **34 in line with** conforming to **35 lay** *or* **put on the line a** to speak frankly and directly ▷ **b** to risk (one's career or reputation) on something ▷ *vb* **lining, lined 36** to mark with a line or lines **37** to be or form a border: *the square was lined with stalls selling snacks* **38** to place in or form a row, series, or alignment ▷ See also **lines, line-up** ▶ HISTORY Old French *ligne* + Old English *līn* **> lined** *adj*

line² *vb* **lining, lined 1** to attach an inside layer to **2** to cover the inside of: *the works of Shakespeare lined his walls* **3 line one's pockets** to make a lot of money, esp. dishonestly ▶ HISTORY Latin *linum* flax

lineage (**lin**-ee-ij) *n* direct descent from an ancestor

lineal *adj* **1** being in a direct line of descent from an ancestor **2** of or derived from direct descent **3** linear ▶ HISTORY Latin *linea* line

lineament *n* (often *pl*) a facial outline or feature ▶ HISTORY Latin *lineare* to draw a line

linear (**lin**-ee-er) *adj* **1** of or in lines **2** of or relating to length **3** represented by a line or lines **> linearity** *n*

linear measure *n* a unit or system of units for the measurement of length

lineation (lin-ee-**ay**-shun) *n* **1** the act of marking with lines **2** an arrangement of lines

line dancing *n* a form of dancing performed by rows of people to country and western music

line drawing *n* a drawing formed with lines

line graph *n maths* a graph where each value is plotted as a point, joined by a straight line to the points on either side of it

linen *n* **1** a hard-wearing fabric woven from the spun fibres of flax **2** articles, such as sheets or tablecloths, made from linen cloth or from cotton ▶ HISTORY Latin *linum* flax

483

line of best fit *n maths* a straight line drawn on a graph, which shows the general trend of the varying values plotted there

line of latitude *n* an imaginary line circling the earth horizontally, joining all the points with a given latitude

line of longitude *n* an imaginary line circling the earth vertically, joining all the points with a given longitude

line printer *n* an electromechanical device that prints a line of characters at a time: used in printing and in computer systems

liner¹ *n* **1** a passenger ship or aircraft, esp. one that is part of a commercial fleet **2** Also called: **eyeliner** a cosmetic used to outline the eyes

liner² *n* something used as a lining: *a plastic bin liner*

lines *pl n* **1** the words of a theatrical role: *shaky sets, fluffed lines, and wooden plots* **2** *informal, chiefly Brit* a marriage certificate: *marriage lines* **3** a school punishment of writing out the same sentence or phrase a specified number of times **4 read between the lines** to find an implicit meaning in addition to the obvious one

linesman *n, pl* **-men 1** an official who helps the referee or umpire in various sports, by indicating when the ball has gone out of play **2** a person who maintains railway, electricity, or telephone lines

line-up *n* **1** people or things assembled for a particular purpose: *the Christmas TV line-up* **2** the members of such an assembly ▷ *vb* **line up 3** to form or organize a line-up

ling¹ *n, pl* **ling** *or* **lings** a fish with a long slender body ▶ HISTORY probably Low German

ling² *n* heather ▶ HISTORY Old Norse *lyng*

linger *vb* **1** to delay or prolong departure **2** to survive in a weakened condition for some time before death **3** to spend a long time doing or considering something ▶ HISTORY Old English *lengan* prolong > **lingering** *adj*

lingerie (lan-zher-ee) *n* women's underwear and nightwear ▶ HISTORY French, from Latin *lineus* linen

lingo *n, pl* **-goes** *informal* any foreign or unfamiliar language or jargon ▶ HISTORY perhaps from LINGUA FRANCA

lingua franca *n, pl* **lingua francas** *or* **linguae francae 1** a language used for communication among people of different mother tongues **2** any system of communication providing mutual understanding ▶ HISTORY Italian: Frankish tongue

lingual *adj* **1** *anat* of the tongue **2** articulated with the tongue **3** *rare* of language or languages > **lingually** *adv*

linguist *n* **1** a person who is skilled in foreign languages **2** a person who studies linguistics ▶ HISTORY Latin *lingua* tongue

linguistic *adj* **1** of language **2** of linguistics > **linguistically** *adv*

linguistics *n* the scientific study of language

liniment *n* a medicated oily liquid applied to the skin to relieve pain or stiffness ▶ HISTORY Latin *linere* to smear

lining *n* **1** material used to line a garment or curtain **2** any interior covering: *the lining of the womb*

link *n* **1** any of the separate rings that form a chain **2** an emotional or logical relationship between people or things; association **3** a connecting part or episode **4** a type of communications connection: *a rail link; radio link* ▷ *vb* **5** (often foll. by *up*) to connect with or as if with links **6** to connect by association ▶ HISTORY from Old Norse

linkage *n* **1** the act of linking or the state of being linked **2** a system of links

links *pl n* a golf course ▶ HISTORY Old English *hlincas*, plural of *hlinc* ridge

link-up *n* a joining together of two systems or groups

Linnean system *n biol* the system of classification of plants and animals using binomial Latin names ▶ HISTORY after Carolus *Linnaeus*, Swedish botanist

linnet *n* a brownish finch: the male has a red breast and forehead ▶ HISTORY Old French *linotte*, from Latin *līnum* flax (because the bird feeds on flaxseeds)

lino *n* short for **linoleum**

linocut *n* **1** a design cut in relief in linoleum mounted on a block of wood **2** a print made from such a block

linoleum *n* a floor covering made of hessian or jute with a smooth decorative coating of powdered cork ▶ HISTORY Latin *linum* flax + *oleum* oil

Linotype *n trademark* a typesetting machine that casts an entire line of text on one piece of metal

linseed *n* the seed of the flax plant ▶ HISTORY Old English *līn* flax + *sǣd* seed

linseed oil *n* a yellow oil extracted from flax seeds and used in making paints, inks, linoleum, and varnish

lint *n* **1** an absorbent material with raised fibres on one side, used to dress wounds **2** tiny shreds of yarn or cloth; fluff ▶ HISTORY probably Latin *linteus* made of linen, from *linum* flax

lintel *n* a horizontal beam over a door or window ▶ HISTORY probably ultimately from Latin *limes* boundary

lion *n* **1** a large animal of the cat family found in Africa and India, with a tawny yellow coat and, in the male, a shaggy mane **2** a courageous and strong person **3 the lion's share** the largest portion ▶ HISTORY Latin *leo* > **lioness** *fem n*

lion-hearted *adj* very brave; courageous

lionize *or* **-ise** *vb* **-izing, -ized** *or* **-ising, -ised** to treat as a celebrity

lip *n* **1** *anat* either of the two fleshy folds surrounding the mouth **2** any structure resembling a lip, such as the rim of a jug **3** *slang* impudent talk or backchat **4 bite one's lip** to avoid showing feelings of anger or distress **5 keep a stiff upper lip** to maintain one's composure during a time of trouble **6 lick** *or* **smack one's lips** to anticipate or

recall something with glee or relish ▶ **HISTORY** Old English *lippa*

lipase *n biochem* any of a group of enzymes that digest fat and are produced in the stomach and pancreas and occur in seeds

lipid *n biochem* any of a group of organic compounds including fats, oils, waxes, and sterols ▶ **HISTORY** Greek *lipos* fat

lipoprotein *n biochem* any of a group of proteins that help transport lipids in the bloodstream

liposuction *n* a cosmetic surgical operation in which fat is removed from the body by suction

lip-read *vb* **-reading, -read** to interpret speech by lip-reading

lip-reading *n* a method used by deaf people to understand spoken words by interpreting movements of the speaker's lips ▶ **lip-reader** *n*

lip service *n* **pay lip service to** to appear to support or obey something publicly while actually disregarding it

lipstick *n* a cosmetic in the form of a stick, for colouring the lips

liquefied natural gas *n* a mixture of various gases, esp. methane, liquefied for transportation and used as engine fuel. Abbrev: **LNG**

liquefy *vb* **-fies, -fying, -fied** (esp. of a gas) to make or become liquid ▶ **HISTORY** Latin *liquefacere* to make liquid > **liquefaction** *n*

liqueur (lik-**cure**) *n* a highly flavoured sweetened alcoholic spirit, intended to be drunk after a meal ▶ **HISTORY** French

liquid *n* **1** a substance in a physical state which can change shape but not size ▷ *adj* **2** of or being a liquid: *liquid medicines* **3** shining and clear: *liquid sunlight days* **4** flowing, fluent, or smooth **5** (of assets) in the form of money or easily convertible into money ▶ **HISTORY** Latin *liquere* to be fluid

liquidate *vb* **-dating, -dated** **1** to settle or pay off (a debt or claim) **2** to dissolve a company and divide its assets among creditors **3** to convert (assets) into cash **4** to eliminate or kill

liquidation *n* **1a** the dissolving of a company by selling its assets to pay off its debts **b go into liquidation** (of a business firm) to have its affairs so terminated **2** destruction; elimination

liquidator *n* an official appointed to liquidate a business

liquid-crystal display *n* a display of numbers, characters, or images, esp. on a calculator, using cells containing a liquid with crystalline properties, that change their reflectivity when an electric field is applied to them

liquidity *n* the state of being able to meet financial obligations

liquidize *or* **-dise** *vb* **-izing, -ized** *or* **-ising, -ised** **1** to make or become liquid; liquefy **2** to process (food) in a liquidizer to make it liquid

liquidizer *or* **-diser** *n* a kitchen appliance with blades for liquidizing food

liquid measure *n* a unit or system of units for measuring volumes of liquids or their containers

liquid oxygen *n* oxygen liquefied by cooling: used in rocket fuels

liquid paraffin *n* an oily liquid obtained by petroleum distillation and used as a laxative

liquor *n* **1** spirits or other alcoholic drinks **2** any liquid in which food has been cooked ▶ **HISTORY** Latin *liquere* to be liquid

liquorice *or US & Canad* **licorice** (lik-ker-iss) *n* **1** a chewy black sweet with a strong flavour **2** the dried black root of a Mediterranean plant, used as a laxative and in confectionery ▶ **HISTORY** Greek *glukus* sweet + *rhiza* root

lira *n, pl* **lire** *or* **liras** **1** a former monetary unit of Italy **2** the standard monetary unit of Turkey ▶ **HISTORY** Italian, from Latin *libra* pound

lisle (rhymes with **mile**) *n* a strong fine cotton thread or fabric, formerly used to make stockings ▶ **HISTORY** after *Lisle* (now Lille), in France

lisp *n* **1** a speech defect in which *s* and *z* are pronounced like the *th* sounds in English *thin* and *then* respectively ▷ *vb* **2** to speak with a lisp ▶ **HISTORY** Old English *wlisp* lisping (imitative)

LISP *n* a high-level computer programming language suitable for work in artificial intelligence ▶ **HISTORY** *lis(t) p(rocessing)*

lissom *or* **lissome** *adj* slim and graceful and agile in movement ▶ **HISTORY** variant of *lithesome*, from *lithe* + *-some* of a specific nature

list¹ *n* **1** an item-by-item record of names or things, usually written one below the other ▷ *vb* **2** to make a list of **3** to include in a list ▶ **HISTORY** Old English *liste*

list² *vb* **1** (esp. of ships) to lean to one side ▷ *n* **2** a leaning to one side: *to speak a list to starboard* ▶ **HISTORY** origin unknown

listed building *n* (in Britain and Australia) a building protected from demolition or alteration because of its special historical or architectural interest

listen *vb* **1** to concentrate on hearing something **2** to take heed or pay attention: *listen, let me explain* ▶ **HISTORY** Old English *hlysnan* > **listener** *n*

listen in *vb* (often foll. by *on* or *to*) to listen secretly to; eavesdrop

listeriosis *n* a serious form of food poisoning, caused by bacteria of the genus *Listeria* ▶ **HISTORY** after Joseph Lister, surgeon

listing *n* **1** a list or an entry in a list **2 listings** lists of films, concerts, etc printed in newspapers and magazines, and showing details such as times and venues

listless *adj* lacking interest or energy ▶ **HISTORY** obsolete *list* desire > **listlessly** *adv*

list price *n* the selling price of merchandise as quoted in a catalogue or advertisement

lists *pl n* **1** *history* the enclosed field of combat at a tournament **2 enter the lists** to engage in a conflict or controversy ▶ **HISTORY** plural of Old English *liste* border

lit *vb* a past of **light¹ light²**

litany *n, pl* **-nies** **1** *Christianity* a prayer consisting of a series of invocations, each followed by the same

little

Depending on what you are describing, you can choose from any of the following alternatives instead of the overused word **little**.

DEFINITION 1

- If you are describing an object or the physical size of something, you could try: **dainty** sandwiches and cakes • **dwarf** tulips • a **mini** laptop • **miniature** toy boats • **minute** particles of soil • **pygmy** goats • a **skimpy** bikini

• a **small** table • **tiny** pieces • a **wee** bit of cake

- If you are describing someone's height, you could try: **dainty** Japanese girl • his **diminutive** stature • **petite** women • too **short** • a short, **squat** figure • a **tiny** woman • a **wee** guy

DEFINITION 2

- If you are describing someone's age, you could try: my **baby** sister • her **infant** son • two **small** kids • a **young** child

---

response **2** any tedious recital: *a litany of complaints* ▶ HISTORY Late Greek *litaneia* prayer

litchi *n* same as **lychee**

liter *n US* same as **litre**

literacy *n* **1** the ability to read and write **2** the ability to use language effectively

literal *adj* **1** in exact accordance with the explicit meaning of a word or text **2** word for word: *a literal translation* **3** dull or unimaginative: *she's very, very literal and flat in how she interprets what she sees* **4** true; actual ▷ *n* **5** a misprint or misspelling in a text ▶ HISTORY Latin *littera* letter > **literally** *adv*

literalism *n* the tendency to take words and statements in their literal sense > **literalist** *n*

literary *adj* **1** of or characteristic of literature: *literary criticism* **2** knowledgeable about literature **3** (of a word) used chiefly in written work; not colloquial ▶ HISTORY Latin *litterarius* concerning reading and writing > **literariness** *n*

literary canon *n literature* a set of works that are considered to be important and of great literary value: *the most sublime works of the English literary canon*

literary theory *n literature* a collective term for the many different innovative approaches to studying and analysing texts which have been advanced over the years

literate *adj* **1** able to read and write **2** educated ▷ *n* **3** a literate person ▶ HISTORY Latin *litteratus* learned

literati *pl n* literary or scholarly people ▶ HISTORY Latin

literature *n* **1** written material such as poetry, novels, or essays **2** the body of written work of a particular culture, country, or era: *Elizabethan literature* **3** written or printed matter of a particular type or genre: *medical literature* **4** the art or profession of a writer **5** *informal* printed matter on any subject ▶ HISTORY Latin *litteratura* writing

lithe *adj* attractively graceful and supple in movement ▶ HISTORY Old English *līthe* (in the sense: gentle; later: supple)

lithium *n chem* a soft silvery element of the alkali metal series: the lightest known metal. Symbol: Li ▶ HISTORY Greek *lithos* stone

litho *n, pl* **-thos** *adj, adv* short for **lithography, lithograph, lithographic, lithographically**

lithograph *n* **1** a print made by lithography ▷ *vb* **2** to reproduce (pictures or text) by lithography > **lithographic** *adj* > **lithographically** *adv*

lithography (lith-**og**-ra-fee) *n* a method of printing from a metal or stone surface on which the printing areas are made ink-receptive ▶ HISTORY Greek *lithos* stone + *graphein* to write > **lithographer** *n*

lithosphere *n geol* the rigid outer layer of the earth, comprising the earth's crust and the solid upper part of the mantle. Compare **asthenosphere**

Lithuanian *adj* **1** from Lithuania ▷ *n* **2** a person from Lithuania **3** the language of Lithuania

litigant *n* a person involved in a lawsuit

litigate *vb* **-gating, -gated 1** to bring or contest a lawsuit **2** to engage in legal proceedings ▶ HISTORY Latin *lis, lit-* lawsuit + *agere* to carry on > **litigator** *n*

litigation *n* the process of bringing or contesting a lawsuit

litigious (lit-**ij**-uss) *adj* frequently going to law

litmus *n* a soluble powder obtained from lichens, which is turned red by acids and blue by alkalis. Paper treated with it (**litmus paper**) is used as an indicator in chemistry ▶ HISTORY perhaps Scandinavian

litmus test *n* something that is regarded as a simple and accurate test of a particular thing, such as a person's attitude to an issue

litotes *n, pl* **-tes** *literature* understatement used for effect, for example 'She was not a little upset', meaning 'She was extremely upset' ▶ HISTORY Greek *litos* small

litre *or US* **liter** *n* a measure of volume equivalent to 1 cubic decimetre ▶ HISTORY Greek *litra* a unit of weight

litter *n* **1** small items of rubbish carelessly dropped in public places **2** a disordered or untidy collection of objects **3** a group of animals produced at one birth **4** straw or hay used as bedding for animals **5** dry material used to line a receptacle in which a domestic cat can urinate and defecate **6** (esp. formerly) a bed or seat held between parallel poles and used for carrying people ▷ *vb* **7** to strew with litter **8** to scatter or be scattered in an untidy fashion **9** (of animals) to give birth to offspring

10 to provide (an animal) with straw or hay for bedding ▸ HISTORY Latin *lectus* bed

little *adj* **1** of small or less than average size **2** young: *a little boy* **3** endearingly familiar: *he was a sweet little man* **4** contemptible, mean, or disagreeable: *she's got one of her horrible little friends to stay* **5** a small quantity, extent, or duration of: *there was little money circulating; I could see little evidence of it* ▷ *adv* **6** (usually preceded by *a*) to a small extent or degree; not a lot: *to sleep a little* **7** not at all, or hardly: *army life varied little as the years passed* **8** not much or often: *we go there very little now* **9 little by little** by small degrees ▷ *n* **10 make little of** to treat as insignificant: *one episode in their history is made little of in the guide books* **11 think little of** to have a low opinion of ▷ See also **less, lesser, least** ▸ HISTORY Old English *lȳtel*. See WORD FOCUS **little**

little people *pl n folklore* small supernatural beings, such as elves

littoral *adj* **1** of or by the shore ▷ *n* **2** a coastal region ▸ HISTORY Latin *litus* shore

liturgy *n, pl* **-gies** the forms of public services officially prescribed by a Church ▸ HISTORY Greek *leitourgia* > **liturgical** *adj*

live¹ *vb* **living, lived** **1** to show the characteristics of life; be alive **2** to remain alive or in existence **3** to exist in a specified way: *to live at ease* **4** to have one's home: *he went to live in Switzerland* **5** to continue or last: *his childhood had always lived inside him* **6** (foll. by *on, upon* or *by*) to support one's style of life: *forest dwellers who live by extracting rubber* **7** (foll. by *with*) to endure the effects (of a crime or mistake); tolerate **8** to pass or spend (one's life) **9** to enjoy life to the full: *he's the kind of person who knows how to live* **10** to put into practice in one's daily life: *the freedom to live his own life as he chooses* **11 live and let live** to be tolerant ▷ See also **live down** ▸ HISTORY Old English *libban, lifian*

live² *adj* **1** alive; living **2** *radio, television* transmitted at the time of performance, rather than being prerecorded: *a live broadcast* **3** actual: *I was able to speak to a real live Hurricane pilot* **4** (of a recording) recorded during a performance **5** connected to a source of electric power: *a live cable* **6** of current interest; controversial: *the document has become a live political issue* **7** loaded or capable of exploding: *a live firing exercise using a mortar cannon* **8** (of a coal or ember) glowing or burning ▷ *adv* **9** during, at, or in the form of a live performance ▸ HISTORY shortened from *on live* alive

live down *vb* to withstand people's reactions to a crime or mistake until they forget it

livelihood *n* one's job or other source of income

livelong (**liv**-long) *adj chiefly poetic* long or seemingly long: *all the livelong day*

lively *adj* **-lier, -liest** **1** full of life or vigour **2** vivacious or animated **3** vivid > **liveliness** *n*

liver¹ *n* **1** a large glandular organ which secretes bile, balances nutrients, and removes certain poisons from the body **2** the liver of certain animals used as food ▸ HISTORY Old English *lifer*

liver² *n* a person who lives in a specified way: *a fast liver*

liveried *adj* wearing livery

liverish *adj* **1** *informal* having a disorder of the liver **2** feeling disagreeable and slightly irritable

Liverpudlian *adj* **1** of Liverpool, a city in NW England ▷ *n* **2** a person from Liverpool

liverwort *n* a plant growing in wet places and resembling green seaweeds or leafy mosses ▸ HISTORY late Old English *liferwyrt*

livery *n, pl* **-eries** **1** the identifying uniform of a servant **2** distinctive dress or outward appearance **3** the stabling, keeping, or hiring out of horses for money ▸ HISTORY Old French *livrée* allocation

lives *n* the plural of **life**

livestock *n* animals kept on a farm

live together *vb* (of an unmarried couple) to live in the same house; cohabit

live up to *vb* to fulfil (an expectation, obligation, or principle)

live wire *n* **1** *informal* an energetic person **2** a wire carrying an electric current

livid *adj* **1** *informal* extremely angry **2** of a dark grey or purple colour: *livid bruises* ▸ HISTORY Latin *livere* to be black and blue

living *adj* **1** possessing life; not dead or inanimate **2** currently in use or valid: *a living alliance* **3** seeming to be real: *a living doll* **4** (of people or animals) existing in the present age **5** very: *the living image* **6** of or like everyday life: *living costs* **7** of or involving those now alive: *one of our greatest living actors* ▷ *n* **8** the condition of being alive **9** the manner of one's life: *high living* **10** one's financial means **11** *Church of England* a benefice

living room *n* a room in a private house or flat used for relaxation and entertainment

living wage *n* a wage adequate for a worker to live on and support a family in reasonable comfort

living will *n* a document that states that a person who becomes terminally ill does not want their life to be prolonged by artificial means

lizard *n* a reptile with an elongated body, four limbs, and a long tail ▸ HISTORY Latin *lacerta*

llama *n* a South American mammal of the camel family that is used as a beast of burden and is valued for its woolly fleece ▸ HISTORY from a Native American language

LLB Bachelor of Laws ▸ HISTORY Latin *Legum Baccalaureus*

LLD Doctor of Laws ▸ HISTORY Latin *Legum Doctor*

LLM Master of Laws ▸ HISTORY Latin *Legum Magister*

LNG liquefied natural gas

lo *interj old-fashioned* look! see!: *lo and behold!* ▸ HISTORY Old English *lā*

loa (**loh**-ah) *n, pl* **loa** or **loas** any of a number of spirits in the voodoo religion of Haiti

loach *n* a freshwater fish with a long narrow body and barbels around the mouth ▸ HISTORY Old French *loche*

load *n* **1** something to be borne or conveyed; weight **2** the amount borne or conveyed

3 something that weighs down or burdens: *I have enough of a load to carry right now* **4** *electronics* the power delivered by a machine, generator, or circuit **5** an external force applied to a component or mechanism **6 a load of** *informal* a quantity of: *a load of half-truths* **7 get a load of** *informal* to pay attention to ▷ *vb* **8** to place cargo or goods upon (a ship or vehicle) **9** to burden or oppress **10** to supply in abundance: *other treats are loaded with fat* **11** to cause to be biased: *the dice are loaded* **12** to put ammunition into (a firearm) **13** *photog* to insert film in (a camera) **14** to weight or bias (a roulette wheel or dice) **15** *computers* to transfer (a program) to a memory ▷ See also **loads ▶ HISTORY** Old English *lād* course; in meaning, influenced by LADE > **loader** *n*

loaded *adj* **1** carrying a load **2** charged with ammunition **3** (of a question or statement) containing a hidden trap or implication **4** (of dice or a roulette wheel) weighted or otherwise biased **5** *slang* wealthy **6** *slang, chiefly US & Canad* drunk

loads *pl n informal* (often foll. by *of*) a lot

loadstar *n* same as **lodestar**

loadstone *n* same as **lodestone**

loaf¹ *n, pl* **loaves 1** a shaped mass of baked bread **2** any shaped or moulded mass of food, such as cooked meat **3** *slang* the head; common sense: *use your loaf!* **▶ HISTORY** Old English *hlāf*

loaf² *vb* to loiter or lounge around in an idle way **▶ HISTORY** perhaps from *loafer*

loafer *n* **1** a person who avoids work; idler **2** a moccasin-like shoe **▶ HISTORY** perhaps German *Landläufer* vagabond

loam *n* fertile soil consisting of sand, clay, and decaying organic material **▶ HISTORY** Old English *lām* > **loamy** *adj*

loan *n* **1** money lent at interest for a fixed period of time **2** the act of lending: *I am grateful to her for the loan of her book* **3** property lent **4 on loan** lent out; borrowed ▷ *vb* **5** to lend (something, esp. money) **▶ HISTORY** Old Norse *lān*

loan shark *n* a person who lends money at an extremely high interest rate, esp. illegally

loath *or* **loth** (rhymes with **both**) *adj* (usually foll. by *to*) reluctant or unwilling **▶ HISTORY** Old English *lāth* (in the sense: hostile)

loathe *vb* **loathing, loathed** to feel strong disgust for **▶ HISTORY** Old English *lāthiān*

loathing *n* strong disgust

loathsome *adj* causing loathing

loaves *n* the plural of **loaf¹**

lob *sport n* **1** a ball struck or bowled in a high arc ▷ *vb* **lobbing, lobbed 2** to hit or kick (a ball) in a high arc **3** *informal* to throw **▶ HISTORY** probably Low German

lobar (**loh**-ber) *adj* of or affecting a lobe

lobate *adj* with or like lobes

lobby *n, pl* **-bies 1** a room or corridor used as an entrance hall or vestibule **2** a group which attempts to influence legislators on behalf of a particular interest **3** *chiefly Brit* a hall in a legislative building used for meetings between legislators

and members of the public **4** *chiefly Brit* one of two corridors in a legislative building in which members vote ▷ *vb* **-bies, -bying, -bied 5** to attempt to influence (legislators) in the formulation of policy **▶ HISTORY** Old High German *lauba* arbor

lobbyist *n* a person who lobbies on behalf of a particular interest

lobe *n* **1** any rounded projection **2** the fleshy lower part of the external ear **3** any subdivision of a bodily organ **▶ HISTORY** Greek *lobos* lobe of the ear or of the liver

lobelia *n* a plant with blue, red, white, or yellow five-lobed flowers **▶ HISTORY** Matthias de *Lobel*, botanist

lobola *n* *S African* an African custom by which a bridegroom's family makes a payment in cattle or cash to the bride's family shortly before the marriage **▶ HISTORY** Nguni (language group of southern Africa) *ukulobola* to give bride price

lobotomy *n, pl* **-mies** the surgical cutting of nerves in the frontal lobe of the brain to treat severe mental disorders **▶ HISTORY** Greek *lobos* lobe + *tomē* a cutting

lobster *n, pl* **-sters** *or* **-ster 1** a large edible crustacean with large pincers and a long tail, which turns red when boiled **2** its edible flesh **▶ HISTORY** Old English *loppestre*, from *loppe* spider

lobster pot *n* a round basket made of open slats, used to catch lobsters

lobule *n* a small lobe

local *adj* **1** of or concerning a particular area **2** restricted to a particular place **3** *med* of, affecting, or confined to a limited area or part: *a local anaesthetic* **4** (of a train or bus) stopping at all stations or stops ▷ *n* **5** an inhabitant of a particular locality: *we swim, sunbathe, meet the locals, unwind* **6** *Brit, informal* a pub close to one's home **▶ HISTORY** Latin *locus* place > **locally** *adv*

local anaesthetic *n* *med* See **anaesthesia**

local authority *n* the governing body of a county, district, or region

locale (loh-**kahl**) *n* the place where something happens or has happened **▶ HISTORY** French, from Latin *locus* place

local government *n* the government of the affairs of counties, towns, and districts by locally elected political bodies

locality *n, pl* **-ties 1** a neighbourhood or area **2** the site or scene of an event

localize *or* **-ise** *vb* **-izing, -ized** *or* **-ising, -ised** to restrict (something) to a particular place

local relief *n* *geog* the difference between the highest and lowest land levels in a given area

locate *vb* **-cating, -cated 1** to discover the whereabouts of; find **2** to situate or build: *located around the corner from the church* **3** to become established or settled

location *n* **1** a site or position; situation **2** the act of locating or the state of being located: *make their location and rescue a top priority* **3** a place outside a studio where filming is done: *shot on location*

I

4 (in South Africa) a Black African or Coloured township ▶ HISTORY Latin *locare* to place

loc. cit. (in textual annotation) in the place cited ▶ HISTORY Latin *loco citato*

loch *n Scot* **1** a lake **2** a long narrow arm of the sea ▶ HISTORY Gaelic

loci (loh-sigh) *n* the plural of **locus**

lock¹ *n* **1** a device for fastening a door, drawer, lid, etc. and preventing unauthorized access **2** a section of a canal or river closed off by gates between which the water level can be altered to aid boats moving from one level to the next **3** *Brit & NZ* the extent to which a vehicle's front wheels will turn: *they adopted more steering lock* **4** the interlocking of parts **5** a mechanism that fires a gun **6 lock, stock, and barrel** completely; entirely **7** a wrestling hold **8** Also called: **lock forward** *rugby* a player in the second row of the scrum ▷ *vb* **9** to fasten or become fastened to prevent entry or exit **10** to secure (a building) by locking all doors and windows **11** to fix or become fixed together securely **12** to become or cause to become immovable: *just before your knees lock* **13** to clasp or entangle in a struggle or embrace ▷ See also **lock up** ▶ HISTORY Old English *loc*

lock² *n* **1** a strand or curl of hair **2 locks** *chiefly literary* hair ▶ HISTORY Old English *loc*

locker *n* a small compartment with a lock, used for temporarily storing clothes, valuables, or luggage

locket *n* a small hinged ornamental pendant that holds a picture or keepsake ▶ HISTORY French *loquet* latch

lockjaw *n pathol* a nontechnical name for **trismus, tetanus**

locksmith *n* a person who makes or repairs locks

lock up *vb* **1** to imprison **2** to secure a building by locking all the doors and windows ▷ *n* **lockup 3** a jail **4** *Brit* a garage or store separate from the main premises **5** *Brit* a small shop with no attached quarters for the owner ▷ *adj* **lock-up 6** *Brit & NZ* (of premises) without living quarters: *a lock-up garage*

loco¹ *n, pl* **locos** *informal* a locomotive

loco² *adj slang, chiefly US* insane ▶ HISTORY Spanish: crazy

locomotion *n* the act or power of moving ▶ HISTORY Latin *loco* from a place + MOTION

locomotive *n* **1** a self-propelled engine for pulling trains ▷ *adj* **2** of locomotion

locomotor *adj* of or relating to locomotion: *locomotor skills*

locule *or* **loculus** *n, pl* **locules** *or* **loculi** *biol* **1** any of the chambers of an ovary or anther **2** any small hollow space or chamber

locum *n* a person who stands in temporarily for a doctor or member of the clergy ▶ HISTORY Medieval Latin *locum tenens* (someone) holding the place (of another)

locus (loh-kuss) *n, pl* **loci 1** an area or place where something happens **2** *maths* a set of points or lines whose location satisfies or is determined by one or more specified conditions: *the locus of points*

equidistant from a given point is a circle ▶ HISTORY Latin

locus standi *n law* the right of a party to appear and be heard before a court ▶ HISTORY Latin: a place for standing

locust *n* **1** an African insect, related to the grasshopper, which travels in vast swarms, stripping large areas of vegetation **2** a North American leguminous tree with prickly branches; the carob tree ▶ HISTORY Latin *locusta*

lode *n* a vein of metallic ore ▶ HISTORY Old English *lād* course

lodestar *n* **1** a star, esp. the North Star, used in navigation or astronomy as a point of reference **2** something that serves as a guide

lodestone *n* **1 a** magnetic iron ore **b** a piece of this, used as a magnet **2** a person or thing regarded as a focus of attraction

lodge *n* **1** *chiefly Brit* the gatekeeper's house at the entrance to the grounds of a country mansion **2** a house or cabin used occasionally by hunters, skiers, etc.: *a hunting lodge* **3** *chiefly Brit* a room used by porters in a university or college **4** a local branch of certain societies **5** a beaver's home ▷ *vb* **lodging, lodged 6** to provide or be provided with rented accommodation **7** to live temporarily in rented accommodation **8** to embed or be embedded: *the bullet lodged in his brain* **9** to leave for safety or storage: *a report was lodged with the local police station* **10** to bring (a charge or accusation) against someone: *the Brazilians lodged a complaint* **11** (often foll. by *in* or *with*) to place (authority or power) in the control (of someone) ▶ HISTORY Old French *loge*

lodger *n* a person who pays rent in return for accommodation in someone else's home

lodging *n* **1** a temporary residence: *where might I find a night's lodging?* **2 lodgings** a rented room or rooms in another person's home

loess (loh-iss) *n* a fine-grained soil, found mainly in river valleys, originally deposited by the wind ▶ HISTORY Swiss German *lösch* loose

loft *n* **1** the space inside a roof **2** a gallery in a church **3** a room over a stable used to store hay **4** a raised house or coop in which pigeons are kept **5** *golf* **a** the angle of the face of the club used to elevate a ball **b** the height reached by a struck ball ▷ *vb* **6** *sport* to strike or kick (a ball) high in the air ▶ HISTORY Old Norse *lopt* air, ceiling

lofty *adj* **loftier, loftiest 1** of majestic or imposing height **2** morally admirable: *lofty ideals* **3** unpleasantly superior: *a lofty contempt* > **loftily** *adv* > **loftiness** *n*

log¹ *n* **1** a section of a felled tree stripped of branches **2 a** a detailed record of a voyage of a ship or aircraft **b** a record of the hours flown by pilots and aircrews **c** a book in which these records are made; logbook **3** a device consisting of a float with an attached line, formerly used to measure the speed of a ship **4 sleep like a log** to sleep without stirring ▷ *vb* **logging, logged 5** to saw logs from (trees) **6** to enter (a distance or event) in a logbook 489 or log ▷ See also **log in, log out** ▶ HISTORY origin unknown

log² n short for **logarithm**

loganberry n, pl **-ries** a purplish-red fruit, similar to a raspberry, that grows on a trailing prickly plant ▶ HISTORY after J. H. *Logan*, who first grew it

logarithm n the exponent indicating the power to which a fixed number, the base, must be raised to obtain a given number or variable ▶ HISTORY Greek *logos* ratio + *arithmos* number > **logarithmic** adj

logbook n **1** a book containing the official record of trips made by a ship or aircraft **2** *Brit, informal* the registration document of a car

loggerhead n **1** a large-headed turtle occurring in most seas **2 at loggerheads** engaged in dispute or confrontation ▶ HISTORY probably dialect *logger* wooden block + HEAD

loggia (**loj**-ya) n a covered gallery on the side of a building ▶ HISTORY Italian

logging n the work of felling, trimming, and transporting timber > **logger** n

logic n **1** the branch of philosophy that analyses the patterns of reasoning **2** a particular system of reasoning **3** reasoned thought or argument, as distinguished from irrationality **4** the interdependence of a series of events or facts **5** *electronics, computers* the principles underlying the units in a computer system that produce results from data ▶ HISTORY Greek *logikos* concerning speech or reasoning

logical adj **1** relating to or characteristic of logic **2** using or deduced from the principles of logic: *a logical conclusion* **3** capable of or using clear and valid reasoning **4** reasonable because of facts or events: *the logical choice* > **logically** adv

logical relations pl n (in language) the logical linking of ideas and arguments by means of connectives such as *and, but, because,* and *therefore*

logic gate n *electronics* same as **gate** (sense 4)

logician n a person who specializes in or is skilled at logic

log in or **on** vb to gain entrance to a computer system by keying in a special command

logistics n the detailed planning and organization of a large complex operation, such as a military campaign ▶ HISTORY French *loger* to lodge > **logistical** or **logistic** adj > **logistically** adv

log jam n *chiefly US & Canad* **1** a blockage caused by the crowding together of logs floating in a river **2** a deadlock

logo (**loh**-go) n, pl **logos** a special design that identifies a company or an organization and appears on all its products, printed material, etc. ▶ HISTORY shortened from *logotype* badge, symbol

log out or **off** vb to exit from a computer system by keying in a special command

-logy n combining form **1** indicating the science or study of: *musicology* **2** indicating writing or discourse: *trilogy; phraseology* ▶ HISTORY Greek *logos* word > **-logical** or **-logic** adj combining form > **-logist** n combining form

loin n **1** the part of the body between the pelvis and the ribs **2** a cut of meat from this part of an animal ▷ See also **loins** ▶ HISTORY Old French *loigne*

loincloth n a piece of cloth covering only the loins

loins pl n **1** the hips and the inner surface of the legs where they join the body **2** *euphemistic* the genitals

loiter vb to stand or wait aimlessly or idly ▶ HISTORY perhaps Middle Dutch *lōteren* to wobble

loll vb **1** to lounge in a lazy manner **2** to hang loosely: *a wet lolling tongue; his head lolled back and forth* ▶ HISTORY perhaps imitative

lollipop n **1** a boiled sweet stuck on a small wooden stick **2** *Brit* an ice lolly ▶ HISTORY perhaps dialect *lolly* the tongue + POP²

lollipop man or **lady** n *Brit, informal* a person holding a circular sign on a pole who stops traffic to enable children to cross the road safely

lollop vb *chiefly Brit* to walk or run with a clumsy or relaxed bouncing movement ▶ HISTORY probably *loll* + *-op*, as in *gallop*

lolly n, pl **-lies** **1** *informal* a lollipop **2** *Brit* short for **ice lolly** **3** *Brit, Austral & NZ, slang* money **4** *Austral & NZ, informal* a sweet ▶ HISTORY shortened from *lollipop*

Londoner n a person from London

London pride n a rock plant with a rosette of leaves and pink flowers

lone adj **1** solitary: *a lone figure* **2** isolated: *a lone isle guarded by the great Atlantic swell* **3** *Brit* unmarried or widowed: *a lone parent* ▶ HISTORY from the mistaken division of *alone* into *a lone*

lonely adj **-lier, -liest** **1** unhappy as a result of solitude **2** resulting from the state of being alone: *command can be a lonely business* **3** isolated and not much visited by people: *a lonely beach* > **loneliness** n

loner n *informal* a person who prefers to be alone

lonesome adj **1** *chiefly US & Canad* lonely **2** causing feelings of loneliness: *it was lonesome up here on the mountain*

long¹ adj **1** having relatively great length in space or time **2** having greater than the average or expected range, extent, or duration: *a long session of talks* **3** seeming to occupy a greater time than is really so: *she was quiet a long moment* **4** of a specified extent or duration: *trimmed to about 2 cm long* **5** consisting of a large number of parts: *a long list* **6** *phonetics, prosody* (of a vowel) of relatively considerable duration **7** from end to end; lengthwise **8** *finance* having large holdings of securities or commodities in anticipation of rising prices **9 in the long run** ultimately; after or over a period of time **10 long on** *informal* plentifully supplied or endowed with: *long on show-biz gossip* ▷ adv **11** for a certain time or period: *how long have we got?* **12** for or during an extensive period of time: *to talk long into the night* **13** a considerable amount of time: *long after I met you;*

long ago **14 as** or **so long as a** for or during the same length of time that
b provided that; if ▷ *n* **15** anything that is long **16 before long** soon **17 for long** for a long time **18 the long and the short of it** the essential points or facts ▶ HISTORY Old English *lang* > **longish** *adj*

long² *vb* to have a strong desire for something or to do something: *I longed for a baby; the more I think of him the more I long to see him* ▶ HISTORY Old English *langian*

long. longitude

longboat *n* **1** the largest boat carried aboard a commercial ship **2** same as **longship**

longbow *n* a large powerful hand-drawn bow

long-distance *adj* **1** covering relatively long distances: *a long-distance race* **2** (of telephone calls) connecting points relatively far apart

longevity (lon-**jev**-it-ee) *n* long life ▶ HISTORY Latin *longus* long + *aevum* age

long face *n* a glum expression

longhand *n* ordinary handwriting, as opposed to typing or shorthand

longhorn *n* a British breed of beef cattle with long curved horns

longing *n* **1** a strong feeling of wanting something one is unlikely ever to have ▷ *adj* **2** having or showing desire: *longing glances* > **longingly** *adv*

longitude *n* distance in degrees east or west of the prime meridian at 0° ▶ HISTORY Latin *longitudo* length

longitudinal *adj* **1** of longitude or length **2** placed or extended lengthways

longitudinal dune *n geog* a long dune lying parallel to the direction of the prevailing wind

longitudinal wave *n physics* a wave that is propagated in the same direction as the displacement of the transmitting medium

long johns *pl n informal* long underpants

long jump *n* an athletic contest of jumping the greatest length from a fixed mark

long-life *adj* (of milk, batteries, etc.) lasting longer than the regular kind

long-lived *adj* living or lasting for a long time

long-playing *adj old-fashioned* of or relating to an LP

long-range *adj* **1** of or extending into the future: *a long-range economic forecast* **2** (of vehicles, aircraft, or weapons) capable of covering great distances

longship *n* a narrow open boat with oars and a square sail, used by the Vikings

longshore drift *n* the movement of material along a beach, due to waves approaching the shore at an oblique angle

longshoreman *n, pl* **-men** *US & Canad* a docker

long shot *n* **1** an undertaking, guess, or possibility with little chance of success **2** a bet against heavy odds **3 not by a long shot** not by any means: *she wasn't beaten, not by a long shot*

long-sighted *adj* **1** able to see only distant objects in focus **2** far-sighted

long-standing *adj* existing for a long time

long-suffering *adj* enduring trouble or unhappiness without complaint

long-term *adj* **1** lasting or extending over a long time: *a long-term commitment* ▷ *n* **long term 2 in the long term** over a long period of time: *in the long term the cost of energy will have to go up*

long wave *n* a radio wave with a wavelength greater than 1000 metres

longways or *US & Canad* **longwise** *adv* lengthways

long-winded *adj* tiresomely long > **long-windedness** *n*

loo *n, pl* **loos** *Brit & NZ, informal* a toilet ▶ HISTORY perhaps from French *lieu d'aisance* water closet

loofah *n* a long rough-textured bath sponge made from the dried pod of a gourd ▶ HISTORY Arabic *lūf*

look *vb* **1** (often foll. by *at*) to direct the eyes (towards): *he turned to look at her* **2** (often foll. by *at*) to consider: *we shall now look at some problems* **3** to give the impression of being; seem: *Luxembourg's timetable looks a winner* **4** to face in a particular direction: *Morgan's Rock looks south* **5** (foll. by *for*) to search or seek: *the department looks for reputable firms* **6** (foll. by *into*) to carry out an investigation **7** to direct a look at (someone) in a specified way: *she looks at Teresina suspiciously* **8** to match in appearance with (something): *looking your best* **9** to expect or hope (to do something): *we would look to derive a procedure that would account for most cases* **10 look alive** or **lively** or **sharp** or **smart** to hurry up; get busy **11 look here** an expression used to attract someone's attention or add emphasis to a statement ▷ *n* **12** an instance of looking: *a look of icy contempt* **13** a view or sight (of something): *take a look at my view* **14** (often *pl*) appearance to the eye or mind; aspect: *I'm not happy with the look of things here; better than you by the looks of it* **15** style or fashion: *the look made famous by the great Russian* ▷ *conj* **16** an expression demanding attention or showing annoyance: *look, I won't be coming back* ▷ See also **look after** ▶ HISTORY Old English *lōcian* > **looker** *n*
See WORD FOCUS **look** on page 492

look after *vb* to take care of

lookalike *n* a person or thing that is the double of another, often well-known, person or thing

look forward to *vb* to anticipate with pleasure

look-in *informal n* **1** a chance to be chosen or participate: *before anyone else gets a look-in* ▷ *vb* **look in 2** to pay a short visit

looking glass *n* a mirror

look on *vb* **1** to be a spectator **2** to consider or regard: *I just looked on her as a friend* > **looker-on** *n*

lookout *n* **1** the act of watching for danger or for an opportunity: *on the lookout for attack* **2** a person or people keeping such a watch **3** a viewpoint from which a watch is kept **4** *informal* worry or concern: *that is my lookout rather than theirs* **5** *chiefly Brit* chances or prospect: *it's a bad lookout for Europe* ▷ *vb* **look out 6** to be careful **7** to watch out for: *look out particularly for oils that have been flavoured* **8** to find and take out: *little time to look out clothes*

look

All of the following words mean to **look**, but each one has an extra shade of meaning which makes it a more expressive substitute for the word **look** in particular situations or contexts.

DEFINITION 1

- If you **glance**, **peek**, or **peep** at something, you look at it quickly, and often secretly: He **glanced** at his watch as she spoke. • She **peeked** at him through the curtains. • He **peeped** at me to see if I was watching him.
- If you **scan** something written or printed, you look at it quickly: She **scanned** the advertisement pages of the newspapers.
- If you **eye** or **regard** someone or something, you look at them carefully: The waiters **eyed** him with suspicion. • He **regarded** me curiously.
- If you **gaze** or **stare** at someone or something, you look at them steadily for a long time, for example because you find them interesting or because you are thinking about something else. **Staring** is often thought to be rude, but **gazing** is not: She sat **gazing** into the fire for a long time. • They **stared** silently into each other's eyes.
- If you **observe** or **watch** someone or something, you look at them for a period of time to see what they are doing or what is happening: A man was **observing** him from across the square. • I hate people **watching** me while I eat.

- If you **survey** or **view** someone or something, you look at the whole of them carefully: He stood up and **surveyed** the crowd. • The guests went to **view** the presents, which were set out on a table.
- If you **examine**, **scrutinize**, or **study** something, you look at it very carefully, often to find out information from it: He **examined** the document carefully. • He **scrutinized** her passport and stamped it. • We **studied** the menu for several minutes.
- If you **glare**, **glower**, or **scowl** at someone, you stare at them angrily: He **glared** resentfully at me. • She stood **glowering** at me with her arms crossed. • She **scowled** at the two men as they came into the room.
- If you **peer** or **squint** at something, you try to see it more clearly by narrowing or screwing up your eyes as you look at it: He was **peering** at me through the keyhole. • She **squinted** at the whiteboard, trying to read what was on it.
- If you **gape** at someone or something, you look at them in surprise, usually with your mouth open: She was **gaping** at the wreckage, lost for words.
- If you **goggle** at someone or something, you look at them with your eyes wide open, usually because you are surprised by them: He **goggled** at me in disbelief.

---

that she might need **9** (foll. by *on* or *over*) to face in a particular direction: *looking out over the courtyard* **look up** *vb* **1** to discover or confirm by checking in a reference book **2** to improve: *things were looking up* **3 look up to** to have respect for: *she looked up to him as a kind of father* **4** to visit (a person): *I'll look you up when I'm in town*

loom¹ *n* a machine for weaving yarn into cloth ▶ HISTORY variant of Old English *gelōma* tool

loom² *vb* **1** to appear indistinctly, esp. as a tall and threatening shape **2** (of an event) to seem ominously close ▶ HISTORY perhaps East Frisian *lomen* to move slowly

loon¹ *n US & Canad* same as **diver** (sense 3) ▶ HISTORY Scandinavian

loon² *n informal* a simple-minded or stupid person

loony *slang adj* **loonier**, **looniest** **1** insane **2** foolish or ridiculous ▷ *n*, *pl* **loonies** **3** a foolish or insane person ▶ HISTORY shortened from *lunatic*

loop *n* **1** the rounded shape formed by a curved line that crosses itself: *a loop of the highway* **2** any round or oval-shaped thing that is closed or nearly closed **3** *electronics* a closed circuit through which a signal can circulate **4** a flight manoeuvre in which an aircraft flies vertically in a complete circle **5** a continuous strip of film or tape **6** *computers* a series of instructions in a program, performed repeatedly

until some specified condition is satisfied ▷ *vb* **7** to make into a loop **8** to fasten or encircle with a loop **9** Also: **loop the loop** to fly or be flown vertically in a complete circle ▶ HISTORY origin unknown

loophole *n* an ambiguity or omission in the law, which enables one to evade it

loose *adj* **1** (of clothing) not close-fitting: *the jacket loose and unbuttoned* **2** free or released from confinement or restraint **3** not tight, fastened, fixed, or tense **4** not bundled, fastened, or put in a container: *loose tobacco* **5** inexact or imprecise: *a loose translation* **6** (of cash) accessible: *a lot of the loose money is floating around the city* **7** old-fashioned sexually promiscuous **8** lacking a sense of propriety: *loose talk* **9 at a loose end** bored because one has nothing to do ▷ *n* **10 the loose** *rugby* the part of play when the forwards close round the ball in a ruck or loose scrum **11 on the loose** free from confinement or restraint ▷ *adv* **12** in a loose manner; loosely ▷ *vb* **loosing**, **loosed** **13** to free or release from restraint or obligation: *he loosed the dogs* **14** to unfasten or untie: *the guards loosed his arms* **15** to make or become less strict, tight, firmly attached, or compact **16** to let fly (a bullet, arrow, or other missile) ▶ HISTORY Old Norse *lauss* free > **loosely** *adv* > **looseness** *n*

loosebox *n* an enclosed stall with a door in which an animal can be kept

loose-leaf *adj* (of a binder) allowing the removal and addition of pages

loosen *vb* **1** to make or become less tight: *loosen and relax the ankle* **2** (often foll. by *up*) to make or become less firm, compact, or rigid: *massage is used first to loosen up the muscles* **3** to untie **4** (often foll. by *up*) to make or become less strict: *the finance minister loosened up financial controls*

loot *n* **1** goods stolen in wartime or during riots; plunder **2** *informal* money ▷ *vb* **3** to plunder (a city) during war or riots **4** to steal (money or goods) during war or riots ▶ HISTORY Hindi *lūt* > **looter** *n*

lop *vb* **lopping, lopped** (usually foll. by *off*) **1** to cut (parts) off a tree or body **2** to cut out or eliminate any unnecessary parts: *some parts of the legislature were lopped off* ▶ HISTORY Middle English *loppe* branches cut off

lope *vb* **loping, loped 1** to move or run with a long easy stride ▷ *n* **2** a long steady gait or stride ▶ HISTORY Old Norse *hlaupa* to leap

lop-eared *adj* (of animals) having ears that droop

lopsided *adj* greater in weight, height, or size on one side

loquacious *adj* talkative ▶ HISTORY Latin *loqui* to speak > **loquacity** *n*

lord *n* **1** a person with power or authority over others, such as a monarch or master **2** a male member of the nobility **3** (in medieval Europe) a feudal superior **4 my lord** a respectful form of address used to a judge, bishop, or nobleman ▷ *vb* **5 lord it over someone** to act in a superior manner towards someone ▶ HISTORY Old English *hlāford* bread keeper

Lord *n* **1** *Christianity* a title given to God or Jesus Christ **2** *Brit* a title given to certain male peers **3** *Brit* a title given to certain high officials and judges ▷ *interj* **4** an exclamation of dismay or surprise: *Good Lord!*

Lord Chancellor *n* *Brit government* the cabinet minister who is head of the judiciary and Speaker of the House of Lords

Lord Lieutenant *n* **1** (in Britain) the representative of the Crown in a county **2** (formerly) the British viceroy in Ireland

lordly *adj* **-lier, -liest 1** haughty or arrogant **2** of or suitable to a lord > **lordliness** *n*

Lord Mayor *n* the mayor in the City of London, in certain other English boroughs, and in some Australian cities

Lord Privy Seal *n* (in Britain) the senior cabinet minister without official duties

Lords *n* **the Lords** short for **House of Lords**

lordship *n* the position or authority of a lord

Lordship *n* (preceded by *Your* or *His*) *Brit* a title used to address or refer to a bishop, a judge of the high court, or any peer except a duke

Lord's Prayer *n* **the Lord's Prayer** the prayer taught by Jesus Christ to his disciples

Lords Spiritual *pl n* (in Britain) the Anglican archbishops and senior bishops who are members of the House of Lords

Lord's Supper *n* **the Lord's Supper** same as **Holy Communion**

Lords Temporal *pl n* (in Britain) the peers other than bishops in their capacity as members of the House of Lords

lore *n* collective knowledge or wisdom on a particular subject ▶ HISTORY Old English *lār*

lorgnette (lor-**nyet**) *n* a pair of spectacles or opera glasses mounted on a long handle ▶ HISTORY French, from *lorgner* to squint

lorikeet *n* a small brightly coloured Australian parrot

lorry *n*, *pl* **-ries** *Brit & S African* a large motor vehicle for transporting heavy loads ▶ HISTORY perhaps dialect *lurry* to pull

lose *vb* **losing, lost 1** to come to be without, through carelessness or by accident or theft **2** to fail to keep or maintain: *to lose control* **3** to suffer the loss of: *he will lose his redundancy money* **4** to get rid of: *I've lost a stone this summer* **5** to fail to get or make use of: *Lysenko never lost a chance to show his erudition* **6** to be defeated in a fight or competition **7** to fail to see, hear, or understand: *she lost sight of him* **8** to waste: *so I'd lost a fortune* **9** to go astray: *psychologists lose the trail* **10** to allow to go astray or out of sight: *he lost, at the Gare de Lyon, a case with most of his early manuscripts* **11** to cause the loss of: *I came in to have the gear attended to, which lost me a lap* **12** to absorb or engross: *lost in thought* **13** to die or cause the death of: *two lost as yacht sinks in storm* **14** to outdistance or escape from: *there's some satisfaction in knowing that they've lost us* **15** (of a timepiece) to run slow (by a specified amount) ▶ HISTORY Old English *losian* to perish

loser *n* **1** a person or thing that loses **2** *informal* a person or thing that seems destined to fail: *he's a bit of a loser*

loss *n* **1** the act or an instance of losing **2** the person, thing, or amount lost: *the only loss was a sleeping-bag* **3** the disadvantage or deprivation resulting from losing: *a loss of sovereignty* **4 at a loss a** uncertain what to do; bewildered **b** with income less than outlay: *they cannot afford to run branches at a loss* ▶ HISTORY Old English *lōsian* to be destroyed

loss leader *n* an article offered at a low price to attract customers

lost *vb* **1** the past of **lose** ▷ *adj* **2** unable to find one's way **3** unable to be found or recovered **4** confused or bewildered: *she seemed a bit lost* **5** (sometimes foll. by *on*) not used, noticed, or understood by: *not that the propaganda value of the game was lost on the authorities* **6** no longer possessed or existing: *lost credit* **7** (foll. by *in*) engrossed (in): *he remained lost in his own thoughts* **8** morally fallen: *a lost woman* **9** damned: *a lost soul*

lot *pron* **1 a lot** a great number or quantity: *not that there was a lot to tell; a lot of people* ▷ *n* **2** a collection of things or people: *your lot have wasted enough time* **3** destiny or fortune: *the refugees did not choose their lot* **4** any object, such as a straw or slip of paper, drawn from others at random to make a selection or choice: *they could only be split by the drawing of lots; the casting by lots* **5** the use of lots in making a choice: *chosen by lot* **6** an item or set of items for sale in an auction **7** *US, Canad, Austral & NZ* an area of land: *to the parking lot* **8 a bad lot** an unpleasant or disreputable person **9 cast** or **throw in one's lot with someone** to join with voluntarily and share the fortunes of someone **10 the lot** the entire amount or number ▷ *adv* **11** (preceded by *a*) *informal* to a considerable extent, degree, or amount: *steroids are used a lot in weightlifting* ▷ See also **lots** ▶ HISTORY Old English *hlot*

loth (rhymes with **both**) *adj* same as **loath**

lotion *n* a liquid preparation having a soothing, cleansing, or antiseptic action, applied to the skin ▶ HISTORY Latin *lotio* a washing

lots *informal pl n* **1** (often foll. by *of*) great numbers or quantities: *lots of friends; you can read lots into Nostradamus* ▷ *adv* **2** a great deal

lottery *n, pl* **-teries 1** a method of raising money by selling tickets by which a winner is selected at random **2** a venture whose outcome is a matter of luck: *hospital treatment is a lottery* ▶ HISTORY Middle Dutch *loterije*

lotto *n* **1** a game of chance similar to bingo **2 Lotto** *Brit, NZ & S African* national lottery ▶ HISTORY Italian

lotus *n* **1** (in Greek mythology) a fruit that induces dreamy forgetfulness in those who eat it **2** any of several water lilies of tropical Africa and Asia, regarded as sacred **3** a symbolic representation of such a plant ▶ HISTORY Greek *lōtos*

lotus position *n* a seated cross-legged position with each foot on top of the opposite thigh, used in yoga and meditation

loud *adj* **1** (of sound) relatively great in volume: *loud applause* **2** making or able to make sounds of relatively great volume: *a loud voice* **3** insistent and emphatic: *loud appeals* **4** (of colours or patterns) harsh to look at **5** noisy, vulgar, and offensive ▷ *adv* **6** in a loud manner **7 out loud** audibly ▶ HISTORY Old English *hlud* > **loudly** *adv* > **loudness** *n*

loud-hailer *n* a portable loudspeaker with a built-in amplifier and microphone

loudspeaker *n* a device for converting electrical signals into sounds

lough *n Irish* **1** a lake **2** a long narrow arm of the sea ▶ HISTORY Irish *loch* lake

lounge *n* **1** a living room in a private house **2** a communal room in a hotel, ship, or airport, used for waiting or relaxing in **3** the act of lounging ▷ *vb* **lounging, lounged 4** (often foll. by *about* or *around*) to sit or lie in a relaxed manner **5** to pass time lazily or idly ▶ HISTORY origin unknown

lounge suit *n* a man's suit for daytime wear

lour *vb* same as **lower²**

lourie (rhymes with **dowry**) or **loerie** *n* a type of African bird with either crimson or grey plumage ▶ HISTORY Afrikaans, from Malay

louse *n* **1** (*pl* **lice**) a wingless blood-sucking insect that feeds off man and some animals **2** (*pl* **louses**)

slang an unpleasant or dishonourable person ▶ HISTORY Old English *lūs*

lousy *adj* **lousier, lousiest 1** *slang* very mean or unpleasant **2** *slang* inferior or bad **3** *slang* ill or unwell **4** infested with lice

lout *n* a crude or oafish person; boor ▶ HISTORY perhaps Old English *lūtan* to stoop > **loutish** *adj*

louvre or *US* **louver** (**loo**-ver) *n* **a** any of a set of horizontal slats in a door or window, slanted to admit air but not rain **b** the slats and frame supporting them ▶ HISTORY Old French *lovier* > **louvred** or *US* **louvered** *adj*

lovage *n* a European herb with greenish-white flowers ▶ HISTORY Old French *luvesche*, from Latin *ligusticum*, literally: Ligurian (plant)

love *vb* **loving, loved 1** to have a great affection for a person or thing **2** to have passionate desire for someone **3** to like (to do something) very much ▷ *n* **4** an intense emotion of affection towards a person or thing **5** a deep feeling of romantic attraction **6** wholehearted liking for or pleasure in something **7** a beloved person: often used as an endearment **8** *Brit, informal* a commonplace term of address, not necessarily restricted to people one knows or has regard for **9** (in tennis, squash, etc.) a score of zero **10 fall in love** to become in love **11 for love or money** in any circumstances **12 in love** feeling a strong emotional and romantic attraction **13 make love to a** to have sexual intercourse with **b** *now archaic* to court ▶ HISTORY Old English *lufu* > **lovable** or **loveable** *adj*

love affair *n* a romantic relationship between two people

lovebird *n* any of several small African parrots often kept as cage birds

love child *n* euphemistic a child whose parents have not been married to each other

loveless *adj* without love: *a loveless marriage*

love-lies-bleeding *n* a plant with drooping spikes of small red flowers

love life *n* a person's romantic relationships

lovelorn *adj* miserable because of unreturned love or unhappiness in love

lovely *adj* **-lier, -liest 1** very attractive or beautiful **2** highly pleasing or enjoyable: *thanks for a lovely evening* ▷ *n, pl* **-lies 3** *slang* an attractive woman: *curvaceous lovelies* > **loveliness** *n*

lovemaking *n* **1** sexual play and activity **2** *archaic* courtship

lover *n* **1** (often *pl*) either of the people involved in a love affair **2** someone who loves a specified person or thing: *an animal lover*

loving *adj* feeling or showing love and affection > **lovingly** *adv*

low¹ *adj* **1** having a relatively small distance from base to top: *a low wall* **2** of less than usual amount, degree, quality, or cost: *low score; low inflation* **3** situated at a relatively short distance above the ground, sea level, or the horizon: *heavy weather with low driving cloud* **4** (of numbers) small **5** involving or containing a relatively small amount of something: *low-alcohol summer drinks* **6** having little value or quality: *it sounds as if your self-confidence is low* **7** coarse or vulgar: *that's a low blow* **8** inferior in culture or status **9** in a weakened physical or mental state **10** with a hushed tone: *in a low, scared voice* **11** low-necked: *a low evening gown* **12** *music* of or having a relatively low pitch **13** (of latitudes) situated not far north or south of the equator **14** having little or no money **15** unfavourable: *he has a low opinion of Ford* **16** deep: *a low bow* **17** (of a gear) providing a relatively low speed ▷ *adv* **18** in a low position, level, or degree: *the pilot flew low over the area* **19** at a low pitch; deeply: *he's singing very low* **20** cheaply: *the bank is having to buy high and sell low* **21 lay low a** to make (someone) fall by a blow **b** to overcome or destroy **22 lie low** to keep or be concealed or quiet ▷ *n* **23** a low position, level, or degree: *shares hit a new low* **24** an area of low atmospheric pressure; depression ▶ **HISTORY** Old Norse *lāgr* **> lowness** *n*

low² *n* **1** Also: **lowing** the sound uttered by cattle; moo ▷ *vb* **2** to make a mooing sound ▶ **HISTORY** Old English *hlōwan*

lowbrow *disparaging n* **1** a person with uncultivated or nonintellectual tastes ▷ *adj* **2** of or for such a person

Low Church *n* a section of the Church of England which stresses evangelical beliefs and practices **> Low-Church** *adj*

Low Countries *pl n* Belgium, Luxembourg, and the Netherlands

low-down *informal adj* **1** mean, underhand, and dishonest ▷ *n* **lowdown 2 the lowdown** information

lower¹ *adj* **1** being below one or more other things: *the lower branches* **2** reduced in amount or value: *lower rates* **3 Lower** *geol* denoting the early part of a period or formation ▷ *vb* **4** to cause or allow to move down: *she lowered her head* **5** to behave in a way that damages one's self-respect: *she'd never lowered herself enough to make a call* **6** to lessen or become less: *the cholesterol was lowered by medication* **7** to make quieter or reduce the pitch of

lower² *or* **lour** *vb* (of the sky or weather) to be overcast and menacing ▶ **HISTORY** Middle English *louren* to scowl **> lowering** *or* **louring** *adj*

lower case *n* (in printing) small letters, as opposed to capital letters **> lower-case** *adj*

lower class *n* the class with the lowest position in society **> lower-class** *adj*

lower house *n* one of the houses of a parliament that has two chambers: usually the larger and more representative

lowest common denominator *n maths* the smallest integer or polynomial that is exactly divisible by each denominator of a set of fractions

lowest common multiple *n maths* the smallest number or quantity that is exactly divisible by each member of a set of numbers or quantities

low frequency *n* any radio frequency lying between 300 and 30 kilohertz

Low German *n* a language of N Germany, spoken in rural areas

low-key *or* **low-keyed** *adj* **1** restrained or subdued **2** having a low intensity or tone

lowland *n* **1** relatively low ground **2** (often *pl*) a low generally flat region ▷ *adj* **3** of a lowland or lowlands **> lowlander** *n*

Lowland *adj* of the Lowlands or the dialects of English spoken there **> Lowlander** *n*

lowly *adj* **-lier, -liest 1** humble in position or status **2** simple and unpretentious **> lowliness** *n*

Low Mass *n* a simplified form of Mass that is spoken rather than sung

low profile *n* a deliberate shunning of publicity: *he kept a low profile* **> low-profile** *adj*

low-spirited *adj* depressed or dejected

low tide *n* the tide at its lowest level or the time at which it reaches this

low water *n* **1** low tide **2** the lowest level that a stretch of water reaches

loyal *adj* **1** faithful to one's friends, country, or government **2** of or expressing loyalty: *the loyal toast* ▶ **HISTORY** Latin *legalis* legal **> loyally** *adv*

loyalist *n* a patriotic supporter of the sovereign or government **> loyalism** *n*

Loyalist *n* (in Northern Ireland) any of the Protestants wishing to retain Ulster's link with Britain

loyalty *n, pl* **-ties 1** the quality of being loyal **2** a feeling of friendship or duty towards someone or something

loyalty card *n* a swipe card issued by a supermarket or chain store to a customer, used to record credit points awarded for money spent in the store

lozenge *n* **1** *med* a medicated tablet held in the mouth until it has dissolved **2** *geom* a rhombus ▶ **HISTORY** Old French *losange*

LP *n* a long-playing record or CD

L-plate *n Brit & Austral* a red 'L' on a white square attached to a motor vehicle to indicate that the driver is a learner

Lr *chem* lawrencium

LSD *n* lysergic acid diethylamide; an illegal hallucinogenic drug

Lt Lieutenant

Ltd *Brit* Limited (Liability)

Lu *chem* lutetium

LUB *maths* least upper bound

lubricant *n* a lubricating substance, such as oil

lubricate (loo-brik-ate) *vb* **-cating, -cated 1** to cover with an oily substance to lessen friction **2** to make greasy, slippery, or smooth ▶ **HISTORY** Latin *lubricare* to make slippery **> lubrication** *n*

lubricious (loo-**brish**-uss) *adj formal or literary* lewd ▶ **HISTORY** Latin *lubricus* slippery

lucerne *n Brit & Austral* same as **alfalfa**

lucid *adj* **1** clear and easily understood **2** capable of clear thought, particularly between periods of insanity or delirium **3** shining or glowing ▶ **HISTORY** Latin *lucidus* full of light **> lucidity** *n* **> lucidly** *adv* 495

Lucifer *n* Satan ▶ **HISTORY** Latin: light-bearer, from *lux* light + *ferre* to bear

luck *n* 1 events that are subject to chance; fortune, good or bad 2 success or good fortune 3 **down on one's luck** lacking good fortune to the extent of suffering hardship 4 **no such luck** *informal* unfortunately not 5 **try one's luck** to attempt something that is uncertain ▶ **HISTORY** Middle Dutch *luc*

luckless *adj written* unfortunate or unlucky

lucky *adj* **luckier, luckiest** 1 having or bringing good fortune 2 happening by chance, esp. as desired > **luckily** *adv*

lucky dip *n Brit, Austral & NZ* a box filled with sawdust containing small prizes for which children search

lucrative *adj* profitable

lucre (**loo**-ker) *n usually facetious* money or wealth: *filthy lucre* ▶ **HISTORY** Latin *lucrum* gain

Luddite *n Brit history* 1 any of the textile workers opposed to mechanization, who organized machine-breaking between 1811 and 1816 2 any opponent of industrial change or innovation ▷ *adj* 3 of the Luddites ▶ **HISTORY** after Ned *Ludd*, who destroyed machinery

luderick *n* an Australian fish, usu. black or dark brown in colour

ludicrous *adj* absurd or ridiculous ▶ **HISTORY** Latin *ludus* game > **ludicrously** *adv*

ludo *n Brit & Austral* a simple board game in which players move counters forward by throwing dice ▶ **HISTORY** Latin: I play

luff *vb* 1 *naut* to sail (a ship) into the wind 2 to move the jib of a crane in order to shift a load ▶ **HISTORY** Old French *lof*

lug¹ *vb* **lugging, lugged** to carry or drag with great effort ▶ **HISTORY** probably from Old Norse

lug² *n* 1 a projecting piece by which something is connected, supported, or lifted 2 *informal or Scot* an ear ▶ **HISTORY** Scots: ear

luggage *n* suitcases, trunks, and bags ▶ **HISTORY** perhaps LUG¹ + -*age*, as in *baggage*

lugger *n naut* a small working boat with an oblong sail ▶ **HISTORY** origin unknown

lugubrious (loo-**goo**-bree-uss) *adj* mournful or gloomy ▶ **HISTORY** Latin *lugere* to grieve

lugworm *n* a large worm which lives in burrows on sandy shores and is often used as bait by fishermen ▶ **HISTORY** origin unknown

lukewarm *adj* 1 (of a liquid) moderately warm; tepid 2 lacking enthusiasm or conviction ▶ **HISTORY** probably from Old English *hlēow* warm

lull *vb* 1 to soothe (a person or animal) by soft sounds or motions 2 to calm (fears or suspicions) by deception ▷ *n* 3 a short period of calm ▶ **HISTORY** perhaps imitative of crooning sounds

lullaby *n, pl* **-bies** a quiet song to lull a child to sleep ▶ **HISTORY** perhaps a blend of *lull* + *goodbye*

lumbago (lum-**bay**-go) *n* pain in the lower back; low backache ▶ **HISTORY** Latin *lumbus* loin

lumbar *adj* relating to the lower back ▶ **HISTORY** Latin *lumbus* loin

lumbar puncture *n med* insertion of a hollow needle into the lower spinal cord to withdraw fluid for diagnosis

lumber¹ *n* 1 *Brit* unwanted disused household articles 2 *chiefly US & Canad* logs; sawn timber ▷ *vb* 3 *informal* to burden with something unpleasant: *somebody gets lumbered with the extra costs* 4 to fill up with useless household articles 5 *chiefly US & Canad* to convert trees into marketable timber ▶ **HISTORY** perhaps from LUMBER²

lumber² *vb* to move awkwardly and heavily ▶ **HISTORY** Middle English *lomeren* > **lumbering** *adj*

lumberjack *n* (esp. in North America) a person who fells trees and prepares the timber for transport

lumen *n, pl* **-mens** or **-mina** *anat* a passage, duct, or cavity in a tubular organ

luminary *n, pl* **-naries** 1 a a famous person b an expert in a particular subject 2 *literary* something, such as the sun or moon, that gives off light

luminescence *n physics* the emission of light at low temperatures by any process other than burning > **luminescent** *adj*

luminous *adj* 1 reflecting or giving off light: *luminous colours* 2 *not in technical use* luminescent: *luminous sparklers* 3 enlightening or wise ▶ **HISTORY** Latin *lumen* light > **luminosity** *n*

lump¹ *n* 1 a small solid mass without definite shape 2 *pathol* any small swelling or tumour 3 *informal* an awkward, heavy, or stupid person 4 **a lump in one's throat** a tight dry feeling in one's throat, usually caused by great emotion 5 **the lump** *Brit* self-employed workers in the building trade considered collectively ▷ *adj* 6 in the form of a lump or lumps: *lump sugar* ▷ *vb* 7 (often foll. by *together*) to consider as a single group, often without justification 8 to grow into lumps or become lumpy ▶ **HISTORY** probably related to Scandinavian dialect: block

lump² *vb* **lump it** *informal* to accept something irrespective of personal preference: *if you don't like it, you can lump it* ▶ **HISTORY** origin unknown

lumpectomy *n, pl* **-mies** surgical removal of a tumour in a breast ▶ **HISTORY** *lump* + Greek *tomē* a cutting

lumpish *adj* stupid, clumsy, or heavy > **lumpishness** *n*

lump sum *n* a relatively large sum of money, paid at one time

lumpy *adj* **lumpier, lumpiest** full of or having lumps > **lumpiness** *n*

lunacy *n, pl* **-cies** 1 foolishness 2 (formerly) any severe mental illness

lunar *adj* relating to the moon: *lunar eclipse* ▶ **HISTORY** Latin *luna* the moon

lunar calendar *n* a calendar based on the cycle of the moon's phases

lunatic *adj* 1 foolish; eccentric 2 *old-fashioned* insane ▷ *n* 3 a foolish or annoying person 4 *old-fashioned* a person who is insane ▶ **HISTORY** Latin *luna* moon

lunatic asylum n old-fashioned, offensive a psychiatric hospital

lunch n 1 a meal eaten during the middle of the day ▷ vb 2 to eat lunch ▶ HISTORY shortened from luncheon

luncheon n a lunch, often a formal one ▶ HISTORY probably variant of nuncheon, from Middle English none noon + schench drink

luncheon meat n a ground mixture of meat (often pork) and cereal, usually tinned

luncheon voucher n Brit a voucher for a specified amount issued to employees and accepted by some restaurants as payment for food

lung n the part of the body that allows an animal or bird to breathe air. Humans have two lungs, contained within the chest cavity ▶ HISTORY Old English lungen

lunge n 1 a sudden forward motion 2 fencing a thrust made by advancing the front foot and straightening the back leg ▷ vb lunging, lunged 3 to move with a lunge 4 fencing to make a lunge ▶ HISTORY French allonger to stretch out (one's arm)

lungfish n, pl -fish or -fishes a freshwater fish with an air-breathing lung

lupin n a garden plant with large spikes of brightly coloured flowers and flattened pods ▶ HISTORY Latin lupinus wolfish; from the belief that it ravenously exhausted the soil

lupine adj of or like a wolf ▶ HISTORY Latin lupus wolf

lupus n an ulcerous skin disease ▶ HISTORY Latin: wolf; so called because it rapidly eats away the affected part

lurch¹ vb 1 to lean or tilt suddenly to one side 2 to stagger ▷ n 3 a lurching movement ▶ HISTORY origin unknown

lurch² n leave someone in the lurch to abandon someone in trouble ▶ HISTORY French lourche, a game similar to backgammon

lure vb luring, lured 1 (sometimes foll. by away or into) to tempt or attract by the promise of reward ▷ n 2 a person or thing that lures 3 angling a brightly coloured artificial spinning bait 4 falconry a feathered decoy to which small pieces of meat can be attached ▶ HISTORY Old French loirre falconer's lure

lurid adj 1 vivid in shocking detail; sensational: magazines whose lurid covers sickened him 2 glaring in colour: a lurid red tartan 3 horrible in savagery or violence: reporting lurid crimes ▶ HISTORY Latin luridus pale yellow > **luridly** adv

lurk vb 1 to move stealthily or be concealed, esp. for evil purposes 2 to be present in an unobtrusive way; be latent ▶ HISTORY probably frequentative of lour

luscious (lush-uss) adj 1 extremely pleasurable to taste or smell 2 very attractive ▶ HISTORY perhaps short for delicious

lush¹ adj 1 (of vegetation) growing thickly and healthily 2 luxurious, elaborate, or opulent ▶ HISTORY Latin laxus loose

lush² n slang an alcoholic ▶ HISTORY origin unknown

lust n 1 a strong sexual desire 2 a strong desire or drive: a lust for power ▷ vb 3 (often foll. by after or for) to have a passionate desire (for) ▶ HISTORY Old English > **lustful** adj > **lustfully** adv

lustre or US **luster** n 1 soft shining light reflected from a surface; sheen 2 great splendour or glory 3 a shiny metallic surface on some pottery and porcelain ▶ HISTORY Latin lustrare to make bright > **lustrous** adj

lusty adj lustier, lustiest 1 healthy and full of strength and energy 2 strong or invigorating > **lustily** adv > **lustiness** n

lute n an ancient plucked stringed instrument with a long fingerboard and a body shaped like a half pear ▶ HISTORY Arabic al ʿūd, literally: the wood

lutetium (loo-**tee**-shee-um) n chem a silvery-white metallic element of the lanthanide series. Symbol: Lu ▶ HISTORY Lutetia, ancient name of Paris

Lutheran n 1 a follower of Martin Luther (1483–1546), German leader of the Reformation, or a member of a Lutheran Church ▷ adj 2 of or relating to Luther, his doctrines, or any of the Churches that follow these doctrines > **Lutheranism** n

luvvie or **luvvy** n, pl -vies facetious a person who is involved in acting or the theatre

lux n, pl lux the SI unit of illumination ▶ HISTORY Latin: light

Luxembourger n a person from Luxembourg

luxuriant adj 1 rich and abundant; lush: luxuriant foliage 2 very elaborate or ornate ▶ HISTORY Latin luxuriare to abound to excess > **luxuriance** n > **luxuriantly** adv

luxuriate vb -ating, -ated 1 luxuriate in to take self-indulgent pleasure in; revel in 2 to flourish profusely

luxurious adj 1 characterized by luxury 2 enjoying or devoted to luxury > **luxuriously** adv

luxury n, pl -ries 1 indulgence in rich and sumptuous living 2 something considered an indulgence rather than a necessity ▷ adj 3 relating to, indicating, or supplying luxury: a luxury hotel ▶ HISTORY Latin luxuria excess

LV (in Britain) luncheon voucher

lx lux

lyceum n (now chiefly in the names of buildings) a public building for events such as concerts and lectures ▶ HISTORY Latin: a school in ancient Athens

lychee (lie-**chee**) n a Chinese fruit with a whitish juicy pulp ▶ HISTORY Cantonese lai chi

lych gate or **lich gate** n a roofed gate to a churchyard, formerly used as a temporary shelter for a coffin ▶ HISTORY Old English līc corpse

Lycra n trademark a synthetic elastic fabric used for tight-fitting garments, such as swimsuits

lye n 1 a caustic solution obtained from wood ash 2 a concentrated solution of sodium hydroxide or potassium hydroxide ▶ HISTORY Old English lēag

lying *vb* the present participle of **lie¹ lie²**

lying-in *n, pl* **lyings-in** *old-fashioned* confinement in childbirth

lymph *n* the almost colourless body fluid containing chiefly white blood cells ▶ **HISTORY** Latin *lympha* water > **lymphatic** *adj*

lymphatic system *n* a network of fine vessels by which lymph circulates throughout the body

lymph node *n* any of many bean-shaped masses of tissue in the lymphatic system that help to protect against infection

lymphocyte *n* a type of white blood cell ▶ **HISTORY** lymph + Greek *kutos* vessel

lynch *vb* (of a mob) to kill (a person) for some supposed offence without a trial ▶ **HISTORY** after Captain William *Lynch* of Virginia, US > **lynching** *n*

lynchpin *n* same as **linchpin**

lynx *n, pl* **lynxes** *or* **lynx** a mammal of the cat family, with grey-brown mottled fur, tufted ears, and a short tail ▶ **HISTORY** Greek *lunx*

lyre *n* an ancient Greek U-shaped stringed instrument, similar to a harp but plucked with a plectrum ▶ **HISTORY** Greek *lura*

lyrebird *n* an Australian bird, the male of which spreads its tail into the shape of a lyre during courtship

lyric *adj* **1** (of poetry) **a** expressing the writer's personal feelings **b** having the form and manner of a song **2** of or relating to such poetry **3** (of a singing voice) light and melodic ▷ *n* **4** a short poem of songlike quality **5** **lyrics** the words of a popular song: *Cole invests all her lyrics with a touch of drama* ▶ **HISTORY** Greek *lura* lyre > **lyrically** *adv*

lyrical *adj* **1** same as **lyric** (senses 1, 2) **2** enthusiastic or effusive

lyricism *n* **1** the quality or style of lyric poetry **2** emotional outpouring

lyricist *n* a person who writes the words for a song, opera, or musical

lysozyme *n* *biochem* an enzyme that occurs in tears, some body tissues, and egg whites

l

Mm

m 1 metre(s) **2** mile(s) **3** milli- **4** million **5** minute(s)

M 1 mach **2** *currency* mark(s) **3** medium **4** mega- **5** (in Britain) motorway **6** the Roman numeral for 1000

m. 1 male **2** married **3** masculine **4** meridian **5** month

M. 1 Majesty **2** Master **3** (in titles) Member **4** (*pl* **MM.** *or* **MM**) Monsieur

ma *n* an informal word for mother

MA 1 Massachusetts **2** Master of Arts

ma'am *n* short for **madam** (sense 1)

maas (mahs) *n S African* thick soured milk ▶ HISTORY Nguni (language group of southern Africa) *amasi* milk

Mabo decision *n Austral law* the 1992 decision of the High Court of Australia that abolished the legal concept of *terra nullius*

mac *or* **mack** *n Brit, informal* a mackintosh

macabre (mak-**kahb**-ra) *adj* strange and horrible; gruesome ▶ HISTORY French

macadam *n* a road surface made of compressed layers of small broken stones, esp. one bound together with tar or asphalt ▶ HISTORY after John McAdam, engineer

macadamia (mak-a-**day**-mee-a) *n* an Australian tree with edible nuts ▶ HISTORY after John Macadam, Australian chemist

macadamize *or* **-ise** *vb* **-izing, -ized** *or* **-ising, -ised** to pave a road with macadam

macaque (mak-**kahk**) *n* any of various Asian and African monkeys with cheek pouches and either a short tail or no tail ▶ HISTORY W African *makaku*

macaroni *n, pl* **-nis** *or* **-nies 1** pasta tubes made from wheat flour **2** (in 18th-century Britain) a man who was excessively concerned with his clothes and appearance ▶ HISTORY Italian (dialect) *maccarone*

macaroon *n* a sweet biscuit made of ground almonds ▶ HISTORY French *macaron*

macaw *n* a large tropical American parrot with a long tail and brightly coloured feathers ▶ HISTORY Portuguese *macau*

mace¹ *n* **1** a ceremonial staff carried by certain officials **2** a club with a spiked metal head used in the Middle Ages ▶ HISTORY probably Vulgar Latin *mattea*

mace² *n* a spice made from the dried outer casing of the nutmeg ▶ HISTORY Latin *macir*

macerate (**mass**-er-ate) *vb* **-ating, -ated** to soften or be softened by soaking ▶ HISTORY Latin *macerare* to soften > **macerated** *adj* > **maceration** *n*

Mach (mak) *n* a unit for expressing the speed of an aircraft as a multiple of the speed of sound: *an airliner capable of cruising at Mach 2*. See also **Mach number**

machete (mash-**ett**-ee) *n* a broad heavy knife used for cutting or as a weapon ▶ HISTORY Spanish

Machiavellian (mak-ee-a-**vel**-yan) *adj* cleverly deceitful and unscrupulous ▶ HISTORY after Machiavelli, political philosopher > **Machiavellianism** *n*

machinations (mak-in-**nay**-shunz) *pl n* cunning schemes or plots to gain power or harm an opponent: *the machinations of a power-hungry institution* ▶ HISTORY Latin *machinari* to plan

machine *n* **1** an assembly of components arranged so as to perform a particular task and usually powered by electricity **2** a vehicle, such as a car or aircraft **3** a system within an organization that controls activities and policies: *the party machine* ▷ *vb* **-chining, -chined 4** to shape, cut, or make something using a machine ▶ HISTORY Latin *machina* > **machinable** *adj*

machine code *or* **language** *n* instructions for a computer in binary or hexadecimal code that require no conversion or translation by the computer

machine gun *n* **1** a rapid-firing automatic gun, using small-arms ammunition ▷ *vb* **machine-gun, -gunning, -gunned 2** to shoot or fire at with a machine gun

machine-readable *adj* in a form suitable for processing by a computer

machinery *n, pl* **-eries 1** machines, machine parts, or machine systems collectively **2** the mechanism of a machine **3** the organization and procedures by which a system functions: *the machinery of international politics*

machine shop *n* a workshop in which machine tools are operated

machine tool *n* a power-driven machine, such as a lathe, for cutting and shaping metal, wood, or plastic

machinist *n* **1** a person who operates machines to cut or process materials **2** a maker or repairer of machines

machismo (mak-**izz**-moh) *n* strong or exaggerated masculinity ▶ HISTORY Mexican Spanish *macho* male

Mach number (mak) *n* the ratio of the speed of a body in a particular medium to the speed of sound in that medium ▶ HISTORY after Ernst *Mach*, physicist

macho (**match**-oh) *adj* **1** strongly or exaggeratedly masculine ▷ *n* **2** strong or exaggerated masculinity ▶ HISTORY from *machismo*

mack *n Brit, informal* same as **mac**

mackerel *n, pl* **-rel** *or* **-rels** an edible sea fish ▶ HISTORY Old French *maquerel*

m

mackintosh or **macintosh** n Brit **1** a raincoat made of rubberized cloth **2** any raincoat ▶ HISTORY after Charles *Macintosh*, who invented it

macramé (mak-**rah**-mee) n **1** the art of knotting and weaving coarse thread into patterns **2** ornaments made in this way ▶ HISTORY Turkish *makrama* towel

macro- or before a vowel **macr-** combining form large, long, or great: *macroscopic* ▶ HISTORY Greek *makros*

macrobiotics n a dietary system that advocates whole grains and vegetables grown without chemical additives ▶ HISTORY Greek *makros* long + *biōtikos* life > **macrobiotic** adj

macrocarpa n a large Californian coniferous tree, used in New Zealand and elsewhere as a windbreak on farms and for rough timber ▶ HISTORY Greek *makros* large + *karpos* fruit

macrocosm n a complex structure, such as the universe or society, regarded as a whole ▶ HISTORY Greek *makros kosmos* great world

macroeconomics n the branch of economics concerned with the relationships between aggregates, such as consumption and investment, in a large economic system > **macroeconomic** adj

macromolecule n any very large molecule, such as a protein or synthetic polymer

macron n a mark (¯) placed over a letter to represent a long vowel ▶ HISTORY Greek *makros* long

macronutrient n any substance, such as carbon, hydrogen, or oxygen, that is required in large amounts for healthy development

macroscopic adj **1** large enough to be visible to the naked eye **2** concerned with large units ▶ HISTORY Greek *makros* large + *skopein* to look at

macula (**mak**-kew-la) n, pl **-ulae** (-yew-lee) anat a small spot or area of distinct colour, such as a freckle ▶ HISTORY Latin

mad adj **madder, maddest 1** mentally deranged; insane **2** extremely foolish; senseless: *that was a mad thing to do!* **3** informal angry or annoyed: *he's mad at her for the unjust accusation* **4** extremely excited or confused: *a mad rush* **5** (of animals) **a** unusually ferocious: *a mad bear* **b** afflicted with rabies **6 mad about** or **on** or **over** wildly enthusiastic about or fond of **7 like mad** informal with great energy, enthusiasm, or haste ▶ HISTORY Old English *gemǣded* made insane > **madness** n

MAD mil mutually assured destruction: a theory of nuclear deterrence whereby each side in a conflict has the capacity to destroy the other in retaliation for a nuclear attack

madam n, pl **madams 1** (pl **mesdames**) (may-**dam**) a polite term of address for a woman **2** a woman who runs a brothel **3** Brit & Austral, informal, spoken a spoilt or pert girl: *she is a thoroughly precocious little madam if ever there was one* ▶ HISTORY Old French *ma dame* my lady

madame (mad-**dam**) n, pl **mesdames** (may-**dam**) a French form of address equivalent to *Mrs*

madcap adj **1** impulsive, reckless, or unlikely to succeed: *a madcap expansion of council bureaucracy* ▷ n **2** an impulsive or reckless person

mad cow disease n informal same as **BSE**

madden vb to make or become mad or angry > **maddening** adj

madder n **1** a plant with small yellow flowers and a red fleshy root **2** a dark reddish-purple dye formerly obtained from its root **3** an artificial pigment of this colour ▶ HISTORY Old English *mædere*

made vb **1** the past of **make** ▷ adj **2** produced or shaped as specified: *handmade* **3 get** or **have it made** informal to be assured of success

Madeira (mad-**deer**-a) n a fortified white wine from Madeira, an island in the N Atlantic

Madeira cake n a type of rich sponge cake

mademoiselle (mad-mwah-**zel**) n, pl **mesdemoiselles** (maid-mwah-**zel**) **1** a French form of address equivalent to *Miss* **2** a French teacher or governess

made-up adj **1** invented or fictitious **2** wearing make-up **3** put together: *some made-up carpet shampoo* **4** (of a road) surfaced with tarmac or concrete

madhouse n **1** informal a state of uproar or confusion **2** old-fashioned, sometimes offensive a psychiatric hospital

madly adv **1** in an insane or foolish manner **2** with great speed and energy **3** informal extremely or excessively: *she was madly in love with him*

madman or fem **madwoman** n, pl **-men** or **-women** a person who is insane

Madonna n **1** chiefly RC Church the Virgin Mary **2** a picture or statue of the Virgin Mary ▶ HISTORY Italian: my lady

madrigal n a type of 16th- or 17th-century part song for unaccompanied voices ▶ HISTORY Medieval Latin *matricale* primitive > **madrigalist** n

maelstrom (**male**-strom) n **1** a large powerful whirlpool **2** any confused, violent, and destructive turmoil: *a maelstrom of adulterous passion* ▶ HISTORY Old Dutch *malen* to whirl round + *stroom* stream

maenad (**mean**-ad) n **1** classical history a female disciple of Dionysus, the Greek god of wine **2** a frenzied woman ▶ HISTORY Greek *mainas* madwoman

maestro (**my**-stroh) n, pl **-tri** or **-tros 1** a distinguished musician or conductor **2** any master of an art: *Milan's maestro of minimalism* ▶ HISTORY Italian: master

mae west n slang an inflatable life jacket ▶ HISTORY after *Mae West*, actress renowned for her large bust

Mafia n **the Mafia** a secret criminal organization founded in Sicily, and carried to the US by Italian immigrants ▶ HISTORY Sicilian dialect, literally: hostility to the law

mafioso (maf-fee-**oh**-so) n, pl **-sos** or **-si** (-see) a member of the Mafia

mag n short for **magazine** (sense 1)

magazine n **1** a periodic paperback publication containing written pieces and illustrations

m

2 a television or radio programme made up of short nonfictional items **3** a metal case holding several cartridges used in some firearms **4** a rack for automatically feeding slides through a projector **5** a place for storing weapons, explosives, or military equipment ▶ HISTORY Arabic *makhāzin* storehouses

magenta (maj-**jen**-ta) *adj* deep purplish-red ▶ HISTORY after *Magenta*, Italy

maggot *n* the limbless larva of various insects, esp. the housefly and blowfly ▶ HISTORY earlier *mathek* > **maggoty** *adj*

magi (**maje**-eye) *pl n, sing* **magus** (**may**-guss) **1** See **magus 2 the three Magi** *Christianity* the wise men from the East who came to worship the infant Jesus (Matthew 2:1–12) ▶ HISTORY see MAGUS

magic *n* **1** the supposed power to make things happen by using supernatural means **2** tricks done to entertain; conjuring **3** any mysterious or extraordinary quality or power: *the magic of Placido Domingo* **4 like magic** very quickly ▷ *adj also* **magical 5** of magic **6** possessing or considered to possess mysterious powers **7** unaccountably enchanting **8** *informal* wonderful or marvellous ▷ *vb* **-icking, -icked 9** to transform or produce as if by magic: *he had magicked up a gourmet meal at a moment's notice* ▶ HISTORY Greek *magikē* witchcraft > **magically** *adv*

magician *n* **1** a conjuror **2** a person with magic powers

magic lantern *n* an early type of slide projector

Maginot line (**mazh**-in-oh) *n history* a line of fortifications built by France to defend its border with Germany prior to World War II ▶ HISTORY after André *Maginot*, French minister of war when fortifications were begun in 1929

magisterial *adj* **1** commanding and authoritative **2** of a magistrate ▶ HISTORY Latin *magister* master > **magisterially** *adv*

magistracy *n, pl* **-cies 1** the office or function of a magistrate **2** magistrates collectively

magistrate *n* **1** a public officer concerned with the administration of law **2** same as **justice of the peace 3** *Austral & NZ* a former name for **district court judge** ▶ HISTORY Latin *magister* master

magistrates' court *n law* a court that deals with minor crimes, certain civil actions, and preliminary hearings

magma *n, pl* **-mas** or **-mata** hot molten rock within the earth's crust which sometimes finds its way to the surface, where it solidifies to form igneous rock ▶ HISTORY Greek: salve made by kneading

Magna Carta *n English history* the charter granted by King John at Runnymede in 1215, recognizing the rights and privileges of the barons, church, and freemen ▶ HISTORY Medieval Latin: great charter

magnanimous *adj* generous and forgiving, esp. towards a defeated enemy ▶ HISTORY Latin *magnanimus* great-souled > **magnanimity** *n* > **magnanimously** *adv*

magnate *n* an influential or wealthy person, esp. in industry ▶ HISTORY Late Latin *magnates* great men

magnesia *n* a white tasteless substance used as an antacid and laxative; magnesium oxide ▶ HISTORY Greek *Magnēsia* of *Magnēs*, ancient mineral-rich region

magnesium *n chem* a light silvery-white metallic element that burns with a very bright white flame. Symbol: Mg ▶ HISTORY from *magnesia*

magnesium sulphate *n chem* a colourless crystalline compound used in medicine, fertilizers, and manufacturing

magnet *n* **1** a piece of iron, steel, or lodestone that has the property of attracting iron to it **2** a person or thing that exerts a great attraction: *these woods are a magnet for bird watchers* ▶ HISTORY Greek *magnēs*

magnetic *adj* **1** of, producing, or operated by means of magnetism **2** of or like a magnet **3** capable of being made into a magnet **4** exerting a powerful attraction: *political leaders of magnetic appeal* > **magnetically** *adv*

magnetic anomaly *n geog* a disturbance in the strength of the earth's magnetic field owing to the magnetism of rocks in the crust

magnetic disk *n* a computer storage disk

magnetic field *n* an area around a magnet in which its power of attraction is felt

magnetic field line *n physics* one of many lines describing the structure of a magnetic field in three dimensions. Field lines converge where the magnetic force is strong, near the poles, and spread out where it is weak

magnetic needle *n* a slender magnetized rod used in certain instruments, such as the magnetic compass, for indicating the direction of a magnetic field

magnetic north *n* the direction in which a compass needle points, at an angle from the direction of true (geographic) north

magnetic pole *n* either of two variable points on the earth's surface towards which a magnetic needle points

magnetic storm *n* a sudden severe disturbance of the earth's magnetic field, caused by emission of charged particles from the sun

magnetic tape *n* a long plastic strip coated with a magnetic substance, used to record sound or video signals or to store information in computers

magnetism *n* **1** the property of attraction displayed by magnets **2** powerful personal charm **3** the branch of physics concerned with magnetic phenomena

magnetite *n* a black magnetizable mineral that is an important source of iron

magnetize or **-ise** *vb* **-izing, -ized** or **-ising, -ised 1** to make a substance or object magnetic **2** to attract strongly: *he was magnetized by her smile* > **magnetizable** or **-isable** *adj* > **magnetization** or **-isation** *n*

m

magneto (mag-**nee**-toe) *n, pl* **-tos** a small electric generator in which the magnetic field is produced by a permanent magnet, esp. one used to provide the spark in an internal-combustion engine ▶ HISTORY short for *magnetoelectric generator*

magnetron *n* an electronic valve used with a magnetic field to generate microwave oscillations, used. esp. in radar ▶ HISTORY *magnet + electron*

Magnificat *n Christianity* the hymn of the Virgin Mary (Luke 1:46—55), used as a canticle ▶ HISTORY from its opening word

magnification *n* **1** the act of magnifying or the state of being magnified **2** the degree to which something is magnified **3** a magnified copy of something

magnificent *adj* **1** splendid or impressive in appearance **2** superb or very fine: *a magnificent performance* ▶ HISTORY Latin *magnificus* great in deeds > **magnificence** *n* > **magnificently** *adv*

magnify *vb* **-fies, -fying, -fied 1** to make something look bigger than it really is, for instance by using a lens or microscope **2** to make something seem more important than it really is; exaggerate: *you are magnifying the problem out of all proportion* **3** to make something sound louder than it really is: *the stethoscope magnifies internal body sounds* **4** *archaic* to glorify or praise ▶ HISTORY Latin *magnificare* to praise > **magnified** *adj*

magnifying glass *or* **magnifier** *n* a convex lens used to produce an enlarged image of an object

magnitude *n* **1** relative importance: *an evil of the first magnitude* **2** relative size or extent **3** *astron* the apparent brightness of a celestial body expressed on a numerical scale on which bright stars have a low value ▶ HISTORY Latin *magnitudo* size

magnolia *n* an Asian and North American tree or shrub with white, pink, purple, or yellow showy flowers ▶ HISTORY after Pierre *Magnol*, botanist

magnox *n* an alloy composed mainly of magnesium, used in fuel elements of some nuclear reactors (**magnox reactors**) ▶ HISTORY from *mag(nesium) n(o) ox(idation)*

magnum *n, pl* **-nums** a wine bottle of twice the normal size, holding 1.5 litres ▶ HISTORY Latin: a big thing

magnum opus *n* a great work of art or literature, esp. the greatest single work of an artist ▶ HISTORY Latin

magpie *n* **1** a bird of the crow family with black-and-white plumage, a long tail, and a chattering call **2** any of various similar Australian birds, such as the butcherbird **3** *Brit* a person who hoards small objects ▶ HISTORY from *Mag*, diminutive of *Margaret + pie*, obsolete name for the magpie

magus (**may**-guss) *n, pl* **magi** (**maje**-eye) **1** a Zoroastrian priest **2** an astrologer or magician of ancient times ▶ HISTORY Old Persian: magician

Magyar *n* **1** a member of the main ethnic group of Hungary **2** the Hungarian language ▷ *adj* **3** of the Magyars

maharaja *or* **maharajah** *n* the head of one of the royal families which formerly ruled parts of India ▶ HISTORY Hindi: great raja

maharani *or* **maharanee** *n* the wife of a maharaja ▶ HISTORY Hindi: great rani

maharishi *n Hinduism* a teacher of religious and mystical knowledge ▶ HISTORY Hindi: great sage

mahatma *n* a person revered for his holiness or wisdom: often used as a title or form of address: *Mahatma Gandhi* ▶ HISTORY Sanskrit *mahā* great + *ātman* soul

mah jong *or* **mah-jongg** *n* a game of Chinese origin, played using tiles bearing various designs, in which the players try to obtain a winning combination of tiles ▶ HISTORY Chinese, literally: sparrows

mahogany *n, pl* **-nies 1** the hard reddish-brown wood of any of several tropical trees ▷ *adj* **2** reddish-brown: *wonderful mahogany tones* ▶ HISTORY origin unknown

mahout (ma-**howt**) *n* (in India and the East Indies) an elephant driver or keeper ▶ HISTORY Hindi *mahāut*

maid *n* **1** a female servant **2** *archaic or literary* a young unmarried girl; maiden ▶ HISTORY form of *maiden*

maiden *n* **1** *archaic or literary* a young unmarried girl, esp. a virgin **2** *horse racing* a horse that has never won a race ▷ *adj* **3** unmarried: *a maiden aunt* **4** first or earliest: *maiden voyage* ▶ HISTORY Old English *mægden* > **maidenhood** *n* > **maidenly** *adj*

maidenhair fern *n* a fern with delicate hairlike fronds of small pale green leaflets

maidenhead *n* **1** the hymen **2** virginity or maidenhood

maiden name *n* a woman's surname before marriage

maiden over *n cricket* an over in which no runs are scored

mail¹ *n* **1** letters and packages transported and delivered by the post office **2** the postal system **3** a single collection or delivery of mail **4** a train, ship, or aircraft that carries mail **5** short for **e-mail** ▷ *vb* **6** *chiefly US & Canad* to send by mail **7** to contact or send by e-mail ▶ HISTORY Old French *male* bag

mail² *n* flexible armour made of riveted metal rings or links ▶ HISTORY Old French *maille* mesh > **mailed** *adj*

mailbox *n* **1** *US, Canad & Austral* a box outside a house into which the postman puts letters for the occupiers of the house **2** a computer directory in which e-mail messages are stored

mail coach *n history* a fast stagecoach designed primarily for carrying mail

mailing list *n* a register of names and addresses to which information or advertising matter is sent by post or e-mail

mail merge *n computers* a word-processing facility that can produce personalized letters by combining data from two different files

mail order *n* a system of buying and selling goods by post

m

mailshot *n Brit* a posting of circulars, leaflets, or other advertising to a selected large number of people at once

maim *vb* to injure badly or cruelly, with some permanent damage resulting ▶ HISTORY Old French *mahaignier* to wound

main *adj* **1** chief or principal ▷ *n* **2** a principal pipe or line in a system used to distribute water, electricity, or gas **3 mains** the main distribution network for water, gas, or electricity **4** great strength or force: *with might and main* **5** *literary* the open ocean **6 in the main** on the whole ▶ HISTORY Old English *mægen* strength

mainbrace *n naut* **1** the rope that controls the movement of the spar of a ship's mainsail **2 splice the mainbrace** See **splice**

main clause *n grammar* a clause that can stand alone as a sentence

mainframe *n computers* a high-speed general-purpose computer, with a large storage capacity

mainland *n* the main part of a land mass as opposed to an island

mainland territories *pl n* the Caribbean countries located in Central and South America: Belize, Guyana, French Guiana, and Surinam

main line *n* **1** *railways* the chief route between two points, usually fed by branch lines ▷ *vb* **2** *slang* to inject a drug into a vein

mainly *adv* for the most part; principally

mainmast *n naut* the chief mast of a sailing vessel with two or more masts

mainsail *n naut* the largest and lowermost sail on the mainmast

mainspring *n* **1** *written* the chief cause or motive of something: *the mainspring of a dynamic economy* **2** the chief spring of a watch or clock

mainstay *n* **1** a chief support **2** *naut* a rope securing a mainmast

mainstream *n* **1** the people or things representing the most common or generally accepted ideas and styles in a society, art form, etc.: *the mainstream of academic life* **2** the main current of a river ▷ *adj* **3** belonging to the social or cultural mainstream: *mainstream American movies*

mainstreeting *n Canad* the practice of a politician walking about a town or city to try to gain votes

maintain *vb* **1** to continue or keep in existence: *we must maintain good relations with them* **2** to keep in proper or good condition: *an expensive car to maintain* **3** to sustain or keep up a particular level or speed: *he set off at a high speed, but couldn't maintain it all the way* **4** to enable a person to have the money, food, and other things he or she needs to live: *the money maintained us for a month* **5** to assert: *he had always maintained that he never wanted children* **6** to defend against contradiction; uphold: *he maintained his innocence* ▶ HISTORY from Latin *manu tenere* to hold in the hand

maintenance *n* **1** the act of maintaining or the state of being maintained **2** the process of keeping a car, building, etc. in good condition **3** *law*

financial provision ordered to be made by way of periodical payments or a lump sum, usually for a separated or divorced spouse

maisonette *n Brit & S African* a flat with more than one floor ▶ HISTORY French, diminutive of *maison* house

maize *n* a type of corn grown for its large yellow edible grains, which are used for food and as a source of oil. See also **sweet corn** ▶ HISTORY Spanish *maiz*

Maj. Major

majestic *adj* beautiful, dignified, and impressive > **majestically** *adv*

majesty *n* **1** great dignity and grandeur **2** supreme power or authority ▶ HISTORY Latin *majestas*

Majesty *n, pl* **-ties** (preceded by *Your, His* or *Her*) a title used to address or refer to a sovereign or the wife or widow of a sovereign

Maj. Gen. Major General

majolica *or* **maiolica** *n* a type of porous pottery glazed with bright metallic oxides. It was extensively made in Renaissance Italy ▶ HISTORY Italian, from Late Latin *Majorica* Majorca

major *adj* **1** greater in size, frequency, or importance than others of the same kind: *the major political parties* **2** very serious or significant: *a major investigation* **3** main or principal: *a major road* **4** *music* (of a scale) **a** having notes separated by a whole tone, except for the third and fourth notes, and seventh and eighth notes, which are separated by a semitone **b** of or based on the major scale: *the key of D minor* ▷ *n* **5** a middle-ranking military officer **6** *music* a major key, chord, mode, or scale **7** a person who has reached the age of legal majority **8** *US, Canad, S African, Austral & NZ* the principal field of study of a student ▷ *vb* **9 major in** *US, Canad, S African, Austral & NZ* to study as one's principal subject: *he majored in economics* ▶ HISTORY Latin: greater

major-domo *n, pl* **-mos** the chief steward or butler of a great household ▶ HISTORY Medieval Latin *major domus* head of the household

majorette *n* one of a group of girls who practise formation marching and baton twirling

major general *n* a senior military officer

majority *n, pl* **-ties** **1** the greater number or part of something **2** (in an election) the number of votes or seats by which the strongest party or candidate beats the combined opposition or the runner-up **3** the largest party or group that votes together in a meeting, council, or parliament **4** the age at which a person legally becomes an adult **5 in the majority** forming or part of the group of people or things made up of more than half of a larger group ▶ HISTORY Medieval Latin *majoritas*

make *vb* **making, made** **1** to create, construct, establish, or draw up; bring into being: *houses made of stone*; *he will have to make a will* **2** to cause to do or be; compel or induce: *please make her go away* **3** to bring about or produce: *don't make a noise* **4** to carry out or perform: *he made his first trip to China in 1987*; *she made an obscene gesture* **5** to appoint: *they made*

m

him caretaker manager **6** to come into a specified state or condition: *to make merry* **7** to become: *she will make a good diplomat* **8** to cause or ensure the success of: *that news has made my day* **9** to amount to: *5 and 5 make 10* **10** to earn or be paid: *they must be making a fortune* **11** to have the qualities of or be suitable for: *what makes this book such a good read?* **12** to prepare for use: *she forgot to make her bed* **13** to be the essential element in: *confidence makes a good salesman* **14** to use for a specified purpose: *they will make this town their base* **15** to deliver: *he made a very good speech* **16** to consider to be: *what time do you make it?* **17** to cause to seem or represent as being: *her girlish pigtails made her look younger than she was; she made the experience sound most unpleasant* **18** to acquire: *she doesn't make friends easily* **19** to engage in: *they made war on the Turks* **20** to travel a certain distance or to a certain place: *we can make at least three miles before it gets dark* **21** to arrive in time for: *he didn't make the first act of the play* **22** to win or score: *he made a break of 125* **23** *informal* to gain a place or position on or in: *to make the headlines* **24 make a day** *or* **night of it** to cause an activity to last a day or night **25 make eyes at** *old-fashioned* to flirt with or ogle **26 make it** *informal* **a** to be able to attend: *I'm afraid I can't make it to your party* **b** to be successful **27 make like** *slang, chiefly US & Canad* **a** to imitate **b** to pretend **28 make to** *or* **as if to** *or* **as though** *written* to act with the intention or with a show of doing something: *she made as if to hit him* ▷ *n* **29** a manufacturer; brand: *what make of car is that?* **30** the way in which something is made **31 on the make** *slang* out for profit or conquest ▷ See also **make for** ▶ HISTORY Old English *macian* > **maker** *n*

make do *vb* to manage with an inferior alternative

make for *vb* **1** to head towards **2** to prepare to attack **3** to help bring about: *this will make for a spectacular race*

make out *vb* **1** to manage to see or hear **2** to understand **3** to write out: *how shall I make out the cheque?* **4** to attempt to establish or prove: *she made me out to be a crook* **5** to pretend: *he made out that he could play the piano* **6** to manage or get on: *how did you make out in the exam?*

make over *vb* **1** to renovate or remodel: *she made over the dress to fit her sister* ▷ *n* **makeover 2** a complete remodelling **3** a series of alterations, including beauty treatments and new clothes, intended to make an improvement to someone's appearance

Maker *n* a title given to God

makeshift *adj* serving as a temporary substitute

make-up *n* **1** cosmetics, such as powder or lipstick **2** the cosmetics used by an actor to adapt his or her appearance **3** the arrangement of the parts of something **4** mental or physical constitution ▷ *vb* **make up 5** to form or constitute: *these arguments make up the case for the defence* **6** to devise or compose, sometimes with the intent to deceive: *she was well known for making up stories about herself* **7** to supply what is lacking in; complete: *I'll make up*

the difference **8** Also: **make it up** to settle differences amicably **9 make up for** to compensate for: *one good year can make up for several bad ones* **10** to apply cosmetics to the face **11 make up to** *informal* **a** to make friendly overtures to **b** to flirt with

makeweight *n* an unimportant person or thing added to make up a lack

making *n* **1** the act or process of producing something **2 be the making of** to cause the success of **3 in the making** in the process of becoming or being made

makings *pl n* **have the makings of** to have the potential, qualities, or materials necessary to make or become something: *it had the makings of a classic showdown*

mako *n, pl* **makos** a powerful shark of the Atlantic and Pacific Oceans ▶ HISTORY Māori

mal- *combining form* bad or badly; wrong or wrongly: *maladjusted; malfunction* ▶ HISTORY Latin *malus* bad, *male* badly

malachite (**mal**-a-kite) *n* a green mineral used as a source of copper, and for making ornaments ▶ HISTORY Greek *molokhitis*

maladjustment *n psychol* a failure to meet the demands of society, such as coping with problems and social relationships > **maladjusted** *adj*

maladroit (mal-a-**droyt**) *adj* clumsy, awkward, or tactless ▶ HISTORY French *mal* badly + ADROIT > **maladroitly** *adv* > **maladroitness** *n*

malady (**mal**-a-dee) *n, pl* **-dies** *old-fashioned* any disease or illness ▶ HISTORY Vulgar Latin *male habitus* in poor condition

malaise (mal-**laze**) *n* **1** a vague feeling of unease, illness, or depression **2** a complex of problems affecting a country, economy, etc.: *Belgium's political malaise* ▶ HISTORY Old French *mal* bad + *aise* ease

malapropism *n* the comic misuse of a word by confusion with one which sounds similar, for example *under the affluence of alcohol* ▶ HISTORY after Mrs *Malaprop* in Sheridan's play *The Rivals*

malaria *n* a disease with recurring attacks of fever, caused by the bite of some types of mosquito ▶ HISTORY Italian *mala aria* bad air > **malarial** *adj*

Malay *n* **1** a member of a people living chiefly in Malaysia and Indonesia **2** the language of this people ▷ *adj* **3** of the Malays or their language

Malayan *adj* **1** of Malaya ▷ *n* **2** a person from Malaya

Malaysian *adj* **1** of Malaysia ▷ *n* **2** a person from Malaysia

malcontent *n* a person who is discontented with the existing situation ▶ HISTORY Old French

male *adj* **1** of the sex that can fertilize female reproductive cells **2** of or characteristic of a man **3** for or composed of men or boys: *a male choir* **4** (of flowers) bearing stamens but lacking a pistil **5** *electronics, engineering* having a projecting part or parts that fit into a hollow counterpart: *a male plug* ▷ *n* **6** a male person, animal, or plant ▶ HISTORY Latin *masculus* masculine > **maleness** *n*

m

male chauvinism *n* the belief, held by some men, that men are better and more important than women ▶ **male chauvinist** *n, adj*

malediction (mal-lid-**dik**-shun) *n* the utterance of a curse against someone or something ▶ HISTORY Latin *maledictio* a reviling > **maledictory** *adj*

malefactor (**mal**-if-act-or) *n* a criminal or wrongdoer ▶ HISTORY Latin *malefacere* to do evil > **malefaction** *n*

malevolent (mal-**lev**-a-lent) *adj* wishing evil to others; malicious ▶ HISTORY Latin *malevolens* > **malevolence** *n* > **malevolently** *adv*

malfeasance (mal-**fee**-zanss) *n* *law* wrongful or illegal behaviour, esp. by a public official ▶ HISTORY Old French *mal faisant* evil-doing

malformation *n* **1** the condition of being faulty or abnormal in form or shape **2** *pathol,* written a deformity, esp. when congenital > **malformed** *adj*

malfunction *vb* **1** to fail to function properly or fail to function at all ▷ *n* **2** failure to function properly or failure to function at all

malice (**mal**-iss) *n* the desire to do harm or cause mischief to others ▶ HISTORY Latin *malus* evil > **malicious** *adj* > **maliciously** *adv*

malice aforethought *n* *law* a deliberate intention to do something unlawful

malign (mal-**line**) *vb* **1** to say unpleasant and untrue things about someone; slander ▷ *adj* **2** evil in influence or effect ▶ HISTORY Latin *malignus* spiteful

malignant (mal-**lig**-nant) *adj* **1** seeking to harm others **2** tending to cause great harm; injurious **3** *pathol* (of a tumour) uncontrollable or resistant to therapy ▶ HISTORY Late Latin *malignare* to behave spitefully > **malignancy** *n*

malignity (mal-**lig**-nit-ee) *n* the condition of being malign or deadly

malinger (mal-**ling**-ger) *vb* to pretend to be ill, or exaggerate how ill one is, to avoid work ▶ HISTORY French *malingre* sickly > **malingerer** *n*

mall (**mawl**) *n* **1** *US, Canad, Austral & NZ* short for **shopping mall 2** a shaded avenue, esp. one open to the public ▶ HISTORY after *the Mall,* an avenue in St James's Park, London

mallard *n, pl* **-lard** *or* **-lards** a common N hemisphere duck, the male of which has a dark green head ▶ HISTORY Old French *mallart*

malleable (**mal**-lee-a-bl) *adj* **1** (esp. of metal) capable of being hammered or pressed into shape without breaking **2** *written* able to be influenced ▶ HISTORY Medieval Latin *malleabilis* > **malleability** *n* > **malleably** *adv*

mallee *n* a low-growing eucalypt found in dry regions of Australia

mallet *n* **1** a hammer with a large wooden head **2** a long stick with a head like a hammer used to strike the ball in croquet or polo ▶ HISTORY Old French *maillet* wooden hammer

mallow *n* any of a group of plants, with purple, pink, or white flowers ▶ HISTORY Latin *malva*

malnourished *adj* physically weak due to lack of healthy food

malnutrition *n* physical weakness resulting from insufficient food or an unbalanced diet

malodorous (mal-**lode**-or-uss) *adj* having an unpleasant smell: *the malodorous sludge of Boston harbour*

Malpighian body (mal-**pig**-ee-an) *n* *anat* a cluster of capillaries at the end of each tubule of the kidney ▶ HISTORY after Marcello *Malpighi,* Italian physiologist

malpractice *n* illegal, unethical, or negligent professional conduct

malt *n* **1** grain, such as barley, that is kiln-dried after it has been germinated by soaking in water **2** See **malt whisky** ▷ *vb* **3** to make into or become malt **4** to make from malt or to add malt to ▶ HISTORY Old English *mealt* > **malted** *adj* > **malty** *adj*

Maltese *adj* **1** of Malta ▷ *n* **2** (*pl* **-tese**) a person from Malta **3** the language of Malta

Maltese cross *n* a cross with triangular arms that taper towards the centre, sometimes with the outer sides curving in

Malthusian (malth-**yew**-zee-an) *adj* of the theory stating that increases in population tend to exceed increases in the food supply and that therefore sexual restraint should be exercised ▶ HISTORY after T. R. *Malthus,* economist

maltose *n* a sugar formed by the action of enzymes on starch ▶ HISTORY *malt* + *-ose* indicating a sugar

maltreat *vb* to treat badly, cruelly, or violently ▶ HISTORY French *maltraiter* > **maltreatment** *n*

malt whisky *n* whisky made from malted barley

malware *n* *computers* a program designed specifically to damage or disrupt a system, such as a virus

mama *or esp US* **mamma** (mam-**mah**) *n* *old-fashioned, informal* same as **mother** ▶ HISTORY reduplication of childish syllable *ma*

mamba *n* a very poisonous tree snake found in tropical and Southern Africa ▶ HISTORY Zulu *im-amba*

mambo *n, pl* **-bos** a Latin American dance resembling the rumba ▶ HISTORY American Spanish

mammal *n* a warm-blooded animal, such as a human being, dog, or whale, the female of which produces milk to feed her babies ▶ HISTORY Latin *mamma* breast > **mammalian** *adj, n*

mammary *adj* of the breasts or milk-producing glands ▶ HISTORY Latin *mamma* breast

mammary gland *n* any of the milk-producing glands in mammals, such as a woman's breast or a cow's udder

mammon *n* wealth regarded as a source of evil and corruption, personified in the New Testament as a false god (**Mammon**) ▶ HISTORY New Testament Greek *mammōnas* wealth

mammoth *n* **1** a large extinct elephant with a hairy coat and long curved tusks ▷ *adj* **2** gigantic ▶ HISTORY Russian *mamot*

m

man *n, pl* **men 1** an adult male human being, as distinguished from a woman **2** a human being of either sex; person: *all men are born equal* **3** human beings collectively; mankind. *Related adjective:* **anthropoid 4** a human being regarded as representative of a particular period or category: *Neanderthal man* **5** an adult male human being with qualities associated with the male, such as courage or virility: *take it like a man* **6** an employee, servant, or representative **7** a member of the armed forces who is not an officer **8** a member of a group or team **9** a husband, boyfriend, or male lover **10** a movable piece in various games, such as draughts **11** *S African, slang* any person: used as a term of address **12 as one man** with unanimous action or response **13 he's your man** he's the person needed **14 man and boy** from childhood **15 sort out the men from the boys** to discover who can cope with difficult or dangerous situations and who cannot **16 to a man** without exception ▷ *vb* **manning, manned 17** to provide with sufficient people for operation or defence **18** to take one's place at or near in readiness for action ▶ HISTORY Old English *mann*
> **manhood** *n*

mana *n NZ* authority, influence, and prestige

manacle (**man**-a-kl) *n* **1** a metal ring or chain put round the wrists or ankles, used to restrict the movements of a prisoner or convict ▷ *vb* **-cling, -cled 2** to put manacles on ▶ HISTORY Latin *manus* hand

manage *vb* **-aging, -aged 1** to succeed in doing something: *we finally managed to sell our old house* **2** to be in charge of; administer: *the company is badly managed* **3** to have room or time for: *can you manage lunch tomorrow?* **4** to keep under control: *she disapproved of taking drugs to manage stress* **5** to struggle on despite difficulties, esp. financial ones: *most people cannot manage on a cleaner's salary* ▶ HISTORY Italian *maneggiare* to train (esp. horses)
> **manageable** *adj*

management *n* **1** the people responsible for running an organization or business **2** managers or employers collectively **3** the technique or practice of managing or controlling

manager *n* **1** a person who manages an organization or business **2** a person in charge of a sports team **3** a person who controls the business affairs of an entertainer > **manageress** *fem n*

managerial *adj* of a manager or management

managing director *n* the senior director of a company, who has overall responsibility for the way it is run

mañana (man-**yah**-na) *n, adv* **a** tomorrow **b** some other and later time ▶ HISTORY Spanish

man-at-arms *n, pl* **men-at-arms** a soldier, esp. a medieval soldier

manatee *n* a large plant-eating mammal occurring in tropical coastal waters of the Atlantic ▶ HISTORY Carib *Manattouï*

Manchu *n, pl* **-chus** *or* **-chu** a member of a Mongoloid people of Manchuria, a region of NE China, who conquered China in the 17th century, ruling until 1912

Mancunian (man-**kew**-nee-an) *adj* **1** of Manchester, a city in NW England ▷ *n* **2** a person from Manchester ▶ HISTORY Medieval Latin *Mancunium* Manchester

mandala *n Hindu and Buddhist art* a circular design symbolizing the universe ▶ HISTORY Sanskrit: circle

mandamus *n, pl* **mandamuses** *law* an order from a superior court commanding a body or public official to carry out a public duty ▶ HISTORY Latin: we command, from *mandāre*

mandarin *n* **1** (in the Chinese Empire) a member of a senior grade of the bureaucracy **2** a high-ranking official with extensive powers **3** a person of standing and influence, esp. in literary or intellectual circles **4** a small citrus fruit resembling the tangerine ▶ HISTORY Sanskrit *mantrin* counsellor

Mandarin Chinese *or* **Mandarin** *n* the official language of China since 1917

mandate *n* **1** an official or authoritative command to carry out a particular task: *the UN force's mandate does not allow it to intervene* **2** *politics* the political authority given to a government or an elected representative through an electoral victory **3** Also: **mandated territory** (formerly) a territory administered by one country on behalf of an international body ▷ *vb* **-dating, -dated 4** to delegate authority to **5** to assign territory to a nation under a mandate ▶ HISTORY Latin *mandare* to command

mandatory *adj* **1** obligatory; compulsory **2** having the nature or powers of a mandate
> **mandatorily** *adv*

mandible *n* **1** the lower jawbone of a vertebrate **2** either of the jawlike mouthparts of an insect **3** either part of the bill of a bird, esp. the lower part ▶ HISTORY Late Latin *mandibula* jaw

mandir (**mun**-dee-uh) *n* a Hindu temple ▶ HISTORY Hindi

mandolin *n* a musical instrument with four pairs of strings stretched over a small light body, usually played with a plectrum ▶ HISTORY Italian *mandolino* small lute

mandrake *n* a plant with a forked root. It was formerly thought to have magic powers and a narcotic was prepared from its root ▶ HISTORY Latin *mandragoras*

mandrel *or* **mandril** *n* **1** a spindle on which the object being worked on is supported in a lathe **2** a shaft on which a machining tool is mounted ▶ HISTORY perhaps from French *mandrin* lathe

mandrill *n* a monkey of W Africa. The male has red and blue markings on its face and buttocks ▶ HISTORY *man* + *drill* an Old-World monkey

mane *n* **1** the long hair that grows from the neck in such mammals as the lion and horse **2** long thick human hair ▶ HISTORY Old English *manu*
> **maned** *adj*

manful *adj* determined and brave > **manfully** *adv*

manganese *n chem* a brittle greyish-white metallic element used in making steel. Symbol: Mn ▶ HISTORY probably altered form of Medieval Latin *magnesia*

mange *n* a skin disease of domestic animals, characterized by itching and loss of hair ▶ HISTORY Old French *mangeue* itch

mangelwurzel *n* a variety of beet with a large yellowish root ▶ HISTORY German *Mangold* beet + *Wurzel* root

manger *n* a trough in a stable or barn from which horses or cattle feed ▶ HISTORY Old French *maingeure*

mangetout (**mawnzh**-too) *n* a variety of garden pea with an edible pod ▶ HISTORY French: eat all

mangle[1] *vb* **-gling, -gled 1** to destroy or damage by crushing and twisting **2** to spoil ▶ HISTORY Norman French *mangler* > **mangled** *adj*

mangle[2] *n* **1** a machine for pressing or squeezing water out of washed clothes, consisting of two heavy rollers between which the clothes are passed ▷ *vb* **-gling, -gled 2** to put through a mangle ▶ HISTORY Dutch *mangel*

mango *n, pl* **-goes** *or* **-gos** the egg-shaped edible fruit of a tropical Asian tree, with a smooth rind and sweet juicy flesh ▶ HISTORY Malay *mangā*

mangrove *n* a tropical evergreen tree or shrub with intertwining aerial roots that forms dense thickets along coasts ▶ HISTORY older *mangrow* (changed through influence of *grove*), from Portuguese *mangue*

mangy *adj* **-gier, -giest 1** having mange **2** scruffy or shabby > **mangily** *adv* > **manginess** *n*

manhandle *vb* **-handling, -handled 1** to handle or push someone about roughly **2** to move something by manpower rather than by machinery

manhole *n* a hole with a detachable cover, through which a person can enter a sewer or pipe to inspect or repair it

man-hour *n* a unit of work in industry, equal to the work done by one person in one hour

manhunt *n* an organized search, usually by police, for a wanted man or fugitive

mania *n* **1** an obsessional enthusiasm or liking **2** a mental disorder characterized by great or violent excitement ▶ HISTORY Greek: madness

-mania *n combining form* indicating extreme or abnormal excitement aroused by something: *kleptomania*

maniac *n* **1** a wild disorderly person **2** a person who has a great craving or enthusiasm for something ▶ HISTORY Late Latin *maniacus* belonging to madness > **maniacal** (man-**eye**-ak-kl) *adj*

manic *adj* **1** extremely excited or energetic; frenzied: *manic, cavorting dancers* **2** of, involving, or affected by mania: *deep depression broken by periods of manic excitement*

manic-depressive *psychiatry adj* **1** denoting a mental disorder characterized by an alternation between extreme euphoria and deep depression ▷ *n* **2** a person afflicted with this disorder

manicure *n* **1** cosmetic care of the hands and fingernails ▷ *vb* **-curing, -cured 2** to care for the fingernails and hands ▶ HISTORY Latin *manus* hand + *cura* care > **manicurist** *n*

manifest *adj* **1** easily noticed, obvious ▷ *vb* **2** to reveal or display: *an additional symptom now manifested itself* **3** to show by the way one behaves: *he manifested great personal bravery* **4** (of a disembodied spirit) to appear in visible form ▷ *n* **5** a customs document containing particulars of a ship and its cargo **6** a list of the cargo and passengers on an aeroplane ▶ HISTORY Latin *manifestus* plain > **manifestation** *n*

manifest destiny *n history* the 19th-century doctrine that territorial expansion of the United States was both justified and divinely ordained

manifesto *n, pl* **-tos** *or* **-toes** a public declaration of intent or policy issued by a group of people, for instance by a political party ▶ HISTORY Italian

manifold *adj* **1** *formal* numerous and varied: *her talents are manifold* ▷ *n* **2** a pipe with a number of inlets or outlets, esp. one in a car engine ▶ HISTORY Old English *manigfeald*

manikin *n* **1** a little man; dwarf or child **2** a model of the human body ▶ HISTORY Dutch *manneken*

manila *or* **manilla** *n* a strong usually brown paper used to make envelopes ▶ HISTORY after *Manila*, in the Philippines

man in the street *n* the average person

manioc *n* same as **cassava** ▶ HISTORY S American Indian *mandioca*

manipulate *vb* **-lating, -lated 1** to handle or use skilfully **2** to control something or someone cleverly or deviously ▶ HISTORY Latin *manipulus* handful > **manipulation** *n* > **manipulator** *n* > **manipulative** *adj*

mankind *n* **1** human beings collectively **2** men collectively

manly *adj* **-lier, -liest 1** possessing qualities, such as vigour or courage, traditionally regarded as appropriate to a man; masculine **2** characteristic of a man > **manliness** *n*

man-made *adj* made by humans; artificial

manna *n* **1** *Bible* the miraculous food which sustained the Israelites in the wilderness (Exodus 16:14–36) **2** a windfall: *manna from heaven* ▶ HISTORY Hebrew *mān*

manned *adj* having a human staff or crew: *thirty years of manned space flight*

mannequin *n* **1** a woman who wears the clothes displayed at a fashion show; model **2** a life-size dummy of the human body used to fit or display clothes ▶ HISTORY French

manner *n* **1** the way a thing happens or is done **2** a person's bearing and behaviour **3** the style or customary way of doing something: *sculpture in the Greek manner* **4** type or kind **5 in a manner of speaking** in a way; so to speak **6 to the manner born** naturally fitted to a specified role or activity ▶ HISTORY Old French *maniere*

m

507

mannered *adj* **1** (of speech or behaviour) unnaturally formal and put on to impress others **2** having manners as specified: *ill-mannered*

mannerism *n* **1** a distinctive and individual gesture way or way of speaking **2** excessive use of a distinctive or affected manner, esp. in art or literature

mannerly *adj* well-mannered and polite > **mannerliness** *n*

manners *pl n* **1** a person's social conduct viewed in the light of whether it is regarded as polite or acceptable or not: *his manners leave something to be desired; shockingly bad manners* **2** a socially acceptable way of behaving: *it's not manners to point*

mannish *adj* (of a woman) displaying qualities regarded as typical of a man

manoeuvre *or US* **maneuver** (man-**noo**-ver) *vb* **-vring, -vred** *or US* **-vering, -vered 1** to move or do something with dexterity and skill: *she manoeuvred the car easily into the parking space* **2** to manipulate a situation in order to gain some advantage **3** to perform a manoeuvre or manoeuvres ▷ *n* **4** a movement or action requiring dexterity and skill **5** a contrived, complicated, and possibly deceptive plan or action **6 manoeuvres** military or naval exercises, usually on a large scale **7** a change in course of a ship or aircraft, esp. a complicated one **8 room for manoeuvre** the possibility of changing one's plans or behaviour if it becomes necessary or desirable ▶ HISTORY French, from Medieval Latin *manuopera* manual work > **manoeuvrable** *or US* **maneuverable** *adj* > **manoeuvrability** *or US* **maneuverability** *n*

man-of-war *n, pl* **men-of-war 1** a warship **2** short for **Portuguese man-of-war**

manor *n* **1** (in medieval Europe) the lands and property controlled by a lord **2** *Brit* a large country house and its lands **3** *Brit, slang* an area of operation, esp. of a local police force ▶ HISTORY Old French *manoir* dwelling > **manorial** *adj*

manpower *n* the number of people needed or available for a job

manqué (**mong**-kay) *adj* unfulfilled; would-be: *an actor manqué* ▶ HISTORY French, literally: having missed

manse *n* the house provided for a minister of some Christian denominations ▶ HISTORY Medieval Latin *mansus* dwelling

manservant *n, pl* **menservants** a male servant, esp. a valet

mansion *n* **1** a large and imposing house **2 Mansions** *Brit* a name given to some blocks of flats as part of their address: *18 Wilton Mansions* ▶ HISTORY Latin *mansio* a remaining

manslaughter *n* *law* the unlawful but not deliberately planned killing of one human being by another

mantel *n* a wooden, stone, or iron frame around a fireplace ▶ HISTORY variant of *mantle*

mantelpiece *n* a shelf above a fireplace often forming part of the mantel. Also: **mantel shelf, chimneypiece**

mantilla *n* a woman's lace or silk scarf covering the shoulders and head, worn esp. in Spain ▶ HISTORY Spanish *manta* cloak

mantis *n, pl* **-tises** *or* **-tes** a carnivorous insect, resembling a grasshopper, that rests with the first pair of legs raised as if in prayer. Also: **praying mantis** ▶ HISTORY Greek: prophet

mantissa *n* the part of a common logarithm consisting of the decimal point and the figures following it: *the mantissa of 2.4771 is .4771* ▶ HISTORY Latin: something added

mantle *n* **1** *old-fashioned* a loose wrap or cloak **2** *written* anything that covers completely or envelops: *a mantle of snow covered the ground* **3** *written* the responsibilities and duties which go with a particular job or position: *he refuses to accept the mantle of leader* **4** a small mesh dome used to increase illumination in a gas or oil lamp by becoming incandescent **5** *geol* the part of the earth between the crust and the core ▷ *vb* **-tling, -tled 6** to spread over or become spread over: *mountains mantled in lush vegetation* ▶ HISTORY Latin *mantellum* little cloak

mantra *n* **1** *Hinduism, Buddhism* any sacred word or syllable used as an object of concentration **2** *Hinduism* a Vedic psalm of praise ▶ HISTORY Sanskrit: speech, instrument of thought

manual *adj* **1** of a hand or hands: *manual dexterity* **2** physical as opposed to mental: *manual labour* **3** operated or done by human labour rather than automatic or computer-aided means: *a manual gearbox* ▷ *n* **4** a book of instructions or information **5** *music* one of the keyboards on an organ ▶ HISTORY Latin *manus* hand > **manually** *adv*

manufacture *vb* **-turing, -tured 1** to process or make goods on a large scale, esp. using machinery **2** to invent or concoct evidence, an excuse, etc. ▷ *n* **3** the production of goods, esp. by industrial processes ▶ HISTORY Latin *manus* hand + *facere* to make > **manufacturer** *n* > **manufacturing** *n, adj*

manuka (**mah**-nook-a) *n* a New Zealand tree with strong elastic wood and aromatic leaves ▶ HISTORY Māori

manure *n* **1** animal excrement used as a fertilizer ▷ *vb* **-nuring, -nured 2** to spread manure upon fields or soil ▶ HISTORY Anglo-French *mainoverer*

manuscript *n* **1** a book or other document written by hand **2** the original handwritten or typed version of a book or article submitted by an author for publication ▶ HISTORY Medieval Latin *manuscriptus* handwritten

Manx *adj* **1** of the Isle of Man ▷ *n* **2** an almost extinct Celtic language of the Isle of Man ▷ *pl n* **3 the Manx** the people of the Isle of Man ▶ HISTORY Scandinavian > **Manxman** *n* > **Manxwoman** *n*

Manx cat *n* a short-haired breed of cat without a tail

many *adj* **1** a large number of; numerous: *many times; many people think the government is incompetent* ▷ *pron* **2** a number of people or things,

m

esp. a large one: *have as many as you want* **3 many a** each of a considerable number of: *many a man* ▷ *n* **4 the many** the majority of mankind, esp. the common people ▶ **HISTORY** Old English *manig*

Maoism *n* Communism as interpreted in the theories and policies of Mao Tse-tung (1893–1976), Chinese statesman > **Maoist** *n*, *adj*

Māori *n* **1** (*pl* **-ri** or **-ris**) a member of the Polynesian people living in New Zealand since before the arrival of European settlers **2** the language of this people ▷ *adj* **3** of this people or their language

map *n* **1** a diagrammatic representation of the earth's surface or part of it, showing the geographical distributions or positions of features such as roads, towns, relief, and rainfall **2** a diagrammatic representation of the stars or of the surface of a celestial body **3** *maths* same as **function 4 put on the map** to make (a town or company) well-known: *William Morris put Kelmscott on the map* ▷ *vb* **mapping, mapped 5** to make a map of **6** *maths* to represent or transform (a function, figure, or set) ▷ See also **map out** ▶ **HISTORY** Latin *mappa* cloth

maple *n* **1** any of various trees or shrubs with five-pointed leaves and winged seeds borne in pairs **2** the hard wood of any of these trees ▷ See also **sugar maple** ▶ **HISTORY** Old English *mapeltrēow* maple tree

maple syrup *n* a very sweet syrup made from the sap of the sugar maple

map out *vb* to plan or design

mapping *n* *maths* same as **function**

map projection *n* *geog* a representation of or a means of representing a globe or celestial sphere or part of it on a flat map

maquis (mah-**kee**) *n*, *pl* **-quis** (-**kee**) **1** the French underground movement that fought against the German occupying forces in World War II **2** a type of shrubby, mostly evergreen, vegetation found in coastal regions of the Mediterranean area ▶ **HISTORY** French

mar *vb* **marring, marred** to spoil or be the one bad feature of: *Sicily's coastline is marred by high-rise hotels* ▶ **HISTORY** Old English *merran*

Mar. March

marabou *n* **1** a large black-and-white African stork **2** the soft white down of this bird, used to trim hats, etc. ▶ **HISTORY** Arabic *murābit* holy man

maraca (mar-**rak**-a) *n* a shaken percussion instrument, usually one of a pair, consisting of a gourd or plastic shell filled with dried seeds or pebbles ▶ **HISTORY** Brazilian Portuguese

marae (mar-**rye**) *n* *NZ* **1** an enclosed space in front of a Māori meeting house **2** a Māori meeting house and its buildings ▶ **HISTORY** Māori

maraschino cherry *n* a cherry preserved in maraschino

marasmus *n* *pathol* general emaciation and wasting

marathon *n* **1** a race on foot of 26 miles 385 yards (42.195 km) **2** any long or arduous task or event ▷ *adj* **3** of or relating to a race on foot of 26 miles

385 yards (42.195 km): *marathon runners* **4** long and arduous: *a marathon nine hour meeting* ▶ **HISTORY** referring to the feat of the messenger said to have run 26 miles from Marathon to Athens to bring the news of victory in 490 BC

marble *n* **1** a hard limestone rock, which usually has a mottled appearance and can be given a high polish **2** a block of marble or work of art made of marble **3** a small round glass ball used in playing marbles ▷ *vb* **-bling, -bled 4** to mottle with variegated streaks in imitation of marble ▶ **HISTORY** Greek *marmaros* > **marbled** *adj*

marbling *n* **1** a mottled effect or pattern resembling marble **2** the streaks of fat in lean meat

marcasite *n* **1** a pale yellow form of iron pyrites used in jewellery **2** a cut and polished form of steel used for making jewellery ▶ **HISTORY** Arabic *marqashītā*

march[1] *vb* **1** to walk with very regular steps, like a soldier **2** to walk in a quick and determined manner, esp. when angry: *he marched into the kitchen without knocking* **3** to make a person or group proceed: *he was marched back to his cell* **4** (of an army, procession, etc.) to walk as an organized group: *the demonstrators marched down the main street* **5** to advance or progress steadily: *time marches on* ▷ *n* **6** a regular stride **7** a long or exhausting walk **8** the steady development or progress of something: *the continuous march of industrial development* **9** a distance covered by marching **10** an organized protest in which a large group of people walk somewhere together: *a march against racial violence* **11** a piece of music suitable for marching to **12 steal a march on** to gain an advantage over, esp. by a trick ▶ **HISTORY** Old French *marchier* to tread > **marcher** *n* > **marching** *adj*

march[2] *n* **1** a border or boundary **2** the land lying along a border or boundary, often of disputed ownership ▶ **HISTORY** Old French *marche*

March *n* the third month of the year ▶ **HISTORY** Latin *Martius* (month) of Mars

March hare *n* a hare during its breeding season in March, noted for its wild and excitable behaviour

marching girl *n* *NZ* a girl who does team formation marching as a sport

marching orders *pl n* **1** *informal* dismissal, esp. from employment **2** military orders, giving instructions about a march

marchioness (marsh-on-**ness**) *n* **1** a woman who holds the rank of marquis or marquess **2** the wife or widow of a marquis or marquess ▶ **HISTORY** Medieval Latin *marchionissa*

Mardi Gras (**mar**-dee **grah**) *n* the festival of Shrove Tuesday, celebrated in some cities with great revelry ▶ **HISTORY** French: fat Tuesday

mare[1] *n* the adult female of a horse or zebra ▶ **HISTORY** Old English *mere*

mare[2] (**mar**-ray) *n*, *pl* **maria** one of many huge dry plains on the surface of the moon or Mars, visible as dark markings ▶ **HISTORY** Latin: sea

509

mark

WORD FOCUS

Mark is rather a vague word. Depending on what you are referring to, there are a number of more interesting synonyms which you can use in its place.

DEFINITION 1
- If you would like to describe a stain, you could try: an ink **blot** • a **line** of dirt • a lipstick **smudge** • a grease **spot** • a **streak** of mud
- If you would like to describe a damaged area on a surface, you could try: slight **blemishes** • purple **blotches** • cuts and **bruises** • a tiny **dent** • little **nicks** on his chin • a jagged **scar** • a long **scratch**

DEFINITION 2
- If you would like to describe a sign that indicates something, you could try: the company's **emblem** • the Papal **insignia** • corporate **logo** • zodiac **sign** • a flag bearing a national **symbol**

DEFINITION 3
- If you would like to describe a written or printed symbol, you could try: Chinese **characters** • a multiplication **sign** • the paragraph **symbol**

DEFINITION 4
- If you would like to describe a grade, you could

try: good **grades** • compare **percentages** • high **score** in the exam

DEFINITION 5
- If you would like to describe something that indicates position, you could try: up to third **level** • a **marker** of distance • the halfway **point** • middle **stage**

DEFINITION 6
- If you would like to describe something that is an indication of something, you could try: a **gesture** of goodwill • an **indication** of his regard • a **sign** of respect • a **symbol** of mourning • a **token** of our friendship

DEFINITION 7
- If you would like to describe a goal, you could try: our final **aim** • achieve our **end** • reach the **goal** • meet my **objective** • hit the **target**

DEFINITION 8
- If you would like to describe a characteristic of something, you could try: the essential **attributes** • a defining **characteristic** • fundamental **features** • the hallmark • a **measure** • a **symptom** • a common **trait**

---

m

margarine n a butter substitute made from vegetable and animal fats ▶ HISTORY Greek *margaron* pearl

marge n *Brit & Austral, informal* margarine

margin n **1** an edge, rim, or border: *we came to the margin of the wood; people on the margin of society* **2** the blank space surrounding the text on a page **3** an additional amount or one beyond the minimum necessary: *the margin of victory was seven lengths; a small margin of error* **4** *chiefly Austral* a payment made in addition to a basic wage, esp. for special skill or responsibility **5** a limit beyond which something can no longer exist or function: *the margin of physical survival* **6** *econ* the minimum return below which an enterprise becomes unprofitable ▶ HISTORY Latin *margo* border

marginal *adj* **1** of, in, on, or forming a margin **2** not important; insignificant: *he remained a rather marginal political figure* **3** close to a limit, esp. a lower limit: *marginal legal ability* **4** *econ* relating to goods or services produced and sold at the margin of profitability: *marginal cost* **5** *politics* of or designating a constituency in which elections tend to be won by small margins: *a marginal seat* **6** designating agricultural land on the edge of fertile areas ▷ n **7** *politics, chiefly Brit & NZ* a marginal constituency > **marginally** *adv*

marginalia *pl n* notes in the margin of a book, manuscript, or letter

margrave n (formerly) a German nobleman ranking above a count ▶ HISTORY Middle Dutch *markgrave* count of the frontier

marguerite n a garden plant with flowers resembling large daisies ▶ HISTORY French: daisy

marigold n any of various plants cultivated for their yellow or orange flowers ▶ HISTORY from *Mary* (the Virgin) + *gold*

marijuana *or* **marihuana** (mar-ree-**wah**-na) n the dried leaves and flowers of the hemp plant, used as a drug, esp. in cigarettes ▶ HISTORY Mexican Spanish

marimba n a percussion instrument consisting of a set of hardwood plates placed over tuned metal resonators, played with soft-headed sticks ▶ HISTORY West African

marina n a harbour for yachts and other pleasure boats ▶ HISTORY Latin: marine

marinade n **1** a mixture of oil, wine, vinegar, etc. in which meat or fish is soaked before cooking ▷ *vb* **-nading, -naded** **2** same as **marinate** ▶ HISTORY French

marinate *vb* **-nating, -nated** to soak in marinade ▶ HISTORY Italian *marinare* to pickle > **marinated** *adj*

marine *adj* **1** of, found in, or relating to the sea **2** of shipping or navigation **3** used or adapted for use at sea ▷ n **4** (esp. in Britain and the US) a soldier trained for land and sea combat **5** a country's shipping or navy collectively: *the merchant marine* ▶ HISTORY Latin *marinus* of the sea

mariner (**mar**-in-er) n a sailor

marionette n a puppet whose limbs are moved by strings ▶ HISTORY French, from the name *Marion*

marital *adj* of or relating to marriage ▶ HISTORY Latin *maritus* married > **maritally** *adv*

maritime *adj* **1** of or relating to shipping **2** of, near, or living near the sea ▶ HISTORY Latin *maritimus* of the sea

marjoram *n* a plant with sweet-scented leaves, used for seasoning food and in salads ▶ HISTORY Medieval Latin *marjorana*

mark¹ *n* **1** a visible impression on a surface, such as a spot or scratch **2** a sign, symbol, or other indication that distinguishes something **3** a written or printed symbol, as used for punctuation **4** a letter, number, or percentage used to grade academic work **5** a thing that indicates position; marker **6** an indication of some quality: *a mark of respect* **7** a target or goal **8** impression or influence: *this book displays the mark of its author's admiration of Kafka* **9** (in trade names) a particular model or type of a vehicle, machine, etc.: *the Ford Escort Mark Two* **10** one of the temperature settings at which a gas oven can work: *bake at gas mark 5 for 30 minutes* **11 make one's mark** to achieve recognition **12 on your mark** *or* **marks** a command given to runners in a race to prepare themselves at the starting line **13 up to the mark** meeting the desired standard ▷ *vb* **14** to make a visible impression, trace, or stain on **15** to have a tendency to become dirty, scratched, or damaged: *this material marks easily* **16** to characterize or distinguish: *the gritty determination that has marked his career* **17** to designate someone as a particular type of person: *she would now be marked as a troublemaker* **18** to label, esp. to indicate price **19** to celebrate or commemorate an occasion or its anniversary: *a series of concerts to mark the 200th anniversary of Mozart's death* **20** to pay attention to: *mark my words* **21** to observe or notice **22** to grade or evaluate academic work **23** *sport* to stay close to an opponent to hamper his or her play **24 mark off** *or* **out** to set boundaries or limits on **25 mark time a** to move the feet alternately as in marching but without advancing **b** to wait for something more interesting to happen ▷ See also **markdown, mark-up** ▶ HISTORY Old English *mearc* See WORD FOCUS **mark**

mark² *n* See **Deutschmark** ▶ HISTORY Old English *marc* unit of weight of precious metal

markdown *n* **1** a price reduction ▷ *vb* **mark down 2** to reduce in price **3** to make a written note of: *she marked down the number of the getaway car*

marked *adj* **1** obvious or noticeable: *a marked improvement* **2** singled out, esp. as the target of attack: *a marked man* > **markedly** (mark-id-lee) *adv*

marker *n* **1** an object used to show the position of something **2** Also called: **marker pen** a thick felt-tipped pen used for drawing and colouring

market *n* **1** an occasion at which people meet to buy and sell merchandise **2** a place at which a market is held **3** the buying and selling of goods and services, esp. when unrestrained by political or social considerations: *the market has been brought* into health care **4** the trading opportunities provided by a particular group of people: *the youth market* **5** demand for a particular product **6** short for **stock market 7 be in the market for** to wish to buy **8 on the market** available for purchase **9 seller's** (*or* **buyer's**) **market** a market characterized by excess demand (or supply) and thus favourable to sellers (or buyers) ▷ *adj* **10** of, relating to, or controlled by the buying and selling of goods and services, esp. when unrestrained by political or social considerations: *a market economy* ▷ *vb* **-keting, -keted 11** to offer or produce for sale **12** to promote or advertise (a product) ▶ HISTORY Latin *mercari* to trade > **marketable** *adj*

market forces *pl n* the effect of supply and demand on trading within a free market

market garden *n chiefly Brit & NZ* a place where fruit and vegetables are grown for sale > **market gardener** *n*

marketing *n* the part of a business which controls the way that goods or services are sold

marketing mix *n marketing* the variables, such as price, promotion, and service, managed by an organization to influence demand for a product or service

market maker *n Stock Exchange* a dealer in securities on the London Stock Exchange who can also deal with the public as a broker

market-oriented *adj marketing* focusing on consumers rather than on the products

marketplace *n* **1** a place where a public market is held **2** the commercial world of buying and selling

market price *n* the prevailing price at which goods may be bought or sold

market research *n* the study of customers' wants and purchases, and of the forces influencing them

market segmentation *n marketing* the division of a market into identifiable groups to improve the effectiveness of a marketing strategy

market share *n marketing* the percentage of a total market, in terms of either value or volume, accounted for by the sales of a specific brand

market-test *vb* to put (a section of a public-sector service) out to tender, often before full privatization

market town *n chiefly Brit* the main town in an agricultural area, usually one where a market is regularly held

marking *n* **1** the arrangement of colours on an animal or plant **2** the assessment and correction of pupils' or students' written work by teachers

marksman *n, pl* **-men** a person skilled in shooting > **marksmanship** *n*

mark-up *n* **1** an amount added to the cost of something to provide the seller with a profit ▷ *vb* **mark up 2** to increase the cost of something by an amount or percentage in order to make a profit

marl *n* a fine-grained rock consisting of clay, limestone, and silt used as a fertilizer ▶ HISTORY Late Latin *margila* > **marly** *adj*

marlin *n*, *pl* **-lin** *or* **-lins** a large fish with a long spear-like upper jaw, found in warm and tropical seas ▶ HISTORY after *marlinspike* (because of its long jaw)

marlinspike *or* **marlinespike** (**mar**-lin-spike) *n naut* a pointed metal tool used in separating strands of rope ▶ HISTORY Dutch *marlijn* light rope + SPIKE

marmalade *n* a jam made from citrus fruits, esp. oranges ▶ HISTORY Portuguese *marmelo* quince

marmoreal (mar-**more**-ee-al) *adj* of or like marble ▶ HISTORY Latin *marmoreus*

marmoset *n* a small South American monkey with a long bushy tail ▶ HISTORY Old French *marmouset* grotesque figure

marmot *n* any of various burrowing rodents of Europe, Asia, and North America. They are heavily built and have coarse fur ▶ HISTORY French *marmotte*

maroon[1] *vb* **1** to abandon someone in a deserted area, esp. on an island **2** to isolate in a helpless situation: *we're marooned here until the snow stops* ▷ *n* **Maroon 3** a descendant of a group of runaway slaves living in the Caribbean or Guyana ▶ HISTORY American Spanish *cimarrón* wild > **marooned** *adj*

maroon[2] *adj* **1** dark purplish-red ▷ *n* **2** an exploding firework or flare used as a warning signal ▶ HISTORY French: chestnut

marque (**mark**) *n* a brand of product, esp. of a car ▶ HISTORY French

marquee *n* a large tent used for a party, exhibition, etc. ▶ HISTORY invented singular form of MARQUISE

marquess (**mar**-kwiss) *n* **1** (in the British Isles) a nobleman ranking between a duke and an earl **2** See **marquis**

marquetry *n*, *pl* **-quetries** a pattern of inlaid veneers of wood or metal used chiefly as ornamentation in furniture ▶ HISTORY Old French *marqueter* to inlay

marquis *n*, *pl* **-quises** *or* **-quis** (in various countries) a nobleman ranking above a count, corresponding to a British marquess ▶ HISTORY Old French *marchis* count of the frontier

marquise (mar-**keez**) *n* **1** (in various countries) a marchioness **2** a gemstone cut in a pointed oval shape ▶ HISTORY French

marram grass *n* a grass that grows on sandy shores: often planted to stabilize sand dunes ▶ HISTORY Old Norse *marálmr*

marriage *n* **1** the state or relationship of being husband and wife: *the institution of marriage* **2** the contract made by a man and woman to live as husband and wife. *Related adjectives:* **connubial, nuptial 3** the ceremony formalizing this union; wedding **4** a close union or relationship: *the marriage of scientific knowledge and industry*

marriageable *adj* suitable for marriage, usually with reference to age

married *adj* **1** having a husband or wife **2** of marriage or married people: *married life* ▷ *n* **3 marrieds** married people: *young marrieds*

marrow *n* **1** the fatty tissue that fills the cavities of bones **2** short for **vegetable marrow** ▶ HISTORY Old English *mærg*

marry[1] *vb* **-ries, -rying, -ried 1** to take (someone) as one's husband or wife **2** to join or give in marriage **3** Also: **marry up** to fit together or unite; join: *their playing marries Irish traditional music and rock* ▶ HISTORY Latin *maritare*

marry[2] *interj archaic* an exclamation of surprise or anger ▶ HISTORY euphemistic for the Virgin *Mary*

Mars *n* **1** the Roman god of war **2** the fourth planet from the sun

Marseillaise (mar-say-**yaze**) *n* **the Marseillaise** the French national anthem ▶ HISTORY French *(chanson) marseillaise* (song) of Marseilles (first sung in Paris by the battalion of Marseilles)

marsh *n* low poorly drained land that is wet, muddy, and sometimes flooded ▶ HISTORY Old English *merisc* > **marshy** *adj*

marshal *n* **1** (in some armies and air forces) an officer of the highest rank: *Field Marshal* **2** an officer who organizes or controls ceremonies or public events **3** US the chief police or fire officer in some states **4** (formerly in England) an officer of the royal family or court ▷ *vb* **-shalling, -shalled** *or US* **-shaling, -shaled 5** to arrange in order: *she marshalled her facts and came to a conclusion* **6** to assemble and organize people or vehicles in readiness for onward movement **7** to guide or lead, esp. in a ceremonious way: *she marshalled them towards the lecture theatre* ▶ HISTORY Old French *mareschal* > **marshalcy** *n*

marshalling yard *n railways* a place where railway wagons are shunted and made up into trains

Marshal of the Royal Air Force *n* the highest rank in the Royal Air Force

marsh gas *n* a gas largely composed of methane formed when plants decay in the absence of air

marshland *n* land consisting of marshes

marshmallow *n* a spongy pink or white sweet

marsh mallow *n* a plant that grows in salt marshes and has pale pink flowers. It was formerly used to make marshmallows

marsupial (mar-**soop**-ee-al) *n* **1** a mammal, such as a kangaroo or an opossum, the female of which carries her babies in a pouch at the front of her body until they reach a mature state ▷ *adj* **2** of or like a marsupial ▶ HISTORY Latin *marsupium* purse

mart *n* a market or trading centre ▶ HISTORY Middle Dutch: market

Martello tower *n* a round tower used for coastal defence, formerly much used in Europe ▶ HISTORY after Cape *Mortella* in Corsica

marten *n*, *pl* **-tens** *or* **-ten 1** any of several agile weasel-like mammals with bushy tails and golden-brown to blackish fur **2** the fur of these animals ▶ HISTORY Middle Dutch *martren*

martial *adj* of or characteristic of war, soldiers, or the military life: *martial music* ▶ HISTORY Latin *martialis* of Mars, god of war

m

martial art *n* any of various philosophies and techniques of self-defence originating in the Far East, such as judo or karate

martial law *n* rule of law maintained by military forces in the absence of civil law

Martian (**marsh**-an) *adj* **1** of the planet Mars ▷ *n* **2** an inhabitant of Mars, in science fiction

martin *n* a bird of the swallow family with a square or slightly forked tail ▶ **HISTORY** probably after St *Martin*, because the birds were believed to migrate at Martinmas

martinet *n* a person who maintains strict discipline ▶ **HISTORY** after General *Martinet*, drillmaster under Louis XIV

martingale *n* a strap from the reins to the girth of a horse, preventing it from carrying its head too high ▶ **HISTORY** French

martini *n* **1** (often cap) *trademark* an Italian vermouth **2** a cocktail of gin and vermouth

Martinmas *n* the feast of St Martin on November 11: a quarter day in Scotland

martyr *n* **1** a person who chooses to die rather than renounce his or her religious beliefs **2** a person who suffers greatly or dies for a cause or belief **3 a martyr to** suffering constantly from: *a martyr to arthritis* ▷ *vb* **4** to make a martyr of ▶ **HISTORY** Late Greek *martur*- witness > **martyrdom** *n*

marvel *vb* **-velling, -velled** *or US* **-veling, -veled** **1** to be filled with surprise or wonder ▷ *n* **2** something that causes wonder ▶ **HISTORY** Old French *merveille*

marvellous *or US* **marvelous** *adj* **1** excellent or splendid: *a marvellous idea* **2** causing great wonder or surprise; extraordinary: *electricity is a marvellous thing* > **marvellously** *or US* **marvelously** *adv*

Marxism *n* the economic and political theories of Karl Marx (1818–83), German political philosopher, which argue that class struggle is the basic agency of historical change, and that capitalism will be superseded by communism > **Marxist** *n, adj*

marzipan *n* a mixture made from ground almonds, sugar, and egg whites that is put on top of cakes or used to make sweets ▶ **HISTORY** Italian *marzapane*

masc. masculine

mascara *n* a cosmetic for darkening the eyelashes ▶ **HISTORY** Spanish: mask

mascot *n* a person, animal, or thing considered to bring good luck ▶ **HISTORY** French *mascotte*

masculine *adj* **1** possessing qualities or characteristics considered typical of or appropriate to a man; manly **2** unwomanly; not feminine **3** *grammar* denoting a gender of nouns that includes some male animate things **4** *prosody* denoting a rhyme between pairs of single final stressed syllables ▶ **HISTORY** Latin *masculinus* > **masculinity** *n*

maser *n* a device for amplifying microwaves, working on the same principle as a laser ▶ **HISTORY** m(icrowave) a(mplification by) s(timulated) e(mission of) r(adiation)

mash *n* **1** a soft pulpy mass **2** *agriculture* bran, meal, or malt mixed with warm water and used as food for horses, cattle, or poultry **3** *Brit, informal* mashed potatoes ▷ *vb* **4** to beat or crush into a mash ▶ **HISTORY** Old English *mæsc*- > **mashed** *adj*

mask *n* **1** any covering for the whole or a part of the face worn for amusement, protection, or disguise **2** behaviour that hides one's true feelings: *his mask of detachment* **3** *surgery* a sterile gauze covering for the nose and mouth worn to minimize the spread of germs **4** a device placed over the nose and mouth to facilitate or prevent inhalation of a gas **5** a moulded likeness of a face or head, such as a death mask **6** the face or head of an animal such as a fox ▷ *vb* **7** to cover with or put on a mask **8** to hide or disguise: *a high brick wall that masked the front of the building* **9** to cover so as to protect ▶ **HISTORY** Arabic *maskharah* clown > **masked** *adj*

masking tape *n* an adhesive tape used to protect surfaces surrounding an area to be painted

masochism (**mass**-oh-kiz-zum) *n* **1** *psychiatry* a condition in which pleasure is obtained from feeling pain or from being humiliated **2** a tendency to take pleasure from one's own suffering > **masochist** *n, adj* > **masochistic** *adj*

■ **WORD HISTORY**
■ 'Masochism' derives its name from the
■ Austrian novelist Leopold von Sacher *Masoch*
■ (1836–1895), who wrote about the pleasures
■ of masochism.

mason *n* a person skilled in building with stone ▶ **HISTORY** Old French *masson*

Masonic *adj* of Freemasons or Freemasonry

masonry *n* **1** stonework or brickwork **2** the craft of a mason

masque (**mask**) *n* a dramatic entertainment of the 16th to 17th centuries, consisting of dancing, dialogue, and song ▶ **HISTORY** variant of *mask* > **masquer** *n*

masquerade (mask-er-**aid**) *vb* **-ading, -aded** **1** to pretend to be someone or something else ▷ *n* **2** an attempt to keep secret the real identity or nature of something: *he was unable to keep up his masquerade as the war's victor* **3** a party at which the guests wear masks and costumes ▶ **HISTORY** Spanish *mascara* mask

mass *n* **1** a large body of something without a definite shape **2** a collection of the component parts of something: *a mass of fibres* **3** a large amount or number, as of people **4** the main part or majority **5** the size of a body; bulk **6** *physics* a physical quantity expressing the amount of matter in a body **7** (in painting or drawing) an area of unified colour, shade, or intensity ▷ *adj* **8** done or occurring on a large scale: *mass hysteria* **9** consisting of a mass or large number, esp. of people: *a mass meeting* ▷ *vb* **10** to join together into a mass ▷ See also **masses** ▶ **HISTORY** Latin *massa* > **massed** *adj*

Mass *n* **1** (in the Roman Catholic Church and certain other Christian churches) a service in which bread and wine are consecrated to represent the body and blood of Christ **2** a musical setting of parts of this service ▶ HISTORY Church Latin *missa*

massacre (**mass**-a-ker) *n* **1** the wanton or savage killing of large numbers of people **2** *informal* an overwhelming defeat ▷ *vb* **-cring, -cred 3** to kill people indiscriminately in large numbers **4** *informal* to defeat overwhelmingly ▶ HISTORY Old French

massage (**mass**-ahzh) *n* **1** the kneading or rubbing of parts of the body to reduce pain or stiffness or help relaxation ▷ *vb* **-saging, -saged 2** to give a massage to **3** to manipulate (statistics or evidence) to produce a desired result ▶ HISTORY French *masser* to rub

massasauga (mass-a-**saw**-ga) *n* a North American venomous snake with a horny rattle at the end of the tail ▶ HISTORY after the *Missisauga* River, Ontario, Canada

masses *pl n* **1 the masses** ordinary people as a group **2 masses of** *informal*, *chiefly Brit* a great number or quantity of: *masses of food*

masseur (mass-**ur**) *or fem* **masseuse** (mass-**uhz**) *n* a person who gives massages

massif (**mass**-seef) *n* a series of connected masses of rock forming a mountain range ▶ HISTORY French

massive *adj* **1** (of objects) large, bulky, heavy, and usually solid **2** impressive or imposing **3** intensive or considerable: *a massive overdose* ▶ HISTORY French *massif* > **massively** *adv*

mass-market *adj* of, for, or appealing to a large number of people; popular: *mass-market newspapers*

mass media *pl n* the means of communication that reach large numbers of people, such as television, newspapers, and radio

mass movement *n geol* a general term for movement of rocks and sediment down a slope as a result of gravity and the action of water

mass noun *n grammar* a noun that refers to a substance rather than to an individual object, e.g. *water* as opposed to *lake*; mass nouns can be preceded by *some, a lot of, much*, and *more*

mass number *n* the total number of protons and neutrons in the nucleus of an atom

mass-produce *vb* **-producing, -produced** to manufacture standardized goods on a large scale by extensive use of machinery > **mass-produced** *adj* > **mass-production** *n*

mass spectrometer *n* an instrument for analysing the composition of a sample of material, in which ions, produced from the sample, are separated by electric or magnetic fields according to their ratios of charge to mass

mast¹ *n* **1** *naut* a vertical pole for supporting sails, radar equipment, etc., above the deck of a ship **2** a tall upright pole used as an aerial for radio or television broadcasting: *a television mast* **3 before the mast** *naut* as an apprentice seaman ▶ HISTORY Old English *mæst*

mast² *n* the fruit of forest trees, such as beech or oak, used as food for pigs ▶ HISTORY Old English *mæst*

mastectomy (mass-**tek**-tom-ee) *n, pl* **-mies** surgical removal of a breast ▶ HISTORY Greek *mastos* breast + *tomē* a cutting

master *n* **1** the man who has authority over others, such as the head of a household, the employer of servants, or the owner of slaves or animals **2** a person with exceptional skill at a certain thing: *B.B. King is a master of the blues* **3** a person who has complete control of a situation: *the master of his portfolio* **4** an original copy or tape from which duplicates are made **5** a craftsman fully qualified to practise his trade and to train others: *a master builder* **6** a player of a game, esp. chess or bridge, who has won a specified number of tournament games **7** a highly regarded teacher or leader **8** a graduate holding a master's degree **9** the chief officer aboard a merchant ship **10** *chiefly Brit* a male teacher **11** the superior person or side in a contest **12** the heir apparent of a Scottish viscount or baron: *the Master of Ballantrae* ▷ *adj* **13** overall or controlling: *master plan* **14** designating a mechanism that controls others: *master switch* **15** main or principal: *master bedroom* ▷ *vb* **16** to become thoroughly proficient in **17** to overcome or defeat ▶ HISTORY Latin *magister* teacher

master aircrew *n* a rank in the Royal Air Force, equal to warrant officer

masterful *adj* **1** showing great skill **2** domineering or authoritarian > **masterfully** *adv*

master key *n* a key that opens all the locks of a set; passkey

masterly *adj* showing great skill; expert

mastermind *vb* **1** to plan and direct a complex task or project ▷ *n* **2** a person who plans and directs a complex task or project

Master of Arts *n* a degree, usually postgraduate in a nonscientific subject, or a person holding this degree

master of ceremonies *n* a person who presides over a public ceremony, formal dinner, or entertainment, introducing the events and performers

Master of Science *n* a degree, usually postgraduate, in a scientific subject, or a person holding this degree

Master of the Rolls *n* (in England) the senior civil judge in the country and the head of the Public Record Office

masterpiece *or* **masterwork** *n* **1** an outstanding work or performance **2** the most outstanding piece of work of an artist or craftsman

masterstroke *n* an outstanding piece of strategy, skill, or talent

mastery *n, pl* **-teries 1** outstanding skill or expertise **2** complete power or control: *he had complete mastery over the country*

masthead *n* **1** *naut* the highest part of a mast **2** the name of a newspaper or periodical printed at the top of the front page

mastic *n* **1** an aromatic resin obtained from a Mediterranean tree and used to make varnishes and lacquers **2** any of several putty-like substances used as a filler, adhesive, or seal ▶ **HISTORY** Greek *mastikhē*

masticate *vb* **-cating, -cated** to chew food ▶ **HISTORY** Greek *mastikhan* to grind the teeth > **mastication** *n*

mastiff *n* a large powerful short-haired dog, usually fawn or brown with dark streaks ▶ **HISTORY** Latin *mansuetus* tame

mastitis *n* inflammation of the breast

mastodon *n* an extinct elephant-like mammal ▶ **HISTORY** New Latin, literally: breast-tooth, referring to the nipple-shaped projections on the teeth

mastoid *adj* **1** shaped like a nipple or breast ▷ *n* **2** a nipple-like projection of bone behind the ear **3** *informal* mastoiditis ▶ **HISTORY** Greek *mastos* breast

mastoiditis *n* inflammation of the mastoid

mat¹ *n* **1 a** a thick flat piece of fabric used as a floor covering, a place to wipe one's shoes, etc. **2** a small pad of material used to protect a surface from heat or scratches from an object placed upon it **3** a large piece of thick padded material put on the floor as a surface for wrestling, gymnastics, etc. ▷ *vb* **matting, matted 4** to tangle or become tangled into a dense mass ▶ **HISTORY** Old English *matte*

mat² *adj* same as **matt** ▶ **HISTORY** French, literally: dead

matador *n* the bullfighter armed with a sword, who attempts to kill the bull ▶ **HISTORY** Spanish, from *matar* to kill

matai *n* a New Zealand tree, the wood of which is used for timber for building ▶ **HISTORY** Māori

match¹ *n* **1** a formal game or sports event in which people or teams compete **2** a person or thing able to provide competition for another: *he has met his match* **3** a person or thing that resembles, harmonizes with, or is equivalent to another: *the colours aren't a perfect match, but they're close enough; white wine is not a good match for steak* **4** a person or thing that is an exact copy or equal of another **5** a partnership between a man and a woman, as in marriage **6** a person regarded as a possible partner in marriage: *for any number of men she would have been a good match* ▷ *vb* **7** to fit parts together **8** to resemble, harmonize with, or equal one another or something else: *our bedroom curtains match the bedspread; she walked at a speed that he could barely match* **9** to find a match for **10 match with** or **against a** to compare in order to determine which is the superior **b** to arrange a competition between ▶ **HISTORY** Old English *gemæcca* spouse > **matching** *adj*

match² *n* **1** a thin strip of wood or cardboard tipped with a chemical that ignites when scraped against a rough or specially treated surface **2** a fuse used to fire cannons' explosives ▶ **HISTORY** Old French *meiche*

matchbox *n* a small box for holding matches

match-fit *adj sport* in good physical condition for competing in a match

matchless *adj* unequalled

matchmaker *n* a person who introduces people in the hope that they will form a couple > **matchmaking** *n, adj*

match play *n golf* scoring according to the number of holes won and lost

match point *n sport* the final point needed to win a match

matchstick *n* **1** the wooden part of a match ▷ *adj* **2** (esp. of drawn figures) thin and straight: *little matchstick men*

matchwood *n* **1** wood suitable for making matches **2** splinters

mate¹ *n* **1 a** *informal, chiefly Brit, Austral & NZ* a friend: often used as a term of address between males: *I spotted my mate Jimmy McCrae at the other end of the bar; that's all right, mate* **b** an associate or colleague: *a classmate; the governor's running mate* **2** the sexual partner of an animal **3** a marriage partner **4** *naut* any officer below the master on a commercial ship **5** (in some trades) an assistant: *a plumber's mate* **6** one of a pair of matching items ▷ *vb* **mating, mated 7** to pair (a male and female animal) or (of animals) to pair for breeding **8** to marry **9** to join as a pair ▶ **HISTORY** Low German

mate² *n, vb* **mating, mated** *chess* same as **checkmate**

material *n* **1** the substance of which a thing is made **2** cloth **3** ideas or notes that a finished work may be based on: *the material of the story resembles an incident in his own life* ▷ *adj* **4** concerned with or composed of physical matter or substance; not relating to spiritual or abstract things: *the material universe* **5** of or affecting economic or physical wellbeing: *material prosperity* **6** relevant or pertinent: *material evidence* ▷ See also **materials** ▶ **HISTORY** Latin *materia* matter

materialism *n* **1** excessive interest in and desire for money or possessions **2** the belief that only the material world exists > **materialist** *n, adj* > **materialistic** *adj*

materiality *n chiefly law* the quality of being relevant to the issue before court

materialize or **-ise** *vb* **-izing, -ized** or **-ising, -ised 1** *not universally accepted* to become fact; actually happen: *the promised pay rise never materialized* **2** to appear after being invisible: *trees materialized out of the gloom* **3** to take shape: *after hours of talks, a plan began to materialize* > **materialization** or **-isation** *n*

materially *adv* to a significant extent: *we were not materially affected*

material process *n functional grammar* an action or process specified by a verb group. Compare **mental process, relational process, verbal process**

materials *pl n* the equipment necessary for a particular activity: *building materials*

materiel (mat-ear-ee-**ell**) *n* the materials and equipment of an organization, esp. of a military force ▶ **HISTORY** French

maternal *adj* 1 of or characteristic of a mother 2 related through the mother's side of the family: *his maternal uncle* ▸ HISTORY Latin *mater* mother > **maternally** *adv*

maternity *n* 1 motherhood 2 motherliness ▷ *adj* 3 relating to women during pregnancy or childbirth: *maternity leave*

mate's rates *pl n informal* reduced charges offered to a friend or colleague

matey *adj Brit, informal* friendly or intimate

math *n US & Canad, informal* short for **mathematics**

mathematical *adj* 1 using, used in, or relating to mathematics 2 having the precision of mathematics > **mathematically** *adv*

mathematician *n* an expert or specialist in mathematics

mathematics *n* 1 a group of related sciences, including algebra, geometry, and calculus, which use a specialized notation to study number, quantity, shape, and space 2 numerical calculations involved in the solution of a problem ▸ HISTORY Greek *mathēma* a science

maths *n Brit & Austral, informal* short for **mathematics**

matinee (**mat-in-nay**) *n* an afternoon performance of a play or film ▸ HISTORY French

matins *n* an early morning service in various Christian Churches ▸ HISTORY Latin *matutinus* of the morning

matriarch (**mate-ree-ark**) *n* the female head of a tribe or family ▸ HISTORY Latin *mater* mother + Greek *arkhein* to rule > **matriarchal** *adj*

matriarchy *n, pl* **-chies** a form of social organization in which a female is head of the family or society, and descent and kinship are traced through the female line

matrices (**may-triss-seez**) *n* a plural of **matrix**

matricide *n* 1 the act of killing one's mother 2 a person who kills his or her mother ▸ HISTORY Latin *mater* mother + *caedere* to kill > **matricidal** *adj*

matriculate *vb* **-lating, -lated** to enrol or be enrolled in a college or university ▸ HISTORY Medieval Latin *matriculare* to register > **matriculation** *n*

matrilineal (mat-rill-**in**-ee-al) *adj* relating to descent through the female line

matrimony *n* the state of being married ▸ HISTORY Latin *matrimonium* wedlock > **matrimonial** *adj*

matrix (**may-trix**) *n, pl* **-trices** or **-trixes** 1 the context or framework in which something is formed or develops: *a highly complex matrix of overlapping interests* 2 the rock in which fossils or pebbles are embedded 3 a mould, esp. one used in printing 4 *maths* a rectangular array of elements set out in rows and columns ▸ HISTORY Latin: womb

matron *n* 1 a staid or dignified married woman 2 a woman in charge of the domestic or medical arrangements in an institution 3 *Brit* (formerly)

the administrative head of the nursing staff in a hospital ▸ HISTORY Latin *matrona* > **matronly** *adj*

matt or **matte** *adj* having a dull surface rather than a shiny one

matted *adj* tangled into a thick mass

matter *n* 1 the substance of which something, esp. a physical object, is made; material 2 substance that occupies space and has mass, as distinguished from substance that is mental or spiritual 3 substance of a specified type: *vegetable matter* 4 an event, situation, or subject: *a matter of taste; the break-in is a matter for the police* 5 a quantity or amount: *a matter of a few pounds* 6 the content of written or verbal material as distinct from its style or form 7 written material in general: *advertising matter* 8 a secretion or discharge, such as pus 9 **for that matter** as regards that 10 **no matter** regardless of; irrespective of: *you have to leave, no matter what she thinks* 11 **the matter** wrong; the trouble: *there's nothing the matter* ▷ *vb* 12 to be of importance ▷ *interj* **no matter** 13 it is unimportant ▸ HISTORY Latin *materia* cause, substance

matter of fact *n* 1 **as a matter of fact** actually; in fact ▷ *adj* **matter-of-fact** 2 unimaginative or emotionless: *he conducted the executions in a completely matter-of-fact manner*

matting *n* a coarsely woven fabric used as a floor covering

mattock *n* a type of large pick that has one flat, horizontal end to its blade, used for loosening soil ▸ HISTORY Old English *mattuc*

mattress *n* a large flat cushion with a strong cover, filled with cotton, foam rubber, etc., and often including coiled springs, used as a bed ▸ HISTORY Arabic *almatrah* place where something is thrown

maturation *n* the process of becoming mature

mature *adj* 1 fully developed physically or mentally; grown-up 2 (of plans or theories) fully considered and thought-out 3 sensible and balanced in personality and emotional behaviour 4 due or payable: *a mature insurance policy* 5 (of fruit, wine, or cheese) ripe or fully aged ▷ *vb* **-turing, -tured** 6 to make or become mature 7 (of bills or bonds) to become due for payment or repayment ▸ HISTORY Latin *maturus* early, developed > **maturity** *n*

matzo *n, pl* **matzos** a large very thin biscuit of unleavened bread, traditionally eaten by Jews during Passover ▸ HISTORY Hebrew *matsāh*

maudlin *adj* foolishly or tearfully sentimental, esp. as a result of drinking ▸ HISTORY Middle English *Maudelen* Mary Magdalene, often shown weeping

maul *vb* 1 to tear with the claws: *she was badly mauled by a lion* 2 to criticize a play, performance, etc. severely: *the film was mauled by the critics* 3 to handle roughly or clumsily ▷ *n* 4 *rugby* a loose scrum ▸ HISTORY Latin *malleus* hammer

maunder *vb* to move, talk, or act aimlessly or idly ▸ HISTORY origin unknown

m

Maundy Thursday *n Christianity* the Thursday before Easter observed as a commemoration of the Last Supper ▶ HISTORY Latin *mandatum* commandment

mausoleum (maw-so-lee-um) *n* a large stately tomb ▶ HISTORY Greek *mausōleion* the tomb of king Mausolus

mauve *adj* light purple ▶ HISTORY Latin *malva* mallow

maverick *n* 1 a person of independent or unorthodox views 2 (in the US and Canada) an unbranded stray calf ▷ *adj* 3 (of a person or his or her views) independent and unorthodox ▶ HISTORY after Samuel A. *Maverick*, Texas rancher

maw *n* the mouth, throat, or stomach of an animal ▶ HISTORY Old English *maga*

mawkish *adj* foolishly or embarrassingly sentimental ▶ HISTORY obsolete *mawk* maggot > **mawkishness** *n*

max. maximum

maxilla *n, pl* **-lae** 1 the upper jawbone of a vertebrate 2 any part of the mouth in insects and other arthropods ▶ HISTORY Latin: jaw > **maxillary** *adj*

maxim *n* a brief expression of a general truth, principle, or rule of conduct ▶ HISTORY Latin *maxima*, in the phrase *maxima propositio* basic axiom

maximal *adj* of or being a maximum; the greatest possible

maximize *or* **-ise** *vb* **-izing, -ized** *or* **-ising, -ised** to make as high or great as possible; increase to a maximum > **maximization** *or* **-isation** *n*

maximum *n, pl* **-mums** *or* **-ma** 1 the greatest possible amount or degree: *he gave the police the maximum of cooperation* 2 the greatest amount recorded, allowed, or reached: *keep to a maximum of two drinks a day* ▷ *adj* 3 of, being, or showing a maximum or maximums: *maximum speed* ▶ HISTORY Latin: greatest

maxwell *n* the cgs unit of magnetic flux ▶ HISTORY after J. C. *Maxwell*, physicist

may¹ *vb, past* **might** 1 an auxiliary expressing that permission is requested by or granted to someone: *she may leave* 2 an auxiliary expressing the possibility that something could happen: *problems which may well have tragic consequences* 3 an auxiliary expressing ability or capacity, esp. in questions: *may I help you?* 4 an auxiliary expressing a strong wish: *long may she reign* ▶ HISTORY Old English *mæg*, from *magan* to be able

may² *or* **may tree** *n Brit* same as **hawthorn** ▶ HISTORY from *May*

May *n* the fifth month of the year ▶ HISTORY probably from *Maia*, Roman goddess

Maya *n* 1 (*pl* **-ya** *or* **-yas**) a member of an indigenous people of Central America, who once had an advanced civilization 2 the language of this people > **Mayan** *n, adj*

maybe *adv* perhaps

Mayday *n* the international radio distress signal ▶ HISTORY phonetic spelling of French *m'aidez* help me

May Day *n* the first day of May, traditionally a celebration of the coming of spring

mayfly *n, pl* **-flies** a short-lived insect with large transparent wings

mayhem *n* 1 any violent destruction or confusion: *a driver caused motorway mayhem* 2 *law* the maiming of a person ▶ HISTORY Anglo-French *mahem* injury

mayonnaise *n* a thick creamy sauce made from egg yolks, oil, and vinegar ▶ HISTORY French

mayor *n* the civic head of a municipal council in many countries ▶ HISTORY Latin *maior* greater > **mayoral** *adj*

mayoralty *n, pl* **-ties** the office or term of office of a mayor

mayoress *n* 1 *chiefly Brit* the wife of a mayor 2 a female mayor

maypole *n* a tall pole around which people dance during May-Day celebrations

maze *n* 1 a complex network of paths or passages designed to puzzle people who try and find their way through or out of it 2 a puzzle in which the player must trace a path through a complex network of lines without touching or crossing any of them 3 any confusing network or system: *a maze of regulations* ▶ HISTORY from *amaze*

mazurka *n* 1 a lively Polish dance in triple time 2 music for this dance ▶ HISTORY Polish

mb millibar

Mb *computers* megabyte

MB 1 Bachelor of Medicine 2 Manitoba

MBE (in Britain) Member of the Order of the British Empire

MC 1 Master of Ceremonies 2 (in the US) Member of Congress 3 (in Britain) Military Cross

MCC (in Britain) Marylebone Cricket Club

MCh Master of Surgery ▶ HISTORY Latin *Magister Chirurgiae*

Md *chem* mendelevium

MD 1 Doctor of Medicine ▶ HISTORY Latin *Medicinae Doctor* 2 Managing Director 3 Maryland

MDC more developed country

MDF medium-density fibreboard: a wood-substitute material used in interior decoration

MDMA methylenedioxymethamphetamine: the chemical name for the drug ecstasy

me¹ *pron* (objective) 1 refers to the speaker or writer: *that hurts me* ▷ *n* 2 *informal* the personality of the speaker or writer or something that expresses it: *the real me* ▶ HISTORY Old English *mē*

me² *or* **mi** *n music* (in tonic sol-fa) the third note of any ascending major scale

ME 1 Maine 2 Middle English 3 myalgic encephalomyelitis: see **chronic fatigue syndrome**

mead¹ *n* a wine-like alcoholic drink made from honey, often with spices added ▶ HISTORY Old English *meodu*

mead² *n archaic or poetic* a meadow ▶ HISTORY Old English *mæd*

meadow *n* 1 a grassy field used for hay or for grazing animals 2 a low-lying piece of grassland, often near a river ▶ HISTORY Old English *mædwe*

517

meadowsweet n a plant with dense heads of small fragrant cream-coloured flowers

meagre or US **meager** adj **1** not enough in amount or extent: *meagre wages* **2** thin or emaciated ▶ HISTORY Old French *maigre*

meal¹ n **1** any of the regular occasions, such as breakfast or dinner, when food is served and eaten **2** the food served and eaten **3 make a meal of** *informal* to perform (a task) with unnecessarily great effort ▶ HISTORY Old English *mǣl* measure, set time, meal

meal² n **1** the edible part of a grain or bean pulse (excluding wheat) ground to a coarse powder **2** *Scot* oatmeal **3** *chiefly US* maize flour ▶ HISTORY Old English *melu* > **mealy** adj

mealie or **mielie** n (often pl) *S African* same as **maize** ▶ HISTORY Afrikaans, from Latin *milium* millet

meals-on-wheels n a service taking hot meals to elderly or disabled people in their own homes

meal ticket n *slang* a person or situation providing a source of livelihood or income ▶ HISTORY from original US sense of ticket entitling holder to a meal

mealy-mouthed adj unwilling or afraid to speak plainly

mean¹ vb **meaning, meant 1** to intend to convey or express: *what do you mean by that?* **2** to denote, represent, or signify: *a red light means 'stop!'; 'gravid' is a technical term meaning 'pregnant'* **3** to intend: *I meant to phone you earlier, but didn't have time* **4** to say or do in all seriousness: *the boss means what she says* **5** to have the importance specified: *music means everything to him* **6** to destine or design for a certain person or purpose: *those sweets weren't meant for you* **7** to produce, cause, or result in: *major road works will mean long traffic delays* **8** to foretell: *those black clouds mean rain* **9 mean well** to have good intentions ▶ HISTORY Old English *mǣnan*

mean² adj **1** not willing to give or use much of something, esp. money: *she was noticeably mean; don't be mean with the butter* **2** unkind or spiteful: *a mean trick* **3** *informal* ashamed: *she felt mean about not letting the children stay out late* **4** *informal, chiefly US, Canad & Austral* bad-tempered or vicious **5** shabby and poor: *a mean little room* **6** *slang* excellent or skilful: *he plays a mean trumpet* **7 no mean a** of high quality: *no mean player* **b** difficult: *no mean feat* ▶ HISTORY Old English *gemǣne* common > **meanly** adv > **meanness** n

mean³ n **1** the middle point, state, or course between limits or extremes **2** *maths* **a** the mid-point between the highest and lowest number in a set **b** the average ▷ adj **3** intermediate in size or quantity **4** occurring halfway between extremes or limits; average ▶ HISTORY Late Latin *medianus* median

meander (mee-and-er) vb **1** (of a river, road, etc.) to follow a winding course **2** to wander without definite aim or direction ▷ n **3** *geog* a curve or bend, as in a river **4** a winding course or movement ▶ HISTORY Greek *Maiandros* the River Maeander

mean deviation n *statistics* the difference between an observed value of a variable and its mean

meanie or **meany** n *informal* **1** *chiefly* Brit a miserly person **2** *chiefly US* a nasty ill-tempered person

meaning n **1** the sense or significance of a word, sentence, or symbol **2** the inner, symbolic, or true interpretation or message: *the meaning of the New Testament*

meaningful adj **1** serious and important: *a meaningful relationship* **2** intended to express a feeling or opinion: *a meaningful pause*

meaningless adj having no meaning or purpose; futile

means n **1** the medium, method, or instrument used to obtain a result or achieve an end: *a means of transport* ▷ pl n **2** income: *a man of means* **3 by all means** without hesitation or doubt; certainly **4 by means of** with the use or help of **5 by no** or **not by any means** on no account; in no way

mean sea level n (in the UK) the sea level used by the Ordnance Survey as a datum level, determined at Newlyn in Cornwall. See **sea level**

means test n the checking of a person's income to determine whether he or she qualifies for financial aid > **means-tested** adj

meant vb the past of **mean¹**

meantime n **1** the intervening period: *in the meantime* ▷ adv **2** same as **meanwhile**

mean time or **mean solar time** n the times, at a particular place, measured so as to give 24-hour days (mean solar days) throughout a year

meanwhile adv **1** during the intervening period **2** at the same time, esp. in another place

measles n a highly contagious viral disease common in children, characterized by fever and a rash of small red spots ▷ See also **German measles** ▶ HISTORY Low German *masele* spot on the skin

measly adj **-slier, -sliest 1** *informal* too small in quantity or value **2** having or relating to measles

measure n **1** the size, quantity, or degree of something, as discovered by measurement or calculation **2** a device for measuring distance, volume, etc., such as a graduated scale or container **3** a system or unit of measurement: *the joule is a measure of energy* **4** an amount of alcoholic drink, esp. that served as standard in a bar **5** degree or extent: *a measure of success* **6** a particular action intended to achieve an effect: *radical measures are needed to cut unemployment* **7** a legislative bill, act, or resolution **8** *music* same as **bar¹** (sense 9) **9** *prosody* poetic rhythm or metre **10** *prosody* a metrical foot **11** *old-fashioned* a dance **12 for good measure** as an extra precaution or beyond requirements ▷ vb **-uring, -ured 13** to determine the size, amount, etc. of by measurement: *he measured the room for a new carpet* **14** to indicate or record the size, speed, force, etc.

m

of: *this dial measures the pressure in the pipe* **15** to have the size, quantity, etc. specified: *the room measures six feet* **16** to estimate or assess: *you cannot measure intelligence purely by exam results* **17** to function as a measurement of: *the ohm measures electrical resistance* **18** to bring into competition or conflict with: *he measured his strength against that of his opponent* ▷ See also **measures** ▶ HISTORY Latin *mensura* > **measurable** *adj*

measured *adj* **1** slow or stately **2** carefully considered; deliberate

measurement *n* **1** the act or process of measuring **2** an amount, extent, or size determined by measuring **3** a system or unit used for measuring: *the kilometre is the standard measurement of distance in most countries* **4 measurements** the size of a person's waist, chest, hips, etc., used when buying clothes

measures *pl n* rock strata that contain a particular type of deposit: *coal measures*

meat *n* **1** the flesh of animals used as food **2** the essence or gist: *get to the meat of your lecture as quickly as possible* ▶ HISTORY Old English *mete* > **meatless** *adj*

meaty *adj* **meatier, meatiest 1** of, like, or full of meat **2** heavily built; fleshy or brawny **3** full of import or interest: *a meaty historical drama*

Mecca *n* **1** the holy city of Islam **2** a place that attracts many visitors

mechanic *n* a person skilled in maintaining or operating machinery or motors ▶ HISTORY Greek *mēkhanē* machine

mechanical *adj* **1** made, performed, or operated by machinery **2** able to understand how machines work and how to repair or maintain them **3 a** (of an action) done without thought or feeling **b** (of a task) not requiring any thought; routine or repetitive **4** of or involving the science of mechanics > **mechanically** *adv*

mechanical digestion *n biol* the process of food being broken down into smaller pieces, esp. by the teeth, chewing and grinding it

mechanical drawing *n* a drawing to scale of a machine or architectural plan from which dimensions can be taken

mechanical engineering *n* the branch of engineering concerned with the design, construction, and operation of machines

mechanics *n* **1** the scientific study of motion and force **2** the science of designing, constructing, and operating machines ▷ *pl n* **3** the technical aspects of something

mechanism *n* **1** a system of moving parts that performs some function, esp. in a machine **2** any mechanical device or part of such a device **3** a process or technique: *the body's defence mechanisms* > **mechanistic** *adj*

mechanize *or* **-nise** *vb* **-nizing, -nized** *or* **-nising, -nised 1** to equip a factory or industry with machinery **2** to make mechanical or automatic **3** *mil* to equip an army with armoured vehicles > **mechanization** *or* **-nisation** *n*

med. **1** medical **2** medicine **3** medieval **4** medium

MEd Master of Education

medal *n* a small flat piece of metal bearing an inscription or image, given as an award or in commemoration of some outstanding event ▶ HISTORY French *médaille*

medallion *n* **1** a disc-shaped ornament worn on a chain round the neck **2** a large medal **3** a circular decorative device used in architecture ▶ HISTORY Italian *medaglia* medal

medallist *or US* **medalist** *n chiefly sport* a winner of a medal or medals

MEDC more economically developed country

meddle *vb* **-dling, -dled** to interfere annoyingly ▶ HISTORY Old French *medler* > **meddler** *n* > **meddlesome** *adj*

media *n* **1** a plural of **medium 2 the media** the mass media collectively ▷ *adj* **3** of or relating to the mass media: *media hype*

mediaeval (med-ee-**eve**-al) *adj* same as **medieval**

media event *n* an event that is staged for or exploited by the mass media

medial (**mee**-dee-al) *adj* of or situated in the middle ▶ HISTORY Latin *medius* middle > **medially** *adv*

median *n* **1** a middle point, plane, or part **2** *geom* a straight line joining one corner of a triangle to the midpoint of the opposite side **3** *statistics* the middle value in a frequency distribution, below and above which lie values with equal total frequencies ▶ HISTORY Latin *medius* middle

median strip *n US, Canad & NZ* the strip that separates the two sides of a motorway or dual carriageway

mediate (**mee**-dee-ate) *vb* **-ating, -ated 1** to intervene between people or in a dispute in order to bring about agreement **2** to resolve differences by mediation **3** to be changed slightly by (an experience or event): *clients' attitudes to social workers have often been mediated by their past experiences* ▶ HISTORY Late Latin *mediare* to be in the middle > **mediator** *n*

mediation *n law* the act of mediating; intercession between people, states, etc. in an attempt to reconcile disputed matters

medic *n informal* a doctor, medical orderly, or medical student ▶ HISTORY from MEDICAL

medical *adj* **1** of or relating to the science of medicine or to the treatment of persons without surgery ▷ *n* **2** *informal* a medical examination ▶ HISTORY Latin *medicus* physician > **medically** *adv*

medical certificate *n* **1** a doctor's certificate giving evidence of a person's unfitness for work **2** a document stating the result of a satisfactory medical examination

medicament (mid-**dik**-a-ment) *n* a medicine

medicate *vb* **-cating, -cated 1** to treat a patient with a medicine **2** to add a medication to (a bandage, shampoo, etc.) ▶ HISTORY Latin *medicare* to heal > **medicative** *adj*

medication n **1** treatment with drugs or remedies **2** a drug or remedy

medicinal (mid-**diss**-in-al) adj relating to or having therapeutic properties > **medicinally** adv

medicine n **1** any substance used in treating or alleviating the symptoms of disease **2** the science of preventing, diagnosing, or curing disease **3** any nonsurgical branch of medical science **4 take one's medicine** to accept a deserved punishment ▶ HISTORY Latin medicina (ars) (art) of healing

medicine man n (among certain peoples) a person believed to have supernatural powers of healing

medico n, pl **-cos** informal a doctor or medical student

medieval or **mediaeval** (med-ee-**eve**-al) adj **1** of, relating to, or in the style of the Middle Ages **2** informal old-fashioned or primitive ▶ HISTORY New Latin medium aevum the middle age > **medievalist** or **mediaevalist** n

Medieval Greek n the Greek language from the 7th to 13th century AD

Medieval Latin n the Latin language as used throughout Europe in the Middle Ages

mediocre (mee-dee-**oak**-er) adj not very high quality; average or second rate ▶ HISTORY Latin mediocris moderate > **mediocrity** (mee-dee-**ok**-rit-ee) n

meditate vb **-tating, -tated 1** to think about something deeply: he meditated on the problem **2** to reflect deeply on spiritual matters **3** to plan, consider, or think of doing something ▶ HISTORY Latin meditari to reflect upon > **meditative** adj > **meditator** n

meditation n **1** the act of meditating; reflection **2** contemplation of spiritual matters, esp. as a religious practice

Mediterranean adj of the Mediterranean Sea, lying between S Europe, N Africa, and SW Asia, or the surrounding region ▶ HISTORY Latin medius middle + terra land

Mediterranean climate n geog a climate type having mild, dry, hot summers and short, humid, cool winters found around the Mediterranean and in other regions between the same latitudes

medium adj **1** midway between extremes of size, amount, or degree: fry over a medium heat; a man of medium height ▷ n, pl **-dia** or **-diums 2** a middle state, degree, or condition: the happy medium **3** a substance which has a particular effect or can be used for a particular purpose: linseed oil is used as a thinning medium for oil paint **4** a means for communicating information or news to the public **5** a person who can supposedly communicate with the dead **6** the substance or surroundings in which an organism naturally lives or grows **7** art the category of a work of art, as determined by its materials: his works in the photographic medium ▶ HISTORY Latin medius middle

medium wave n a radio wave with a wavelength between 100 and 1000 metres

medlar n the apple-like fruit of a small Eurasian tree, which is not edible until it has begun to decay ▶ HISTORY Old French medlier

medley n **1** a mixture of various elements **2** a musical composition consisting of various tunes arranged as a continuous whole **3** swimming a race in which a different stroke is used for each length ▶ HISTORY Old French, from medler to mix, quarrel

medulla (mid-**dull**-la) n, pl **-las** or **-lae** (-lee) **1** anat the innermost part of an organ or structure **2** anat the lower stalklike section of the brain **3** bot the central pith of a plant stem ▶ HISTORY Latin: marrow > **medullary** adj

medulla oblongata n anat the lower stalklike section of the brain

medusa (mid-**dew**-za) n, pl **-sas** or **-sae** (-zee) jellyfish ▶ HISTORY Medusa, in Greek mythology, who had snakes for hair

meek adj quiet, and ready to do what other people say ▶ HISTORY related to Old Norse mjūkr amenable > **meekly** adv

meerkat n a South African mongoose ▶ HISTORY Dutch: sea-cat

meerschaum (**meer**-shum) n **1** a white, heat-resistant, claylike mineral **2** a tobacco pipe with a bowl made of this mineral ▶ HISTORY German Meerschaum, literally: sea foam

meet[1] vb **meeting, met 1** to be in or come to the same place at the same time as, either by arrangement or by accident: I met him in town **2** to come into contact with something or each other: his head met the ground with a crack; the town where the Rhine and the Moselle meet **3** to come to or be at the place of arrival of: he met his train at noon **4** to make the acquaintance of or be introduced to someone or each other **5** (of people) to gather together for a purpose: the board meets once a week **6** to compete, play, or fight against **7** to cope with effectively; satisfy: they were unable to meet his demands **8** to pay for (something): it is difficult to meet the cost of medical insurance **9** Also: **meet with** to experience or suffer: he met his death at the Somme **10 more to this than meets the eye** there is more involved in this than appears ▷ n **11** a sports meeting **12** chiefly Brit the assembly of hounds and huntsmen prior to a hunt ▶ HISTORY Old English mētan

meet[2] adj archaic proper, fitting, or correct: meet and proper ▶ HISTORY Old English gemǣte

meeting n **1** an act of coming together: a meeting was fixed for the following day **2** an assembly or gathering of people: the meeting voted in favour **3** a sporting competition, as of athletes, or of horse racing

meg n informal short for **megabyte**

mega adj slang extremely good, great, or successful

mega- combining form **1** denoting 10^6: megawatt **2** (in computer technology) denoting 2^{20} (1,048,576): megabyte **3** large or great: megalith **4** informal very great: megastar ▶ HISTORY Greek megas huge, powerful

megabyte n computers 2^{20} or 1 048 576 bytes

megadeath n the death of a million people, esp. in a nuclear war or attack

megahertz *n, pl* **megahertz** one million hertz; one million cycles per second

megajoule *n* one million joules

megalith *n* a very large stone, esp. one forming part of a prehistoric monument > **megalithic** *adj*

megalomania *n* **1** an obsessional delusion of power and importance **2** *informal* a craving for power ▶ HISTORY Greek *megas* great + *mania* madness > **megalomaniac** *adj, n*

megalopolis *n* an urban complex, usually comprising several large towns ▶ HISTORY Greek *megas* great + *polis* city > **megalopolitan** *adj, n*

megaphone *n* a funnel-shaped instrument used to make someone's voice sound louder, esp. out of doors

megapode *n* any of various ground-living birds of Australia, New Guinea, and adjacent islands. Their eggs incubate in mounds of sand or rotting vegetation ▶ HISTORY Greek *megas* great + *-podos* -footed

megaton *n* **1** one million tons **2** an explosive power, esp. of a nuclear weapon, equal to the power of one million tons of TNT

megavolt *n* one million volts

megawatt *n* one million watts

meiosis (my-**oh**-siss) *n, pl* **-ses** (-seez) a type of cell division in which reproductive cells are produced, each containing half the chromosome number of the parent nucleus ▶ HISTORY Greek *meiōn* less

Meissner's corpuscle *n anat* a tiny touch receptor in the palms, soles, and lips that is sensitive to light pressure ▶ HISTORY after Georg *Meissner*, German anatomist

meitnerium *n chem* an element artificially produced in small quantities by high-energy ion bombardment. Symbol: Mt ▶ HISTORY after Lise *Meitner*, physicist

melaleuca (mel-a-**loo**-ka) *n* an Australian shrub or tree with a white trunk and black branches ▶ HISTORY Greek *melas* black + *leukos* white

melamine *n* a colourless crystalline compound used in making synthetic resins ▶ HISTORY German *Melamin*

melancholia (mel-an-**kole**-lee-a) *n* an old name for **depression** (sense 1)

melancholy (mel-an-kol-lee) *n, pl* **-cholies** **1** a tendency to gloominess or depression **2** a sad thoughtful state of mind ▷ *adj* **3** characterized by, causing, or expressing sadness ▶ HISTORY Greek *melas* black + *kholē* bile > **melancholic** *adj, n*

melange (may-**lahnzh**) *n anat* a mixture or assortment: *a melange of historical facts and legends* ▶ HISTORY French *mêler* to mix

melanin *n* a black pigment present in the hair, skin, and eyes of humans and animals ▶ HISTORY Greek *melas* black

melanoma *n, pl* **-mas** *or* **-mata** *pathol* a tumour composed of dark-coloured cells, occurring in some skin cancers ▶ HISTORY Greek *melas* black + *-oma*, modelled on *carcinoma*

Melba toast *n* very thin crisp toast ▶ HISTORY after Dame Nellie *Melba*, singer

mellifluous (mel-**lif**-flew-uss) *adj* (of sound) smooth and sweet ▶ HISTORY Latin *mel* honey + *fluere* to flow

mellow *adj* **1** (esp. of colours, light, or sounds) soft or rich: *the mellow stillness of a sunny Sunday morning* **2** kind-hearted, esp. through maturity or old age **3** genial and relaxed, for instance through the effects of alcohol or good food **4** (esp. of fruits) sweet, ripe, and full-flavoured **5** (esp. of wine or cheese) having developed a full, smooth flavour as a result of maturing **6** (of soil) soft and loamy ▷ *vb* **7** to make or become mellow **8** (foll. by *out*) to make or become calm and relaxed ▶ HISTORY origin unknown

melodic (mel-**lod**-ik) *adj* **1** of or relating to melody **2** tuneful and pleasant to the ear; melodious > **melodically** *adv*

melodious (mel-**lode**-ee-uss) *adj* **1** pleasant to the ear: *he gave a melodious chuckle* **2** tuneful and melodic > **melodiousness** *n*

melodrama *n* **1** a play or film full of extravagant action and emotion **2** overdramatic emotion or behaviour ▶ HISTORY Greek *melos* song + *drama* drama

melodramatic *adj* characterized by or reminiscent of melodrama > **melodramatics** *pl n* ▶ HISTORY Greek *melos* song + *drama* drama

melody *n, pl* **-dies** **1** *music* a succession of notes forming a distinctive sequence; tune **2** sounds that are pleasant because of their tone or arrangement, esp. words of poetry ▶ HISTORY Greek *melōidia*

melon *n* any of various large edible fruits which have a hard rind and juicy flesh ▶ HISTORY Greek *mēlon* apple

Melpomene (mel-**pom**-in-nee) *n Greek myth* the Muse of tragedy

melt *vb* **1** to change from a solid into a liquid as a result of the action of heat **2** to dissolve: *these sweets melt in the mouth* **3** Also: **melt away** to diminish and finally disappear; fade away: *he felt his inner doubts melt away* **4** to blend so that it is impossible to tell where one thing ends and another begins: *they melted into the trees until the gamekeeper had passed* **5** to make or become emotional or sentimental; soften: *she melted into tears* ▶ HISTORY Old English *meltan* to digest > **meltingly** *adv*

meltdown *n* **1** (in a nuclear reactor) the melting of the fuel rods, with the possible escape of radioactivity **2** *informal* a sudden disastrous failure **3** *informal* a process of irreversible decline

melting point *n* the temperature at which a solid turns into a liquid

melting pot *n* a place or situation in which many races, ideas, etc. are mixed

member *n* **1** a person who belongs to a group or organization such as a club or political party **2** any part of a plant or animal, such as a limb or petal **3** a Member of Parliament: *the member for Glasgow Central* ▷ *adj* **4** (of a country or group) belonging to an organization or alliance: *a summit of the member countries' heads of state is due* ▶ HISTORY Latin *membrum* limb, part

521

Member of Parliament *n* a person who has been elected to the House of Commons or the equivalent assembly in another country

membership *n* **1** the members of an organization collectively **2** the number of members **3** the state of being a member

membrane *n* a thin flexible tissue that covers, lines, or connects plant and animal organs or cells ▶ HISTORY Latin *membrana* skin covering a part of the body > **membranous** *adj*

meme *n* a video, photo, or story that is viewed by many internet users, and often altered by them for humorous effect ▶ HISTORY possibly from *mimic*

memento *n, pl* **-tos** *or* **-toes** something that reminds one of past events; a souvenir ▶ HISTORY Latin, imperative of *meminisse* to remember

memento mori *n, pl* **memento mori** an object intended to remind people of death ▶ HISTORY Latin: remember you must die

memo *n, pl* **memos** short for **memorandum**

memoir (**mem**-wahr) *n* a biography or historical account based on personal knowledge ▶ HISTORY Latin *memoria* memory

memoirs *pl n* **1** a collection of reminiscences about a period or series of events, written from personal experience **2** an autobiography

memorabilia *pl n, sing* **-rabile** objects connected with famous people or events

memorable *adj* worth remembering or easily remembered because it is very special or important ▶ HISTORY Latin *memorare* to remember > **memorably** *adv*

memorandum *n, pl* **-dums** *or* **-da** **1** a note sent by one person or department to another within a business organization **2** a note of things to be remembered **3** *law* a short written summary of the terms of a transaction ▶ HISTORY Latin: (something) to be remembered

memorial *n* **1** something, such as a statue, built or displayed to preserve the memory of someone or something: *a war memorial* ▷ *adj* **2** in memory of someone or something: *a memorial service* ▶ HISTORY Late Latin *memoriale* a reminder

memorize *or* **-rise** *vb* **-rizing, -rized** *or* **-rising, -rised** to commit to memory; learn by heart

memory *n, pl* **-ries** **1** the ability of the mind to store and recall past sensations, thoughts, and knowledge: *she can do it from memory* **2** the sum of everything retained by the mind **3** a particular recollection of an event or person: *he started awake with a sudden memory* **4** the length of time one can remember: *my memory doesn't go that far back* **5** commemoration: *in memory of our leader* **6** a person's reputation after death: *a conductor of fond memory* **7** a part of a computer in which information is stored ▶ HISTORY Latin *memoria*

memory card *n* a small removable data storage device, used in mobile phones, digital cameras, etc.

memory stick *n* same as **flash drive**

memsahib *n* (formerly, in India) a term of respect used for a European married woman ▶ HISTORY *ma'am* + *sahib*

men *n* the plural of **man**

menace *vb* **-acing, -aced** **1** to threaten with violence or danger ▷ *n* **2** a threat; a source of danger **3** *informal* an annoying person or thing; nuisance ▶ HISTORY Latin *minax* threatening > **menacing** *adj*

menagerie (min-**naj**-er-ee) *n* a collection of wild animals kept for exhibition ▶ HISTORY French

mend *vb* **1** to repair something broken or not working **2** to heal or recover: *a wound like that will take a while to mend* **3** (esp. of behaviour) to improve; make or become better: *if you don't mend your ways you'll be in serious trouble* ▷ *n* **4** a mended area, esp. on a garment **5** **on the mend** regaining one's health ▶ HISTORY from *amend*

mendacity *n* the tendency to be untruthful ▶ HISTORY Latin *mendax* untruthful > **mendacious** *adj*

mendelevium *n chem* an artificially produced radioactive element. Symbol: Md ▶ HISTORY after D. I. *Mendeleyev*, chemist

Mendel's laws *pl n* the principles of heredity proposed by Gregor Mendel (1822–84), Austrian monk and botanist > **Mendelism** *n*

mendicant *adj* **1** begging **2** (of a monk, nun, etc.) dependent on charity for food ▷ *n* **3** a mendicant friar **4** a beggar ▶ HISTORY Latin *mendicus* beggar

menfolk *pl n* men collectively, esp. the men of a particular family

menhir (**men**-hear) *n* a single standing stone, dating from prehistoric times ▶ HISTORY Breton *men* stone + *hir* long

menial (**mean**-nee-al) *adj* **1** involving or doing boring work of low status ▷ *n* **2** a domestic servant ▶ HISTORY Old French *meinie* household

meninges (min-in-jeez) *pl n, sing* **meninx** (**mean**-inks) the three membranes that surround the brain and spinal cord ▶ HISTORY Greek, plural of *meninx* membrane

meningitis (men-in-**jite**-iss) *n* inflammation of the meninges, caused by infection and causing severe headache, fever, and rigidity of the neck muscles

meniscus *n, pl* **-nisci** *or* **-niscuses** **1** the curved upper surface of a liquid standing in a tube, produced by the surface tension **2** a crescent-shaped lens ▶ HISTORY Greek *mēniskos* crescent

menopause *n* the period during which a woman's menstrual cycle ceases, normally at an age of 45 to 55 ▶ HISTORY Greek *mēn* month + *pausis* halt > **menopausal** *adj*

menorah (min-**or**-a) *n Judaism* a seven-branched candelabrum used as an emblem of Judaism ▶ HISTORY Hebrew: candlestick

menses (**men**-seez) *n* same as **menstruation** ▶ HISTORY Latin, plural of *mensis* month

Menshevik (men-shiv-ick) *or* **Menshevist** *n history* a member of the moderate wing of the Russian Social Democratic Party, advocating gradual reform to achieve socialism. Compare **Bolshevik** ▶ HISTORY Russian: minority, from *menshe* less, from *malo* few > **Menshevism** *n*

mens rea *n law* the criminal intent, negligence, or other legally indefensible state of mind that must be proved for a defendant to be convicted of a crime. Compare **actus reus** ▶ HISTORY Latin: guilty mind

menstrual *adj* of or relating to menstruation: *the menstrual cycle*

menstruate *vb* **-ating, -ated** to undergo menstruation ▶ HISTORY Latin *menstruare*, from *mensis* month

menstruation *n* the approximately monthly discharge of blood from the womb in women of childbearing age who are not pregnant

mensuration *n* **1** the study of the measurement of geometric magnitudes such as length **2** the act or process of measuring ▶ HISTORY Latin *mensura* measure

mental *adj* **1** of, done by, or involving the mind: *mental alertness* **2** done in the mind without using speech or writing: *mental arithmetic* **3** affected by mental illness: *a mental patient* **4** concerned with mental illness: *a mental hospital* **5** *slang* extremely foolish or eccentric ▶ HISTORY Latin *mens* mind > **mentally** *adv*

mental age *n* the age which a person is considered to have reached in thinking ability, judged by comparing his or her ability with the average for people of various ages: *a twenty-one-year-old woman with a mental age of only ten*

mental handicap *n old-fashioned, often offensive* any intellectual disability resulting from injury to or abnormal development of the brain > **mentally handicapped** *adj*

mental illness *n* any of various disorders in which a person's thoughts, emotions, or behaviour are so abnormal as to cause suffering to himself or herself, or other people

mentality *n*, *pl* **-ties** a particular attitude or way of thinking: *the traditional civil-service mentality*

mental map *n* a person's individual perception of the world around them, both locally and much further afield, and of how one place links to another

mental process *n functional grammar* the process of thinking, reflecting, or feeling as specified by a verb group. Compare **material process, relational process, verbal process**

menthol *n* an organic compound found in peppermint oil and used as an antiseptic, decongestant, and painkiller ▶ HISTORY Latin *mentha* mint > **mentholated** *adj*

mention *vb* **1** to refer to or speak about briefly or incidentally **2** to include in a report, list, etc., because of high standards or an outstanding achievement: *the hotel is mentioned in all the guidebooks; he was twice mentioned in dispatches during the war* **3** **not to mention (something)** to say nothing of (something too obvious to mention) ▷ *n* **4** a slight reference or allusion **5** a recognition or acknowledgment of high quality or an outstanding achievement ▶ HISTORY Latin *mentio* a calling to mind

mento *n*, *pl* **-tos** a traditional Jamaican song or ballad similar to a calypso

mentor *n* an adviser or guide ▶ HISTORY *Mentor*, adviser of Telemachus in Homer's *Odyssey* > **mentorship** *n*

menu *n* **1** a list of dishes served at a meal or that can be ordered in a restaurant **2** a list of options displayed on a visual display unit from which the operator can choose ▶ HISTORY French: small, detailed (list)

MEP (in Britain) Member of the European Parliament

Mercalli scale *n geol* a scale for expressing the intensity of an earthquake, ranging from 1 (rarely felt) to 12 (total destruction). Compare **Richter scale** ▶ HISTORY after Giuseppe *Mercalli* (1850–1914), Italian volcanologist and seismologist

mercantile *adj* of trade or traders; commercial ▶ HISTORY Italian *mercante* merchant

Mercator projection (mer-**kate**-er) *n geog* a way of drawing maps in which latitude and longitude form a rectangular grid, scale being exaggerated with increasing distance from the equator ▶ HISTORY after G. *Mercator*, cartographer

mercenary *n*, *pl* **-naries** **1** a soldier who fights for a foreign army for money ▷ *adj* **2** motivated by greed or the desire for gain: *calculating and mercenary businessmen* **3** of or relating to a mercenary or mercenaries ▶ HISTORY Latin *merces* wages

mercerized or **-ised** *adj* (of cotton) treated with an alkali to make it strong and shiny ▶ HISTORY after John *Mercer*, maker of textiles

merchandise *n* **1** goods for buying, selling, or trading with; commodities ▷ *vb* **-dising, -dised** **2** to engage in the commercial purchase and sale of goods or services; trade

merchandising *n* **1** the selection and display of goods in a retail outlet **2** commercial goods, esp. ones issued to exploit the popularity of a pop group, sporting event, etc.

merchant *n* **1** a person who buys and sells goods in large quantities and usually of one type: *a wine merchant* **2** *chiefly Scot, US & Canad* a person engaged in retail trade; shopkeeper **3** a person dealing in something undesirable: *a gossip merchant* ▷ *adj* **4** of ships involved in commercial trade or their crews: *a merchant sailor; the British merchant fleet* ▶ HISTORY Latin *mercari* to trade

merchant bank *n* a financial institution that deals primarily with foreign trade and business finance > **merchant banker** *n*

merchantman *n*, *pl* **-men** a merchant ship

merchant navy *n* the ships or crew engaged in a nation's commercial shipping

merciful *adj* **1** (of an act or event) giving relief from pain or suffering: *after months of illness, death came as a merciful release* **2** showing or giving mercy; compassionate > **mercifully** *adv*

merciless *adj* without mercy; pitiless, cruel, or heartless > **mercilessly** *adv*

mercurial (mer-**cure**-ee-al) *adj* **1** lively and unpredictable: *a mercurial and temperamental chess player* **2** of or containing mercury ▶ HISTORY Latin *mercurialis*

mercuric *adj* of or containing mercury in the divalent state

mercurous *adj* of or containing mercury in the monovalent state

mercury *n, pl* **-ries** *chem* a silvery toxic metal, the only element liquid at normal temperatures, used in thermometers, barometers, lamps, and dental amalgams. Symbol: Hg ▶ HISTORY Latin *Mercurius*, messenger of Jupiter

Mercury *n* **1** *Roman myth* the messenger of the gods **2** the second smallest planet and the one nearest the sun

mercy *n, pl* **-cies** **1** compassionate treatment of or attitude towards an offender or enemy who is in one's power **2** the power to show mercy: *they threw themselves on the King's mercy* **3** a relieving or welcome occurrence or act: *it was a mercy you turned up when you did* **4 at the mercy of** in the power of ▷ *adj* **5** done or undertaken in an attempt to relieve suffering or bring help: *a mercy mission* ▶ HISTORY Latin *merces* recompense

mercy killing *n* same as **euthanasia**

mere¹ *adj* nothing more than: *the election in Slovenia seems a mere formality* ▶ HISTORY Latin *merus* pure > **merely** *adv*

mere² *n* *Brit, dialect or archaic* a lake ▶ HISTORY Old English: sea, lake

meretricious *adj* superficially or garishly attractive but of no real value ▶ HISTORY Latin *meretrix* prostitute

merganser (mer-**gan**-ser) *n, pl* **-sers** *or* **-ser** a large crested marine diving duck ▶ HISTORY Latin *mergere* to plunge + *anser* goose

merge *vb* **merging, merged** **1** to combine, esp. so as to become part of a larger whole: *the two airlines merged in 1983* **2** to blend gradually, without any sudden change being apparent: *late afternoon merged imperceptibly into early evening* ▶ HISTORY Latin *mergere* to plunge

merger *n* the act of merging, esp. the combination of two or more companies

meridian *n* **1** one of the imaginary lines joining the north and south poles at right angles to the equator, designated by degrees of longitude from 0° at Greenwich to 180° **2** (in acupuncture, etc.) any of various channels through which vital energy is believed to circulate round the body ▶ HISTORY Latin *meridies* midday

meridional *adj* **1** of or along a meridian **2** of or in the south, esp. the south of Europe

meringue (mer-**rang**) *n* **1** stiffly beaten egg whites mixed with sugar and baked **2** a small cake made from this mixture ▶ HISTORY French

merino *n, pl* **-nos** **1** a sheep with long fine wool, originally reared in Spain **2** the yarn made from this wool ▶ HISTORY Spanish

meristem *n* *bot* a plant tissue whose cells divide and differentiate to form the tissues and organs of the plant ▶ HISTORY from Greek *meristos* divided

meristematic tissue *n* *bot* plant tissue responsible for growth, whose cells divide to form the tissues and organs of the plant

merit *n* **1** worth or superior quality; excellence: *the film had two sequels, neither of much merit* **2** an admirable or advantageous quality: *the relative merits of film and video as a medium of communication* **3 have the merit of** to have a positive feature or advantage that the alternatives do not have: *the first version has the merit of being short* **4 on its merits** on its intrinsic qualities or virtues ▷ *vb* **-iting, -ited 5** to be worthy of; deserve: *the issue merits much fuller discussion* ▶ HISTORY Latin *meritum* reward

meritocracy (mer-it-**tok**-rass-ee) *n, pl* **-cies** a social system in which power is held by the most talented or intelligent people > **meritocrat** *n* > **meritocratic** *adj*

meritorious *adj* deserving praise for being good or worthwhile ▶ HISTORY Latin *meritorius* earning money

merlin *n* a small falcon with dark plumage ▶ HISTORY Old French *esmerillon*

mermaid *n* an imaginary sea creature with a woman's head and upper body and a fish's tail ▶ HISTORY *mere* sea + *maid* > **merman** *masc n*

merry *adj* **-rier, -riest 1** cheerful and jolly **2** *Brit & Austral, informal* slightly drunk **3 make merry** to take part in noisy cheerful celebrations or fun ▶ HISTORY Old English *merige* agreeable > **merrily** *adv* > **merriment** *n*

merry-go-round *n* **1** a fairground roundabout **2** a whirl of activity

merrymaking *n* noisy cheerful celebrations or fun > **merrymaker** *n*

mesa *n* a flat-topped hill found in arid regions ▶ HISTORY Spanish: table

mescal (mess-**kal**) *n* **1** a globe-shaped cactus without spines found in Mexico and the southwestern US **2** a Mexican alcoholic spirit similar to tequila ▶ HISTORY Mexican Indian *mexcalli*

mescaline *n* a hallucinogenic drug derived from the button-like top of the mescal cactus

mesdames (may-**dam**) *n* the plural of **madame** or **madam** (sense 1)

mesdemoiselles (maid-mwah-**zel**) *n* the plural of **mademoiselle**

mesembryanthemum *n* a low-growing plant with fleshy leaves and bright daisy-like flowers ▶ HISTORY Greek *mesēmbria* noon + *anthemon* flower

mesentery *n, pl* **-teries** *anat* the double layer of peritoneum that is attached to the back wall of the abdominal cavity

mesh *n* **1** a material resembling a net made from intersecting strands with a space between each strand **2** an open space between the strands of a net or network: *the minimum permitted size of fishing net mesh* **3** (often pl) the strands surrounding these spaces **4** anything that ensnares or holds like a net ▷ *adj* **5** made from mesh: *a wire mesh fence* ▷ *vb* **6** to entangle or become entangled **7** (of gear teeth) to engage or interlock **8** to fit together closely or work in harmony: *she schedules her holidays to mesh with theirs* ▶ HISTORY probably Dutch *maesche*

mesmerize *or* **-ise** *vb* **-izing, -ized** *or* **-ising, -ised** **1** to fascinate and hold spellbound: *his voice had the entire audience mesmerized* **2** *archaic* to hypnotize > **mesmerism** *n* > **mesmerizing** *adj*

Mesolithic (mess-oh-**lith**-ik) *adj* of the middle period of the Stone Age, in Europe from about 12,000 to 3000 BC ▶ HISTORY Greek *mesos* middle + *lithos* stone

mesomorph *n* *physiol* a person with a muscular body build. Compare **ectomorph, endomorph** ▶ HISTORY Greek *misos* middle + *morphē* shape > **mesomorphic** *adj*

meson (**mee**-zon) *n* *physics* any of a group of elementary particles that has a mass between those of an electron and a proton ▶ HISTORY Greek *mesos* middle + *-on*, indicating an elementary particle

mesophyll *n* *bot* the soft chlorophyll-containing tissue of a leaf between the upper and lower layers of epidermis > **mesophyllic** *or* **mesophyllous** *adj*

mesosphere (mess-oh-sfeer) *n* the atmospheric layer above the stratosphere

Mesozoic (mess-oh-**zoh**-ik) *adj* *geol* of the geological era that began 225 million years ago and lasted about 155 million years, during which the dinosaurs emerged, flourished, then became extinct ▶ HISTORY Greek *mesos* middle + *zōion* animal

mess *n* **1** a state of untidiness or confusion, esp. a dirty or unpleasant one: *the house was in a mess* **2** a confused and difficult situation; muddle: *the firm is in a terrible financial mess* **3** *informal* a dirty or untidy person or thing: *there was a nasty burnt mess in the saucepan* **4** a building providing catering, and sometimes recreation, facilities for service personnel **5** a group of service personnel who regularly eat together **6** *old-fashioned* a portion of soft or runny food: *a mess of pottage* ⊳ *vb* **7** (of service personnel) to eat in a group ▶ HISTORY Old French *mes* dish of food

message *n* **1** a communication from one person or group to another **2** an implicit meaning or moral, as in a work of art **3** a religious or political belief that someone attempts to communicate to others: *paintings with a fierce feminist message* **4** **get the message** *informal* to understand ▶ HISTORY Old French, from Latin *mittere* to send

message board *n* a discussion forum on the internet

messaging *n* the sending of a message by any form of electronic communication: *text messaging*

messenger *n* a person who takes messages from one person or group to another ▶ HISTORY Old French *messagier*

Messiah *n* **1** *Judaism* the awaited king of the Jews, who will be sent by God to free them **2** *Christianity* Jesus Christ, when regarded in this role **3** a liberator of a country or people ▶ HISTORY Hebrew *māshīach* anointed

Messianic *adj* **1** of or relating to a Messiah, or the arrival on Earth of a Messiah **2** **messianic** of or relating to the belief that someone or something will bring about a complete transformation of the existing social order: *a messianic zeal for the free market*

messieurs (may-**syuh**) *n* the plural of **monsieur**

mess kit *n* a soldier's eating utensils for use in the field

Messrs (**mess**-erz) *n* the plural of **Mr**

messy *adj* **messier, messiest** **1** dirty or untidy **2** unpleasantly confused or complicated: *the messy, uncontrollable world of real life* > **messily** *adv* > **messiness** *n*

met *vb* the past of **meet¹**

Met *adj* **1** Meteorological: *the Met Office* ⊳ *n* **2** **the Met** the Metropolitan Police, who operate in London

metabolism (met-**tab**-ol-liz-zum) *n* the chemical processes that occur in living organisms, resulting in growth, production of energy, and elimination of waste ▶ HISTORY Greek *metaballein* to change > **metabolic** *adj*

metabolize *or* **-lise** *vb* **-lizing, -lized** *or* **-lising, -lised** to produce or be produced by metabolism

metacarpus *n, pl* **-pi** the set of five long bones in the hand between the wrist and the fingers ▶ HISTORY Greek *meta* after + *karpos* wrist > **metacarpal** *adj, n*

metafiction *n* *literature* fiction that draws attention to its fictional status and the conventions and nature of fiction

metal *n* **1 a** *chem* a chemical element, such as iron or copper, that reflects light and can be shaped, forms positive ions, and is a good conductor of heat and electricity **b** an alloy, such as brass or steel, containing one or more of these elements **2** short for **road metal 3** *informal* short for **heavy metal 4 metals** the rails of a railway ⊳ *adj* **5** made of metal ▶ HISTORY Greek *metallon* mine

metalanguage *n* the language or system of symbols used to discuss another language or system

metalled *or US* **metaled** *adj* (of a road) surfaced with crushed rock or small stones: *a metalled driveway*

metallic *adj* **1** of or consisting of metal **2** sounding like two pieces of metal hitting each other: *a metallic click* **3** (of a voice) harsh, unpleasant, and unemotional **4** shining like metal: *metallic paint* **5** (of a taste) unpleasantly harsh and bitter

metallic bond *n* *chem* the covalent bonding between atoms in metals, in which the valence electrons are free to move through the crystal

metalliferous *adj* containing a metallic element ▶ HISTORY Latin *metallum* metal + *ferre* to bear

metallography *n* the study of the composition and structure of metals

metalloid *n* *chem* a nonmetallic element, such as arsenic or silicon, that has some of the properties of a metal

metallurgy n the scientific study of the structure, properties, extraction, and refining of metals ▶ HISTORY metal + Greek -urgia, from ergon work > **metallurgical** adj > **metallurgist** n

metal oxide n chem the substance formed when a base metal reacts with oxygen

metal road n NZ an unsealed road covered in gravel

metalwork n 1 the craft of making articles from metal 2 articles made from metal 3 the metal part of something > **metalworker** n

metamorphic adj 1 (of rocks) altered considerably from the original structure and composition by pressure and heat 2 of metamorphosis or metamorphism

metamorphic rock n geol rock that has been altered over time by pressure and heat

metamorphism n the process by which metamorphic rocks are formed

metamorphose vb -phosing, -phosed to change from one state or thing into something different: the media personality metamorphosed into society hostess

metamorphosis (met-a-**mor**-foss-is) n, pl -**ses** (-seez) 1 a complete change of physical form or substance 2 a complete change of character or appearance 3 zool the change of form that accompanies transformation into an adult in certain animals, for example the butterfly or frog ▶ HISTORY Greek: transformation, from meta after + morphē form

metaphor n a figure of speech in which a word or phrase is applied to an object or action that it does not literally apply to in order to imply a resemblance, for example he is a lion in battle ▶ HISTORY Greek metapherein to transfer > **metaphorical** adj > **metaphorically** adv

metaphysical adj 1 of metaphysics 2 abstract, abstruse, or unduly theoretical

Metaphysical adj denoting certain 17th-century poets who combined intense feeling with elaborate imagery

metaphysics n 1 the philosophical study of the nature of reality 2 abstract or subtle discussion or reasoning ▶ HISTORY Greek ta meta ta phusika the things after the physics, from the arrangement of subjects treated in the works of Aristotle

metastasis (mit-**tass**-tiss-iss) n, pl -**ses** (-seez) 1 pathol the spreading of a disease, esp. cancer, from one part of the body to another 2 the spreading of a problem into new areas ▶ HISTORY Greek: transition > **metastasize** or -**sise** vb

metatarsus n, pl -**si** the set of five long bones in the foot between the toes and the ankle ▶ HISTORY Greek meta after + tarsos instep > **metatarsal** adj, n

metathesis (mit-**tath**-iss-iss) n, pl -**ses** (-seez) the transposition of two sounds or letters in a word ▶ HISTORY Greek metatithenai to transpose

metazoan (met-a-**zoh**-an) n 1 any animal having a body composed of many cells: includes all animals except sponges and protozoans ▷ adj 2 of the metazoans ▶ HISTORY New Latin Metazoa

meteor n 1 a small piece of rock or metal that has entered the earth's atmosphere from space 2 Also: **shooting star** the bright streak of light appearing in the sky due to a piece of rock or metal burning up because of friction as it falls through the atmosphere ▶ HISTORY Greek meteōros lofty

meteoric (meet-ee-**or**-rik) adj 1 of or relating to meteors 2 brilliant and very rapid: his meteoric rise to power > **meteorically** adv

meteorite n the rocklike remains of a meteoroid that has collided with the earth

meteoroid n any of the small celestial bodies that are thought to orbit the sun. When they enter the earth's atmosphere, they become visible as meteors

meteorol. or **meteor.** 1 meteorological 2 meteorology

meteorology n the study of the earth's atmosphere and weather-forming processes, esp. for weather forecasting > **meteorological** adj > **meteorologist** n

meter¹ n 1 any device that measures and records the quantity or number of units of something that was used during a specified period or is being used at that moment: a gas meter 2 short for **parking meter** ▷ vb 3 to measure the amount of something used or a rate of flow with a meter ▶ HISTORY Old English metan to measure

meter² n US same as **metre¹**, **metre²**

-meter n combining form 1 indicating an instrument for measuring: barometer 2 prosody indicating a verse having a specified number of feet: pentameter ▶ HISTORY Greek metron measure

methadone n a drug similar to morphine, sometimes prescribed as a heroin substitute ▶ HISTORY (di)meth(yl) + a(mino) + d(iphenyl) + -one, indicating a ketone

methanal n same as **formaldehyde**

methane n a colourless odourless flammable gas, the main constituent of natural gas ▶ HISTORY meth(yl) + -ane, indicating an alkane

methane series n a series of saturated hydrocarbons with the general formula C_nH_{2n+2}

methanol n a colourless poisonous liquid used as a solvent and fuel. Also: **methyl alcohol** ▶ HISTORY methane + -ol, indicating alcohol

methinks vb, past **methought** archaic it seems to me that

method n 1 a way of doing something, esp. a systematic or regular one 2 orderliness of thought or action 3 the techniques of a particular field or subject ▶ HISTORY Greek methodos, literally: a going after

Method n an acting technique in which the actor bases his or her role on the inner motivation of the character played

methodical adj careful, well-organized, and systematic > **methodically** adv

Methodist n 1 a member of any of the Christian Nonconformist denominations that derive from the beliefs and practices of John Wesley and his followers ▷ *adj* **2** of or relating to Methodists or their Church > **Methodism** *n*

methodology *n*, *pl* **-gies 1** the system of methods and principles used in a particular discipline **2** the philosophical study of method > **methodological** *adj*

meths *n Brit, Austral & NZ, informal* methylated spirits

methyl *adj* of or containing the monovalent saturated hydrocarbon group of atoms CH3–: *methyl mercury* ▶ HISTORY from *methylene*

methyl alcohol *n* same as **methanol**

methylate *vb* **-ating, -ated** to mix with methanol

methylated spirits *n* alcohol that has been rendered undrinkable by the addition of methanol and a violet dye, used as a solvent or as a fuel for small lamps or heaters. Also: **methylated spirit**

methylene *adj* of, consisting of, or containing the divalent group of atoms –CH2–: *a methylene group or radical* ▶ HISTORY Greek *methu* wine + *hulē* wood + *-ene*, indicating a double bond

meticulous *adj* very precise about details; careful and thorough ▶ HISTORY Latin *meticulosus* fearful > **meticulously** *adv* > **meticulousness** *n*

metonymy (mit-**on**-im-ee) *n*, *pl* **-mies** a figure of speech in which one thing is replaced by another associated with it, for instance the use of *Downing Street* to mean the *British government* ▶ HISTORY Greek *meta-*, indicating change + *onoma* name

metre¹ *or US* **meter** *n* the basic SI unit of length, equal to 100 centimetres (39.37 inches): *the majority of people are between one and a half and two metres tall* ▶ HISTORY same as METRE²

metre² *or US* **meter** *n* **1** *prosody* the rhythmic arrangement of syllables in verse, usually according to the number and kind of feet in a line **2** *music, chiefly US* the rhythmic arrangement of the beat in a piece of music ▶ HISTORY Greek *metron* measure

metre-kilogram-second *n* See **mks units**

metric *adj* of or relating to the metre or metric system: *use either all metric or all imperial measurements*

metrical *or* **metric** *adj* **1** of or relating to measurement **2** of or in poetic metre > **metrically** *adv*

metric system *n* any decimal system of units based on the metre. For scientific purposes SI units are used

metric ton *n* (not in technical use) a tonne

metro *n*, *pl* **-ros** an urban, usually underground, railway system in certain cities, such as Paris ▶ HISTORY French, from *chemin de fer métropolitain* metropolitan railway

metronome *n* a device which indicates the speed music should be played at by producing a clicking sound from a pendulum with an adjustable period of swing ▶ HISTORY Greek *metron* measure + *nomos* law

metropolis (mit-**trop**-oh-liss) *n* the main city of a country or region ▶ HISTORY Greek *mētēr* mother + *polis* city

metropolitan *adj* **1** of or characteristic of a metropolis **2** of or consisting of a city and its suburbs: *the Tokyo metropolitan region* **3** of or belonging to the home territories of a country, as opposed to overseas territories: *metropolitan France* ▷ *n* **4** *Christianity* the senior member of the clergy, esp. an archbishop, in charge of an ecclesiastical province **5** an inhabitant of a large city

-metry *n combining form* indicating the process or science of measuring: *geometry* ▶ HISTORY Greek *metron* measure > **-metric** *adj combining form*

mettle *n* **1** courage or spirit: *the lack of mettle evident among British politicians* **2** character or abilities: *the mettle saints are made of* **3 on one's mettle** roused to making one's best efforts ▶ HISTORY variant of *metal*

MeV million electronvolts (10^6 electronvolts)

mew¹ *n* **1** the characteristic high-pitched cry of a cat; miaow ▷ *vb* **2** to make such a sound ▶ HISTORY imitative

mew² *n* a seagull ▶ HISTORY Old English *mǣw*

mews *chiefly Brit n* **1** a yard or street lined by buildings originally used as stables but now often converted into dwellings ▷ *adj* **2** (of a flat or house) located in a mews: *a mews cottage* ▶ HISTORY plural of *mew*, originally referring to royal stables built on the site of hawks' mews (cages)

Mex. 1 Mexican **2** Mexico

Mexican *adj* **1** of Mexico ▷ *n* **2** a person from Mexico

mezzanine (**mez**-zan-een) *n* an intermediate storey, esp. one between the ground and first floor ▶ HISTORY Italian *mezzano* middle

mezzo (**met**-so) *adv* **1** *music* moderately; quite: *mezzo-forte* ▷ *n*, *pl* **-zos 2** short for **mezzo-soprano** ▶ HISTORY Italian: half

mezzo-soprano *n*, *pl* **-nos 1** a female voice lower than soprano but higher than contralto **2** a singer with such a voice

mezzotint (**met**-so-tint) *n* **1** a method of engraving done by scraping and burnishing the roughened surface of a copper plate **2** a print made from a plate so treated ▶ HISTORY Italian *mezzotinto* half tint

mg milligram

Mg *chem* magnesium

Mgr 1 manager **2** monseigneur **3** monsignor

MHR (in Australia) Member of the House of Representatives

MHz megahertz

mi *n music* same as **me²**

MI Michigan

MI5 Military Intelligence, section five; the part of the British security services which combats spying and subversion in Britain

MI6 Military Intelligence, section six; the part of the British security services which spies on other countries. Also called: **SIS**

miaow (mee-**ow**) *n* **1** the characteristic high-pitched cry of a cat; mew ▷ *vb* **2** to make such a sound

miasma (mee-**azz**-ma) *n, pl* -**mata** *or* -**mas** an unwholesome or foreboding atmosphere ▸ HISTORY Greek: defilement

mica (**my**-ka) *n* any of a group of minerals consisting of flakelike crystals of aluminium or potassium silicates. They have a high resistance to electricity and heat ▸ HISTORY Latin: crumb

mice *n* the plural of **mouse**

Mich. Michigan

Michaelmas (**mik**-kl-mass) *n* Sept 29, the feast of St Michael the archangel: one of the four quarter days in England, Ireland, and Wales

Michaelmas daisy *n Brit* a garden plant with small daisy-shaped purple, pink, or white flowers in autumn

mickey *n* **take the mickey (out of)** *informal* to tease (someone) ▸ HISTORY origin unknown

micro *n, pl* **micros** short for **microcomputer, microprocessor**

micro- *or* **micr-** *combining form* **1** small or minute: *microdot* **2** involving the use of a microscope: *microscopy* **3** denoting 10⁻⁶: *microsecond* ▸ HISTORY Greek *mikros* small

microbe *n* any microscopic organism, esp. a disease-causing bacterium ▸ HISTORY MICRO- + Greek *bios* life > **microbial** *or* **microbic** *adj*

microbiology *n* the branch of biology involving the study of microorganisms

microblog *n* a blog in which there is a limitation on the length of individual postings > **microblogger** *n* > **microblogging** *n*

microchemistry *n* chemical experimentation with minute quantities of material

microchip *n* a tiny wafer of semiconductor material, such as silicon, containing an integrated circuit. Often shortened to: **chip**

microcircuit *n* a miniature electronic circuit in which a number of permanently connected components are contained in one small chip of semiconducting material

microclimate *n meteorol* the atmospheric conditions affecting an individual or a small group of organisms, esp. when they differ from the climate of the rest of the community

microcomputer *n* a compact computer in which the central processing unit is contained in one or more silicon chips

microcosm *n* **1** a miniature representation of something: *this area is a microcosm of France as a whole* **2** man regarded as epitomizing the universe **3 in microcosm** on a small scale ▸ HISTORY Greek *mikros kosmos* little world > **microcosmic** *adj*

microdot *n* a greatly reduced photographic copy (about the size of a pinhead) of a document

microeconomics *n* the branch of economics concerned with particular commodities, firms, or individuals and the relationships between them

microelectronics *n* the branch of electronics concerned with microcircuits

microfiche (**my**-kroh-feesh) *n* same as **fiche** ▸ HISTORY French, from MICRO- + *fiche* small card

microfilm *n* **1** a strip of film on which books or documents can be recorded in miniaturized form ▷ *vb* **2** to photograph a page or document on microfilm

microlight *or* **microlite** *n* a very small private aircraft with large wings

micrometer (my-**krom**-it-er) *n* an instrument for the accurate measurement of small distances or angles

microminiaturization *or* -**isation** *n* the production and use of very small electronic components

micron (**my**-kron) *n* a unit of length equal to one millionth of a metre ▸ HISTORY Greek *mikros* small

micronutrient *n* any substance, such as a vitamin, essential for healthy development but required only in minute amounts

microorganism *n* any organism of microscopic size, such as a virus or bacterium

microphone *n* a device for converting sound into electrical energy

microprocessor *n computers* a single integrated circuit which acts as the central processing unit in a small computer

microscope *n* **1** an optical instrument that uses a lens or combination of lenses to produce a greatly magnified image of a small, close object **2** any instrument, such as the electron microscope, for producing a greatly magnified visual image of a small object

microscopic *adj* **1** too small to be seen except with a microscope **2** very small; minute **3** of or using a microscope > **microscopically** *adv*

microscopy *n* the use of microscopes

microsecond *n* one millionth of a second

microstructure *n* a structure on a microscopic scale, such as that of a metal or a cell

microsurgery *n* intricate surgery performed using a special microscope and miniature precision instruments

microwave *n* **1** an electromagnetic wave with a wavelength of between 0.3 and 0.001 metres: used in radar and cooking **2** short for **microwave oven** ▷ *vb* -**waving, -waved** **3** to cook in a microwave oven

microwave oven *n* a type of cooker which uses microwaves to cook food quickly

micturate *vb* -**rating, -rated** to urinate ▸ HISTORY Latin *micturire* to desire to urinate > **micturition** *n*

mid¹ *n archaic* the middle ▸ HISTORY Old English

mid² *or* **'mid** *prep poetic* amid

mid- *combining form* indicating a middle part, point, time, or position: *midday; mid-June; mid-Victorian*

midair *n* some point above ground level, in the air

midbrain *n anat* the part of the brain that develops from the middle portion of the embryonic brain

midday *n* **1** twelve o'clock in the day; noon **2** the middle part of the day, from late morning to early afternoon: *the midday sun*

m

midden n Brit & Austral a dunghill or pile of refuse ▶ HISTORY from Old Norse

middle n 1 an area or point equal in distance from the ends or edges of a place: *a hotel in the middle of town* 2 the time between the first part and last part of an event or period of time: *the middle of June; the film got a bit boring in the middle* 3 the part of the body around the stomach; waist 4 **in the middle of** busy doing something: *I'm in the middle of washing the dishes* ▷ adj 5 equally distant from the ends or outer edges of something; central: *the middle finger* 6 having an equal number of elder and younger brothers and sisters: *he was the middle child of three* 7 intermediate in status or situation: *middle management* 8 avoiding extremes; moderate: *we must find a middle course between authoritarianism and anarchy* ▶ HISTORY Old English *middel*

middle age n the period of life between youth and old age, usually considered to occur between the ages of 40 and 60 > **middle-aged** adj

Middle Ages n European history 1 (broadly) the period from the fall of the W Roman Empire in 476 AD to the Italian Renaissance 2 (narrowly) the period from about 1000 AD to the 15th century

Middle America n the US middle class, esp. those groups that are politically conservative

middle C n music the note written on the first ledger line below the treble staff or the first ledger line above the bass staff. On a piano it is near the middle of the keyboard

middle class n 1 the social class between the working and upper classes. It consists of business and professional people ▷ adj **middle-class** 2 of or characteristic of the middle class

middle-distance adj 1 athletics of or being a race of a length between the sprints and the distance events, esp. the 800 or 1500 metres: *a middle-distance runner* ▷ n **middle distance** 2 the part of a painting between the foreground and the far distance

middle ear n the sound-conducting part of the ear immediately inside the eardrum

Middle East n the area around the E Mediterranean, esp. Israel and the Arab countries from Turkey to North Africa and eastwards to Iran > **Middle Eastern** adj

Middle England n a characterization of a predominantly middle-class, middle-income section of British society, living mainly in suburban and rural England

Middle English n the English language from about 1100 to about 1450

Middle High German n High German from about 1200 to about 1500

Middle Low German n Low German from about 1200 to about 1500

middleman n, pl **-men** 1 a trader who buys from the producer and sells to the consumer 2 an intermediary or go-between

middle-of-the-road adj 1 not extreme, esp. in political views; moderate 2 of or denoting popular music of wide general appeal

middle school n (in England and Wales) a school for children aged between 8 or 9 and 12 or 13

middleweight n a professional boxer weighing up to 160 pounds (72.5 kg) or an amateur weighing up to 75 kg

middling adj 1 neither very good nor very bad 2 moderate in size 3 **fair to middling** neither good nor bad, esp. in health ▷ adv 4 informal moderately: *middling well*

midfield n soccer the area between the two opposing defences

midge n a small mosquito-like biting insect occurring in dancing swarms, esp. near water ▶ HISTORY Old English *mycge*

midget adj 1 much smaller than normal: *a midget submarine* ▷ n 2 offensive a very small person ▶ HISTORY *midge* + *-et* small

midi- combining form of medium or middle size or length: *a midi-skirt*

midi system n a complete set of compact hi-fi sound equipment designed as a single unit

midland n the central or inland part of a country

Midlands n 1 **the Midlands** the central counties of England ▷ adj 2 of, in, or from the central counties of England: *a Midlands engineering firm*

midnight n 1 the middle of the night; 12 o'clock at night ▷ adj 2 happening or apparent at midnight or in the middle of the night: *midnight Mass* 3 **burn the midnight oil** to work or study late into the night

midnight sun n the sun visible at midnight during the summer inside the Arctic and Antarctic circles

mid-ocean ridge n geol a linear landform, between 200 and 20,000 km in length, found on the ocean floor at the boundary between tectonic plates

mid-off n cricket the fielding position on the off side closest to the bowler

mid-on n cricket the fielding position on the on side closest to the bowler

midpoint n 1 the point on a line equally distant from either end 2 a point in time halfway between the beginning and end of an event

midriff n 1 the middle part of the human body between waist and chest 2 anat same as **diaphragm** (sense 1) ▶ HISTORY Old English *midhrif* mid belly

midshipman n, pl **-men** a naval officer of the lowest commissioned rank

midships adv, adj naut See **amidships**

midst n 1 **in our midst** among us 2 **in the midst of** a surrounded by b at a point during

midsummer n 1 the middle or height of summer 2 same as **summer solstice**

Midsummer's Day or **Midsummer Day** n June 24, the feast of St John the Baptist: one of the four quarter days in England, Ireland, and Wales

midway adj 1 in or at the middle of the distance; halfway: *the midway point* ▷ adv 2 to the middle of the distance

m

mid-wicket *n cricket* the fielding position on the on side, roughly the same distance from both wickets, and halfway towards the boundary

midwife *n, pl* **-wives** a person qualified to deliver babies and to care for women before, during, and after childbirth ▶ HISTORY Old English *mid* with + *wif* woman > **midwifery** (mid-**wiff**-fer-ree) *n*

midwinter *n* **1** the middle or depth of winter **2** same as **winter solstice**

mien (**mean**) *n literary* a person's manner, bearing, or appearance ▶ HISTORY probably from obsolete *demean* appearance

mifepristone (mi-**fep**-riss-tone) *n* a technical name for **abortion pill**

miffed *adj informal* offended or upset ▶ HISTORY perhaps imitative of bad temper

might¹ *vb* **1** an auxiliary expressing the past tense or subjunctive mood of **may¹**: *he might have come* **2** an auxiliary expressing possibility: *he might well have gone already*. See **may¹** (sense 2) ▶ HISTORY Old English *mihte*

might² *n* **1** great power, strength, or vigour **2 with all one's might** using all one's strength and energy **3 (with) might and main** See **main** ▶ HISTORY Old English *miht*

mighty *adj* **mightier, mightiest 1** powerful or strong **2** very great in extent or importance ▷ *adv* **3** *informal, chiefly US, Canad & Austral* very: *mighty hungry* > **mightily** *adv* > **mightiness** *n*

mignonette (min-yon-**net**) *n* a plant with spikes of small fragrant greenish-white flowers ▶ HISTORY French, diminutive of *mignon* dainty

migraine (**mee**-grain) *n* a throbbing headache usually affecting only one side of the head and commonly accompanied by nausea and visual disturbances

■ **WORD HISTORY**
■ 'Migraine' comes via French from Latin
■ *hēmicrānia*, meaning 'pain in half the head',
■ from Greek *hemi-*, meaning 'half', and *kranion*,
■ meaning 'cranium, skull'.

migrant *n* **1** a person or animal that moves from one place to another ▷ *adj* **2** moving from one place to another: *migrant farm labourers*

migrate *vb* **-grating, -grated 1** to go from one place to settle in another, esp. in a foreign country **2** (of living creatures, esp. birds) to journey between different habitats at specific times of the year ▶ HISTORY Latin *migrare* to change one's abode > **migration** *n* > **migratory** *adj*

mikado *n, pl* **-dos** *archaic* the Japanese emperor ▶ HISTORY Japanese

mike *n informal* a microphone

mil *n photog* short for **millimetre**: *35-mil film* ▶ HISTORY Latin *millesimus* thousandth

milch (miltch) *adj chiefly Brit* (esp. of cattle) kept for milk ▶ HISTORY Old English *-milce* (in compounds)

mild *adj* **1** (of a taste or sensation) not strong; bland **2** gentle or temperate in character, climate, or behaviour **3** not extreme; moderate: *mild criticism of senior officers* **4** feeble; unassertive: *a mild protest*

▷ *n* **5** *Brit* a dark beer flavoured with fewer hops than bitter ▶ HISTORY Old English *milde*

mildew *n* **1** a disease of plants caused by a parasitic fungus **2** same as **mould²** ▷ *vb* **3** to affect or become affected with mildew ▶ HISTORY Old English *mildēaw* honey dew > **mildewy** *adj*

mild steel *n* strong tough steel containing a small quantity of carbon

mile *n* **1** Also: **statute mile** a unit of length used in the UK, the US, and certain other countries, equal to 1760 yards. 1 mile is equivalent to 1.60934 kilometres **2** See **nautical mile 3** Also: **miles** *informal* a great distance; great deal: *he missed by miles* **4** a race extending over a mile ▷ *adv* **5 miles** very much: *it's miles better than their first album*

■ **WORD HISTORY**
■ In Roman times, a mile was equal to a
■ thousand paces. In Latin, 'one thousand paces'
■ is *mīlia passuum*, from *mille*, meaning 'a
■ thousand' (the same Latin word as is found
■ in English words such as 'millennium' and
■ 'millimetre').

mileage *n* **1** a distance expressed in miles **2** the total number of miles that a motor vehicle has travelled **3** the number of miles a motor vehicle will travel on one gallon of fuel **4** *informal* the usefulness or benefit of something: *the opposition is trying to make political mileage out of the issue*

mileometer *or* **milometer** (mile-**om**-it-er) *n Brit* a device that records the number of miles that a vehicle has travelled

milepost *n chiefly US & Canad* a signpost that shows the distance in miles to or from a place

milestone *n* **1** a stone pillar that shows the distance in miles to or from a place **2** a significant event in a life or history: *a milestone in Turkish-Bulgarian relations*

milfoil *n* same as **yarrow** ▶ HISTORY Latin *mille* thousand + *folium* leaf

milieu (**meal**-yuh) *n, pl* **milieux** *or* **milieus** (**meal**-yuhz) the social and cultural environment in which a person or thing exists: *the film takes for its milieu an apparently wholesome small town* ▶ HISTORY French

militant *adj* **1** very active or aggressive in the support of a cause **2** *formal* warring; engaged in warfare ▷ *n* **3** a militant person ▶ HISTORY Latin *militare* to be a soldier > **militancy** *n* > **militantly** *adv*

militarism *n* the pursuit of policies intended to create and maintain aggressive and influential armed forces > **militarist** *n, adj* > **militaristic** *adj*

militarized *or* **-ised** *adj* occupied by armed forces: *one of the most heavily militarized borders in the world* > **militarization** *or* **-isation** *n*

military *adj* **1** of or relating to the armed forces or war **2** of or characteristic of soldiers ▷ *n* **3 the military** the armed services, esp. the army ▶ HISTORY Latin *miles* soldier > **militarily** *adv*

military police *n* a corps within an army that performs police duties

militate *vb* **-tating, -tated** (of facts or events) to have a strong influence or effect: *our position militated against counter-attacks*

militia (mill-**ish**-a) *n* a military force of trained civilians enlisted for use in emergency only ▶ HISTORY Latin: soldiery > **militiaman** *n*

milk *n* **1 a** a whitish fluid secreted by the mammary glands of mature female mammals and used for feeding their young **b** the milk of cows, goats, etc., used by humans as a food and to make cheese, butter, and yogurt **2** any similar fluid, such as the juice of a coconut ▷ *vb* **3** to draw milk from the udder of a cow or other animal **4** to extract as much money, help, or value as possible from: *he was accused of milking the situation for his own ends* ▶ HISTORY Old English *milc* > **milker** *n* > **milkiness** *n* > **milky** *adj*

milk bar *n* (formerly) a snack bar at which milk drinks and light refreshments are served

milk float *n* Brit a small electrically powered vehicle used to deliver milk to houses

milkmaid *n* a girl or woman who milks cows

milkman *n, pl* **-men** Brit, Austral & NZ a man who delivers milk to people's houses

milk of magnesia *n* a suspension of magnesium hydroxide in water, used as an antacid and laxative

milk pudding *n* chiefly Brit & Austral a pudding made by cooking milk with a grain, esp. rice

milk round *n* **1** Brit & NZ a route along which a milkman regularly delivers milk **2** Brit a regular series of visits made by recruitment officers from industry to colleges

milksop *n* a feeble or ineffectual man or youth

Milky Way *n* **1** the diffuse band of light stretching across the night sky that consists of millions of distant stars in our galaxy **2** the galaxy in which the Earth is situated ▶ HISTORY translation of Latin *via lactea*

mill *n* **1** a building where grain is crushed and ground to make flour **2** a factory, esp. one which processes raw materials: *a steel mill* **3** any of various processing or manufacturing machines, esp. one that grinds, presses, or rolls **4** a small device for grinding solids: *a pepper mill* **5 go** or **be put through the mill** to have an unpleasant experience or ordeal ▷ *vb* **6** to grind, press, or process in or as if in a mill **7** to groove or flute the edge of a coin **8** to move about in a confused manner: *the corridor was full of people milling about* ▶ HISTORY Latin *molere* to grind

millennium (mill-**en**-nee-um) *n, pl* **-nia** (-nee-a) or **-niums 1** a period of one thousand years **2 the Millennium** Christianity the period of a thousand years of Christ's awaited reign upon earth **3** a future period of peace and happiness ▶ HISTORY Latin *mille* thousand + *annus* year > **millennial** *adj*

millennium bug *n* computers any software problem arising from the change in date at the start of the 21st century

millepede *n* same as **millipede**

miller *n* history a person who owns or operates a mill, esp. a corn mill

miller's thumb *n* a small freshwater European fish with a flattened body ▶ HISTORY from the alleged likeness of the fish's head to a thumb

millesimal (mill-**less**-im-al) *adj* **1** denoting or consisting of a thousandth ▷ *n* **2** a thousandth part of something ▶ HISTORY Latin *millesimus*

millet *n* a cereal grass cultivated for its edible grain and as animal fodder ▶ HISTORY Latin *milium*

milli- *combining form* denoting 10^{-3}: *millimetre* ▶ HISTORY Latin *mille* thousand

milliard *n* Brit (no longer in technical use) a thousand million ▶ HISTORY French

millibar *n* a unit of atmospheric pressure equal to 100 newtons per square metre

milligram or **milligramme** *n* one thousandth of a gram ▶ HISTORY French

millilitre or US **milliliter** *n* a measure of volume equivalent to one thousandth of a litre

millimetre or US **millimeter** *n* a unit of length equal to one thousandth of a metre

milliner *n* a person who makes or sells women's hats ▶ HISTORY originally *Milaner* a native of *Milan*, once famous for its fancy goods > **millinery** *n*

million *n, pl* **-lions** or **-lion 1** the number equal to one thousand thousands: 1 000 000 or 10^6 **2** (often pl) informal an extremely large but unspecified number: *I've got a million things to do today* ▶ HISTORY early Italian *millione* > **millionth** *n, adj*

millionaire *n* a person who has money or property worth at least a million pounds, dollars, etc. > **millionairess** *fem n*

millipede or **millepede** *n* a small crawling animal with a cylindrical many-segmented body, each segment of which bears two pairs of legs ▶ HISTORY Latin *mille* thousand + *pes* foot

millisecond *n* one thousandth of a second

millstone *n* **1** one of a pair of heavy flat stones that are rotated one against the other to grind grain **2** a heavy burden of responsibility or obligation: *the debt had become a millstone round his neck*

millwheel *n* a water wheel that drives a mill

milometer (mile-**om**-it-er) *n* same as **mileometer**

milt *n* the male reproductive gland, sperm, or semen of a fish ▶ HISTORY Old English *milte* spleen

mime *n* **1** a style of acting using only gesture and bodily movement and not words **2** a performer specializing in this **3** a performance in this style ▷ *vb* **miming, mimed 4** to express or describe something in actions or gestures without using speech **5** (of musicians) to pretend to be singing or playing music that is actually prerecorded ▶ HISTORY Greek *mimos* imitator > **mimer** *n*

mimetic (mim-**met**-ik) *adj* **1** imitating or representing something: *most photographs are mimetic representations of the real world* **2** biol of or showing mimicry ▶ HISTORY Greek *mimeisthai* to imitate

mimic *vb* **-icking, -icked 1** to imitate (a person or a way of acting or speaking), esp. to entertain or make fun of **2** to take on the appearance of: *certain flies mimic wasps* **3** to copy closely or in a servile manner: *social climbers in the colonies began to mimic their conquerors* ▷ *n* **4** a person or an animal, such as a parrot, that is clever at mimicking ▶ HISTORY Greek *mimikos*

mimicry *n, pl* **-ries 1** the act or art of copying or imitating closely **2** *biol* the resemblance shown by one animal species to another dangerous or inedible one, which protects it from predators

mimosa *n* a tropical shrub with ball-like clusters of yellow flowers and leaves sensitive to touch and light ▶ HISTORY Latin *mimus* mime, because the plant's sensitivity to touch imitates the similar reaction of animals

min. 1 minimum or minutes

Min. 1 Minister **2** Ministry

minaret *n* a slender tower of a mosque with one or more balconies ▶ HISTORY Arabic *manārat* lamp

minatory *adj* threatening or menacing ▶ HISTORY Latin *minari* to threaten

mince *vb* **mincing, minced 1** to chop, grind, or cut into very small pieces **2** to walk or speak in an affected dainty manner **3 not mince one's words** to be direct and to the point rather than making an effort to avoid upsetting people ▷ *n* **4** *chiefly Brit & NZ* minced meat ▶ HISTORY Old French *mincier*, from Late Latin *minutia* smallness > **minced** *adj* > **mincer** *n*

mincemeat *n* **1** a mixture of dried fruit and spices used for filling pies **2 make mincemeat of** *informal* to defeat completely

mince pie *n* a small round pastry tart filled with mincemeat

mincing *adj* (of a person or their style of walking or speaking) affectedly elegant

mind *n* **1** the part of a person responsible for thought, feelings, and intention. *Related adjective:* **mental 2** intelligence as opposed to feelings or wishes **3** memory or recollection: *his name didn't spring to mind immediately* **4** a person considered as an intellectual being: *one of Europe's greatest minds* **5** the condition or state of a person's feelings or thoughts: *a confused state of mind* **6** an intention or desire: *I have a mind to go* **7** attention or thoughts: *keep your mind on the job* **8** a sound mental state; sanity: *he's out of his mind* **9 change one's mind** to alter one's decision or opinion **10 give someone a piece of one's mind** to scold someone severely **11 in two minds** undecided or wavering **12 make up one's mind** to reach a decision **13 on one's mind** in one's thoughts **14 to my mind** in my opinion ▷ *vb* **15** to take offence at: *do you mind if I open a window?* **16** to pay attention to: *to mind one's own business* **17** to make certain; ensure: *mind you tell him* **18** to take care of: *mind the shop* **19** to be cautious or careful about: *mind how you go* **20** *dialect* to remember ▶ HISTORY Old English *gemynd*

minded *adj* having a mind or inclination as specified: *commercially minded*

minder *n* **1** *slang* an aide or assistant, esp. one employed as a bodyguard or public relations officer for someone **2** short for **child minder**

mindful *adj* **mindful of** being aware of and taking into account: *the company is ever mindful of the need to find new markets*

mindless *adj* **1** stupid or careless **2** requiring little or no intellectual effort **3** heedless: *mindless of the risks involved* > **mindlessly** *adv* > **mindlessness** *n*

Mind Map *n trademark* a method of representing ideas in a diagram, with related concepts arranged around a core concept

mine¹ *pron* **1** something or someone belonging to or associated with me: *that's mine* **2 of mine** belonging to or associated with me: *it's a great favourite of mine* ▷ *adj* **3** *archaic* same as **my**: *mine eyes; mine host* ▶ HISTORY Old English *mīn*

mine² *n* **1** a place where minerals, esp. coal, ores, or precious stones, are dug from the ground **2** a type of bomb placed in water or under the ground, and designed to destroy ships, vehicles, or people passing over or near it **3** a profitable source or abundant supply: *a mine of information* ▷ *vb* **mining, mined 4** to dig minerals from the ground: *lead has been mined here for over three centuries* **5** to dig a hole or tunnel, esp. in order to obtain minerals **6** to place explosive mines in or on: *the retreating troops had mined the bridge* ▶ HISTORY Old French

mine dump *n* S African a large mound of waste material from gold-mining operations

minefield *n* **1** an area of ground or water containing explosive mines **2** a subject or situation full of hidden problems

minelayer *n* a warship or aircraft for carrying and laying mines

miner *n* a person who works in a mine, esp. a coal mine

mineral *n* **1** a naturally occurring solid inorganic substance with a characteristic chemical composition and structure **2** any inorganic matter **3** any substance obtained by mining, esp. a metal ore **4** *Brit* a soft drink containing carbonated water and flavourings ▷ *adj* **5** of, containing, or resembling minerals ▶ HISTORY Medieval Latin *minera* mine, ore

mineral acid *n* any acid which can be produced from a mineral

mineralogy (min-er-**al**-a-jee) *n* the scientific study of minerals > **mineralogical** *adj* > **mineralogist** *n*

mineral water *n* water containing dissolved mineral salts or gases

minestrone (min-ness-**strone**-ee) *n* a soup made from a variety of vegetables and pasta ▶ HISTORY Italian, from *minestrare* to serve

minesweeper *n* a naval vessel equipped to clear mines

Ming *adj* of or relating to Chinese porcelain from the time of the Ming dynasty, which ruled China from 1368 to 1644

minger n Brit, informal an unattractive person > **minging** adj

mingle vb **-gling, -gled** 1 to mix or blend 2 to associate or mix with a group of people: *the performers mingled with the audience after the show* ▶ HISTORY Old English *mengan* to mix

mingy adj **-gier, -giest** Brit & NZ, informal mean or miserly ▶ HISTORY probably a blend of *mean* + *stingy*

mini adj 1 small; miniature 2 (of a skirt or dress) very short ▷ n, pl **minis** 3 something very small of its kind, esp. a miniskirt

mini- combining form smaller or shorter than the standard size: *minibus; miniseries* ▶ HISTORY from *miniature* + *minimum*

miniature n 1 a model or representation on a very small scale 2 a very small painting, esp. a portrait 3 a very small bottle of whisky or other spirits, which can hold 50 millilitres 4 **in miniature** on a small scale ▷ adj 5 much smaller than usual; small-scale ▶ HISTORY Medieval Latin *miniare* to paint red (in illuminating manuscripts), from *minium* red lead > **miniaturist** n

miniaturize or **-ise** vb **-izing, -ized** or **-ising, -ised** to make a very small version of something, esp. electronic components > **miniaturization** or **-isation** n

minibus n a small bus

minicab n Brit an ordinary car used as a taxi

minicomputer n a small digital computer which is more powerful than a microcomputer

minidisc n a small recordable compact disc

minim n 1 a unit of fluid measure equal to one sixtieth of a drachm 2 music a note with the time value of half a semibreve ▶ HISTORY Latin *minimus* smallest

minimal adj of the least possible quantity or degree

minimalism n 1 a type of music based on the repetition of simple elements 2 a design or style using the simplest and fewest elements to create the maximum effect > **minimalist** adj, n

minimize or **-mise** vb **-mizing, -mized** or **-mising, -mised** 1 to reduce to the lowest possible degree or amount: *these measures should help minimize our costs* 2 to regard or treat as less important than it really is; belittle: *I don't want to minimize the importance of her contribution*

minimum n, pl **-mums** or **-ma** 1 the least possible amount, degree, or quantity: *fry the burgers in the minimum of oil* 2 the least amount recorded, allowed, or reached: *soak the beans for a minimum of eight hours* ▷ adj 3 of, being, or showing a minimum or minimums: *the minimum age* ▶ HISTORY Latin *minimus* least

minimum lending rate n (formerly) the minimum rate at which the Bank of England would lend money: replaced in 1981 by the base rate

minimum wage n the lowest wage that an employer is permitted to pay by law or union contract

mining n 1 the act, process, or industry of extracting coal or ores from the earth 2 mil the process of laying mines

minion n a servile assistant ▶ HISTORY French *mignon* darling

miniseries n, pl **-series** a television programme in several parts that is shown on consecutive days over a short period

miniskirt n a very short skirt

minister n 1 (esp. in Presbyterian and some Nonconformist Churches) a member of the clergy 2 a head of a government department 3 a diplomat with a lower rank than an ambassador ▷ vb 4 **minister to** to attend to the needs of ▶ HISTORY Latin: servant > **ministerial** adj

minister of state n (in the British Parliament) a minister, usually below cabinet rank, appointed to assist a senior minister

Minister of the Crown n Brit any Government minister of cabinet rank

ministry n, pl **-tries** 1 the profession or duties of a minister of religion 2 ministers considered as a group 3 a a government department headed by a minister b the buildings of such a department

mink n, pl **mink** or **minks** 1 a mammal of Europe, Asia, and North America, resembling a large stoat 2 its highly valued fur 3 a garment made of this, esp. a woman's coat or stole ▶ HISTORY Scandinavian

minneola n a juicy citrus fruit that is a cross between a tangerine and a grapefruit

minnow n, pl **-nows** or **-now** a small slender European freshwater fish ▶ HISTORY Old English *myne*

Minoan (min-**no**-an) adj of or denoting the Bronze Age culture of Crete from about 3000 BC to about 1100 BC ▶ HISTORY *Minos*, in Greek mythology, king of Crete

minor adj 1 lesser or secondary in size, frequency, or importance than others of the same kind: *a minor poet* 2 not very serious or significant: *minor injuries* 3 music a (of a scale) having a semitone between the second and third and fifth and sixth notes (**natural minor**) b of or based on the minor scale: *his quintet in C minor; a minor third* ▷ n 4 a person below the age of legal majority 5 US, Canad & Austral education a subsidiary subject 6 music a minor key, chord, mode, or scale ▷ vb 7 **minor in** US, Canad & Austral education to study as a subsidiary subject: *to minor in politics* ▶ HISTORY Latin: less, smaller

minority n, pl **-ties** 1 the smaller of two parts, factions, or groups 2 a group that is different, esp. racially or politically, from a larger group of which it is a part 3 **in the minority** forming or part of the group of people or things made up of less than half of a larger group ▷ adj 4 relating to or being a minority: *a minority sport*

Minotaur n Greek myth a monster with the head of a bull and the body of a man ▶ HISTORY Greek *Minōtauros*

m

minster *n Brit* any of certain cathedrals and large churches, usually originally connected to a monastery ▷ **HISTORY** Church Latin *monasterium* monastery

minstrel *n* **1** a medieval singer and musician **2** a performer in a minstrel show ▷ **HISTORY** Old French *menestral*

minstrel show *n* a theatrical entertainment consisting of songs and dances performed by actors wearing black face make-up

mint¹ *n* **1** any of various plants with aromatic leaves used for seasoning and flavouring **2** a sweet flavoured with mint ▷ **HISTORY** Greek *minthē* > **minty** *adj*

mint² *n* **1** a factory where the official coins of a country are made **2** a very large amount of money ▷ *adj* **3 in mint condition** in perfect condition; as if new ▷ *vb* **4** to make coins by stamping metal **5** to invent or create: *no-one knows who first minted the term 'yuppie'* ▷ **HISTORY** Latin *moneta* money, mint

minuet (min-new-**wet**) *n* **1** a stately court dance of the 17th and 18th centuries in triple time **2** music for this dance ▷ **HISTORY** French *menuet* dance

minus *prep* **1** reduced by the subtraction of: *six minus two equals four* **2** *informal* without or lacking: *he returned minus his jacket* ▷ *adj* **3** indicating or involving subtraction: *a minus sign* **4** Also: **negative** less than zero: *it's minus eight degrees in Montreal today* **5** *education* slightly below the standard of a particular grade: *a C minus for maths* ▷ *n* **6** short for **minus sign** **7** a negative quantity **8** *informal* something detrimental or negative ▷ **HISTORY** Latin, neuter of *minor* less

minuscule (**min**-niss-skyool) *adj* very small ▷ **HISTORY** Latin *(littera) minuscula* very small (letter)

minus sign *n* the symbol –, indicating subtraction, a negative quantity, or a negative electrical charge

minute¹ *n* **1** 60 seconds; one sixtieth of an hour **2** any very short period of time; moment: *I'll be with you in a minute* **3** the distance that can be travelled in a minute: *it's about ten minutes away* **4** a measure of angle equal to one sixtieth of a degree **5 up to the minute** the very latest or newest ▷ *vb* **-uting, -uted** **6** to record in minutes: *the decision was minuted in 1990* ▷ See also **minutes** ▷ **HISTORY** Medieval Latin *minuta*, noun use of Latin *minutus* minute (small)

minute² *adj* **1** very small; tiny **2** precise or detailed: *a minute examination* ▷ **HISTORY** Latin *minutus*, past participle of *minuere* to diminish > **minutely** *adv*

minutes *pl n* an official record of the proceedings of a meeting or conference

minutiae (my-**new**-shee-eye) *pl n*, *sing* **-tia** trifling or precise details ▷ **HISTORY** Late Latin, plural of *minutia* smallness

minx *n* a bold or flirtatious girl ▷ **HISTORY** origin unknown

Miocene (**my**-oh-seen) *adj geol* of the epoch of geological time about 25 million years ago ▷ **HISTORY** Greek *meiōn* less + *kainos* new

miracle *n* **1** an event contrary to the laws of nature and attributed to a supernatural cause **2** any amazing and fortunate event: *it's a miracle that no-one was killed in the accident* **3** a marvellous example of something: *a miracle of organization* ▷ **HISTORY** Latin *mirari* to wonder at

miracle play *n* a medieval play based on a biblical story or the life of a saint

miraculous *adj* **1** like a miracle **2** surprising or remarkable

mirage (mir-**rahzh**) *n* **1** an image of a distant object or sheet of water, often inverted or distorted, caused by atmospheric refraction by hot air **2** something illusory: *the mirage of economic recovery* ▷ **HISTORY** French, from *(se) mirer* to be reflected

mire *n* **1** a boggy or marshy area **2** mud, muck, or dirt **3** an unpleasant or difficult situation that is difficult to get out of: *the country sank deeper into the economic mire* ▷ *vb* **miring, mired** **4** to sink or be stuck in a mire: *the company has been mired in financial scandal* ▷ **HISTORY** Old Norse *mȳrr*

mirror *n* **1** a sheet of glass with a metal coating on its back that reflects an image of an object placed in front of it **2** a thing that reflects or depicts something else ▷ *vb* **3** to reflect or represent faithfully: *the book inevitably mirrors my own interests* ▷ **HISTORY** Latin *mirari* to wonder at

mirror image *n* an image or object that has left and right reversed as if seen in a mirror

mirth *n* laughter, gaiety, or merriment ▷ **HISTORY** Old English *myrgth* > **mirthful** *adj* > **mirthless** *adj*

mis- *prefix* **1** wrong or bad; wrongly or badly: *misunderstanding; mislead* **2** lack of; not: *mistrust* ▷ **HISTORY** Old English *mis(se)-*

misadventure *n* **1** an unlucky event; misfortune **2** *law* accidental death not due to crime or negligence

misalliance *n* an unsuitable alliance or marriage

misanthrope (**miz**-zan-thrope) *or* **misanthropist** (miz-**zan**-throp-ist) *n* a person who dislikes or distrusts people in general ▷ **HISTORY** Greek *misos* hatred + *anthrōpos* man > **misanthropic** (miz-zan-**throp**-ik) *adj* > **misanthropy** (miz-**zan**-throp-ee) *n*

misapprehend *vb* to misunderstand > **misapprehension** *n*

misappropriate *vb* **-ating, -ated** to take and use money dishonestly > **misappropriation** *n*

misbehave *vb* **-having, -haved** to behave badly > **misbehaviour** *or US* **misbehavior** *n*

miscalculate *vb* **-lating, -lated** to calculate or judge wrongly: *we miscalculated the strength of the opposition* > **miscalculation** *n*

miscarriage *n* **1** spontaneous premature expulsion of a fetus from the womb, esp. before the 20th week of pregnancy **2** an act of mismanagement or failure: *a miscarriage of justice*

miscarry *vb* **-ries, -rying, -ried** **1** to expel a fetus prematurely from the womb **2** to fail

miscast *vb* **-casting, -cast** to cast a role or an actor in a play or film inappropriately: *the role of the* *avaricious boss was miscast; she was miscast as Cassandra*

miscegenation (miss-ij-in-**nay**-shun) *n* interbreeding of races, esp. where differences of colour are involved ▶ HISTORY Latin *miscere* to mingle + *genus* race

miscellaneous (miss-sel-**lane**-ee-uss) *adj* composed of or containing a variety of things; mixed or assorted ▶ HISTORY Latin *miscere* to mix

miscellany (miss-**sell**-a-nee) *n*, *pl* **-nies** written a mixed assortment of items

mischance *n* **1** bad luck **2** an unlucky event or accident

mischief *n* **1** annoying but not malicious behaviour that causes trouble or irritation **2** an inclination to tease **3** injury or harm caused by a person or thing ▶ HISTORY Old French *meschief*, from *mes*- mis- + *chef* end

mischievous (miss-chiv-uss) *adj* **1** full of mischief **2** teasing; slightly malicious **3** intended to cause harm: *a purveyor of mischievous disinformation* > **mischievously** *adv*

miscible (**miss**-sib-bl) *adj* able to be mixed: *miscible with water* ▶ HISTORY Latin *miscere* to mix > **miscibility** *n*

misconceived *adj* false, mistaken, or badly thought-out: *a misconceived conception of loyalty*

misconception *n* a false or mistaken view, idea, or belief

misconduct *n* behaviour, such as adultery or professional negligence, that is regarded as immoral or unethical

misconstrue *vb* **-struing, -strued** to interpret mistakenly > **misconstruction** *n*

miscreant (**miss**-kree-ant) *n* a wrongdoer or villain ▶ HISTORY Old French *mescreant* unbelieving

misdeed *n* an evil or illegal action

misdemeanour *or US* **misdemeanor** *n* **1** a minor wrongdoing **2** *criminal law* (formerly) an offence less serious than a felony

misdirect *vb* to give someone wrong directions or instructions > **misdirection** *n*

mise en scène (**meez**-orn-sen) *n* **1** the arrangement of properties, scenery, etc. in a play **2** the objects so arranged; stage setting ▶ HISTORY French: putting on stage

miser *n* a person who hoards money and hates spending it: *I'm married to a miser* ▶ HISTORY Latin: wretched > **miserly** *adj*

miserable *adj* **1** unhappy or depressed; wretched **2** causing misery or discomfort: *a miserable existence* **3** sordid or squalid: *miserable living conditions* **4** mean or ungenerous: *a miserable pension* ▶ HISTORY Latin *miserabilis* > **miserableness** *n* > **miserably** *adv*

misericord *n* a ledge projecting from the underside of the hinged seat of a choir stall in a church, which the occupant can rest against while standing ▶ HISTORY Latin *miserere* to pity + *cor* heart

misery *n*, *pl* **-eries** **1** intense unhappiness or suffering **2** something which causes such unhappiness **3** squalid or poverty-stricken

conditions **4** *Brit, informal* a person who is habitually depressed: *he is such a misery* ▶ HISTORY Latin *miser* wretched

misfire *vb* **-firing, -fired** **1** (of a firearm) to fail to fire as expected **2** (of a motor engine or vehicle) to fail to fire at the appropriate time **3** to fail to have the intended result; go wrong: *he was injured when a practical joke misfired* ▷ *n* **4** the act or an instance of misfiring

misfit *n* a person who is not suited to the role, social group, etc. he or she finds himself or herself in

misfortune *n* **1** bad luck **2** an unfortunate event

misgivings *pl n* feelings of uncertainty, fear, or doubt

misgovern *vb* to govern badly > **misgovernment** *n*

misguided *adj* mistaken or unwise

mishandle *vb* **-dling, -dled** to handle or treat badly or inefficiently

mishap *n* a minor accident

mishear *vb* **-hearing, -heard** to fail to hear (what someone says) correctly

mishit *sport n* **1** a faulty shot, kick, or stroke ▷ *vb* **-hitting, -hit** **2** to hit or kick (a ball) with a faulty stroke

mishmash *n* a confused collection or mixture ▶ HISTORY reduplication of *mash*

misinform *vb* to give incorrect information to > **misinformation** *n*

misinterpret *vb* to understand or represent (something) wrongly: *the press misinterpreted the President's remarks* > **misinterpretation** *n*

misjudge *vb* **-judging, -judged** to judge wrongly or unfairly > **misjudgment** *or* **misjudgement** *n*

mislay *vb* **-lays, -laying, -laid** to lose (something) temporarily, esp. by forgetting where it is

mislead *vb* **-leading, -led** to give false or confusing information to

misleading *adj* giving a false or confusing impression: *misleading use of statistical data*

mismanage *vb* **-aging, -aged** to organize or run (something) badly > **mismanagement** *n*

misnomer (miss-**no**-mer) *n* **1** an incorrect or unsuitable name for a person or thing **2** the use of the wrong name ▶ HISTORY Old French *mesnommer* to misname

misogyny (miss-**oj**-in-ee) *n* hatred of women ▶ HISTORY Greek *misos* hatred + *gunē* woman > **misogynist** *n* > **misogynous** *adj*

misperception *n* **1** the act of misunderstanding something **2** an incorrect understanding of something

misplace *vb* **-placing, -placed** **1** to lose something temporarily by forgetting where it was placed **2** to put something in the wrong place

misprint *n* **1** an error in printing ▷ *vb* **2** to print a letter incorrectly

misprision *n* *law* the concealment of the commission of a felony or an act of treason ▶ HISTORY Old French *mesprision* error

m

mispronounce *vb* **-nouncing, -nounced** to pronounce a word or name wrongly > **mispronunciation** *n*

misquote *vb* **-quoting, -quoted** to quote inaccurately > **misquotation** *n*

misread *vb* **-reading, -read 1** to misinterpret or misunderstand: *he misread her politeness as approval* **2** to read incorrectly

misrepresent *vb* to represent wrongly or inaccurately

misrepresentation *n law* inaccurate or untrue information given to induce someone into entering into a contract; if proved, misrepresentation is grounds for voiding the contract

misrule *vb* **-ruling, -ruled 1** to govern inefficiently or without justice ▷ *n* **2** inefficient or unjust government **3** disorder or lawlessness

miss¹ *vb* **1** to fail to notice, see, or hear: *it's right at the top of the hill, so you can't miss it; I missed what he said because I was talking at the time* **2** to fail to hit something aimed at: *he threw a stone at the dog but missed* **3** to fail to achieve or reach: *they narrowly missed promotion last season* **4** to fail to take advantage of: *he never missed a chance to make money* **5** to fail or be unable to be present: *he had missed the last three meetings* **6** to be too late for: *we missed the bus and had to walk* **7** to fail to take advantage of: *he never missed a chance to make money* **8** to discover or regret the loss or absence of: *the boys miss their father when he's away on business* **9** to escape or avoid narrowly: *it missed the helicopter's rotors by inches* ▷ *n* **10** a failure to hit, reach, etc.: *an easy miss in the second frame gave his opponent the advantage* **11 give something a miss** to decide not to do, go to, or take part in something: *I'll give the pub a miss and have a quiet night in* ▷ See also **miss out** ▸ **HISTORY** Old English *missan*

miss² *n informal* an unmarried woman or girl ▸ **HISTORY** from *mistress*

Miss *n* a title of a girl or unmarried woman, usually used before the surname: *Miss Brown to you*

missal *n RC Church* a book containing the prayers and rites of the Masses for a complete year ▸ **HISTORY** Church Latin *missale*, from *missa* Mass

misshapen *adj* badly shaped; deformed

missile *n* **1** a rocket with an exploding warhead, used as a weapon **2** an object or weapon that is thrown, launched, or fired at a target ▸ **HISTORY** Latin *mittere* to send

missing *adj* **1** not in its proper or usual place and unable to be found **2** not able to be traced and not known to be dead: *seven men were reported missing after the raid* **3** not included in something although it perhaps should have been: *two things are missing from the report*

missing link *n* **1** any missing section or part in a series **2 the missing link** a hypothetical extinct animal, formerly thought to be intermediate between the apes and man

mission *n* **1** a specific task or duty assigned to a person or group of people **2** a task or duty that a

person believes he or she must achieve; vocation: *he felt it was his mission to pass on his knowledge to other people* **3** a group of people representing or working for a particular country or organization in a foreign country: *the UN peacekeeping mission* **4** a group of people sent by a church to a foreign country to do religious and social work **5** the place in which a church or government mission is based **6** the dispatch of aircraft or spacecraft to achieve a particular task **7** a charitable centre that offers shelter or aid to poor or homeless people **8** *S African* a long and difficult process ▸ **HISTORY** Latin *mittere* to send

missionary *n, pl* **-aries 1** a person sent abroad by a church to do religious and social work ▷ *adj* **2** of or relating to missionaries: *missionary work* **3** resulting from a desire to convert people to one's own beliefs: *missionary zeal*

mission statement *n* an official statement of the aims and objectives of a business or other organization

missive *n* a formal or official letter ▸ **HISTORY** Latin *mittere* to send

miss out *vb* **1** to leave out or overlook **2 miss out on** to fail to take part in (something enjoyable or beneficial): *she'd missed out on going to university*

misspell *vb* **-spelling, -spelt** *or* **-spelled** to spell a word wrongly > **misspelling** *n*

missus *or* **missis** *n* **1** *Brit, Austral & NZ, informal* one's wife or the wife of the person addressed or referred to: *the missus is a fabulous cook* **2** an informal term of address for a woman ▸ **HISTORY** spoken version of *mistress*

mist *n* **1** a thin fog **2** a fine spray of liquid, such as that produced by an aerosol container **3** condensed water vapour on a surface **4** something that causes haziness or lack of clarity, such as a film of tears ▷ *vb* **5** to cover or be covered with mist: *the windscreen has misted up again; his eyes misted over and he shook with rage* ▸ **HISTORY** Old English > **misty** *adj* > **mistiness** *n*

mistake *n* **1** an error or blunder **2** a misconception or misunderstanding ▷ *vb* **-taking, -took, -taken 3** to misunderstand or misinterpret: *the chaplain quite mistook her meaning* **4** to confuse a person or thing with another: *they saw the HMS Sheffield and mistook her for the Bismarck* **5** to choose badly or incorrectly: *he mistook his path* ▸ **HISTORY** Old Norse *mistaka* to take erroneously

mistaken *adj* **1** wrong in opinion or judgment **2** arising from error in opinion or judgment: *a mistaken viewpoint*

mister *n* an informal form of address for a man ▸ **HISTORY** variant of *master*

Mister *n* the full form of **Mr**

mistime *vb* **-timing, -timed** to do or say at the wrong time

mistle thrush *or* **missel thrush** *n* a large European thrush with a brown back and spotted breast ▸ **HISTORY** Old English *mistel* mistletoe

mistletoe *n* a Eurasian evergreen shrub with waxy white berries, which grows as a parasite on

m

various trees ▸ HISTORY Old English *misteltān*, from *mistel* mistletoe + *tān* twig

mistral *n* a strong cold dry northerly wind of S France ▸ HISTORY Provençal, from Latin *magistralis* masterful

mistreat *vb* to treat badly > **mistreatment** *n*

mistress *n* 1 a woman who has a continuing sexual relationship with a man who is usually married to somebody else 2 a woman in a position of authority, ownership, or control 3 a woman having control over something specified: *she is a mistress of disguise* 4 *chiefly Brit* a female teacher ▸ HISTORY Old French *maistresse*

mistrial *n law* a trial which is invalid because of some error

mistrust *vb* 1 to have doubts or suspicions about ▷ *n* 2 lack of trust > **mistrustful** *adj* > **mistrustfully** *adv*

misunderstand *vb* **-standing, -stood** to fail to understand properly

misunderstanding *n* 1 a failure to understand properly 2 a disagreement

misuse *n* 1 incorrect, improper, or careless use: *misuse of drugs* 2 cruel or inhumane treatment ▷ *vb* **-using, -used** 3 to use wrongly 4 to treat badly or harshly

mite¹ *n* any of numerous very small creatures of the spider family some of which live as parasites ▸ HISTORY Old English *mīte*

mite² *n* 1 a very small creature or thing 2 a very small sum of money 3 **a mite** *informal* somewhat: *the main course was a mite bland* ▸ HISTORY Middle Dutch *mīte*

mitigate *vb* **-gating, -gated** to make less severe or harsh ▸ HISTORY Latin *mitis* mild + *agere* to make > **mitigating** *adj*

mitigation *n* 1 the act of making something less severe or harsh 2 *law* **a** (in a criminal case) a plea for sentence reduction in view of certain circumstances **b** (in a civil case) the obligation for an injured party to try to limit any losses they may suffer

mitochondrion *n, pl* **-dria** *biol* a small spherical or rodlike body found in the cytoplasm of most cells ▸ HISTORY Greek *mitos* thread + *khondrion* grain

mitosis *n* a type of cell division in which the nucleus divides into two nuclei each containing the same number of chromosomes as the parent nucleus ▸ HISTORY Greek *mitos* thread

mitre *or US* **miter** (my-ter) *n* 1 *Christianity* the headdress of a bishop or abbot, consisting of a tall pointed cleft cap 2 Also: **mitre joint** a corner joint formed by cutting bevels of equal angles at the ends of each piece of material ▷ *vb* **-tring, -tred** *or* **-tering, -tered** 3 to join with a mitre joint ▸ HISTORY Greek *mitra* turban

mitt *n* 1 a glovelike hand covering that does not cover the fingers 2 short for **mitten** 3 *slang* a hand 4 a baseball glove ▸ HISTORY from *mitten*

mitten *n* a glove with one section for the thumb and a single section for the fingers ▸ HISTORY Old French *mitaine*

mix *vb* 1 to combine or blend into one mass or substance: *mix the water, yeast, and flour into a smooth dough* 2 to be able to combine into one substance: *oil and water do not mix* 3 to form by combining different substances: *to mix cement* 4 to do at the same time: *to mix business and pleasure* 5 to be outgoing in social situations: *he mixed well* 6 *music* to balance and adjust individual performers' parts to make an overall sound by electronic means ▷ *n* 7 something produced by mixing; mixture 8 a mixture of ingredients, esp. one commercially prepared for making a cake 9 *music* the sound produced by mixing ▷ See also **mix-up** ▸ HISTORY Latin *miscere* > **mixed** *adj*

mixed blessing *n* an event or situation with both advantages and disadvantages

mixed doubles *pl n tennis, badminton* a doubles game with a man and a woman as partners on each side

mixed economy *n* an economy in which some companies are privately owned and others are owned by the government

mixed farming *n* farming involving both the growing of crops and the keeping of livestock > **mixed farm** *n*

mixed grill *n* a dish of several kinds of grilled meat, tomatoes, and mushrooms

mixed market *n econ* an economic system in which there are both privately owned and government-controlled businesses

mixed metaphor *n* a combination of incongruous metaphors, such as *when the Nazi jackboots sing their swan song*

mixed number *n maths* a figure that includes a whole number and a fraction

mixer *n* 1 a kitchen appliance, usually electrical, used for mixing foods 2 any of various other devices or machines used for mixing things: *a cement mixer* 3 a nonalcoholic drink such as tonic water or ginger ale that is mixed with an alcoholic drink 4 *informal* a person considered in relation to his or her ability to mix socially: *he's not a good mixer*

mixture *n* 1 something produced by blending or combining other things: *top with the cheese and breadcrumb mixture* 2 a combination of different things, such as feelings: *he speaks of her with a mixture of loyalty and regret* 3 *chem* a substance consisting of two or more substances mixed together without any chemical bonding between them

mix-up *n* 1 a confused condition or situation ▷ *vb* **mix up** 2 to make into a mixture 3 to confuse: *he mixes Ryan up with Lee* 4 **mixed up in** involved in (an activity or group, esp. one that is illegal): *she's mixed up in a drugs racket*

mizzenmast *n naut* (on a vessel with three or more masts) the third mast from the bow ▸ HISTORY Italian *mezzano* middle + MAST

MJ megajoule

Mk (in trade names) mark

mks units *pl n* a metric system of units based on the metre, kilogram, and second: it forms the basis of the SI units

ml 1 millilitre(s) **2** mile(s)

MLitt Master of Letters ▸ HISTORY Latin *Magister Litterarum*

Mlle *or* **Mlle.** *pl* **Mlles** *or* **Mlles.** the French equivalent of *Miss* ▸ HISTORY from *Mademoiselle*

MLR minimum lending rate

mm millimetre(s)

Mme *pl* **Mmes** the French equivalent of *Mrs*
▸ HISTORY from *Madame, Mesdames*

MMR a combined vaccine against measles, mumps, and rubella, given to very young children

Mn *chem* manganese

MN Minnesota

mnemonic (nim-**on**-ik) *n* **1** something, for instance a verse, intended to help the memory ▷ *adj* **2** aiding or meant to aid one's memory
▸ HISTORY Greek *mnēmōn* mindful
> **mnemonically** *adv*

mo *n* informal, spoken, chiefly Brit short for **moment** (sense 1)

Mo *chem* molybdenum

MO 1 Medical Officer **2** Missouri

m.o. *or* **MO 1** mail order **2** money order

moa *n* a recently extinct large flightless bird of New Zealand that resembled the ostrich ▸ HISTORY Māori

moan *n* **1** a low prolonged cry of pain or suffering **2** any similar sound, esp. that made by the wind **3** *informal* a grumble or complaint ▷ *vb* **4** to make a low cry of, or talk in a way suggesting, pain or suffering: *he moaned in pain* **5** to make a sound like a moan: *the wind moaned through the trees* **6** *informal* to grumble or complain ▸ HISTORY Old English *mǣnan* to grieve over > **moaner** *n*

moat *n* a wide ditch, originally filled with water, surrounding a fortified place such as a castle
▸ HISTORY Old French *motte* mound

mob *n* **1** a riotous or disorderly crowd of people **2** *informal* any group of people **3** the masses **4** *slang* a gang of criminals ▷ *vb* **mobbing, mobbed 5** to attack in a group resembling a mob **6** to surround in a crowd to acclaim or attack: *she was mobbed by her fans when she left the theatre* ▸ HISTORY shortened from Latin *mobile vulgus* the fickle populace

mobile *adj* **1** able to move or be moved: *mobile toilets* **2** changing quickly in expression: *a mobile face* **3** *sociol* (of individuals or social groups) moving within and between classes, occupations, and localities ▷ *n* **4** a light structure suspended in midair with delicately balanced parts that are set in motion by air currents **5** short for **mobile phone**
▸ HISTORY Latin *mobilis* > **mobility** *n*

mobile home *n* a large caravan, usually staying in one place, which people live in permanently

mobile phone *n* a portable telephone powered by batteries

mobilize *or* **-lise** *vb* **-lizing, -lized** *or* **-lising, -lised 1** to prepare for war or another emergency by organizing resources and the armed services **2** to organize for a purpose: *we must mobilize local residents behind our campaign* > **mobilization** *or* **-lisation** *n*

moccasin *n* **1** a type of soft leather shoe traditionally worn by some Native American peoples **2** a soft leather shoe with a raised seam at the front above the toe ▸ HISTORY American Indian

mocha (**mock**-a) *n* **1** a dark brown coffee originally imported from the port of Mocha in Arabia **2** a flavouring made from coffee and chocolate

mock *vb* **1** to behave with scorn or contempt towards a person or thing: *her husband mocked her attempts to educate herself* **2** to imitate or mimic, esp. in fun **3** to defy or frustrate: *the team mocked the visitors' attempts to score* ▷ *n* **4 mocks** informal (in England and Wales) school examinations taken as practice before public exams ▷ *adj* **5** sham or imitation: *mock Georgian windows* **6** serving as an imitation or substitute, esp. for practice purposes: *a mock battle* ▷ See also **mock-up** ▸ HISTORY Old French *mocquer* > **mocking** *n, adj*

mockers *pl n* **put the mockers on** Brit, Austral & NZ, *informal* to ruin the chances of success of
▸ HISTORY perhaps from *mock*

mockery *n, pl* **-eries 1** ridicule, contempt, or derision **2** a person, thing, or action that is so worthless that it seems like a parody: *the interview was a mockery from start to finish* **3 make a mockery of something** to make something appear worthless or foolish: *the judge's decision makes a mockery of the law*

mock-heroic *adj* literature, prosody (of a literary work, esp. a poem) imitating the style of heroic poetry in order to satirize an unheroic subject

mockingbird *n* an American songbird which can mimic the song of other birds

mock orange *n* a shrub with white fragrant flowers like those of the orange

mock-up *n* a working full-scale model of a machine or apparatus for test or research purposes

mod[1] *n* Brit a member of a group of teenagers, originally in the mid-1960s, who were very clothes-conscious and rode motor scooters
▸ HISTORY from *modernist*

mod[2] *n* an annual Highland Gaelic meeting with musical and literary competitions ▸ HISTORY Gaelic *mòd* assembly

MOD (in Britain) Ministry of Defence

mod. 1 moderate **2** modern

modal (**mode**-al) *adj* **1** of or relating to mode or manner **2** *grammar* (of a verb form or auxiliary verb) expressing possibility, intention, or necessity rather than actuality: 'can', 'might', and 'will' are examples of modal verbs in English **3** *music* of or relating to a mode

modal class *n* statistics the class with the highest frequency

modality *n, pl* **-ties 1** the condition of being modal **2** a quality, attribute, or circumstance that denotes mode, mood, or manner

mod cons *pl n* informal modern conveniences, such as hot water and heating

mode *n* **1** a manner or way of doing, acting, or existing **2** a particular fashion or style **3** *music* any of the various scales of notes within one octave

4 *maths* the most frequently occurring of a range of values ▶ HISTORY Latin *modus* manner

model *n* **1** a three-dimensional representation, usually on a smaller scale, of a device or structure: *an architect's model of the proposed new housing estate* **2** an example or pattern that people might want to follow: *her success makes her an excellent role model for other young Black women* **3** an outstanding example of its kind: *the report is a model of clarity* **4** a person who poses for a sculptor, painter, or photographer **5** a person who wears clothes to display them to prospective buyers; mannequin **6** a design or style of a particular product: *the cheapest model of this car has a 1300cc engine* **7** a theoretical description of the way a system or process works: *a working model of the human immune system* **8** *maths* a simplified description of a system, used to make predictions ▷ *adj* **9** excellent or perfect: *a model husband* **10** being a small-scale representation of: *a model aeroplane* ▷ *vb* **-elling, -elled** *or US* **-eling, -eled** **11** to make a model of: *he modelled a plane out of balsa wood* **12** to plan or create according to a model or models: *it had a constitution modelled on that of the United States* **13** to display (clothing and accessories) as a mannequin **14** to pose for a sculptor, painter, or photographer **15** *maths* to devise a model of a system ▶ HISTORY Latin *modulus*, diminutive of *modus* mode

modem (**mode**-em) *n computers* a device for transmitting information between two computers by a telephone line, consisting of a modulator that converts computer signals into audio signals and a corresponding demodulator ▶ HISTORY from *mo(dulator) dem(odulator)*

moderate *adj* **1** not extreme or excessive: *a man of moderate views; moderate consumption of alcohol* **2** (of a size, rate, intensity, etc.) towards the middle of the range of possible values: *a moderate-sized garden; a moderate breeze* **3** of average quality or extent: *moderate success* ▷ *n* **4** a person who holds moderate views, esp. in politics ▷ *vb* **-ating, -ated** **5** to make or become less extreme or violent: *he has moderated his opinions since then* **6** to preside over a meeting, discussion, etc. ▶ HISTORY Latin *moderari* to restrain > **moderately** *adv*

moderation *n* **1** the quality of being moderate **2** the act of moderating **3 in moderation** within moderate or reasonable limits

moderato (mod-er-**ah**-toe) *adv music* **1** at a moderate speed **2** with restraint: *allegro moderato* ▶ HISTORY Italian

moderator *n* **1** *Presbyterian Church* a minister appointed to preside over a Church court, synod, or general assembly **2** a person who presides over a public or legislative assembly **3** a material, such as heavy water, used for slowing down neutrons in nuclear reactors

modern *adj* **1** of the present or a recent time; contemporary: *there have been very few outbreaks of the disease in modern times* **2** using the latest techniques, equipment, etc.; up-to-date: *modern and efficient railways* **3** of contemporary styles or schools of art, literature, and music, esp. those of an experimental kind* ▷ *n* **4** a contemporary person ▶ HISTORY Late Latin *modernus*, from *modus* mode > **modernity** *n*

Modern English *n* the English language since about 1450

modernism *n* a early- and mid-20th-century movement in art, literature, and music that rejected traditional styles and techniques > **modernist** *n, adj*

modernize *or-***ise** *vb* **-izing, -ized** *or-***ising, -ised** **1** to make modern in style, methods, or equipment: *a commitment to modernizing industry* **2** to adopt modern ways or ideas > **modernization** *or* **-isation** *n*

modern languages *pl n* the languages spoken in present-day Europe, with the exception of English

modern pentathlon *n* an athletic contest consisting of five different events: horse riding with jumps, fencing with electric épée, freestyle swimming, pistol shooting, and cross-country running

modest *adj* **1** having a humble opinion of oneself or one's accomplishments **2** not extreme or excessive: *a modest increase in inflation* **3** not ostentatious or pretentious: *a modest flat in the suburbs* **4** shy or easily embarrassed **5** old-fashioned (esp. of clothes) not revealing much of the body: *a modest dress* ▶ HISTORY Latin *modestus* moderate > **modestly** *adv* > **modesty** *n*

modicum *n* a small amount ▶ HISTORY Latin: a little way

modifier *n grammar* a word or phrase that makes the sense of another word more specific: for example, the noun *garage* is a modifier of *door* in *garage door*

modify *vb* **-fies, -fying, -fied** **1** to change or alter slightly **2** to make less extreme or uncompromising **3** *grammar* (of a word or phrase) to act as a modifier to another word or phrase ▶ HISTORY Latin *modus* measure + *facere* to make > **modification** *n*

modish (**mode**-ish) *adj* in the current fashion or style > **modishly** *adv*

modulate *vb* **-lating, -lated** **1** *written* to change the tone, pitch, or volume of (one's voice) **2** *formal* to adjust or regulate the degree of the hormone which modulates the development of the sexual organs **3** *music* to change from one key to another **4** *physics, electronics* to superimpose the amplitude, frequency, or phase of a wave or signal onto another wave or signal ▶ HISTORY Latin *modulari* to modulate > **modulation** *n* > **modulator** *n*

module *n* **1** a standard self-contained unit, such as an assembly of electronic components or a standardized piece of furniture, that can be used in combination with other units **2** *astronautics* a self-contained separable unit making up a spacecraft **3** *education* a short course of study that together with other such courses counts towards

539

a qualification ▶ HISTORY Latin *modulus*, diminutive of *modus* mode > **modular** *adj*

modulus *n*, *pl* -**li** *physics* a coefficient expressing a specified property, for instance elasticity, of a specified substance ▶ HISTORY Latin

modus operandi (mode-uss op-er-**an**-die) *n*, *pl* **modi operandi** (mode-eye) method of operating ▶ HISTORY Latin

modus vivendi (mode-uss viv-**venn**-die) *n*, *pl* **modi vivendi** (mode-eye) a working arrangement between conflicting interests ▶ HISTORY Latin: way of living

moggy *or* **mog** *n*, *pl* **moggies** *or* **mogs** *Brit, Austral & NZ, slang* a cat ▶ HISTORY dialect *mog*, originally a pet name for a cow

mogul (moh-gl) *n* an important or powerful person

Mogul *adj* of or relating to a Muslim dynasty of Indian emperors established in 1526 ▶ HISTORY Persian *mughul* Mongolian

MOH (in Britain) Medical Officer of Health

mohair *n* 1 the long soft silky hair of the Angora goat 2 a fabric made from yarn of this hair and cotton or wool ▶ HISTORY Arabic *mukhayyar*, literally: choice

Mohammed *or* **Muhammad** *n* the prophet who founded Islam

Mohawk *n* 1 a member of a N American Indian people formerly living along the Mohawk river 2 the language of this people

mohican *n* a punk hairstyle in which the head is shaved at the sides and the remaining strip of hair is worn stiffly erect and often brightly coloured ▶ HISTORY after the *Mohicans*, a Native American people

Mohican *n* 1 (*pl* -**cans** *or* -**can**) a member of a N American Indian people formerly living along the Hudson river 2 the language of this people

Mohorovičić discontinuity *n geol* the boundary between the earth's crust and mantle, across which there is a sudden change in the velocity of seismic waves ▶ HISTORY named after Andrija *Mohorovičić* (1857–1936), Croatian geologist

moiety (**moy**-it-ee) *n*, *pl* -**ties** *archaic* 1 a half 2 one of two parts or divisions of something ▶ HISTORY Old French *moitié*

moiré (**mwahr**-ray) *adj* 1 having a watered or wavelike pattern ▷ *n* 2 such a pattern, impressed on fabrics 3 a fabric, usually silk, with such a pattern 4 Also: **moiré pattern** a pattern seen when two geometrical patterns, such as grids, are visually superimposed ▶ HISTORY French

moist *adj* slightly damp or wet ▶ HISTORY Old French

moisten *vb* to make or become moist

moisture *n* water diffused as vapour or condensed on or in objects

moisturize *or* -**ise** *vb* -**izing**, -**ized** *or* -**ising**, -**ised** to add moisture to the air or the skin > **moisturizer** *or* -**iser** *n*

mojo *n*, *pl* -**jos** *or* -**joes** *slang* 1 an amulet, charm, or magic spell 2 uncanny personal power or influence ▶ HISTORY from West African

moke *n* 1 *Brit, slang* a donkey 2 *Austral & NZ* a horse of inferior quality ▶ HISTORY origin unknown

moksha *n Hinduism* freedom from the cycle of reincarnation into a state of bliss ▶ HISTORY Sanskrit

mol *chem* mole

mol. 1 molecular 2 molecule

molar *n* 1 a large back tooth specialized for crushing and chewing food ▷ *adj* 2 of any of these teeth ▶ HISTORY Latin *mola* millstone

molasses *n* 1 the thick brown bitter syrup obtained from sugar during refining 2 *US & Canad* same as **treacle** ▶ HISTORY Portuguese *melaço*

mole[1] *n* a small dark raised spot on the skin

mole[2] *n* 1 a small burrowing mammal with velvety dark fur and forelimbs specialized for digging 2 *informal* a spy who has infiltrated an organization and become a trusted member of it ▶ HISTORY Middle Dutch *mol*

mole[3] *n chem* the basic SI unit of amount of substance: the amount that contains as many elementary entities as there are atoms in 0.012 kilogram of carbon-12 ▶ HISTORY German *Mol*, short for *Molekül* molecule

mole[4] *n* 1 a breakwater 2 a harbour protected by a breakwater ▶ HISTORY Latin *moles* mass

molecular (mol-**lek**-yew-lar) *adj* of or relating to molecules

molecular compound *n chem* a compound in which the atoms are linked by covalent bonds to form molecules

molecular formula *n chem* a chemical formula indicating the number and type of atoms in a molecule, but not its structure: NH_3 *is the molecular formula of ammonia*

molecular weight *n chem* the sum of all the atomic weights of the atoms in a molecule

molecule (**mol**-lik-kyool) *n* 1 the simplest unit of a chemical compound that can exist, consisting of two or more atoms held together by chemical bonds 2 a very small particle ▶ HISTORY New Latin *molecula*, diminutive of Latin *moles* mass

molehill *n* 1 the small mound of earth thrown up by a burrowing mole 2 **make a mountain out of a molehill** to exaggerate an unimportant matter out of all proportion

molest *vb* 1 to accost or attack someone 2 to disturb or injure, esp. by using or threatening violence: *killing, capturing, or molesting the local wildlife was strictly forbidden* ▶ HISTORY Latin *molestare* to annoy > **molestation** *n* > **molester** *n*

moll *n slang* a gangster's female accomplice or girlfriend ▶ HISTORY from *Moll*, familiar form of *Mary*

mollify *vb* -**fies**, -**fying**, -**fied** to make someone less angry or upset; soothe: *he sought to mollify his critics* ▶ HISTORY Latin *mollis* soft + *facere* to make > **mollification** *n*

mollusc *or US* **mollusk** *n* an invertebrate with a soft unsegmented body and often a shell, such as a snail, mussel, or octopus ▶ HISTORY Latin *molluscus*

m

mollycoddle vb **-coddling, -coddled** to give an excessive amount of care and protection to ▶ HISTORY from *Molly*, girl's name + *coddle*

Molotov cocktail n a simple bomb made from a bottle filled with petrol and a cloth wick; petrol bomb ▶ HISTORY after V. M. *Molotov*, Soviet statesman

molt vb, n US same as **moult**

molten adj so hot that it has melted and formed a liquid: *molten metal*

molto adv music very: *allegro molto; molto adagio* ▶ HISTORY Italian

molybdenum (mol-**lib**-din-um) n chem a very hard silvery-white metallic element used in alloys, esp. to harden and strengthen steels. Symbol: Mo ▶ HISTORY Greek *molubdos* lead

mom n informal, chiefly US, Canad & S African same as **mother**

moment n **1** a short period of time **2** a specific instant or point in time: *at that moment the phone rang* **3 the moment** the present point of time: *for the moment he is out of prison* **4** importance, significance, or value: *a matter of greatest moment* **5** physics **a** a tendency to produce motion, esp. rotation about a point or axis **b** the product of a physical quantity, such as force or mass, and its distance from a fixed reference point ▶ HISTORY Latin *momentum* movement

momentary adj lasting for only a moment; temporary > **momentarily** adv

momentous (moh-**men**-tuss) adj of great significance > **momentousness** n

momentum (moh-**men**-tum) n **1** the impetus to go forward, develop, or get stronger: *the campaign steadily gathered support and momentum* **2** the impetus of a moving body: *the sledge gathered momentum as it slid ever faster down the slope* **3** physics the product of a body's mass and its velocity ▶ HISTORY Latin: movement

Mon. Monday

mon- combining form See **mono-**

monad n **1** philosophy any fundamental singular metaphysical entity **2** a single-celled organism **3** an atom, ion, or radical with a valency of one ▶ HISTORY Greek *monas* unit

monandrous adj **1** biol having only one stamen in each flower **2** having only one male sexual partner over a period of time ▶ HISTORY Greek *monos* sole + *anēr* man

monarch n a sovereign head of state, esp. a king, queen, or emperor, who rules by hereditary right ▶ HISTORY Greek *monos* sole + *arkhos* ruler > **monarchical** or **monarchic** adj

monarchy n, pl **-chies 1** a form of government in which supreme authority is held by a single hereditary ruler, such as a king **2** a country reigned over by a monarch

monastery n, pl **-teries** the building or group of buildings where a community of monks lives ▶ HISTORY Greek *monazein* to live alone

monastic adj **1** of or relating to monasteries, monks, or nuns **2** (of a way of life) simple and austere; ascetic > **monasticism** n

monatomic adj chem **1** (of an element) consisting of single atoms **2** (of a compound or molecule) having only one atom or group that can be replaced in a reaction

Monday n the second day of the week, and the first day of the working week ▶ HISTORY Old English *mōnandæg* moon's day

monetarism n **1** the theory that inflation is caused by an excess quantity of money in an economy **2** an economic policy based on this theory and a belief in the efficiency of free market forces > **monetarist** n, adj

monetary adj of money or currency ▶ HISTORY Latin *moneta* money

money n **1** a means of payment and measure of value: *some cultures used to use shells as money* **2** the official currency, in the form of banknotes or coins, issued by a government **3 moneys** or **monies** law, old-fashioned a financial sum or income **4** an unspecified amount of wealth: *money to lend* **5** informal a rich person or rich people: *he married money* **6 for one's money** in one's opinion **7 one's money's worth** full value for the money one has paid for something **8 put money on** to place a bet on. Related adjective: **pecuniary** ▶ HISTORY Latin *moneta*

moneybags n informal a very rich person

moneychanger n a person engaged in the business of exchanging currencies or money

moneyed or **monied** adj having a great deal of money; rich

moneylender n a person who lends money at interest as a living

moneymaker n **1** a person whose chief concern is to make money **2** a person or thing that is or might be profitable > **moneymaking** adj, n

-monger n combining form **1** indicating a trader or dealer: *an ironmonger* **2** indicating a promoter of something: *a warmonger* ▶ HISTORY Old English *mangere*

mongol n offensive (not in technical use) a person affected by Down's syndrome > **mongoloid** n, adj

Mongolian adj **1** of Mongolia ▷ n **2** a person from Mongolia **3** the language of Mongolia

mongolism n offensive a former name (not in technical use) for **Down's syndrome** ▶ HISTORY the condition produces facial features similar to those of the Mongoloid peoples

Mongoloid adj of a major racial group of mankind, characterized by yellowish skin, straight black hair, and slanting eyes: includes most of the people of SE Asia, E Asia, and the Arctic area of N America

mongoose n, pl **-gooses** a small long-tailed predatory mammal of Asia and Africa that kills snakes ▶ HISTORY from Marathi (a language of India) *mangūs*

mongrel n **1** a dog of mixed breeding **2** something made up of things from a variety of sources: *despite using components from three other cars, this new model is no mongrel* ▷ adj **3** of mixed breeding or

m

origin: *a mongrel race* ▶ HISTORY from obsolete *mong* mixture

monied *adj* same as **moneyed**

monies *n law, old-fashioned* a plural of **money**

moniker *n slang* a person's name or nickname ▶ HISTORY from Shelta *munnik*, altered from Irish Gaelic *ainm* name

monism *n philosophy* the doctrine that reality consists of only one basic substance or element, such as mind or matter ▶ HISTORY Greek *monos* sole > **monist** *n, adj*

monition *n* a warning or caution ▶ HISTORY Latin *monere* to warn

monitor *n* **1** a person or device that warns, checks, controls, or keeps a continuous record of something **2** *Brit, Austral & NZ* a pupil assisting a teacher with various duties **3** a screen used to display certain kinds of information, for example in airports or television studios **4** a large predatory lizard inhabiting warm regions of Africa, Asia, and Australia ▷ *vb* **5** to act as a monitor of **6** to observe or record the condition or performance of a person or thing **7** to check (a broadcast) for acceptable quality or content ▶ HISTORY Latin *monere* to advise > **monitorial** *adj*

monk *n* a male member of a religious community bound by vows of poverty, chastity, and obedience. *Related adjective:* **monastic** ▶ HISTORY Greek *monos* alone > **monkish** *adj*

monkey *n* **1** any long-tailed primate that is not a lemur or tarsier **2** (loosely) any primate that is not a human **3** a naughty or mischievous child **4** *slang* £500 or $500 **5 give a monkey's** *Brit, slang* to care about or regard as important: *who gives a monkey's what he thinks?* ▷ *vb* **6 monkey around** or **about with** to meddle or tinker with ▶ HISTORY origin unknown

monkey nut *n Brit* a peanut

monkey puzzle *n* a South American coniferous tree with branches shaped like a candelabrum and stiff sharp leaves

monkey wrench *n chiefly Brit* a wrench with adjustable jaws

monkshood *n* a poisonous plant with hooded blue-purple flowers

mono *adj* **1** short for **monophonic** ▷ *n* **2** monophonic sound

mono- or before a vowel **mon-** *combining form* **1** one; single: *monorail; monolingual* **2** *chem* indicating that a chemical compound contains a single specified atom or group: *monoxide* ▶ HISTORY Greek *monos* alone

monobasic *adj chem* (of an acid, such as hydrogen chloride) having only one replaceable hydrogen atom per molecule

monochromatic *adj* (of light or other electromagnetic radiation) having only one wavelength

monochrome *adj* **1** *photog, television* black-and-white ▷ *n* **2** a painting or drawing done in a range of tones of a single colour ▶ HISTORY Greek *monokhrōmos* of one colour

monocle (mon-a-kl) *n* (formerly) a lens worn for correcting defective sight in one eye only, held in position by the facial muscles ▶ HISTORY MONO- + Latin *oculus* eye > **monocled** *adj*

monoclinal *adj geol* (of folds) inclining in one direction

monocline *n geol* a fold in stratified rocks in which the strata are inclined in one direction from the horizontal ▶ HISTORY MONO- + Greek *klinein* to lean

monoclinic *adj crystallog* of the crystal system characterized by three unequal axes, one pair of which are not at right angles to each other

monoclonal antibody *n* an antibody produced from a single clone of cells grown in a culture

monocoque (mon-a-cock) *n* a vehicle body moulded from a single piece of material with no separate load-bearing parts ▶ HISTORY French

monocotyledon (mon-no-kot-ill-**leed**-on) *n* any flowering plant with a single embryonic seed leaf, such as the grasses, lilies, palms, and orchids

monocropping *n* the practice of growing the same crop on the same land year after year

monocular *adj* having or intended for the use of only one eye ▶ HISTORY Late Latin *monoculus* one-eyed

monoculture *n* the continuous growing of one type of crop

monody *n, pl* **-dies 1** (in Greek tragedy) an ode sung by a single actor **2** *music* a style of composition consisting of a single vocal part, usually with accompaniment ▶ HISTORY MONO- + Greek *aeidein* to sing > **monodist** *n*

monoecious (mon-ee-shuss) *adj* **1** (of some flowering plants) having the male and female reproductive organs in separate flowers on the same plant **2** (of some animals and lower plants) hermaphrodite ▶ HISTORY MONO- + Greek *oikos* house

monogamy *n* the state or practice of having only one husband or wife at a time ▶ HISTORY MONO- + Greek *gamos* marriage > **monogamous** *adj*

monogram *n* a design of one or more letters, esp. initials, on clothing, stationery, etc. ▶ HISTORY Greek *monogrammatos* consisting of one letter

monograph *n* a paper, book, or other work concerned with a single subject or aspect of a subject

monolingual *adj* knowing or expressed in only one language

monolith *n* **1** a large block of stone **2** a statue, obelisk, or column cut from one block of stone **3** something which can be regarded as forming one large, single whole: *the Christian religion should not be thought of as a monolith* ▶ HISTORY Greek *monolithos* made from a single stone > **monolithic** *adj*

monologue *n* **1** a long speech made by one actor in a play or film; soliloquy **2** a dramatic piece for a single performer **3** any long speech by one person, esp. one which prevents other people talking or expressing their views ▶ HISTORY Greek *monologos* speaking alone

monomania n an obsession with one thing or idea > **monomaniac** n, adj

monomer n chem a compound whose molecules can join together to form a polymer

monometer n poetry a line of poetry consisting of one metrical foot > **monometrical** adj

monomial n maths an expression consisting of a single term, such as 5ax ▶ HISTORY MONO- + (BIN)OMIAL

mononucleosis (mon-oh-new-klee-**oh**-siss) n **infectious mononucleosis** same as **glandular fever**

monophonic adj (of a system of broadcasting, recording, or reproducing sound) using only one channel between source and loudspeaker. Short form: **mono**

monoplane n an aeroplane with only one pair of wings

monopolize or **-lise** vb **-lizing, -lized** or **-lising, -lised** 1 to have full control or use of, to the exclusion of others 2 to hold exclusive control of a market or supply

monopoly n, pl **-lies** 1 exclusive control of the market supply of a product or service 2 **a** an enterprise exercising this control **b** the product or service so controlled 3 law the exclusive right granted to a person or company by the state to trade in a specified commodity or area 4 exclusive control, possession, or use of something ▶ HISTORY MONO- + Greek pōlein to sell > **monopolist** n > **monopolistic** adj

monorail n a single-rail railway

monosaccharide n a simple sugar, such as glucose, that cannot be broken down into other sugars

monosodium glutamate n a substance which enhances protein flavours: used as a food additive

monosyllable n a word of one syllable > **monosyllabic** adj

monotheism n the belief or doctrine that there is only one God > **monotheist** n, adj > **monotheistic** adj

monotone n 1 a single unvaried pitch level in speech or sound 2 a way of speaking which lacks variety of pitch or expression: he rambled on in a dull monotone 3 lack of variety in style or expression ▷ adj 4 unvarying

monotonous adj tedious because of lack of variety > **monotonously** adv

monotony n, pl **-nies** 1 wearisome routine; dullness 2 lack of variety in pitch or tone

monounsaturated adj of a group of vegetable oils, such as olive oil, that have a neutral effect on cholesterol in the body

monovalent adj chem 1 having a valency of one 2 having only one valency > **monovalence** or **monovalency** n

monoxide n an oxide that contains one oxygen atom per molecule

Monseigneur (mon-sen-**nyur**) n, pl **Messeigneurs** (may-sen-**nyur**) a title given to

French prelates and princes ▶ HISTORY French, literally: my lord

monsieur (muss-**syuh**) n, pl **messieurs** (may-**syuh**) a French form of address equivalent to sir or Mr ▶ HISTORY French, literally: my lord

Monsignor n, pl **Monsignors** or **Monsignori** RC Church a title given to certain senior clergymen ▶ HISTORY Italian

monsoon n 1 a seasonal wind of S Asia which blows from the southwest in summer and from the northeast in winter 2 the rainy season when the SW monsoon blows, from about April to October ▶ HISTORY Arabic mawsim season

monsoon bucket n NZ a large container for water carried by helicopter and used to extinguish bush and scrub fires

mons pubis (monz **pew**-biss) n, pl **montes pubis** (**mon**-teez) the fatty flesh in human males over the junction of the pubic bones ▶ HISTORY New Latin: hill of the pubes

monster n 1 an imaginary beast, usually frightening in appearance 2 a very large person, animal, or thing 3 an exceptionally cruel or wicked person 4 a person, animal, or plant with a marked deformity ▶ HISTORY Latin monstrum portent

monstrance n RC Church a vessel in which the consecrated Host is exposed for adoration ▶ HISTORY Latin monstrare to show

monstrosity n, pl **-ties** 1 an outrageous or ugly person or thing 2 the state or quality of being monstrous

monstrous adj 1 hideous or unnatural in size or character 2 atrocious, unjust, or shocking: the President described the invasion as monstrous 3 huge 4 of or like a monster 5 (of plants and animals) abnormal in structure > **monstrously** adv

mons veneris (monz **ven**-er-iss) n, pl **montes veneris** (**mon**-teez) the fatty flesh in human females over the junction of the pubic bones ▶ HISTORY New Latin: hill of Venus

montage (**mon**-tahzh) n 1 a picture made by combining material from various sources, such as other pictures or photographs 2 the technique of producing pictures in this way 3 a method of film editing by juxtaposition or partial superimposition of several shots to form a single image 4 a film sequence of this kind ▶ HISTORY French

month n 1 one of the twelve divisions (**calendar months**) of the calendar year 2 a period of time extending from one date to a corresponding date in the next calendar month 3 a period of four weeks or of 30 days ▶ HISTORY Old English mōnath

monthly adj 1 happening or payable once every month: a monthly magazine 2 lasting or valid for a month: a monthly travel pass ▷ adv 3 once a month ▷ n, pl **-lies** 4 a magazine published once a month

monument n 1 something, such as a statue or building, erected in commemoration of a person or event 2 an ancient building which is regarded as an important part of a country's history 3 an exceptional 543 example of the results of something: *the whole town is a monument to bad 60s architecture* ▶ HISTORY Latin *monumentum*

monumental *adj* **1** large, impressive, or likely to last or be remembered for a long time: *a monumental three-volume biography* **2** of or being a monument **3** *informal* extreme: *a monumental gamble*

moo *n* **1** the characteristic deep long sound made by a cow ▷ *vb* **2** to make this sound; low

mooch *vb slang* **1** to loiter or walk aimlessly **2** to cadge or scrounge ▶ HISTORY perhaps Old French *muchier* to skulk

mood¹ *n* **1** a temporary state of mind or temper: *a happy mood* **2** a sullen or gloomy state of mind, esp. when temporary: *she's in a mood* **3** a prevailing atmosphere or feeling: *the current mood of disenchantment with politics* **4 in the mood** inclined to do or have (something) ▶ HISTORY Old English *mōd* mind, feeling

mood² *n grammar* a form of a verb indicating whether the verb expresses a fact (indicative mood), a wish or supposition (subjunctive mood), or a command (imperative mood) ▶ HISTORY same as MOOD¹

mood board *n* a board used (esp. by designers) on which samples of various colours and textures, images, etc. are mounted to inspire creations

moody *adj* **moodier, moodiest** **1** sullen, sulky, or gloomy **2** temperamental or changeable > **moodily** *adv* > **moodiness** *n*

Moog *n music trademark* a type of synthesizer ▶ HISTORY after Robert *Moog*, engineer

mooi *adj* S.*African, slang* pleasing or nice ▶ HISTORY Afrikaans

moon *n* **1** the natural satellite of the earth. *Related adjective:* **lunar 2** this satellite as it is seen during its revolution around the earth, esp. at one of its phases: *new moon; full moon* **3** any natural satellite of a planet **4** a month **5 over the moon** *informal* extremely happy; ecstatic ▷ *vb* **6 moon about** or **around** to be idle in a listless or dreamy way ▶ HISTORY Old English *mōna* > **moonless** *adj*

moonbeam *n* a ray of moonlight

moonlight *n* **1** light from the sun received on earth after reflection by the moon ▷ *adj* **2** illuminated by the moon: *a moonlight walk* ▷ *vb* **-lighting, -lighted 3** *informal* to work at a secondary job, esp. illegally > **moonlighter** *n*

moonlight flit *n Brit & Austral, informal* a hurried departure at night to avoid paying rent

moonlit *adj* illuminated by the moon

moonscape *n* the surface of the moon or a picture or model of it

moonshine *n* **1** *US & Canad* illegally distilled or smuggled whisky **2** foolish or nonsensical talk or thought

moonshot *n* the launching of a spacecraft to the moon

moonstone *n* a white translucent form of feldspar, used as a gem

moonstruck *adj* slightly mad or odd, as if affected by the moon

moony *adj* **moonier, mooniest** *Brit, Austral & NZ, informal* dreamy or listless

moor¹ *n Brit* an expanse of open uncultivated ground covered with heather, coarse grass, and bracken ▶ HISTORY Old English *mōr*

moor² *vb* to secure (a ship or boat) with cables, ropes, or anchors so that it remains in one place ▶ HISTORY Germanic > **moorage** *n*

Moor *n* a member of a Muslim people of North Africa who ruled Spain between the 8th and 15th centuries ▶ HISTORY Greek *Mauros*

moorhen *n* a waterfowl with black plumage and a red bill

mooring *n* a place where a ship or boat can be tied up or anchored

moorings *pl n naut* the ropes and anchors used in mooring a vessel

Moorish *adj* **1** of or relating to the Moors **2** of a style of architecture used in Spain from the 13th to the 16th century, characterized by the horseshoe arch

moorland *n Brit* an area of moor

moose *n, pl* **moose** a large North American deer with large flattened antlers; the American elk ▶ HISTORY from a Native American language

moot *adj* **1** subject or open to debate: *a moot point* ▷ *vb* **2** to suggest or bring up for debate: *a compromise proposal, involving building fewer flats, was mooted* ▷ *n* **3** (in Anglo-Saxon England) a local administrative assembly ▶ HISTORY Old English *gemōt*

mop *n* **1** a tool with a head made of twists of cotton or sponge and a long handle used for washing or polishing floors **2** a similar tool, except smaller and without a long handle, used to wash dishes **3** a thick untidy mass of hair ▷ *vb* **mopping, mopped 4** to clean or soak up with or as if with a mop: *she mopped her brow with a handkerchief* ▷ See also **mop up** ▶ HISTORY Latin *mappa* napkin

mope *vb* **moping, moped 1** to be gloomy or apathetic **2** to walk around in a gloomy and aimless manner ▶ HISTORY perhaps from obsolete *mope* fool

moped *n* a light motorcycle not over 50cc ▶ HISTORY *motor* + *pedal*

mopoke *n* **1** a small spotted owl of Australia and New Zealand **2** *Austral, slang* a slow or lugubrious person ▶ HISTORY imitative of the bird's cry

mop up *vb* **1** to clean with a mop **2** *informal* to complete the last remaining stages of a job **3** *mil* to clear remaining enemy forces after a battle, by killing them or taking them prisoner

moraine *n* a ridge or mound formed from debris deposited by a glacier ▶ HISTORY French

moral *adj* **1** concerned with or relating to the distinction between good and bad or right and wrong behaviour: *moral sense* **2** based on a sense of right and wrong: *moral duty* **3** (of support or a victory) psychological rather than practical ▷ *n* **4** a lesson about right or wrong behaviour

m

that is shown in a fable or event **5 morals** principles of behaviour in accordance with standards of right and wrong ▶ HISTORY Latin *moralis* relating to morals or customs > **morally** *adv*

morale (mor-**rahl**) *n* the degree of confidence or optimism of a person or group ▶ HISTORY French

moralist *n* **1** a person who has a strong sense of right and wrong **2** someone who criticizes other people for not doing what he or she thinks is morally correct > **moralistic** *adj*

morality *n, pl* -**ties** **1** good moral conduct **2** the degree to which something is morally acceptable: *we discussed the morality of fox-hunting* **3** a system of moral principles

morality play *n* a medieval type of drama concerned with the conflict between personified virtues and vices

moralize *or* -**ise** *vb* -**izing**, -**ized** *or* -**ising**, -**ised** **1** to discuss or consider something in the light of one's own moral beliefs, esp. with disapproval **2** to interpret or explain in a moral sense **3** to improve the morals of

moral philosophy *n* the branch of philosophy dealing with ethics

morass *n* **1** a tract of swampy low-lying land **2** a disordered, confusing, or muddled state of affairs ▶ HISTORY Old French *marais* marsh

moratorium *n, pl* -**ria** *or* -**riums** **1** a legally authorized postponement of the payment of a debt **2** an agreed suspension of activity ▶ HISTORY Latin *mora* delay

moray *n* a large marine eel marked with brilliant colours ▶ HISTORY Greek *muraina*

morbid *adj* **1** having an unusual interest in death or unpleasant events **2** *med* relating to or characterized by disease ▶ HISTORY Latin *morbus* illness > **morbidity** *n* > **morbidly** *adv*

mordant *adj* **1** sarcastic or caustic: *mordant wit* ▷ *n* **2** a substance used in dyeing to fix colours **3** an acid or other corrosive fluid used to etch lines on a printing plate ▶ HISTORY Latin *mordere* to bite

more *adj* **1** the comparative of **much, many**: *more joy than you know; even more are leaving the country* **2** additional or further: *no more apples* **3 more of** to a greater extent or degree: *more of a nuisance* ▷ *adv* **4** used to form the comparative of some adjectives and adverbs: *more quickly* **5** the comparative of **much**: *people listen to the radio more now* **6 more or less a** as an estimate; approximately **b** to an unspecified extent or degree: *the film was a disaster, more or less* ▶ HISTORY Old English *māra*

morel *n* an edible mushroom with a pitted cap ▶ HISTORY French *morille*

morello *n, pl* -**los** a variety of small very dark sour cherry ▶ HISTORY Italian: blackish

moreover *adv* in addition to what has already been said

morepork *n chiefly NZ* same as **mopoke**

mores (**more**-rayz) *pl n* the customs and conventions embodying the fundamental values of a community ▶ HISTORY Latin: customs

Moreton Bay bug *n* an Australian flattish edible shellfish

morganatic *adj* of or designating a marriage between a person of high rank and a person of low rank, by which the latter is not elevated to the higher rank and any children have no rights to inherit the higher party's titles or property ▶ HISTORY Medieval Latin *morganaticum* morning-gift after consummation representing the husband's only liability

morgue *n* **1** a mortuary **2** *informal* a store of clippings and back numbers used for reference in a newspaper ▶ HISTORY French

moribund *adj* **1** near death **2** no longer performing effectively or usefully: *Romania's moribund economy* ▶ HISTORY Latin *mori* to die

Mormon *n* **1** a member of the Church of Jesus Christ of Latter-day Saints, founded in 1830 in New York by Joseph Smith ▷ *adj* **2** of the Mormons, their Church, or their beliefs > **Mormonism** *n*

morn *n poetic* morning ▶ HISTORY Old English *morgen*

mornay *adj* served with a cheese sauce: *haddock mornay* ▶ HISTORY after Philippe de *Mornay*, Huguenot leader

morning *n* **1** the first part of the day, ending at noon **2** daybreak; dawn **3 the morning after** *informal* the after effects of excess, esp. a hangover ▷ *adj* **4** of or in the morning: *morning coffee* ▶ HISTORY from *morn*, on the model of *evening*

morning dress *n* formal daytime dress for men, consisting of a frock coat with the front cut away (**morning coat**), usually with grey trousers and top hat

morning-glory *n, pl* -**ries** a tropical climbing plant with trumpet-shaped blue, pink, or white flowers, which close in late afternoon

morning sickness *n* nausea occurring shortly after rising in early pregnancy

morning star *n* a planet, usually Venus, seen just before sunrise

Moroccan *adj* **1** of Morocco ▷ *n* **2** a person from Morocco

morocco *n* a fine soft leather made from goatskins ▶ HISTORY after *Morocco*, where it was originally made

moron *n* **1** *informal, derogatory* a foolish or stupid person **2** *offensive* (formerly) a person having an intelligence quotient of between 50 and 70 ▶ HISTORY Greek *mōros* foolish > **moronic** *adj*

morose (mor-**rohss**) *adj* ill-tempered, sullen, and unwilling to talk very much ▶ HISTORY Latin *morosus* peevish > **morosely** *adv*

morpheme *n linguistics* a speech element having a meaning or grammatical function that cannot be subdivided into further such elements

morphine *or* **morphia** *n* a drug extracted from opium: used in medicine as an anaesthetic and sedative ▶ HISTORY *Morpheus*, in Greek mythology, the god of sleep and dreams

morphing *n* a computer technique used for graphics and in films, in which one image is

545

gradually transformed into another image without individual changes being noticeable in the process ▶ HISTORY from METAMORPHOSIS

morphology n the science of forms and structures of organisms or words > **morphological** adj

morris dance n an old English folk dance performed by men (**morris men**) who wear a traditional costume decorated with bells ▶ HISTORY Middle English *moreys daunce* Moorish dance

morrow n **the morrow** old-fashioned or poetic **1** the next day **2** the morning ▶ HISTORY Old English *morgen* morning

Morse code n a code formerly used internationally for transmitting messages, in which letters and numbers are represented by groups of dots and dashes, or by shorter and longer sounds ▶ HISTORY after Samuel *Morse*, inventor

morsel n a small piece of something, esp. of food ▶ HISTORY Old French *mors* a bite

mortal adj **1** (of living beings, esp. humans) destined to die sometime rather than living forever **2** causing death; fatal: *a mortal wound* **3** deadly or unrelenting: *he is my mortal enemy* **4** of or resulting from the fear of death: *mortal terror* **5** of or involving life or the world: *the hangman's noose ended his mortal existence* **6** great or very intense: *mortal pain* **7** informal conceivable or possible: *there was no mortal reason to leave* **8** slang long and tedious: *for three mortal hours* ▷ n **9** a human being ▶ HISTORY Latin *mors* death > **mortally** adv

mortality n, pl **-ties 1** the condition of being mortal **2** great loss of life, as in war or disaster **3** the number of deaths in a given period

mortal sin n Christianity a sin that will lead to damnation unless repented of

mortar n **1** a small cannon that fires shells in high arcs **2** a mixture of cement or lime or both with sand and water, used to hold bricks or stones together **3** a vessel, usually bowl-shaped, in which substances are crushed with a pestle ▷ vb **4** to fire on with mortars **5** to join bricks or stones with mortar ▶ HISTORY Latin *mortarium* basin in which mortar is mixed

mortarboard n **1** a black tasselled academic cap with a flat square top **2** a small square board with a handle on the underside for carrying mortar

mortgage n **1** an agreement under which a person borrows money to buy property, esp. a house, and the lender can take possession of the property if the borrower fails to repay the money **2** a loan obtained under such an agreement: *a mortgage of three times one's income* **3** a regular repayment of money borrowed under such an agreement: *the monthly mortgage on the building* ▷ vb **-gaging, -gaged 4** to pledge a house or other property as security for the repayment of a loan ▷ adj **5** of or relating to a mortgage: *a mortgage payment* ▶ HISTORY Old French, literally: dead pledge

mortgagee n the person or organization who lends money in a mortgage agreement

mortgagor or **-ger** n the person who borrows money in a mortgage agreement

mortice or **mortise** (**more**-tiss) n **1** a slot or recess cut into a piece of wood or stone to receive a matching projection (tenon) on another piece, or a mortice lock ▷ vb **-ticing, -ticed** or **-tising, -tised 2** to cut a slot or recess in a piece of wood or stone **3** to join two pieces of wood or stone by means of a mortice and tenon ▶ HISTORY Old French *mortoise*

mortice lock n a lock set into the edge of a door so that the mechanism of the lock is enclosed by the door

mortify vb **-fies, -fying, -fied 1** to make someone feel ashamed or embarrassed **2** Christianity to subdue one's emotions, the body, etc. by self-denial **3** (of flesh) to become gangrenous ▶ HISTORY Latin *mors* death + *facere* to do > **mortification** n > **mortifying** adj

mortuary n, pl **-aries** a building or room where dead bodies are kept before cremation or burial ▶ HISTORY Latin *mortuarius* of the dead

morula (**morr**-yoo-la) n embryology a solid ball of cells resulting from cleavage of a fertilized ovum

mosaic (moh-**zay**-ik) n a design or decoration made up of small pieces of coloured glass or stone ▶ HISTORY Greek *mouseios* of the Muses

Mosaic adj of or relating to Moses or the laws and traditions ascribed to him

mosey vb **mosey along** or **on** Brit, Austral & NZ, informal to walk slowly and casually; amble ▶ HISTORY origin unknown

Moslem n, pl **-lems** or **-lem** adj same as **Muslim**

mosque n a Muslim place of worship ▶ HISTORY Arabic *masjid* temple

mosquito n, pl **-toes** or **-tos** a two-winged insect, the females of which pierce the skin of humans and animals to suck their blood ▶ HISTORY Spanish, diminutive of *mosca* fly

moss n **1** a very small flowerless plant typically growing in dense mats on trees, rocks, or moist ground **2** Scot & N English a peat bog or marsh ▶ HISTORY Old English *mos* swamp > **mossy** adj

mossie n S African the common sparrow ▶ HISTORY Afrikaans

moss rose n a variety of rose that has a mossy stem and fragrant pink flowers

most n **1** the greatest number or degree: *the most I can ever remember being paid* **2** the majority: *most of his records are dreadful* **3 at (the) most** at the maximum: *she is fifteen at the most* **4 make the most of** to use to the best advantage: *they made the most of their chances* ▷ adj **5** of or being the majority of a group of things or people or the largest part of something: *most people don't share your views* **6 the most** the superlative of **many, much**: *he has the most talent* ▷ adv **7 the most** used to form the superlative of some adjectives and adverbs: *the most beautiful women in the world* **8** the superlative of **much**: *what do you like most about* *your job?* **9** very; exceedingly: *a most unfortunate accident* ▶ HISTORY Old English *mâst* or *mǽst*

mostly *adv* **1** almost entirely; generally: *the men at the party were mostly young* **2** on many or most occasions; usually: *rattlesnakes mostly hunt at night*

Most Reverend *n* (in Britain) a courtesy title applied to archbishops

MOT **1** *Brit* short for **MOT test** **2** *Brit* the certificate showing that a vehicle has passed its MOT test **3** *NZ* Ministry of Transport

mote *n* a tiny speck ▶ HISTORY Old English *mot*

motel *n* a roadside hotel for motorists ▶ HISTORY blend of MOTOR + HOTEL

motet (moh-**tet**) *n* a religious song for a choir in which several voices, usually unaccompanied, sing contrasting parts simultaneously ▶ HISTORY Old French, diminutive of *mot* word

moth *n* any of numerous chiefly nocturnal insects resembling butterflies that typically have stout bodies and do not have club-shaped antennae ▶ HISTORY Old English *moththe*

mothball *n* **1** a small ball of camphor or naphthalene placed in stored clothing to repel clothes moths **2 put in mothballs** to postpone work on ▷ *vb* **3** to take something out of operation but maintain it for future use **4** to postpone work on

moth-eaten *adj* **1** decayed or scruffy **2** eaten away by or as if by moths: *a moth-eaten suit*

mother *n* **1** a female who has given birth to offspring **2** a person's own mother **3** a title given to certain members of female religious orders **4** motherly qualities, such as maternal affection: *it appealed to the mother in her* **5 the mother of** a female or thing that creates, founds, or protects something: *the mother of modern feminism; necessity is the mother of invention* **6 the mother of all** *informal* the greatest example of its kind: *the mother of all parties* ▷ *adj* **7** of or relating to a female or thing that creates, founds, or protects something: *our mother company is in New York* **8** native or innate: *mother wit* ▷ *vb* **9** to give birth to or produce **10** to nurture or protect ▶ HISTORY Old English *mōdor* > **motherless** *adj* > **motherly** *adj*

Mother Carey's chicken *n* same as **stormy petrel** ▶ HISTORY origin unknown

mother country *n* **1** the original country of colonists or settlers **2** a person's native country

motherhood *n* the state of being a mother

Mothering Sunday *n* **1** (in Britain and S Africa) the fourth Sunday in Lent, when mothers traditionally receive presents from their children **2** (in Australia) the second Sunday in May, when mothers traditionally receive presents from their children. Also called: **Mother's Day**

mother-in-law *n, pl* **mothers-in-law** the mother of one's wife or husband

motherland *n* a person's native country

mother-of-pearl *n* a hard iridescent substance that forms the inner layer of the shells of certain molluscs, such as the oyster

Mother's Day *n* **1** See **Mothering Sunday** **2** *US & Canad* the second Sunday in May, observed as a day in honour of mothers

mother superior *n, pl* **mother superiors** or **mothers superior** the head of a community of nuns

mother tongue *n* the language first learned by a child

motif (moh-**teef**) *n* **1** a distinctive idea, esp. a theme elaborated on in a piece of music or literature **2** a recurring shape in a design **3** a single decoration, such as a symbol or name on a piece of clothing ▶ HISTORY French

motile *adj* capable of independent movement ▶ HISTORY Latin *movere* to move > **motility** *n*

motion *n* **1** the process of continual change in the position of an object; movement: *the motion of the earth round the sun. Related adjective:* **kinetic** **2** a movement or gesture: *he made stabbing motions with the spear* **3** a way or style of moving: *massage the back with steady circular motions* **4** a formal proposal to be discussed and voted on in a debate or meeting **5** *Brit* **a** the evacuation of the bowels **b** excrement **6 go through the motions** to do something mechanically or without sincerity **7 set in motion** to make operational or start functioning ▷ *vb* **8** to signal or direct a person by a movement or gesture: *she motioned to me to sit down* ▶ HISTORY Latin *movere* to move > **motionless** *adj*

motion picture *n* *US & Canad* a film; movie

motivate *vb* **-vating, -vated** **1** to give a reason or inspiration for a course of action to someone: *he was motivated purely by greed* **2** to inspire and encourage (someone) to do something: *a good teacher must motivate her pupils* > **motivation** *n*

motive *n* **1** the reason, whether conscious or unconscious, for a certain course of action **2** same as **motif** (sense 2) ▷ *adj* **3** of or causing motion: *a motive force* ▶ HISTORY Late Latin *motivus* moving

motive power *n* **1** any source of energy used to produce motion **2** the means of supplying power to an engine or vehicle

motley *adj* **1** made up of people or things of different types: *a motley assortment of mules, donkeys, and camels* **2** multicoloured ▷ *n* **3** history the costume of a jester ▶ HISTORY perhaps Old English *mot* speck

motocross *n* the sport of motorcycle racing across rough ground ▶ HISTORY *moto(r)* + *cross(-country)*

motor *n* **1** the engine, esp. an internal-combustion engine, of a vehicle **2** a machine that converts energy, esp. electrical energy, into mechanical energy **3** *chiefly Brit, informal* a car ▷ *adj* **4** *chiefly Brit* of or relating to cars and other vehicles powered by petrol or diesel engines: *the motor industry* **5** powered by or relating to a motor: *a new synthetic motor oil* **6** *physiol* producing or causing motion ▷ *vb* **7** to travel by car **8** *informal* to move fast ▶ HISTORY Latin *movere* to move

motorbicycle *n* **1** a motorcycle **2** a moped

motorbike *n* *informal* a motorcycle

547

motorboat *n* any boat powered by a motor

motorcade *n* a procession of cars carrying an important person or people ▶ HISTORY *motor* + *(caval)cade*

motorcar *n* a more formal word for **car**

motorcycle *n* a two-wheeled vehicle driven by an engine > **motorcyclist** *n*

motorist *n* a driver of a car

motorize *or* **-ise** *vb* **-izing, -ized** *or* **-ising, -ised** to equip with a motor

motorman *n, pl* **-men** *Brit, Austral & NZ* the driver of an electric train

motor scooter *n* a light motorcycle with small wheels and an enclosed engine

motor vehicle *n* a road vehicle driven by an engine

motorway *n* *Brit, Austral & NZ* a dual carriageway for fast-moving traffic, with no stopping permitted and no crossroads

motte *n* *history* a mound on which a castle was built ▶ HISTORY Old French

MOT test *n* (in Britain) a compulsory annual test of the roadworthiness of motor vehicles over three years old

mottled *adj* coloured with streaks or blotches of different shades ▶ HISTORY from *motley* > **mottling** *n*

motto *n, pl* **-toes** *or* **-tos** **1** a short saying expressing the guiding maxim or ideal of a family or organization, esp. when part of a coat of arms **2** a verse or maxim contained in a paper cracker **3** a quotation prefacing a book or chapter of a book ▶ HISTORY Italian

mould¹ *or US* **mold** *n* **1** a shaped hollow container into which a liquid material is poured so that it can set in a particular shape: *pour the mixture into a buttered mould, cover, and steam for two hours* **2** a shape, nature, or type: *an orthodox Communist in the Stalinist mould* **3** a framework around which something is constructed or shaped: *the heated glass is shaped round a mould inside a kiln* **4** something, esp. a food, made in or on a mould: *salmon mould* ▷ *vb* **5** to make in a mould **6** to shape or form: *a figure moulded out of clay* **7** to influence or direct: *cultural factors moulding our everyday life* ▶ HISTORY Latin *modulus* a small measure

mould² *or US* **mold** *n* a coating or discoloration caused by various fungi that develop in a damp atmosphere on food, fabrics, and walls ▶ HISTORY Northern English dialect *mowlde* mouldy

mould³ *or US* **mold** *n* loose soil, esp. when rich in organic matter: *leaf mould* ▶ HISTORY Old English *molde*

mouldboard *or US* **moldboard** *n* the curved blade of a plough, which turns over the furrow

moulder *or US* **molder** *vb* to crumble or cause to crumble, as through decay: *John Brown's body lies mouldering in the grave* ▶ HISTORY from MOULD³

moulding *or US* **molding** *n* a shaped ornamental edging

mouldy *or US* **moldy** *adj* **-dier, -diest** **1** covered with mould **2** stale or musty, esp. from age or lack of use **3** *slang* dull or boring

moult *or US* **molt** *vb* **1** (of birds and animals) to shed feathers, hair, or skin so that they can be replaced by a new growth ▷ *n* **2** the periodic process of moulting ▶ HISTORY Latin *mutare* to change

mound *n* **1** a heap of earth, debris, etc. **2** any heap or pile **3** a small natural hill ▶ HISTORY origin unknown

mount¹ *vb* **1** to climb or ascend: *he mounted the stairs to his flat* **2** to get up on a horse, a platform, etc. **3** Also: **mount up** to increase or accumulate: *costs do mount up; the tension mounted* **4** to fix onto a backing, setting, or support: *sensors mounted on motorway bridges* **5** to organize and stage (a campaign, a play, etc.): *the Allies mounted a counterattack on the eastern front* ▷ *n* **6** a backing, setting, or support onto which something is fixed: *a diamond set in a gold mount* **7** a horse for riding: *none of his mounts at yesterday's race meeting finished better than third* ▶ HISTORY same as MOUNT²

mount² *n* a mountain or hill: used in literature and (when cap.) in proper names: *Mount Etna* ▶ HISTORY Latin *mons* mountain

mountain *n* **1** a very large, high, and steep hill: *the highest mountain in the Alps* **2** a huge heap or mass: *a mountain of papers* **3** a surplus of a commodity, esp. in the European Union: *a butter mountain* ▷ *adj* **4** of, found on, or for use on a mountain or mountains: *a mountain village* ▶ HISTORY Latin *mons*

mountain ash *n* a tree with clusters of small white flowers and bright red berries; rowan

mountain bike *n* a type of bicycle with straight handlebars and heavy-duty tyres, originally designed for use over rough hilly ground

mountain cat *n* any of various wild animals of the cat family, such as the bobcat, lynx, or puma

mountaineer *n* **1** a person who climbs mountains ▷ *vb* **2** to climb mountains > **mountaineering** *n*

mountain goat *n* a wild goat inhabiting mountainous regions

mountain lion *n* a puma

mountainous *adj* **1** having many mountains: *a mountainous region* **2** like a mountain or mountains, esp. in size: *mountainous waves*

mountain oyster *n* *NZ, informal* a sheep's testicle eaten as food

mountain range *n* a series of adjoining mountains or of lines of mountains of similar origin

mountain sickness *n* nausea, headache, and shortness of breath caused by climbing to high altitudes

mountebank *n* **1** (formerly) a person who sold quack medicines in public places **2** a charlatan or fake ▶ HISTORY Italian *montambanco* a climber on a bench

Mountie *or* **Mounty** *n, pl* **Mounties** *informal* a member of the Royal Canadian Mounted Police ▶ HISTORY from *mounted*

mourn *vb* to feel or express sadness for the death or loss of someone or something ▶ HISTORY Old English *murnan* > **mourner** *n*

m

mournful *adj* **1** feeling or expressing grief and sadness: *he stood by, a mournful expression on his face* **2** (of a sound) suggestive or reminiscent of grief or sadness: *the locomotive gave a mournful bellow* > **mournfully** *adv*

mourning *n* **1** sorrow or grief, esp. over a death **2** the conventional symbols of grief for a death, such as the wearing of black **3** the period of time during which a death is officially mourned ▷ *adj* **4** of or relating to mourning

mouse *n*, *pl* **mice 1** a small long-tailed rodent similar to but smaller than a rat **2** a quiet, timid, or cowardly person **3** *computers* a hand-held device used to control cursor movements and computing functions without keying ▷ *vb* **mousing, moused 4** *rare* to stalk and catch mice ▶ HISTORY Old English *mūs*

mouser *n* a cat or other animal that is used to catch mice

mousetrap *n* **1** a spring-loaded trap for killing mice **2** *Brit, informal* cheese of mediocre quality

moussaka *n* a dish originating in the Balkan States, consisting of meat, aubergines, and tomatoes, topped with cheese sauce ▶ HISTORY Modern Greek

mousse *n* **1** a light creamy dessert made with eggs, cream, and fruit set with gelatine **2** a similar dish made from fish or meat ▶ HISTORY French: froth

moustache *or US* **mustache** *n* unshaved hair growing on the upper lip ▶ HISTORY French, from Italian *mostaccio*

mousy *or* **mousey** *adj* **mousier, mousiest 1** (of hair) dull light brown in colour **2** shy or ineffectual > **mousiness** *n*

mouth *n*, *pl* **mouths 1** the opening through which many animals take in food and issue sounds **2** the visible part of the mouth; lips **3** a person regarded as a consumer of food: *three mouths to feed* **4** a particular manner of speaking: *a foul mouth* **5** *informal* boastful, rude, or excessive talk: *she is all mouth* **6** the point where a river issues into a sea or lake **7** an opening, such as that of a bottle, tunnel, or gun **8 down in the mouth** in low spirits ▷ *vb* **9** to form (words) with movements of the lips but without speaking **10** to speak or say (something) insincerely, esp. in public: *ministers mouthing platitudes* ▶ HISTORY Old English *mūth*

mouthful *n*, *pl* **-fuls 1** the amount of food or drink put into the mouth at any one time when eating or drinking **2** a long word, phrase, or name that is difficult to say **3** *Brit, informal* an abusive response: *I asked him to move and he just gave me a mouthful*

mouth organ *n* same as **harmonica**

mouthpiece *n* **1** the part of a wind instrument into which the player blows **2** the part of a telephone receiver into which a person speaks **3** a person or publication expressing the views of an organization

mouthwash *n* a medicated solution for gargling and cleansing the mouth

movable *or* **moveable** *adj* **1** able to be moved; not fixed **2** (of a festival, esp. Easter) varying in date from year to year ▷ *n* **3 movables** movable articles, esp. furniture

move *vb* **moving, moved 1** to go or take from one place to another; change in position: *I moved your books off the table* **2** to start to live or work in a different place: *I moved to Brighton from Bristol last year* **3** to be or cause to be in motion: *the trees were moving in the wind; the car moved slowly down the road* **4** to act or begin to act: *the government plans to move to reduce crime* **5** to cause or prompt to do something: *public opinion moved the President to act* **6** to change the time when something is scheduled to happen: *can I move the appointment to Friday afternoon, please?* **7** to arouse affection, pity, or compassion in; touch: *her story moved me to tears* **8** to change, progress, or develop in a specified way: *the conversation moved to more personal matters* **9** to suggest a proposal formally, as in a debate: *to move a motion* **10** to spend most of one's time with a specified social group: *they both move in theatrical, arty circles* **11** (in board games) to change the position of a piece **12** (of machines) to work or operate **13 a** (of the bowels) to excrete waste **b** to cause the bowels to excrete waste **14** (of merchandise) to be disposed of by being bought **15** to travel quickly: *this car can really move* **16 move heaven and earth** to do everything possible to achieve a result ▷ *n* **17** the act of moving; movement **18** one of a sequence of actions, usually part of a plan: *the first real move towards disarmament* **19** the act of moving one's home or place of business **20** (in board games) **a** a player's turn to move his piece **b** a manoeuvre of a piece **21 get a move on** *informal* to hurry up **22 make a move** *informal* **a** to prepare or begin to leave a place to go somewhere else: *we'd better make a move if we want to be home before dark* **b** to do something which will produce a response: *neither of us wanted to make the first move* **23 on the move** travelling from place to place ▶ HISTORY Latin *movere*
See WORD FOCUS **move** on page 550

movement *n* **1** the act, process, or an instance of moving **2** the manner of moving: *their movement is jerky* **3 a** a group of people with a common ideology **b** the organized action and campaigning of such a group: *a successful movement to abolish child labour* **4** a trend or tendency: *a movement towards shorter working hours* **5** *finance* a change in the price or value of shares, a currency, etc.: *adverse currency movements* **6** *music* a principal self-contained section of a large-scale work, such as a symphony **7 movements** a person's location and activities during a specific time: *police were trying to piece together the recent movements of the two men* **8 a** the evacuation of the bowels **b** the matter evacuated **9** the mechanism which drives and regulates a watch or clock

mover *n* **1** a person or animal that moves in a particular way: *a slow mover* **2** the person who first puts forward a proposal **3** *US & Canad* a removal firm or a person who works for one

m

move

Move is not a very expressive word. If you can use a more descriptive substitute to say something about the way in which a person or thing moves, it will give your writing variety and interest.

DEFINITION 1

- When a person **crawls**, they move forwards on their hands and knees: As he tried to **crawl** away, his captors heard him.
- When an insect **crawls** somewhere, it moves there quite slowly: I watched the moth **crawl** up the outside of the lampshade.
- If a person or animal **creeps** somewhere, they move quietly and slowly: I tried to **creep** upstairs without being heard.
- To **inch** somewhere means to move there very carefully and slowly: He began to **inch** along the ledge.
- If you **edge** somewhere, you move very slowly in that direction: He **edged** closer to the telephone.
- If a person or animal **slithers** somewhere, they move by sliding along the ground in an uneven way: Robert lost his footing and **slithered** down the bank. • The snake **slithered** into the water.
- If you **wriggle** somewhere, for example through a small gap, you move there by twisting and turning your body: I **wriggled** through a gap in the fence.
- When people or small animals **scamper** or **scuttle** somewhere, they move there quickly with small, light steps: The children got off the bus and **scampered** into the playground. • The crabs **scuttled** along the muddy bank.
- When people or small animals **scurry** somewhere, they move there quickly and hurriedly, often because they are frightened: The attack began, sending residents **scurrying** for cover.

- If you **hurry**, **race**, or **rush** somewhere, you go there as quickly as you can: Claire **hurried** along the road. • He **raced** across town to the hospital. • A schoolgirl **rushed** into a burning building to save a baby.
- If you **hasten** somewhere, you hurry there: He **hastened** along the corridor to Grace's room.
- If you **dash**, **dart**, or **shoot** somewhere, you run or go there quickly and suddenly: She jumped up and **dashed** out of the room. • The girl turned and **darted** away through the trees. • They had almost reached the boat when a figure **shot** past them.
- If you say that someone or something **flies** in a particular direction, you are emphasizing that they move there with a lot of speed and force: I **flew** downstairs to answer the door.
- If you **tear** somewhere, you move there very quickly, often in an uncontrolled or dangerous way: Without looking to the left or right, he **tore** off down the road.
- When you **run**, you move quickly because you are in a hurry to get somewhere: I excused myself and **ran** back to the telephone.
- If you **jog**, you run slowly: She **jogged** off in the direction he had indicated.
- If you **sprint**, you run as fast as you can over a short distance: The sergeant **sprinted** to the car.
- If you **gallop**, you run somewhere very quickly: They were **galloping** round the garden playing football.
- If a person or animal **bolts**, they suddenly start to run very fast, often because something has frightened them: I made some excuse and **bolted** towards the exit.
- If a group of animals or people **stampede**, they run in a wild, uncontrolled way: The crowd **stampeded** out of the hall.

---

movie n 1 informal a cinema film 2 **the movies** the cinema: I want to go to the movies tonight

moving adj 1 arousing or touching the emotions: a moving account of her son's death 2 changing or capable of changing position: a moving target > **movingly** adv

moving staircase or **stairway** n an escalator

mow vb **mowing, mowed, mowed** or **mown** 1 to cut down grass or crops: a tractor chugged along, mowing hay 2 to cut the growing vegetation of a field or lawn: to mow a meadow ▶ HISTORY Old English māwan > **mower** n

mow down vb to kill in large numbers, esp. by gunfire

mozzarella (mot-sa-**rel**-la) n a moist white curd cheese originally made in Italy from buffalo milk ▶ HISTORY Italian

MP 1 Member of Parliament 2 Military Police 3 Mounted Police

MP3 MPEG-1 Audio Layer 3: a digital compression format created by the Motion Picture Expert Group, used to compress audio files to a fraction of their original size without loss of sound quality

MP4 MPEG-4 Part 14: software created by the Motion Picture Expert Group for transmitting data streams to a receiving device in real time

MPEG n computing **a** a standard compressed file format used for audio and video files **b** a file in this format ▶ HISTORY from Motion Picture Experts Group

mpg miles per gallon

mph miles per hour

MPhil Master of Philosophy

MPV multipurpose vehicle

Mr n, pl **Messrs** a title used before a man's name or before some office that he holds: Mr Pickwick; Mr President ▶ HISTORY from mister

MRI *med* magnetic resonance imaging: a diagnostic technique using high-frequency radio waves: *an MRI scan*

Mrs *n, pl* **Mrs** *or* **Mesdames** a title used before the name of a married woman ▶ **HISTORY** from *mistress*

ms millisecond(s)

Ms (**mizz**) *n* a title used before the name of a woman to avoid indicating whether she is married or not

MS 1 Mississippi **2** multiple sclerosis

MS. *or* **ms.** *pl* **MSS** *or* **mss** manuscript

MSc Master of Science

MSG monosodium glutamate

MSM mainstream media

MSP (in Britain) Member of the Scottish Parliament

MST Mountain Standard Time

mt megaton

Mt¹ Mount: *Mt Everest*

Mt² *chem* meitnerium

MT Montana

mt. megaton

MTech (in the US) Master of Technology

much *adj* **more, most 1** a large amount or degree of: *there isn't much wine left* ▷ *n* **2** a large amount or degree **3 a bit much** *informal* rather excessive **4 make much of a** to make sense of: *he couldn't make much of her letter* **b** to give importance to: *the press made much of the story* **5 not much of** not to any appreciable degree or extent: *he's not much of a cook* **6 not up to much** *informal* of a low standard: *this beer is not up to much* ▷ *adv* **7** considerably: *I'm much better now* **8** practically or nearly: *it's much the same* **9** often or a great deal: *that doesn't happen much these days* **10 (as) much as** even though; although: *much as I'd like to, I can't come* ▷ See also **more, most** ▶ **HISTORY** Old English *mycel*

muchness *n* **much of a muchness** *Brit & NZ* very similar

mucilage (**mew**-sill-ij) *n* **1** a sticky substance used as an adhesive, such as gum or glue **2** a glutinous substance secreted by certain plants ▶ **HISTORY** Late Latin *mucilago* mouldy juice > **mucilaginous** *adj*

muck *n* **1** dirt or filth **2** farmyard dung or decaying vegetable matter **3** *slang, chiefly Brit & NZ* something of poor quality; rubbish: *I don't want to eat this muck* **4 make a muck of** *slang, chiefly Brit & NZ* to ruin or spoil ▷ *vb* **5** to spread manure upon ▷ See also **muck about, muck in,** etc. ▶ **HISTORY** probably Old Norse

muck about *or* **around** *vb slang* **1** to waste time by misbehaving or being silly **2 muck about with** to interfere with, annoy, or waste the time of

muck in *vb Brit & NZ, slang* to share duties or work with other people

muck out *vb* to clean (a barn, stable, etc.)

muckraking *n* seeking out and exposing scandal relating to well-known people > **muckraker** *n*

mucksweat *n Brit, informal* profuse sweat

muck up *vb informal* to ruin, spoil, or do very badly: *I mucked up my driving test*

mucky *adj* dirty or muddy: *don't come in here with your mucky boots on!*

mucosa *n* same as **mucous membrane** ▶ **HISTORY** Latin *mucosus* slimy > **mucosal** *adj*

mucous membrane *n* a mucus-secreting tissue that lines body cavities or passages

mucus (**mew**-kuss) *n* the slimy protective secretion of the mucous membranes ▶ **HISTORY** Latin: nasal secretions > **mucosity** *n* > **mucous** *adj*

mucus glands *pl n zool* glands that produce mucus

mud *n* **1** soft wet earth, as found on the ground after rain or at the bottom of ponds **2 (someone's) name is mud** *informal* (someone) is disgraced **3 throw mud at** *informal* to slander or vilify ▷ *adj* **4** made from mud or dried mud: *a mud hut* ▶ **HISTORY** probably Low German *mudde*

mud bath *n* **1** a medicinal bath in heated mud **2** a dirty or muddy place, occasion, or state: *heavy rain turned the pitch into a mud bath*

muddle *n* **1** a state of untidiness or confusion: *the files are in a terrible muddle* **2** a state of mental confusion or uncertainty: *the government are in a muddle over the economy* ▷ *vb* **-dling, -dled 3** Also: **muddle up** to mix up or confuse (objects or items): *you've got your books all muddled up with mine* **4** to make (someone) confused: *don't muddle her with too many suggestions* ▶ **HISTORY** perhaps Middle Dutch *moddelen* to make muddy > **muddled** *adj*

muddleheaded *adj* mentally confused or vague

muddy *adj* **-dier, -diest 1** covered or filled with mud **2** not clear or bright: *muddy colours* **3** cloudy: *a muddy liquid* **4** (esp. of thoughts) confused or vague ▷ *vb* **-dies, -dying, -died 5** to make muddy **6** to make a situation or issue less clear: *the allegations of misconduct only serve to muddy the issue* > **muddily** *adv*

mud flat *n* an area of low muddy land that is covered at high tide but not at low tide

mudflow *n geol* a flow of soil mixed with water down a steep unstable slope

mudguard *n* a curved part of a bicycle or other vehicle attached above the wheels to reduce the amount of water or mud thrown up by them

mudslinging *n* the making of malicious personal attacks on an opponent, esp. in politics > **mudslinger** *n*

muesli (**mewz**-lee) *n* a mixture of rolled oats, nuts, and dried fruit, usually eaten with milk ▶ **HISTORY** Swiss German

muezzin (moo-**ezz**-in) *n Islam* the official of a mosque who calls the faithful to prayer from the minaret ▶ **HISTORY** Arabic *mu'adhdhin*

muff¹ *n* a tube of fur or cloth into which the hands are placed for warmth ▶ **HISTORY** probably Dutch *mof*

muff² *vb* **1** to do (something) badly: *I muffed my chance to make a good impression* **2** to bungle (a shot or catch) ▶ **HISTORY** origin unknown

muffin *n* **1** a small domed spongy cake made with eggs and baking powder **2** a thick round baked

muffle *n* yeast roll, usually toasted and served with butter ▶ HISTORY origin unknown

muffle *vb* **-fling, -fled 1** to deaden (a sound or noise), esp. by wrapping the source of it in something: *the sound was muffled by the double glazing* **2** to wrap up in a scarf or coat for warmth **3** to censor or restrict: *an attempt to muffle criticism* ▶ HISTORY probably Old French *moufle* mitten ▷ **muffled** *adj*

muffler *n* **1** *Brit* a thick scarf worn for warmth **2** a device to deaden sound, esp. one on a car exhaust; silencer

mufti *n* civilian clothes worn by a person who normally wears a military uniform ▶ HISTORY from *Mufti*, Muslim religious leader

mug¹ *n* **1** a large drinking cup with a handle **2** the quantity held by a mug or its contents: *a mug of coffee* ▶ HISTORY probably Scandinavian

mug² *n* **1** *slang* a person's face or mouth: *keep your ugly mug out of this* **2** *slang* a gullible person, esp. one who is swindled easily **3 a mug's game** a worthless activity ▶ HISTORY perhaps same as MUG¹

mug³ *vb* **mugging, mugged** to attack someone in order to rob them ▷ **mugger** *n* ▷ **mugging** *n*

muggins *n slang* **a** a stupid or gullible person **b** a title used humorously to refer to oneself ▶ HISTORY probably from surname *Muggins*

muggy *adj* **-gier, -giest** (of weather or air) unpleasantly warm and humid ▶ HISTORY dialect *mug* drizzle ▷ **mugginess** *n*

mug shot *n informal* a photograph of a person's face, esp. one resembling a police-file picture

mug up *vb Brit, slang* to study a subject hard, esp. for an exam ▶ HISTORY origin unknown

Muhammad *n* same as **Mohammed**

mujaheddin *or* **mujahedeen** (moo-ja-hed-**deen**) *pl n* fundamentalist Muslim guerrillas ▶ HISTORY Arabic *mujāhidīn* fighters

mulatto (mew-**lat**-toe) *n, pl* **-tos** *or* **-toes** *old-fashioned, offensive* a person with one Black and one White parent ▶ HISTORY Spanish *mulato* young mule

mulberry *n, pl* **-ries 1** a tree with edible blackberry-like fruit, the leaves of which are used to feed silkworms **2** the fruit of any of these trees ▷ *adj* **3** dark purple ▶ HISTORY Latin *morum*

mulch *n* **1** a mixture of half-rotten vegetable matter and peat used to protect the roots of plants or enrich the soil ▷ *vb* **2** to cover soil with mulch ▶ HISTORY obsolete *mulch* soft

mule¹ *n* **1** the sterile offspring of a male donkey and a female horse **2** a machine that spins cotton into yarn ▶ HISTORY Latin *mulus*

mule² *n* a backless shoe or slipper ▶ HISTORY Latin *mulleus* a magistrate's shoe

muleteer *n* a person who drives mules

mulga *n* **1** an Australian acacia shrub growing in desert regions **2** *Austral* the outback ▶ HISTORY Aboriginal

552 **mulish** *adj* stubborn; obstinate

mull *n Scot* a promontory or headland: *the Mull of Galloway* ▶ HISTORY probably Gaelic *maol*

mullah *n* (formerly) a Muslim scholar, teacher, or religious leader ▶ HISTORY Arabic *mawlā* master

mulled *adj* (of wine or ale) flavoured with sugar and spices and served hot ▶ HISTORY origin unknown

mullet *n, pl* **mullets** *or* **mullet** any of various marine food fishes ▶ HISTORY Greek *mullos*

mulligatawny *n* a curry-flavoured soup of Anglo-Indian origin ▶ HISTORY Tamil *milakutanni* pepper water

mullion *n* a slender vertical bar between the casements or panes of a window ▶ HISTORY Old French *moinel* ▷ **mullioned** *adj*

mulloway *n* a large Australian sea fish, valued for sport and food

multi- *combining form* **1** many or much: *multimillion* **2** more than one: *multistorey* ▶ HISTORY Latin *multus* much, many

multicellular *adj biol* consisting of more than one cell

multicoloured *adj* having many colours: *multicoloured balls of wool*

multicultural *adj* of or for the cultures of several different races ▷ **multiculturalism** *n*

multidirectional *adj* **1** moving in several directions **2** working in several different ways: *a multidirectional learning experience*

multi-ethnic *adj* of or consisting of various different races

multifarious (mull-tee-**fare**-ee-uss) *adj* many and varied: *multifarious religious movements and political divisions sprang up around this time* ▶ HISTORY Late Latin *multifarius* manifold

multiflora rose *n* a climbing rose with clusters of small fragrant flowers

multilateral *adj* of or involving more than two nations or parties: *multilateral trade negotiations*

multilingual *adj* **1** able to speak more than two languages **2** written or expressed in more than two languages: *a multilingual leaflet*

multimedia *pl n* **1** the combined use of media such as television and slides ▷ *adj* **2** *computers* of or relating to systems that can manipulate data in a variety of forms, such as sound, graphics, or text

multimillionaire *n* a person who has money or property worth several million pounds, dollars, etc.

multinational *adj* **1** (of a large business company) operating in several countries **2** involving people from several countries: *a multinational peacekeeping force* ▷ *n* **3** a large company operating in several countries

multiparous (mull-**tip**-a-russ) *adj* producing many offspring at one birth ▶ HISTORY New Latin *multiparus*

multiple *adj* **1** having or involving more than one part, individual, or element ▷ *n* **2** a number or polynomial which can be divided by another specified one an exact number of times: *6 is a multiple of 2* ▶ HISTORY Latin *multiplus* > **multiply** *adv*

multiple-choice *adj* (of a test or question) giving a number of possible answers out of which the correct one must be chosen

multiple sclerosis *n* a chronic progressive disease of the central nervous system, resulting in speech and visual disorders, tremor, muscular incoordination, and partial paralysis

multiplex *n, pl* **-plexes 1** a purpose-built complex containing several cinemas and usually restaurants and bars ▷ *adj* **2** having many elements; complex ▶ HISTORY Latin: having many folds

multiplicand *n* a number to be multiplied by another number (the **multiplier**)

multiplication *n* **1** a mathematical operation, equivalent to adding a number to itself a specified number of times. For instance, 4 multiplied by 3 equals 12 (i.e. 4+4+4) **2** the act of multiplying or state of being multiplied

multiplication sign *n* the symbol ×, placed between numbers to be multiplied

multiplication table *n* a table giving the results of multiplying two numbers together

multiplicity *n, pl* **-ties 1** a large number or great variety **2** the state of being multiple

multiplier *n* a number by which another number (the **multiplicand**) is multiplied

multiply *vb* **-plies, -plying, -plied 1** to increase or cause to increase in number, quantity, or degree **2** to combine numbers or quantities by multiplication **3** to increase in number by reproduction ▶ HISTORY Latin *multiplicare*

multipurpose *adj* having many uses: *a giant multipurpose enterprise*

multipurpose vehicle *n* a large car, similar to a van, designed to carry up to eight passengers

multiracial *adj* consisting of or involving people of many races: *a multiracial society* > **multiracialism** *n*

multistage *adj* (of a rocket or missile) having several stages, each of which can be jettisoned after it has burnt out

multistorey *adj* (of a building) having many storeys

multitrack *adj* (in sound recording) using tape containing two or more tracks

multitude *n* **1** a large number of people or things: *a multitude of different pressure groups* **2 the multitude** *written* the common people ▶ HISTORY Latin *multitudo* > **multitudinous** *adj*

multi-user *adj* (of a computer) capable of being used by several people at once

mum¹ *n* *chiefly Brit, informal* same as **mother** ▶ HISTORY a child's word

mum² *adj* **1 keep mum** remain silent **2 mum's the word** keep quiet (about something) ▶ HISTORY suggestive of closed lips

mumble *vb* **-bling, -bled 1** to speak or say something indistinctly, with the mouth partly

closed: *I could hear him mumbling under his breath* ▷ *n* **2** an indistinct or low utterance or sound ▶ HISTORY Middle English *momelen*, from MUM²

mumbo jumbo *n* **1** meaningless language; nonsense or gibberish **2** foolish religious ritual or incantation ▶ HISTORY probably from West African *mama dyumbo*, name of a tribal god

mummer *n* one of a group of masked performers in a folk play or mime ▶ HISTORY Old French *momer* to mime

mummery *n, pl* **-meries 1** a performance by mummers **2** hypocritical or ostentatious ceremony

mummified *adj* (of a body) preserved as a mummy > **mummification** *n*

mummy¹ *n, pl* **-mies** *chiefly Brit* an embalmed body as prepared for burial in ancient Egypt ▶ HISTORY Persian *mūm* wax

mummy² *n, pl* **-mies** a child's word for **mother** ▶ HISTORY variant of MUM¹

mumps *n* an infectious viral disease in which the glands below the ear become swollen and painful ▶ HISTORY obsolete *mump* to grimace

munch *vb* to chew noisily and steadily ▶ HISTORY imitative

mundane *adj* **1** everyday, ordinary, and therefore not very interesting **2** relating to the world or worldly matters ▶ HISTORY Latin *mundus* world

mung bean *n* an E Asian bean plant grown for its edible seeds which are used as a source of bean sprouts ▶ HISTORY Tamil *mūngu*

municipal *adj* of or relating to a town or city or its local government ▶ HISTORY Latin *municipium* a free town

municipality *n, pl* **-ties 1** a city, town, or district enjoying local self-government **2** the governing body of such a unit

munificent (mew-**niff**-fiss-sent) *adj* very generous ▶ HISTORY Latin *munus* gift + *facere* to make > **munificence** *n*

muniments (mew-nim-ments) *pl n* *law* the title deeds and other documentary evidence relating to the title to land ▶ HISTORY Latin *munire* to defend

munitions (mew-**nish**-unz) *pl n* military equipment and stores, esp. ammunition

munted *adj* *NZ, slang* **1** destroyed or ruined **2** abnormal or peculiar

muon (**mew**-on) *n* a positive or negative elementary particle with a mass 207 times that of an electron ▶ HISTORY short for *mu meson*

mural (**myoor**-al) *n* **1** a large painting on a wall ▷ *adj* **2** of or relating to a wall ▶ HISTORY Latin *murus* wall > **muralist** *n*

murder *n* **1** the unlawful intentional killing of one human being by another **2** *informal* something dangerous, difficult, or unpleasant: *shopping on Christmas Eve is murder* **3 cry blue murder** *informal* to make an outcry **4 get away with murder** *informal* to do as one pleases without ever being punished ▷ *vb* **5** to kill someone intentionally and unlawfully **6** *informal* to ruin a piece of music or drama by performing it very badly: *he absolutely murdered that song* **7** *informal* to beat decisively

▶ HISTORY Old English *morthor* > **murderer** *n*
> **murderess** *fem n* > **murderous** *adj*

murk *n* thick gloomy darkness ▶ HISTORY Old Norse *myrkr* darkness

murky *adj* **murkier, murkiest** 1 gloomy or dark 2 cloudy or hard to see through: *a murky stagnant pond* 3 obscure and suspicious; shady: *murky goings-on; his murky past* > **murkily** *adv*
> **murkiness** *n*

murmur *vb* 1 to speak or say in a quiet indistinct way 2 to complain ▷ *n* 3 a continuous low indistinct sound, such as that of a distant conversation 4 an indistinct utterance: *a murmur of protest* 5 a complaint or grumble: *he left without a murmur* 6 *med* any abnormal soft blowing sound heard usually over the chest: *a heart murmur*
▶ HISTORY Latin *murmurare* to rumble
> **murmuring** *n, adj* > **murmurous** *adj*

murrain (**murr**-rin) *n* any plaguelike disease in cattle ▶ HISTORY Old French *morir* to die

murti (**moor**-ti) *n Hinduism* an image or idol of a god ▶ HISTORY Sanskrit

mus. 1 museum 2 music 3 musical

muscle *n* 1 a tissue in the body composed of bundles of elongated cells which produce movement in an organ or part by contracting or relaxing 2 an organ composed of muscle tissue: *the heart is essentially just another muscle* 3 strength or force: *we do not have the political muscle to force through these reforms* ▷ *vb* **-cling, -cled** 4 **muscle in** to force one's way into a situation; intrude: *I don't like the way he's trying to muscle in here* ▶ HISTORY Medical Latin *musculus* little mouse

muscle-bound *adj* having overdeveloped and inelastic muscles

muscleman *n, pl* **-men** 1 a man with highly developed muscles 2 a henchman employed to intimidate or use violence upon victims

Muscovite *adj* 1 of Moscow, a city in Russia ▷ *n* 2 a person from Moscow

muscular *adj* 1 having well-developed muscles; brawny 2 of or consisting of muscle: *great muscular effort is needed* 3 forceful or powerful: *a muscular account of Schumann's Fourth Symphony*
> **muscularity** *n*

muscular dystrophy *n* a hereditary disease in which the muscles gradually weaken and waste away

musculature *n* the arrangement of muscles in an organ, part, or organism

muse¹ *vb* **musing, mused** *written* to think deeply and at length about: *she mused unhappily on how right her sister had been* ▶ HISTORY Old French *muser*

muse² *n* a force or person, esp. a woman, that inspires a creative artist ▶ HISTORY Greek *Mousa* a Muse

Muses *pl n Greek myth* the nine sister goddesses, each of whom was the protector of a different art or science

museum *n* a building where objects of historical, artistic, or scientific interest are exhibited and preserved

■ 'Museum' comes from Greek *mouseion*,
■ meaning the 'home of the Muses', the
■ goddesses of the arts and sciences.
■ The first building to be given this name
■ was a university building built in Alexandria
■ in Egypt about 300 BC.

museum piece *n informal* a very old or old-fashioned object or building

mush¹ *n* 1 a soft pulpy mass 2 *informal* cloying sentimentality ▶ HISTORY obsolete *moose* porridge

mush² *Canad interj* 1 an order to dogs in a sled team to start up or go faster ▷ *vb* 2 to travel by or drive a dogsled ▶ HISTORY perhaps from imperative of French *marcher* to advance

mushroom *n* 1 an edible fungus consisting of a cap at the end of a stem 2 something resembling a mushroom in shape or rapid growth ▷ *vb* 3 to grow rapidly: *consumer debt mushroomed rapidly in 1989* ▶ HISTORY Late Latin *mussirio*

mushroom cloud *n* the large mushroom-shaped cloud produced by a nuclear explosion

mushy *adj* **mushier, mushiest** 1 soft and pulpy 2 *informal* excessively sentimental

music *n* 1 an art form consisting of sequences of sounds organized melodically, harmonically, and rhythmically 2 such sounds, esp. when produced by singing or musical instruments 3 any written or printed representation of musical sounds: *I can't read music* 4 any sequence of sounds perceived as pleasing or harmonious 5 **face the music** *informal* to confront the consequences of one's actions 6 **music to one's ears** something, such as a piece of news, that one is pleased to hear ▶ HISTORY Greek *mousikē (tekhnē)* (art) in the protection of the Muses

musical *adj* 1 of or used in music 2 talented in or fond of music 3 pleasant-sounding; harmonious: *musical laughter* 4 involving or set to music: *a musical biography of Judy Garland* ▷ *n* 5 a play or film that has dialogue interspersed with songs and dances > **musicality** *n* > **musically** *adv*

music centre *n Brit* a single hi-fi unit containing a turntable, radio, compact disc player, and cassette player

music hall *n chiefly Brit* (formerly) 1 a variety entertainment consisting of songs and comic turns 2 a theatre at which such entertainments were staged

musician *n* a person who plays or composes music, esp. as a profession

musicianship *n* the technical and interpretive skills involved in singing or playing music: *the piano part is simple but performed with great musicianship*

musicology *n* the scholarly study of music > **musicologist** *n*

musk *n* 1 a strong-smelling glandular secretion of the male musk deer, used in perfumery 2 any similar substance produced by animals or plants, or manufactured synthetically ▶ HISTORY Persian *mushk*

musk deer *n* a small central Asian mountain deer

muskeg *n chiefly Canad* an area of undrained boggy land ▶ HISTORY Native American: grassy swamp

musket *n* a long-barrelled muzzle-loading gun fired from the shoulder, a forerunner of the rifle ▶ HISTORY Italian *moschetto* arrow, earlier: sparrow hawk > **musketeer** *n*

muskmelon *n* any of several varieties of melon, such as the cantaloupe and honeydew

musk ox *n* a large ox that has a dark shaggy coat, downward-curving horns and emits a musky smell

muskrat *n, pl* **-rats** *or* **-rat** **1** a North American beaver-like amphibious rodent **2** the brown fur of this animal

musk rose *n* a Mediterranean rose, cultivated for its white musk-scented flowers

musky *adj* **muskier, muskiest** having a heady sweet smell > **muskiness** *n*

Muslim *or* **Moslem** *n, pl* **-lims, -lim** *or* **-lems, -lem** **1** a follower of the religion of Islam ▷ *adj* **2** of or relating to Islam ▶ HISTORY Arabic, literally: one who surrenders

muslin *n* a very fine plain-weave cotton fabric ▶ HISTORY French *mousseline*

musquash *n* muskrat fur ▶ HISTORY from a Native American language

mussel *n* an edible shellfish, with a dark slightly elongated hinged shell, which lives attached to rocks ▶ HISTORY Latin *musculus*, diminutive of *mus* mouse

must¹ *vb* **1** an auxiliary expressing the need or necessity to do something: *I must go to the shops* **2** an auxiliary expressing obligation or requirement: *you must not smoke in here* **3** an auxiliary expressing the probable correctness of a statement: *he must be finished by now* **4** an auxiliary expressing inevitability: *all good things must come to an end* **5** an auxiliary expressing determination: *I must try and finish this* **6** an auxiliary expressing conviction or certainty on the part of the speaker: *you must be kidding!* ▷ *n* **7** an essential or necessary thing: *strong boots are a must for hill walking* ▶ HISTORY Old English *mōste*, past tense of *mōtan* to be allowed or obliged

must² *n* the pressed juice of grapes or other fruit ready for fermentation ▶ HISTORY Latin *mustum* new wine

mustang *n* a small breed of horse, often wild or half wild, found in the southwestern US ▶ HISTORY Mexican Spanish *mestengo*

mustard *n* **1** a hot, spicy paste made from the powdered seeds of any of a family of plants **2** any of these plants, which have yellow flowers and slender pods ▷ *adj* **3** brownish-yellow ▶ HISTORY Old French *moustarde*

mustard gas *n* an oily liquid with poisonous vapour used in chemical warfare, esp. in World War I, which can cause blindness, burns, and sometimes death

mustard plaster *n med* a mixture of powdered black mustard seeds applied to the skin

muster *vb* **1** to summon or gather: *I put as much disbelief in my expression as I could muster* **2** to call or be called together for duty or inspection: *the battalion mustered on the bank of the river* ▷ *n* **3** an assembly of military personnel for duty or inspection **4** a collection, assembly, or gathering **5 pass muster** to be acceptable ▶ HISTORY Latin *monstrare* to show

musty *adj* **-tier, -tiest** **1** smelling or tasting old, stale, or mouldy **2** old-fashioned, dull, or hackneyed: *musty ideas* ▶ HISTORY perhaps variant of obsolete *moisty* > **mustily** *adv* > **mustiness** *n*

mutable (**mew**-tab-bl) *adj* able to or tending to change ▶ HISTORY Latin *mutare* to change > **mutability** *n*

mutagen (**mew**-ta-jen) *n* any substance that can induce genetic mutation ▶ HISTORY MUTATION + *-gen* (suffix) producing > **mutagenic** *adj*

mutagenesis (mew-ta-**jen**-iss-iss) *n* the origin and development of a genetic mutation ▶ HISTORY MUTATION + GENESIS

mutant (**mew**-tant) *n* **1** an animal, organism, or gene that has undergone mutation ▷ *adj* **2** of or resulting from mutation

mutate (mew-**tate**) *vb* **-tating, -tated** to undergo or cause to undergo mutation ▶ HISTORY Latin *mutare* to change

mutation (mew-**tay**-shun) *n* **1** a change or alteration **2** a change in the chromosomes or genes of a cell which may affect the structure and development of the resultant offspring **3** a physical characteristic in an organism resulting from this type of chromosomal change

mute *adj* **1** not giving out sound or speech; silent **2** *offensive* unable to speak **3** unspoken or unexpressed: *she shot him a look of mute entreaty* **4** (of a letter in a word) silent: *the 'k' in 'know' is mute* ▷ *n* **5** *offensive* a person who is unable to speak **6** any of various devices used to soften the tone of stringed or brass instruments ▷ *vb* **muting, muted** **7** to reduce the volume or soften the tone of (a musical instrument) by means of a mute or soft pedal **8** to reduce the volume of (a sound): *the double glazing muted the noise* ▶ HISTORY Latin *mutus* silent > **mutely** *adv* > **muteness** *n*

muted *adj* **1** (of a sound or colour) softened: *a muted pink shirt* **2** (of an emotion or action) subdued or restrained: *his response was muted* **3** (of a musical instrument) being played while fitted with a mute: *muted trumpet*

mute swan *n* the swan most commonly seen in Britain, which has a pure white plumage and an orange-red bill

muti (**moo**-tee) *n S African* medicine, esp. herbal ▶ HISTORY Zulu

mutilate (**mew**-till-ate) *vb* **-lating, -lated** **1** to injure by tearing or cutting off a limb or essential part; maim **2** to damage a book or text so as to render it unintelligible **3** to spoil or damage severely: *why did he mutilate his favourite books and leave ours alone?* ▶ HISTORY Latin *mutilare* to cut off > **mutilated** *adj* > **mutilation** *n* > **mutilator** *n*

mutineer *n* a person who mutinies

m

555

mutinous *adj* **1** openly rebellious **2** characteristic or indicative of mutiny

mutiny (mew-tin-ee) *n, pl* **-nies** **1** open rebellion against authority, esp. by sailors or soldiers against their officers ▷ *vb* **-nies, -nying, -nied** **2** to engage in mutiny: *soldiers who had mutinied and taken control* ▶ HISTORY Old French *mutin* rebellious

mutt *n slang* **1** a foolish or stupid person **2** a mongrel dog ▶ HISTORY from *muttonhead*

mutter *vb* **1** to say something or speak in a low and indistinct tone: *he muttered an excuse* **2** to grumble ▷ *n* **3** a muttered sound or complaint ▶ HISTORY Middle English *moteren* > **muttering** *n, adj*

mutton *n* **1** the flesh of mature sheep, used as food **2** **mutton dressed as lamb** an older woman dressed up to look young ▶ HISTORY Medieval Latin *multo* sheep

mutton bird *n* **1** *Austral* a migratory sea bird with dark plumage **2** *NZ* any of a number of migratory sea birds, the young of which are a Māori delicacy

mutual (mew-chew-al) *adj* **1** experienced or expressed by each of two or more people about the other; reciprocal: *mutual respect* **2** common to or shared by two or more people: *a mutual friend* **3** denoting an organization, such as an insurance company, in which the policyholders or investors share the profits and expenses and there are no shareholders ▶ HISTORY Latin *mutuus* reciprocal > **mutuality** *n* > **mutually** *adv*

mutually exclusive events *pl n maths* (in probability) two events that cannot occur at the same time

Muzak *n trademark* recorded light music played in places such as restaurants and shops

muzzle *n* **1** the projecting part of an animal's face, usually the jaws and nose **2** a guard, made of plastic or strap of strong material, fitted over an animal's nose and jaws to prevent it biting or eating **3** the front end of a gun barrel ▷ *vb* **-zling, -zled** **4** to prevent from being heard or noticed: *an attempt to muzzle the press* **5** to put a muzzle on (an animal) ▶ HISTORY Old French *muse* snout

muzzy *adj* **-zier, -ziest** **1** confused and groggy: *he felt muzzy and hung over* **2** blurred or hazy: *the picture was muzzy and out of focus* ▶ HISTORY origin unknown > **muzzily** *adv* > **muzziness** *n*

MV megavolt

MW **1** megawatt **2** *radio* medium wave

Mx *physics* maxwell

my *adj* **1** of, belonging to, or associated with the speaker or writer (me): *my own way of doing things* **2** used in various forms of address: *my lord* ▷ *interj* **3** *spoken* an exclamation of surprise or awe: *my, how you've grown!* ▶ HISTORY variant of Old English *mīn*

myalism *n* a kind of witchcraft practised in the Caribbean ▶ HISTORY probably of W African origin > **myalist** *n*

myall *n* an Australian acacia with hard scented wood ▶ HISTORY Aboriginal

mycelium (mice-eel-lee-um) *n, pl* **-lia** (-lee-a) the mass forming the body of a fungus ▶ HISTORY Greek *mukēs* mushroom + *hēlos* nail

Mycenaean (mice-in-ee-an) *adj* of or relating to the Aegean civilization of Mycenae, a city in S Greece (1400–1100 BC)

mycology *n* the study of fungi ▶ HISTORY Greek *mukēs* mushroom + -LOGY

myelin (my-ill-in) *n* a white tissue forming an insulating sheath around certain nerve fibres ▶ HISTORY Greek *muelos* marrow

myeloma (my-ill-oh-ma) *n, pl* **-mas** or **-mata** (-ma-ta) a tumour of the bone marrow ▶ HISTORY Greek *muelos* marrow + -*oma*, modelled on *carcinoma*

mynah or **myna** *n* a tropical Asian starling which can mimic human speech ▶ HISTORY Hindi *mainā*

myocardium *n, pl* **-dia** the muscular tissue of the heart ▶ HISTORY Greek *mus* muscle + *kardia* heart > **myocardial** *adj*

myopia (my-oh-pee-a) *n* inability to see distant objects clearly because the images are focused in front of the retina; short-sightedness ▶ HISTORY Greek *muōps* short-sighted > **myopic** (my-op-ik) *adj*

myriad (mir-ree-ad) *adj* **1** innumerable: *the myriad demands of the modern world* ▷ *n* **2** a large indefinite number: *myriads of tiny yellow flowers* ▶ HISTORY Greek *murias* ten thousand

myriapod *n* an invertebrate with a long segmented body and many legs, such as a centipede ▶ HISTORY Greek *murias* ten thousand + *pous* foot

myrrh (mur) *n* the aromatic resin of an African or Asian shrub or tree, used in perfume, incense, and medicine ▶ HISTORY Greek *murrha*

myrtle (mur-tl) *n* an evergreen shrub with pink or white flowers and aromatic blue-black berries ▶ HISTORY Greek *murtos*

myself *pron* **1** the reflexive form of *I* or *me*: *I really enjoyed myself at the party* **2** I or me in person, as distinct from anyone else: *I myself know of no answer* **3** my usual self: *I'm not myself today*

mysterious *adj* **1** of unknown cause or nature: *a mysterious illness* **2** creating a feeling of strangeness, curiosity, or wonder: *a fascinating and mysterious old woman* > **mysteriously** *adv*

mystery *n, pl* **-teries** **1** an unexplained or inexplicable event or phenomenon **2** a person or thing that arouses curiosity or suspense because of an unknown, obscure, or enigmatic quality **3** a story or film which arouses suspense and curiosity because of facts concealed until a religious rite, such as the Eucharist in Christianity ▶ HISTORY Greek *mustērion* secret rites

mystery play *n* (in the Middle Ages) a type of drama based on the life of Christ

mystic *n* **1** a person who achieves mystical experience ▷ *adj* **2** same as **mystical** ▶ HISTORY Greek *mustēs* one who has been initiated

mystical *adj* **1** relating to or characteristic of mysticism **2** *Christianity* having a sacred significance that is beyond human understanding **3** having occult or metaphysical significance > **mystically** *adv*

mysticism *n* **1** belief in or experience of a reality beyond normal human understanding or experience **2** the use of prayer and meditation in an attempt to achieve direct intuitive experience of the divine

mystify *vb* **-fies, -fying, -fied 1** to confuse, bewilder, or puzzle: *his success mystifies many in the fashion industry* **2** to make obscure: *it is important for us not to mystify the function of the scientist* > **mystification** *n* > **mystifying** *adj*

mystique (miss-**steek**) *n* an aura of mystery, power, and awe that surrounds a person or thing

myth *n* **1 a** a story about superhuman beings of an earlier age, usually of how natural phenomena or social customs came into existence **b** same as **mythology** (senses 1, 2) **2 a** an idea or explanation which is widely held but untrue or unproven: *the myth that the USA is a classless society* **b** a person or thing whose existence is fictional or unproven: *the Loch Ness Monster is a myth* ▶ **HISTORY** Greek *muthos* fable

mythical *or* **mythic** *adj* **1** of or relating to myth **2** imaginary or fictitious > **mythically** *adv*

mythology *n*, *pl* **-gies 1** myths collectively, esp. those associated with a particular culture or person **2** a body of stories about a person, institution, etc. **3** the study of myths > **mythological** *adj*

myxoedema *or US* **myxedema** (mix-id-**deem**-a) *n* a disease caused by an underactive thyroid gland, characterized by puffy eyes, face, and hands, and mental sluggishness ▶ **HISTORY** Greek *muxa* mucus + *oidēma* swelling

myxomatosis (mix-a-mat-**oh**-siss) *n* an infectious and usually fatal viral disease of rabbits causing swellings and tumours ▶ **HISTORY** Greek *muxa* mucus + *-ōma* denoting tumour + *-osis* denoting disease

m

Nn

n¹ 1 nano- **2** neutron

n² *n* **1** *maths* a number whose value is not stated: *two to the power n* ▷ *adj* **2** an indefinite number of: *there are n objects in the box* > **nth** *adj*

N *chess* knight **2** *chem* nitrogen **3** *physics* newton(s) **4** North(ern) **5** nuclear: *N plant*

n. **1** neuter **2** noun **3** number

N. **1** National(ist) **2** Navy **3** New **4** Norse

Na *chem* sodium ▶ **HISTORY** Latin *natrium*

NA North America

n/a not applicable: used to indicate that a question on a form is not relevant to the person filling it in

Naafi *n* **1** *Brit* Navy, Army, and Air Force Institutes **2** a canteen or shop run by this organization, esp. for military personnel

naan *n* same as **nan bread**

naartjie (**nahr**-chee) *n* *S African* a tangerine ▶ **HISTORY** Afrikaans

nab *vb* **nabbing, nabbed** *informal* **1** to arrest (someone) **2** to catch (someone) doing something wrong ▶ **HISTORY** perhaps Scandinavian

nabob (**nay**-bob) *n* *informal* a rich or important person ▶ **HISTORY** Hindi *nawwāb; see* NAWAB

nacelle (nah-**sell**) *n* a streamlined enclosure on an aircraft, esp. one housing an engine ▶ **HISTORY** French: small boat

nacho *n, pl* **nachos** *Mexican cookery* a snack of a piece of tortilla topped with cheese, peppers, etc.

nacre (**nay**-ker) *n* mother-of-pearl ▶ **HISTORY** Arabic *naqqārah* shell, drum > **nacreous** *adj*

nadir *n* **1** the point in the sky directly below an observer and opposite the zenith **2** the lowest or worst point of anything: *I had touched the very nadir of despair* ▶ **HISTORY** Arabic *nazīr as-samt,* literally: opposite the zenith

naevus *or US* **nevus** (**nee**-vuss) *n, pl* **-vi** a birthmark or mole ▶ **HISTORY** Latin

naff *adj* *Brit, slang* in poor taste: *naff frocks and trouser suits* ▶ **HISTORY** perhaps back slang from *fan,* short for FANNY > **naffness** *n*

nag¹ *vb* **nagging, nagged** **1** to scold or find fault constantly **2** **nag at** to be a constant source of discomfort or worry to ▷ *n* **3** a person who nags ▶ **HISTORY** Scandinavian > **nagging** *adj, n*

nag² *n* **1** *often disparaging* an old horse **2** a small riding horse ▶ **HISTORY** Germanic

naiad (**nye**-ad) *n, pl* **naiads** *or* **naiades** (**nye**-ad-deez) *Greek myth* a water nymph ▶ **HISTORY** Greek *nāias*

nail *n* **1** a piece of metal with a point at one end and a head at the other, hit with a hammer to join two objects together **2** the hard covering of the upper tips of the fingers and toes **3** **hit the nail on the head** to say something exactly correct or accurate **4** **on the nail** at once: *he paid always in cash, always on the nail* ▷ *vb* **5** to attach (something) with nails **6** *informal* to arrest or catch (someone) ▶ **HISTORY** Old English *nægl*

naive (nye-**eev**) *adj* **1** innocent and gullible **2** simple and lacking sophistication: *naive art* ▶ **HISTORY** French, from Latin *nativus* native > **naively** *adv*

naivety (nye-**eev**-tee) *or* **naïveté** *n* the state or quality of being naive

naked *adj* **1** without clothes **2** *written* not concealed: *naked aggression* **3** without any covering: *it was dimly lit by naked bulbs* **4** **the naked eye** the eye unassisted by any optical instrument: *difficult to spot with the naked eye* ▶ **HISTORY** Old English *nacod* > **nakedly** *adv* > **nakedness** *n*

namby-pamby *adj* *Brit, Austral & NZ* excessively sentimental or prim ▶ **HISTORY** nickname of Ambrose Phillips, 18th-century pastoral poet

name *n* **1** a word or term by which a person or thing is known. *Related adjective:* **nominal** **2** reputation, esp. a good one: *he was making a name for himself* **3** a famous person: *she's a big name now* **4** **call someone names** *or* **a name** to insult someone by using rude words to describe him or her **5** **in name only** not possessing the powers or status implied by one's title: *a leadership in name only* **6** **in the name of a** for the sake of: *in the name of decency* **b** by the authority of: *in the name of the law* **7** **name of the game** the most significant or important aspect of something: *survival is the name of the game in wartime* **8** **to one's name** in one's possession: *she hasn't a penny to her name* ▷ *vb* **naming, named** **9** to give a name to **10** to refer to by name: *he refused to name his source* **11** to fix or specify: *he named a time for the meeting* **12** to appoint: *she was named Journalist of the Year* **13** to ban (an MP) from the House of Commons by mentioning him or her formally by name as being guilty of disorderly conduct **14** **name names** to cite people in order to blame or accuse them ▶ **HISTORY** Old English *nama*

name day *n* *RC Church* the feast day of a saint whose name one bears

name-dropping *n* *informal* the practice of referring to famous people as though they were friends, in order to impress others

nameless *adj* **1** without a name **2** unspecified: *the individual concerned had better remain nameless* **3** too horrible to speak about: *the nameless dread*

namely *adv* that is to say

nameplate *n* a small sign on or next to a door giving the occupant's name and, sometimes, profession

namesake *n* *written* a person or thing with the same name as another ▶ **HISTORY** probably originally *for the name's sake*

nan bread or **naan** n a slightly leavened Indian bread in a large flat leaf shape ▶ HISTORY Hindi

nanny n, pl -nies 1 a woman whose job is looking after young children ▷ vb **nannies, nannying, nannied** 2 to nurse or look after someone else's children 3 to be too protective towards (someone) ▶ HISTORY child's name for a nurse

nanny goat n a female goat

nano- combining form denoting one thousand millionth (10^{-9}): nanosecond ▶ HISTORY Latin nanus dwarf

nap[1] n 1 a short sleep ▷ vb **napping, napped** 2 to have a short sleep 3 **catch someone napping** to catch someone unprepared: they don't want to be caught napping when the army moves again ▶ HISTORY Old English hnappian

nap[2] n the raised fibres of velvet or similar cloth ▶ HISTORY probably Middle Dutch noppe

nap[3] n 1 a card game similar to whist 2 horse racing a tipster's choice for a certain winner ▷ vb **napping, napped** 3 horse racing to name (a horse) as a likely winner ▶ HISTORY shortened from Napoleon

napalm n 1 a highly inflammable jellied petrol, used in firebombs and flame-throwers ▷ vb 2 to attack (people or places) with napalm ▶ HISTORY na(phthene) + palm(itate) salt of palmitic acid

nape n the back of the neck ▶ HISTORY origin unknown

naphtha n chem a liquid mixture distilled from coal tar or petroleum: used as a solvent and in petrol ▶ HISTORY Greek

naphthalene n chem a white crystalline substance distilled from coal tar or petroleum, used in mothballs, dyes, and explosives ▶ HISTORY naphtha + alcohol + -ene

napkin n 1 a piece of cloth or paper for wiping the mouth or protecting the clothes while eating 2 same as **sanitary towel** ▶ HISTORY Latin mappa cloth

nappy n, pl -pies Brit & NZ a piece of soft absorbent material, usually disposable, wrapped around the waist and between the legs of a baby to absorb its urine and excrement ▶ HISTORY from napkin

narcissism n an exceptional interest in or admiration for oneself ▶ HISTORY after Narcissus, a youth in Greek mythology, who fell in love with his reflection > **narcissistic** adj

narcissus (nahr-**siss**-uss) n, pl -**cissi** (-**siss**-eye) a yellow, orange, or white flower related to the daffodil ▶ HISTORY Greek narkissos, perhaps from narkē numbness, because of narcotic properties attributed to the plant

narcosis n unconsciousness caused by a narcotic or general anaesthetic ▶ HISTORY Greek narkē numbness

narcotic n 1 a drug, such as opium or morphine, that produces numbness and drowsiness, used medicinally but addictive ▷ adj 2 of narcotics or narcosis ▶ HISTORY Greek narkē numbness

nark slang vb 1 to annoy ▷ n 2 an informer or spy: copper's nark 3 Brit someone who complains in an irritating or whining manner ▶ HISTORY probably from Romany nāk nose

narky adj **narkier, narkiest** slang irritable, complaining, or sarcastic

narrate vb -rating, -rated 1 to tell (a story); relate 2 to speak the words accompanying and telling what is happening in a film or TV programme ▶ HISTORY Latin narrare to recount

narration n 1 a narrating 2 a narrated account or story

narrative n 1 an account of events 2 the part of a literary work that relates events ▷ adj 3 telling a story 4 of narration

narrative genre n literature a form of writing or speech in which the writer or speaker tells a story

narrative voice n literature the style or character of the person telling the story or relating events in a work of literature

narrator n literature 1 a person telling a story 2 (in novels) the fictional character or authorial voice relating events

narrow adj 1 small in breadth in comparison to length 2 limited in range, extent, or outlook: a narrow circle of academics 3 with little margin: a narrow advantage ▷ vb 4 to make or become narrow 5 **narrow down** to restrict or limit: the search can be narrowed down to a single room ▷ See also **narrows** ▶ HISTORY Old English nearu > **narrowly** adv > **narrowness** n

narrow boat n Brit a long bargelike canal boat

narrow-minded adj bigoted, intolerant, or prejudiced > **narrow-mindedness** n

narrows pl n a narrow part of a strait, river, or current

narwhal n an arctic whale with a long spiral tusk ▶ HISTORY Old Norse nāhvalr, from nār corpse + hvalr whale

NASA (in the US) National Aeronautics and Space Administration

nasal adj 1 of the nose 2 (of a sound) pronounced with air passing through the nose 3 (of a voice) characterized by nasal sounds ▶ HISTORY Latin nasus nose > **nasally** adv

nascent adj formal starting to grow or develop ▶ HISTORY Latin nasci to be born

nastic movement n physiol a response of plant parts that is independent of the direction of the external stimulus

nasturtium n a plant with yellow, red, or orange trumpet-shaped flowers ▶ HISTORY Latin: kind of cress

nasty adj -tier, -tiest 1 unpleasant: a nasty odour 2 dangerous or painful: a nasty burn 3 (of a person) spiteful or ill-natured ▷ n, pl -ties 4 something unpleasant: video nasties ▶ HISTORY probably related to Dutch nestig dirty > **nastily** adv > **nastiness** n

nat. 1 national 2 nationalist

natal (**nay**-tl) adj of or relating to birth ▶ HISTORY Latin natalis of one's birth

natality n statistics, chiefly US same as **birth rate**

nation n 1 a large body of people of one or more cultures or races, organized into a single state: a major industrialized nation 2 ethnography a

559

federation of Native American tribes ▶ HISTORY Latin *natio* birth, tribe

national *adj* **1** of or serving a nation as a whole **2** characteristic of a particular nation: *the national character* ▷ *n* **3** a citizen of a particular country: *Belgian nationals* **4** a national newspaper > **nationally** *adv*

national anthem *n* a patriotic song adopted by a nation for use on public occasions

National Curriculum *n* (in England and Wales) the curriculum of subjects taught in state schools since 1989

national debt *n* the total outstanding borrowings of a nation's central government

National Estate *n* **the National Estate** Australia's national inventory of places of natural or cultural interest to be protected for the future

national grid *n Brit & NZ* **1** a network of high-voltage power lines linking major electric power stations **2** the arrangement of vertical and horizontal lines on an ordnance survey map

National Health Service *n* (in Britain) the system of national medical services financed mainly by taxation

national insurance *n* (in Britain) state insurance based on contributions from employees and employers, providing payments to people who are unemployed, sick, and retired

nationalism *n* **1** a policy of national independence **2** patriotism, sometimes to an excessive degree > **nationalist** *n, adj* > **nationalistic** *adj*

nationality *n, pl* **-ties** **1** the fact of being a citizen of a particular nation **2** a group of people of the same race: *young men of all nationalities*

nationalize *or* **-ise** *vb* **-izing, -ized** *or* **-ising, -ised** to put (an industry or a company) under state control > **nationalization** *or* **-isation** *n*

national park *n* an area of countryside protected by a national government for its scenic or environmental importance

national service *n chiefly Brit* compulsory military service

National Socialism *n German history* the doctrines and practices of the Nazis, involving the supremacy of Hitler, anti-Semitism, state control of the economy, and national expansion > **National Socialist** *n, adj*

national superannuation *n NZ* a government pension paid to people of 65 years and over; retirement pension

national symbol *n* any symbol, such as a flag, animal, plant, etc., representing a country, its people, or its culture

nationhood *n* the state of being an independent country

nation-state *n politics* an independent state inhabited by the people of one nation only

nationwide *adj* covering or available to the whole of a nation

native *adj* **1** relating to a place where a person was born: *native land* **2** born in a specified place:

a native New Yorker **3** **native to** originating in: *a plant native to alpine regions* **4** natural or inborn: *native genius* **5** relating to the original inhabitants of a country: *archaeology may uncover magnificent native artefacts* **6** **go native** (of a settler) to adopt the lifestyle of the local population ▷ *n* **7** a person born in a specified place: *a native of Palermo* **8** an indigenous animal or plant: *the saffron crocus is a native of Asia Minor* **9** a member of the original race of a country, as opposed to colonial immigrants ▶ HISTORY Latin *nativus* innate, natural, from *nasci* to be born

Native American *n* same as **American Indian**

native bear *n Austral* same as **koala**

native companion *n Austral* same as **brolga**

native dog *n Austral* a dingo

native title *n Austral law* title that recognizes the indigenous inhabitants as the rightful owners of the land

nativity *n, pl* **-ties** birth or origin ▶ HISTORY Late Latin *nativitas* birth

Nativity *n Christianity* **1** the birth of Jesus Christ **2** the feast of Christmas celebrating this

NATO *or* **Nato** North Atlantic Treaty Organization: an international organization established for purposes of collective security

natter *Brit & NZ, informal vb* **1** to talk idly and at length ▷ *n* **2** a long idle chat ▶ HISTORY dialect *gnatter* to grumble, imitative

natterjack *n* a greyish-brown toad with reddish warty lumps ▶ HISTORY origin unknown

natty *adj* **-tier, -tiest** *informal* smart and spruce ▶ HISTORY dialect *net* neat > **nattily** *adv*

natural *adj* **1** as is normal or to be expected: *the natural consequence* **2** genuine or spontaneous **3** of, according to, existing in, or produced by nature: *natural disasters* **4** not acquired; inborn: *their natural enthusiasm* **5** not created by human beings: *the natural environment* **6** not synthetic: *natural fibres such as wool* **7** (of a parent) not adoptive **8** (of a child) illegitimate **9** *music* not sharp or flat: *F natural* ▷ *n* **10** *informal* a person with an inborn talent or skill: *she's a natural at bridge* **11** *music* a note that is neither sharp nor flat > **naturalness** *n*

natural gas *n* a gaseous mixture, consisting mainly of methane, found below ground; used widely as a fuel

natural hazard *n* any natural event such as an earthquake, hurricane, flood, forest fire, or outbreak of disease that could threaten the lives and livelihood of those caught up in it

natural history *n* the study of animals and plants in the wild

naturalism *n* a movement in art and literature advocating detailed realism > **naturalistic** *adj*

naturalist *n* **1** a student of natural history **2** a person who advocates or practises naturalism

naturalize *or* **-ise** *vb* **-izing, -ized** *or* **-ising, -ised** **1** to give citizenship to (a person born in another country) **2** to introduce (a plant or animal) into another region **3** to cause (a foreign word or custom) to be adopted

natural justice *n law* the principles and procedures that govern the adjudication of disputes between people or organizations, chief among which are that the adjudication should be unbiased and given in good faith, and that each party should have equal access to the tribunal and should be aware of arguments and documents adduced by the other

natural law *n philosophy* **1** an ethical belief or system of beliefs supposed to be inherent in human nature and discoverable by reason rather than revelation **2** a law of nature **3** the philosophical doctrine that the authority of the legal system or of certain laws derives from their justifiability by reason, and that a legal system which cannot be so justified has no authority

natural logarithm *n* a logarithm which has the irrational number e as a base

naturally *adv* **1** of course; surely **2** in a natural or normal way **3** instinctively

natural number *n* a positive integer, such as 1, 2, 3, 4, etc.

natural philosophy *n old-fashioned* physics

natural radiation *n physics* radiation that occurs freely in nature

natural resources *pl n* naturally occurring materials such as coal, oil, and minerals

natural science *n* any of the sciences dealing with the study of the physical world, such as biology, physics, chemistry, and geology

natural selection *n* a process by which only those creatures and plants well adapted to their environment survive

natural vegetation *n* the plants that grow without human help in a particular location

natural wastage *n chiefly Brit* a reduction in the number of employees through not replacing those who leave, rather than by dismissing employees or making them redundant

nature *n* **1** the whole system of the existence, forces, and events of the physical world that are not controlled by human beings **2** fundamental or essential qualities: *the theory and nature of science* **3** kind or sort: *problems of a financial nature* **4** temperament or personality: *an amiable and pleasant nature* **5 by nature** essentially: *he was by nature a cautious man* **6 in the nature of** essentially; by way of: *it was in the nature of a debate rather than an argument* ▶ HISTORY Latin *natura*, from *nasci* to be born

nature reserve *n* an area of land that is preserved and managed in order to protect its animal and plant life

nature study *n* the study of animals and plants by direct observation

naturism *n* same as **nudism** > **naturist** *n, adj*

naught *n* **1** *archaic or literary* nothing **2** *chiefly US* the figure 0 ▷ *adv* **3** *archaic or literary* not at all: *I care naught* ▶ HISTORY Old English *nāwiht*

naughty *adj* **-tier, -tiest** **1** (of children) mischievous or disobedient **2** mildly indecent: *naughty lingerie* ▶ HISTORY (originally: needy, poor) from *naught* > **naughtily** *adv* > **naughtiness** *n*

nausea (naw-zee-a) *n* **1** the feeling of being about to vomit **2** disgust ▶ HISTORY Greek: seasickness, from *naus* ship

nauseate *vb* **-ating, -ated** **1** to cause (someone) to feel sick **2** to arouse feelings of disgust in (someone) > **nauseating** *adj*

nauseous *adj* **1** as if about to be sick: *he felt nauseous* **2** sickening

nautical *adj* of the sea, ships, or navigation ▶ HISTORY Greek *nautikos*, from *naus* ship

nautical mile *n* a unit of length, used in navigation, standardized as 6080 feet

nautilus *n, pl* **-luses** *or* **-li** a sea creature with a shell and tentacles ▶ HISTORY Greek *nautilos* sailor

naval *adj* of or relating to a navy or ships ▶ HISTORY Latin *navis* ship

nave[1] *n* the long central part of a church ▶ HISTORY Latin *navis* ship, from the similarity in shape

nave[2] *n* the hub of a wheel ▶ HISTORY Old English *nafu, nafa*

navel *n* the slight hollow in the centre of the abdomen, where the umbilical cord was attached ▶ HISTORY Old English *nafela*

navel orange *n* a sweet orange that has a navel-like hollow at the top

navigable *adj* **1** wide, deep, or safe enough to be sailed through **2** able to be steered

navigate *vb* **-gating, -gated** **1** to direct or plot the course or position of a ship or aircraft **2** to travel over or through safely: *your cousin, who's just navigated the Amazon* **3** *informal* to direct (oneself) carefully or safely: *he navigated his unsteady way to the bar* **4** (of a passenger in a vehicle) to read the map and give directions to the driver **5** to move around and find material on (the internet, a website, etc.) ▶ HISTORY Latin *navis* ship + *agere* to drive > **navigation** *n* > **navigational** *adj* > **navigator** *n*

navvy *n, pl* **-vies** *Brit & Austral, informal* a labourer on a building site or road ▶ HISTORY from *navigator* builder of a *navigation* (in the sense: canal)

navy *n, pl* **-vies** **1** the branch of a country's armed services comprising warships with their crews, and all their supporting services **2** the warships of a nation ▷ *adj* **3** short for **navy-blue** ▶ HISTORY Latin *navis* ship

navy-blue *adj* very dark blue ▶ HISTORY from the colour of the British naval uniform

nawab (na-**wahb**) *n* (formerly) a Muslim ruler or powerful landowner in India ▶ HISTORY Hindi *nawwāb*, from Arabic *nuwwāb*, plural of *na'ib* viceroy

nay *interj* **1** *old-fashioned* no ▷ *n* **2** a person who votes against a motion ▷ *adv* **3** used for emphasis: *I want, nay, need to know* ▶ HISTORY Old Norse *nei*

Nazarene *n* **1 the Nazarene** Jesus Christ **2** *old-fashioned* a Christian **3** a person from Nazareth, a town in N Israel ▷ *adj* **4** of Nazareth

Nazi *n, pl* **-zis** **1** a member of the fascist National Socialist German Workers' Party, which came to power in Germany in 1933 under Adolf Hitler ▷ *adj* **2** of or relating to the Nazis ▶ HISTORY German,

n

phonetic spelling of the first two syllables of *Nationalsozialist* National Socialist ▸ **Nazism** *n*

nb *cricket* no-ball

Nb *chem* niobium

NB 1 New Brunswick **2** note well ▸ **HISTORY** Latin *nota bene*

NC 1 North Carolina **2** *Brit education* National Curriculum

NCO noncommissioned officer

Nd *chem* neodymium

ND North Dakota

Ne *chem* neon

NE 1 Nebraska **2** northeast(ern)

ne- *combining form* same as **neo-**: *Nearctic*

Neanderthal (nee-**ann**-der-tahl) *adj* **1** of a type of primitive man that lived in Europe before 12,000 BC **2** *informal* with excessively conservative views: *his notoriously Neanderthal attitude to women* ▸ **HISTORY** after *Neandertal*, a valley in Germany

neap *n* short for **neap tide** ▸ **HISTORY** Old English, as in *nēpflōd* neap tide

Neapolitan *adj* **1** of Naples, a city in SW Italy ▷ *n* **2** a person from Naples ▸ **HISTORY** Greek *Neapolis* new town

neap tide *n* a tide that occurs at the first and last quarter of the moon when there is the smallest rise and fall in tidal level

near *prep* **1** at or to a place or time not far away from ▷ *adv* **2** at or to a place or time not far away **3** short for **nearly**: *the pain damn near crippled him* ▷ *adj* **4** at or in a place or time not far away: *in the near future* **5** closely connected or intimate: *a near relation* **6** almost being the thing specified: *a mood of near rebellion* ▷ *vb* **7** to draw close (to): *the participants are nearing agreement* ▷ *n* **8** the left side of a horse or vehicle ▸ **HISTORY** Old English *nēar*, comparative of *nēah* close > **nearness** *n*

nearby *adj, adv* not far away

Near East *n* same as **Middle East**

nearly *adv* **1** almost **2** **not nearly** nowhere near: *it's not nearly as easy as it looks*

near-market research *n* scientific research that is not to develop a specific product but which has commercial value

near miss *n* **1** any attempt that just fails to succeed **2** an incident in which two aircraft or vehicles narrowly avoid collision **3** a bomb or shot that does not quite hit the target

nearside *n* **1** *chiefly Brit* the side of a vehicle that is nearer the kerb **2** the left side of an animal

near-sighted *adj* same as **short-sighted**

neat *adj* **1** clean and tidy **2** smoothly or competently done: *a neat answer* **3** (of alcoholic drinks) undiluted **4** *slang, chiefly US & Canad* admirable; excellent ▸ **HISTORY** Latin *nitidus* clean > **neatly** *adv* > **neatness** *n*

neaten *vb* to make neat

neb *n* *archaic or dialect* the beak of a bird or the nose of an animal ▸ **HISTORY** Old English *nebb*

nebula (**neb**-yew-la) *n*, *pl* **-lae** (-lee) *astron* a hazy cloud of particles and gases ▸ **HISTORY** Latin: mist, cloud > **nebular** *adj*

nebulize *or* **-ise** *vb* **-izing**, **-ized** *or* **-ising**, **-ised** to turn (a liquid) into a fine spray

nebulizer *or* **-iser** *n* a device which turns a drug from a liquid into a fine spray which can be inhaled

nebulous *adj* vague and unclear: *a nebulous concept*

NEC (in Britain) National Executive Committee

necessaries *pl n* essential items: *the necessaries and comforts of life*

necessarily *adv* **1** as a certainty: *the factors were not necessarily connected with one another* **2** inevitably: *tourism is an industry that has a necessarily close connection with governments*

necessary *adj* **1** needed in order to obtain the desired result: *the necessary skills* **2** certain or unavoidable: *the necessary consequences* ▷ *n* **3 the necessary** *informal* the money required for a particular purpose **4 do the necessary** *informal* to do something that is necessary in a particular situation ▷ See also **necessaries** ▸ **HISTORY** Latin *necessarius* indispensable

necessitate *vb* **-tating**, **-tated** to compel or require

necessitous *adj* *literary* very needy

necessity *n*, *pl* **-ties** **1** a set of circumstances that inevitably requires a certain result: *the necessity to maintain safety standards* **2** something needed: *the daily necessities* **3** great poverty **4 of necessity** inevitably

neck *n* **1** the part of the body connecting the head with the rest of the body **2** the part of a garment around the neck **3** the long narrow part of a bottle or violin **4** the length of a horse's head and neck taken as the distance by which one horse beats another in a race: *to win by a neck* **5** *informal* impudence **6 by a neck** by a very small margin: *she held on to win by a neck* **7 get it in the neck** *informal* to be reprimanded or punished severely **8 neck and neck** absolutely level in a race or competition **9 neck of the woods** *informal* a particular area: *how did they get to this neck of the woods?* **10 stick one's neck out** *informal* to risk criticism or ridicule by speaking one's mind **11 up to one's neck in** *informal* deeply involved in: *he was up to his neck in the scandal* ▷ *vb* **12** *informal* (of two people) to kiss each other passionately ▸ **HISTORY** Old English *hnecca*

neckerchief *n* a piece of cloth worn tied round the neck ▸ **HISTORY** neck + kerchief

necklace *n* a decorative piece of jewellery worn round the neck

neckline *n* the shape or position of the upper edge of a dress or top

necktie *n* US same as **tie** (sense 5)

necromancy (**neck**-rome-man-see) *n* **1** communication with the dead **2** sorcery ▸ **HISTORY** Greek *nekros* corpse + *mantis* prophet > **necromancer** *n*

necropolis (neck-**rop**-pol-liss) *n* a cemetery ▸ **HISTORY** Greek *nekros* dead + *polis* city

necrosis *n* **1** *biol, med* the death of cells in the body, as from an interruption of the blood supply

2 *bot* death of plant tissue due to disease or frost ▶ HISTORY Greek *nekros* corpse > **necrotic** *adj*

nectar *n* **1** a sugary fluid produced by flowers and collected by bees **2** *classical myth* the drink of the gods **3** any delicious drink ▶ HISTORY Greek *nektar*

nectarine *n* a smooth-skinned variety of peach ▶ HISTORY apparently from *nectar*

NEDC (formerly) National Economic Development Council. Also (informal): **Neddy**

née *prep* indicating the maiden name of a married woman: *Jane Gray (née Blandish)* ▶ HISTORY French, past participle (feminine) of *naître* to be born

need *vb* **1** to require or be in want of: *they desperately need success* **2** to be obliged: *the government may need to impose a statutory levy* **3** used to express necessity or obligation and does not add -s when used with singular nouns or pronouns: *need he go?* ▷ *n* **4** the condition of lacking something: *he has need of a new coat* **5** a requirement: *the need for closer economic co-operation* **6** necessity: *there was no need for an explanation* **7** poverty or destitution: *the money will go to those areas where need is greatest* **8** distress: *help has been given to those in need* ▷ See also **needs** ▶ HISTORY Old English *nēad*, *nied*

needful *adj* **1** necessary or required ▷ *n* **2 the needful** *informal* what is necessary, usually money

needle *n* **1** a pointed slender piece of metal with a hole in it through which thread is passed for sewing **2** a long pointed rod used in knitting **3** same as **stylus 4** *med* the long hollow pointed part of a hypodermic syringe, which is inserted into the body **5** a pointer on the scale of a measuring instrument **6** a long narrow stiff leaf: *pine needles* **7** *Brit, informal* intense rivalry or ill-feeling in a sports match **8** short for **magnetic needle 9 have** or **get the needle** *Brit, informal* to be annoyed ▷ *vb* **-dling, -dled 10** *informal* to goad or provoke ▶ HISTORY Old English *nǣdl*

needlecord *n* a fine-ribbed corduroy fabric

needlepoint *n* **1** embroidery done on canvas **2** lace made by needles on a paper pattern

needless *adj* not required; unnecessary > **needlessly** *adv*

needlework *n* sewing and embroidery

needs *adv* **1** necessarily: *they must needs be admired* ▷ *pl n* **2** what is required

needy *adj* **needier, neediest** in need of financial support

ne'er *adv poetic* never

ne'er-do-well *n* **1** an irresponsible or lazy person ▷ *adj* **2** useless; worthless

nefarious (nif-**fair**-ee-uss) *adj literary* evil; wicked ▶ HISTORY Latin *ne* not + *fas* divine law

neg. negative

negate *vb* **-gating, -gated 1** to cause to have no value or effect: *his prejudices largely negate his accomplishments* **2** to deny the existence of ▶ HISTORY Latin *negare*

negation *n* **1** the opposite or absence of something **2** a negative thing or condition **3** a negating

negative *adj* **1** expressing a refusal or denial: *a negative response* **2** lacking positive qualities, such as enthusiasm or optimism **3** *med* indicating absence of the condition for which a test was made **4** *physics* **a** (of an electric charge) having the same electrical charge as an electron **b** (of a body or system) having a negative electric charge; having an excess of electrons **5** same as **minus** (sense 4) **6** measured in a direction opposite to that regarded as positive **7** short for **electronegative 8** of a photographic negative ▷ *n* **9** a statement or act of denial or refusal **10** *photog* a piece of photographic film, exposed and developed, bearing an image with a reversal of tones or colours, from which positive prints are made **11** a word or expression with a negative meaning, such as *not* **12** a quantity less than zero **13 in the negative** indicating denial or refusal > **negatively** *adv*

negative equity *n* the holding of a property of fallen value which is worth less than the amount of mortgage still unpaid

negativism *n* a tendency to be unconstructively critical > **negativist** *n, adj*

neglect *vb* **1** to fail to give due care or attention to: *she had neglected her child* **2** to fail (to do something) through carelessness: *he neglected to greet his guests* **3** to disregard: *he neglected his duty* ▷ *n* **4** lack of due care or attention: *the city had a look of shabbiness and neglect* **5** the state of being neglected ▶ HISTORY Latin *neglegere*

neglectful *adj* not paying enough care or attention: *abusive and neglectful parents*

negligee (**neg**-lee-zhay) *n* a woman's light, usually lace-trimmed dressing gown ▶ HISTORY French

negligence *n* neglect or carelessness > **negligent** *adj* > **negligently** *adv*

negligible *adj* so small or unimportant as to be not worth considering

negotiable *adj* **1** able to be changed or agreed by discussion **2** (of a bill of exchange or promissory note) legally transferable

negotiate *vb* **-ating, -ated 1** to talk with others in order to reach (an agreement) **2** to succeed in passing round or over (a place or a problem) ▶ HISTORY Latin *negotium* business, from *nec* not + *otium* leisure > **negotiation** *n* > **negotiator** *n*

Negro *old-fashioned n, pl* **-groes** *offensive* **1** a member of any of the Black peoples originating in Africa ▷ *adj* **2** of these peoples ▶ HISTORY Latin *niger* black

Negroid *adj* of or relating to the Black peoples originating in Africa

Negro spiritual *n old-fashioned* same as **spiritual** (sense 4)

neigh *n* **1** the high-pitched sound made by a horse ▷ *vb* **2** to make this sound ▶ HISTORY Old English *hnǣgan*

neighbour or US **neighbor** *n* **1** a person who lives near or next to another **2** a person, thing, or country near or next to another ▶ HISTORY Old English *nēah* near + *būr*, *gebūr* dweller

n

neighbourhood or US **neighborhood** n
1 a district where people live **2** the immediate
environment; surroundings **3** the people in a
district **4 in the neighbourhood of** approximately
▷ adj **5** in and for a district: *our neighbourhood cinema*

neighbouring or US **neighboring** adj situated
nearby: *the neighbouring island*

neighbourly or US **neighborly** adj kind,
friendly, and helpful

neither adj **1** not one nor the other (of two):
neither enterprise went well ▷ pron **2** not one nor the
other (of two): *neither completed the full term* ▷ conj
3 a used preceding alternatives joined by nor;
sparing neither strength nor courage **b** same as **nor**
(sense 2) ▷ adv **4** *not standard* same as **either**
(sense 4) ▶ HISTORY Old English *nāwther*

nelson n a wrestling hold in which a wrestler
places his arm or arms under his opponent's arm or
arms from behind and exerts pressure with his
palms on the back of his opponent's neck
▶ HISTORY from a proper name

nematode n a slender unsegmented cylindrical
worm ▶ HISTORY Greek *nēma* thread + *eidos* shape

nemesis (nem-miss-iss) n, pl **-ses** (-seez) a means
of retribution or vengeance ▶ HISTORY Greek
nemein to distribute what is due

neo- combining form new, recent, or a modern form
of: *neoclassicism; neo-Nazi* ▶ HISTORY Greek *neos*
new

neoclassicism n a late 18th- and early
19th-century style of art and architecture, based
on ancient Roman and Greek models
> **neoclassical** adj

neocolonialism n political control wielded by
one country over another through control of its
economy > **neocolonial** adj

neodymium n chem a toxic silvery-white metallic
element of the lanthanide series. Symbol: Nd
▶ HISTORY NEO- + *didymium*, a compound originally
thought to be an element

Neolithic adj of the period that lasted in Europe
from about 4000 to 2400 BC, characterized by
primitive farming and the use of polished stone
and flint tools and weapons ▶ HISTORY NEO-
+ Greek *lithos* stone

neologism (nee-**ol**-a-jiz-zum) n a newly coined
word, or an established word used in a new sense
▶ HISTORY NEO- + Greek *logos* word

neon n **1** chem a colourless odourless rare gas, used
in illuminated signs and lights. Symbol: Ne ▷ adj
2 of or illuminated by neon: *a flashing neon sign*
▶ HISTORY Greek: new

neonatal adj relating to the first few weeks of a
baby's life > **neonate** n

neon light n a glass tube containing neon, which
gives a pink or red glow when a voltage is applied

neophyte n formal **1** a beginner **2** a person newly
converted to a religious faith **3** a novice in a
religious order ▶ HISTORY Greek *neos* new + *phuton*
a plant

NEP history New Economic Policy: an economic
programme in the former Soviet Union from 1921 to

1928 that allowed limited private ownership and
commerce

Nepali (nip-**paw**-lee) or **Nepalese** (nep-pal-**leez**)
adj **1** of Nepal ▷ n **2** (pl **-pali, -palis** or **-palese**) a
person from Nepal **3** the language of Nepal

nephew n a son of one's sister or brother
▶ HISTORY Latin *nepos*

nephritis (nif-**frite**-tiss) n inflammation of the
kidney ▶ HISTORY Greek *nephros* kidney

nepotism (**nep**-a-tiz-zum) n favouritism shown
to relatives and friends by those with power
▶ HISTORY Italian *nepote* nephew

Neptune n **1** the Roman god of the sea **2** the
eighth planet from the sun

neptunium n chem a silvery metallic element
synthesized in the production of plutonium.
Symbol: Np ▶ HISTORY after *Neptune*, the planet

nerd or **nurd** n slang **1** a boring or unpopular
person, esp. one who is obsessed with a particular
subject: *a computer nerd* **2** a stupid and feeble
person ▶ HISTORY origin unknown > **nerdish** or
nurdish adj

nervate adj (of leaves) with veins

nerve n **1** a cordlike bundle of fibres that conducts
impulses between the brain and other parts of the
body **2** bravery and determination **3** informal
impudence: *you've got a nerve!* **4 lose one's nerve**
to lose self-confidence and become afraid about
what one is doing **5 strain every nerve** to make
every effort (to do something) ▷ vb **nerving,
nerved 6** written **nerve oneself** to prepare oneself
(to do something difficult or unpleasant) ▷ See also
nerves ▶ HISTORY Latin *nervus*

nerve cell n same as **neuron**

nerve centre n **1** a place from which a system or
organization is controlled **2** a group of nerve cells
associated with a specific function

nerve gas n a poisonous gas which affects the
nervous system

nerveless adj **1** (of fingers or hands) without
feeling; numb **2** (of a person) fearless

nerve-racking or **nerve-wracking** adj very
distressing or harrowing

nerves pl n informal **1** anxiety or tension: *nerves can
often be the cause of wedding-day hitches* **2** the ability
or inability to remain calm in a difficult situation:
his nerves are in a shocking state **3 get on someone's
nerves** to irritate someone

nervous adj **1** apprehensive or worried **2** excitable;
highly strung **3** of or relating to the nerves: *the
nervous system* > **nervously** adv > **nervousness** n

nervous breakdown n a mental illness in
which the sufferer ceases to function properly, and
experiences symptoms including tiredness,
anxiety, and deep depression

nervous system n the brain, spinal column, and
nerves, which together control thought, feeling,
and movement. See **neuron**

nervy adj **nervier, nerviest** Brit & Austral, informal
excitable or nervous

ness n Brit a headland or cape ▶ HISTORY
Old English *næs*

-ness *n suffix* indicating state, condition, or quality: *greatness; selfishness* ▶ HISTORY Old English *-nes*

nest *n* **1** a place or structure in which birds or other animals lay eggs or give birth to young **2** a cosy or secluded place **3** a set of things of graduated sizes designed to fit together: *a nest of tables* ▷ *vb* **4** to make or inhabit a nest **5** (of a set of objects) to fit one inside another **6** *computers* to position (data) within other data at different ranks or levels ▶ HISTORY Old English

nest egg *n* a fund of money kept in reserve

nestle *vb* **-tling, -tled** **1** to snuggle or cuddle closely **2** to be in a sheltered position ▶ HISTORY Old English *nestlian*

nestling *n* a young bird not yet able to fly

net¹ *n* **1** a very fine fabric made from intersecting strands of material with a space between each strand **2** a piece of net, used to protect or hold things or to trap animals **3** (in certain sports) a strip of net over which the ball or shuttlecock must be hit **4** the goal in soccer or hockey **5** a strategy intended to trap people: *innocent fans were caught in the police net* **6** *maths* the shape that a three-dimensional figure would make if it were laid out flat **7** *informal* short for **internet** ▷ *vb* **netting, netted** **8** to catch (a fish or other animal) in a net ▶ HISTORY Old English *net(t)*

net² *or* **nett** *adj* **1** remaining after all deductions, as for taxes and expenses: *net income* **2** (of weight) excluding the weight of wrapping or container **3** final or conclusive: *the net effect* ▷ *vb* **netting, netted** **4** to yield or earn as a clear profit ▶ HISTORY French: *neat*

netball *n* a team game, usually played by women, in which a ball has to be thrown through a net hanging from a ring at the top of a pole

nether *adj* old-fashioned lower or under: *nether regions* ▶ HISTORY Old English *nithera*, literally: further down

nethermost *adj* lowest

net profit *n* gross profit minus all operating expenses such as wages and overheads

nett *adj, vb* same as **net²**

netting *n* a fabric or structure made of net

nettle *n* **1** a plant with stinging hairs on the leaves **2 grasp the nettle** to attempt something unpleasant with boldness and courage ▶ HISTORY Old English *netele*

nettled *adj* irritated or annoyed

nettle rash *n* a skin condition, usually caused by an allergy, in which itchy red or white raised patches appear

network *n* **1** a system of intersecting lines, roads, veins, etc. **2** an interconnecting group or system: *a network of sympathizers and safe houses* **3** *radio, television* a group of broadcasting stations that all transmit the same programme at the same time **4** *electronics, computers* a system of interconnected components or circuits ▷ *vb* **5** *radio, television* to broadcast (a programme) over a network

neural *adj* of a nerve or the nervous system

neuralgia *n* severe pain along a nerve
> **neuralgic** *adj*

neuritis (nyoor-**rite**-tiss) *n* inflammation of a nerve or nerves, often causing pain and loss of function in the affected part

neurology *n med* the scientific study of the nervous system > **neurological** *adj* > **neurologist** *n*

neuron *or* **neurone** *n* a cell specialized to conduct nerve impulses ▶ HISTORY Greek

neurosis (nyoor-**oh**-siss) *n, pl* **-ses** (-seez) a mental disorder producing hysteria, anxiety, depression, or obsessive behaviour

neurosurgery *n med* the branch of surgery concerned with the nervous system
> **neurosurgeon** *n* > **neurosurgical** *adj*

neurotic *adj* **1** tending to be emotionally unstable **2** afflicted by neurosis ▷ *n* **3** a person afflicted with a neurosis or tending to be emotionally unstable

neurotransmitter *n biochem* a chemical by which a nerve cell communicates with another nerve cell or with a muscle

neuter *adj* **1** *grammar* denoting a gender of nouns which are neither male nor female **2** (of animals and plants) sexually underdeveloped ▷ *n* **3** *grammar* **a** the neuter gender **b** a neuter noun **4** a sexually underdeveloped female insect, such as a worker bee **5** a castrated animal ▷ *vb* **6** to castrate (an animal) ▶ HISTORY Latin *ne* not + *uter* either (of two)

neutral *adj* **1** not taking any side in a war or dispute **2** of or belonging to a neutral party or country **3** not displaying any emotions or opinions **4** (of a colour) not definite or striking **5** *chem* neither acidic nor alkaline **6** *physics* having zero charge or potential ▷ *n* **7** a neutral person or nation **8** the position of the controls of a gearbox that leaves the gears unconnected to the engine ▶ HISTORY Latin *neutralis* of neuter gender
> **neutrality** *n*

neutralize *or* **-ise** *vb* **-izing, -ized** *or* **-ising, -ised** **1** to make electrically or chemically neutral **2** to make ineffective by counteracting **3** to make (a country) neutral by international agreement

neutrino (new-**tree**-no) *n, pl* **-nos** *physics* an elementary particle with no mass or electrical charge ▶ HISTORY Italian diminutive of *neutrone* neutron

neutron *n physics* a neutral elementary particle of about the same mass as a proton ▶ HISTORY from *neutral*, on the model of *electron*

neutron bomb *n* a nuclear weapon designed to kill people and animals while leaving buildings virtually undamaged

never *adv* **1** at no time; not ever **2** certainly not; not at all **3** Also: **well I never!** *spoken* surely not! ▶ HISTORY Old English *næfre*

never-ending *adj* long and boring

nevermore *adv literary* never again

never-never *n* **the never-never** *informal* hire-purchase: *they are buying it on the never-never*

never-never land *n* an imaginary idyllic place

nevertheless *adv* in spite of that 565

new

Depending on which sense of **new** you mean, there are a number of alternatives which you can use to vary your writing and make it more interesting.

DEFINITION 1
- If you would like to describe something that has been recently made, you could try: the company's most **advanced** drugs • a **brand new** car
  - the **current** gossip • **fresh** footprints
  - **ground-breaking** discovery • all the **latest** films
  - most **recent** novel • **ultra-modern** shopping mall • **up-to-date** computers • **up-to-the-minute** information

DEFINITION 2
- If you would like to describe something that has not existed before, you could try: **fresh** challenges
  - a **novel** approach • **original** thinking

DEFINITION 3
- If you would like to describe something that has

been recently discovered, you could try: a **newly discovered** planet • **previously unseen** evidence

DEFINITION 4
- If you would like to describe someone or something that has been recently introduced, you could try: **inexperienced** in this field
  - **newbie** computer user (*informal*) • a **recent** recruit • a **rookie** cop (*informal*)

DEFINITION 5
- If you would like to describe someone or something that is additional, you could try: **added** responsibilities • **extra** resources • **fresh** skills
  - **new-found** ability • **supplementary** tasks

DEFINITION 6
- If you would like to describe something that is unfamiliar, you could try: a completely **different** idea • a **novel** way • an **original** idea • a **strange** country • the **unaccustomed** experience
  - visiting **unfamiliar** places • completely **unknown**

new *adj* **1** recently made, brought into being, or acquired: *a new car* **2** of a kind never before existing; novel: *a new approach to monetary policy* **3** recently discovered: *testing new drugs* **4** recently introduced to or inexperienced in a place or situation: *new to this game* **5** fresh; additional: *you can acquire new skills* **6** unknown: *this is new to me* **7** (of a cycle) beginning again: *a new era* **8** (of crops) harvested early: *new potatoes* **9** changed for the better: *she returned a new woman* ▷ *adv* **10** recently, newly: *new-laid eggs* ▷ See also **news** ▶ HISTORY Old English *nīowe* > **newish** *adj* > **newness** *n* See WORD FOCUS **new**

New Age *n* **1** a philosophy, originating in the late 1980s, characterized by a belief in alternative medicine, astrology, and spiritualism ▷ *adj* **2** of the New Age: *New Age therapies* > **New Ager** *n*

New Australian *n* *Austral* an Australian name for a recent immigrant, esp. one from Europe

newbie *n* *informal* a person new to a job, club, etc.

newborn *adj* recently or just born

new chum *n* *Austral & NZ, archaic informal* a recent British immigrant

newcomer *n* a recent arrival or participant

newel *n* **1** Also called: **newel post** the post at the top or bottom of a flight of stairs that supports the handrail **2** the central pillar of a winding staircase ▶ HISTORY Old French *nouel* knob

newfangled *adj* objectionably or unnecessarily modern ▶ HISTORY Middle English *newefangel* liking new things

new-found *adj* newly or recently discovered

New Jerusalem *n* *Christianity* heaven

New Latin *n* the form of Latin used since the Renaissance, mainly for scientific names

newly *adv* **1** recently **2** again; anew

newlyweds *pl n* a recently married couple

new maths *n* *Brit* an approach to mathematics in which basic set theory is introduced at an elementary level

new moon *n* the moon when it appears as a narrow crescent at the beginning of its cycle

news *n* **1** important or interesting new happenings **2** information about such events, reported in the mass media **3** **the news** a television or radio programme presenting such information **4** interesting or important new information: *it's news to me* **5** a person or thing widely reported in the mass media: *reggae is suddenly big news again*

news agency *n* an organization that collects news reports and sells them to newspapers, magazines, and TV and radio stations

newsagent *n* *Brit* a shopkeeper who sells newspapers and magazines

newscast *n* a radio or television broadcast of the news > **newscaster** *n*

news conference *n* same as **press conference**

newsflash *n* a brief item of important news, which interrupts a radio or television programme

newsgroup *n* *computers* a forum where subscribers exchange information about a specific subject by e-mail

newsletter *n* a periodical bulletin issued to members of a group

newspaper *n* a weekly or daily publication consisting of folded sheets and containing news, features, and advertisements

newsprint *n* an inexpensive wood-pulp paper used for newspapers

newsreader *n* a news announcer on radio or television

newsreel *n* a short film with a commentary which presents current events

newsroom *n* a room in a newspaper office or radio or television station where news is received and prepared for publication or broadcasting

nice

WORD FOCUS

When you are writing or talking and you are going to use the word **nice**, try to think of a more descriptive and interesting word instead. Here are some ideas for words and phrases that you might use to describe different aspects of people and things.

DEFINITION 1

- If you are describing someone's appearance, you could try: an **attractive** lady • looking very **beautiful** • a very **cute** baby • He was **dishy**. • Her son is **good-looking**. • She's really **gorgeous**. • a very **handsome** young man • a **lovely** woman • You look very **pretty**.
- If you are describing an object, place, or view, you could try: **beautiful** little antique shop • **charming** little fishing village • **delightful** place • **lovely** ornamental garden • a **pretty** room
- If you are describing an item of clothing, you could try: **chic** designer frock • very **elegant** dress • a **fetching** outfit • a **smart** navy-blue suit • such **stylish** clothes

- If you are describing an event or occasion, you could try: very **agreeable** • a **delightful** time • much more **enjoyable** • such a **fantastic** party • a **lovely** holiday • a very **pleasant** experience • a **pleasurable** sensation
- If you are describing someone's personality, you could try: very **amiable** man • very **considerate** towards his sisters • very **friendly** to strangers • unfailingly **good-natured** • **kind** to everyone • a **kindly** old man • an immensely **likeable** chap • a very **thoughtful** gesture
- If you are describing food or drink, you could try: **appetizing** smell • some **delectable** raspberries • **delicious** food • **luscious** peaches • **mouth-watering** dessert • serving **tasty** dishes
- If you are describing the weather, you could try: a **beautiful** morning • The weather is **fine**. • a **glorious** day
- If you are describing a room, flat, or house, you could try: a **comfortable** home • a **cosy** house • a **homely** atmosphere • a very **relaxing** room

---

New Style *n* the present method of reckoning dates using the Gregorian calendar

newsworthy *adj* sufficiently interesting to be reported as news

newsy *adj* **newsier, newsiest** (of a letter) full of news

newt *n* a small amphibious creature with a long slender body and tail and short legs

■ **WORD HISTORY**

■ The newt owes its name to a mistake by speakers
■ of English round about the 15th century, who
■ wrongly understood 'an ewt' (from Old English
■ *eveta* or *efeta*) to be 'a newt'. In some English
■ dialects, this mistake did not happen and newts
■ are called 'efts'. Interestingly, the opposite
■ process can be seen to have taken place in the
■ name of the adder: 'an adder' comes from 'a
■ nadder', from Old English *nædre*, meaning 'snake'.

New Testament *n* the second part of the Christian Bible, dealing with the life and teachings of Christ and his followers

newton *n* the SI unit of force that gives an acceleration of 1 metre per second per second to a mass of 1 kilogram ▶ HISTORY after Sir Isaac *Newton*, scientist

new town *n* (in Britain) a town planned as a complete unit and built with government sponsorship

New World *n* **the New World** the western hemisphere of the world, esp. the Americas

New Year *n* the first day or days of the year in various calendars, usually a holiday

New Zealander *n* a person from New Zealand

next *adj* **1** immediately following: *the next generation* **2** immediately adjoining: *in the next room* **3** closest to in degree: *the next-best thing* ▷ *adv* **4** at a time immediately to follow: *the patient to be examined next* **5 next to a** adjacent to: *the house next to ours* **b** following in degree: *next to my wife, I love you most* **c** almost: *the evidence is next to totally useless*
▶ HISTORY Old English *nēhst*, superlative of *nēah* near

next door *adj, adv* in, at, or to the adjacent house or flat

next of kin *n* a person's closest relative or relatives

nexus *n, pl* **nexus 1** a connection or link **2** a connected group or series ▶ HISTORY Latin, from *nectere* to bind

NF Newfoundland

ngati (nah-tee) *n, pl* **ngati** NZ (occurring as part of the tribe name) a tribe or clan ▶ HISTORY Māori

NH New Hampshire

NHS (in Britain) National Health Service

Ni *chem* nickel

NI 1 (in Britain) National Insurance **2** Northern Ireland

niacin *n* a vitamin of the B complex that occurs in milk, liver, and yeast. Also called: **nicotinic acid**
▶ HISTORY from *ni(cotinic) ac(id)* + *-in* denoting a chemical substance

nib *n* the writing point of a pen ▶ HISTORY origin unknown

nibble *vb* **-bling, -bled 1** to take little bites (of) **2** to bite gently: *she nibbled at her lower lip* ▷ *n* **3** a little bite **4** a light hurried meal ▶ HISTORY related to Low German *nibbelen*

nibs *n* **his** *or* **her nibs** *slang* a mock title used of an important or self-important person ▶ HISTORY origin unknown

NICAM near-instantaneous companding system: a technique for coding audio signals into digital form

nice *adj* **1** pleasant **2** kind: *it's really nice of you to worry about me* **3** good or satisfactory: *a nice clean*

567

operation **4** subtle: *a nice distinction* ▶ HISTORY Old French: simple, silly > **nicely** *adv* > **niceness** *n*
See WORD FOCUS on page 567

nicety *n, pl* **-ties 1** a subtle point: *the niceties of our arguments* **2** a refinement or delicacy: *social niceties* **3 to a nicety** precisely

niche (**neesh**) *n* **1** a recess in a wall for a statue or ornament **2** a position exactly suitable for the person occupying it: *perhaps I will find my niche in a desk job* ▷ *adj* **3** of or aimed at a specialist group or market: *niche retailing ventures* ▶ HISTORY Old French *nichier* to nest

nick *vb* **1** to make a small cut in **2** *chiefly Brit, slang* to steal **3** *chiefly Brit, slang* to arrest ▷ *n* **4** a small notch or cut **5** *slang* a prison or police station **6** *informal* condition: *in good nick* **7 in the nick of time** just in time ▶ HISTORY perhaps Middle English *nocke* nock

nickel *n* **1** *chem* a silvery-white metallic element that is often used in alloys. Symbol: Ni **2** a US or Canadian coin worth five cents ▶ HISTORY German *Kupfernickel* nickel ore, literally: copper demon; it was mistakenly thought to contain copper

nickelodeon *n US* an early type of jukebox ▶ HISTORY *nickel* + (*mel*)*odeon*

nickel silver *n* an alloy containing copper, zinc, and nickel

nicker *n, pl* **nicker** *Brit, slang* a pound sterling ▶ HISTORY origin unknown

nickname *n* **1** a familiar, pet, or derisory name given to a person or place ▷ *vb* **-naming, -named** **2** to call (a person or place) by a nickname: *Gaius Caesar Augustus Germanicus, nicknamed Caligula* ▶ HISTORY mistaken division of *an ekename* an additional name

nickpoint *n* a variant spelling (esp. US) of **knickpoint**

nicotine *n* a poisonous alkaloid found in tobacco ▶ HISTORY after J. Nicot, who introduced tobacco into France > **nicotinic** *adj*

nictitating membrane *n* (in reptiles, birds, and some mammals) a thin fold of skin under the eyelid that can be drawn across the eye

niece *n* a daughter of one's sister or brother ▶ HISTORY Latin *neptis* granddaughter

nifty *adj* **-tier, -tiest** *informal* neat or smart ▶ HISTORY origin unknown

Nigerian *adj* **1** of Nigeria ▷ *n* **2** a person from Nigeria

niggard *n* a stingy person ▶ HISTORY perhaps from Old Norse

niggardly *adj* not generous: *it pays its staff on a niggardly scale* > **niggardliness** *n*

nigger *n* offensive a Black person ▶ HISTORY Spanish *negro*

niggle *vb* **-gling, -gled 1** to worry slightly **2** to find fault continually ▷ *n* **3** a small worry or doubt **4** a trivial objection or complaint ▶ HISTORY Scandinavian > **niggling** *adj*

nigh *adj, adv, prep archaic, poetic* near ▶ HISTORY Old English *nēah, nēh*

night *n* **1** the period of darkness that occurs each

24 hours, between sunset and sunrise **2** the period between sunset and bedtime; evening **3** the time between bedtime and morning **4** nightfall or dusk **5** an evening designated for a specific activity: *opening night* **6 make a night of it** to celebrate the whole evening. *Related adjective:* **nocturnal** *adj* **7** of, occurring, or working at night: *the night sky* ▶ HISTORY Old English *niht*

nightcap *n* **1** a drink taken just before bedtime **2** a soft cap formerly worn in bed

nightclub *n* a place of entertainment open until late at night, offering drink and dancing

nightdress *n* a loose dress worn in bed by women or girls

nightfall *n* the approach of darkness; dusk

nightgown *n* same as **nightdress**

nightie *n* *informal* short for **nightdress**

nightingale *n* a small bird with a musical song, usually heard at night ▶ HISTORY Old English *nihtegale*, literally: night singer

nightjar *n* a nocturnal bird with a harsh cry ▶ HISTORY *night* + JAR² (so called from its harsh cry)

nightlife *n* the entertainment and social activities available at night in a town or city

night-light *n* a dim light left on overnight

nightly *adj* **1** happening each night ▷ *adv* **2** each night

nightmare *n* **1** a terrifying or deeply distressing dream **2** a terrifying or unpleasant experience **3** a thing that is feared: *wheels and loose straps are a baggage handler's nightmare* > **nightmarish** *adj*

■ **WORD HISTORY**
■ 'Nightmare' comes from *night* and Old English
■ *mare*, meaning 'evil spirit'.

night safe *n* a safe built into the outside wall of a bank, in which customers can deposit money when the bank is closed

night school *n* an educational institution that holds classes in the evening

nightshade *n* a plant which produces poisonous berries with bell-shaped flowers ▶ HISTORY Old English *nihtscada*

nightshirt *n* a long loose shirtlike garment worn in bed

night-time *n* the time from sunset to sunrise

nihilism (**nye**-ill-liz-zum) *n* a total rejection of all established authority and institutions ▶ HISTORY Latin *nihil* nothing > **nihilist** *n, adj* > **nihilistic** *adj*

-nik *suffix* forming nouns indicating a person associated with a particular state or quality: *refusenik* ▶ HISTORY Russian

nil *n* nothing: esp. as a score in games ▶ HISTORY Latin

nimble *adj* **1** agile and quick in movement **2** mentally alert or acute ▶ HISTORY Old English *nǣmel* quick to grasp + *numol* quick at seizing > **nimbly** *adv*

nimbostratus (nim-boh-**stray**-tuss) *n, pl* **-ti** (-tie) *meteorol* a dark-coloured rain-bearing stratus cloud

nimbus *n, pl* **-bi** or **-buses 1** a dark grey rain cloud **2** a halo ▶ HISTORY Latin: cloud

nincompoop n informal a stupid person ▶ HISTORY origin unknown

nine n 1 the cardinal number that is the sum of one and eight 2 a numeral, 9 or IX, representing this number 3 something representing or consisting of nine units 4 **dressed up to the nines** informal elaborately dressed ▷ adj 5 amounting to nine: nine men ▶ HISTORY Old English nigon > **ninth** adj, n

ninefold adj 1 having nine times as many or as much 2 having nine parts ▷ adv 3 by nine times as much or as many

nine night n a Jamaican funerary tradition in which family and friends gather in the deceased person's home for nine consecutive nights until the eve of the burial, celebrating the person's life with food, drink, music, and dancing

ninepins n the game of skittles

nineteen n 1 the cardinal number that is the sum of ten and nine 2 a numeral, 19 or XIX, representing this number 3 something representing or consisting of nineteen units 4 **talk nineteen to the dozen** to talk very fast ▷ adj 5 amounting to nineteen: nineteen years > **nineteenth** adj, n

nineteenth hole n golf, slang the bar in a golf clubhouse ▶ HISTORY from its being the next objective after a standard 18-hole round

ninety n, pl **-ties** 1 the cardinal number that is the product of ten and nine 2 a numeral, 90 or XC, representing this number 3 something representing or consisting of ninety units 4 **nineties** the numbers 90 to 99, esp. when used to refer to a year of someone's life or of a century ▷ adj 5 amounting to ninety: ninety degrees > **ninetieth** adj, n

niobium n chem a white superconductive metallic element. Symbol: Nb ▶ HISTORY Latin after Niobe (daughter of Tantalus); because it occurred in tantalite

nip¹ vb **nipping, nipped** 1 informal to hurry 2 to pinch or squeeze 3 to bite lightly 4 (of the cold) to affect (someone) with a stinging sensation 5 to check the growth of (something): a trite script nips all hope in the bud ▷ n 6 a pinch or light bite 7 sharp coldness: a nip in the air ▶ HISTORY perhaps from Old Norse

nip² n a small drink of spirits ▶ HISTORY from nipperkin a vessel holding a half-pint or less

nipper n Brit, Austral & NZ, informal a small child

nipple n 1 the small projection in the centre of each breast, which in females contains the outlet of the milk ducts 2 a small projection through which oil or grease can be put into a machine or component ▶ HISTORY perhaps from neb peak, tip

nippy adj **-pier, -piest** 1 (of weather) frosty or chilly 2 informal quick or nimble 3 (of a motor vehicle) small and relatively powerful

nirvana (near-**vah**-na) n Buddhism, Hinduism the ultimate state of spiritual enlightenment and bliss attained by extinction of all desires and individual existence ▶ HISTORY Sanskrit: extinction

nisi (nye-sigh) adj See **decree nisi**

Nissen hut n chiefly Brit a tunnel-shaped military shelter made of corrugated steel ▶ HISTORY after Lt Col. Peter Nissen, mining engineer

nit¹ n the egg or larva of a louse ▶ HISTORY Old English hnitu

nit² n informal short for **nitwit**

nit-picking informal n 1 a concern with insignificant details, usually with the intention of finding fault ▷ adj 2 showing such concern

nitrate chem n 1 a salt or ester of nitric acid 2 a fertilizer containing nitrate salts ▷ vb **-trating, -trated** 3 to treat with nitric acid or a nitrate 4 to convert or be converted into a nitrate > **nitration** n

nitre or US **niter** n chem same as **potassium nitrate** ▶ HISTORY Latin nitrum

nitric adj chem of or containing nitrogen

nitric acid n chem a colourless corrosive liquid widely used in industry

nitride n chem a compound of nitrogen with a more electropositive element

nitrify vb **-fies, -fying, -fied** chem 1 to treat (a substance) or cause (a substance) to react with nitrogen 2 to treat (soil) with nitrates 3 to convert (ammonium compounds) into nitrates by oxidation > **nitrification** n

nitrite n chem a salt or ester of nitrous acid

nitro- or before a vowel **nitr-** combining form 1 indicating that a chemical compound contains the univalent group, $-NO_2$: nitrobenzene 2 indicating a chemical compound which is a nitrate ester: nitrocellulose ▶ HISTORY Greek nitron nitre

nitrogen (**nite**-roj-jen) n chem a colourless odourless gas that forms four-fifths of the air and is an essential part of all animal and plant life. Symbol: N > **nitrogenous** adj

nitrogen cycle n the natural cycle by which nitrates in the soil, derived from dead organic matter, are absorbed by plants and reduced to nitrates again when the plants and the animals feeding on them die and decay

nitrogen fixation n the conversion of atmospheric nitrogen into nitrogen compounds by soil bacteria

nitroglycerine or **nitroglycerin** n chem a thick pale yellow explosive liquid made from glycerol and nitric and sulphuric acids

nitrous adj chem derived from or containing nitrogen in a low valency state

nitrous acid n chem a weak acid known only in solution and in the form of nitrite salts

nitrous oxide n chem a colourless gas used as an anaesthetic

nitty-gritty n **the nitty-gritty** informal the basic facts of a matter or situation ▶ HISTORY perhaps rhyming compound from grit

nitwit n informal a stupid person ▶ HISTORY perhaps NIT¹ + WIT¹

NJ New Jersey

nkosi (ing-**koss**-ee) n S African a term of address to a superior; master; chief ▶ HISTORY Nguni

(language group of southern Africa) *inkosi* chief
NM New Mexico

no¹ *interj* **1** used to express denial, disagreement, or refusal ▷ *n, pl* **noes** *or* **nos 2** an answer or vote of *no* **3** a person who answers or votes *no* ▶ HISTORY Old English *nā*

no² *adj* **1** not any, not a, or not one: *I have no money; no comment* **2** not at all: *he's no exception* **3** not: *no taller than a child* **4 no way!** an expression of emphatic refusal or denial ▶ HISTORY Old English *nān* none

No³ *or* **Noh** *n, pl* **No** *or* **Noh** the stylized classical drama of Japan, using music and dancing ▶ HISTORY Japanese *nō* talent

No² *chem* nobelium

No. *or* **no.** *pl* **Nos.** *or* **nos.** number ▶ HISTORY French *numéro*

n.o. *cricket* not out

nob *n chiefly Brit, slang* a person of wealth or social distinction ▶ HISTORY origin unknown

no-ball *n cricket* an improperly bowled ball, for which the batting side scores a run. Abbrev: **nb**

nobble *vb* **-bling, -bled** *Brit & Austral, slang* **1** to attract the attention of (someone) in order to talk to him or her **2** to bribe or threaten **3** to disable (a racehorse) to stop it from winning **4** to steal ▶ HISTORY *a nobbler*, a false division of *an hobbler* one who hobbles horses

nobelium *n chem* a radioactive element produced artificially from curium. Symbol: No ▶ HISTORY after *Nobel* Institute, Stockholm, where it was discovered

Nobel prize (no-**bell**) *n* a prize for outstanding contributions to chemistry, physics, physiology and medicine, literature, economics, and peace that may be awarded annually ▶ HISTORY after Alfred *Nobel*, chemist and philanthropist

nobility *n* **1** the quality of being noble; dignity **2** the class of people who hold titles and high social rank

noble *adj* **1** having or showing high moral qualities: *a noble cause* **2** belonging to a class of people who hold titles and high social rank **3** impressive and magnificent: *a noble beast* **4** *chem* (of certain metals) resisting oxidation ▷ *n* **5** a person who holds a title and high social rank ▶ HISTORY Latin *nobilis*, originally capable of being known, hence well-known > **nobly** *adv*

noble gas *n* any of the unreactive gases helium, neon, argon, krypton, xenon, and radon

nobleman *or fem* **noblewoman** *n, pl* **-men** *or* **-women** a person of noble rank

noblesse oblige (no-**bless** oh-**bleezh**) *n often ironic* the supposed obligation of the nobility to be honourable and generous ▶ HISTORY French, literally: nobility obliges

nobody *pron* **1** no person; no-one ▷ *n, pl* **-bodies 2** a person of no importance

nock *n* **1** a notch on an arrow that fits on the bowstring **2** a groove at either end of a bow that holds the bowstring ▶ HISTORY related to Swedish *nock* tip

no-claims bonus *or* **no-claim bonus** *n* a reduction in the cost of an insurance policy made if no claims have been made in a specified period

nocturnal *adj* **1** of the night **2** (of animals) active at night ▶ HISTORY Latin *nox* night

nocturne *n* a short dreamy piece of music

nod *vb* **nodding, nodded 1** to lower and raise (one's head) briefly, to express agreement or greeting **2** to express by nodding: *he nodded his approval* **3** to sway or bend forwards and back **4** to let one's head fall forward with sleep **5 nodding acquaintance** a slight knowledge (of a subject or person) ▷ *n* **6** a quick down-and-up movement of the head, in agreement **7 land of Nod** an imaginary land of sleep ▶ HISTORY origin unknown

noddle *n chiefly Brit, informal* the head or brains ▶ HISTORY origin unknown

noddy *n, pl* **-dies 1** a tropical tern with a dark plumage **2** a fool ▶ HISTORY perhaps from obsolete *noddy* foolish, drowsy

node *n* **1** *bot* the point on a plant stem from which the leaves grow **2** *maths* a point at which a curve crosses itself **3** a knot or knob **4** *physics* a point in a vibrating body at which there is practically no vibration **5** *anat* any natural bulge or swelling: *lymph node* **6** *astron* either of the two points at which the orbit of a body intersects the path of the sun or the orbit of another body ▶ HISTORY Latin *nodus* knot > **nodal** *adj*

nod off *vb informal* to fall asleep

nodule *n* **1** a small rounded lump or node **2** a rounded mineral growth on the root of a plant such as clover ▶ HISTORY Latin *nodulus* > **nodular** *adj*

Noel *n* same as **Christmas** ▶ HISTORY French, from Latin *natalis* a birthday

nog *n* an alcoholic drink containing beaten egg ▶ HISTORY origin unknown

noggin *n* **1** *informal* the head **2** a small quantity of spirits ▶ HISTORY origin unknown

no-go area *n* a district that is barricaded off so that the police or army can enter only by force

noise *n* **1** a sound, usually a loud or disturbing one **2** loud shouting; din **3** an undesired electrical disturbance in a signal **4** unwanted or irrelevant elements in a visual image: *removing noise from pictures* **5 noises** conventional utterances conveying a reaction: *he made the appropriate noises* ▷ *vb* **noising, noised 6 be noised abroad** (of news or gossip) to be spread ▶ HISTORY Latin *nausea* seasickness

noiseless *adj* making little or no sound > **noiselessly** *adv*

noise pollution *n* annoying or harmful noise in an environment

noisome *adj formal* **1** (of smells) offensive **2** extremely unpleasant ▶ HISTORY obsolete *noy*, variant of *annoy*

noisy *adj* **noisier, noisiest 1** making a lot of noise **2** (of a place) full of noise > **noisily** *adv*

nomad *n* **1** a member of a tribe who move

from place to place to find pasture and food
2 a wanderer ▶ HISTORY Greek *nomas* wandering
for pasture > **nomadic** *adj*

no-man's-land *n* land between boundaries,
esp. an unoccupied zone between opposing
forces

nom de plume *n, pl* **noms de plume** same as
pen name ▶ HISTORY French

nomenclature (no-**men**-klatch-er) *n formal* the
system of names used in a particular subject
▶ HISTORY Latin *nomenclatura* list of names

nominal *adj* **1** in name only: *nominal independence*
2 very small in comparison with real worth: *a
nominal amount of aid* ▶ HISTORY Latin *nomen* name
> **nominally** *adv*

nominalism *n* the philosophical theory that a
general word, such as *dog*, is merely a name and
does not denote a real object > **nominalist** *n*

nominalization *or* **-lisation** *n grammar* the
use of an abstract noun rather than the verb or
adjective from which it derives, as in *he had a shave*
rather than *he shaved*; also used to refer to the noun
itself

nominal value *n* same as **par value**

nominate *vb* **-nating, -nated** **1** to propose
(someone) as a candidate **2** to appoint (someone)
to an office or position ▶ HISTORY Latin *nomen*
name > **nomination** *n*

nominative *or* **nominative case** *n grammar* a
grammatical case in some languages that
identifies the subject of a verb ▶ HISTORY Latin
nominativus belonging to naming

nominee *n* a person who is nominated to an office
or as a candidate

non- *prefix* **1** indicating negation: *nonexistent*
2 indicating refusal or failure: *noncooperation*
3 indicating exclusion from a specified class:
nonfiction **4** indicating lack or absence: *nonevent*
▶ HISTORY Latin *non* not

nonage *n* **1** *law* the state of being under full legal
age for various actions **2** a period of immaturity

nonagenarian *n* a person who is from 90 to 99
years old ▶ HISTORY Latin *nonaginta* ninety

nonaggression *n* the policy of not attacking .
other countries

nonagon *n geom* a figure with nine sides
> **nonagonal** *adj*

nonalcoholic *adj* containing no alcohol

nonaligned *adj* (of a country) not part of a major
alliance or power bloc > **nonalignment** *n*

nonbelligerent *adj* (of a country) not taking
part in a war

nonce *n* **for the nonce** for the present ▶ HISTORY
a mistaken division of *for then anes*, for the once

nonce word *n* a word coined for a single
occasion

nonchalant (**non**-shall-ant) *adj* casually
unconcerned or indifferent ▶ HISTORY French,
from *nonchaloir* to lack warmth > **nonchalance** *n*
> **nonchalantly** *adv*

non-com *n* short for **noncommissioned officer**

noncombatant *n* a member of the armed forces

whose duties do not include fighting, such as a
chaplain or surgeon

noncommissioned officer *n* (in the armed
forces) a person who is appointed as a subordinate
officer, from the lower ranks, rather than by a
commission

noncommittal *adj* not committing oneself to
any particular opinion

non compos mentis *adj* of unsound mind
▶ HISTORY Latin: not in control of one's mind

nonconductor *n* a substance that is a poor
conductor of heat, electricity, or sound

nonconformist *n* **1** a person who does not
conform to generally accepted patterns of
behaviour or thought ▷ *adj* **2** (of behaviour or
ideas) not conforming to accepted patterns
> **nonconformity** *n*

Nonconformist *n* **1** a member of a Protestant
group separated from the Church of England
▷ *adj* **2** of or relating to Nonconformists

noncontributory *adj Brit* denoting a pension
scheme for employees, the premiums of which are
paid entirely by the employer

non-cooperation *n* the refusal to do more than
is legally or contractually required of one

nondescript *adj* lacking outstanding features
▶ HISTORY NON- + Latin *descriptus*, past participle of
describere to copy

none *pron* **1** not any: *none of the men was represented
by a lawyer; none of it meant anything to him*
2 no-one; nobody: *none could deny it* **3** **none the** in
no degree: *her parents were none the wiser* ▶ HISTORY
Old English *nān*, literally: not one

nonentity (non-**enn**-tit-tee) *n, pl* **-ties** an
insignificant person or thing

nonessential *adj* not absolutely necessary

nonetheless *adv* despite that; however

nonevent *n* a disappointing or insignificant
occurrence that was expected to be important

nonexistent *adj* not existing in a particular place
> **nonexistence** *n*

nonferrous *adj* **1** denoting a metal other than iron
2 not containing iron

nonfiction *n* writing that deals with facts or real
events

nonflammable *adj* not easily set on fire

nonintervention *n* refusal to intervene in the
affairs of others

noniron *adj* not requiring ironing

non-magnetic material *n physics* any material
that cannot be magnetized

nonmetal *n chem* a chemical element that forms
acidic oxides and is a poor conductor of heat and
electricity > **nonmetallic** *adj*

non-nuclear *adj* not involving or using nuclear
power or weapons

nonpareil (non-par-**rail**) *n* a person or thing that
is unsurpassed ▶ HISTORY French, from
NON- + *pareil* similar

nonpartisan *adj* not supporting any single
political party

nonpayment *n* failure to pay money owed

571

nonplussed *or US* **nonplused** *adj* perplexed
▶ HISTORY Latin *non plus* no further

non-profit-making *adj* not intended to make a profit

nonproliferation *n* limitation of the production or spread of something such as nuclear or chemical weapons

non-renewable resources *pl n environmental science* resources that cannot be replaced or take millions of years to form, such as iron, copper, oil, and coal. Compare **renewable resources**

nonrepresentational *adj art* same as **abstract**

nonresident *n* a person who does not live in a particular country or place

nonsectarian *adj* not confined to any specific subdivision of a religious group

nonsense *n* **1** something that has or makes no sense **2** unintelligible language **3** foolish behaviour > **nonsensical** *adj*

non sequitur (sek-wit-tur) *n* a statement having little or no relation to what preceded it ▶ HISTORY Latin: it does not follow

nonsmoker *n* **1** a person who does not smoke **2** a train carriage in which smoking is forbidden

nonsmoking *or* **no-smoking** *adj* denoting an area in which smoking is forbidden

nonstandard *adj* denoting words, expressions, or pronunciations that are not regarded as correct by educated native speakers of a language

nonstarter *n* a person or an idea that has little chance of success

nonstick *adj* (of cooking utensils) coated with a substance that food will not stick to when cooked

nonstop *adj, adv* without a stop: *two weeks of nonstop rain; most days his phone rings nonstop*

nontoxic *adj* not poisonous

nonunion *adj* **1** (of a company) not employing trade union members: *a nonunion shop* **2** (of a person) not belonging to a trade union

nonverbal *adj* not spoken: *nonverbal communication like gestures and facial expressions*

nonviolent *adj* using peaceful methods to bring about change > **nonviolence** *n*

nonvoter *n* **1** a person who does not vote **2** a person not eligible to vote

nonvoting *adj finance* (of shares in a company) not entitling the holder to vote at company meetings

non-White *adj* **1** belonging to a race of people not European in origin ▷ *n* **2** a member of one of these races

noodles *pl n* ribbon-like strips of pasta ▶ HISTORY German *Nudeln*

nook *n* **1** a corner or recess **2** a secluded or sheltered place ▶ HISTORY origin unknown

noon *n* the middle of the day; 12 o'clock ▶ HISTORY Latin *nona (hora)* ninth hour (originally 3 p.m., the ninth hour from sunrise)

noonday *adj* happening or appearing at noon

no-one *or* **no one** *pron* no person; nobody

572 **noose** *n* a loop in the end of a rope, tied with a

slipknot, such as one used to hang people ▶ HISTORY Latin *nodus* knot

nor *conj* **1** used to join alternatives, the first of which is preceded by *neither*; and not: *neither willing nor able* **2** and not … either: *he had not arrived yet, nor had any of the models* ▶ HISTORY contraction of Old English *nōther*

nordic *adj skiing* of competitions in cross-country racing and ski-jumping

Nordic *adj* of Scandinavia or its typically tall, blond, and blue-eyed people ▶ HISTORY French *nordique* of the north

norm *n* a standard that is required or regarded as normal ▶ HISTORY Latin *norma* carpenter's square

normal *adj* **1** usual, regular, or typical: *the study of normal behaviour* **2** free from mental or physical disorder **3** *geom* same as **perpendicular** (sense 1) ▷ *n* **4** the usual, regular, or typical state, degree, or form **5** *geom* a perpendicular line or plane ▶ HISTORY Latin *normalis* conforming to the carpenter's square > **normality** *or esp US* **normalcy** *n*

normal fault *n geol* a fault in which rock on one side of the fault drops in relation to the other. Compare **reverse fault**

normalize *or* **-ise** *vb* **-izing, -ized** *or* **-ising, -ised** **1** to make or become normal **2** to bring into conformity with a standard

normally *adv* **1** as a rule; usually **2** in a normal manner

Norman *n* **1** a person from Normandy in N France, esp. one of the people who conquered England in 1066 **2** same as **Norman French** ▷ *adj* **3** of the Normans or their dialect of French **4** of Normandy **5** of a style of architecture used in Britain from the Norman Conquest until the 12th century, with rounded arches and massive masonry walls

Norman French *n* the medieval Norman and English dialect of Old French

normative *adj* of or establishing a norm or standard: *a normative model*

Norn *n Norse myth* any of the three virgin goddesses of fate ▶ HISTORY Old Norse

Norse *adj* **1** of ancient and medieval Scandinavia **2** of Norway ▷ *n* **3 a** the N group of Germanic languages spoken in Scandinavia **b** any one of these languages, esp. in their ancient or medieval forms

Norseman *n, pl* **-men** same as **Viking**

north *n* **1** one of the four cardinal points of the compass, at 0° or 360° **2** the direction along a meridian towards the North Pole **3** the direction in which a compass needle points; magnetic north **4 the north** any area lying in or towards the north ▷ *adj* **5** in or towards the north **6** (esp. of the wind) from the north ▷ *adv* **7** in, to, or towards the north ▶ HISTORY Old English

North *n* **1 the North a** the northern part of England, generally regarded as reaching the southern boundaries of Yorkshire, Derbyshire, and Cheshire **b** (in the US) the states north of the Mason-Dixon Line that were known as the Free States during the

Civil War **c** the economically and technically advanced countries of the world ▷ *adj* **2** of or denoting the northern part of a country or area

northeast *n* **1** the direction midway between north and east **2 the northeast** any area lying in or towards the northeast ▷ *adj also* **northeastern 3** (sometimes cap) of or denoting that part of a country or area which lies in the northeast **4** situated in, moving towards, or facing the northeast **5** (esp. of the wind) from the northeast ▷ *adv* **6** in, to, or towards the northeast > **northeasterly** *adj, adv, n*

northeaster *n* a strong wind or storm from the northeast

northerly *adj* **1** of or in the north ▷ *adv, adj* **2** towards the north **3** from the north

northern *adj* **1** situated in or towards the north **2** facing or moving towards the north **3** (sometimes cap) of or characteristic of the north or North > **northernmost** *adj*

northern hemisphere *n geog* that half of the globe lying north of the equator

northern lights *pl n* same as **aurora borealis**

northing *n geog* a latitudinal grid line. Compare **easting**

Northman *n, pl* **-men** same as **Viking**

North Pole *n* the northernmost point on the earth's axis, at a latitude of 90°N, which has very low temperatures

North Star *n* **the North Star** same as **Pole Star**

northward *adj, adv also* **northwards 1** towards the north ▷ *n* **2** the northward part or direction

northwest *n* **1** the direction midway between north and west **2 the northwest** any area lying in or towards the northwest ▷ *adj also* **northwestern 3** (sometimes cap) of or denoting that part of a country or area which lies in the northwest **4** situated in, moving towards, or facing the northwest **5** (esp. of the wind) from the northwest ▷ *adv* **6** in, to, or towards the northwest > **northwesterly** *adj, adv, n*

northwester *n* a strong wind or storm from the northwest

Norwegian *adj* **1** of Norway ▷ *n* **2** a person from Norway **3** the language of Norway

nor'wester *n NZ* a hot dry wind

nose *n* **1** the organ situated above the mouth, used for smelling and breathing **2** the sense of smell **3** the front part of a vehicle **4** the distinctive smell of a wine or perfume **5** instinctive skill in finding something: *he had a nose for media events* **6 get up someone's nose** *informal* to annoy someone **7 keep one's nose clean** to stay out of trouble **8 look down one's nose at** *informal* to be haughty towards **9 pay through the nose** *informal* to pay a high price **10 put someone's nose out of joint** *informal* to make someone envious by doing what he or she would have liked to do or had expected to do **11 rub someone's nose in it** *informal* to remind someone unkindly of a failing or error **12 turn up one's nose at** *informal* to show contempt for **13 win by a nose** to win by a narrow margin ▷ *vb*

nosing, nosed 14 to move forward slowly and carefully **15** to pry or snoop **16 nose out** to discover by searching or prying ▶ HISTORY Old English *nosu*

nosebag *n* a bag containing feed, fastened around the head of a horse

nosebleed *n* bleeding from the nose

nose cone *n* the cone-shaped front section of a missile or spacecraft

nose dive *n* **1** (of an aircraft) a sudden plunge with the nose pointing downwards **2** *informal* a sudden drop: *when we fail our self-confidence takes a nose dive* ▷ *vb* **nose-dive, -diving, -dived 3** to take a nose dive

nosegay *n* a small bunch of flowers ▶ HISTORY *nose* + *gay* (archaic) toy

nosey *or* **nosy** *adj* **nosier, nosiest** *informal* prying or inquisitive > **nosiness** *n*

nosey parker *n Brit & S African, informal* a prying person ▶ HISTORY arbitrary use of surname *Parker*

nosh *Brit, Austral & NZ, slang n* **1** food ▷ *vb* **2** to eat ▶ HISTORY Yiddish

nosh-up *n Brit, slang* a large meal

nostalgia *n* **1** a sentimental yearning for the past **2** homesickness ▶ HISTORY Greek *nostos* a return home + *algos* pain > **nostalgic** *adj* > **nostalgically** *adv*

nostril *n* either of the two openings at the end of the nose ▶ HISTORY Old English *nosu* nose + *thyrel* hole

nostrum *n* **1** a quack medicine **2** a favourite remedy ▶ HISTORY Latin: our own (make)

nosy *adj* **nosier, nosiest** same as **nosey**

not *adv* **1** used to negate the sentence, phrase, or word that it modifies: *I will not stand for it* **2 not that** which is not to say that: *not that I've ever heard him complain* ▶ HISTORY Old English *nāwiht*, from *nā* no + *wiht* creature, thing

nota bene (**note**-a **ben**-nay) note well; take note ▶ HISTORY Latin

notable (**note**-a-bl) *adj* **1** worthy of being noted; remarkable ▷ *n* **2** a person of distinction ▶ HISTORY Latin *notare* to note > **notably** *adv*

notary *or* **notary public** (**note**-a-ree) *n, pl* **notaries** *or* **notaries public** a public official, usually a solicitor, who is legally authorized to attest and certify documents ▶ HISTORY Latin *notarius* one who makes notes, a clerk

notation (no-**tay**-shun) *n* **1** representation of numbers or quantities in a system by a series of symbols **2** a set of such symbols ▶ HISTORY Latin *notare* to note

notch *n* **1** a V-shaped cut **2** *informal* a step or level: *the economy moved up another notch* ▷ *vb* **3** to cut a notch in **4 notch up** *informal* to score or achieve: *he notched up a hat trick of wins*

■ **WORD HISTORY**
■ Like 'newt', which comes from the mistaken
■ division of 'an ewt' into 'a newt', the word
■ 'notch' arose from the mistaken division of *an*
■ *otch* (from Old French *oche*, meaning 'notch')
■ into 'a notch'.

573

note n **1** a brief informal letter **2** a brief record in writing for future reference **3** a critical comment or explanation in a book **4** an official written communication, as from a government or from a doctor **5** short for **banknote 6** Brit & NZ a musical sound of a particular pitch **7** a written symbol representing the pitch and duration of a musical sound **8** chiefly Brit a key on a piano, organ, or other keyboard instrument **9** a particular feeling or atmosphere: an optimistic note **10** a distinctive vocal sound, as of a type of animal **11** a sound used as a signal or warning: the note to retreat was sounded **12** short for **promissory note 13 of note a** distinguished or famous **b** important: nothing of note **14 strike the right note** to behave appropriately **15 take note of** to pay attention to ▷ vb **noting, noted 16** to notice; pay attention to: such criticism should be noted **17** to make a written note of **18** to remark upon: I note that you do not wear shoes ▶ HISTORY Latin nota sign

notebook n a book for writing in

notebook computer n a portable computer approximately the size of a sheet of A4 paper

noted adj well-known: a noted scholar

notelet n a folded card with a printed design on the front, for writing informal letters

notepaper n paper used for writing letters

noteworthy adj worth noting; remarkable

nothing pron **1** not anything: I felt nothing **2** a matter of no importance: don't worry, it's nothing **3** absence of meaning, value, or worth: the industry shrank to almost nothing **4** the figure o **5 have** or **be nothing to do with** to have no connection with **6 nothing but** not something other than; only **7 nothing doing** informal an expression of dismissal or refusal **8 nothing less than** downright: nothing less than complete withdrawal **9 think nothing of something** to regard something as easy or natural ▷ adv **10** not at all: he looked nothing like his brother ▷ n **11** informal a person or thing of no importance or significance ▶ HISTORY Old English nāthing, nān thing

nothingness n **1** nonexistence **2** total insignificance

notice n **1** observation or attention: to attract notice **2** a displayed placard or announcement giving information **3** advance notification of something such as intention to end a contract of employment: she handed in her notice **4** a theatrical or literary review **5 take notice** to pay attention **6 take no notice of** to ignore or disregard **7 at short notice** with very little notification ▷ vb **-ticing, -ticed 8** to become aware (of) **9** to point out or remark upon ▶ HISTORY Latin notus known

noticeable adj easily seen or detected > **noticeably** adv

notice board n a board on which notices are displayed

notifiable adj having to be reported to the authorities: a notifiable disease

notification n **1** the act of notifying someone of something **2** a formal announcement

notify vb **-fies, -fying, -fied** to inform ▶ HISTORY Latin notus known + facere to make

notion n **1** an idea or opinion **2** a whim ▶ HISTORY Latin notio a becoming acquainted

notional adj hypothetical, imaginary, or unreal: a notional dividend payment

notorious adj well known for some bad reason ▶ HISTORY Medieval Latin notorius well-known > **notoriety** n > **notoriously** adv

not proven adj a verdict in Scottish courts, given when there is insufficient evidence to convict the accused

no-trump cards n **1** a bid or hand without trumps ▷ adj **2** (of a hand) suitable for playing without trumps

notwithstanding prep **1** in spite of ▷ adv **2** nevertheless

nougat n a hard chewy pink or white sweet containing chopped nuts ▶ HISTORY French, from Latin nux nut

nought n **1** the figure o ▷ n, adv **2** same as **naught** ▶ HISTORY Old English nōwiht, from ne not, no + ōwiht something

noughties pl n informal the decade from 2000 to 2009

noun n a word that refers to a person, place, or thing ▶ HISTORY Latin nomen name

noun group or **phrase** n grammar a noun, pronoun, or group of words containing one or more of these that acts as the subject, object, or complement of a verb, or as the object of a preposition, e.g. my late wife and I in my late wife and I read a lot

nourish vb **1** to provide with the food necessary for life and growth **2** to encourage or foster (an idea or feeling) ▶ HISTORY Latin nutrire to feed > **nourishing** adj

nourishment n the food needed to nourish the body

nous n old-fashioned, slang common sense ▶ HISTORY Greek: mind

nouveau riche (noo-voh reesh) n, pl **nouveaux riches** (noo-voh reesh) a person who has become wealthy recently and is regarded as vulgar ▶ HISTORY French: new rich

nouvelle cuisine (noo-vell kwee-zeen) n a style of preparing and presenting food with light sauces and unusual combinations of flavours ▶ HISTORY French: new cooking

Nov. November

nova n, pl **-vae** or **-vas** a star that undergoes an explosion and fast increase of brightness, then gradually decreases to its original brightness ▶ HISTORY New Latin nova (stella) new (star)

novel[1] n a long fictional story in book form ▶ HISTORY Latin novella (narratio) new (story)

novel[2] adj fresh, new, or original: a novel approach ▶ HISTORY Latin novus new

novelette n a short novel, usually one regarded as trivial or sentimental

novelist n a writer of novels

novella n, pl **-las** a short narrative tale or short novel ▶ HISTORY Italian

novelty *n, pl* **-ties** **1** the quality of being new and interesting **2** a new or unusual experience or thing **3** a small cheap toy or trinket

November *n* the eleventh month of the year ▶ HISTORY Latin: ninth month

novena (no-**vee**-na) *n, pl* **-nas** *or* **-nae** (-nee) *RC Church* a set of prayers or services on nine consecutive days ▶ HISTORY Latin *novem* nine

novice (**nov**-viss) *n* **1** a beginner **2** a person who has entered a religious order but has not yet taken vows ▶ HISTORY Latin *novus* new

novitiate *or* **noviciate** *n* **1** the period of being a novice **2** the part of a monastery or convent where the novices live

now *adv* **1** at or for the present time **2** immediately: *bring it now* **3** in these times; nowadays **4** given the present circumstances: *now do you understand why?* **5** *spoken* **a** used as a hesitation word: *now, I can't really say* **b** used for emphasis: *now listen to this* **c** used at the end of a command: *run along now* **6 just now** *spoken* **a** very recently: *he left just now* **b** very soon: *I'm going just now* **7 now and again** *or* **then** occasionally **8** *spoken* **now now!** an exclamation used to tell someone off or to calm someone ▷ *conj* **9** Also: **now that** seeing that: *now you're here, you can help me* ▷ *n* **10** the present time: *now is the time to go* ▶ HISTORY Old English *nū*

nowadays *adv* in these times

Nowell *n* same as **Noel**

nowhere *adv* **1** in, at, or to no place **2 getting nowhere** *informal* making no progress **3 nowhere near** far from: *the stadium is nowhere near completion* ▷ *n* **4 in the middle of nowhere** (of a place) completely isolated

noxious *adj* **1** poisonous or harmful **2** extremely unpleasant ▶ HISTORY Latin *noxius* harmful

nozzle *n* a projecting spout from which fluid is discharged ▶ HISTORY diminutive of *nose*

Np *chem* neptunium

nr near

NS **1** New Style (method of reckoning dates) **2** Nova Scotia

NSPCC (in Britain) National Society for the Prevention of Cruelty to Children

NSW New South Wales

NT **1** (in Britain) National Trust **2** New Testament **3** Northern Territory **4** Nunavut

nth *adj* See **n²**

nuance (**new**-ahnss) *n* a subtle difference, as in colour, meaning, or tone ▶ HISTORY French

nub *n* the point or gist: *this is the nub of his theory* ▶ HISTORY Middle Low German *knubbe* knob

nubile (**new**-bile) *adj* (of a young woman) **1** physically attractive **2** old enough for marriage ▶ HISTORY Latin *nubere* to marry

nuclear *adj* **1** of nuclear weapons or energy **2** of an atomic nucleus: *nuclear fission*

nuclear bomb *n* a bomb whose force is due to uncontrolled nuclear fusion or fission

nuclear energy *n* energy released during a nuclear reaction as a result of fission or fusion

nuclear family *n* *sociol, anthropol* a family consisting only of parents and their offspring

nuclear fission *n* *nuclear physics* the splitting of an atomic nucleus, either spontaneously or by bombardment by a neutron: used in atomic bombs and nuclear power plants

nuclear fusion *n* *nuclear physics* the combination of two nuclei to form a heavier nucleus with the release of energy: used in hydrogen bombs

nuclear physics *n* the branch of physics concerned with the structure of the nucleus and the behaviour of its particles

nuclear power *n* power produced by a nuclear reactor

nuclear reaction *n* *physics* a process in which the structure and energy content of an atomic nucleus is changed by interaction with another nucleus or particle

nuclear reactor *n* *nuclear physics* a device in which a nuclear reaction is maintained and controlled to produce nuclear energy

nuclear winter *n* a theoretical period of low temperatures and little light that has been suggested would occur after a nuclear war

nucleate *adj* **1** having a nucleus ▷ *vb* **-ating, -ated** **2** to form a nucleus

nucleated settlement *n* a pattern of settlement in which dwellings are clustered together as in villages and towns. Compare **dispersed settlement**

nuclei (**new**-klee-eye) *n* the plural of **nucleus**

nucleic acid *n* *biochem* a complex compound, such as DNA or RNA, found in all living cells

nucleolus *n, pl* **-li** *biol* a small rounded body within a resting nucleus that is involved in protein synthesis

nucleon *n* *physics* a proton or neutron

nucleonics *n* the branch of physics concerned with the applications of nuclear energy > **nucleonic** *adj*

nucleoplasm *n* *biol* the protoplasm that makes up the nucleus of a plant or animal cell

nucleoside *n* *biochem* a compound containing a purine or pyrimidine base linked to a sugar

nucleotide *n* *biochem* a compound consisting of a nucleoside linked to phosphoric acid

nucleus *n, pl* **-clei** **1** *physics* the positively charged centre of an atom, made of protons and neutrons, about which electrons orbit **2** a central thing around which others are grouped **3** a centre of growth or development: *the nucleus of a new relationship* **4** *biol* the part of a cell that contains the chromosomes and associated molecules that control the characteristics and growth of the cell **5** *chem* a fundamental group of atoms in a molecule serving as the base structure for related compounds ▶ HISTORY Latin: kernel

nude *adj* **1** completely undressed ▷ *n* **2** a naked figure in painting, sculpture, or photography **3 in the nude** naked ▶ HISTORY Latin *nudus* > **nudity** *n*

nudge *vb* **nudging, nudged** **1** to push (someone) gently with the elbow to get attention **2** to push (something or someone) lightly **3** to persuade (someone) gently ▷ *vb* **4** a gentle poke or push ▶ **HISTORY** origin unknown

nudism *n* the practice of not wearing clothes, for reasons of health > **nudist** *n, adj*

nugatory (**new**-gat-tree) *adj formal* **1** of little value **2** not valid: *their rejection rendered the treaty nugatory* ▶ **HISTORY** Latin *nugae* trifling things

nugget *n* **1** a small lump of gold in its natural state **2** something small but valuable: *a nugget of useful knowledge* ▷ *vb* **3** *NZ & S African* to polish footwear ▶ **HISTORY** origin unknown

nuisance *n* **1** a person or thing that causes annoyance or bother ▷ *adj* **2** causing annoyance or bother: *nuisance calls* ▶ **HISTORY** Old French *nuire* to injure

NUJ (in Britain) National Union of Journalists

nuke *slang vb* **nuking, nuked** **1** to attack with nuclear weapons ▷ *n* **2** a nuclear bomb

null *adj* **1 null and void** not legally valid **2 null set** *maths* a set with no members ▶ **HISTORY** Latin *nullus* none > **nullity** *n*

nulla-nulla *n* a wooden club used by Australian Aborigines

nullify *vb* **-fies, -fying, -fied** **1** to make (something) ineffective **2** to make (something) legally void ▶ **HISTORY** Latin *nullus* of no account + *facere* to make > **nullification** *n*

numb *adj* **1** deprived of feeling through cold, shock, or fear **2** unable to move; paralysed ▷ *vb* **3** to make numb ▶ **HISTORY** Middle English *nomen*, literally: taken (with paralysis) > **numbly** *adv* > **numbness** *n*

numbat *n* a small Australian marsupial with a long snout and tongue

number *n* **1** a concept of quantity that is or can be derived from a single unit, a sum of units, or zero **2** the word or symbol used to represent a number **3** a numeral or string of numerals used to identify a person or thing: *an account number* **4** the person or thing so identified: *he was seeded number two* **5** a sum or quantity: *a very large number of people have telephoned* **6** one of a series, as of a magazine **7** a self-contained piece of pop or jazz music **8** a group of people: *one of their number might be willing* **9** *informal* an admired article: *that little number is by Dior* **10** *grammar* classification of words depending on how many people or things are referred to **11 any number of** many **12 beyond** or **without number** innumerable **13 have someone's number** *informal* to have discovered someone's true character or intentions **14 one's number is up** *Brit & Austral, informal* one is about to die ▷ *vb* **15** to count **16** to assign a number to: *numbered seats* **17** to add up to: *the illustrations numbered well over 50* **18** to include in a group **19 one's days are numbered** something unpleasant, such as death, is likely to happen to one soon ▶ **HISTORY** Latin *numerus*

number crunching *n computers* the large-scale processing of numerical data

numberless *adj* too many to be counted

number one *n* **1** *informal* oneself: *he looks after number one* **2** *informal* the bestselling pop recording in any one week ▷ *adj* **3** first in importance, urgency, or quality: *he's their number one suspect*

numberplate *n* a plate on a motor vehicle showing the registration number

numbskull *or* **numskull** *n* a stupid person

numeral *n* a word or symbol used to express a sum or quantity ▶ **HISTORY** Latin *numerus* number

numerate *adj* able to do basic arithmetic > **numeracy** *n*

numeration *n* **1** the act or process of numbering or counting **2** a system of numbering

numerator *n maths* the number above the line in a fraction

numerical *or* **numeric** *adj* measured or expressed in numbers > **numerically** *adv*

numerology *n* the study of numbers and of their supposed influence on human affairs

numerous *adj* **1** many: *they carried out numerous bombings* **2** consisting of a large number of people or things

numinous *adj formal* **1** arousing spiritual or religious emotions **2** mysterious or awe-inspiring ▶ **HISTORY** Latin *numen* divine will

numismatics *n* the study or collection of coins or medals ▶ **HISTORY** Greek *nomisma* piece of currency > **numismatist** *n*

numskull *n* same as **numbskull**

nun *n* a female member of a religious order ▶ **HISTORY** Late Latin *nonna*

nunatak *n geog* an isolated mountain peak projecting through the surface of surrounding glacial ice and supporting a distinct fauna and flora after recession of the ice ▶ **HISTORY** via Danish from Inuktitut

nuncio *n, pl* **-cios** *RC Church* a papal ambassador ▶ **HISTORY** Latin *nuntius* messenger

nunnery *n, pl* **-neries** a convent

nuptial *adj* relating to marriage: *a nuptial blessing* ▶ **HISTORY** Latin *nuptiae* marriage

nuptials *pl n* a wedding

nurd *n slang* same as **nerd**

nurse *n* **1** a person trained to look after sick people, usually in a hospital ▷ *vb* **nursing, nursed** **2** to look after (a sick person) **3** to breast-feed (a baby) **4** (of a baby) to feed at its mother's breast **5** to try to cure (an ailment) **6** to harbour or foster (a feeling) **7** to clasp fondly: *she nursed her drink* ▶ **HISTORY** Latin *nutrire* to nourish > **nursing** *n, adj*

nursery *n, pl* **-ries** **1** a room in a house where children sleep or play **2** a place where children are taken care of when their parents are at work **3** a place where plants are grown for sale

nurseryman *n, pl* **-men** a person who raises plants and trees for sale

nursery rhyme *n* a short traditional verse or song for children

nursery school *n* a school for young children from three to five years old

nursery slopes *pl n* gentle slopes used by beginners in skiing

nursing home *n* a private hospital or home for people who are old or ill

nursing officer *n* (in Britain) the administrative head of the nursing staff of a hospital

nurture *n* **1** the act or process of promoting the development of a child or young plant ▷ *vb* **-turing, -tured 2** to promote or encourage the development of ▶ HISTORY Latin *nutrire* to nourish

nut *n* **1** a dry one-seeded fruit that grows inside a hard shell **2** the edible inner part of such a fruit **3** a small piece of metal with a hole in it, that screws on to a bolt **4** *slang* an eccentric or insane person **5** *slang* the head **6** *slang* an enthusiast: *a health nut* **7** *Brit* a small piece of coal **8 do one's nut** *Brit & Austral, slang* to be very angry **9 a tough nut to crack** a person or thing that presents difficulties ▷ See also **nuts** ▶ HISTORY Old English *hnutu*

NUT (in Britain & S Africa) National Union of Teachers

nutcracker *n* a device for cracking the shells of nuts. Also: **nutcrackers**

nuthatch *n* a songbird that feeds on insects, seeds, and nuts ▶ HISTORY Middle English *notehache* nut hatchet, because it splits nuts

nutmeg *n* a spice made from the seed of a tropical tree ▶ HISTORY Old French *nois muguede* musk-scented nut

nutria (**new**-tree-a) *n* the fur of the coypu ▶ HISTORY Latin *lutra* otter

nutrient (**new**-tree-ent) *n* **1** a substance that provides nourishment ▷ *adj* **2** providing nourishment ▶ HISTORY Latin *nutrire* to nourish

nutriment (**new**-tree-ment) *n* the food or nourishment required by all living things to grow and stay healthy ▶ HISTORY Latin *nutrimentum*

nutrition (new-**trish**-un) *n* **1** the process of taking in and absorbing nutrients **2** the process of being nourished **3** the study of nutrition ▶ HISTORY Latin *nutrire* to nourish > **nutritional** *adj* > **nutritionist** *n*

nutritious *adj* providing nourishment ▶ HISTORY Latin *nutrix* nurse

nutritive *adj* of nutrition; nutritious

nuts *adj slang* **1** insane **2 nuts about** very fond of

nuts and bolts *pl n informal* the essential or practical details: *the nuts and bolts of photography*

nutshell *n* **in a nutshell** in essence; briefly

nutter *n Brit & NZ, slang* an insane person

nutty *adj* **-tier, -tiest 1** containing or resembling nuts **2** *slang* insane or eccentric > **nuttiness** *n*

nux vomica *n* the seed of a tree, containing strychnine ▶ HISTORY Medieval Latin: vomiting nut

nuzzle *vb* **-zling, -zled** to push or rub gently with the nose or snout ▶ HISTORY from *nose*

NV Nevada

nvCJD new-variant Creutzfeldt-Jakob disease

NW northwest(ern)

NWT Northwest Territories (of Canada)

NY *or* **N.Y.** New York

nylon *n* a synthetic material used for clothing and many other products ▶ HISTORY originally a trademark

nylons *pl n* stockings made of nylon

nymph *n* **1** *myth* a spirit of nature, represented as a beautiful young woman **2** the larva of certain insects, resembling the adult form **3** *chiefly poetic* a beautiful young woman ▶ HISTORY Greek *numphē*

NZ *or* **N.Z.** New Zealand

NZE New Zealand English

NZRFU New Zealand Rugby Football Union

NZSE40 Index New Zealand Stock Exchange 40 Index

n

Oo

O¹ 1 *chem* oxygen **2** Old **3** *spoken* same as **nought**

O² *interj* same as **oh**

o. *or* **O.** old

o' *prep informal or old-fashioned* of: *a cup o' tea*

OA Order of Australia

oaf *n* a stupid or clumsy person ▶ HISTORY variant of Old English *ælf* elf > **oafish** *adj*

oak *n* **1** a large forest tree with hard wood, acorns as fruits, and leaves with rounded projections **2** the wood of this tree, used as building timber and for making furniture ▶ HISTORY Old English *āc* > **oaken** *adj*

oak apple *or* **gall** *n* a brownish round lump or ball produced on oak trees by certain wasps

oakum *n* loose fibre obtained by unravelling old rope, used for filling cracks in wooden ships ▶ HISTORY Old English *ācumba*, literally: off-combings

OAM Medal of the Order of Australia

OAP (in Britain) old age pensioner

oar *n* **1** a long pole with a broad blade, used for rowing a boat **2 put** *or* **stick one's oar in** to interfere or interrupt ▶ HISTORY Old English *ār*

oarsman *or fem* **oarswoman** *n, pl* -**men** *or* -**women** a person who rows > **oarsmanship** *n*

oasis *n, pl* -**ses 1** a fertile patch in a desert **2** a place or situation offering relief in the midst of difficulty ▶ HISTORY Greek

oast *n chiefly Brit* an oven for drying hops ▶ HISTORY Old English *āst*

oast house *n chiefly Brit* a building containing ovens for drying hops

oat *n* **1** a hard cereal grown as food **2 oats** the edible grain of this cereal ▶ HISTORY Old English *āte* > **oaten** *adj*

oatcake *n* a thin unsweetened biscuit made of oatmeal

oath *n, pl* **oaths 1** a solemn promise, esp. to tell the truth in a court of law **2** *written* an offensive or blasphemous expression; a swearword **3 on** *or* **under oath** having made a solemn promise to tell the truth, esp. in a court of law ▶ HISTORY Old English *āth*

oath of allegiance *n* a solemn promise of loyalty to a monarch or a country

oatmeal *n* **1** a coarse flour made by grinding oats ▷ *adj* **2** greyish-yellow

obbligato (ob-lig-**gah**-toe) *music adj* **1** not to be omitted in performance ▷ *n, pl* -**tos 2** an essential part or accompaniment: *an aria with bassoon obbligato* ▶ HISTORY Italian

obdurate *adj* not to be persuaded; hardhearted or obstinate ▶ HISTORY Latin *obdurare* to make hard > **obduracy** *n*

OBE (in Britain) Officer of the Order of the British Empire

obeah (oh-**bee**-ya) *n* **1** a kind of African witchcraft practised in the West Indies **2** a charm used in this practice ▶ HISTORY of West African origin

obeah man *n* a practitioner of obeah

obedient *adj* obeying or willing to obey ▶ HISTORY Latin *oboediens* > **obedience** *n* > **obediently** *adv*

obeisance (oh-**bay**-sanss) *n formal* **1** an attitude of respect or humble obedience **2** a bow or curtsy showing this attitude ▶ HISTORY Old French *obéissant* obeying > **obeisant** *adj*

obelisk (**ob**-bill-isk) *n* **1** a four-sided stone pillar that tapers to a pyramid at the top **2** *printing* same as **dagger** (sense 2) ▶ HISTORY Greek *obeliskos* a little spit

obese (oh-**beess**) *adj* very fat ▶ HISTORY Latin *obesus* > **obesity** *n*

obey *vb* **1** to carry out instructions or orders; be obedient **2** to act in accordance with one's feelings, an impulse, etc.: *I had obeyed the impulse to open the gate and had walked up the drive* ▶ HISTORY Latin *oboedire*

obfuscate *vb* -**cating,** -**cated** *formal* to make something unnecessarily difficult to understand ▶ HISTORY Latin *ob*- (intensive) + *fuscare* to blacken > **obfuscation** *n* > **obfuscatory** *adj*

obiter dictum *n, pl* **obiter dicta 1** *law* an observation by a judge on a point of law not directly in issue in the case before him and thus neither requiring his decision nor serving as a precedent, but nevertheless of persuasive authority **2** any comment or remark made in passing ▶ HISTORY Latin: something said in passing

obituary *n, pl* -**aries** a published announcement of a death, usually with a short biography of the dead person ▶ HISTORY Latin *obitus* death > **obituarist** *n*

obj. 1 objection **2** *grammar* object(ive)

object¹ *n* **1** a thing that can be touched or seen **2** a person or thing seen as a focus for feelings, actions, or thought: *she had become for him an object of compassion* **3** an aim or purpose: *the main object of the exercise* **4** *philosophy* that which can be perceived by the mind, as contrasted with the thinking subject **5** *grammar* a noun, pronoun, or other noun group that receives the action of a verb or is governed by a preposition, such as *the bottle* in *she threw the bottle* **6 no object** not a hindrance or obstacle: *money's no object* ▶ HISTORY Late Latin *objectus* something thrown before (the mind)

object² *vb* **1** to express disapproval or opposition: *my colleagues objected strongly to further delays* **2** to state as one's reason for opposing: *he objected that his small staff would be unable to handle the added work* ▶ HISTORY Latin *ob*- against + *jacere* to throw > **objector** *n*

objection n 1 an expression or feeling of opposition or disapproval 2 a reason for opposing something: *the planning officer had raised no objection to the proposals*

objectionable adj offensive or unacceptable

objective n 1 an aim or purpose: *the objective is to highlight the environmental threat to the planet* 2 grammar same as **objective case** 3 optics the lens nearest to the object observed in an optical instrument ▷ adj 4 not distorted by personal feelings or bias: *I have tried to be as objective as possible in my presentation* 5 of or relating to actual facts as opposed to thoughts or feelings: *stand back and try to take a more objective view of your life as a whole* 6 existing independently of the mind; real > **objectival** adj > **objectively** adv > **objectivity** n

objective case n grammar a grammatical case in some languages that identifies the direct object of a verb or preposition

objective shot n films, television a camera shot taken from a neutral position rather than from the angle of vision of one of the characters in the scene. Compare **subjective shot**

object lesson n a practical demonstration of some principle or ideal

objet d'art (**ob**-zhay **dahr**) n, pl **objets d'art** (**ob**-zhay **dahr**) a small object considered to be of artistic worth ▶ HISTORY French: object of art

oblate adj geom (of a sphere) flattened at the poles: *the oblate spheroid of the earth* ▶ HISTORY New Latin *oblatus* lengthened

oblation n 1 Christianity the offering of bread and wine to God at Communion 2 any offering made for religious purposes ▶ HISTORY Medieval Latin *oblatus* offered > **oblational** adj

obligated adj being morally or legally bound to do something: *they are obligated to provide temporary accommodation* > **obligative** adj

obligation n 1 a moral or legal duty 2 the binding power of such a duty: *I feel under some obligation to help you with your education* 3 a sense of being in debt because of a service or favour: *I don't want him marrying me out of obligation*

obligatory adj required or compulsory because of custom or law

oblige vb **obliging, obliged** 1 to compel someone by legal, moral, or physical means to do something 2 to make (someone) indebted or grateful for a favour: *I am obliged to you for your help* 3 to do a favour to someone: *she obliged the guests with a song* ▶ HISTORY Latin *ob-* towards + *ligare* to bind

obliging adj written willing to be helpful > **obligingly** adv

oblique (oh-**bleak**) adj 1 at an angle; slanting 2 geom (of lines or planes) neither perpendicular nor parallel to one another 3 indirect or evasive: *only oblique references have been made to the anti-government unrest* ▷ n 4 same as **solidus** ▶ HISTORY Latin *obliquus* > **obliquely** adv > **obliqueness** n

oblique angle n an angle that is not a right angle or any multiple of a right angle

obliterate vb **-rating, -rated** to destroy every trace of; wipe out completely ▶ HISTORY Latin *oblitterare* to erase > **obliteration** n

oblivion n 1 the condition of being forgotten or disregarded: *the Marxist-Leninist wing of the party looks set to sink into oblivion* 2 the state of being unaware or unconscious: *guests seemed to feel a social obligation to drink themselves into oblivion* ▶ HISTORY Latin *oblivio* forgetfulness

oblivious adj unaware or unconscious: *oblivious of her soaking clothes; I was oblivious to the beauty* > **obliviousness** n

oblong adj 1 having an elongated, rectangular shape ▷ n 2 a figure or object having this shape ▶ HISTORY Latin *oblongus*

obloquy (**ob**-lock-wee) n, pl **-quies** formal 1 abusive statements or blame: *the British press was held up to moral obloquy* 2 disgrace brought about by this: *the punishment of lifelong public obloquy and private embarrassment* ▶ HISTORY Latin *obloquium* contradiction

obnoxious adj extremely unpleasant ▶ HISTORY Latin *obnoxius* > **obnoxiousness** n

oboe n a double-reeded woodwind instrument with a penetrating nasal tone > **oboist** n

■ **WORD HISTORY**
■ 'Oboe' comes from French *haut bois*, meaning
■ 'high wood', a reference to the instrument's
■ relatively high pitch compared to other
■ instruments of the woodwind family.

obscene adj 1 offensive to accepted standards of decency or modesty 2 law tending to deprave or corrupt: *an obscene publication* 3 disgusting: *a great dark obscene pool of blood* ▶ HISTORY Latin *obscenus* inauspicious > **obscenity** n

obscure adj 1 not well-known: *the concerts feature several obscure artists* 2 not easily understood: *the contracts are written in obscure language* 3 unclear or indistinct ▷ vb **-scuring, -scured** 4 to make unclear or vague; hide: *no amount of bluster could obscure the fact that the prime minister had run out of excuses* 5 to cover or cloud over ▶ HISTORY Latin *obscurus* dark > **obscuration** n > **obscurity** n

obsequies (**ob**-sick-weez) pl n, sing **-quy** formal funeral rites ▶ HISTORY Medieval Latin *obsequiae*

obsequious (ob-**seek**-wee-uss) adj being overattentive in order to gain favour ▶ HISTORY Latin *obsequiosus* compliant > **obsequiousness** n

observance n 1 the observing of a law or custom 2 a ritual, ceremony, or practice, esp. of a religion

observant adj quick to notice details around one; sharp-eyed

observation n 1 the act of watching or the state of being watched 2 a comment or remark 3 detailed examination of something before analysis, diagnosis, or interpretation: *you may be admitted to hospital for observation and rest* 4 the facts learned from observing 5 the ability to notice things: *she has good powers of observation* > **observational** adj

observatory n, pl **-ries** a building specially designed and equipped for studying the weather and the stars

observe *vb* **-serving, -served** **1** to see or notice: *it is worth observing that old Chinese maps and charts usually show south at the top* **2** to watch (something) carefully **3** to make scientific examinations of **4** to remark: *the speaker observed that times had changed* **5** to keep (a law or custom) ▶ HISTORY Latin *observare* > **observable** *adj*

observer *n* **1** a person who observes **2** a person allowed to attend a meeting without being allowed to participate in any way

obsessed *adj* thinking about someone or something all the time: *he had become obsessed with her* ▶ HISTORY Latin *obsessus* besieged > **obsessive** *adj, n*

obsession *n* **1** something that preoccupies a person to the exclusion of other things: *his principal obsession was with trying to economize* **2** psychiatry a persistent idea or impulse, often associated with anxiety and mental illness > **obsessional** *adj*

obsidian *n* a dark glassy volcanic rock ▶ HISTORY after *Obsius*, the discoverer of a stone resembling obsidian

obsolescent *adj* becoming obsolete or out of date > **obsolescence** *n*

obsolete *adj* no longer used; out of date ▶ HISTORY Latin *obsoletus* worn out

obstacle *n* **1** a situation or event that prevents something being done: *there are obstacles which could slow the development of a vaccine* **2** a person or thing that hinders movement ▶ HISTORY Latin *obstaculum*, from *ob-* against + *stare* to stand

obstetrician *n* a doctor who specializes in obstetrics

obstetrics *n* the branch of medicine concerned with pregnancy and childbirth ▶ HISTORY Latin *obstetrix* a midwife > **obstetric** *adj*

obstinate *adj* **1** keeping stubbornly to a particular opinion or course of action **2** difficult to treat or deal with: *obstinate weeds* ▶ HISTORY Latin *obstinatus* > **obstinacy** *n* > **obstinately** *adv*

obstreperous *adj* noisy and difficult to control: *her obstreperous teenage son* ▶ HISTORY Latin *ob-* against + *strepere* to roar

obstruct *vb* **1** to block a way with an obstacle **2** to make progress or activity difficult: *this government will never obstruct the course of justice* **3** to block a clear view of ▶ HISTORY Latin *obstructus* built against

obstruction *n* **1** a person or thing that obstructs **2** the act of obstructing or being obstructed **3** *sport* the act of unfairly impeding an opposing player

obstructionist *n* a person who deliberately obstructs legal or parliamentary business > **obstructionism** *n*

obstructive *adj* deliberately causing difficulties or delays > **obstructively** *adv* > **obstructiveness** *n*

obtain *vb* **1** to gain possession of; get **2** *formal* to be customary or accepted: *silence obtains from eight in the evening* ▶ HISTORY Latin *obtinere* to take hold of > **obtainable** *adj*

obtrude *vb* **-truding, -truded** **1** to push oneself or one's opinions on others in an unwelcome way **2** to be or make unpleasantly noticeable ▶ HISTORY Latin *obtrudere* > **obtrusion** *n*

obtrusive *adj* unpleasantly noticeable: *the music should fit your mood, it shouldn't be too obtrusive* > **obtrusiveness** *n*

obtuse *adj* **1** mentally slow or emotionally insensitive **2** *maths* (of an angle) between 90° and 180° **3** not sharp or pointed; blunt ▶ HISTORY Latin *obtusus* dulled > **obtuseness** *n*

obverse *n* **1** a counterpart or opposite: *his true personality being the obverse of his outer image* **2** the side of a coin that bears the main design **3** the front, top, or main surface of anything ▶ HISTORY Latin *obversus* turned towards

obviate *vb* **-ating, -ated** *formal* to avoid or prevent (a need or difficulty): *a mediator will obviate the need for independent legal advice* ▶ HISTORY Latin *obviare*

obvious *adj* **1** easy to see or understand ▷ *n* **2** state the obvious to say something that is unnecessary or already known: *he is prone to stating the obvious* ▶ HISTORY Latin *obvius* > **obviously** *adv* > **obviousness** *n*

ocarina *n* a small egg-shaped wind instrument with a mouthpiece and finger holes ▶ HISTORY Italian: little goose

occasion *n* **1** a particular event or the time at which it happens **2** a need or reason to do or be something: *we barely knew him and never had occasion to speak of him* **3** a suitable time or opportunity to do something **4** a special event, time, or celebration: *a wedding day is a truly special occasion* **5** on occasion every so often **6** rise to the occasion to meet the special demands of a situation ▷ *vb* **7** *formal* to cause, esp. incidentally ▶ HISTORY Latin *occasio* a falling down

occasional *adj* happening from time to time; not frequent or regular > **occasionally** *adv*

Occident *n* the western hemisphere, esp. Europe and America ▶ HISTORY Latin *occidere* to fall (with reference to the setting sun) > **Occidental** *adj*

occipital lobe *n* *physiol* the rear part of each hemisphere of the brain

occiput (**ox**-sip-putt) *n* *anat* the back of the head or skull ▶ HISTORY Latin *ob-* at the back of + *caput* head > **occipital** *adj*

occlude *vb* **-cluding, -cluded** *formal* **1** to block or stop up a passage or opening: *the arteries are occluded by deposits of plaque* **2** to shut in or out: *slowly occluding him from Nash's vision* **3** *chem* (of a solid) to absorb and retain a gas or other substance ▶ HISTORY Latin *occludere* > **occlusion** *n*

occluded front *n* *meteorol* the front formed when the cold front of a depression overtakes a warm front, raising the warm air from ground level

occult *adj* **1** involving mystical or supernatural phenomena or powers **2** beyond ordinary human understanding **3** secret or mysterious ▷ *n* **4** the occult the knowledge and study of occult phenomena and powers ▶ HISTORY Latin *occultus* hidden, secret

occupancy *n, pl* **-cies 1** the act of occupying a property **2** the period of time during which one is an occupant of a property

occupant *n* a person occupying a property, position, or place

occupation *n* **1** a person's job or profession **2** any activity on which someone's time is spent: *a pleasant and rewarding occupation* **3** the control of a country by a foreign military power **4** the act of occupying or the state of being occupied: *the occupation of Kuwait* > **occupational** *adj*

occupational hazard *n* something unpleasant that occurs due to your job: *frequent colds are an occupational hazard in teaching*

occupational therapy *n* treatment of people with physical, emotional, or social problems using purposeful activity to help them overcome or learn to accept their problems

occupier *n Brit* the person who lives in a particular house, whether as owner or tenant

occupy *vb* **-pies, -pying, -pied 1** to live, stay, or work in (a house, flat, or office) **2** to keep (someone or someone's mind) busy **3** to take up (time or space) **4** to move in and take control of (a country or other place): *soldiers have occupied the country's television station* **5** to fill or hold (a position or office) ▶ **HISTORY** Latin *occupare* to seize hold of

occur *vb* **-curring, -curred 1** to happen **2** to be found or be present; exist **3 occur to** to come into the mind of ▶ **HISTORY** Latin *occurrere* to run up to

occurrence *n* **1** something that happens **2** the fact of occurring: *the likelihood of its occurrence increases with age*

ocean *n* **1** the vast area of salt water covering about 70 per cent of the earth's surface **2** one of the five principal divisions of this, the Atlantic, Pacific, Indian, Arctic, and Antarctic **3** *informal* a huge quantity or expanse: *oceans of replies* **4** *literary* the sea ▶ **HISTORY** from *Oceanus*, Greek god of the stream believed to flow round the earth > **oceanic** *adj*

ocean current *n geog* a movement of water in the sea in a particular direction

ocean-going *adj* (of a ship or boat) suited for travel on the open ocean

oceanic crust *n geol* the solid outer shell of the earth found beneath ocean basins and composed of basalt and sedimentary layers

oceanic plate *n geol* part of the earth's crust that lies under the sea

oceanography *n* the study of oceans and their environment > **oceanographer** *n* > **oceanographic** *adj*

ocean trench *n geol* a deep trench found at the edge of an ocean basin caused by the moving of tectonic plates

ocelot (**oss**-ill-lot) *n* a large cat of Central and South America with a dark-spotted yellow-grey coat ▶ **HISTORY** Mexican Indian *ocelotl* jaguar

oche (**ok**-kee) *n darts* a mark on the floor behind which a player must stand when throwing a dart ▶ **HISTORY** origin unknown

ochre *or US* **ocher** (**oak**-er) *n* **1** a yellow or reddish-brown earth used in paints or dyes ▷ *adj* **2** moderate yellow-orange to orange ▶ **HISTORY** Greek *ōkhros* pale yellow

o'clock *adv* used after a number between one and twelve to specify an hour: *five o'clock in the morning*

OCR optical character reader *or* recognition

Oct. October

octagon *n* a geometric figure with eight sides ▶ **HISTORY** Greek *oktagōnos* having eight angles > **octagonal** *adj*

octahedron (ok-ta-**heed**-ron) *n, pl* **-drons** *or* **-dra** a solid figure with eight plane faces

octane *n* a liquid hydrocarbon found in petroleum

octane number *or* **rating** *n* a number indicating the quality of a petrol

octave *n* **1 a** the musical interval between the first note and the eighth note of a major or minor scale **b** the higher of these two notes **c** the series of notes filling this interval **2** *prosody* a rhythmic group of eight lines of verse ▶ **HISTORY** Latin *octo* eight

octavo *n, pl* **-vos 1** a book size resulting from folding a sheet of paper of a standard size to form eight leaves **2** a book or sheet of this size ▶ **HISTORY** New Latin *in octavo* in an eighth (of a sheet)

octet *n* **1** a group of eight instrumentalists or singers **2** a piece of music for eight performers ▶ **HISTORY** Latin *octo* eight

October *n* the tenth month of the year ▶ **HISTORY** Latin *octo* eight, since it was originally the eighth month in Roman reckoning

Octobrist *n history* a member of a Russian political party favouring the constitutional reforms granted in a manifesto issued by Nicholas II in Oct. 1905

octogenarian *n* **1** a person between 80 and 89 years old ▷ *adj* **2** between 80 and 89 years old ▶ **HISTORY** Latin *octogenarius* containing eighty

octopus *n, pl* **-puses** a sea creature with a soft oval body and eight long tentacles with suckers ▶ **HISTORY** Greek *oktōpous* having eight feet

ocular *adj* of or relating to the eyes or sight ▶ **HISTORY** Latin *oculus* eye

oculist *n old-fashioned* an ophthalmologist

OD *informal n* **1** an overdose of a drug ▷ *vb* **OD'ing, OD'd 2** to take an overdose of a drug

odd *adj* **1** unusual or peculiar: *his increasingly odd behaviour* **2** occasional or incidental: *the odd letter from a friend abroad, the occasional postcard from a chum* **3** leftover or additional: *we use up odd pieces of fabric to make up jerseys in wild designs* **4** (of a number) not divisible by two **5** being part of a pair or set when the other or others are missing: *the drawer was full of odd socks* **6** somewhat more than the round number specified: *I had known him for the past twenty-odd years* **7 odd man** *or* **one out** a person or thing excluded from others forming a group or unit ▷ See also **odds** ▶ **HISTORY** Old Norse *oddi* angle, point, third or odd number > **oddly** *adv* > **oddness** *n*

581

oddball n informal a strange or eccentric person

oddity n, pl **-ties** 1 an odd person or thing 2 a peculiar characteristic 3 the quality of being or appearing unusual or strange

oddments pl n odd pieces or things; leftovers: oddments of wool

odds pl n 1 the probability, expressed as a ratio, that something will or will not happen: the odds against an acquittal had stabilized at six to four 2 the difference, expressed as a ratio, between the money placed on a bet and the amount that would be received as winning payment: the current odds are ten to one 3 the likelihood that a certain state of affairs will be so: the odds are that you are going to fail 4 the advantage that one contender is judged to have over another: the odds are in his favour 5 **it makes no odds** Brit & Austral it does not matter 6 **at odds** on bad terms 7 **over the odds** more than is expected or necessary

odds and ends pl n small, usually unimportant, objects, jobs to be done, etc.: I have brought a few odds and ends with me

ode n a lyric poem, usually addressed to a particular subject, with lines of varying lengths and metres ▶ HISTORY Greek ōidē song

odious adj offensive or hateful: I steeled myself for the odious task ▶ HISTORY see ODIUM
> **odiousness** n

odium (oh-dee-um) n formal widespread dislike or disapproval of a person or action ▶ HISTORY Latin

odometer (odd-**om**-it-er) n US & Canad same as **mileometer** ▶ HISTORY Greek hodos way + -METER

odour or US **odor** n a particular and distinctive scent or smell ▶ HISTORY Latin odor > **odorous** adj
> **odourless** adj

odyssey (odd-iss-ee) n a long eventful journey
- ■ **WORD HISTORY**
- ■ The Odyssey is one of the two great poems
- ■ attributed to the Greek poet Homer. It
- ■ describes the ten-year homeward journey of
- ■ the Greek hero Odysseus, king of Ithaca, after
- ■ the Trojan War.

OE NZ, informal overseas experience: he's away on his OE

OECD Organization for Economic Cooperation and Development

OECS Organization of Eastern Caribbean States

oedema or **edema** (id-**deem**-a) n, pl **-mata** pathol an abnormal accumulation of fluid in the tissues of the body, causing swelling ▶ HISTORY Greek oidēma swelling

Oedipus complex (ee-dip-puss) n psychoanal the usually unconscious sexual desire of a child, esp. a male child, for the parent of the opposite sex
> **oedipal** adj

o'er prep, adv poetic over

oesophagus (ee-**soff**-a-guss) n, pl **-gi** (-guy) the tube through which food travels from the throat to the stomach; gullet ▶ HISTORY Greek oisophagos
> **oesophageal** adj

oestrogen (**ee**-stra-jen) n a female sex hormone that controls the reproductive cycle, and prepares the body for pregnancy ▶ HISTORY from oestrus + -gen (suffix) producing

oestrus (ee-struss) n a regularly occurring period of fertility and sexual receptivity in the reproductive cycle of most female mammals, except humans; heat ▶ HISTORY Greek oistros gadfly, hence frenzy

of prep 1 belonging to; situated in or coming from; because of: the inhabitants of former East Germany; I saw five people die of chronic hepatitis 2 used after words or phrases expressing quantities: a pint of milk 3 specifying an amount or value: we had to release the bombs at a height of 400 metres 4 made up of, containing, or characterized by: a length of rope; she is a woman of enviable beauty 5 used to link a verbal noun with a following noun or noun phrase that is either the subject or the object of the verb: the sudden slipping of the plates of the Earth's crust; the bombing of civilian targets 6 at a given distance or space of time from: you can still find wood within a mile of the village; he had been within hours of leaving for Romania 7 used to specify or give more information about: the city of Glasgow; a meeting on the subject of regional security 8 about or concerning: speaking of boycotts 9 US before the hour of: about quarter of eight in the evening ▶ HISTORY Old English

Ofcom n (in Britain) Office of Communications: a government body regulating the telecommunications industries

off prep 1 so as to be no longer in contact with: take the wok off the heat 2 so as to be no longer attached to or associated with: making use of benefit disqualification to terrorize the unemployed off the register 3 away from: he was driven off the road 4 situated near to or leading away from: they were laying out a bombing range off the coast 5 no longer having a liking for: she's gone off you lately 6 no longer using: he was off heroin for a year ▷ adv 7 so as to deactivate or disengage: turn off the gas supply 8 a so as to get rid of: he was flying at midnight so he had to sleep off his hangover b as a reduction in price: she took twenty per cent off 9 spent away from work or other duties: it was the assistant manager's day off 10 away; at a distance: the men dashed back to their car and sped off 11 away in the future: the date was six weeks off 12 so as to be no longer taking place: the investigation was hastily called off 13 removed from contact with something: he took the jacket off 14 **off and on** occasionally; not regularly or continuously: we lived together off and on ▷ adj 15 not on; no longer operating: her bedroom light was off 16 cancelled or postponed: the deal is off and your deposit will be returned in full 17 in a specified condition, esp. regarding money or provisions: a married man with four children is better off on the dole; how are you off for money? 18 not up to the usual standard: an off year for good wine 19 no longer on the menu: haddock is off 20 (of food or drink) having gone bad or sour: this milk is off ▷ n 21 cricket the side of the field to the right of a right-handed batsman when he is facing the bowler ▶ HISTORY variant of of

offal *n* the edible internal parts of an animal, such as the heart or liver ▶ **HISTORY** *off + fall*, referring to parts cut off

offal pit *or* **hole** *n* NZ a place on a farm for the disposal of animal offal

offbeat *adj* unusual, unconventional, or eccentric

off-break *n* cricket a bowled ball that spins from off to leg on pitching

off colour *adj* **1** slightly ill; unwell **2** slightly indecent: *an off colour joke*

offcut *n* a piece of paper, wood, or fabric remaining after the main pieces have been cut; remnant

offence *or* US **offense** *n* **1** law a breaking of a law or rule; a crime **2** annoyance or anger **3** a cause of annoyance or anger **4 give offence** to cause to feel upset or angry **5 take offence** to feel hurt or offended

offend *vb* **1** to hurt the feelings of (a person); insult **2** to be disagreeable to; disgust: *the lady was offended by what she saw* **3** to commit a crime ▶ **HISTORY** Latin *offendere* > **offender** *n* > **offending** *adj*

offensive *adj* **1** unpleasant or disgusting to the senses: *there was an offensive smell of beer* **2** causing annoyance or anger; insulting **3** for the purpose of attack rather than defence ▷ *n* **4** an attitude or position of aggression: *to go on the offensive* **5** an attack or hostile action: *troops had launched a major offensive against the rebel forces* > **offensively** *adv*

offer *vb* **1** to present for acceptance or rejection: *I offered her a lift* **2** to provide: *this department offers a wide range of courses* **3** to present itself: *if an opportunity should offer* **4** to be willing (to do something): *his father offered to pay his tuition* **5** to put forward (a proposal, information, or opinion) for consideration: *may I offer a different view?* **6** to present for sale **7** to propose as payment; bid **8** to present (a prayer or sacrifice) as an act of worship **9** to show readiness for: *to offer resistance* ▷ *n* **10** something that is offered **11** the act of offering ▶ **HISTORY** Latin *offerre* to present

offering *n* **1** something that is offered **2** a contribution to the funds of a religious organization **3** a sacrifice to a god

offertory *n, pl* **-tories** Christianity **1** the part of a church service when the bread and wine for communion are offered for consecration **2** the collection of money at this service **3** the prayers said or sung while the worshippers' offerings are being brought to the altar

offhand *adj also* **offhanded** **1** curt or casual in manner: *I felt calm enough to adopt a casual offhand manner* ▷ *adv* **2** without preparation: *I don't know offhand why that should be so* > **offhandedly** *adv* > **offhandedness** *n*

office *n* **1** a room, set of rooms, or building in which business, professional duties, or clerical work are carried out **2** a department of an organization dealing with particular business: *cheque books were sent from the printer to the bank's sorting office* **3** the group of people working in an office: *she assured him that the office was running smoothly* **4** a government department or agency: *Office of Fair Trading* **5** a position of trust or authority, as in a government: *he would not seek a second term of office* **6** a place where tickets, information, or some service can be obtained: *why don't you give the ticket office a ring?* **7** Christianity a religious ceremony or service **8 good offices** the help given by someone to someone else: *Syria's good offices finally led to the release of two western hostages* **9 in** *or* **out of office** (of a government) in or out of power ▶ **HISTORY** Latin *officium* service, duty

officer *n* **1** a person in the armed services, or on a non-naval ship, who holds a position of authority **2** a policeman or policewoman **3** a person holding a position of authority in a government or organization

official *adj* **1** of an office or position of authority: *I'm not here in any official capacity* **2** approved by or derived from authority: *there has been no official announcement* **3** formal or ceremonial: *he was speaking at an official dinner in Warsaw* ▷ *n* **4** a person holding a position of authority > **officially** *adv*

officialdom *n* officials or bureaucrats collectively

official language *n* any language used within the government of a country

Official Receiver *n* Brit an officer appointed by the government to deal with the affairs of a bankrupt person or company

officiate *vb* **-ating, -ated** **1** to perform the duties of an office; act in an official capacity: *the referee will officiate at the match* **2** to conduct a religious or other ceremony: *the priest officiated at the wedding* > **officiation** *n* > **officiator** *n*

officious *adj* offering unwanted advice or services; interfering ▶ **HISTORY** Latin *officiosus* kindly > **officiousness** *n*

offing *n* **1** the part of the sea that can be seen from the shore **2 in the offing** Brit, Austral & NZ not far off; likely to occur soon

off key *adj, adv* music out of tune

off-licence *n* Brit a shop or a counter in a shop where alcoholic drink is sold for drinking elsewhere

offline *or* **off-line** *adj* **1** (of computer equipment) not directly connected to or controlled by the central processing unit of a computer **2** not connected to the internet

off-load *vb* to get rid of (something unpleasant), usually by giving it to someone else: *you take all the credit and off-load all the blame*

off-putting *adj* informal rather unpleasant or disturbing: *it can be very off-putting when you first visit a social security office*

off-road *adj* (of a motor vehicle) designed for use away from public roads

off-roader *n* a motor vehicle designed for use away from public roads

offset *vb* **-setting, -set** **1** to cancel out or compensate for **2** to print (something) using the offset process ▷ *n* **3** a printing method in which the impression is made onto a surface, such as a rubber roller, which transfers it to the paper **4** *bot* a short runner in certain plants that produces roots and shoots at the tip

offshoot *n* **1** a shoot growing from the main stem of a plant **2** something that has developed from something else

offshore *adj, adv* **1** away from or at some distance from the shore ▷ *adj* **2** sited or conducted at sea: *he reversed his position on offshore drilling*

offside *adj, adv* **1** *sport* (of a player) in a position illegally ahead of the ball when it is played ▷ *n* **2** *chiefly Brit* the side of a vehicle nearest the centre of the road

offspring *n* **1** the immediate descendant or descendants of a person or animal **2** a product, outcome, or result: *the women's liberation movement was the offspring of the 1960s*

Ofgem *n* (in Britain) Office of Gas and Electricity Markets: the body which regulates the power supply industries

Oflot *n* (in Britain) Office of the National Lottery: the body which oversees the running of the National Lottery

Ofsted *n* (in Britain) Office for Standards in Education: the body which assesses the educational standards of schools in England and Wales

oft *adv old-fashioned or poetic* short for **often** ▶ HISTORY Old English

often *adv* **1** frequently; much of the time **2 as often as not** quite frequently **3 every so often** occasionally **4 more often than not** in more than half the instances ▶ HISTORY Middle English variant of *oft*

Ofwat *n* (in Britain) Office of Water Services: the body which regulates the activities of the water companies in England and Wales

ogee arch (**oh**-jee) *n* a pointed arch made with an S-shaped curve on each side ▶ HISTORY probably from Old French

ogle *vb* **ogling, ogled** to stare at (someone) lustfully ▶ HISTORY probably from Low German *oegeln*

O grade *n* (formerly) **1** the basic level of the Scottish Certificate of Education **2** a pass in a particular subject at O grade: *she has eight O grades*

ogre *n* **1** (in folklore) a man-eating giant **2** any monstrous or cruel person ▶ HISTORY French > **ogreish** *adj* > **ogress** *fem n*

oh *interj spoken* an exclamation of surprise, pain, pleasure, fear, or annoyance

OH Ohio

ohm *n* the SI unit of electrical resistance ▶ HISTORY after Georg Simon *Ohm*, physicist

OHMS (in Britain and the Commonwealth) On Her (or His) Majesty's Service

Ohm's law *n electronics* the principle that the electric current passing through a conductor is directly proportional to the potential difference across it, provided that the temperature remains constant ▶ HISTORY named after Georg Simon Ohm, German physicist

oil *n* **1** any of a number of viscous liquids with a smooth sticky feel, which are usually flammable, insoluble in water, and are obtained from plants, animals, or mineral deposits by synthesis **2** same as **petroleum 3** a substance derived from petroleum and used for lubrication **4** *Brit* paraffin as a domestic fuel **5** oil colour or paint **6** an oil painting ▷ *vb* **7** to lubricate with oil or apply oil to **8 oil the wheels** to make things run smoothly ▶ HISTORY Latin *oleum* (olive) oil

oilcloth *n* a cotton fabric treated with oil or a synthetic resin to make it waterproof, formerly used esp. for tablecloths

oilfield *n* an area containing reserves of oil

oilfired *adj* using oil as fuel

oil paint *n* a thick paint made of pigment ground in linseed oil

oil painting *n* **1** a picture painted with oil paints **2** the art of painting with oil paints

oil rig *n* a structure used as a base when drilling an oil well

oil-seed rape *n* same as **rape²**

oilskin *n* **1** a thick cotton fabric treated with oil to make it waterproof **2** a protective outer garment made of this fabric

oil slick *n* a mass of floating oil covering an area of water

oil well *n* a well bored into the earth or sea bed to a supply of oil

oily *adj* **oilier, oiliest 1** soaked or covered with oil **2** of, containing, or like oil **3** attempting to gain favour by insincere behaviour and flattery > **oiliness** *n*

ointment *n* a smooth greasy substance applied to the skin to heal or protect, or as a cosmetic: *home-made creams and ointments* ▶ HISTORY Latin *unguentum* unguent

OK Oklahoma

O.K. or **OK** *informal interj* **1** an expression of approval or agreement ▷ *adj, adv* **2** in good or satisfactory condition ▷ *vb* **O.K.ing, O.K.ed** or **OKing, OKed 3** to approve or endorse ▷ *n, pl* **O.K.s** or **OKs 4** approval or agreement ▶ HISTORY perhaps from *o(ll) k(orrect)*, jocular alteration of *all correct*

okapi (oh-**kah**-pee) *n, pl* **-pis** or **-pi** an African mammal related to the giraffe, but with a shorter neck, a reddish coat, and white stripes on the legs ▶ HISTORY from a Central African word

okay *interj, adj, adv, vb, n* same as **O.K.**

okra *n* a tall plant with long green pods that are used as food ▶ HISTORY West African

old *adj* **1** having lived or existed for a long time: *the old woman; burning witches is one old custom I've no desire to see revived* **2** of or relating to advanced years or a long life: *I twisted my knee as I tried to squat and cursed old age* **3** worn with age or use: *the old bathroom fittings* **4** having lived or existed for a specified period: *he is 60 years old* **5** the earlier or earliest of two or more things with the same name: *the old edition; the Old Testament*

o

old

Depending on which sense of old you mean, there are a number of alternatives which you can use to vary your writing and make it more interesting.

DEFINITION 1

• If you are describing someone who has lived for a long time, you could try: an **aged** grandparent • an **elderly** man • a **venerable** father-figure
• If you are describing something that existed a long time ago, you could try: relics of **ancient** cultures • rituals of a **bygone** civilization • **early** days • in **olden** times • those **remote** days

DEFINITION 2

• If you are talking about something relating to advanced years, you could try: **geriatric** ward • the **grey** pound • **senior** citizens

DEFINITION 3

• If you are describing something that is worn with age, you could try: **decayed** food • **dilapidated** house • **ragged** clothes • **ruined** building • **shabby** furniture • **tatty** curtains • **tumbledown** cottage • **worn** carpets • **worn-out** equipment

DEFINITION 4

• If you are talking about something that has existed for a specified period, you could try: twenty years **of age**

DEFINITION 5

• If you are talking about the earliest of two or more things, you could try: **earliest** edition • **first** printing • **oldest** example

DEFINITION 6

• If you are designating the earliest form of

a language, you could try: **ancient** Greek
• **earliest recorded** Latin

DEFINITION 7

• If you are describing someone or something familiar, you could try: the same **clichéd** phrases • **familiar** scenario • **overused** words • **tired** arguments • **trite** expressions • the **usual** excuses

DEFINITION 8

• If you are using old to express affection, you could try: That's just like **dear** Lydia. • Well done, **dearest** Tom.

DEFINITION 9

• If you are describing something that is out of date, you could try: **antiquated** teaching methods • **archaic** practices • very much **behind the times** • **dated** TV shows • **obsolete** technology • an **old-fashioned** style • **outdated** attitudes • working with **outmoded** equipment • a phone that is **out of date** • That kind of music is **passé**.

DEFINITION 10

• If you are describing someone or something that existed before another thing, you could try: an **earlier** version • his **ex-**girlfriend • my **former** teacher • the **one-time** president • **past** grievances • **previous** tenants • **prior** criminal convictions

DEFINITION 11

• If you are describing someone or something of long standing, you could try: a **long-established** company • **long-standing** acquaintance • **time-honoured** custom

o

---

6 designating the form of a language in which the earliest known records are written: *Old English* **7** familiar through long acquaintance or repetition: *an old acquaintance; the legalization argument is an old and familiar one* **8** dear: used as a term of affection or familiarity: *always rely on old Tom to turn out* **9** out of date; unfashionable **10** former or previous: *my old housekeeper lent me some money* **11** of long standing: *he's an old and respected member of staff* **12 good old days** an earlier period of time regarded as better than the present ▷ *n* **13** an earlier or past time: *in days of old* ▶ HISTORY Old English *eald* > **oldish** *adj*
See WORD FOCUS **old**

old age pension *n* a former name for **retirement pension** > **old age pensioner** *n*

Old Bailey *n* the Central Criminal Court of England

olden *adj* archaic or poetic old: *in the olden days the girls were married young*

Old English *n* the English language of the Anglo-Saxons, spoken from the fifth century AD to about 1100. Also called: **Anglo-Saxon**

Old English sheepdog *n* a large sheepdog with thick shaggy hair

old-fashioned *adj* **1** in the style of a previous period; outdated: *she wore her hair in a strangely old-fashioned tight hairdo* **2** favouring or denoting the styles or ideas of a former time: *old-fashioned values*

old flame *n* informal, old-fashioned a person with whom one once had a romantic relationship

Old French *n* the French language in its earliest forms, from about the 9th century up to about 1400

old guard *n* a group of people in an organization who have traditional values: *the company's old guard is making way for a new, more youthful team* ▶ HISTORY after Napoleon's imperial guard

old hand *n* a skilled or experienced person

old hat *adj* old-fashioned or dull

Old High German *n* a group of West Germanic dialects that developed into modern German; High German up to about 1200

old identity *n* NZ a well-known local person who has lived in an area for a long time

oldie *n* informal an old song, film, or person

old lady *n* informal one's mother or wife

old maid *n* **1** a woman regarded as unlikely ever to marry; spinster **2** informal a prim, fussy, or excessively cautious person

585

old man *n* **1** *informal* one's father or husband **2** an affectionate form of address used to a man

old master *n* **1** one of the great European painters of the period 1500 to 1800 **2** a painting by one of these

old moon *n* a phase of the moon between last quarter and new moon, when it appears as a waning crescent

Old Nick *n informal* Satan

old school tie *n* the system of mutual help supposed to operate among the former pupils of independent schools

Old Style *n* the former method of reckoning dates using the Julian calendar

Old Testament *n* the first part of the Christian Bible, containing the sacred Scriptures of the Hebrews

Old World *n* that part of the world that was known to Europeans before the discovery of the Americas; the eastern hemisphere

oleaginous (oh-lee-**aj**-in-uss) *adj* like or producing oil; oily ▶ HISTORY Latin *oleaginus*

oleander (oh-lee-**ann**-der) *n* an evergreen Mediterranean shrub with fragrant white, pink, or purple flowers ▶ HISTORY Medieval Latin

O level *n* (formerly in England and Wales) **1** the basic level of the General Certificate of Education **2** a pass in a particular subject at O level: *a very intelligent young woman with ten O levels*

olfactory *adj* of the sense of smell ▶ HISTORY Latin *olere* to smell + *facere* to make

oligarchy (**ol**-lee-gark-ee) *n, pl* **-chies** **1** government by a small group of people **2** a state governed this way **3** a small group of people governing such a state ▶ HISTORY Greek *oligos* few + *arkhein* to rule > **oligarchic** *or* **oligarchical** *adj*

Oligocene (**ol**-lig-go-seen) *adj geol* of the epoch of geological time about 35 million years ago ▶ HISTORY Greek *oligos* little + *kainos* new

oligopoly *n, pl* **-lies** *econ* a market situation in which control over the supply of a commodity is held by a small number of producers ▶ HISTORY Greek *oligos* few + *pōlein* to sell

olive *n* **1** an evergreen Mediterranean tree **2** the small green or black bitter-tasting fruit of this tree ▷ *adj* **3** short for **olive-green** ▶ HISTORY Latin *oliva*

olive branch *n* a peace offering: *I should offer some kind of olive branch and get in touch with them*

olive-green *adj* deep yellowish-green

Olympiad *n* **1** a staging of the modern Olympic Games **2** an international contest in chess or other games

Olympian *adj* **1** of Mount Olympus or the classical Greek gods **2** majestic or godlike ▷ *n* **3** a competitor in the Olympic Games **4** a god of Mount Olympus

Olympic *adj* of the Olympic Games

Olympic Games *n* **1** an ancient Greek festival, held every fourth year in honour of Zeus, consisting of games and festivities **2** Also called: **the Olympics** the modern revival of these games,

consisting of international athletic and sporting contests held every four years in a selected country

Om *or* **Aum** (rhymes with **home**) *n Hinduism* a sacred syllable typifying the gods Brahma, Vishnu, and Shiva ▶ HISTORY Sanskrit

OM Order of Merit (a Brit. title)

ombudsman *n, pl* **-men** an official who investigates citizens' complaints against the government or its servants ▶ HISTORY Swedish: commissioner

omega *n* **1** the 24th and last letter of the Greek alphabet (Ω, ω) **2** the ending or last of a series

omelette *or esp US* **omelet** *n* a dish of beaten eggs cooked in a flat pan and often folded round a savoury filling ▶ HISTORY French

omen *n* **1** a thing or occurrence regarded as a sign of future happiness or disaster **2** prophetic significance: *birds of ill omen* ▶ HISTORY Latin

ominous *adj* warning of evil ▶ HISTORY Latin *ominosus* > **ominously** *adv*

omission *n* **1** something that has been left out or passed over **2** an act of missing out or failing to do something: *we regret the omission of these and the names of the other fine artists*

omit *vb* **omitting, omitted** **1** to fail to include; leave out **2** to fail (to do something) ▶ HISTORY Latin *omittere*

omnibus *n, pl* **-buses** **1** a collection of works by one author or several works on a similar topic, reprinted in one volume **2** Also called: **omnibus edition** a television or radio programme consisting of two or more episodes of a serial broadcast earlier in the week **3** *old-fashioned* a bus ▷ *adj* **4** consisting of or dealing with several different things at once: *this year's version of an omnibus crime bill* ▶ HISTORY Latin, literally: for all

omnipotent (om-**nip**-a-tent) *adj* having very great or unlimited power ▶ HISTORY Latin *omnipotens* all-powerful > **omnipotence** *n*

omnipresent *adj* (esp. of a god) present in all places at the same time ▶ HISTORY Latin *omnis* all + *praesens* present > **omnipresence** *n*

omniscient (om-**niss**-ee-ent) *adj formal* knowing or seeming to know everything ▶ HISTORY Latin *omnis* all + *scire* to know > **omniscience** *n*

omniscient point of view *n literature* a narrative style where the storyteller's point of view is not limited to that of a particular character

omnivore (**om**-niv-vore) *n* an animal that eats any type of food

omnivorous (om-**niv**-or-uss) *adj* **1** eating any type of food **2** taking in everything indiscriminately: *his omnivorous sociability has meant constant hard work for his wife* ▶ HISTORY Latin *omnivorus* all-devouring

on *prep* **1** in contact with or at the surface of: *let the cakes stand in the tins on a wire rack; she had dirt on her dress* **2** attached to: *a piece of paper on a clipboard* **3** carried with: *the message found on her* **4** near to or along the side of: *the hotel is on the coast* **5** within the time limits of (a day or date): *they returned to*

Moscow on 22nd September **6** being performed upon or relayed through the medium of: *a construction of refined sounds played on special musical instruments; what's on television?* **7** at the occasion of: *she had received numerous letters congratulating her on her election* **8** immediately after or at the same time as: *check with the tourist office on arrival* **9** through the use of: *an extraordinarily vigorous man who thrives on physical activity; the program runs on the Unix operating system* **10** regularly taking (a drug): *she's on the pill* **11** by means of (a mode of transport): *his only way up the hill had to be on foot; they get around on bicycles* **12** in the process or course of: *he is away on a climbing expedition; coal miners have been on strike for six weeks* **13** concerned with or relating to: *ten million viewers watched the recent series on homelessness* **14** (of a statement or action) having as basis or grounds: *I have it on good authority* **15** charged to: *all drinks are on the house for the rest of the evening* **16** staked as a bet: *I'll have a bet on the favourite* ▷ *adv* **17** in operation; functioning: *the lights had been left on all night* **18** attached to, surrounding, or placed in contact with something: *they escaped with nothing on except sleeveless shirts and shorts* **19** taking place: *what do you have on tonight?* **20** continuously or persistently: *the crisis must not be allowed to drag on indefinitely* **21** forwards or further: *they trudged on* **22 on and off** occasionally; not regularly or continuously **23 on and on** without ceasing; continually ▷ *adj* **24** *informal* performing: *who's on next?* **25** *informal* definitely taking place: *is the party still on?* **26** *informal*, *written* tolerable, practicable, or acceptable: *I'm not going, that's just not on* **27 on at** *spoken, informal* nagging: *he was always on at her to stop smoking* ▷ *n* **28** *cricket* the side of the field to the left of a right-handed batsman when he is facing the bowler ▶ HISTORY Old English *an, on*

ON Ontario

onager *n, pl* **-gri** or **-gers** a wild ass of Persia ▶ HISTORY Greek *onagros*

ONC (in Britain) Ordinary National Certificate

once *adv* **1** one time; on one occasion only **2** at some past time, but no longer: *I was in love once* **3** by one degree (of relationship): *he was Deirdre's cousin once removed* **4 once and for all** conclusively; for the last time **5 once in a while** occasionally; now and then **6 once or twice** a few times **7 once upon a time** used to begin fairy tales and children's stories ▷ *conj* **8** as soon as: *once you have learned good grammar you can leave it to nature and forget it* ▷ *n* **9** one occasion or case: *once is enough* **10 all at once a** suddenly **b** simultaneously **11 at once a** immediately **b** simultaneously **12 for once** this time, even if at no other time ▶ HISTORY Middle English *ones, anes*

once-over *n informal* a quick examination or appraisal

oncogene (**ong**-koh-jean) *n* a gene, present in all cells, that when abnormally activated can cause cancer ▶ HISTORY Greek *onkos* tumour + *-gen* (suffix) producing

oncoming *adj* coming nearer in space or time; approaching: *oncoming traffic*

OND (in Britain) Ordinary National Diploma

one *adj, n* **1** single or lone (person or thing); not two or more: *one civilian has died and thirty-three have been injured* **2** only or unique (person or thing): *he is the one to make correct judgments and influence the public; she was unique, inimitable, one of a kind* **3** a specified (person or thing) as distinct from another or others of its kind: *place one hand under the knee and the other under the ankle; which one is correct?* **4 one or two** a few ▷ *adj* **5** a certain, indefinite, or unspecified (time): *one day he would learn the truth about her* **6** *informal*, emphatic a: *we're on to one hell of a story* ▷ *pron* **7** an indefinite person regarded as typical of every person: *one can always hope that there won't be an accident* **8** any indefinite person: *one can catch fine trout in this stream* **9** I or me: *one only wonders what he has against the dogs* ▷ *n* **10** the smallest natural number and first cardinal number **11** a numeral, 1 or I, representing this number **12** something representing or consisting of one unit **13** *informal* a joke or story: *have you heard the one about the actress and the bishop?* **14 (all) in one** combined or united **15 all one** of no consequence: *leave if you want to, it's all one to me* **16 at one with** in agreement or harmony with **17 one and all** everyone, without exception **18 one by one** one at a time; individually ▶ HISTORY Old English *ān*

one-armed bandit *n informal* a fruit machine operated by pulling down a lever at one side

one-dimensional *adj* **1** having only one of the dimensions of height, length, or width **2** completely lacking in depth or complexity: *her characters are one-dimensional stereotypes*

one-liner *n informal* a short joke or witty remark

oneness *n* **1** agreement **2** uniqueness **3** sameness

one-night stand *n* **1** *informal* a sexual encounter lasting only one evening or night **2** a performance given only once at any one place

one-off *n* something that happens or is made only once

onerous (**own**-er-uss) *adj* (of a task) difficult to carry out ▶ HISTORY Latin *onus* load
> **onerousness** *n*

oneself *pron* **1** the reflexive form of *one* **2** one's normal or usual self: *one doesn't feel oneself after such an experience*

one-sided *adj* **1** considering or favouring only one side of a matter: *it is a one-sided debate* **2** having all the advantage on one side: *it was a one-sided match with Brazil missing a succession of chances*

one-to-one *adj* **1** (of two or more things) corresponding exactly **2** denoting a relationship or encounter in which someone is involved with only one other person: *one-to-one meetings* **3** *maths* involving the pairing of each member of one set with only one member of another set, without remainder

one-way *adj* **1** moving or allowing travel in one direction only: *the town centre has a baffling one-way system* **2** involving no reciprocal obligation or action: *he does not get anything back out of the one-way relationship*

ongoing *adj* in progress; continuing: *there are still ongoing discussions about the future role of NATO*

onion *n* **1** a vegetable with an edible bulb with a strong smell and taste **2 know one's onions** *Brit & NZ, slang* to be fully acquainted with a subject ▶ HISTORY Latin *unio* > **oniony** *adj*

onion skin peeling *n geol* the effect that weathering can have on sedimentary rocks, where the surface is worn away to reveal successive layers

online *or* **on-line** *adj* **1** (of computer equipment) directly connected to and controlled by the central processing unit of a computer **2** of or relating to the internet: *online shopping* ▷ *adv* **3** connected to the internet: *I'll find a gift online*

onlooker *n* a person who observes without taking part > **onlooking** *adj*

only *adj* **1** alone of its or their kind: *I will be talking to the only journalist to have been inside the prison* **2** (of a child) having no brothers or sisters **3** unique by virtue of superiority; best: *first class is the only way to travel* **4 one and only** incomparable: *the one and only Diana Ross* ▷ *adv* **5** without anyone or anything else being included; alone: *only you can decide if you can abide by this compromise* **6** merely or just: *it's only Henry* **7** no more or no greater than: *I was talking to a priest only a minute ago* **8** merely: *they had only to turn up to win the competition* **9** not earlier than; not until: *I've only found out today why you wouldn't come* **10 if only** *or* **if ... only** used to introduce a wish or hope **11 only too** extremely: *they were only too willing to do anything to help* ▷ *conj* **12** but or however: *those countries are going through the same cycle, only a little later than us* ▶ HISTORY Old English *ānlīc*

o.n.o. or near(est) offer

onomatopoeia (on-a-mat-a-**pee**-a) *n literature* use of a word that imitates the sound it represents, such as *hiss* ▶ HISTORY Greek *onoma* name + *poiein* to make > **onomatopoeic** *or* **onomatopoetic** *adj*

onset *n* a start; beginning

onside *adj, adv sport* (of a player) in a legal position, for example, behind the ball or with a required number of opponents between oneself and the opposing team's goal line

onslaught *n* a violent attack ▶ HISTORY Middle Dutch *aenslag*

onto *or* **on to** *prep* **1** to a position that is on: *step onto the train* **2** having discovered or become aware of: *the police are onto us* **3** into contact with: *get onto the factory*

ontology *n philosophy* the study of the nature of being ▶ HISTORY Greek *ōn* being + -LOGY > **ontological** *adj*

onus (**own**-uss) *n, pl* **onuses** a responsibility, task, or burden: *the courts put the onus on parents* ▶ HISTORY Latin: burden

onus of proof *n, pl* **onuses** *law* the obligation to provide evidence that will convince the court or jury of the truth of one's contention if the case is to succeed; in criminal cases, the *onus of proof* lies

with the prosecution and in civil cases, it lies with the plaintiff. Also: **burden of proof** ▶ HISTORY Latin: burden

onward *adj* **1** directed or moving forward ▷ *adv also* **onwards 2** continuing; progressing

onyx *n* a kind of quartz with alternating coloured layers, used as a gemstone ▶ HISTORY Greek: fingernail (so called from its veined appearance)

oodles *pl n informal* great quantities: *he has shown he can raise oodles of cash* ▶ HISTORY origin unknown

oogenesis (oh-a-**jen**-iss-iss) *n biol* the formation and development of ova

oolite (**oh**-a-lite) *n* a limestone made up of tiny grains of calcium carbonate ▶ HISTORY New Latin *oolites*, literally: egg stone > **oolitic** *adj*

oom *n S African* a title of respect used to refer to an elderly man ▶ HISTORY Afrikaans, literally: uncle

oops *interj* an exclamation of surprise or of apology when someone has a slight accident or makes a mistake

OOS occupational overuse syndrome: pain caused by repeated awkward movements while at work

ooze^1 *vb* **oozing, oozed 1** to flow or leak out slowly; seep **2** (of a substance) to discharge moisture **3** to overflow with (a feeling or quality): *he oozes confidence* ▷ *n* **4** a slow flowing or leaking ▶ HISTORY Old English *wōs* juice > **oozy** *adj*

ooze^2 *n* a soft thin mud, such as that found at the bottom of a lake, river, or sea ▶ HISTORY Old English *wāse* mud

op. opus

opacity (ohp-**ass**-it-tee) *n, pl* **-ties 1** the state or quality of being opaque **2** the quality of being difficult to understand; unintelligibility

opal *n* a precious stone, usually milky or bluish in colour, with shimmering changing reflections ▶ HISTORY Greek *opallios*

opalescent *adj* having shimmering changing reflections, like opal > **opalescence** *n*

opaque *adj* **1** not able to be seen through; not transparent or translucent **2** hard to understand; unintelligible ▶ HISTORY Latin *opacus* shady

op art *n* a style of abstract art concerned with optical effects such as the illusion of movement

op. cit. (op sit) (in textual annotations) in the work cited ▶ HISTORY Latin *opere citato*

OPEC Organization of Petroleum-Exporting Countries

open *adj* **1** not closed, fastened, or blocked up: *the doctor's office was open* **2** not enclosed, covered, or wrapped: *the parcel was open* **3** extended, expanded, or unfolded: *an open flower* **4** ready for business: *some of the crafts rooms and photography shops are open all night* **5** (of a job) available: *all the positions on the council should be open to females* **6** unobstructed by buildings or trees: *we lived in a small market town surrounded by open countryside* **7** free to all to join in, enter, or use: *there was an open competition and I was appointed* **8** (of a season or period) not restricted for purposes of hunting game of various kinds **9** not decided or finalized: *the legality of these sales is still an open question*

10 ready to consider new ideas: *I was able to approach their problem with an open mind* **11** honest and frank **12** generous: *she has given me love and the open hand* **13** exposed to view; blatant: *there has never been such sustained and open criticism of the President* **14** unprotected; susceptible: *a change of policy which would leave vulnerable youths open to exploitation* **15** having spaces or gaps: *open ranks; an open texture* **16** *computers* designed to an internationally agreed standard to allow communication between computers irrespective of size or manufacturer **17** *music* **a** (of a string) not stopped with the finger **b** (of a note) played on such a string **18** *sport* (of a goal or court) unguarded or relatively unprotected **19** (of a wound) exposed to the air ▷ *vb* **20** to make or become open: *it was easy to open the back door and to slip noiselessly outside; she knelt and tried to open the drawer* **21** to set or be set in action; start: *the US will have to open talks on Palestinian rights; I want to open a dress shop* **22** to arrange for (a bank account), usually by making an initial deposit **23** to declare open ceremonially or officially ▷ *n* **24 the open** any wide or unobstructed area **25** *sport* a competition which anyone may enter ▶ HISTORY Old English
> **opener** *n* > **openly** *adv* > **openness** *n*

open air *n* the place or space where the air is unenclosed; outdoors

opencast mining *n Brit & Austral* mining by excavating from the surface ▶ HISTORY *open* + archaic *cast* ditch, cutting

open circuit *n electronics* an incomplete electrical circuit in which no current flows

open day *n* a special occasion on which a school, university, or other institution is open for the public to visit

open-ended *adj* **1** without definite limits; unrestricted: *the schedule is open-ended* **2** (of an activity) done without the aim of attaining a particular result or decision: *the dangers of open-ended military involvement*

open-handed *adj* generous

open-hearted *adj* **1** kind or generous **2** willing to speak one's mind; candid

open-heart surgery *n* surgical repair of the heart during which the heart is exposed and the blood circulation is maintained mechanically

open house *n* a situation in which people allow friends or visitors to come to their house whenever they want to

opening *n* **1** the beginning or first part of something **2** the first performance of a theatrical production **3** a chance or opportunity: *an opening into show business* **4** a hole or gap

opening time *n Brit & Austral* the time at which public houses can legally open for business

open letter *n* a letter, esp. one of protest, addressed to an individual but published in a newspaper or magazine for all to read

open market *n* a process by which prices are decided by supply and demand and goods are sold anywhere

open-minded *adj* willing to consider new ideas; unprejudiced

open-plan *adj* having no or few dividing walls between areas: *the house includes an open-plan living room and dining area*

open prison *n* a prison in which the prisoners are not locked up, thus extending the range of work they can do

open-range *adj agriculture* of or relating to the grazing of farm animals on unfenced pasture

open source *n* intellectual property, esp. computer source code, that is made freely available to the general public

Open University *n* (in Britain) a university teaching by means of broadcasts, online materials, correspondence courses, and summer schools

open up *vb* **1** to make or become accessible: *the Berlin Wall came down and opened up new territory for dramatists* **2** to speak freely or without self-restraint **3** to start firing a gun or guns **4** *informal* to increase the speed of (a vehicle)

open verdict *n* a finding by a coroner's jury of death without stating the cause

opera[1] *n* **1** a dramatic work in which most or all of the text is sung to orchestral accompaniment **2** the branch of music or drama relating to operas **3** a group that produces or performs operas **4** a theatre where opera is performed ▶ HISTORY Latin: work

opera[2] *n* a plural of **opus**

operable *adj* **1** capable of being treated by a surgical operation **2** capable of being operated or put into practice > **operability** *n*

opera glasses *pl n* small low-powered binoculars used by audiences in theatres

operand *n maths* a quantity, variable, or function upon which an operation is performed

operate *vb* **-ating, -ated 1** to work **2** to control the working of (a machine) **3** to manage, direct, or run (a business or system) **4** to perform a surgical operation (upon a person or animal) **5** to conduct military or naval operations ▶ HISTORY Latin *operari* to work

operatic *adj* **1** of or relating to opera **2** overdramatic or exaggerated: *he was about to go out with his operatic strut*

operating system *n* the software controlling a computer

operating theatre *or US* **room** *n* a room in which surgical operations are performed

operation *n* **1** the act or method of operating **2** the condition of being in action: *there are twenty teleworking centres in operation around the country* **3** an action or series of actions done to produce a particular result: *a large-scale police operation has been in place to manage the heavy traffic* **4** *surgery* a surgical procedure carried out to remove, replace, or repair a diseased or damaged part of the body **5** a military or naval manoeuvre **6** *maths* any procedure, such as addition, in which a number is derived from another number or numbers by applying specific rules

o

operational *adj* **1** in working order and ready for use **2** of or relating to an action done to produce a particular result

operations research *n* the analysis of problems in business and industry. Also called: **operational research**

operative (**op**-rat-tiv) *adj* **1** in force, effect, or operation: *these pension provisions became operative from 1978* **2** (of a word) particularly relevant or significant: *'if' is the operative word* **3** of or relating to a surgical operation ▷ *n* **4** a worker with a special skill

operator *n* **1** a person who operates a machine or instrument, esp. a telephone switchboard **2** a person who runs a business: *your tour operator will arrange a visa for you* **3** *informal* a person who manipulates affairs and other people: *she considered him a shrewd operator who only liked to appear to be simple* **4** *maths* any symbol, term, or letter used to indicate or express a specific operation or process

operculum (oh-**perk**-yew-lum) *n*, *pl* **-la** (-la) or **-lums** a covering flap or lidlike structure in animals or plants ▶ HISTORY Latin: lid

operetta *n* a type of comic or light-hearted opera

ophiolite suite *n* *geol* a group of rock types frequently found together and originating in the oceanic crust

ophthalmia *n* inflammation of the eyeball or conjunctiva ▶ HISTORY Greek *ophthalmos* eye

ophthalmic *adj* of or relating to the eye

ophthalmic optician *n* See **optician** (sense 1)

ophthalmology *n* the branch of medicine concerned with the eye and its diseases > **ophthalmologist** *n*

ophthalmoscope *n* an instrument for examining the interior of the eye

opiate (oh-pee-ate) *n* **1** a narcotic or sedative drug containing opium **2** something that causes mental dullness or inactivity

opine *vb* **opining, opined** *formal* to hold or express an opinion: *he opined that the navy would have to start again from the beginning* ▶ HISTORY Latin *opinari*

opinion *n* **1** belief not founded on certainty or proof but on what seems probable **2** evaluation or estimation of a person or thing: *they seemed to share my high opinion of her* **3** a judgment given by an expert: *medical opinion* **4** **a matter of opinion** a point open to question ▶ HISTORY Latin *opinio* belief

opinionated *adj* holding very strong opinions which one is convinced are right

opinion evidence *n* *law* evidence in which a witness expresses an opinion; such evidence is only admissible in the case of expert witnesses

opinion poll *n* same as **poll** (sense 1)

opium (oh-pee-um) *n* an addictive narcotic drug made from the seed capsules of the opium poppy and used in medicine as a painkiller and sedative ▶ HISTORY Latin: poppy juice

opossum *n*, *pl* **-sums** or **-sum 1** a thick-furred American marsupial, with a long snout and a hairless prehensile tail **2** *Austral & NZ* a similar Australian animal, such as a phalanger ▶ HISTORY Native American *aposoum*

opponent *n* a person who opposes another in a contest, battle, or argument ▶ HISTORY Latin *opponere* to oppose

opportune *adj* *formal* **1** happening at a time that is suitable or advantageous: *there was an opportune knock at the door* **2** (of time) suitable for a particular purpose: *I have arrived at a very opportune moment* ▶ HISTORY Latin *opportunus*, from *ob-* to + *portus* harbour (originally: coming to the harbour, obtaining timely protection)

opportunist *n* **1** a person who adapts his or her actions to take advantage of opportunities and circumstances without regard for principles ▷ *adj* **2** taking advantage of opportunities and circumstances in this way > **opportunism** *n* > **opportunistic** *adj*

opportunity *n*, *pl* **-ties 1** a favourable combination of circumstances **2** a good chance or prospect

opportunity cost *n* *econ* the benefit that could have been gained from an alternative use of the same resource

opportunity shop *n* *Austral & NZ* a shop selling second-hand clothes, sometimes for charity. Sometimes shortened to: **op-shop**

opposable *adj* *zool* (of the thumb) capable of touching the tip of all the other fingers

oppose *vb* **-posing, -posed 1** Also: **be opposed to** to be against (something or someone) in speech or action **2 as opposed to** in strong contrast with: *I'm a realist as opposed to a theorist* ▶ HISTORY Latin *opponere* > **opposing** *adj*

opposite *adj* **1** situated on the other or further side **2** facing or going in contrary directions: *he saw another small craft heading the opposite way* **3** completely different: *I have a different, in fact, opposite view on this subject* **4** *maths* (of a side in a triangle) facing a specified angle ▷ *n* **5** a person or thing that is opposite; antithesis ▷ *prep* **6** facing; across from ▷ *adv* **7** in an opposite position: *fragments smashed through the windows of the house opposite*

opposition *n* **1** the act of opposing or being opposed **2** hostility, resistance, or disagreement **3** a person or group antagonistic or opposed to another **4** a political party or group opposed to the ruling party or Government: *leader of the opposition* **5** *astrol* a diametrically opposite position of two heavenly bodies

oppress *vb* **1** to put down or control by cruelty or force **2** to make anxious or uncomfortable ▶ HISTORY Latin *ob-* against + *premere* to press > **oppression** *n* > **oppressor** *n*

oppressive *adj* **1** cruel, harsh, or tyrannical **2** uncomfortable or depressing: *a small flat can become rather oppressive* **3** (of weather) hot and humid > **oppressiveness** *n*

opprobrium (op-**probe**-ree-um) *n* *formal* **1** the state of being abused or scornfully criticized

o

2 a cause of disgrace or shame ▸ **HISTORY** Latin *ob-* against + *probrum* a shameful act
> **opprobrious** *adj*

op-shop *n Austral & NZ* short for **opportunity shop**

opt *vb* to show preference (for) or choose (to do something) ▸ **HISTORY** Latin *optare* to choose

optic *adj* of the eye or vision ▸ **HISTORY** Greek *optos* visible

optical *adj* **1** of or involving light or optics **2** of the eye or the sense of sight; optic **3** (of a lens) helping vision

optical character reader *n* a computer device enabling letters and numbers to be optically scanned and input to a storage device

optical fibre *n* a thin flexible glass fibre used in fibre optics to transmit information

optician *n* **1** Also called: **ophthalmic optician** a person who is qualified to examine the eyes and prescribe and supply spectacles and contact lenses **2** Also called: **dispensing optician** a person who supplies and fits spectacle frames and lenses, but is not qualified to prescribe lenses

optic nerve *n* a cranial nerve of vertebrates that conducts nerve impulses from the retina of the eye to the brain

optics *n* the science dealing with light and vision

optimal *adj* best or most favourable

optimism *n* **1** the tendency to take the most hopeful view in all matters **2** *philosophy* the doctrine of the ultimate triumph of good over evil ▸ **HISTORY** Latin *optimus* best > **optimist** *n* > **optimistic** *adj* > **optimistically** *adv*

optimize or **-mise** *vb* **-mizing, -mized** or **-mising, -mised** to make the most of

optimum *n, pl* **-ma** or **-mums 1** the most favourable conditions or best compromise possible ▷ *adj* **2** most favourable or advantageous; best: *balance is a critical part of an optimum diet* ▸ **HISTORY** Latin: the best (thing)

option *n* **1** the power or liberty to choose: *we have no option other than to fully comply* **2** something that is or may be chosen: *the menu includes a vegetarian option* **3** an exclusive right, usually for a limited period, to buy or sell something at a future date: *a producer could extend his option on the material for another six months* **4 keep** or **leave one's options open** not to commit oneself **5 soft option** an easy alternative ▷ *vb* **6** to obtain or grant an option on: *the film rights are optioned by an international film director* ▸ **HISTORY** Latin *optare* to choose

optional *adj* possible but not compulsory; open to choice

optometrist (op-**tom**-met-trist) *n* a person qualified to examine the eyes and prescribe and supply spectacles and contact lenses
> **optometry** *n*

opt out *vb* **1** (often foll. by *of*) to choose not to be involved (in) or part (of), used esp. of schools and hospitals that leave the public sector ▷ *n* **opt-out 2** the act of opting out, esp. of a local authority administration

opulent (**op**-pew-lent) *adj* **1** having or indicating wealth **2** abundant or plentiful ▸ **HISTORY** Latin *opulens* > **opulence** *n*

opus (**oh**-puss) *n, pl* **opuses** or **opera** an artistic creation, esp. a musical work by a particular composer, numbered in order of publication: *Beethoven's opus 61* ▸ **HISTORY** Latin: a work

or *conj* **1** used to join alternatives: *do you want to go out or stay at home?* **2** used to join rephrasings of the same thing: *twelve, or a dozen* ▸ **HISTORY** Middle English contraction of *other*

OR Oregon

oracle *n* **1** a shrine in ancient Greece or Rome at which gods were consulted through the medium of a priest or priestess for advice or prophecy **2** a prophecy or statement made by an oracle **3** any person believed to indicate future action with infallible authority ▸ **HISTORY** Latin *oraculum*

oracular *adj* **1** of or like an oracle **2** wise and prophetic **3** mysterious or ambiguous

oral *adj* **1** spoken or verbal; using spoken words **2** of or for use in the mouth: *an oral thermometer* **3** (of a drug) to be taken by mouth: *an oral contraceptive* ▷ *n* **4** an examination in which the questions and answers are spoken rather than written ▸ **HISTORY** Latin *os, oris* mouth > **orally** *adv*

orange *n* **1** a round reddish-yellow juicy citrus fruit **2** the evergreen tree on which it grows **3** a colour between red and yellow; the colour of an orange ▷ *adj* **4** of a colour between red and yellow ▸ **HISTORY** Arabic *nāranj*

orangeade *n Brit* a usually fizzy orange-flavoured drink

orange blossom *n* the flowers of the orange tree, traditionally worn by brides

Orangeman *n, pl* **-men** a member of a political society founded in Ireland in 1795 to uphold Protestantism ▸ **HISTORY** after William, prince of *Orange*, later William III

orangery *n, pl* **-eries** a conservatory or greenhouse in which orange trees are grown in cooler climates

orang-utan or **orang-utang** *n* a large ape of the forests of Sumatra and Borneo, with shaggy reddish-brown hair and long arms ▸ **HISTORY** Malay *ōrang* man + *hūtan* forest

oration *n* a formal or ceremonial public speech ▸ **HISTORY** Latin *oratio*

orator (**or**-rat-tor) *n* a person who gives an oration, esp. one skilled in persuasive public speaking

oratorio (or-rat-**tor**-ee-oh) *n, pl* **-rios** a musical composition for soloists, chorus, and orchestra, based on a religious theme ▸ **HISTORY** Italian

oratory[1] (**or**-rat-tree) *n* the art or skill of public speaking ▸ **HISTORY** Latin *(ars) oratoria* (the art of) public speaking

oratory[2] *n, pl* **-ries** a small room or building set apart for private prayer ▸ **HISTORY** Latin *orare* to pray

orb *n* **1** an ornamental sphere with a cross on top, carried by a king or queen in important ceremonies

O

2 a sphere; globe **3** *poetic* the eye **4** *obsolete or poetic* a heavenly body, such as the sun ▷ **HISTORY** Latin *orbis* circle, disc

orbit *n* **1** the curved path followed by something, such as a heavenly body or spacecraft, in its motion around another body **2** a range or sphere of action or influence **3** *anat* the eye socket ▷ *vb* **-biting, -bited 4** to move around (a heavenly body) in an orbit **5** to send (a satellite or spacecraft) into orbit ▷ **HISTORY** Latin *orbis* circle > **orbital** *adj*

Orcadian *n* **1** a person from the Orkneys ▷ *adj* **2** of the Orkneys ▷ **HISTORY** Latin *Orcades* the Orkney Islands

orchard *n* an area of land on which fruit trees are grown ▷ **HISTORY** Old English *orceard*

orchestra *n* **1** a large group of musicians whose members play a variety of different instruments **2** Also called: **orchestra pit** the space, in front of or under the stage, reserved for musicians in a theatre ▷ **HISTORY** Greek: the space in the theatre for the chorus > **orchestral** *adj*

orchestrate *vb* **-trating, -trated 1** to score or arrange (a piece of music) for orchestra **2** to arrange (something) in order to produce a particular result: *he had orchestrated today's meeting* > **orchestration** *n*

orchid *n* a plant having flowers of unusual shapes and beautiful colours, usually with one lip-shaped petal which is larger than the other two ▷ **HISTORY** Greek *orkhis* testicle, because of the shape of its roots

ordain *vb* **1** to make (someone) a member of the clergy **2** *formal* to decree or order with authority ▷ **HISTORY** Late Latin *ordinare* > **ordainment** *n*

ordeal *n* **1** a severe or trying experience **2** *history* a method of trial in which the accused person was subjected to physical danger ▷ **HISTORY** Old English *ordāl, ordēl* verdict

order *n* **1** an instruction that must be obeyed; command **2** a state in which everything is arranged logically, comprehensibly, or naturally: *she strove to keep more order in the house* **3** an arrangement of things in succession; sequence: *group them by letter and then put them in numerical order* **4** an established or customary system of society: *there is an opportunity here for a new world order* **5** a peaceful or harmonious condition of society: *riot police were called in to restore order* **6 a** an instruction to supply something in return for payment: *the waitress came to take their order* **b** the thing or things supplied **7** a written instruction to pay money: *post the coupon below with a cheque or postal order* **8** a social class: *the result will be harmful to society as a whole and to the lower orders in particular* **9** *biol* one of the groups into which a class is divided, containing one or more families **10** kind or sort: *the orchestra played superbly and the singing was of the highest order* **11** Also called: **religious order** a religious community of monks or nuns **12** a group of people who have been awarded a particular honour: *the Order of the Garter* **13** the office or rank of a Christian minister: *he studied for* the priesthood as a young man, but never took Holy Orders **14** the procedure and rules followed by an assembly or meeting: *a point of order* **15** one of the five major classical styles of architecture, classified by the type of columns used **16 a tall order** something difficult or demanding **17 in order a** in sequence **b** properly arranged: *everything is in order for your trip* **c** appropriate or fitting **18 in order that** so that **19 in order to** so that it is possible to: *a healthy diet is necessary in order to keep fit* **20 in** or **of the order of** amounting approximately to: *summer temperatures are usually in the order of thirty-five degrees* **21 keep order** to ensure that people obey the law or behave in an acceptable manner **22 on order** having been ordered but not yet delivered **23 out of order a** not in sequence **b** not working: *the lift was out of order, so we had to use the stairs* **c** not following the rules or customary procedure: *the chairperson ruled the motion out of order* **24 to order** according to a buyer's specifications ▷ *vb* **25** to command or instruct (to do something): *she ordered her son to wash the dishes; the police ordered her into the house* **26** to request (something) to be supplied in return for payment: *I ordered a new car three weeks ago, but it hasn't been delivered yet* **27** to arrange (things) methodically or in their proper places ▷ *interj* **28** an exclamation demanding that orderly behaviour be restored ▷ **HISTORY** Latin *ordo*

ordered pair *n maths* an ordered set of only two elements: *the ordered pair a,b does not equal b,a unless a = b*

ordered set *n maths* a sequence of elements, usually enclosed in angle brackets, which must appear in a particular order to maintain the same value: *a, b, c is an ordered set and is therefore not equal to c, b, a*

orderly *adj* **1** tidy or well-organized: *they evacuated the building in an orderly manner* **2** well-behaved; law-abiding ▷ *n, pl* **-lies 3** *med* a male hospital attendant **4** *mil* a soldier whose duty is to carry orders or perform minor tasks for a more senior officer > **orderliness** *n*

order of combinations *n maths* (in transformational geometry) the number of members of a set organized into specified groups without regard to order in the group

order of operations *n maths* the conventional order in which multiple mathematical operations should be performed: brackets, exponents, division and multiplication (left to right), addition and subtraction (left to right)

order of reactivity *n chem* a list of chemical elements arranged according to how reactive they are

order paper *n* a list indicating the order of business, esp. in Parliament

ordinal number *n* a number indicating position in a sequence, such as *first, second, third*

ordinance *n* an official rule or order ▷ **HISTORY** Latin *ordinare* to set in order

ordinarily *adv* in circumstances; usually; normally

o

ordinary *adj* **1** usual or normal: *it was an ordinary working day for them* **2** not special or different in any way: *what do ordinary Germans feel about reunification?* **3** dull or unexciting: *the restaurant charged very high prices for very ordinary cooking* ▷ *n, pl* **-naries** **4** *RC Church* the parts of the Mass that do not vary from day to day **5** **out of the ordinary** unusual ▶ HISTORY Latin *ordinarius* orderly

Ordinary level *n* (in Britain) the formal name for **O level**

ordinary rating *n* a rank in the Royal Navy equivalent to that of a private in the army

ordinary seaman *n Brit, Austral & NZ* a seaman of the lowest rank

ordinary shares *pl n Brit & Austral* shares issued by a company entitling their holders to a dividend according to the profits of the company and to a claim on net assets

ordinate *n maths* the vertical coordinate of a point in a two-dimensional system of coordinates ▶ HISTORY Latin *ordinare* to arrange in order

ordination *n* the act or ceremony of making someone a member of the clergy

ordnance *n* **1** weapons and other military supplies **2** **the ordnance** a government department dealing with military supplies ▶ HISTORY variant of *ordinance*

Ordnance Survey *n* the British government organization that produces detailed maps of Britain and Ireland

Ordovician (or-doe-**vish**-ee-an) *adj geol* of the period of geological time about 500 million years ago ▶ HISTORY Latin *Ordovices*, ancient Celtic tribe in N Wales

ordure *n* excrement; dung ▶ HISTORY Old French *ord* dirty

ore *n* rock or mineral from which valuable substances such as metals can be extracted ▶ HISTORY Old English *ār, ōra*

oregano (or-rig-**gah**-no) *n* a sweet-smelling herb used as seasoning ▶ HISTORY Greek *origanon* an aromatic herb

organ *n* **1** a part in animals and plants that is adapted to perform a particular function, for example the heart or lungs **2 a** a musical keyboard instrument which produces sound by forcing air through pipes of a variety of lengths **b** Also called: **electric organ** a keyboard instrument which produces similar sounds electronically **3** a means of communication, such as a newspaper issued by a specialist group or party ▶ HISTORY Greek *organon* tool

organdie *n* a fine, slightly stiff cotton fabric ▶ HISTORY French *organdi*

organelle *n chem* a structural and functional unit such as a mitochondrion, in a cell or unicellular organism

organ-grinder *n* (formerly) an entertainer who played a barrel organ in the streets

organic *adj* **1** of, produced by, or found in plants or animals: *the rocks were carefully searched for organic remains* **2** not using, or grown without, artificial

fertilizers or pesticides: *organic vegetables; an organic farm* **3** *chem* of or belonging to the class of chemical compounds that are formed from carbon **4** (of change or development) gradual and natural rather than sudden or forced **5** made up of many different parts which contribute to the way in which the whole society or structure works: *an organic whole* ▷ *n* **6** food produced without artificial fertilizers or pesticides > **organically** *adv*

organic chemistry *n chem* the branch of chemistry dealing with carbon compounds

organic farming *n agriculture* farming without using artificial fertilizers and pesticides

organism *n* **1** an animal or plant **2** anything resembling a living creature in structure, behaviour, or complexity: *cities are more complicated organisms than farming villages*

organist *n* a person who plays the organ

organization *or* **-isation** *n* **1** an organized group of people, such as a club, society, union, or business **2** the act of organizing: *setting up the European tour took a lot of organization* **3** the structure and arrangement of the different parts of something: *the report recommended radical changes in the organization of the social services department* **4** the state of being organized: *the material in this essay lacks any sort of organization* > **organizational** *or* **-isational** *adj*

organization chart *n business* a chart showing the structure and relationships of the positions within an organization

organize *or* **-ise** *vb* **-izing, -ized** *or* **-ising, -ised** **1** to plan and arrange (something): *we organized a protest meeting in the village hall* **2** to arrange systematically: *the files are organized in alphabetical order and by date* **3** to form, join, or recruit (people) into a trade union: *the seasonal nature of tourism makes it difficult for hotel workers to organize* ▶ HISTORY Medieval Latin *organizare* > **organizer** *or* **-iser** *n*

organized *or* **-ised** *adj* **1** planned and controlled on a large scale and involving many people: *organized crime* **2** orderly and efficient: *a highly organized campaign* **3** (of the workers in a factory or office) belonging to a trade union: *socialism is especially popular among organized labour*

orgasm *n* the most intense point of pleasure and excitement during sexual activity ▶ HISTORY Greek *orgasmos* > **orgasmic** *adj*

orgy *n, pl* **-gies** **1** a wild party involving promiscuous activity and excessive drinking **2** an act of immoderate or frenzied indulgence: *the rioters were engaged in an orgy of destruction* ▶ HISTORY Greek *orgia* secret rites > **orgiastic** *adj*

oriel window *or* **oriel** *n* a window built out from the wall of a house at an upper level ▶ HISTORY Old French *oriol* gallery

orient *vb* **1** to adjust or align (oneself or one's ideas) according to surroundings or circumstances: *new employees can take some time to orient themselves to the company's procedures* **2** to position or set (a map or chart) with relation to the points of the compass 593 or other specific directions **3 be oriented to** or **towards** to work or act with a particular aim, idea, or person in mind: *many people feel that Britain is too much oriented to the Americans* ▷ n **4** *poetic* the east ▶ HISTORY Latin *oriens* rising (sun)

Orient n **the Orient** East Asia

Oriental adj of the Orient

orientate vb **-tating, -tated** same as **orient**

-orientated or **-oriented** adj combining form interested in or directed towards the thing specified: *career-orientated women*

orientation n **1** the activities and aims that a person or organization is interested in: *the course has a practical rather than theoretical orientation* **2** the position of an object with relation to the points of the compass or other specific directions: *the room's southerly orientation means that it receives a lot of light* ▷ adj **3** of or providing information or training needed to understand a new situation or environment: *nearly every college has an orientation programme*

orienteering n a sport in which contestants race on foot over a cross-country course consisting of checkpoints found with the aid of a map and compass ▶ HISTORY Swedish *orientering*

orifice (**or**-rif-fiss) n an opening or hole through which something can pass, esp. one in the body such as the mouth or anus ▶ HISTORY Latin *os* mouth + *facere* to make

origami (or-rig-**gah**-mee) n the art, originally Japanese, of folding paper intricately into decorative shapes ▶ HISTORY Japanese *ori* a fold + *kami* paper

origin n **1** the point, source, or event from which something develops: *the origin of the term 'jazz' is obscure; the war had its origin in the clash between rival nationalists* **2** the country, race, or social class of a person's parents or ancestors: *an Australian of Greek origin; he was proud of his working-class origins* **3** *maths* the point at which the horizontal and vertical axes intersect ▶ HISTORY Latin *origo* beginning

original adj **1** first or earliest: *the dining room also has attractive original beams* **2** fresh and unusual; not copied from or based on something else: *the composer's work has created some original and attractive choreography* **3** able to think of or carry out new ideas or concepts: *he is an excitingly original writer* **4** being the first and genuine form of something, from which a copy or translation is made: *all French recipes were translated from the original abridged versions* ▷ n **5** the first and genuine form of something, from which others are copied or translated: *the original is in the British Museum* **6** a person or thing used as a model in art or literature: *she claimed to be the original on whom Lawrence based Lady Chatterley* > **originality** n > **originally** adv

original jurisdiction n *law* a court's power to hear a case for the first time rather than on appeal: *it is both a court of original jurisdiction and an appellate court*

original sin n a state of sin believed by some Christians to be inborn in all human beings as a result of Adam's disobedience

originate vb **-nating, -nated** to come or bring (something) into existence: *humans probably originated in East Africa* > **origination** n > **originator** n

oriole n a songbird with a long pointed bill and a mostly yellow-and-black plumage ▶ HISTORY Latin *aureolus* golden

orisha (uh-**rish**-uh) n any of the minor gods or spirits of traditional Yoruba religion and its Caribbean and S American offshoots ▶ HISTORY Yoruba

ormolu n a gold-coloured alloy of copper, tin, or zinc, used to decorate furniture and other articles ▶ HISTORY French *or moulu* ground gold

ornament n **1** anything that adorns someone or something; decoration: *the room's only ornament was a dim, oily picture of the Holy Family* **2** decorations collectively: *he had no watch, nor ornament of any kind* **3** a small decorative object: *I hit a garden ornament while parking* **4** a person whose character or talent makes them an asset to society or the group to which they belong: *an ornament of the firm* **5** *music* a note or group of notes which embellishes the melody but is not an integral part of it, for instance a trill ▷ vb **6** to decorate or adorn: *the hall had a high ceiling, ornamented with plaster fruits and flowers* ▶ HISTORY Latin *ornamentum* > **ornamental** adj > **ornamentation** n > **ornamented** adj

ornate adj **1** heavily or elaborately decorated: *an ornate ceiling painted with allegorical figures* **2** (of style in writing) overelaborate; using many literary expressions ▶ HISTORY Latin *ornare* to decorate > **ornately** adv

ornithology n the study of birds ▶ HISTORY Greek *ornis* bird > **ornithological** adj > **ornithologist** n

orogeny or **orogenesis** n *geol* the formation of mountain ranges > **orogenic** or **orogenetic** adj

orographic rain n *meteorol* rain that results from moist air being forced to rise by the effects of hills or mountains

orographic rainfall n *meteorol* rainfall resulting from moist air being forced up over mountain ranges where it cools and condenses

orphan n **1** a child whose parents are dead ▷ vb **2** to cause (someone) to become an orphan: *she was orphaned at 16 when her parents died in a car crash* ▶ HISTORY Greek *orphanos*

orphanage n a children's home for orphans and abandoned children

orphaned adj having no living parents

orrery n, pl **-ries** a mechanical model of the solar system in which the planets can be moved around the sun ▶ HISTORY originally made for Earl of *Orrery*

orris n **1** a kind of iris that has fragrant roots **2** Also: **orrisroot** the root of this plant prepared and used as perfume ▶ HISTORY variant of *iris*

orthodontics n the branch of dentistry concerned with correcting irregularities of the

o

teeth ▶ HISTORY Greek *orthos* straight + *odōn* tooth > **orthodontic** *adj* > **orthodontist** *n*

orthodox *adj* conforming to traditional or established standards in religion, behaviour, or attitudes: *orthodox medicine; the concerto has a more orthodox structure than is usual for this composer* ▶ HISTORY Greek *orthos* correct + *doxa* belief > **orthodoxy** *n*

Orthodox *adj* 1 of the Orthodox Church of Eastern Europe 2 of or being the form of Judaism characterized by traditional interpretation of and strict adherence to Mosaic Law: *an Orthodox Jew*

Orthodox Church *n* the Christian Church dominant in Eastern Europe, which has the Greek Patriarch of Constantinople as its head

orthography *n* 1 spelling considered to be correct: *British and American orthography is different in many cases* 2 the study of spelling ▶ HISTORY Greek *orthos* correct + *graphein* to write > **orthographic** *adj*

orthopaedics *or US* **orthopedics** *n* the branch of surgery concerned with disorders of the bones and joints ▶ HISTORY Greek *orthos* straight + *pais* child > **orthopaedic** *or US* **orthopedic** *adj* > **orthopaedist** *or US* **orthopedist** *n*

ortolan *n* a small European songbird eaten as a delicacy ▶ HISTORY Latin *hortulus* a little garden

oryx *n* any of various large straight-horned African antelopes

Os *chem* osmium

OS 1 (in Britain) Ordnance Survey 2 outsize(d)

Oscar *n trademark* an award in the form of a small gold statuette awarded annually in the US for outstanding achievements in various aspects of the film industry: *he won an Oscar for Best Supporting Actor in 1974* ▶ HISTORY said to have been named after a remark made by an official that it reminded her of her uncle Oscar

oscillate (**oss**-ill-late) *vb* **-lating, -lated** 1 to swing repeatedly back and forth: *its wings oscillate up and down many times a second* 2 to waver between two extremes of opinion, attitude, or behaviour: *the government oscillates between a desire for reform and a desire to keep its powers intact* 3 *physics* (of an electric current) to vary between minimum and maximum values ▶ HISTORY Latin *oscillare* to swing > **oscillation** *n* > **oscillator** *n*

oscilloscope (oss-**sill**-oh-scope) *n* an instrument that produces a visual representation of an oscillating electric current on the screen of a cathode-ray tube

osier (**oh**-zee-er) *n* 1 a willow tree whose flexible branches or twigs are used for making baskets and furniture 2 a twig or branch from this tree ▶ HISTORY Old French

osmium *n chem* a very hard brittle bluish-white metal, the heaviest known element. Symbol: Os ▶ HISTORY Greek *osmē* smell, from its penetrating odour

osmoregulation *n zool* the adjustment of the osmotic pressure of a cell or organism in relation to the surrounding fluid

osmosis *n* 1 the diffusion of liquids through a membrane until they are mixed 2 the process by which people or ideas influence each other gradually and subtly ▶ HISTORY Greek *ōsmos* push > **osmotic** *adj*

osprey *n* a large fish-eating bird of prey, with a dark back and whitish head and underparts ▶ HISTORY Old French *ospres*, apparently from Latin *ossifraga*, literally: bone-breaker

osseous *adj* consisting of or like bone ▶ HISTORY Latin *os* bone

ossify *vb* **-fies, -fying, -fied** 1 to change into bone; harden 2 to become rigid, inflexible, or unprogressive: *ossified traditions* ▶ HISTORY Latin *os* bone + *facere* to make > **ossification** *n*

ostensible *adj* apparent or seeming; alleged: *our ostensible common interest is boats* ▶ HISTORY Latin *ostendere* to show > **ostensibly** *adv*

ostensive *adj* directly showing or pointing out: *he gave ostensive definitions to things* ▶ HISTORY Latin *ostendere* to show

ostentation *n* pretentious, showy, or vulgar display: *she felt the gold taps in the bathroom were tasteless ostentation* > **ostentatious** *adj* > **ostentatiously** *adv*

osteoarthritis (ost-ee-oh-arth-**rite**-iss) *n* chronic inflammation of the joints, causing pain and stiffness ▶ HISTORY Greek *osteon* bone + ARTHRITIS > **osteoarthritic** *adj*

osteopathy *n* a system of healing based on the manipulation of bones or muscles ▶ HISTORY Greek *osteon* bone + *patheia* suffering > **osteopath** *n*

osteoporosis (ost-ee-oh-pore-**oh**-siss) *n* brittleness of the bones, caused by lack of calcium ▶ HISTORY Greek *osteon* bone + *poros* passage

ostinato *n, pl* **-tos** *music* a persistently repeated phrase or rhythm ▶ HISTORY Italian, from Latin *obstinatus* obstinate

ostler *n* (formerly) a stableman at an inn ▶ HISTORY variant of *hostler*, from *hostel*

ostracize *or* **-cise** *vb* **-cizing, -cized** *or* **-cising, -cised** to exclude or banish (a person) from a particular group or from society: *he was ostracized from his family when his affair became known* ▶ HISTORY Greek *ostrakizein* to select someone for banishment by voting on potsherds > **ostracism** *n*

ostrich *n* 1 a large African bird which runs fast but cannot fly, and has a long neck, long legs, and soft dark feathers 2 a person who refuses to recognize an unpleasant truth: *he accused the Minister of being 'an ostrich with its head stuck in the sand, while all around him unemployment soars'* ▶ HISTORY Greek *strouthion*

OT Old Testament

OTC (in Britain) Officers' Training Corps

OTE *chiefly Brit* (esp. in job adverts) on target earnings: the minimum amount of money a salesman is expected to make

other *adj* 1 remaining (one or ones) in a group of which one or some have been specified: *she wasn't getting on with the other children* 2 being a different

595

one or ones from the one or ones already specified or understood: *other people might not be so tolerant of your behaviour; are you sure it's not in your other pocket?* **3** refers to a place or time which is not the one the speaker or writer is in: *results in other countries have been most encouraging* **4** additional; further: *there is one other thing for the government to do* **5 every other** alternate: *the doctor sees me every other week* **6 other than a** apart from: *he knew little of the country other than it was Muslim* **b** different from: *treatment other than a hearing aid will be possible for those with inner ear deafness* **7 or other** used to add vagueness to the preceding word or phrase: *he could take some evening course or other which could lead to an extra qualification; he was called away from the house on some pretext or other* **8 the other day** a few days ago ▷ *n* **9** an additional person or thing: *show me one other* **10 others** people apart from the person who is being spoken or written about: *she devoted her entire life to helping others* **11 the others** the people or things remaining in a group of which one or some have been specified: *I can't speak for the others* ▷ *adv* **12** otherwise; differently: *they couldn't behave other than they do* ▶ HISTORY Old English *ōther*
> otherness *n*

other ranks *pl n Brit & Austral* (in the armed forces) all those who do not hold a commissioned rank

otherwise *conj* **1** or else; if not, then: *I was fifty but said I was forty, otherwise I'd never have got a job* ▷ *adv written* **2** differently: *it was fruitless to pretend or to hope otherwise* **3** in other respects: *shrewd psychological twists perk up an otherwise predictable story line* ▷ *adj* **4** different: *circumstances beyond our control dictated that it should be otherwise* ▷ *pron* **5 or otherwise** or not; or the opposite: *he didn't want company, talkative or otherwise*

otherworldly *adj* **1** concerned with spiritual rather than practical matters: *his otherworldly manner concealed a ruthless business mind* **2** mystical or supernatural: *this part of Italy has an otherworldly beauty*

otiose (oh-tee-oze) *adj* serving no useful purpose: *such a strike is almost otiose* ▶ HISTORY Latin *otiosus* leisured

OTT *Brit & S African, slang* over the top

otter *n* a small freshwater fish-eating animal with smooth brown fur, a streamlined body, and webbed feet ▶ HISTORY Old English *otor*

ottoman *n, pl* **-mans** a storage chest with a padded lid for use as a seat ▶ HISTORY French *ottomane*, feminine of *Ottoman*

Ottoman *adj* **1** *history* of the Ottomans or the Ottoman Empire, the Turkish empire which lasted from the late 13th century until the end of World War I, and at its height included the Balkans and much of N Africa ▷ *n, pl* **-mans** **2** a member of a Turkish people who formed the basis of this empire ▶ HISTORY Arabic *Othmāni*

ou (oh) *n S African, slang* a man, bloke, or chap ▶ HISTORY Afrikaans

OU 1 the Open University **2** Oxford University

oubaas (oh-bahss) *n S African* a man in authority ▶ HISTORY Afrikaans *ou* man + *baas* boss

oubliette (oo-blee-ett) *n history* a dungeon, the only entrance to which is a trap door in the ceiling ▶ HISTORY French *oublier* to forget

ouch *interj* an exclamation of sharp sudden pain

ought *vb* **1** used to express duty or obligation: *she ought to tell this to the police* **2** used to express advisability: *we ought to get the roof repaired before the attics get any damper* **3** used to express probability or expectation: *a good lawyer ought to be able to fix it for you* **4** used to express a desire on the part of the speaker: *you ought to have a good breakfast before you hit the road* ▶ HISTORY Old English *āhte*, past tense of *āgan* to owe

Ouija board *or* **Ouija** (weej-a) *n trademark* a board on which are marked the letters of the alphabet. Answers to questions are spelt out by a pointer, which is supposedly guided by spirits ▶ HISTORY French *oui* yes + German *ja* yes

ouma (oh-mah) *n S African* **1** grandmother, often as a title with a surname **2** *slang* any elderly woman ▶ HISTORY Afrikaans

ounce *n* **1** a unit of weight equal to one sixteenth of a pound or 28.4 grams **2** short for **fluid ounce** **3** a small amount: *you haven't got one ounce of control over her* ▶ HISTORY Latin *uncia* a twelfth

OUP (in Northern Ireland) Official Unionist Party

oupa (oh-pah) *n S African* **1** grandfather, often as a title with a surname **2** *slang* any elderly man ▶ HISTORY Afrikaans

our *adj* **1** of, belonging to, or associated with us: *our daughter* **2** a formal word for *my* used by monarchs ▶ HISTORY Old English *ūre*

Our Father *n* same as the **Lord's Prayer**

ours *pron* **1** something belonging to us: *ours are smaller guns than those; the money is ours* **2 of ours** belonging to or associated with us: *my wife and a friend of ours had both deserted me*

ourselves *pron* **1 a** the reflexive form of *we* or *us*: *we humiliated ourselves* **b** used for emphasis: *we ourselves will finish it* **2** our usual selves: *we've not been feeling quite ourselves since the accident* **3** *not standard* used instead of *we* or *us* in compound noun phrases: *other people and ourselves*

ousel *n* same as **ouzel**

oust *vb* to force (someone) out of a position; expel: *the coup which ousted the President* ▶ HISTORY Anglo-Norman *ouster*

ouster *n US* an act or instance of forcing someone out of a position: *the demonstrators called for the ouster of the police chief*

out *adv, adj* **1** away from the inside of a place: *she took her purse out; inspection of the eggs should be done when the hen is out of the nest* **2** away from one's home or place of work for a short time: *I called earlier but you were out; a search party is out looking for survivors* **3** no longer burning, shining, or functioning: *he switched the light out; the living-room fire went out while we were next door eating* **4** used up; not having any more of: *their supplies ran out after* two weeks; we're out of milk **5** public; revealed: *our dirty little secret is out* **6** available to the public: *her biography will be out in December* **7** (of the sun, stars, or moon) visible *the roses are out early this year* **9** not in fashion or current usage: *trying to be trendy is out* **10** excluded from consideration: *cost cutting is out of the question* **11** not allowed: *smoking on duty is out* **12 out for** or **to** wanting or intent on (something or doing something): *the young soldiers were out for revenge; they're out to get me* **13** *sport* (of a player in a sport like cricket or baseball) no longer batting because he or she has been dismissed by being caught, bowled, etc. **14** on strike **15** in or into a state of unconsciousness: *he went outside and passed out in an alley* **16** used to indicate a burst of activity as indicated by a verb: *war broke out in the Gulf* **17** out of existence: *the mistakes were scored out* **18** to the fullest extent: *spread out* **19** loudly; clearly: *he cried out in shock and pain* **20** to a conclusion; completely: *she'd worked it out for herself* **21** existing: *the friendliest dog out* **22** inaccurate or incorrect: *the estimate was out by sixty pounds* **23** not in office or authority: *she was finally voted out as party leader* **24** (of a period of time) completed: *before the year is out* **25** openly homosexual: *I came out as a lesbian when I was still in my teens* **26** old-fashioned (of a young woman) in or into upper-class society life: *Lucinda had a large party when she came out* **27 out of a** at or to a point outside: *the train pulled out of the station* **b** away from; not in: *they're out of touch with reality; out of focus* **c** because of; motivated by: *out of jealousy* **d** from (a material or source): *made out of plastic* **e** no longer in a specified state or condition: *out of work; out of practice* ▷ *adj* **28** *informal* not concealing one's homosexuality ▷ *prep* **29** *US, not standard* out of; out through: *he ran out the door* ▷ *interj* **30 a** an exclamation of dismissal **b** (in signalling and radio) an expression used to signal that the speaker is signing off: *over and out!* ▷ *vb* **31** *informal* to expose (a public figure) as being homosexual **32** *informal* to reveal something embarrassing or unknown about (a person): *he was outed as a talented goal scorer* ▶ HISTORY Old English *ūt*

out- *prefix* **1** excelling or surpassing in a particular action: *outlast; outlive* **2** at or from a point away; outside: *outpost; outpatient* **3** going away; outward: *outcrop; outgrowth*

outage *n* a period of power failure

outback *n* the remote bush country of Australia

outbid *vb* **-bidding, -bidded** or **-bid** to offer a higher price than (another person)

outboard motor *n* a portable petrol engine that can be attached externally to the stern of a boat to propel it

outbox *n computers* a folder in which outgoing messages are stored

outbreak *n* a sudden occurrence of disease or war

outbuilding *n* same as **outhouse**

outburst *n* **1** a sudden strong expression of emotion, esp. of anger: *such emotional outbursts do nothing to help calm discussion of the matter*

2 a sudden period of violent activity: *this sudden outburst of violence has come as a shock*

outcast *n* a person who is rejected or excluded from a particular group or from society

outclass *vb* to surpass (someone) in performance or quality

outcome *n* the result or consequence of something

outcrop *n* part of a rock formation that sticks out of the earth

outcry *n, pl* **-cries** a widespread or vehement protest: *there was great popular outcry against the plan for a dual carriageway*

outdated *adj* old-fashioned or obsolete

outdo *vb* **-doing, -did, -done** to be more successful or better than (someone or something) in performance: *this car easily outdoes its rivals when it comes to comfort*

outdoor *adj* **1** taking place, existing, or intended for use in the open air: *have a swim at the beach or outdoor pool; she was just taking off her outdoor clothing* **2** fond of the outdoors: *Paul was a butch outdoor type*

outdoors *adv* **1** in the open air; outside: *he hardly ever went outdoors* ▷ *n* **2** the world outside or far away from buildings; the open air: *he'd forgotten his fear of the outdoors*

outer *adj* **1** on the outside; external: *the building's outer walls were painted pale pink* **2** further from the middle: *the outer suburbs* ▷ *n* **3** *archery* **a** the white outermost ring on a target **b** a shot that hits this ring

outermost *adj* furthest from the centre or middle

outer space *n* space beyond the atmosphere of the earth

outface *vb* **-facing, -faced** to subdue or disconcert (someone) by staring

outfall *n Brit, Austral & NZ* the mouth of a river, drain, or pipe: *the survey measured pollution levels near sewer outfalls*

outfield *n* **1** *cricket* the area of the field far from the pitch **2** *baseball* the area of the playing field beyond the lines connecting first, second, and third bases > **outfielder** *n*

outfit *n* **1** a set of clothes worn together **2** *informal* a group of people working together as a unit **3** a set of equipment for a particular task; kit: *a complete anti-snakebite outfit*

outfitter *n old-fashioned* a shop or person that sells men's clothes

outflank *vb* **1** to go around and beyond the side of (an enemy army) **2** to get the better of (someone)

outgoing *adj* **1** leaving: *some members of the outgoing government continued to attend the peace talks* **2** friendly and sociable

outgoings *pl n* expenses

outgrow *vb* **-growing, -grew, -grown** **1** to grow too large for (clothes or shoes): *it's amazing how quickly children outgrow their clothes* **2** to lose (a way of behaving or thinking) in the course of becoming more mature: *most teenagers outgrow their*

597

moodiness as they near adulthood **3** to grow larger or faster than (someone or something): *the weeds threatened to outgrow and choke the rice plants*

outgrowth *n* **1** a natural development or consequence: *he argued that religion was an outgrowth of magic* **2** a thing growing out of a main body; offshoot

outhouse *n* a building near to, but separate from, a main building

outing *n* a trip or excursion

outlandish *adj* extremely unconventional; bizarre

outlast *vb* to last longer than

outlaw *n* **1** *history* a criminal who has been deprived of legal protection and rights ▷ *vb* **2** to make (something) illegal: *racial discrimination was formally outlawed* **3** *history* to make (someone) an outlaw > **outlawed** *adj*

outlay *n* the money, effort, or time spent on something

outlet *n* **1** a means of expressing one's feelings: *the shock would give her an outlet for her own grief* **2 a** a market for a product: *there is a huge sales outlet for personal computers* **b** a shop or organization selling the goods of a particular producer or wholesaler or manufacturer: *her own brand is now sold to outlets throughout the world* **3** an opening permitting escape or release: *make sure the exhaust outlet is not blocked*

outlier *n* **1** a person, thing, or part situated away from a main body **2** *statistics* a point in a sample widely separated from the main cluster of points in the sample

outline *n* **1** a general explanation or description of something, which does not give all the details: *the course gave a brief outline of twentieth-century music* **2 outlines** the important features of something: *the outlines of his theory are correct, we just need to fill in the details* **3** the general shape of something, esp. when only the profile and not the details are visible: *it was still light enough to see the outline of the distant mountains* **4** a drawing showing only the external lines of an object ▷ *vb* **-lining, -lined** **5** to give the main features or general idea of (something): *I outlined what we had done and what we had still to do* **6** to show the general shape of an object but not its details, as light does coming from behind an object: *we could see the towers of the city outlined against the night sky*

outlive *vb* **-living, -lived** **1** to live longer than (someone): *she only outlived her husband by a few months* **2** to live beyond (a date or period): *the sparrow outlived the winter* **3 outlive its usefulness** to be no longer useful or necessary: *some argued that the organization had outlived its usefulness*

outlook *n* **1** a general attitude to life: *my whole outlook on life had changed* **2** the probable condition or outcome of something: *the economic outlook is not good* **3** the weather forecast for the next few days: *the outlook for the weekend* **4** the view from a place: *a dreary outlook of chimneys and smoke*

outlying *adj* far away from the main area

outmanoeuvre *or US* **outmaneuver** *vb* **-vring, -vred** *or* **-vering, -vered** to gain an advantage over (someone) by skilful dealing: *the management outmanoeuvred us into accepting redundancies*

outmoded *adj* no longer fashionable or accepted

outnumber *vb* to exceed in number: *they were outnumbered by fifty to one*

out-of-date *adj, adv* old-fashioned; outmoded

out of pocket *adj* having lost or spent money: *I was ten pounds out of pocket after paying for their drinks*

out-of-the-way *adj* remote and isolated: *an out-of-the-way village in the Bavarian Forest*

outpatient *n* a patient who visits a hospital for treatment but does not stay there overnight

outpost *n* a small settlement in a distant part of the country or in a foreign country, which is used for military or trading purposes

outpouring *n* **1** a great amount of something that is produced very rapidly: *a prolific outpouring of ideas and energy* **2** a passionate outburst: *the hysterical outpourings of fanatics*

output *n* **1** the amount of something that is made or produced: *our weekly output has increased by 240 tonnes* **2** *electronics* the power, voltage, or current delivered by a circuit or component **3** *computers* the information produced by a computer ▷ *vb* **-putting, -putted** *or* **-put** **4** *computers* to produce (data) at the end of a process

outrage *n* **1** deep indignation, anger, or resentment: *she felt a sense of outrage that he should abandon her like that* **2** an extremely vicious or cruel act; gross violation of decency, morality, or honour: *there have been reports of another bombing outrage in the capital* ▷ *vb* **-raging, -raged** **3** to cause deep indignation, anger, or resentment in (someone): *they were outraged by the news of the assassination* ▶ HISTORY French *outré* beyond

outrageous *adj* **1** unusual and shocking: *his sense of humour made him say and do the most outrageous things* **2** shocking and socially or morally unacceptable: *I will fight these outrageous accusations of corruption in the courts if necessary* > **outrageously** *adv*

outré (**oo**-tray) *adj* eccentric and rather shocking ▶ HISTORY French: having gone beyond

outrider *n* a person who rides a motorcycle or horse in front of or beside an official vehicle as an attendant or guard

outrigger *n* **1** a stabilizing framework projecting from the side of a boat or canoe **2** a boat or canoe equipped with such a framework

outright *adj* **1** complete; total: *he is close to an outright victory* **2** straightforward and direct: *outright hostility* ▷ *adv* **3** completely: *the film was banned outright* **4** instantly: *my driver was killed outright* **5** openly: *ask her outright why she treated you as she did*

outrun *vb* **-running, -ran, -run** **1** to run faster or further than (someone) **2** to develop faster than (something): *the population of the city is in danger of outrunning the supply of houses*

outsell vb **-selling, -sold** to be sold in greater quantities than: CDs were outselling cassettes

outset n a start; beginning: we never really hit it off from the outset

outshine vb **-shining, -shone** to be better than (someone) at something: by university she had begun to outshine me in sports

outside prep **1** on or to the exterior of: a crowd gathered outside the court **2** beyond the limits of: it was outside my experience and beyond my ability **3** apart from; other than: no-one knows outside us ▷ adj **4** on or of the outside: an outside light is also a good idea **5** remote; unlikely: I still had an outside chance of the title **6** coming from outside a particular group or organization: the patient had been subjected to outside influences **7** of or being the lane in a road which is further from the side than other lanes going in the same direction: he was doing 120 in the outside lane ▷ adv **8** outside a specified thing or place; out of doors: we went outside to get some fresh air **9** slang not in prison ▷ n **10** the external side or surface of something **11 at the outside** informal at the very most: I'll be away four days at the outside

outside broadcast n radio, television a broadcast not made from a studio

outsider n **1** a person excluded from a group **2** a contestant thought unlikely to win

outsize adj **1** Also: **outsized** very large or larger than normal ▷ n **2** an outsize garment

outskirts pl n the parts of a town or city that are furthest from the centre: an office in the northernmost outskirts of Glasgow

outsmart vb informal same as **outwit**

outsource vb **1** to subcontract (work) to another company **2** to buy (components for a product) rather than manufacture them

outspan S African n **1** an area on a farm kept available for travellers to rest and refresh their animals ▷ vb **-spanning, -spanned 2** to unharness or unyoke (animals) **3** to relax ▶ HISTORY Afrikaans uit out + spannen to stretch

outspoken adj **1** saying exactly what one thinks: an outspoken critic of human rights abuses **2** spoken candidly: she is known for her outspoken views > **outspokenness** n

outstanding adj **1** very good; excellent: an outstanding performance **2** still to be dealt with or paid: outstanding bills; a few outstanding problems have to be put right **3** very obvious or important: there are significant exceptions, of which oil is the outstanding example > **outstandingly** adv

outstation n a station or post in a remote region

outstay vb same as **overstay**

outstretched adj extended or stretched out as far as possible: he pushed a wad of drachma notes into the young man's outstretched hand

outstrip vb **-stripping, -stripped 1** to surpass (someone) in a particular activity: his newspapers outstrip all others in vulgarity **2** to go faster than (someone)

outtake n an unreleased take from a recording session, film, or television programme

out-tray n a shallow basket in an office for collecting letters and documents that are to be sent out

outvote vb **-voting, -voted** to defeat (someone) by getting more votes than him or her

outward adj **1** apparent or superficial: to outward appearances the house is largely unchanged today **2** of or relating to the outside: outward shape **3** (of a journey) away from a place to which one intends to return ▷ adv also **outwards 4** in an outward direction; towards the outside > **outwardly** adv

outweigh vb **1** to be more important, significant, or influential than: these niggles are outweighed by the excellent cooking and service **2** to be heavier than

outwit vb **-witting, -witted** to gain an advantage over (someone) by cunning or ingenuity

outworks pl n mil defences which lie outside the main fortifications of a fort, etc.

outworn adj (of a belief or custom) old-fashioned and no longer of any use or relevance: there is no point in pandering to outworn superstition

ouzel or **ousel** (ooze-el) n same as **dipper** (sense 2) ▶ HISTORY Old English ōsle

ouzo (ooze-oh) n, pl **ouzos** a strong aniseed-flavoured alcoholic drink from Greece ▶ HISTORY Modern Greek ouzon

ova n the plural of **ovum**

oval adj **1** egg-shaped ▷ n **2** anything that is oval in shape, such as a sports ground ▶ HISTORY Latin ovum egg

ovary n, pl **-ries 1** a reproductive organ in women and female animals in which eggs are produced **2** bot the lower part of a pistil, containing the ovules ▶ HISTORY Latin ovum egg > **ovarian** adj

ovate adj shaped like an egg: the tree has bluish-green, ovate leaves ▶ HISTORY Latin ovatus egg-shaped

ovation n an enthusiastic round of applause ▶ HISTORY Latin ovatio rejoicing

oven n **1** an enclosed heated compartment or container for baking or roasting food, or for drying or firing ceramics ▷ vb **2** to cook in an oven ▶ HISTORY Old English ofen

over prep **1** directly above; across the top or upper surface of: set the frying pan over a low heat **2** on or to the other side of: the pilot flew over the blue waters **3** during or throughout (a period of time): over the next few months it became clear what was happening **4** throughout the whole extent of: the effects are being felt all over the country now **5** by means of (an instrument of telecommunication): there was an announcement over the Tannoy system **6** more than: she had met him over a year ago **7** concerning; about: there has been much argument over these figures **8** while occupied in: I'll tell you over dinner tonight **9** having recovered from the effects of: he appeared to be over his niggling injury problems **10 all over someone** informal extremely affectionate or attentive towards someone **11 over and above** added to; in addition to ▷ adv **12** in a state,

O

599

condition, or position over something: *to climb over* **13** onto its side: *the jug toppled over* **14** at or to a point across an intervening space: *she carried him over to the other side of the river* **15** covering the whole area: *there's poverty the world over* **16** from beginning to end: *to read a document over* **17 all over a** finished **b** over one's entire body **c** typically: *that's him all over* **18 over again** once more **19 over and over (again)** repeatedly ▷ *interj* **20** (in signalling and radio) it is now your turn to speak ▷ *adj* **21** finished; no longer in progress: *the second round of voting is over* ▷ *adv, adj* **22** remaining; surplus: *there wasn't any money left over* ▷ *n* **23** cricket **a** a series of six balls bowled by a bowler from the same end of the pitch **b** the play during this ▶ HISTORY Old English *ofer*

over- *prefix* **1** excessive or excessively: *overcharge; overdue* **2** superior in rank: *overlord* **3** indicating location or movement above: *overhang* **4** downwards from above: *overthrow*

overact *vb* to act in an exaggerated way

overactive *adj* more active than is normal or desirable: *an overactive thyroid gland*

overall *adj* **1** from one end to the other: *the overall length* **2** including everything; total: *the overall cost* ▷ *adv* **3** in general; on the whole: *overall, I think this is the better car* ▷ *n* **4** Brit & NZ a coat-shaped work garment worn over ordinary clothes as a protection against dirt **5 overalls** work trousers with a bib and braces or jacket attached, worn over ordinary clothes as a protection against dirt and wear

overarm *sport adj* **1** bowled, thrown, or performed with the arm raised above the shoulder ▷ *adv* **2** with the arm raised above the shoulder

overawe *vb* **-awing, -awed** to affect (someone) with an overpowering sense of awe: *he was overawed by the prospect of meeting the Prime Minister*

overbalance *vb* **-ancing, -anced** to lose one's balance

overbearing *adj* **1** imposing one's views in an unpleasant or forceful manner **2** of particular or overriding importance: *an overbearing need*

overblown *adj* inflated or excessive: *humiliation comes from having overblown expectations for yourself*

overboard *adv* **1** from a boat or ship into the water: *many passengers drowned when they jumped overboard to escape the flames* **2 go overboard** *informal* **a** to be extremely enthusiastic **b** to go to extremes **3 throw overboard** to reject or abandon (an idea or a plan)

overburden *vb* to have more of something than it is possible to cope with: *the city's streets are already overburdened by rush-hour motorists*

overcast *adj* (of the sky or weather) cloudy

overcharge *vb* **-charging, -charged** to charge too high a price

overcoat *n* a warm heavy coat worn in cold weather

overcome *vb* **-coming, -came, -come 1** to deal successfully with or control (a problem or feeling): *once I'd overcome my initial nerves I discovered*

hang-gliding was great fun **2** (of an emotion or a feeling) to affect (someone) strongly or make (someone) powerless: *he was overcome by a sudden surge of jealousy* **3** to defeat (someone) in a conflict

overcompensate *vb* **-sating, -sated** to attempt to make up for or cancel out (something) to an unnecessary degree: *when bookings dropped slightly, the company overcompensated by slashing the price of its holidays by 50%*

overcrowded *adj* containing more people or things than is desirable: *overcrowded commuter trains*

overcrowding *n* the cramming of too many people into too small a space: *prison overcrowding and poor conditions*

overdo *vb* **-doing, -did, -done 1** to do (something) to excess **2** to exaggerate (something) **3** to cook (something) too long **4 overdo it** or **things** to do something to a greater degree than is advisable or healthy

overdose *n* **1** a larger dose of a drug than is safe: *she tried to kill herself with an overdose of alcohol and drugs* ▷ *vb* **-dosing, -dosed 2** to take more of a drug than is safe, either accidentally or deliberately: *this drug is rarely prescribed because it is easy to overdose fatally on it*

overdraft *n* **1** the withdrawal of more money from a bank account than there is in it **2** the amount of money withdrawn thus

overdraw *vb* **-drawing, -drew, -drawn** to withdraw more money from a bank account than is in it

overdrawn *adj* **1** having overdrawn one's bank account **2** (of an account) in debit

overdressed *adj* wearing clothes which are too elaborate or formal for the occasion

overdrive *n* **1** a very high gear in a motor vehicle, used at high speeds to reduce wear **2** a state of great activity or excitement: *the government propaganda machine went into overdrive to try to play down the Minister's comments*

overdub *vb* **-dubbing, -dubbed 1** to add (new sounds) to a track in such a way that the old and the new sounds can be heard ▷ *n* **2** a sound or series of sounds added by this method

overdue *adj* **1** not having arrived or happened by the time expected or desired: *a reassessment of policy on this issue is long overdue* **2** (of money) not having been paid by the required date: *by this time his rent was three weeks overdue* **3** (of a library book) not having been returned to the library by the required date

overestimate *vb* **-mating, -mated** to believe something or someone to be bigger, more important, or better than is the case
> **overestimation** *n*

overexposed *adj* (of a photograph) too light in colour because the film has been exposed to light for too long

overfish *vb* **-fishing, -fished** to fish intensively in an area of water so that fish species, numbers, etc. are excessively reduced

overflow *vb* **-flowing, -flowed** *or formerly* **-flown** **1** to flow over (a brim) **2** to be filled beyond capacity so as to spill over **3 overflow with** to be filled with (an emotion): *a letter overflowing with passion and ardour* ▷ *n* **4** something that overflows, usually a liquid **5** an outlet that enables surplus liquid to be drained off **6** the amount by which a limit or capacity is exceeded ▷ *adj* **7** of or being a subsidiary thing for use when there is no room left in the main one: *an overflow car park*

overgraze *vb* **-grazing, -grazed** to graze (land) too intensively so that it is damaged and no longer provides nourishment

overgrown *adj* covered over with plants or weeds: *they headed up the overgrown and winding trail*

overhang *vb* **-hanging, -hung** **1** to project or hang over beyond (something) ▷ *n* **2** an overhanging part or object

overhaul *vb* **1** to examine (a system or an idea) carefully for faults **2** to make repairs or adjustments to (a vehicle or machine) **3** to overtake (a vehicle or person) ▷ *n* **4** a thorough examination and repair

overhead *adj, adv* above head height

overheads *pl n* the general costs of running a business, such as rent, electricity, and stationery

overhear *vb* **-hearing, -heard** to hear (a speaker or remark) unintentionally or without the knowledge of the speaker

overheat *vb* **1** to make or become too hot **2** to cause (an economy) to tend towards inflation **3 become overheated** (of a person, discussion, etc.) to become angry or agitated: *the Colonel becomes overheated if he sees the term 'Ms' in the newspaper*

overjoyed *adj* extremely pleased

overkill *n* any treatment that is greater than that required: *the overkill in negative propaganda resulted in this upsurge*

overlap *vb* **-lapping, -lapped** **1** (of two things) to share part of the same space as or lie partly over (each other): *slice the meat and lay it in overlapping slices in a serving dish* **2** to coincide partly in time or subject: *their careers have overlapped for the last ten years* ▷ *n* **3** a part that overlaps **4** the amount or length of something overlapping

overlay *vb* **-laying, -laid** **1** to cover (a surface) with an applied decoration: *a woollen cloth overlaid with gold and silver embroidery* ▷ *n* **2** something that is laid over something else; a covering **3** an applied decoration or layer, for example of gold leaf

overleaf *adv* on the other side of the page

overlie *vb* **-lying, -lay, -lain** to lie on or cover (something or someone): *a thin layer of black dust overlay everything*

overload *vb* **1** to put too large a load on or in (something): *the aircraft was dangerously overloaded* **2** to cause (a transport system) to be unable to function properly because too many people or vehicles are using it: *Heathrow Airport was already overloaded by 1972* **3** to try to put more electricity

through a system than the system can cope with ▷ *n* **4** an excessive load

overlook *vb* **1** to fail to notice (something) **2** to disregard or ignore (misbehaviour or a fault): *I'm prepared to overlook your failure, but don't do it again* **3** to give a view of (something) from above: *a cliff overlooking the Atlantic*

overly *adv* too; excessively

overman *vb* **-manning, -manned** to provide with too many staff: *the company is not overmanned overall, but it has too many managers and not enough productive workers* > **overmanned** *adj* > **overmanning** *n*

overmuch *adv, adj* too much; very much

overnight *adv* **1** during the night **2** in or as if in the course of one night; suddenly: *we are not saying that a change like this would happen overnight* ▷ *adj* **3** done in, occurring in, or lasting the night: *the army has ordered an overnight curfew* **4** staying for one night: *overnight guests* **5** for use during a single night: *should I pack an overnight case?* **6** happening very quickly; sudden: *he doesn't expect the programme to be an overnight success*

overpass *n* same as **flyover**

overplay *vb* **1** to overemphasize (something) **2 overplay one's hand** to overestimate the worth or strength of one's position

overpopulation *n* the population of an area in too large numbers

overpower *vb* **1** to conquer or subdue (someone) by superior force **2** to have such a strong effect on (someone) as to make him or her helpless or ineffective: *I was so appalled, so overpowered by my guilt and my shame that I was unable to speak* > **overpowering** *adj*

overrate *vb* to have too high an opinion of: *the director's role was seriously overrated*

overreach *vb* **overreach oneself** to fail by trying to be too clever or achieve too much: *he built up a successful media empire before he overreached himself and lost much of his fortune*

overreact *vb* to react more strongly or forcefully than is necessary: *allergies happen when the body overreacts to a harmless substance* > **overreaction** *n*

override *vb* **-riding, -rode, -ridden** **1** to set aside or disregard (a person or a person's decisions) by having superior authority or power: *the managing director can override any decision he doesn't like* **2** to be more important than or replace (something): *unsurprisingly the day-to-day struggle for survival overrode all moral considerations* > **overriding** *adj*

overrule *vb* **-ruling, -ruled** **1** to reverse the decision of (a person or organization with less power): *the President overruled the hardliners in the party who wanted to use force* **2** to rule or decide against (an argument or decision): *the initial judgment was overruled by the Supreme Court*

overrun *vb* **-running, -ran, -run** **1** to conquer (territory) rapidly by force of numbers **2** to spread over (a place) rapidly: *dirty tenements, overrun by lice, rats, and roaches* **3** to extend or run beyond a set limit: *Tuesday's lunch overran by three-quarters of an hour*

overseas *adv* **1** across the sea; abroad ▷ *adj* **2** of, to, from, or in a distant country or countries ▷ *n* **3** *informal* a foreign country or foreign countries collectively

oversee *vb* **-seeing, -saw, -seen** to watch over and direct (someone or something); supervise > **overseer** *n*

oversell *vb* **-selling, -sold** to exaggerate the merits or abilities of

overshadow *vb* **1** to make (someone or something) seem insignificant or less important by comparison **2** to sadden the atmosphere of: *news of their team-mate's injury overshadowed the victory celebrations*

overshoe *n* a protective shoe worn over an ordinary shoe

overshoot *vb* **-shooting, -shot** to go beyond (a mark or target): *the plane overshot the main runway*

overshot *adj* (of a water wheel) driven by a flow of water that passes over the wheel

oversight *n* a mistake caused by not noticing something

oversleep *vb* **-sleeping, -slept** to sleep beyond the intended time for getting up

overspill *n* *Brit* the rehousing of people from crowded cities in smaller towns

overstate *vb* **-stating, -stated** to state (something) too strongly; overemphasize > **overstatement** *n*

overstay *vb* **overstay one's welcome** to stay as a guest longer than one's host or hostess would like

overstayer *n* a person who remains in a country after their permit has expired

overstep *vb* **-stepping, -stepped** **1** to go beyond the limits of what is thought acceptable: *he had overstepped his authority by acting without consulting his superiors* **2** **overstep the mark** to go too far and behave in an unacceptable way

oversubscribe *vb* **-scribing, -scribed** to apply for or try to buy more of something than is available: *the company's new share offer was heavily oversubscribed* > **oversubscription** *n*

overt *adj* done or shown in an open and obvious way: *jurors were now looking at the defendant with overt hostility* ▶ HISTORY Old French > **overtly** *adv*

overtake *vb* **-taking, -took, -taken** **1** *chiefly Brit* to move past (another vehicle or person) travelling in the same direction **2** to do better than (someone) after catching up with him or her **3** to come upon (someone) suddenly or unexpectedly: *a mortal tiredness overtook him*

overtax *vb* **1** to impose too great a strain on: *a singer who had overtaxed her voice* **2** to tax (people) too heavily

overthrow *vb* **-throwing, -threw, -thrown** **1** to defeat and replace (a ruler or government) by force **2** to replace (standards or values) ▷ *n* **3** downfall or destruction: *the overthrow of the US-backed dictatorship*

overtime *n* **1** work at a regular job done in addition to regular working hours **2** pay for such work ▷ *adv* **3** in addition to one's regular working hours: *she had been working overtime and she fell asleep at the wheel*

overtone *n* **1** an additional meaning or hint: *I don't want to deny that from time to time there are political overtones* **2** *music, acoustics* any of the tones, with the exception of the principal or lowest one, that make up a musical sound

overture *n* **1** *music* **a** a piece of orchestral music played at the beginning of an opera, oratorio, ballet, musical comedy, or film, often containing the main musical themes of the work **b** a one-movement orchestral piece, usually having a descriptive or evocative title: *the 1812 Overture* **2** **overtures** opening moves towards a new relationship or agreement: *the German government made a variety of friendly overtures towards the French* ▶ HISTORY Late Latin *apertura* opening

overturn *vb* **1** to turn over or upside down **2** to overrule or reverse (a legal decision) **3** to overthrow or destroy (a government)

overview *n* a general survey

overweening *adj* (of opinions or qualities) excessive or immoderate: *your modesty is a cover for your overweening conceit* ▶ HISTORY obsolete *ween* to think

overweight *adj* **1** (of a person) weighing more than is healthy **2** weighing more than is usual or permitted

overwhelm *vb* **1** to overpower the thoughts, emotions, or senses of (someone): *we were overwhelmed with grief* **2** to overcome (people) with irresistible force: *gang violence has overwhelmed an ailing police force* > **overwhelming** *adj* > **overwhelmingly** *adv*

overwinter *vb* **1** to spend winter in a particular place **2** *biol* to remain alive through winter > **overwintering** *n*

overwork *vb* **1** to work too hard or too long **2** to use (something) too much: *the phrase 'every parent's nightmare' is an overworked platitude* ▷ *n* **3** excessive work

overwrite *vb* **-writing, -wrote, -written** **1** to record on a storage medium, such as a magnetic disk, thus destroying what was originally recorded there **2** to write (something) in an excessively ornate style

overwrought *adj* tense, nervous, and agitated

oviduct *n* *anat* the tube through which eggs are conveyed from an ovary ▶ HISTORY Latin *ovum* egg + *ducere* to lead

oviform *adj* *biol* shaped like an egg ▶ HISTORY Latin *ovum* egg + *forma* shape

ovine *adj* of or like a sheep ▶ HISTORY Latin *ovis* sheep

oviparous (oh-**vip**-par-uss) *adj* *zool* producing eggs that hatch outside the body of the mother ▶ HISTORY Latin *ovum* egg + *-parus* bearing

ovoid (**oh**-void) *adj* egg-shaped

O

ovulate (**ov**-yew-late) *vb* **-lating, -lated** *biol* to produce or release eggs from an ovary
> **ovulation** *n*

ovule *n* **1** *bot* the part of a plant that contains the egg cell and develops into the seed after fertilization **2** *zool* an immature ovum ▶ HISTORY Latin *ovum* egg

ovum (**oh**-vum) *n*, *pl* **ova** an unfertilized female egg cell ▶ HISTORY Latin: egg

owe *vb* **owing, owed 1** to be under an obligation to pay an amount of money to (someone): *he owes me a lot of money* **2** to feel an obligation to do or give: *I think I owe you an apology* **3 owe something to** to have something as a result of: *many serving officers owe their present position to the former president* ▶ HISTORY Old English *āgan* to have

owl *n* a bird of prey which has a flat face, large eyes, and a small hooked beak, and which is active at night ▶ HISTORY Old English *ūle* > **owlish** *adj*

own *adj* (preceded by a possessive) **1** used to emphasize that something belongs to a particular person: *rely on your own instincts* ▷ *pron* (preceded by a possessive) **2** the one or ones belonging to a particular person: *I had one of my own* **3** the people that someone feels loyalty to, esp. relations: *we all look after our own around here* **4 come into one's own** to fulfil one's potential **5 hold one's own** to have the necessary ability to deal successfully with a situation: *he chose a partner who could hold her own with the best* **6 on one's own a** without help: *you'll never manage to lift that on your own* **b** by oneself; alone: *he lives on his own in a flat in town* ▷ *vb* **7** to have (something) as one's possession: *he owns homes in four countries* **8** Also: **own up** to confess or admit: *I must own up to a great horror of war*
▶ HISTORY Old English *āgen* > **owner** *n*
> **ownership** *n*

ownership flat *n* NZ a flat owned by the occupier

own goal *n* **1** *sport* a goal scored by a player accidentally playing the ball into his or her own team's net **2** *informal* any action that results in disadvantage to the person who took it or to his or her associates: *the minister's admission was the latest in a series of own goals by the government*

ox *n*, *pl* **oxen** a castrated bull used for pulling heavy loads and for meat ▶ HISTORY Old English *oxa*

oxalic acid *n* a colourless poisonous acid found in many plants ▶ HISTORY Latin *oxalis* garden sorrel

oxbow lake *n* *geog* a crescent-shaped lake on the flood plain of a river and constituting the remnant of a former meander

Oxbridge *n* *Brit* the British universities of Oxford and Cambridge considered together

oxen *n* the plural of **ox**

Oxfam Oxford Committee for Famine Relief

oxidation *n* the act or process of oxidizing

oxide *n* *chem* a compound of oxygen with another element ▶ HISTORY French

-oxide *suffix chem* indicating a compound of oxygen: *carbon dioxide*

oxidize *or* **-dise** *vb* **-dizing, -dized** *or* **-dising, -dised** *chem* to react chemically with oxygen, as in burning or rusting > **oxidation** *or* **-disation** *n*

oxidizing agent *or* **oxidising agent** *n* *chem* a substance that oxidizes another substance, being itself reduced in the process. Common oxidizing agents are oxygen, hydrogen peroxide, and ferric salts

Oxon. (in degree titles) of Oxford University ▶ HISTORY Latin *Oxoniensis*

oxyacetylene *n* a mixture of oxygen and acetylene, used in blowlamps for cutting or welding metals at high temperatures

oxygen *n* *chem* a colourless odourless gaseous element essential to life processes and to combustion. Symbol: O ▶ HISTORY Greek *oxus* sharp + *-genēs* producing: from former belief that all acids contained oxygen

oxygenate *vb* **-ating, -ated** to add oxygen to: *to oxygenate blood*

oxygen cycle *n* the process by which oxygen is produced and used: plants create oxygen, animals take in oxygen and release carbon dioxide, and plants then take in carbon dioxide

oxygen mask *n* a small bowl-shaped object which is connected via a pipe to an cylinder of oxygen and can be placed over a person's nose and mouth to help him or her breathe

oxygen tent *n* *med* a transparent enclosure covering a bedridden patient, into which oxygen is released to aid breathing

oxymoron (ox-see-**more**-on) *n* a figure of speech that combines two apparently contradictory terms, for example *cruel kindness* ▶ HISTORY Greek *oxus* sharp + *mōros* stupid

oyez *or* **oyes** *interj* a cry usually uttered three times by a public crier or court official calling for silence and attention ▶ HISTORY Old French *oiez!* hear!

oyster *n* **1** an edible shellfish, some types of which produce pearls **2 the world is your oyster** you are in a position where there is every possible chance of personal advancement and satisfaction ▷ *adj* **3** greyish-white ▶ HISTORY Greek *ostreon*

oystercatcher *n* a wading bird with black-and-white plumage and a long stout red bill

oz *or* **oz.** ounce ▶ HISTORY Italian *onza*

Oz *n* *slang* Australia

ozone *n* **1** a form of oxygen with a strong odour, formed by an electric discharge in the atmosphere **2** *informal* clean bracing air, as found at the seaside ▶ HISTORY Greek *ozein* to smell

ozone depletion *n* *environmental science* thinning of the ozone layer caused by atmospheric pollutants

ozone hole *n* *environmental science* a severe depletion of ozone in the ozone layer above Antarctica

ozone layer *n* *environmental science* a layer of ozone in the upper atmosphere that absorbs harmful ultraviolet rays from the sun

o

Pp

p¹ or **P** n, pl **p's, P's** or **Ps 1** the 16th letter of the English alphabet **2 mind one's p's and q's** to be careful to behave correctly and use polite language

p² 1 Brit, Austral & NZ penny 2 Brit pence

P 1 chem phosphorus 2 (on road signs) parking 3 chess pawn

p. 1 (pl **pp.**) page 2 per

pa¹ n informal father

pa² n NZ (formerly) a fortified Māori settlement

Pa 1 chem protactinium 2 physics pascal

PA 1 Pennsylvania 2 personal assistant 3 public-address system

p.a. yearly ▶ HISTORY Latin per annum

pace¹ n 1 a a single step in walking b the length of a step 2 speed of walking or running 3 speed of doing some other activity: efforts to accelerate the pace of change are unlikely to succeed 4 manner of walking 5 **keep pace with** to advance at the same speed as 6 **put someone through his** or **her paces** to test someone's ability 7 **set the pace** to determine the speed at which a group advances ▷ vb **pacing, paced** 8 to walk with regular steps, often in anxiety or impatience: he paced up and down the foyer impatiently 9 to set the speed for (the competitors) in a race 10 **pace out** to measure by paces ▶ HISTORY Latin passus step

pace² prep with due respect to: used to express polite disagreement ▶ HISTORY Latin, from pax peace

pacemaker n 1 an electronic device positioned in the body, next to the heart, to regulate the heartbeat 2 a competitor who, by leading a race, causes it to be run at a particular speed

pachyderm (pak-ee-durm) n a large thick-skinned mammal, such as an elephant or rhinoceros ▶ HISTORY Greek pakhus thick + derma skin

Pacific adj of the Pacific Ocean, the world's largest and deepest ocean, lying between Asia and Australia and America, or its islands

pacifist n a person who is totally opposed to violence and refuses to take part in war > **pacifism** n

pacify vb **-fies, -fying, -fied** to soothe or calm ▶ HISTORY Old French pacifier; see PACIFIC > **pacification** n

Pacinian corpuscle n anat a sensory nerve ending that is sensitive to pressure and vibration ▶ HISTORY from Felippo Pacini, Italian anatomist

pack¹ n 1 a bundle or load carried on the back 2 Brit & NZ a complete set of playing cards 3 a group of animals that hunt together: a pack of hounds 4 rugby the forwards of a team 5 any collection of people or things: a pack of lies 6 chiefly US & Canad same as **packet** (sense 1) 7 an organized group of Cub Scouts or Brownie Guides 8 same as **rucksack** or **backpack** 9 Also called: **face pack** a cream treatment that cleanses and tones the skin ▷ vb 10 to put (articles) in a case or container for moving 11 to roll (articles) up into a bundle 12 to press tightly together; cram: thousands of people packed into the city's main square 13 (foll. by off) to send away hastily: their young son came in to say good night and was packed off to bed 14 slang to be able to deliver a specified amount of unexpected or violent force or power: the film's unexpected ending packs quite a punch 15 US, informal to carry (a gun) habitually 16 **send someone packing** informal to dismiss someone abruptly ▷ See also **pack in, pack up** ▶ HISTORY origin unknown

pack² vb to fill (a committee, jury, or audience) with one's own supporters ▶ HISTORY perhaps from pact

package n 1 a small parcel 2 Also: **package deal** a deal in which separate items are presented together as a unit 3 US & Canad same as **packet** (sense 1) ▷ vb **-aging, -aged** 4 to put (something) into a package > **packaging** n

package holiday n a holiday in which everything is arranged by one company for a fixed price

packet n 1 a container, together with its contents: a packet of crisps 2 a small parcel 3 Also: **packet boat** a boat that transports mail, passengers, or goods on a fixed short route 4 slang a large sum of money: she was paid a packet 5 computers a unit into which a larger piece of data is broken down for more efficient transmission ▶ HISTORY Old French pacquet

packhorse n a horse used to carry goods

pack ice n geog a large area of floating ice, consisting of pieces that have become massed together

pack in vb informal to stop doing (something): I'm going to pack it in and resign

packing n material, such as paper or plastic, used to protect packed goods

pack up vb 1 to put (articles) in a bag or case before leaving 2 informal to stop doing (something) 3 (of a machine) to break down

pact n a formal agreement between two or more parties ▶ HISTORY Latin pactum

pad¹ n 1 a thick piece of soft material used for comfort, shape, protection, or absorption 2 a number of sheets of paper fastened together along one edge 3 the fleshy cushioned underpart of an animal's paw 4 a level area or flat-topped structure, from which rockets are launched or helicopters take off 5 the floating leaf of the water lily 6 slang a person's residence ▷ vb **padding, padded** 7 to fill (something) out with soft material for comfort, shape, or protection **8 pad out** to lengthen (a speech or piece of writing) with unnecessary words or pieces of information ▶ HISTORY origin unknown

pad² *vb* **padding, padded 1** to walk with a soft or muffled step **2** to travel (a route) on foot: *men padding the streets in cheap sneakers* ▶ HISTORY Middle Dutch *pad* path

padding *n* **1** any soft material used to pad something **2** unnecessary information put into a speech or written work to make it longer

paddle¹ *n* **1** a short light oar with a flat blade at one or both ends **2** a paddle wheel used to move a boat **3** a blade of a water wheel or paddle wheel ▷ *vb* **-dling, -dled 4** to move (a boat) with a paddle **5** to swim with short rapid strokes, like a dog **6** *US & Canad, informal* to spank ▶ HISTORY origin unknown

paddle² *vb* **-dling, -dled 1** to walk barefoot in shallow water **2** to dabble (one's fingers, hands, or feet) in water ▷ *n* **3** the act of paddling in water ▶ HISTORY origin unknown

paddle steamer *n* a ship propelled by paddle wheels turned by a steam engine

paddle wheel *n* a large wheel fitted with paddles, turned by an engine to propel a ship

paddock *n* **1** a small enclosed field for horses **2** (in horse racing) the enclosure in which horses are paraded and mounted before a race **3** *Austral & NZ* any area of fenced land ▶ HISTORY Old English *pearruc* enclosure

paddy¹ *n, pl* **-dies 1** Also: **paddy field** a field planted with rice **2** rice as a growing crop or when harvested but not yet milled ▶ HISTORY Malay *pādī*

paddy² *n, pl* **-dies** *Brit & NZ, informal* a fit of temper ▶ HISTORY from *Paddy*, informal name for an Irishman

pademelon, paddymelon (pad-ee-mel-an) *n* a small Australian wallaby

padkos (pudd-koss) *n* *S African* snacks and provisions for a journey ▶ HISTORY Afrikaans, literally: road food

padlock *n* **1** a detachable lock with a hinged hoop fastened through a ring on the object to be secured ▷ *vb* **2** to fasten (something) with a padlock ▶ HISTORY origin unknown

padre (pah-dray) *n* *informal* a chaplain to the armed forces ▶ HISTORY via Spanish or Italian from Latin *pater* father

paean (pee-an) *n* *literary* an expression of praise or joy ▶ HISTORY Greek *paian* hymn to Apollo

paediatrician *or US* **pediatrician** *n* a doctor who specializes in children's diseases

paediatrics *or US* **pediatrics** *n* the branch of medicine concerned with children and their diseases ▶ HISTORY Greek *pais, paid-* child + *iatros* physician > **paediatric** *or US* **pediatric** *adj*

paedophile *or US* **pedophile** *n* a person who is sexually attracted to children

paedophilia *or US* **pedophilia** *n* the condition of being sexually attracted to children ▶ HISTORY Greek *pais, paid-* child + *philos* loving

paella (pie-**ell**-a) *n* a Spanish dish made from rice, shellfish, chicken, and vegetables ▶ HISTORY Catalan

pagan *adj* **1** having, being, or relating to religious beliefs, esp. ancient ones, which are not part of any of the world's major religions: *this was the site of a pagan temple to the sun* **2** irreligious ▷ *n* **3** a person who does not belong to any of the world's major religions **4** a person without any religion ▶ HISTORY Church Latin *paganus* civilian (hence not a soldier of Christ) > **paganism** *n*

page¹ *n* **1** one side of one of the leaves of a book, newspaper, or magazine **2** one of the leaves of a book, newspaper, or magazine **3** *literary* a period or event: *a new page in the country's political history* **4** a screenful of information from a website or teletext service ▶ HISTORY Latin *pagina*

page² *n* **1** a small boy who attends a bride at her wedding **2** a youth employed to run errands for the guests in a hotel or club **3** *medieval history* a boy in training for knighthood ▷ *vb* **paging, paged 4** to summon (a person), by bleeper or loudspeaker, in order to pass on a message ▶ HISTORY Greek *pais* child

pageant *n* **1** an outdoor show portraying scenes from history **2** any magnificent display or procession ▶ HISTORY perhaps from Latin *pagina* scene of a play

pageantry *n* spectacular display or ceremony

pageboy *n* **1** a hairstyle in which the hair is smooth and the same medium length with the ends curled under **2** same as **page²** (senses 1, 2)

pagination *n* the numbering in sequence of the pages of a book or manuscript > **paginate** *vb*

pagoda *n* a pyramid-shaped Asian temple or tower ▶ HISTORY Portuguese *pagode*

paid *vb* **1** past of **pay 2 put paid to** to end or destroy: *a knee injury put paid to his promising sporting career*

pail *n* **1** a bucket **2** Also called: **pailful** the amount contained in a pail: *a pail of water* ▶ HISTORY Old English *pægel*

pain *n* **1** physical hurt or discomfort caused by injury or illness **2** emotional suffering **3 on pain of** subject to the penalty of: *orders which their soldiers were bound to follow on pain of death* **4** Also called: **pain in the neck** *informal* a person or thing that is annoying or irritating ▷ *vb* **5** to cause (a person) physical or mental suffering **6** *informal* to annoy; irritate ▷ See also **pains** ▶ HISTORY Latin *poena* punishment > **painless** *adj*

painful *adj* **1** causing pain or distress: *painful inflammation of the joints; he began the painful task of making funeral arrangements* **2** affected with pain: *the symptoms include fever and painful joints* **3** tedious or difficult: *the hours passed with painful slowness* **4** *informal* extremely bad: *a painful so-called comedy* > **painfully** *adv*

painkiller *n* a drug that relieves pain

pains *pl n* care or trouble: *they are at great pains to appear realistic and responsible*

painstaking *adj* extremely careful and thorough > **painstakingly** *adv*

p

paint n **1** a coloured substance, spread on a surface with a brush or a roller, that forms a hard coating **2** a dry film of paint on a surface **3** *informal* face make-up ▷ vb **4** to apply paint to paper or canvas to make (a picture) of **5** to coat (a surface) with paint **6** to describe vividly in words: *the survey paints a dismal picture of growing hunger and disease* **7** to apply make-up to (the face) **8** to apply (liquid) to (a surface): *paint the varnish on and leave it to dry for at least four hours* **9 paint the town red** *informal* to celebrate in a lively way ▶ HISTORY Latin *pingere* to paint

painted lady n a butterfly with pale brownish-red mottled wings

painter¹ n **1** an artist who paints pictures **2** a person who paints surfaces of buildings as a trade

painter² n a rope attached to the bow of a boat for tying it up ▶ HISTORY probably from Old French *penteur* strong rope

painting n **1** a picture produced by using paint **2** the art of producing pictures by applying paints to paper or canvas **3** the act of applying paint to a surface

pair n **1** two identical or similar things matched for use together: *a pair of shoes* **2** two people, animals, or things used or grouped together: *a pair of tickets* **3** an object consisting of two identical or similar parts joined together: *a pair of jeans* **4** a male and a female animal of the same species kept for breeding purposes **5** *Parliament* two opposed members who both agree not to vote on a specified motion **6** two playing cards of the same denomination **7** one member of a matching pair: *I can't find the pair to this glove* ▷ vb **8** to group (people or things) in twos **9 pair off** to separate into groups of two ▶ HISTORY Latin *par* equal

paisley pattern or **paisley** n a detailed pattern of small curving shapes, used in fabric ▶ HISTORY after *Paisley*, town in Scotland

pajamas pl n US pyjamas

pakeha (pah-kee-hah) n, pl **pakeha** or **pakehas** NZ a person of European descent, as distinct from a Māori ▶ HISTORY Māori

Pakistani adj **1** of Pakistan ▷ n **2** a person from Pakistan

pal *informal* n **1** a close friend ▷ vb **palling, palled 2 pal up with** to become friends with ▶ HISTORY Romany: brother

palace n **1** the official residence of a king, queen, president, or archbishop **2** a large and richly furnished building ▶ HISTORY Latin *Palatium* Palatine, the site of the palace of the emperors in Rome

paladin n **1** one of the legendary twelve peers of Charlemagne's court **2** (formerly) a knight who did battle for a king or queen ▶ HISTORY Italian *paladino*

palaeo- or US **paleo-** combining form old, ancient, or prehistoric: *palaeobotany*

Palaeocene or US **Paleocene** (pal-ee-oh-seen) adj geol of the epoch of geological time about 65 million years ago ▶ HISTORY Greek *palaeo-* ancient + *kainos* new

palaeography or US **paleography** (pal-ee-**og**-ra-fee) n the study of ancient handwriting ▶ HISTORY Greek *palaeo-* ancient + -GRAPHY

Palaeolithic or US **Paleolithic** (pal-ee-oh-**lith**-ik) adj of the period from about 2.5 to 3 million years ago until about 12 000 BC during which primitive man emerged and unpolished chipped stone tools were made ▶ HISTORY Greek *palaeo-* ancient + *lithos* stone

palaeontology or US **paleontology** (pal-ee-on-**tol**-a-jee) n the study of past geological periods and fossils ▶ HISTORY Greek *palaeo-* ancient + *ōn, ont-* being + -LOGY > **palaeontologist** or US **paleontologist** n

Palaeozoic or US **Paleozoic** (pal-ee-oh-**zoh**-ik) adj geol of the geological era that lasted from about 600 million years ago to 230 million years ago ▶ HISTORY Greek *palaeo-* ancient + *zōion* animal

Palagi (pa-**lang**-gee) n, pl **-gis** NZ the Samoan name for a pakeha

palanquin (pal-an-**keen**) n (formerly, in the Orient) a covered bed in which someone could be carried on the shoulders of four men ▶ HISTORY Portuguese *palanquim*

palatable adj **1** (of food or drink) pleasant to taste **2** (of an experience or idea) acceptable or satisfactory

palate n **1** the roof of the mouth **2** the sense of taste: *a range of dishes to tempt every palate* ▶ HISTORY Latin *palatum*

palatial adj like a palace; magnificent: *his palatial home*

palatinate n a territory ruled by a palatine prince or noble or a count palatine

palatine adj possessing royal prerogatives: *a count palatine* ▶ HISTORY Latin *palatium* palace

palaver (pal-**lah**-ver) n time-consuming fuss: *all the palaver involved in obtaining a visa* ▶ HISTORY Portuguese *palavra* talk

pale¹ adj **1** (of a colour) whitish and not very strong: *pale yellow* **2** (of a complexion) having a whitish appearance, usually because of illness, shock, or fear **3** lacking brightness or colour: *the pale, chill light of an October afternoon* ▷ vb **paling, paled 4** to become pale or paler: *the girl paled at the news* ▶ HISTORY Latin *pallidus* > **paleness** n

pale² n **1** a wooden post used in fences **2 a** a fence made of pales **b** a boundary **3 beyond the pale** outside the limits of social convention: *the destruction of forests is beyond the pale* ▶ HISTORY Latin *palus* stake

Palestinian adj **1** of Palestine, an area in the Middle East between the Jordan River and the Mediterranean ▷ n **2** an Arab from this area, esp. one living in Israel or Israeli-occupied territory or as a refugee

palette n **1** a flat board used by artists to mix paints **2** the range of colours characteristic of a particular artist or school of painting: *he uses a cool palette with no strong red* **3** the range of colours or patterns that can be displayed on the visual display unit of a computer ▶ HISTORY French

p

palette knife *n* a spatula with a thin flexible blade used in painting or cookery

palindrome *n* a word or phrase that reads the same backwards or forwards, such as *able was I ere I saw Elba* ▶ HISTORY Greek *palindromos* running back again

paling *n* 1 a fence made of pales 2 pales collectively 3 a single pale

palisade *n* 1 a fence made of stakes driven into the ground 2 one of the stakes used in such a fence ▶ HISTORY Latin *palus* stake

palisade cell *n* *bot* a cell containing many chloroplasts, situated below the outer epidermis of a leaf blade

pall[1] *n* 1 a cloth spread over a coffin 2 a coffin at a funeral ceremony 3 a dark heavy covering: *a pall of smoke and dust hung in the air* 4 a depressing atmosphere: *a pall hung on them all after his death* ▶ HISTORY Latin *pallium* cloak

pall[2] *vb* to become boring or uninteresting, esp. by continuing for too long: *any pleasure had palled long before the two-hour programme was over* ▶ HISTORY variant of *appal*

Palladian *adj* of a style of architecture characterized by symmetry and the revival and development of ancient Roman styles ▶ HISTORY after Andrea *Palladio*, Italian architect

palladium *n* *chem* a rare silvery-white element of the platinum metal group, used in jewellery. Symbol: Pd ▶ HISTORY after the asteroid *Pallas*

pallbearer *n* a person who helps to carry or who escorts the coffin at a funeral

pallet[1] *n* a straw-filled mattress or bed ▶ HISTORY Latin *palea* straw

pallet[2] *n* 1 a tool with a flat, sometimes flexible, blade used for shaping pottery 2 a portable platform for storing and moving goods ▶ HISTORY Latin *pala* spade

palliasse *n* a straw-filled mattress; pallet ▶ HISTORY French *paillasse*

palliate *vb* -ating, -ated 1 to lessen the severity of (pain or disease) without curing it 2 to cause (an offence) to seem less serious ▶ HISTORY Latin *pallium* a cloak

palliative *adj* 1 relieving without curing ▷ *n* 2 something that palliates, such as a sedative drug 3 something that alleviates or lessens a problem: *equal pay was a palliative for the growing unrest among women*

pallid *adj* 1 lacking colour, brightness, or vigour: *a pallid autumn sun* 2 lacking energy or vitality; insipid: *many militants find the party's socialism too pallid* ▶ HISTORY Latin *pallidus*

pallor *n* paleness of complexion, usually because of illness, shock, or fear ▶ HISTORY Latin: whiteness

pally *adj* -lier, -liest *informal* on friendly terms

palm[1] *n* 1 the inner surface of the hand from the wrist to the base of the fingers 2 the part of a glove that covers the palm 3 **in the palm of one's hand** at one's mercy or command: *he had the jury in the palm of his hand* ▷ *vb* 4 to hide (something) in the hand: *he palmed the key* ▷ See also **palm off** ▶ HISTORY Latin *palma*

palm[2] *or* **palm tree** *n* a tropical or subtropical tree with a straight unbranched trunk crowned with long pointed leaves ▶ HISTORY Latin *palma*, from the likeness of its spreading fronds to a hand

palmate *adj* shaped like an open hand: *palmate leaves*

palmcorder *n* a small camcorder which can be held in the palm of the hand

palmetto *n, pl* -tos a small palm tree with fan-shaped leaves ▶ HISTORY Spanish *palmito* a little palm

palmistry *n* fortune-telling by examining the lines and bumps of the hand > **palmist** *n*

palm off *vb* 1 to get rid of (someone or something) by passing it on to another: *the risk has to be shared with subcontractors, not simply palmed off on them* 2 to divert (someone) by a lie or excuse: *Mark was palmed off with a series of excuses*

palm oil *n* an oil obtained from the fruit of certain palm trees, used as an edible fat and in soap

Palm Sunday *n* the Sunday before Easter

palmtop *adj* (of a computer) small enough to be held in the hand

palomino *n, pl* -nos a golden or cream horse with a white mane and tail ▶ HISTORY Spanish: dovelike

palpable *adj* 1 obvious: *palpable nonsense* 2 (of a feeling or an atmosphere) so intense that it seems capable of being touched: *an air of palpable gloom hung over him* ▶ HISTORY Latin *palpare* to touch > **palpably** *adv*

palpate *vb* -pating, -pated *med* to examine (an area of the body) by touching ▶ HISTORY Latin *palpare* to stroke > **palpation** *n*

palpitate *vb* -tating, -tated 1 (of the heart) to beat rapidly 2 to flutter or tremble ▶ HISTORY Latin *palpitare* > **palpitation** *n*

palsy (pawl-zee) *n* *pathol* paralysis of a specified type: *cerebral palsy* ▶ HISTORY Old French *paralisie* > **palsied** *adj*

paltry *adj* -trier, -triest insignificant ▶ HISTORY Low Germanic *palter, paltrig* ragged

pampas *n* the extensive grassy plains of South America ▶ HISTORY Native American *bamba* plain

pampas grass *n* a South American grass with large feathery silver-coloured flower branches

pamper *vb* to treat (someone) with excessive indulgence or care; spoil ▶ HISTORY Germanic

pamphlet *n* a thin paper-covered booklet, often on a subject of current interest ▶ HISTORY Medieval Latin *Pamphilus*, title of a poem

pamphleteer *n* a person who writes or issues pamphlets

pan[1] *n* 1 a wide long-handled metal container used in cooking 2 any of various similar containers used in industry, etc. 3 either of the two dishes on a set of scales 4 *Brit* the bowl of a lavatory 5 a natural or artificial hollow in the ground: *a saltpan* 6 (in the Caribbean) the indented top from an oil drum used as the treble drum in a steel band ▷ *vb* **panning, panned** 7 to sift gold from (a river) in a shallow pan

P

8 *informal* to criticize harshly: *his first film was panned by the critics* ▷ See also **pan out** ▶ HISTORY Old English *panne*

pan² *vb* **panning, panned 1** to move (a film camera) to follow a moving object or to take in a whole scene ▷ *n* **2** the act of panning ▶ HISTORY from *panoramic*

pan- *combining form* including or relating to all parts or members: *Pan-American* ▶ HISTORY Greek

panacea (pan-a-**see**-a) *n* a remedy for all diseases or problems ▶ HISTORY Greek *pan*- all + *akos* remedy

panache (pan-**ash**) *n* a confident and stylish manner: *the orchestra played with great panache* ▶ HISTORY Old Italian *pennacchio* feather

panama hat *or* **panama** *n* a straw hat with a rounded crown and a wide brim

Pan-American *adj* of North, South, and Central America collectively

panatella *n* a long slender cigar ▶ HISTORY American Spanish *panetela* long thin biscuit

pancake *n* **1** a thin flat circle of fried batter **2** Also called: **pancake landing** an aircraft landing made by levelling out a few feet from the ground and then dropping onto it

Pancake Day *n* Shrove Tuesday, when people traditionally eat pancakes

panchromatic *adj photog* (of an emulsion or film) sensitive to light of all colours

pancreas (**pang**-kree-ass) *n* a large gland behind the stomach that produces insulin and aids digestion ▶ HISTORY Greek *pan*- all + *kreas* flesh > **pancreatic** *adj*

pancreatic juice *n physiol* the clear alkaline secretion of the pancreas

panda *n* **1** Also called: **giant panda** a large black-and-white bearlike animal from the high mountain bamboo forests of China **2** Also called: **lesser panda, red panda** a raccoon-like animal of the mountain forests of S Asia, with a reddish-brown coat and ringed tail ▶ HISTORY Nepalese

panda car *n* Brit a police patrol car

pandemic *adj* (of a disease) occurring over a wide geographical area ▶ HISTORY Greek *pandēmos* general

pandemonium *n* wild confusion; uproar

- **WORD HISTORY**
- *Pandemonium* is the capital of Hell in John
- Milton's poem 'Paradise Lost'. The word
- 'pandemonium' comes from Greek *pan*,
- meaning 'all', and *daimōn*, meaning 'demon'
- or 'spirit'.

pander *vb* (foll. by *to*) to indulge (a person or his or her desires): *he pandered to popular fears* ▶ HISTORY after *Pandarus*, in legend, the procurer of Cressida for Troilus

pandit *n Hinduism* same as **pundit** (sense 2)

p & p Brit postage and packing

pane *n* a sheet of glass in a window or door ▶ HISTORY Latin *pannus* rag

panegyric (pan-ee-**jirr**-rik) *n* a formal speech or piece of writing that praises a person or event ▶ HISTORY Greek *panēguris* public gathering

panel *n* **1** a distinct section of a larger surface area, such as that in a door **2** any distinct section of something formed from a sheet of material, such as part of a car body **3** a piece of material inserted in a garment **4** a group of people acting as a team, such as in a quiz or a discussion before an audience **5** *law* **a** a list of jurors **b** the people on a jury **6** short for **instrument panel** ▷ *adj* **7** of a group acting as a panel: *a panel game* ▷ *vb* **-elling, -elled** *or US* **-eling, -eled 8** to cover or decorate with panels ▶ HISTORY Old French: portion

panel beater *n* a person who repairs damage to car bodies

panelling *or US* **paneling** *n* panels collectively, such as on a wall or ceiling

panellist *or US* **panelist** *n* a member of a panel, usually on radio or television

panel van *n* Austral & NZ a small van

pang *n* a sudden sharp feeling of pain or sadness ▶ HISTORY Germanic

Pangaea (pan-**jee**-a) *n geol* the ancient supercontinent, comprising all the present continents joined together

pangolin *n* an animal of tropical countries with a scaly body and a long snout for feeding on ants and termites. Also called: **scaly anteater** ▶ HISTORY Malay *peng-gōling*

panic *n* **1** a sudden overwhelming feeling of terror or anxiety, sometimes affecting a whole group of people ▷ *adj* **2** of or resulting from such terror: *panic measures* ▷ *vb* **-icking, -icked 3** to feel or cause to feel panic ▶ HISTORY Greek *panikos* emanating from *Pan*, god of the fields > **panicky** *adj*

panicle *n bot* a loose, irregularly branched cluster of flowers, such as in the oat ▶ HISTORY Latin *panicula* tuft

panic-stricken *adj* affected by panic

panini *n, pl* **-ni** *or* **-nis** Italian bread, usually served grilled with a filling ▶ HISTORY Italian, plural of *panino* bread roll

pannier *n* **1** one of a pair of bags fixed on either side of the back wheel of a bicycle or motorcycle **2** one of a pair of large baskets slung over a beast of burden ▶ HISTORY Old French *panier*

panoply (**pan**-a-plee) *n* a magnificent array: *ambassadors equipped with the full panoply of diplomatic bags, codes and cyphers* ▶ HISTORY Greek *pan*- all + *hopla* armour

panorama *n* **1** a wide unbroken view in all directions: *the beautiful panorama of the Cornish coast* **2** a wide or comprehensive survey of a subject: *the panorama of American life* **3** a picture of a scene unrolled before spectators a part at a time so as to appear continuous ▶ HISTORY Greek *pan*- all + *horama* view > **panoramic** *adj*

pan out *vb* **1** *informal* to work out; result: *Parker's research did not pan out too well* **2** (of gravel) to yield gold by panning

pansy *n, pl* **-sies 1** a garden plant whose flowers have rounded white, yellow, or purple velvety petals ▶ HISTORY Old French *pensée* thought

pant *vb* **1** to breathe with noisy gasps after exertion **2** to say (something) while breathing in this way **3** (foll. by *for*) to have a frantic desire for ▷ *n* **4** the act of panting ▶ **HISTORY** Greek *phantasioun* to have visions

pantaloons *pl n* baggy trousers gathered at the ankles ▶ **HISTORY** French *pantalon* trousers

pantechnicon *n Brit* a large van used for furniture removals ▶ **HISTORY** Greek *pan-* all + *tekhnē* art; originally a London bazaar later used as a furniture warehouse

pantheism *n* **1** the belief that God is present in everything **2** readiness to worship all gods > **pantheist** *n* > **pantheistic** *adj*

pantheon *n* **1** (in ancient Greece or Rome) a temple built to honour all the gods **2** all the gods of a particular creed: *the Celtic pantheon of horse gods* **3** *written* a group of very important people: *he deserves a place in the pantheon of social reformers* ▶ **HISTORY** Greek *pan-* all + *theos* god

panther *n* a leopard, usually a black one ▶ **HISTORY** Greek

panties *pl n* women's or children's underpants

pantihose *pl n US & Austral* women's tights

pantile *n* a roofing tile, with an S-shaped cross section ▶ **HISTORY** PAN¹ + *tile*

panto *n, pl* **-tos** *Brit, informal* short for **pantomime** (sense 1)

pantograph *n* **1** an instrument for copying drawings or maps to any scale **2** a device on the roof of an electric train to carry the current from an overhead wire ▶ **HISTORY** Greek *pant-* all + *graphein* to write

pantomime *n* **1** (in Britain) a play based on a fairy tale and performed at Christmas time **2** a theatrical entertainment in which words are replaced by gestures and bodily actions **3** *informal, chiefly Brit* a confused or farcical situation ▶ **HISTORY** Greek *pantomīmos*

pantry *n, pl* **-tries** a small room or large cupboard in which food is kept ▶ **HISTORY** Latin *panis* bread

pants *pl n* **1** *Brit* an undergarment with two leg holes, covering the body from the waist or hips to the thighs **2** *US, Canad, Austral & NZ* trousers or shorts **3 bore** or **scare the pants off someone** *informal* to bore or scare someone very much ▶ **HISTORY** shortened from *pantaloons*

pantyhose *pl n NZ & Austral* women's tights

pap¹ *n* **1** a soft food for babies or invalids **2** worthless or oversimplified entertainment or information **3** *S African* maize porridge ▶ **HISTORY** Latin *pappare* to eat

pap² *n* *old-fashioned, Scot & N English dialect* a nipple or teat ▶ **HISTORY** from Old Norse

papa (pap-**pah**) *n old-fashioned, informal* father ▶ **HISTORY** French

Papa Bois (**bwah**) *n* (in the folklore of Trinidad and Tobago) a character who is the protector of the forests, their animals, and plants ▶ **HISTORY** French, literally: daddy forest

papacy (**pay**-pa-see) *n, pl* **-cies 1** the office or term of office of a pope **2** the system of government in the Roman Catholic Church that has the pope as its head ▶ **HISTORY** Medieval Latin *papa* pope

papal *adj* of the pope or the papacy

paparazzo (pap-a-**rat**-so) *n, pl* **-razzi** (-**rat**-see) a freelance photographer who specializes in taking shots of famous people without their knowledge or consent ▶ **HISTORY** Italian

papaya (pap-**pie**-a) *n* a large green fruit with a sweet yellow flesh that grows in the West Indies ▶ **HISTORY** Spanish

paper *n* **1** a flexible material made in sheets from wood pulp or other fibres and used for writing on, decorating walls, or wrapping parcels **2** short for **newspaper** or **wallpaper 3 papers** documents, such as a passport, which can identify the bearer **4** a set of examination questions **5 papers** the collected diaries or letters of someone's private or public life **6** a lecture or an essay on a specific subject **7 on paper** in theory, as opposed to fact: *countless ideas which look good on paper just don't work in practice* ▷ *adj* **8** made of paper: *paper towels; a paper bag* **9** recorded on paper but not yet existing in practice: *a paper profit of more than $50 million* ▷ *vb* **10** to cover (walls) with wallpaper ▶ **HISTORY** Latin *papyrus* > **papery** *adj*

paperback *n* **1** a book with covers made of flexible card ▷ *adj* **2** of a paperback or publication of paperbacks: *a paperback novel*

paperhanger *n* a person who hangs wallpaper as an occupation

paperknife *n, pl* **-knives** a knife-shaped object with a blunt blade for opening sealed envelopes

paper money *n* banknotes, rather than coins

paperweight *n* a small heavy object placed on top of loose papers to prevent them from scattering

paperwork *n* clerical work, such as the writing of reports or letters

papier-mâché (pap-yay **mash**-ay) *n* **1** a hard substance made of layers of paper mixed with paste and moulded when moist ▷ *adj* **2** made of papier-mâché ▶ **HISTORY** French, literally: chewed paper

papilla (pap-**pill**-a) *n, pl* **-lae** (-lee) *biol* a small projection of tissue at the base of a hair, tooth, or feather ▶ **HISTORY** Latin: nipple > **papillary** *adj*

papist *n, adj usually offensive* same as **Roman Catholic** ▶ **HISTORY** Church Latin *papa* pope

papoose *n* a Native American baby ▶ **HISTORY** Native American *papoos*

paprika *n* a mild powdered seasoning made from red peppers ▶ **HISTORY** Hungarian

Pap test or **smear** *n med* same as **cervical smear** ▶ **HISTORY** after George Papanicolaou, anatomist

papyrus (pap-**ire**-uss) *n, pl* **-ri** (-rye) or **-ruses 1** a tall water plant of Africa **2** a kind of paper made from the stem of this plant, used by the ancient Egyptians, Greeks, and Romans **3** an ancient document written on this paper ▶ **HISTORY** Greek *papuros* reed

par *n* **1** the usual or average condition: *I feel slightly below par most of the time* **2 on a par with** equal or equivalent to: *an environmental disaster on a par with Chernobyl* **3** *golf* a standard score for a hole or course that a good player should make: *four under par with two holes to play* **4** *finance* the established value of the unit of one national currency in terms of the unit of another **5** *commerce* short for **par value** **6** **par for the course** to be expected: *random acts of violence were par for the course in the capital* ▸ HISTORY Latin: equal

par. **1** paragraph **2** parenthesis

para *n* *informal* **1** a paratrooper **2** a paragraph

para- *or before a vowel* **par-** *prefix* **1** beside or near: *parameter* **2** beyond: *parapsychology* **3** resembling: *paratyphoid fever* ▸ HISTORY Greek

parable *n* a short story that uses familiar situations to illustrate a religious or moral point ▸ HISTORY Greek *parabolē* analogy

parabola (par-**ab**-bol-a) *n* *geom* an open plane curve formed by the intersection of a cone by a plane parallel to its side ▸ HISTORY Greek *parabolē* a setting alongside > **parabolic** *adj*

paracetamol *n* a mild pain-relieving drug ▸ HISTORY from *para-acetamidophenol*

parachute *n* **1** a large fabric canopy connected by a harness, that slows the descent of a person or package from an aircraft ▹ *vb* **-chuting, -chuted** **2** to land or to drop (supplies or troops) by parachute from an aircraft ▸ HISTORY French > **parachutist** *n*

parade *n* **1** an ordered march or procession **2** a public promenade or street of shops **3** a blatant but sometimes insincere display: *a man who made a parade of liking his own company best* ▹ *vb* **-rading, -raded** **4** to exhibit or flaunt: *he neither paraded nor disguised his devout faith* **5** to walk or march, esp. in a procession ▸ HISTORY French: a making ready

parade ground *n* a place where soldiers assemble ready for inspection or display

paradigm (**par**-a-dime) *n* a model or example: *his experience is a paradigm for the young artist* ▸ HISTORY Greek *paradeigma* pattern

paradise *n* **1** heaven; where the good go after death **2** the Garden of Eden **3** any place or condition that fulfils a person's desires ▸ HISTORY Greek *paradeisos* garden

paradise duck *n* a New Zealand duck with bright feathers

paradox *n* **1** a statement that seems self-contradictory but may be true: *it's a strange paradox that a musician must practise improvising to become a good improviser* **2** a self-contradictory proposition, such as *I always tell lies* **3** a person or thing that is made up of contradictory elements ▸ HISTORY Greek *paradoxos* opposed to existing notions > **paradoxical** *adj* > **paradoxically** *adv*

paraffin *n* **1** *Brit* a liquid mixture distilled from petroleum or shale and used as a fuel or solvent **2** *chem* the former name for **alkane** ▸ HISTORY Latin *parum* too little + *affinis* adjacent; so called from its chemical inertia

paraffin wax *n* a white waxlike substance distilled from petroleum and used to make candles and as a sealing agent

paragon *n* a model of perfection: *a paragon of female integrity and determination* ▸ HISTORY Old Italian *paragone* comparison

paragraph *n* **1** a section of a piece of writing, usually devoted to one idea, which begins on a new line and is often indented **2** *printing* the character ¶, used to indicate the beginning of a new paragraph ▹ *vb* **3** to put (a piece of writing) into paragraphs ▸ HISTORY Greek *paragraphos* line drawing attention to part of a text

parakeet *n* a small colourful parrot with a long tail ▸ HISTORY Spanish *periquito* parrot

paralegal *n* a person trained to assist lawyers but not qualified to practise law

parallax *n* an apparent change in an object's position due to a change in the observer's position ▸ HISTORY Greek *parallaxis* change

parallel *adj* **1** separated by an equal distance at every point: *parallel lines; a path parallel to the main road* **2** precisely corresponding: *we decide our salaries by comparison with parallel jobs in other charities* **3** *computers* operating on several items of information or instructions at the same time ▹ *n* **4** *maths* one of a set of parallel lines or planes **5** something with similar features to another **6** a comparison; similarity between two things: *she attempted to excuse herself by drawing a parallel between her behaviour and ours* **7** Also called: **parallel of latitude** any of the imaginary lines around the earth parallel to the equator, marking degrees of latitude **8** *printing* the character ‖, used as a reference mark ▹ *vb* **9** to correspond to: *the increase in smoking is paralleled by an increase in lung cancer* ▸ HISTORY Greek *parallēlos* alongside one another

parallel bars *pl n* *gymnastics* a pair of wooden bars on upright posts used for various exercises

parallel circuit *n* *electronics* an electrical circuit in which the current divides into two or more paths of the same voltage, before joining to complete the circuit

parallelepiped (par-a-lel-ee-**pipe**-ed) *n* *geom* a solid shape whose six faces are parallelograms ▸ HISTORY Greek *parallēlos* parallel + *epipedon* plane surface

parallelism *n* **1** the state of being parallel **2** a close likeness

parallelogram *n* *geom* a plane figure whose opposite sides are parallel and equal in length ▸ HISTORY Greek *parallēlos* parallel + *grammē* line

paralyse *or US* **-lyze** *vb* **-lysing, -lysed** *or* **-lyzing, -lyzed** **1** *pathol* to affect with paralysis **2** to make immobile: *he was paralysed by fear* ▸ HISTORY French *paralyser*

paralysis *n* **1** *pathol* inability to move all or part of the body due to damage to the nervous system **2** a state of inactivity: *the economic chaos and political paralysis into which the country has sunk* ▸ HISTORY Greek *paralusis*, from *para-* beyond + *lusis* a loosening

paralytic adj **1** of or relating to paralysis **2** Brit, informal very drunk ▷ n **3** a person who is paralysed

paramecium (par-a-**mee**-see-um) n, pl **-cia** (-see-a) a single-celled animal which lives in ponds, puddles, and sewage filters and swims by means of cilia

paramedic n a person, such as a member of an ambulance crew, whose work supplements that of the medical profession > **paramedical** adj

parameter (par-**am**-it-er) n **1** maths an arbitrary constant that determines the specific form of a mathematical expression, such as a and b in $y = ax^2 + b$ **2** informal any limiting factor: exchange rates are allowed to fluctuate only within designated parameters ▶ HISTORY Greek para beside + metron measure

paramilitary adj denoting a group of people organized on military lines

paramount adj of the greatest importance ▶ HISTORY Old French par by + -amont above

paramour n old-fashioned an adulterous lover ▶ HISTORY Old French, literally: through love

paranoia n **1** a mental disorder which causes delusions of grandeur or of persecution **2** informal intense fear or suspicion, usually unfounded ▶ HISTORY Greek para- beyond + noos mind > **paranoid** or **paranoiac** adj, n

paranormal adj beyond normal scientific explanation ▷ n **2 the paranormal** paranormal happenings or matters generally

parapet n **1** a low wall or railing along the edge of a balcony or roof **2** mil a mound of sandbags in front of a trench to conceal and protect troops from fire ▶ HISTORY Italian parapetto

paraphernalia n various articles or bits of equipment

- **WORD HISTORY**
- In Latin a married woman's parapherna or
- paraphernālia was her personal property, what
- she herself owned as opposed to her dowry.
- The words come from Greek para, meaning
- 'beside', and phernē, meaning 'dowry'.

paraphrase n **1** an expression of a statement or text in other words ▷ vb **-phrasing, -phrased** **2** to put (a statement or text) into other words ▶ HISTORY Greek paraphrazein to recount

paraplegia (par-a-**pleej**-ya) n pathol paralysis of the lower half of the body ▶ HISTORY Greek: a blow on one side > **paraplegic** adj, n

parapsychology n the study of mental phenomena such as telepathy

Paraquat n trademark an extremely poisonous weedkiller

parasite n **1** an animal or plant that lives in or on another from which it obtains nourishment **2** a person who habitually lives at the expense of others; sponger > **parasitic** adj

- **WORD HISTORY**
- 'Parasite' comes from Greek parasitos, meaning
- 'someone who lives at another's expense', from
- para beside + sitos grain.

parasol n an umbrella-like sunshade ▶ HISTORY French

paratrooper n a member of the paratroops

paratroops pl n troops trained to be dropped by parachute into a battle area

paratyphoid fever n a disease resembling but less severe than typhoid fever

parboil vb to boil (food) until partially cooked ▶ HISTORY Late Latin perbullire to boil thoroughly; modern meaning due to confusion of par- with part

parcel n **1** something wrapped up; a package **2** a group of people or things sharing something in common: a parcel of fools **3** a distinct portion of land: he was the recipient of a substantial parcel of land ▷ vb **-celling, -celled** or US **-celing, -celed** **4** (often foll. by up) to wrap (something) up into a parcel **5** (foll. by out) to divide (something) into portions: the children were parcelled out to relatives ▶ HISTORY Old French parcelle

parch vb **1** to deprive (something) of water; dry up: the summer sun parched the hills **2** to make (someone) very thirsty: I'm parched. Have we got any lemonade? ▶ HISTORY origin unknown

parchment n **1** a thick smooth material made from animal skin and used for writing on **2** a manuscript made of this material **3** a stiff yellowish paper resembling parchment ▶ HISTORY Greek pergamēnē, from Pergamēnos of Pergamum (where parchment was made)

pardon vb **1** to forgive or excuse: I hope you'll pardon the wait ▷ n **2** forgiveness **3** official release from punishment for a crime ▷ interj spoken **4** Also: **pardon me, I beg your pardon a** sorry; excuse me **b** what did you say? ▶ HISTORY Medieval Latin perdonare to forgive freely > **pardonable** adj

pare vb **paring, pared 1** to peel (the outer layer) from (something): thinly pare the rind from the grapefruit **2** to trim or cut the edge of **3** to decrease bit by bit: the government is prepared to pare down the armed forces ▶ HISTORY Latin parare to make ready

parent n **1** a father or mother **2** a person acting as a father or mother; guardian **3** a plant or animal that has produced one or more plants or animals ▶ HISTORY Latin parens, from parere to bring forth > **parental** adj > **parenthood** n

parentage n ancestry or family

parent company n a company that owns a number of smaller companies

parenthesis (par-**en**-thiss-iss) n, pl **-ses** (-seez) **1** a word or phrase inserted into a passage, and marked off by brackets or dashes **2** Also called: **bracket** either of a pair of characters ( ), used to enclose such a phrase ▶ HISTORY Greek: something placed in besides > **parenthetical** adj > **parenthetically** adv

parenting n the activity of bringing up children

parenting order n law **a** England and Wales an order requiring a parent or parents of a young offender or truant to attend guidance sessions **b** Austral (in cases of parental disagreement) an order specifying arrangements for a child's residence, visiting rights, and other matters such as schooling

par excellence adv beyond comparison: *this book justifies its claim to be a reference work par excellence* ▶ HISTORY French

pariah (par-**rye**-a) n a social outcast: *the man they regard as a pariah* ▶ HISTORY Tamil *paraiyan* drummer

parietal (par-**rye**-it-al) adj *anat, biol* of or forming the walls of a body cavity: *the parietal bones of the skull* ▶ HISTORY Latin *paries* wall

paring n something that has been cut off something

parish n **1** an area that has its own church and a priest or pastor. *Related adjective:* **parochial 2** the people who live in a parish **3** an administrative division ▶ HISTORY Greek *paroikos* neighbour

parish clerk n a person who assists in various church duties

parish council n (in England and, formerly, Wales) the administrative body of a parish. See **parish** (sense 3)

parishioner n a person who lives in a particular parish

parish register n a book in which the births, baptisms, marriages, and deaths in a parish are recorded

parity n **1** equality, for example of rank or pay **2** close or exact equivalence: *the company maintained parity with the competition* **3** *finance* equivalence between the units of currency of two countries ▶ HISTORY Latin *par* equal

park n **1** a large area of open land for recreational use by the public **2** a piece of open land for public recreation in a town **3** *Brit* a large area of private land surrounding a country house **4** an area designed to accommodate a number of related enterprises: *a science park* **5** *US & Canad* a playing field or sports stadium **6 the park** *Brit, informal* the pitch in soccer ▷ vb **7** to stop and leave (a vehicle) temporarily: *I parked between the two cars already outside; police vans were parked on every street corner* **8** *informal* to leave or put (someone or something) somewhere: *she parked herself on the sofa and stayed there all evening* ▶ HISTORY Germanic > **parking** n

parka n a long jacket with a quilted lining and a fur-trimmed hood ▶ HISTORY from Aleutian (language of Aleutian Islands, off Alaska): skin

park and ride n a transportation scheme in which travellers park their private vehicles some distance away from a city centre, tourist attraction, etc. and complete the journey by public transport

parking meter n a coin-operated device beside a parking space that indicates how long a vehicle may be left parked

parking ticket n the notice of a fine served on a motorist for a parking offence

Parkinson's disease or **Parkinsonism** n a progressive disorder of the central nervous system which causes tremor, rigidity, and impaired muscular coordination ▶ HISTORY after J. Parkinson, surgeon

Parkinson's law n the notion that work expands to fill the time available for its completion ▶ HISTORY after C. N. *Parkinson*, historian and writer

parkland n grassland with scattered trees

parky adj **parkier, parkiest** *Brit, informal* (of the weather) chilly ▶ HISTORY origin unknown

parlance n the manner of speaking associated with a particular group or subject: *he had, in Marxist parlance, a 'petit bourgeois' mentality* ▶ HISTORY French *parler* to talk

parley *old-fashioned* n **1** a discussion between members of opposing sides to decide terms of agreement ▷ vb **2** to have a parley ▶ HISTORY French *parler* to talk

parliament n a law-making assembly of a country ▶ HISTORY Old French *parlement*, from *parler* to speak

Parliament n **1** the highest law-making authority in Britain, consisting of the House of Commons, the House of Lords, and the sovereign **2** the equivalent law-making authority in another country

parliamentarian n an expert in parliamentary procedures

parliamentary adj **1** of or from a parliament: *parliamentary elections* **2** conforming to the procedures of a parliament: *parliamentary language*

parliamentary privilege n *in Parliament* the special rights enjoyed by Members of Parliament to enable them to carry out their duties; these include immunity from civil action if they make defamatory comments in Parliament

parlour or US **parlor** n **1** *old-fashioned* a living room for receiving visitors **2** a room or shop equipped as a place of business: *an ice-cream parlour* ▶ HISTORY Old French *parler* to speak

parlous adj *archaic or humorous* dangerously bad; dire: *the parlous state of the economy* ▶ HISTORY variant of *perilous*

Parmesan (par-miz-zan) n a hard strong-flavoured cheese used grated on pasta dishes and soups ▶ HISTORY Italian *parmegiano* of Parma, Italy

parochial adj **1** narrow in outlook; provincial **2** of or relating to a parish ▶ HISTORY see PARISH > **parochialism** n

parody n, pl **-dies 1** a piece of music or literature that mimics the style of another composer or author in a humorous way **2** something done so badly that it seems like an intentional mockery ▷ vb **-dies, -dying, -died 3** to make a parody of ▶ HISTORY Greek *paroidia* satirical poem > **parodist** n

parol *law* adj **1** expressed or given by word of mouth: *parol evidence* **2** (of a contract, lease, etc.) made orally or in writing but not under seal ▷ n **3** an oral statement; word of mouth (now only in the phrase *by parol*) ▶ HISTORY Old French *parole* speech

parole n *law* **1** the freeing of a prisoner before his or her sentence has run out, on condition that he or she behaves well **2** a promise given by a prisoner to behave well if granted liberty or partial liberty **3 on parole** conditionally released from prison ▷ vb **-roling, -roled 4** to place (a person) on parole ▶ HISTORY Old French *parole d'honneur* word of honour

parotid gland n anat either of a pair of salivary glands in front of and below the ears ▶ HISTORY Greek *para-* near + *ous* ear

paroxysm n **1** an uncontrollable outburst of emotion: *a paroxysm of grief* **2** pathol **a** a sudden attack or recurrence of a disease **b** a fit or convulsion ▶ HISTORY Greek *paroxunein* to goad > **paroxysmal** adj

parquet (par-kay) n **1** a floor covering made of blocks of wood ▷ vb **2** to cover (a floor) with parquetry ▶ HISTORY Old French: small enclosure

parquetry (par-kit-tree) n pieces of wood arranged in a geometric pattern, used to cover floors

parr n a salmon up to two years of age ▶ HISTORY origin unknown

parricide n **1** a person who kills one of his or her parents **2** the act of killing either of one's parents ▶ HISTORY Latin *parricidium* murder of a parent or relative > **parricidal** adj

parrot n **1** a tropical bird with a short hooked beak, bright plumage, and an ability to mimic human speech **2** a person who repeats or imitates someone else's words **3 sick as a parrot** usually facetious extremely disappointed ▷ vb **-roting, -roted 4** to repeat or imitate (someone else's words) without understanding them ▶ HISTORY probably from French *paroquet*

parrot fever n same as **psittacosis**

parrotfish n a brightly coloured sea fish

parry vb **-ries, -rying, -ried 1** to ward off (an attack) **2** to avoid answering (questions) in a clever way ▷ n, pl **-ries 3** an instance of parrying **4** a skilful evasion of a question ▶ HISTORY French *parer* to ward off

parse (parz) vb **parsing, parsed** to analyse (a sentence or the words in a sentence) grammatically ▶ HISTORY Latin *pars (orationis)* part (of speech)

parsec n a unit of astronomical distance equivalent to 3.0857×10^{16} metres or 3.262 light years ▶ HISTORY *parallax* + *second* (of time)

parsimony n formal extreme caution in spending ▶ HISTORY Latin *parcimonia* > **parsimonious** adj

parsley n a herb with curled pleasant-smelling leaves, used for seasoning and decorating food ▶ HISTORY Middle English *persely*

parsnip n a long tapering cream-coloured root vegetable ▶ HISTORY Latin *pastinaca*

parson n **1** a parish priest in the Church of England **2** any member of the clergy **3** NZ a nonconformist minister ▶ HISTORY Latin *persona* personage

parsonage n the residence of a parson, provided by the parish

parson's nose n the rump of a fowl when cooked

part n **1** a piece or portion **2** one of several equal divisions: *a salad dressing made with two parts oil to*

one part vinegar **3** an actor's role in a play **4** a person's duty: *his ancestors had done their part nobly and well at Bannockburn* **5** an involvement in or contribution to something: *he was jailed for his part in the fraud* **6** a region or area: *he's well known in these parts; the weather in this part of the country is extreme* **7** anat an area of the body **8** a component that can be replaced in a vehicle or machine **9** US, Canad & Austral same as **parting** (sense 2) **10** music a melodic line assigned to one or more instrumentalists or singers **11 for my part** as far as I am concerned **12 for the most part** generally **13 in part** to some degree; partly **14 on the part of** on behalf of **15 part and parcel of** an essential ingredient of **16 play a part a** to pretend to be what one is not **b** (foll. by *in*) to have something to do with: *examinations play a large part in education and in schools* **17 take part in** to participate in **18 take someone's part** to support someone, for example in an argument **19 take something in good part** to respond to (teasing or criticism) with good humour ▷ vb **20** to divide or separate from one another: *her lips parted in laughter; the cord parted with a pop* **21** to go away from one another: *we parted with handshakes all round* **22 part with** to give up: *check carefully before you part with your cash* **23 part from** to cause (someone) to give up: *I was astonished at the way Henry parted his audience from their money* **24** to split: *the path parts here* **25** to arrange (the hair) in such a way that a line of scalp is left showing ▷ adv **26** to some extent; partly: *this book is part history, part travelogue* ▷ See also **parts** ▶ HISTORY Latin *pars* a part

partake vb **-taking, -took, -taken 1 partake of** to take (food or drink) **2 partake in** to take part in ▶ HISTORY from earlier *part taker*

parterre n **1** a formally patterned flower garden **2** the pit of a theatre ▶ HISTORY French

parthenocarpy n biol the development of fruit without fertilization or formation of seeds

partial adj **1** relating to only a part; not complete: *partial deafness* **2** biased: *religious programmes can be as partial as they like* **3 partial to** having a particular liking for ▶ HISTORY Latin *pars* part > **partiality** n > **partially** adv

participant n **1** one who takes part in something **2** functional grammar any person or thing, as specified by a noun group, that performs or is the object of an action

participate vb **-pating, -pated • participate in** to become actively involved in ▶ HISTORY Latin *pars* part + *capere* to take > **participation** n > **participatory** adj

participle n grammar a form of a verb that is used in compound tenses or as an adjective. See also **present participle, past participle** ▶ HISTORY Latin *pars* part + *capere* to take > **participial** adj

particle n **1** an extremely small piece or amount: *clean thoroughly to remove all particles of dirt* **2** grammar an uninflected part of speech, such as an interjection or preposition **3** physics a minute piece of matter, such as an electron or proton ▶ HISTORY Latin *pars* part

particular *adj* **1** of, belonging to, or being one person or thing; specific: *the particular type of tuition on offer* **2** exceptional or special: *the report voices particular concern over the state of the country's manufacturing industry* **3** providing specific details or circumstances: *a particular account* **4** difficult to please; fussy ▷ *n* **5** a separate distinct item as opposed to a generalization: *moving from the general to the particular* **6** an item of information; detail: *she refused to go into particulars* **7** **in particular** especially or exactly: *three painters in particular were responsible for these developments* ▶ HISTORY Latin *particula* a small part > **particularly** *adv*

particularize *or* **-ise** *vb* **-izing, -ized** *or* **-ising, -ised** to give details about (something) > **particularization** *or* **-isation** *n*

parting *n* **1** a departure or leave-taking **2** *Brit & NZ* the line of scalp showing when sections of hair are combed in opposite directions **3** the act of dividing (something): *the parting of the Red Sea*

partisan *n* **1** a person who supports a particular cause or party **2** a member of an armed resistance group within occupied territory ▷ *adj* **3** prejudiced or one-sided ▶ HISTORY Old Italian *partigiano* > **partisanship** *n*

partition *n* **1** a large screen or thin wall that divides a room **2** the division of a country into two or more independent countries ▷ *vb* **3** to separate (a room) into sections: *the shower is partitioned off from the rest of the bathroom* **4** to divide (a country) into separate self-governing parts: *the subcontinent was partitioned into India and Pakistan* ▶ HISTORY Latin *partire* to divide

partitive *grammar adj* **1** (of a noun) referring to part of something. The phrase *some of the butter* is a partitive construction ▷ *n* **2** a partitive word, such as *some* or *any* ▶ HISTORY Latin *partire* to divide

partly *adv* not completely

partner *n* **1** either member of a couple in a relationship **2** a member of a business partnership **3** one of a pair of dancers or of players on the same side in a game: *her bridge partner* **4** an ally or companion: *the country's main European trading partner* ▷ *vb* **5** to be the partner of (someone) ▶ HISTORY Middle English *parcener* joint inheritor

partnership *n* **1** a relationship in which two or more people or organizations work together in a business venture **2** the condition of being a partner

part of speech *n* *grammar* a class of words, such as a noun, verb, or adjective, sharing important syntactic or semantic features

partridge *n, pl* **-tridges** *or* **-tridge** a game bird with an orange-brown head, greyish neck, and a short rust-coloured tail ▶ HISTORY Latin *perdix*

parts *pl n literary* abilities or talents: *a man of many parts*

part song *n* a song composed in harmonized parts

part-time *adj* **1** for less than the normal full working time: *a part-time job* ▷ *adv* **part time**

2 on a part-time basis: *he works part time* > **part-timer** *n*

parturient *adj formal* giving birth ▶ HISTORY Latin *parturire* to be in labour

parturition *n* the process of giving birth ▶ HISTORY Latin *parturire* to be in labour

party *n, pl* **-ties 1** a social gathering for pleasure **2** a group of people involved in the same activity: *a search party* **3** a group of people sharing a common political aim **4** the person or people who take part in or are involved in something, esp. a legal action or dispute: *a judge in a wig and gown who will decide who the guilty party is* **5** *informal, humorous* a person: *he's an odd old party* ▷ *vb* **-ties, -tying, -tied** **6** *informal* to celebrate; have a good time ▶ HISTORY Old French *partie* part

party line *n* **1** the policies of a political party **2** a telephone line shared by two or more subscribers

party wall *n* *property law* a common wall separating two properties

par value *n* the value printed on a share certificate or bond at the time of its issue

parvenu *or fem* **parvenue** (par-ven-new) *n* a person newly risen to a position of power or wealth who is considered to lack culture or education ▶ HISTORY French

pascal *n* the SI unit of pressure; the pressure exerted on an area of 1 square metre by a force of 1 newton ▶ HISTORY after B. *Pascal*, mathematician & scientist

Pascal *n* a high-level computer programming language developed as a teaching language ▶ HISTORY after B. *Pascal*, mathematician & scientist

paschal (**pask**-l) *adj* **1** of or relating to the Passover **2** of or relating to Easter ▶ HISTORY Hebrew *pesah* Passover

pas de deux (pah de **duh**) *n, pl* **pas de deux** *ballet* a dance for two people ▶ HISTORY French: step for two

pasha *n* (formerly) a high official of the Ottoman Empire: placed after a name when used as a title ▶ HISTORY Turkish *paşa*

pashmina (pash-**meen**-a) *n* a shawl or scarf made from fine soft goat's wool ▶ HISTORY Persian

pas op (**pass** op) *interj* *S African* beware ▶ HISTORY Afrikaans

paspalum (pass-**pale**-um) *n* *Austral & NZ* a type of grass with wide leaves

pasqueflower *n* a small purple-flowered plant of Europe and Asia ▶ HISTORY French *passefleur*, changed to *pasqueflower* Easter flower, because it blooms at Easter

pass *vb* **1** to go by or past (a person or thing) **2** to continue or extend in a particular direction: *the road to Camerino passes through some fine scenery* **3** to go through or cause (something) to go through (an obstacle or barrier): *the bullet passed through his head* **4** to be successful in (a test or examination) **5** to spend (time) or (of time) go by: *the time passed surprisingly quickly* **6** to hand over or be handed over: *she passed me her glass* **7** to be inherited by: *his mother's small estate had passed to him after her death* **8** *sport* to hit, kick, or throw (the ball) to another player **9** (of a law-making body) to agree to (a law or proposal): *the bill was passed by parliament last week* **10** to pronounce (judgment): *the court is expected to pass sentence later today* **11** to move onwards or over: *a flicker of amusement passed over his face* **12** to exceed: *Australia's population has just passed the 23 million mark* **13** to go without comment: *the insult passed unnoticed* **14** to choose not to answer a question or not to make a bid or a play in card games **15** to discharge (urine, etc.) from the body **16** to come to an end or disappear: *the madness will soon pass* **17** (foll. by *for* or *as*) to be likely to be mistaken for (someone or something else): *the few sunny days that pass for summer in this country* **18** *old-fashioned* to take place: *what passed at the meeting?* **19 pass away** or **on** *euphemistic* to die ▷ *n* **20** a successful result in an examination or test **21** *sport* the transfer of a ball from one player to another **22** a route through a range of mountains where there is a gap between peaks **23** a permit or licence **24** *mil* a document authorizing leave of absence **25** *Bridge etc.* an instance of choosing not to answer a question or not to make a bid or a play in card games **26 make a pass at** *informal* to try to persuade (someone) to have sex **27 a pretty pass** a bad state of affairs ▷ See also **pass off, pass out,** etc. ▶ HISTORY Latin *passus* step

passable *adj* **1** adequate or acceptable: *passable if hardly faultless German* **2** (of a road, path, etc.) capable of being travelled along: *most main roads are passable with care despite the snow* **> passably** *adv*

passage *n* **1** a channel or opening providing a way through **2** a hall or corridor **3** a section of a written work, speech, or piece of music **4** a journey by ship **5** the act of passing from one place or condition to another: *Ireland faced a tough passage to qualify for the World Cup finals* **6** the right or freedom to pass: *the aid convoys were guaranteed safe passage through rebel-held areas* **7** the establishing of a law by a law-making body ▶ HISTORY Old French *passer* to pass

passageway *n* corridor or passage

passbook *n* **1** a book issued by a bank or building society for recording deposits and withdrawals **2** *S African* formerly, an official identity document

passé (pas-say) *adj* out-of-date: *smoking is a bit passé these days* ▶ HISTORY French

passenger *n* **1** a person travelling in a vehicle driven by someone else **2** *Brit & NZ* a member of a team who does not take an equal share of the work: *you'll have to pull your weight – we can't afford passengers* ▶ HISTORY Old French *passager* passing

passer-by *n, pl* **passers-by** a person who is walking past someone or something

passerine *adj* **1** belonging to an order of perching birds that includes the larks, finches, and starlings ▷ *n* **2** any bird of this order ▶ HISTORY Latin *passer* sparrow

passim *adv* throughout: used to indicate that what is referred to occurs frequently in a particular piece of writing ▶ HISTORY Latin

passing *adj* **1** momentary or short-lived: *a passing fad* **2** casual or superficial: *a passing resemblance* ▷ *n* **3** *euphemistic* death **4** the ending of something: *the passing of the old order in Eastern Europe* **5 in passing** briefly and without going into detail; incidentally: *this fact is only noted in passing*

passion *n* **1** intense love **2** any strongly felt emotion **3** a strong enthusiasm for something: *a passion for football* **4** the object of an intense desire or enthusiasm: *flying is his abiding passion* ▶ HISTORY Latin *pati* to suffer **> passionless** *adj*

Passion *n* the sufferings of Christ from the Last Supper to his death on the cross

passionate *adj* **1** showing intense desire **2** capable of or revealing intense emotion: *a passionate speech* **> passionately** *adv*

passionflower *n* a tropical plant with brightly coloured showy flowers ▶ HISTORY parts of the flowers are said to resemble the instruments of the Crucifixion

passion fruit *n* the edible egg-shaped fruit of the passionflower

Passion play *n* a play about the Passion of Christ

passive *adj* **1** not taking an active part **2** submissive and receptive to outside forces **3** *grammar* denoting a form of verbs used to indicate that the subject is the recipient of the action, as *was broken* in *The glass was broken by that boy over there* **4** *chem* (of a substance) chemically unreactive ▷ *n* **5** *grammar* the passive form of a verb ▶ HISTORY Latin *passivus* capable of suffering **> passively** *adv* **> passivity** *n*

passive resistance *n* resistance to a government or the law by nonviolent acts such as fasting, peaceful demonstrations, or refusing to cooperate

passive smoking *n* the unwilling inhalation of smoke from other people's cigarettes by a nonsmoker

passive voice *n* *grammar* a set of verb forms used to indicate that the subject is the recipient of the action, for example *was discovered* in *penicillin was discovered by Fleming*. Compare **active voice**

passkey *n* **1** a private key **2** same as **master key** or **skeleton key**

pass law *n* (formerly in South Africa) a law restricting the movement of Black Africans

pass off *vb* **1** to present (something or oneself) under false pretences: *women who passed themselves off effectively as men* **2** to come to a gradual end: *the effects of the gas passed off relatively peacefully* **3** to take place: *the main demonstration passed off peacefully*

pass out *vb* **1** *informal* to become unconscious; faint **2** *Brit* (of an officer cadet) to qualify for a military commission

pass over *vb* **1** to take no notice of; disregard: *she claims she had been passed over for promotion because she is a woman* **2** to ignore or not discuss: *this disaster cannot be passed over lightly*

P

Passover *n* an eight-day Jewish festival commemorating the sparing of the Israelites in Egypt ▶ HISTORY *pass over*, translation of Hebrew *pesah*

passport *n* **1** an official document issued by a government, which identifies the holder and grants him or her permission to travel abroad **2** an asset that gains a person admission or acceptance: *good qualifications are no automatic passport to a job* ▶ HISTORY French *passer* to pass + *port* port

pass up *vb informal* to let (something) go by; disregard: *am I passing up my one chance to be really happy?*

password *n* **1** a secret word or phrase that ensures admission by proving identity or membership **2** *computing* a sequence of keystrokes that a particular user must enter in order to access part of a computer system

past *adj* **1** of the time before the present: *the past history of the world* **2** no longer in existence: *past happiness* **3** immediately previous: *the past year* **4** former: *a past president* **5** *grammar* indicating a tense of verbs used to describe actions that have been begun or completed at the time of speaking ▷ *n* **6 the past** the period of time before the present: *a familiar face from the past* **7** the history of a person or nation **8** an earlier disreputable period of someone's life: *a woman with a bit of a past* **9** *grammar* **a** the past tense **b** a verb in the past tense ▷ *adv* **10** at a time before the present; ago: *three years past* ▷ *prep* **11** beyond in time: *it's past midnight* **12** beyond in place: *a procession of mourners filed past the coffin* **13** beyond the limit of: *riches past his wildest dreams* **14 not put it past someone** to consider someone capable of (a particular action): *I wouldn't put it past him to double-cross us* **15 past it** *informal* unable to do the things one could when younger ▶ HISTORY from *pass*

pasta *n* a type of food, such as spaghetti, that is made from a dough of flour and water and formed into different shapes ▶ HISTORY Italian

paste *n* **1** a soft moist mixture, such as toothpaste **2** an adhesive made from water and flour or starch, for use with paper **3** a smooth creamy preparation of fish, meat, or vegetables for spreading on bread: *sausage paste* **4** *Brit & NZ* dough for making pastry **5** a hard shiny glass used to make imitation gems ▷ *vb* **pasting, pasted 6** to attach by paste: *she bought a scrapbook and carefully pasted in it all her clippings* **7** *computers* to insert (information copied from a different document) in a document **8** *slang* to beat or defeat (someone) ▶ HISTORY Greek *pastē* barley porridge

pasteboard *n* a stiff board made by pasting layers of paper together

pastel *n* **1 a** a crayon made of ground pigment bound with gum **b** a picture drawn with such crayons **2** a pale delicate colour ▷ *adj* **3** (of a colour) pale and delicate: *pastel pink* ▶ HISTORY Latin *pasta* paste

pastern *n* the part of a horse's foot between the fetlock and the hoof ▶ HISTORY Old French *pasture* a tether

paste-up *n printing* a sheet of paper or board with artwork and proofs pasted on it, which is photographed prior to making a plate

pasteurize *or* **-ise** *vb* **-izing, -ized** *or* **-ising, -ised** to destroy bacteria (in beverages or solid foods) by a special heating process ▶ HISTORY after Louis Pasteur, chemist ▶ **pasteurization** *or* **-isation** *n*

pastiche (past-**eesh**) *n* a work of art that mixes styles or copies the style of another artist ▶ HISTORY French

pastille *n* a small fruit-flavoured and sometimes medicated sweet ▶ HISTORY Latin *pastillus* small loaf

pastime *n* an activity which makes time pass pleasantly

pasting *n* **1** *slang* a thrashing or heavy defeat **2** *informal* strong criticism

past master *n* a person with a talent for or experience in a particular activity: *a past master at manipulating the media*

pastor *n* a member of the clergy in charge of a congregation ▶ HISTORY Latin: shepherd

pastoral *adj* **1** of or depicting country life or scenery **2** (of land) used for pasture **3** of or relating to a member of the clergy or his or her duties **4** of or relating to shepherds or their work ▷ *n* **5** a literary work, picture, or piece of music portraying country life **6** a letter from a bishop to the clergy or people of his diocese ▶ HISTORY Latin *pastor* shepherd

pastoral farming *n agriculture* the rearing of sheep and cattle as a business

pastoralism *n* a system of agriculture in dry grassland regions based on raising stock such as cattle, sheep, or goats ▶ **pastoralist** *n*

past participle *n grammar* a form of verb used with an auxiliary verb to form compound past tenses and passives; also used to modify nouns: *spoken is the past participle of speak*

past perfect *or* **past perfect tense** *n grammar* a compound tense formed, in English, using *had* plus a past participle: *had eaten is the past perfect of eat*

pastrami *n* highly seasoned smoked beef ▶ HISTORY Yiddish

pastry *n* **1** a dough of flour, water, and fat **2** (*pl* **-tries**) an individual cake or pie **3** baked foods, such as tarts, made with this dough ▶ HISTORY from *paste*

past tense *n grammar* a tense of verbs used when the action took place at some time in the past; in the sentence, *I telephoned her earlier, telephoned* is in a past tense

pasturage *n* **1** the business of grazing cattle **2** same as **pasture**

pasture *n* **1** land covered with grass, suitable for grazing by farm animals **2** the grass growing on this land ▶ HISTORY Latin *pascere* to feed

pasty[1] (pay-stee) *adj* **pastier, pastiest** (of the complexion) pale and unhealthy-looking

pasty[2] (past-ee) *n, pl* **pasties** a round of pastry folded over a filling of meat and vegetables ▶ HISTORY Old French *pastée*

p

pat¹ vb **patting, patted 1** to tap (someone or something) lightly with the hand **2** to shape (something) with a flat instrument or the palm of the hand **3 pat someone on the back** informal to congratulate someone ▷ n **4** a gentle tap or stroke **5** a small shaped lump of something soft, such as butter **6 pat on the back** informal an indication of approval ▶ HISTORY probably imitative

pat² adv **1** Also: **off pat** thoroughly learned: he had all his answers off pat **2 stand pat** chiefly US & Canad to stick firmly to a belief or decision ▷ adj **3** quick, ready, or glib: a pat generalization ▶ HISTORY perhaps adverbial use ('with a light stroke') of PAT¹

patch n **1** a piece of material used to cover a hole in a garment **2** a small contrasting section: there was a bald patch on the top of his head **3** a small plot of land **4** med a protective covering for an injured eye **5** a scrap or remnant **6** the area under someone's supervision, such as a policeman or social worker **7 a bad patch** a difficult time **8 not a patch on** not nearly as good as ▷ vb **9** to mend (a garment) with a patch **10 patch up a** to mend (something) hurriedly or carelessly **b** to make up (a quarrel) **11 patch together** to produce (something) by piecing parts together hurriedly or carelessly ▶ HISTORY perhaps from French pieche piece

patchwork n **1** needlework done by sewing together pieces of different materials **2** something made up of various parts

patchy adj **patchier, patchiest 1** of uneven quality or intensity: since then her career has been patchy **2** having or forming patches

pate n old-fashioned or humorous the head or the crown of the head ▶ HISTORY origin unknown

pâté (pat-ay) n a spread of finely minced meat, fish, or vegetables often served as a starter ▶ HISTORY French

patella (pat-**tell**-a) n, pl **-lae** (-lee) anat kneecap ▶ HISTORY Latin > **patellar** adj

paten (**pat**-in) n a plate, usually made of silver or gold, used for the bread at Communion ▶ HISTORY Latin patina pan

patent n **1 a** an official document granting the exclusive right to make, use, and sell an invention for a limited period **b** the right granted by such a document **2** an invention protected by a patent ▷ adj **3** open or available for inspection: letters patent **4** obvious: their scorn was patent to everyone **5** concerning protection of or appointment by a patent **6** (of food, drugs, etc.) made or held under a patent ▷ vb **7** to obtain a patent for (an invention) ▶ HISTORY Latin patere to lie open

patent leather n leather processed with lacquer to give a hard glossy surface

patently adv clearly and obviously: an outdated and patently absurd promise

patent medicine n a medicine with a patent, available without a prescription

Patent Office n a government department that issues patents

paternal adj **1** fatherly: paternal authority **2** related through one's father: his paternal grandmother ▶ HISTORY Latin pater father > **paternally** adv

paternalism n authority exercised in a way that limits individual responsibility ▶ HISTORY Latin pater father > **paternalistic** adj

paternity n **1** the fact or state of being a father **2** descent or derivation from a father

paternity suit n legal proceedings, usually brought by an unmarried mother, in order to gain legal recognition that a particular man is the father of her child

Paternoster n RC Church the Lord's Prayer ▶ HISTORY Latin pater noster our father

path n, pl **paths 1** a road or way, often a narrow trodden track **2** a surfaced walk, such as through a garden **3** the course or direction in which something moves: his car skidded into the path of an oncoming lorry **4** a course of conduct: the path of reconciliation and forgiveness ▶ HISTORY Old English pæth

pathetic adj **1** arousing pity or sympathy **2** distressingly inadequate: his pathetic attempt to maintain a stiff upper lip failed ▶ HISTORY Greek pathos suffering > **pathetically** adv

pathetic fallacy n (in literature) the presentation of inanimate objects in nature as possessing human feelings

pathname n computers a description of the sequence of directories leading to a particular file or directory

pathogen n any agent, such as a bacterium, that can cause disease ▶ HISTORY Greek pathos suffering + -gen (suffix) producing > **pathogenic** adj

pathological adj **1** of or relating to pathology **2** informal compulsively motivated: pathological jealousy

pathology n the branch of medicine that studies diseases ▶ HISTORY Greek pathos suffering + -LOGY > **pathologist** n

pathos n the power, for example in literature, of arousing feelings of pity or sorrow ▶ HISTORY Greek: suffering

pathway n a path

patience n **1** the capacity for calmly enduring difficult situations: the endless patience of the nurses **2** the ability to wait calmly for something to happen without complaining or giving up: he urged the international community to have patience to allow sanctions to work **3** Brit & NZ a card game for one player only ▶ HISTORY Latin pati to suffer

patient adj **1** enduring difficult situations with an even temper **2** persevering or diligent: his years of patient work may finally pay off ▷ n **3** a person who is receiving medical care > **patiently** adv

patina n **1** a film formed on the surface of a metal **2** the sheen on the surface of an old object, caused by age and much handling ▶ HISTORY Italian: coating

patio n, pl **-tios 1** a paved area adjoining a house: a barbecue on the patio **2** an open inner courtyard in a Spanish or Spanish-American house ▶ HISTORY Spanish: courtyard

patois (pat-wah) n, pl **patois** (pat-wahz) **1** a regional dialect of a language **2** the jargon of a particular group ▶ HISTORY Old French: rustic speech

patrial n (in Britain, formerly) a person with a right by statute to live in the United Kingdom, and so not subject to immigration control ▶ HISTORY Latin *patria* native land

patriarch n **1** the male head of a tribe or family **2** *Bible* any of the men regarded as the fathers of the human race or of the Hebrew people **3 a** *RC Church* the pope **b** *Eastern Orthodox Church* a highest-ranking bishop **4** an old man who is respected ▶ HISTORY Church Latin *patriarcha* > **patriarchal** *adj*

patriarchate n the office, jurisdiction, or residence of a patriarch

patriarchy n **1** a form of social organization in which males hold most of the power **2** (pl **-chies**) a society governed by such a system

patrician n **1** a member of the nobility of ancient Rome **2** an aristocrat **3** a person of refined conduct and tastes ▷ *adj* **4** (in ancient Rome) of or relating to patricians **5** aristocratic ▶ HISTORY Latin *patricius* noble

patricide n **1** the act of killing one's father **2** a person who kills his or her father ▶ HISTORY Latin *pater* father + *caedere* to kill > **patricidal** *adj*

patrimony n, pl **-nies** an inheritance from one's father or other ancestor ▶ HISTORY Latin *patrimonium* paternal inheritance

patriot n a person who loves his or her country and passionately supports its interests ▶ HISTORY Greek *patris* native land > **patriotic** *adj* > **patriotically** *adv* > **patriotism** n

patrol n **1** the action of going round an area or building at regular intervals for purposes of security or observation **2** a person or group that carries out such an action **3** a group of soldiers or ships involved in patrolling a particular area **4** a division of a troop of Scouts or Guides ▷ *vb* **-trolling, -trolled** **5** to engage in a patrol of (a place): *peacekeepers patrolled several areas of the city* ▶ HISTORY French *patrouiller*

patrol car n a police car used for patrolling streets

patron n **1** a person who financially supports artists, writers, musicians, or charities **2** a regular customer of a shop, hotel, etc. ▶ HISTORY Latin *patronus* protector

patronage n **1** the support or custom given by a patron **2** (in politics) the ability or power to appoint people to jobs **3** a condescending manner

patronize or **-ise** *vb* **-izing, -ized** or **-ising, -ised** **1** to treat (someone) in a condescending way **2** to be a patron of > **patronizing** or **-ising** *adj* > **patronizingly** or **-isingly** *adv*

patron saint n a saint regarded as the particular guardian of a country or a group of people

patronymic n a name derived from one's father's or a male ancestor ▶ HISTORY Greek *patēr* father + *onoma* name

patter¹ *vb* **1** to make repeated light tapping sounds **2** to walk with quick soft steps ▷ *n* **3** a quick succession of light tapping sounds, such as by feet: *the steady patter of rain against the window* ▶ HISTORY from PAT¹

patter² n **1** the glib rapid speech of comedians or salesmen **2** chatter **3** the jargon of a particular group ▷ *vb* **4** to speak glibly and rapidly ▶ HISTORY Latin *pater* in *Pater Noster* Our Father

pattern n **1** an arrangement of repeated parts or decorative designs **2** a regular recognizable way that something is done: *I followed a normal eating pattern* **3** a plan or diagram used as a guide to making something: *a knitting pattern* **4** a model worthy of imitation: *a pattern of kindness* **5** a representative sample ▷ *vb* **6** (foll. by *after* or *on*) to model: *an orchestra patterned after Count Basie's* ▶ HISTORY Medieval Latin *patronus* example

patterned n having a decorative pattern on it: *a selection of plain and patterned fabrics*

patty n, pl **-ties** a small round pie filled with meat or vegetables ▶ HISTORY French *pâté*

paua (pah-ooh-uh) n an edible shellfish of New Zealand, which has a pearly shell used for jewellery ▶ HISTORY Māori

paucity n *formal* **1** scarcity **2** smallness of amount or number ▶ HISTORY Latin *paucus* few

paunch n a protruding belly or abdomen ▶ HISTORY Latin *pantices* bowels > **paunchy** *adj*

pauper n *old-fashioned* **1** a person who is extremely poor **2** (formerly) a person supported by public charity ▶ HISTORY Latin: poor

pause *vb* **pausing, paused** **1** to stop doing (something) for a short time **2** to hesitate: *she answered him without pausing* ▷ *n* **3** a temporary stop or rest in speech or action **4** *music* a continuation of a note or rest beyond its normal length **5 give someone pause** to cause someone to hesitate: *it gave him pause for reflection* ▶ HISTORY Greek *pausis*

pavane (pav-van) n **1** a slow and stately dance of the 16th and 17th centuries **2** music for this dance ▶ HISTORY Spanish *pavana*

pave *vb* **paving, paved** **1** to cover (a road or area of ground) with a firm surface to make it suitable for walking or travelling on **2 pave the way for** to prepare or make easier: *the arrests paved the way for the biggest-ever Mafia trial* ▶ HISTORY Old French *paver*

pavement n **1** a hard-surfaced path for pedestrians, alongside and a little higher than a road **2** the material used in paving **3** *US* the surface of a road ▶ HISTORY Latin *pavimentum* hard floor

pavilion n **1** a building at a sports ground, esp. a cricket pitch, in which players can wash and change **2** an open building or temporary structure used for exhibitions **3** a summerhouse or other decorative shelter **4** a large ornate tent ▶ HISTORY Latin *papilio* butterfly, tent

P

paving *n* **1** a paved surface **2** material used for a pavement

pavlova *n* a meringue cake topped with whipped cream and fruit ▶ HISTORY after Anna *Pavlova*, ballerina

paw *n* **1** a four-legged mammal's foot with claws and pads **2** *informal* a hand ▷ *vb* **3** to scrape or hit with the paws **4** *informal* to touch or caress (someone) in a rough or overfamiliar manner ▶ HISTORY Germanic

pawl *n* a pivoted lever shaped to engage with a ratchet to prevent motion in a particular direction ▶ HISTORY Dutch *pal*

pawn¹ *vb* **1** to deposit (an article) as security for money borrowed **2** to stake or risk: *I will pawn my honour on this matter* ▷ *n* **3** an article deposited as security **4** the condition of being so deposited: *in pawn* ▶ HISTORY Old French *pan* security

pawn² *n* **1** a chessman of the lowest value, usually able to move only one square forward at a time **2** a person or thing manipulated by someone else: *our city is just a pawn in their power games* ▶ HISTORY Anglo-Norman *poun*, from Medieval Latin *pedo* infantryman

pawnbroker *n* a person licensed to lend money on goods deposited > **pawnbroking** *n*

Pawnee *n*, *pl* **Pawnees** *or* **Pawnee 1** a member of a group of Native American peoples, formerly living in Nebraska and Kansas, now chiefly in Oklahoma **2** the language of these peoples

pawnshop *n* the premises of a pawnbroker

pawpaw (paw-paw) *n* same as **papaya**

pax *n* **1** *chiefly RC Church* the kiss of peace ▷ *interj* **2** *Brit, school slang* a call signalling a desire to end hostilities ▶ HISTORY Latin: peace

pay *vb* **pays, paying, paid 1** to give (money) in return for goods or services: *Willie paid for the drinks; nurses are not very well paid* **2** to settle (a debt or obligation) by giving or doing something: *he has paid his debt to society* **3** to suffer: *she paid dearly for her mistake* **4** to give (a compliment, regards, attention, etc.) **5** to profit or benefit (someone): *it doesn't always pay to be honest* **6** to make (a visit or call) **7** to yield a return of: *the account pays 5% interest* **8 pay one's way a** to contribute one's share of expenses **b** to remain solvent without outside help ▷ *n* **9** money given in return for work or services; a salary or wage **10 in the pay of** employed by ▷ See also **pay back** ▶ HISTORY Latin *pacare* to appease

payable *adj* **1** (often foll. by *on*) due to be paid: *the instalments are payable on the third of each month* **2** that is capable of being paid: *pensions are payable to those disabled during the wars*

pay back *vb* **1** to repay (a loan) **2** to make (someone) suffer for a wrong he or she has done you: *I want to pay him back for all the suffering he's caused me*

pay bed *n* (in Britain) a bed in a hospital used by a patient who is paying for treatment

PAYE (in Britain, Australia, and New Zealand) pay as you earn; a system by which income tax is deducted by employers and paid directly to the government

payee *n* the person to whom a cheque or money order is made out

paying guest *n* *euphemistic* a lodger

payload *n* **1** the amount of passengers, cargo, or bombs which an aircraft can carry **2** the part of a cargo which earns revenue **3** the explosive power of a warhead or bomb carried by a missile or aircraft

paymaster *n* an official responsible for the payment of wages and salaries

payment *n* **1** the act of paying **2** a sum of money paid **3** something given in return; punishment or reward

pay off *vb* **1** to pay the complete amount of (a debt) **2** to pay (someone) all that is due in wages and dismiss him or her from employment **3** to turn out successfully: *her persistence finally paid off* **4** *informal* to give a bribe to ▷ *n* **payoff 5** *informal* the climax or outcome of events **6** *informal* a bribe **7** the final payment of a debt **8** the final settlement, esp. in retribution: *the payoff came when the gang besieged the squealer's house*

payola *n* *informal* a bribe to secure special treatment, esp. to promote a commercial product

pay out *vb* **1** to spend (money) on a particular thing **2** to release (a rope) gradually, bit by bit ▷ *n* **payout 3** a sum of money paid out

payphone *n* a coin-operated telephone

payroll *n* a list of employees, giving the salary or wage of each

Pb *chem* lead ▶ HISTORY New Latin *plumbum*

pc 1 per cent **2** postcard

PC 1 personal computer **2** (in Britain) Police Constable **3** *informal* short for **politically correct 4** (in Britain) Privy Council *or* Counsellor **5** (in Canada) Progressive Conservative

pd paid

Pd *chem* palladium

PDA personal digital assistant

PDF *n* *computers* Portable Document Format: a format for viewing documents

PE 1 physical education **2** Prince Edward Island

pea *n* **1** an annual climbing plant with green pods containing green seeds **2** the seed of this plant, eaten as a vegetable ▶ HISTORY from *pease* (incorrectly assumed to be a plural)

peace *n* **1** stillness or silence **2** absence of mental anxiety: *peace of mind* **3** absence of war **4** harmony between people or groups **5** a treaty marking the end of a war **6** law and order within a state: *a breach of the peace* **7 at peace a** dead: *the old lady is at peace now* **b** in a state of harmony or serenity **8 hold** *or* **keep one's peace** to keep silent **9 keep the peace** to maintain law and order ▶ HISTORY Latin *pax*

peaceable *adj* *written* **1** inclined towards peace **2** tranquil or calm

peace dividend *n* additional money available to a government from cuts in defence expenditure because of the end of a period of hostilities

619

peaceful *adj* **1** not in a state of war or disagreement **2** calm or tranquil > **peacefully** *adv*

peacekeeper *n* **1** a person who tries to avert arguments between people **2** a soldier whose job is to prevent further fighting between hostile forces in an area: *UN peacekeepers*

peacemaker *n* a person who brings about peace, esp. between others

peace offering *n* something given or said in order to restore peace: *I bought Mum some flowers as a peace offering*

peace pipe *n* a long decorated pipe smoked by Native Americans, esp. as a token of peace

peach *n* **1** a soft juicy fruit with a downy skin, yellowish-orange sweet flesh, and a single stone **2** *informal* a person or thing that is especially pleasing: *a peach of a goal* ▷ *adj* **3** pale pinkish-orange ▶ HISTORY Latin *Persicum malum* Persian apple

peacock *n*, *pl* **-cocks** *or* **-cock** **1** a large male bird of the pheasant family with a crested head and a very large fanlike tail with blue and green eyelike spots **2** a vain strutting person ▶ HISTORY Latin *pavo* peacock + COCK > **peahen** *fem n*

peafowl *n* a peacock or peahen

peak *n* **1** a pointed tip or projection: *the peak of the roof* **2 a** the pointed summit of a mountain **b** a mountain with a pointed summit **3** the point of greatest success or achievement: *the peak of his career* **4** a projecting piece on the front of some caps ▷ *vb* **5** to form or reach a peak ▷ *adj* **6** of or relating to a period of greatest demand: *hotels are generally dearer in peak season* ▶ HISTORY perhaps from *pike* (the weapon)

peaked *adj* having a peak

peak load *n* the maximum load on an electrical power-supply system

peaky *adj* **peakier, peakiest** pale and sickly ▶ HISTORY origin unknown

peal *n* **1** a long loud echoing sound, such as of bells or thunder ▷ *vb* **2** to sound with a peal or peals ▶ HISTORY Middle English *pele*

peanut *n* a plant with edible nutlike seeds which ripen underground

pear *n* **1** a sweet juicy fruit with a narrow top and a rounded base **2 go pear-shaped** *informal* to go wrong: *the plan started to go pear-shaped* ▶ HISTORY Latin *pirum*

pearl *n* **1** a hard smooth greyish-white rounded object found inside the shell of a clam or oyster and much valued as a gem **2** See **mother-of-pearl** **3** a person or thing that is like a pearl in beauty or value ▷ *adj* **4** of, made of, or set with pearl or mother-of-pearl ▷ *vb* **5** to set with or as if with pearls **6** to shape into or assume a pearl-like form or colour **7** to dive for pearls ▶ HISTORY Latin *perna* sea mussel

pearl barley *n* barley ground into small round grains, used in soups and stews

pearly *adj* **pearlier, pearliest** **1** resembling a pearl, esp. in lustre **2** decorated with pearls or mother-of-pearl

peasant *n* **1** a member of a low social class employed in agricultural labour **2** *informal* an uncouth or uncultured person ▶ HISTORY Old French *paisant*

peasantry *n* peasants as a class

pease *n*, *pl* **pease** *archaic or dialect* same as **pea** ▶ HISTORY Old English *pise, pease*

pease pudding *n* (esp. in Britain) a dish of split peas that have been soaked and boiled

peasouper *n* *informal, chiefly Brit* thick dirty yellowish fog

peat *n* decaying vegetable matter found in uplands and bogs and used as a fuel (when dried) and as a fertilizer ▶ HISTORY perhaps Celtic

pebble *n* **1** a small smooth rounded stone, esp. one worn by the action of water ▷ *vb* **-bling, -bled** **2** to cover with pebbles ▶ HISTORY Old English *papolstān* pebble stone > **pebbly** *adj*

pebble dash *n* *Brit & Austral* a finish for external walls consisting of small stones set in plaster

pec *n* *informal* a pectoral muscle: *a gigolo with flowing blond locks and rippling pecs*

pecan (pee-kan) *n* a smooth oval nut with a sweet oily kernel that grows on hickory trees in the Southern US ▶ HISTORY Native American *paccan*

peccadillo *n*, *pl* **-loes** *or* **-los** *written* a trivial misdeed ▶ HISTORY Spanish *pecadillo*, from Latin *peccare* to sin

peccary *n*, *pl* **-ries** *or* **-ry** a piglike animal of American forests ▶ HISTORY Carib

peck¹ *vb* **1** to strike or pick up with the beak **2** *informal* to kiss (a person) quickly and lightly **3 peck at** to eat slowly and reluctantly: *pecking away at your lunch* ▷ *n* **4** a quick light blow from a bird's beak **5** a mark made by such a blow **6** *informal* a quick light kiss ▶ HISTORY origin unknown

peck² *n* an obsolete unit of liquid measure equal to one quarter of a bushel or 2 gallons (9.1 litres) ▶ HISTORY Anglo-Norman

pecker *n* **keep one's pecker up** *Brit & NZ, slang* to remain cheerful

pecking order *n* the order of seniority or power in a group: *she came from a family low in the social pecking order*

peckish *adj* *informal* feeling slightly hungry

pectin *n* *biochem* a water-soluble carbohydrate that occurs in ripe fruit: used in the manufacture of jams because of its ability to gel ▶ HISTORY Greek *pēktos* congealed

pectoral *adj* **1** of or relating to the chest, breast, or thorax: *pectoral fins* **2** worn on the breast or chest: *a pectoral cross* ▷ *n* **3** a pectoral organ or part, esp. a muscle or fin ▶ HISTORY Latin *pectus* breast

pectoral fin *n* a fin, just behind the head in fishes, that helps to control the direction of movement

peculate *vb* **-lating, -lated** *literary* to embezzle (public money) ▶ HISTORY Latin *peculari* > **peculation** *n*

peculiar *adj* **1** strange or odd: *a peculiar idea* **2** distinct or special **3** (foll. by *to*) belonging exclusively (to): *a fish peculiar to these waters*

▶ **HISTORY** Latin *peculiaris* concerning private property

peculiarity *n*, *pl* **-ties** **1** a strange or unusual habit; eccentricity **2** a distinguishing trait **3** the state or quality of being peculiar

pecuniary *adj* **1** of or relating to money **2** *law* (of an offence) involving a monetary penalty ▶ **HISTORY** Latin *pecunia* money

pedagogue *or US sometimes* **pedagog** *n* a teacher, esp. a pedantic one ▶ **HISTORY** Greek *pais* boy + *agōgos* leader > **pedagogic** *adj*

pedagogy (**ped**-a-goj-ee) *n* the principles, practice, or profession of teaching

pedal[1] *n* **1** a foot-operated lever used to control a vehicle or machine, or to modify the tone of a musical instrument ▷ *vb* **-alling, -alled** *or US* **-aling, -aled** **2** to propel (a bicycle) by operating the pedals **3** to operate the pedals of an organ or piano ▶ **HISTORY** Latin *pedalis*, from *pes* foot

pedal[2] *adj* of or relating to the foot or the feet ▶ **HISTORY** Latin *pedalis*, from *pes* foot

pedant *n* a person who is concerned chiefly with insignificant detail or who relies too much on academic learning ▶ **HISTORY** Italian *pedante* teacher > **pedantic** *adj* > **pedantically** *adv*

pedantry *n*, *pl* **-ries** the practice of being a pedant, esp. in the minute observance of petty rules or details

peddle *vb* **-dling, -dled** **1** to sell (goods) from place to place **2** to sell illegal drugs **3** to advocate (an idea or information) persistently: *the version of events being peddled by his opponents* ▶ **HISTORY** from *pedlar*

pedestal *n* **1** a base that supports something, such as a statue **2 put someone on a pedestal** to admire someone very much ▶ **HISTORY** Old Italian *piedestallo*

pedestal rock *n* *geol* an isolated rock that is wider at the top than at the bottom, sometimes resembling a mushroom

pedestrian *n* **1** a person who travels on foot ▷ *adj* **2** dull or commonplace: *a pedestrian performance* ▶ **HISTORY** Latin *pes* foot

pedestrian crossing *n* *Brit & Austral* a path across a road marked as a crossing for pedestrians

pedestrianize *or* **-ise** *vb* **-izing, -ized** *or* **-ising, -ised** to convert (a street or shopping area) into an area for pedestrians only

pedestrian precinct *n* *Brit* an area of a town for pedestrians only, esp. an area of shops

pedicure *n* medical or cosmetic treatment of the feet ▶ **HISTORY** Latin *pes* foot + *curare* to care for

pedigree *n* **1** the line of descent of a purebred animal **2** a document recording this **3** a genealogical table, esp. one indicating pure ancestry ▶ **HISTORY** Old French *pie de grue* crane's foot, alluding to the spreading lines used in a genealogical chart

pediment *n* a triangular part over a door, as used in classical architecture ▶ **HISTORY** obsolete *periment*, perhaps workman's corruption of *pyramid*

pedlar *or esp US* **peddler** *n* a person who peddles ▶ **HISTORY** Middle English *ped* basket

pedometer (pid-**dom**-it-er) *n* a device that measures the distance walked by recording the number of steps taken ▶ **HISTORY** Latin *pes* foot + **METER**

peds *pl n* *geol, agriculture* clusters of soil particles regarded as units in soil analysis

peduncle *n* **1** *bot* a plant stalk bearing a flower cluster or solitary flower **2** *anat, pathol* any stalklike structure ▶ **HISTORY** Latin *pediculus* little foot > **peduncular** *adj*

pee *informal vb* **peeing, peed** **1** to urinate ▷ *n* **2** urine **3** the act of urinating ▶ **HISTORY** euphemistic for *piss*

peek *vb* **1** to glance quickly or secretly ▷ *n* **2** such a glance ▶ **HISTORY** Middle English *pike*

peel *vb* **1** to remove the skin or rind of (a fruit or vegetable) **2** to come off in flakes **3** (of a person or part of the body) to shed skin in flakes as a result of sunburn ▷ *n* **4** the skin or rind of a fruit, etc. ▶ **HISTORY** Latin *pilare* to make bald

peelings *pl n* strips of skin or rind that have been peeled off: *potato peelings*

peel off *vb* **1** to remove or be removed by peeling: *this softens the paint, which can then be peeled off* **2** *slang* to take off one's clothes or a piece of clothing **3** to leave a group of moving people, vehicles, etc. by taking a course that curves away to one side: *two aircraft peeled off to attack the enemy bombers*

peen *n* the end of a hammer head opposite the striking face, often rounded or wedge-shaped ▶ **HISTORY** origin unknown

peep[1] *vb* **1** to look slyly or quickly, such as through a small opening or from a hidden place **2** to appear partially or briefly: *the sun peeped through the clouds* ▷ *n* **3** a quick or sly look **4** the first appearance: *the peep of dawn* ▶ **HISTORY** variant of *peek*

peep[2] *vb* **1** (esp. of young birds) to make small shrill noises ▷ *n* **2** a peeping sound ▶ **HISTORY** imitative

Peeping Tom *n* a man who furtively observes women undressing ▶ **HISTORY** after the tailor who, according to legend, peeped at Lady Godiva when she rode naked through Coventry

peer[1] *n* **1** a member of a nobility **2** a person who holds any of the five grades of the British nobility: duke, marquess, earl, viscount, and baron **3** a person of equal social standing, rank, age, etc.: *he is greatly respected by his peers in the arts world* ▶ **HISTORY** Latin *par* equal

peer[2] *vb* **1** to look intently or as if with difficulty: *Walter peered anxiously at his father's face* **2** to appear dimly: *the sun peered through the fog* ▶ **HISTORY** Flemish *pieren* to look with narrowed eyes

peerage *Brit n* **1** the whole body of peers; aristocracy **2** the position, rank, or title of a peer

peeress *n* **1** (in Britain) a woman holding the rank of a peer **2** the wife or widow of a peer

peer group *n* a social group composed of people of similar age and status

peerless *adj* having no equals; unsurpassed

p

621

peer pressure *n* pressure to conform to the opinions and behaviour of people of one's own age or status

peevish *adj* fretful or irritable ▸ HISTORY origin unknown > **peevishly** *adv*

peewee *n* a black-and-white Australian bird

peewit *or* **pewit** *n* same as **lapwing** ▸ HISTORY imitative of its call

peg *n* **1** a small pin or bolt used to join two parts together, to fasten, or to mark **2** a hook or knob for hanging things on **3** *music* a pin on a stringed instrument which can be turned to tune the string wound around it **4** Also called: **clothes peg** a split or hinged pin for fastening wet clothes to a line to dry **5** *Brit* a small drink of spirits **6** an opportunity or pretext for doing something: *the play's subject matter provides a perfect peg for a discussion of issues like morality and faith* **7 bring** *or* **take (someone) down a peg** to lower the pride of (someone) **8 off the peg** *Brit & NZ* (of clothes) ready-to-wear, as opposed to tailor-made ▹ *vb* **pegging, pegged 9** to insert a peg into **10** to secure with pegs: *the balloon was pegged down to stop it drifting away* **11** to mark (a score) with pegs, as in some card games **12** *chiefly Brit* to work steadily: *he pegged away at his job for years* **13** to fix or maintain something, such as prices, at a particular level or value: *a fixed rate mortgage, pegged at 9.6 per cent* ▸ HISTORY Low Germanic *pegge*

peggy square *n NZ* a small hand-knitted square

peignoir (**pay**-nwahr) *n* a woman's light dressing gown ▸ HISTORY French

pejorative (pij-**jor**-a-tiv) *adj* **1** (of a word or expression) having an insulting or critical sense ▹ *n* **2** a pejorative word or expression ▸ HISTORY Late Latin *pejorare* to make worse

peke *n informal* a Pekingese dog

Pekingese *or* **Pekinese** *n* **1** (*pl* **-ese**) a small dog with a long straight coat, curled plumed tail, and short wrinkled muzzle **2** the dialect of Mandarin Chinese spoken in Beijing

pelargonium *n* a plant with circular leaves and red, pink, or white flowers: includes many cultivated geraniums ▸ HISTORY Greek *pelargos* stork

pelican *n* a large water bird with a pouch beneath its long bill for holding fish ▸ HISTORY Greek *pelekan*

pelican crossing *n* (in Britain) a type of road crossing with a pedestrian-operated traffic-light system ▸ HISTORY from *pe(destrian) li(ght) con(trolled) crossing*, with *-con* adapted to *-can* of *pelican*

pellagra *n pathol* a disease caused by a diet lacking in vitamin B, which results in scaling of the skin, diarrhoea, and mental disorder ▸ HISTORY Italian, from *pelle* skin + Greek *agra* paroxysm

pellet *n* **1** a small round ball, esp. of compressed matter **2 a** an imitation bullet used in toy guns **b** a piece of small shot **3** a small pill ▸ HISTORY Latin *pila* ball

pell-mell *adv* **1** in a confused headlong rush: *the hounds ran pell-mell into the yard* **2** in a disorderly manner: *the things were piled pell-mell in the room* ▸ HISTORY Old French *pesle-mesle*

pellucid *adj literary* **1** transparent or translucent **2** extremely clear in style and meaning ▸ HISTORY Latin *pellucidus*

pelmet *n* a board or piece of fabric used to conceal the curtain rail ▸ HISTORY probably from French *palmette* palm-leaf decoration on cornice moulding

pelt[1] *vb* **1** to throw (missiles) at **2** (foll. by *along* etc.) to hurry **3** to rain heavily ▹ *n* **4** a blow **5 at full pelt** very quickly: *she ran down the street at full pelt* ▸ HISTORY origin unknown

pelt[2] *n* the skin or fur of an animal, esp. as material for clothing or rugs: *the lucrative international trade in beaver pelts* ▸ HISTORY probably from Latin *pellis* skin

pelvis *n, pl* **-vises** *or* **-ves 1** the framework of bones at the base of the spine, to which the hips are attached **2** the bones that form this structure ▸ HISTORY Latin: basin > **pelvic** *adj*

pen[1] *n* **1** an instrument for writing or drawing using ink. See also **ballpoint, fountain pen 2 the pen** writing as an occupation ▹ *vb* **penning, penned 3** to write or compose ▸ HISTORY Latin *penna* feather

pen[2] *n* **1** an enclosure in which domestic animals are kept **2** any place of confinement ▹ *vb* **penning, penned** *or* **pent 3** to enclose (animals) in a pen **4 penned in** being or feeling trapped or confined: *she stood penned in by bodies at the front of the crowd* ▸ HISTORY Old English *penn*

pen[3] *n US & Canad, informal* short for **penitentiary** (sense 1)

pen[4] *n* a female swan ▸ HISTORY origin unknown

Pen. Peninsula

penal (**pee**-nal) *adj* **1** of or relating to punishment **2** used as a place of punishment: *a penal institution* ▸ HISTORY Latin *poena* penalty > **penally** *adv*

penal code *n* the body of laws relating to crime and punishment

penal colony *n history* a colony established for the containment and punishment of convicted criminals and benefitting from their forced labour

penalize *or* **-ise** *vb* **-izing, -ized** *or* **-ising, -ised 1** to impose a penalty on (someone) for breaking a law or rule **2** to inflict a disadvantage on: *why should I be penalized just because I'm a woman?* > **penalization** *or* **-isation** *n*

penal settlement *n* a place to which convicted criminals are banished as a punishment for their crimes

penalty *n, pl* **-ties 1** a legal punishment for a crime or offence **2** loss or suffering as a result of one's own action: *we are now paying the penalty for neglecting to keep our equipment up to date* **3** *sport, games, etc.* a handicap awarded against a player or team for illegal play, such as a free shot at goal by the opposing team ▸ HISTORY Latin *poena*

penalty box *n* **1** Also called: **penalty area** *soccer* a rectangular area in front of the goal, within which a penalty is awarded for a serious foul by the defending team **2** *ice hockey* a bench for players serving time penalties

penalty corner n *hockey* a free hit from the goal line taken by the attacking side

penalty shoot-out n *sport* a method of deciding the winner of a drawn match, in which players from each team attempt to score with a penalty shot

penance n **1** voluntary self-punishment to make amends for a sin **2** *RC Church* a sacrament in which repentant sinners are forgiven provided they confess their sins to a priest and perform a penance ▶ HISTORY Latin *paenitentia* repentance

pence n a plural of **penny**

penchant (**pon**-shon) n strong inclination or liking: *a stylish woman with a penchant for dark glasses* ▶ HISTORY French

pencil n **1** a rod of graphite encased in wood which is used for writing or drawing ▷ vb **-cilling, -cilled** or US **-ciling, -ciled** **2** to draw, colour, write, or mark with a pencil **3 pencil in** to note, arrange, or include provisionally or tentatively ▶ HISTORY Latin *penicillus* painter's brush

pendant n **a** an ornament worn on a chain round the neck: *a beautiful pearl pendant* **b** an ornament that hangs from a piece of jewellery ▶ HISTORY Latin *pendere* to hang down

pendent adj *literary* **1** dangling **2** jutting ▶ HISTORY see PENDANT

pending prep **1** while waiting for ▷ adj **2** not yet decided or settled **3** imminent: *these developments have been pending for some time*

pendulous adj *literary* hanging downwards and swinging freely ▶ HISTORY Latin *pendere* to hang down

pendulum n **1** a weight suspended so it swings freely under the influence of gravity **2** such a device used to regulate a clock mechanism **3** a movement from one attitude or belief towards its opposite: *the pendulum has swung back to more punitive measures*

peneplain or **peneplane** n *geog* a relatively flat land surface produced by erosion ▶ HISTORY Latin *paene* almost + PLAIN

penetrate vb **-trating, -trated** **1** to find or force a way into or through **2** to diffuse through; permeate: *the smell of cooking penetrated through to the sitting room* **3** to see through: *the sunlight did not penetrate the thick canopy of leaves* **4** (of a man) to insert the penis into the vagina of (a woman) **5** to grasp the meaning of (a principle, etc.) ▶ HISTORY Latin *penetrare* > **penetrable** adj > **penetrative** adj

penetrating adj tending to or able to penetrate: *a penetrating mind; a penetrating voice*

penetration n **1** the act or an instance of penetrating **2** the ability or power to penetrate **3** keen insight or perception

pen friend n a person with whom one exchanges letters, often a person in another country whom one has not met

penguin n a flightless black-and-white sea bird with webbed feet and wings modified as flippers for swimming ▶ HISTORY origin unknown

penicillin n an antibiotic used to treat diseases caused by bacteria ▶ HISTORY Latin *pencillus* tuft of hairs

peninsula n a narrow strip of land projecting from the mainland into a sea or lake ▶ HISTORY Latin, literally: almost an island > **peninsular** adj

penis n, pl **-nises** or **-nes** the organ of copulation in higher vertebrates, also used for urinating in many mammals ▶ HISTORY Latin > **penile** adj

penitent adj **1** feeling regret for one's sins; repentant ▷ n **2** a person who is penitent ▶ HISTORY Church Latin *paenitens* regretting > **penitence** n

penitential adj of, showing, or as a penance

penitentiary n, pl **-ries** **1** (in the US and Canada) a state or federal prison ▷ adj **2** of or for penance **3** used for punishment and reformation: *the penitentiary system* ▶ HISTORY Latin *paenitens* penitent

penknife n, pl **-knives** a small knife with one or more blades that fold into the handle

pen name n a name used by a writer instead of his or her real name; nom de plume

pennant n **1** a long narrow flag, esp. one used by ships as identification or for signalling **2** *chiefly US, Canad & Austral* a flag indicating the winning of a championship in certain sports ▶ HISTORY probably a blend of *pendant* + *pennon*

penniless adj very poor

pennon n **1** a long flag, often tapering and divided at the end, originally a knight's personal flag **2** a small tapering or triangular flag flown by a ship or boat ▶ HISTORY Latin *penna* feather

penny n, pl **pennies** or **pence** **1** a British bronze coin worth one hundredth of a pound **2** a former British and Australian coin worth one twelfth of a shilling **3** (pl **pennies**) *US & Canad* a cent **4** *informal, chiefly Brit* the least amount of money: *I don't have a penny* **5 a pretty penny** *informal* a considerable sum of money **6 spend a penny** *Brit & NZ, informal* to urinate **7 the penny dropped** *informal* the explanation of something was finally understood ▶ HISTORY Old English *penig, pening*

penny-dreadful n, pl **-fuls** *Brit, informal* a cheap, often lurid book or magazine

penny-farthing n *Brit* an early type of bicycle with a large front wheel and a small rear wheel

penny-pinching adj **1** excessively careful with money; miserly ▷ n **2** miserliness > **penny-pincher** n

pennyroyal n a Eurasian plant with hairy leaves and small mauve flowers, which provides an aromatic oil used in medicine ▶ HISTORY Old French *pouliol* pennyroyal + *royal* royal

pennywort n a Eurasian rock plant with whitish-green tubular flowers and rounded leaves

penology (pee-**nol**-a-jee) n the study of the punishment of criminals and of prison management ▶ HISTORY Greek *poinē* punishment

pension¹ n **1** a regular payment made by the state or a former employer to a person who has retired or to a widowed or disabled person ▷ vb **2** to grant

P

a pension to ▶ HISTORY Latin *pensio* a payment
> **pensionable** *adj* > **pensioner** *n*

pension² (**pon**-syon) *n* (in France and some other countries) a relatively cheap boarding house ▶ HISTORY French: extended meaning of *pension* grant

pension off *vb* to cause (someone) to retire from a job and pay him or her a pension

pensive *adj* deeply thoughtful, often with a tinge of sadness ▶ HISTORY Latin *pensare* to consider > **pensively** *adv*

penta- *combining form* five: *pentagon; pentameter* ▶ HISTORY Greek *pente*

pentacle *n* same as **pentagram** ▶ HISTORY Italian *pentacolo* something having five corners

pentagon *n* *geom* a figure with five sides > **pentagonal** *adj*

Pentagon *n* a five-sided building that houses the headquarters of the US Department of Defense

pentagram *n* a star-shaped figure with five points

pentameter (pen-**tam**-it-er) *n* a line of poetry consisting of five metrical feet

Pentateuch (**pent**-a-tyuke) *n* the first five books of the Old Testament ▶ HISTORY Greek *pente* five + *teukhos* scroll case > **Pentateuchal** *adj*

pentatonic scale *n* *music* a scale consisting of five notes

pentavalent *adj* *chem* having a valency of five

Pentecost *n* a Christian festival occurring on Whit Sunday celebrating the descent of the Holy Ghost to the apostles ▶ HISTORY Greek *pentēkostē* fiftieth (day after the Resurrection)

Pentecostal *adj* relating to any of the Christian groups that have a charismatic and fundamentalist approach to Christianity

penthouse *n* a luxurious flat built on the top floor or roof of a building ▶ HISTORY Middle English *pentis*, later *penthouse*, from Latin *appendere* to hang from

pent-up *adj* not released; repressed: *full of pent-up emotional violence*

penultimate *adj* second last

penumbra *n*, *pl* -**brae** or -**bras** 1 the partially shadowed region which surrounds the full shadow in an eclipse 2 *literary* a partial shadow ▶ HISTORY Latin *paene* almost + *umbra* shadow > **penumbral** *adj*

penurious *adj* *formal* 1 niggardly with money 2 lacking money or means

penury *n* *formal* 1 extreme poverty 2 extreme scarcity ▶ HISTORY Latin *penuria*

peon *n* a Spanish-American farm labourer or unskilled worker ▶ HISTORY Spanish

peony *n*, *pl* -**nies** a garden plant with showy pink, red, white, or yellow flowers ▶ HISTORY Greek *paiōnia*

people *pl n* 1 persons collectively or in general 2 a group of persons considered together: *old people suffer from anaemia more often than younger people do* 3 (*pl* -**ples**) the persons living in a particular country: *the American people* 4 one's family or

ancestors: *her people originally came from Skye* 5 **the people a** the mass of ordinary persons without rank or privileges **b** the body of persons in a country who are entitled to vote ▷ *vb* -**pling, -pled** 6 to provide with inhabitants: *the centre of the continent is sparsely peopled* ▶ HISTORY Latin *populus*

people carrier *n* same as **multipurpose vehicle**

people mover *n* *Brit, Austral & NZ* same as **multipurpose vehicle**

pep *n* 1 high spirits, energy, or vitality ▷ *vb* **pepping, pepped** 2 **pep up** to make more lively or interesting: *the company has spent thousands trying to pep up its image* ▶ HISTORY short for *pepper*

pepper *n* 1 a sharp hot condiment obtained from the fruit of an East Indian climbing plant 2 Also called: **capsicum** a colourful tropical fruit used as a vegetable and a condiment ▷ *vb* 3 to season with pepper 4 to sprinkle liberally: *his speech is heavily peppered with Americanisms* 5 to pelt with small missiles ▶ HISTORY Greek *peperi*

peppercorn *n* the small dried berry of the pepper plant

peppercorn rent *n* *Brit* a rent that is very low or nominal

pepper mill *n* a small hand mill used to grind peppercorns

peppermint *n* 1 a mint plant which produces a pungent oil, used as a flavouring 2 a sweet flavoured with peppermint

peppery *adj* 1 tasting of pepper 2 irritable

pep pill *n* *informal* a tablet containing a stimulant drug

pepsin *n* an enzyme produced in the stomach, which, when activated by acid, breaks down proteins ▶ HISTORY Greek *peptein* to digest

pep talk *n* *informal* a talk designed to increase confidence and enthusiasm

peptic *adj* 1 of or relating to digestion 2 of or caused by pepsin or the action of the digestive juices: *a peptic ulcer* ▶ HISTORY Greek *peptein* to digest

peptic ulcer *n* an ulcer in the stomach or duodenum

peptide *n* *chem* a compound consisting of two or more amino acids linked by chemical bonding between the amino group of one and the carboxyl group of another

per *prep* 1 for every: *three pence per pound; 30 pounds per week* 2 by; through 3 **as per** according to: *proceed as per the instructions* 4 **as per usual** or **as per normal** *informal* as usual ▶ HISTORY Latin: by, for each

perambulate *vb* -**lating, -lated** *formal* to walk about (a place) ▶ HISTORY Latin *per-* through + *ambulare* to walk > **perambulation** *n*

perambulator *n* *formal* same as **pram**

per annum *adv* in each year ▶ HISTORY Latin

per capita *adj*, *adv* of or for each person: *the average per capita wage has increased* ▶ HISTORY Latin, literally: according to heads

perceive *vb* -**ceiving, -ceived** 1 to become aware of (something) through the senses

2 to understand or grasp ► HISTORY Latin *percipere* to seize entirely > **perceivable** *adj*

per cent *adv* **1** in each hundred. Symbol: %
▷ *n also* **percent 2** a percentage or proportion ► HISTORY Medieval Latin *per centum* out of every hundred

percentage *n* **1** proportion or rate per hundred parts **2** any proportion in relation to the whole: *a small percentage of the population* **3** *informal* profit or advantage

percentage error *n maths* the difference between the predicted value and the actual value of a quantity, expressed as a percentage

percentile *n* one of 99 actual or notional values of a variable dividing its distribution into 100 groups with equal frequencies

perceptible *adj* able to be perceived; recognizable > **perceptibly** *adv*

perception *n* **1** the act of perceiving **2** insight or intuition: *his acute perception of other people's emotions* **3** the ability to perceive **4** way of viewing: *advertising affects the customer's perception of a product* ► HISTORY Latin *perceptio* comprehension > **perceptual** *adj*

perceptive *adj* **1** observant **2** able to perceive > **perceptively** *adv* > **perceptiveness** *n*

perch[1] *n* **1** a branch or other resting place above ground for a bird **2** any raised resting place: *from his perch on the bar stool* ▷ *vb* **3** (of birds) to alight or rest on a perch: *it fluttered to the branch and perched there for a moment* **4** to place or position precariously: *he was perched uneasily on the edge of his chair* ► HISTORY Latin *pertica* long staff

perch[2] *n, pl* **perch** *or* **perches 1** a spiny-finned edible freshwater fish of Europe and North America **2** any of various similar or related fishes ► HISTORY Greek *perkē*

perchance *adv archaic or poetic* **1** perhaps **2** by chance ► HISTORY Anglo-French *par chance*

percipient *adj formal* quick at perceiving; observant ► HISTORY Latin *percipiens* observing > **percipience** *n*

percolate *vb* **-lating, -lated 1** to pass or filter through very small holes: *the light percolating through the stained-glass windows cast coloured patterns on the floor* **2** to spread gradually: *his theories percolated through the academic community* **3** to make (coffee) or (of coffee) to be made in a percolator ► HISTORY Latin *per-* through + *colare* to strain > **percolation** *n*

percolator *n* a coffeepot in which boiling water is forced up through a tube and filters down through the coffee grounds into a container

percussion *n* **1** the striking of one thing against another **2** *music* percussion instruments collectively ► HISTORY Latin *percutere* to hit > **percussive** *adj*

percussion instrument *n* a musical instrument, such as the drums, that produces a sound when struck directly

percussionist *n music* a person who plays percussion instruments

perdition *n* **1** *Christianity* final and unalterable spiritual ruin; damnation **2** same as **hell** ► HISTORY Late Latin *perditio* ruin

peregrine falcon *n* a European falcon with dark plumage on the back and wings and lighter underparts ► HISTORY Latin *peregrinus* foreign

peremptory *adj* **1** urgent or commanding: *a peremptory knock on the door* **2** expecting immediate obedience without any discussion: *he gave peremptory instructions to his son* **3** dogmatic ► HISTORY Latin *peremptorius* decisive > **peremptorily** *adv*

perennial *adj* **1** lasting throughout the year or through many years ▷ *n* **2** a plant that continues its growth for at least three years ► HISTORY Latin *per-* through + *annus* year

perestroika *n* (in the late 1980s) the policy of restructuring the Soviet economy and political system ► HISTORY Russian: reconstruction

perfect *adj* **1** having all essential elements **2** faultless: *a perfect circle* **3** correct or precise: *perfect timing* **4** utter or absolute: *a perfect stranger* **5** excellent in all respects: *a perfect day* **6** *maths* exactly divisible into equal integral or polynomial roots: *36 is a perfect square* **7** *grammar* denoting a tense of verbs used to describe a completed action ▷ *n* **8** *grammar* the perfect tense ▷ *vb* (per-**fect**) **9** to improve to one's satisfaction: *he is in Paris to perfect his French* **10** to make fully accomplished: *he perfected the system* ► HISTORY Latin *perficere* to complete > **perfectly** *adv*

perfect flower *n bot* a flower with functional stamens and pistils

perfection *n* the state or quality of being perfect ► HISTORY Latin *perfectio* a completing

perfectionism *n* the demand for the highest standard of excellence > **perfectionist** *n, adj*

perfect tense *n* **1** same as **present perfect 2** one of the tenses used to refer to the time leading up either to the present or to a particular point in the past. See also **past perfect**

perfidious *adj literary* treacherous or deceitful ► HISTORY Latin *perfidus* > **perfidy** *n*

perforate *vb* **-rating, -rated 1** to make a hole or holes in **2** to punch rows of holes between (stamps) for ease of separation ► HISTORY Latin *per-* through + *forare* to pierce > **perforable** *adj* > **perforator** *n*

perforation *n* **1** a hole or holes made in something **2** a series of punched holes, such as that between individual stamps

perforce *adv formal* of necessity ► HISTORY Old French *par force*

perform *vb* **1** to carry out (an action): *the hospital performs more than a hundred such operations each year* **2** to present (a play or concert): *he performed a couple of songs from his new album* **3** to fulfil: *you have performed the first of two conditions* ► HISTORY Old French *parfournir* > **performable** *adj* > **performer** *n*

performance *n* **1** the act or process of performing **2** an artistic or dramatic production:

P

625

the concert includes the first performance of a new trumpet concerto **3** manner or quality of functioning: *the car's overall performance is excellent* **4** *informal* conduct or behaviour, esp. when distasteful: *what did you mean by that performance at the restaurant?*

perfume *n* **1** a liquid cosmetic worn for its pleasant smell **2** a fragrant smell ▷ *vb* **-fuming, -fumed 3** to impart a perfume to ▶ HISTORY French *parfum*, from Latin *per* through + *fumare* to smoke > **perfumed** *adj*

perfumer *n* a person who makes or sells perfume > **perfumery** *n*

perfunctory *adj formal* done only as a matter of routine: *he gave his wife a perfunctory kiss* ▶ HISTORY Late Latin *perfunctorius* negligent > **perfunctorily** *adv* > **perfunctoriness** *n*

perfuse *vb* **-fusing, -fused 1** to permeate (a liquid, colour, etc.) through or over (something) **2** *surgery* to pass (a fluid) through tissue

pergola *n* an arched trellis or framework that supports climbing plants ▶ HISTORY Italian

perhaps *adv* **1** possibly; maybe **2** approximately; roughly: *it would have taken perhaps three or four minutes* ▶ HISTORY earlier *perhappes*, from *per* by + *happes* chance

perianth *n bot* the outer part of a flower ▶ HISTORY Greek *peri-* around + *anthos* flower

pericardium *n, pl* **-dia** the membranous sac enclosing the heart ▶ HISTORY Greek *peri-* around + *kardia* heart > **pericardial** *adj*

pericarp *n bot* the part of a fruit enclosing the seed that develops from the wall of the ovary ▶ HISTORY Greek *peri-* around + *karpos* fruit

perigee *n astron* the point in its orbit around the earth when the moon or a satellite is nearest the earth ▶ HISTORY Greek *peri-* near + *gē* earth

periglacial *adj geog* relating to a region bordering a glacier: *periglacial climate*

perihelion *n, pl* **-lia** *astron* the point in its orbit around the sun when a planet or comet is nearest the sun ▶ HISTORY Greek *peri-* near + *hēlios* sun

peril *n* great danger or jeopardy ▶ HISTORY Latin *periculum* > **perilous** *adj*

perilymph *n physiol* the fluid that fills the space between the membranous and bony labyrinths of the internal ear

perimeter (per-**rim**-it-er) *n* **1** *maths* **a** the curve or line enclosing a plane area **b** the length of this curve or line **2** any boundary around something ▶ HISTORY Latin *perimetros*

perinatal *adj* of or occurring in the period from about three months before to one month after birth ▶ HISTORY Greek *peri-* around + Latin *natus* born

perineum (per-rin-**nee**-um) *n, pl* **-nea** (-**nee**-a) *anat* the region of the body between the anus and the genitals ▶ HISTORY Greek *perinaion* > **perineal** *adj*

perineurium *n anat* the connective tissue forming a sheath around a single bundle of nerve fibres

period *n* **1** a portion of time: *six inches of rain fell in a 24-hour period* **2** a portion of time specified in some way: *the President's first period of office* **3** an occurrence of menstruation **4** *geol* a unit of geological time during which a system of rocks is formed: *the Jurassic period* **5** a division of time at school, college, or university when a particular subject is taught **6** *physics, maths* the time taken to complete one cycle of a regularly recurring phenomenon **7** *chem* one of the horizontal rows of elements in the periodic table **8** *chiefly US & Canad* same as **full stop** ▷ *adj* **9** dating from or in the style of an earlier time: *a performance on period instruments* ▶ HISTORY Greek *periodos* circuit

periodic *adj* recurring at intervals > **periodically** *adv* > **periodicity** *n*

periodical *n* **1** a publication issued at regular intervals, usually monthly or weekly ▷ *adj* **2** of or relating to such publications **3** periodic or occasional

periodic law *n chem* the principle that the chemical properties of the elements are periodic functions of their atomic numbers

periodic table *n chem* a table of the elements, arranged in order of increasing atomic number, based on the periodic law

peripatetic (per-rip-a-**tet**-ik) *adj* **1** travelling from place to place **2** *Brit* employed in two or more educational establishments and travelling from one to another: *a peripatetic violin teacher* ▷ *n* **3** a peripatetic person ▶ HISTORY Greek *peripatein* to pace to and fro

peripheral (per-**if**-er-al) *adj* **1** not relating to the most important part of something; incidental **2** of or relating to a periphery ▷ *n* **3** *computers* any device, such as a disk or modem, concerned with input/output or storage

periphery (per-**if**-er-ee) *n, pl* **-eries 1** the boundary or edge of an area or group: *slums sprouted up on the periphery of the city* **2** fringes of a field of activity: *less developed countries on the periphery of the capitalist system* ▶ HISTORY Greek *peri-* around + *pherein* to bear

periscope *n* an optical instrument used, esp. in submarines, to give a view of objects on a different level ▶ HISTORY Greek *periskopein* to look around

perish *vb* **1** *written* to be destroyed or die **2** to cause to suffer: *we were perished with cold* **3** to rot or cause to rot: *to prevent your swimsuit from perishing, rinse it in clean water before it dries* ▶ HISTORY Latin *perire* to pass away entirely

perishable *adj* **1** liable to rot ▷ *n* **2** (often pl) a perishable article, esp. food

perishing *adj* **1** (of weather) *informal* extremely cold **2** *slang* confounded or blasted: *get rid of the perishing lot!*

peristalsis (per-riss-**tal**-siss) *n, pl* **-ses** (-seez) *physiol* the wavelike involuntary muscular contractions of the walls of the digestive tract ▶ HISTORY Greek *peri-* around + *stalsis* compression > **peristaltic** *adj*

P

peritoneum (per-rit-toe-**nee**-um) *n*, *pl* **-nea** (-**nee**-a) *or* **-neums** a serous sac that lines the walls of the abdominal cavity and covers the abdominal organs ▶ HISTORY Greek *peritonos* stretched around > **peritoneal** *adj*

peritonitis (per-rit-tone-**ite**-iss) *n* inflammation of the peritoneum, causing severe abdominal pain

periwinkle¹ *n* same as **winkle** (sense 1) ▶ HISTORY origin unknown

periwinkle² *n* a Eurasian evergreen plant with trailing stems and blue flowers ▶ HISTORY Old English *perwince*

perjure *vb* **-juring, -jured • perjure oneself** *criminal law* to deliberately give false evidence while under oath ▶ HISTORY Latin *perjurare* > **perjurer** *n*

perjury (**per**-jer-ee) *n*, *pl* **-juries** *criminal law* the act of deliberately giving false evidence while under oath ▶ HISTORY Latin *perjurium* a false oath

perk¹ *n informal* an incidental benefit gained from a job, such as a company car ▶ HISTORY short for *perquisite*

perk² *vb informal* short for **percolate** (sense 3)

perk up *vb* **1** to make or become more cheerful **2** to rise or cause to rise briskly: *the dog's ears perked up suddenly* ▶ HISTORY origin unknown

perky *adj* **perkier, perkiest** **1** jaunty or lively **2** confident or spirited

Perl *n* a computer programming language that is used for text manipulation, esp. on the World Wide Web ▶ HISTORY practical extraction and report language

perlemoen (**per**-la-moon) *n S African* same as **abalone** ▶ HISTORY Afrikaans, from Dutch

perm¹ *n* **1** a hairstyle with long-lasting waves or curls produced by treating the hair with chemicals ▷ *vb* **2** to give a perm to (hair)

perm² *n informal* short for **permutation** (sense 4)

permafrost *n* ground that is permanently frozen ▶ HISTORY perma(nent) + frost

permanent *adj* **1** existing or intended to exist forever: *a permanent solution* **2** not expected to change: *a permanent condition* ▶ HISTORY Latin *permanens* continuing > **permanence** *n* > **permanently** *adv*

permanent health insurance *n law* a form of insurance that provides up to 75 per cent of a person's salary in case of prolonged illness or disability

permanent magnet *n physics* a magnet that retains its magnetism after the magnetic field producing it is removed

permanganate *n* a salt of an acid containing manganese, used as a disinfectant

permeability *n* **1** the state or quality of being permeable **2** *geol* the degree to which a substance such as sandstone or granite is capable of transmitting fluids

permeable *adj* capable of being permeated, esp. by liquids

permeate *vb* **-ating, -ated** **1** to penetrate or spread throughout (something): *his mystical philosophy permeates everything he creates* **2** to pass through or cause to pass through by osmosis or diffusion: *the rain permeated her anorak* ▶ HISTORY Latin *permeare* > **permeation** *n*

Permian *adj geol* of the period of geological time about 280 million years ago ▶ HISTORY after *Perm*, Russian port

permissible *adj* permitted or allowable > **permissibility** *n*

permission *n* authorization to do something

permissive *adj* tolerant or lenient: *the so-called permissive society* > **permissiveness** *n*

permit *vb* (per-**mit**) **-mitting, -mitted** *written* **1** to allow (something) to be done or to happen: *smoking is not permitted in the office* **2** to allow (someone) to do something: *her father does not permit her to eat sweets* **3** to allow the possibility (of): *they saw each other as often as time and circumstances permitted* ▷ *n* (**per**-mit) **4** an official document granting permission to do something ▶ HISTORY Latin *permittere*

permutation *n* **1** *maths* an ordered arrangement of the numbers or terms of a set into specified groups: *the permutations of a, b, and c, taken two at a time, are ab, ba, ac, ca, bc, cb* **2** a combination of items made by reordering **3** a transformation **4** a fixed combination for selections of results on football pools ▶ HISTORY Latin *permutare* to change thoroughly

pernicious *adj formal* **1** wicked or malicious: *pernicious lies* **2** causing grave harm; deadly ▶ HISTORY Latin *perniciēs* ruin

pernicious anaemia *n* a severe form of anaemia resulting in a reduction of the red blood cells, weakness, and a sore tongue

pernickety *adj informal* **1** excessively fussy about details **2** (of a task) requiring close attention ▶ HISTORY origin unknown

peroration *n formal* the concluding part of a speech which sums up the points made previously ▶ HISTORY Latin *peroratio*

peroxide *n* **1** hydrogen peroxide used as a hair bleach **2** any of a class of metallic oxides, such as sodium peroxide, Na_2O_2 ▷ *adj* **3** bleached with or resembling peroxide: *a peroxide blonde* ▷ *vb* **-iding, -ided** **4** to bleach (the hair) with peroxide

perpendicular *adj* **1** at right angles to a given line or surface **2** upright; vertical **3** denoting a style of English Gothic architecture characterized by vertical lines ▷ *n* **4** *geom* a line or plane perpendicular to another ▶ HISTORY Latin *perpendiculum* a plumb line > **perpendicularity** *n*

perpendicular bisector *n maths* a perpendicular line or segment that passes through the midpoint of a segment

perpetrate *vb* **-trating, -trated** to perform or be responsible for (a deception or crime) ▶ HISTORY Latin *perpetrare* > **perpetration** *n* > **perpetrator** *n*

perpetual *adj* **1** never ending or never changing: *Mexico's colourful scenery and nearly perpetual sunshine* **2** continually repeated: *his mother's perpetual worries about his health* ▶ HISTORY Latin *perpetualis* > **perpetually** *adv*

P

perpetual motion *n* motion of a hypothetical mechanism that continues indefinitely without any external source of energy

perpetuate *vb* **-ating, -ated** to cause to continue: *images that perpetuate racial stereotypes* ▶ HISTORY Latin *perpetuare* to continue without interruption > **perpetuation** *n*

perpetuity *n, pl* **-ties** **1** eternity **2** the state of being perpetual **3** something perpetual, such as a pension that is payable indefinitely **4 in perpetuity** forever ▶ HISTORY Latin *perpetuitas* continuity

perplex *vb* **1** to puzzle or bewilder **2** to complicate: *this merely perplexes the issue* ▶ HISTORY Latin *perplexus* entangled > **perplexing** *adj*

perplexity *n, pl* **-ties** **1** the state of being perplexed **2** something that perplexes

perquisite *n formal* same as **perk¹** ▶ HISTORY Latin *perquirere* to seek earnestly for something

perry *n, pl* **-ries** an alcoholic drink made from fermented pear juice ▶ HISTORY Old French *peré*

per se (per **say**) *adv* in itself ▶ HISTORY Latin

persecute *vb* **-cuting, -cuted** **1** to oppress or maltreat (someone), because of race or religion **2** to harass (someone) persistently ▶ HISTORY Latin *persequi* to take vengeance upon > **persecution** *n* > **persecutor** *n*

perseverance *n* continued steady belief or efforts; persistence

persevere *vb* **-severing, -severed** (often foll. by *with* or *in*) to continue to make an effort despite difficulties ▶ HISTORY Latin *perseverus* very strict

Persian *adj* **1** of ancient Persia or modern Iran ▷ *n* **2** a person from Persia (now Iran) **3** the language of Iran or of Persia

Persian carpet *n* a hand-made carpet or rug with flowing or geometric designs in rich colours

Persian cat *n* a long-haired variety of domestic cat

Persian lamb *n* **1** a black loosely curled fur from the karakul lamb **2** a karakul lamb

persimmon *n* a sweet red tropical fruit ▶ HISTORY from a Native American language

persist *vb* **1** to continue without interruption: *if the symptoms persist, see your doctor* **2** (often foll. by *in* or *with*) to continue obstinately despite opposition: *she persisted in using these controversial methods* ▶ HISTORY Latin *persistere*

persistent *adj* **1** unrelenting: *persistent rain* **2** showing persistence: *she was a persistent woman* > **persistence** *n* > **persistently** *adv*

persistent vegetative state *n med* an irreversible condition, resulting from brain damage, characterized by lack of consciousness, thought, and feeling, although reflex activities continue

person *n, pl* **people** *or* **persons** **1** an individual human being **2** the body of a human being: *he was found to have a knife concealed about his person* **3** *grammar* a category into which pronouns and forms of verbs are subdivided to show whether they refer to the speaker, the person addressed, or some other individual or thing **4 in person** actually doing something or being somewhere oneself: *I had the chance to hear her speak in person* ▶ HISTORY Latin *persona* mask

-person *n combining form* sometimes used instead of *man* and *woman* or *lady*: *chairperson*

persona (per-**soh**-na) *n, pl* **-nae** (-nee) the personality that a person adopts and presents to other people ▶ HISTORY Latin: mask

personable *adj* pleasant in appearance and personality

personage *n* **1** an important or distinguished person **2** any person

personal *adj* **1** of the private aspects of a person's life: *redundancy can put an enormous strain on personal relationships* **2** of a person's body: *personal hygiene* **3** belonging to, or for the sole use of, a particular individual: *he disappeared, leaving his passport, diary and other personal belongings in his flat* **4** undertaken by an individual: *the sponsorship deal requires him to make a number of personal appearances for publicity purposes* **5** offensive in respect of an individual's personality or intimate affairs: *he has suffered a lifetime of personal remarks about his weight* **6** having the attributes of an individual conscious being: *a personal God* **7** *grammar* of person **8** *law* of movable property, such as money

personal assistant *n* a person who is employed to help someone with his or her work, esp. the secretarial and administrative aspects of it

personal column *n* a newspaper column containing personal messages and advertisements

personal computer *n* a small computer used for word processing or computer games

personality *n, pl* **-ties** **1** *psychol* the distinctive characteristics which make an individual unique **2** the distinctive character of a person which makes him or her socially attractive: *some people find him lacking in personality and a bit colourless* **3** a well-known person in a certain field; celebrity **4** a remarkable person: *she is a personality to be reckoned with* **5** (often pl) an offensive personal remark: *the argument never degenerated into personalities*

personalize *or* **-ise** *vb* **-izing, -ized** *or* **-ising, -ised** **1** to base (an argument or discussion) around people's characters rather than on abstract arguments **2** to mark (stationery or clothing) with a person's initials or name **3** same as **personify**

personally *adv* **1** without the help of others: *she had seen to it personally that permission was granted* **2** in one's own opinion: *personally, I think it's overrated* **3** as if referring to oneself: *yes, he was rather rude but it's not worth taking it personally* **4** as a person: *I don't like him personally, but he's fine to work with*

personal organizer *n* **1** a diary for storing personal records, appointments, etc. **2** a pocket-sized electronic device that performs the same functions

personal pronoun *n grammar* a pronoun such as *I, you, he, she, it, we,* and *they* that represents a definite person or thing

p

personal stereo *n chiefly Brit* a small portable audio cassette player used with lightweight headphones

personate *vb* **-ating, -ated** *criminal law* to assume the identity of (another person) with intent to deceive > **personation** *n*

personification *n* **1** the attribution of human characteristics to things, abstract ideas, etc. **2** the representation of an abstract quality or idea in the form of a person, creature, etc., as in art and literature. **3** a person or thing that personifies **4** a person or thing regarded as the embodiment of a quality: *he is the personification of optimism*

personify *vb* **-fies, -fying, -fied** **1** to give human characteristics to (a thing or abstraction) **2** to represent (an abstract quality) in human or animal form **3** (of a person or thing) to represent (an abstract quality), as in art **4** to be the embodiment of: *she can be charm personified*

personnel *n* **1** the people employed in an organization or for a service **2** the department in an organization that appoints or keeps records of employees **3** (in the armed forces) people, as opposed to machinery or equipment ▶ **HISTORY** French

perspective *n* **1** a way of regarding situations or facts and judging their relative importance: *the female perspective on love* **2** objectivity: *Kay's problems helped me put my minor worries into perspective* **3** a method of drawing that gives the effect of solidity and relative distances and sizes **4** the appearance of objects or buildings relative to each other, determined by their distance from the viewer ▶ **HISTORY** Latin *perspicere* to inspect carefully

Perspex *n trademark* a clear acrylic resin used as a substitute for glass

perspicacious *adj formal* acutely perceptive or discerning ▶ **HISTORY** Latin *perspicax* > **perspicacity** *n*

perspiration *n* **1** the salty fluid secreted by the sweat glands of the skin; sweat **2** the act of sweating

perspire *vb* **-spiring, -spired** to sweat ▶ **HISTORY** Latin *per-* through + *spirare* to breathe

persuade *vb* **-suading, -suaded** **1** to make (someone) do something by reason or charm: *we tried to persuade him not to come up the mountain with us* **2** to cause to believe; convince: *persuading people of the need for enforced environmental protection may be difficult* ▶ **HISTORY** Latin *persuadere* > **persuadable** *adj*

persuasion *n* **1** the act of persuading **2** the power to persuade **3** a set of beliefs; creed: *the Roman Catholic persuasion; literary intellectuals of the modernist persuasion*

persuasive *adj* able to persuade: *a persuasive argument* > **persuasively** *adv*

persuasive language *n* a type of language in which speakers and writers try to influence others often by appealing to their feelings, desires, and prejudices

pert *adj* saucy or impudent ▶ **HISTORY** Latin *apertus* open

pertain *vb* (often foll. by *to*) **1** to have reference or relevance: *the notes pertaining to the case* **2** to be appropriate: *the product pertains to real user needs* **3** to belong (to) or be a part (of) ▶ **HISTORY** Latin *pertinere*

pertinacious *adj* **1** doggedly resolute in purpose or belief **2** stubbornly persistent ▶ **HISTORY** Latin *per-* (intensive) + *tenax* clinging > **pertinacity** *n*

pertinent *adj* relating to the matter at hand; relevant ▶ **HISTORY** Latin *pertinens* > **pertinence** *n*

perturb *vb* **1** to disturb the composure of **2** to throw into disorder ▶ **HISTORY** Latin *perturbare* to confuse

perturbation *n literary* anxiety or worry

peruse *vb* **-rusing, -rused** **1** to read or examine with care **2** to browse or read in a leisurely way ▶ **HISTORY** *per-* (intensive) + *use* > **perusal** *n*

pervade *vb* **-vading, -vaded** to spread through or throughout (something) ▶ **HISTORY** Latin *per-* through + *vadere* to go > **pervasion** *n* > **pervasive** *adj*

perverse *adj* **1** deliberately acting in a way different from what is regarded as normal or proper **2** wayward or contrary; obstinate ▶ **HISTORY** Latin *perversus* turned the wrong way > **perversely** *adv* > **perversity** *n*

perversion *n* **1** any abnormal means of obtaining satisfaction **2** the act of perverting

pervert *vb* **1** to use wrongly or badly **2** to interpret wrongly or badly; distort **3** to lead (someone) into abnormal behaviour; corrupt **4** to debase ▷ *n* **5** a person who practises sexual perversion ▶ **HISTORY** Latin *pervertere* to turn the wrong way > **perverted** *adj*

pervious *adj* **1** able to be penetrated; permeable: *the thin walls were pervious to the slightest sound* **2** receptive to new ideas; open-minded ▶ **HISTORY** Latin *per-* through + *via* a way

Pesach *or* **Pesah** (pay-sahk) *n* same as **Passover**

peseta (pess-**say**-ta) *n* a former monetary unit of Spain ▶ **HISTORY** Spanish

peso (**pay**-so) *n, pl* **-sos** the standard monetary unit of Chile, Colombia, Cuba, the Dominican Republic, Mexico, the Philippines, and Uruguay ▶ **HISTORY** Spanish: weight

pessary *n, pl* **-ries** *med* **1** a device worn in the vagina, either as a support for the uterus or as a contraceptive **2** a vaginal suppository ▶ **HISTORY** Greek *pessos* plug

pessimism *n* **1** the tendency to expect the worst in all things **2** the doctrine of the ultimate triumph of evil over good ▶ **HISTORY** Latin *pessimus* worst > **pessimist** *n* > **pessimistic** *adj* > **pessimistically** *adv*

pest *n* **1** an annoying person or thing; nuisance **2** any organism that damages crops, or injures or irritates livestock or man ▶ **HISTORY** Latin *pestis* plague

pester *vb* to annoy or nag continually ▶ **HISTORY** Old French *empestrer* to hobble (a horse)

P

pesticide n a chemical used to destroy pests, esp. insects ▶ HISTORY *pest* + Latin *caedere* to kill

pestilence n *literary* any deadly epidemic disease, such as the plague

pestilent adj **1** annoying or irritating **2** highly destructive morally or physically **3** likely to cause infectious disease ▶ HISTORY Latin *pestis* plague > **pestilential** adj

pestle n a club-shaped instrument for grinding or pounding substances in a mortar ▶ HISTORY Old French *pestel*

pet¹ n **1** a tame animal kept for companionship or pleasure **2** a person who is favoured or indulged: *teacher's pet* ▷ adj **3** kept as a pet: *a pet hamster* **4** of or for pet animals: *pet food* **5** strongly felt or particularly cherished: *a pet hatred; he would not stand by and let his pet project be abandoned* ▷ vb **petting, petted 6** to treat as a pet; pamper **7** to pat or stroke affectionately **8** *informal* (of two people) to caress each other in an erotic manner ▶ HISTORY origin unknown

pet² n a fit of sulkiness ▶ HISTORY origin unknown

petal n any of the brightly coloured leaflike parts which form the head of a flower ▶ HISTORY Greek *petalon* leaf > **petalled** adj

petard n **1** (formerly) a device containing explosives used to break through a wall or door **2 hoist with one's own petard** being the victim of one's own schemes ▶ HISTORY French: firework

peter out vb to come gradually to an end: *the road petered out into a rutted track* ▶ HISTORY origin unknown

pethidine (peth-id-een) n a white crystalline water-soluble drug used to relieve pain ▶ HISTORY perhaps a blend of *piperidine* + *ethyl*

petiole n *bot* the stalk which attaches a leaf to a plant ▶ HISTORY Latin *petiolus* little foot

petit bourgeois (pet-ee boor-zhwah) n, pl **petits bourgeois** (pet-ee boor-zhwahz) the lower middle class ▶ HISTORY French

petite (pit-eat) adj (of a woman) small and dainty ▶ HISTORY French

petition n **1** a document signed by a large number of people requesting some form of action from a government or other authority **2** any formal request to a higher authority **3** *law* a formal application in writing made to a court asking for some specific judicial action: *she filed a petition for divorce* ▷ vb **4** to address or present a petition to (a government or to someone in authority): *he petitioned the Crown for mercy* **5** (foll. by *for*) to seek by petition: *the firm's creditors petitioned for liquidation* ▶ HISTORY Latin *petere* to seek > **petitioner** n

petit mal (pet-ee mal) n a mild form of epilepsy in which there are periods of loss of consciousness for up to 30 seconds ▶ HISTORY French: little illness

petrel n a sea bird with a hooked bill and tubular nostrils, such as the albatross, storm petrel, or shearwater ▶ HISTORY variant of earlier *pitteral*

Petri dish (pet-ree) n a shallow dish used in laboratories, esp. for producing cultures of bacteria ▶ HISTORY after J. R. *Petri*, bacteriologist

petrify vb **-fies, -fying, -fied 1** to stun or daze with fear: *he was petrified of going to jail* **2** (of organic material) to turn to stone **3** to make or become unable to change or develop: *a society petrified by outmoded conventions* ▶ HISTORY Greek *petra* stone > **petrification** n

petrochemical n a substance, such as acetone, obtained from petroleum > **petrochemistry** n

petrodollar n money earned by a country by exporting petroleum

petroglyph n a drawing or carving on rock, esp. a prehistoric one ▶ HISTORY Greek *petra* stone + *gluphē* carving

petrol n a volatile flammable liquid obtained from petroleum and used as a fuel for internal-combustion engines ▶ HISTORY see PETROLEUM

petrolatum (pet-rol-late-um) n a translucent jelly-like substance obtained from petroleum: used as a lubricant and in medicine as an ointment base

petrol bomb n a simple grenade consisting of a bottle filled with petrol. A piece of cloth is put in the neck of the bottle and set alight just before the bomb is thrown

petroleum n a dark-coloured thick flammable crude oil occurring in sedimentary rocks, consisting mainly of hydrocarbons: the source of petrol and paraffin ▶ HISTORY Latin *petra* stone + *oleum* oil

petroleum jelly n same as **petrolatum**

petrol station n *Brit* same as **filling station**

petticoat n a woman's underskirt ▶ HISTORY from *petty* + *coat*

pettifogging adj excessively concerned with unimportant detail ▶ HISTORY origin unknown > **pettifogger** n

petty adj **-tier, -tiest 1** trivial or unimportant: *petty details* **2** small-minded: *petty spite* **3** low in importance: *petty criminals* ▶ HISTORY French *petit* little > **pettily** adv > **pettiness** n

petty apartheid n (formerly, in South Africa) a form of apartheid as applied in trivial or everyday situations

petty cash n a small cash fund for minor incidental expenses

petty officer n a noncommissioned officer in the navy

petulant adj unreasonably irritable or peevish ▶ HISTORY Latin *petulans* bold > **petulance** n > **petulantly** adv

petunia n a tropical American plant with pink, white, or purple funnel-shaped flowers ▶ HISTORY obsolete French *petun* variety of tobacco

pew n **1** (in a church) **a** a long benchlike seat with a back, used by the congregation **b** an enclosed compartment reserved for the use of a family or group **2 take a pew** take a seat ▶ HISTORY Greek *pous* foot

pewter n **1** an alloy containing tin, lead, and sometimes copper and antimony **2** dishes or kitchen utensils made from pewter ▶ HISTORY Old French *peaultre*

p

PG indicating a film certified for viewing by anyone, but which contains scenes that may be unsuitable for children, for whom parental guidance is necessary

pH *n* potential of hydrogen; a measure of the acidity or alkalinity of a solution

phagocyte (**fag**-go-site) *n* a cell or protozoan that engulfs particles, such as microorganisms ▶ HISTORY Greek *phagein* to eat + *kutos* vessel

phalanger *n* an Australian marsupial with dense fur and a long tail ▶ HISTORY Greek *phalaggion* spider's web, referring to its webbed hind toes

phalanx (**fal**-lanks) *n, pl* **phalanxes** *or* **phalanges** (fal-**lan**-jeez) **1** any closely grouped mass of people: *a solid phalanx of reporters and photographers* **2** a number of people united for a common purpose **3** an ancient Greek battle formation of infantry in close ranks ▶ HISTORY Greek

phallic *adj* of or resembling a phallus: *a phallic symbol*

phallus (**fal**-luss) *n, pl* **-luses** *or* **-li** (-lie) **1** same as **penis 2** an image of the penis as a symbol of reproductive power ▶ HISTORY Greek *phallos*

phantasm *n* **1** a phantom **2** an unreal vision; illusion ▶ HISTORY Greek *phantasma* > **phantasmal** *adj*

phantasmagoria *n* a shifting medley of dreamlike figures ▶ HISTORY probably from French *fantasmagorie* production of phantoms > **phantasmagoric** *adj*

phantasy *n, pl* **-sies** *archaic* same as **fantasy**

phantom *n* **1** an apparition or spectre **2** the visible representation of something abstract, such as in a dream or hallucination: *the phantom of liberty* ▷ *adj* **3** deceptive or unreal: *she regularly took days off for what her bosses considered phantom illnesses* ▶ HISTORY Latin *phantasma*

Pharaoh (**fare**-oh) *n* the title of the ancient Egyptian kings ▶ HISTORY Egyptian *pr-'o* great house

Pharisee *n* **1** a member of an ancient Jewish sect teaching strict observance of Jewish traditions **2** (often not cap) a self-righteous or hypocritical person ▶ HISTORY Hebrew *pārūsh* separated > **Pharisaic** *adj*

pharmaceutical *adj* of or relating to drugs or pharmacy

pharmaceutics *n* same as **pharmacy** (sense 1)

pharmacist *n* a person qualified to prepare and dispense drugs

pharmacology *n* the science or study of drugs > **pharmacological** *adj* > **pharmacologist** *n*

pharmacopoeia (far-ma-koh-**pee**-a) *n* an authoritative book containing a list of medicinal drugs along with their uses, preparation, and dosages ▶ HISTORY Greek *pharmakopoiia* art of preparing drugs

pharmacy *n* **1** the preparation and dispensing of drugs **2** (*pl* **-cies**) a dispensary ▶ HISTORY Greek *pharmakon* drug

pharming *n* the practice of redirecting computer users from legitimate websites to fraudulent ones, in order to trick them into revealing confidential data ▶ HISTORY altered from FARMING

pharyngitis (far-rin-**jite**-iss) *n* inflammation of the pharynx, causing a sore throat

pharynx (**far**-rinks) *n, pl* **pharynges** (far-**rin**-jeez) *or* **pharynxes** the part of the alimentary canal between the mouth and the oesophagus ▶ HISTORY Greek *pharunx* throat > **pharyngeal** *adj*

phase *n* **1** any distinct or characteristic stage in a sequence of events: *these two recordings sum up two distinct phases in the singer's career* **2** *astron* one of the recurring shapes of the portion of the moon, Mercury, or Venus illuminated by the sun **3** *physics* a particular stage in a periodic process or phenomenon **4** *physics* **in** *or* **out of phase** (of two waves or signals) reaching or not reaching corresponding phases at the same time ▷ *vb* **phasing, phased 5** to do or introduce gradually: *the redundancies will be phased over two years* ▶ HISTORY Greek *phasis* aspect

phase in *vb* to introduce in a gradual or cautious manner: *the scheme was phased in over seven years*

PhD Doctor of Philosophy

pheasant *n* a long-tailed bird with a brightly coloured plumage in the male: native to Asia but introduced elsewhere ▶ HISTORY Latin *phasianus*

phenobarbitone *or* **phenobarbital** *n* a sedative used to treat insomnia and epilepsy

phenol *n* a white crystalline derivative of benzene, used as an antiseptic and disinfectant and in the manufacture of resins, explosives, and pharmaceutical substances ▶ HISTORY Greek *phaino-* shining; because originally prepared from illuminating gas

phenolphtalein (fee-noll-**fthal**-ee-in) *n chem* a colourless crystalline compound used in medicine as a laxative and in chemistry as an indicator

phenomenal *adj* **1** extraordinary or outstanding: *a phenomenal success* **2** of or relating to a phenomenon > **phenomenally** *adv*

phenomenalism *n* *philosophy* the doctrine that all knowledge comes from sense perception > **phenomenalist** *n, adj*

phenomenon *n, pl* **-ena** *or* **-enons 1** anything that can be perceived as an occurrence or fact **2** any remarkable occurrence or person ▶ HISTORY Greek *phainomenon*, from *phainesthai* to appear

phenotype *n* the physical form of an organism as determined by the interaction of its genetic make-up and its environment

phenyl (**fee**-nile) *adj* of, containing, or consisting of the monovalent group C_6H_5, derived from benzene: *a phenyl group*

phew *interj* an exclamation of relief, surprise, disbelief, or weariness

phial *n* a small bottle for liquid medicine ▶ HISTORY Greek *phialē* wide shallow vessel

phil. 1 philharmonic **2** philosophy

philadelphus *n* a shrub grown for its strongly scented showy flowers ▶ HISTORY Greek *philadelphon*, literally: loving one's brother

P

philanthropy *n, pl* **-pies 1** the practice of helping people less well-off than oneself **2** love of mankind in general ▶ HISTORY Greek *philanthrōpia* love of mankind > **philanthropic** *adj* > **philanthropist** *n*

philately (fill-**lat**-a-lee) *n* the collection and study of postage stamps ▶ HISTORY Greek *philos* loving + *ateleia* exemption from tax > **philatelist** *n*

philharmonic *adj* **1** fond of music ▷ *n* **2** a specific choir, orchestra, or musical society: *the Vienna Philharmonic* ▶ HISTORY French *philharmonique*

philippic *n* a bitter verbal attack ▶ HISTORY after the orations of Demosthenes against Philip of Macedon

Philippine *adj, n* same as **Filipino**

philistine *n* **1** a person who is hostile towards culture and the arts ▷ *adj* **2** boorishly uncultured > **philistinism** *n*

Philistine *n* a member of the non-Semitic people who inhabited ancient Palestine

philology *n* the science of the structure and development of languages ▶ HISTORY Greek *philologia* love of language > **philological** *adj* > **philologist** *n*

philosopher *n* **1** a person who studies philosophy **2** a person who remains calm and stoical in the face of difficulties or disappointments

philosopher's stone *n* a substance thought by alchemists to be capable of changing base metals into gold

philosophical *or* **philosophic** *adj* **1** of or relating to philosophy or philosophers **2** calm and stoical in the face of difficulties or disappointments > **philosophically** *adv*

philosophize *or* **-phise** *vb* **-phizing, -phized** *or* **-phising, -phised** to discuss in a philosophical manner > **philosophizer** *or* **-phiser** *n*

philosophy *n, pl* **-phies 1** the academic study of knowledge, thought, and the meaning of life **2** the particular doctrines of a specific individual or school relating to these issues: *the philosophy of John Locke* **3** any system of beliefs or values **4** a personal outlook or viewpoint ▶ HISTORY Greek *philosophia* love of wisdom

philtre *or US* **philter** *n* a drink supposed to arouse desire ▶ HISTORY Greek *philtron* love potion

phishing *n* the practice of tricking computer users into revealing personal details, esp. of financial data ▶ HISTORY altered from FISHING

phlebitis (fleb-**bite**-iss) *n* inflammation of a vein, usually in the legs ▶ HISTORY Greek *phleps* vein > **phlebitic** *adj*

phlegm (flem) *n* **1** the thick yellowish substance secreted by the walls of the respiratory tract **2** apathy or stolidity **3** calmness ▶ HISTORY Greek *phlegma* > **phlegmy** *adj*

phlegmatic (fleg-**mat**-ik) *adj* having an unemotional disposition

phloem (**flow**-em) *n bot* the plant tissue that acts as a path for the distribution of food substances to all parts of the plant ▶ HISTORY Greek *phloos* bark

phlox *n, pl* **phlox** *or* **phloxes** a plant with clusters of white, red, or purple flowers ▶ HISTORY Greek, literally: flame

phobia *n psychiatry* an intense and irrational fear of a given situation or thing ▶ HISTORY Greek *phobos* fear > **phobic** *adj, n*

Phoenician (fon-**nee**-shun) *adj* **1** of Phoenicia, an ancient E Mediterranean country ▷ *n* **2** a person from Phoenicia

phoenix *n* a legendary Arabian bird said to set fire to itself and rise anew from the ashes every 500 years ▶ HISTORY Greek *phoinix*

phone *n, vb* **phoning, phoned** short for **telephone**

phonecard *n* a card used instead of coins to operate certain public telephones

phone-in *n Brit, Austral & S African* a radio or television programme in which telephone questions or comments from the public are broadcast live as part of a discussion

phoneme *n linguistics* one of the set of speech sounds in any given language that serve to distinguish one word from another ▶ HISTORY Greek *phōnēma* sound, speech > **phonemic** *adj*

phonemics *n* the classification and analysis of the phonemes of a language

phonetic *adj* **1** of phonetics **2** denoting any perceptible distinction between one speech sound and another **3** conforming to pronunciation: *phonetic spelling* ▶ HISTORY Greek *phōnein* to make sounds, speak > **phonetically** *adv*

phonetics *n* the study of speech processes, including the production, perception, and analysis of speech sounds

phoney *or esp US* **phony** *informal adj* **-nier, -niest 1** not genuine: *a phoney Belgian 50-franc coin* **2** (of a person) insincere or pretentious ▷ *n, pl* **-neys** *or esp US* **-nies 3** an insincere or pretentious person **4** something that is not genuine ▶ HISTORY origin unknown

phonics *n* (functioning as sing) a method of teaching people to read by training them to associate letters with their phonetic values > **phonic** *adj* > **phonically** *adv*

phonograph *n* **1** an early form of record player capable of recording and reproducing sound on wax cylinders **2** *US & Canad* a record player ▶ HISTORY Greek *phonē* sound + *graphein* to write

phonology *n, pl* **-gies 1** the study of the sound system in a language **2** such a sound system ▶ HISTORY Greek *phonē* sound, voice + -LOGY > **phonological** *adj*

phosgene (**foz**-jean) *n* a poisonous gas used in warfare ▶ HISTORY Greek *phōs* light + *-genēs* born

phosphate *n* **1** any salt or ester of any phosphoric acid **2** (often pl) chemical fertilizer containing phosphorous compounds > **phosphatic** *adj*

phosphor *n* a substance capable of emitting light when irradiated with particles of electromagnetic radiation ▶ HISTORY Greek *phōsphoros* phosphorus'

phosphoresce *vb* **-rescing, -resced** to exhibit phosphorescence

phosphorescence *n* **1** *physics* a fluorescence that persists after the bombarding radiation producing it has stopped **2** the light emitted in phosphorescence > **phosphorescent** *adj*

phosphoric *adj* of or containing phosphorus in the pentavalent state

phosphorous *adj* of or containing phosphorus in the trivalent state

phosphorus *n* *chem* a toxic flammable nonmetallic element which appears luminous in the dark. It exists in two forms, white and red. Symbol: P ▶ HISTORY Greek *phōsphoros* light-bringing

photo *n*, *pl* **-tos** short for **photograph**

photo- *combining form* **1** of or produced by light: *photosynthesis* **2** indicating a photographic process: *photolithography* ▶ HISTORY Greek *phōs*, *phōt-* light

photocell *n* a cell which produces a current or voltage when exposed to light or other electromagnetic radiation

photochemical smog *n* *environmental science* a kind of smog caused by chemical reactions involving light, ozone, and pollutants that occurs in big cities

photocopier *n* a machine using light-sensitive photographic materials to reproduce written, printed, or graphic work

photocopy *n*, *pl* **-copies** **1** a photographic reproduction of written, printed, or graphic work ▷ *vb* **-copies, -copying, -copied** **2** to reproduce on photographic material

photoelectric *adj* of or concerned with electric or electronic effects caused by light or other electromagnetic radiation > **photoelectricity** *n*

photo finish *n* a finish of a race in which contestants are so close that a photograph is needed to decide the result

Photofit *n* *trademark* a picture of someone wanted by the police which has been made by combining photographs of different facial features resembling those of the wanted person

photoflash *n* same as **flashbulb**

photoflood *n* a highly incandescent electric lamp used for indoor photography and television

photogenic *adj* **1** (esp. of a person) always looking attractive in photographs **2** *biol* producing or emitting light

photograph *n* **1** a picture made by the chemical action of light on sensitive film ▷ *vb* **2** to take a photograph of

photographic *adj* **1** of or like photography or a photograph **2** (of a person's memory) able to retain facts or appearances in precise detail > **photographically** *adv*

photographic image *n* **1** a photograph **2** the way something or someone is presented in a photograph

photography *n* **1** the process of recording images on sensitized material by the action of light **2** the practice of taking photographs > **photographer** *n*

photogravure *n* a process in which an etched metal plate for printing is produced by photography ▶ HISTORY PHOTO- + French *gravure* engraving

photojournalism *n* journalism in which photographs are the predominant feature > **photojournalist** *n*

photolithography *n* a lithographic printing process using photographically made plates > **photolithographer** *n*

photometer (foe-**tom**-it-er) *n* an instrument used to measure the intensity of light

photometry (foe-**tom**-it-tree) *n* the branch of physics concerned with the measurement of the intensity of light > **photometrist** *n*

photomontage (foe-toe-mon-**tahzh**) *n* **1** the combination of several photographs to produce one picture **2** a picture produced in this way

photon *n* *physics* a quantum of electromagnetic radiation energy, such as light, having both particle and wave behaviour

photoreceptor *n* *zool*, *physiol* a light-sensitive cell or organ that conveys impulses through a sensory neuron

photosensitive *adj* sensitive to electromagnetic radiation, esp. light

photostat *n* **1** a type of photocopying machine or process **2** any copy made by such a machine ▷ *vb* **-statting, -statted** *or* **-stating, -stated** **3** to make a photostat copy (of)

photosynthesis *n* *biol*, *geog* (in plants) the process by which a green plant uses sunlight to build up carbohydrate reserves > **photosynthesize** *or* **-sise** *vb* > **photosynthetic** *adj*

phototropism (foe-toe-**trope**-iz-zum) *n* the growth of plants towards a source of light ▶ HISTORY PHOTO- + Greek *tropos* turn > **phototropic** *adj*

phrasal verb *n* a phrase that consists of a verb plus an adverb or preposition, esp. one whose meaning cannot be deduced from its parts, such as *take in* meaning *deceive*

phrase *n* **1** a group of words forming a unit of meaning in a sentence **2** an idiomatic or original expression **3** *music* a small group of notes forming a coherent unit of melody ▷ *vb* **phrasing, phrased** **4** to express orally or in a phrase: *I could have phrased that better* **5** *music* to divide (a melodic line or part) into musical phrases, esp. in performance ▶ HISTORY Greek *phrasis* speech > **phrasal** *adj*

phrase book *n* a book containing frequently used expressions and their equivalent in a foreign language

phraseology *n*, *pl* **-gies** the manner in which words or phrases are used

phrasing *n* **1** the exact words used to say or write something **2** the way in which someone who is performing a piece of music or reading aloud divides up the work being performed by pausing slightly in appropriate places

phrenology *n* (formerly) the study of the shape and size of the skull as a means of finding out a person's character and mental ability ▶ HISTORY Greek *phrēn* mind + -LOGY > **phrenological** *adj* > **phrenologist** *n*

pH-scale *n* *chem* a method of measuring the acidity or alkalinity of a solution

p

phut *informal n* **1** a representation of a muffled explosive sound ▷ *adv* **2 go phut** to break down or collapse ▶ HISTORY imitative

phylactery *n, pl* **-teries** *Judaism* either of the pair of square cases containing biblical passages, worn by Jewish men on the left arm and head during weekday morning prayers ▶ HISTORY Greek *phulaktērion* safeguard

phylum *n, pl* **-la** *biol* one of the major groups into which the animal and plant kingdoms are divided, containing one or more classes ▶ HISTORY Greek *phulon* race

physical *adj* **1** of the body, as distinguished from the mind or spirit **2** of material things or nature: *the physical world* **3** of or concerned with matter and energy **4** of or relating to physics
> **physically** *adv*

physical education *n* training and practice in sports and gymnastics

physical geography *n* the branch of geography that deals with the natural features of the earth's surface

physical jerks *pl n* *Brit & Austral, informal* repetitive keep-fit exercises

physical science *n* any of the sciences concerned with nonliving matter, such as physics, chemistry, astronomy, and geology

physical theatre *n* any form of theatre in which the bodily movements of actors are the main means of conveying a story

physical weathering *n* *geol* damage such as erosion, caused to rocks as a result of being exposed to wind, water, or ice

physician *n* **1** a medical doctor **2** *archaic* a healer ▶ HISTORY Greek *phusis* nature

physicist *n* a person versed in or studying physics

physics *n* **1** the branch of science concerned with the properties of matter and energy and the relationships between them **2** physical properties of behaviour: *the physics of the electron* ▶ HISTORY translation of Greek *ta phusika* natural things

physio *n* **1** short for **physiotherapy 2** (*pl* **physios**) short for **physiotherapist**

physiognomy (fiz-ee-**on**-om-ee) *n* **1** a person's face considered as an indication of personality **2** the outward appearance of something: *the changed physiognomy of the forests* ▶ HISTORY Greek *phusis* nature + *gnōmōn* judge

physiography *n* same as **physical geography**
> **physiographic** *adj* ▶ HISTORY Greek *phusis* nature + -GRAPHY

physiology *n* **1** the branch of science concerned with the functioning of organisms **2** the processes and functions of all or part of an organism ▶ HISTORY Greek *phusis* nature + -LOGY
> **physiologist** *n* > **physiological** *adj*

physiotherapy *n* the treatment of disease or injury by physical means, such as massage or exercises, rather than by drugs > **physiotherapist** *n* ▶ HISTORY physio- (prefix) physical + *therapy*

physique *n* person's bodily build and muscular development ▶ HISTORY French

pi *n, pl* **pis 1** the 16th letter in the Greek alphabet (Π, π) **2** *maths* a number that is the ratio of the circumference of a circle to its diameter; approximate value: 3.141 592. Symbol: π

pianica *n* a wind instrument with a small keyboard and a mouthpiece

pianissimo *adj, adv* *music* to be performed very quietly ▶ HISTORY Italian

pianist *n* a person who plays the piano

piano¹ *n, pl* **-anos** a musical instrument played by depressing keys that cause hammers to strike strings and produce audible vibrations ▶ HISTORY short for *pianoforte*

piano² *adj, adv* *music* to be performed softly ▶ HISTORY Italian

Pianola (pee-an-**oh**-la) *n* *trademark* a type of mechanical piano, the music for which is encoded in perforations in a paper roll

piazza *n* **1** a large open square in an Italian town **2** *chiefly Brit* a covered passageway or gallery ▶ HISTORY Italian: marketplace

pibroch (**pee**-brok) *n* a form of music for Scottish bagpipes, consisting of a theme and variations ▶ HISTORY Gaelic *piobaireachd*

pic *n, pl* **pics** or **pix** *informal* a photograph or illustration

pica (**pie**-ka) *n* **1** a size of printer's type giving 6 lines to the inch **2** a size of typewriter type that has 10 characters to the inch ▶ HISTORY Latin *pica* magpie; sense connection obscure

picador *n* *bullfighting* a horseman who wounds the bull with a lance to weaken it ▶ HISTORY Spanish

picaresque *adj* of or relating to a type of fiction in which the hero, a rogue, goes through a series of episodic adventures ▶ HISTORY Spanish *pícaro* a rogue

piccalilli *n* a pickle of mixed vegetables in a mustard sauce ▶ HISTORY origin unknown

piccanin *n* *S African, offensive* a Black African child ▶ HISTORY variant of *piccaninny*

piccolo *n, pl* **-los** a woodwind instrument an octave higher than the flute ▶ HISTORY Italian: small

pick¹ *vb* **1** to choose or select **2** to gather (fruit, berries, or crops) from (a tree, bush, or field) **3** to remove loose particles from: *she picked some bits of fluff off her sleeve* **4** (foll. by *at*) to nibble (at) without appetite **5** to provoke (an argument or fight) deliberately **6** to separate (strands or fibres), as in weaving **7** to steal from (someone's pocket) **8** to open (a lock) with an instrument other than a key **9** to make (one's way) carefully on foot: *they picked their way through the rubble* **10 pick and choose** to select fastidiously or fussily ▷ *n* **11** choice: *take your pick* **12** the best: *the pick of the country's young cricketers* ▷ See also **pick off, pick on**, etc. ▶ HISTORY Middle English *piken*

pick² *n* **1** a tool with a handle and a long curved steel head, used for loosening soil or breaking rocks **2** any tool used for picking, such as an ice pick or toothpick **3** a plectrum ▷ *vb* **4** to pierce or break up (a hard surface) with a pick ▶ HISTORY perhaps a variant of PIKE²

pickaxe *or US* **pickax** *n* a large pick

picket *n* **1** a person or group standing outside a workplace to dissuade strikebreakers from entering **2** a small unit of troops posted to give early warning of attack **3** a pointed stake that is driven into the ground to support a fence ▷ *vb* **-eting, -eted 4** to act as pickets outside (a workplace) ▶ HISTORY Old French *piquer* to prick

picket line *n* a line of people acting as pickets

pickings *pl n* money or profits acquired easily

pickle *n* **1** (often *pl*) food, esp. vegetables preserved in vinegar or brine **2** a liquid or marinade, such as spiced vinegar, for preserving vegetables, meat, or fish **3** *informal* an awkward or difficult situation: *to be in a pickle; they are in a pickle over what to do with toxic waste* ▷ *vb* **-ling, -led 4** to preserve or treat in a pickling liquid ▶ HISTORY probably Middle Dutch *pekel*

pickled *adj* **1** (of food) preserved in a pickling liquid **2** *informal* drunk

pick-me-up *n informal* a tonic, esp. a special drink taken as a stimulant

pick off *vb* to aim at and shoot (people or things) one by one

pick on *vb* to continually treat someone unfairly

pick out *vb* **1** to select for use or special consideration: *she picked out a wide gold wedding ring* **2** to distinguish (an object from its surroundings), such as in painting: *the wall panels are light brown, with their edges picked out in gold* **3** to recognize (a person or thing): *the culprit was picked out at a police identification parade* **4** to play (a tune) tentatively, as by ear

pickpocket *n* a person who steals from the pockets of others in public places

pick up *vb* **1** to lift or raise: *he picked up his glass* **2** to obtain or purchase: *a couple of pictures she had picked up in a flea market in Paris* **3** to improve in health or condition: *the tourist trade has picked up after the slump caused by the Gulf War* **4** to learn as one goes along: *she had a good ear and picked up languages quickly* **5** to raise (oneself) after a fall or setback: *she picked herself up and got on with her life* **6** to resume; return to **7** to accept the responsibility for paying (a bill) **8** to collect or give a lift to (passengers or goods) **9** *informal* to become acquainted with for a sexual purpose **10** *informal* to arrest **11** to receive (sounds or signals)

pick-up *n* **1** a small truck with an open body used for light deliveries **2** *informal* **a** a stop to collect passengers or goods **b** the people or things collected **3** a device which converts vibrations into electrical signals, such as that to which a record player stylus is attached

picky *adj* **pickier, pickiest** *Brit, Austral & NZ, informal* fussy; finicky

picnic *n* **1** an excursion on which people bring food to be eaten in the open air **2** an informal meal eaten out-of-doors **3 no picnic** *informal* a hard or disagreeable task ▷ *vb* **-nicking, -nicked 4** to eat or take part in a picnic ▶ HISTORY French *piquenique* > **picnicker** *n*

pico- *combining form* denoting 10⁻¹²: *picofarad* ▶ HISTORY Spanish *pico* small quantity

picot (**peek**-oh) *n* any of a pattern of small loops, for example on lace

Pict *n* a member of any of the peoples who lived in N Britain in the first to the fourth centuries AD ▶ HISTORY Late Latin *Picti* painted men > **Pictish** *adj*

pictograph *n* **1** a picture or symbol standing for a word or group of words, as in written Chinese **2** Also called: **pictogram** a chart on which symbols are used to represent values **3** ▶ HISTORY Latin *pingere* to paint > **pictographic** *adj*

pictorial *adj* **1** relating to or expressed by pictures ▷ *n* **2** a periodical containing many pictures ▶ HISTORY Latin *pingere* to paint

picture *n* **1** a visual representation produced on a surface, such as in a photograph or painting **2** a mental image: *neither had any clear picture of whom they were looking for* **3** a description or account of a situation considered as an observable scene: *the reports do not provide an accurate picture of the spread of AIDS* **4** a person or thing resembling another: *he is the picture of a perfect host* **5** a person or scene typifying a particular state: *his face was a picture of dejection* **6** the image on a television screen **7** a cinema film **8 the pictures** a cinema or film show **9 in the picture** informed about a situation ▷ *vb* **-turing, -tured 10** to visualize or imagine **11** to describe or depict vividly: *a documentary that had pictured the police as good-natured dolts* **12** to put in a picture or make a picture of: *the women pictured above are all the same age* ▶ HISTORY Latin *pingere* to paint

picture rail *n* the rail near the top of a wall from which pictures are hung

picturesque *adj* **1** visually pleasing, as in being striking or quaint: *a small picturesque harbour* **2** (of language) graphic or vivid ▶ HISTORY French *pittoresque*

picture window *n* a large window with a single pane of glass, usually facing a view

piddle *vb* **-dling, -dled** *informal* **1** to urinate **2 piddle about** *or* **around** *or* **away** to spend (one's) time) aimlessly: *we have been piddling around for seven months* ▶ HISTORY origin unknown

piddling *adj informal* petty or trivial: *piddling amounts of money*

pidgin *n* a language made up of elements of two or more languages and used between the speakers of the languages involved ▶ HISTORY supposed Chinese pronunciation of *business*

pidgin English *n* a pidgin in which one of the languages involved is English

pie *n* **1** a sweet or savoury filling baked in pastry **2 pie in the sky** illusory hope or promise of some future good ▶ HISTORY origin unknown

piebald *adj* **1** marked in two colours, esp. black and white ▷ *n* **2** a black-and-white horse ▶ HISTORY dialect *pie* magpie + BALD

piece *n* **1** a separate bit or part **2** an instance or occurrence: *a piece of luck* **3** an example or

p

specimen of a style or type: *each piece of furniture is crafted from native red pine by traditional methods* **4** a literary, musical, or artistic composition **5** a coin: *a fifty-pence piece* **6** a firearm or cannon **7** a small object used in playing various games: *a chess piece* **8 go to pieces** (of a person) to lose control of oneself; have a breakdown ▷ *vb* **piecing, pieced 9** (often foll. by *together*) to fit or assemble bit by bit **10** (often foll. by *up*) to patch or make up (a garment) by adding pieces ▶ HISTORY Middle English *pece*

pièce de résistance (**pyess** de ray-**zeest**-onss) *n* the most outstanding item in a series ▶ HISTORY French

piecemeal *adv* **1** bit by bit; gradually ▷ *adj* **2** fragmentary or unsystematic: *a piecemeal approach* ▶ HISTORY Middle English *pece* piece + *-mele* a measure

piece rate *n business* a fixed rate paid according to the quantity produced

piecework *n* work paid for according to the quantity produced

pie chart *n* a circular graph divided into sectors proportional to the sizes of the quantities represented

pied *adj* having markings of two or more colours ▶ HISTORY dialect *pie* magpie

pied-à-terre (**pyay**-da-**tair**) *n, pl* **pieds-à-terre** (**pyay**-da-**tair**) a flat or other lodging for occasional use ▶ HISTORY French, literally: foot on (the) ground

pie-eyed *adj slang* drunk

pier *n* **1** a structure with a deck that is built out over water and used as a landing place or promenade **2** a pillar or support that bears heavy loads **3** the part of a wall between two adjacent openings ▶ HISTORY Middle English *per*

pierce *vb* **piercing, pierced 1** to make a hole in (something) with a sharp point **2** to force (a way) through (something) **3** (of light) to shine through (darkness) **4** (of sounds or cries) to sound sharply through (the silence) **5** to penetrate: *the cold pierced the air* ▶ HISTORY Old French *percer* > **piercing** *adj*

Pierrot (**pier**-roe) *n* a male character from French pantomime with a whitened face, white costume, and pointed hat

pietism *n* exaggerated piety

piety *n, pl* **-ties 1** dutiful devotion to God and observance of religious principles **2** the quality of being pious **3** a pious action or saying ▶ HISTORY Latin *pietas*

piezoelectric effect (pie-eez-oh-ill-**ek**-trik) *or* **piezoelectricity** *n physics* **a** the production of electricity by applying a mechanical stress to certain crystals **b** the converse effect in which stress is produced in a crystal as a result of an applied voltage ▶ HISTORY Greek *piezein* to press

piffle *n informal* nonsense ▶ HISTORY origin unknown

pig *n* **1** a mammal with a long head, a snout, and bristle-covered skin, which is kept and killed for pork, ham, and bacon. *Related adjective:* **porcine 2** *informal* a dirty, greedy, or bad-mannered person **3** *offensive slang* a policeman **4** a mass of metal cast into a simple shape **5** *Brit, informal* something that is difficult or unpleasant: *the coast is a pig for little boats* **6 a pig in a poke** something bought or received without previous sight or knowledge **7 make a pig of oneself** *informal* to overeat ▷ *vb* **pigging, pigged 8** (of a sow) to give birth **9** (often foll. by *out*) *slang* to eat greedily or to excess: *she had pigged out on pizza before the show* ▶ HISTORY Middle English *pigge*

pigeon¹ *n* **1** a bird which has a heavy body, small head, and short legs, and is usually grey in colour **2** *slang* a victim or dupe ▶ HISTORY Old French *pijon* young dove

pigeon² *n informal* concern or responsibility: *this is our pigeon – there's nothing to keep you* ▶ HISTORY from *pidgin*

pigeonhole *n* **1** a small compartment, such as in a bureau, for filing papers ▷ *vb* **-holing, -holed 2** to classify or categorize **3** to put aside

pigeon-toed *adj* with the toes or feet turned inwards

piggery *n, pl* **-geries** a place where pigs are kept

piggish *adj* **1** like a pig in appetite or manners **2** stubborn > **piggishness** *n*

piggy *n, pl* **-gies 1** a child's word for a **pig** ▷ *adj* **-gier, -giest 2** same as **piggish**

piggyback *or* **pickaback** *n* **1** a ride on the back and shoulders of another person ▷ *adv, adj* **2** on the back and shoulders of another person

piggy bank *n* a child's bank shaped like a pig with a slot for coins

pig-headed *adj* stupidly stubborn

pig iron *n* crude iron produced in a blast furnace and poured into moulds

piglet *n* a young pig

pigment *n* **1** any substance which gives colour to paint or dye **2** a substance which occurs in plant or animal tissue and produces a characteristic colour ▶ HISTORY Latin *pigmentum* > **pigmentary** *adj*

pigmentation *n* colouring in plants, animals, or humans, caused by the presence of pigments

Pigmy *n, pl* **-mies** same as **Pygmy**

pigsty *or US & Canad* **pigpen** *n, pl* **-sties 1** a pen for pigs **2** *Brit & Austral* an untidy place

pigswill *n* waste food or other edible matter fed to pigs

pigtail *n* a plait of hair or one of two plaits on either side of the face

pike¹ *n, pl* **pike** *or* **pikes** a large predatory freshwater fish with a broad flat snout, strong teeth, and a long body covered with small scales ▶ HISTORY Old English *pīc* point, from the shape of its jaw

pike² *n* a medieval weapon consisting of a metal spearhead on a long pole ▶ HISTORY Old English *pīc* point > **pikeman** *n*

pikelet *n Austral & NZ* a small thick pancake

piker *n Austral & NZ, slang* shirker

p

pilaster *n* a shallow rectangular column attached to the face of a wall ▶ HISTORY Latin *pila* pillar > **pilastered** *adj*

pilau *or* **pilaf** *n* a Middle Eastern dish, consisting of rice flavoured with spices and cooked in stock, to which meat, poultry, or fish may be added ▶ HISTORY Turkish *pilāw*

pilchard *n* a small edible sea fish of the herring family, with a rounded body covered with large scales ▶ HISTORY origin unknown

pile[1] *n* **1** a collection of objects laid on top of one another **2** *informal* a large amount: *boxing has made him a pile of money; I've got piles of work to do* **3** same as **pyre** **4** a large building or group of buildings **5** *physics* a nuclear reactor ▷ *vb* **piling, piled** **6** (often foll. by *up*) to collect or be collected into a pile: *snow piled up in the drive* **7** (foll. by *in, into, off, out* etc.) to move in a group, often in a hurried manner: *the crew piled into the van* **8** **pile it on** *informal* to exaggerate ▶ HISTORY Latin *pila* stone pier

pile[2] *n* a long heavy beam driven into the ground as a foundation for a structure ▶ HISTORY Latin *pilum*

pile[3] *n* the fibres in a fabric that stand up or out from the weave, such as in carpeting or velvet ▶ HISTORY Latin *pilus* hair

pile-driver *n* a machine that drives piles into the ground

piles *pl n* swollen veins in the rectum; haemorrhoids ▶ HISTORY Latin *pilae* balls

pilfer *vb* to steal (minor items) in small quantities ▶ HISTORY Old French *pelfre* booty

pilgrim *n* **1** a person who journeys to a holy place **2** any wayfarer ▶ HISTORY Latin *peregrinus* foreign

pilgrimage *n* **1** a journey to a shrine or other holy place **2** a journey or long search made for sentimental reasons: *a sentimental pilgrimage to the poet's birthplace*

Pilgrim Fathers *pl n* the English Puritans who founded Plymouth Colony in SE Massachusetts (1620)

pill *n* **1** a small mass of medicine intended to be swallowed whole **2** **the pill** *informal* an oral contraceptive taken by a woman **3** something unpleasant that must be endured: *her reinstatement was a bitter pill to swallow; the pill was sweetened by a reduction in interest* ▶ HISTORY Latin *pilula* a little ball

pillage *vb* **-laging, -laged** **1** to steal property violently, often in war ▷ *n* **2** the act of pillaging **3** something obtained by pillaging; booty ▶ HISTORY Old French *piller* to despoil

pillar *n* **1** an upright support of stone, brick, or metal; column **2** something resembling this: *a pillar of smoke* **3** a prominent supporter or member: *a pillar of society* **4** **from pillar to post** from one place to another ▶ HISTORY Latin *pila*

pillar box *n* (in Britain) a red pillar-shaped public letter box situated in the street

pillbox *n* **1** a box for pills **2** a small enclosed fort of reinforced concrete **3** a small round hat

pillion *n* **1** a seat for a passenger behind the rider of a motorcycle or horse ▷ *adv* **2** on a pillion: *the motorbike on which he was riding pillion* ▶ HISTORY from Gaelic

pillory *n, pl* **-ries** **1** *history* a wooden frame in which offenders were locked by the neck and wrists and exposed to public abuse and ridicule ▷ *vb* **-ries, -rying, -ried** **2** to expose to public ridicule **3** to punish by putting in a pillory ▶ HISTORY Old French *pilori*

pillow *n* **1** a cloth bag stuffed with feathers, polyester fibre, or pieces of foam rubber used to support the head in bed ▷ *vb* **2** to rest (one's head) on or as if on a pillow: *he pillowed his head in her lap* ▶ HISTORY Old English *pylwe*

pillowcase *or* **pillowslip** *n* a removable washable cover for a pillow

pilot *n* **1** a person who is qualified to fly an aircraft or spacecraft **2** a person employed to steer a ship into or out of a port **3** a person who acts as a guide ▷ *adj* **4** serving as a test or trial: *a pilot scheme* **5** serving as a guide: *a pilot beacon* ▷ *vb* **-loting, -loted** **6** to act as pilot of **7** to guide or lead (a project or people): *the legislation was piloted through its committee stage* ▶ HISTORY French *pilote*

pilot light *n* a small flame that lights the main burner of a gas appliance

pilot officer *n* the most junior commissioned rank in certain air forces

pimento *n, pl* **-tos** same as **allspice** or **pimiento** ▶ HISTORY Spanish *pimiento* pepper plant

pimiento (pim-**yen**-toe) *n, pl* **-tos** a Spanish pepper with a red fruit used as a vegetable ▶ HISTORY variant of PIMENTO

pimp *n* **1** a man who obtains customers for a prostitute, in return for a share of his or her earnings ▷ *vb* **2** to act as a pimp ▶ HISTORY origin unknown

pimpernel *n* a plant, such as the scarlet pimpernel, typically having small star-shaped flowers ▶ HISTORY Old French *pimpernelle*

pimple *n* a small swollen infected spot on the skin ▶ HISTORY Middle English > **pimpled** *adj* > **pimply** *adj*

pin *n* **1** a short stiff straight piece of wire with a pointed end and a rounded head: used mainly for fastening **2** short for **cotter pin, hairpin, rolling pin, safety pin** **3** a wooden or metal peg **4** a pin-shaped brooch **5** (in various bowling games) a club-shaped wooden object set up in groups as a target **6** a clip that prevents a hand grenade from exploding until it is removed or released **7** *golf* the flagpole marking the hole on a green **8** *informal* a leg ▷ *vb* **pinning, pinned** **9** to fasten with a pin or pins **10** to seize and hold fast: *they pinned his arms behind his back* **11** **pin something on someone** *informal* to place the blame for something on someone: *corruption charges are the easiest to pin on former dictators* ▷ See also **pin down** ▶ HISTORY Old English *pinn*

PIN Personal Identity Number: a code number used in conjunction with a bank card to enable an account holder to use certain computerized systems, such as cash dispensers

pinafore *n* **1** *chiefly Brit* an apron with a bib **2** a dress with a sleeveless bodice or bib top, worn over a jumper or blouse ▶ **HISTORY** *pin* + *afore* in front

pinball *n* an electrically operated table game in which the player shoots a small ball through several hazards

pince-nez (panss-**nay**) *n, pl* **pince-nez** glasses that are held in place only by means of a clip over the bridge of the nose ▶ **HISTORY** French, literally: pinch-nose

pincers *pl n* **1** a gripping tool consisting of two hinged arms and curved jaws **2** the jointed grasping arms of crabs and lobsters ▶ **HISTORY** Old French *pincier* to pinch

pinch *vb* **1** to squeeze (something, esp. flesh) between a finger and thumb **2** to squeeze by being too tight: *shoes that pinch* **3** to cause stinging pain to: *the cold pinched his face* **4** to make thin or drawn-looking, such as from grief or cold **5** *informal* to steal **6** *informal* to arrest **7** (usually foll. by *out* or *back*) to remove the tips of (a plant shoot) to correct or encourage growth ▷ *n* **8** a squeeze or sustained nip **9** the quantity that can be taken up between a thumb and finger: *a pinch of ground ginger* **10** extreme stress or need: *most companies are feeling the pinch of recession* **11 at a pinch** if absolutely necessary **12 feel the pinch** to be forced to economize ▶ **HISTORY** probably from Old French

pinchbeck *n* **1** an alloy of copper and zinc, used as imitation gold ▷ *adj* **2** sham or cheap ▶ **HISTORY** after C. Pinchbeck, watchmaker who invented the alloy

pincushion *n* a small cushion in which pins are stuck ready for use

pin down *vb* **1** to force (someone) to make a decision or carry out a promise **2** to define clearly: *the courts have found it difficult to pin down what exactly obscenity is*

pine¹ *n* **1** an evergreen tree with long needle-shaped leaves and brown cones **2** the light-coloured wood of this tree **3** (in the Caribbean) short for **pineapple** ▶ **HISTORY** Latin *pinus*

pine² *vb* **pining, pined 1** (often foll. by *for*) to feel great longing (for) **2** (often foll. by *away*) to become ill or thin through grief or longing ▶ **HISTORY** Old English *pīnian* to torture

pineal gland or **body** (pin-ee-al) *n* a small cone-shaped gland at the base of the brain ▶ **HISTORY** Latin *pinea* pine cone

pineapple *n* a large tropical fruit with juicy flesh and a thick hard skin ▶ **HISTORY** Middle English *pinappel* pine cone

pine cone *n* the woody seed case of a pine tree

pine marten *n* a mammal of N European and Asian coniferous woods, with dark brown fur and a creamy-yellow patch on the throat

ping *n* **1** a short high-pitched sound, such as of a bullet striking metal ▷ *vb* **2** to make such a noise ▶ **HISTORY** imitative

pinger *n* a device that makes a pinging sound, esp. a timer

pingo *n geog* (in Arctic regions) a cone-shaped ice mound covered with soil and vegetation, formed by the freezing and expansion of water under the ground ▶ **HISTORY** Inuktitut

Ping-Pong *n trademark* same as **table tennis**

pinion¹ *n* **1** *chiefly poetic* a bird's wing **2** the outer part of a bird's wing including the flight feathers ▷ *vb* **3** to immobilize (someone) by holding or tying his or her arms **4** to confine ▶ **HISTORY** Latin *pinna* wing

pinion² *n* a cogwheel that engages with a larger wheel or rack ▶ **HISTORY** French *pignon*

pink¹ *n* **1** a colour between red and white **2** anything pink, such as pink paint or pink clothing: *packaged in pink* **3** a garden plant with pink, red, or white fragrant flowers **4 in the pink** in good health ▷ *adj* **5** of a colour between red and white **6** *Brit, Austral & S African, informal* having mild left-wing sympathies **7** *informal* relating to homosexuals or homosexuality: *the pink vote* ▷ *vb* **8** same as **knock** (sense 7) ▶ **HISTORY** origin unknown > **pinkish** or **pinky** *adj*

pink² *vb* to cut with pinking shears ▶ **HISTORY** perhaps from Low German

pinkie or **pinky** *n, pl* **-ies** *Scot, US, Canad & NZ* the little finger ▶ **HISTORY** Dutch *pinkje*

pinking shears *pl n* scissors with a serrated edge that give a wavy edge to material cut and so prevent fraying

pin money *n* a small amount of extra money earned to buy small luxuries

pinna *n anat* the external part of the ear

pinnace *n* a ship's boat ▶ **HISTORY** French *pinace*

pinnacle *n* **1** the highest point of fame or success **2** a towering peak of a mountain **3** a slender spire ▶ **HISTORY** Latin *pinna* wing

pinnate *adj bot* (of compound leaves) having leaflets growing opposite each other in pairs ▶ **HISTORY** Latin *pinna* feather

pinotage (**pin**-oh-tazh) *n* a red wine blended from the Pinot Noir and Hermitage grapes that is unique to South Africa

pinpoint *vb* **1** to locate or identify exactly: *we've pinpointed the fault* ▷ *adj* **2** exact: *pinpoint accuracy*

pinprick *n* a small irritation or annoyance

pins and needles *pl n informal* a tingling sensation in a part of the body

pinstripe *n* (in textiles) a very narrow stripe in fabric or the fabric itself

pint *n* **1** *Brit* a unit of liquid measure equal to one eighth of an Imperial gallon (0.568 litre) **2** *US* a unit of liquid measure equal to one eighth of a US gallon (0.473 litre) **3** *Brit, informal* a pint of beer ▶ **HISTORY** Old French *pinte*

pinta *n Brit, informal* a pint of milk ▶ **HISTORY** phonetic rendering of *pint of*

pintail *n, pl* **-tails** or **-tail** a greyish-brown duck with a pointed tail

pintle *n* a pin or bolt forming the pivot of a hinge ▶ **HISTORY** Old English *pintel* penis

pinto US & Canad adj **1** marked with patches of white; piebald ▷ n, pl **-tos 2** a pinto horse ▶ HISTORY American Spanish

pin tuck n a narrow, ornamental fold used on shirt fronts and dress bodices

pin-up n **1** informal a picture of an attractive person **2** slang a person who has appeared in such a picture: your favourite pin-up **3** a photograph of a famous personality

pinwheel n same as **Catherine wheel**

Pinyin n a system of spelling used to represent Chinese in Roman letters

pion or **pi meson** n physics any of three subatomic particles which are classified as mesons

pioneer n **1** an explorer or settler of a new land or region **2** an originator or developer of something new ▷ vb **3** to be a pioneer (in or of) **4** to initiate or develop: the new technique was pioneered in France ▶ HISTORY Old French paonier infantryman

pious adj **1** religious or devout **2** insincerely reverent; sanctimonious ▶ HISTORY Latin pius > **piousness** n

pip[1] n the seed of a fleshy fruit, such as an apple or pear ▶ HISTORY short for pippin

pip[2] n **1** a short high-pitched sound used as a time signal on radio **2** any of the spots on a playing card, dice, or domino **3** informal the emblem worn on the shoulder by junior officers in the British Army, indicating their rank ▶ HISTORY imitative

pip[3] n **1** a contagious disease of poultry **2** facetious slang a minor human ailment **3 give someone the pip** Brit, NZ & S African, slang to annoy someone: it really gives me the pip **4 get** or **have the pip** NZ, slang to sulk ▶ HISTORY Middle Dutch pippe

pip[4] vb **pipping, pipped • pip someone at the post** Brit & NZ, slang to defeat someone whose success seems certain ▶ HISTORY probably from PIP[2]

pipe n **1** a long tube for conveying water, oil, or gas **2 a** a tube with a small bowl at the end for smoking tobacco **b** the amount of tobacco that fills the bowl of a pipe **3 put that in your pipe and smoke it** informal accept that fact if you can **4** zool, bot any of various hollow organs, such as the respiratory passage of certain animals **5 a** a tubular instrument in which air vibrates and produces a musical sound **b** any of the tubular devices on an organ **6 the pipes** See **bagpipes 7** a boatswain's whistle ▷ vb **piping, piped 8** to play (music) on a pipe **9** to summon or lead by a pipe: to pipe in the haggis **10 a** to signal orders to (the crew) by a boatswain's pipe **b** to signal the arrival or departure of: he piped his entire ship's company on deck **11** written to utter in a shrill tone **12** to convey (water, oil, or gas) by pipe **13** to force cream or icing through a shaped nozzle to decorate food ▷ See also **pipe down, pipe up** ▶ HISTORY Old English pīpe

pipeclay n a fine white pure clay, used in tobacco pipes and pottery and to whiten leather and similar materials

pipe cleaner n a short length of wire covered with tiny tufts of yarn: used to clean the stem of a tobacco pipe

piped music n light music played as background music in public places

pipe down vb informal to stop talking or making noise

pipe dream n a fanciful or impossible plan or hope ▶ HISTORY alluding to dreams produced by smoking an opium pipe

pipeline n **1** a long pipe for transporting oil, water, or gas **2** a means of communication **3 in the pipeline** in preparation

piper n a person who plays a pipe or bagpipes

pipette n a slender glass tube for transferring or measuring out liquids ▶ HISTORY French: little pipe

pipe up vb to speak up unexpectedly

pipi n, pl **pipi** or **pipis 1** Austral an Australian mollusc of sandy beaches widely used as bait **2** NZ an edible shellfish of New Zealand ▶ HISTORY Māori

piping n **1** a system of pipes **2** a string of icing or cream used to decorate cakes and desserts **3** a thin strip of covered cord or material, used to edge hems or cushions **4** the sound of a pipe or bagpipes **5** written a shrill voice or whistling sound: a dove's cool piping ▷ adj **6** making a shrill sound ▷ adv **7 piping hot** extremely hot

pipistrelle n a type of small brownish bat found throughout the world ▶ HISTORY Italian pipistrello

pipit n a small songbird with a brownish speckled plumage and a long tail ▶ HISTORY probably imitative

pippin n a type of eating apple ▶ HISTORY Old French pepin

piquant (pee-kant) adj written **1** having a spicy taste **2** stimulating to the mind: love was a forbidden piquant secret ▶ HISTORY French, literally: prickling > **piquancy** n

pique (peek) n **1** a feeling of resentment or irritation, such as from hurt pride ▷ vb **piquing, piqued 2** to hurt (someone's) pride **3** to excite (curiosity or interest) ▶ HISTORY French piquer to prick

piqué (pee-kay) n a stiff ribbed fabric of cotton, silk, or spun rayon ▶ HISTORY French: pricked

piquet (pik-ket) n a card game for two people played with a reduced pack ▶ HISTORY French

piracy n, pl **-cies 1** Brit & NZ robbery on the seas **2** a crime, such as hijacking, committed aboard a ship or aircraft **3** the unauthorized use of patented or copyrighted material

piranha n a small fierce freshwater fish of tropical America, with strong jaws and sharp teeth ▶ HISTORY S American Indian: fish with teeth

pirate n **1** a person who commits piracy **2** a vessel used by pirates **3** a person who illegally sells or publishes someone else's literary or artistic work **4** a person or group of people who broadcast illegally ▷ vb **-rating, -rated 5** to sell or reproduce (artistic work, ideas, etc.) illegally ▶ HISTORY Greek peira an attack > **piratical** adj

pirouette n **1** a body spin performed on the toes or the ball of the foot ▷ vb **-etting, -etted 2** to perform a pirouette ▸ HISTORY French

piscatorial adj formal of or relating to fish, fishing, or fishermen ▸ HISTORY Latin piscatorius

Pisces n astrol the twelfth sign of the zodiac; the Fishes ▸ HISTORY Latin

pisciculture (piss-ee-cult-cher) n formal the rearing and breeding of fish under controlled conditions ▸ HISTORY Latin piscis fish

piscine (piss-sign) adj of or resembling a fish ▸ HISTORY Latin piscis fish

pistachio n, pl **-chios** a Mediterranean nut with a hard shell and an edible green kernel ▸ HISTORY Persian pistah

piste (peest) n a slope or course for skiing ▸ HISTORY French

pistil n the seed-bearing part of a flower ▸ HISTORY Latin pistillum pestle

pistillate adj bot (of plants) having pistils

pistol n a short-barrelled handgun ▸ HISTORY Czech pišt'ala

piston n a cylindrical part that slides to and fro in a hollow cylinder: in an engine it is attached by a rod to other parts, thus its movement causes the other parts to move ▸ HISTORY Old Italian pistone

pit¹ n **1** a large deep opening in the ground **2** a coal mine **3** anat **a** a small natural depression on the surface of a body or organ **b** the floor of any natural bodily cavity: the pit of the stomach **4** pathol a pockmark **5** a concealed danger or difficulty **6** an area at the side of a motor-racing track for servicing or refuelling vehicles **7** the pit hell **8** the area occupied by the orchestra in a theatre **9** an enclosure for fighting animals or birds **10** the back of the ground floor of a theatre **11** same as **pitfall** (sense 2) ▷ vb **pitting, pitted 12** (often foll. by against) to match in opposition, esp. as antagonists: sister pitted against sister **13** to mark with small dents or scars **14** to place or bury in a pit **15 pit one's wits against** to compete against in a test or contest ▷ See also **pits** ▸ HISTORY Old English pytt

pit² chiefly US & Canad n **1** the stone of various fruits ▷ vb **pitting, pitted 2** to remove the stone from (a fruit) ▸ HISTORY Dutch: kernel

pitapat adv **1** with quick light taps ▷ n **2** such taps ▸ HISTORY imitative

pit bull terrier n a strong muscular terrier with a short coat

pitch¹ vb **1** to hurl or throw **2** to set up (a tent or camp) **3** to slope or fall forwards or downwards: she pitched forwards like a diver **4** (of a ship or plane) to dip and raise its back and front alternately **5** to set the level or tone of: his ambitions were pitched too high **6** to aim to sell (a product) to a specified market or on a specified basis **7** music to sing or play (a note or interval) accurately ▷ n **8** chiefly Brit (in many sports) the field of play **9** a level of emotion: children can wind their parents up to a pitch of anger and guilt **10** the degree or angle of slope **11** the distance between corresponding points or adjacent threads on a screw thread **12** the pitching motion of a ship or plane **13** music the highness or lowness of a note in relation to other notes: low pitch **14** the act or manner of pitching a ball **15** chiefly Brit the place where a street or market trader regularly sells **16** slang a persuasive sales talk, esp. one routinely repeated ▷ See also **pitch in, pitch into** ▸ HISTORY Middle English picchen

pitch² n **1** a thick sticky substance formed from coal tar and used for paving or waterproofing **2** any similar substance, such as asphalt, occurring as a natural deposit ▷ vb **3** to apply pitch to ▸ HISTORY Old English pic

pitch-black adj extremely dark; unlit: it was a wild night, pitch-black, with howling gales

pitchblende n a blackish mineral which is the principal source of uranium and radium ▸ HISTORY German Pechblende

pitch-dark adj extremely or completely dark

pitched battle n a fierce fight

pitcher¹ n a large jug, usually rounded with a narrow neck ▸ HISTORY Old French pichier

pitcher² n baseball the player on the fielding team who throws the ball to the batter

pitcher plant n a plant with pitcher-like leaves that attract and trap insects, which are then digested

pitchfork n **1** a long-handled fork with two or three long curved prongs for tossing hay ▷ vb **2** to use a pitchfork on (something)

pitch in vb to cooperate or contribute

pitch into vb informal to attack (someone) physically or verbally

pitch pine n a pine tree of North America: a source of turpentine and pitch

piteous adj written arousing or deserving pity: the piteous mewing of an injured kitten > **piteousness** n

pitfall n **1** an unsuspected difficulty or danger **2** a trap in the form of a concealed pit, designed to catch men or wild animals ▸ HISTORY Old English pytt pit + fealle trap

pith n **1** the soft white lining inside the rind of fruits such as the orange **2** the essential part: policy, though, isn't the pith of what happened yesterday **3** the soft spongy tissue in the centre of the stem of certain plants ▸ HISTORY Old English pitha

pithead n the top of a mine shaft and the buildings and hoisting gear around it

pith helmet n a lightweight hat made from the pith of the sola, an E Indian swamp plant, that is worn for protection from the sun

pithy adj **pithier, pithiest 1** written terse and full of meaning **2** of, resembling, or full of pith > **pithiness** n

pitiable adj written arousing or deserving pity or contempt > **pitiableness** n

pitiful adj arousing or deserving great pity or contempt > **pitifully** adv > **pitifulness** n

pitiless adj feeling no pity or mercy > **pitilessly** adv

piton (peet-on) n mountaineering a metal spike that may be driven into a crack and used to secure a rope ▸ HISTORY French

pits *pl n* **the pits** *slang, spoken* the worst possible person, place, or thing ▶ HISTORY perhaps from *armpits*

pitta bread *or* **pitta** *n* a flat rounded slightly leavened bread, originally from the Middle East ▶ HISTORY Modern Greek *pitta* a cake

pittance *n* a very small amount of money ▶ HISTORY Old French *pietance* ration

pitter-patter *n* **1** the sound of light rapid taps or pats, such as of rain drops ▷ *vb* **2** to make such a sound

pituitary *or* **pituitary gland** *n* the gland at the base of the brain which secretes hormones that affect skeletal growth, development of the sex glands, and other functions of the body ▶ HISTORY Late Latin *pituitarius* slimy

pity *n, pl* **pities 1** sorrow felt for the sufferings of others **2 have** *or* **take pity on** to have sympathy or show mercy for **3** a cause of regret: *it's a great pity he did not live longer* ▷ *vb* **pities, pitying, pitied 4** to feel pity for ▶ HISTORY Latin *pietas* duty > **pitying** *adj*

pivot *n* **1** a central shaft around which something turns **2** the central person or thing necessary for progress or success ▷ *vb* **-oting, -oted 3** to turn on or provide with a pivot ▶ HISTORY Old French

pivotal *adj* **1** of crucial importance **2** of or acting as a pivot

pix *n informal* a plural of **pic**

pixel *n photog* the smallest constituent element of an image, as on a visual display unit ▶ HISTORY from PIX + EL(EMENT)

pixie *or* **pixy** *n, pl* **pixies** (in folklore) a fairy or elf

pizza *n* a dish of Italian origin consisting of a baked disc of dough covered with a wide variety of savoury toppings ▶ HISTORY Italian

pizzazz *or* **pizazz** *n informal* an attractive combination of energy and style ▶ HISTORY origin obscure

pizzicato (pit-see-**kah**-toe) *adj, adv music* (in music for the violin family) to be plucked with the finger ▶ HISTORY Italian: pinched

Pl. (in street names) Place

plaas *n S African* a farm ▶ HISTORY Afrikaans

placard *n* **1** a notice that is paraded in public ▷ *vb* **2** to attach placards to ▶ HISTORY Old French *plaquart*

placate *vb* **-cating, -cated** to calm (someone) to stop him or her feeling angry or upset ▶ HISTORY Latin *placare* > **placatory** *adj*

place *n* **1** a particular part of a space or of a surface **2** a geographical point, such as a town or city **3** a position or rank in a sequence or order **4** an open square lined with houses in a city or town **5** space or room **6** a house or living quarters: *he's buying his own place* **7** any building or area set aside for a specific purpose **8** the point reached in reading or speaking: *her finger was pressed to the page as if marking her place* **9** right or duty: *it's not my place to do their job for them* **10** appointment, position, or job: *she won a place at university* **11** position, condition, or state: *you know what your place in the world is* **12** a space or seat, as at a dining table **13** *maths* the relative position of a digit in a number **14 all over the place** in disorder or disarray **15 go places** *informal* to become successful **16 in** *or* **out of place** in or out of the proper or customary position **17 in place of a** instead of: *leeks can be used in place of the broccoli* **b** in exchange for: *he gave her it in place of her ring* **18 know one's place** to be aware of one's inferior position **19 put someone in his** *or* **her place** to humble someone who is arrogant, conceited, etc. **20 take place** to happen or occur **21 take the place of** to be a substitute for ▷ *vb* **placing, placed 22** to put in a particular or appropriate place **23** to find or indicate the place of: *I bet you the media couldn't have placed Neath on the map before the by-election* **24** to identify or classify by linking with an appropriate context: *I felt I should know him, but could not quite place him* **25** to make (an order or bet) **26** to find a home or job for (someone) **27** (often foll. by *with*) to put under the care (of) **28** (of a racehorse, greyhound, athlete, etc.) to arrive in first, second, third, or sometimes fourth place ▶ HISTORY Latin *platea* courtyard

placebo (plas-**see**-bo) *n, pl* **-bos** *or* **-boes** *med* an inactive substance given to a patient usually to compare its effects with those of a real drug but sometimes for the psychological benefit gained by the patient through believing that he or she is receiving treatment ▶ HISTORY Latin: I shall please

place kick *n rugby, American football, etc.* a kick in which the ball is placed in position before it is kicked

placement *n* **1** arrangement or position **2** a temporary job which someone is given as part of a training course: *many pupils have been on work placements with local businesses* **3** the act or an instance of finding someone a job or a home: *the main task of the adoption agency is to find the best family placement for each child*

placenta (plass-**ent**-a) *n, pl* **-tas** *or* **-tae** the organ formed in the womb of most mammals during pregnancy, providing oxygen and nutrients for the fetus ▶ HISTORY Latin, from Greek *plakoeis* flat cake > **placental** *adj*

place of worship *n* a building where people go to practise their religion

place setting *n* the cutlery, crockery, and glassware laid for one person at a dining table

placid *adj* having a calm appearance or nature: *placid waters; a placid temperament* ▶ HISTORY Latin *placidus* peaceful > **placidity** *or* **placidness** *n* > **placidly** *adv*

placket *n dressmaking* an opening at the waist of a dress or skirt for buttons or zips or for access to a pocket ▶ HISTORY perhaps from Medieval Dutch *plackaet* breastplate

plagiarize *or* **-rise** (**play**-jer-ize) *vb* **-rizing, -rized** *or* **-rising, -rised** to steal ideas or passages from (another's work) and present them as one's own ▶ HISTORY Latin *plagium* kidnapping > **plagiarism** *n* > **plagiarizer** *or* **-riser** *n*

plague n **1** any widespread and usually highly contagious disease with a high fatality rate **2** an infectious disease of rodents transmitted to man by the bite of the rat flea; bubonic plague **3** something that afflicts or harasses: *a plague of locusts* **4** *informal* a nuisance ▷ vb **plaguing, plagued 5** to afflict or harass: *a playing career plagued by injury* **6** *informal* to annoy or pester ▶ HISTORY Latin *plaga* a blow

plaice n, pl **plaice** or **plaices** an edible European flatfish with a brown body marked with red or orange spots ▶ HISTORY Greek *platus* flat

plaid n **1** a long piece of tartan cloth worn over the shoulder as part of Highland costume **2** a crisscross weave or cloth ▶ HISTORY Scottish Gaelic *plaide*

Plaid Cymru (plide **kumm**-ree) n the Welsh nationalist party ▶ HISTORY Welsh

plain adj **1** flat or smooth **2** easily understood: *he made it plain what he wanted from me* **3** honest or blunt: *the plain fact is that my mother has no time for me* **4** without adornment: *a plain brown envelope* **5** not good-looking **6** (of fabric) without pattern or of simple weave **7** lowly, esp. in social rank or education: *the plain people of Ireland* **8** knitting of or done in plain stitch ▷ n **9** a level stretch of country **10** a simple stitch in knitting made by passing the wool round the front of the needle ▷ adv **11** clearly or simply: *that's just plain stupid!* ▶ HISTORY Latin *planus* level, clear > **plainly** adv > **plainness** n

plain clothes pl n ordinary clothes, as opposed to uniform, worn by a detective on duty

plain sailing n **1** *informal* smooth or easy progress **2** *naut* sailing in a body of water that is unobstructed; clear sailing

plainsong n the style of unaccompanied choral music used in the medieval Church, esp. in Gregorian chant ▶ HISTORY translation of Medieval Latin *cantus planus*

plain speaking n saying exactly what one thinks > **plain-spoken** adj

plaint n **1** *archaic* a complaint or lamentation **2** *law* a statement in writing of grounds of complaint made to a court of law ▶ HISTORY Old French *plainte*

plaintiff n a person who sues in a court of law ▶ HISTORY Old French *plaintif* complaining

plaintive adj sad and mournful ▶ HISTORY Old French *plaintif* grieving > **plaintively** adv

plait (platt) n **1** a length of hair that has been plaited ▷ vb **2** to intertwine (strands or strips) in a pattern ▶ HISTORY Latin *plicare* to fold

plan n **1** a method thought out for doing or achieving something **2** a detailed drawing to scale of a horizontal section through a building **3** an outline or sketch ▷ vb **planning, planned 4** to form a plan (for) **5** to make a plan of (a building) **6** to intend ▶ HISTORY Latin *planus* flat

plane¹ n **1** an aeroplane **2** *maths* a flat surface in which a straight line joining any two of its points lies entirely on that surface **3** a level surface: *an inclined plane* **4** a level of existence or attainment: *her ambition was set on a higher plane than pulling pints in a pub* ▷ adj **5** level or flat **6** *maths* lying entirely in one plane ▷ vb **planing, planed 7** to glide or skim: *they planed over the ice* ▶ HISTORY Latin *planum* level surface

plane² n **1** a tool with a steel blade for smoothing timber ▷ vb **planing, planed 2** to smooth (timber) using a plane **3** (often foll. by *away* or *off*) to remove using a plane ▶ HISTORY Latin *planare* to level

planet n any of the eight celestial bodies, Mercury, Venus, Earth, Mars, Jupiter, Saturn, Uranus, or Neptune, that revolve around the sun in oval-shaped orbits ▶ HISTORY Greek *planaein* to wander > **planetary** adj

planetarium n, pl **-iums** or **-ia 1** an instrument for projecting images of the sun, moon, stars, and planets onto a domed ceiling **2** a building in which such an instrument is housed

planetoid (plan-it-oid) n See **asteroid**

plane tree or **plane** n a tree with rounded heads of fruit and leaves with pointed lobes ▶ HISTORY Greek *platus* wide (because of its broad leaves)

plangent (**plan**-jent) adj (of sounds) mournful and resounding

plank n **1** a long flat piece of sawn timber **2** one of the policies in a political party's programme **3 walk the plank** to be forced by sailors to walk to one's death off the end of a plank jutting out from the side of a ship ▶ HISTORY Late Latin *planca* board

plankton n the small drifting plants and animals on the surface layer of a sea or lake ▶ HISTORY Greek *planktos* wandering

planned market n *econ* an economic system in which the government controls the factors of production

planner n **1** a person who makes plans, esp. for the development of a town, building, etc. **2** a chart for recording future appointments, etc.

planning permission n formal permission granted by a local authority for the construction, alteration, or change of use of a building

plant n **1** a living organism that grows in the ground and lacks the power of movement **2** the land, building, and equipment used in an industry or business **3** a factory or workshop **4** mobile mechanical equipment for construction or road-making **5** *informal* a thing positioned secretly for discovery by someone else, often in order to incriminate an innocent person ▷ vb **6** to set (seeds or crops) into the ground to grow: *it's the wrong time of year for planting roses* **7** to place firmly in position: *I planted my chair beside hers* **8** to introduce into someone's mind: *once Wendy had planted the idea in the minds of the owners, they quite fancied selling* **9** *slang* to deliver (a blow or kiss) **10** *informal* to position or hide (someone) in order to deceive or observe **11** *informal* to hide or secrete (something), usually for some illegal purpose or in order to incriminate someone ▶ HISTORY Old English

plantae (**plahn**-tee) pl n *bot* the plant kingdom

plantain¹ *n* a plant with a rosette of broad leaves and a slender spike of small greenish flowers ▶ HISTORY Latin *planta* sole of the foot

plantain² *n* **1** a large tropical fruit like a green-skinned banana **2** the tree on which this fruit grows ▶ HISTORY Spanish *platano*

plantation *n* **1** an estate, esp. in tropical countries, where cash crops such as rubber or coffee are grown on a large scale **2** a group of cultivated trees or plants **3** (formerly) a colony of settlers

planter *n* **1** the owner or manager of a plantation **2** a decorative pot for house plants

plantigrade *adj* walking on the entire sole of the foot, as humans and bears do ▶ HISTORY Latin *planta* sole of the foot + *gradus* a step

plant succession *n geog* the natural process by which one plant community succeeds another

plaque *n* **1** a commemorative inscribed stone or metal plate **2** Also called: **dental plaque** a filmy deposit on teeth, consisting of mucus, bacteria, and food, that causes decay ▶ HISTORY French

plasma *n* **1** the clear yellowish fluid portion of blood which contains the corpuscles and cells **2** a sterilized preparation of such fluid, taken from the blood, for use in transfusions **3** a former name for **protoplasm 4** *physics* a hot ionized gas containing positive ions and free electrons ▶ HISTORY Greek: something moulded

plasmalemma *n biol* a very thin membrane that surrounds the cytoplasm of a cell

plasma screen *n* a type of flat screen on a television or a visual display unit in which the image is created by an electric current passing through many gas-filled cells

plasmolysis *n biol* the shrinkage of protoplasm away from the cell walls that occurs as a result of excessive water loss

plaster *n* **1** a mixture of lime, sand, and water that is applied to a wall or ceiling as a soft paste and dries as a hard coating **2** *Brit, Austral & NZ* an adhesive strip of material for dressing a cut or wound **3** short for **mustard plaster, plaster of Paris** ▷ *vb* **4** to coat (a wall or ceiling) with plaster **5** to apply like plaster: *he plastered his face with shaving cream* **6** to cause to lie flat or to adhere: *his hair was plastered to his forehead* ▶ HISTORY Greek *emplastron* healing dressing > **plasterer** *n*

plasterboard *n* a thin rigid board, made of plaster compressed between two layers of fibreboard, used to form or cover interior walls

plaster cast *n med* a casing around a limb, often made of plaster of Paris, for preventing broken bones from moving while they heal

plastered *adj slang* drunk

plaster of Paris *n* a white powder that sets to a hard solid when mixed with water, used for making sculptures and casts for setting broken limbs

plastic *n* **1** any of a large number of synthetic materials that can be moulded when soft and then set **2** *informal* Also called: **plastic money** credit cards, etc. as opposed to cash ▷ *adj* **3** made of plastic **4** easily influenced **5** capable of being moulded or formed **6** of moulding or modelling: *the plastic arts* **7** *slang* superficially attractive yet artificial or false: *glamorous models with plastic smiles* ▶ HISTORY Greek *plastikos* mouldable > **plasticity** *n*

plastic bullet *n* a solid PVC cylinder fired by the police in riot control

plastic explosive *n* an adhesive jelly-like explosive substance

Plasticine *n trademark* a soft coloured material used, esp. by children, for modelling

plasticizer *or* **-ciser** *n* a substance added to a plastic material to soften it and improve flexibility

plastic surgery *n* the branch of surgery concerned with the repair or reconstruction of missing, injured, or malformed tissues or parts > **plastic surgeon** *n*

plate *n* **1** a shallow dish made of porcelain, earthenware, glass, etc. on which food is served **2** Also called: **plateful** the contents of a plate **3** a shallow dish for receiving a collection in church **4** flat metal of even thickness obtained by rolling **5** a thin coating of metal usually on another metal **6** dishes or cutlery made of gold or silver **7** a sheet of metal, plastic, or rubber having a printing surface produced by a process such as stereotyping **8** a print taken from such a sheet or from a woodcut **9** a thin flat sheet of a substance, such as glass **10** a small piece of metal or plastic with an inscription, fixed to another surface: *a brass name plate* **11** *photog* a sheet of glass coated with photographic emulsion on which an image can be formed by exposure to light **12** *informal* same as **denture 13** *anat* any flat platelike structure **14** a cup awarded to the winner of a sporting contest, esp. a horse race **15** any of the rigid layers of the earth's crust **16 have a lot on one's plate** to have many pressing things to deal with **17 on a plate** acquired without trouble: *he got the job handed to him on a plate* ▷ *vb* **plating, plated 18** to coat (a metal surface) with a thin layer of another metal **19** to cover with metal plates, usually for protection **20** to form (metal) into plate, usually by rolling ▶ HISTORY Old French: something flat

plateau *n* (plat-oh) *n, pl* **-eaus** *or* **-eaux** (-ohs) **1** a wide level area of high land **2** a relatively long period of stability: *the body temperature rises to a plateau that it keeps until shortly before bedtime* ▷ *vb* **3** to remain stable for a long period ▶ HISTORY French

plated *adj* coated with a layer of metal

plate glass *n* glass produced in thin sheets, used for windows and mirrors

platelet *n* a minute particle occurring in the blood of vertebrates and involved in the clotting of the blood

platen *n* **1** the roller on a typewriter, against which the keys strike **2** a flat plate in a printing press that presses the paper against the type ▶ HISTORY Old French *platine*

P

plate tectonics n geol (functioning as sing) the study of the earth's crust with reference to the theory that the lithosphere is divided into rigid blocks (plates) that float on semimolten rock and are thus able to interact with each other at their boundaries

platform n **1** a raised floor **2** a raised area at a railway station where passengers get on or off the trains **3** the declared aims of a political party **4** the thick raised sole of some shoes **5** a type of computer hardware or operating system ▷ **HISTORY** French plat flat + forme layout

platform game n a type of computer game that is played by moving a figure on the screen through a series of obstacles

plating n **1** a coating of metal **2** a layer or covering of metal plates

platinum n a silvery-white metallic element, very resistant to heat and chemicals: used in jewellery, laboratory apparatus, electrical contacts, dentistry, electroplating, and as a catalyst. Symbol: Pt ▷ **HISTORY** Spanish platina silvery element

platinum blonde n a girl or woman with silvery-blonde hair

platitude n a trite or unoriginal remark: it's a platitude, but people need people ▷ **HISTORY** French: flatness > **platitudinous** adj

platonic adj friendly or affectionate but without physical desire: platonic love

- ■ **WORD HISTORY**
- ■ 'Platonic' comes from the name of the Greek
- ■ philosopher Plato (428–347 BC). The concept of
- ■ 'platonic love' between people of opposite sexes
- ■ is based on a passage in one of his writings.

Platonic adj of the philosopher Plato or his teachings

Platonism (**plate**-on-iz-zum) n the teachings of Plato (?427–?347 BC), Greek philosopher, and his followers > **Platonist** n

platoon n mil a subunit of a company, usually comprising three sections of ten to twelve men ▷ **HISTORY** French peloton little ball, group of men

platteland n **the platteland** (in South Africa) the country districts or rural areas ▷ **HISTORY** Afrikaans

platter n a large shallow, usually oval, dish ▷ **HISTORY** Anglo-Norman plater

platypus or **duck-billed platypus** n, pl **-puses** an Australian egg-laying amphibious mammal, with dense fur, webbed feet, and a ducklike bill ▷ **HISTORY** Greek platus flat + pous foot

plausible adj **1** apparently reasonable or true: a plausible excuse **2** apparently trustworthy or believable: he is an extraordinarily plausible liar ▷ **HISTORY** Latin plausibilis worthy of applause > **plausibility** n > **plausibly** adv

play vb **1** to occupy oneself in (a sport or recreation) **2** to compete against (someone) in a sport or game: I saw Brazil play Argentina recently **3** to fulfil (a particular role) in a team game: he usually plays in midfield **4** (often foll. by about or around) to behave carelessly: he's only playing with your affections, you know **5** to act the part (of) in a dramatic piece: he has played Hamlet to packed Broadway houses **6** to perform (a dramatic piece) **7 a** to perform (music) on an instrument **b** to be able to perform on (a musical instrument): she plays the bassoon **8** to send out (water) or cause to send out water: they played a hose across the wrecked building **9** to cause (a radio, etc.) to emit sound **10** to move freely or quickly: the light played across the water **11** Stock Exchange to speculate for gain in (a market) **12** angling to tire (a hooked fish) by alternately letting out and reeling in the line **13** to put (a card) into play **14** to gamble **15 play fair** or **false with** to act fairly or unfairly with **16 play for time** to gain time to one's advantage by the use of delaying tactics **17 play into the hands of** to act unwittingly to the advantage of (an opponent) ▷ n **18 a** a dramatic piece written for performance by actors **b** the performance of such a piece **19** games or other activity undertaken for pleasure **20** the playing of a game or the time during which a game is in progress: rain stopped play **21** conduct: fair play **22** gambling **23** activity or operation: radio allows full play to your imagination **24** scope for freedom of movement: there was a lot of play in the rope **25** free or rapidly shifting motion: the play of light on the water **26** fun or jest: I used to throw cushions at her in play **27 in** or **out of play** (of a ball in a game) in or not in a position for continuing play according to the rules **28 make a play for** informal to make an obvious attempt to gain (something) ▷ See also **playback** ▷ **HISTORY** Old English plega, plegan > **playable** adj

playa (**plah**-ya) n geog (in the US) a temporary lake, or its dry often salty bed, in a desert basin ▷ **HISTORY** Spanish: shore, from Late Latin plagia, from Greek plagios slanting, from plagos side

playback n **1** the playing of a recording ▷ vb **play back 2** to listen to or watch (something recorded)

playbill n a poster or bill advertising a play

playboy n a rich man who devotes himself to such pleasures as nightclubs and female company

playcentre n NZ a centre for preschool children run by parents

play down vb to minimize the importance of: she played down the problems of the company

player n **1** a person who takes part in a game or sport **2** a person who plays a musical instrument **3** informal a leading participant in a particular field or activity: one of the key players in Chinese politics **4** an actor

playful adj **1** good-natured and humorous: a playful remark **2** full of high spirits and fun: a playful child > **playfully** adv

playgoer n a person who goes often to the theatre

playground n **1** an outdoor area for children's play, either with swings and slides, or adjoining a school **2** a place or activity enjoyed by a specified person or group: they oppose turning the island into a tourist playground

playgroup *n* a regular meeting of infants for supervised creative play

playhouse *n* a theatre

playing field *n* (sometimes pl) *Brit & NZ* a field or open space used for sport

play-lunch *n* *Austral & NZ* a child's mid-morning snack at school

playmaker *n* *sport* a player who creates scoring opportunities for his or her team-mates

play off *vb* **1** to set (two people) against each other for one's own ends: *she delighted in playing one parent off against the other* **2** to take part in a play-off ▷ *n* **play-off 3** *sport* an extra contest to decide the winner when there is a tie **4** *chiefly US & Canad* a contest or series of games to determine a championship

play on *vb* to exploit (the feelings or weakness of another): *he played on my sympathy*

play on words *n* same as **pun**

playpen *n* a small portable enclosure in which a young child can safely be left to play

playschool *n* a nursery group for preschool children

PlayStation *n* *trademark* a type of video-game console

plaything *n* **1** a toy **2** a person regarded or treated as a toy

playtime *n* a time for play or recreation, such as a school break

play up *vb* **1** to highlight: *the temptation is to play up the sensational aspects of the story* **2** *Brit & Austral, informal* to behave in an unruly way **3** to give (one) trouble or not be working properly: *my back's playing me up again; the photocopier's started to play up* **4 play up to** to try to please by flattery

playwright *n* a person who writes plays

plaza *n* **1** an open public square, usually in Spain **2** *chiefly US & Canad* a modern shopping complex ▶ HISTORY Spanish

PLC *or* **plc** (in Britain) Public Limited Company

plea *n* **1** an emotional appeal **2** *law* a statement by or on behalf of a defendant **3** an excuse: *his plea of poverty rings a little hollow* ▶ HISTORY Anglo-Norman *plai*

plea bargaining *n* *law* the process whereby the prosecution, defence, and sometimes the judge, come to an agreement in which the accused agrees to plead guilty to a lesser charge in return for more serious charges being dropped

plead *vb* **pleading, pleaded, plead** *or esp Scot & US* **pled 1** (sometimes foll. by *with*) to ask with deep feeling **2** to give as an excuse: *whenever she invites him to dinner, he pleads a prior engagement* **3** *law* to declare oneself to be (guilty or not guilty) of the charge made against one **4** *law* to present (a case) in a court of law ▶ HISTORY Latin *placere* to please

pleadings *pl n* *law* the formal written statements presented by the plaintiff and defendant in a lawsuit

pleasant *adj* **1** pleasing or enjoyable: *what a pleasant surprise* **2** having pleasing manners or appearance: *he was a pleasant boy* ▶ HISTORY Old French *plaisant* > **pleasantly** *adv*

pleasantry *n, pl* **-ries 1** (often pl) a polite or jocular remark: *we exchanged pleasantries about the weather* **2** agreeable jocularity ▶ HISTORY French *plaisanterie*

please *vb* **pleasing, pleased 1** to give pleasure or satisfaction to (a person) **2** to regard as suitable or satisfying: *he can get almost anyone he pleases to work with him* **3 if you please** if you wish, sometimes used in ironic exclamation **4 pleased with** happy because of **5 please oneself** to do as one likes ▷ *adv* **6** used in making polite requests or pleading: *please sit down* **7 yes please** a polite phrase used to accept an offer or invitation ▶ HISTORY Latin *placere* > **pleased** *adj*

pleasing *adj* giving pleasure

pleasurable *adj* enjoyable or agreeable > **pleasurably** *adv*

pleasure *n* **1** a feeling of happiness and contentment: *the pleasure of hearing good music* **2** something that gives enjoyment: *his garden was his only pleasure* **3** the activity of enjoying oneself: *business before pleasure* **4** a person's preference ▶ HISTORY Old French *plaisir*

pleat *n* **1** a fold formed by doubling back fabric and pressing or stitching into place ▷ *vb* **2** to arrange (material) in pleats ▶ HISTORY variant of *plait*

pleb *n* *Brit, informal, often offensive* a common vulgar person

plebeian (pleb-**ee**-an) *adj* **1** of the lower social classes **2** unrefined: *plebeian tastes* ▷ *n* **3** one of the common people, usually in ancient Rome **4** a coarse or unrefined person ▶ HISTORY Latin *plebs* the common people of ancient Rome

plebiscite (**pleb**-iss-ite) *n* a direct vote by all the electorate on an issue of national importance ▶ HISTORY Latin *plebiscitum* decree of the people

plectrum *n, pl* **-trums** *or* **-tra** an implement for plucking the strings of a guitar or similar instrument ▶ HISTORY Greek *plektron*

pledge *n* **1** a solemn promise **2 a** something valuable given as a guarantee that a promise will be kept or a debt paid **b** the condition of being used as security: *in pledge* **3** a token: *a pledge of good faith* **4** an assurance of support or goodwill, given by drinking a toast: *we drank a pledge to their success* **5 take** *or* **sign the pledge** to vow not to drink alcohol ▷ *vb* **pledging, pledged 6** to promise solemnly **7** to bind by or as if by a pledge: *I was pledged to secrecy* **8** to give (one's word or property) as a guarantee **9** to drink a toast to (a person or cause) ▶ HISTORY Old French *plege*

Pleiocene *adj, n* same as **Pliocene**

Pleistocene (**ply**-stow-seen) *adj* *geol* of the epoch of geological time from about 1.6 million to 10 000 years ago ▶ HISTORY Greek *pleistos* most + *kainos* recent

plenary *adj* **1** (of an assembly) attended by all the members **2** full or complete: *plenary powers* ▶ HISTORY Latin *plenus* full

plenipotentiary *adj* **1** (usually of a diplomat) invested with full authority ▷ *n, pl* **-aries 2** a diplomat or representative who has full authority

P

to transact business ▶ HISTORY Latin *plenus* full + *potentia* power

plenitude *n literary* **1** abundance **2** fullness or completeness ▶ HISTORY Latin *plenus* full

plenteous *adj literary* **1** abundant: *a plenteous supply* **2** producing abundantly: *a plenteous harvest*

plentiful *adj* existing in large amounts or numbers > **plentifully** *adv*

plenty *n, pl* **-ties 1** (often foll. by *of*) a great number or amount: *plenty of time* **2** abundance: *an age of plenty* ▷ *adj* **3** very many: *there's plenty more fish in the sea* ▷ *adv* **4** *informal* more than adequately: *that's plenty fast enough for me* ▶ HISTORY Latin *plenus* full

pleonasm *n rhetoric* **1** the use of more words than necessary, such as *a tiny little child* **2** an unnecessary word or phrase ▶ HISTORY Greek *pleonasmos* excess > **pleonastic** *adj*

plethora *n* an excess ▶ HISTORY Greek *plēthōra* fullness

pleura (ploor-a) *n, pl* **pleurae** (ploor-ee) *anat* the thin transparent membrane enveloping the lungs ▶ HISTORY Greek: side, rib > **pleural** *adj*

pleurisy *n* inflammation of the pleura, making breathing painful > **pleuritic** *adj, n*

plexus *n, pl* **-uses** *or* **-us** a complex network of nerves or blood vessels ▶ HISTORY Latin *plectere* to braid

pliable *adj* **1** easily bent: *pliable branches* **2** easily influenced: *his easy and pliable nature* > **pliability** *n*

pliant *adj* **1** easily bent; supple: *pliant young willow and hazel twigs* **2** easily influenced: *he was a far more pliant subordinate than his predecessor* ▶ HISTORY Old French *plier* to fold > **pliancy** *n*

pliers *pl n* a gripping tool consisting of two hinged arms usually with serrated jaws ▶ HISTORY from PLY[1]

plight[1] *n* a dangerous or difficult situation: *the plight of the British hostages* ▶ HISTORY Old French *pleit* fold, and probably influenced by Old English *pliht* peril

plight[2] *vb* **plight one's troth** *old-fashioned* to make a promise to marry ▶ HISTORY Old English *pliht* peril

Plimsoll line *n* a line on the hull of a ship showing the level that the water should reach if the ship is properly loaded ▶ HISTORY after Samuel *Plimsoll*, who advocated its adoption

plimsolls *pl n Brit* light rubber-soled canvas sports shoes ▶ HISTORY from the resemblance of the sole to a Plimsoll line

plinth *n* **1** a base on which a statue stands **2** the slab that forms the base of a column or pedestal ▶ HISTORY Greek *plinthos* brick

Pliocene *or* **Pleiocene** (ply-oh-seen) *adj geol* of the epoch of geological time about 10 million years ago ▶ HISTORY Greek *pleiōn* more + *kainos* recent

PLO Palestine Liberation Organization

plod *vb* **plodding, plodded 1** to walk with heavy slow steps **2** to work slowly and steadily ▷ *n* **3** the act of plodding **4** *Brit, slang* a policeman ▶ HISTORY imitative > **plodder** *n*

plonk[1] *vb* **1** to put down heavily and carelessly: *he plonked himself down on the sofa* ▷ *n* **2** the act or sound of plonking ▶ HISTORY variant of *plunk*

plonk[2] *n informal* cheap inferior wine ▶ HISTORY origin unknown

plop *n* **1** the sound made by an object dropping into water without a splash ▷ *vb* **plopping, plopped 2** to drop with such a sound: *a tear rolled down his cheek and plopped into his soup* **3** to fall or be placed heavily or carelessly: *we plopped down on the bed and went straight to sleep* ▶ HISTORY imitative

plosive *phonetics adj* **1** pronounced with a sudden release of breath ▷ *n* **2** a plosive consonant ▶ HISTORY French *explosif* explosive

plot[1] *n* **1** a secret plan for an illegal purpose **2** the story of a play, novel, or film ▷ *vb* **plotting, plotted 3** to plan secretly; conspire **4** to mark (a course) on a map **5** to make a plan or map of **6 a** to locate (points) on a graph by means of coordinates **b** to draw (a curve) through these points **7** to construct the plot of (a play, novel, or film) ▶ HISTORY from PLOT[2], influenced by obsolete *complot* conspiracy > **plotter** *n*

plot[2] *n* a small piece of land: *there was a small vegetable plot in the garden* ▶ HISTORY Old English

plough *or esp US* **plow** *n* **1** an agricultural tool for cutting or turning over the earth **2** a similar tool used for clearing snow ▷ *vb* **3** to turn over (the soil) with a plough **4** to make (furrows or grooves) in (something) with or as if with a plough **5** (sometimes foll. by *through*) to move (through something) in the manner of a plough: *the ship ploughed through the water* **6** (foll. by *through*) to work at slowly or perseveringly **7** to invest (money): *he ploughed the profits back into the business* **8 plough into** (of a vehicle, plane, etc.) to run uncontrollably into (something): *the aircraft ploughed into a motorway embankment* ▶ HISTORY Old English *plōg* plough land

Plough *n* **the Plough** the group of the seven brightest stars in the constellation Ursa Major

ploughman *or esp US* **plowman** *n, pl* **-men** a man who ploughs

ploughman's lunch *n* a snack lunch consisting of bread and cheese with pickle

ploughshare *or esp US* **plowshare** *n* the cutting blade of a plough

plover *n* a shore bird with a round head, straight bill, and long pointed wings ▶ HISTORY Old French *plovier* rainbird

plow *n, vb US* same as **plough**

ploy *n* a manoeuvre designed to gain an advantage in a situation: *a cheap political ploy* ▶ HISTORY from obsolete noun sense of *employ*, meaning an occupation

pluck *vb* **1** *written* to pull or pick off **2** to pull out the feathers of (a bird for cooking) **3** (foll. by *off, away*) to pull (something) forcibly or violently (from something or someone) **4** to sound the strings of (a musical instrument) with the fingers or a plectrum **5** *slang* to swindle ▷ *n* **6** courage **7** a pull or tug **8** the heart, liver, and lungs of an animal used for food ▶ HISTORY Old English *pluccian*

pluck up vb to summon up (courage)

plucky adj **pluckier, pluckiest** courageous
> **pluckily** adv > **pluckiness** n

plug n **1** an object used to block up holes or waste pipes **2** a device with one or more pins which connects an appliance to an electricity supply **3** informal a favourable mention of a product, etc., for example on television, to encourage people to buy it **4** See **spark plug 5** a piece of tobacco for chewing ▷ vb **plugging, plugged 6** to block or seal (a hole or gap) with a plug **7** informal to make frequent favourable mentions of (a product, etc.), for example on television **8** slang to shoot: he lifted the rifle and plugged the deer **9** slang to punch **10** (foll. by along, away etc.) informal to work steadily ▶ HISTORY Middle Dutch plugge

plug in vb to connect (an electrical appliance) to a power source by pushing a plug into a socket

plum n **1** an oval dark red or yellow fruit with a stone in the middle, that grows on a small tree **2** a raisin, as used in a cake or pudding **3** informal something of a superior or desirable kind ▷ adj **4** made from plums: plum cake **5** dark reddish-purple **6** very desirable: plum targets for attack ▶ HISTORY Old English plūme

plumage n the feathers of a bird ▶ HISTORY Old French plume feather

plumb vb **1** to understand (something obscure): to plumb a mystery **2 plumb the depths** to experience the worst extremes of: to plumb the depths of despair **3** to test the alignment of or make vertical with a plumb line **4** (foll. by in or into) to connect (an appliance or fixture) to a water pipe or drainage system: the shower should be plumbed in professionally ▷ n **5** a lead weight hanging at the end of a string and used to test the depth of water or to test whether something is vertical **6 out of plumb** not vertical ▷ adv **7** vertical or perpendicular **8** informal, spoken, chiefly US utterly: plumb stupid **9** informal exactly: plumb in the centre ▶ HISTORY Latin plumbum lead

plumber n a person who fits and repairs pipes and fixtures for water, drainage, or gas systems ▶ HISTORY Old French plommier worker in lead

plumbing n **1** the pipes and fixtures used in a water, drainage, or gas system **2** the trade or work of a plumber

plumb line n a string with a metal weight at one end, used to test the depth of water or to test whether something is vertical

plume n **1** a large ornamental feather **2** a group of feathers worn as a badge or ornament on a hat **3** something like a plume: a plume of smoke ▷ vb **pluming, plumed 4** to adorn with plumes **5** (of a bird) to preen (its feathers) **6** (foll. by on or upon) to be proud of oneself or one's achievements, esp. unjustifiably: she was pluming herself on her figure ▶ HISTORY Old French

plummet vb **-meting, -meted 1** to plunge downward ▷ n **2** the weight on a plumb line or fishing line ▶ HISTORY Old French plommet ball of lead

plump¹ adj **1** full or rounded: until puberty I was really quite plump ▷ vb **2** (often foll. by up or out) to make (something) fuller or rounder: she plumped up the cushions on the couch ▶ HISTORY Middle Dutch plomp blunt > **plumpness** n

plump² vb **1** (often foll. by down, into) to drop or sit suddenly and heavily: he plumped down on the seat **2 plump for** to choose one from a selection ▷ n **3** a heavy abrupt fall or the sound of this ▷ adv **4** suddenly or heavily **5** directly: the plane landed plump in the middle of the field **6** in a blunt, direct, or decisive manner ▶ HISTORY probably imitative

plum pudding n Brit & Austral a boiled or steamed pudding made with flour, suet, and dried fruit

plumule n bot the embryonic shoot of a seed-bearing plant

plunder vb **1** to seize (valuables or goods) from (a place) by force, usually in wartime; loot ▷ n **2** anything plundered; booty **3** the act of plundering; pillage ▶ HISTORY probably from Dutch plunderen

plunge vb **plunging, plunged 1** (usually foll. by into) to thrust or throw (something or oneself) forcibly or suddenly: they plunged into the sea; he plunged the knife in to the hilt **2** to throw or be thrown into a certain condition: the room was plunged into darkness **3** (usually foll. by into) to involve or become involved deeply (in) **4** to move swiftly or impetuously **5** to descend very suddenly or steeply: temperatures were plunging **6** informal to gamble recklessly ▷ n **7** a leap or dive **8** informal a swim **9** a pitching motion **10 take the plunge** informal to make a risky decision which cannot be reversed later ▶ HISTORY Old French plongier

plunge pool n geog a pool at the base of a waterfall carved out by the action of the water

plunger n **1** a rubber suction cup used to clear blocked drains **2** a device with a plunging motion; piston

plunk vb **1** to pluck the strings of (an instrument) to produce a twanging sound **2** (often foll. by down) to drop or be dropped heavily ▷ n **3** the act or sound of plunking ▶ HISTORY imitative

plunket baby n NZ a baby brought up according to the principles of the Plunket Society > **plunket nurse** NZ a nurse working for the Plunket Society

Plunket Society n NZ an organization for the care of mothers and babies

pluperfect or **pluperfect tense** n grammar same as **past perfect** ▶ HISTORY Latin plus quam perfectum more than perfect

plural adj **1** of or consisting of more than one **2** grammar denoting a word indicating more than one ▷ n **3** grammar **a** the plural number **b** a plural form ▶ HISTORY Latin plus more

pluralism n **1** the existence and toleration in a society of a variety of groups of different ethnic origins, cultures, or religions **2** the holding of more than one office by a person > **pluralist** n, adj > **pluralistic** adj

plurality n, pl **-ties 1** the state of being plural **2** maths a number greater than one **3** a large number **4** a majority

P

647

pluralize or **-ise** vb **-izing, -ized** or **-ising, -ised** to make or become plural

plus prep **1** increased by the addition of: *four plus two* **2** with the addition of: *a good salary, plus a company car* ▷ adj **3** indicating addition: *a plus sign* **4** maths same as **positive** (sense 7) **5** on the positive part of a scale **6** indicating the positive side of an electrical circuit **7** involving advantage: *a plus factor* **8** informal having a value above the value stated: *it must be worth a thousand pounds plus* **9** slightly above a specified standard: *he received a B plus for his essay* ▷ n **10** a plus sign (+), indicating addition **11** a positive quantity **12** informal something positive or an advantage **13** a gain, surplus, or advantage ▶ HISTORY Latin: more

plus fours pl n men's baggy knickerbockers gathered in at the knee, now only worn for hunting or golf ▶ HISTORY because made with four inches of material to hang over at the knee

plush n **1** a velvety fabric with a long soft pile, used for furniture coverings ▷ adj **2** Also: **plushy** informal luxurious ▶ HISTORY French *pluche*

plus-one n informal someone who accompanies an invited person to a social function

Pluto n **1** classical myth the god of the underworld **2** the second-largest dwarf planet in the solar system. It was classified as a planet until 2006, when it was reclassified

plutocracy n, pl **-cies** **1** government by the wealthy **2** a state ruled by the wealthy **3** a group that exercises power on account of its wealth ▶ HISTORY Greek *ploutos* wealth + *-kratia* rule > **plutocratic** adj

plutocrat n a person who is powerful because of being very rich

plutonic adj (of igneous rocks) formed from molten rock that has cooled and solidified below the earth's surface ▶ HISTORY after the Greek god *Pluto*

plutonium n chem a toxic radioactive metallic element, used in nuclear reactors and weapons. Symbol: Pu ▶ HISTORY after *Pluto*, because Pluto lies beyond Neptune and plutonium was discovered soon after neptunium

pluvial adj geog, geol of or due to the action of rain ▶ HISTORY Latin *pluvia* rain

ply[1] vb **plies, plying, plied** **1** to work at (a job or trade) **2** to use (a tool) **3** (usually foll. by *with*) to provide (with) or subject (to) persistently: *he plied us with drink; he plied me with questions* **4** to work steadily **5** (of a ship) to travel regularly along (a route): *to ply the trade routes* ▶ HISTORY Middle English *plye*, short for *aplye* to apply

ply[2] n, pl **plies** **1** a layer or thickness, such as of fabric or wood **2** one of the strands twisted together to make rope or yarn ▶ HISTORY Old French *pli* fold

Plymouth Brethren pl n a Puritanical religious sect with no organized ministry

plywood n a board made of thin layers of wood glued together under pressure, with the grain of one layer at right angles to the grain of the next

Pm chem promethium

PM **1** prime minister **2** Postmaster **3** Paymaster

p.m. **1** after noon ▶ HISTORY Latin *post meridiem* **2** postmortem (examination)

PMG **1** Postmaster General **2** Paymaster General

PMS premenstrual syndrome

PMT premenstrual tension

pneumatic adj **1** operated by compressed air: *pneumatic drill* **2** containing compressed air: *a pneumatic tyre* **3** of or concerned with air, gases, or wind ▶ HISTORY Greek *pneuma* breath, wind

pneumatics n the branch of physics concerned with the mechanical properties of air and other gases

pneumonia n inflammation of one or both lungs ▶ HISTORY Greek *pneumōn* lung

Po chem polonium

PO **1** Also: **p.o.** Brit postal order **2** Post Office **3** petty officer **4** Pilot Officer

poach[1] vb **1** to catch (game or fish) illegally on someone else's land **2 a** to encroach on (someone's rights or duties) **b** to steal (an idea, employee, or player) ▶ HISTORY Old French *pocher* > **poacher** n

poach[2] vb to simmer (food) very gently in liquid ▶ HISTORY Old French *pochier* to enclose in a bag

pock n **1** a pus-filled blister resulting from smallpox **2** a pockmark ▶ HISTORY Old English *pocc*

pocket n **1** a small pouch sewn into clothing for carrying small articles **2** any pouchlike container, esp. for catching balls at the edge of a snooker table **3** a small isolated area or group: *a pocket of resistance* **4** a cavity in the earth, such as one containing ore **5 in one's pocket** under one's control **6 out of pocket** having made a loss ▷ vb **-eting, -eted** **7** to put into one's pocket **8** to take secretly or dishonestly **9** billiards etc. to drive (a ball) into a pocket **10** to conceal or suppress: *he pocketed his pride and asked for help* ▷ adj **11** small: *a pocket edition* ▶ HISTORY Anglo-Norman *poket* a little bag

pocket borough n (before the Reform Act of 1832) an English borough constituency controlled by one person or family

pocketknife n, pl **-knives** a small knife with one or more blades that fold into the handle; penknife

pocket money n **1** a small weekly sum of money given to children by parents **2** money for small personal expenses

pockmarked adj **1** (of the skin) marked with pitted scars after the healing of smallpox **2** (of a surface) covered in many small hollows: *the building is pockmarked with bullet holes* > **pockmark** n

pod n **1 a** a long narrow seedcase containing peas, beans, etc. **b** the seedcase as distinct from the seeds ▷ vb **podding, podded** **2** to remove the pod from ▶ HISTORY origin unknown

podcast n **1** an audio file similar to a radio broadcast, which can be downloaded and listened to on a computer, music player, etc. ▷ vb **-casting, -cast** or **-casted** **2** to create such files and make them available for downloading ▶ HISTORY from (1) POD + (BROAD)CAST > **podcasting** n

podgy *adj* **podgier, podgiest** short and fat ▶ HISTORY from *podge* a short plump person > **podginess** *n*

podium *n, pl* **-diums** *or* **-dia** 1 a small raised platform used by conductors or speakers 2 a plinth that supports a colonnade or wall ▶ HISTORY Latin: platform

podzol *or* **podsol** *n geol* a type of soil characteristic of coniferous forest regions having a greyish-white colour in its upper layers from which certain minerals have leached ▶ HISTORY Russian: ash ground, from *pod* ground + *zola* ashes

poem *n* 1 a literary work, often in verse, usually dealing with emotional or descriptive themes in a rhythmic form 2 a literary work that is not in verse but deals with emotional or descriptive themes in a rhythmic form: *a prose poem* 3 anything like a poem in beauty or effect: *his painting is a poem on creation* ▶ HISTORY Greek *poiēma* something created

poesy *n archaic* poetry

poet *n* 1 a writer of poetry 2 a person with great imagination and creativity ▶ HISTORY Greek *poiētēs* maker, poet

poetaster *n* a writer of inferior verse

poetic *or* **poetical** *adj* 1 like poetry, by being expressive or imaginative 2 of poetry or poets 3 recounted in verse

poetic justice *n* an appropriate punishment or reward for previous actions

poetic licence *n* freedom from the normal rules of language or truth, as in poetry

poet laureate *n, pl* **poets laureate** *Brit* the poet selected by the British sovereign to write poems on important occasions

poetry *n* 1 poems in general 2 the art or craft of writing poems 3 a poetic quality that prompts an emotional response: *her acting was full of poetry* ▶ HISTORY Latin *poeta* poet

po-faced *adj* wearing a disapproving stern expression ▶ HISTORY perhaps from PO + POKER-FACED

pogey *or* **pogy** (**pohg**-ee) *n, pl* **pogeys** *or* **pogies** *Canad, slang* 1 financial or other relief given to unemployed people by the government; dole 2 unemployment insurance ▶ HISTORY from earlier *pogie* workhouse

pogo stick *n* a pole with steps for the feet and a spring at the bottom, so that the user can bounce up, down, and along on it ▶ HISTORY origin unknown

pogrom *n* an organized persecution and massacre ▶ HISTORY Russian: destruction

poi *n NZ* a ball of woven flax swung rhythmically by Māori women during poi dances ▶ HISTORY Māori

poi dance *n NZ* a women's formation dance that involves singing and twirling a poi

poignant *adj* 1 sharply painful to the feelings: *a poignant reminder* 2 cutting: *poignant wit* 3 pertinent in mental appeal: *a poignant subject* ▶ HISTORY Latin *pungens* pricking > **poignancy** *n*

poinsettia *n* a shrub of Mexico and Central America, widely grown for its showy scarlet bracts, which resemble petals ▶ HISTORY after J. P. Poinsett, US Minister to Mexico

point *n* 1 the essential idea in an argument or discussion: *I agreed with the point he made* 2 a reason or aim: *what is the point of this exercise?* 3 a detail or item 4 a characteristic: *he thinks his good points* 5 a location or position 6 a dot or tiny mark 7 a dot used as a decimal point or a full stop 8 the sharp tip of anything: *the point of the spear* 9 a headland: *the soaring cliffs at Dwerja Point in the southwest of the island* 10 *maths* a geometric element having a position located by coordinates, but no magnitude 11 a specific condition or degree: *freezing point* 12 a moment: *at that point he left* 13 (often *pl*) any of the extremities, such as the tail, ears, or feet, of a domestic animal 14 (often *pl*) *ballet* the tip of the toes 15 a single unit for measuring something such as value, or of scoring in a game 16 *printing* a unit of measurement equal to one twelfth of a pica 17 *navigation* one of the 32 direction marks on the compass 18 *cricket* a fielding position at right angles to the batsman on the off side 19 either of the two electrical contacts that make or break the circuit in the distributor of a motor vehicle 20 *Brit, Austral & NZ* (often *pl*) a movable section of railway track used to direct a train from one line to another 21 *Brit* short for **power point** 22 *boxing* a mark awarded for a scoring blow or knockdown 23 **beside the point** irrelevant 24 **make a point of a** to make a habit of (something) **b** to do (something) because one thinks it important 25 **on** *or* **at the point of** about to; on the verge of: *on the point of leaving* 26 **to the point** relevant 27 **up to a point** not completely ▷ *vb* 28 (usually foll. by *at* or *to*) to show the position or direction of something by extending a finger or other pointed object towards it 29 (usually foll. by *at* or *to*) to single out one person or thing from among several: *all the symptoms pointed to epilepsy* 30 to direct or face in a specific direction: *point me in the right direction* 31 to finish or repair the joints in brickwork with mortar or cement 32 (of gun dogs) to show where game is lying by standing rigidly with the muzzle turned towards it ▶ HISTORY Latin *pungere* to pierce

point-blank *adj* 1 fired at a very close target 2 plain or blunt: *a point-blank refusal to discuss the matter* ▷ *adv* 3 directly or bluntly: *the Minister was asked point-blank if he intended to resign* ▶ HISTORY point + blank (centre spot of an archery target)

point duty *n* the control of traffic by a policeman at a road junction

pointed *adj* 1 having a sharp tip 2 cutting or incisive: *pointed wit* 3 obviously directed at a particular person: *a pointed remark* 4 emphasized or obvious: *pointed ignorance* > **pointedly** *adv*

pointer *n* 1 something that is a helpful indicator of how a situation has arisen or may turn out: *a significant pointer to the likely resumption of talks* 2 an indicator on a measuring instrument 3 a long stick **649**

p

used by teachers, to point out particular features on a map, chart, etc. **4** a large smooth-coated gun dog

pointillism (**pwan**-till-iz-zum) *n* a technique used by some impressionist painters, in which dots of colour are placed side by side so that they merge when seen from a distance ▶ HISTORY French > **pointillist** *n, adj*

pointless *adj* without meaning or purpose

point of order *n, pl* **points of order** an objection in a meeting to the departure from the proper procedure

point of view *n, pl* **points of view** **1** a mental viewpoint or attitude: *she refuses to see the other person's point of view* **2** a way of considering something: *a scientific point of view* **3** the mental position from which a story is observed or narrated

point-to-point *n Brit* a steeplechase organized by a hunt

poise *n* **1** dignified manner **2** physical balance: *the poise of a natural model* **3** mental balance: *he recovered his poise* ▷ *vb* **poising, poised 4** to be balanced or suspended **5** to hold in readiness: *to poise a lance* ▶ HISTORY Old French *pois* weight

poised *adj* **1** absolutely ready **2** behaving with or showing poise

poison *n* **1** a substance that causes death or injury when swallowed or absorbed **2** something that destroys or corrupts: *the poison of Nazism* ▷ *vb* **3** to give poison to someone **4** to add poison to something **5** to have a harmful or evil effect on **6** (foll. by *against*) to turn (a person's mind) against: *he poisoned her mind against me* ▶ HISTORY Latin *potio* a drink, esp. a poisonous one > **poisoner** *n*

poison ivy *n* a North American climbing plant that causes an itching rash if it touches the skin

poisonous *adj* **1** of or like a poison **2** malicious

poison-pen letter *n* a malicious anonymous letter

poke¹ *vb* **poking, poked 1** to jab or prod with an elbow, finger, etc. **2** to make a hole by poking **3** (sometimes foll. by *at*) to thrust (at): *she poked at the food with her fork* **4** (usually foll. by *in, through*) to thrust forward or out: *yellow hair poked from beneath his cap* **5** to stir (a fire) by poking **6** (often foll. by *about* or *around*) to search or pry **7 poke one's nose into** to meddle in ▷ *n* **8** a jab or prod ▶ HISTORY Low German & Middle Dutch *poken*

poke² *n* **1** *dialect* a pocket or bag **2 a pig in a poke** See **pig** ▶ HISTORY Old French *poque*

poker¹ *n* a metal rod with a handle for stirring a fire

poker² *n* a card game of bluff and skill in which players bet on the hands dealt ▶ HISTORY origin unknown

pokerwork *n* the art of producing pictures or designs on wood by burning it with a heated metal point

poky *adj* **pokier, pokiest** (of a room) small and cramped ▶ HISTORY from POKE¹ (in slang sense: to confine) > **pokiness** *n*

pol. **1** political **2** politics

polar *adj* **1** of or near either of the earth's poles or the area inside the Arctic or Antarctic Circles **2** of or having a pole or polarity **3** directly opposite in tendency or nature: *polar opposites*

polar bear *n* a white bear of coastal regions of the North Pole

polar circle *n* the Arctic or Antarctic Circle

polarity *n, pl* **-ties 1** the state of having two directly opposite tendencies or opinions **2** the condition of a body which has opposing physical properties, usually magnetic poles or electric charge **3** the particular state of a part with polarity: *an electrode with positive polarity*

polarization *or* **-isation** *n* **1** the condition of having or giving polarity **2** *physics* the condition in which waves of light or other radiation are restricted to certain directions of vibration

polarize *or* **-ise** *vb* **-izing, -ized** *or* **-ising, -ised** **1** to cause people to adopt directly opposite opinions: *political opinion had polarized since the restoration of democracy* **2** to have or give polarity or polarization

Polaroid *n* *trademark* **1** a type of plastic that polarizes light: used in sunglasses to eliminate glare **2 Polaroid camera** a camera that produces a finished print by developing and processing it inside the camera within a few seconds **3 Polaroids** sunglasses with Polaroid plastic lenses

polder *n* a stretch of land reclaimed from the sea ▶ HISTORY Middle Dutch *polre*

pole¹ *n* **1** a long slender rounded piece of wood, metal, or other material **2 up the pole** *Brit, Austral & NZ, informal* **a** slightly mad **b** in a predicament ▶ HISTORY Latin *palus* a stake

pole² *n* **1** either end of the earth's axis of rotation. See also **North Pole, South Pole 2** *physics* **a** either of the opposite forces of a magnet **b** either of two points at which there are opposite electric charges **3** either of two directly opposite tendencies or opinions **4 poles apart** having widely divergent opinions or tastes ▶ HISTORY Greek *polos* pivot

Pole *n* a person from Poland

poleaxe *or US* **poleax** *vb* **-axing, -axed 1** to hit or stun with a heavy blow ▷ *n* **2** an axe formerly used in battle or used by a butcher ▶ HISTORY Middle English *pollax* battle-axe

polecat *n, pl* **-cats** *or* **-cat 1** a dark brown mammal like a weasel that gives off a foul smell **2** *US* a skunk ▶ HISTORY origin unknown

polemic (pol-**em**-ik) *n* **1** a fierce attack on or defence of a particular opinion, belief, etc.: *anti-capitalist polemic* ▷ *adj also* **polemical 2** of or involving dispute or controversy ▶ HISTORY Greek *polemos* war > **polemicist** *n*

polemics *n* the art of dispute

pole position *n* **1** (in motor racing) the starting position on the inside of the front row, generally considered the best one **2** an advantageous starting position

Pole Star *n* **the Pole Star** the star closest to the N celestial pole

pole vault *n* **1 the pole vault** a field event in which competitors try to clear a high bar with the aid of a very flexible long pole ▷ *vb* **pole-vault** **2** to perform or compete in the pole vault > **pole-vaulter** *n*

police *n* **1** (often preceded by *the*) the organized civil force in a state which keeps law and order **2** the men and women who are members of such a force **3** an organized body with a similar function: *security police* ▷ *vb* **-licing, -liced** **4** to maintain order or control by means of a police force or similar body ▶ HISTORY French, from Latin *politia* administration

police dog *n* a dog trained to help the police

policeman *or fem* **policewoman** *n, pl* **-men** *or* **-women** a member of a police force

police procedural *n* a novel, film, or television drama that deals with police work

police state *n* a state in which a government controls people's freedom through the police

police station *n* the office of the police force of a district

policy¹ *n, pl* **-cies 1** a plan of action adopted by a person, group, or government **2** *archaic* wisdom or prudence ▶ HISTORY Old French *policie*, from Latin *politia* administration

policy² *n, pl* **-cies** a document containing an insurance contract ▶ HISTORY Old French *police* certificate > **policyholder** *n*

polio *n* short for **poliomyelitis**

poliomyelitis (pole-ee-oh-my-el-**lite**-iss) *n* a viral disease which affects the brain and spinal cord, often causing paralysis ▶ HISTORY Greek *polios* grey + *muelos* marrow

polish *vb* **1** to make smooth and shiny by rubbing **2** to perfect or complete: *media experts he had hired to polish his image* **3** to make or become elegant or refined: *not having polished his south London accent didn't help his career* ▷ *n* **4** a substance used for polishing **5** a shine or gloss **6** elegance or refinement ▶ HISTORY Latin *polire* to polish

Polish *adj* **1** of Poland ▷ *n* **2** the language of Poland

polished *adj* **1** accomplished: *a polished actor* **2** done or performed well or professionally: *a polished performance*

polish off *vb informal* **1** to finish completely **2** to dispose of or kill

Politburo *n* formerly, the chief decision-making committee of a Communist country ▶ HISTORY Russian

polite *adj* **1** having good manners; courteous **2** cultivated or refined: *polite society* **3** socially correct but insincere: *he smiled a polite response and stifled an urge to scream* ▶ HISTORY Latin *politus* polished > **politely** *adv* > **politeness** *n*

politic *adj* **1** wise or possibly advantageous: *I didn't feel it was politic to mention it* **2** artful or shrewd: *a politic manager* **3** crafty; cunning: *a politic old scoundrel* **4** *archaic* political. See also **body politic** ▶ HISTORY Old French *politique*, from Greek *polis* city

political *adj* **1** of the state, government, or public administration **2** relating to or interested in politics: *she was always a very political person* **3** of the parties and the partisan aspects of politics: *the government blames political opponents for fanning the unrest* > **politically** *adv*

political cartoon *n* a cartoon that satirizes or makes observations about recent political events

politically correct *adj* displaying progressive attitudes, esp. in using vocabulary which is intended to avoid any implied prejudice

political prisoner *n* a person imprisoned for holding particular political beliefs

political science *n* the study of the state, government, and politics > **political scientist** *n*

politician *n* a person actively engaged in politics, esp. a member of parliament

politicize *or* **-cise** *vb* **-cizing, -cized** *or* **-cising, -cised 1** to make political or politically aware **2** to take part in political discussion or activity > **politicization** *or* **-cisation** *n*

politics *n* **1** (functioning as sing) the art and science of government **2** (functioning as pl) political opinions or sympathies: *his conservative politics* **3** (functioning as pl) political activities or affairs: *party politics* **4** (functioning as sing) the business or profession of politics **5** (functioning as sing or pl) any activity concerned with the acquisition of power: *company politics are often vicious*

polity *n, pl* **-ties** *formal* **1** a politically organized state, church, or society **2** a form of government of a state, church, or society ▶ HISTORY Greek *politeia* citizenship, from *polis* city

polka *n* **1** a lively 19th-century dance **2** music for this dance ▷ *vb* **-kaing, -kaed 3** to dance a polka ▶ HISTORY Czech *pulka* half-step

polka dots *pl n* a regular pattern of small bold spots on a fabric

poll *n* **1** Also called: **opinion poll** the questioning of a random sample of people to find out the general opinion **2** the casting, recording, or counting of votes in an election **3** the result of such a voting: *a marginal poll* **4** the head ▷ *vb* **5** to receive (a certain number of votes) **6** to record the votes of: *he polled the whole town* **7** to question (a person, etc.) as part of an opinion poll **8** to vote in an election **9** to clip or shear **10** to remove or cut short the horns of (cattle) ▶ HISTORY Middle Low German *polle* hair, head, top of a tree

pollack *or* **pollock** *n, pl* **-lacks** *or* **-lack, -locks** *or* **-lock** a food fish related to the cod, found in northern seas ▶ HISTORY origin unknown

pollard *n* **1** an animal that has shed its horns or has had them removed **2** a tree with its top cut off to encourage a more bushy growth ▷ *vb* **3** to cut off the top of (a tree) to make it grow bushy ▶ HISTORY see POLL > **pollarded** *adj*

pollen *n* a fine powder produced by flowers to fertilize other flowers of the same species ▶ HISTORY Latin: powder

651

pollen count *n* a measure of the amount of pollen in the air over a 24-hour period, often published as a warning to hay fever sufferers

pollinate *vb* **-nating, -nated** to fertilize by the transfer of pollen > **pollination** *n*

polling booth *n* a compartment in which a voter can mark his or her ballot paper in private during an election

polling station *n* a building where voters go during an election to cast their votes

pollster *n* a person who conducts opinion polls

poll tax *n* any tax levied per head of adult population, esp. the tax which replaced previous rates (in Scotland from 1989 and England and Wales from 1990, until 1993)

pollutant *n* a substance that pollutes, usually the chemical waste of an industrial process

pollute *vb* **-luting, -luted 1** to contaminate with poisonous or harmful substances **2** to corrupt morally ▸ **HISTORY** Latin *polluere* to defile

pollution *n* **1** *environmental science* harmful or poisonous substances introduced into an environment **2** the act of polluting or the state of being polluted

polo *n* **1** a game like hockey played on horseback with long-handled mallets and a wooden ball **2** short for **water polo** ▸ **HISTORY** Tibetan *pulu* ball

polonaise *n* **1** a stately Polish dance **2** music for this dance ▸ **HISTORY** French *danse polonaise* Polish dance

polo neck *n* a sweater with a high tight turned-over collar

polonium *n* *chem* a rare radioactive element found in trace amounts in uranium ores. Symbol: Po ▸ **HISTORY** Medieval Latin *Polonia* Poland; in honour of the nationality of its discoverer, Marie Curie

polo shirt *n* a cotton short-sleeved shirt with a collar and three-button opening at the neck

poltergeist *n* a spirit believed to be responsible for noises and acts of mischief, such as throwing objects about ▸ **HISTORY** German *poltern* to be noisy + *Geist* ghost

poltroon *n* *obsolete* a complete coward ▸ **HISTORY** Old Italian *poltrone* lazy good-for-nothing

poly *n*, *pl* **polys** *informal* short for **polytechnic**

poly- *combining form* many or much: *polyhedron; polysyllabic* ▸ **HISTORY** Greek *polus*

polyandry *n* the practice of having more than one husband at the same time ▸ **HISTORY** Greek *polus* many + *anēr* man > **polyandrous** *adj*

polyanthus *n*, *pl* **-thuses** a hybrid garden primrose with brightly coloured flowers ▸ **HISTORY** Greek: having many flowers

polychromatic *adj* **1** having many colours **2** (of radiation) containing more than one wavelength

polyester *n* a synthetic material used to make plastics and textile fibres

polyethylene *n* same as **polythene**

polygamy (pol-**ig**-a-mee) *n* the practice of having more than one wife or husband at the same time ▸ **HISTORY** Greek *polus* many + *gamos* marriage > **polygamist** *n* > **polygamous** *adj*

polyglot *adj* **1** able to speak many languages **2** written in or using many languages ▷ *n* **3** a person who can speak many languages ▸ **HISTORY** Greek *poluglōttos* many-tongued

polygon *n* a geometrical figure with three or more sides and angles ▸ **HISTORY** Greek *polugōnon* figure with many angles > **polygonal** *adj*

polygraph *n* an instrument for recording pulse rate and perspiration, often used as a lie detector ▸ **HISTORY** Greek *polugraphos* writing copiously

polygyny *n* the practice of having more than one wife at the same time ▸ **HISTORY** Greek *polus* many + *gunē* woman > **polygynous** *adj*

polyhedron *n*, *pl* **-drons** or **-dra** a solid figure with four or more sides ▸ **HISTORY** Greek *polus* many + *hedron* side > **polyhedral** *adj*

Polyhymnia *n* *Greek myth* the Muse of singing, mime, and sacred dance

polymath *n* a person of great and varied learning ▸ **HISTORY** Greek *polumathēs* having much knowledge

polymer *n* a natural or synthetic compound with large molecules made up of simple molecules of the same kind

polymeric *adj* of or being a polymer: *polymeric materials such as PVC* ▸ **HISTORY** Greek *polumerēs* having many parts

polymerization *or* **-isation** *n* the process of forming a polymer > **polymerize** *or* **-ise** *vb*

polymorphous *or* **polymorphic** *adj* having, or passing through many different forms or stages ▸ **HISTORY** Greek *polus* many + *morphē* form

Polynesian *adj* **1** of Polynesia ▷ *n* **2** a person from Polynesia **3** any of the languages of Polynesia

polynomial *maths adj* **1** consisting of two or more terms ▷ *n* **2** an algebraic expression consisting of the sum of a number of terms

polyp *n* **1** *zool* a small sea creature that has a hollow cylindrical body with a ring of tentacles around the mouth **2** *pathol* a small growth on the surface of a mucous membrane ▸ **HISTORY** Greek *polupous* having many feet

polypeptide *n* *biochem* a polymer made up of amino acids chemically linked together

polyphonic *adj* *music* consisting of several melodies played together

polyphony (pol-**if**-on-ee) *n*, *pl* **-nies** polyphonic style of composition or a piece of music using it ▸ **HISTORY** Greek *poluphōnia* diversity of tones

polysaccharide *n* a carbohydrate which consists of a number of linked sugar molecules, such as starch or cellulose

polystyrene *n* a synthetic material used esp. as white rigid foam for insulating and packing

polysyllabic *adj* **1** having more than two syllables: *polysyllabic words* **2** containing a marked number of words of more than two syllables: *polysyllabic language*

polysyllable *n* a word having more than two syllables

polytechnic *n* **1** (in New Zealand and formerly in Britain) college offering courses in many subjects

p

at and below degree level ▷ *adj* **2** of or relating to technical instruction ▶ HISTORY Greek *polutekhnos* skilled in many arts

polytheism *n* belief in more than one god > **polytheistic** *adj* > **polytheist** *n*

polythene *n* a light plastic material made from ethylene, usually made into thin sheets or bags

polyunsaturated *adj* of a group of fats that are less likely to contribute to the build-up of cholesterol in the body

polyurethane *n* a synthetic material used esp. in paints

polyvinyl chloride *n* See **PVC**

pom same as **pommy**

pomade *n* a perfumed oil put on the hair to make it smooth and shiny, esp. formerly ▶ HISTORY French *pommade*

pomander *n* **1** a mixture of sweet-smelling substances in a container, used to perfume drawers or cupboards **2** a container for such a mixture ▶ HISTORY Medieval Latin *pomum ambrae* apple of amber

pomegranate *n* a round tropical fruit with a tough reddish rind containing many seeds in a juicy red pulp ▶ HISTORY Latin *pomum* apple + *granatus* full of seeds

pomelo (pom-ill-oh) *n, pl* **-los** the edible yellow fruit, like a grapefruit, of a tropical tree ▶ HISTORY Dutch *pompelmoes*

Pomeranian *n* a toy dog with a long straight silky coat ▶ HISTORY after *Pomerania*, region of N central Europe

pomfret (pum-frit) *or* **pomfret-cake** *n* a small black rounded liquorice sweet ▶ HISTORY from *Pomfret*, earlier form of *Pontefract*, Yorks., where originally made

pommel *n* **1** the raised part on the front of a saddle **2** a knob at the top of a sword handle ▷ *vb* **-melling, -melled** *or US* **-meling, -meled 3** same as **pummel** ▶ HISTORY Old French *pomel* knob

pommy *n, pl* **-mies** (sometimes cap) *slang* a word used by Australians and New Zealanders for a British person. Sometimes shortened to: **pom** ▶ HISTORY origin unknown

pomp *n* **1** stately display or ceremony **2** ostentatious display ▶ HISTORY Greek *pompē* procession

pompom *n* **1** a decorative ball of tufted silk or wool **2** the small round flower head of some dahlias and chrysanthemums ▶ HISTORY French

pompous *adj* **1** foolishly dignified or self-important **2** foolishly grand in style: *a pompous speech* > **pomposity** *n* > **pompously** *adv*

ponce *offensive slang, chiefly Brit n* **1** an effeminate man **2** same as **pimp** ▷ *vb* **poncing, ponced 3** (often foll. by *around* or *about*) *Brit & Austral* to act stupidly or waste time ▶ HISTORY from Polari, an English slang derived from the Mediterranean ports

poncho *n, pl* **-chos** a type of cloak made of a piece of cloth with a hole in the middle for the head ▶ HISTORY American Spanish

pond *n* a pool of still water ▶ HISTORY Middle English *ponde* enclosure

ponder *vb* (sometimes foll. by *on* or *over*) to consider thoroughly or deeply ▶ HISTORY Latin *ponderare* to weigh, consider > **ponderable** *adj*

ponderous *adj* **1** serious and dull: *much of the film is ponderous and pretentious* **2** heavy or huge **3** *written* (of movement) slow and clumsy ▶ HISTORY Latin *ponderosus* of great weight

pondok *or* **pondokkie** *n* (in southern Africa) a crudely made house or shack ▶ HISTORY Malay *pondók* leaf house

pondweed *n* a plant which grows in ponds and slow streams

pong *Brit & Austral, informal n* **1** a strong unpleasant smell ▷ *vb* **2** to give off a strong unpleasant smell ▶ HISTORY origin unknown > **pongy** *adj*

ponga (pong-a) *n* a tall New Zealand tree fern with large leathery leaves ▶ HISTORY Māori

pons *n, pl* **pontes** *anat* a bridge of connective tissue

pontiff *n* the Pope ▶ HISTORY Latin *pontifex* high priest

pontifical *adj* **1** of a pontiff **2** pompous or dogmatic in manner

pontificate *vb* **-cating, -cated 1** to speak in a dogmatic manner **2** to officiate as a pontiff ▷ *n* **3** the term of office of a Pope

pontoon¹ *n* a floating platform used to support a bridge ▶ HISTORY Latin *ponto* punt

pontoon² *n* a card game in which players try to obtain sets of cards worth 21 points ▶ HISTORY probably an alteration of French *vingt-et-un* twenty-one

pony *n, pl* **-nies** a breed of small horse ▶ HISTORY Scots *powney*, perhaps from Latin *pullus* young animal, foal

ponytail *n* a hairstyle in which the hair is tied in a bunch at the back of the head and hangs down like a tail

pony trekking *n* the pastime of riding ponies cross-country

poodle *n* a dog with curly hair, which is sometimes clipped ▶ HISTORY German *Pudel*

pooh *interj* an exclamation of disdain, scorn, or disgust

pooh-pooh *vb* to express disdain or scorn for

pool¹ *n* **1** a small body of still water **2** a small body of spilt liquid: *a pool of blood* **3** See **swimming pool 4** a deep part of a stream or river ▶ HISTORY Old English *pōl*

pool² *n* **1** a shared fund of resources or workers: *a typing pool* **2** a billiard game in which all the balls are potted with the cue ball **3** the combined stakes of those betting in many gambling games **4** *commerce* a group of producers who agree to maintain output levels and high prices ▷ *vb* **5** to put into a common fund ▶ HISTORY French *poule*, literally: hen used to signify stakes in a card game

pool and riffle sequence *n* *geog* the natural alternating pattern of deep pools and fast flowing shallows found in rivers and streams

p

pools *pl n* **the pools** *chiefly Brit* a nationwide mainly postal form of gambling which bets on the results of football matches

poop *n naut* a raised part at the back of a sailing ship ▶ **HISTORY** Latin *puppis*

pooped *adj US, Canad, Austral & NZ, slang* exhausted or tired: *if I wasn't so pooped I'd run and have a look at it* ▶ **HISTORY** Middle English *poupen* to blow

poor *adj* **1** having little money and few possessions **2** less than is necessary or expected: *it was a poor reward for all his effort* **3** (sometimes foll. by *in*) lacking in (something): *a food which is rich in energy but poor in vitamins* **4** inferior: *poor quality* **5** disappointing or disagreeable: *a poor play* **6** pitiable; unlucky: *poor John is ill* **7 poor man's (something)** a cheaper substitute for (something): *pewter, sometimes known as poor man's silver* ▶ **HISTORY** Latin *pauper*

poorhouse *n* same as **workhouse**

poor law *n English history* a law providing for support of poor people from parish funds

poorly *adv* **1** badly ▷ *adj* **2** *informal* rather ill

poor White *n often offensive* a poverty-stricken White person, usually in the southern US or South Africa

pop¹ *vb* **popping, popped 1** to make or cause to make a small explosive sound **2** (often foll. by *in*, *out*) *informal* to enter or leave briefly or suddenly: *his mother popped out to buy him an ice cream* **3** to place suddenly or unexpectedly: *Benny popped a sweet into his mouth* **4** to burst with a small explosive sound **5** (of the eyes) to protrude **6** *informal* to pawn **7 pop the question** *informal* to propose marriage ▷ *n* **8** a light sharp explosive sound **9** *Brit, informal* a nonalcoholic fizzy drink ▷ *adv* **10** with a pop ▶ **HISTORY** imitative

pop² *n* **1** music of general appeal, esp. to young people, that usually has a strong rhythm and uses electrical amplification ▷ *adj* **2** relating to pop music: *a pop concert* **3** *informal* short for **popular**

pop³ *n informal* **1** father **2** an old man

pop art *n* a movement in modern art that uses the methods, styles, and themes of popular culture and mass media

popcorn *n* grains of maize heated until they puff up and burst

Pope *n* the bishop of Rome as head of the Roman Catholic Church ▶ **HISTORY** Greek *pappas* father

popery (**pope**-er-ee) *n offensive* Roman Catholicism

popeyed *adj* **1** staring in astonishment **2** having bulging eyes

popinjay *n* a conceited or talkative person ▶ **HISTORY** Arabic *babaghā* parrot

popish (**pope**-ish) *adj offensive* relating to Roman Catholicism

poplar *n* a tall slender tree with light soft wood, triangular leaves, and catkins ▶ **HISTORY** Latin *populus*

poplin *n* a strong plain-woven fabric, usually of cotton, with fine ribbing ▶ **HISTORY** French *papeline*

poppadom *or* **poppadum** *n* a thin round crisp fried Indian bread ▶ **HISTORY** Hindi

poppet *n* a term of affection for a small child or sweetheart ▶ **HISTORY** variant of *puppet*

popping crease *n cricket* a line in front of and parallel with the wicket where the batsman stands ▶ **HISTORY** from obsolete *pop* to hit

poppy *n, pl* **-pies 1** a plant with showy red, orange, or white flowers **2** a drug, such as opium, obtained from these plants **3** an artificial red poppy worn to mark Remembrance Sunday and in New Zealand to mark Anzac Day ▷ *adj* **4** reddish-orange ▶ **HISTORY** Old English *popæg*

poppycock *n informal* nonsense ▶ **HISTORY** Dutch dialect *pappekak*, literally: soft excrement

populace *n* the common people; masses ▶ **HISTORY** Latin *populus*

popular *adj* **1** widely liked or admired **2** (often foll. by *with*) liked by a particular person or group: *the bay is popular with windsurfers and water-skiers* **3** common among the general public: *the groundswell of popular feeling* **4** designed to appeal to a mass audience: *an attack on him in the popular press* ▶ **HISTORY** Latin *popularis* of the people > **popularity** *n* > **popularly** *adv*

popular front *n* a left-wing group or party opposed to fascism

popularize *or* **-ise** *vb* **-izing, -ized** *or* **-ising, -ised 1** to make popular **2** to make easily understandable > **popularization** *or* **-isation** *n*

populate *vb* **-lating, -lated 1** (often passive) to live in: *a mountainous region populated mainly by Armenians* **2** to provide with inhabitants ▶ **HISTORY** Latin *populus* people > **populated** *adj*

population *n* **1** all the inhabitants of a place **2** the number of such inhabitants **3** all the people of a particular class in a place: *the bulk of the rural population lives in poverty* **4** *ecology* a group of individuals of the same species inhabiting a given area: *a population of grey seals*

population density *n statistics* a statistic showing the number of people living within a given area

population distribution *n geog* the way in which people settle more or less densely in different areas

population pyramid *n statistics* a pyramid-shaped diagram showing the age distribution of a population: the youngest are represented by a rectangle at the base, the oldest by one at the apex

population size *n geog* the number of people living in a particular area

populism *n* a political strategy based on a calculated appeal to the interests or prejudices of ordinary people: *they preach a heady message of populism and religion* > **populist** *adj, n*

populous *adj* containing many inhabitants

pop-up *adj* **1** (of an appliance) characterized by or having a mechanism that springs upwards: *a pop-up toaster* **2** (of a book) having pages that rise when opened to create a three-dimensional image **3** (of a menu on a computer screen, etc.) suddenly

appearing when an option is selected ▷ *n*
4 something that appears over or above the open
window on a computer screen

porangi (pore-ang-ee) *adj NZ, informal* crazy; mad
▶ **HISTORY** Māori

porbeagle *n* a kind of shark

porcelain *n* **1** a delicate type of china **2** an object
or objects made of this ▶ **HISTORY** French
porcelaine, from Italian *porcellana* cowrie shell

porch *n* a covered approach to the entrance of a
building ▶ **HISTORY** French *porche*

porcine *adj* of or like a pig ▶ **HISTORY** Latin *porcus*
a pig

porcupine *n* a large rodent covered with long
pointed quills ▶ **HISTORY** Middle English *porc
despyne* pig with spines

pore¹ *vb* **poring, pored • pore over** to examine or
study intently: *a wife who pored over account books
and ledgers all day* ▶ **HISTORY** Middle English *pouren*

pore² *n* **1** a small opening in the skin or surface of
an animal or plant **2** any small hole, such as a tiny
gap in a rock ▶ **HISTORY** Greek *poros* passage, pore

poriferan (por-**riff**-er-an) *n biol* a sponge
▶ **HISTORY** from New Latin *porifer* bearing pores

pork *n* the flesh of pigs used as food ▶ **HISTORY**
Latin *porcus* pig

porker *n* a pig fattened for food

porn or **porno** *n, adj informal* short for
pornography, pornographic

pornography *n* writings, pictures, or films
designed to be sexually exciting ▶ **HISTORY** Greek
pornographos writing of prostitutes
> **pornographer** *n* > **pornographic** *adj*

porosity *n science* the state or condition of being
porous

porous *adj* **1** allowing air and liquids to be
absorbed **2** *biol, geol* having pores ▶ **HISTORY** Late
Latin *porus* passage, pore

porphyry (**por**-fir-ee) *n, pl* **-ries** a reddish-purple
rock with large crystals of feldspar in it ▶ **HISTORY**
Greek *porphuros* purple > **porphyritic** *adj*

porpoise *n, pl* **-poises** or **-poise** a small mammal
of the whale family with a blunt snout ▶ **HISTORY**
Latin *porcus* pig + *piscis* fish

porridge *n* **1** a dish made of oatmeal or other
cereal, cooked in water or milk **2** *chiefly Brit, slang* a
term of imprisonment ▶ **HISTORY** variant of *pottage*

port¹ *n* a town with a harbour where ships can load
and unload ▶ **HISTORY** Latin *portus*

port² *n* **1** the left side of an aircraft or ship when
facing the front of it ▷ *vb* **2** to turn or be turned
towards the port ▶ **HISTORY** origin unknown

port³ *n* a strong sweet fortified wine, usually dark
red ▶ **HISTORY** after *Oporto*, Portugal, from where
it came originally

port⁴ *n* **1** *naut* **a** an opening with a watertight door
in the side of a ship, used for loading, etc. **b** See
porthole **2** *electronics* a logical circuit for the input
and output of data ▶ **HISTORY** Latin *porta* gate

port⁵ *vb computers* to change (programs) from one
system to another ▶ **HISTORY** probably from PORT⁴

portable *adj* **1** easily carried ▷ *n* **2** an article

designed to be easily carried, such as a television
▶ **HISTORY** Latin *portare* to carry > **portability** *n*

portage *n* **1** the transporting of boats and supplies
overland between navigable waterways **2** the
route used for such transport ▷ *vb* **-taging,
-taged** **3** to transport (boats and supplies) in this
way ▶ **HISTORY** French

portal *n* **1** *literary* a large and impressive gateway or
doorway **2** *computers* an internet site providing
links to other sites ▶ **HISTORY** Latin *porta* gate

portcullis *n* an iron grating suspended in a castle
gateway, that can be lowered to bar the entrance
▶ **HISTORY** Old French *porte coleïce* sliding gate

portend *vb* to be an omen of: *the 0.5 percent
increase certainly portends higher inflation ahead*
▶ **HISTORY** Latin *portendere* to indicate

portent *n* **1** a sign of a future event **2** great or
ominous significance: *matters of great portent*
3 a marvel ▶ **HISTORY** Latin *portentum* sign

portentous *adj* **1** of great or ominous significance
2 self-important or pompous: *there was nothing
portentous or solemn about him*

porter¹ *n* **1** a man employed to carry luggage at a
railway station or hotel **2** a hospital worker who
transfers patients between rooms ▶ **HISTORY** Latin
portare to carry > **porterage** *n*

porter² *n chiefly Brit* a doorman or gatekeeper of a
building ▶ **HISTORY** Latin *porta* door

porter³ *n Brit* a dark sweet ale brewed from black
malt ▶ **HISTORY** short for *porter's ale*

porterhouse *n* a thick choice beef steak. Also
called: **porterhouse steak** ▶ **HISTORY** formerly,
a place that served porter, beer, and sometimes
meals

portfolio *n, pl* **-os** **1** a flat case for carrying maps,
drawings, or papers **2** selected examples, such as
drawings or photographs, that show an artist's
recent work **3** the area of responsibility of the head
of a government department: *the defence portfolio*
4 Minister without portfolio a cabinet minister
without responsibility for a government
department **5** a list of investments held by an
investor ▶ **HISTORY** Italian *portafoglio*

porthole *n* a small round window in a ship or
aircraft

portico *n, pl* **-coes** or **-cos** a porch or covered
walkway with columns supporting the roof
▶ **HISTORY** Italian, from Latin *porticus*

portion *n* **1** a part of a whole **2** a part belonging to
a person or group **3** a helping of food served to one
person **4** *law* a dowry **5** *literary* someone's fate or
destiny: *utter disaster was my portion* ▷ *vb* **6** to divide
(something) into shares ▶ **HISTORY** Latin *portio*

portion out *vb* to distribute or share (something)
among a group of people: *the British portioned out
the oil-rich lands to various sheikhs*

portly *adj* **-lier, -liest** stout or rather fat ▶ **HISTORY**
from *port* (in the sense: deportment)

portmanteau *n, pl* **-teaus** or **-teaux** *old-fashioned*
a large suitcase made of stiff leather that opens
out into two compartments ▶ **HISTORY** French:
cloak carrier

p

portmanteau word n a word made by joining together the beginning and end of two other words, such as *brunch*. Also called: **blend**

portrait n **1** a painting, drawing, or photograph of a person, often only of the face **2** a description ▶ HISTORY French > **portraitist** n

portraiture n **1** the art of making portraits **2** a description **3 a** a portrait **b** portraits collectively

portray vb to describe or represent (someone) by artistic means, such as in writing or on film ▶ HISTORY Old French *portraire* to depict > **portrayal** n

Portuguese adj **1** of Portugal ▷ n **2** (pl **-guese**) a person from Portugal **3** the language of Portugal and Brazil

Portuguese man-of-war n a large sea creature like a jellyfish, with long stinging tentacles

pose vb **posing, posed 1** to take up a particular position to be photographed or drawn **2** to behave in an affected way in order to impress others **3** (often foll. by *as*) to pretend to be (someone one is not) **4** to create or be (a problem, threat, etc.): *dressing complicated wounds has always posed a problem for doctors* **5** to put forward or ask: *the question you posed earlier* ▷ n **6** a position taken up for an artist or photographer **7** behaviour adopted for effect ▶ HISTORY Old French *poser* to set in place

Poseidon n *Greek myth* the god of the sea

poser[1] n **1** *Brit, Austral & NZ, informal* a person who likes to be seen in trendy clothes in fashionable places **2** a person who poses

poser[2] n a baffling question

poseur n a person who behaves in an affected way in order to impress others ▶ HISTORY French

posh adj *informal, chiefly Brit* **1** smart or elegant **2** upper-class ▶ HISTORY probably from obsolete slang *posh* a dandy

posit (pozz-it) vb **-iting, -ited** to lay down as a basis for argument: *the archetypes posited by modern psychology* ▶ HISTORY Latin *ponere* to place

position n **1** place or location: *the hotel is in an elevated position above the River Wye* **2** the proper or usual place **3** the way in which a person or thing is placed or arranged: *an upright position* **4** point of view; attitude: *the Catholic Church's position on contraception* **5** social status, esp. high social standing **6** a job; appointment **7** *sport* a player's allotted role or place in the playing area **8 in a position to** able to: *you were not in a position to repay the money* **9** *mil* a place occupied for tactical reasons ▷ vb **10** to put in the proper or usual place; locate ▶ HISTORY Latin *ponere* to place > **positional** adj

positive adj **1** expressing certainty: *a positive answer* **2** definite or certain: *are you absolutely positive about the date?* **3** tending to emphasize what is good; constructive: *positive thinking* **4** tending towards progress or improvement: *investment that could have a positive impact on the company's fortunes* **5** *philosophy* constructive rather than sceptical **6** *informal* complete; downright:

a positive delight **7** *maths* having a value greater than zero: *a positive number* **8** *grammar* denoting the unmodified form of an adjective as opposed to its comparative or superlative form **9** *physics* (of an electric charge) having an opposite charge to that of an electron **10** *physics* short for **electropositive 11** *med* (of the result of an examination or test) indicating the presence of a suspected condition or organism ▷ n **12** something positive **13** *maths* a quantity greater than zero **14** *photog* a print showing an image whose colours and tones correspond to those of the original subject **15** *grammar* the positive degree of an adjective or adverb **16** a positive object, such as a terminal in a cell ▶ HISTORY Late Latin *positivus* > **positively** adv > **positiveness** or **positivity** n

positive discrimination n the provision of special opportunities for a disadvantaged group

positive vetting n *Brit* the thorough checking of all aspects of a person's life to ensure his or her suitability for a position that may involve national security

positivism n a system of philosophy that accepts only things that can be seen or proved > **positivist** n, adj

positron n *physics* the antiparticle of the electron, having the same mass but an equal and opposite charge ▶ HISTORY *posi(tive)* + *(elec)tron*

posse (poss-ee) n **1** *US* a selected group of men on whom the sheriff may call for assistance **2** *informal* a group of friends or associates: *a posse of reporters* **3** (in W Canada) a troop of horses and riders who perform at rodeos ▶ HISTORY Latin: to be able

possess vb **1** to have as one's property; own **2** to have a quality or attribute: *he possessed an innate elegance, authority, and wit on screen* **3** to gain control over or dominate: *absolute terror possessed her* ▶ HISTORY Latin *possidere* > **possessor** n

possessed adj **1** (foll. by *of*) owning or having: *he is possessed of a calm maturity far beyond his years* **2** under the influence of a powerful force, such as a spirit or strong emotion: *possessed by the devil; she was possessed by a frenzied urge to get out of Moscow*

possession n **1** the state of possessing; ownership: *how had this compromising picture come into the possession of the press?* **2** anything that is possessed **3 possessions** wealth or property **4** the state of being controlled by or as if by evil spirits **5** the occupancy of land or property: *troops had taken possession of the airport* **6** a territory subject to a foreign state **7** the criminal offence of having something illegal on one's person: *arrested for drug dealing and possession* **8** *sport* control of the ball by a team or player: *City had most of the possession, but couldn't score*

possessive adj **1** of possession **2** desiring excessively to possess or dominate: *a possessive husband* **3** *grammar* denoting a form of a noun or pronoun used to convey possession, as *my* or *Harry's*: *a possessive pronoun* ▷ n **4** *grammar* **a** the possessive case **b** a word in the possessive case > **possessiveness** n

possessive case n grammar (in some languages) a grammatical case used to indicate a relation of ownership

possibility n, pl **-ties** 1 the state of being possible 2 anything that is possible 3 a competitor or candidate with a chance of success 4 a future prospect or potential: *all sorts of possibilities began to open up*

possible adj 1 capable of existing, happening, or proving true: *the earliest possible time* 2 capable of being done: *I am grateful to the library staff for making this work possible* 3 having potential: *a possible buyer* 4 feasible but less than probable: *it's possible that's what he meant, but I doubt it* ▷ n 5 same as **possibility** (sense 3) ▶ HISTORY Latin *possibilis*

possibly adv 1 perhaps or maybe 2 by any means; at all: *he can't possibly come*

possum n 1 informal an opossum 2 Austral & NZ a phalanger 3 **play possum** to pretend to be dead, ignorant, or asleep in order to deceive an opponent

post¹ n 1 an official system of mail delivery 2 letters or packages that are transported and delivered by the Post Office; mail 3 a single collection or delivery of mail 4 a postbox or post office: *take this to the post* 5 computers a message or article published on a website ▷ vb 6 to send by post 7 computers to publish (a message or article) on a website 8 book-keeping **a** to enter (an item) in a ledger **b** (often foll. by up) to enter all paper items in (a ledger) 9 **keep someone posted** to inform someone regularly of the latest news ▶ HISTORY Latin *posita* something placed

post² n 1 a length of wood, metal, or concrete fixed upright to support or mark something 2 horse racing **a** either of two upright poles marking the beginning and end of a racecourse **b** the finish of a horse race ▷ vb 3 (sometimes foll. by up) to put up (a notice) in a public place 4 to publish (a name) on a list ▶ HISTORY Latin *postis*

post³ n 1 a position to which a person is appointed; job 2 a position to which a soldier or guard is assigned for duty 3 a permanent military establishment 4 Brit either of two military bugle calls (**first post** and **last post**) giving notice of the time to retire for the night ▷ vb 5 Brit & Austral to send (someone) to a new place to work 6 to assign to or station at a particular place or position: *guards were posted at the doors* ▶ HISTORY French *poste*, from Latin *ponere* to place

post- prefix 1 after in time: *postgraduate* 2 behind: *postorbital* ▶ HISTORY Latin

postage n the charge for sending a piece of mail by post

postal adj of a Post Office or the mail-delivery service

postal order n Brit & Austral a written money order sent by post and cashed at a post office by the person who receives it

postbag n 1 chiefly Brit a mailbag 2 the mail received by a magazine, radio programme, or public figure

postbox n same as **letter box** (sense 2)

postcard n a card, often with a picture on one side, for sending a message by post without an envelope

postcode n a system of letters and numbers used to aid the sorting of mail

postdate vb **-dating, -dated** 1 to write a future date on (a cheque or document) 2 to occur at a later date than 3 to assign a date to (an event or period) that is later than its previously assigned date

poster n 1 a large notice displayed in a public place as an advertisement 2 a large printed picture

poste restante n a post-office department where mail is kept until it is called for ▶ HISTORY French, literally: mail remaining

posterior n 1 formal or humorous the buttocks ▷ adj 2 at the back of or behind something: *posterior leg muscles* 3 coming after in a series or time ▶ HISTORY Latin: latter

posterity n 1 future generations 2 all of one's descendants ▶ HISTORY Latin *posterus* coming after

postern n a small back door or gate ▶ HISTORY Old French *posterne*

post-free adv, adj 1 Brit & Austral with the postage prepaid 2 free of postal charge

postgraduate n 1 a person who is studying for a more advanced qualification after obtaining a degree ▷ adj 2 of or for postgraduates

posthaste adv with great speed

posthumous (poss-tume-uss) adj 1 happening after one's death 2 born after the death of one's father 3 (of a book) published after the author's death ▶ HISTORY Latin *postumus* the last > **posthumously** adv

postie n Scot, Austral & NZ, informal a postman

postilion or **postillion** n (esp. formerly) a person who rides one of a pair of horses drawing a coach ▶ HISTORY French *postillon*

postimpressionism n a movement in painting in France at the end of the 19th century which rejected Impressionism but adapted its use of pure colour to paint with greater subjective emotion > **postimpressionist** n, adj

posting n 1 a job to which someone is assigned by his or her employer which involves moving to a particular town or country: *Bonn was his third posting overseas* 2 computers a message sent to a bulletin board, website, etc. and intended for access by every user

postman or fem **postwoman** n, pl **-men** or **-women** a person who collects and delivers mail as a profession

postmark n 1 an official mark stamped on mail, showing the place and date of posting ▷ vb 2 to put such a mark on (mail)

postmaster n 1 Also (fem): **postmistress** an official in charge of a post office 2 the person who manages the e-mail at a site

postmaster general n, pl **postmasters general** the executive head of the postal service

postmortem n 1 In full: **postmortem examination** medical examination of a dead body   657 to discover the cause of death **2** analysis of a recent event: *a postmortem on the party's recent appalling by-election results* ▷ *adj* **3** occurring after death ▶ HISTORY Latin, literally: after death

postnatal *adj* occurring after childbirth: *postnatal depression*

post office *n* a building where stamps are sold and postal business is conducted

Post Office *n* a government department responsible for postal services

postoperative *adj* of or occurring in the period after a surgical operation

postpone *vb* **-poning, -poned** to put off until a future time ▶ HISTORY Latin *postponere* to put after > **postponement** *n*

postpositive *adj grammar* (of an adjective) placed after the word it modifies

postscript *n* a message added at the end of a letter, after the signature ▶ HISTORY Late Latin *postscribere* to write after

postulant *n* an applicant for admission to a religious order ▶ HISTORY Latin *postulare* to ask

postulate *formal vb* **-lating, -lated** **1** to assume to be true as the basis of an argument or theory **2** to ask, demand, or claim ▷ *n* **3** something postulated ▶ HISTORY Latin *postulare* to ask for > **postulation** *n*

posture *n* **1** a position or way in which a person stands, walks, etc.: *good posture* **2** a mental attitude: *a cooperative posture* **3** an affected attitude: *an intellectual posture* ▷ *vb* **-turing, -tured** **4** to behave in an exaggerated way to attract attention **5** to assume an affected attitude ▶ HISTORY Latin *positura* > **postural** *adj*

posy *n, pl* **-sies** a small bunch of flowers ▶ HISTORY variant of *poesy*

pot¹ *n* **1** a round deep container, often with a handle and lid, used for cooking **2** the amount that a pot will hold **3** short for **flowerpot, teapot** **4** a handmade piece of pottery **5** *billiards etc.* a shot by which a ball is pocketed **6** a chamber pot **7** the money in the pool in gambling games **8** (often *pl*) *informal* a large sum of money **9** *informal* a cup or other trophy **10** See **potbelly** **11** **go to pot** to go to ruin ▷ *vb* **potting, potted** **12** to put (a plant) in soil in a flowerpot **13** *billiards etc.* to pocket (a ball) **14** to preserve (food) in a pot **15** to shoot (game) for food rather than for sport **16** to shoot casually or without careful aim **17** *informal* to capture or win ▶ HISTORY Old English *pott*

pot² *n slang* cannabis ▶ HISTORY perhaps from Mexican Indian *potiguaya*

potable (pote-a-bl) *adj formal* drinkable ▶ HISTORY Latin *potare* to drink

potash *n* **1** potassium carbonate, used as fertilizer **2** a compound containing potassium: *permanganate of potash* ▶ HISTORY from *pot ashes*, because originally obtained by evaporating the lye of wood ashes in pots

potassium *n chem* a light silvery element of the alkali metal group. Symbol: K ▶ HISTORY New Latin *potassa* potash

potassium nitrate *n* a crystalline compound used in gunpowders, fertilizers, and as a preservative for foods (**E252**)

potato *n, pl* **-toes** **1** a starchy vegetable that grows underground **2** the plant from which this vegetable is obtained ▶ HISTORY Spanish *patata*, from a Native American language

potato beetle *n* same as **Colorado beetle**

potbelly *n, pl* **-lies** **1** a bulging belly **2** a person with such a belly

potboiler *n informal* an inferior work of art produced quickly to make money

pot-bound *adj* (of a pot plant) having roots too big for its pot, so that it is unable to grow further

poteen *or* **poitín** *n* (in Ireland) illegally made alcoholic drink ▶ HISTORY Irish *poitín* little pot

potent *adj* **1** having great power or influence **2** (of arguments) persuasive or forceful **3** highly effective: *a potent poison* **4** (of a male) capable of having sexual intercourse ▶ HISTORY Latin *potens* able > **potency** *n*

potentate *n* a ruler or monarch ▶ HISTORY Latin *potens* powerful

potential *adj* **1 a** possible but not yet actual: *potential buyers* **b** capable of being or becoming; latent: *potential danger* ▷ *n* **2** ability or talent not yet in full use: *she has great potential as a painter* **3** In full: **electric potential** the work required to transfer a unit positive electric charge from an infinite distance to a given point ▶ HISTORY Latin *potentia* power > **potentially** *adv*

potential difference *n* the difference in electric potential between two points in an electric field, measured in volts

potential energy *n* the energy which an object has stored up because of its position

potentiality *n, pl* **-ties** latent capacity for becoming or developing

potherb *n* a plant whose leaves, flowers, or stems are used in cooking

pothole *n* **1** a hole in the surface of a road **2** a deep hole in a limestone area

potholing *n* the sport of exploring underground caves ▶ **potholer** *n*

pothook *n* **1** an S-shaped hook for suspending a pot over a fire **2** an S-shaped mark in handwriting

potion *n* a drink of medicine, poison, or some supposedly magic liquid ▶ HISTORY Latin *potio* a drink, esp. a poisonous one

potoroo *n, pl* **-roos** an Australian leaping rodent

potpourri (po-poor-ee) *n, pl* **-ris** **1** a fragrant mixture of dried flower petals **2** an assortment or medley ▶ HISTORY French, literally: rotten pot

Potsdam Conference *n history* a conference held in 1945 between British, US, and Soviet leaders, to establish principles for the Allied occupation of Germany after World War II

potsherd *n* a broken piece of pottery ▶ HISTORY *pot* + *schoord* piece of broken crockery

pot shot *n* **1** a shot taken without careful aim **2** a shot fired at an animal within easy range

pottage *n* a thick soup or stew ▶ HISTORY Old French *potage* contents of a pot

potted *adj* **1** grown in a pot: *potted plant* **2** cooked or preserved in a pot: *potted shrimps* **3** *informal* shortened or abridged: *a potted history*

potter¹ *n* a person who makes pottery

potter² *or esp US & Canad* **putter** *vb* **1 potter about** *or* **around** *or* **away** to be busy in a pleasant but aimless way: *he potters away doing God knows what all day* **2** to move with little energy or direction: *I saw him pottering off to see to his canaries* ▶ HISTORY Old English *potian* to thrust

pottery *n, pl* **-teries 1** articles made from baked clay **2** a place where such articles are made **3** the craft of making such articles

potting shed *n* a garden hut in which plants are put in flowerpots and potting materials are stored

potty¹ *adj* **-tier, -tiest** *informal* **1** slightly crazy **2** trivial or insignificant **3** (foll. by *about*) very keen (on) ▶ HISTORY origin unknown > **pottiness** *n*

potty² *n, pl* **-ties** a bowl used as a toilet by a small child

pouch *n* **1** a small bag **2** a baglike pocket in various animals, such as the cheek fold in hamsters ▷ *vb* **3** to place in or as if in a pouch **4** to make or be made into a pouch ▶ HISTORY Old French *poche* bag

pouf *or* **pouffe** (**poof**) *n* a large solid cushion used as a seat ▶ HISTORY French

poulterer *n Brit* a person who sells poultry

poultice (**pole**-tiss) *n med* a moist dressing, often heated, applied to painful and swollen parts of the body ▶ HISTORY Latin *puls* a thick porridge

poultry *n* domestic fowls ▶ HISTORY Old French *pouletrie*

pounce *vb* **pouncing, pounced 1** (often foll. by *on* or *upon*) to spring upon suddenly to attack or capture ▷ *n* **2** the act of pouncing; a spring or swoop ▶ HISTORY origin unknown

pound¹ *n* **1** the standard monetary unit of the United Kingdom and some other countries, made up of 100 pence. Official name: **pound sterling** **2** the standard monetary unit of various other countries, such as Egypt and Syria **3** a unit of weight made up of 16 ounces and equal to 0.454 kilograms ▶ HISTORY Old English *pund*

pound² *vb* **1** (sometimes foll. by *on* or *at*) to hit heavily and repeatedly **2** to crush to pieces or to powder **3** (foll. by *out*) to produce, by typing heavily **4** (of the heart) to throb heavily **5** to run with heavy steps ▶ HISTORY Old English *pūnian*

pound³ *n* an enclosure for stray dogs or officially removed vehicles ▶ HISTORY Old English *pund-*

poundage *n* **1** a charge of so much per pound of weight **2** a charge of so much per pound sterling

-pounder *n combining form* **1** something weighing a specified number of pounds: *a 200-pounder* **2** something worth a specified number of pounds: *a ten-pounder* **3** a gun that discharges a shell weighing a specified number of pounds: *a two-pounder*

pour *vb* **1** to flow or cause to flow out in a stream **2** to rain heavily **3** to be given or obtained in large amounts: *foreign aid is pouring into Iran* **4** to move together in large numbers: *the fans poured onto the pitch* ▶ HISTORY origin unknown

pout *vb* **1** to thrust out (the lips) sullenly or provocatively **2** to swell out; protrude ▷ *n* **3** a pouting ▶ HISTORY origin unknown

pouter *n* a breed of domestic pigeon that can puff out its crop

poverty *n* **1** the state of lacking adequate food or money **2** lack or scarcity: *a poverty of information* **3** inferior quality or inadequacy: *the poverty of political debate in this country* ▶ HISTORY Old French *poverté*

poverty line *n* the minimum income considered necessary to be able to live

poverty-stricken *adj* extremely poor

poverty trap *n Brit, Austral & NZ* the situation of being unable to raise one's living standard because any extra income would result in state benefits being reduced or withdrawn

pow *interj* an exclamation to indicate that a collision or explosion has taken place

POW prisoner of war

powder *n* **1** a substance in the form of tiny loose particles **2** a medicine or cosmetic in this form ▷ *vb* **3** to cover or sprinkle with powder ▶ HISTORY Old French *poldre*, from Latin *pulvis* dust > **powdery** *adj*

powdered *adj* **1** sold in the form of a powder, esp. one which has been formed by grinding or drying the original material: *powdered milk* **2** covered or made up with a cosmetic in the form of a powder: *liveried footmen in powdered wigs*

powder puff *n* a soft pad used to apply cosmetic powder to the skin

powder room *n* a ladies' cloakroom or toilet

power *n* **1** ability to do something **2** (often pl) a specific ability or faculty **3** political, financial, or social force or authority: *men's use of power over women in a subordinate position in the workforce; economic power is the bedrock of political power* **4** a position of control, esp. over the running of a country: *he seized power in a coup in 1966* **5** a state with political, industrial, or military strength **6** a person or group having authority **7** a prerogative or privilege: *the power of veto* **8** official or legal authority **9** *maths* the value of a number or quantity raised to some exponent **10** *physics, engineering* a measure of the rate of doing work expressed as the work done per unit time **11** the rate at which electrical energy is fed into or taken from a device or system, measured in watts **12** mechanical energy as opposed to manual labour **13** a particular form of energy: *nuclear power* **14** the magnifying capacity of a lens or optical system **15** *informal* a great deal: *a power of good* **16 the powers that be** established authority ▷ *vb* **17** to supply with power ▷ *adj* **18** producing or using electrical energy: *a large selection of power tools* ▶ HISTORY Anglo-Norman *poer*

power cut *n* a temporary interruption in the supply of electricity

powerful *adj* **1** having great power **2** extremely effective: *a powerful drug* > **powerfully** *adv* > **powerfulness** *n*

powerhouse *n* **1** *informal* a forceful person or thing **2** an electrical generating station

powerless *adj* without control or authority > **powerlessly** *adv* > **powerlessness** *n*

power of attorney *n* **1** legal authority to act for another person **2** the document conferring such authority

power point *n* an electrical socket fitted into a wall for plugging in electrical appliances

power pole *n* *Austral & NZ* a pole carrying an overhead power line

power-sharing *n* a political arrangement in which opposing groups in a society participate in government

power station *n* an installation for generating and distributing electricity

power steering *n* a type of steering in vehicles in which the turning of the steering wheel is assisted by power from the engine

power supply *n* *science* a source of energy such as electricity, gas, etc.

powwow *n* **1** a talk or meeting **2** a meeting of Native Americans of N America ▷ *vb* **3** to hold a powwow ▶ **HISTORY** from a Native American language

pox *n* **1** a disease in which pus-filled blisters or pimples form on the skin **2 the pox** *informal* syphilis ▶ **HISTORY** changed from *pocks*, plural of *pock*

pp 1 past participle **2** (in signing documents on behalf of someone else) by delegation to ▶ **HISTORY** Latin *per procurationem*

pp. pages

PPS 1 parliamentary private secretary **2** additional postscript ▶ **HISTORY** Latin *post postscriptum*

PPTA (in New Zealand) Post Primary Teachers Association

PQ 1 Province of Quebec **2** (in Canada) Parti Québecois

PQE *n* **1** post-qualification education **2** post-qualification experience

pr *pl* **prs** pair

Pr *chem* praseodymium

PR 1 proportional representation **2** public relations

pr. 1 price **2** pronoun

practicable *adj* **1** capable of being done **2** usable ▶ **HISTORY** French *praticable* > **practicability** *n*

practical *adj* **1** involving experience or actual use rather than theory **2** concerned with everyday matters: *the kind of practical and emotional upheaval that divorce can bring* **3** sensible, useful, and effective rather than fashionable or attractive: *it's a marvellous design, because it's comfortable, it's practical, and it actually looks good* **4** involving the simple basics: *practical skills* **5** being very close to (a state); virtual: *it's a practical certainty* ▷ *n* **6** an examination or lesson in which something has to be made or done ▶ **HISTORY** Greek *praktikos*, from *prassein* to experience > **practicality** *n* > **practically** *adv*

practical joke *n* a trick intended to make someone look foolish > **practical joker** *n*

practice *n* **1** something done regularly or repeatedly **2** repetition of an activity in order to gain skill: *regular practice is essential if you want to play an instrument well* **3** the business or surgery of a doctor or lawyer **4** the act of doing something: *I'm not sure how effective these methods will be when put into practice* **5 in practice a** what actually happens as distinct from what is supposed to happen: *many ideas which look good on paper just don't work in practice* **b** skilled in something through having had a lot of regular recent experience at it: *I still go shooting, just to keep in practice* **6 out of practice** not having had much regular recent experience at an activity: *although out of practice, I still love playing my violin* ▶ **HISTORY** Greek *praktikē* practical work

practise *or US* **practice** *vb* **-tising, -tised** *or US* **-ticing, -ticed 1** to do repeatedly in order to gain skill **2** to take part in or follow (a religion, etc.): *none of them practise Islam* **3** to work at (a profession): *he originally intended to practise medicine* **4** to do regularly: *they practise meditation* ▶ **HISTORY** Greek *prattein* to do

practitioner *n* a person who practises a profession

praetor (**pree**-tor) *n* (in ancient Rome) a senior magistrate ranking just below the consuls ▶ **HISTORY** Latin > **praetorian** *adj, n*

pragmatic *adj* **1** concerned with practical consequences rather than theory **2** *philosophy* of pragmatism ▶ **HISTORY** Greek *pragmatikos* > **pragmatically** *adv*

pragmatism *n* **1** policy dictated by practical consequences rather than by theory **2** *philosophy* the doctrine that the content of a concept consists only in its practical applicability > **pragmatist** *n, adj*

Prague Spring *n* *history* a period in 1968 when Alexander Dubček, first secretary of the Czechoslovak Communist Party, attempted to reform communism in Czechoslovakia. His reforms were brought to an end by Soviet occupation

prairie *n* (often *pl*) a large treeless area of grassland of North America ▶ **HISTORY** French, from Latin *pratum* meadow

prairie dog *n* a rodent that lives in burrows in the N American prairies

praise *vb* **praising, praised 1** to express admiration or approval for **2** to express thanks and worship to (one's God) ▷ *n* **3** the expression of admiration or approval **4 sing someone's praises** to praise someone highly ▶ **HISTORY** Latin *pretium* prize

praiseworthy *adj* deserving praise; commendable

praline (**prah**-leen) *n* a sweet made of nuts with caramelized sugar ▶ **HISTORY** French

pram *n* a four-wheeled carriage for a baby, pushed by a person on foot ▶ **HISTORY** altered from *perambulator*

prance *vb* **prancing, pranced 1** to walk with exaggerated movements **2** (of an animal) to move with high springing steps ▷ *n* **3** the act of prancing ▶ **HISTORY** origin unknown

prang *old-fashioned slang n* **1** a crash in an aircraft or car ▷ *vb* **2** to crash or damage (an aircraft or car) ▶ HISTORY perhaps imitative

prank *n* a mischievous trick ▶ HISTORY origin unknown > **prankster** *n*

praseodymium (pray-zee-oh-**dim**-ee-um) *n* *chem* a silvery-white element of the lanthanide series of metals. Symbol: Pr ▶ HISTORY New Latin

prat *n* *Brit, Austral & NZ, slang* an incompetent or ineffectual person ▶ HISTORY probably special use of earlier *prat* buttocks, origin unknown

prattle *vb* **-tling, -tled 1** to chatter in a foolish or childish way ▷ *n* **2** foolish or childish talk ▶ HISTORY Middle Low German *pratelen* to chatter

prawn *n* a small edible shellfish ▶ HISTORY origin unknown

praxis *n* **1** practice as opposed to the theory **2** accepted practice or custom ▶ HISTORY Greek: deed, action

pray *vb* **1** to say prayers (to one's God) **2** to ask earnestly; beg ▷ *adv* **3** *archaic* I beg you; please: *pray, leave us alone* ▶ HISTORY Latin *precari* to implore

prayer[1] *n* **1** a thanksgiving or an appeal spoken to one's God **2** a set form of words used in praying: *the Lord's Prayer* **3** an earnest request **4** the practice of praying: *call the faithful to prayer* **5** (often pl) a form of devotion spent mainly praying: *morning prayers* **6** something prayed for

prayer[2] *n* a person who prays

prayer book *n* a book of prayers used in church or at home

prayer mat *or* **prayer rug** *n* the small carpet on which a Muslim performs his or her daily prayers

prayer wheel *n* *Buddhism* (in Tibet) a cylinder inscribed with prayers, each turning of which is counted as an uttered prayer

praying mantis *n* same as **mantis**

pre- *prefix* before in time or position: *predate; pre-eminent* ▶ HISTORY Latin *prae*

preach *vb* **1** to talk on a religious theme as part of a church service **2** to speak in support of (something) in a moralizing way ▶ HISTORY Latin *praedicare* to proclaim

preacher *n* a person who preaches

preamble *n* an introduction that comes before something spoken or written ▶ HISTORY Latin *prae* before + *ambulare* to walk

prearranged *adj* arranged beforehand > **prearrangement** *n*

prebend *n* **1** the allowance paid by a cathedral or collegiate church to a canon or member of the chapter **2** the land or tithe from which this is paid ▶ HISTORY Old French *prébende* > **prebendal** *adj*

prebendary *n, pl* **-daries** a member of the clergy who is a member of the chapter of a cathedral

Precambrian *or* **Pre-Cambrian** *adj* *geol* of the earliest geological era, lasting from about 4500 million years ago to 600 million years ago

precancerous *adj* relating to cells that show signs that they may develop cancer

precarious *adj* (of a position or situation) dangerous or insecure ▶ HISTORY Latin *precarius* obtained by begging > **precariously** *adv*

precaution *n* an action taken in advance to prevent an undesirable event ▶ HISTORY Latin *prae* before + *cavere* to beware > **precautionary** *adj*

precede *vb* **-ceding, -ceded** to go or be before (someone or something) in time, place, or rank ▶ HISTORY Latin *praecedere*

precedence (**press**-ee-denss) *n* formal order of rank or position

precedent *n* **1** a previous occurrence used to justify taking the same action in later similar situations **2** *law* a judicial decision that serves as an authority for deciding a later case ▷ *adj* **3** preceding

precentor *n* a person who leads the singing in church services ▶ HISTORY Latin *prae* before + *canere* to sing

precept *n* **1** a rule of conduct **2** a rule for morals **3** *law* a writ or warrant ▶ HISTORY Latin *praeceptum* > **preceptive** *adj*

preceptor *n* *rare* an instructor > **preceptorial** *adj*

precession *n* **1** the act of preceding **2** the motion of a spinning body, in which the axis of rotation sweeps out a cone **3** **precession of the equinoxes** the slightly earlier occurrence of the equinoxes each year ▶ HISTORY Latin *praecedere* to precede

precinct *n* **1** *Brit, Austral & S African* an area in a town closed to traffic: *a shopping precinct* **2** *Brit, Austral & S African* an enclosed area around a building **3** *US* an administrative area of a city ▶ HISTORY Latin *praecingere* to surround

precincts *pl n* the surrounding region

precious *adj* **1** very costly or valuable: *precious jewellery* **2** loved and treasured **3** very affected in speech, manners, or behaviour **4** *informal* worthless: *nothing is too good for his precious dog* ▷ *adv* **5** *informal* very: *there's precious little to do in this town* ▶ HISTORY Latin *pretiosus* valuable

precious metal *n* gold, silver, or platinum

precious stone *n* a rare mineral, such as diamond, ruby, or opal, that is highly valued as a gem

precipice *n* the very steep face of a cliff ▶ HISTORY Latin *praecipitium* steep place

precipitant *adj* **1** hasty or rash **2** rushing or falling rapidly ▷ *n* **3** something which helps bring about an event or condition: *stressful events are often the precipitant for a manic attack*

precipitate *vb* **-tating, -tated 1** to cause to happen earlier than expected: *the scandal could bring the government down, precipitating a general election* **2** to condense or cause to condense and fall as snow or rain **3** *chem* to cause to be deposited in solid form from a solution **4** to throw from a height: *the encircled soldiers chose to precipitate themselves into the ocean* ▷ *adj* **5** done rashly or hastily **6** rushing ahead ▷ *n* **7** *chem* a precipitated solid ▶ HISTORY Latin *praecipitare* to throw down headlong

p

precipitation n **1** the formation of a chemical precipitate **2** meteorol **a** rain, hail, snow, or sleet formed by condensation of water vapour in the atmosphere **b** the falling of these **3** rash haste: *they decamped with the utmost precipitation*

precipitous adj **1** very steep: *precipitous cliffs* **2** very quick and severe: *a precipitous decline* **3** rapid and unplanned; hasty: *European governments urged the Americans not to make a precipitous decision*

précis (**pray**-see) n, pl **précis 1** a short summary of a longer text ▷ vb **2** to make a précis of ▶ HISTORY French

precise adj **1** particular or exact: *this precise moment* **2** strictly correct in amount or value: *precise measurements* **3** working with total accuracy: *precise instruments* **4** strict in observing rules or standards ▶ HISTORY Latin *prae* before + *caedere* to cut > **precisely** adv

precision n **1** the quality of being precise ▷ adj **2** accurate: *precision engineering*

preclude vb **-cluding, -cluded** formal to make impossible to happen ▶ HISTORY Latin *prae* before + *claudere* to close

precocious adj having developed or matured early or too soon ▶ HISTORY Latin *prae* early + *coquere* to ripen > **precocity** n

precognition n psychol the alleged ability to foresee future events ▶ HISTORY Latin *praecognoscere* to foresee

preconceived adj (of ideas, etc.) formed without real experience or reliable information > **preconception** n

precondition n something that is necessary before something else can come about

precursor n **1** something that comes before and signals something to follow; a forerunner **2** a predecessor ▶ HISTORY Latin *praecursor* one who runs in front

pred. predicate

predacious adj (of animals) habitually hunting and killing other animals for food ▶ HISTORY Latin *praeda* plunder

predate vb **-dating, -dated 1** to occur at an earlier date than **2** to write a date on (a document) that is earlier than the actual date

predator n an animal that kills and eats other animals

predatory (**pred**-a-tree) adj **1** (of animals) habitually hunting and killing other animals for food **2** eager to gain at the expense of others ▶ HISTORY Latin *praedari* to pillage

predecease vb **-ceasing, -ceased** to die before (someone else)

predecessor n **1** a person who precedes another in an office or position **2** an ancestor **3** something that precedes something else: *the library will be more extravagant than its predecessors* ▶ HISTORY Latin *prae* before + *decedere* to go away

predestination n Christian theol the belief that future events have already been decided by God

predestined adj Christian theol determined in advance by God ▶ HISTORY Latin *praedestinare* to resolve beforehand

predicable adj capable of being predicated

predicament n an embarrassing or difficult situation ▶ HISTORY See PREDICATE

predicant (**pred**-ik-ant) adj **1** of preaching ▷ n **2** a member of a religious order founded for preaching, usually a Dominican ▶ HISTORY Latin *praedicans* preaching

predicate n **1** grammar the part of a sentence in which something is said about the subject **2** logic something that is asserted about the subject of a proposition ▷ vb **-cating, -cated 3** to base or found: *political aims which are predicated upon a feminist view of women's oppression* **4** to declare or assert: *forecasters predicated that the rainfall would end by 10am today* **5** logic to assert (something) about the subject of a proposition ▶ HISTORY Latin *praedicare* to assert publicly > **predication** n > **predicative** adj

predict vb to tell about in advance; prophesy ▶ HISTORY Latin *praedicere* > **predictable** adj > **predictably** adv > **predictor** n

prediction n **1** the act of forecasting in advance **2** something that is forecast in advance

predictive adj **1** relating to or able to make predictions **2** (of a word processer) able to complete words after only part of a word has been keyed

predikant (pred-ik-**ant**) n a minister in the Dutch Reformed Church in South Africa ▶ HISTORY Dutch

predilection n formal a preference or liking ▶ HISTORY French *prédilection*

predispose vb **-posing, -posed** (often foll. by to) **1** to influence (someone) in favour of something: *some scientists' social class background predisposes them to view the natural world in a certain way* **2** to make (someone) susceptible to something: *a high-fat diet appears to predispose men towards heart disease* > **predisposition** n

predominant adj being more important or noticeable than others: *improved living conditions probably played the predominant role in reducing disease in the nineteenth century* > **predominance** n > **predominantly** adv

predominate vb **-nating, -nated 1** to be the most important or controlling aspect or part: *the image of brutal repression that has tended to predominate since the protests were crushed* **2** to form the greatest part or be most common: *women predominate in this gathering* ▶ HISTORY Latin *prae* before + *dominari* to rule

pre-eminent adj outstanding > **pre-eminence** n

pre-empt vb to prevent an action by doing something which makes it pointless or impossible: *he pre-empted his expulsion from the party by resigning*

pre-emption n law the purchase of or right to buy property in advance of others ▶ HISTORY Medieval Latin *praeemere* to buy beforehand

pre-emptive adj mil designed to damage or destroy an enemy's attacking strength before it can be used: *a pre-emptive strike*

preen *vb* **1** (of birds) to clean or trim (feathers) with the beak **2** to smarten (oneself) carefully **3** (often foll. by *on*) to be self-satisfied ▷ HISTORY Middle English *preinen*

prefab *n* a prefabricated house

prefabricated *adj* (of a building) made in shaped sections for quick assembly

preface (**pref**-iss) *n* **1** an introduction to a book, usually explaining its intention or content **2** anything introductory ▷ *vb* **-acing, -aced 3** to say or do something before proceeding to the main part **4** to act as a preface to ▷ HISTORY Latin *praefari* to say in advance

prefatory *adj* concerning a preface ▷ HISTORY Latin *praefari* to say in advance

prefect *n* **1** *Brit, Austral & NZ* a senior pupil in a school with limited power over the behaviour of other pupils **2** (in some countries) the chief administrative officer in a department ▷ HISTORY Latin *praefectus* one put in charge

prefecture *n* the office or area of authority of a prefect

prefer *vb* **-ferring, -ferred 1** to like better: *most people prefer television to reading books* **2** *law* to put (charges) before a court for judgment **3** (often passive) to promote over another or others ▷ HISTORY Latin *praeferre* to carry in front, prefer

preferable *adj* more desirable or suitable > **preferably** *adv*

preference *n* **1** a liking for one thing above the rest **2** a person or thing preferred

preference shares *pl n finance* shares in a company that entitle their owners to receive dividends from profits before ordinary shareholders although the rate of dividend is generally lower than that declared on ordinary shares

preferential *adj* **1** showing preference: *preferential treatment* **2** indicating a special favourable status in business affairs: *the President is to renew China's preferential trading status* **3** indicating a voting system which allows voters to rank candidates in order of preference: *a multi-option referendum with preferential voting*

preferment *n* promotion to a higher position

prefigure *vb* **-uring, -ured 1** to represent or suggest in advance **2** to imagine beforehand

prefix *n* **1** *grammar* a letter or group of letters put at the beginning of a word to make a new word, such as *un-* in *unhappy* **2** a title put before a name, such as *Mr* ▷ *vb* **3** *grammar* to add (a letter or group of letters) as a prefix to the beginning of a word **4** to put before

pregnant *adj* **1** carrying a fetus or fetuses within the womb **2** full of meaning or significance: *a pregnant pause* ▷ HISTORY Latin *praegnans* > **pregnancy** *n*

prehensile *adj* capable of curling round objects and grasping them: *a prehensile tail* ▷ HISTORY Latin *prehendere* to grasp

prehistoric *adj* of man's development before the appearance of the written word > **prehistory** *n*

preindustrial *adj* of a time before the mechanization of industry

prejudge *vb* **-judging, -judged** to judge before knowing all the facts

prejudice *n* **1** an unreasonable or unfair dislike or preference **2** intolerance of or dislike for people because they belong to a specific race, religion, or group: *class prejudice* **3** the act or condition of holding such opinions **4** harm or detriment: *conduct to the prejudice of good order and military discipline* **5 without prejudice** *law* without harm to an existing right or claim ▷ *vb* **-dicing, -diced 6** to cause (someone) to have a prejudice **7** to harm: *the incident prejudiced his campaign* ▷ HISTORY Latin *prae* before + *judicium* sentence

prejudicial *adj* harmful; damaging

prelacy *n, pl* **-cies 1 a** the office or status of a prelate **b** prelates collectively **2** *often offensive* government of the Church by prelates

prelate (**prel**-it) *n* a high-ranking member of the clergy, such as a bishop ▷ HISTORY Church Latin *praelatus*, from Latin *praeferre* to hold in special esteem

preliminary *adj* **1** occurring before or in preparation; introductory ▷ *n, pl* **-naries 2** an action or event occurring before or in preparation for an activity: *the discussions are a preliminary to the main negotiations* **3** a qualifying contest held before a main competition ▷ HISTORY Latin *prae* before + *limen* threshold

prelims *pl n* **1** the pages of a book, such as the title page and contents, which come before the main text **2** the first public examinations in some universities ▷ HISTORY a contraction of *preliminaries*

prelude (**prel**-yewd) *n* **1 a** an introductory movement in music **b** a short piece of music for piano or organ **2** an event introducing or preceding the main event ▷ *vb* **-uding, -uded 3** to act as a prelude to (something) **4** to introduce by a prelude ▷ HISTORY Latin *prae* before + *ludere* to play

premarital *adj* occurring before marriage

premature *adj* **1** happening or done before the normal or expected time: *premature ageing* **2** impulsive or hasty: *a premature judgment* **3** (of a baby) born weeks before the date when it was due to be born ▷ HISTORY Latin *prae* in advance + *maturus* ripe > **prematurely** *adv*

premedication *n surgery* any drugs given to prepare a patient for a general anaesthetic

premeditated *adj* planned in advance > **premeditation** *n*

premenstrual *adj* occurring or experienced before a menstrual period

premenstrual syndrome *or* **tension** *n* symptoms, such as nervous tension, that may be experienced because of hormonal changes in the days before a menstrual period starts

premier *n* **1** a prime minister **2** a head of government of a Canadian province or Australian state ▷ *adj* **3** first in importance or rank: *Torbay, Devon's premier resort* **4** first in occurrence ▷ HISTORY Latin *primus* first > **premiership** *n*

premiere n **1** the first public performance of a film, play, or opera ▷ vb **-ering, -ered 2** to give a premiere of: *the play was premiered last year in Johannesburg* ▶ HISTORY French, feminine of *premier* first

premise or **premiss** n *logic* a statement that is assumed to be true and is used as a basis for an argument ▶ HISTORY Medieval Latin *praemissa* sent on before

premises pl n **1** a piece of land together with its buildings **2** *law* (in a deed) the matters referred to previously

premium n **1** an extra sum of money added to a standard rate, price, or wage: *the superior taste persuades me to pay the premium for bottled water* **2** the (regular) amount paid for an insurance policy **3** the amount above the usual value at which something sells: *some even pay a premium of up to 15 per cent for the privilege* **4** great value or regard: *we do put a very high premium on common sense* **5 at a premium a** in great demand, usually because of scarcity **b** at a higher price than usual ▶ HISTORY Latin *praemium* prize

Premium Savings Bonds pl n (in Britain) savings certificates issued by the government, on which no interest is paid, but there is a monthly draw for cash prizes. Also called: **premium bonds**

premonition n a feeling that something unpleasant is going to happen; foreboding ▶ HISTORY Latin *prae* before + *monere* to warn > **premonitory** adj

prenatal adj before birth; during pregnancy

preoccupy vb **-pies, -pying, -pied** to fill the thoughts or mind of (someone) to the exclusion of other things ▶ HISTORY Latin *praeoccupare* to capture in advance > **preoccupation** n

preordained adj decreed or determined in advance

prep n *Brit, informal* short for **preparation** (sense 4)

prep. **1** preparation **2** preparatory **3** preposition

prepacked adj (of goods) sold already wrapped

prepaid adj paid for in advance

preparation n **1** the act of preparing or being prepared **2** (often pl) something done in order to prepare for something else: *to make preparations for a wedding* **3** something that is prepared, such as a medicine **4** *Brit, old-fashioned* **a** homework **b** the period reserved for this

preparatory (prip-**par**-a-tree) adj **1** preparing for: *a preparatory meeting to organize the negotiations* **2** introductory **3 preparatory to** before: *Jack cleared his throat preparatory to speaking*

preparatory school n **1** *Brit & S African* a private school for children between the ages of 6 and 13, generally preparing pupils for public school **2** (in the US) a private secondary school preparing pupils for college

prepare vb **-paring, -pared 1** to make or get ready: *the army prepared for battle* **2** to put together using parts or ingredients: *he had spent most of the afternoon preparing the meal* **3** to equip or outfit, as for an expedition **4 be prepared to** to be willing

and able to: *I'm not prepared to say* ▶ HISTORY Latin *prae* before + *parare* to make ready

preponderant adj greater in amount, force, or influence > **preponderance** n

preposition n a word used before a noun or pronoun to relate it to the other words, for example *in* in *he is in the car* ▶ HISTORY Latin *praepositio* a putting before > **prepositional** adj

prepossessing adj making a favourable impression; attractive

preposterous adj utterly absurd ▶ HISTORY Latin *praeposterus* reversed

prep school n *informal* See **preparatory school**

prepuce (pree-pyewss) n **1** the retractable fold of skin covering the tip of the penis; foreskin **2** the retractable fold of skin covering the tip of the clitoris ▶ HISTORY Latin *praeputium*

Pre-Raphaelite (pree-**raff**-a-lite) n **1** a member of a group of painters in the nineteenth century who revived the style considered typical of Italian painting before Raphael ▷ adj **2** of or in the manner of Pre-Raphaelite painting and painters

prerequisite n **1** something that is required before something else is possible ▷ adj **2** required before something else is possible

prerogative n a special privilege or right ▶ HISTORY Latin *praerogativa* privilege

pres. **1** present (time) **2** presidential

Pres. President

presage (press-ij) vb **-aging, -aged 1** to be a warning or sign of something about to happen: *the windless air presaged disaster* ▷ n **2** an omen **3** a misgiving ▶ HISTORY Latin *praesagire* to perceive beforehand

presbyopia n *med* a gradual inability of the eye to focus on nearby objects ▶ HISTORY Greek *presbus* old man + *ōps* eye

presbyter n **1** (in some Episcopal Churches) an official with administrative and priestly duties **2** (in the Presbyterian Church) an elder ▶ HISTORY Greek *presbuteros* an older man > **presbyterial** adj

presbyterian adj **1** of or designating Church government by lay elders ▷ n **2** someone who supports this type of Church government > **presbyterianism** n

Presbyterian adj **1** of any of the Protestant Churches governed by lay elders ▷ n **2** a member of a Presbyterian Church > **Presbyterianism** n

presbytery n, pl **-teries 1** *Presbyterian Church* a local Church court **2** *RC Church* the residence of a parish priest **3** elders collectively **4** the part of a church east of the choir; a sanctuary ▶ HISTORY see PRESBYTER

preschool adj of or for children below the age of five: *a preschool playgroup*

prescience (press-ee-enss) n *formal* knowledge of events before they happen ▶ HISTORY Latin *praescire* to know beforehand > **prescient** adj

prescribe vb **-scribing, -scribed 1** *med* to recommend the use of (a medicine or other remedy) **2** to lay down as a rule ▶ HISTORY Latin *praescribere* to write previously

prescription *n* **1 a** written instructions from a doctor for the preparation and use of a medicine **b** the medicine prescribed **2** written instructions from an optician specifying the lenses needed to correct bad eyesight **3** a prescribing ▶ HISTORY Legal Latin *praescriptio* an order

prescriptive *adj* **1** laying down rules **2** based on tradition

presence *n* **1** the fact of being in a specified place: *the test detects the presence of sugar in the urine* **2** impressive personal appearance or bearing: *a person of dignified and commanding presence* **3** the company or nearness of a person: *she seemed completely unaware of my presence* **4** mil a force stationed in another country: *the American-led military presence in the Gulf* **5** an invisible spirit felt to be nearby: *I felt a presence in the room* ▶ HISTORY Latin *praesentia* a being before

presence of mind *n* the ability to stay calm and act sensibly in a crisis

present¹ *adj* **1** being in a specified place: *he had been present at the birth of his son* **2** existing or happening now **3** current: *the present exchange rate* **4** grammar of a verb tense used when the action described is happening now ▷ *n* **5** grammar the present tense **6 at present** now **7 for the present** for now; temporarily **8 the present** the time being; now ▷ See also **presents** ▶ HISTORY Latin *praesens*

present² *n* (**prez**-int) **1** a gift ▷ *vb* (pri-**zent**) **2** to introduce (a person) formally to another **3** to introduce to the public: *the Museum of Modern Art is presenting a retrospective of his work* **4** to introduce and compere (a radio or television show) **5** to show or exhibit: *they took advantage of every tax dodge that presented itself* **6** to bring about: *the case presented a large number of legal difficulties* **7** to put forward or submit: *they presented a petition to the Prime Minister* **8** to give or offer formally: *he was presented with a watch to celebrate his twenty-five years with the company* **9** to hand over for action or payment: *to present a bill* **10** to portray in a particular way: *her lawyer presented her as a naive woman who had got into bad company* **11** to aim (a weapon) **12 present arms** to salute with one's weapon ▶ HISTORY Latin *praesentare* to exhibit

presentable *adj* **1** fit to be seen by or introduced to other people **2** acceptable: *the team reached a presentable total* **> presentability** *n*

presentation *n* **1** the act of presenting or being presented **2** the manner of presenting **3** a formal ceremony in which an award is made **4** a public performance, such as a play or a ballet

presenter *n* a person who introduces a radio or television show and links the items in it

presentiment (priz-**zen**-tim-ent) *n* a sense that something unpleasant is about to happen; premonition ▶ HISTORY obsolete French *pressentir* to sense beforehand

presently *adv* **1** soon: *you will understand presently* **2** chiefly Scot, US & Canad at the moment: *these methods are presently being developed*

present participle *n* grammar a form of verb, in English ending in -*ing*, that is used both adjectivally, to describe action happening at the same time as that of the main verb, and in continuous tenses

present perfect or **present perfect tense** *n* grammar a compound tense formed, in English, using *have* or *has* plus a past participle: *have/has eaten* is the present perfect of *eat*

presents *pl n* law used in a deed or document to refer to itself: *know all men by these presents*

present tense *n* grammar a verb tense used to describe action which is happening now

preservative *n* **1** a chemical added to foods to prevent decay ▷ *adj* **2** preventing decay

preserve *vb* **-serving, -served 1** to keep safe from change or extinction; protect: *we are interested in preserving world peace* **2** to protect from decay or damage: *the carefully preserved village of Cregneish* **3** to treat (food) in order to prevent it from decaying **4** to maintain; keep up: *the 1.2% increase in earnings needed to preserve living standards* ▷ *n* **5** an area of interest restricted to a particular person or group: *working-class preserves such as pigeon racing* **6** (usually pl) fruit preserved by cooking in sugar **7** an area where game is kept for private hunting or fishing ▶ HISTORY Latin *prae* before + *servare* to keep safe **> preservation** *n*

preset *vb* **-setting, -set 1** to set the timer on a piece of equipment so that it starts to work at a specific time ▷ *adj* **2** (of equipment) with the controls set in advance

preshrunk *adj* (of fabric or a garment) having been shrunk during manufacture so that further shrinkage will not occur when washed

preside *vb* **-siding, -sided 1** to chair a meeting **2** to exercise authority: *he presided over the burning of the books* ▶ HISTORY Latin *praesidere* to superintend

presidency *n, pl* **-cies** the office or term of a president

president *n* **1** the head of state of a republic, esp. of the US **2** the head of a company, society, or institution **3** a person who presides over a meeting **4** the head of certain establishments of higher education ▶ HISTORY Late Latin *praesidens* ruler **> presidential** *adj*

presidium *n* (in Communist countries) a permanent administrative committee ▶ HISTORY Russian *prezidium*

press¹ *vb* **1** to apply weight or force to: *he pressed the button on the camera* **2** to squeeze: *she pressed his hand* **3** to compress to alter in shape **4** to smooth out creases by applying pressure or heat **5** to make (objects) from soft material by pressing with a mould **6** to crush to force out (juice) **7** to urge (someone) insistently: *they pressed for an answer* **8** to force or compel: *I was pressed into playing rugby at school* **9** to plead or put forward strongly: *they intend to press their claim for damages in the courts* **10** to be urgent: *time presses* **11** (sometimes foll. by *on* or *forward*) to continue in a determined way:

they pressed on with their journey **12** to crowd; push: *shoppers press along the pavements* **13 pressed for** short of: *pressed for time* ▷ *n* **14** any machine that exerts pressure to form or cut materials or to extract liquids or compress solids **15** the art or process of printing **16 go to press** to go to be printed: *when is this book going to press?* **17 the press a** news media collectively, esp. newspapers **b** journalists collectively **18** the opinions and reviews in the newspapers: *the government is not receiving a good press at the moment* **19** the act of pressing or state of being pressed: *at the press of a button* **20** a crowd: *a press of people at the exit* **21** a cupboard for storing clothes or linen ▶ HISTORY Old French *presser*

press² *vb* **1** to recruit (men) forcibly for military service **2** to use for a purpose other than intended: *press into service* ▶ HISTORY from *prest* to recruit soldiers

press agent *n* a person employed to obtain favourable publicity for an individual or organization

press box *n* a room at a sports ground reserved for reporters

press conference *n* an interview for reporters given by a famous person

press gallery *n* an area for newspaper reporters, esp. in a parliament

press gang *n* **1** (formerly) a group of men used to capture men and boys and force them to join the navy ▷ *vb* **press-gang 2** to force (a person) to join the navy by a press gang **3** to persuade (someone) to do something that he or she does not want to do: *he was press-ganged into joining the family business*

pressing *adj* **1** demanding immediate attention ▷ *n* **2** a large number of records or CDs produced at one time

press stud *n* Brit a fastener in which one part with a projecting knob snaps into a hole on another part

press-up *n* an exercise in which the body is raised from and lowered to the floor by straightening and bending the arms

pressure *n* **1** the state of pressing or being pressed **2** the application of force by one body on the surface of another **3** urgent claims or demands: *to work under pressure* **4** a condition that is hard to bear: *the pressure of grief* **5** physics the force applied to a unit area of a surface **6 bring pressure to bear on** to use influence or authority to persuade ▷ *vb* **-suring, -sured 7** to persuade forcefully: *he was pressured into resignation* ▶ HISTORY Late Latin *pressura* a pressing, from Latin *premere* to press

pressure cooker *n* an airtight pot which cooks food quickly by steam under pressure > **pressure-cook** *vb*

pressure gradient *n* meteorol the decrease in atmospheric pressure per unit of horizontal distance, shown on a synoptic chart by the spacing of the isobars

pressure group *n* a group that tries to influence policies or public opinion

pressurize or **-ise** *vb* **-izing, -ized** or **-ising, -ised 1** to increase the pressure in (an aircraft cabin, etc.) in order to maintain approximately atmospheric pressure when the external pressure is low **2** to make insistent demands of (someone): *do not be pressurized into making a decision* > **pressurization** or **-isation** *n*

prestidigitation *n* formal same as **sleight of hand** ▶ HISTORY French > **prestidigitator** *n*

prestige *n* **1** high status or respect resulting from success or achievements: *a symbol of French power and prestige* **2** the power to impress: *a humdrum family car with no prestige* ▶ HISTORY Latin *praestigiae* tricks > **prestigious** *adj*

presto music adv, adj **1** very fast ▷ *n, pl* **-tos 2** a passage to be played very quickly ▶ HISTORY Italian

presumably *adv* one supposes or guesses; probably: *he emerged from what was presumably the kitchen carrying a tray*

presume *vb* **-suming, -sumed 1** to take (something) for granted: *I presume he's dead* **2** to dare (to): *I would not presume to lecture you on medical matters, Dr Jacobs* **3** (foll. by on or upon) to rely or depend: *don't presume on his agreement* **4** (foll. by on or upon) to take advantage (of): *I'm afraid I presumed on Aunt Ginny's generosity* ▶ HISTORY Latin *praesumere* to take in advance > **presumedly** *adv* > **presuming** *adj*

presumption *n* **1** the act of presuming **2** a basis on which an assumption is made **3** bold insolent behaviour **4** a belief or assumption based on reasonable evidence > **presumptive** *adj*

presumptuous *adj* bold and insolent

presuppose *vb* **-posing, -posed 1** to require as a previous condition in order to be true: *the idea of integration presupposes a disintegrated state* **2** to take for granted > **presupposition** *n*

pretence or US **pretense** *n* **1** an action or claim that could mislead people into believing something which is not true: *the pretence that many unemployed people are on 'training schemes'* **2** a false display; affectation: *she abandoned all pretence of work and watched me* **3** a claim, esp. a false one, to a right, title, or distinction **4** make-believe **5** a pretext: *they were placed in a ghetto on the pretence that they would be safe there*

pretend *vb* **1** to claim or give the appearance of (something untrue): *he pretended to be asleep* **2** to make believe: *the children pretended to be pop stars* **3** (foll. by to) to present a claim, esp. a doubtful one: *to pretend to the throne* ▶ HISTORY Latin *praetendere* to stretch forth, feign

pretender *n* a person who makes a false or disputed claim to a throne or title

pretension *n* (often pl) a false claim to merit or importance

pretentious *adj* **1** making (unjustified) claims to special merit or importance: *many critics thought her work and ideas pretentious and empty* **2** vulgarly showy; ostentatious: *a family restaurant with no pretentious furnishing*

preterite or esp US **preterit** (pret-er-it) grammar *n* Also **preterite tense 1** a past tense of verbs, such as *jumped, swam* **2** a verb in this tense ▷ *adj* **3** expressing such a past tense ▶ **HISTORY** Late Latin *praeteritum (tempus)* past (time)

preternatural *adj* beyond what is natural; supernatural ▶ **HISTORY** Latin *praeter naturam* beyond the scope of nature

pretext *n* a false reason given to hide the real one: *delivering the book had been a good pretext for seeing her again* ▶ **HISTORY** Latin *praetextum* disguise, from *praetexere* to weave in front

pretty *adj* **-tier, -tiest 1** attractive in a delicate or graceful way **2** pleasant to look at **3** *informal, often ironic* excellent or fine: *well, this is a pretty state of affairs to have got into* ▷ *adv* **4** *informal* fairly: *I think he and Nicholas got on pretty well* **5 sitting pretty** *informal* in a favourable state ▶ **HISTORY** Old English *prættig* clever > **prettily** *adv* > **prettiness** *n*

pretzel *n* a brittle salted biscuit in the shape of a knot ▶ **HISTORY** from German

Pre-U *n* (in Britain) a public examination for secondary school pupils wishing to enter university, offered as an alternative to A level

prevail *vb* **1** (often foll. by *over* or *against*) to prove superior; gain mastery: *moderate nationalists have until now prevailed over the radicals* **2** to be the most important feature: *a casual good-natured mood prevailed* **3** to be generally established: *this attitude has prevailed for many years* **4 prevail on** or **upon** to succeed in persuading: *he had easily been prevailed upon to accept a lift* ▶ **HISTORY** Latin *praevalere* to be superior in strength

prevailing *adj* **1** widespread: *the prevailing mood* **2** most usual: *elsewhere, the prevailing weather will vary*

prevailing wind *n meteorol* the most frequent wind direction over a given period

prevalent *adj* widespread or common > **prevalence** *n*

prevaricate *vb* **-cating, -cated** to avoid giving a direct or truthful answer ▶ **HISTORY** Latin *praevaricari* to walk crookedly > **prevarication** *n* > **prevaricator** *n*

prevent *vb* **1** to keep from happening: *vitamin C prevented scurvy* (often foll. by *from*) to keep (someone from doing something): *circumstances prevented her from coming* ▶ **HISTORY** Latin *praevenire* > **preventable** *adj* > **prevention** *n*

preventive *adj* **1** intended to prevent or hinder **2** *med* tending to prevent disease ▷ *n* **3** something that serves to prevent **4** *med* any drug or agent that tends to prevent disease. Also: **preventative**

preview *n* **1** an opportunity to see a film, exhibition, or play before it is shown to the public ▷ *vb* **2** to view in advance

previous *adj* **1** coming or happening before **2** *informal* happening too soon; premature: *such criticism is a bit previous because no definite decision has yet been taken* **3 previous to** before ▶ **HISTORY** Latin *praevius* leading the way > **previously** *adv*

prey *n* **1** an animal hunted and killed for food by another animal **2** the victim of a hostile person,

influence, emotion, or illness: *children are falling prey to the disease* **3 bird** or **beast of prey** a bird or animal that kills and eats other birds or animals ▷ *vb* (often foll. by *on* or *upon*) **4** to hunt and kill for food **5** to worry or obsess: *it preyed on his conscience* **6** to make a victim (of others), by profiting at their expense ▶ **HISTORY** Old French *preie*

price *n* **1** the amount of money for which a thing is bought or sold **2** the cost at which something is obtained: *the price of making the wrong decision* **3** *gambling* odds **4 at any price** whatever the price or cost **5 at a price** at a high price **6 what price (something)?** what are the chances of (something) happening now? ▷ *vb* **pricing, priced** **7** to fix the price of **8** to discover the price of ▶ **HISTORY** Latin *pretium*

price-fixing *n* the setting of prices by agreement among producers and distributors

priceless *adj* **1** extremely valuable **2** *informal* extremely amusing

pricey *adj* **pricier, priciest** *informal* expensive

prick *vb* **1** to pierce lightly with a sharp point **2** to cause a piercing sensation (in): *a needle pricked her finger* **3** to cause a sharp emotional pain (in): *the film pricked our consciences about the plight of the Afghan refugees* **4 prick up one's ears a** (of a dog) to make the ears stand erect **b** (of a person) to listen attentively ▷ *n* **5** a sudden sharp pain caused by pricking **6** a mark made by a sharp point **7** a sharp emotional pain: *a prick of conscience* ▶ **HISTORY** Old English *prica* point, puncture

prickle *n* **1** *bot* a thorn or spike on a plant **2** a pricking or stinging sensation ▷ *vb* **-ling, -led 3** to feel a stinging sensation ▶ **HISTORY** Old English *pricel*

prickly *adj* **-lier, -liest 1** having prickles **2** tingling or stinging: *he had a prickly feeling down his back* **3** touchy or irritable: *Canadians are notoriously prickly about being taken for Americans*

prickly heat *n* an itchy rash that occurs in very hot moist weather

prickly pear *n* **1** a tropical cactus with edible oval fruit **2** the fruit of this plant

pride *n* **1** a feeling of satisfaction about one's achievements **2** an excessively high opinion of oneself **3** satisfaction in one's own or another's success or achievements: *his obvious pride in his son's achievements* **4** a sense of dignity and self-respect: *he must swallow his pride and ally himself with his political enemies* **5** one of the better or most admirable parts of something: *the pride of the main courses is the Japanese fish and vegetable tempura* **6** a group of lions **7 pride and joy** the main source of pride: *the car was his pride and joy* **8 pride of place** the most important position ▷ *vb* **priding, prided 9** (foll. by *on* or *upon*) to take pride in (oneself) for ▶ **HISTORY** Old English *prȳde*

priest *n* **1** (in the Christian Church) a person ordained to administer the sacraments and preach **2** a minister of any religion **3** an official who performs religious ceremonies ▶ **HISTORY** Old English *prēost*, apparently from *presbyter* > **priestess** *fem n* > **priesthood** *n* > **priestly** *adj*

prig *n* a person who is smugly self-righteous and narrow-minded ▶ HISTORY origin unknown > **priggish** *adj* > **priggishness** *n*

prim *adj* **primmer, primmest** affectedly proper, or formal, and rather prudish ▶ HISTORY origin unknown > **primly** *adv*

prima ballerina *n* a leading female ballet dancer ▶ HISTORY Italian: first ballerina

primacy *n, pl* **-cies** 1 the state of being first in rank, grade, or order 2 *Christianity* the office of an archbishop

prima donna *n, pl* **prima donnas** 1 a leading female opera singer 2 *informal* a temperamental person ▶ HISTORY Italian: first lady

primaeval *adj* same as **primeval**

prima facie (**prime**-a **fay**-shee) *adj, adv* as it seems at first ▶ HISTORY Latin

prima-facie case *n law* a case in which the evidence against someone is sufficient for it to succeed unless the evidence can be rebutted. A finding by a magistrate that there is a prima facie case to answer means that a case will proceed to a higher court

prima-facie evidence *n law* evidence that is sufficient to establish a fact or to raise a presumption of the truth unless controverted

primal *adj* 1 of basic causes or origins 2 chief or most important ▶ HISTORY Latin *primus* first

primarily *adv* 1 chiefly or mainly 2 originally

primary *adj* 1 first in importance 2 first in position or time, as in a series: *he argued that the country was only in the primary stage of socialism* 3 fundamental or basic: *the new policy will put the emphasis on primary health care rather than hospital care* 4 being the first stage; elementary: *all new recruits participated in the same primary training courses* 5 relating to the education of children up to the age of 11 or 12 6 (of an industry) involving the obtaining of raw materials 7 (of the flight feathers of a bird's wing) outer and longest 8 being the part of an electric circuit in which a changing current causes a current in a neighbouring circuit: *a primary coil* ▷ *n, pl* **-ries** 9 a person or thing that is first in position, time, or importance 10 (in the US) an election in which the voters of a state choose a candidate for office. Full name: **primary election** 11 a primary school 12 a primary colour 13 any of the outer and longest flight feathers of a bird's wing 14 a primary part of an electric circuit ▶ HISTORY Latin *primarius* principal

primary accent *or* **stress** *n linguistics* the strongest accent in a word

primary colours *pl n* 1 *physics* the colours red, green, and blue from which all other colours can be obtained by mixing 2 *art* the colours red, yellow, and blue from which all other colours can be obtained by mixing

primary consumer *n biol* a herbivore. Compare **primary producer, secondary consumer, tertiary consumer**

primary differentiation *n marketing* the real or illusory distinction between competing products in a market

primary industry *n econ, business* an industry concerned with the growing, collecting, or extracting of raw materials. Compare **secondary industry, tertiary industry, quaternary industry**

primary producer *n biol* an organism such as a plant that converts inorganic matter into organic matter and serves as food for a primary consumer. Compare **primary consumer**

primary production *n econ* the process of producing raw materials for industry

primary school *n* 1 (in England and Wales) a school for children between the ages of 5 and 11 2 (in Scotland, Australia and New Zealand) a school for children between the ages of 5 and 12 3 (in the US and Canada) a school equivalent to the first three or four grades of elementary school

primary source *n* a document, diary, or artefact that was created at the time being studied and that offers first-hand evidence of something. Compare **secondary source**

primate[1] *n* a mammal with flexible hands and feet and a highly developed brain, such as a monkey, an ape, or a human being

primate[2] *n* an archbishop ▶ HISTORY Latin *primas* principal

primate city *n geog* the most important city in a country or region in population, economic, and general terms, and one that is likely to be twice the size of the next most important city

prime *adj* 1 first in importance: *the prime aim* 2 of the highest quality: *prime beef* 3 typical: *a prime example* ▷ *n* 4 the time when a thing is at its best 5 a period of power, vigour, and activity: *he was in the prime of life* 6 *maths* short for **prime number** ▷ *vb* **priming, primed** 7 to give (someone) information in advance to prepare him or her 8 to prepare (a surface) for painting 9 to prepare (a gun or mine) before detonating or firing 10 to fill (a pump) with its working fluid, to expel air from it before starting 11 to prepare (something) ▶ HISTORY Latin *primus* first

prime meridian *n* the 0° meridian from which the other meridians are worked out, usually taken to pass through Greenwich

prime minister *n* the leader of a government

prime mover *n* a person or thing which was important in helping create an idea, situation, etc.: *he was the prime mover behind the coup*

prime number *n* an integer that cannot be divided into other integers but is only divisible by itself or 1, such as 2, 3, 5, 7, and 11

primer[1] *n* 1 a substance applied to a surface as a base coat or sealer 2 a device for detonating the main charge in a gun or mine ▶ HISTORY see PRIME (verb)

primer[2] *n* an introductory text, such as a school textbook ▶ HISTORY Medieval Latin *primarius (liber)* a first (book)

prime stock *n NZ* livestock in peak condition and ready for killing

primeval (prime-**ee**-val) *adj* of the earliest age of the world ▶ HISTORY Latin *primus* first + *aevum* age

primitive *adj* **1** of or belonging to the beginning **2** *biol* of an early stage in development: *primitive amphibians* **3** characteristic of an early simple state, esp. in being crude or basic: *a primitive dwelling* ▷ *n* **4** a primitive person or thing **5** a painter of any era whose work appears childlike or untrained **6** a work by such an artist ▶ HISTORY Latin *primitivus* earliest of its kind

primogeniture *n* **1** *formal* the state of being the first-born child **2** *law* the right of an eldest son to inherit all the property of his parents ▶ HISTORY Medieval Latin *primogenitura* birth of a first child

primordial *adj formal* existing at or from the beginning ▶ HISTORY Late Latin *primordialis* original

primrose *n* **1** a wild plant which has pale yellow flowers in spring ▷ *adj* **2** Also: **primrose yellow** pale yellow **3** of primroses ▶ HISTORY Medieval Latin *prima rosa* first rose

primula *n* a type of primrose with brightly coloured funnel-shaped flowers ▶ HISTORY Medieval Latin *primula (veris)* little first one (of the spring)

Primus *n* *trademark* a portable paraffin cooking stove, used esp. by campers

prince *n* **1** a male member of a royal family, esp. the son of the king or queen **2** the male ruler of a small country **3** an outstanding member of a specified group: *Dryden, that prince of poets* ▶ HISTORY Latin *princeps* first man, ruler

prince consort *n* the husband of a queen, who is himself a prince

princely *adj* **-lier, -liest** **1** of or characteristic of a prince **2** generous or lavish

Prince of Wales *n* the eldest son of the British sovereign

princess *n* **1** a female member of a royal family, esp. the daughter of the king or queen **2** the wife of a prince

Princess Royal *n* a title sometimes given to the eldest daughter of the British sovereign

principal *adj* **1** first in importance, rank, or value: *salt is the principal source of sodium in our diets; the Republic's two principal parties* ▷ *n* **2** the head of a school or other educational institution **3** a person who holds one of the most important positions in an organization: *she became a principal in the home finance department* **4** the leading actor in a play **5** *law* **a** a person who engages another to act as his or her agent **b** a person who takes an active part in a crime **c** the person held responsible for fulfilling an obligation **6** *finance* **a** capital or property, as contrasted with income **b** the original amount of a debt on which interest is calculated ▶ HISTORY Latin *principalis* chief ▶ **principally** *adv*

principal boy *n* *Brit* the leading male role in a pantomime, traditionally played by a woman

principal clause *n* the same as **main clause**

principality *n, pl* **-ties** a territory ruled by a prince

principal parts *pl n* *grammar* the main verb forms, from which all other verb forms may be deduced

principle *n* **1** a moral rule guiding personal conduct: *he'd stoop to anything – he has no principles* **2** a set of such moral rules: *a man of principle* **3** a basic or general truth: *the principle of freedom of expression* **4** a basic law or rule underlying a particular theory or philosophy: *the government has been deceitful and has violated basic principles of democracy* **5** a general law in science: *the principle of the conservation of mass* **6** *chem* a constituent of a substance that determines its characteristics **7** **in principle** in theory though not always in practice **8** **on principle** because of one's beliefs ▶ HISTORY Latin *principium* beginning, basic tenet

principle of moments *n* *physics* the relationship between the forces on either side of a pivot

print *vb* **1** to reproduce (a newspaper, book, etc.) in large quantities by mechanical or electronic means **2** to reproduce (text or pictures) by applying ink to paper **3** to write in letters that are not joined up **4** to stamp (fabric) with a design **5** to produce (a photograph) from a negative **6** to fix in the mind or memory ▷ *n* **7** printed content, such as newsprint **8** a printed publication, such as a book **9** **in print a** in printed or published form **b** (of a book) available from a publisher **10** **out of print** no longer available from a publisher **11** a picture printed from an engraved plate or wood block **12** printed text, with regard to the typeface: *italic print* **13** a photograph produced from a negative **14** a fabric with a printed design **15** a mark made by pressing something onto a surface **16** See **fingerprint** ▷ See also **print out** ▶ HISTORY Old French *preindre* to make an impression

printed circuit *n* an electronic circuit in which the wiring is a metallic coating printed on a thin insulating board

printer *n* **1** a person or business engaged in printing **2** a machine that prints **3** *computers* a machine that prints out results on paper

printing *n* **1** the process of producing printed matter **2** printed text **3** all the copies of a book printed at one time **4** a form of writing in which the letters are not joined together

printmaking *n* an artistic technique that consists of making a series of pictures from an original, or from a specially prepared surface > **printmaker** *n*

print out *vb* **1** *computers* to produce (printed information) ▷ *n* **print-out** *or* **printout** **2** printed information from a computer

prior[1] *adj* **1** previous: *prior knowledge* **2** **prior to** before ▶ HISTORY Latin: previous

prior[2] *n* **1** the head monk in a priory **2** the abbot's deputy in a monastery ▶ HISTORY Late Latin: head > **prioress** *fem n*

priority *n, pl* **-ties** **1** the most important thing that must be dealt with first **2** the right to be or go before others

p

priory n, pl **-ories** a religious house where certain orders of monks or nuns live

prise or **prize** vb **prising, prised** or **prizing, prized** to force open or out by levering ▶ HISTORY Old French *prise* a taking

prism n **1** a transparent block, often with triangular ends and rectangular sides, used to disperse light into a spectrum or refract it in optical instruments **2** maths a polyhedron with parallel bases and sides that are parallelograms ▶ HISTORY Greek *prisma* something shaped by sawing

prismatic adj **1** of or shaped like a prism **2** exhibiting bright spectral colours; rainbow-like: *prismatic light*

prison n **1** a public building used to hold convicted criminals and accused people awaiting trial **2** any place of confinement ▶ HISTORY Old French *prisun*, from Latin *prensio* a capturing

prisoner n **1** a person kept in prison as a punishment for a crime, or while awaiting trial **2** a person confined by any restraints: *he's a prisoner of his own past* **3 take (someone) prisoner** to capture and hold (someone) as a prisoner

prisoner of war n a serviceman captured by an enemy in wartime

prissy adj **-sier, -siest** prim and prudish ▶ HISTORY probably from *prim* + *sissy* > **prissily** adv

pristine adj **1** completely new, clean, and pure: *pristine white plates* **2** of or involving the original, unchanged, and unspoilt period or state: *the viewing of wild game in its pristine natural state* ▶ HISTORY Latin *pristinus* primitive

privacy n **1** the condition of being private **2** secrecy

private adj **1** not for general or public use: *a private bathroom* **2** confidential or secret: *a private conversation* **3** involving someone's domestic and personal life rather than his or her work or business: *what I do in my private life is none of your business* **4** owned or paid for by individuals rather than by the government: *private enterprise* **5** not publicly known: *they had private reasons for the decision* **6** having no public office, rank, or position: *the Red Cross received donations from private citizens* **7** (of a place) quiet and secluded: *the garden is completely private* **8** (of a person) quiet and retiring: *she was private – her life was her own* ▷ n **9** a soldier of the lowest rank in the army **10 in private** in secret ▶ HISTORY Latin *privatus* belonging to one individual, withdrawn from public life > **privately** adv

private bill n a bill presented to Parliament on behalf of a private individual or corporation

private company n a limited company that does not issue shares for public subscription

private detective n a person hired by a client to do detective work

privateer n **1** a privately owned armed vessel authorized by the government to take part in a war **2** a captain of such a ship

private income n income from sources other than employment, such as investment

private law n law the branch of law that deals with the rights and duties of private individuals and the relations between them. Compare **public law**

private member n a Member of Parliament who is not a government minister

private member's bill n law a law proposed by a Member of Parliament who is not a government minister

private parts or **privates** pl n euphemistic the genitals

private school n a school controlled by a private body, accepting mostly fee-paying pupils

private sector n the part of a country's economy that consists of privately owned enterprises

privation n formal loss or lack of the necessities of life ▶ HISTORY Latin *privatio* deprivation

privative (priv-a-tiv) adj **1** causing privation **2** grammar expressing lack or absence, for example *-less* and *un-*

privatize or **-ise** vb **-izing, -ized** or **-ising, -ised** to sell (a state-owned company) to individuals or a private company > **privatization** or **-isation** n

privet n a bushy evergreen shrub used for hedges ▶ HISTORY origin unknown

privilege n **1** a benefit or advantage granted only to certain people: *a privilege of rank* **2** the opportunity to do something which gives you great satisfaction and which most people never have the chance to do: *I had the privilege of meeting the Queen when she visited our school* **3** the power and advantages that come with great wealth or high social class: *the use of violence to protect class privilege and thwart popular democracy* ▶ HISTORY Latin *privilegium* law relevant to rights of an individual

privileged adj enjoying a special right or immunity

privity of contract n law the legal principle (in some countries including England) that only the parties to a contract have the right to take legal action to enforce it

privy adj **privier, priviest 1 privy to** sharing in the knowledge of something secret **2** archaic secret ▷ n, pl **privies** obsolete a toilet, esp. an outside one ▶ HISTORY Old French *privé* something private

Privy Council n **1** the private council of the British king or queen **2** (in Canada) a formal body of advisers of the governor general > **Privy Counsellor** n

privy purse n an allowance voted by Parliament for the private expenses of the king or queen

privy seal n (in Britain) a seal affixed to certain documents of state

prize¹ n **1** something of value, such as a trophy, given to the winner of a contest or game **2** something given to the winner of any game of chance, lottery, etc. **3** something striven for ▷ adj **4** winning or likely to win a prize: *a prize bull* ▶ HISTORY Old French *prise* a capture

prize² vb **prizing, prized** to value highly ▶ HISTORY Old French *preisier* to praise

prizefight *n* a boxing match for a prize or purse
> **prizefighter** *n*

pro¹ *adv* **1** in favour of a motion, etc. ▷ *prep* **2** in favour of ▷ *n, pl* **pros 3** (usually pl) an argument or vote in favour of a proposal or motion ▷ See also **pros and cons** ▶ **HISTORY** Latin: in favour of

pro² *n, pl* **pros** *adj informal* **1** short for **professional 2** a prostitute

PRO public relations officer

pro-¹ *prefix* **1** in favour of; supporting: *pro-Chinese* **2** acting as a substitute for: *pronoun* ▶ **HISTORY** Latin

pro-² *prefix* before in time or position: *proboscis* ▶ **HISTORY** Greek

proactive *adj* tending to initiate change rather than reacting to events

probability *n, pl* **-ties 1** the condition of being probable **2** an event or other thing that is likely to happen or be true **3** *statistics* a measure of the likelihood of an event happening

probable *adj* **1** likely to happen or be true **2** most likely: *the probable cause of the accident* ▷ *n* **3** a person who is likely to be chosen for a team, event, etc. ▶ **HISTORY** Latin *probabilis* that may be proved

probably *adv* in all likelihood or probability: *the wedding's probably going to be in late August*

probate *n* **1** the process of officially proving the validity of a will **2** the official certificate stating that a will is genuine ▶ **HISTORY** Latin *probare* to inspect

probation *n* **1** a system of dealing with offenders, esp. juvenile ones, by placing them under supervision **2** **on probation** **a** under the supervision of a probation officer **b** undergoing a test or trial period, such as at the start of a new job ▶ **HISTORY** Latin *probare* to test > **probationary** *adj*

probationer *n* a person on probation

probation officer *n* an officer of a court who supervises offenders placed on probation

probe *vb* **probing, probed 1** to search into closely **2** to poke or examine (something) with or as if with a probe: *he probed carefully with his fingertips* ▷ *n* **3** *surgery* a slender instrument for exploring a wound, etc. **4** a thorough inquiry, such as one into corrupt practices **5** See **space probe** ▶ **HISTORY** Latin *probare* to test

probiotic *n* **1** a bacterium that protects the body from harmful bacteria ▷ *adj* **2** relating to probiotics: *probiotic yogurts*

probity *n formal* honesty; integrity ▶ **HISTORY** Latin *probitas* honesty

problem *n* **1** something or someone that is difficult to deal with **2** a puzzle or question set for solving **3** *maths* a statement requiring a solution usually by means of several operations ▷ *adj* **4** of a literary work that deals with difficult moral questions: *a problem play* **5** difficult to deal with or creating difficulties for others: *a problem child* ▶ **HISTORY** Greek *problēma* something put forward

problematic *or* **problematical** *adj* difficult to solve or deal with

proboscis (pro-**boss**-iss) *n* **1** a long flexible trunk or snout, such as an elephant's **2** the elongated mouth part of certain insects ▶ **HISTORY** Greek *proboskis* trunk of an elephant

procedural genre *n* a form of writing or speech in which the writer or speaker explains the procedures to follow in order to do something

procedure *n* **1** a way of doing something, esp. an established method **2** the established form of conducting the business of a legislature > **procedural** *adj*

proceed *vb* **1** to advance or carry on, esp. after stopping **2** (often foll. by *with*) to start or continue doing: *he proceeded to pour himself a large whisky* **3** *formal* to walk or go **4** (often foll. by *against*) to start a legal action **5** *formal* to arise from: *their mutual dislike proceeded from differences of political opinion* ▶ **HISTORY** Latin *procedere* to advance

proceeding *n* **1** an act or course of action **2** **proceedings** the events of an occasion: *millions watched the proceedings on television* **3** **proceedings** the minutes of the meetings of a society **4** **proceedings** legal action

proceeds *pl n* the amount of money obtained from an event or activity

process¹ *n* **1** a series of actions or changes: *a process of genuine national reconciliation* **2** a series of natural developments which result in an overall change: *the ageing process* **3** a method of doing or producing something: *the various production processes use up huge amounts of water* **4** **in the process of** during or in the course of **5 a** a summons to appear in court **b** an action at law **6** a natural outgrowth or projection of a part or organism ▷ *vb* **7** to handle or prepare by a special method of manufacture **8** *computers* to perform operations on (data) in order to obtain the required information ▶ **HISTORY** Latin *processus* an advancing

process² *vb* to move in an orderly or ceremonial group: *the cult members processed through the streets to the music of tambourines*

processed *adj* (of food) treated by adding colouring, preservatives, etc. to improve its appearance or the period it will stay edible: *processed cheese*

procession *n* **1** a line of people or vehicles moving forwards in an orderly or ceremonial manner **2** the act of proceeding in a regular formation ▶ **HISTORY** Latin *processio* a marching forwards

processional *adj* **1** of or suitable for a procession: *the processional route* ▷ *n* **2** *Christianity* a hymn sung as the clergy enter church

processor *n* **1** *computers* same as **central processing unit 2** a person or thing that carries out a process

proclaim *vb* **1** to announce publicly; declare: *Greece was proclaimed an independent kingdom in 1832* **2** to indicate plainly: *the sharp hard glint in the eye proclaimed her determination* ▶ **HISTORY** Latin *proclamare* to shout aloud > **proclamation** *n*

proclivity *n, pl* **-ties** *formal* a tendency or inclination ▶ **HISTORY** Latin *proclivitas*

p

procrastinate *vb* **-nating, -nated** to put off (an action) until later; delay ▶ HISTORY Latin *procrastinare* to postpone until tomorrow
> **procrastination** *n* > **procrastinator** *n*

procreate *vb* **-ating, -ated** *formal* to produce (offspring) ▶ HISTORY Latin *procreare*
> **procreative** *adj* > **procreation** *n*

Procrustean *adj* ruthlessly enforcing uniformity ▶ HISTORY after *Procrustes*, robber in Greek myth who fitted travellers into his bed by stretching or lopping off their limbs

proctor *n* a member of the staff of certain universities having duties including the enforcement of discipline ▶ HISTORY syncopated variant of *procurator* > **proctorial** *adj*

procurator fiscal *n* (in Scotland) a legal officer who acts as public prosecutor and coroner

procure *vb* **-curing, -cured 1** to get or provide: *it remained very difficult to procure food and fuel* **2** to obtain (people) to act as prostitutes ▶ HISTORY Latin *procurare* to look after > **procurement** *n*

procurer *n* a person who obtains people to act as prostitutes

prod *vb* **prodding, prodded 1** to poke with a pointed object **2** to rouse (someone) to action ▷ *n* **3** the act of prodding **4** a reminder ▶ HISTORY origin unknown

prodigal *adj* **1** recklessly wasteful or extravagant **2 prodigal of** lavish with: *you are prodigal of both your toil and your talent* ▷ *n* **3** a person who squanders money ▶ HISTORY Latin *prodigere* to squander > **prodigality** *n*

prodigious *adj* **1** very large or immense **2** wonderful or amazing ▶ HISTORY Latin *prodigiosus* marvellous

prodigy *n, pl* **-gies 1** a person, esp. a child, with marvellous talent **2** anything that is a cause of wonder ▶ HISTORY Latin *prodigium* an unnatural happening

produce *vb* **-ducing, -duced 1** to bring (something) into existence **2** to present to view: *he produced his passport* **3** to make: *this area produces much of Spain's best wine* **4** to give birth to **5** to present on stage, film, or television: *the girls and boys write and produce their own plays* **6** to act as producer of ▷ *n* **7** food grown for sale: *farm produce* **8** something produced ▶ HISTORY Latin *producere* to bring forward > **producible** *adj*

producer *n* **1** a person with the financial and administrative responsibility for a film or television programme **2** *Brit & NZ* a person responsible for the artistic direction of a play **3** a person who supervises the arrangement, performance, and mixing of a recording **4** a person or thing that produces **5** *econ* a person or business that generates goods for sale **6** *biol* an organism, esp. a green plant, that builds up its own tissues from simple inorganic compounds and is itself a food source for other organisms. Compare **consumer**

product *n* **1** something produced **2** a consequence: *their skill was the product of hours of training* **3** *maths* the result achieved by multiplication

product differentiation *n marketing* the real or illusory distinction between competing products in a market

production *n* **1** the act of producing **2** anything that is produced **3** the amount produced or the rate at which it is produced **4** *econ* the creation or manufacture of goods and services **5** any work created as a result of literary or artistic effort **6** the presentation of a play, opera, etc. **7** *Brit & NZ* the artistic direction of a play **8** the overall sound of a recording

production designer *n films, television* the person responsible for a film's look and design, which includes sets, props, costumes, and location

production line *n* a system in a factory in which an item being manufactured is moved from machine to machine by conveyor belt, and each machine carries out one step in the manufacture of the item

production unit *n films, television* the director, camera crew, sound and lighting teams, and everyone else responsible for providing the necessary expertise and technical support involved in making a film or TV programme

productive *adj* **1** producing or having the power to produce **2** yielding favourable results **3** *econ* producing goods and services that have exchange value: *the country's productive capacity* **4** (foll. by *of*) resulting in: *a period highly productive of books and ideas* > **productivity** *n*

product life-cycle *n business* the progress of a product from its initial development, its introduction to the market, the growth and decline of its sales, and its redevelopment or ultimate withdrawal from the market

product line *n marketing* a group of related products marketed by the same company

product-oriented *adj marketing* focusing on the design and development of products

product placement *n* the practice of a company of paying for its product to appear prominently in a film or television programme

product range *n marketing* all of the products marketed by a company

proem (pro-em) *n formal* an introduction or preface ▶ HISTORY Greek *pro-* before + *oimē* song

Prof. Professor

profane *adj* **1** showing disrespect for religion or something sacred **2** secular **3** coarse or blasphemous: *profane language* ▷ *vb* **-faning, -faned 4** to treat (something sacred) with irreverence **5** to put to an unworthy use ▶ HISTORY Latin *profanus* outside the temple > **profanation** *n*

profanity *n, pl* **-ties 1** the quality of being profane **2** coarse or blasphemous action or speech

profess *vb* **1** to claim (something as true), often falsely: *he professes not to want the job of prime minister* **2** to acknowledge openly: *he professed great relief at getting some rest* **3** to have as one's belief or religion: *most Indonesians profess the Islamic faith* ▶ HISTORY Latin *profiteri* to confess openly > **professed** *adj*

profession n 1 a type of work that requires special training, such as in law or medicine 2 the people employed in such an occupation 3 a declaration of a belief or feeling: *a profession of faith* ▶ HISTORY Latin *professio* public acknowledgment

professional adj 1 of a profession 2 taking part in an activity, such as sport or music, as a means of livelihood 3 displaying a high level of competence or skill: *a professional and polished performance* 4 undertaken or performed by people who are paid: *professional golf* ▷ n 5 a professional person > **professionalism** n > **professionally** adv

professor n 1 the highest rank of teacher in a university 2 *chiefly US & Canad* any teacher in a university or college 3 *rare* a person who professes his or her opinions or beliefs ▶ HISTORY Latin: a public teacher > **professorial** adj > **professorship** n

proffer vb *formal* to offer for acceptance ▶ HISTORY Old French *proffrir*

proficient adj skilled; expert ▶ HISTORY Latin *proficere* to make progress > **proficiency** n

profile n 1 an outline, esp. of the human face, as seen from the side 2 a short biographical sketch ▶ HISTORY Italian *profilo*

profiling n the practice of categorizing people and predicting their behaviour according to characteristics such as race or age

profit n 1 (often pl) money gained in business or trade 2 a benefit or advantage ▷ vb **-iting, -ited** 3 to gain a profit or advantage: *we do not want to profit from someone else's problems* ▶ HISTORY Latin *proficere* to make progress

profitable adj making profit > **profitability** n > **profitably** adv

profit and loss n *finance* an account compiled at the end of a financial year showing that year's income and expenses and indicating gross and net profit

profiteer n 1 a person who makes excessive profits at the expense of the public ▷ vb 2 to make excessive profits > **profiteering** n

profit-sharing n a system in which a portion of the net profit of a business is shared among its employees

profligate adj 1 recklessly extravagant 2 shamelessly immoral ▷ n 3 a profligate person ▶ HISTORY Latin *profligatus* corrupt > **profligacy** n

pro forma adj 1 laying down a set form ▷ adv 2 performed in a set manner ▶ HISTORY Latin: for form's sake

pro forma invoice n *commerce* an invoice issued before an order is placed or before the goods are delivered, giving all the details and the cost of the goods

profound adj 1 showing or needing great knowledge: *a profound knowledge of Greek literature* 2 strongly felt; intense: *profound relief* 3 extensive: *profound changes* 4 situated at or having a great depth ▶ HISTORY Latin *profundus* deep > **profoundly** adv > **profundity** n

profuse adj 1 plentiful or abundant: *he broke out in a profuse sweat* 2 (often foll. by *in*) generous in the giving (of): *he was profuse in his apologies* ▶ HISTORY Latin *profundere* to pour lavishly > **profusely** adv > **profusion** n

progenitor (pro-**jen**-it-er) n 1 a direct ancestor 2 an originator or founder ▶ HISTORY Latin: ancestor

progeny (**proj**-in-ee) n, pl **-nies** 1 offspring; descendants 2 an outcome ▶ HISTORY Latin *progenies* lineage

progesterone n a hormone, produced in the ovary, that prepares the womb for pregnancy and prevents further ovulation ▶ HISTORY PRO-[1] + *ge(station)* + *ster(ol)* + *-one*

prognathous adj having a projecting lower jaw

prognosis n, pl **-noses** 1 *med* a forecast about the course or outcome of an illness 2 any forecast ▶ HISTORY Greek: knowledge beforehand

program n 1 a sequence of coded instructions which enables a computer to perform various tasks ▷ vb **-gramming, -grammed** 2 to arrange (data) so that it can be processed by a computer 3 to feed a program into (a computer) > **programmer** n

programmable or **programable** adj capable of being programmed for computer processing

programme or US **program** n 1 a planned series of events 2 a broadcast on radio or television 3 a printed list of items or performers in an entertainment ▷ vb **-gramming, -grammed** or US **-graming, -gramed** 4 to schedule (something) as a programme ▶ HISTORY Greek *programma* written public notice > **programmatic** adj

programming language n a language system by which instructions to a computer are coded that is understood by both user and computer

progress n 1 improvement or development 2 movement forward or advance 3 **in progress** taking place ▷ vb 4 to become more advanced or skilful 5 to move forward ▶ HISTORY Latin *progressus* a going forwards

progression n 1 the act of progressing; advancement 2 the act or an instance of moving from one thing in a sequence to the next 3 *maths* a sequence of numbers in which each term differs from the succeeding term by a fixed ratio

progressive adj 1 favouring political or social reform 2 happening gradually: *a progressive illness* 3 (of a dance, card game, etc) involving a regular change of partners ▷ n 4 a person who favours political or social reform > **progressively** adv

prohibit vb **-iting, -ited** 1 to forbid by law or other authority 2 to hinder or prevent: *the paucity of information prohibits us from drawing reliable conclusions* ▶ HISTORY Latin *prohibere* to prevent > **prohibitor** n

prohibition n 1 the act of forbidding 2 a legal ban on the sale or drinking of alcohol 3 an order or decree that forbids > **prohibitionist** n

Prohibition n the period (1920–33) when making, selling, and transporting alcohol was banned in the US > **Prohibitionist** n

prohibitive adj **1** (esp. of prices) too high to be affordable **2** prohibiting or tending to prohibit: *a prohibitive distance*

project n **1** a proposal or plan **2** a detailed study of a particular subject ▷ vb **3** to make a prediction based on known data and observations **4** to cause (an image) to appear on a surface **5** to communicate (an impression): *he wants to project an image of a deep-thinking articulate gentleman* **6** to jut out **7** to cause (one's voice) to be heard clearly at a distance **8** to transport in the imagination: *it's hard to project oneself into his situation* ▶ HISTORY Latin *proicere* to throw down

projectile n **1** an object thrown as a weapon or fired from a gun ▷ adj **2** designed to be thrown forwards **3** projecting forwards ▶ HISTORY New Latin *projectilis* jutting forwards

projection n **1** a part that juts out **2** a forecast based on known data **3** the process of showing film on a screen **4** the representation on a flat surface of a three-dimensional figure or curved line

projectionist n a person who operates a film projector

projector n an apparatus for projecting photographic images, film, or slides onto a screen

prokaryotic adj biol denoting an organism that has cells in each of which the genetic material is in a single filament of DNA

prolapse pathol n **1** Also: **prolapsus** the slipping down of an internal organ of the body from its normal position ▷ vb **-lapsing, -lapsed** **2** (of an internal organ) to slip from its normal position ▶ HISTORY Latin *prolabi* to slide along

prolapsed adj pathol (of an internal organ) having slipped from its normal position

prolate adj geom having a polar diameter which is longer than the equatorial diameter ▶ HISTORY Latin *prolatus* enlarged

prole n chiefly Brit, offensive slang a proletarian

proletarian (pro-lit-**air**-ee-an) adj **1** of the proletariat ▷ n **2** a member of the proletariat

proletariat (pro-lit-**air**-ee-at) n the working class ▶ HISTORY Latin *proletarius* one whose only contribution to the state was his offspring

proliferate vb **-ating, -ated** **1** to increase rapidly in numbers **2** to grow or reproduce (new parts, such as cells) rapidly ▶ HISTORY Latin *proles* offspring + *ferre* to bear > **proliferation** n

prolific adj **1** producing a constant creative output: *a prolific author* **2** producing fruit or offspring in abundance **3** (often foll. by in or of) rich or fruitful ▶ HISTORY Latin *proles* offspring > **prolifically** adv

prolix adj (of a speech or piece of writing) overlong and boring ▶ HISTORY Latin *prolixus* stretched out widely > **prolixity** n

prologue or US often **prolog** n **1** an introduction to a play or book **2** an event that comes before another: *this success was a happy prologue to their transatlantic tour* ▶ HISTORY Greek pro- before + *logos* discourse

prolong vb to make (something) last longer ▶ HISTORY Late Latin *prolongare* > **prolongation** n

prom n **1** Brit short for **promenade** (sense 1), **promenade concert** **2** US & Canad, informal a formal dance held at a high school or college

PROM n computers Programmable Read Only Memory

promenade n **1** chiefly Brit a paved walkway along the seafront at a holiday resort **2** old-fashioned a leisurely walk for pleasure or display ▷ vb **-nading, -naded** **3** old-fashioned to take a leisurely walk ▶ HISTORY French

promenade concert n a concert at which some of the audience stand rather than sit

promethium (pro-**meeth**-ee-um) n chem an artificial radioactive element of the lanthanide series. Symbol: Pm ▶ HISTORY from *Prometheus*, in Greek mythology, the Titan who gave fire to mankind

prominent adj **1** standing out from the surroundings; noticeable **2** widely known; famous **3** jutting or projecting outwards: *prominent eyes* ▶ HISTORY Latin *prominere* to jut out > **prominence** n > **prominently** adv

promiscuous adj **1** taking part in many casual sexual relationships **2** formal consisting of different elements mingled indiscriminately ▶ HISTORY Latin *promiscuus* indiscriminate > **promiscuity** n

promise vb **-ising, -ised** **1** to say that one will definitely do or not do something: *I promise I'll have it finished by the end of the week* **2** to undertake to give (something to someone): *he promised me a car for my birthday* **3** to show signs of; seem likely: *she promises to be a fine singer* **4** to assure (someone) of the certainty of something: *everything's fine, I promise you* ▷ n **5** an undertaking to do or not do something **6** indication of future success: *a young player who shows great promise* ▶ HISTORY Latin *promissum* a promise

Promised Land n **1** Bible the land of Canaan **2** any longed-for place where one expects to find greater happiness

promising adj likely to succeed or turn out well

promissory note n commerce, chiefly US a written promise to pay a stated sum of money to a particular person on a certain date or on demand

promo n, pl **-mos** informal an item produced to promote a product, esp. a video used to promote a pop recording

promontory n, pl **-ries** a point of high land that juts out into the sea ▶ HISTORY Latin *promunturium* headland

promote vb **-moting, -moted** **1** to encourage the progress or success of: *all attempts to promote a lasting ceasefire have failed* **2** to raise to a higher rank or position **3** to encourage the sale of (a product) by advertising **4** to work for: *he actively promoted reform* ▶ HISTORY Latin *promovere* to push onwards > **promotion** n > **promotional** adj

promoter n **1** a person who helps to organize and finance an event, esp. a sports one **2** a person or thing that encourages the progress or success of: *a promoter of terrorism*

prompt *vb* **1** to cause (an action); bring about: *the killings prompted an anti-Mafia crackdown* **2** to motivate or cause someone to do something: *I still don't know what prompted me to go* **3** to remind (an actor) of lines forgotten during a performance **4** to refresh the memory of ▷ *adj* **5** done without delay **6** quick to act ▷ *adv* **7** *informal* punctually: *at 8 o'clock prompt* ▷ *n* **8** anything that serves to remind ▸ HISTORY Latin *promptus* evident > **promptly** *adv* > **promptness** *n*

prompter *n* a person offstage who reminds the actors of forgotten lines

promulgate *vb* **-gating, -gated 1** to put (a law or decree) into effect by announcing it officially **2** to make widely known ▸ HISTORY Latin *promulgare* > **promulgation** *n* > **promulgator** *n*

pron. 1 pronoun **2** pronunciation

prone *adj* **1** having a tendency to be affected by or do something: *I am prone to indigestion* **2** lying face downwards; prostrate ▸ HISTORY Latin *pronus* bent forward

prong *n* a long pointed projection from an instrument or tool such as a fork ▸ HISTORY Middle English

pronominal *adj grammar* relating to or playing the part of a pronoun

pronoun *n* a word, such as *she* or *it*, that replaces a noun or noun phrase that has already been or is about to be mentioned ▸ HISTORY Latin *pronomen*

pronounce *vb* **-nouncing, -nounced 1** to speak (a sound or sounds), esp. clearly or in a certain way **2** to announce or declare officially: *I now pronounce you man and wife* **3** to declare as one's judgment: *he pronounced the wine drinkable* ▸ HISTORY Latin *pronuntiare* to announce > **pronounceable** *adj*

pronounced *adj* very noticeable: *he speaks with a pronounced lisp*

pronouncement *n* a formal announcement

pronto *adv informal* at once ▸ HISTORY Spanish: quick

pronunciation *n* **1** the recognized way to pronounce sounds in a given language **2** the way in which someone pronounces words

proof *n* **1** any evidence that confirms that something is true or exists **2** *law* the total evidence upon which a court bases its verdict **3** *maths, logic* a sequence of steps or statements that establishes the truth of a proposition **4** the act of testing the truth of something **5** an early copy of printed matter for checking before final production **6** *photog* a trial print from a negative **7** (esp. formerly) a defined level of alcoholic content used as a standard measure for comparing the alcoholic strength of other liquids: *Moldavian ruby port, seventeen degrees proof* ▷ *adj* **8** (foll. by *against*) *written* able to withstand: *proof against tears* **9** (esp. formerly) having a level of alcoholic content used as a standard measure for comparing the alcoholic strength of other liquids ▷ *vb* **10** to take a proof from (type matter) **11** to render (something) proof, esp. to waterproof ▸ HISTORY Old French *preuve* a test

proofread *vb* **-reading, -read** to read and correct (printer's proofs) > **proofreader** *n*

prop[1] *vb* **propping, propped** (often foll. by *up*) **1** to support (something or someone) in an upright position: *she was propped up by pillows* **2** to sustain or support: *the type of measures necessary to prop up the sagging US economy* **3** (often foll. by *against*) to place or lean ▷ *n* **4** something that gives rigid support, such as a pole **5** a person or thing giving moral support ▸ HISTORY perhaps from Middle Dutch *proppe*

prop[2] *n* a movable object used on the set of a film or play

prop[3] *n informal* a propeller

prop. 1 proper(ly) **2** property **3** proposition **4** proprietor

propaganda *n* **1** the organized promotion of information to assist or damage the cause of a government or movement **2** such information ▸ HISTORY Italian > **propagandist** *n, adj*

propagate *vb* **-gating, -gated 1** to spread (information or ideas) **2** *biol* to reproduce or breed **3** *horticulture* to produce (plants) **4** *physics* to transmit, esp. in the form of a wave: *the electrical signal is propagated through a specialized group of conducting fibres* ▸ HISTORY Latin *propagare* to increase (plants) by cuttings > **propagation** *n* > **propagator** *n*

propane *n* a flammable gas found in petroleum and used as a fuel ▸ HISTORY from *propionic (acid)*

propel *vb* **-pelling, -pelled** to cause to move forwards ▸ HISTORY Latin *propellere* > **propellant** *n, adj*

propeller *n* a revolving shaft with blades to drive a ship or aircraft

propene *n* same as **propylene**

propensity *n, pl* **-ties** *formal* a natural tendency: *his problem had always been a propensity to live beyond his means* ▸ HISTORY Latin *propensus* inclined to

proper *adj* **1** real or genuine: *a proper home* **2** appropriate or usual: *good wine must have the proper balance of sugar and acid* **3** suited to a particular purpose: *they set out without any proper climbing gear* **4** correct in behaviour: *in many societies it is not considered proper for a woman to show her legs* **5** excessively moral: *she was very strait-laced and proper* **6** being or forming the main or central part of something: *a suburb some miles west of the city proper* **7** *Brit, Austral & NZ, informal* complete: *you made him look a proper fool* ▸ HISTORY Latin *proprius* special > **properly** *adv*

proper fraction *n* a fraction in which the numerator has a lower absolute value than the denominator, for example ½

proper noun *or* **name** *n grammar* the name of a person or place, for example *Iceland* or *Patrick*. Compare **common noun**

property *n, pl* **-ties 1** something owned **2** *law* the right to possess, use, and dispose of anything **3** possessions collectively **4** land or buildings owned by someone **5** a quality or attribute: *the oils* 675 have healing properties **6** same as **prop²** ▶ HISTORY Latin *proprius* one's own

prophecy *n*, *pl* **-cies 1** a prediction **2 a** a message revealing God's will **b** the act of uttering such a message **3** the function or activity of a prophet

prophesy *vb* **-sies, -sying, -sied** to foretell

prophet *n* **1** a person supposedly chosen by God to pass on His message **2** a person who predicts the future: *a prophet of doom* **3** a spokesman for, or advocate of, some cause: *a prophet of revolution* ▶ HISTORY Greek *prophētēs* one who declares the divine will > **prophetess** *fem n*

Prophet *n* **the Prophet** the main name used for Mohammed, the founder of Islam

prophetic *adj* **1** foretelling what will happen **2** of the nature of a prophecy > **prophetically** *adv*

prophylactic *adj* **1** preventing disease ▷ *n* **2** a drug or device that prevents disease **3** *chiefly US* a condom ▶ HISTORY Greek *prophulassein* to guard by taking advance measures

propitiate *vb* **-ating, -ated** to appease (someone, esp. a god or spirit); make well disposed ▶ HISTORY Latin *propitiare* > **propitiable** *adj* > **propitiation** *n* > **propitiator** *n* > **propitiatory** *adj*

propitious *adj* **1** favourable or auspicious: *a propitious moment* **2** likely to prove favourable; advantageous: *his origins were not propitious for a literary career* ▶ HISTORY Latin *propitius* well disposed

proponent *n* a person who argues in favour of something ▶ HISTORY Latin *proponere* to propose

proportion *n* **1** relative size or extent: *a large proportion of our revenue comes from advertisements* **2** correct relationship between parts **3** a part considered with respect to the whole: *the proportion of women in the total workforce* **4 proportions** written dimensions or size: *a building of vast proportions* **5** *maths* a relationship between four numbers in which the ratio of the first pair equals the ratio of the second pair **6 in proportion a** comparable in size, rate of increase, etc. **b** without exaggerating ▷ *vb* **7** to adjust in relative amount or size: *the size of the crops are very rarely proportioned to the wants of the inhabitants* **8** to cause to be harmonious in relationship of parts ▶ HISTORY Latin *pro portione*, literally: for (its, one's) portion

proportional *adj* **1** being in proportion ▷ *n* **2** *maths* an unknown term in a proportion, for example in $a/b = c/x$, x is the fourth proportional > **proportionally** *adv* > **proportionality** *n*

proportional representation *n* the representation of political parties in parliament in proportion to the votes they win

proportionate *adj* being in proper proportion > **proportionately** *adv*

proposal *n* **1** the act of proposing **2** a suggestion put forward for consideration **3** an offer of marriage

propose *vb* **-posing, -posed 1** to put forward (a plan) for consideration **2** to nominate (someone) for a position **3** to intend (to do something): *I don't propose to waste any more time discussing it* **4** to ask people to drink a toast **5** (often foll. by *to*) to make an offer of marriage ▶ HISTORY Old French *proposer*, from Latin *proponere* to display

proposition *n* **1** a proposal or offer **2** *logic* a statement that affirms or denies something and is capable of being true or false **3** *maths* a statement or theorem, usually containing its proof **4** *informal* a person or matter to be dealt with: *even among experienced climbers the mountain is considered a tough proposition* **5** *informal* an invitation to engage in sexual intercourse ▷ *vb* **6** to invite (someone) to engage in sexual intercourse ▶ HISTORY Latin *propositio* a setting forth

propound *vb* to put forward for consideration ▶ HISTORY Latin *proponere* to set forth

proprietary *adj* **1** denoting a product manufactured and distributed under a trade name **2** possessive: *she watched them with a proprietary eye* **3** privately owned and controlled ▶ HISTORY Late Latin *proprietarius* an owner

proprietor *n* an owner of a business establishment > **proprietress** *fem n* > **proprietorial** *adj*

propriety *n*, *pl* **-ties 1** the quality or state of being appropriate or fitting **2** correct conduct **3 the proprieties** the standards of behaviour considered correct by polite society ▶ HISTORY Old French *propriété*, from Latin *proprius* one's own

propulsion *n* **1** a force that moves (something) forward **2** the act of propelling or the state of being propelled ▶ HISTORY Latin *propellere* to propel > **propulsive** *adj*

propylene *or* **propene** *n* a gas found in petroleum and used to produce many organic compounds ▶ HISTORY from *propionic (acid)*

pro rata *adv*, *adj* in proportion ▶ HISTORY Medieval Latin

prorogue *vb* **-roguing, -rogued** to suspend (parliament) without dissolving it ▶ HISTORY Latin *prorogare*, literally: to ask publicly > **prorogation** *n*

prosaic (pro-**zay**-ik) *adj* **1** lacking imagination; dull **2** having the characteristics of prose > **prosaically** *adv*

pros and cons *pl n* the advantages and disadvantages of a situation ▶ HISTORY Latin *pro* for + *con(tra)* against

proscenium *n*, *pl* **-nia** *or* **-niums** *theatre* the arch in a theatre separating the stage from the auditorium ▶ HISTORY Greek *pro* before + *skēnē* scene

proscribe *vb* **-scribing, -scribed 1** to condemn or prohibit (something) **2** to outlaw or banish ▶ HISTORY Latin *proscribere* to put up a public notice > **proscription** *n* > **proscriptive** *adj*

prose *n* **1** ordinary spoken or written language in contrast to poetry **2** a passage set for translation into a foreign language **3** commonplace or dull talk ▷ *vb* **prosing, prosed 4** to speak or write in a tedious style ▶ HISTORY Latin *prosa oratio* straightforward speech

p

prosecute *vb* **-cuting, -cuted** **1** to bring a criminal charge against (someone) **2** to continue to do (something): *the business of prosecuting a cold war through propaganda* **3 a** to seek redress by legal proceedings **b** to institute or conduct a prosecution ▸ HISTORY Latin *prosequi* to follow > **prosecutor** *n*

prosecution *n* **1** the bringing of criminal charges against (someone) **2** the institution and conduct of legal proceedings against a person **3** the lawyers acting for the Crown to put the case against a person **4** the carrying out of something begun

proselyte (**pross**-ill-ite) *n* a recent convert ▸ HISTORY Greek *prosēlutos* recent arrival, convert > **proselytism** *n*

proselytize *or* **-ise** (**pross**-ill-it-ize) *vb* **-izing, -ized** *or* **-ising, -ised** to attempt to convert (someone)

prosody (**pross**-a-dee) *n* **1** the study of poetic metre and techniques **2** the vocal patterns in a language ▸ HISTORY Greek *prosōidia* song set to music > **prosodic** *adj* > **prosodist** *n*

prospect *n* **1** (usually pl) a probability of future success: *a job with impossible workloads and poor career prospects* **2** expectation, or something anticipated: *she was terrified at the prospect of bringing up two babies on her own* **3** old-fashioned a view or scene: *a prospect of spires, domes, and towers* ▹ *vb* **4** (sometimes foll. by *for*) to search for gold or other valuable minerals ▸ HISTORY Latin *prospectus* distant view

prospective *adj* **1** future: *prospective customers* **2** expected or likely: *the prospective loss* > **prospectively** *adv*

prospector *n* a person who searches for gold or other valuable minerals

prospectus *n, pl* **-tuses** a booklet produced by a university, company, etc. giving details about it and its activities

prosper *vb* to be successful ▸ HISTORY Latin *prosperare* to succeed

prosperity *n* success and wealth

prosperous *adj* wealthy and successful

prostate *n* a gland in male mammals that surrounds the neck of the bladder. Also called: **prostate gland** ▸ HISTORY Greek *prostatēs* something standing in front (of the bladder)

prosthesis (pross-**theess**-iss) *n, pl* **-ses** (-seez) *surgery* **a** the replacement of a missing body part with an artificial substitute **b** an artificial body part such as a limb, eye, or tooth ▸ HISTORY Greek: an addition > **prosthetic** *adj*

prostitute *n* **1** a person who offers sexual intercourse in return for payment ▹ *vb* **-tuting, -tuted** **2** to offer (oneself or another) in sexual intercourse for money **3** to offer (oneself or one's talent) for unworthy purposes ▸ HISTORY Latin *pro-* in public + *statuere* to cause to stand > **prostitution** *n*

prostrate *adj* **1** lying face downwards **2** physically or emotionally exhausted ▹ *vb* **-trating, -trated** **3** to lie face downwards **4** to exhaust physically or emotionally ▸ HISTORY Latin *prosternere* to throw to the ground > **prostration** *n*

Prot. **1** Protectorate **2** Protestant

protactinium *n chem* a toxic radioactive metallic element. Symbol: Pa

protagonist *n* **1** a supporter of a cause: *a great protagonist of the ideas and principles of mutuality* **2** the leading character in a play or story ▸ HISTORY Greek *prōtos* first + *agōnistēs* actor

protea (pro-**tee**-a) *n* an African shrub with showy heads of flowers ▸ HISTORY after *Proteus*, a sea god who could take many shapes

protean (pro-**tee**-an) *adj* capable of constantly changing shape or form: *he is a protean stylist who can move from blues to ballads with consummate ease* ▸ HISTORY after *Proteus*; see PROTEA

protect *vb* **1** to defend from trouble, harm, or loss **2** *econ* to assist (domestic industries) by taxing imports ▸ HISTORY Latin *protegere* to cover before

protection *n* **1** the act of protecting or the condition of being protected **2** something that keeps (one) safe **3 a** the charging of taxes on imports, to protect domestic industries **b** Also called: **protectionism** the policy of such taxation **4** *informal* Also called: **protection money** money paid to gangsters to avoid attack or damage > **protectionism** *n* > **protectionist** *n, adj*

protective *adj* **1** giving protection: *protective clothing* **2** tending or wishing to protect someone > **protectively** *adv* > **protectiveness** *n*

protector *n* **1** a person or thing that protects **2** *history* a person who acts for the king or queen during his or her childhood, absence, or incapacity > **protectress** *fem n*

protectorate *n* **1** a territory largely controlled by a stronger state **2** the office or term of office of a protector

protégé *or fem* **protégée** (pro-tizh-ay) *n* a person who is protected and helped by another ▸ HISTORY French *protéger* to protect

protein *n* any of a large group of nitrogenous compounds that are essential for life ▸ HISTORY Greek *prōteios* primary

pro tempore *adv, adj* for the time being. Often shortened to: **pro tem**

protest *n* **1** public, often organized, demonstration of objection **2** a strong objection **3** a formal statement declaring that a debtor has dishonoured a bill **4** the act of protesting ▹ *vb* **5** to take part in a public demonstration to express one's support for or disapproval of an action, proposal, etc.: *the workers marched through the city to protest against the closure of their factory* **6** to disagree or object: *'I'm OK,' she protested* **7** to assert in a formal or solemn manner: *all three repeatedly protested their innocence* **8** US & NZ to object forcefully to: *students and teachers have protested the budget reductions* ▸ HISTORY Latin *protestari* to make a formal declaration > **protestant** *adj, n* > **protester** *n*

Protestant *n* **1** a follower of any of the Christian Churches that separated from the Roman Catholic

Church in the sixteenth century ▷ *adj* **2** of or relating to any of these Churches or their followers > **Protestantism** *n*

protestation *n formal* a strong declaration

protist *n biol* an organism belonging to a kingdom that includes bacteria, algae, and fungi and that is distinct from plants and animals

protium *n* the most common isotope of hydrogen, with a mass number of 1 ▶ HISTORY from Greek *prōtos* first

proto- *or sometimes before a vowel* **prot-** *combining form* **1** first: *protomartyr* **2** original: *prototype* ▶ HISTORY Greek *prōtos* first

protocol *n* **1** the rules of behaviour for formal occasions **2** a record of an agreement in international negotiations **3** *computers* a standardized format for exchanging data, esp. between different computer systems ▶ HISTORY Late Greek *prōtokollon* sheet glued to the front of a manuscript

proton (**pro-**ton) *n* a positively charged elementary particle, found in the nucleus of an atom ▶ HISTORY Greek *prōtos* first

protoplasm *n biol* a complex colourless substance forming the living contents of a cell ▶ HISTORY Greek *prōtos* first + *plasma* form > **protoplasmic** *adj*

prototype *n* **1** an early model of a product, which is tested so that the design can be changed if necessary **2** a person or thing that serves as an example of a type

protozoan (pro-toe-**zoe**-an) *n*, *pl* **-zoa** a very tiny single-celled invertebrate, such as an amoeba. Also: **protozoon** ▶ HISTORY Greek *prōtos* first + *zoion* animal

protract *vb* to lengthen or extend (a situation, etc.) ▶ HISTORY Latin *protrahere* to prolong > **protracted** *adj* > **protraction** *n*

protractor *n* an instrument for measuring angles, usually a flat semicircular piece of plastic

protrude *vb* **-truding, -truded** to stick out or project ▶ HISTORY PRO-² + Latin *trudere* to thrust > **protrusion** *n* > **protrusive** *adj*

protuberant *adj* swelling out; bulging ▶ HISTORY Late Latin *protuberare* to swell > **protuberance** *n*

proud *adj* **1** feeling pleasure or satisfaction: *she was proud of her daughter's success* **2** feeling honoured **3** haughty or arrogant **4** causing pride: *the city's proud history* **5** dignified: *too proud to accept charity* **6** (of a surface or edge) projecting or protruding ▷ *adv* **7 do someone proud** to entertain someone on a grand scale: *Mum did us all proud last Christmas* ▶ HISTORY Old French *prud, prod* brave > **proudly** *adv*

proud flesh *n* a mass of tissue formed around a healing wound

prove *vb* **proving, proved; proved** *or* **proven** **1** to establish the validity of: *such a claim is difficult to prove scientifically* **2** to demonstrate or test: *the autopsy proved that she had drowned* **3** *law* to establish the genuineness of (a will) **4** to show (oneself) to be: *he proved equal to the task* **5** to be

found to be: *it proved to be a trap* **6** (of dough) to rise in a warm place before baking ▶ HISTORY Latin *probare* to test > **provable** *adj*

proven *vb* **1** a past participle of **prove 2** See **not proven** ▷ *adj* **3** known from experience to work: *a proven ability to make money*

provenance (**prov**-in-anss) *n* a place of origin ▶ HISTORY French

Provençal (prov-on-**sahl**) *adj* **1** of Provence, in SE France ▷ *n* **2** a language of Provence **3** a person from Provence

provender *n old-fashioned* fodder for livestock ▶ HISTORY Old French *provendre*

proverb *n* a short memorable saying that expresses a truth or gives a warning, for example *half a loaf is better than no bread* ▶ HISTORY Latin *proverbium*

proverbial *adj* **1** well-known because commonly or traditionally referred to **2** of a proverb > **proverbially** *adv*

provide *vb* **-viding, -vided** **1** to make available **2** to afford; yield: *social activities providing the opportunity to meet new people* **3** (often foll. by *for* or *against*) to take careful precautions: *we provide for the possibility of illness in the examination regulations* **4** (foll. by *for*) to support financially: *both parents should be expected to provide for their children* **5** *formal* **provide for** (of a law, treaty, etc.) to make possible: *a bill providing for stiffer penalties for racial discrimination* ▶ HISTORY Latin *providere* to provide for > **provider** *n*

providence *n* **1** God or nature seen as a protective force that oversees people's lives **2** the foresight shown by a person in the management of his or her affairs

Providence *n Christianity* God, esp. as showing foreseeing care of his creatures

provident *adj* **1** thrifty **2** showing foresight ▶ HISTORY Latin *providens* foreseeing

providential *adj* fortunate, as if through divine involvement

provident society *n* same as **friendly society**

providing *or* **provided** *conj* on condition (that): *the deal is on, providing he passes his medical*

province *n* **1** a territory governed as a unit of a country or empire **2** an area of learning, activity, etc. **3 the provinces** those parts of a country lying outside the capital ▶ HISTORY Latin *provincia* conquered territory

provincial *adj* **1** of a province **2** unsophisticated or narrow-minded **3** *NZ* denoting a football team representing a province ▷ *n* **4** an unsophisticated person **5** a person from a province or the provinces > **provincialism** *n*

provision *n* **1** the act of supplying something **2** something supplied **3 provisions** food and other necessities **4** a condition incorporated in a document **5 make provision for** to make arrangements for beforehand: *many restaurants still make no provision for children* ▷ *vb* **6** to supply with provisions ▶ HISTORY Latin *provisio* a providing

provisional *adj* temporary or conditional: *a provisional diagnosis* > **provisionally** *adv*

Provisional *n* a member of the Provisional IRA or Sinn Féin

proviso (pro-**vize**-oh) *n*, *pl* **-sos** or **-soes** a condition or stipulation ▶ HISTORY Medieval Latin *proviso quod* it being provided that > **provisory** *adj*

provocation *n* 1 the act of provoking or inciting 2 something that causes indignation or anger

provocative *adj* provoking or inciting: *a provocative remark* > **provocatively** *adv*

provoke *vb* **-voking, -voked** 1 to deliberately act in a way intended to anger someone: *waving a red cape, Delgado provoked the animal into charging* 2 to incite or stimulate: *the army seems to have provoked this latest confrontation* 3 (often foll. by into) to cause a person to react in a particular, often angry, way: *keeping your true motives hidden may provoke others into being just as two-faced with you* 4 to bring about: *the case has provoked furious public debate* ▶ HISTORY Latin *provocare* to call forth > **provoking** *adj*

provost *n* 1 the head of certain university colleges or schools 2 the chief councillor of a Scottish town ▶ HISTORY Old English *profost*

provost marshal *n* the officer in charge of military police in a camp or city

prow *n* the bow of a vessel ▶ HISTORY Greek *prōra*

prowess *n* 1 superior skill or ability 2 bravery or fearlessness ▶ HISTORY Old French *proesce*

prowl *vb* 1 (sometimes foll. by around or about) to move stealthily around (a place) as if in search of prey or plunder ▷ *n* 2 the act of prowling 3 **on the prowl** moving around stealthily ▶ HISTORY origin unknown > **prowler** *n*

proxemics *n* *zool* the study of spatial relationships between humans or between animals of the same species

proximate *adj* 1 next or nearest in space or time 2 very near 3 immediately coming before or following in a series 4 approximate ▶ HISTORY Latin *proximus* next

proximity *n* 1 nearness in space or time 2 nearness or closeness in a series ▶ HISTORY Latin *proximitas* closeness

proxy *n*, *pl* **proxies** 1 a person authorized to act on behalf of someone else: *the firm's creditors can vote either in person or by proxy* 2 the authority to act on behalf of someone else ▶ HISTORY Latin *procuratio* procuration

Prozac *n* *trademark* an antidepressant drug

prude *n* a person who is excessively modest or prim ▶ HISTORY Old French *prode femme* respectable woman > **prudery** *n* > **prudish** *adj*

prudent *adj* 1 sensible and careful 2 discreet or cautious 3 exercising good judgment ▶ HISTORY Latin *prudens* far-sighted > **prudence** *n* > **prudently** *adv*

prudential *adj* *old-fashioned* showing prudence: *prudential reasons* > **prudentially** *adv*

prune[1] *n* a purplish-black partially dried plum ▶ HISTORY Latin *prunum* plum

prune[2] *vb* **pruning, pruned** 1 to cut off dead or surplus branches of (a tree or shrub) 2 to shorten or reduce ▶ HISTORY Old French *proignier* to clip

prurient *adj* excessively interested in sexual matters ▶ HISTORY Latin *prurire* to lust after, itch > **prurience** *n*

Prussian *adj* 1 of Prussia, a former German state ▷ *n* 2 a person from Prussia

prussic acid *n* the extremely poisonous solution of hydrogen cyanide ▶ HISTORY French *acide prussique* Prussian acid

pry *vb* **pries, prying, pried** (often foll. by into) to make an impertinent or uninvited inquiry (about a private matter) ▶ HISTORY origin unknown

PS 1 Also: **ps** postscript 2 private secretary

PSA (in New Zealand) Public Service Association

psalm *n* (often cap) any of the sacred songs that make up a book (Psalms) of the Old Testament ▶ HISTORY Greek *psalmos* song accompanied on the harp

psalmist *n* a writer of psalms

psalmody *n*, *pl* **-dies** the singing of sacred music

Psalter *n* 1 the Book of Psalms 2 a book containing a version of Psalms ▶ HISTORY Greek *psaltērion* stringed instrument

psaltery *n*, *pl* **-teries** an ancient musical instrument played by plucking strings

PSBR (in Britain) public sector borrowing requirement: the money needed by the public sector of the economy for items not paid for by income

psephology (sef-**fol**-a-jee) *n* the statistical and sociological study of elections ▶ HISTORY Greek *psephos* pebble, vote + -LOGY > **psephologist** *n*

pseud *n* *informal* a pretentious person

pseudo *adj* *informal* not genuine

pseudo- or *sometimes before a vowel* **pseud-** *combining form* false, pretending, or unauthentic: *pseudo-intellectual* ▶ HISTORY Greek *pseudēs* false

pseudonym *n* a fictitious name adopted, esp. by an author ▶ HISTORY Greek *pseudēs* false + *onoma* name > **pseudonymity** *n* > **pseudonymous** *adj*

psittacosis *n* a viral disease of parrots that can be passed on to humans ▶ HISTORY Greek *psittakos* a parrot

psoriasis (so-**rye**-a-siss) *n* a skin disease with reddish spots and patches covered with silvery scales ▶ HISTORY Greek: itching disease

PST Pacific Standard Time

PSV (in Britain, formerly) public service vehicle

psyche *n* the human mind or soul ▶ HISTORY Greek *psukhē* breath, soul

psychedelic *adj* 1 denoting a drug that causes hallucinations 2 *informal* having vivid colours and complex patterns similar to those experienced during hallucinations ▶ HISTORY Greek *psukhē* mind + *delos* visible

psychiatry *n* the branch of medicine concerned with the study and treatment of mental health problems > **psychiatric** *adj* > **psychiatrist** *n*

psychic *adj* 1 having mental powers which cannot be explained by natural laws 2 relating to the mind ▷ *n* 3 a person who has psychic powers > **psychical** *adj*

psycho *informal n, pl* **-chos 1** same as **psychopath**
▷ *adj* **2** same as **psychopathic**

psycho- *or sometimes before a vowel* **psych-**
combining form indicating the mind or mental
processes: *psychology; psychosomatic* ▶ HISTORY
Greek *psukhē* spirit, breath

psychoactive *adj* capable of affecting mental
activity: *a psychoactive drug*

psychoanalyse *or esp US* **-lyze** *vb* **-lysing,
-lysed** *or* **-lyzing, -lyzed** to examine or treat (a
person) by psychoanalysis

psychoanalysis *n* a method of treating mental
and emotional disorders by discussion and analysis
of the patient's thoughts and feelings
> **psychoanalyst** *n* > **psychoanalytical** *or*
psychoanalytic *adj*

psychogenic *adj psychol* (esp. of disorders or
symptoms) of mental, rather than organic, origin

psychological *adj* **1** relating to the mind or
mental activity **2** relating to psychology **3** having
its origin in the mind: *his backaches are purely
psychological* > **psychologically** *adv*

psychological moment *n* the best time for
achieving the desired response or effect

psychological warfare *n* the military
application of psychology, esp. to influence morale
in time of war

psychology *n, pl* **-gies 1** the scientific study of all
forms of human and animal behaviour **2** *informal*
the mental make-up of a person > **psychologist** *n*

psychopath *n* a person with a personality
disorder which may cause him or her to commit
antisocial and sometimes violent acts
> **psychopathic** *adj*

psychopathology *n* the scientific study of
mental disorders

psychopathy (sike-**op**-ath-ee) *n* any mental
disorder or disease

psychosis (sike-**oh**-siss) *n, pl* **-ses** (-seez) a severe
mental disorder in which the sufferer's contact
with reality becomes highly distorted: *a classic case
of psychosis* > **psychotic** *adj*

psychosomatic *adj* (of a physical disorder)
thought to have psychological causes, such as
stress

psychotherapy *n* the treatment of nervous
disorders by psychological methods
> **psychotherapeutic** *adj* > **psychotherapist** *n*

psych up *vb* to prepare (oneself or another)
mentally for a contest or task

pt 1 part **2** past tense **3** point **4** port **5** pro tempore

Pt *chem* platinum

PT *old-fashioned* physical training

pt. pint

PTA Parent-Teacher Association

ptarmigan (**tar**-mig-an) *n* a bird of the grouse
family that turns white in winter

Pte. *mil* private

pterodactyl (terr-roe-**dak**-til) *n* an extinct flying
reptile with batlike wings ▶ HISTORY Greek *pteron*
wing + *daktulos* finger

PTO *or* **pto** please turn over

Ptolemaic (tol-lim-**may**-ik) *adj* relating to
Ptolemy, the 2nd-century AD Greek astronomer, or
to his belief that the earth was in the centre of the
universe

ptomaine *or* **ptomain** (**toe**-main) *n* any of a
group of poisonous alkaloids found in decaying
matter ▶ HISTORY Greek *ptoma* corpse

Pty *Austral & S African* Proprietary

Pu *chem* plutonium

pub *n* **1** *chiefly Brit* a building with a licensed bar
where alcoholic drinks may be bought and drunk
2 *Austral & NZ* a hotel

pub. 1 public **2** publication **3** published **4** publisher
5 publishing

puberty (**pew**-ber-tee) *n* the beginning of sexual
maturity ▶ HISTORY Latin *pubertas* maturity
> **pubertal** *adj*

pubes (**pew**-beez) *n, pl* **pubes 1** the region above
the genitals **2** the plural of **pubis** ▶ HISTORY Latin

pubescent *adj* **1** arriving or arrived at puberty
2 covered with down, as some plants and animals
▶ HISTORY Latin *pubescere* to reach manhood
> **pubescence** *n*

pubic (**pew**-bik) *adj* of or relating to the pubes or
pubis: *pubic hair*

pubis *n, pl* **-bes** one of the three sections of the
hipbone that forms part of the pelvis ▶ HISTORY
New Latin *os pubis* bone of the pubes

public *adj* **1** relating to the people as a whole
2 open to all: *public gardens* **3** well-known: *a public
figure* **4** performed or made openly: *public
proclamation* **5** maintained by and for the
community: *a public library* **6** open, acknowledged,
or notorious: *a public scandal* **7 go public a** (of a
private company) to offer shares for sale to the
public: *few German firms have gone public in recent
years* **b** to make information, plans, etc. known:
*the group would not have gone public with its
suspicions unless it was fully convinced of them* ▷ *n*
8 the community or people in general **9** a
particular section of the community: *the racing
public* ▶ HISTORY Latin *publicus* > **publicly** *adv*

public-address system *n* a system of
microphones, amplifiers, and loudspeakers for
increasing the sound level of speech or music at
public gatherings

publican *n Brit, Austral & NZ* a person who owns or
runs a pub

publication *n* **1** the publishing of a printed work
2 any printed work offered for sale **3** the act of
making information known to the public

public bar *n* a bar in a hotel or pub which is
cheaper and more basically furnished than the
lounge or saloon bar

public company *or* **public limited
company** *n* a limited company whose shares
may be purchased by the public

public domain *n* the status of a publication or
invention that is not under copyright and is
available for the public to use freely

public enemy *n* a notorious person who is
considered a danger to the public

public house n 1 Brit a pub 2 US & Canad an inn or small hotel

publicist n a person, such as a press agent or journalist, who publicizes something

publicity n 1 the process or information used to arouse public attention 2 the public interest so aroused

publicize or **-cise** vb **-cizing, -cized** or **-cising, -cised** to bring to public attention

public law n law the branch of law that deals with relations between a state and its individual members. Compare **private law**

public lending right n the right of authors to receive payment when their books are borrowed from public libraries

public prosecutor n law an official in charge of prosecuting important cases

public relations n the practice of gaining the public's goodwill and approval for an organization

public school n 1 (in England and Wales) a private independent fee-paying secondary school 2 (in certain Canadian provinces) a public elementary school as distinguished from a separate school 3 (in the US and other countries) any school that is part of a free local educational system

public sector n the part of a country's economy that consists of state-owned industries and services

public servant n 1 an elected or appointed holder of a public office 2 Austral & NZ a civil servant

public service n Austral & NZ the civil service

public-spirited adj having or showing an active interest in the good of the community

public transport n a system of buses, trains, etc., running on fixed routes, on which the public may travel

public utility n an organization that supplies water, gas, or electricity to the public

publish vb 1 to produce and issue (printed matter) for sale 2 to have one's written work issued for publication 3 to announce formally or in public ▶ HISTORY Latin publicare to make public > **publishing** n

publisher n 1 a company or person that publishes books, periodicals, music, etc. 2 US & Canad the proprietor of a newspaper

puce adj dark brownish-purple: his face suddenly turned puce with futile rage ▶ HISTORY French couleur puce flea colour

puck¹ n a small disc of hard rubber used in ice hockey ▶ HISTORY origin unknown

puck² n a mischievous or evil spirit ▶ HISTORY Old English pūca > **puckish** adj

pucker vb 1 to gather into wrinkles ▷ n 2 a wrinkle or crease ▶ HISTORY origin unknown

pudding n 1 a dessert, esp. a cooked one served hot 2 a savoury dish with pastry or batter: steak-and-kidney pudding 3 a sausage-like mass of meat: black pudding ▶ HISTORY Middle English poding

puddle n 1 a small pool of water, esp. of rain 2 a worked mixture of wet clay and sand that is impervious to water ▷ vb **-dling, -dled** 3 to make (clay, etc.) into puddle 4 to subject (iron) to puddling ▶ HISTORY Middle English podel > **puddly** adj

pudenda pl n the human genitals, esp. of a female ▶ HISTORY Latin: the shameful (parts)

puerile adj silly and childish ▶ HISTORY Latin puer a boy > **puerility** n

puerperal (pew-**er**-per-al) adj concerning the period following childbirth ▶ HISTORY Latin puerperium childbirth

puerperal fever n a serious, formerly widespread, form of blood poisoning caused by infection during childbirth

puerperium (pure-**peer**-ee-um) n the period after childbirth

puff n 1 a short quick blast of breath, wind, or smoke 2 the amount of wind or smoke released in a puff 3 the sound made by a puff 4 **out of puff** out of breath: by the third flight of stairs she was out of puff 5 an act of inhaling and expelling cigarette smoke 6 a light pastry usually filled with cream and jam ▷ vb 7 to blow or breathe in short quick blasts 8 (often foll. by out) to cause to be out of breath 9 to take draws at (a cigarette) 10 to move with or by the emission of puffs: the steam train puffed up the incline 11 (often foll. by up or out) to swell ▶ HISTORY Old English pyffan > **puffy** adj

puff adder n a large venomous African viper whose body swells when alarmed

puffball n a ball-shaped fungus that sends out a cloud of brown spores when mature

puffin n a black-and-white sea bird with a brightly coloured beak ▶ HISTORY origin unknown

puff pastry or US **puff paste** n a light flaky pastry

pug n a small dog with a smooth coat, lightly curled tail, and a short wrinkled nose ▶ HISTORY origin unknown

pugilist (**pew**-jil-ist) n a boxer ▶ HISTORY Latin pugil a boxer > **pugilism** n > **pugilistic** adj

pugnacious adj ready and eager to fight ▶ HISTORY Latin pugnax > **pugnacity** n

pug nose n a short stubby upturned nose ▶ HISTORY from pug (the dog) > **pug-nosed** adj

puissance n a showjumping competition that tests a horse's ability to jump large obstacles ▶ HISTORY see PUISSANT

puke slang vb **puking, puked** 1 to vomit ▷ n 2 the act of vomiting 3 the matter vomited ▶ HISTORY probably imitative

pukeko (poo-kek-oh) n, pl **-kos** a brightly coloured New Zealand wading bird ▶ HISTORY Māori

pukka adj 1 properly done, constructed, etc. 2 genuine or real ▶ HISTORY Hindi pakkā firm

pulchritude n formal or literary physical beauty ▶ HISTORY Latin pulchritudo > **pulchritudinous** adj

pull vb 1 to exert force on (an object) to draw it towards the source of the force 2 to strain or stretch 3 to remove or extract: he pulled a crumpled tenner from his pocket 4 informal to draw out (a weapon) for use: he pulled a knife on his attacker

5 *informal* to attract: *the game is expected to pull a large crowd* **6** (usually foll. by *on* or *at*) to drink or inhale deeply: *he pulled on his pipe* **7** to possess or exercise the power to move: *this car doesn't pull well on hills* **8** to withdraw or remove: *the board pulled their support* **9** *printing* to take (a proof) from type **10** *golf, baseball, etc.* to hit (a ball) away from the direction in which the player intended to hit it **11** *cricket* to hit (a ball) to the leg side **12** to row (a boat) or take a stroke of (an oar) in rowing **13 pull a face** to make a grimace **14 pull a fast one** *slang* to play a sly trick **15 pull apart** or **to pieces** to criticize harshly **16 pull (one's) punches** to limit the force of one's criticisms or blows ▷ *n* **17** the act of pulling **18** the force used in pulling: *the pull of the moon affects the tides* **19** the act of taking in drink or smoke **20** *printing* a proof taken from type **21** something used for pulling, such as a handle **22** *informal* power or influence: *his uncle is chairman of the company, so he has quite a lot of pull* **23** *informal* the power to attract attention or support **24** a single stroke of an oar in rowing **25** the act of pulling the ball in golf, cricket, etc. ▷ See also **pull in** ▸ HISTORY Old English *pullian*

pullet *n* a hen less than one year old ▸ HISTORY Old French *poulet* chicken

pulley *n* a wheel with a grooved rim in which a belt, chain, or piece of rope runs in order to lift weights by a downward pull ▸ HISTORY Old French *polie*

pull in *vb* **1** Also: **pull over** (of a motor vehicle) to draw in to the side of the road **2** (often foll. by *to*) to reach a destination: *the train pulled in to the station* **3** to attract: *his appearance will pull in the crowds* **4** *Brit, Austral & NZ, slang* to arrest **5** to earn (money): *he pulls in at least thirty thousand a year*

Pullman *n, pl* **-mans** *chiefly Brit* a luxurious railway coach ▸ HISTORY after G. M. *Pullman*, its inventor

pull off *vb informal* to succeed in accomplishing (something difficult): *super-heroes who pull off the impossible*

pull out *vb* **1** (of a motor vehicle) **a** to draw away from the side of the road **b** to move out from behind another vehicle to overtake **2** to depart: *the train pulled out of the station* **3** to withdraw: *several companies have pulled out of the student market* **4** to remove by pulling **5** to abandon a situation

pullover *n* a sweater that is pulled on over the head

pull through *vb* to survive or recover, esp. after a serious illness

pull up *vb* **1** (of a motor vehicle) to stop **2** to remove by the roots **3** to rebuke

pulmonary *adj* **1** of or affecting the lungs **2** having lungs or lunglike organs ▸ HISTORY Latin *pulmo* a lung

pulmonary vein *n anat* a vein that conveys blood from the heart to the lungs

pulp *n* **1** a soft wet substance made from matter which has been crushed or beaten: *mash the strawberries to a pulp* **2** the soft fleshy part of a fruit or vegetable: *halve the tomatoes then scoop the seeds*

and pulp into a bowl **3** printed or recorded material with little depth or designed to shock: *pulp fiction; a DJ churned out disco pulp* ▷ *vb* **4** to reduce a material to pulp: *he began to pulp the orange in his fingers* ▸ HISTORY Latin *pulpa* > **pulpy** *adj*

pulpit *n* **1** a raised platform in churches used for preaching **2** (usually preceded by *the*) preaching or the clergy ▸ HISTORY Latin *pulpitum* a platform

pulpwood *n* pine, spruce, or any other soft wood used to make paper

pulsar *n* a very small star which emits regular pulses of radio waves ▸ HISTORY from *puls(ating st)ar*

pulsate *vb* **-sating, -sated** **1** to expand and contract rhythmically, like a heartbeat **2** to quiver or vibrate: *the images pulsate with energy and light* **3** *physics* to vary in intensity or magnitude ▸ HISTORY Latin *pulsare* to push > **pulsation** *n*

pulse¹ *n* **1** *physiol* **a** the regular beating of blood through the arteries at each heartbeat **b** a single such beat **2** *physics, electronics* a sudden change in a quantity, such as a voltage, that is normally constant in a system **3** a regular beat or vibration **4** bustle or excitement: *the lively pulse of a city* **5** the feelings or thoughts of a group as they can be measured: *the political pulse of the capital* ▷ *vb* **pulsing, pulsed** **6** to beat, throb, or vibrate ▸ HISTORY Latin *pulsus* a beating

pulse² *n* the edible seeds of pod-bearing plants, such as peas, beans, and lentils ▸ HISTORY Latin *puls* pottage of pulse

pulverize or **-ise** *vb* **-izing, -ized** or **-ising, -ised** **1** to reduce to fine particles by crushing or grinding **2** to destroy completely ▸ HISTORY Latin *pulvis* dust > **pulverization** or **-isation** *n*

puma *n* a large American wild cat with a plain greyish-brown coat and a long tail ▸ HISTORY S American Indian

pumice (**pumm**-iss) *n* a light porous stone used for scouring and for removing hard skin. Also called: **pumice stone** ▸ HISTORY Old French *pomis*

pummel *vb* **-melling, -melled** or US **-meling, -meled** to strike repeatedly with the fists ▸ HISTORY see POMMEL

pump¹ *n* **1** a device to force a gas or liquid to move in a particular direction ▷ *vb* **2** (sometimes foll. by *from, out, etc.*) to raise or drive (air, liquid, etc.) with a pump, esp. into or from something **3** (usually foll. by *in* or *into*) to supply in large amounts: *pumping money into the economy* **4** to operate (a handle, etc.) in the manner of a pump: *he was warmly applauded, and his hand was pumped by well-wishers* **5** to obtain information from (someone) by persistent questioning **6 pump iron** *slang* to exercise with weights; do body-building exercises ▸ HISTORY Middle Dutch *pumpe* pipe

pump² *n* **1** *chiefly Brit* a shoe with a rubber sole, used in games such as tennis; plimsoll **2** *chiefly Brit* a low-cut low-heeled shoe, worn for dancing ▸ HISTORY origin unknown

pumpernickel *n* a slightly sour black bread made of coarse rye flour ▸ HISTORY from German

P

pumpkin *n* **1** a large round fruit with a thick orange rind, pulpy flesh, and many seeds **2** the creeping plant that bears this fruit ▶ HISTORY Greek *pepōn* ripe

pun *n* **1** the use of words to exploit double meanings for humorous effect, for example *my dog's a champion boxer* ▷ *vb* **punning, punned 2** to make puns ▶ HISTORY origin unknown

punch¹ *vb* **1** to strike at with a clenched fist ▷ *n* **2** a blow with the fist **3** *informal* point or vigour: *the jokes are mildly amusing but lack any real punch* ▶ HISTORY probably variant of *pounce* to stamp

punch² *n* **1** a tool or machine for shaping, piercing, or engraving **2** *computers* a device for making holes in a card or paper tape ▷ *vb* **3** to pierce, cut, stamp, shape, or drive with a punch ▶ HISTORY Latin *pungere* to prick

punch³ *n* a mixed drink containing fruit juice and, usually, alcoholic liquor, generally hot and spiced ▶ HISTORY origin unknown

Punch *n* the main character in the children's puppet show, Punch and Judy

punchbowl *n* a large bowl for serving punch

punch-drunk *adj* dazed and confused through suffering repeated blows to the head

punched card or *esp US* **punch card** *n* *computers* a card on which data can be coded in the form of punched holes

Punchinello *n, pl* **-los** or **-loes** a clown from Italian puppet shows, the origin of Punch ▶ HISTORY Italian *Polecenella*

punchline *n* the last line of a joke or funny story that gives it its point

punch-up *n* *informal* a fight or brawl

punchy *adj* **punchier, punchiest** *informal* effective or forceful: *learn to compose short concise punchy letters*

punctilious *adj formal* **1** paying careful attention to correct social behaviour **2** attentive to detail ▶ HISTORY Latin *punctum* a point > **punctiliously** *adv*

punctual *adj* **1** arriving or taking place at an arranged time **2** (of a person) always keeping exactly to arranged times ▶ HISTORY Medieval Latin *punctualis* concerning detail > **punctuality** *n* > **punctually** *adv*

punctuate *vb* **-ating, -ated** **1** to insert punctuation marks into (a written text) **2** *written* to interrupt at frequent intervals: *the meeting was punctuated by heckling* **3** to emphasize: *he punctuated the question by pressing the muzzle into the pilot's neck* ▶ HISTORY Latin *pungere* to puncture

punctuation *n* **1** the use of symbols, such as commas, to indicate speech patterns and meaning not otherwise shown by the written language **2** the symbols used for this purpose

punctuation mark *n* any of the signs used in punctuation, such as a comma

puncture *n* **1** a small hole made by a sharp object **2** a tear and loss of pressure in a tyre **3** the act of puncturing or perforating ▷ *vb* **-turing, -tured 4** to pierce a hole in (something) with a sharp

object **5** to cause (a tyre, etc.) to lose pressure by piercing ▶ HISTORY Latin *pungere* to prick

pundit *n* **1** an expert on a subject who often speaks or writes about it for a non-specialist audience: *Spain's leading sports pundit, who hosts two TV programmes* **2** a Hindu scholar learned in Sanskrit, religion, philosophy, or law ▶ HISTORY Hindi *pandit*

pungent *adj* **1** having a strong sharp bitter smell or taste **2** (of speech or writing) biting; critical ▶ HISTORY Latin *pungens* piercing > **pungency** *n*

punish *vb* **1** to force (someone) to undergo a penalty for some crime or misbehaviour **2** to inflict punishment for (some crime or misbehaviour) **3** to treat harshly, esp. by overexertion: *he continued to punish himself in the gym* ▶ HISTORY Latin *punire* > **punishable** *adj* > **punishing** *adj*

punishment *n* **1** a penalty for a crime or offence **2** the act of punishing or state of being punished **3** *informal* rough physical treatment: *the boxer's face could not withstand further punishment*

punitive (pew-nit-tiv) *adj* relating to punishment: *punitive measures*

punk *n* **1** a worthless person **2** a youth movement of the late 1970s, characterized by anti-Establishment slogans, short spiky hair, and the wearing of worthless articles such as safety pins for decoration **3** short for **punk rock 4** a follower of the punk movement or of punk rock ▷ *adj* **5** relating to the punk youth movement of the late 1970s: *a punk band* **6** worthless or insignificant ▶ HISTORY origin unknown

punkah or **punka** *n* (in India) a ceiling fan made of a cloth stretched over a rectangular frame ▶ HISTORY Hindi *pankhā*

punk rock *n* rock music of the punk youth movement of the late 1970s, characterized by energy and aggressive lyrics and performance > **punk rocker** *n*

punnet *n* a small basket for fruit ▶ HISTORY origin unknown

punster *n* a person who is fond of making puns

punt¹ *n* **1** an open flat-bottomed boat, propelled by a pole ▷ *vb* **2** to propel (a punt) by pushing with a pole on the bottom of a river ▶ HISTORY Latin *ponto*

punt² *n* **1** a kick in certain sports, such as rugby, in which the ball is dropped and kicked before it hits the ground ▷ *vb* **2** to kick (a ball) using a punt ▶ HISTORY origin unknown

punt³ *chiefly Brit vb* **1** to gamble or bet ▷ *n* **2** a gamble or bet, esp. against the bank, such as in roulette **3 take a punt at** *Austral & NZ* to make an attempt at ▶ HISTORY French *ponter*

punt⁴ *n* a former monetary unit of the Republic of Ireland

punter *n* **1** a person who places a bet **2** *Brit, Austral & NZ, informal* any member of the public, esp. when a customer: *the punters are flocking into the sales*

puny *adj* **-nier, -niest** small and weakly ▶ HISTORY Old French *puisné* born later

pup *n* **1 a** a young dog; puppy **b** the young of various other animals, such as the seal ▷ *vb* **pupping, pupped 2** (of dogs, seals, etc.) to give birth to pups 683

pupa (pew-pa) *n*, *pl* **-pae** (-pee) *or* **-pas** an insect at the stage of development between larva and adult ▶ **HISTORY** Latin: a doll > **pupal** *adj*

pupil[1] *n* a student who is taught by a teacher ▶ **HISTORY** Latin *pupus* a child

pupil[2] *n* the dark circular opening at the centre of the iris of the eye ▶ **HISTORY** Latin *pupilla*, diminutive of *pupa* doll; from the tiny reflections in the eye

puppet *n* **1** a small doll or figure moved by strings attached to its limbs or by the hand inserted in its cloth body **2** a person or state that appears independent but is controlled by another: *the former cabinet ministers have denied that they are puppets of a foreign government* ▶ **HISTORY** Latin *pupa* doll

puppeteer *n* a person who operates puppets

puppy *n*, *pl* **-pies** **1** a young dog **2** *informal*, *contemptuous* a brash or conceited young man ▶ **HISTORY** Old French *popée* doll > **puppyish** *adj*

puppy fat *n* fatty tissue that develops in childhood or adolescence and usually disappears with maturity

purblind *adj* **1** partly or nearly blind **2** lacking in understanding ▶ **HISTORY** *pure* (that is, utterly) blind

purchase *vb* **-chasing, -chased** **1** to obtain (goods) by payment **2** to obtain by effort or sacrifice: *he had purchased his freedom at the expense of his principles* ▷ *n* **3** something that is bought **4** the act of buying **5** the mechanical advantage achieved by a lever **6** a firm leverage or grip ▶ **HISTORY** Old French *porchacier* to strive to obtain > **purchaser** *n*

purchasing cycle *n* *commerce* the practice of consecutive purchasing

purchasing function *n* *commerce* the acquisition of the materials and services that are required in the running of a company

purdah *n* the custom in some Muslim and Hindu communities of keeping women in seclusion, with clothing that conceals them completely when they go out ▶ **HISTORY** Hindi *parda* veil

pure *adj* **1** not mixed with any other materials or elements: *pure wool* **2** free from tainting or polluting matter: *pure water* **3** innocent: *pure love* **4** complete: *Pamela's presence on that particular flight was pure chance* **5** (of a subject) studied in its theoretical aspects rather than for its practical applications: *pure mathematics* **6** of unmixed descent ▶ **HISTORY** Latin *purus* unstained > **purely** *adv* > **pureness** *n*

purebred *adj* denoting a pure strain obtained through many generations of controlled breeding

puree (pure-ray) *n* **1** a smooth thick pulp of sieved fruit, vegetables, meat, or fish ▷ *vb* **-reeing, -reed** **2** to make (foods) into a puree ▶ **HISTORY** French

purgative *med* *n* **1** a medicine for emptying the bowels ▷ *adj* **2** causing emptying of the bowels

purgatory *n* **1** *chiefly RC Church* a place in which the souls of those who have died undergo limited suffering for their sins on earth before they go to

heaven **2** a situation of temporary suffering or torment: *it was purgatory living in the same house as him* ▶ **HISTORY** Latin *purgare* to purify > **purgatorial** *adj*

purge *vb* **purging, purged** **1** to rid (something) of undesirable qualities **2** to rid (an organization, etc.) of undesirable people: *the party was purged* **3 a** to empty (the bowels) **b** to cause (a person) to empty his or her bowels **4 a** *law* to clear (a person) of a charge **b** to free (oneself) of guilt by showing repentance **5** to be purified ▷ *n* **6** the act or process of purging **7** the removal of undesirables from a state, organization, or political party **8** a medicine that empties the bowels ▶ **HISTORY** Latin *purgare* to purify

purify *vb* **-fies, -fying, -fied** **1** to free (something) of harmful or inferior matter **2** to free (a person) from sin or guilt **3** to make clean, for example in a religious ceremony ▶ **HISTORY** Latin *purus* pure + *facere* to make > **purification** *n*

purism *n* strict insistence on the correct usage or style, such as in grammar or art > **purist** *adj*, *n* > **puristic** *adj*

puritan *n* **1** a person who follows strict moral or religious principles ▷ *adj* **2** of or like a puritan: *he maintained a streak of puritan self-denial* ▶ **HISTORY** Late Latin *puritas* purity > **puritanism** *n*

Puritan *history* *n* **1** a member of the extreme English Protestants who wished to strip the Church of England of most of its rituals ▷ *adj* **2** of or relating to the Puritans > **Puritanism** *n*

puritanical *adj* **1** *usually disparaging* strict in moral or religious outlook **2** (sometimes cap) of or relating to a puritan or the Puritans > **puritanically** *adv*

purity *n* the state or quality of being pure

purl[1] *n* **1** a knitting stitch made by doing a plain stitch backwards **2** a decorative border, such as of lace ▷ *vb* **3** to knit in purl stitch ▶ **HISTORY** dialect *pirl* to twist into a cord

purl[2] *vb* *literary* (of a stream) to flow with a gentle movement and a murmuring sound ▶ **HISTORY** probably imitative

purlieu (per-lyoo) *n* **1** *English history* land on the edge of a royal forest **2** (usually pl) *literary* a neighbouring area; outskirts **3** (often pl) *literary* a place one frequents: *the committee was the purlieu of civil servants* ▶ **HISTORY** Anglo-French *puralé* a going through

purloin *vb* *formal* to steal ▶ **HISTORY** Old French *porloigner* to put at a distance

purple *n* **1** a colour between red and blue **2** cloth of this colour, often used to symbolize royalty or nobility **3** the official robe of a cardinal **4** anything purple, such as purple paint or purple clothing: *a large lady, unwisely dressed in purple* ▷ *adj* **5** of a colour between red and blue **6** (of writing) excessively elaborate: *purple prose* ▶ **HISTORY** Greek *porphura* the purple fish (murex) > **purplish** *adj*

purple heart *n* *informal, chiefly Brit* a heart-shaped purple tablet consisting mainly of amphetamine

P

Purple Heart *n* a decoration awarded to members of the US Armed Forces wounded in action

purport *vb* **1** to claim to be or do something, esp. falsely: *painkillers may actually cause the headaches they purport to cure* **2** (of speech or writing) to signify or imply ▷ *n* **3** meaning or significance ▶ HISTORY Old French *porporter* to convey

purpose *n* **1** the reason for which anything is done, created, or exists **2** a fixed design or idea that is the object of an action **3** determination: *his easy manner only lightly conceals a clear sense of purpose* **4** practical advantage or use: *we debated senseless points of dogma for hours to no fruitful purpose* **5 on purpose** intentionally ▷ *vb* **-posing, -posed** **6** to intend or determine to do (something) ▶ HISTORY Old French *porposer* to plan

purposeful *adj* with a fixed and definite purpose; determined > **purposefully** *adv*

purposely *adv* on purpose

purr *vb* **1** (esp. of cats) to make a low vibrant sound, usually considered as expressing pleasure **2** to express (pleasure) by this sound or by a sound suggestive of purring ▷ *n* **3** a purring sound ▶ HISTORY imitative

purse *n* **1** a small pouch for carrying money **2** US, Canad, Austral & NZ a woman's handbag **3** wealth or resources: *the public purse appeared bottomless* **4** a sum of money that is offered as a prize ▷ *vb* **pursing, pursed** **5** to pull (the lips) into a small rounded shape ▶ HISTORY Old English *purs*

purser *n* an officer aboard a ship who keeps the accounts

purse strings *pl n* **hold the purse strings** to control the spending of a particular family, group, etc.

pursue *vb* **-suing, -sued** **1** to follow (a person, vehicle, or animal) in order to capture or overtake **2** to try hard to achieve (some desire or aim) **3** to follow the guidelines of (a plan or policy) **4** to apply oneself to (studies or interests) **5** to follow persistently or seek to become acquainted with: *was his desire to pursue and marry Carol based purely on her looks?* **6** to continue to discuss or argue (a point or subject) ▶ HISTORY Old French *poursivre* > **pursuer** *n*

pursuit *n* **1** the act of pursuing **2** an occupation or pastime

pursuivant (**purse**-iv-ant) *n* the lowest rank of heraldic officer ▶ HISTORY Old French

purulent (**pure**-yew-lent) *adj* of, relating to, or containing pus ▶ HISTORY Latin *purulentus* > **purulence** *n*

purvey *vb* **1** to sell or provide (foodstuffs) **2** to provide or make available: *the foreign ministry used him to purvey sensitive items of diplomatic news* ▶ HISTORY Old French *porveeir* to provide > **purveyor** *n*

purview *n* **1** scope of operation: *each designation falls under the purview of a different ministry* **2** breadth or range of outlook: *he hopes that the purview of science will be widened* ▶ HISTORY Anglo-Norman *purveu*

pus *n* the yellowish fluid that comes from inflamed or infected tissue ▶ HISTORY Latin

push *vb* **1** (sometimes foll. by *off, away*) to apply steady force to in order to move **2** to thrust (one's way) through something, such as a crowd **3** (sometimes foll. by *for*) to be an advocate or promoter (of): *there are many groups you can join to push for change* **4** to spur or drive (oneself or another person) in order to achieve more effort or better results: *you must be careful not to push your children too hard* **5** *informal* to sell (narcotic drugs) illegally ▷ *n* **6** the act of pushing; thrust **7** *informal* drive or determination: *everything depends on him having the push to obtain the money* **8** *informal* a special effort to achieve something: *when this push spent itself it was obvious the bid had failed* **9 the push** *Brit & NZ, informal* dismissal from employment ▶ HISTORY Latin *pulsare*

push-bike *n* *Brit, Austral & NZ, informal* a bicycle

push button *n* **1** an electrical switch operated by pressing a button ▷ *adj* **push-button** **2** operated by a push button: *a push-button radio*

pushchair *n* *Brit* a small folding chair on wheels in which a small child can be wheeled around: *escalators are difficult with pushchairs*

pusher *n* *informal* a person who sells illegal drugs

pushover *n* *informal* **1** something that is easily achieved **2** a person, team, etc. that is easily taken advantage of or defeated

push-start *vb* **1** to start (a motor vehicle) by pushing it, thus turning the engine ▷ *n* **2** this process

pushy *adj* **pushier, pushiest** *informal* offensively assertive or ambitious

pusillanimous *adj* *formal* timid and cowardly: *pusillanimous behaviour* ▶ HISTORY Latin *pusillus* weak + *animus* courage > **pusillanimity** *n*

puss *n* **1** *informal* a cat **2** *slang* a girl or woman ▶ HISTORY probably Low German

pussy¹ *n, pl* **pussies** Also called: **pussycat** *informal* a cat ▶ HISTORY from *puss*

pussy² *adj* **-sier, -siest** containing or full of pus

pussyfoot *vb* *informal* **1** to move about stealthily **2** to avoid committing oneself: *don't let's pussyfoot about naming the hit man*

pussy willow *n* a willow tree with silvery silky catkins

pustulate *vb* **-lating, -lated** to form into pustules

pustule *n* a small inflamed raised area of skin containing pus ▶ HISTORY Latin *pustula* a blister > **pustular** *adj*

put *vb* **putting, put** **1** to cause to be (in a position or place): *he put the book on the table* **2** to cause to be (in a state or condition): *what can be done to put things right?* **3** to lay (blame, emphasis, etc.) on a person or thing: *don't try to put the blame on someone else!* **4** to set or commit (to an action, task, or duty), esp. by force: *she put him to work weeding the garden* **5** to estimate or judge: *I wouldn't put him in the same class as Verdi as a composer* **6** (foll. by *to*) to utilize: *he put his culinary skills to good use when he opened a restaurant* **7** to express: *he didn't put it quite* 685 as crudely as that **8** to make (an end or limit): *opponents claim the scheme will put an end to much of the sailing and boating in the area* **9** to present for consideration; propose: *he put the question to the committee* **10** to invest (money) in or expend (time or energy) on: *they put a lot of money into the sport* **11** to throw or cast: *put the shot* ▷ *n* **12** a throw, esp. in putting the shot ▷ See also **put about, put across**, etc. ▸ HISTORY Middle English *puten* to push

put about *vb* **1** to make widely known: *a rumour was put about that he had been drunk* **2** *naut* to change course

put across *vb* to communicate successfully: *he's not very good at putting his ideas across*

putative (**pew**-tat-iv) *adj formal* **1** commonly regarded as being: *the desire of the putative father to establish his possible paternity* **2** considered to exist or have existed; inferred: *a putative earlier form* ▸ HISTORY Latin *putare* to consider

put away *vb* **1** to save: *it takes a lot of discipline to put away for your old age* **2** *informal* to lock up in a prison or other institution: *we have enough evidence to put him away for life* **3** *informal* to eat or drink in large amounts: *he put away three beers and three huge shots of brandy*

put down *vb* **1** to make a written record of **2** to repress: *the rising was put down with revolting cruelty* **3** to consider: *I'd put him down as a complete fool* **4** to attribute: *the government's defeat in the election can be put down to a general desire for change* **5** to put (an animal) to death **6** *slang* to belittle or humiliate ▷ *n* **put-down 7** *informal* a cruelly crushing remark

put in *vb* **1** to devote (time or effort): *the competitors who did best were the ones who had put in some practice* **2** (often foll. by *for*) to apply (for a job) **3** to submit: *they have put in an official complaint* **4** *naut* to bring a vessel into port

put off *vb* **1** to postpone: *ministers have put off making a decision until next month* **2** to evade (a person) by delay: *they tried to put him off, but he came anyway* **3** to cause extreme dislike in: *he was put off by her appearance* **4** to cause to lose interest in: *the accident put him off driving*

put on *vb* **1** to dress oneself in **2** to adopt (an attitude or feeling) insincerely: *I don't see why you have to put on that fake American accent* **3** to present (a play or show) **4** to add: *I've put on nearly a stone since September* **5** to cause (an electrical device) to function: *she put on the light* **6** to bet (money) on a horse race or game **7** to impose: *the government has put a tax on gas*

put out *vb* **1 a** to annoy or anger **b** to disturb or confuse **2** to extinguish (a fire, light, etc.) **3** to inconvenience (someone): *I hope I'm not putting you out* **4** to select or lay out for use: *she put out two clean cloths in the kitchen* **5** to publish or broadcast: *she put out a statement denying the rumours* **6** to dislocate: *he put his back out digging the garden*

put over *vb informal* to communicate (facts or information)

putrefy *vb* **-fies, -fying, -fied** *formal* (of organic matter) to rot and produce an offensive smell ▸ HISTORY Latin *putrefacere* > **putrefaction** *n*

putrescent *adj formal* becoming putrid; rotting: *putrescent toadstools* ▸ HISTORY Latin *putrescere* to become rotten > **putrescence** *n*

putrid *adj* **1** (of organic matter) rotting: *putrid meat* **2** sickening or foul: *a putrid stench* **3** *informal* deficient in quality or value: *a penchant for putrid puns* **4** morally corrupt ▸ HISTORY Latin *putrere* to be rotten > **putridity** *n*

putsch *n* a violent and sudden political revolt: *an attempted putsch against the general* ▸ HISTORY from German

putt *golf n* **1** a stroke on the green with a putter to roll the ball into or near the hole ▷ *vb* **2** to strike (the ball) in this way ▸ HISTORY Scot

putter *n golf* a club, usually with a short shaft, for putting

put through *vb* **1** to connect by telephone: *I'm sorry, you've been put through to the wrong extension* **2** to carry out to a conclusion

putting green *n* (on a golf course) the area of closely mown grass around the hole

putty *n, pl* **-ties 1** a stiff paste used to fix glass into frames and fill cracks in woodwork ▷ *vb* **-ties, -tying, -tied 2** to fix or fill with putty ▸ HISTORY French *potée* a potful

put up *vb* **1** to build or erect: *I want to put up some shelves in the living room* **2** to accommodate or be accommodated at: *can you put me up for tonight?* **3** to increase (prices) **4** to submit (a plan, case, etc.) **5** to offer: *the factory is being put up for sale* **6** to give: *they put up a good fight* **7** to provide (money) for: *they put up 35 per cent of the film's budget* **8** to nominate or be nominated as a candidate: *the party have yet to decide whether to put up a candidate* **9 put up to** to incite to: *I wonder who put them up to it?* **10 put up with** *informal* to endure or tolerate ▷ *adj* **put-up 11** *informal* dishonestly or craftily prearranged: *a put-up job*

puzzle *vb* **-zling, -zled 1** to baffle or bewilder **2 puzzle out** to solve (a problem) by mental effort **3 puzzle over** to think deeply about in an attempt to understand: *he puzzled over the squiggles and curves on the paper* ▷ *n* **4** a problem that cannot be easily solved **5** a toy, game, or question presenting a problem that requires skill or ingenuity for its solution ▸ HISTORY origin unknown

> **puzzlement** *n* > **puzzled** *adj* > **puzzler** *n* > **puzzling** *adj*

PVC polyvinyl chloride

PVS persistent vegetative state

PW policewoman

PWR pressurized-water reactor

pyaemia *or* **pyemia** *n med* blood poisoning with pus-forming microorganisms in the blood ▸ HISTORY Greek *puon* pus + *haima* blood

pye-dog *or* **pi-dog** *n* a half-wild Asian dog with no owner ▸ HISTORY Hindi *pāhī* outsider

pygmy *n, pl* **-mies 1** something that is a very small example of its type **2** an abnormally undersized person **3** a person of little importance or significance ▷ *adj* **4** very small: *the pygmy anteater* ▶ HISTORY Greek *pugmaios* undersized

Pygmy *n, pl* **-mies** a member of one of the very short peoples of Equatorial Africa

pyjamas *or US* **pajamas** *pl n* a loose-fitting jacket or top and trousers worn to sleep in

- ■ **WORD HISTORY**
- ■ 'Pyjamas' comes from Persian *pāy jāma*,
- ■ meaning 'leg clothing'.

pylon *n* a large vertical steel tower-like structure supporting high-tension electrical cables ▶ HISTORY Greek *pulōn* a gateway

pylorus *n, pl* **-ri** *anat* the small circular opening at the base of the stomach through which partially digested food passes to the duodenum

pyorrhoea *or esp US* **pyorrhea** (pire-**ree**-a) *n med* a discharge of pus, esp. in disease of the gums or tooth sockets ▶ HISTORY Greek *puon* pus + *rhein* to flow

pyramid *n* **1** a huge stone building with a square base and four sloping triangular sides meeting in a point, such as the royal tombs built by the ancient Egyptians **2** *maths* a solid figure with a polygonal base and triangular sides that meet in a common vertex ▶ HISTORY Greek *puramis* > **pyramidal** *adj*

pyramid of numbers *n biol* the graduated decrease in numbers at each stage in a food chain

pyramid selling *n* the practice of selling distributors batches of goods which they then subdivide and sell to other distributors, this process continuing until the final distributors are left with a stock that is unsaleable except at a loss

pyre *n* a pile of wood for cremating a corpse ▶ HISTORY Greek *pur* fire

pyrethrum (pie-**reeth**-rum) *n* **1** a Eurasian chrysanthemum with white, pink, red, or purple flowers **2** an insecticide prepared from dried

pyrethrum flowers ▶ HISTORY Greek *purethron*

pyretic (pie-**ret**-ik) *adj pathol* of, relating to, or characterized by fever ▶ HISTORY Greek *puretos* fever

Pyrex *n trademark* a variety of heat-resistant glassware used in cookery and chemical apparatus

pyrite (**pie**-rite) *n* a yellow mineral consisting of iron sulphide in cubic crystalline form. Formula: FeS_2 ▶ HISTORY Latin *pyrites* flint

pyrites (pie-**rite**-eez) *n, pl* **-tes** **1** same as **pyrite** **2** a disulphide of a metal, esp. of copper and tin

pyroclastic *adj geol* formed from the solid fragments ejected during a volcanic eruption: *the pyroclastic flows coming down the slope of a volcano*

pyromania *n psychiatry* the uncontrollable impulse and practice of setting things on fire ▶ HISTORY Greek *pur* fire + *mania* madness > **pyromaniac** *n, adj*

pyrotechnics *n* **1** the art of making fireworks **2** a firework display **3** a brilliant display of skill: *all those courtroom pyrotechnics* ▶ HISTORY Greek *pur* fire + *tekhnē* art > **pyrotechnic** *adj*

Pyrrhic victory (**pir**-ik) *n* a victory in which the victor's losses are as great as those of the defeated ▶ HISTORY after *Pyrrhus*, who defeated the Romans in 279 BC but suffered heavy losses

Pythagoras' theorem (pie-**thag**-or-ass) *n* the theorem that in a right-angled triangle the square of the length of the hypotenuse equals the sum of the squares of the other two sides ▶ HISTORY after *Pythagoras*, Greek philosopher and mathematician

python *n* a large nonpoisonous snake of Australia, Africa, and S Asia which kills its prey by crushing it with its body ▶ HISTORY after *Python*, a dragon killed by Apollo

pyx *n Christianity* any receptacle in which the bread used in Holy Communion is kept ▶ HISTORY Latin *pyxis* small box

p

Qq

Q 1 *chess* queen 2 question

q. 1 quart 2 quarter 3 question 4 quire

Q. 1 Queen 2 question

QC 1 Queen's Counsel 2 Quebec

QED which was to be shown or proved ▶ HISTORY Latin *quod erat demonstrandum*

QLD *or* **Qld** Queensland

QM Quartermaster

qr. *pl* **qrs.** 1 quarter 2 quire

QR code *n trademark* a type of bar code that can be read both horizontally and vertically, allowing large amounts of information to be encoded in it

qt *pl* **qt** *or* **qts** quart

q.t. *n* **on the q.t.** *informal* secretly

qua (**kwah**) *prep* in the capacity of; by virtue of being ▶ HISTORY Latin

quack¹ *vb* 1 (of a duck) to utter a harsh guttural sound 2 to make a noise like a duck ▷ *n* 3 the sound made by a duck ▶ HISTORY imitative

quack² *n* 1 an unqualified person who claims medical knowledge 2 *Brit, Austral & NZ, informal* a doctor ▶ HISTORY short for *quacksalver*, from Dutch
> **quackery** *n*

quad¹ *n* short for **quadrangle** (sense 1)

quad² *n informal* a quadruplet

quad³ *n* 1 quadraphonics ▷ *adj* 2 quadraphonic

quad bike *or* **quad** *n* a vehicle like a small motorcycle, with four large wheels, designed for agricultural and sporting uses

quadrangle *n* 1 a rectangular courtyard with buildings on all four sides 2 *geom* a figure consisting of four points connected by four lines ▶ HISTORY Late Latin *quadrangulum*
> **quadrangular** *adj*

quadrant *n* 1 *geom* a a quarter of the circumference of a circle b the area enclosed by two perpendicular radii of a circle c any of the four sections into which a plane is divided by two coordinate axes 2 a piece of a mechanism in the form of a quarter circle 3 an instrument formerly used in astronomy and navigation for measuring the altitudes of stars ▶ HISTORY Latin *quadrans* a quarter

quadraphonic *adj* using four independent channels to reproduce or record sound
> **quadraphonics** *n*

quadrat *n ecology* an area of vegetation, usually one square metre, selected at random for the study of plants in the surrounding area

quadrate *n* 1 a cube or square, or a square or cubelike object ▷ *vb* **-rating, -rated** 2 to make square or rectangular ▶ HISTORY Latin *quadrare* to make square

quadratic *maths n* 1 Also called: **quadratic equation** an equation in which the variable is raised to the power of two, but nowhere raised to a higher power: *solve the quadratic equation $2x^2–3x–6=3$* ▷ *adj* 2 of or relating to the second power

quadratic function *n maths* a function of the second power, which has a graph called a parabola

quadrat sampling *n ecology* the process of making assumptions about a large area of a habitat based on the information that can be learnt about a smaller, randomly selected area within it, usually one square metre

quadrennial *adj* 1 occurring every four years 2 lasting four years

quadri- *or before a vowel* **quadr-** *combining form* four: *quadrilateral* ▶ HISTORY Latin

quadriceps *n anat* a muscle at the front of the thigh ▶ HISTORY New Latin

quadrilateral *adj* 1 having four sides ▷ *n* 2 a polygon with four sides

quadrille *n* 1 a square dance for four couples 2 music for this dance ▶ HISTORY Spanish *cuadrilla*

quadrillion *n, pl* **-lions** *or* **-lion** 1 (in Britain, France, and Germany) the number represented as one followed by 24 zeros (10^{24}) 2 (in the US and Canada) the number represented as one followed by 15 zeros (10^{15}) ▶ HISTORY French *quadrillon*

quadriplegia *n* paralysis of all four limbs ▶ HISTORY QUADRI- + Greek *plēssein* to strike
> **quadriplegic** *adj, n*

quadruped (**kwod**-roo-ped) *n* an animal, esp. a mammal, that has four legs ▶ HISTORY Latin *quadru-* four + *pes* foot

quadruple *vb* **-pling, -pled** 1 to multiply by four ▷ *adj* 2 four times as much or as many 3 consisting of four parts 4 *music* having four beats in each bar ▷ *n* 5 a quantity or number four times as great as another ▶ HISTORY Latin *quadru-* four + *-plus* -fold

quadruplet *n* one of four children born at one birth

quaff (**kwoff**) *vb old-fashioned* to drink heartily or in one draught ▶ HISTORY perhaps imitative

quagga *n, pl* **-gas** *or* **-ga** a recently extinct zebra, striped only on the head and shoulders ▶ HISTORY Hottentot *qŭagga*

quagmire (**kwog**-mire) *n* a soft wet area of land that gives way under the feet; bog ▶ HISTORY from *quag* bog + *mire*

quail¹ *n, pl* **quails** *or* **quail** a small game bird of the partridge family ▶ HISTORY Old French *quaille*

quail² *vb* to shrink back with fear; cower ▶ HISTORY origin unknown

quaint *adj* attractively unusual, esp. in an old-fashioned style ▶ HISTORY Old French *cointe*, from Latin *cognitus* known

quake *vb* **quaking, quaked** 1 to shake or tremble with or as if with fear 2 to shudder because of instability ▷ *n* **3** *informal* an earthquake ▶ HISTORY Old English *cwacian*

Quaker *n* a member of a Christian sect, the Religious Society of Friends ▶ HISTORY originally an offensive nickname > **Quakerism** *n*

qualification *n* **1** an official record of achievement awarded on the successful completion of a course of training or passing of an examination **2** an ability, quality, or attribute, esp. one that fits a person to perform a particular job or task **3** a condition that modifies or limits; restriction **4** the act of qualifying or being qualified

qualified *adj* **1** having successfully completed a training course or passed the exams necessary in order to be entitled to work in a particular profession: *a qualified lawyer* **2** having the abilities, qualities, or attributes necessary to perform a particular job or task **3** having completed a training or degree course and gained the relevant certificates **4** limited or restricted; not wholehearted: *the mission was only a qualified success*

qualifier *n* **1** a person or thing that qualifies, esp. a contestant in a competition who wins a preliminary heat or contest and so earns the right to take part in the next round **2** a preliminary heat or contest **3** *grammar* another word for **modifier**

qualify *vb* **-fies, -fying, -fied 1** to have the abilities or attributes required in order to do or have something, such as a job: *he qualified as a teacher; she did not qualify for a State pension at that time* **2** to moderate or restrict (a statement one has made) **3** to describe or be described as having a particular quality: *it was neither witty nor subtle enough to qualify as a spoof* **4** to be successful in one stage of a competition and as a result progress to the next stage: *Lewis failed to qualify for the 100 metres* **5** *grammar* to modify the sense of (a word) ▶ HISTORY Latin *qualis* of what kind + *facere* to make

qualitative *adj* involving or relating to distinctions based on quality

qualitative analysis *n chem* analysis of a substance to determine its constituents

qualitative observation *n science* scientific study in which descriptive information is collected

quality *n, pl* **-ties 1** degree or standard of excellence **2** a distinguishing characteristic or attribute **3** the basic character or nature of something **4** a feature of personality **5** (formerly) high social status ▷ *adj* **6** excellent or superior: *a quality product* ▶ HISTORY Latin *qualis* of what sort

quality assurance *n commerce* the process of verifying that a product conforms to required standards, often performed by an independent assessor

quality control *n* checking of the relative quality of a manufactured product, usually by testing samples

qualm (kwahm) *n* **1** a pang of conscience; scruple **2** a sudden sensation of misgiving **3** a sudden feeling of sickness or nausea ▶ HISTORY Old English *cwealm* death or plague

quandary *n, pl* **-ries** a situation in which it is difficult to decide what to do; predicament; dilemma ▶ HISTORY origin unknown

quandong (kwon-dong) *n* **1** a small Australian tree with edible fruit and nuts used in preserves **2** an Australian tree with pale timber

quango *n, pl* **-gos** *chiefly Brit* a semipublic government-financed administrative body whose members are appointed by the government ▶ HISTORY qu(asi-)a(utonomous) n(on)g(overnmental) o(rganization)

quangocracy *n, pl* **-cies a** the influence held by quangos **b** quangos collectively

quantify *vb* **-fies, -fying, -fied** to discover or express the quantity of ▶ HISTORY Latin *quantus* how much + *facere* to make > **quantifiable** *adj* > **quantification** *n*

quantitative *adj* **1** involving considerations of amount or size **2** capable of being measured

quantitative analysis *n chem* analysis of a substance to determine the proportions of its constituents

quantitative observation *n science* scientific study in which numerical information is collected

quantity *n, pl* **-ties 1** a specified or definite amount or number **2** the aspect of anything that can be measured, weighed, or counted **3** a large amount **4** *maths* an entity having a magnitude that may be denoted by a numerical expression ▶ HISTORY Latin *quantus* how much

quantity surveyor *n* a person who estimates the cost of the materials and labour necessary for a construction job

quantum *n, pl* **-ta 1** an amount or quantity, esp. a specific amount **2** *physics* the smallest quantity of some physical property that a system can possess ▷ *adj* **3** of or designating a major breakthrough or sudden advance: *a quantum leap in business computing* ▶ HISTORY Latin *quantus* how much

quantum theory *n* a theory concerning the behaviour of physical systems based on the idea that they can only possess certain properties, such as energy and angular momentum, in discrete amounts (quanta)

quarantine *n* **1** a period of isolation, esp. of people or animals arriving from abroad, to prevent the spread of disease ▷ *vb* **-tining, -tined 2** to isolate in or as if in quarantine ▶ HISTORY Italian *quarantina* period of forty days

quark *n physics* the hypothetical elementary particle supposed to be a fundamental unit of all baryons and mesons ▶ HISTORY special use of a word coined by James Joyce in the novel *Finnegans Wake*

quarrel *n* **1** an angry disagreement; argument **2** a cause of dispute; grievance ▷ *vb* **-relling, -relled** or *US* **-reling, -reled** (often foll. by *with*) **3** to engage in a disagreement or dispute; argue **4** to find fault; complain ▶ HISTORY Latin *querella* complaint

quarrelsome *adj* inclined to quarrel or disagree

quarry[1] *n, pl* **-ries 1** a place where stone is dug from the surface of the earth ▷ *vb* **-ries, -rying,**

q

-ried 2 to extract (stone) from a quarry ▶ HISTORY Old French *quarriere*

quarry² *n, pl* **-ries 1** an animal that is being hunted; prey **2** anything pursued ▶ HISTORY Middle English *quirre* entrails offered to the hounds

quart *n* a unit of liquid measure equal to one quarter of a gallon or two pints (1.136 litres) ▶ HISTORY Latin *quartus* fourth

quarter *n* **1** one of four equal parts of something such as an object or quantity **2** the fraction equal to one divided by four (¼) **3** a fourth part of a year; three months **4** *Brit, informal* a unit of weight equal to four ounces (113.4 grams) **5** a region or district of a town or city: *the French quarter of New Orleans* **6** a region, direction, or point of the compass **7** *US & Canad* a coin worth 25 cents **8** short for **quarter-hour 9** *astron* **a** one fourth of the moon's period of revolution around the earth **b** either of two phases of the moon when half of the lighted surface is visible **10** (sometimes pl) an unspecified person or group of people: *it met stiff opposition in some quarters* **11** mercy or pity shown to a defeated opponent: *no quarter was asked or given* **12** any of the four limbs of a quadruped ▷ *vb* **13** to divide into four equal parts **14** (formerly) to dismember (a human body) **15** to billet or be billeted in lodgings **16** *heraldry* to divide (a shield) into four separate bearings ▷ *adj* **17** being or consisting of one of four equal parts ▷ See also **quarters** ▶ HISTORY Latin *quartus* fourth

quarterback *n* a player in American football who directs attacking play

quarter day *n Brit* any of four days in the year when certain payments become due

quarterdeck *n naut* the rear part of the upper deck of a ship, traditionally for official or ceremonial use

quarterfinal *n* the round before the semifinal in a competition

quarter-hour *n* **1** a period of 15 minutes **2** either of the points of time 15 minutes before or after the hour

quarterlight *n Brit* a small pivoted window in the door of a car for ventilation

quarterly *adj* **1** occurring, done, due, or issued at intervals of three months ▷ *n, pl* **-lies 2** a periodical issued every three months ▷ *adv* **3** once every three months

quartermaster *n* **1** a military officer responsible for accommodation, food, and equipment **2** a naval officer responsible for navigation

quarters *pl n* accommodation, esp. as provided for military personnel

quarter sessions *n* (formerly) a court with limited jurisdiction, held four times a year

quartet *n* **1** a group of four singers or instrumentalists **2** a piece of music for four performers **3** *written* any group of four ▶ HISTORY Italian *quarto* fourth

quartile *n* **1** one of three values of a variable dividing its distribution into four groups with equal frequencies ▷ *adj* **2** of a quartile

quarto *n, pl* **-tos** a book size resulting from folding a sheet of paper into four leaves or eight pages ▶ HISTORY New Latin *in quarto* in quarter

quartz *n* a hard glossy mineral consisting of crystalline silicon dioxide ▶ HISTORY German *Quarz*

quartz crystal *n* a thin plate or rod cut from a piece of quartz and ground so that it vibrates at a particular frequency

quartzite *n geol* **1** a very hard metamorphic rock consisting of a mosaic of intergrown quartz crystals **2** a white or grey sandstone composed of quartz

quasar (**kway**-zar) *n* any of a class of extremely distant starlike objects that are powerful sources of radio waves and other forms of energy ▶ HISTORY *quas(i-stell)ar (radio source)*

quash *vb* **1** to officially reject (something, such as a judgment or decision) as invalid **2** to defeat or suppress forcefully and completely ▶ HISTORY Latin *quassare* to shake

quasi- (**kway**-zie) *combining form* **1** almost but not really; seemingly: *a quasi-religious cult* **2** resembling but not actually being; so-called: *a quasi-scholar* ▶ HISTORY Latin: as if

quassia (**kwosh**-a) *n* **1** a tropical American tree with bitter bark and wood **2** the wood of this tree or a bitter compound extracted from it, used in insecticides ▶ HISTORY after Graman *Quassi*, who discovered its medicinal value

quaternary *adj* consisting of four parts ▶ HISTORY Latin *quaterni* by fours

Quaternary *adj geol* of the most recent period of geological time, which started about one million years ago

quaternary industry *n econ, business* an industry concerned with providing the specialist knowledge and skills for the other economic sectors. Compare **primary industry, secondary industry, tertiary industry**

quatrain *n* a stanza or poem of four lines ▶ HISTORY French, from Latin *quattuor* four

quatrefoil *n* **1** a leaf composed of four leaflets **2** *archit* a carved ornament of four arcs about a common centre ▶ HISTORY Old French *quatre* four + *-foil* leaflet

quattrocento (kwat-roe-**chen**-toe) *n* the 15th century, esp. in reference to Renaissance Italian art ▶ HISTORY Italian: four hundred (short for fourteen hundred)

quaver *vb* **1** (esp. of the voice) to quiver or tremble **2** to say or sing (something) with a trembling voice ▷ *n* **3** *music* a note having the time value of an eighth of a semibreve **4** a tremulous sound or note ▶ HISTORY Germanic > **quavering** *adj*

quay (**kee**) *n* a wharf built parallel to the shoreline ▶ HISTORY Old French *kai*

queasy *adj* **-sier, -siest 1** having the feeling that one is about to vomit; nauseous **2** feeling or causing uneasiness ▶ HISTORY origin unknown > **queasily** *adv* > **queasiness** *n*

queen *n* **1** a female sovereign who is the official ruler or head of state **2** the wife of a king

3 a woman, thing, or place considered the best or most important of her or its kind: *the rose is considered the queen of garden flowers* **4** the only fertile female in a colony of bees, wasps, or ants **5** a playing card with a picture of a queen on it **6** a chessman, able to move in a straight line in any direction ▷ *vb* **7** *chess* to promote (a pawn) to a queen when it reaches the eighth rank **8 queen it** *informal* to behave in an overbearing manner: *she is more beautiful than ever and still queening it over everybody* ▶ HISTORY Old English *cwēn*
> **queenly** *adj*

queen consort *n* the wife of a reigning king

queen mother *n* the widow of a former king who is also the mother of the reigning sovereign

queen post *n* *building* one of a pair of vertical posts that connect the tie beam of a truss to the principal rafters of a roof

Queensberry rules *pl n* **1** the code of rules followed in modern boxing **2** *informal* gentlemanly conduct, esp. in a dispute ▶ HISTORY after the ninth Marquess of *Queensberry*, who originated the rules

Queen's Counsel *n* **1** (in Britain, Australia, and New Zealand) a barrister or advocate appointed Counsel to the Crown **2** (in Canada and New Zealand) an honorary title bestowed on lawyers with long experience

Queen's English *n* correctly spoken and written British English

queen's evidence *n* *English law* evidence given for the Crown against former associates in crime by an accomplice

queen's highway *n* **1** (in Britain) any public road or right of way **2** (in Canada) a main road maintained by the provincial government

queer *adj* **1** not normal or usual; odd or strange **2** dubious; shady **3** *Brit* faint, giddy, or queasy **4** *informal, usually offensive* homosexual **5** *informal* eccentric or slightly mad ▷ *n* **6** *informal, usually offensive* a homosexual ▷ *vb* **7 queer someone's pitch** *informal* to spoil or thwart someone's chances of something ▶ HISTORY origin unknown

quell *vb* **1** to suppress (rebellion or unrest); subdue **2** to overcome or allay ▶ HISTORY Old English *cwellan* to kill

quench *vb* **1** to satisfy (one's thirst) **2** to put out; extinguish **3** to suppress or subdue **4** *metallurgy* to cool (hot metal) by plunging it into cold water ▶ HISTORY Old English *ācwencan* to extinguish

quern *n* a stone hand mill for grinding corn ▶ HISTORY Old English *cweorn*

querulous (**kwer**-yew-luss) *adj* complaining; whining or peevish ▶ HISTORY Latin *queri* to complain > **querulously** *adv*

query *n, pl* **-ries 1** a question, esp. one expressing doubt **2** a question mark ▷ *vb* **-ries, -rying, -ried 3** to express uncertainty, doubt, or an objection concerning (something) **4** to express as a query; ask ▶ HISTORY Latin *quaere* ask!

quest *n* **1** a looking for or seeking; search **2** the object of a search; a goal or target ▷ *vb* **3 quest for** to go in search of **4** (of dogs) to search for game ▶ HISTORY Old French *queste*

question *n* **1** a form of words addressed to a person in order to obtain an answer; interrogative sentence **2** a point at issue: *they were silent on the question of social justice* **3** a difficulty or uncertainty **4 a** an act of asking **b** an investigation into some problem **5** a motion presented for debate **6 beyond (all) question** beyond (any) doubt **7 call something into question a** to make something the subject of disagreement **b** to cast doubt upon the validity or truth of something **8 in question** under discussion: *the area in question was not contaminated* **9 out of the question** beyond consideration; impossible ▷ *vb* **10** to put a question or questions to (a person); interrogate **11** to make (something) the subject of dispute **12** to express uncertainty; doubt ▶ HISTORY Latin *quaestio*

questionable *adj* **1** (esp. of a person's morality or honesty) doubtful **2** of disputable value or authority > **questionably** *adv*

question mark *n* **1** the punctuation mark (?), used at the end of questions **2** a doubt or uncertainty: *a question mark still hangs over their success*

question master *n* *Brit* the person chairing a radio or television quiz or panel game

questionnaire *n* a set of questions on a form, used to collect statistical information or opinions from people

question on notice *n* *Austral politics* a question submitted in writing to a minister and answered in writing

question tag *n* *grammar* a clause added on to another clause to invite the hearer's agreement or disagreement, such as *isn't it* in *the bread's on the table, isn't it?*

question time *n* (in some parliamentary bodies) the time set aside each day for questions to government ministers

question without notice *n* *Austral politics* a question put orally to a minister usually without prior warning as to the content of it

queue *n* **1** a line of people or vehicles waiting for something ▷ *vb* **queuing** or **queueing, queued 2** (often foll. by *up*) to form or remain in a line while waiting ▶ HISTORY Latin *cauda* tail

quibble *vb* **-bling, -bled 1** to make trivial objections ▷ *n* **2** a trivial objection or equivocation, esp. one used to avoid an issue **3** *archaic* a pun ▶ HISTORY origin unknown

quiche (**keesh**) *n* a savoury flan with an egg custard filling to which cheese, bacon, or vegetables are added ▶ HISTORY French

quick *adj* **1** characterized by rapidity of movement or action; fast **2** lasting or taking a short time **3** immediate or prompt: *her quick action minimized the damage* **4** eager or ready to perform (an action): *quick to condemn* **5** responsive to stimulation; alert; lively: *they were impressed by his quick mind* **6** easily excited or aroused: *he is impulsive and has a quick*

q

691

temper **7** nimble in one's movements or actions; deft: *she has quick hands* ▷ *n* **8** any area of sensitive flesh, esp. that under a nail **9 cut someone to the quick** to hurt someone's feelings deeply **10 the quick** *archaic* living people ▷ *adv* **11** in a rapid manner; swiftly ▶ HISTORY Old English *cwicu* living > **quickly** *adv* > **quickness** *n*

quick-change artist *n* an actor or entertainer who undertakes several rapid changes of costume during a performance

quicken *vb* **1** to make or become faster; accelerate **2** to impart to or receive vigour or enthusiasm: *science quickens the imagination* **3 a** (of a fetus) to begin to show signs of life **b** (of a pregnant woman) to reach the stage of pregnancy at which movements of the fetus can be felt

quickie *informal n* **1** anything made or done rapidly ▷ *adj* **2** made or done rapidly: *a quickie divorce*

quicklime *n* a white caustic solid, mainly composed of calcium oxide, used in the manufacture of glass and steel

quicksand *n* a deep mass of loose wet sand that submerges anything on top of it

quickset *chiefly Brit adj* **1** (of plants or cuttings) planted so as to form a hedge ▷ *n* **2** a hedge composed of such plants

quicksilver *n* the metal mercury

quickstep *n* **1** a modern ballroom dance in rapid quadruple time **2** music for this dance

quid¹ *n, pl* **quid** *Brit, slang* **1** a pound (sterling) **2 be quids in** to be in a very favourable or advantageous position ▶ HISTORY origin unknown

quid² *n* a piece of tobacco for chewing ▶ HISTORY Old English *cwidu* chewing resin

quiddity *n, pl* **-ties 1** the essential nature of something **2** a petty or trifling distinction ▶ HISTORY Latin *quid* what

quid pro quo *n, pl* **quid pro quos** one thing, esp. an advantage or object, given in exchange for another ▶ HISTORY Latin: something for something

quiescent (kwee-**ess**-ent) *adj formal* quiet, inactive, or dormant ▶ HISTORY Latin *quiescere* to rest > **quiescence** *n*

quiet *adj* **1** characterized by an absence of noise **2** calm or tranquil: *the sea is quiet today* **3** untroubled: *a quiet life* **4** not busy: *business is quiet this morning* **5** private or secret: *I had a quiet word with her* **6** free from anger, impatience, or other extreme emotion **7** not showy: *quiet colours; a quiet wedding* **8** modest or reserved: *quiet humour* ▷ *n* **9** the state of being silent, peaceful, or untroubled **10 on the quiet** without other people knowing ▷ *vb* **11** to make or become calm or silent ▶ HISTORY Latin *quies* repose > **quietly** *adv* > **quietness** *n*

quieten *vb Brit & NZ* **1** (often foll. by *down*) to make or become calm or silent **2** to allay (fear or doubts)

quietism *n formal* passivity and calmness of mind towards external events > **quietist** *n, adj*

quietude *n formal* quietness, peace, or tranquillity

quietus *n, pl* **-tuses 1** *literary* a release from life; death **2** the discharge or settlement of debts or duties ▶ HISTORY Latin *quietus est*, literally: he is at rest

quiff *n Brit* a tuft of hair brushed up above the forehead ▶ HISTORY origin unknown

quill *n* **1** Also called: **quill pen** a feather made into a pen **2 a** any of the large stiff feathers of the wing or tail of a bird **b** the hollow stem of a feather **3** any of the stiff hollow spines of a porcupine or hedgehog ▶ HISTORY origin unknown

quilt *n* **1** a cover for a bed, consisting of a soft filling sewn between two layers of material, usually with crisscross seams **2** a continental quilt; duvet ▷ *vb* **3** to stitch together two layers of (fabric) with padding between them ▶ HISTORY Old French *coilte* mattress > **quilted** *adj*

quin *n* a quintuplet

quince *n* the acid-tasting pear-shaped fruit of an Asian tree, used in preserves ▶ HISTORY Greek *kudōnion*

quincunx *n* a group of five objects arranged in the shape of a rectangle with one at each corner and the fifth in the centre ▶ HISTORY Latin: five twelfths; in ancient Rome, this was a coin marked with five spots

quinine *n* a bitter drug extracted from cinchona bark, used as a tonic and formerly in malaria therapy ▶ HISTORY Spanish *quina* cinchona bark

quinquennial *adj* occurring once every five years or over a period of five years

quinquereme *n* an ancient Roman galley with five banks of oars ▶ HISTORY Latin *quinque* five + *remus* oar

quinsy *n* inflammation of the tonsils and throat, with abscesses ▶ HISTORY Greek *kuōn* dog + *ankhein* to strangle

quint *n US & Canad* a quintuplet

quintain *history n* **1** a post or target set up for jousting practice for medieval knights **2** the exercise of tilting at such a target

quintal *n* **1** a unit of weight equal to (esp. in Britain) 112 pounds (50.85 kg) or (esp. in US) 100 pounds (45.36 kg) **2** a unit of weight equal to 100 kilograms ▶ HISTORY Arabic *qintār*

quintessence *n* **1** the most perfect representation of a quality or state **2** an extract of a substance containing its central nature in its most concentrated form ▶ HISTORY Medieval Latin *quinta essentia* the fifth essence > **quintessential** *adj*

quintet *n* **1** a group of five singers or instrumentalists **2** a piece of music for five performers **3** any group of five ▶ HISTORY Italian *quintetto*

quintillion *n, pl* **-lions** *or* **-lion 1** (in Britain, France, and Germany) the number represented as one followed by 30 zeros (10^{30}) **2** (in the US and Canada) the number represented as one followed by 18 zeros (10^{18}) ▶ HISTORY Latin *quintus* fifth

quintuple *vb* **-pling, -pled 1** to multiply by five ▷ *adj* **2** five times as much or as many **3** consisting of five parts ▷ *n* **4** a quantity or number five times as great as another ► **HISTORY** Latin *quintus* fifth + *-plus* -fold

quintuplet *n* one of five children born at one birth

quip *n* **1** a witty saying ▷ *vb* **quipping, quipped 2** *written* to make a quip ► **HISTORY** probably from Latin *quippe* indeed, to be sure

quire *n* a set of 24 or 25 sheets of paper ► **HISTORY** Old French *quaier*

quirk *n* **1** a peculiarity of character; mannerism or foible **2** an unexpected twist or turn: *a strange quirk of fate* ► **HISTORY** origin unknown > **quirky** *adj*

quisling *n* a traitor who aids an occupying enemy force; collaborator ► **HISTORY** after Vidkun *Quisling*, Norwegian collaborator with the Nazis

quit *vb* **quitting, quit 1** to stop (doing something) **2** to resign (from): *the Prime Minister's decision to quit; he quit his job as a salesman* **3** to leave (a place) ► **HISTORY** Old French *quitter* > **quitter** *n*

quite *adv* **1** (not used with a negative) to a greater than average extent; somewhat: *he found her quite attractive* **2** absolutely: *you're quite right* **3** in actuality; truly **4 quite a** or **an** of an exceptional kind: *she is quite a girl* **5 quite something** a remarkable thing or person ▷ *interj* **6** *spoken* an expression used to indicate agreement ► **HISTORY** adverbial use of *quite* (adjective) quit, free of

quits *adj informal* **1** on an equal footing **2 call it quits** to end a dispute or contest, agreeing that honours are even

quittance *n* **1** release from debt or other obligation **2** a document certifying this ► **HISTORY** Old French *quitter* to release from obligation

quiver[1] *vb* **1** to shake with a tremulous movement; tremble ▷ *n* **2** a shaking or trembling ► **HISTORY** obsolete *cwiver* quick, nimble > **quivering** *adj*

quiver[2] *n* a case for holding or carrying arrows ► **HISTORY** Old French *cuivre*

quixotic (kwik-**sot**-ik) *adj* unrealistically optimistic or chivalrous ► **HISTORY** after Don *Quixote* in Cervantes' romance > **quixotically** *adv*

quiz *n, pl* **quizzes 1** an entertainment in which the knowledge of the players is tested by a series of questions **2** any set of quick questions designed to test knowledge **3** an investigation by close questioning ▷ *vb* **quizzing, quizzed 4** to investigate by close questioning; interrogate ► **HISTORY** origin unknown

quizzical *adj* questioning and mocking or supercilious: *the question elicits a quizzical expression* > **quizzically** *adv*

quod *n Brit, slang* a jail ► **HISTORY** origin unknown

quoin *n* **1** an external corner of a wall **2** the stone forming the outer corner of a wall; a cornerstone **3** a wedge ► **HISTORY** variant of *coin* (in former sense of corner)

quoit *n* a large ring used in the game of quoits ► **HISTORY** origin unknown

quokka *n* a small Australian wallaby

quondam *adj formal* of an earlier time; former: *her quondam employers* ► **HISTORY** Latin

quorate *adj* having or being a quorum: *the meeting is now quorate*

quorum *n* the minimum number of members required to be present in a meeting or assembly before any business can be transacted ► **HISTORY** Latin, literally: of whom

quota *n* **1** the share that is due from, due to, or allocated to a person or group **2** the prescribed number or quantity allowed, required, or admitted ► **HISTORY** Latin *quotus* of what number

quotation *n* **1** a written or spoken passage repeated exactly in a later work, speech, or conversation, usually with an acknowledgment of its source **2** the act of quoting **3** an estimate of costs submitted by a contractor to a prospective client

quotation marks *pl n* the punctuation marks used to begin and end a quotation, either " and " or ' and '

quote *vb* **quoting, quoted 1** to repeat (words) exactly from (an earlier work, speech, or conversation), usually with an acknowledgment of their source **2** to state a price for goods or a job of work **3** to put quotation marks round (words) ▷ *n* **4** *informal* a quotation **5 quotes** *informal* quotation marks ▷ *interj* **6** *spoken* an expression used to indicate that the words that follow are a quotation ► **HISTORY** Medieval Latin *quotare* to assign reference numbers to passages > **quotable** *adj*

quoth *vb archaic* (foll. by *I, he* or *she*) said ► **HISTORY** Old English *cwæth*

quotidian *adj* **1** daily **2** *literary* commonplace **3** (esp. of fever) recurring daily ► **HISTORY** Latin *quotidianus*

quotient *n* the result of the division of one number or quantity by another ► **HISTORY** Latin *quotiens* how often

Quran *or* **Qur'an** (koo-**rahn**) *n* same as **Koran**

q.v. (denoting a cross-reference) which (word, item, etc.) see ► **HISTORY** New Latin *quod vide*

qwerty *or* **QWERTY keyboard** *n* the standard English language typewriter or computer keyboard with the characters q, w, e, r, t, and y at the top left of the keyboard

q

Rr

r **1** radius **2** ratio **3** right **4** *cricket* run(s)

R **1** *chem* radical **2** Regina **3** Registered Trademark **4** *physics, electronics* resistance **5** Rex **6** River **7** *chess* rook

Ra *chem* radium

RA **1** rear admiral **2** (in Britain) Royal Academy **3** (in Britain) Royal Artillery

RAAF Royal Australian Air Force

rabbi (**rab**-bye) *n, pl* **-bis** **1** the spiritual leader of a Jewish congregation **2** an expert in or teacher of Jewish Law ▶ **HISTORY** Hebrew: my master > **rabbinical** *adj*

rabbit *n, pl* **-bits** *or* **-bit** **1** a common burrowing mammal with long ears and a short fluffy tail ▷ *vb* **-biting, -bited** **2** *informal* to talk too much: *he keeps rabbiting on about interrogation* ▶ **HISTORY** origin unknown

rabbit ears *pl n* *Austral & NZ* an indoor television aerial

rabbit fence *n* *Austral & NZ* a fence to prevent the spread of rabbits

rabble *n* **1** a disorderly crowd of noisy people **2** **the rabble** *contemptuous* the common people ▶ **HISTORY** origin unknown

rabble-rouser *n* a person who stirs up the feelings of the mob > **rabble-rousing** *adj, n*

Rabelaisian *adj* characterized by broad, often bawdy humour and sharp satire ▶ **HISTORY** after the work of the French writer, François *Rabelais*

rabid *adj* **1** fanatical: *a rabid separatist* **2** having rabies ▶ **HISTORY** Latin *rabidus* frenzied > **rabidity** *n*

rabies (**ray**-beez) *n* *pathol* a fatal infectious viral disease of the nervous system transmitted by dogs and certain other animals ▶ **HISTORY** Latin: madness

RAC (in Britain) Royal Automobile Club

raccoon *or* **racoon** *n, pl* **-coons** *or* **-coon** a small American mammal with a long striped tail ▶ **HISTORY** from a Native American language

race¹ *n* **1** a contest of speed **2** any competition or rivalry: *the arms race* **3** a rapid current of water **4** a channel of a stream: *a mill race* **5** *Austral & NZ* a narrow passage through which sheep pass individually, as to a sheep dip ▷ *vb* **racing, raced** **6** to take part in a contest of speed with (someone) **7** to enter (an animal or vehicle) in a race: *to race greyhounds* **8** to travel as fast as possible **9** (of an engine) to run faster than normal **10** (of the heart) to beat faster than normal ▷ See also **races**

▶ **HISTORY** Old Norse *rās* running > **racer** *n* > **racing** *adj, n*

race² *n* **1** a group of people of common ancestry with distinguishing physical features, such as skin colour or build **2** **the human race** human beings collectively **3** a group of animals or plants having common characteristics that distinguish them from other members of the same species ▶ **HISTORY** Italian *razza*

race caller *n* *Austral & NZ* a professional horse-racing commentator

racecourse *n* a long broad track on which horses are raced

racehorse *n* a horse specially bred for racing

raceme (rass-**eem**) *n* *bot* a cluster of flowers along a central stem, as in the foxglove ▶ **HISTORY** Latin *racemus* bunch of grapes

race relations *pl n* the relations between members of two or more races within a single community

race riot *n* a riot involving violence between people of different races

races *pl n* **the races** a series of contests of speed between horses or greyhounds over a fixed course

racetrack *n* **1** a circuit used for races between cars, bicycles, or runners **2** *US & Canad* a racecourse

racial *adj* **1** relating to the division of the human species into races **2** typically associated with any such group **3** relating to differences between the races: *racial discrimination* > **racially** *adv*

racism *or* **racialism** *n* **1** hostile or oppressive behaviour towards people because they belong to a different race **2** the belief that some races are innately superior to others because of hereditary characteristics > **racist** *or* **racialist** *n, adj*

rack¹ *n* **1** a framework for holding particular articles, such as coats or luggage **2** a straight bar with teeth on its edge, to work with a cogwheel **3** **the rack** *history* an instrument of torture that stretched the body of the victim ▷ *vb* **4** to cause great suffering to: *Germany was racked by food riots* **5** **rack one's brains** to try very hard to think of something ▶ **HISTORY** probably from Middle Dutch *rec* framework

rack² *n* **go to rack and ruin** to be destroyed through neglect ▶ **HISTORY** variant of WRACK¹

rack³ *vb* to clear (wine or beer) by siphoning it off from the dregs

rack⁴ *n* the neck or rib part of a joint of meat

rack-and-pinion *n* a device for converting rotary into linear motion and vice versa, in which a gearwheel (the pinion) engages with a flat toothed bar (the rack)

racket¹ *n* **1** a noisy disturbance **2** an illegal activity done to make money **3** *slang* a business or occupation: *I've been in the racket since I was sixteen* ▷ *vb* **-eting, -eted** **4** to make a commotion ▶ **HISTORY** probably imitative > **rackety** *adj*

racket² *or* **racquet** *n* a bat consisting of an oval frame surrounding a mesh of strings, with a handle, used in tennis, badminton, and squash ▷ See also **rackets** ▶ **HISTORY** French *raquette*

racketeer *n* a person who makes money from illegal activities > **racketeering** *n*

rackets *n* a game similar to squash, played by two or four people

raconteur (rak-on-**tur**) *n* a person skilled in telling stories ▶ HISTORY French

racoon *n*, *pl* **-coons** or **-coon** same as **raccoon**

racquet *n* same as **racket²**

racy *adj* **racier, raciest 1** slightly shocking **2** spirited or lively > **racily** *adv* > **raciness** *n*

rad radian

RADA (in Britain) Royal Academy of Dramatic Art

radar *n* **1** a method of detecting the position and velocity of a distant object by bouncing a narrow beam of extremely high-frequency radio pulses off it **2** the equipment used in this ▶ HISTORY *ra(dio) d(etecting) a(nd) r(anging)*

raddle *vb* **-dling, -dled** *Austral & NZ* to mark (sheep) for identification

raddled *adj* (of a person) untidy or run-down in appearance ▶ HISTORY from *rud* red ochre

radial *adj* **1** spreading out from a common central point **2** of a radius or ray **3** short for **radial-ply 4** *anat* of the forearm: *a radial nerve* ▷ *n* **5** a radial-ply tyre > **radially** *adv*

radial-ply *adj* (of a tyre) having the fabric cords in the outer casing running radially to enable the sidewalls to be flexible

radian *n* an SI unit of plane angle; the angle between two radii of a circle that cut off on the circumference an arc equal in length to the radius

radiant *adj* **1** characterized by health and happiness: *radiant good looks* **2** shining **3** emitted as radiation: *radiant heat* **4** sending out heat by radiation: *radiant heaters* ▶ HISTORY Latin *radiare* to shine > **radiance** *n* > **radiantly** *adv*

radiant energy *n* energy that is emitted or propagated in the form of particles or electromagnetic radiation

radiate *vb* **-ating, -ated 1** to spread out from a central point **2** to show (an emotion or quality) to a great degree: *she radiated competence and composure* **3** to emit or be emitted as radiation ▷ *adj* **4** having rays or a radial structure ▶ HISTORY Latin *radiare* to emit rays

radiation *n* **1** *physics* **a** the emission of energy as particles, electromagnetic waves, or sound **b** the particles or waves emitted **2** the process of radiating

radiation sickness *n* illness caused by overexposure to radioactive material or X-rays

radiator *n* **1** *Brit* a device for heating a room or building, consisting of a series of pipes containing hot water **2** a device for cooling an internal-combustion engine, consisting of thin-walled tubes containing water **3** *Austral & NZ* an electric fire

radical *adj* **1** favouring fundamental change in political or social conditions: *a radical student movement* **2** of the essential nature of a room or thing; fundamental: *a radical fault* **3** searching or thorough: *a radical interpretation* **4** *maths* of or

containing roots of numbers or quantities ▷ *n* **5** a person who favours fundamental change in existing institutions or in political, social, or economic conditions **6** *maths* a root of a number or quantity, such as $\sqrt[3]{5}$, $\sqrt{x}$ **7** *chem* an atom or group of atoms which acts as a unit during chemical reactions ▶ HISTORY Latin *radix* a root > **radicalism** *n* > **radically** *adv*

radical sign *n* the symbol √ placed before a number or quantity to indicate the extraction of a root, esp. a square root. The value of a higher root is indicated by a raised digit in front of the symbol, as in $\sqrt[3]{}$

radicchio (rad-**deek**-ee-oh) *n*, *pl* **-chios** an Italian variety of chicory, with purple leaves streaked with white that are eaten raw in salads

radicle *n* *bot* **a** the part of the embryo of seed-bearing plants that develops into the main root **b** a very small root or rootlike part ▶ HISTORY Latin *radix* root

radii *n* a plural of **radius**

radio *n*, *pl* **-dios 1** the use of electromagnetic waves for broadcasting or two-way communication without the use of linking wires **2** an electronic device for converting radio signals into sounds **3** a communications device for sending and receiving messages using radio waves **4** sound broadcasting ▷ *vb* **5** to transmit (a message) by radio ▷ *adj* **6** of, relating to, or using radio broadcasting or radio signals: *a radio interview* **7** using or producing electromagnetic waves in the range used for radio signals: *radio astronomy* ▶ HISTORY Latin *radius* ray

radio- *combining form* **1** denoting radio **2** denoting radioactivity or radiation: *radiocarbon*

radioactive *adj* showing or using radioactivity

radioactivity *n* the spontaneous emission of radiation from atomic nuclei. The radiation can consist of alpha or beta particles, or gamma rays

radio astronomy *n* astronomy using a radio telescope to analyse signals received from radio sources in space

radiocarbon *n* a radioactive isotope of carbon, esp. carbon-14

radiocarbon dating *n* same as **carbon dating**

radiochemistry *n* the chemistry of radioactive substances

radio-controlled *adj* controlled by signals sent by radio

radio frequency *n* any electromagnetic frequency that lies in the range 10 kilohertz to 300,000 megahertz and can be used for broadcasting

radiogram *n* *Brit* an old-fashioned combined radio and record player

radiograph *n* an image produced on a special photographic film or plate by radiation, usually by X-rays

radiography (ray-dee-**og**-ra-fee) *n* the production of radiographs for use in medicine and industry > **radiographer** *n*

radioisotope *n* a radioactive isotope

radiology (ray-dee-**ol**-a-jee) *n* the use of X-rays and radioactive substances in the diagnosis and treatment of disease > **radiologist** *n*

radioscopy (ray-dee-**oss**-kop-ee) *n* examination of a person or object by means of a fluorescent screen and an X-ray source

radiosonde *n* an airborne instrument to send meteorological information back to earth by radio ▶ HISTORY RADIO- + French *sonde* sounding line

radiotelegraphy *n* telegraphy in which messages are transmitted by radio waves

radiotelephone *n* a telephone which sends and receives messages using radio waves rather than wires > **radiotelephony** *n*

radio telescope *n* an instrument used in radio astronomy to pick up and analyse radio waves from space

radiotherapy *n* the treatment of disease, esp. cancer, by radiation

radio wave *n* an electromagnetic wave of radio frequency

radish *n* a small hot-flavoured red root vegetable eaten raw in salads ▶ HISTORY Latin *radix* root

radium *n chem* a highly radioactive luminescent metallic element, found in pitchblende. Symbol: Ra ▶ HISTORY Latin *radius* ray

radius (**ray**-dee-uss) *n, pl* **-dii** (-dee-eye) *or* **-diuses 1** a straight line joining the centre of a circle to any point on the circumference **2** the length of this line **3** *anat* the outer, slightly shorter of the two bones of the forearm **4** a circular area of a specified size round a central point: *within a seven-mile radius of the club* ▶ HISTORY Latin: ray, spoke

radon (**ray**-don) *n chem* a colourless radioactive element of the noble gas group. Symbol: Rn ▶ HISTORY from *radium*

RAF (in Britain) Royal Air Force

Rafferty *or* **Rafferty's rules** *pl n Austral & NZ, slang* no rules at all ▶ HISTORY origin unknown

raffia *n* a fibre obtained from the leaves of a palm tree, used for weaving ▶ HISTORY Malagasy

raffish *adj written* unconventional or slightly disreputable ▶ HISTORY obsolete *raff* rubbish

raffle *n* **1** a lottery, often to raise money for charity, in which the prizes are goods rather than money ▷ *vb* **-fling, -fled 2** to offer as a prize in a raffle ▶ HISTORY Old French

raft *n* a floating platform of logs or planks tied together ▶ HISTORY Old Norse *raptr* rafter

rafter *n* any of the parallel sloping beams that form the framework of a roof ▶ HISTORY Old English

rag¹ *n* **1** a small piece of cloth **2** *Brit, Austral & NZ, informal* a newspaper **3 rags** old tattered clothing **4 from rags to riches** from being extremely poor to being extremely wealthy ▶ HISTORY probably formed from *ragged*, from Old Norse *raggi*

rag² *Brit vb* **ragging, ragged 1** to tease **2** to play rough practical jokes on ▷ *n* **3** a boisterous practical joke ▷ *adj* **4** (in British universities and colleges) of various events organized to raise money for charity: *a rag week* ▶ HISTORY origin unknown

rag³ *n* a piece of ragtime music

ragamuffin *n* a ragged dirty child ▶ HISTORY probably from RAG¹

ragbag *n* a confused mixture: *the traditional ragbag of art traders*

rage *n* **1** intense anger or passion **2** a fashion or craze: *the dance was the rage of Europe* **3** aggressive behaviour associated with a specified activity or environment: *road rage; school rage* **4 all the rage** *informal* very popular **5** *Austral & NZ, informal* a dance or party ▷ *vb* **raging, raged 6** to feel or show intense anger **7** to proceed violently and without restraint: *the argument was still raging* ▶ HISTORY Latin *rabies* madness

ragged (**rag**-gid) *adj* **1** dressed in shabby or torn clothes **2** (of clothes) tattered and torn **3** having a rough or uneven surface or edge **4** neglected or untidy: *the ragged stone-built village*

ragged robin *n* a plant that has pink or white flowers with ragged petals

raglan *adj* **1** (of a sleeve) joined to the garment by diagonal seams from the collar to the underarm **2** (of a garment) with this style of sleeve ▶ HISTORY after Lord *Raglan*

ragout (rag-**goo**) *n* a richly seasoned stew of meat and vegetables ▶ HISTORY French

ragtime *n* a style of jazz piano music with a syncopated melody ▶ HISTORY probably *ragged time*

rag trade *n Brit, Austral & NZ, informal* the clothing business

ragwort *n* a plant with ragged leaves and yellow flowers

raid *n* **1** a sudden surprise attack: *a bombing raid* **2** a surprise visit by police searching for people or goods: *a drugs raid* ▷ *vb* **3** to make a raid on **4** to sneak into (a place) in order to steal ▶ HISTORY Old English *rād* military expedition > **raider** *n*

rail¹ *n* **1** a horizontal bar supported by vertical posts, used as a fence or barrier **2** a horizontal bar on which to hang things: *a curtain rail* **3** one of a pair of parallel bars that serve as a running surface for the wheels of a train **4** railway: *by car or by rail* **5 go off the rails** to start behaving improperly or eccentrically ▷ *vb* **6** to fence (an area) with rails ▶ HISTORY Old French *raille* rod

rail² *vb written* **rail against** or **at** to complain bitterly or loudly about ▶ HISTORY Old French *railler* to mock

rail³ *n* a small wading marsh bird ▶ HISTORY Old French *raale*

railcard *n Brit* an identity card, which pensioners or young people can buy, entitling them to cheaper rail travel

railhead *n* **1** a terminal of a railway **2** the farthest point reached by completed track on an unfinished railway

railing *n* a fence made of rails supported by posts

raillery *n, pl* **-leries** good-natured teasing ▶ HISTORY French *railler* to tease

railroad *n* **1** *US* a railway ▷ *vb* **2** *informal* to force (a person) into an action with haste or by unfair means

r

railway *n* **1** a track composed of a line of parallel metal rails fixed to sleepers, on which trains run **2** any track on which the wheels of a vehicle may run: *a cable railway* **3** the rolling stock, buildings, and tracks used in such a transport system **4** the organization responsible for operating a railway network

raiment *n archaic or poetic* clothing ▶ HISTORY from *arrayment*

rain *n* **1 a** water falling from the sky in drops formed by the condensation of water vapour in the atmosphere **b** a fall of rain. *Related adjective:* **pluvial** **2** a large quantity of anything falling rapidly: *a rain of stones descended on the police* **3 (come) rain or shine** regardless of circumstances **4 right as rain** *informal* perfectly all right ▷ *vb* **5** to fall as rain: *it's raining back home* **6** to fall rapidly and in large quantities: *steel rungs and sawdust raining down* **7 rained off** cancelled or postponed because of rain. US and Canad term: **rained out** ▷ See also **rains** ▶ HISTORY Old English *regn* > **rainy** *adj*

rainbird *n S African* a common name for **Burchell's coucal**, a bird whose call is believed to be a sign of impending rain

rainbow *n* an arched display in the sky of the colours of the spectrum, caused by the refraction and reflection of the sun's rays through rain

rainbow nation *n* the South African nation

rainbow trout *n* a freshwater trout with black spots and two red stripes

raincoat *n* a coat made of a waterproof material

rainfall *n* the amount of rain, hail, or snow in a specified place and time

rainforest *n* dense forest found in tropical areas of heavy rainfall

rain gauge *n meteorol* an instrument for measuring rainfall or snowfall, consisting of a cylinder covered by a funnel-like lid

rains *pl n* **the rains** the season in the tropics when there is a lot of rain

rain shadow *n meteorol* the relatively dry area on the leeward side of high ground in the path of rain-bearing winds

rainstorm *n* a storm with heavy rain

rainwater *n* water from rain

rainy day *n* a future time of need, esp. financial need

raise *vb* **raising, raised** **1** to lift to a higher position or level **2** to place in an upright position **3** to increase in amount, quality, or intensity: *to raise interest rates* **4** to collect or gather together: *to raise additional capital; to raise an army* **5** to cause to be expressed: *to raise a smile* **6** to stir up **7** to bring up: *to raise a family* **8** to grow: *to raise a crop* **9** to put forward for consideration: *they raised controversial issues* **10** to arouse from sleep or death **11** to build: *to raise a barn* **12** to bring to an end: *to raise a siege* **13** to establish radio communications with: *we raised Moscow last night* **14** to advance in rank; promote **15** *maths* to multiply (a number) by itself a specified number of times: *8 is 2 raised to the power 3* **16** to cause (dough) to rise, as by the addition of

yeast **17** *cards* to bet more than (the previous player) **18 raise Cain a** to create a disturbance **b** to protest vehemently ▷ *n* **19** *US, Canad & NZ* an increase in pay ▶ HISTORY Old Norse *reisa*

raised *adj* higher than the surrounding area: *a small raised platform*

raised beach *n geog* a wave-cut platform raised above the shoreline by a relative fall in the water level

raisin *n* a dried grape ▶ HISTORY Old French: grape

raison d'être (ray-zon **det**-ra) *n, pl* **raisons d'être** (ray-zon **det**-ra) reason or justification for existence ▶ HISTORY French

raita (**rye**-ta) *n* an Indian dish of chopped cucumber, mint, etc. in yogurt, served with curry ▶ HISTORY Hindi

Raj *n* **the Raj** the British government in India before 1947 ▶ HISTORY Hindi

raja *or* **rajah** *n history* an Indian prince or ruler ▶ HISTORY Hindi

rake¹ *n* **1** a farm or garden tool consisting of a row of teeth set in a headpiece attached to a long shaft and used for gathering leaves or straw, or for smoothing loose earth **2** any of various implements similar in shape or function ▷ *vb* **raking, raked** **3** to scrape or gather with a rake **4** to smooth (a surface) with a rake **5** Also: **rake out** to clear (ashes) from (a fire) **6 rake together** *or* **up** to gather (items or people) with difficulty, as from a limited supply **7** to search or examine carefully: *raking over the past is not always popular* **8** to direct (gunfire) along the length of (a target): *the machine guns raked up and down their line* **9** to scrape or graze: *he raked the tip of his shoe across the pavement* ▷ See also **rake-off** ▶ HISTORY Old English *raca*

rake² *n* an immoral man ▶ HISTORY short for *rakehell*

rake³ *n* **1** the degree to which an object slopes ▷ *vb* **raking, raked** **2** to slope from the vertical, esp. (of a ship's mast) towards the stern **3** to construct with a backward slope ▶ HISTORY origin unknown

raked *adj* (of a surface) sloping so that it is higher at the back than at the front

rake-off *n slang* a share of profits, esp. an illegal one

rake up *vb* to bring back memories of (a forgotten unpleasant event): *she doesn't want to rake up the past*

rakish¹ (**ray**-kish) *adj* dashing or jaunty: *a hat which he wore at a rakish angle* ▶ HISTORY probably from RAKE³

rakish² *adj* immoral: *a rakish life of drinking and womanizing* ▶ HISTORY from RAKE² > **rakishly** *adv*

rallentando *music adj, adv* **1** becoming slower ▷ *n* **2** a passage in which the music becomes slower ▶ HISTORY Italian

rally¹ *n, pl* **-lies** **1** a large gathering of people for a meeting **2** a marked recovery of strength, as during illness **3** *Stock Exchange* a sharp increase in price or trading activity after a decline **4** *tennis, squash, etc.* an exchange of several shots before one player wins the point **5** a car-driving competition

r

on public roads ▷ *vb* **-lies, -lying, -lied**
6 to bring or come together after being dispersed
7 to bring or come together for a common cause
8 to summon up (one's strength or spirits)
9 to recover (sometimes only temporarily) from an illness **10** *Stock Exchange* to increase sharply after a decline ▶ HISTORY Old French *rallier*

rally² *vb* **-lies, -lying, -lied** to mock or tease (someone) in a good-natured way ▶ HISTORY Old French *railler* to tease

rally round *vb* to group together to help someone

ram *n* **1** an uncastrated adult male sheep **2** a hydraulically or pneumatically driven piston **3** the falling weight of a pile driver **4** short for **battering ram** ▷ *vb* **ramming, rammed 5** to strike against with force **6** to force or drive: *he rammed his sword into the man's belly* **7** to stuff or cram **8 ram something home** to make something clear or obvious: *to ram home the message* **9 ram something down someone's throat** to put forward or emphasize an argument or idea with excessive force ▶ HISTORY Old English *ramm*

RAM *computers* random access memory: a temporary storage space which loses its contents when the computer is switched off

Rama *n* a Hindu god, the incarnation of Vishnu

Ramadan *n* **1** the ninth month of the Muslim year, 30 days long, during which strict fasting is observed from sunrise to sunset **2** the fast itself

ramble *vb* **-bling, -bled 1** to walk for relaxation, sometimes with no particular direction **2** to speak or write in a confused style **3** to grow or develop in a random fashion ▷ *n* **4** a walk, esp. in the countryside ▶ HISTORY Middle English *romblen*

rambler *n* **1** a person who takes country walks **2** a climbing rose

rambling *adj* **1** long and irregularly shaped: *a rambling 14th-century church* **2** (of speech or writing) confused and long-winded ▷ *n* **3** the activity of going for long walks in the country

RAMC Royal Army Medical Corps

ramekin (**ram**-ik-in) *n* a small container for baking and serving one portion of food ▶ HISTORY French *ramequin*

ramification *n* **1 ramifications** the consequences or complications resulting from an action **2** a structure of branching parts

ramp *n* **1** a slope that joins two surfaces at different levels **2** a place where the level of a road surface changes because of road works **3** a movable stairway by which passengers enter and leave an aircraft **4** *Brit* a small hump on a road to make traffic slow down ▶ HISTORY Old French *ramper* to crawl, rear

rampage *vb* **-paging, -paged 1** to rush about violently ▷ *n* **2 on the rampage** behaving violently or destructively ▶ HISTORY Scots

rampant *adj* **1** growing or spreading uncontrollably **2** *heraldry* (of a beast) standing on the hind legs, the right foreleg raised above the left: *a lion rampant* ▶ HISTORY Old French *ramper* to crawl, rear

rampart *n* a mound of earth or wall built to protect a fort or city ▶ HISTORY Old French

ram raid *n informal* a raid on a shop in which a stolen car is driven into the window > **ram raider** *n*

ramrod *n* **1** a long thin rod for cleaning the barrel of a gun or forcing gunpowder into an old-fashioned gun ▷ *adj* **2** (of someone's posture) very straight and upright

ramshackle *adj* badly made or cared for: *a curious ramshackle building* ▶ HISTORY obsolete *ransackle* to ransack

ran *vb* the past tense of **run**

RAN Royal Australian Navy

ranch *n* **1** a large cattle farm in the American West **2** *chiefly US & Canad* a large farm for the rearing of a particular kind of livestock or crop: *he owned a yak ranch in Tibet* ▷ *vb* **3** to run a ranch ▶ HISTORY Mexican Spanish *rancho* small farm > **rancher** *n*

ranchslider *n NZ* a glazed sliding door usually opening onto an outside terrace

rancid *adj* (of fatty foods) stale and having an offensive smell ▶ HISTORY Latin *rancidus* > **rancidity** *n*

rancour *or US* **rancor** *n* deep bitter hate ▶ HISTORY Old French > **rancorous** *adj*

rand *n* the standard monetary unit of the Republic of South Africa ▶ HISTORY from *Witwatersrand*, S Transvaal, referring to the gold-mining there

R & B rhythm and blues

R & D research and development

random *adj* **1** lacking any definite plan or prearranged order: *a random sample* ▷ *n* **2 at random** not following any prearranged order ▶ HISTORY Old French *randir* to gallop > **randomly** *adv* > **randomness** *n*

random access *n* a method of reading data from a computer file without having to read through the file from the beginning

ranee *n* same as **rani**

rang *vb* the past tense of **ring¹**

rangatira (rung-a-**teer**-a) *n NZ* a Māori chief of either sex ▶ HISTORY Māori

range *n* **1** the limits within which a person or thing can function effectively: *academic ability range* **2 a** the maximum effective distance of a projectile fired from a weapon **b** the distance between a target and a weapon **3** the total distance which a ship, aircraft, or vehicle can travel without taking on fresh fuel **4** the difference in pitch between the highest and lowest note of a voice or musical instrument **5** a whole set of related things: *a range of treatments was available* **6** the total products of a manufacturer, designer, or stockist: *the latest skin-care range* **7** the limits within which something can lie: *a range of prices* **8** *US & Canad* an extensive tract of open land on which livestock can graze **9** a chain of mountains **10** an area set aside for shooting practice or rocket testing **11** a large cooking stove with one or more ovens **12** *maths* the set of values that a function or variable can take ▷ *vb* **ranging, ranged 13** to vary between one point and another **14** to cover a specified period or

r

specified things: *attitudes ranged from sympathy to indifference* **15** to roam (over) **16** to establish or be situated in a line or series **17** to put into a specific category: *they ranged themselves with the opposition* ▶ HISTORY Old French: row

rangefinder *n* an instrument for finding how far away an object is

ranger *n* **1** an official in charge of a park or nature reserve **2** *US* an armed trooper employed to police a State or district: *a Texas ranger*

Ranger or **Ranger Guide** *n Brit & Austral* a member of the senior branch of the Guides

rangy (**rain**-jee) *adj* **rangier, rangiest** *written* having long slender limbs

rani or **ranee** *n* the wife or widow of a raja ▶ HISTORY Hindi

rank¹ *n* **1** a position within a social organization: *the rank of superintendent* **2** high social or other standing: *accusations were made against people of high rank* **3** a person's social class: *it was too grand for someone of his lowly rank* **4** the position of an item in any ordering or sequence **5** a line or row of people or things **6** *Brit, NZ & S African* a place where taxis wait to be hired **7** a line of people, esp. soldiers, positioned one beside the other **8** any of the eight horizontal rows of squares on a chessboard **9 close ranks** to maintain solidarity **10 pull rank** to get one's own way by virtue of one's superior position **11 rank and file** the ordinary people or members of a group **12 the ranks** the common soldiers ▷ *vb* **13** to give or hold a specific position in an organization or group **14** to arrange in rows or lines **15** to arrange in sequence: *it ranks a lowly 19th worldwide* **16** to be important: *the legendary coronation stone ranks high in the hearts of patriots* ▶ HISTORY Old French *ranc*

rank² *adj* **1** complete or absolute: *rank incompetence* **2** *written* smelling offensively strong **3** growing too quickly: *rank weeds* ▶ HISTORY Old English *ranc* straight, proud

rankle *vb* **-kling, -kled** to continue to cause resentment or bitterness ▶ HISTORY Old French *draoncle* ulcer

rank-size rule *n geog, sociol* the theory proposed by George Zipf in 1949 according to which a country's second city will be half the size of its primate city while its third major city will be a third of its size, and so on

ransack *vb* **1** to search through every part of (a place or thing) **2** to plunder or pillage ▶ HISTORY Old Norse *rann* house + *saka* to search

ransom *n* **1** the money demanded in return for the release of someone who has been kidnapped **2 hold to ransom a** to keep (a prisoner) in confinement until payment is received **b** to attempt to force (a person) to do something ▷ *vb* **3** to pay money to obtain the release of (a prisoner) **4** to set free (a prisoner) in return for money ▶ HISTORY Old French *ransoun* > **ransomer** *n*

rant *vb* **1** to talk in a loud and excited way ▷ *n* **2** loud excited speech ▶ HISTORY Dutch *ranten* to rave > **ranting** *adj, n*

ranunculus *n, pl* **-luses** or **-li** a genus of plants including the buttercup ▶ HISTORY Latin *rana* frog

RAOC Royal Army Ordnance Corps

rap¹ *vb* **rapping, rapped** **1** to hit with a sharp quick blow **2** to knock loudly and sharply **3 rap out** to utter in sharp rapid speech: *he rapped out his address* **4** to perform a rhythmic monologue with musical backing **5** *slang* to talk in a relaxed and friendly way **6** to rebuke or criticize sharply **7 rap over the knuckles** to reprimand ▷ *n* **8** a sharp quick blow or the sound produced by it **9** a fast rhythmic monologue over a musical backing **10** a sharp rebuke or criticism **11** *slang* a legal charge: *a murder rap* **12 take the rap** *slang* to suffer the punishment for a crime, whether guilty or not ▶ HISTORY probably from Old Norse > **rapper** *n*

rap² *n* **not care a rap** to not care in the least: *she didn't care a rap for us* ▶ HISTORY probably from *ropaire*, counterfeit coin formerly current in Ireland

rapacious *adj* **1** greedy or grasping **2** (of animals or birds) living by catching prey ▶ HISTORY Latin *rapax* > **rapacity** *n*

rape¹ *vb* **raping, raped** **1** to force (someone) to submit to sexual intercourse ▷ *n* **2** the act of raping **3** any violation or abuse: *the rape of the country's natural resources* ▶ HISTORY Latin *rapere* to seize > **rapist** *n*

rape² *n* a yellow-flowered plant cultivated for its seeds (**rapeseed**), which yield a useful oil (**rape oil**), and as a fodder plant ▶ HISTORY Latin *rapum* turnip

rapid *adj* **1** (of an action) taking or lasting a short time **2** acting or moving quickly: *a rapid advance* ▶ HISTORY Latin *rapidus* > **rapidly** *adv* > **rapidity** *n*

rapid eye movement *n* the movement of the eyeballs while a person is dreaming

rapids *pl n* part of a river where the water is very fast and turbulent

rapier (**ray**-pyer) *n* a long narrow two-edged sword ▶ HISTORY Old French *espee rapiere* rasping sword

rapine (**rap**-pine) *n* pillage or plundering ▶ HISTORY Latin *rapina*

rapport (rap-**pore**) *n* a sympathetic relationship or understanding ▶ HISTORY French

rapprochement (rap-**prosh**-mong) *n* a re-establishment of friendly relations: *the policy of rapprochement with Eastern Europe* ▶ HISTORY French

rapscallion *n old-fashioned* a rascal or rogue ▶ HISTORY earlier *rascallion*

rapt *adj* **1** totally engrossed: *rapt attention* **2** arising from or showing rapture: *with a rapt look on his face* ▶ HISTORY Latin *raptus* carried away

raptor *n* any bird of prey ▶ HISTORY Latin: robber > **raptorial** *adj*

rapture *n* **1** extreme happiness or delight **2 raptures** *written* ecstatic joy: *they will be in raptures over the rugged scenery* ▶ HISTORY Latin *raptus* carried away > **rapturous** *adj*

rare¹ *adj* **1** uncommon or unusual: *a rare plant* **2** not happening or done very often: *a rare appearance in*

r

London **3** of uncommonly high quality: *a rare beauty* **4** (of air at high altitudes) having low density; thin ▸ HISTORY Latin *rarus* sparse

rare² *adj* (of meat) very lightly cooked ▸ HISTORY Old English *hrēr*

rarebit *n* short for **Welsh rarebit**

rare earth *n chem* **1** any oxide of a lanthanide. **2** Also called: **rare-earth element** any element of the lanthanide series

rarefied (rare-if-ide) *adj* **1** highly specialized: *the rarefied world of classical ballet* **2** (of air) thin **3** exalted in character: *the rarefied heights of academic excellence*

rarely *adv* **1** hardly ever **2** to an unusual degree; exceptionally

raring *adj* **raring to do something** keen and willing to do something ▸ HISTORY *rare*, variant of REAR²

rarity *n, pl* **-ties 1** something that is valuable because it is unusual **2** the state of being rare

rascal *n* **1** a scoundrel or rogue **2** a mischievous child ▸ HISTORY Old French *rascaille* rabble > **rascally** *adj*

rase *vb* **rasing, rased** same as **raze**

rash¹ *adj* acting or done without proper thought or consideration; hasty: *rash actions* ▸ HISTORY Old High German *rasc* hurried, clever > **rashly** *adv* > **rashness** *n*

rash² *n* **1** an outbreak of spots or patches on the skin, caused by illness or allergy **2** an outbreak of occurrences: *a rash of censorship trials* ▸ HISTORY Old French *rasche*

rasher *n* a thin slice of bacon ▸ HISTORY origin unknown

rasp *n* **1** a harsh grating noise **2** a coarse file with rows of raised teeth ▷ *vb* **3** to say or speak in a grating voice **4** to make a harsh grating noise **5** to scrape or rub (something) roughly **6** to irritate (one's nerves) ▸ HISTORY Old French *raspe*

raspberry *n, pl* **-ries 1** the red fruit of a prickly shrub of Europe and North America **2** *informal* a spluttering noise made with the tongue and lips to express contempt: *she blew a loud raspberry* ▸ HISTORY origin unknown

Rasta *n informal* short for **Rastafarian**

Rastafari *n* **1** the Rastafarian movement ▷ *adj* **2** of this movement or its followers

Rastafarian *n* **1** a follower of a religious movement of Jamaican origin that regards Ras Tafari, the former emperor of Ethiopia, Haile Selassie, as God ▷ *adj* **2** of this movement or its followers

rat *n* **1** a long-tailed rodent, similar to but larger than a mouse **2** *informal* someone who is disloyal or treacherous **3 smell a rat** to detect something suspicious ▷ *vb* **ratting, ratted 4 rat on a** to betray (someone): *good friends don't rat on each other* **b** to go back on (an agreement): *his ex-wife claims he ratted on their divorce settlement* **5** to hunt and kill rats ▸ HISTORY Old English *ræt*

ratafia (rat-a-**fee**-a) *n* **1** a liqueur made from fruit **2** *chiefly Brit* an almond-flavoured biscuit ▸ HISTORY West Indian Creole French

rat-arsed *adj Brit & Austral, slang* drunk

ratatouille (rat-a-**twee**) *n* a vegetable casserole made of stewed tomatoes, aubergines, etc. ▸ HISTORY French

ratchet *n* **1** a device in which a toothed rack or wheel is engaged by a pivoted lever which permits motion in one direction only **2** the toothed rack or wheel in such a device ▸ HISTORY French *rochet*

rate¹ *n* **1** a quantity or amount considered in relation to or measured against another quantity or amount: *he was publishing at the rate of about 10 books a year* **2** a price or charge with reference to a standard or scale: *an exchange rate* **3** the speed of progress or change: *crime is increasing at an alarming rate* **4** a charge made per unit for a commodity or service **5** See **rates 6** relative quality: *a third-rate power* **7 at any rate** in any case ▷ *vb* **rating, rated 8** to assign a position on any scale of relative values: *he is rated as one of the top caterers in the country* **9** to estimate the value of: *we rate your services highly* **10** to consider or regard: *it could hardly be rated a success* **11** to be worthy of: *it barely rates a mention* **12** *informal* to have a high opinion of: *the cognoscenti have always rated his political skills* ▸ HISTORY Medieval Latin *rata*

rate² *vb* **rating, rated** to scold or criticize severely ▸ HISTORY origin unknown

rateable *adj* **1** able to be rated or evaluated **2** liable to payment of rates

ratepayer *n* a person who pays local rates on a building

rates *pl n* (in some countries) a tax on property levied by a local authority

rather *adv* **1** fairly: *that was a rather narrow escape* **2** to a limited extent: *I rather thought that was the case* **3** more truly or appropriately: *they tend to be cat rather than dog people* **4** more willingly: *I would rather go straight home* ▷ *interj* **5** an expression of strong affirmation: *Is it worth seeing? Rather!* ▸ HISTORY Old English *hrathor*, comparative of *hrathe* ready, quick

ratify *vb* **-fies, -fying, -fied** to give formal approval to ▸ HISTORY Latin *ratus* fixed + *facere* to make > **ratification** *n*

rating *n* **1** a valuation or assessment **2** a classification according to order or grade **3** a noncommissioned sailor **4 ratings** the size of the audience for a television or radio programme

ratio *n, pl* **-tios 1** the relationship between two numbers or amounts expressed as a proportion: *a ratio of one instructor to every five pupils* **2** *maths* a quotient of two numbers or quantities ▸ HISTORY Latin: a reckoning

ratio decidendi *n law* the legal principle on which a particular judicial decision is based ▸ HISTORY Latin: reason for deciding

ration *n* **1** a fixed allowance of something that is scarce, such as food or petrol in wartime **2 rations** a fixed daily allowance of food, such as that given to a soldier ▷ *vb* **3** to restrict the distribution of (something): *the government has rationed petrol* **4** to distribute a fixed amount of something to (each person in a group) ▸ HISTORY Latin *ratio* reckoning > **rationing** *n*

rational *adj* **1** reasonable or sensible **2** using reason or logic in thinking out a problem **3** capable of reasoning: *man is a rational being* **4** sane: *rational behaviour* **5** *maths* able to be expressed as a ratio of two integers: *a rational number* ▶ HISTORY Latin *rationalis* > **rationality** *n* > **rationally** *adv*

rationale (rash-a-**nahl**) *n* the reason for an action or belief

rationalism *n* the philosophy that regards reason as the only basis for beliefs or actions > **rationalist** *n* > **rationalistic** *adj*

rationalize or **-ise** *vb* **-izing, -ized** or **-ising, -ised** **1** to find reasons to justify or explain (one's actions) **2** to apply logic or reason to (something) **3** to get rid of unnecessary equipment or staff to make (a business) more efficient > **rationalization** or **-isation** *n*

rational number *n* any real number that can be expressed in the form a/b, where a and b are integers and b is not zero, as 7 or ⅔

ratpack *n* *slang* the members of the press who pursue celebrities and give wide coverage of their private lives: *the royal ratpack*

rat race *n* a continual routine of hectic competitive activity: *get out of the rat race for a while*

rattan *n* a climbing palm with tough stems used for wickerwork and canes ▶ HISTORY Malay *rōtan*

rattle *vb* **-tling, -tled** **1** to make a rapid succession of short sharp sounds, such as when loose pellets are shaken in a container **2** to send, move, or drive with such a sound: *rain rattled against the window* **3** to shake briskly causing sharp sounds **4** *informal* to frighten or confuse **5 rattle off** *or* **out** to recite perfunctorily or rapidly **6 rattle on** *or* **away** to talk quickly and at length about something unimportant **7 rattle through** to do (something) very quickly: *she rattled through a translation* ▷ *n* **8** a rapid succession of short sharp sounds **9** a baby's toy filled with small pellets that rattle when shaken ▶ HISTORY Middle Dutch *ratelen* > **rattly** *adj*

rattlesnake *n* a poisonous snake with loose horny segments on the tail that make a rattling sound

rattling *adv informal, old-fashioned* very: *a rattling good yarn*

ratty *adj* **-tier, -tiest** **1** *informal* cross and irritable **2** *informal* (of the hair) straggly and greasy > **rattily** *adv* > **rattiness** *n*

raucous *adj* loud and harsh ▶ HISTORY Latin *raucus*

raunchy *adj* **-chier, -chiest** *slang* sexy or earthy ▶ HISTORY origin unknown

ravage *vb* **-aging, -aged** **1** to cause extensive damage to ▷ *n* **2 ravages** the damaging effects: *the ravages of weather and pollution* ▶ HISTORY Old French *ravir* to snatch away

rave *vb* **raving, raved** **1** to talk in a wild or incoherent manner **2** *informal* to write or speak (about) with great enthusiasm ▷ *n* **3** *informal* an enthusiastically favourable review **4** *slang* a professionally organized large-scale party with electronic dance music **5** a name given to various

types of dance music, such as techno, that feature a fast electronic rhythm ▶ HISTORY probably from Old French *resver* to wander

ravel *vb* **-elling, -elled** *or US* **-eling, -eled** **1** to tangle or become entangled **2** (of a fabric) to fray out in loose ends; unravel ▶ HISTORY Middle Dutch *ravelen*

raven *n* **1** a large bird of the crow family with shiny black feathers ▷ *adj* **2** (of hair) shiny black ▶ HISTORY Old English *hræfn*

ravening *adj* (of animals) hungrily searching for prey

ravenous *adj* **1** very hungry **2** ravening ▶ HISTORY Old French *ravineux* > **ravenously** *adv*

raver *n* *slang* **1** *Brit, Austral & S African* a person who leads a wild or uninhibited social life **2** a person who enjoys rave music and goes to raves

ravine (rav-**veen**) *n* a deep narrow steep-sided valley worn by a stream ▶ HISTORY Old French: torrent

raving *adj* **1** delirious **2** *informal* great or exceptional: *a raving beauty* ▷ *adv* **3** to an excessive degree: *raving mad* ▷ *n* **4 ravings** frenzied or wildly extravagant talk

ravioli *pl n* small squares of pasta with a savoury filling, such as meat or cheese ▶ HISTORY Italian

ravish *vb* **1** to enrapture or delight: *tourists ravished by our brilliant costumes* **2** *literary* to rape ▶ HISTORY Latin *rapere* to seize > **ravishment** *n*

ravishing *adj* lovely or delightful > **ravishingly** *adv*

raw *adj* **1** (of food) not cooked **2** in an unfinished or unrefined state: *raw sewage* **3** not selected or modified: *raw data* **4** (of the skin or a wound) painful, with the surface scraped away **5** untrained or inexperienced: *a raw recruit* **6** (of the weather) harshly cold and damp **7** frank or realistic: *a raw reality* **8 raw deal** *informal* unfair or dishonest treatment ▷ *n* **9 in the raw a** *informal* naked **b** in a natural and uncivilized state: *to see life in the raw* **10 on the raw** *Brit, informal* sensitive to upset: *my nerves are on the raw today* ▶ HISTORY Old English *hrēaw*

rawhide *n* **1** untanned hide **2** a whip or rope made of strips of this

ray¹ *n* **1** a narrow beam of light **2** any of a set of lines spreading from a central point **3** a slight indication: *a ray of hope* **4** *maths* a straight line extending from a point **5** a thin beam of electromagnetic radiation or particles **6** any of the spines that support the fin of a fish ▶ HISTORY Old French *rai*

ray² *n* a sea fish related to the sharks, with a flattened body and a long whiplike tail ▶ HISTORY Old French *raie*

ray³ *n* *music* (in tonic sol-fa) the second note of any ascending major scale

rayon *n* a textile fibre or fabric made from cellulose ▶ HISTORY French

raze *or* **rase** *vb* **razing, razed** *or* **rasing, rased** to destroy (buildings or a town) completely ▶ HISTORY Old French *raser*

r

razoo n, pl **-zoos** Austral & NZ, informal an imaginary coin: *we haven't got a brass razoo* ▶ HISTORY origin unknown

razor n an implement with a sharp blade, used for shaving ▶ HISTORY Old French *raseor*

razorbill n a black-and-white sea bird with a stout sideways flattened bill

razor shell n **1** a burrowing shellfish with a long narrow shell **2** this shell

razor wire n strong wire with pieces of sharp metal set across it at intervals

razzle-dazzle or **razzmatazz** n slang **1** noisy or showy fuss or activity **2** a spree or frolic ▶ HISTORY rhyming compound from *dazzle*

Rb chem rubidium

RC **1** Red Cross **2** Roman Catholic

Rd road

re¹ prep with reference to ▶ HISTORY Latin *res* thing

re² n music same as **ray³**

Re chem rhenium

RE **1** Religious Education **2** Royal Engineers

re- prefix **1** indicating repetition of an action: *remarry* **2** indicating return to a previous condition: *renew* ▶ HISTORY Latin

reach vb **1** to arrive at or get to (a place) **2** to make a movement (towards), as if to grasp or touch: *she reached for her bag* **3** to succeed in touching: *I can't reach that shelf unless I stand on a chair* **4** to make contact or communication with: *to reach a wider audience* **5** to extend as far as (a point or place): *to reach the ceiling* **6** to come to (a certain condition or situation): *to reach a compromise* **7** to arrive at or amount to (an amount or value): *temperatures in Greece reached 35° yesterday* **8** informal to give (something to a person) with the outstretched hand ▷ n **9** the extent or distance of reaching: *within easy reach* **10** the range of influence or power: *it symbolized America's global reach* **11 reaches** a section of river, land, or sky: *the quieter reaches of the upper Thames* ▶ HISTORY Old English *rǣcan* > **reachable** adj

react vb **1** (of a person or thing) to act in response to another person, a stimulus, or a situation **2 react against** to act in an opposing or contrary manner **3** chem to undergo a chemical reaction **4** physics to exert an equal force in the opposite direction to an acting force ▶ HISTORY Late Latin *reagere*

reactance n electricity the resistance to the flow of an alternating current caused by the inductance or capacitance of the circuit

reactant n a substance that participates in a chemical reaction

reaction n **1** a physical or emotional response to a stimulus **2** any action resisting another **3** opposition to change **4** med any effect produced by a drug or by a substance (allergen) to which a person is allergic **5** chem a process that involves changes in the structure and energy content of atoms, molecules, or ions **6** the equal and opposite force that acts on a body whenever it exerts a force on another body **7 reactions** someone's ability to act in response to something that happens

reactionary adj **1** opposed to political or social change ▷ n, pl **-aries** **2** a person opposed to radical change

reaction rate n physics the rate of fission that occurs in a nuclear reactor

reactive adj **1** readily taking part in chemical reactions: *ozone is a highly reactive form of oxygen gas* **2** of or having a reactance **3** responsive to stimulus > **reactively** adv > **reactivity** n

reactor n short for **nuclear reactor**

read vb **reading, read** **1** to look at and understand or take in (written or printed matter) **2** to look at and say aloud **3** to have a certain wording: *the memorandum read as follows* **4** to interpret in a specified way: *it can be read as satire* **5** to interpret the significance or meaning of: *an astrologer who reads Tarot* **6** to register or show: *the meter reads 100* **7** to make out the true nature or mood of: *she had read his thoughts* **8** to interpret (signs, characters, etc.) other than by visual means: *to read Braille* **9** to have sufficient knowledge of (a language) to understand the written word **10** to undertake a course of study in (a subject): *to read economics* **11** to gain knowledge by reading: *he read about the war* **12** to hear and understand, esp. when using a two-way radio: *we are reading you loud and clear* **13** computers to obtain (data) from a storage device, such as magnetic tape ▷ n **14** matter suitable for reading: *this book is a very good read* **15** a spell of reading ▷ See also **read out** ▶ HISTORY Old English *rǣdan* to advise, explain

readable adj **1** enjoyable to read **2** (of handwriting or print) legible

reader n **1** a person who reads **2** a person who reads aloud in public **3** a person who reads and judges manuscripts sent to a publisher **4** a book of texts for those learning a foreign language **5** Brit a member of staff below a professor but above a senior lecturer at a university **6** a proofreader **7** short for **lay reader**

readership n all the readers collectively of a publication or author: *a new format would alienate its readership*

reading n **1** the act of reading **2** ability to read: *disputes over methods of teaching reading* **3** material for reading **4** a public recital of a literary work **5** a measurement indicated by a gauge or dial **6** Parliamentary procedure one of the three stages in the passage of a bill through a legislative assembly **7** the form of a particular word or passage in a given text **8** an interpretation of a situation or something said ▷ adj **9** of or for reading: *reading glasses*

readjust vb to adapt to a new situation > **readjustment** n

readmit vb **-mitting, -mitted** to let (a person or country) back into a place or organization > **readmission** n

read out vb **1** to read (something) aloud **2** to retrieve (information) from a computer memory ▷ n **read-out** **3** the information retrieved from a computer memory

r

read-write head *n computers* an electromagnet that can both read and write information on a magnetic tape or disk

ready *adj* **readier, readiest** **1** prepared for use or action **2** prompt or eager: *the ready use of corporal punishment* **3** quick or intelligent: *a ready wit* **4** **ready to** on the point of or liable to: *ready to pounce* **5** easily available: *his ready tears* ▷ *n* **6** *informal* same as **ready money** **7** **at the ready** poised for use: *with pen at the ready* ▷ *vb* **readies, readying, readied** **8** to make ready; prepare ▶ HISTORY Old English *(ge)ræde* > **readily** *adv* > **readiness** *n*

ready-made *adj* **1** for immediate use by any customer **2** extremely convenient or ideally suited: *a ready-made audience*

ready money *n* cash for immediate use. Also: **the ready, the readies**

reaffirm *vb* to state again > **reaffirmation** *n*

reafforest *vb* to plant new trees in (an area that was formerly forested) > **reafforestation** *n*

reagent (ree-**age**-ent) *n* a chemical substance that reacts with another, used to detect the presence of the other

real¹ *adj* **1** existing or occurring in the physical world **2** actual: *the real agenda* **3** important or serious: *the real challenge* **4** rightly so called: *a real friend* **5** genuine: *the council has no real authority* **6** (of food or drink) made in a traditional way to ensure the best flavour **7** *maths* involving or containing real numbers alone **8** relating to immovable property such as land or buildings: *real estate* **9** *econ* (of prices or incomes) considered in terms of purchasing power rather than nominal currency value **10** **the real thing** the genuine article, not a substitute or imitation ▶ HISTORY Latin *res* thing

real² *n* a former small Spanish or Spanish-American silver coin ▶ HISTORY Spanish, literally: royal

real ale *n chiefly Brit* beer that has fermented in the barrel

real depth *n physics* the depth at which an object actually is

real estate *n* immovable property, esp. land and houses

realism *n* **1** awareness or acceptance of things as they are, as opposed to the abstract or ideal **2** a style in art or literature that attempts to show the world as it really is **3** *philosophy* the theory that physical objects continue to exist whether they are perceived or not > **realist** *n* > **realistic** *adj* > **realistically** *adv*

reality *n, pl* **-ties** **1** the state of things as they are or appear to be, rather than as one might wish them to be **2** something that is real **3** the state of being real **4** **in reality** in fact

reality TV *n* television programmes focusing on members of the public living in conditions created especially by the programme makers

realize *or* **-ise** *vb* **-izing, -ized** *or* **-ising, -ised** **1** to be aware of or grasp the significance of **2** to achieve (a plan or ambition) **3** to convert (property or goods) into cash **4** (of goods or property) to sell

for (a certain sum): *this table realized a large sum at auction* **5** to produce (a complete work of art) from an idea or draft > **realizable** *or* **-isable** *adj* > **realization** *or* **-isation** *n*

really *adv* **1** truly: *really boring* **2** in reality: *it's really quite harmless* ▷ *interj* **3** spoken an exclamation of dismay, doubt, or surprise

realm *n* **1** a kingdom **2** a field of interest or study: *the realm of science* ▶ HISTORY Old French *reialme*

real number *n* any rational or irrational number

real property *n* immovable property, esp. land and houses

real tennis *n* an ancient form of tennis played in a four-walled indoor court

real-time *adj* (of a computer system) processing data as it is received

realty *n* same as **real estate**

ream *n* **1** a number of sheets of paper, now equal to 500 or 516 sheets (20 quires) **2** **reams** *informal* a large quantity (of written material): *reams of verse* ▶ HISTORY Arabic *rizmah* bale

reap *vb* **1** to cut and gather (a harvest) **2** to receive as the result of a previous activity: *reap the benefits of our efforts* ▶ HISTORY Old English *riopan*

reaper *n* **1** a person who reaps or a machine for reaping **2** **the grim reaper** death

reappear *vb* to come back into view > **reappearance** *n*

reappraise *vb* **-praising, -praised** to consider or review (something) to see if changes are needed > **reappraisal** *n*

rear¹ *n* **1** the back part **2** the area or position that lies at the back **3** *informal* the buttocks **4** **bring up the rear** to come last ▷ *adj* **5** of or in the rear: *the rear carriage* ▶ HISTORY Old French *rer*

rear² *vb* **1** to care for and educate (children) until maturity **2** to breed (animals) or grow (plants) **3** (of a horse) to lift the front legs in the air and stand nearly upright **4** to place or lift (something) upright ▶ HISTORY Old English *ræran*

rear admiral *n* a high-ranking naval officer

rearguard *n* **1** the troops who protect the rear of a military formation **2** **rearguard action** an effort to prevent or postpone something that is unavoidable

rear light *or* **rear lamp** *n* a red light, usually one of a pair, attached to the rear of a vehicle. Also called: **tail-light, tail lamp**

rearm *vb* **1** to arm again **2** to equip with better weapons > **rearmament** *n*

rearmost *adj* nearest the back

rearrange *vb* **-ranging, -ranged** to organize differently > **rearrangement** *n*

rear-view mirror *n* a mirror on a motor vehicle enabling the driver to see the traffic behind

rearward *adj* **1** in the rear ▷ *adv also* **rearwards** **2** towards the rear

reason *n* **1** a cause or motive for a belief or action: *he had two reasons for his dark mood* **2** the ability to think or argue rationally **3** an argument in favour of or a justification for something: *there is every reason to encourage people to keep fit* **4** sanity

r

5 by reason of because of **6 within reason** within moderate or justifiable bounds **7 it stands to reason** it is logical or obvious ▷ *vb* **8** to think logically in forming conclusions **9 reason with** to persuade by logical arguments into doing something **10 reason out** to work out (a problem) by reasoning ▶ HISTORY Latin *reri* to think

reasonable *adj* **1** sensible **2** not making unfair demands **3** logical: *a reasonable explanation* **4** moderate in price **5** average: *a reasonable amount of luck* > **reasonably** *adv* > **reasonableness** *n*

reassess *vb* to reconsider the value or importance of > **reassessment** *n*

reassure *vb* **-assuring, -assured** to relieve (someone) of anxieties > **reassurance** *n* > **reassuring** *adj*

rebate[1] *n* a refund or discount ▶ HISTORY Old French *rabattre* to beat down

rebate[2] *or* **rabbet** *n* **1** a groove cut into a piece of timber into which another piece fits ▷ *vb* **-bating, -bated** *or* **-beting, -beted** **2** to cut a rabbet in **3** to join (pieces of timber) with a rabbet ▶ HISTORY Old French *rabattre* to beat down

rebel *vb* **-belling, -belled** **1** to fight against the ruling power **2** to reject accepted conventions of behaviour ▷ *n* **3** a person who rebels **4** a person who rejects accepted conventions of behaviour ▷ *adj* **5** rebelling: *rebel councillors* ▶ HISTORY Latin *re-* again + *bellum* war

rebellion *n* **1** organized opposition to a government or other authority involving the use of violence **2** nonviolent opposition to a government or other authority: *a Tory backbenchers' rebellion* **3** rejection of accepted conventions of behaviour ▶ HISTORY Latin *rebellio*

rebellious *adj* rebelling or showing a tendency towards rebellion > **rebelliously** *adv*

rebirth *n* a revival or renaissance: *the rebirth of their nation*

reboot *vb* to shut down and then restart (a computer system)

rebore *or* **reboring** *n* the boring of a cylinder to restore its true shape

reborn *adj* active again after a period of inactivity

rebound *vb* **1** to spring back from a sudden impact **2** (of a plan or action) to misfire so as to hurt the person responsible ▷ *n* **3** the act of rebounding **4 on the rebound** *informal* while recovering from rejection: *she married him on the rebound*

rebrand *vb* to change or update the image of (an organization or product)

rebuff *vb* **1** to snub and reject an offer or suggestion ▷ *n* **2** a blunt refusal; snub ▶ HISTORY Old French *rebuffer*

rebuke *vb* **-buking, -buked** **1** to scold sternly ▷ *n* **2** a stern scolding ▶ HISTORY Old French *rebuker*

rebus (ree-buss) *n, pl* **-buses** a puzzle consisting of pictures and symbols representing syllables and words ▶ HISTORY Latin: by things

rebut *vb* **-butting, -butted** to prove that (a claim) is untrue ▶ HISTORY Old French *reboter* > **rebuttal** *n*

recalcitrant *adj* wilfully disobedient ▶ HISTORY Latin *re-* again + *calcitrare* to kick > **recalcitrance** *n*

recall *vb* **1** to bring back to mind **2** to order to return **3** to annul or cancel ▷ *n* **4** the ability to remember things **5** an order to return

recant *vb* to take back (a former belief or statement) publicly ▶ HISTORY Latin *re-* again + *cantare* to sing > **recantation** *n*

recap *informal vb* **-capping, -capped** **1** to recapitulate ▷ *n* **2** a recapitulation

recapitulate *vb* **-lating, -lated** to restate the main points of (an argument or speech) ▶ HISTORY Late Latin *recapitulare*, literally: to put back under headings

recapitulation *n* **1** the act of recapitulating **2** *music* the repeating of earlier themes, esp. in the final section of a movement

recapture *vb* **-turing, -tured** **1** to relive vividly (a former experience or sensation): *they recaptured some of those first feelings* **2** to capture again ▷ *n* **3** the act of recapturing

recast *vb* **-casting, -cast** **1** to give a new form or shape to: *he found the organization wholly recast* **2** to change the actors or singers in (a play, musical, or opera) **3** to rework (a piece of writing or music): *she has recast most of my book*

recce *chiefly Brit, slang vb* **-ceing, -ced** *or* **-ceed** **1** to reconnoitre ▷ *n* **2** reconnaissance

recede *vb* **-ceding, -ceded** **1** to withdraw from a point or limit: *the tide had receded* **2** to become more distant: *the threat of intervention had receded* **3** (of a man's hair) to stop growing at the temples and above the forehead **4** to slope backwards: *a receding chin* ▶ HISTORY Latin *recedere* to go back

receipt *n* **1** a written acknowledgment that money or goods have been received **2** the act of receiving **3** receipts money taken in over a particular period by a shop or business ▶ HISTORY Old French *receite*

receive *vb* **-ceiving, -ceived** **1** to get (something offered or sent to one) **2** to experience: *he received a knife wound* **3** to greet (guests) **4** to have (an honour) bestowed: *he received the Order of the Garter* **5** to admit (a person) to a society or condition: *he was received into the Church* **6** to convert (incoming radio or television signals) into sounds or pictures **7** to be informed of (news) **8** to react to: *the article was well received* **9** to support or sustain (the weight of something) **10** *tennis etc.* to play at the other end from the server **11** *Brit & NZ* to buy and sell stolen goods ▶ HISTORY Latin *recipere*

received *adj* generally accepted or believed: *contrary to received wisdom*

Received Pronunciation *n* the accent of standard Southern British English

receiver *n* **1** a person who receives something **2** the detachable part of a telephone that is held to the ear **3** the equipment in a telephone, radio, or television that converts the incoming signals into sound or pictures **4** a person appointed by a court to manage property of a bankrupt **5** a person who receives stolen goods knowing they have been stolen

receivership n law the state of being administered by a receiver: *the company went into receivership*

recent adj **1** having happened lately **2** new ▸ HISTORY Latin *recens* fresh > **recently** adv

Recent adj same as **Holocene**

receptacle n **1** an object used to contain something **2** bot the enlarged or modified tip of the flower stalk that bears the flower ▸ HISTORY Latin *receptaculum* store-place

reception n **1** an area in an office, hotel, etc. where visitors are received or reservations dealt with **2** a formal party for guests, esp. after a wedding **3** the manner in which something is received: *an enthusiastic reception* **4** the act of formally welcoming **5** radio, television the quality of a received broadcast: *the reception was poor*

receptionist n a person employed to receive guests or clients and deal with reservations and appointments

reception room n a room in a private house suitable for entertaining guests

receptive adj willing to consider and accept new ideas or suggestions > **receptivity** or **receptiveness** n

receptor n physiol a sensory nerve ending that changes specific stimuli into nerve impulses

recess n **1** a space, such as an alcove, set back in a wall **2** a holiday between sessions of work **3** recesses secret hidden places: *the recesses of her brain* **4** US & Canad a break between classes at a school ▸ HISTORY Latin *recessus* a retreat

recessed adj hidden or placed in a recess

recession n **1** a period of economic difficulty when little is being bought or sold **2** the act of receding

recessional n a hymn sung as the clergy and choir withdraw after a church service

recessive adj **1** tending to recede **2** genetics (in a pair of genes) designating a gene that has a characteristic which will only be passed on if the other gene has the same characteristic

recharge vb **-charging, -charged** to cause (a battery) to take in and store electricity again > **rechargeable** adj

recherché (rish-**air**-shay) adj **1** studiedly refined or elegant **2** known only to connoisseurs ▸ HISTORY French: thoroughly sought after

recidivism n habitual relapse into crime ▸ HISTORY Latin *recidivus* falling back > **recidivist** n, adj

recipe n **1** a list of ingredients and directions for making a particular dish **2** a method for achieving something: *a recipe for industrial chaos* ▸ HISTORY Latin, literally: take (it)!

recipient n a person who receives something

reciprocal (ris-**sip**-pro-kl) adj **1** done or felt by each of two people or groups to or about the other: *a reciprocal agreement* **2** given or done in return: *a reciprocal invitation* **3** grammar (of a pronoun) indicating that action is given and received by each subject, for example, *each other* in *they started to shout at each other* ▹ n **4** Also called: **inverse** maths a number or quantity that when multiplied by a given number or quantity gives a product of one: *the reciprocal of 2 is 0.5* ▸ HISTORY Latin *reciprocus* alternating > **reciprocally** adv

reciprocal function n maths a function that includes a reciprocal

reciprocal ratio n maths the reciprocal of the ratio of two numbers or quantities

reciprocate vb **-cating, -cated 1** to give or feel in return: *not everyone reciprocated his enthusiasm* **2** (of a machine part) to move backwards and forwards > **reciprocation** n

reciprocity n **1** reciprocal action or relation **2** a mutual exchange of commercial or other privileges

recital (ris-**site**-al) n **1** a musical performance by a soloist or soloists **2** the act of reciting something learned or prepared **3** written a narration or description: *she plagued her with the recital of constant ailments and illnesses*

recitation n **1** the act of reciting poetry or prose from memory **2** written something recited

recitative (ress-it-a-**teev**) n a narrative passage in an opera or oratorio, reflecting the natural rhythms of speech ▸ HISTORY Italian *recitativo*

recite vb **-citing, -cited 1** to repeat (a poem or passage) aloud from memory before an audience **2** to give a detailed account of ▸ HISTORY Latin *recitare*

reckless adj **1** having no regard for danger or consequences: *reckless behaviour* **2** law carrying a serious and foreseeable risk: *she was charged with reckless driving* ▸ HISTORY Old English *recceleās*

recklessness n **1** a lack of regard for danger or consequences: *it seems foolhardy to the point of recklessness* **2** law acts that are unreasonable and carry a serious foreseeable risk

reckon vb **1** informal to be of the opinion: *she reckoned she could find them* **2** to consider: *he reckoned himself a failure* **3** to calculate or compute **4** to expect **5** reckon with or without to take into account or fail to take into account: *there is this ancestral hatred to reckon with* **6** reckon on or upon to rely on or expect: *they can't reckon on your automatic support* ▸ HISTORY Old English *(ge) recenian* recount

reckoning n **1** counting or calculating: *by his reckoning, he owed him money* **2** retribution for one's actions: *the moment of reckoning came* **3** settlement of an account or bill

reclaim vb **1** to get back possession of: *the club is now trying to reclaim the money from the blockaders* **2** to convert (unusable or submerged land) into land suitable for farming or building on **3** to recover (useful substances) from waste products ▸ HISTORY Latin *reclamare* to cry out > **reclamation** n

recline vb **-clining, -clined** to rest in a leaning position ▸ HISTORY Latin *reclinare*

reclining adj (of a seat) with a back that can be adjusted to slope at various angles

recluse n a person who lives alone and avoids people ▸ HISTORY Late Latin *recludere* to shut away > **reclusive** adj

r

705

recognition n **1** the act of recognizing **2** acceptance or acknowledgment **3** formal acknowledgment of a government or of the independence of a country **4 in recognition of** as a token of thanks for

recognizance or **recognisance** (rik-**og**-nizz-anss) n law **a** an undertaking made before a court or magistrate to do something specified, such as to appear in court on a stated day **b** a sum of money promised as a guarantee of this undertaking ▶ HISTORY Old French reconoissance

recognize or **-nise** vb **-nizing, -nized** or **-nising, -nised 1** to identify (a person or thing) as someone or something already known **2** to accept or be aware of (a fact or problem): to recognize change **3** to acknowledge formally the status or legality of (something or someone): an organization recognized by the UN **4** to show approval or appreciation of (something) **5** to make formal acknowledgment of (a claim or duty): I must ask for her to be recognized as a hostile witness ▶ HISTORY Latin re- again + cognoscere to know
> **recognizable** or **-isable** adj

recoil vb **1** to jerk or spring back **2** to draw back in fear or horror **3** (of an action) to go wrong so as to hurt the person responsible ▷ n **4** the backward movement of a gun when fired **5** the act of recoiling ▶ HISTORY Old French reculer

recollect vb to remember ▶ HISTORY Latin recolligere to gather again > **recollection** n

recombinant (ree-**kom**-bin-ant) adj genetics produced by the combining of genetic material from more than one origin

recombinant DNA n biol DNA molecules extracted from different sources and chemically joined together

recommend vb **1** to advise as the best course or choice **2** to praise or commend: I would wholeheartedly recommend his books **3** to make attractive or advisable: she has everything to recommend her ▶ HISTORY Latin re- again + commendare to commend > **recommendation** n

recompense vb **-pensing, -pensed 1** to pay or reward for work or help **2** to compensate or make up for loss or injury ▷ n **3** compensation for loss or injury **4** reward or repayment ▶ HISTORY Latin re- again + compensare to balance

reconcile vb **-ciling, -ciled 1** to make (two apparently conflicting things) compatible or consistent with each other: in many cases science and religion are reconciled **2** to re-establish friendly relations with (a person or people) or between (people) **3** to accept or cause to accept (an unpleasant situation): we reconciled ourselves to a change ▶ HISTORY Latin reconciliare

reconciliation n **1** the state of being reconciled **2** the act of reconciling people or groups **3** S African a political term emphasizing the need to acknowledge the wrongs of the past

recondite adj formal **1** requiring special knowledge **2** dealing with abstruse or profound subjects ▶ HISTORY Latin reconditus hidden away

recondition vb to restore to good condition or working order: a reconditioned engine
> **reconditioned** adj

reconnaissance (rik-**kon**-iss-anss) n **1** the process of obtaining information about the position and movements of an enemy **2** a preliminary inspection ▶ HISTORY French

reconnoitre or US **reconnoiter** (rek-a-**noy**-ter) vb to make a reconnaissance of ▶ HISTORY obsolete French reconnoître

reconsider vb to think about again, with a view to changing one's policy or course of action
> **reconsideration** n

reconstitute vb **-tuting, -tuted 1** to reorganize in a slightly different form **2** to restore (dried food) to its former state by adding water
> **reconstitution** n

reconstruct vb **1** to build again **2** to reorganize: three works proved useful in reconstructing the training routine **3** to form a picture of (a past event, esp. a crime) by piecing together evidence
> **reconstruction** n

record n (**rek**-ord) **1** a document or other thing that preserves information **2 records** information or data on a subject collected over a long period: dental records **3** a thin disc of a plastic material upon which sound has been recorded in a continuous spiral groove on each side **4** the best recorded achievement in some field: her score set a Games record **5** the known facts about a person's achievements **6** a list of crimes of which an accused person has previously been convicted **7** anything serving as evidence or as a memorial: the First World War is a record of human folly **8** computers a group of data or piece of information preserved as a unit in machine-readable form **9 for the record** for the sake of strict factual accuracy **10 go on record** to state one's views publicly **11 have a record** to have previous criminal convictions **12 off the record** not for publication **13 on record a** stated in a public document **b** publicly known ▷ adj **14** the highest or lowest, or best or worst ever achieved: record losses ▷ vb (rik-**kord**) **15** to put in writing to preserve the true facts: to record the minutes of a meeting **16** to preserve (sound, TV programmes, etc.) on plastic disc, magnetic tape, etc. for reproduction on a playback device **17** to show or register ▶ HISTORY Latin recordari to remember

recorded delivery n a postal service by which an official receipt is obtained for the posting and delivery of a letter or parcel

recorder n **1** a person or machine that records, e.g. a tape recorder **2** music a wind instrument, blown through the end with finger-holes and a reedlike tone **3** (in England and Wales) a barrister or solicitor appointed to sit as a part-time judge in the crown court

recording n **1** something that has been recorded **2** the process of storing sounds or visual signals for later use

record player n a device for reproducing the sounds stored on a record

r

recount *vb* to tell the story or details of ▶ HISTORY Old French *reconter*

re-count *vb* **1** to count again ▷ *n* **2** a second or further count, esp. of votes in an election

recount genre *n* a form of writing or speech in which the writer or speaker relates events as they happened and in chronological order

recoup (rik-**koop**) *vb* **1** to regain or make good (a loss) **2** to reimburse or compensate (someone) for a loss ▶ HISTORY Old French *recouper* to cut back > **recoupment** *n*

recourse *n* **1** a source of help or course of action that is turned to when in difficulty **2 have recourse to** to turn to (a source of help or course of action) ▶ HISTORY Latin *re*- back + *currere* to run

recover *vb* **1** (of a person) to regain health, spirits, or composure **2** to regain a former and better condition: *real wages have recovered from the recession* **3** to find again or obtain the return of (something lost) **4** to get back or make good (expense or loss) **5** to obtain (useful substances) from waste **6** *law* to gain (something) by the judgment of a court: *it should be possible to recover damages* ▶ HISTORY Latin *recuperare* > **recoverable** *adj*

recovery *n, pl* **-eries 1** the act of recovering from sickness, a shock, or a setback **2** restoration to a former and better condition **3** the regaining of something lost **4** the extraction of useful substances from waste

re-create *vb* **-creating, -created** to make happen or exist again > **re-creation** *n*

recreation *n* an activity done for pleasure or relaxation ▶ HISTORY Latin *recreare* to refresh > **recreational** *adj*

recreation ground *n* an area of publicly owned land where sports and games may be played

recrimination *n* accusations made by two people or groups about each other: *bitter recrimination* ▶ HISTORY Latin *re*- back + *criminari* to accuse > **recriminatory** *adj*

recrudescence *n literary* an outbreak of trouble or a disease after a period of quiet ▶ HISTORY Latin *re*- again + *crudus* bloody, raw

recruit *vb* **1** to enlist (people) for military service **2** to enrol or obtain (members or support) ▷ *n* **3** a newly joined member of a military service **4** a new member or supporter ▶ HISTORY French *recrute* new growth > **recruitment** *n*

rectal *adj* of the rectum

rectangle *n* an oblong shape with four straight sides and four right angles ▶ HISTORY Latin *rectus* straight + *angulus* angle > **rectangular** *adj*

rectify *vb* **-fies, -fying, -fied 1** to put right; correct **2** *chem* to separate (a substance) from a mixture by distillation **3** *electricity* to convert (alternating current) into direct current ▶ HISTORY Latin *rectus* straight + *facere* to make > **rectification** *n* > **rectifier** *n*

rectilinear (rek-tee-**lin**-ee-er) *adj formal* **1** in a straight line **2** bounded by or formed of straight lines

rectitude *n* moral or religious correctness: *a model of rectitude* ▶ HISTORY Latin *rectus* right

recto *n, pl* **-tos 1** the right-hand page of a book **2** the front of a sheet of printed paper ▶ HISTORY Latin: on the right

rector *n* **1** *Church of England* a member of the clergy in charge of a parish **2** *RC Church* a cleric in charge of a college or congregation **3** *chiefly Brit* the head of certain academic institutions **4** (in Scotland) a high-ranking official in a university, elected by the students ▶ HISTORY Latin: director > **rectorship** *n*

rectory *n, pl* **-ries** the house of a rector

rectum *n, pl* **-tums** or **-ta** the lower part of the alimentary canal, ending in the anus ▶ HISTORY Latin: straight

recumbent *adj* lying down ▶ HISTORY Latin *recumbere* to lie back

recuperate *vb* **-ating, -ated** to recover from illness or exhaustion ▶ HISTORY Latin *recuperare* > **recuperation** *n* > **recuperative** *adj*

recur *vb* **-curring, -curred 1** to happen or occur again **2** (of a thought or feeling) to come back to the mind ▶ HISTORY Latin *re*- again + *currere* to run > **recurrence** *n* > **recurrent** *adj* > **recurring** *adj*

recurring decimal *n* a rational number that contains a pattern of digits repeated indefinitely after the decimal point: *1 divided by 11 gives the recurring decimal 0.09090909...*

recusant (**rek**-yew-zant) *n* **1** *history* a Roman Catholic who did not attend the services of the Church of England **2** a person who refuses to obey authority ▶ HISTORY Latin *recusans* refusing > **recusancy** *n*

recyclable *adj* capable of being reused either in its current state or after reprocessing

recyclable resource *n environmental science* a resource such as a mineral, paper, or man-made substance that can be reclaimed at the end of its current use and used for or reprocessed into something else

recycle *vb* **-cling, -cled 1** to reprocess (something already used) for further use: *public demand for recycled paper* **2** to pass (a substance) through a system again for further use > **recycling** *n*

red *adj* **redder, reddest 1** of a colour varying from crimson to orange; of the colour of blood **2** reddish in colour or having parts or marks that are reddish: *red deer* **3** flushed in the face from anger or shame **4** (of the eyes) bloodshot **5** (of wine) made from black grapes and coloured by their skins ▷ *n* **6** the colour red; the colour of blood **7** anything red, such as red clothing or red paint: *she had dressed in red* **8 in the red** *informal* in debt **9 see red** *informal* to become very angry ▶ HISTORY Old English *rēad* > **redness** *n* > **reddish** *adj*

Red *informal n* **1** a Communist or socialist ▷ *adj* **2** Communist or socialist

red admiral *n* a butterfly with black wings with red and white markings

redback spider *n* a small venomous Australian spider with a red stripe on the back of the abdomen

red blood cell *n* same as **erythrocyte**

red-blooded *adj informal* vigorous or virile

707

redbreast n a robin

redbrick adj (of a university in Britain) founded in the late 19th or early 20th century

red card soccer n **1** a piece of red pasteboard raised by a referee to indicate that a player has been sent off ▷ vb **red-card 2** to send off (a player)

red carpet n very special treatment given to an important guest

redcoat n **1** history a British soldier **2** Canad, informal a Mountie

Red Crescent n the name and symbol used by the Red Cross in Muslim countries

Red Cross n an international organization (**Red Cross Society**) which helps victims of war or natural disaster

redcurrant n a very small red edible fruit that grows in bunches on a bush

red deer n a large deer of Europe and Asia, which has a reddish-brown coat and a short tail

redden vb written **1** to make or become red or redder **2** to blush

redeem vb **1** to make up for **2** to reinstate (oneself) in someone's good opinion: he missed a penalty but redeemed himself by setting up the winning goal **3** Christianity (of Christ as Saviour) to free (humanity) from sin by death on the Cross **4** to buy back: she didn't have the money to redeem it **5** to pay off (a loan or debt) **6** to convert (bonds or shares) into cash **7** to exchange (coupons) for goods **8** to fulfil (a promise): I vowed to abide by the bill and have redeemed my pledge ▶ HISTORY Latin re- back + emere to buy > **redeemable** adj > **redeemer** n

Redeemer n **the Redeemer** Christianity Jesus Christ

redeeming adj making up for faults or deficiencies: the soundtrack is the film's only redeeming feature

redemption n **1** the act of redeeming **2** the state of being redeemed **3** Christianity deliverance from sin through the incarnation and death of Christ > **redemptive** adj

redeploy vb to assign (people) to new positions or tasks > **redeployment** n

redevelop vb to rebuild or renovate (an area or building) > **redeveloper** n > **redevelopment** n

redfish n, pl -**fish** or -**fishes** Canad same as **kokanee**

red flag n **1** a symbol of revolution **2** a warning of danger

red-handed adj **catch someone red-handed** to catch someone in the act of doing something wrong or illegal

red hat n the broad-brimmed crimson hat given to cardinals as the symbol of their rank

redhead n a person with reddish hair > **redheaded** adj

red herring n something which diverts attention from the main issue

red-hot adj **1** (of metal) glowing hot **2** extremely hot **3** very keen or excited **4** furious: one of those red-hot blazes of temper **5** very recent or topical: red-hot information

red-hot poker n a garden plant with spikes of red or yellow flowers

Red Indian n, adj offensive Native American

redirect vb **1** to send in a new direction or course **2** to send (mail) to a different address

red lead n a bright-red poisonous insoluble oxide of lead

red-letter day n a memorably important or happy occasion ▶ HISTORY from the red letters in ecclesiastical calendars to indicate saints' days

red light n **1** a traffic signal to stop **2** a danger signal

red-light district n an area where many prostitutes work

red meat n meat, such as beef or lamb, that is dark brown when cooked

redolent adj **redolent of** or **with 1** reminiscent or suggestive of: a castle redolent of historical novels **2** smelling of: the warm heavy air was redolent of sea and flowers ▶ HISTORY Latin redolens > **redolence** n

redouble vb -**bling, -bled 1** to make or become much greater: the party will have to redouble its efforts **2** Bridge to double (an opponent's double)

redoubt n **1** a small fort defending a hill top or pass **2** a stronghold ▶ HISTORY French redoute

redoubtable adj to be feared and respected: the redoubtable Mr Brooks ▶ HISTORY Old French redouter to dread > **redoubtably** adv

redound vb **1 redound to** to have an advantageous or disadvantageous effect on: individual rights redound to the common good **2 redound on** or **upon** to recoil or rebound on ▶ HISTORY Latin redundare to stream over

redox n a chemical reaction between two substances, in which one is oxidized and the other reduced

red pepper n **1** the red ripe fruit of the sweet pepper, eaten as a vegetable **2** same as **cayenne pepper**

redraft vb to write a second copy of (a letter, proposal, essay, etc.)

red rag n something that infuriates or provokes: a red rag to businessmen ▶ HISTORY so called because red objects supposedly infuriate bulls

redress vb **1** to make amends for **2** to adjust in order to make fair or equal: to redress the balance ▷ n **3** compensation or reparation **4** the setting right of a wrong ▶ HISTORY Old French redrecier to set up again

red salmon n a salmon with reddish flesh

redshank n a large common European sandpiper with red legs

red shift n the appearance of lines in the spectrum of distant stars nearer the red end of the spectrum than on earth: used to calculate the velocity of objects in relation to the earth

redskin n informal, offensive a Native American ▶ HISTORY so called because one now extinct tribe painted themselves with red ochre

red squirrel n a reddish-brown squirrel of Europe and Asia

redstart *n* **1** a European songbird of the thrush family, the male of which has an orange-brown tail and breast **2** a North American warbler ▶ HISTORY Old English *rēad* red + *steort* tail

red tape *n* time-consuming official rules or procedure ▶ HISTORY from the red tape used to bind official government documents

reduce *vb* **-ducing, -duced 1** to bring down or lower: *monitoring could reduce the number of perinatal deaths* **2** to weaken or lessen: *vegetarian diets reduce cancer risk* **3** to bring by force or necessity to some state or action: *it reduced her to helpless laughter* **4** to slim **5** to set out systematically as an aid to understanding: *reducing the problem to three main issues* **6** *cookery* to thicken (a sauce) by boiling away some of its liquid **7** to impoverish: *to be in reduced circumstances* **8** *chem* **a** to undergo a chemical reaction with hydrogen **b** to lose oxygen atoms **c** to increase the number of electrons **9** *maths* to simplify the form of (an expression or equation), esp. by substitution of one term by another ▶ HISTORY Latin *reducere* to bring back
> **reducible** *adj*

reducing agent *n chem* a substance that reduces another substance in a chemical reaction, being itself oxidized in the process

reduction *n* **1** the act of reducing **2** the amount by which something is reduced **3** a reduced form of an original, such as a copy of a document on a smaller scale > **reductive** *adj*

reduction formula *n maths* a formula expressing the values of a trigonometric function of any angle greater than 90° in terms of a function of an acute angle

redundant *adj* **1** deprived of one's job because it is no longer necessary or sufficiently profitable **2** surplus to requirements ▶ HISTORY Latin *redundans* overflowing > **redundancy** *n*

reduplicate *vb* **-cating, -cated** to make double; repeat

redwood *n* a giant Californian conifer with reddish bark

re-echo *vb* **-oing, -oed** to echo over and over again

reed *n* **1** a tall grass that grows in swamps and shallow water **2** a straight hollow stem of this plant **3** *music* **a** a thin piece of cane or metal in certain wind instruments, which vibrates producing a musical note when the instrument is blown **b** a wind instrument or organ pipe that sounds by means of a reed ▶ HISTORY Old English *hrēod*

reedy *adj* **reedier, reediest 1** harsh or thin in tone: *his reedy, hesitant voice* **2** (of a place) full of reeds > **reedily** *adv* > **reediness** *n*

reef¹ *n* **1** a ridge of rock, sand, or coral, lying just beneath the surface of the sea: *a coral reef* **2** a vein of ore ▶ HISTORY Middle Dutch *ref*

reef² *naut n* **1** the part of a sail which can be rolled up to reduce its area ▷ *vb* **2** to reduce the area of (sail) by taking in a reef ▶ HISTORY Middle Dutch *rif*

reefer *n* **1** Also called: **reefer jacket** a man's short heavy double-breasted woollen jacket **2** *old-fashioned, slang* a hand-rolled cigarette containing cannabis ▶ HISTORY from the cigarette's resemblance to the rolled reef of a sail

reef knot *n* a knot consisting of two overhand knots turned opposite ways

reek *vb* **1** to give off a strong unpleasant smell **2 reek of** to give a strong suggestion of: *the scene had reeked of insincerity* **3** *dialect* to give off smoke or fumes ▷ *n* **4** a strong unpleasant smell **5** *dialect* smoke or steam ▶ HISTORY Old English *rēocan*

reel¹ *n* **1** a cylindrical object or frame that turns on an axis and onto which film, tape, wire, or thread is wound **2** a winding device attached to a fishing rod, used for casting and winding in the line **3** a roll of film for projection ▷ *vb* **4 reel in** to wind or draw in on a reel ▶ HISTORY Old English *hrēol*

reel² *vb* **1** to move unsteadily or spin round, as if about to fall **2** to be in a state of confusion or stress: *my mind was still reeling* ▶ HISTORY probably from REEL¹

reel³ *n* **1** a lively Scottish dance **2** music for this dance ▶ HISTORY from REEL²

re-elect *vb* to vote for (someone) to retain his or her position, for example as a Member of Parliament > **re-election** *n*

reel off *vb* to recite or write fluently or quickly

re-enter *vb* **1** to come back into (a place, esp. a country) **2** (of a spacecraft) to return into (the earth's atmosphere) > **re-entry** *n*

re-entrant *n geog* a small valley forming an indentation in a hillside

reeve *n* **1** *English history* the local representative of the king in a shire until the early 11th century **2** (in medieval England) a steward who supervised the daily affairs of a manor **3** *Canad government* (in some provinces) a president of a local council ▶ HISTORY Old English *gerēfa*

re-examine *vb* **-examining, -examined** to inspect or investigate again > **re-examination** *n*

ref *n informal* the referee in a sport

refectory *n, pl* **-ries** a dining hall in a religious or academic institution ▶ HISTORY Latin *refectus* refreshed

refectory table *n* a long narrow dining table supported by two trestles

refer *vb* **-ferring, -ferred • refer to 1** to mention or allude to **2** to be relevant or relate to: *the word 'cancer' refers to many quite specific different diseases* **3** to seek information from: *he referred to his notes* **4** to direct the attention of (someone) for information: *the reader is referred to the introduction* **5** to direct (a patient or client) to another doctor or agency: *her GP referred her to a specialist* **6** to hand over for consideration or decision: *to refer a complaint to another department* ▶ HISTORY Latin *re-* back + *ferre* to carry > **referable** or **referrable** *adj* > **referral** *n*

referee *n* **1** the umpire in various sports, such as football and boxing **2** a person who is willing to provide a reference for someone for a job

r

3 a person referred to for a decision or opinion in a dispute ▷ *vb* **-eeing, -eed 4** to act as a referee

reference *n* **1** the act of referring **2** a mention: *this book contains several references to the Civil War* **3** direction to a passage elsewhere in a book or to another book **4** a book or passage referred to **5** a written testimonial regarding one's character or capabilities **6** a person referred to for such a testimonial **7** relation or restriction, esp. to or by membership of a specific group: *without reference to sex or age* **8 with reference to** concerning ▷ *adj* **9** containing information or facts: *reference books* > **referential** *adj*

referendum *n, pl* **-dums** *or* **-da** a direct vote of the electorate on a question of importance ▶ HISTORY Latin: something to be carried back

refill *vb* **1** to fill (something) again ▷ *n* **2** a second or subsequent filling: *I held out my glass for a refill* **3** a replacement supply of something in a permanent container > **refillable** *adj*

refine *vb* **-fining, -fined 1** to make free from impurities; purify **2** to improve: *surgical techniques are constantly being refined* **3** to separate (a mixture) into pure constituents: *molasses is a residual syrup obtained during sugar refining*

refined *adj* **1** cultured or polite **2** freed from impurities **3** highly developed and effective: *refined intelligence tests*

refinement *n* **1** an improvement to something, such as a piece of equipment **2** fineness of taste or manners **3** a subtle point or distinction **4** the act of refining

refinery *n, pl* **-eries** a factory for purifying a raw material, such as sugar or oil

refit *vb* **-fitting, -fitted 1** to make (a ship) ready for use again by repairing or re-equipping ▷ *n* **2** a repair or re-equipping for further use

reflation *n* an increase in the supply of money and credit designed to encourage economic activity ▶ HISTORY RE- + *-flation*, as in *inflation* > **reflate** *vb* > **reflationary** *adj*

reflect *vb* **1** (of a surface or object) to throw back (light, heat, or sound) **2** (of a mirror) to form an image of (something) by reflection **3** to show: *many of her books reflect her obsession with fine art* **4** to consider carefully **5 reflect on** *or* **upon** to cause to be regarded in a specified way: *the incident reflects very badly on me* **6** to bring as a consequence: *the programme reflected great credit on the technicians* ▶ HISTORY Latin *re-* back + *flectere* to bend

reflecting telescope *n* a telescope in which the initial image is formed by a concave mirror

reflection *n* **1** the act of reflecting **2** the return of rays of light, heat, or sound **3** an image of a an object given back in a mirror **4** careful or long consideration **5 on reflection** after careful consideration or reconsideration **6** discredit or blame: *it's a sad reflection on modern morality* **7** *maths* a transformation of a shape in which right and left, or top and bottom, are reversed

reflection in the x-axis *n maths* a reflection in which a shape is reversed along the x-axis

reflection in the y-axis *n maths* a reflection in which a shape is reversed along the y-axis

reflective *adj* **1** *written* characterized by quiet thought or contemplation **2** capable of reflecting: *a reflective coating*

reflector *n* **1** a polished surface for reflecting light **2** a reflecting telescope

reflex *n* **1** an immediate involuntary response to a given stimulus **2** a mechanical response to a particular situation, involving no conscious decision **3** an image produced by reflection ▷ *adj* **4** of or caused by a reflex: *a reflex action* **5** reflected **6** *maths* (of an angle) between 180° and 360° ▶ HISTORY Latin *reflexus* bent back

reflex arc *n physiol* the neural pathway over which impulses travel to produce a reflex action

reflex camera *n* a camera which uses a mirror to channel light from a lens to the viewfinder, so that the image seen is the same as the image photographed

reflexive *adj* **1** *grammar* denoting a pronoun that refers back to the subject of a sentence or clause. Thus, in *that man thinks a great deal of himself*, the pronoun *himself* is reflexive **2** *grammar* denoting a verb used with a reflexive pronoun as its direct object, as in *to dress oneself* **3** *physiol* of or relating to a reflex ▷ *n* **4** a reflexive pronoun or verb

reflexology *n* foot massage as a therapy in alternative medicine > **reflexologist** *n*

reforest *vb* same as **reafforest**

reform *n* **1** correction of abuses or malpractices: *a programme of economic reforms* **2** improvement of morals or behaviour ▷ *vb* **3** to improve (a law or institution) by correcting abuses **4** to give up or cause to give up a bad habit or way of life ▶ HISTORY Latin *reformare* to form again > **reformative** *adj* > **reformer** *n*

reformation (ref-fer-**may**-shun) *n* **1** a reforming **2 the Reformation** a religious movement in 16th-century Europe that began as an attempt to reform the Roman Catholic Church and resulted in the establishment of the Protestant Churches

reformatory *n, pl* **-ries** (formerly) a place where young offenders were sent to be reformed

Reformed *adj* of a Protestant Church, esp. a Calvinist one

reformist *adj* **1** advocating reform rather than abolition, esp. of a religion or a political movement ▷ *n* **2** a person advocating reform

refract *vb* to cause light, heat, or sound to undergo refraction ▶ HISTORY Latin *re-* back + *frangere* to break > **refractive** *adj* > **refractor** *n*

refracted ray *n physics* a ray of light that has undergone refraction

refracting telescope *n* a type of telescope in which the image is formed by a set of lenses. Also called: **refractor**

refraction *n physics* **1** the change in direction of a wave, such as light or sound, in passing from one medium to another in which it has a different velocity **2** the amount by which a wave is refracted

refractory *adj* **1** *formal* stubborn or rebellious **2** *med* not responding to treatment **3** (of a material) able to withstand high temperatures without fusion or decomposition

refrain[1] *vb* **refrain from** to keep oneself from (doing) ▶ HISTORY Latin *refrenare* to check with a bridle

refrain[2] *n* **1** a frequently repeated part of a song **2** a much repeated saying or idea ▶ HISTORY Latin *refringere* to break into pieces

refrangible *adj* capable of being refracted

refresh *vb* **1** to revive or reinvigorate, for example through rest, drink, or food **2** to stimulate (the memory) ▶ HISTORY Old French *refreschir* > **refresher** *n*

refresher course *n* a course designed to improve or update a person's knowledge of a subject

refreshing *adj* **1** having a reviving effect **2** pleasantly different or new: *refreshing candour*

refreshment *n* **1** the act of refreshing **2 refreshments** snacks and drinks served as a light meal

refrigerant *n* **1** a fluid capable of vaporizing at low temperatures, used in refrigerators ▷ *adj* **2** causing cooling or freezing

refrigerate *vb* **-ating, -ated** to chill or freeze in order to preserve ▶ HISTORY Latin *refrigerare* to make cold > **refrigeration** *n*

refrigerator *n* the full name for **fridge**

refuel *vb* **-elling, -elled** *or US* **-eling, -eled** to supply or be supplied with fresh fuel

refuge *n* **1** shelter or protection from danger or hardship **2** a place, person, or thing that offers protection or help ▶ HISTORY Latin *re-* back + *fugere* to escape

refugee *n* a person who has fled from some danger, such as war or political persecution

refulgent *adj* *literary* shining brightly ▶ HISTORY Latin *refulgere* to reflect > **refulgence** *n*

refund *vb* **1** to give back (money) **2** to pay back (a person) ▷ *n* **3** return of money to a purchaser or the amount returned ▶ HISTORY Latin *re-* back + *fundere* to pour > **refundable** *adj*

refurbish *vb* to renovate and brighten up > **refurbishment** *n*

refusal *n* **1** the act of refusing **2** the opportunity to reject or accept: *he was given first refusal on all three scripts*

refuse[1] *vb* **-fusing, -fused** **1** to be determined not (to do something): *he refuses to consider it* **2** to decline to give or allow (something) to (someone): *if the judge refuses bail, he'll appeal* **3** to decline to accept (something offered): *he refused the captaincy* **4** (of a horse) to be unwilling to jump a fence ▶ HISTORY Latin *refundere* to pour back

refuse[2] *n* anything thrown away; rubbish ▶ HISTORY Old French *refuser* to refuse

refusenik *n* **1** (formerly) a Jew in the USSR who was refused permission to emigrate **2** a person who refuses to obey a law or cooperate with the government because of strong beliefs

refute *vb* **-futing, -futed** to prove (a statement or theory) to be false or incorrect ▶ HISTORY Latin *refutare* > **refutation** *n*

reg *n* *geol* an area of desert covered with loose stones

regain *vb* **1** to get back or recover **2** to reach again: *to regain the shore*

regal *adj* **1** of or fit for a king or queen **2** splendid and dignified; magnificent: *a luxury cruise liner on her serene and regal way around the better ports* ▶ HISTORY Latin *regalis* > **regality** *n* > **regally** *adv*

regale *vb* **-galing, -galed** **1** to give delight or amusement to: *she would regale her friends with stories* **2** to provide with abundant food or drink ▶ HISTORY French *régaler*

regalia *n* the ceremonial emblems or robes of royalty or high office ▶ HISTORY Medieval Latin: royal privileges

regard *vb* **1** to look upon or think of in a specified way: *angina can therefore be regarded as heart cramp* **2** to look closely or attentively at (something or someone) **3** to take notice of: *he has never regarded the conventions* **4 as regards** on the subject of ▷ *n* **5** respect or affection: *you haven't a high regard for her opinion* **6** attention: *he eats what he wants with no regard to health* **7** a gaze or look **8** reference or connection: *with regard to my complaint* **9 regards** an expression of goodwill: *give her my regards* ▶ HISTORY Old French *regarder* to look at, care about

regarding *prep* on the subject of; relating to

regardless *adj* **1 regardless of** taking no notice of: *the illness can affect anyone regardless of their social class* ▷ *adv* **2** in spite of everything: *I carried on regardless*

regatta *n* a series of races of boats or yachts ▶ HISTORY obsolete Italian *rigatta* contest

regency *n, pl* **-cies** **1** government by a regent **2** the status of a regent **3** a period when a regent is in power ▶ HISTORY Latin *regere* to rule

Regency *adj* of the regency (1811–20) of the Prince of Wales (later George IV) or the styles of architecture or furniture produced during it

regenerate *vb* (ri-**jen**-er-ate) **-ating, -ated** **1** to undergo or cause to undergo physical, economic, or spiritual renewal **2** to come or bring into existence once again **3** to replace (lost or damaged tissues or organs) by new growth ▷ *adj* (ri-**jen**-er-it) **4** physically, economically, or spiritually renewed > **regeneration** *n* > **regenerative** *adj*

regent *n* **1** the ruler of a country during the childhood, absence, or illness of its monarch **2** *US & Canad* a member of the governing board of certain schools and colleges ▷ *adj* **3** acting as a regent: *the Prince Regent* ▶ HISTORY Latin *regere* to rule

reggae *n* a type of popular music of Jamaican origin with a strong beat ▶ HISTORY West Indian

regicide *n* **1** the killing of a king **2** a person who kills a king ▶ HISTORY Latin *rex* king + *caedere* to kill

regime (ray-**zheem**) *n* **1** a system of government **2** a particular administration: *the corrupt regime* **3** *med* a regimen ▶ HISTORY French

r

regimen *n* a prescribed system of diet and exercise ▶ HISTORY Latin: guidance

regiment *n* **1** an organized body of troops as a unit in the army **2** a large number or group ▶ HISTORY Late Latin *regimentum* government > **regimental** *adj*

regimentals *pl n* **1** the uniform and insignia of a regiment **2** military uniform

regimental sergeant major *n mil* the senior warrant officer in a regiment or battalion

regimented *adj* very strictly controlled: *the regimented confines of the school* > **regimentation** *n*

Regina *n* queen: now used chiefly in documents and inscriptions ▶ HISTORY Latin

region *n* **1** an administrative division of a country **2** an area considered as a unit for geographical or social reasons **3** a sphere of activity or interest **4** a part of the body: *the lumbar region* **5 in the region of** approximately: *in the region of 100,000 troops* **6 the regions** the parts of a country away from the capital: *discord between Moscow and the regions* ▶ HISTORY Latin *regio* > **regional** *adj*

regionalism *n* **1** the division of a country or organization into geographical regions each having some autonomy **2** loyalty to one's home region

register *n* **1** an official list recording names, events, or transactions **2** the book in which such a list is written **3** a device that records data, totals sums of money, etc.: *a cash register* **4** a style of speaking or writing, such as slang, used in particular circumstances or social situations **5** *music* **a** the timbre characteristic of a certain manner of voice production **b** any of the stops on an organ in respect of its tonal quality: *the flute register* ▷ *vb* **6** to enter (an event, person's name, ownership, etc.) in a register **7** to show on a scale or other measuring instrument **8** to show in a person's face or bearing: *his face registered surprise* **9** *informal* to have an effect or make an impression: *the news did not register at first* **10** to have a letter or parcel insured against loss by the Post Office: *registered mail* ▶ HISTORY Medieval Latin *registrum* > **registration** *n*

register office *n Brit* a government office where civil marriages are performed and births, marriages, and deaths are recorded

registrar *n* **1** a person who keeps official records **2** an official responsible for student records and enrolment in a college **3** a hospital doctor senior to a houseman but junior to a consultant

registration document *n Brit & Austral* a document giving identification details of a vehicle, including its owner's name

registration number *n* a sequence of letters and numbers given to a motor vehicle when it is registered, displayed on numberplates at the front and rear

registry *n, pl* **-tries 1** a place where official records are kept **2** the registration of a ship's country of origin: *a ship of Liberian registry*

registry office *n Brit & NZ* same as **register office**

Regius professor (reej-yuss) *n Brit* a person appointed by the Crown to a university chair founded by a royal patron ▶ HISTORY Latin *regius* royal

regolith *n geol* the layer of loose material covering the bedrock of the earth and moon, etc., comprising soil, sand, rock fragments, volcanic ash, glacial drift, etc. ▶ HISTORY Greek *rhēgos* covering, blanket + *lithos* stone

regress *vb* **1** to return to a former and worse condition ▷ *n* **2** return to a former and worse condition ▶ HISTORY Latin *regredi* to go back > **regressive** *adj*

regression *n* **1** the act of regressing **2** *psychol* the use by an adult of behaviour more appropriate to a child

regret *vb* **-gretting, -gretted 1** to feel sorry or upset about **2** to express apology or distress: *we regret any misunderstanding caused* ▷ *n* **3** a feeling of repentance, guilt, or sorrow **4 regrets** a polite expression of refusal: *she had sent her regrets* ▶ HISTORY Old French *regreter* > **regretful** *adj* > **regretfully** *adv* > **regrettable** *adj* > **regrettably** *adv*

regroup *vb* **1** to reorganize (military forces) after an attack or a defeat **2** to rearrange into a new grouping

regular *adj* **1** normal, customary, or usual **2** symmetrical or even: *regular features* **3** according to a uniform principle, arrangement, or order **4** occurring at fixed or prearranged intervals: *we run regular advertisements in the press* **5** following a set rule or normal practice **6** *grammar* following the usual pattern of formation in a language: *regular verbs* **7** of or serving in the permanent military services: *the regular armed forces* **8** *maths* (of a polygon) having all its sides and angles the same **9** officially qualified or recognized: *he's not a regular doctor* **10** *informal* not constipated: *eating fresh vegetables helps keep you regular* **11** *US & Canad, informal* likeable: *a regular guy* **12** complete or utter: *a regular fool* **13** subject to the rule of an established religious community: *canons regular* ▷ *n* **14** a professional long-term serviceman in a military unit **15** *informal* a frequent customer or visitor ▶ HISTORY Latin *regula* ruler, model > **regularity** *n* > **regularize** *or* **-ise** *vb* > **regularly** *adv*

regulate *vb* **-lating, -lated 1** to control by means of rules: *a code of practice to regulate advertising by schools* **2** to adjust slightly: *he had to take drugs to regulate his heartbeat* ▶ HISTORY Late Latin *regulare* to control > **regulatory** *adj*

regulation *n* **1** a rule that governs procedure or behaviour **2** the act of regulating ▷ *adj* **3** in accordance with rules or conventions: *dressed in the orchestra's regulation black tie*

regulator *n* **1** a mechanism that automatically controls pressure, temperature, etc. **2** the mechanism by which the speed of a clock is regulated **3** *econ* a person or body appointed by the government to ensure that a particular industry or utility offers choice and value to consumers

r

regurgitate *vb* **-tating, -tated 1** to vomit **2** (of some birds and animals) to bring back (partly digested food) to the mouth to feed the young **3** to reproduce (ideas or facts) without understanding them ▶ HISTORY Medieval Latin *re-* back + *gurgitare* to flood > **regurgitation** *n*

rehabilitate *vb* **-tating, -tated 1** to help (a person) to readapt to society after illness or imprisonment **2** to restore to a former position or rank **3** to restore the good reputation of ▶ HISTORY Medieval Latin *rehabilitare* to restore > **rehabilitation** *n*

rehash *vb* **1** to use (old or already used ideas) in a slightly different form without real improvement ▷ *n* **2** old ideas presented in a new form ▶ HISTORY *re-* again + *hash* to chop into pieces

rehearse *vb* **-hearsing, -hearsed 1** to practise (a play, concert, etc.) for public performance **2** to repeat aloud: *he rehearsed his familiar views on the press* **3** to train (a person) for public performance ▶ HISTORY Old French *rehercier* to harrow a second time > **rehearsal** *n* > **rehearser** *n*

rehouse *vb* **-housing, -housed** to provide with a new and better home

Reich (**rike**) *n* the former German state, esp. the Nazi dictatorship in Germany from 1933–45 (**Third Reich**) ▶ HISTORY German: kingdom

reign *n* **1** the period during which a monarch is the official ruler of a country **2** a period during which a person or thing is dominant: *a reign of terror* ▷ *vb* **3** to rule (a country) **4** to be supreme: *a sense of confusion reigns in the capital* ▶ HISTORY Old French *reigne*

reimburse *vb* **-bursing, -bursed** to repay (someone) for (expenses or losses) ▶ HISTORY Medieval Latin *imbursare* to put in a moneybag > **reimbursement** *n*

rein *n* **1 reins a** long narrow straps attached to a bit to control a horse **b** narrow straps attached to a harness to control a young child **c** means of control: *to take up the reins of government* **2 give (a) free rein** to allow a considerable amount of freedom **3 keep a tight rein on** to control carefully: *we have to keep a tight rein on expenditure* ▷ *vb* **4** to restrain or halt with reins **5** to control or limit: *public spending was reined in* ▶ HISTORY Old French *resne*

reincarnate *vb* **-nating, -nated** to be born again in a different body: *souls may be reincarnated in human forms*

reincarnation *n* **1** the belief that after death the soul is reborn in another body **2** an instance of rebirth in another body **3** reappearance in a new form of a principle or idea: *he was the reincarnation of the old Republican Party isolationist*

reindeer *n, pl* **-deer** or **-deers** a deer with large branched antlers that lives in the arctic regions ▶ HISTORY Old Norse *hreindȳri*

reinforce *vb* **-inforcing, -inforced 1** to give added emphasis to (an idea or feeling): *his tired face reinforced his own weariness* **2** to make physically stronger or harder: *the plastic panels were reinforced* with carbon fibre **3** to give added support to (a military force) by providing more men or equipment: *the army garrison had been reinforced with helicopters* ▶ HISTORY French *renforcer* > **reinforcement** *n*

reinforced concrete *n* concrete with steel bars or mesh embedded in it to strengthen it

reinstate *vb* **-stating, -stated 1** to restore to a former rank or status **2** to cause to exist or be important again: *reinstate some semblance of order* > **reinstatement** *n*

reiterate *vb* **-ating, -ated** *formal* to repeat again and again ▶ HISTORY Latin *reiterare* > **reiteration** *n*

reject *vb* **1** to refuse to accept, use, or believe **2** to deny to (a person) the feelings hoped for: *the boy had been rejected by his mother* **3** to pass over or throw out as useless **4** (of an organism) to fail to accept (a tissue graft or organ transplant) ▷ *n* **5** a person or thing rejected as not up to standard ▶ HISTORY Latin *reicere* to throw back > **rejection** *n*

rejig *vb* **-jigging, -jigged 1** to re-equip (a factory or plant) **2** *informal* to rearrange or manipulate, sometimes in an unscrupulous way: *the promoter hastily rejigged the running order*

rejoice *vb* **-joicing, -joiced** to feel or express great happiness ▶ HISTORY Old French *resjoir* > **rejoicing** *n*

rejoin[1] *vb* to come together with (someone or something) again

rejoin[2] *vb* *written* to reply in a sharp or witty way ▶ HISTORY Old French *rejoindre*

rejoinder *n* a sharp or witty reply

rejuvenate *vb* **-nating, -nated 1** to give back youth or vitality to **2** *geol* to cause (a river) to begin eroding more vigorously to a new lower base level, usually because of uplift of the land ▶ HISTORY Latin *re-* again + *juvenis* young

rekindle *vb* **-dling, -dled** to arouse (former emotions or interests)

relapse *vb* **-lapsing, -lapsed 1** to fall back into bad habits or illness ▷ *n* **2** the act of relapsing **3** the return of ill health after an apparent or partial recovery ▶ HISTORY Latin *re-* back + *labi* to slip

relate *vb* **-lating, -lated 1** to establish a relation between **2** to have reference or relation to **3** to have an understanding (of people or ideas): *the inability to relate to others* **4** to tell (a story) or describe (an event) ▶ HISTORY Latin *relatus* brought back

related *adj* **1** linked by kinship or marriage **2** connected or associated: *salts and related compounds*

relation *n* **1** the connection between things or people **2** a person who is connected by blood or marriage **3** connection by blood or marriage **4** an account or narrative **5 in** or **with relation to** with reference to: *an inquiry into export controls in relation to Iraq*

relational process *n* *functional grammar* the process of being or possessing as specified by a verb group. Compare **material process, mental process, verbal process**

713

relations *pl n* **1** social or political dealings between individuals or groups **2** family or relatives **3** *euphemistic* sexual intercourse

relationship *n* **1** the dealings and feelings that exist between people or groups **2** an emotional or romantic affair **3** the connection between two things: *the relationship between exercise and mental health* **4** association by blood or marriage

relative *adj* **1** true to a certain degree or extent: *a zone of relative affluence* **2** having significance only in relation to something else: *time is relative* **3 relative to** in proportion to: *it will benefit from high growth in earnings relative to prices* **4** respective: *the relative qualities of speed and accuracy* **5** relevant: *the facts relative to the enquiry* **6** *grammar* of a clause (**relative clause**) that modifies a noun or pronoun occurring earlier in the sentence **7** *grammar* of or belonging to a class of words, such as *who*, *which*, or *that*, which function as conjunctions introducing relative clauses ▷ *n* **8** a person who is related by blood or marriage > **relatively** *adv*

relative atomic mass *n* same as **atomic weight**

relative clause *n* *grammar* a subordinate clause, often beginning with *who*, *whom*, *which*, *whose*, or *that*, that gives information about or defines the person or thing mentioned immediately before

relative density *n* *physics* the ratio of the density of a substance such as water, under specified conditions. Compare **specific gravity**

relative frequency *n* *statistics* an estimate of probability based on the ratio of the actual number of favourable events to the total possible number of events

relative pronoun *n* *grammar* one of the pronouns *who*, *whom*, *whose*, *which*, or *that* when they introduce additional or defining information about a person or thing just mentioned, as in the example, *the man who masterminded the campaign*

relativity *n* **1** either of two theories developed by Albert Einstein, the **special theory of relativity**, which requires that the laws of physics shall be the same as seen by any two different observers in uniform relative motion, and the **general theory of relativity**, which considers observers with relative acceleration and leads to a theory of gravitation **2** the state of being relative

relax *vb* **1** to make or become less tense, looser, or less rigid **2** to ease up from effort or attention **3** to make (rules or discipline) less strict **4** to become more friendly **5** to lessen the intensity of: *he relaxed his vigilance in the lulls between attacks* ▶ HISTORY Latin *relaxare* to loosen > **relaxed** *adj*

relaxation *n* **1** rest after work or effort **2** a form of recreation: *his favoured form of relaxation was walking on the local moors* **3** the act of relaxing

relay *n* **1** a fresh set of people or animals relieving others **2** short for **relay race** **3** an automatic device that controls a valve or switch, esp. one in which a small change in current or voltage controls the switching on or off of circuits **4** *radio* a combination of a receiver and transmitter designed to receive radio signals and retransmit them ▷ *vb* **5** to pass on (a message) **6** to retransmit (a signal) by means of a relay **7** *Brit* to broadcast (a performance or event) as it happens ▶ HISTORY Old French *relaier* to leave behind

relay race *n* a race between teams in which each contestant covers a specified portion of the distance

release *vb* **-leasing, -leased** **1** to free (a person or animal) from captivity or imprisonment **2** to free (someone) from obligation or duty **3** to free (something) from (one's grip) **4** to allow news or information to be made public or available **5** to allow (something) to move freely: *she released the handbrake* **6** to issue (a recording, film, or book) for sale or public showing: *the single was originally released six years ago* **7** to give out (heat, energy, radiation, etc.): *the explosion released a cloud of toxic gas* ▷ *n* **8** the act of freeing or state of being freed **9** a statement to the press **10** the act of issuing for sale or publication **11** something issued for sale or public showing ▶ HISTORY Old French *relesser*

relegate *vb* **-gating, -gated** **1** to put in a less important position **2** to demote (a sports team) to a lower division: *four clubs were relegated from the first division* ▶ HISTORY Latin *re-* back + *legare* to send > **relegation** *n*

relent *vb* **1** to change one's mind about some decision **2** to become milder or less severe: *the weather relented* ▶ HISTORY Latin *re-* back + *lentare* to bend

relentless *adj* **1** never stopping or reducing in severity: *relentless deterioration in standards* **2** (of a person) determined and pitiless

relevant *adj* to do with the matter in hand ▶ HISTORY Medieval Latin *relevans* > **relevance** *n*

reliable *adj* able to be trusted > **reliability** *n* > **reliably** *adv*

reliance *n* the state of relying on or trusting (a person or thing) > **reliant** *adj*

relic *n* **1** an object or custom that has survived from the past **2** something valued for its past associations **3 relics** remaining parts or traces **4** *RC Church, Eastern Church* a body part or possession of a saint, venerated as holy ▶ HISTORY Latin *reliquiae* remains

relict *n* *archaic* **1** a relic **2** a widow ▶ HISTORY Latin *relictus* left behind

relief *n* **1** a feeling of cheerfulness that follows the removal of anxiety, pain, or distress **2** a temporary pause in anxiety, pain, or distress **3** money, food, or clothing given to people in special need: *disaster relief* **4** the act of freeing a besieged town or fortress: *the relief of Mafeking* **5** a person who replaces another at some task or duty **6** a bus, plane, etc. that carries additional passengers when a scheduled service is full **7** Also called: **relievo** *sculpture, archit* the projection of a carved design from the surface **8** any vivid effect resulting from contrast: *a welcome relief* **9** the difference between the highest and lowest level: *study the map of relief and the rainfall map* **10 on relief** *US &*

Canad (of people) in receipt of government aid because of personal need ▶ **HISTORY** Old French *relever* to relieve

relief map *n* a map showing the shape and height of the land surface by contours and shading

relief rainfall *n meteorol* rain that occurs when air has been blown over the sea and is then forced up over an area of high land. The air then cools and the moisture in the air condenses and rain falls

relieve *vb* **-lieving, -lieved 1** to lessen (pain, distress, boredom, etc.) **2** to bring assistance to (someone in need): *a plan to relieve those facing hunger* **3** to free (someone) from an obligation: *a further attempt to relieve the taxpayers of their burdens* **4** to take over the duties of (someone): *the night nurse came in to relieve her* **5** to free (a besieged town or fort) **6 relieve oneself** to urinate or defecate **7** to set off by contrast: *painted walls are marginally relieved by some abstract prints* **8** *informal* to take from: *the prince had relieved him of his duties* ▶ **HISTORY** Latin *re-* again + *levare* to lighten **> relieved** *adj*

religion *n* **1** belief in or worship of a supernatural power or powers considered to be divine or to have control of human destiny **2** any formal expression of such belief: *the Christian religion* **3** *chiefly RC Church* the way of life entered upon by monks and nuns: *to enter religion* ▶ **HISTORY** Latin *religio*

religious *adj* **1** of religion **2** pious or devout **3** scrupulous or conscientious: *religious attention to detail* **4** *Christianity* relating to the way of life of monks and nuns ▷ *n* **5** *Christianity* a monk or nun **> religiously** *adv*

relinquish *vb formal* **1** to give up: *that hope has to be relinquished* **2** to renounce (a claim or right) **3** to release one's hold on ▶ **HISTORY** Latin *relinquere* **> relinquishment** *n*

reliquary (rel-lik-wer-ee) *n, pl* **-quaries** a container for relics of saints

relish *vb* **1** to savour or enjoy (an experience) to the full **2** to anticipate eagerly ▷ *n* **3** liking or enjoyment: *he has an enormous relish for life* **4** pleasurable anticipation: *his early relish for a new challenge* **5** an appetizing or spicy food, such as a pickle, added to a main dish to improve its flavour **6** a zestful quality: *he tells stories with great relish* ▶ **HISTORY** earlier *reles* aftertaste

relive *vb* **-living, -lived** to experience (a sensation or event) again, esp. in the imagination

relocate *vb* **-cating, -cated** to move or be moved to a new place of work **> relocation** *n*

reluctance *n* **1** unwillingness to do something **2** *physics* a measure of the resistance of a closed magnetic circuit to a magnetic flux ▶ **HISTORY** Latin *reluctari* to resist

reluctant *adj* unwilling or disinclined **> reluctantly** *adv*

rely *vb* **-lies, -lying, -lied · rely on** or **upon a** to be dependent on: *the organization relies on voluntary contributions* **b** to have trust or confidence in: *you can rely on his judgment* ▶ **HISTORY** Old French *relier* to fasten together

REM rapid eye movement

remain *vb* **1** to continue to be: *the situation remains alarming* **2** to stay behind or in the same place: *to remain at home* **3** to be left after use or the passage of time **4** to be left to be done, said, etc.: *whether this will be a long-term trend remains to be seen* ▶ **HISTORY** Latin *remanere*

remainder *n* **1** a part or portion that is left after use or the passage of time: *we ate some biscuits and the remainder of the jam* **2** *maths* **a** the amount left over when one quantity cannot be exactly divided by another: *for 10 ÷ 3, the remainder is 1* **b** the amount left over when one quantity is subtracted from another **3** a number of copies of a book sold cheaply because it has been impossible to sell them at full price ▷ *vb* **4** to sell (copies of a book) as a remainder

remains *pl n* **1** parts left over from something after use or the passage of time: *the remains of the old Roman fortress* **2** a corpse

remand *vb* **1** *law* to send (a prisoner or accused person) back into custody or put on bail before trial ▷ *n* **2** the sending of a person back into custody or putting on bail before trial **3 on remand** in custody or on bail awaiting trial ▶ **HISTORY** Latin *re-* back + *mandare* to command

remand centre *n* (in Britain) a place where accused people are detained while awaiting trial

remark *vb* **1** to pass a casual comment (about) **2** to say **3** to observe or notice ▷ *n* **4** a brief casually expressed thought or opinion ▶ **HISTORY** Old French *remarquer* to observe

remarkable *adj* **1** worthy of note or attention: *a remarkable career* **2** striking or extraordinary: *a thing of remarkable beauty* **> remarkably** *adv*

remarry *vb* **-ries, -rying, -ried** to marry again following a divorce or the death of one's previous spouse **> remarriage** *n*

REME Royal Electrical and Mechanical Engineers

remedial *adj* **1** providing or intended as a remedy **2** of special teaching for slow learners: *remedial classes* **> remedially** *adv*

remedy *n, pl* **-edies 1** a drug or treatment for curing pain or disease **2** a way of solving a problem: *every statesman promised a remedy for unemployment* ▷ *vb* **-edies, -edying, -edied 3** to put right or improve ▶ **HISTORY** Latin *remedium* a cure **> remediable** *adj*

remember *vb* **1** to become aware of (something forgotten) again **2** to keep (an idea, intention, etc.) in one's mind: *remember to write* **3** to give money to (someone), as in a will or in tipping **4 remember to** to mention (a person's name) to another person, by way of greeting: *remember me to her* **5** to commemorate: *we are here to remember the dead* ▶ **HISTORY** Latin *re-* again + *memor* mindful

remembrance *n* **1** a memory **2** a memento or keepsake **3** the act of honouring some past event or person

Remembrance Day *n* **1** (in Britain) Remembrance Sunday **2** (in Canada and Australia) a statutory holiday observed on November 11 in memory of the dead of both World Wars

r

715

Remembrance Sunday n (in Britain) the Sunday closest to November 11th, on which the dead of both World Wars are commemorated

remind vb 1 to cause to remember: *remind her that she was on duty* 2 to put in mind (of someone or something): *you remind me of Alice in Wonderland*

reminder n 1 *written* something that recalls the past 2 a note to remind a person of something not done

reminisce vb **-niscing, -nisced** to talk or write about old times or past experiences

reminiscence n 1 the act of recalling or narrating past experiences 2 something remembered from the past 3 **reminiscences** stories about a person's life, often presented in a book

reminiscent adj 1 **reminiscent of** reminding or suggestive of 2 characterized by reminiscence ▶ HISTORY Latin *reminisci* to call to mind

remiss adj *formal* careless in attention to duty or responsibility ▶ HISTORY Latin *remissus*

remission n 1 a reduction in the length of a prison term 2 forgiveness for sin 3 easing of intensity of the symptoms of a disease 4 a release from an obligation

remit vb (rim-**mitt**) **-mitting, -mitted** 1 to send (money) for goods or services 2 to cancel (a punishment or debt) 3 *law* to send back (a case) to a lower court for further consideration 4 to slacken or ease off 5 *archaic* to forgive (crime or sins) ▷ n (**ree**-mitt) 6 area of authority: *within the review body's remit* ▶ HISTORY Latin *re-* back + *mittere* to send

remittance n money sent as payment

remittent adj (of a disease) periodically less severe

remix vb 1 to change the relative prominence of each performer's part of (a recording) ▷ n 2 a remixed version of a recording

remnant n 1 a part left over 2 a piece of material from the end of a roll 3 a surviving trace or vestige: *the authorities drafted in the military to crush any remnant of protest* ▶ HISTORY Old French *remenant* remaining

remonstrance n *formal* a strong protest about something

remonstrate vb **-strating, -strated** *formal* to argue in protest or objection: *the player remonstrated loudly with the official* ▶ HISTORY Latin *re-* again + *monstrare* to show > **remonstration** n

remorse n a sense of deep regret and guilt for something one did ▶ HISTORY Medieval Latin *remorsus* a gnawing > **remorseful** adj

remorseless adj 1 constantly unkind and lacking pity: *remorseless fate* 2 continually intense: *the superintendent's remorseless gaze*

remote adj 1 far away 2 far from civilization 3 distant in time 4 not relevant: *the issues seem remote from the general population* 5 (of a person's manner) aloof or abstracted 6 slight or faint: *a remote possibility* 7 operated from a distance; remote-controlled: *a remote manipulator arm* ▶ HISTORY Latin *remotus* far removed > **remotely** adv

remote control n control of an apparatus from a distance by radio or electrical signals > **remote-controlled** adj

remote sensing n the use of an instrument, such as a radar device or camera, to scan the earth or another planet from space in order to collect data about some aspect of it > **remote-sensing** adj

remould vb 1 to change completely: *to remould the country* 2 *Brit* to bond a new tread onto the casing of (a worn pneumatic tyre) ▷ n 3 *Brit* a tyre made by this process

removable adj capable of being removed from a place or released from another object: *a farmer's truck with removable wooden sides*

removal n 1 the act of removing or state of being removed 2 the process of moving one's possessions from a previous address to a new one

remove vb **-moving, -moved** 1 *written* to take away and place elsewhere 2 *written* to take (clothing) off 3 to get rid of 4 to dismiss (someone) from office 5 *formal* to change the location of one's home or place of business ▷ n 6 the degree of difference: *one remove away from complete rebuttal* 7 *Brit* (in certain schools) a class or form designed to prepare pupils for senior classes ▶ HISTORY Old French *removoir*

removed adj 1 very different or distant: *madness seemed far removed from the sunny order of things* 2 separated by a degree of descent: *the child of a person's first cousin is their first cousin once removed*

remunerate vb **-ating, -ated** *formal* to reward or pay for work or service ▶ HISTORY Latin *remunerari* > **remuneration** n > **remunerative** adj

renaissance n a renewal of interest or creativity in an area: *a complete renaissance in maze building* ▶ HISTORY French

Renaissance n 1 **the Renaissance** the great revival of art, literature, and learning in Europe in the 14th, 15th, and 16th centuries ▷ adj 2 of or from the Renaissance

renal (**ree**-nal) adj of the kidneys ▶ HISTORY Latin *renes* kidneys

renascent adj *literary* becoming active or vigorous again: *renascent nationalism* ▶ HISTORY Latin *renasci* to be born again > **renascence** n

rend vb **rending, rent** *literary* 1 to tear violently 2 (of a sound) to break (the silence) with a shrill or piercing tone ▶ HISTORY Old English *rendan*

render vb 1 to cause to become: *he was rendered unconscious by his wound* 2 to give or provide (aid, a service, etc.) 3 *formal* to present or submit (a bill) 4 to translate 5 to represent in painting, music, or acting 6 to yield or give: *he rendered up his soul to God* 7 to cover with plaster 8 to melt down (fat) ▶ HISTORY Old French *rendre* > **rendering** n

rendezvous (**ron**-day-voo) n, pl **-vous** (-vooz) 1 an appointment to meet at a specified time and place 2 a place where people meet ▷ vb 3 to meet at a specified time or place ▶ HISTORY French

rendition n *formal* 1 a performance of a piece of music or a dramatic role 2 a translation

renegade *n* a person who deserts a cause for another ▶ **HISTORY** Spanish *renegado*

renege (rin-**nayg**) *vb* **-neging, -neged** to go back (on an agreement or promise): *the politicians reneged on every promise* ▶ **HISTORY** Medieval Latin *renegare* to renounce

renew *vb* **1** to begin again **2** to take up again after a break: *they wanted to renew diplomatic ties* **3** to make valid again: *we didn't renew the lease* **4** to grow again **5** to restore to a new or fresh condition **6** to replace (an old or worn-out part or piece) **7** to restate or reaffirm (a promise) > **renewal** *n*

renewable *adj* **1** able to be renewed ▷ *pl n* **renewables 2** sources of alternative energy, such as wind and wave power

renewable resources *pl n environmental science* resources that can easily be replaced or that can be replaced through good management, such as quick-growing species of tree. Compare **non-renewable resources**

rennet *n* a substance prepared from the stomachs of calves and used for curdling milk to make cheese ▶ **HISTORY** Old English *gerinnan* to curdle

renounce *vb* **-nouncing, -nounced 1** to give up (a belief or habit) voluntarily **2** to give up formally (a claim or right): *he would renounce his rights to the throne* ▶ **HISTORY** Latin *renuntiare*

renovate *vb* **-vating, -vated** to restore to good condition ▶ **HISTORY** Latin *re-* again + *novare* to make new > **renovation** *n* > **renovator** *n*

renown *n* widespread good reputation ▶ **HISTORY** Old French *renom*

renowned *adj* famous

rent¹ *vb* **1** to give or have use of (land, a building, a machine, etc.) in return for periodic payments ▷ *n* **2** a payment made periodically for the use of land, a building, a machine, etc. ▶ **HISTORY** Old French *rente* revenue

rent² *n* **1** a slit made by tearing ▷ *vb* **2** the past of **rend**

rent-a- *prefix* **1** denoting a rental service: *rent-a-car* **2** *derogatory* denoting a person or group that performs a function as if hired from a rental service: *rent-a-mob*

rental *n* **1** the amount paid or received as rent ▷ *adj* **2** of or relating to rent

rentier (**ron**-tee-ay) *n* a person who lives off unearned income such as rents or interest

renunciation *n* **1** the act or an instance of renouncing **2** a formal declaration renouncing something

reorganize *or* **-ise** *vb* **-izing, -ized** *or* **-ising, -ised** to organize in a new and more efficient way > **reorganization** *or* **-isation** *n*

rep¹ *n theatre* short for **repertory company**

rep² *n* **1** a sales representative **2** someone elected to represent a group of people: *the union rep* **3** *NZ, informal* a rugby player selected to represent his district

repair¹ *vb* **1** to restore (something damaged or broken) to good condition or working order **2** to make up for (a mistake or injury) **3** to heal (a breach or division) in (something): *he is attempting to repair his country's relations with America* ▷ *n* **4** the act, task, or process of repairing **5** a part that has been repaired **6** state or condition: *many museums may have to close because they are in such bad repair* ▶ **HISTORY** Latin *re-* again + *parare* to make ready > **repairable** *adj*

repair² *vb* **repair to** to go to (a place) ▶ **HISTORY** Latin *re-* back + *patria* fatherland

reparation *n* **1** the act of making up for loss or injury **2** **reparations** compensation paid by a defeated nation after a war for the damage and injuries it caused ▶ **HISTORY** Latin *reparare* to repair

repartee *n* **1** conversation consisting of witty remarks **2** a sharp witty remark made as a reply ▶ **HISTORY** French *repartie*

repast *n literary* a meal ▶ **HISTORY** Old French *repaistre* to feed

repatriate *vb* **-ating, -ated 1** to send back (a person) to the country of his or her birth or citizenship ▷ *n* **2** a person who has been repatriated: *Algerian repatriates* ▶ **HISTORY** Latin *re-* back + *patria* fatherland > **repatriation** *n*

repay *vb* **-paying, -paid 1** to refund or reimburse **2** to make a return for (something): *to repay hospitality* > **repayable** *adj* > **repayment** *n*

repeal *vb* **1** to cancel (a law) officially ▷ *n* **2** the act of repealing: *the repeal of repressive legislation* ▶ **HISTORY** Old French *repeler* > **repealable** *adj*

repeat *vb* **1** to say, write, or do again **2** to tell to another person (the secrets told to one by someone else) **3** to recite (a poem, etc.) from memory **4** to occur more than once: *this pattern repeats itself many times* **5** (of food) to be tasted again after eating as the result of belching **6** to say (the words or sounds) uttered by someone else; echo ▷ *n* **7** the act or an instance of repeating **8** a word, action, pattern, etc. that is repeated **9** *radio, television* a broadcast of a programme which has been broadcast before **10** *music* a passage that is an exact restatement of the passage preceding it ▶ **HISTORY** Latin *repetere* to seek again > **repeated** *adj* > **repeatedly** *adv* > **repeatable** *adj*

repeater *n* **1** a gun capable of firing several shots without reloading **2** a clock or watch which strikes the hour or quarter-hour just past, when a spring is pressed

repeat reading *n science* the practice of taking a measurement more than once and then using an average of those results as a value, for example on a graph

repel *vb* **-pelling, -pelled 1** to cause (someone) to feel disgusted **2** to force or drive back (someone or something) **3** to be effective in keeping away or controlling: *these buzzers are claimed to repel female mosquitoes* **4** to fail to mix with or absorb: *water and oil repel each other* **5** to reject or spurn: *she repelled his advances* ▶ **HISTORY** Latin *re-* back + *pellere* to push

repellent *adj* **1** disgusting or distasteful **2** resisting water, etc. ▷ *n* **3** a chemical used to keep insects or other creatures away

r

repent *vb* to feel regret for (something bad one has done) ▶ HISTORY Old French *repentir* > **repentance** *n* > **repentant** *adj*

repercussion *n* 1 **repercussions** results or consequences of an action or event 2 an echo or reverberation ▶ HISTORY Latin *repercutere* to strike back

repertoire *n* 1 all the works that a company or performer can perform 2 the entire stock of skills or techniques that someone or something, such as a computer, is capable of: *a superb repertoire of shots* ▶ HISTORY French

repertory *n, pl* -**ries** 1 same as **repertoire** (sense 2) 2 short for **repertory company** ▶ HISTORY Late Latin *repertorium* storehouse

repertory company *n* a permanent theatre company producing a succession of plays

repetition *n* 1 the act of repeating 2 a thing that is repeated 3 a replica or copy > **repetitious** *adj* > **repetitive** *adj*

rephrase *vb* -**phrasing, -phrased** to express in different words > **rephrasing** *n*

repine *vb* -**pining, -pined** *literary* to be worried or discontented ▶ HISTORY RE- + PINE²

replace *vb* -**placing, -placed** 1 to take the place of 2 to substitute a person or thing for (another): *we need to replace that chair* 3 to put (something) back in its rightful place

replacement *n* 1 the act or process of replacing 2 a person or thing that replaces another

replay *n* 1 a showing again of a sequence of action immediately after it happens 2 a second sports match played because an earlier game was drawn ▷ *vb* 3 to play (a recording, match, etc.) again

replenish *vb* to make full or complete again by supplying what has been used up ▶ HISTORY Old French *replenir* > **replenishment** *n*

replete *adj* 1 pleasantly full of food and drink 2 well supplied: *a world replete with true horror* ▶ HISTORY Latin *repletus* > **repletion** *n*

replica *n* an exact copy ▶ HISTORY Italian, literally: a reply

replicate *vb* -**cating, -cated** to make or be an exact copy of; reproduce ▶ HISTORY Latin *replicatus* bent back > **replication** *n*

reply *vb* -**plies, -plying, -plied** 1 to make answer (to) in words or writing or by an action 2 to say (something) in answer: *she replied that she did not believe him* ▷ *n, pl* -**plies** 3 an answer or response ▶ HISTORY Old French *replier* to fold again

report *vb* 1 to give an account (of) 2 to give an account of the results of an investigation (into): *the commission is to report on global warming* 3 to make a formal report on (a subject) 4 to make a formal complaint about 5 to present (oneself) at an appointed place or for a specific purpose: *report to the manager's office* 6 **report to** to be responsible to and under the authority of 7 to act as a reporter ▷ *n* 8 an account prepared after investigation and published or broadcast 9 an account of the discussions of a committee or other group of people: *I have the report of the mining union* 10 a story for which there is no absolute proof: *according to report, he is not dead* 11 Brit & NZ a statement on the progress of a schoolchild 12 a loud bang made by a gun or explosion 13 comment on a person's character or actions: *he is of good report here* ▶ HISTORY Latin *re-* back + *portare* to carry > **reportedly** *adv*

reported speech *n* *grammar* a report of what someone said that gives the content of the speech without repeating the exact words

reporter *n* a person who gathers news for a newspaper or broadcasting organization

report genre *n* a form of writing or speech in which the writer or speaker presents information in the form of a report

repose¹ *n* 1 a state of quiet restfulness 2 calmness or composure 3 sleep ▷ *vb* -**posing, -posed** 4 to lie or lay down at rest 5 to lie when dead ▶ HISTORY Old French *reposer*

repose² *vb* -**posing, -posed** to put (trust) in a person or thing ▶ HISTORY Latin *reponere* to store up

reposition *vb* to place in a different position

repository *n, pl* -**ries** 1 a place or container in which things can be stored for safety: *a repository for national treasures* 2 a person to whom a secret is entrusted ▶ HISTORY Latin *repositorium*

repossess *vb* (of a lender) to take back (property) from a customer who is behind with payments, for example mortgage repayments > **repossession** *n*

reprehend *vb* to find fault with ▶ HISTORY Latin *reprehendere*

reprehensible *adj* deserving criticism: *Willie's reprehensible behaviour*

represent *vb* 1 to act as the authorized delegate for (a person, country, etc.): *she represented her country at the Olympic Games* 2 to act as a substitute for 3 to stand as an equivalent of 4 to be a means of expressing: *the lights are relit to represent resurrection* 5 to display the characteristics of: *romanticism in music is represented by Liszt* 6 to describe as having a specified character or quality: *the magical bird was often represented as having two heads* 7 to state or explain 8 to present an image of through a picture or sculpture 9 to bring clearly before the mind ▶ HISTORY Latin *repraesentare* to exhibit

representation *n* 1 the state of being represented 2 anything that represents, such as a pictorial portrait 3 **representations** formal statements made to an official body by a person making a complaint > **representational** *adj*

representative *n* 1 a person chosen to act for or represent a group 2 a person who tries to sell the products or services of a firm 3 a typical example ▷ *adj* 4 typical of a class or kind 5 representing 6 including examples of all the interests or types in a group 7 acting as deputy for another 8 of a political system in which people choose a person to make decisions on their behalf

representative action *n* *law* a legal action undertaken by one or more people representing the interests of a large group of people with the same grievance

representative democracy *n* a political system in which policy decisions are taken by representatives who have been elected by the people. Compare **direct democracy**

repress *vb* **1** to keep (feelings) under control **2** to restrict the freedom of: *he continued to repress his people* **3** *psychol* to banish (unpleasant thoughts) from one's conscious mind ▶ HISTORY Latin *reprimere* to press back > **repression** *n* > **repressive** *adj*

reprieve *vb* **-prieving, -prieved 1** to postpone the execution of (a condemned person) **2** to give temporary relief to ▷ *n* **3** a postponement or cancellation of a punishment **4** a warrant granting a postponement or cancellation **5** a temporary relief from pain or harm ▶ HISTORY Old French *repris* (something) taken back

reprimand *vb* **1** to blame (someone) officially for a fault ▷ *n* **2** an instance of blaming someone officially ▶ HISTORY French *réprimande*

reprint *vb* **1** to print further copies of (a book) ▷ *n* **2** a reprinted copy

reprisal *n* an act of taking revenge: *many residents say they are living in fear of reprisals by the army* ▶ HISTORY Old French *reprisaille*

reprise (rip-**preez**) *music n* **1** the repeating of an earlier theme ▷ *vb* **-prising, -prised 2** *written* to repeat an earlier theme

reproach *n* **1** blame or rebuke **2** a scolding **3 beyond reproach** beyond criticism ▷ *vb* **4** to express disapproval of (someone's actions) ▶ HISTORY Old French *reprochier* > **reproachful** *adj*

reprobate (**rep**-roh-bate) *n* **1** an unprincipled bad person ▷ *adj* **2** morally unprincipled ▶ HISTORY Late Latin *reprobatus* held in disfavour

reprobation *n* *literary* disapproval or blame

reproduce *vb* **-ducing, -duced 1** to make a copy or representation of **2** *biol* to produce offspring **3** to re-create > **reproducible** *adj*

reproduction *n* **1** *biol* a process by which an animal or plant produces one or more individuals similar to itself **2** a copy of a work of art **3** the quality of sound from an audio system **4** the act or process of reproducing ▷ *adj* **5** made in imitation of an earlier style: *reproduction furniture* > **reproductive** *adj*

reproof *n* a severe blaming of someone for a fault

reprove *vb* **-proving, -proved** to speak severely to (someone) about a fault ▶ HISTORY Old French *reprover* > **reprovingly** *adv*

reptile *n* **1** a cold-blooded animal, such as a tortoise, snake, or crocodile, that has an outer covering of horny scales or plates and lays eggs **2** a contemptible grovelling person ▶ HISTORY Late Latin *reptilis* creeping > **reptilian** *adj*

republic *n* **1** a form of government in which the people or their elected representatives possess the supreme power **2** a country in which the head of state is an elected or nominated president ▶ HISTORY Latin *respublica*, literally: the public thing

republican *adj* **1** of or supporting a republic ▷ *n* **2** a person who supports or advocates a republic > **republicanism** *n*

Republican *adj* **1** belonging to the Republican Party, the more conservative of the two main political parties in the US **2** belonging to the Irish Republican Army ▷ *n* **3** a member or supporter of the Republican Party in the US **4** a member or supporter of the Irish Republican Army > **Republicanism** *n*

repudiate (rip-**pew**-dee-ate) *vb* **-ating, -ated 1** *written* to reject the authority or validity of **2** *written* to disown (a person) **3** to refuse to acknowledge or pay (a debt) ▶ HISTORY Latin *repudium* divorce > **repudiation** *n*

repugnant *adj* offensive or disgusting ▶ HISTORY Latin *repugnans* resisting > **repugnance** *n*

repulse *vb* **-pulsing, -pulsed 1** to be disgusting to: *this act of feminist rage repulsed as many as it delighted* **2** to drive (an army) back **3** to reject with coldness or discourtesy: *she repulsed his advances* ▷ *n* **4** a driving back **5** a cold discourteous rejection or refusal ▶ HISTORY Latin *repellere*

repulsion *n* **1** a feeling of disgust or aversion **2** *physics* a force separating two objects, such as the force between two like electric charges

repulsive *adj* **1** disgusting or distasteful **2** *physics* of repulsion > **repulsively** *adv*

reputable (**rep**-pew-tab-bl) *adj* trustworthy or respectable > **reputably** *adv*

reputation *n* **1** the opinion generally held of a person or thing **2** a high opinion generally held about a person or thing **3** notoriety or fame, esp. for some specified characteristic ▶ HISTORY Latin *reputatio*

repute *n* good reputation: *a sculptor of international repute* ▶ HISTORY Latin *reputare* to think over

reputed *adj* supposed or rumoured: *the island was reputed to have held a Roman temple; the reputed murderess* > **reputedly** *adv*

request *vb* **1** to ask for or politely demand: *we requested a formal meeting with the committee* ▷ *n* **2** the act or an instance of asking for something: *a polite request* **3** something asked for **4 on request** if asked for: *most companies will send samples on request* ▶ HISTORY Old French *requeste*

Requiem (**rek**-wee-em) *n* **1** *RC Church* a Mass celebrated for the dead **2** a musical setting of this Mass ▶ HISTORY Latin *requies* rest

require *vb* **-quiring, -quired 1** to need **2** to be a necessary condition: *the decision requires a logical common-sense approach* **3** to insist upon **4** to order or command: *family doctors are required to produce annual reports* ▶ HISTORY Latin *requirere* to seek to know

requirement *n* **1** something demanded or imposed as an obligation **2** a specific need or want

requisite (**rek**-wizz-it) *adj* **1** absolutely essential ▷ *n* **2** something essential ▶ HISTORY Latin *requisitus* sought after

requisition *vb* **1** to demand and take for use, esp. for military or public use ▷ *n* **2** a formal request or demand for the use of something **3** the act of taking something over, esp. for military or public use **4** a formal written demand

requite *vb* **-quiting, -quited** to return to someone (the same treatment or feeling as received): *an Australian who requites her love* ▶ HISTORY *re-* back + obsolete *quite* to repay > **requital** *n*

reredos (rear-doss) *n* a screen or wall decoration at the back of an altar ▶ HISTORY Old French *arere* behind + *dos* back

rerun *n* **1** a film or programme that is broadcast again **2** a race that is run again ▷ *vb* **-running, -ran, -run 3** to put on (a film or programme) again **4** to run (a race) again

resale *n* the selling again of something purchased

reschedule *vb* **-uling, -uled 1** to change the time, date, or schedule of: *the show has been rescheduled for August* **2** to arrange a revised schedule for repayment of (a debt)

rescind *vb* to annul or repeal ▶ HISTORY Latin *rescindere* to cut off

rescission *n* **1** the act of rescinding **2** *law* the right to have a contract set aside if it has been entered into mistakenly, as a result of misrepresentation, undue influence, etc.

rescue *vb* **-cuing, -cued 1** to bring (someone or something) out of danger or trouble ▷ *n* **2** the act or an instance of rescuing ▶ HISTORY Old French *rescourre* > **rescuer** *n*

research *n* **1** systematic investigation to establish facts or collect information on a subject ▷ *vb* **2** to carry out investigations into (a subject) ▶ HISTORY Old French *recercher* to search again > **researcher** *n*

resemble *vb* **-bling, -bled** to be or look like ▶ HISTORY Old French *resembler* > **resemblance** *n*

resent *vb* to feel bitter or indignant about ▶ HISTORY French *ressentir* > **resentful** *adj* > **resentment** *n*

reservation *n* **1** a doubt: *his only reservation was, did he have the stamina?* **2** an exception or limitation that prevents one's wholehearted acceptance: *work I admire without reservation* **3** a seat, room, etc. that has been reserved **4** (esp. in the US) an area of land set aside for American Indian peoples: *the Cherokee reservation* **5** *Brit* short for **central reservation**

reserve *vb* **-serving, -served 1** to keep back or set aside for future use **2** to obtain by arranging beforehand: *I phoned to reserve two tickets* **3** to keep for oneself: *the association reserves the right to charge a fee* **4** to delay announcing (a legal judgment) ▷ *n* **5** something kept back or set aside for future use **6** the state or condition of being reserved: *we're keeping these two in reserve* **7** *sport* a substitute **8** an area of publicly owned land used for sport, etc.: *a wildlife reserve* **9** the hiding of one's feelings and personality **10** the part of a nation's armed services not in active service **11 reserves** *finance* money or assets held by a bank or business to meet future expenses **12** *Canad* an Indian reservation ▶ HISTORY Latin *reservare* to keep

reserved *adj* **1** not showing one's feelings **2** set aside for use by a particular person

reserve price *n* the minimum price acceptable to the owner of property being auctioned or sold

reservist *n* a member of a nation's military reserve

reservoir *n* **1** a natural or artificial lake for storing water for community use **2** a large supply of something: *a vast reservoir of youthful enthusiasm* ▶ HISTORY French *réservoir*

reshuffle *n* **1** a reorganization of jobs in a government or company ▷ *vb* **-fling, -fled 2** to reorganize jobs or duties in a government or company

reside *vb* **-siding, -sided** *formal* **1** to live permanently (in a place): *my daughter resides in Europe* **2** to be present (in): *desire resides in the unconscious* ▶ HISTORY Latin *residere* to sit back

residence *n* **1** a person's home or house **2** a large imposing house **3** the fact of residing in a place **4** a period of residing in a place **5 in residence a** living in a particular place: *the Monarch was not in residence* **b** (of an artist) working for a set period at a college, gallery, etc.: *composer in residence*

residence order *n* *law* a court order specifying with which party a child shall live

resident *n* **1** a person who lives in a place **2** a bird or animal that does not migrate ▷ *adj* **3** living in a place **4** living at a place in order to carry out a job: *a resident custodian* **5** employed for one's specialized abilities: *the Museum's resident expert on 17th-century Dutch art* **6** (of birds and animals) not in the habit of migrating

residential *adj* **1** (of a part of a town) consisting mainly of houses **2** providing living accommodation: *residential clubs for homeless boys*

residential school *n* a government boarding school in N Canada for Indian and Inuit students

residual *adj* **1** of or being a remainder ▷ *n* **2** something left over as a residue

residue *n* **1** what is left over after something has been removed **2** *law* what is left of an estate after the discharge of debts and distribution of specific gifts ▶ HISTORY Latin *residuus* remaining over

residuum *n*, *pl* **-ua** same as **residue**

resign *vb* **1** to give up office or a job **2** to accept (an unpleasant fact): *he resigned himself to the inevitable* **3** to give up (a right or claim) ▶ HISTORY Latin *resignare* to unseal, destroy

resignation *n* **1** the act of resigning **2** a formal document stating one's intention to resign **3** passive endurance of difficulties: *full of quiet resignation*

resigned *adj* content to endure something unpleasant > **resignedly** *adv*

resilient *adj* **1** (of a person) recovering easily and quickly from misfortune or illness **2** (of an object) capable of regaining its original shape or position after bending or stretching ▶ HISTORY Latin *resilire* to jump back > **resilience** *n*

resin (rezz-in) *n* **1** a solid or semisolid substance obtained from certain plants: *cannabis resin* **2** a similar substance produced synthetically ▶ HISTORY Latin *resina* > **resinous** *adj*

resist *vb* **1** to stand firm against or oppose: *the party's old guard continue to resist economic reform* **2** to refrain from in spite of temptation: *I couldn't resist a huge portion of almond cake* **3** to refuse to comply with: *to resist arrest* **4** to be proof against: *airport design should be strengthened to help resist explosion* ▶ HISTORY Latin *resistere* > **resistible** *adj*

resistance *n* **1** the act of resisting **2** the capacity to withstand something, esp. the body's natural capacity to withstand disease **3** *electricity* the opposition to a flow of electric current through a circuit, component, or substance **4** any force that slows or hampers movement: *wind resistance* **5 line of least resistance** the easiest, but not necessarily the best, course of action > **resistant** *adj, n*

Resistance *n* **the Resistance** an illegal organization fighting for national liberty in a country under enemy occupation

resistor *n* an electrical component designed to introduce a known value of resistance into a circuit

resit *vb* **-sitting, -sat 1** to sit (an examination) again ▷ *n* **2** an examination which one must sit again

resolute *adj* firm in purpose or belief ▶ HISTORY Latin *resolutus* > **resolutely** *adv*

resolution *n* **1** firmness or determination **2** a decision to do something **3** a formal expression of opinion by a meeting **4** the act of resolving **5** *music* the process in harmony whereby a dissonant note or chord is followed by a consonant one **6** the ability of a television to reproduce fine detail **7** *physics* Also called: **resolving power** the ability of a telescope or microscope to produce separate images of closely placed objects

resolve *vb* **-solving, -solved 1** to decide or determine firmly **2** to express (an opinion) formally by a vote **3** to separate or cause to separate into constituent parts **4** to find the answer or solution to **5** to explain away or dispel: *to resolve the controversy* **6** *music* to follow (a dissonant note or chord) by one producing a consonance **7** *physics* to distinguish between (separate parts) of (an image) as in a microscope, telescope, or other optical instrument ▷ *n* **8** absolute determination: *he spoke of his resolve to deal with the problem of terrorism* ▶ HISTORY Latin *resolvere* to unfasten, reveal

resolved *adj* determined

resonance *n* **1** the condition or quality of being resonant **2** sound produced by a body vibrating in sympathy with a neighbouring source of sound ▶ HISTORY Latin *resonare* to resound

resonant *adj* **1** resounding or re-echoing **2** producing resonance: *the resonant cavities of the mouth* **3** full of resonance: *his voice is a resonant baritone*

resonate *vb* **-nating, -nated** to resound or cause to resound > **resonator** *n*

resort *vb* **1 resort to** to have recourse to for help, use, etc.: *some people have resorted to begging for food* **2** to go, esp. often or habitually: *to resort to the beach* ▷ *n* **3** a place to which many people go for holidays **4** the use of something as a means or aid **5 last resort** the last possible course of action open to a person ▶ HISTORY Old French *resortir* to come out again

resound (riz-**zownd**) *vb* **1** to ring or echo with sound **2** (of sounds) to echo or ring **3** to be widely known: *his fame resounded throughout India* ▶ HISTORY Latin *resonare* to sound again

resounding *adj* **1** echoing **2** clear and emphatic: *he won a resounding victory* > **resoundingly** *adv*

resource *n* **1 resources** sources of economic wealth, esp. of a country or business enterprise: *mineral resources* **2 resources** money available for use **3** something resorted to for aid or support: *he saw the university as a resource for the community* **4** the ability to deal with problems: *a man of resource* **5** a means of doing something: *resistance was their only resource* ▶ HISTORY Old French *resourdre* to spring up again

resourceful *adj* capable and full of initiative > **resourcefulness** *n*

respect *n* **1** consideration: *respect for my feelings* **2** an attitude of deference or esteem **3** the state of being honoured or esteemed **4** a detail or characteristic: *in virtually all respects boys develop more slowly than girls* **5 in respect of** or **with respect to** in reference or relation to **6 respects** polite greetings: *he paid his respects to her and left* ▷ *vb* **7** to have an attitude of esteem towards: *she is the person I most respect and wish to emulate* **8** to pay proper attention or consideration to: *he called on rebel groups to respect a ceasefire* ▶ HISTORY Latin *respicere* to pay attention to > **respecter** *n*

respectable *adj* **1** worthy of respect **2** having good social standing or reputation **3** relatively or fairly good: *they obtained respectable results* **4** fit to be seen by other people > **respectability** *n* > **respectably** *adv*

respectful *adj* full of or showing respect > **respectfully** *adv*

respecting *prep* on the subject of

respective *adj* relating separately to each of several people or things: *the culprits will be repatriated to their respective countries*

respectively *adv* (in listing things that refer to another list) separately in the order given: *Diotema and Mantinea were tutors to Pythagoras and Socrates respectively*

respiration (ress-per-**ray**-shun) *n* **1** breathing **2** the process in living organisms of taking in oxygen and giving out carbon dioxide **3** the breakdown of complex organic substances that takes place in the cells of animals and plants, producing energy and carbon dioxide > **respiratory** *adj*

respirator *n* **1** a device worn over the mouth and nose to prevent the breathing in of poisonous fumes **2** an apparatus for providing artificial respiration

respire *vb* **-spiring, -spired 1** to breathe **2** to undergo respiration ▶ HISTORY Latin *respirare* to exhale

r

respite n **1** an interval of rest: *I allowed myself a six-month respite to enjoy my family* **2** a temporary delay ▸ HISTORY Old French *respit*

resplendent adj **1** brilliant or splendid in appearance **2** shining ▸ HISTORY Latin *re-* again + *splendere* to shine > **resplendence** n

respond vb **1** to state or utter (something) in reply **2** to act in reply: *the government must respond accordingly to our recommendations* **3** to react favourably: *most headaches will respond to the use of relaxants* ▸ HISTORY Old French *respondre*

respondent n *law* a person against whom a petition is brought

response n **1** the act of responding **2** a reply or reaction **3** a reaction to stimulation of the nervous system **4 responses** *Christianity* the words recited or sung in reply to the priest at a church service

responsibility n, pl **-ties 1** the state of being responsible **2** a person or thing for which one is responsible

responsible adj **1 a responsible for** having control or authority over **b** being the agent or cause (of some action): *only a small number of students were responsible for the disturbances* **2 responsible to** being accountable for one's actions and decisions to: *management should be made more responsible to shareholders* **3** rational and accountable for one's own actions **4** (of a position or duty) involving decision and accountability ▸ HISTORY Latin *respondere* to respond > **responsibly** adv

responsive adj reacting quickly or favourably to something > **responsiveness** n

respray n a new coat of paint applied to a vehicle

rest¹ n **1** relaxation from exertion or labour **2** a period of inactivity **3** relief or refreshment **4** calm **5** death regarded as repose: *now he has gone to his eternal rest* **6 at rest a** not moving **b** calm **c** dead **d** asleep **7** a pause or interval **8** a mark in a musical score indicating a pause lasting a specific time **9** a thing or place on which to put something for support or to steady it **10 lay to rest** to bury (a dead person) ▷ vb **11** to become or make refreshed **12** to position (oneself, etc.) for rest or relaxation **13** to place for support or steadying: *he slumped forward to rest his head on his forearms* **14** to depend or rely: *his presidency rested on the outcome of the crisis* **15** written to direct (one's eyes) or (of one's eyes) to be directed: *she rested her gaze on the face of the statue* **16** to be at ease **17** to cease or cause to cease from motion or exertion **18** to remain without further attention or action: *she refused to let the matter rest* **19** law to finish the introduction of evidence in (a case) **20** to put (pastry) in a cool place to allow the gluten to contract ▸ HISTORY Old English *ræst, reste*

rest² n **1 the rest a** something left; remainder **b** the others: *the rest of the world* ▷ vb **2** to continue to be (as specified): *your conscience can rest easy* ▸ HISTORY Old French *rester* to remain

rest area n *Austral & NZ* a motorist's stopping place off a highway, equipped with tables and seats

restaurant n a place where meals are prepared and served to customers ▸ HISTORY French

restaurant car n *Brit & Austral* a railway coach in which meals are served

restaurateur (rest-er-a-**tur**) n a person who owns or runs a restaurant

rest-cure n a rest taken as part of a course of medical treatment

restful adj relaxing or soothing

restitution n **1** the act of giving back something that has been lost or stolen **2** law compensation for loss or injury ▸ HISTORY Latin *restituere* to rebuild

restive adj **1** restless or uneasy **2** impatient of control or authority ▸ HISTORY Old French *restif* balky

restless adj **1** bored or dissatisfied **2** unable to stay still or quiet **3** not restful: *a restless sleep* > **restlessly** adv > **restlessness** n

restoration n **1** the act of restoring to a former or original condition, place, etc. **2** the giving back of something lost or stolen **3** something restored, replaced, or reconstructed **4** a model or representation of a ruin or extinct animal **5 the Restoration** *Brit* the re-establishment of the monarchy in 1660 or the reign of Charles II (1660–85)

restorative (rist-**or**-a-tiv) adj **1** giving back health or good spirits ▷ n **2** a food or medicine that gives back health or good spirits

restore vb **-storing, -stored 1** to return (something) to its original or former condition **2** to bring back to health or good spirits **3** to return (something lost or stolen) to its owner **4** to re-enforce or re-establish: *he must restore confidence in himself and his government; they worked to restore the monarchy* **5** to reconstruct (a ruin, extinct animal, etc.) ▸ HISTORY Latin *restaurare* to rebuild > **restorer** n

restrain vb **1** to hold (someone) back from some action **2** to limit or restrict: *restrain any tendency to impulse-buy* **3** to deprive (someone) of liberty ▸ HISTORY Latin *re-* back + *stringere* to draw

restrained adj not displaying emotion

restraining order n *law* a court order prohibiting a person from doing something such as making contact with a specified individual or going to a particular place

restraint n **1** something that restrains **2** the ability to control one's impulses or passions **3** a restraining or being restrained

restrict vb to confine or keep within certain limits ▸ HISTORY Latin *restrictus* bound up > **restrictive** adj

restriction n a rule or situation that limits or controls something or someone: *operating under severe financial restrictions*

restrictive practice n *Brit & Austral* **1** a trading agreement against the public interest **2** a practice of a union or other group tending to limit the freedom of other workers or employers

rest room n *US, Canad & Austral* a toilet in a public building

restructure *vb* **-turing, -tured** to organize in a different way: *to restructure the world economy*

result *n* **1** the outcome or consequence of an action, policy, etc. **2** the final score of a sporting contest **3** a number or value obtained by solving a mathematical problem **4** a favourable result, esp. a victory or success: *the best chance of a result is at Cheltenham* **5 results** the marks or grades obtained in an examination ▷ *vb* **6 result from** to be the outcome or consequence of: *poverty resulting from high unemployment* **7 result in** to end in (a specified way): *negotiations which resulted in the Treaty of Paris* ▶ **HISTORY** Latin *resultare* to spring from

resultant *adj* **1** arising as a result: *the resultant publicity* ▷ *n* **2** maths, physics a single vector that is the vector sum of two or more other vectors, such as a force which results from two other forces acting on a single point

resume *vb* **-suming, -sumed** *written* **1** to begin again or go on with (something interrupted) **2** to occupy again or recover: *he will resume his party posts today* ▶ **HISTORY** Latin *resumere*

résumé (**rezz**-yew-may) *n* **1** a short descriptive summary **2** *US, Canad & Austral* a curriculum vitae ▶ **HISTORY** French

resumption *n* the act of resuming or beginning again

resurgence *n* a rising again to vigour: *worldwide religious resurgence* ▶ **HISTORY** Latin *resurgere* to rise again > **resurgent** *adj*

resurrect *vb* **1** to bring or be brought back to life from death **2** to bring back into use or activity

resurrection *n* **1** a return to life by a dead person **2** revival or renewal **3 the Resurrection a** *Christian theol* the rising again of Christ from the tomb three days after his death **b** the rising again from the dead of all people at the Last Judgment ▶ **HISTORY** Latin *resurgere* to rise again

resuscitate (ris-**suss**-it-tate) *vb* **-tating, -tated** to restore to consciousness ▶ **HISTORY** Latin *re-* again + *suscitare* to raise > **resuscitation** *n*

retail *n* **1** the sale of goods individually or in small quantities to the public ▷ *adj* **2** of or engaged in such selling: *auctioneers have been successful in cornering the retail market* **3** in small amounts or at a retail price ▷ *vb* **4** to sell or be sold in small quantities to the public **5** to relate (gossip or scandal) in detail: *he gleefully retailed the story* ▶ **HISTORY** Old French *re-* again + *taillier* to cut > **retailer** *n*

retain *vb* **1** to keep in one's possession **2** to be able to hold or contain: *with this method the salmon retains its flavour and texture* **3** *law* to engage the services of (a barrister) by payment of a preliminary fee **4** (of a person) to be able to remember (something) without difficulty **5** to hold in position ▶ **HISTORY** Latin *retinere* to hold back

retainer *n* **1** a fee paid in advance to engage someone's services **2** *Brit, Austral & NZ* a reduced rent paid for a room or flat to reserve it for future use **3** a servant who has been with a family for a long time

retake *vb* **-taking, -took, -taken** **1** to recapture: *to retake Jerusalem* **2** to take something, such as an examination or vote, again ▷ *n* **3** *films* a rephotographed scene

retaliate *vb* **-ating, -ated** **1** to repay some injury or wrong in kind **2** to cast (accusations) back upon a person ▶ **HISTORY** Latin *re-* back + *talis* of such kind > **retaliation** *n* > **retaliatory** *adj*

retard *vb* to delay or slow down (the progress or development of something) ▶ **HISTORY** Latin *retardare* > **retardant** *n, adj* > **retardation** *n*

retarded *adj* old-fashioned, offensive underdeveloped mentally

retch *vb* **1** to undergo spasms of the stomach as if one is vomiting ▷ *n* **2** an involuntary spasm of the stomach ▶ **HISTORY** Old English *hræcan*

retention *n* **1** the act of retaining or state of being retained **2** the capacity to remember **3** *pathol* the abnormal holding of something within the body, esp. fluid > **retentive** *adj*

rethink *vb* **-thinking, -thought** **1** to think about (something) again with a view to changing one's tactics ▷ *n* **2** the act or an instance of thinking again

reticent *adj* not willing to say or tell much ▶ **HISTORY** Latin *reticere* to keep silent > **reticence** *n*

reticulate *adj* in the form of a network or having a network of parts: *a reticulate leaf* ▶ **HISTORY** Late Latin *reticulatus* like a net > **reticulation** *n*

retina *n, pl* **-nas** *or* **-nae** the light-sensitive inner lining of the back of the eyeball ▶ **HISTORY** Medieval Latin > **retinal** *adj*

retinue *n* a band of attendants accompanying an important person ▶ **HISTORY** Old French *retenue*

retire *vb* **-tiring, -tired** **1** to give up or to cause (a person) to give up work, esp. on reaching pensionable age **2** to go away into seclusion **3** to go to bed **4** to withdraw from a sporting contest, esp. because of injury **5** to pull back (troops) from battle or (of troops) to fall back ▶ **HISTORY** French *retirer* > **retired** *adj* > **retirement** *n*

retirement pension *n* *Brit* a regular payment made by the state or a former employer to a retired person over a specified age

retiring *adj* very shy

retort[1] *vb* **1** *written* to reply quickly, wittily, or angrily **2** *written* to use (an argument) against its originator ▷ *n* **3** a sharp, angry, or witty reply **4** an argument used against its originator ▶ **HISTORY** Latin *re-* back + *torquere* to twist, wrench

retort[2] *n* **1** a glass vessel with a long tapering neck that is bent down, used for distillation **2** a vessel used for heating ores in the production of metals or heating coal to produce gas ▶ **HISTORY** see RETORT[1]

retouch *vb* to restore or improve (a painting or photograph) with new touches

retrace *vb* **-tracing, -traced** **1** to go back over (one's steps or a route) **2** to go over (a story) from the beginning

r

723

retract *vb* **1** to withdraw (a statement, charge, etc.) as invalid or unjustified **2** to go back on (a promise or agreement) **3** to draw in (a part or appendage): *the rear wheels are retracted for tight spaces* ▶ HISTORY Latin *retractare* to withdraw > **retraction** *n*

retractile *adj* capable of being drawn in: *the retractile claws of a cat*

retread *vb* **-treading, -treaded** **1** to bond a new tread onto (a worn tyre) ▷ *n* **2** a remoulded tyre

retreat *vb* **1** *mil* to withdraw or retire in the face of or from action with an enemy **2** to retire or withdraw to seclusion or shelter **3** to alter one's opinion about something ▷ *n* **4** the act of retreating or withdrawing **5** *mil* **a** a withdrawal or retirement in the face of the enemy **b** a bugle call signifying withdrawal or retirement **6** a place to which one may retire, esp. for religious contemplation **7** a period of seclusion, esp. for religious contemplation **8** the act of altering one's opinion about something ▶ HISTORY Old French *retret*

retrench *vb* to reduce expenditure ▶ HISTORY Old French *re-* off + *trenchier* to cut > **retrenchment** *n*

retrial *n* a second trial of a defendant in a court of law

retribution *n* punishment or vengeance for evil deeds ▶ HISTORY Latin *re-* back + *tribuere* to pay > **retributive** *adj*

retrieve *vb* **-trieving, -trieved** **1** to get or fetch back again **2** to bring back to a more satisfactory state: *his attempt to retrieve the situation* **3** to rescue or save **4** to recover (stored information) from a computer system **5** (of dogs) to find and fetch (shot birds and animals) **6** to remember ▷ *n* **7** the chance of being retrieved: *beyond retrieve* ▶ HISTORY Old French *retrover* > **retrievable** *adj* > **retrieval** *n*

retriever *n* a dog trained to retrieve shot birds and animals

retro *adj* associated with or revived from the past: *swap sandals for heeled mules to complete the retro look*

retro- *prefix* **1** back or backwards: *retroactive* **2** located behind: *retrochoir* ▶ HISTORY Latin

retroactive *adj* effective from a date in the past: *justice through retroactive legislation is never justice*

retrograde *adj* **1** tending towards an earlier worse condition **2** moving or bending backwards **3** (esp. of order) reverse or inverse ▷ *vb* **-grading, -graded** **4** to go backwards or deteriorate ▶ HISTORY Latin *retro-* backwards + *gradi* to walk

retrogress *vb* to go back to an earlier worse condition ▶ HISTORY Latin *retrogressus* having moved backwards > **retrogression** *n* > **retrogressive** *adj*

retrorocket *n* a small rocket on a larger rocket or a spacecraft, that produces thrust in the opposite direction to the direction of flight in order to slow down

retrospect *n* **in retrospect** when looking back on the past ▶ HISTORY Latin *retrospicere* to look back

retrospective *adj* **1** looking back in time **2** applying from a date in the past: *retrospective*

legislation ▷ *n* **3** an exhibition of an artist's life's work

retroussé (rit-**troo**-say) *adj* (of a nose) turned upwards ▶ HISTORY French

retsina *n* a Greek wine flavoured with resin ▶ HISTORY Modern Greek

return *vb* **1** to come back to a former place or state **2** to give, put, or send back **3** to repay with something of equivalent value: *she returned the compliment* **4** *sport* to hit, throw, or play (a ball) back **5** to recur or reappear: *as he relaxed his appetite returned* **6** to come back or revert in thought or speech: *let's return to what he said* **7** to earn or yield (profit or interest) **8** to answer or reply **9** to vote into office **10** *law* (of a jury) to deliver (a verdict) ▷ *n* **11** the act or an instance of coming back **12** the act of being returned **13** replacement or restoration: *the return of law and order* **14** something that is given or sent back **15** *sport* the act of playing or throwing a ball back **16** a recurrence or reappearance: *the return of tuberculosis* **17** the yield or profit from an investment or venture **18** a statement of one's taxable income (a **tax return**) **19** an answer or reply **20** *Brit, Austral & NZ* short for **return ticket** **21 in return** in exchange **22 returns** statement of the votes counted at an election **23 by return (of post)** *Brit* by the next post back to the sender **24 many happy returns (of the day)** a conventional birthday greeting ▷ *adj* **25** of or being a return: *the team is keen on a return match* ▶ HISTORY Old French *retorner* > **returnable** *adj*

returning officer *n* an official in charge of conducting an election in a constituency

return ticket *n* *Brit, Austral & NZ* a ticket allowing a passenger to travel to a place and back

reunify *vb* **-fies, -fying, -fied** to bring together again something previously divided > **reunification** *n*

reunion *n* **1** a gathering of people who have been apart **2** the act of coming together again

reunite *vb* **-niting, -nited** to bring or come together again after a separation

reuse *n* **1** the act of using something again ▷ *vb* **-using, -used** **2** to use again > **reusable** *adj*

rev *informal* *n* **1** revolution per minute (of an engine) ▷ *vb* **revving, revved** **2** to increase the speed of revolution of (an engine)

Rev. Reverend

revalue *vb* **-valuing, -valued** to adjust the exchange value of (a currency) upwards > **revaluation** *n*

revamp *vb* to patch up or renovate

Revd. Reverend

reveal *vb* **1** to disclose or divulge (a secret) **2** to expose to view or show (something concealed) **3** (of God) to disclose (divine truths) ▶ HISTORY Latin *revelare* to unveil

revealing *adj* **1** disclosing information that one did not know: *she made several revealing remarks during the interview* **2** (of clothes) showing more of the body than is usual

reveille (riv-**val**-ee) *n* a signal given by a bugle or drum to awaken soldiers or sailors in the morning ▶ HISTORY French *réveillez!* awake!

revel *vb* **-elling, -elled** *or US* **-eling, -eled 1 revel in** to take pleasure or wallow in: *he would revel in his victory* **2** to take part in noisy festivities ▷ *n* **3 revels** noisy merrymaking ▶ HISTORY Old French *reveler* > **reveller** *n*

revelation *n* **1** the act of making known a truth that was previously secret **2** a fact newly made known **3** a person or experience that proves to be different from expectations: *New York State could prove a revelation to first-time visitors* **4** Christianity God's disclosure of his own nature and his purpose for mankind

Revelation *or* **Revelations** *n informal* the last book of the New Testament, containing visionary descriptions of heaven, and of the end of the world

revelry *n, pl* **-ries** noisy or unrestrained merrymaking

revenge *n* **1** vengeance for wrongs or injury received **2** something done as a means of vengeance ▷ *vb* **-venging, -venged 3** to inflict equivalent injury or damage for (injury received) **4** to take vengeance for (oneself or another) ▶ HISTORY Old French *revenger* > **revengeful** *adj*

revenue *n* **1** income, esp. that obtained by a government from taxation **2** a government department responsible for collecting taxes ▶ HISTORY Old French *revenir* to return

reverberate *vb* **-ating, -ated 1** to resound or re-echo **2** to reflect or be reflected many times ▶ HISTORY Latin *re-* again + *verberare* to beat > **reverberation** *n*

revere *vb* **-vering, -vered** to be in awe of and respect deeply ▶ HISTORY Latin *revereri*

reverence *n* profound respect > **reverential** *adj*

Reverence *n* **Your** *or* **His Reverence** a title sometimes used for a Roman Catholic priest

reverend *adj* **1** worthy of reverence **2** relating to or designating a member of the clergy ▷ *n* **3** *informal* a member of the clergy

Reverend *adj* a title of respect for a member of the clergy

reverent *adj* feeling or expressing reverence

reverie *n* absent-minded daydream ▶ HISTORY Old French *resverie* wildness

revers (riv-**veer**) *n, pl* **-vers** the turned-back lining of part of a garment, such as the lapel or cuff ▶ HISTORY French

reverse *vb* **-versing, -versed 1** to turn or set in an opposite direction, order, or position **2** to change into something different or contrary: *the Cabinet intends to reverse the trend of recent polls* **3** to move backwards or in an opposite direction: *as he started to reverse the car, the bomb exploded* **4** to run (machinery) in the opposite direction to normal **5** to turn inside out **6** *law* to revoke or set aside (a judgment or decree) **7 reverse the charges** to make a telephone call at the recipient's expense ▷ *n* **8** the opposite or contrary of something **9** the back or rear side of something **10** a change to an

opposite position, state, or direction **11** a change for the worse **12** the gear by which a motor vehicle can be made to go backwards **13** the side of a coin bearing a secondary design **14 in reverse** in an opposite or backward direction **15 the reverse of** not at all: *the result was the reverse of his expectations* ▷ *adj* **16** opposite or contrary in direction, position, etc. **17** denoting the gear by which a motor vehicle can be made to go backwards ▶ HISTORY Latin *reversus* turned back > **reversal** *n*

reverse fault *n geol* a fault in which rock on one side of the fault is pushed up higher than the other. Compare **normal fault**

reversible *adj* **1** capable of being reversed: *the effect of the operation may not be reversible* **2** (of a garment) made so that either side may be used as the outer side

reversible reaction *n chem, physics* a reaction that is capable of producing either of two possible states and changing from one to the other

reversing lights *pl n* a pair of lights on the rear of a motor vehicle that go on when the vehicle is moving backwards

reversion *n* **1** a return to an earlier condition, practice, or belief **2** *biol* the return of individuals or organs to a more primitive condition or type **3** the rightful passing of property to the owner or designated heir

revert *vb* **1** to go back to a former state **2** *biol* (of individuals or organs) to return to a more primitive, earlier, or simpler condition or type **3** *written* to come back to a subject **4** *property law* (of an estate) to return to its former owner ▶ HISTORY Latin *revertere*

review *n* **1** a critical assessment of a book, film, etc. **2** a publication containing such articles **3** a general survey or report: *the new curriculum is to be set up a year after the conclusions of the review are due* **4** a formal or official inspection **5** the act or an instance of reviewing **6** a second consideration; re-examination **7** a retrospective survey **8** *law* a re-examination of a case ▷ *vb* **9** to hold or write a review of **10** to examine again: *the committee will review the ban in the summer* **11** to look back upon (a period of time or sequence of events): *he reviewed his achievements with pride* **12** to inspect formally or officially: *when he reviewed the troops they cheered him* **13** *law* to re-examine (a decision) judicially ▶ HISTORY Latin *re-* again + *videre* to see

reviewer *n* a person who writes reviews of books, films, etc.

revile *vb* **-viling, -viled** to be abusively scornful of: *his works were reviled and admired in equal measure* ▶ HISTORY Old French *reviler*

revise *vb* **-vising, -vised 1** to change or alter: *he grudgingly revised his opinion* **2** to prepare a new edition of (a previously printed work) **3** to read (something) several times in order to learn it in preparation for an examination ▶ HISTORY Latin *re-* again + *visere* to inspect

Revised Version *n* a revision of the Authorized Version of the Bible published between 1881 and 1885

r

725

revision *n* **1** the act or process of revising **2** a corrected or new version of a book, article, etc.

revisionism *n* **1** (in Marxist ideology) any dangerous departure from the true interpretation of Marx's teachings **2** the advocacy of revision of some political theory > **revisionist** *n, adj*

revival *n* **1** a reviving or being revived **2** a reawakening of religious faith **3** a new production of a play that has not been recently performed **4** a renewed use or interest in: *there has been an Art Deco revival*

revivalism *n* a movement that seeks to revive religious faith > **revivalist** *n, adj*

revive *vb* **-viving, -vived** **1** to make or become lively or active again **2** to bring or be brought back to life, consciousness, or strength: *revived by a drop of whisky* **3** *theatre* to put on a new production of (an old play) ▶ **HISTORY** Latin *re-* again + *vivere* to live

revoke *vb* **-voking, -voked** **1** to take back or cancel (an agreement, will, etc.) **2** *cards* to break a rule by failing to follow suit when able to do so ▷ *n* **3** *cards* the act of revoking ▶ **HISTORY** Latin *revocare* to call back > **revocation** *n*

revolt *n* **1** a rebellion or uprising against authority **2 in revolt** in the state of rebelling ▷ *vb* **3** to rise up in rebellion against authority **4** to cause to feel disgust ▶ **HISTORY** French *révolter*

revolting *adj* horrible and disgusting

revolution *n* **1** the overthrow of a regime or political system by the governed **2** (in Marxist theory) the transition from one system of production in a society to the next **3** a far-reaching and drastic change **4 a** movement in or as if in a circle **b** one complete turn in a circle: *33 revolutions per minute* ▶ **HISTORY** Latin *revolvere* to revolve

revolutionary *adj* **1** of or like a revolution **2** advocating or engaged in revolution **3** radically new or different: *they have designed revolutionary new materials to build power stations* ▷ *n, pl* **-aries** **4** a person who advocates or engages in revolution

revolutionize *or* **-ise** *vb* **-izing, -ized** *or* **-ising, -ised** to bring about a radical change in

revolve *vb* **-volving, -volved** **1** to move or cause to move around a centre **2 revolve around** to be centred or focused upon: *the campaign revolves around one man* **3** to occur periodically or in cycles **4** to consider or be considered ▶ **HISTORY** Latin *revolvere* > **revolvable** *adj*

revolver *n* a pistol with a revolving cylinder that allows several shots to be fired without reloading

revolving door *n* a door with four leaves at right angles to each other, revolving about a vertical axis

revue *n* a theatrical entertainment with topical sketches and songs ▶ **HISTORY** French

revulsion *n* a violent feeling of disgust ▶ **HISTORY** Latin *revulsio* a pulling away

reward *n* **1** something given in return for a service **2** a sum of money offered for finding a criminal or missing property **3** something received in return for good or evil: *sacrifice provided its own reward* ▷ *vb* **4** to give something to (someone) for a service rendered ▶ **HISTORY** Old French *rewarder* to regard

rewarding *adj* giving personal satisfaction: *my most professionally rewarding experience*

rewarewa (ray-wa-**ray**-wa) *n* a tall New Zealand tree with reddish wood ▶ **HISTORY** Māori

rewind *vb* **-winding, -wound** to run (a tape or film) back to an earlier point in order to replay

rewire *vb* **-wiring, -wired** to provide (a house, engine, etc.) with new wiring

rewrite *vb* **-writing, -wrote, -written** **1** to write again in a different way ▷ *n* **2** something rewritten

Rex *n* king: now used chiefly in documents and inscriptions ▶ **HISTORY** Latin

Rf *chem* rutherfordium

RFC Rugby Football Club

RGN (in Britain) Registered General Nurse

Rh **1** *chem* rhodium **2** See **Rh factor**

rhapsodize *or* **-dise** *vb* **-dizing, -dized** *or* **-dising, -dised** to speak or write with extravagant enthusiasm

rhapsody *n, pl* **-dies** **1** *music* a freely structured and emotional piece of music **2** an expression of ecstatic enthusiasm ▶ **HISTORY** Greek *rhaptein* to sew together + *ōidē* song > **rhapsodic** *adj*

rhea (**ree**-a) *n* a large fast-running flightless bird of South America, similar to the ostrich ▶ **HISTORY** after *Rhea*, mother of Zeus

rheme *n linguistics* everything in a sentence that is not the theme; the part of the sentence that adds most new information. Compare **theme** (sense 5) ▶ **HISTORY** Greek *rhēma* that which is said

rhenium *n chem* a silvery-white metallic element with a high melting point. Symbol: Re ▶ **HISTORY** Latin *Rhenus* the Rhine

rheostat *n* a variable resistor in an electrical circuit, such as one used to dim lights ▶ **HISTORY** Greek *rheos* flow + *-statēs* stationary > **rheostatic** *adj*

rhesus factor (**ree**-suss) *n* See **Rh factor**

rhesus monkey *n* a small long-tailed monkey of S Asia ▶ **HISTORY** Greek *Rhesos*, mythical Thracian king

rhetoric (**ret**-a-rik) *n* **1** the art of using speech or writing to persuade or influence **2** artificial or exaggerated language: *there's been no shortage of soaring rhetoric at this summit* ▶ **HISTORY** Greek *rhētorikē* (*tekhnē*) (art) of rhetoric

rhetorical (rit-**tor**-ik-kl) *adj* **1** concerned with effect or style rather than content or meaning; bombastic **2** of or relating to rhetoric or oratory > **rhetorically** *adv*

rhetorical device *n* any device used by speakers or writers to give more impact to their speech or writing, for example the use of repetition or direct address

rhetorical question *n* a question to which no answer is required, used for dramatic effect, for example *who knows?*

rheum (**room**) *n* a watery discharge from the eyes or nose ▶ **HISTORY** Greek *rheuma* a flow > **rheumy** *adj*

rheumatic *adj* **1** caused by or affected by rheumatism ▷ *n* **2** a person suffering from rheumatism > **rheumatically** *adv*

r

rheumatic fever *n* a disease with inflammation and pain in the joints

rheumatics *n informal* rheumatism

rheumatism *n* any painful disorder of joints, muscles, or connective tissue ▶ HISTORY Greek *rheuma* a flow

rheumatoid *adj* (of symptoms) resembling rheumatism

rheumatoid arthritis *n* a chronic disease causing painful swelling of the joints

Rh factor *n* an antigen commonly found in human blood: the terms **Rh positive** and **Rh negative** are used to indicate its presence or absence ▶ HISTORY after the rhesus monkey, in which it was first discovered

rhinestone *n* an imitation diamond made of glass ▶ HISTORY originally made at Strasbourg, on the Rhine

rhino *n*, *pl* **-nos** *or* **-no** a rhinoceros

rhinoceros *n*, *pl* **-oses** *or* **-os** a large plant-eating mammal of SE Asia and Africa with one or two horns on the nose and a very thick skin

- ■ **WORD HISTORY**
- ■ 'Rhinoceros' came into English via Latin from
- ■ Greek *rhinokerōs*, from *rhino-*, meaning 'of the
- ■ nose', and *keras*, meaning 'horn'.

rhizome *n* a thick horizontal underground stem whose buds develop into new plants ▶ HISTORY Greek *rhiza* a root

rhodium *n chem* a hard silvery-white metallic element, used to harden platinum and palladium. Symbol: Rh ▶ HISTORY Greek *rhodon* rose, from the pink colour of its compounds

rhododendron *n* an evergreen shrub with clusters of showy flowers ▶ HISTORY Greek *rhodon* rose + *dendron* tree

rhodopsin *n physiol* a red pigment in the rods of the retina of the eye

rhombohedron (rom-boh-**heed**-ron) *n*, *pl* **-drons** *or* **-dra** (-dra) a six-sided prism whose sides are parallelograms ▶ HISTORY RHOMBUS + Greek *-edron* -sided

rhomboid *n* **1** a parallelogram with adjacent sides of unequal length. It resembles a rectangle but does not have 90° angles ▷ *adj also* **rhomboidal** **2** having such a shape ▶ HISTORY Greek *rhomboeidēs* shaped like a rhombus

rhombus (rom-buss) *n*, *pl* **-buses** *or* **-bi** (-bye) a parallelogram with sides of equal length but no right angles ▶ HISTORY Greek *rhombos* something that spins > **rhombic** *adj*

rhubarb *n* **1** a large-leaved plant with long green and red stalks which can be cooked and eaten **2** a related plant of central Asia, whose root can be dried and used as a laxative or astringent ▷ *interj*, *n* **3** the noise made by actors to simulate conversation, esp. by repeating the word *rhubarb* ▶ HISTORY Old French *reubarbe*

rhyme *n* **1** sameness of the final sounds in lines of verse or in words **2** a word that is identical to another in its final sound: '*while*' is a rhyme for '*mile*' **3** a piece of poetry with corresponding sounds at the ends of the lines **4 rhyme or reason** sense or meaning ▷ *vb* **rhyming, rhymed 5** (of a word) to form a rhyme with another word **6** to compose (verse) in a metrical structure ▶ HISTORY Old French *rime*; spelling influenced by *rhythm*

rhyme scheme *or* **pattern** *n poetry* the system of rhymes used by a poet in a particular work

rhymester *n* a mediocre poet

rhyming couplet *n poetry* two lines of verse which rhyme and usually have the same metre

rhyming slang *n* slang in which a word is replaced by another word or phrase that rhymes with it, e.g. *apples and pears* meaning *stairs*

rhythm *n* **1** any regular movement or beat: *the side-effects can cause changes in the rhythm of the heart beat* **2** any regular pattern that occurs over a period of time: *the seasonal rhythm of the agricultural year* **3 a** the arrangement of the durations of and stress on the notes of a piece of music, usually laid out in regular groups (**bars**) of beats **b** any specific arrangement of such groupings: *waltz rhythm* **4** (in poetry) the arrangement of words to form a regular pattern of stresses ▶ HISTORY Greek *rhuthmos* > **rhythmic** *or* **rhythmical** *adj* > **rhythmically** *adv*

rhythm and blues *n* a kind of popular music of Black American origin, derived from and influenced by the blues

rhythm method *n* a method of contraception in which intercourse is avoided at times when conception is most likely

RI Rhode Island

ria *n* a long narrow inlet of the sea coast, being a former valley that was submerged by the sea ▶ HISTORY Spanish *ría* estuary

rialto *n*, *pl* **-tos** a market or exchange ▶ HISTORY after the *Rialto*, the business centre of medieval Venice

rib¹ *n* **1** one of the curved bones forming the framework of the upper part of the body and attached to the spinal column **2** a cut of meat including one or more ribs **3** a curved supporting part, such as in the hull of a boat **4** one of a series of raised rows in knitted fabric ▷ *vb* **ribbing, ribbed 5** to provide or support with ribs **6** to knit to form a rib pattern ▶ HISTORY Old English *ribb* > **ribbed** *adj*

rib² *vb* **ribbing, ribbed** *informal* to tease or ridicule ▶ HISTORY short for *rib-tickle* > **ribbing** *n*

ribald *adj* coarse or obscene in a humorous or mocking way ▶ HISTORY Old French *ribauld* > **ribaldry** *n*

ribbing *n* **1** a pattern of ribs in knitted material **2** a framework or structure of ribs

ribbon *n* **1** a narrow strip of fine material used for trimming, tying, etc. **2** a long narrow strip of inked cloth or plastic used to produce print in a typewriter **3** a small strip of coloured cloth worn as a badge or as a symbol of an award **4** a long thin strip: *a ribbon of white water* **5 ribbons** ragged strips or shreds: *his clothes were torn to ribbons; his credibility was shot to ribbons* ▶ HISTORY Old French *riban*

r

727

ribbon development *n Brit & Austral* the building of houses along a main road

ribbonwood *n* a small evergreen tree of New Zealand

ribcage *n* the bony structure formed by the ribs that encloses the lungs

riboflavin (rye-boe-**flay**-vin) *n* a vitamin of the B complex that occurs in green vegetables, milk, fish, eggs, liver, and kidney: used as a yellow or orange food colouring (**E101**). Also called: **vitamin B2** ▶ HISTORY *ribose*, a sugar + Latin *flavus* yellow

ribonucleic acid *n* the full name of **RNA**

ribosome *n biol* a minute particle in the cytoplasm of cells that contains RNA and protein and is the site of protein synthesis > **ribosomal** *adj*

rice *n* **1** the edible grain of an erect grass that grows on wet ground in warm climates ▷ *vb* **ricing, riced 2** *US & Canad* to sieve (potatoes or other vegetables) to a coarse mashed consistency ▶ HISTORY Greek *orūza*

rice paper *n* **1** a thin edible paper made from rice straw **2** a thin Chinese paper made from the rice-paper plant, the pith of which is flattened into sheets

rich *adj* **1** owning a lot of money or property **2** well supplied (with a desirable substance or quality): *a country rich with cultural interest* **3** having an abundance of natural resources, minerals, etc.: *a land rich in unexploited minerals* **4** producing abundantly: *the island is a blend of hilly moorland and rich farmland* **5** luxuriant or prolific: *the meadows rich with corn* **6** (of food) containing much fat or sugar **7** having a full-bodied flavour: *a gloriously rich Cabernet-dominated wine* **8** (of colour) intense or vivid: *her hair had a rich auburn tint* **9** (of sound or a voice) full or resonant **10** very amusing or ridiculous: *a rich joke* **11** (of a fuel-air mixture) containing a relatively high proportion of fuel ▶ HISTORY Old English *rīce* (originally of people, with sense: great, mighty) > **richness** *n*

riches *pl n* valuable possessions or desirable substances: *the unexpected riches of Georgian culture*

richly *adv* **1** in a rich or elaborate manner: *the rooms are richly decorated with a variety of classical motifs* **2** fully and appropriately: *he left the field to a richly deserved standing ovation*

Richter scale *n geol* a scale for expressing the magnitude of an earthquake, ranging from 0 to over 8. Compare **Mercalli scale** ▶ HISTORY after Charles *Richter*, seismologist

rick¹ *n* a large stack of hay or straw ▶ HISTORY Old English *hrēac*

rick² *vb* **1** to wrench or sprain (a joint) ▷ *n* **2** a wrench or sprain of a joint ▶ HISTORY variant of *wrick*

rickets *n* a disease of children, caused by a deficiency of vitamin D and characterized by softening of developing bone, and hence bow legs ▶ HISTORY origin unknown

rickety *adj* **1** likely to collapse or break: *a rickety wooden table* **2** resembling or afflicted with rickets > **ricketiness** *n*

rickshaw *or* **ricksha** *n* **1** a small two-wheeled passenger vehicle pulled by one or two people, used in parts of Asia **2** a similar vehicle with three wheels, propelled by a person pedalling ▶ HISTORY Japanese *jinrikisha*

ricochet (**rik**-osh-ay) *vb* **-cheting, -cheted** *or* **-chetting, -chetted 1** (of a bullet) to rebound from a surface ▷ *n* **2** the motion or sound of a rebounding bullet ▶ HISTORY French

rid *vb* **ridding, rid** *or* **ridded 1 rid of** to relieve (oneself) or make a place free of (something undesirable) **2 get rid of** to relieve or free oneself of (something undesirable) ▶ HISTORY Old Norse *rythja*

ridden *vb* **1** the past participle of **ride** ▷ *adj* **2** afflicted or affected by the thing specified: *the police found three bullet-ridden bodies*

riddle¹ *n* **1** a question, puzzle, or verse phrased so that ingenuity is required to find the answer or meaning **2** a puzzling person or thing ▷ *vb* **-dling, -dled 3** to speak in riddles ▶ HISTORY Old English *rǣdels(e)*

riddle² *vb* **-dling, -dled 1** to pierce with many holes **2** to put through a sieve ▷ *n* **3** a coarse sieve ▶ HISTORY Old English *hriddel* a sieve

ride *vb* **riding, rode, ridden 1** to sit on and control the movements of (a horse or other animal) **2** to sit on and propel (a bicycle or motorcycle) **3** to travel on or in a vehicle: *he rides around in a chauffeur-driven Rolls-Royce* **4** to travel over: *they rode the countryside in search of shelter* **5** to travel through or be carried across (sea, sky, etc.): *the moon was riding high* **6** *US & Canad* to cause to be carried: *to ride someone out of town* **7** (of a vessel) to lie at anchor **8** to tyrannize over or dominate: *she was ridden by fear* **9 be riding on** to be dependent on (something) for success: *a lot is riding on the profits of the film* **10** *informal* to continue undisturbed: *let it ride* **11 riding high** popular and successful ▷ *n* **12** a journey on a bicycle, on horseback, or in a vehicle **13** transport in a vehicle: *most of us have been told not to accept rides from strangers* **14** the type of movement experienced in a vehicle: *a bumpy ride* **15** a path for riding on horseback **16 take for a ride** *informal* to cheat or deceive ▶ HISTORY Old English *rīdan*

ride out *vb* to survive (a period of difficulty or danger) successfully

rider *n* **1** a person who rides **2** an extra clause or condition added to a document

ride up *vb* (of a garment) to move up from the proper position

ridge *n* **1** a long narrow raised land formation with sloping sides **2** a long narrow raised strip on a flat surface **3** the top of a roof where the two sloping sides meet **4** *meteorol* an elongated area of high pressure ▶ HISTORY Old English *hrycg* > **ridged** *adj* > **ridgy** *adj*

ridicule *n* **1** language or behaviour intended to humiliate or mock ▷ *vb* **-culing, -culed 2** to make fun of or mock ▶ HISTORY Latin *ridere* to laugh

ridiculous *adj* worthy of or causing ridicule

riding¹ *n* the art or practice of horsemanship

riding² *n* **1 Riding** any of the three former administrative divisions of Yorkshire: North Riding, East Riding, and West Riding **2** *Canad* an electoral constituency ▸ HISTORY Old English *thriding* a third

riesling *n* a medium-dry white wine ▸ HISTORY from German

rife *adj* **1** widespread or common **2 rife with** full of: *the media is rife with speculation* ▸ HISTORY Old English *rífe*

riff *n* *jazz, rock* a short series of chords ▸ HISTORY probably from REFRAIN²

riffle *vb* **-fling, -fled 1** to flick through (papers or pages) quickly: *I riffled through the rest of the memos* ▸ *n* **2** *US & Canad* **a** a rapid in a stream **b** a rocky shoal causing a rapid **c** a ripple on water **3** a riffling ▸ HISTORY probably from *ruffle*

riffraff *n* worthless or disreputable people ▸ HISTORY Old French *rif et raf*

rifle¹ *n* **1** a firearm having a long barrel with a spirally grooved interior, which gives the bullet a spinning motion and thus greater accuracy over a longer range **2 Rifles** a unit of soldiers equipped with rifles: *the Burma Rifles* ▸ *vb* **-fling, -fled 3** to cut spiral grooves inside the barrel of (a gun) ▸ HISTORY Old French *rifler* to scratch ▸ **rifled** *adj*

rifle² *vb* **-fling, -fled 1** to search (a house or safe) and steal from it **2** to steal and carry off: *he rifled whatever valuables he could lay his hands on* ▸ HISTORY Old French *rifler* to plunder, scratch

rift *n* **1** a break in friendly relations between people or groups of people **2** a gap or space made by splitting ▸ HISTORY Old Norse

rift valley *n* a long narrow valley resulting from the subsidence of land between two faults

rig *vb* **rigging, rigged 1** to arrange in a dishonest way, for profit or advantage: *he claimed that the poll was rigged* **2** to set up or prepare (something) hastily ready for use **3** *naut* to equip (a vessel or mast) with (sails or rigging) ▸ *n* **4** an apparatus for drilling for oil and gas **5** *naut* the arrangement of the sails and masts of a vessel **6** apparatus or equipment **7** *informal* an outfit of clothes **8** *US, Canad & Austral* an articulated lorry ▸ See also **rig up** ▸ HISTORY Scandinavian

rigging *n* the ropes and cables supporting a ship's masts and sails

right *adj* **1** morally or legally acceptable or correct: *his conduct seemed reasonable, even right* **2** correct or true: *the customer is always right* **3** appropriate, suitable, or proper: *there were problems involved in finding the right candidate* **4** most favourable or convenient: *she waited until the right moment to broach the subject* **5** in a satisfactory condition: *things are right again now* **6** accurate: *is that clock right?* **7** correct in opinion or judgment **8** sound in mind or body **9** of or on the side of something or someone that faces east when the front is turned towards the north **10** conservative or reactionary: *it was alleged he was an agent of the right wing* **11** *geom* formed by or containing a line or plane perpendicular to another line or plane: *a right angle* **12** of or on the side of cloth worn or facing outwards **13 in one's right mind** sane **14 on the right side of a** in favour with: *you'd better stay on the right side of him* **b** younger than: *he's still on the right side of fifty* **15 she'll be right** *Austral & NZ, informal* that's all right; not to worry **16 too right** *informal, spoken* an exclamation of agreement ▸ *adv* **17** correctly: *if we change the structure of local government we must do it right* **18** in the appropriate manner: *do it right next time!* **19** straight or directly: *let's go right to bed* **20** in the direction of the east from the point of view of a person or thing facing north **21** all the way: *he drove right up to the gate* **22** without delay: *I'll be right over* **23** exactly or precisely: *right here* **24** fittingly: *it serves him right* **25** to good or favourable advantage: *it all came out right in the end* ▸ *n* **26** a freedom or power that is morally or legally due to a person: *the defendant had an absolute right to a fair trial* **27** anything that accords with the principles of legal or moral justice **28 in the right** the state of being in accordance with reason or truth **29** the right side, direction, or part: *the right of the army* **30 the Right** the supporters or advocates of conservatism or reaction: *the rise of the far Right in France* **31** *boxing* a punch with the right hand **32 rights** *finance* the privilege of a company's shareholders to subscribe for new issues of the company's shares on advantageous terms **33 by right** *or* **rights** properly: *by rights he should have won* **34 in one's own right** having a claim or title oneself rather than through marriage or other connection **35 to rights** consistent with justice or orderly arrangement: *he put the matter to rights* ▸ *vb* **36** to bring or come back to a normal or correct state **37** to bring or come back to a vertical position: *he slipped and righted himself at once* **38** to compensate for or redress: *there is a wrong to be righted* **39** to make (something) accord with truth or facts ▸ *interj* **40** *spoken* an expression of agreement or compliance ▸ HISTORY Old English *riht*

right angle *n* **1** an angle of 90° or π/2 radians **2 at right angles** perpendicular or perpendicularly > **right-angled** *adj*

right-angled triangle *n* a triangle with one angle which is a right angle

right away *adv* without delay

right-branching sentence *n* *grammar* a sentence in which most of the information comes after the main verb in the main clause. Compare **left-branching sentence**

righteous (**rye**-chuss) *adj* **1** moral, just, or virtuous: *the lieutenant was a righteous cop* **2** morally justifiable or right: *her eyes were blazing with righteous indignation* ▸ HISTORY Old English *rihtwís* > **righteousness** *n*

rightful *adj* **1** in accordance with what is right **2** having a legally or morally just claim: *he is the rightful heir to her fortune* **3** held by virtue of a legal or just claim: *these moves will restore them to their rightful homes* > **rightfully** *adv* > **rightfulness** *n*

right-handed *adj* **1** more adept with the right hand than with the left **2** made for or by the right hand **3** turning from left to right

r

729

rightist *adj* **1** of the political right or its principles ▷ *n* **2** a supporter of the political right > **rightism** *n*

rightly *adv* **1** in accordance with the true facts or justice **2** with good reason: *he was rightly praised for his constancy*

right-minded *or* **right-thinking** *adj* holding opinions or principles considered acceptable by the speaker

right of way *n, pl* **rights of way** **1** the right of one vehicle or ship to go before another **2 a** the legal right of someone to pass over someone else's land **b** the path used by this right

Right Reverend *adj* (in Britain) a title of respect for a bishop

right whale *n* a large grey or black whalebone whale with a large head ▶ HISTORY origin unknown

right-wing *adj* **1** conservative or reactionary: *there's a very fast-growing right-wing feeling in our country* **2** belonging to the more conservative part of a political party: *a group of right-wing Labour MPs* ▷ *n* **right wing 3** (often cap) the more conservative or reactionary section, esp. of a political party: *the Right Wing of the Conservative Party* **4** *sport* **a** the right-hand side of the field of play **b** a player positioned in this area in certain games > **right-winger** *n*

rigid *adj* **1** inflexible or strict: *the talks will be general without a rigid agenda* **2** physically unyielding or stiff: *use only rigid plastic containers* ▶ HISTORY Latin *rigidus* > **rigidity** *n* > **rigidly** *adv*

rigmarole *n* **1** a long complicated procedure **2** a set of incoherent or pointless statements ▶ HISTORY earlier *ragman roll* a list

rigor mortis *n* the stiffness of joints and muscles of a dead body ▶ HISTORY Latin: rigidity of death

rigorous *adj* **1** harsh, strict, or severe: *rigorous enforcement of the libel laws* **2** severely accurate: *rigorous scientific testing*

rigour *or US* **rigor** *n* **1** a severe or cruel circumstance: *the rigours of forced labour* **2** strictness in judgment or conduct **3** harsh but just treatment ▶ HISTORY Latin *rigor*

rig up *vb* to set up or build temporarily: *they rigged up a loudspeaker system*

rile *vb* **riling, riled 1** to annoy or anger **2** *US & Canad* to stir up (a liquid) ▶ HISTORY variant of *roil* to agitate

rill *n* a small stream ▶ HISTORY Low German *rille*

rim *n* **1** the raised edge of an object **2** the outer part of a wheel to which the tyre is attached ▶ HISTORY Old English *rima* > **rimless** *adj*

rime¹ *literary n* **1** frost formed by the freezing of water droplets in fog onto solid objects ▷ *vb* **riming, rimed 2** to cover with rime or something resembling it ▶ HISTORY Old English *hrīm* > **rimy** *adj*

rime² *n, vb* **riming, rimed** *archaic* same as **rhyme**

rind *n* a hard outer layer on fruits, bacon, or cheese ▶ HISTORY Old English *rinde*

ring¹ *vb* **ringing, rang, rung 1** to give out a clear resonant sound, like that of a bell **2** to cause (a bell) to give out a ringing sound or (of a bell) to give out such a sound **3** *chiefly Brit & NZ* to call (a person) by telephone **4 ring for** to call by means of a bell: *ring for the maid* **5** (of a building or place) to be filled with sound: *the church rang with singing* **6** (of the ears) to have the sensation of humming or ringing **7** *slang* to change the identity of (a stolen vehicle) by using the licence plate or serial number of another, usually disused, vehicle **8 ring a bell** to bring something to the mind or memory: *the name doesn't ring a bell* **9 ring down the curtain a** to lower the curtain at the end of a theatrical performance **b ring down the curtain on** to put an end to **10 ring true** *or* **false** to give the impression of being true *or* false ▷ *n* **11** the act of or a sound made by ringing **12** a sound produced by or sounding like a bell **13** *informal, chiefly Brit & NZ* a telephone call **14** an inherent quality: *it has the ring of possibility to it* ▷ See also **ring in, ring off**, etc. ▶ HISTORY Old English *hringan*

ring² *n* **1** a circular band of a precious metal worn on the finger **2** any object or mark that is circular in shape **3** a group of people or things standing or arranged in a circle: *a ring of standing stones* **4** a circular path or course: *crowds of people walking round in a ring* **5** a circular enclosure where circus acts perform or livestock is sold at a market **6** a square raised platform, marked off by ropes, in which contestants box or wrestle **7** a group of people, usually illegal, who control a specified market: *a drugs ring* **8** *chem* a closed loop of atoms in a molecule **9** one of the systems of circular bands orbiting the planets Saturn, Uranus, and Jupiter **10 the ring** the sport of boxing **11 throw one's hat in the ring** to announce one's intention to be a candidate or contestant **12 run rings around** *informal* to outclass completely ▷ *vb* **ringing, ringed 13** to put a ring round **14** to mark (a bird) with a ring or clip for subsequent identification **15** to kill (a tree) by cutting the bark round the trunk **16** to fit a ring in the nose of (a bull, etc.) so that it can be led easily ▶ HISTORY Old English *hring* > **ringed** *adj*

ring binder *n* a loose-leaf binder with metal rings that can be opened to insert perforated paper

ringdove *n* a wood pigeon

ringer *n* **1** *Brit, Austral & NZ* Also called: **dead ringer** a person or thing that is almost identical to another **2** *slang* a stolen vehicle the identity of which has been changed by the use of the licence plate or serial number of another, usually disused, vehicle

ring finger *n* the third finger, esp. of the left hand, on which a wedding ring is worn

ring in *vb* to report to someone by telephone

ringleader *n* a person who leads others in illegal or mischievous actions

ringlet *n* a lock of hair hanging down in a spiral curl > **ringleted** *adj*

ring main *n* a domestic electrical supply in which outlet sockets are connected to the mains supply through a continuous closed circuit (**ring circuit**)

r

ringmaster *n* the master of ceremonies in a circus

ring off *vb chiefly Brit & NZ* to end a telephone conversation by replacing the receiver

ring road *n Brit, Austral & S African* a main road that bypasses a town or town centre

ringside *n* **1** the row of seats nearest a boxing or wrestling ring ▷ *adj* **2** providing a close uninterrupted view: *a ringside seat for the election*

ringtail *n Austral* a possum with a curling tail used to grip branches while climbing

ringtone *n* a musical tune played by a mobile phone when it receives a call

ring up *vb* **1** to make a telephone call to **2** to record on a cash register **3 ring up the curtain a** to begin a theatrical performance **b ring up the curtain on** to make a start on

ringworm *n* a fungal infection of the skin producing itchy patches

rink *n* **1** a sheet of ice for skating on, usually indoors **2** an area for roller-skating on **3** a building for ice-skating or roller-skating **4** (in bowls or curling) **a** a strip of grass or ice on which a game is played **b** the players on one side in a game ▶ HISTORY Old French *renc* row

rinkhals (**rink**-hals) *n, pl* **-hals** *or* **-halses** a highly venomous snake of Southern Africa capable of spitting its venom accurately at its victim's eyes ▶ HISTORY Afrikaans

rinse *vb* **rinsing, rinsed** **1** to remove soap or shampoo from (clothes, dishes, or hair) by washing it out with clean water **2** to wash lightly, esp. without soap **3** to cleanse the mouth by swirling water or mouthwash in it and then spitting the liquid out **4** *hairdressing* to give a tint to (hair) ▷ *n* **5** the act or an instance of rinsing **6** *hairdressing* a liquid to tint hair: *a blue rinse* ▶ HISTORY Old French *rincer*

riot *n* **1** a disturbance made by an unruly mob **2** *Brit, Austral & NZ* an occasion of lively enjoyment **3** a dazzling display: *the pansies provided the essential riot of colour* **4** *slang* a very amusing person or thing **5 read the riot act** to reprimand severely **6 run riot a** to behave without restraint **b** (of plants) to grow profusely ▷ *vb* **7** to take part in a riot ▶ HISTORY Old French *riote* dispute > **rioter** *n* > **rioting** *n*

riotous *adj* **1** unrestrained and excessive: *riotous decadence* **2** unruly or rebellious **3** characterized by unrestrained merriment: *riotous celebration*

rip¹ *vb* **ripping, ripped** **1** to tear or be torn violently or roughly **2** to remove hastily or roughly **3** *informal* to move violently or hurriedly **4 let rip** to act or speak without restraint ▷ *n* **5** a tear or split ▷ See also **rip off** ▶ HISTORY origin unknown

rip² *n* short for **riptide**

RIP may he, she, or they rest in peace ▶ HISTORY Latin *requiescat* or *requiescant in pace*

riparian (rip-**pair**-ee-an) *adj formal* of or on the bank of a river ▶ HISTORY Latin *ripa* river bank

ripcord *n* a cord pulled to open a parachute from its pack

ripe *adj* **1** mature enough to be eaten or used: *a round ripe apple* **2** fully developed in mind or body **3** suitable: *wait until the time is ripe* **4 ripe for** ready or eager to (undertake or undergo an action): *China was ripe for revolution* **5 ripe old age** an elderly but healthy age ▶ HISTORY Old English *rīpe*

ripen *vb* **1** to make or become ripe **2** to mature

rip off *slang vb* **1** to cheat by overcharging **2** to steal (something) ▷ *n* **rip-off** **3** a grossly overpriced article **4** the act of stealing or cheating

riposte (rip-**posst**) *n* **1** *written* a swift clever reply **2** *fencing* a counterattack made immediately after a successful parry ▷ *vb* **-posting, -posted** **3** *written* to make a riposte ▶ HISTORY French

ripple *n* **1** a slight wave on the surface of water **2** a slight ruffling of a surface **3** a sound like water flowing gently in ripples: *a ripple of applause* **4** vanilla ice cream with stripes of another ice cream through it: *raspberry ripple* ▷ *vb* **-pling, -pled** **5** to form ripples or flow with a waving motion **6** (of sounds) to rise and fall gently ▶ HISTORY origin unknown > **rippling** *adj*

rip-roaring *adj informal* boisterous and exciting

ripsaw *n* a handsaw for cutting along the grain of timber

riptide *n geog* **1** Also: **rip** a stretch of turbulent water in the sea, caused by the meeting of currents **2** Also: **rip current** a strong current, esp. one flowing outwards from the shore

rise *vb* **rising, rose, risen** **1** to get up from a lying, sitting, or kneeling position **2** to get out of bed, esp. to begin one's day: *she rises at 5 a.m. every day to look after her horse* **3** to move from a lower to a higher position or place **4** to appear above the horizon: *as the sun rises higher the mist disappears* **5** to slope upwards: *the road crossed the valley then rose to a low ridge* **6** to increase in height or level: *the tide rose* **7** to swell up: *dough rises* **8** to increase in strength or degree: *frustration is rising amongst sections of the population* **9** to increase in amount or value: *living costs are rising at an annual rate of nine per cent* **10** *informal* to respond (to a challenge or remark) **11** to revolt: *the people rose against their oppressors* **12** (of a court or parliament) to adjourn **13** to be resurrected **14** to become erect or rigid: *the hairs on his neck rose in fear* **15** to originate: *that river rises in the mountains* **16** *angling* (of fish) to come to the surface of the water ▷ *n* **17** the act or an instance of rising **18** a piece of rising ground **19** an increase in wages **20** an increase in amount, cost, or quantity **21** an increase in height **22** an increase in status or position **23** an increase in degree or intensity **24** the vertical height of a step or of a flight of stairs **25 get** or **take a rise out of** *slang* to provoke an angry reaction from **26 give rise to** to cause the development of ▶ HISTORY Old English *rīsan*

riser *n* **1** a person who rises from bed: *an early riser* **2** the vertical part of a step

risible (riz-zib-bl) *adj formal* ridiculous ▶ HISTORY Latin *ridere* to laugh

rising *n* **1** a rebellion ▷ *adj* **2** increasing in rank or maturity

731

risk *n* **1** the possibility of bringing about misfortune or loss **2** a person or thing considered as a potential hazard: *in parts of the world transfusions carry the risk of infection* **3 at risk** in a dangerous situation **4 take** *or* **run a risk** to act without regard to the danger involved ▷ *vb* **5** to act in spite of the possibility of (injury or loss): *if they clamp down they risk a revolution* **6** to expose to danger or loss ▶ **HISTORY** French *risque* > **risky** *adj*

risk assessment *n* *business* an analysis of the level of risk attached to a particular activity

risotto *n, pl* **-tos** a dish of rice cooked in stock with vegetables, meat, etc. ▶ **HISTORY** Italian

risqué (**risk**-ay) *adj* making slightly rude references to sex: *risqué humour* ▶ **HISTORY** French *risquer* to risk

rissole *n* a mixture of minced cooked meat coated in egg and breadcrumbs and fried ▶ **HISTORY** French

ritardando *adj, adv* same as **rallentando** ▶ **HISTORY** Italian

rite *n* **1** a formal act which forms part of a religious ceremony: *the rite of burial* **2** a custom that is carried out within a particular group: *the barbaric rites of public execution* **3** a particular body of such acts, esp. of a particular Christian Church: *the traditional Anglican rite* ▶ **HISTORY** Latin *ritus*

rite of passage *n* a ceremony or event that marks an important change in a person's life

ritual *n* **1** a religious or other ceremony involving a series of fixed actions performed in a certain order **2** these ceremonies collectively: *people need ritual* **3** regular repeated action or behaviour **4** stereotyped activity or behaviour ▷ *adj* **5** of or like rituals > **ritually** *adv*

ritualism *n* exaggerated emphasis on the importance of rites and ceremonies > **ritualistic** *adj* > **ritualistically** *adv*

ritzy *adj* **ritzier, ritziest** *slang* luxurious or elegant ▶ **HISTORY** after the hotels established by César Ritz

rival *n* **1** a person or group that competes with another for the same object or in the same field **2** a person or thing that is considered the equal of another: *she is without rival in the field of physics* ▷ *adj* **3** in the position of a rival ▷ *vb* **-valling, -valled** *or* US **-valing, -valed** **4** to be the equal or near equal of: *his inarticulateness was rivalled only by that of his brother* **5** to try to equal or surpass ▶ **HISTORY** Latin *rivalis*, literally: one who shares the same brook

rivalry *n, pl* **-ries** active competition between people or groups

riven *adj old-fashioned* **1** split apart: *the party is riven by factions* **2** torn to shreds ▶ **HISTORY** Old Norse *rīfa* to tear, rend

river *n* **1** a large natural stream of fresh water flowing along a definite course into the sea, a lake, or a larger river. *Related adjective:* **fluvial** **2** an abundant stream or flow: *rivers of blood* ▶ **HISTORY** Old French *riviere*

river basin *n* *geog* the catchment area of a river and its tributaries

river profile *n* *geog* a cross-sectional representation mapping the height above sea level of a river at different points along its length and showing variations in slope and river bed

river terrace *n* *geog* an area of flat land that was part of an earlier higher flood plain when the river bed was higher

rivet (**riv**-vit) *n* **1** a short metal pin for fastening metal plates, with a head at one end, the other end being hammered flat after being put through holes in the plates ▷ *vb* **-eting, -eted** **2** to join by riveting **3** to cause a person's attention to be fixed in fascination or horror: *he was riveted by the story* ▶ **HISTORY** Old French *river* to fasten > **riveter** *n*

riveting *adj* very interesting or exciting

rivulet *n* a small stream ▶ **HISTORY** Latin *rivus* stream

RM 1 Royal Mail **2** Royal Marines **3** (in Canada) Rural Municipality **4** (in Canada) Regional Municipality

RME (in England and Wales) Religious and Moral Education

Rn *chem* radon

RN 1 (in Canada and New Zealand) Registered Nurse **2** (in Britain) Royal Navy

RNA *n* *biochem* ribonucleic acid: any of a group of nucleic acids, present in all living cells, that play an essential role in the synthesis of proteins

RNZ Radio New Zealand

RNZAF Royal New Zealand Air Force

RNZN Royal New Zealand Navy

roach¹ *n, pl* **roaches** *or* **roach** a European freshwater food fish ▶ **HISTORY** Old French *roche*

roach² *n chiefly US & Canad* a cockroach

road *n* **1** a route, usually surfaced, used by travellers and vehicles to get from one place to another **2** a street **3** a way or course: *on the road to recovery* **4** *naut* same as **roadstead** **5 one for the road** *informal* a last alcoholic drink before leaving **6 on the road** travelling about ▶ **HISTORY** Old English *rād*

roadblock *n* a barrier set up across a road by the police or military, in order to stop and check vehicles

road hog *n informal* a selfish or aggressive driver

roadholding *n* the extent to which a vehicle is stable and does not skid on bends or wet roads

roadhouse *n* a pub or restaurant at the side of a road

roadie *n Brit, Austral & NZ, informal* a person who transports and sets up equipment for a band

road map *n* **1** a map for drivers that shows roads, distances, and other features in an area **2** a plan for future actions: *a road map for peace*

road metal *n Brit, Austral & NZ* crushed rock or broken stone used in building roads

road rage *n* aggressive behaviour by a motorist in response to the actions of another road user

road show *n* **1** *radio* a live broadcast from a radio van taking a particular programme on a tour of the country **2** a group of entertainers on tour

roadside *n* **1** the edge of a road ▷ *adj* **2** by the edge or side of a road: *a roadside café*

roadstead *n naut* a partly sheltered anchorage

roadster *n* an open car with only two seats

road tax *n* (in Britain) a tax paid on vehicles used on the roads

road test *n* **1** a test of something, such as a vehicle in actual use ▷ *vb* **road-test** **2** to test (a vehicle, etc.) in actual use

roadway *n* the part of a road that is used by vehicles

roadworks *pl n* repairs to a road or cable under a road, esp. when they block part of the road

roadworthy *adj* (of a motor vehicle) mechanically sound > **roadworthiness** *n*

roam *vb* to walk about with no fixed purpose or direction ▶ HISTORY origin unknown

roan *adj* **1** (of a horse) having a brown or black coat sprinkled with white hairs ▷ *n* **2** a horse with such a coat ▶ HISTORY Spanish *roano*

roar *vb* **1** (of lions and other animals) to make loud growling cries **2** *written* to shout (something) with a loud deep cry: *'Don't do that!' he roared at me* **3** *written* to make a very loud noise: *the engine roared* **4** to laugh in a loud hearty manner **5** (of a fire) to burn fiercely with a roaring sound ▷ *n* **6** a roaring noise: *there was a roar as the train came in* **7** a loud deep cry, uttered by a person or crowd, esp. in anger or triumph: *a roar of approval came from the crowd* ▶ HISTORY Old English *rārian*

roaring *adj* **1 a roaring trade** a brisk and profitable business ▷ *adv* **2 roaring drunk** noisily or boisterously drunk

Roaring Forties *pl n* **the Roaring Forties** *geog* the areas of ocean between 40° and 50° latitude in the S Hemisphere, noted for gale-force winds

roast *vb* **1** to cook (food) by dry heat in an oven or over a fire **2** to brown over dry (coffee or nuts) by exposure to heat **3** to make or be extremely hot **4** *informal* to criticize severely ▷ *n* **5** a roasted joint of meat ▷ *adj* **6** cooked by roasting. *roast beef* ▶ HISTORY Old French *rostir* > **roaster** *n*

roasting *informal adj* **1** extremely hot ▷ *n* **2** severe criticism or scolding

rob *vb* **robbing, robbed** **1** to take something from (a person or place) illegally **2** to deprive, esp. of something deserved: *I can't forgive him for robbing me of an Olympic gold* ▶ HISTORY Old French *rober* > **robber** *n*

robbery *n, pl* **-beries** **1** *criminal law* the stealing of property from a person by using or threatening to use force **2** the act or an instance of robbing

robe *n* **1** a long loose flowing garment **2** a dressing gown or bathrobe ▷ *vb* **robing, robed** **3** to put a robe on ▶ HISTORY Old French

robin *n* **1** Also called: **robin redbreast** a small Old World songbird with a brown back and an orange-red breast and face **2** a North American thrush similar to but larger than the Old World robin ▶ HISTORY arbitrary use of name *Robin*

robot *n* **1** a machine programmed to perform specific tasks in a human manner, esp. one with a human shape **2** a person of machine-like efficiency **3** *S African* a set of traffic lights > **robotic** *adj*

robotics *n* the science of designing, building, and using robots

robust *adj* **1** very strong and healthy **2** sturdily built: *the new generation of robust lasers* **3** requiring or displaying physical strength: *robust tackles* ▶ HISTORY Latin *robur* an oak, strength

roc *n* (in Arabian legend) a bird of enormous size and power ▶ HISTORY Persian *rukh*

rock¹ *n* **1** *geol* the mass of mineral matter that makes up part of the earth's crust; stone **2** a large rugged mass of stone **3** *chiefly US, Canad & Austral* a stone **4** *Brit* a hard, often peppermint-flavoured sweet, usually in the shape of a long stick **5** a person or thing on which one can always depend: *your loyalty is a rock* **6** *slang* a precious jewel **7 on the rocks a** (of a marriage) about to end **b** (of an alcoholic drink) served with ice ▶ HISTORY Old French *roche*

rock² *vb* **1** to move from side to side or backwards and forwards **2** to shake or move (something) violently **3** to feel or cause to feel shock: *key events have rocked both countries* **4** to dance to or play rock music **5** *slang* to be very good ▷ *n* **6** Also called: **rock music** a style of pop music with a heavy beat **7** a rocking motion ▷ *adj* **8** of or relating to rock music ▶ HISTORY Old English *roccian*

rock and roll *or* **rock'n'roll** *n* a type of pop music originating in the 1950s as a blend of rhythm and blues and country and western

rock bottom *n* the lowest possible level

rock cake *n* a small fruit cake with a rough surface

rock crystal *n* a pure transparent colourless quartz

rock cycle *n geol* the cycle of change which rocks are subjected to, including being uplifted, eroded, transported, deposited, and possibly metamorphosed

rock dove *n* a common dove from which domestic and wild pigeons are descended

rocker *n* **1** a rocking chair **2** either of two curved supports on which a rocking chair stands **3** a rock music performer or fan **4 off one's rocker** *slang* crazy

rockery *n, pl* **-eries** a garden built of rocks and soil, for growing rock plants

rocket *n* **1** a self-propelling device, usually cylindrical, which produces thrust by expelling through a nozzle the gases produced by burning fuel, such as one used as a firework or distress signal **2** any vehicle propelled by a rocket engine, as a weapon or carrying a spacecraft **3** *informal* a severe reprimand: *my sister gave me a rocket for writing such dangerous nonsense* ▷ *vb* **-eting, -eted** **4** to increase rapidly: *within six years their turnover had rocketed* **5** to attack with rockets ▶ HISTORY Italian *rochetto* little distaff

rocketry *n* the science and technology of the design and operation of rockets

rock garden *n* a garden featuring rocks or rockeries

rocking chair *n* a chair set on curving supports so that the sitter may rock backwards and forwards

rocking horse *n* a toy horse mounted on a pair of rocking supports on which a child can rock to and fro

rock melon *n* US, Austral & NZ same as **cantaloupe**

rock plant *n* a plant that grows on rocks or in rocky ground

rock salmon *n* Brit a former term for dogfish when used as a food

rock salt *n* common salt as a naturally occurring solid mineral

rock tripe *n* Canad any edible lichen that grows on rocks

rocky¹ *adj* **rockier, rockiest** covered with rocks: *rocky and sandy shores* > **rockiness** *n*

rocky² *adj* **rockier, rockiest** shaky or unstable: *a rocky relationship* > **rockiness** *n*

rococo (rok-**koe**-koe) *adj* **1** relating to an 18th-century style of architecture, decoration, and music characterized by elaborate ornamentation **2** excessively elaborate in style ▶ **HISTORY** French

rod *n* **1** a thin straight pole made of wood or metal **2** a cane used to beat people as a punishment **3** a type of cell in the retina, sensitive to dim light ▶ **HISTORY** Old English *rodd* > **rodlike** *adj*

rode *vb* the past tense of **ride**

rodent *n* a small mammal with teeth specialized for gnawing, such as a rat, mouse, or squirrel ▶ **HISTORY** Latin *rodere* to gnaw > **rodent-like** *adj*

rodeo *n, pl* **-deos** a display of the skills of cowboys, including bareback riding ▶ **HISTORY** Spanish

roe¹ *n* the ovary and eggs of a female fish, sometimes eaten as food ▶ **HISTORY** Middle Dutch *roge*

roe² *or* **roe deer** *n* a small graceful deer with short antlers ▶ **HISTORY** Old English *rā(ha)*

roentgen (**ront**-gan) *n* a unit measuring a radiation dose ▶ **HISTORY** after the German physicist *Roentgen*, who discovered X-rays

roger *interj* **1** (used in signalling) message received and understood **2** an expression of agreement ▶ **HISTORY** from the name *Roger*, representing R for *received*

rogue *n* **1** a dishonest or unprincipled person **2** a mischievous person **3** a crop plant which is inferior, diseased, or of a different variety **4** an inferior or defective specimen ▷ *adj* **5** (of a wild animal) having a savage temper and living apart from the herd: *a rogue elephant* **6** inferior or defective: *rogue heroin* ▶ **HISTORY** origin unknown > **roguish** *adj*

roguery *n, pl* **-gueries** dishonest or immoral behaviour

rogues' gallery *n* a collection of photographs of known criminals kept by the police for identification purposes

roister *vb* old-fashioned to enjoy oneself noisily and boisterously ▶ **HISTORY** Old French *rustre* lout > **roisterer** *n*

role *n* **1** a task or function: *their role in international relations* **2** an actor's part in a production ▶ **HISTORY** French

role model *n* a person regarded by others, esp. younger people, as a good example to follow

role play *n* activity in which a person improvises a role or part

roll *vb* **1** to move along by turning over and over **2** to move along on wheels or rollers **3** to curl or make by curling into a ball or tube **4** to move along in an undulating movement **5** to rotate wholly or partially: *he would snort in derision, roll his eyes, and heave a deep sigh* **6** to spread out flat or smooth with a roller or rolling pin: *roll the pastry out thinly* **7** (of a ship or aircraft) to turn from side to side around the longitudinal axis **8** to operate or begin to operate: *the cameras continued to roll as she pulled up to the nightclub* **9** to make a continuous deep reverberating sound: *the thunder rolled* **10** to walk in a swaying manner: *the drunks came rolling home* **11** to appear like a series of waves: *mountain ranges rolling away in every direction* **12** to pass or elapse: *watching the time roll away* **13** (of animals) to turn onto the back and kick **14** to trill or cause to be trilled: *she rolled her r's* **15** to throw (dice) ▷ *n* **16** the act or an instance of rolling **17** anything rolled up into a tube: *a roll of paper towels* **18** a small cake of bread for one person **19** a flat pastry or cake rolled up with a meat, jam, or other filling **20** an official list or register of names: *the electoral roll; the voters' roll* **21** a complete rotation about its longitudinal axis by an aircraft **22** a continuous deep reverberating sound: *the roll of musketry* **23** a swaying or unsteady movement or gait **24** a rounded mass: *rolls of fat* **25** a very rapid beating of the sticks on a drum **26** **on a roll** slang experiencing continued good luck or success **27** **strike off the roll** to expel from membership of a professional association ▶ **HISTORY** Old French *roler*

roll call *n* the reading aloud of an official list of names, to check who is present

rolled gold *n* a metal, such as brass, coated with a thin layer of gold

roller *n* **1** a rotating cylinder used for smoothing, supporting a thing to be moved, spreading paint, etc. **2** a small tube around which hair may be wound in order to make it curly **3** a long heavy wave of the sea **4** a cylinder fitted on pivots, used to enable heavy objects to be easily moved

Rollerblade *n* trademark a type of roller skate in which the wheels are set in a single straight line under the boot

roller coaster *n* (at a funfair) a narrow railway with open carriages, sharp curves, and steep slopes

roller skate *n* **1** a shoe with four small wheels that enable the wearer to glide swiftly over a floor ▷ *vb* **roller-skate, -skating, -skated** **2** to move on roller skates > **roller skater** *n*

rollicking *adj* boisterously carefree: *a rollicking read* ▶ **HISTORY** origin unknown

rolling *adj* **1** having gentle rising and falling slopes: *rolling hills* **2** (of a walk) slow and swaying **3** subject to regular review and updating: *a 10-year rolling programme* **4** progressing by stages or in succession: *a rolling campaign*

rolling mill *n* **1** a factory where metal ingots are passed between rollers to produce sheets or bars of the required shape **2** a machine with rollers for doing this

rolling pin *n* a cylinder with handles at both ends used for rolling pastry

rolling stock *n* the locomotives and coaches of a railway

rolling stone *n* a restless or wandering person

rollmop *n* a herring fillet rolled around onion slices and pickled ▶ **HISTORY** German *rollen* to roll + *Mops* pug dog

roll of honour *n* a list of those who have died in war for their country

roll-on/roll-off *adj Brit, Austral & NZ* denoting a ship designed so that vehicles can be driven straight on and straight off

roll-top *adj* (of a desk) having a slatted wooden panel that can be pulled down over the writing surface when not in use

roll up *vb* **1** to form into a cylindrical shape: *roll up a length of black material* **2** *informal* to arrive ▷ *n* **roll-up** **3** *Brit, informal* a cigarette made by the smoker from loose tobacco and cigarette papers

roly-poly *adj* **1** plump or chubby ▷ *n, pl* **-lies** **2** *Brit* a strip of suet pastry spread with jam, rolled up, and baked or steamed ▶ **HISTORY** probably from *roll*

ROM *n computers* read only memory: a storage device that holds data permanently and cannot be altered by the programmer

roman *adj* **1** in or relating to the vertical style of printing type used for most printed matter ▷ *n* **2** roman type ▶ **HISTORY** so called because the style of letters is that used in ancient Roman inscriptions

Roman *adj* **1** of Rome, a city in Italy, or its inhabitants in ancient or modern times **2** of Roman Catholicism or the Roman Catholic Church ▷ *n* **3** a person from ancient or modern Rome

Roman alphabet *n* the alphabet evolved by the ancient Romans for writing Latin, used for writing most of the languages of W Europe, including English

Roman candle *n* a firework that produces a steady stream of coloured sparks ▶ **HISTORY** it originated in Italy

Roman Catholic *adj* **1** of the Roman Catholic Church ▷ *n* **2** a member of this Church > **Roman Catholicism** *n*

Roman Catholic Church *n* the Christian Church over which the pope presides

romance *n* **1** a love affair: *a failed romance* **2** love, esp. romantic love idealized for its purity or beauty **3** a spirit of or inclination for adventure or mystery **4** a mysterious or sentimental quality **5** a story or film dealing with love, usually in an idealized way **6** a story or film dealing with events and characters remote from ordinary life **7** an extravagant, absurd, or fantastic account **8** a medieval narrative dealing with adventures of chivalrous heroes ▷ *vb* **-mancing, -manced 9** to tell extravagant or improbable lies ▶ **HISTORY** Old French *romans*

Romance *adj* of the languages derived from Latin, such as French, Spanish, and Italian

Romanesque *adj* of or in the style of architecture used in Europe from the 9th to the 12th century, characterized by rounded arches and massive walls

Romanian *adj* **1** of Romania ▷ *n* **2** a person from Romania **3** the language of Romania

Roman nose *n* a nose with a high prominent bridge

Roman numerals *pl n* the letters used as numerals by the Romans, used occasionally today: I (= 1), V (= 5), X (= 10), L (= 50), C (= 100), D (= 500), and M (= 1000). VI = 6 (V + I) but IV = 4 (V − I)

Roman system *n* a system for numerical representation originating in ancient Rome. See also **Roman numerals**

romantic *adj* **1** of or dealing with love **2** idealistic but impractical: *a romantic notion* **3** evoking or given to thoughts and feelings of love: *romantic images* **4 Romantic** relating to a movement in European art, music, and literature in the late 18th and early 19th centuries, characterized by an emphasis on feeling and content rather than order and form ▷ *n* **5** a person who is idealistic or amorous **6** a person who likes or produces artistic works in the style of Romanticism > **romantically** *adv*

romanticism *n* **1** idealistic but unrealistic thoughts and feelings **2 Romanticism** the spirit and style of the Romantic art, music, and literature of the late 18th and early 19th centuries > **romanticist** *n*

romanticize *or* **-cise** *vb* **-cizing, -cized** *or* **-cising, -cised** to describe or regard (something or someone) in an unrealistic and idealized way: *the Victorian legacy of romanticizing family life*

Romany *n* **1** (*pl* **-nies**) a Gypsy **2** the language of the Gypsies ▶ **HISTORY** Romany *romani* (adjective) Gypsy

Romeo *n, pl* **Romeos** an ardent male lover ▶ **HISTORY** after the hero of Shakespeare's *Romeo and Juliet*

romp *vb* **1** to play or run about wildly or joyfully **2 romp home** *or* **in** to win a race or other competition easily **3 romp through** to do (something) quickly and easily ▷ *n* **4** a noisy or boisterous game or prank ▶ **HISTORY** probably from Old French *ramper* to crawl, climb

rompers *pl n* Also called: **romper suit** a one-piece baby garment combining trousers and a top

rondavel *n S African* a small circular building with a cone-shaped roof ▶ **HISTORY** origin unknown

735

rondeau (**ron**-doe) *n, pl* **-deaux** (-doe) a poem consisting of 13 or 10 lines with the opening words of the first line used as a refrain ► HISTORY Old French

rondo *n, pl* **-dos** a piece of music with a leading theme continually returned to: often forms the last movement of a sonata or concerto ► HISTORY Italian

roo *n, pl* **roos** *Austral, informal* a kangaroo

rood *n* **1** *Christianity* the Cross **2** a crucifix ► HISTORY Old English *rōd*

rood screen *n* (in a church) a screen separating the nave from the choir

roof *n, pl* **roofs** **1** a structure that covers or forms the top of a building **2** the top covering of a vehicle, oven, or other structure **3** the highest part of the mouth or a cave **4** **hit** *or* **go through the roof** *informal* to get extremely angry **5** **raise the roof** *informal* to be very noisy ▷ *vb* **6** to put a roof on ► HISTORY Old English *hrōf*

roof rack *n* a rack for carrying luggage attached to the roof of a car

rooibos (**roy**-boss) *n* *S African* a kind of tea made from the leaves of a South African wild shrub. Also called: **rooibos tea, bush tea** ► HISTORY Afrikaans *rooi* red + *bos* bush

rooinek (**roy**-neck) *n* *S African* a contemptuous name for an Englishman ► HISTORY Afrikaans *rooi* red + *nek* neck

rook[1] *n* **1** a large European black bird of the crow family ▷ *vb* **2** *old-fashioned, slang* to cheat or swindle ► HISTORY Old English *hrōc*

rook[2] *n* a chessman that may move any number of unoccupied squares in a straight line, horizontally or vertically; castle ► HISTORY Arabic *rukhkh*

rookery *n, pl* **-eries** **1** a group of nesting rooks **2** a colony of penguins or seals

rookie *n* *informal* a newcomer without much experience ► HISTORY changed from *recruit*

room *n* **1** an area within a building enclosed by a floor, a ceiling, and walls **2** the people present in a room: *the whole room was laughing* **3** unoccupied or unobstructed space: *there wasn't enough room* **4** **room for** opportunity or scope for: *there was no room for acts of heroism* **5** **rooms** lodgings ▷ *vb* **6** *US* to occupy or share a rented room: *I roomed with him for five years* ► HISTORY Old English *rūm*

roomy *adj* **roomier, roomiest** with plenty of space inside: *a roomy entrance hall* > **roominess** *n*

roost *n* **1** a place where birds rest or sleep ▷ *vb* **2** to rest or sleep on a roost **3** **come home to roost** to have unfavourable repercussions **4** **rule the roost** to have authority over people in a particular place ► HISTORY Old English *hrōst*

rooster *n* *chiefly US, Canad & Austral* the male of the domestic fowl; a cock

root[1] *n* **1** the part of a plant that anchors the rest of the plant in the ground and absorbs water and mineral salts from the soil **2** a plant with an edible root, such as a carrot **3** *anat* the part of a tooth, hair, or nail that is below the skin **4** **roots** a person's sense of belonging in a place, esp. the

one in which he or she was brought up **5** source or origin **6** the essential part or nature of something: *the root of a problem* **7** *linguistics* the form of a word from which other words and forms are derived **8** *maths* a quantity that when multiplied by itself a certain number of times equals a given quantity: *what is the cube root of 1000?* **9** Also called: **solution** *maths* a number that when substituted for the variable satisfies a given equation **10** **root and branch** written entirely or utterly. *Related adjective:* **radical** *vb* **11** Also: **take root** to establish a root and begin to grow **12** Also: **take root** to become established or embedded ► HISTORY Old English *rōt*

root[2] *vb* **1** *Brit* to dig up the earth in search of food, using the snout: *dogs were rooting in the rushes for bones* **2** *informal* to search vigorously but unsystematically: *she was rooting around in her large untidy purse* ► HISTORY Old English *wrōtan*

root crop *n* a crop, such as potato or turnip, cultivated for its roots

root for *vb* *informal* to give support to (a team or contestant) ► HISTORY origin unknown

rootle *vb* **-ling, -led** *Brit* same as **root**[2]

rootless *adj* having no sense of belonging: *a rootless city dweller*

root mean square *n* the square root of the average of the squares of a set of numbers or quantities, for example *the root mean square of* 1, 2, and 4 is $\sqrt{[(1^2 + 2^2 + 4^2)/3]} = \sqrt{7}$

root out *vb* to get rid of completely: *a major drive to root out corruption*

rootstock *n* same as **rhizome**

rope *n* **1** a fairly thick cord made of intertwined fibres or wire **2** a row of objects fastened to form a line: *a 20-inch rope of pearls* **3** **know the ropes** to have a thorough understanding of a particular activity **4** **the rope** a rope noose used for hanging someone **b** death by hanging ▷ *vb* **roping, roped** **5** to tie with a rope **6** **rope off** to enclose or divide with a rope ► HISTORY Old English *rāp*

rope in *vb* to persuade to take part in some activity

ropey *or* **ropy** *adj* **ropier, ropiest** *Brit, informal* **1** poor or unsatisfactory in quality: *a ropey performance* **2** slightly unwell > **ropiness** *n*

Roquefort *n* a strong blue-veined cheese made from ewes' and goats' milk ► HISTORY after *Roquefort*, village in S France

rorqual *n* a whalebone whale with a fin on the back ► HISTORY Norwegian *rörhval*

Rorschach test (**ror**-shahk) *n* *psychol* a personality test consisting of a number of unstructured inkblots for interpretation ► HISTORY after H. *Rorschach*, psychiatrist

rort *Austral, informal* *n* **1** a dishonest scheme ▷ *vb* **2** to take unfair advantage of something

rosaceous *adj* of or belonging to a family of plants typically having five-petalled flowers, which includes the rose, strawberry, and many fruit trees

rosary *n, pl* **-saries** *RC Church* **1** a series of prayers counted on a string of beads **2** a string of beads used to count these prayers as they are recited ▸ HISTORY Latin *rosarium* rose garden

rose¹ *n* **1** a shrub or climbing plant with prickly stems and fragrant flowers **2** the flower of any of these plants **3** a plant similar to this, such as the Christmas rose **4** a perforated cap fitted to a watering can or hose, causing the water to come out in a spray **5 bed of roses** a situation of comfort or ease ▷ *adj* **6** reddish-pink ▸ HISTORY Latin *rosa*

rose² *vb* the past tense of **rise**

rosé (roe-zay) *n* a pink wine ▸ HISTORY French

roseate (roe-zee-ate) *adj* **1** of the colour rose or pink **2** excessively optimistic

rosebud *n* a rose which has not yet fully opened

rosehip *n* the berry-like fruit of a rose plant

rosella *n* a type of Australian parrot

rosemary *n, pl* **-maries** an aromatic European shrub widely cultivated for its grey-green evergreen leaves, which are used in cookery and perfumes ▸ HISTORY Latin *ros* dew + *marinus* marine

rosette *n* a rose-shaped decoration, esp. a circular bunch of ribbons

rose window *n* a circular window with spokes branching out from the centre to form a symmetrical roselike pattern

rosewood *n* a fragrant dark wood used to make furniture

Rosh Hashanah *or* **Rosh Hashana** *n* the festival celebrating the Jewish New Year ▸ HISTORY Hebrew: beginning of the year

rosin (rozz-in) *n* **1** a translucent brittle substance produced from turpentine and used for treating the bows of stringed instruments ▷ *vb* **2** to apply rosin to ▸ HISTORY variant of *resin*

roster *n* **1** a list showing the order in which people are to perform a duty ▷ *vb* **2** to place on a roster ▸ HISTORY Dutch *rooster* grating or list

rostrum *n, pl* **-trums** *or* **-tra** a platform or stage ▸ HISTORY Latin: beak

rosy *adj* **rosier, rosiest 1** of the colour rose or pink: *rosy cheeks* **2** hopeful or promising: *the analysis revealed a far from rosy picture* > **rosiness** *n*

rot *vb* **rotting, rotted 1** to decay or cause to decay **2** to deteriorate slowly, mentally and physically: *I thought he was either dead or rotting in a Chinese jail* ▷ *n* **3** the process of rotting or the state of being rotten **4** something decomposed **5** short for **dry rot 6** a plant or animal disease which causes decay of the tissues **7** nonsense ▸ HISTORY Old English *rotian*

rota *n* a list of people who take it in turn to do a particular task ▸ HISTORY Latin: a wheel

rotary *adj* **1** revolving **2** operating by rotation ▷ *n, pl* **-ries 3** US & Canad a traffic roundabout

Rotary Club *n* a club that is part of **Rotary International**, an international association of professional and businesspeople who raise money for charity > **Rotarian** *n, adj*

rotate *vb* **-tating, -tated 1** to turn around a centre or pivot **2** to follow or cause to follow a set sequence **3** to regularly change the type of crop

grown on a piece of land in order to preserve the fertility of the soil ▸ HISTORY Latin *rota* wheel

rotation *n* **1** the act of rotating; rotary motion **2** a regular cycle of events in a set order or sequence **3** *agriculture* a planned sequence of cropping according to which the crops grown in successive seasons on the same land are varied so as to make a balanced demand on its resources of fertility **4** the spinning motion of a body, such as a planet, about an internal axis **5** *maths* **a** a circular motion of a configuration about a given point, without a change in shape **b** a transformation in which the coordinate axes are rotated by a fixed angle about the origin > **rotational** *adj*

Rotavator *n trademark* a mechanical cultivator with rotary blades

rote *adj* **1** done by routine repetition: *rote learning* ▷ *n* **2 by rote** by repetition: *we learned by rote* ▸ HISTORY origin unknown

roti *n, pl* **rotis** a type of flat bread eaten in the Caribbean and in India

rotisserie *n* a rotating spit on which meat and poultry can be cooked ▸ HISTORY French

rotor *n* **1** the rotating part of a machine or device, such as the revolving arm of the distributor of an internal-combustion engine **2** a rotating device with blades projecting from a hub which produces thrust to lift a helicopter

rotten *adj* **1** decomposing or decaying: *rotten vegetables* **2** breaking up through age or hard use: *the window frames are rotten* **3** *informal* very bad: *what rotten luck!* **4** morally corrupt: *this country's politics are rotten and out of date* **5** *informal* miserably unwell: *I had glandular fever and spent that year feeling rotten* **6** *informal* distressed and embarrassed: *I'm feeling rotten as a matter of fact, rotten and guilty* ▷ *adv* **7** *informal* extremely; very much: *men fancy her rotten* ▸ HISTORY Old Norse *rotinn*

rotter *n chiefly Brit, old-fashioned slang* a despicable person

Rottweiler (rot-vile-er) *n* a large sturdy dog with a smooth black-and-tan coat and a docked tail ▸ HISTORY *Rottweil*, German city where it was first bred

rotund (roe-tund) *adj* **1** round and plump **2** (of speech) pompous or grand ▸ HISTORY Latin *rotundus* > **rotundity** *n* > **rotundly** *adv*

rotunda *n* a circular building or room, esp. with a dome ▸ HISTORY Italian *rotonda*

rouble *or* **ruble** (roo-bl) *n* the standard monetary unit of Russia and Tadzhikistan ▸ HISTORY Russian *rubl*

roué (roo-ay) *n* a man who leads a sensual and immoral life ▸ HISTORY French

rouge *n* **1** a red cosmetic for adding colour to the cheeks ▷ *vb* **rouging, rouged 2** to apply rouge to ▸ HISTORY French: red

rough *adj* **1** not smooth; uneven or irregular **2** not using enough care or gentleness **3** difficult or unpleasant: *tomorrow will be a rough day* **4** approximate: *a rough guess* **5** violent or stormy **6** troubled by violence or crime: *he lived in a rough* area **7** incomplete or basic: *a rough draft* **8** lacking refinement: *a rough shelter* **9** (of ground) covered with scrub or rubble **10** harsh or grating to the ear **11** harsh or sharp: *the rough interrogation of my father* **12** unfair: *rough luck* **13** *informal* ill: *Feeling rough? A good stiff drink will soon fix that!* **14** shaggy or hairy: *the rough wool of her sweater* **15** (of work, etc.) requiring physical rather than mental effort: *wear gloves for any rough work* ▷ *vb* **16** to make rough **17** **rough it** *informal* to live without the usual comforts of life ▷ *n* **18** rough ground **19** a sketch or preliminary piece of artwork **20** *informal* a violent person **21** **in rough** in an unfinished or crude state **22** **the rough** *golf* the part of the course beside the fairways where the grass is untrimmed **23** the unpleasant side of something: *you have to take the rough with the smooth* ▷ *adv* **24** roughly **25** **sleep rough** to spend the night in the open without shelter ▷ See also **rough out** ▸ HISTORY Old English *rūh* > **roughly** *adv*

roughage *n* the coarse indigestible constituents of food, which help digestion

rough-and-ready *adj* **1** hastily prepared but adequate for the purpose **2** (of a person) without formality or refinement

rough-and-tumble *n* **1** a playful fight **2** a disorderly situation

roughcast *n* **1** a mixture of plaster and small stones for outside walls ▷ *vb* **-casting, -cast** **2** to put roughcast on (a wall)

roughen *vb* to make or become rough

rough-hewn *adj* roughly shaped or cut without being properly finished

roughhouse *n* *slang* rough or noisy behaviour

roughneck *n* *slang* **1** a violent person **2** a worker on an oil rig

rough out *vb* to prepare (a sketch or report) in preliminary form: *he offered to rough out some designs for the sets*

roughshod *adv* **ride roughshod over** to act with complete disregard for

roulette *n* a gambling game in which a ball is dropped onto a revolving wheel with numbered coloured slots ▸ HISTORY French

round *adj* **1** having a flat circular shape, like a hoop **2** having the shape of a ball **3** curved; not angular **4** involving or using circular motion **5** complete **6** *maths* **a** forming or expressed by a whole number, with no fraction **b** expressed to the nearest ten, hundred, or thousand: *in round figures* ▷ *adv* **7** on all or most sides **8** on or outside the circumference or perimeter: *ponds which are steeply sided all round* **9** in rotation or revolution: *she swung round on me* **10** by a circuitous route: *the road to the farm goes round by the pond* **11** to all members of a group: *handing cigarettes round* **12** to a specific place: *the boys invited him round* **13** **all year round** throughout the year ▷ *prep* **14** surrounding or encircling: *wrap your sash round the wound* **15** on all or most sides of: *the man turned in a circle, looking all round him* **16** on or outside the circumference or perimeter of **17** from place to place in: *a trip round the island in an ancient*

bus **18** reached by making a partial circuit about: *just round the corner* **19** revolving about: *if you have two bodies in orbit, they orbit round their common centre of gravity* ▷ *vb* **20** to move round: *as he rounded the last corner, he raised a fist* ▷ *n* **21** a round shape or object **22** a session: *a round of talks* **23** a series: *the petty round of domestic matters* **24** a series of calls: *a paper round* **25** **the daily round** the usual activities of a person's day **26** a playing of all the holes on a golf course **27** a stage of a competition: *the first round of the Portuguese Open* **28** one of a number of periods in a boxing or wrestling match **29** a single turn of play by each player in a card game **30** a number of drinks bought at one time for a group of people **31** a bullet or shell for a gun **32** a single discharge by a gun **33** *music* a part song in which the voices follow each other at equal intervals **34** circular movement **35** **a** a single slice of bread **b** a serving of sandwiches made from two complete slices of bread **36** a general outburst: *a round of applause* **37** **in the round a** in full detail **b** *theatre* with the audience all round the stage **38** **go the rounds** (of information or infection) to be passed around from person to person ▸ HISTORY Old French *ront*

roundabout *n* **1** a road junction in which traffic moves in one direction around a central island **2** a revolving circular platform, often with seats, on which people ride for amusement ▷ *adj* **3** not straightforward: *the roundabout sea route; she thought of asking about it in a roundabout way* ▷ *adv, prep* **round about** **4** approximately: *round about 1900*

round character *n* *literature* a character in a story who is well-developed and interesting, changing as the story progresses and therefore wholly convincing

roundel *n* **1** a circular identifying mark on military aircraft **2** a small circular object ▸ HISTORY Old French *rondel* little circle

roundelay *n* a song in which a line or phrase is repeated as a refrain ▸ HISTORY Old French *rondelet*

rounders *n* *Brit & NZ* a bat and ball game in which players run between posts after hitting the ball

Roundhead *n* *English history* a supporter of Parliament against Charles I during the Civil War ▸ HISTORY referring to their short-cut hair

roundly *adv* bluntly or thoroughly: *the Church roundly criticized the bill*

round on *vb* to attack or reply to (someone) with sudden irritation or anger

round robin *n* **1** a petition with the signatures in a circle to disguise the order of signing **2** a tournament in which each player plays against every other player

round-shouldered *adj* denoting poor posture with drooping shoulders and a slight forward bending of the back

round table *n* a meeting of people on equal terms for discussion

Round Table *n* **1** (in Arthurian legend) the table of King Arthur, shaped so that his knights could sit around as equals **2** one of an organization of clubs of young business and professional men who meet in order to further charitable work

round-the-clock *adj* throughout the day and night

round trip *n* a journey to a place and back again

round up *vb* **1** to gather together: *the police had rounded up a circle of drug users* **2** to raise (a number) to the nearest whole number or ten, hundred, or thousand above it ▷ *n* **roundup** **3** a summary or discussion of news and information **4** the act of gathering together livestock or people

roundworm *n* a worm that is a common intestinal parasite of man

rouse¹ *vb* **rousing, roused** **1** to wake up **2** to provoke or excite: *his temper was roused and he had a gun* **3** **rouse oneself** to become energetic ▶ **HISTORY** origin unknown

rouse² (rhymes with **mouse**) *vb* (foll. by on) Austral to scold or rebuke

rouseabout *n* Austral & NZ a labourer in a shearing shed

rousing *adj* lively or vigorous: *a rousing speech*

roustabout *n* **1** an unskilled labourer on an oil rig **2** Austral & NZ another word for **rouseabout**

rout¹ *n* **1** an overwhelming defeat **2** a disorderly retreat **3** a noisy rabble ▷ *vb* **4** to defeat and put to flight ▶ **HISTORY** Anglo-Norman *rute*

rout² *vb* **1** to find by searching **2** to drive out: *the dissidents had been routed out* **3** to dig (something) up ▶ **HISTORY** variant of ROOT²

route *n* **1** the choice of roads taken to get to a place **2** a fixed path followed by buses, trains, etc. between two places **3** a chosen way or method: *the route to prosperity* ▷ *vb* **routeing, routed** **4** to send by a particular route ▶ **HISTORY** Old French *rute*

routemarch *n* mil a long training march

router *n* computers a device that allows data to be moved efficiently between two points on a network

routine *n* **1** a usual or regular method of procedure **2** the boring repetition of tasks: *mindless routine* **3** a set sequence of dance steps **4** computers a program or part of a program performing a specific function: *an input routine* ▷ *adj* **5** relating to or characteristic of routine ▶ **HISTORY** Old French *route* a customary way

roux (roo) *n* a cooked mixture of fat and flour used as a basis for sauces ▶ **HISTORY** French: brownish

rove *vb* **roving, roved** **1** to wander about (a place) **2** (of the eyes) to look around ▶ **HISTORY** probably from Old Norse > **rover** *n*

row¹ (rhymes with **know**) *n* **1** an arrangement of people or things in a line: *a row of shops* **2** a line of seats in a cinema or theatre **3** Brit a street lined with identical houses **4** maths a horizontal line of numbers **5** **in a row** in succession: *five championships in a row* ▶ **HISTORY** Old English *rāw, rēw*

row² (rhymes with **know**) *vb* **1** to propel (a boat) by using oars **2** to carry (people or goods) in a rowing boat **3** to take part in the racing of rowing boats as

a sport ▷ *n* **4** an act or spell of rowing **5** an excursion in a rowing boat ▶ **HISTORY** Old English *rōwan* > **rowing** *n*

row³ (rhymes with **cow**) *informal n* **1** a noisy quarrel **2** a controversy or dispute: *the row over Europe* **3** a noisy disturbance: *go to the insurance offices and kick up a row about your money* **4** a reprimand ▷ *vb* **5** to quarrel noisily ▶ **HISTORY** origin unknown

rowan *n* a European tree with white flowers and red berries; mountain ash ▶ **HISTORY** Scandinavian

rowdy *adj* **-dier, -diest** **1** rough, noisy, or disorderly ▷ *n, pl* **-dies** **2** a person like this ▶ **HISTORY** origin unknown > **rowdily** *adv*

rowel (rhymes with **towel**) *n* a small spiked wheel at the end of a spur ▶ **HISTORY** Old French *roel* a little wheel

rowing boat *n* a small pleasure boat propelled by oars. Usual US and Canad word: **rowboat**

rowlock (rol-luk) *n* a swivelling device attached to the top of the side of a boat that holds an oar in place

royal *adj* **1** of or relating to a king or queen or a member of his or her family: *the royal yacht* **2** **Royal** supported by or in the service of royalty: *the Royal Society of Medicine* **3** very grand: *royal treatment* ▷ *n* **4** informal a king or queen or a member of his or her family ▶ **HISTORY** Old French *roial* > **royally** *adv*

Royal Air Force *n* the air force of the United Kingdom

royal assent *n* law (in Britain) the formal signing of an Act of Parliament by the sovereign, by which it becomes law

royalist *n* **1** a supporter of a monarch or monarchy ▷ *adj* **2** of or relating to royalists > **royalism** *n*

royal jelly *n* a substance secreted by worker bees and fed to all larvae when very young and to larvae destined to become queens throughout their growth

Royal Marines *pl n* Brit a corps of soldiers specially trained in amphibious warfare

royalty *n, pl* **-ties** **1** royal people **2** the rank or power of a king or queen **3** a percentage of the revenue from the sale of a book, performance of a work, use of a patented invention or of land, paid to the author, inventor, or owner

royal warrant *n* an authorization to a tradesman to supply goods to a royal household

RP Received Pronunciation

RPI (in Britain) retail price index: a measure of the changes in the average level of retail prices of selected goods

rpm revolutions per minute

RR **1** Right Reverend **2** US & Canad rural route

RSA **1** Republic of South Africa **2** (in New Zealand) Returned Services Association **3** Royal Scottish Academy **4** Royal Society of Arts

RSI repetitive strain injury: pain in the arm caused by repeated awkward movements, such as in typing

RSM (in Britain) regimental sergeant major

RSPCA (in Britain) Royal Society for the Prevention of Cruelty to Animals

RSS *n* Rich Site Summary (*or* Really Simple Syndication): a way of allowing internet users to receive updates from selected websites on their browsers

RSVP please reply ▸ HISTORY French *répondez s'il vous plaît*

Rt Hon. Right Honourable: a title of respect for a Privy Councillor, certain peers, and the Lord Mayor or Lord Provost of certain cities

Ru *chem* ruthenium

RU486 *n* the technical name for **abortion pill**

rub *vb* **rubbing, rubbed 1** to apply pressure and friction to (something) with a circular or backwards-and-forwards movement **2** to move (something) with pressure along or against (a surface) **3** to clean, polish, or dry by rubbing **4** to spread with pressure, esp. so that it can be absorbed: *rub beeswax into all polishable surfaces* **5** to chafe or fray through rubbing **6** to mix (fat) into flour with the fingertips, as in making pastry **7 rub it in** to emphasize an unpleasant fact **8 rub up the wrong way** to annoy ▷ *n* **9** the act of rubbing **10 the rub** the obstacle or difficulty: *there's the rub* ▷ See also **rub along** ▸ HISTORY origin unknown

rub along *vb* **1** to have a friendly relationship **2** to continue in spite of difficulties

rubato *music n, pl* **-tos 1** flexibility of tempo in performance: *his playing brought much beautifully felt but never sentimental rubato to the music* ▷ *adj, adv* **2** to be played with a flexible tempo ▸ HISTORY Italian, literally: robbed

rubber¹ *n* **1** an elastic material obtained from the latex of certain plants, such as the rubber tree **2** a similar substance produced synthetically **3** a piece of rubber used for erasing something written **4** *US, slang* a condom **5 rubbers** *US* rubber-coated waterproof overshoes ▷ *adj* **6** made of or producing rubber ▸ HISTORY the tree was so named because its product was used for rubbing out writing > **rubbery** *adj*

rubber² *n* **1** *Bridge, whist* a match of three games **2** a series of matches or games in various sports ▸ HISTORY origin unknown

rubberize *or* **-ise** *vb* **-izing, -ized** *or* **-ising, -ised** to coat or treat with rubber

rubberneck *US & NZ, slang vb* **1** to stare in a naive or foolish manner ▷ *n* **2** a person who stares inquisitively **3** a sightseer or tourist

rubber plant *n* **1** a large house plant with glossy leathery leaves **2** same as **rubber tree**

rubber stamp *n* **1** a device used for imprinting dates or signatures on forms or invoices **2** automatic authorization of something **3** a person or body that gives official approval to decisions taken elsewhere but has no real power ▷ *vb* **rubber-stamp 4** *informal* to approve automatically

rubber tree *n* a tropical tree cultivated for its latex, which is the major source of commercial rubber

rubbish *n* **1** discarded or waste matter **2** anything worthless or of poor quality: *the rubbish on television*

3 foolish words or speech ▷ *vb* **4** *informal* to criticize ▸ HISTORY origin unknown > **rubbishy** *adj*

rubble *n* **1** debris from ruined buildings **2** pieces of broken stones or bricks ▸ HISTORY origin unknown

rubella (roo-**bell**-a) *n* a mild contagious viral disease characterized by cough, sore throat, and skin rash. Also called: **German measles** ▸ HISTORY Latin *rubellus* reddish

Rubicon (**roo**-bik-on) *n* **cross the Rubicon** to commit oneself to a course of action which cannot be altered ▸ HISTORY a stream in N Italy: by leading his army across it, Julius Caesar caused civil war in Rome in 49 BC

rubicund (**roo**-bik-kund) *adj* *old-fashioned* of a reddish colour ▸ HISTORY Latin *rubicundus*

rubidium (roo-**bid**-ee-um) *n* *chem* a soft highly reactive radioactive metallic element used in electronic valves, photocells, and special glass. Symbol: Rb ▸ HISTORY Latin *rubidus* red

rub off *vb* **1** to remove or be removed by rubbing: *rub the skins off the hazelnuts* **2** to have an effect through close association: *glamour can rub off on you by association*

rub out *vb* **1** to remove or be removed with a rubber **2** *US, slang* to murder

rubric (**roo**-brik) *n* **1** a set of rules of conduct or procedure, esp. one for the conduct of Christian church services **2** a title or heading in a book ▸ HISTORY Latin *ruber* red

ruby *n, pl* **-bies 1** a deep red transparent precious gemstone ▷ *adj* **2** deep red **3** denoting a fortieth anniversary: *a ruby wedding* ▸ HISTORY Latin *ruber* red

ruche *n* a strip of pleated or frilled lace or ribbon used to decorate clothes ▸ HISTORY French, literally: beehive

ruck¹ *n* **1 the ruck** ordinary people, often in a crowd **2** *rugby* a loose scrum that forms around the ball when it is on the ground ▸ HISTORY probably from Old Norse

ruck² *n* **1** a wrinkle or crease ▷ *vb* **2** to wrinkle or crease: *the toe of his shoe had rucked up one corner of the pale rug* ▸ HISTORY Scandinavian

rucksack *n* *Brit, Austral & S African* a large bag, with two straps, carried on the back ▸ HISTORY from German

rudder *n* **1** *naut* a vertical hinged piece that projects into the water at the stern, used to steer a boat **2** a vertical control surface attached to the rear of the fin used to steer an aircraft ▸ HISTORY Old English *rōther* > **rudderless** *adj*

ruddy *adj* **-dier, -diest 1** (of the complexion) having a healthy reddish colour **2** red or pink: *a ruddy glow* ▷ *adv, adj* **3** *informal* bloody: *too ruddy slow; I just went through the ruddy ceiling* ▸ HISTORY Old English *rudig*

rude *adj* **1** insulting or impolite **2** vulgar or obscene: *rude words* **3** unexpected and unpleasant: *we received a rude awakening* **4** roughly or crudely made: *the rude hovels* **5** robust or sturdy: *the very picture of rude health* **6** lacking refinement ▸ HISTORY Latin *rudis* > **rudely** *adv* > **rudeness** *n*

r

rudiment *n* **1 rudiments a** the simplest and most basic stages of a subject: *the rudiments of painting* **b** a partially developed version of something: *the rudiments of a democratic society* **2** *biol* an organ or part that is incompletely developed or no longer functions ▶ HISTORY Latin *rudimentum* > **rudimentary** *adj*

rue¹ *vb* **ruing, rued** *literary* to feel regret for ▶ HISTORY Old English *hrēowan*

rue² *n* an aromatic shrub with bitter evergreen leaves formerly used in medicine ▶ HISTORY Greek *rhutē*

rueful *adj* feeling or expressing sorrow or regret: *a rueful smile* > **ruefully** *adv*

ruff¹ *n* **1** a circular pleated or fluted cloth collar **2** a natural growth of long or coloured hair or feathers around the necks of certain animals or birds **3** a bird of the sandpiper family ▶ HISTORY from *ruffle*

ruff² *n, vb* *cards* same as **trump¹** (senses 1, 2) ▶ HISTORY Old French *roffle*

ruffian *n* a violent lawless person ▶ HISTORY Old French *rufien*

Ruffini's organs *pl n* *anat* a sensory nerve ending that is sensitive to heat ▶ HISTORY from Angelo *Ruffini*, Italian anatomist

ruffle *vb* **-fling, -fled 1** to disturb the smoothness of: *the wind was ruffling Dad's hair* **2** to annoy or irritate **3** (of a bird) to erect (its feathers) in anger or display **4** to flick (cards or pages) rapidly ▷ *n* **5** a strip of pleated material used as a trim ▶ HISTORY Germanic

rufous *adj* (of birds or animals) reddish-brown ▶ HISTORY Latin *rufus*

rug *n* **1** a small carpet **2** a thick woollen blanket **3** *slang* a wig **4 pull the rug out from under** to betray or leave defenceless ▶ HISTORY Scandinavian

rugby *or* **rugby football** *n* a form of football played with an oval ball in which the handling and carrying of the ball is permitted ▶ HISTORY after the public school at *Rugby*, where it was first played

rugby league *n* a form of rugby played between teams of 13 players

rugby union *n* a form of rugby played between teams of 15 players

rugged (**rug**-gid) *adj* **1** rocky or steep: *the rugged mountains of Sicily's interior* **2** with an uneven or jagged surface **3** (of the face) strong-featured **4** rough, sturdy, or determined in character **5** (of equipment or machines) designed to withstand rough treatment or use in rough conditions ▶ HISTORY probably from Old Norse

rugger *n* *chiefly Brit, informal* rugby

ruin *vb* **1** to destroy or spoil completely: *the suit was ruined* **2** to cause (someone) to lose money: *the first war ruined him* ▷ *n* **3** the state of being destroyed or decayed **4** loss of wealth or position **5** a destroyed or decayed building or town **6** something that is severely damaged: *my heart was an aching ruin* ▶ HISTORY Latin *ruina* a falling down

ruination *n* **1** the act of ruining or the state of being ruined **2** something that causes ruin

ruinous *adj* **1** causing ruin or destruction **2** more expensive than can reasonably be afforded: *ruinous rates of exchange* > **ruinously** *adv*

rule *n* **1** a statement of what is allowed, for example in a game or procedure **2** a customary form or procedure: *he has his own rule: be firm, be clear, but never be rude* **3 the rule** the common order of things: *humanitarian gestures were more the exception than the rule* **4** the exercise of governmental authority or control: *the rule of President Marcos* **5** the period of time in which a monarch or government has power: *four decades of Communist rule* **6** a device with a straight edge for guiding or measuring: *a slide rule* **7** *printing* a long thin line or dash **8** *Christianity* a systematic body of laws and customs followed by members of a religious order **9** *law* an order by a court or judge **10 as a rule** usually ▷ *vb* **ruling, ruled 11** to govern (people or a political unit) **12** to be pre-eminent or superior **13** to be customary or prevalent: *chaos ruled as the scene turned into one of total confusion* **14** to decide authoritatively: *the judges ruled that men could be prosecuted for rape offences against their wives* **15** to mark with straight parallel lines or one straight line **16** to restrain or control ▶ HISTORY Old French *riule*

rule of law *n* *law* the principle that everyone is subject to the law

rule of thumb *n* a rough and practical approach, based on experience, rather than theory

rule out *vb* **1** to dismiss from consideration **2** to make impossible

ruler *n* **1** a person who rules or commands **2** a strip of wood, metal, or plastic, with straight edges, used for measuring and drawing straight lines

ruling *adj* **1** controlling or exercising authority **2** predominant ▷ *n* **3** a decision of someone in authority

rum¹ *n* alcoholic drink made from sugar cane ▶ HISTORY origin unknown

rum² *adj* **rummer, rummest** *Brit, slang* strange or unusual ▶ HISTORY origin unknown

Rumanian *adj, n* same as **Romanian**

rumba *n* **1** a rhythmic and syncopated dance of Cuban origin **2** music for this dance ▶ HISTORY Spanish

rumble *vb* **-bling, -bled 1** to make or cause to make a deep echoing sound: *thunder rumbled overhead* **2** to move with such a sound: *a slow freight train rumbled past* **3** *Brit, slang* to find out about (someone or something): *his real identity was rumbled* ▷ *n* **4** a deep resonant sound **5** *slang* a gang fight ▶ HISTORY probably from Middle Dutch *rummelen* > **rumbling** *adj, n*

rumbustious *adj* boisterous or unruly ▶ HISTORY probably variant of *robustious*

ruminant *n* **1** a mammal that chews the cud, such as cattle, sheep, deer, goats, and camels ▷ *adj* **2** of ruminants **3** meditating or contemplating in a slow quiet way

ruminate *vb* **-nating, -nated 1** (of ruminants) to chew (the cud) **2** to meditate or ponder ▶ HISTORY

Latin *ruminare* to chew the cud **> rumination** *n* **> ruminative** *adj*

rummage *vb* **-maging, -maged 1** to search untidily ▷ *n* **2** an untidy search through a collection of things ▶ **HISTORY** Old French *arrumage* to stow cargo

rummy *n* a card game based on collecting sets and sequences ▶ **HISTORY** origin unknown

rumour *or US* **rumor** *n* **1** information, often a mixture of truth and untruth, told by one person to another **2** gossip or common talk ▷ *vb* **3 be rumoured** to be circulated as a rumour: *he is rumoured to have at least 53 yachts* ▶ **HISTORY** Latin *rumor*

rump *n* **1** a person's buttocks **2** the rear part of an animal's or bird's body **3** Also called: **rump steak** a cut of beef from the rump **4** a small core of members within a group who remain loyal to it: *the rump of the once-influential communist party* ▶ **HISTORY** probably from Old Norse

rumple *vb* **-pling, -pled** to make or become crumpled or dishevelled ▶ **HISTORY** Middle Dutch *rompelen*

rumpus *n, pl* **-puses** a noisy or confused commotion ▶ **HISTORY** origin unknown

run *vb* **running, ran, run 1** to move on foot at a rapid pace **2** to pass over (a distance or route) in running: *being a man isn't about running the fastest mile* **3** to take part in (a race): *I ran a decent race* **4** to carry out as if by running: *he is running errands for his big brother* **5** to flee **6** to travel somewhere in a vehicle **7** to give a lift to (someone) in a vehicle: *one wet day I ran her down to the service* **8** to drive or maintain and operate (a vehicle) **9** to travel regularly between places on a route: *trains running through the night* **10** to move or pass quickly: *he ran his hand across his forehead* **11** to function or cause to function: *run the film backwards* **12** to manage: *he ran a small hotel* **13** to continue in a particular direction or for a particular time or distance: *a road running alongside the Nile; a performing arts festival running in the city for six weeks* **14** *law* to have legal force or effect: *the lease runs for two more years* **15** to be subjected to or affected by: *she ran a high risk of losing her hair* **16** to tend or incline: *he was of medium height and running to fat* **17** to recur persistently or be inherent: *the capacity for infidelity ran in the genes* **18** to flow or cause (liquids) to flow: *sweat ran down her face* **19** to dissolve and spread: *the soles of the shoes peeled off and the colours ran* **20** (of stitches) to unravel **21** to spread or circulate: *rumours ran around quickly* **22** to publish or be published in a newspaper or magazine: *our local newspaper ran a story on the appeal* **23** *chiefly US & Canad* to stand as a candidate for political or other office: *he has formally announced his decision to run for the office of President* **24** to get past or through: *the oil tanker was hit as it tried to run the blockade* **25** to smuggle (goods, esp. arms) **26** (of fish) to migrate upstream from the sea, esp. in order to spawn **27** *cricket* to score (a run or number of runs) by hitting the ball and running between the wickets ▷ *n* **28** the act or an instance of running: *he broke into a run* **29** a distance covered by running or a period of running: *it's a short run of about 20 km* **30** a trip in a vehicle, esp. for pleasure: *our only treat is a run in the car to Dartmoor* **31** free and unrestricted access: *he had the run of the house* **32 a** a period of time during which a machine or computer operates **b** the amount of work performed in such a period **33** a continuous or sustained period: *a run of seven defeats* **34** a continuous sequence of performances: *the play had a long run* **35** *cards* a sequence of winning cards in one suit: *a run of spades* **36** type, class, or category: *he had nothing in common with the usual run of terrorists* **37** a continuous and urgent demand: *a run on the pound* **38** a series of unravelled stitches, esp. in tights **39** a steeply inclined course, esp. a snow-covered one used for skiing **40** an enclosure for domestic fowls or other animals: *the chicken run* **41** (esp. in Australia and New Zealand) a tract of land for grazing livestock **42** the migration of fish upstream in order to spawn **43** *music* a rapid scalelike passage of notes **44** *cricket* a score of one, normally achieved by both batsmen running from one end of the wicket to the other after one of them has hit the ball **45** *baseball* an instance of a batter touching all four bases safely, thereby scoring **46 a run for one's money** *informal* **a** a close competition **b** pleasure or success from an activity **47 in the long run** as an eventual outcome **48 on the run** escaping from arrest **49 the runs** *slang* diarrhoea ▷ See also **runabout, run across**, etc. ▶ **HISTORY** Old English *runnen*

runabout *n* **1** a small car used for short journeys ▷ *vb* **run about 2** to move busily from place to place

run across *vb* to meet unexpectedly by chance

run away *vb* **1** to go away **2** to escape **3** (of a horse) to gallop away uncontrollably: *the horse ran away with him* **4 run away with a** to abscond or elope with: *I ran away with David* **b** to escape from the control of: *he let his imagination run away with him* **c** to win easily or be certain of victory in (a competition): *the Spaniards at one stage seemed to be running away with the match* ▷ *n* **runaway 5** a person or animal that runs away ▷ *adj* **runaway 6** no longer under control: *a runaway train* **7** (of a race or victory) easily won

run down *vb* **1** to be rude about: *he is busy running us down and insulting other Europeans* **2** to reduce in number or size: *it should be possible to run down the existing hospitals almost entirely* **3** (of a device such as a clock or battery) to lose power gradually and cease to function **4** to hit and knock to the ground with a moving vehicle **5** to pursue and find or capture: *while I was there, Moscow ran me down, convinced I was ready to defect* ▷ *adj* **run-down 6** tired or ill **7** shabby or dilapidated ▷ *n* **rundown 8** a reduction in number or size **9** a brief review or summary

rune *n* **1** any of the characters of the earliest Germanic alphabet **2** an obscure piece of writing using mysterious symbols ▶ **HISTORY** Old Norse *rūn* secret **> runic** *adj*

r

rung[1] *n* **1** one of the bars forming the steps of a ladder **2** a crosspiece between the legs of a chair ▶ HISTORY Old English *hrung*

rung[2] *vb* the past participle of **ring**[1]

run-holder *n* Austral & NZ the owner or manager of a sheep or cattle station

run in *vb* **1** to run (an engine) gently, usually when it is new **2** *informal* to arrest ▶ *n* **run-in** *informal* **3** an argument or quarrel **4** an approach to the end of an event: *the run-in for the championship*

run into *vb* **1** to be beset by: *the mission has run into difficulty* **2** to meet unexpectedly **3** to extend to: *businessmen denied losses running into the thousands* **4** to collide with

runnel *n* *literary* a small stream ▶ HISTORY Old English *rynele*

runner *n* **1** a competitor in a race **2** a messenger for a firm **3** a person involved in smuggling **4 a** either of the strips of metal or wood on which a sledge runs **b** the blade of an ice skate **5 bot** a slender horizontal stem of a plant, such as the strawberry, that grows along the surface of the soil and produces new roots and shoots **6** a long strip of cloth used to decorate a table or as a rug **7** a roller or guide for a sliding component **8 do a runner** *slang* to run away to escape trouble or to avoid paying for something

runner bean *n* the edible pod and seeds of a type of climbing bean plant

runner-up *n*, *pl* **runners-up** a person who comes second in a competition

running *adj* **1** maintained continuously: *a running battle* **2** without interruption: *for the third day running* **3** flowing: *rinse them under cold running water* **b** supplied through a tap: *there is no electricity, no running water, and no telephone* **4** operating: *running costs* **5** discharging pus: *a running sore* **6** accomplished at a run: *a running jump* **7** moving or slipping easily, as a rope or a knot ▶ *n* **8** the act of moving or flowing quickly **9** management or organization: *the running of the farm* **10** the operation or maintenance of a machine **11 in** or **out of the running** having or not having a good chance in a competition **12 make the running** to set the pace in a competition or race

running board *n* a board along the side of a vehicle, for help in stepping into it

running head *n* *printing* a heading printed at the top of every page of a book

running mate *n* **1** US a candidate for the lesser of two linked positions, esp. a candidate for the vice-presidency **2** a horse that pairs another in a team

running repairs *pl n* repairs that are done without greatly disrupting operations

runny *adj* **-nier, -niest 1** tending to flow: *a runny egg* **2** producing moisture: *a runny nose*

run off *vb* **1** to leave quickly **2 run off with a** to run away in order to marry or live with **b** to steal **3** to produce (copies of a document) on a machine **4** to drain (liquid) or (of liquid) to be drained ▶ *n* **run-off 5** an extra race or contest to decide the winner after a tie **6** *geog* that portion of rainfall that runs into streams as surface water rather than being absorbed into ground water or evaporating **7** NZ grazing land for cattle

run-of-the-mill *adj* ordinary or average

run-on line *n* *prosody* a line that is not complete at the end of a line of poetry but continues onto the next line without a pause

run out *vb* **1** to use up or (of a supply) to be used up: *we soon ran out of gas* **2** to become invalid: *my passport has run out* **3 run out on** *informal* to desert or abandon **4** *cricket* to dismiss (a running batsman) by breaking the wicket with the ball while he is running between the wickets ▶ *n* **run-out 5** *cricket* dismissal of a batsman by running him out

run over *vb* **1** to knock down (a person) with a moving vehicle **2** to overflow **3** to examine hastily

runt *n* **1** the smallest and weakest young animal in a litter **2** an undersized or inferior person ▶ HISTORY origin unknown

run up *vb* **1** to amass: *running up massive debts* **2** to make by sewing together quickly **3 run up against** to experience (difficulties) ▶ *n* **run-up 4** the time just before an event: *the run-up to the elections*

runway *n* a hard level roadway where aircraft take off and land

rupee *n* the standard monetary unit of a number of countries including India and Pakistan ▶ HISTORY Hindi *rupaīyā*

rupture *n* **1** the act of breaking or the state of being broken **2** a breach of peaceful or friendly relations **3** *pathol* a hernia ▶ *vb* **-turing, -tured 4** to break or burst **5** to cause a breach in relations or friendship **6** to affect or be affected with a hernia ▶ HISTORY Latin *rumpere* to burst forth

rural *adj* in or of the countryside ▶ HISTORY Latin *ruralis*

rural dean *n* *chiefly Brit* a member of the clergy with authority over a group of parishes

rural urban fringe *n* *geog* the area around the very edge of a town or city

ruse (**rooz**) *n* an action or plan intended to mislead someone ▶ HISTORY Old French

rush[1] *vb* **1** to move or do very quickly **2** to force (someone) to act hastily **3** to make a sudden attack upon (a person or place): *scores of pubescent girls rushed the stage* **4** to proceed or approach in a reckless manner **5** to come or flow quickly or suddenly: *the water rushed in, and the next instant the boat was swamped* ▶ *n* **6** a sudden quick or violent movement **7** Brit, Austral & NZ a sudden demand or need **8** a sudden surge towards someone or something: *the gold rush* **9** a sudden surge of sensation **10** a sudden flow of air or liquid **11 rushes** (in film-making) the initial prints of a scene before editing ▶ *adj* **12** done with speed or urgency: *a rush job* ▶ HISTORY Old French *ruser* to put to flight

rush[2] *n* a plant which grows in wet places and has a slender pithy stem ▶ HISTORY Old English *risce, rysce* > **rushy** *adj*

r

rush hour *n* a period at the beginning and end of the working day when large numbers of people are travelling to or from work

rusk *n* a hard brown crisp biscuit, often used for feeding babies ▶ HISTORY Spanish or Portuguese *rosca* screw, bread shaped in a twist

russet *adj* **1** *literary* reddish-brown: *a disarray of russet curls* ▷ *n* **2** an apple with a rough reddish-brown skin ▶ HISTORY Latin *russus*

Russian *adj* **1** of Russia ▷ *n* **2** a person from Russia **3** the official language of Russia and, formerly, of the Soviet Union

Russian roulette *n* an act of bravado in which a person spins the cylinder of a revolver loaded with only one cartridge and presses the trigger with the barrel against his or her own head

rust *n* **1** a reddish-brown oxide coating formed on iron or steel by the action of oxygen and moisture **2** a fungal disease of plants which produces a reddish-brown discolouration ▷ *adj* **3** reddish-brown ▷ *vb* **4** to become coated with a layer of rust **5** to deteriorate through lack of use: *my brain had rusted up* ▶ HISTORY Old English *rūst*

rustic *adj* **1** of or resembling country people **2** of or living in the country **3** crude, awkward, or uncouth **4** made of untrimmed branches: *rustic furniture* ▷ *n* **5** a person from the country ▶ HISTORY Latin *rusticus* > **rusticity** *n*

rusticate *vb* **-cating, -cated 1** *Brit* to send (a student) down from university for a specified time as a punishment **2** to retire to the country **3** to make or become rustic ▶ HISTORY Latin *rus* the country

rustle¹ *vb* **-tling, -tled 1** to make a low crisp whispering sound: *the leaves rustled in the breeze* ▷ *n* **2** this sound ▶ HISTORY Old English *hrūxlian*

rustle² *vb* **-tling, -tled** *chiefly US & Canad* to steal (livestock) ▶ HISTORY probably from RUSTLE¹ (in the sense: to move with a quiet sound) > **rustler** *n*

rustle up *vb* *informal* to prepare or find at short notice: *Bob rustled up a meal*

rusty *adj* **rustier, rustiest 1** affected by rust: *a rusty old freighter* **2** reddish-brown **3** out of practice in a skill or subject: *your skills may be a little rusty, but your past experience will more than make up for that* > **rustily** *adv* > **rustiness** *n*

rut¹ *n* **1** a groove or furrow in a soft road, caused by wheels **2** dull settled habits or way of living: *his career was in a rut* ▶ HISTORY probably from French *route* road

rut² *n* **1** a recurrent period of sexual excitement in certain male ruminants ▷ *vb* **rutting, rutted 2** (of male ruminants) to be in a period of sexual excitement ▶ HISTORY Old French *rut* noise, roar

ruthenium *n* *chem* a rare hard brittle white metallic element. Symbol: Ru ▶ HISTORY Medieval Latin *Ruthenia* Russia, where it was discovered

rutherfordium *n* *chem* an artificially produced radioactive element. Symbol: Rf ▶ HISTORY after E. *Rutherford*, physicist

ruthless *adj* **1** feeling or showing no mercy **2** thorough and forceful, regardless of effect: *the ruthless pursuit of cost-effectiveness* ▶ HISTORY *ruth* pity > **ruthlessly** *adv* > **ruthlessness** *n*

RV Revised Version (of the Bible)

rye *n* **1** a tall grasslike cereal grown for its light brown grain **2** the grain of this plant **3** Also called: **rye whiskey** whisky distilled from rye ▶ HISTORY Old English *ryge*

rye-grass *n* any of several grasses grown for fodder

r

Ss

s second (of time)

S 1 South(ern) 2 *chem* sulphur 3 *physics* siemens

-'s *suffix* 1 forming the possessive singular of nouns and some pronouns: *woman's; one's* 2 forming the possessive plural of nouns whose plurals do not end in -s: *children's* 3 forming the plural of numbers, letters, or symbols: *20's* 4 *informal* contraction of *is* or *has*: *it's over* 5 *informal* contraction of *us* with *let*: *let's go*

SA 1 Salvation Army 2 South Africa 3 South America 4 South Australia

SAA South African Airways

Sabbath *n* 1 Saturday, observed by Jews as the day of worship and rest 2 Sunday, observed by Christians as the day of worship and rest ▶ HISTORY Hebrew *shābath* to rest

sabbatical *adj* 1 denoting a period of leave granted at intervals to university teachers for rest, study, or travel: *a sabbatical year* ▷ *n* 2 a sabbatical period ▶ HISTORY see SABBATH

SABC South African Broadcasting Corporation

sable *n, pl* **-bles** *or* **-ble** 1 a marten of N Asia, N Europe, and America, with dark brown luxuriant fur 2 the highly valued fur of this animal, used to make coats and hats ▷ *adj* 3 dark brown-to-black ▶ HISTORY Slavic

sable antelope *n* a large black African antelope with stout backward-curving horns

sabot (**sab**-oh) *n* a heavy wooden or wooden-soled shoe; clog ▶ HISTORY French

sabotage *n* 1 the deliberate destruction or damage of equipment, for example by enemy agents or dissatisfied employees 2 deliberate obstruction of or damage to a cause or effort ▷ *vb* **-taging, -taged** 3 to destroy or disrupt by sabotage ▶ HISTORY French

saboteur *n* a person who commits sabotage ▶ HISTORY French

sabre *or US* **saber** *n* 1 a heavy single-edged cavalry sword with a curved blade 2 a light sword used in fencing, with a narrow V-shaped blade ▶ HISTORY German (dialect) *Sabel*

sac *n* a pouch or pouchlike part in an animal or plant ▶ HISTORY Latin *saccus*

saccharin *n* an artificial sweetener ▶ HISTORY Greek *sakkharon* sugar

saccharine *adj* 1 excessively sweet or sentimental: *saccharine ballads* 2 like or containing sugar or saccharin

sacerdotal *adj formal* of priests or the priesthood ▶ HISTORY Latin *sacerdos* priest

sachet *n* 1 a small sealed usually plastic envelope containing a small portion of a substance such as shampoo 2 a small soft bag of perfumed powder, placed in drawers to scent clothing ▶ HISTORY French

sack¹ *n* 1 a large bag made of coarse cloth or thick paper and used for carrying or storing goods 2 the amount contained in a sack 3 **the sack** *informal* dismissal from employment 4 *slang* bed 5 **hit the sack** *slang* to go to bed ▷ *vb* 6 *informal* to dismiss from employment ▶ HISTORY Greek *sakkos* > **sacklike** *adj*

sack² *n* 1 the plundering of a captured town or city by an army or mob ▷ *vb* 2 to plunder and partially destroy (a town or city) ▶ HISTORY French *mettre à sac* to put (loot) in a sack

sackcloth *n* 1 same as **sacking** 2 garments made of such cloth, worn formerly to indicate mourning 3 **sackcloth and ashes** an exaggerated attempt to apologize or compensate for a mistake or wrongdoing

sacking *n* coarse cloth woven from flax, hemp, or jute, and used to make sacks

sacrament *n* 1 a symbolic religious ceremony in the Christian Church, such as baptism or communion 2 Holy Communion 3 something regarded as sacred ▶ HISTORY Latin *sacrare* to consecrate > **sacramental** *adj*

sacred *adj* 1 exclusively devoted to a god or gods; holy 2 connected with religion or intended for religious use: *sacred music* 3 regarded as too important to be changed or interfered with: *sacred principles of free speech* 4 **sacred to** dedicated to: *the site is sacred to Vishnu* ▶ HISTORY Latin *sacer* holy

sacred cow *n informal* a person, custom, belief, or institution regarded as being beyond criticism ▶ HISTORY alluding to the Hindu belief that cattle are sacred

sacrifice *n* 1 a surrender of something of value in order to gain something more desirable or prevent some evil 2 a ritual killing of a person or animal as an offering to a god 3 a symbolic offering of something to a god 4 the person or animal killed or offered ▷ *vb* **-ficing, -ficed** 5 to make a sacrifice (of) 6 *chess* to permit or force one's opponent to capture (a piece) as a tactical move ▶ HISTORY Latin *sacer* holy + *facere* to make > **sacrificial** *adj*

sacrilege *n* 1 the misuse of or disrespect shown to something sacred 2 disrespect for a person who is widely admired or a belief that is widely accepted: *it is a sacrilege to offend democracy* ▶ HISTORY Latin *sacrilegus* temple robber > **sacrilegious** *adj*

sacristan *n* a person in charge of the contents of a church; sexton ▶ HISTORY Latin *sacer* holy

sacristy *n, pl* **-ties** a room attached to a church or chapel where the sacred objects are kept

sacrosanct *adj* regarded as too important to be criticized or changed: *weekend rest days were considered sacrosanct by staff* ▶ HISTORY Latin *sacer* holy + *sanctus* hallowed > **sacrosanctity** *n*

S

sacrum (**say**-krum) *n, pl* **-cra** *anat* the large wedge-shaped bone in the lower part of the back ▷ **HISTORY** Latin *os sacrum* holy bone, because it was used in sacrifices

sad *adj* **sadder, saddest** **1** feeling sorrow; unhappy **2** causing, suggesting, or expressing sorrow: *a sad story* **3** deplorably bad: *the garden was in a sad state* **4** regrettable: *it's rather sad he can't be with us* **5** *Brit, informal* ridiculously pathetic: *a sad, boring little wimp* **6** **pack a sad** *NZ, slang* to express sadness or displeasure strongly ▷ **HISTORY** Old English *sæd* weary > **sadly** *adv* > **sadness** *n*

sadden *vb* to make (someone) sad

saddle *n* **1** a seat for a rider, usually made of leather, placed on a horse's back and secured under its belly **2** a similar seat on a bicycle, motorcycle, or tractor **3** a cut of meat, esp. mutton, consisting of both loins **4** **in the saddle** in a position of control ▷ *vb* **-dling, -dled** **5** to put a saddle on (a horse): *we saddled up at dawn* **6** **saddle with** to burden with (a responsibility): *he was also saddled with debt* ▷ **HISTORY** Old English *sadol, sadul*

saddleback *n* **1** an animal with a marking resembling a saddle on its back **2** a hill with a concave outline at the top > **saddle-backed** *adj*

saddlebag *n* a pouch or small bag attached to the saddle of a horse, bicycle, or motorcycle

saddler *n* a person who makes, deals in, or repairs saddles and other leather equipment for horses

saddlery *n, pl* **-dleries** **1** saddles and harness for horses collectively **2** the work or place of work of a saddler

saddo *n, pl* **-dos, -does** *Brit, informal* a socially inadequate or pathetic person

Sadducee (**sad**-yew-see) *n* *Judaism* a member of an ancient Jewish sect that denied the resurrection of the dead and accepted only the traditional written law

sadhu (**sah**-doo) *n* a Hindu wandering holy man ▷ **HISTORY** Sanskrit

sadism (**say**-diz-zum) *n* the gaining of pleasure from infliction of suffering on another person ▷ **HISTORY** after the Marquis de *Sade*, soldier & writer > **sadist** *n* > **sadistic** *adj* > **sadistically** *adv*

sadomasochism *n* the combination of sadistic and masochistic elements in one person, characterized by both submissive and aggressive periods in relationships with others > **sadomasochist** *n* > **sadomasochistic** *adj*

s.a.e. *Brit, Austral & NZ* stamped addressed envelope

safari *n, pl* **-ris** an overland expedition for hunting or observing animals, esp. in Africa ▷ **HISTORY** Swahili: journey

safari park *n* an enclosed park in which wild animals are kept uncaged in the open and can be viewed by the public from cars or buses

safe *adj* **1** giving security or protection from harm: *a safe environment* **2** free from danger: *she doesn't feel safe* **3** taking or involving no risks: *a safe bet* **4** not dangerous: *the beef is safe to eat* **5** **on the safe side** as a precaution ▷ *n* **6** a strong metal container

with a secure lock, for storing money or valuables ▷ **HISTORY** Old French *salf* > **safely** *adv*

safe-conduct *n* **1** a document giving official permission to travel through a dangerous region, esp. in time of war **2** the protection given by such a document

safeguard *vb* **1** to protect (something) from being harmed or destroyed ▷ *n* **2** a person or thing that ensures protection against danger or harm: *safeguards to prevent air collisions*

safekeeping *n* protection from theft or damage: *I put my money in a bank for safekeeping*

safe sex *or* **safer sex** *n* nonpenetrative sex, or intercourse using a condom, intended to prevent the spread of AIDS

safety *n* **1** the quality or state of being free from danger **2** shelter: *they swam to safety*

safety belt *n* same as **seat belt**

safety curtain *n* a fireproof curtain that can be lowered to separate the auditorium from the stage in a theatre to prevent the spread of a fire

safety lamp *n* a miner's oil lamp designed to prevent it from igniting combustible gas

safety net *n* **1** a large net under a trapeze or high wire to catch performers if they fall **2** something that can be relied on for help in the event of difficulties: *the social security safety net*

safety pin *n* a pin bent back on itself so that it forms a spring, with the point shielded by a guard when closed

safety valve *n* **1** a valve in a boiler or machine that allows fluid or gases to escape at excess pressure **2** an outlet that allows one to express strong feelings without harming or offending other people: *sport acted as a safety valve for his pent-up frustrations*

Saffir-Simpson Hurricane Scale *n* *meteorol* a scale for measuring the strength of an hurricane, according to its speed and potential to cause damage ▷ **HISTORY** after Herbert *Saffir* (1917–2007), American civil engineer, and Robert *Simpson* (1912–2014), American meteorologist

safflower *n* a thistle-like plant with orange-yellow flowers, which yields a dye and an oil used in paints, medicines, and cooking ▷ **HISTORY** Old French *saffleur*

saffron *n* **1** a type of crocus with purple or white flowers with orange stigmas **2** the dried orange-coloured stigmas of this plant, used for colouring or flavouring ▷ *adj* **3** orange-yellow ▷ **HISTORY** Arabic *za'farān*

sag *vb* **sagging, sagged** **1** to sink in the middle, under weight or pressure: *the bed sagged nearly to the floor* **2** (of courage or spirits) to weaken or tire **3** (of clothes) to hang loosely or unevenly **4** to fall in value: *the stock market sagged* ▷ *n* **5** the act or state of sagging ▷ **HISTORY** from Old Norse > **saggy** *adj*

saga (**sah**-ga) *n* **1** a medieval Scandinavian legend telling the adventures of a hero or a family **2** *informal* a long story or series of events: *the long-running saga of the hostage issue* ▷ **HISTORY** Old Norse

S

sagacious *adj formal* wise or sensible ▶ HISTORY Latin *sagax* > **sagaciously** *adv* > **sagacity** *n*

sage¹ *n* **1** a person, esp. an old man, regarded as being very wise ▷ *adj* **2** very wise or knowledgeable, esp. as the result of age or experience

■ **WORD HISTORY**
■ In this sense, 'sage' comes via French from Latin
■ *sapere*, meaning 'to be wise'.

sage² *n* **1** a Mediterranean plant with grey-green leaves which are used in cooking for flavouring **2** short for **sagebrush**

■ **WORD HISTORY**
■ In this sense, 'sage' comes from Latin *salvus*,
■ meaning 'healthy', because of the supposed
■ medicinal properties of the plant.

sagebrush *n* an aromatic plant of W North America, with silver-green leaves and large clusters of small white flowers

Sagittarius *n astrol* the ninth sign of the zodiac; the Archer ▶ HISTORY Latin

sago *n* an edible starch from the powdered pith of the sago palm tree, used for puddings and as a thickening agent ▶ HISTORY Malay *sāgū*

sahib *n* an Indian term of address equivalent to *sir*, formerly used as a mark of respect to a European man ▶ HISTORY Urdu

said *adj* **1** named or mentioned already: *she had heard that the said lady was also a medium* ▷ *vb* **2** the past of **say**

sail *n* **1** a sheet of canvas or other fabric, spread on rigging to catch the wind and move a ship over water **2** a voyage on such a ship: *a relaxing sail across the lake* **3** a ship or ships with sails: *to travel by sail* **4** one of the revolving arms of a windmill **5 set sail** to begin a voyage by water **6 under sail a** under way **b** with sail hoisted ▷ *vb* **7** to travel in a boat or ship: *to sail around the world* **8** to begin a voyage: *he hoped to sail at eleven* **9** (of a ship) to move over the water **10** to navigate (a ship): *she sailed the schooner up the channel* **11** to sail over: *he had already sailed the Pacific* **12** to move along smoothly **13 sail into** *informal* to make a violent attack on **14 sail through** to progress quickly or effortlessly: *the top seed sailed through to the second round* ▶ HISTORY Old English *segl*

sailboard *n* a board with a mast and a single sail, used for windsurfing

sailcloth *n* **1** the fabric used for making sails **2** a canvas-like cloth used for clothing

sailfish *n, pl* **-fish** *or* **-fishes** a large tropical game fish, with a long sail-like fin on its back

sailor *n* **1** any member of a ship's crew, esp. one below the rank of officer **2** a person considered as liable or not liable to seasickness: *a good sailor*

sainfoin (**san**-foin) *n* a Eurasian plant with pink flowers, widely grown as feed for grazing farm animals ▶ HISTORY Medieval Latin *sanum faenum* wholesome hay

saint *n* **1** a person who after death is formally recognized by a Christian Church as deserving special honour because of having lived a very holy life **2** an exceptionally good person ▶ HISTORY Latin *sanctus* holy > **sainthood** *n* > **saintlike** *adj*

Saint Bernard *n* a very large dog with a dense red-and-white coat, formerly used as a mountain-rescue dog

Saint John's wort *n* a plant with yellow flowers

saintly *adj* behaving in a very good, patient, or holy way > **saintliness** *n*

Saint Vitus's dance *n pathol* a nontechnical name for **chorea**

saithe *n* *Brit* a dark-coloured food fish found in northern seas ▶ HISTORY Old Norse *seithr* coalfish

sake¹ *n* **1 for someone's** *or* **one's own sake** for the benefit or interest of someone or oneself **2 for the sake of something** for the purpose of obtaining or achieving something **3 for its own sake** for the enjoyment obtained by doing something **4** used in various exclamations of annoyance, impatience, or urgency: *for God's sake* ▶ HISTORY Old English *sacu* lawsuit (hence, a cause)

sake² *or* **saki** (**sah**-kee) *n* a Japanese alcoholic drink made from fermented rice ▶ HISTORY Japanese

salaam (sal-**ahm**) *n* **1** a Muslim greeting consisting of a deep bow with the right palm on the forehead **2** a greeting signifying peace ▷ *vb* **3** to make a salaam (to) ▶ HISTORY Arabic *salām* peace

salacious *adj* **1** having an excessive interest in sex **2** (of books, films, or jokes) concerned with sex in an unnecessarily detailed way ▶ HISTORY Latin *salax* fond of leaping > **salaciousness** *n*

salad *n* a dish of raw vegetables, often served with a dressing, eaten as a separate course or as part of a main course ▶ HISTORY Old French *salade*

salad days *pl n* a period of youth and inexperience

salad dressing *n* a sauce for salad, such as oil and vinegar or mayonnaise

salamander *n* **1** a tailed amphibian which looks like a lizard **2** a mythical creature supposed to live in fire ▶ HISTORY Greek *salamandra*

salami *n* a highly spiced sausage, usually flavoured with garlic ▶ HISTORY Italian

salaried *adj* earning or providing a salary: *a salaried employee, a salaried position*

salary *n, pl* **-ries** a fixed regular payment made by an employer, usually monthly, for professional or office work ▶ HISTORY Latin *salarium* the sum given to Roman soldiers to buy salt

salat *n* *Islam* a prayer that Muslims say five times a day ▶ HISTORY Arabic

sale *n* **1** the exchange of goods or property for an agreed sum of money **2** the amount sold **3** an event at which goods are sold at reduced prices **4** an auction **5 sales** the department dealing with selling its company's products ▶ HISTORY Old English *sala*

saleable *or US* **salable** *adj* fit for selling or capable of being sold > **saleability** *or US* **salability** *n*

saleroom *n* *chiefly Brit* a room where objects are displayed for sale by auction

salesman *n, pl* **-men** a man who sells goods in a shop

salesmanship *n* the technique of or skill in selling

salesperson *n, pl* **-people** *or* **-persons** a person who sells goods in a shop

sales pitch *or* **talk** *n* persuasive talk used by a salesperson in persuading a customer to buy something

saleswoman *n, pl* **-women** a woman who sells goods in a shop

saleyard *n Austral & NZ* an area with pens for holding animals before auction

salicylic acid (sal-liss-**ill**-ik) *n* a white crystalline substance used to make aspirin and as a fungicide ▷ HISTORY Latin *salix* willow

salient (**say**-lee-ent) *adj* **1** (of points or facts) most important: *the salient points of his speech* ▷ *n* **2** *mil* a projection of the forward line of an army into enemy-held territory ▷ HISTORY Latin *salire* to leap

saline (**say**-line) *adj* **1** of or containing salt: *a saline flavour* **2** *med* of or relating to a saline: *a saline drip* ▷ *n* **3** *med* a solution of sodium chloride and water ▷ HISTORY Latin *sal* salt

salinity *n chem* the condition of containing salt or the degree to which something contains salt

saliva (sal-**lie**-va) *n* the watery fluid secreted by glands in the mouth, which aids digestion ▷ HISTORY Latin > **salivary** *adj*

salivate *vb* **-vating, -vated** to produce saliva, esp. an excessive amount > **salivation** *n*

sallee *n Austral* **1** a SE Australian eucalyptus with a pale grey bark **2** an acacia tree. Also: **snow gum**

sallow *adj* (of human skin) of an unhealthy pale or yellowish colour ▷ HISTORY Old English *salu* > **sallowness** *n*

sally *n, pl* **-lies 1** a witty remark **2** a sudden brief attack by troops **3** an excursion ▷ *vb* **-lies, -lying, -lied 4 sally forth a** to set out on a journey **b** to set out in an energetic manner ▷ HISTORY Latin *salire* to leap

salmon *n, pl* **-ons** *or* **-on** a large pink-fleshed fish which is highly valued for food and sport: *salmon live in the sea but return to fresh water to spawn* ▷ HISTORY Latin *salmo*

salmonella (sal-mon-**ell**-a) *n* a kind of bacteria that can cause food poisoning ▷ HISTORY after Daniel E. *Salmon*, veterinary surgeon

salon *n* **1** a commercial establishment in which hairdressers or fashion designers carry on their business **2** an elegant room in a large house in which guests are received **3** an informal gathering, esp. in the 18th, 19th, and early 20th centuries, of major literary, artistic, and political figures in a fashionable household **4** an art exhibition ▷ HISTORY French

saloon *n* **1** a two-door or four-door car with a fixed roof **2** a comfortable but more expensive bar in a pub or hotel **3** a large public room on a passenger ship **4** *chiefly US & Canad* a place where alcoholic drink is sold and consumed ▷ HISTORY from *salon*

salsa *n* **1** a lively Puerto Rican dance **2** big-band music accompanying this dance ▷ HISTORY Spanish, literally: sauce

salsify *n, pl* **-fies** a Mediterranean plant with a long white edible root ▷ HISTORY Italian *sassefrica*

salt *n* **1** sodium chloride, a white crystalline substance, used for seasoning and preserving food **2** *chem* a crystalline solid compound formed from an acid by replacing its hydrogen with a metal **3** lively wit: *his humour added salt to the discussion* **4 old salt** an experienced sailor **5 rub salt into someone's wounds** to make an unpleasant situation even worse for someone **6 salt of the earth** a person or people regarded as the finest of their kind **7 take something with a pinch of salt** to refuse to believe something is completely true or accurate **8 worth one's salt** worthy of one's pay; efficient ▷ *vb* **9** to season or preserve with salt **10** to scatter salt over (an iced road or path) to melt the ice ▷ *adj* **11** preserved in or tasting of salt: *salt beef* ▷ See also **salt away, salts** ▷ HISTORY Old English *sealt* > **salted** *adj*

SALT Strategic Arms Limitation Talks *or* Treaty

saltation *n* **1** *biol* an abrupt variation in the appearance of an organism, species, etc. **2** *geog* the leaping movement of sand or soil particles carried in water or by the wind **3** a sudden abrupt movement ▷ HISTORY Latin *saltātiō* a dance, from *saltāre* to leap about

salt away *vb* to hoard or save (money) for the future

saltbush *n bot* a shrub that grows in alkaline desert regions

saltfish *n, pl* **-fish** *or* **-fishes** (in the Caribbean) cod which has been preserved by being coated with salt and then dried

saltire *n* **1** *heraldry* a diagonal cross on a shield **2** the national flag of Scotland, a white diagonal cross on a blue background

salt lake *n geog* a highly saline inland lake

salt lick *n* **1** a place where wild animals go to lick salt deposits **2** a block of salt given to domestic animals to lick

saltpan *n geog* a shallow basin, usually in a desert region, containing salt, gypsum, etc. that was deposited from an evaporated salt lake

saltpetre *or US* **saltpeter** *n* same as **potassium nitrate** ▷ HISTORY Latin *sal petrae* salt of rock

salts *pl n* **1** *med* mineral salts used as a medicine **2 like a dose of salts** *informal* very quickly

saltwater *adj* of or inhabiting salt water, esp. the sea: *saltwater fish*

salty *adj* **saltier, saltiest 1** of, tasting of, or containing salt **2** (esp. of humour) sharp and witty > **saltiness** *n*

salubrious *adj* favourable to health ▷ HISTORY Latin *salus* health > **salubrity** *n*

Saluki *n* a tall hound with a smooth coat and long fringes on the ears and tail ▷ HISTORY from *Saluq*, ancient Arabian city

salutary *adj* **1** (of an experience) producing a beneficial result despite being unpleasant:

a salutary reminder **2** promoting health ▶ HISTORY Latin *salutaris* wholesome

salutation *n* formal a greeting by words or actions ▶ HISTORY Latin *salutare* to greet

salute *vb* **-luting, -luted 1** to greet with friendly words or gestures of respect, such as bowing **2** to acknowledge with praise: *the statement salutes the changes of the past year* **3** *mil* to pay formal respect to (someone) by raising the right hand to the forehead ▷ *n* **4** the act of saluting as a formal military gesture of respect **5** the act of firing guns as a military greeting of honour ▶ HISTORY Latin *salutare* to greet

salvage *n* **1** the rescue of a ship or its cargo from loss at sea **2** the saving of any goods or property from destruction or waste **3** the goods or property so saved **4** compensation paid for the salvage of a ship or its cargo ▷ *vb* **-vaging, -vaged 5** to save (goods or property) from shipwreck, destruction, or waste **6** to gain (something beneficial) from a failure: *it's too late to salvage anything from the whole dismal display* ▶ HISTORY Latin *salvare* to save
> **salvageable** *adj*

salvation *n* **1** the act of preserving someone or something from harm **2** a person or thing that preserves from harm **3** *Christianity* the fact or state of being saved from the influence or consequences of sin ▶ HISTORY Latin *salvatio* saved

Salvation Army *n* a Christian body organized on military lines for working among disadvantaged people and spreading the Christian faith

salve *n* **1** an ointment for wounds **2** anything that heals or soothes ▷ *vb* **salving, salved 3 salve one's conscience** to do something in order to feel less guilty ▶ HISTORY Old English *sealf*

salver *n* a tray, usually a silver one, on which something is presented ▶ HISTORY Spanish *salva* tray from which the king's taster sampled food

salvia *n* any small plant or shrub of the sage genus ▶ HISTORY Latin

salvo *n, pl* **-vos** *or* **-voes 1** a simultaneous discharge of guns in battle or on a ceremonial occasion **2** an outburst of applause or questions ▶ HISTORY Italian *salva*, from Latin *salve!* greetings!

sal volatile (**sal** vol-**at**-ill-ee) *n* a solution of ammonium carbonate, used as smelling salts ▶ HISTORY New Latin: volatile salt

SAM surface-to-air missile

Samaritan *n* **1** short for **Good Samaritan 2** a member of a voluntary organization (**the Samaritans**) which offers counselling to people in despair, esp. by telephone

samarium *n* chem a silvery metallic element of the rare-earth series. Symbol: Sm ▶ HISTORY after Col. von *Samarski*, Russian inspector of mines

samba *n, pl* **-bas 1** a lively Brazilian dance **2** music for this dance ▶ HISTORY Portuguese

same *adj* (usually preceded by *the*) **1** being the very one: *she is wearing the same hat* **2** being the one previously referred to: *it causes problems for the same reason* **3** alike in kind or quantity: *the same age* **4** unchanged in character or nature: *his attitude is*

the same as ever **5 all the same** *or* **just the same** nevertheless; even so **6 be all the same** to be a matter of indifference: *it was all the same to me* ▷ *adv* **7** in the same way; similarly: *I felt much the same* ▷ *n* **8 the same** something that is like something else in kind or quantity: *this is basically much more of the same* ▶ HISTORY Old Norse *samr*
> **sameness** *n*

samizdat *n* (in the former Soviet Union) a system of secret printing and distribution of banned literature ▶ HISTORY Russian

samovar *n* a Russian metal tea urn in which the water is heated by an inner container ▶ HISTORY Russian

Samoyed *n* a dog with a thick white coat and a tightly curled tail ▶ HISTORY Russian *Samoed*

sampan *n* a small flat-bottomed boat with oars, used esp. in China ▶ HISTORY Chinese *san* three + *pan* board

samphire *n* a plant found on rocks by the seashore ▶ HISTORY French *herbe de Saint Pierre* Saint Peter's herb

sample *n* **1** a small part of anything, taken as being representative of a whole ▷ *vb* **-pling, -pled 2** to take a sample or samples of **3** *music* **a** to take a short extract from (one record) and mix it into a different backing track **b** to record (a sound) and feed it into a computerized synthesizer so that it can be reproduced at any pitch ▶ HISTORY Latin *exemplum*

sampler *n* **1** a piece of embroidery done to show the embroiderer's skill in using many different stitches **2** *music* a piece of electronic equipment used for sampling

sampling *n* **1** *statistics* the process of selecting a small random group and assuming that it is a representative sample of a much bigger group **2** *music* the process of taking a short musical extract and mixing it into a different backing track

samsara *n* **1** *Hinduism* the endless cycle of birth, death, and rebirth **2** *Buddhism* the rebirth of a person ▶ HISTORY Sanskrit, literally: a passing through

Samson *n* a man of outstanding physical strength ▶ HISTORY from the biblical character who was renowned for his strength

samurai *n, pl* **-rai** a member of the aristocratic warrior caste of feudal Japan ▶ HISTORY Japanese

sanatorium *or US* **sanitarium** *n, pl* **-riums** *or* **-ria 1** an institution providing medical treatment and rest for invalids or convalescents **2** *Brit* a room in a boarding school where sick pupils may be treated ▶ HISTORY Latin *sanare* to heal

sanctify *vb* **-fies, -fying, -fied 1** to make holy **2** to free from sin **3** to approve (an action or practice) as religiously binding: *she is trying to make amends for her marriage not being sanctified* ▶ HISTORY Latin *sanctus* holy + *facere* to make
> **sanctification** *n*

sanctimonious *adj* pretending to be very religious and virtuous ▶ HISTORY Latin *sanctimonia* sanctity

S

sanction n **1** permission granted by authority: *official sanction* **2** support or approval: *they could not exist without his sanction* **3** something that gives binding force to a law, such as a penalty for breaking it or a reward for obeying it **4 sanctions** coercive measures, such as boycotts and trade embargoes, taken by one or more states against another guilty of violating international law ▷ *vb* **5** to officially approve of or allow: *they do not want to sanction direct payments* **6** to confirm or ratify ▶ HISTORY Latin *sancire* to decree

sanctity n the quality of something considered so holy or important it must be respected totally: *the sanctity of the Sabbath; the sanctity of marriage*

sanctuary n, *pl* -**aries 1** a holy place, such as a consecrated building or shrine **2** the part of a church nearest the main altar **3** a place of refuge or protection for someone who is being chased or hunted **4** refuge or safety: *the sanctuary of your own home* **5** a place, protected by law, where animals can live and breed without interference ▶ HISTORY Latin *sanctus* holy

sanctum n, *pl* -**tums** or -**ta 1** a sacred or holy place **2** a room or place of total privacy ▶ HISTORY Latin

sand n **1** a powdery substance consisting of very small rock or mineral grains, found on the seashore and in deserts **2 sands** a large sandy area, esp. on the seashore or in a desert ▷ *vb* **3** to smooth or polish the surface of (something) with sandpaper or a sander **4** to fill with sand: *the channel sanded up* ▶ HISTORY Old English

sandal n a light shoe consisting of a sole held on the foot by thongs or straps ▶ HISTORY Greek *sandalon* > **sandalled** or US **sandaled** adj

sandalwood n **1** the hard light-coloured wood of a S Asian or Australian tree, which is used for carving and for incense, and which yields an aromatic oil used in perfumes **2** a tree yielding this wood ▶ HISTORY Sanskrit *candana*

sandbag n **1** a sack filled with sand used to make a temporary defence against gunfire or flood water ▷ *vb* -**bagging, -bagged 2** to protect or strengthen with sandbags

sandbank or **sand bar** n a bank of sand in a sea or river that may be exposed at low tide

sandblast n **1** a jet of sand blown from a nozzle under air or steam pressure ▷ *vb* **2** to clean or decorate (a surface) with a sandblast > **sandblaster** n

sand castle n a model of a castle made from sand

sander n a power-driven tool for smoothing surfaces, removing layers of paint from walls, etc.

sand martin n a small brown European songbird which nests in tunnels bored in sand or river banks

sandpaper n **1** a strong paper coated with sand or other abrasive material for smoothing or polishing a surface ▷ *vb* **2** to smooth or polish (a surface) with sandpaper

sandpiper n a wading shore bird with a long bill and slender legs

sandshoes *pl n* light canvas shoes with rubber soles

sandstone n a sedimentary rock consisting mainly of sand grains, much used in building

sandstorm n a strong wind that whips up clouds of sand, esp. in a desert

sandwich n **1** two or more slices of bread, usually buttered, with a layer of food between them ▷ *vb* **2** to place between two other things: *shops sandwiched between flats*

■ **WORD HISTORY**
■ Sandwiches are named after John Montagu
■ (1718–1792), the 4th Earl of Sandwich, who was
■ in the habit of spending whole days at
■ gambling tables. Since he did not want to leave
■ the tables to eat, he asked waiters to bring him
■ meals in the form of meat placed between two
■ slices of bread.

sandwich board n one of two connected boards that are hung over the shoulders in front of and behind a person to display advertisements

sandwich course n Brit an educational course consisting of alternate periods of study and industrial work

sandy adj **sandier, sandiest 1** resembling, containing, or covered with sand **2** (of hair) reddish-yellow > **sandiness** n

sane adj **1** having a normal healthy mind **2** sensible or well-judged: *sane advice* ▶ HISTORY Latin *sanus* healthy

sang vb the past tense of **sing**

sang-froid (sahng-**frwah**) n composure and calmness in a difficult situation ▶ HISTORY French, literally: cold blood

sangoma (sang-**go**-ma) n S African a witch doctor ▶ HISTORY Nguni (language group of southern Africa) *isangoma* a diviner

sangria n a Spanish drink of red wine, sugar, and orange or lemon juice ▶ HISTORY Spanish: a bleeding

sanguinary adj formal **1** (of a battle or fight) involving much violence and bloodshed **2** (of a person) eager to see violence and bloodshed **3** of or stained with blood ▶ HISTORY Latin *sanguinarius*

sanguine adj **1** cheerful and confident **2** (of the complexion) ruddy ▶ HISTORY Latin *sanguineus* bloody

Sanhedrin (**san**-id-rin) n Judaism the highest court and supreme council of the ancient Jewish nation

sanitary adj **1** promoting health by getting rid of dirt and germs **2** free from dirt or germs; hygienic ▶ HISTORY Latin *sanitas* health

sanitary towel or esp US **napkin** n a pad worn externally by women during menstruation to absorb the flow of blood

sanitation n **1** the use of sanitary measures to maintain public health **2** the drainage and disposal of sewage

sanity n **1** the state of having a normal healthy mind **2** good sense or soundness of judgment ▶ HISTORY Latin *sanitas* health

sank vb the past tense of **sink**

sans-culotte (sanz-kew-**lot**) *n* a revolutionary extremist ▶ HISTORY French, literally: without knee breeches, because during the French Revolution the revolutionaries wore trousers

Sanskrit *n* the classical literary language of India, used since ancient times for religious purposes ▶ HISTORY Sanskrit *samskrta* perfected > **Sanskritic** *adj*

Santa Claus *n* the legendary patron saint of children, who brings presents to children on Christmas Eve, commonly identified with Saint Nicholas

Santeria (san-ta-**ree**-ya) *n* a Caribbean religion combining elements of traditional African religion and Roman Catholicism ▶ HISTORY Spanish, literally: holiness

santero *n* **-ros** a priest of Santeria

sap¹ *n* **1** a thin liquid that circulates in a plant, carrying food and water **2** *slang* a gullible person ▷ *vb* **sapping, sapped 3** to drain of sap ▶ HISTORY Old English *sæp*

sap² *vb* **sapping, sapped 1** to weaken or exhaust the strength or confidence of **2** to undermine (an enemy position) by digging saps ▷ *n* **3** a deep and narrow trench used to approach or undermine an enemy position ▶ HISTORY Italian *zappa* spade

sapient (**say**-pee-ent) *adj often ironic* having great wisdom or sound judgment ▶ HISTORY Latin *sapere* to taste, know > **sapience** *n*

sapling *n* a young tree

saponify *vb* **-fies, -fying, -fied** *chem* to convert (a fat) into a soap by treatment with alkali ▶ HISTORY Latin *sapo* soap > **saponification** *n*

sapper *n* **1** a soldier who digs trenches **2** (in the British Army) a private of the Royal Engineers

sapphire *n* **1** a transparent blue precious stone ▷ *adj* **2** deep blue ▶ HISTORY Greek *sappheiros*

sappy *adj* **-pier, -piest** (of plants) full of sap

saprophyte *n* *biol* any plant, such as a fungus, that lives and feeds on dead organic matter ▶ HISTORY Greek *sapros* rotten + *phuton* plant

sarabande *or* **saraband** *n* **1** a stately slow Spanish dance **2** music for this dance ▶ HISTORY Spanish *zarabanda*

Saracen *n* **1** an Arab or Muslim who opposed the Crusades ▷ *adj* **2** of the Saracens ▶ HISTORY Late Greek *Sarakēnos*

sarcasm *n* **1** mocking or ironic language intended to insult someone **2** the use or tone of such language ▶ HISTORY Greek *sarkazein* to rend the flesh

sarcastic *adj* **1** full of or showing sarcasm **2** tending to use sarcasm: *a sarcastic critic* > **sarcastically** *adv*

sarcoma *n* *pathol* a malignant tumour beginning in connective tissue ▶ HISTORY Greek *sarkōma* fleshy growth

sarcophagus (sahr-**koff**-a-guss) *n*, *pl* **-gi** (-guy) *or* **-guses** a stone or marble coffin or tomb, esp. one bearing sculpture or inscriptions ▶ HISTORY Greek *sarkophagos* flesh-devouring

sardine *n*, *pl* **-dines** *or* **-dine 1** a small fish of the herring family, often preserved in tightly packed tins **2 like sardines** very closely crowded together ▶ HISTORY Latin *sardina*

sardonic *adj* (of behaviour) mocking or scornful ▶ HISTORY Greek *sardonios* > **sardonically** *adv*

sardonyx *n* a type of gemstone with alternating reddish-brown and white parallel bands ▶ HISTORY Greek *sardonux*

sargassum *n* a floating brown seaweed with long stringy fronds containing air sacs ▶ HISTORY Portuguese *sargaço*

sarge *n* *informal* sergeant

sari *or* **saree** *n*, *pl* **-ris** *or* **-rees** the traditional dress of Hindu women, consisting of a very long piece of cloth swathed around the body with one end over the shoulder ▶ HISTORY Hindi

sarking *n* *Scot, N English, Austral & NZ* flat planking supporting the roof cladding of a building ▶ HISTORY Scots *sark* shirt

sarky *adj* **-kier, -kiest** *Brit & NZ, informal* sarcastic

sarmie *n* *S African, children's slang* a sandwich

sarong *n* a garment worn by Malaysian men and women, consisting of a long piece of cloth tucked around the waist or under the armpits ▶ HISTORY Malay

sarsaparilla *n* a nonalcoholic drink prepared from the roots of a tropical American climbing plant ▶ HISTORY Spanish *sarzaparrilla*

sartorial *adj* *formal* of men's clothes or tailoring: *sartorial elegance* ▶ HISTORY Latin *sartor* a tailor

SAS (in Britain) Special Air Service

sash¹ *n* a long piece of cloth worn around the waist or over one shoulder, usually as a symbol of rank ▶ HISTORY Arabic *shāsh* muslin

sash² *n* **1** a frame that contains the panes of a window or door **2** a complete frame together with panes of glass ▶ HISTORY French *châssis* a frame

sash window *n* a window consisting of two sashes placed one above the other so that the window can be opened by sliding one frame over the front of the other

sassafras *n* a tree of North America, with aromatic bark used medicinally and as a flavouring ▶ HISTORY Spanish *sasafras*

Sassenach *n* *Scot & occasionally Irish* an English person ▶ HISTORY Gaelic *Sassunach*

sat *vb* the past of **sit**

Sat. Saturday

Satan *n* the Devil ▶ HISTORY Hebrew: plotter

satanic *adj* **1** of Satan **2** supremely evil or wicked

Satanism *n* the worship of Satan > **Satanist** *n, adj*

satchel *n* a small bag, usually with a shoulder strap ▶ HISTORY Old French *sachel*

sate *vb* **sating, sated** to satisfy (a desire or appetite) fully ▶ HISTORY Old English *sadian*

satellite *n* **1** a man-made device orbiting the earth or another planet, used in communications or to collect scientific information **2** a heavenly body orbiting a planet or star: *the earth is a satellite of the sun* **3** a country controlled by or dependent on a more powerful one ▷ *adj* **4** of, used in, or relating

S

to the transmission of television signals from a satellite to the home: *satellite TV; a satellite dish* ▶ HISTORY Latin *satelles* an attendant

satellite imagery *n* pictures of earth taken and transmitted from space

satellite town *n* a subordinate community dependent upon a larger adjacent city

satiate (**say**-she-ate) *vb* -**ating**, -**ated** to provide with more than enough, so as to disgust or weary: *enough cakes to satiate several children* ▶ HISTORY Latin *satiare* > **satiable** *adj* > **satiation** *n*

satiety (sat-**tie**-a-tee) *n formal* the feeling of having had too much

satin *n* **1** a fabric, usually made from silk or rayon, closely woven to give a smooth glossy surface on one side ▷ *adj* **2** like satin in texture: *satin polyurethane varnish* ▶ HISTORY Arabic *zaitūnī* > **satiny** *adj*

satinwood *n* **1** a hard wood with a satiny texture, used in fine furniture **2** the East Indian tree yielding this wood

satire *n* **1** the use of ridicule to expose incompetence, evil, or corruption **2** a play, novel, or poem containing satire ▶ HISTORY Latin *satira* a mixture > **satirical** *adj*

satirist *n* **1** a writer of satire **2** a person who uses satire

satirize *or* **-rise** *vb* -**rizing**, -**rized** *or* -**rising**, -**rised** to ridicule (a person or thing) by means of satire > **satirization** *or* -**risation** *n*

satisfaction *n* **1** the pleasure obtained from the fulfilment of a desire **2** something that brings fulfilment: *craft workers get satisfaction from their work* **3** compensation or an apology for a wrong done: *consumers unable to get satisfaction from their energy suppliers*

satisfactory *adj* **1** adequate or acceptable **2** giving satisfaction > **satisfactorily** *adv*

satisfy *vb* -**fies**, -**fying**, -**fied** **1** to fulfil the desires or needs of (a person): *his answer didn't satisfy me* **2** to provide sufficiently for (a need or desire): *to satisfy public demand* **3** to convince: *that trip did seem to satisfy her that he was dead* **4** to fulfil the requirements of: *unable to satisfy the conditions set by the commission* ▶ HISTORY Latin *satis* enough + *facere* to make > **satisfiable** *adj* > **satisfying** *adj*

satnav *n motoring, informal* satellite navigation

satrap *n* (in ancient Persia) a provincial governor or subordinate ruler ▶ HISTORY Old Persian *khshathrapāvan*, literally: protector of the land

SATs *Brit* standard assessment tasks

satsuma *n* a small loose-skinned variety of orange with easily separable segments ▶ HISTORY *Satsuma*, former province of Japan

saturate *vb* -**rating**, -**rated** **1** to soak completely **2** to fill so completely that no more can be added: *saturating the area with their men* **3** *chem* to combine (a substance) or (of a substance) to be combined with the greatest possible amount of another substance ▶ HISTORY Latin *saturare*

saturated solution *n chem* a solution containing the maximum amount of solute that can normally be dissolved in it at a particular temperature and pressure

saturation *n* **1** the process or state that occurs when one substance is filled so full of another substance that no more can be added **2** *mil* the use of very heavy force, esp. bombing, against an area

saturation point *n* **1** the point at which the maximum amount of a substance has been absorbed **2** the point at which some capacity is at its fullest; limit: *the market is close to saturation point*

Saturday *n* the seventh day of the week ▶ HISTORY Latin *Saturni dies* day of Saturn

Saturn *n* **1** the Roman god of agriculture and vegetation **2** the sixth planet from the sun, second largest in the solar system, around which revolve concentric rings

Saturnalia *n, pl* -**lia** *or* -**lias** **1** the ancient Roman festival of Saturn, renowned for its unrestrained revelry **2** *saturnalia* a wild party or orgy ▶ HISTORY Latin *Saturnalis* relating to Saturn

saturnine *adj* having a gloomy temperament or appearance ▶ HISTORY Latin *Saturnus* Saturn, from the gloomy influence attributed to the planet

satyr *n Greek myth* a woodland god represented as having a man's body with the ears, horns, tail, and legs of a goat ▶ HISTORY Greek *saturos*

sauce *n* **1** a liquid added to food to enhance its flavour **2** anything that adds interest or zest **3** *chiefly Brit, informal* impudent language or behaviour ▶ HISTORY Latin *salsus* salted

saucepan *n* a metal pan with a long handle and often a lid, used for cooking food·

saucer *n* **1** a small round dish on which a cup is set **2** something shaped like a saucer ▶ HISTORY Old French *saussier* container for sauce > **saucerful** *n*

saucy *adj* **saucier**, **sauciest** **1** cheeky or slightly rude in an amusing and light-hearted way **2** jaunty and boldly smart: *a saucy hat* > **sauciness** *n*

sauerkraut *n* a German dish of finely shredded pickled cabbage ▶ HISTORY German *sauer* sour + *Kraut* cabbage

sauna *n* **1** a Finnish-style hot steam bath, usually followed by a cold plunge **2** the place in which such a bath is taken ▶ HISTORY Finnish

saunter *vb* **1** to walk in a leisurely manner; stroll ▷ *n* **2** a leisurely pace or stroll ▶ HISTORY origin unknown

saurian *adj* of or resembling a lizard ▶ HISTORY Greek *sauros* lizard

sausage *n* **1** finely minced meat mixed with fat, cereal, and seasonings, in a tube-shaped casing **2** an object shaped like a sausage **3 not a sausage** *informal* nothing at all ▶ HISTORY Old French *saussiche*

sausage dog *n informal* same as **dachshund**

sausage roll *n* a roll of sausage meat in pastry

sausage sizzle *n Austral & NZ* an event at which sausages are barbecued, often to raise money for a school or other organization

sauté (**so**-tay) *vb* -**téing** *or* -**téeing**, -**téed** **1** to fry (food) quickly in a little fat ▷ *n* **2** a dish of sautéed food ▷ *adj* **3** sautéed until lightly brown: *sauté potatoes* ▶ HISTORY French: tossed

savage adj **1** wild and untamed: *savage tigers* **2** fierce and cruel: *savage cries* **3** (of peoples) uncivilized or primitive: *savage tribes* **4** rude, crude, and violent: *savage behaviour on the terraces* **5** (of terrain) wild and uncultivated ▷ n **6** a member of an uncivilized or primitive society **7** a fierce or vicious person ▷ vb **-aging, -aged** **8** to attack ferociously and wound: *savaged by a wild dog* **9** to criticize extremely severely: *savaged by the press for incompetence* ▶ HISTORY Latin *silvaticus* belonging to a wood > **savagely** adv

savagery n, pl **-ries** viciousness and cruelty

savannah or **savanna** n geog (in Africa) open grasslands, usually with scattered bushes or trees ▶ HISTORY Spanish *zavana*

savant n a very wise and knowledgeable man ▶ HISTORY French > **savante** fem n

save¹ vb **saving, saved** **1** to rescue or preserve (a person or thing) from danger or harm **2** to avoid the spending, waste, or loss of (something): *an appeal on television for the public to save energy* **3** to set aside or reserve (money or goods) for future use: *I'm saving for a vintage Mercedes* **4** to treat with care so as to preserve **5** to prevent the necessity for: *a chance saved him from having to make up his mind* **6** sport to prevent (a goal) by stopping (a ball or puck) **7** Christianity to free (someone) from the influence or consequences of sin ▷ n **8** sport the act of saving a goal **9** computers an instruction to write information from the memory onto a tape or disk ▶ HISTORY Old French *salver* > **savable** or **saveable** adj > **saver** n

save² old-fashioned prep **1** (often foll. by for) with the exception of: *the stage was empty save for a single chair* ▷ conj **2** but ▶ HISTORY Middle English *sauf*

save as you earn n (in Britain) a savings scheme operated by the government, in which regular deposits are made into a savings account from a salary

saveloy n Brit, Austral & NZ a highly seasoned smoked sausage made from salted pork ▶ HISTORY Italian *cervellato*

saving n **1** preservation from destruction or danger **2** a reduction in the amount of time or money used **3 savings** money saved for future use ▷ adj **4** tending to rescue or preserve ▷ prep **5** with the exception of

saving grace n a good quality in a person that prevents him or her from being entirely bad or worthless

saviour or US **savior** n a person who rescues another person or a thing from danger or harm ▶ HISTORY Church Latin *Salvator* the Saviour

Saviour or US **Savior** n Christianity Jesus Christ, regarded as the saviour of people from sin

savoir-faire (sav-wahr-**fair**) n the ability to say and do the right thing in any situation ▶ HISTORY French

savory n, pl **-vories** an aromatic plant whose leaves are used in cooking ▶ HISTORY Latin *satureia*

savour or US **savor** vb **1** to enjoy and appreciate (food or drink) slowly **2** to enjoy (a pleasure) for as long as possible: *an experience to be savoured* **3 savour of a** to have a suggestion of: *that could savour of ostentation* **b** to possess the taste or smell of: *the vegetables savoured of coriander* ▷ n **4** the taste or smell of something **5** a slight but distinctive quality or trace ▶ HISTORY Latin *sapor* taste

savoury or US **savory** adj **1** salty or spicy: *savoury foods* **2** attractive to the sense of taste or smell **3** pleasant or acceptable: *one of the book's less savoury characters* ▷ n, pl **-ries** **4** chiefly Brit a savoury dish served before or after a meal > **savouriness** or US **savoriness** n

savoy n a cabbage with a compact head and wrinkled leaves ▶ HISTORY after the Savoy region in France

savvy slang vb **-vies, -vying, -vied** **1** to understand ▷ n **2** understanding or common sense ▶ HISTORY corruption of Spanish *sabe (usted)* (you) know

saw¹ n **1** a cutting tool with a toothed metal blade or edge, either operated by hand or powered by electricity ▷ vb **sawing, sawed; sawed** or **sawn** **2** to cut with or as if with a saw **3** to form by sawing **4** to move (an object) from side to side as if moving a saw ▶ HISTORY Old English *sagu*

saw² vb the past tense of **see¹**

saw³ n old-fashioned a wise saying or proverb ▶ HISTORY Old English *sagu* a saying

saw doctor n NZ a sawmill specialist who sharpens and services saw blades

sawdust n particles of wood formed by sawing

sawfish n, pl **-fish** or **-fishes** a sharklike ray with a long toothed snout resembling a saw

sawhorse n Austral & NZ a structure for supporting wood that is being sawn

sawmill n a factory where timber is sawn into planks

sawyer n a person who saws timber for a living

sax n informal short for **saxophone**

saxifrage n an alpine rock plant with small white, yellow, purple, or pink flowers ▶ HISTORY Late Latin *saxifraga*, literally: rock breaker

Saxon n **1** a member of a West Germanic people who raided and settled parts of Britain in the fifth and sixth centuries AD **2** any of the West Germanic dialects spoken by the ancient Saxons ▷ adj **3** of the ancient Saxons or their language ▶ HISTORY Late Latin *Saxon-, Saxo*

saxophone n a brass wind instrument with keys and a curved metal body > **saxophonist** n

■ **WORD HISTORY**
■ The saxophone is named after its inventor
■ Adolphe Sax (1814-1894), a French musical-
■ instrument maker. Sax invented a number of
■ other musical instruments, including the
■ saxhorn, the sax-tromba, and the saxtuba.

say vb **saying, said** **1** to speak or utter **2** to express (an idea) in words: *I can't say what I feel* **3** to state (an opinion or fact) positively: *I say you are wrong* **4** to indicate or show: *the clock says ten to nine* **5** to recite: *to say grace* **6** to report or allege: *they say we*

say

There are a number of more interesting or creative words you can use in place of the basic verbs say, speak, and talk, if you want to describe the way in which a person says something.

DEFINITION 1

• If you **mention** something, you say something about it, usually briefly: He never **mentioned** that he had a new job.

• If you **observe** that something is the case, you make a comment about it, especially when it is something you have noticed or thought about a lot: "He's a very loyal friend," Daniel **observed**.

• If you **announce** something, you tell people about it publicly or officially: "We've bought a house!" she **announced**.

• If someone **asserts** a fact or belief, they state it firmly: "The facts are clear," the Prime Minister **asserted**.

• If you **declare** that something is true, you say that it is true in a firm, deliberate way: "I'm absolutely thrilled with the result," he **declared**.

• If you **put in** a remark, you interrupt someone or add to what they have said with the remark: "Not that it's any of your business," Max **put in**.

• When you **chat**, they talk to each other in a friendly and informal way: We were just **chatting** in the corridor.

• If you **converse** with someone, you talk to them: They were **conversing** in German.

• When people **natter**, they talk casually for a long time about unimportant things: The three of them were still **nattering** when I left.

• If you **gossip** with someone, you talk informally, especially about other people or events: We sat and **gossiped** well into the evening.

• If you **explain** something, you give details about it so that it can be understood: "We weren't married at that point," she **explained**.

• If you **ask** something, you say it in the form of a question because you want to know the answer: "How is Frank?" he **asked**.

• If you **inquire** about something, you ask for information about it: "Is something wrong?" he **inquired**.

• To **query** or **question** means to ask a question: "Can I help you?" the assistant **queried**. • "What if something goes wrong?" he **questioned** anxiously.

• When you **answer** or **reply** to someone who has just spoken, you say something back to them: "When are you leaving?" she asked. "Tomorrow," he **answered**. • "That's a nice car," he commented. "Thanks," she **replied**.

• When you **respond** to something that has been said, you react to it by saying something yourself: "Are you well enough to carry on?"

"Of course," she **responded** scornfully.

• To **retort** means to reply angrily to someone: "I don't agree," Liz said. "Who cares what you think?" he **retorted**.

• If someone **babbles**, they talk in a confused or excited way: "I'm so excited I don't know what I'm doing," she **babbled**.

• If you **chatter**, you talk quickly and excitedly about things which are not important: Everyone was **chattering** away in different languages.

• If you **gabble**, you say things so quickly that it is difficult for people to understand you: The child sat on his knee and **gabbled** excitedly.

• If you **prattle**, you talk a great deal about something unimportant: He was **prattling** on about this girl he had met the day before.

• If someone **rambles**, they talk but do not make much sense because they keep going off the subject: The old man **rambled** about his feud with his neighbours.

• If someone **breathes** something, they say it very quietly: "Oh, thank God you're here," he **breathed**.

• When you **whisper**, you say something very quietly, using your breath rather than your throat: "Keep your voice down," I **whispered**.

• If you **hiss** something, you say it forcefully in a whisper: "Stay here and don't make a sound," he **hissed**.

• If you **mumble**, you speak very quietly and not at all clearly, so that your words are hard to make out: "I didn't know I was meant to do it," she **mumbled**.

• If you **murmur** something, you speak very quietly, so that not many people can hear you: "How convenient," I **murmured**.

• If you **mutter**, you speak very quietly, often because you are complaining about something: "Oh great," he **muttered**, "That's all I need."

• If you **croak** something, you say it in a low, rough voice: "Water!" he **croaked**.

• If you **grunt** something, you say it in a low voice, often because you are annoyed or not interested: "Rubbish," I **grunted**, "You just didn't try hard enough."

• If you **rasp** something, you say it in a harsh, unpleasant voice: "Get into the car," he **rasped**.

• If you **groan** or **moan** something, you say it in a low voice, usually because you are unhappy or in pain: "My leg – I think it's broken," Eric **groaned**. • "I can't stand it any longer," she **moaned**.

• When someone **growls** something, they say it in a low, rough, and angry voice: "I ought to kill you for this," Sharpe **growled**.

• If you **snap** at someone, you speak to them in a sharp, unfriendly way: "Of course you can't have it," he **snapped**.

shall have rain today **7** to suppose as an example or possibility: *let us say that he is lying* **8** to convey by means of artistic expression: *what does the artist have to say in this picture?* **9** to make a case for: *there is much to be said for it* **10 go without saying** to be so obvious as to need no explanation **11 to say the least** at the very least ▷ *adv* **12** approximately: *there were, say, 20 people present* **13** for example: *choose a number, say, four* ▷ *n* **14** the right or chance to speak: *the opposition has hardly had a say in these affairs* **15** authority, esp. to influence a decision: *he has a lot of say* ▶ **HISTORY** Old English *secgan* See WORD FOCUS **say**

SAYE (in Britain) save as you earn

saying *n* a well-known phrase or sentence expressing a belief or a truth

Sb *chem* antimony ▶ **HISTORY** New Latin *stibium*

Sc *chem* scandium

SC South Carolina

scab *n* **1** the dried crusty surface of a healing skin wound or sore **2** *disparaging* a person who refuses to support a trade union's actions, and continues to work during a strike **3** a contagious disease of sheep, caused by a mite **4** a fungal disease of plants ▷ *vb* **scabbing, scabbed** **5** to become covered with a scab **6** *disparaging* to work as a scab ▶ **HISTORY** Old English *sceabb*

scabbard *n* a holder for a sword or dagger ▶ **HISTORY** Middle English *scauberc*

scabby *adj* **-bier, -biest 1** *pathol* covered with scabs **2** *informal* mean or despicable > **scabbiness** *n*

scabies (**skay**-beez) *n* a contagious skin infection caused by a mite, characterized by intense itching ▶ **HISTORY** Latin *scabere* to scratch

scabious (**skay**-bee-uss) *n* a plant with showy blue, red, or whitish dome-shaped flower heads ▶ **HISTORY** Medieval Latin *scabiosa herba* the scabies plant

scabrous (**skay**-bruss) *adj* **1** rough and scaly **2** indecent or crude: *scabrous stand-up comedy* ▶ **HISTORY** Latin *scaber* rough

scaffold *n* **1** a temporary framework used to support workmen and materials during the construction or repair of a building **2** a raised wooden platform on which criminals are hanged; gallows ▶ **HISTORY** Old French *eschaffaut*

scaffolding *n* **1** a scaffold or scaffolds **2** the building materials used to make scaffolds

scalar *maths n* **1** a quantity, such as time or temperature, that has magnitude but not direction ▷ *adj* **2** having magnitude but not direction ▶ **HISTORY** Latin *scala* ladder

scald *vb* **1** to burn with hot liquid or steam **2** to sterilize with boiling water **3** to heat (a liquid) almost to boiling point ▷ *n* **4** a burn caused by scalding ▶ **HISTORY** Late Latin *excaldare* to wash in warm water

scale¹ *n* **1** one of the thin flat overlapping plates covering the bodies of fishes and reptiles **2** a thin flat piece or flake **3** a coating which sometimes forms in kettles and hot-water pipes in areas

where the water is hard **4** tartar formed on the teeth ▷ *vb* **scaling, scaled 5** to remove the scales or coating from **6** to peel off in flakes or scales **7** to cover or become covered with scales ▶ **HISTORY** Old French *escale* > **scaly** *adj*

scale² *n* **1** (often *pl*) a machine or device for weighing **2** one of the pans of a balance **3 tip the scales** to have a decisive influence **4 tip the scales at** to amount in weight to ▶ **HISTORY** Old Norse *skål* bowl

scale³ *n* **1** a sequence of marks at regular intervals, used as a reference in making measurements **2** a measuring instrument with such a scale **3** the ratio between the size of something real and that of a representation of it: *the map has a scale of 1:10 000* **4** a series of degrees or graded system of things: *the Western wage scale for the same work* **5** a relative degree or extent: *growing flowers on a very small scale* **6** *music* a sequence of notes taken in ascending or descending order, esp. within one octave **7** *maths* the notation of a given number system: *the decimal scale* ▷ *vb* **scaling, scaled 8** *written* to climb to the top of (an object or height): *the men scaled a wall* **9 scale up** or **down** to increase or reduce proportionately in size: *the design can easily be scaled up; after five days the search was scaled down* ▶ **HISTORY** Latin *scala* ladder

scale drawing *n* a drawing whose proportions are exactly the same as those of the object represented

scalene *adj maths* (of a triangle) having all sides of unequal length ▶ **HISTORY** Greek *skalēnos*

scallion *n* a spring onion ▶ **HISTORY** Anglo-French *scalun*

scallop *n* **1** an edible marine mollusc with two fluted fan-shaped shells **2** a single shell of this mollusc **3** one of a series of small curves along an edge ▶ **HISTORY** Old French *escalope* shell > **scalloping** *n*

scalloped *adj* decorated with small curves along the edge

scallywag *n informal* a badly behaved but likeable person; rascal ▶ **HISTORY** origin unknown

scalp *n* **1** *anat* the skin and hair covering the top of the head **2** (formerly among Native Americans of N America) a part of this removed as a trophy from a slain enemy ▷ *vb* **3** to cut the scalp from **4** *informal, chiefly US* to buy and resell so as to make a high or quick profit ▶ **HISTORY** probably from Old Norse *skálpr* sheath

scalpel *n* a small surgical knife with a very sharp thin blade ▶ **HISTORY** Latin *scalper* a knife

scam *n slang* a stratagem for gain; a swindle

scamp *n* a mischievous person, esp. a child ▶ **HISTORY** probably from Middle Dutch *schampen* to decamp

scamper *vb* **1** to run about hurriedly or quickly ▷ *n* **2** the act of scampering ▶ **HISTORY** see SCAMP

scampi *n* large prawns, usually eaten fried in breadcrumbs ▶ **HISTORY** Italian

scan *vb* **scanning, scanned 1** to scrutinize carefully **2** to glance over quickly **3** *prosody* to analyse (verse) by examining its rhythmic structure **4** *prosody* (of a line or verse) to be metrically correct **5** to examine or search (an area) by systematically moving a beam of light or electrons, or a radar or sonar beam over it **6** *med* to obtain an image of (a part of the body) by means of ultrasound or a scanner ▷ *n* **7** an instance of scanning ▶ HISTORY Latin *scandere* to climb

scandal *n* **1** a disgraceful action or event: *the chairman resigned after a loans scandal* **2** shame or outrage arising from a disgraceful action or event: *the figures were a national scandal* **3** malicious gossip ▶ HISTORY Greek *skandalon* a trap > **scandalous** *adj* > **scandalously** *adv*

scandalize *or* **-ise** *vb* **-izing, -ized** *or* **-ising, -ised** to shock or be shocked by improper behaviour

scandalmonger *n* a person who spreads or enjoys scandal or gossip

Scandinavian *adj* **1** of Scandinavia (Norway, Sweden, Denmark, and often Finland, Iceland, and the Faeroe Islands) ▷ *n* **2** a person from Scandinavia **3** the northern group of Germanic languages, consisting of Swedish, Danish, Norwegian, Icelandic, and Faeroese

scandium *n chem* a rare silvery-white metallic element. Symbol: Sc ▶ HISTORY Latin *Scandia* Scandinavia, where discovered

scanner *n* **1** an aerial or similar device designed to transmit or receive signals, esp. radar signals **2** a device used in medical diagnosis to obtain an image of an internal organ or part **3** *computing* a device connected to a computer, which enables printed material, including text and pictures, to be scanned and converted into a form that can be stored in a computer

scansion *n* the metrical scanning of verse

scant *adj* scarcely sufficient: *some issues will get scant attention* ▶ HISTORY Old Norse *skamt* short

scanty *adj* **scantier, scantiest** barely sufficient or not sufficient > **scantily** *adv* > **scantiness** *n*

scapegoat *n* **1** a person made to bear the blame for others ▷ *vb* **2** to make a scapegoat of ▶ HISTORY *escape* + *goat*, coined to translate Biblical Hebrew *azāzēl*, probably goat for Azazel, mistakenly thought to mean 'goat that escapes'

scapula (**skap**-pew-la) *n, pl* **-lae** (-lee) the technical name for **shoulder blade** ▶ HISTORY Late Latin: shoulder

scapular *adj* **1** *anat* of the scapula ▷ *n* **2** a loose sleeveless garment worn by monks over their habits

scar¹ *n* **1** a mark left on the skin following the healing of a wound **2** a permanent effect on a person's character resulting from emotional distress **3** a mark on a plant where a leaf was formerly attached **4** a mark of damage ▷ *vb* **scarring, scarred 5** to mark or become marked with a scar ▶ HISTORY Greek *eskhara* scab

scar² *n* a bare craggy rock formation ▶ HISTORY Old Norse *sker* low reef

scarab *n* **1** the black dung-beetle, regarded by the ancient Egyptians as divine **2** an image or carving of this beetle ▶ HISTORY Latin *scarabaeus*

scarce *adj* **1** insufficient to meet the demand: *scarce water resources* **2** not common; rarely found **3 make oneself scarce** *informal* to go away ▷ *adv* **4** *archaic or literary* scarcely ▶ HISTORY Old French *scars*

scarcely *adv* **1** hardly at all **2** *often ironic* probably or definitely not: *that is scarcely justification for your actions*

scarcity *n, pl* **-ties** an inadequate supply

scare *vb* **scaring, scared 1** to frighten or be frightened **2 scare away** *or* **off** to drive away by frightening ▷ *n* **3** a sudden attack of fear or alarm: *you gave me a scare* **4** a period of general fear or alarm: *the latest AIDS scare* ▶ HISTORY Old Norse *skirra*

scarecrow *n* **1** an object, usually in the shape of a man, made out of sticks and old clothes, to scare birds away from crops **2** *informal* a raggedly dressed person

scaremonger *n* a person who starts or spreads rumours of disaster to frighten people > **scaremongering** *n*

scarf¹ *n, pl* **scarves** *or* **scarfs** a piece of material worn around the head, neck, or shoulders ▶ HISTORY origin unknown

scarf² *n, pl* **scarfs 1** a joint between two pieces of timber made by notching the ends and strapping or gluing the two pieces together ▷ *vb* **2** to join (two pieces of timber) by means of a scarf ▶ HISTORY probably from Old Norse

scarify *vb* **-fies, -fying, -fied 1** *surgery* to make slight incisions in (the skin) **2** *agriculture* to break up and loosen (topsoil) **3** to criticize without mercy ▶ HISTORY Latin *scarifare* to scratch open > **scarification** *n*

scarlatina *n* the technical name for **scarlet fever** ▶ HISTORY Italian *scarlatto* scarlet

scarlet *adj* bright red ▶ HISTORY Old French *escarlate* fine cloth

scarlet fever *n* an acute contagious disease characterized by fever, a sore throat, and a red rash on the body

scarp *n* **1** a steep slope or ridge of rock **2** *fortifications* the side of a ditch cut nearest to a rampart ▶ HISTORY Italian *scarpa*

scarper *vb* *chiefly Brit, slang* to run away or escape ▶ HISTORY origin unknown

Scart *or* **SCART** *n electronics* a plug-and-socket system which carries pictures and sound, used in home entertainment systems

scary *adj* **scarier, scariest** *informal* quite frightening

scat¹ *vb* **scatting, scatted** *informal* to go away in haste ▶ HISTORY origin unknown

scat² *n* **1** a type of jazz singing using improvised vocal sounds instead of words ▷ *vb* **scatting, scatted 2** to sing jazz in this way ▶ HISTORY perhaps imitative

scathing *adj* harshly critical: *there was a scathing review of the play in the paper* ▶ HISTORY Old Norse *skathi* harm > **scathingly** *adv*

scatology *n* preoccupation with obscenity, esp. with references to excrement ▶ HISTORY Greek *skat-* excrement + -LOGY > **scatological** *adj*

scatter *vb* **1** to throw about in various directions: *scatter some oatmeal on top of the cake* **2** to separate and move in various directions; disperse: *the infantry were scattering* ▷ *n* **3** the act of scattering **4** a number of objects scattered about ▶ HISTORY probably variant of *shatter*

scatterbrain *n* a person who is incapable of serious thought or concentration > **scatterbrained** *adj*

scatter diagram *n statistics* a graph with points plotted along two axes at right angles to each other to show the relationship between two variable quantities

scatty *adj* **-tier, -tiest** *informal* rather absent-minded ▶ HISTORY from *scatterbrained* > **scattiness** *n*

scavenge *vb* **-enging, -enged** to search for (anything usable) among discarded material

scavenger *n* **1** a person who collects things discarded by others **2** any animal that feeds on discarded or decaying matter ▶ HISTORY Old French *escauwer* to scrutinize

SCE (in Scotland) Scottish Certificate of Education

scenario *n*, *pl* **-narios 1** a summary of the plot and characters of a play or film **2** an imagined sequence of future events: *the likeliest scenario is another general election* ▶ HISTORY Italian

scene *n* **1** the place where an action or event, real or imaginary, occurs **2** an incident or situation, real or imaginary, esp. as described or represented **3** a division of an act of a play, in which the setting is fixed and the action is continuous **4** *films* a shot or series of shots that constitutes a unit of the action **5** the backcloths or screens used to represent a location in a play or film set **6** the view of a place or landscape **7** a display of emotion or loss of temper in public: *you do not want to cause a scene* **8** *informal* a particular activity or aspect of life, and all the things associated with it: *the club scene* **9 behind the scenes a** backstage **b** in secret or in private ▶ HISTORY Greek *skēnē* tent, stage

scenery *n* **1** the natural features of a landscape **2** *theatre* the painted backcloths or screens used to represent a location in a theatre or studio

scenic *adj* **1** of or having beautiful natural scenery: *untouched scenic areas* **2** of the stage or stage scenery: *scenic artists*

scent *n* **1** a distinctive smell, esp. a pleasant one **2** a smell left in passing, by which a person or animal may be traced **3** a trail or series of clues by which something is followed: *he must have got on to the scent of the story through you* **4** perfume ▷ *vb* **5** to become aware of by smelling **6** to suspect: *he scented the beginnings of irritation in the car* **7** to fill with odour or fragrance ▶ HISTORY Old French *sentir* to sense > **scented** *adj*

sceptic *or US* **skeptic** (skep-tik) *n* **1** a person who habitually doubts generally accepted beliefs **2** a person who doubts the truth of a religion > **sceptical** *or US* **skeptical** *adj* > **sceptically** *or US* **skeptically** *adv* > **scepticism** *or US* **skepticism** *n*

■ **WORD HISTORY**
■ The Sceptics were a school of philosophers in
■ ancient Greece who believed that nothing
■ could be known for certain. The word 'sceptic'
■ comes from the Greek word *skeptikos*, meaning
■ 'someone who considers', from the verb
■ *skeptesthai* meaning 'to consider'.

sceptre *or US* **scepter** *n* an ornamental rod symbolizing royal power ▶ HISTORY Greek *skeptron* staff > **sceptred** *or US* **sceptered** *adj*

Schadenfreude (shah-den-froy-da) *n* one person's delight in another's misfortune ▶ HISTORY German *Schaden* harm + *Freude* joy

schedule *n* **1** a timed plan of procedure for a project **2** a list of details or items: *the schedule of priorities* **3** a timetable ▷ *vb* **-uling, -uled 4** to plan and arrange (something) to happen at a certain time **5** to make a schedule or include in a schedule ▶ HISTORY Latin *scheda* sheet of paper

schema *n*, *pl* **-mata** an outline of a plan or theory ▶ HISTORY Greek: form

schematic *adj* presented as a diagram or plan > **schematically** *adv*

schematize *or* **-tise** *vb* **-tizing, -tized** *or* **-tising, -tised** to form into or arrange in a systematic arrangement or plan

scheme *n* **1** a systematic plan for a course of action **2** a systematic arrangement of parts or features: *colour scheme* **3** a secret plot **4** a chart, diagram, or outline **5** a plan formally adopted by a government or organization: *a pension scheme* ▷ *vb* **scheming, schemed 6** to plan in an underhand manner ▶ HISTORY Greek *skhēma* form > **schemer** *n* > **scheming** *adj*, *n*

scherzo (skairt-so) *n*, *pl* **-zos** a quick lively piece of music, often the second or third movement in a sonata or symphony ▶ HISTORY Italian: joke

schilling *n* a former monetary unit of Austria ▶ HISTORY from German: shilling

schism (skizz-um) *n* the division of a group, esp. a religious group, into opposing factions, due to differences in doctrine ▶ HISTORY Greek *skhizein* to split > **schismatic** *adj*

schist (skist) *n* a crystalline rock which splits into thin layers ▶ HISTORY Greek *skhizein* to split

schistosomiasis (shiss-ta-so-**my**-a-siss) *n* same as **bilharzia**

schizo (skit-so) *offensive adj* **1** schizophrenic ▷ *n*, *pl* **-os 2** a schizophrenic person

schizoid *adj* **1** *psychol* having a personality disorder characterized by extreme shyness and extreme sensitivity **2** *informal* characterized by conflicting or contradictory ideas or attitudes ▷ *n* **3** *offensive* a person who has a schizoid personality

schizophrenia *n* **1** a psychotic disorder characterized by withdrawal from reality, hallucinations, or emotional instability **2** *informal*

behaviour that seems to be motivated by contradictory or conflicting principles ▶ HISTORY Greek *skhizein* to split + *phrēn* mind
> **schizophrenic** *adj, n*

Schlieffen Plan (**shlee**-fen) *n history* a plan devised in 1905 by Count von Schlieffen, intended to ensure German victory over a Franco-Russian alliance by holding off Russia with minimal strength and swiftly defeating France by a massive flanking movement through the Low Countries

schmaltz *n* excessive sentimentality, esp. in music ▶ HISTORY Yiddish: melted fat > **schmaltzy** *adj*

schnapps *n* a strong dry alcoholic drink distilled from potatoes ▶ HISTORY German *Schnaps*

schnitzel *n* a thin slice of meat, esp. veal ▶ HISTORY German: cutlet

scholar *n* 1 a person who studies an academic subject 2 a student who has a scholarship 3 a pupil ▶ HISTORY Latin *schola* school > **scholarly** *adj*

scholarship *n* 1 academic achievement; learning gained by serious study 2 financial aid provided for a scholar because of academic merit

scholastic *adj* 1 of schools, scholars, or education 2 of or relating to scholasticism ▷ *n* 3 a scholarly person 4 a disciple or adherent of scholasticism ▶ HISTORY Greek *skholastikos* devoted to learning

scholasticism *n* the system of philosophy, theology, and teaching that dominated medieval Europe and was based on the writings of Aristotle

school¹ *n* 1 a place where children are educated 2 the staff and pupils of a school 3 a regular session of instruction in a school: *we stayed behind after school* 4 a faculty or department specializing in a particular subject: *the dental school* 5 a place or sphere of activity that instructs: *the school of hard knocks* 6 a group of artists, writers, or thinkers, linked by the same style, teachers, or methods 7 *informal* a group assembled for a common purpose, such as gambling: *a card school* ▷ *vb* 8 *written* to educate or train: *she schooled herself to be as ambitious as her sister* ▶ HISTORY Greek *skholē* leisure spent in the pursuit of knowledge

school² *n* a group of sea-living animals that swim together, such as fish, whales, or dolphins ▶ HISTORY Old English *scolu* shoal

schoolboy *n* a boy attending school

schooling *n* the education a person receives at school

schoolmaster *or fem* **schoolmistress** *n* a person who teaches in or runs a school

schoolteacher *n* a person who teaches in a school

school year *n* 1 a twelve-month period, usually of three terms, during which pupils remain in the same class 2 the time during this period when the school is open

schooner *n* 1 a sailing ship with at least two masts, one at the back and one at the front 2 *Brit* a large glass for sherry 3 *US, Canad, Austral & NZ* a large glass for beer ▶ HISTORY origin unknown

schottische *n* 1 a 19th-century German dance resembling a slow polka 2 music for this dance

▶ HISTORY German *der schottische Tanz* the Scottish dance

schuss (**shooss**) *n skiing* a straight high-speed downhill run ▶ HISTORY from German

sciatic *adj* 1 *anat* of the hip or the hipbone 2 of or afflicted with sciatica: *a sciatic injury* ▶ HISTORY Greek *iskhia* hip joint

sciatica *n* severe pain in the large nerve in the back of the leg

sciatic nerve *n anat* the long nerve from the back of the thigh down to the calf

science *n* 1 the study of the nature and behaviour of the physical universe, based on observation, experiment, and measurement 2 the knowledge obtained by these methods 3 any particular branch of this knowledge: *medical science* 4 any body of knowledge organized in a way resembling that of the physical sciences but concerned with other subjects: *political science* ▶ HISTORY Latin *scientia* knowledge

science fiction *n* stories and films that make imaginative use of scientific knowledge or theories

science park *n* an area where scientific research and commercial development are carried on in cooperation

scientific *adj* 1 relating to science or a particular science: *scientific discovery* 2 done in a systematic way, using experiments or tests > **scientifically** *adv*

scientific method *n science* a system of understanding and gaining knowledge in which some aspect of the universe is observed, and a description, called a hypothesis, is made and used to make predictions. Those predictions are then tested by experiments. The hypothesis is adjusted in the light of the results

scientist *n* a person who studies or practises a science

sci-fi *n* short for **science fiction**

scimitar *n* a curved oriental sword ▶ HISTORY probably from Persian *shimshīr*

scintillate *vb* **-lating, -lated** to give off (sparks); sparkle ▶ HISTORY Latin *scintilla* a spark
> **scintillation** *n*

scintillating *adj* (of conversation or humour) very lively and amusing

scion (**sy**-on) *n* 1 a descendant or young member of a family 2 a shoot of a plant for grafting onto another plant ▶ HISTORY Old French *cion*

sciophyte *n bot* any plant that grows best in the shade ▶ HISTORY via Latin from Greek *skia* shade + -PHYTE

scissors *pl n* a cutting instrument held in one hand, with two crossed blades pivoted so that they close together on what is to be cut ▶ HISTORY Old French *cisoires*

sclera (**skleer**-a) *n biol* the tough white substance that forms the outer covering of the eyeball ▶ HISTORY Greek *sklēros* hard

sclerosis (skleer-**oh**-siss) *n, pl* **-ses** (-seez) *pathol* an abnormal hardening or thickening of body tissues, esp. of the nervous system or the inner wall of arteries ▸ HISTORY Greek *sklērōsis* a hardening

sclerotic (skleer-**rot**-ik) *adj* **1** of or relating to the sclera **2** of, relating to, or having sclerosis

scoff[1] *vb* **1** (often foll. by *at*) to speak in a scornful and mocking way about (something) ▷ *n* **2** a mocking expression; jeer ▸ HISTORY probably from Old Norse > **scoffing** *adj, n*

scoff[2] *vb informal* to eat (food) fast and greedily ▸ HISTORY variant of *scaff* food

scold *vb* **1** to find fault with or rebuke (a person) harshly **2** *old-fashioned* to use harsh or abusive language ▷ *n* **3** a person, esp. a woman, who constantly scolds ▸ HISTORY from Old Norse *skāld* > **scolding** *n*

scollop *n, vb* same as **scallop**

sconce *n* a bracket fixed to a wall for holding candles or lights ▸ HISTORY Late Latin *absconsa* dark lantern

scone *n* a small plain cake baked in an oven or on a griddle ▸ HISTORY Scots

scoop *n* **1** a spoonlike tool with a deep bowl, used for handling loose or soft materials such as flour or ice cream **2** the deep shovel of a mechanical digger **3** the amount taken up by a scoop **4** the act of scooping or dredging **5** a news story reported in one newspaper before all the others ▷ *vb* **6** (often foll. by *up*) to take up and remove (something) with or as if with a scoop **7 scoop out** to hollow out with or as if with a scoop **8** to beat (rival newspapers) in reporting a news item ▸ HISTORY Germanic

scoot *vb* to leave or move quickly ▸ HISTORY origin unknown

scooter *n* **1** a child's small cycle which is ridden by pushing the ground with one foot **2** a light motorcycle with a small engine

scope *n* **1** opportunity for using abilities: *ample scope for creative work* **2** range of view or grasp: *that is outside my scope* **3** the area covered by an activity or topic: *the scope of his essay was vast* ▸ HISTORY Greek *skopos* target

scorbutic (score-**byewt**-ik) *adj* of or having scurvy ▸ HISTORY Medieval Latin *scorbutus*

scorch *vb* **1** to burn or become burnt slightly on the surface **2** to parch or shrivel from heat **3** *informal* to criticize harshly ▷ *n* **4** a slight burn **5** a mark caused by the application of excessive heat ▸ HISTORY probably from Old Norse *skorpna* to shrivel up > **scorching** *adj*

scorcher *n informal* a very hot day

score *n* **1** the total number of points made by a side or individual in a game **2** the act of scoring a point or points: *there was no score and three minutes remained* **3 the score** *informal* the actual situation: *what's the score on this business?* **4** *old-fashioned, written* a group or set of twenty: *three score years and ten* **5 scores of** *written* lots of: *we received scores of letters* **6** *music* a written version of a piece of music showing parts for each musician **7 a** the incidental music for a film or play **b** the songs and music for a stage or film musical **8** a mark or

scratch **9** a record of money due: *what's the score for the drinks?* **10** an amount recorded as due **11** a reason: *some objections were made on the score of sentiment* **12** a grievance: *a score to settle* **13 over the score** *informal* excessive or unfair ▷ *vb* **scoring, scored 14** to gain (a point or points) in a game or contest **15** to make a total score of **16** to keep a record of the score (of) **17** to be worth (a certain number of points) in a game: *red aces score twenty* **18** to make cuts or lines in or on **19** to arrange (a piece of music) for specific instruments or voices **20** to write the music for (a film or play) **21** *written* to achieve (success or an advantage): *your idea scored with the boss* ▸ HISTORY Old English *scora*

scoreboard *n sport* a board for displaying the score of a game or match

score off *vb* to make a clever or insulting reply to what someone has just said: *they spent the evening scoring off each other*

scorer *n* **1** a player of a sport who scores a goal, run, or point: *Ireland's record goal scorer has announced his retirement* **2** a person who keeps note of the score of a match or competition as it is being played

scoria (**score**-ee-a) *n* **1** *geol* a mass of solidified lava containing many cavities **2** refuse left after ore has been smelted ▸ HISTORY Latin: dross

scorn *n* **1** open contempt for a person or thing ▷ *vb* **2** to treat with contempt: *she attacked the government for scorning her profession* **3** to refuse to have or do (something) because it is felt to be undesirable or wrong: *youths who scorn traditional morals* ▸ HISTORY Old French *escharnir* > **scornful** *adj* > **scornfully** *adv*

Scorpio *n astrol* the eighth sign of the zodiac; the Scorpion ▸ HISTORY Latin

scorpion *n* a small lobster-shaped animal with a sting at the end of a jointed tail ▸ HISTORY Greek *skorpios*

Scot *n* a person from Scotland

scotch *vb* **1** to put an end to: *she had scotched the idea of bingo in the church* **2** to wound without killing ▸ HISTORY origin unknown

Scotch[1] *not universally accepted adj* **1** same as **Scottish** ▷ *pl n* **2 the Scotch** the Scots

Scotch[2] *n* whisky distilled in Scotland from fermented malted barley

Scotch broth *n Brit* a thick soup made from mutton or beef stock, vegetables, and pearl barley

Scotch egg *n Brit & NZ* a hard-boiled egg encased in sausage meat and breadcrumbs, and fried

Scotch mist *n* a heavy wet mist or drizzle

scot-free *adv, adj* without harm or punishment: *the real crooks got off scot-free* ▸ HISTORY obsolete *scot* a tax

Scotland Yard *n* the headquarters of the police force of metropolitan London

Scots *adj* **1** of Scotland ▷ *n* **2** any of the English dialects spoken or written in Scotland

Scotsman *or fem* **Scotswoman** *n, pl* **-men** *or* **-women** a person from Scotland

Scots pine n **1** a coniferous tree found in Europe and Asia, with needle-like leaves and brown cones **2** the wood of this tree

Scotticism n a Scottish expression or word

Scottish adj of Scotland

scoundrel n old-fashioned a person who cheats and deceives ▶ HISTORY origin unknown

scour¹ vb **1** to clean or polish (a surface) by rubbing with something rough **2** to clear (a channel) by the force of water ▷ n **3** the act of scouring ▶ HISTORY Old French escurer > **scourer** n

scour² vb **1** to search thoroughly and energetically: he had scoured auction salerooms **2** to move quickly over (land) in search or pursuit ▶ HISTORY probably from Old Norse skūr shower

scourge n **1** a person who or thing that causes affliction or suffering **2** a whip formerly used for punishing people ▷ vb **scourging, scourged 3** to cause severe suffering to **4** to whip ▶ HISTORY Latin excoriare to whip

Scouse Brit, informal n **1** Also called: **Scouser** a person from Liverpool **2** the Liverpool dialect ▷ adj **3** of Liverpool, its people, or their dialect ▶ HISTORY from lobscouse a sailor's stew

scout n **1** mil a person sent to find out the position of the enemy **2** same as **talent scout 3** the act or an instance of scouting ▷ vb **4** to examine or observe (something) in order to obtain information **5 scout about** or **around** to go in search (of) ▶ HISTORY Old French ascouter to listen to

Scout or **scout** n a member of the Scout Association, an organization for boys and girls, which aims to develop character and promote outdoor activities > **Scouting** n

scowl vb **1** to have an angry or bad-tempered facial expression ▷ n **2** an angry or bad-tempered facial expression ▶ HISTORY probably from Old Norse

scrabble vb **-bling, -bled 1** to scrape at or grope for something with hands, feet, or claws: scrabbling with his feet to find a foothold **2** to move one's hands about in order to find something one cannot see: scrabbling in her handbag for a comb ▶ HISTORY Middle Dutch schrabbelen

scrag n **1** the thin end of a neck of veal or mutton **2** a thin or scrawny person or animal ▶ HISTORY perhaps variant of crag

scraggy adj **-gier, -giest** unpleasantly thin and bony > **scragginess** n

scram¹ vb **scramming, scrammed** informal to leave very quickly ▶ HISTORY from scramble

scram² n **1** an emergency shutdown of a nuclear reactor ▷ vb **scramming, scrammed 2** (of a nuclear reactor) to shut down or be shut down in an emergency ▶ HISTORY perhaps from SCRAM¹

scramble vb **-bling, -bled 1** to climb or crawl hurriedly by using the hands to aid movement **2** to go hurriedly or in a disorderly manner **3** to compete with others in a rough and undignified way: spectators scrambled for the best seats **4** to jumble together in a haphazard manner **5** to cook (eggs that have been whisked up with milk) in a pan **6** mil (of a crew or aircraft) to take off quickly in an emergency **7** to make (transmitted speech) unintelligible by the use of an electronic scrambler ▷ n **8** the act of scrambling **9** a climb or trek over difficult ground **10** a rough and undignified struggle to gain possession of something **11** mil an immediate takeoff of crew or aircraft in an emergency **12** Brit a motorcycle race across rough open ground ▶ HISTORY blend of SCRABBLE + RAMP

scrambler n an electronic device that makes broadcast or telephone messages unintelligible without a special receiver

scrap¹ n **1** a small piece of something larger; fragment **2** waste material or used articles, often collected and reprocessed **3 scraps** pieces of leftover food ▷ vb **scrapping, scrapped 4** to discard as useless ▶ HISTORY Old Norse skrap

scrap² informal n **1** a fight or quarrel ▷ vb **scrapping, scrapped 2** to quarrel or fight ▶ HISTORY perhaps from scrape

scrapbook n a book of blank pages in which newspaper cuttings or pictures are stuck

scrape vb **scraping, scraped 1** to move (a rough or sharp object) across (a surface) **2** (often foll. by away or off) to remove (a layer) by rubbing **3** to produce a grating sound by rubbing against (something else) **4** to injure or damage by scraping: he had scraped his knees **5 scrimp and scrape** See **scrimp** (sense 2) ▷ n **6** the act or sound of scraping **7** a scraped place: a scrape on the car door **8** informal an awkward or embarrassing situation **9** informal a conflict or struggle ▶ HISTORY Old English scrapian > **scraper** n

scrape through vb to succeed in or survive with difficulty: both teams had scraped through their semifinals

scrappy adj **-pier, -piest** badly organized or done: a scrappy draft of a chapter of my thesis

scratch vb **1** to mark or cut (the surface of something) with a rough or sharp instrument **2** (often foll. by at, out) to tear or dig with the nails or claws **3** to scrape (the surface of the skin) with the nails to relieve itching **4** to rub against (the skin) causing a slight cut **5** to make or cause to make a grating sound **6** (sometimes foll. by out) to erase or cross out **7** to withdraw from a race or (in the US) an election ▷ n **8** the act of scratching **9** a slight cut on a person's or an animal's body **10** a mark made by scratching **11** a slight grating sound **12 from scratch** informal from the very beginning **13 not up to scratch** informal not up to standard ▷ adj **14** put together at short notice: a scratch team **15** sport with no handicap allowed: a scratch golfer ▶ HISTORY Germanic > **scratchy** adj

scratchcard n a ticket that reveals whether or not the holder is eligible for a prize when the surface is removed by scratching

scratching n music a sound produced when the record groove in contact with the stylus of a record player is moved back and forth by hand

scrawl vb **1** to write carelessly or hastily ▷ n **2** careless or scribbled writing ▶ HISTORY perhaps blend of SPRAWL + CRAWL > **scrawly** adj

scrawny *adj* **scrawnier, scrawniest** very thin and bony ▶ HISTORY dialect *scranny* > **scrawniness** *n*

scream *vb* **1** to make a sharp piercing cry or sound because of fear or pain **2** *written* (of a machine) to make a high-pitched noise **3** to laugh wildly **4** to utter with a scream: *he screamed abuse up into the sky* **5** to be unpleasantly conspicuous: *bad news screaming out from the headlines* ▷ *n* **6** a sharp piercing cry or sound, esp. of fear or pain **7** *informal* a very funny person or thing ▶ HISTORY Germanic

scree *n* a pile of rock fragments at the foot of a cliff or hill, often forming a sloping heap ▶ HISTORY Old English *scrīthan* to slip

screech¹ *n* **1** a shrill or high-pitched sound or cry ▷ *vb* **2** to utter a shrill cry ▶ HISTORY earlier *scritch*, imitative > **screechy** *adj*

screech² *n* *Canad* a dark rum ▶ HISTORY origin unknown

screech owl *n* **1** *Brit* same as **barn owl** **2** a small North American barn owl

screed *n* a long tiresome speech or piece of writing ▶ HISTORY probably from Old English *scrēade* shred

screen *n* **1** the blank surface of a television set, VDU, or radar receiver, on which a visible image is formed **2** the white surface on which films or slides are projected **3** **the screen** the film industry or films collectively **4** a light movable frame, panel, or partition used to shelter, divide, or conceal **5** anything that shelters, protects, or conceals: *a screen of leaves blocking out the sun* **6** a frame containing a mesh that is used to keep out insects ▷ *vb* **7** (sometimes foll. by *off*) to shelter, protect, or conceal with or as if with a screen **8** to test or check (an individual or group) so as to assess suitability for a task or to detect the presence of a disease or weapons: *women screened for breast cancer* **9** to show (a film) in the cinema or show (a programme) on television ▶ HISTORY Old French *escren*

screenplay *n* the script for a film, including instructions for sets and camera work

screen saver *n* *computers* software that produces changing images on a monitor when the computer is operating but idle

screenshot *n* an image created by copying part or all of the display on a computer screen at a particular moment

screenwriter *n* a person who writes screenplays

screw *n* **1** a metal pin with a spiral ridge along its length, twisted into materials to fasten them together **2** a threaded cylindrical rod that engages with a similarly threaded cylindrical hole **3** a thread in a cylindrical hole corresponding with the one on the screw with which it is designed to engage **4** anything resembling a screw in shape **5** *slang* a prison guard **6** **have a screw loose** *informal* to be insane **7** **put the screws on** *slang* to use force on or threatening behaviour against ▷ *vb* **8** to rotate (a screw or bolt) so as to drive it into or draw it out of a material **9** to twist or turn: *she screwed up the sheet of paper* **10** to attach or fasten with or as if

with a screw or screws **11** *informal* to take advantage of, esp. illegally: *screwed by big business* **12** *informal* to distort or contort: *his face was screwed up in pain* **13** (often foll. by *out of*) *informal* to force out of; extort **14** **have one's head screwed on the right way** *informal* to be sensible ▷ See also **screw up** ▶ HISTORY French *escroe*

screwdriver *n* **1** a tool used for turning screws, consisting of a long thin metal rod with a flattened tip that fits into a slot in the head of the screw **2** a drink consisting of orange juice and vodka

screw up *vb* **1** *informal* to mishandle or spoil (something): *that screws up all my arrangements* **2** to twist out of shape or distort **3** **screw up one's courage** to force oneself to be brave > **screwed-up** *adj*

screwy *adj* **screwier, screwiest** *informal* crazy or eccentric

scribble *vb* **-bling, -bled** **1** to write or draw quickly and roughly **2** to make meaningless or illegible marks (on) ▷ *n* **3** something written or drawn quickly or roughly **4** meaningless or illegible marks ▶ HISTORY Latin *scribere* to write > **scribbler** *n* > **scribbly** *adj*

scribe *n* **1** a person who made handwritten copies of manuscripts or documents before the invention of printing **2** *Bible* a recognized scholar and teacher of the Jewish Law ▶ HISTORY Latin *scriba* clerk

scrimmage *n* **1** a rough or disorderly struggle ▷ *vb* **-maging, -maged** **2** to take part in a scrimmage ▶ HISTORY earlier *scrimish*

scrimp *vb* **1** to be very sparing in the use of something: *they were scrimping by on the last of the potatoes* **2** **scrimp and save** or **scrape** to spend as little money as possible ▶ HISTORY Scots

scrip¹ *n* *finance* a certificate representing a claim to shares or stocks ▶ HISTORY short for *subscription receipt*

scrip² or **script** *n* *informal* a medical prescription ▶ HISTORY from PRESCRIPTION

script *n* **1** the text of a play, TV programme, or film for the use of performers **2** an alphabet or system of writing: *Cyrillic script* **3** a candidate's answer paper in an examination **4** handwriting **5** a typeface which looks like handwriting ▷ *vb* **6** to write a script for ▶ HISTORY Latin *scriptum* something written

scripture *n* the sacred writings of a religion ▶ HISTORY Latin *scriptura* written material > **scriptural** *adj*

Scripture *n* *Christianity* the Old and New Testaments

scriptwriter *n* a person who writes scripts, esp. for a film or TV programme > **scriptwriting** *n*

scrofula *n* *no longer in technical use* tuberculosis of the lymphatic glands ▶ HISTORY Medieval Latin > **scrofulous** *adj*

scroggin *n* *NZ* a mixture of nuts and dried fruits

scroll *n* **1** a roll of parchment or paper, usually inscribed with writing **2** an ancient book in the form of a roll of parchment, papyrus, or paper **3** a decorative carving or moulding resembling a scroll

▷ *vb* **4** *computers* to move (text) on a screen in order to view a section that cannot be fitted into a single display ▶ HISTORY Middle English *scrowle*

Scrooge *n* a mean or miserly person ▶ HISTORY after a character in Dickens' story *A Christmas Carol*

scrotum *n* the pouch of skin containing the testicles in most male mammals ▶ HISTORY Latin

scrounge *vb* **scrounging, scrounged** *informal* to get (something) by asking for it rather than buying it or working for it ▶ HISTORY dialect *scrunge* to steal > **scrounger** *n*

scrub¹ *vb* **scrubbing, scrubbed 1** to rub (something) hard in order to clean it **2** to remove (dirt) by rubbing with a brush and water **3 scrub up** (of a surgeon) to wash the hands and arms thoroughly before operating **4** *informal* to delete or cancel (an idea or plan) ▷ *n* **5** the act of scrubbing ▶ HISTORY Middle Low German *schrubben* or Middle Dutch *schrobben*

scrub² *n* **1** vegetation consisting of stunted trees or bushes growing in a dry area **2** an area of dry land covered with such vegetation ▷ *adj* **3** stunted or inferior: *scrub pines* ▶ HISTORY variant of *shrub*

scrubber *n* a device that removes pollutants from the gases that are produced when coal is burned industrially

scrubby *adj* **-bier, -biest 1** (of land) rough, dry, and covered with scrub **2** (of plants) stunted **3** *Brit, informal* shabby or untidy

scruff¹ *n* the nape of the neck: *the sergeant had him by the scruff of the neck* ▶ HISTORY perhaps from Old Norse *skoft* hair

scruff² *n* *informal* a very untidy person

scruffy *adj* **scruffier, scruffiest** dirty and untidy in appearance

scrum *n* **1** *rugby* a formation in which players from each side form a tight pack and push against each other in an attempt to get the ball which is thrown on the ground between them **2** *informal* a disorderly struggle ▷ *vb* **scrumming, scrummed 3** (usually foll. by *down*) *rugby* to form a scrum ▶ HISTORY from *scrummage*

scrum half *n* *rugby* a player who puts in the ball at scrums and tries to regain its possession in order to pass it to his team's backs

scrummage *n, vb* **-maging, -maged 1** *rugby* same as **scrum 2** same as **scrimmage** ▶ HISTORY variant of *scrimmage*

scrump *vb* *Brit, dialect* to steal (apples) from an orchard or garden ▶ HISTORY variant of *scrimp*

scrumptious *adj* *informal* delicious or very attractive ▶ HISTORY probably changed from *sumptuous*

scrumpy *n* *Brit* a rough dry cider brewed in the West Country of England ▶ HISTORY dialect *scrump* withered apples

scrunch *vb* **1** to press or crush noisily or be pressed or crushed noisily ▷ *n* **2** the act or sound of scrunching: *the scrunch of tyres on gravel* ▶ HISTORY variant of *crunch*

scrunchie *n* a loop of elastic covered loosely with fabric, used to hold the hair in a ponytail

scruple *n* **1** a doubt or hesitation as to what is morally right in a certain situation: *he had no scruples about the drug trade* ▷ *vb* **-pling, -pled 2** to have doubts (about), esp. on moral grounds ▶ HISTORY Latin *scrupulus* a small weight

scrupulous *adj* **1** taking great care to do what is fair, honest, or morally right **2** very careful or precise: *scrupulous attention to detail* ▶ HISTORY Latin *scrupulosus* > **scrupulously** *adv*

scrutineer *n* a person who examines, esp. one who scrutinizes the conduct of an election poll

scrutinize *or* **-nise** *vb* **-nizing, -nized** *or* **-nising, -nised** to examine carefully or in minute detail

scrutiny *n, pl* **-nies 1** very careful study or observation **2** a searching look ▶ HISTORY Late Latin *scrutari* to search

scuba (**skew**-ba) *n* an apparatus used in skin diving, consisting of cylinders containing compressed air attached to a breathing apparatus ▶ HISTORY s(*elf*-)c(*ontained*) u(*nderwater*) b(*reathing*) a(*pparatus*)

scud *vb* **scudding, scudded 1** (esp. of clouds) to move along quickly **2** *naut* to run before a gale ▷ *n* **3** the act of scudding **4** spray, rain, or clouds driven by the wind ▶ HISTORY probably Scandinavian

scuff *vb* **1** to drag (the feet) while walking **2** to scrape (one's shoes) by doing so ▷ *n* **3** a mark caused by scuffing **4** the act or sound of scuffing ▶ HISTORY probably imitative

scuffle *vb* **-fling, -fled 1** to fight in a disorderly manner ▷ *n* **2** a short disorganized fight **3** a scuffling sound ▶ HISTORY Scandinavian

scull *n* **1** a single oar moved from side to side over the back of a boat **2** one of a pair of small oars, both of which are pulled by one oarsman **3** a racing boat rowed by one oarsman pulling two oars ▷ *vb* **4** to row (a boat) with a scull ▶ HISTORY origin unknown > **sculler** *n*

scullery *n, pl* **-leries** *chiefly Brit* a small room where washing-up and other kitchen work is done ▶ HISTORY Anglo-Norman *squillerie*

sculpt *vb* same as **sculpture**

sculptor *or fem* **sculptress** *n* a person who makes sculptures

sculpture *n* **1** the art of making figures or designs in wood, plaster, stone, or metal **2** works or a work made in this way ▷ *vb* **-turing, -tured 3** to carve (a material) into figures or designs **4** to represent (a person or thing) in sculpture **5** to form or be formed in the manner of sculpture: *limestone sculptured by fast-flowing streams* ▶ HISTORY Latin *sculptura* a carving > **sculptural** *adj*

scum *n* **1** a layer of impure or waste matter that forms on the surface of a liquid: *the build-up of soap scum* **2** a person or people regarded as worthless or criminal ▷ *vb* **scumming, scummed 3** to remove scum from **4** *rare* to form a layer of or become covered with scum ▶ HISTORY Germanic > **scummy** *adj*

scungy (**skun**-jee) *adj* **scungier, scungiest** *Austral & NZ, slang* miserable, sordid, or dirty ▶ HISTORY origin unknown

S

scupper[1] *n naut* a drain or spout in a ship's side allowing water on the deck to flow overboard ► HISTORY origin unknown

scupper[2] *vb* **1** *Brit & NZ, slang* to defeat or ruin: *a deliberate attempt to scupper the peace talks* **2** to sink (one's ship) deliberately ► HISTORY origin unknown

scurf *n* **1** same as **dandruff 2** any flaky or scaly matter sticking to or peeling off a surface ► HISTORY Old English > **scurfy** *adj*

scurrilous *adj* untrue or unfair, insulting, and designed to damage a person's reputation: *scurrilous allegations* ► HISTORY Latin *scurra* buffoon > **scurrility** *n*

scurry *vb* **-ries, -rying, -ried 1** *written* to run quickly with short steps ▷ *n, pl* **-ries 2** a quick hurrying movement or the sound of this movement **3** a short shower of rain or snow ► HISTORY probably from *hurry-scurry*

scurvy *n* **1** a disease caused by a lack of vitamin C, resulting in weakness, spongy gums, and bleeding beneath the skin ▷ *adj* **-vier, -viest 2** *old-fashioned* deserving contempt ► HISTORY from *scurf* > **scurviness** *n*

scut *n* the short tail of animals such as the deer and rabbit ► HISTORY probably from Old Norse

scuttle[1] *n* same as **coal scuttle** ► HISTORY Latin *scutella* bowl

scuttle[2] *vb* **-tling, -tled 1** to run with short quick steps ▷ *n* **2** a hurried pace or run ► HISTORY probably from *scud*

scuttle[3] *vb* **-tling, -tled 1** *naut* to cause (a ship) to sink by making holes in the sides or bottom **2** to ruin (hopes or plans) or have them ruined: *a new policy scuttled by popular resistance* ▷ *n* **3** *naut* a small hatch in a ship's deck or side ► HISTORY Spanish *escotilla* a small opening

scythe *n* **1** a long-handled tool for cutting grass or grain, with a curved sharpened blade that is swung parallel to the ground ▷ *vb* **scything, scythed 2** to cut (grass or grain) with a scythe ► HISTORY Old English *sigthe*

SD South Dakota

SDI Strategic Defense Initiative

SDLP (in Northern Ireland) Social Democratic and Labour Party

Se *chem* selenium

SE southeast(ern)

sea *n* **1 the sea** the mass of salt water that covers three-quarters of the earth's surface **2 a** one of the smaller areas of this. *the Irish Sea* **b** a large inland area of water: *the Caspian Sea* **3** the area on or close to the edge of the sea, esp. as a place where holidays are taken: *a day by the sea* **4** strong and uneven swirling movement of waves: *rough seas* **5** anything resembling the sea in size or movement: *a sea of red and yellow flags* **6 at sea a** on the ocean **b** in a state of confusion or uncertainty **7 go to sea** to become a sailor **8 put out to sea** to start a sea voyage ► HISTORY Old English *sǣ*

sea anchor *n naut* a canvas-covered frame, dragged in the water behind a ship to slow it down or reduce drifting

sea anemone *n* a marine animal with a round body and rings of tentacles which trap food from the water

sea bird *n* a bird that lives on or near the sea

seaboard *n* land bordering on the sea

seaborgium *n chem* a synthetic element. Symbol: Sg ► HISTORY after Glenn *Seaborg*, physicist and chemist

sea breeze *n meteorol* a breeze blowing inland from the sea, usually during the day, caused by the land heating faster than the sea and cooler air from the sea flowing to replace rising warmer air from the land. Compare **land breeze**

sea cow *n* **1** a whalelike mammal such as a dugong or manatee **2** *archaic* a walrus

sea dog *n* an experienced or old sailor

seafaring *adj* **1** travelling by sea **2** *written* working as a sailor ▷ *n* **3** the act of travelling by sea **4** the work of a sailor

seafloor spreading *n geol* a series of processes in which new oceanic lithosphere is created at oceanic ridges, spreads away from the ridges, and returns to the earth's interior

seafood *n* edible saltwater fish or shellfish

seafront *n* a built-up area facing the sea

seagoing *adj* built for travelling on the sea

seagull *n* same as **gull**

sea horse *n* a small marine fish with a horselike head, which swims upright

sea kale *n* a European coastal plant with broad fleshy leaves and asparagus-like shoots that can be eaten

seal[1] *n* **1** a special design impressed on a piece of wax, lead, or paper, fixed to a letter or document as a mark of authentication **2** a stamp or signet ring engraved with a design to form such an impression **3** a substance placed over an envelope or container, so that it cannot be opened without the seal being broken **4** something that serves as an official confirmation of approval: *seal of approval* **5** any substance or device used to close an opening tightly **6 set the seal on** *written* to confirm something: *the experience set the seal on their friendship* ▷ *vb* **7** to close or secure with or as if with a seal: *once the manuscripts were sealed up, they were forgotten about* **8 seal off** to enclose or isolate (a place) completely **9** to close tightly so as to make airtight or watertight **10** to inject a compound around the edges of (something) to make it airtight or watertight **11** to attach a seal to or stamp with a seal **12** *written* to finalize or authorize **13 seal one's fate** to make sure one dies or fails **14 seal one's lips** to promise not to reveal a secret ► HISTORY Latin *signum* a sign > **sealable** *adj*

seal[2] *n* **1** a fish-eating mammal with four flippers, which lives in the sea but comes ashore to breed **2** sealskin ▷ *vb* **3** to hunt seals ► HISTORY Old English *seolh*

sealant *n* any substance, such as wax, used for sealing, esp. to make airtight or watertight

sea legs *pl n informal* the ability to maintain one's balance on board ship and to avoid being seasick

sea level *n geog* the average level of the sea's surface in relation to the land

sealing wax *n* a hard material made of shellac and turpentine, which softens when heated and which is used to make a seal

sea lion *n* a type of large seal found in the Pacific Ocean

Sea Lord *n* (in Britain) a naval officer on the admiralty board of the Ministry of Defence

sealskin *n* the skin or prepared fur of a seal, used to make coats

seam *n* **1** the line along which pieces of fabric are joined by stitching **2** a ridge or line made by joining two edges: *the seam between the old and the new buildings* **3** a long narrow layer of coal, marble, or ore formed between layers of other rocks **4** a mark or line like a seam, such as a wrinkle or scar ▷ *adj* **5** *cricket* of a style of bowling in which the bowler uses the stitched seam round the ball in order to make it swing in flight and after touching the ground: *a seam bowler* ▷ *vb* **6** to join together by or as if by a seam **7** to mark with furrows or wrinkles ▶ HISTORY Old English *sēam*

seaman *n, pl* **-men 1** a man ranking below an officer in a navy **2** a sailor

seamer *or* **seam bowler** *n cricket* a fast bowler who makes the ball bounce on its seam so that it will change direction

seamless *adj* **1** (of a garment) without seams **2** continuous or flowing: *a seamless performance* > **seamlessness** *n*

seamstress *n* a woman who sews, esp. professionally

seamy *adj* **seamier, seamiest** involving the sordid and unpleasant aspects of life, such as crime, prostitution, poverty, and violence > **seaminess** *n*

seance *or* **séance** (**say**-onss) *n* a meeting at which a spiritualist attempts to communicate with the spirits of the dead ▶ HISTORY French

seaplane *n* an aircraft that is designed to land on and take off from water

seaport *n* a port that is accessible to seagoing vessels

sear *vb* **1** to scorch or burn the surface of **2** to cause to wither ▶ HISTORY Old English *sēarian* to become withered

search *vb* **1** to look through (a place) thoroughly in order to find someone or something **2** to examine (a person) for hidden objects **3** to look at or examine (something) closely: *I searched my heart for one good thing she had done* **4 search out** to find by searching **5** to make a search **6 search me** *informal* I don't know ▷ *n* **7** an attempt to find something by looking somewhere ▶ HISTORY Old French *cerchier*

search engine *n computers* an internet service enabling users to search for items of interest

searching *adj* keen or thorough: *a searching analysis* > **searchingly** *adv*

searchlight *n* **1** a light with a powerful beam that can be shone in any direction **2** the beam of light produced by this device

search warrant *n* a legal document allowing a policeman to enter and search premises

seascape *n* a drawing, painting, or photograph of a scene at sea

seashell *n* the empty shell of a marine mollusc

seashore *n* land bordering on the sea

seasick *adj* suffering from nausea and dizziness caused by the movement of a ship at sea > **seasickness** *n*

seaside *n* an area, esp. a holiday resort, bordering on the sea

season *n* **1** one of the four divisions of the year (spring, summer, autumn, and winter), each of which has characteristic weather conditions **2** a period of the year characterized by particular conditions or activities: *the typhoon season; the football season* **3** the period during which any particular species of animal, bird, or fish is legally permitted to be caught or killed: *the deer season* **4** any definite or indefinite period: *the busy season* **5** any period during which a show or play is performed at one venue: *the show ran for three seasons* **6 in season a** (of game) permitted to be killed **b** (of fresh food) readily available **c** (of animals) ready to mate ▷ *vb* **7** to add herbs, salt, pepper, or spice to (food) in order to enhance the flavour **8** (in the preparation of timber) to dry and harden **9** to make experienced: *old men seasoned by living* ▶ HISTORY Latin *satio* a sowing > **seasoned** *adj*

seasonable *adj* **1** suitable for the season: *a seasonable Christmas snow scene* **2** coming or happening just at the right time: *seasonable advice*

seasonal *adj* of or depending on a certain season or seasons of the year: *seasonal employment* > **seasonally** *adv*

seasoning *n* something that is added to food to enhance the flavour

season ticket *n* a ticket for a series of events or number of journeys, usually bought at a reduced rate

seat *n* **1** a piece of furniture designed for sitting on, such as a chair **2** the part of a chair or other piece of furniture on which one sits **3** a place to sit in a theatre, esp. one that requires a ticket: *there were two empty front-row seats at the pageant* **4** the buttocks **5** the part of a garment covering the buttocks **6** the part or surface on which an object rests **7** the place or centre in which something is based: *the seat of government* **8** *Brit* a country mansion **9** a membership or the right to membership of a legislative or administrative body: *a seat on the council* **10** *chiefly Brit* a parliamentary constituency **11** the manner in which a rider sits on a horse ▷ *vb* **12** to bring to or place on a seat **13** to provide seats for: *the dining hall seats 150 people* **14** to set firmly in place ▶ HISTORY Old English *gesete*

seat belt *n* a strap attached to a car or aircraft seat, worn across the body to prevent a person being thrown forward in the event of a collision

seating *n* **1** seats which are provided somewhere, esp. in a public place: *the grandstand has seating for*

S

10 000; *hard plastic seating* ▷ *adj* **2** of or relating to the provision of places to sit: *the delegation leader complained about the seating arrangements*

sea urchin *n* a small sea animal with a round body enclosed in a spiny shell

seaweed *n* any plant growing in the sea or on the seashore

seaworthy *adj* (of a ship) in a fit condition for a sea voyage > **seaworthiness** *n*

sebaceous *adj* of, like, or secreting fat ▶ HISTORY Latin *sebum* tallow

sebaceous glands *pl n* the small glands in the skin that secrete oil into hair follicles and onto most of the body surface

sebum (**see**-bum) *n* the oily substance secreted by the sebaceous glands ▶ HISTORY Latin: tallow

sec¹ *adj* (of wines) dry ▶ HISTORY French

sec² *n informal* a second (of time): *hang on a sec*

sec³ secant

sec. **1** second (of time) **2** secondary **3** secretary

secant (**seek**-ant) *n* **1** (in trigonometry) the ratio of the length of the hypotenuse to the length of the adjacent side in a right-angled triangle; the reciprocal of cosine **2** a straight line that intersects a curve ▶ HISTORY Latin *secare* to cut

secateurs *pl n* a small pair of gardening shears for pruning ▶ HISTORY French

secede *vb* **-ceding, -ceded** to make a formal withdrawal of membership from a political alliance, federation, or group: *it will secede from the federation within six months* ▶ HISTORY Latin *se-* apart + *cedere* to go

secession *n* the act of seceding > **secessionism** *n* > **secessionist** *n, adj*

seclude *vb* **-cluding, -cluded** **1** to remove from contact with others **2** to shut off or screen from view ▶ HISTORY Latin *secludere*

secluded *adj* **1** kept apart from the company of others: *a secluded private life* **2** private and sheltered: *a secluded cottage*

seclusion *n* the state of being secluded; privacy: *the seclusion of his winter retreat*

second¹ *adj* **1** coming directly after the first in order **2** rated, graded, or ranked between the first and third levels **3** alternate: *every second Saturday* **4** another of the same kind; additional: *a second chance* **5** resembling or comparable to a person or event from the past: *a second Virgin Mary* **6** of lesser importance or position; inferior **7** denoting the second lowest forward gear in a motor vehicle **8** *music* denoting a musical part, voice, or instrument subordinate to or lower in pitch than another (the first): *the second tenors* **9 at second hand** by hearsay ▷ *n* **10** a person or thing that is second **11** *Brit education* an honours degree of the second class **12** the second lowest forward gear in a motor vehicle **13** (in boxing or duelling) an attendant who looks after a boxer or duellist **14 seconds a** *informal* a second helping of food or the second course of a meal **b** goods that are sold cheaply because they are slightly faulty ▷ *vb* **15** to give aid or backing to **16** (in boxing or duelling) to

act as second to (a boxer or duellist) **17** to express formal support for (a motion proposed in a meeting) ▷ *adv* **18** Also: **secondly** in the second place ▶ HISTORY Latin *secundus* next in order

second² *n* **1** the basic SI unit of time, equal to ⅟₆₀ of a minute **2** ⅟₆₀ of a minute of angle **3** a very short period of time ▶ HISTORY Latin *pars minuta secunda* the second small part (a minute being the first small part of an hour)

second³ (sik-**kond**) *vb Brit & NZ* to transfer (a person) temporarily to another job ▶ HISTORY French *en second* in second rank > **secondment** *n*

secondary *adj* **1** below the first in rank or importance: *a secondary consideration* **2** coming next after the first: *secondary cancers* **3** derived from or depending on what is primary or first: *a secondary source* **4** of or relating to the education of people between the ages of 11 and 18 or, in New Zealand, between 13 and 18: *secondary education* **5** (of an industry) involving the manufacture of goods from raw materials ▷ *n, pl* **-aries** **6** a person or thing that is secondary

secondary consumer *n biol* an animal that eats herbivores. Compare **primary consumer, tertiary consumer**

secondary industry *n econ, business* an industry concerned with manufacturing and the processing of raw materials. Compare **primary industry, tertiary industry, quaternary industry**

secondary production *n econ* the process of converting raw materials into products for consumers

secondary source *n* a description, commentary, or analysis of something not experienced personally but which is based on someone else's experiences, descriptions, work, etc. Compare **primary source**

second-best *adj* **1** next to the best ▷ *adv* **second best** **2 come off second best** *informal* to fail to win against someone ▷ *n* **second best** **3** an inferior alternative

second chamber *n* the upper house of a two-chamber system of government

second class *n* **1** the class or grade next in value, rank, or quality to the first ▷ *adj* **second-class** **2** of the class or grade next to the best in value, rank, or quality **3** shoddy or inferior **4** denoting the class of accommodation in a hotel or on a train, aircraft, or ship, lower in quality and price than first class **5** (of mail) sent by a cheaper type of postage and taking slightly longer to arrive than first-class mail ▷ *adv* **6** by second-class mail, transport, etc.

Second Coming *n* the prophesied return of Christ to earth at the Last Judgment

second-degree burn *n* a burn in which blisters appear on the skin

second fiddle *n informal* a person who has a secondary status

second-hand *adj* **1** previously owned or used **2** not from an original source or one's own experience: *second-hand opinions* **3** dealing in or selling goods that are not new: *second-hand*

S

furniture shops ▷ *adv* **4** from a source of previously owned or used goods: *they preferred to buy second-hand* **5** not directly or from one's own experience: *his knowledge had been gleaned second-hand*

second lieutenant *n* an officer holding the lowest commissioned rank in an army or navy

secondly *adv* same as **second¹** (sense 18)

second nature *n* a habit or characteristic practised for so long that it seems to be part of one's character

second person *n* *grammar* the form of a pronoun or verb used to refer to the person or people being addressed, as in *you see*

second-person narration *n* *literature* a narrative style in which the author addresses the reader directly using the pronoun *you*

second-rate *adj* **1** not of the highest quality; mediocre **2** second in importance or rank: *a second-rate citizen*

second sight *n* the supposed ability to foresee the future or see actions taking place elsewhere

second-strike *adj* *mil* (of a nuclear weapon) to be used in a counterattack in response to a nuclear attack

second thoughts *pl n* a revised opinion or idea on a matter already considered

second wind *n* **1** the return of comfortable breathing following difficult or strenuous exercise **2** renewed ability to continue in an effort

secrecy *n, pl* **-cies** **1** the state of being secret **2** the ability or tendency to keep things secret

secret *adj* **1** kept hidden or separate from the knowledge of all or all but a few others **2** secretive: *she had become a secret drinker* **3** operating without the knowledge of outsiders: *secret organizations* ▷ *n* **4** something kept or to be kept hidden **5** something unrevealed; a mystery: *the secrets of nature* **6** an underlying explanation or reason: *the secret of great-looking hair* **7** **in secret** without the knowledge of others ▶ **HISTORY** Latin *secretus* concealed > **secretly** *adv*

secret agent *n* a person employed by a government to find out the military and political secrets of other governments

secretariat *n* **1 a** an office responsible for the secretarial, clerical, and administrative affairs of a legislative body or international organization **b** the staff of such an office or department **2** the premises of a secretariat ▶ **HISTORY** French

secretary *n, pl* **-taries** **1** a person who handles correspondence, keeps records, and does general clerical work for an individual or organization **2** the official manager of the day-to-day business of a society, club, or committee **3** (in Britain) a senior civil servant who assists a government minister **4** (in the US) the head of a government administrative department ▶ **HISTORY** Medieval Latin *secretarius* someone entrusted with secrets > **secretarial** *adj*

secretary bird *n* a large long-legged African bird of prey

secretary-general *n, pl* **secretaries-general** the chief administrative official of a legislative body or international organization

secretary of state *n* **1** (in Britain) the head of a major government department **2** (in the US) the head of the government department in charge of foreign affairs

secret ballot *n* a system of voting in which all votes are cast in secret

secrete¹ *vb* **-creting, -creted** (of a cell, organ, or gland) to produce and release (a substance) > **secretory** (sik-**reet**-or-ee) *adj*

secrete² *vb* **-creting, -creted** to put in a hiding place ▶ **HISTORY** variant of obsolete *secret* to hide away

secretin (sick-**ree**-tin) *n* *biochem* a peptic hormone secreted in the duodenum and jejunum when food passes to the stomach

secretion *n* **1** a substance that is released from a cell, organ, or gland **2** the process involved in producing and releasing such a substance ▶ **HISTORY** Latin *secretio* a separation

secretive *adj* hiding feelings and intentions > **secretively** *adv*

secret police *n* a police force that operates secretly to suppress opposition to the government

secret service *n* a government agency or department that conducts intelligence or counterintelligence operations

sect *n* **1** a subdivision of a larger religious or political group, esp. one regarded as extreme in its beliefs or practices **2** a group of people with a common interest or philosophy ▶ **HISTORY** Latin *secta* faction

sectarian *adj* **1** of or belonging to a sect **2** narrow-minded as a result of supporting a particular sect ▷ *n* **3** a member of a sect > **sectarianism** *n*

section *n* **1** a part cut off or separated from the main body of something: *a non-smoking section* **2** a part or subdivision of a piece of writing or a book: *the business section* **3** a distinct part of a country or community: *the Arabic section* **4** *surgery* the act or process of cutting or separating by cutting **5** *geom* a plane surface formed by cutting through a solid **6** short for **Caesarean section** **7** *NZ* a plot of land for building on **8** *Austral & NZ* a fare stage on a bus ▷ *vb* **9** to cut or divide into sections **10** to commit (a mentally disturbed person) to a psychiatric hospital ▶ **HISTORY** Latin *secare* to cut

sectional *adj* **1** concerned with a particular area or group within a country or community, esp. to the exclusion of others: *narrow sectional interests* **2** made of sections **3** of a section

sector *n* **1** a part or subdivision, esp. of a society or an economy: *the public sector* **2** *geom* either portion of a circle bounded by two radii and the arc cut off by them **3** a portion into which an area is divided for military operations ▶ **HISTORY** Latin: a cutter

secular *adj* **1** relating to worldly as opposed to sacred things **2** not connected with religion or the church **3** (of clerics) not bound by religious vows to

S

a monastic or other order ▶ HISTORY Late Latin *saecularis*

secularism *n* the belief that religion should have no place in civil affairs > **secularist** *n, adj*

secularize *or* **-ise** *vb* **-izing, -ized** *or* **-ising, -ised** to change (something, such as education) so that it is no longer connected with religion or the Church > **secularization** *or* **-isation** *n*

secure *adj* **1** free from danger or damage **2** free from fear, doubt, or care **3** tightly locked or well protected **4** fixed or tied firmly in position **5** able to be relied on: *secure profits* ▷ *vb* **-curing, -cured 6** to obtain: *to secure a change in German policy* **7** to make or become free from danger or fear **8** to make safe from loss, theft, or attack **9** to guarantee (payment of a loan) by giving something as security ▶ HISTORY Latin *securus* free from care > **securely** *adv*

security *n, pl* **-ties 1** precautions taken to ensure against theft, espionage, or other danger **2** the state of being free from danger, damage, or worry **3** assured freedom from poverty: *the security of a weekly pay cheque* **4** a certificate of ownership, such as a share, stock, or bond **5** something given or pledged to guarantee payment of a loan

security risk *n* someone or something thought to be a threat to state security

sedan *n US, Canad, Austral & NZ* a saloon car ▶ HISTORY origin unknown

sedan chair *n* an enclosed chair for one passenger, carried on poles by two bearers, commonly used in the 17th and 18th centuries

sedate¹ *adj* **1** quiet, calm, and dignified **2** slow or unhurried: *a sedate walk to the beach* ▶ HISTORY Latin *sedare* to soothe > **sedately** *adv*

sedate² *vb* **-dating, -dated** to calm down or make sleepy by giving a sedative drug to

sedation *n* **1** a state of calm, esp. when brought about by sedatives **2** the administration of a sedative

sedative *adj* **1** having a soothing or calming effect ▷ *n* **2** *med* a sedative drug or agent that makes people sleep or calm down ▶ HISTORY Latin *sedatus* assuaged

sedentary (**sed**-en-tree) *adj* **1** done sitting down and involving very little exercise: *a sedentary job* **2** tending to sit about without taking much exercise ▶ HISTORY Latin *sedere* to sit

sedge *n* a coarse grasslike plant growing on wet ground ▶ HISTORY Old English *secg* > **sedgy** *adj*

sedge warbler *n* a European songbird living in marshy areas

sediment *n* **1** matter that settles to the bottom of a liquid **2** material that has been deposited by water, ice, or wind ▶ HISTORY Latin *sedimentum* a settling

sedimentary layer *n geol* a layer within a sedimentary rock

sedimentary rock *n geol* rock that forms as mineral and organic materials, deposited by wind, water, and ice, and gradually built up in layers

sedimentation *n geol* the process in which layers of mineral and organic materials are deposited by water, ice, or wind

sedition *n* speech, writing, or behaviour intended to encourage rebellion or resistance against the government ▶ HISTORY Latin *seditio* discord > **seditionary** *n, adj* > **seditious** *adj*

seduce *vb* **-ducing, -duced 1** to persuade to have sexual intercourse **2** to tempt into wrongdoing ▶ HISTORY Latin *seducere* to lead apart > **seduction** *n*

seductive *adj* **1** (of a woman) sexually attractive **2** very attractive or tempting: *a seductive argument* > **seductively** *adv* > **seductiveness** *n*

sedulous *adj* diligent or painstaking: *a sedulous concern with the achievements of western thought* ▶ HISTORY Latin *sedulus* > **sedulously** *adv*

sedum *n* a rock plant with thick clusters of white, yellow, or pink flowers ▶ HISTORY Latin

see¹ *vb* **seeing, saw, seen 1** to look at or recognize with the eyes **2** to understand: *I explained the problem but he could not see it* **3** to perceive or be aware of: *she had never seen him so angry* **4** to view, watch, or attend: *we had barely seen a dozen movies in our lives* **5** to foresee: *they could see what their fate was to be* **6** to find out (a fact): *I was ringing to see whether you'd got it* **7** to make sure (of something) or take care (of something): *see that he is never in a position to do these things again; you must see to it* **8** to consider or decide: *see if you can come next week* **9** to have experience of: *he had seen active service in the revolution* **10** to meet or pay a visit to: *I see my specialist every three months* **11** to receive: *the Prime Minister will see the deputation now* **12** to frequent the company of: *we've been seeing each other since then* **13** to accompany: *she saw him to the door* **14** to refer to or look up: *see page 35* **15** (in gambling, esp. in poker) to match (another player's bet) or match the bet of (another player) by staking an equal sum **16 see fit** to consider it proper (to do something): *I did not see fit to send them home* **17 see you** *or* **see you later** *or* **be seeing you** an expression of farewell ▷ See also **see about** ▶ HISTORY Old English *sēon*

see² *n* the diocese of a bishop or the place within it where his cathedral is situated ▶ HISTORY Latin *sedes* a seat

see about *vb* **1** to take care of: *I'll see about some coffee* **2** to investigate: *to see about a new car*

seed *n* **1** *bot* the mature fertilized grain of a plant, containing an embryo ready for germination. Related adjective: **seminal 2** such seeds used for sowing **3** the source, beginning, or origin of anything: *the seeds of dissent* **4** *chiefly Bible* descendants; offspring: *the seed of David* **5** *sport* a player ranked according to his or her ability **6 go** *or* **run to seed a** (of plants) to produce and shed seeds after flowering **b** to lose strength or usefulness ▷ *vb* **7** to plant (seeds) in (soil) **8** (of plants) to produce or shed seeds **9** to remove the seeds from (fruit or plants) **10** to scatter silver iodide in (clouds) in order to cause rain **11** to arrange (the draw of a tournament) so that outstanding teams or players will not meet in the early rounds ▶ **HISTORY** Old English *sǣd* > **seedless** *adj*

seedbed *n* **1** an area of soil prepared for the growing of seedlings before they are transplanted **2** the place where something develops: *a seedbed of immorality*

seedling *n* a plant produced from a seed, esp. a very young plant

seed pod *n bot* a carpel or pistil enclosing the seeds of a plant, esp. a flowering plant

seedy *adj* **seedier, seediest** **1** shabby in appearance: *a seedy cinema* **2** *informal* physically unwell **3** (of a plant) at the stage of producing seeds > **seediness** *n*

seeing *n* **1** the sense or faculty of sight ▷ *conj* **2** (often foll. by *that*) in light of the fact (that)

seek *vb* **seeking, sought** **1** to try to find by searching: *to seek employment* **2** to try to obtain: *to seek a diplomatic solution* **3** to try (to do something): *we seek to establish a stable relationship* ▶ **HISTORY** Old English *sēcan*

seem *vb* **1** to appear to the mind or eye; give the impression of: *the car seems to be running well* **2** to appear to be: *there seems no need for all this nonsense* **3** to have the impression: *I seem to remember you were there too* ▶ **HISTORY** Old Norse *sōma* to be suitable

seeming *adj* apparent but not real: *his seeming willingness to participate* > **seemingly** *adv*

seemly *adj* **-lier, -liest** *formal* proper or fitting

seen *vb* the past participle of **see¹**

see off *vb* **1** to be present at the departure of (a person going on a journey): *your sisters came to see you off* **2** *informal* to cause to leave or depart, esp. by force

seep *vb* to leak through slowly; ooze ▶ **HISTORY** Old English *sīpian* > **seepage** *n*

seer *n* a person who can supposedly see into the future

seersucker *n* a light cotton fabric with a slightly crinkled surface ▶ **HISTORY** Hindi *śīrśakar*

seesaw *n* **1** a plank balanced in the middle so that two people seated on the ends can ride up and down by pushing on the ground with their feet **2** an up-and-down or back-and-forth movement ▷ *vb* **3** to move up and down or back and forth alternately ▶ **HISTORY** reduplication of *saw*, alluding to the movement from side to side, as in sawing

seethe *vb* **seething, seethed** **1** to be in a state of extreme anger or indignation without publicly showing these feelings **2** (of a liquid) to boil or foam ▶ **HISTORY** Old English *sēothan* > **seething** *adj*

see through *vb* **1** to perceive the true nature of: *it was difficult to see through people* **2** to remain with until the end or completion: *not all of them saw it through* **3** to help out in a time of need or trouble: *he helped see her through her divorce* ▷ *adj* **see-through** **4** (of clothing) made of thin cloth so that the wearer's body or underclothes are visible

segment *n* **1** one of several parts or sections into which an object is divided **2** *maths* **a** a part of a circle cut off by an intersecting line **b** a part of a sphere cut off by an intersecting plane or planes ▷ *vb* **3** to cut or divide into segments ▶ **HISTORY** Latin *segmentum* > **segmental** *adj* > **segmentation** *n*

segregate *vb* **-gating, -gated** **1** to set apart from others or from the main group **2** to impose segregation on (a racial or minority group) ▶ **HISTORY** Latin *se-* apart + *grex* a flock

segregation *n* **1** the practice or policy of creating separate facilities within the same society for the use of a racial or minority group **2** the act of segregating > **segregational** *adj* > **segregationist** *n*

seigneur *n* a feudal lord, esp. in France ▶ **HISTORY** Old French > **seigneurial** *adj*

seine (**sane**) *n* **1** a large fishing net that hangs vertically in the water by means of floats at the top and weights at the bottom ▷ *vb* **seining, seined** **2** to catch (fish) using this net ▶ **HISTORY** Old English *segne*

seismic *adj* relating to or caused by earthquakes ▶ **HISTORY** Greek *seismos* earthquake

seismic wave *n physics* an earth vibration caused by an earthquake or explosion

seismograph *n* an instrument that records the intensity and duration of earthquakes ▶ **HISTORY** Greek *seismos* earthquake + -GRAPH > **seismographer** *n* > **seismography** *n*

seismology *n* the branch of geology concerned with the study of earthquakes ▶ **HISTORY** Greek *seismos* earthquake + -LOGY > **seismologist** *n*

seismometer *n* same as **seismograph**

seize *vb* **seizing, seized** **1** to take hold of forcibly or quickly; grab **2** to take immediate advantage of: *real journalists would have seized the opportunity* **3** to take legal possession of **4** (sometimes foll. by *on* or *upon*) to understand quickly: *she immediately seized his idea* **5** to occupy or fill the mind of suddenly: *a wild frenzy seized her* **6** to take by force or capture: *the rebels seized a tank factory* **7** (often foll. by *up*) (of mechanical parts) to become jammed through overheating ▶ **HISTORY** Old French *saisir*

seizure *n* **1** *pathol* a sudden violent attack of an illness, such as an epileptic convulsion **2** the act of seizing: *a seizure of drug traffickers' assets*

seldom *adv* rarely; not often ▶ **HISTORY** Old English *seldon*

select *vb* **1** to choose (someone or something) in preference to another or others ▷ *adj* **2** chosen in preference to others **3** restricted to a particular group; exclusive: *a select audience* ▶ **HISTORY** Latin *seligere* to sort > **selector** *n*

select committee *n Government* a small committee of Members of Parliament, set up to investigate and report on a specified matter

selection *n* **1** a selecting or being selected **2** a thing or number of things that have been selected **3** a range from which something may be selected: *a good selection of reasonably priced wines* **4** *biol* the

S

process by which certain organisms or individuals are reproduced and survive in preference to others

selective *adj* **1** tending to choose carefully or characterized by careful choice: *they were selective in their reading* **2** of or characterized by selection > **selectively** *adv* > **selectivity** *n*

selective breeding *n agriculture, horticulture* the practice of producing animals or plants from particular specimens or individuals with particular inherited characteristics

selenium *n chem* a nonmetallic element used in photocells, solar cells, and in xerography. Symbol: Se ▶ HISTORY Greek *selēnē* moon

self *n, pl* **selves** **1** the distinct individuality or identity of a person or thing **2** a person's typical bodily make-up or personal characteristics: *back to my old self after the scare* **3** one's own welfare or interests: *he only thinks of self* **4** an individual's consciousness of his or her own identity or being ▷ *pron* **5** not standard myself, yourself, himself, or herself: *setting goals for self and others* ▶ HISTORY Old English

self- *combining form* **1** of oneself or itself: *self-defence* **2** by, to, in, due to, for, or from the self: *self-employed; self-respect* **3** automatic or automatically: *self-propelled*

self-absorption *n* preoccupation with oneself to the exclusion of others > **self-absorbed** *adj*

self-addressed *adj* addressed for return to the sender

self-assertion *n* the act of putting forward one's own opinions or demanding one's rights, esp. in an aggressive or confident manner > **self-assertive** *adj*

self-catering *adj* (of accommodation) for tenants providing and preparing their own food

self-centred *or US* **self-centered** *adj* totally preoccupied with one's own concerns

self-coloured *or US* **self-colored** *adj* **1** having only a single and uniform colour: *a self-coloured tie* **2** (of cloth or wool) having the natural or original colour

self-confessed *adj* according to one's own admission: *a self-confessed addict*

self-confidence *n* confidence in oneself, one's abilities, or one's judgment > **self-confident** *adj*

self-conscious *adj* embarrassed or ill at ease through being unduly aware of oneself as the object of the attention of others > **self-consciously** *adv* > **self-consciousness** *n*

self-contained *adj* **1** containing within itself all parts necessary for completeness **2** (of a flat) having its own kitchen, bathroom, and toilet not shared by others

self-control *n* the ability to control one's feelings, emotions, or reactions > **self-controlled** *adj*

self-defence *or US* **self-defense** *n* **1** the act or skill of defending oneself against physical attack **2** the act of defending one's actions, ideas, or rights

self-determination *n* **1** the ability to make a decision for oneself without influence from outside **2** the right of a nation or people to determine its

own form of government > **self-determined** *adj*

self-discipline *n* the power to control one's own feelings and actions, esp. in order to improve oneself

self-employed *adj* earning one's living in one's own business, rather than as the employee of another

self-esteem *n* respect for or a favourable opinion of oneself

self-evident *adj* so obvious that no proof or explanation is needed > **self-evidently** *adv*

self-government *n* the government of a country, nation, or community by its own people > **self-governing** *adj*

self-help *n* **1** the use of one's own abilities and resources to help oneself without relying on the assistance of others **2** the practice of solving one's problems within a group of people with similar problems

selfie *n informal* a photograph taken by pointing the camera at oneself

self-important *adj* having an unduly high opinion of one's own importance > **self-importance** *n*

self-improvement *n* the improvement of one's education, status, etc. by one's own efforts

self-indulgent *adj* tending to allow oneself to have or do things that one enjoys > **self-indulgence** *n*

self-interest *n* **1** one's personal interest or advantage **2** the pursuit of one's own interest > **self-interested** *adj*

selfish *adj* **1** caring too much about oneself and not enough about others **2** (of behaviour or attitude) motivated by self-interest > **selfishly** *adv* > **selfishness** *n*

selfless *adj* putting other people's interests before one's own > **selflessly** *adv* > **selflessness** *n*

self-made *adj* having achieved wealth or status by one's own efforts

self-opinionated *adj* clinging stubbornly to one's own opinions

self-pollination *n bot* the transfer of pollen from the anthers to the stigma of the same flower

self-possessed *adj* having control of one's emotions or behaviour, esp. in difficult situations > **self-possession** *n*

self-propelled *adj* **1** (of a vehicle) driven by its own engine rather than drawn by a locomotive, horse, etc. **2** (of a rocket launcher or artillery piece) mounted on a motor vehicle > **self-propelling** *adj*

self-raising *adj* (of flour) having a raising agent, such as baking powder, already added

self-respect *n* a feeling of confidence and pride in one's own abilities and worth > **self-respecting** *adj*

self-righteous *adj* thinking oneself more virtuous than others > **self-righteousness** *n*

selfsame *adj* the very same: *this was the selfsame woman I'd met on the train*

self-satisfied *adj* smug and complacently satisfied with oneself or one's own actions > **self-satisfaction** *n*

S

self-seeking *n* **1** the act or an instance of seeking one's own profit or interests ▷ *adj* **2** inclined to promote only one's own profit or interests: *self-seeking politicians* > **self-seeker** *n*

self-service *adj* **1** of or denoting a shop or restaurant where the customers serve themselves and then pay a cashier ▷ *n* **2** the practice of serving oneself and then paying a cashier

self-starter *n* **1** an electric motor used to start an internal-combustion engine **2** a person who is strongly motivated and shows initiative at work

self-styled *adj* using a title or name that one has given oneself, esp. without right or justification; so-called: *the self-styled leader of the rebellion*

self-sufficient *adj* able to provide for or support oneself without the help of others > **self-sufficiency** *n*

self-willed *adj* stubbornly determined to have one's own way, esp. at the expense of others

sell *vb* **selling, sold 1** to exchange (something) for money **2** to deal in (objects or property): *he sells used cars* **3** to give up or surrender for a price or reward: *to sell one's honour* **4 sell for** to have a specified price: *they sell for 10 pence each* **5** to promote the sale of (objects or property): *sensational stories sell magazines* **6** to gain acceptance of: *he'll sell an idea to a producer* **7** to be in demand on the market: *his books did not sell well enough* **8 sell down the river** *informal* to betray **9 sell oneself a** to convince someone else of one's potential or worth **b** to give up one's moral standards for a price or reward **10 sell someone short** *informal* to undervalue someone ▷ *n* **11** the act or an instance of selling: *the hard sell* ▷ See also **sell off, sell out, sell up** ▶ HISTORY Old English *sellan* to give, deliver > **seller** *n*

sell-by date *n* **1** *Brit* the date printed on packaged food specifying the date after which the food should not be sold **2 past one's sell-by date** beyond one's prime

sell off *vb* to sell (remaining items) at reduced prices

Sellotape *n* **1** *trademark* a type of transparent adhesive tape ▷ *vb* **-taping, -taped 2** to seal or stick using adhesive tape

sell out *vb* **1** to dispose of (something) completely by selling **2** *informal* to betray in order to gain an advantage or benefit ▷ *n* **sellout 3** *informal* a performance of a show, etc. for which all tickets are sold **4** a commercial success **5** *informal* a betrayal

sell-through *adj* of the sale of prerecorded DVDs, without their first being for hire only

sell up *vb* *chiefly Brit & Austral* to sell all one's goods or property

selvage *or* **selvedge** *n* a specially woven edge on a length of fabric to prevent it from unravelling ▶ HISTORY SELF + EDGE > **selvaged** *adj*

selves *n* the plural of **self**

semantic *adj* **1** of or relating to the meanings of words **2** of or relating to semantics ▶ HISTORY Greek *sēma* a sign > **semantically** *adv*

semantics *n* the branch of linguistics that deals with the study of meaning

semaphore *n* **1** a system of signalling by holding two flags in different positions to represent letters of the alphabet ▷ *vb* **-phoring, -phored 2** to signal (information) by semaphore ▶ HISTORY Greek *sēma* a signal + *-phoros* carrying

semblance *n* outward or superficial appearance: *some semblance of order had been established* ▶ HISTORY Old French *sembler* to seem

semen *n* the thick whitish fluid containing spermatozoa that is produced by the male reproductive organs and ejaculated from the penis ▶ HISTORY Latin: seed

semester *n* either of two divisions of the academic year ▶ HISTORY Latin *semestris* half-yearly

semi *n* *Brit, Austral & S African, informal* short for **semidetached** (sense 2)

semi- *prefix* **1** half: *semicircle* **2** partly or almost: *semiprofessional* **3** occurring twice in a specified period: *semiweekly* ▶ HISTORY Latin

semiarid *adj* denoting land that lies on the edges of a desert but has a slightly higher rainfall (above 300 mm) so that some farming is possible

semi-autonomous *adj* having a degree of self-government without being fully independent

semibreve *n* *music* a note, now the longest in common use, with a time value that may be divided by any power of 2 to give all other notes

semicircle *n* **1** one half of a circle **2** anything having the shape or form of half a circle > **semicircular** *adj*

semicolon *n* the punctuation mark (;) used to separate clauses or items in a list, or to indicate a pause longer than that of a comma and shorter than that of a full stop

semiconductor *n* *physics* a substance, such as silicon, which has an electrical conductivity that increases with temperature

semidetached *adj* **1** (of a house) joined to another house on one side by a common wall ▷ *n* **2** *Brit* a semidetached house: *the mock Georgian semidetached*

semifinal *n* the round before the final in a competition > **semifinalist** *n*

seminal *adj* **1** highly original and influential: *seminal thinkers* **2** potentially capable of development **3** of semen: *seminal fluid* **4** *biol* of seed ▶ HISTORY Latin *semen* seed

seminar *n* **1** a small group of students meeting regularly under the guidance of a tutor for study and discussion **2** one such meeting ▶ HISTORY Latin *seminarium* a nursery garden

seminary *n*, *pl* **-naries** a college for the training of priests ▶ HISTORY Latin *seminarium* a nursery garden > **seminarian** *n*

seminiferous *n* *biol* containing, conveying, or producing semen: *seminiferous tubules*

semiotics *n* the study of human communication, esp. communication using signs and symbols ▶ HISTORY Greek *sēmeion* a sign > **semiotic** *adj*

S

semipermeable *adj* (of a cell membrane) allowing small molecules to pass through but not large ones

semiprecious *adj* (of certain stones) having less value than a precious stone

semiquaver *n* *music* a note having the time value of one-sixteenth of a semibreve

semirigid *adj* (of an airship) maintaining shape by means of a main supporting keel and internal gas pressure

semiskilled *adj* partly skilled or trained but not sufficiently so to perform specialized work

Semite *n* a member of the group of peoples who speak a Semitic language, such as the Jews and Arabs ▶ HISTORY New Latin *semita* descendant of Shem, eldest of Noah's sons

Semitic *n* **1** a group of languages that includes Arabic, Hebrew, and Aramaic ▷ *adj* **2** of this group of languages **3** of any of the peoples speaking a Semitic language, esp. the Jews or the Arabs **4** same as **Jewish**

semitone *n* the smallest interval between two notes in Western music represented on a piano by the difference in pitch between any two adjacent keys > **semitonic** *adj*

semitrailer *n* *Austral* a large truck in two separate sections joined by a pivoted bar. Also called: **semi**

semitropical *adj* bordering on the tropics; nearly tropical > **semitropics** *pl n*

semivowel *n* *phonetics* a vowel-like sound that acts like a consonant, such as the sound *w* in *well*

semolina *n* the large hard grains of wheat left after flour has been milled, used for making puddings and pasta ▶ HISTORY Italian *semolino*

SEN (in Britain) State Enrolled Nurse

Sen. *or* **sen.** **1** senate **2** senator **3** senior

senate *n* the main governing body at some universities ▶ HISTORY Latin *senatus* council of the elders

Senate *n* the upper chamber of the legislatures of Australia, the US, Canada, and many other countries

senator *n* a member of a Senate > **senatorial** *adj*

send *vb* **sending, sent** **1** to cause (a person or thing) to go or be taken or transmitted to another place: *send a cheque or postal order* **2 send for** to dispatch a request or command for (someone or something): *she had sent for me* **3** to cause to go to a place or point: *the bullet sent him flying into the air* **4** to bring to a state or condition: *his schemes to send her mad* **5** to cause to happen or come: *the thunderstorm sent by the gods* **6** *old-fashioned, slang* to move to excitement or rapture: *this music really sends me* ▶ HISTORY Old English *sendan* > **sender** *n*

send down *vb* **1** *Brit* to expel from a university **2** *informal* to send to prison

sendoff *n* **1** *informal* a show of good wishes to a person about to set off on a journey or start a new career ▷ *vb* **send off** **2** to dispatch (something, such as a letter) **3** *sport* (of a referee) to dismiss (a player) from the field of play for some offence

send up *informal vb* **1** to make fun of by doing an imitation or parody ▷ *n* **send-up** **2** a parody or imitation

senescent *adj* *formal* growing old ▶ HISTORY Latin *senescere* to grow old > **senescence** *n*

seneschal (**sen**-ish-al) *n* *history* a steward of the household of a medieval prince or nobleman ▶ HISTORY Old French

senile *adj* mentally or physically weak or infirm on account of old age ▶ HISTORY Latin *senex* an old man > **senility** *n*

senior *adj* **1** higher in rank or length of service **2** older in years: *senior citizens* **3** *education* of or designating more advanced or older pupils or students ▷ *n* **4** a senior person ▶ HISTORY Latin: older

senior aircraftman *n* an ordinary rank in the Royal Air Force

senior citizen *n* an old person, esp. a pensioner

seniority *n, pl* **-ties** **1** the state of being senior **2** degree of power or importance in an organization from length of continuous service

senior service *n* *Brit* the Royal Navy

senna *n* **1** a tropical plant with yellow flowers and long pods **2** the dried leaves and pods of this plant, used as a laxative ▶ HISTORY Arabic *sanā*

señor (sen-**nyor**) *n* a Spanish form of address equivalent to *sir* or *Mr*

señora (sen-**nyor**-a) *n* a Spanish form of address equivalent to *madam* or *Mrs*

señorita (sen-nyor-**ee**-ta) *n* a Spanish form of address equivalent to *madam* or *Miss*

sensation *n* **1** the power of feeling things physically: *I lose all sensation in my hands* **2** a physical feeling: *a burning sensation in the throat* **3** a general feeling or awareness: *a sensation of vague resentment* **4** a state of excitement: *imagine the sensation in Washington!* **5** an exciting person or thing: *you'll be a sensation* ▶ HISTORY Late Latin *sensatus* endowed with feelings

sensational *adj* **1** causing intense feelings of shock, anger, or excitement: *sensational allegations* **2** *informal* extremely good: *the views are sensational* **3** of the senses or sensation > **sensationally** *adv*

sensationalism *n* the deliberate use of sensational language or subject matter to arouse feelings of shock, anger, or excitement > **sensationalist** *adj, n*

sense *n* **1** any of the faculties (sight, hearing, touch, taste, and smell) by which the mind receives information about the external world or the state of the body **2** the ability to perceive **3** a feeling perceived through one of the senses: *a sense of warmth* **4** a mental perception or awareness: *a sense of security* **5** an ability to make moral judgments: *a sense of honour* **6** (usually pl) sound practical judgment or intelligence: *a man lost his senses and killed his wife* **7** a reason or purpose: *no sense in continuing* **8** a general meaning: *he couldn't understand every word but he got the sense of what they were saying* **9** a specific meaning; definition: *the three senses of the word* **10 make sense** to be

understandable or practical ▷ vb **sensing, sensed**
11 to perceive without the evidence of the senses:
he sensed that she was impressed **12** to perceive
through the senses ▶ HISTORY Latin *sentire* to feel

senseless *adj* **1** having no meaning or purpose:
a senseless act of violence **2** unconscious
> **senselessly** *adv* > **senselessness** *n*

sense organ *n* a part of the body that receives
stimuli and transmits them as sensations to the
brain

sensibility *n, pl* **-ties 1** (often pl) the ability to
experience deep feelings **2** (usually pl) the
tendency to be influenced or offended: *its sheer
callousness offended her sensibilities* **3** the ability to
perceive or feel

sensible *adj* **1** having or showing good sense or
judgment **2** (of clothing and footwear) practical
and hard-wearing **3** capable of receiving sensation
4 capable of being perceived by the senses
5 perceptible to the mind **6** *literary* aware: *sensible
of your kindness* ▶ HISTORY Latin *sentire* to feel
> **sensibly** *adv*

sensitive *adj* **1** easily hurt; tender **2** responsive to
feelings and moods **3** responsive to external
stimuli or impressions **4** easily offended or shocked
5 (of a subject or issue) liable to arouse controversy
or strong feelings **6** (of an instrument) capable of
registering small differences or changes in
amounts **7** *photog* responding readily to light:
a sensitive emulsion **8** *chiefly US* connected with
matters affecting national security ▶ HISTORY
Latin *sentire* to feel > **sensitively** *adv*
> **sensitivity** *n*

sensitize *or* **-tise** *vb* **-tizing, -tized** *or* **-tising,
-tised** to make sensitive > **sensitization** *or*
-tisation *n*

sensor *n* a device that detects or measures a
physical property, such as radiation

sensory *adj* relating to the physical senses

sensual *adj* **1** giving pleasure to the body and
senses rather than the mind: *soft sensual music*
2 having a strong liking for physical pleasures **3** of
the body and senses rather than the mind or soul
▶ HISTORY Latin *sensus* feeling > **sensualist** *n*

sensuality *n* **1** the quality or state of being
sensual **2** enjoyment of physical pleasures

sensuous *adj* **1** pleasing to the senses of the mind
or body: *the sensuous rhythms of the drums* **2** (of a
person) appreciating qualities perceived by the
senses > **sensuously** *adv*

sent *vb* the past of **send**

sentence *n* **1** a sequence of words constituting a
statement, question, or a command that begins
with a capital letter and ends with a full stop when
written down **2 a** the decision of a law court as to
what punishment is passed on a convicted person
b the punishment passed on a convicted person
▷ *vb* **-tencing, -tenced 3** to pronounce sentence
on (a convicted person) in a lawcourt ▶ HISTORY
Latin *sententia* a way of thinking > **sentential** *adj*

sententious *adj formal* **1** trying to sound wise
2 making pompous remarks about morality

▶ HISTORY Latin *sententiosus* full of meaning
> **sententiously** *adv*

sentient (**sen**-tee-ent, **sen**-shent) *adj* capable of
perception and feeling ▶ HISTORY Latin *sentiens*
feeling > **sentience** *n*

sentiment *n* **1** a mental attitude based on a
mixture of thoughts and feelings: *anti-American
sentiment* **2** (often pl) a thought, opinion, or
attitude expressed in words: *his sentiments were
echoed by subsequent speakers* **3** feelings such as
tenderness, romance, and sadness, esp. when
exaggerated: *a man without the softness of sentiment*
▶ HISTORY Latin *sentire* to feel

sentimental *adj* **1** feeling or expressing
tenderness, romance, or sadness to an
exaggerated extent **2** appealing to the emotions,
esp. to romantic feelings: *she kept the ring for
sentimental reasons* > **sentimentalism** *n*
> **sentimentalist** *n* > **sentimentality** *n*
> **sentimentally** *adv*

sentimentalize *or* **-ise** *vb* **-izing, -ized** *or*
-ising, -ised to make sentimental or behave
sentimentally

sentinel *n old-fashioned* a sentry ▶ HISTORY Old
French *sentinelle*

sentry *n, pl* **-tries** a soldier who keeps watch and
guards a camp or building ▶ HISTORY perhaps from
obsolete *centrinel* sentinel

sentry box *n* a small shelter with an open front in
which a sentry stands during bad weather

sepal *n bot* a leaflike division of the calyx of a flower
▶ HISTORY New Latin *sepalum*

separable *adj* able to be separated

separate *vb* **-rating, -rated 1** to act as a barrier
between: *the narrow stretch of water which separates
Europe from Asia* **2** to part or be parted from a mass
or group **3** to distinguish: *it's what separates the
women from the boys* **4** to divide or be divided into
component parts **5** to sever or be severed **6** (of a
couple) to stop living together ▷ *adj* **7** existing or
considered independently: *a separate issue* **8** set
apart from the main body or mass **9** distinct or
individual ▶ HISTORY Latin *separare* > **separately**
adv > **separateness** *n* > **separator** *n*

separates *pl n Brit, Austral & NZ* clothes, such as
skirts, blouses, and trousers, that only cover part
of the body and are designed to be worn together
or separately

separate school *n* (in certain Canadian
provinces) a school for a large religious minority
financed by provincial grants in addition to the
education tax

separation *n* **1** the act of separating: *the
separation of child from mother* **2** *family law* the living
apart of a married couple without divorce **3** a
mark, line, or object that separates one thing from
another

separation of powers *n law* the doctrine that
power should be separated rather than
concentrated to safeguard individual rights, as in
the separate branches for executive, legislative,
and judicial powers

separatist *n* a person who advocates the separation of his or her own group from an organization or country ▶ **separatism** *n*

sepia *adj* dark reddish-brown, like the colour of very old photographs ▶ HISTORY Latin: a cuttlefish

sepoy *n* (formerly) an Indian soldier in the service of the British ▶ HISTORY Urdu *sipāhī*

sepsis *n* poisoning caused by the presence of pus-forming bacteria in the body ▶ HISTORY Greek: a rotting

sept *n* a clan, esp. in Ireland or Scotland ▶ HISTORY perhaps variant of *sect*

Sept. September

September *n* the ninth month of the year ▶ HISTORY Latin: the seventh (month)

septet *n* **1** a group of seven performers **2** a piece of music for seven performers ▶ HISTORY Latin *septem* seven

septic *adj* of or caused by harmful bacteria ▶ **septicity** *n*

septicaemia or **septicemia** (sep-tis-see-mee-a) *n* an infection of the blood which develops in a wound ▶ HISTORY Greek *sēptos* decayed + *haima* blood

septic tank *n* a tank in which sewage is decomposed by the action of bacteria

septuagenarian *n* **1** a person who is between 70 and 79 years old ▷ *adj* **2** between 70 and 79 years old ▶ HISTORY Latin *septuaginta* seventy

Septuagint (**sept**-yew-a-jint) *n* the ancient Greek version of the Old Testament, including the Apocrypha ▶ HISTORY Latin *septuaginta* seventy

septum *n, pl* **-ta** *biol, anat* a dividing partition between two tissues or cavities, such as in the nose ▶ HISTORY Latin *saeptum* wall

septuple *vb* **-pling, -pled** **1** to multiply by seven ▷ *adj* **2** seven times as much or as many **3** consisting of seven parts ▷ *n* **4** a quantity or number seven times as great as another ▶ HISTORY Latin *septem* seven

sepulchral (sip-**pulk**-ral) *adj* **1** gloomy and solemn, like a tomb or grave **2** of a sepulchre

sepulchre or US **sepulcher** (**sep**-pulk-er) *n* **1** a burial vault, tomb, or grave ▷ *vb* **-chring** or US **-chering, -chred** or US **-chered** **2** to bury in a sepulchre ▶ HISTORY Latin *sepulcrum*

sequel *n* **1** a novel, play, or film that continues the story of an earlier one **2** anything that happens after or as a result of something else: *there was an amusing sequel to this incident* ▶ HISTORY Latin *sequi* to follow

sequence *n* **1** an arrangement of two or more things in a successive order **2** the successive order of two or more things: *chronological sequence* **3** an action or event that follows another or others **4** *maths* an ordered set of numbers or other quantities in one-to-one correspondence with the integers 1 to *n* **5** a section of a film forming a single uninterrupted episode **6** to arrange in a sequence ▶ HISTORY Latin *sequi* to follow

sequence of events *n* the order in which several related things happen

sequential *adj* happening in a fixed order or sequence

sequester *vb* **1** to seclude: *he could sequester himself in his own home* **2** *law* same as **sequestrate** ▶ HISTORY Late Latin *sequestrare* to surrender for safekeeping

sequestrate *vb* **-trating, -trated** *law* to confiscate (property) temporarily until creditors are satisfied or a court order is complied with ▶ **sequestrator** *n*

sequestration *n* **1** the act of sequestering or the state of being sequestered **2** *law* the sequestering of property **3** *chem* the effective removal of ions from a solution by coordination with another type of ion or molecule to form complexes

sequin *n* a small piece of shiny metal foil used to decorate clothes ▶ HISTORY Italian *zecchino* ▶ **sequined** *adj*

sequoia *n* a giant Californian coniferous tree ▶ HISTORY after *Sequoya*, a Native American scholar

seraglio (sir-**ah**-lee-oh) *n, pl* **-raglios** **1** the part of a Muslim house or palace where the owner's wives live **2** a Turkish sultan's palace ▶ HISTORY Italian *serraglio* animal cage

seraph *n, pl* **-aphim** *theol* a member of the highest order of angels ▶ HISTORY from Hebrew ▶ **seraphic** *adj*

Serb *adj, n* same as **Serbian**

Serbian *adj* **1** of Serbia ▷ *n* **2** a person from Serbia **3** the dialect of Serbo-Croat spoken in Serbia

Serbo-Croat or **Serbo-Croatian** *n* **1** the chief official language of Serbia and Croatia ▷ *adj* **2** of this language

serenade *n* **1** a piece of music played or sung to a woman by a lover **2** a piece of music suitable for this **3** an orchestral suite for a small ensemble ▷ *vb* **-nading, -naded** **4** to sing or play a serenade to (someone) ▶ HISTORY French

serendipity *n* the gift of making fortunate discoveries by accident ▶ HISTORY from the fairy tale *The Three Princes of Serendip*, in which the heroes possess this gift

serene *adj* **1** peaceful or calm **2** (of the sky) clear or bright ▶ HISTORY Latin *serenus* ▶ **serenely** *adv* ▶ **serenity** *n*

serf *n* (esp. in medieval Europe) a labourer who could not leave the land on which he worked ▶ HISTORY Latin *servus* a slave ▶ **serfdom** *n*

serge *n* a strong fabric made of wool, cotton, silk, or rayon, used for clothing ▶ HISTORY Old French *sarge*

sergeant *n* **1** a noncommissioned officer in the armed forces **2** (in Britain and Australia) a police officer ranking between constable and inspector ▶ HISTORY Old French *sergent*

sergeant at arms *n* a parliamentary or court officer responsible for keeping order

sergeant major *n* a noncommissioned officer of the highest rank in the army

serial *n* **1** a story published or broadcast in instalments at regular intervals **2** a publication that is regularly issued and consecutively

773

numbered ▷ *adj* **3** of, in, or forming a series: *serial pregnancies* **4** published or presented as a serial ▶ **HISTORY** Latin *series* series > **serially** *adv*

serialize *or* **-ise** *vb* **-izing, -ized** *or* **-ising, -ised** to publish or present in the form of a serial > **serialization** *or* **-isation** *n*

serial killer *n* a person who commits a number of murders

series *n*, *pl* **-ries 1** a group or succession of related things **2** a set of radio or television programmes dealing with the same subject, esp. one having the same characters but different stories **3** *maths* the sum of a finite or infinite sequence of numbers or quantities **4** *electronics* an arrangement of two or more components connected in a circuit so that the same current flows in turn through each of them: *a number of resistors in series* **5** *geol* a set of layers that represent the rocks formed during an epoch ▶ **HISTORY** Latin: a row

series circuit *n electronics* an electrical circuit in which two or more components are connected in such a way that the same current can flow through each of them in turn

serious *adj* **1** giving cause for concern: *the situation is serious* **2** concerned with important matters: *there are some serious questions that need to be answered* **3** not cheerful; grave: *I am a serious person* **4** in earnest; sincere: *he believes we are serious* **5** requiring concentration: *a serious book* **6** *informal* impressive because of its substantial quantity or quality: *serious money* ▶ **HISTORY** Latin *serius* > **seriously** *adv* > **seriousness** *n*

serjeant *n* same as **sergeant**

sermon *n* **1** a speech on a religious or moral subject given by a member of the clergy as part of a church service **2** *disparaging* a serious talk on behaviour, morals, or duty, esp. a long and tedious one ▶ **HISTORY** Latin *sermo* discourse

seropositive (seer-oh-**poz**-zit-iv) *adj* (of a person whose blood has been tested for a specific disease, such as AIDS) showing a significant level of serum antibodies, indicating the presence of the disease

serotonin (ser-roe-**tone**-in) *n biochem* a compound that occurs in the brain, intestines, and blood platelets and acts as a neurotransmitter

serous (**seer**-uss) *adj* of, containing, or like serum

serpent *n* **1** *literary* a snake **2** a devious person ▶ **HISTORY** Latin *serpens* a creeping thing

serpentine¹ *adj* twisting like a snake

serpentine² *n* a soft green or brownish-red mineral ▶ **HISTORY** so named from its snakelike patterns

serrated *adj* having a notched or sawlike edge ▶ **HISTORY** Latin *serratus* saw-shaped > **serration** *n*

serried *adj literary* in close formation: *the serried ranks of fans* ▶ **HISTORY** Old French *serré* close-packed

serum (**seer**-um) *n* **1** the yellowish watery fluid left after blood has clotted **2** this fluid from the blood of immunized animals used for inoculation or vaccination **3** *physiol*, *zool* any clear watery animal fluid ▶ **HISTORY** Latin: whey

serval *n* a slender African wild cat with black-spotted tawny fur

servant *n* **1** a person employed to do household work for another person **2** a person or thing that is useful or provides a service: *a distinguished servant of this country* ▶ **HISTORY** Old French: serving

serve *vb* **serving, served 1** to be of service to (a person, community, or cause); help **2** to perform an official duty or duties: *he served on several university committees* **3** to attend to (customers) in a shop **4** to provide (guests) with food or drink: *he served dinner guests German wine* **5** to provide (food or drink) for customers: *breakfast is served from 7 a.m.* **6** to provide with something needed by the public: *the community served by the school* **7** to work as a servant for (a person) **8** to go through (a period of police or military service, apprenticeship, or imprisonment) **9** to meet the needs of: *they serve a purpose* **10** to perform a function: *the attacks only served to strengthen their resolve* **11** (of a male animal) to mate with (a female animal) **12** *tennis, squash, etc.* to put (the ball) into play **13** to deliver (a legal document) to (a person) **14** **serve someone right** *informal* to be what someone deserves, esp. for doing something stupid or wrong ▷ *n* **15** *tennis, squash, etc.* short for **service** (sense 12) ▶ **HISTORY** Latin *servus* a slave

server *n* **1** a person who serves **2** *computers* a computer or program that supplies data to other machines on a network

service *n* **1** an act of help or assistance **2** an organization or system that provides something needed by the public: *a consumer information service* **3** a department of public employment and its employees: *the diplomatic service* **4** the installation or maintenance of goods provided by a dealer after a sale **5** availability for use by the public: *the new plane could be in service within fifteen years* **6** a regular check made on a machine or vehicle in which parts are tested, cleaned, or replaced if worn **7** the serving of guests or customers: *service is included on the wine list* **8** one of the branches of the armed forces **9** the serving of food: *silver service* **10** a set of dishes, cups, and plates for use at table **11** a formal religious ceremony **12** *tennis, squash, etc.* **a** the act, manner, or right of serving the ball **b** the game in which a particular player serves: *she dropped only one point on her service* ▷ *adj* **13** of or for the use of servants or employees: *a service elevator* **14** serving the public rather than producing goods: *the service sector* ▷ *vb* **-vicing, -viced 15** to provide service or services to **16** to check and repair (a vehicle or machine) **17** (of a male animal) to mate with (a female animal) ▷ See also **services** ▶ **HISTORY** Latin *servitium* condition of a slave

serviceable *adj* **1** performing effectively: *serviceable boots* **2** able or ready to be used: *five remaining serviceable aircraft* > **serviceability** *n*

service area *n* a place on a motorway with a garage, restaurants, and toilets

service charge *n* a percentage added to a bill in a hotel or restaurant to pay for service

S

service flat *n* a flat where domestic services are provided by the management

service industry *n econ, business* an industry that serves the public rather than producing goods

serviceman *n, pl* **-men 1** a person in the armed services **2** a man employed to service and maintain equipment ▸ *n* **servicewoman** *fem n*

service road *n Brit & Austral* a narrow road running parallel to a main road that provides access to houses and shops situated along its length

services *pl n* **1** work performed in a job: *the OBE for her services to the community* **2 the services** the armed forces **3** a system of providing the public with something it needs, such as gas or water

service station *n* **1** a place that sells fuel, oil, and spare parts for motor vehicles **2** same as **service area**

serviette *n* a table napkin ▸ **HISTORY** Old French

servile *adj* **1** too eager to obey people; fawning **2** of or suitable for a slave ▸ **HISTORY** Latin *servus* slave > **servility** *n*

serving *n* a portion of food

servitude *n formal* **1** slavery or bondage **2** the state or condition of being completely dominated ▸ **HISTORY** Latin *servus* a slave

servomechanism *n* a device which converts a small force into a larger force, used esp. in steering mechanisms

sesame (**sess**-am-ee) *n* a plant of the East Indies, grown for its seeds and oil, which are used in cooking ▸ **HISTORY** Greek

sessile *adj* **1** (of flowers or leaves) having no stalk **2** (of animals such as the barnacle) fixed in one position ▸ **HISTORY** Latin *sessilis* concerning sitting

session *n* **1** any period devoted to a particular activity **2** a meeting of a court, parliament, or council **3** a series or period of such meetings **4** a school or university term or year ▸ **HISTORY** Latin *sessio* a sitting > **sessional** *adj*

sestet *n* **1** *prosody* the last six lines of a sonnet **2** same as **sextet** (sense 1) ▸ **HISTORY** Italian *sesto* sixth

set¹ *vb* **setting, set 1** to put in a specified position or state: *I set him free* **2 set to** *or* **on** to bring (something) into contact with (something else): *three prisoners set fire to their cells* **3** to put into order or make ready: *set the table* **4** to make or become firm or rigid: *before the eggs begin to set* **5** to put (a broken bone) or (of a broken bone) to be put into a normal position for healing **6** to adjust (a clock or other instrument) to a particular position **7** to arrange or establish: *to set a date for diplomatic talks; it set the standards of performance* **8** to prescribe or assign (a task or material for study): *the examiners have set 'Paradise Lost'* **9** to arrange (hair) while wet, so that it dries in position **10** to place a jewel in (a setting): *a ring set with diamonds* **11** to provide music for (a poem or other text to be sung) **12** *printing* **a** to arrange (type) for printing **b** to put (text) into type **13** to arrange (a stage or television studio) with scenery and props **14 set to** *or* **on** to value

(something) at a specified price or worth: *he set a high price on his services* **15** (of the sun or moon) to disappear beneath the horizon **16** (of plants) to produce (fruits or seeds) or (of fruits or seeds) to develop **17** to place (a hen) on (eggs) to incubate them **18** (of a gun dog) to turn in the direction of game birds ▸ *n* **19** the act of setting **20** a condition of firmness or hardness **21** manner of standing; posture: *the set of his shoulders* **22** the scenery and other props used in a play or film **23** same as **sett** ▸ *adj* **24** fixed or established by authority or agreement: *set hours of work* **25** rigid or inflexible: *she is set in her ways* **26** unmoving; fixed: *a set expression on his face* **27** conventional or stereotyped: *she made her apology in set phrases* **28 set in** (of a scene or story) represented as happening at a certain time or place: *a European film set in Africa* **29 set on** *or* **upon** determined to (do or achieve something): *why are you so set upon avoiding me?* **30** ready: *all set to go* **31** (of material for study) prescribed for students' preparation for an examination ▸ **HISTORY** Old English *settan*

set² *n* **1** a number of objects or people grouped or belonging together: *a set of slides* **2** a group of people who associate with each other or have similar interests: *the tennis set* **3** *maths* a collection of numbers or objects that satisfy a given condition or share a property **4** a television or piece of radio equipment **5** *sport* a group of games or points in a match, of which the winner must win a certain number **6** a series of songs or tunes performed by a musician or group on a given occasion: *the front row spent the rest of the set craning their necks* ▸ **HISTORY** Old French *sette*

set back *vb* **1** to delay or hinder **2** *informal* to cost (a person) a specified amount ▸ *n* **setback** **3** anything that delays progress

set off *vb* **1** to start a journey **2** to cause (a person) to act or do something, such as laugh **3** to cause to explode **4** to act as a contrast to: *blue suits you, sets off the colour of your hair*

set piece *n* **1** a work of literature, music, or art, intended to create an impressive effect **2** *football, hockey, etc.* an attacking move from a corner or free kick

set square *n* a thin flat piece of plastic or metal in the shape of a right-angled triangle, used in technical drawing

sett *or* **set** *n* **1** a badger's burrow **2** a small rectangular paving block made of stone ▸ **HISTORY** variant of **SET¹** (noun)

settee *n* a seat, for two or more people, with a back and usually with arms; couch ▸ **HISTORY** from **SETTLE²**

setter *n* a large long-haired dog originally bred for hunting

set theory *n maths* the branch of mathematics concerned with the properties and interrelationships of sets

setting *n* **1** the surroundings in which something is set **2** the scenery, properties, or background used to create the location for a stage play or film

S

3 a piece of music written for the words of a text **4** the decorative metalwork in which a gem is set **5** the plates and cutlery for a single place at a table **6** one of the positions or levels to which the controls of a machine can be adjusted

settle¹ *vb* **-tling, -tled 1** to put in order: *he settled his affairs before he died* **2** to arrange or be arranged firmly or comfortably: *he settled into his own chair by the fire* **3** to come down to rest: *a bird settled on top of the hedge* **4** to establish or become established as a resident: *they eventually settled in Glasgow* **5** to establish or become established in a way of life or a job **6** to migrate to (a country) and form a community; colonize **7** to make or become quiet, calm, or stable **8** to cause (sediment) to sink to the bottom in a liquid or (of sediment) to sink thus **9** to subside: *the dust settled* **10** (sometimes foll. by *up*) to pay off (a bill or debt) **11** to decide or dispose of: *to settle an argument* **12** (often foll. by *on* or *upon*) to agree or fix: *they settled on an elementary code* **13** (usually foll. by *on* or *upon*) to give (a title or property) to a person by gift or legal deed: *he settled his property on his wife* **14** to decide (a legal dispute) by agreement without court action: *they settled out of court* ▶ HISTORY Old English *setlan*

settle² *n* a long wooden bench with a high back and arms, sometimes having a storage space under the seat ▶ HISTORY Old English *setl*

settle down *vb* **1** to make or become quiet and orderly **2 settle down to** to remove all distractions and concentrate on: *we settled down to a favourite movie* **3** to adopt an orderly and routine way of life, esp. after marriage

settle for *vb* to accept or agree to in spite of dissatisfaction

settlement *n* **1** an act of settling **2** a place newly settled; colony **3** subsidence of all or part of a building **4** an official agreement ending a dispute **5** *law* **a** an arrangement by which property is transferred to a person's possession **b** the deed transferring such property

settler *n* a person who settles in a new country or a colony

set to *vb* **1** to begin working **2** to start fighting ▷ *n* **set-to 3** *informal* a brief disagreement or fight

set-top box *n* a device which converts the signals from a digital television broadcast into a form which can be viewed on a standard television set

set up *vb* **1** to build or construct: *the soldiers had actually set up a munitions factory* **2** to put into a position of power or wealth **3** to begin or enable (someone) to begin (a new venture): *he set up a small shop* **4** to begin or produce: *to set up a nuclear chain reaction* **5** to establish: *Broad set up a world record* **6** *informal* to cause (a person) to be blamed or accused **7** to restore the health of: *a pub lunch set me up nicely* ▷ *n* **setup 8** *informal* the way in which anything is organized or arranged **9** *slang* an event the result of which is prearranged

seven *n* **1** the cardinal number that is the sum of one and six **2** a numeral, 7 or VII, representing this number **3** something representing or consisting of

seven units ▷ *adj* **4** amounting to seven: *seven weeks* ▶ HISTORY Old English *seofon* > **seventh** *adj*, *n*

seven seas *pl n old-fashioned* all the oceans of the world

seventeen *n* **1** the cardinal number that is the sum of ten and seven **2** a numeral, 17 or XVII, representing this number **3** something representing or consisting of seventeen units ▷ *adj* **4** amounting to seventeen: *seventeen children* > **seventeenth** *adj*, *n*

seventh heaven *n* a state of supreme happiness

seventy *n*, *pl* **-ties 1** the cardinal number that is the product of ten and seven **2** a numeral, 70 or LXX, representing this number **3** something representing or consisting of seventy units ▷ *adj* **4** amounting to seventy: *seventy countries* > **seventieth** *adj*, *n*

sever *vb* **1** to cut right through or cut off (something): *it accidentally severed the electrical cable* **2** to break off (a tie or relationship) ▶ HISTORY Latin *separare* to separate > **severable** *adj* > **severance** *n*

several *adj* **1** more than a few: *I spoke to several doctors* **2** *formal* various or separate: *the members with their several occupations* **3** *formal* distinct or different: *misfortune visited her three several times* ▶ HISTORY Medieval Latin *separalis*

severally *adv* *formal* individually or separately: *the Western nations severally rather than jointly decided that they would have to act without Russia*

severance pay *n* compensation paid by a firm to an employee who has to leave because the job he or she was appointed to do no longer exists

severe *adj* **1** strict or harsh in the treatment of others: *a severe parent* **2** serious in appearance or manner: *a severe look; a severe hairdo* **3** very intense or unpleasant: *severe chest pains; the punishments are severe* **4** causing discomfort by its harshness: *severe frost* **5** hard to perform or accomplish: *a severe challenge* ▶ HISTORY Latin *severus* > **severely** *adv* > **severity** *n*

Seville orange *n* a bitter orange used to make marmalade ▶ HISTORY after *Seville* in Spain

sew *vb* **sewing, sewed; sewn** *or* **sewed 1** to join with thread repeatedly passed through with a needle **2** to attach, fasten, or close by sewing ▶ HISTORY Old English *sēowan*

sewage *n* waste matter or excrement carried away in sewers or drains

sewage farm *n* a place where sewage is treated so that it can be used as manure or disposed of safely

sewer *n* a drain or pipe, usually underground, used to carry away surface water or sewage ▶ HISTORY Old French *essever* to drain

sewerage *n* **1** a system of sewers **2** the removal of surface water or sewage by means of sewers

sewn *vb* a past participle of **sew**

sex *n* **1** the state of being either male or female **2** either of the two categories, male or female, into which organisms are divided **3** sexual intercourse **4** feelings or behaviour connected with having sex or the desire to have sex **5** sexual matters in general ▷ *adj* **6** of sexual matters: *sex education* **7** based on or resulting from the difference between the sexes: *sex discrimination* ▷ *vb* **8** to find out the sex of (an animal) ▶ HISTORY Latin *sexus*

sexagenarian *n* **1** a person who is between 60 and 69 years old ▷ *adj* **2** between 60 and 69 years old ▶ HISTORY Latin *sexaginta* sixty

sex cell *n biol* a cell that can begin a reproductive process

sex chromosome *n* either of the chromosomes that determine the sex of an animal

sexism *n* discrimination against the members of one sex, usually women > **sexist** *n, adj*

sexless *adj* **1** neither male nor female **2** having no sexual desires

sextant *n* an instrument used in navigation for measuring angular distance, for example between the sun and the horizon, to calculate the position of a ship or aircraft ▶ HISTORY Latin *sextans* one sixth of a unit

sextet *n* **1** a group of six performers **2** a piece of music for six performers **3** a group of six people or things ▶ HISTORY variant of *sestet*

sexton *n* a person employed to look after a church and its churchyard ▶ HISTORY Medieval Latin *sacristanus* sacristan

sextuplet *n* one of six children born at one birth

sexual *adj* **1** of or characterized by sex **2** (of reproduction) characterized by the union of male and female reproductive cells **3** of or relating to the differences between males and females > **sexuality** *n* > **sexually** *adv*

sexual harassment *n* the unwelcome directing of sexual remarks, looks, or advances, usually at a woman in the workplace

sexual intercourse *n* the sexual act in which the male's erect penis is inserted into the female's vagina, usually followed by the ejaculation of semen

sex up *vb informal* to make (something) more exciting

sexy *adj* **sexier, sexiest** *informal* **1** sexually exciting or attractive: *a sexy voice* **2** interesting, exciting, or trendy: *a sexy project; a sexy new car* > **sexiness** *n*

SF *or* **sf** science fiction

SFA Scottish Football Association

SFO (in Britain) Serious Fraud Office

sforzando (sfort-**san**-doh) *music adj, adv* **1** to be sung or played with a sudden, strong emphasis ▷ *n* **2** a symbol (>) written above a note to indicate that it should be sung or played in this way ▶ HISTORY Italian

Sg *chem* seaborgium

Sgt. Sergeant

sh *interj* be quiet!

Shabbat *n, pl* **Shabbatot** another word for **Sabbath** (sense 1) ▶ HISTORY Hebrew

shabby *adj* **-bier, -biest** **1** old and worn in appearance **2** wearing worn and dirty clothes **3** behaving in a mean or unfair way: *shabby manoeuvres* ▶ HISTORY Old English *sceabb* scab > **shabbily** *adv* > **shabbiness** *n*

shack *n* **1** a roughly built hut ▷ *vb* **2** **shack up with** *slang* to live with (a lover) ▶ HISTORY perhaps from dialect *shackly* ramshackle

shackle *n* **1** one of a pair of metal rings joined by a chain for securing someone's wrists or ankles **2** **shackles** anything that confines or restricts freedom: *free from the shackles of its feudal past* **3** a metal loop or link closed by a bolt, used for securing ropes or chains ▷ *vb* **-ling, -led** **4** to fasten with shackles **5** to restrict or hamper: *an economy shackled by central control* ▶ HISTORY Old English *sceacel*

shad *n, pl* **shad** *or* **shads** a herring-like food fish ▶ HISTORY Old English *sceadd*

shade *n* **1** relative darkness produced by blocking out sunlight **2** a place sheltered from the sun by trees, buildings, etc. **3** something used to provide a shield or protection from a direct source of light, such as a lamp shade **4** a shaded area in a painting or drawing **5** any of the different hues of a colour: *a much darker shade of grey* **6** a slight amount: *a shade of reluctance* **7** **put someone** *or* **something in the shade** to be so impressive as to make another person or thing seem unimportant by comparison **8** *literary* a ghost ▷ *vb* **shading, shaded** **9** to screen or protect from heat or light **10** to make darker or dimmer **11** to represent (a darker area) in (a painting or drawing), by graded areas of tone, lines, or dots **12** to change slightly or by degrees ▶ HISTORY Old English *sceadu*

shades *pl n* **1** *slang* sunglasses **2** **shades of** a reminder of: *shades of Margaret Thatcher*

shading *n* the graded areas of tone, lines, or dots, indicating light and dark in a painting or drawing

shadow *n* **1** a dark image or shape cast on a surface when something stands between a light and the surface **2** a patch of shade **3** the dark portions of a picture **4** a hint or faint trace: *a shadow of a doubt* **5** a person less powerful or vigorous than his or her former self **6** a threatening influence: *news of the murder cast a shadow over the village* **7** a person who always accompanies another **8** a person who trails another in secret, such as a detective ▷ *adj* **9** *Brit & Austral* designating a member or members of the main opposition party in Parliament who would hold ministerial office if their party were in power: *the shadow chancellor* ▷ *vb* **10** to cast a shade or shadow over **11** to make dark or gloomy **12** to follow or trail secretly ▶ HISTORY Old English *sceadwe*

shadow-box *vb boxing* to box against an imaginary opponent for practice > **shadow-boxing** *n*

shadowy *adj* **1** (of a place) full of shadows; shady **2** faint or dark like a shadow: *a shadowy figure* **3** mysterious or not well known: *the shadowy world of espionage*

shady *adj* **shadier, shadiest** **1** full of shade; shaded **2** giving or casting shade **3** *informal* of doubtful honesty or legality: *shady business dealings* > **shadiness** *n*

S

shaft n **1 a** a spear or arrow **b** its long narrow stem **2 shaft of wit** or **humour** a clever or amusing remark **3** a ray or streak of light **4** the long straight narrow handle of a tool or golf club **5** a revolving rod in a machine that transmits motion or power **6** one of the bars between which an animal is harnessed to a vehicle **7** archit the middle part of a column or pier, between the base and the capital **8** a vertical passageway through a building for a lift **9** a vertical passageway into a mine ▶ HISTORY Old English sceaft

shag¹ n **1** coarse shredded tobacco **2** a matted tangle of hair or wool ▷ adj **3** (of a carpet) having long thick woollen threads ▶ HISTORY Old English sceacga

shag² n a kind of cormorant ▶ HISTORY special use of SHAG¹ (with reference to its crest)

shaggy adj **-gier, -giest 1** having or covered with rough unkempt fur, hair, or wool: shaggy cattle **2** rough and untidy > **shagginess** n

shagreen n **1** the skin of a shark, used as an abrasive **2** a rough grainy leather made from certain animal hides ▶ HISTORY French chagrin

shah n a ruler of certain Middle Eastern countries, esp. (formerly) Iran ▶ HISTORY Persian: king

shahada n Islam a declaration of faith, repeated every day by Muslims ▶ HISTORY Arabic

shake vb **shaking, shook, shaken 1** to move up and down or back and forth with short quick movements **2** to be or make unsteady **3** (of a voice) to tremble because of anger or nervousness **4** to clasp or grasp (the hand) of (a person) in greeting or agreement: they shook hands **5 shake on it** informal to shake hands in agreement or reconciliation **6** to wave vigorously and angrily: he shook his fist **7** (often foll. by up) to frighten or unsettle **8** to shock, disturb, or upset: he was badly shaken but unharmed **9** to undermine or weaken: a team whose morale had been badly shaken **10** US & Canad, informal to get rid of **11** music to perform a trill on (a note) **12 shake one's head** to indicate disagreement or disapproval by moving the head from side to side ▷ n **13** the act or an instance of shaking **14** a tremor or vibration **15 the shakes** informal a state of uncontrollable trembling **16** informal a very short period of time: in half a shake **17** music same as **trill** (sense 1) ▷ See also **shake down, shake off, shake up** ▶ HISTORY Old English sceacan

shake down vb **1** to go to bed, esp. in a makeshift bed ▷ n **shakedown 2** a makeshift bed

shake off vb **1** to remove or get rid of: I have been trying to shake off the stigma for some time **2** to escape from; get away from: they switched to a blue car in a bid to shake off reporters

shaker n **1** a container used for shaking a powdered substance onto something: a flour shaker **2** a container in which the ingredients of alcoholic drinks are shaken together

Shakespearean or **Shakespearian** adj **1** of William Shakespeare, English dramatist and poet, or his works ▷ n **2** a student of or specialist in Shakespeare's works

shake up vb **1** to mix by shaking **2** to reorganize drastically **3** informal to shock mentally or physically: the thunderstorm really shook me up ▷ n **shake-up 4** informal a radical reorganization, such as the reorganization of employees in a company

shaky adj **shakier, shakiest 1** weak and unsteady, esp. due to illness or shock **2** uncertain or doubtful: their prospects are shaky **3** tending to shake or tremble > **shakily** adv

shale n a flaky sedimentary rock formed by compression of successive layers of clay ▶ HISTORY Old English scealu shell

shall vb, past **should 1** (esp. with I or we as subject) used as an auxiliary to make the future tense: we shall see you tomorrow **2** (with you, he, she, it, they, or a noun as subject) **a** used as an auxiliary to indicate determination on the part of the speaker: you shall pay for this! **b** used as an auxiliary to indicate compulsion or obligation, now esp. in official documents **3** (with I or we as subject) used as an auxiliary in questions asking for advice or agreement: what shall we do now?; shall I shut the door? ▶ HISTORY Old English sceal

shallot (shal-**lot**) n a small, onion-like plant used in cooking for flavouring ▶ HISTORY Old French eschaloigne

shallow adj **1** having little depth **2** not involving sincere feelings or serious thought **3** (of breathing) consisting of short breaths ▷ n **4** (often pl) a shallow place in a body of water ▶ HISTORY Middle English shalow > **shallowness** n

sham n **1** anything that is not genuine or is not what it appears to be **2** a person who pretends to be something other than he or she is ▷ adj **3** not real or genuine ▷ vb **shamming, shammed 4** to fake or feign (something); pretend: he made a point of shamming nervousness ▶ HISTORY origin unknown

shaman (**sham**-man) n **1** a priest of shamanism **2** a medicine man or witch doctor of a similar religion ▶ HISTORY Russian

shamanism (**sham**-man-iz-zum) n a religion of northern Asia, based on a belief in good and evil spirits who can be influenced or controlled only by the shamans > **shamanist** n, adj

shamble vb **-bling, -bled 1** to walk or move along in an awkward shuffling way ▷ n **2** an awkward or shuffling walk ▶ HISTORY perhaps from shambles, referring to legs of a meat vendor's table > **shambling** adj, n

shambles n **1** a disorderly or badly organized event or place: the bathroom was a shambles **2** chiefly Brit a butcher's slaughterhouse **3** old-fashioned any scene of great slaughter ▶ HISTORY Middle English shamble table used by meat vendors

shambolic adj informal completely disorganized

shame n **1** a painful emotion resulting from an awareness of having done something wrong or foolish **2** capacity to feel such an emotion: have they no shame? **3** loss of respect; disgrace **4** a person or thing that causes this **5** a cause for regret or disappointment: it's a shame to rush back **6 put to shame** to show up as being inferior by

S

comparison: *his essay put mine to shame* ▷ *interj* **7** *S African, informal* **a** an expression of sympathy **b** an expression of pleasure or endearment ▷ *vb* **shaming, shamed 8** to cause to feel shame **9** to bring shame on **10** (often foll. by *into*) to force someone to do something by making him or her feel ashamed not to: *he was finally shamed into paying the bill* ▶ **HISTORY** Old English *scamu*

shamefaced *adj* embarrassed or guilty ▶ **HISTORY** earlier *shamefast* **> shamefacedly** *adv*

shameful *adj* causing or deserving shame: *a shameful lack of concern* **> shamefully** *adv*

shameless *adj* **1** having no sense of shame: *a shameless manipulator* **2** without decency or modesty: *a shameless attempt to stifle democracy* **> shamelessly** *adv*

shammy *n, pl* **-mies** *informal* a piece of chamois leather ▶ **HISTORY** variant of *chamois*

shampoo *n* **1** a soapy liquid used to wash the hair **2** a similar liquid for washing carpets or upholstery **3** the process of shampooing ▷ *vb* **-pooing, -pooed 4** to wash (the hair, carpets, or upholstery) with shampoo

■ **WORD HISTORY**
■ A shampoo was originally a massage rather
■ than a wash. The word 'shampoo' is derived
■ from the Hindi verb *chāmpnā*, meaning 'to
■ press, knead, or massage'.

shamrock *n* a small clover-like plant with three round leaves on each stem: the national emblem of Ireland ▶ **HISTORY** Irish Gaelic *seamróg*

shandy *n, pl* **-dies** a drink made of beer and lemonade ▶ **HISTORY** origin unknown

shanghai *slang vb* **-haiing, -haied 1** to force or trick (someone) into doing something **2** *history* to kidnap (a man) and force him to serve at sea **3** *Austral & NZ* to shoot with a catapult ▷ *n* **4** *Austral & NZ* a catapult ▶ **HISTORY** senses 1 and 2 after the city of *Shanghai*; senses 3 and 4 from Scots dialect *shangie, shangan* cleft stick

Shango *n* **1** an African religious cult surviving in some parts of the Caribbean ▷ *adj* **2** of or relating to Shango: *Shango rituals*

shank *n* **1** the part of the leg between the knee and the ankle **2** a cut of meat from the top part of an animal's shank **3** the long narrow part of a tool, key, spoon, etc. ▶ **HISTORY** Old English *scanca*

shan't shall not

shantung *n* a heavy Chinese silk with a knobbly surface ▶ **HISTORY** after province of NE China

shanty¹ *n, pl* **-ties** a small rough hut; crude dwelling ▶ **HISTORY** Canadian French *chantier* cabin built in a lumber camp

shanty² *or* **chanty** *n, pl* **-ties** a rhythmic song originally sung by sailors when working ▶ **HISTORY** French *chanter* to sing

shantytown *n* a town of poor people living in shanties

shape *n* **1** the outward form of an object, produced by its outline **2** the figure or outline of the body of a person **3** organized or definite form: *to preserve the union in its present shape* **4** the specific form that

anything takes on: *a gold locket in the shape of a heart* **5** pattern or mould **6** condition or state of efficiency: *in poor shape* **7 take shape** to assume a definite form ▷ *vb* **shaping, shaped 8** (often foll. by *into* or *up*) to receive or cause to receive shape or form: *spinach shaped into a ball* **9** to mould into a particular pattern or form **10** to devise or develop: *to shape a system of free trade* ▷ See also **shape up** ▶ **HISTORY** Old English *gesceap*, literally: that which is created

shapeless *adj* **1** (of a person or object) lacking a pleasing shape: *a shapeless dress* **2** having no definite shape or form: *a shapeless mound* **> shapelessness** *n*

shapely *adj* **-lier, -liest** (esp. of a woman's body or legs) pleasing or attractive in shape **> shapeliness** *n*

shape up *vb informal* **1** to progress or develop satisfactorily **2** to develop a definite or proper form **3** to start working efficiently or behaving properly: *shape up or face the sack*

shard *n* a broken piece or fragment of pottery, glass, or metal ▶ **HISTORY** Old English *sceard*

share¹ *n* **1** a part or portion of something that belongs to or is contributed by a person or group **2** (often *pl*) any of the equal parts into which the capital stock of a company is divided ▷ *vb* **sharing, shared 3** (often foll. by *out*) to divide and distribute **4** to receive or contribute a portion of: *we shared a bottle of mineral water* **5** to join with another or others in the use of (something): *a programme about four women sharing a house* **6** to go through (a similar experience) as others: *we have all shared the nightmare of toothache* **7** to tell others about (something) **8** to have the same (beliefs or opinions) as others: *universal values shared by both east and west* ▶ **HISTORY** Old English *scearu*

share² *n* short for **ploughshare** ▶ **HISTORY** Old English *scear*

shareholder *n* the owner of one or more shares in a company

sharemilker *n* *NZ* a person who works on a dairy farm belonging to someone else and gets a share of the proceeds from the sale of the milk

shareware *n* *computers* software available to all users without the need for a licence and for which a token fee is requested

shark *n* **1** a large, usually predatory fish with a long body, two dorsal fins, and rows of sharp teeth **2** *disparaging* a person who swindles or extorts money from other people ▶ **HISTORY** origin unknown

sharkskin *n* a smooth glossy fabric used for sportswear

sharp *adj* **1** having a keen cutting edge **2** tapering to an edge or point **3** involving a sudden change in direction: *a sharp bend on a road; a sharp rise in prices* **4** moving, acting, or reacting quickly: *sharp reflexes* **5** clearly defined: *a sharp contrast* **6** quick to notice or understand things; keen-witted **7** clever in an underhand way: *sharp practices* **8** bitter or harsh:

a sharp response **9** shrill or penetrating: *a sharp cry of horror* **10** having a bitter or sour taste **11** (of pain or cold) acute or biting: *a sharp gust of wind* **12** *music* **a** (of a note) raised in pitch by one semitone: *F sharp* **b** (of an instrument or voice) out of tune by being too high in pitch **13** *informal* neat and stylish: *a sharp dresser* ▷ *adv* **14** promptly **15** exactly: *at ten o'clock sharp* **16** *music* **a** higher than a standard pitch **b** out of tune by being too high in pitch: *she sings sharp* ▷ *n* **17** *music* **a** an accidental that raises the pitch of a note by one semitone. Symbol: ♯ **b** a note affected by this accidental **18** *informal* a cheat; cardsharp ▶ HISTORY Old English *scearp*
> **sharpish** *adj* > **sharply** *adv* > **sharpness** *n*

sharpen *vb* to make or become sharp or sharper
> **sharpener** *n*

sharper *n* a person who cheats or swindles; fraud

sharpshooter *n* a skilled marksman

shatter *vb* **1** to break suddenly into many small pieces **2** to damage badly or destroy: *to shatter American confidence* **3** to upset (someone) greatly: *the whole experience shattered me* ▶ HISTORY origin unknown > **shattering** *adj*

shattered *adj informal* **1** completely exhausted **2** badly upset: *he was shattered by the separation*

shave *vb* **shaving, shaved; shaved** *or* **shaven** **1** to remove (the beard or hair) from (the face, head, or body) by using a razor or shaver **2** to remove thin slices from (wood or other material) with a sharp cutting tool **3** to touch (someone or something) lightly in passing ▷ *n* **4** the act or an instance of shaving **5** the removal of hair from a man's face by a razor **6** a tool for cutting off thin slices **7 close shave** *informal* a narrow escape
▶ HISTORY Old English *sceafan*

shaver *n* **1** an electrically powered razor **2** *old-fashioned* a young boy

Shavian (**shave**-ee-an) *adj* **1** of or like George Bernard Shaw, Irish dramatist noted for his sharp wit, or his works ▷ *n* **2** an admirer of Shaw or his works

shawl *n* a piece of woollen cloth worn over the head or shoulders by a woman or wrapped around a baby ▶ HISTORY Persian *shāl*

she *pron* **1** (refers to) the female person or animal previously mentioned or in question: *she is my sister* **2** (refers to) something regarded as female, such as a car, ship, or nation ▷ *n* **3** a female person or animal ▶ HISTORY Old English *sīe*

sheaf *n, pl* **sheaves** **1** a bundle of papers tied together **2** a bundle of reaped corn tied together ▷ *vb* **3** to bind or tie into a sheaf ▶ HISTORY Old English *scēaf*

shear *vb* **shearing, sheared** *or Austral & NZ* sometimes **shore; sheared** *or* **shorn** **1** to remove (the fleece) of (a sheep) by cutting or clipping **2** to cut or cut through (something) with shears or a sharp instrument **3** *engineering* to cause (a part) to break or (of a part) to break through strain or twisting ▷ *n* **4** breakage caused through strain or twisting ▷ See also **shears** ▶ HISTORY Old English *sceran* > **shearer** *n*

shearing shed *n Austral & NZ* a farm building with equipment for shearing sheep

shears *pl n* **1** large scissors, used for sheep shearing **2** a large scissor-like cutting tool with flat blades, used for cutting hedges

sheath *n, pl* **sheaths** **1** a case or covering for the blade of a knife or sword **2** *biol* a structure that encloses or protects **3** *Brit, Austral & NZ* same as **condom 4** a close-fitting dress ▶ HISTORY Old English *scēath*

sheathe *vb* **sheathing, sheathed** **1** to insert (a knife or sword) into a sheath **2** to cover with a sheath or sheathing

sheaves *n* the plural of **sheaf**

shebeen *or* **shebean** *n Scot, Irish & S African* a place where alcoholic drink is sold illegally ▶ HISTORY Irish Gaelic *síbín* beer of poor quality

shed¹ *n* **1** a small, roughly made building used for storing garden tools, etc. **2** a large barnlike building used for various purposes at factories, train stations, etc.: *a locomotive shed* ▶ HISTORY Old English *sced*

shed² *vb* **shedding, shed** **1** to get rid of: *250 workers shed by the company* **2 shed tears** to cry **3 shed light on** to make (a problem or situation) easier to understand **4** to cast off (skin, hair, or leaves): *the trees were already beginning to shed their leaves* **5** to cause to flow off: *this coat sheds water* **6** to separate or divide (a group of sheep) ▶ HISTORY Old English *sc(e)ādan*

sheen *n* a glistening brightness on the surface of something: *grass with a sheen of dew on it* ▶ HISTORY Old English *sciēne*

sheep *n, pl* **sheep** **1** a cud-chewing mammal with a thick woolly coat, kept for its wool or meat. *Related adjective:* **ovine 2** a timid person **3 like sheep** (of a group of people) allowing a single person to dictate their actions or beliefs **4 separate the sheep from the goats** to pick out the members of a group who are superior in some respects
▶ HISTORY Old English *scēap* > **sheeplike** *adj*

sheep-dip *n* **1** a liquid disinfectant and insecticide in which sheep are immersed **2** a deep trough containing such a liquid

sheepdog *n* **1** a dog used for herding sheep **2** a breed of dog reared originally for herding sheep

sheepfold *n* a pen or enclosure for sheep

sheepish *adj* embarrassed because of feeling foolish > **sheepishly** *adv*

sheepskin *n* the skin of a sheep with the wool still attached, used to make clothing and rugs

sheer¹ *adj* **1** absolute; complete: *sheer amazement* **2** perpendicular; very steep: *the sheer rock face* **3** (of textiles) light, delicate, and see-through ▷ *adv* **4** steeply: *the cliff drops sheer to the sea* ▶ HISTORY Old English *scīr*

sheer² *vb* **sheer off** *or* **away (from) a** to change course suddenly **b** to avoid an unpleasant person, thing, or topic ▶ HISTORY origin unknown

sheet¹ *n* **1** a large rectangular piece of cloth used as an inner bed cover **2** a thin piece of material such as paper or glass, usually rectangular **3** a broad

continuous surface or layer: *a sheet of ice*
4 a newspaper ▷ *vb* **5** to provide with, cover, or
wrap in a sheet **6** (often foll. by *down*) to rain very
heavily ▶ **HISTORY** Old English *scīete*

sheet² *n naut* a line or rope for controlling the
position of a sail ▶ **HISTORY** Old English *scēata*
corner of a sail

sheet anchor *n* **1** *naut* a large strong anchor for
use in an emergency **2** a person or thing that can
always be relied on

sheet erosion *n geol* the wearing away of a layer
of surface soil due to rainwater run-off

sheeting *n* any material from which sheets are
made

sheet lightning *n meteorol* lightning that
appears as a broad sheet, caused by the reflection
of more distant lightning

sheet metal *n* metal formed into a thin sheet by
rolling or hammering

sheikh or **sheik** (**shake**) *n* (in Muslim countries)
a the head of an Arab tribe, village, or family
b a religious leader ▶ **HISTORY** Arabic *shaykh* old
man > **sheikhdom** or **sheikdom** *n*

sheila *n Austral & NZ, old-fashioned informal* a girl or
woman ▶ **HISTORY** from the girl's name *Sheila*

shekel *n* **1** the monetary unit of Israel **2 shekels**
informal money ▶ **HISTORY** Hebrew *sheqel*

shelduck or *masc* **sheldrake** *n*, *pl* **-ducks, -duck**
or **-drakes, -drake** a large brightly coloured wild
duck of Europe and Asia ▶ **HISTORY** probably from
dialect *sheld* pied

shelf *n*, *pl* **shelves** **1** a board fixed horizontally
against a wall or in a cupboard, for holding things
2 a projecting layer of ice or rock on land or in the
sea **3 off the shelf** (of products in shops) sold as
standard **4 on the shelf** put aside or abandoned;
used esp. of unmarried women considered to be
past the age of marriage ▶ **HISTORY** Old English
scylfe ship's deck

shelf life *n* the length of time a packaged product
will remain fresh or usable

shell *n* **1** the protective outer layer of an egg, fruit,
or nut **2** the hard outer covering of an animal such
as a crab or tortoise **3** any hard outer case **4** the
external structure of a building, car, or ship, esp.
one that is unfinished or gutted by fire **5** an
explosive artillery projectile that can be fired from
a large gun **6** a small-arms cartridge **7** *rowing* a
very light narrow racing boat **8 come** or **bring out
of one's shell** to become or help to become less
shy and reserved ▷ *vb* **9** to remove the shell or husk
from **10** to attack with artillery shells ▷ See also
shell out ▶ **HISTORY** Old English *sciell*
> **shell-like** *adj*

shellac *n* **1** a yellowish resin used in varnishes and
polishes **2** a varnish made by dissolving shellac in
alcohol ▷ *vb* **-lacking, -lacked** **3** to coat with
shellac ▶ **HISTORY** *shell* + *lac*

shellfish *n*, *pl* **-fish** or **-fishes** a sea-living
animal, esp. one that can be eaten, having
a shell

shell out *vb informal* to pay out or hand over (money)

shell shock *n* a nervous disorder characterized by
anxiety and depression that occurs as a result of
lengthy exposure to battle conditions > **shell-
shocked** *adj*

shell suit *n Brit* a lightweight tracksuit made of a
waterproof nylon layer over a cotton layer

Shelta *n* a secret language based on Gaelic, used
by some travelling people in Ireland and Britain
▶ **HISTORY** origin unknown

shelter *n* **1** something that provides cover or
protection from weather or danger **2** the
protection given by such a cover ▷ *vb* **3** to take
cover from bad weather **4** to provide with a place
to live or a hiding place: *dissidents were sheltered in
foreign embassies* ▶ **HISTORY** origin unknown

sheltered *adj* **1** protected from wind and rain
2 protected from unpleasant or upsetting
experiences: *a sheltered childhood* **3** specially
designed to provide a safe environment for
people who are elderly or disabled: *sheltered
housing*

shelve¹ *vb* **shelving, shelved** **1** to put aside or
postpone: *to shelve a project* **2** to place (something,
such as a book) on a shelf **3** to provide with
shelves: *to shelve a cupboard* **4** to dismiss (someone)
from active service ▶ **HISTORY** from *shelves*, plural
of *shelf*

shelve² *vb* **shelving, shelved** to slope away
gradually ▶ **HISTORY** origin unknown

shelves *n* the plural of **shelf**

shelving *n* **1** material for shelves **2** shelves
collectively

shenanigans *pl n informal* **1** mischief or nonsense
2 trickery or deception ▶ **HISTORY** origin
unknown

shepherd *n* **1** a person employed to tend sheep
2 *Christianity* a member of the clergy when
considered as the moral and spiritual guide of the
people in the parish ▷ *vb* **3** to guide or watch over
(people) ▶ **HISTORY** SHEEP + HERD > **shepherdess**
fem n

shepherd's pie *n* a baked dish of minced meat
covered with mashed potato

sherbet *n* **1** *Brit, Austral & NZ* a fruit-flavoured
slightly fizzy powder, eaten as a sweet or used to
make a drink **2** *US, Canad & S African* same as **sorbet**
▶ **HISTORY** Turkish *şerbet*

sheriff *n* **1** (in the US) the chief elected law-
enforcement officer in a county **2** (in Canada) a
municipal officer who enforces court orders and
escorts convicted criminals to prison **3** (in England
and Wales) the chief executive officer of the Crown
in a county, having chiefly ceremonial duties **4** (in
Scotland) a judge in a sheriff court **5** (*in Australia*)
an officer of the Supreme Court ▶ **HISTORY** Old
English *scīrgerēfa*

sheriff court *n* (in Scotland) a court having
powers to try all but the most serious crimes and
to deal with most civil actions

Sherpa *n*, *pl* **-pas** or **-pa** a member of a
Tibetan people living on the southern slopes
of the Himalayas

S

sherry *n, pl* **-ries** a pale or dark brown fortified wine, originally from southern Spain

- ■ **WORD HISTORY**
- ■ 'Sherry' is named after the town of Jerez de la
- ■ Frontera in southwestern Spain, where it was
- ■ first made.

Shetland pony *n* a very small sturdy breed of pony with a long shaggy mane and tail

shibboleth *n* **1** a slogan or catch phrase, usually considered outworn, that characterizes a particular party or sect: *the shibboleth of Western strategy* **2** a custom, phrase, or use of language that reliably distinguishes a member of one group or class from another ▶ **HISTORY** word used in the Old Testament by the Gileadites as a test word for the Ephraimites, who could not pronounce *sh*

shickered *adj* *Austral & NZ, old-fashioned, slang* drunk ▶ **HISTORY** Yiddish *shicker* liquor

shied *vb* the past of **shy¹**, **shy²**

shield *n* **1** a piece of defensive armour carried in the hand or on the arm to protect the body from blows or missiles **2** any person or thing that protects, hides, or defends: *a wind shield* **3** *heraldry* a representation of a shield used for displaying a coat of arms **4** anything that resembles a shield in shape, such as a trophy in a sports competition ▷ *vb* **5** to protect, hide, or defend (someone or something) from danger or harm: *an industry shielded from competition* ▶ **HISTORY** Old English *scield*

shield volcano *n geol* a broad volcano built up from the repeated nonexplosive eruption of basalt to form a low dome or shield, usually having a large crater at the summit

shift *vb* **1** to move from one place or position to another **2** to pass (blame or responsibility) onto someone else: *he was trying to shift the blame to me* **3** to change (gear) in a motor vehicle **4** to remove or be removed: *no detergent can shift these stains* **5** *US* to change for another or others **6** *slang* to move quickly ▷ *n* **7** the act or an instance of shifting **8 a** a group of workers who work during a specific period **b** the period of time worked by such a group **9** a method or scheme **10** a loose-fitting straight underskirt or dress ▶ **HISTORY** Old English *sciftan*

shifting cultivation *n agriculture* **1** a cultivation system based on the rotations of fields rather than of crops, allowing land to lie fallow and regain fertility **2** a cultivation system which entails moving to and clearing new land once the fertility of the current land is exhausted

shiftless *adj* lacking in ambition or initiative

shifty *adj* **shiftier**, **shiftiest** looking deceitful and not to be trusted > **shiftiness** *n*

shillelagh (shil-**lay**-lee) *n* (in Ireland) a heavy club ▶ **HISTORY** Irish Gaelic *sail* cudgel + *éille* thong

shilling *n* **1** a former British coin worth one twentieth of a pound, replaced by the 5p piece in 1970 **2** a former Australian coin, worth one twentieth of a pound **3** the standard monetary unit in several E African countries ▶ **HISTORY** Old English *scilling*

shillyshally *vb* **-shallies**, **-shallying**, **-shallied** *informal* to be indecisive ▶ **HISTORY** shill I shall I, reduplication of *shall I*

shim *n* **1** a thin strip of material placed between two close surfaces to fill a gap ▷ *vb* **shimming**, **shimmed** **2** to fit or fill up with a shim ▶ **HISTORY** origin unknown

shimmer *vb* **1** to shine with a faint unsteady light ▷ *n* **2** a faint unsteady light ▶ **HISTORY** Old English *scimerian* > **shimmering** or **shimmery** *adj*

shin *n* **1** the front part of the lower leg **2** a cut of beef including the lower foreleg ▷ *vb* **shinning**, **shinned** **3 shin up** to climb (something, such as a rope or pole) by gripping with the hands or arms and the legs and hauling oneself up ▶ **HISTORY** Old English *scinu*

shinbone *n* the nontechnical name for **tibia**

shindig or **shindy** *n, pl* **-digs** or **-dies** *slang* **1** a noisy party or dance **2** a quarrel or brawl ▶ **HISTORY** variant of *shinty*

shine *vb* **shining**, **shone** **1** to give off or reflect light **2** to direct the light of (a lamp or torch): *I shone a torch at the ceiling* **3** (*pt & pp* **shined**) to make clean and bright by polishing: *they earned money by shining shoes* **4** to be very good at something: *she shone in most subjects; she shone at school* **5** to appear very bright and clear: *her hair shone like gold* ▷ *n* **6** brightness or lustre **7 take a shine to someone** *informal* to take a liking to someone ▶ **HISTORY** Old English *scīnan*

shiner *n informal* a black eye

shingle¹ *n* **1** a thin rectangular tile laid with others in overlapping rows to cover a roof or a wall **2** a woman's short-cropped hairstyle ▷ *vb* **-gling**, **-gled** **3** to cover (a roof or a wall) with shingles **4** to cut (the hair) in a short-cropped style ▶ **HISTORY** Latin *scindere* to split

shingle² *n* coarse gravel found on beaches ▶ **HISTORY** Scandinavian

shingles *n* a disease causing a rash of small blisters along a nerve ▶ **HISTORY** Medieval Latin *cingulum* girdle

shingle slide *n NZ* the loose stones on a steep slope

Shinto *n* a Japanese religion in which ancestors and nature spirits are worshipped ▶ **HISTORY** Japanese: the way of the gods > **Shintoism** *n* > **Shintoist** *n, adj*

shinty *n Scot* **1** a game like hockey but with taller goals **2** (*pl* **-ties**) the stick used in this game ▶ **HISTORY** perhaps Scottish Gaelic *sinteag* a pace

shiny *adj* **shinier**, **shiniest** **1** bright and polished **2** (of clothes or material) worn to a smooth and glossy state by continual wear or rubbing

ship *n* **1** a large seagoing vessel with engines or sails **2** short for **airship**, **spaceship 3 when one's ship comes in** when one has become successful ▷ *vb* **shipping**, **shipped** **4** to send or transport by any carrier, esp. a ship **5** *naut* to take in (water) over the side **6** to bring or go aboard a vessel: *to ship oars* **7** (often foll. by *off*) *informal* to send away: *they were shipped off to foreign countries* **8** to be hired to serve aboard a ship: *I shipped aboard a Liverpool liner* ▶ **HISTORY** Old English *scip*

shipmate *n* a sailor who serves on the same ship as another

shipment *n* **1** goods shipped together as part of the same lot: *a shipment of arms* **2** the act of shipping cargo

shipping *n* **1** the business of transporting freight, esp. by ship **2** ships collectively: *all shipping should stay clear of the harbour*

shipshape *adj* **1** neat or orderly ▷ *adv* **2** in a neat and orderly manner

shipwreck *n* **1** the destruction of a ship at sea **2** the remains of a wrecked ship **3** ruin or destruction: *the shipwreck of the old science* ▷ *vb* **4** to wreck or destroy (a ship) **5** to bring to ruin or destruction

shipyard *n* a place where ships are built and repaired

shire *n* **1** Brit a county **2** Austral a rural area with an elected council **3 the Shires** the Midland counties of England ▶ **HISTORY** Old English *scīr* office

shire horse *n* a large powerful breed of working horse

shirk *vb* to avoid doing (work or a duty) ▶ **HISTORY** probably from German *Schurke* rogue > **shirker** *n*

shirt *n* **1** an item of clothing worn on the upper part of the body, usually with a collar and sleeves and buttoning up the front **2 keep your shirt on** *informal* keep your temper **3 put one's shirt on something** *informal* to bet all one has on something ▶ **HISTORY** Old English *scyrte*

shirty *adj* **shirtier, shirtiest** *slang, chiefly Brit & NZ* bad-tempered or annoyed

shish kebab *n* a dish of small pieces of meat and vegetables grilled on a skewer ▶ **HISTORY** Turkish *şiş kebabı*

Shiva *n* a Hindu god, the Destroyer

shiver¹ *vb* **1** to tremble from cold or fear ▷ *n* **2** a tremble caused by cold or fear **3 the shivers** a fit of shivering through fear or illness ▶ **HISTORY** Middle English *chiveren* > **shivering** *n, adj* > **shivery** *adj*

shiver² *vb* **1** to break into fragments ▷ *n* **2** a splintered piece ▶ **HISTORY** Germanic

shoal¹ *n* **1** a large group of fish swimming together **2** a large group of people or things ▶ **HISTORY** Old English *scolu*

shoal² *n* **1** a stretch of shallow water **2** a sandbank or rocky area, esp. one that can be seen at low water ▷ *vb* **3** to make or become shallow ▶ **HISTORY** Old English *sceald* shallow

shock¹ *vb* **1** to cause (someone) to experience extreme horror, disgust, or astonishment: *the similarity shocked me* **2** to cause a state of shock in (a person) ▷ *n* **3** a sudden and violent blow or impact **4 a** a sudden and violent emotional disturbance **b** something causing this **5** *pathol* a condition in which a person's blood cannot flow properly because of severe injury, burns, or fright **6** pain and muscular spasm caused by an electric current passing through a person's body ▶ **HISTORY** Old French *choc* > **shocker** *n*

shock² *n* **1** a number of grain sheaves set on end in a field to dry ▷ *vb* **2** to set up (sheaves) in shocks ▶ **HISTORY** probably Germanic

shock³ *n* written a thick bushy mass of hair ▶ **HISTORY** origin unknown

shock absorber *n* any device designed to absorb mechanical shock, esp. one fitted to a motor vehicle to reduce the effects of travelling over bumpy surfaces

shocking *adj* **1** *informal* very bad or terrible: *a shocking match at Leicester* **2** causing dismay or disgust: *a shocking lack of concern* **3 shocking pink** (of) a very bright shade of pink

shock jock *n* a radio disc jockey who is deliberately controversial or provocative

shock therapy *or* **treatment** *n* the treatment of certain mental conditions by passing an electric current through the patient's brain

shod *vb* past tense and past participle of **shoe**

shoddy *adj* **-dier, -diest** **1** made or done badly or carelessly: *shoddy goods* **2** of poor quality; shabby ▶ **HISTORY** origin unknown > **shoddily** *adv* > **shoddiness** *n*

shoe *n* **1** one of a matching pair of coverings shaped to fit the foot, made of leather or other strong material and ending below the ankle **2** anything resembling a shoe in shape, function, or position **3** short for **horseshoe 4 be in a person's shoes** *informal* to be in another person's situation ▷ *vb* **shoeing, shod 5** to fit (a horse) with horseshoes ▶ **HISTORY** Old English *scōh*

shoehorn *n* a smooth curved piece of metal or plastic inserted at the heel of a shoe to ease the foot into it

shoelace *n* a cord for fastening shoes

shoestring *n* **1** same as **shoelace 2** *informal* a very small amount of money: *the theatre will be run on a shoestring*

shoetree *n* a long piece of metal, plastic, or wood, put into a shoe or boot to keep its shape

shogun (**show-gun**) *n history* **1** (in Japan from the 8th century AD) a chief military commander **2** (in Japan from the late 12th to the late 19th century) any of a line of hereditary military dictators who relegated the emperors to a position of purely theoretical supremacy ▶ **HISTORY** Japanese, from Chinese *chiang chün* general, from *chiang* to lead + *chün* army

Shomer Shabbat *or* **Shomer Shabbos** *n, pl* **Shomrei Shabbat** *or* **Shomrei Shabbos** *Judaism* a person who observes the Jewish Sabbath ▶ **HISTORY** Hebrew

shone *vb* a past of **shine**

shonky *adj* **-kier, -kiest** *Austral & NZ, informal* unreliable or unsound

shoo *interj* **1** go away!: used to drive away unwanted or annoying animals or people ▷ *vb* **shooing, shooed 2** to drive away by crying 'shoo' ▶ **HISTORY** imitative

shook *vb* the past tense of **shake**

shoot *vb* **shooting, shot 1** to hit, wound, or kill with a missile fired from a weapon **2** to fire

S

short

WORD FOCUS

Some words used to describe a person who is **short** can be more hurtful or insulting than others.

DEFINITION 2

- A **little** or **small** person is not large in physical size: *She was too* **little** *to reach the books on the top shelf.* • *She is* **small** *for her age.*
- A **diminutive** person is very small: *a* **diminutive** *figure standing at the entrance*
- A **tiny** person is extremely small: *Though she was* **tiny***, she had a loud voice.*

- If you describe a woman as **petite**, you are politely saying that she is small and slender. This is a complimentary word: *a* **petite** *blonde woman*
- If you describe someone as **dumpy**, you mean that they are short and fat. This is an uncomplimentary word: *a* **dumpy** *woman in a baggy tracksuit*
- If you **describe** someone as **squat**, you mean that they are short and thick, usually in an unattractive way: *Eddie was a short,* **squat** *fellow in his mid-forties.*

(a missile or missiles) from a weapon **3** to fire (a weapon) **4** to hunt game with a gun for sport **5** to send out or be sent out quickly and aggressively: *he shot questions at her* **6** to move very rapidly: *the car shot forward* **7** to go or pass quickly over or through: *he was trying to shoot the white water* **8** to slide or push into or out of a fastening: *she shot the bolt quickly* **9** (of a plant) to sprout (a new growth) **10** to photograph or film **11** *sport* to hit or kick the ball at goal ▷ *n* **12** the act of shooting **13** a new growth or sprout of a plant **14** *chiefly Brit* a meeting or party organized for hunting game with guns **15** an area where game can be hunted with guns **16** *informal* a photographic assignment: *a fashion shoot in New York* ▶ HISTORY Old English *scēotan*

shooting star *n informal* a meteor

shooting stick *n* a walking stick with a spike at one end and a folding seat at the other

shop *n* **1** a place for the sale of goods and services **2** a place where a specified type of work is done; workshop: *a repair shop* **3 all over the shop** *informal* scattered everywhere: *his papers were all over the shop* **4 shut up shop** to close business at the end of the day or permanently **5 talk shop** *informal* to discuss one's business or work on a social occasion ▷ *vb* **shopping, shopped 6** (often foll. by *for*) to visit a shop or shops in order to buy (goods) **7** *Brit, Austral & NZ, slang* to inform on (someone), esp. to the police ▶ HISTORY Old English *sceoppa* stall > **shopper** *n*

shop around *vb informal* **1** to visit a number of shops or stores to compare goods and prices **2** to consider a number of possibilities before making a choice

shop assistant *n* a person who serves in a shop

shop floor *n* **1** the production area of a factory **2** workers, esp. factory workers, as opposed to management

shopkeeper *n* a person who owns or manages a shop > **shopkeeping** *n*

shoplifter *n* a customer who steals goods from a shop > **shoplifting** *n*

shopping *n* **1** the act of going to shops and buying things **2** things that have been bought in shops

shopping centre *n* **1** a complex of stores, restaurants, and sometimes banks, usually under

the same roof **2** the area of a town where most of the shops are situated

shopping mall *n* a large enclosed shopping centre

shopping plaza *n chiefly US, Canad & Austral* a shopping centre, usually a small group of stores built as a strip

shop steward *n* a trade-union official elected by his or her fellow workers to be their representative in dealing with their employer

shopwalker *n Brit* (esp. formerly) a person employed by a department store to assist sales personnel and help customers

shore¹ *n* **1** the land along the edge of a sea, lake, or wide river. *Related adjective:* **littoral 2** land, as opposed to water: *150 yards from shore* **3 shores** a country: *foreign shores* ▶ HISTORY probably from Middle Low German, Middle Dutch *schōre*

shore² *n* **1** a prop placed under or against something as a support ▷ *vb* **shoring, shored 2 shore up a** to prop up (an unsteady building or wall) with a strong support **b** to strengthen or support (something weak): *lower interest rates to shore up the economy* ▶ HISTORY Middle Dutch *schōre*

shoreline *n* the edge of a sea, lake, or wide river

shorn *vb* a past participle of **shear**

short *adj* **1** of little length; not long **2** of little height; not tall **3** not lasting long **4** not enough: *the number of places laid at the table was short by four* **5 short of** or **on** lacking in: *short of cash; short on detail* **6** concise: *a short book* **7** (of drinks) consisting chiefly of a spirit, such as whisky **8** (of someone's memory) lacking the ability to retain a lot of facts **9** (of a person's manner) abrupt and rather rude: *Kemp was short with her* **10** (of betting odds) almost even **11** *finance* **a** not possessing at the time of sale the stocks or commodities one sells **b** relating to such sales, which depend on falling prices for profit **12** *phonetics* (of a vowel) of relatively short duration **13** (of pastry) crumbly in texture **14 in short supply** scarce **15 short and sweet** brief and to the point **16 short for** a shortened form of ▷ *adv* **17** abruptly: *to stop short* **18 be caught short** to have a sudden need to go to the toilet **19 go short** not to have enough **20 short of** except: *they want nothing short of his removal from power* ▷ *n* **21** a drink

of spirits **22** a short film shown before the main feature in a cinema **23** same as **short circuit** **24 for short** *informal* as a shortened form: *cystic fibrosis, CF for short* **25 in short** briefly ▷ *vb* **26** to short-circuit ▷ See also **shorts** ▶ HISTORY Old English *sceort* > **shortness** *n*
See WORD FOCUS **short**

shortage *n* not enough of something needed

shortbread *n* a rich crumbly biscuit made with butter

shortcake *n* **1** shortbread **2** a dessert made of layers of biscuit or cake filled with fruit and cream

short-change *vb* **-changing, -changed** **1** to give (someone) less than the correct change **2** *slang* to treat (someone), unfairly, esp. by giving less than is expected

short circuit *n* **1** a faulty or accidental connection in an electric circuit, which deflects current through a path of low resistance, usually causing the failure of the circuit ▷ *vb* **short-circuit** **2** to develop a short circuit **3** to bypass (a procedure): *she wrote to them direct and short-circuited the job agency* **4** to hinder or frustrate (a plan)

shortcoming *n* a fault or weakness

short cut *n* **1** a route that is shorter than the usual one **2** a way of saving time or effort

shorten *vb* to make or become short or shorter

shortfall *n* **1** a failure to meet a requirement **2** the amount of such a failure; deficit

shorthand *n* a system of rapid writing using simple strokes and other symbols to represent words or phrases

short-handed *adj* (of a company or organization) lacking enough staff to do the required work

shorthand typist *n* Brit & Austral a person skilled in the use of shorthand and in typing

shorthorn *n* a member of a breed of cattle with short horns

short list *n* **1** Also called (Scot): **short leet** a list of suitable candidates for a job or prize, from which the successful candidate will be selected ▷ *vb* **short-list** **2** to put (someone) on a short list

short-lived *adj* lasting only for a short time: *his authority was short-lived*

shortly *adv* **1** in a short time; soon **2** spoken in a cross and impatient manner

shorts *pl n* **1** trousers reaching the top of the thigh or partway to the knee **2** *chiefly US & Canad* men's underpants

short shrift *n* brief and unsympathetic treatment

short-sighted *adj* **1** unable to see faraway things clearly **2** not taking likely future developments into account: *a short-sighted approach to the problem* > **short-sightedness** *n*

short story *n* literature a fictional narrative of shorter length than the novel

short-tempered *adj* easily angered

short-term *adj* of, for, or lasting a short time

short-termism *n* the tendency to concentrate on short-term gains, often at the expense of long-term success

short wave *n* a radio wave with a wavelength in the range 10–100 metres

shot¹ *n* **1** the act or an instance of firing a gun or rifle **2** *sport* the act or an instance of hitting, kicking, or throwing the ball **3** small round lead pellets used in shotguns **4** a person with specified skill in shooting: *my father was quite a good shot* **5** *informal* an attempt: *a second shot at writing a better treaty* **6** *informal* a guess **7 a** a single photograph **b** an uninterrupted sequence of film taken by a single camera **8** *informal* an injection of a vaccine or narcotic drug **9** *informal* a drink of spirits **10** the launching of a rocket or spacecraft to a specified destination: *a moon shot* **11** *sport* a heavy metal ball used in the shot put **12 like a shot** without hesitating **13 shot in the arm** *informal* something that brings back energy or confidence **14 shot in the dark** a wild guess ▶ HISTORY Old English *scot*

shot² *vb* **1** the past of **shoot** ▷ *adj* **2** (of textiles) woven to give a changing colour effect **3** streaked with colour: *dark hair shot with streaks of grey*

shotgun *n* a gun for firing a charge of shot at short range

shot length *n* films, television the time that a particular camera shot remains on view

shot put *n* an athletic event in which contestants hurl a heavy metal ball called a shot as far as possible > **shot-putter** *n*

should *vb* **1** the past tense of **shall**: used to indicate that an action is considered by the speaker to be obligatory (*you should go*) or to form the subjunctive mood (*I should like to see you; if I should die; should I be late, start without me*) ▶ HISTORY Old English *sceolde*

shoulder *n* **1** the part of the body where the arm, wing, or foreleg joins the trunk **2** a cut of meat including the upper part of the foreleg **3** the part of an item of clothing that covers the shoulder **4** the strip of unpaved land that borders a road **5 a shoulder to cry on** a person one turns to for sympathy with one's troubles **6 put one's shoulder to the wheel** *informal* to work very hard **7 rub shoulders with someone** *informal* to mix with someone socially **8 shoulder to shoulder a** side by side **b** working together ▷ *vb* **9** to accept (blame or responsibility) **10** to push with one's shoulder: *he shouldered his way through the crowd* **11** to lift or carry on one's shoulders **12 shoulder arms** *mil* to bring one's rifle vertically close to one's right side ▶ HISTORY Old English *sculdor*

shoulder blade *n* either of two large flat triangular bones, one on each side of the back part of the shoulder

shouldn't should not

shout *n* **1** a loud call or cry **2** *informal* one's turn to buy a round of drinks ▷ *vb* **3** to cry out loudly **4** *Austral & NZ,* *informal* to treat (someone) to (something, such as a drink) ▶ HISTORY probably from Old Norse *skūta* taunt

shout down *vb* to silence (someone) by talking loudly

785

shove *vb* **shoving, shoved** **1** to give a violent push to **2** to push (one's way) roughly **3** *informal* to put (something) somewhere quickly and carelessly: *shove it into the boot* ▷ *n* **4** a rough push ▶ HISTORY Old English *scūfan*

shovel *n* **1** a tool for lifting or moving loose material, consisting of a broad blade attached to a large handle **2** a machine or part of a machine resembling a shovel in function ▷ *vb* **-elling, -elled** *or US* **-eling, -eled** **3** to lift or move (loose material) with a shovel **4** to put away large quantities of (something) quickly: *shovelling food into their mouths* ▶ HISTORY Old English *scofl*

shove off *vb informal* to go away; depart

show *vb* **showing, showed; shown** *or* **showed** **1** to make, be, or become visible or noticeable: *to show an interest; excitement showed on everyone's face* **2** to present for inspection: *someone showed me the plans* **3** to demonstrate or prove: *evidence showed that this was the most economical way* **4** to instruct by demonstration: *she showed me how to feed the pullets* **5** to indicate: *the device shows changes in the pressure* **6** to behave towards (someone) in a particular way: *to show mercy* **7** to exhibit or display (works of art): *three artists are showing at the gallery* **8** to present (a film or play) or (of a film or play) to be presented **9** to guide or escort: *he offered to show me around* **10** *informal* to arrive ▷ *n* **11** a theatrical or other entertainment: *a magic show* **12** a display or exhibition: *a show of paintings* **13** something done to create an impression: *a show of indignation* **14** vain and conspicuous display: *it was nothing but show* **15** *slang, chiefly Brit* a thing or affair: *jolly good show* ▷ See also **show off, show up** ▶ HISTORY Old English *scēawian*

show business *n* the entertainment industry. Also (*informal*): **show biz**

showcase *n* **1** a setting in which something is displayed to best advantage: *a showcase for young opera singers* **2** a glass case used to display objects in a museum or shop ▷ *vb* **-casing, -cased** to exhibit or display

showdown *n informal* a major confrontation that settles a dispute

shower *n* **1 a** a kind of bathing in which a person stands upright and is sprayed with water from a nozzle **b** a device, room, or booth for such bathing **2** a brief period of rain, hail, sleet, or snow **3** a sudden fall of many small light objects: *a shower of loose gravel* **4** *Brit, slang* a worthless or contemptible group of people **5** *US, Canad, Austral & NZ* a party held to honour and present gifts to a prospective bride or prospective mother ▷ *vb* **6** to take a shower **7** to sprinkle with or as if with a shower: *the walkers were showered by volcanic ash* **8** to present (someone) with things liberally: *he showered her with presents* ▶ HISTORY Old English *scūr* > **showery** *adj*

showing *n* **1** a presentation, exhibition, or display **2** manner of presentation

showjumping *n* the sport of riding horses in competitions to demonstrate skill in jumping > **showjumper** *n*

showman *n, pl* **-men** **1** a person skilled at presenting anything in an effective manner **2** a person who presents or produces a show > **showmanship** *n*

shown *vb* a past participle of **show**

show off *vb* **1** to exhibit or display (something) so as to invite admiration: *he was eager to show off his new car* **2** *informal* to flaunt skills, knowledge, or looks in order to attract attention or impress people ▷ *n* **show-off** **3** *informal* a person who flaunts his or her skills, knowledge, or looks in order to attract attention or impress people

showpiece *n* **1** anything displayed or exhibited **2** something admired as a fine example of its type: *an orchestral showpiece*

showroom *n* a room in which goods for sale, esp. cars or electrical or gas appliances, are on display

show trial *n* a trial conducted primarily to make a particular impression on the public or on other nations

show up *vb* **1** to reveal or be revealed clearly **2** to expose the faults or defects of (someone or something) by comparison **3** *informal* to put (someone) to shame; embarrass **4** *informal* to arrive

showy *adj* **showier, showiest** **1** colourful, bright in appearance, and very noticeable, and perhaps rather vulgar: *showy jewellery* **2** making an imposing display > **showily** *adv* > **showiness** *n*

shrank *vb* a past tense of **shrink**

shrapnel *n* **1** an artillery shell containing a number of small pellets or bullets which it is designed to scatter on explosion **2** fragments from this type of shell

■ **WORD HISTORY**
■ 'Shrapnel' is named after Henry *Shrapnel*
■ (1761–1842), the English artillery officer who
■ invented it.

shred *n* **1** a long narrow strip torn off something **2** a very small amount: *not a shred of truth* ▷ *vb* **shredding, shredded** *or* **shred** **3** to tear into shreds ▶ HISTORY Old English *scrēad* > **shredder** *n*

shrew *n* **1** a small mouselike animal with a long snout **2** a bad-tempered nagging woman ▶ HISTORY Old English *scrēawa* > **shrewish** *adj*

shrewd *adj* intelligent and making good judgments ▶ HISTORY from *shrew* (obsolete verb) to curse, from *shrew* > **shrewdly** *adv* > **shrewdness** *n*

shriek *n* **1** a high-pitched scream ▷ *vb* **2** to utter (words or sounds) in a high-pitched tone ▶ HISTORY probably from Old Norse *skrǣkja* to screech

shrike *n* a bird with a heavy hooked bill, which kills small animals by dashing them on thorns ▶ HISTORY Old English *scrīc* thrush

shrill *adj* **1** (of a sound) sharp and high-pitched ▷ *vb* **2** *written* to utter (words or sounds) in a shrill tone ▶ HISTORY origin unknown > **shrillness** *n* > **shrilly** *adv*

shrimp *n* **1** a small edible shellfish with a long tail and a pair of pincers **2** *informal* a small person ▷ *vb* **3** to fish for shrimps ▶ HISTORY probably Germanic

S

shrine *n* **1** a place of worship associated with a sacred person or object **2** a container for sacred relics **3** the tomb of a saint or other holy person **4** a place that is visited and honoured because of its association with a famous person or event: *he'd come to worship at the shrine of Mozart* ▶ HISTORY Latin *scrinium* bookcase

shrink *vb* **shrinking, shrank** *or* **shrunk; shrunk** *or* **shrunken 1** to become or cause to become smaller, sometimes because of wetness, heat, or cold **2 shrink from a** to withdraw or move away from through fear: *they didn't shrink from danger* **b** to feel great reluctance (to perform a task or duty) ▷ *n* **3** *slang* a psychiatrist ▶ HISTORY Old English *scrincan*

shrinkage *n* **1** the fact of shrinking **2** the amount by which anything decreases in size, value, or weight

shrink-wrap *vb* **-wrapping, -wrapped** to package (a product) in a flexible plastic wrapping which shrinks about its contours to seal it

shrivel *vb* **-elling, -elled** *or US* **-eling, -eled** to become dry and withered ▶ HISTORY probably Scandinavian

shroud *n* **1** a piece of cloth used to wrap a dead body **2** anything that hides things: *a shroud of smoke* ▷ *vb* **3** to hide or obscure (something): *shrouded in uncertainty; shrouded by smog* ▶ HISTORY Old English *scrūd* garment

Shrove Tuesday *n* the day before Ash Wednesday ▶ HISTORY Old English *scrīfan* to confess one's sins

shrub *n* a woody plant, smaller than a tree, with several stems instead of a trunk ▶ HISTORY Old English *scrybb* > **shrubby** *adj*

shrubbery *n, pl* **-beries 1** an area planted with shrubs **2** shrubs collectively

shrug *vb* **shrugging, shrugged 1** to draw up and drop (the shoulders) as a sign of indifference or doubt ▷ *n* **2** the action of shrugging ▶ HISTORY origin unknown

shrug off *vb* **1** to treat (a matter) as unimportant **2** to get rid of (someone)

shrunk *vb* a past tense and past participle of **shrink**

shrunken *vb* **1** a past participle of **shrink** ▷ *adj* **2** reduced in size

shudder *vb* **1** to shake or tremble suddenly and violently from horror or fear **2** (of a machine) to shake violently ▷ *n* **3** a shiver of fear or horror ▶ HISTORY Middle Low German *schōderen*

shuffle *vb* **-fling, -fled 1** to walk or move (the feet) with a slow dragging motion **2** to mix together in a jumbled mass: *the chairman shuffled his papers* **3** to mix up (playing cards) so as to change their order ▷ *n* **4** an instance of shuffling **5** a rearrangement: *a shuffle of top management* **6** a dance with short dragging movements of the feet ▶ HISTORY probably from Low German *schüffeln*

shun *vb* **shunning, shunned** to avoid deliberately ▶ HISTORY Old English *scunian*

shunt *vb* **1** to move (objects or people) to a different position **2** *railways* to transfer (engines or carriages) from track to track ▷ *n* **3** the act of shunting **4** a railway point **5** *electronics* a conductor connected in parallel across a part of a circuit to divert a known fraction of the current **6** *informal* a collision where one vehicle runs into the back of another ▶ HISTORY perhaps from Middle English *shunen* to shun

shush *interj* **1** be quiet!; hush! ▷ *vb* **2** to quiet (someone) by saying 'shush' ▶ HISTORY imitative

shut *vb* **shutting, shut 1** to move (something) so as to cover an opening: *shut the door* **2** to close (something) by bringing together the parts: *Ridley shut the folder* **3 shut up** to close or lock the doors of: *let's shut up the shop* **4 shut in** to confine or enclose **5 shut out** to prevent from entering **6** (of a shop or other establishment) to stop operating for the day: *the late-night rush after the pubs shut* ▷ *adj* **7** closed or fastened ▷ See also **shutdown** ▶ HISTORY Old English *scyttan*

shutdown *n* **1** the closing of a factory, shop, or other business ▷ *vb* **shut down 2** to discontinue operations permanently

shuteye *n slang* sleep

shutter *n* **1** a hinged doorlike cover, usually one of a pair, for closing off a window **2 put up the shutters** to close business at the end of the day or permanently **3** *photog* a device in a camera that opens to allow light through the lens so as to expose the film when a photograph is taken ▷ *vb* **4** to close or equip with a shutter or shutters

shuttle *n* **1** a bus, train, or aircraft that makes frequent journeys between two places which are fairly near to each other **2** a bobbin-like device used in weaving to pass the weft thread between the warp threads **3** a small bobbin-like device used to hold the thread in a sewing machine ▷ *vb* **-tling, -tled 4** to travel back and forth ▶ HISTORY Old English *scytel* dart, arrow

shuttlecock *n* a rounded piece of cork or plastic with feathers stuck in one end, struck to and fro in badminton

shut up *vb* **1** *informal* to stop talking or cause (someone) to stop talking: often used in commands **2** to confine or imprison (someone)

shy¹ *adj* **1** not at ease in the company of others **2** easily frightened; timid **3 shy of** cautious or wary of **4** reluctant or unwilling: *camera-shy; workshy* ▷ *vb* **shies, shying, shied 5** to move back or aside suddenly from fear: *with a terrified whinny the horse shied* **6 shy away from** to draw back from (doing something), through lack of confidence ▷ *n, pl* **shies 7** a sudden movement back or aside from fear ▶ HISTORY Old English *scēoh* > **shyly** *adv* > **shyness** *n*

shy² *vb* **shies, shying, shied 1** to throw (something) ▷ *n, pl* **shies 2** a quick throw ▶ HISTORY Germanic

Shylock *n* an unsympathetic and demanding person to whom one owes money ▶ HISTORY after the heartless usurer in Shakespeare's *The Merchant of Venice*

si *n music* same as **te**

787

S

Si *chem* silicon

SI See **SI unit**

Siamese *n, pl* **-mese 1** same as **Siamese cat** ▷ *adj,
n, pl* **-mese 2** (formerly) same as **Thai**

Siamese cat *n* a breed of cat with cream fur, dark
ears and face, and blue eyes

Siamese twins *pl n* twins born joined together at
some part of the body. Technical name: **conjoined
twins**

sibilant *adj* **1** having a hissing sound ▷ *n* **2** *phonetics*
a consonant, such as *s* or *z*, that is pronounced
with a hissing sound ▶ HISTORY Latin *sibilare* to
hiss

sibling *n* a brother or sister ▶ HISTORY Old English:
a relative

sibyl *n* (in ancient Greece and Rome) a prophetess
▶ HISTORY Greek *Sibulla* > **sibylline** *adj*

sic¹ *adv* thus: inserted in brackets in a text to
indicate that an odd spelling or reading is in fact
what was written, even though it is or appears to
be wrong ▶ HISTORY Latin

sic² *vb* **sicking, sicked 1** to attack: used only in
commands to a dog **2** to urge (a dog) to attack
(someone) ▶ HISTORY dialect variant of *seek*

sick *adj* **1** vomiting or likely to vomit **2** physically or
mentally unwell **3** of or for ill people: *sick pay*
4 deeply affected with mental or spiritual distress:
sick at heart **5** mentally disturbed **6** *informal* making
fun of death, illness, or misfortune: *a sick joke* **7 sick
of** *or* **sick and tired of** *informal* disgusted by or
weary of: *I'm sick of this town* ▷ *n, vb* **8** *informal* same
as **vomit** ▶ HISTORY Old English *sēoc*

sickbay *n* a room for the treatment of sick people,
for example on a ship

sicken *vb* **1** to make (someone) feel nauseated or
disgusted **2 sicken for** to show symptoms of (an
illness)

sickle *n* a tool for cutting grass and grain crops,
with a curved blade and a short handle ▶ HISTORY
Old English *sicol*

sickly *adj* **-lier, -liest 1** weak and unhealthy **2** (of a
person) looking pale and unwell: *sickly pallor*
3 unpleasant to smell, taste, or look at **4** showing
excessive emotion in a weak and rather pathetic
way: *a sickly tune* ▷ *adv* **5** suggesting sickness: *sickly
pale* > **sickliness** *n*

sickness *n* **1** a particular illness or disease: *sleeping
sickness* **2** the state of being ill or unhealthy: *absent
from work due to sickness* **3** a feeling of queasiness in
the stomach followed by vomiting

side *n* **1** a line or surface that borders anything
2 *geom* a line forming part of the perimeter of a
plane figure: *a square has four sides* **3** either of two
parts into which an object, surface, or area can be
divided: *the right side and the left side* **4** either of the
two surfaces of a flat object: *write on both sides of
the page* **5** the sloping part of a hill or bank **6** either
the left or the right half of the body, esp. the area
around the waist: *he took a nine millimetre bullet in
the side* **7** the area immediately next to a person or
thing: *at the side of my bed* **8** a place within an area
identified by reference to a central point: *the south*

side of the island **9** the area at the edge of
something, as opposed to the centre: *the far side of
the square* **10** aspect or part: *there is a positive side to
truancy* **11** one of two or more contesting groups or
teams: *the two sides will meet in the final* **12** a
position held in opposition to another in a dispute
13 a line of descent through one parent: *a relative on
his father's side* **14** *informal* a television channel
15 *Brit, slang* conceit or cheek: *to put on side* **16 on
one side** apart from the rest **17 on the side** in
addition to a person's main work: *she did a little
public speaking on the side* **18 side by side** close
together **19 side by side with** beside or near to
20 take sides to support one party in a dispute
against another ▷ *adj* **21** situated at the side: *the
side entrance* **22** less important: *a side issue* ▷ *vb*
siding, sided 23 side with to support (one party
in a dispute) ▶ HISTORY Old English *sīde*

sidebar *n* *computers* (on a web page or other
display) a vertical column appearing beside the
main display area and providing additional
information

sideboard *n* a piece of furniture for a dining room,
with drawers, cupboards, and shelves to hold
tableware

sideboards *or esp US & Canad* **sideburns** *pl n* a
man's whiskers grown down either side of the face
in front of the ears

sidecar *n* a small passenger car attached to the
side of a motorcycle

side effect *n* **1** a usually unwanted effect caused
by a drug in addition to its intended one **2** any
additional effect, usually an undesirable one: *the
unforeseen side effects of the end of the Cold War*

sidekick *n* *informal* a close friend or associate

sidelight *n* **1** *Brit* either of two small lights at the
front of a motor vehicle **2** either of the two
navigational lights used by ships at night

sideline *n* an extra job in addition to one's main
job

sidelines *pl n* **1** *sport* **a** the lines that mark the side
boundaries of a playing area **b** the area just outside
the playing area, where substitute players sit **2 on
the sidelines a** only passively involved: *on the
sidelines of the modern world* **b** waiting to join in an
activity

sidelong *adj* **1** directed to the side; oblique ▷ *adv*
2 from the side; obliquely

sidereal (side-**eer**-ee-al) *adj* of or determined with
reference to the stars: *the sidereal time* ▶ HISTORY
Latin *sidus* a star

side-saddle *n* **1** a riding saddle originally designed
for women in skirts, allowing the rider to sit with
both legs on the same side of the horse ▷ *adv* **2** on
a side-saddle

sideshow *n* **1** an event or incident considered less
important than another: *a mere sideshow compared
to the war on the Russian front* **2** a small show or
entertainment offered along with the main show
at a circus or fair

sidestep *vb* **-stepping, -stepped 1** to step out of
the way of (something) **2** to dodge (an issue) ▷ *n*

S

side step 3 a movement to one side, such as in dancing or boxing

sidetrack vb to distract (someone) from a main subject

sidewalk n US & Canad a raised space alongside a road, for pedestrians

sideways adv 1 moving, facing, or inclining towards one side 2 from one side; obliquely 3 with one side forward ▷ adj 4 moving or directed to or from one side

siding n a short stretch of railway track connected to a main line, used for loading and unloading freight and storing engines and carriages

sidle vb -dling, -dled to walk slowly and carefully, not wanting to be noticed ▶ HISTORY obsolete sideling sideways

SIDS sudden infant death syndrome; cot death

siege n 1 a military operation carried out to capture a place by surrounding and blockading it 2 a similar operation carried out by police, for example to force people out of a place 3 **lay siege to** to subject (a place) to a siege ▶ HISTORY Old French sege a seat

Siegfried line (**seeg**-freed) n history the line of fortifications built by Germany prior to and during World War II opposite the Maginot line in France

siemens n, pl **siemens** the SI unit of electrical conductance ▶ HISTORY after E. W. von Siemens, engineer

sienna n 1 a natural earth used as a reddish-brown or yellowish-brown pigment ▷ adj 2 **burnt sienna** reddish-brown 3 **raw sienna** yellowish-brown ▶ HISTORY after Siena, Italian city

sierra n a range of mountains with jagged peaks in Spain or America ▶ HISTORY Spanish, literally: saw

sies (siss) interj S African, informal same as **sis²**

siesta n an afternoon nap, taken in hot countries ▶ HISTORY Spanish

sieve (siv) n 1 a utensil with a mesh through which a substance is sifted or strained ▷ vb **sieving, sieved** 2 to sift or strain through a sieve ▶ HISTORY Old English sife

sift vb 1 to sieve (a powdery substance) in order to remove the coarser particles 2 to examine (information or evidence) carefully to select what is important ▶ HISTORY Old English siftan

sigh vb 1 to draw in and audibly let out a deep breath as an expression of sadness, tiredness, longing, or relief 2 to make a sound resembling this 3 **sigh for** to long for 4 to say (something) with a sigh ▷ n 5 the act or sound of sighing ▶ HISTORY Old English sīcan

sight n 1 the ability to see; vision. Related adjective: **visual** 2 an instance of seeing 3 the range of vision: the cemetery was out of sight 4 anything that is seen 5 point of view; judgment: nothing has changed in my sight 6 informal anything unpleasant to see: she looked a sight in the streetlamps 7 a device for guiding the eye in aiming a gun or making an observation with an optical instrument 8 an aim or observation made with such a device 9 **sights**

anything worth seeing: the great sights of Barcelona 10 **a sight** informal a great deal: it's a sight warmer than in the hall 11 **a sight for sore eyes** a welcome sight 12 **catch sight of** to glimpse 13 **know someone by sight** to be able to recognize someone without having ever been introduced 14 **lose sight of a** to be unable to see (something) any longer **b** to forget: we lose sight of priorities 15 **on sight** as soon as someone or something is seen 16 **set one's sights on** to have (a specified goal) in mind 17 **sight unseen** without having seen the object concerned: he would have taken it sight unseen ▷ vb 18 to see (someone or something) briefly or suddenly: the two suspicious vessels were sighted 19 to aim (a firearm) using the sight ▶ HISTORY Old English sihth

sighted adj not blind

sightless adj blind

sight-read vb -reading, -read to sing or play (music in a printed form) without previous preparation > **sight-reading** n

sightscreen n cricket a large white screen placed near the boundary behind the bowler, which helps the batsman see the ball

sightseeing n informal visiting famous or interesting sights in a place > **sightseer** n

sigma n 1 the 18th letter in the Greek alphabet (Σ, ς) 2 maths the symbol Σ, indicating summation

sign n 1 something that indicates a fact or condition that is not immediately or outwardly observable: a sign of tension 2 a gesture, mark, or symbol intended to convey an idea or information 3 a board or placard displayed in public and intended to advertise, inform, or warn 4 a conventional mark or symbol that has a specific meaning, for example £ for pounds 5 maths **a** any symbol used to indicate an operation: a minus sign **b** a symbol used to indicate whether a number or expression is positive or negative 6 a visible indication: no sign of the enemy 7 an omen 8 med any evidence of the presence of a disease or disorder 9 astrol short for **sign of the zodiac** ▷ vb 10 to write (one's name) on (a document or letter) to show its authenticity or one's agreement 11 to communicate using sign language 12 to make a sign to someone so as to convey an idea or information 13 to engage or be engaged by signing a contract: he signed for another team ▶ HISTORY Latin signum

signage n signs collectively, esp. street signs or signs giving directions

signal n 1 any sign, gesture, sound, or action used to communicate information 2 anything that causes immediate action: this is the signal for a detailed examination of the risk 3 **a** a variable voltage, current, or electromagnetic wave, by which information is conveyed through an electronic circuit **b** the information so conveyed ▷ adj 4 formal very important: a signal triumph for the government ▷ vb -nalling, -nalled or US -naling, -naled 5 to communicate (information) by signal ▶ HISTORY Latin signum sign > **signally** adv

signal box *n* a building from which railway signals are operated

signalman *n*, *pl* **-men** a railwayman in charge of the signals and points within a section

signatory (**sig**-na-tree) *n*, *pl* **-ries 1** a person, organization, or state that has signed a document such as a treaty ▷ *adj* **2** having signed a document or treaty

signature *n* **1** a person's name written by himself or herself, used in signing something **2** a distinctive characteristic that identifies a person or animal **3** *music* a sign at the beginning of a piece to show key or time **4** *printing* a sheet of paper printed with several pages, which when folded becomes a section of a book ▶ **HISTORY** Latin *signare* to sign

signature tune *n* a piece of music used to introduce a particular television or radio programme

signboard *n* a board carrying a sign or notice, often to advertise a business or product

signet *n* a small seal used to make documents official ▶ **HISTORY** Medieval Latin *signetum*

signet ring *n* a finger ring engraved with an initial or other emblem

significance *n* **1** the effect something is likely to have on other things: *an event of important significance in British history* **2** meaning: *the occult significance of the symbol*

significant *adj* **1** very important **2** having or expressing a meaning > **significantly** *adv*

significant figures *pl n* *maths* **1** the figures of a number that express a magnitude to a specified degree of accuracy: *3.141 59 to four significant figures is 3.142* **2** the number of such figures: *3.142 has four significant figures*

signify *vb* **-fies, -fying, -fied 1** to indicate or suggest **2** to stand as a symbol or sign for: *a blue line on the map signified a river* **3** to be important ▶ **HISTORY** Latin *signum* a mark + *facere* to make

signing *n* a system of communication using hand and arm movements, such as one used by deaf people. Also called: **sign language**

sign off *vb* to announce the end of a radio or television programme

sign of the zodiac *n* *astrol* any of the 12 areas into which the zodiac is divided

sign on *vb* **1** *Brit & Austral* to register and report regularly at an unemployment-benefit office **2** to commit oneself to a job or activity by signing a form or contract

signor (see-**nyor**) *n* an Italian form of address equivalent to *sir* or *Mr*

signora (see-**nyor**-a) *n* an Italian form of address equivalent to *madam* or *Mrs*

signorina (see-nyor-**ee**-na) *n* an Italian form of address equivalent to *madam* or *Miss*

signpost *n* **1** a road sign displaying information, such as the distance to the next town **2** an indication as to how an event is likely to develop or advice on what course of action should be taken ▷ *vb* **3** to mark (the way) with signposts

Sikh (**seek**) *n* **1** a member of an Indian religion that teaches that there is only one God ▷ *adj* **2** of the Sikhs or their religious beliefs or customs ▶ **HISTORY** Hindi: disciple > **Sikhism** *n*

silage (**sile**-ij) *n* a fodder crop harvested while green and partially fermented in a silo

silence *n* **1** the state or quality of being silent **2** the absence of sound **3** refusal or failure to speak or communicate when expected: *he's broken his silence on the issue* ▷ *vb* **-lencing, -lenced 4** to cause (someone or something) to become silent **5** to put a stop to: *a way of silencing criticism*

silencer *n* any device designed to reduce noise, for example one fitted to the exhaust system of a motor vehicle or one fitted to the muzzle of a gun

silent *adj* **1** tending to speak very little **2** failing to speak or communicate when expected: *they remained silent as minutes passed* **3** producing no noise: *the silent room* **4** not spoken: *silent reproach* **5** (of a letter) used in the spelling of a word but not pronounced, such as the *k* in *know* **6** (of a film) having no soundtrack ▶ **HISTORY** Latin *silere* to be quiet > **silently** *adv*

silent partner *n* business, chiefly *US & Canad* same as **sleeping partner**

silhouette *n* **1** the outline of a dark shape seen against a light background **2** an outline drawing, often a profile portrait, filled in with black ▷ *vb* **-etting, -etted 3** to show (something) in silhouette ▶ **HISTORY** after E. de *Silhouette*, politician

silica *n* a hard glossy mineral, silicon dioxide, which occurs naturally as quartz and is used in the manufacture of glass ▶ **HISTORY** Latin *silex* hard stone

silicate *n* *mineral* a compound of silicon, oxygen, and a metal

silicon *n* **1** *chem* a brittle non-metallic element: used in transistors, solar cells, and alloys. Symbol: Si ▷ *adj* **2** denoting an area of a country that contains much high-technology industry: *the Silicon Glen* ▶ **HISTORY** from *silica*

silicon chip *n* same as **chip** (sense 3)

silicone *n* *chem* a tough synthetic material made from silicon and used in lubricants, paints, and resins

silicosis *n* *pathol* a lung disease caused by breathing in silica dust

silk *n* **1** the fine soft fibre produced by a silkworm **2** thread or fabric made from this fibre **3** silks clothing made of this **4** *Brit* **a** the gown worn by a Queen's (or King's) Counsel **b** *informal* a Queen's (or King's) Counsel **c** **take silk** to become a Queen's (or King's) Counsel ▶ **HISTORY** Old English *sioloc*

silken *adj* **1** made of silk **2** *literary* smooth and soft: *her silken hair*

silkworm *n* a caterpillar that spins a cocoon of silk

silky *adj* **silkier, silkiest 1** soft, smooth, and shiny **2** (of a voice or manner) smooth and elegant > **silkiness** *n*

sill *n* **1** a shelf at the bottom of a window, either inside or outside a room **2** the lower horizontal part of a window or door frame ▶ HISTORY Old English *syll*

silly *adj* **-lier, -liest 1** behaving in a foolish or childish way **2** *old-fashioned* unable to think sensibly, as if from a blow **3** *cricket* (of a fielding position) near the batsman's wicket: *silly mid-off* ▷ *n, pl* **-lies 4** *informal* a foolish person ▶ HISTORY Old English *sǣlig* (unattested) happy > **silliness** *n*

silo *n, pl* **-los 1** an airtight pit or tower in which silage or grain is made and stored **2** an underground structure in which missile systems are sited for protection ▶ HISTORY Spanish

silt *n* **1** a fine sediment of mud or clay deposited by moving water ▷ *vb* **2 silt up** to fill or choke up with silt: *the channels have been silted up* ▶ HISTORY probably Old Norse

Silurian (sile-**yoor**-ee-an) *adj geol* of the period of geological time about 425 million years ago, during which fishes first appeared ▶ HISTORY after *Silures*, a Welsh tribe who opposed the Romans

silvan *adj* same as **sylvan**

silver *n* **1** a precious greyish-white metallic element: used in jewellery, tableware, and coins. Symbol: Ag **2** a coin or coins made of silver **3** any household articles made of silver **4** short for **silver medal** ▷ *adj* **5** greyish-white: *silver hair* **6** (of anniversaries) the 25th in a series: *Silver Jubilee; silver wedding* ▷ *vb* **7** to coat with silver or a silvery substance: *a company that silvers their own mirrors* **8** to cause (something) to become silvery in colour: *the sun silvered the tarmac* ▶ HISTORY Old English *siolfor*

silverbeet *n* *Austral & NZ* a beet of Australia and New Zealand with edible spinach-like leaves

silver birch *n* a tree with silvery-white peeling bark

silverfish *n, pl* **-fish** *or* **-fishes 1** a small wingless silver-coloured insect **2** a silver-coloured fish

silver medal *n* a medal of silver awarded to a competitor who comes second in a contest or race

silver plate *n* **1** a thin layer of silver deposited on a base metal **2** articles, such as tableware, made of silver plate > **silver-plate** *vb*

silver screen *n* *informal* films collectively or the film industry

silverside *n* a cut of beef from below the rump and above the leg

silversmith *n* a craftsman who makes or repairs items made of silver

silver thaw *n* *Canad* **1** a freezing rainstorm **2** same as **glitter** (sense 7)

silvery *adj* **1** having the appearance or colour of silver: *her silvery eyes* **2** having a clear ringing sound: *a cascade of silvery notes*

silviculture *n* the cultivation of forest trees ▶ HISTORY Latin *silva* woodland + CULTURE

sim *n* a computer game that simulates an activity such as flying or playing a sport

simian *adj* **1** of or resembling a monkey or ape ▷ *n* **2** a monkey or ape ▶ HISTORY Latin *simia* an ape

similar *adj* **1** alike but not identical **2** *geom* (of two or more figures) different in size or position, but

with exactly the same shape ▶ HISTORY Latin *similis* > **similarity** *n* > **similarly** *adv*

simile (**sim**-ill-ee) *n* a figure of speech that likens one thing to another of a different category, introduced by *as* or *like* ▶ HISTORY Latin: something similar

similitude *n* *formal* likeness; similarity

simmer *vb* **1** to cook (food) gently at just below boiling point **2** (of violence or conflict) to threaten to break out: *revolt simmering among rural MPs* ▷ *n* **3** the state of simmering ▶ HISTORY perhaps imitative

simmer down *vb informal* to calm down after being angry

simnel cake *n* *Brit* a fruit cake with marzipan, traditionally eaten during Lent or at Easter ▶ HISTORY Latin *simila* fine flour

simony (**sime**-on-ee) *n* *Christianity* the practice of buying or selling Church benefits such as pardons ▶ HISTORY after *Simon Magus*, a biblical sorcerer who tried to buy magical powers

simoom *n* a hot suffocating sand-laden desert wind ▶ HISTORY Arabic *samūm* poisonous

simper *vb* **1** to smile in a silly and mannered way **2** to say (something) with a simper ▷ *n* **3** a simpering smile ▶ HISTORY origin unknown > **simpering** *adj*

simple *adj* **1** easy to understand or do: *in simple English; simple exercises* **2** plain and not elaborate: *a simple red skirt; a simple answer* **3** not combined or complex: *simple diagnostic equipment* **4** leading an uncomplicated life: *I am a simple man myself* **5** sincere or frank: *a simple apology* **6** of humble background: *the simple country girl* **7** *informal* lacking in intelligence **8** straightforward: *a simple matter of choice* **9** *music* denoting a time where the number of beats per bar may be two, three, or four ▶ HISTORY Latin *simplex* plain > **simplicity** *n*

simple fraction *n* *maths* a fraction in which the numerator and denominator are both whole numbers

simple fracture *n* a fracture in which the broken bone does not pierce the skin

simple interest *n* *finance* interest paid only on the original amount of a debt

simple-minded *adj* **1** (of people) naive and unsophisticated **2** (of opinions or explanations) not taking the complexity of an issue or subject into account > **simple-mindedness** *n*

simple sentence *n* *grammar* a sentence consisting of a single main clause

simpleton *n* a foolish or stupid person

simplify *vb* **-fies, -fying, -fied 1** to make (something) less complicated **2** *maths* to reduce (an equation or fraction) to its simplest form ▶ HISTORY Latin *simplus* simple + *facere* to make > **simplification** *n*

simplistic *adj* (of an opinion or interpretation) too simple or naive

simply *adv* **1** in a simple manner: *an interesting book, simply written* **2** merely; just: *he's simply too slow* **3** absolutely: *a simply enormous success*

791

simulate vb **-lating, -lated** 1 to pretend to feel or perform (an emotion or action); imitate: *I tried to simulate anger* 2 to imitate the conditions of (a situation), as in carrying out an experiment: *we can then simulate global warming* 3 to have the appearance of: *the wood had been painted to simulate stone* ▶ HISTORY Latin *simulare* to copy
> **simulated** adj > **simulation** n

simulator n a device that simulates specific conditions for the purposes of research or training: *a flight simulator*

simultaneous adj occurring or existing at the same time ▶ HISTORY Latin *simul* at the same time
> **simultaneously** adv > **simultaneity** n

simultaneous equations pl n maths a set of equations that are all satisfied by the same values of the variables, the number of variables being equal to the number of equations

sin[1] n 1 the breaking of a religious or moral law 2 any offence against a principle or standard 3 **live in sin** old-fashioned, informal (of an unmarried couple) to live together ▷ vb **sinning, sinned** 4 to commit a sin ▶ HISTORY Old English *synn*
> **sinner** n

sin[2] maths sine

sin bin n slang (in ice hockey etc.) the area in which players must sit for a specified period after committing a serious foul

since prep 1 during the period of time after: *one of their worst winters since 1945* ▷ conj 2 continuously from the time given: *they've been standing in line ever since she arrived* 3 for the reason that; because ▷ adv 4 from that time: *I have often been asked since* ▶ HISTORY Old English *siththan*

sincere adj genuine and honest: *sincere concern* ▶ HISTORY Latin *sincerus* > **sincerely** adv
> **sincerity** n

sine n (in trigonometry) the ratio of the length of the opposite side to that of the hypotenuse in a right-angled triangle ▶ HISTORY Latin *sinus* a bend

sinecure (**sin**-ee-cure) n a paid job that involves very little work or responsibility ▶ HISTORY Latin *sine* without + *cura* care

sine die (**sin**-ay **dee**-ay) adv without fixing a day for future action or meeting ▶ HISTORY Latin, literally: without a day

sine qua non (**sin**-ay kwah **non**) n an essential requirement ▶ HISTORY Latin, literally: without which not

sinew n 1 anat a tough fibrous cord connecting muscle to bone 2 literary physical strength ▶ HISTORY Old English *sinu, seonu*

sinewy adj lean and muscular

sinful adj 1 having committed or tending to commit sin: *I am a sinful man* 2 being a sin; wicked: *sinful acts*

sing vb **singing, sang, sung** 1 to produce musical sounds with the voice 2 to perform (a song) 3 (of certain birds and insects) to make musical calls 4 **sing of** to tell a story in song about: *the minstrels sang of courtly love* 5 to make a humming, ringing, or whistling sound: *the arrow sang past his ear*

6 (of one's ears) to be filled with a continuous ringing sound 7 to bring (someone) to a given state by singing: *I sang him to sleep* 8 slang, chiefly US to act as an informer ▶ HISTORY Old English *singan*
> **singer** n > **singing** adj, n

singe vb **singeing, singed** 1 to burn slightly without setting alight; scorch: *it singed his sheepskin* ▷ n 2 a slight burn ▶ HISTORY Old English *sengan*

Singhalese n, pl **-lese** adj same as **Sinhalese**

singing telegram n 1 a service by which a person is employed to present greetings to someone on a special occasion by singing 2 the greetings presented in this way 3 the person who presents the greetings

single adj 1 existing alone; solitary: *the cottage's single chimney* 2 distinct from others of the same kind: *every single housing society* 3 designed for one user: *a single room* 4 unmarried 5 even one: *there was not a single bathroom* 6 (of a flower) having only one circle of petals 7 **single combat** a duel or fight involving two individuals ▷ n 8 a hotel bedroom for one person 9 a short music recording with one main song 10 cricket a hit from which one run is scored 11 a Brit a pound note or coin b US & Canad a dollar bill 12 a ticket valid for a one-way journey only ▷ vb **-gling, -gled** 13 **single out** to select from a group of people or things: *the judge had singled him out for praise* ▷ See also **singles** ▶ HISTORY Old French *sengle*

single-breasted adj (of a jacket or coat) having the fronts overlapping only slightly and with one row of buttons

single-decker n Brit, informal a bus with only one passenger deck

single entry n a book-keeping system in which all transactions are entered in one account only

single file n a line of people, one behind the other

single-handed adj, adv unaided or working alone: *the first single-handed sail in my boat; she had to take on the world single-handed* > **single-handedly** adv

single-minded adj having one purpose or aim only; dedicated > **single-mindedly** adv
> **single-mindedness** n

single-parent family n a family consisting of one parent and his or her child or children living together, the other parent being dead or permanently absent

singles pl n sport a match played with one person on each side

singles bar n a bar that is a social meeting place for single people

singlet n Brit & NZ a man's sleeveless vest

singleton n cards the only card of a particular suit held by a player

singly adv one at a time; one by one

singsong n 1 Brit & NZ an informal group singing session ▷ adj 2 (of a voice) having a repetitive rise and fall in tone

singular adj 1 grammar (of a word or form) denoting only one person or thing: *a singular noun*

S

2 remarkable; extraordinary: *one of the singular achievements* **3** unusual; odd: *a lovable but very singular old woman* ▷ *n* **4** *grammar* the singular form of a word ▶ HISTORY Latin *singularis* single > **singularity** *n* > **singularly** *adv*

Sinhalese *or* **Singhalese** *n* **1** (*pl* **-lese**) a member of a people living mainly in Sri Lanka **2** the language of this people ▷ *adj* **3** of this people ▷ See also **Sri Lankan**

sinister *adj* **1** threatening or suggesting evil or harm: *a sinister conspiracy* **2** *heraldry* of, on, or starting from the bearer's left side

■ **WORD HISTORY**
■ In Latin *sinister* means 'left' or 'on the left-hand
■ side'. The word came to have its 'sinister'
■ meaning because the left side was considered
■ unlucky.

sink *vb* **sinking, sank, sunk** *or* **sunken 1** to submerge (in liquid) **2** to cause (a ship) to submerge by attacking it with bombs, torpedoes, etc. **3** to appear to descend towards or below the horizon **4** to make or become lower in amount or value: *sterling sank to a record low against the euro* **5** *written* to move or fall into a lower position, esp. due to tiredness or weakness: *she sank back in her chair* **6 sink into** to pass into a lower state or condition, esp. an unpleasant one: *to sink into debt* **7** *written* (of a voice) to become quieter **8** to become weaker in health **9** to dig (something sharp) into a solid object: *she sank her teeth into the steak* **10** *informal* to drink (a number of alcoholic drinks) **11** to dig, drill, or excavate (a hole or shaft) **12** to drive (a stake) into the ground **13 sink in** *or* **into** to invest (money) in (a venture) **14** *golf, snooker* to hit (the ball) into the hole or pocket: *he finally sank the shot for a bogey* ▷ *n* **15** a fixed basin in a kitchen or bathroom, with a water supply and drainpipe ▷ *adj* **16** *informal* (of a housing estate or school) deprived or having low standards of achievement ▶ HISTORY Old English *sincan*

sinker *n* a weight attached to a fishing line or net to cause it to sink in water

sinkhole *n geol* Also called (esp. Brit): **swallow hole** a depression in the ground surface, esp. in limestone, where a surface stream disappears underground

sink in *vb* (of a fact) to become fully understood: *the euphoria started to wear off as the implications of it all sank in*

sinking fund *n* a fund set aside to repay a long-term debt

Sinn Féin (shin *fane*) *n* an Irish Republican political movement linked to the IRA ▶ HISTORY Irish Gaelic: we ourselves

Sino- *combining form* Chinese: *Sino-European*; *Sinology* ▶ HISTORY Late Latin *Sinae* the Chinese

Sinology (sine-**ol**-a-jee) *n* the study of Chinese history, language, and culture > **Sinologist** *n*

SI notation *n maths* scientific notation: a standard system for the representation of numbers or quantities

sinuous *adj literary* **1** full of curves **2** having smooth twisting movements: *sinuous dances* ▶ HISTORY Latin *sinuosus* winding > **sinuosity** *n*

sinus (**sine**-uss) *n anat* a hollow space in bone, such as one in the skull opening into a nasal cavity ▶ HISTORY Latin: a curve

sinusitis *n* inflammation of the membrane lining a sinus, esp. a nasal sinus

Sioux (**soo**) *n* **1** (*pl* **Sioux**) a member of a group of Native American peoples, formerly living over a wide area from Lake Michigan to the Rocky Mountains **2** any of the languages of these peoples

sip *vb* **sipping, sipped 1** to drink (a liquid) in small mouthfuls ▷ *n* **2** an amount sipped **3** an instance of sipping ▶ HISTORY probably from Low German *sippen*

siphon *or* **syphon** *n* **1** a tube which uses air pressure to draw liquid from a container ▷ *vb* **2 siphon off a** to draw (liquid) off through a siphon **b** to redirect (resources or money), esp. dishonestly, into other projects or bank accounts ▶ HISTORY Greek

sir *n* a polite term of address for a man ▶ HISTORY variant of SIRE

Sir *n* a title placed before the name of a knight or baronet: *Sir David Attenborough*

sire *n* **1** a male parent of a horse or other domestic animal **2** *archaic* a respectful form of address used to a king ▷ *vb* **siring, sired 3** to father ▶ HISTORY Old French

siren *n* **1** a device that gives out a loud wailing sound as a warning or signal **2 Siren** *Greek myth* a sea nymph whose singing lured sailors to destruction on the rocks **3** a woman who is attractive but dangerous to men

■ **WORD HISTORY**
■ The Sirens in Greek mythology were sea
■ nymphs who had beautiful voices and sang in
■ order to lure sailors to their deaths on the rocks
■ where the nymphs lived.

sirloin *n* a prime cut of beef from the upper part of the loin ▶ HISTORY Old French *surlonge*

sirocco *n, pl* **-cos** a hot stifling wind blowing from N Africa into S Europe ▶ HISTORY Italian

sis¹ *n informal* short for **sister**

sis² *or* **sies** (siss) *interj S African, informal* an exclamation of disgust ▶ HISTORY Afrikaans

SIS Secret Intelligence Service: same as **MI6**

sisal (**size**-al) *n* a stiff fibre obtained from a Mexican plant and used for making rope ▶ HISTORY after *Sisal*, a port in Mexico

siskin *n* a yellow-and-black finch ▶ HISTORY Middle Dutch *siseken*

sissy *or* **cissy** *n, pl* **-sies 1** an effeminate, weak, or cowardly person ▷ *adj* **2** effeminate, weak, or cowardly ▶ HISTORY from SIS¹

sister *n* **1** a woman or girl having the same parents as another person **2** a female fellow member of a group, race, or profession **3** a female nurse in charge of a ward **4** *chiefly RC Church* a nun ▷ *adj* **5** of the same class, origin, or design, as another: *its sister paper* ▶ HISTORY Old English *sweostor*

sisterhood *n* **1** the state of being sisters or like sisters **2** a religious group of women **3** a group of women united by a common interest or belief

sister-in-law *n*, *pl* **sisters-in-law** **1** the sister of one's husband or wife **2** one's brother's wife

sisterly *adj* of or like a sister; affectionate

Siswati *n* a language of Swaziland

sit *vb* **sitting, sat** **1** to rest one's body upright on the buttocks: *she had to sit on the ground* **2** to cause (someone) to rest in such a position: *they sat their grandfather in the shade* **3** (of an animal) to rest with the rear part of its body lowered to the ground **4** (of a bird) to perch or roost **5 sit on** (of a bird) to cover its eggs so as to hatch them **6** *written* to be located: *the bank sits in the middle of the village* **7** to pose for a painting or photograph **8** to occupy a seat in some official capacity: *no police representatives will sit on the committee* **9** (of a parliament or court) to be in session **10** to remain unused: *his car sat in the garage* **11** (of clothes) to fit or hang in a certain way: *that dress sits well on you* **12** to take (an examination): *he's sitting his finals* **13** (in combination) to look after a specified person or thing for someone else: *is someone going to dog-sit for you?* **14 sit for** *chiefly Brit* to be a candidate for (a qualification): *he sat for a degree in medicine* **15 sit tight** *informal* **a** to wait patiently **b** to maintain one's position firmly ▷ See also **sit down** ▶ HISTORY Old English *sittan*

sitar *n* an Indian stringed musical instrument with a long neck and a rounded body ▶ HISTORY Hindi

sitcom *n* *informal* (on television or radio) a comedy series involving the same characters in various everyday situations: *yet another unfunny sitcom set in Liverpool*

sit down *vb* **1** to adopt or cause (someone) to adopt a sitting position **2 sit down under** to suffer (insults or humiliations) without resistance ▷ *n* **sit-down** **3** a short rest sitting down ▷ *adj* **sit-down** **4** (of a meal) eaten while sitting down at a table

site *n* **1** the piece of ground where something was, is, or is intended to be located: *a building site; a car park is to be built on the site of a Roman fort* **2** same as **website** ▷ *vb* **siting, sited** **3** to locate (something) on a specific site ▶ HISTORY Latin *situs* position

sit-in *n* **1** a protest in which the demonstrators sit in a public place and refuse to move ▷ *vb* **sit in** **2 sit in for** to stand in as a substitute for (someone) **3 sit in on** to be present at (a meeting) as an observer

sitka spruce *n* a tall North American spruce tree, now often grown in Britain ▶ HISTORY after *Sitka*, a town in Alaska

sit on *vb* *informal* to delay action on: *they are sitting on their information*

sit out *vb* **1** to endure to the end: *just sit it out, and it will pass eventually* **2** to take no part in (a dance or game)

sitter *n* **1** a person posing for his or her portrait or photograph **2** same as **baby-sitter** **3** (in combination) a person who looks after a specified person or thing for someone else: *a house-sitter*

sitting *n* **1** a continuous period of being seated at some activity: *you may not be able to complete it in one sitting* **2** one of the times when a meal is served, when there is not enough space for everyone to eat at the same time: *the second sitting* **3** a period of posing for a painting or photograph **4** a meeting of an official body to conduct business ▷ *adj* **5** current: *a sitting member of Congress* **6** seated: *a sitting position*

sitting room *n* a room in a house or flat where people sit and relax

sitting tenant *n* a tenant occupying a house or flat

situate *vb* **-ating, -ated** *formal* to place ▶ HISTORY Late Latin *situare* to position

situation *n* **1 a** state of affairs **b** a complex or critical state of affairs **2** location and surroundings **3** social or financial circumstances **4** a position of employment

situation comedy *n* same as **sitcom**

SI unit *n* any of the units (metre, kilogram, second, ampere, kelvin, candela, mole, and those derived from them) adopted for international use under the Système International d'Unités, now employed for all scientific and most technical purposes

Siva *n* same as **Shiva**

six *n* **1** the cardinal number that is the sum of one and five **2** a numeral, 6 or VI, representing this number **3** something representing or consisting of six units **4** *cricket* a score of six runs, obtained by hitting the ball so that it crosses the boundary without bouncing **5 at sixes and sevens** in a state of confusion **6 knock someone for six** *informal* to upset or overwhelm someone completely **7 six of one and half a dozen of the other** a situation in which there is no real difference between the alternatives ▷ *adj* **8** amounting to six: *six days* ▶ HISTORY Old English *siex* > **sixth** *adj, n*

sixfold *adj* **1** having six times as many or as much **2** composed of six parts ▷ *adv* **3** by six times as many or as much

six-pack *n* *informal* **1** a package containing six units, esp. six cans of beer **2** a highly developed set of abdominal muscles in a man

sixpence *n* (formerly) a small British, Australian & New Zealand coin worth six old pennies, or 2½ pence

sixteen *n* **1** the cardinal number that is the sum of ten and six **2** a numeral, 16 or XVI, representing this number **3** something representing or consisting of sixteen units ▷ *adj* **4** amounting to sixteen: *sixteen years* > **sixteenth** *adj, n*

sixth form *n* (in England and Wales) the most senior form in a secondary school, in which pupils over sixteen may take A levels or retake GCSEs > **sixth-former** *n*

sixth sense *n* the supposed ability of knowing something instinctively without having any evidence for it

sixty *n*, *pl* **-ties** **1** the cardinal number that is the product of ten and six **2** a numeral, 60 or LX, representing this number **3** something representing or consisting of sixty units ▷ *adj* **4** amounting to sixty: *sixty seconds* > **sixtieth** *adj, n*

sizable *or* **sizeable** *adj* quite large

size¹ *n* **1** the dimensions, amount, or extent of something **2** large dimensions, amount, or extent: *I was overwhelmed by the sheer size of the city* **3** one of a series of standard measurements for goods: *he takes size 11 shoes* **4** *informal* state of affairs as summarized: *that's about the size of it* ▷ *vb* **sizing, sized 5** to sort (things) according to size ▶ HISTORY Old French *sise*

size² *n* **1** a thin gluey substance that is used as a sealer ▷ *vb* **sizing, sized 2** to treat (a surface) with size ▶ HISTORY origin unknown

size up *vb informal* to make an assessment of (a person or situation)

sizzle *vb* **-zling, -zled 1** to make a hissing sound like the sound of frying fat **2** *informal* to be very hot: *the city was sizzling in a hot summer spell* **3** *informal* to be very angry ▷ *n* **4** a hissing sound ▶ HISTORY imitative > **sizzling** *adj*

sjambok (**sham**-bock) *S African* *n* **1** a whip or riding crop made of hide ▷ *vb* **-bokking, -bokked 2** to beat with a sjambok ▶ HISTORY Malay *tjambok*

SK Saskatchewan

skanky *adj slang* **1** dirty or unattractive **2** promiscuous

skate¹ *n* **1** same as **ice skate, roller skate 2 get one's skates on** *informal* to hurry ▷ *vb* **skating, skated 3** to glide on or as if on skates **4 skate on thin ice** to place oneself in a dangerous situation ▶ HISTORY Old French *éschasse* stilt > **skater** *n* > **skating** *n*

skate² *n, pl* **skate** *or* **skates** a large edible marine fish with a broad flat body ▶ HISTORY Old Norse *skata*

skateboard *n* **1** a narrow board mounted on roller-skate wheels, usually ridden while standing up ▷ *vb* **2** to ride on a skateboard > **skateboarding** *n*

skean-dhu (**skee**-an-**doo**) *n* a dagger worn in the sock as part of Highland dress ▶ HISTORY Gaelic *sgian* knife + *dhu* black

skedaddle *vb* **-dling, -dled** *informal* to run off hastily ▶ HISTORY origin unknown

skein *n* **1** a length of yarn or thread wound in a loose coil **2** a flock of geese in flight ▶ HISTORY Old French *escaigne*

skeleton *n* **1** the hard framework of bones that supports and protects the organs and muscles of the body **2** the essential framework of any structure: *a metal skeleton supporting the roof and floors* **3** *informal* an extremely thin person or animal **4** an outline consisting of bare essentials: *the mere skeleton of a script* **5 skeleton in the cupboard** *or* **closet** an embarrassing or scandalous fact from the past that is kept secret ▷ *adj* **6** reduced to a minimum: *a skeleton staff* ▶ HISTORY Greek: something dried up > **skeletal** *adj*

skeleton key *n* a key designed so that it can open many different locks

skelm *n* *S African, informal* a villain or crook ▶ HISTORY Afrikaans

skerry *n, pl* **-ries** *Scot* a rocky island or reef ▶ HISTORY Old Norse *sker*

sketch *n* **1** a quick rough drawing **2** a brief descriptive piece of writing **3** a short funny piece of acting forming part of a show **4** any brief outline ▷ *vb* **5** to make a quick rough drawing (of) **6 sketch out** to make a brief description of: *they sketched out plans for the invasion* ▶ HISTORY Greek *skhedios* unprepared

sketchbook *n* a book of blank pages for sketching on

sketchy *adj* **sketchier, sketchiest** giving only a rough or incomplete description > **sketchily** *adv*

skew *adj* **1** having a slanting position ▷ *n* **2** a slanting position ▷ *vb* **3** to take or cause to take a slanting position: *our boat skewed off course* ▶ HISTORY Old French *escuer* to shun

skewbald *adj* **1** marked with patches of white and another colour ▷ *n* **2** a horse with this marking ▶ HISTORY origin unknown

skewed *adj* distorted or biased because of prejudice or lack of information: *a skewed conception of religion*

skewer *n* **1** a long pin for holding meat together during cooking ▷ *vb* **2** to fasten or pierce with or as if with a skewer ▶ HISTORY probably from dialect *skiver*

ski *n, pl* **skis** *or* **ski 1** one of a pair of long runners that are used, fastened to boots, for gliding over snow ▷ *vb* **skiing, skied** *or* **ski'd 2** to travel on skis ▶ HISTORY Norwegian > **skier** *n* > **skiing** *n*

skid *vb* **skidding, skidded 1** (of a vehicle or person) to slide sideways while in motion ▷ *n* **2** an instance of skidding ▶ HISTORY origin unknown

skid row *n* *slang, chiefly US & Canad* a poor and neglected area of a city, inhabited by down-and-outs

skiff *n* a small narrow boat for one person ▶ HISTORY French *esquif*

skilful *or US* **skillful** *adj* having or showing skill > **skilfully** *or US* **skillfully** *adv*

skill *n* **1** special ability or expertise enabling one to perform an activity very well **2** something, such as a trade, requiring special training or expertise ▶ HISTORY Old Norse *skil* distinction > **skilled** *adj*

skillet *n* **1** a small frying pan **2** *chiefly Brit* a long-handled cooking pot ▶ HISTORY origin unknown

skim *vb* **skimming, skimmed 1** to remove (floating material) from the surface of (a liquid): *skim any impurities off the surface* **2** to glide smoothly over (a surface) **3** to throw (a flat stone) across a surface, so that it bounces: *two men skimmed stones on the surface of the sea* **4** (often foll. by *through*) to read (a piece of writing) quickly and without taking in the details ▶ HISTORY Middle English *skimmen*

skimp *vb* **1** to be extremely sparing or supply (someone) sparingly **2** to do (something) carelessly or with inadequate materials ▶ HISTORY perhaps a combination of SCANT + SCRIMP

skimpy *adj* **skimpier, skimpiest** inadequate in amount or size; scant

skin *n* **1** the tissue forming the outer covering of the body **2** a person's complexion: *sallow skin* **3** any outer layer or covering: *potato skin* **4** a thin solid layer on the surface of a liquid: *custard with a thick skin on it* **5** the outer covering of a furry animal, removed and prepared for use **6** a container for liquids, made from animal skin **7 by the skin of one's teeth** by a narrow margin **8 get under one's skin** *informal* to annoy one **9 no skin off one's nose** *informal* not a matter that concerns one **10 save one's skin** to save one from death or harm **11 skin and bone** extremely thin **12 thick** *or* **thin skin** an insensitive *or* sensitive nature ▷ *vb* **skinning, skinned 13** to remove the outer covering from (a dead animal) **14** to injure (a part of the body) by scraping some of the skin off: *I had skinned my knuckles* **15** *slang* to swindle ▶ HISTORY Old English *scinn* ▷ **skinless** *adj*

skin-deep *adj* not of real importance; superficial: *beauty is only skin-deep*

skin diving *n* underwater swimming using only light breathing apparatus and without a special diving suit ▷ **skin-diver** *n*

skin flick *n slang* a pornographic film

skinflint *n* a very mean person ▶ HISTORY referring to a person so greedy that he or she would skin (swindle) a flint

skin graft *n* a piece of skin removed from one part of the body and surgically grafted at the site of a severe burn or other injury

skinhead *n* **1** a member of a group of White youths, noted for their closely cropped hair, aggressive behaviour, and overt racism **2** a closely cropped hairstyle

skinny *adj* **-nier, -niest** extremely thin

skint *adj slang* without money, esp. only temporarily ▶ HISTORY variant of *skinned*

skintight *adj* (of garments) fitting tightly over the body; clinging

skip¹ *vb* **skipping, skipped 1** to move lightly by hopping from one foot to the other **2** to jump over a skipping-rope **3** to cause (a stone) to skim over a surface or (of a stone) to move in this way **4** to pass over or miss out; omit: *I skipped a few paragraphs* **5 skip through** *informal* to read or deal with (something) quickly or without great effort or concentration **6 skip it!** *informal* it doesn't matter! **7** *informal* to miss deliberately: *she skipped the class* **8** *informal, chiefly US, Canad & Austral* to leave (a place) in a hurry: *he skipped town three years later* ▷ *n* **9** a skipping movement or action ▶ HISTORY probably from Old Norse

skip² *n* **1** a large open container for transporting building materials or rubbish **2** a cage used as a lift in mines ▶ HISTORY variant of *skep* a beehive

skipper *n* **1** the captain of a ship or aircraft **2** the captain of a sporting team ▷ *vb* **3** to be the captain of ▶ HISTORY Middle Low German, Middle Dutch *schipper* shipper

skipping *n* the act of jumping over a rope held either by the person jumping or by two other people, as a game or for exercise

skirl *Scot & N English, dialect n* **1** the sound of bagpipes ▷ *vb* **2** (of bagpipes) to give out a shrill sound ▶ HISTORY probably from Old Norse

skirmish *n* **1** a brief or minor fight or argument ▷ *vb* **2** to take part in a skirmish ▶ HISTORY Old French *eskirmir*

skirt *n* **1** a woman's or girl's garment hanging from the waist **2** the part of a dress or coat below the waist **3** a circular hanging flap, for example round the base of a hovercraft **4** *Brit & NZ* a cut of beef from the flank **5 bit of skirt** *offensive slang* a girl or woman ▷ *vb* **6** to lie along or form the edge of (something): *a track skirting the foot of the mountain* **7** to go around the outer edge of (something): *we skirted the township* **8** to avoid dealing with (an issue): *I was skirting around the real issues* ▶ HISTORY Old Norse *skyrta* shirt

skirting board *n* a narrow board round the bottom of an interior wall where it joins the floor

skit *n* a short funny or satirical sketch ▶ HISTORY probably Scandinavian

skite *Austral & NZ vb* **1** to boast ▷ *n* **2** a boast

skittish *adj* **1** playful or lively **2** (of a horse) excitable and easily frightened ▶ HISTORY probably from Old Norse

skittle *n* **1** a bottle-shaped object used as a target in a game of skittles **2 skittles** a bowling game in which players knock over as many skittles as possible by rolling a wooden ball at them ▶ HISTORY origin unknown

skive *vb* **skiving, skived** (often foll. by *off*) *Brit, informal* to avoid work or responsibility ▶ HISTORY origin unknown ▷ **skiver** *n*

skivvy *n, pl* **-vies 1** *chiefly Brit, often disparaging* a female servant who does menial work; drudge **2** *Austral & NZ* a garment resembling a sweater with long sleeves and a polo neck ▷ *vb* **-vies, -vying, -vied 3** to work as a skivvy ▶ HISTORY origin unknown

skolly *or* **skollie** *n, pl* **-lies** *S African* a hooligan, usually one of a gang ▶ HISTORY origin unknown

skua *n* a large predatory gull living in cold marine regions ▶ HISTORY Faeroese *skúgvur*

skulduggery *or US* **skullduggery** *n informal, written* underhand dealing to achieve an aim ▶ HISTORY origin unknown

skulk *vb* **1** to move stealthily, so as to avoid notice **2** to lie in hiding; lurk ▶ HISTORY from Old Norse

skull *n* **1** the bony framework of the head **2** *informal* the head or mind: *that would have penetrated even your thick skull* ▶ HISTORY probably from Old Norse

skullcap *n* a closely fitting brimless cap

skunk *n, pl* **skunks** *or* **skunk 1** a mammal with a black-and-white coat and bushy tail, which gives out a foul-smelling fluid when attacked **2** *informal* an unpleasant or unfair person ▶ HISTORY from a Native American language

sky *n, pl* **skies 1** the upper atmosphere as seen from earth **2 praise to the skies** praise rather excessively ▷ *vb* **skies, skying, skied 3** *informal* to hit (a ball) high in the air: *the blond-haired forward skied the ball high over the bar* ▶ HISTORY Old Norse *skȳ* cloud

skydiving *n* the sport of jumping from an aircraft and falling freely or performing manoeuvres before opening the parachute > **skydiver** *n*

skyjack *vb* to hijack (an aircraft) ▶ HISTORY SKY + HIJACK

skylark *n* **1** a lark that sings while soaring at a great height ▷ *vb* **2** *old-fashioned* to play or frolic

skylight *n* a window placed in a roof or ceiling to let in daylight

skyline *n* **1** the line at which the earth and sky appear to meet **2** the outline of buildings, trees, or hills, seen against the sky

Skype *n* **1** *trademark* a system that enables audiovisual communication over the internet ▷ *vb* **2** to call (someone) using Skype

skyrocket *n* **1** same as **rocket** (sense 1) ▷ *vb* **2** *informal* to rise very quickly

skyscraper *n* a very tall building

slab *n* a broad flat thick piece of wood, stone, or other material ▶ HISTORY origin unknown

slack¹ *adj* **1** not tight, tense, or taut: *the slack jaw hung open* **2** careless in one's work **3** (esp. of water) moving slowly **4** (of trade) not busy ▷ *n* **5** a part that is slack or hangs loose: *take up the slack* **6** a period of less busy activity ▷ *vb* **7** to neglect (one's work or duty) **8** (often foll. by *off*) to loosen or slacken ▷ See also **slacks** ▶ HISTORY Old English *slæc, sleac* > **slackness** *n*

slack² *n* small pieces of coal with a high ash content ▶ HISTORY probably Middle Low German *slecke*

slacken *vb* (often foll. by *off*) **1** to make or become looser **2** to make or become slower or less intense: *to slacken the pace of reform*

slacker *n* a person who evades work or duty; shirker

slacks *pl n old-fashioned* casual trousers

slag *n* **1** the waste material left after metal has been smelted ▷ *vb* **slagging, slagged 2** *Brit, Austral & NZ, slang* to criticize in an unpleasant way: *I don't think anyone can slag it off* ▶ HISTORY Middle Low German *slagge* > **slagging** *n* > **slaggy** *adj*

slag heap *n* a pile of waste matter from metal smelting or coal mining

slain *vb* the past participle of **slay**

slake *vb* **slaking, slaked 1** *literary* to satisfy (thirst or desire) **2** to add water to (lime) to produce calcium hydroxide ▶ HISTORY Old English *slacian*

slalom *n* *skiing, canoeing* a race over a winding course marked by artificial obstacles ▶ HISTORY Norwegian

slam¹ *vb* **slamming, slammed 1** to close violently and noisily **2** to throw (something) down violently **3** *slang* to criticize harshly: *his new proposals were slammed by the opposition* **4** to strike with violent force: *he slammed the ball into the back of the net* ▷ *n* **5** the act or noise of slamming ▶ HISTORY Scandinavian

slam² *n* the winning of all (**grand slam**) or all but one (**little slam**) of the 13 tricks at bridge ▶ HISTORY origin unknown

slam dunk *n* **1** *basketball* a scoring shot in which a player jumps up and forces the ball down through the basket **2** *informal* a task so easy that success in it is deemed a certainty **3** *informal* an overwhelming victory or success ▷ *vb* **slam-dunk 4** *basketball* to jump up and force (the ball) through the basket **5** *informal* **a** to defeat decisively **b** to achieve an overwhelming victory or success

slammer *n* **the slammer** *slang* prison

slander *n* **1** *law* a false and damaging statement about a person **2** the crime of making such a statement ▷ *vb* **3** to utter slander (about) ▶ HISTORY Old French *escandle* > **slanderous** *adj*

slang *n* **1** informal language not used in formal speech or writing and often restricted to a particular social group or profession ▷ *vb* **2** to use insulting language to (someone) ▶ HISTORY origin unknown > **slangy** *adj*

slanging match *n* an angry quarrel in which people trade insults

slant *vb* **1** to lean at an angle; slope **2** to write or present (information) in a biased way ▷ *n* **3** a sloping line or position **4** a point of view, esp. a biased one: *a right-wing slant on the story* **5 on a** or **the slant** sloping ▷ *adj* **6** oblique; sloping ▶ HISTORY Scandinavian > **slanting** *adj* > **slantwise** *adv*

slap *n* **1** a sharp blow or smack with something flat, such as the open hand **2** the sound made by or as if by such a blow **3 a slap in the face** an unexpected rejection or insult **4 a slap on the back** congratulations ▷ *vb* **slapping, slapped 5** to strike sharply with something flat, such as the open hand **6** to bring (something) down forcefully: *he slapped down a fiver* **7** (usually foll. by *against*) to strike (something) with a slapping sound **8** *informal, chiefly Brit & NZ* to cover with quickly or carelessly: *she slapped on some make-up* **9 slap on the back** to congratulate ▷ *adv informal* **10** exactly: *slap in the middle* **11 slap into** forcibly or abruptly into: *he ran slap into the guard* ▶ HISTORY Low German *slapp*

slap-bang *adv informal, chiefly Brit & Austral* **1** directly or exactly: *he's on holiday in LA and has run slap-bang into a famous face* **2** forcefully and abruptly: *he'd gone and run slap-bang into the watchman*

slapdash *adv* **1** carelessly or hastily ▷ *adj* **2** careless or hasty

slap-happy *adj* **-pier, -piest** *informal* cheerfully careless

slapstick *n* rough and high-spirited comedy in which the characters behave childishly

slap-up *adj Brit, informal* (esp. of meals) large and expensive

slash *vb* **1** to cut (a person or thing) with sharp sweeping strokes **2** to make large gashes in: *I slashed the tyres of his van* **3** to reduce drastically: *to slash costs* **4** to criticize harshly ▷ *n* **5** a sharp sweeping stroke **6** a cut made by such a stroke **7** same as **solidus 8** *Brit, slang* the act of urinating ▶ **HISTORY** origin unknown

slash and burn *n* a farming method in which trees and crops are cut and burned in order to plant new crops

slasher *n Austral & NZ* a tool or tractor-drawn machine used for cutting scrub or undergrowth in the bush

slat *n* a narrow thin strip of wood or metal, such as used in a Venetian blind ▶ **HISTORY** Old French *esclat* splinter

slate¹ *n* **1** a dark grey rock that can be easily split into thin layers and is used as a roofing material **2** a roofing tile of slate **3** (formerly) a writing tablet of slate **4** *chiefly US & Canad* a list of candidates in an election **5 wipe the slate clean** to forget about past mistakes or failures and start afresh **6 on the slate** *Brit & Austral, informal* on credit ▷ *vb* **slating, slated 7** to cover (a roof) with slates **8** *chiefly US* to plan or schedule: *another exercise is slated for tomorrow* ▶ **HISTORY** Old French *esclate* fragment > **slaty** *adj*

slate² *vb* **slating, slated** *informal, chiefly Brit & Austral* to criticize harshly: *the new series was slated by the critics* ▶ **HISTORY** probably from Old French *esclat* fragment > **slating** *n*

slattern *n old-fashioned* a dirty and untidy woman ▶ **HISTORY** probably from dialect *slatter* to slop > **slatternliness** *n* > **slatternly** *adj*

slaughter *n* **1** the indiscriminate or brutal killing of large numbers of people **2** the savage killing of a person **3** the killing of animals for food ▷ *vb* **4** to kill indiscriminately or in large numbers **5** to kill brutally **6** to kill (animals) for food **7** *informal* (in sport) to defeat easily ▶ **HISTORY** Old English *sleaht*

slaughterhouse *n* a place where animals are killed for food

Slav *n* a member of any of the peoples of E Europe or the former Soviet Union who speak a Slavonic language ▶ **HISTORY** Medieval Latin *Sclavus* a captive Slav

slave *n* **1** a person legally owned by another for whom he or she has to work without freedom, pay, or rights **2** a person under the domination of another or of some habit or influence: *a slave to party doctrine* **3** *informal* a badly-paid person doing menial tasks ▷ *vb* **slaving, slaved 4** (often foll. by *away* or *over*) to work very hard for little or no money

- ■ **WORD HISTORY**
- ■ 'Slave' is derived from Latin *Sclavus*, meaning
- ■ 'a Slav', because the Slavonic races were
- ■ frequently conquered and enslaved during
- ■ the Middle Ages.

slave-driver *n* **1** a person who makes people work very hard **2** (esp. formerly) a person forcing slaves to work

slaver¹ (**slay**-ver) *n* **1** (esp. formerly) a dealer in slaves **2** *history* a ship used in the slave trade

slaver² (**slav**-ver) *vb* **1** to dribble saliva **2** (often foll. by *over*) to drool (over someone), making flattering

remarks ▷ *n* **3** saliva dribbling from the mouth **4** *informal* nonsense ▶ **HISTORY** probably from Low German

slavery *n* **1** the state or condition of being a slave **2** the practice of owning slaves **3** hard work with little reward

slave trade *n* the buying and selling of slaves, esp. the transportation of Black Africans to America and the Caribbean from the 16th to the 19th centuries

slavish *adj* **1** of or like a slave **2** imitating or copying exactly without any originality: *a slavish adherence to the conventions of Italian opera* > **slavishly** *adv*

Slavonic *or esp US* **Slavic** *n* **1** a group of languages including Bulgarian, Russian, Polish, and Czech ▷ *adj* **2** of this group of languages **3** of the people who speak these languages

slay *vb* **slaying, slew, slain** *archaic or literary* to kill, esp. violently ▶ **HISTORY** Old English *slēan* > **slayer** *n*

sleaze *n informal* behaviour in public life considered immoral, dishonest, or disreputable: *political sleaze*

sleazy *adj* **-zier, -ziest** dirty, run-down, and not respectable: *a sleazy hotel* ▶ **HISTORY** origin unknown > **sleaziness** *n*

sledge¹ *or esp US & Canad* **sled** *n* **1** a vehicle mounted on runners, drawn by horses or dogs, for transporting people or goods over snow **2** a light wooden frame used, esp. by children, for sliding over snow ▷ *vb* **sledging, sledged 3** to travel by sledge ▶ **HISTORY** Middle Dutch *sleedse*

sledge² *n* short for **sledgehammer**

sledgehammer *n* **1** a large heavy hammer with a long handle, used for breaking rocks and concrete ▷ *adj* **2** crushingly powerful: *the sledgehammer approach* ▶ **HISTORY** Old English *slecg* a large hammer

sleek *adj* **1** smooth, shiny, and glossy: *sleek blond hair* **2** (of a person) elegantly dressed ▶ **HISTORY** variant of *slick*

sleep *n* **1** a state of rest during which the eyes are closed, the muscles and nerves are relaxed, and the mind is unconscious **2** a period spent sleeping **3** the substance sometimes found in the corner of the eyes after sleep **4** a state of inactivity, like sleep **5** *poetic* death ▷ *vb* **sleeping, slept 6** to be in or as in the state of sleep **7** to be inactive or unaware: *their defence slept as we scored another try* **8** to have sleeping accommodation for (a certain number): *the villa sleeps ten* **9** *poetic* to be dead **10 sleep on it** to delay making a decision about something until the next day, in order to think about it ▷ See also **sleep in** ▶ **HISTORY** Old English *slǣpan*

sleeper *n* **1** a railway sleeping car or compartment **2** one of the blocks supporting the rails on a railway track **3** a small plain gold ring worn in a pierced ear lobe to prevent the hole from closing up **4** *informal* a person or thing that achieves success after an initial period of obscurity

sleep in *vb* to sleep longer than usual

sleeping bag *n* a large well-padded bag for sleeping in, esp. outdoors

sleeping partner *n* a partner in a business who shares in the financing but does not take part in its management

sleeping pill *n* a pill containing a drug that induces sleep

sleeping policeman *n Brit* a bump built across a road to prevent motorists from driving too fast

sleeping sickness *n* an infectious, usually fatal, African disease transmitted by the bite of the tsetse fly, causing fever and sluggishness

sleepless *adj* **1** (of a night) during which one does not sleep **2** unable to sleep **3** *chiefly poetic* always active > **sleeplessness** *n*

sleepout *n NZ* a small building for sleeping in

sleepover *n* an occasion when a person, esp. a child, stays overnight at a friend's house

sleepwalk *vb* to walk while asleep > **sleepwalker** *n* > **sleepwalking** *n*

sleep with *vb* to have sexual intercourse and, usually, spend the night with

sleepy *adj* **sleepier, sleepiest 1** tired and ready for sleep **2** (of a place) without activity or excitement: *a sleepy little town* > **sleepily** *adv*

sleet *n* **1** partly melting snow or hail or (esp. US) partly frozen rain ▷ *vb* **2** to fall as sleet ▶ **HISTORY** Germanic

sleeve *n* **1** the part of a garment covering the arm **2** a tubelike part which fits over or completely encloses another part **3** a flat cardboard container to protect a gramophone record **4 up one's sleeve** secretly ready: *he has a few more surprises up his sleeve* ▶ **HISTORY** Old English *slīefe, slēfe* > **sleeveless** *adj*

sleigh *n* **1** same as **sledge¹** (sense 1) ▷ *vb* **2** to travel by sleigh ▶ **HISTORY** Dutch *slee*

sleight of hand *n* **1** the skilful use of the hands when performing magic tricks **2** the performance of such tricks

slender *adj* **1** *written* (esp. of a person's figure) slim and graceful **2** of small width relative to length or height **3** *written* small or inadequate in amount or size: *a slender advantage* ▶ **HISTORY** origin unknown

slept *vb* the past of **sleep**

sleuth (rhymes with **tooth**) *n informal* a detective
- **WORD HISTORY**
- 'Sleuth' is a shortened form of *sleuthhound*,
- meaning a 'tracker dog'. It denoted a dog, such
- as a bloodhound, that can follow trails. The
- 'sleuth' part of the word comes from Old Norse
- *sloth*, meaning 'track'.

slew¹ *vb* the past tense of **slay**

slew² *or esp US* **slue** *vb* **1** to slide or skid sideways: *the bus slewed across the road* ▷ *n* **2** the act of slewing ▶ **HISTORY** origin unknown

slice *n* **1** a thin flat piece or wedge cut from something: *a slice of tomato* **2** a share or portion: *the biggest slice of their income* **3** a kitchen tool having a broad flat blade: *a fish slice* **4** *sport* a shot that causes the ball to go to one side, rather than straight ahead ▷ *vb* **slicing, sliced 5** to cut (something) into slices **6** (usually foll. by *through*) to cut through cleanly and effortlessly, with or as if with a knife **7** (usually foll. by *off, from* or *away*) to cut or be cut (from) a larger piece **8** *sport* to play (a ball) with a slice ▶ **HISTORY** Old French *esclice* a piece split off

slick *adj* **1** (esp. of speech) easy and persuasive: *a slick answer* **2** skilfully devised or executed: *a slick marketing effort* **3** *informal, chiefly US & Canad* shrewd; sly **4** *informal* well-made and attractive, but superficial: *a slick publication* **5** *chiefly US & Canad* slippery ▷ *n* **6** a slippery area, esp. a patch of oil floating on water ▷ *vb* **7** to make smooth or shiny: *long hair slicked back with gel* ▶ **HISTORY** probably from Old Norse

slide *vb* **sliding, slid, slid 1** to move smoothly along a surface in continual contact with it: *doors that slide open* **2** to slip: *he slid on his back* **3** (usually foll. by *into, out of* or *away from*) to pass or move smoothly and quietly: *she slid out of her seat* **4** (usually foll. by *into*) to go (into a specified condition) gradually: *the republic will slide into political anarchy* **5** (of a currency) to lose value gradually **6 let slide** to allow to change to a worse state by neglect: *past chairmen have undoubtedly let things slide* ▷ *n* **7** the act or an instance of sliding **8** a small glass plate on which specimens are placed for study under a microscope **9** a photograph on a transparent base, mounted in a frame, that can be viewed by means of a projector **10** a smooth surface, such as ice, for sliding on **11** a structure with a steep smooth slope for sliding down in playgrounds **12** *chiefly Brit* an ornamental clip to hold hair in place **13** the sliding curved tube of a trombone that is moved in and out to allow different notes to be played ▶ **HISTORY** Old English *slīdan*

slide rule *n* a device formerly used to make mathematical calculations consisting of two strips, one sliding along a central groove in the other, each strip graduated in two or more logarithmic scales of numbers

slide show *n* **1** a display of photographic transparencies using a slide projector **2** any display in the form of a series of static images, such as on a computer screen

sliding scale *n* a variable scale according to which things such as wages or prices alter in response to changes in other factors

slight *adj* **1** small in quantity or extent: *a slight improvement* **2** not very important or lacking in substance: *her political career was honourable but relatively slight* **3** slim and delicate ▷ *vb* **4** to insult (someone) by behaving rudely; snub ▷ *n* **5** an act of snubbing (someone) ▶ **HISTORY** Old Norse *slēttr* smooth > **slightly** *adv*

slim *adj* **slimmer, slimmest 1** (of a person) attractively thin **2** small in width relative to height or length: *a slim book* **3** poor; meagre: *a slim chance of progress* ▷ *vb* **4** to make or become slim by diets and exercise **5** to reduce in size: *that would slim the overheads* ▶ **HISTORY** Dutch: crafty > **slimmer** *n* > **slimming** *n*

Slim n the E African name for **AIDS** ▶ HISTORY from its wasting effects

slime n **1** soft runny mud or any sticky substance, esp. when disgusting or unpleasant **2** a thick, sticky substance produced by some fish, slugs, and fungi ▶ HISTORY Old English *slīm*

slimy adj **slimier, slimiest 1** of, like, or covered with slime **2** pleasant and friendly in an insincere way

sling¹ n **1** med a wide piece of cloth suspended from the neck for supporting an injured hand or arm **2** a rope or strap by which something may be lifted **3** a simple weapon consisting of a strap tied to cords, in which a stone is whirled and then released ▷ vb **slinging, slung 4** informal to throw **5** to carry or hang loosely from or as if from a sling: *her shoulder bag was slung across her chest* **6** to hurl with or as if with a sling ▶ HISTORY probably from Old Norse

sling² n a sweetened mixed drink with a spirit base: *gin sling* ▶ HISTORY origin unknown

slingback n a shoe with a strap instead of a complete covering for the heel

sling off at vb Austral & NZ, informal to mock and jeer

slink vb **slinking, slunk** to move or act in a quiet and secretive way from fear or guilt ▶ HISTORY Old English *slincan*

slinky adj **slinkier, slinkiest** informal **1** (of clothes) figure-hugging **2** moving in an alluring way

slip¹ vb **slipping, slipped 1** to lose balance and slide unexpectedly: *he slipped on some leaves* **2** to let loose or be let loose: *the rope slipped from his fingers* **3** to move smoothly and easily: *small enough to slip into a pocket* **4** to place quickly or stealthily: *he slipped the pistol back into his holster* **5** to put on or take off easily or quickly: *we had slipped off our sandals* **6** to pass out of (the mind or memory) **7** to move or pass quickly and without being noticed: *we slipped out of the ballroom* **8** to make a mistake **9** to decline in health or mental ability **10** to become worse or lower: *sales had slipped below the level for June of last year* **11** to dislocate (a disc in the spine) **12** to pass (a stitch) from one needle to another without knitting it **13** let slip a to allow to escape b to say unintentionally ▷ n **14** a slipping **15** a mistake or oversight: *one slip in concentration that cost us the game* **16** a woman's sleeveless undergarment, worn under a dress **17** same as **slipway 18** cricket a fielding position a little behind and to the offside of the wicketkeeper **19** give someone the slip to escape from someone ▷ See also **slip up** ▶ HISTORY Middle Low German or Dutch *slippen*

slip² n **1** a small piece of paper: *the registration slip* **2** a cutting taken from a plant **3** a young slim person: *a slip of a girl* ▶ HISTORY probably Middle Low German, Middle Dutch *slippe* to cut

slip³ n clay mixed with water to a thin paste, used for decorating or patching a ceramic piece ▶ HISTORY Old English *slyppe* slime

slipe n NZ wool removed from the pelt of a slaughtered sheep by immersion in a chemical bath ▶ HISTORY Middle English *slype* to skin

slipknot n a nooselike knot tied so that it will slip along the rope round which it is made

slip-off slope n geol the gently sloping inside bank of a meandering stream that builds up as a result of sedimentary deposits from slower-moving water on this side

slip-on adj **1** (of a garment or shoe) without laces or buttons so as to be easily and quickly put on ▷ n **2** a slip-on garment or shoe

slipped disc n pathol a painful condition in which one of the discs which connects the bones of the spine becomes displaced and presses on a nerve

slipper n a light soft shoe for indoor wear > **slippered** adj

slippery adj **1** liable or tending to cause objects to slip: *the road was slippery* **2** liable to slip from one's grasp: *a bar of slippery soap* **3** not to be trusted: *slippery politicians* > **slipperiness** n

slippy adj **-pier, -piest** informal or dialect same as **slippery** (senses 1, 2) > **slippiness** n

slip road n Brit a short road connecting a motorway to another road

slipshod adj **1** (of an action) done in a careless way without attention to detail: *a slipshod piece of research* **2** (of a person's appearance) untidy and slovenly

slip-slop n S African same as **flip-flop**

slipstream n the stream of air forced backwards by an aircraft or car

slip up informal vb **1** to make a mistake ▷ n **slip-up 2** a mistake

slipway n a large ramp that slopes down from the shore into the water, on which a ship is built or repaired and from which it is launched

slit n **1** a long narrow cut or opening ▷ vb **slitting, slit 2** to make a straight long cut in (something) ▶ HISTORY Old English *slītan* to slice

slither vb **1** to move or slide unsteadily, such as on a slippery surface **2** to move along the ground in a twisting way: *a snake slithered towards the tree* ▷ n **3** a slithering movement ▶ HISTORY Old English *slid(e)rian* > **slithery** adj

sliver (**sliv**-ver) n **1** a small thin piece that is cut or broken off lengthwise ▷ vb **2** to cut into slivers ▶ HISTORY obsolete *sliven* to split

Sloane Ranger n informal (in Britain) a young upper-class woman having a home in London and in the country, characterized as wearing expensive informal clothes ▶ HISTORY from *Sloane* Square, London + *Lone Ranger*, cowboy hero

slob n informal a lazy and untidy person ▶ HISTORY Irish Gaelic *slab* mud > **slobbish** adj

slobber vb **1** to dribble (liquid or saliva) from the mouth **2 slobber over** to behave in an excessively sentimental way towards (someone) ▷ n **3** liquid or saliva spilt from the mouth ▶ HISTORY Middle Low German, Middle Dutch *slubberen* > **slobbery** adj

slob ice n Canad sludgy masses of floating sea ice

sloe n **1** the small sour blue-black fruit of the blackthorn **2** same as **blackthorn** ▶ HISTORY Old English *slāh*

S

slog *vb* **slogging, slogged 1** to work hard and steadily **2** to make one's way with difficulty: *we slogged our way through the snow* **3** to hit hard ▷ *n* **4** long exhausting work **5** a long and difficult walk: *a slog through heather and bracken* **6** a heavy blow ▶ HISTORY origin unknown

slogan *n* a catchword or phrase used in politics or advertising

■ **WORD HISTORY**
■ 'Slogan' is derived from Gaelic *sluagh-ghairm*, ■ which means 'war cry'.

sloop *n* a small sailing ship with a single mast ▶ HISTORY Dutch *sloep*

slop *vb* **slopping, slopped 1** (often foll. by *about*) to splash or spill (liquid) **2 slop over** *informal, chiefly US & Canad* to be excessively sentimental ▷ *n* **3** a puddle of spilt liquid **4 slops** liquid refuse and waste food used to feed animals, esp. pigs **5** (often pl) *informal* liquid food ▶ HISTORY Old English *-sloppe*

slope *n* **1** a stretch of ground where one end is higher than the other **2 slopes** hills or foothills **3** any slanting surface **4** the angle of such a slant ▷ *vb* **sloping, sloped 5** to slant or cause to slant **6** (esp. of natural features) to have one end or part higher than another: *the bank sloped sharply down to the river* **7 slope off** or **away** *informal* to go quietly and quickly in order to avoid something or someone **8 slope arms** *mil* (formerly) to hold (a rifle) in a sloping position against the shoulder ▶ HISTORY origin unknown

slop out *vb* (of prisoners) to empty chamber pots and collect water

sloppy *adj* **-pier, -piest 1** *informal* careless or untidy: *sloppy workmanship* **2** *informal* excessively sentimental and romantic **3** wet; slushy > **sloppily** *adv* > **sloppiness** *n*

slosh *n, vb* **1** *informal* to throw or pour (liquid) carelessly **2** (often foll. by *about* or *around*) *informal* **a** to shake or stir (something) in a liquid **b** (of a person) to splash (around) in water or mud **3** (usually foll. by *about* or *around*) *informal* to shake (a container of liquid) or (of liquid in a container) to be shaken **4** *Brit, slang* to deal a heavy blow to ▷ *vb* **5** the sound of splashing liquid **6** slush **5** *Brit, slang* a heavy blow ▶ HISTORY variant of SLUSH > **sloshy** *adj*

sloshed *adj slang, chiefly Brit & Austral* drunk

slot *n* **1** a narrow opening or groove, such as one in a vending machine for inserting a coin **2** *informal* a place in a series or scheme: *the late-night slot when people stop watching TV* ▷ *vb* **slotting, slotted 3** to make a slot or slots in **4** (usually foll. by *in* or *into*) to fit or be fitted into a slot: *I slotted my card into the machine* ▶ HISTORY Old French *esclot* the depression of the breastbone

sloth (rhymes with **both**) *n* **1** a slow-moving shaggy-coated animal of Central and South America, which hangs upside down in trees by its long arms and feeds on vegetation **2** *formal* laziness, esp. regarding work ▶ HISTORY Old English *slǣwth*

slothful *adj* lazy and unwilling to work

slot machine *n* a machine, esp. for vending food and cigarettes or featuring an electronic game on which to gamble, worked by placing a coin in a slot

slouch *vb* **1** to sit, stand, or move with a drooping posture ▷ *n* **2** a drooping posture **3 be no slouch** *informal* be very good or talented: *he was no slouch himself as a negotiator* ▶ HISTORY origin unknown

slough¹ (rhymes with **now**) *n* **1** a swamp or marshy area **2** (rhymes with **blue**) *US & Canad* a large hole where water collects **3** despair or hopeless depression ▶ HISTORY Old English *slōh*

slough² (**sluff**) *n* **1** any outer covering that is shed, such as the dead outer layer of the skin of a snake ▷ *vb* **slough off 2** to shed (an outer covering) or (of an outer covering) to be shed: *the dead cells would slough off* **3** *written* to get rid of (something unwanted or unnecessary): *she tried hard to slough off her old personality* ▶ HISTORY Germanic

Slovak *adj* **1** of Slovakia ▷ *n* **2** a person from Slovakia **3** the language of Slovakia

sloven *n* a person who is always untidy or careless in appearance or behaviour ▶ HISTORY origin unknown

Slovene *adj also* **Slovenian 1** of Slovenia ▷ *n* **2** Also: **Slovenian** a person from Slovenia **3** the language of Slovenia

slovenly *adj* **1** always unclean or untidy **2** negligent and careless: *to write in such a slovenly style* ▷ *adv* **3** in a slovenly manner > **slovenliness** *n*

slow *adj* **1** taking a longer time than is usual or expected **2** lacking speed: *slow movements* **3** adapted to or producing slow movement: *the slow lane* **4** (of a clock or watch) showing a time earlier than the correct time **5** not quick to understand: *slow on the uptake* **6** dull or uninteresting: *the play was very slow* **7** not easily aroused: *he is slow to anger* **8** (of business) not busy; slack **9** (of a fire or oven) giving off low heat **10** *photog* requiring a relatively long time of exposure: *a slow film* ▷ *adv* **11** in a slow manner ▷ *vb* **12** (often foll. by *up* or *down*) to decrease or cause to decrease in speed or activity ▶ HISTORY Old English *slāw* sluggish > **slowly** *adv*

slowcoach *n informal* a person who moves or works slowly

slow motion *n* **1** *films, television* action that is made to appear slower than normal by filming at a faster rate or by replaying a recording more slowly ▷ *adj* **slow-motion 2** of or relating to such action **3** moving at considerably less than usual speed

slow virus *n* a type of virus that is present in the body for a long time before it becomes active or infectious

slowworm *n* a legless lizard with a brownish-grey snakelike body

sludge *n* **1** soft mud or snow **2** any muddy or slushy sediment **3** sewage ▶ HISTORY probably related to SLUSH > **sludgy** *adj*

slug¹ *n* a mollusc like a snail but without a shell ▶ HISTORY probably from Old Norse

S

slug² n 1 a bullet 2 printing a line of type produced by a Linotype machine 3 informal a mouthful of alcoholic drink, esp. spirits: he poured out a large slug of Scotch ▶ HISTORY probably from SLUG¹ (with allusion to the shape of the animal)

slug³ vb **slugging, slugged** 1 chiefly US & Canad to hit very hard ▷ n 2 US & Canad a heavy blow ▶ HISTORY probably from SLUG² (bullet)

sluggard n old-fashioned a very lazy person ▶ HISTORY Middle English slogarde

sluggish adj 1 lacking energy 2 moving or working at slower than the normal rate: the sluggish waters of the canal

sluice n 1 a channel that carries a rapid current of water, with a sluicegate to control the flow 2 the water controlled by a sluicegate 3 same as **sluicegate** 4 mining a sloping trough for washing ore ▷ vb **sluicing, sluiced** 5 to draw off or drain with a sluice 6 to wash with a stream of water 7 (often foll. by away or out) (of water) to run or flow from or as if from a sluice ▶ HISTORY Old French escluse

sluicegate n a valve or gate fitted to a sluice to control the rate of flow of water

slum n 1 an overcrowded and badly maintained house 2 (often pl) a poor rundown overpopulated section of a city ▷ vb **slumming, slummed** 3 to visit slums, esp. for curiosity 4 **slum it** to temporarily and deliberately experience poorer places or conditions ▶ HISTORY origin unknown > **slummy** adj

slumber literary vb 1 to sleep ▷ n 2 sleep ▶ HISTORY Old English slūma > **slumbering** adj

slump vb 1 (of commercial activity or prices) to decline suddenly 2 to sink or fall heavily and suddenly: she slumped back with exhaustion ▷ n 3 a severe decline in commercial activity or prices; depression 4 a sudden or marked decline or failure: a slump in demand for oil ▶ HISTORY probably Scandinavian

slung vb the past of **sling¹**

slunk vb the past of **slink**

slur vb **slurring, slurred** 1 to pronounce or say (words) unclearly 2 to make insulting remarks about 3 music to sing or play (successive notes) smoothly by moving from one to the other without a break 4 (often foll. by over) to treat hastily or carelessly ▷ n 5 an insulting remark intended to damage someone's reputation 6 a slurring of words 7 music a a slurring of successive notes b the curved line (⌢ or ⌣) indicating this ▶ HISTORY probably from Middle Low German

slurp informal vb 1 to eat or drink (something) noisily ▷ n 2 a slurping sound ▶ HISTORY Middle Dutch slorpen to sip

slurry n, pl **-ries** a thin watery mixture of something such as cement or mud ▶ HISTORY Middle English slory

slush n 1 any watery muddy substance, esp. melting snow 2 informal sloppily sentimental language or writing ▶ HISTORY origin unknown > **slushy** adj

slush fund n a fund for financing political or commercial corruption

sly adj **slyer, slyest** or **slier, sliest** 1 (of a person's remarks or gestures) indicating that he or she knows something of which other people may be unaware: she had the feeling they were poking sly fun at her 2 secretive and skilled at deception: a sly trickster 3 roguish: sly comedy ▷ n 4 **on the sly** secretively: they were smoking on the sly behind the shed ▶ HISTORY Old Norse slœgr clever > **slyly** adv

Sm chem samarium

smack¹ vb 1 to slap sharply 2 to strike loudly or to be struck loudly 3 to open and close (the lips) loudly to show pleasure or anticipation ▷ n 4 a sharp loud slap, or the sound of such a slap 5 a loud kiss 6 a sharp sound made by the lips in enjoyment 7 **smack in the eye** informal a snub or rejection ▷ adv informal 8 directly; squarely: smack in the middle 9 sharply and unexpectedly: he ran smack into one of the men ▶ HISTORY probably imitative

smack² n 1 a slight flavour or suggestion (of something): the smack of loss of self-control 2 slang heroin ▷ vb 3 **smack of a** to have a slight smell or flavour of (something) b to have a suggestion of (something): it smacks of discrimination ▶ HISTORY Old English smæc

smack³ n a small single-masted fishing vessel ▶ HISTORY Dutch smak

smacker n slang 1 a loud kiss 2 a pound note or dollar bill

small adj 1 not large in size or amount 2 of little importance or on a minor scale: a small detail 3 mean, ungenerous, or petty: a small mind 4 modest or humble: small beginnings 5 **feel small** to be humiliated 6 (of a child or animal) young; not mature 7 unimportant or trivial: a small matter 8 (of a letter) written or printed in lower case rather than as a capital ▷ adv 9 into small pieces: cut it small ▷ n 10 the small narrow part of the back 11 **smalls** informal, chiefly Brit underwear ▶ HISTORY Old English smæl > **smallish** adj > **smallness** n See WORD FOCUS **small**

small change n coins of low value

small fry pl n 1 people regarded as unimportant 2 young children

small goods pl n Austral & NZ meats bought from a delicatessen, such as sausages

smallholding n a piece of agricultural land smaller than a farm > **smallholder** n

small hours pl n the early hours of the morning, after midnight and before dawn

small intestine n anat the narrow, longer part of the alimentary canal, in which digestion is completed

small-minded adj having narrow selfish attitudes; petty

smallpox n a contagious disease causing fever, a rash, and blisters which usually leave permanent scars

small print n details in a contract or document printed in small type, esp. when considered as containing important information that people may regret not reading

S

small

WORD FOCUS

Depending on which sense of **small** you mean, there are a number of alternatives which you can use to vary your writing and make it more interesting.

DEFINITION 1

- If you are describing an object or the physical size of something, you could try: **dainty** cakes and sandwiches. • a **miniature** camera • a pair of **minuscule** shorts • Only a **minute** amount is needed. • The living room is **tiny**.
- If you are describing an area, you could try: only a **short** distance from the station • squeeze through a **narrow** space • a **restricted** habitat
- If you are describing the size of a person, you could try: a **diminutive** figure • a **dumpy** woman • too **little** to reach • **petite** blonde woman • a **short**, squat fellow • She was **tiny**.

DEFINITION 2

- If you are describing something on a minor scale, you could try: such a fuss over such a **little** thing • a **minor** detail • It will only make a **slight** difference.

DEFINITION 3

- If you are describing something mean or petty, you could try: a **mean** thing to do • started

mean-spirited rumours • a **narrow-minded** attitude • **petty** jealousy • **shabby** behaviour • **small-minded** prejudices • **ungenerous** thoughts

DEFINITION 4

- If you are describing something such as a business, you could try: **humble** corner shop • The company started from **modest** beginnings. • a **small-scale** cheese industry • an **unpretentious** restaurant

DEFINITION 5

- If you feel small, you could say that you: are **ashamed** • are **deflated** • are **embarrassed** • feel **foolish** • feel **humble** • are **humiliated** • feel **stupid** • feel **worthless**

DEFINITION 6

- If you are describing someone's age, you could try: my **baby** sister • an **infant** prodigy • when you were **little** • a **young** child

DEFINITION 7

- If you are describing something of no importance, you could try: a seemingly **inconsequential** event • an **insignificant** village • The impact will be **negligible**. • over the most **petty** things • These are **trifling** objections. • bogged down in **trivial** details • a comparatively **unimportant** event

small-scale adj of limited size or scope

small talk n light conversation for social occasions

small-time adj informal operating on a limited scale; minor: a small-time smuggler

smarmy adj smarmier, smarmiest unpleasantly flattering or polite

smart adj 1 clean and neatly dressed 2 intelligent and shrewd 3 quick and witty in speech: a smart talker 4 (of places or events) fashionable; chic: smart restaurants 5 vigorous or brisk: a smart pace 6 causing a sharp stinging pain 7 (of a machine or system) using computer technology in a way that simulates human intelligence: a smart bomb ▷ vb 8 to feel or cause a sharp stinging physical or mental pain: I was still smarting from the insult ▷ n 9 a stinging pain or feeling ▷ adv 10 in a smart manner ▶ HISTORY Old English smeortan be painful > **smartly** adv > **smartness** n

smart aleck n informal a person who thinks he or she is an expert on every subject; know-all

smart card n a plastic card with integrated circuits used for storing and processing computer data

smarten vb (usually foll. by up) to make or become smart

smartphone n a mobile phone that allows access to the internet

smash vb 1 to break into pieces violently and noisily 2 (often foll. by against, through or into) to

throw or crash (against) violently, causing shattering: his head smashed against a window 3 to hit or collide forcefully and suddenly 4 racket sports to hit (the ball) fast and powerfully with an overhead stroke 5 to defeat or destroy: the police had smashed a major drug ring ▷ n 6 an act or sound of smashing 7 a violent collision of vehicles 8 racket sports a fast and powerful overhead stroke 9 informal a show, record or film which is very popular with the public ▷ adv 10 with a smash ▶ HISTORY probably imitative

smasher n informal, chiefly Brit a person or thing that is very attractive or outstanding

smashing adj informal, chiefly Brit excellent or first-rate

smash-up informal n 1 a bad collision or crash involving motor vehicles ▷ vb **smash up** 2 to damage to the point of complete destruction: two men smashed up a bar

smattering n a slight or superficial knowledge: I knew a smattering of Russian

smear vb 1 to spread with a greasy or sticky substance 2 to apply (a greasy or sticky substance) thickly 3 to rub so as to produce a smudge 4 to spread false and damaging rumours (about) ▷ n 5 a dirty mark or smudge 6 a false but damaging rumour spread by a rival or enemy 7 med a small amount of a substance smeared onto a glass slide for examination under a microscope ▶ HISTORY Old English smeoru a smear > **smeary** adj

smear test *n med* same as **Pap test**

smell *vb* **smelling, smelt** *or* **smelled** **1** to perceive the scent of (a substance) with the nose **2** to have a specified kind of smell: *it smells fruity; your supper smells good* **3** (often foll. by *of*) to emit an odour (of): *the place smells of milk and babies* **4** to give off an unpleasant odour **5** (often foll. by *out*) to detect through instinct: *I smell trouble* **6** to use the sense of smell; sniff **7 smell of** to indicate or suggest: *anything that smells of devaluation* ▷ *n* **8** the sense by which scents or odours are perceived. *Related adjective:* **olfactory 9** an odour or scent **10** the act of smelling ▶ **HISTORY** origin unknown

smelling salts *pl n* a preparation containing crystals of ammonium carbonate, used to revive a person feeling faint

smelly *adj* **smellier, smelliest** having a nasty smell > **smelliness** *n*

smelt[1] *vb* to extract (a metal) from (an ore) by heating ▶ **HISTORY** Middle Low German, Middle Dutch *smelten*

smelt[2] *n, pl* **smelt** *or* **smelts** a small silvery food fish ▶ **HISTORY** Old English *smylt*

smelt[3] *vb* a past tense and past participle of **smell**

smelter *n* an industrial plant in which smelting is carried out

smile *n* **1** a facial expression in which the corners of the mouth are turned up, showing amusement or friendliness ▷ *vb* **smiling, smiled 2** to give a smile **3 smile at a** to look at with a kindly expression **b** to look with amusement at **4 smile on** *or* **upon** to regard favourably: *fortune smiled on us today* **5** to express by a smile: *he smiled a comrade's greeting* ▶ **HISTORY** probably from Old Norse

smiley *adj* **1** cheerful **2** depicting a smile ▷ *n* **3** same as **emoticon**

smirch *vb* **1** to disgrace **2** to dirty or soil ▷ *n* **3** a disgrace **4** a smear or stain ▶ **HISTORY** origin unknown

smirk *n* **1** a smug smile ▷ *vb* **2** to give such a smile ▶ **HISTORY** Old English *smearcian*

smite *vb* **smiting, smote; smitten** *or* **smit** *archaic biblical* **1** to strike with a heavy blow **2** to affect severely: *hunger smites him again* **3** to burden with an affliction in order to punish: *God smote the enemies of the righteous* **4 smite on** to strike abruptly and with force: *the sun smote down on him* ▶ **HISTORY** Old English *smītan*

smith *n* **1** a person who works in metal: *goldsmith* **2** See **blacksmith** ▶ **HISTORY** Old English

smithereens *pl n* shattered fragments ▶ **HISTORY** Irish Gaelic *smidirín*

smithy *n, pl* **smithies** the workshop of a blacksmith; forge

smitten *vb* **1** a past participle of **smite** ▷ *adj* **2** deeply affected by love (for)

smock *n* **1** a loose overall worn to protect the clothes **2** a loose blouselike garment worn by women **3** a loose protective overgarment decorated with smocking, worn formerly by farm workers ▷ *vb* **4** to gather (material) by sewing in a honeycomb pattern ▶ **HISTORY** Old English *smocc*

smocking *n* ornamental needlework used to gather material

smog *n* a mixture of smoke and fog that occurs in some industrial areas ▶ **HISTORY** SMOKE + FOG > **smoggy** *adj*

smoke *n* **1** the cloudy mass that rises from something burning **2** the act of smoking tobacco **3** *informal* a cigarette or cigar **4 go up in smoke a** to come to nothing **b** to burn up vigorously ▷ *vb* **smoking, smoked 5** to give off smoke: *a smoking fireplace* **6 a** to draw the smoke of (burning tobacco) into the mouth and exhale it again **b** to do this habitually **7** to cure (meat, cheese, or fish) by treating with smoke ▶ **HISTORY** Old English *smoca*

smokeless *adj* having or producing little or no smoke: *smokeless fuel*

smokeless zone *n* an area where only smokeless fuels may be used

smoke out *vb* **1** to drive (a person or animal) out of a hiding place by filling it with smoke **2** to bring (someone) out of secrecy and into the open: *they smoked out the plotters*

smoker *n* **1** a person who habitually smokes tobacco **2** a train compartment where smoking is permitted

smoke screen *n* **1** something said or done to hide the truth **2** *mil* a cloud of smoke used to provide cover for manoeuvres

smokestack *n* a tall chimney that carries smoke away from a factory

smoko *or* **smokeho** (**smoke**-oh) *n, pl* **-kos** *or* **-hos** *Austral & NZ, informal* **1** a short break from work for tea or a cigarette **2** refreshment taken during this break

smoky *adj* **smokier, smokiest 1** filled with or giving off smoke, sometimes excessively: *smoky coal or wood fires* **2** having the colour of smoke **3** having the taste or smell of smoke **4** made dirty or hazy by smoke > **smokiness** *n*

smolt *n* a young salmon at the stage when it migrates from fresh water to the sea ▶ **HISTORY** Scots

smooch *slang vb* **1** (of two people) to kiss and cuddle **2** *Brit* to dance very slowly with one's arms around another person or (of two people) to dance together in such a way ▷ *n* **3** the act of smooching ▶ **HISTORY** dialect *smouch*, imitative

smoodge *or* **smooge** *vb* **smoodging** *or* **smooging, smoodged** *or* **smooged** *Austral & NZ* **1** same as **smooch** (sense 1) **2** to attempt to gain favour through flattery

smooth *adj* **1** having an even surface with no roughness, bumps, or holes **2** without obstructions or difficulties: *smooth progress towards an agreement* **3** without lumps: *a smooth paste* **4** free from jolts and bumps: *a smooth landing* **5** not harsh in taste; mellow: *an excellent smooth wine* **6** charming or persuasive but possibly insincere ▷ *adv* **7** in a smooth manner ▷ *vb* **8** (often foll. by *down*) to make or become even or without roughness **9** (often foll. by *out* or *away*) to remove in order to make smooth: *smoothing out the creases*

s

10 to make calm; soothe **11** to make easier: *Moscow smoothed the path to democracy* ▷ *n* **12** the smooth part of something **13** the act of smoothing ▶ HISTORY Old English *smōth* > **smoothly** *adv*

smoothie *n* **1** *slang* a man who is so confident, well-dressed, and charming that one is suspicious of his motives and doubts his honesty **2** a smooth thick drink made from fresh fruit and yoghurt, ice cream, or milk

smorgasbord *n* a variety of savoury dishes served as hors d'oeuvres or as a buffet meal ▶ HISTORY Swedish

smote *vb* the past tense of **smite**

smother *vb* **1** to extinguish (a fire) by covering so as to cut it off from the air **2** to suffocate **3** to surround or overwhelm (with): *she smothered him with her idea of affection* **4** to suppress or stifle: *he smothered an ironic chuckle* **5** to cover over thickly: *ice cream smothered with sauce* ▶ HISTORY Old English *smorian* to suffocate

smoulder or US **smolder** *vb* **1** to burn slowly without flames, usually giving off smoke **2** (of emotions) to exist in a suppressed state without being released ▶ HISTORY origin unknown

SMS short message system: used for sending data to mobile phones

smudge *vb* **smudging, smudged** **1** to make or become smeared or soiled ▷ *n* **2** a smear or dirty mark **3** a blurred form or area: *the dull smudge of a ship* ▶ HISTORY origin unknown > **smudgy** *adj*

smug *adj* **smugger, smuggest** very pleased with oneself; self-satisfied ▶ HISTORY Germanic > **smugly** *adv* > **smugness** *n*

smuggle *vb* **-gling, -gled** **1** to import or export (goods that are prohibited or subject to taxation) secretly **2** (often foll. by *into* or *out of*) to bring or take secretly: *he was smuggled out of the country unnoticed* ▶ HISTORY Low German *smukkelen* > **smuggler** *n* > **smuggling** *n*

smut *n* **1** stories, pictures, or jokes relating to sex or nudity **2** a speck of soot or a dark mark left by soot **3** a disease of cereals, in which black sooty masses cover the affected parts ▶ HISTORY Old English *smitte* > **smutty** *adj*

Sn *chem* tin ▶ HISTORY New Latin *stannum*

snack *n* a light quick meal eaten between or in place of main meals ▶ HISTORY probably from Middle Dutch *snacken*

snack bar *n* a place where light meals or snacks are sold

snaffle *n* **1** a mouthpiece for controlling a horse ▷ *vb* **-fling, -fled** **2** *Brit, Austral & NZ, informal* to steal or take **3** to fit or control (a horse) with a snaffle ▶ HISTORY origin unknown

snafu (snaf-**foo**) *chiefly mil, slang n* **1** confusion or chaos regarded as the normal state ▷ *adj* **2** confused or muddled up, as usual ▶ HISTORY s(ituation) n(ormal): a(ll) f(ucked) u(p)

snag *n* **1** a small problem or difficulty: *one possible snag in his plans* **2** a sharp projecting point that may catch on things **3** a small hole in a fabric caused by a sharp object **4** a tree stump in a river bed that is a

danger to navigation ▷ *vb* **snagging, snagged** **5** to tear or catch on a snag ▶ HISTORY Scandinavian

snail *n* a slow-moving mollusc with a spiral shell ▶ HISTORY Old English *snæg(e)l*

snail mail *informal n* **1** conventional post, as opposed to e-mail **2** the conventional postal system ▷ *vb* **snail-mail 3** to send by the conventional postal system, rather than by e-mail

snail's pace *n* a very slow speed

snake *n* **1** a long scaly limbless reptile **2** Also: **snake in the grass** a person, esp. a colleague or friend, who secretly acts against one ▷ *vb* **snaking, snaked 3** to glide or move in a winding course, like a snake ▶ HISTORY Old English *snaca*

snakebite *n* **1** the bite of a snake **2** a drink of cider and lager

snake charmer *n* an entertainer who appears to hypnotize snakes by playing music

snaky *adj* **snakier, snakiest 1** twisting or winding **2** treacherous

snap *vb* **snapping, snapped 1** to break suddenly, esp. with a sharp sound **2** to make or cause to make a sudden sharp cracking sound: *he snapped his fingers* **3** to move or close with a sudden sharp sound: *I snapped the lid shut* **4** to move in a sudden or abrupt way **5** to give way or collapse suddenly under strain: *one day someone's temper will snap* **6** to panic when a situation becomes too difficult to cope with: *he could snap at any moment* **7** (often foll. by *at* or *up*) to seize suddenly or quickly **8** (often foll. by *at*) (of animals) to bite suddenly **9** to speak (words) sharply and angrily **10** to take a photograph of **11** **snap one's fingers at** *informal* to defy or dismiss contemptuously **12** **snap out of it** *informal* to recover quickly, esp. from depression or anger ▷ *n* **13** the act of breaking suddenly or the sound of a sudden breakage **14** a sudden sharp sound **15** a clasp or fastener that closes with a snapping sound **16** a sudden grab or bite **17** a thin crisp biscuit: *brandy snaps* **18** *informal* an informal photograph taken with a simple camera **19** See **cold snap 20** *Brit & NZ* a card game in which the word *snap* is called when two similar cards are turned up ▷ *adj* **21** done on the spur of the moment: *snap judgments* ▷ *adv* **22** with a snap ▷ *interj* **23** *spoken* **a** *cards* the word called while playing snap **b** a cry used to draw attention to the similarity of two things ▷ See also **snap up** ▶ HISTORY Middle Dutch *snappen* to seize

snapdragon *n* a plant with spikes of colourful flowers that can open and shut like a mouth; antirrhinum

snapper *n* a food fish of Australia and New Zealand with a pinkish body covered with blue spots

snappy *adj* **-pier, -piest 1** smart and fashionable: *snappy designs* **2** Also: **snappish** (of someone's behaviour) irritable, unfriendly, and cross **3** brisk or lively: *short snappy movements* **4** **make it snappy** *slang* hurry up! > **snappiness** *n*

snapshot *n* same as **snap** (sense 18)

snap up *vb* to take advantage of eagerly and quickly: *the tickets have been snapped up*

snare¹ *n* **1** a trap for birds or small animals, usually a flexible loop that is drawn tight around the prey **2** anything that traps someone or something unawares ▷ *vb* **snaring, snared** **3** to catch in or as if in a snare ▶ HISTORY Old English *snear*

snare² *n music* a set of strings fitted against the lower head of a snare drum, which produces a rattling sound when the drum is beaten ▶ HISTORY Middle Dutch *snaer* or Middle Low German *snare* string

snare drum *n music* a small drum fitted with a snare

snarl¹ *vb* **1** (of an animal) to growl fiercely with bared teeth **2** to speak or say (something) fiercely: *he snarled out a command to a subordinate* ▷ *n* **3** a fierce growl or facial expression **4** the act of snarling ▶ HISTORY Germanic

snarl² *n* **1** a complicated or confused state **2** a tangled mass ▷ *vb* **3 snarl up** to become, be, or make confused or complicated: *the postal service was snarled up at Christmas* ▶ HISTORY from Old Norse

snarl-up *n informal* a confused, disorganized situation such as a traffic jam

snatch *vb* **1** to seize or grasp (something) suddenly: *she snatched the paper* **2** (usually foll. by *at*) to attempt to seize suddenly **3** to take hurriedly: *these players had snatched a few hours sleep* **4** to remove suddenly: *she snatched her hand away* ▷ *n* **5** an act of snatching **6** a small piece or incomplete part: *snatches of song* **7** a brief spell: *snatches of sleep* **8** *slang, chiefly US* an act of kidnapping **9** *Brit, slang* a robbery: *a wages snatch* ▶ HISTORY Middle English *snacchen*

snazzy *adj* **-zier, -ziest** *informal* (esp. of clothes) stylish and flashy ▶ HISTORY origin unknown

sneak *vb* **1** to move quietly, trying not to be noticed **2** to behave in a cowardly or underhand manner **3** to bring, take, or put secretly: *we sneaked him over the border* **4** *informal, chiefly Brit & NZ* (esp. in schools) to tell tales ▷ *n* **5** a person who acts in an underhand or cowardly manner ▷ *adj* **6** without warning: *a sneak attack* ▶ HISTORY Old English *snīcan* to creep > **sneaky** *adj*

sneakers *pl n US, Canad, Austral & NZ* canvas shoes with rubber soles

sneaking *adj* **1** slight but nagging: *a sneaking suspicion* **2** secret: *a sneaking admiration* **3** acting in a cowardly and furtive way

sneak thief *n* a burglar who sneaks into houses through open doors and windows

sneer *n* **1** a facial expression showing distaste or contempt, typically with a curled upper lip **2** a remark showing distaste or contempt ▷ *vb* **3** to make a facial expression of scorn or contempt **4** to say (something) in a scornful manner ▶ HISTORY origin unknown > **sneering** *adj, n*

sneeze *vb* **sneezing, sneezed** **1** to expel air from the nose suddenly and without control, esp. as the result of irritation in the nostrils ▷ *n* **2** the act or sound of sneezing ▶ HISTORY Old English *fnēosan* (unattested)

sneeze at *vb informal* to ignore or dismiss lightly: *the money's not to be sneezed at*

snib *n Scot & NZ* the catch of a door or window

snick *n* **1** a small cut in something; notch **2** *cricket* a glancing blow off the edge of the bat ▷ *vb* **3** to make a small cut or notch in (something) **4** *cricket* to hit (the ball) with a snick ▶ HISTORY probably Scandinavian

snicker *n, vb. chiefly US & Canad* same as **snigger** ▶ HISTORY probably imitative

snide *or* **snidey** *adj* (of comments) critical in an unfair and nasty way ▶ HISTORY origin unknown

sniff *vb* **1** to inhale through the nose in short audible breaths **2** (often foll. by *at*) to smell by sniffing ▷ *n* **3** the act or sound of sniffing ▶ HISTORY imitative > **sniffer** *n*

sniff at *vb* to express contempt or dislike for

sniffer dog *n* a police dog trained to locate drugs or explosives by smell

sniffle *vb* **-fling, -fled** **1** to sniff repeatedly when the nasal passages are blocked up ▷ *n* **2** the act or sound of sniffling

sniffles *or* **snuffles** *pl n* **the sniffles** *informal* a cold in the head

snifter *n* **1** *informal* a small quantity of alcoholic drink **2** a pear-shaped brandy glass ▶ HISTORY origin unknown

snig *vb* **snigging, snigged** *Austral & NZ* to drag (a felled log) by a chain or cable ▶ HISTORY English dialect

snigger *n* **1** a quiet and disrespectful laugh kept to oneself ▷ *vb* **2** to utter such a laugh ▶ HISTORY variant of *snicker*

snip *vb* **snipping, snipped** **1** to cut with small quick strokes with scissors or shears ▷ *n* **2** *informal, chiefly Brit* a bargain **3** the act or sound of snipping **4** a small piece snipped off **5** a small cut made by snipping ▶ HISTORY Low German, Dutch *snippen*

snipe *n, pl* **snipe** *or* **snipes** **1** a wading bird with a long straight bill ▷ *vb* **sniping, sniped** **2** (often foll. by *at*) to shoot (someone) from a place of hiding **3** (often foll. by *at*) to make critical remarks about ▶ HISTORY Old Norse *snīpa* > **sniper** *n*

snippet *n* a small scrap or fragment: *the odd snippet of knowledge*

snitch *slang vb* **1** to act as an informer **2** to steal small amounts ▷ *n* **3** an informer ▶ HISTORY origin unknown

snitchy *adj* **snitchier, snitchiest** *NZ, informal* bad-tempered or irritable

snivel *vb* **-elling, -elled** *or US* **-eling, -eled** **1** to cry and sniff in a self-pitying way **2** to say (something) tearfully; whine **3** to have a runny nose ▷ *n* **4** the act of snivelling ▶ HISTORY Middle English *snivelen*

snob *n* **1** a person who tries to associate with those of higher social status and who hates those of a lower social status **2** a person who feels smugly superior with regard to his or her tastes or interests: *a cultural snob* ▶ HISTORY origin unknown > **snobbery** *n* > **snobbish** *adj*

S

snoek (**snook**) *n* a South African edible marine fish ▶ HISTORY Afrikaans, from Dutch: pike

snoep (**snoop**) *adj* S African, informal mean or tight-fisted ▶ HISTORY Afrikaans: greedy

snog Brit, NZ & S African, slang *vb* **snogging, snogged 1** to kiss and cuddle ▷ *n* **2** the act of kissing and cuddling ▶ HISTORY origin unknown

snood *n* a pouchlike that loosely holding a woman's hair at the back ▶ HISTORY Old English *snōd*

snook *n* **cock a snook at** Brit **a** to make a rude gesture at (someone) by putting one thumb to the nose with the fingers of the hand outstretched **b** to show contempt for (someone in authority) without fear of punishment ▶ HISTORY origin unknown

snooker *n* **1** a game played on a billiard table with 15 red balls, six balls of other colours, and a white cue ball **2** a shot in which the cue ball is left in a position such that another ball blocks the target ball ▷ *vb* **3** to leave (an opponent) in an unfavourable position by playing a snooker **4** to put someone in a position where he or she can do nothing ▶ HISTORY origin unknown

snoop informal *vb* **1** (often foll. by *about* or *around*) to pry into the private business of others ▷ *n* **2** the act of snooping ▶ HISTORY Dutch *snoepen* to eat furtively > **snooper** *n* > **snoopy** *adj*

snooty *adj* **snootier, snootiest** informal behaving as if superior to other people; snobbish ▶ HISTORY from *snoot* nose

snooze informal *vb* **snoozing, snoozed 1** to take a brief light sleep ▷ *n* **2** a nap ▶ HISTORY origin unknown

snore *vb* **snoring, snored 1** to breathe with snorting sounds while asleep ▷ *n* **2** the act or sound of snoring ▶ HISTORY imitative

snorkel *n* **1** a tube allowing a swimmer to breathe while face down on the surface of the water **2** a device supplying air to a submarine when under water ▷ *vb* **-kelling, -kelled** or US **-keling, -keled 3** to swim with a snorkel ▶ HISTORY German *Schnorchel*

snort *vb* **1** to exhale air noisily through the nostrils **2** to express contempt or annoyance by snorting **3** to say with a snort **4** slang to inhale a powdered drug through the nostrils ▷ *n* **5** a loud exhalation of air through the nostrils to express contempt or annoyance: *Clare gave a snort of disgust* ▶ HISTORY Middle English *snorten*

snot *n* usually considered vulgar **1** mucus from the nose **2** slang an annoying or disgusting person ▶ HISTORY Old English *gesnot*

snotty *adj* **-tier, -tiest** considered vulgar **1** dirty with nasal discharge **2** having a proud and superior attitude **3** slang contemptible; nasty > **snottiness** *n*

snout *n* **1** the projecting nose and jaws of an animal **2** anything projecting like a snout: *the snout of a gun* **3** slang a person's nose ▶ HISTORY Germanic

snow *n* **1** frozen vapour falling from the sky in flakes **2** a layer of snow on the ground **3** a falling of snow **4** slang cocaine ▷ *vb* **5** (with it as subject) to be the case that snow is falling: *it's snowing today* **6 be snowed in** or **be snowed up** or **be snowed over** to be covered by or confined with a heavy fall of snow **7** to fall as or like snow **8 be snowed under** to be overwhelmed, esp. with paperwork ▶ HISTORY Old English *snāw* > **snowy** *adj*

snowball *n* **1** snow pressed into a ball for throwing ▷ *vb* **2** to increase rapidly in size or importance: *production snowballed between 1950 and 1970* **3** to throw snowballs at

snowberry *n, pl* **-ries** a shrub grown for its white berries

snow-blind *adj* blinded for a short time by the intense reflection of sunlight from snow > **snow blindness** *n*

snowboard *n* a shaped board, like a skateboard without wheels, on which a person stands to slide across the snow > **snowboarding** *n*

snowbound *adj* shut in or blocked off by snow

snowcap *n* a cap of snow on top of a mountain > **snowcapped** *adj*

snowdrift *n* a bank of deep snow driven together by the wind

snowdrop *n* a plant with small drooping white bell-shaped flowers

snowfall *n* **1** a fall of snow **2** meteorol the amount of snow that falls in a specified place and time

snowflake *n* a single crystal of snow

snow goose *n* a North American goose with white feathers and black wing tips

snow gum *n* same as **sallee**

snow line *n* geog (on a mountain) the altitude above which there is permanent snow

snowman *n, pl* **-men** a figure like a person, made of packed snow

snowmobile *n* a motor vehicle for travelling on snow, esp. one with caterpillar tracks and front skis

snowplough or esp US **snowplow** *n* a vehicle for clearing away snow

snowstorm *n* a storm with heavy snow

SNP Scottish National Party

snub *vb* **snubbing, snubbed 1** to insult (someone) deliberately ▷ *n* **2** a deliberately insulting act or remark ▷ *adj* **3** (of a nose) short and turned up ▶ HISTORY Old Norse *snubba* to scold

snub-nosed *adj* having a short turned-up nose

snuff¹ *vb* **1** to inhale through the nose **2** (esp. of an animal) to examine by sniffing ▷ *n* **3** a sniff ▶ HISTORY probably Middle Dutch *snuffen* to snuffle

snuff² *n* finely powdered tobacco for sniffing up the nostrils ▶ HISTORY Dutch *snuf*

snuff³ *vb* **1** (often foll. by *out*) to put out (a candle) **2** to cut off the charred part of (a candle wick) **3** (usually foll. by *out*) informal to put an end to **4 snuff it** Brit & Austral, informal to die ▷ *n* **5** the burned portion of the wick of a candle ▶ HISTORY origin unknown

snuffle *vb* **-fling, -fled 1** to breathe noisily or with difficulty **2** to say or speak through the nose

3 to cry and sniff in a self-pitying way ▷ *n* **4** an act or the sound of snuffling ▶ HISTORY Low German or Dutch *snuffelen* > **snuffly** *adj*

snug *adj* **snugger, snuggest 1** comfortably warm and well protected; cosy: *safe and snug in their homes* **2** small but comfortable: *a snug office* **3** fitting closely and comfortably ▷ *n* **4** (in Britain and Ireland) a small room in a pub ▶ HISTORY Swedish *snygg* tidy > **snugly** *adv*

snuggle *vb* **-gling, -gled** to nestle into (a person or thing) for warmth or from affection ▶ HISTORY from SNUG

so¹ *adv* **1** to such an extent: *the river is so dirty that it smells* **2** to the same extent as: *she is not so old as you* **3** extremely: *it's so lovely* **4** also: *I can speak Spanish and so can you* **5** thereupon: *and so we ended up in France* **6** in the state or manner expressed or implied: *they're happy and will remain so* **7 and so on** or **forth** and continuing similarly **8 or so** approximately: *fifty or so people came to see me* **9 so be it** an expression of agreement or resignation **10 so much a** a certain degree or amount (of) **b** a lot (of): *it's just so much nonsense* **11 so much for a** no more need be said about **b** used to express contempt for something that has failed: *so much for all our plans* ▷ *conj* (often foll. by *that*) **12** in order (that): *to die so that you might live* **13** with the consequence (that): *he was late home, so that there was trouble* **14 so as** in order (to): *to diet so as to lose weight* **15** not universally accepted in consequence: *she wasn't needed, so she left* **16 so what!** *informal* that is unimportant ▷ *pron* **17** used to substitute for a clause or sentence, which may be understood: *you'll stop because I said so* ▷ *adj* **18** true: *it can't be so* ▷ *interj* **19** an exclamation of surprise or triumph ▶ HISTORY Old English *swā*

so² *n music* same as **soh**

soak *vb* **1** to put or lie in a liquid so as to become thoroughly wet **2** (usually foll. by *in* or *into*) (of a liquid) to penetrate or permeate **3** (usually foll. by *in* or *up*) to take in; absorb: *white clay soaks up excess oil* ▷ *n* **4** a soaking or being soaked **5** *slang* a person who drinks very heavily ▶ HISTORY Old English *sōcian* > **soaking** *n, adj*

so-and-so *n, pl* **so-and-sos** *informal* **1** a person whose name is not specified **2** *euphemistic* a person regarded as unpleasant; a name used in place of a swear word: *you're a dirty so-and-so*

soap *n* **1** a compound of alkali and fat, used with water as a cleaning agent **2** *informal* short for **soap opera** ▷ *vb* **3** to apply soap to ▶ HISTORY Old English *sāpe*

soapbox *n* a crate used as a platform for making speeches

soap opera *n* an on-going television or radio serial about the daily lives of a group of people ▶ HISTORY so called because manufacturers of soap were typical sponsors

soapstone *n* a soft mineral used for making table tops and ornaments

soapsuds *pl n* foam or lather produced when soap is mixed with water

soapy *adj* **soapier, soapiest 1** containing or covered with soap: *a soapy liquid* **2** like soap in texture, smell, or taste: *the cheese had a soapy taste* **3** *slang* flattering or persuasive > **soapiness** *n*

soar *vb* **1** to rise or fly upwards into the air **2** (of a bird or aircraft) to glide while maintaining altitude **3** to rise or increase suddenly above the usual level: *television ratings soared* ▶ HISTORY Old French *essorer*

sob *vb* **sobbing, sobbed 1** to cry noisily, breathing in short gasps **2** to speak with sobs ▷ *n* **3** the act or sound of sobbing ▶ HISTORY probably from Low German

sober *adj* **1** not drunk **2** tending to drink only moderate quantities of alcohol **3** serious and thoughtful: *a sober and serious fellow* **4** (of colours) plain and dull **5** free from exaggeration: *a fairly sober version of what happened* ▷ *vb* **6** (usually foll. by *up*) to make or become less drunk ▶ HISTORY Latin *sobrius* > **sobering** *adj*

sobriety *n* the state of being sober

sobriquet *or* **soubriquet** (**so**-brik-ay) *n written* a nickname ▶ HISTORY French *soubriquet*

sob story *n* a tale of personal misfortune or bad luck intended to arouse sympathy

Soc. *or* **soc.** **1** socialist **2** society

soca (**soah**-ka) *n* a mixture of soul and calypso music typical of the E Caribbean ▶ HISTORY blend of SOUL + CALYPSO

so-called *adj* called (in the speaker's opinion, wrongly) by that name: *so-called military experts*

soccer *n* a game in which two teams of eleven players try to kick or head a ball into their opponents' goal, only the goalkeeper on either side being allowed to touch the ball with his hands

∎ **WORD HISTORY**

∎ 'Soccer' is formed from *Association Football*.

sociable *adj* **1** friendly and enjoying other people's company **2** (of an occasion) providing the opportunity for relaxed and friendly companionship > **sociability** *n* > **sociably** *adv*

social *adj* **1** living or preferring to live in a community rather than alone **2** of or relating to human society or organization **3** of the way people live and work together in groups: *social organization* **4** of or for companionship or communal activities: *social clubs* **5** of or engaged in social services: *a social worker* **6** relating to a certain class of society: *social misfits* **7** (of certain species of insects) living together in organized colonies: *social bees* ▷ *n* **8** an informal gathering ▶ HISTORY Latin *socius* a comrade > **socially** *adv*

Social Charter *n* a proposed declaration of the rights, minimum wages, etc. of workers in the European Union

social climber *n* a person who tries to associate with people from a higher social class in the hope that he or she will be thought also to be upper-class

social contract *or* **compact** *n* an agreement among individuals to cooperate for greater security, which results in the loss of some personal liberties

S

social democrat *n* **1** a person who is in favour of a market or mixed economy but believes the State must play an active role in ensuring social justice and equality of opportunity **2** (formerly) a person who believed in the gradual transformation of capitalism into democratic socialism > **social democracy** *n*

social exclusion *n sociol* the failure of society to provide certain people with those rights normally available to its members, such as employment, health care, education, etc.

social inclusion *n sociol* the provision of certain rights to all people in society, such as employment, health care, education, etc.

social intelligence *n* the ability to form rewarding relationships with other people

socialism *n* a political and economic theory or system in which the means of production, distribution, and exchange are owned by the community collectively, usually through the state > **socialist** *n, adj*

socialite *n* a person who goes to many events attended by the rich, famous, and fashionable

socialize *or* **-ise** *vb* **-izing, -ized** *or* **-ising, -ised** **1** to meet others socially **2** to prepare for life in society **3** *chiefly US* to organize along socialist principles > **socialization** *or* **-isation** *n*

social market *n* an economic system in which industry and commerce are run by private enterprise within limits set by the government to ensure equality of opportunity and social responsibility

social media *pl n* agencies, such as websites and applications, that facilitate social networking

social networking *n* interaction between subscribers to a website, typically involving the forming or joining of groups based around shared interests, or publishing content so that a specified group of subscribers can access it

social science *n* the systematic study of society and of human relationships within society > **social scientist** *n*

social security *n* state provision for the welfare of people who are elderly, unemployed, or sick, through pensions and other financial aid

social services *pl n* welfare services provided by local authorities or a state agency for people with particular social needs

social skills *pl n* the level of ability a person has for communicating with and getting along with other people

social studies *n* the study of how people live and organize themselves in society

social welfare *n* **1** social services provided by a state for the benefit of its citizens **2** (in New Zealand) a government department concerned with pensions and benefits for elderly and disabled people, etc.

social work *n* social services that give help and advice to elderly people, disabled people, and families with problems > **social worker** *n*

society *n, pl* **-ties** **1** human beings considered as a group **2** a group of people forming a single community with its own distinctive culture and institutions **3** the structure, culture, and institutions of such a group **4** an organized group of people sharing a common aim or interest: *a dramatic society* **5** the rich and fashionable class of society collectively **6** *old-fashioned* companionship: *I enjoy her society* ▶ HISTORY Latin *societas* > **societal** *adj*

Society of Jesus *n* the religious order of the Jesuits

sociocultural *adj* relating to both social and cultural issues

socioeconomic *adj* of or involving economic and social factors

sociology *n* the study of the development, organization, functioning, and classification of human societies > **sociological** *adj* > **sociologist** *n*

sociopolitical *adj* of or involving political and social factors

sock[1] *n* **1** a cloth covering for the foot, reaching to between the ankle and knee and worn inside a shoe **2** **pull one's socks up** *Brit & NZ, informal* to make a determined effort to improve **3** **put a sock in it** *slang* be quiet! ▶ HISTORY Greek *sukkhos* a light shoe

sock[2] *slang vb* **1** to hit hard ▷ *n* **2** a hard blow ▶ HISTORY origin unknown

socket *n* **1** a device into which an electric plug can be inserted in order to make a connection in a circuit **2** *anat* a bony hollow into which a part or structure fits: *the hip socket* ▶ HISTORY Anglo-Norman *soket* a little ploughshare

Socratic *adj* of the Greek philosopher Socrates, or his teachings

Socratic method *n philosophy* the method of instruction used by Socrates, in which a series of questions and answers lead to a logical conclusion

sod[1] *n* **1** a piece of grass-covered surface soil; turf **2** *poetic* the ground ▶ HISTORY Low German

sod[2] *slang, chiefly Brit* *n* **1** an unpleasant person **2** *jocular* a person, esp. an unlucky one: *the poor sod hasn't been out for weeks* **3** **sod all** *slang* nothing ▷ *interj* **4** **sod it** an exclamation of annoyance ▶ HISTORY from *sodomite* > **sodding** *adj*

soda *n* **1** a simple compound of sodium, such as sodium carbonate or sodium bicarbonate **2** same as **soda water** **3** *US & Canad* a sweet fizzy drink ▶ HISTORY perhaps from Arabic

soda fountain *n US & Canad* **1** a counter that serves soft drinks and snacks **2** a device dispensing soda water

soda lime *n chem* a solid mixture of sodium and calcium hydroxides used to absorb carbon dioxide and dry gases

soda water *n* a fizzy drink made by charging water with carbon dioxide under pressure

sodden *adj* **1** soaking wet **2** (of someone's senses) dulled, esp. by excessive drinking ▶ HISTORY *soden*, obsolete past participle of *seethe*

sodium *n chem* a very reactive soft silvery-white metallic element. Symbol: Na ▶ HISTORY from SODA

S

809

sodium bicarbonate *n* a white soluble crystalline compound used in fizzy drinks, baking powder, and in medicine as an antacid

sodium carbonate *n* a colourless or white soluble crystalline compound used in the manufacture of glass, ceramics, soap, and paper, and as a cleansing agent

sodium chlorate *n* a colourless crystalline compound used as a bleaching agent, antiseptic, and weedkiller

sodium chloride *n* common table salt; a soluble colourless crystalline compound widely used as a seasoning and preservative for food and in the manufacture of chemicals, glass, and soap

sodium hydroxide *n* a white strongly alkaline solid used in the manufacture of rayon, paper, aluminium, and soap

sodomite *n* a person who practises sodomy

sodomy *n* anal intercourse committed by a man with another man or a woman ▶ HISTORY after *Sodom*, Biblical city, noted for its depravity

sofa *n* a long comfortable seat with back and arms for two or more people

■ **WORD HISTORY**
■ 'Sofa' comes from Arabic *suffah*, meaning 'an upholstered raised platform'.

soft *adj* **1** easy to dent, shape, or cut: *soft material* **2** not hard; giving way easily under pressure: *a soft bed* **3** fine, smooth, or fluffy to the touch: *soft fur* **4** (of music or sounds) quiet and pleasing **5** (of light or colour) not excessively bright or harsh **6** (of a breeze or climate) temperate, mild, or pleasant **7** with smooth curves rather than sharp edges: *soft focus* **8** kind or lenient, often to excess **9** easy to influence or make demands on: *he's a soft touch* **10** *informal* feeble or silly; simple: *soft in the head* **11** not strong or able to endure hardship **12** (of a drug) nonaddictive **13** *informal* requiring little effort; easy: *a soft option* **14** *chem* (of water) relatively free of mineral salts and therefore easily able to make soap lather **15** loving and tender: *soft words* **16** *phonetics* denoting the consonants *c* and *g* when they are pronounced sibilantly, as in *cent* and *germ* **17** **soft on a** lenient towards: *he was accused of being soft on criminals* **b** experiencing romantic love for ▷ *adv* **18** softly: *to speak soft* ▷ *interj* **19** *archaic* quiet! ▶ HISTORY Old English *sōfte* > **softly** *adv*

softball *n* a game similar to baseball, played using a larger softer ball

soft coal *n* same as **bituminous coal**

soft drink *n* a nonalcoholic drink

soften *vb* **1** to make or become soft or softer **2** to make or become more sympathetic and less critical: *the farmers softened their opposition to the legislation* **3** to lessen the severity or difficulty of: *foreign relief softened the hardship of a terrible winter* > **softener** *n*

soft furnishings *pl n* curtains, hangings, rugs, and covers

softie or **softy** *n, pl* **softies** *informal* a person who is easily hurt or upset

soft news *n* news stories based on analysis and interpretation rather than substance and real events, or entertaining stories dealing human-interest topics and events of local interest. Compare **hard news**

soft option *n* the easiest of a number of choices

soft palate *n* the fleshy part at the back of the roof of the mouth

soft-pedal *vb* **-alling, -alled** *or US* **-aling, -aled** **1** to deliberately avoid emphasizing (something): *he was soft-pedalling the question of tax increases* ▷ *n* **soft pedal 2** a pedal on a piano that softens the tone

soft sell *n* a method of selling based on subtle suggestion and gentle persuasion

soft-soap *vb informal* to flatter (a person)

soft touch *n informal* a person who is easily persuaded to perform favours for, or lend money to, other people

software *n computers* the programs used with a computer

softwood *n* the wood of coniferous trees

soggy *adj* **-gier, -giest 1** soaked with liquid: *a soggy running track* **2** moist and heavy: *a soggy sandwich* ▶ HISTORY probably from dialect *sog* marsh > **sogginess** *n*

soh *n music* the fifth note of any ascending major scale

soigné or fem **soignée** (swah-nyay) *adj* neat, elegant, and well-dressed: *the soignée deputy editor of Vogue* ▶ HISTORY French

soil[1] *n* **1** the top layer of the land surface of the earth **2** a specific type of this material: *sandy soil* **3** land, country, or region: *the first US side to lose on home soil* ▶ HISTORY Latin *solium* a seat, confused with *solum* the ground

soil[2] *vb* **1** to make or become dirty or stained **2** to bring disgrace upon: *he's soiled our reputation* ▷ *n* **3** a soiled spot **4** refuse, manure, or excrement ▶ HISTORY Old French *soillier*

soil creep *n geol* the gradual downhill movement of soil and loose rock material on a slope

soil profile *n geol* the layers of soil between the surface and the bedrock seen in cross section

soil texture *n geol, agriculture* the texture of soil to the touch, dependent on the relative amounts of clay, sand, etc. in it

soiree (swah-ray) *n* an evening social gathering ▶ HISTORY French

sojourn (soj-urn) *literary n* **1** a short stay in a place ▷ *vb* **2** to stay temporarily: *he sojourned in Basle during a short illness* ▶ HISTORY Old French *sojorner*

sol[1] *n music* same as **soh**

sol[2] *n chem* a liquid colloidal solution

solace (sol-iss) *n* **1** comfort in misery or disappointment: *it drove him to seek increasing solace in alcohol* **2** something that gives comfort or consolation: *his music was a solace to me during my illness* ▷ *vb* **-acing, -aced 3** to give comfort or cheer to (a person) in time of sorrow or distress ▶ HISTORY Old French *solas*

solar adj **1** of the sun: a solar eclipse **2** operating by or using the energy of the sun: solar cell ▶ HISTORY Latin sol the sun

solarium n, pl **-lariums** or **-laria** a place with beds equipped with ultraviolet lights used for giving people an artificial suntan ▶ HISTORY Latin: a terrace

solar plexus n **1** anat a network of nerves behind the stomach **2** not in technical use the vulnerable part of the stomach beneath the diaphragm

solar power n science heat radiation from the sun converted into electrical power

solar system n the system containing the sun and the planets, comets, and asteroids that go round it

sold vb **1** the past of **sell** ▷ adj **2 sold on** slang enthusiastic and uncritical about

solder n **1** an alloy used for joining two metal surfaces by melting the alloy so that it forms a thin layer between the surfaces ▷ vb **2** to join or mend or be joined or mended with solder ▶ HISTORY Latin solidare to strengthen

soldering iron n a hand tool with a copper tip that is heated and used to melt and apply solder

soldier n **1 a** a person who serves or has served in an army **b** a person who is not an officer in an army ▷ vb **2** to serve as a soldier ▶ HISTORY Old French soudier > **soldierly** adj

soldier of fortune n a man who seeks money or adventure as a soldier; mercenary

soldier on vb to continue one's efforts despite difficulties or pressure

sole¹ adj **1** being the only one; only **2** not shared; exclusive: sole ownership ▶ HISTORY Latin solus alone

sole² n **1** the underside of the foot **2** the underside of a shoe **3** the lower surface of an object ▷ vb **soling, soled 4** to provide (a shoe) with a sole ▶ HISTORY Latin solea sandal

sole³ n, pl **sole** or **soles** an edible marine flatfish ▶ HISTORY Latin solea a sandal (from the fish's shape)

sole charge school n NZ a country school with only one teacher

solecism (**sol**-iss-iz-zum) n formal **1** a minor grammatical mistake in speech or writing **2** an action considered not to be good manners ▶ HISTORY Greek soloikos speaking incorrectly > **solecistic** adj

solely adv **1** only; completely: an action intended solely to line his own pockets **2** without others

solemn adj **1** very serious; deeply sincere: my solemn promise **2** marked by ceremony or formality: a solemn ritual **3** serious or glum: a solemn look on her face ▶ HISTORY Latin sollemnis appointed > **solemnly** adv

solemnity n, pl **-ties 1** the state or quality of being solemn **2** a solemn ceremony or ritual

solemnize or **-nise** vb **-nizing, -nized** or **-nising, -nised 1** to celebrate or perform (a ceremony, esp. of marriage) **2** to make solemn or serious > **solemnization** or **-nisation** n

solenoid (**sole**-in-oid) n a coil of wire, usually cylindrical, in which a magnetic field is set up by passing a current through it ▶ HISTORY French solénoïde > **solenoidal** adj

sole proprietor or **sole trader** n a person who owns their own business and does not have any partners or shareholders

sol-fa n short for **tonic sol-fa**

solicit vb **1** formal to seek or request, esp. formally: she was brushed aside when soliciting his support for the vote **2** to approach (a person) with an offer of sex in return for money ▶ HISTORY Latin sollicitare to harass > **solicitation** n

solicitor n Brit, Austral & NZ a lawyer who advises clients on matters of law, draws up legal documents, and prepares cases for barristers

Solicitor General n, pl **Solicitors General** (in Britain) the law officer of the Crown ranking next to the Attorney General (in Scotland to the Lord Advocate) and acting as his assistant

solicitous adj formal **1** anxious about someone's welfare **2** eager ▶ HISTORY Latin sollicitus anxious > **solicitousness** n

solicitude n formal anxiety or concern for someone's welfare

solid adj **1** (of a substance) in a physical state in which it resists changes in size and shape; not liquid or gaseous **2** consisting of matter all through; not hollow **3** of the same substance all through: solid gold **4** firm, strong, or substantial: the solid door of a farmhouse **5** proved or provable: solid evidence **6** law-abiding and respectable: solid family men **7** (of a meal or food) substantial **8** without interruption; continuous or unbroken: solid bombardment **9** financially sound: a solid institution **10** strongly united or established: a solid marriage **11** geom having or relating to three dimensions **12** adequate; sound, but not brilliant: a solid career **13** of a single uniform colour or tone ▷ n **14** geom a three-dimensional shape **15** a solid substance ▶ HISTORY Latin solidus firm > **solidity** n > **solidly** adv

solidarity n, pl **-ties** agreement in interests or aims among members of a group; total unity

solid geometry n the branch of geometry concerned with three-dimensional figures

solidify vb **-fies, -fying, -fied 1** to make or become solid or hard **2** to make or become strong or unlikely to change: a move that solidified the allegiance of our followers > **solidification** n

solid-state adj (of an electronic device) using a semiconductor component, such as a transistor or silicon chip, in which current flow is through solid material, rather than a valve or mechanical part, in which current flow is through a vacuum

solidus n, pl **-di** a short oblique stroke used in text to separate items, such as and/or

soliloquize or **-quise** vb **-quizing, -quized** or **-quising, -quised** to say a soliloquy

soliloquy n, pl **-quies** a speech made by a person while alone, esp. in a play ▶ HISTORY Latin solus sole + loqui to speak

S

811

solipsism n philosophy the doctrine that the self is the only thing known to exist ▶ HISTORY Latin solus alone + ipse self > **solipsist** n

solitaire n **1** a game played by one person, involving moving and taking pegs in a pegboard with the object of being left with only one **2** a gem, esp. a diamond, set alone in a ring **3** chiefly US patience (the card game) ▶ HISTORY French

solitary adj **1** experienced or performed alone: a solitary dinner **2** living a life of solitude: a solitary child **3** single; alone: the solitary cigarette in the ashtray **4** having few friends; lonely **5** (of a place) without people; empty ▷ n, pl **-taries 6** a person who lives on his or her own; hermit **7** informal short for **solitary confinement**: I can't put him back in solitary ▶ HISTORY Latin solitarius > **solitariness** n

solitary confinement n isolation of a prisoner in a special cell

solitude n the state of being alone

solo n, pl **-los 1** a piece of music or section of a piece of music for one performer: a trumpet solo **2** any performance by an individual without assistance **3** Also: **solo whist** a card game in which each person plays on his or her own ▷ adj **4** performed by an individual without assistance: a solo dance ▷ adv **5** by oneself; alone: to fly solo across the Atlantic ▶ HISTORY Latin solus alone > **soloist** n

Solomon n any person considered to be very wise ▶ HISTORY after 10th-century BC king of Israel

Solomon's seal n a plant with greenish flowers and long waxy leaves

so long interj **1** informal farewell; goodbye ▷ adv **2** S African, slang for the time being; meanwhile

solo parent n NZ a parent bringing up a child or children alone

solstice n either the shortest day of the year (**winter solstice**) or the longest day of the year (**summer solstice**) ▶ HISTORY Latin solstitium the standing still of the sun

soluble adj **1** (of a substance) capable of being dissolved **2** (of a mystery or problem) capable of being solved > **solubility** n

solute n chem the substance in a solution that is dissolved ▶ HISTORY Latin solutus free

solution n **1** a specific answer to or way of answering a problem **2** the act or process of solving a problem **3** chem a mixture of two or more substances in which the molecules or atoms of the substances are completely dispersed **4** the act or process of forming a solution **5** the state of being dissolved: the sugar is held in solution ▶ HISTORY Latin solutio an unloosing

solve vb **solving, solved** to find the explanation for or solution to (a mystery or problem) ▶ HISTORY Latin solvere to loosen > **solvable** adj

solvent adj **1** having enough money to pay off one's debts **2** (of a liquid) capable of dissolving other substances ▷ n **3** a liquid capable of dissolving other substances ▶ HISTORY Latin solvens releasing > **solvency** n

solvent abuse n the deliberate inhaling of intoxicating fumes from certain solvents

somatic adj of or relating to the body as distinct from the mind: somatic symptoms ▶ HISTORY Greek sōma the body

sombre or US **somber** adj **1** serious, sad, or gloomy: a sombre message **2** (of a place) dim or gloomy **3** (of colour or clothes) dull or dark ▶ HISTORY Latin sub umbra shade > **sombrely** or US **somberly** adv

sombrero n, pl **-ros** a wide-brimmed Mexican hat ▶ HISTORY Spanish

some adj **1** unknown or unspecified: some man called for you **2** an unknown or unspecified quantity or number of: I've got some money **3 a** a considerable number or amount of: he lived some years afterwards **b** a little: show some respect **4** informal an impressive or remarkable: that was some game! ▷ pron **5** certain unknown or unspecified people or things: some can teach and others can't **6** an unknown or unspecified quantity of something or number of people or things: he will sell some in his pub ▷ adv **7** approximately: some thirty pounds ▶ HISTORY Old English sum

somebody pron **1** some person; someone ▷ n, pl **-bodies 2** a person of great importance: he was a somebody

somehow adv **1** in some unspecified way **2** for some unknown reason: somehow I can't do it

someone pron some person; somebody

somersault n **1** a leap or roll in which the head is placed on the ground and the trunk and legs are turned over it ▷ vb **2** to perform a somersault ▶ HISTORY Old French soubresault

something pron **1** an unspecified or unknown thing; some thing: there was something wrong **2** an unspecified or unknown amount: something less than a hundred **3** an impressive or important person, thing, or event: isn't that something? **4 something else** slang, chiefly US a remarkable person or thing ▷ adv **5** to some degree; somewhat: he looks something like me

-something n combining form a person whose age can be approximately expressed by a specific decade: twenty-somethings ▶ HISTORY from the US television series thirtysomething

sometime adv **1** at some unspecified point of time ▷ adj **2** former: a sometime actress

sometimes adv now and then; from time to time

somewhat adv rather; a bit: somewhat surprising

somewhere adv **1** in, to, or at some unknown or unspecified place, point, or amount: somewhere down south; somewhere between 35 and 45 per cent **2 getting somewhere** informal making progress

somnambulism n formal the condition of walking in one's sleep ▶ HISTORY Latin somnus sleep + ambulare to walk > **somnambulist** n

somnolent adj formal drowsy; sleepy ▶ HISTORY Latin somnus sleep > **somnolence** n

son n **1** a male offspring **2** a form of address for a man or boy who is younger than the speaker **3** a male who comes from a certain place or one closely connected with a certain thing: a good son of the church. Related adjective: **filial** ▶ HISTORY Old English sunu

Son *n Christianity* the second member of the Trinity, Jesus Christ

sonar *n* a device that locates objects by the reflection of sound waves: used in underwater navigation and target detection ▶ HISTORY so(und) na(vigation and) r(anging)

sonata *n* a piece of classical music, usually in three or more movements, for piano or for another instrument with or without piano ▶ HISTORY Italian

son et lumière (sonn ay loom-yair) *n* an entertainment staged at night at a famous building or historical site, at which its history is described by a speaker accompanied by lighting effects and music ▶ HISTORY French, literally: sound and light

song *n* **1** a piece of music with words, composed for the voice **2** the tuneful call made by certain birds or insects **3** the act or process of singing: *he broke into song* **4 for a song** at a bargain price **5 make a song and dance** *Brit & NZ, informal* to make an unnecessary fuss ▶ HISTORY Old English *sang*

songbird *n* any bird that has a musical call

songololo (song-gol-**loll**-o) *n, pl* **-los** *S African* a kind of millipede ▶ HISTORY Nguni (language group of southern Africa) *ukusonga* to roll up

songstress *n* a female singer of popular songs

song thrush *n* a common thrush that repeats each note of its song

sonic *adj* of, involving, or producing sound ▶ HISTORY Latin *sonus* sound

sonic barrier *n* same as **sound barrier**

sonic boom *n* a loud explosive sound caused by the shock wave of an aircraft travelling at supersonic speed

son-in-law *n, pl* **sons-in-law** the husband of one's daughter

sonnet *n prosody* a verse form consisting of 14 lines with a fixed rhyme scheme and rhythm pattern ▶ HISTORY Old Provençal *sonet* a little poem

sonny *n* a familiar, often patronizing, term of address to a boy or man

sonorous *adj* **1** (of a sound) deep or rich **2** (of speech) using language that is unnecessarily complicated and difficult to understand; pompous ▶ HISTORY Latin *sonor* a noise > **sonority** *n*

soon *adv* **1** in or after a short time; before long **2 as soon as** at the very moment that: *as soon as he had closed the door* **3 as soon ... as** used to indicate that the first alternative is slightly preferable to the second: *they'd just as soon die for him as live* ▶ HISTORY Old English *sōna*

sooner *adv* **1** the comparative of **soon**: *I only wish I'd been back sooner* **2** rather; in preference: *he would sooner leave the party than break with me* **3 no sooner ... than** immediately after or when: *no sooner had he spoken than the stench drifted up* **4 sooner or later** eventually

soot *n* a black powder formed by the incomplete burning of organic substances such as coal ▶ HISTORY Old English *sōt* > **sooty** *adj*

soothe *vb* **soothing, soothed** **1** to make (a worried or angry person) calm and relaxed **2** (of an ointment or cream) to relieve (pain) ▶ HISTORY Old English *sōthian* to prove > **soothing** *adj*

soothsayer *n* a person who makes predictions about the future; prophet

sop *n* **1** a small bribe or concession given or made to someone to keep them from causing trouble: *a sop to her conscience* **2** *informal* a stupid or weak person **3 sops** food soaked in a liquid before being eaten ▷ *vb* **sopping, sopped** **4 sop up** to soak up or absorb (liquid) ▶ HISTORY Old English *sopp*

sophism *n* an argument that seems reasonable but is actually false and misleading ▶ HISTORY Greek *sophisma* ingenious trick

sophist *n* a person who uses clever but false arguments ▶ HISTORY Greek *sophistēs* a wise man > **sophistic** *adj*

sophisticate *vb* **-cating, -cated** **1** to make (someone) less natural or innocent, such as by education **2** to make (a machine or method) more complex or refined ▷ *n* **3** a sophisticated person ▶ HISTORY Latin *sophisticus* sophistic > **sophistication** *n*

sophisticated *adj* **1** having or appealing to fashionable and refined tastes and habits: *a sophisticated restaurant* **2** intelligent, knowledgeable, or able to appreciate culture and the arts: *a sophisticated concert audience* **3** (of machines or methods) complex and using advanced technology

sophistry *n* **1** the practice of using arguments which seem clever but are actually false and misleading **2** (*pl* **-ries**) an instance of this

sophomore *n chiefly US & Canad* a second-year student at a secondary (high) school or college ▶ HISTORY probably from earlier *sophum*, variant of *sophism*

soporific *adj* **1** causing sleep ▷ *n* **2** a drug that causes sleep ▶ HISTORY Latin *sopor* sleep

sopping *adj* completely soaked; wet through. Also: **sopping wet**

soppy *adj* **-pier, -piest** *informal* foolishly sentimental: *a soppy love song* > **soppily** *adv*

soprano *n, pl* **-pranos** **1** the highest adult female voice **2** the voice of a young boy before puberty **3** a singer with such a voice **4** the highest or second highest instrument in a family of instruments ▷ *adj* **5** denoting a musical instrument that is the highest or second highest pitched in its family: *the soprano saxophone* **6** of or relating to the highest female voice, or the voice of a young boy: *the part is quite possibly the most demanding soprano role Wagner ever wrote* ▶ HISTORY Italian

sorbet *n* a flavoured water ice ▶ HISTORY French, from Arabic *sharbah* a drink

sorcerer *or fem* **sorceress** *n* a person who uses magic powers; a wizard ▶ HISTORY Old French *sorcier*

sorcery *n, pl* **-ceries** witchcraft or magic ▶ HISTORY Old French *sorcerie*

S

813

sordid *adj* **1** dirty, depressing, and squalid: *a sordid backstreet in a slum area* **2** relating to sex in a crude or unpleasant way: *the sordid details of his affair* **3** involving immoral and selfish behaviour: *the sordid history of the slave trade* ▶ HISTORY Latin *sordidus*

sore *adj* **1** (of a wound, injury, etc.) painfully sensitive; tender **2** causing annoyance and resentment: *a sore point* **3** upset and angered: *she's still sore about last night* **4** *literary* urgent; pressing: *in sore need of firm government* ▷ *n* **5** a painful or sensitive wound or injury ▷ *adv* **6 sore afraid** *archaic* greatly frightened ▶ HISTORY Old English *sār*

sorely *adv* greatly: *sorely disappointed*

sorghum *n* a grass grown for grain and as a source of syrup ▶ HISTORY Italian *sorgo*

sorority *n, pl* **-ties** *chiefly US* a society of female students ▶ HISTORY Latin *soror* sister

sorrel *n* a plant with bitter-tasting leaves which are used in salads and sauces ▶ HISTORY Old French *surele*

sorrow *n* **1** deep sadness or regret, associated with death or sympathy for another's misfortune **2** a particular cause of this ▷ *vb* **3** *literary* to feel deep sadness about (death or another's misfortunes); mourn ▶ HISTORY Old English *sorg* > **sorrowful** *adj* > **sorrowfully** *adv*

sorry *adj* **-rier, -riest 1** (often foll. by *for* or *about*) feeling or expressing pity, sympathy, grief, or regret: *I'm sorry about this* **2** in bad mental or physical condition: *a sorry state* **3** poor: *a sorry performance* ▷ *interj* **4** an exclamation expressing apology or asking someone to repeat what he or she has said ▶ HISTORY Old English *sārig*

sort *n* **1** a class, group, or kind sharing certain characteristics or qualities **2** *informal* a type of character: *she was a good sort* **3** a more or less adequate example: *a sort of dream machine* **4 of sorts** *or* **of a sort a** of poor quality: *she was wearing a uniform of sorts* **b** of a kind not quite as intended or desired: *it was a reward, of sorts, for my efforts* **5 out of sorts** not in normal good health or temper **6 sort of** as it were; rather: *I sort of quit; sort of insensitive* ▷ *vb* **7** to arrange (things or people) according to class or type **8** to put (something) into working order; fix **9** to arrange (computer information) by machine in an order the user finds convenient ▶ HISTORY Latin *sors* fate

sortie *n* **1** a short or relatively short return trip **2** (of troops) a raid into enemy territory **3** an operational flight made by a military aircraft ▷ *vb* **-tieing, -tied 4** to make a sortie ▶ HISTORY French

sort out *vb* **1** to find a solution to (a problem): *did they sort out the mess?* **2** to take or separate (things or people) from a larger group: *to sort out the wheat from the chaff* **3** to organize (things or people) into an orderly and disciplined group **4** *informal* to punish or tell off (someone)

SOS *n* **1** an international code signal of distress in which the letters SOS are repeatedly spelt out in Morse code **2** *informal* any call for help

so-so *informal adj* **1** neither good nor bad ▷ *adv* **2** in an average or indifferent way

sot *n* a person who is frequently drunk ▶ HISTORY Old English *sott* > **sottish** *adj*

sotto voce (**sot**-toe **voe**-chay) *adv* with a soft voice ▶ HISTORY Italian

sou *n* **1** a former French coin of low value **2** *old-fashioned* a very small amount of money: *the tax man never saw a sou from this income* ▶ HISTORY French

soubrette (soo-**brett**) *n* a minor female role in comedy, often that of a pert maid ▶ HISTORY French

soubriquet *n* same as **sobriquet**

soufflé (**soo**-flay) *n* a light fluffy dish made with beaten egg whites and other ingredients such as cheese or chocolate ▶ HISTORY French

sough (rhymes with **now**) *vb literary* (of the wind) to make a sighing sound ▶ HISTORY Old English *swōgan*

sought (**sawt**) *vb* the past of **seek**

souk (**sook**) *n* an open-air marketplace in Muslim countries ▶ HISTORY Arabic *sūq*

soul *n* **1** the spiritual part of a person, regarded as the centre of personality, intellect, will, and emotions: believed by many to survive the body after death **2** the essential part or fundamental nature of anything: *the soul of contemporary America* **3** deep and sincere feelings: *you've got no soul* **4** Also called: **soul music** a type of Black music using blues and elements of jazz, gospel, and pop **5** a person regarded as a good example of some quality: *the soul of prudence* **6** a person: *there was hardly a soul there* **7 the life and soul** *informal* a person who is lively, entertaining, and fun to be with: *the life and soul of the campus* ▶ HISTORY Old English *sāwol*

soul-destroying *adj* (of an occupation or situation) very boring and repetitive

soulful *adj* expressing deep feelings: *a soulful performance of one of Tchaikovsky's songs*

soulless *adj* **1** lacking human qualities; mechanical: *soulless materialism* **2** (of a person) lacking in sensitivity or emotion

soul-searching *n* deep examination of one's actions and feelings

sound[1] *n* **1** anything that can be heard; noise **2** *physics* mechanical vibrations that travel in waves through the air, water, etc. **3** the sensation produced by such vibrations in the organs of hearing **4** the impression one has of something: *I didn't really like the sound of it* **5 sounds** *slang* music, esp. rock, jazz, or pop ▷ *vb* **6** to make or cause (an instrument, etc.) to make a sound **7** to announce (something) by a sound: *guns sound the end of the two minutes silence* **8** to make a noise with a certain quality: *her voice sounded shrill* **9** to suggest (a particular idea or quality): *his argument sounded false* **10** to pronounce (something) clearly: *to sound one's r's* ▶ HISTORY Latin *sonus*

sound[2] *adj* **1** free from damage, injury, or decay; in good condition **2** firm or substantial: *sound* documentary evidence **3** financially safe or stable: *a sound investment* **4** showing good judgment or reasoning; wise: *sound advice* **5** morally correct; honest **6** (of sleep) deep and uninterrupted **7** thorough: *a sound defeat* ▷ *adv* **8 sound asleep** in a deep sleep ▸ HISTORY Old English *sund* > **soundly** *adv*

sound³ *vb* **1** to measure the depth of (a well, the sea, etc.) **2** *med* to examine (a part of the body) by tapping or with a stethoscope ▸ HISTORY Old French *sonder*

sound⁴ *n* a channel between two larger areas of sea or between an island and the mainland ▸ HISTORY Old English *sund*

sound barrier *n* a sudden increase in the force of air against an aircraft flying at or above the speed of sound

sound bite *n* a short pithy sentence or phrase extracted from a longer speech for use on television or radio: *complicated political messages cannot be properly reduced to fifteen-second sound bites*

sound effects *pl n* sounds artificially produced to make a play, a radio play, more realistic

sounding board *n* a person or group used to test a new idea or policy

soundings *pl n* **1** measurements of the depth of a river, lake, or sea **2** questions asked of someone in order to find out his or her opinion: *soundings among colleagues had revealed enthusiasm for the plan*

sound mixer *n* **1** (in cinema and television) an audio engineer responsible for the overall sound mix, including dialogue, music, and sound effects **2** an electronic device for mixing sounds

soundproof *adj* **1** (of a room) built so that no sound can get in or out ▷ *vb* **2** to make (a room) soundproof

sound recordist *n* (in cinema and television) the person who operates the audio recording equipment

soundtrack *n* the recorded sound accompaniment to a film

sound wave *n* a wave that carries sound

soup *n* **1** a food made by cooking meat, fish, or vegetables in a stock **2 in the soup** *slang* in trouble or difficulties ▸ HISTORY Old French *soupe* > **soupy** *adj*

soupçon (**soop**-sonn) *n* a slight amount; dash ▸ HISTORY French

souped-up *adj slang* (of a car, motorbike, or engine) adjusted so as to be faster or more powerful than normal

soup kitchen *n* a place where food and drink are served to needy people

sour *adj* **1** having a sharp biting taste like the taste of lemon juice or vinegar **2** made acid or bad, such as when milk ferments **3** (of a person's mood) bad-tempered and unfriendly **4 go** *or* **turn sour** to become less enjoyable or happy: *the dream has turned sour* ▷ *vb* **5** to make or become less enjoyable or friendly: *relations soured shortly after the war* ▸ HISTORY Old English *sūr* > **sourly** *adv*

source *n* **1** the origin or starting point: *the source of discontent among fishermen* **2** any person, book, or organization that provides information for a news report or for research **3** the area or spring where a river or stream begins ▷ *vb* **4** (foll. by *from*) to originate from ▸ HISTORY Latin *surgere* to rise

sour cream *n* cream soured by bacteria for use in cooking

sour grapes *n* the attitude of pretending to hate something because one cannot have it oneself

souse *vb* **sousing, soused** **1** to plunge (something) into water or other liquid **2** to drench **3** to steep or cook (food) in a marinade ▷ *n* **4** the liquid used in pickling **5** the act or process of sousing ▸ HISTORY Old French *sous*

soused *adj slang* drunk

soutane (soo-**tan**) *n RC Church* a priest's robe ▸ HISTORY French

south *n* **1** one of the four cardinal points of the compass, at 180° from north **2** the direction along a line of latitude towards the South Pole **3 the south** any area lying in or towards the south ▷ *adj* **4** situated in, moving towards, or facing the south **5** (esp. of the wind) from the south ▷ *adv* **6** in, to, or towards the south ▸ HISTORY Old English *sūth*

South *n* **1 the South a** the southern part of England **b** (in the US) the Southern states that formed the Confederacy during the Civil War **c** the countries of the world that are not technically and economically advanced ▷ *adj* **2** of or denoting the southern part of a country, area, etc.

South African *adj* **1** of the Republic of South Africa ▷ *n* **2** a person from the Republic of South Africa

southeast *n* **1** the direction midway between south and east **2 the southeast** any area lying in or towards the southeast ▷ *adj also* **southeastern** **3** of or denoting that part of a country or area which lies in the southeast **4** situated in, moving towards, or facing the southeast **5** (esp. of the wind) from the southeast ▷ *adv* **6** in, to, or towards the southeast > **southeasterly** *adj, adv, n*

southeaster *n* a strong wind or storm from the southeast

southerly *adj* **1** of or in the south ▷ *adv, adj* **2** towards the south **3** from the south: *light southerly winds*

southern *adj* **1** situated in or towards the south **2** facing or moving towards the south **3** (sometimes cap) of or characteristic of the south or South > **southernmost** *adj*

southern hemisphere *n geog* that half of the globe lying south of the equator

southern lights *pl n* same as **aurora australis**

southern oscillation *n meteorol* a regularly occurring alternation in atmospheric pressures between the Indonesian region and the eastern tropical Pacific which gives rise to *El Niño* and *La Niña*

southpaw *informal n* **1** any left-handed person, esp. a boxer ▷ *adj* **2** left-handed

South Pole n the southernmost point on the earth's axis, at a latitude of 90°S, which has very low temperatures

South Seas pl n the seas south of the equator

southward adj, adv also **southwards 1** towards the south ▷ n **2** the southward part or direction

southwest n **1** the direction midway between west and south **2 the southwest** any area lying in or towards the southwest ▷ adj also **southwestern 3** of or denoting that part of a country or area which lies in the southwest **4** situated in, moving towards, or facing the southwest **5** (esp. of the wind) from the southwest ▷ adv **6** in, to, or towards the southwest > **southwesterly** adj, adv, n

southwester n a strong wind or storm from the southwest

souvenir n an object that reminds one of a certain place, occasion, or person; memento ▶ HISTORY French

sou'wester n **1** a seaman's hat with a broad brim that covers the back of the neck **2** same as **southwester** ▶ HISTORY a contraction of SOUTHWESTER

sovereign n **1** the Royal ruler of a country **2** a former British gold coin worth one pound sterling ▷ adj **3** independent of outside authority; not governed by another country: a sovereign nation **4** supreme in rank or authority: a sovereign queen **5** old-fashioned excellent or outstanding: a sovereign remedy for epilepsy ▶ HISTORY Old French soverain

sovereignty n, pl **-ties 1** the political power a nation has to govern itself **2** the position or authority of the most powerful institution in a country **3** the position or authority of a sovereign

soviet n (in the former Soviet Union) an elected government council at the local, regional, and national levels ▶ HISTORY Russian sovyet

Soviet adj **1** of the former Soviet Union ▷ n **2** a person from the former Soviet Union

sow¹ vb **sowing, sowed; sown** or **sowed 1** to scatter or plant (seed) in or on (the ground) so that it may grow: sow sweet peas in pots; farmers sow their fields with fewer varieties **2** to implant or introduce: to sow confusion among the other members ▶ HISTORY Old English sāwan

sow² n a female adult pig ▶ HISTORY Old English sugu

soya bean or US & Canad **soybean** n a plant whose bean is used for food and as a source of oil ▶ HISTORY Japanese shōyu

soy sauce n a salty dark brown sauce made from fermented soya beans, used in Chinese cookery

sozzled adj Brit, Austral & NZ, informal drunk ▶ HISTORY origin unknown

spa n a mineral-water spring or a resort where such a spring is found ▶ HISTORY after Spa, a watering place in Belgium

space n **1** the unlimited three-dimensional expanse in which all objects exist **2** an interval of distance or time between two points, objects, or events **3** a blank portion or area **4** unoccupied area or room: barely enough space to walk around **5** the region beyond the earth's atmosphere containing other planets, stars, and galaxies; the universe ▷ vb **spacing, spaced 6** to place or arrange (things) at intervals or with spaces between them ▶ HISTORY Latin spatium

space age n **1** the period in which the exploration of space has become possible ▷ adj **space-age 2** very modern, futuristic, or using the latest technology: a space-age helmet

space-bar n a bar on a keyboard that is pressed in order to leave a space between words or letters

space capsule n the part of a spacecraft in which the crew live and work

spacecraft n a vehicle that can be used for travel in space

spaceman or fem **spacewoman** n, pl **-men** or fem **-women** a person who travels in space

space probe n a small vehicle equipped to gather scientific information, normally transmitted back to earth by radio, about a planet or conditions in space

spaceship n (in science fiction) a spacecraft used for travel between planets and galaxies

space shuttle n a manned reusable spacecraft designed for making regular flights

space station n a large manned artificial satellite used as a base for scientific research in space and for people travelling in space

spacesuit n a sealed protective suit worn by astronauts

space-time or **space-time continuum** n physics the four-dimensional continuum having three space coordinates and one time coordinate that together completely specify the location of an object or an event

spacious adj having or providing a lot of space; roomy > **spaciousness** n

spade¹ n **1** a tool for digging, with a flat steel blade and a long wooden handle **2 call a spade a spade** to speak plainly and frankly ▶ HISTORY Old English spadu

spade² n **1 a spades** the suit of playing cards marked with a black leaf-shaped symbol **b** a card with one or more of these symbols on it **2** offensive a Black person **3 in spades** informal in plenty: all you need is talent in spades ▶ HISTORY Italian spada sword, used as an emblem on playing cards

spadework n dull or routine work done as preparation for a project or activity

spadix (spade-ix) n, pl **spadices** (spade-**ice**-eez) bot a spike of small flowers on a fleshy stem ▶ HISTORY Greek: torn-off frond

spaghetti n pasta in the form of long strings ▶ HISTORY Italian

spaghetti junction n a junction between motorways with a large number of intersecting roads ▶ HISTORY from the nickname of the Gravelly Hill Interchange, Birmingham

spaghetti western n a cowboy film made in Europe by an Italian director

spam *computers, slang n* **1** unsolicited messages sent to multiple recipients ▷ *vb* **spamming, spammed** **2** to send unsolicited messages to multiple recipients ▶ HISTORY from the repeated use of the word *Spam* in a popular sketch from the British television show *Monty Python's Flying Circus*

span *n* **1** the interval or distance between two points, such as the ends of a bridge **2** the complete extent: *that span of time* **3** short for **wingspan** **4** a unit of length based on the width of a stretched hand, usually taken as nine inches (23 cms) ▷ *vb* **spanning, spanned** **5** to stretch or extend across, over, or around: *her career spanned fifty years; to span the Danube* ▶ HISTORY Old English *spann*

spangle *n* **1** a small piece of shiny material used as a decoration on clothes or hair; sequin ▷ *vb* **-gling, -gled** **2** to cover or decorate (something) with spangles ▶ HISTORY Middle English *spange* clasp

Spaniard *n* a person from Spain

spaniel *n* a dog with long drooping ears and a silky coat ▶ HISTORY Old French *espaigneul* Spanish (dog)

Spanish *adj* **1** of Spain ▷ *n* **2** the official language of Spain, Mexico, and most countries of South and Central America ▷ *pl n* **3 the Spanish** the people of Spain

Spanish fly *n* a beetle, the dried body of which is used in medicine

Spanish Main *n* **1** the N coast of South America **2** the Caribbean Sea, the S part of which was frequented by pirates

spank *vb* **1** to slap (someone) with the open hand, on the buttocks or legs ▷ *n* **2** such a slap ▶ HISTORY probably imitative

spanking[1] *n* a series of spanks, usually as a punishment for children

spanking[2] *adj* **1** *informal* outstandingly fine or smart: *spanking new uniforms* **2** very fast: *a spanking pace*

spanner *n* **1** a tool for gripping and turning a nut or bolt **2 throw a spanner in the works** *Brit & NZ, informal* to cause a problem that prevents things from running smoothly ▶ HISTORY German *spannen* to stretch

span of control *n business* the area of responsibility or activity of a particular person or organization

spanspek *n S African* a cantaloupe melon ▶ HISTORY Afrikaans

spar[1] *n* a pole used as a ship's mast, boom, or yard ▶ HISTORY Old Norse *sperra* beam

spar[2] *vb* **sparring, sparred** **1** *boxing, martial arts* to fight using light blows for practice **2** to argue with someone ▷ *n* **3** an argument ▶ HISTORY Old English

spar[3] *n* a light-coloured, crystalline, easily split mineral ▶ HISTORY Middle Low German

spare *adj* **1** extra to what is needed: *there are some spare chairs at the back* **2** able to be used when needed: *a spare parking space* **3** (of a person) tall and thin **4** (of a style) plain and without unnecessary decoration or details; austere: *a spare but beautiful*

novel **5** *Brit, slang* frantic with anger or worry: *the boss went spare* ▷ *n* **6** an extra thing kept in case it is needed ▷ *vb* **sparing, spared** **7** to stop from killing, punishing, or injuring (someone) **8** to protect (someone) from something unpleasant: *spare me the sermon* **9** to be able to afford or give: *can you spare me a moment to talk?* **10 not spare oneself** to try one's hardest **11 to spare** more than is required: *a few hours to spare* ▶ HISTORY Old English *sparian*

spare tyre *n* **1** an additional tyre kept in a motor vehicle in case of puncture **2** *slang* a roll of fat just above the waist

sparing *adj* (sometimes foll. by *of*) economical (with): *she was mercifully sparing in her use of jargon* > **sparingly** *adv*

spark *n* **1** a fiery particle thrown out from a fire or caused by friction **2** a short flash of light followed by a sharp crackling noise, produced by a sudden electrical discharge through the air **3** a trace or hint: *a spark of goodwill* **4** liveliness, enthusiasm, or humour: *that spark in her eye* ▷ *vb* **5** to give off sparks **6** to cause to start; trigger: *the incident sparked off an angry exchange* ▶ HISTORY Old English *spearca*

sparkie *n NZ, informal* electrician

sparkle *vb* **-kling, -kled** **1** to glitter with many bright points of light **2** (of wine or mineral water) to be slightly fizzy **3** to be lively, witty, and intelligent ▷ *n* **4** a small bright point of light **5** liveliness and wit ▶ HISTORY Middle English *sparklen*

sparkler *n* **1** a type of hand-held firework that throws out sparks **2** *informal* a sparkling gem; esp. a diamond

spark plug *n* a device in an internal-combustion engine that ignites the fuel by producing an electric spark

sparrow *n* a very common small brown or grey bird which feeds on seeds and insects ▶ HISTORY Old English *spearwa*

sparrowhawk *n* a small hawk which preys on smaller birds

sparse *adj* small in amount and spread out widely: *a sparse population* ▶ HISTORY Latin *sparsus* > **sparsely** *adv*

Spartan *adj* **1** of or relating to the ancient Greek city of Sparta **2** (of a way of life) strict or simple and with no luxuries: *Spartan accommodation* ▷ *n* **3** a citizen of Sparta **4** a person who leads a strict or simple life without luxuries

■ **WORD HISTORY**
■ 'Spartan' means 'belonging to *Sparta*', a city in
■ ancient Greece whose inhabitants were
■ famous for their discipline, military skill, and
■ stern and plain way of life. Compare the word
■ history for **laconic**.

spasm *n* **1** a sudden tightening of the muscles, over which one has no control **2** *written* a sudden burst of activity or feeling: *a spasm of applause; sudden spasms of anger* ▶ HISTORY Greek *spasmos* a cramp

spasmodic *adj* taking place in sudden short spells: *spasmodic bouts of illness* > **spasmodically** *adv*

spastic *n* old-fashioned, offensive **1** a person who has cerebral palsy, and therefore has difficulty controlling his or her muscles ▷ *adj* **2** affected by involuntary muscle contractions: *a spastic colon* **3** old-fashioned, offensive suffering from cerebral palsy ▸ **HISTORY** Greek *spasmos* a cramp

spat¹ *n* a slight quarrel ▸ **HISTORY** probably imitative

spat² *vb* a past of **spit**¹

spate *n* **1** a large number of things happening within a period of time: *a spate of bombings* **2** a fast flow or outpouring: *an incomprehensible spate of words* **3 in spate** chiefly Brit (of a river) flooded ▸ **HISTORY** origin unknown

spathe *n* bot a large leaf that surrounds the base of a flower cluster ▸ **HISTORY** Greek *spathē* a blade

spatial *adj* of or relating to size, area, or position: *spatial dimensions* > **spatially** *adv*

spatial analysis *n* geog analytical processes that use geographical data for modelling, looking at the suitability of areas for particular purposes, and making predictions about the future

spatial patterns *pl n* geog the distribution and arrangement of given elements in an area and how they interrelate

spats *pl n* cloth or leather coverings formerly worn by men over the ankle and instep ▸ **HISTORY** obsolete *spatterdash* a long gaiter

spatter *vb* **1** to scatter or splash (a substance, esp. a liquid) in scattered drops: *spattering mud in all directions* **2** to sprinkle (an object or surface) with a liquid ▷ *n* **3** the sound of spattering **4** something spattered, such as a spot or splash ▸ **HISTORY** imitative

spatula *n* a utensil with a broad flat blade, used in cooking and by doctors ▸ **HISTORY** Latin: a broad piece

spawn *n* **1** the jelly-like mass of eggs laid by fish, amphibians, or molluscs ▷ *vb* **2** (of fish, amphibians, or molluscs) to lay eggs **3** to cause (something) to be created: *the depressed economy spawned the riots* ▸ **HISTORY** Anglo-Norman *espaundre*

spay *vb* to remove the ovaries from (a female animal) ▸ **HISTORY** Old French *espeer* to cut with the sword

speak *vb* **speaking, spoke, spoken 1** to say words; talk **2** to communicate or express (something) in words **3** to give a speech or lecture **4** to know how to talk in (a specified language): *I don't speak French* **5 on speaking terms** on good terms; friendly **6 so to speak** as it were **7 speak one's mind** to express one's opinions honestly and plainly **8 to speak of** of a significant nature: *no licensing laws to speak of* ▸ **HISTORY** Old English *specan*

speaker *n* **1** a person who speaks, esp. someone making a speech **2** a person who speaks a particular language: *a fluent Tibetan and English speaker* **3** same as **loudspeaker**

Speaker *n* the official chairman of a law-making body: *the Speaker of the House*

spear¹ *n* **1** a weapon consisting of a long pole with a sharp point ▷ *vb* **2** to pierce (someone or something) with a spear or other pointed object: *she took her fork and speared an oyster from its shell* ▸ **HISTORY** Old English *spere*

spear² *n* **1** a slender shoot, such as of grass **2** a single stalk of broccoli or asparagus ▸ **HISTORY** probably variant of *spire*

spearhead *vb* **1** to lead (an attack or a campaign) ▷ *n* **2** the leading force in an attack or campaign

spearmint *n* a minty flavouring used for sweets and toothpaste, which comes from a purple-flowered plant

spec *n* **on spec** informal as a risk or gamble: *I still tend to buy on spec*

special *adj* **1** distinguished from or better than others of its kind: *a special occasion* **2** designed or reserved for a specific purpose: *special equipment* **3** not usual; different from normal: *a special case* **4** particular or primary: *a special interest in gifted children* **5** relating to the education of children with disabilities: *a special school* ▷ *n* **6** a product, TV programme, etc., which is only available or shown at a certain time: *a two-hour Christmas special live from Hollywood* **7** a meal, usually at a low price, in a bar or restaurant **8** short for **special constable** ▸ **HISTORY** Latin *specialis* > **specially** *adv*

Special Branch *n* (in Britain and S Africa) the department of the police force that is concerned with political security

special constable *n* (in Britain) a person recruited for occasional police duties, such as in an emergency

special delivery *n* the delivery of a piece of mail outside the time of a scheduled delivery, for an extra fee

special effects *pl n* films techniques used in the production of scenes that cannot be achieved by normal methods: *the special effects and make-up are totally convincing*

specialist *n* **1** a person who is an expert in a particular activity or subject **2** a doctor who concentrates on treating one particular category of diseases or the diseases of one particular part of the body: *an eye specialist* ▷ *adj* **3** particular to or concentrating on one subject or activity: *a specialist comic shop*

speciality *or esp US & Canad* **specialty** *n, pl* **-ties 1** a special interest or skill **2** a service, product, or type of food specialized in

specialize *or* **-ise** *vb* **-izing, -ized** *or* **-ising, -ised 1** to concentrate all one's efforts on studying a particular subject, occupation, or activity: *an expert who specializes in transport* **2** to modify (something) for a special use or purpose: *plants have evolved and specialized in every type of habitat* > **specialization** *or* **-isation** *n*

special licence *n* Brit a licence allowing a marriage to take place without following all the usual legal procedures

S

specialty n, pl -ties chiefly US & Canad same as **speciality**

specie n coins as distinct from paper money ▶ HISTORY Latin in specie in kind

species n, pl -cies biol one of the groups into which a genus is divided, the members of which are able to interbreed ▶ HISTORY Latin: appearance

specific adj 1 particular or definite: a specific area of economic policy 2 precise and exact: try and be more specific ▷ n 3 specifics particular qualities or aspects of something: the specifics of the situation 4 med any drug used to treat a particular disease ▶ HISTORY Latin species kind + facere to make > **specifically** adv > **specificity** n

specification n 1 a detailed description of features in the design of something: engines built to racing specification 2 a requirement or detail which is clearly stated: the main specification was that a good degree was required 3 the specifying of something

specific gravity n physics the ratio of the density of a substance to the density of water

specific heat capacity n physics the quantity of heat required to raise the temperature of unit mass of a substance by one degree centigrade

specific performance n law a remedy awarded by a court requiring a person to fulfil obligations under a contract where damages are an insufficient remedy

specify vb -fies, -fying, -fied 1 to state or describe (something) clearly 2 to state (something) as a condition: the rules specify the number of prisoners to be kept in each cell ▶ HISTORY Medieval Latin specificare to describe

specimen n 1 an individual or part regarded as typical of its group or class 2 med a sample of tissue, blood, or urine taken for analysis 3 informal, written a person: I'm quite a healthy specimen ▶ HISTORY Latin: mark, proof

specious (spee-shuss) adj apparently correct or true, but actually wrong or false ▶ HISTORY Latin species outward appearance

speck n 1 a very small mark or spot 2 a small or tiny piece of something: a speck of fluff ▶ HISTORY Old English specca

speckle vb -ling, -led 1 to mark (something) with speckles ▷ n 2 a small mark or spot, such as on the skin or on an egg ▶ HISTORY Middle Dutch spekkel > **speckled** adj

specs pl n informal short for **spectacles**

spectacle n 1 a strange, interesting, or ridiculous scene 2 an impressive public show: the opening ceremony of the Olympics was an impressive spectacle 3 **make a spectacle of oneself** to draw attention to oneself by behaving foolishly ▶ HISTORY Latin spectare to watch

spectacles pl n a pair of glasses for correcting faulty vision

spectacular adj 1 impressive, grand, or dramatic ▷ n 2 a spectacular show > **spectacularly** adv

spectate vb -tating, -tated to be a spectator; watch

spectator n a person viewing anything; onlooker ▶ HISTORY Latin spectare to watch

spectator ion n chem an ion which is present in a mixture but plays no part in a reaction

spectre or US **specter** n 1 a ghost 2 an unpleasant or menacing vision in one's imagination: the spectre of famine ▶ HISTORY Latin spectrum > **spectral** adj

spectrometer (speck-**trom**-it-er) n physics an instrument for producing a spectrum, usually one in which wavelength, energy, or intensity can be measured

spectroscope n physics an instrument for forming or recording a spectrum by passing a light ray through a prism or grating

spectrum n, pl -tra 1 physics the distribution of colours produced when white light is dispersed by a prism or grating: violet, indigo, blue, green, yellow, orange, and red 2 physics the whole range of electromagnetic radiation with respect to its wavelength or frequency 3 a range or scale of anything such as opinions or emotions ▶ HISTORY Latin: image

speculate vb -lating, -lated 1 to form opinions about something, esp. its future consequences, based on the information available; conjecture: it is too early to speculate about Jackie getting married 2 to buy securities or property in the hope of selling them at a profit ▶ HISTORY Latin speculari to spy out > **speculation** n > **speculative** adj > **speculator** n

speculative buying n commerce the practice of buying in materials in a greater quantity than current requirements demand while prices are low, with the expectation of a future rise in prices

sped vb a past of **speed**

speech n 1 the ability to speak: the loss of speech 2 spoken language: Doran's lack of coherent speech 3 a talk given to an audience: a speech to parliament 4 a person's manner of speaking: her speech was extremely slow 5 a national or regional language or dialect: Canadian speech ▶ HISTORY Old English spēc

speech band n (in Trinidad and Tobago) a group of performers, dressed as stock characters, who recite rhyming speeches to a musical accompaniment

speech bubble n an area in the main body of a cartoon where the words of a character are written; this area is shaped so that the words appear to come from the character's mouth

speech day n Brit & Austral (in schools) an annual day on which prizes are presented and speeches are made by guest speakers

speechify vb -fies, -fying, -fied to make a dull or pompous speech

speechless adj 1 unable to speak for a short time because of great emotion or shock 2 unable to be expressed in words: speechless disbelief

speech therapy n the treatment of people with speech problems

speed n 1 the quality of acting or moving fast; swiftness 2 the rate at which something moves or

S

happens **3** a gear ratio in a motor vehicle or bicycle: *five-speed gearbox* **4** *photog* a measure of the sensitivity to light of a particular type of film **5** *slang* amphetamine **6 at speed** quickly **7 up to speed a** operating at an acceptable level **b** in possession of all the necessary information ▷ *vb* **speeding, sped** *or* **speeded 8** to move or go somewhere quickly **9** to drive a motor vehicle faster than the legal limit ▷ See also **speed up** ▶ HISTORY Old English *spēd* (originally: success)

speedboat *n* a high-speed motorboat

speed camera *n* *Brit, Austral & NZ* a camera for photographing vehicles breaking the speed limit

speed limit *n* the maximum speed at which a vehicle may legally travel on a particular road

speedo *n, pl* **speedos** *informal* a speedometer

speedometer *n* a dial in a vehicle which shows the speed of travel

speed up *vb* to accelerate

speedway *n* **1** the sport of racing on light powerful motorcycles round cinder tracks **2** *US, Canad & NZ* the track or stadium where such races are held

speedwell *n* a small blue or pinkish-white flower

speedy *adj* **speedier, speediest 1** done without delay **2** (of a vehicle) able to travel fast > **speedily** *adv*

speleology *n* the scientific study of caves ▶ HISTORY Latin *spelaeum* cave

spell¹ *vb* **spelling, spelt** *or* **spelled 1** to write or name in correct order the letters that make up (a word): *how do you spell that name?* **2** (of letters) to make up (a word): *c-a-t spells cat* **3** to indicate (a particular result): *share price slump spells disaster* ▷ See also **spell out** ▶ HISTORY Old French *espeller*

spell² *n* **1** a sequence of words used to perform magic **2** the effect of a spell: *the wizard's spell was broken* **3 under someone's spell** fascinated by someone ▶ HISTORY Old English *spell* speech

spell³ *n* **1** a period of time of weather or activity: *the dry spell; a short spell in prison* **2** a period of duty after which one person or group relieves another **3** *Scot, Austral & NZ* a period of rest ▶ HISTORY Old English *spelian* to take the place of

spellbound *adj* completely fascinated; as if in a trance

spellchecker *n* *computers* a program that highlights any word in a word-processed document that is not recognized as being correctly spelt

spelling *n* **1** the way a word is spelt: *the British spelling of 'theatre'* **2** a person's ability to spell: *my spelling used to be excellent*

spell out *vb* **1** to make (something) as easy to understand as possible: *to spell out the implications* **2** to read with difficulty, working out each word letter by letter

spelt *vb* a past of **spell¹**

spend *vb* **spending, spent 1** to pay out (money) **2** to pass (time) in a specific way or place: *I spent a year in Budapest* **3** to concentrate (effort) on an activity: *a lot of energy was spent organizing the*

holiday **4** to use up completely: *the hurricane spent its force* ▶ HISTORY Latin *expendere* > **spending** *n*

spendthrift *n* **1** a person who spends money wastefully ▷ *adj* **2** of or like a spendthrift: *a spendthrift policy*

spent *vb* **1** the past of **spend** ▷ *adj* **2** used up or exhausted

sperm *n* **1** (*pl* **sperms** *or* **sperm**) one of the male reproductive cells released in the semen during ejaculation **2** same as **semen** ▶ HISTORY Greek *sperma*

spermaceti (sper-ma-**set**-ee) *n* a white waxy substance obtained from the sperm whale ▶ HISTORY Medieval Latin *sperma ceti* whale's sperm

spermatogenesis *n* *biol* the formation and development of spermatozoa in the testis

spermatozoid (spur-mat-o-**zoh**-id) *n* *bot* a small male gamete produced by a lower plant

spermatozoon (sper-ma-toe-**zoe**-on) *n, pl* **-zoa**, same as **sperm** (sense 1) ▶ HISTORY Greek *sperma* seed + *zōion* animal

spermicide *n* a substance, esp. a cream or jelly, that kills sperm, used as a means of contraception ▶ HISTORY SPERM + Latin *caedere* to kill > **spermicidal** *adj*

sperm oil *n* an oil obtained from the head of the sperm whale, used as a lubricant

sperm whale *n* a large whale which is hunted for spermaceti and ambergris ▶ HISTORY short for SPERMACETI WHALE

spew *vb* **1** to vomit **2** to send or be sent out in a stream: *the hydrant spewed a tidal wave of water* ▶ HISTORY Old English *spīwan*

SPF sun protection factor

sphagnum *n* a moss which is found in bogs and which decays to form peat ▶ HISTORY Greek *sphagnos*

sphere *n* **1** *geom* a round solid figure in which every point on the surface is equally distant from the centre **2** an object having this shape, such as a planet **3** a particular field of activity **4** people of the same rank or with shared interests: *a humbler social sphere* ▶ HISTORY Greek *sphaira*

spherical *adj* shaped like a sphere

spheroid *n* *geom* a solid figure that is almost but not exactly a sphere

sphincter *n* *anat* a ring of muscle surrounding the opening of a hollow organ and contracting to close it ▶ HISTORY Greek *sphingein* to grip tightly

sphinx *n* **1** one of the huge statues built by the ancient Egyptians, with the body of a lion and the head of a man **2** a mysterious person

Sphinx *n* **1** the huge statue of a sphinx near the pyramids at El Gīza in Egypt **2** *Greek myth* a monster with a woman's head and a lion's body, who set a riddle for travellers, killing them when they failed to answer it. Oedipus answered the riddle and the Sphinx then killed herself ▶ HISTORY Greek

spice *n* **1 a** an aromatic substance, such as ginger or cinnamon, used as flavouring **b** such substances collectively **2** something that makes life or an activity more exciting ▷ *vb* **spicing, spiced**

3 to flavour (food) with spices **4** to add excitement or interest to (something): *they spiced their letters with pointed demands* ▶ HISTORY Old French *espice*

spick-and-span *adj* very neat and clean ▶ HISTORY obsolete *spick* spike + *span-new* absolutely new, like a freshly cut spike

spicy *adj* **spicier, spiciest 1** strongly flavoured with spices **2** *informal* slightly scandalous: *spicy new story lines*

spider *n* a small eight-legged creature, many species of which weave webs in which to trap insects for food ▶ HISTORY Old English *spīthra*
> **spidery** *adj*

spider monkey *n* a tree-living monkey with very long legs, a long tail, and a small head

spiel *n* a prepared speech made to persuade someone to buy or do something ▶ HISTORY German *Spiel* play

spigot *n* **1** a stopper for the vent hole of a cask **2** a wooden tap fitted to a cask ▶ HISTORY probably from Latin *spica* a point

spike[1] *n* **1** a sharp-pointed metal object: *a high fence with iron spikes* **2** anything long and pointed: *a hedgehog bristling with spikes* **3** a long metal nail **4 spikes** sports shoes with metal spikes on the soles for greater grip ▷ *vb* **spiking, spiked 5** to secure or supply (something) with spikes: *spiked shoes* **6** to drive a spike or spikes into **7** to add alcohol to (a drink) ▶ HISTORY Middle English *spyk*
> **spiky** *adj*

spike[2] *n bot* **1** an arrangement of flowers attached at the base to a long stem **2** an ear of grain ▶ HISTORY Latin *spica* ear of corn

spikenard *n* **1** a fragrant Indian plant with rose-purple flowers **2** an ointment obtained from this plant ▶ HISTORY Medieval Latin *spica nardi*

spill[1] *vb* **spilling, spilt** or **spilled 1** to pour from or as from a container by accident **2** (of large numbers of people) to come out of a place: *rival groups spilled out from the station* **3** *written* to shed (blood) **4 spill the beans** *informal* to give away a secret ▷ *n* **5** *informal* a fall from a motorbike, bike, or horse, esp. in a competition **6** an amount of liquid spilt ▶ HISTORY Old English *spillan* to destroy
> **spillage** *n*

spill[2] *n* a splinter of wood or strip of paper for lighting pipes or fires ▶ HISTORY Germanic

spin *vb* **spinning, spun 1** to revolve or cause to revolve quickly **2** to draw out and twist (fibres, such as silk or cotton) into thread **3** (of a spider or silkworm) to form (a web or cocoon) from a silky fibre that comes out of the body **4 spin a yarn** to tell an unlikely story **5** *sport* to throw, hit, or kick (a ball) so that it spins and changes direction or changes speed on bouncing **6** same as **spin-dry 7** to grow dizzy: *her head was spinning* **8** *informal* to present information in a way that creates a favourable impression ▷ *n* **9** a fast rotating motion **10** a flight manoeuvre in which an aircraft flies in a downward spiral **11** *sport* a spinning motion given to a ball **12** *informal* a short car drive taken for pleasure **13** *informal* the presenting of information

in a way that creates a favourable impression ▷ See also **spin out** ▶ HISTORY Old English *spinnan*
> **spinning** *n*

spina bifida *n* a condition in which part of the spinal cord protrudes through a gap in the backbone, sometimes causing paralysis ▶ HISTORY New Latin: split spine

spinach *n* a dark green leafy vegetable ▶ HISTORY Arabic *isfānākh*

spinal column *n* same as **spine** (sense 1)

spinal cord *n* the thick cord of nerve tissue within the spine, which connects the brain to the nerves of the body

spin bowler *n cricket* same as **spinner** (sense 1a)

spindle *n* **1** a rotating rod that acts as an axle **2** a rod with a notch in the top for drawing out, twisting and winding the thread in spinning ▶ HISTORY Old English *spinel*

spindly *adj* **-dlier, -dliest** tall, thin, and frail

spin doctor *n informal* a person who provides a favourable slant to a news item or policy on behalf of a political personality or party ▶ HISTORY from the spin given to a ball in sport to make it go in the desired direction

spindrift *n* spray blown up from the sea ▶ HISTORY Scots variant of *spoondrift*, from *spoon* to scud + DRIFT

spin-dry *vb* **-dries, -drying, -dried** to dry (clothes) in a spin-dryer

spin-dryer *n* a device that removes water from washed clothes by spinning them in a perforated drum

spine *n* **1** the row of bony segments that surround and protect the spinal cord **2** the back of a book, record sleeve, or dvd case **3** a sharp point on the body of an animal or on a plant ▶ HISTORY Latin *spina* thorn > **spinal** *adj*

spine-chiller *n* a frightening film or story
> **spine-chilling** *adj*

spineless *adj* **1** behaving in a cowardly way **2** (of an animal) having no spine

spinet *n* a small harpsichord ▶ HISTORY Italian *spinetta*

spinifex *n* a coarse spiny Australian grass

spinnaker *n* a large triangular sail on a racing yacht ▶ HISTORY probably from *spin*, but traditionally from Sphinx, the yacht that first used this type of sail

spinner *n* **1** *cricket* **a** a bowler who specializes in spinning the ball with his or her fingers to make it change direction when it bounces or strikes the batsman's bat **b** a ball that is bowled with a spinning motion **2** a small round object used in angling to attract fish to the bait by spinning in the water **3** a person who makes thread by spinning

spinneret *n* an organ through which silk threads come out of the body of a spider or insect

spinney *n chiefly Brit* a small wood: *the hollow tree in the spinney* ▶ HISTORY Old French *espinei*

spinning jenny *n* an early type of spinning frame with several spindles

spinning wheel *n* a wheel-like machine for

spinning at home, having one hand- or foot-operated spindle

spin-off *n* **1** a product or development that unexpectedly results from activities designed to achieve something else: *new energy sources could occur as a spin-off from the space effort* **2** a television series involving some of the characters from an earlier successful series

spin out *vb* **1** to take longer than necessary to do (something) **2** to make (money) last as long as possible

spinster *n* an unmarried woman > **spinsterish** *adj*

■ **WORD HISTORY**
■ A 'spinster' was originally a spinner, that is, a
■ person - not necessarily a woman - whose
■ occupation was spinning. It is said that a young
■ woman was not considered fit to be a wife until
■ she had spun a certain amount of household
■ linen. Hence, the word came to designate an
■ unmarried woman.

spiny *adj* **spinier, spiniest** (of animals or plants) covered with spines

spiracle (**spire**-a-kl) *n zool* a small blowhole for breathing through, such as that of a whale ▸ **HISTORY** Latin *spiraculum* vent

spiraea *or esp US* **spirea** (spire-**ee**-a) *n* a plant with small white or pink flowers ▸ **HISTORY** Greek *speiraia*

spiral *n* **1** *geom* a plane curve formed by a point winding about a fixed point at an ever-increasing distance from it **2** something that follows a winding course or that has a twisting form **3** *econ* a continuous upward or downward movement in economic activity or prices ▷ *adj* **4** having the shape of a spiral: *a spiral staircase* ▷ *vb* **-ralling, -ralled** *or US* **-raling, -raled** **5** to follow a spiral course or be in the shape of a spiral **6** to increase or decrease with steady acceleration: *oil prices continue to spiral* ▸ **HISTORY** Latin *spira* a coil > **spirally** *adv*

spire *n* the tall cone-shaped structure on the top of a church ▸ **HISTORY** Old English *spīr* blade

spirillum *n, pl* **-la** *biol* a bacterium with a curved or spirally twisted body

spirit¹ *n* **1** the nonphysical aspect of a person concerned with profound thoughts and emotions **2** the nonphysical part of a person believed to live on after death **3** a shared feeling: *a spirit of fun and adventure* **4** mood or attitude: *fighting spirit* **5** a person's character or temperament: *the indomitable spirit of the Polish people* **6** liveliness shown in what a person does: *it has been undertaken with spirit* **7** the feelings that motivate someone to survive in difficult times or live according to his or her beliefs: *someone had broken his spirit* **8 spirits** an emotional state: *in good spirits* **9** the way in which something, such as a law or an agreement, was intended to be interpreted: *they acted against the spirit of the treaty* **10** a supernatural being, such as a ghost ▷ *vb* **-iting, -ited** **11 spirit away** *or* **off** *written* to carry (someone or something) off mysteriously or secretly ▸ **HISTORY** Latin *spiritus* breath, spirit

spirit² *n* **1** (usually pl) distilled alcoholic liquor, such as whisky or gin **2** *chem* **a** a solution of ethanol obtained by distillation **b** the essence of a substance, extracted as a liquid by distillation **3** *pharmacol* a solution of a volatile oil in alcohol ▸ **HISTORY** special use of SPIRIT¹

spirited *adj* **1** showing liveliness or courage: *a spirited rendition of Schubert's ninth symphony; a spirited defence of the government's policy* **2** characterized by the mood as specified: *high-spirited; mean-spirited*

spirit lamp *n* a lamp that burns methylated or other spirits instead of oil

spirit level *n* a device for checking whether a surface is level, consisting of a block of wood or metal containing a tube partially filled with liquid set so that the air bubble in it rests between two marks on the tube when the block is level

spiritual *adj* **1** relating to a person's beliefs as opposed to his or her physical or material needs **2** relating to religious beliefs **3 one's spiritual home** the place where one feels one belongs ▷ *n* **4** Also called: **Negro spiritual** a type of religious folk song originally sung by Black slaves in the American South > **spirituality** *n* > **spiritually** *adv*

spiritualism *n* the belief that the spirits of the dead can communicate with the living > **spiritualist** *n*

spirituous *adj* containing alcohol

spirogyra (spire-oh-**jire**-a) *n* a green freshwater plant that floats on the surface of ponds and ditches ▸ **HISTORY** Greek *speira* a coil + *guros* a circle

spit¹ *vb* **spitting, spat** *or* **spit** **1** to force saliva out of one's mouth **2** to force (something) out of one's mouth: *he spat tobacco into an old coffee can* **3** (of a fire or hot fat) to throw out sparks or particles violently and explosively **4** to rain very lightly **5** (often foll. by *out*) *written* to say (words) in a violent angry way **6** to show contempt or hatred by spitting **7 spit it out!** *informal* a command given to someone to say what is on his or her mind ▷ *n* **8** same as **spittle 9** *informal, chiefly Brit* same as **spitting image** ▸ **HISTORY** Old English *spittan*

spit² *n* **1** a pointed rod for skewering and roasting meat over a fire or in an oven **2** a long narrow strip of land jutting out into the sea ▸ **HISTORY** Old English *spitu*

spite *n* **1** deliberate nastiness **2 in spite of** regardless of: *he loved them in spite of their shortcomings* ▷ *vb* **spiting, spited** **3** to annoy (someone) deliberately, out of spite: *it was to spite his father* ▸ **HISTORY** variant of DESPITE > **spiteful** *adj* > **spitefully** *adv*

spitfire *n* a woman or girl who is easily angered

spitting image *n informal* a person who looks very like someone else ▸ **HISTORY** from *spit* likeness

spittle *n* the fluid that is produced in the mouth; saliva ▸ **HISTORY** Old English *spǣtl* saliva

spittoon *n* a bowl for people to spit into

spitz *n* a stockily built dog with a pointed face, erect ears, and a tightly curled tail ▸ **HISTORY** from German

S

spiv n *Brit, Austral & NZ, slang* a smartly dressed man who makes a living by underhand dealings; black marketeer ▶ **HISTORY** dialect *spiving* smart

splash vb **1** to scatter (liquid) on (something) **2** to cause (liquid) to fall or (of liquid) to be scattered in drops **3** to display (a photograph or story) prominently in a newspaper ▷ n **4** a splashing sound **5** an amount splashed **6** a patch (of colour or light) **7 make a splash** *informal* to attract a lot of attention **8** a small amount of liquid added to a drink ▶ **HISTORY** alteration of *plash*

splashdown n **1** the landing of a spacecraft on water at the end of a flight ▷ vb **splash down** **2** (of a spacecraft) to make a splashdown

splash out vb to spend a lot of money on a treat or luxury: *she planned to splash out on a good holiday*

splatter vb **1** to splash (something or someone) with small blobs ▷ n **2** a splash of liquid

splatter movie n *slang* a film in which the main feature is the graphic and gory murder of numerous victims

splay vb to spread out, with ends spreading out in different directions: *her hair splayed over the pillow* ▶ **HISTORY** short for DISPLAY

spleen n **1** a spongy organ near the stomach, which filters bacteria from the blood **2** spitefulness or bad temper: *we vent our spleen on drug barons* ▶ **HISTORY** Greek *splēn*

spleenwort n a kind of fern that grows on walls

splendid adj **1** very good: *a splendid match* **2** beautiful or impressive: *a splendid palace* ▶ **HISTORY** Latin *splendere* to shine
> **splendidly** adv

splendour or US **splendor** n **1** beauty or impressiveness **2 splendours** the impressive or beautiful features of something: *the splendours of the Emperor's Palace*

splenetic adj *literary* irritable or bad-tempered ▶ **HISTORY** from SPLEEN

splice vb **splicing, spliced 1** to join up the trimmed ends of (two pieces of wire, film, or tape) with an adhesive material **2** to join (two ropes) by interweaving the ends **3 get spliced** *informal* to get married ▶ **HISTORY** probably from Middle Dutch *splissen*

splint n a piece of wood used to support a broken bone ▶ **HISTORY** Middle Low German *splinte*

splinter n **1** a small thin sharp piece broken off, esp. from wood ▷ vb **2** to break or be broken into small sharp fragments ▶ **HISTORY** Middle Dutch

splinter group n a number of members of an organization, who split from the main body and form an independent group of their own

split vb **splitting, split 1** to break or cause (something) to break into separate pieces **2** to separate (a piece) or (of a piece) to be separated from (something) **3** (of a group) to separate into smaller groups, through disagreement: *the council is split over rent increases* **4** (often foll. by up) to divide (something) among two or more people **5** *slang* to leave a place **6 split on** *slang* to betray; inform: *he didn't tell tales or split on him* **7 split one's**

sides to laugh a great deal ▷ n **8** a gap or rift caused by splitting **9** a division in a group or the smaller group resulting from such a division **10** a dessert of sliced fruit and ice cream, covered with whipped cream and nuts: *banana split* ▷ adj **11** having a split or splits: *split ends* ▷ See also **splits** ▶ **HISTORY** Middle Dutch *splitten*

split infinitive n (in English grammar) an infinitive used with another word between *to* and the verb, as in *to really finish it*. This is often thought to be incorrect

split-level adj (of a house or room) having the floor level of one part about half a storey above that of the other

split personality n **1** the tendency to change mood very quickly **2** a disorder in which a person's mind appears to have separated into two or more personalities

splits n (in gymnastics and dancing) the act of sitting with both legs outstretched, pointing in opposite directions, and at right angles to the body

split second n **1** an extremely short period of time; instant ▷ adj **split-second 2** made in an extremely short time: *split-second timing*

splitting adj (of a headache) extremely painful

splodge or US **splotch** n **1** a large uneven spot or stain ▷ vb **splodging, splodged 2** to mark (something) with a splodge or splodges ▶ **HISTORY** alteration of earlier *splotch*

splurge n **1** a bout of spending money extravagantly ▷ vb **splurging, splurged 2** (foll. by *on*) to spend (money) extravagantly: *they rushed out to splurge their pocket money on chocolate* ▶ **HISTORY** origin unknown

splutter vb **1** to spit out (something) from the mouth when choking or laughing **2** to say (words) with spitting sounds when choking or in a rage **3** to throw out or to be thrown out explosively: *sparks spluttered from the fire* ▷ n **4** the act or noise of spluttering ▶ **HISTORY** variant of SPUTTER

spoil vb **spoiling, spoilt** or **spoiled 1** to make (something) less valuable, beautiful, or useful **2** to weaken the character of (a child) by giving it all it wants **3** (of yourself) to indulge one's desires: *go ahead and spoil yourself* **4** (of food) to become unfit for consumption **5 be spoiling for** to have an aggressive urge for: *he is spoiling for a fight* ▷ See also **spoils** ▶ **HISTORY** Latin *spolium* booty

spoiler n **1** a device fitted to an aircraft wing to increase drag and reduce lift **2** a similar device fitted to a car

spoils pl n **1** valuables seized during war **2** the rewards and benefits of having political power

spoilsport n *informal* a person who spoils the enjoyment of other people

spoke¹ vb the past tense of **speak**

spoke² n **1** a bar joining the centre of a wheel to the rim **2 put a spoke in someone's wheel** *Brit & NZ* to create a difficulty for someone ▶ **HISTORY** Old English *spāca*

spoken vb **1** the past participle of **speak** ▷ adj **2** said in speech: *spoken commands* **3** having speech as specified: *quiet-spoken* **4 spoken for** engaged or reserved

spokesman, spokesperson *or* **spokeswoman** *n*, *pl* **-men, -people** *or* **-women** a person chosen to speak on behalf of another person or group

spoliation *n* the act or an instance of plundering: *the spoliation of the countryside* ▶ HISTORY Latin *spoliare* to plunder

spondee *n prosody* a metrical foot of two long syllables ▶ HISTORY Greek *spondē* ritual offering of drink > **spondaic** *adj*

sponge *n* **1** a sea animal with a porous absorbent elastic skeleton **2** the skeleton of a sponge, or a piece of artificial sponge, used for bathing or cleaning **3** a soft absorbent material like a sponge **4** Also called: **sponge cake** a light cake made of eggs, sugar, and flour **5** Also called: **sponge pudding** *Brit & Austral* a light steamed or baked spongy pudding **6** a rub with a wet sponge ▷ *vb* **sponging, sponged 7** (often foll. by *down*) to clean (something) by rubbing it with a wet sponge **8** to remove (marks) by rubbing them with a wet sponge **9** (usually foll. by *off* or *on*) to get (something) from someone by taking advantage of his or her generosity: *stop sponging off the rest of us!* ▶ HISTORY Greek *spongia* > **spongy** *adj*

sponge bag *n* a small waterproof bag for holding toiletries when travelling

sponger *n informal, offensive* a person who lives off other people by continually taking advantage of their generosity

sponsor *n* **1** a person or group that promotes another person or group in an activity or the activity itself, either for profit or for charity **2** *chiefly US & Canad* a person or firm that pays the costs of a radio or television programme in return for advertising time **3** a person who presents and supports a proposal or suggestion **4** a person who makes certain promises on behalf of a person being baptized and takes responsibility for his or her Christian upbringing ▷ *vb* **5** to act as a sponsor for (someone or something) ▶ HISTORY Latin *spondere* to promise solemnly > **sponsored** *adj* > **sponsorship** *n*

spontaneous *adj* **1** not planned or arranged; impulsive: *a spontaneous celebration* **2** occurring through natural processes without outside influence: *a spontaneous explosion* ▶ HISTORY Latin *sponte* voluntarily > **spontaneously** *adv* > **spontaneity** *n*

spontaneous combustion *n chem* the bursting into flame of a substance as a result of internal oxidation processes, without heat from an outside source

spoof *informal n* **1** an imitation of a film, TV programme, etc., that exaggerates in an amusing way the most memorable features of the original **2** a good-humoured trick or deception ▷ *vb* **3** to fool (a person) with a trick or deception ▶ HISTORY made-up word

spook *informal n* **1** a ghost **2** a strange and frightening person ▷ *vb US, Canad & Austral* **3** to frighten: *it was the wind that spooked her* ▶ HISTORY Dutch > **spooky** *adj*

spool *n* a cylinder around which film, thread, or tape can be wound ▶ HISTORY Germanic

spoon *n* **1** a small shallow bowl attached to a handle, used for eating, stirring, or serving food **2 be born with a silver spoon in one's mouth** to be born into a very rich and respected family ▷ *vb* **3** to scoop up (food or liquid) with a spoon **4** *old-fashioned slang* to kiss and cuddle ▶ HISTORY Old English *spōn* splinter

spoonbill *n* a wading bird with a long flat bill

spoonerism *n* the accidental changing over of the first sounds of a pair of words, often with an amusing result, such as *hush my brat* for *brush my hat* ▶ HISTORY after W. A. *Spooner*, clergyman

spoon-feed *vb* **-feeding, -fed 1** to feed (someone, usually a baby) using a spoon **2** to give (someone) too much help

spoor *n* the trail of an animal ▶ HISTORY Afrikaans

sporadic *adj* happening at irregular intervals; intermittent: *sporadic bursts of gunfire* ▶ HISTORY Greek *sporas* scattered > **sporadically** *adv*

spore *n* a reproductive body, produced by nonflowering plants and bacteria, that develops into a new individual ▶ HISTORY Greek *spora* a sowing

sporran *n* a large pouch worn hanging from a belt in front of the kilt in Scottish Highland dress ▶ HISTORY Scottish Gaelic *sporan* purse

sport *n* **1** an activity for exercise, pleasure, or competition: *your favourite sport* **2** such activities collectively: *the minister for sport* **3** the enjoyment gained from a pastime: *just for the sport of it* **4** playful or good-humoured joking: *I only did it in sport* **5** *informal* a person who accepts defeat or teasing cheerfully **6 make sport of someone** to make fun of someone **7** an animal or plant that is very different from others of the same species, usually because of a mutation **8** *Austral & NZ, informal* a term of address between males ▷ *vb* **9** *informal, written* to wear proudly: *sporting a pair of bright yellow shorts* ▷ See also **sports** ▶ HISTORY variant of Middle English *disporten* to disport

sporting *adj* **1** of sport **2** behaving in a fair and decent way **3 a sporting chance** a reasonable likelihood of happening: *a sporting chance of winning*

sportive *adj* playful or high-spirited

sports *adj* **1** of or used in sports: *a sports arena* ▷ *n* **2** Also called: **sports day** *Brit* a meeting held at a school or college for competitions in athletic events

sports car *n* a fast car with a low body and usually seating only two people

sports jacket *n* a man's casual jacket, usually made of tweed. Also called: *US, Austral & NZ* **sports coat**

sportsman *n*, *pl* **-men 1** a man who plays sports **2** a person who plays by the rules, is fair, and

s

accepts defeat with good humour > **sportsman-like** adj > **sportsmanship** n

sportswoman n, pl **-women** a woman who plays sports

sporty adj **sportier, sportiest 1** (of a person) interested in sport **2** (of clothes) suitable for sport **3** (of a car) small and fast > **sportily** adv > **sportiness** n

spot n **1** a small mark on a surface, which has a different colour or texture from its surroundings **2** a location: *a spot where they could sit* **3** a small mark or pimple on the skin **4** a feature of something that has the attribute mentioned: *the one bright spot in his whole day; the high spot of our trip* **5** informal, chiefly Brit, Austral & NZ a small amount: *a spot of bother* **6** informal an awkward situation: *I'm sometimes in a spot* **7** a part of a show, TV programme, etc. reserved for a specific performer or type of entertainment **8** short for **spotlight** (sense 1) **9 in a tight spot** in a difficult situation **10 knock spots off someone** to be much better than someone **11 on the spot a** immediately: *he decided on the spot to fly down* **b** at the place in question: *the expert weapons man on the spot* **c** in an awkward situation: *the British government will be put on the spot* **12 soft spot** a special affection for someone: *a soft spot for older men* ▷ vb **spotting, spotted 13** to see (something or someone) suddenly **14** to put stains or spots on (something) **15** (of some fabrics) to be prone to marking by liquids: *silk spots easily* **16** to take note of (the numbers of trains or planes observed) **17** (of scouts, agents, etc.) to look out for (talented but unknown actors, sportspersons, etc.) **18** Brit to rain lightly ▶ **HISTORY** from German

spot check n a quick unplanned inspection

spot height n geog a mark on a map indicating the height of a hill, mountain, etc.

spotless adj **1** perfectly clean **2** free from moral flaws: *a spotless reputation* > **spotlessly** adv

spotlight n **1** a powerful light focused so as to light up a small area **2 the spotlight** the centre of attention: *the spotlight moved to the president* ▷ vb **-lighting, -lit** or **-lighted 3** to direct a spotlight on (something) **4** to focus attention on (something)

spot-on adj informal absolutely correct; very accurate: *they're spot-on in terms of style*

spotted adj **1** having a pattern of spots **2** marked with stains

spotter n a person whose hobby is watching for and noting numbers or types of trains or planes

spotty adj **-tier, -tiest 1** covered with spots or pimples **2** not consistent; irregular in quality: *a rather spotty performance* > **spottiness** n

spouse n a person's partner in marriage ▶ **HISTORY** Latin *sponsus, sponsa* betrothed man or woman

spout vb **1** (of a liquid or flames) to pour out in a stream or jet **2** informal to talk about (something) in a boring way or without much thought ▷ n **3** a projecting tube or lip for pouring liquids . **4** a stream or jet of liquid: *a spout of steaming water* **5 up the spout** slang **a** ruined or lost: *the motor*

industry is up the spout **b** pregnant ▶ **HISTORY** Middle English *spouten*

spouting n NZ **a** a rainwater downpipe on the outside of a building **b** such pipes collectively

sprain vb **1** to injure (a joint) by a sudden twist ▷ n **2** this injury, which causes swelling and temporary disability ▶ **HISTORY** origin unknown

sprang vb a past tense of **spring**

sprat n a small edible fish like a herring ▶ **HISTORY** Old English *sprott*

sprawl vb **1** to sit or lie with one's arms and legs spread out **2** to spread out untidily over a large area: *the pulp mill sprawled over the narrow flats* ▷ n **3** the part of a city or town that has not been planned and spreads out untidily over a large area: *the huge Los Angeles sprawl* ▶ **HISTORY** Old English *spreawlian* > **sprawling** adj

spray¹ n **1** fine drops of a liquid **2 a** a liquid under pressure designed to be discharged in fine drops from an aerosol or atomizer: *hair spray* **b** the aerosol or atomizer itself **3** a number of small objects flying through the air: *a spray of bullets* ▷ vb **4** to scatter in fine drops **5** to squirt (a liquid) from an aerosol or atomizer **6** to cover with a spray: *spray the crops* ▶ **HISTORY** Middle Dutch *spräien* > **sprayer** n

spray² n **1** a sprig or branch with buds, leaves, flowers, or berries **2** an ornament or design like this ▶ **HISTORY** Germanic

spray gun n a device for spraying fine drops of paint, etc.

spread vb **spreading, spread 1** to open out or unfold to the fullest width: *spread the material out* **2** to extend over a larger expanse: *the subsequent unrest spread countrywide* **3** to apply as a coating: *spread the paste evenly over your skin* **4** to be displayed to its fullest extent: *the shining bay spread out below* **5** to send or be sent out in all directions or to many people: *the news spread quickly; the sandflies that spread the disease* **6** to distribute or be distributed evenly: *we were advised to spread the workload over the whole year* ▷ n **7** a spreading; distribution, dispersion, or expansion: *the spread of higher education* **8** informal a large meal **9** informal the wingspan of an aircraft or bird **10** informal, chiefly US & Canad a ranch or other large area of land **11** a soft food which can be spread: *cheese spread* **12** two facing pages in a book or magazine **13** a widening of the hips and waist: *middle-age spread* ▶ **HISTORY** Old English *sprædan*

spread-eagled adj with arms and legs outstretched

spreadsheet n a computer program for manipulating figures, used for financial planning

spree n a session of overindulgence, usually in drinking or spending money ▶ **HISTORY** Scots *spreath* plundered cattle

sprig n **1** a shoot, twig, or sprout **2** an ornamental device like this **3** NZ a stud on the sole of a soccer or rugby boot ▶ **HISTORY** Germanic > **sprigged** adj

sprightly adj **-lier, -liest** lively and active ▶ **HISTORY** obsolete *spright*, variant of SPRITE > **sprightliness** n

spring *vb* **springing, sprang** *or* **sprung; sprung**
1 to jump suddenly upwards or forwards **2** to return or be returned into natural shape from a forced position by elasticity: *the coil sprang back* **3** to cause (something) to happen unexpectedly: *the national coach sprang a surprise* **4** (usually foll. by *from*) to originate; be descended: *this motivation springs from their inborn curiosity; Truman sprang from ordinary people* **5** (often foll. by *up*) to come into being or appear suddenly: *new courses will spring up* **6** to provide (something, such as a mattress) with springs **7** *informal* to arrange the escape of (someone) from prison ▷ *n* **8** the season between winter and summer **9** a leap or jump **10** a coil which can be compressed, stretched, or bent and then return to its original shape when released **11** a natural pool forming the source of a stream **12** elasticity ▶ HISTORY Old English *springan* > **springlike** *adj*

spring balance *or esp US* **spring scale** *n* a device that indicates the weight of an object by the extension of a spring to which the object is attached

springboard *n* **1** a flexible board used to gain height or momentum in diving or gymnastics **2** anything that makes it possible for an activity to begin: *the meeting acted as a springboard for future negotiations*

springbok *n, pl* **-bok** *or* **-boks 1** a S African antelope which moves in leaps **2** a person who has represented S Africa in a national sports team ▶ HISTORY Afrikaans

spring chicken *n* **1** *chiefly US & S African* a young chicken, which is tender for cooking **2 he** *or* **she is no spring chicken** *informal* he *or* she is no longer young

spring-clean *vb* **1** to clean (a house) thoroughly, traditionally at the end of winter ▷ *n* **2** an instance of this > **spring-cleaning** *n*

spring onion *n* a small onion with a tiny bulb and long green leaves, eaten in salads

spring tide *n* either of the two tides at or just after new moon and full moon: the greatest rise and fall in tidal level

springtime *n* the season of spring

springy *adj* **springier, springiest** (of an object) having the quality of returning to its original shape after being pressed or pulled > **springiness** *n*

sprinkle *vb* **-kling, -kled 1** to scatter (liquid or powder) in tiny drops over (something) **2** to distribute over (something): *a dozen mud huts sprinkled around it* ▶ HISTORY probably from Middle Dutch *sprenkelen* > **sprinkler** *n*

sprinkling *n* a small quantity or amount: *a sprinkling of diamonds*

sprint *n* **1** *athletics* **a** a short race run at top speed **b** a fast run at the end of a longer race **2** any quick run ▷ *vb* **3** to run or cycle a short distance at top speed ▶ HISTORY Scandinavian > **sprinter** *n*

sprit *n naut* a light pole set diagonally across a sail to extend it ▶ HISTORY Old English *sprēot*

sprite *n* **1** (in folklore) a fairy or elf **2** an icon in a computer game which can be manoeuvred around the screen ▶ HISTORY Latin *spiritus* spirit

spritsail *n naut* a sail mounted on a sprit

sprocket *n* **1** Also called: **sprocket wheel** a wheel with teeth on the rim, that drives or is driven by a chain **2** a cylindrical wheel with teeth on one or both rims for pulling film through a camera or projector ▶ HISTORY origin unknown

sprout *vb* **1** (of a plant or seed) to produce (new leaves or shoots) **2** (often foll. by *up*) to begin to grow or develop ▷ *n* **3** a new shoot or bud **4** same as **Brussels sprout** ▶ HISTORY Old English *sprūtan*

spruce[1] *n* **1** an evergreen pyramid-shaped tree with needle-like leaves **2** the light-coloured wood of this tree ▶ HISTORY obsolete *Spruce* Prussia

spruce[2] *adj* neat and smart ▶ HISTORY perhaps from *Spruce leather*; see SPRUCE[1]

spruce up *vb* **sprucing, spruced** to make neat and smart

sprung *vb* a past tense and the past participle of **spring**

spry *adj* **spryer, spryest** *or* **sprier, spriest** active and lively; nimble ▶ HISTORY origin unknown

spud *n informal* a potato ▶ HISTORY obsolete *spudde* short knife

spume *n literary* **1** foam or froth on the sea ▷ *vb* **spuming, spumed 2** (of the sea) to foam or froth ▶ HISTORY Latin *spuma*

spun *vb* **1** the past of **spin** ▷ *adj* **2** made by spinning: *spun sugar; spun silk*

spunk *n old-fashioned, informal* courage or spirit ▶ HISTORY Scottish Gaelic *spong* tinder, sponge > **spunky** *adj*

spur *n* **1** an incentive to get something done **2** a sharp spiked wheel on the heel of a rider's boot used to urge the horse on **3** a sharp horny part sticking out from a cock's leg **4** a ridge sticking out from a mountain side **5 on the spur of the moment** suddenly and without planning; on impulse **6 win one's spurs** to prove one's ability ▷ *vb* **spurring, spurred 7** (often foll. by *on*) to encourage (someone) ▶ HISTORY Old English *spura*

spurge *n* a plant with milky sap and small flowers ▶ HISTORY Latin *expurgare* to cleanse

spurious *adj* not genuine or real ▶ HISTORY Latin *spurius* of illegitimate birth

spurn *vb* to reject (a person or thing) with contempt ▶ HISTORY Old English *spurnan*

spurt *vb* **1** to gush or cause (something) to gush out in a sudden powerful stream or jet **2** to make a sudden effort ▷ *n* **3** a short burst of activity, speed, or energy **4** a sudden powerful stream or jet ▶ HISTORY origin unknown

sputnik *n* a Russian artificial satellite ▶ HISTORY Russian, literally: fellow traveller

sputter *vb, n* same as **splutter** ▶ HISTORY Dutch *sputteren*, imitative

sputum *n, pl* **-ta** saliva, usually mixed with mucus ▶ HISTORY Latin

spy *n, pl* **spies 1** a person employed to find out secret information about other countries or organizations **2** a person who secretly keeps watch on others ▷ *vb* **spies, spying, spied 3** (foll. by *on*) to keep a secret watch on someone **4** to work as a spy **5** to catch sight of (someone or something); notice ▶ HISTORY Old French *espier*

spyglass *n* a small telescope

spyware *n* *computers* software secretly installed via the internet to gather and transmit information about the user

sq. square

SQL *n* a computer programming language that is used for database management ▶ HISTORY *structured query language*

squab *n*, *pl* **squabs** or **squab** a young bird yet to leave the nest ▶ HISTORY probably Germanic

squabble *vb* **-bling, -bled 1** to quarrel over a small matter ▷ *n* **2** a petty quarrel ▶ HISTORY probably Scandinavian

squad *n* **1** the smallest military formation, usually a dozen soldiers **2** any small group of people working together: *the fraud squad* **3** *sport* a number of players from which a team is to be selected ▶ HISTORY Old French *esquade*

squadron *n* the basic unit of an air force ▶ HISTORY Italian *squadrone* soldiers drawn up in square formation

squadron leader *n* a fairly senior commissioned officer in the air force; the rank above flight lieutenant

squalid *adj* **1** dirty, untidy, and in bad condition **2** unpleasant, selfish, and often dishonest: *this squalid affair* ▶ HISTORY Latin *squalidus*

squall¹ *n* a sudden strong wind or short violent storm ▶ HISTORY perhaps a special use of SQUALL²

squall² *vb* **1** to cry noisily; yell ▷ *n* **2** a noisy cry or yell ▶ HISTORY probably Scandinavian

squalor *n* **1** dirty, poor, and untidy physical conditions **2** the condition of being squalid ▶ HISTORY Latin

squander *vb* to waste (money or resources) ▶ HISTORY origin unknown

square *n* **1** a geometric figure with four equal sides and four right angles **2** anything of this shape **3** an open area in a town bordered by buildings or streets **4** *maths* the number produced when a number is multiplied by itself: *9 is the square of 3, written 3²* **5** *informal* a person who is dull or unfashionable **6 go back to square one** to return to the start because of failure or lack of progress ▷ *adj* **7** being a square in shape **8 a** having the same area as that of a square with sides of a specified length: *2,500 square metres of hillside* **b** denoting a square having a specified length on each side: *a cell of only four square metres* **9** straight or level: *I don't think that painting is square* **10** fair and honest: *a square deal* **11** *informal* dull or unfashionable **12** having all debts or accounts settled: *if I give you 50 pence, then we'll be square* **13 all square** on equal terms; even in score **14 square peg in a round hole** *informal* a misfit ▷ *vb* **squaring, squared 15** *maths* to multiply (a number or quantity) by itself **16** to position so as to be straight or level:

bravely he squared his shoulders **17** to settle (a debt or account) **18** to level the score in (a game) **19** to be or cause to be consistent: *it would not have squared with her image* ▷ *adv* **20** *informal* same as **squarely** ▷ See also **square up** ▶ HISTORY Old French *esquare*

square-bashing *n* *Brit mil, slang* marching and other drill on a parade ground

square bracket *n* either of a pair of characters [ ], used to separate a section of writing or printing from the main text

square dance *n* a country dance in which the couples are arranged in squares

square leg *n* *cricket* a fielding position on the on side, at right angles to the batsman

squarely *adv* **1** directly; straight: *he looked her squarely in the eye* **2** in an honest and frank way: *you should face squarely anything that worries you*

square meal *n* a meal which is large enough to leave the eater feeling full: *we gave him his first square meal in days*

square proportion *n* *maths* a relationship between two variables in which one is proportional to the square of the other

square-rigged *adj* *naut* having sails set at right angles to the keel

square root *n* a number that when multiplied by itself gives a given number: *the square roots of 4 are 2 and –2*

square up *vb* **1** to settle bills or debts **2 square up to** to prepare to confront (a problem or a person)

squash¹ *vb* **1** to press or squeeze (something) so as to flatten it **2** to overcome (a difficult situation), often with force **3 squash in** or **into** to push or force (oneself or a thing) into a confined space **4** to humiliate (someone) with a sarcastic reply ▷ *n* **5** *Brit & Austral* a drink made from fruit juice or fruit syrup diluted with water **6** a crowd of people in a confined space **7** Also called: **squash rackets** a game for two players played in an enclosed court with a small rubber ball and long-handled rackets ▶ HISTORY Old French *esquasser*

squash² *n*, *pl* **squashes** or **squash** *US & Canad* a marrow-like vegetable ▶ HISTORY from a Native American language

squashy *adj* **squashier, squashiest** soft and easily squashed

squat *vb* **squatting, squatted 1** to crouch with the knees bent and the weight on the feet **2** *law* to occupy an unused building to which one has no legal right ▷ *adj* **3** short and thick ▷ *n* **4** a building occupied by squatters ▶ HISTORY Old French *esquater*

squatter *n* an illegal occupier of an unused building

squaw *n* *offensive* a Native American woman of N America ▶ HISTORY from a Native American language

squawk *n* **1** a loud harsh cry, esp. one made by a bird **2** *informal* a loud complaint ▷ *vb* **3** to make a squawk ▶ HISTORY imitative

squeak *n* **1** a short high-pitched cry or sound **2 a narrow squeak** *informal* a narrow escape or success ▷ *vb* **3** to make a squeak **4 squeak through** *or* **by** to pass (an examination), but only just ▶ HISTORY probably Scandinavian > **squeaky** *adj* > **squeakiness** *n*

squeal *n* **1** a long high-pitched yelp ▷ *vb* **2** to make a squeal **3** *slang* to inform on someone to the police **4** *informal, chiefly Brit* to complain loudly ▶ HISTORY Middle English *squelen*, imitative > **squealer** *n*

squeamish *adj* easily shocked or upset by unpleasant sights or events ▶ HISTORY Anglo-French *escoymous*

squeegee *n* a tool with a rubber blade used for wiping away excess water from a surface ▶ HISTORY probably imitative

squeeze *vb* **squeezing, squeezed 1** to grip or press (something) firmly **2** to crush or press (something) so as to extract (a liquid): *squeeze the tomato and strain the juice; freshly squeezed lemon juice* **3** to push (oneself or a thing) into a confined space **4** to hug (someone) closely **5** to obtain (something) by great effort or force: *to squeeze the last dollar out of every deal* ▷ *n* **6** a squeezing **7** a hug **8** a crush of people in a confined space **9** *chiefly Brit & NZ* a restriction on borrowing made by a government to control price inflation **10** an amount extracted by squeezing: *a squeeze of lime* **11 put the squeeze on someone** *informal* to put pressure on someone in order to obtain something ▶ HISTORY Old English *cwȳsan*

squelch *vb* **1** to make a wet sucking noise, such as by walking through mud **2** *informal* to silence (someone) with a sarcastic or wounding reply ▷ *n* **3** a squelching sound ▶ HISTORY imitative > **squelchy** *adj*

squib *n* **1** a firework that burns with a hissing noise before exploding **2 damp squib** something expected to be exciting or successful but turning out to be a disappointment ▶ HISTORY probably imitative of a light explosion

squid *n, pl* **squid** *or* **squids** a sea creature with ten tentacles and a long soft body ▶ HISTORY origin unknown

squiffy *adj* **-fier, -fiest** *Brit, informal* slightly drunk: *a bit squiffy* ▶ HISTORY origin unknown

squiggle *n* a wavy line ▶ HISTORY perhaps SQUIRM + WIGGLE > **squiggly** *adj*

squill *n* a Mediterranean plant of the lily family ▶ HISTORY Greek *skilla*

squint *vb* **1** to have eyes which face in different directions **2** to glance sideways ▷ *n* **3** an eye disorder in which one or both eyes turn inwards or outwards from the nose **4** *informal* a quick look; glance: *take a squint at the map* ▷ *adj* **5** *informal* not straight; crooked ▶ HISTORY short for *asquint*

squire *n* **1** a country gentleman in England, usually the main landowner in a country community **2** *informal, chiefly Brit* a term of address used by one man to another **3** *history* a knight's young attendant ▷ *vb* **squiring, squired 4** *old-fashioned* (of a man) to escort (a woman) ▶ HISTORY Old French *esquier*

squirm *vb* **1** to wriggle **2** to feel embarrassed or guilty ▷ *n* **3** a wriggling movement ▶ HISTORY imitative

squirrel *n* a small bushy-tailed animal that lives in trees ▶ HISTORY Greek *skiouros*, from *skia* shadow + *oura* tail

squirt *vb* **1** to force (a liquid) or (of a liquid) to be forced out of a narrow opening **2** to cover or spatter (a person or thing) with liquid in this way ▷ *n* **3** a jet of liquid **4** a squirting **5** *informal* a small or insignificant person ▶ HISTORY imitative

squish *vb* **1** to crush (something) with a soft squelching sound **2** to make a squelching sound ▷ *n* **3** a soft squelching sound ▶ HISTORY imitative > **squishy** *adj*

Sr 1 (after a name) senior **2** Señor **3** *chem* strontium

Sri Lankan *adj* **1** of Sri Lanka ▷ *n* **2** a person from Sri Lanka

SRN (formerly in Britain) State Registered Nurse

SS 1 an organization in the Nazi party that provided Hitler's bodyguard, security forces, and concentration-camp guards ▶ HISTORY German *Schutzstaffel* protection squad **2** steamship

St 1 Saint **2** Street

st. stone (in weight)

stab *vb* **stabbing, stabbed 1** to pierce with a sharp pointed instrument **2** (often foll. by *at*) to make a thrust (at); jab **3 stab someone in the back** to do harm to someone by betraying him or her ▷ *n* **4** a stabbing **5** a sudden, usually unpleasant, sensation: *a stab of jealousy* **6** *informal* an attempt: *you've got to have a stab at it* **7 stab in the back** an act of betrayal that harms a person ▶ HISTORY Middle English *stabbe* stab wound > **stabbing** *n*

stability *n* the quality of being stable: *the security and stability of married life*

stabilize *or* **-lise** *vb* **-lizing, -lized** *or* **-lising, -lised** to make or become stable or more stable > **stabilization** *or* **-lisation** *n*

stabilizer *or* **-liser** *n* **1** a device for stabilizing a child's bicycle, an aircraft, or a ship **2** a substance added to food to preserve its texture

stable¹ *n* **1** a building where horses are kept **2** an organization that breeds and trains racehorses **3** an organization that manages or trains several entertainers or athletes ▷ *vb* **-bling, -bled 4** to put or keep (a horse) in a stable ▶ HISTORY Latin *stabulum* shed

stable² *adj* **1** steady in position or balance; firm **2** lasting and not likely to experience any sudden changes: *a stable environment* **3** having a calm personality; not moody **4** *physics* (of an elementary particle) not subject to decay **5** *chem* (of a chemical compound) not easily decomposed ▶ HISTORY Latin *stabilis* steady

staccato (stak-**ah**-toe) *adj* **1** *music* (of notes) short and separate **2** consisting of short abrupt sounds: *the staccato sound of high-heels on the stairs* ▷ *adv* **3** in a staccato manner ▶ HISTORY Italian

stack *n* **1** a pile of things, one on top of the other **2** a large neat pile of hay or straw **3 stacks** a large amount: *there's still stacks for us to do* **4** same as

S

smokestack 5 an area in a computer memory for temporary storage ▷ *vb* **6** to place (things) in a stack **7** to load or fill (something) up with piles of objects: *Henry was watching her stack the dishwasher* **8** to control (a number of aircraft) waiting to land at an airport so that each flies at a different altitude ▸ HISTORY Old Norse *stakkr* haystack

stadium *n, pl* **-diums** *or* **-dia** a large sports arena with tiered rows of seats for spectators ▸ HISTORY Greek *stadion*

staff *n, pl for senses* 1 & 2 **staffs**; *for senses* 3 & 4 **staffs** *or* **staves 1** the people employed in a company, school, or organization **2** *mil* the officers appointed to assist a commander **3** a stick with some special use, such as a walking stick or an emblem of authority **4** *music* a set of five horizontal lines on which music is written and which, along with a clef, indicates pitch ▷ *vb* **5** to provide (a company, school, or organization) with a staff ▸ HISTORY Old English *stæf*

staff nurse *n* (in Britain) a qualified nurse ranking just below a sister or charge nurse

staff sergeant *n* *mil* a noncommissioned officer in an army or in the US Air Force or Marine Corps

staff turnover *n* *business* the number of workers employed by a firm in a given period to replace those who have left

stag *n* the adult male of a deer ▸ HISTORY Old English *stagga*

stag beetle *n* a beetle with large branched jaws

stage *n* **1** a step or period of development, growth, or progress **2** the platform in a theatre where actors perform **3 the stage** the theatre as a profession **4** the scene of an event or action **5** a part of a journey: *the last stage of his tour around France* **6** short for **stagecoach 7** *Brit & Austral* a division of a bus route for which there is a fixed fare ▷ *vb* **staging, staged 8** to present (a dramatic production) on stage: *to stage 'Hamlet'* **9** to organize and carry out (an event) ▸ HISTORY Old French *estage* position

stagecoach *n* a large four-wheeled horse-drawn vehicle formerly used to carry passengers and mail on a regular route

stage direction *n* an instruction to an actor, written into the script of a play

stage door *n* a door at a theatre leading backstage

stage fright *n* feelings of fear and nervousness felt by a person about to appear in front of an audience

stagehand *n* a person who sets the stage and moves props in a theatre

stage-manage *vb* **-managing, -managed** to arrange (an event) from behind the scenes

stage manager *n* a person who supervises the stage arrangements of a production at a theatre

stage-struck *adj* having a great desire to act

stage whisper *n* **1** a loud whisper from an actor, intended to be heard by the audience **2** any loud whisper that is intended to be overheard

stagflation *n* inflation combined with stagnant or falling output and employment ▸ HISTORY STAGNATION + INFLATION

stagger *vb* **1** to walk unsteadily **2** to amaze or shock (someone): *it staggered her that there was any liaison between them* **3** to arrange (events) so as not to happen at the same time: *staggered elections* ▷ *n* **4** a staggering ▸ HISTORY dialect *stacker* > **staggering** *adj* > **staggeringly** *adv*

staggers *n* a disease of horses and other domestic animals that causes staggering

stagnant *adj* **1** (of water) stale from not moving **2** unsuccessful or dull from lack of change or development ▸ HISTORY Latin *stagnans*

stagnate *vb* **-nating, -nated** to become inactive or unchanging: *people in old age only stagnate when they have no interests* > **stagnation** *n*

stagy *or US* **stagey** *adj* **stagier, stagiest** too theatrical or dramatic

staid *adj* serious, rather dull, and old-fashioned in behaviour or appearance ▸ HISTORY obsolete past participle of STAY

stain *vb* **1** to discolour (something) with marks that are not easily removed **2** to dye (something) with a lasting pigment ▷ *n* **3** a mark or discoloration that is not easily removed **4** an incident in someone's life that has damaged his or her reputation: *a stain on his character* **5** a liquid used to penetrate the surface of a material, such as wood, and colour it without covering up the surface or grain ▸ HISTORY Middle English *steynen*

stainless steel *n* a type of steel that does not rust, as it contains large amounts of chromium

stair *n* **1** one step in a flight of stairs **2** a series of steps: *he fled down the back stair* ▷ See also **stairs** ▸ HISTORY Old English *stæger*

staircase *n* a flight of stairs, usually with a handrail or banisters

stairs *pl n* a flight of steps going from one level to another, usually indoors

stairway *n* a staircase

stake¹ *n* **1** a stick or metal bar driven into the ground as part of a fence or as a support or marker **2 be burned at the stake** to be executed by being tied to a stake in the centre of a pile of wood that is then set on fire ▷ *vb* **staking, staked 3** to lay (a claim) to land or rights **4** to support (something, such as a plant) with a stake ▸ HISTORY Old English *staca* stake, post

stake² *n* **1** the money that a player must risk in order to take part in a gambling game or make a bet **2** an interest, usually financial, held in something: *a 50% stake in a new consortium* **3 at stake** at risk **4 stakes a** the money that a player has available for gambling **b** a prize in a race or contest **c** a horse race in which all owners of competing horses contribute to the prize ▷ *vb* **staking, staked 5** to risk (something, such as money) on a result **6** to give financial support to (a business) ▸ HISTORY origin unknown

stakeholder *n* **1** a person or group not owning shares in an enterprise but having an interest in its

S

operations, such as the employees, customers, or local community ▷ *adj* **2** relating to policies intended to allow people to participate in decisions made by enterprises in which they have a stake: *stakeholder economy*

stakeout *n* **1** *slang, chiefly US & Canad* a police surveillance of an area or house ▷ *vb* **stake out** **2** *slang, chiefly US & Canad* to keep an area or house under surveillance **3** to surround (a piece of land) with stakes

stalactite *n* an icicle-shaped mass of calcium carbonate hanging from the roof of a cave: formed by continually dripping water ▶ HISTORY Greek *stalaktos* dripping

stalagmite *n* a large pointed mass of calcium carbonate sticking up from the floor of a cave: formed by continually dripping water from a stalactite ▶ HISTORY Greek *stalagmos* dripping

stale *adj* **1** (esp. of food) no longer fresh, having being kept too long **2** (of air) stagnant and having an unpleasant smell **3** lacking in enthusiasm or ideas through overwork or lack of variety **4** uninteresting from having been done or seen too many times: *such achievements now seem stale today* **5** no longer new: *her war had become stale news* ▶ HISTORY probably from Old French *estale* motionless > **staleness** *n*

stalemate *n* **1** a chess position in which any of a player's moves would place his king in check: in this position the game ends in a draw **2** a situation in which further action by two opposing forces is impossible or will not achieve anything; deadlock ▶ HISTORY obsolete *stale* standing place + CHECKMATE

Stalinism *n* the policies associated with Joseph Stalin, general secretary of the Communist Party of the Soviet Union 1922–53, which resulted in rapid industrialization, state terror as a means of political control, and the abolition of collective leadership > **Stalinist** *n, adj*

stalk¹ *n* **1** the main stem of a plant **2** a stem that joins a leaf or flower to the main stem of a plant ▶ HISTORY probably from Old English *stalu* upright piece of wood

stalk² *vb* **1** to follow (an animal or person) quietly and secretly in order to catch or kill them **2** to pursue persistently and, sometimes, attack (a person with whom one is obsessed, often a celebrity) **3** to spread over (a place) in a menacing way: *danger stalked the streets* **4** to walk in an angry, arrogant, or stiff way ▶ HISTORY Old English *bestealcian* > **stalker** *n*

stalking-horse *n* something or someone used to hide a true purpose; pretext

stall¹ *n* **1** a small stand for the display and sale of goods **2** a compartment in a stable or shed for a single animal **3** any small room or compartment: *a shower stall* ▷ *vb* **4** to stop (a motor vehicle or its engine) or (of a motor vehicle or its engine) to stop, by incorrect use of the clutch or incorrect adjustment of the fuel mixture ▶ HISTORY Old English *steall* a place for standing

stall² *vb* to employ delaying tactics towards (someone); be evasive ▶ HISTORY Anglo-French *estale* bird used as a decoy

stallion *n* an uncastrated male horse, usually used for breeding ▶ HISTORY Old French *estalon*

stalls *n* **1** the seats on the ground floor of a theatre or cinema **2** (in a church) a row of seats, divided by armrests or a small screen, for the choir or clergy

stalwart (**stawl**-wart) *adj* **1** strong and sturdy **2** loyal and reliable ▷ *n* **3** a hard-working and loyal supporter: *local party stalwarts* ▶ HISTORY Old English *stǣlwirthe* serviceable

stamen *n* the part of a flower that produces pollen ▶ HISTORY Latin: the warp in an upright loom

stamina *n* energy and strength sustained while performing an activity over a long time ▶ HISTORY Latin: the threads of life spun out by the Fates, hence energy

stammer *vb* **1** to speak or say (something) with involuntary pauses or repetition, as a result of a speech disorder or through fear or nervousness ▷ *n* **2** a speech disorder characterized by involuntary repetitions and pauses ▶ HISTORY Old English *stamerian*

stamp *n* **1** a printed paper label attached to a piece of mail to show that the required postage has been paid **2** a token issued by a shop or business after a purchase that can be saved and exchanged for other goods sold by that shop or business **3** the action or an act of stamping **4** an instrument for stamping a design or words **5** a design, device, or mark that has been stamped **6** a characteristic feature: *the stamp of inevitability* **7** *Brit, informal* a national insurance contribution, formerly recorded by a stamp on an official card **8** type or class: *men of his stamp* ▷ *vb* **9** (often foll. by *on*) to bring (one's foot) down heavily **10** to walk with heavy or noisy footsteps **11** to characterize: *a performance that stamped him as a star* **12** **stamp on** to subdue or restrain: *all of which have stamped on dissent* **13** to impress or mark (a pattern or sign) on **14** to mark (something) with an official seal or device **15** to have a strong effect on: *a picture vividly stamped on memory* **16** to stick a stamp on (an envelope or parcel) ▶ HISTORY probably from Old English *stampian*

stampede *n* **1** a sudden rush of frightened animals or of a crowd ▷ *vb* **-peding, -peded** **2** to run away in a stampede ▶ HISTORY Spanish *estampar* to stamp

stamping ground *n* a favourite meeting place

stamp out *vb* **1** to put an end to (something) by force; suppress: *an attempt to stamp out democracy* **2** to put out by stamping: *I stamped out my cigarette*

stance *n* **1** an attitude towards a particular matter: *a tough stance in the trade talks* **2** the manner and position in which a person stands **3** *sport* the position taken when about to play the ball ▶ HISTORY Latin *stare* to stand

stanch (**stahnch**) *vb* same as **staunch²** ▶ HISTORY Old French *estanchier*

S

stanchion *n* a vertical pole or bar used as a support ▶ HISTORY Old French *estanchon*

stand *vb* **standing, stood** **1** to be upright **2** to rise to an upright position **3** to place (something) upright **4** *written* to be situated: *the property stands in a prime position* **5** to have a specified height when standing: *the structure stands sixty feet above the river* **6** to be in a specified position: *Turkey stands to gain handsomely* **7** to be in a specified state or condition: *how he stands in comparison to others* **8** to remain unchanged or valid: *the Conservatives were forced to let much of the legislation stand* **9 stand at** (of a score or an account) to be in the specified position: *now the total stands at nine* **10** to tolerate or bear: *Christopher can't stand him* **11** to survive: *stand the test of time* **12** (often foll. by *for*) to be a candidate: *to stand for president* **13** *informal* to buy: *to stand someone a drink* **14 stand a chance** to have a chance of succeeding **15 stand one's ground** to face a difficult situation bravely **16 stand trial** to be tried in a law court ▷ *n* **17** a stall or counter selling goods: *the hot dog stand* **18** a structure at a sports ground where people can sit or stand **19** the act or an instance of standing **20** a firmly held opinion: *its firm stand on sanctions* **21** *US & Austral* a place in a law court where a witness stands **22** a rack on which coats and hats may be hung **23** a small table or piece of furniture where articles may be placed or stored: *an umbrella stand* **24** an effort to defend oneself or one's beliefs against attack or criticism: *a last stand against superior forces* **25** *cricket* a long period at the wicket by two batsmen **26** See **one-night stand** ▷ See also **stand by**, **stand down**, etc. ▶ HISTORY Old English *standan*

standard *n* **1** a level of quality: *cuisine of a high standard* **2** an accepted example of something against which others are judged or measured: *the work was good by any standard* **3** a moral principle of behaviour **4** a flag of a nation or cause **5** an upright pole or beam used as a support: *a lamp standard* **6** a song that has remained popular for many years ▷ *adj* **7** of a usual, medium, or accepted kind: *a standard cost* **8** of recognized authority: *a standard reference book* **9** denoting pronunciations or grammar regarded as correct and acceptable by educated native speakers ▶ HISTORY Old French *estandart* gathering place

standard assessment tasks *pl n* (in Britain) national standardized tests for assessing school pupils

standard-bearer *n* **1** a leader of a movement or party **2** a person who carries a flag in battle or in a march

Standard English *n* the style of English that is regarded as correct and acceptable by educated native speakers

standard form *n* *maths* the expression of numbers as multiples of suitable powers of the base of the counting system and so not always employing the decimal point strictly between the integral and fractional parts of the number: 123.45 *can be written in standard form as* 1.2345×10^2

standardize *or* **-ise** *vb* **-izing, -ized** *or* **-ising, -ised** to make (things) standard: *to standardize the preparation process* > **standardization** *or* **-isation** *n*

standard lamp *n* a tall electric lamp that has a shade and stands on a base

standard of living *n* the level of comfort and wealth of a person, group, or country

standard of proof *n* *law* the degree of proof required for a case to be proved; in a criminal case, the standard is *beyond reasonable doubt*, while in a civil case, the standard is the lower *balance of probabilities*

standard time *n* the official local time of a region or country determined by the distance from Greenwich of a line of longitude passing through the area

stand by *vb* **1** to be available and ready to act if needed: *stand by for firing* **2** to be present as an onlooker or without taking any action: *the military police stood by watching idly* **3** to be faithful to: *his wife will stand by him* ▷ *n* **stand-by** **4** a person or thing that is ready for use or can be relied on in an emergency **5 on stand-by** ready for action or use ▷ *adj* **stand-by 6** not booked in advance but subject to availability: *stand-by planes*

stand down *vb* to resign or withdraw, often in favour of another

stand for *vb* **1** to represent: *AIDS stands for Acquired Immune Deficiency Syndrome* **2** to support and represent (an idea or a belief): *to stand for liberty and truth* **3** *informal* to tolerate or bear: *I won't stand for this!*

stand in *vb* **1** to act as a substitute: *she stood in for her father* ▷ *n* **stand-in 2** a person who acts as a substitute for another

standing *adj* **1** permanent, fixed, or lasting: *it was a standing joke* **2** used to stand in or on: *standing room only* **3** *athletics* (of a jump or the start of a race) begun from a standing position ▷ *n* **4** social or financial status or reputation: *her international standing* **5** *written* duration: *a friendship of at least ten years' standing*

standing committee *n* *Government* a permanent committee appointed to deal with a specified subject

standing order *n* **1** an instruction to a bank to pay a fixed amount to a person or organization at regular intervals **2** a rule or order governing the procedure of an organization

standoffish *adj* behaving in a formal and unfriendly way

stand out *vb* **1** to be more impressive or important than others of the same kind: *his passing ability stood out in this game* **2** to be noticeable because of looking different: *her long fair hair made her stand out from the rest* **3** to refuse to agree or comply: *a hero who stood out against foreign domination*

standpipe *n* *chiefly Brit* a temporary vertical pipe installed in a street and supplying water when household water supplies are cut off

standpoint *n* a point of view from which a matter is considered

S

standstill *n* a complete stoppage or halt: *all traffic came to a standstill*

stand to *vb* **1** *mil* to take up positions in order to defend against attack **2 stand to reason** to be obvious or logical: *it stands to reason you will play better*

stand up *vb* **1** to rise to one's feet **2** *informal* to fail to keep a date with (a boyfriend or girlfriend): *sometimes he would stand me up* **3** to be accepted as satisfactory or true: *the decision would not stand up in court* **4 stand up for** to support or defend **5 stand up to a** to confront or resist (someone) bravely **b** to withstand and endure (something, such as criticism) ▷ *adj* **stand-up 6** (of a comedian) telling jokes alone to an audience **7** done while standing: *a stand-up breakfast* **8** (of a fight or row) angry and unrestrained ▷ *n* **stand-up 9** stand-up comedy or a stand-up comedian

stank *vb* a past tense of **stink**

Stanley knife *n* *trademark* a type of knife with a thick metal handle with a short, very sharp, replaceable blade ▶ HISTORY after F. T. *Stanley*, businessman

stanza *n* *prosody* a verse of a poem ▶ HISTORY Italian: halting place

staphylococcus (staff-ill-oh-**kok**-uss) *n, pl* **-cocci** (-**kok**-eye) a bacterium occurring in clusters and including many species that cause disease ▶ HISTORY Greek *staphulē* bunch of grapes + *kokkos* berry

staple¹ *n* **1** a short length of wire bent into a square U-shape, used to fasten papers or secure things ▷ *vb* **-pling, -pled 2** to secure (things) with staples ▶ HISTORY Old English *stapol* prop

staple² *adj* **1** of prime importance; principal: *the staple diet of a country* ▷ *n* **2** something that forms a main part of the product, consumption, or trade of a region **3** a main constituent of anything: *the personal reflections which make up the staple of the book* ▶ HISTORY Middle Dutch *stapel* warehouse

stapler *n* a device used to fasten things together with a staple

star *n* **1** a planet or meteor visible in the clear night sky as a point of light **2** a hot gaseous mass, such as the sun, that radiates energy as heat and light, or in some cases as radio waves and X-rays. *Related adjectives:* **astral, sidereal, stellar 3 stars** same as **horoscope** (sense 1) **4** an emblem with five or more radiating points, often used as a symbol of rank or an award: *the RAC awarded the hotel three stars* **5** same as **asterisk 6** a famous person from the sports, acting, or music professions **7 see stars** to see flashes of light after a blow on the head ▷ *vb* **starring, starred 8** to feature (an actor or actress) or (of an actor or actress) to be featured as a star: *he's starred in dozens of films* **9** to mark (something) with a star or stars ▶ HISTORY Old English *steorra*

starboard *n* **1** the right side of an aeroplane or ship when facing forwards ▷ *adj* **2** of or on the starboard

starch *n* **1** a carbohydrate forming the main food element in bread, potatoes, and rice: in solution with water it is used to stiffen fabric **2** food containing a large amount of starch ▷ *vb* **3** to stiffen (cloth) with starch ▶ HISTORY Old English *sterced* stiffened

starchy *adj* **starchier, starchiest 1** of or containing starch **2** (of a person's behaviour) very formal and humourless

stardom *n* the status of a star in the entertainment or sport world

stare *vb* **staring, stared 1** (often foll. by *at*) to look at for a long time **2 stare one in the face** to be glaringly obvious ▷ *n* **3** a long fixed look ▶ HISTORY Old English *starian*

starfish *n, pl* **-fish** or **-fishes** a star-shaped sea creature with a flat body and five limbs

star fruit *n* same as **carambola**

stark *adj* **1** harsh, unpleasant, and plain: *a stark choice* **2** grim, desolate, and lacking any beautiful features: *the stark landscapes* **3** utter; absolute: *in stark contrast* ▷ *adv* **4** completely: *stark staring bonkers* ▶ HISTORY Old English *stearc* stiff > **starkly** *adv* > **starkness** *n*

stark-naked *adj* completely naked. Also (informal): **starkers** ▶ HISTORY Middle English *stert naket*, literally: tail naked

starlet *n* a young actress who has the potential to become a star

starlight *n* the light that comes from the stars

starling *n* a common songbird with shiny blackish feathers and a short tail ▶ HISTORY Old English *stærlinc*

Star of David *n* a symbol of Judaism, consisting of a star formed by two interlaced equilateral triangles

starry *adj* **-rier, -riest 1** (of a sky or night) full of or lit by stars **2** of or like a star or stars: *a starry cast*

starry-eyed *adj* full of unrealistic hopes and dreams; naive

Stars and Stripes *n* the national flag of the United States of America

star sign *n* *astrol* the sign of the zodiac under which a person was born

star-studded *adj* featuring many well-known performers: *a star-studded premiere*

start *vb* **1** to begin (something or to do something): *to start a war; we've already started building* **2** to set or be set in motion: *he started the van* **3** to make a sudden involuntary movement from fright or surprise; jump **4** to establish; set up: *to start a state lottery* **5** to support (someone) in the first part of a career or activity **6** *Brit, informal* to begin quarrelling or causing a disturbance: *don't start with me* **7 to start with** in the first place ▷ *n* **8** the first part of something **9** the place or time at which something begins **10** a signal to begin, such as in a race **11** a lead or advantage, either in time or distance, in a competitive activity: *he had an hour's start on me* **12** a slight involuntary movement from fright or surprise: *I awoke with a start* **13** an opportunity to enter a career or begin a project **14 for a start** in the first place ▸ HISTORY Old English *styrtan*

starter *n* **1** *chiefly Brit* the first course of a meal **2 for starters** *slang* in the first place **3** a device for starting an internal-combustion engine **4** a person who signals the start of a race **5** a competitor in a race or contest **6 under starter's orders** (of competitors in a race) waiting for the signal to start

startle *vb* **-tling, -tled** to slightly surprise or frighten someone ▸ HISTORY Old English *steartlian* to kick, struggle > **startling** *adj*

start up *vb* **1** to come or cause (something, such as a business) to come into being; found **2** to set (something) in motion: *she started up the car*

starve *vb* **starving, starved 1** to die from lack of food **2** to deliberately prevent (a person or animal) from having any food **3** *informal* to be very hungry: *we're both starving* **4 starve of** to deprive (someone) of something needed: *the heart is starved of oxygen* **5 starve into** to force someone into a specified state by starving: *an attempt to starve him into submission* ▸ HISTORY Old English *steorfan* to die > **starvation** *n*

stash *informal vb* **1** (often foll. by *away*) to store (money or valuables) in a secret place for safekeeping ▷ *n* **2** a secret store, usually of illegal drugs, or the place where this is hidden ▸ HISTORY origin unknown

state *n* **1** the condition or circumstances of a person or thing **2** *physics* the structure, form, or constitution of something: *a solid state* **3** a sovereign political power or community **4** the territory of such a community **5** the sphere of power in such a community: *matters of state* **6** (often cap) one of a number of areas or communities having their own governments and forming a federation under a sovereign government, such as in the US or Australia **7** (often cap) the government, civil service, and armed forces **8 in a state** *informal* in an emotional or very worried condition **9 lie in state** (of a body) to be placed on public view before burial **10 state of affairs** circumstances or condition: *this wonderful state of affairs* **11** grand and luxurious lifestyle, as enjoyed by royalty, aristocrats, or the wealthy: *living in state* ▷ *adj* **12** controlled or financed by a state: *state ownership* **13** of or concerning the State: *state secrets* **14** involving ceremony: *a state visit* ▷ *vb* **stating, stated 15** to express (something) in words ▸ HISTORY Latin *stare* to stand

State Enrolled Nurse *n* (in Britain) a nurse who has completed a two-year training course

statehouse *n NZ* a rented house built by the government

stateless *adj* not belonging to any country: *stateless refugees*

stately *adj* **-lier, -liest** having a dignified, impressive, and graceful appearance or manner: *the Rolls-Royce approached him at a stately speed* > **stateliness** *n*

statement *n* **1** something stated, usually a formal prepared announcement or reply **2** an account prepared by a bank at regular intervals for a client to show all credits and debits and the balance at the end of the period **3** an account containing a summary of bills or invoices and showing the total amount due **4** the act of stating

statement of claim *n law* (in a civil case) the formal written statement made by a plaintiff setting out his or her allegations and the remedy sought

State Registered Nurse *n* (formerly in Britain) a nurse who has completed an extensive three-year training course

stateroom *n* **1** a private room on a ship **2** *chiefly Brit* a large room in a palace, etc. used on ceremonial occasions

States *pl n* **the States** *informal* the United States of America

state school *n* a school funded by the state, in which education is free

statesman *n, pl* **-men** an experienced and respected political leader > **statesmanship** *n*

static *adj* **1** not active, changing, or moving; stationary **2** *physics* (of a weight, force, or pressure) acting but causing no movement **3** *physics* of forces that do not produce movement ▷ *n* **4** hissing or crackling or a speckled picture caused by interference in the reception of radio or television transmissions **5** electric sparks or crackling produced by friction ▸ HISTORY Greek *statikos* causing to stand

statics *n* the branch of mechanics concerned with the forces producing a state of equilibrium

station *n* **1** a place along a route or line at which a bus or train stops to pick up passengers or goods **2** the headquarters of an organization such as the police or fire service **3** a building with special equipment for some particular purpose: *power station; a filling station* **4** a television or radio channel **5** *mil* a place of duty **6** position in society: *he had ideas above his station* **7** *Austral & NZ* a large sheep or cattle farm **8** the place or position where a person is assigned to stand: *every man stood at his station* ▷ *vb* **9** to assign (someone) to a station ▸ HISTORY Latin *statio* a standing still

stationary *adj* not moving: *a line of stationary traffic* ▸ HISTORY Latin *stationarius*

stationer *n* a person or shop selling stationery ▸ HISTORY Medieval Latin *stationarius* a person having a regular station, hence a shopkeeper

stationery *n* writing materials, such as paper, envelopes, and pens

stationmaster *n* the senior official in charge of a railway station

Stations of the Cross *pl n RC Church* **1** a series of 14 crosses with pictures or carvings, arranged around the walls of a church, to commemorate

14 stages in Christ's journey to Calvary **2** a series of 14 prayers relating to each of these stages

station wagon *n US, Austral & NZ* an estate car

statistic *n* a numerical fact collected and classified systematically > **statistical** *adj* > **statistically** *adv* > **statistician** *n*

statistics *n* **1** the science dealing with the collection, classification, and interpretation of numerical information ⊳ *pl n* **2** numerical information which has been collected, classified, and interpreted ▶ HISTORY originally: science dealing with facts of a state, from New Latin *statisticus* concerning state affairs

statuary *n* statues collectively

statue *n* a sculpture of a human or animal figure, usually life-size or larger ▶ HISTORY Latin *statuere* to set up

statuesque (stat-yoo-**esk**) *adj written* (of a woman) tall and well-proportioned; like a classical statue

statuette *n* a small statue

stature *n* **1** height and size of a person **2** the reputation of a person or their achievements: *a batsman of international stature* **3** moral or intellectual distinction ▶ HISTORY Latin *stare* to stand

status *n* **1** a person's position in society **2** the esteem in which people hold a person: *priests feel they have lost some of their status in society* **3** the legal or official standing or classification of a person or country: *the status of refugees; Ireland's non-aligned status* **4** degree of importance ▶ HISTORY Latin: posture

status quo *n* the existing state of affairs ▶ HISTORY literally: the state in which

status symbol *n* a possession regarded as a mark of social position or wealth

statute *n* **1** a law made by a government and expressed in a formal document **2** a permanent rule made by a company or other institution ▶ HISTORY Latin *statuere* to set up, decree

statute law *n* **1** a law made by a government **2** such laws collectively

statutory *adj* **1** required or authorized by law **2** (of an offence) declared by law to be punishable

staunch¹ *adj* strong and loyal: *a staunch supporter* ▶ HISTORY Old French *estanche* > **staunchly** *adv*

staunch² or **stanch** *vb* to stop the flow of (blood) from someone's body

stave *n* **1** one of the long strips of wood joined together to form a barrel or bucket **2** a stick carried as a symbol of office **3** a verse of a poem **4** *music* same as **staff** ⊳ *vb* **staving, stove 5 stave in** to burst a hole in (something) ▶ HISTORY from *staves*, plural of STAFF

stave off *vb* **staving, staved** to delay (something) for a short time: *to stave off political rebellion*

staves *n* a plural of **staff, stave**

stay¹ *vb* **1** to continue or remain in a place, position, or condition: *to stay away; to stay inside* **2** to lodge as a guest or visitor temporarily: *we stay with friends*

3 *Scot & S African* to reside permanently; live **4** to endure (something testing or difficult): *you have stayed the course this long* ⊳ *n* **5** the period spent in one place **6** the postponement of an order of a court of law: *a stay of execution* ▶ HISTORY Old French *ester*

stay² *n* something that supports or steadies something, such as a prop or buttress ▶ HISTORY Old French *estaye*

stay³ *n* a rope or chain supporting a ship's mast or funnel ▶ HISTORY Old English *stæg*

stay-at-home *adj* **1** (of a person) enjoying a quiet, settled, and unadventurous life ⊳ *n* **2** a stay-at-home person

staying power *n* endurance to complete something undertaken; stamina

STD 1 sexually transmitted disease **2** *Brit, Austral & S African* subscriber trunk dialling **3** *NZ* subscriber toll dialling

stead *n* **1 stand someone in good stead** to be useful to someone in the future **2** *rare* the function or position that should be taken by another: *I cannot let you rule in my stead* ▶ HISTORY Old English *stede*

steadfast *adj* dedicated and unwavering > **steadfastly** *adv* > **steadfastness** *n*

steady *adj* **steadier, steadiest 1** firm and not shaking **2** without much change or variation: *we're on a steady course* **3** continuous: *a steady decline* **4** not easily excited; sober **5** regular; habitual: *the steady drinking of alcohol* ⊳ *vb* **steadies, steadying, steadied 6** to make or become steady ⊳ *adv* **7** in a steady manner **8 go steady** *informal* to date one person regularly ⊳ *n, pl* **steadies 9** *informal* one's regular boyfriend or girlfriend ⊳ *interj* **10** a warning to keep calm or be careful ▶ HISTORY from *stead* > **steadily** *adv* > **steadiness** *n*

steady state *n physics* the condition of a system when all or most changes or disturbances have been eliminated from it

steak *n* **1** a lean piece of beef for grilling or frying **2** a cut of beef for braising or stewing **3** a thick slice of pork, veal, or fish ▶ HISTORY Old Norse *steik* roast

steakhouse *n* a restaurant that specializes in steaks

steal *vb* **stealing, stole, stolen 1** to take (something) from someone without permission or unlawfully **2** to use (someone else's ideas or work) without acknowledgment **3** to move quietly and carefully, not wanting to be noticed: *my father stole up behind her* **4 steal the show** (of a performer) to draw the audience's attention to oneself and away from the other performers **5** to obtain or do (something) stealthily: *I stole a glance behind* ⊳ *n* **6** *US, Canad & NZ, informal* something acquired easily or at little cost ▶ HISTORY Old English *stelan*

stealth *n* **1** moving carefully and quietly, so as to avoid being seen **2** cunning or underhand behaviour ▶ HISTORY Old English *stelan* to steal > **stealthy** *adj* > **stealthily** *adv*

stealth tax n Brit & Austral an indirect tax, such as a tax on fuel or pension plans, esp. one of which people are unaware or one that is felt to be unfair

steam n **1** the vapour into which water changes when boiled **2** the mist formed when such vapour condenses in the atmosphere **3** informal power, energy, or speed **4 let off steam** informal to release pent-up energy or feelings **5 pick up steam** informal to gather momentum ▷ adj **6** operated, heated, or powered by steam: a steam train ▷ vb **7** to give off steam **8** (of a vehicle) to move by steam power **9** informal to proceed quickly and often forcefully **10** to cook (food) in steam **11** to treat (something) with steam, such as in cleaning or pressing clothes **12 steam open** or **off** to use steam in order to open or remove (something): let me steam open this letter ▶ HISTORY Old English stēam

steam engine n an engine worked by steam

steamer n **1** a boat or ship driven by steam engines **2** a container with holes in the bottom, used to cook food by steam

steam iron n an electric iron that uses steam to take creases out of clothes

steamroller n **1** a steam-powered vehicle with heavy rollers used for flattening road surfaces during road-making ▷ vb **2** to make (someone) do what one wants by overpowering force

steamy adj **steamier, steamiest 1** full of steam **2** informal (of books, films, etc.) erotic

steatite (stee-a-tite) n same as **soapstone** ▶ HISTORY Greek stear fat

steed n archaic or literary a horse ▶ HISTORY Old English stēda stallion

steel n **1** an alloy of iron and carbon, often with small quantities of other elements **2** a steel rod used for sharpening knives **3** courage and mental toughness ▷ vb **4** to prepare (oneself) for coping with something unpleasant: he had steeled himself to accept the fact ▶ HISTORY Old English stēli > **steely** adj

steel band n music a band of people playing on metal drums, popular in the West Indies

steel drum n a drum made from the head of an oil drum, hammered or embossed to create a certain note, played in a steel band. Also called: **steel pan**

steel wool n a mass of fine steel fibres, used for cleaning metal surfaces

steelworks n a factory where steel is made > **steelworker** n

steep¹ adj **1** having a sharp slope **2** informal (of a fee, price, or demand) unreasonably high; excessive ▶ HISTORY Old English stēap > **steeply** adv > **steepness** n

steep² vb **1** to soak or be soaked in a liquid in order to soften or cleanse **2 steeped in** filled with: an industry steeped in tradition ▶ HISTORY Old English stēpan

steeple n a tall ornamental tower on a church roof ▶ HISTORY Old English stēpel

steeplechase n **1** a horse race over a course with fences to be jumped **2** a track race in which the runners have to leap hurdles and a water jump ▷ vb **-chasing, -chased 3** to race in a steeplechase

■ **WORD HISTORY**
■ A 'steeplechase' was originally a horse race
■ across country using a distant church steeple
■ as the landmark to aim for as the finishing
■ point of the race.

steeplejack n a person who repairs steeples and chimneys

steer¹ vb **1** to direct the course of (a vehicle or vessel) with a steering wheel or rudder **2** to direct the movements or course of (a person, conversation, or activity) **3** to follow (a specified course): the Dutch government steered a middle course **4 steer clear of** to avoid ▶ HISTORY Old English stīeran

steer² n a castrated male ox or bull ▶ HISTORY Old English stēor

steerage n **1** the cheapest accommodation on a passenger ship **2** steering

steering committee n a committee set up to prepare and arrange topics to be discussed, and the order of business, for a government, etc.

steering wheel n a wheel turned by the driver of a vehicle in order to change direction

stein (stine) n an earthenware beer mug ▶ HISTORY German Stein, literally: stone

stela (steal-a) or **stele** (steal-ee) n, pl **stelae** (steal-ee) or **steles** an upright stone slab or column decorated with figures or inscriptions, common in prehistoric times ▶ HISTORY Greek stēlē

stellar adj **1** relating to the stars **2** informal outstanding or immense: stellar profits ▶ HISTORY Latin stella star

stem¹ n **1** the long thin central part of a plant **2** a stalk that bears a flower, fruit, or leaf **3** the long slender part of anything, such as a wineglass **4** linguistics the form of a word that remains after removal of all inflectional endings ▷ vb **stemming, stemmed 5 stem from** originate from: this tradition stems from pre-Christian times ▶ HISTORY Old English stemn

stem² vb **stemming, stemmed** to stop or hinder the spread of (something): to stem the flow of firearms ▶ HISTORY Old Norse stemma

stem-and-leaf-diagram n a histogram in which the data points in each class interval are listed in order

stem cell n histology an undifferentiated embryonic cell that gives rise to specialized cells, such as blood, bone, etc.

stench n a strong and very unpleasant smell ▶ HISTORY Old English stenc

stencil n **1** a thin sheet with a cut-out pattern through which ink or paint passes to form the pattern on the surface below **2** a design or letters made in this way ▷ vb **-cilling, -cilled** or US **-ciling, -ciled 3** to make (a design or letters) with a stencil ▶ HISTORY Old French estenceler to decorate brightly

Sten gun n a light sub-machine-gun ▶ HISTORY S & T (initials of the inventors) + -en, as in Bren gun

S

stenographer n US & Canad a shorthand typist ▶ HISTORY Greek *stenos* narrow + *graphein* to write

stent n a surgical implant used to keep an artery open

stentorian adj (of the voice) very loud: *a stentorian tone* ▶ HISTORY after *Stentor*, a herald in Greek mythology

step n 1 the act of moving and setting down one's foot, such as when walking 2 the distance covered by such a movement 3 the sound made by such a movement 4 one of a sequence of foot movements that make up a dance 5 one of a sequence of actions taken in order to achieve a goal 6 a degree or rank in a series or scale 7 a flat surface for placing the foot on when going up or down 8 manner of walking: *he moved with a purposeful step* 9 **steps a** a flight of stairs, usually out of doors **b** same as **stepladder** 10 a short easily travelled distance: *Mexico and Brazil were only a step away* 11 **break step** to stop marching in step 12 **in step a** marching or dancing in time or at the same pace as other people **b** informal in agreement: *in step with the West on this issue* 13 **out of step a** not marching or dancing in time or at the same pace as other people **b** informal not in agreement: *out of step with the political mood* 14 **step by step** gradually 15 **take steps** to do what is necessary (to achieve something) 16 **watch one's step a** informal to behave with caution **b** to walk carefully ▷ vb **stepping, stepped** 17 to move by taking a step, such as in walking 18 to walk a short distance: *please step this way* 19 **step into** to enter (a situation) apparently without difficulty: *she stepped into a life of luxury* ▷ See also **step down, step in**, etc. ▶ HISTORY Old English *stepe, stæpe*

stepbrother n a son of one's stepmother or stepfather

stepchild n, pl **-children** a stepson or stepdaughter

stepdaughter n a daughter of one's husband or wife by an earlier relationship

step down vb informal to resign from a position

step-down transformer n electronics a transformer that reduces voltage

stepfather n a man who has married one's mother after the death or divorce of one's father

stephanotis (stef-fan-**note**-iss) n a tropical climbing shrub with sweet-smelling white flowers ▶ HISTORY Greek: fit for a crown

step in vb informal to intervene (in a quarrel or difficult situation)

stepladder n a small folding portable ladder with a supporting frame

stepmother n a woman who has married one's father after the death or divorce of one's mother

step-parent n a stepfather or stepmother

steppes pl n geog wide grassy plains without trees ▶ HISTORY Old Russian *step* lowland

stepping stone n 1 one of a series of stones acting as footrests for crossing a stream 2 a stage in a person's progress towards a goal: *it was a big stepping stone in his career*

stepsister n a daughter of one's stepmother or stepfather

stepson n a son of one's husband or wife by an earlier relationship

step up vb informal to increase (something) by stages; accelerate

step-up transformer n electronics a transformer that raises voltage

stereo adj 1 (of a sound system) using two or more separate microphones to feed two or more loudspeakers through separate channels ▷ n, pl **stereos** 2 a music system in which sound is directed through two speakers 3 sound broadcast or played in stereo

stereophonic adj same as **stereo** (sense 1) ▶ HISTORY Greek *stereos* solid + *phōnē* sound

stereoscopic adj having a three-dimensional effect: *stereoscopic vision*

stereotype n 1 a set of characteristics or a fixed idea considered to represent a particular kind of person 2 an idea or convention that has grown stale through fixed usage ▷ vb **-typing, -typed** 3 to form a standard image or idea of (a type of person) ▶ HISTORY Greek *stereos* solid + TYPE

sterile adj 1 free from germs 2 unable to produce offspring 3 (of plants) not producing or bearing seeds 4 lacking inspiration or energy; unproductive ▶ HISTORY Latin *sterilis* > **sterility** n

sterilize or **-lise** vb **-lizing, -lized** or **-lising, -lised** to make sterile > **sterilization** or **-lisation** n

sterling n 1 British money: *sterling fell by almost a cent* ▷ adj 2 genuine and reliable; first-class: *he has a reputation for sterling honesty* ▶ HISTORY probably Old English *steorra* star, referring to a small star on early Norman pennies

sterling silver n 1 an alloy containing at least 92.5 per cent of silver 2 articles made of sterling silver

stern[1] adj 1 strict and serious: *he's a very stern taskmaster* 2 difficult and often unpleasant: *the stern demands of the day* 3 (of a facial expression) severe and disapproving ▶ HISTORY Old English *styrne* > **sternly** adv

stern[2] n the rear part of a boat or ship ▶ HISTORY Old Norse *stjörn* steering

sternum n, pl **-na** or **-nums** a long flat bone in the front of the body, to which the collarbone and most of the ribs are attached ▶ HISTORY Greek *sternon*

steroid n biochem an organic compound containing a carbon ring system, such as sterols and many hormones

sterol n biochem a natural insoluble alcohol such as cholesterol and ergosterol ▶ HISTORY shortened from *cholesterol, ergosterol*, etc.

stertorous adj (of breathing) laboured and noisy ▶ HISTORY Latin *stertere* to snore

stet vb **stetting, stetted** 1 used as an instruction to indicate to a printer that certain deleted matter is to be kept 2 to mark (matter) in this way ▶ HISTORY Latin, literally: let it stand

S

stethoscope *n med* an instrument for listening to the sounds made inside the body, consisting of a hollow disc that transmits the sound through hollow tubes to earpieces ▸ **HISTORY** Greek *stēthos* breast + *skopein* to look at

Stetson *n trademark* a felt hat with a broad brim and high crown, worn mainly by cowboys ▸ **HISTORY** after John *Stetson*, American hat maker

stevedore *n chiefly US* a person employed to load or unload ships ▸ **HISTORY** Spanish *estibador* a packer

stew *n* **1** a dish of meat, fish, or other food, cooked slowly in a closed pot **2 in a stew** *informal* in a troubled or worried state ▷ *vb* **3** to cook by long slow simmering in a closed pot **4** *informal* (of a person) to be too hot **5** to cause (tea) to become bitter or (of tea) to become bitter through infusing for too long **6 stew in one's own juice** to suffer, without help, the results of one's actions ▸ **HISTORY** Middle English *stuen* to take a very hot bath

steward *n* **1** a person who looks after passengers and serves meals on a ship or aircraft **2** an official who helps to supervise a public event, such as a race **3** a person who administers someone else's property **4** a person who manages the eating arrangements, staff, or service at a club or hotel **5** See **shop steward** ▷ *vb* **6** to act as a steward (of) ▸ **HISTORY** Old English *stigweard* hall keeper

stewardess *n* a female steward on an aircraft or ship

stewardship *n* the responsibility of looking after something, such as property

stick¹ *n* **1** a small thin branch of a tree **2 a** a long thin piece of wood **b** such a piece of wood shaped for a special purpose: *a walking stick; a hockey stick* **3** a piece of something shaped like a stick: *a stick of cinnamon* **4** *slang* verbal abuse, criticism: *they gave me a lot of stick* **5 the sticks** a country area considered backward or unsophisticated: *places out in the sticks* **6 sticks** pieces of furniture: *these few sticks are all I have* **7** *informal* a person: *not a bad old stick* **8 get hold of the wrong end of the stick** to misunderstand a situation or an explanation completely ▸ **HISTORY** Old English *sticca*

stick² *vb* **sticking, stuck 1** to push (a pointed object) or (of a pointed object) to be pushed into another object **2** to fasten (something) in position by pins, nails, or glue: *she just stuck the label on* **3** to extend beyond something else; protrude: *he stuck his head out of the door* **4** *informal* to place (something) in a specified position: *stick it in the oven* **5** to fasten or be fastened by or as if by an adhesive **6** to come or be brought to a standstill: *stuck in a rut; two army lorries stuck behind us* **7** to remain for a long time: *the room that sticks in my mind the most* **8** *slang, chiefly Brit* to tolerate; abide: *you couldn't stick it for more than two days* **9** (in the Caribbean) to hesitate or waste time **10 be stuck** *informal* to be at a loss; to be baffled or puzzled: *I'm stuck; stuck for words* ▷ See also **stick around** ▸ **HISTORY** Old English *stician*

stick around *vb informal* to remain in a place, often when waiting for something

sticker *n* a small piece of paper with a picture or writing on it that can be stuck to a surface

sticking plaster *n* a piece of adhesive material used for covering slight wounds

stick insect *n* a tropical insect with a long thin body and legs, which looks like a twig

stick-in-the-mud *n informal* a person who is unwilling to try anything new or do anything exciting

stickleback *n* a small fish with sharp spines along its back ▸ **HISTORY** Old English *sticel* prick, sting + BACK

stickler *n* a person who insists on something: *a stickler for punctuality*

stick-up *n slang, chiefly US* a robbery at gunpoint; hold-up

stick up for *vb informal* to support or defend (oneself, another person, or a principle)

sticky *adj* **stickier, stickiest 1** covered with a substance that sticks to other things: *sticky little fingers* **2** intended to stick to a surface: *sticky labels* **3** *informal* difficult or painful: *a sticky meeting* **4** (of weather) unpleasantly warm and humid > **stickiness** *n*

stiff *adj* **1** firm and not easily bent **2** moving with pain or difficulty: *stiff and aching joints* **3** not moving easily: *the door is stiff* **4** difficult or severe: *a stiff challenge; stiff penalties* **5** formal and not relaxed **6** fairly firm in consistency; thick **7** powerful: *a stiff breeze* **8** (of a drink) containing a lot of alcohol ▷ *n* **9** *slang* a corpse ▷ *adv* **10** completely or utterly: *I was bored stiff* ▸ **HISTORY** Old English *stif* > **stiffly** *adv* > **stiffness** *n*

stiffen *vb* to make or become stiff or stiffer

stiff-necked *adj* proud and stubborn

stifle *vb* **-fling, -fled 1** to stop oneself from expressing (a yawn or cry) **2** to stop (something) from continuing: *the new leadership stifled all internal debate* **3** to feel discomfort and difficulty in breathing **4** to kill (someone) by preventing him or her from breathing ▸ **HISTORY** probably from Old French *estouffer* to smother

stifling *adj* uncomfortably hot and stuffy

stigma *n, pl* **stigmas** *or* **stigmata 1** a mark of social disgrace: *a stigma attached to being redundant* **2** *bot* the part of a flower that receives pollen **3 stigmata** Christianity marks resembling the wounds of the crucified Christ, believed to appear on the bodies of certain people ▸ **HISTORY** Greek: brand

stigmatize *or* **-tise** *vb* **-tizing, -tized** *or* **-tising, -tised** to regard as being shameful

stile *n* a set of steps in a wall or fence to allow people, but not animals, to pass over ▸ **HISTORY** Old English *stigel*

stiletto *n, pl* **-tos 1** Also called: **spike heel, stiletto heel** a high narrow heel on a woman's shoe or a shoe with such a heel **2** a small dagger with a slender tapered blade ▸ **HISTORY** Italian: little dagger

S

still¹ *adv* **1** continuing now or in the future as in the past: *she still loved the theatre* **2** up to this or that time; yet **3** even or yet: *still more pressure on the government* **4** even then; nevertheless: *the baby has been fed and still cries* **5** quietly or without movement: *keep still* ▷ *adj* **6** motionless; stationary **7** undisturbed; silent and calm **8** (of a soft drink) not fizzy ▷ *n* **9** poetic silence or tranquillity: *the still of night* **10** a still photograph from a film ▷ *vb* **11** to make or become quiet or calm **12** to relieve or end: *Fowler stilled his conscience* ▸ HISTORY Old English *stille* > **stillness** *n*

still² *n* an apparatus for distilling spirits ▸ HISTORY Latin *stilla* a drip

stillborn *adj* **1** (of a baby) dead at birth **2** (of an idea or plan) completely unsuccessful > **stillbirth** *n*

still life *n, pl* **still lifes 1** a painting or drawing of objects such as fruit or flowers **2** this kind of painting or drawing

stilt *n* **1** either of a pair of long poles with footrests for walking raised from the ground **2** a long post or column used with others to support a building above ground level ▸ HISTORY Middle English *stilte*

stilted *adj* (of speech, writing, or behaviour) formal or pompous; not flowing continuously or naturally

Stilton *n* trademark a strong-flavoured blue-veined cheese ▸ HISTORY named after *Stilton*, Cambridgeshire

stimulant *n* **1** a drug, food, or drink that makes the body work faster, increases heart rate, and makes sleeping difficult **2** any stimulating thing ▷ *adj* **3** stimulating

stimulate *vb* **-lating, -lated 1** to encourage to start or progress further: *a cut in interest rates should help stimulate economic recovery* **2** to fill (a person) with ideas or enthusiasm: *books satisfy a part of the intellect that needs to be stimulated* **3** *physiol* to excite (a nerve or organ) with a stimulus ▸ HISTORY Latin *stimulare* > **stimulation** *n*

stimulus (**stim**-myew-luss) *n, pl* **-li** (-lie) **1** something that acts as an incentive to (someone) **2** something, such as a drug or electrical impulse, that is capable of causing a response in a person or an animal ▸ HISTORY Latin: a cattle goad

sting *vb* **stinging, stung 1** (of certain animals and plants) to inflict a wound on (someone) by the injection of poison **2** to cause (someone) to feel a sharp physical pain: *her hand was stinging* **3** to offend or upset (someone) with a critical remark: *I was stung by what he said* **4** to provoke (a response) by angering: *the consulate would be stung into convulsive action* **5** *informal* to cheat (someone) by overcharging ▷ *n* **6** a skin wound caused by stinging **7** pain caused by or as if by a sting **8** a mental pain: *the sting of memory* **9** the sharp pointed organ of certain animals or plants used to inject poison **10** *slang* a deceptive trick **11** *slang* a trap set up by the police to entice a person to commit a crime, thereby producing evidence ▸ HISTORY Old English *stingan* > **stinging** *adj*

stinging nettle *n* same as **nettle** (sense 1)

stingray *n* a flat fish with a jagged whiplike tail capable of inflicting painful wounds

stingy *adj* **-gier, -giest** very mean ▸ HISTORY perhaps from *stinge*, dialect variant of STING > **stinginess** *n*

stink *n* **1** a strong unpleasant smell **2** **make** or **create** or **kick up a stink** *slang* to make a fuss ▷ *vb* **stinking, stank** or **stunk; stunk 3** to give off a strong unpleasant smell **4** *slang* to be thoroughly bad or unpleasant: *the script stinks, the casting stinks* ▸ HISTORY Old English *stincan* > **stinky** *adj*

stink bomb *n* a small glass globe used by practical jokers: it releases a liquid with a strong unpleasant smell when broken

stinker *n* *slang* a difficult or very unpleasant person or thing

stinking *adj* **1** having a strong unpleasant smell **2** *informal* unpleasant or disgusting ▷ *adv* **3** **stinking rich** *informal* very wealthy

stink out *vb* **1** to drive (people) away by a foul smell **2** *Brit & NZ* to cause (a place) to stink: *I won't have it stinking the car out!*

stint *vb* **1** to be miserly with (something): *don't stint on paper napkins* ▷ *n* **2** a given amount of work ▸ HISTORY Old English *styntan* to blunt

stipend (**sty**-pend) *n* a regular salary or allowance, esp. that paid to a member of the clergy ▸ HISTORY Latin *stipendium* tax > **stipendiary** *adj*

stipple *vb* **-pling, -pled** to draw, engrave, or paint (something) using dots or flecks ▸ HISTORY Dutch *stippelen*

stipulate *vb* **-lating, -lated** to specify (something) as a condition of an agreement ▸ HISTORY Latin *stipulari* > **stipulation** *n*

stir¹ *vb* **stirring, stirred 1** to mix up (a liquid) by moving a spoon or stick around in it **2** *written* to move slightly **3** **stir from** to depart from (one's usual or preferred place) **4** to get up after sleeping **5** *written* to excite or move (someone) emotionally **6** to move (oneself) quickly or vigorously; exert (oneself) **7** to wake up: *to stir someone from sleep* ▷ *n* **8** a stirring **9** a strong reaction, usually of excitement: *she created a stir wherever she went* ▷ See also **stir up** ▸ HISTORY Old English *styrian*

stir² *n* chiefly US, slang prison: *in stir* ▸ HISTORY Romany *stariben* prison

stir-crazy *adj* *slang* mentally disturbed as a result of being in prison

stir-fry *vb* **-fries, -frying, -fried 1** to cook (food) quickly by stirring it in a wok or frying pan over a high heat ▷ *n, pl* **-fries 2** a dish cooked in this way

stirrer *n* *informal* a person who deliberately causes trouble

stirrup *n* a metal loop attached to a saddle for supporting a rider's foot ▸ HISTORY Old English *stig* step + *rāp* rope

stirrup pump *n* a hand-operated pump, the base of which is placed in a bucket of water: used in fighting fires

stir up *vb* **1** to cause (leaves or dust) to rise up and swirl around **2** to set (something) in motion: *that fact has stirred up resentment*

S

stitch n **1** a link made by drawing a thread through material with a needle **2** a loop of yarn formed around a needle or hook in knitting or crocheting **3** a particular kind of stitch **4** informal a link of thread joining the edges of a wound together **5** a sharp pain in the side caused by running or exercising **6 in stitches** informal laughing uncontrollably **7 not a stitch** informal no clothes at all ▷ vb **8** to sew or fasten (something) with stitches ▶ HISTORY Old English stice sting > **stitching** n

stitch up vb **1** to join by stitching **2** slang to incriminate by manufacturing evidence **3** slang to prearrange in a clandestine manner ▷ n **stitch-up 4** slang a matter that has been prearranged clandestinely

stoat n a small brown N European mammal related to the weasel: in winter it has a white coat and is then known as an ermine ▶ HISTORY origin unknown

stock n **1** the total amount of goods kept on the premises of a shop or business **2** a supply of something stored for future use **3** finance **a** the money raised by a company through selling shares entitling their holders to dividends, partial ownership, and usually voting rights **b** the proportion of this money held by an individual shareholder **c** the shares of a specified company or industry **4** farm animals bred and kept for their meat, skins, etc. **5** the original type from which a particular race, family, or group is descended **6** the handle of a rifle, held by the firer against the shoulder **7** a liquid produced by simmering meat, fish, bones, or vegetables, and used to make soups and sauces **8** a kind of plant grown for its brightly coloured flowers **9** old-fashioned the degree of status a person has **10** See **laughing stock 11 in stock** stored on the premises or available for sale or use **12 out of stock** not immediately available for sale or use **13 take stock** to think carefully about a situation before making a decision ▷ adj **14** staple; standard: stock sizes in clothes **15** being a cliché; hackneyed: the stock answer ▷ vb **16** to keep (goods) for sale **17** to obtain a store of (something) for future use or sale: to stock up on food **18** to supply (a farm) with animals or (a lake or stream) with fish ▷ See also **stocks** ▶ HISTORY Old English stocc tree trunk

stockade n an enclosure or barrier of large wooden posts ▶ HISTORY Spanish estacada

stockbreeder n a person who breeds or rears farm animals

stockbroker n a person who buys and sells stocks and shares for customers and receives a percentage of their profits > **stockbroking** n

stock car n a car that has been strengthened and modified for a form of racing in which the cars often collide

stock exchange n **1 a** a highly organized market for the purchase and sale of stocks and shares, operated by professional stockbrokers and market makers according to fixed rules **b** a place where stocks and shares are traded **2** the prices or trading activity of a stock exchange: the stock exchange has been rising

stockholder n an owner of some of a company's stock

stockinette n a machine-knitted elastic fabric ▶ HISTORY perhaps from stocking-net

stocking n a long piece of close-fitting nylon or knitted yarn covering the foot and part or all of a woman's leg ▶ HISTORY dialect stock stocking

stocking stitch n alternate rows of plain and purl in knitting

stock in trade n a person's typical behaviour or usual work: practicality is the farmer's stock in trade

stockist n commerce, Brit a dealer who stocks a particular product

stock market n same as **stock exchange**

stockpile vb **-piling, -piled 1** to store a large quantity of (something) for future use ▷ n **2** a large store gathered for future use

stockpot n Brit & NZ a pot in which stock for soup is made

stockroom n a room in which a stock of goods is kept in a shop or factory

stock route n Austral & NZ a route designated for droving farm animals, so as to avoid traffic

stocks pl n history an instrument of punishment consisting of a heavy wooden frame with holes in which the feet, hands, or head of an offender were locked

stock-still adv absolutely still; motionlessly

stocktaking n **1** the counting and valuing of goods in a shop or business **2** a reassessment of a person's current situation and prospects

stocky adj **stockier, stockiest** (of a person) short but well-built > **stockily** adv > **stockiness** n

stockyard n a large yard with pens or covered buildings where farm animals are sold

stodge n Brit, Austral & NZ, informal heavy and filling starchy food ▶ HISTORY perhaps blend of STUFF + podge a short plump person

stodgy adj **stodgier, stodgiest 1** (of food) full of starch and very filling **2** (of a person) dull, serious, or excessively formal ▶ HISTORY from STODGE > **stodginess** n

stoep (stoop) n (in South Africa) a verandah ▶ HISTORY Afrikaans

stoic (**stow**-ik) n **1** a person who suffers great difficulties without showing his or her emotions ▷ adj **2** same as **stoical**

■ **WORD HISTORY**

■ 'Stoic' behaviour mirrors that advocated by the
■ Stoics.

Stoic n **1** a member of the ancient Greek school of philosophy which believed that virtue and happiness could be achieved only by calmly accepting Fate ▷ adj **2** of or relating to the Stoics ▶ HISTORY Greek stoa porch > **Stoicism** n

stoical adj suffering great difficulties without showing one's emotions

stoke vb **stoking, stoked 1** to feed and tend (a fire or furnace) **2** to excite or encourage (a strong

839

emotion) in oneself or someone else ▶ HISTORY from STOKER

stokehold *n naut* the hold for a ship's boilers; fire room

stoker *n* a person employed to tend a furnace on a ship or train powered by steam ▶ HISTORY Dutch *stoken* to stoke

stole¹ *vb* the past tense of **steal**

stole² *n* a long scarf or shawl, worn by women ▶ HISTORY Greek *stolē* clothing

stolen *vb* the past participle of **steal**

stolid *adj* showing little or no emotion or interest in anything ▶ HISTORY Latin *stolidus* dull > **stolidity** *n* > **stolidly** *adv*

stolon *n bot* same as **runner** (sense 5)

stoma (stow-ma) *n*, *pl* **stomata** (stow-ma-ta) **1** *bot* a pore in a plant leaf that controls the passage of gases into and out of the plant **2** *zool* a mouth or mouthlike part ▶ HISTORY Greek: mouth

stomach *n* **1** an organ inside the body in which food is stored until it has been partially digested **2** the front of the body around the waist **3** desire or appetite: *he still has the stomach for a fight* ▷ *vb* **4** to put up with: *liberals could not stomach the rest of the package* ▶ HISTORY Greek *stoma* mouth

stomachache *n* pain in the stomach, such as from indigestion. Also called: **stomach upset, upset stomach**

stomacher *n history* a decorative V-shaped panel of stiff material worn over the chest and stomach mainly by women

stomach pump *n med* a pump with a long tube used for removing the contents of a person's stomach, for instance after he or she has swallowed poison

stomp *vb* to tread or stamp heavily ▶ HISTORY variant of STAMP

stompie *n S African, slang* **1** a cigarette butt **2** a short man ▶ HISTORY Afrikaans *stomp* stump

stone *n* **1** the hard nonmetallic material of which rocks are made **2** a small lump of rock **3** Also called: **gemstone** a precious or semiprecious stone that has been cut and polished **4** a piece of rock used for some particular purpose: *gravestone; millstone* **5** the hard central part of fruits such as the peach or date **6** (*pl* **stone**) *Brit* a unit of weight equal to 14 pounds or 6.350 kilograms **7** *pathol* a hard deposit formed in the kidney or bladder **8 heart of stone** a hard or unemotional personality **9 leave no stone unturned** to do everything possible to achieve something ▷ *adj* **10** made of stoneware: *the polished stone planter* ▷ *vb* **stoning, stoned** **11** to throw stones at (someone), for example as a punishment **12** to remove the stones from (a fruit) ▶ HISTORY Old English *stān*

Stone Age *n* a phase of human culture identified by the use of tools made of stone

stonechat *n* a songbird that has black feathers and a reddish-brown breast ▶ HISTORY from its cry, which sounds like clattering pebbles

stone-cold *adj* **1** completely cold ▷ *adv* **2 stone-cold sober** completely sober

stoned *adj slang* under the influence of drugs or alcohol

stone-deaf *adj* completely deaf

stone fruit *n* same as **drupe**

stonewall *vb* **1** to deliberately prolong a discussion by being long-winded or evasive **2** *cricket* (of a batsman) to play defensively

stoneware *n* a hard type of pottery, fired at a very high temperature

stonework *n* any structure or part of a building made of stone

stonkered *adj NZ, slang* completely exhausted or beaten; whacked ▶ HISTORY from *stonker* to beat, of unknown origin

stony or **stoney** *adj* **stonier, stoniest** **1** (of ground) rough and covered with stones: *the stony path* **2** (of a face, voice, or attitude) unfriendly and unsympathetic > **stonily** *adv*

stony-broke *adj slang* completely without money

stood *vb* the past of **stand**

stooge *n* **1** an actor who feeds lines to a comedian or acts as the butt of his or her jokes **2** *slang* someone who is taken advantage of by someone in a superior position ▶ HISTORY origin unknown

stool *n* **1** a seat with legs but no back **2** waste matter from the bowels ▶ HISTORY Old English *stōl*

stool pigeon *n* an informer for the police

stoop¹ *vb* **1** to bend (the body) forward and downward **2** to stand or walk with head and shoulders habitually bent forward **3 stoop to** to lower one's normal standards of behaviour; degrade oneself: *no journalist would stoop to faking* ▷ *n* **4** the act, position, or habit of stooping ▶ HISTORY Old English *stūpian* > **stooping** *adj*

stoop² *n US* an open porch or small platform with steps leading up to it at the entrance to a building ▶ HISTORY Dutch *stoep*

stop *vb* **stopping, stopped** **1** to cease doing (something); discontinue **2** to cause (something moving) to halt or (of something moving) to come to a halt **3** to prevent the continuance or completion of (something) **4** (often foll. by *from*) to prevent or restrain: *I stopped her from going on any further* **5** to keep back: *no agreement to stop arms supplies* **6 stop up** to block or plug: *to stop up a pipe* **7** to stay or rest: *we stopped at a camp site for a change* **8** to instruct a bank not to honour (a cheque) **9** to deduct (money) from pay **10** *informal* to receive (a blow or hit) **11** *music* to alter the vibrating length of (a string on a violin, guitar, etc.) by pressing down on it at some point with the finger **12 stop at nothing** to be prepared to do anything; be ruthless ▷ *n* **13** prevention of movement or progress: *you can put a stop to it quite easily* **14** the act of stopping or the state of being stopped: *the car lurched to a stop* **15** a place where something halts or pauses: *a bus stop* **16** the act or an instance of blocking or obstructing **17** a device that prevents, limits, or ends the motion of a mechanism or moving part **18** *Brit* a full stop **19** *music* a knob on an organ that is operated to allow sets of pipes to sound

20 pull out all the stops to make a great effort
▶ HISTORY Old English *stoppian* (unattested)

stopbank *n NZ* an embankment to prevent flooding

stopcock *n* a valve used to control or stop the flow of a fluid in a pipe

stopgap *n* a thing that serves as a substitute for a short time until replaced by something more suitable

stopover *n* **1** a break in a journey ▷ *vb* **stop over** **2** to make a stopover

stoppage *n* **1** the act of stopping something or the state of being stopped: *a heart stoppage* **2** a deduction of money, such as taxation, from pay **3** an organized stopping of work during industrial action

stoppage time *n chiefly Brit* same as **injury time**

stopper *n* a plug for closing a bottle, pipe, etc.

stop press *n* news items inserted into a newspaper after the printing has been started

stopwatch *n* a watch which can be stopped instantly for exact timing of a sporting event

storage *n* **1** the act of storing or the state of being stored **2** space for storing **3** the place where something is stored **4** *computers* the process of storing information in a computer

storage device *n* a piece of computer equipment, such as a magnetic tape or a disk in or on which information can be stored

storage heater *n* an electric device that accumulates and radiates heat generated by cheap off-peak electricity

store *vb* **storing, stored 1** to keep, set aside, or gather (things) for future use **2** to place furniture or other possessions in a warehouse for safekeeping **3** to supply or stock (certain goods) **4** *computers* to enter or keep (information) in a storage device ▷ *n* **5** a shop (in Britain usually a large one) **6** a large supply or stock kept for future use **7** short for **department store 8** a storage place, such as a warehouse **9** *computers, chiefly Brit* same as **memory** (sense 7) **10 in store** about to happen; forthcoming: *you've got a treat in store* **11 set great store by something** to value something as important ▷ See also **stores** ▶ HISTORY Old French *estor*

stores *pl n* supply or stock of food and other essentials for a journey

storey *or esp US* **story** *n, pl* **-reys** *or* **-ries** a floor or level of a building ▶ HISTORY Anglo-Latin *historia* picture, probably from the pictures on medieval windows

stork *n* a large wading bird with very long legs, a long bill, and white-and-black feathers ▶ HISTORY Old English *storc*

storm *n* **1** a violent weather condition of strong winds, rain, hail, thunder, lightning, etc. **2** a violent disturbance or quarrel: *a storm of protest from the opposition* **3** (usually foll. by *of*) a heavy discharge of bullets or missiles **4 take a place by storm a** to capture or overrun a place by a violent attack **b** to surprise people, but receive their praise,

by being extremely successful at something ▷ *vb* **5** to attack or capture (a place) suddenly and violently **6** *written* to shout angrily **7** to move or rush violently or angrily: *she stormed into the study* ▶ HISTORY Old English

storm centre *n* **1** the centre of a storm, where pressure is lowest **2** the centre of any disturbance or trouble

storm surge *n geog* an occasion when ocean water is driven inland due to extreme weather conditions and significant flooding occurs

storm trooper *n* a member of the paramilitary wing of the Nazi Party

stormy *adj* **stormier, stormiest 1** (of weather) violent with dark skies, heavy rain or snow, and strong winds **2** involving violent emotions: *a stormy affair*

stormy petrel *or* **storm petrel** *n* **1** a small sea bird with dark feathers and paler underparts **2** a person who brings trouble

story¹ *n, pl* **-ries 1** a description of a chain of events told or written in prose or verse **2** Also called: **short story** a piece of fiction, shorter and usually less detailed than a novel **3** Also called: **story line** the plot of a book or film **4** a news report **5** the event or material for such a report **6** *informal* a lie ▶ HISTORY Latin *historia*

story² *n, pl* **-ries** *chiefly US* same as **storey**

storyboard *n films, television* a series of sketches or photographs showing the sequence of shots or images planned for a film

storybook *n* **1** a book containing stories for children ▷ *adj* **2** better or happier than in real life: *a storybook romance*

story line *n* the plot of a book, film, etc.

storyteller *n* a person who tells stories > **storytelling** *n*

stoup *or* **stoop** (stoop) *n* a small basin in a church for holy water ▶ HISTORY from Old Norse

stoush *Austral & NZ, slang vb* **1** to hit or punch (someone) ▷ *n* **2** fighting or violence ▶ HISTORY origin unknown

stout *adj* **1** solidly built or fat **2** strong and sturdy: *stout footwear* **3** brave or determined: *we met unexpectedly stout resistance* ▷ *n* **4** strong dark beer ▶ HISTORY Old French *estout* bold > **stoutly** *adv*

stove¹ *n* **1** same as **cooker** (sense 1) **2** any apparatus for heating, such as a kiln ▶ HISTORY Old English *stofa* bathroom

stove² *vb* a past tense and past participle of **stave**

stovepipe *n* a pipe that takes fumes and smoke away from a stove

stow *vb* (often foll. by *away*) to pack or store (something) ▶ HISTORY Old English *stōwian* to keep

stowage *n* **1** space, room, or a charge for stowing goods **2** the act of stowing

stowaway *n* **1** a person who hides aboard a ship or aircraft in order to travel free ▷ *vb* **stow away 2** to travel in such a way: *he stowed away on a ferry*

strabismus *n pathol* same as **squint** (sense 3) ▶ HISTORY Greek *strabismos*

straddle *vb* **-dling, -dled 1** to have one leg or part on each side of (something) **2** *US & Canad, informal* to be in favour of both sides of (an issue or argument) ▶ **HISTORY** from *stride*

strafe *vb* **strafing, strafed** to machine-gun (an enemy) from the air ▶ **HISTORY** German *strafen* to punish

straggle *vb* **-gling, -gled 1** to spread out in an untidy and rambling way: *the town straggled off to the east* **2** to linger behind or wander from a main line or part ▶ **HISTORY** origin unknown
> **straggler** *n* > **straggly** *adj*

straight *adj* **1** continuing in the same direction without bending; not curved or crooked **2** even, level, or upright **3** in keeping with the facts; accurate **4** outright or candid: *a straight rejection* **5** in continuous succession **6** (of an alcoholic drink) undiluted **7** not wavy or curly: *straight hair* **8** in good order **9** (of a play or acting style) straightforward or serious **10** honest, respectable, or reliable **11** *slang* heterosexual **12** *slang* conventional in views, customs, or appearance **13** *informal* no longer owing or being owed something: *if you buy the next round we'll be straight* ▷ *adv* **14** in a straight line or direct course **15** immediately; at once: *get straight back here* **16** in a level or upright position: *he sat up straight* **17** continuously; uninterruptedly: *we waited for three hours straight* **18** (often foll. by *out*) frankly; candidly: *she asked me straight out* **19 go straight** *informal* to reform after having been a criminal **20 straight away** *or* **straightaway** at once ▷ *n* **21** a straight line, form, part, or position **22** *Brit* a straight part of a racetrack **23** *slang* a heterosexual person ▶ **HISTORY** Old English *streccan* to stretch

straighten *vb* (sometimes foll. by *up* or *out*) **1** to make or become straight **2** to make (something) neat or tidy

straight face *n* a serious facial expression which hides a desire to laugh > **straight-faced** *adj*

straightforward *adj* **1** (of a person) honest, frank, and open **2** *Brit & NZ* (of a task) easy to do

straight man *n* an actor who acts as the butt of a comedian's jokes

strain¹ *n* **1** tension or tiredness resulting from overwork or worry **2** tension between people or organizations: *there are signs of strain between the economic superpowers* **3** an intense physical or mental effort **4** the damage resulting from excessive physical exertion **5** a great demand on the emotions, strength, or resources **6** a way of speaking: *he would have gone on in this strain for some time* **7** *physics* the change in dimension of a body caused by outside forces **8 strains** *music* a theme, melody, or tune ▷ *vb* **9** to subject (someone) to mental tension or stress **10** to make an intense effort: *the rest were straining to follow the conversation* **11** to use (resources) to, or beyond, their limits **12** to injure or damage (oneself or a part of one's body) by overexertion: *he appeared to have strained a muscle* **13** to pour (a substance) through a sieve or filter **14 strain at** to push, pull, or work with

violent effort on (something) **15** to draw (something) taut or be drawn taut ▶ **HISTORY** Latin *stringere* to bind tightly

strain² *n* **1** a group of animals or plants within a species or variety, distinguished by one or more minor characteristics **2** a trace or streak: *a strain of ruthlessness in their play* ▶ **HISTORY** Old English *strēon*

strained *adj* **1** (of an action, expression, etc.) not natural or spontaneous **2** (of an atmosphere, relationship, etc.) not relaxed; tense

strainer *n* a sieve used for straining sauces, vegetables, or tea

strait *n* **1** (often pl) a narrow channel of the sea linking two larger areas of sea **2 straits** a position of extreme difficulty: *in desperate straits* ▶ **HISTORY** Old French *estreit* narrow

straitened *adj* **in straitened circumstances** not having much money

straitjacket *n* **1** a strong canvas jacket with long sleeves used to bind the arms of a violent person **2** anything which holds back or restricts development or freedom: *exporters are wrapped in a straitjacket of regulations*

strait-laced *or* **straight-laced** *adj* having a strict code of moral standards; puritanical

strand¹ *vb* **1** to leave or drive (ships or fish) ashore **2** to leave (someone) helpless, for example without transport or money ▷ *n* **3** *chiefly poetic* a shore or beach ▶ **HISTORY** Old English

strand² *n* **1** one of the individual fibres of string or wire that form a rope, cord, or cable **2** a single length of string, hair, wool, or wire **3** a string of pearls or beads **4** a part of something; element: *the many disparate strands of the Anglican Church* ▶ **HISTORY** origin unknown

strange *adj* **1** odd or unexpected **2** not known, seen, or experienced before; unfamiliar **3 strange to** inexperienced (in) or unaccustomed (to): *they are in some degree strange to it* ▶ **HISTORY** Latin *extraneus* foreign > **strangely** *adv* > **strangeness** *n*

stranger *n* **1** any person whom one does not know **2** a person who is new to a particular place **3 stranger to** a person who is unfamiliar with or new to something: *Paul is no stranger to lavish spending*

strangle *vb* **-gling, -gled 1** to kill (someone) by pressing his or her windpipe; throttle **2** to prevent the growth or development of: *another attempt at strangling national identity* **3** to stifle (a voice, cry, or laugh) by swallowing suddenly: *the words were strangled by sobs* ▶ **HISTORY** Greek *strangalē* a halter > **strangler** *n*

stranglehold *n* **1** a wrestling hold in which a wrestler's arms are pressed against his opponent's windpipe **2** complete power or control over a person or situation

strangulate *vb* **-lating, -lated 1** *pathol* to constrict (a hollow organ or vessel) so as to stop the flow of air or blood through it: *a badly strangulated hernia* **2** same as **strangle** > **strangulation** *n*

strap *n* **1** a strip of strong flexible material used for carrying, lifting, fastening, or holding things in place **2** a loop of leather or rubber, hanging from the roof in a bus or train for standing passengers to hold on to **3 the strap** a beating with a strap as a punishment ▷ *vb* **strapping, strapped 4** to tie or bind (something) with a strap ▸ **HISTORY** variant of STROP

strapping *adj* tall, strong, and healthy-looking: *a strapping young lad* ▸ **HISTORY** from *strap* (in the archaic sense: to work vigorously)

strata *n* the plural of **stratum**

stratagem *n* a clever plan to deceive an enemy ▸ **HISTORY** Greek *stratēgos* a general

strata title *n Austral law* a system of registered ownership of space in multistorey buildings, to be equivalent to the ownership of the land of a single-storey building. NZ equivalent: **stratum title**

strategic (strat-**ee**-jik) *adj* **1** planned to achieve an advantage; tactical **2** (of weapons, esp. missiles) directed against an enemy's homeland rather than used on a battlefield > **strategically** *adv*

strategy *n, pl* **-gies 1** a long-term plan for success, such as in politics or business **2** the art of the planning and conduct of a war ▸ **HISTORY** Greek *stratēgia* function of a general > **strategist** *n*

strath *n Scot* a flat river valley ▸ **HISTORY** Scottish & Irish Gaelic *srath*

strathspey *n* **1** a Scottish dance with gliding steps, slower than a reel **2** music for this dance ▸ **HISTORY** after *Strathspey*, valley of the River Spey

stratified *adj* **1** (of rocks) formed in horizontal layers of different materials **2** *sociol* (of a society) divided into different classes or groups ▸ **HISTORY** New Latin *stratificare* to form in layers
> **stratification** *n*

stratocumulus (strat-oh-**kew**-myew-luss) *n, pl* **-li** (-lie) *meteorol* an unbroken stretch of dark grey cloud

stratosphere *n* the atmospheric layer between about 15 and 50 km above the earth

strato-volcano *n, pl* **-noes** *or* **-nos** *geol* Also: **composite cone** a steep cone-shaped volcano composed of alternate layers of viscous lava and pyroclastic material

stratum (strah-tum) *n, pl* **-ta** (-ta) **1** any of the distinct layers into which certain rocks are divided **2** a layer of ocean or atmosphere marked off naturally or decided arbitrarily by man **3** a social class ▸ **HISTORY** Latin: something strewn

stratus (stray-tuss) *n, pl* **-ti** (-tie) a grey layer cloud ▸ **HISTORY** Latin: strewn

straw *n* **1** dried stalks of threshed grain, such as wheat or barley **2** a single stalk of straw **3** a long thin hollow paper or plastic tube, used for sucking up liquids into the mouth **4 clutch at straws** to turn in desperation to something with little chance of success **5 draw the short straw** to be the person chosen to perform an unpleasant task ▷ *adj* **6** made of straw: *straw baskets* ▸ **HISTORY** Old English *strēaw*

strawberry *n, pl* **-ries** a sweet fleshy red fruit with small seeds on the outside ▸ **HISTORY** Old English *strēawberige*

strawberry mark *n* a red birthmark

straw-coloured *adj* pale yellow: *straw-coloured hair*

straw poll *or* **vote** *n* an unofficial poll or vote taken to find out the opinion of a group or the public on some issue

stray *vb* **1** to wander away from the correct path or from a given area **2** to move away from the point or lose concentration **3** to fail to live up to certain moral standards: *her man had strayed* ▷ *n* **4** a domestic animal that has wandered away from its home **5** *old-fashioned* a lost or homeless child ▷ *adj* **6** (of a domestic animal) having wandered away from its home **7** random or separated from the main group of things of their kind: *stray bombs and rockets* ▸ **HISTORY** Old French *estraier*

streak *n* **1** a long thin stripe or trace of some contrasting colour **2** (of lightning) a sudden flash **3** a quality or characteristic: *a nasty streak* **4** a short stretch of good or bad luck: *a losing streak* **5** *informal* an instance of running naked through a public place ▷ *vb* **6** to mark (something) with a streak or streaks: *sweat streaking the grime of his face* **7** to move quickly in a straight line **8** *informal* to run naked through a public place ▸ **HISTORY** Old English *strica* > **streaked** *or* **streaky** *adj* > **streaker** *n*

stream *n* **1** a small river **2** any steady flow of water or other liquid **3** something that resembles a stream in moving continuously in a line or particular direction: *the stream of traffic* **4** a fast and continuous flow of speech: *the constant stream of jargon* **5** *Brit, Austral & NZ* a class of school children grouped together because of similar ability ▷ *vb* **6** to pour in a continuous flow: *rain streamed down her cheeks* **7** (of a crowd of people or traffic or a herd of animals) to move in unbroken succession **8** to float freely or with a waving motion: *a flimsy pink dress that streamed out behind her* **9** to send video or audio material over the internet so that the receiving system can play it almost simultaneously **10** *Brit, Austral & NZ* to group (school children) in streams ▸ **HISTORY** Old English *strēam* > **streaming** *n* > **streamlet** *n*

streamer *n* **1** a long coiled ribbon of coloured paper that unrolls when tossed **2** a long narrow flag

streamline *vb* **-lining, -lined 1** to improve (something) by removing the parts that are least useful or profitable **2** to make (an aircraft, boat, or vehicle) less resistant to flowing air or water by improving its shape > **streamlined** *adj*

stream of consciousness *n literature* a literary technique that reveals the flow of thoughts and feelings of characters through long passages of soliloquy

stream order *n geog* a system for classifying streams in a drainage basin whereby streams without tributaries are classified as *first order,*

S

843

the streams they flow into, *second order*, and the streams these flow into, *third order*, etc.

street *n* **1** a public road that is usually lined with buildings, esp. in a town: *Sauchiehall Street* **2** the part of the road between the pavements, used by vehicles **3** the people living in a particular street **4 on the streets** homeless **5 right up one's street** *informal* just what one knows or likes best **6 streets ahead of** *informal* superior to or more advanced than ▶ HISTORY Old English *strǣt*

streetcar *n* US & Canad a tram

street child *n*, *pl* **street children** a homeless child who lives on the streets

street furniture *n* equipment, such as street lights and pillar boxes, placed in the street for the benefit of the public

street theatre *n* dramatic entertainments performed in shopping precincts

street value *n* the price that would be paid for goods, esp. illegal ones such as drugs, by the final user: *cocaine with a street value of £2m was seized at Heathrow airport*

streetwalker *n* a prostitute who tries to find customers in the streets

streetwise *adj* knowing how to survive or succeed in poor and often criminal sections of big cities

strength *n* **1** the state or quality of being physically or mentally strong **2** the ability to withstand great force, stress, or pressure **3** something regarded as valuable or a source of power: *his chief strength is rocketry* **4** potency or effectiveness, such as of a drink or drug **5** power to convince: *the strength of this argument* **6** degree of intensity or concentration of colour, light, sound, or flavour: *a strong cheese* **7** the total number of people in a group: *at full strength; 50 000 men below strength* **8 go from strength to strength** to have ever-increasing success **9 on the strength of** on the basis of or relying upon ▶ HISTORY Old English *strengthu*

strengthen *vb* to make (something) stronger or become stronger

strength of evidence *n science* a measure of how strongly a hypothesis is supported by the results of experiments or tests

strenuous *adj* requiring or involving the use of great energy or effort ▶ HISTORY Latin *strenuus* brisk > **strenuously** *adv*

streptococcus (strep-toe-**kok**-uss) *n*, *pl* **-cocci** (-**kok**-eye) a bacterium occurring in chains and including many species that cause disease ▶ HISTORY Greek *streptos* crooked + *kokkos* berry

streptomycin *n med* an antibiotic used in the treatment of tuberculosis and other bacterial infections ▶ HISTORY Greek *streptos* crooked + *mukēs* fungus

stress *n* **1** mental, emotional, or physical strain or tension **2** special emphasis or significance **3** emphasis placed upon a syllable by pronouncing it more loudly than those that surround it **4** *physics* force producing a change in shape or volume ▷ *vb*

5 to give emphasis to (a point or subject): *she stressed how difficult it had been* **6** to pronounce (a word or syllable) more loudly than those surrounding it ▶ HISTORY shortened from *distress* > **stressful** *adj*

stressed-out *adj informal* suffering from anxiety or tension

stretch *vb* **1 stretch over** *or* **for** to extend or spread over (a specified distance): *the flood barrier stretches for several miles* **2** to draw out or extend (something) or to be drawn out or extended in length or area **3** to distort or lengthen (something) or to be distorted or lengthened permanently **4** to extend (the limbs or body), for example when one has just woken up **5** (often foll. by *out, forward*) to reach or hold out (a part of one's body) **6** to reach or suspend (a rope, etc.) from one place to another **7** to draw (something) tight; tighten **8** (usually foll. by *over*) to extend in time: *a dinner which stretched over three consecutive evenings* **9** to put a great strain upon (one's money or resources) **10** to make do with (limited resources): *the Walkers decided to stretch their budget* **11** to extend (someone) to the limit of his or her abilities **12** to extend (someone) to the limit of his or her tolerance **13 stretch a point** to make an exception not usually made ▷ *n* **14** the act of stretching **15** a large or continuous expanse or distance: *this stretch of desert* **16** extent in time **17** a term of imprisonment **18 at a stretch** *chiefly Brit & NZ* **a** with some difficulty; by making a special effort **b** at one time: *for hours at a stretch they had no conversation* ▷ *adj* **19** (of clothes) able to be stretched without permanently losing shape: *a stretch suit* ▶ HISTORY Old English *streccan* > **stretchy** *adj*

stretcher *n* a frame covered with canvas, on which an ill or injured person is carried

stretcher-bearer *n* a person who helps to carry a stretcher

strew *vb* **strewing, strewed, strewn** to scatter (things) over a surface ▶ HISTORY Old English *streowian*

strewth *interj informal* an expression of surprise or alarm ▶ HISTORY alteration of *God's truth*

stria (**strye**-a) *n*, *pl* **striae** (**strye**-ee) *geol* a scratch or groove on the surface of a rock crystal ▶ HISTORY Latin: a groove

striation *n* **1** an arrangement or pattern of striae **2** same as **stria** > **striated** *adj*

stricken *adj* badly affected by disease, pain, grief, etc.: *flood-stricken areas* ▶ HISTORY past participle of STRIKE

strict *adj* **1** severely correct in attention to behaviour or morality: *a strict disciplinarian* **2** following carefully and exactly a set of rules: *she is a strict vegetarian* **3** (of a rule or law) very precise and requiring total obedience: *a strict code of practice* **4** (of a meaning) exact: *this is not, in the strictest sense, a biography* **5** (of a punishment, etc.) harsh or severe **6** complete; absolute: *strict obedience* ▶ HISTORY Latin *strictus* drawn tight > **strictly** *adv* > **strictness** *n*

strict liability offence n law an offence in which the prosecution need only prove actus reus but not mens rea

stricture n formal a severe criticism ▶ HISTORY Latin strictura contraction

stride n 1 a long step or pace 2 the length of such a step 3 a striding walk 4 progress or development: he has made great strides in regaining his confidence 5 a regular pace or rate of progress: it put me off my stride 6 **take something in one's stride** to do something without difficulty or effort ▷ vb **striding, strode, stridden** 7 to walk with long steps or paces 8 **stride over** or **across** to cross (over a space or an obstacle) with a stride ▶ HISTORY Old English strídan

strident adj 1 (of a voice or sound) loud and harsh 2 loud, persistent, and forceful: a strident critic of the establishment ▶ HISTORY Latin stridens > **stridency** n

strife n angry or violent struggle; conflict ▶ HISTORY Old French estrif

strike vb **striking, struck** 1 (of employees) to stop work collectively as a protest against working conditions, low pay, etc. 2 to hit (someone) 3 to cause (something) to come into sudden or violent contact with something 4 **strike at** to attack (someone or something) 5 to cause (a match) to light by friction 6 to sound (a specific note) on a musical instrument 7 (of a clock) to indicate (a time) by the sound of a bell 8 to affect (someone) deeply in a particular way: he never struck me as the supportive type 9 to enter the mind of: a brilliant thought struck me 10 (of a poisonous snake) to injure by biting 11 (past participle **struck** or **stricken**) to change into (a different state): struck blind 12 to be noticed by; catch: the heavy smell of incense struck my nostrils 13 to arrive at (something) suddenly or unexpectedly: to strike on a solution 14 to afflict (someone) with a disease: she has been struck down by breast cancer 15 to discover a source of (gold, oil, etc.) 16 to reach (something) by agreement: to strike a deal 17 to take up (a posture or an attitude) 18 to take apart or pack up: to strike camp 19 to make (a coin) by stamping it 20 **strike home** to achieve the desired effect 21 **strike it rich** informal to have an unexpected financial success ▷ n 22 a stopping of work, as a protest against working conditions, low pay, etc.: a one-day strike 23 an act or instance of striking 24 a military attack, esp. an air attack on a target on land or at sea: a pre-emptive strike 25 baseball a pitched ball swung at and missed by the batter 26 tenpin bowling the knocking down of all the pins with one bowl 27 the discovery of a source of gold, oil, etc. 28 geol the horizontal direction of a fault, rock stratum, etc. ▷ See also **strike up** ▶ HISTORY Old English strícan

strikebreaker n a person who tries to make a strike fail by working or by taking the place of those on strike

striker n 1 a person who is on strike 2 soccer an attacking player

strike-slip fault n geol a fault in which rock on one side or on both sides of a fault scrapes along sideways in relation to the other

strike up vb 1 to begin (a conversation or friendship) 2 (of a band or an orchestra) to begin to play

striking adj 1 attracting attention; impressive: her striking appearance 2 very noticeable: a striking difference > **strikingly** adv

Strimmer n trademark an electrical tool for trimming the edges of lawns

Strine n a humorous transliteration of Australian pronunciation, as in Gloria Soame for glorious home ▶ HISTORY a jocular rendering of the Australian pronunciation of Australian

string n 1 thin cord or twine used for tying, hanging, or binding things 2 a group of objects threaded on a single strand: a string of pearls 3 a series of things or events: a string of wins 4 a tightly stretched wire or cord on a musical instrument, such as the guitar, violin, or piano, that produces sound when vibrated 5 **the strings** music a violins, violas, cellos, and double basses collectively b the section of an orchestra consisting of such instruments 6 a group of characters that can be treated as a unit by a computer program 7 **with no strings attached** (of an offer) without complications or conditions 8 **pull strings** informal to use one's power or influence, esp. secretly or unofficially ▷ adj 9 composed of stringlike strands woven in a large mesh: a string bag ▷ vb **stringing, strung** 10 to hang or stretch (something) from one point to another 11 to provide (something) with a string or strings 12 to thread (beads) on a string 13 to extend in a line or series: towns strung out along the valley ▶ HISTORY Old English streng > **stringlike** adj

string along vb informal 1 **string along with** to accompany: I'll string along with you 2 to deceive (someone) over a period of time: she had only been stringing him along

string bean n same as **runner bean**

string course n archit an ornamental projecting band along a wall

stringed adj (of musical instruments) having strings

stringent (strin-jent) adj requiring strict attention to rules or detail: all have particularly stringent environmental laws ▶ HISTORY Latin stringere to bind > **stringency** n

stringer n 1 archit a long horizontal timber beam that connects upright posts 2 a journalist employed by a newspaper on a part-time basis to cover a particular town or area

string quartet n music 1 a group of musicians consisting of two violins, one viola, and one cello 2 a piece of music composed for such a group

string up vb informal to kill (a person) by hanging

stringy adj **stringier, stringiest** 1 thin and rough: stringy hair 2 (of meat or other food) tough and fibrous

S

845

stringy-bark *n* an Australian eucalyptus with a fibrous bark

strip[1] *vb* **stripping, stripped 1** to take (the covering or clothes) off (oneself, another person, or thing) **2 a** to undress completely **b** to perform a striptease **3** to empty (a building) of all furniture **4** to take something away from (someone): *they were stripped of their possessions* **5** to remove (paint) from (a surface or furniture): *she stripped the plaster from the kitchen walls* **6** (often foll. by *down*) to dismantle (an engine or a mechanism) into individual parts ▷ *n* **7** the act or an instance of undressing or of performing a striptease ▸ **HISTORY** Old English *bestrīepan* to plunder

strip[1] *n* **1** a long narrow piece of something **2** short for **airstrip 3** *Brit, Austral & NZ* the clothes a sports team plays in ▸ **HISTORY** Middle Dutch *strīpe* stripe

strip cartoon *n* a sequence of drawings in a newspaper or magazine, telling an amusing story or an adventure

stripe[1] *n* **1** a long band of colour that differs from the surrounding material **2** a chevron or band worn on a uniform to indicate rank ▷ *vb* **striping, striped 3** to mark (something) with stripes ▸ **HISTORY** probably from Middle Dutch *strīpe* > **striped, stripy** *or* **stripey** *adj*

stripe[2] *n* a stroke from a whip, rod, or cane ▸ **HISTORY** from Middle Low German *strippe*

strip lighting *n* a method of electric lighting that uses fluorescent lamps in long glass tubes

stripling *n* a teenage boy or young man

stripper *n* **1** a person who performs a striptease **2** a tool or liquid for removing paint or varnish

strip-search *vb* **1** (of police, customs officials, etc.) to strip (a prisoner or suspect) naked to search him or her for drugs or smuggled goods ▷ *n* **2** a search that involves stripping a person naked

striptease *n* an entertainment in which a person gradually undresses to music

strive *vb* **striving, strove, striven** to make a great effort: *to strive for a peaceful settlement* ▸ **HISTORY** Old French *estriver*

strobe *n* short for **strobe lighting** or **stroboscope**

strobe lighting *n* a flashing beam of very bright light produced by a perforated disc rotating in front of a light source

stroboscope *n* an instrument producing a very bright flashing light which makes moving people appear stationary ▸ **HISTORY** Greek *strobos* a whirling + *skopein* to look at

strode *vb* the past tense of **stride**

stroke *vb* **stroking, stroked 1** to touch or brush lightly or gently ▷ *n* **2** a light touch or caress with the fingers **3** *pathol* rupture of a blood vessel in the brain resulting in loss of consciousness, often followed by paralysis and damage to speech **4** a blow, knock, or hit **5** an action or occurrence of the kind specified: *a fantastic stroke of luck; a stroke of intuition* **6 a** the striking of a clock **b** the hour registered by this: *at the stroke of twelve* **7** a mark made by a pen or paintbrush **8** same as **solidus**:

used esp. when dictating or reading aloud **9** the hitting of the ball in sports such as golf or cricket **10** any one of the repeated movements used by a swimmer **11** a particular style of swimming, such as the crawl **12** a single pull on the oars in rowing **13 at a stroke** with one action **14 not a stroke (of work)** no work at all ▸ **HISTORY** Old English *strācian*

stroll *vb* **1** to walk about in a leisurely manner ▷ *n* **2** a leisurely walk ▸ **HISTORY** probably from dialect German *strollen*

strong *adj* **stronger, strongest 1** having physical power **2** not easily broken or injured; solid or robust **3** great in degree or intensity; not faint or feeble: *a strong voice; a strong smell of explosive* **4** (of arguments) supported by evidence; convincing **5** concentrated; not weak or diluted **6** having a powerful taste or smell: *strong perfume* **7** (of language) using swear words **8** (of a person) self-confident: *a strong personality* **9** committed or fervent: *a strong believer in free trade* **10** important or having a lot of power or influence: *a strong left-wing tendency within the university* **11** very competent at a particular activity: *they sent a very strong team to the Olympics* **12** containing or having a specified number: *the 700-strong workforce* **13** (of an accent) distinct and indicating where the speaker comes from **14** (of a relationship) stable and likely to last **15** having an extreme or drastic effect: *strong discipline* **16** (of a colour) very bright and intense **17** (of a wind, current, or earthquake) moving fast or intensely **18** (of an economy, an industry, a currency, etc.) growing, successful, or increasing in value ▷ *adv* **19 going strong** *informal* working or performing well; thriving ▸ **HISTORY** Old English *strang* > **strongly** *adv*

See **WORD FOCUS strong**

strong-arm *adj informal* involving physical force or violence: *strong-arm tactics*

stronghold *n* **1** an area in which a particular belief is shared by many people: *a Labour stronghold* **2** a place that is well defended; fortress

strong point *n* something at which one is very good: *diplomacy wasn't his strong point*

strongroom *n* a specially designed room in which valuables are locked for safety

strontium *n chem* a soft silvery-white metallic element: the radioactive isotope **strontium-90** is used in nuclear power sources and is a hazardous nuclear fallout product. Symbol: Sr ▸ **HISTORY** after *Strontian*, in Scotland, where it was discovered

strop *n* a leather strap for sharpening razors ▸ **HISTORY** Greek *strophos* cord

strophe *n* **1** *poetry* the first of two metrical systems used alternately within a poem **2** *drama* the movement made by a chorus during the first part of a choral ode in an ancient Greek drama ▷ See also **antistrophe, epode**

stroppy *adj* **-pier, -piest** *informal* bad-tempered or deliberately awkward ▸ **HISTORY** from *obstreperous*

strove *vb* the past tense of **strive**

struck *vb* a past of **strike**

strong

Strong is an overused word. Depending on what you are referring to, there are many substitutes which you can use in its place to add variety and interest to your writing.

DEFINITION 1

- If you are describing a person who has powerful muscles, you could try: He was tall and **athletic**.
  - a **brawny** young rugby player • a big, **burly** man
  - She was lean and **muscular**. • a **powerful** bodybuilder • a big, **strapping** fellow • a fit, **well-built** runner
- If you are describing a person who is in good physical condition, you could try: She is positively **blooming** with health. • It won't be long till you're **fit** again. • a **healthy** child • He's **in good condition**.
  - a **robust** child • in **sound** physical condition

DEFINITION 2

- If you are describing an object that is able to withstand rough treatment, you could try: made of **durable** plastic • **hard-wearing** cotton overalls
  - a **heavy-duty** canvas bag • **reinforced** concrete supports • a camera mounted on a **sturdy** tripod
  - a **substantial** boat with a powerful rigging
  - a **tough** vehicle designed for all terrains • You need a **well-built** fence all round the garden.

DEFINITION 3

- If you are describing something that is not weak or feeble, you could try: **fierce** competition
  - **forceful** opinions • an **intense** battle
  - a **powerful** voice • a **vigorous** performance
- If you are describing feelings which are great in degree or intensity, you could try: **acute** feelings of self-consciousness • a **deep** resentment
  - my **fervent** hope • He inspires **fierce** loyalty.
  - an **intense** dislike • a **keen** interest in cricket
  - a **passionate** belief • his **profound** distrust
  - His announcement sparked off **vehement** criticism. • His plans met with **violent** hostility.

DEFINITION 4

- If you are describing an argument which is convincing or supported by a lot of evidence, you could try: a **compelling** case • a **convincing** theory • some **effective** arguments against war
  - **persuasive** reasons justifying the move • a **sound** case for using organically-grown produce
  - the most **telling** condemnation of the system

DEFINITION 5

- If you are describing a concentrated substance, you could try: **concentrated** bleach • **powerful** medicine • **pure** poison • **undiluted** acid

DEFINITION 6

- If you are describing something with a very powerful smell, you could try: an **overpowering** aftershave • a **powerful** smell of ammonia
  - the **pungent** aroma of oregano
- If you are describing food or drink that has a powerful flavour, you could try: a **hot** curry

- the **overpowering** taste of chillies • a **piquant** sauce • a **powerful** aniseed flavour • the **sharp** taste of pickles • **spicy** foods

DEFINITION 7

- If you are talking about bad language, you could try: **foul** language • **obscene** lyrics • **offensive** slang • **rude** words • **vulgar** terms

DEFINITION 8

- If you are describing a person who is confident and courageous, you could try: Be **brave**.
  - a **courageous** leader • a **plucky** schoolgirl
  - You've always been **resilient**. • feisty, **self-confident** people • You have to be **tough**.

DEFINITION 9

- If you are describing a person who is committed and fervent, you could try: **ardent** admirer
  - **enthusiastic** fan • **fervent** nationalist • **fierce** critic • a **keen** follower • **passionate** advocate
  - **staunch** defender of the regime • **steadfast** patriot • **vehement** opponent • **zealous** campaigner

DEFINITION 10

- If you are describing someone or something with a lot of influence, you could try: **dominant** political figures • **influential** group • **powerful** factions

DEFINITION 11

- If you are describing someone or something very competent, you could try: **capable** players
  - **formidable** opposition • a **skilful** side

DEFINITION 12

- If you are talking about something with a specified number of members, you could try: eleven-**man** team • 30-**member** squad • ten-**person** delegation • four-**piece** band • 200-**plus** workforce • seven-**woman** group

DEFINITION 13

- If you are describing a person's accent as being very noticeable, you could try: a **distinct** American drawl • a **marked** West country accent • his **noticeable** southern accent
  - her **unmistakeable** Spanish accent

DEFINITION 14

- If you are describing a relationship as being stable, you could try: **enduring** love • **firm** bonds
  - **lasting** feelings • a **secure** family life • a **solid** friendship • **sound** foundations • a **stable** marriage • a **steady** relationship

DEFINITION 15

- If you are describing something with a drastic effect, you could try: **decisive** action • **drastic** changes • **extreme** measures • a **firm** rule
  - **forceful** impact • **incisive** acts • **severe** cuts
  - **strict** discipline • **vigorous** cost-cutting

DEFINITION 16

- If you are describing very bright colours, you could try: **bold** colours • **bright** reds and blues
  - **brilliant** jewel colours • **glaring** red dress
  - shirts with **loud** patterns

S

structural *adj* **1** of or having structure or a structure **2** of or forming part of the structure of a building **3** *chem* of or involving the arrangement of atoms in molecules: *a structural formula* **> structurally** *adv*

structural control *n geog* the way that underlying geographical features affect drainage and topography

structuralism *n* an approach to social sciences and to literature which sees changes in the subject as caused and organized by a hidden set of universal rules **> structuralist** *n, adj*

structure *n* **1** something that has been built or organized **2** the way the individual parts of something are made, built, or organized into a whole **3** the pattern of interrelationships within an organization, society, etc. **4** an organized method of working, thinking, or behaving **5** *chem* the arrangement of atoms in a molecule of a chemical compound **6** *geol* the way in which a rock is made up of its component parts ▷ *vb* **-turing, -tured 7** to arrange (something) into an organized system or pattern: *a structured school curriculum* ▸ HISTORY Latin *structura*

strudel *n* a thin sheet of filled dough rolled up and baked: *apple strudel* ▸ HISTORY from German

struggle *vb* **-gling, -gled 1** to work or strive: *the old regime struggled for power; he struggled to keep the conversation flowing* **2** to move about violently in an attempt to escape from something restricting **3** to fight with someone, often for possession of something **4** to go or progress with difficulty **5 struggle on** to manage to do (something) with difficulty ▷ *n* **6** something requiring a lot of exertion or effort to achieve **7** a fight or battle **8 the struggle** *S African* the concerted opposition to apartheid ▸ HISTORY origin unknown **> struggling** *adj*

strum *vb* **strumming, strummed 1** to play (a stringed instrument) by sweeping the thumb or a plectrum across the strings **2** to play (a tune) in this way ▸ HISTORY probably imitative

strumpet *n archaic* a prostitute or promiscuous woman ▸ HISTORY origin unknown

strung *vb* the past of **string**

strut *vb* **strutting, strutted 1** to walk in a stiff proud way with head high and shoulders back; swagger ▷ *n* **2** a piece of wood or metal that forms part of the framework of a structure ▸ HISTORY Old English *strūtian* to stand stiffly

strychnine (**strik**-neen) *n* a very poisonous drug formerly used in small quantities as a stimulant ▸ HISTORY Greek *strukhnos* nightshade

Stuart *adj* of or relating to the royal house that ruled Scotland from 1371 to 1714 and England from 1603 to 1714

stub *n* **1** a short piece remaining after something has been used: *a cigarette stub* **2** the section of a ticket or cheque which the purchaser keeps as a receipt ▷ *vb* **stubbing, stubbed 3** to strike (one's toe or foot) painfully against a hard surface **4 stub out** to put out (a cigarette or cigar) by pressing the end against a surface ▸ HISTORY Old English *stubb*

stubble *n* **1** the short stalks left in a field where a crop has been harvested **2** the short bristly hair on the chin of a man who has not shaved for a while ▸ HISTORY Old French *estuble* **> stubbly** *adj*

stubble-jumper *n Canad, slang* a prairie grain farmer

stubborn *adj* **1** refusing to agree or give in **2** persistent and determined **3** difficult to handle, treat, or overcome: *the most stubborn dandruff* ▸ HISTORY origin unknown **> stubbornly** *adv* **> stubbornness** *n*

stubby *adj* **-bier, -biest** short and broad

stucco *n* **1** plaster used for coating or decorating outside walls ▷ *vb* **-coing, -coed 2** to apply stucco to (a building) ▸ HISTORY Italian

stuck *vb* **1** the past of **stick²** ▷ *adj* **2** *informal* baffled by a problem or unable to find an answer to a question **3 be stuck on** *slang* to feel a strong attraction to; be infatuated with **4 get stuck in** *informal* to perform a task with determination

stuck-up *adj informal* proud or snobbish

stud¹ *n* **1** a small piece of metal attached to a surface for decoration **2** a fastener consisting of two discs at either end of a short bar, usually used with clothes **3** one of several small round objects attached to the sole of a football boot to give better grip ▷ *vb* **studding, studded 4** to decorate or cover (something) with or as if with studs: *apartment houses studded with satellite dishes* ▸ HISTORY Old English *studu*

stud² *n* **1** a male animal, esp. a stallion kept for breeding **2** Also: **stud farm** a place where animals are bred **3** the state of being kept for breeding purposes ▸ HISTORY Old English *stōd*

student *n* **1** a person following a course of study in a school, college, or university **2** a person who makes a thorough study of a subject: *a keen student of opinion polls* ▸ HISTORY Latin *studens* diligent

studied *adj* carefully practised or planned: *studied calm*

studio *n, pl* **-dios 1** a room in which an artist, photographer, or musician works **2** a room used to record television or radio programmes or to make films or records **3 studios** the premises of a radio, television, record, or film company ▸ HISTORY Italian

studio flat *n Brit* a flat with one main room and, usually, a small kitchen and bathroom. Also called: **studio apartment**

studious (**styoo**-dee-uss) *adj* **1** serious, thoughtful, and hard-working **2** precise, careful, or deliberate ▸ HISTORY Latin *studiosus* devoted to **> studiously** *adv*

study *vb* **studies, studying, studied 1** to be engaged in the learning or understanding of (a subject) **2** to investigate or examine (something) by observation and research **3** to look at (something or someone) closely; scrutinize ▷ *n, pl* **studies 4** the act or process of studying **5** a room used for studying, reading, or writing **6** (often pl) work relating to a particular area of learning: *environmental studies* **7** an investigation and

S

analysis of a particular subject **8** a paper or book produced as a result of study **9** a work of art, such as a drawing, done for practice or in preparation for another work **10** a musical composition designed to develop playing technique ▶ **HISTORY** Latin *studium* zeal

stuff *n* **1** substance or material **2** any collection of unnamed things **3** the raw material of something **4** subject matter, skill, etc.: *this journalist knew his stuff* **5** woollen fabric **6 do one's stuff** *informal* to do what is expected of one ▷ *vb* **7** to pack or fill (something) completely; cram **8** to force, shove, or squeeze (something somewhere): *I stuffed it in my briefcase* **9** to fill (food such as poultry or tomatoes) with a seasoned mixture **10** to fill (a dead animal's skin) with material so as to restore the shape of the live animal **11** *slang* to frustrate or defeat **12 get stuffed!** *Brit, Austral & NZ, slang* an exclamation of anger or annoyance with someone **13 stuff oneself** *or* **one's face** to eat a large amount of food ▶ **HISTORY** Old French *estoffe*

stuffing *n* **1** a mixture of ingredients with which poultry or meat is stuffed before cooking **2** the material used to fill and give shape to soft toys, pillows, furniture, etc.; padding

stuffy *adj* **-ier, -iest** **1** lacking fresh air **2** old-fashioned and very formal: *an image of stuffy tradition* > **stuffiness** *n*

stultify *vb* **-fies, -fying, -fied** to dull (the mind) by boring routine ▶ **HISTORY** Latin *stultus* stupid + *facere* to make > **stultifying** *adj*

stumble *vb* **-bling, -bled** **1** to trip and almost fall while walking or running **2** to walk in an unsteady or unsure way **3** to make mistakes or hesitate in speech **4 stumble across** *or* **on** *or* **upon** to encounter or discover (someone or something) by accident ▷ *n* **5** an act of stumbling ▶ **HISTORY** Middle English *stomble*

stumbling block *n* any obstacle that prevents something from taking place or progressing

stump *n* **1** the base of a tree trunk left standing after the tree has been cut down or has fallen **2** the part of something, such as a tooth or limb, that remains after a larger part has been removed **3** *cricket* any of three upright wooden sticks that, with two bails laid across them, form a wicket ▷ *vb* **4** to baffle or confuse (someone) **5** *cricket* to dismiss (a batsman) by breaking his wicket with the ball **6** *chiefly US & Canad* to campaign or canvass (an area), by political speech-making **7** to walk with heavy steps; trudge ▶ **HISTORY** Middle Low German

stump up *vb Brit, informal* to give (the money required)

stumpy *adj* **stumpier, stumpiest** short and thick like a stump; stubby

stun *vb* **stunning, stunned** **1** to shock or astonish (someone) so that he or she is unable to speak or act **2** (of a heavy blow or fall) to make (a person or an animal) unconscious ▶ **HISTORY** Old French *estoner* to daze

stung *vb* the past of **sting**

stunk *vb* a past of **stink**

stunner *n Brit, Austral & NZ, informal* a person or thing of great beauty

stunning *adj informal* very attractive or impressive > **stunningly** *adv*

stunt¹ *vb* to prevent or slow down (the growth or development) of a plant, animal, or person ▶ **HISTORY** Old English: foolish > **stunted** *adj*

stunt² *n* **1** an acrobatic or dangerous piece of action in a film or television programme **2** anything spectacular or unusual done to gain publicity ▷ *adj* **3** of or relating to acrobatic or dangerous pieces of action in films or television programmes: *a stunt man* ▶ **HISTORY** origin unknown

stupefaction *n* the state of being unable to think clearly because of tiredness or boredom

stupefy *vb* **-pefies, -pefying, -pefied** **1** to make (someone) feel so bored and tired that he or she is unable to think clearly **2** to confuse or astound (someone) ▶ **HISTORY** Old French *stupefier* > **stupefying** *adj*

stupendous *adj* very large or impressive ▶ **HISTORY** Latin *stupere* to be amazed > **stupendously** *adv*

stupid *adj* **1** lacking in common sense or intelligence **2** trivial, silly, or childish: *we got into a stupid quarrel* **3** unable to think clearly; dazed: *stupid with tiredness* ▶ **HISTORY** Latin *stupidus* > **stupidity** *n* > **stupidly** *adv*

stupor *n* a state of near unconsciousness in which a person is unable to behave normally or think clearly ▶ **HISTORY** Latin

sturdy *adj* **-dier, -diest** **1** (of a person) healthy, strong, and unlikely to tire or become injured **2** (of a piece of furniture, shoes, etc.) strongly built or made ▶ **HISTORY** Old French *estordi* dazed > **sturdily** *adv*

sturgeon *n* a bony fish from which caviar is obtained ▶ **HISTORY** Old French *estourgeon*

stutter *vb* **1** to speak (a word or phrase) with involuntary repetition of initial consonants ▷ *n* **2** the tendency to involuntarily repeat initial consonants while speaking ▶ **HISTORY** Middle English *stutten* > **stuttering** *n*

sty *n, pl* **sties** a pen in which pigs are kept ▶ **HISTORY** Old English *stīg*

stye *or* **sty** *n, pl* **styes** *or* **sties** inflammation of a gland at the base of an eyelash ▶ **HISTORY** Old English *stīgend* swelling + *ye* eye

Stygian (**stij**-jee-an) *adj chiefly literary* dark or gloomy ▶ **HISTORY** after the *Styx*, a river in Hades

style *n* **1** a form of appearance, design, or production: *I like that style of dress* **2** the way in which something is done: *a new style of command* **3** elegance or refinement of manners and dress: *he has bags of style* **4** a distinctive manner of expression in words, music, painting, etc.: *a painting in the Expressionist style* **5** popular fashion in dress and looks: *the old ones had gone out of style* **6** a fashionable or showy way of life: *the newly rich could dine in style* **7** the particular kind of spelling,

S

849

punctuation, and design followed in a book, journal, or publishing house **8** *bot* the stemlike part of a flower that bears the stigma ▷ *vb* **styling, styled 9** to design, shape, or tailor: *neatly styled hair* **10** to name or call: *Walsh, who styled himself the Memory Man* ▶ HISTORY Latin *stilus* writing implement

style manual *n* a manual containing standardized rules and examples of punctuation, typography, etc., for writers, editors, and printers working for an organization or organizations

stylish *adj* smart, fashionable, and attracting attention > **stylishly** *adv*

stylist *n* **1** a hairdresser who styles hair **2** a person who performs, writes, or acts with great attention to the particular style he or she employs

stylistic *adj* of the techniques used in creating or performing a work of art: *there are many stylistic problems facing the performers of Baroque music* > **stylistically** *adv*

stylus *n* a needle-like device in the pick-up arm of a record player that rests in the groove in the record and picks up the sound signals ▶ HISTORY Latin *stilus* writing implement

stymie *vb* **-mieing, -mied 1** to hinder or foil (someone): *the President was stymied by a reluctant Congress* ▷ *n, pl* **-mies 2** *golf* (formerly) a situation in which an opponent's ball is blocking the line between the hole and the ball about to be played ▶ HISTORY origin unknown

styptic *adj* **1** used to stop bleeding: *a styptic pencil* ▷ *n* **2** a styptic drug ▶ HISTORY Greek *stuphein* to contract

suave (**swahv**) *adj* (esp. of a man) smooth, confident, and sophisticated ▶ HISTORY Latin *suavis* sweet > **suavely** *adv*

sub *n* **1** short for **subeditor, submarine, subscription, substitute 2** *Brit, informal* an advance payment of wages or salary. Formal term: **subsistence allowance** ▷ *vb* **subbing, subbed 3** to act as a substitute

sub- *or before r* **sur-** *prefix* **1** situated under or beneath: *subterranean* **2** secondary in rank; subordinate: *sublieutenant; surrogate* **3** falling short of; less than or imperfectly: *subarctic; subhuman* **4** forming a subdivision or less important part: *subcommittee* ▶ HISTORY Latin

subaltern *n* a British army officer below the rank of captain ▶ HISTORY Latin *sub-* under + *alter* another

subatomic *adj* *physics* of, relating to, or being one of the particles making up an atom

subclavian vein *n* *anat* a vein situated below the clavicle

subclimax *n* *biol, geog* a stage in the development of the natural plant community of an area in which progress to climax vegetation is inhibited by factors other than the weather. Compare **climax vegetation**

subcommittee *n* a small committee consisting of members of a larger committee and which is set up to look into a particular matter

subconscious *adj* **1** happening or existing without one's awareness ▷ *n* **2** *psychol* the part of the mind that contains memories and motives of which one is not aware but which can influence one's behaviour > **subconsciously** *adv*

subcontinent *n* a large land mass that is a distinct part of a continent, such as India is of Asia

subcontract *n* **1** a secondary contract by which the main contractor for a job puts work out to another company ▷ *vb* **2** to let out (work) on a subcontract > **subcontractor** *n*

subculture *n* a group of people within a society or class with a distinct pattern of behaviour, beliefs, and attitudes

subcutaneous (sub-cute-**ayn**-ee-uss) *adj* *med* beneath the skin

subdivide *vb* **-viding, -vided** to divide (a part of something) into smaller parts > **subdivision** *n*

subduction *n* *geol* the process of one tectonic plate sliding under another, resulting in earthquakes and volcanic eruptions

subdue *vb* **-duing, -dued 1** to overcome and bring (a person or people) under control by persuasion or force **2** to make (feelings, colour, or lighting) less intense ▶ HISTORY Latin *subducere* to remove

subeditor *n* a person who checks and edits text for a newspaper or other publication

subgroup *n* a small group that is part of a larger group

subheading *n* the heading of a subdivision of a piece of writing

subhuman *adj* lacking the intelligence or decency expected of a human being

subject *n* **1** the person, thing, or topic being dealt with or discussed **2** any branch of learning considered as a course of study **3** a person, object, idea, or scene portrayed in a work of art **4** *grammar* a word or phrase that represents the person or thing performing the action of the verb in a sentence; for example, *the cat* in the sentence *The cat catches mice* **5** a person or thing that undergoes an experiment or treatment **6** a person under the rule of a monarch or government: *Zambian subjects* ▷ *adj* **7** being under the rule of a monarch or government: *a subject race* **8 subject to a** showing a tendency towards: *they are expensive and subject to over-runs in cost and time* **b** exposed or vulnerable to: *subject to ridicule* **c** conditional upon: *pay is subject to negotiation* ▷ *adv* **9 subject to** under the condition that something takes place: *my visit was agreed subject to certain conditions* ▷ *vb* (sub-**ject**) **10 subject to a** to cause (someone) to experience (something unpleasant): *they were subjected to beatings* **b** to bring under the control or authority of: *to subject a soldier to discipline* ▶ HISTORY Latin *subjectus* brought under > **subjection** *n*

subjective *adj* **1** of or based on a person's emotions or prejudices ▷ *n* **2** *grammar* the grammatical case in certain languages that identifies the subject of a verb > **subjectively** *adv*

S

subjective case *n grammar* a grammatical case in some languages that identifies the subject of a verb

subjective shot *n films, television* a camera shot taken from the angle of vision of one of the characters in the scene rather than from a neutral position. Compare **objective shot**

sub judice (sub **joo**-diss-ee) *adj* before a court of law: *he declined to comment on the case saying it was sub judice* ▶ HISTORY Latin

subjugate *vb* **-gating, -gated** to bring (a group of people) under one's control ▶ HISTORY Latin *sub-* under + *jugum* yoke > **subjugation** *n*

subjunctive *grammar adj* **1** denoting a mood of verbs used when the content of the clause is being doubted, supposed, or feared true, for example *were* in the sentence *I'd be careful if I were you* ▷ *n* **2** the subjunctive mood ▶ HISTORY Latin *subjungere* to add to

sublet *vb* **-letting, -let** to rent out (property which one is renting from someone else)

sublieutenant *n* a junior officer in a navy

sublimate *vb* **-mating, -mated** *psychol* to direct the energy of (a strong desire) into activities that are socially more acceptable ▶ HISTORY Latin *sublimare* to elevate

sublimation *n* **1** the act of sublimating **2** *chem, physics* the process of subliming

sublime *adj* **1** causing deep emotions and feelings of wonder or joy **2** without equal; supreme **3** of great moral, artistic, or spiritual value ▷ *n* **4 the sublime** something that is sublime ▷ *vb* **-liming, -limed 5** *chem, physics* to change directly from a solid to a vapour without first melting ▶ HISTORY Latin *sublimis* lofty > **sublimely** *adv*

subliminal *adj* resulting from or relating to mental processes of which the individual is not aware: *the subliminal message* ▶ HISTORY Latin *sub* below + *limen* threshold

sub-machine-gun *n* a portable automatic or semiautomatic gun with a short barrel

submarine *n* **1** a vessel which can operate below the surface of the sea ▷ *adj* **2** existing or located below the surface of the sea: *submarine cables* > **submariner** *n*

submaxillary *adj anat* of the lower jaw

submerge *vb* **-merging, -merged 1** to put or go below the surface of water or another liquid **2** to involve totally: *she submerged herself in her work* ▶ HISTORY Latin *submergere* > **submersion** *n*

submersible *adj* **1** capable of operating under water ▷ *n* **2** a small vessel designed to operate under water

submission *n* **1** an act or instance of submitting **2** something submitted, such as a proposal **3** the state in which someone has to accept the control of another person

submissive *adj* showing quiet obedience > **submissively** *adv* > **submissiveness** *n*

submit *vb* **-mitting, -mitted 1** to accept the will of another person or a superior force **2** to send (an application or proposal) to someone for judgment or consideration **3** to be voluntarily subjected (to medical or psychiatric treatment) ▶ HISTORY Latin *submittere* to place under

submucosa *n*, *pl* **-sae** *anat* the connective tissue beneath a mucous membrane

subnormal *adj* **1** less than the normal: *subnormal white blood cells* **2** *no longer in technical use* having a lower than average intelligence ▷ *n* **3** *no longer in technical use* a subnormal person

subordinate *adj* **1** of lesser rank or importance ▷ *n* **2** a person or thing that is of lesser rank or importance ▷ *vb* **-nating, -nated 3** (usually foll. by *to*) to regard (something) as less important than another: *the army's interests were subordinated to those of the air force* ▶ HISTORY Latin *sub-* lower + *ordo* rank > **subordination** *n*

subordinate clause *n grammar* a clause that functions as an adjective, an adverb, or a noun rather than one that functions as a sentence in its own right

subordinating conjunction *or* **subordinate conjunction** *n grammar* a conjunction that introduces subordinate clauses, such as *if, because, although,* and *until*

suborn *vb formal* to bribe or incite (a person) to commit a wrongful act ▶ HISTORY Latin *subornare*

subplot *n* a secondary plot in a novel, play, or film

subpoena (sub-**pee**-na) *n* **1** a legal document requiring a person to appear before a court of law at a specified time ▷ *vb* **-naing, -naed 2** to summon (someone) with a subpoena ▶ HISTORY Latin: under penalty

sub-post office *n* (in Britain) a post office which is run by a self-employed agent for the Post Office

sub rosa (sub **rose**-a) *adv literary* in secret ▶ HISTORY Latin, literally: under the rose; in ancient times a rose was hung over a table as a mark of secrecy

subroutine *n* a section of a computer program that is stored only once but can be used at several different points in the program

sub-Saharan *adj* in or relating to Africa south of the Sahara desert

subscribe *vb* **-scribing, -scribed 1** (usually foll. by *to*) to pay (money) as a contribution (to a charity, for a magazine, etc.) at regular intervals **2 subscribe to** to give support or approval: *I do not subscribe to this view* ▶ HISTORY Latin *subscribere* to write underneath > **subscriber** *n*

subscriber trunk dialling *n Brit, Austral & S African* a system allowing telephone users to obtain trunk calls by dialling direct without the help of an operator

subscript *printing adj* **1** (of a character) written or printed below the line ▷ *n* **2** a subscript character

subscription *n* **1** a payment for issues of a publication over a specified period of time **2** money paid or promised, such as to a charity or the fund raised in this way **3** *Brit, Austral & NZ* the membership fees paid to a society **4** an advance order for a new product

S

851

subsection *n* any of the smaller parts into which a section may be divided

subsequent *adj* occurring after; succeeding ▶ HISTORY Latin *subsequens* > **subsequently** *adv*

subservient *adj* **1** overeager to carry out someone else's wishes **2** of less importance or rank: *the subservient role of women in society* ▶ HISTORY Latin *subserviens* > **subservience** *n*

subset *n* a mathematical set contained within a larger set

subside *vb* **-siding, -sided** **1** to become less loud, excited, or violent **2** to sink to a lower level **3** (of the surface of the earth) to cave in; collapse ▶ HISTORY Latin *subsidere* to settle down > **subsidence** *n*

subsidiarity *n* the principle of taking political decisions at the lowest practical level

subsidiary *n, pl* **-aries** **1** Also called: **subsidiary company** a company which is at least half owned by another company **2** a person or thing that is of lesser importance ▷ *adj* **3** of lesser importance; subordinate ▶ HISTORY Latin *subsidiarius* supporting

subsidize *or* **-dise** *vb* **-dizing, -dized** *or* **-dising, -dised** to aid or support (an industry, a person, a public service, or a venture) with money

subsidy *n, pl* **-dies** **1** financial aid supplied by a government, for example to industry, or for public welfare **2** any financial aid, grant, or contribution ▶ HISTORY Latin *subsidium* assistance

subsist *vb* **subsist on** to manage to live: *to subsist on a diet of sausage rolls* ▶ HISTORY Latin *subsistere* to stand firm > **subsistence** *n*

subsistence farming *n* *agriculture* a type of farming in which most of the produce is consumed by the farmer and his or her family

subsoil *n* the layer of soil beneath the surface soil

subsonic *adj* being or moving at a speed below that of sound

substance *n* **1** the basic matter of which a thing consists **2** a specific type of matter with definite or fairly definite chemical composition: *a fatty substance* **3** the essential meaning of a speech, thought, or written article **4** important or meaningful quality: *the only evidence of substance against him* **5** material possessions or wealth: *a woman of substance* **6** **in substance** with regard to the most important points ▶ HISTORY Latin *substantia*

substantial *adj* **1** of a considerable size or value: *a substantial amount of money* **2** (of food or a meal) large and filling **3** solid or strong: *substantial brick pillars* **4** *formal* available to the senses; real: *substantial evidence* **5** of or relating to the basic material substance of a thing > **substantially** *adv*

substantiate *vb* **-ating, -ated** to establish (a story) as genuine > **substantiation** *n*

substantive *n* **1** *grammar* a noun or pronoun used in place of a noun ▷ *adj* **2** having importance or significance: *substantive negotiations between management and staff* **3** of or being the essential element of a thing ▶ HISTORY Latin *substare* to stand beneath

substitute *vb* **-tuting, -tuted** **1** (often foll. by *for*) to take the place of or put in place of another person or thing **2** *chem* to replace (an atom or group in a molecule) with (another atom or group) ▷ *n* **3** a person or thing that takes the place of another, such as a player who takes the place of a team-mate ▶ HISTORY Latin *substituere*

substitution *n* **1** the act of substituting **2** *maths* the replacing of the term of an equation by another that is known to have the same value in order to simplify the equation

substitution reaction *n* *chem* the replacing of an atom or group in a molecule by another atom or group

substrate *n* *biol* the substance upon which an enzyme acts ▶ HISTORY Latin *substratus* strewn beneath

subsume *vb* **-suming, -sumed** *formal* to include (something) under a larger classification or group: *an attempt to subsume fascism and communism under a general concept of totalitarianism* ▶ HISTORY Latin *sub-* under + *sumere* to take

subtenant *n* a person who rents property from a tenant > **subtenancy** *n*

subtend *vb* *geom* to be opposite (an angle or side) ▶ HISTORY Latin *subtendere* to extend beneath

subterfuge *n* a trick or deception used to achieve an objective ▶ HISTORY Latin *subterfugere* to escape by stealth

subterranean *adj* **1** found or operating below the surface of the earth **2** existing or working in a concealed or mysterious way: *the resistance movement worked largely by subterranean methods* ▶ HISTORY Latin *sub* beneath + *terra* earth

subtext *n* **1** an underlying theme in a piece of writing **2** a message which is not stated directly but can be inferred

subtitle *n* **1** **subtitles** *films* a written translation at the bottom of the picture in a film with foreign dialogue **2** a secondary title given to a book or play ▷ *vb* **-tling, -tled** **3** to provide subtitles for (a film) or a subtitle for (a book or play)

subtle *adj* **1** not immediately obvious: *a subtle change in his views* **2** (of a colour, taste, or smell) delicate or faint: *the subtle aroma* **3** using shrewd and indirect methods to achieve an objective **4** having or requiring the ability to make fine distinctions: *a subtle argument* ▶ HISTORY Latin *subtilis* finely woven > **subtly** *adv*

subtlety *n* **1** (*pl* **-ties**) a fine distinction **2** the state or quality of being subtle

subtract *vb* **1** *maths* to take (one number or quantity) away from another **2** to remove (a part of something) from the whole ▶ HISTORY Latin *subtrahere* to draw away from beneath > **subtraction** *n*

subtribe *n* *sociol* a subdivision of a tribe

subtropical *adj* of the region lying between the tropics and temperate lands

suburb *n* a residential district on the outskirts of a city or town ▶ HISTORY Latin *sub-* close to + *urbs* a city

S

suburban adj **1** of, in, or inhabiting a suburb **2** mildly disparaging conventional and unexciting

suburbanite n a person who lives in a suburb

suburbia n suburbs or the people living in them considered as a distinct community or class in society

subvention n formal a grant or subsidy, for example one from a government ▸ HISTORY Late Latin subventio assistance

subversion n the act or an instance of attempting to weaken or overthrow a government or an institution

subversive adj **1** intended or intending to weaken or overthrow a government or an institution ▹ n **2** a person engaged in subversive activities

subvert vb to bring about the downfall of (something existing by a system of law, such as a government) ▸ HISTORY Latin subvertere to overturn

subway n **1** Brit & Austral an underground passage for pedestrians to cross a road or railway **2** an underground railway

subzero adj lower than zero: subzero temperatures

succeed vb **1** to achieve an aim **2** to turn out satisfactorily: Grandfather's plan succeeded **3** to do well in a specified field: how to succeed in show biz **4** to come next in order after (someone or something): the first shock had been succeeded by a different kind of gloom **5** to take over (a position) from (someone): Henry VIII succeeded to the throne in 1509; he will be succeeded as president by his deputy ▸ HISTORY Latin succedere to follow after > **succeeding** adj

success n **1** the achievement of something attempted **2** the attainment of wealth, fame, or position **3** a person or thing that is successful ▸ HISTORY Latin successus an outcome

successful adj **1** having a favourable outcome **2** having attained fame, wealth, or position > **successfully** adv

succession n **1** a number of people or things following one another in order **2** the act or right by which one person succeeds another in a position **3** biol, geog the change in the types of plant occupying a given area that takes place over time **4 in succession** one after another: the third time in succession

successive adj following another or others without interruption: eleven successive victories > **successively** adv

successor n a person or thing that follows another, esp. a person who takes over another's job or position

succinct adj brief and clear: a succinct answer to this question ▸ HISTORY Latin succinctus > **succinctly** adv

succour or US **succor** n **1** help in time of difficulty ▹ vb **2** to give aid to (someone in time of difficulty) ▸ HISTORY Latin succurrere to hurry to help

succulent adj **1** (of food) juicy and delicious **2** (of plants) having thick fleshy leaves or stems ▹ n **3** a plant that can exist in very dry conditions by using water stored in its fleshy tissues ▸ HISTORY Latin sucus juice > **succulence** n

succumb vb **succumb to a** to give way to the force of or desire for (something) **b** to die of (a disease) ▸ HISTORY Latin succumbere

such adj **1** of the sort specified or understood: such places **2** so great or so much: such a mess ▹ adv **3** extremely: such a powerful friend ▹ pron **4** a person or thing of the sort specified or understood: such is the law of the land; fruitcakes and puddings and such **5 as such** in itself or themselves: the Nordic countries are not lifting sanctions as such **6 such as** for example: other socialist groups, such as the Fabians ▸ HISTORY Old English swilc

suchlike n **1** such or similar things: shampoos, talcs, and suchlike ▹ adj **2** of such a kind; similar: astrology and suchlike nonsense

suck vb **1** to draw (a liquid) into the mouth through pursed lips **2** to take (something) into the mouth and moisten, dissolve, or roll it around with the tongue: suck a mint **3** to extract liquid from (a solid food): he sat sucking orange segments **4** to draw in (fluid) as if by sucking: the mussel sucks in water **5** to drink milk from (a mother's breast); suckle **6** (often foll. by down, in) to draw (a thing or person somewhere) with a powerful force **7** slang to be contemptible or disgusting ▹ n **8** a sucking ▸ HISTORY Old English sūcan

sucker n **1** slang a person who is easily deceived or swindled **2** slang a person who cannot resist something: he's a sucker for fast cars **3** zool a part of the body of certain animals that is used for sucking or sticking to a surface **4** a rubber cup-shaped device attached to objects allowing them to stick to a surface by suction **5** bot a strong shoot coming from a mature plant's root or the base of its main stem

suckle vb **-ling, -led** to give (a baby or young animal) milk from the breast or udder or (of a baby or young animal) to suck milk from its mother's breast or udder

suckling n a baby or young animal that is still sucking milk from its mother's breast or udder

suck up to vb informal to flatter (a person in authority) in order to get something, such as praise or promotion

sucrose (soo-kroze) n chem sugar ▸ HISTORY French sucre sugar

suction n **1** the act or process of sucking **2** the force produced by drawing air out of a space to make a vacuum that will suck in a substance from another space ▸ HISTORY Latin sugere to suck

Sudanese adj **1** of the Sudan ▹ n, pl **-nese 2** a person from the Sudan

sudden adj **1** occurring or performed quickly and without warning ▹ n **2 all of a sudden** without warning; unexpectedly ▸ HISTORY Latin subitus unexpected > **suddenly** adv > **suddenness** n

sudden death n sport an extra period of play to decide the winner of a tied competition: the first player or team to go into the lead is the winner

sudden infant death syndrome n same as **cot death**

853

sudoku (soo-**doh**-koo) *n* a logic puzzle involving the insertion of numbers in a square so that none is repeated in any row, column, or internal square ▶ HISTORY from Japanese

sudorific (syoo-dor-**if**-ik) *adj* **1** causing sweating ▷ *n* **2** a drug that causes sweating ▶ HISTORY Latin *sudor* sweat + *facere* to make

suds *pl n* the bubbles on the surface of water in which soap or detergent has been dissolved; lather ▶ HISTORY probably from Middle Dutch *sudse* marsh

sue *vb* **suing, sued** to start legal proceedings (against): *we want to sue the council; he sued for custody of the three children* ▶ HISTORY Latin *sequi* to follow

suede *n* a leather with a fine velvet-like surface on one side

■ **WORD HISTORY**

■ In French, *gants de Suède* means 'gloves from Sweden'. The gloves were called 'Swedish gloves' because they were first made there.

suet *n* a hard fat obtained from sheep and cattle and used for making pastry and puddings ▶ HISTORY Old French *seu*

suffer *vb* **1** to undergo or be subjected to (physical pain or mental distress) **2 suffer from** to be badly affected by (an illness): *he was suffering from depression* **3** to become worse in quality; deteriorate: *his work suffered during their divorce* **4** to tolerate: *he suffers no fools* **5** to be set at a disadvantage: *the strongest of them suffers by comparison* ▶ HISTORY Latin *sufferre* > **sufferer** *n* > **suffering** *n*

sufferance *n* **on sufferance** tolerated with reluctance: *I was there on sufferance and all knew it*

suffice (suf-**fice**) *vb* **-ficing, -ficed 1** to be enough or satisfactory for a purpose **2 suffice it to say ...** it is enough to say ...: *suffice it to say that AIDS is on the increase* ▶ HISTORY Latin *sufficere*

sufficiency *n, pl* **-cies** an adequate amount

sufficient *adj* enough to meet a need or purpose; adequate ▶ HISTORY Latin *sufficiens* > **sufficiently** *adv*

suffix *grammar n* **1** a letter or letters added to the end of a word to form another word, such as -s and -ness in *dogs* and *softness* ▷ *vb* **2** to add (a letter or letters) to the end of a word to form another word ▶ HISTORY Latin *suffixus* fastened below

suffocate *vb* **-cating, -cated 1** to kill or die through lack of oxygen, such as by blockage of the air passage **2** to feel uncomfortable from heat and lack of air ▶ HISTORY Latin *suffocare* > **suffocating** *adj* > **suffocation** *n*

suffragan *n* a bishop appointed to assist an archbishop ▶ HISTORY Medieval Latin *suffragium* assistance

suffrage *n* the right to vote in public elections ▶ HISTORY Latin *suffragium*

suffragette *n* (in Britain at the beginning of the 20th century) a woman who campaigned militantly for women to be given the right to vote in public elections

suffragist *n* (in Britain at the beginning of the 20th century) a person who campaigned for women to be given the right to vote in public elections

suffuse *vb* **-fusing, -fused** to spread through or over (something): *the dawn suffused the sky with a cold grey wash* ▶ HISTORY Latin *suffusus* overspread with > **suffusion** *n*

sugar *n* **1** a sweet carbohydrate, usually in the form of white or brown crystals, which is found in many plants and is used to sweeten food and drinks **2** short for **sugar cane 3** *informal, chiefly US & Canad* a term of affection ▷ *vb* **4** to add sugar to (food or drink) to make it sweet **5** to cover with sugar: *sugared almonds* **6 sugar the pill** to make something unpleasant more tolerable by adding something pleasant ▶ HISTORY Old French *çucre*, from Sanskrit *śarkarā* > **sugared** *adj*

sugar beet *n* a beet grown for the sugar obtained from its roots

sugar cane *n* a tropical grass grown for the sugar obtained from its tall stout canes

sugar daddy *n* an elderly man who gives a young woman money and gifts in return for her company

sugar glider *n* a common Australian phalanger that glides from tree to tree feeding on insects and nectar

sugar maple *n* a North American maple tree, grown as a source of sugar, which is extracted from the sap

sugary *adj* **1** of, like, or containing sugar: *sugary snacks* **2** (of behaviour or language) very pleasant but probably not sincere: *sugary sentiment* > **sugariness** *n*

suggest *vb* **1** to put forward (a plan or an idea) for consideration: *he didn't suggest a meeting* **2** to bring (a person or thing) to the mind by the association of ideas: *a man whose very name suggests blandness* **3** to give a hint of: *her grey eyes suggesting a livelier mood than usual* ▶ HISTORY Latin *suggerere* to bring up

suggestible *adj* easily influenced by other people's ideas

suggestion *n* **1** something that is suggested **2** a hint or indication: *the entire castle gave no suggestion of period* **3** *psychol* the process whereby the presentation of an idea to a receptive individual leads to the acceptance of that idea

suggestive *adj* **1** (of remarks or gestures) causing people to think of sex **2 suggestive of** communicating a hint of

suicidal *adj* **1** wanting to commit suicide **2** likely to lead to danger or death: *a suicidal attempt to rescue her son* **3** likely to destroy one's own career or future: *it would be suicidal for them to ignore public opinion*

suicide *n* **1** the act of killing oneself deliberately: *he tried to commit suicide* **2** a person who kills himself or herself intentionally **3** the self-inflicted ruin of one's own career or future: *such a cut would be political suicide* ▶ HISTORY Latin *sui* of oneself + *caedere* to kill

S

suit *n* **1** a set of clothes of the same material designed to be worn together, usually a jacket with matching trousers or skirt **2** an outfit worn for a specific purpose: *a diving suit* **3** a legal action taken against someone; lawsuit **4** any of the four types of card in a pack of playing cards: spades, hearts, diamonds, or clubs **5** *slang* a business executive or white-collar worker **6 follow suit** to act in the same way as someone else **7 strong suit** *or* **strongest suit** something one excels in ▷ *vb* **8** to be fit or appropriate for: *that colour suits you* **9** to be acceptable to (someone) **10 suit oneself** to do what one wants without considering other people ▶ HISTORY Old French *sieute* set of things > **suited** *adj*

suitable *adj* appropriate for a particular function or occasion; proper > **suitability** *n* > **suitably** *adv*

suitcase *n* a large portable travelling case for clothing

suite *n* **1** a set of connected rooms in a hotel **2** a matching set of furniture, for example two armchairs and a settee **3** *music* a composition of several movements in the same key ▶ HISTORY French

suitor *n* **1** *old-fashioned* a man who wants to marry a woman **2** *law* a person who starts legal proceedings against someone; plaintiff ▶ HISTORY Latin *secutor* follower

Sukkoth (**sook**-oat) *n* an eight-day Jewish harvest festival, commemorating the period when the Israelites lived in the wilderness

sulk *vb* **1** to be silent and moody as a way of showing anger or resentment: *I went home and sulked for two days* ▷ *n* **2** a mood in which one shows anger or resentment by being silent and moody: *he was just in a sulk*

sulky *adj* **sulkier, sulkiest** moody or silent because of anger or resentment ▶ HISTORY perhaps from obsolete *sulke* sluggish > **sulkily** *adv* > **sulkiness** *n*

sullen *adj* unwilling to talk or be sociable; sulky ▶ HISTORY Latin *solus* alone > **sullenly** *adv* > **sullenness** *n*

sully *vb* **-lies, -lying, -lied 1** to ruin (someone's reputation) **2** to spoil or make dirty: *the stream had been sullied by the smelter's pollution* ▶ HISTORY probably from French *souiller* to soil

sulpha *or US* **sulfa drug** *n pharmacol* any of a group of sulphonamides that prevent the growth of bacteria: used to treat bacterial infections

sulphate *or US* **sulfate** *n chem* a salt or ester of sulphuric acid

sulphide *or US* **sulfide** *n chem* a compound of sulphur with another element

sulphite *or US* **sulfite** *n chem* any salt or ester of sulphurous acid

sulphonamide *or US* **sulfonamide** (sulf-**on**-a-mide) *n pharmacol* any of a class of organic compounds that prevent the growth of bacteria

sulphur *or US* **sulfur** *n chem* a light yellow, highly inflammable, nonmetallic element used in the production of sulphuric acid, in the vulcanization of rubber, and in medicine. Symbol: S ▶ HISTORY Latin *sulfur* > **sulphuric** *or US* **sulfuric** *adj*

sulphur dioxide *n chem* a strong-smelling colourless soluble gas, used in the manufacture of sulphuric acid and in the preservation of foodstuffs

sulphureous *or US* **sulfureous** (sulf-**yoor**-ee-uss) *adj* same as **sulphurous** (sense 1)

sulphuric acid *n chem* a colourless dense oily corrosive liquid used in the manufacture of fertilizers and explosives

sulphurize *or* **-rise** *or US* **sulfurize** (sulf-yoor-rise) *vb* **-rizing, -rized** *or* **-rising, -rised** *chem* to combine with or treat (something) with sulphur or a sulphur compound

sulphurous *or US* **sulfurous** *adj chem* **1** of or resembling sulphur **2** containing sulphur, esp. with a valence of four

sultan *n* the sovereign of a Muslim country ▶ HISTORY Arabic: rule

sultana *n* **1** the dried fruit of a small white seedless grape **2** a sultan's wife, mother, daughter, or concubine ▶ HISTORY Italian

sultanate *n* **1** the territory ruled by a sultan **2** the office or rank of a sultan

sultry *adj* **-trier, -triest** *written* **1** (of weather or climate) very hot and humid **2** suggesting hidden passion: *a sultry brunette* ▶ HISTORY obsolete *sulter* to swelter

sum *n* **1** the result of the addition of numbers or quantities **2** one or more columns or rows of numbers to be added, subtracted, multiplied, or divided **3** a quantity of money: *they can win enormous sums* **4 in sum** as a summary; in short: *in sum, it's been a bad week for the government* ▷ *adj* **5** complete or final: *the sum total* ▷ *vb* **summing, summed 6** See **sum up** ▶ HISTORY Latin *summa* the top, sum

summarize *or* **-rise** *vb* **-rizing, -rized** *or* **-rising, -rised** to give a short account of (something)

summary *n, pl* **-maries 1** a brief account giving the main points of something ▷ *adj* **2** performed quickly, without formality or attention to details: *a summary judgment* ▶ HISTORY Latin *summarium* > **summarily** *adv*

summary offence *n law* a minor criminal offence for which the defendant is tried before a magistrate. Compare **indictable offence**

summation *n* **1** a summary of what has just been done or said **2** the process of working out a sum; addition **3** the result of such a process

summer *n* **1** the warmest season of the year, between spring and autumn **2** *literary* a time of youth, success, or happiness ▶ HISTORY Old English *sumor* > **summery** *adj*

summerhouse *n* a small building in a garden, used for shade in the summer

summer school *n* an academic course held during the summer

summer solstice *n* the time at which the sun is at its northernmost point in the sky (southernmost point in the S hemisphere), appearing at noon at its highest altitude above the horizon. It occurs about June 21 (December 22 in the S hemisphere)

summertime *n* the period or season of summer

summing-up *n* **1** a summary of the main points of an argument, speech, or piece of writing **2** concluding statements made by a judge to the jury before they retire to consider their verdict

summit *n* **1** the highest point or part of a mountain or hill **2** the highest possible degree or state; peak or climax: *the summit of success* **3** a meeting of heads of governments or other high officials ▶ HISTORY Old French *somet*

summon *vb* **1** to order (someone) to come **2** send for (someone) to appear in court **3** to call upon (someone) to do something: *the authorities had summoned the relatives to be available* **4** to convene (a meeting) **5** (often foll. by *up*) to call into action (one's strength, courage, etc.); muster ▶ HISTORY Latin *summonere* to give a discreet reminder

summons *n, pl* **-monses 1** a call or an order to attend a specified place at a specified time **2** an official order requiring a person to attend court, either to answer a charge or to give evidence ▷ *vb* **3** to order (someone) to appear in court: *three others had been summonsed for questioning*

sumo *n* the national style of wrestling of Japan, in which two contestants of great height and weight attempt to force each other out of the ring ▶ HISTORY Japanese

sump *n* **1** a container in an internal-combustion engine into which oil can drain **2** same as **cesspool** **3** *mining* a hollow at the bottom of a shaft where water collects ▶ HISTORY Middle Dutch *somp* marsh

sumptuary *adj* controlling expenditure or extravagant use of resources ▶ HISTORY Latin *sumptuarius* concerning expense

sumptuous *adj* magnificent and very expensive; splendid: *sumptuous decoration* ▶ HISTORY Latin *sumptuosus* costly

sum up *vb* **1** to give a short account of (the main points of an argument, speech, or piece of writing) **2** to form a quick opinion of: *how well you have summed me up!*

sun *n* **1** the star that is the source of heat and light for the planets in the solar system. *Related adjective:* **solar 2** any star around which a system of planets revolves **3** the heat and light received from the sun; sunshine **4** **catch the sun** to become slightly suntanned **5** **under the sun** on earth; at all: *there are no free lunches under the sun* ▷ *vb* **sunning, sunned 6** **sun oneself** to lie, sit, or walk in the sunshine on a warm day ▶ HISTORY Old English *sunne* > **sunless** *adj*

Sun. Sunday

sunbathe *vb* **-bathing, -bathed** to lie or sit in the sunshine, in order to get a suntan > **sunbather** *n* > **sunbathing** *n*

sunbeam *n* a ray of sunlight

sunburn *n* painful reddening of the skin caused by overexposure to the sun > **sunburnt** or **sunburned** *adj*

sundae *n* ice cream topped with a sweet sauce, nuts, whipped cream, and fruit ▶ HISTORY origin unknown

Sunday *n* the first day of the week and the Christian day of worship ▶ HISTORY Old English *sunnandæg* day of the sun

Sunday school *n* a school for teaching children about Christianity, usually held in a church hall on Sunday

sundial *n* a device used for telling the time during the hours of sunlight, consisting of a pointer that casts a shadow onto a surface marked in hours

sundown *n* US sunset

sundries *pl n* several things of various sorts

sundry *adj* **1** several or various; miscellaneous ▷ *pron* **2** **all and sundry** everybody ▶ HISTORY Old English *syndrig* separate

sunfish *n, pl* **-fish** or **-fishes** a large sea fish with a rounded body

sunflower *n* **1** a very tall plant with large yellow flowers **2** **sunflower seed oil** the oil extracted from sunflower seeds, used as a salad oil and in margarine

sung *vb* the past participle of **sing**

sunglasses *pl n* glasses with darkened lenses that protect the eyes from bright sunlight

sunk *vb* a past participle of **sink**

sunken *vb* **1** a past participle of **sink** ▷ *adj* **2** (of a person's cheeks, eyes, or chest) curving inward due to old age or bad health **3** situated at a lower level than the surrounding or usual one: *the sunken garden* **4** situated under water; submerged: *sunken ships*

sun lamp *n* a lamp that gives off ultraviolet rays, used for muscular therapy or for giving people an artificial suntan

sunlight *n* the light that comes from the sun > **sunlit** *adj*

Sunnah *n* the body of traditional Islamic law ▶ HISTORY Arabic

sunny *adj* **-nier, -niest 1** full of or lit up by sunshine **2** cheerful and happy

sunrise *n* **1** the daily appearance of the sun above the horizon **2** the time at which the sun rises

sunrise industry *n* any of the fast-developing high-technology industries, such as electronics

sunroof *n* a panel in the roof of a car that may be opened to let in air or sunshine

sunset *n* **1** the daily disappearance of the sun below the horizon **2** the time at which the sun sets

sunshine *n* **1** the light and warmth from the sun **2** a light-hearted term of address

sunspot *n* **1** *informal* a sunny holiday resort **2** a dark cool patch on the surface of the sun **3** *Austral* a small area of skin damage caused by exposure to the sun

sunstroke *n* a condition caused by spending too much time exposed to intensely hot sunlight and producing high fever and sometimes loss of consciousness

suntan *n* a brownish colouring of the skin caused by exposure to the sun or a sun lamp > **suntanned** *adj*

sun-up *n* US & Austral sunrise

S

sup[1] *vb* **supping, supped** **1** to take (liquid) by swallowing a little at a time ▷ *n* **2** a sip ▸ **HISTORY** Old English *sūpan*

sup[2] *vb* **supping, supped** *archaic* to have supper ▸ **HISTORY** Old French *soper*

super *informal adj* **1** very good or very nice: *they had a super holiday* ▷ *n* **2** *Austral & NZ, informal* superannuation **3** *Austral & NZ, informal* superphosphate ▸ **HISTORY** Latin: above

super- *prefix* **1** above or over: *superscript* **2** outstanding: *superstar* **3** of greater size, extent, or quality: *supermarket* ▸ **HISTORY** Latin

superannuated *adj* **1** discharged with a pension, owing to age or illness **2** too old to be useful; obsolete ▸ **HISTORY** Medieval Latin *superannatus* aged more than one year

superannuation *n* **a** a regular payment made by an employee into a pension fund **b** the pension finally paid

superb *adj* extremely good or impressive ▸ **HISTORY** Latin *superbus* distinguished > **superbly** *adv*

Super Bowl *n American football* the championship game held annually between the best team of the American Football Conference and that of the National Football Conference

superbug *n informal* a bacterium resistant to antibiotics

supercharge *vb* **-charging, -charged** **1** to increase the power of (an internal-combustion engine) with a supercharger **2** to charge (the atmosphere, a remark, etc.) with an excess amount of (tension, emotion, etc.) **3** to apply pressure to (a fluid); pressurize

supercharger *n* a device that increases the power of an internal-combustion engine by forcing extra air into it

supercilious *adj* behaving in a superior and arrogant manner ▸ **HISTORY** Latin *supercilium* eyebrow > **superciliously** *adv* > **superciliousness** *n*

superconductivity *n physics* the ability of certain substances to conduct electric current with almost no resistance at very low temperatures > **superconducting** *adj* > **superconductor** *n*

supercontinent *n* a huge landmass thought to have existed in the geological past and to have split into smaller landmasses and formed the present continents

superego *n, pl* **-gos** *psychoanal* that part of the unconscious mind that governs a person's ideas concerning what is right and wrong

supererogation *n* the act of doing more work than is required ▸ **HISTORY** Latin *supererogare* to spend over and above

superficial *adj* **1** not careful or thorough: *a superficial analysis* **2** only outwardly apparent rather than genuine or actual: *those are merely superficial differences* **3** (of a person) lacking deep emotions or serious interests; shallow **4** of, near, or forming the surface: *the gash was superficial*

▸ **HISTORY** Late Latin *superficialis* > **superficiality** *n* > **superficially** *adv*

superfluous (soo-**per**-flew-uss) *adj* more than is sufficient or required ▸ **HISTORY** Latin *superfluus* overflowing > **superfluity** *n*

superglue *n* an extremely strong and quick-drying glue

supergrass *n Brit, Austral & NZ* an informer who names a large number of people as terrorists or criminals, esp. one who gives this information in order to avoid being put on trial

superhuman *adj* beyond normal human ability or experience: *a superhuman effort*

superimpose *vb* **-posing, -posed** to set or place (something) on or over something else

superintend *vb* to supervise (a person or an activity) ▸ **HISTORY** Latin *super-* above + *intendere* to give attention to

superintendent *n* **1** a senior police officer **2** a person who directs and manages an organization or office

superior *adj* **1** greater in quality, quantity, or usefulness **2** higher in rank, position, or status: *he was reprimanded by a superior officer* **3** believing oneself to be better than others **4** of very high quality or respectability: *superior merchandise* **5** *formal* placed higher up: *damage to the superior surface of the wing* **6** *printing* (of a character) written or printed above the line ▷ *n* **7** a person of greater rank or status **8** See **mother superior** ▸ **HISTORY** Latin *superus* placed above > **superiority** *n*

superior court *n law* **1** a higher court not subject to control by any other court except by way of appeal **2** *US* (in several states) a court of general jurisdiction ranking above the inferior courts and below courts of last resort

superlative (soo-**per**-lat-iv) *adj* **1** of outstanding quality; supreme **2** *grammar* denoting the form of an adjective or adverb that expresses the highest degree of quality ▷ *n* **3** the highest quality **4** *grammar* the superlative form of an adjective or adverb ▸ **HISTORY** Old French *superlatif*

superman *n, pl* **-men** any man with great physical or mental powers

supermarket *n* a large self-service shop selling food and household goods

supermodel *n* a famous and highly-paid fashion model

supernatural *adj* **1** of or relating to things that cannot be explained by science, such as clairvoyance, ghosts, etc. ▷ *n* **2 the supernatural** forces, occurrences, and beings that cannot be explained by science

supernova *n, pl* **-vae** *or* **-vas** a star that explodes and, for a few days, becomes one hundred million times brighter than the sun

supernumerary *adj* **1** exceeding the required or regular number; extra **2** employed as a substitute or assistant ▷ *n, pl* **-aries** **3** a person or thing that exceeds the required or regular number **4** a substitute or assistant **5** an actor who has no lines to say ▸ **HISTORY** Latin *super-* above + *numerus* number

S

857

superphosphate n a chemical fertilizer, esp. one made by treating rock phosphate with sulphuric acid

superpower n a country of very great military and economic power, such as the US

superscript printing adj **1** (of a character) written or printed above the line ▷ n **2** a superscript character

supersede vb **-seding, -seded 1** to take the place of (something old-fashioned or less appropriate): cavalry was superseded by armoured vehicles **2** to replace (someone) in function or office ▶ HISTORY Latin supersedere to sit above

supersonic adj being, having, or capable of a speed greater than the speed of sound

superstar n an extremely popular and famous entertainer or sportsperson > **superstardom** n

superstate n a large state, esp. one created from a federation of states

superstition n **1** irrational belief in magic and the powers that supposedly bring good luck or bad luck **2** a belief or practice based on this ▶ HISTORY Latin superstitio > **superstitious** adj

superstore n a large supermarket

superstructure n **1** any structure or concept built on something else **2** naut any structure above the main deck of a ship

supertanker n a very large fast tanker

supertax n an extra tax on incomes above a certain level

supervene vb **-vening, -vened** to happen as an unexpected development ▶ HISTORY Latin supervenire to come upon > **supervention** n

supervise vb **-vising, -vised 1** to direct the performance or operation of (an activity or a process) **2** to watch over (people) so as to ensure appropriate behaviour ▶ HISTORY Latin super- over + videre to see > **supervision** n > **supervisor** n > **supervisory** adj

supine (**soo**-pine) adj **1** formal lying on one's back **2** offering no resistance; submissive: the team's supine surrender to Manchester United ▶ HISTORY Latin supinus

supper n **1** an evening meal **2** a late evening snack ▶ HISTORY Old French soper

supplant vb to take the place of (someone or something) ▶ HISTORY Latin supplantare to trip up

supple adj **1** (of a person) moving and bending easily and gracefully **2** (of a material or object) soft and bending easily without breaking ▶ HISTORY Latin supplex bowed > **suppleness** n

supplement n **1** an addition designed to make something more adequate **2** a magazine distributed free with a newspaper **3** a section added to a publication to supply further information or correct errors **4** (of money) an additional payment to obtain special services ▷ vb **5** to provide an addition to (something), esp. in order to make up for an inadequacy: a Saturday job to supplement her grant ▶ HISTORY Latin supplementum > **supplementary** adj

supplementary angle n geom either of two angles whose sum is 180 degrees

supplicant n formal a person who makes a humble request ▶ HISTORY Latin supplicans beseeching

supplication n formal a humble request for help ▶ HISTORY Latin supplicare to beg on one's knees

supply vb **-plies, -plying, -plied 1** to provide with something required: Nigeria may supply them with oil ▷ n, pl **-plies 2** the act of providing something **3** an amount available for use; stock: electricity supply **4 supplies** food and equipment needed for a trip or military campaign **5** econ the amount of a commodity that producers are willing and able to offer for sale at a specified price: supply and demand **6** a person who acts as a temporary substitute ▷ adj **7** acting as a temporary substitute: supply teachers ▶ HISTORY Latin supplere to complete > **supplier** n

support vb **1** to carry the weight of (a thing or person) **2** to provide the necessities of life for (a family or person) **3** to give practical or emotional help to (someone) **4** to give approval to (a cause, idea, or political party) **5** to take an active interest in and be loyal to (a particular football or other sports team) **6** to establish the truthfulness or accuracy of (a theory or statement) by providing new facts **7** to speak in a debate in favour of (a motion) **8** (in a concert) to perform earlier than (the main attraction) **9** films, theatre to play a less important role to (the leading actor or actress) ▷ n **10** the act of supporting or the condition of being supported **11** a thing that bears the weight of an object from below **12** a person who gives someone practical or emotional help **13** the means of providing the necessities of life for a family or person **14** a band and entertainer not topping the bill ▶ HISTORY Latin supportare to bring > **supportive** adj

supporter n a person who supports a sports team, politician, etc.

suppose vb **-posing, -posed 1** to presume (something) to be true without certain knowledge: I suppose it will be in the papers **2** to consider (something) as a possible suggestion for the sake of discussion: suppose you're arrested on a misdemeanour **3** (of a theory) to depend on the truth or existence of: this scenario supposes that he would do so ▶ HISTORY Latin supponere to substitute

supposed adj **1 supposed to** expected to: spies aren't supposed to be nice **2** presumed to be true without certain knowledge; doubtful: the supposed wonders of drug therapy > **supposedly** adv

supposition n **1** an idea or a statement believed or assumed to be true **2** the act of supposing: much of it is based on supposition

suppository n, pl **-ries** med a medicine in solid form that is inserted into the vagina or rectum and left to dissolve ▶ HISTORY Latin suppositus placed beneath

suppress vb **1** to put an end to (something) by physical or legal force **2** to prevent the circulation

s

or publication of (information or books) **3** to hold (an emotion or a response) in check; restrain: *he could barely suppress a groan* **4** *electronics* to reduce or eliminate (interference) in a circuit ▶ **HISTORY** Latin *suppressus* held down > **suppression** *n*

suppressant *n* a drug that suppresses an action: *a cough suppressant*

suppurate *vb* **-rating, -rated** *pathol* (of a wound or sore) to produce or leak pus ▶ **HISTORY** Latin *suppurare*

supremacy *n* **1** supreme power; dominance **2** the state or quality of being superior

supreme *adj* **1** of highest status or power: *the Supreme Council* **2** of highest quality or importance: *a supreme player* **3** greatest in degree; extreme: *supreme happiness* ▶ **HISTORY** Latin *supremus* highest > **supremely** *adv*

Supreme Being *n* the highest or greatest being; God

Supreme Court *n law* **1** (in the US) the highest Federal court, possessing final appellate jurisdiction and exercising supervisory jurisdiction over the lower courts **2** (in many states) the highest state court

supremo *n*, *pl* **-mos** *Brit & Austral, informal* a person in overall authority

sur-¹ *prefix* over; above; beyond: *surcharge; surrealism* ▶ **HISTORY** Old French

sur-² *prefix* See **sub-**

surcharge *n* **1** a charge in addition to the usual payment or tax **2** an excessive sum charged, often unlawfully ▷ *vb* **-charging, -charged** **3** to charge (someone) an additional sum or tax **4** to overcharge (someone) for something

surd *maths n* **1** an irrational number ▷ *adj* **2** of or relating to a surd ▶ **HISTORY** Latin *surdus* muffled

sure *adj* **1** free from doubt or uncertainty (in regard to a belief): *she was sure that she was still at home; I am sure he didn't mean it* **2** **sure of** having no doubt, such as of the occurrence of a future state or event: *sure of winning the point* **3** reliable or accurate: *a sure sign of dry rot* **4** bound inevitably (to be or do something); certain: *his aggressive style is sure to please the American fans* **5** **sure of** or **about** happy to put one's trust in (someone): *I'm still not quite sure about her* **6** **sure of oneself** confident in one's own abilities and opinions **7** not open to doubt: *sure proof* **8** bound to be or occur; inevitable: *victory is sure* **9** physically secure: *a sure footing* **10** **be sure** to be careful or certain: *be sure to label each jar* **11** **for sure** without a doubt **12** **make sure** to make certain: *make sure there is no-one in the car* **13** **sure enough** *informal* in fact: *sure enough, this is happening* **14** **to be sure** it has to be acknowledged; admittedly ▷ *adv* **15** *informal, chiefly US & Canad* without question; certainly: *it sure is bad news* ▷ *interj* **16** *informal* willingly; yes ▶ **HISTORY** Old French *seur* > **sureness** *n*

sure-fire *adj informal* certain to succeed: *a sure-fire cure*

sure-footed *adj* **1** unlikely to fall, slip, or stumble **2** unlikely to make a mistake

surely *adv* **1** am I not right in thinking that?; I am sure that: *surely you can see that?* **2** without doubt: *without support they will surely fail* **3** **slowly but surely** gradually but noticeably ▷ *interj* **4** *chiefly US & Canad* willingly; yes

surety *n*, *pl* **-ties** **1** a person who takes legal responsibility for the fulfilment of another's debt or obligation **2** security given as a guarantee that an obligation will be met ▶ **HISTORY** Latin *securitas* security

surf *n* **1** foam caused by waves breaking on the shore or on a reef ▷ *vb* **2** to take part in surfing **3** to move rapidly through a particular medium: *surfing the internet* **4** *informal* to be carried on top of something: *that guy's surfing the audience* ▶ **HISTORY** probably variant of *sough* > **surfer** *n*

surface *n* **1** the outside or top of an object **2** the size of such an area **3** material covering the surface of an object **4** the outward appearance as opposed to the real or hidden nature of something: *on the surface the idea seems attractive* **5** *geom* **a** the complete boundary of a solid figure **b** something that has length and breadth but no thickness **6** the uppermost level of the land or sea **7** **come to the surface** to become apparent after being hidden ▷ *vb* **-facing, -faced** **8** to become apparent or widely known **9** to rise to the surface of water **10** to give (an area) a particular kind of surface **11** *informal* to get up out of bed ▶ **HISTORY** French

surface area *n chem* the area that is exposed for a chemical reaction to take place

surface tension *n physics* a property of liquids, caused by molecular forces, that leads to the apparent presence of a surface film and to rising and falling in contact with solids

surfboard *n* a long narrow board used in surfing

surfeit *n formal* **1** an excessive amount **2** excessive eating or drinking **3** an uncomfortably full or sickened feeling caused by eating or drinking too much ▶ **HISTORY** French *sourfait*

surfing *n* the sport of riding towards shore on the crest of a wave by standing or lying on a surfboard

surge *n* **1** a sudden powerful increase: *a surge in spending* **2** a strong rolling movement of the sea **3** a heavy rolling motion or sound: *a great surge of people* ▷ *vb* **surging, surged** **4** to move forward strongly and suddenly **5** (of the sea) to rise or roll with a heavy swelling motion ▶ **HISTORY** Latin *surgere* to rise

surgeon *n* a medical doctor who specializes in surgery

surgery *n*, *pl* **-geries** **1** medical treatment in which a person's body is cut open by a surgeon in order to treat or remove the problem part **2** *Brit* a place where, or time when, a doctor or dentist can be consulted **3** *Brit* a time when an MP or councillor can be consulted ▶ **HISTORY** Greek *kheir* hand + *ergon* work

surgical *adj* involving or used in surgery > **surgically** *adv*

surgical spirit *n* methylated spirit used medically for cleaning wounds and sterilizing equipment

S

surly *adj* **-lier, -liest** *written* bad-tempered and rude ▶ HISTORY from obsolete *sirly* haughty

surmise *vb* **-mising, -mised 1** to guess (something) from incomplete or uncertain evidence ▷ *n* **2** a conclusion based on incomplete or uncertain evidence ▶ HISTORY Old French *surmettre* to accuse

surmount *vb* **1** to overcome (a problem) **2** to be situated on top of (something): *the island is surmounted by a huge black castle* ▶ HISTORY Old French *surmonter* > **surmountable** *adj*

surname *n* a family name as opposed to a first or Christian name ▶ HISTORY Old French *sur-* over + *nom* name

surpass *vb* **1** to be greater in extent than or superior in achievement to (something or someone) **2 surpass oneself** or **expectations** to go beyond the limit of what was expected ▶ HISTORY French *surpasser*

surplice *n* a loose knee-length garment with wide sleeves, worn by members of the clergy and choristers ▶ HISTORY Old French *sourpelis*

surplus *n* **1** a quantity or amount left over in excess of what is required **2** *accounting* an excess of income over spending ▷ *adj* **3** being in excess; extra: *surplus to requirements* ▶ HISTORY Old French

surprise *n* **1** the act of taking someone unawares: *the element of surprise* **2** a sudden or unexpected event, gift, etc.: *this is a nice surprise* **3** the feeling of being surprised; astonishment: *to our great surprise* **4 take someone by surprise** to capture someone unexpectedly or catch someone unprepared ▷ *adj* **5** causing surprise: *a surprise attack* ▷ *vb* **-prising, -prised 6** to cause (someone) to feel amazement or wonder **7** to come upon or discover (someone) unexpectedly or suddenly **8** to capture or attack (someone) suddenly and without warning **9 surprise into** to provoke (someone) to unintended action by a trick or deception ▶ HISTORY Old French *surprendre* to overtake > **surprised** *adj* > **surprising** *adj* > **surprisingly** *adv*

surreal *adj* very strange or dreamlike; bizarre

surrealism *n* a movement in art and literature in the 1920s, involving the combination of images that would not normally be found together, as if in a dream ▶ HISTORY French *surréalisme* > **surrealist** *n, adj* > **surrealistic** *adj*

surrender *vb* **1** to give oneself up physically to an enemy after defeat **2** to give (something) up to another, under pressure or on demand: *the rebels surrendered their arms* **3** to give (something) up voluntarily to another: *he was surrendering his own chance for the championship* **4** to give in to a temptation or an influence ▷ *n* **5** the act or instance of surrendering ▶ HISTORY Old French *surrendre*

surreptitious *adj* done in secret or without permission: *surreptitious moments of bliss* ▶ HISTORY Latin *surrepticius* furtive > **surreptitiously** *adv*

860 **surrogate** *n* **1** a person or thing acting as a

substitute ▷ *adj* **2** acting as a substitute: *a surrogate father* ▶ HISTORY Latin *surrogare* to substitute

surrogate mother *n* a woman who gives birth to a child on behalf of a couple who cannot have a baby themselves, usually by artificial insemination > **surrogate motherhood** or **surrogacy** *n*

surround *vb* **1** to encircle or enclose (something or someone) **2** to exist around (someone or something): *the family members who surround him* ▷ *n* **3** *chiefly Brit* a border, such as the area of uncovered floor between the walls of a room and the carpet ▶ HISTORY Old French *suronder* > **surrounding** *adj*

surroundings *pl n* the area and environment around a person, place, or thing

surtax *n* an extra tax on incomes above a certain level

surveillance *n* close observation of a person suspected of being a spy or a criminal ▶ HISTORY French

survey *vb* **1** to view or consider (something) as a whole: *she surveyed her purchases anxiously* **2** to make a detailed map of (an area of land) by measuring or calculating distances and height **3** *Brit* to inspect (a building) to assess its condition and value **4** to make a detailed investigation of the behaviour, opinions, etc. of (a group of people) ▷ *n* **5** a detailed investigation of the behaviour, opinions, etc. of a group of people **6** the act of making a detailed map of an area of land by measuring or calculating distance and height **7** *Brit* an inspection of a building to assess its condition and value ▶ HISTORY French *surveoir* > **surveying** *n* > **surveyor** *n*

survival *n* **1** the condition of having survived something **2** a person or thing that continues to exist in the present despite being from an earlier time, such as a custom ▷ *adj* **3** of, relating to, or assisting the act of surviving: *survival suits*

survive *vb* **-viving, -vived 1** to continue to live or exist after (a passage of time or a difficult or dangerous experience) **2** to live after the death of (another) ▶ HISTORY Old French *sourvivre* > **survivor** *n*

susceptibility *n, pl* **-ties 1** the quality or condition of being easily affected or influenced by something **2 susceptibilities** emotional feelings

susceptible *adj* **1 susceptible to a** giving in easily to: *susceptible to political pressure* **b** vulnerable to (a disease or injury): *susceptible to pneumonia* **2** easily affected emotionally; impressionable ▶ HISTORY Late Latin *susceptibilis*

sushi (**soo**-shee) *n* a Japanese dish consisting of small cakes of cold rice with a topping of raw fish ▶ HISTORY Japanese

suspect *vb* **1** to believe (someone) to be guilty without having any proof **2** to think (something) to be false or doubtful: *he suspected her intent* **3** to believe (something) to be the case; think probable: *I suspect he had another reason* ▷ *n* **4** a person who is believed guilty of a specified offence ▷ *adj* **5** not to be trusted or relied upon: *her commitment to the* cause has always been suspect ▶ HISTORY Latin *suspicere* to mistrust

suspend vb **1** to hang (something) from a high place **2** to cause (something) to remain floating or hanging: *a huge orange sun suspended above the horizon* **3** to cause (something) to stop temporarily: *the discussions have been suspended* **4** to remove (someone) temporarily from a job or position, usually as a punishment ▶ HISTORY Latin *suspendere*

suspended animation n a state in which the body's functions are slowed down to a minimum for a period of time, such as by freezing or hibernation

suspended sentence n a sentence of imprisonment that is not served by an offender unless he or she commits a further offence during a specified time

suspenders pl n **1 a** elastic straps attached to a belt or corset, with fasteners for holding up women's stockings **b** similar fasteners attached to garters for holding up men's socks **2** US & Canad braces

suspense n **1** a state of anxiety or uncertainty: *Sue and I stared at each other in suspense* **2** excitement felt at the approach of the climax of a book, film, or play: *action and suspense abound in this thriller* ▶ HISTORY Medieval Latin *suspensum* delay > **suspenseful** adj

suspension n **1** the delaying or stopping temporarily of something: *the suspension of the talks* **2** temporary removal from a job or position, usually as a punishment **3** the act of suspending or the state of being suspended **4** a system of springs and shock absorbers that supports the body of a vehicle **5** a device, usually a wire or spring, that suspends or supports something, such as the pendulum of a clock **6** chem a mixture in which fine solid or liquid particles are suspended in a fluid

suspension bridge n a bridge suspended from cables that hang between two towers and are secured at both ends

suspicion n **1** the act or an instance of suspecting; belief without sure proof that something is wrong **2** a feeling of mistrust **3** written a slight trace: *the merest suspicion of a threat* **4 above suspicion** not possibly guilty of anything, through having a good reputation **5 under suspicion** suspected of doing something wrong ▶ HISTORY Latin *suspicio* distrust

suspicious adj **1** causing one to suspect something is wrong: *suspicious activities* **2** unwilling to trust: *I'm suspicious of his motives* > **suspiciously** adv

suss out vb Brit, Austral & NZ, slang to work out (a situation or a person's character), using one's intuition ▶ HISTORY from *suspect*

sustain vb **1** to maintain or continue for a period of time: *I managed to sustain a conversation* **2** to keep up the strength or energy of (someone): *one mouthful of water to sustain him; the merest drop of comfort to sustain me* **3** to suffer (an injury or loss): *he sustained a spinal injury* **4** to support (something)

from below **5** to support or agree with (a decision or statement): *objection sustained* ▶ HISTORY Latin *sustinere* to hold up > **sustained** adj

sustainable adj **1** capable of being sustained **2** (of economic development or energy sources) capable of being maintained at a steady level without exhausting natural resources or causing ecological damage: *sustainable development* > **sustainability** n

sustenance n means of maintaining health or life; food and drink

suture (soo-tcher) n surgery a stitch made with catgut or silk thread, to join the edges of a wound together ▶ HISTORY Latin *suere* to sew

SUV sport (or sports) utility vehicle

suzerain n **1** a state or sovereign that has some degree of control over a dependent state **2** (formerly) a person who had power over many people ▶ HISTORY French > **suzerainty** n

svelte adj attractively or gracefully slim; slender ▶ HISTORY French

SW 1 southwest(ern) **2** short wave

swab n **1** med a small piece of cotton wool used for applying medication or cleansing a wound ▷ vb **swabbing, swabbed 2** to clean or apply medication to (a wound) with a swab **3** to clean (the deck of a ship) with a mop ▶ HISTORY probably from Middle Dutch *swabbe* mop

swaddle vb **-dling, -dled** to wrap (a baby) in swaddling clothes ▶ HISTORY Old English *swæthel* swaddling clothes

swaddling clothes pl n long strips of cloth formerly wrapped round a newborn baby

swag n **1** slang stolen property **2** Austral & NZ, informal (formerly) a swagman's pack containing personal belongings ▶ HISTORY probably Scandinavian

swagger vb **1** to walk or behave in an arrogant manner ▷ n **2** an arrogant walk or manner ▶ HISTORY probably from *swag*

swagger stick n a short cane carried by army officers

swagman n, pl **-men** Austral & NZ, informal a labourer who carries his personal possessions in a pack while looking for work

Swahili (swah-**heel**-ee) n a language of E Africa that is an official language of Kenya and Tanzania ▶ HISTORY Arabic *sawāhil* coasts

swain n archaic or poetic **1** a male lover or admirer **2** a young man from the countryside ▶ HISTORY Old English *swān* swineherd

swallow¹ vb **1** to pass (food, drink, etc.) through the mouth and gullet to the stomach **2** informal to believe (something) trustingly: *I was supposed to swallow the lie* **3** not to show: *I believe they should swallow their pride* **4** to make a gulping movement in the throat, such as when nervous **5** to put up with (an insult) without answering back **6 be swallowed up** to be taken into and made a part of something: *the old centre was being swallowed up by new estates* ▷ n **7** the act of swallowing **8** the amount swallowed at any single time; mouthful ▶ HISTORY Old English *swelgan*

swallow² *n* a small migratory bird with long pointed wings and a forked tail ▶ HISTORY Old English *swealwe*

swallow hole *n esp. Brit* same as **sinkhole**

swallowtail *n* **1** a butterfly with a long tail-like part on each hind wing **2** the forked tail of a swallow or similar bird

swam *vb* the past tense of **swim**

swami (swah-mee) *n* a Hindu religious teacher ▶ HISTORY Hindi *svāmī*

swamp *n* **1** an area of permanently waterlogged land; bog ▷ *vb* **2** *naut* to cause (a boat) to sink or fill with water **3** to overwhelm (a person or place) with more than can be dealt with or accommodated ▶ HISTORY probably from Middle Dutch *somp* > **swampy** *adj*

swan *n* **1** a large, usually white, water bird with a long neck ▷ *vb* **swanning, swanned 2 swan around** *or* **about** *informal* to wander about without purpose, but with an air of superiority ▶ HISTORY Old English

swank *informal vb* **1** to show off or boast ▷ *n* **2** showing off or boasting ▶ HISTORY origin unknown > **swanky** *adj*

swanndri (swan-dry) *n trademark, NZ* a weatherproof woollen shirt or jacket. Also called: **swannie**

swan song *n* the last public act of a person before retirement or death

swap *or* **swop** *vb* **swapping, swapped 1** to exchange (something) for something else ▷ *n* **2** an exchange ▶ HISTORY originally, to shake hands on a bargain, strike: probably imitative

SWAPO *or* **Swapo** South-West Africa People's Organization

sward *n* a stretch of turf or grass ▶ HISTORY Old English *sweard* skin

swarm¹ *n* **1** a group of bees, led by a queen, that has left the hive to make a new home **2** a large mass of insects or other small animals **3** a moving mass of people ▷ *vb* **4** to move quickly and in large numbers: *the place is swarming with cops* ▶ HISTORY Old English *swearm*

swarm² *vb* **swarm up** to climb (a ladder or rope) by gripping it with the hands and feet: *the boys swarmed up the rigging* ▶ HISTORY origin unknown

swarthy *adj* **swarthier, swarthiest** having a dark complexion ▶ HISTORY obsolete *swarty*

swash (swosh) *n* the rush of water up a beach following each break of the waves ▶ HISTORY probably imitative

swashbuckling *adj* having the exciting manner or behaviour of pirates, esp. those depicted in films > **swashbuckler** *n*

- ■ **WORD HISTORY**
- ■ *Swashbuckling* originally meant 'making a noise
- ■ by "swashing" or banging your sword against
- ■ your "buckler" or shield'.

swastika *n* **1** a primitive religious symbol in the shape of a Greek cross with the ends of the arms bent at right angles **2** this symbol with clockwise arms as the emblem of Nazi Germany ▶ HISTORY Sanskrit *svastika*

swat *vb* **swatting, swatted 1** to hit sharply: *swatting the ball with confidence* ▷ *n* **2** a sharp blow ▶ HISTORY dialect variant of *squat*

swatch *n* **1** a sample of cloth **2** a collection of such samples ▶ HISTORY origin unknown

swath (swawth) *n* same as **swathe** ▶ HISTORY Old English *swæth*

swathe *vb* **swathing, swathed 1** to wrap a bandage, garment, or piece of cloth around (a person or part of the body) ▷ *n* **2** a long strip of cloth wrapped around something **3** the width of one sweep of a scythe or of the blade of a mowing machine **4** the strip cut in one sweep **5** the quantity of cut crops left in one sweep **6** a long narrow strip of land ▶ HISTORY Old English *swathian*

sway *vb* **1** to swing to and fro: *red poppies swayed in the faint breeze* **2** to lean to one side and then the other: *entire rows swayed in time* **3** to be unable to decide between two or more opinions **4** to influence (someone) in his or her opinion or judgment ▷ *n* **5** power or influence **6** a swinging or leaning movement **7 hold sway** to have power or influence ▶ HISTORY probably from Old Norse *sveigja* to bend

swear *vb* **swearing, swore, sworn 1** to use words considered obscene or blasphemous **2** to promise solemnly on oath; vow: *Sally and Peter swore to love and cherish each other* **3 swear by** to have complete confidence in (something) **4** to state (something) earnestly: *I swear he was all right* **5** to give evidence on oath in a law court ▶ HISTORY Old English *swerian*

swear in *vb* to make (someone) take an oath when taking up an official position or entering the witness box to give evidence in court: *a new federal president was sworn in*

swearword *n* a word considered rude or blasphemous

sweat *n* **1** the salty liquid that comes out of the skin's pores during strenuous activity in excessive heat or when afraid **2** the state or condition of sweating: *he worked up a sweat* **3** *slang* hard work or effort: *climbing to the crest of Ward Hill was a sweat* **4 in a sweat** *informal* in a state of worry **5 no sweat** *slang* no problem ▷ *vb* **sweating, sweat** *or* **sweated 6** to have sweat come through the skin's pores, as a result of strenuous activity, excessive heat, nervousness, or fear **7** *informal* to suffer anxiety or distress **8 sweat blood** *informal* **a** to work very hard **b** to be filled with anxiety ▷ See also **sweats** ▶ HISTORY Old English *swætan* > **sweaty** *adj*

sweatband *n* a piece of cloth tied around the forehead or around the wrist to absorb sweat during strenuous physical activity

sweater *n* a warm knitted piece of clothing covering the upper part of the body

sweat out *vb* **sweat it out** *informal* to endure an unpleasant situation for a time, hoping for an improvement

S

sweats *pl n* sweatshirts and sweat suit trousers collectively

sweatshirt *n* a long-sleeved casual top made of knitted cotton or cotton mixture

sweatshop *n* a workshop where employees work long hours in poor conditions for low pay

swede *n* a round root vegetable with a purplish-brown skin and yellow flesh ▶ HISTORY introduced from Sweden in the 18th century

Swede *n* a person from Sweden

Swedish *adj* 1 of Sweden ▷ *n* 2 the language of Sweden

sweep *vb* **sweeping, swept** 1 to clean (a floor or chimney) with a brush 2 (often foll. by *up*) to remove or collect (dirt or rubbish) with a brush 3 *written* to move smoothly and quickly: *the car swept into the drive* 4 to spread rapidly across or through (a place): *the wave of democracy that had swept through Eastern Europe* 5 *written* to move in a proud and majestic fashion: *the boss himself swept into the hall* 6 *written* to direct (one's eyes, line of fire, etc.) over (a place or target) 7 **sweep away** or **off** to overwhelm (someone) emotionally: *I've been swept away by my fears* 8 to brush or lightly touch (a surface): *the dress swept along the ground* 9 to clear away or get rid of (something) suddenly or forcefully: *these doubts were quickly swept aside; bridges have been swept away by the floods* 10 to stretch out gracefully or majestically, esp. in a wide circle: *the hills swept down into the green valley* 11 to win overwhelmingly in an election: *the umbrella party which swept these elections* 12 **sweep the board** to win every event or prize in a contest ▷ *n* 13 the act or an instance of sweeping 14 a swift or steady movement: *the wide sweep of the shoulders* 15 a wide expanse: *the whole sweep of the bay* 16 any curving line or contour, such as a driveway 17 short for **sweepstake** 18 *chiefly Brit* same as **chimney sweep** 19 **make a clean sweep** to win an overwhelming victory ▶ HISTORY Middle English *swepen*

sweeper *n* 1 a device used to sweep carpets, consisting of a long handle attached to a revolving brush 2 *soccer* a defensive player usually positioned in front of the goalkeeper

sweeping *adj* 1 affecting many people to a great extent: *sweeping financial reforms* 2 (of a statement) making general assumptions about an issue without considering the details 3 decisive or overwhelming: *to suffer sweeping losses* 4 taking in a wide area: *a sweeping view of the area*

sweepstake or *esp US* **sweepstakes** *n* 1 a lottery in which the stakes of the participants make up the prize 2 a horse race involving such a lottery ▶ HISTORY originally referring to someone who *sweeps* or takes all the stakes in a game

sweet *adj* 1 tasting of or like sugar 2 kind and charming: *that was really sweet of you* 3 attractive and delightful: *a sweet child* 4 (of a sound) pleasant and tuneful: *sweet music* 5 (of wine) having a high sugar content; not dry 6 fresh, clear, and clean: *sweet water; sweet air* 7 **sweet on someone** fond of

or infatuated with someone ▷ *n* 8 *Brit, Austral & NZ* a shaped piece of confectionery consisting mainly of sugar 9 *Brit, Austral & NZ* a dessert ▶ HISTORY Old English *swēte* > **sweetly** *adv* > **sweetness** *n*

sweetbread *n* the meat obtained from the pancreas of a calf or lamb

sweetbrier *n* a wild rose with sweet-smelling leaves and pink flowers

sweet corn *n* 1 a kind of maize with sweet yellow kernels, eaten as a vegetable when young 2 the sweet kernels removed from the maize cob, cooked as a vegetable

sweeten *vb* 1 to make (food or drink) sweet or sweeter 2 to be nice to (someone) in order to ensure cooperation 3 to make (an offer or a proposal) more acceptable

sweetener *n* 1 a sweetening agent that does not contain sugar 2 *Brit, Austral & NZ, slang* an inducement offered to someone in order to persuade them to accept an offer or business deal

sweetheart *n* 1 an affectionate name to call someone 2 *old-fashioned* one's boyfriend or girlfriend 3 *informal* a lovable or generous person

sweetie *n* *informal* 1 an affectionate name to call someone 2 *Brit & NZ* same as **sweet** (sense 8) 3 *chiefly Brit* a lovable or generous person

sweetmeat *n* *old-fashioned* a small delicacy preserved in sugar

sweet pea *n* a climbing plant with sweet-smelling pastel-coloured flowers

sweet pepper *n* the large bell-shaped fruit of the pepper plant, which is eaten unripe (**green pepper**) or ripe (**red pepper**) as a vegetable

sweet potato *n* a root vegetable, grown in the tropics, with pinkish-brown skin and yellow flesh

sweet spot *n* *sport* the centre area of a racquet, club, etc., from which the cleanest shots are made

sweet-talk *informal vb* 1 to persuade (someone) by flattery: *I thought I could sweet-talk you into teaching me* ▷ *n* **sweet talk** 2 insincere flattery intended to persuade

sweet tooth *n* a strong liking for sweet foods

sweet william *n* a garden plant with clusters of white, pink, red, or purple flowers

swell *vb* **swelling, swelled; swollen** or **swelled** 1 (of a part of the body) to grow in size as a result of injury or infection: *his face swelled and became pale* 2 to increase in size as a result of being filled with air or liquid: *a balloon swells if you force in more air* 3 to grow or cause (something) to grow in size, numbers, amount, or degree: *Israel's population is swelling* 4 (of an emotion) to become more intense: *his anger swelled within him* 5 (of the seas) to rise in waves 6 (of a sound) to become gradually louder and then die away ▷ *n* 7 the waving movement of the surface of the open sea 8 an increase in size, numbers, amount, or degree 9 a bulge 10 *old-fashioned, informal* a person who is wealthy, upper class, and fashionably dressed 11 *music* an increase in sound followed by an immediate dying away ▷ *adj* 12 *slang, chiefly US* excellent or fine ▶ HISTORY Old English *swellan*

S

swelling n an enlargement of a part of the body as the result of injury or infection

swelter vb **1** to feel uncomfortable under extreme heat ▷ n **2** a hot and uncomfortable condition: *they left the city swelter for the beach* ▶ HISTORY Old English *sweltan* to die

sweltering adj uncomfortably hot: *a sweltering summer*

swept vb the past of **sweep**

swerve vb **swerving, swerved 1** to turn aside from a course sharply or suddenly ▷ n **2** the act of swerving ▶ HISTORY Old English *sweorfan* to scour

swift adj **1** moving or able to move quickly; fast **2** happening or performed quickly or suddenly: *a swift glance this way* **3 swift to** prompt to (do something): *swift to retaliate* ▷ n **4** a small fast-flying insect-eating bird with long wings ▶ HISTORY Old English > **swiftly** adv > **swiftness** n

swig informal n **1** a large swallow or deep drink, esp. from a bottle ▷ vb **swigging, swigged 2** to drink (some liquid) in large swallows, esp. from a bottle ▶ HISTORY origin unknown

swill vb **1** to drink large quantities of (an alcoholic drink) **2** (often foll. by *out*) chiefly Brit & NZ to rinse (something) in large amounts of water ▷ n **3** a liquid mixture containing waste food, fed to pigs **4** a deep drink, esp. of beer ▶ HISTORY Old English *swilian* to wash out

swim vb **swimming, swam, swum 1** to move along in water by movements of the arms and legs, or (in the case of fish) tail and fins **2** to cover (a stretch of water) in this way: *the first person to swim the Atlantic* **3** to float on a liquid: *flies swimming on the milk* **4** to be affected by dizziness: *his head was swimming* **5** (of the objects in someone's vision) to appear to spin or move around: *the faces of the nurses swam around her* **6** (often foll. by *in* or *with*) to be covered or flooded with liquid: *a steak swimming in gravy* ▷ n **7** the act, an instance, or a period of swimming **8 in the swim** informal fashionable or active in social or political activities ▶ HISTORY Old English *swimman* > **swimmer** n > **swimming** n

swimming bath n an indoor swimming pool

swimming costume or **bathing costume** n chiefly Brit, Austral & NZ same as **swimsuit**

swimmingly adv successfully, effortlessly, or well: *everything went swimmingly*

swimming pool n a large hole in the ground, tiled and filled with water for swimming in

swimsuit n a woman's swimming garment that leaves the arms and legs bare

swindle vb **-dling, -dled 1** to cheat (someone) out of money **2** to obtain (money) from someone by fraud ▷ n **3** an instance of cheating someone out of money ▶ HISTORY German *schwindeln* > **swindler** n

swine n **1** a mean or unpleasant person **2** (pl **swine**) same as **pig** ▶ HISTORY Old English *swīn* > **swinish** adj

swine flu n **1** a form of influenza occurring in swine caused by a virus capable of spreading to humans

swing vb **swinging, swung 1** to move backwards and forwards; sway **2** to pivot or cause (something) to pivot from a fixed point such as a hinge: *the door swung open* **3** to move in a sweeping curve: *the headlights swung along the street* **4** to alter one's opinion or mood suddenly **5** to hang so as to be able to turn freely **6** old-fashioned, slang to be hanged: *you'll swing for this!* **7** informal to manipulate or influence successfully: *it may help to swing the election* **8** (often foll. by *at*) to hit out with a sweeping motion **9** old-fashioned to play (music) in the style of swing **10** old-fashioned, slang to be lively and modern ▷ n **11** the act of swinging **12** a sweeping stroke or punch **13** a seat hanging from two chains or ropes on which a person may swing back and forth **14** popular dance music played by big bands in the 1930s and 1940s **15** informal the normal pace at which an activity, such as work, happens: *I'm into the swing of things now* **16** a sudden or extreme change, for example in some business activity or voting pattern **17 go with a swing** to go well; be successful **18 in full swing** at the height of activity ▶ HISTORY Old English *swingan*

swingboat n a boat-shaped carriage for swinging in at a fairground

swing bridge n a bridge that can be swung open to let ships pass through

swingeing (**swin**-jing) adj chiefly Brit severe or causing hardship: *swingeing spending cuts*

swipe vb **swiping, swiped 1** informal to try to hit (someone or something) with a sweeping blow: *he swiped at a boy who ran forward* **2** slang to steal (something) **3** to pass (a credit or debit card) through a machine which electronically interprets the information stored in the card **4** to move a finger across a touchscreen on an electronic device as a means of inputting a command ▷ n **5** informal a hard blow ▶ HISTORY origin unknown

swirl vb **1** to turn round and round with a twisting motion ▷ n **2** a twisting or spinning motion **3** a twisting shape ▶ HISTORY probably from Dutch *zwirrelen* > **swirling** adj

swish vb **1** to move with or cause (something) to make a whistling or hissing sound ▷ n **2** a hissing or rustling sound or movement: *she turned with a swish of her skirt* ▷ adj **3** informal, chiefly Brit, Austral & NZ smart and fashionable ▶ HISTORY imitative

Swiss adj **1** of Switzerland ▷ n, pl **Swiss 2** a person from Switzerland

Swiss ball n a very large inflatable ball made of strong elastic rubber, used for physical exercise and physiotherapy

swiss roll n a sponge cake spread with jam or cream and rolled up

switch n **1** a device for opening or closing an electric circuit **2** a sudden quick change **3** an exchange or swap **4** a flexible rod or twig, used for punishment **5** US & Canad a pair of movable rails for diverting moving trains from one track to another ▷ vb **6** to change quickly and suddenly **7** to exchange (places) or swap (something for

S

something else) **8** *chiefly US & Canad* to transfer (rolling stock) from one railway track to another ▶ **HISTORY** probably from Middle Dutch *swijch* twig

switchback *n* a steep mountain road, railway, or track which rises and falls sharply many times

switchboard *n* the place in a telephone exchange or office building where telephone calls are connected

swivel *vb* **-elling, -elled** *or US* **-eling, -eled 1** to turn on or swing round on a central point ▷ *n* **2** a coupling device which allows an attached object to turn freely ▶ **HISTORY** Old English *swīfan* to turn

swizz *n Brit, NZ & S African, informal* a swindle or disappointment ▶ **HISTORY** origin unknown

swizzle stick *n* a small stick used to stir cocktails

swollen *vb* **1** a past participle of **swell** ▷ *adj* **2** enlarged by swelling

swoon *vb* **1** *literary* to faint because of shock or strong emotion **2** to be deeply affected by passion for (someone): *you've swooned over a string of rotten men* ▷ *n* **3** *literary* a faint ▶ **HISTORY** Old English *geswōgen* insensible > **swooning** *adj*

swoop *vb* **1** (usually foll. by *down*) to move quickly through the air in a downward curve: *an owl swooped down from its perch* **2** (usually foll. by *on*) to move suddenly and quickly towards (a place) in order to attack, arrest, or question the people inside: *nine police cars and vans swooped on the premises* ▷ *n* **3** the act of swooping ▶ **HISTORY** Old English *swāpan* to sweep

swop *n, vb* **swopping, swopped** same as **swap**

sword *n* **1** a weapon with a long sharp blade and a short handle **2 the sword a** military power **b** death; destruction: *we will put them to the sword* **3 cross swords** to have a disagreement with someone ▶ **HISTORY** Old English *sweord*

sword dance *n* a dance in which the performer dances over swords on the ground

swordfish *n, pl* **-fish** *or* **-fishes** a large fish with a very long upper jaw that resembles a sword

swordsman *n, pl* **-men** a person who is skilled in the use of a sword > **swordsmanship** *n*

swore *vb* the past tense of **swear**

sworn *vb* **1** the past participle of **swear** ▷ *adj* **2** bound by or as if by an oath: *a sworn enemy*

swot[1] *informal vb* **swotting, swotted 1** (often foll. by *up*) to study (a subject) very hard, esp. for an exam; cram ▷ *n* **2** a person who works or studies hard ▶ **HISTORY** variant of *sweat*

swot[2] *n, vb* **swotting, swotted** same as **swat**

swum *vb* the past participle of **swim**

swung *vb* the past of **swing**

sybarite (**sib**-bar-ite) *n* **1** a lover of luxury and pleasure ▷ *adj* **2** luxurious or sensuous ▶ **HISTORY** after *Sybaris*, ancient Greek colony in S Italy, famed for its luxury > **sybaritic** *adj*

sycamore *n* **1** a tree with five-pointed leaves and two-winged fruits **2** *US & Canad* an American plane tree ▶ **HISTORY** Latin *sycomorus*

sycophant *n* a person who uses flattery to win favour from people with power or influence ▶ **HISTORY** Greek *sukophantēs* > **sycophancy** *n* > **sycophantic** *adj*

syllabic *adj* of or relating to syllables

syllabify *vb* **-fies, -fying, -fied** to divide (a word) into syllables > **syllabification** *n*

syllable *n* **1** a part of a word which is pronounced as a unit, which contains a single vowel sound, and which may or may not contain consonants: for example, 'paper' has two syllables **2** the least mention: *without a syllable about what went on* **3 in words of one syllable** simply and plainly ▶ **HISTORY** Greek *sullabē*

syllabub *n Brit & Austral* a dessert made from milk or cream beaten with sugar, wine, and lemon juice ▶ **HISTORY** origin unknown

syllabus (**sill**-lab-buss) *n, pl* **-buses** *or* **-bi** (-bye) **a** the subjects studied for a particular course **b** a list of these subjects ▶ **HISTORY** Late Latin

syllogism *n* a form of reasoning consisting of two premises and a conclusion, for example *some temples are in ruins; all ruins are fascinating; so some temples are fascinating* ▶ **HISTORY** Greek *sullogismos* > **syllogistic** *adj*

sylph *n* **1** a slender graceful girl or young woman **2** an imaginary creature believed to live in the air ▶ **HISTORY** New Latin *sylphus* > **sylphlike** *adj*

sylvan *or* **silvan** *adj chiefly poetic* of or consisting of woods or forests ▶ **HISTORY** Latin *silva* forest

symbiosis *n* **1** *biol* a close association of two different animal or plant species living together to their mutual benefit **2** a similar relationship between different individuals or groups: *the symbiosis of the coal and railway industries* ▶ **HISTORY** Greek: a living together > **symbiotic** *adj*

symbol *n* **1** something that represents or stands for something else, usually an object used to represent something abstract **2** a letter, figure, or sign used in mathematics, music, etc. to represent a quantity, operation, function, etc. ▶ **HISTORY** Greek *sumbolon* sign

symbolic *adj* **1** of or relating to a symbol or symbols **2** being a symbol of something > **symbolically** *adv*

symbolism *n* **1** the representation of something by the use of symbols **2** an art movement involving the use of symbols to express mystical or abstract ideas > **symbolist** *adj, n*

symbolize *or* **-ise** *vb* **-izing, -ized** *or* **-ising, -ised 1** to be a symbol of (something) **2** to represent with a symbol > **symbolization** *or* **-isation** *n*

symmetry *n, pl* **-tries 1** the state of having two halves that are mirror images of each other **2** beauty resulting from a balanced arrangement of parts ▶ **HISTORY** Greek *summetria* proportion > **symmetrical** *adj* > **symmetrically** *adv*

sympathetic *adj* **1** feeling or showing kindness and understanding **2** (of a person) likeable and appealing: *the film's only sympathetic character* **3 sympathetic to** showing agreement with or willing to lend support to: *sympathetic to the movement* > **sympathetically** *adv*

sympathize *or* **-thise** *vb* **-thizing, -thized** *or* **-thising, -thised** • **sympathize with a** to feel or express sympathy for: *I sympathized with this fear*

865

b to agree with or support: *Pitt sympathized with these objectives* ▷ **sympathizer** *or* **-thiser** *n*

sympathy *n, pl* **-thies 1** (often foll. by *for*) understanding of other people's problems; compassion **2 sympathy with** agreement with someone's feelings or interests: *we have every sympathy with how she felt* **3** (often pl) feelings of loyalty or support for an idea or a cause: *was this where her sympathies lay?* **4** mutual affection or understanding between two people or a person and an animal ▶ HISTORY Greek *sympatheia*

symphony *n, pl* **-nies 1** a large-scale orchestral composition with several movements **2** an orchestral movement in a vocal work such as an oratorio **3** short for **symphony orchestra 4** anything that has a pleasing arrangement of colours or shapes: *the garden was a symphony of coloured bunting* ▶ HISTORY Greek *sun-* together + *phōnē* sound ▷ **symphonic** *adj*

symphony orchestra *n music* a large orchestra that performs symphonies

symposium *n, pl* **-sia** *or* **-siums 1** a conference at which experts or academics discuss a particular subject **2** a collection of essays on a particular subject ▶ HISTORY Greek *sumposion* a drinking party

symptom *n* **1** *med* a sign indicating the presence of an illness or disease **2** anything that is taken as an indication that something is wrong: *a growing symptom of grave social injustice* ▶ HISTORY Greek *sumptōma* chance ▷ **symptomatic** *adj*

synagogue *n* a building for Jewish religious services and religious instruction ▶ HISTORY Greek *sunagōgē* a gathering

synapse *n anat* a gap where nerve impulses pass between two nerve cells ▶ HISTORY Greek *sunapsis* junction

sync *or* **synch** *films, television, computers, informal vb* **1** to synchronize ▷ *n* **2** synchronization: *the film and sound are in sync*

synchromesh *adj* **1** (of a gearbox) having a system of clutches that synchronizes the speeds of the gearwheels before they engage ▷ *n* **2** a gear system having these features ▶ HISTORY *synchronized mesh*

synchronism *n* the quality or condition of occurrence at the same time or rate

synchronize *or* **-nise** *vb* **-nizing, -nized** *or* **-nising, -nised 1** (of two or more people) to perform (an action) at the same time: *a synchronized withdrawal of Allied forces* **2** to cause (two or more clocks or watches) to show the same time **3** *films* to match (the soundtrack and the action of a film) precisely ▷ **synchronization** *or* **-nisation** *n*

synchronous *adj* occurring at the same time and rate ▶ HISTORY Greek *sun-* together + *khronos* time ▷ **synchrony** *n*

synclinal *adj geol* (of folds, structures) dipping towards each other

syncline *n geol* a downward slope of stratified rock in which the layers dip towards each other from either side

syncopate *vb* **-pating, -pated** *music* to stress the weak beats in (a rhythm or a piece of music) instead of the strong beats ▶ HISTORY Medieval Latin *syncopare* to omit a letter or syllable ▷ **syncopation** *n*

syncope (**sing**-kop-ee) *n* **1** *med* a faint **2** *linguistics* the omission of sounds or letters from the middle of a word, as in *ne'er* for *never* ▶ HISTORY Greek *sunkopē* a cutting off

syndic *n Brit* a business or legal agent of some universities or other institutions ▶ HISTORY Greek *sundikos* defendant's advocate

syndicalism *n* a movement advocating seizure of economic and political power by the industrial working class by means of industrial action, esp. general strikes ▷ **syndicalist** *n*

syndicate *n* **1** a group of people or firms organized to undertake a joint project **2** an association of individuals who control organized crime **3** a news agency that sells articles and photographs to a number of newspapers for simultaneous publication ▷ *vb* **-cating, -cated 4** to sell (articles and photographs) to several newspapers for simultaneous publication **5** to form a syndicate of (people) ▶ HISTORY Old French *syndicat* ▷ **syndication** *n*

syndrome *n* **1** *med* a combination of signs and symptoms that indicate a particular disease **2** a set of characteristics indicating the existence of a particular condition or problem ▶ HISTORY Greek *sundromē*, literally: a running together

synecdoche (sin-**neck**-dock-ee) *n* a figure of speech in which a part is substituted for a whole or a whole for a part, as in *50 head of cattle* for *50 cows* ▶ HISTORY Greek *sunekdokhē*

synergy *n* the potential ability for individuals or groups to be more successful working together than on their own ▶ HISTORY Greek *sunergos*

synod *n* a special church council which meets regularly to discuss church affairs ▶ HISTORY Greek *sunodos*

synonym *n* a word that means the same as another word, such as *bucket* and *pail* ▶ HISTORY Greek *sun-* together + *onoma* name

synonymous *adj* **synonymous with a** having the same meaning as **b** closely associated with: *a family whose name had been synonymous with fine jewellery*

synopsis (sin-**op**-siss) *n, pl* **-ses** (-seez) a brief review or outline of a subject; summary: *they have sent me a monthly synopsis of the plot* ▶ HISTORY Greek *sunopsis*

synoptic *adj* **1** of or relating to a synopsis **2** *Bible* of or relating to the Gospels of Matthew, Mark, and Luke ▷ **synoptically** *adv*

synoptic chart *n meteorol* a weather chart showing the distribution of meteorological conditions over a wide area at a given time

synovia (sine-**oh**-vee-a) *n med* a clear thick fluid that lubricates the body joints ▶ HISTORY New Latin ▷ **synovial** *adj*

syntax *n* the grammatical rules of a language and the way in which words are arranged to form phrases and sentences ▶ HISTORY Greek *suntassein* to put in order > **syntactic** or **syntactical** *adj*

synthesis (sinth-iss-siss) *n*, *pl* **-ses** (-seez) **1** the process of combining objects or ideas into a complex whole **2** the combination produced by such a process **3** *chem* the process of producing a compound by one or more chemical reactions, usually from simpler starting materials ▶ HISTORY Greek *sunthesis*

synthesize or **-sise** *vb* **-sizing, -sized** or **-sising, -sised 1** to combine (objects or ideas) into a complex whole **2** to produce (a compound) by synthesis

synthesizer *n* a keyboard instrument in which speech, music, or other sounds are produced electronically

synthetic *adj* **1** (of a substance or material) made artificially by chemical reaction **2** not sincere or genuine: *synthetic compassion* ▷ *n* **3** a synthetic substance or material ▶ HISTORY Greek *sunthetikos* expert in putting together > **synthetically** *adv*

syphilis *n* a sexually transmitted disease that causes sores on the genitals and eventually on other parts of the body ▶ HISTORY *Syphilis*, hero of a 16th-century Latin poem > **syphilitic** *adj*

syphon *n*, *vb* same as **siphon**

Syrian *adj* **1** of Syria ▷ *n* **2** a person from Syria

syringa *n* same as **mock orange** or **lilac** ▶ HISTORY Greek *surinx* tube (its hollow stems were used for pipes)

syringe *n* **1** *med* a device used for withdrawing or injecting fluids, consisting of a hollow cylinder of glass or plastic, a tightly fitting piston, and a hollow needle ▷ *vb* **-ringing, -ringed 2** to wash out, inject, or spray with a syringe: *a harmless blue dye is syringed into the uterus* ▶ HISTORY Greek *surinx* tube

syrup *n* **1** a solution of sugar dissolved in water and often flavoured with fruit juice: used for sweetening fruit, etc. **2** a thick sweet liquid food made from sugar or molasses: *maple syrup*

3 a liquid medicine containing a sugar solution: *cough syrup* ▶ HISTORY Arabic *sharāb* a drink

syrupy *adj* **1** (of a liquid) thick or sweet **2** excessively sentimental: *a soundtrack of syrupy violins*

system *n* **1** a method or set of methods for doing or organizing something: *a new system of production or distribution* **2** orderliness or routine; an ordered manner: *there is no system in his work* **3** the manner in which an institution or aspect of society has been arranged: *the Scottish legal system* **4** **the system** the government and state regarded as exploiting, restricting, and repressing individuals **5** the manner in which the parts of something fit or function together; structure: *disruption of the earth's weather system* **6** any scheme or set of rules used to classify, explain, or calculate: *the Newtonian system of physics* **7** a network of communications, transportation, or distribution **8** *biol* an animal considered as a whole **9** *biol* a set of organs or structures that together perform some function: *the immune system* **10** one's physical or mental constitution: *the intrusion of the ME virus into my system; to get the hate out of my system* **11** an assembly of electronic or mechanical parts forming a self-contained unit: *an alarm system* ▶ HISTORY Greek *sustēma*

systematic *adj* following a fixed plan and done in an efficient and methodical way: *a systematic approach to teaching* > **systematically** *adv*

systematize or **-tise** *vb* **-tizing, -tized** or **-tising, -tised** to arrange (information) in a system > **systematization** or **-tisation** *n*

systemic *adj* *biol* (of a poison, disease, etc.) affecting the entire animal or body > **systemically** *adv*

systems analysis *n* the analysis of the requirements of a task and the expression of these in a form that enables a computer to perform the task > **systems analyst** *n*

systole (siss-tol-ee) *n* *physiol* contraction of the heart, during which blood is pumped into the arteries ▶ HISTORY Greek *sustolē* > **systolic** *adj*

S

Tt

t¹ *or* **T** *n, pl* **t's, T's** *or* **Ts** **1** the 20th letter of the English alphabet **2 to a T** a in every detail: *that's her to a T* **b** perfectly: *that dress suits you to a T*

t² tonne(s)

T **1** *chem* tritium **2** tera-

t. **1** temperature **2** ton(s)

ta *interj Brit, Austral & NZ, informal* thank you ▶ **HISTORY** imitative of baby talk

Ta *chem* tantalum

TA (in Britain) Territorial Army

tab¹ *n* **1** a small flap of material, esp. one on a garment for decoration or for fastening to a button **2** any similar flap, such as a piece of paper attached to a file for identification **3** *chiefly US & Canad.* a bill, esp. for a meal or drinks **4 keep tabs on** *informal* to keep a watchful eye on ▶ **HISTORY** origin unknown

tab² *n* short for **tabulator**

TAB (in New Zealand) Totalisator Agency Board

tabard *n* **1** a sleeveless jacket, esp. one worn by a medieval knight over his armour **2** a short coat bearing the coat of arms of the sovereign, worn by a herald ▶ **HISTORY** Old French *tabart*

Tabasco *n trademark* a very hot red sauce made from peppers

tabby *n, pl* **-bies** **1** a cat whose fur has dark stripes or wavy markings on a lighter background ▷ *adj* **2** having dark stripes or wavy markings on a lighter background ▶ **HISTORY** from the girl's name *Tabitha*, influenced by *tabby*, old kind of striped silk

tabernacle *n* **1 the Tabernacle** *Bible* the portable sanctuary in which the ancient Israelites carried the Ark of the Covenant **2** any place of Christian worship that is not called a church **3** *RC Church* a receptacle in which the Blessed Sacrament is kept ▶ **HISTORY** Latin *tabernaculum* a tent

tabla *n, pl* **-bla** *or* **-blas** one of a pair of Indian drums played with the hands ▶ **HISTORY** Hindi, from Arabic: drum

table *n* **1** a piece of furniture consisting of a flat top supported by legs: *a coffee table* **2** a set of facts or figures arranged in rows and columns: *a league table* **3** a group of people sitting round a table for a meal, game, etc.: *the whole table laughed* **4** *formal* the food provided at a meal or in a particular house: *he keeps a good table* **5 turn the tables** to cause a complete reversal of circumstances ▷ *vb* **-bling, -bled** **6** *Brit & Austral* to submit (a motion)

for discussion by a meeting **7** *US* to suspend discussion of (a proposal) indefinitely ▶ **HISTORY** Latin *tabula* a writing tablet

tableau (**tab**-loh) *n, pl* **-leaux** (-loh) a silent motionless group of people arranged to represent a scene from history, legend, or literature ▶ **HISTORY** French

tablecloth *n* a cloth for covering the top of a table, esp. during meals

table d'hôte (**tah**-bla **dote**) *adj* **1** (of a meal) consisting of a set number of courses with a limited choice of dishes offered at a fixed price ▷ *n, pl* **tables d'hôte** (**tah**-bla **dote**) **2** a table d'hôte meal or menu ▶ **HISTORY** French: the host's table

table football *n Brit* a game based on soccer, played on a table with sets of miniature human figures mounted on rods allowing them to be tilted or spun to strike the ball. US and Canad. equivalent: **foosball**

tableland *n* a flat area of high ground; plateau

tablespoon *n* **1** a spoon, larger than a dessertspoon, used for serving food **2** Also called: **tablespoonful** the amount contained in such a spoon **3** a unit of capacity used in cooking, equal to half a fluid ounce

tablet *n* **1** a pill consisting of a compressed medicinal substance **2** a flattish cake of some substance, such as soap **3** a slab of stone, wood, etc., used for writing on before the invention of paper **4** an inscribed piece of stone, wood, etc. that is fixed to a wall as a memorial: *a tablet in memory of those who died* **5** a small mobile personal computer with a screen that is manipulated by swiping or tapping with the hand ▶ **HISTORY** Latin *tabula* a board

table tennis *n* a game resembling a miniature form of tennis played on a table with bats and a small light ball

tabloid *n* a newspaper with fairly small pages, usually with many photographs and a concise and often sensational style ▶ **HISTORY** from *tablet*

taboo *or* **tabu** *n, pl* **-boos** *or* **-bus** **1** a restriction or prohibition resulting from social or other conventions **2** a ritual prohibition, esp. of something that is considered holy or unclean ▷ *adj* **3** forbidden or disapproved of: *a taboo subject* ▶ **HISTORY** Tongan *tapu*

tabor *n* a small drum used esp. in the Middle Ages, struck with one hand while the other held a pipe ▶ **HISTORY** Old French *tabour*

tabular *adj* arranged in parallel columns so as to form a table ▶ **HISTORY** Latin *tabula* a board

tabulate *vb* **-lating, -lated** to arrange (information) in rows and columns > **tabulation** *n*

tabulator *n* a key on a typewriter or word processor that sets stops so that data can be arranged and presented in columns

tachograph *n* a device that measures the speed of a vehicle and the distance that it covers, and produces a record (**tachogram**) of its readings ▶ **HISTORY** Greek *takhos* speed + -GRAPH

tachometer *n* a device for measuring speed, esp. that of a revolving shaft ▶ HISTORY Greek *takhos* speed + -METER

tacit (**tass**-it) *adj* understood or implied without actually being stated: *tacit support* ▶ HISTORY Latin *tacitus* silent

taciturn (**tass**-it-turn) *adj* habitually silent, reserved, or uncommunicative ▶ HISTORY Latin *tacere* to be silent > **taciturnity** *n*

tack¹ *n* **1** a short sharp-pointed nail with a large flat head **2** *Brit & NZ* a long loose temporary stitch used in dressmaking ▷ *vb* **3** to fasten (something) with a tack or tacks: *the carpet needs to be tacked down* **4** *Brit & NZ* to sew (something) with long loose temporary stitches ▷ See also **tack on** ▶ HISTORY Middle English *tak* fastening, nail

tack² *n* **1** *naut* the course of a boat sailing obliquely into the wind, expressed in terms of the side of the boat against which the wind is blowing: *on the port tack* **2** a course of action or a policy: *telling her to get off my back hadn't worked, so I took a different tack* ▷ *vb* **3** *naut* to steer (a boat) on a zigzag course, so as to make progress against the wind ▶ HISTORY from *tack* rope used to secure a sail

tack³ *n* riding harness for horses, including saddles and bridles ▶ HISTORY from *tackle*

tackies *or* **takkies** *pl n*, *sing* **tacky** *S African, informal* tennis shoes or plimsolls ▶ HISTORY origin unknown

tackle *vb* **-ling, -led 1** to deal with (a problem or task) in a determined way **2** to confront (someone) about something: *I intend to tackle both management and union on this issue* **3** to attack and fight (a person or animal) **4** *sport* to attempt to get the ball away from (an opposing player) ▷ *n* **5** *sport* an attempt to get the ball away from an opposing player **6** the equipment required for a particular sport or occupation: *fishing tackle* **7** a set of ropes and pulleys for lifting heavy weights **8** *naut* the ropes and other rigging aboard a ship ▶ HISTORY Middle English

tack on *vb* to attach or add (something) to something that is already complete: *an elegant mansion with a modern extension tacked on at the back*

tacky¹ *adj* **tackier, tackiest** slightly sticky ▶ HISTORY earlier *tack* stickiness > **tackiness** *n*

tacky² *adj* **tackier, tackiest** *informal* **1** vulgar and tasteless: *tacky commercialism* **2** shabby or shoddy: *tacky streets* ▶ HISTORY origin unknown > **tackiness** *n*

taco (**tah**-koh) *n*, *pl* **tacos** *Mexican cookery* a tortilla folded into a roll with a filling and usually fried ▶ HISTORY from Mexican Spanish, from Spanish: literally, a bite to eat

tact *n* **1** a sense of the best and most considerate way to deal with people so as not to upset them **2** skill in handling difficult situations ▶ HISTORY Latin *tactus* a touching > **tactful** *adj* > **tactfully** *adv* > **tactless** *adj* > **tactlessly** *adv* > **tactlessness** *n*

tactic *n* a move or method used to achieve an aim or task: *he has perfected dissent as a tactic to further his career*. See also **tactics**

tactical *adj* **1** of or employing tactics: *a tactical advantage* **2** (of missiles, bombing, etc.) for use in limited military operations > **tactically** *adv*

tactical voting *n* (in an election) the practice of voting for a candidate or party one would not normally support in an attempt to prevent an even less acceptable candidate or party being elected

tactics *n* **1** *mil* the science of the detailed direction of forces in battle to achieve an aim or task ▷ *pl n* **2** the plans and methods used to achieve a particular short-term aim ▶ HISTORY Greek *tassein* to arrange > **tactician** *n*

tactile *adj* of or having a sense of touch: *the tactile sense* ▶ HISTORY Latin *tactilis*

tadpole *n* the aquatic larva of a frog or toad, which develops from a limbless tailed form with external gills into a form with internal gills, limbs, and a reduced tail ▶ HISTORY Middle English *tadde* toad + *pol* head

TAFE (in Australia) Technical and Further Education

taffeta *n* a thin shiny silk or rayon fabric used esp. for women's clothes ▶ HISTORY Persian *tāftah* spun

taffrail *n* *naut* a rail at the back of a ship or boat ▶ HISTORY Dutch *taffereel* panel

tag¹ *n* **1** a piece of paper, leather, etc. for attaching to something as a mark or label: *the price tag* **2** a point of metal or plastic at the end of a cord or lace **3** a brief trite quotation **4** an electronic device worn by a prisoner under house arrest so that his or her movements can be monitored **5** *slang* a graffito consisting of a nickname or personal symbol ▷ *vb* **tagging, tagged 6** to mark with a tag ▷ See also **tag along** ▶ HISTORY origin unknown

tag² *n* **1** a children's game in which one player chases the others in an attempt to touch one of them, who will then become the chaser ▷ *vb* **tagging, tagged 2** to catch and touch (another child) in the game of tag ▷ Also: **tig** ▶ HISTORY origin unknown

Tagalog (tag-**gah**-log) *n* a language spoken in the Philippines

tag along *vb* to accompany someone, esp. when uninvited: *I tagged along behind the gang*

tagetes (taj-**eet**-eez) *n*, *pl* **-tes** any of a genus of plants with yellow or orange flowers, including the French and African marigolds ▶ HISTORY Latin *Tages*, a god of ancient Etruria

tagliatelle (tal-yat-**tell**-ee) *n* a form of pasta made in narrow strips ▶ HISTORY Italian

taiga (**tie**-ga) *n* the belt of coniferous forest extending across much of subarctic North America, Europe, and Asia

tail¹ *n* **1** the rear part of an animal's body, usually forming a long thin flexible part attached to the trunk. *Related adjective:* **caudal 2** any long thin part projecting or hanging from the back or end of something: *the waiter produced menus from beneath the tail of his coat* **3** the last part: *the tail of the* procession **4** the rear part of an aircraft **5** *astron* the luminous stream of gas and dust particles driven from the head of a comet when it is close to the sun **6** *informal* a person employed to follow and spy upon another **7 turn tail** to run away **8 with one's tail between one's legs** completely defeated and demoralized ▷ *adj* **9** at the back: *tail feathers* ▷ *vb* **10** *informal* to follow (someone) stealthily ▷ See also **tail off, tails** ▶ HISTORY Old English *tægel* > **tailless** *adj*

tail² *n law* the limitation of an estate or interest to a person and his or her descendants ▶ HISTORY Old French *taille* a division

tailback *n Brit* a queue of traffic stretching back from an obstruction

tailboard *n* a removable or hinged rear board on a lorry or trailer

tail coat *n* a man's black coat which stops at the hips at the front and has a long back split into two below the waist

tailgate *n* **1** same as **tailboard 2** a door at the rear of a hatchback vehicle ▷ *vb* **3** to drive very close behind (a vehicle) > **tailgater** *n*

tail-light *or* **tail lamp** *n* same as **rear light**

tail off *or* **away** *vb* **1** to decrease gradually: *orders tailed off* **2** (of someone's voice) to become gradually quieter and then silent

tailor *n* **1** a person who makes, repairs, or alters outer garments, esp. menswear. *Related adjective:* **sartorial** *vb* **2** to cut or style (a garment) to satisfy specific requirements **3** to adapt (something) so as to make it suitable: *activities are tailored to participants' capabilities* ▶ HISTORY Old French *taillier* to cut > **tailored** *adj*

tailorbird *n* a tropical Asian warbler that builds a nest by sewing together large leaves using plant fibres

tailor-made *adj* **1** (of clothing) made by a tailor to fit exactly **2** perfect for a particular purpose: *I'm tailor-made for the role*

tailpipe *n* a pipe from which exhaust gases are discharged, esp. in a motor vehicle

tailplane *n* a small horizontal wing at the tail of an aircraft to help keep it stable

tails *pl n* **1** *informal* same as **tail coat** ▷ *interj, adv* **2** with the side of a coin uppermost that does not have a portrait of a head on it

tailspin *n* **1** *aeronautics* same as **spin** (sense 10) **2** *informal* a state of confusion or panic

tailwind *n* a wind blowing from behind an aircraft or vehicle

taint *vb* **1** to spoil or contaminate by an undesirable quality: *tainted by corruption* ▷ *n* **2** a defect or flaw **3** a trace of contamination or infection ▶ HISTORY Old French *teindre* to dye > **tainted** *adj*

taipan *n* a large poisonous Australian snake ▶ HISTORY Aboriginal

take *vb* **taking, took, taken 1** to remove from a place, usually by grasping with the hand: *he took a fifty-dollar note from his wallet* **2** to accompany or escort: *he took me home* **3** to use as a means of transport: *we took a taxi* **4** to conduct or lead: *that*

road takes you to Kingston **5** to obtain possession of (something), often dishonestly: *they had taken everything most precious to us* **6** to seize or capture: *her husband had been taken by the rebels* **7** (in games such as chess or cards) to win or capture (a piece, trick, etc.) **8** to choose or select (something to use or buy): *I'll take the green one, please* **9** to put an end to: *he took his own life* **10** to require (time, resources, or ability): *this would have taken years to set up* **11** to use as a particular case: *take a friend of mine, for example* **12** to find and make use of (a seat, flat, etc.) **13** to accept the duties of: *the legitimate government will take office* **14** to receive in a specified way: *my mother took it calmly* **15** to receive and make use of: *she took the opportunity to splash her heated face* **16** to eat or drink: *all food substances are toxic if taken in excess* **17** to perform (an action, esp. a beneficial one): *she took a deep breath* **18** to accept (something that is offered or given): *she took a job as a waitress* **19** to put into effect: *taking military action* **20** to make (a photograph) **21** to write down or copy: *taking notes* **22** to work at or study: *taking painting lessons* **23** to do or sit (a test, exam, etc.) **24** to begin to experience or feel: *he took an interest in psychoanalysis* **25** to accept (responsibility, blame, or credit) **26** to accept as valid: *I take your point* **27** to stand up to or endure: *I can't take this harassment any more* **28** to wear a particular size of shoes or clothes: *what size of shoes do you take?* **29** to have a capacity of or room for: *the Concert Hall can take about 2500 people* **30** to ascertain by measuring: *she comes after breakfast to take her pulse and temperature* **31** to subtract or deduct: *take seven from eleven* **32** to aim or direct: *he took a few steps towards the door* **33** (of a shop, club, etc.) to make (a specified amount of money) from sales, tickets, etc.: *films that take no money at the box office* **34** to have or produce the intended effect: *the dye hasn't taken on your shoes* **35** (of seedlings) to start growing successfully **36 take account of** *or* **take into account** See **account** (sense 9) **37 take advantage of** See **advantage** (sense 4) **38 take care** See **care** (sense 10) **39 take care of** See **care** (sense 11) **40 take it** to assume or believe: *I take it that means they don't want to leave* **41 take part in** See **part** (sense 17) **42 take place** See **place** (sense 20) **43 take upon oneself** to assume the right or duty (to do something) **44 take your time** use as much time as you need ▷ *n* **45** *films, music* one of a series of recordings from which the best will be selected **46** *informal, chiefly US* a version or interpretation: *Minnelli's bleak take on the story* ▷ See also **take after, take against**, etc. ▶ HISTORY Old English *tacan*

take after *vb* to resemble in appearance or character: *he takes after his grandfather*

take against *vb informal* to start to dislike, esp. for no good reason: *I took against her right from the start*

take away *vb* **1** to remove or subtract: *the lymph glands are taken away and examined under a microscope* **2** to detract from or lessen the value of (something):

t

the fact that he beat his wife doesn't take away from his merits as a writer ▷ *prep* **3** minus: *six take away two is four* ▷ *adj* **takeaway 4** *Brit, Austral & NZ* sold for consumption away from the premises: *takeaway food* ▷ *n* **takeaway** *Brit, Austral & NZ* **5** a shop or restaurant that sells such food **6** a meal sold for consumption away from the premises

take-home pay *n* the remainder of one's pay after income tax and other compulsory deductions have been made

take in *vb* **1** to understand: *I was too tired to take in all of what was being said* **2** *informal* to cheat or deceive: *don't be taken in by his charming manner* **3** to include: *this tour takes in the romance and history of Salzburg, Vienna, and Munich* **4** to receive into one's house: *his widowed mother lived by taking in boarders* **5** to make (clothing) smaller by altering the seams **6** *biol* to absorb (a substance) **7** to go to: *taking in a movie*

take off *vb* **1** to remove (a garment) **2** (of an aircraft) to become airborne **3** *informal* to set out on a journey: *taking off for the Highlands* **4** *informal* to become successful or popular: *the song took off after being used in a film* **5** to deduct (an amount) from a price or total **6** to withdraw or put an end to: *the bus service has been taken off because of lack of demand* **7** *informal* to mimic (someone) ▷ *n* **takeoff 8** the act or process of making an aircraft airborne **9** *informal* an act of mimicry

take up *vb* **1** to occupy or fill (space or time): *looking after the baby takes up most of my time* **2** to adopt the study, practice, or activity of: *I took up architecture* **3** to shorten (a garment) **4** to accept (an offer): *I'd like to take up your offer of help* **5 take up on a** to accept what is offered by (someone): *I might just take you up on that offer* **b** to discuss (something) further with (someone): *I'd like to take you up on that last point* **6 take up with a** to discuss (an issue) with (someone): *take up the matter with the District Council more seriously* **b** to begin to be friendly and spend time with (someone): *he'd already taken up with the woman he would marry*

taking *adj* charming, fascinating, or intriguing

takings *pl n* receipts; earnings

talc *or* **talcum** *n* **1** same as **talcum powder 2** a soft mineral, consisting of magnesium silicate, used in the manufacture of ceramics, paints, and talcum powder ▸ HISTORY Persian *talk*

talcum powder *n* a powder made of purified talc, usually scented, used to dry or perfume the body

tale *n* **1** a report, account, or story: *everyone had their own tale to tell about the flood* **2** a malicious piece of gossip **3 tell tales a** to tell fanciful lies **b** to report malicious stories or trivial complaints, esp. to someone in authority **4 tell a tale** to reveal something important **5 tell its own tale** to be self-evident ▸ HISTORY Old English *talu*

talent *n* **1** a natural ability to do something well: *the boy has a real talent for writing* **2** a person or people with such ability: *he is the major talent in*

Italian fashion **3** any of various ancient units of weight and money ▸ HISTORY Greek *talanton* unit of money > **talented** *adj*

talent scout *n* a person whose occupation is the search for talented people, such as sportsmen or performers, for work as professionals

talisman *n, pl* **-mans** a stone or other small object, usually inscribed or carved, believed to protect the wearer from evil influences ▸ HISTORY Medieval Greek *telesma* ritual > **talismanic** *adj*

talk *vb* **1** to express one's thoughts or feelings by means of spoken words **2** to exchange ideas or opinions about something: *they were talking about where they would go on holiday* **3** to give voice to; utter: *he was talking rubbish* **4** to discuss: *the political leaders were talking peace* **5** to reveal information: *she was ready to talk* **6** to be able to speak (a language or style) in conversation: *the ferry was full of people talking French* **7** to spread rumours or gossip **8** to be effective or persuasive: *money talks* **9** to get into a particular condition or state of mind by talking: *I had talked myself hoarse* **10 now you're talking** *informal* at last you're saying something agreeable **11 you can** *or* **can't talk** *informal* you are in no position to comment or criticize ▷ *n* **12** a speech or lecture: *a talk on local government reform* **13** an exchange of ideas or thoughts: *we had a talk about our holiday plans* **14** idle chatter, gossip, or rumour **15** (often *pl*) a conference, discussion, or negotiation ▷ See also **talk back, talk down**, etc. ▸ HISTORY Middle English *talkien* > **talker** *n*

talkative *adj* given to talking a great deal

talkback *n NZ* a broadcast in which telephone comments or questions from the public are transmitted live

talk back *vb* to answer (someone) rudely or cheekily

talk down *vb* **1 talk down to** to speak to (someone) in a patronizing manner **2** to give instructions to (an aircraft) by radio to enable it to land

talkie *n informal* an early film with a soundtrack

talking-to *n informal* a scolding or telling-off

talk into *vb* to persuade (someone) to do something by talking to him or her: *don't let anyone talk you into buying things you don't want*

talk out *vb* **1** to resolve (a problem) by talking: *we won't reach a compromise unless we can talk out our differences* **2** *Brit* to block (a bill) in parliament by discussing it for so long that there is no time to vote on it **3 talk out of** to dissuade (someone) from doing something by talking to him or her

tall *adj* **1** of greater than average height **2** having a specified height: *five feet tall* ▸ HISTORY Middle English

tallboy *n Brit* a high chest of drawers made in two sections placed one on top of the other

tall order *n informal* a difficult or unreasonable request

tallow *n* a hard fatty animal fat used in making soap and candles

tall poppy syndrome *n Austral & NZ, informal* a tendency to disparage any person who is conspicuously successful

tall story *n informal* an unlikely and probably untrue tale

tally *vb* **-lies, -lying, -lied** **1** to agree with or be consistent with something else: *this description didn't seem to me to tally with what we saw* **2** to keep score ▷ *n, pl* **-lies 3** any record of debit, credit, the score in a game, etc. **4** an identifying label or mark **5** a stick used (esp. formerly) as a record of the amount of a debt according to the notches cut in it ▶ HISTORY Latin *talea* a stick

tally-ho *interj* the cry of a participant at a hunt when the quarry is sighted

tally table *n maths* a table where data is recorded as a series of marks that each represent a certain number

Talmud *n Judaism* the primary source of Jewish religious law ▶ HISTORY Hebrew *talmūdh* instruction > **Talmudic** *adj* > **Talmudist** *n*

talon *n* a sharply hooked claw, such as that of a bird of prey ▶ HISTORY Latin *talus* ankle

tamarillo *n, pl* **-los** a shrub with a red oval edible fruit

tamarind *n* a tropical evergreen tree with fruit whose acid pulp is used as a food and to make beverages and medicines ▶ HISTORY Arabic *tamr hindī* Indian date

tamarisk *n* a tree or shrub of the Mediterranean region and S Asia, with scalelike leaves, slender branches, and feathery flower clusters ▶ HISTORY Latin *tamarix*

tambourine *n music* a percussion instrument consisting of a single drum skin stretched over a circular wooden frame with pairs of metal discs that jingle when it is struck or shaken ▶ HISTORY from Old French

tambrin *n* (in Trinidad and Tobago) a kind of shallow drum made of goatskin ▶ HISTORY from *tambourine*

t

tame *adj* **1** (of an animal) **a** changed by humans from a wild state into a domesticated state **b** not afraid of or aggressive towards humans **2** (of a person) tending to do what one is told without questioning or criticizing it **3** mild and unexciting: *the love scenes are fairly tame by modern standards* ▷ *vb* **taming, tamed 4** to make (an animal) tame; domesticate **5** to bring under control; make less extreme or dangerous: *many previously deadly diseases have been tamed by antibiotics* ▶ HISTORY Old English *tam*

Tamil *n* **1** (*pl* **-ils** or **-il**) a member of a people of S India and Sri Lanka **2** the language of the Tamils ▷ *adj* **3** of the Tamils

tam-o'-shanter *n* a Scottish brimless woollen cap with a bobble in the centre ▶ HISTORY after the hero of Robert Burns's poem *Tam o' Shanter*

tamp *vb* to force or pack (something) down by tapping it several times: *he tamped the bowl of his pipe* ▶ HISTORY probably from obsolete *tampin* plug for gun's muzzle

tamper *vb* (foll. by *with*) **1** to interfere or meddle with without permission: *someone has been tampering with the locks* **2** to attempt to influence someone, esp. by bribery: *an attempt to tamper with the jury* ▶ HISTORY alteration of *temper* (verb)

tampon *n* an absorbent plug of cotton wool inserted into the vagina during menstruation ▶ HISTORY French

tan¹ *n* **1** a brown coloration of the skin caused by exposure to ultraviolet rays, esp. those of the sun ▷ *vb* **tanning, tanned 2** (of a person or his or her skin) to go brown after exposure to ultraviolet rays **3** to convert (a skin or hide) into leather by treating it with a tanning agent **4** *slang* to beat or flog ▷ *adj* **5** yellowish-brown ▶ HISTORY Medieval Latin *tannare*

tan² *maths* tangent

tandem *n* **1** a bicycle with two sets of pedals and two saddles, arranged one behind the other for two riders **2 in tandem** together or in conjunction: *the two drugs work in tandem to combat the disease* ▷ *adv* **3** one behind the other: *Jim and Ruth arrived, riding tandem* ▶ HISTORY Latin *tandem* at length

tandoor *n* a type of clay oven used in India, Pakistan, and parts of the Middle East

tandoori *adj* cooked in a tandoor: *tandoori chicken*

tang *n* **1** a strong sharp taste or smell: *we could already smell the tang of the distant sea* **2** a trace or hint of something: *there was a tang of cloves in the apple pie* **3** the pointed end of a tool, such as a knife or chisel, which fits into the handle ▶ HISTORY Old Norse *tangi* point > **tangy** *adj*

tangata whenua (**tang**-ah-tah **fen**-noo-ah) *pl n NZ* **1** the original Polynesian settlers in New Zealand **2** descendants of the original Polynesian settlers ▶ HISTORY Māori: people of the land

tangent *n* **1** a line, curve, or plane that touches another curve or surface at one point but does not cross it **2** (in trigonometry) the ratio of the length of the opposite side to that of the adjacent side of a right-angled triangle **3 go off at a tangent** suddenly take a completely different line of thought or action ▷ *adj* **4** of or involving a tangent **5** touching at a single point ▶ HISTORY Latin *linea tangens* the touching line

tangential *adj* **1** only having an indirect or superficial relevance: *Hitler's vegetarianism only has a tangential link with the policies of the Nazis* **2** of or being a tangent: *a street tangential to the market square* > **tangentially** *adv*

tangerine *n* **1** the small orange-like fruit, with a sweet juicy flesh, of an Asian tree ▷ *adj* **2** reddish-orange ▶ HISTORY *Tangier*, a port in Morocco

tangi (**tang**-ee) *n NZ* **1** a Māori funeral ceremony **2** *informal* a lamentation

tangible *adj* **1** able to be touched; material or physical **2** real or substantial: *tangible results* ▶ HISTORY Latin *tangere* to touch > **tangibility** *n* > **tangibly** *adv*

tangle *n* **1** a confused or complicated mass of things, such as hair or fibres, knotted or coiled

together: *a tangle of wires* **2** a complicated problem or situation ▷ *vb* **-gling, -gled 3** to twist (things, such as hair or fibres) together in a confused mass **4** to come into conflict: *the last thing she wanted was to tangle with the police* **5** to catch or trap in a net, ropes, etc.: *the string of the kite had got tangled in the branches* ▸ **HISTORY** Middle English *tangilen*
> **tangled** *adj*

tango *n, pl* **-gos 1** a Latin-American dance characterized by long gliding steps and sudden pauses **2** music for this dance ▷ *vb* **-going, -goed 3** to perform this dance ▸ **HISTORY** American Spanish

tangram *n* a Chinese puzzle in which a square, cut into a parallelogram, a square, and five triangles, is formed into figures

taniwha (**tun**-ee-fah) *n NZ* a mythical Māori monster that lives in rivers and lakes ▸ **HISTORY** Māori

tank *n* **1** a large container for storing liquids or gases **2** an armoured combat vehicle moving on tracks and armed with guns **3** Also called:
tankful the quantity contained in a tank
▸ **HISTORY** Gujarati (language of W India) *tānkh* artificial lake

tankard *n* a large one-handled beer-mug, sometimes fitted with a hinged lid ▸ **HISTORY** Middle English

tanker *n* a ship or lorry for carrying liquid in bulk: *an oil tanker*

tank farming *n* same as **hydroponics** > **tank farmer** *n*

tannery *n, pl* **-neries** a place or building where skins and hides are tanned

tannic *adj* of, containing, or produced from tannin or tannic acid

tannie (**tun**-nee) *n S African* a title of respect used to refer to an elderly woman ▸ **HISTORY** Afrikaans, literally: aunt

tannin *n* a yellowish compound found in many plants, such as tea and grapes, and used in tanning and dyeing. Also called: **tannic acid**

Tannoy *n trademark, Brit* a type of public-address system

tansy *n, pl* **-sies** a plant with yellow flowers in flat-topped clusters ▸ **HISTORY** Greek *athanasia* immortality

tantalize *or* **-lise** *vb* **-lizing, -lized** *or* **-lising, -lised** to tease or make frustrated, for example by tormenting (someone) with the sight of something that he or she wants but cannot have ▸ **HISTORY** after *Tantalus*, a mythological king condemned to stand in water that receded when he tried to drink it and under fruit that moved away when he reached for it > **tantalizing** *or* **-lising** *adj* > **tantalizingly** *or* **-lisingly** *adv*

tantalum *n chem* a hard greyish-white metallic element that resists corrosion. Symbol: Ta ▸ **HISTORY** after *Tantalus* (see **TANTALIZE**), from the metal's incapacity to absorb acids

tantamount *adj* **tantamount to** equivalent in effect to: *the raid was tantamount to a declaration of*

war ▸ **HISTORY** Anglo-French *tant amunter* to amount to as much

tantrum *n* a childish outburst of bad temper ▸ **HISTORY** origin unknown

Taoiseach (**tee**-shack) *n* the prime minister of the Irish Republic

Taoism *n* a Chinese system of religion and philosophy advocating a simple honest life and noninterference with the course of natural events > **Taoist** *n, adj*

tap[1] *vb* **tapping, tapped 1** to knock lightly and usually repeatedly: *she tapped gently on the door* **2** to make a rhythmic sound with the hands or feet by lightly and repeatedly hitting a surface with them: *he was tapping one foot to the music* ▷ *n* **3** a light blow or knock, or the sound made by it **4** the metal piece attached to the toe or heel of a shoe used for tap-dancing **5** same as **tap-dancing** ▸ **HISTORY** Middle English *tappen*

tap[2] *n* **1** *Brit, Austral & NZ* a valve by which the flow of a liquid or gas from a pipe can be controlled. Usual US word: **faucet 2** a stopper to plug a cask or barrel **3** a concealed listening or recording device connected to a telephone **4** *med* the withdrawal of fluid from a bodily cavity: *a spinal tap* **5 on tap a** *informal* ready for use **b** (of drinks) on draught rather than in bottles ▷ *vb* **tapping, tapped 6** to listen in on (a telephone conversation) secretly by making an illegal connection **7** to obtain something useful or desirable from (something): *a new way of tapping the sun's energy* **8** to withdraw liquid from (something) as if through a tap: *to tap a cask of wine* **9** to cut into (a tree) and draw off sap from it **10** *Brit, Austral & NZ, informal* to obtain (money or information) from (someone) **11** *informal* to make an illicit attempt to recruit (a player or employee bound by an existing contract) ▸ **HISTORY** Old English *tæppa*

tap-dancing *n* a style of dancing in which the performer wears shoes with metal plates on the heels and toes that make a rhythmic sound on the stage as he or she dances > **tap dance** *n* > **tap-dancer** *n*

tape *n* **1** a long thin strip of cotton or linen used for tying or fastening: *a parcel tied with pink tape* **2 a** short for **magnetic tape b** a spool or cassette containing magnetic tape, and used for recording or playing sound or video signals: *he put a tape into his stereo* **c** the music, speech, or pictures which have been recorded on a particular cassette or spool of magnetic tape **3** a narrow strip of plastic which has one side coated with an adhesive substance and is used to stick paper, etc. together: *sticky tape* **4** a string stretched across the track at the end of a race course **5** short for **tape measure** ▷ *vb* **taping, taped 6** Also: **tape-record** to record (speech, music, etc.) on magnetic tape **7** to bind or fasten with tape **8 have a person** *or* **situation taped** *Brit & Austral, informal* to have full understanding and control of a person or situation ▸ **HISTORY** Old English *tæppe*

t

tape measure n a tape or length of metal marked off in centimetres or inches, used for measuring

taper vb 1 to become narrower towards one end 2 **taper off** to make or become gradually less: *treatment should be tapered off gradually* ▷ n 3 a long thin fast-burning candle 4 a narrowing ▸ HISTORY Old English *tapor*

tape recorder n an electrical device used for recording and reproducing sounds on magnetic tape

tape recording n 1 the act of recording sounds on magnetic tape 2 the magnetic tape used for this: *a tape recording of the interview* 3 the sounds so recorded

tape streamer n computers a device that enables data to be copied byte by byte from a hard disk onto magnetic tape for storage

tapestry n, pl **-tries** 1 a heavy woven fabric, often in the form of a picture, used for wall hangings or furnishings 2 same as **needlepoint** (sense 1) 3 a colourful and complicated situation that is made up of many different kinds of things: *the rich tapestry of Hindustani music* ▸ HISTORY Old French *tapisserie* carpeting

tapeworm n a long flat parasitic worm that inhabits the intestines of vertebrates, including man

tapioca n a beadlike starch made from cassava root, used in puddings ▸ HISTORY S American Indian *tipioca* pressed-out juice

tapir (**tape**-er) n a piglike mammal of South and Central America and SE Asia, with a long snout, three-toed hind legs, and four-toed forelegs ▸ HISTORY S American Indian *tapiira*

tappet n a short steel rod in an engine which moves up and down, transferring movement from one part of the machine to another ▸ HISTORY from TAP¹

taproot n the main root of plants such as the dandelion, which grows straight down and bears smaller lateral roots

tar¹ n 1 a dark sticky substance obtained by distilling organic matter such as coal, wood, or peat 2 same as **coal tar** ▷ vb **tarring, tarred** 3 to coat with tar 4 **tar and feather** to cover (someone) with tar and feathers as a punishment 5 **tarred with the same brush** having, or regarded as having, the same faults ▸ HISTORY Old English *teoru* > **tarry** adj

tar² n informal a seaman ▸ HISTORY short for *tarpaulin*

tarakihi (tarr-a-kee-hee) or **terakihi** (terr-a-kee-hee) n a common edible sea fish of New Zealand waters ▸ HISTORY Māori

taramasalata n a creamy pale pink pâté, made from the eggs of fish, esp. smoked cod's roe, and served as an hors d'oeuvre ▸ HISTORY Modern Greek

tarantella n 1 a peasant dance from S Italy 2 music for this dance ▸ HISTORY Italian

tarantula n 1 a large hairy spider of tropical America with a poisonous bite 2 a large hairy spider of S Europe ▸ HISTORY Medieval Latin

tardy adj **-dier, -diest** 1 occurring later than it is expected to or than it should: *he spent the weekend writing tardy thank-you letters* 2 slow in progress, growth, etc.: *we made tardy progress across the ice* ▷ n, pl **tardies** (in the Caribbean) a pupil who arrives late at school ▸ HISTORY Latin *tardus* slow > **tardily** adv > **tardiness** n

tare¹ n 1 the weight of the wrapping or container in which goods are packed 2 the weight of a vehicle without its cargo or passengers ▸ HISTORY Arabic *tarhah* something discarded

tare² n 1 any of various vetch plants of Eurasia and N Africa 2 Bible a weed, thought to be the darnel ▸ HISTORY origin unknown

target n 1 the object or person that a weapon, ball, etc. is aimed at: *the station was an easy target for an air attack* 2 an object at which an archer or marksman aims, usually a round flat surface marked with circles 3 a fixed goal or objective: *our sales figures are well below target* 4 a person or thing at which criticism or ridicule is directed: *the Chancellor has been the target of much of the criticism* ▷ vb **-geting, -geted** 5 to direct: *an advertising campaign targeted at gay men* 6 to aim (a missile) ▸ HISTORY Old French *targette* a little shield

target audience n the group of people at whom a particular film, show, or advertisement is aimed

tariff n 1 a a tax levied by a government on imports or occasionally exports b a list of such taxes 2 a list of fixed prices, for example in a hotel 3 chiefly Brit a method of charging for services such as gas and electricity by setting a price per unit ▸ HISTORY Arabic *ta'rīfa* to inform

Tarmac n 1 trademark a paving material made of crushed stone bound with a mixture of tar and bitumen, used for a road or airport runway 2 **the tarmac** the area of an airport where planes wait, taxi, and take off or land: *we had to wait for an hour on the tarmac* ▷ vb **tarmac, -macking, -macked** 3 to apply Tarmac to (a surface)

- ■ **WORD HISTORY**
- ■ 'Tarmac' is short for *tarmacadam*, from the
- ■ surname of John McAdam (1756-1836), the
- ■ Scottish road engineer who greatly improved
- ■ the state of British roads and invented the
- ■ process of making road surfaces from a layer of
- ■ small stones on top of larger stones.

tarn n chiefly Brit a small mountain lake ▸ HISTORY from Old Norse

tarnish vb 1 (of a metal) to become stained or less bright, esp. by exposure to air or moisture 2 to damage or taint: *the affair could tarnish the reputation of the prime minister* ▷ n 3 a tarnished condition, surface, or film on a surface ▸ HISTORY Old French *ternir* to make dull > **tarnished** adj

taro n, pl **-ros** a plant with a large edible rootstock ▸ HISTORY Tahitian & Polynesian

tarot (tarr-oh) n 1 a special pack of cards, now used mainly for fortune-telling 2 a card in a tarot pack with a distinctive symbolic design ▸ HISTORY French

t

tarpaulin n 1 a heavy waterproof canvas coated with tar, wax, or paint 2 a sheet of this canvas, used as a waterproof covering ▶ HISTORY probably from TAR¹ + PALL¹

tarragon n a European herb with narrow leaves which are used as seasoning in cooking ▶ HISTORY Old French *targon*

tarry vb **-ries, -rying, -ried** old-fashioned 1 to delay or linger: *I have no plans to tarry longer than necessary* 2 to stay briefly: *most people tarried only a few hours before moving on* ▶ HISTORY origin unknown

tarsal anat adj 1 of the tarsus or tarsi ▷ n 2 a bone of the tarsus

tarseal n NZ 1 the bitumen surface of a road 2 **the tarseal** the main highway

tarsier n a small nocturnal primate of the E Indies which has very large eyes

tarsus n, pl **-si** 1 the bones of the ankle and heel collectively 2 the corresponding part in other mammals and in amphibians and reptiles ▶ HISTORY Greek *tarsos* flat surface, instep

tart¹ n 1 a pastry case, often having no top crust, with a sweet filling, such as jam or custard 2 chiefly US a small open pie with a fruit filling ▶ HISTORY Old French *tarte*

tart² adj 1 (of a flavour) sour or bitter 2 sharp and hurtful: *he made a rather tart comment* ▶ HISTORY Old English *teart* rough > **tartly** adv > **tartness** n

tartan n 1 a design of straight lines, crossing at right angles to give a chequered appearance, esp. one associated with a Scottish clan 2 a fabric with this design ▶ HISTORY origin unknown

tartar¹ n 1 a hard deposit on the teeth 2 a brownish-red substance deposited in a cask during the fermentation of wine ▶ HISTORY Medieval Greek *tartaron*

tartar² n a fearsome or formidable person ▶ HISTORY from *Tartar*

Tartar or **Tatar** n 1 a member of a Mongoloid people who established a powerful state in central Asia in the 13th century, now scattered throughout Russia and central Asia ▷ adj 2 of the Tartars ▶ HISTORY Persian *Tātār*

tartaric adj of or derived from tartar or tartaric acid

tartaric acid n a colourless crystalline acid which is found in many fruits

tartrazine (**tar**-traz-zeen) n an artificial yellow dye used as a food additive

tart up vb Brit, informal 1 to decorate in a cheap and flashy way: *the shops were tarted up for Christmas* 2 to try to make (oneself) look smart and attractive

task n 1 a specific piece of work required to be done 2 an unpleasant or difficult job or duty 3 **take to task** to criticize or rebuke ▶ HISTORY Old French *tasche*

task force n 1 a temporary grouping of military units formed to undertake a specific mission 2 any organization set up to carry out a continuing task

taskmaster n a person who enforces hard or continuous work

Tasmanian devil n a small flesh-eating marsupial of Tasmania

Tasmanian tiger n same as **thylacine**

Tass n (formerly) the principal news agency of the Soviet Union

tassel n a tuft of loose threads secured by a knot or knob, used to decorate a cushion, piece of clothing, etc. ▶ HISTORY Old French

taste n 1 the sense by which the flavour of a substance is distinguished by the taste buds 2 the sensation experienced by means of the taste buds 3 a small amount eaten, sipped, or tried on the tongue 4 a brief experience of something: *a taste of the planter's life* 5 a liking for something: *a taste for puns* 6 the ability to appreciate what is beautiful and excellent: *she's got very good taste in clothes* 7 a person's typical preferences as displayed by what they choose to buy, enjoy, etc.: *the film was good but a bit violent for my taste* 8 the quality of not being offensive or bad-mannered: *that remark was in rather poor taste* ▷ vb **tasting, tasted** 9 to distinguish the taste of (a substance) by means of the taste buds: *I've got a stinking cold and can't taste anything* 10 to take a small amount of (a food or liquid) into the mouth, esp. in order to test the flavour 11 to have a flavour or taste as specified: *the pizza tastes delicious* 12 to have a brief experience of (something): *they have tasted democracy and they won't let go* ▶ HISTORY Old French *taster*

taste bud n any of the cells on the surface of the tongue, by means of which the sensation of taste is experienced

tasteful adj having or showing good social or aesthetic taste: *tasteful decor* > **tastefully** adv

tasteless adj 1 lacking in flavour: *the canteen serves cold, tasteless pizzas* 2 lacking social or aesthetic taste: *a room full of tasteless ornaments; a tasteless remark* > **tastelessly** adv > **tastelessness** n

taster n 1 a person employed to test the quality of food or drink by tasting it 2 a sample of something intended to indicate what the entire thing is like: *the entrance hall was filled with flowers, giving a taster of the splendours in the main exhibition*

tasty adj **tastier, tastiest** having a pleasant flavour

tat n Brit tatty or tasteless articles

Tatar n, adj same as **Tartar**

tater n Brit, dialect a potato

tattered adj 1 ragged or torn: *a tattered old book* 2 wearing ragged or torn clothing: *the tattered refugees*

tatters pl n 1 torn ragged clothing 2 **in tatters** a (of clothing) torn in several places b (of an argument, plan, etc.) completely destroyed

tattle vb **-tling, -tled** 1 to gossip or chatter ▷ n 2 gossip or chatter ▶ HISTORY Middle Dutch *tatelen* > **tattler** n

tattoo¹ n, pl **-toos** 1 a picture or design made on someone's body by pricking small holes in the skin and filling them with indelible dye ▷ vb **-tooing, -tooed** 2 to make pictures or designs on (a person's skin) by pricking and staining it with indelible colours ▶ HISTORY Tahitian *tatau* > **tattooed** *adj* > **tattooist** *n*

tattoo² *n, pl* **-toos** **1** (formerly) a signal by drum or bugle ordering soldiers to return to their quarters **2** a military display or pageant **3** any drumming or tapping ▶ HISTORY Dutch *taptoe*

tatty *adj* **-tier, -tiest** worn out, shabby, or unkempt ▶ HISTORY Scots

taught *vb* the past of **teach**

taunt *vb* **1** to tease or provoke (someone) with jeering remarks ▷ *n* **2** a jeering remark ▶ HISTORY French *tant pour tant* like for like > **taunting** *adj*

Taurus *n astrol* the second sign of the zodiac; the Bull ▶ HISTORY Latin

taut *adj* **1** stretched tight: *the cable must be taut* **2** showing nervous strain: *he was looking taut and anxious* **3** (of a film or piece of writing) having no unnecessary or irrelevant details: *a taut thriller* ▶ HISTORY Middle English *tought*

tauten *vb* to make or become taut

tautology *n, pl* **-gies** the use of words which merely repeat something already stated, as in *reverse back* ▶ HISTORY Greek *tautologia* > **tautological** or **tautologous** *adj*

tavern *n* **1** *old-fashioned* a pub **2** *US, Canad, Austral & NZ* a place licensed for the sale and consumption of alcoholic drink ▶ HISTORY Latin *taberna* hut

tawdry *adj* **-drier, -driest** cheap, showy, and of poor quality: *tawdry Christmas decorations* ▶ HISTORY Middle English *seynt Audries lace*, finery sold at the fair of St *Audrey*

tawny *adj* brown to brownish-orange ▶ HISTORY Old French *tané*

tawny owl *n* a European owl having a reddish-brown plumage and a round head

tawse *n Scot* a leather strap with one end cut into thongs, formerly used by schoolteachers to hit children who had misbehaved ▶ HISTORY probably plural of obsolete *taw* strip of leather

tax *n* **1** a compulsory payment to a government to raise revenue, levied on income, property, or goods and services ▷ *vb* **2** to levy a tax on (people, companies, etc.) **3** to make heavy demands on: *the task taxed his ingenuity and patience* **4 tax someone with** to accuse someone of: *he was taxed with parochialism and meanness* ▶ HISTORY Latin *taxare* to appraise > **taxable** *adj* > **taxing** *adj*

taxation *n* the levying of taxes or the condition of being taxed

tax avoidance *n* reduction of tax liability by lawful methods

tax-deductible *adj* legally deductible from income or wealth before tax assessment

tax evasion *n* reduction of tax liability by illegal methods

tax-free *adj* not needing to have tax paid on it: *a tax-free lump sum*

tax haven *n* a country or state having a lower rate of taxation than elsewhere

taxi *n, pl* **taxis** **1** Also called: **cab, taxicab** a car that may be hired, along with its driver, to carry

passengers to any specified destination ▷ *vb* **taxiing, taxied** **2** (of an aircraft) to move along the ground, esp. before takeoff and after landing ▶ HISTORY *taximeter cab*

taxidermy *n* the art of preparing, stuffing, and mounting animal skins so that they have a lifelike appearance ▶ HISTORY Greek *taxis* arrangement + *derma* skin > **taxidermist** *n*

taxi rank *n Brit* a place where taxis wait to be hired

taxman *n, pl* **-men** **1** a collector of taxes **2** *informal* a tax-collecting body personified: *he was convicted of conspiring to cheat the taxman*

taxonomic group *n biol* a group of organisms that have been classified according to their structure, origin, etc.

taxonomy *n* **1** the branch of biology concerned with the classification of plants and animals into groups based on their similarities and differences **2** the science or practice of classification ▶ HISTORY Greek *taxis* order + *nomia* law > **taxonomic** *adj* > **taxonomist** *n*

taxpayer *n* a person or organization that pays taxes

tax relief *n* a reduction in the amount of tax a person or company has to pay

tax return *n* a declaration of personal income used as a basis for assessing an individual's liability for taxation

tax year *n* a period of twelve months used by a government as a basis for calculating taxes

Tb *chem* terbium

TB tuberculosis

T-bone steak *n* a large choice steak cut from the sirloin of beef, containing a T-shaped bone

tbs. or **tbsp.** tablespoon(ful)

Tc *chem* technetium

TCP/IP Transmission Control Protocol/Internet Protocol

te *n music* (in tonic sol-fa) the seventh note of any ascending major scale

Te *chem* tellurium

tea *n* **1 a** a drink made by infusing the dried chopped leaves of an Asian shrub in boiling water: *would you like a cup of tea?* **b** the dried chopped leaves of an Asian shrub used to make this drink: *could you get some tea at the grocer's?* **c** the Asian shrub on which these leaves grow **2** *Brit, Austral & NZ* the main evening meal **3** *chiefly Brit* a light meal eaten in mid-afternoon, usually consisting of tea and cakes, sometimes with sandwiches **4** a drink like tea made from other plants: *mint tea* ▶ HISTORY Ancient Chinese *d'a*

tea bag *n* a small bag containing tea leaves, infused in boiling water to make tea

teach *vb* **teaching, taught** **1** to tell or show (someone) how to do something **2** to give instruction or lessons in (a subject) to (students) **3** to cause to learn or understand: *life has taught me to seize the day* **4 teach someone a lesson** to warn or punish someone: *a bully has to be taught a lesson* ▶ HISTORY Old English *tǣcan* > **teachable** *adj*

t

teacher *n* a person whose job is to teach others, esp. children

teaching *n* **1** the art or profession of a teacher **2 teachings** the ideas and principles taught by a person, school of thought, etc.: *the teachings of the Catholic Church*

teaching hospital *n* a hospital attached to a medical school, in which students are taught and given supervised practical experience

tea cloth *n Brit* same as **tea towel**

tea cosy *n* a covering for a teapot to keep the contents hot

teacup *n* **1** a cup out of which tea may be drunk **2** Also called: **teacupful** the amount a teacup will hold

teahouse *n* a restaurant, esp. in Japan or China, where tea and light refreshments are served

teak *n* the hard yellowish-brown wood of an East Indian tree, used for furniture making ▶ HISTORY Malayalam (a language of S India) *tēkka*

teal *n*, *pl* **teals** *or* **teal** a small freshwater duck related to the mallard ▶ HISTORY Middle English *tele*

team *n* **1** a group of players forming one of the sides in a sporting contest **2** a group of people organized to work together: *a team of scientists* **3** two or more animals working together: *a sledge pulled by a team of dogs* ▷ *vb* **4 team up with** to join with (someone) in order to work together **5 team with** to match (something) with something else: *navy skirts teamed with various coloured blouses* ▶ HISTORY Old English *tēam* offspring

team spirit *n* willingness to cooperate as part of a team

teamster *n* **1** *US & Canad* a lorry driver **2** (formerly) a driver of a team of horses

teamwork *n* the cooperative work done by a team

teapot *n* a container with a lid, spout, and handle, in which tea is made and from which it is served

tear¹ *n* **1** Also called: **teardrop** a drop of salty fluid appearing in and falling from the eye. *Related adjectives:* **lacrimal, lachrymal, lacrymal 2 in tears** weeping ▶ HISTORY Old English *tēar*

tear² *vb* **tearing, tore, torn 1** to rip a hole in (something): *I tore my jumper on a nail* **2** to pull apart or to pieces: *eagles have powerful beaks for tearing flesh* **3** to hurry or rush **4** to remove or take by force: *the sacred things torn from the temples of Inca worshippers* **5 tear at someone's heartstrings** to cause someone distress or anguish **6** to injure (a muscle or ligament) by moving or twisting it violently ▷ *n* **7** a hole or split ▶ HISTORY Old English *teran*

tear duct *n* a short tube in the inner corner of the eyelid, through which tears drain into the nose

tearful *adj* weeping or about to weep
> **tearfully** *adv*

tear gas *n* a gas that stings the eyes and causes temporary blindness, used in warfare and to control riots

tear-jerker *n informal* an excessively sentimental film or book

tearoom *n* **1** *chiefly Brit* a restaurant where tea and light refreshments are served **2** *NZ* a room in a school or university where hot drinks are served

tease *vb* **teasing, teased 1** to make fun of (someone) in a provocative and often playful manner **2** to arouse sexual desire in (someone) with no intention of satisfying it **3** to raise the nap of (a fabric) with a teasel ▷ **4** a person who teases **5** a piece of teasing behaviour ▷ See also **tease out** ▶ HISTORY Old English *tǣsan*
> **teasing** *adj*

teasel, teazel *or* **teazle** *n* **1** a plant of Eurasia and N Africa, with prickly heads of yellow or purple flowers **2** the dried flower head of a teasel, used, esp. formerly, for raising the nap of cloth ▶ HISTORY Old English *tǣsel*

tease out *vb* **1** to comb (hair, flax, or wool) so as to remove any tangles **2** to extract information with difficulty: *it's not easy to tease out the differences between anxiety and depression*

teaser *n* **1** a difficult question **2** a preliminary advertisement in a campaign that makes people curious to know what product is being advertised

teaspoon *n* **1** a small spoon used for stirring tea or coffee **2** Also called: **teaspoonful** the amount contained in such a spoon **3** a unit of capacity used in cooking etc., equal to 5 ml

teat *n* **1** the nipple of a breast or udder **2** something resembling a teat such as the rubber mouthpiece of a feeding bottle ▶ HISTORY Old French *tete*

tea towel *or* **tea cloth** *n Brit* a towel for drying dishes

tea tree *n* a tree of Australia and New Zealand that yields an oil used as an antiseptic

tech *n informal* a technical college

techie *informal n* **1** a person who is skilled in the use of technology ▷ *adj* **2** relating to or skilled in the use of technology

technetium (tek-**neesh**-ee-um) *n chem* a silvery-grey metallic element, produced artificially, esp. by the fission of uranium. Symbol: Tc ▶ HISTORY Greek *tekhnētos* man-made

technical *adj* **1** of or specializing in industrial, practical, or mechanical arts and applied sciences: *a technical school* **2** skilled in practical activities rather than abstract thinking **3** relating to a particular field of activity: *technical jargon* **4** according to the letter of the law: *a last-minute penalty awarded to the Irish for a technical offence* **5** showing technique: *technical perfection*
> **technically** *adv*

technical college *n Brit & Austral* an institution for further education that provides courses in art and technical subjects

technical drawing *n* drawing done by a draughtsman with compasses, T-squares, etc.

technicality *n*, *pl* **-ties 1** a petty formal point arising from a strict interpretation of the law or a set of rules: *the case was dismissed on a legal*

t

technicality **2** a detail of the method used to do something: *the technicalities of making a recording*

technical knockout *n* *boxing* a judgment of a knockout given when a boxer is, in the referee's opinion, too badly beaten to continue without risk of serious injury

technician *n* a person skilled in a particular technical field: *oil technicians*

Technicolor *n* *trademark* a process of producing colour film for the cinema by superimposing synchronized films of the same scene, each having a different colour filter

technikon *n* *S African* a technical college

technique *n* **1** a method or skill used for a particular task: *modern management techniques* **2** proficiency in a practical or mechanical skill: *he lacks the technique to be a good player* ▶ HISTORY Greek *tekhnē* skill

techno *n* a type of very fast disco music, using electronic sounds and having a strong technological influence

techno- *combining form* of or relating to technology: *technocrat* ▶ HISTORY Greek *tekhnē* skill

technocracy *n, pl* **-cies** government by scientists, engineers, and other experts ▶ HISTORY Greek *tekhnē* skill + *kratos* power > **technocrat** *n* > **technocratic** *adj*

technology *n, pl* **-gies** **1** the application of practical or mechanical sciences to industry or commerce **2** the scientific methods or devices used in a particular field: *the latest aircraft technology* ▶ HISTORY Greek *tekhnologia* systematic treatment > **technological** *adj* > **technologist** *n*

technophobia *n* fear of using technological devices, such as computers > **technophobe** *n* > **technophobic** *adj*

tectonic *adj* **1** denoting or relating to building **2** *geol* **a** (of landforms, etc.) resulting from distortion of the earth's crust due to forces within it **b** (of processes, movements, etc.) occurring within the earth's crust and causing structural deformation ▶ HISTORY Late Latin *tectonicus*, from Greek *tektonikos* belonging to carpentry, from *tektōn* a builder

tectonic plate *n* *geol* a large section of the earth's crust

tectonics *n* *geol* the study of the earth's crust and the forces that produce changes in it ▶ HISTORY Greek *tektōn* a builder

ted¹ *vb* **tedding, tedded** to shake out (hay), so as to dry it ▶ HISTORY Old Norse *tethja*

ted² *n* *Brit, informal* short for **teddy boy**

teddy¹ *n, pl* **-dies** short for **teddy bear**

teddy² *n, pl* **-dies** a woman's one-piece undergarment incorporating a camisole top and French knickers ▶ HISTORY origin unknown

teddy bear *n* a stuffed toy bear

■ **WORD HISTORY**
■ 'Teddy bears' are named after the American
■ president Theodore (Teddy) Roosevelt
■ (1859-1919), who was keen on bear-hunting.

teddy boy *n* (in Britain, esp. in the mid-1950s) a youth who wore mock Edwardian fashions ▶ HISTORY *Teddy*, from *Edward*

Te Deum (tee **dee**-um) *n* *Christianity* an ancient Latin hymn beginning Te Deum Laudamus (we praise thee, O God)

tedious *adj* boring and uninteresting > **tediously** *adv* > **tediousness** *n*

tedium *n* the state of being bored or the quality of being boring: *the tedium of a nine-to-five white-collar job* ▶ HISTORY Latin *taedium*

tee *n* **1 a** a support for a golf ball, usually a small wooden or plastic peg, used when teeing off **2** an area on a golf course from which the first stroke of a hole is made **3** a mark used as a target in certain games such as curling and quoits ▷ See also **tee off** ▶ HISTORY origin unknown

teem¹ *vb* **teem with** to have a great number of: *the woods were teeming with snakes and bears* ▶ HISTORY Old English *tēman* to produce offspring

teem² *vb* (of rain) to pour down in torrents ▶ HISTORY Old Norse *tœma*

teenage *adj* **1** (of a person) aged between 13 and 19 **2** typical of or designed for people aged between 13 and 19: *teenage fashions*

teenager *n* a person between the ages of 13 and 19

teens *pl n* **1** the years of a person's life between the ages of 13 and 19 **2** all the numbers that end in *-teen*

teeny *adj* **-nier, -niest** *informal* extremely small ▶ HISTORY variant of *tiny*

tee off *vb* **teeing, teed** *golf* to hit (the ball) from a tee at the start of a hole

teepee *n* same as **tepee**

teeter *vb* to wobble or move unsteadily ▶ HISTORY Middle English *titeren*

teeth *n* **1** the plural of **tooth 2** the power to produce a desired effect: *resolution 672 had no teeth* **3 armed to the teeth** very heavily armed **4 get one's teeth into** to become engrossed in **5 in the teeth of** in spite of: *trying to run a business in the teeth of the recession*

teethe *vb* **teething, teethed** (of a baby) to grow his or her first teeth

teething troubles *pl n* problems arising during the early stages of a project

teetotal *adj* never drinking alcohol ▶ HISTORY reduplication of *t* + *total* > **teetotaller** *n*

TEFL Teaching of English as a Foreign Language

Teflon *n* *trademark* a substance used for nonstick coatings on saucepans, etc.

tel. telephone

tele- *combining form* **1** at or over a distance: *telecommunications* **2** television: *telegenic* **3** via telephone or television: *teleconference* ▶ HISTORY Greek *tēle* far

telecommunications *n* communications using electronic equipment, such as telephones, radio, and television

telecommuting *n* same as **teleworking**

telegram *n* (formerly) a message transmitted by telegraph

t

telegraph n **1** (formerly) a system by which information could be transmitted over a distance, using electrical signals sent along a cable ▷ vb **2** (formerly) to send (a message) by telegraph **3** to give advance notice of (something), esp. unintentionally: *the twist in the plot was telegraphed long in advance* **4** *Canad, informal* to cast (a vote) illegally by impersonating a registered voter > **telegraphic** adj > **telegraphist** n

telegraphy n (formerly) the science or use of a telegraph

telekinesis n movement of a body by thought or willpower, without the application of a physical force > **telekinetic** adj

Telemessage n *trademark, Brit* a message sent by telephone or telex and delivered in printed form

telemetry n the use of electronic devices to record or measure a distant event and transmit the data to a receiver > **telemetric** adj

teleology n **1** *philosophy* the doctrine that there is evidence of purpose or design in the universe **2** *biol* the belief that natural phenomena have a predetermined purpose and are not determined by mechanical laws ▶ HISTORY Greek *telos* end + -LOGY > **teleological** adj > **teleologist** n

telepathy n the direct communication of thoughts and feelings between minds without the need to use normal means such as speech, writing, or touch ▶ HISTORY Greek *tēle* far + *pathos* suffering > **telepathic** adj > **telepathically** adv

telephone n **1** a piece of equipment for transmitting speech, consisting of a microphone and receiver mounted on a handset: *the telephone was ringing* **2** the worldwide system of communications using telephones: *reports came in by telephone* ▷ vb **-phoning, -phoned 3** to call or talk to (a person) by telephone ▷ adj **4** of or using a telephone: *a telephone call* ▶ HISTORY Greek *tēle* far + *phōnē* voice > **telephonic** adj

telephone box n an enclosure from which a paid telephone call can be made

telephone directory n a book listing the names, addresses, and telephone numbers of subscribers in a particular area

telephonist n a person who operates a telephone switchboard

telephony n a system of telecommunications for the transmission of speech or other sounds

telephoto lens n a lens fitted to a camera to produce a magnified image of a distant object

teleprinter n *Brit* an apparatus, similar to a typewriter, by which typed messages are sent and received by wire

Teleprompter n *trademark* a device for displaying a script under a television camera, so that a speaker can read it while appearing to look at the camera

telesales n the selling of a commodity or service by telephone

telescope n **1** an optical instrument for making distant objects appear closer by use of a combination of lenses **2** See **radio telescope** ▷ vb **-scoping, -scoped 3** to shorten (something) while still keeping the important parts: *a hundred years of change has been telescoped into five years* ▶ HISTORY New Latin *telescopium* far-seeing instrument > **telescopic** adj

teletext n a Videotex service in which information is broadcast by a television station and received on a specially equipped television set

Teletype n *trademark* a type of teleprinter

televangelist n *US* an evangelical preacher who appears regularly on television, preaching the gospel and appealing for donations from viewers ▶ HISTORY tele(vision) + (e)vangelist

televise vb **-vising, -vised** to show (a programme or event) on television

television n **1** the system or process of producing a moving image with accompanying sound on a distant screen **2** Also called: **television set** a device for receiving broadcast signals and converting them into sound and pictures **3** the content of television programmes: *some people think that television is too violent nowadays* ▷ adj **4** of or relating to television: *a television interview* > **televisual** adj

teleworking n the use of home computers, telephones, etc. to enable a person to work from home while maintaining contact with colleagues or customers > **teleworker** n

telex n **1** an international communication service which sends messages by teleprinter **2** a teleprinter used in such a service **3** a message sent by telex ▷ vb **4** to transmit (a message) by telex ▶ HISTORY tel(eprinter) ex(change)

tell vb **telling, told 1** to make known in words; notify: *I told her what had happened* **2** to order or instruct (someone to do something): *he had been told to wait in the lobby* **3** to give an account (of an event or situation): *the President had been told of the developments* **4** to communicate by words: *he was woken at 5 a.m. to be told the news* **5** to discover, distinguish, or discern: *she could tell that he was not sorry* **6** to have or produce an impact or effect: *the pressure had begun to tell on him* **7** *informal* to reveal secrets or gossip **8 tell the time** to read the time from a clock **9 you're telling me** *slang* I know that very well ▷ See also **tell off** ▶ HISTORY Old English *tellan*

teller n **1** a narrator **2** a bank cashier **3** a person appointed to count votes

telling adj having a marked effect or impact: *to inflict telling damage on the enemy*

tell off vb *informal* to reprimand or scold (someone) > **telling-off** n

telltale n **1** a person who tells tales about others ▷ adj **2** giving away information: *examining the hands for telltale signs of age*

tellurian adj of the earth ▶ HISTORY Latin *tellus* the earth

tellurium n *chem* a brittle silvery-white nonmetallic element. Symbol: Te ▶ HISTORY Latin *tellus* the earth

telly n, pl **-lies** informal short for **television**

TEM science transmission electron microscope

temazepam (ti-**maz**-i-pam) n (sometimes cap) a sedative in the form of a gel-like capsule, which is taken orally or melted and injected by drug users

temerity (tim-**merr**-it-tee) n boldness or audacity ▶ HISTORY Latin temere at random

temp Brit, informal n **1** a person, esp. a secretary, employed on a temporary basis ▷ vb **2** to work as a temp

temp. **1** temperature **2** temporary

temper n **1** a sudden outburst of anger: she stormed out in a temper **2** a tendency to have sudden outbursts of anger: you've got a temper all right **3** a mental condition of moderation and calm: he lost his temper **4** a person's frame of mind: he was in a bad temper ▷ vb **5** to modify so as to make less extreme or more acceptable: past militancy has been tempered with compassion and caring **6** to reduce the brittleness of (a hardened metal) by reheating it and allowing it to cool **7** music to adjust the frequency differences between the notes of a scale on (a keyboard instrument) ▶ HISTORY Latin temperare to mix

tempera n a painting medium for powdered pigments, consisting usually of egg yolk and water ▶ HISTORY Italian temperare to mingle

temperament n a person's character or disposition ▶ HISTORY Latin temperamentum a mixing

temperamental adj **1** (of a person) tending to be moody and have sudden outbursts of anger **2** informal working erratically and inconsistently; unreliable: the temperamental microphone **3** of or relating to a person's temperament: we discussed temperamental and developmental differences > **temperamentally** adv

temperance n **1** restraint or moderation, esp. in yielding to one's appetites or desires **2** abstinence from alcoholic drink ▶ HISTORY Latin temperare to regulate

temperate adj **1** (of a climate) never extremely hot or extremely cold **2** mild or moderate in quality or character: try to be more temperate in your statements ▶ HISTORY Latin temperatus

Temperate Zone n geog those parts of the earth's surface lying between the Arctic Circle and the tropic of Cancer and between the Antarctic Circle and the tropic of Capricorn. Compare **Frigid Zone, Torrid Zone**

temperature n **1** the hotness or coldness of something, as measured on a scale that has one or more fixed reference points **2** chem the average kinetic energy of the atoms or molecules of a substance **3** informal an abnormally high body temperature **4** the strength of feeling among a group of people: his remarks are likely to raise the political temperature considerably ▶ HISTORY Latin temperatura proportion

temperature inversion n meteorol the condition in which layers of warmer air lie above cooler air

tempest n literary a violent wind or storm ▶ HISTORY Latin tempestas

tempestuous adj **1** violent or stormy **2** extremely emotional or passionate: a tempestuous relationship > **tempestuously** adv

template n a wood or metal pattern, used to help cut out shapes accurately ▶ HISTORY from temple a part in a loom that keeps the cloth stretched

temple¹ n a building or place used for the worship of a god or gods ▶ HISTORY Latin templum

temple² n the region on each side of the head in front of the ear and above the cheek bone ▶ HISTORY Latin tempus

tempo (**tem**-po) n, pl **-pi** (-pee) or **-pos** **1** rate or pace: the slow tempo of change in an overwhelmingly rural country **2** the speed at which a piece of music is played or meant to be played ▶ HISTORY Italian

temporal¹ adj **1** of or relating to time **2** of secular as opposed to spiritual or religious affairs: in the Middle Ages the Pope had temporal as well as spiritual power **3** not permanent or eternal: a temporal view of drugs as the No. 1 social problem ▶ HISTORY Latin tempus time

temporal² adj anat of or near the temple or temples

temporal bone n either of two compound bones forming the sides of the skull

temporary adj lasting only for a short time; not permanent: temporary accommodation ▶ HISTORY Latin temporarius > **temporarily** adv

temporary deafness n pathol an inability to hear which is not permanent

temporary magnet n physics a magnet that loses its magnetization after the magnetic field producing it has been removed

temporize or **-rise** vb **-rizing, -rized** or **-rising, -rised** **1** to delay, act evasively, or protract a negotiation in order to gain time or avoid making a decision: 'Well,' I temporized, 'I'll have to ask your mother' **2** to adapt oneself to circumstances, as by temporary or apparent agreement ▶ HISTORY Latin tempus time

tempt vb **1** to entice (someone) to do something, esp. something morally wrong or unwise: can I tempt you to have another whisky? **2** to allure or attract: she was tempted by the glamour of a modelling career **3 be tempted** to want to do something while knowing it would be wrong or inappropriate to do so: many youngsters are tempted to experiment with drugs **4 tempt fate** or **providence** to take foolish or unnecessary risks ▶ HISTORY Latin temptare to test > **tempter** n > **temptress** fem n

temptation n **1** the act of tempting or the state of being tempted **2** a person or thing that tempts

tempting adj attractive or inviting: it's tempting to say I told you so > **temptingly** adv

ten n **1** the cardinal number that is the sum of one and nine **2** a numeral, 10 or X, representing this number **3** something representing or consisting of ten units ▷ adj **4** amounting to ten: ten years ▶ HISTORY Old English tēn > **tenth** adj, n

t

tenable *adj* **1** able to be upheld or maintained: *a tenable strategy* **2** (of a job) intended to be held by a person for a particular length of time: *the post will be tenable for three years in the first instance* ▸ HISTORY Latin *tenere* to hold > **tenability** *n* > **tenably** *adv*

tenacious *adj* **1** holding firmly: *a tenacious grasp* **2** stubborn or persistent: *tenacious support* ▸ HISTORY Latin *tenere* to hold > **tenaciously** *adv* > **tenacity** *n*

tenancy *n, pl* **-cies 1** the temporary possession or use of lands or property owned by somebody else, in return for payment **2** the period of holding or occupying such property

tenant *n* **1** a person who pays rent for the use of land or property **2** any holder or occupant ▸ HISTORY Old French: one who is holding

tenant farmer *n* a person who farms land rented from somebody else

tenantry *n* old-fashioned tenants collectively

tench *n* a European freshwater game fish of the carp family ▸ HISTORY Old French *tenche*

Ten Commandments *pl n Bible* the commandments given by God to Moses on Mount Sinai, summarizing the basic obligations of people towards God and their fellow humans

tend[1] *vb* to be inclined (to take a particular kind of action or to be in a particular condition) as a rule: *she tends to be rather absent-minded* ▸ HISTORY Latin *tendere* to stretch

tend[2] *vb* **1** to take care of: *it is she who tends his wounds* **2** **tend to** to attend to: *excuse me, I have to tend to the other guests* ▸ HISTORY variant of *attend*

tendency *n, pl* **-cies 1** an inclination to act in a particular way **2** the general course or drift of something **3** a faction, esp. within a political party ▸ HISTORY Latin *tendere* to stretch

tendentious *adj* expressing a particular viewpoint or opinion, esp. a controversial one, in very strong terms: *a somewhat tendentious reading of French history* > **tendentiously** *adv*

tender[1] *adj* **1** (of cooked food) having softened and become easy to chew or cut **2** gentle and kind: *tender loving care* **3** vulnerable or sensitive: *at the tender age of 9* **4** painful when touched: *his wrist was swollen and tender* ▸ HISTORY Old French *tendre* > **tenderly** *adv* > **tenderness** *n*

tender[2] *vb* **1** to present or offer: *he tendered his resignation* **2** to make a formal offer or estimate for a job or contract: *contractors tendering for government work* ▷ *n* **3** a formal offer to supply specified goods or services at a stated cost or rate: *the government invited tenders to run television and radio services* ▸ HISTORY Latin *tendere* to extend > **tenderer** *n* > **tendering** *n*

tender[3] *n* **1** a small boat that brings supplies to larger vessels in a port **2** a wagon attached to the rear of a steam locomotive that carries the fuel and water ▸ HISTORY variant of *attender*

tenderize or **-ise** *vb* **-izing, -ized** or **-ising, -ised** to make (meat) tender, by pounding it or adding a substance to break down the fibres > **tenderizer** or **-iser** *n*

tenderloin *n* a tender cut of pork from between the sirloin and ribs

tendon *n* a band of tough tissue that attaches a muscle to a bone ▸ HISTORY Medieval Latin *tendo*

tendril *n* a threadlike leaf or stem by which a climbing plant attaches itself to a support ▸ HISTORY probably from Old French *tendron*

tenement *n* a large building divided into several different flats ▸ HISTORY Latin *tenere* to hold

tenet (**ten**-nit) *n* a principle on which a belief or doctrine is based ▸ HISTORY Latin, literally: he (it) holds

tenfold *adj* **1** having ten times as many or as much **2** composed of ten parts ▷ *adv* **3** by ten times as many or as much

tenner *n* Brit, Austral & NZ, informal **1** a ten-pound or ten-dollar note **2** the sum of ten pounds or ten dollars: *it's worth a tenner at least*

tennis *n* a game played between two players or pairs of players who use a racket to hit a ball to and fro over a net on a rectangular court ▷ See also **lawn tennis, real tennis, table tennis** ▸ HISTORY probably from Anglo-French *tenetz* hold!

tennis elbow *n* inflammation of the elbow, typically caused by exertion in playing tennis

tenon *n* a projecting end of a piece of wood, formed to fit into a corresponding slot in another piece ▸ HISTORY Old French

tenor *n* **1 a** the second highest male voice, between alto and baritone **b** a singer with such a voice **c** a saxophone, horn, or other musical instrument between the alto and baritone or bass **2** a general meaning or character: *it was clear from the tenor of the meeting that the chairman's actions are very unpopular* ▷ *adj* **3** denoting a musical instrument between alto and baritone: *a tenor saxophone* **4** of or relating to the second highest male voice: *his voice lacks the range needed for the tenor role* ▸ HISTORY Old French *tenour*

tenpin bowling *n* a game in which players try to knock over ten skittles by rolling a ball at them

tense[1] *adj* **1** having, showing, or causing mental or emotional strain: *the tense atmosphere* **2** stretched tight: *tense muscles* ▷ *vb* **tensing, tensed** **3** Also: **tense up** to make or become tense ▸ HISTORY Latin *tensus* taut > **tensely** *adv* > **tenseness** *n*

tense[2] *n grammar* the form of a verb that indicates whether the action referred to in the sentence is located in the past, the present, or the future: *'ate' is the past tense of 'to eat'* ▸ HISTORY Old French *tens* time

tensile *adj* of or relating to tension or being stretched: *the properties of metals are normally measured under tensile stress*

tensile strength *n* a measure of the ability of a material to withstand lengthwise stress, expressed as the greatest stress that the material can stand without breaking

tension *n* **1** a situation or condition of hostility, suspense, or uneasiness: *a renewed state of tension* between old enemies **2** mental or emotional strain: *nervous tension* **3** a force that stretches or the state or degree of being stretched tight: *keep tension on the line until the fish comes within range of the net* **4** *physics* a force that tends to produce an elongation of a body or structure **5** *physics* voltage, electromotive force, or potential difference ▶ HISTORY Latin *tensio*

tensional plate boundary *n geol* a place where the edges of two tectonic plates move away from each other

tent *n* **1** a portable shelter made of canvas or other fabric supported on poles, stretched out, and fastened to the ground by pegs and ropes **2** See **oxygen tent** ▶ HISTORY Old French *tente*

tentacle *n* **1** a flexible organ that grows near the mouth in many invertebrates and is used for feeding, grasping, etc. **2 tentacles** the unseen methods by which an organization or idea, esp. a sinister one, influences people and events: *the tentacles of the secret police* ▶ HISTORY Latin *tentare* to feel > **tentacled** *adj*

tentative *adj* **1** provisional or unconfirmed: *a tentative agreement* **2** hesitant, uncertain, or cautious: *their rather tentative approach* ▶ HISTORY Latin *tentare* to test > **tentatively** *adv* > **tentativeness** *n*

tenterhooks *pl n* **on tenterhooks** in a state of tension or suspense ▶ HISTORY Latin *tentus* stretched + HOOK

tenth *adj, n* See **ten**

tenuous *adj* insignificant or flimsy: *there is only the most tenuous evidence for it* ▶ HISTORY Latin *tenuis* > **tenuously** *adv*

tenure *n* **1** the holding of an office or position **2** the length of time an office or position lasts **3** the holding of a teaching position at a university on a permanent basis **4** the legal right to live in a place or to use land or buildings for a period of time ▶ HISTORY Latin *tenere* to hold

tepee *or* **teepee** (**tee**-pee) *n* a cone-shaped tent of animal skins, formerly used by Native Americans ▶ HISTORY Sioux *tīpī*

tepid *adj* **1** slightly warm **2** lacking enthusiasm: *tepid applause* ▶ HISTORY Latin *tepidus* > **tepidity** *n* > **tepidly** *adv*

tequila *n* a Mexican alcoholic spirit distilled from the agave plant ▶ HISTORY after *Tequila*, district in Mexico

tera- *combining form* denoting one million million (10^{12}): *terameter* ▶ HISTORY Greek *teras* monster

teratology (terr-a-**tol**-a-jee) *n* the branch of medicine concerned with the development of physical abnormalities during the fetal or early embryonic stage ▶ HISTORY Greek *teras* monster + -LOGY

terbium *n chem* a soft silvery-grey element of the lanthanide series of metals. Symbol: Tb ▶ HISTORY after *Ytterby*, Sweden, where discovered

tercentenary *or* **tercentennial** *adj* **1** marking a 300th anniversary ▷ *n, pl* -**tenaries** *or* -**tennials**

882

2 a 300th anniversary ▶ HISTORY Latin *ter* three times + CENTENARY

teredo (ter-**ree**-doh) *n, pl* -**dos** *or* -**dines** (-din-eez) a marine mollusc that bores into and destroys submerged timber ▶ HISTORY Greek *terēdōn* wood-boring worm

term *n* **1** a word or expression, esp. one used in a specialized field of knowledge: *he coined the term 'inferiority complex'* **2** a limited period of time: *a four-year prison term; Obama's second term as President* **3** one of the periods of the year when a school, university, or college is open or a lawcourt holds sessions **4** the period of pregnancy when childbirth is imminent **5** *maths* any distinct quantity making up a fraction or proportion, or contained in a sequence, series, etc. **6** *logic* any of the three subjects or predicates occurring in a syllogism **7 full term** the end of a specific period of time: *the agony of carrying the child to full term* ▷ *vb* **8** to name, call, or describe as being: *social workers tend to be termed lefties* ▷ See also **terms** ▶ HISTORY Latin *terminus* end

termagant *n literary* an unpleasant, aggressive, and overbearing woman ▶ HISTORY earlier *Tervagaunt*, after an arrogant character in medieval mystery plays

terminable *adj* capable of being terminated: *his terminable interest in the property* > **terminability** *n*

terminal *adj* **1** (of an illness) ending in death **2** situated at an end, terminus, or boundary: *the terminal joints of the fingers* **3** *informal* extreme or severe: *terminal boredom* ▷ *n* **4** a place where vehicles, passengers, or goods begin or end a journey: *the ferry terminal* **5** a point at which current enters or leaves an electrical device **6** *computers* a device, usually a keyboard and a visual display unit, having input/output links with a computer ▶ HISTORY Latin *terminus* end > **terminally** *adv*

terminal velocity *n physics* the maximum velocity reached by a body falling under gravity through a liquid or gas, esp. the atmosphere

terminate *vb* -**nating**, -**nated** **1** to bring or come to an end: *his flying career was terminated by this crash* **2** to put an end to (a pregnancy) by inducing an abortion **3** (of the route of a train, bus, etc.) to stop at a particular place and not go any farther: *this train terminates at Leicester* ▶ HISTORY Latin *terminare* to set boundaries > **termination** *n*

terminology *n, pl* -**gies** the specialized words and expressions relating to a particular subject > **terminological** *adj* > **terminologist** *n*

terminus (**term**-in-nuss) *n, pl* -**ni** (-nye) *or* -**nuses** the station or town at one end of a railway line or bus route: *Vienna's Westbahnhof is the terminus for trains to France* ▶ HISTORY Latin: end

termite *n* a whitish antlike insect of warm and tropical regions that destroys timber ▶ HISTORY New Latin *termites* white ants

term of office *n* the period time a person serves in a post to which he or she has been elected

terms *pl n* **1** the actual language or mode of presentation used: *the video explains in simple terms*

t

how the new tax works **2** the conditions of an agreement **3** mutual relationship or standing of a specified nature: *he is on first-name terms with many of the directors* **4 come to terms with** to learn to accept (an unpleasant or difficult situation) **5 in terms of** as expressed by; with regard to: *he is the best cricketer we have got in terms of pure ability*

tern *n* a gull-like sea bird with a forked tail and long narrow wings ▶ HISTORY Old Norse *therna*

ternary *adj* **1** consisting of three items or groups of three items **2** *maths* (of a number system) to the base three ▶ HISTORY Latin *ternarius*

Terpsichore (turp-**sick**-or-ee) *n* *Greek myth* the Muse of dance

Terpsichorean (turp-sick-or-**ee**-an) *adj often facetious* of or relating to dancing ▶ HISTORY from *Terpsichore*, the Muse of dance in Greek mythology

terrace *n* **1** a row of houses, usually identical and joined together by common dividing walls, or the street onto which they face **2** a paved area alongside a building **3** a horizontal flat area of ground, often one of a series in a slope **4 the terraces** or **terracing** *Brit & NZ* a tiered area in a stadium where spectators stand ▷ *vb* **-racing, -raced 5** to make into terraces ▶ HISTORY Latin *terra* earth

terracotta *n* **1** a hard unglazed brownish-red earthenware used for pottery ▷ *adj* **2** made of terracotta **3** brownish-orange ▶ HISTORY Italian, literally: baked earth

terra firma *n* the ground, as opposed to the sea ▶ HISTORY Latin

terrain *n* an area of ground, esp. with reference to its physical character: *mountainous terrain* ▶ HISTORY Latin *terra* earth

terra nullius *n* *international law* land belonging to nobody, and therefore available to an occupier; used in the past to justify land acquisition in Australia ▶ HISTORY Latin See also **Mabo decision**

terrapin *n* a small turtle-like reptile of N America that lives in fresh water and on land ▶ HISTORY from a Native American language

terrarium *n* **1** an enclosed area or container where small land animals are kept **2** a glass container in which plants are grown ▶ HISTORY Latin *terra* earth

terrazzo *n, pl* **-zos** a floor made by setting marble chips into a layer of mortar and polishing the surface ▶ HISTORY Italian: terrace

terrestrial *adj* **1** of the planet earth **2** of the land as opposed to the sea or air **3** (of animals and plants) living or growing on the land **4** *television* denoting or using a signal sent from a transmitter on land, rather than by satellite ▶ HISTORY Latin *terra* earth

terrible *adj* **1** very serious or extreme: *war is a terrible thing* **2** *informal* very bad, unpleasant, or unsatisfactory: *terrible books* **3** causing fear ▶ HISTORY Latin *terribilis* > **terribly** *adv*

terrier *n* any of several small active breeds of dog, originally trained to hunt animals living

underground ▶ HISTORY Old French *chien terrier* earth dog

terrific *adj* **1** very great or intense: *a terrific blow on the head* **2** *informal* very good; excellent: *a terrific book* ▶ HISTORY Latin *terrere* to frighten > **terrifically** *adv*

terrify *vb* **-fies, -fying, -fied** to frighten greatly ▶ HISTORY Latin *terrificare* > **terrified** *adj* > **terrifyingly** *adv* > **terrifying** *adj*

terrine (terr-**reen**) *n* **1** an oval earthenware cooking dish with a tightly fitting lid **2** the food cooked or served in such a dish, esp. pâté ▶ HISTORY earlier form of *tureen*

territorial *adj* **1** of or relating to a territory or territories **2** of or concerned with the ownership and control of an area of land or water: *a territorial dispute* **3** (of an animal or bird) establishing and defending an area which it will not let other animals or birds into: *the baboon is a territorial species* **4** of or relating to a territorial army > **territoriality** *n* > **territorially** *adv*

Territorial *n* a member of a Territorial Army

Territorial Army *n* (in Britain) a reserve army whose members are not full-time soldiers but undergo military training in their spare time so that they can be called upon in an emergency

territorial waters *pl n* the part of the sea near to a country's coast which is under the control of the government of that country

territory *n, pl* **-ries 1** any tract of land; district: *mountainous territory* **2** the geographical area under the control of a particular government: *the islands are Japanese territory* **3** an area inhabited and defended by a particular animal or pair of animals **4** an area of knowledge or experience: *all this is familiar territory to readers of her recent novels* **5** a country or region under the control of a foreign country: *a French Overseas Territory* **6** a region of a country, esp. of a federal state, that enjoys less autonomy and a lower status than most constituent parts of the state ▶ HISTORY Latin *territorium* land surrounding a town

terror *n* **1** very great fear, panic, or dread **2** a person or thing that inspires great dread **3** *Brit, Austral & NZ, informal* a troublesome person, esp. a child ▶ HISTORY Latin

terrorism *n* the systematic use of violence and intimidation to achieve political ends > **terrorist** *n, adj*

terrorize or **-ise** *vb* **-izing, -ized** or **-ising, -ised 1** to control or force (someone) to do something by violence, fear, threats, etc.: *he was terrorized into withdrawing his accusations* **2** to make (someone) very frightened > **terrorization** or **-isation** *n* > **terrorizer** or **-iser** *n*

terry *n* a fabric covered on both sides with small uncut loops, used for towelling and nappies ▶ HISTORY origin unknown

terse *adj* **1** neatly brief and concise **2** curt or abrupt ▶ HISTORY Latin *tersus* precise > **tersely** *adv* > **terseness** *n*

883

tertiary (**tur**-shar-ee) *adj* **1** third in degree, order, etc. **2** (of education) at university or college level **3** (of an industry) involving services, such as transport and financial services, as opposed to manufacture ▶ HISTORY Latin *tertius*

Tertiary *adj geol* of the period of geological time lasting from about 65 million years ago to 600 000 years ago

tertiary consumer *n biol* an animal that eats other carnivores. Compare **primary consumer, secondary consumer**

tertiary industry *n econ, business* an industry concerned with providing a service. Compare **primary industry, secondary industry, quaternary industry**

tertiary production *n econ* the provision of services which help to support the primary and secondary sectors. Tertiary production includes administration, transportation, financial services, education, health care, etc.

Terylene *n trademark* a synthetic polyester fibre or fabric

TESL Teaching of English as a Second Language

tessellated *adj* paved or inlaid with a mosaic of small tiles ▶ HISTORY Latin *tessellatus* checked

tessellation *n maths* the fitting together exactly of identical shapes

tessera *n, pl* -**serae** a small square tile used in mosaics ▶ HISTORY Latin

test¹ *vb* **1** to try (something) out to ascertain its worth, safety, or endurance: *the company has never tested its products on animals* **2** to carry out an examination on (a substance, material, or system) in order to discover whether a particular substance, component, or feature is present: *baby foods are regularly tested for pesticides* **3** to put under severe strain: *the long delay tested my patience* **4** to achieve a result in a test which indicates the presence or absence of something: *he tested positive for cocaine* ▷ *n* **5** a method, practice, or examination designed to test a person or thing **6** a series of questions or problems designed to test a specific skill or knowledge: *a spelling test* **7** a chemical reaction or physical procedure for testing the composition or other qualities of a substance **8** **Test** *sport* short for **Test match 9 put to the test** to use (something) in order to gauge its usefulness or effectiveness ▶ HISTORY Latin *testum* earthen vessel > **testable** *adj* > **testing** *adj*

test² *n* the hard outer covering of certain invertebrates ▶ HISTORY Latin *testa* shell

testa (**tess**-ta) *n, pl* -**tae** (-tee) the hard outer layer of a seed ▶ HISTORY Latin: shell

testaceous (test-**ay**-shuss) *adj biol* of or having a hard continuous shell ▶ HISTORY Latin *testaceus*, from TESTA

testament *n* **1** something which provides proof of a fact about someone or something: *the size of the audience was an immediate testament to his appeal* **2** *law* a formal statement of how a person wants his or her property to be disposed of after his or her death: *last will and testament* ▶ HISTORY Latin *testis* a witness > **testamentary** *adj*

Testament *n* either of the two main parts of the Bible, the Old Testament or the New Testament

testate *law adj* **1** having left a legally valid will at death ▷ *n* **2** a person who dies and leaves a legally valid will ▶ HISTORY Latin *testari* to make a will > **testacy** *n*

testator (test-**tay**-tor) *or fem* **testatrix** (test-**tay**-triks) *n law* a person who has made a will, esp. one who has died testate

test case *n* a legal action that serves as a precedent in deciding similar succeeding cases

testicle *n* either of the two male reproductive glands, in most mammals enclosed within the scrotum, that produce spermatozoa ▶ HISTORY Latin *testis* a witness (to masculinity)

testify *vb* -**fies**, -**fying**, -**fied** **1** *law* to declare or give evidence under oath, esp. in court **2 testify to** to be evidence of: *a piece of paper testifying to their educational qualifications* ▶ HISTORY Latin *testis* witness

testimonial *n* **1** a recommendation of the character or worth of a person or thing **2** a tribute given for services or achievements ▷ *adj* **3** of a testimony or testimonial: *a testimonial match*

testimony *n, pl* -**nies** **1** a declaration of truth or fact **2** *law* evidence given by a witness, esp. in court under oath **3** evidence proving or supporting something: *that they are still talking is a testimony to their 20-year friendship* ▶ HISTORY Latin *testimonium*

testis *n, pl* -**tes** same as **testicle**

Test match *n* (in various sports, esp. cricket) an international match, esp. one of a series

testosterone *n* a steroid male sex hormone secreted by the testicles

test paper *n* **1** the question sheet of a test **2** *chem* paper impregnated with an indicator for use in chemical tests

test pilot *n* a pilot who flies aircraft of new design to test their performance in the air

test tube *n* a cylindrical round-bottomed glass tube open at one end, which is used in scientific experiments

test-tube baby *n* **1** a fetus that has developed from an ovum fertilized in an artificial womb **2** a baby conceived by artificial insemination

testy *adj* -**tier**, -**tiest** irritable or touchy ▶ HISTORY Anglo-Norman *testif* headstrong > **testily** *adv* > **testiness** *n*

tetanus *n* an acute infectious disease in which toxins released from a bacterium cause muscular spasms and convulsions ▶ HISTORY Greek *tetanos*

tetchy *adj* **tetchier, tetchiest** cross, irritable, or touchy ▶ HISTORY probably from obsolete *tetch* defect > **tetchily** *adv* > **tetchiness** *n*

tête-à-tête *n, pl* -**têtes** *or* -**tête 1** a private conversation between two people ▷ *adv* **2** together in private: *they dined tête-à-tête* ▶ HISTORY French, literally: head to head

tether *n* **1** a rope or chain for tying an animal to a fence, post, etc., so that it cannot move away from a particular place **2 at the end of one's tether** at the limit of one's patience or endurance ▷ *vb* **3** to tie with a tether ▶ HISTORY Old Norse *tjōthr*

tetra- *combining form* four: *tetrapod*

tetrad *n* a group or series of four ▶ HISTORY Greek *tetras*

tetraethyl lead *n* a colourless oily insoluble liquid used in petrol to prevent knocking

tetragon *n* a shape with four angles and four sides ▶ HISTORY Greek *tetragōnon* > **tetragonal** *adj*

tetrahedron (tet-ra-**heed**-ron) *n*, *pl* **-drons** or **-dra** a solid figure with four triangular plane faces ▶ HISTORY Late Greek *tetraedron* > **tetrahedral** *adj*

tetralogy *n*, *pl* **-gies** a series of four related books, dramas, operas, etc. ▶ HISTORY Greek *tetralogia*

tetrameter (tet-**tram**-it-er) *n* **1** *prosody* a line of verse consisting of four metrical feet **2** verse consisting of such lines ▶ HISTORY Greek *tetra-* four + METER

Teuton (**tew**-tonn) *n* **1** a member of an ancient Germanic people of N Europe **2** a member of any people speaking a Germanic language, esp. a German ▷ *adj* **3** Teutonic ▶ HISTORY Latin *Teutoni* the Teutons

Teutonic (tew-**tonn**-ik) *adj* **1** characteristic of or relating to the Germans **2** of the ancient Teutons

text *n* **1** the main body of a printed or written work as distinct from items such as notes or illustrations **2** any written material, such as words displayed on a visual display unit **3** the written version of the words of a speech, broadcast, or recording: *an advance text of the remarks the president will deliver tonight* **4** a short passage of the Bible used as a starting point for a sermon **5** a book required as part of a course of study: *shelves full of sociology texts* **6** short for **text message** ▷ *vb* **7** to send (a text message) by mobile phone **8** to contact (a person) by means of a text message ▶ HISTORY Latin *texere* to compose

textbook *n* **1** a book of facts about a subject used by someone who is studying that subject ▷ *adj* **2** perfect or exemplary: *a textbook example of an emergency descent*

textile *n* **1** any fabric or cloth, esp. a woven one ▷ *adj* **2** of or relating to fabrics or their production: *the world textile market* ▶ HISTORY Latin *textilis* woven

text message *n* **1** a message sent in text form, esp. by means of a mobile phone **2** a message appearing on a computer screen > **text messaging** *n*

text type *n* one of the categories according to which texts can typically be grouped

textual *adj* of, based on, or relating to, a text or texts > **textually** *adv*

texture *n* **1** the structure, appearance, and feel of a substance: *curtains of many textures and colours* **2** the overall sound of a piece of music, resulting from the way the different instrumental parts in it are combined: *a big orchestra weaving rich textures*

▷ *vb* **-turing, -tured 3** to give a distinctive texture to (something) ▶ HISTORY Latin *texere* to weave > **textural** *adj*

Th *chem* thorium

Thai *adj* **1** of Thailand ▷ *n* **2** (*pl* **Thais** or **Thai**) a person from Thailand **3** the main language of Thailand

Thalia *n* Greek myth the Muse of comedy

thalidomide (thal-**lid**-oh-mide) *n* a drug formerly used as a sedative and hypnotic but withdrawn from use when found to cause abnormalities in developing fetuses ▶ HISTORY *thali(mi)do(glutari)mide*

thallium *n* *chem* a soft highly toxic white metallic element. Symbol: Tl ▶ HISTORY Greek *thallos* a green shoot; from the green line in its spectrum

than *conj*, *prep* **1** used to introduce the second element of a comparison, the first element of which expresses difference: *the radio is smaller than a cigarette packet* **2** used to state a number, quantity, or value in approximate terms by contrasting it with another number, quantity, or value: *temperatures lower than 25 degrees* **3** used after the adverbs *rather* and *sooner* to introduce a rejected alternative: *fruit is examined by hand, rather than by machine* ▶ HISTORY Old English *thanne*

thane *n* **1** (in Anglo-Saxon England) a nobleman who held land from the king or from a superior nobleman in return for certain services **2** (in medieval Scotland) a person of rank holding land from the king ▶ HISTORY Old English *thegn*

thank *vb* **1** to convey feelings of gratitude to: *he thanked the nursing staff for saving his life* **2** to hold responsible: *he has his father to thank for his familiarity with the film world* **3 thank you** a polite response or expression of gratitude **4 thank goodness** or **thank heavens** or **thank God** an exclamation of relief ▶ HISTORY Old English *thancian*

thankful *adj* grateful and appreciative > **thankfully** *adv*

thankless *adj* unrewarding or unappreciated: *she took on the thankless task of organizing the office Xmas lunch* > **thanklessly** *adv* > **thanklessness** *n*

thanks *pl n* **1** an expression of appreciation or gratitude **2 thanks to** because of: *the birth went very smoothly, thanks to the help of the GHQ medical officer* ▷ *interj* **3** *informal* an exclamation expressing gratitude

thanksgiving *n* a formal public expression of thanks to God

Thanksgiving Day *n* (in North America) an annual holiday celebrated on the fourth Thursday of November in the United States and on the second Monday of October in Canada

that *adj* **1** used preceding a noun that has been mentioned or is already familiar: *he'd have to give up on that idea* **2** used preceding a noun that denotes something more remote: *that book on the top shelf* ▷ *pron* **3** used to denote something already mentioned or understood: *that's right* **4** used to denote a more remote person or thing: *is that him*

885

over there? **5** used to introduce a restrictive relative clause: *a problem that has to be overcome* **6 and all that** *or* **and that** *informal* and similar or related things: *import cutting and all that* **7 that is a** to be precise **b** in other words **8** *spoken* **that's that** there is no more to be said or done ▷ *conj* **9** used to introduce a clause: *he denied that the country was suffering from famine* **10** used, usually after *so*, to introduce a clause of purpose: *he turns his face away from her so that she shall not see his tears* **11** used to introduce a clause of result: *a scene so sickening and horrible that it is impossible to describe it* ▷ *adv* **12** Also: **all that** *informal* very or particularly: *the fines imposed have not been that large* ▶ HISTORY Old English *thæt*

thatch *n* **1** Also called: **thatching** a roofing material that consists of straw or reeds **2** a roof made of such a material **3** a mass of thick untidy hair on someone's head ▷ *vb* **4** to cover with thatch ▶ HISTORY Old English *theccan* to cover > **thatched** *adj* > **thatcher** *n*

thaw *vb* **1** to melt or cause to melt: *snow thawing in the gutter* **2** (of frozen food) to become or cause to become unfrozen; defrost **3** (of weather) to be warm enough to cause ice or snow to melt: *it's starting to thaw* **4** to become more relaxed or friendly: *only with Llewelyn did he thaw, let his defences down* ▷ *n* **5** the act or process of thawing **6** a spell of relatively warm weather, causing snow or ice to melt ▶ HISTORY Old English *thawian*

the¹ *adj* (definite article) **1** used preceding a noun that has been previously specified or is a matter of common knowledge: *those involved in the search* **2** used to indicate a particular person or object: *the man called Frank turned to look at it* **3** used preceding certain nouns associated with one's culture, society, or community: *to comply with the law* **4** used preceding an adjective that is functioning as a collective noun: *the young* **5** used preceding titles and certain proper nouns: *the Middle East* **6** used preceding an adjective or noun in certain names or titles: *Alexander the Great* **7** used preceding a noun to make it refer to its class as a whole: *cultivation of the coca plant* **8** used instead of *my, your, her,* etc. with parts of the body: *swelling of tissues in the brain* **9** the best or most remarkable: *it's THE place in town for good Mexican food* ▶ HISTORY Old English *thē*

the² *adv* used in front of each of two things which are being compared to show how they increase or decrease in relation to each other: *the smaller the baby, the lower its chances of survival* ▶ HISTORY Old English *thē*

theatre *or US* **theater** *n* **1** a building designed for the performance of plays, operas, etc. **2** a large room or hall with tiered seats for an audience: *a lecture theatre* **3** a room in a hospital equipped for surgical operations **4 the theatre** drama and acting in general **5** a region in which a war or conflict takes place: *a potential theatre of war close to Russian borders* **6** *US, Austral & NZ* same as **cinema** (sense 1) ▶ HISTORY Greek *theatron*

theatre in the round *n, pl* **theatres in the round** a theatre with seats arranged around a central acting area

theatre of the absurd *n drama* drama in which normal conventions and dramatic structure are ignored or modified in order to present life as irrational or meaningless

Theatresports *n trademark* competitive improvised theatre involving teams

theatrical *adj* **1** of or relating to the theatre or dramatic performances **2** exaggerated and affected in manner or behaviour > **theatricality** *n* > **theatrically** *adv*

theatricals *pl n* dramatic performances, esp. as given by amateurs

thee *pron old-fashioned* the objective form of **thou¹**

theft *n* **1** the act or an instance of stealing: *he reported the theft of his passport* **2** the crime of stealing: *he had a number of convictions for theft* ▶ HISTORY Old English *thēofth*

their *adj* of or associated with them: *owning their own land; two girls on their way to school* ▶ HISTORY Old Norse *theira*

theirs *pron* **1** something or someone belonging to or associated with them: *it was their fault, not theirs* **2 of theirs** belonging to them

theism (**thee**-iz-zum) *n* **1** belief in one God as the creator of everything in the universe **2** belief in the existence of a God or gods ▶ HISTORY Greek *theos* god > **theist** *n, adj* > **theistic** *adj*

them *pron* (objective) refers to things or people other than the speaker or people addressed: *I want you to give this to them* ▶ HISTORY Old English *thǣm*

theme *n* **1** the main idea or topic in a discussion or lecture **2** (in literature, music, or art) an idea, image, or motif, repeated or developed throughout a work or throughout an artist's career **3** *music* a group of notes forming a recognizable melodic unit, used as the basis of part or all of a composition **4** a short essay, esp. one set as an exercise for a student **5** *grammar* the first major constituent of a sentence, usually but not necessarily the subject. Compare **rheme** ▶ HISTORY Greek *thema* > **thematic** *adj* > **thematically** *adv*

theme park *n* an area planned as a leisure attraction in which all the displays and activities are based on a particular theme, story, or idea: *a Wild West theme park*

themselves *pron* **1 a** the reflexive form of *they* or *them: two men barricaded themselves into a cell* **b** used for emphasis: *among the targets were police officers themselves* **2** their normal or usual selves: *they don't seem themselves these days*

then *adv* **1** at that time: *he was then at the height of his sporting career* **2** after that: *let's eat first and then we can explore the town* **3** in that case: *then why did he work for you?* ▷ *pron* **4** that time: *since then the list of grievances has steadily grown* ▷ *adj* **5** existing or functioning at that time: *the then Defence Minister* ▶ HISTORY Old English *thænne, thanne*

thence *adv formal* **1** from that place: *the train went south into Switzerland, and thence on to Italy* **2** for that reason; therefore ▶ HISTORY Middle English *thannes*

theocracy *n, pl* **-cies** **1** government by a god or by priests **2** a community under such government ▶ HISTORY Greek *theos* god + *kratos* power > **theocrat** *n* > **theocratic** *adj* > **theocratically** *adv*

theodolite (thee-**odd**-oh-lite) *n* an instrument used in surveying for measuring horizontal and vertical angles ▶ HISTORY origin unknown

theologian *n* a person versed in the study of theology

theology *n, pl* **-gies** **1** the systematic study of religions and religious beliefs **2** a specific system, form, or branch of this study: *Muslim theology* ▶ HISTORY Greek *theos* god + -LOGY > **theological** *adj* > **theologically** *adv*

theorem *n* a proposition, esp. in maths, that can be proved by reasoning from the basic principles of a subject ▶ HISTORY Greek *theōrein* to view

theoretical *or* **theoretic** *adj* **1** based on or concerned with the ideas and abstract principles relating to a particular subject rather than its practical uses: *theoretical physics* **2** existing in theory but perhaps not in reality: *the secret service is under the theoretical control of the government* > **theoretically** *adv*

theorize *or* **-rise** *vb* **-rizing, -rized** *or* **-rising, -rised** to produce or use theories; speculate > **theorist** *n*

theory *n, pl* **-ries** **1** a set of ideas, based on evidence and careful reasoning, which offers an explanation of how something works or why something happens, but has not been completely proved: *the theory of cosmology* **2** the ideas and abstract knowledge relating to something: *political theory* **3** an idea or opinion: *it's only a theory, admittedly, but I think it's worth pursuing* **4** **in theory** in an ideal or hypothetical situation: *in theory, the tax is supposed to limit inflation* ▶ HISTORY Greek *theōria* a sight

theosophy *n* a religious or philosophical system claiming to be based on an intuitive insight into the divine nature ▶ HISTORY Greek *theos* god + *sophia* wisdom > **theosophical** *adj* > **theosophist** *n*

therapeutic (ther-rap-**pew**-tik) *adj* of or relating to the treatment and cure of disease ▶ HISTORY Greek *therapeuein* to minister to > **therapeutically** *adv*

therapeutics *n* the branch of medicine concerned with the treatment of disease

therapy *n, pl* **-pies** the treatment of a person's physical, mental, or social problems ▶ HISTORY Greek *therapeia* attendance > **therapist** *n*

there *adv* **1** in, at, or to that place or position: *he won't be there* **2** in that respect: *you're right there* **3** **there and then** immediately and without delay: *he walked out there and then* ▷ *adj* **4** **not all there** *informal* stupid or silly ▷ *pron* **5** that place: *to return from there* **6** used as a grammatical subject when the true subject follows the verb, esp. the verb 'to be': *there are no children in the house* **7** **so there!** *informal* an exclamation, used esp. by children, that usually follows a declaration of refusal or defiance: *you can't come, so there!* **8** **there you are** *or* **go** *spoken* **a** an expression used when handing a person something **b** an exclamation of satisfaction or vindication ▷ *interj* **9** *spoken* an expression of sympathy, for example when consoling a child: *there, there, pet!* ▶ HISTORY Old English *thær*

thereabouts *or US* **thereabout** *adv* near that place, time, amount, etc.: *meet me at three o'clock or thereabouts; Methuselah lived 900 years or thereabouts*

thereafter *adv formal* from that time onwards

thereby *adv formal* by that means or consequently

therefore *adv* for that reason: *the training is long, and therefore expensive*

therein *adv formal* in or into that place or thing

thereof *adv formal* of or concerning that or it

thereto *adv formal* **1** to that or it **2** Also: **thereunto** in addition to that

thereupon *adv formal* immediately after that; at that point

therm *n* Brit a unit of heat equal to $1.055\,056 \times 10^8$ joules ▶ HISTORY Greek *thermē* heat

thermal *adj* **1** of, caused by, or generating heat **2** hot or warm: *thermal springs* **3** (of garments) specially made so as to have exceptional heat-retaining qualities: *thermal underwear* ▷ *n* **4** a column of rising air caused by uneven heating of the land surface, and used by gliders and birds to gain height

thermal conductivity *n physics* a measure of the ability of a substance to conduct heat

thermionic valve *or esp US & Canad* **thermionic tube** *n* an electronic valve in which electrons are emitted from a heated rather than a cold cathode

thermistor (therm-**mist**-or) *n physics* a metal-oxide rod whose resistance falls as temperature rises, used in electronic circuits and as a thermometer

thermocouple *n* a device for measuring temperature, consisting of a pair of wires of different metals joined at both ends

thermodynamics *n* the branch of physical science concerned with the relationship between heat and other forms of energy

thermoelectric *or* **thermoelectrical** *adj* of or relating to the conversion of heat energy to electrical energy

thermometer *n* an instrument used to measure temperature, esp. one in which a thin column of liquid, such as mercury, expands and contracts within a sealed tube marked with a temperature scale

thermonuclear *adj* **1** (of a nuclear reaction) involving a nuclear fusion reaction of a type which occurs at very high temperatures **2** (of a weapon) giving off energy as the result of a thermonuclear reaction **3** involving thermonuclear weapons

thermoplastic *adj* 1 (of a material, esp. a synthetic plastic) becoming soft when heated and rehardening on cooling ▷ *n* 2 a synthetic plastic or resin, such as polystyrene

Thermos *or* **Thermos flask** *n trademark* a type of stoppered vacuum flask used to preserve the temperature of its contents

thermosetting *adj* (of a material, esp. a synthetic plastic) hardening permanently after one application of heat and pressure

thermosphere *n geog* an atmospheric layer lying between the mesosphere and the exosphere

thermostat *n* a device which automatically regulates the temperature of central heating, an oven, etc. by switching it off or on when it reaches or drops below a particular temperature > **thermostatic** *adj* > **thermostatically** *adv*

thesaurus (thiss-**sore**-uss) *n, pl* **-ruses** *or* **-ri** a book containing lists of synonyms and related words ▶ HISTORY Greek *thēsauros* a treasury

these *adj, pron* the plural of **this**

thesis (**theess**-siss) *n, pl* **-ses** (-seez) 1 a written work resulting from original research, esp. one submitted for a higher degree in a university 2 an opinion supported by reasoned argument: *it is the author's thesis that Britain has yet to come to terms with the loss of its Empire* 3 *logic* an unproved statement put forward as a premise in an argument ▶ HISTORY Greek: a placing

Thespian *n* 1 *often facetious* an actor or actress ▷ *adj* 2 of or relating to drama and the theatre ▶ HISTORY after *Thespis*, a Greek poet

they *pron* (subjective) 1 (refers to) people or things other than the speaker or people addressed: *they both giggled* 2 (refers to) people in general: *they say he beats his wife* 3 *informal* (refers to) an individual person, whose sex is either not known or not regarded as important: *someone could have a nasty accident if they tripped over that* ▶ HISTORY Old Norse *their*

thiamine *or* **thiamin** *n* vitamin B1, a vitamin found in the outer coat of rice and other grains, a deficiency of which leads to nervous disorders and beriberi ▶ HISTORY Greek *theion* sulphur + VITAMIN

thick *adj* 1 having a relatively great distance between opposite surfaces: *thick slices* 2 having a specified distance between opposite surfaces: *fifty metres thick* 3 having a dense consistency: *thick fog* 4 consisting of a lot of things grouped closely together: *thick forest* 5 (of clothes) made of heavy cloth or wool: *a thick jumper* 6 *informal* stupid, slow, or insensitive 7 (of an accent) very noticeable: *each word was pronounced in a thick Dutch accent* 8 Also: **thick as thieves** *informal* very friendly 9 **a bit thick** *Brit, informal* unfair or unreasonable: *£2 an hour? that's a bit thick!* 10 **thick with** a covered with a lot of: *glass panels thick with dust* b (of a voice) throaty and hard to make out: *his voice was thick with emotion* ▷ *adv* 11 in order to produce something thick: *the machine sliced the potatoes too thick* 12 **lay it on thick** *informal* a to exaggerate a story b to flatter someone excessively 13 **thick and fast** quickly and in large numbers: *theories were flying thick and fast* ▷ *n* 14 **the thick** the most intense or active part: *in the thick of the fighting* 15 **through thick and thin** in good times and bad ▶ HISTORY Old English *thicce* > **thickly** *adv*

thicken *vb* 1 to make or become thick or thicker 2 to become more complicated: *the plot thickens* > **thickener** *n*

thicket *n* a dense growth of small trees or shrubs ▶ HISTORY Old English *thiccet*

thickhead *n slang* a stupid or ignorant person > **thickheaded** *adj*

thickness *n* 1 the state or quality of being thick 2 the dimension through an object, as opposed to length or width 3 a layer: *several thicknesses of brown paper*

thickset *adj* 1 stocky in build 2 planted or placed close together

thick-skinned *adj* insensitive to criticism or hints; not easily upset

thief *n, pl* **thieves** a person who steals something from another ▶ HISTORY Old English *thēof* > **thievish** *adj*

thieve *vb* **thieving, thieved** to steal other people's possessions ▶ HISTORY Old English *thēofian* > **thieving** *adj*

thigh *n* the part of the human leg between the hip and the knee ▶ HISTORY Old English *thēh*

thighbone *n* same as **femur**

thimble *n* a small metal or plastic cap used to protect the end of the finger from the needle when sewing ▶ HISTORY Old English *thȳmel* thumbstall

thin *adj* **thinner, thinnest** 1 having a relatively small distance between opposite surfaces: *a thin mattress* 2 much narrower than it is long: *push a thin stick up the pipe in order to clear it* 3 (of a person or animal) having no excess body fat 4 made up of only a few, widely separated, people or things: *thin hair* 5 not dense: *a thin liquid* 6 unconvincing because badly thought out or badly presented: *the evidence against him was extremely thin* 7 (of a voice) high-pitched and not very loud: *a thin squeaky voice* ▷ *adv* 8 in order to produce something thin: *roll the dough very thin* ▷ *vb* **thinning, thinned** 9 to make or become thin or sparse ▶ HISTORY Old English *thynne* > **thinly** *adv* > **thinness** *n*
See WORD FOCUS **thin**

thine *old-fashioned adj* 1 (preceding a vowel) of or associated with you (thou): *if thine eye offend thee, pluck it out!* ▷ *pron* 2 something belonging to you (thou): *the victory shall be thine* ▶ HISTORY Old English *thīn*

thing *n* 1 any physical object that is not alive: *there are very few jobs left where people actually make things* 2 an object, fact, circumstance, or concept considered as being a separate entity: *that would be a terrible thing to do* 3 an object or entity that cannot or need not be precisely named: *squares and circles and things* 4 *informal* a person or animal: *pretty little thing, isn't she?* 5 a possession, article of clothing, etc.: *have you brought your swimming things?* 6 *informal* a preoccupation or obsession:

t

thin

Some words which you might use to describe someone who is **thin** are complimentary, some are neutral, and others are definitely uncomplimentary.

DEFINITION 3
- A **slender** person is attractively thin and graceful: *a tall,* **slender** *lady in a straw hat*
- A **slim** person has an attractively thin and well-shaped body: *a pretty,* **slim** *girl with blue eyes*
- A **slight** person has a fairly thin and delicate-looking body: *He is a* **slight***, bespectacled, intellectual figure.*
- A **light** person does not weigh very much: *You need to be* **light** *to be a dancer.*
- Someone who is **spare** is tall and not at all fat: *She was thin and* **spare***, with a sharp, intelligent face.*
- If you describe someone as **lean**, you mean that they are thin but look strong and healthy: *Like most athletes, she was* **lean** *and muscular.*

- If you say someone is **lanky**, you mean that they are tall and thin and move rather awkwardly: *He had grown into a* **lanky** *teenager.*
- A **skinny** person is extremely thin, in a way that you find unattractive: *I don't think these* **skinny** *supermodels are at all attractive.*
- If you say a person is **scraggy** or **scrawny**, you mean that they look unattractive because they are so thin: *a* **scraggy** *old man • a* **scrawny** *child of fifteen*
- Someone who is **bony** has very little flesh covering their bones: *a* **bony** *old woman dressed in black*
- If someone is **underweight**, they are too thin and therefore not healthy: *Nearly a third of the girls were severely* **underweight***.*
- A person or animal that is **emaciated** is very thin and weak from illness or lack of food: **emaciated** *prisoners*

---

they have this thing about policemen **7** *informal* **do one's own thing** to engage in an activity or mode of behaviour satisfying to one's personality **8 make a thing of** to exaggerate the importance of **9 the thing** the latest fashion ▶ HISTORY Old English: *assembly*

think *vb* **thinking, thought 1** to consider, judge, or believe: *I think that it is scandalous* **2** to make use of the mind, for example in order to make a decision: *I'll need to think about what I'm going to do* **3** to engage in conscious thought: *that made me think* **4** to be considerate enough or remember (to do something): *no other company had thought to bring high tech down to the user* **5 think much** or **a lot of** to have a favourable opinion of: *I don't think much of the new design* **6 think of a** to remember or recollect: *I couldn't think of your surname* **b** to conceive of or formulate: *for a long time he couldn't think of a response* **7 think twice** to consider something carefully before making a decision ▷ *n* **8** *informal* a careful open-minded assessment: *she had a long hard think* ▷ See also **think up** ▶ HISTORY Old English *thencan* > **thinker** *n*

thinking *n* **1** opinion or judgment: *contrary to all fashionable thinking* **2** the process of thought ▷ *adj* **3** using intelligent thought: *the thinking man's sport*

think-tank *n informal* a group of experts employed to study specific problems

think up *vb* to invent or devise

thinner *n* a solvent, such as turpentine, added to paint or varnish to dilute it

thin-skinned *adj* sensitive to criticism or hints; easily upset

third *adj* **1** of or being number three in a series **2** rated, graded, or ranked below the second level **3** denoting the third from lowest forward gear in a motor vehicle ▷ *n* **4** one of three equal parts of something **5** the fraction equal to one divided by

three ($\frac{1}{3}$) **6** the third from lowest forward gear in a motor vehicle **7** *Brit* an honours degree of the third and usually the lowest class **8** *music* the interval between one note and the note four semitones (**major third**) or three semitones (**minor third**) higher or lower than it ▷ *adv* **9** Also: **thirdly** in the third place ▶ HISTORY Old English *thirda*

third class *n* **1** the class or grade next in value, rank, or quality after the second ▷ *adj* **third-class 2** of the class or grade next in value, rank, or quality after the second

third degree *n informal* torture or bullying, esp. as used to extort confessions or information

third-degree burn *n* a burn in which both the surface and the underlying layers of the skin are destroyed

third man *n cricket* a fielding position on the off side, near the boundary behind the batsman's wicket

third party *n* **1** a person who is involved in an event, legal proceeding, agreement, or other transaction only by chance or indirectly ▷ *adj* **third-party 2** *insurance* providing protection against liability caused by accidental injury or death of other people: *third-party cover*

third person *n* the form of a pronoun or verb used to refer to something or someone other than the speaker or the person or people being addressed, as in *he understands* or *they understand*

third-person narration *n literature* a narrative style in which the author describes events happening to another person, using the pronouns *he, she, it,* and *they*

Third Reich *n* See **Reich**

Third World *n* the developing countries of Africa, Asia, and Latin America collectively

thirst *n* **1** a desire to drink, accompanied by a feeling of dryness in the mouth and throat

2 a craving or yearning: *a thirst for knowledge* ▷ *vb* **3** to feel a thirst ▶ HISTORY Old English *thurst*

thirsty *adj* **thirstier, thirstiest 1** feeling a desire to drink **2** causing thirst: *morris dancing is thirsty work* **3 thirsty for** feeling an eager desire for: *thirsty for information* > **thirstily** *adv*

thirteen *n* **1** the cardinal number that is the sum of ten and three **2** a numeral, 13 or XIII, representing this number **3** something representing or consisting of thirteen units ▷ *adj* **4** amounting to thirteen: *thirteen people* > **thirteenth** *adj, n*

thirty *n, pl* **-ties 1** the cardinal number that is the product of ten and three **2** a numeral, 30 or XXX, representing this number **3** something representing or consisting of thirty units ▷ *adj* **4** amounting to thirty: *thirty miles* > **thirtieth** *adj, n*

Thirty-nine Articles *pl n* a set of formulas defining the doctrinal position of the Church of England

this *adj* **1** used preceding a noun referring to something or someone that is closer: *on this side of the Channel* **2** used preceding a noun that has ust been mentioned or is understood: *this text has two chief goals* **3** used to refer to something about to be mentioned: *NPR's Anne Garrels has this report* **4** used to refer to the present time or occasion: *this week's edition of the newspaper* **5** *informal* used instead of *a* or *the* in telling a story: *I saw this big brown bear* ▷ *pron* **6** used to denote a person or thing that is relatively close: *black coral like this* **7** used to denote something already mentioned or understood: *this didn't seem fair to me* **8** used to denote something about to be mentioned: *listen to this* **9** the present time or occasion: *after this it was impossible to talk to him about his feelings* **10 this and that** various unspecified and trivial events or facts ▶ HISTORY Old English *thes, thēos, this* (masculine, feminine, and neuter singular)

thistle *n* a plant with prickly-edged leaves, dense flower heads, and feathery hairs on the seeds ▶ HISTORY Old English *thīstel* > **thistly** *adj*

thistledown *n* the mass of feathery plumed seeds produced by a thistle

thither *adv formal* to or towards that place ▶ HISTORY Old English *thider*

tho' or **tho** *conj, adv US or poetic* same as **though**

thole¹ or **tholepin** *n* one of a pair of wooden pins set upright in the gunwale on either side of a rowing boat to serve as a fulcrum in rowing ▶ HISTORY Old English *tholl*

thole² *vb* **tholing, tholed** *Scot & N English* to bear or put up with

thong *n* **1** a thin strip of leather or other material **2** *US, Canad & Austral* same as **flip-flop** **3** a skimpy article of beachwear consisting of thin strips of leather or cloth attached to a piece of material that covers the genitals while leaving the buttocks bare ▶ HISTORY Old English *thwang*

Thor *n Norse myth* the god of thunder

thorax (**thaw**-racks) *n, pl* **thoraxes** or **thoraces** (**thaw**-rass-seez) **1** the part of the human body enclosed by the ribs **2** the part of an insect's body between the head and abdomen ▶ HISTORY Greek: breastplate, chest > **thoracic** *adj*

thorium *n chem* a silvery-white radioactive metallic element. It is used in electronic equipment and as a nuclear power source. Symbol: Th ▶ HISTORY after *Thor*, Norse god of thunder

thorn *n* **1** a sharp pointed woody projection from a stem or leaf **2** any of various trees or shrubs having thorns, esp. the hawthorn **3 a thorn in one's side** or **flesh** a source of irritation: *he was sufficiently bright at school to become a thorn in the side of his maths teacher* ▶ HISTORY Old English > **thornless** *adj*

thorny *adj* **thornier, thorniest 1** covered with thorns **2** difficult or unpleasant: *a thorny issue*

thorough *adj* **1** carried out completely and carefully: *he needs a thorough checkup by the doctor* **2** (of a person) painstakingly careful: *he is very thorough if rather unimaginative* **3** great in extent or degree; utter: *a thorough disgrace* ▶ HISTORY Old English *thurh* through > **thoroughly** *adv* > **thoroughness** *n*

thoroughbred *adj* **1** obtained through successive generations of selective breeding: *thoroughbred horses* ▷ *n* **2** a pedigree animal, esp. a horse

thoroughfare *n* a way through from one place to another: *the great thoroughfare from the Castle to the Palace of Holyrood*

thoroughgoing *adj* **1** extremely thorough **2** absolute or complete: *a thoroughgoing hatred*

those *adj, pron* the plural of **that** ▶ HISTORY Old English *thās*, plural of *this*

thou¹ *pron old-fashioned* same as **you**: used when talking to one person ▶ HISTORY Old English *thū*

thou² *n, pl* **thou** *informal* **1** one thousandth of an inch **2** a thousand

though *conj* **1** despite the fact that: *he was smiling with relief and happiness, though the tears still flowed down his cheeks* ▷ *adv* **2** nevertheless or however: *he can't dance – he sings well, though* ▶ HISTORY Old English *thēah*

thought *vb* **1** the past of **think** ▷ *n* **2** the act or process of thinking **3** a concept or idea **4** ideas typical of a particular time or place: *the development of Western intellectual thought* **5** detailed consideration: *he appeared to give some sort of thought to the question* **6** an intention, hope, or reason for doing something: *his first thought was to call the guard and have the man arrested* ▶ HISTORY Old English *thōht*

thoughtful *adj* **1** considerate in the treatment of other people **2** showing careful thought: *a thoughtful and scholarly book* **3** quiet, serious, and deep in thought > **thoughtfully** *adv* > **thoughtfulness** *n*

thoughtless *adj* not considerate of the feelings of other people > **thoughtlessly** *adv* > **thoughtlessness** *n*

t

thousand *n, pl* **-sands** *or* **-sand** **1** the cardinal number that is the product of ten and one hundred **2** a numeral, 1000 or 10³, representing this number **3** a very large but unspecified number: *thousands of bees swarmed out of the hive* **4** something representing or consisting of 1000 units ▷ *adj* **5** amounting to a thousand: *a thousand members* ▶ HISTORY Old English *thūsend* > **thousandth** *adj, n*

thrall *n* the state of being completely in the power of, or spellbound by, a person or thing: *he was held in thrall by her almost supernatural beauty* ▶ HISTORY Old English *thrǣl* slave

thrash *vb* **1** to beat (someone), esp. with a stick or whip **2** to defeat totally: *the All Blacks thrashed England 24-3* **3** to move about in a wild manner: *his legs stuck and he fell sideways, thrashing about wildly* **4** same as **thresh** ▷ *n* **5** *informal* a party ▷ See also **thrash out** ▶ HISTORY Old English *therscan*

thrashing *n* a severe beating

thrash out *vb* to discuss (a problem or difficulty) fully in order to come to an agreement or decision about it: *we must arrange a meeting to thrash out the details of the scheme*

thread *n* **1** a fine strand or fibre of some material **2** a fine cord of twisted yarns, esp. of cotton, used in sewing or weaving **3** something acting as the continuous link or theme of a whole: *the thread of the story* **4** the spiral ridge on a screw, bolt, or nut **5** a very small amount (of something): *there was a thread of nervousness in his voice* **6** a very thin seam of coal or vein of ore ▷ *pl n* **threads** **7** *chiefly US, slang* clothes ▷ *vb* **8** to pass thread through the eye of (a needle) before sewing with it **9** to string together: *plastic beads threaded on lengths of nylon line* **10** to make (one's way) through a crowd of people or group of objects: *she threaded and pushed her way through the crowds* ▶ HISTORY Old English *thrǣd* > **threadlike** *adj*

threadbare *adj* **1** (of cloth, clothing, or a carpet) having the nap worn off so that the threads are exposed **2** having been used or expressed so often as to be no longer interesting: *threadbare ideas* **3** wearing shabby worn-out clothes

threadworm *n* a small threadlike worm that is a parasite of humans

threat *n* **1** a declaration of an intention to inflict harm: *they carried out their threat to kill the hostages* **2** a strong possibility of something dangerous or unpleasant happening: *the wet weather will bring a threat of flooding* **3** a person or thing that is regarded as dangerous and likely to inflict harm: *unemployment is a serious threat to the social order* ▶ HISTORY Old English *thrēat*

threaten *vb* **1** to express a threat to (someone): *he threatened John with the sack* **2** to be a threat to: *he was worried about anything that might threaten the health of his child* **3** to be a menacing indication of (something): *the early summer threatened drought* > **threatening** *adj* > **threateningly** *adv*

three *n* **1** the cardinal number that is the sum of one and two **2** a numeral, 3 or III, representing this number **3** something representing or consisting of three units ▷ *adj* **4** amounting to three: *three days* ▶ HISTORY Old English *thrēo*

three-decker *n* **1** a warship with guns on three decks **2** anything that has three levels, layers, or tiers

three-dimensional *or* **3-D** *adj* **1** having three dimensions **2** lifelike or realistic: *all the characters are three-dimensional*

threefold *adj* **1** having three times as many or as much **2** composed of three parts ▷ *adv* **3** by three times as many or as much

three-ply *adj* made of three thicknesses, layers, or strands

three-point turn *n* a complete turn of a motor vehicle using forward and reverse gears alternately, and completed after only three movements

three-quarter *adj* **1** amounting to three out of four equal parts of something **2** being three quarters of the normal length: *a three-quarter-length coat* ▷ *n* **3** *rugby* any of the four players between the fullback and the halfbacks

three Rs *pl n* reading, writing, and arithmetic regarded as the three fundamental skills to be taught in primary schools ▶ HISTORY humorous spelling of *reading, 'riting, and 'rithmetic*

threesome *n* a group of three people

threnody *n, pl* **threnodies** *formal* a lament for the dead ▶ HISTORY Greek *thrēnōidia* > **threnodic** *adj* > **threnodist** *n*

thresh *vb* **1** to beat (stalks of ripe corn, rice, etc.), either with a hand tool or by machine to separate the grain from the husks and straw **2 thresh about** to toss and turn ▶ HISTORY Old English *therscan*

thresher *n* any of a genus of large sharks occurring in tropical and temperate seas. They have a very long whiplike tail

threshold *n* **1** the lower horizontal part of an entrance or doorway, esp. one made of stone or hardwood **2** any doorway or entrance: *he had never been over the threshold of a pub before* **3** the starting point of an experience, event, or venture: *she was on the threshold of a glorious career* **4** the point at which something begins to take effect or be noticeable: *the threshold for basic rate tax; he has a low boredom threshold* ▶ HISTORY Old English *therscold*

threw *vb* the past tense of **throw**

thrice *adv literary* **1** three times: *twice or thrice in a lifetime* **2** three times as big, much, etc.: *his vegetables are thrice the size of mine* ▶ HISTORY Old English *thrīwa, thrīga*

thrift *n* **1** wisdom and caution with money **2** a low-growing plant of Europe, W Asia, and North America, with narrow leaves and round heads of pink or white flowers ▶ HISTORY Old Norse: success > **thriftless** *adj*

thrifty *adj* **thriftier, thriftiest** not wasteful with money > **thriftily** *adv* > **thriftiness** *n*

thrill *n* **1** a sudden sensation of excitement and pleasure: *he felt a thrill of excitement* **2** a situation producing such a sensation: *all the thrills of rafting the meandering Dordogne* **3** a sudden trembling sensation caused by fear or emotional shock ▷ *vb* **4** to feel or cause to feel a thrill **5** to vibrate or quiver ▶ HISTORY Old English *thȳrlian* to pierce > **thrilling** *adj*

thriller *n* a book, film, or play depicting crime, mystery, or espionage in an atmosphere of excitement and suspense

thrips *n, pl* **thrips** a small slender-bodied insect with piercing mouthparts that feeds on plant sap ▶ HISTORY Greek: woodworm

thrive *vb* **thriving; thrived** *or* **throve; thrived** *or* **thriven 1** to do well; be successful: *Munich has thrived as a centre of European commerce* **2** to grow strongly and vigorously: *the vine can thrive in the most unlikely soils* ▶ HISTORY Old Norse *thrīfask* to grasp for oneself

throat *n* **1** the passage from the mouth and nose to the stomach and lungs **2** the front part of the neck **3 at each other's throats** quarrelling or fighting with each other **4 cut one's own throat** to bring about one's own ruin **5 ram** *or* **force something down someone's throat** to insist that someone listen to or accept something **6 stick in one's throat** to be hard to accept: *his arrogance really sticks in my throat* ▶ HISTORY Old English *throtu*

throaty *adj* **throatier, throatiest 1** hoarse and suggestive of a sore throat: *a throaty 40 fags-a-day bark* **2** deep, husky, or guttural: *she gives a deliciously throaty laugh*

throb *vb* **throbbing, throbbed 1** to pulsate or beat repeatedly, esp. with abnormally strong force: *her eardrums were throbbing with pain* **2** (of engines, drums, etc.) to have a strong rhythmic vibration or beat ▷ *n* **3** the act or sensation of throbbing: *he felt a throb of fear; the throb of the engines* ▶ HISTORY imitative > **throbbing** *adj, n*

throes *pl n* **1** violent pangs, pain, or convulsions: *an animal in its death throes* **2 in the throes of** struggling to cope with (something difficult or disruptive): *in the throes of a civil war* ▶ HISTORY Old English *thrāwu* threat

thrombosis (throm-**boh**-siss) *n, pl* **-ses** (-seez) coagulation of the blood in the heart or in a blood vessel, forming a blood clot ▶ HISTORY Greek: curdling

throne *n* **1** the ceremonial seat occupied by a monarch or bishop on occasions of state **2** the rank or power of a monarch: *she came to the throne after her father was murdered* ▶ HISTORY Greek *thronos*

throng *n* **1** a great number of people or things crowded together ▷ *vb* **2** to gather in or fill (a place) in large numbers: *streets thronged with shoppers* ▶ HISTORY Old English *gethrang*

throstle *n* *poetic* a song thrush ▶ HISTORY Old English

throttle *n* **1** a device that controls the fuel-and-air mixture entering an engine ▷ *vb* **-tling, -tled 2** to kill or injure (someone) by squeezing his or

her throat **3** to suppress or censor: *the government is trying to throttle dissent* ▶ HISTORY Middle English *throtel* throat

through *prep* **1** going in at one side and coming out at the other side of: *he drove through the west of the city* **2** occupying or visiting several points scattered around in (an area): *a journey through the Scottish Highlands* **3** as a result of: *diminished responsibility through temporary insanity* **4** during: *driving for five hours through the night* **5** for all of (a period): *it rained all through that summer* **6** *chiefly US* up to and including: *from Monday through Saturday* ▷ *adj* **7** finished: *I'm through with history* **8** (on a telephone line) connected **9** no longer able to function successfully in some specified capacity: *as a journalist, you're through* **10** (of a train, plane flight, etc.) going directly to a place, so that passengers do not have to change: *the first ever through train between Singapore and Bangkok* ▷ *adv* **11** through a thing, place, or period of time: *the script gives up around halfway through* **12** extremely or absolutely: *I'm soaked through* **13 through and through** to the greatest possible extent: *the boards are rotten through and through* ▶ HISTORY Old English *thurh*

throughout *prep* **1** through the whole of (a place or a period of time): *radio stations throughout the UK* ▷ *adv* **2** through the whole of a place or a period of time: *I led both races throughout*

throughput *n* the amount of material processed in a given period, esp. by a computer

throve *vb* a past tense of **thrive**

throw *vb* **throwing, threw, thrown 1** to hurl (something) through the air, esp. with a rapid motion of the arm **2** to put or move suddenly, carelessly, or violently: *she threw her arms round his neck* **3** to bring into a specified state or condition, esp. suddenly: *the invasion threw the region into turmoil* **4** to move (a switch or lever) so as to engage or disengage a mechanism **5** to cause (someone) to fall: *I'm riding the horse that threw me* **6 a** to tip (dice) out onto a flat surface **b** to obtain (a specified number) in this way: *one throws a 3 and the other throws a 5* **7** to shape (clay) on a potter's wheel **8** to give (a party) **9** *informal* to confuse or disconcert: *the question threw me* **10** to direct or cast (a look, light, etc.): *the lamp threw a shadow on the ceiling* **11** to project (the voice) so as to make it appear to come from somewhere else **12** *informal* to lose (a contest) deliberately **13 throw a punch** to strike, or attempt to strike, someone with one's fist **14 throw oneself at** to behave in a way which makes it clear that one is trying to win the affection of (someone) **15 throw oneself into** to involve oneself enthusiastically in **16 throw oneself on** to rely entirely upon (someone's goodwill, etc.): *the president threw himself on the mercy of the American people* ▷ *n* **17** the act or an instance of throwing **18** the distance thrown: *a throw of 90 metres* **19** (in sports such as wrestling or judo) a move which causes one's opponent to fall to the floor **20** a decorative blanket or cover **21 a throw** each: *we drank our way through a couple* *of bottles of claret at £12.50 a throw* ▷ See also **throwaway, throwback**, etc. ▶ HISTORY Old English *thrāwan* to turn, torment

throwaway *adj* **1** *chiefly Brit & NZ* said or done incidentally: *a throwaway line* **2** designed to be discarded after use: *throwaway cups* ▷ *vb* **throw away 3** to get rid of or discard: *try to recycle glass bottles instead of simply throwing them away* **4** to fail to make good use of: *she threw away the chance of a brilliant career when she got married*

throwback *n* **1** a person or thing that is like something that existed or was common long ago: *his ideas were a throwback to old colonial attitudes* ▷ *vb* **throw back 2** to remind someone of (something he or she said or did previously) in order to upset him or her: *he threw back at me everything I'd said the week before*

throw in *vb* **1** to add at no additional cost: *buy pancakes and the chef will throw in a free coffee* **2** to contribute (a remark) in a discussion **3** **throw in the towel** *informal* to give in; accept defeat ▷ *n* **throw-in 4** *soccer etc.* the act of putting the ball back into play when it has gone over one of the sidelines, by throwing it over one's head with both hands

throw up *vb* **1** *informal* to vomit **2** to give up or abandon: *he would threaten to throw up his job* **3** to construct (a building or structure) hastily **4** to produce: *these links are throwing up fresh opportunities*

thrum *vb* **thrumming, thrummed 1** to strum rhythmically but without expression on (a musical instrument) **2** to make a low beating or humming sound: *the air conditioner thrummed* ▷ *n* **3** a repetitive strumming ▶ HISTORY imitative

thrush¹ *n* any of a large group of songbirds, esp. one having a brown plumage with a spotted breast, such as the mistle thrush and song thrush ▶ HISTORY Old English *thrȳsce*

thrush² *n* **1** a fungal disease, esp. of infants, in which whitish spots form on the mouth, throat, and lips **2** a genital infection caused by the same fungus ▶ HISTORY origin unknown

thrust *vb* **thrusting, thrust 1** to push (someone or something) with force: *he took him by the arm and thrust him towards the door* **2** to force (someone) into some condition or situation: *the unemployed have been thrust into the front line of politics* **3** to force (one's way) through a crowd, forest, etc.: *Edward thrust his way towards them* **4** to stick out or up: *she thrust out her lower lip* ▷ *n* **5** a forceful drive, push, stab, or lunge: *the thrust of his spear* **6** a force, esp. one that produces motion **7** the propulsive force produced by the pressure of air and gas forced out of a jet engine or rocket engine **8** the essential or most forceful part: *the main thrust of the report* **9** *physics* a continuous pressure exerted by one part of an object against another **10** *informal* intellectual or emotional drive; forcefulness: *thanks to the ingenuity and enterprising thrust of this company* ▶ HISTORY Old Norse *thrȳsta*

thud *n* **1** a dull heavy sound **2** a blow or fall that causes such a sound ▷ *vb* **thudding, thudded 3** to make or cause to make such a sound ▶ HISTORY Old English *thyddan* to strike

thug *n* a tough and violent man, esp. a criminal ▶ HISTORY Hindi *thag* thief > **thuggery** *n* > **thuggish** *adj*

thulium *n* *chem* a silvery-grey element of the lanthanide series. Symbol: Tm ▶ HISTORY after *Thule*, a region thought by ancient geographers to be northernmost in the world

thumb *n* **1** the short thick finger of the hand set apart from the others **2** the part of a glove shaped to fit the thumb **3** **all thumbs** very clumsy **4** **thumbs down** an indication of refusal or disapproval **5** **thumbs up** an indication of encouragement or approval **6** **under someone's thumb** completely under someone else's control ▷ *vb* **7** to touch, mark, or move with the thumb: *he thumbed the volume switch to maximum* **8** to attempt to obtain (a lift in a motor vehicle) by signalling with the thumb: *he thumbed a lift to the station* **9** **thumb one's nose at** to behave in a way that shows one's contempt or disregard for: *her mother had always thumbed her nose at convention* **10** **thumb through** to flip the pages of (a book or magazine) in order to glance at the contents ▶ HISTORY Old English *thūma*

thumb index *n* a series of notches cut into the fore-edge of a book to facilitate quick reference

thumbnail *n* **1** the nail of the thumb ▷ *adj* **2** concise and brief: *a thumbnail sketch*

thumbscrew *n* (formerly) an instrument of torture that pinches or crushes the thumbs

thump *n* **1** the sound of something heavy hitting a comparatively soft surface **2** a heavy blow with the hand ▷ *vb* **3** to place (something) on or bang against (something) with a loud dull sound: *she thumped the table aggressively* **4** to hit or punch (someone): *stop that at once or I'll thump you!* **5** to throb or beat violently: *he could feel his heart thumping* ▶ HISTORY imitative

thumping *adj* *slang* huge or excessive: *a thumping majority*

thunder *n* **1** a loud cracking or deep rumbling noise caused by the rapid expansion of atmospheric gases that are suddenly heated by lightning **2** any loud booming sound: *the thunder of heavy gunfire* **3** **steal someone's thunder** to lessen the effect of someone's idea or action by anticipating it ▷ *vb* **4** to make a loud noise like thunder: *an explosion thundered through the shaft* **5** *written* to speak in a loud, angry manner: *'Get out of here this instant!' he thundered* **6** to move fast, heavily, and noisily: *a lorry thundered by* ▶ HISTORY Old English *thunor* > **thundery** *adj*

thunderbolt *n* **1** a flash of lightning accompanying thunder **2** something sudden and unexpected: *his career has been no thunderbolt* **3** *myth* a weapon thrown to earth by certain gods **4** *sport* a very fast-moving shot or serve

thunderclap *n* **1** a loud outburst of thunder **2** something as violent or unexpected as a clap of thunder

thundercloud *n* a large dark electrically charged cloud associated with thunderstorms

thunderous *adj* **1** resembling thunder in loudness: *thunderous applause* **2** threatening or angry: *a thunderous scowl*

thunderstorm *n* a storm with thunder and lightning and usually heavy rain or hail

thunderstruck *adj* amazed or shocked

thurible (**thyoor**-rib-bl) *n* same as **censer** ▶ HISTORY Latin *turibulum*

Thurs. Thursday

Thursday *n* the fifth day of the week ▶ HISTORY Old English *Thursdæg* Thor's day

thus *adv* **1** as a result or consequence: *the platforms provided a new floor and thus improved and enlarged the premises* **2** in this manner: *I sat thus for nearly half an hour* **3** to such a degree: *the competition has been almost bereft of surprise thus far* ▶ HISTORY Old English

thwack *vb* **1** to beat with something flat ▷ *n* **2 a** a blow with something flat **b** the sound made by it ▶ HISTORY imitative

thwart *vb* **1** to prevent or foil: *they inflicted such severe losses that they thwarted the invasion* ▷ *n* **2** the seat across a boat where the rower sits ▶ HISTORY Old Norse *thvert* across

thy *adj old-fashioned* belonging to or associated in some way with you (thou): *love thy neighbour* ▶ HISTORY variant of *thine*

thylacine *n* an extinct doglike Tasmanian marsupial

thyme (**time**) *n* a small shrub with white, pink, or red flowers and scented leaves used for seasoning food ▶ HISTORY Greek *thumon*

thymine *n biochem* a white crystalline pyrimidine base found in DNA

thymol *n* a white crystalline substance obtained from thyme, used as a fungicide and an antiseptic

thymus (**thigh**-muss) *n*, *pl* **-muses** *or* **-mi** (-my) *anat* a small gland situated near the base of the neck ▶ HISTORY Greek *thumos* sweetbread

thyroid *anat adj* **1** of or relating to the thyroid gland **2** of or relating to the largest cartilage of the larynx, which forms the Adam's apple in men ▷ *n* **3** the thyroid gland ▶ HISTORY Greek *thureos* oblong shield

thyroid gland *n anat* an endocrine gland that secretes hormones that control metabolism and body growth

thyself *pron archaic* the reflexive form of **thou**[1]

ti *n music* same as **te**

Ti *chem* titanium

tiara *n* **1** a semicircular jewelled headdress worn by some women on formal occasions **2** the triple-tiered crown sometimes worn by the pope ▶ HISTORY Greek

tibia (**tib**-ee-a) *n*, *pl* **tibiae** (**tib**-ee-ee) *or* **tibias** the inner and thicker of the two bones of the human leg below the knee; shinbone ▶ HISTORY Latin: leg, pipe > **tibial** *adj*

tic *n* a spasmodic muscular twitch ▶ HISTORY French

tick[1] *n* **1** a mark (✓) used to check off or indicate the correctness of something **2** a recurrent metallic tapping or clicking sound, such as that made by a clock **3** *informal* a moment or instant: *won't be a tick* ▷ *vb* **4** to mark or check with a tick **5** to produce a recurrent tapping sound or indicate by such a sound: *the clock ticked away* **6 what makes someone tick** *informal* the basic motivation of a person ▷ See also **tick off, tick over** ▶ HISTORY Low German *tikk* touch

tick[2] *n* a small parasitic creature typically living on the skin of warm-blooded animals and feeding on the blood and tissues of their hosts: *a sheep tick* ▶ HISTORY Old English *ticca*

tick[3] *n Brit & NZ, informal* account or credit: *a spending spree that was financed on tick* ▶ HISTORY from *ticket*

ticker *n slang* the heart

ticker tape *n* (formerly) a continuous paper tape on which current stock quotations were printed by machine

ticket *n* **1** a printed piece of paper or cardboard showing that the holder is entitled to certain rights, such as travel on a train or bus or entry to a place of public entertainment **2** a label or tag attached to an article showing information such as its price and size **3** an official notification of a parking or traffic offence **4** the declared policy of a political party **5 that's (just) the ticket** *informal* that's the right or appropriate thing ▷ *vb* **-eting, -eted 6** to issue or attach a ticket or tickets to ▶ HISTORY Old French *etiquet*

tickets *pl n S African, informal* death or ruin; the end

ticking *n* a strong cotton fabric, often striped, used esp. for mattress and pillow covers ▶ HISTORY probably from Middle Dutch *tīke*

tickle *vb* **-ling, -led 1** to touch or stroke (someone), so as to produce laughter or a twitching sensation **2** to itch or tingle **3** to amuse or please **4 tickled pink** *or* **to death** *informal* greatly pleased **5 tickle someone's fancy** to appeal to or amuse someone ▷ *n* **6** a sensation of light stroking or itching: *a tickle in the throat* **7** the act of tickling **8** *Canad* (in the Atlantic Provinces) a narrow strait ▶ HISTORY Middle English *titelen*

ticklish *adj* **1** sensitive to being tickled **2** delicate or difficult: *a ticklish problem*

tick off *vb* **1** to mark with a tick, esp. to show that an item on a list has been dealt with **2** *informal* to reprimand or scold (someone) > **ticking-off** *n*

tick over *vb* **1** (of an engine) to run at low speed with the transmission disengaged **2** to run smoothly without any major changes: *the business is just ticking over*

ticktack *n Brit & Austral* a system of sign language, mainly using the hands, by which bookmakers transmit their odds to each other at race courses

tidal *adj* **1** (of a river, lake, or sea) having tides **2** of or relating to tides: *a tidal surge*

tidal energy *n physics* energy obtained by harnessing tidal power

tidal flat *n* a level area that is covered with water at high tide

tidal wave *n* **1** *not in technical use* same as **tsunami** **2** an unusually large incoming wave, often caused by high winds and spring tides **3** a forceful and widespread movement in public opinion, action, etc.: *a tidal wave of scandals and embezzlement*

tiddler *n informal* **1** a very small fish, esp. a stickleback **2** a small child ▶ HISTORY perhaps from TIDDLY[1]

tiddly[1] *adj* **-dlier, -dliest** *Brit* very small ▶ HISTORY childish variant of *little*

tiddly[2] *adj* **-dlier, -dliest** *informal, chiefly Brit* slightly drunk ▶ HISTORY origin unknown

tiddlywinks *n* a game in which players try to flick discs of plastic into a cup ▶ HISTORY origin unknown

tide *n* **1** the alternate rise and fall of sea level caused by the gravitational pull of the sun and moon **2** the current caused by these changes in level: *I got caught by the tide and almost drowned* **3** a widespread tendency or movement: *the rising tide of nationalism* **4** *literary or old-fashioned* a season or time: *Yuletide* ▶ HISTORY Old English *tīd* time

tideline *n* the mark or line left by the tide when it retreats from its highest point

tidemark *n* **1** a mark left by the highest or lowest point of a tide **2** *chiefly Brit & NZ* a line of dirt left round a bath after the water has been drained away **3** *informal, chiefly Brit* a dirty mark on the skin, indicating the extent to which someone has washed

tide over *vb* **tiding, tided** to help (someone) to get through a period of difficulty or distress: *they need some form of Social Security to tide them over*

tidings *pl n* information or news ▶ HISTORY Old English *tīdung*

tidy *adj* **-dier, -diest 1** neat and orderly **2** *Brit, Austral & NZ, informal* quite large: *a tidy sum of money* ▷ *vb* **-dies, -dying, -died 3** to put (things) in their proper place; make neat: *I've tidied up the toys under the bed* ▷ *n, pl* **-dies 4** a small container for odds and ends ▶ HISTORY (originally: timely, excellent) from *tide* > **tidily** *adv* > **tidiness** *n*

tie *vb* **tying, tied 1** to fasten or be fastened with string, rope, etc.: *a parcel tied with string* **2** to make a knot or bow in (something): *hang on while I tie my laces* **3** to restrict or limit: *they had children and were consequently tied to the school holidays* **4** to equal the score of a competitor or fellow candidate: *three players tied for second place* ▷ *n* **5** a long narrow piece of material worn, esp. by men, under the collar of a shirt, tied in a knot close to the throat with the ends hanging down the front **6** a bond or link: *he still has close ties to the town where he grew up* **7** a string, wire, etc. with which something is tied **8** *Brit sport* a match in a knockout competition: *whoever wins the tie will play Australia in the semifinals*

9 a a result in a match or competition in which the scores or times of some of the competitors are the same: *a tie for second place* **b** the match or competition in which the scores or results are equal **10** a regular commitment that limits a person's freedom: *it's a bit of a tie having to visit him every day* **11** something which supports or links parts of a structure **12** *US & Canad* a sleeper on a railway track **13** *music* a curved line connecting two notes of the same pitch indicating that the sound is to be prolonged for their joint time value ▷ See also **tie in, tie up** ▶ HISTORY Old English *tīgan*

tie-break *or* **tie-breaker** *n* an extra game or question that decides the result of a contest that has ended in a draw

tied *adj* *Brit* **1** (of a public house) allowed to sell beer from only one particular brewery **2** (of a house) rented out to the tenant for as long as he or she is employed by the owner

tie in *vb* **1** to have or cause to have a close link or connection: *there's no evidence to tie this killing in with the murder of Mrs McGowan* ▷ *n* **tie-in 2** a link or connection **3** a book or other product that is linked with a film or TV programme

tier *n* one of a set of rows placed one above and behind the other, such as theatre seats ▶ HISTORY Old French *tire*

tie up *vb* **1** to bind (someone or something) securely with string or rope **2** to moor (a vessel) **3** to commit (money etc.) so that it is unavailable for other uses: *people don't want to tie up their savings for a long period* ▷ *n* **tie-up 4** a link or connection

tiff *n* a minor quarrel ▶ HISTORY origin unknown

tiger *n* **1** a large Asian mammal of the cat family which has a tawny yellow coat with black stripes **2** a dynamic, forceful, or cruel person **3** a country, esp. in E Asia, that is achieving rapid economic growth ▶ HISTORY Greek *tigris*

tiger lily *n* a lily of China and Japan with black-spotted orange flowers

tiger moth *n* a moth with conspicuously striped and spotted wings

tiger snake *n* a highly venomous brown-and-yellow Australian snake

tight *adj* **1** stretched or drawn taut: *loosening up of tight muscles* **2** closely fitting: *wearing a jacket that was too tight for him* **3** made, fixed, or closed firmly and securely: *a tight band* **4** constructed so as to prevent the passage of water, air, etc.: *watertight; airtight* **5** cramped and allowing very little room for movement: *they squeezed him into the tight space* **6** unyielding or stringent: *tight security* **7** (of a situation) difficult or dangerous **8** allowing only the minimum time or money for doing something: *we have been working to a tight schedule* **9** *Brit, Austral & NZ, informal* mean or miserly **10** (of a match or game) very close or even **11** *informal* drunk **12** (of a corner or turn) turning through a large angle in a short distance: *the boat skidded round in a tight turn* ▷ *adv* **13** in a close, firm, or secure way: *they held each other tight* ▶ HISTORY Old Norse *thēttr* of close texture > **tightly** *adv* > **tightness** *n*

t

tighten *vb* to make or become tight or tighter

tight-lipped *adj* **1** unwilling to give any information; secretive: *the Minister remained tight-lipped when it came to answering the press's questions* **2** with the lips pressed tightly together, as through anger: *tight-lipped determination*

tightrope *n* a rope stretched taut on which acrobats perform

tights *pl n* a one-piece clinging garment covering the body from the waist to the feet, worn by women and also by acrobats, dancers, etc.

tigress *n* **1** a female tiger **2** a fierce, cruel, or passionate woman

tiki (**tee**-kee) *n* a Māori greenstone neck ornament in the form of a fetus ▶ HISTORY Māori

tikka *adj Indian cookery* (of meat) marinated in spices and then dry-roasted: *chicken tikka*

tilde *n* a mark (~) used in some languages to indicate that the letter over which it is placed is pronounced in a certain way, as in Spanish *señor* ▶ HISTORY Spanish

tile *n* **1** a thin piece of ceramic, plastic, etc. used with others to cover a surface such as a floor or wall **2** a rectangular block used as a playing piece in mah jong and other games **3 on the tiles** *informal* out having a good time and drinking a lot ▷ *vb* **tiling, tiled** **4** to cover (a surface) with tiles ▶ HISTORY Latin *tegula* > **tiled** *adj* > **tiler** *n*

tiling *n* **1** tiles collectively **2** something made of or surfaced with tiles

till¹ *conj, prep* same as **until** ▶ HISTORY Old English *til*

till² *vb* to cultivate (land) for the raising of crops: *they sowed, tilled, and harvested all year* ▶ HISTORY Old English *tilian* to try, obtain > **tillable** *adj* > **tiller** *n*

till³ *n* a box or drawer into which money taken from customers is put, now usually part of a cash register ▶ HISTORY origin unknown

tillage *n* **1** the act, process, or art of tilling **2** tilled land

tiller *n naut* a handle used to turn the rudder when steering a boat ▶ HISTORY Anglo-French *teiler* beam of a loom

tillite *n geol* sedimentary rock composed of consolidated glacial sediment

tilt *vb* **1** to move into a sloping position with one end or side higher than the other: *Dave tilted his chair back on two legs* **2** to move (part of the body) slightly upwards or to the side: *Marie tilted her head back* **3** to become more influenced by a particular idea or group: *the party is tilting more and more to the right* **4** to compete against someone in a jousting contest ▷ *n* **5** a slope or angle: *a tilt to one side* **6** the act of tilting **7** (esp. in medieval Europe) **a** a jousting contest **b** a thrust with a lance delivered during a tournament **8** an attempt to win a contest: *a tilt at the world title* **9 at full tilt** at full speed or force ▶ HISTORY Old English *tealtian*

tilth *n* **1** the tilling of land **2** the condition of land that has been tilled

timber *n* **1** wood as a building material **2** trees collectively **3** a wooden beam in the frame of a house, boat, etc. ▷ *adj* **4** made out of timber: *timber houses* **5** of or involved in the production or sale of wood as a building material: *a timber merchant* ▶ HISTORY Old English > **timbered** *adj* > **timbering** *n*

timber line *n* the geographical limit beyond which trees will not grow

timbre (**tam**-bra) *n* the distinctive quality of sound produced by a particular voice or musical instrument ▶ HISTORY French

timbrel *n chiefly biblical* a tambourine ▶ HISTORY Old French

time *n* **1** the past, present, and future regarded as a continuous whole. *Related adjective:* **temporal** **2** *physics* a quantity measuring duration, measured with reference to the rotation of the earth or from the vibrations of certain atoms **3** a specific point in time expressed in hours and minutes: *what time are you going?* **4** a system of reckoning for expressing time: *the deadline is 5:00 Eastern Time today* **5** an unspecified interval; a while: *some recover for a time and then relapse* **6** an instance or occasion: *when was the last time you saw it?* **7** a sufficient interval or period: *I need time to think* **8** an occasion or period of specified quality: *they'd had a lovely time* **9** a suitable moment: *the time has come to make peace* **10** a period or point marked by specific attributes or events: *in Victorian times* **11** *Brit* the time at which licensed premises are required by law to stop selling alcoholic drinks **12** the rate of pay for work done in normal working hours: *you get double time for working on a Sunday* **13 a** the system of combining beats in music into successive groupings by which the rhythm of the music is established **b** a specific system having a specific number of beats in each grouping or bar: *duple time* **14 against time** in an effort to complete something in a limited period **15 ahead of time** before the deadline **16 at one time a** once or formerly **b** simultaneously **17 at the same time a** simultaneously **b** nevertheless or however **18 at times** sometimes **19 beat time** to indicate the tempo of a piece of music by waving a baton, hand, etc. **20 do time** *informal* to serve a term in jail **21 for the time being** for the moment; temporarily **22 from time to time** at intervals; occasionally **23 have no time for** to have no patience with **24 in no time** very quickly **25 in one's own time a** outside paid working hours **b** at the speed of one's choice **26 in time a** early or at the appointed time: *he made it to the hospital in time for the baby's arrival* **b** eventually: *in time, the children of intelligent parents will come to dominate* **c** *music* at a correct metrical or rhythmic pulse **27 make time** to find an opportunity **28 on time** at the expected or scheduled time **29 pass the time** to occupy oneself when there is nothing else to do: *they pass their time watching game shows on television* **30 pass the time of day** to have a short casual conversation (with someone) **31 time and**

t

again frequently **32 time of one's life** a memorably enjoyable time **33 time out of mind** from long before anyone can remember ▷ *vb*
timing, timed 34 to measure the speed or duration of: *my Porsche was timed at 128 mph* **35** to set a time for: *the attack was timed for 6 a.m* **36** to do (something) at a suitable time: *her entry could not have been better timed* ▷ *adj* **37** operating automatically at or for a set time: *an electrical time switch* ▷ *interj* **38** the word called out by a publican signalling that it is closing time ▷ See also **times** ▶ **HISTORY** Old English *tīma*

time-and-motion study *n* the analysis of work procedures to work out the most efficient methods of operation

time capsule *n* a container holding articles representative of the current age, buried for discovery in the future

time exposure *n* a photograph produced by exposing film for a relatively long period, usually a few seconds

time-honoured *adj* having been used or done for a long time and established by custom

time-lapse photography *n photog* the technique of photographing a slow process, such as a flower opening, by taking pictures at regular intervals and then viewing them as a film at normal speed

timeless *adj* **1** unaffected by time or by changes in fashion, society, etc.: *the timeless appeal of tailored wool jackets* **2** eternal and everlasting: *the timeless universal reality behind all religions* > **timelessness** *n*

timeline *n* a graphic representation showing the passage of time as a line

timely *adj* **-lier, -liest** *adv* at the right or an appropriate time

time-out *n* **1** *sport, chiefly US, Canad & Austral* an interruption in play during which players rest, discuss tactics, etc. **2 take time out** to take a break from a job or activity

timepiece *n* a device, such as a clock or watch, which measures and indicates time

timer *n* a device for measuring time, esp. a switch or regulator that causes a mechanism to operate at a specific time

times *prep* multiplied by: *ten times four is forty*

timescale *n* the period of time within which events occur or are due to occur

timeserver *n* a person who changes his or her views in order to gain support or favour

time sharing *n* **1** a system of part ownership of a property for use as a holiday home whereby each participant owns the property for a particular period every year **2** a system by which users at different terminals of a computer can communicate with it at the same time

time signature *n music* a sign, usually consisting of two figures placed after the key signature, that indicates the number and length of beats in the bar

timetable *n* **1** a plan of the times when a job or activity should be done: *the timetable for the Royal Visit* **2** a list of departure and arrival times of trains

or buses: *a timetable hung on the wall beside the ticket office* **3** a plan of the times when different subjects or classes are taught in a school or college: *a heavy timetable of lectures and practical classes* ▷ *vb* **-tabling, -tabled 4** to set a time when a particular thing should be done: *the meeting is timetabled for 3 o'clock*

time value *n music* the duration of a note relative to other notes in a composition and considered in relation to the basic tempo

time warp *n* an imagined distortion of the progress of time, so that, for instance, events from the past seem to be happening in the present

time zone *n geog* a region throughout which the same standard time is used

timid *adj* **1** lacking courage or self-confidence: *a timid youth* **2** indicating shyness or fear: *a timid and embarrassed smile* ▶ **HISTORY** Latin *timere* to fear > **timidity** *n* > **timidly** *adv*

timing *n* the ability to judge when to do or say something so as to make the best effect, for instance in the theatre, in playing an instrument, or in hitting a ball in sport

timorous (**tim**-mor-uss) *adj literary* lacking courage or self-confidence: *a reclusive timorous creature* ▶ **HISTORY** Latin *timor* fear > **timorously** *adv*

timpani *or* **tympani** (**tim**-pan-ee) *pl n* a set of kettledrums ▶ **HISTORY** Italian > **timpanist** *or* **tympanist** *n*

tin *n* **1** a soft silvery-white metallic element. Symbol: Sn **2** a sealed airtight metal container used for preserving and storing food or drink: *a cupboard full of packets and tins* **3** any metal container: *a tin of paint* **4** the contents of a tin **5** *Brit, Austral & NZ* galvanized iron, used to make roofs ▷ *vb* **tinning, tinned 6** to put (food) into tins ▶ **HISTORY** Old English

tincture *n* a medicine consisting of a small amount of a drug dissolved in alcohol ▶ **HISTORY** Latin *tinctura* a dyeing

tinder *n* dry wood or other easily burning material used to start a fire ▶ **HISTORY** Old English *tynder* > **tindery** *adj*

tinderbox *n* (formerly) a small box for tinder, esp. one fitted with a flint and steel which could be used to make a spark

tine *n* a slender prong of a fork or a deer's antler ▶ **HISTORY** Old English *tind* > **tined** *adj*

tinfoil *n* a paper-thin sheet of metal, used for wrapping foodstuffs

ting *n* a high metallic sound such as that made by a small bell ▶ **HISTORY** imitative

tinge *n* **1** a slight tint or colouring: *his skin had an unhealthy greyish tinge* **2** a very small amount: *both goals had a tinge of fortune* ▷ *vb* **tingeing** *or* **tinging, tinged 3** to colour or tint faintly: *the sunset tinged the lake with pink* **4 tinged with** having a small amount of a particular quality: *the victory was tinged with sadness* ▶ **HISTORY** Latin *tingere* to colour

tingle *vb* **-gling, -gled 1** to feel a mild prickling or stinging sensation, as from cold or excitement ▷ *n*

2 a mild prickling or stinging feeling ▸ HISTORY probably a variant of *tinkle* > **tingling** *adj* > **tingly** *adj*

tinker *n* **1** (esp. formerly) a travelling mender of pots and pans **2** *Scot & Irish, often derogatory* a Gypsy **3** a mischievous child ▹ *vb* **4 tinker with** to try to repair or improve (something) by making lots of minor adjustments ▸ HISTORY origin unknown

tinkle *vb* **-kling, -kled 1** to ring with a high tinny sound like a small bell ▹ *n* **2** a high clear ringing sound **3** *Brit, informal* a telephone call ▸ HISTORY imitative > **tinkly** *adj*

tinned *adj* (of food) preserved by being sealed in a tin

tinny¹ *adj* **-nier, -niest 1** (of a sound) high, thin, and metallic: *the tinny sound of a transistor radio* **2** cheap or shoddy: *a tinny East European car*

tinny² *adj* **-nier, -niest** *Austral & NZ, slang* lucky

tin-opener *n* a small tool for opening tins

tin plate *n* thin steel sheet coated with a layer of tin to protect it from corrosion

tinpot *adj informal* worthless or unimportant: *a tinpot dictator*

tinsel *n* **1** a decoration consisting of a piece of metallic thread with thin strips of metal foil attached along its length **2** anything cheap, showy, and gaudy: *all their tinsel and show counts for nothing* ▹ *adj* **3** made of or decorated with tinsel **4** cheap, showy, and gaudy ▸ HISTORY Latin *scintilla* a spark > **tinselly** *adj*

tint *n* **1** a shade of a colour, esp. a pale one: *his eyes had a yellow tint* **2** a colour that is softened by the addition of white: *a room decorated in pastel tints* **3** a dye for the hair ▹ *vb* **4** to give a tint to (something, such as hair) ▸ HISTORY Latin *tingere* to colour

tintinnabulation *n* the ringing or pealing of bells ▸ HISTORY Latin *tintinnare* to tinkle

tiny *adj* **tinier, tiniest** very small ▸ HISTORY origin unknown

tip¹ *n* **1** a narrow or pointed end of something: *the northern tip of Japan* **2** a small piece attached to the end or bottom of something: *boot tips keep boots from getting scuffed* ▹ *vb* **tipping, tipped 3** to make or form a tip on: *the long strips that hang down are tipped with silver cones* ▸ HISTORY Old Norse *typpi* > **tipped** *adj*

tip² *n* **1** an amount of money given to someone, such as a waiter, in return for service **2** a helpful hint or warning: *here are some sensible tips to help you avoid sunburn* **3** a piece of inside information, esp. in betting or investing ▹ *vb* **tipping, tipped 4** to give a tip to ▸ HISTORY origin unknown

tip³ *vb* **tipping, tipped 1** to tilt: *he tipped back his chair* **2 tip over** to tilt so as to overturn or fall: *the box tipped over and the clothes in it spilled out* **3** *Brit* to dump (rubbish) **4** to pour out (the contents of a container): *he tipped the water from the basin down the sink* ▹ *n* **5** a rubbish dump ▸ HISTORY origin unknown

tippet *n* a scarflike piece of fur, often made from a whole animal skin, worn, esp. formerly, round a woman's shoulders ▸ HISTORY probably from TIP¹

tipple *vb* **-pling, -pled 1** to drink alcohol regularly, esp. in small quantities ▹ *n* **2** an alcoholic drink ▸ HISTORY origin unknown > **tippler** *n*

tipstaff *n* **1** a court official **2** a metal-tipped staff formerly used as a symbol of office

tipster *n* a person who sells tips to people betting on horse races or speculating on the stock market

tipsy *adj* **-sier, -siest** slightly drunk ▸ HISTORY from TIP³ > **tipsiness** *n*

tiptoe *vb* **-toeing, -toed 1** to walk quietly with the heels off the ground ▹ *n* **2 on tiptoe** on the tips of the toes or on the ball of the foot and the toes: *I stood on tiptoe*

tiptop *adj, adv* of the highest quality or condition

TIR International Road Transport ▸ HISTORY French *Transports Internationaux Routiers*

tirade *n* a long angry speech or denunciation ▸ HISTORY French

tire¹ *vb* **tiring, tired 1** to reduce the energy of, as by exertion: *she could still do things that would tire women half her age* **2** to become wearied or bored: *he simply stopped talking when he tired of my questions* ▸ HISTORY Old English *tēorian* > **tiring** *adj*

tire² *n* *US* same as **tyre**

tired *adj* **1** weary or exhausted: *they were tired after their long journey* **2** bored with or no longer interested in something: *I'm tired of staying in watching TV every night* **3** having been used so often as to be no longer interesting: *you haven't fallen for that tired old line, have you?* > **tiredness** *n*

tireless *adj* energetic and determined: *a tireless worker for charity* > **tirelessly** *adv*

tiresome *adj* boring and irritating

tissue *n* **1** a group of cells in an animal or plant with a similar structure and function: *muscular tissue forms 42% of the body tissue* **2** a thin piece of soft absorbent paper used as a disposable handkerchief, towel, etc. **3** an interwoven series: *a tissue of lies* ▸ HISTORY Old French *tissu* woven cloth

tit¹ *n* any of various small European songbirds, such as the bluetit, that feed on insects and seeds ▸ HISTORY Middle English *tite* little

tit² *n* a teat or nipple ▸ HISTORY Old English *titt*

titan *n* a person of great strength, importance, or size: *one of the titans of the computer industry*

■ **WORD HISTORY**

■ In Greek mythology, the *Titans* were a family of
■ twelve giants, the children of Uranus and Gaia.

titanic *adj* having or requiring colossal strength: *a titanic struggle*

titanium *n* *chem* a strong white metallic element used in the manufacture of strong lightweight alloys, esp. aircraft parts. Symbol: Ti ▸ HISTORY from *titan*

titbit *or esp US* **tidbit** *n* **1** a tasty small piece of food **2** a pleasing scrap of scandal: *an interesting titbit of gossip* ▸ HISTORY origin unknown

tit-for-tat *adj* done in return or retaliation for a similar act: *a spate of tit-for-tat killings* ▸ HISTORY earlier *tip for tap*

tithe *n* **1** one tenth of one's income or produce paid to the church as a tax **2** a tenth or very small part

t

of anything: *he had accomplished only a tithe of his great dream* ▷ *vb* **tithing, tithed 3** to demand a tithe from **4** to pay a tithe or tithes ▶ HISTORY Old English *teogotha* > **tithable** *adj*

tithe barn *n* a large barn where, formerly, the agricultural tithe of a parish was stored

Titian (**tish**-un) *adj* (of hair) reddish-yellow ▶ HISTORY from *Titian*, Italian painter, because he often used this hair colour in his paintings

titillate *vb* **-lating, -lated** to arouse or excite pleasurably ▶ HISTORY Latin *titillare* > **titillating** *adj* > **titillation** *n*

titivate *vb* **-vating, -vated** to make smarter or neater ▶ HISTORY perhaps from *tidy* + *cultivate* > **titivation** *n*

title *n* **1** the distinctive name of a book, film, recording, etc.: *his first album bore the title 'Safe as Milk'* **2** a descriptive name or heading of a section of a book, speech, etc. **3** a book or periodical: *publishers were averaging a total of 500 new titles annually* **4** a name or epithet signifying rank, office, or function: *the job bears the title Assistant Divisional Administrator* **5** a formal designation, such as *Mrs* or *Dr* **6** *sport* a championship: *the Italians have won the title* **7** *law* the legal right to possession of property ▶ HISTORY Latin *titulus*

titled *adj* having a title such as 'Lady' or 'Sir' which indicates a high social rank

title deed *n* a document containing evidence of a person's legal right or title to property, esp. a house or land

titleholder *n* a person who holds a title, esp. a sporting championship

title role *n* the role of the character after whom a play or film is named

titmouse *n, pl* **-mice** same as **tit¹** ▶ HISTORY Middle English *tite* little + MOUSE

titrate (**tite**-rate) *vb* **-trating, -trated** *chem* to measure the volume or concentration of (a solution) by titration ▶ HISTORY French *titrer*

titration *n chem* an operation in which a measured amount of one solution is added to a known quantity of another solution until the reaction between the two is complete. If the concentration of one solution is known, that of the other can be calculated

titter *vb* **1** to snigger, esp. derisively or in a suppressed way ▷ *n* **2** a suppressed laugh or snigger ▶ HISTORY imitative

tittle-tattle *n* **1** idle chat or gossip ▷ *vb* **-tattling, -tattled 2** to chatter or gossip

titular *adj* **1** in name only: *titular head of state* **2** of or having a title

tizzy *n, pl* **-zies** *informal* a state of confusion or excitement ▶ HISTORY origin unknown

T-junction *n* a junction where one road joins another at right angles but does not cross it

Tl *chem* thallium

Tm *chem* thulium

TN Tennessee

TNT *n* 2,4,6-trinitrotoluene: a type of powerful explosive

to *prep* **1** used to indicate the destination of the subject or object of an action: *he went to the theatre* **2** used to introduce the indirect object of a verb: *talk to him* **3** used to introduce the infinitive of a verb: *I'm going to lie down* **4** as far as or until: *from September 11 to October 25* **5** used to indicate that two things have an equivalent value: *there are 16 ounces to the pound* **6** against or onto: *I put my ear to the door* **7** before the hour of: *17 minutes to midnight* **8** accompanied by: *dancing to a live band* **9** as compared with: *four goals to nil* **10** used to indicate a resulting condition: *burnt to death* **11** working for or employed by: *he was an official interpreter to the government of Nepal* **12** in commemoration of: *a memorial to the victims of the disaster* ▷ *adv* **13** towards a closed position: *push the door to* ▶ HISTORY Old English *tō*

toad *n* **1** an amphibian which resembles a frog, but has a warty skin and spends more time on dry land **2** a loathsome person ▶ HISTORY Old English *tādige*

toadflax *n* a plant with narrow leaves and yellow-orange flowers

toad-in-the-hole *n Brit & NZ* a dish made of sausages baked in a batter

toadstool *n* any of various poisonous funguses consisting of a caplike top on a stem

toady *n, pl* **toadies 1** a person who flatters and ingratiates himself or herself in a fawning way: *a spineless political toady* ▷ *vb* **toadies, toadying, toadied 2** to fawn on and flatter (someone) ▶ HISTORY shortened from *toadeater*, originally a quack's assistant who pretended to eat toads; hence a flatterer > **toadyism** *n*

to and fro *adv, adj also* **to-and-fro 1** back and forth: *he moved his head to and fro as if dodging blows* **2** from one place to another and then back again: *the ferry sailed to and fro across the river* > **toing and froing** *n*

toast¹ *n* **1** sliced bread browned by exposure to heat ▷ *vb* **2** to brown (bread) under a grill or over a fire **3** to warm or be warmed: *toasting his feet at the fire* ▶ HISTORY Latin *tostus* parched

toast² *n* **1** a proposal of health or success given to a person or thing and marked by people raising glasses and drinking together **2** a person or thing that is honoured: *his success made him the toast of the British film industry* ▷ *vb* **3** to propose or drink a toast to (a person or thing) ▶ HISTORY from the spiced toast formerly put in wine

toaster *n* an electrical device for toasting bread

tobacco *n, pl* **-cos** *or* **-coes** an American plant with large leaves which are dried for smoking, or chewing, or made into snuff ▶ HISTORY Spanish *tabaco*

tobacconist *n Brit & Austral* a person or shop that sells tobacco, cigarettes, pipes, etc.

Tobagonian *adj* **1** of Tobago ▷ *n* **2** a person from Tobago

toboggan *n* **1** a long narrow sledge used for sliding over snow and ice ▷ *vb* **2** to ride on a toboggan ▶ HISTORY from a Native American language

t

toby n, pl **-bies** NZ a water stopcock at the boundary of a street and house section ▶ HISTORY origin unknown

toby jug n chiefly Brit a beer mug or jug in the form of a stout seated man wearing a three-cornered hat and smoking a pipe ▶ HISTORY from the name Tobias

toccata (tok-**kah**-ta) n a piece of fast music for the organ, harpsichord, or piano, usually in a rhythmically free style ▶ HISTORY Italian

Toc H n a society formed after World War I to encourage Christian comradeship ▶ HISTORY from obsolete telegraphic code for T.H., initials of Talbot House, Poperinge, Belgium, its original headquarters

tod n **on one's tod** Brit, slang by oneself; alone ▶ HISTORY rhyming slang Tod Sloan/own

today n **1** this day, as distinct from yesterday or tomorrow **2** the present age: in today's world ▷ adv **3** during or on this day: I hope you're feeling better today **4** nowadays: this is one of the most reliable cars available today ▶ HISTORY Old English tō dæge, literally: on this day

toddle vb **-dling, -dled 1** to walk with short unsteady steps, like a young child **2 toddle off** jocular to depart: he toddled off to bed ▷ n **3** the act or an instance of walking with short unsteady steps ▶ HISTORY origin unknown

toddler n a young child who has only just learned how to walk

toddy n, pl **-dies** a drink made from spirits, esp. whisky, hot water, sugar, and usually lemon juice ▶ HISTORY Hindi tārī juice of the palmyra palm

to-do n, pl **-dos** Brit, Austral & NZ a commotion, fuss, or quarrel

toe n **1** any one of the digits of the foot **2** the part of a shoe or sock covering the toes **3 on one's toes** alert **4 tread on someone's toes** to offend a person, esp. by trespassing on his or her field of responsibility ▷ vb **toeing, toed 5** to touch or kick with the toe **6 toe the line** to conform to expected attitudes or standards ▶ HISTORY Old English tā

toecap n a reinforced covering for the toe of a boot or shoe

toehold n **1** a small space on a rock, mountain, etc. which can be used to support the toe of the foot in climbing **2** any means of gaining access or advantage: the French car industry has lost its last toehold in America

toenail n a thin hard clear plate covering part of the upper surface of the end of each toe

toerag n Brit, slang a contemptible or despicable person

toff n Brit, slang a well-dressed or upper-class person ▶ HISTORY perhaps from tuft, nickname for a titled student at Oxford University wearing a cap with a gold tassel

toffee n **1** a sticky chewy sweet made by boiling sugar with water and butter **2 can't (do something) for toffee** informal is not competent or talented at (doing something): she couldn't dance for toffee ▶ HISTORY earlier taffy

toffee-apple n an apple fixed on a stick and coated with a thin layer of toffee

toffee-nosed adj slang snobbish or conceited

tofu n a food with a soft cheeselike consistency made from unfermented soya-bean curd ▶ HISTORY Japanese

tog n a unit for measuring the insulating power of duvets

toga (**toe**-ga) n a garment worn by citizens of ancient Rome, consisting of a piece of cloth draped around the body ▶ HISTORY Latin > **togaed** adj

together adv **1** with cooperation between people or organizations: we started a company together **2** in or into contact with each other: he clasped his hands together **3** in or into one place: the family gets together to talk **4** at the same time: 'Disgusting,' said Julie and Alice together **5** considered collectively: the properties together were worth more as a unit **6** old-fashioned continuously: working for eight hours together **7 together with** in addition to ▷ adj **8** slang self-possessed, competent, and well-organized ▶ HISTORY Old English tōgædere

toggle n **1** a bar-shaped button inserted through a loop for fastening coats, etc. **2** computers a key on a keyboard which, when pressed, will turn a feature on if it is currently off, and turn it off if it is currently on **3** short for **toggle switch** (sense 1) ▶ HISTORY origin unknown

toggle switch n **1** an electric switch with a projecting lever that is moved in a particular way to open or close a circuit **2** same as **toggle** (sense 2)

togs pl n **1** Brit, Austral & NZ, informal clothes **2** Austral, NZ & Irish a swimming costume ▶ HISTORY probably from toga

toheroa (toe-a-**roe**-a) n a large edible mollusc of New Zealand with a distinctive flavour ▶ HISTORY Māori

tohunga (toe-hung-a) n NZ a Māori priest ▶ HISTORY Māori

toil n **1** hard or exhausting work: hours of toil beneath the Catalan sun ▷ vb **2** to work hard: workers toiling in the fields to produce tea for westerners to drink **3** to move slowly and with difficulty, for instance because of exhaustion or the steepness of a slope: Joanna toiled up the steps to the church ▶ HISTORY Anglo-French toiler to struggle

toilet n **1 a** a bowl fitted with a water-flushing device and connected to a drain, for receiving and disposing of urine and faeces **b** a room with such a fitment **2** old-fashioned the act of dressing and preparing oneself ▶ HISTORY French toilette dress

toilet paper n thin absorbent paper used for cleaning oneself after defecation or urination

toiletry n, pl **-ries** an object or cosmetic used in making up, dressing, etc.

toilet water n liquid perfume lighter than cologne

token n **1** a symbol, sign, or indication of something: as a token of respect **2** a gift voucher that can be used as payment for goods of a specified value **3** a metal or plastic disc, such as a

t

substitute for currency for use in a slot machine **4 by the same token** in the same way as something mentioned previously ▷ *adj* **5** intended to create an impression but having no real importance: *as a token gesture of goodwill* ▶ HISTORY Old English *tācen*

tokenism *n* the practice of making only a token effort or doing no more than the minimum, esp. in order to comply with a law > **tokenist** *adj*

told *vb* the past of **tell**

tolerable *adj* **1** able to be put up with; bearable **2** *informal* fairly good > **tolerably** *adv*

tolerance *n* **1** the quality of accepting other people's rights to their own opinions, beliefs, or actions **2** capacity to endure something, esp. pain or hardship **3** the ability of a substance to withstand heat, stress, etc. without damage **4** *med* the capacity to endure the effects of a continued or increasing dose of a drug, poison, etc. **5** an acceptable degree of variation in a measurement or value: *the bodywork of the car is precision-engineered with a tolerance of 0.01 millimetres*

tolerant *adj* **1** accepting of the beliefs, actions, etc. of other people **2 tolerant of** able to withstand (heat, stress, etc.) without damage

tolerate *vb* **-ating, -ated 1** to allow something to exist or happen, even though one does not approve of it: *you must learn to tolerate opinions other than your own* **2** to put up with (someone or something): *he found the pain hard to tolerate* ▶ HISTORY Latin *tolerare* to sustain > **toleration** *n*

toll[1] *vb* **1** to ring (a bell) slowly and regularly **2** to announce by tolling: *the bells tolled the Queen's death* ▷ *n* **3** the slow regular ringing of a bell ▶ HISTORY origin unknown

toll[2] *n* **1** a charge for the use of certain roads and bridges: *the Skye bridge toll* **2** loss or damage from a disaster: *the annual death toll on the roads is about 4500* **3 take a** or **its toll** to have a severe and damaging effect: *the continued stress had taken a toll on her health* ▶ HISTORY Old English *toln*

tolu (tol-**loo**) *n* a sweet-smelling balsam obtained from a South American tree, used in medicine and perfume ▶ HISTORY after *Santiago de Tolu,* Colombia

toluene *n* a flammable liquid obtained from petroleum and coal tar and used as a solvent and in the manufacture of dyes, explosives, etc. ▶ HISTORY previously obtained from tolu

tom *n* **1** a male cat ▷ *adj* **2** (of an animal) male: *a tom turkey* ▶ HISTORY from *Thomas*

tomahawk *n* a fighting axe used by the Native Americans of N America ▶ HISTORY from a Native American language

tomato *n, pl* **-toes 1** a red fleshy juicy fruit with many edible seeds, eaten in salads, as a vegetable, etc. **2** the plant, originally from South America, on which this fruit grows ▶ HISTORY S American Indian *tomatl*

tomb *n* **1** a place for the burial of a corpse **2** a monument over a grave **3 the tomb** *poetic* death ▶ HISTORY Greek *tumbos*

tombola *n* Brit a type of lottery, in which tickets are drawn from a revolving drum ▶ HISTORY Italian

tombolo *n, pl* **-los** *geog* a narrow sand or shingle bar linking a small island with another island or the mainland ▶ HISTORY Italian, from Latin *tumulus* mound

tomboy *n* a girl who behaves or dresses like a boy

tombstone *n* a gravestone

tome *n* a large heavy book ▶ HISTORY Greek *tomos* a slice

tomfoolery *n* foolish behaviour

Tommy *n, pl* **-mies** Brit, old-fashioned, informal a private in the British Army ▶ HISTORY originally *Thomas Atkins,* name used in specimen copies of official forms

Tommy gun *n* a type of light sub-machine-gun ▶ HISTORY in full *Thompson sub-machine-gun,* from the name of the manufacturer

tomorrow *n* **1** the day after today: *tomorrow's meeting has been cancelled* **2** the future: *the struggle to build a better tomorrow* ▷ *adv* **3** on the day after today: *the festival starts tomorrow* **4** at some time in the future: *they live today as millions more will live tomorrow* ▶ HISTORY Old English *tō morgenne*

tomtit *n* Brit a small European bird that eats insects and seeds

tom-tom *n* a long narrow drum beaten with the hands ▶ HISTORY Hindi *tamtam*

ton[1] *n* **1** Brit a unit of weight equal to 2240 pounds or 1016.046 kilograms **2** US & Canad a unit of weight equal to 2000 pounds or 907.184 kilograms **3** See **metric ton 4 come down on someone like a ton of bricks** *informal* to scold someone very severely ▷ *adv* **5 tons** *informal* a lot: *I've got tons of things to do before going on holiday* ▶ HISTORY variant of *tun*

ton[2] *n* slang, chiefly Brit a hundred miles per hour ▶ HISTORY special use of TON[1]

tonal *adj* **1** *music* written in a key **2** of or relating to tone or tonality

tonality *n, pl* **-ties 1** *music* the presence of a musical key in a composition **2** the overall scheme of colours and tones in a painting

tone *n* **1** sound with reference to its pitch, timbre, or volume **2** US & Canad same as **note** (sense 6) **3** *music* an interval of two semitones, such as that between doh and ray in tonic sol-fa **4** the quality or character of a sound: *her tone was angry* **5** general aspect, quality, or style: *the tone of the conversation made him queasy* **6** high quality or style: *my car with its patches of rust lowered the tone of the neighbourhood* **7** the quality of a given colour, as modified by mixture with white or black; shade or tint **8** *physiol* the natural firmness of the tissues and normal functioning of bodily organs in health ▷ *vb* **toning, toned 9** to be of a matching or similar tone **10** to give a tone to or correct the tone of ▷ See also **tone down, tone up** ▶ HISTORY Greek *tonos* > **toneless** *adj* > **tonelessly** *adv*

tone-deaf *adj* unable to distinguish subtle differences in musical pitch

tone down *vb* to moderate in tone: *I sensed some reserve in his manner, so I toned down my enthusiasm*

tone poem n music an extended orchestral composition based on nonmusical material, such as a work of literature or a fairy tale

toner n **1** a cosmetic applied to the skin to reduce oiliness **2** a powdered chemical that forms the image produced by a photocopier

tone up vb to make or become more vigorous, healthy, etc.: muscle tissue can be toned up

tong n (formerly) a secret society of Chinese Americans ▶ HISTORY Chinese (Cantonese) t'ong meeting place

tongs pl n a tool for grasping or lifting, consisting of two long metal or wooden arms, joined with a hinge or flexible metal strip at one end ▶ HISTORY Old English tange

tongue n **1** a movable mass of muscular tissue attached to the floor of the mouth, used for tasting, eating, and speaking **2** a language, dialect, or idiom: the Scots tongue **3** the ability to speak: taken aback, she could not find her tongue **4** a manner of speaking: a sharp tongue **5** the tongue of certain animals used as food **6** a narrow strip of something that extends outwards: a narrow tongue of flame **7** a flap of leather on a shoe **8** the clapper of a bell **9** a projecting strip along an edge of a board that is made to fit a groove in another board **10 hold one's tongue** to keep quiet **11 on the tip of one's tongue** about to come to mind **12 with (one's) tongue in one's cheek** with insincere or ironical intent ▶ HISTORY Old English tunge

tongue-tie n a congenital condition in which movement of the tongue is limited as the result of the fold of skin under the tongue extending too close to the front of the tongue

tongue-tied adj speechless, esp. with embarrassment or shyness

tongue twister n a sentence or phrase that is difficult to say clearly and quickly, such as the sixth sick sheikh's sixth sheep's sick

tonguing n a technique of playing a wind instrument by obstructing and uncovering the air passage through the lips with the tongue

tonic n **1** a medicine that improves the functioning of the body or increases the feeling of wellbeing **2** anything that enlivens or strengthens: his dry humour was a stimulating tonic **3** Also called: **tonic water** a carbonated beverage containing quinine and often mixed with alcoholic drinks: gin and tonic **4** music the first note of a major or minor scale and the tonal centre of a piece composed in a particular key ▷ adj **5** having an invigorating or refreshing effect: a tonic bath **6** music of the first note of a major or minor scale ▶ HISTORY Greek tonikos concerning tone

tonic sol-fa n a method of teaching music, by which syllables are used as names for the notes of the major scale in any key

tonight n **1** the night or evening of this present day: tonight's programme examines the rise of poverty in the 1990s ▷ adv **2** in or during the night or evening of this day: I want to go out dancing tonight

902 ▶ HISTORY Old English tōniht

toning table n an exercise table, parts of which move mechanically to exercise specific parts of the body of the person lying on it

tonnage n **1** the capacity of a merchant ship expressed in tons **2** the weight of the cargo of a merchant ship **3** the total amount of shipping of a port or nation

tonne (tunn) n a unit of mass equal to 1000 kg or 2204.6 pounds ▶ HISTORY French

tonoplast n bot the membrane that encloses a vacuole in a plant cell

tonsil n either of two small oval lumps of spongy tissue situated one on each side of the back of the mouth ▶ HISTORY Latin tonsillae tonsils
> **tonsillar** adj

tonsillectomy n, pl **-mies** surgical removal of the tonsils ▶ HISTORY TONSIL + Greek ek- out + tomē a cutting

tonsillitis n inflammation of the tonsils, causing a sore throat and fever

tonsure n **1** (in certain religions and monastic orders) **a** the shaving of the head or the crown of the head only **b** the part of the head left bare by shaving ▷ vb **-suring, -sured 2** to shave the head of ▶ HISTORY Latin tonsura a clipping
> **tonsured** adj

too adv **1** as well or also: I'll miss you, too **2** in or to an excessive degree: it's too noisy in here **3** extremely: you're too kind **4** US, Canad & Austral, informal used to emphasize contradiction of a negative statement: You didn't! – I did too! ▶ HISTORY Old English tō

took vb the past tense of **take**

tool n **1 a** an implement, such as a hammer, saw, or spade, that is used by hand to help do a particular type of work **b** a power-driven instrument: machine tool **2** the cutting part of such an instrument **3** a person used to perform dishonourable or unpleasant tasks for another: the government is acting as a tool of big business **4** any object, skill, etc. used for a particular task or in a particular job: a skilled therapist can use photographs as tools ▷ vb **5** to work, cut, or form (something) with a tool ▶ HISTORY Old English tōl

toolbar n computers a row of buttons displayed on a computer screen, allowing the user to select various functions

toot n **1** a short hooting sound ▷ vb **2** to give or cause to give a short blast, hoot, or whistle: motorists tooted their car horns ▶ HISTORY imitative

tooth n, pl **teeth 1** one of the bonelike projections in the jaws of most vertebrates that are used for biting, tearing, or chewing **2** one of the sharp projections on the edge of a comb, saw, zip, etc. **3 long in the tooth** old or ageing **4 a sweet tooth** a liking for sweet food **5 tooth and nail** with great vigour and determination: the union would oppose compulsory redundancies tooth and nail ▷ See also **teeth** ▶ HISTORY Old English tōth

toothless adj **1** having no teeth **2** having no real power: the proposed Commission will not be as toothless as scoffers suggest

t

toothpaste *n* a paste used for cleaning the teeth, applied with a toothbrush

toothpick *n* a small wooden or plastic stick used for extracting pieces of food from between the teeth

tooth powder *n* a powder used for cleaning the teeth, applied with a toothbrush

top¹ *n* **1** the highest point or part of anything: *the top of the stairs* **2** the most important or successful position: *at the top of the agenda* **3** a lid or cap that fits on to one end of something, esp. to close it: *he unscrewed the top from a quart of ale* **4** the highest degree or point: *the two people at the top of the Party* **5** the most important person or people in an organization: *the top of the military establishment* **6** the loudest or highest pitch: *she cheered and sang at the top of her voice* **7** a garment, esp. for a woman, that extends from the shoulders to the waist or hips **8** the part of a plant that is above ground: *nettle tops* **9** same as **top gear** **10** **off the top of one's head** without previous preparation or careful thought **11** **on top of a** in addition to: *the average member of staff will get 25% on top of salary* **b** *informal* in complete control of: *we're on top of our costs and expenses and looking for other opportunities* **12** **over the top a** lacking restraint or a sense of proportion: *you went over the top when you called her a religious maniac* **b** *mil* over the edge of a trench ▷ *adj* **13** at, of, or being the top: *men still hold most of the top jobs in industry* ▷ *vb* **topping, topped** **14** to put on top of (something): *top your salad with a mild dressing* **15** to reach or pass the top of **16** to be at the top of: *her biggest hit topped the charts for six weeks* **17** to exceed or surpass: *his estimated fortune tops £2 billion* **18** **top and tail a** to trim off the ends of (fruit or vegetables) before cooking **b** to wash only a baby's face and bottom ▷ See also **top up** ▶ HISTORY Old English *topp*

top² *n* **1** a toy that is spun on its pointed base **2** **sleep like a top** to sleep very soundly ▶ HISTORY Old English

topaz (**toe**-pazz) *n* a hard glassy yellow, pink, or colourless mineral used in making jewellery ▶ HISTORY Greek *topazos*

top brass *pl n* the most important or high-ranking officials or leaders

top-down reading *n* an approach to reading and understanding involving using historical or other background clues as well as reading for gist to gain an overview of a text. Compare **bottom-up reading**

top dressing *n* a layer of fertilizer or manure spread on the surface of land > **top-dress** *vb*

tope¹ *vb* **toping, toped** to drink (alcohol), usually in large quantities ▶ HISTORY perhaps from French *toper* to take a bet > **toper** *n*

tope² *n* a small grey shark of European coastal waters ▶ HISTORY origin unknown

topee *or* **topi** (**toe**-pee) *n* same as **pith helmet** ▶ HISTORY Hindi *topī* hat

top gear *n* the highest forward ratio of a gearbox in a motor vehicle

top hat *n* a man's hat with a tall cylindrical crown and narrow brim, now only worn for some formal occasions

top-heavy *adj* unstable through being overloaded at the top

topiary (**tope**-yar-ee) *n* **1** the art of trimming trees or bushes into artificial decorative shapes **2** trees or bushes trimmed into decorative shapes ▷ *adj* **3** of or relating to topiary ▶ HISTORY Latin *topia* decorative garden work > **topiarist** *n*

topic *n* a subject of a speech, book, conversation, etc. ▶ HISTORY Greek *topos* place

topical *adj* of or relating to current affairs > **topicality** *n* > **topically** *adv*

topknot *n* a crest, tuft, decorative bow, etc. on the top of the head

topless *adj* of or relating to women wearing costumes that do not cover the breasts: *topless bars*

topmost *adj* at or nearest the top

top-notch *adj informal* excellent or superb: *top-notch entertainment*

topographic map *n* a map that shows natural and significant features of the landscape and uses contour lines to show elevations

topography *n, pl* **-phies** **1** the surface features of a region, such as its hills, valleys, or rivers: *the islands are fragile, with a topography constantly changed by wind and wave* **2** the study or description of such surface features **3** the representation of these features on a map ▶ HISTORY Greek *topos* a place + -GRAPHY > **topographer** *n* > **topographical** *adj*

topology *n* a branch of geometry describing the properties of a figure that are unaffected by continuous distortion ▶ HISTORY Greek *topos* a place + -LOGY > **topological** *adj*

topping *n* a sauce or garnish for food

topple *vb* **-pling, -pled** **1** to fall over or cause (something) to fall over, esp. from a height: *he staggered back against the railing and toppled over into the river* **2** to overthrow or oust: *few believe the scandal will topple the government* ▶ HISTORY from TOP¹ (verb)

top-secret *adj* (of military or government information) classified as needing the highest level of secrecy and security

top slicing *n* the act of using a specific part of a sum of money for a special purpose, such as assessing a taxable gain

topsoil *n* the surface layer of soil

topsy-turvy *adj* **1** upside down **2** in a state of confusion ▷ *adv* **3** in a topsy-turvy manner ▶ HISTORY probably *top* + obsolete *tervy* to turn upside down

top up *vb* **1** to refill (a container), usually to the brim: *I topped up his glass* **2** to add to (an amount) in order to make it sufficient: *the grant can be topped up by a student loan* ▷ *n* **top-up** **3** another serving of a drink in the glass that was used for the first one: *anyone want a top-up?* ▷ *adj* **top-up** **4** serving to top something up: *a top-up loan*

toque (**toke**) *n* **1** a woman's small round brimless hat **2** *Canad* same as **tuque** (sense 2) ▶ HISTORY French

t

tor *n chiefly Brit* a high hill, esp. a bare rocky one ▶ **HISTORY** Old English *torr*

Torah *n* the whole body of traditional Jewish teaching, including the Oral Law ▶ **HISTORY** Hebrew: precept

torch *n* **1** *Brit* a small portable electric lamp powered by batteries **2** a wooden shaft dipped in wax or tallow and set alight **3** anything regarded as a source of enlightenment, guidance, etc.: *a torch of hope* **4 carry a torch for** to be in love with (someone), esp. unrequitedly ▷ *vb* **5** *informal* to deliberately set (a building) on fire ▶ **HISTORY** Old French *torche* handful of twisted straw

tore *vb* the past tense of **tear²**

toreador (torr-ee-a-dor) *n* a bullfighter, esp. one on horseback ▶ **HISTORY** Spanish

torment *vb* **1** to cause (someone) great pain or suffering **2** to tease or pester (a person or animal) in an annoying or cruel way ▷ *n* **3** physical or mental pain **4** a source of pain or suffering ▶ **HISTORY** Latin *tormentum* > **tormentor** *n*

tormentil *n* a creeping plant with yellow four-petalled flowers ▶ **HISTORY** Old French *tormentille*

torn *vb* **1** the past participle of **tear²** ▷ *adj* **2** split or cut **3** divided or undecided, as in preference: *torn between two lovers*

tornado *n, pl* **-dos** or **-does** a rapidly whirling column of air, usually characterized by a dark funnel-shaped cloud causing damage along its path ▶ **HISTORY** Spanish *tronada* thunderstorm

torpedo *n, pl* **-does 1** a cylindrical self-propelled weapon carrying explosives that is launched from aircraft, ships, or submarines and follows an underwater path to hit its target ▷ *vb* **-doing, -doed 2** to attack or hit (a ship) with one or a number of torpedoes **3** to destroy or wreck: *the Prime Minister warned his party against torpedoing the bill* ▶ **HISTORY** Latin: crampfish (whose electric discharges can cause numbness)

torpedo boat *n* (formerly) a small high-speed warship for torpedo attacks

torpid *adj* **1** sluggish or dull: *he has a rather torpid intellect* **2** (of a hibernating animal) dormant ▶ **HISTORY** Latin *torpere* to be numb

torpor *n* drowsiness and apathy

torque (tork) *n* **1** a force that causes rotation around a central point such as an axle **2** an ancient Celtic necklace or armband made of twisted metal ▶ **HISTORY** Latin *torques* necklace, from *torquere* to twist

torr *n, pl* **torr** a unit of pressure equal to one millimetre of mercury (133.3 newtons per square metre) ▶ **HISTORY** after E. *Torricelli*, physicist

Torrens title *n Austral law* legal title to land based on record of registration rather than on title deeds ▶ **HISTORY** from Sir Robert Richard *Torrens* (1814—84), who introduced the system as premier of South Australia in 1857

torrent *n* **1** a fast or violent stream, esp. of water **2** a rapid flow of questions, abuse, etc. ▶ **HISTORY** Latin *torrens*

torrential *adj* (of rain) very heavy

torrid *adj* **1** (of weather) so hot and dry as to parch or scorch **2** (of land) arid or parched **3** highly charged emotionally: *a torrid affair* ▶ **HISTORY** Latin *torrere* to scorch

Torrid Zone *n geog* those parts of the earth's surface lying between the tropics of Cancer and Capricorn. Compare **Frigid Zone, Temperate Zone**

torsion *n* the twisting of a part by equal forces being applied at both ends but in opposite directions ▶ **HISTORY** Latin *torquere* to twist > **torsional** *adj*

torso *n, pl* **-sos 1** the trunk of the human body **2** a statue of a nude human trunk, esp. without the head or limbs ▶ **HISTORY** Italian: stalk, stump

tort *n law* a civil wrong or injury, for which an action for damages may be brought ▶ **HISTORY** Latin *torquere* to twist

tortilla *n Mexican cookery* a kind of thin pancake made from corn meal ▶ **HISTORY** Spanish: little cake

tortoise *n* a land reptile with a heavy dome-shaped shell into which it can withdraw its head and legs ▶ **HISTORY** Medieval Latin *tortuca*

tortoiseshell *n* **1** the horny yellow-and-brown mottled shell of a sea turtle, used for making ornaments and jewellery **2** a domestic cat with black, cream, and brownish markings **3** a butterfly which has orange-brown wings with black markings ▷ *adj* **4** made of tortoiseshell

tortuous *adj* **1** twisted or winding: *a tortuous route* **2** devious or cunning: *months of tortuous negotiations*

torture *vb* **-turing, -tured 1** to cause (someone) extreme physical pain, esp. to extract information, etc.: *suspects were regularly tortured and murdered by the secret police* **2** to cause (someone) mental anguish ▷ *n* **3** physical or mental anguish **4** the practice of torturing a person **5** something which causes great mental distress: *she was going through the torture of a collapsing marriage* ▶ **HISTORY** Latin *torquere* to twist > **tortured** *adj* > **torturer** *n* > **torturous** *adj*

Tory *n, pl* **-ries 1** a member or supporter of the Conservative Party in Great Britain or Canada **2** *history* a member of the English political party that supported the Church and Crown and traditional political structures and opposed the Whigs ▷ *adj* **3** of or relating to a Tory or Tories > **Toryism** *n*

■ **WORD HISTORY**
■ 'Tory' comes from Irish *toraidhe* or *toiridhe*,
■ meaning 'outlaw' or 'robber'. The name was
■ first given to Irish outlaws who harassed the
■ English in Ireland, and then came to be applied
■ to members of the English political faction that
■ opposed the exclusion of the Roman Catholic
■ James, Duke of York, from succession to the
■ throne. Thereafter 'Tory' remained as a political
■ label for those of a conservative outlook, as
■ opposed to the more reformist Whigs.

t

tosa (**toe**-za) *n* a large reddish dog, originally bred for fighting ▶ HISTORY after a province on the Japanese island of Skikoku

toss *vb* **1** to throw (something) lightly **2** to fling or be flung about, esp. in a violent way: *the salty sea breeze tossing the branches of the palms* **3** to coat (food) with a dressing by gentle stirring or mixing: *her technique for tossing Caesar salad* **4** (of a horse) to throw (its rider) **5** to move (one's head) suddenly backwards, as in impatience **6** to throw up (a coin) to decide between alternatives by guessing which side will land uppermost **7 toss and turn** to be restless when trying to sleep ▷ *n* **8** the act or an instance of tossing **9** the act of deciding between alternatives by throwing up a coin and guessing which side will land uppermost: *Essex won the toss and decided to bat first* **10 argue the toss** to waste time and energy arguing about an unimportant point **11 not give a toss** *informal* not to care at all ▷ See also **toss up** ▶ HISTORY Scandinavian

toss up *vb* **1** to spin (a coin) in the air in order to decide between alternatives by guessing which side will land uppermost ▷ *n* **toss-up 2** an instance of tossing up a coin **3** *informal* an even chance or risk: *if it's a toss-up for a top position, he gives it to the woman*

tot *n* **1** a very young child **2** a small drink of spirits ▶ HISTORY origin unknown

total *n* **1** the whole, esp. regarded as the sum of a number of parts **2 in total** overall: *the company employs over 700 people in total* ▷ *adj* **3** complete: *a total ban on alcohol* **4** being or related to a total: *the total number of deaths* ▷ *vb* **-talling, -talled** *or US* **-taling, -taled 5** to amount to: *the firm's losses totalled more than $2 billion* **6** to add up: *purchases are totalled with a pencil and a notepad* ▶ HISTORY Latin *totus* all > **totally** *adv*

total internal reflection *n physics* the complete reflection of a light ray at the boundary of two media, when the ray is in the medium with greater refractive index

totalitarian *adj* **1** of a political system in which there is only one party, which allows no opposition and attempts to control everything: *a totalitarian state* ▷ *n* **2** a person who is in favour of totalitarian policies > **totalitarianism** *n*

totality *n, pl* **-ties 1** the whole amount **2** the state of being total

totalizator, totalizer *or* **totalisator, totaliser** *n* a machine for operating a system of betting on a racecourse in which money is paid out to the winners in proportion to their stakes

total war *n* a war in which all economic and military resources are mobilized as part of the war effort and in which the whole of the population is involved

tote[1] *vb* **toting, toted** *informal* **1** to carry or wear (a gun) **2** to haul or carry ▶ HISTORY origin unknown

tote[2] *n* **the tote** *informal* short for **totalizator**

totem *n* **1** (esp. among Native Americans) an object or animal symbolizing a clan or family **2** a representation of such an object ▶ HISTORY from a Native American language > **totemic** *adj* > **totemism** *n*

totem pole *n* a pole carved or painted with totemic figures set up by certain Native Americans as a tribal symbol

totter *vb* **1** to move in an unsteady manner **2** to sway or shake as if about to fall **3** to be failing, unstable, or precarious: *the world was tottering on the edge of war* ▶ HISTORY origin unknown

toucan *n* a tropical American fruit-eating bird with a large brightly coloured bill ▶ HISTORY Portuguese *tucano*

touch *vb* **1** to cause or permit a part of the body to come into contact with (someone or something): *the baking tin is too hot to touch* **2** to tap, feel, or strike (someone or something): *he touched me on the shoulder* **3** to come or bring (something) into contact with (something else): *the plane's wheels touched the runway* **4** to move or disturb by handling: *we shouldn't touch anything before the police arrive* **5** to have an effect on: *millions of people's lives had been touched by their music* **6** to produce an emotional response in: *the painful truth of it touched her* **7** to eat or drink: *she hardly ever touched alcohol* **8** to compare to in quality or attainment; equal or match: *nothing can touch them for scope and detail* **9** *Brit, Austral & NZ, slang* to ask (someone) for a loan or gift of money **10** to strike, harm, or molest: *I never touched him!* **11 touch on** or **upon** to allude to briefly or in passing: *these two issues may be touched upon during the talks* ▷ *n* **12** the sense by which the texture and other qualities of objects can be experienced when they come in contact with a part of the body surface, esp. the tips of the fingers. *Related adjective:* **tactile 13** the feel or texture of an object as perceived by this sense: *she enjoyed the touch of the damp grass on her feet* **14** the act or an instance of something coming into contact with the body: *he remembered the touch of her hand* **15** a gentle push, tap, or caress: *the switch takes only the merest touch to operate* **16** a small amount; trace: *a touch of luxury* **17** a particular manner or style of doing something: *his songs always reveal his keen melodic touch* **18** a detail of some work: *final touches were now being put to the plans* **19** a slight attack: *a touch of dysentery* **20** (in sports such as football or rugby) the area outside the lines marking the side of the pitch: *he kicked the ball into touch* **21** the technique of fingering a keyboard instrument **22 a touch** slightly or marginally: *it's nice, but a touch expensive* **23 in touch a** regularly speaking to, writing to, or visiting someone **b** having up-to-date knowledge or understanding of a situation or trend **24 lose touch a** to gradually stop speaking to, writing to, or visiting someone **b** to stop having up-to-date knowledge or understanding of a situation or trend **25 out of touch a** no longer speaking to, writing to, or visiting someone **b** no longer having up-to-date knowledge or understanding of a situation or trend ▷ See also **touchdown** ▶ HISTORY Old French *tochier*

touch and go *adj* risky or critical: *it was touch and go whether the mission would succeed*

touchdown *n* **1** the moment at which a landing aircraft or spacecraft comes into contact with the landing surface **2** *American football* a scoring move in which an attacking player takes the ball into the area behind his opponents' goal ▷ *vb* **touch down** **3** (of an aircraft or spacecraft) to land

touché (too-**shay**) *interj* **1** an acknowledgment that a remark or witty reply has been effective **2** an acknowledgment of a scoring hit in fencing ▶ HISTORY French, literally: touched

touched *adj* **1** moved to sympathy or emotion: *I was touched by her understanding* **2** slightly mad: *she's a bit touched*

touching *adj* **1** arousing tender feelings ▷ *prep* **2** relating to or concerning: *she might talk about matters touching both of them*

touchline *n* either of the lines marking the side of the playing area in certain games, such as rugby

touchpad *n* (esp. on laptop computers) a small flat surface which is sensitive to touch, used to control an on-screen cursor

touchscreen *n* a visual display unit screen that allows the user to give commands to the computer by touching parts of the screen

touchstone *n* a standard by which judgment is made: *this restaurant is the touchstone for genuine Italian cookery in Leeds*

touch-type *vb* **-typing, -typed** to type without looking at the keyboard > **touch-typist** *n*

touchy *adj* **touchier, touchiest** **1** easily upset or irritated: *he is a touchy and quick-tempered man* **2** requiring careful and tactful handling: *a touchy subject* > **touchiness** *n*

touchy-feely *adj informal, sometimes derogatory* sensitive and caring

tough *adj* **1** strong and difficult to break, cut, or tear: *this fabric is tough and water-resistant* **2** (of meat or other food) difficult to cut and chew; not tender **3** physically or mentally strong and able to cope with hardship: *a tough, uncompromising woman, unwilling to take no for an answer* **4** rough or violent: *a tough and ruthless mercenary* **5** strict and firm: *the country's tough drugs laws* **6** difficult or troublesome to do or deal with: *a tough task* **7 tough luck!** *informal* an expression of lack of sympathy for someone else's problems ▷ *n* **8** a rough, vicious, or violent person ▷ *vb* **9 tough it out** *informal* to endure a difficult situation until it improves: *criticism of his performance has reinforced his desire to tough it out* ▶ HISTORY Old English *tōh* > **toughness** *n*

toughen *vb* to make or become tough or tougher

toupee (too-pay) *n* a hairpiece worn by men to cover a bald place ▶ HISTORY French *toupet* forelock

tour *n* **1** an extended journey visiting places of interest along the route **2** a trip, by a band, theatre company, etc. to perform in several places **3** an overseas trip made by a cricket team, rugby team, etc. to play in several places **4** *mil* a period of service, esp. in one place: *the regiment has served several tours in Northern Ireland* ▷ *vb* **5** to make a tour of (a place) ▶ HISTORY Old French: a turn

tour de force *n, pl* **tours de force** a masterly or brilliant stroke or achievement ▶ HISTORY French, literally: feat of skill or strength

tourism *n* tourist travel, esp. when regarded as an industry

tourist *n* **1** a person who travels for pleasure, usually sightseeing and staying in hotels **2** a member of a sports team which is visiting a country to play a series of matches: *the tourists were bowled out for 135* **3** the lowest class of accommodation on a passenger ship ▷ *adj* **4** of or relating to tourists or tourism: *a popular tourist attraction* **5** of the lowest class of accommodation on a passenger ship or aircraft

touristy *adj informal, often disparaging* full of tourists or tourist attractions

tourmaline *n* a hard crystalline mineral used in jewellery and electrical equipment ▶ HISTORY German *Turmalin*

tournament *n* **1** a sporting competition in which contestants play a series of games to determine an overall winner **2** Also: **tourney** *medieval history* a contest in which mounted knights fought for a prize ▶ HISTORY Old French *torneiement*

tourniquet (**tour**-nick-kay) *n med* a strip of cloth tied tightly round an arm or leg to stop bleeding from an artery ▶ HISTORY French

tout (rhymes with **shout**) *vb* **1** to seek (business, customers, etc.) or try to sell (goods), esp. in a persistent or direct manner: *he went from door to door touting for business* **2** to put forward or recommend (a person or thing) as a good or suitable example or candidate: *the plant was once touted as a showcase factory* ▷ *n* **3** a person who sells tickets for a heavily booked event at inflated prices ▶ HISTORY Old English *tȳtan* to peep

tow¹ *vb* **1** to pull or drag (a vehicle), esp. by means of a rope or cable ▷ *n* **2** the act or an instance of towing **3 in tow** *informal* in one's company or one's charge or under one's influence: *she had an older man in tow* **4 on tow** (of a vehicle) being towed ▶ HISTORY Old English *togian*

tow² *n* fibres of hemp, flax, jute, etc. prepared for spinning ▶ HISTORY Old English *tōw*

towards *or chiefly US* **toward** *prep* **1** in the direction of: *towards the lake* **2** with regard to: *hostility towards the President* **3** as a contribution to: *the profits will go towards three projects* **4** just before: *towards evening*

towbar *n* a rigid metal bar attached to the back of a vehicle, from which a trailer or caravan can be towed

towel *n* **1** a piece of absorbent cloth or paper used for drying things **2 throw in the towel** See **throw in** (sense 3) ▷ *vb* **-elling, -elled** *or US* **-eling, -eled** **3** to dry or wipe with a towel ▶ HISTORY Old French *toaille*

towelling *or US* **toweling** *n* a soft, fairly thick fabric used to make towels and dressing gowns

t

tower *n* **1** a tall, usually square or circular structure, sometimes part of a larger building and usually built for a specific purpose **2 tower of strength** a person who supports or comforts someone else at a time of difficulty ▷ *vb* **3 tower over** to be much taller than: *sheer walls of limestone towered over us* ▶ HISTORY Latin *turris*

tower block *n Brit* a very tall building divided into flats or offices

towering *adj* **1** very tall **2** very impressive or important: *his towering presence on stage* **3** very intense: *in a towering rage*

town *n* **1** a large group of houses, shops, factories, etc., smaller than a city and larger than a village. *Related adjective:* **urban 2** the nearest town or the chief town of an area: *people from town rarely went out to the farm* **3** the central area of a town where most of the shops and offices are: *we're going to a pub in town tonight* **4** the people of a town: *the town is split over the plans for a bypass* **5** built-up areas in general, as opposed to the countryside: *migration from the country to the town* **6 go to town** to make a supreme or unrestricted effort **7 on the town** visiting nightclubs, restaurants, etc.: *we'd a night on the town to celebrate her promotion* ▶ HISTORY Old English *tūn* village

town clerk *n* (currently in Australia and in Britain until 1974) the chief administrative officer of a town

town crier *n* (formerly) a person employed to make public announcements in the streets

town hall *n* a large building in a town often containing the council offices and a hall for public meetings

town house *n* **1** a terraced house in an urban area, esp. an up-market one **2** a person's town residence as distinct from his or her country residence

town planning *n* the comprehensive planning of the physical and social development of a town

township *n* **1** a small town **2** (in South Africa) a planned urban settlement of Black Africans or Coloureds **3** (in the US and Canada) a small unit of local government, often consisting of a town and the area surrounding it **4** (in Canada) a land-survey area, usually 36 square miles (93 square kilometres)

townsman *n*, *pl* **-men** an inhabitant of a town > **townswoman** *fem n*

townspeople *or* **townsfolk** *pl n* the people who live in a town

towpath *n* a path beside a canal or river, formerly used by horses pulling barges

towrope *n* a rope or cable used for towing a vehicle or vessel

toxaemia *or US* **toxemia** (tox-**seem**-ya) *n* **1** a form of blood poisoning caused by toxins released by bacteria at a wound or other site of infection **2** a condition in pregnant women characterized by high blood pressure ▶ HISTORY Greek *toxicon* poison + *haima* blood > **toxaemic** *or US* **toxemic** *adj*

toxic *adj* **1** poisonous: *toxic fumes* **2** caused by poison: *toxic effects* ▶ HISTORY Greek *toxikon* (*pharmakon*) (poison) used on arrows > **toxicity** *n*

toxicology *n* the branch of science concerned with poisons and their effects > **toxicological** *adj* > **toxicologist** *n*

toxin *n* **1** any of various poisonous substances produced by microorganisms and causing certain diseases **2** any other poisonous substance of plant or animal origin

toy *n* **1** an object designed for children to play with, such as a doll or model car **2** an object that adults use for entertainment rather than for a serious purpose: *I do use my computer: it's not just a toy* ▷ *adj* **3** being an imitation or model of something for children to play with: *a toy aeroplane* **4** (of a dog) of a variety much smaller than is normal for that breed: *a toy poodle* ▷ See also **toy with** ▶ HISTORY origin unknown

toy-toy *or* **toyi-toyi** *S African n* **1** a dance expressing defiance and protest ▷ *vb* **2** to dance in this way ▶ HISTORY origin uncertain

toy with *vb* **1** to consider an idea without being serious about it or being able to decide about it: *I've been toying with the idea of setting up my own firm* **2** to keep moving (an object) about with one's fingers, esp. when thinking about something else: *Jessica sat toying with her glass*

trace *vb* **tracing, traced 1** to locate or work out (the cause or source of something): *he traced the trouble to a faulty connection* **2** to find (something or someone that was missing): *the police were unable to trace her missing husband* **3** to discover or describe the progress or development of (something): *throughout the 19th century we can trace the development of more complex machinery* **4** to copy (a design, map, etc.) by putting a piece of transparent paper over it and following the lines which show through the paper with a pencil **5** to make the outline of (a shape or pattern): *his index finger was tracing circles on the arm of the chair* ▷ *n* **6** a mark, footprint, or other sign that shows that a person, animal, or thing has been in a particular place: *the police could find no trace of the missing van* **7** an amount of something so small that it is barely noticeable: *I detected a trace of jealousy in her voice* **8** a remnant of something: *traces of an Iron-Age fort remain visible* **9** a pattern made on a screen or a piece of paper by a device that is measuring or detecting something: *a baffling radar trace* ▶ HISTORY French *tracier* > **traceable** *adj*

trace element *n* a chemical element that occurs in very small amounts in soil, water, etc. and is essential for healthy growth

tracer *n* **1** a projectile that can be observed when in flight by the burning of chemical substances in its base **2** *med* an element or other substance introduced into the body to study metabolic processes

tracery *n*, *pl* **-eries 1** a pattern of interlacing lines, esp. one in a stained glass window **2** any fine lacy pattern resembling this

traces *pl n* **1** the two side straps that connect a horse's harness to the vehicle being pulled **2 kick over the traces** to escape or defy control ▶ HISTORY Old French *trait*

t

907

trachea (track-**kee**-a) *n*, *pl* **-cheae** (-**kee**-ee) *anat*, *zool* the tube that carries inhaled air from the throat to the lungs ▶ HISTORY Greek

tracheotomy (track-ee-**ot**-a-mee) *n*, *pl* **-mies** a surgical incision into the trachea, as performed when the air passage has been blocked ▶ HISTORY TRACHEA + Greek *tomē* a cutting

trachoma (track-**oh**-ma) *n* a chronic contagious disease of the eye characterized by inflammation of the inner surface of the lids and the formation of scar tissue ▶ HISTORY Greek *trakhōma* roughness

tracing *n* **1** a copy of something, such as a map, made by tracing **2** a line traced by a recording instrument

track *n* **1** a rough road or path: *a farm track* **2** the mark or trail left by something that has passed by: *the fox didn't leave any tracks* **3** a rail or pair of parallel rails on which a vehicle, such as a train, runs **4** a course for running or racing on: *a running track* **5** a separate song or piece of music on a record, tape, or CD: *Dolphy switches back to bass clarinet for the final track* **6** a course of action, thought, etc.: *I don't think you're on the right track at all* **7** an endless band on the wheels of a tank, bulldozer, etc. to enable it to move across rough ground **8 keep** or **lose track of** to follow or fail to follow the course or progress of **9 off the beaten track** in an isolated location: *the village where she lives is a bit off the beaten track* ▷ *vb* **10** to follow the trail of (a person or animal) **11** to follow the flight path of (a satellite etc.) by picking up signals transmitted or reflected by it **12** *films* to follow (a moving object) while filming ▷ See also **track down, tracks** ▶ HISTORY Old French *trac* > **tracker** *n*

track and field *n* **1** track events and field events ▷ *adj* **track-and-field 2** relating to both track events and field events: *track-and-field competitions*

trackball or **trackerball** *n computers* **1** a device consisting of a small ball mounted in a cup, which can be moved to control an on-screen cursor

track down *vb* to find (someone or something) by tracking or pursuing

tracker dog *n* a dog specially trained to search for missing people

track event *n* a competition in athletics, such as sprinting, that takes place on a running track. Compare **field event**

track record *n informal* the past record of the accomplishments and failures of a person or organization

tracks *pl n* **1** marks, such as footprints, left by someone or something that has passed **2 in one's tracks** on the very spot where one is standing: *those words stopped her in her tracks* **3 make tracks** to leave or depart: *it was time to start making tracks*

track shoe *n* a light running shoe fitted with steel spikes for better grip

tracksuit *n* a warm loose-fitting suit worn by athletes etc., esp. during training

tract¹ *n* **1** a large area, esp. of land: *an extensive tract of moorland* **2** *anat* a system of organs or glands that

has a particular function: *the urinary tract*
▶ HISTORY Latin *tractus* a stretching out

tract² *n* a pamphlet, esp. a religious one ▶ HISTORY Latin *tractatus*

tractable *adj formal* easy to control, manage, or deal with: *he could easily manage his tractable and worshipping younger brother* ▶ HISTORY Latin *tractare* to manage > **tractability** *n*

traction *n* **1** pulling, esp. by engine power: *the increased use of electric traction* **2** *med* the application of a steady pull on an injured limb using a system of weights and pulleys or splints: *he was in traction for weeks following the accident* **3** the grip that the wheels of a vehicle have on the ground: *four-wheel drive gives much better traction in wet or icy conditions* ▶ HISTORY Latin *tractus* dragged

traction engine *n* a heavy steam-powered vehicle used, esp. formerly, for drawing heavy loads along roads or over rough ground

traction load *n geol* the solid material that is carried along the bed of a river

tractor *n* a motor vehicle with large rear wheels, used to pull heavy loads, esp. farm machinery ▶ HISTORY Late Latin: one who pulls

trade *n* **1** the buying and selling of goods and services **2** a person's job, esp. a craft requiring skill: *he's a plumber by trade* **3** the people and practices of an industry, craft, or business **4** amount of custom or commercial dealings: *a brisk trade in second-hand weapons* **5** a specified market or business: *the wool trade* **6 trades** the trade winds ▷ *vb* **trading, traded 7** to buy and sell (goods) **8** to exchange: *he traded a job in New York for a life as a cowboy* **9** to engage in trade **10** to deal or do business (with) ▷ See also **trade-in, trade-off** ▶ HISTORY Low German: track, hence a regular business > **tradable** or **tradeable** *adj* > **trader** *n* > **trading** *n*

trade-in *n* **1** a used article given in part payment for the purchase of a new article ▷ *vb* **trade in 2** to give (a used article) as part payment for a new article

trade magazine *n publishing* a periodical containing news articles and information specific to a trade or profession

trademark *n* **1a** the name or other symbol used by a manufacturer to distinguish his or her products from those of competitors **b Registered Trademark** one that is officially registered and legally protected **2** any distinctive sign or mark of a person or thing: *the designer bars which have become the trademark of the city*

trade name *n* **1** the name used by a trade to refer to a product or range of products **2** the name under which a commercial enterprise operates in business

trade-off *n* an exchange, esp. as a compromise: *there is often a trade-off between manpower costs and computer costs*

tradescantia (trad-dess-**kan**-shee-a) *n* a widely cultivated plant with striped leaves ▶ HISTORY after John *Tradescant*, botanist

trade secret n a secret formula, technique, or process known and used to advantage by only one manufacturer

tradesman n, pl **-men 1** a skilled worker, such as an electrician or painter **2** a shopkeeper
> **tradeswoman** fem n

Trades Union Congress n (in Britain and S Africa) the major association of trade unions, which includes all the larger unions

trade union or **trades union** n a society of workers formed to protect and improve their working conditions, pay, etc. > **trade unionism** or **trades unionism** n > **trade unionist** or **trades unionist** n

trade wind n meteorol a wind blowing steadily towards the equator either from the northeast in the N hemisphere or the southeast in the S hemisphere

trading estate n chiefly Brit a large area in which a number of commercial or industrial firms are situated

tradition n **1** the handing down from generation to generation of customs, beliefs, etc. **2** the unwritten body of beliefs, customs, etc. handed down from generation to generation **3** a custom or practice of long standing **4 in the tradition of** having many features similar to those of a person or thing in the past: a thriller writer in the tradition of Chandler ▶ HISTORY Latin traditio a handing down

traditional adj of, relating to, or being a tradition
> **traditionally** adv

traditional grammar n rules and terminology for language analysis based on parts of speech. Compare **functional grammar**

traditionalist n a person who supports established customs or beliefs > **traditionalism** n

traduce vb **-ducing, -duced** formal to speak badly of (someone) ▶ HISTORY Latin traducere to lead over, disgrace > **traducement** n > **traducer** n

traffic n **1** the vehicles travelling on roads **2** the movement of vehicles or people in a particular place or for a particular purpose: air traffic **3** trade, esp. of an illicit kind: drug traffic **4** the exchange of ideas between people or organizations: a lively traffic in ideas ▷ vb **-ficking, -ficked 5** to carry on trade or business, esp. of an illicit kind: he confessed to trafficking in gold and ivory ▶ HISTORY Old French trafique > **trafficker** n > **trafficking** n

traffic calming n chiefly Brit the use of devices, such as bends and humps in the road, designed to slow down traffic, esp. in residential areas

traffic island n a raised area in the middle of a road designed as a guide for traffic flow and to provide a stopping place for pedestrians crossing

traffic warden n Brit a person employed to supervise road traffic and report traffic offences

tragedian (traj-**jee**-dee-an) or fem **tragedienne** (traj-jee-dee-**enn**) n **1** an actor who specializes in tragic roles **2** a writer of tragedy

tragedy n, pl **-dies 1** a shocking or sad event **2** a serious play, film, or opera in which the main character is destroyed by a combination of a personal failing and adverse circumstances
▶ HISTORY Greek tragōidia

tragic adj **1** sad and distressing because it involves death or suffering: she was blinded in a tragic accident **2** of or like a tragedy: a tragic hero **3** sad or mournful: a tragic melody > **tragically** adv

tragic flaw adj theatre the character failing in a tragic hero that brings about his downfall

tragicomedy n, pl **-dies** a play or other written work having both comic and tragic elements
> **tragicomic** adj

trail n **1** a rough path across open country or through a forest **2** a route along a series of roads or paths that has been specially planned to let people see or do particular things: a nature trail through the woods **3** a print, mark, or scent left by a person, animal, or object: a trail of blood was found down three flights of stairs **4** something that trails behind: a vapour trail **5** a sequence of results from an event: a trail of mishaps ▷ vb **6** to drag or stream along the ground or through the air behind someone or something: part of her sari trailed behind her on the floor **7** to lag behind (a person or thing): Max had arrived as well, trailing behind the others **8** to follow or hunt (an animal or person), usually secretly, by following the marks or tracks he, she, or it has made: the police had trailed him the length and breadth of the country **9** to be falling behind in a race, match or competition: they trailed 2-1 at half-time **10** to move wearily or slowly: we spent the afternoon trailing round the shops ▶ HISTORY Old French trailler to tow

trailer n **1** a road vehicle, usually two-wheeled, towed by a motor vehicle and used for carrying goods, transporting boats, etc.: ahead of us was a tractor, drawing a trailer laden with dung **2** the rear section of an articulated lorry **3** an extract or series of extracts from a film, TV or radio programme, used to advertise it **4** US & Canad same as **caravan** (sense 1)

trailing adj (of a plant) having a long stem which spreads over the ground or hangs loosely: trailing ivy

train vb **1** to instruct (someone) in a skill: soldiers are trained to obey orders unquestioningly **2** to learn the skills needed to do a particular job or activity: she was training to be a computer programmer **3** to do exercises and prepare for a specific purpose: he was training for a marathon **4** to focus on or aim at (something): the warship kept its guns trained on the trawler **5** to discipline (an animal) to obey commands or perform tricks **6** to tie or prune (a plant) so that it grows in a particular way: he had trained the roses to grow up the wall ▷ n **7** a line of railway coaches or wagons coupled together and drawn by a engine **8** a sequence or series: following an earlier train of thought **9** the long back section of a dress that trails along the floor **10 in its train** as a consequence: economic mismanagement brought unemployment and inflation in its train **11 in train** actually happening or being done: the programme of reforms set in train by the new government ▷ adj

909

12 of or by a train: *the long train journey north* ▶ HISTORY Old French *trahiner*

trainee *n* **1** a person undergoing training ▷ *adj* **2** (of a person) undergoing training: *a trainee journalist*

trainer *n* **1** a person who coaches a person or team in a sport **2** a person who trains racehorses **3** an aircraft used for training pilots **4** *Brit* a flat-soled sports shoe of the style used by athletes when training

training *n* the process of bringing a person to an agreed standard of proficiency by practice and instruction

train spotter *n Brit* **1** a person who collects the numbers of railway locomotives **2** *informal* a person who is obsessed with trivial details, esp. of a subject generally considered uninteresting

traipse *informal vb* **traipsing, traipsed 1** to walk heavily or tiredly ▷ *n* **2** a long or tiring walk ▶ HISTORY origin unknown

trait *n* a characteristic feature or quality of a person or thing ▶ HISTORY French

traitor *n* a person who betrays friends, a country, a cause, etc. ▶ HISTORY Latin *tradere* to hand over > **traitorous** *adj* > **traitress** *fem n*

trajectory *n, pl* **-ries** the path described by an object moving in air or space, esp. the curved path of a projectile ▶ HISTORY Latin *trajectus* cast over

tram *n* an electrically driven public transport vehicle that runs on rails laid into the road and takes its power from an overhead cable ▶ HISTORY probably from Low German *traam* beam

tramlines *pl n* **1** the tracks on which a tram runs **2** the outer markings along the sides of a tennis or badminton court

trammel *vb* **-elling, -elled** *or US* **-eling, -eled 1** to hinder or restrict: *trammelled by family responsibilities* ▷ *pl n* **2** **trammels** things that hinder or restrict someone: *the trammels of social respectability* ▶ HISTORY Old French *tramail* three-mesh net

tramp *vb* **1** to walk long and far; hike **2** to walk heavily or firmly across or through (a place): *she tramped slowly up the beach* ▷ *n* **3** a homeless person who travels about on foot, living by begging or doing casual work **4** a long hard walk; hike: *we went for a long tramp over the downs* **5** the sound of heavy regular footsteps: *we could hear the tramp of the marching soldiers* **6** a small cargo ship that does not run on a regular schedule **7** *US, Canad, Austral & NZ, slang* a promiscuous woman ▶ HISTORY probably from Middle Low German *trampen*

tramping *n NZ* the leisure activity of walking in the bush > **tramper** *n*

trample *vb* **-pling, -pled 1** Also: **trample on** to tread on and crush: *three children were trampled to death when the crowd panicked and ran* **2 trample on** to treat (a person or his or her rights or feelings) with disregard or contempt ▶ HISTORY from *tramp*

trampoline *n* **1** a tough canvas sheet suspended by springs or cords from a frame, which acrobats, gymnasts, etc. bounce on ▷ *vb* **-lining, -lined 2** to exercise on a trampoline ▶ HISTORY Italian *trampolino*

trance *n* **1** a hypnotic state resembling sleep in which a person is unable to move or act of his or her own will **2** a dazed or stunned state ▶ HISTORY Latin *transire* to go over

tranche (**trahnsh**) *n* an instalment or portion, esp. of a loan or share issue: *the new shares will be offered in four tranches around the world*

trannie *or* **tranny** *n, pl* **-nies** *informal, chiefly Brit* transistor radio

tranquil *adj* calm, peaceful, or quiet ▶ HISTORY Latin *tranquillus* > **tranquilly** *adv*

tranquillity *or US sometimes* **tranquility** *n* a state of calmness or peace

tranquillize, -lise *or US* **tranquilize** *vb* **-lizing, -lized** *or* **-lising, -lised 1** to make or become calm or calmer **2** to give (someone) a drug to make them calm or calmer > **tranquillization, -lisation** *or US* **tranquilization** *n* > **tranquillizing, -lising** *or US* **tranquilizing** *adj*

tranquillizer, -liser *or US* **tranquilizer** *n* a drug that calms someone suffering from anxiety, tension, etc.

trans. **1** transitive **2** translated

trans- *prefix* **1** across, beyond, crossing, or on the other side of: *transnational* **2** changing thoroughly: *transliterate* ▶ HISTORY Latin

transact *vb* to do, conduct, or negotiate (a business deal) ▶ HISTORY Latin *transigere* to drive through

transaction *n* **1** something that is transacted, esp. a business deal **2 transactions** the records of the proceedings of a society, etc.: *an article on land use in the Niagara area taken from the 'Transactions of the Royal Canadian Institute'*

transalpine *adj* beyond the Alps, esp. as viewed from Italy

transatlantic *adj* **1** on or from the other side of the Atlantic **2** crossing the Atlantic

transceiver *n* a device which transmits and receives radio or electronic signals ▶ HISTORY *trans(mitter)* + *(re)ceiver*

transcend *vb* **1** to go above or beyond what is expected or normal: *a vital party issue that transcends traditional party loyalties* **2** to overcome or be superior to: *to transcend all difficulties* ▶ HISTORY Latin *transcendere* to climb over

transcendent *adj* **1** above or beyond what is expected or normal **2** *theol* (of God) having existence outside the created world > **transcendence** *n*

transcendental *adj* **1** above or beyond what is expected or normal **2** *philosophy* based on intuition or innate belief rather than experience **3** supernatural or mystical > **transcendentally** *adv*

transcendentalism *n* any system of philosophy that seeks to discover the nature of reality by examining the processes of thought rather than the things thought about, or that emphasizes intuition as a means to knowledge > **transcendentalist** *n, adj*

transcendental meditation *n* *trademark* a technique, based on Hindu traditions, for relaxing and refreshing the mind and body through the silent repetition of a special formula of words

transcribe *vb* **-scribing, -scribed 1** to write, type, or print out (a text) fully from a speech or notes **2** to make an electrical recording of (a programme or speech) for a later broadcast **3** *music* to rewrite (a piece of music) for an instrument other than that originally intended ▶ **HISTORY** Latin *transcribere* > **transcriber** *n*

transcript *n* **1** a written, typed, or printed copy made by transcribing **2** *chiefly US & Canad* an official record of a student's school progress

transducer *n* any device, such as a microphone or electric motor, that converts one form of energy into another ▶ **HISTORY** Latin *transducere* to lead across

transect *n* *biol* a sample strip of land used to monitor plant distribution and animal populations within a given area

transept *n* either of the two shorter wings of a cross-shaped church ▶ **HISTORY** Latin *trans-* across + *saeptum* enclosure

transfer *vb* **-ferring, -ferred 1** to change or move from one thing, person, place, etc. to another: *he was transferred from prison to hospital* **2** to move (money or property) from the control of one person or organization to that of another: *the money has been transferred into your account* **3** (of a football club) to sell or release (a player) to another club: *he was transferred to Juventus for a world record fee* **4** to move (a drawing or design) from one surface to another ▷ *n* **5** the act, process, or system of transferring, or the state of being transferred **6** a person or thing that transfers or is transferred **7** a design or drawing that is transferred from one surface to another **8** the moving of (money or property) from the control of one person or organization to that of another ▶ **HISTORY** Latin *trans* across + *ferre* to carry > **transferable** *or* **transferrable** *adj* > **transference** *n*

transfer station *n* *NZ* a depot where rubbish is sorted for recycling

transfiguration *n* a transfiguring or being transfigured

Transfiguration *n* **1** *New Testament* the change in the appearance of Christ on the mountain **2** the Church festival held in commemoration of this on August 6

transfigure *vb* **-uring, -ured 1** to change or cause to change in appearance **2** to become or cause to become more exalted ▶ **HISTORY** Latin *trans-* beyond + *figura* appearance

transfix *vb* **-fixing, -fixed 1** to make (someone) motionless, esp. with horror or shock: *they stood transfixed and revolted by what they saw* **2** to pierce (a person or animal) through with a pointed object: *the Pharaoh is shown transfixing enemies with arrows from a moving chariot* ▶ **HISTORY** Latin *transfigere* to pierce through

transform *vb* **1** to change completely in form or function: *the last forty years have seen the country transformed from a peasant economy to a major industrial power* **2** to change so as to make better or more attractive: *most religions claim to be able to transform people's lives* **3** to convert (one form of energy) to another **4** *maths* to change the form of (an equation, expression, etc.) without changing its value **5** to change (an alternating current or voltage) using a transformer ▶ **HISTORY** Latin *transformare*

transformation *n* **1** a change or alteration, esp. a radical one **2** the act of transforming or the state of being transformed **3** *S African* a political slogan for demographic change in the power struggle **4** *n* *geom* the mapping, or movement, of all the points of a figure in a plane according to a common operation. Some transformations, like dilation, affect the size of the figure, while others, called isometries, preserve the size of the figure

transformer *n* a device that transfers an alternating current from one circuit to one or more other circuits, usually with a change of voltage

transfuse *vb* **-fusing, -fused 1** to inject (blood or other fluid) into a blood vessel **2** *literary* to transmit or instil ▶ **HISTORY** Latin *transfundere* to pour out

transfusion *n* **1** the injection of blood, blood plasma, etc. into the blood vessels of a patient **2** the act of transferring something: *a transfusion of new funds*

transgress *vb* *formal* **1** to break (a law or rule) **2** to overstep (a limit): *he had never before been known to transgress the very slowest of walks* ▶ **HISTORY** Latin *trans* beyond + *gradi* to step > **transgression** *n* > **transgressor** *n*

transhumance *n* *agriculture* the seasonal migration of livestock to suitable grazing grounds ▶ **HISTORY** French *transhumer* to change one's pastures, from Spanish *trashumar*, from Latin TRANS- + *humus* ground

transient *adj* **1** lasting for a short time only: *she had a number of transient relationships with fellow students* **2** (of a person) not remaining in a place for a long time: *the transient population of the inner city* ▷ *n* **3** a transient person or thing ▶ **HISTORY** Latin *transiens* going over > **transience** *n*

transistor *n* **1** a semiconductor device used to amplify and control electric currents **2** *informal* a small portable radio containing transistors ▶ **HISTORY** *transfer + resistor*

transistorized *or* **-ised** *adj* (of an electronic device) using transistors

transit *n* **1** the moving or carrying of goods or people from one place to another **2** a route or means of transport: *transit by road* **3** *astron* the apparent passage of a celestial body across the meridian **4 in transit** while travelling or being taken from one place to another: *in transit the fruit can be damaged* ▷ *adj* **5** indicating a place or building where people wait or goods are kept between different stages of a journey: *a transit lounge for passengers who are changing planes* ▶ HISTORY Latin *transitus* a going over

transition *n* **1** the process of changing from one state or stage to another: *the transition from dictatorship to democracy* **2** *music* a movement from one key to another ▶ HISTORY Latin *transitio* a going over > **transitional** *adj*

transition element *or* **metal** *n chem* any element belonging to one of three series of elements with atomic numbers between 21 and 30, 39 and 48, and 57 and 80 (**transition series**). They tend to have more than one valency and to form complexes

transitive *adj grammar* denoting a verb which takes a direct object

transitive verb *n grammar* a verb which takes a direct object: *'to raise' is a transitive verb.* Compare **intransitive verb**

transitory *adj* lasting only for a short time

translate *vb* **-lating, -lated 1 a** to change (something spoken or written in one language) into another **b** to be capable of being changed from one language into another: *puns do not translate well* **2** to express (something) in a different way, for instance by using a different measurement system or less technical language: *the temperature is 30° Celsius, or if we translate into Fahrenheit, 86°* **3** to transform or convert, for instance by putting an idea into practice: *cheap crops translate into lower feed prices* **4** to interpret the significance of (a gesture, action, etc.): *I gave him what I hoped would be translated as a thoughtful look* **5** to act as a translator: *I had to translate for a party of visiting Greeks* ▶ HISTORY Latin *translatus* carried over > **translatable** *adj* > **translator** *n*

translation *n* **1** a piece of writing or speech that has been translated into another language **2** the act of translating something **3** the expression of something in a different way or form: *the book's plot was radically altered during its translation to film* **4** *maths* a transformation in which the origin of a coordinate system is moved to another position so that each axis retains the same direction > **translational** *adj*

transliterate *vb* **-ating, -ated** to write or spell (a word, etc.) into corresponding letters of another alphabet ▶ HISTORY Latin *trans-* across + *littera* letter > **transliteration** *n*

translucent *adj* allowing light to pass through, but not transparent ▶ HISTORY Latin *translucere* to shine through > **translucency** *or* **translucence** *n*

transmigrate *vb* **-grating, -grated** (of a soul) to pass from one body into another at death > **transmigration** *n*

transmission *n* **1** the sending or passing of something, such as a message or disease from one place or person to another **2** something that is transmitted, esp. a radio or television broadcast **3** a system of shafts and gears that transmits power from the engine to the driving wheels of a motor vehicle

transmit *vb* **-mitting, -mitted 1** to pass (something, such as a message or disease) from one place or person to another **2 a** to send out (signals) by means of radio waves **b** to broadcast (a radio or television programme) **3** to allow the passage of (particles, energy, etc.): *water transmits sound better than air* **4** to transfer (a force, motion, etc.) from one part of a mechanical system to another: *the chain of the bike transmits the motion of the pedals to the rear wheel* ▶ HISTORY Latin *transmittere* to send across > **transmittable** *adj*

transmitter *n* **1** a piece of equipment used for broadcasting radio or television programmes **2** a person or thing that transmits something

transmogrify *vb* **-fies, -fying, -fied** *jocular* to change or transform (someone or something) into a different shape or appearance, esp. a grotesque or bizarre one ▶ HISTORY origin unknown > **transmogrification** *n*

transmute *vb* **-muting, -muted** to change the form or nature of: *self-contempt is transmuted into hatred of others* ▶ HISTORY Latin *transmutare* to shift > **transmutation** *n*

transom *n* **1** a horizontal bar across a window **2** a horizontal bar that separates a door from a window over it ▶ HISTORY Old French *traversin*

transparency *n, pl* **-cies 1** the state of being transparent **2** a positive photograph on transparent film, usually mounted in a frame or between glass plates, which can be viewed with the use of a slide projector

transparent *adj* **1** able to be seen through; clear **2** easy to understand or recognize; obvious: *transparent honesty* ▶ HISTORY Latin *trans-* through + *parere* to appear > **transparently** *adv*

transpiration *n bot* (in plants) water loss through pores known as *stomata*

transpire *vb* **-spiring, -spired 1** to come to light; become known **2** *not universally accepted* to happen or occur **3** *physiol* to give off (water or vapour) through the pores of the skin, etc. **4** (of plants) to lose (water vapour) through the stomata ▶ HISTORY Latin *trans-* through + *spirare* to breathe

transplant *vb* **1** *surgery* to transfer (an organ or tissue) from one part of the body or from one person to another **2** to remove or transfer (esp. a plant) from one place to another ▷ *n* **3** *surgery* **a** the procedure involved in transferring an organ or tissue **b** the organ or tissue transplanted > **transplantation** *n*

transponder *n* a type of radio or radar transmitter-receiver that transmits signals automatically when it receives predetermined signals ▶ HISTORY *transmitter* + *responder*

transport *vb* **1** to carry or move (people or goods) from one place to another, esp. over some distance **2** *history* to exile (a criminal) to a penal colony **3** to have a strong emotional effect on: *transported by joy* ▷ *n* **4** the business or system of transporting goods or people: *public transport* **5** *Brit* freight vehicles generally **6** a vehicle used to transport troops **7** a transporting or being transported

8 ecstasy or rapture: *transports of delight*
▶ HISTORY Latin *trans-* across + *portare* to carry
> **transportable** *adj*

transportation *n* **1** a means or system of transporting **2** the act of transporting or the state of being transported **3** *history* deportation to a penal colony

transporter *n* a large vehicle used for carrying cars from the factory to garages for sale

transpose *vb* **-posing, -posed 1** to change the order of (letters, words, or sentences) **2** *music* to play (notes, music, etc.) in a different key **3** *maths* to move (a term) from one side of an equation to the other with a corresponding reversal in sign: *transposing 3 in x − 3 = 6 gives x = 6 + 3* ▶ HISTORY Old French *transposer* > **transposition** *n*

transsexual *or* **transexual** *n* **1** a person who believes that his or her true identity is of the opposite sex **2** a person who has had medical treatment to alter his or her sexual characteristics to those of the opposite sex

transubstantiation *n* *Christianity* the doctrine that the bread and wine consecrated in Communion change into the substance of Christ's body and blood ▶ HISTORY Latin *trans-* over + *substantia* substance

transuranic (tranz-yoor-**ran**-ik) *adj chem* (of an element) having an atomic number greater than that of uranium

transversal *n* *geom* a line intersecting two or more other lines

transverse *adj* crossing from side to side: *the transverse arches in the main hall of the college* ▶ HISTORY Latin *transvertere* to turn across

transverse dune *n* *geog* a dune that lies at right angles to the direction of the prevailing wind with a gentle slope facing the wind and a steeper slope on the other side

transverse wave *n* *physics* a wave that is propagated at right angles to the direction of displacement of the transmitting field or medium

transvestite *n* a person, esp. a man, who wears clothes of the opposite sex ▶ HISTORY Latin *trans-* across + *vestitus* clothed > **transvestism** *n*

trap *n* **1** a device or hole in which something, esp. an animal, is caught: *a fox trap* **2** a plan for tricking a person into being caught unawares **3** a situation from which it is difficult to escape: *caught in the poverty trap* **4** a bend in a pipe that contains standing water to prevent the passage of gases **5** a boxlike stall in which greyhounds are enclosed before the start of a race **6** a device that hurls clay pigeons into the air to be fired at **7** a light two-wheeled carriage: *a pony and trap* **8** *Brit, Austral & NZ, slang* the mouth: *shut your trap!* ▷ *vb* **trapping, trapped 9** to catch (an animal) in a trap **10** to catch (someone) by a trick: *the police trapped the drug dealers by posing as potential customers* **11** to hold or confine in an unpleasant situation from which it is difficult to escape: *trapped in the rubble of collapsed buildings* ▶ HISTORY Old English *træppe*

trap-door spider *n* a spider that builds a silk-lined hole in the ground closed by a hinged door of earth and silk

trapeze *n* a horizontal bar suspended from two ropes, used by circus acrobats ▶ HISTORY French

trapezium *n, pl* **-ziums** *or* **-zia 1** a quadrilateral having two parallel sides of unequal length **2** *chiefly US & Canad* a quadrilateral having neither pair of sides parallel ▶ HISTORY Greek *trapeza* table > **trapezial** *adj*

trapezoid (**trap**-piz-zoid) *n* **1** a quadrilateral having neither pair of sides parallel **2** *US & Canad* same as **trapezium** (sense 1) ▶ HISTORY Greek *trapeza* table

trapper *n* a person who traps animals, esp. for their furs or skins

trappings *pl n* **1** the accessories that symbolize a condition, office, etc.: *the trappings of power* **2** ceremonial harness for a horse or other animal ▶ HISTORY probably from Old French *drap* cloth

Trappist *n* a member of an order of Christian monks who follow a rule of strict silence

trash *n* **1** foolish ideas or talk; nonsense **2** *US, Canad, NZ & S African* unwanted objects; rubbish **3** *chiefly US, Canad & NZ* a worthless person or group of people ▷ *vb* **4** *slang* to attack or destroy maliciously: *we've never trashed a hotel room* ▶ HISTORY origin unknown > **trashy** *adj*

trauma (**traw**-ma) *n* **1** *psychol* an emotional shock that may have long-lasting effects **2** *pathol* any bodily injury or wound ▶ HISTORY Greek: a wound > **traumatic** *adj* > **traumatically** *adv* > **traumatize** *or* **-ise** *vb*

travail *n* *literary* painful or exceptionally hard work ▶ HISTORY Old French *travaillier*

travel *vb* **-elling, -elled** *or US* **-eling, -eled 1** to go or move from one place to another **2** to go or journey through or across (an area, region, etc.): *Margaret travelled widely when she was in New Zealand* **3** to go at a specified speed or for a specified distance: *the car was travelling at 30 mph* **4** to go from place to place as a salesman **5** (of perishable goods) to withstand a journey: *not all wines travel well* **6** (of light or sound) to be transmitted or carried from one place to another: *sound travels a long distance in these conditions* **7** (of a machine or part) to move in a fixed path **8** (of a vehicle) *informal* to move rapidly ▷ *n* **9** the act or a means of travelling: *air travel has changed the way people live* **10** a tour or journey: *his travels took him to Dublin* **11** the distance moved by a mechanical part, such as the stroke of a piston ▶ HISTORY Old French *travaillier* to travail

travel agency *n* an agency that arranges flights, hotel accommodation, etc. for tourists > **travel agent** *n*

traveller *or US* **traveler** *n* **1** a person who travels, esp. habitually **2** a travelling salesman **3** a Gypsy

traveller's cheque *or US* **traveler's check** *n* a cheque sold by a bank, travel agency, etc., which the buyer signs on purchase and can cash abroad by re-signing it

t

913

travelogue *or US* **travelog** *n* a film or lecture on travels and travelling

traverse *vb* **-ersing, -ersed** 1 to move over or back and forth over; cross: *he once traversed San Francisco harbour in a balloon* 2 to reach across 3 to walk, climb, or ski diagonally up or down a slope ▷ *n* 4 something being or lying across, such as a crossbar 5 the act or an instance of traversing or crossing 6 a path or road across ▷ *adj* 7 being or lying across ▶ HISTORY Latin *transversus* turned across > **traversal** *n*

travesty *n, pl* **-ties** 1 a grotesque imitation or mockery: *a travesty of justice* ▷ *vb* **-ties, -tying, -tied** 2 to make or be a travesty of ▶ HISTORY French *travesti* disguised

travois (trav-**voy**) *n, pl* **-vois** (-**voyz**) *Canad* a sled used for dragging logs ▶ HISTORY Canadian French

trawl *n* 1 a large net, usually in the shape of a sock or bag, dragged at deep levels behind a fishing boat ▷ *vb* 2 to fish using such a net ▶ HISTORY Middle Dutch *traghelen* to drag

trawler *n* a ship used for trawling

tray *n* 1 a flat board of wood, plastic, or metal, usually with a rim, on which things can be carried 2 an open receptacle for office correspondence ▶ HISTORY Old English *trieg*

TRC *n* (in S Africa) Truth and Reconciliation Commission: a commission which encourages people who committed human rights abuses or acts of terror during the apartheid era to reveal the truth about their crimes in return for immunity from prosecution

treacherous *adj* 1 disloyal and untrustworthy: *he was cruel, treacherous, and unscrupulous* 2 unreliable or dangerous, esp. because of sudden changes: *the tides here can be very treacherous* > **treacherously** *adv*

treachery *n, pl* **-eries** the act or an instance of wilful betrayal ▶ HISTORY Old French *trecherie*

treacle *n* a thick dark syrup obtained during the refining of sugar ▶ HISTORY Latin *theriaca* antidote to poison > **treacly** *adj*

tread *vb* **treading, trod; trodden** *or* **trod** 1 to set one's foot down on or in something: *he trod on some dog's dirt* 2 to crush or squash by treading (on): *treading on a biscuit* 3 to walk along (a path or road) 4 **tread carefully** *or* **warily** to proceed in a delicate or tactful manner 5 **tread water** to stay afloat in an upright position by moving the legs in a walking motion ▷ *n* 6 a way of walking or the sound of walking: *he walked, with a heavy tread, up the stairs* 7 the top surface of a step in a staircase 8 the pattern of grooves in the outer surface of a tyre that helps it grip the road 9 the part of a shoe that is generally in contact with the ground ▶ HISTORY Old English *tredan*

treadle (**tred**-dl) *n* a lever operated by the foot to turn a wheel ▶ HISTORY Old English *tredan* to tread

treadmill *n* 1 (formerly) an apparatus turned by the weight of men or animals climbing steps on a revolving cylinder or wheel 2 a dreary routine: *they are chained to the treadmill of a job* 3 an exercise machine that consists of a continuous moving belt on which to walk or jog

treason *n* 1 betrayal of one's sovereign or country, esp. by attempting to overthrow the government 2 any treachery or betrayal ▶ HISTORY Latin *traditio* a handing over > **treasonable** *adj* > **treasonous** *adj*

treasure *n* 1 a collection of wealth, esp. in the form of money, precious metals, or gems 2 a valuable painting, ornament, or other object: *the museum has many art treasures* 3 *informal* a person who is highly valued: *she can turn her hand to anything, she's a perfect treasure* ▷ *vb* **-uring, -ured** 4 to cherish (someone or something) ▶ HISTORY Greek *thēsauros*

treasurer *n* a person appointed to look after the funds of a society or other organization

treasure-trove *n law* any articles, such as coins or valuable objects, found hidden and without any evidence of ownership ▶ HISTORY Anglo-French *tresor trové* treasure found

treasury *n, pl* **-uries** 1 a storage place for treasure 2 the revenues or funds of a government or organization

Treasury *n* (in various countries) the government department in charge of finance

treat *vb* 1 to deal with or regard in a certain manner: *her love for a man who treats her abominably* 2 to attempt to cure or lessen the symptoms of (an illness or injury or a person suffering from it): *the drug is prescribed to treat asthma* 3 to subject to a chemical or industrial process: *the wood should be treated with a preservative* 4 to provide (someone) with something as a treat: *I'll treat you to an ice cream* 5 **treat of** to deal with (something) in writing or speaking: *this book treats of a most abstruse subject* ▷ *n* 6 a celebration, entertainment, gift, or meal given for or to someone and paid for by someone else 7 any delightful surprise or specially pleasant occasion ▶ HISTORY Old French *tretier* > **treatable** *adj*

treatise (**treat**-izz) *n* a formal piece of writing that deals systematically with a particular subject ▶ HISTORY Anglo-French *tretiz*

treatment *n* 1 the medical or surgical care given to a patient 2 a way of handling a person or thing: *the party has had unfair treatment in the press*

treaty *n, pl* **-ties** 1 a formal written agreement between two or more states, such as an alliance or trade arrangement: *the Treaty of Rome established the Common Market* 2 an agreement between two parties concerning the purchase of property ▶ HISTORY Old French *traité*

Treaty of Versailles (ver-**sigh**) *n history* the treaty of 1919 imposed upon Germany by the Allies, except for the USA and the Soviet Union

treble *adj* 1 three times as much or as many 2 of or denoting a soprano voice or part or a high-pitched instrument ▷ *n* 3 a soprano voice or part or a high-pitched instrument 4 of the highest range of musical notes: *these loudspeakers give excellent treble*

t

reproduction ▷ vb **-bling, -bled** 5 to make or become three times as much or as many: *sales have trebled in three years* ▶ HISTORY Latin *triplus* threefold > **trebly** *adv*

treble clef *n music* the clef that establishes G a fifth above middle C as being on the second line of the staff

tree *n* 1 any large woody perennial plant with a distinct trunk and usually having leaves and branches. *Related adjective:* **arboreal** 2 See **family tree, shoetree** 3 **at the top of the tree** in the highest position of a profession ▶ HISTORY Old English *trēow* > **treeless** *adj*

tree creeper *n* a small songbird of the N hemisphere that creeps up trees to feed on insects

tree diagram *n maths* a branching diagram showing the probability of various events

tree fern *n* any of numerous large tropical ferns with a trunklike stem

tree kangaroo *n* a tree-living kangaroo of New Guinea and N Australia

tree line *n* same as **timber line**

tree surgery *n* the treatment of damaged trees by filling cavities, applying braces, etc. > **tree surgeon** *n*

tree tomato *n* same as **tamarillo**

trefoil (**tref**-foil) *n* 1 a plant, such as clover, with leaves divided into three smaller leaves 2 *archit* a carved ornament with a shape like such leaves ▶ HISTORY Latin *trifolium* three-leaved herb > **trefoiled** *adj*

trek *n* 1 a long and often difficult journey, esp. on foot 2 *S African* a journey or stage of a journey, esp. a migration by ox wagon ▷ vb **trekking, trekked** 3 to make a trek ▶ HISTORY Afrikaans

trellis *n* a frame made of vertical and horizontal strips of wood, esp. one used to support climbing plants ▶ HISTORY Old French *treliz* fabric of open texture > **trelliswork** *n*

tremble *vb* **-bling, -bled** 1 to shake with short slight movements: *her hands trembled uncontrollably; he felt the ground trembling beneath him* 2 to experience fear or anxiety: *his parents trembled with apprehension about his future* 3 (of the voice) to sound uncertain or unsteady, for instance through pain or emotion ▷ *n* 4 the act or an instance of trembling ▶ HISTORY Latin *tremere* > **trembling** *adj*

tremendous *adj* 1 very large or impressive: *a tremendous amount of money* 2 very exciting or unusual: *a tremendous feeling of elation* 3 very good or pleasing: *my wife has given me tremendous support* ▶ HISTORY Latin *tremendus* terrible > **tremendously** *adv*

tremolo *n, pl* **-los** *music* 1 (in playing the violin or other stringed instrument) the rapid repetition of a note or notes to produce a trembling effect 2 (in singing) a fluctuation in pitch ▶ HISTORY Italian: quavering

tremor *n* 1 an involuntary shudder or vibration: *the slight tremor of excitement* 2 a minor earthquake ▶ HISTORY Latin

tremulous *adj literary* trembling, as from fear or excitement: *I managed a tremulous smile* ▶ HISTORY Latin *tremere* to shake > **tremulously** *adv*

trench *n* 1 a long narrow ditch in the ground, such as one for laying a pipe in 2 a long deep ditch used by soldiers for protection in a war: *my grandfather fought in the trenches in the First World War* ▷ *adj* 3 of or involving military trenches: *trench warfare* ▶ HISTORY Old French *trenche* something cut

trenchant *adj* 1 keen or incisive: *a trenchant screenplay* 2 vigorous and effective: *the prime minister's trenchant adoption of this issue* ▶ HISTORY Old French: cutting > **trenchancy** *n*

trench coat *n* a belted raincoat similar in style to a military officer's coat

trencher *n history* a wooden board on which food was served or cut ▶ HISTORY Old French *trencheoir*

trencherman *n, pl* **-men** a person who enjoys food; hearty eater

trench warfare *n* a type of warfare in which opposing armies face each other in entrenched positions

trend *n* 1 general tendency or direction: *an accelerating trend towards part-time employment* 2 fashionable style: *she set a trend for wearing lingerie as outer garments* ▷ vb 3 to take a certain trend 4 to be widely discussed on a social media site ▶ HISTORY Old English *trendan* to turn

trendsetter *n* a person or thing that creates, or may create, a new fashion > **trendsetting** *adj*

trendy *informal adj* **trendier, trendiest** 1 consciously fashionable: *a flat in Glasgow's trendy West End* ▷ *n, pl* **trendies** 2 a trendy person: *a media trendy* > **trendily** *adv* > **trendiness** *n*

trepidation *n formal* a state of fear or anxiety ▶ HISTORY Latin *trepidatio*

trespass *vb* 1 to go onto somebody else's property without permission ▷ *n* 2 the act or an instance of trespassing 3 *old-fashioned* a sin or wrong-doing ▷ See also **trespass on** ▶ HISTORY Old French *trespas* a passage > **trespasser** *n*

trespass on *or* **upon** *vb formal* to take unfair advantage of (someone's friendship, patience, etc.): *I won't trespass upon your hospitality any longer*

tresses *pl n* a woman's long flowing hair ▶ HISTORY Old French *trece*

trestle *n* 1 a support for one end of a table or beam, consisting of two rectangular frameworks or sets of legs which are joined at the top but not the bottom 2 Also called: **trestle table** a table consisting of a board supported by a trestle at each end ▶ HISTORY Old French *trestel*

trevally (**trih-val**-lee) *n, pl* **-lies** *Austral & NZ* any of various food and game fishes ▶ HISTORY probably alteration of *cavalla*, species of tropical fish

trews *pl n chiefly Brit* close-fitting trousers of tartan cloth ▶ HISTORY Scottish Gaelic *triubhas*

tri- *combining form* 1 three or thrice: *trilingual* 2 occurring every three: *triweekly* ▶ HISTORY Latin *tres*

triad *n* 1 a group of three 2 *music* a three-note chord consisting of a note and the third and fifth above it ▶ HISTORY Greek *trias* > **triadic** *adj*

Triad *n* a Chinese secret society involved in criminal activities, such as drug trafficking

trial *n* **1** *law* an investigation of a case in front of a judge to decide whether a person is innocent or guilty of a crime by questioning him or her and considering the evidence **2** the act or an instance of trying or proving; test or experiment: *the new drug is undergoing clinical trials* **3** an annoying or frustrating person or thing: *young children can be a great trial at times* **4** a motorcycling competition in which the skills of the riders are tested over rough ground **5 trials** a sporting competition for individual people or animals: *horse trials* **6 on trial a** undergoing trial, esp. before a court of law **b** being tested, for example before a commitment to purchase: *I only have the car out on trial* ▷ *adj* **7** on a temporary basis while being tried out or tested: *a trial run* ▷ *vb* **8** to test or make experimental use of: *the idea has been trialled in several schools* ▶ HISTORY Anglo-French *trier* to try

trial and error *n* a method of discovery based on practical experiment and experience rather than on theory: *raising her children has been a matter of trial and error*

trial balance *n* *book-keeping* a statement of all the debit and credit balances in the double-entry ledger

triallist *or* **trialist** *n* **1** a person who takes part in a competition **2** *sport* a person who takes part in a preliminary match or heat held to determine selection for a team or event

triangle *n* **1** a geometric figure with three sides and three angles **2** any object shaped like a triangle: *a triangle of streets running up from the river* **3** *music* a percussion instrument that consists of a metal bar bent into a triangular shape, played by striking it with a metal stick **4** any situation involving three people or points of view: *an awkward love triangle* ▶ HISTORY TRI- + Latin *angulus* corner > **triangular** *adj*

triangulate *vb* **-lating, -lated** to survey (an area) by dividing it into triangles

triangulation *n* a method of surveying in which an area is divided into triangles, one side (the base line) and all angles of which are measured and the lengths of the other lines calculated by trigonometry

Triassic *adj* *geol* of the period of geological time about 230 million years ago ▶ HISTORY Latin *trias* triad

tribalism *n* loyalty to a tribe, esp. as opposed to a modern political entity such as a state

tribe *n* **1** a group of families or clans believed to have a common ancestor **2** *informal* a group of people who do the same type of thing: *a tribe of German yachtsmen* ▶ HISTORY Latin *tribus* > **tribal** *adj*

tribesman *n, pl* **-men** a member of a tribe

tribulation *n* great distress: *the tribulations of a deserted wife* ▶ HISTORY Latin *tribulare* to afflict

tribunal *n* **1** a special court or committee that is appointed to deal with a particular problem: *an industrial tribunal investigating allegations of unfair dismissal* **2** a court of justice ▶ HISTORY Latin *tribunus* tribune

tribune *n* **1** a person who upholds public rights **2** (in ancient Rome) an officer elected by the plebs to protect their interests ▶ HISTORY Latin *tribunus*

tributary *n, pl* **-taries 1** a stream or river that flows into a larger one: *Frankfurt lies on the River Main, a tributary of the Rhine* **2** a person, nation, or people that pays tribute ▷ *adj* **3** (of a stream or river) flowing into a larger stream **4** paying tribute: *Egypt was formerly a tributary province of the Turkish Empire*

tribute *n* **1** something given, done, or said as a mark of respect or admiration **2** a payment by one ruler or state to another, usually as an acknowledgment of submission **3** something that shows the merits of a particular quality of a person or thing: *the car's low fuel consumption is a tribute to the quality of its engine* ▶ HISTORY Latin *tributum*

trice *n* **in a trice** in a moment: *she was back in a trice* ▶ HISTORY originally, at one tug, from *trice* to haul up

triceps *n* the muscle at the back of the upper arm ▶ HISTORY Latin

trichology (trick-**ol**-a-jee) *n* the branch of medicine concerned with the hair and its diseases ▶ HISTORY Greek *thrix* hair > **trichologist** *n*

trichromatic *or* **trichromic** *adj* **1** having or involving three colours **2** of or having normal colour vision > **trichromatism** *n*

trick *n* **1** a deceitful or cunning action or plan: *she was willing to use any dirty trick to get what she wanted* **2** a joke or prank: *he loves playing tricks on his sister* **3** a clever way of doing something, learned from experience: *an old campers' trick is to use three thin blankets rather than one thick one* **4** an illusory or magical feat or device **5** a simple feat learned by an animal or person **6** a deceptive illusion: *a trick of the light* **7** a habit or mannerism: *she had a trick of saying 'oh dear'* **8** *cards* a batch of cards played in turn and won by the person playing the highest card **9 do the trick** *informal* to produce the desired result **10 how's tricks?** *slang* how are you? ▷ *vb* **11** to defraud, deceive, or cheat (someone) ▶ HISTORY Old French *trique* > **trickery** *n*

trickle *vb* **-ling, -led 1** to flow or cause to flow in a thin stream or drops: *tears trickled down her cheeks* **2** to move slowly or in small groups: *voters trickled to the polls* ▷ *n* **3** a thin, irregular, or slow flow of something: *a trickle of blood* ▶ HISTORY probably imitative

trickle-down *adj* of the theory that granting concessions like tax cuts to the rich will benefit all levels of society by stimulating the economy

trickster *n* a person who deceives or plays tricks

tricky *adj* **trickier, trickiest 1** involving snags or difficulties: *a tricky task* **2** needing careful handling: *a tricky situation* **3** sly or wily: *a tricky customer* > **trickily** *adv* > **trickiness** *n*

t

tricolour *or US* **tricolor** (**trick**-kol-lor) *n* a flag with three equal stripes in different colours, esp. the French or Irish national flags

tricuspid *adj anat* having three points, cusps, or segments: *a tricuspid valve*

tricycle *n* a three-wheeled cycle > **tricyclist** *n*

trident *n* a three-pronged spear ▶ HISTORY Latin *tridens* three-pronged

triennial *adj* occurring every three years ▶ HISTORY TRI- + Latin *annus* year > **triennially** *adv*

trifle¹ *n* **1** a thing of little or no value or significance **2** *Brit, Austral & NZ* a cold dessert made of sponge cake spread with jam or fruit, soaked in sherry, covered with custard and cream **3 a trifle** to a small extent or degree; slightly: *he is a trifle eccentric* ▶ HISTORY Old French *trufle* mockery

trifle² *vb* **trifling, trifled • trifle with** to treat (a person or his or her feelings) with disdain or disregard

trifling *adj* insignificant, petty, or frivolous: *a trifling misunderstanding*

trig. trigonometry

trigger *n* **1** a small lever that releases a catch on a gun or machine **2** any event that sets a course of action in motion: *his murder was the trigger for a night of rioting* ▷ *vb* **3** Also: **trigger off** to set (an action or process) in motion: *various factors can trigger off a migraine* ▶ HISTORY Dutch *trekker*

trigger-happy *adj informal* too ready or willing to use guns or violence: *trigger-happy border guards*

trigonometric function *n maths* a function of an angle expressed as a ratio of two of the sides of a right-angled triangle containing the angle

trigonometry *n* the branch of mathematics concerned with the relations of sides and angles of triangles, which is used in surveying, navigation, etc. ▶ HISTORY Greek *trigōnon* triangle

trig point *n* a point on a hilltop, etc., used for triangulation by a surveyor

trike *n informal* a tricycle

trilateral *adj* having three sides

trilby *n, pl* **-bies** a man's soft felt hat with an indented crown ▶ HISTORY after *Trilby*, the heroine of a novel by George Du Maurier

trill *n* **1** *music* a rapid alternation between a note and the note above it **2** a shrill warbling sound made by some birds: *the canary's high trills* ▷ *vb* **3** (of a bird) to make a shrill warbling sound **4** (of a person) to talk or laugh in a high-pitched musical voice ▶ HISTORY Italian *trillo*

trillion *n* **-lions** *or* **-lion 1** the number represented as one followed by twelve zeros (10^{12}); a million million **2** (in Britain, originally) the number represented as one followed by eighteen zeros (10^{18}); a million million million ▷ *adj* **3** amounting to a trillion: *a trillion dollars* ▶ HISTORY French > **trillionth** *n, adj*

trillium *n* a plant of Asia and North America that has three leaves at the top of the stem with a single white, pink, or purple three-petalled flower ▶ HISTORY New Latin

trilobite (**trile**-oh-bite) *n* a small prehistoric marine arthropod, found as a fossil ▶ HISTORY Greek *trilobos* having three lobes

trilogy (**trill**-a-jee) *n, pl* **-gies** a series of three books, plays, etc. which form a related group but are each complete works in themselves ▶ HISTORY Greek *trilogia*

trim *adj* **trimmer, trimmest 1** neat and spruce in appearance: *trim lace curtains* **2** attractively slim: *his body was trim and athletic* ▷ *vb* **trimming, trimmed 3** to make (something) neater by cutting it slightly without changing its basic shape: *his white beard was neatly trimmed* **4** to adorn or decorate (something, such as a garment) with lace, ribbons, etc.: *a cotton camisole neatly trimmed with lace* **5 a** to adjust the balance of (a ship or aircraft) by shifting cargo, etc. **b** to adjust (a ship's sails) to take advantage of the wind **6** to reduce or lower the size of: *the company has trimmed its pretax profits forecast by $2.3 million* **7** to alter (a plan or policy) by removing parts which seem unnecessary or unpopular: *the government would rather trim its policies than lose the election* **8 trim off** *or* **away** to cut so as to remove: *trim off most of the fat before cooking the meat* ▷ *n* **9** a decoration or adornment: *a black suit with scarlet trim* **10** the upholstery and decorative facings of a car's interior **11** good physical condition: *he had always kept himself in trim* **12** a haircut that neatens but does not alter the existing hairstyle ▶ HISTORY Old English *trymman* to strengthen

trimaran (**trime**-a-ran) *n* a boat with one smaller hull on each side of the main hull ▶ HISTORY tri- + (cata)maran

trimeter *n poetry* a verse line consisting of three metrical feet

trimming *n* **1** an extra piece added to a garment for decoration: *a pink nightie with lace trimming* **2 trimmings** usual or traditional accompaniments: *bacon and eggs with all the trimmings*

Trimurti *n* the three chief gods of later Hinduism: Brahma, Vishnu, and Siva ▶ HISTORY Sanskrit

Trini *adj, n informal* same as **Trinidadian**

Trinidadian *adj* **1** of Trinidad ▷ *n* **2** a person from Trinidad

Trinitarian *n* **1** a person who believes in the doctrine of the Trinity ▷ *adj* **2** of or relating to the Trinity > **Trinitarianism** *n*

trinitrotoluene *n* the full name for **TNT**

trinity *n, pl* **-ties** a group of three people or things ▶ HISTORY Latin *trinus* triple

Trinity *n Christianity* the union of three persons, the Father, Son, and Holy Spirit, in one God

trinket *n* a small or worthless ornament or piece of jewellery ▶ HISTORY origin unknown

trio *n, pl* **trios 1** a group of three people or things **2** a group of three instrumentalists or singers **3** a piece of music for three performers ▶ HISTORY Italian

t

trip *n* **1** a journey to a place and back, esp. for pleasure: *they took a coach trip round the island* **2** a false step; stumble **3** the act of causing someone to stumble or fall by catching his or her foot with one's own **4** *informal* a hallucinogenic drug experience **5** a catch on a mechanism that acts as a switch ▷ *vb* **tripping, tripped 6** Also: **trip up** to stumble or cause (someone) to stumble **7** Also: **trip up** to trap or catch (someone) in a mistake **8** to walk lightly and quickly, with a dancelike motion: *I could see Amelia tripping along beside him* **9** *informal* to experience the effects of a hallucinogenic drug ▶ HISTORY Old French *triper* to tread

tripartite *adj* involving or composed of three people or parts: *tripartite system of government* > **tripartism** *n*

tripe *n* **1** the stomach lining of a cow or pig used as a food **2** *Brit, Austral & NZ, informal* nonsense or rubbish ▶ HISTORY Old French

tripeptide *n* *biochem* a protein consisting of three linked amino acids

Tripitaka (trip-it-**tah**-ka) *n* the three collections of books making up the Buddhist scriptures ▶ HISTORY Pali (an ancient language of India) *tri* three + *pitaka* basket

triple *adj* **1** made up of three parts or things: *a triple murder* **2** (of musical time or rhythm) having three beats in each bar **3** three times as great or as much: *a triple brandy* ▷ *vb* **-pling, -pled 4** to make or become three times as much or as many: *the company has tripled its sales over the past five years* ▷ *n* **5** something that is, or contains, three times as much as normal **6** a group of three ▶ HISTORY Latin *triplus* > **triply** *adv*

Triple Entente *n* *history* the understanding between Britain, France, and Russia that developed between 1894 and 1907, which became a formal alliance on the outbreak of World War I

triple jump *n* an athletic event in which the competitor has to perform a hop, a step, and a jump in a continuous movement

triple point *n* *chem* the temperature and pressure at which a substance can exist as a solid, liquid, and gas

triplet *n* **1** one of three children born at one birth **2** a group of three musical notes played in the time that two would normally take **3** a group or set of three similar things

triplicate *adj* **1** triple ▷ *vb* **-cating, -cated 2** to multiply or be multiplied by three ▷ *n* **3 in triplicate** written out three times: *my request to interview the commander had to be made in triplicate* ▶ HISTORY Latin *triplicare* to triple > **triplication** *n*

tripod (**tripe**-pod) *n* **1** a three-legged stand to which a camera can be attached to hold it steady **2** a three-legged stool, table, etc. ▶ HISTORY TRI- + Greek *pous* a foot

tripos (**tripe**-poss) *n* *Brit* the final honours degree examinations at Cambridge University ▶ HISTORY Latin *tripus* tripod

tripper *n* *chiefly Brit* a tourist

triptych (**trip**-tick) *n* a set of three pictures or panels, usually hinged together and often used as an altarpiece ▶ HISTORY TRI- + Greek *ptux* plate

trireme (**try**-ream) *n* an ancient Greek warship with three rows of oars on each side ▶ HISTORY TRI- + Latin *remus* oar

trismus *n* *pathol* the state of being unable to open the mouth because of sustained contractions of the jaw muscles, caused by tetanus. Nontechnical name: **lockjaw** ▶ HISTORY Greek *trismos* a grinding

trite *adj* (of a remark or idea) commonplace and unoriginal ▶ HISTORY Latin *tritus* worn down

tritium *n* a radioactive isotope of hydrogen. Symbol: T or ^{3}H ▶ HISTORY Greek *tritos* third

triumph *n* **1** the feeling of great happiness resulting from a victory or major achievement **2** an outstanding success, achievement, or victory: *the concert was a musical triumph* **3** (in ancient Rome) a procession held in honour of a victorious general ▷ *vb* **4** to gain control or success: *triumphing over adversity* **5** to rejoice over a victory ▶ HISTORY Latin *triumphus* > **triumphal** *adj*

triumphant *adj* **1** feeling or displaying triumph: *her smile was triumphant* **2** celebrating a victory or success: *the general's triumphant tour round the city* > **triumphantly** *adv*

triumvir (try-**umm**-vir) *n* (esp. in ancient Rome) a member of a triumvirate ▶ HISTORY Latin

triumvirate (try-**umm**-vir-rit) *n* **1** a group of three people, organizations, etc. in joint control of something: *the triumvirate of great orchestras which dominates classical music in Europe* **2** (in ancient Rome) a board of three officials jointly responsible for some task

trivalent *adj* *chem* **1** having a valency of three **2** having three valencies > **trivalency** *n*

trivet (**triv**-vit) *n* **1** a three-legged stand for holding a pot, kettle, etc. over a fire **2** a short metal stand on which hot dishes are placed on a table ▶ HISTORY Old English *trefet*

trivia *n* petty and unimportant things or details

trivial *adj* of little importance: *a trivial matter* ▶ HISTORY Latin *trivialis* common > **triviality** *n* > **trivially** *adv*

trivialize *or* **-ise** *vb* **-izing, -ized** *or* **-ising, -ised** to make (something) seem less important or complex than it is

trochee (**troke**-ee) *n* *prosody* a metrical foot of one long and one short syllable ▶ HISTORY Greek *trekhein* to run > **trochaic** *adj*

trod *vb* the past tense and a past participle of **tread**

trodden *vb* a past participle of **tread**

troglodyte *n* a person who lives in a cave ▶ HISTORY Greek *trōglodutēs* one who enters caves

troika *n* **1** a Russian coach or sleigh drawn by three horses abreast **2** a group of three people in authority: *a troika of European foreign ministers* ▶ HISTORY Russian

Trojan *adj* **1** of ancient Troy or its people ▷ *n* **2** a person from ancient Troy **3** a hard-working person

t

Trojan Horse *n* **1** *Greek myth* the huge wooden hollow figure of a horse used by the Greeks to enter Troy **2** a trap or trick intended to undermine an enemy

troll¹ *n* (in Scandinavian folklore) a supernatural dwarf or giant that dwells in a cave or mountain ▶ HISTORY Old Norse: demon

troll² *vb* **1** *angling* to fish by dragging a lure through the water **2** to make deliberately provocative and offensive comments on social media ▷ *n* **3** a person who trolls on social media ▶ HISTORY Old French *troller* to run about

trolley *n* **1** *Brit* a small table on casters used for carrying food or drink **2** *Brit* a wheeled cart or stand used for moving heavy items, such as shopping in a supermarket or luggage at a railway station **3** *Brit* See **trolley bus 4** *US & Canad* See **trolley car 5** a device, such as a wheel that collects the current from an overhead wire, to drive the motor of an electric vehicle **6** *Brit & Austral* a low truck running on rails, used in factories, mines, etc. ▶ HISTORY probably from TROLL²

trolley bus *n* a bus powered by electricity from two overhead wires but not running on rails

trolley car *n* *US & Canad* same as **tram**

trollop *n* *derogatory* a promiscuous or slovenly woman ▶ HISTORY origin unknown

trombone *n* a brass musical instrument with a sliding tube which is moved in or out to alter the note played ▶ HISTORY Italian > **trombonist** *n*

trompe l'oeil (tromp **luh**-ee) *n, pl* **trompe l'oeils** (tromp **luh**-ee) **1** a painting, etc. giving a convincing illusion that the objects represented are real **2** an effect of this kind ▶ HISTORY French, literally: deception of the eye

troop *n* **1** a large group: *a troop of dogs* **2 troops** soldiers: *troops have been maintaining an unusually high profile* **3** a subdivision of a cavalry or armoured regiment **4** a large group of Scouts made up of several patrols ▷ *vb* **5** to move in a crowd: *we trooped into the room after her* **6** *mil, chiefly Brit & Austral* to parade (a flag or banner) ceremonially: *trooping the colour* ▶ HISTORY French *troupe*

trooper *n* **1** a soldier in a cavalry regiment **2** *US & Austral* a mounted policeman **3** *US* a state policeman **4** a cavalry horse **5** *informal, chiefly Brit* a troopship

troopship *n* a ship used to transport military personnel

trope *n* a word or expression used in a figurative sense ▶ HISTORY Greek *tropos* style, turn

trophic *adj* *biol* of or relating to nutrition ▶ HISTORY Greek *trophikos*, from *trophē* food, from *trephein* to feed

trophic level *n* *biol* position (of an organism) in the food chain, as determined by whether it is a primary producer, a primary consumer, a secondary consumer, or a tertiary consumer

trophy *n, pl* **-phies 1** a cup, shield, etc. given as a prize **2** a memento of success, esp. one taken in war or hunting: *stuffed animal heads and other hunting trophies* ▷ *adj* **3** *informal* regarded as a highly desirable symbol of wealth or success: *a trophy wife* ▶ HISTORY Greek *tropaion*

tropic *n* **1** either of the lines of latitude at about 23½°N (**tropic of Cancer**) and 23½°S (**tropic of Capricorn**) of the equator **2 the tropics** that part of the earth's surface between the tropics of Cancer and Capricorn: *the intense heat and humidity of the tropics* ▶ HISTORY Greek *tropos* a turn; from the belief that the sun turned back at the solstices

-tropic *combining form physiol* turning or developing in response to a certain stimulus: *heliotropic*

tropical *adj* belonging to, typical of, or located in, the tropics: *tropical rainforests* > **tropically** *adv*

tropism *n* the tendency of a plant or animal to turn or curve in response to an external stimulus ▶ HISTORY Greek *tropos* a turn

troposphere *n* the lowest layer of the earth's atmosphere, about 18 kilometres (11 miles) thick at the equator to about 6 km (4 miles) at the Poles ▶ HISTORY Greek *tropos* a turn + SPHERE

trot *vb* **trotting, trotted 1** (of a horse) to move in a manner faster than a walk but slower than a gallop, in which diagonally opposite legs come down together **2** (of a person) to move fairly quickly, with small quick steps ▷ *n* **3** a medium-paced gait of a horse, in which diagonally opposite legs come down together **4** a steady brisk pace **5 on the trot** *informal* one after the other: *ten years on the trot* **6 the trots** *slang* diarrhoea ▷ See also **trot out** ▶ HISTORY Old French

Trot *n* *chiefly Brit, informal* a follower of Trotsky

troth (rhymes with **growth**) *n* *archaic* **1** a pledge of fidelity, esp. a betrothal **2 in troth** truly ▶ HISTORY Old English *trēowth*

trot out *vb* *informal* to repeat (old information or ideas) without fresh thought: *the government trots out the same excuse every time*

Trotskyist *or* **Trotskyite** *adj* **1** of the theories of Leon Trotsky (1879–1940), Russian Communist, which call for a worldwide revolution by the proletariat ▷ *n* **2** a supporter of Trotsky or his theories > **Trotskyism** *n*

trotter *n* **1** the foot of a pig **2** a horse that is specially trained to trot fast

troubadour (**troo**-bad-oor) *n* a travelling poet and singer in S France or N Italy from the 11th to the 13th century who wrote chiefly on courtly love ▶ HISTORY French

trouble *n* **1** difficulties or problems: *I'd trouble finding somewhere to park* **2** a cause of distress, disturbance, or pain: *we must be sensitive to the troubles of other people* **3** disease or a problem with one's health: *ear trouble* **4** a state of disorder, ill-feeling, or unrest: *the police had orders to intervene at the first sign of trouble* **5** effort or exertion to do something: *they didn't even take the trouble to see the film before banning it* **6** a personal weakness or cause of annoyance: *his trouble is that he's constitutionally jealous* **7 in trouble a** likely to be punished for something one has done: *in trouble* with the public prosecutor **b** pregnant when not married **8 more trouble than it's worth** involving a lot of time or effort for very little reward: *making your own pasta is more trouble than it's worth* ▷ *vb* **-bling, -bled 9** to cause trouble to **10** to make an effort or exert oneself: *he dismissed the letters as forgeries without troubling to examine them* **11** to cause inconvenience or discomfort to: *sorry to trouble you!* ▶ HISTORY Old French *troubler* > **troubled** *adj*

troublemaker *n* a person who causes trouble, esp. between people > **troublemaking** *adj, n*

troubleshooter *n* a person employed to locate and deal with faults or problems > **troubleshooting** *n, adj*

troublesome *adj* causing trouble

trouble spot *n* a place where there is frequent fighting or violence: *the Balkans have long been one of the major European trouble spots*

troublous *adj literary* unsettled or agitated

trough (troff) *n* **1** a long open container, esp. one for animals' food or water **2** a narrow channel between two waves or ridges **3** a low point in a pattern that has regular high and low points: *the trough of the slump in pupil numbers was in 1985* **4** *meteorol* a long narrow area of low pressure **5** a narrow channel or gutter ▶ HISTORY Old English *trōh*

trounce *vb* **trouncing, trounced** to defeat (someone) utterly ▶ HISTORY origin unknown

troupe (troop) *n* a company of actors or other performers ▶ HISTORY French

trouper *n* **1** a member of a troupe **2** an experienced person: *like the old trouper he is, he timed his entry to perfection*

trouser *adj* **1** of or relating to trousers: *trouser legs* ▷ *vb* **2** *Brit, slang* to take (something, esp. money), often surreptitiously or unlawfully

trousers *pl n* a garment that covers the body from the waist to the ankles or knees with a separate tube-shaped section for each leg ▶ HISTORY Scottish Gaelic *triubhas* trews

trousseau (troo-so) *n, pl* **-seaux** (-so) the clothes, linen, and other possessions collected by a bride for her marriage ▶ HISTORY Old French

trout *n, pl* **trout** or **trouts** any of various game fishes related to the salmon and found chiefly in fresh water in northern regions ▶ HISTORY Old English *trūht*

trowel *n* **1** a hand tool resembling a small spade with a curved blade, used by gardeners for lifting plants, etc. **2** a similar tool with a flat metal blade, used for spreading cement or plaster on a surface ▶ HISTORY Latin *trulla* a scoop

troy weight or **troy** *n* a system of weights used for precious metals and gemstones in which one pound equals twelve ounces ▶ HISTORY after the city of *Troyes*, France, where first used

truant *n* **1** a pupil who stays away from school without permission **2 play truant** to stay away from school without permission ▷ *adj* **3** being or

relating to a truant: *a truant schoolkid* ▶ HISTORY Old French: vagabond > **truancy** *n*

truce *n* a temporary agreement to stop fighting or quarreling ▶ HISTORY plural of Old English *trēow* pledge

truck¹ *n* **1** *Brit* a railway wagon for carrying freight **2** a large motor vehicle for transporting heavy loads **3** any wheeled vehicle used to move goods ▷ *vb* **4** *chiefly US* to transport goods in a truck ▶ HISTORY perhaps from *truckle* a small wheel

truck² *n* **1** *history* the payment of wages in goods rather than in money **2 have no truck with** to refuse to be involved with: *the opposition will have no truck with the planned cut in pensions* ▶ HISTORY Old French *troquer* (unattested) to barter

truckie *n Austral & NZ, informal* a truck driver

truckle bed *n chiefly Brit* a low bed on wheels, stored under a larger bed

truculent (truck-yew-lent) *adj* defiantly aggressive or bad-tempered ▶ HISTORY Latin *trux* fierce > **truculence** *n* > **truculently** *adv*

trudge *vb* **trudging, trudged 1** to walk or plod heavily or wearily ▷ *n* **2** a long tiring walk ▶ HISTORY origin unknown

true *adj* **truer, truest 1** in accordance with the truth or facts; factual: *not all of the stories about her are true* **2** real or genuine: *he didn't want to reveal his true feelings* **3** faithful and loyal: *a true friend* **4** accurate or precise: *he looked through the telescopic sight until he was convinced his aim was true* **5** (of a compass bearing) according to the earth's geographical rather than magnetic poles: *true north* **6 come true** to actually happen: *fortunately his gloomy prediction didn't come true* **7 in** or **out of true** in or not in correct alignment ▷ *adv* **8** truthfully or rightly: *I'd like to move to Edinburgh, true, but I'd need to get a job there first* ▶ HISTORY Old English *trīewe*

true-blue *adj* **1** staunchly loyal ▷ *n* **true blue 2** *chiefly Brit & Austral* a staunch royalist or Conservative

truelove *n* the person that one loves

true north *n* the direction from any point along a meridian towards the North Pole

truffle *n* **1** a round fungus which grows underground and is regarded as a delicacy **2** Also called: **rum truffle** a sweet flavoured with chocolate or rum ▶ HISTORY French *truffe*

trug *n Brit* a long shallow basket for carrying garden tools, flowers, etc. ▶ HISTORY perhaps variant of *trough*

truism *n* a statement that is clearly true and well known

truly *adv* **1** in a true, just, or faithful manner **2** really: *a truly awful poem*

trump¹ *n* **1** same as **trump card** ▷ *vb* **2** *cards* to beat a card by playing a card which belongs to a suit which outranks it **3** to outdo or surpass: *she trumped his news by announcing that she had been picked for the Olympic team* ▷ See also **trumps** ▶ HISTORY variant of *triumph*

t

trump² *n archaic or literary* **1** a trumpet or the sound produced by one **2 the last trump** the final trumpet call on the Day of Judgment ▶ HISTORY Old French *trompe*

trump card *n* **1** any card from the suit that ranks higher than any other suit in one particular game **2** an advantage, weapon, etc. that is kept in reserve until needed: *the President hoped to use his experience of foreign affairs as a trump card in the election*

trumped up *adj* (of charges, excuses, etc.) made up in order to deceive

trumpery *n, pl* **-eries** **1** something useless or worthless ▷ *adj* **2** useless or worthless ▶ HISTORY Old French *tromperie* deceit

trumpet *n* **1** a valved brass musical instrument consisting of a narrow tube ending in a flare **2** a loud sound such as that of a trumpet: *the elephant gave a loud trumpet* **3 blow one's own trumpet** to boast about one's own skills or good qualities ▷ *vb* **-peting, -peted** **4** to proclaim or state forcefully: *almost every one of the party's loudly trumpeted election claims is untrue* **5** (of an elephant) to make a loud cry ▶ HISTORY Old French *trompette* > **trumpeter** *n*

trumps *pl n* **1** *cards* any one of the four suits that outranks all the other suits for the duration of a deal or game **2 turn up trumps** (of a person) to bring about a happy or successful conclusion, esp. unexpectedly

truncate *vb* **-cating, -cated** to shorten by cutting ▶ HISTORY Latin *truncare* > **truncated** *adj* > **truncation** *n*

truncheon *n chiefly Brit* a stick carried by a police officer as a weapon ▶ HISTORY Old French *tronchon* stump

trundle *vb* **-dling, -dled** to move heavily on or as if on wheels: *a bus trundled along the drive* ▶ HISTORY Old English *tryndel* circular or spherical object

trundle bed *n* *US, Canad & NZ* a low bed on wheels, stored under a larger bed

trundler *n* **1** *NZ* a golf or shopping trolley **2** a child's pushchair

trunk *n* **1** the main stem of a tree **2** a large strong case or box used to contain clothes when travelling and for storage **3** a person's body excluding the head, neck, and limbs; torso **4** the long nose of an elephant **5** *US* the boot of a car ▷ See also **trunks** ▶ HISTORY Latin *truncus*

trunk call *n* *old-fashioned* a long-distance telephone call

trunk line *n* the main route or routes on a railway

trunk road *n* *Brit* a main road, esp. one maintained by the central government

trunks *pl n* shorts worn by a man for swimming

trunk stream *n geog* the main stream in a drainage basin

truss *vb* **1** *written* to tie or bind (someone) up **2** to bind the wings and legs of (a fowl) before cooking ▷ *n* **3** *med* a device for holding a hernia in place **4** a framework of wood or metal used to support a roof, bridge, etc. **5** a cluster of flowers or fruit

growing at the end of a single stalk ▶ HISTORY Old French *trousse*

trust *vb* **1** to believe that (someone) is honest and means no harm: *my father warned me never to trust strangers* **2** to feel that (something) is safe and reliable: *I don't trust those new gadgets* **3** to entrust (someone) with important information or valuables: *she's not somebody I would trust with this sort of secret* **4** to believe that (someone) is likely to do something safely and reliably: *I wouldn't trust anyone else to look after my child properly* **5** to believe (a story, account, etc.) **6** to expect, hope, or suppose: *I trust you've made your brother welcome here* ▷ *n* **7** confidence in the truth, worth, reliability, etc. of a person or thing; faith: *he knew that his father had great trust in him* **8** the obligation of someone in a responsible position: *he was in a position of trust as her substitute father* **9 a** a legal arrangement whereby one person looks after property, money, etc. on another's behalf **b** property that is the subject of such an arrangement **10** (in Britain) a self-governing hospital, group of hospitals, or other body that operates as an independent commercial unit within the National Health Service **11** *chiefly US & Canad* a group of companies joined together to control the market for any commodity ▷ *adj* **12** of or relating to a trust or trusts: *trust status* ▶ HISTORY Old Norse *traust* help, support, confidence

trustee *n* **1** a person who administers property on someone else's behalf **2** a member of a board that manages the affairs of an institution or organization

trustful *or* **trusting** *adj* characterized by a readiness to trust others > **trustfully** *or* **trustingly** *adv*

trust fund *n* money, securities, etc. held in trust

trustworthy *adj* (of a person) honest, reliable, or dependable

trusty *adj* **trustier, trustiest** **1** faithful or reliable: *his trusty steed* ▷ *n, pl* **trusties** **2** a trustworthy convict to whom special privileges are granted

truth *n* **1** the quality of being true, genuine, or factual: *there is no truth in the allegations* **2** something that is true: *he finally learned the truth about his parents' marriage* **3** a proven or verified fact, principle, etc.: *some profound truths about biology have come to light* ▶ HISTORY Old English *triewth*

truthful *adj* **1** telling the truth; honest **2** true; based on facts: *a truthful answer* > **truthfully** *adv* > **truthfulness** *n*

try *vb* **tries, trying, tried** **1** to make an effort or attempt: *you must try to understand* **2** to sample or test (something) to see how enjoyable, good, or useful it is: *I tried smoking once but didn't like it* **3** to put strain or stress on (someone's patience) **4** to give pain, affliction, or vexation to: *sometimes when I've been sorely tried, my temper gets a little out of hand* **5 a** to investigate (a case) in a court of law **b** to hear evidence in order to determine the guilt or innocence of (a person) ▷ *n*, *pl* **tries 6** an attempt or effort **7** *rugby* a score made by placing the ball down behind the opposing team's goal line ▶ HISTORY Old French *trier* to sort

trying *adj* upsetting, difficult, or annoying

tryst *n* *archaic or literary* **1** an arrangement to meet, esp. secretly **2** a meeting, esp. a secret one with a lover, or the place where such a meeting takes place ▶ HISTORY Old French *triste* lookout post

tsar *or* **czar** (**zahr**) *n* (until 1917) the emperor of Russia. Also: **tzar** ▶ HISTORY Russian, ultimately from CAESAR > **tsarist** *or* **czarist** *n*

tsarevitch *or* **czarevitch** (**zahr**-rev-itch) *n* the eldest son of a Russian tsar

tsarina *or* **czarina** (zahr-**een**-a) *n* the wife of a Russian tsar

tsetse fly *or* **tzetze fly** (**tset**-see) *n* a bloodsucking African fly whose bite transmits disease, esp. sleeping sickness ▶ HISTORY Tswana (language of southern Africa) *tse tse*

T-shirt *or* **tee-shirt** *n* a short-sleeved casual shirt or top ▶ HISTORY T-shape formed when laid flat

tsotsi (**tsot**-see) *n* *S African* a Black street thug or gang member ▶ HISTORY perhaps from Nguni (language group of southern Africa) *tsotsa* to dress flashily

tsp. teaspoon

T-square *n* a T-shaped ruler used for drawing horizontal lines and to support set squares when drawing vertical and inclined lines

tsunami *n* a large, often destructive, sea wave, usually caused by an earthquake under the sea ▶ HISTORY Japanese

TT 1 teetotal **2** teetotaller **3** tuberculin-tested

tuatara (too-ah-**tah**-rah) *n* a large lizard-like New Zealand reptile ▶ HISTORY Māori *tua* back + *tara* spine

tub *n* **1** a low, wide, usually round container **2** a small plastic or cardboard container for ice cream, etc. **3** *chiefly US* same as **bath** (sense 1) **4** Also called: **tubful** the amount a tub will hold **5** a slow and uncomfortable boat or ship ▶ HISTORY Middle Dutch *tubbe*

tuba (**tube**-a) *n* a low-pitched brass musical instrument with valves ▶ HISTORY Latin

tubby *adj* **-bier, -biest** (of a person) fat and short > **tubbiness** *n*

tube *n* **1** a long hollow cylindrical object, used for the passage of fluids or as a container **2** a flexible cylinder of soft metal or plastic closed with a cap, used to hold substances such as toothpaste **3** *anat* any hollow cylindrical structure: *the Fallopian tubes* **4 the tube** *Brit* the underground railway system in London **5** *electronics* See **cathode-ray tube** **6** *slang, chiefly US* a television set ▶ HISTORY Latin *tubus* > **tubeless** *adj*

tuber (**tube**-er) *n* a fleshy underground root of a plant such as a potato ▶ HISTORY Latin: hump

tubercle (**tube**-er-kl) *n* **1** a small rounded swelling **2** any abnormal hard swelling, esp. one characteristic of tuberculosis ▶ HISTORY Latin *tuberculum* a little swelling

tubercular (tube-**berk**-yew-lar) *or* **tuberculous** *adj* **1** of or symptomatic of tuberculosis **2** of or relating to a tubercle

tuberculin (tube-**berk**-yew-lin) *n* a sterile liquid prepared from cultures of the tubercle bacillus and used in the diagnosis of tuberculosis

tuberculin-tested *adj* (of milk) produced by cows that have been certified as free of tuberculosis

tuberculosis (tube-berk-yew-**lohss**-iss) *n* an infectious disease characterized by the formation of tubercles, esp. in the lungs

tuberous (**tube**-er-uss) *adj* (of plants) forming, bearing, or resembling a tuber or tubers

tubing (**tube**-ing) *n* **1** a length of tube **2** a system of tubes

tubular (**tube**-yew-lar) *adj* **1** having the shape of a tube or tubes **2** of or relating to a tube or tubing

tubule (**tube**-yewl) *n* any small tubular structure, esp. in an animal or plant

TUC (in Britain and S Africa) Trades Union Congress

tuck *vb* **1** to push or fold into a small space or between two surfaces: *she tucked the letter into her handbag* **2** to thrust the loose ends or sides of (something) into a confining space, so as to make it neat and secure: *he tucked his shirt back into his trousers* **3** to make a tuck or tucks in (a garment) ▷ *n* **4** a pleat or fold in a part of a garment, usually stitched down **5** *Brit, informal* food, esp. cakes and sweets ▶ HISTORY Old English *tūcian* to torment

tuck away *vb* *informal* **1** to eat (a large amount of food) **2** to store (something) in a safe place: *we knew he had some money tucked away somewhere* **3** to have a quiet, rarely disturbed or visited location: *the chapel is tucked away in a side street*

tucker *n* **1** a detachable yoke of lace, linen, etc., formerly worn over the breast of a low-cut dress **2** *Austral & NZ, informal* food **3 one's best bib and tucker** *informal* one's best clothes

Tudor *adj* **1** of or in the reign of the English royal house ruling from 1485 to 1603 **2** denoting a style of architecture characterized by half-timbered houses: *a Tudor cottage*

Tues. Tuesday

Tuesday *n* the third day of the week ▶ HISTORY Old English *tīwesdæg* day of Tyr, Norse god

tufa (**tew**-fa) *n* a porous rock formed of calcium carbonate deposited from springs ▶ HISTORY Italian *tufo*

tuff *n* *geol* a porous rock formed from volcanic dust or ash ▶ HISTORY Old French *tuf*

tuffet *n* a small mound or low seat ▶ HISTORY from *tuft*

tuft *n* a bunch of feathers, grass, hair, threads, etc., held together at the base ▶ HISTORY probably from Old French *tufe* > **tufted** *adj* > **tufty** *adj*

tug *vb* **tugging, tugged 1** to pull or drag with a sharp or powerful movement: *she tugged at my arm* **2** to tow (a ship or boat) by means of a tug ▷ *n* **3** a strong pull or jerk **4** Also called: **tugboat** a boat with a powerful engine, used for towing barges, ships, etc. ▶ HISTORY Middle English *tuggen*

tuition *n* **1** instruction, esp. that received individually or in a small group **2** the payment for instruction, esp. in colleges or universities ▶ HISTORY Latin *tueri* to watch over

tulip *n* **1** a plant which produces bright cup-shaped flowers in spring **2** the flower or bulb

■ **WORD HISTORY**

■ 'Tulip' comes from Turkish *tülbend*, meaning

■ 'turban', because of the shape of the flowers.

tulip tree *n* a North American tree with tulip-shaped greenish-yellow flowers and long conelike fruits

tulle (**tewl**) *n* a fine net fabric of silk, rayon, etc., used to make evening dresses ▶ HISTORY French

tumble *vb* **-bling, -bled 1** to fall or cause to fall, esp. awkwardly or violently: *chairs tumbled over* **2** to roll or twist, esp. in playing: *they rolled and tumbled as wild beasts* **3** to decrease in value suddenly: *interest rates tumbled* **4** to move in a quick and uncontrolled manner: *I tumbled into my apartment and slammed the door* **5** to disturb, rumple, or toss around: *she was all tumbled by the fall* **6** to perform leaps or somersaults ▷ *n* **7** a fall, esp. an awkward or violent one: *he took a tumble down the stairs* **8** a somersault ▷ See also **tumble to** ▶ HISTORY Old English *tumbian* dance, jump > **tumbled** *adj*

tumbledown *adj* (of a building) falling to pieces; dilapidated

tumbler *n* **1 a** a flat-bottomed drinking glass with no handle or stem **b** the amount a tumbler will hold **2** a person who performs somersaults and other acrobatic feats **3** a part of the mechanism of a lock

tumble to *vb* to understand or become aware of: *how did he tumble to this?*

tumbril *n* a farm cart that tilts backwards to empty its load, which was used to take condemned prisoners to the guillotine during the French Revolution ▶ HISTORY Old French *tumberel*

tumescent (tew-**mess**-ent) *adj* swollen or becoming swollen

tumid (**tew**-mid) *adj rare* **1** (of an organ or part of the body) enlarged or swollen **2** pompous or fulsome in style: *a tumid tome* ▶ HISTORY Latin *tumere* to swell > **tumidity** *n*

tummy *n, pl* **-mies** an informal or childish word for **stomach**

tumour *or US* **tumor** (**tew**-mer) *n pathol* **a** any abnormal swelling **b** a mass of tissue formed by a new growth of cells ▶ HISTORY Latin *tumere* to swell > **tumorous** *adj*

tumult (**tew**-mult) *n* **1** a loud confused noise, such as one produced by a crowd **2** a state of confusion and excitement: *a tumult of emotions* ▶ HISTORY Latin *tumultus*

tumultuous (tew-**mull**-tew-uss) *adj* **1** exciting, confused, or turbulent: *this week's tumultuous events* **2** unruly, noisy, or excited: *a tumultuous welcome*

tumulus (**tew**-myew-luss) *n, pl* **-li** (-lie) *archaeol, no longer in technical use* a burial mound ▶ HISTORY Latin: a hillock

tun *n* a large beer cask ▶ HISTORY Old English *tunne*

tuna (**tune**-a) *n, pl* **-na** *or* **-nas 1** a large marine spiny-finned fish **2** the flesh of this fish, often tinned for food ▶ HISTORY American Spanish

tundra *n* a vast treeless Arctic region with permanently frozen subsoil ▶ HISTORY Russian

tune *n* **1** a melody, esp. one for which harmony is not essential **2** the correct musical pitch: *many of the notes are out of tune* **3 call the tune** to be in control of the proceedings **4 change one's tune** to alter one's attitude or tone of speech **5 in** *or* **out of tune with** in *or* not in agreement or sympathy with: *in tune with public opinion* **6 to the tune of** *informal* to the amount or extent of ▷ *vb* **tuning, tuned 7** to adjust (a musical instrument) so each string, key, etc. produces the right note **8** to make small adjustments to (an engine, machine, etc.) to obtain the proper or desired performance **9** to adjust (a radio or television) to receive a particular station or programme: *the radio was tuned to the local station* ▷ See also **tune in, tune up** ▶ HISTORY variant of *tone* > **tuner** *n*

tuneful *adj* having a pleasant tune > **tunefully** *adv*

tune in *vb* **1** to adjust (a radio or television) to receive (a station or programme) **2 tuned in to** *slang* aware of or knowledgeable about: *tuned in to European cinema*

tuneless *adj* having no melody or tune

tune up *vb* **1** to adjust (a musical instrument) to a particular pitch **2** to adjust the engine of a car, etc. to improve its performance

tungsten *n chem* a hard greyish-white metallic element. Symbol: W ▶ HISTORY Swedish *tung* heavy + *sten* stone

tunic *n* **1** a close-fitting jacket forming part of some uniforms **2** a loose-fitting knee-length garment ▶ HISTORY Latin *tunica*

tuning fork *n* a two-pronged metal fork that when struck produces a pure note of constant specified pitch

tunnel *n* **1** an underground passageway, esp. one for trains or cars **2** any passage or channel through or under something: *the carpal tunnel* ▷ *vb* **-nelling, -nelled** *or US* **-neling, -neled 3** to make one's way through or under (something) by digging a tunnel: *ten men succeeded in tunnelling out of the prisoner-of-war camp* **4** to dig a tunnel (through or under something): *the idea of tunnelling under the English Channel has been around for a long time* ▶ HISTORY Old French *tonel* cask

tunnel vision *n* **1** a condition in which a person is unable to see things that are not straight in front **2** narrowness of viewpoint resulting from concentration on only one aspect of a subject or situation

tunny *n, pl* **-nies** *or* **-ny** same as **tuna** ▶ HISTORY Latin *thunnus*

tup *n chiefly Brit* a male sheep ▶ HISTORY origin unknown

tupik (**too**-pick) *n* a tent of seal or caribou skin used for shelter by the Inuit in summer ▶ HISTORY Inuit *tupiq*

t

tuque n Canad **1** a knitted cap with a long tapering end **2** a close-fitting knitted hat often with a tassel or pompom

turban n **1** a head-covering worn by a Muslim, Hindu, or Sikh man, consisting of a long piece of cloth wound round the head **2** any head-covering resembling this ▶ HISTORY Turkish tülbend > **turbaned** adj

turbid adj literary (of water or air) full of mud or dirt, and frequently swirling around: the turbid stream of the Loire ▶ HISTORY Latin turbare to agitate > **turbidity** n

turbine n a machine in which power is produced by a stream of water, air, etc. that pushes the blades of a wheel and causes it to rotate ▶ HISTORY Latin turbo whirlwind

turbocharger n a device that increases the power of an internal-combustion engine by using the exhaust gases to drive a turbine > **turbocharged** adj

turbofan n a type of engine in which a large fan driven by a turbine forces air rearwards to increase the propulsive thrust

turbojet n **1** a gas turbine in which the exhaust gases provide the propulsive thrust to drive an aircraft **2** an aircraft powered by turbojet engines

turboprop n an aircraft propulsion unit where the propeller is driven by a gas turbine

turbot n, pl **-bot** or **-bots** a European flatfish, highly valued as a food fish ▶ HISTORY Old French tourbot

turbulence n **1** a state or condition of confusion, movement, or agitation **2** meteorol instability in the atmosphere causing gusty air currents

turbulent adj **1** involving a lot of sudden changes and conflicting elements: the city has had a turbulent history **2** (of people) wild and unruly: a harsh mountain tribe inhabited by a score of turbulent tribes **3** (of water or air) full of violent unpredictable currents: the turbulent ocean ▶ HISTORY Latin turba confusion

tureen n a large deep dish with a lid, used for serving soups ▶ HISTORY French terrine earthenware vessel

turf n, pl **turfs** or **turves 1** a layer of thick even grass with roots and soil attached: a short turf rich in wild flowers **2** a piece cut from this layer: we spent the afternoon digging turves **3** informal **a** the area where a person lives and feels at home: my boyhood turf of east Cork **b** a person's area of knowledge or influence: when Kate is at work, she's on her own turf **4 the turf a** a track where horse races are run **b** horse racing as a sport or industry **5** same as **peat** ▷ vb **6** to cover (an area of ground) with pieces of turf ▷ See also **turf out** ▶ HISTORY Old English

turf accountant n Brit same as **bookmaker**

turf out vb informal to throw (someone or something) out: the residents fear a new landlord might push up rents and turf them out of their homes

turgid (tur-jid) adj **1** (of language) pompous, boring, and hard to understand **2** (of water or mud) unpleasantly thick and brown ▶ HISTORY Latin turgere to swell > **turgidity** n

turgor n biol the normal rigid state of a cell, caused by pressure of the cell contents against the cell wall or membrane

Turk n a person from Turkey

turkey n, pl **-keys** or **-key 1** a large bird of North America bred for its meat **2** informal, chiefly US & Canad something, esp. a theatrical production, that fails **3 cold turkey** slang a method of curing drug addiction by abrupt withdrawal of all doses **4 talk turkey** informal, chiefly US & Canad to discuss, esp. business, frankly and practically ▶ HISTORY used at first of the African guinea fowl (because it was brought through Turkish territory), later applied by mistake to the American bird

Turkic n a family of Asian languages including Turkish and Azerbaijani

Turkish adj **1** of Turkey ▷ n **2** the language of Turkey

Turkish bath n **1** a type of bath in which the bather sweats freely in hot dry air, is then washed, often massaged, and has a cold plunge or shower **2 Turkish baths** an establishment for such baths

Turkish delight n a jelly-like sweet flavoured with flower essences, usually cut into cubes and covered in icing sugar

turmeric n **1** a tropical Asian plant with yellow flowers and an aromatic underground stem **2** a yellow spice obtained from the root of this plant ▶ HISTORY Old French terre merite meritorious earth

turmoil n disorder, agitation, or confusion: a period of political turmoil and uncertainty ▶ HISTORY origin unknown

turn vb **1** to move to face in another direction **2** to rotate or move round **3** to operate (a switch, key, etc.) by twisting it **4** to aim or point (something) in a particular direction: they turned their guns on the crowd **5** to change in course or direction: the van turned right into Victoria Road **6** (of a road, river, etc.) to have a bend or curve in it **7** to perform or do (something) with a rotating movement: a small boy was turning somersaults **8** to change so as to become: he turned pale **9** to reach, pass, or progress beyond in age, time, etc.: she had just turned fourteen **10** to find (a particular page) in a book: turn to page 78 **11** to look at the other side of: turning the pages of a book **12** to shape (wood, metal, etc.) on a lathe **13** (of leaves) to change colour in autumn **14** to make or become sour: the milk is starting to turn **15** to affect or be affected with nausea or giddiness: that would turn the strongest stomach **16** (of the tide) to start coming in or going out **17 turn against** to stop liking (something or someone one previously liked): people turned against her because she became so dictatorial **18 turn into** to become or change, or cause to become or change, into: my mother turned our house into four apartments **19 turn loose** to set (an animal or a person) free **20 turn someone's head** to affect someone mentally or emotionally **21 turn to a** to direct or apply (one's attention or thoughts) to **b** to stop doing or using one thing and start doing or using (another): *I turned to photography from writing* **c** to appeal or apply to (someone) for help, advice, etc. ▷ *n* **22** the act of turning **23** a movement of complete or partial rotation: *a turn of the dial* **24** a change of direction or position **25** same as **turning** (sense 1) **26** the right or opportunity to do something in an agreed order or succession: *it was her turn to play next* **27** a change in something that is happening or being done: *events took an unhappy turn* **28** a period of action, work, etc. **29** a short walk, ride, or excursion **30** natural inclination: *a liberal turn of mind* **31** distinctive form or style: *she'd a nice turn of phrase* **32** a deed that helps or hinders someone: *I'm trying to do you a good turn* **33** a twist, bend, or distortion in shape **34** a slight attack of an illness: *she's just having one of her turns* **35** *music* a melodic ornament that alternates the main note with the notes above and below it, beginning with the note above, in a variety of sequences **36** a short theatrical act: *tonight's star turn* **37** *informal* a shock or surprise: *you gave me rather a turn* **38 done to a turn** *informal* cooked perfectly **39 turn and turn about** one after another; alternately ▷ See also **turn down, turn in**, etc. ▶ HISTORY Old English *tyrnan* > **turner** *n*

turnaround *or* **turnabout** *n* a complete change or reversal: *a prompt economic turnaround*

turncoat *n* a person who deserts one cause or party to join an opposing one

turn down *vb* **1** to reduce (the volume, brightness, or temperature of something): *turn the heat down* **2** to reject or refuse: *the invitation was turned down* **3** to fold down (sheets, etc.)

turn in *vb informal* **1** to go to bed for the night **2** to hand in: *turning in my essay* **3** to hand (a suspect or criminal) over to the police: *his own brother turned him in*

turning *n* **1** a road, river, or path that turns off the main way **2** the point where such a way turns off **3** the process of turning objects on a lathe

turning circle *n* the smallest circle in which a vehicle can turn

turning effect *n physics* a tendency to produce motion, esp. rotation about a point or axis. Also called **moment**

turning point *n* a moment when a decisive change occurs

turnip *n* a vegetable with a large yellow or white edible root ▶ HISTORY Latin *napus*

turnkey *n old-fashioned* a jailer

turn off *vb* **1** to leave (a road or path): *turning off the main road* **2** (of a road or path) to lead away from (another road or path): *a main street with alleys twisting and turning off it* **3** to cause (something) to stop operating by turning a knob, pushing a button, etc. **4** *informal* to cause disgust or loss of interest in (someone): *keeping kids from getting turned off by mathematics* ▷ *n* **turn-off** **5** a road or other way branching off from the main thoroughfare **6** *informal* a person or thing that causes dislike

turn on *vb* **1** to cause (something) to operate by turning a knob, pushing a button, etc.: *turn on the radio, please* **2** to attack (someone), esp. without warning: *the Labrador turned on me* **3** *informal* to produce suddenly or automatically: *turning on that bland smile* **4** *slang* to arouse or excite **5** to depend or hinge on: *the match turned on three double faults by Murray* ▷ *n* **turn-on** **6** *slang* a person or thing that excites or arouses

turn out *vb* **1** to cause (something, esp. a light) to stop operating by moving a switch **2** to produce or create: *turning out two hits a year* **3** to force (someone) out of a place or position: *turned out of office* **4** to empty the contents of (something): *the police ordered him to turn out his pockets* **5** to be discovered or found (to be or do something): *he turned out to be a Finn* **6** to end up or result: *how interesting to see how it all turned out!* **7** to dress and groom: *she is always very well turned out* **8** to assemble or gather: *crowds turned out to see him* **9 turn out for** *informal* to make an appearance, esp. in a sporting competition: *he was asked to turn out for Liverpool* ▷ *n* **turnout** **10** a number of people attending an event: *there has been a high turnout of voters in elections in Bulgaria* **11** the quantity or amount produced

turn over *vb* **1** to change position, esp. so as to reverse top and bottom **2** to shift position, for instance by rolling onto one's side: *he turned over and went straight to sleep* **3** to consider carefully: *as I walked, I turned her story over* **4** to give (something) to someone who has a right to it or to the authorities: *the police ordered him to turn over the files to them* **5** (of an engine) to start or function correctly: *when he pressed the starter button, the engine turned over at once* **6** *slang* to rob: *the house had been turned over while they were out* ▷ *n* **turnover** **7 a** the amount of business done by a company during a specified period **b** the rate at which stock in trade is sold and replenished **8** a small pastry case filled with fruit or jam: *an apple turnover* **9** the number of workers employed by a firm in a given period to replace those who have left

turnpike *n* **1** *history* a barrier across a road to prevent vehicles or pedestrians passing until a charge (toll) had been paid **2** *US* a motorway for use of which a toll is charged ▶ HISTORY *turn* + *pike* a spike

turnstile *n* a mechanical barrier with arms that are turned to admit one person at a time

turntable *n* **1** the circular platform in a record player that rotates the record while it is being played **2** a circular platform used for turning locomotives and cars

turn up *vb* **1** to arrive or appear: *few people turned up* **2** to find or discover or be found or discovered: *a medical checkup has only turned up a sinus infection* **3** to increase the flow, volume, etc. of: *he turned up the radio* ▷ *n* **turn-up** **4** *Brit* the turned-up fold at the bottom of some trouser legs **5 a turn-up for the books** *informal* an unexpected happening

925

turpentine n **1** a strong-smelling colourless oil distilled from the resin of some coniferous trees, and used for thinning paint, for cleaning, and in medicine **2** a semisolid mixture of resin and oil obtained from various conifers, which is the main source of commercial turpentine **3** not in technical usage any one of a number of thinners for paints and varnishes, consisting of fractions of petroleum ▶ HISTORY Latin terebinthina

turpitude n formal depravity or wickedness: newspapers owned by proprietors whose moral turpitude far exceeded anything chronicled in their pages ▶ HISTORY Latin turpitudo ugliness

turps n short for **turpentine** (senses 1, 3)

turquoise adj **1** greenish-blue ▷ n **2** a greenish-blue precious stone ▶ HISTORY Old French turqueise Turkish (stone)

turret n **1** a small tower that projects from the wall of a building, esp. a castle **2** (on a tank or warship) a rotating structure on which guns are mounted **3** (on a machine tool) a turret-like steel structure with tools projecting from it that can be rotated to bring each tool to bear on the work ▶ HISTORY Latin turris tower > **turreted** adj

turtle n **1** an aquatic reptile with a flattened shell enclosing the body and flipper-like limbs adapted for swimming **2** **turn turtle** (of a boat) to capsize ▶ HISTORY French tortue tortoise

turtledove n an Old World dove noted for its soft cooing and devotion to its mate ▶ HISTORY Old English turtla

turtleneck n a round high close-fitting neck on a sweater or a sweater with such a neck

Tuscan adj of a style of classical architecture characterized by unfluted columns ▶ HISTORY from Tuscany, a region in central Italy

tusk n a long pointed tooth in the elephant, walrus, and certain other mammals ▶ HISTORY Old English tūsc > **tusked** adj

tussle n **1** an energetic fight, struggle, or argument: she resigned following a protracted boardroom tussle ▷ vb **-sling, -sled 2** to fight or struggle energetically ▶ HISTORY Middle English tusen to pull

tussock n a dense tuft of grass or other vegetation ▶ HISTORY origin unknown > **tussocky** adj

tutelage (**tew**-till-lij) n formal **1** instruction or guidance, esp. by a tutor **2** the state of being supervised by a guardian or tutor ▶ HISTORY Latin tueri to watch over

tutelary (**tew**-till-lar-ee) adj literary **1** having the role of guardian or protector **2** of a guardian

tutor n **1** a teacher, usually one instructing individual pupils **2** (at a college or university) a member of staff responsible for the teaching and supervision of a certain number of students ▷ vb **3** to act as a tutor to (someone) ▶ HISTORY Latin: a watcher > **tutorship** n

tutorial n **1** a period of intensive tuition given by a tutor to an individual student or to a small group of students ▷ adj **2** of or relating to a tutor

tutti adj, adv music to be performed by the whole orchestra, choir, etc. ▶ HISTORY Italian

tutti-frutti n, pl **-fruttis** an ice cream or other sweet food containing small pieces of candied or fresh fruits ▶ HISTORY Italian, literally: all the fruits

tutu n a very short skirt worn by ballerinas, made of projecting layers of stiffened material ▶ HISTORY French

tuxedo n, pl **-dos** US, Canad & Austral a dinner jacket ▶ HISTORY after a country club in Tuxedo Park, New York

TV television

TVEI Brit technical and vocational educational initiative: a national educational scheme in which pupils gain practical experience in technology and industry, often through work placement

twaddle n **1** silly, trivial, or pretentious talk or writing ▷ vb **-dling, -dled 2** to talk or write in a silly or pretentious way ▶ HISTORY earlier twattle

twain adj, n archaic two ▶ HISTORY Old English twēgen

twang n **1** a sharp ringing sound produced by or as if by the plucking of a taut string **2** a strongly nasal quality in a person's speech: a high-pitched Texas twang ▷ vb **3** to make or cause to make a twang: a bunch of angels twanging harps ▶ HISTORY imitative > **twangy** adj

tweak vb **1** to twist or pinch with a sharp or sudden movement: she tweaked his ear **2** informal to make a minor alteration to (something) ▷ n **3** the act of tweaking **4** informal a minor alteration ▶ HISTORY Old English twiccian

twee adj informal excessively sentimental, sweet, or pretty ▶ HISTORY from tweet, affected pronunciation of sweet

tweed n **1** a thick woollen cloth produced originally in Scotland **2 tweeds** a suit made of tweed ▶ HISTORY probably from tweel, Scots variant of twill

tweedy adj **tweedier, tweediest 1** of, made of, or resembling tweed **2** showing a fondness for a hearty outdoor life, often associated with wearers of tweeds

tweet interj **1** an imitation of the thin chirping sound made by small birds ▷ vb **2** to make this sound **3** to write a short message on the Twitter website ▷ n **4** a thin chirping sound **5** a short message posted on the Twitter website ▶ HISTORY imitative

tweeter n a loudspeaker used in high-fidelity systems for the reproduction of high audio frequencies

tweezers pl n a small pincer-like tool used for tasks such as handling small objects or plucking out hairs ▶ HISTORY obsolete tweeze case of instruments

twelfth adj **1** of or being number twelve in a series ▷ n **2** number twelve in a series **3** one of twelve equal parts of something

Twelfth Day n Jan 6, the twelfth day after Christmas and the feast of the Epiphany

t

Twelfth Night n **a** the evening of Jan 5, the eve of Twelfth Day **b** the evening of Twelfth Day itself

twelve n **1** the cardinal number that is the sum of ten and two **2** a numeral, 12 or XII, representing this number **3** something representing or consisting of twelve units ▷ adj **4** amounting to twelve: *twelve months* ▶ HISTORY Old English *twelf*

twenty n, pl **-ties 1** the cardinal number that is the product of ten and two **2** a numeral, 20 or XX, representing this number **3** something representing or consisting of twenty units ▷ adj **4** amounting to twenty: *twenty minutes* > **twentieth** adj, n

twenty-four-seven or **24/7** adv US & Brit, informal constantly or all the time: *consultants would no longer be available 24/7* ▶ HISTORY from twenty-four hours a day, seven days a week

twerp or **twirp** n informal a silly, stupid, or contemptible person ▶ HISTORY origin unknown

twice adv **1** two times; on two occasions or in two cases: *I've met her only twice* **2** double in degree or quantity: *twice as big* ▶ HISTORY Old English *twiwa*

twiddle vb **-dling, -dled 1** to twirl or fiddle, often in an idle way: *twiddling the knobs of a radio* **2 twiddle one's thumbs a** to rotate one's thumbs around one another, when bored or impatient **b** to be bored, with nothing to do ▷ n **3** an unnecessary decoration, esp. a curly one ▶ HISTORY probably *twirl* + *fiddle*

twig¹ n a small branch or shoot of a tree ▶ HISTORY Old English *twigge* > **twiggy** adj

twig² vb **twigging, twigged** Brit informal to realize or understand: *I should have twigged it earlier* ▶ HISTORY origin unknown

twilight n **1** the soft dim light that occurs when the sun is just below the horizon after sunset **2** the period in which this light occurs: *soon after twilight we started marching again* **3** a period in which strength, importance, etc. is gradually declining: *the twilight of his political career* ▷ adj **4** of or relating to the period towards the end of the day: *the twilight shift* **5** of or being a period of decline: *he spent most of his twilight years working on a history of France* **6** denoting irregularity and obscurity: *a twilight existence* ▶ HISTORY Old English *twi-* half + LIGHT > **twilit** adj

twilight zone n any indefinite or intermediate condition or area: *the twilight zone between sleep and wakefulness*

twill n a fabric woven to produce an effect of parallel diagonal lines or ribs in the cloth ▶ HISTORY Old English *twilic* having a double thread

twin n **1** one of a pair of people or animals conceived at the same time **2** one of a pair of people or things that are identical or very similar ▷ vb **twinning, twinned 3** to pair or be paired together ▶ HISTORY Old English *twinn*

twine n **1** string or cord made by twisting fibres together ▷ vb **twining, twined 2** to twist or wind together: *she twined the flowers into a garland* **3 twine round** or **around** to twist or wind around:

she twined her arms around her neck ▶ HISTORY Old English *twīn*

twinge n **1** a sudden brief darting or stabbing pain **2** a sharp emotional pang: *a twinge of conscience* ▶ HISTORY Old English *twengan* to pinch

twinkle vb **-kling, -kled 1** to shine brightly and intermittently; sparkle **2** (of the eyes) to sparkle, esp. with amusement or delight ▷ n **3** a flickering brightness; sparkle ▶ HISTORY Old English *twinclian*

twin town n a town that has cultural and social links with a foreign town: *Nuremberg is one of Glasgow's twin towns*

twirl vb **1** to move around rapidly and repeatedly in a circle **2** to twist, wind, or twiddle, often idly: *twirling the glass in her hand* ▷ n **3** a whirl or twist **4** a written flourish ▶ HISTORY origin unknown

twist vb **1** to turn one end or part while the other end or parts remain still or turn in the opposite direction: *never twist or wring woollen garments* **2** to distort or be distorted **3** to wind or twine: *the wire had been twisted twice* **4** to force or be forced out of the natural form or position: *I twisted my knee* **5** to change the meaning of; distort: *he'd twisted the truth to make himself look good* **6** to revolve or rotate: *he twisted the switch to turn the radio off* **7** to wrench with a turning action: *he twisted the wheel sharply* **8** to follow a winding course: *the road twisted as it climbed* **9** to dance the twist **10 twist someone's arm** to persuade or coerce someone ▷ n **11** the act of twisting: *she gave a dainty little twist to her parasol* **12** something formed by or as if by twisting: *there's a twist in the cable* **13** a decisive change of direction, aim, meaning, or character: *the latest revelations give a new twist to the company's boardroom wranglings* **14** an unexpected development in a story, play, or film **15** a bend: *a twist of the mountain road* **16** a distortion of the original shape or form **17** a jerky pull, wrench, or turn **18 the twist** a dance popular in the 1960s, in which dancers vigorously twist the hips **19 round the twist** Brit slang mad or eccentric ▶ HISTORY Old English > **twisty** adj

twisted adj (of a person) cruel or perverted

twister n Brit a swindling or dishonest person

twit¹ vb **twitting, twitted** Brit to poke fun at (someone) ▶ HISTORY Old English *ætwītan*

twit² n informal a foolish or stupid person ▶ HISTORY from TWIT¹

twitch vb **1** (of a person or part of a person's body) to move in a jerky spasmodic way: *his left eyelid twitched involuntarily* **2** to pull (something) with a quick jerky movement: *she twitched the curtains shut* ▷ n **3** a sharp jerking movement, esp. one caused by a nervous condition ▶ HISTORY Old English *twiccian* to pluck

twitter vb **1** (esp. of a bird) to utter a succession of chirping sounds **2** to talk rapidly and nervously in a high-pitched voice: *novelists who twittered about how much they admired him* **3** to write a short message on the Twitter website ▷ n **4** the act or

t

sound of twittering **5 Twitter** *trademark* a website where people can post short messages about their current activities **6 in a twitter** in a state of nervous excitement ▶ **HISTORY** imitative
> **twitterer** *n* > **twittering** *n* > **twittery** *adj*

two *n* **1** the cardinal number that is the sum of one and one **2** a numeral, 2 or II, representing this number **3** something representing or consisting of two units **4 in two** in or into two parts: *cut the cake in two and take a bit each* **5 put two and two together** to reach an obvious conclusion by considering the evidence available **6 that makes two of us** the same applies to me ▷ *adj* **7** amounting to two: *two years* ▶ **HISTORY** Old English *twā*

twoccing *or* **twocking** *n Brit, slang* the act of breaking into a motor vehicle and driving it away ▶ **HISTORY** from *T(aking)W(ithout) O(wner's) C(onsent)*, the legal offence > **twoccer** *or* **twocker** *n*

two-dimensional *adj* **1** having two dimensions **2** somewhat lacking in depth or complexity: *a modern audience is unable to tolerate two-dimensional characters*

two-edged *adj* **1** (of a remark) having both a favourable and an unfavourable interpretation, such as *she looks nice when she smiles* **2** (of a knife, saw, etc.) having two cutting edges

two-faced *adj* deceitful or hypocritical: *he's a two-faced liar and opportunist*

twofold *adj* **1** having twice as many or as much **2** composed of two parts ▷ *adv* **3** by twice as many or as much

twopence *or* **tuppence** (**tup**-pence) *n Brit* **1** the sum of two pennies **2** the slightest amount: *I don't care twopence who your father is*

two-ply *adj* made of two thicknesses, layers, or strands

two-stroke *adj* of an internal-combustion engine whose piston makes two strokes for every explosion

two-time *vb* **-timing, -timed** *informal* to deceive (a lover) by having an affair with someone else > **two-timer** *n*

two-way *adj* **1** moving in, or allowing movement in, two opposite directions: *two-way traffic* **2** involving mutual involvement or cooperation: *two-way communication* **3** (of a radio or transmitter) capable of both transmission and reception of messages

TX Texas

tycoon *n* a businessman of great wealth and power

> ■ **WORD HISTORY**
> ■ 'Tycoon' comes from Japanese *taikun*, meaning
> ■ 'great lord'. It was a term of respect given to the
> ■ Japanese shoguns, the hereditary military
> ■ commanders who were for centuries the real
> ■ rulers of Japan although nominally subordinate
> ■ to the emperors.

tyke *or* **tike** *n* **1** *Brit, Austral & NZ, informal* a small or cheeky child **2** *Brit, dialect* a rough ill-mannered person ▶ **HISTORY** Old Norse *tík* bitch

tympanic membrane *n anat* the thin membrane separating the external ear from the middle ear; eardrum

tympanum *n, pl* **-nums** *or* **-na 1** *anat* **a** the cavity of the middle ear **b** same as **tympanic membrane 2** *archit* the recessed space between the arch and the lintel above a door ▶ **HISTORY** Greek *tumpanon* drum > **tympanic** *adj*

Tynwald (**tin**-wold) *n* the Parliament of the Isle of Man ▶ **HISTORY** Old Norse *thing* assembly + *vollr* field

type *n* **1** a kind, class, or category of things, all of which have something in common **2** a subdivision of a particular class; sort: *it is more alcoholic than most wines of this type* **3** the general characteristics distinguishing a particular group: *the old-fashioned type of nanny* **4** *informal* a person, esp. of a specified kind: *a seagoing type* **5** a block with a raised character on it used for printing **6** text printed from type; print ▷ *vb* **typing, typed 7** to write using a typewriter or keyboard **8** to be a symbol of or typify **9** to decide the type of; classify ▶ **HISTORY** Greek *tupos* image

typecast *vb* **-casting, -cast** to cast (an actor or actress) in the same kind of role continually

typeface *n* the size and style of printing used in a book, magazine, etc.

typescript *n* any typewritten document

typeset *vb* **-setting, -set** *printing* to set (text for printing) in type

typewriter *n* a machine which prints a letter or other character when the appropriate key is pressed

typhoid *pathol n* **1** short for **typhoid fever** ▷ *adj* **2** of or relating to typhoid fever: *typhoid vaccines*

typhoid fever *n* an acute infectious disease characterized by high fever, spots, abdominal pain, etc. It is spread by contaminated food or water

typhoon *n* a violent tropical storm, esp. one in the China Seas or W Pacific ▶ **HISTORY** Chinese *tai fung* great wind

typhus *n* an acute infectious disease transmitted by lice or mites and characterized by high fever, skin rash, and severe headache ▶ **HISTORY** Greek *tuphos* fever

typical *adj* **1** being or serving as a representative example of a particular type; characteristic: *a typical working day* **2** considered to be an example of some undesirable trait: *it was typical that he should start talking almost before he was inside the room* ▶ **HISTORY** Greek *tupos* image
> **typically** *adv*

typify *vb* **-fies, -fying, -fied 1** to be typical of or characterize: *the beers made here typify all that is best about the independent brewing sector* **2** to symbolize or represent: *a number of dissident intellectuals, typified by Andrei Sakharov*

typing *n* **1** the work or activity of using a typewriter or keyboard **2** the skill of using a keyboard quickly and accurately

typist *n* a person who types letters, reports, etc., esp. for a living

typography *n* **1** the art or craft of printing **2** the style or quality of printing and layout in a book, magazine, etc. **>** **typographical** *adj* **>** **typographically** *adv*

tyrannical *adj* of or like a tyrant; unjust and oppressive

tyrannize *or* **-ise** *vb* **-nizing, -nized** *or* **-nising, -nised** to rule or exercise power (over) in a cruel or oppressive manner: *he dominated and tyrannized his younger brother*

tyrannosaurus *or* **tyrannosaur** (tirr-ran-oh-**sore**-uss) *n* a large two-footed flesh-eating dinosaur common in North America in Cretaceous times ▶ HISTORY Greek *turannos* tyrant + *sauros* lizard

tyranny *n, pl* **-nies 1 a** a government by a tyrant **b** oppressive and unjust government by more than one person **2** the condition or state of being dominated or controlled by something that makes unpleasant or harsh demands: *the tyranny of fashion drives many women to diet although they are not overweight* **>** **tyrannous** *adj*

tyrant *n* **1** a person who governs oppressively, unjustly, and arbitrarily **2** any person who exercises authority in a tyrannical manner: *a domestic tyrant* ▶ HISTORY Greek *turannos*

tyre *or US* **tire** *n* a ring of rubber, usually filled with air but sometimes solid, fitted round the rim of a wheel of a road vehicle to grip the road ▶ HISTORY earlier *tire*, probably archaic variant of *attire*

tyro *n, pl* **-ros** a novice or beginner ▶ HISTORY Latin *tiro* recruit

tzar *n* same as **tsar**

tzetze fly *n* same as **tsetse fly**

929

Uu

U 1 (in Britain) universal (used to describe a film certified as suitable for viewing by anyone) **2** *chem* uranium *adj* **3** *Brit, informal* (of language or behaviour) characteristic of the upper class

ubiquitous (yew-**bik**-wit-uss) *adj* being or seeming to be everywhere at once ▶ **HISTORY** Latin *ubique* everywhere > **ubiquity** *n*

U-boat *n history* a German submarine ▶ **HISTORY** German *Unterseeboot* undersea boat

Ubuntu *n S African* humanity or fellow feeling; kindness ▶ **HISTORY** Nguni (language group of southern Africa)

UC *printing* upper case

UCAS (in Britain) Universities and Colleges Admissions Service

UCCA (formerly, in Britain) Universities Central Council on Admissions

udder *n* the large baglike milk-producing gland of cows, sheep, or goats, with two or more teats ▶ **HISTORY** Old English *ūder*

UDHR Universal Declaration of Human Rights: a list of 30 fundamental human rights published by the United Nations in 1948

UDI Unilateral Declaration of Independence

UEFA Union of European Football Associations

UFO unidentified flying object

ugh (uhh) *interj* an exclamation of disgust, annoyance, or dislike

UGLI *n, pl* **-LIS** *or* **-LIES** *trademark* a yellow citrus fruit: a cross between a tangerine, grapefruit, and orange ▶ **HISTORY** probably an alteration of *ugly*, from its wrinkled skin

ugly *adj* **uglier, ugliest 1** so unattractive as to be unpleasant to look at **2** very unpleasant and involving violence or aggression: *an ugly incident in which one man was stabbed* **3** repulsive or displeasing: *ugly rumours* **4** bad-tempered or sullen: *an ugly mood* ▶ **HISTORY** Old Norse *uggligr* dreadful > **ugliness** *n*

UHF *radio* ultrahigh frequency

UHT ultra-heat-treated (milk or cream)

UK United Kingdom

ukase (yew-**kaze**) *n* (in imperial Russia) a decree from the tsar ▶ **HISTORY** Russian *ukaz*

Ukrainian *adj* **1** of the Ukraine ▷ *n* **2** a person from the Ukraine **3** the language of the Ukraine

ukulele *or* **ukelele** (yew-kal-**lay**-lee) *n* a small four-stringed guitar ▶ **HISTORY** Hawaiian, literally: jumping flea

ulcer *n* an open sore on the surface of the skin or a mucous membrane ▶ **HISTORY** Latin *ulcus*

ulcerated *adj* made or becoming ulcerous > **ulceration** *n*

ulcerous *adj* of, like, or characterized by ulcers

ulna *n, pl* **-nae** *or* **-nas** the inner and longer of the two bones of the human forearm or of the forelimb in other vertebrates ▶ **HISTORY** Latin: elbow > **ulnar** *adj*

ulnar nerve *n anat* a nerve situated along the inner side of the arm and passing close to the surface of the skin near the elbow

ulster *n* a man's heavy double-breasted overcoat ▶ **HISTORY** *Ulster*, the northernmost province of Ireland

Ulsterman *or fem* **Ulsterwoman** *n, pl* **-men** *or* **-women** a person from Ulster

ulterior (ult-**ear**-ee-or) *adj* (of an aim, reason, etc.) concealed or hidden: *an ulterior motive* ▶ **HISTORY** Latin: further

ultimate *adj* **1** final in a series or process: *predictions about the ultimate destination of modern art* **2** highest, supreme, or unchallengeable: *he has the ultimate power to dismiss the Prime Minister* **3** fundamental or essential: *a believer in the ultimate goodness of man* **4** most extreme: *genocide is the ultimate abuse of human rights* **5** final or total: *she should be able to estimate the ultimate cost* ▷ *n* **6 the ultimate** in the best example of: *the ultimate in luxury holidays* ▶ **HISTORY** Latin *ultimus* last, distant > **ultimately** *adv*

ultimatum (ult-im-**may**-tum) *n* a final warning to someone that they must agree to certain conditions or requirements, or else action will be taken against them: *Britain declared war after the Nazis rejected the ultimatum to withdraw from Poland*

ultra *n* a person who has extreme or immoderate beliefs or opinions ▶ **HISTORY** Latin: beyond

ultra- *prefix* **1** beyond a specified extent, range, or limit: *ultrasonic* **2** extremely: *ultraleftist* ▶ **HISTORY** Latin

ultraconservative *adj* **1** highly reactionary ▷ *n* **2** a highly reactionary person

ultrahigh frequency *n* a radio frequency between 3000 and 300 megahertz

ultramarine *n* **1** a blue pigment originally made from lapis lazuli ▷ *adj* **2** vivid blue

- ■ **WORD HISTORY**
- ■ 'Ultramarine' comes from Latin *ultramarinus*,
- ■ meaning 'from beyond the sea'. It was given
- ■ this name because the blue mineral, lapis
- ■ lazuli, that the pigment was made from was
- ■ imported from Asia.

ultramontane *adj* **1** on the other side of the mountains, usually the Alps, from the speaker or writer **2** of a movement in the Roman Catholic Church which favours supreme papal authority ▷ *n* **3** a person from beyond the Alps **4** a member of the ultramontane party of the Roman Catholic Church

ultrasonic *adj* of or producing sound waves with higher frequencies than humans can hear > **ultrasonically** *adv*

ultrasonics *n* the branch of physics concerned with ultrasonic waves

ultrasound *n* ultrasonic waves, used in echo sounding, medical diagnosis, and therapy

ultrasound scan *n* an examination of an internal bodily structure by the use of ultrasonic waves, esp. for diagnosing abnormality in a fetus

ultraviolet *n* **1** the part of the electromagnetic spectrum with wavelengths shorter than light but longer than X-rays ▷ *adj* **2** of or consisting of radiation lying in the ultraviolet: *ultraviolet light*

ultraviolet radiation *n science* the damaging ultraviolet light waves from the sun that can cause sunburn in humans

ultra vires (**ul**-tra-**vire**-reez) *adv, adj law* beyond the legal power of a person or organization ▶ HISTORY Latin, literally: beyond strength

ululate (**yewl**-yew-late) *vb literary* **-lating, -lated** to howl or wail ▶ HISTORY Latin *ululare*
> **ululation** *n*

umbel *n* a type of compound flower in which the flowers arise from the same point in the main stem and have stalks of the same length, to give a cluster with the youngest flowers at the centre ▶ HISTORY Latin *umbella* a sunshade
> **umbellate** *adj*

umbelliferous *adj* of or denoting a plant with flowers in umbels, such as fennel, parsley, carrot, or parsnip ▶ HISTORY Latin *umbella* a sunshade + *ferre* to bear

umber *n* **1** a type of dark brown earth containing ferric oxide (rust) ▷ *adj* **2** dark brown to reddish-brown ▶ HISTORY French (*terre d'*)*ombre* or Italian (*terra di*) *ombra* shadow (earth)

umbilical (um-**bill**-ik-kl) *adj* of or like the navel or the umbilical cord

umbilical cord *n* the long flexible cordlike structure that connects a fetus to the placenta

umbilicus (um-**bill**-ik-kuss) *n, pl* **-ci** *anat* the navel ▶ HISTORY Latin: navel, centre

umbra *n, pl* **-brae** *or* **-bras** a shadow, usually the shadow cast by the moon onto the earth during a solar eclipse ▶ HISTORY Latin: shade

umbrage *n* **take umbrage** to take offence ▶ HISTORY Latin *umbra* shade

umbrella *n* **1** a portable device used for protection against rain, consisting of a light canopy supported on a collapsible metal frame mounted on a central rod **2** a single organization, idea, etc. that contains or covers many different organizations or ideas **3** anything that has the effect of a protective screen or general cover: *under the umbrella of the Helsinki security conference* ▷ *adj* **4** containing or covering many different organizations, ideas, etc.: *an umbrella group of nationalists and anti-communists* ▶ HISTORY Italian *ombrella*, from *ombra* shade > **umbrella-like** *adj*

umiak, oomiak *or* **oomiac** (**oo**-mee-ak) *n* a large open boat made of stretched skins, used by the Inuit ▶ HISTORY Inuit

umlaut (**oom**-lout) *n* **1** the mark (¨) placed over a vowel, esp. in German, indicating a change in its sound **2** (esp. in Germanic languages) the change of a vowel brought about by the influence of a vowel in the next syllable ▶ HISTORY German, from *um* around + *Laut* sound

umlungu (oom-**loong**-goo) *n S African* a White man: used esp. as a term of address ▶ HISTORY Nguni (language group of southern Africa)

umpire *n* **1** an official who ensures that the people taking part in a game follow the rules; referee ▷ *vb* **-piring, -pired** **2** to act as umpire in a game ▶ HISTORY Old French *nomper* not one of a pair

umpteen *adj informal* very many: *the centre of umpteen scandals* ▶ HISTORY *umpty* a great deal + *-teen* ten > **umpteenth** *n, adj*

UN United Nations

un-[1] *prefix* (freely used with adjectives, participles, and their derivative adverbs and nouns: less frequently used with certain other nouns) not; contrary to; opposite of: *uncertain; untidiness; unbelief; untruth* ▶ HISTORY Old English *on-, un-*

un-[2] *prefix* forming verbs **1** denoting reversal of an action or state: *uncover; untie* **2** denoting removal from, release, or deprivation: *unharness* ▶ HISTORY Old English *un-, on-*

unabated *adv* without any reduction in force: *the storm continued unabated*

unable *adj* **unable to** not having the power, ability, or authority to; not able to

unaccented syllable *n* see **unstressed syllable**

unaccountable *adj* **1** without any sensible explanation: *for some unaccountable reason I got on the wrong bus* **2** not having to justify or answer for one's actions to other people: *the secret service remains unaccountable to the public*
> **unaccountably** *adv*

unadulterated *adj* **1** completely pure, with nothing added: *fresh unadulterated spring water* **2** (of an emotion) not mixed with anything else: *a look of unadulterated terror*

unaffected[1] *adj* unpretentious, natural, or sincere

unaffected[2] *adj* not influenced or changed

unalienable *adj law* same as **inalienable**

unanimous (yew-**nan**-im-uss) *adj* **1** in complete agreement **2** characterized by complete agreement: *unanimous approval* ▶ HISTORY Latin *unus* one + *animus* mind > **unanimity** *n*
> **unanimously** *adv*

unannounced *adv* without warning: *she turned up unannounced*

unapproachable *adj* discouraging friendliness; aloof

unarmed *adj* **1** not carrying any weapons: *they were shooting unarmed peasants* **2** not using any weapons: *unarmed combat*

unassailable *adj* not able to be destroyed or overcome: *an unassailable lead*

unassuming *adj* modest or unpretentious

unattached *adj* **1** not connected with any specific body or group **2** not engaged or married

unavailing *adj* useless or futile

u

unavoidable adj unable to be avoided or prevented > **unavoidably** adv

unaware adj 1 not aware or conscious: *unaware of my surroundings* ▷ adv 2 not universally accepted same as **unawares**

unawares adv 1 by surprise: *death had taken him unawares* 2 without knowing: *had he passed her, all unawares?*

unbalanced adj 1 lacking balance 2 mentally deranged 3 biased; one-sided: *his unbalanced summing-up*

unbearable adj not able to be endured > **unbearably** adv

unbecoming adj 1 unattractive or unsuitable: *unbecoming garments* 2 not proper or appropriate to a person or position: *acts unbecoming of university students*

unbeknown adv (foll. by *to*) without the knowledge of (a person): *unbeknown to her family she had acquired modern ways*. Also (esp. Brit): **unbeknownst** ▶ HISTORY archaic *beknown* known

unbelievable adj 1 too unlikely to be believed 2 extremely impressive; marvellous 3 *informal* terrible or shocking > **unbelievably** adv

unbeliever n a person who does not believe in a religion

unbend vb **-bending, -bent** to become less strict or more informal in one's attitudes or behaviour

unbending adj rigid or inflexible: *an unbending routine*

unbiased adj not having or showing prejudice or favouritism; impartial

unbidden adj *literary* not ordered or asked; voluntary or spontaneous: *unbidden thoughts came into Catherine's mind*

unborn adj not yet born

unbosom vb to relieve oneself of secrets or feelings by telling someone ▶ HISTORY UN-[2] + *bosom* (in the sense: centre of the emotions)

unbridled adj (of feelings or behaviour) not restrained or controlled in any way: *unbridled passion*

unbroken adj 1 complete or whole 2 continuous: *I slept for eight unbroken hours* 3 not disturbed or upset: *an unbroken night* 4 (of a record) not improved upon 5 (of animals, esp. horses) not tamed

unburden vb to relieve one's mind or oneself of a worry or trouble by telling someone about it

uncalled-for adj unnecessary or unwarranted: *uncalled-for comments*

uncanny adj 1 weird or mysterious: *an uncanny silence* 2 beyond what is normal: *an uncanny eye for detail* > **uncannily** adv > **uncanniness** n

unceremonious adj 1 relaxed and informal: *she greeted him with unceremonious friendliness* 2 abrupt or rude: *the answer was an unceremonious 'no'* > **unceremoniously** adv

uncertain adj 1 not able to be accurately known or predicted: *an uncertain future* 2 not definitely decided: *they are uncertain about the date* 3 not to be depended upon: *an uncertain career* 4 changeable: *an uncertain sky* > **uncertainty** n

uncharacteristic adj not typical > **uncharacteristically** adv

uncharitable adj unkind or harsh > **uncharitably** adv

uncharted adj 1 (of an area of sea or land) not having had a map made of it, esp. because it is unexplored 2 unknown or unfamiliar: *a whole uncharted universe of emotions*

unchristian *or* **un-Christian** adj not in accordance with Christian principles

uncial (un-see-al) adj 1 of or written in letters that resemble modern capitals, as used in Greek and Latin manuscripts of the third to ninth centuries ▷ n 2 an uncial letter or manuscript ▶ HISTORY Late Latin *unciales litterae* letters an inch long

uncivilized *or* **-ised** adj 1 (of a tribe or people) not yet civilized 2 lacking culture or sophistication

unclassified adj 1 not arranged in any specific order or grouping 2 (of official information) not secret

uncle n 1 a brother of one's father or mother 2 the husband of one's aunt 3 a child's term of address for a male friend of its parents 4 *slang* a pawnbroker ▶ HISTORY Latin *avunculus*

unclean adj lacking moral, spiritual, or physical cleanliness

Uncle Sam n a personification of the government of the United States ▶ HISTORY apparently a humorous interpretation of the letters stamped on army supply boxes during the War of 1812: *US*

uncomfortable adj 1 not physically relaxed: *he was forced to sit in an uncomfortable cross-legged position* 2 not comfortable to be in or use: *an uncomfortable chair* 3 causing discomfort or unease: *the uncomfortable truth* > **uncomfortably** adv

uncommon adj 1 not happening or encountered often 2 in excess of what is normal: *an uncommon amount of powder*

uncommonly adv 1 in an unusual manner or degree 2 extremely: *an uncommonly good humour*

uncompromising adj not prepared to compromise; inflexible > **uncompromisingly** adv

unconcerned adj 1 not interested in something and not wanting to become involved 2 not worried or troubled > **unconcernedly** (un-kon-**sern**-id-lee) adv

unconditional adj without conditions or limitations: *an unconditional ceasefire* > **unconditionally** adv

unconscionable adj 1 unscrupulous or unprincipled: *an unconscionable charmer* 2 excessive in amount or degree: *unconscionable number of social obligations*

unconscious adj 1 unable to notice or respond to things which one would normally be aware of through the senses; insensible or comatose 2 not aware of one's actions or behaviour: *unconscious of* his failure **3** not realized or intended: *unconscious duplicity* **4** coming from or produced by the unconscious: *unconscious mental processes* ▷ *n* **5** *psychoanal* the part of the mind containing instincts, impulses, and ideas that are not available for direct examination > **unconsciously** *adv* > **unconsciousness** *n*

unconstitutional *adj* forbidden by the rules or laws which state how an organization or country must function

unconventional *adj* not conforming to accepted rules or standards

uncooperative *adj* not willing to help other people with what they are trying to do

uncoordinated *adj* **1** not joining or functioning together properly to form a whole **2** (of a person) not able to control his or her movements properly; clumsy

uncountable *adj* existing in such large numbers that it is impossible to say how many there are: *uncountable millions*

uncouth *adj* lacking in good manners, refinement, or grace ▶ **HISTORY** Old English *un-* not + *cūth* familiar

uncover *vb* **1** to remove the cover or top from **2** to reveal or disclose: *they have uncovered a plot to overthrow the government* > **uncovered** *adj*

uncrowned *adj* **1** having the powers, but not the title, of royalty **2** (of a king or queen) not yet crowned

UNCTAD *econ* United Nations Conference on Trade and Development

unction *n* **1** *chiefly RC & Eastern Churches* the act of anointing with oil in sacramental ceremonies **2** oily charm **3** an ointment **4** anything soothing ▶ **HISTORY** Latin *unguere* to anoint

unctuous *adj* pretending to be kind and concerned but obviously not sincere ▶ **HISTORY** Latin *unctum* ointment

undecided *adj* **1** not having made up one's mind **2** (of an issue or problem) not agreed or decided upon

undeniable *adj* **1** unquestionably true **2** of unquestionable excellence: *of undeniable character* > **undeniably** *adv*

under *prep* **1** directly below; on, to, or beneath the underside or base of: *under the bed* **2** less than: *in just under an hour* **3** lower in rank than: *under a general* **4** subject to the supervision, control, or influence of: *under communism for 45 years* **5** in or subject to certain circumstances or conditions: *the bridge is still under construction; under battle conditions* **6** in (a specified category): *he had filed Kafka's 'The Trial' under crime stories* **7** known by: *under their own names* **8** planted with: *a field under corn* **9** powered by: *under sail* ▷ *adv* **10** below; to a position underneath ▶ **HISTORY** Old English

under- *prefix* **1** below or beneath: *underarm; underground* **2** insufficient or insufficiently: *underemployed* **3** of lesser importance or lower rank: *undersecretary* **4** indicating secrecy or deception: *underhand*

underachieve *vb* **-achieving, -achieved** to fail to achieve a performance appropriate to one's age or talents > **underachiever** *n*

underactive *adj* less active than is normal or desirable: *an underactive thyroid gland*

underage *adj* below the required or standard age, usually below the legal age for voting or drinking

underarm *adj* **1** *sport* denoting a style of throwing, bowling, or serving in which the hand is swung below shoulder level **2** below the arm ▷ *adv* **3** in an underarm style

underbelly *n*, *pl* **-lies 1** the part of an animal's belly nearest the ground **2** a vulnerable or unprotected part, aspect, or region

underbrush *n US, Canad & Austral* same as **undergrowth**

undercarriage *n* **1** the wheels, shock absorbers, and struts that support an aircraft on the ground and enable it to take off and land **2** the framework supporting the body of a vehicle

undercharge *vb* **-charging, -charged** to charge too little for something

underclass *n* a class beneath the usual social scale consisting of the most disadvantaged people, such as the long-term unemployed

underclothes *pl n* same as **underwear**. Also called: **underclothing**

undercoat *n* **1** a coat of paint applied before the top coat **2** *zool* a layer of soft fur beneath the outer fur of animals such as the otter ▷ *vb* **3** to apply an undercoat to a surface

undercover *adj* done or acting in secret: *an undercover investigation*

undercurrent *n* **1** a current that is not apparent at the surface **2** an underlying opinion or emotion

undercut *vb* **-cutting, -cut 1** to charge less than a competitor in order to obtain trade **2** to undermine or render less effective: *the latest fighting undercuts diplomatic attempts to find a peaceful solution* **3** to cut away the under part of something

underdeveloped *adj* **1** immature or undersized **2** (of a country or its economy) lacking the finance, industries, and organization necessary to advance

underdog *n* a person or team in a weak or underprivileged position

underdone *adj* insufficiently or lightly cooked

underemployment *n* the state of not having enough work > **underemployed** *adj*, *n*

underestimate *vb* **-mating, -mated 1** to make too low an estimate of: *the trust had underestimated the cost of work* **2** to not be aware or take account of the full abilities or potential of: *the police had underestimated him* ▷ *n* **3** too low an estimate > **underestimation** *n*

underexpose *vb* **-posing, -posed** *photog* to expose (a film, plate, or paper) for too short a time or with insufficient light > **underexposure** *n*

underfelt *n* thick felt laid under a carpet to increase insulation

u

underfoot *adv* **1** underneath the feet; on the ground **2 trample** or **crush underfoot a** to damage or destroy by stepping on **b** to treat with contempt

undergarment *n* a garment worn under clothes

undergo *vb* **-going, -went, -gone** to experience, endure, or sustain: *he underwent a three-hour operation* ▶ HISTORY Old English *undergān*

undergraduate *n* a person studying at a university for a first degree

underground *adj, adv* **1** occurring, situated, used, or going below ground level **2** secret or secretly: *an underground organization; several political parties had to operate underground for many years* **3** (of art, film, music, etc.) avant-garde, experimental, or subversive ▷ *n* **4** a movement dedicated to overthrowing a government or occupation forces **5** (often preceded by *the*) an electric passenger railway operated in underground tunnels

undergrowth *n* small trees and bushes growing beneath taller trees in a wood or forest

underhand *adj also* **underhanded 1** sly, deceitful, and secretive **2** *sport* same as **underarm** ▷ *adv* **3** in an underhand manner or style

underinsurance *n* *insurance* inadequate insurance cover

underlay *n* felt or rubber laid under a carpet to increase insulation and resilience

underlie *vb* **-lying, -lay, -lain 1** to lie or be placed under **2** to be the foundation, cause, or basis of: *the basic unity which underlies all religion*

underline *vb* **-lining, -lined 1** to put a line under **2** to emphasize

underling *n* *derogatory* a subordinate

underlying *adj* **1** not obvious but detectable: *the deeper and underlying aim of her travels* **2** fundamental; basic: *an underlying belief* **3** lying under: *the underlying layers of the skin*

undermine *vb* **-mining, -mined 1** to weaken gradually or insidiously: *morphia had undermined his grasp of reality* **2** (of the sea or wind) to wear away the base of cliffs

- **WORD HISTORY**
- 'Undermining' is originally a military term,
- denoting the practice in warfare of digging
- mines or tunnels under enemy fortifications in
- order to make them collapse.

underneath *prep, adv* **1** under or beneath ▷ *adj* **2** lower ▷ *n* **3** a lower part or surface ▶ HISTORY Old English *underneothan*

underpants *pl n* a man's undergarment covering the body from the waist or hips to the thighs

underpass *n* **1** a section of a road that passes under another road or a railway line **2** a subway for pedestrians

underpin *vb* **-pinning, -pinned 1** to give strength or support to: *the principles that underpin his political convictions* **2** to support from beneath with a prop: *to underpin a wall* **> underpinning** *n*

underplay *vb* to achieve (an effect) by deliberate lack of emphasis

underprivileged *adj* **1** lacking the rights and advantages of other members of society; deprived ▷ *n* **2 the underprivileged** underprivileged people regarded as a group

underrate *vb* **-rating, -rated** to not be aware or take account of the full abilities or potential of **> underrated** *adj*

undersea *adj, adv* below the surface of the sea

underseal *n* **1** a special coating applied to the underside of a motor vehicle to prevent corrosion ▷ *vb* **2** to apply such a coating to a motor vehicle

undersecretary *n, pl* **-taries** a senior civil servant or junior minister in a government department

undersell *vb* **-selling, -sold** to sell at a price lower than that of another seller

undershoot *vb* **-shooting, -shot** *aviation* to land an aircraft short of a runway

underside *n* the bottom or lower surface

undersized *adj* smaller than normal

underskirt *n* a skirtlike garment worn under a skirt or dress; petticoat

understand *vb* **-standing, -stood 1** to know and comprehend the nature or meaning of: *I understand what you are saying* **2** to know what is happening or why it is happening: *in order to understand the problems that can occur* **3** to assume, infer, or believe: *I understand he is based in this town* **4** to know how to translate or read: *don't you understand Russian?* **5** to be sympathetic to or compatible with: *she needed him to understand her completely* ▶ HISTORY Old English *understandan* **> understandable** *adj* **> understandably** *adv*

understanding *n* **1** the ability to learn, judge, or make decisions **2** a personal opinion or interpretation of a subject: *my understanding of what he said* **3** a mutual agreement, usually an informal or private one ▷ *adj* **4** kind, sympathetic, or tolerant towards people

understate *vb* **-stating, -stated 1** to describe or portray something in restrained terms, often to obtain an ironic effect **2** to state that something, such as a number, is less than it is **> understatement** *n*

understudy *n, pl* **-studies 1** an actor who studies a part so as to be able to replace the usual actor if necessary **2** anyone who is trained to take the place of another if necessary ▷ *vb* **-studies, -studying, -studied 3** to act as an understudy to

undertake *vb* **-taking, -took, -taken 1** to agree to or commit oneself to something or to do something: *I undertook the worst job in gardening* **2** to promise to do something

undertaker *n* a person whose job is to look after the bodies of people who have died and to organize funerals

undertaking *n* **1** a task or enterprise **2** an agreement to do something **3** *informal* the practice of overtaking on an inner lane a vehicle which is travelling in an outer lane

undertone n 1 a quiet tone of voice 2 something which suggests an underlying quality or feeling: *an undertone of anger*

undertow n a strong undercurrent flowing in a different direction from the surface current, such as in the sea

undervalue vb **-valuing, -valued** to value a person or thing at less than the true worth or importance

underwater adj 1 situated, occurring, or for use under the surface of the sea, a lake, or a river ▷ adv 2 beneath the surface of the sea, a lake, or a river

under way adj 1 in progress; taking place: *this test is already under way* 2 naut in motion in the direction headed

underwear n clothing worn under other garments, usually next to the skin

underweight adj weighing less than is average, expected, or healthy

underworld n 1 criminals and their associates 2 *classical myth* the regions below the earth's surface regarded as the abode of the dead

underwrite vb **-writing, -wrote, -written** 1 to accept financial responsibility for a commercial project or enterprise 2 to sign and issue an insurance policy, thus accepting liability 3 to support > **underwriter** n

undesirable adj 1 not desirable or pleasant; objectionable ▷ n 2 a person considered undesirable

undies pl n Brit, Austral & NZ, informal women's underwear

undiluted adj 1 (of a liquid) not having any water added to it; concentrated 2 not mixed with any other feeling or quality: *undiluted hatred*

undistinguished adj not particularly good or bad; mediocre

undo vb **-doing, -did, -done** 1 to open, unwrap, or untie 2 to reverse the effects of: *all the work of the congress would be undone* 3 to cause the downfall of

undoing n 1 ruin; downfall 2 the cause of someone's downfall: *his confidence was his undoing*

undone¹ adj not done or completed; unfinished

undone² adj 1 ruined; destroyed 2 unfastened; untied

undoubted adj beyond doubt; certain or indisputable > **undoubtedly** adv

undress vb 1 to take off the clothes of oneself or another ▷ n 2 **in a state of undress** naked or nearly naked 3 informal or ordinary working clothes or uniform > **undressed** adj

undue adj greater than is reasonable; excessive: *undue attention*

undulate vb **-lating, -lated** 1 to move gently and slowly from side to side or up and down 2 to have a wavy shape or appearance ▶ **HISTORY** Latin *unda* a wave > **undulation** n

unduly adv excessively

undying adj never ending; eternal

unearned income n income from property or investments rather than work

unearth vb 1 to discover by searching 2 to dig up out of the earth

unearthly adj 1 strange, unnatural, or eerie: *unearthly beauty* 2 ridiculous or unreasonable: *the unearthly hour of seven in the morning* > **unearthliness** n

unease n 1 anxiety or nervousness: *my unease grew when she was not back by midnight* 2 dissatisfaction or tension: *unease about the government's handling of the affair*

uneasy adj 1 (of a person) anxious or apprehensive 2 (of a condition) precarious or insecure: *an uneasy peace* 3 (of a thought or feeling) disquieting > **uneasily** adv > **uneasiness** n

uneatable adj (of food) so rotten or unattractive as to be unfit to eat

uneconomic adj not producing enough profit

unemployed adj 1 without paid employment; out of work 2 not being used; idle ▷ pl n 3 people who are out of work: *the long-term unemployed*

unemployment n 1 the condition of being unemployed 2 the number of unemployed workers: *unemployment rose again last month*

unemployment benefit n (formerly, in the British National Insurance scheme, and currently, in New Zealand) a regular payment to an unemployed person

unequivocal adj completely clear in meaning; unambiguous > **unequivocally** adv

unerring adj never mistaken; consistently accurate

UNESCO United Nations Educational, Scientific, and Cultural Organization

uneven adj 1 (of a surface) not level or flat 2 not consistent in quality: *an uneven performance* 3 not parallel, straight, or horizontal 4 not fairly matched: *the uneven battle*

unexceptionable adj not likely to be criticized or objected to

unexceptional adj usual, ordinary, or normal

unexpected adj surprising or unforeseen > **unexpectedly** adv

unexpurgated adj (of a piece of writing) not censored by having allegedly offensive passages removed

unfailing adj continuous or reliable: *his unfailing enthusiasm* > **unfailingly** adv

unfair adj 1 unequal or unjust 2 dishonest or unethical > **unfairly** adv > **unfairness** n

unfaithful adj 1 not loyal to one's romantic partner 2 not true to a promise or vow > **unfaithfulness** n

unfathomable adj too strange or complicated to be understood: *pugs exert a powerful, unfathomable hold over their owners*

unfavourable or US **unfavorable** adj 1 making a successful or positive outcome unlikely: *unfavourable weather conditions* 2 disapproving: *an unfavourable opinion* > **unfavourably** or US **unfavorably** adv

unfeeling adj written without sympathy; callous

u

935

unfit *adj* **1** unqualified for or incapable of a particular role or task: *an unfit mother; he was unfit to drive* **2** unsuitable: *this meat is unfit for human consumption* **3** in poor physical condition

unflappable *adj informal* (of a person) not easily upset > **unflappability** *n*

unfledged *adj* **1** (of a young bird) not having developed adult feathers **2** immature and inexperienced

unfold *vb* **1** to open or spread out from a folded state **2** to reveal or be revealed: *a terrible truth unfolds* **3** to develop or be developed: *the novel unfolds through their recollections*

unforeseen *adj* surprising because not expected

unforgettable *adj* making such a strong impression that it is impossible to forget > **unforgettably** *adv*

unfortunate *adj* **1** caused or accompanied by bad luck: *an unfortunate coincidence* **2** having bad luck: *my unfortunate daughter* **3** regrettable or unsuitable: *an unfortunate choice of phrase* ▷ *n* **4** an unlucky person > **unfortunately** *adv*

unfounded *adj* (of ideas, fears, or allegations) not based on facts or evidence

unfreeze *vb* **-freezing, -froze, -frozen** **1** to thaw or cause to thaw **2** to relax restrictions or controls on (trade, the transfer of money, etc.): *Congress is considering unfreezing US aid to Jordan*

unfrock *vb* to deprive a person in holy orders of the status of a priest

unfurl *vb* to unroll or spread out (an umbrella, flag, or sail) or (of an umbrella, flag, or sail) to be unrolled or spread out

ungainly *adj* **-lier, -liest** lacking grace when moving ▶ **HISTORY** dialect *gainly* graceful > **ungainliness** *n*

ungodly *adj* **-lier, -liest** **1** wicked or sinful **2** *informal* unreasonable or outrageous: *at this ungodly hour* > **ungodliness** *n*

ungovernable *adj* **1** (of an emotion) not able to be controlled or restrained: *an ungovernable rage* **2** (of a country or area) not able to be effectively governed, esp. because of unrest or violence: *years of religious conflict had made much of the island ungovernable*

ungrammatical *adj* not following the rules of grammar

ungrateful *adj* not showing or offering thanks for a favour or compliment

unguarded *adj* **1** unprotected **2** open or frank: *one unguarded briefing* **3** incautious or careless: *an unguarded moment*

unguent (**ung**-gwent) *n literary* an ointment ▶ **HISTORY** Latin *unguere* to anoint

ungulate (**ung**-gyew-lit) *n* a hoofed mammal ▶ **HISTORY** Latin *ungula* hoof

unhallowed *adj* **1** not consecrated or holy: *unhallowed ground* **2** sinful or wicked

unhand *vb old-fashioned or literary* to release from one's grasp

unhappy *adj* **-pier, -piest** **1** sad or depressed **2** unfortunate or wretched > **unhappily** *adv* > **unhappiness** *n*

unhealthy *adj* **-healthier, -healthiest** **1** likely to cause illness or poor health: *unhealthy foods such as hamburger and chips* **2** not very fit or well **3** caused by or looking as if caused by poor health: *a thin unhealthy look about him* **4** morbid or unwholesome: *an unhealthy interest in computer fraud* > **unhealthiness** *n*

unheard-of *adj* **1** without precedent: *an unheard-of phenomenon* **2** highly offensive: *unheard-of behaviour*

unhinge *vb* **-hinging, -hinged** to make a person mentally deranged or unbalanced > **unhinged** *adj*

unholy *adj* **-lier, -liest** **1** immoral or wicked **2** *informal* outrageous or unnatural: *this unholy mess* > **unholiness** *n*

uni *n Brit, Austral & NZ, informal* short for **university**

uni- *combining form* of, consisting of, or having only one: *unilateral* ▶ **HISTORY** Latin *unus* one

unicameral *adj* of or having a single legislative chamber: *Denmark's unicameral parliament, known as the Folketing*

UNICEF United Nations Children's Fund

unicellular *adj* (of organisms) consisting of a single cell

unicorn *n* a legendary creature resembling a white horse with one horn growing from its forehead ▶ **HISTORY** Latin *unus* one + *cornu* a horn

unicycle *n* a one-wheeled vehicle driven by pedals, used in a circus > **unicyclist** *n*

uniform *n* **1** a special identifying set of clothes for the members of an organization, such as soldiers ▷ *adj* **2** regular and even throughout: *the mixture must be beaten to a uniform consistency* **3** alike or like: *uniform green metal filing cabinets* ▶ **HISTORY** Latin *unus* one + *forma* shape > **uniformity** *n* > **uniformly** *adv*

unify *vb* **-fies, -fying, -fied** to make or become one; unite ▶ **HISTORY** Latin *unus* one + *facere* to make > **unification** *n*

unilateral *adj* made or done by only one person or group: *unilateral action* > **unilateralism** *n*

unimpeachable *adj* completely honest and reliable

uninhabitable *n* not capable of being lived in

uninsurable *adj* insurance considered to be too great a risk for insurance cover

uninterested *adj* having or showing no interest in someone or something

union *n* **1** the act of merging two or more things to become one, or the state of being merged in such a way **2** short for **trade union** **3** an association of individuals or groups for a common purpose: *the Scripture Union* **4 a** an association or society: *the Students' union* **b** the buildings of such an organization **5** marriage **6** *maths* a set containing all the members of two given sets **7** (in 19th-century England) a workhouse maintained by a number of parishes ▷ *adj* **8** of a trade union ▶ **HISTORY** Latin *unus* one

unionism *n* **1** the principles of trade unions **2** adherence to the principles of trade unions > **unionist** *n, adj*

Unionist *n* a supporter of union between Britain and Northern Ireland

unionize *or* **-ise** *vb* **-izing, -ized** *or* **-ising, -ised** to organize workers into a trade union > **unionization** *or* **-isation** *n*

Union Jack *or* **Union flag** *n* the national flag of the United Kingdom, combining the crosses of Saint George, Saint Andrew, and Saint Patrick

unique (yew-**neek**) *adj* **1** being the only one of a particular type **2 unique to** concerning or belonging to a particular person, thing, or group: *certain dishes are unique to this restaurant* **3** without equal or like **4** *informal* remarkable ▶ HISTORY Latin *unicus* unparalleled > **uniquely** *adv*

unisex *adj* (of clothing, a hairstyle, or hairdressers) designed for both sexes

unisexual *adj* **1** of one sex only **2** (of an organism) having either male or female reproductive organs but not both

unison *n* **1 in unison** at the same time as another person or other people: *smiling and nodding in unison* **2** complete agreement: *to act in unison* **3** *music* a style, technique, or passage in which all the performers sing or play the same notes at the same time ▶ HISTORY Latin *unus* one + *sonus* sound

UNISON *n* a British trade union consisting mainly of council and hospital workers

unit *n* **1** a single undivided entity or whole **2** a group or individual regarded as a basic element of a larger whole: *the clan was the basic unit of Highland society* **3** a mechanical part or small device that does a particular job: *a waste disposal unit* **4** a team of people that performs a specific function, and often also their buildings and equipment: *a combat unit* **5** a standard amount of a physical quantity, such as length or energy, used to express magnitudes of that quantity: *the year as a unit of time* **6** *maths* the digit or position immediately to the left of the decimal point **7** a piece of furniture designed to be fitted with other similar pieces: *bedroom units* **8** *NZ* a self-propelled railcar **9** *Austral & NZ* short for **home unit** ▶ HISTORY from *unity*

Unitarian *n* **1** a person who believes that God is one being and rejects the Trinity ▷ *adj* **2** of Unitarians or Unitarianism > **Unitarianism** *n*

unitary *adj* **1** consisting of a single undivided whole: *a unitary state* **2** of a unit or units

unit cost *n* the actual cost of producing one article

unite *vb* **uniting, united 1** to make or become an integrated whole: *conception occurs when a sperm unites with the egg* **2** to form an association or alliance: *the opposition parties unite to fight against privatization* **3** to possess (a combination of qualities) at the same time: *he manages to unite charm and ruthlessness* ▶ HISTORY Latin *unus* one

united *adj* **1** produced by two or more people or things in combination: *a united effort*

2 in agreement: *we are united in our opposition to these proposals* **3** in association or alliance

United Kingdom *n* a kingdom of NW Europe, consisting of the island of Great Britain together with Northern Ireland

United Nations *n* an international organization of independent states, formed to promote peace and international security

unit price *n* the price charged per unit

unit trust *n* *Brit & Austral* an investment trust that issues units for public sale and invests the money in many different businesses

unity *n, pl* **-ties 1** the state of being one **2** mutual agreement: *unity of intention* **3** the state of being a single thing that is composed of separate parts, organizations, etc.: *moves towards church unity* **4** *maths* the number or numeral one ▶ HISTORY Latin *unus* one

Univ. University

univalent *adj* *chem* same as **monovalent**

universal *adj* **1** of or relating to everyone in the world or everyone in a particular place or society: *the introduction of universal primary education* **2** of, relating to, or affecting the entire world or universe: *the universal laws of physics* **3** true and relevant at all times and in all situations: *there may be no single universal solution* ▷ *n* **4** something which exists or is true in all places and all situations: *universals such as beauty and justice* > **universality** *n* > **universally** *adv*

universal joint *or* **coupling** *n* a form of coupling between two rotating shafts allowing freedom of movement in all directions

universe *n* **1** the whole of all existing matter, energy, and space **2** the world ▶ HISTORY Latin *universum* the whole world

university *n, pl* **-ties 1** an institution of higher education with authority to award degrees **2** the buildings, members, staff, or campus of a university ▶ HISTORY Medieval Latin *universitas* group of scholars

Unix (yew-**nicks**) *n* *trademark* an operating system found on many types of computer

unkempt *adj* **1** (of the hair) uncombed or dishevelled **2** untidy or slovenly: *an unkempt appearance* ▶ HISTORY Old English *uncembed*, from *cemban* to comb

unkind *adj* unsympathetic or cruel > **unkindly** *adv* > **unkindness** *n*

unknown *adj* **1** not known, understood, or recognized **2** not famous: *a young and then unknown actor* **3 unknown quantity** a person or thing whose action or effect is unknown or unpredictable ▷ *n* **4** an unknown person, quantity, or thing **5** *maths* a variable whose value is to be discovered by solving an equation ▷ *adv* **6 unknown to someone** without someone being aware: *unknown to him, the starboard engine had dropped off*

unlawful *adj* not permitted by law; illegal

unleaded *adj* (of petrol) containing less tetraethyl lead, in order to reduce environmental pollution

unleash *vb* to set loose or cause (something bad): *to unleash war*

unleavened (un-**lev**-vend) *adj* (of bread) made without yeast or leavening

unless *conj* except under the circumstances that; except on the condition that: *you can't get in unless you can prove you're over eighteen*

unlettered *adj* uneducated or illiterate

unlike *adj* **1** not similar; different ▷ *prep* **2** not like or typical of: *unlike his brother, he could not control his weight* > **unlikeness** *n*

unlikely *adj* not likely; improbable > **unlikeliness** *n*

unlikely outcome *n statistics* an outcome which falls at the opposite end of a likelihood scale from a certain chance

unlimited *adj* **1** apparently endless: *there was unlimited coffee* **2** not restricted or limited: *unlimited access to the rest of the palace*

unlisted *adj* **1** not entered on a list **2** (of securities) not quoted on a stock exchange **3** *Austral, US & Canad* not listed in a telephone directory by request

unload *vb* **1** to remove cargo from a ship, lorry, or plane **2** to express worries or problems by telling someone about them **3** to remove the ammunition from a gun

unlooked-for *adj* unexpected or unforeseen

unlucky *adj* **1** having bad luck or misfortune: *an unlucky man* **2** caused by bad luck or misfortune: *an unlucky coincidence* **3** regarded as likely to bring about bad luck: *an unlucky number* > **unluckily** *adv*

unman *vb* **-manning, -manned** **1** to cause to lose courage or nerve **2** to make effeminate

unmanned *adj* **1** having no personnel or crew: *the border posts were unmanned* **2** (of an aircraft or spacecraft) operated by automatic or remote control

unmarried *adj* not married

unmask *vb* **1** to remove the mask or disguise from **2** to expose or reveal the true nature or character of

unmentionable *adj* unsuitable as a topic of conversation

unmistakable *or* **unmistakeable** *adj* clear or unambiguous > **unmistakably** *or* **unmistakeably** *adv*

unmitigated *adj* **1** not reduced or lessened in severity or intensity **2** total and complete: *unmitigated boredom*

unmoved *adj* not affected by emotion; indifferent

unnatural *adj* **1** strange and slightly frightening because it is not usual; abnormal: *an unnatural silence* **2** not in accordance with accepted standards of behaviour: *an unnatural relationship* **3** affected or forced: *a determined smile which seemed unnatural* **4** inhuman or monstrous: *unnatural evils* > **unnaturally** *adv*

unnecessary *adj* not essential, or more than is essential > **unnecessarily** *adv*

unnerve *vb* **-nerving, -nerved** to cause to lose courage, confidence, or self-control: *he unnerves me* > **unnerving** *adj*

unnumbered *adj* **1** countless; too many to count **2** not counted or given a number

UNO United Nations Organization

unobtrusive *adj* not drawing attention to oneself or itself; inconspicuous

unoccupied *adj* **1** (of a building) without occupants **2** unemployed or idle **3** (of an area or country) not overrun by foreign troops

unofficial *adj* **1** not authorized or approved by the relevant organization or person: *an unofficial strike* **2** not confirmed officially: *unofficial reports of the minister's resignation*

unorganized *or* **-nised** *adj* **1** not arranged into an organized system or structure **2** (of workers) not unionized

unorthodox *adj* **1** (of ideas, methods, etc.) unconventional and not generally accepted **2** (of a person) not conventional in beliefs, behaviour, etc.

unpack *vb* **1** to remove the packed contents of a case **2** to take something out of a packed container

unpaid *adj* **1** without a salary or wage: *unpaid overtime* **2** still to be paid: *unpaid bills*

unpalatable *adj* **1** (of food) unpleasant to taste **2** (of a fact, idea, etc.) unpleasant and hard to accept

unparalleled *adj* not equalled; supreme

unparliamentary *adj* not consistent with parliamentary procedure or practice

unpick *vb* to undo the stitches of a piece of sewing

unplayable *adj sport* **1** (of a ball) thrown too fast or too skilfully to be hit **2** (of a pitch or course) too badly affected by rain or frost to be used

unpleasant *adj* not pleasant or agreeable > **unpleasantly** *adv* > **unpleasantness** *n*

unplug *vb* **-plugging, -plugged** to disconnect a piece of electrical equipment by taking the plug out of the socket

unpopular *adj* generally disliked or disapproved of > **unpopularity** *n*

unprecedented *adj* never having happened before: *an unprecedented decision*

unprepossessing *adj* not very attractive or appealing

unpretentious *adj* modest, unassuming, and down-to-earth

unprincipled *adj* lacking moral principles; unscrupulous

unprintable *adj* unsuitable for printing for reasons of obscenity, libel, or indecency

unproductive *adj* not producing any worthwhile results: *unproductive talks*

unprofessional *adj* not behaving according to the standards expected of a member of a particular profession

unprofitable *adj* **1** not making a profit **2** not producing any worthwhile results: *an unprofitable line of thinking*

unputdownable *adj* (of a book, usually a novel) so gripping that one wants to read it at one sitting

unqualified *adj* **1** lacking the necessary qualifications **2** having no conditions or

u

limitations: *an unqualified denial* **3** total or complete: *unqualified admiration*

unquestionable *adj* not to be doubted; indisputable > **unquestionably** *adv*

unquote *interj spoken* an expression used to indicate the end of a quotation that was introduced with the word 'quote'

unravel *vb* **-elling, -elled** *or US* **-eling, -eled** **1** to separate something knitted or woven into individual strands **2** to become separated into individual strands **3** to explain or solve: *we unravelled the secrets*

unreactive *adj* (of a substance) not readily partaking in chemical reactions

unreadable *adj* **1** unable to be read or deciphered; illegible **2** too difficult or dull to read

unreal *adj* **1** existing only in the imagination or giving the impression of doing so: *an unreal quality* **2** insincere or artificial > **unreality** *n*

unreasonable *adj* **1** unfair and excessive: *an unreasonable request* **2** refusing to listen to reason > **unreasonably** *adv*

unrecognized *or* **-ised** *adj* not properly identified or acknowledged: *her talents went unrecognized during her lifetime*

unremitting *adj* never slackening or stopping

unrequited *adj* (of love) not returned

unreserved *adj* **1** complete and without holding back any doubts: *unreserved support* **2** open and forthcoming in manner **3** not booked or not able to be booked: *all the seats are unreserved* > **unreservedly** (un-riz-**zerv**-id-lee) *adv*

unrest *n* **1** a rebellious state of discontent **2** an uneasy or troubled state

unrighteous *adj* sinful or wicked

unrivalled *or US* **unrivaled** *adj* having no equal; matchless

unroll *vb* **1** to open out or unwind: *I unrolled the map* **2** (of a series of events or period of time) to happen or be revealed or remembered one after the other

unruffled *adj* **1** calm and unperturbed **2** smooth and still: *unruffled ponds*

unruly *adj* **-lier, -liest** difficult to control or organize; disobedient or undisciplined > **unruliness** *n*

unsafe *adj* **1** dangerous **2** (of a criminal conviction) based on inadequate or false evidence

unsaturated *adj* **1** *chem* (of an organic compound) containing a double or triple bond and therefore capable of combining with other substances **2** (of a fat, esp. a vegetable fat) containing a high proportion of fatty acids with double bonds

unsavoury *or US* **unsavory** *adj* objectionable or distasteful: *an unsavoury divorce*

unscathed *adj* not harmed or injured

unscrupulous *adj* prepared to act in a dishonest or immoral manner

unseasonable *adj* **1** (of the weather) inappropriate for the season **2** inappropriate or unusual for the time of year: *an unseasonable dip in the sea*

unseat *vb* **1** to throw or displace from a seat or saddle **2** to depose from office or position

unseemly *adj* not according to expected standards of behaviour > **unseemliness** *n*

unseen *adj* **1** hidden or invisible: *an unseen organist was practising* **2** mysterious or supernatural: *unseen powers* ▷ *adv* **3** without being seen; unnoticed: *the thief entered unseen* ▷ *n* **4** a passage which is given to students for translation without them having seen it in advance

unsettled *adj* **1** lacking order or stability: *an unsettled time* **2** disturbed and restless: *your child will feel unsettled and insecure* **3** constantly changing or moving from place to place: *his wandering unsettled life* **4** (of an argument or dispute) not resolved **5** (of a debt or bill) not yet paid

unshakable *or* **unshakeable** *adj* (of beliefs) utterly firm and unwavering

unsightly *adj* unpleasant to look at; ugly > **unsightliness** *n*

unsigned *adj* (of a letter, etc.) anonymous

unskilled *adj* having no skills or no special skills

unsocial *adj* **1** not fond of the company of other people **2** (of the hours of work of a job) falling outside the normal working day

unsolicited *adj* not requested or invited: *unsolicited advice*

unsound *adj* **1** unhealthy or unstable: *of unsound mind* **2** based on faulty ideas: *unsound judgment* **3** not firm: *unsound foundations* **4** not financially reliable: *his business plan was unsound*

unspeakable *adj* **1** incapable of expression in words: *unspeakable gratitude* **2** indescribably bad or evil: *unspeakable atrocities* > **unspeakably** *adv*

unstable *adj* **1** not firmly fixed and likely to wobble or fall: *an unstable pile of books* **2** likely to change suddenly and create difficulties or danger: *the unstable political climate* **3** (of a person) having abrupt changes of mood or behaviour **4** *chem, physics* readily decomposing

unsteady *adj* **1** not securely fixed: *unsteady metal posts* **2** (of a manner of walking, standing, or holding) shaky or staggering > **unsteadily** *adv* > **unsteadiness** *n*

unstinting *adj* generous and gladly given: *unstinting praise*

unstressed syllable *n linguistics* a part of a word that is not stressed when it is pronounced

unstructured *adj* without formal or systematic organization

unstuck *adj* **1** freed from being stuck, glued, or fastened **2 come unstuck** to suffer failure or disaster

unstudied *adj* natural or spontaneous: *her unstudied elegance and grace*

unsuccessful *adj* not achieving success

unsuitable *adj* not right or appropriate for a particular purpose

unsuited *adj* **1** not appropriate for a particular task or situation: *a likeable man unsuited to a military career* **2** (of a couple) having different personalities or tastes and unlikely to form a lasting relationship: *they are totally unsuited to each other*

unsung *adj written* not appreciated or honoured: *an unsung hero*

unswerving *adj* not turning aside; constant

unsympathetic *adj* **1** not feeling or showing sympathy **2** unpleasant and unlikeable **3** (foll. by *to*) opposed or hostile to

untapped *adj* not yet used or exploited: *untapped mineral reserves*

untaught *adj* **1** without training or education **2** acquired without instruction

untenable *adj* (of a theory, idea, etc.) impossible to defend in an argument

unthinkable *adj* **1** so shocking or unpleasant that one cannot believe it to be true **2** unimaginable or inconceivable

untidy *adj* **-dier, -diest** not neat; messy and disordered > **untidily** *adv* > **untidiness** *n*

untie *vb* **-tying, -tied** to unfasten or free someone or something that is tied

until *conj* **1** up to a time that: *he lifted the wire until it was taut* **2** before (a time or event): *until the present crisis, they weren't allowed into the country* ▷ *prep* **3** (often preceded by *up*) in or throughout the period before: *up until then I'd never thought about having kids* **4** before: *Baker does not get to Israel until Sunday* ▶ HISTORY earlier *untill*

untimely *adj* **1** occurring before the expected or normal time: *his untimely death* **2** inappropriate to the occasion or time: *an untimely idea to raise at the United Nations* > **untimeliness** *n*

unto *prep archaic* to ▶ HISTORY from Old Norse

untold *adj* **1** incapable of description: *untold misery* **2** incalculably great in number or quantity: *untold millions* **3** not told

untouchable *adj* **1** above criticism, suspicion, or punishment **2** unable to be touched ▷ *n* **3** *offensive* a member of the lowest class in India, whose touch was formerly regarded as defiling to the four main castes

untoward *adj* **1** causing misfortune or annoyance **2** unfavourable: *untoward reactions* **3** out of the ordinary; out of the way: *nothing untoward had happened*

untried *adj* **1** not yet used, done, or tested **2** (of a prisoner) not yet put on trial

untrue *adj* **1** incorrect or false **2** disloyal or unfaithful

untruth *n* a statement that is not true; lie

untruthful *adj* **1** (of a person) given to lying **2** (of a statement) not true > **untruthfully** *adv*

untutored *adj* **1** without formal education **2** lacking sophistication or refinement

unusual *adj* uncommon or extraordinary > **unusually** *adv*

unutterable *adj written* incapable of being expressed in words > **unutterably** *adv*

unvarnished *adj* not elaborated upon; plain: *an unvarnished account of literary life*

unveil *vb* **1** to ceremonially remove the cover from a new picture, plaque, etc. **2** to make

public a secret **3** to remove the veil from one's own or another person's face

unveiling *n* **1** a ceremony involving the removal of a veil covering a new picture, statue, plaque, etc. **2** the presentation of something for the first time

unvoiced *adj* **1** not expressed or spoken **2** *phonetics* voiceless

unwarranted *adj* not justified or necessary

unwell *adj* not healthy; ill

unwieldy *adj* too heavy, large, or awkward to be easily handled

unwilling *adj* **1** reluctant **2** done or said with reluctance > **unwillingly** *adv* > **unwillingness** *n*

unwind *vb* **-winding, -wound** **1** to slacken, undo, or unravel: *Paul started to unwind the bandage* **2** to relax after a busy or tense time: *we go out to unwind after work*

unwitting *adj* **1** not intentional **2** not knowing or conscious ▶ HISTORY Old English *unwitende* > **unwittingly** *adv*

unwonted *adj* out of the ordinary; unusual

unworthy *adj* **1** (often foll. by *of*) not deserving or meriting: *a person deemed unworthy of membership* **2** (often foll. by *of*) beneath the level considered befitting (to): *unworthy of a prime minister* **3** lacking merit or value > **unworthiness** *n*

unwrap *vb* **-wrapping, -wrapped** to remove the wrapping from something or (of something wrapped) to have the covering removed

unwritten *adj* **1** not printed or in writing **2** operating only through custom: *an unwritten code of conduct*

up *prep* **1** indicating movement to a higher position: *go up the stairs* **2** at a higher or further level or position in or on: *a shop up the road* ▷ *adv* **3** to an upward, higher, or erect position: *the men straightened up from their digging* **4** indicating readiness for an activity: *up and about* **5** indicating intensity or completion of an action: *he tore up the cheque* **6** to the place referred to or where the speaker is: *a man came up to me* **7 a** *mostly spoken* to a more important place: *up to the city* **b** *mostly spoken* to a more northerly place: *pensioners who were going up to Norway* **c** to or at university **8** above the horizon: *the sun came up* **9** appearing for trial: *up before the judge* **10** having gained: *ten pounds up on the deal* **11** higher in price: *beer has gone up again* **12 all up with someone** *informal* over for or hopeless for someone **13 something's up** *informal* something strange is happening **14 up against** having to cope with: *look what we're up against now* **15 up for** being a candidate or applicant for: *he's up for the job* **16 up to a** occupied with; scheming: *she's up to no good* **b** dependent upon: *the decision is up to you* **c** equal to or capable of: *are you up to playing in the final?* **d** as far as: *up to his neck in mud* **e** as many as: *up to two years' credit* **f** comparable with: *not up to my usual standard* **17 what's up?** *informal* **a** what is the matter? **b** what is happening? ▷ *adj* **18** of a high or higher position **19** out of bed: *aren't you up yet?* **20** (of a period of time) over or completed: *the* examiner announced that their time was up **21** of or relating to a train going to a more important place: *the up platform* ▷ *vb* **upping, upped** **22** to increase or raise **23 up and** *informal* to do something suddenly: *he upped and left her* ▷ *n* **24** a high point: *every couple has ups and downs* **25 on the up and up** *informal* **a** *US* trustworthy or honest **b** *Brit, Austral & NZ* on an upward trend: *our firm's on the up and up* ▶ HISTORY Old English *upp*

up-and-coming *adj* likely to be successful in the future; promising

upbeat *adj* **1** *informal* cheerful and optimistic: *the upbeat atmosphere of a thriving metropolis* ▷ *n* **2** *music* **a** an unaccented beat **b** the upward gesture of a conductor's baton indicating this

upbraid *vb* to scold or reproach ▶ HISTORY Old English *upbrēdan*

upbringing *n* the education of a person during his or her formative years

upcountry *adj* **1** of or from the interior of a country ▷ *adv* **2** towards or in the interior of a country

update *vb* **-dating, -dated** to bring up to date

upend *vb* to turn or set or become turned or set on end

upfront *adj* **1** open and frank ▷ *adv, adj* **2** (of money) paid out at the beginning of a business arrangement

upgrade *vb* **-grading, -graded** **1** to promote a person or job to a higher rank **2** to raise in value, importance, or esteem

upheaval *n* a strong, sudden, or violent disturbance

uphill *adj* **1** sloping or leading upwards **2** requiring a great deal of effort: *an uphill struggle* ▷ *adv* **3** up a slope ▷ *n* **4** *S African* a difficulty

uphold *vb* **-holding, -held** **1** to maintain or defend against opposition **2** to give moral support to > **upholder** *n*

upholster *vb* to fit chairs or sofas with padding, springs, and covering > **upholstered** *adj* > **upholsterer** *n*

upholstery *n* the padding, springs, and covering of a chair or sofa

upkeep *n* **1** the act or process of keeping something in good repair **2** the cost of maintenance

upland *adj* of or in an area of high or relatively high ground: *an upland wilderness*

uplands *pl n* an area of high or relatively high ground: *the uplands of Nepal*

uplift *vb* **1** to raise or lift up **2** to raise morally or spiritually **3** *Scot* to collect or pick up ▷ *n* **4** the act or process of bettering moral, social, or cultural conditions > **uplifting** *adj*

upload *vb* to transfer (data or a program) from one's own computer into the memory of another computer

up-market *adj* expensive and of superior quality

upon *prep* **1** on **2** up and on: *they climbed upon his lap for comfort* ▶ HISTORY *up + on*

upper *adj* **1** higher or highest in physical position,

wealth, rank, or status **2 Upper** *geol* denoting the late part of a period or formation: *Upper Cretaceous* ▷ *n* **3** the part of a shoe above the sole **4 on one's uppers** *Brit, Austral & NZ, informal* very poor; penniless

upper-case *adj* denoting capital letters as used in printed or typed matter

upper class *n* **1** the highest social class; aristocracy ▷ *adj* **upper-class 2** of the upper class

upper crust *n* *Brit, Austral & NZ, informal* the upper class

uppercut *n* a short swinging upward punch delivered to the chin

upper hand *n* the position of control: *the hardliners have gained the upper hand*

Upper House *n* the smaller and less representative chamber of a two-chamber parliament, for example the House of Lords or a Senate

uppermost *adj* **1** highest in position, power, or importance ▷ *adv* **2** in or into the highest place or position

uppish *adj* *Brit, informal* uppity

uppity *adj* *informal* snobbish, arrogant, or presumptuous ▶ HISTORY *up* + fanciful ending

upright *adj* **1** vertical or erect **2** honest or just ▷ *adv* **3** vertically or in an erect position ▷ *n* **4** a vertical support, such as a post **5** the state of being vertical > **uprightness** *n*

uprising *n* a revolt or rebellion

uproar *n* **1** a commotion or disturbance characterized by loud noise and confusion **2** angry public criticism or debates: *the decision to close the railway led to an uproar*

uproarious *adj* **1** very funny **2** (of laughter) loud and boisterous

uproot *vb* **1** to pull up by or as if by the roots **2** to displace (a person or people) from their native or usual surroundings **3** to remove or destroy utterly: *we must uproot all remnants of feudalism*

ups and downs *pl n* alternating periods of good and bad luck or high and low spirits

upset *adj* **1** emotionally or physically disturbed or distressed ▷ *vb* **-setting, -set 2** to turn or tip over **3** to disrupt the normal state or progress of: *bad weather upset their plans* **4** to disturb mentally or emotionally **5** to make physically ill: *it still seems to upset my stomach* ▷ *n* **6** an unexpected defeat or reversal, as in a contest or plans **7** a disturbance or disorder of the emotions, mind, or body > **upsetting** *adj*

upset price *n* *chiefly Scot, US & Canad* the lowest price acceptable for something that is for sale by auction, usually a house

upshot *n* the final result or conclusion; outcome ▶ HISTORY *up + shot*

upside down *adj* **1** with the bottom where the top would normally be; inverted **2** *informal* confused or jumbled ▷ *adv* **3** in an inverted fashion **4** in a chaotic manner or into a chaotic state: *recent events have changed many people's lives upside down* ▶ HISTORY by folk etymology, from *upsodown*

upstage *adv* **1** on, at, or to the rear of the stage ▷ *adj* **2** at the back half of the stage ▷ *vb* **-staging, -staged 3** to move upstage of another actor, forcing him or her to turn away from the audience **4** *informal* to draw attention to oneself and away from someone else

upstairs *adv* **1** to or on an upper floor of a building **2** *informal* to or into a higher rank or office ▷ *n* **3** an upper floor ▷ *adj* **4** situated on an upper floor: *an upstairs bedroom*

upstanding *adj* **1** of good character **2** upright and vigorous in build

upstart *n* a person who has risen suddenly to a position of power and behaves arrogantly

upstream *adv, adj* in or towards the higher part of a stream; against the current

upsurge *n* a rapid rise or swell

upswing *n* **1** *econ* a recovery period in the trade cycle **2** any increase or improvement

uptake *n* **1 quick** *or* **slow on the uptake** *informal* quick *or* slow to understand or learn **2** the use or consumption of something by a machine or part of the body: *the uptake of oxygen into the blood*

upthrust *n* **1** an upward push **2** *geol* a violent upheaval of the earth's surface

uptight *adj informal* **1** nervously tense, irritable, or angry **2** unable to express one's feelings

up-to-date *adj* modern or fashionable: *an up-to-date kitchen*

upturn *n* **1** an upward trend or improvement ▷ *vb* **2** to turn or cause to turn over or upside down

UPVC unplasticized polyvinyl chloride

upward *adj* directed or moving towards a higher place or level ▷ *adv also* **upwards 2** from a lower to a higher place, level, or condition **3 upward** *or* **upwards of** more than (the stated figure): *a crowd estimated at upward of one hundred thousand people*

upward mobility *n* movement from a lower to a higher economic and social status

upwind *adv* **1** into or against the wind **2** towards or on the side where the wind is blowing ▷ *adj* **3** going against the wind **4** on the windward side

Urania *n* *Greek myth* the Muse of astronomy

uranium (yew-**rain**-ee-um) *n* *chem* a radioactive silvery-white metallic element of the actinide series. It is used chiefly as a source of nuclear energy by fission of the radioisotope **uranium 235**. Symbol: U ▸ HISTORY from *Uranus*, from the fact that the element was discovered soon after the planet

Uranus *n* **1** *Greek myth* a god; the personification of the sky **2** the seventh planet from the sun ▸ HISTORY Greek *Ouranos* heaven

urban *adj* **1** of or living in a city or town **2** relating to modern pop music of African-American origin, such as hip-hop ▸ HISTORY Latin *urbs* city

urban decay *n* deterioration in an area of a town or city characterized by lack of maintenance, poor infrastructure, vandalism, etc.

urbane *adj* polite, elegant, and sophisticated in manner ▸ HISTORY Latin *urbanus* of the town

urban heat island *n* *geog* an area of heat intensification in a city caused by ultra-violet light rays becoming trapped by atmospheric pollution

urban hierarchy *n* the ranking of cities, towns, and villages by size and provision of services

urbanity *n* the quality of being urbane

urbanize *or* **-ise** *vb* **-izing, -ized** *or* **-ising, -ised 1** to make a rural area more industrialized and urban **2** *geog* to cause people to move out of rural areas and settle in cities > **urbanization** *or* **-isation** *n*

urban morphology *n* *geog, civil engineering* the shape and structure of a town or city

urban renewal *n* *civil engineering* the process of redeveloping dilapidated or no longer functional urban areas

urban sprawl *n* *civil engineering* the part of a city or town that has not been planned and spreads out untidily over a large area

urchin *n* **1** a mischievous child **2** See **sea urchin** ▸ HISTORY Latin *ericius* hedgehog

Urdu (**oor**-doo) *n* an Indic language of the Indo-European family which is an official language of Pakistan and is also spoken in India ▸ HISTORY Hindustani (*zabāni*) *urdū* (language of the) camp

urea (**yew**-ree-a) *n* a white soluble crystalline compound found in urine ▸ HISTORY Greek *ouron* urine

ureter (yew-**reet**-er) *n* the tube that carries urine from the kidney to the bladder ▸ HISTORY Greek *ourein* to urinate

urethra (yew-**reeth**-ra) *n* the tube that in most mammals carries urine from the bladder out of the body ▸ HISTORY Greek *ourein* to urinate

urethritis (yew-rith-**rite**-iss) *n* inflammation of the urethra causing a discharge and painful urination > **urethritic** *adj*

urge *n* **1** a strong impulse, inner drive, or yearning ▷ *vb* **urging, urged 2** to plead with or press someone to do something: *he urged his readers to do the same* **3** to advocate earnestly and persistently: *I have long urged this change* **4** to force or hasten onwards: *something very powerful urged him on* ▸ HISTORY Latin *urgere*

urgent *adj* **1** requiring speedy action or attention: *an urgent inquiry* **2** earnest and forceful: *she heard loud urgent voices in the corridor* ▸ HISTORY Latin *urgere* to urge > **urgency** *n* > **urgently** *adv*

uric (**yew**-rik) *adj* of or derived from urine

uric acid *n* a white odourless crystalline acid present in the blood and urine

urinal *n* **1** a sanitary fitting, used by men for urination **2** a room containing urinals

urinary *adj* *anat* of urine or the organs that secrete and pass urine

urinary bladder *n* a membranous sac that can expand in which urine excreted from the kidneys is stored

urinate *vb* **-nating, -nated** to excrete urine > **urination** *n*

urine *n* the pale yellow fluid excreted by the kidneys, containing waste products from the

u

blood. It is stored in the bladder and discharged through the urethra ▶ HISTORY Latin *urina*

urinogenital (yew-rin-oh-**jen**-it-al) *adj* same as **urogenital**

URL uniform resource locator: a standardized address of a location on the internet

urn *n* **1** a vaselike container, usually with a foot and a rounded body **2** a vase used as a container for the ashes of the dead **3** a large metal container, with a tap, used for making and holding tea or coffee ▶ HISTORY Latin *urna*

urogenital (yew-roh-**jen**-it-al) *or* **urinogenital** *adj* of the urinary and genital organs and their functions. Also: **genitourinary**

urology (yew-**rol**-a-jee) *n* the branch of medicine concerned with the urinary system and its diseases

ursine *adj* of or like a bear ▶ HISTORY Latin *ursus* a bear

us *pron* (objective) **1** refers to the speaker or writer and another person or other people: *the bond between us* **2** refers to all people or people in general: *this table shows us the tides* **3** *informal, spoken* me: *give us a kiss!* **4** *formal* same as **me**: used by monarchs ▶ HISTORY Old English *ūs*

US *or* **U.S.** United States

USA *or* **U.S.A.** United States of America

usable *adj* able to be used > **usability** *n*

usage *n* **1** regular or constant use: *a move to reduce pesticide usage* **2** the way in which a word is actually used in a language **3** a particular meaning or use that a word can have ▶ HISTORY Latin *usus* a use

USB Universal Serial Bus: a standard for connecting sockets on computers

use *vb* **using, used** **1** to put into service or action; employ for a given purpose: *use a garden fork to mix them together* **2** to choose or employ regularly: *what sort of toothpaste do you use?* **3** to take advantage of; exploit: *I used Jason and he used me* **4** to consume or expend: *a manufacturing plant uses 1000 tonnes of steel a month* ▷ *n* **5** the act or fact of using or being used: *large-scale use of pesticides* **6** the ability or permission to use **7** need or opportunity to use: *the Colombian government had no use for them* **8** usefulness or advantage: *there is no use in complaining* **9** the purpose for which something is used **10 have no use for a** to have no need of **b** to have a contemptuous dislike for **11 make use of a** *written* to employ; use **b** to exploit (a person) ▶ HISTORY Latin *usus* having used > **user** *n*

use-by date *n* the date on packaged food after which it should not be sold

used *adj* second-hand: *it was a used car*

used to *adj* **1** accustomed to: *I am used to being a medical guinea pig* ▷ *vb* **2** used as an auxiliary to express habitual or accustomed actions or states taking place in the past but not continuing to be the case in the present: *he used to vanish into his studio for days*

useful *adj* **1** able to be used advantageously or for several purposes **2** *informal* commendable or capable: *a useful hurdler* > **usefully** *adv* > **usefulness** *n*

useless *adj* **1** having no practical use **2** *informal* ineffectual, weak, or stupid: *I'm useless at most things* > **uselessly** *adv* > **uselessness** *n*

user-friendly *adj* easy to familiarize oneself with, understand, and use

username *n* *computers* a name entered into a computer, usually in combination with a password, to identify the user

U-shaped valley *n* a steep-sided valley caused by glacial erosion

usher *n* **1** an official who shows people to their seats, as in a church **2** a person who acts as doorkeeper in a court of law ▷ *vb* **3** to conduct or escort **4** (foll. by *in*) to happen immediately before something or cause it to happen; herald: *the French Revolution ushered in a new age* ▶ HISTORY Old French *huissier* doorkeeper

usherette *n* a woman assistant in a cinema, who shows people to their seats

USP *marketing* unique selling proposition (*or* point)

USSR Union of Soviet Socialist Republics: a former state in E Europe and N Asia, covering the area now composed of Russia, the Ukraine, Kazakhstan and a number of smaller states

usual *adj* **1** of the most normal, frequent, or regular type: *the usual assortment of stories* ▷ *n* **2** ordinary or commonplace events: *the dirt was nothing out of the usual* **3 as usual** as happens normally **4 the usual** *informal* the habitual or usual drink ▶ HISTORY Latin *usus* use > **usually** *adv*

usurp (yewz-**zurp**) *vb* to seize a position or power without authority ▶ HISTORY Latin *usurpare* to take into use > **usurpation** *n* > **usurper** *n*

usury (**yewz**-yoor-ree) *n, pl* **-ries** *old-fashioned* **1** the practice of loaning money at an exorbitant rate of interest **2** an unlawfully high rate of interest ▶ HISTORY Latin *usura* usage > **usurer** *n*

UT Utah

ute *n* *Austral & NZ, informal* a utility truck

utensil *n* a tool or container for practical use: *cooking utensils* ▶ HISTORY Latin *utensilia* necessaries

uterine *adj* of or affecting the womb

uterus (**yew**-ter-russ) *n, pl* **uteri** (**yew**-ter-rye) *anat* a hollow muscular organ in the pelvic cavity of female mammals, which houses the developing fetus; womb ▶ HISTORY Latin

utilitarian *adj* **1** useful rather than beautiful **2** of utilitarianism ▷ *n* **3** an advocate of utilitarianism

utilitarianism *n* *ethics* the doctrine that the right thing to do is that which brings about the greatest good for the greatest number

utility *n, pl* **-ties** **1** usefulness **2** something useful **3** a public service, such as water or electricity ▷ *adj* **4** designed for use rather than beauty: *utility fabrics* ▶ HISTORY Latin *utilitas* usefulness, from *uti* to use

utility room *n* a room with equipment for domestic work like washing and ironing

utility truck *n* *Austral & NZ* a small truck with an open body and low sides

utilize *or* **-lise** *vb* **-lizing, -lized** *or* **-lising, -lised** to make practical or worthwhile use of > **utilization** *or* **-lisation** *n*

u

utmost *adj* **1** of the greatest possible degree or amount: *the utmost seriousness* **2** at the furthest limit: *the utmost point* ▷ *n* **3** the greatest possible degree or amount: *I was doing my utmost to comply* ▶ HISTORY Old English *ūtemest*

utmost good faith *n* *insurance* a principle used in insurance contracts, legally obliging all parties to reveal to the others any information that might influence the others' decision to enter into the contract

Utopia (yew-**tope**-ee-a) *n* any real or imaginary society, place, or state considered to be perfect or ideal ▶ HISTORY coined by Sir Thomas More in 1516 as the title of his book that described an imaginary island representing the perfect society, literally: no place, from Greek *ou* not + *topos* a place > **Utopian** *adj*

utter¹ *vb* **1** to express something in sounds or words: *she hadn't uttered a single word* **2** *criminal law* to put counterfeit money or forged cheques into circulation ▶ HISTORY Middle Dutch *ūteren* to make known

utter² *adj* total or absolute: *utter amazement*

▶ HISTORY Old English *ūtera* outer > **utterly** *adv*

utterance *n* **1** something expressed in speech or writing **2** the expression in words of ideas, thoughts, or feelings

uttermost *adj*, *n* same as **utmost**

U-turn *n* **1** a turn, made by a vehicle, in the shape of a U, resulting in a reversal of direction **2** a complete change in policy

UV ultraviolet

UV-A *or* **UVA** *n* ultraviolet radiation with a range of 320-380 nanometres

UV-B *or* **UVB** *n* ultraviolet radiation with a range of 280-320 nanometres

uvula (**yew**-view-la) *n*, *pl* **-las** *or* **-lae** the small fleshy part of the soft palate that hangs in the back of the throat ▶ HISTORY Medieval Latin, literally: a little grape > **uvular** *adj*

UWI University of the West Indies: a public university system serving 18 English-speaking countries of the Caribbean

uxorious (ux-**or**-ee-uss) *adj* excessively fond of or dependent on one's wife ▶ HISTORY Latin *uxor* wife

u

Vv

V 1 *chem* vanadium **2** volt **3** the Roman numeral for five

V. 1 verb **2** verse **3** versus **4** volume

VA Virginia

vacancy *n, pl* **-cies 1** an unoccupied job or position: *he had heard of a vacancy for a librarian* **2** an unoccupied room in a hotel or guesthouse: *the last hotel we tried had a vacancy* **3** the state of being unoccupied

vacant *adj* **1** (of a toilet, room, etc.) unoccupied or not being used: *I sat down in a vacant chair* **2** (of a job or position) unfilled at the present time **3** having or suggesting a lack of interest or understanding: *he sat there staring at me with a vacant look* **4** (of a period of time) not set aside for any particular activity: *two slots in his programme have been left vacant* ▶ HISTORY Latin *vacare* to be empty > **vacantly** *adv*

vacate *vb* **-cating, -cated 1** to cause (something) to be empty by leaving: *do you wish us to vacate the room?* **2** to give up (a job or position)

vacation *n* **1** *Brit & S African* a time of the year when the universities or law courts are closed **2** *US, Canad & Austral* same as **holiday** (sense 2) ▶ HISTORY Latin *vacatio* freedom

vaccinate *vb* **-nating, -nated** to inject (someone) with a vaccine in order to protect them against a disease: *children vaccinated against meningitis* > **vaccination** *n*

vaccine *n* **1** *med* a substance made from the germs that cause a disease which is given to people to prevent them getting the disease **2** *computers* a piece of software that detects and removes computer viruses from a system

■ **WORD HISTORY**

■ 'Vaccine' comes from Latin *vacca*, meaning
■ 'a cow'. At a time when many people were dying
■ of smallpox, the English surgeon Edward Jenner
■ (1749-1823) noted that people who had
■ contracted cowpox, a relatively mild disease
■ caught from cattle, were immune to smallpox.
■ He therefore advocated inoculation with the
■ cowpox virus as a means of immunizing
■ against smallpox.

vacillate (**vass**-ill-late) *vb* **-lating, -lated** to keep changing one's mind or opinions about something: *he vacillated between republican and monarchist sentiments* ▶ HISTORY Latin *vacillare* to sway > **vacillation** *n*

vacuity *n* an absence of intelligent thought or ideas: *I suggested to one of his advisers that his vacuity was a handicap in these debates*

vacuole (**vack**-yew-ohl) *n biol* a fluid-filled cavity in the cytoplasm of a cell

vacuous *adj* **1** lacking in intelligent ideas **2** showing no sign of intelligence or understanding: *her smile was vacuous but without malice* ▶ HISTORY Latin *vacuus* empty

vacuum *n, pl* **vacuums** *or* **vacua 1** a space which contains no air or other gas **2** a vacant place or position that needs to be filled by someone or something else: *the army moved in to fill the power vacuum* **3** short for **vacuum cleaner** ▷ *vb* **4** to clean (something) with a vacuum cleaner ▶ HISTORY Latin *vacuus* empty

vacuum cleaner *n* an electric machine which sucks up dust and dirt from carpets and upholstery > **vacuum cleaning** *n*

vacuum flask *n* a double-walled flask with a vacuum between the walls that keeps drinks hot or cold

vacuum-packed *adj* (of food) packed in an airtight container in order to preserve freshness

vacuum tube *or* **valve** *n* same as **valve** (sense 3)

vagabond *n* a person who travels from place to place and has no fixed home or job ▶ HISTORY Latin *vagari* to roam

vagary (**vaig**-a-ree) *n, pl* **-garies** an unpredictable change in a situation or in someone's behaviour: *I was unused to the vagaries of the retailer's world* ▶ HISTORY probably from Latin *vagari* to roam

vagina (vaj-**jine**-a) *n* the passage in most female mammals that extends from the neck of the womb to the external genitals ▶ HISTORY Latin: sheath > **vaginal** *adj*

vagrant (**vaig**-rant) *n* **1** a person who moves from place to place and has no regular home or job **2** wandering about ▶ HISTORY probably from Old French *waucrant* > **vagrancy** *n*

vague *adj* **1** not expressed or explained clearly: *he thought of his instructions, so vague and imprecise* **2** deliberately withholding information: *he was rather vague about the whole deal* **3** (of a sound or shape) unable to be heard or seen clearly: *he heard some vague sound from downstairs* **4** (of a person) not concentrating or thinking clearly: *she was mumbling to herself in a vague way* **5** not clearly established or known: *it was a vague rumour which would fade away and be forgotten* ▶ HISTORY Latin *vagus* wandering > **vaguely** *adv* > **vagueness** *n*

vain *adj* **1** excessively proud of one's appearance or achievements **2** senseless or unsuccessful: *he made a vain attempt to lighten the atmosphere* ▷ *n* **3 in vain** without achieving the desired effects or results: *the old man searched in vain for his son* ▶ HISTORY Latin *vanus* > **vainly** *adv*

vainglorious *adj* boastful or proud: *his vainglorious posturing had earned him numerous powerful enemies*

valance (**val**-lenss) *n* a short piece of decorative material hung round the edge of a bed or above a window ▶ HISTORY perhaps after *Valence* in SE France

vale *n literary* a valley ▶ HISTORY Latin *vallis* valley

valediction (val-lid-**dik**-shun) *n* a farewell speech ▶ HISTORY Latin *vale* farewell + *dicere* to say > **valedictory** *adj*

valence (**vale**-enss) *n chem* the ability of atoms and chemical groups to form compounds

valency *or esp US & Canad* **valence** *n, pl* **-cies** *or* **-ces** *chem* the number of atoms of hydrogen that an atom or chemical group is able to combine with in forming compounds ▶ HISTORY Latin *valere* to be strong

valentine *n* **1** a card sent, often anonymously, as an expression of love on Saint Valentine's Day, February 14 **2** the person to whom one sends such a card ▶ HISTORY after Saint *Valentine*

valerian *n* a plant with small white or pinkish flowers and a medicinal root ▶ HISTORY Medieval Latin *valeriana (herba)* (herb) of Valerius

valet *n* **1** a male servant employed to look after another man ▷ *vb* **-eting, -eted 2** to act as a valet (for) **3** to clean the bodywork and interior of (a car) as a professional service ▶ HISTORY Old French *vaslet* page

valetudinarian (val-lit-yew-din-**air**-ee-an) *n* **1** a person who is chronically sick **2** a person who continually worries about his or her health ▶ HISTORY Latin *valetudo* state of health > **valetudinarianism** *n*

Valhalla *n Norse myth* the great hall of Odin where warriors who die as heroes in battle dwell eternally ▶ HISTORY Old Norse *valr* slain warriors + *höll* hall

valiant *adj* very brave: *it was a valiant attempt to rescue the struggling victim* ▶ HISTORY Latin *valere* to be strong > **valiantly** *adv*

valid *adj* **1** based on sound reasoning: *I think that's a very valid question* **2** legally acceptable: *she must produce a valid driving licence* **3** important or serious enough to say or do: *religious broadcasting has a valid purpose* ▶ HISTORY Latin *validus* robust > **validity** *n*

validate *vb* **-dating, -dated 1** to prove (a claim or statement) to be true or correct **2** to give legal force or official confirmation to > **validation** *n*

valise (val-**leez**) *n old-fashioned* a small suitcase ▶ HISTORY via French from Italian *valigia*

Valium *n trademark* a drug used as a tranquillizer

Valkyrie (**val**-keer-ee) *n Norse myth* any of the beautiful maidens who take the dead heroes to Valhalla ▶ HISTORY Old Norse *valr* slain warriors + *kyrja* chooser

valley *n* a long stretch of land between hills, often with a river flowing through it ▶ HISTORY Latin *vallis*

valour *or US* **valor** *n literary* great bravery, esp. in battle ▶ HISTORY Latin *valere* to be strong > **valorous** *adj*

valuable *adj* **1** worth a large amount of money: *his house was furnished with valuable antique furniture* **2** of great use or importance: *the investigations will* provide valuable information ▷ *n* **3 valuables** valuable articles of personal property, such as jewellery

valuation *n* **1** a formal assessment of how much something is worth: *they will arrange a valuation on your house* **2** the price arrived at by the process of valuing

value *n* **1** the desirability of something, often in terms of its usefulness or exchangeability **2** an amount of money considered to be a fair exchange for something: *50 kilos of cocaine with a high street value* **3** something worth the money it cost: *the set meal was value for money* **4 values** the moral principles and beliefs of a person or group **5** *maths* a particular number or quantity represented by a figure or symbol **6** *music* short for **time value** ▷ *vb* **-uing, -ued 7** to assess the worth or desirability of (something) **8** to hold (someone or something) in high regard ▶ HISTORY Latin *valere* to be worth > **valued** *adj* > **valueless** *adj* > **valuer** *n*

value-added tax *n Brit & S African* See **VAT**

value judgment *n* a personal opinion about something based on an individual's beliefs and not on facts which can be checked or proved

valve *n* **1** a part attached to a pipe or tube which controls the flow of gas or liquid **2** *anat* a small flap in a hollow organ, such as the heart, that controls the flow and direction of blood **3** a closed tube through which electrons move in a vacuum **4** *zool* one of the hinged shells of an oyster or clam **5** *music* a device on some brass instruments by which the effective length of the tube may be varied ▶ HISTORY Latin *valva* a folding door

valvular *adj* of or relating to valves: *valvular heart disease*

vamp¹ *informal n* **1** a sexually attractive woman who seduces men ▷ *vb* **2** (of a woman) to seduce (a man) ▶ HISTORY short for *vampire*

vamp² *vb* **vamp up** to make (a story, piece of music, etc.) seem new by inventing additional parts ▶ HISTORY Old French *avantpié* the front part of a shoe

vampire *n* (in European folklore) a corpse that rises nightly from its grave to drink the blood of living people ▶ HISTORY from Magyar

vampire bat *n* a bat of Central and South America that feeds on the blood of birds and mammals

van¹ *n* **1** a road vehicle with a roof and no side windows used to transport goods **2** *Brit* a closed railway wagon used to transport luggage, goods, or mail ▶ HISTORY shortened from *caravan*

van² *n* short for **vanguard**

vanadium *n chem* a silvery-white metallic element used to toughen steel. Symbol: V ▶ HISTORY Old Norse *Vanadís*, epithet of the goddess Freya

Van Allen belt *n* either of two belts of charged particles which surround the Earth ▶ HISTORY after J. A. *Van Allen*, physicist

vandal *n* someone who deliberately causes damage to personal or public property ▶ HISTORY from the name of a Germanic tribe of the 3rd and 4th centuries AD > **vandalism** *n*

vandalize *or* **-ise** *vb* **-izing, -ized** *or* **-ising, -ised** to cause damage to (personal or public property) deliberately

Van de Graaf generator *n physics* a device for producing high electrostatic potentials (up to 15 million volts), consisting of a hollow metal sphere on which a charge is accumulated from a continuous moving belt of insulating material ▶ HISTORY after R. J. *Van de Graaf*, US physicist

Van der Hum *n* S African a liqueur made from tangerines ▶ HISTORY origin uncertain but possibly derived from the humorous uncertainty of the name, equivalent of *whatshisname*

vane *n* **1** one of the blades forming part of the wheel of a windmill, a screw propeller, etc. **2** short for **weather vane** ▶ HISTORY Old English *fana*

vanguard *n* **1** the leading division or units of an army **2** the most advanced group or position in scientific research, a movement, etc.: *a distinguished architect in the vanguard of his profession* ▶ HISTORY Old French *avant-garde* advance guard

vanilla *n* **1** a flavouring for food such as ice cream, which comes from the pods of a tropical plant **2** a flavouring extract prepared from the beans of this plant and used in cooking ▷ *adj* **3** flavoured with vanilla: *vanilla essence* **4** *slang* ordinary or conventional: *a vanilla kind of guy* ▶ HISTORY Spanish *vainilla* pod

vanish *vb* **1** to disappear suddenly: *the choppers vanished from radar screens at dawn yesterday* **2** to cease to exist: *the old landmarks had vanished* ▶ HISTORY Latin *evanescere* to evaporate

vanishing point *n* the point in the distance where parallel lines appear to meet

vanity *n* **1** a feeling of pride about one's appearance or ability **2** (*pl* **-ties**) something about which one is vain: *it's one of my vanities that I can guess scents* ▶ HISTORY Latin *vanitas* emptiness

vanity case *n* a small bag for holding cosmetics

vanquish *vb literary* to defeat (someone) in a battle, contest, or argument ▶ HISTORY Latin *vincere*

vantage *n* a state, position, or opportunity offering advantage ▶ HISTORY Old French *avantage* advantage

vape *vb* **vaping, vaped** to inhale vapour from an e-cigarette

vapid *adj* dull and uninteresting: *their publications were vapid and amateurish* ▶ HISTORY Latin *vapidus* > **vapidity** *n*

vapor *n* US same as **vapour**

vaporize *or* **-ise** *vb* **-izing, -ized** *or* **-ising, -ised** (of a liquid or solid) to change into vapour > **vaporization** *or* **-isation** *n*

vaporous *adj* resembling or full of vapour

vapour *or* US **vapor** *n* **1** a mass of tiny drops of water or other liquids in the air, which appear as a mist **2** the gaseous form of a substance that is usually a liquid or a solid **3 the vapours** *old-fashioned* a feeling of faintness, dizziness, and depression ▶ HISTORY Latin *vapor*

variable *adj* **1** likely to change at any time: *variable weather* **2** *maths* having a range of possible values ▷ *n* **3** something that is subject to variation **4** *maths* an expression that can be assigned any of a set of values ▶ HISTORY Latin *variare* to diversify > **variability** *n* > **variably** *adv*

variable cost *n econ* a cost of production that varies directly with output. Compare **fixed cost**

variance *n* **at variance** not in agreement: *the real record is at variance with the public record*

variant *adj* **1** differing from a standard or type: *variant spellings* ▷ *n* **2** something that differs from a standard or type

variation *n* **1** something presented in a slightly different form: *his books are all variations on a basic theme* **2** a change in level, amount, or quantity: *there was a variation in the figures* **3** *music* the repetition of a simple tune with the addition of new harmonies or a change in rhythm: *Variations on a Hussar's Song*

varicose *adj* of or resulting from varicose veins: *a varicose ulcer* ▶ HISTORY Latin *varix* a swollen vein

varicose veins *pl n* veins, usually in the legs, which have become knotted, swollen, and sometimes painful

varied *adj* of different types, sizes, or quantities: *these young men and women would be of varied backgrounds*

variegated *adj* having patches or streaks of different colours: *variegated holly* > **variegation** *n*

variety *n, pl* **-ties** **1** the state of being diverse or various **2** different things of the same kind: *I'm cooking the mince with a variety of vegetables* **3** a particular type of something in the same general category: *this variety of pear is extremely juicy* **4** *taxonomy* a race whose distinct characters do not justify classification as a separate species **5** a type of entertainment consisting of short unrelated acts, such as singing, dancing, and comedy ▶ HISTORY Latin *varietas*

varifocal *adj* of a lens that is gradated to permit any length of vision between near and distant

varifocals *pl n* a pair of spectacles with varifocal lenses

various *adj* **1** several different: *there are various possible answers to this question* **2** of different kinds: *the causes of high blood pressure are various and complicated* ▶ HISTORY Latin *varius* changing > **variously** *adv*

varlet *n archaic* **1** a menial servant **2** a rascal ▶ HISTORY Old French *vaslet*

varnish *n* **1** a liquid painted onto a surface to give it a hard glossy finish **2** a smooth surface, coated with or as if with varnish **3** an artificial, superficial, or deceptively pleasing manner or appearance: *those who aspired to become civil servants acquired a varnish of university education* ▷ *vb* **4** to apply varnish to **5** to try to make (something unpleasant) appear more attractive: *when did we*

V

start equivocating, camouflaging, varnishing the truth? ▶ **HISTORY** Old French vernis

varsity n, pl **-ties** old-fashioned informal short for **university**

vary vb **varies, varying, varied** **1** to change in appearance, character, or form **2** to be different or cause to be different: the age of appearance of underarm and body hair varies greatly from person to person **3** to give variety to: you can vary the type of exercise you do **4** to change in accordance with another variable: an individual's calorie requirement varies with age, sex, and physical activity ▶ **HISTORY** Latin varius changing > **varying** adj

vas n, pl **vasa** anat, zool a vessel or tube that carries a fluid ▶ **HISTORY** Latin: vessel

vascular adj biol, anat of or relating to the vessels that conduct and circulate body fluids such as blood or sap ▶ **HISTORY** Latin vas vessel

vas deferens n, pl **vasa deferentia** anat either of the two ducts that convey sperm from the testicles to the penis ▶ **HISTORY** Latin vas vessel + deferens carrying away

vase n a glass or pottery jar used as an ornament or for holding cut flowers ▶ **HISTORY** Latin vas vessel

vasectomy n, pl **-mies** surgical removal of all or part of the vas deferens as a method of contraception ▶ **HISTORY** VAS + Greek ek- out + tomē a cutting

Vaseline n trademark petroleum jelly, used as an ointment or a lubricant

vasoconstriction n anat the narrowing of the walls of blood vessels ▶ **HISTORY** Latin vas vessel + constringere to bind together
> **vasoconstrictor** n

vasodilation or **vasodilatation** n anat the widening of the walls of blood vessels ▶ **HISTORY** Latin vas vessel + dilatare to spread out
> **vasodilator** n

vassal n **1** (in feudal society) a man who gave military service to a lord in return for protection and often land **2** written a person, nation, or state dominated by another ▶ **HISTORY** Medieval Latin vassus servant > **vassalage** n

vast adj unusually large in size, degree, or number ▶ **HISTORY** Latin vastus deserted > **vastly** adv
> **vastness** n

vat n a large container for holding or storing liquids ▶ **HISTORY** Old English fæt

VAT (in Britain and S Africa) value-added tax: a tax levied on the difference between the cost of materials and the selling price of a commodity or service

Vatican n **1** the Pope's palace, in Rome **2** the authority of the Pope ▶ **HISTORY** Latin Vaticanus (mons) Vatican (hill)

vaudeville n variety entertainment consisting of short acts such as song-and-dance routines and comic turns ▶ **HISTORY** French

vault[1] n **1** a secure room where money and other valuables are stored safely **2** an underground burial chamber **3** an arched structure that forms a roof or ceiling **4** a cellar for storing wine ▶ **HISTORY** Old French voute, voulte

vault[2] vb **1** to jump over (something) by resting one's hands on it or by using a long pole ▷ n **2** the act of vaulting ▶ **HISTORY** Italian voltare to turn
> **vaulter** n

vaulted adj being or having an arched roof: an atmospheric vaulted dining room

vaunt vb **1** to describe or display (one's success or possessions) boastfully ▷ n **2** a boast ▶ **HISTORY** Latin vanus vain > **vaunted** adj

vb verb

VC **1** Vice Chancellor **2** Victoria Cross **3** history Vietcong: the Communist-led guerrilla force of South Vietnam

vCJD variant Creutzfeldt-Jakob disease

VCR video cassette recorder

VD venereal disease

VDU visual display unit

veal n the meat from a calf, used as food ▶ **HISTORY** Latin vitulus calf

vector n **1** maths a variable quantity, such as force, that has magnitude and direction **2** pathol an animal, usually an insect, that carries a disease-producing microorganism from person to person ▶ **HISTORY** Latin: carrier

Veda (**vay**-da) n any or all of the most ancient sacred writings of Hinduism ▶ **HISTORY** Sanskrit: knowledge > **Vedic** adj

veer vb **1** to change direction suddenly: the plane veered off the runway and careered through the perimeter fence **2** to change from one position or opinion to another: her feelings veered from tenderness to sudden spurts of genuine love ▷ n **3** a change of course or direction ▶ **HISTORY** Old French virer

veg n informal a vegetable or vegetables

vegan (**vee**-gan) n a person who does not eat meat, fish, or any animal products such as cheese or butter

vegetable n **1** a plant, such as potato or cauliflower, with parts that are used as food **2** offensive someone who is unable to move or think, as a result of brain damage ▷ adj **3** of or like plants or vegetables ▶ **HISTORY** Late Latin vegetabilis animating

vegetable marrow n a long green vegetable which can be cooked and eaten

vegetable oil n any of a group of oils that are obtained from plants

vegetal adj of or relating to plant life

vegetarian n **1** a person who does not eat meat or fish ▷ adj **2** excluding meat and fish: a vegetarian diet > **vegetarianism** n

vegetate vb **-tating, -tated** to live in a dull and boring way with no mental stimulation

vegetation n plant life as a whole

vegetation cover n the type and number of plants growing in a particular area

vegetative adj **1** of or relating to plant life or plant growth **2** (of reproduction) characterized by asexual processes

vehement *adj* **1** expressing strong feelings or opinions **2** (of actions or gestures) performed with great force or energy ▶ HISTORY Latin *vehemens* ardent > **vehemence** *n* > **vehemently** *adv*

vehicle *n* **1** a machine such as a bus or car for transporting people or goods **2** something used to achieve a particular purpose or as a means of expression: *the newspaper was a vehicle for explaining government policies* **3** *pharmacol* an inactive substance mixed with the active ingredient in a medicine **4** a liquid, such as oil, in which a pigment is mixed before it is applied to a surface ▶ HISTORY Latin *vehere* to carry > **vehicular** *adj*

veil *n* **1** a piece of thin cloth, usually as part of a hat or headdress, used to cover a woman's face **2** something that conceals the truth: *a veil of secrecy* **3 take the veil** to become a nun ▷ *vb* **4** to cover or conceal with or as if with a veil ▶ HISTORY Latin *velum* a covering

veiled *adj* (of a comment or remark) presented in a disguised form: *it was a thinly veiled criticism*

vein *n* **1** any of the tubes that carry blood to the heart **2** a thin line in a leaf or in an insect's wing **3** a clearly defined layer of ore or mineral in rock **4** an irregular streak of colour in marble, wood, or cheese **5** a distinctive trait or quality in speech or writing: *critics have exposed a strong vein of moralism in the poem* **6** a temporary mood: *we're in a very humorous vein tonight* ▶ HISTORY Latin *vena* > **veined** *adj*

Velcro *n trademark* a type of fastening consisting of one piece of fabric with tiny hooked threads and another with a coarse surface that sticks to it

veld *or* **veldt** *n* the open country of South Africa, including landscapes which are grassy, bushy, or thinly forested ▶ HISTORY Afrikaans: field

veldskoen *n* same as **velskoen**

vellum *n* **1** a fine calf, kid, or lamb parchment **2** a strong good-quality paper that resembles vellum ▶ HISTORY Old French *velin* of a calf

velocipede (vel-**loss**-sip-peed) *n* an early form of bicycle ▶ HISTORY Latin *velox* swift + *pes* foot

velocity (vel-**loss**-it-ee) *n, pl* -**ties** the speed at which something is moving in a particular direction ▶ HISTORY Latin *velox* swift

velour *or* **velours** (vel-**loor**) *n* a silk or cotton cloth similar to velvet ▶ HISTORY Latin *villus* shaggy hair

velskoen *or* **veldskoen** (**fell**-skoon) *n S African* a sturdy ankle boot ▶ HISTORY Afrikaans

velvet *n* **1** a fabric with a thick close soft pile on one side **2** the furry covering of the newly formed antlers of a deer ▷ *adj* **3** made of velvet **4** soft or smooth like velvet **5 an iron fist** *or* **hand in a velvet glove** determination concealed by a gentle manner ▶ HISTORY Old French, from Latin *villus* shaggy hair > **velvety** *adj*

velveteen *n* a cotton fabric that resembles velvet

vena cava (vee-na **kay**-va) *n, pl* **venae cavae** (vee-nee **kay**-vee) *anat* either one of the two large veins that convey blood to the heart

venal (**vee**-nal) *adj* **1** willing to accept bribes in return for acting dishonestly: *venal politicians* **2** associated with corruption or bribery: *venal greed* ▶ HISTORY Latin *venum* sale > **venality** *n*

vend *vb* to sell (goods) ▶ HISTORY Latin *vendere* to sell

Venda *n* **1** (*pl* -**da** *or* -**das**) a member of a Negroid people of southern Africa, living chiefly in NE South Africa **2** the language of this people

vendetta *n* **1** a long-lasting quarrel between people or organizations in which they attempt to harm each other: *it's an inexplicable vendetta against the firm and its directors* **2** a private feud between families in which members of one family kill members of the other family in revenge for earlier murders ▶ HISTORY Italian

vending machine *n* a machine that automatically dispenses food, drinks, or cigarettes when money is inserted

vendor *n* **1** a person who sells goods such as newspapers or hamburgers from a stall or cart **2** any person or business selling something **3** *chiefly law* a person who sells property

veneer *n* **1** a thin layer of wood or plastic used to cover the surface of something made of cheaper material **2** a deceptive but convincing appearance: *nobody penetrated his veneer of modest charm* ▶ HISTORY Old French *fournir* to furnish

venerable *adj* **1** (of a person) entitled to respect because of great age or wisdom **2** (of an object) impressive because it is old or important historically **3** *RC Church* a title given to a dead person who is going to be declared a saint **4** *Church of England* a title given to an archdeacon ▶ HISTORY Latin *venerari* to venerate

venerate *vb* -**ating, -ated** to hold (someone) in deep respect ▶ HISTORY Latin *venerari* > **venerator** *n*

veneration *n* a feeling of awe or great respect: *George Gershwin is worthy of the veneration accorded his classical counterparts*

venereal (vin-**ear**-ee-al) *adj* **1** transmitted by sexual intercourse: *venereal infections* **2** of the genitals: *venereal warts* ▶ HISTORY Latin *venus* sexual love

venereal disease *n* a disease, such as syphilis, transmitted by sexual intercourse

Venetian *adj* **1** of Venice, a port in NE Italy ▷ *n* **2** a person from Venice

Venetian blind *n* a window blind made of thin horizontal slats

vengeance *n* **1** the act of killing, injuring, or harming someone for revenge **2 with a vengeance** to a much greater extent or with much greater force than expected: *my career was beginning to take off with a vengeance* ▶ HISTORY Old French, from Latin *vindicare* to punish

vengeful *adj* wanting revenge

venial (**veen**-ee-al) *adj* easily excused or forgiven: *venial sins* ▶ HISTORY Latin *venia* forgiveness

venison *n* the flesh of a deer, used as food ▶ HISTORY Old French *venaison*

949

Venn diagram n maths a drawing which uses circles to show the relationships between different sets ▶ HISTORY after John Venn, logician

venom n 1 a feeling of great bitterness or anger towards someone 2 the poison that certain snakes and scorpions inject when they bite or sting ▶ HISTORY Latin *venenum* poison, love potion > **venomous** adj > **venomously** adv

venous (**vee**-nuss) adj of or relating to veins ▶ HISTORY Latin *vena* vein

vent¹ n 1 a small opening in something through which fresh air can enter and fumes can be released 2 the shaft of a volcano through which lava and gases erupt 3 the anal opening of a bird or other small animal 4 **give vent to** to release (an emotion) in an outburst: *she gave vent to her misery and loneliness* ▷ vb 5 to release or express freely: *consumers vented their anger on the group by boycotting its products* 6 to make vents in ▶ HISTORY Old French *esventer* to blow out

vent² n a vertical slit in the lower hem of a jacket ▶ HISTORY Latin *findere* to cleave

ventilate vb **-lating, -lated** 1 to let fresh air into (a room or building) 2 to discuss (ideas or feelings) openly: *ultra-rightists ventilated anti-Semitic sentiments* ▶ HISTORY Latin *ventilare* to fan

ventilation n 1 the act or process of ventilating 2 a system in a building that provides a supply of fresh air 3 biol the process by which oxygen is added to the blood through the lungs

ventilator n an opening or device, such as a fan, used to let fresh air into a room or building

ventral adj relating to the front part of the body ▶ HISTORY Latin *venter* abdomen > **ventrally** adv

ventricle n anat 1 a chamber of the heart that pumps blood to the arteries 2 any one of the four main cavities of the brain ▶ HISTORY Latin *ventriculus* > **ventricular** adj

ventriloquism n the ability to speak without moving the lips so that the words appear to come from another person or from another part of the room ▶ HISTORY Latin *venter* belly + *loqui* to speak > **ventriloquist** n

venture n 1 a project or activity that is risky or of uncertain outcome 2 a business operation in which there is the risk of loss as well as the opportunity for profit ▷ vb **-turing, -tured** 3 to do something that involves risk or danger: *I thought it wise to venture into foreign trade* 4 *written* to dare to express (an opinion) 5 to go to an unknown or dangerous place 6 to dare (to do something): *you have asked me so often to come to your place that I ventured to drop in* ▶ HISTORY variant of *adventure* > **venturer** n

venture capital n capital that is provided for a new commercial enterprise by individuals or organizations other than those who own the enterprise

venturesome adj willing to take risks

venue n a place where an organized gathering, such as a concert or a sporting event, is held ▶ HISTORY Latin *venire* to come

Venus n 1 the Roman goddess of love 2 the planet second nearest to the sun

Venus's flytrap or **Venus flytrap** n a plant that traps and digests insects between hinged leaves

veracious adj habitually truthful ▶ HISTORY Latin *verus* true

veracity n 1 habitual truthfulness 2 accuracy

verandah or **veranda** n 1 an open porch attached to a house 2 NZ a continuous overhead canopy outside shops that gives shelter to pedestrians ▶ HISTORY Portuguese *varanda* railing

verb n a word that is used to indicate the occurrence or performance of an action or the existence of a state, for example *run, make,* or *do* ▶ HISTORY Latin *verbum* word

verbal adj 1 of or relating to words: *verbal skills* 2 spoken rather than written: *a verbal agreement* 3 grammar of or relating to a verb > **verbally** adv

verbalize or **-ise** vb **-izing, -ized** or **-ising, -ised** to express (an idea or feeling) in words

verbal noun n grammar a noun derived from a verb, for example *smoking* in the sentence *smoking is bad for you*

verbal process n functional grammar the process of saying, stating or exclaiming, etc., as specified by a verb group. Compare **material process, mental process, relational process**

verbatim (verb-**bait**-im) adv, adj using exactly the same words: *a verbatim account of events* ▶ HISTORY Medieval Latin: word by word

verbena n a plant with red, white, or purple sweet-smelling flowers ▶ HISTORY Latin: sacred bough used by the priest in religious acts

verbiage n the excessive use of words ▶ HISTORY Latin *verbum* word

verbose (verb-**bohss**) adj using more words than is necessary > **verbosity** n

verdant adj literary covered with green vegetation ▶ HISTORY from Latin *viridis* green

verdict n 1 the decision made by a jury about the guilt or innocence of a defendant 2 an opinion formed after examining the facts ▶ HISTORY Latin *vere dictum* truly spoken

verdigris (ver-dig-reess) n a green or bluish coating which forms on copper, brass, or bronze that has been exposed to damp ▶ HISTORY Old French *vert de Grice* green of Greece

verdure n literary flourishing green vegetation ▶ HISTORY from Latin *viridis* green

verge¹ n 1 a grass border along a road 2 **on the verge of** having almost reached (a point or condition) 3 an edge or rim ▷ vb **verging, verged** 4 **verge on** to be near to: *she was verging on hysteria* ▶ HISTORY Latin *virga* rod

verge² vb **verging, verged** to move in a specified direction: *verging towards the Irish Sea* ▶ HISTORY Latin *vergere*

verger n chiefly Church of England 1 a church official who acts as caretaker 2 an official who carries the rod of office before a bishop or dean in ceremonies and processions ▶ HISTORY Latin *virga* rod, twig

verify vb **-fies, -fying, -fied 1** to check the truth of (something) by investigation **2** to prove (something) to be true ▶ HISTORY Latin *verus* true + *facere* to make > **verifiable** adj > **verification** n

verily adv archaic truly: *for verily, this was their destiny* ▶ HISTORY from *very*

verisimilitude n the appearance of truth or reality ▶ HISTORY Latin *verus* true + *similitudo* similitude

veritable adj rightly called; real: *a veritable mine of information* > **veritably** adv

verity n, pl **-ties** a true statement or principle ▶ HISTORY Latin *verus* true

vermicelli (ver-me-**chell**-ee) n **1** very fine strands of pasta, used in soups **2** tiny chocolate strands used as a topping for cakes or ice cream ▶ HISTORY Italian: little worms

vermiform adj shaped like a worm

vermiform appendix n anat same as **appendix**

vermilion adj **1** orange-red ▷ n **2** mercuric sulphide, used as an orange-red pigment; cinnabar ▶ HISTORY Late Latin *vermiculus* insect from which red dye was prepared

vermin pl n **1** small animals collectively, such as insects and rodents, that spread disease and damage crops **2** unpleasant people ▶ HISTORY Latin *vermis* worm > **verminous** adj

vermouth (**ver**-muth) n a wine flavoured with herbs ▶ HISTORY German *Wermut* wormwood

vernacular (ver-**nak**-yew-lar) n **1** the commonly spoken language or dialect of a particular people or place ▷ adj **2** in or using the vernacular ▶ HISTORY Latin *vernaculus* belonging to a household slave

vernal adj of or occurring in spring ▶ HISTORY Latin *ver* spring > **vernally** adv

vernier (**ver**-nee-er) n a small movable scale in certain measuring instruments such as theodolites, used to obtain a fractional reading of one of the divisions on the main scale ▶ HISTORY after Paul *Vernier*, mathematician

veronica n a plant with small blue, pink, or white flowers ▶ HISTORY perhaps from the name *Veronica*

verruca (ver-**roo**-ka) n pathol a wart, usually on the sole of the foot ▶ HISTORY Latin: wart

versatile adj having many different skills or uses ▶ HISTORY Latin *versare* to turn > **versatility** n

verse n **1** a division of a poem or song **2** poetry as distinct from prose **3** one of the short sections into which chapters of the books of the Bible are divided **4** a poem ▶ HISTORY Latin *versus* furrow, literally: a turning (of the plough)

versify vb **-fies, -fying, -fied 1** to put (something) into verse **2** to write in verse ▶ HISTORY Latin *versus* verse + *facere* to make > **versification** n > **versifier** n

version n **1** a form of something, such as a piece of writing, with some differences from other forms **2** an account of something from a certain point of view: *so far there's been no official version of the incident* **3** an adaptation, for example of a book or play into a film ▶ HISTORY Latin *vertere* to turn

verso n, pl **-sos 1** the left-hand page of a book **2** the back of a sheet of printed paper ▶ HISTORY New Latin *verso (folio)* (the leaf) having been turned

versus prep **1** (in a sporting competition or lawsuit) against **2** in opposition to or in contrast with: *man versus machine* ▶ HISTORY Latin: turned (in the direction of), opposite

vertebra (**ver**-tib-bra) n, pl **-brae** (-bree) one of the bony segments of the spinal column ▶ HISTORY Latin > **vertebral** adj

vertebrate n **1** an animal with a backbone, such as a fish, amphibian, reptile, bird, or mammal ▷ adj **2** having a backbone

vertex (**ver**-tex) n, pl **-tices** (-tiss-seez) **1** the highest point **2** maths **a** the point on a geometric figure where the sides form an angle **b** the highest point of a triangle ▶ HISTORY Latin: top

vertical adj **1** at right angles to the horizon: *the vertical cliff* **2** straight up and down: *a vertical cut* **3** econ of or relating to associated or consecutive, though not identical, stages of industrial activity: *the purchase of a chain of travel agents by a leading tour operator will increase vertical integration in the holiday industry* ▷ n **4** a vertical line or direction ▶ HISTORY from Latin *vertex* top, pole of the sky > **vertically** adv

vertical exaggeration n geog distortion that occurs on cross section diagrams when the units on the vertical axis showing height are bigger than those on the horizontal axis showing distance, making the highs and lows look disproportionately great

vertically opposite angles pl n geom the pair of equal angles between a pair of intersecting lines

vertiginous adj producing dizziness

vertigo n pathol a sensation of dizziness felt because one's balance is disturbed, sometimes experienced when looking down from a high place ▶ HISTORY Latin: a whirling round

vervain n a plant with long slender spikes of purple, blue, or white flowers ▶ HISTORY Latin *verbena* sacred bough

verve n written great enthusiasm or liveliness ▶ HISTORY Latin *verba* words, chatter

very adv **1** used to add emphasis to adjectives and adverbs that are able to be graded: *I'm very happy; he'll be home very soon* ▷ adj **2** used with nouns to give emphasis or exaggerated intensity: *the very end of his visit* ▶ HISTORY Old French *verai* true

very high frequency n a radio-frequency band lying between 30 and 300 megahertz

vesicle n biol **1** a small sac or cavity, esp. one filled with fluid **2** a blister ▶ HISTORY Latin *vesica* bladder, sac

vespers n an evening service in some Christian churches ▶ HISTORY Latin *vesper* the evening star

vessel n **1** a ship or large boat **2** an object used as a container for liquid **3** biol a tubular structure in animals and plants that carries body fluids, such as blood and sap ▶ HISTORY Latin *vas*

951

vest n 1 *Brit* an undergarment covering the top half of the body 2 *US, Canad & Austral* a waistcoat ▷ vb 3 **vest in** to settle (power or property) on: *by the power vested in me, I pronounce you man and wife* 4 **vest with** to bestow on: *the sponsorship has vested these matches with a new interest* ▶ HISTORY Latin *vestis* clothing

vestal adj 1 chaste or pure ▷ n 2 a chaste woman ▶ HISTORY Latin *Vestalis* virgin priestess of the goddess Vesta

vestal virgin n (in ancient Rome) one of the virgin priestesses dedicated to the goddess Vesta and to maintaining the sacred fire in her temple

vested adj *property law* having an existing right to the immediate or future possession of property

vested interest n 1 a strong personal interest someone has in a matter because he or she might benefit from it 2 *property law* an existing right to the immediate or future possession of property

vestibule n a small entrance hall ▶ HISTORY Latin *vestibulum*

vestige (**vest**-ij) n 1 a small amount or trace 2 *biol* an organ or part that is a small nonfunctional remnant of a functional organ in an ancestor ▶ HISTORY Latin *vestigium* track

vestigial (vest-**ij**-ee-al) adj remaining after a larger or more important thing has gone: *a strong seam of vestigial belief*

vestments pl n 1 ceremonial clothes worn by the clergy at religious services 2 robes that show authority or rank ▶ HISTORY Latin *vestire* to clothe

vestry n, pl -tries a room in a church used as an office by the priest or minister ▶ HISTORY probably Old French *vestiarie* wardrobe

vet[1] n 1 short for **veterinary surgeon** ▷ vb **vetting, vetted** 2 to make a careful check of (a person or document) for suitability: *guests have to be vetted and vouched for*

vet[2] n *US, Canad, Austral & NZ* short for **veteran**

vetch n 1 a climbing plant with blue or purple flowers 2 the beanlike fruit of the vetch, used as fodder ▶ HISTORY Latin *vicia*

veteran n 1 a person who has given long service in some capacity 2 a soldier who has seen a lot of active service 3 *US, Canad & Austral* a person who has served in the military forces ▷ adj 4 long-serving: *the veteran American politician* ▶ HISTORY Latin *vetus* old

veteran car n *Brit & Austral* a car built before 1919, esp. before 1905

veterinarian n *US, Canad & Austral* a veterinary surgeon

veterinary adj relating to veterinary science

▪ **WORD HISTORY**

▪ In Latin *veterinae* means 'animals used for pulling carts and ploughs'.

veterinary medicine or **science** n the branch of medicine concerned with the treatment of animals

veterinary surgeon n *Brit* a person qualified to practise veterinary medicine

veto (**vee**-toe) n, pl -toes 1 the power to prevent legislation or action proposed by others: *no single state has a veto* 2 the exercise of this power ▷ vb -toing, -toed 3 to refuse consent to (a proposal, such as a government bill) 4 to prohibit or forbid: *the Sports Minister vetoed the appointments* ▶ HISTORY Latin: I forbid

vex vb to cause (someone) to feel annoyance or irritation ▶ HISTORY Latin *vexare* to jolt (in carrying) > **vexation** n > **vexing** adj

vexatious adj vexing

VHF or **vhf** radio very high frequency

VI Vancouver Island

via prep 1 by way of; through: *he fled to London via Crete* 2 by means of: *working from home and keeping in touch with office life via a video link-up* ▶ HISTORY Latin

viable adj 1 able to be put into practice: *the party has failed to propose a viable alternative* 2 (of seeds or eggs) capable of growth 3 (of a fetus) sufficiently developed to survive outside the uterus ▶ HISTORY Latin *vita* life > **viability** n

viaduct n a bridge for carrying a road or railway across a valley ▶ HISTORY Latin *via* way + *ducere* to bring

vial n same as **phial** ▶ HISTORY Greek *phialē* a bowl

viands pl n *old-fashioned* food ▶ HISTORY Latin *vivenda* things to be lived on

viaticum n, pl -ca or -cums *Christianity* Holy Communion given to a person dying or in danger of death ▶ HISTORY Latin *viaticus* belonging to a journey

vibes pl n *informal* 1 the emotional reactions between people 2 the atmosphere of a place 3 short for **vibraphone**

vibrant (**vibe**-rant) adj 1 full of energy and enthusiasm 2 (of a voice) rich and full of emotion 3 (of a colour) strong and bright ▶ HISTORY Latin *vibrare* to agitate > **vibrancy** n

vibraphone n a musical instrument with metal bars that resonate electronically when hit

vibrate vb -brating, -brated 1 to move backwards and forwards rapidly 2 to have or produce a quivering or echoing sound 3 *physics* to undergo or cause to undergo vibration ▶ HISTORY Latin *vibrare* > **vibratory** adj

vibration n 1 a vibrating 2 *physics* a a periodic motion about an equilibrium position, such as in the production of sound b a single cycle of such a motion

vibrato n, pl -tos *music* a slight rapid fluctuation in the pitch of a note

viburnum (vie-**burn**-um) n a subtropical shrub with white flowers and berry-like fruits ▶ HISTORY Latin

Vic. Victoria (Australian state)

vicar n 1 *Church of England* a priest who is in charge of a parish 2 *RC Church* a church officer acting as deputy to a bishop ▶ HISTORY Latin *vicarius* a deputy > **vicarial** adj

vicarage n the house where a vicar lives

V

vicar apostolic *n, pl* **vicars apostolic** *RC Church* a clergyman with authority in missionary countries

vicar general *n, pl* **vicars general** an official appointed to assist the bishop in his administrative duties

vicarious (vik-**air**-ee-uss) *adj* **1** felt indirectly by imagining what another person experiences: *vicarious satisfaction* **2** undergone or done as the substitute for another: *vicarious adventures* **3** delegated: *vicarious power* ▶ HISTORY Latin *vicarius* substituted > **vicariously** *adv*

vicarious liability *n law* liability of one person for the crimes or torts of another, as in the case of an employer being liable for the actions of an employee

Vicar of Christ *n RC Church* the Pope as Christ's representative on earth

vice¹ *n* **1** an immoral or evil habit or action: *greed is only one of their vices* **2** a habit regarded as a weakness in someone's character: *one of his few vices is cigars* **3** criminal activities involving sex, drugs, or gambling ▶ HISTORY Latin *vitium* a defect

vice² *or US* **vise** *n* a tool with a pair of jaws for holding an object while work is done on it ▶ HISTORY Latin *vitis* vine, plant with spiralling tendrils

vice³ *adj* serving in the place of; being next in importance to: *the vice chairman* ▶ HISTORY Latin *vicis* interchange

vice admiral *n* a senior commissioned officer in certain navies

vice chancellor *n* the chief executive or administrator at a number of universities

vicegerent *n* a person appointed to exercise all or some of the authority of another ▶ HISTORY VICE³ + Latin *gerere* to manage

vice president *n* an officer ranking immediately below a president and serving as his or her deputy > **vice-presidency** *n*

viceregal *adj* **1** of a viceroy **2** *chiefly Austral & NZ* of a governor or governor general

viceroy *n* a governor of a colony or country who represents the monarch ▶ HISTORY VICE³ + French *roi* king

vice squad *n* a police division responsible for the enforcement of gaming and prostitution laws

vice versa *adv* the other way round: *there were attacks on northerners by southerners and vice versa* ▶ HISTORY Latin: relations being reversed

Vichy water (**vee**-shee) *n* a natural mineral water from Vichy in France which is supposed to be good for the health

vicinity (viss-in-it-ee) *n* the area immediately surrounding a place ▶ HISTORY Latin *vicinus* neighbouring

vicious *adj* **1** cruel or violent: *vicious attacks* **2** forceful or ferocious: *she gave the chair a vicious jerk* **3** intended to cause hurt or distress: *vicious letters* **4** (of an animal) fierce or hostile ▶ HISTORY Latin *vitiosus* full of faults > **viciously** *adv* > **viciousness** *n*

vicious circle *n* a situation in which an attempt to resolve one problem creates new problems that recreate the original one

vicissitudes (viss-**iss**-it-yewds) *pl n* changes in circumstance or fortune ▶ HISTORY Latin *vicis* change

victim *n* **1** a person or thing that suffers harm or death **2** a person who is tricked or swindled **3** a living person or animal sacrificed in a religious rite ▶ HISTORY Latin *victima*

victimize *or* **-ise** *vb* **-izing, -ized** *or* **-ising, -ised** to punish or discriminate against (someone) selectively or unfairly > **victimization** *or* **-isation** *n*

victimless crime *n law* a type of crime in which there is no obvious victim or in which the supposed victim willingly participates

victor *n* **1** a person or nation that has defeated an enemy in war **2** the winner of a contest or struggle ▶ HISTORY Latin, from *vincere* to conquer

victoria *n* **1** a large sweet red-and-yellow plum **2** a light four-wheeled horse-drawn carriage with a folding hood ▶ HISTORY after Queen *Victoria*

Victoria Cross *n* the highest decoration for bravery in battle awarded to the British and Commonwealth armed forces

Victorian *adj* **1** of or in the reign of Queen Victoria of Great Britain and Ireland (1837–1901) **2** characterized by prudery or hypocrisy **3** of or relating to Victoria (the state or any of the cities) ▷ *n* **4** a person who lived during the reign of Queen Victoria **5** an inhabitant of Victoria (the state or any of the cities)

victorious *adj* **1** having defeated an enemy or opponent: *the victorious allies* **2** of or characterized by victory: *a victorious smile*

victory *n, pl* **-ries** **1** the winning of a war or battle **2** success attained in a contest or struggle ▶ HISTORY Latin *victoria*

victual *vb* **-ualling, -ualled** *or US* **-ualing, -ualed** *old-fashioned* to supply with or obtain victuals ▶ HISTORY Latin *victus* sustenance > **victualler** *or* *US* **-ualer** *n*

victuals (**vit**-tals) *pl n old-fashioned* food and drink

vide (**vie**-dee) *see*: used to direct a reader to a specified place in a text or in another book ▶ HISTORY Latin

videlicet (vid-**deal**-ee-set) *adv* namely: used to specify items ▶ HISTORY Latin

video *n, pl* **-os** **1** the recording and showing of films and events using a television set, video tapes, and a video recorder **2** short for **video cassette** **3** short for **video cassette recorder** ▷ *vb* **videoing, videoed** **4** to record (a television programme or an event) on video ▷ *adj* **5** relating to or used in producing televised images ▶ HISTORY Latin *videre* to see

video cassette *n* a cassette containing video tape

video cassette recorder *n* a tape recorder for recording and playing back television programmes and films

V

video conferencing *n electronics* a facility that enables participants in distant locations to take part in a conference by means of electronic sound and video communication

video frequency *n* the frequency of a signal conveying the image and synchronizing pulses in a television broadcasting system

video game *n* a game that can be played by using an electronic control to move symbols on the screen of a visual display unit

videophone *n* a communications device by which people can see and speak to each other

video tape *n* **1** magnetic tape used mainly for recording the video-frequency signals of a television programme or film ▷ *vb* **video-tape, -taping, -taped** **2** to record (a film or programme) on video tape

video tape recorder *n* a tape recorder for visual signals, using magnetic tape on open spools

Videotex *n trademark* same as **Viewdata**

videotext *n* a means of providing a written or graphical representation of computerized information on a television screen

vie *vb* **vying, vied** to compete (with someone): *the sisters vied with each other to care for her* ▶ HISTORY probably Old French *envier* to challenge

Vietnamese *adj* **1** of Vietnam ▷ *n* **2** (*pl* **-ese**) a person from Vietnam **3** the language of Vietnam

view *n* **1** an opinion, judgment, or belief: *in my view that doesn't really work* **2** an understanding of or outlook on something: *a specific view of human history* **3** everything that can be seen from a particular place or in a particular direction: *there was a beautiful view from the window* **4** vision or sight, esp. range of vision: *as they turned into the drive, the house came into view* **5** a picture of a scene **6** the act of seeing or observing **7 in view of** taking into consideration **8 on view** exhibited to the public **9 take a dim** *or* **poor view of** to regard (something) unfavourably **10 with a view to** with the intention of ▷ *vb* **11** to consider in a specified manner: *they viewed the visit with apprehension* **12** to examine or inspect (a house or flat) carefully with a view to buying it **13** to look at **14** to watch (television) ▶ HISTORY Latin *videre* to see

Viewdata *n trademark* a videotext service linking users to a computer by telephone, enabling shopping, etc. to be done from home

viewer *n* **1** a person who views something, esp. television **2** a hand-held device for looking at photographic slides

viewfinder *n* a device on a camera that lets the user see what will be included in the photograph

viewpoint *n* **1** same as **point of view** **2** a place where one can stand to get a good view of something

vigil (**vij**-ill) *n* **1** a night-time period of staying awake to look after a sick person, pray, etc. **2** *RC Church, Church of England* the eve of certain major festivals ▶ HISTORY Latin: alert

vigilance *n* careful attention

vigilant *adj* on the watch for trouble or danger ▶ HISTORY Latin *vigilare* to be watchful

vigilante (vij-ill-**ant**-ee) *n* a person who takes it upon himself or herself to enforce the law ▶ HISTORY Spanish, from Latin *vigilare* to keep watch

vignette (vin-**yet**) *n* **1** a short description of the typical features of something **2** a small decorative illustration in a book **3** a photograph or drawing with edges that are shaded off ▶ HISTORY French, literally: little vine (often used to embellish a text)

vigorous *adj* **1** having physical or mental energy **2** displaying or performed with vigour: *vigorous exercise* > **vigorously** *adv*

vigour *or US* **vigor** *n* **1** physical or mental energy **2** forcefulness: *the vigour of his invective astonished MPs* **3** strong healthy growth ▶ HISTORY Latin *vigor*

Viking *n* any of the Scandinavians who raided by sea most of N and W Europe from the 8th to the 11th centuries ▶ HISTORY Old Norse *vikingr*

vile *adj* **1** morally wicked: *a vile act* **2** disgusting: *the vile smell* **3** unpleasant or bad: *a vile day at work* ▶ HISTORY Latin *vilis* cheap > **vilely** *adv* > **vileness** *n*

vilify (**vill**-if-fie) *vb* **-fies, -fying, -fied** to speak very badly of (someone) ▶ HISTORY Latin *vilis* worthless + *facere* to make > **vilification** *n*

villa *n* **1** a large house with gardens **2** *Brit* a house rented to holiday-makers ▶ HISTORY Latin: a farmhouse

village *n* **1** a small group of houses in a country area **2** the inhabitants of such a community ▶ HISTORY Latin *villa* a farmhouse > **villager** *n*

villain *n* **1** a wicked or evil person **2** the main wicked character in a novel or play ▶ HISTORY Late Latin *villanus* worker on a country estate

villainous *adj* of or like a villain

villainy *n*, *pl* **-lainies** evil or vicious behaviour

villein (**vill**-an) *n* (in medieval Europe) a peasant who was directly subject to his lord, to whom he paid dues and services in return for his land ▶ HISTORY see VILLAIN > **villeinage** *n*

villus *n*, *pl* **villi** *zool, anat* **1** any of the numerous finger-like projections of the mucous membrane lining the small intestine of many vertebrates **2** any of the finger-like projections formed in the placenta of mammals ▶ HISTORY from Latin: shaggy hair

vim *n informal* vigour and energy ▶ HISTORY Latin *vis* force

vinaigrette *n* salad dressing made from oil and vinegar with seasonings ▶ HISTORY French

vindicate *vb* **-cating, -cated** **1** to clear (someone) of guilt or suspicion **2** to provide justification for ▶ HISTORY Latin *vindex* claimant > **vindication** *n*

vindictive *adj* **1** maliciously seeking revenge **2** characterized by spite or ill will ▶ HISTORY Latin *vindicare* to avenge > **vindictively** *adv* > **vindictiveness** *n*

vine *n* **1** a plant, such as the grapevine, with long flexible stems that climb by clinging to a support

V

2 the stem of such a plant ▶ HISTORY Latin *vinea* vineyard > **viny** *adj*

vinegar *n* **1** a sour-tasting liquid made by fermentation of beer, wine, or cider, used for salad dressing or for pickling **2** bad temper or spitefulness ▶ HISTORY French *vin* wine + *aigre* sour > **vinegary** *adj*

vineyard (**vinn**-yard) *n* an area of land where grapes are grown ▶ HISTORY Old English *wīngeard*

viniculture *n* the process or business of growing grapes and making wine ▶ HISTORY Latin *vinum* wine + CULTURE > **viniculturist** *n*

vino (**vee**-noh) *n, pl* **-nos** *informal* wine ▶ HISTORY Spanish or Italian: wine

vintage *n* **1** the wine obtained from a particular harvest of grapes **2** the harvest from which such a wine is obtained **3** a time of origin: *an open-necked shirt of uncertain vintage* ▷ *adj* **4** (of wine) of an outstandingly good year **5** representative of the best and most typical: *a vintage Saint Laurent dress* ▶ HISTORY Latin *vindemia*

vintage car *n Brit & Austral* a car built between 1919 and 1930

vintner *n* a wine merchant ▶ HISTORY Latin *vinetum* vineyard

vinyl (**vine**-ill) *n* **1** any of various strong plastics made by the polymerization of vinyl compounds, such as PVC **2** conventional records made of vinyl as opposed to compact discs ▷ *adj* **3** *chem* of or containing the monovalent group of atoms CH_2CH-: *vinyl chloride* **4** of or made of vinyl: *vinyl tiles* ▶ HISTORY Latin *vinum* wine

viol (**vie**-oll) *n* a stringed musical instrument that preceded the violin ▶ HISTORY Old Provençal *viola*

viola[1] (vee-**oh**-la) *n* a bowed stringed instrument of the violin family, slightly larger and lower in pitch than the violin ▶ HISTORY Italian

viola[2] (**vie**-ol-la) *n* a variety of pansy ▶ HISTORY Latin: violet

violate *vb* **-lating, -lated** **1** to break (a law or agreement): *he violated export laws* **2** to disturb rudely or improperly: *these men who were violating her privacy* **3** to treat (a sacred place) disrespectfully **4** to rape ▶ HISTORY Latin *violare* to do violence to > **violation** *n* > **violator** *n*

violence *n* **1** the use of physical force, usually intended to cause injury or destruction **2** great force or strength in action, feeling, or expression ▶ HISTORY Latin *violentus* violent

violent *adj* **1** using or involving physical force with the intention of causing injury or destruction: *violent clashes with government supporters* **2** very intense: *I took a violent dislike to him* **3** sudden and forceful: *a violent explosion* > **violently** *adv*

violet *n* **1** a plant with bluish-purple flowers ▷ *adj* **2** bluish-purple ▶ HISTORY Latin *viola*

violin *n* a musical instrument, the highest member of the violin family, with four strings played with a bow ▶ HISTORY Italian *violino* a little viola

violinist *n* a person who plays the violin

violoncello (vie-oll-on-**chell**-oh) *n, pl* **-los** same as **cello** ▶ HISTORY Italian

VIP very important person

viper *n* a type of poisonous snake ▶ HISTORY Latin *vipera*

virago (vir-**rah**-go) *n, pl* **-goes** or **-gos** an aggressive woman ▶ HISTORY Latin: a manlike maiden

viral (**vie**-ral) *adj* **1** of or caused by a virus **2** (of a video, image, story, etc.) spread quickly and widely among internet users

virgin *n* **1** a person, esp. a woman, who has never had sexual intercourse **2** a person who is inexperienced in a specified field: *a ski virgin* ▷ *adj* **3** not having had sexual intercourse **4** fresh and unused: *a scrap of virgin paper* **5** not yet cultivated, explored, or exploited by people: *virgin territory* ▶ HISTORY Latin *virgo*

Virgin *n* **1** **the Virgin** same as **Virgin Mary** **2** a statue or picture of the Virgin Mary

virginal[1] *adj* **1** like a virgin **2** extremely pure or fresh

virginal[2] *n* an early keyboard instrument like a small harpsichord ▶ HISTORY probably Latin *virginalis* virginal, perhaps because it was played largely by young ladies

Virgin Birth *n Christianity* the doctrine that Jesus Christ was conceived solely by the direct intervention of the Holy Spirit so that Mary remained a virgin

Virginia creeper *n* a climbing plant with leaves that turn red in autumn

virginity *n* the condition or fact of being a virgin

Virgin Mary *n* **the Virgin Mary** *Christianity* Mary, the mother of Christ

Virgo *n astrol* the sixth sign of the zodiac; the Virgin ▶ HISTORY Latin

virile *adj* **1** having traditional male characteristics such as physical strength **2** forceful and energetic: *a virile Highland fling* ▶ HISTORY Latin *virilis* manly > **virility** *n*

virology *n* the branch of medicine concerned with the study of viruses > **virological** *adj*

virtual *adj* **1** having the effect but not the appearance or form of: *the investigation has now come to a virtual standstill* **2** *computers* designed so as to extend the potential of a finite system beyond its immediate limits: *virtual memory* **3** of or relating to virtual reality ▶ HISTORY Latin *virtus* virtue

virtually *adv* almost or nearly: *he is virtually a prisoner in his own palace*

virtual reality *n* a computer-generated environment that seems real to the user

virtue *n* **1** moral goodness **2** a positive moral quality: *the virtue of humility* **3** an advantage or benefit: *the added virtue of being harmless* **4** chastity, esp. in women **5** **by virtue of** by reason of; because of: *they escaped execution by virtue of their high rank* ▶ HISTORY Latin *virtus* manliness

virtuoso *n, pl* **-si** or **-sos** **1** a person with exceptional musical skill **2** a person with exceptional skill in any area ▷ *adj* **3** showing exceptional skill or brilliance ▶ HISTORY Italian: skilled > **virtuosity** *n*

V

virtuous *adj* **1** morally good **2** (of a woman) chaste > **virtuously** *adv*

virulent (**vir**-yew-lent) *adj* **1** extremely bitter or hostile **2 a** (of a microorganism) very infectious **b** (of a disease) having a violent effect **3** extremely poisonous or harmful: *the most virulent poison known to man* ▶ **HISTORY** Latin *virulentus* full of poison > **virulence** *n*

virus *n* **1** a microorganism that is smaller than a bacterium and can cause disease in humans, animals, or plants **2** *informal* a disease caused by a virus **3** *computers* an unsanctioned and self-replicating program which, when activated, corrupts a computer's data and disables its operating system ▶ **HISTORY** Latin: slime, poisonous liquid

visa *n* an official stamp in a passport permitting its holder to travel into or through the country of the government issuing it ▶ **HISTORY** Latin: things seen

visage (**viz**-zij) *n chiefly literary* **1** face **2** appearance ▶ **HISTORY** via Old French from Latin *visus* appearance

vis-à-vis (**veez**-ah-**vee**) *prep* in relation to ▶ **HISTORY** French: face-to-face

viscera (**viss**-er-a) *pl n anat* the large internal organs of the body collectively ▶ **HISTORY** Latin: entrails

visceral *adj* **1** of or affecting the viscera **2** instinctive rather than rational: *visceral hatred*

viscid (**viss**-id) *adj* sticky ▶ **HISTORY** Latin *viscum* mistletoe, birdlime

viscose *n* **1** a sticky solution obtained by dissolving cellulose **2** rayon made from this material ▶ **HISTORY** Latin *viscum* birdlime

viscosity *n, pl* **-ties** **1** the state of being viscous **2** *physics* the extent to which a fluid resists a tendency to flow

viscount (**vie**-count) *n* (in the British Isles) a nobleman ranking below an earl and above a baron ▶ **HISTORY** Old French *visconte* > **viscountcy** *n*

viscountess (**vie**-count-iss) *n* **1** a woman holding the rank of viscount **2** the wife or widow of a viscount

viscous *adj* (of liquids) thick and sticky

vise *n US* same as **vice²**

Vishnu *n* a Hindu god, the Preserver

visibility *n* **1** the range or clarity of vision **2** the condition of being visible

visible *adj* **1** able to be seen **2** able to be perceived by the mind: *a visible and flagrant act of aggression* ▶ **HISTORY** Latin *visibilis* > **visibly** *adv*

vision *n* **1** the ability to see **2** a vivid mental image produced by the imagination: *I kept having visions of him being tortured* **3** a hallucination caused by divine inspiration, madness, or drugs: *visions of God* **4** great perception of future developments **5** the image on a television screen **6** a person or thing of extraordinary beauty ▶ **HISTORY** Latin *visio* sight, from *videre* to see

visionary *adj* **1** showing foresight: *a visionary statesman* **2** idealistic but impractical **3** given to having visions **4** of or like visions ▷ *n, pl* **-aries** **5** a visionary person

visit *vb* **-iting, -ited** **1** to go or come to see (a person or place) **2** to stay with (someone) as a guest **3** *old-fashioned* (of a disease or disaster) to afflict **4 visit on** *or* **upon** to inflict (punishment) on **5 visit with** *US, informal* to chat with (someone) ▷ *n* **6** the act or an instance of visiting **7** a professional or official call **8** a stay as a guest ▶ **HISTORY** Latin *visitare* to go to see

visitant *n* **1** a ghost or apparition **2** a migratory bird temporarily resting in a particular region

visitation *n* **1** an official visit or inspection **2** a punishment or reward from heaven **3** an appearance of a supernatural being

Visitation *n* **a** the visit made by the Virgin Mary to her cousin Elizabeth (Luke 1: 39–56) **b** the Church festival commemorating this, held on July 2

visitor *n* a person who visits a person or place

visitor's book *n* a book in a public building in which people write their names and addresses, and sometimes comments

visor (**vize**-or) *n* **1** a transparent flap on a helmet that can be pulled down to protect the face **2** a small movable screen attached above the windscreen in a vehicle, used as protection against the glare of the sun **3** a peak on a cap ▶ **HISTORY** Old French *vis* face

vista *n* **1** *written* an extensive view **2** *formal* a wide range of possibilities or future events ▶ **HISTORY** Italian

visual *adj* **1** done by or used in seeing **2** capable of being seen ▶ **HISTORY** Latin *visus* sight > **visually** *adv*

visual aids *pl n* objects to be looked at that help the viewer to understand or remember something

visual arts *pl n* the arts of painting, sculpting, photography, etc.

visual display unit *n computers* a device with a screen for displaying data held in a computer

visualize *or* **-ise** *vb* **-izing, -ized** *or* **-ising, -ised** to form a mental image of (something not at that moment visible) > **visualization** *or* **-isation** *n*

visual literacy *n* the ability to interpret and manipulate visual forms of communication

visual text *n* a combination of written material and images, signs, or symbols

vital *adj* **1** essential or highly important: *marriage isn't such a vital part of his life* **2** energetic or lively: *vital youthful manhood* **3** necessary to maintain life: *the vital organs* ▷ *n* **4 vitals** the bodily organs, such as the brain and heart, that are necessary to maintain life ▶ **HISTORY** Latin *vita* life > **vitally** *adv*

vitality *n* physical or mental energy

vital statistics *pl n* **1** population statistics, such as the numbers of births, marriages, and deaths **2** *informal* the measurements of a woman's bust, waist, and hips

vitamin *n* one of a group of substances that occur naturally in certain foods and are essential for normal health and growth ▶ **HISTORY** from Latin *vita* life + AMINE

vitiate (**vish**-ee-ate) *vb* **-ating, -ated 1** to spoil or weaken the effectiveness of (something) **2** to destroy the legal effect of (a contract) ▶ HISTORY Latin *vitiare* to injure > **vitiation** *n*

viticulture *n* the cultivation of grapevines ▶ HISTORY Latin *vitis* vine

vitreous *adj* **1** of or like glass **2** of or relating to the vitreous humour ▶ HISTORY Latin *vitrum* glass

vitreous humour *or* **body** *n* a transparent gelatinous substance that fills the eyeball between the lens and the retina

vitrify *vb* **-fies, -fying, -fied** to change into glass or a glassy substance > **vitrification** *n*

vitriol *n* **1** language expressing bitterness and hatred **2** sulphuric acid ▶ HISTORY Latin *vitrum* glass, referring to the glossy appearance of the sulphates

vitriolic *adj* (of language) severely bitter or harsh

vituperative (vite-**tyew**-pra-tiv) *adj* bitterly abusive ▶ HISTORY Latin *vituperare* to blame > **vituperation** *n*

viva¹ (**vee**-vah) *interj* long live (a specified person or thing) ▶ HISTORY Italian, literally: may (he) live!

viva² (**vive**-ah) *Brit n* **1** an examination in the form of an interview ▷ *vb* **vivaing, vivaed 2** to examine (a candidate) in a spoken interview ▶ HISTORY from VIVA VOCE

vivace (viv-**vah**-chee) *adj music* to be performed in a lively manner ▶ HISTORY Italian

vivacious *adj written* full of energy and enthusiasm ▶ HISTORY Latin *vivax* lively

vivacity *n written* the quality of being vivacious

vivarium *n, pl* **-iums** *or* **-ia** a place where live animals are kept under natural conditions ▶ HISTORY Latin *vivus* alive

viva voce (**vive**-a **voh**-chee) *adv, adj* **1** by word of mouth ▷ *n* **2** same as **viva²** (sense 1) ▶ HISTORY Medieval Latin, literally: with living voice

vivid *adj* **1** very bright: *a vivid blue sky* **2** very clear and detailed: *vivid memories* **3** easily forming lifelike images: *a vivid imagination* ▶ HISTORY Latin *vividus* animated > **vividly** *adv* > **vividness** *n*

vivify *vb* **-fies, -fying, -fied 1** to bring to life **2** to make more vivid or striking ▶ HISTORY Latin *vivus* alive + *facere* to make

viviparous (viv-**vip**-a-russ) *adj* giving birth to living offspring, as most mammals do ▶ HISTORY Latin *vivus* alive + *parere* to bring forth

vivisection *n* the performing of experiments on living animals, involving cutting into or dissecting the body ▶ HISTORY Latin *vivus* living + *sectio* a cutting > **vivisectionist** *n*

vixen *n* **1** a female fox **2** *Brit, Austral & NZ, informal* a spiteful woman ▶ HISTORY related to Old English *fyxe*, feminine of *fox*

vizier (viz-**zeer**) *n* a high official in certain Muslim countries ▶ HISTORY Turkish *vezīr*

vizor *n* same as **visor**

VLF *or* **vlf** *radio* very low frequency

V neck *n* **a** a neck on a garment that comes down to a point, like the letter V **b** a sweater with a neck like this > **V-neck** *or* **V-necked** *adj*

vocab *n* short for **vocabulary**

vocable *n linguistics* a word regarded simply as a sequence of letters or spoken sounds ▶ HISTORY Latin *vocare* to call

vocabulary *n, pl* **-laries 1** all the words that a person knows **2** all the words contained in a language **3** the specialist terms used in a given subject **4** a list of words in another language with their translations **5** a range of symbols or techniques as used in any of the arts or crafts ▶ HISTORY Latin *vocabulum* vocable

vocal *adj* **1** of or relating to the voice: *vocal pitch* **2** expressing one's opinions clearly and openly: *a vocal minority with racist views* ▷ *n* **3 vocals** the singing part of a piece of jazz or pop music ▶ HISTORY Latin *vox* voice > **vocally** *adv*

vocal cords *pl n* either of two pairs of membranous folds in the larynx, of which the lower pair can be made to vibrate and produce sound by forcing air from the lungs over them

vocalist *n* a singer with a jazz band or pop group

vocalize *or* **-ise** *vb* **-izing, -ized** *or* **-ising, -ised 1** to express with or use the voice **2** to make vocal or articulate: *vocalize your discontent* **3** *phonetics* to articulate (a speech sound) with voice

vocation *n* **1** a specified profession or trade **2 a** a special urge to a particular calling or career, esp. a religious one **b** such a calling or career ▶ HISTORY Latin *vocare* to call

vocational *adj* directed towards a particular profession or trade: *vocational training*

vocative *n grammar* a grammatical case used in some languages when addressing a person or thing ▶ HISTORY Latin *vocare* to call

vociferate *vb* **-ating, -ated** to exclaim or cry out about (something) noisily ▶ HISTORY Latin *vox* voice + *ferre* to bear > **vociferation** *n*

vociferous *adj* loud and forceful: *a vociferous minority* > **vociferously** *adv*

VOD *n* video on demand

vodka *n* a clear alcoholic spirit originating in Russia, made from potatoes or grain ▶ HISTORY Russian

voetsak *or* **voetsek** (**foot**-sak) *interj S African, offensive* an expression of dismissal or rejection ▶ HISTORY Afrikaans, from Dutch *voort se ek* forward, I say, commonly applied to animals

vogue *n* **1** the popular style at a given time **2 in vogue** fashionable ▷ *adj* **3** fashionable: *a vogue word* ▶ HISTORY French > **voguish** *adj*

voice *n* **1** the sound made by the vibration of the vocal cords, esp. when modified by the tongue and mouth **2** a distinctive tone of the speech sounds characteristic of a particular person: *he can recognize her voice* **3** the ability to speak or sing: *he had at last found his voice* **4** the condition or quality of a person's voice: *her voice was kind* **5** the musical sound of a singing voice: *what I have is a good voice and a great love of lyrics* **6** the expression of feeling or opinion: *dissenting voices* **7** a right to express an opinion **8** *grammar* a category of the verb that expresses whether it is active or passive **9** *phonetics* the sound characterizing the articulation of several speech sounds, that is produced when the vocal cords are vibrated by the breath **10 with one voice** unanimously ▷ *vb* **voicing, voiced 11** to express verbally: *anyone with an objection has a chance to voice it* **12** to articulate (a speech sound) with voice ▶ HISTORY Latin *vox*

voiced *adj phonetics* articulated with accompanying vibration of the vocal cords, for example 'b' in English

voiceless *adj* **1** *written* without a voice **2** *phonetics* articulated without accompanying vibration of the vocal cords, for example 'p' in English

voice mail *n* an electronic system for the transfer and storage of telephone messages, which can then be dealt with by the user at his or her convenience

voice-over *n films, television* the voice of an unseen commentator heard during a film

void *n* **1** a feeling or condition of loneliness or deprivation **2** an empty space or area ▷ *adj* **3** having no official value or authority, because the terms have been broken or have not been fulfilled: *the race was declared void* **4** *old-fashioned or literary* empty: *behold, the tomb is void!* **5 void of** devoid of or without: *the fact of being punished becomes void of all moral significance* ▷ *vb* **6** to make ineffective or invalid **7** to empty **8** to discharge the contents of (the bowels or bladder) ▶ HISTORY Latin *vacare* to be empty

voile (**voyl**) *n* a light semitransparent dress fabric ▶ HISTORY French: veil

vol. volume

volatile (**voll**-a-tile) *adj* **1** (of circumstances) liable to sudden change **2** (of people) liable to sudden changes of mood and behaviour **3** (of a substance) changing quickly from a solid or liquid form to a vapour ▶ HISTORY Latin *volare* to fly > **volatility** *n*

volatilize *or* **-lise** *vb* **-lizing, -lized** *or* **-lising, -lised** to change from a solid or liquid to a vapour

vol-au-vent (**voll**-oh-von) *n* a very light puff pastry case with a savoury filling ▶ HISTORY French, literally: flight in the wind

volcanic *adj* **1** of or relating to volcanoes **2** displaying sudden violence or anger

volcanic ash *n geol* dust produced by a volcano when it erupts

volcanic plug *n geol* solidified lava in the vent of a volcano

volcano *n, pl* **-noes** *or* **-nos 1** an opening in the earth's crust from which molten lava, ashes, dust, and gases are ejected from below the earth's surface **2** a mountain formed from volcanic material ejected from a vent ▶ HISTORY Italian, from Latin *Volcanus* Vulcan, Roman god of fire

vole *n* a small rodent with a stocky body and a short tail ▶ HISTORY short for *volemouse*, from Old Norse *vollr* field + *mus* mouse

volition *n* **1** the ability to decide things for oneself **2 of one's own volition** through one's own choice ▶ HISTORY Latin *volo* I will

volley *n* **1** the simultaneous firing of several weapons **2** the bullets fired **3** a burst of questions or critical comments **4** *sport* a stroke or kick at a moving ball before it hits the ground ▷ *vb* **5** to fire (weapons) in a volley **6** *sport* to hit or kick (a moving ball) before it hits the ground ▶ HISTORY French *volée* a flight

volleyball *n* a game in which two teams hit a large ball backwards and forwards over a high net with their hands

volt *n* the SI unit of electric potential; the potential difference between two points on a conductor carrying a current of 1 ampere, when the power dissipated between these points is 1 watt ▶ HISTORY after Count Alessandro *Volta*, physicist

volta *n prosody* (in a sonnet) the point where there is a change of mood or argument ▶ HISTORY Italian *volta* a turn

voltage *n* an electromotive force or potential difference expressed in volts

voltaic *adj* same as **galvanic** (sense 1)

volte-face (volt-**fass**) *n, pl* **volte-face** a reversal of opinion ▶ HISTORY via French from Italian *volta* turn + *faccia* face

voltmeter *n* an instrument for measuring voltage

voluble *adj* talking easily and at length ▶ HISTORY Latin *volubilis* turning readily > **volubility** *n* > **volubly** *adv*

volume *n* **1** the magnitude of the three-dimensional space enclosed within or occupied by something **2** an amount or total: *the volume of trade between the two countries* **3** loudness of sound **4** the control on a radio, etc. for adjusting the loudness of sound **5** a book: *a slim volume* **6** one of several books that make up a series **7** a set of issues of a magazine over a specified period ▶ HISTORY Latin *volumen* a roll

volumetric *adj* of or using measurement by volume: *a simple volumetric measurement*

voluminous *adj* **1** (of clothes) large and roomy **2** (of writings) extensive and detailed

voluntary *adj* **1** done or undertaken by free choice: *voluntary repatriation* **2** done or maintained without payment: *voluntary work* **3** (of muscles) having their action controlled by the will ▷ *n, pl* **-taries 4** *music* a composition, usually for organ, played at the beginning or end of a church service ▶ HISTORY Latin *voluntarius* > **voluntarily** *adv*

voluntary sector *n* the part of the economy that consists of non-profit-making organizations, as opposed to the public and private sectors

volunteer *n* **1** a person who offers by choice and without being forced to do something **2** a person who freely undertakes military service ▷ *vb* **3** to offer (oneself or one's services) by choice and without being forced **4** to enlist voluntarily for military service **5** to give (information) willingly **6** to offer the services of (another person)

voluptuary *n, pl* **-aries** a person devoted to luxury and sensual pleasures ▶ HISTORY Latin *voluptas* pleasure

voluptuous *adj* **1** (of a woman) alluring because of the fullness of her figure **2** pleasing to the senses: *voluptuous yellow peaches* > **voluptuously** *adv* > **voluptuousness** *n*

volute *n* a spiral or twisting shape or object, such as a carved spiral scroll on an Ionic capital ► **HISTORY** Latin *volvere* to roll up

vomit *vb* **-iting, -ited 1** to eject (the contents of the stomach) through the mouth **2** to eject or be ejected forcefully ▷ *n* **3** the partly digested food and drink ejected in vomiting ► **HISTORY** Latin *vomitare* to vomit repeatedly

voodoo *n* **1** a religion involving ancestor worship and witchcraft, practised by Black people in the West Indies, esp. in Haiti ▷ *adj* **2** of or relating to voodoo ► **HISTORY** from West African

voorkamer (**foor**-kahm-er) *n* S African the front room of a house ► **HISTORY** Afrikaans

voracious *adj* **1** eating or craving great quantities of food **2** very eager or insatiable in some activity: *a voracious collector* ► **HISTORY** Latin *vorare* to devour > **voraciously** *adv* > **voracity** *n*

vortex (**vor**-tex) *n*, *pl* **-tices** (-tiss-seez) **1** a whirling mass or motion, such as a whirlpool or whirlwind **2** a situation which draws people into it against their will ► **HISTORY** Latin: a whirlpool

votary *n*, *pl* **-ries 1** RC Church, Eastern Churches a person who has dedicated himself or herself to religion by taking vows **2** a person devoted to a cause ► **HISTORY** Latin *votum* a vow

vote *n* **1** a choice made by a participant in a shared decision, esp. in electing a candidate **2** the right to vote **3** the total number of votes cast **4** the opinion of a group of people as determined by voting: *the draft should be put to the vote* **5** a body of votes or voters collectively: *the youth vote* ▷ *vb* **voting, voted 6** to make a choice by vote **7** to authorize or allow by voting **8** to declare oneself as being (something or in favour of something) by voting: *I've always voted Labour* **9** *informal* to declare by common opinion ► **HISTORY** Latin *votum* a solemn promise

vote down *vb* to decide against or defeat in a vote: *a proposed British resolution was voted down*

voter *n* a person who can or does vote

votive *adj* done or given to fulfil a vow ► **HISTORY** Latin *votivus* promised by a vow

vouch *vb* **vouch for a** to give personal assurance about **b** to give supporting evidence for or be proof of ► **HISTORY** Latin *vocare* to call

voucher *n* **1** a ticket or card used instead of money to buy specified goods: *a gift voucher* **2** a document recording a financial transaction ► **HISTORY** Old French *vo(u)cher* to summon

vouchsafe *vb* **-safing, -safed 1** *old-fashioned* to give or grant: *she has powers vouchsafed to few* **2** to offer assurances about; guarantee: *he absolutely vouchsafed your integrity* ► **HISTORY** *vouch* + *safe*

vow *n* **1** a solemn and binding promise **2 take vows** to enter a religious order and commit oneself to its rule of life by the vows of poverty, chastity, and obedience ▷ *vb* **3** to promise or decide solemnly ► **HISTORY** Latin *votum*

vowel *n* **a** a voiced speech sound made with the mouth open and the stream of breath unobstructed by the tongue, teeth, or lips, for example *a* or *e* **b** a letter representing this ► **HISTORY** Latin *vocalis (littera)*, from *vox* voice

vox pop *n* Brit interviews with members of the public on a radio or television programme

vox populi *n* public opinion ► **HISTORY** Latin: the voice of the people

voyage *n* a long journey by sea or in space ▷ *vb* **-aging, -aged 2** to go on a voyage ► **HISTORY** Latin *viaticum* provision for travelling > **voyager** *n*

voyageur (voy-ahzh-**ur**) *n* **1** formerly a French or Métis canoeman who transported furs from trading posts in the North American interior **2** (in Canada) a woodsman, guide, trapper, boatman, or explorer, esp. in the North ► **HISTORY** French: voyager

voyeur (voy-**ur**) *n* a person who obtains pleasure from watching things they should not ► **HISTORY** French, literally: one who sees > **voyeurism** *n* > **voyeuristic** *adj*

VR virtual reality

vrou (**froh**) *n* S African an Afrikaner woman, esp. a married woman ► **HISTORY** Afrikaans

vs versus

VSA (in New Zealand) Voluntary Service Abroad

V-sign *n* **1** (in Britain and Australia) an offensive gesture made by sticking up the index and middle fingers with the palm of the hand inwards **2** a similar gesture with the palm outwards meaning victory or peace

VSO (in Britain) Voluntary Service Overseas

VSOP very special (or superior) old pale: used of brandy or port

VT Vermont

VTOL vertical takeoff and landing

Vulcan *n* the Roman god of fire

vulcanite *n* a hard black rubber produced by vulcanizing natural rubber with sulphur

vulcanize *or* **-ise** *vb* **-izing, -ized** *or* **-ising, -ised** to treat (rubber) with sulphur under heat and pressure to improve elasticity and strength ► **HISTORY** after *Vulcan*, Roman god of fire

vulgar *adj* **1** showing lack of good taste, decency, or refinement **2** denoting a form of a language spoken by the ordinary people, rather than the literary form ► **HISTORY** Latin *vulgus* the common people > **vulgarly** *adv*

vulgar fraction *n* same as **simple fraction**

vulgarian *n* a rich vulgar person

vulgarism *n* a coarse or obscene word or phrase

vulgarity *n*, *pl* **-ties 1** the condition of being vulgar **2** a vulgar action or phrase

vulgarize *or* **-ise** *vb* **-izing, -ized** *or* **-ising, -ised 1** to make vulgar **2** to make (something little known or difficult to understand) popular

Vulgar Latin *n* any of the dialects of Latin spoken in the Roman Empire other than classical Latin

v

959

Vulgate *n* the fourth-century Latin version of the Bible

vulnerable *adj* **1** able to be physically or emotionally hurt **2** easily influenced or tempted **3** *mil* exposed to attack **4** financially weak and likely to fail **5** *Bridge* (of a side that has won one game towards rubber) subject to increased bonuses or penalties ▶ HISTORY Latin *vulnus* a wound > **vulnerability** *n*

vulpine *adj* **1** of or like a fox **2** clever and cunning
▶ HISTORY Latin *vulpes* fox

vulture *n* **1** a very large bird of prey that feeds on the flesh of dead animals **2** a person who profits from the misfortune and weakness of others
▶ HISTORY Latin *vultur*

vulva *n* the external genitals of human females
▶ HISTORY Latin: covering, womb, matrix

vying *vb* the present participle of **vie**

V

960

Ww

w cricket **a** wicket **b** wide

W 1 chem tungsten ▶ HISTORY German Wolfram
2 watt 3 West(ern)

WA 1 Washington (state) 2 Western Australia

wacky adj **wackier, wackiest** slang odd, eccentric,
or crazy: a wacky idea ▶ HISTORY dialect: a fool
> **wackiness** n

wad n 1 a small mass of soft material, such as
cotton wool, used for packing or stuffing
2 a roll or bundle of banknotes or papers
▶ HISTORY Late Latin wadda

wadding n a soft material used for padding or
stuffing

waddle vb **-dling, -dled** 1 to walk with short
steps, rocking slightly from side to side ▷ n
2 a swaying walk ▶ HISTORY from wade

waddy n, pl **-dies** a heavy wooden club used by
Australian Aborigines

wade vb **wading, waded** 1 to walk slowly and
with difficulty through water or mud 2 **wade in**
or **into** to begin doing (something) in an energetic
way: wading into the fray 3 **wade through** to
proceed with difficulty through: a stack of literature
to wade through ▶ HISTORY Old English wadan

wader n a long-legged bird, such as the heron or
stork, that lives near water and feeds on fish. Also
called: **wading bird**

waders pl n long waterproof boots which
completely cover the legs, worn by anglers for
standing in water

wadi (**wod**-dee) n, pl **-dies** a river in N Africa or
Arabia which is dry except in the rainy season
▶ HISTORY Arabic

wafer n 1 a thin crisp sweetened biscuit, often
served with ice cream 2 Christianity a round thin
piece of unleavened bread used at Communion
3 electronics a small thin slice of germanium or
silicon that is separated into numerous individual
components or circuits ▶ HISTORY Old French
waufre

wafer-thin adj very thin: wafer-thin meat

waffle¹ n a square crisp pancake with a gridlike
pattern ▶ HISTORY Dutch wafel

waffle² informal, chiefly Brit, Austral & NZ vb **-fling,
-fled** 1 to speak or write in a vague and wordy
manner ▷ n 2 vague and wordy speech or writing
▶ HISTORY origin unknown

waft vb 1 to move gently through the air as if being
carried by the wind: the scent of summer flowers

gently wafting through my window ▷ n 2 a scent
carried on the air ▶ HISTORY Middle Dutch wachter
guard

wag¹ vb **wagging, wagged** 1 to move rapidly and
repeatedly from side to side or up and down:
Franklin wagged his tail ▷ n 2 an instance of
wagging ▶ HISTORY Old English wagian

wag² n old-fashioned a humorous or witty person
▶ HISTORY origin unknown > **waggish** adj

wage n 1 Also: **wages** the money paid in return for
a person's work, esp. when paid weekly or daily
rather than monthly: a campaign for higher wages
▷ vb **waging, waged** 2 to engage in (a campaign
or war) ▶ HISTORY Old French wagier to pledge

wager n 1 a bet on the outcome of an event or
activity ▷ vb 2 to bet (something, esp. money) on
the outcome of an event or activity ▶ HISTORY Old
French wagier to pledge

waggle vb **-gling, -gled** to move with a rapid
shaking or wobbling motion ▶ HISTORY from WAG¹

wagon or **waggon** n 1 a four-wheeled vehicle
used for carrying heavy loads, sometimes pulled by
a horse or tractor 2 an open railway freight truck
3 a lorry 4 **on the wagon** informal abstaining from
alcoholic drink ▶ HISTORY Dutch wagen > **wagoner**
or **waggoner** n

wagtail n a small songbird of Eurasia and Africa
with a very long tail that wags up and down when
it walks

wahine (wah-**hee**-nay) n NZ a Māori woman, esp.
a wife ▶ HISTORY Māori

wahoo n a food and game fish of tropical seas

waif n a person, esp. a child, who is, or who looks
as if he or she might be, homeless or neglected
▶ HISTORY Anglo-Norman

wail vb 1 to utter a prolonged high-pitched cry of
pain or sorrow ▷ n 2 a prolonged high-pitched cry
of pain or sorrow ▶ HISTORY from Old Norse
> **wailing** n, adj

wain n poetic a farm cart ▶ HISTORY Old English
wægn

wainscot n a wooden covering on the lower half
of the walls of a room. Also: **wainscoting**
▶ HISTORY Middle Low German wagenschot

waist n 1 anat the narrow part of the body between
the ribs and the hips 2 the part of a garment
covering the waist ▶ HISTORY origin unknown

waistband n a band of material sewn on to the
waist of a garment to strengthen it

waistcoat n a sleeveless upper garment which
buttons up the front and is usually worn by men
over a shirt and under a jacket

waistline n 1 an imaginary line around the body at
the narrowest part of the waist 2 the place where
the upper and lower part of a garment are joined
together

wait vb 1 to stay in one place or remain inactive in
expectation of something: the delegates have to wait
for a reply 2 to be temporarily delayed: the
celebrations can wait 3 (of a thing) to be ready or be
in store: waiting for her on the library table was the
latest Jilly Cooper novel ▷ n 4 the act or a period of

w

waiting **5 lie in wait for a** to prepare an ambush for **b** to be ready or be in store for ▷ See also **wait on** ▶ HISTORY Old French *waitier*

Waitangi Day *n* February 6th, the national day of New Zealand commemorating the Treaty Of Waitangi in 1840

waiter *n* a man who serves people with food and drink in a restaurant

waiting list *n* a list of people waiting for something that is not immediately available: *a long waiting list for heart surgery*

wait on *vb* **1** to serve (people) with food and drink in a restaurant **2** to look after the needs of: *they were waited on by a manservant* ▷ *interj* **3** NZ stop! hold on! Also (for senses 1, 2): **wait upon**

waitress *n* **1** a woman who serves people with food and drink in a restaurant ▷ *vb* **2** to work as a waitress

waive *vb* **waiving, waived** to refrain from enforcing or claiming (a rule or right) ▶ HISTORY Old French *weyver*

waiver *n* the act or an instance of voluntarily giving up a claim or right

waka *n* NZ a Māori canoe

wake¹ *vb* **waking, woke, woken** **1** Also: **wake up** to become conscious again or bring (someone) to consciousness again after a sleep **2 wake up** to make (someone) more alert after a period of inactivity **3 wake up to** to become aware of: *the world did not wake up to this tragedy until many people had died* **4 waking hours** the time when a person is awake: *he often used his waking hours to write music* ▷ *n* **5** a watch or vigil held over the body of a dead person during the night before burial ▶ HISTORY Old English *wacian*

wake² *n* **1** the track left by a ship moving through water **2 in the wake of** following soon after: *the arrests come in the wake of the assassination* ▶ HISTORY Scandinavian

wakeful *adj* **1** unable to sleep **2** without sleep: *wakeful nights* **3** alert: *wakeful readiness* > **wakefulness** *n*

waken *vb* to become conscious again or bring (someone) to consciousness again after a sleep

walk *vb* **1** to move on foot at a moderate rate with at least one foot always on the ground **2** to pass through, on, or over on foot: *to walk a short distance* **3** to walk somewhere with (a person or a dog) **4 walking on air** very happy and excited **5 walk the streets** to wander about, esp. when looking for work or when homeless ▷ *n* **6** a short journey on foot, usually for pleasure **7** the action of walking rather than running **8** a manner of walking: *a proud slow walk* **9** a place or route for walking **10 walk of life** social position or profession: *people from all walks of life were drawn to her* ▷ See also **walk into, walkover** ▶ HISTORY Old English *wealcan* > **walker** *n* See WORD FOCUS **walk**

walkabout *n* **1** an occasion when royalty, politicians, or other celebrities walk among and meet the public **2 go walkabout** Austral

a to wander through the bush as a nomad **b** *informal* to be lost or misplaced **c** *informal* to lose one's concentration

walkie-talkie *n* a small combined radio transmitter and receiver that can be carried around by one person

walking stick *n* a stick or cane carried in the hand to assist walking

walk into *vb* to encounter unexpectedly: *the troop reinforcements had walked into a trap*

walk-on *adj* (of a part in a film or play) small and not involving speaking

walkover *n* **1** *informal* an easy victory ▷ *vb* **walk over 2** to mistreat or bully; take advantage of: *if you don't make your mark early, people will walk all over you*

walkway *n* **1** a path designed for use by pedestrians **2** a passage or pathway between two buildings

wall *n* **1** a vertical structure made of stone, brick, or wood, with a length and height much greater than its thickness, used to enclose, divide, or support. *Related adjective:* **mural 2** anything that suggests a wall in function or effect: *a wall of elm trees; a wall of suspicion* **3** *anat* any lining or membrane that encloses a bodily cavity or structure: *cell walls* **4 drive someone up the wall** *slang* to make someone angry or irritated **5 go to the wall** *informal* to be financially ruined **6 have one's back to the wall** *informal* to be in a very difficult situation, with no obvious way out of it ▷ *vb* **7** to surround or enclose (an area) with a wall **8 wall in** or **up** to enclose (someone or something) completely in a room or place ▶ HISTORY Old English *weall* > **walled** *adj*

wallaby *n, pl* **-bies** a marsupial of Australia and New Guinea that resembles a small kangaroo ▶ HISTORY Aboriginal *wolabā*

wallaroo *n* a large stocky Australian kangaroo of rocky regions

wallet *n* a small folding case, usually of leather, for holding paper money and credit cards ▶ HISTORY Germanic

walleye *n* a fish with large staring eyes. Also: **dory**

walleyed *adj* having eyes with an abnormal amount of white showing because of a squint ▶ HISTORY Old Norse *vagleygr*

wallflower *n* **1** a plant grown for its clusters of yellow, orange, red, or purple fragrant flowers **2** *informal* a woman who does not join in the dancing at a party or dance because she has no partner

Walloon (wol-**loon**) *n* **1** a French-speaking person from S Belgium or the neighbouring part of France **2** the French dialect of Belgium ▷ *adj* **3** of the Walloons ▶ HISTORY Germanic

wallop *informal vb* **1** to hit hard ▷ *n* **2** a hard blow ▶ HISTORY Old French *waloper* to gallop

walloping *informal n* **1** a severe physical beating ▷ *adj* **2** large or great: *a walloping amount of sodium*

wallow *vb* **1** to indulge oneself in some emotion: *they wallow in self-pity* **2** to lie or roll about in mud or

walk

There are a number of more interesting or creative words you can use in place of the basic verb walk, if you want to say something about the way in which a person walks.

DEFINITION 1

- If you step in a particular direction, you move your foot in that direction: I stepped carefully over the piles of rubbish.
- If you tread in a particular way, you walk in that way. This is rather a literary word: She trod carefully across the grass.
- If you amble or stroll, you walk in a slow, relaxed way: We ambled along the beach hand in hand.
  • They strolled down the High Street, looking in shop windows.
- If you saunter, you walk in a slow, casual way: He was sauntering along as if he had all the time in the world.
- If you wander, you walk around in a casual way, often without intending to go anywhere in particular: Khachi was wandering aimlessly about in the garden.
- If you tiptoe, you walk very quietly without putting your heels on the ground, so as not to be heard: She slipped out of bed and tiptoed to the window.
- If you toddle, you walk unsteadily, with short quick steps. This word is most often used of babies or small children: My daughter toddles around after me wherever I go.
- If you mince, you walk with quick, small steps in a put-on way: performers mincing around the stage in ridiculous costumes
- If you pace, you walk up and down a small area, usually because you are anxious or impatient: As he waited, he paced nervously around the room.
- If you stride, you walk with quick, long steps: He turned abruptly and strode off down the corridor.
- If you march, you walk quickly and in a determined way, perhaps because you are angry: She marched into the office and demanded to see the manager.
- If you stamp, you put your feet down very hard when you walk, usually because you are angry: "I'm leaving!" he shouted as he stamped out of the room.
- If you flounce, you walk quickly and with exaggerated movements, in a way that shows you are annoyed or upset about something: She flounced out of the room in a huff.
- If you stalk, you walk in a stiff, proud, or angry way: He stalked out of the meeting, slamming the door.
- If you lurch, you walk with sudden, jerky movements: He lurched around the room as if he was drunk.
- If you stagger or totter, you walk very unsteadily: Sick and giddy, he staggered back to his room. • I had to totter around on crutches for six weeks.
- If you reel, you walk about in an unsteady way as if you are going to fall: He lost his balance and reeled back.
- If you stumble, you trip while you are walking and almost fall: I stumbled into the house and called the police.
- If you hike or ramble, you walk some distance in the countryside for pleasure: They hiked along a remote trail. • a relaxing holiday spent rambling over the fells
- If you trek, you make a journey across difficult country by walking: This year we're going trekking in Nepal.
- You can also use trek to describe someone walking rather slowly and unwillingly, usually because they are tired: We trekked all round the shops looking for white shoes.
- If you plod, tramp, or trudge, you walk slowly, with heavy steps, often because you are tired: He plodded about after me, looking bored.
  • They spent all day tramping through the snow.
  • We had to trudge all the way back up the hill.

---

water for pleasure ▷ n **3** the act or an instance of wallowing **4** a muddy place where animals wallow ▶ **HISTORY** Old English *wealwian* to roll (in mud)

wallpaper n **1** a printed or embossed paper for covering the walls of a room ▷ vb **2** to cover (walls) with wallpaper

Wall Street n *finance* a street in New York City where the Stock Exchange and major banks are situated

wall-to-wall *adj* (of carpeting) completely covering a floor

wally n, pl **-lies** Brit, slang a stupid or foolish person ▶ **HISTORY** from the name *Walter*

walnut n **1** an edible nut with a hard, wrinkled, light brown shell **2** a tree on which walnuts grow **3** the light brown wood of a walnut tree, used for making furniture

- **WORD HISTORY**
- 'Walnut' comes from Old English *walh-hnutu*
- meaning 'foreign nut'. The walnut is an Asian
- tree that was not introduced into Britain until
- the 15th or 16th century, and so walnuts
- originally were imported from abroad.

walrus n, pl **-ruses** or **-rus** a mammal of cold northern seas, with two tusks that hang down from the upper jaw, tough thick skin, and coarse whiskers ▶ **HISTORY** Dutch: whale horse

waltz n **1 a** a ballroom dance in triple time in which couples spin round as they progress round the room **2** music for this dance ▷ vb **3** to dance a

waltz 4 *informal* to move in a relaxed and confident way: *he waltzed over to her table to say hello* ▸ HISTORY German *Walzer*

wampum (**wom**-pum) *n* (formerly) money used by Native Americans of N America, made of shells strung or woven together ▸ HISTORY Native American *wampompeag*

wan (rhymes with **swan**) *adj* **wanner, wannest** very pale, as a result of illness or unhappiness ▸ HISTORY Old English *wann* dark > **wanly** *adv*

WAN *n computers* wide area network

wand *n* **1** a rod used by a magician when performing a trick or by a fairy when casting a spell **2** a hand-held electronic device which is pointed at or passed over an item to read the data stored there ▸ HISTORY Old Norse *vöndr*

wander *vb* **1** to walk about in a place without any definite purpose or destination **2** to leave a place where one is supposed to stay: *kids wander off* **3** (of the mind) to lose concentration ▷ *n* **4** the act or an instance of wandering ▸ HISTORY Old English *wandrian* > **wanderer** *n* > **wandering** *adj, n*

wanderlust *n* a great desire to travel

wane *vb* **waning, waned** **1** to decrease gradually in size, strength, or power: *the influence of the extremists is waning* **2** (of the moon) to show a gradually decreasing area of brightness from full moon until new moon ▷ *n* **3 on the wane** decreasing in size, strength, or power: *his fame was on the wane* ▸ HISTORY Old English *wanian* > **waning** *adj*

wangle *vb* **-gling, -gled** *informal* to get (something) by cunning or devious methods: *I've wangled you both an invitation* ▸ HISTORY origin unknown

want *vb* **1** to feel a need or longing for: *I want a job* **2** to wish or desire (to do something): *we did not want to get involved* **3** *Brit, Austral & NZ* to have need of or require (doing or being something): *what will you do when it wants cleaning?* **4** *informal* should or ought (to do something): *the last person you want to hire is someone who is desperate for a job* **5 want for** to be lacking or deficient in: *they were convinced I was wealthy and wanted for nothing* ▷ *n* **6** something that is needed, desired, or lacked: *attempts to satisfy a number of wants* **7** a lack, shortage, or absence: *for want of opportunity* **8 in want of** needing or lacking: *the Chinese peasant farmer may be in want of a roof, a job, a doctor nearby* ▸ HISTORY Old Norse *vanta* to be deficient

wanted *adj* being searched for by the police in connection with a crime that has been committed

wanting *adj* **1** lacking: *I would be wanting in charity if I did not explain the terms* **2** not meeting requirements or expectations: *she compares herself to her sister and finds herself wanting*

wanton *adj* **1** without motive, provocation, or justification: *sheer wanton destruction* **2** (of a person) maliciously and unnecessarily cruel **3** *old-fashioned* (of a woman) sexually unrestrained or immodest ▸ HISTORY Middle English *wantowen* unruly

WAP Wireless Application Protocol: a system that allows mobile phone users to access the internet and other information services

wapiti (**wop**-pit-tee) *n, pl* **-tis** a large North American deer, now also found in New Zealand ▸ HISTORY from a Native American language

war *n* **1** open armed conflict between two or more countries or groups: *this international situation led to war* **2** a particular armed conflict: *the American war in Vietnam* **3** any conflict or contest: *a trade war* **4 have been in the wars** *informal* to look as if one has been in a fight ▷ *adj* **5** relating to war or a war: *the war effort; a war correspondent* ▷ *vb* **warring, warred 6** to conduct a war ▸ HISTORY Old Northern French *werre* > **warring** *adj*

waratah *n* an Australian shrub with crimson flowers

warble *vb* **-bling, -bled** to sing in a high-pitched trilling voice ▸ HISTORY Old French *werbler*

warbler *n* any of various small songbirds

War Communism *n history* the economic policies of the Bolsheviks in the aftermath of the 1917 Russian revolution, consisting of the abolition of private trade, the nationalization of industry, and the forced acquisition of almost all agricultural produce

war crime *n* a crime committed in wartime in violation of the accepted customs, such as ill-treatment of prisoners > **war criminal** *n*

war cry *n* **1** a rallying cry used by combatants in battle **2** a slogan used to rally support for a cause

ward *n* **1** a room in a hospital for patients requiring similar kinds of care: *the maternity ward* **2** one of the districts into which a town, parish, or other area is divided for administration or elections **3** *law* Also called: **ward of court** a person, esp. a child whose parents are dead, who is placed under the control or protection of a guardian or of a court ▷ See also **ward off** ▸ HISTORY Old English *weard* protector > **wardship** *n*

-ward *suffix* **1** (forming adjectives) indicating direction towards: *a backward step* **2** (forming adverbs) *chiefly US & Canad* same as **-wards** ▸ HISTORY Old English *-weard*

warden *n* **1** a person who is in charge of a building, such as a youth hostel, and its occupants **2** a public official who is responsible for the enforcement of certain regulations: *a game warden* **3** the chief officer in charge of a prison ▸ HISTORY Old French *wardein*

warder *or fem* **wardress** *n chiefly Brit* a prison officer ▸ HISTORY Old French *warder* to guard

ward off *vb* to prevent (something unpleasant) from happening or from causing harm: *to ward off the pangs of hunger; to ward off cancer cells*

wardrobe *n* **1** a tall cupboard, with a rail or hooks on which to hang clothes **2** the total collection of articles of clothing belonging to one person: *your autumn wardrobe* **3** the collection of costumes belonging to a theatre or theatrical company ▸ HISTORY Old French *warder* to guard + *robe* robe

W

wardrobe mistress *n* the woman in charge of the costumes in a theatre or theatrical company > **wardrobe master** *masc n*

wardroom *n* the quarters assigned to the officers of a warship, apart from the captain

-wards *or* **-ward** *suffix forming adverbs* indicating direction towards: *a step backwards* ▶ HISTORY Old English *-weardes*

ware *n* articles of the same kind or material: *crystal ware.* See also **wares** ▶ HISTORY Old English *waru*

warehouse *n* a place where goods are stored prior to their sale or distribution

wares *pl n* goods for sale

warfare *n* **1** the act of conducting a war **2** a violent or intense conflict of any kind: *class warfare*

war game *n* **1** a tactical exercise for training military commanders, in which no military units are actually deployed **2** a game in which model soldiers are used to create battles in order to study tactics

warhead *n* the front section of a missile or projectile that contains explosives

warhorse *n* **1** (formerly) a horse used in battle **2** *informal* a veteran soldier or politician

warlike *adj* **1** of or relating to war: *warlike stores and equipment* **2** hostile and eager to have a war: *a warlike nation*

warlock *n* a man who practises black magic ▶ HISTORY Old English *wǣrloga* oath breaker

warlord *n* a military leader of a nation or part of a nation

warm *adj* **1** feeling or having a moderate degree of heat **2** giving heat: *warm clothing* **3** (of colours) predominantly red or yellow in tone **4** kindly or affectionate: *warm embraces* **5** *informal* near to finding a hidden object or guessing facts, for example in a children's game ▷ *vb* **6** to make warm **7 warm to a** to become fonder of: *I warmed to him when he defended me* **b** to become more excited or enthusiastic about: *he had warmed to his theme* ▷ See also **warm up** ▶ HISTORY Old English *wearm* > **warmly** *adv* > **warmness** *n*

warm-blooded *adj* **1** (of an animal, such as a mammal or a bird) having a constant body temperature, usually higher than the surrounding temperature **2** having a passionate nature > **warm-bloodedness** *n*

warm front *n meteorol* the boundary between a warm air mass and the cold air it is replacing

warmonger *n* a person who encourages warlike ideas or advocates war > **warmongering** *n*

warmth *n* **1** the state of being warm **2** affection or cordiality: *the warmth of their friendship*

warm up *vb* **1** to make or become warm or warmer **2** to prepare for a race, sporting contest, or exercise routine by doing gentle exercises immediately beforehand **3** (of an engine or machine) to be started and left running until the working temperature is reached **4** to become more lively: *wait until things warm up* **5** to reheat (food that has already been cooked) ▷ *n* **warm-up 6** a preparatory exercise routine

warn *vb* **1** to make (someone) aware of a possible danger or problem **2** to inform (someone) in advance: *you'd better warn your girlfriend that you'll be working at the weekend* **3 warn off** to advise (someone) to go away or not to do something ▶ HISTORY Old English *wearnian*

warning *n* **1** a hint, threat, or advance notice of a possible danger or problem **2** advice not to do something ▷ *adj* **3** giving or serving as a warning: *warning signs* > **warningly** *adv*

warp *vb* **1** (esp. of wooden objects) to be twisted out of shape, for example by heat or damp **2** to distort or influence in a negative way: *love warps judgment* ▷ *n* **3** a fault or an irregularity in the shape or surface of an object **4** a fault or deviation in someone's character **5** See **time warp 6** the yarns arranged lengthways on a loom through which the weft yarns are woven ▶ HISTORY Old English *wearp* a throw > **warped** *adj*

war paint *n* **1** paint applied to the face and body by certain North American Indians before battle **2** *informal* cosmetics

warpath *n* **on the warpath a** preparing to engage in battle **b** *informal* angry and looking for a fight or conflict

warrant *n* **1** an official authorization for some action or decision: *Scotland Yard today issued a warrant for the arrest of this man* **2** a document that certifies or guarantees something, such as a receipt or licence ▷ *vb* **3** to make necessary: *we've no hard evidence to warrant a murder investigation* ▶ HISTORY Old French *guarant*

warrant officer *n* an officer in certain armed services with a rank between those of commissioned and noncommissioned officers

Warrant of Fitness *n NZ* a six-monthly certificate required for a motor vehicle certifying that it is mechanically sound

warrantor *n* a person or company that provides a warranty

warranty *n, pl* **-ties** a guarantee or assurance that goods meet a specified standard or that the facts in a legal document are as stated ▶ HISTORY Anglo-French *warantie*

warren *n* **1** a series of interconnected underground tunnels in which rabbits live **2** an overcrowded building or area of a city with many narrow passages or streets: *a mountainous concrete warren of apartments* ▶ HISTORY Anglo-French *warenne*

warrigal *Austral n* **1** a dingo ▷ *adj* **2** wild

warrior *n* a person who is engaged in or experienced in war ▶ HISTORY Old French *werreieor*

Warsaw Pact *n history* a military treaty and association of the Soviet Union and its E European allies, formed in 1955 and dissolved in 1991

warship *n* a ship designed for naval warfare

wart *n* **1** a firm abnormal growth on the skin caused by a virus **2 warts and all** including faults: *she loves him warts and all* ▶ HISTORY Old English *weart(e)* > **warty** *adj*

w

warthog *n* a wild African pig with heavy tusks, wartlike lumps on the face, and a mane of coarse hair

wartime *n* **1** a time of war ▷ *adj* **2** of or in a time of war: *the wartime coalition*

wary (**ware**-ree) *adj* **warier, wariest** cautious or on one's guard: *be wary of hitchhikers* ▶ HISTORY Old English *wær* aware, careful > **warily** *adv* > **wariness** *n*

was *vb* (with I, he, she, it, or a singular noun as subject) the past tense of **be** ▶ HISTORY Old English *wæs*

wash *vb* **1** to clean (oneself, part of one's body, or a thing) with soap or detergent and water **2** (of a garment or fabric) to be capable of being washed without damage or loss of colour **3** to move or be moved in a particular direction by water: *houses may be washed away in floods* **4** (of waves) to flow or sweep against or over (a surface or object), often with a lapping sound **5** *chiefly Brit, informal* to be acceptable or believable: *your excuses won't wash with me this time* ▷ *n* **6** the act or process of washing **7** all the clothes, etc. to be washed together on one occasion **8** *written* a thin layer of paint or ink: *a pale wash of blue* **9** the disturbance in the air or water produced at the rear of an aircraft, boat, or other moving object: *we were hit by the wash of a large vessel* **10 come out in the wash** *informal* to become known or apparent in the course of time ▷ See also **wash out, wash up** ▶ HISTORY Old English *wæscan, waxan* > **washable** *adj*

washbasin *n* a small sink in a bathroom, used for washing the face and hands. Also: **wash-hand basin**

washed out *adj* **1** exhausted and lacking in energy **2** faded or colourless

washed up *adj* *informal, chiefly US, Canad, Austral & NZ* no longer as successful or important as previously: *she stands discredited, her career probably washed up*

washer *n* **1** a flat ring of rubber, felt, or metal used to provide a seal under a nut or bolt or in a tap or valve **2** *informal* a washing machine **3** a person who washes things, esp. as a job: *chief cook and bottle washer* **4** *Austral* a small piece of towelling cloth used to wash the face

washing *n* all the clothes, etc. to be washed together on one occasion

washing machine *n* a machine for washing clothes and bed linen in

washing soda *n* crystalline sodium carbonate, used as a cleansing agent

washing-up *n* the act of washing used dishes and cutlery after a meal

wash out *vb* **1** Also: **wash off** to remove or be removed by washing: *the rain washes the red dye out of the cap* **2** to wash the inside of (a container) ▷ *n* **washout 3** *informal* a total failure or disaster **4** *NZ* a part of a road or railway washed away by floodwaters

wash up *vb* **1** to wash used dishes and cutlery after a meal **2** *US & Canad* to wash one's face and hands

wasp *n* a common stinging insect with a slender black-and-yellow striped body ▶ HISTORY Old English *wæsp*

Wasp or **WASP** (in the US and Canada) White Anglo-Saxon Protestant: a person descended from N European, usually Protestant stock, forming a group often considered to be the most dominant and privileged in N American society

waspish *adj* bad-tempered or spiteful: *waspish comments*

wassail *n* **1** (formerly) a toast drunk to a person during festivities **2** a festivity involving a lot of drinking **3** hot spiced beer or mulled wine drunk at such a festivity ▷ *vb* **4 go wassailing** to go from house to house singing carols at Christmas ▶ HISTORY Old Norse *ves heill* be in good health

wastage *n* **1** the act of wasting something or the state of being wasted: *wastage of raw materials* **2** reduction in the size of a workforce by retirement, redundancy, etc.

waste *vb* **wasting, wasted 1** to use up thoughtlessly, carelessly, or unsuccessfully **2** to fail to take advantage of: *let's not waste an opportunity to see the children* **3 be wasted on** to be too good for; not be appreciated by: *fine brandy is wasted on you* **4 waste away** to lose one's strength or health: *wasting away from unrequited love* ▷ *n* **5** the act of wasting something or the state of being wasted: *a waste of time* **6** something that is left over because it is in excess of requirements **7** rubbish: *toxic waste* **8** *physiol* matter discharged from the body as faeces or urine **9 wastes** a region that is wild or uncultivated ▷ *adj* **10** rejected as being useless, unwanted, or worthless: *waste products* **11** not cultivated or productive: *waste ground* **12** *physiol* discharged from the body as faeces or urine: *waste matter* **13 lay waste** or **lay waste to** to devastate or destroy: *the Bikini atoll, laid waste by nuclear tests* ▶ HISTORY Latin *vastare* to lay waste

wasted *adj* **1** unnecessary or unfruitful: *wasted effort* **2** pale, thin, and unhealthy: *the hunched shoulders and the wasted appearance of his body*

wasteful *adj* causing waste: *wasteful expenditure* > **wastefully** *adv*

wasteland *n* **1** a barren or desolate area of land **2** something that is considered spiritually, intellectually, or aesthetically barren: *the TV wasteland*

wastepaper basket *n* a container for paper discarded after use

waster *n* *informal* a lazy or worthless person

wastrel *n* *literary* a lazy or worthless person

watch *vb* **1** to look at or observe closely and attentively **2** to look after (a child or a pet) **3** to maintain a careful interest in or control over: *it reminds me to watch my diet* **4 watch for** to be keenly alert to or cautious about: *the vigilant night watchman hired to watch for thieves* **5 watch it!** be careful! ▷ *n* **6** a small portable timepiece worn strapped to the wrist or in a waistcoat pocket **7** the act or an instance of watching **8** *naut* any of the periods, usually of four hours, during which part of a ship's crew are on duty **9 keep a close watch on** to maintain a careful interest in or control over: *he keeps a close watch on party opinion* **10 keep watch** to be keenly alert to danger; keep guard **11 on the watch** on the lookout ▶ HISTORY Old English *wæccan* > **watcher** *n*

watchable *adj* interesting, enjoyable, or entertaining to watch: *watchable films*

watchdog *n* **1** a dog kept to guard property **2** a person or group that acts as a guard against inefficiency or illegality

watchful *adj* **1** carefully observing everything that happens **2 under the watchful eye of** being closely observed by > **watchfully** *adv* > **watchfulness** *n*

watchman *n, pl*-men a man employed to guard buildings or property

watchtower *n* a tower on which a sentry keeps watch

watchword *n* a slogan or motto: *quality, not quantity, is the watchword*

water *n* **1** a clear colourless tasteless liquid that is essential for plant and animal life, that falls as rain, and forms seas, rivers, and lakes. *Related adjectives:* **aquatic, aqueous 2** any area of this liquid, such as a sea, river, or lake **3** the surface of such an area of water: *four-fifths of an iceberg's mass lie below water* **4** the level of the tide: *at high water* **5** *physiol* **a** any fluid discharged from the body, such as sweat, urine, or tears **b waters** the fluid surrounding a fetus in the womb **6 hold water** (of an argument or idea) to be believable or reasonable **7 of the first water** of the highest quality or the most extreme degree: *he's a scoundrel of the first water* **8 pass water** to urinate **9 water under the bridge** events that are past and done with ▷ *vb* **10** to moisten or soak with water: *keep greenhouse plants well watered* **11** to give (an animal) water to drink **12** (of the eyes) to fill with tears: *our eyes were watering from the fumes* **13** (of the mouth) to fill with saliva in anticipation of food ▷ See also **water down** ▶ HISTORY Old English *wæter* > **waterless** *adj*

waterborne *adj* **1** floating or travelling on water **2** (of a disease, etc.) transported or transmitted by water

water buffalo *n* a large black oxlike draught animal of S Asia, with long backward-curving horns

water chestnut *n* the edible tuber of a Chinese plant, used in Oriental cookery

water closet *n old-fashioned* a toilet. Abbrev: **WC**

watercolour *or US* **watercolor** *n* **1** a kind of paint that is applied with water rather than oil **2** a painting done in watercolours

watercourse *n* the channel or bed of a river or stream

watercress *n* a plant that grows in ponds and streams, with strong-tasting leaves that are used in salads and as a garnish

water cycle *n geog* the circulation of the earth's water, in which water from the sea evaporates,

forms clouds, falls as rain or snow, and returns to the sea by rivers

water down *vb* **1** to weaken (a drink or food) with water **2** to make (a story, plan, or proposal) weaker and less controversial > **watered-down** *adj*

waterfall *n* a cascade of falling water where there is a vertical or almost vertical step in a river

waterfowl *n, pl*-fowl a bird that swims on water, such as a duck or swan

waterfront *n* the area of a town or city next to an area of water, such as a harbour or dockyard

waterhole *n* a pond or pool in a desert or other dry area, used by animals as a drinking place

water ice *n* a dessert made from frozen fruit-flavoured syrup

watering can *n* a container with a handle and a spout with a perforated nozzle, used to sprinkle water over plants

watering hole *n facetious slang* a pub

watering place *n* **1** a place where people or animals can find drinking water **2** *Brit* a spa or seaside resort

water lily *n* a plant with large leaves and showy flowers that float on the surface of an area of water

waterlogged *adj* **1** saturated with water: *waterlogged meadows* **2** (of a boat) having taken in so much water as to be likely to sink

water main *n* a principal supply pipe in an arrangement of pipes for distributing water to houses and other buildings

watermark *n* **1** a mark impressed on paper during manufacture, visible when the paper is held up to the light **2** a line marking the level reached by an area of water

water meadow *n* a meadow that remains fertile by being periodically flooded by a stream

watermelon *n* a large round melon with a hard green rind and sweet watery reddish flesh

water polo *n* a game played in water by two teams of seven swimmers in which each side tries to throw a ball into the opponents' goal

water power *n* the power of flowing or falling water to drive machinery or generate electricity

waterproof *adj* **1** not allowing water to pass through: *waterproof trousers* ▷ *n* **2** *chiefly Brit* a waterproof garment, such as a raincoat ▷ *vb* **3** to make waterproof: *the bridge is having its deck waterproofed*

water quality *n environmental science* a measurement of the amount of pollution in a body of water

water rat *n* same as **water vole**

water rate *n* a charge made for the public supply of water

watershed *n* **1** *geog* **a** the dividing line between two adjacent river systems, such as a ridge **b** *US* same as **drainage basin 2** an important period or factor that serves as a dividing line: *a watershed in history*

waterside *n* the area of land beside a river or lake

W

watersider n NZ a person employed to load and unload ships

water-ski n 1 a type of ski used for gliding over water ▷ vb **-skiing, -skied** or **-ski'd** 2 to ride over water on water-skis while holding a rope towed by a speedboat > **water-skier** n > **water-skiing** n

water softener n a device or substance that removes the minerals that make water hard

waterspout n a tornado occurring over water, which forms a column of water and mist

water table n geog the level below which the ground is saturated with water

watertight adj 1 not letting water through: watertight compartments 2 without loopholes or weak points: a watertight system

water tower n a storage tank mounted on a tower so that water can be distributed at a steady pressure

water vapour n water in a gaseous state, esp. when due to evaporation at a temperature below the boiling point

water vole n a small ratlike animal that can swim and lives on the banks of streams and ponds

waterway n a river, canal, or other navigable channel used as a means of travel or transport

water wheel n a large wheel with vanes set across its rim, which is turned by flowing water to drive machinery

water wings pl n an inflatable rubber device shaped like a pair of wings, which is placed under the arms of a person learning to swim

waterworks n 1 an establishment for storing, purifying, and distributing water for community supply ▷ pl n 2 informal, chiefly Brit, euphemistic the urinary system 3 **turn on the waterworks** informal to begin to cry deliberately, in order to attract attention or gain sympathy

watery adj 1 of, like, or containing water: a watery discharge 2 (of eyes) filled with tears 3 insipid, thin, or weak: a watery sun had appeared

watt (**wott**) n the SI unit of power, equal to the power dissipated by a current of 1 ampere flowing across a potential difference of 1 amp ▶ HISTORY after J. Watt, engineer

wattage n the amount of electrical power, expressed in watts, that an appliance uses or generates

wattle (**wott-tl**) n 1 a frame of rods or stakes interwoven with twigs or branches used to make fences 2 a loose fold of brightly coloured skin hanging from the throat of certain birds and lizards 3 an Australian acacia with spikes of small brightly coloured flowers and flexible branches formerly used for making fences ▷ adj 4 made of, formed by, or covered with wattle: a wattle fence ▶ HISTORY Old English watol

wattle and daub n a building material consisting of interwoven twigs plastered with a mixture of clay and water

wave vb **waving, waved** 1 to move (one's hand) to and fro as a greeting 2 to direct (someone) to move in a particular direction by waving: I waved him on

3 to hold (something) up and move it from side to side in order to attract attention 4 to move freely to and fro: flowers waving in the wind ▷ n 5 one of a sequence of ridges or undulations that moves across the surface of the sea or a lake 6 a curve in the hair 7 a sudden rise in the frequency or intensity of something: a wave of sympathy 8 a widespread movement that advances in a body: a new wave of refugees 9 a prolonged spell of some particular type of weather: a heat wave 10 the act or an instance of waving 11 physics an energy-carrying disturbance travelling through a medium or space by a series of vibrations without any overall movement of matter 12 **make waves** to cause trouble ▷ See also **wave down** ▶ HISTORY Old English wafian

waveband n a range of wavelengths or frequencies used for a particular type of radio transmission

wave-cut notch n geol a groove under the base of a cliff formed by the erosive action of waves

wave-cut platform n geol a flat surface at the base of a cliff formed by the erosive action of waves

wave down vb to signal to (the driver of a vehicle) to stop

wavelength n 1 physics the distance between two points of the same phase in consecutive cycles of a wave 2 the wavelength of the carrier wave used by a particular broadcasting station 3 **on the same wavelength** informal having similar views, feelings, or thoughts

waver vb 1 to hesitate between possibilities; be indecisive 2 to swing from one thing to another: she wavered between annoyance and civility 3 (of a voice or stare) to become unsteady 4 to move back and forth or one way and another: the barrel of the gun began to waver ▶ HISTORY Old Norse vafra to flicker > **wavering** adj

wave refraction n geog the process whereby waves bend as they approach the shore

wavey n Canad a snow goose or other wild goose ▶ HISTORY from a Native American language

wavy adj **wavier, waviest** having curves: wavy hair; a wavy line

wax[1] n 1 a solid fatty or oily substance used for making candles and polish, which softens and melts when heated 2 short for **beeswax** or **sealing wax** 3 physiol a brownish-yellow waxy substance secreted by glands in the ear ▷ vb 4 to coat or polish with wax ▶ HISTORY Old English weax > **waxed** adj > **waxy** adj

wax[2] vb 1 to increase gradually in size, strength, or power: trading has waxed and waned with the economic cycle 2 (of the moon) to show a gradually increasing area of brightness from new moon until full moon 3 to become: he waxed eloquent on the disadvantages of marriage ▶ HISTORY Old English weaxan

waxen adj 1 resembling wax in colour or texture: his face is waxen and pale 2 made of, treated with, or covered with wax: a waxen image

waxeye *n* a small New Zealand bird with a white circle round its eye

waxwork *n* a life-size lifelike wax figure of a famous person

way *n* **1** a manner, method, or means: *a new way of life; a tactful way of finding out* **2** a characteristic style or manner: *we are all special in our own way* **3** **ways** habits or customs: *he had a liking for British ways* **4** an aspect or detail of something: *the tourist industry is in many ways a success story* **5** a choice or option, for example in a vote: *he thought it could go either way* **6** a route or direction: *the shortest way home* **7** a journey: *you could buy a magazine to read on the way* **8** distance: *they are a long way from Paris* **9** space or room for movement or activity: *you won't be in his way* **10** **by the way** spoken incidentally: *by the way, I've decided to leave* **11** **by way of a** serving as: *by way of explanation* **b** by the route of: *I went by way of my family home* **12** **get one's own way** to have things exactly as one wants them to be **13** **give way a** to collapse or break **b** *written* to yield or concede: *I tried to make him understand but he did not give way an inch* **14** **give way to a** to be replaced by: *my first feelings of dismay have given way to comparative complacency* **b** to show (an emotion) unrestrainedly **c** to slow down or stop when driving to let (another driver) pass **15** **go out of one's way** to take considerable trouble: *he had gone out of his way to reassure me* **16** **have it both ways** to enjoy two things that would normally be mutually exclusive **17** **in a bad way** *informal* in a poor state of health or a poor financial state **18** **in a way** in some respects **19** **in no way** not at all **20** **make one's way** to proceed or go: *he decided to make his way back in the dark* **21** **on the way out** *informal* becoming unfashionable **22** **out of the way a** removed or dealt with so as to be no longer a hindrance **b** remote **23** **under way** having started moving or making progress ▷ *adv* **24** *informal* far or by far: *that is way out of line* ▶ HISTORY Old English *weg*

waybill *n* a document stating the nature, origin, and destination of goods being transported

wayfarer *n* *old-fashioned* a traveller

waylay *vb* **-laying, -laid** **1** to lie in wait for and attack **2** to intercept (someone) unexpectedly

way-out *adj* *old-fashioned informal* extremely unconventional

ways and means *pl n* **1** the methods and resources for accomplishing something **2** the money and the methods of raising the money needed for the functioning of a political unit

wayside *adj* **1** *old-fashioned* situated by the side of a road: *wayside shrines* ▷ *n* **2** **fall by the wayside** to be unsuccessful or stop being successful: *thousands of new diets are dreamed up yearly – many fall by the wayside*

wayward *adj* erratic, selfish, or stubborn ▶ HISTORY AWAY + -WARD > **waywardness** *n*

Wb *physics* weber

WC *or* **wc** *n* a toilet

we *pron* (used as the subject of a verb) **1** the speaker or writer and another person or other people: *we arrived in Calais* **2** all people or people in general: *it's an unfair world we live in* **3** *formal* same as **I**: used by monarchs and editors ▶ HISTORY Old English *wē*

weak *adj* **1** lacking in physical or mental strength **2** (of a part of the body) not functioning as well as is normal: *a weak heart* **3** liable to collapse or break: *weak bridges* **4** lacking in importance, influence, or strength: *a weak government* **5** (of a currency or shares) falling in price or characterized by falling prices **6** lacking in moral strength; easily influenced **7** not convincing: *weak arguments* **8** lacking strength or power: *his voice was weak* **9** not having a strong flavour: *weak coffee* ▶ HISTORY Old English *wāc* soft > **weakly** *adv*

weaken *vb* to become or make weak or weaker

weak-kneed *adj* *informal* lacking strength, courage, or resolution

weakling *n* a person who is lacking in physical or mental strength

weak-minded *adj* **1** lacking willpower **2** of low intelligence; foolish

weakness *n* **1** the state of being weak **2** a failing in a person's character: *his weakness is his impetuosity* **3** a self-indulgent liking: *a weakness for gin*

weal¹ *n* a raised mark on the skin produced by a blow ▶ HISTORY from Old English *walu* ridge

weal² *n* *old-fashioned* prosperity or wellbeing: *the public weal* ▶ HISTORY Old English *wela*

wealth *n* **1** the state of being rich **2** a large amount of money and valuable material possessions: *redistribution of wealth* **3** a great amount or number: *a wealth of detail* ▶ HISTORY Middle English *welthe*

wealthy *adj* **wealthier, wealthiest** **1** having a large amount of money and valuable material possessions **2** **wealthy in** having a great amount or number of: *a continent exceptionally wealthy in minerals*

wean *vb* **1** to start giving (a baby or young mammal) food other than its mother's milk **2** to cause (oneself or someone else) to give up a former habit: *they are unable to wean themselves from the tobacco habit* ▶ HISTORY Old English *wenian* to accustom > **weaning** *n*

weapon *n* **1** an object used in fighting, such as a knife or gun **2** anything used to get the better of an opponent: *having a sense of humour is a weapon of self-defence* ▶ HISTORY Old English *wǣpen*

weaponry *n* weapons regarded collectively

wear *vb* **wearing, wore, worn** **1** to carry or have (a garment or jewellery) on one's body as clothing or ornament **2** to have (a particular facial expression): *she wore a scowl of frank antagonism* **3** to style (the hair) in a particular way: *she wears her hair in a braid* **4** to deteriorate or cause to deteriorate by constant use or action **5** *informal* to accept: *he won't be given a top job – the Party wouldn't wear it* **6** **wear thin** to lessen or become weaker: *his patience began to wear thin* **7** **wear well** to remain in good condition for a long time ▷ *n* **8** clothes that are suitable for a particular time or purpose: *evening*

wear; beach wear **9** deterioration from constant or normal use **10** the quality of resisting the effects of constant use ▷ See also **wear off, wear out**
▶ HISTORY Old English *werian* > **wearable** *adj*
> **wearer** *n*

wear and tear *n* damage or loss resulting from ordinary use

wearing *adj* causing exhaustion and sometimes irritation

wearisome *adj* causing fatigue and irritation

wear off *vb* to have a gradual decrease in effect or intensity: *the cocaine injection was beginning to wear off*

wear out *vb* **1** to make or become unfit for use through wear: *he wore out his shoes wandering around Mexico City* **2** *informal* to exhaust: *the afternoon's races and games had worn him out*

weary *adj* **-rier, -riest 1** very tired; lacking energy **2** caused by or suggestive of weariness: *he managed a weary smile* **3** causing exhaustion: *a long weary struggle* **4 weary of** discontented or bored with: *he was weary of the war* ▷ *vb* **-ries, -rying, -ried 5** to make weary **6 weary of** to become discontented or bored with: *he seems to have wearied of her possessiveness* ▶ HISTORY Old English *wērig*
> **wearily** *adv* > **weariness** *n* > **wearying** *adj*

weasel *n, pl* **-sels** *or* **-sel** a small meat-eating mammal with reddish-brown fur, a long body and neck, and short legs ▶ HISTORY Old English *wesle*

weather *n* **1** the day-to-day atmospheric conditions, such as temperature, cloudiness, and rainfall, affecting a specific place **2 make heavy weather of** *informal* to carry out (a task) with great difficulty or needless effort **3 under the weather** *informal* feeling slightly ill ▷ *vb* **4** to undergo or cause to undergo changes, such as discoloration, due to the action of the weather **5** to come safely through (a storm, problem, or difficulty) ▶ HISTORY Old English *weder*

weather balloon *n meteorol* a balloon that carries instruments for collecting meteorological data

weather-beaten *adj* **1** tanned by exposure to the weather: *a crumpled weather-beaten face* **2** worn or damaged as a result of exposure to the weather

weathercock *n* a weather vane in the shape of a cock

weather eye *n* **keep a weather eye on** to keep a careful watch on: *keep a weather eye on your symptoms*

weathering *n* the breakdown of rocks by the action of the weather

weatherman *n, pl* **-men** a man who forecasts the weather on radio or television > **weather girl** *fem n*

weather ship *n meteorol* a ship that carries instruments for collecting meteorological data

weather station *n meteorol* one of a network of meteorological observation posts where information about the weather is recorded

weather vane *n* a metal object on a roof that indicates the direction in which the wind is blowing

weave *vb* **weaving, wove** *or* **weaved, woven** *or* **weaved 1** to form (a fabric) by interlacing yarn on a loom **2** to make (a garment or a blanket) by this process **3** to construct (a basket or fence) by interlacing cane or twigs **4** *written* to compose (a story or plan) by combining separate elements into a whole **5** to move from side to side while going forward: *to weave in and out of lanes* **6 get weaving** *informal* to hurry ▷ *n* **7** the structure or pattern of a woven fabric: *the rough weave of the cloth* ▶ HISTORY Old English *wefan* > **weaver** *n* > **weaving** *n*

web *n* **1** a mesh of fine tough threads built by a spider to trap insects **2** anything that is intricately formed or complex: *a web of relationships* **3** a membrane connecting the toes of some water birds and water-dwelling animals such as frogs **4 the web** (often cap) short for **World Wide Web** ▷ *adj* **5** of or situated on the World Wide Web: *a web server; web pages* ▶ HISTORY Old English *webb* > **webbed** *adj*

Web 2.0 *n computers* the internet viewed as a medium in which interactive experience plays a more important role than simply accessing information

webbing *n* a strong fabric that is woven in strips and used under springs in upholstery or for straps

webcam *n* a camera that transmits still or moving images over the internet

webcast *n* a broadcast of an event over the internet

weber (**vay**-ber) *n* the SI unit of magnetic flux (the strength of a magnetic field over a given area) ▶ HISTORY after W. E. *Weber*, physicist

web-footed *or* **web-toed** *adj* (of certain animals or birds) having webbed feet that aid swimming

weblog *n* See **blog**

webmail *n* an e-mail system that allows account holders to access mail via an internet site rather than by downloading it onto a computer

website *n* a group of connected pages on the World Wide Web containing information on a particular subject

wed *vb* **wedding, wedded** *or* **wed 1** *old-fashioned* to take (a person) as a husband or wife; marry **2** to unite closely: *to wed folklore and magic* ▶ HISTORY Old English *weddian*

Wed. Wednesday

wedded *adj* **1** of marriage: *wedded bliss* **2** firmly in support of an idea or institution: *wedded to the virtues of capitalism*

wedding *n* **1** a marriage ceremony **2** a special wedding anniversary, esp. the 25th (**silver wedding**) or 50th (**golden wedding**)

wedge *n* **1** a block of solid material, esp. wood or metal, that is shaped like a narrow V in cross section and can be pushed or driven between two objects or parts of an object in order to split or secure them **2** a slice shaped like a wedge: *a wedge of quiche* **3** *golf* a club with a wedge-shaped face, used for bunker or pitch shots **4 drive a wedge**

between to cause a split between (people or groups) **5 the thin end of the wedge** anything unimportant in itself that implies the start of something much larger ▷ *vb* **wedging, wedged 6** to secure (something) with a wedge **7** to squeeze into a narrow space: *a book wedged between the bed and the table* ▶ HISTORY Old English *wecg*

wedge-tailed eagle *n* a large brown Australian eagle with a wedge-shaped tail

wedlock *n* **1** the state of being married **2 born out of wedlock** born when one's parents are not legally married ▶ HISTORY Old English *wedlāc*

Wednesday *n* the fourth day of the week ▶ HISTORY Old English *Wōdnes dæg* Woden's day

wee¹ *adj Scot* small or short ▶ HISTORY Old English *wǣg* weight

wee² *Brit, Austral & NZ informal n* **1** an instance of urinating ▷ *vb* **weeing, weed 2** to urinate. Also: **wee-wee** ▶ HISTORY origin unknown

weed *n* **1** any plant that grows wild and profusely, esp. among cultivated plants **2** *slang* **a** marijuana **b the weed** or **the evil weed** tobacco **3** *informal* a thin weak person ▷ *vb* **4** to remove weeds from (a garden) ▷ See also **weed out** ▶ HISTORY Old English *wēod*

weedkiller *n* a chemical or hormonal substance used to kill weeds

weed out *vb* to separate out, remove, or eliminate (an unwanted element): *to weed out the thugs*

weedy *adj* **weedier, weediest 1** *informal* thin or weak: *sick and weedy children* **2** full of weeds: *weedy patches of garden*

week *n* **1** a period of seven consecutive days, esp. one beginning with Sunday **2** a period of seven consecutive days from a specified day: *a week from today* **3** the period of time within a week that is spent at work ▶ HISTORY Old English *wice, wicu*

weekday *n* any day of the week other than Saturday or Sunday

weekend *n* Saturday and Sunday

weekly *adj* **1** happening once a week or every week: *a weekly column* **2** determined or calculated by the week: *weekly earnings* ▷ *adv* **3** once a week or every week: *report to the police weekly* ▷ *n, pl* **-lies 4** a newspaper or magazine issued every week

weep *vb* **weeping, wept 1** to shed tears; cry **2** to ooze liquid: *the skin cracked and wept; the label is weeping black ink in the rain* ▷ *n* **3** a spell of weeping: *together we had a good weep* ▶ HISTORY Old English *wēpan*

weeping willow *n* a willow tree with graceful drooping branches

weepy *informal adj* **weepier, weepiest 1** liable or tending to weep ▷ *n, pl* **weepies 2** a sentimental film or book

weevil *n* a beetle with a long snout that feeds on plants ▶ HISTORY Old English *wifel*

wee-wee *n, vb* **-weeing, -weed** *informal, chiefly Brit* same as **wee²**

weft *n* the yarns woven across the width of the fabric through the lengthways warp yarns ▶ HISTORY Old English

weigh *vb* **1** to have weight as specified: *the tree weighs nearly three tons* **2** to measure the weight of **3** to consider carefully: *the President now has to weigh his options* **4** to be influential: *the authorities did not enter my mind or weigh with me* **5 weigh anchor** to raise a ship's anchor **6 weigh out** to measure out by weight ▷ See also **weigh in** ▶ HISTORY Old English *wegan*

weighbridge *n* a machine for weighing vehicles by means of a metal plate set into a road

weigh in *vb* **1** (of a boxer or jockey) to be weighed to check that one is of the correct weight for the contest **2** *informal* to contribute to a discussion or conversation: *he weighed in with a few sharp comments* ▷ *n* **weigh-in 3** *sport* the occasion of checking the competitors' weight before a boxing match or a horse race

weight *n* **1** the heaviness of an object, substance, or person **2** *physics* the vertical force experienced by a mass as a result of gravitation **3 a** a system of units used to express weight: *metric weight* **b** a unit used to measure weight: *the kilogram is the weight used in the metric system* **4 a** an object of known heaviness used for weighing objects, substances, or people **b** an object of known heaviness used in weight training or weightlifting to strengthen the muscles **5** any heavy load: *with a weight of fish on their backs* **6** force, importance, or influence: *they want their words to carry weight* **7** an oppressive force: *the weight of expectation* **8 pull one's weight** *informal* to do one's full share of a task **9 throw one's weight about** *informal* to act in an aggressive authoritarian manner ▷ *vb* **10** to add weight to; make heavier **11** to slant (a system) so that it favours one side rather than another ▶ HISTORY Old English *wiht*

weighting *n* *Brit* an allowance paid to compensate for higher living costs: *salary includes Inner London weighting*

weightless *adj* **1** seeming to have very little weight or no weight at all **2** seeming not to be affected by gravity, as in the case of astronauts in an orbiting spacecraft > **weightlessness** *n*

weightlifting *n* the sport of lifting barbells of specified weights in a prescribed manner > **weightlifter** *n*

weight training *n* physical exercise using light or heavy weights in order to strengthen the muscles

weighty *adj* **weightier, weightiest 1** important or serious: *weighty matters* **2** very heavy

Weimar Republic (*vie*-mar) *n* *history* the German republic that existed from 1919 till Hitler's accession to power in 1933

weir *n* **1** a low dam that is built across a river to divert the water or control its flow **2** a fencelike trap built across a stream for catching fish in ▶ HISTORY Old English *wer*

weird *adj* **1** strange or bizarre **2** suggestive of the supernatural; uncanny ▶ HISTORY Old English (*ge*) *wyrd* destiny > **weirdly** *adv* > **weirdness** *n*

weirdo *n, pl* **-dos** *informal* a person who behaves in a bizarre or eccentric manner

welch *vb* same as **welsh**

welcome *vb* **-coming, -comed** **1** to greet the arrival of (a guest) cordially **2** to receive or accept (something) gladly: *I would welcome a chance to speak to him* ▷ *n* **3** the act of greeting or receiving someone or something in a specified manner: *the President was given a warm welcome* ▷ *adj* **4** gladly received or admitted: *I wouldn't want to stay where I'm not welcome* **5** encouraged or invited: *you are welcome to join us at one of our social events* **6** bringing pleasure: *a welcome change* **7you're welcome** an expression used to acknowledge someone's thanks ▶ HISTORY Old English *wilcuma* > **welcoming** *adj*

weld *vb* **1** to join (two pieces of metal or plastic) by softening with heat and hammering or by fusion **2** to unite closely: *the diverse ethnic groups had been welded together by the anti-Fascist cause* ▷ *n* **3** a joint formed by welding ▶ HISTORY obsolete *well* to melt, weld > **welder** *n*

welfare *n* **1** health, happiness, prosperity, and general wellbeing **2** financial and other assistance given, usually by the government, to people in need ▶ HISTORY WEL(L)¹ + FARE

welfare state *n* a system in which the government undertakes responsibility for the wellbeing of its population, through unemployment insurance, old age pensions, and other social-security measures

well¹ *adv* **better, best** **1** satisfactorily or pleasingly: *well proportioned* **2** skilfully: *I played well for the last six holes* **3** thoroughly: *make sure the chicken is well cooked* **4** comfortably or prosperously: *he has lived well from his various nautical exploits* **5** suitably or fittingly: *you can't very well refuse* **6** intimately: *darling Robert, I know him so well* **7** favourably: *it will go down very well with all the people who support him* **8** by a considerable margin: *well over half; she left well before tea* **9** very likely: *the claim may well be true* **10** *informal* extremely: *well cool* **11all very well** used ironically to express discontent or annoyance: *that's all very well, but I'm left to pick up the pieces* **12as well a** in addition **b** with equal effect: used to express indifference or reluctance: *I might as well go out* **13as well as** in addition to **14just as well** fortunate or appropriate: *it's just as well I didn't spend all my money* ▷ *adj* **15** in good health: *I'm not feeling well* **16** satisfactory or acceptable: *all was well in the aircraft* ▷ *interj* **17 a** an expression of surprise, indignation, or reproof: *well, what a cheek!* **b** an expression of anticipation in waiting for an answer or remark: *well, what do you think?* ▶ HISTORY Old English *wel*

well² *n* **1** a hole or shaft bored into the earth to tap a supply of water, oil, or gas **2** an open shaft through the floors of a building, used for a staircase ▷ *vb* **3** to flow upwards or outwards: *tears welled up into my eyes* ▶ HISTORY Old English *wella*

well-balanced *adj* sensible and emotionally stable

wellbeing *n* the state of being contented and healthy: *a sense of wellbeing*

well-bred *adj* having good manners; polite

well-built *adj* strong and well-proportioned

well-disposed *adj* inclined to be sympathetic, kindly, or friendly towards a person or idea

well-done *adj* **1** made or accomplished satisfactorily **2** (of food, esp. meat) cooked very thoroughly

well-grounded *adj* having a sound basis in fact: *well-grounded suspicions*

wellhead *n* **1** the source of a well or stream **2** a source, fountainhead, or origin

well-heeled *adj informal* wealthy

wellies *pl n* Brit *&* Austral, *informal* Wellington boots

Wellington boots *or* **wellingtons** *pl n* Brit *&* Austral long rubber boots, worn in wet or muddy conditions ▶ HISTORY after the 1st Duke of Wellington, soldier *&* statesman

well-known *adj* widely known; famous

well-meaning *adj* having or indicating good intentions, usually with unfortunate results

well-nigh *adv* almost: *a well-nigh impossible task*

well-off *adj* **1** moderately wealthy **2** in a fortunate position: *some people don't know when they are well-off*

well-read *adj* having read and learned a lot

well-spoken *adj* having a clear, articulate, and socially acceptable accent and way of speaking

wellspring *n* a source of abundant supply: *the wellspring of truth*

well-to-do *adj* moderately wealthy

well-worn *adj* **1** (of a word or phrase) having lost its meaning or force through being overused **2** having been used so much as to show signs of wear: *well-worn leather*

welsh *or* **welch** *vb* **welsh on** to fail to pay (a debt) or fulfil (an obligation) ▶ HISTORY origin unknown

Welsh *adj* **1** of Wales ▷ *n* **2** a Celtic language spoken in some parts of Wales ▷ *pl n* **3 the Welsh** the people of Wales ▶ HISTORY Old English *Wēlisc, Wēlisc*

Welshman *or fem* **Welshwoman** *n, pl* **-men** *or* **-women** a person from Wales

Welsh rarebit *n* melted cheese, sometimes mixed with milk or seasonings, served on hot toast

welt *n* **1** a raised mark on the skin produced by a blow **2** a raised or strengthened seam in a garment ▶ HISTORY origin unknown

welter *n written* a confused mass or jumble: *a welter of facts* ▶ HISTORY Middle Low German, Middle Dutch *weltern*

welterweight *n* a professional boxer weighing up to 147 pounds (66.5 kg) or an amateur boxer weighing up to 67 kg

wen *n pathol* a cyst on the scalp ▶ HISTORY Old English *wenn*

wench *n old-fashioned* **1** *facetious* a girl or young woman **2** a prostitute or female servant ▶ HISTORY Old English *wencel* child

wend *vb* to make (one's way) in a particular direction: *it's time to wend our way back home* ▶ HISTORY Old English *wendan*

wensleydale *n* a white cheese with a flaky texture ▶ HISTORY after *Wensleydale*, North Yorkshire

went *vb* the past tense of **go**

wept *vb* the past of **weep**

were *vb* the form of the past tense of **be** used after *we, you, they*, or a plural noun, or as a subjunctive in conditional sentences ▶ HISTORY Old English *wēron, wæron*

we're we are

weren't were not

werewolf *n, pl* **-wolves** (in folklore) a person who can turn into a wolf ▶ HISTORY Old English *wer* man + *wulf* wolf

west *n* **1** one of the four cardinal points of the compass, at 270° clockwise from north; the direction along a line of latitude towards the sunset **2 the west** any area lying in or towards the west ▷ *adj* **3** situated in, moving towards, or facing the west **4** (esp. of the wind) from the west ▷ *adv* **5** in, to, or towards the west ▶ HISTORY Old English

West *n* **1 the West a** the western part of the world contrasted historically and culturally with the East **b** (esp. formerly) the non-Communist countries of Europe and America contrasted with the Communist states of the East ▷ *adj* **2** of or denoting the western part of a country or region

westerly *adj* **1** of or in the west ▷ *adv, adj* **2** towards the west **3** from the west: *a westerly wind*

western *adj* **1** situated in or towards the west **2** facing or moving towards the west **3** (sometimes cap) of or characteristic of the west or West ▷ *n* **4** a film or book about cowboys in the western states of the US in the 19th century > **westernmost** *adj*

Western *adj* (esp. formerly) of or characteristic of the Americas and the parts of Europe not under Communist rule

western hemisphere *n* geog the half of the globe that contains the Americas

westernize *or* **-ise** *vb* **-izing, -ized** *or* **-ising, -ised** to influence or make familiar with the customs or practices of the West > **westernization** *or* **-isation** *n*

West Indian *adj* **1** of the West Indies ▷ *n* **2** a person from the West Indies

West Indies Federation *n* a political union (1958–1962) of 10 Caribbean countries that were UK colonies: Antigua and Barbuda, Barbados, Dominica, Grenada, Jamaica, Montserrat, Saint Kitts-Nevis-Anguilla, Saint Lucia, Saint Vincent and the Grenadines, and Trinidad and Tobago

Westminster *n* the British Houses of Parliament

westward *adj, adv also* **westwards** **1** towards the west ▷ *n* **2** the westward part or direction

wet *adj* **wetter, wettest** **1** moistened, covered, or soaked with water or some other liquid **2** not yet dry or solid: *wet paint* **3** rainy: *the weather was cold and wet* **4** Brit & NZ, informal feeble or foolish **5 wet behind the ears** informal immature or inexperienced ▷ *n* **6** rainy weather **7** Brit, informal a feeble or foolish person **8** Brit, informal a Conservative politician who supports moderate

policies ▷ *vb* **wetting, wet** *or* **wetted** **9** to make wet: *wet the brush before applying the paint* **10** to urinate in (one's clothes or bed) **11 wet oneself** to urinate in one's clothes ▶ HISTORY Old English *wǣt* > **wetly** *adv* > **wetness** *n*

wet blanket *n* informal a person whose low spirits or lack of enthusiasm have a depressing effect on others

wet dream *n* an erotic dream accompanied by an emission of semen

wether *n* a male sheep, esp. a castrated one ▶ HISTORY Old English

wetland *n* geog an area of marshy land

wet nurse *n* (esp. formerly) a woman hired to breast-feed another woman's baby

wet suit *n* a close-fitting rubber suit used by skin-divers and yachtsmen to retain body heat

whack *vb* **1** to hit hard: *that lad whacked him over the head with a bottle* ▷ *n* **2** a hard blow or the sound of one: *a whack with a blunt instrument* **3** informal a share: *he took his whack of that money* **4 have a whack** to make an attempt **5 out of whack** informal out of order or out of condition: *my body is just a little out of whack* ▶ HISTORY imitative

whacked *adj* informal completely exhausted

whacking *n* **1** old-fashioned a severe beating ▷ *adv* **2** Brit, Austral & NZ, informal extremely: *a whacking great elm*

whale *n* **1** a very large fishlike sea mammal that breathes through a blowhole on the top of its head **2 have a whale of a time** informal to enjoy oneself very much ▶ HISTORY Old English *hwæl*

whalebone *n* a thin strip of a horny material that hangs from the upper jaw of some whales, formerly used for stiffening corsets

whalebone whale *n* any whale with a double blowhole and strips of whalebone between the jaws instead of teeth, including the right whale and the blue whale

whaler *n* **1** a ship used for hunting whales **2** a person whose job is to hunt whales

whaling *n* the activity of hunting and killing whales for food or oil

wham *interj* informal an expression indicating suddenness or forcefulness: *suddenly, wham! you are caught up right in the middle of it* ▶ HISTORY imitative

wharepuni (**for-rep-poon-ee**) *n* NZ (in a Māori community) a tall carved building used as a guesthouse ▶ HISTORY Māori

wharf *n, pl* **wharves** *or* **wharfs** a platform along the side of a waterfront for docking, loading, and unloading ships ▶ HISTORY Old English *hwearf*

wharfie *n* Austral & NZ a dock labourer

what *pron* **1** used in requesting further information about the identity or categorization of something: *what was he wearing?; I knew what would happen* **2** the person, thing, people, or things that: *all was not what it seemed* **3** used in exclamations to add emphasis: *what a creep!* **4 what for?** for what reason? **5 what have you** other similar or related things: *qualifications, interests, profession, what have you* ▷ *adj* **6** used with a noun in requesting further

W

973

information about the identity or categorization of something: *what difference can it make now?* **7** to any degree or in any amount: *they provided what financial support they could* ▶ **HISTORY** Old English *hwæt*

whatever *pron* **1** everything or anything that: *I can handle whatever comes up* **2** no matter what: *whatever you do, keep your temper* **3** *informal* other similar or related things: *a block of wood, rock, or whatever* **4** an intensive form of *what*, used in questions: *whatever gave you that impression?* ▷ *adj* **5** an intensive form of *what*: *I can take whatever actions I deem necessary* **6** at all: *there is no foundation whatever for such opinions*

whatnot *n informal, spoken* other similar or related things: *groceries, wines, and whatnot*

whatsoever *adj* at all: used for emphasis after a noun phrase that uses words such as *none* or *any*: *there is nothing whatsoever wrong with your heart; it can be used at any time and under any circumstances whatsoever*

wheat *n* **1** a kind of grain used in making flour and pasta **2** the plant from which this grain is obtained ▶ **HISTORY** Old English *hwǣte*

wheatear *n* a small northern songbird with a white rump ▶ **HISTORY** from *white* + *arse*

wheaten *adj* made from the grain or flour of wheat: *wheaten bread*

wheat germ *n* the vitamin-rich middle part of a grain of wheat

wheatmeal *n* a brown flour intermediate between white flour and wholemeal flour

wheedle *vb* **-dling, -dled** **1** to try to persuade (someone) by coaxing or flattery: *wheedling you into giving them their way* **2** to obtain (something) in this way: *she wheedled money out of him* ▶ **HISTORY** origin unknown > **wheedling** *adj, n*

wheel *n* **1** a circular object mounted on a shaft around which it can turn, fixed under vehicles to enable them to move **2** anything like a wheel in shape or function: *the steering wheel; a spinning wheel* **3** something that is repeated in cycles: *the wheel of fashion would turn, and the clothes would be back in style* **4** **at** or **behind the wheel** driving a vehicle ▷ *vb* **5** to push (a bicycle, wheelchair, or pram) along **6** to turn in a circle **7 wheel and deal** to operate shrewdly and sometimes unscrupulously in order to advance one's own interests **8 wheel round** to change direction or turn round suddenly ▷ See also **wheels** ▶ **HISTORY** Old English *hwēol, hweowol*

wheelbarrow *n* a shallow open box for carrying small loads, with a wheel at the front and two handles

wheelbase *n* the distance between the front and back axles of a motor vehicle

wheelchair *n* a special chair on large wheels, for use by people who cannot walk or have difficulty walking

wheel clamp *n* a device fixed onto one wheel of an illegally parked car to prevent the car being driven off

wheelie *n* a manoeuvre on a cycle or skateboard in which the front wheel or wheels are raised off the ground

wheelie bin *n Brit, Austral & NZ* a large container for household rubbish, mounted on wheels so that it can be moved more easily

wheeling and dealing *n* shrewd and sometimes unscrupulous moves made in order to advance one's own interests > **wheeler-dealer** *n*

wheels *pl n* **1** *informal* a car **2** the main force and mechanism of an organization or system: *the wheels of the economy* **3 wheels within wheels** a series of intricately connected events or plots

wheelwright *n* a person whose job is to make and mend wheels

wheeze *vb* **wheezing, wheezed** **1** to breathe with a rasping or whistling sound ▷ *n* **2** a wheezing breath or sound **3** *Brit, old-fashioned slang* a trick or plan: *a glorious tax wheeze* ▶ **HISTORY** probably from Old Norse *hvǣsa* to hiss > **wheezy** *adj*

whelk *n* an edible sea creature with a strong snail-like shell ▶ **HISTORY** Old English *weoloc*

whelp *n* **1** a young wolf or dog **2** *offensive* a youth ▷ *vb* **3** (of a wolf or dog) to give birth ▶ **HISTORY** Old English *hwelp*

when *adv* **1** at what time?: *when are they leaving?* ▷ *conj* **2** at the time at which: *he was twenty when the war started* **3** although: *he drives when he could walk* **4** considering the fact that: *how did you pass the exam when you hadn't studied for it?* ▷ *pron* **5** at which time: *she's at the age when girls get interested in boys* ▶ **HISTORY** Old English *hwanne, hwænne*

whence *conj old-fashioned or poetic* from what place, cause, or origin: *he would then ask them whence they came* ▶ **HISTORY** Middle English *whannes*

whenever *conj* **1** at every or any time that: *the filly was trained to stop whenever a jockey used a whip* ▷ *adv* **2** no matter when: *I am eager to come whenever you suggest* **3** *informal* at an unknown or unspecified time: *the 16th, 17th, or whenever* **4** an intensive form of *when*, used in questions: *if we can't exercise restraint now, whenever can we?*

where *adv* **1** in, at, or to what place, point, or position?: *where are we going?; I know where he found it* ▷ *pron* **2** in, at, or to which place: *he found a sandwich bar where he could get a snack* ▷ *conj* **3** in the place at which: *he should have stayed where he was doing well* ▶ **HISTORY** Old English *hwǣr*

whereabouts *pl n* **1** the place, esp. the approximate place, where a person or thing is: *the whereabouts of the president are unknown* ▷ *adv* **2** approximately where: *whereabouts will you go?*

whereas *conj* but by contrast: *she was crazy about him, whereas for him it was just another affair*

whereby *pron* by or because of which: *the process whereby pests become resistant to pesticides*

wherefore *n* **1 the whys and wherefores** the reasons or explanation: *the whys and wherefores of the war* ▷ *conj* **2** *old-fashioned or formal* for which reason

whereupon conj at which point: they sentenced him to death, whereupon he fainted

wherever pron **1** at, in, or to every place or point which: I got a wonderful reception wherever I went ▷ conj **2** in, to, or at whatever place: wherever they went, the conditions were harsh ▷ adv **3** no matter where: we're going to find him, wherever he is **4** informal at, in, or to an unknown or unspecified place: the jungles of Borneo or wherever **5** an intensive form of where, used in questions: wherever have you been?

wherewithal n the wherewithal the necessary funds, resources, or equipment: the wherewithal for making chemical weapons

whet vb **whetting, whetted 1** whet someone's appetite to increase someone's desire for or interest in something: she gave him just enough information to whet his appetite **2** old-fashioned to sharpen (a knife or other tool) ▶ HISTORY Old English hwettan

whether conj **1** used to introduce an indirect question: he asked him whether he had seen the hunter **2** used to introduce a clause expressing doubt or choice: you are entitled to the assistance of a lawyer, whether or not you can afford one; we learn from experience, whether good or bad ▶ HISTORY Old English hwæther

whetstone n a stone used for sharpening knives or other tools

whew interj an exclamation of relief, surprise, disbelief, or weariness

whey n the watery liquid that separates from the curd when milk is clotted, for example in making cheese ▶ HISTORY Old English hwǣg

which adj **1** used with a noun in requesting that the particular thing being referred to is further identified or distinguished: which way had he gone?; a questionnaire to find out which shops local consumers use **2** any out of several: you have to choose which goods and services you want ▷ pron **3** used in requesting that the particular thing being referred to is further identified or distinguished: which of these occupations would be suitable for you? **4** used in relative clauses referring to a thing rather than a person: a discovery which could have lasting effects **5** and that: her books were all over the dining table, which meant we had to eat in the kitchen ▶ HISTORY Old English hwelc

whichever adj **1** any out of several: choose whichever line you feel more comfortable with **2** no matter which: whichever bridge you take, pause mid-stream for a look up and down the river ▷ pron **3** any one or ones out of several: delete whichever is inapplicable **4** no matter which one or ones: whichever you choose, you must be consistent throughout

whiff n **1** a passing odour: I got a whiff of her perfume **2** a trace or hint: the first whiff of jealousy ▷ vb **3** Brit, informal to have an unpleasant smell ▶ HISTORY imitative > **whiffy** adj

Whig n **1** a member of a British political party of the 18th–19th centuries that sought limited political

and social reform and provided the core of the Liberal Party ▷ adj **2** of or relating to Whigs ▶ HISTORY probably from whiggamore, one of a group of 17th-century Scottish rebels > **Whiggism** n

while conj **1** at the same time that: anti-inflammatory remedies may be used to alleviate the condition while background factors are investigated **2** at some point during the time that: her father had died while she was gone **3** although or whereas: while she tossed and turned, he fell into a dreamless sleep ▷ n **4** a period of time: I'd like to stay a while ▶ HISTORY Old English hwīl

while away vb **whiling, whiled** to pass (time) idly but pleasantly

whilst conj chiefly Brit same as **while**

whim n a sudden, passing, and often fanciful idea ▶ HISTORY origin unknown

whimper vb **1** to cry, complain, or say (something) in a whining plaintive way ▷ n **2** a soft plaintive whine ▶ HISTORY imitative

whimsical adj unusual, playful, and fanciful: a whimsical story > **whimsically** adv

whimsy n **1** (pl **-sies**) a fanciful or playful idea: they thought sparing the rod a foolish whimsy **2** capricious or playful behaviour: sudden flights of whimsy ▶ HISTORY from whim

whin n chiefly Brit same as **gorse** ▶ HISTORY from Old Norse

whine n **1** a long high-pitched plaintive cry or moan **2** a peevish complaint ▷ vb **whining, whined 3** to utter a whine ▶ HISTORY Old English hwīnan > **whiner** n > **whining** adj, n

whinge Brit, Austral & NZ, informal vb **whingeing, whinged 1** to complain in a moaning manner ▷ n **2** a complaint ▶ HISTORY Old English hwinsian to whine > **whinger** n

whinny vb **-nies, -nying, -nied 1** (of a horse) to neigh softly or gently ▷ n, pl **-nies 2** a gentle or low-pitched neigh ▶ HISTORY imitative

whip n **1** a piece of leather or rope attached at one end to a stiff handle, used for hitting people or animals **2 a** a member of a political party who is responsible for urging members to attend Parliament to vote on an important issue **b** a notice sent to members of a political party by the whip, urging them to attend Parliament to vote in a particular way on an important issue **3** a dessert made from egg whites or cream beaten stiff: raspberry whip ▷ vb **whipping, whipped 4** to hit with a whip **5** to hit sharply: strands of hair whipped across her cheeks **6** informal to move or go quickly and suddenly: machine-gun bullets whipped past him **7** to beat (cream or eggs) with a whisk or fork until frothy or stiff **8** to rouse (someone) into a particular condition: politicians and businessmen have whipped themselves into a panic about never-ending recession **9** informal to steal (something) ▷ See also **whip-round** ▶ HISTORY perhaps from Middle Dutch wippen to swing > **whipping** n

whip bird n Austral a bird with a whistle ending in a whipcrack note

whip hand *n* **the whip hand** an advantage or dominating position: *buyers have the whip hand over estate agents*

whiplash *n* **1** a quick lash of a whip **2** short for **whiplash injury**

whiplash injury *n* an injury to the neck resulting from the head being suddenly thrust forward and then snapped back, for example in a car crash

whippet *n* a small slender dog similar to a greyhound ▶ HISTORY perhaps based on *whip it!* move quickly!

whipping boy *n* a person who is expected to take the blame for other people's mistakes or incompetence

whip-round *n informal* an impromptu collection of money

whir *n, vb* **whirring, whirred** same as **whirr**

whirl *vb* **1** to spin or turn round very fast **2** to seem to spin from dizziness or confusion: *my mind whirled with half-formed thoughts* ▷ *n* **3** the act or an instance of whirling: *he grasps her by the waist and gives her a whirl* **4** a round of intense activity: *the social whirl of Paris* **5** a confused state: *my thoughts are in a whirl* **6** **give something a whirl** *informal* to try something new ▶ HISTORY Old Norse *hvirfla* to turn about

whirlpool *n* a powerful circular current of water, into which objects floating nearby are drawn

whirlwind *n* **1** a column of air whirling violently upwards in a spiral ▷ *adj* **2** done or happening much more quickly than usual: *a whirlwind tour of France*

whirr *or* **whir** *n* **1** a prolonged soft whizz or buzz: *the whirr of the fax machine* ▷ *vb* **whirring, whirred** **2** to produce a prolonged soft whizz or buzz ▶ HISTORY probably from Old Norse > **whirring** *n, adj*

whisk *vb* **1** to move or take somewhere swiftly: *I was whisked away in a police car* **2** to brush away lightly: *the waiter whisked the crumbs away with a napkin* **3** to beat (cream or eggs) with a whisk or fork until frothy or stiff ▷ *n* **4** the act or an instance of whisking: *a whisk of a scaly tail* **5** a utensil for beating cream or eggs until frothy or stiff ▶ HISTORY Old Norse *visk* wisp

whisker *n* **1** any of the long stiff hairs that grow out from the sides of the mouth of a cat or other mammal **2** any of the hairs growing on a man's face, esp. on the cheeks or chin **3** **by a whisker** by a very small distance or amount: *we missed him by a whisker* ▶ HISTORY Old Norse *visk* wisp > **whiskered** *or* **whiskery** *adj*

whiskey *n* Irish or American whisky

whisky *n, pl* -**kies** a strong alcoholic drink made by distilling fermented cereals, esp. in Scotland

■ **WORD HISTORY**
■ The word 'whisky' comes from Scottish Gaelic
■ *uisge beatha*, meaning 'water of life'. Whisky is
■ not the only alcoholic 'water of life': 'aqua vitae',
■ which means 'water of life' in Latin, is an old
■ name for brandy, and there is also in
■ Scandinavia a strong alcoholic drink called
■ 'aquavit' or 'akvavit'.

whisper *vb* **1** to speak or say (something) very softly, using the breath instead of the vocal cords **2** to make a low soft rustling sound: *the leaves whispered* ▷ *n* **3** a low soft voice: *her voice sank to a whisper* **4** *informal* a rumour: *I just picked up a whisper on this killing* **5** a low soft rustling sound: *a whisper of breeze in the shrubbery* ▶ HISTORY Old English *hwisprian* > **whispered** *adj*

whist *n* a card game for two pairs of players ▶ HISTORY perhaps from *whisk*, referring to the whisking up of the tricks

whist drive *n* a social gathering where whist is played

whistle *vb* -**tling, -tled** **1** to produce a shrill sound by forcing breath between pursed lips **2** to produce (a tune) by making a series of such sounds **3** to signal (to) by whistling or blowing a whistle: *the doorman whistled a cruising cab* **4** to move with a whistling sound: *a shell whistled through the upper air* **5** (of a kettle or train) to produce a shrill sound caused by steam being forced through a small opening **6** (of a bird) to give a shrill cry **7** **whistle in the dark** to try to keep up one's confidence in spite of being afraid ▷ *n* **8** the act or sound of whistling: *he gave a whistle of astonishment* **9** a metal instrument that is blown down its end to produce a tune, signal, or alarm: *he played the tin whistle; the referee's whistle* **10** a device in a kettle or a train that makes a shrill sound by means of steam under pressure **11** **blow the whistle on** *informal* to reveal and put a stop to (wrongdoing or a wrongdoer): *to blow the whistle on corrupt top-level officials* **12** **wet one's whistle** *informal* to have a drink ▶ HISTORY Old English *hwistlian*

whit *n* **not a whit** not at all: *it does not matter a whit* ▶ HISTORY probably variant of obsolete *wight* a person

Whit *n* **1** short for **Whitsuntide** ▷ *adj* **2** of Whitsuntide: *Whit Monday*

white *adj* **1** having no hue, owing to the reflection of all or almost all light; of the colour of snow **2** pale, because of illness, fear, shock, or another emotion: *white with rage* **3** (of hair) having lost its colour, usually from age **4** (of coffee or tea) with milk or cream **5** (of wine) made from pale grapes or from black grapes separated from their skins **6** denoting flour, or bread made from flour, that has had part of the grain removed ▷ *n* **7** the lightest colour; the colour of snow **8** the clear fluid that surrounds the yolk of an egg **9** *anat* the white part of the eyeball **10** anything white, such as white paint or white clothing: *a room decorated all in white* ▷ See also **whites** ▶ HISTORY Old English *hwīt* > **whiteness** *n* > **whitish** *adj*

White *n* **1** a member of a light-skinned race ▷ *adj* **2** of or relating to a White or Whites

whitebait *n* **1** the young of herrings, sprats, or pilchards, cooked and eaten whole **2** any of various small silvery fishes of Australia and New Zealand and of North American coastal regions of the Pacific

white blood cell *n* same as **leucocyte**

w

white-collar *adj* denoting workers employed in professional and clerical occupations

white-collar crime *n law* criminal activities relating to fraud, embezzlement, tax evasion, and other crimes linked to business and finance rather than to violence, drugs, etc.

white dwarf *n* a small, faint, very dense star

white elephant *n* a possession that is unwanted by its owner

white fish *n* a sea fish with white flesh that is used for food, such as cod or haddock

white flag *n* a signal of surrender or to request a truce

whitefly *n, pl* **-flies** a tiny whitish insect that is harmful to greenhouse plants

white gold *n* a white lustrous hard-wearing alloy containing gold together with platinum or other metals, used in jewellery

white goods *pl n* large household appliances, such as refrigerators and cookers

white heat *n* **1** intense heat that produces a white light **2** *informal* a state of intense emotion: *the white heat of hate*

white-hot *adj* **1** at such a high temperature that white light is produced **2** *informal* in a state of intense emotion: *white-hot agony*

White House *n* the US president and the executive branch of the US government: *the White House reviewed the report* ▶ **HISTORY** after the official home of the US president in Washington DC

white lie *n* a small lie, usually told to avoid hurting someone's feelings

white light *n* light that contains all the wavelengths of the visible spectrum, as in sunlight

white matter *n* the whitish tissue of the brain and spinal cord, consisting mainly of nerve fibres

whiten *vb* to make or become white or whiter > **whitener** *n* > **whitening** *n*

white noise *n* noise that has a wide range of frequencies of uniform intensity

white paper *n Government* an official government report which sets out the government's policy on a specific matter

White Russian (formerly) *adj* **1** of Byelorussia, an administrative division of the W Soviet Union, now Belarus ▷ *n* **2** a person from Byelorussia **3** the language of Byelorussia

whites *pl n* white clothes, as worn for playing cricket

white sauce *n* a thick sauce made from flour, butter, seasonings, and milk or stock

white spirit *n* a colourless liquid obtained from petroleum and used as a substitute for turpentine

White supremacy *n* the theory or belief that White people are superior to people of other races > **White supremacist** *n, adj*

white trash *n derogatory* poor White people living in the United States, esp. in the South

whitewash *n* **1** a mixture of lime or chalk in water, for whitening walls and other surfaces **2** an attempt to conceal the unpleasant truth: *the report was a whitewash* ▷ *vb* **3** to cover with whitewash

4 to conceal the unpleasant truth about > **whitewashed** *adj*

whitewood *n* a light-coloured wood often prepared for staining

whither *conj old-fashioned or poetic* to what place or for what purpose: *they knew not whither they went* ▶ **HISTORY** Old English *hwider, hwæder*

whiting (**white**-ing) *n* **1** a white-fleshed food fish of European seas **2** *Austral* any of several marine food fishes

whitlow *n* an inflamed sore on the end of a finger or toe ▶ **HISTORY** originally *white + flaw*

Whitsun *n* **1** short for **Whitsuntide** ▷ *adj* **2** of Whit Sunday or Whitsuntide

Whit Sunday *n* the seventh Sunday after Easter ▶ **HISTORY** Old English *hwīta sunnandæg* white Sunday

Whitsuntide *n* the week that begins with Whit Sunday

whittle *vb* **-tling, -tled** **1** to make (an object) by cutting or shaving pieces from (a piece of wood) with a small knife **2 whittle down** or **away** to reduce in size or effectiveness gradually: *my self-confidence had been whittled away to almost nothing* ▶ **HISTORY** Old English *thwītan* to cut

whizz or **whiz** *vb* **whizzing, whizzed** **1** to move with a loud humming or buzzing sound: *the bullets whizzed overhead* **2** *informal* to move or go quickly: *the wind surfers fairly whizzed along the water* ▷ *n, pl* **whizzes** **3** a loud humming or buzzing sound **4** *informal* a person who is extremely good at something: *he's a whizz at finance* **5** *slang* amphetamine ▶ **HISTORY** imitative

whizz kid or **whiz kid** *n informal* a person who is outstandingly able and successful for his or her age

who *pron* **1** which person: *who are you?; he didn't know who had started it* **2** used at the beginning of a relative clause referring to a person or people already mentioned: *he is a man who can effect change* ▶ **HISTORY** Old English *hwā*

WHO World Health Organization

whoa *interj* a command used to stop horses or to slow down someone who is moving or talking too fast

whodunnit or **whodunit** (hoo **dun**-nit) *n informal* a novel, play, or film about the solving of a murder mystery

whoever *pron* **1** the person or people who: *whoever bought it for you has to make the claim* **2** no matter who: *I pity him, whoever he is* **3** *informal* other similar or related people or person: *your best friend, your neighbours, or whoever* **4** an intensive form of *who*, used in questions: *whoever thought of such a thing?*

whole *adj* **1** constituting or referring to all of something: *I'd spent my whole allowance by Saturday afternoon* **2** unbroken or undamaged ▷ *adv* **3** in an undivided or unbroken piece: *truffles are cooked whole* **4** *informal* completely or entirely: *a whole new theory of treatment* ▷ *n* **5** all there is of a thing: *the whole of my salary* **6** a collection of parts viewed together as a unit: *taking Great Britain as a whole* **7 on the whole a** taking all things into

W

consideration: *on the whole he has worked about one year out of twelve* **b** in general: *on the whole they were not successful* ▶ HISTORY Old English *hāl* > **wholeness** *n*

wholefood *n* **1** food that has been refined or processed as little as possible ▷ *adj* **2** of or relating to wholefood: *a wholefood diet*

wholehearted *adj* done or given with total sincerity or enthusiasm: *wholehearted support* > **wholeheartedly** *adv*

wholemeal *adj Brit & Austral* **1** (of flour) made from the entire wheat kernel **2** made from wholemeal flour: *wholemeal bread*

whole number *n maths* a number that does not contain a fraction, such as 0, 1, or 2

wholesale *adj, adv* **1** of or by the business of selling goods in large quantities and at lower prices to retailers for resale: *wholesale prices; we buy fruit and vegetables wholesale* **2** on a large scale or indiscriminately: *the wholesale destruction of forests; they were being hunted without mercy and slaughtered wholesale* > **wholesaler** *n*

wholesome *adj* **1** physically beneficial: *wholesome food* **2** morally beneficial: *a wholesome attitude of the mind* ▶ HISTORY from *whole* healthy

wholly *adv* completely or totally

whom *pron* the objective form of *who*: *whom will you tell?; he was devoted to his wife, whom he married in 1960* ▶ HISTORY Old English *hwām*

whoop *vb* **1** written to cry out in excitement or joy **2 whoop it up** *informal* to indulge in a noisy celebration ▷ *n* **3** a loud cry of excitement or joy ▶ HISTORY imitative

whoopee *old-fashioned informal interj* **1** an exclamation of joy or excitement ▷ *n* **2 make whoopee a** to indulge in a noisy celebration **b** to make love

whooping cough *n* an acute infectious disease, mainly affecting children, that causes coughing spasms ending with a shrill crowing sound on breathing in

whoops *interj* an exclamation of mild surprise or of apology

whopper *n informal* **1** an unusually large or impressive example of something: *Deauville's beach is a whopper* **2** a big lie

whopping *informal adj* **1** unusually large: *a whopping 40 per cent* ▷ *adv* **2** extremely: *it's a whopping great gamble*

whore (hore) *n* a prostitute or promiscuous woman: often a term of abuse ▶ HISTORY Old English *hōre*

whorl *n* **1** *bot* a circular arrangement of leaves or flowers round the stem of a plant **2** *zool* a single turn in a spiral shell **3** anything shaped like a coil ▶ HISTORY probably variant of *whirl*

whose *pron* **1** of whom? belonging to whom?: used in direct and indirect questions: *whose idea was it?; I wondered whose it was* **2** of whom or of which: used as a relative pronoun: *Gran had sympathy for anybody whose life had gone wrong* ▶ HISTORY Old English *hwæs*, genitive of *hwā* who and *hwæt* what

why *adv* **1** for what reason?: *why did he marry her?; she avoided asking him why he was there* ▷ *pron* **2** for or because of which: *you can think of all kinds of reasons why you should not believe it* ▷ *n, pl* **whys** **3 the whys and wherefores** See **wherefore** (sense 1) ▷ *interj* **4** an exclamation of surprise, indignation, or impatience: *why, I listen to you on the radio twice a week* ▶ HISTORY Old English *hwȳ, hwī*

WI **1** Wisconsin **2** *Brit & NZ* Women's Institute

wick *n* **1** a cord through the middle of a candle, through which the fuel reaches the flame **2 get on someone's wick** *Brit & Austral, slang* to annoy someone ▶ HISTORY Old English *wēoce*

wicked *adj* **1** morally bad: *the wicked queen in 'Snow White'* **2** playfully mischievous or roguish: *let's be wicked and go skinny-dipping* **3** dangerous or unpleasant: *there was a wicked cut over his eye* **4** *slang* very good ▶ HISTORY Old English *wicca* sorcerer, *wicce* witch > **wickedly** *adv* > **wickedness** *n*

wicker *adj* made of wickerwork: *a wicker chair* ▶ HISTORY from Old Norse

wickerwork *n* a material consisting of slender flexible twigs woven together

wicket *n cricket* **1** either of two sets of three stumps stuck in the ground with two wooden bails resting on top, at which the batsman stands **2** the playing space between these **3** the act or instance of a batsman being got out ▶ HISTORY Old French *wiket*

wicketkeeper *n cricket* the fielder positioned directly behind the wicket

wicking *adj textiles* acting to move moisture by capillary action from the inside to the surface: *wicking fabric*

wide *adj* **1** having a great extent from side to side: *the wide main street* **2** having a specified extent from side to side: *three metres wide* **3** covering or including many different things: *a wide range of services* **4** covering a large distance or extent: *the proposal was voted down by a wide margin* **5** (of eyes) opened fully ▷ *adv* **6** to a large or full extent: *he swung the door wide* **7 far and wide** See **far** (sense 7) ▷ *n* **8** *cricket* a ball bowled outside the batsman's reach, which scores a run for the batting side ▶ HISTORY Old English *wīd* > **widely** *adv* See WORD FOCUS **wide**

wide-angle lens *n* a lens on a camera which can cover a wider angle of view than an ordinary lens

wide-awake *adj* fully awake

wide-eyed *adj* **1** innocent or naive ▷ *adv, adj* **2** surprised or frightened: *wide-eyed astonishment*

widen *vb* to make or become wide or wider

widespread *adj* affecting an extensive area or a large number of people: *widespread damage; widespread public support*

widgeon *n* same as **wigeon**

widget *n* **1** *informal* any small device, the name of which is unknown or forgotten **2** a small device in a beer can which, when the can is opened, releases nitrogen gas into the beer, giving it a head **3** a small computer program that can be installed on and executed from the desktop of a personal computer ▶ HISTORY changed from GADGET

wide

There are a number of ways in which the word **wide** can be used, depending on what you are referring to. But you can make your language more interesting by using one of the following instead.

DEFINITION 1

• If you would like to describe something measuring a large distance from side to side, you could try: **ample** space between the rows • ridiculously **baggy** trousers • His shoulders were **broad**. • an **expansive** play area • The grounds were more **extensive**. • a **full** skirt • an **immense** body of water • in **large** rivers and lakes • I like **roomy** jackets. • a **spacious** kitchen • a **sweeping** view • **vast** stretches of land • a **voluminous** trench coat

DEFINITION 2

• If you are talking about something with a specified distance from side to side, you could try:

three metres **across** • 20cm **from side to side**

DEFINITION 3

• If you would like to describe something that includes many different things, you could try: **broad** range of issues • very **catholic** tastes in music • **comprehensive** guide • an **encyclopedic** knowledge of the subject • **extensive** choice of foods • Treatment of the topic is **exhaustive**. • introduce **far-ranging** reforms • **immense** range of holiday activities • an **inclusive** survey • **large** selection of goods • **vast** range of products • a **wide-ranging** discussion

DEFINITION 4

• If you would like to describe something that covers a large extent, you could try: **ample** scope for the imagination • **extensive** press coverage • **far-reaching** discussions • **general** feeling • **immense** differences • **large** gap in ages • **vast** distance between us

---

widow *n* a woman whose husband has died and who has not remarried ▶ HISTORY Old English *widewe* > **widowhood** *n*

widowed *adj* denoting a person, usually a woman, whose spouse has died and who has not remarried

widower *n* a man whose wife has died and who has not remarried

width *n* **1** the extent or measurement of something from side to side **2** the distance across a rectangular swimming pool, as opposed to its length

wield *vb* **1** to handle or use (a weapon or tool) **2** to exert or maintain (power or influence) ▶ HISTORY Old English *wieldan, wealdan*

wife *n, pl* **wives** the woman to whom a man is married ▶ HISTORY Old English *wīf* > **wifely** *adj*

Wi-Fi *n* a system of wireless access to the internet

wig *n* an artificial head of hair ▶ HISTORY from *periwig*

wigeon *or* **widgeon** *n* a wild marshland duck ▶ HISTORY origin unknown

wigging *n* Brit, old-fashioned slang a reprimand ▶ HISTORY origin unknown

wiggle *vb* **-gling, -gled 1** to move with jerky movements from side to side or up and down: *she wiggled her toes in the cool water* ▷ *n* **2** a wiggling movement or walk ▶ HISTORY Middle Low German, Middle Dutch *wiggelen*

wigwam *n* a N Native American's tent, made of animal skins ▶ HISTORY Native American *wīkwām*

wiki *n computers* a website that can be edited by anyone ▶ HISTORY Hawaiian *wiki wiki* quick

wilco *interj* an expression in signalling and telecommunications, indicating that a message just received will be complied with ▶ HISTORY abbreviation for *I will comply*

wild *adj* **1** (of animals or birds) living in natural surroundings; not domesticated or tame **2** (of plants) growing in a natural state; not cultivated **3** uninhabited and desolate: *wild country* **4** living in a savage or uncivilized way: *a wild mountain man* **5** lacking restraint or control: *a wild party* **6** stormy or violent: *a wild windy October morning* **7** in a state of extreme emotional intensity: *wild with excitement* **8** without reason or substance: *wild accusations* **9 wild about** *informal* very enthusiastic about: *his colleagues aren't all that wild about him* ▷ *adv* **10 run wild** to behave without restraint: *she was allowed to run completely wild* ▷ *n* **11 the wild** a free natural state of living: *creatures of the wild* **12 the wilds** a desolate or uninhabited region: *the wilds of Africa* ▶ HISTORY Old English *wilde* > **wildly** *adv* > **wildness** *n*

wild card *n* **1** *sport* a player or team that is allowed to take part in a competition despite not having met the normal qualifying requirements **2** *computers* a character that can be substituted for any other in a file

wildcat *n, pl* **-cats** *or* **-cat 1** a wild European cat that looks like a domesticated cat but is larger and has a bushy tail **2** *informal* a quick-tempered person ▷ *adj* **3** *chiefly US* risky and financially unsound: *a wildcat operation*

wildcat strike *n* a strike begun by workers spontaneously or without union approval

wildebeest *n, pl* **-beests** *or* **-beest** same as **gnu** ▶ HISTORY Afrikaans

wilderness *n* **1** a wild uninhabited uncultivated region **2** a confused mass or tangle: *a wilderness of long grass and wild flowers* **3** a state of being no longer in a prominent position: *a long spell in the political wilderness* ▶ HISTORY Old English *wildēornes*, from *wildēor* wild beast

wildfire *n* **spread like wildfire** to spread very quickly or uncontrollably

wild flower *n* any flowering plant that grows in an uncultivated state

W

wildfowl *pl n* wild birds, such as grouse and pheasants, that are hunted for sport or food

wild-goose chase *n* a search that has little or no chance of success

wildlife *n* wild animals and plants collectively

wild rice *n* the dark-coloured edible grain of a North American grass that grows on wet ground

Wild West *n* the western US during its settlement, esp. with reference to its lawlessness

wiles *pl n* artful or seductive tricks or ploys ▶ HISTORY from Old Norse *vēl* craft

wilful *or US* **willful** *adj* **1** determined to do things in one's own way: *a wilful and insubordinate child* **2** deliberate and intentional: *wilful misconduct* > **wilfully** *adv*

will¹ *vb, past* **would** **1** used as an auxiliary to make the future tense: *he will go on trial on October 7th* **2** used as an auxiliary to express resolution: *they will not consider giving up territories* **3** used as an auxiliary to express a polite request: *will you please calm down?* **4** used as an auxiliary to express ability: *many essential oils will protect clothing from moths* **5** used as an auxiliary to express probability or expectation: *his followers will be relieved to hear that* **6** used as an auxiliary to express customary practice: *boys will be boys!* **7** used as an auxiliary to express desire: *go in very small steps, if you will* ▶ HISTORY Old English *willan*

will² *n* **1** a strong determination: *a fierce will to survive* **2** desire or wish: *a referendum to determine the will of the people* **3** a document setting out a person's wishes regarding the disposal of his or her property after death **4 at will** when and as one chooses: *customers can withdraw money at will* ▷ *vb* **willing, willed** **5** to try to make (something) happen by wishing very hard for it: *she willed herself not to cry* **6** to wish or desire: *if he wills it, we may meet again* **7** to leave (property) in one's will: *the farm had been willed to her* ▶ HISTORY Old English *willa*

willies *pl n* **give someone the willies** *slang* to make someone nervous or frightened ▶ HISTORY origin unknown

willing *adj* **1** favourably disposed or inclined: *I'm willing to hear what you have to say* **2** keen and obliging: *willing volunteers* > **willingly** *adv* > **willingness** *n*

will-o'-the-wisp *n* **1** someone or something that is elusive or deceptively alluring: *their freedom was just a will-o'-the-wisp* **2** a pale light that is sometimes seen over marshy ground at night ▶ HISTORY *Will*, short for *William* + *wisp* twist of hay burning as a torch

willow *n* a tree that grows near water, with thin flexible branches used in weaving baskets and wood used for making cricket bats ▶ HISTORY Old English *welig*

willowherb *n* a plant with narrow leaves and purplish flowers

willowy *adj* slender and graceful

willpower *n* strong self-disciplined determination to do something

willy-nilly *adv* whether desired or not ▶ HISTORY Old English *wile hē, nyle hē* will he or will he not

willy wagtail *n* *Austral* a black-and-white flycatcher

willy-willy *n* *Austral* a small tropical dust storm ▶ HISTORY from a native Australian language

wilt *vb* **1** (of a flower or plant) to become limp or drooping **2** (of a person) to lose strength or confidence ▶ HISTORY perhaps from obsolete *wilk* to wither

wily *adj* **wilier, wiliest** sly or crafty

wimp *informal n* **1** a feeble ineffective person ▷ *vb* **2 wimp out of** to fail to do (something) through lack of courage ▶ HISTORY origin unknown > **wimpish** *or* **wimpy** *adj*

WIMP *computers* windows, icons, menus (or mice), pointers: denoting a type of user-friendly screen display used on small computers

wimple *n* a piece of cloth draped round the head to frame the face, worn by women in the Middle Ages and now by some nuns ▶ HISTORY Old English *wimpel*

win *vb* **winning, won** **1** to achieve first place in (a competition or race) **2** to gain (a prize or first place) in a competition or race **3** to gain victory in (a battle, argument, or struggle) **4** to gain (sympathy, approval, or support) ▷ *n* **5** *informal* a success, victory, or triumph: *three consecutive wins* ▷ See also **win over** ▶ HISTORY Old English *winnan* > **winnable** *adj*

wince *vb* **wincing, winced** **1** to draw back slightly, as if in sudden pain ▷ *n* **2** the act of wincing ▶ HISTORY Old French *wencier, guenchir* to avoid

winch *n* **1** a lifting or hauling device consisting of a rope or chain wound round a barrel or drum ▷ *vb* **2** to haul or lift using a winch: *two men were winched to safety by a helicopter* ▶ HISTORY Old English *wince* pulley

wind¹ *n* **1** a current of air moving across the earth's surface **2** a trend or force: *the chill wind of change* **3** the power to breathe normally, esp. during or after physical exercise: *if you feel tired during the exercise, persevere – you'll soon get a second wind* **4** *Brit* gas in the stomach or intestines **5** *informal* foolish or empty talk: *political language is designed to give an appearance of solidity to pure wind* **6 break wind** to release intestinal gas through the anus **7 get wind of** *informal* to find out about: *the media finally got wind of her disappearance* ▷ *adj* **8** *music* of or relating to wind instruments: *the wind section* ▷ *vb* **winding, winded** **9** to cause (someone) to be short of breath: *he fell with a thud that left him winded* **10** *Brit* to cause (a baby) to bring up wind after feeding ▶ HISTORY Old English > **windless** *adj*

wind² *vb* **winding, wound** **1** to twist (something flexible) round some object: *a sweatband was wound round his head* **2** to tighten the spring of (a clock or watch) by turning a key or knob **3** to follow a twisting course: *a narrow path wound through the shrubbery* ▷ See also **wind down, wind up** ▶ HISTORY Old English *windan* > **winding** *adj, n*

w

windbag *n slang* a person who talks a lot but says little of interest

windblown *adj* blown about by the wind: *windblown hair*

windbreak *n* a fence or a line of trees that gives protection from the wind by breaking its force

wind down *vb* **1** to move downwards by turning a handle: *he wound down the rear window* **2** (of a clock or watch) to slow down before stopping completely **3** to relax after a stressful or tiring time: *I have not had a chance to wind down from a busy day* **4** to diminish gradually: *trading wound down for the day*

winded *adj* temporarily out of breath after physical exercise or a blow to the stomach

wind energy *n physics* energy obtained by harnessing wind power

windfall *n* **1** a piece of unexpected good fortune, esp. financial gain **2** a fruit blown off a tree by the wind

windfall tax *n* a tax levied on an organization considered to have made excessive profits

wind farm *n* a large group of wind-driven generators for electricity supply

wind gauge *n* same as **anemometer**

Windies *pl n* **the Windies** the international cricket team of the West Indies

winding sheet *n* a sheet in which a dead person is wrapped before being buried

wind instrument *n* a musical instrument, such as a flute, that is played by having air blown into it

windjammer *n history* a large merchant sailing ship

windlass *n* a machine for lifting heavy objects by winding a rope or chain round a barrel or drum driven by a motor ▶ **HISTORY** Old Norse *vindāss*

windmill *n* **1** a building containing machinery for grinding corn or for pumping, driven by sails that are turned by the wind **2** *Brit* a toy consisting of a stick with plastic vanes attached, which revolve in the wind

window *n* **1** an opening in a building or a vehicle containing glass within a framework, which lets in light and enables people to see in or out **2** the display area behind a glass window in a shop **3** a transparent area in an envelope which reveals the address on the letter inside **4** an area on a computer screen that can be manipulated separately from the rest of the display area, for example so that two or more files can be displayed at the same time **5** a period of unbooked time in a diary or schedule ▶ **HISTORY** Old Norse *vindauga* wind eye

window box *n* a long narrow box, placed on a windowsill, in which plants are grown

window-dressing *n* **1** the art of arranging goods in shop windows in such a way as to attract customers **2** an attempt to make something seem better than it is by stressing only its attractive features: *do you think that the president's calling for an investigation is window-dressing, or do you think he actually means to do something?* > **window-dresser** *n*

window-shopping *n* looking at goods in shop windows without intending to buy anything

windowsill *n* a shelf at the bottom of a window, either inside or outside a room

windpipe *n* a nontechnical name for **trachea**

wind-pollination *n bot* pollination by wind-borne pollen

wind rose *n geog* a diagram with radiating lines showing the frequency and strength of winds from each direction affecting a specific place

windscreen *n Brit, Austral & NZ* the sheet of glass that forms the front window of a motor vehicle

windscreen wiper *n Brit, Austral & NZ* an electrically operated blade with a rubber edge that wipes a windscreen clear of rain

windshield *n US & Canad* the sheet of glass that forms the front window of a motor vehicle

windsock *n* a cloth cone mounted on a mast, used esp. at airports to indicate the direction of the wind

wind speed *n meteorol* the strength of the wind. See also **Beaufort scale**

windsurfing *n* the sport of riding on water using a surfboard steered and propelled by an attached sail > **windsurfer** *n*

windswept *adj* **1** exposed to the wind: *the vast windswept plains* **2** blown about by the wind: *his hair was looking a bit windswept*

wind tunnel *n* a chamber through which a stream of air is forced, in order to test the effects of wind on aircraft

wind up *vb* **1** to bring to a conclusion: *we want to wind this conflict up as quickly as possible* **2** *informal* to dissolve (a company) and divide its assets among creditors **3** to tighten the spring of (a clockwork mechanism) by turning a key or knob **4** to move (a car window) upwards by turning a handle **5** *informal* to end up: *to wind up in the hospital* **6** *informal* to make nervous or tense: *as crisis after crisis broke, I became increasingly wound up* **7** *Brit, Austral & NZ, slang* to tease or annoy: *that really used to wind my old man up something rotten* ▷ *adj* **wind-up 8** operated by clockwork: *a wind-up toy* ▷ *n* **wind-up 9** the act of winding someone or something up

windward *chiefly naut adj* **1** of or in the direction from which the wind blows ▷ *n* **2** the windward direction ▷ *adv* **3** towards the wind

windward side *n geog* the side towards the wind

windy *adj* **windier, windiest 1** denoting a time or conditions in which there is a strong wind: *a windy day* **2** exposed to the wind: *the windy graveyard* **3** long-winded or pompous: *his speeches are long and windy* **4** *old-fashioned slang* frightened

wine *n* **1 a** an alcoholic drink produced by the fermenting of grapes with water and sugar **b** an alcoholic drink produced in this way from other fruits or flowers: *dandelion wine* ▷ *adj* **2** dark purplish-red ▷ *vb* **wining, wined 3 wine and dine** to entertain (someone) with wine and fine food ▶ **HISTORY** Latin *vinum*

981

wine bar *n* a bar that specializes in serving wine and usually food

wing *n* **1** one of the limbs or organs of a bird, bat, or insect that are used for flying **2** one of the two winglike supporting parts of an aircraft **3** a projecting part of a building: *converting the unused east wing into a suitable habitation* **4** a faction or group within a political party or other organization: *the youth wing of the African National Congress* **5** *Brit* the part of a car body surrounding the wheels **6** *sport* **a** either of the two sides of the pitch near the touchline **b** same as **winger 7 wings** *theatre* the space offstage to the right or left of the acting area **8 in the wings** ready to step in when needed **9 on the wing** flying **10 spread one's wings** to make fuller use of one's abilities by trying new experiences: *he increasingly spread his wings abroad* **11 take someone under one's wing** to look after someone **12 take wing** to fly away ▷ *vb* **13** to fly: *a lone bird winging its way from the island* **14** to move through the air: *sending a shower of loose gravel winging towards the house* **15** to shoot or wound in the wing or arm **16** to provide with wings ▶ **HISTORY** Old Norse *vængr* > **winged** *adj* > **wingless** *adj*

wing commander *n* a middle-ranking commissioned officer in an air force

winger *n* *sport* a player positioned on a wing

wing nut *n* a threaded nut with two flat projections which allow it to be turned by the thumb and forefinger

wingspan *n* the distance between the wing tips of a bird, insect, bat, or aircraft

wink *vb* **1** to close and open one eye quickly as a signal **2** (of a light) to shine brightly and intermittently; twinkle ▷ *n* **3** the act or an instance of winking, esp. as a signal **4** a twinkling of light **5** *informal* the smallest amount of sleep: *I didn't sleep a wink last night* **6 tip someone the wink** *Brit, Austral & NZ, informal* to give someone a hint or warning ▶ **HISTORY** Old English *wincian*

winkle *n* **1** an edible shellfish with a spirally coiled shell ▷ *vb* **-kling, -kled 2 winkle out** *informal, chiefly Brit* **a** to obtain (information) from someone who is not willing to provide it: *try to winkle the real problem out of them* **b** to coax or force out: *he somehow managed to winkle him out of his room*

winner *n* **1** a person or thing that wins **2** *informal* a person or thing that seems sure to be successful

winning *adj* **1** gaining victory: *the winning side* **2** charming or attractive: *her winning smiles*

winnings *pl n* the money won in a competition or in gambling

winnow *vb* **1** to separate (grain) from (chaff) by a current of air **2** *written* to separate out (an unwanted element): *the committee will need to winnow out the nonsense* ▶ **HISTORY** Old English *windwian*

win over *vb* to gain the support or consent of: *his robust performance won over his critics*

winsome *adj* *literary* charming or attractive: *a winsome smile* ▶ **HISTORY** Old English *wynsum*

winter *n* **1** the coldest season of the year, between autumn and spring ▷ *vb* **2** to spend the winter in a specified place: *wintering in Rome* ▶ **HISTORY** Old English

wintergreen *n* an evergreen shrub from which is obtained a pleasant-smelling oil that is used medicinally and for flavouring

winter solstice *n* the time, about December 22, at which the sun is at its southernmost point in the sky

winter sports *pl n* sports held on snow or ice, such as skiing and skating

wintertime *n* the period or season of winter

wintry *adj* **-trier, -triest 1** of or characteristic of winter: *a cold wintry day* **2** cold or unfriendly: *a wintry smile*

wipe *vb* **wiping, wiped 1** to rub (a surface or object) lightly with a cloth or the hand, in order to remove dirt or liquid from it **2** to remove by wiping: *she made a futile attempt to wipe away her tears* **3** to erase a recording from (a video or audio tape, computer, etc.) ▷ *n* **4** the act or an instance of wiping: *a quick wipe* ▶ **HISTORY** Old English *wīpian*

wipe out *vb* to destroy or get rid of completely: *a hail storm wipes out a wheat crop in five minutes*

wiper *n* short for **windscreen wiper**

wire *n* **1** a slender flexible strand of metal **2** a length of this used to carry electric current in a circuit **3** a long continuous piece of wire or cable connecting points in a telephone or telegraph system **4** *old-fashioned informal* a telegram ▷ *vb* **wiring, wired 5** to fasten with wire **6** to equip (an electrical system, circuit, or component) with wires **7** *informal* to send a telegram **8** to send by telegraph: *they wired the money for a train ticket* ▶ **HISTORY** Old English *wīr*

wired *adj* **1** *slang* excitable or edgy, usually from stimulant intake: *I don't want coffee—I'm wired enough as it is* **2** using computers to send and receive information, esp. via the internet

wire-haired *adj* (of a dog) having a rough wiry coat

wireless *n* **1** *old-fashioned* same as **radio** ▷ *adj* **2** communicating without connecting wires: *wireless communications*

wire netting *n* a net made of wire, used for fencing

wireworm *n* a destructive wormlike beetle larva

wiring *n* the network of wires used in an electrical system, device, or circuit

wiry *adj* **wirier, wiriest 1** (of a person) slim but strong **2** coarse and stiff: *wiry grass*

wisdom *n* **1** the ability to use one's experience and knowledge to make sensible decisions or judgments **2** accumulated knowledge or learning: *the wisdom of Asia and of Africa* ▶ **HISTORY** Old English *wīsdōm*

wisdom tooth *n* any of the four molar teeth, one at the back of each side of the jaw, that are the last of the permanent teeth to come through

wise¹ *adj* **1** possessing or showing wisdom: *a wise move* **2 none the wiser** knowing no more than before: *I left the conference none the wiser* **3 wise to** *informal* aware of or informed about: *they'll get wise to our system; he put him wise to the rumour* ▶ HISTORY Old English *wīs* > **wisely** *adv*

wise² *n* old-fashioned way, manner, or respect: *in no wise* ▶ HISTORY Old English *wīse* manner

-wise *adv suffix* **1** indicating direction or manner: *crabwise* **2** with reference to: *moneywise* ▶ HISTORY Old English *-wisan*

wiseacre *n* a person who wishes to seem wise ▶ HISTORY Middle Dutch *wijsseggher* soothsayer

wisecrack *informal n* **1** a clever, amusing, sometimes unkind remark ▷ *vb* **2** to make such remarks > **wisecracking** *adj*

wish *vb* **1** to want or desire (something impossible or improbable): *he wished he'd kept quiet* **2** to desire or prefer to be or do something: *the next person who wished to speak* **3** to feel or express a hope concerning the welfare, health, or success of: *we wished him well* **4** to greet as specified: *I wished her a Merry Christmas* ▷ *n* **5** a desire, often for something impossible or improbable: *a desperate wish to succeed as a professional artist* **6** something desired or wished for: *your wishes will come true* **7** the expression of a hope for someone's welfare, health, or success: *give him our best wishes* ▶ HISTORY Old English *wȳscan*

wishbone *n* the V-shaped bone above the breastbone of a chicken or turkey

wishful *adj* desirous or longing: *she seemed wishful of prolonging the discussion*

wishful thinking *n* an interpretation of the facts as one would like them to be, rather than as they are: *was it wishful thinking, or had the enemy lost heart?*

wish list *n* a list of things desired by a person or organization: *the government's wish list*

wishy-washy *adj informal* lacking in character, force, or colour

wisp *n* **1** a thin, delicate, or filmy piece or streak: *little wisps of cloud* **2** a small untidy bundle, tuft, or strand: *a wisp of hair* **3** a slight trace: *a wisp of a smile* ▶ HISTORY origin unknown

wispy *adj* **wispier, wispiest** thin, fine, or delicate: *grey wispy hair*

wisteria *n* a climbing plant with large drooping clusters of blue, purple, or white flowers ▶ HISTORY after Caspar *Wistar*, anatomist

wistful *adj* sadly wishing for something lost or unobtainable > **wistfully** *adv* > **wistfulness** *n*

wit¹ *n* **1** the ability to use words or ideas in a clever, amusing, and imaginative way **2** a person possessing this ability **3** practical intelligence: *do credit me with some wit* ▷ See also **wits** ▶ HISTORY Old English *witt*

wit² *vb* **to wit** (used to introduce a statement or explanation) that is to say; namely ▶ HISTORY Old English *witan*

witblits (**vit**-blits) *n S African* an illegally distilled strong alcoholic drink ▶ HISTORY Afrikaans *wit* white + *blits* lightning

witch *n* **1** (in former times) a woman believed to possess evil magic powers **2** a person who

practises magic or sorcery, esp. black magic **3** an ugly or wicked old woman ▶ HISTORY Old English *wicce*

witchcraft *n* the use of magic, esp. for evil purposes

witch doctor *n* a man in certain tribal societies who is believed to possess magical powers, which can be used to cure sickness or to harm people

witchetty grub *n* a wood-boring edible Australian caterpillar

witch hazel *n* a medicinal solution made from the bark and leaves of a N American shrub, which is put on the skin to treat bruises and inflammation

witch-hunt *n* a rigorous campaign to expose and discredit people considered to hold unorthodox views on the pretext of safeguarding the public welfare

with *prep* **1** accompanying; in the company of: *the captain called to the sergeant to come with him* **2** using; by means of: *unlocking the padlock with a key* **3** possessing or having: *a woman with black hair; the patient with angina* **4** concerning or regarding: *be gentle with me* **5** in a manner characterized by: *I know you will handle it with discretion* **6** as a result of: *his voice was hoarse with nervousness* **7** following the line of thought of: *are you with me so far?* **8** having the same opinions as; supporting: *are you with us or against us?* ▶ HISTORY Old English

withdraw *vb* **-drawing, -drew, -drawn 1** to take out or remove: *he withdrew an envelope from his pocket* **2** to remove (money) from a bank account or savings account **3** to leave one place to go to another, usually quieter, place: *he withdrew into his bedroom* **4** (of troops) to leave or be pulled back from the battleground **5** to take back (a statement) formally **6 withdraw from** to give up: *they withdrew from the competition* ▶ HISTORY *with*, in the sense: away from

withdrawal *n* **1** the act or an instance of withdrawing **2** the period that a drug addict goes through after stopping using drugs, during which he or she may experience symptoms such as tremors, sweating, and vomiting ▷ *adj* **3** of or relating to withdrawal from an addictive drug: *withdrawal symptoms*

withdrawn *vb* **1** the past participle of **withdraw** ▷ *adj* **2** extremely reserved or shy

wither *vb* **1** to make or become dried up or shrivelled: *the leaves had withered but not fallen* **2** to fade or waste: *deprived of the nerve supply, the muscles wither* **3** to humiliate (someone) with a scornful look or remark ▶ HISTORY probably variant of *weather* (verb) > **withered** *adj*

withering *adj* (of a look or remark) extremely scornful

withers *pl n* the highest part of the back of a horse, between the shoulders ▶ HISTORY earlier *widersones*

withhold *vb* **-holding, -held** to keep back (information or money)

within *prep* **1** in or inside: *within the hospital grounds* **2** before (a period of time) has passed: *within a*

W

month **3** not beyond: *within the confines of a low budget; he positioned a low table within her reach* ▷ *adv* **4** formal inside or internally: *a glimpse of what was hidden within*

without *prep* **1** not accompanied by: *I can't imagine going through life without him* **2** not using: *our Jeep drove without lights* **3** not possessing or having: *four months without a job; a lot of them came across the border without shoes* **4** in a manner showing a lack of: *without reverence* **5** while not or after not: *she sat without speaking for some while* ▷ *adv* **6** formal outside: *seated on the graveyard without*

withstand *vb* **-standing, -stood** to resist or endure successfully: *our ability to withstand stress*

witless *adj* **1** formal lacking intelligence or sense **2 scared witless** extremely frightened

witness *n* **1** a person who has seen or can give first-hand evidence of some event: *the only witness to a killing* **2** a person who gives evidence in a court of law: *a witness for the defence* **3** a person who confirms the genuineness of a document or signature by adding his or her own signature **4** evidence proving or supporting something: *the Church of England, that historic witness to the power of the Christian faith* **5 bear witness to** to be evidence or proof of: *the high turnout bore witness to the popularity of the contest* ▷ *vb* **6** to see, be present at, or know at first hand: *I have witnessed many motor-racing accidents* **7** to be the scene or setting of: *the 1970s witnessed an enormous increase in international lending* **8** to confirm the genuineness of (a document or signature) by adding one's own signature **9 witness to** formal to confirm: *our aim is to witness to the fact of the empty tomb* ▶ HISTORY Old English *witnes*

witness box *or esp US* **witness stand** *n* the place in a court of law where witnesses stand to give evidence

wits *pl n* **1** the ability to think and act quickly: *when he was sober, his wits were razor-sharp* **2 at one's wits' end** at a loss to know what to do **3 have one's wits about one** to be able to think and act quickly **4 live by** *or* **on one's wits** to gain a livelihood by craftiness rather than by hard work **5 scared out of one's wits** extremely frightened

witter *vb* chiefly Brit, informal to chatter or babble pointlessly or at unnecessary length ▶ HISTORY origin unknown

witticism *n* a witty remark

wittingly *adv* intentionally and knowingly

witty *adj* **-tier, -tiest** clever and amusing > **wittily** *adv*

wives *n* the plural of **wife**

wizard *n* **1** a man in fairy tales who has magic powers **2** a person who is outstandingly gifted in some specified field: *a financial wizard* ▶ HISTORY from *wise*

wizardry *n* **1** magic or sorcery **2** outstanding skill or accomplishment in some specified field: *technological wizardry*

wizened (**wiz**-zend) *adj* shrivelled, wrinkled, or dried up with age

WMD weapon(s) of mass destruction

woad *n* a blue dye obtained from a European plant, used by the ancient Britons as a body dye ▶ HISTORY Old English *wād*

wobbegong *n* an Australian shark with brown-and-white skin

wobble *vb* **-bling, -bled** **1** to move or sway unsteadily **2** to shake: *she was having difficulty in controlling her voice, which wobbled about* ▷ *n* **3** a wobbling movement or sound ▶ HISTORY Low German *wabbeln*

wobbly *adj* **-blier, -bliest** **1** unsteady **2** trembling ▷ *n* **3 throw a wobbly** Brit, slang to become suddenly angry or upset

wodge *n* Brit & NZ, informal a thick lump or chunk: *a wodge of syrupy sponge* ▶ HISTORY from *wedge*

woe *n* **1** literary intense grief **2 woes** written misfortunes or problems: *economic woes* **3 woe betide someone** someone will or would experience misfortune: *woe betide anyone who got in his way* ▶ HISTORY Old English *wā, wǣ*

woebegone *adj* written sad in appearance ▶ HISTORY *woe* + obsolete *bego* to surround

woeful *adj* **1** extremely sad **2** pitiful or deplorable: *a woeful lack of understanding* > **woefully** *adv*

wok *n* a large bowl-shaped metal Chinese cooking pot, used for stir-frying ▶ HISTORY Chinese (Cantonese)

woke *vb* the past tense of **wake¹**

woken *vb* the past participle of **wake¹**

wold *n* a large area of high open rolling country ▶ HISTORY Old English *weald* wood

wolf *n, pl* **wolves** **1** a predatory doglike wild animal which hunts in packs **2** old-fashioned informal a man who habitually tries to seduce women **3 cry wolf** to give false alarms repeatedly: *if you cry wolf too often, people will take no notice* ▷ *vb* **4 wolf down** to eat quickly or greedily: *they will wolf down kidneys but refuse tongue* ▶ HISTORY Old English *wulf*

wolfhound *n* a very large dog, formerly used to hunt wolves

wolf whistle *n* **1** a whistle produced by a man to express admiration of a woman's appearance ▷ *vb* **wolf-whistle, -whistling, -whistled** **2** to produce such a whistle

wolverine *n* a large meat-eating mammal of Eurasia and North America with very thick dark fur ▶ HISTORY earlier *wolvering*, from *wolf*

wolves *n* the plural of **wolf**

woman *n, pl* **women** **1** an adult female human being **2** adult female human beings collectively: *the very image of woman pared of the trappings of 'femininity'* **3** a female servant or domestic help **4** informal a wife or girlfriend ▷ *adj* **5** female: *a woman doctor* ▶ HISTORY Old English *wīfmann*

womanhood *n* **1** the state of being a woman: *young girls approaching womanhood* **2** women collectively: *Asian womanhood*

womanish *adj* (of a man) looking or behaving like a woman

womanizer *or* **-iser** *n* a man who has casual affairs with many women

womanizing or **-ising** n (of a man) the practice of indulging in casual affairs with women

womankind n all women considered as a group

womanly adj possessing qualities generally regarded as typical of, or appropriate to, a woman

womb n the nontechnical name for **uterus**
▶ HISTORY Old English wamb

wombat n a furry heavily-built plant-eating Australian marsupial ▶ HISTORY Aboriginal

women n the plural of **woman**

womenfolk pl n **1** women collectively **2** a group of women, esp. the female members of one's family

Women's Liberation n a movement promoting the removal of inequalities based upon the assumption that men are superior to women. Also called: **women's lib**

won vb the past of **win**

wonder vb **1** to think about something with curiosity or doubt: I wonder why she did that **2** to be amazed: I did wonder at her leaving valuable china on the shelves ▷ n **3** something that causes surprise or awe: it's a wonder she isn't speechless with fright **4** the feeling of surprise or awe caused by something strange: the wonder of travel **5 do** or **work wonders** to achieve spectacularly good results **6 no** or **small wonder** it is not surprising: no wonder you're going broke ▷ adj **7** causing surprise or awe because of spectacular results achieved: a new wonder drug for treating migraine ▶ HISTORY Old English wundor > **wonderingly** adv > **wonderment** n

wonderful adj **1** extremely fine; excellent: I've been offered a wonderful job **2** causing surprise, amazement, or awe: a strange and wonderful phenomenon > **wonderfully** adv

wonderland n **1** an imaginary land of marvels or wonders **2** an actual place of great or strange beauty: the apartment was a wonderland of design and colour

wondrous adj old-fashioned or literary causing surprise or awe; marvellous

wonky adj **-kier, -kiest** Brit, Austral & NZ, slang **1** shaky or unsteady: wonky wheelbarrows; wonky knees **2** insecure or unreliable: his marriage is looking a bit wonky ▶ HISTORY dialect wanky

wont (rhymes with **don't**) old-fashioned, written adj **1** accustomed: most murderers, his police friends were wont to say, were male ▷ n **2** a usual practice: she waded straight in, as was her wont ▶ HISTORY Old English gewunod

won't will not

woo vb **wooing, wooed 1** to coax or urge: it will woo people back into the kitchen **2** old-fashioned to attempt to gain the love of (a woman) ▶ HISTORY Old English wōgian > **wooing** n

wood n **1** the hard fibrous substance beneath the bark in trees and shrubs, which is used in building and carpentry and as fuel. Related adjective: **ligneous 2** an area of trees growing together that is smaller than a forest: a track leading into a wood. Related adjective: **sylvan 3** golf a long-shafted club with a wooden head ▷ adj **4** made of, using, or for use with wood: wood fires ▷ See also **woods**
▶ HISTORY Old English widu, wudu

wood alcohol n same as **methanol**

woodbine n a wild honeysuckle with sweet-smelling yellow flowers

woodcarving n **1** a work of art produced by carving wood **2** the act or craft of carving wood

woodcock n a large game bird with a long straight bill

woodcut n a print made from a block of wood with a design cut into it

woodcutter n a person who cuts down trees or chops wood

wooded adj covered with woods or trees

wooden adj **1** made of wood **2** lacking spirit or animation: the man's expression became wooden > **woodenly** adv

woodland n **1** land that is mostly covered with woods or trees ▷ adj **2** living in woods: woodland birds

woodlouse n, pl **-lice** a very small grey creature with many legs that lives in damp places

woodpecker n a bird with a strong beak with which it bores into trees for insects

wood pulp n pulp made from wood fibre, used to make paper

woodruff n a plant with small sweet-smelling white flowers and sweet-smelling leaves
▶ HISTORY Old English wudurofe

woods pl n closely packed trees forming a forest or wood

woodsman n, pl **-men** a person who lives in a wood or who is skilled at woodwork or carving

woodwind music adj **1** of or denoting a type of wind instrument, such as the oboe ▷ n **2** the woodwind instruments of an orchestra

woodwork n **1** the parts of a room or house that are made of wood, such as the doors and window frames: stark white walls and blue woodwork **2** the art or craft of making objects from wood **3 crawl out of the woodwork** to appear suddenly and make one's feelings known: intellectuals and environmentalists crawled out of the woodwork

woodworm n **1** a beetle larva that bores into wooden furniture or beams **2** the damage caused to wood by these larvae

woody adj **woodier, woodiest 1** (of a plant) having a very hard stem **2** (of an area) covered with woods or trees

woof¹ n same as **weft** ▶ HISTORY Old English ōwef

woof² n an imitation of the bark of a dog

woofer n a loudspeaker used in high-fidelity systems for the reproduction of low audio frequencies

wool n **1** the soft curly hair of sheep and some other animals **2** yarn spun from this, used in weaving and knitting **3** cloth made from this yarn **4 pull the wool over someone's eyes** to deceive someone ▶ HISTORY Old English wull

woolgathering n idle or absent-minded daydreaming

W

985

woollen *or US* **woolen** *adj* **1** made of wool or of a mixture of wool and another material **2** relating to wool: *woollen mills* ▷ *n* **3 woollens** woollen clothes, esp. knitted ones

woolly *or US* **wooly** *adj* **-lier, -liest** **1** made of or like wool **2** confused or indistinct: *woolly ideas* ▷ *n*, *pl* **-lies 3** a woollen garment, such as a sweater

woolshed *n Austral & NZ* a large building in which sheep shearing takes place

woomera *n* a notched stick used by Australian Aborigines to aid the propulsion of a spear

woozy *adj* **woozier, wooziest** *informal* feeling slightly dizzy ▶ HISTORY origin unknown

wop-wops *pl n NZ, informal* remote rural areas

word *n* **1** the smallest single meaningful unit of speech or writing. *Related adjective:* **lexical** ⊳ *n spoken* a brief conversation: *I would like a word with you* **3** a brief statement: *a word of warning* **4** news or information: *let me know if you get word of my wife* **5** a solemn promise: *he had given his word as a rabbi* **6** a command or order: *he had only to say the word and they'd hang him* **7** *computers* a set of bits used to store, transmit, or operate upon an item of information in a computer **8 by word of mouth** by spoken rather than by written means: *their reputation spreads by word of mouth* **9 in a word** briefly or in short: *in a word, we've won* **10 my word!** Also: **upon my word!** *old-fashioned* an exclamation of surprise or amazement **11 take someone at his** *or* **her word** to accept that someone really means what he or she says: *they're willing to take him at his word when he says he'll change* **12 take someone's word for it** to believe what someone says **13 the last word** the closing remark of a conversation or argument, often regarded as settling an issue **14 the last word in** the finest example of: *the last word in comfort* **15 word for word** using exactly the same words: *he repeated almost word for word what had been said* **16 word of honour** a solemn promise ⊳ *vb* **17** to state in words: *the questions have to be carefully worded* ⊳ See also **words** ▶ HISTORY Old English

Word *n* **the Word** the message and teachings contained in the Bible

-word *n combining form* (preceded by **the** and an initial letter) a euphemistic way of referring to a word by its first letter because it is considered to be unmentionable by the user: *the c-word, meaning cancer*

word equation *n chem* the expression of a chemical equation in words rather than using symbols

wording *n* the way in which words are used to express something: *the exact wording of the regulation has still not been worked out*

word-perfect *adj* able to repeat from memory the exact words of a text one has learned

wordplay *n* the making of jokes by clever use of words

word processing *n* the storage and organization of text by electronic means, esp. for business purposes

word processor *n* an electronic machine for word processing, consisting of a keyboard, a VDU incorporating a microprocessor, and a printer

words *pl n* **1** the text of a song, as opposed to the music **2** the text of an actor's part **3 have words** to have an argument or disagreement **4 in other words** expressing the same idea in a different, more understandable, way **5 put into words** to express in speech or writing: *she was reluctant to put her thoughts into words*

wordy *adj* **wordier, wordiest** using too many words, esp. long words: *wordy explanations*

wore *vb* the past tense of **wear**

work *n* **1** physical or mental effort directed to doing or making something **2** paid employment at a job, trade, or profession **3** duties or tasks: *I had to delegate as much work as I could* **4** something done or made as a result of effort: *a work by a major artist* **5** the place where a person is employed: *accidents at work* **6** *physics, old-fashioned* the transfer of energy occurring when a force is applied to move a body **7 at work** working or in action: *the social forces at work in society* ⊳ *adj* **8** of or for work: *work experience* ⊳ *vb* **9** to do work; labour: *no-one worked harder than Arnold* **10** to be employed: *she worked as a waitress* **11** to make (a person or animal) labour **12** to operate (a machine or a piece of equipment) **13** (of a machine or a piece of equipment) to function, esp. effectively: *that clock doesn't work* **14** (of a plan or system) to be successful **15** to cultivate (land) **16** to move gradually into a specific condition or position: *he picked up the shovel, worked it under the ice, and levered it* **17** to make (one's way) with effort: *he worked his way to the top* **18** *informal* to manipulate to one's own advantage: *they could see an angle and they'd know how to work it* ⊳ See also **work off, works,** etc. ▶ HISTORY Old English *weorc*

workable *adj* **1** able to operate efficiently: *a workable solution* **2** able to be used: *a workable mine*

workaday *adj* commonplace or ordinary: *workaday surroundings*

workaholic *n* a person who is obsessed with work

worker *n* **1** a person who works in a specified way: *a hard worker* **2** a person who works at a specific job: *a government worker* **3** an employee, as opposed to an employer **4** a sterile female bee, ant, or wasp that works for the colony

work ethic *n* a belief in the moral value of work

workforce *n* **1** the total number of workers employed by a company **2** the total number of people available for work: *the local workforce*

workhorse *n* a person or thing that does a lot of work, esp. dull or routine work: *this plane is the workhorse of most short-haul airlines*

workhouse *n* (formerly, in England) a public institution where very poor people did work in return for food and accommodation

working *adj* **1** having a job: *the working mother* **2** concerned with, used in, or suitable for work: *working conditions* **3** capable of being operated or used: *a working mechanism* ⊳ *n* **4** a part of a mine or quarry that is or has been used **5 workings** the way that something works: *the workings of the human brain*

working capital *n* the amount of capital that a business has available to meet the day-to-day cash requirements of its operations

working class *n* **1** the social group that consists of people who earn wages, esp. as manual workers ▷ *adj* **working-class 2** of or relating to the working class: *a working-class neighbourhood*

working day *or esp US & Canad* **workday** *n* **1** a day when people normally go to work: *the last working day of the week* **2** the part of the day allocated to work: *the long working day of twelve to fourteen hours*

working party *n* a committee established to investigate a problem

workload *n* the amount of work to be done, esp. in a specified period: *a heavy workload*

workman *n, pl* **-men** a man who is employed to do manual work

workmanship *n* the degree of skill with which an object is made: *shoddy workmanship*

work of art *n* **1** a piece of fine art, such as a painting or sculpture **2** an object or a piece of work that has been exceptionally skilfully made or produced: *the doll was truly a work of art*

work off *vb* to get rid of, usually by effort: *he went along to the tennis club and worked off his pique there*

work out *vb* **1** to solve, find out, or plan by reasoning or calculation: *working out a new budget* **2** to happen in a particular way: *he decided to wait and see how things worked out* **3** to be successful or satisfactory: *the dates never worked out* **4** to take part in physical exercise **5 work out at** to be calculated at (a certain amount): *the return on capital works out at 15 per cent* ▷ *n* **workout 6** a session of physical exercise for training or to keep fit

works *n* **1** a place where something is manufactured: *a chemical works* ▷ *pl n* **2** the sum total of a writer's or artist's achievements considered together: *the works of Goethe* **3 the works** *slang* everything associated with a particular subject or thing: *traditional Indian music, sitars, the works*

worksheet *n* a sheet of paper containing exercises to be completed by a student

workshop *n* **1** a room or building where manufacturing or other manual work is carried on **2** a group of people engaged in intensive study or work in a creative or practical field: *a writers' workshop*

work station *n* **1** an area in an office where one person works **2** *computers* a component of an electronic office system consisting of a VDU and keyboard

worktop *n* a surface in a kitchen, usually the top of a fitted kitchen unit, which is used for food preparation. Also: **work surface**

work-to-rule *n* a form of industrial action in which employees keep strictly to their employers' rules, with the result of reducing the work rate

work up *vb* **1** to make angry, excited, or upset: *he worked himself up into a rage* **2** to build up or develop: *I'd worked up a thirst* **3** to work on (something) in order to improve it: *there was enough material to be worked up into something publishable* **4 work one's way up** to make progress: *he worked his way up in the catering trade* **5 work up to** to develop gradually towards: *the fete worked up to a climax around lunch time*

world *n* **1** the earth as a planet **2** the human race; people generally: *providing food for the world* **3** any planet or moon, esp. one that might be inhabited **4** a particular group of countries or period of history, or its inhabitants: *the Arab world; the post-Cold War world* **5** an area, sphere, or realm considered as a complete environment: *the art world; the world of nature* **6** the total circumstances and experience of a person that make up his or her life: *there may not ever be a place for us in your world* **7 bring into the world** to deliver or give birth to (a baby) **8 come into the world** to be born **9 for all the world** exactly or very much: *they looked for all the world like a pair of newly-weds* **10 in the world** used to emphasize a statement: *she didn't have a worry in the world* **11 man** *or* **woman of the world** a man or woman who is experienced in social or public life **12 worlds apart** very different from each other: *this man and I are worlds apart* ▷ *adj* **13** of or concerning the entire world: *the world championship* ▶ HISTORY Old English w(e)orold

worldly *adj* **-lier, -liest 1** not spiritual; earthly or temporal: *as a simple monk he had no interest in politics and other worldly affairs* **2** of or relating to material things: *all his worldly goods* **3** wise in the ways of the world; sophisticated: *a suave, worldly, charming Frenchman* > **worldliness** *n*

world music *n* popular music of a variety of ethnic origins and styles

World War I *n* the war (1914–18) between the Allies (principally France, Russia, Britain, Italy, Australia, Canada, and the US) and the Central Powers (principally Germany, Austria-Hungary, and Turkey). Also: **First World War**

World War II *n* the war (1939–45) between the Allies (Britain, France, Australia, the US, and the Soviet Union) and the Axis (Germany, Italy, and Japan). Also: **Second World War**

world-weary *adj* no longer finding pleasure in life

worldwide *adj* applying or extending throughout the world

World Wide Web *n* *computers* a vast network of hypertext files, stored on computers throughout the world, that can provide a computer user with information on a huge variety of subjects

worm *n* **1** a small invertebrate animal with a long thin body and no limbs **2** an insect larva that looks like a worm **3** a despicable or weak person **4** a slight trace: *a worm of doubt* **5** a shaft on which a spiral thread has been cut, for example in a gear arrangement in which such a shaft drives a toothed wheel **6** *computers* a type of virus ▷ *vb* **7** to rid (an animal) of worms in its intestines

W

8 worm one's way a to go or move slowly and with difficulty: *I had to worm my way out sideways from the bench* **b** to get oneself into a certain situation or position gradually: *worming your way into my good books* **9 worm out of** to obtain (information) from someone who is not willing to provide it: *it took me weeks to worm the facts out of him* ▷ See also **worms** ▶ HISTORY Old English *wyrm*

WORM *n* computers write once read many (times): an optical disk which enables users to store their own data

wormcast *n* a coil of earth or sand that has been excreted by a burrowing worm

worm-eaten *adj* eaten into by worms: *worm-eaten beams*

wormhole *n* a hole made by a worm in timber, plants, or fruit

worms *n* a disease caused by parasitic worms living in the intestines

wormwood *n* a plant from which a bitter oil formerly used in making absinthe is obtained ▶ HISTORY Old English *wormōd, wermōd*

wormy *adj* **wormier, wormiest** infested with or eaten by worms

worn *vb* **1** the past participle of **wear** ▷ *adj* **2** showing signs of long use or wear: *the worn soles of his boots* **3** looking tired and ill: *that worn pain-creased face*

worn-out *adj* **1** worn or used until threadbare, valueless, or useless **2** completely exhausted: *worn-out by their exertions*

worried *adj* concerned and anxious about things that may happen > **worriedly** *adv*

worry *vb* **-ries, -rying, -ried 1** to be or cause to be anxious or uneasy **2** to annoy or bother: *don't worry yourself with the details* **3** (of a dog) to frighten (sheep or other animals) by chasing and trying to bite them **4 worry away at** to struggle with or work on (a problem) ▷ *n, pl* **-ries 5** a state or feeling of anxiety: *he was beside himself with worry* **6** a cause for anxiety: *having a premature baby is much less of a worry these days* ▶ HISTORY Old English *wyrgan* > **worrier** *n*

worrying *adj* causing concern and anxiety

worse *adj* **1** the comparative of **bad 2 none the worse for** not harmed by (adverse events or circumstances) **3 the worse for wear** *informal* in a poor condition; not at one's best: *returning the worse for wear from the pub* **4 worse off** in a worse condition, esp. financially ▷ *adv* **5 for the worse** into a worse condition: *taking a turn for the worse* ▷ *adv* **6** the comparative of **badly** ▶ HISTORY Old English *wiersa*

worsen *vb* to make or become worse > **worsening** *adj, n*

worship *vb* **-shipping, -shipped** or US **-shiping, -shiped 1** to show profound religious devotion to (one's god), for example by praying **2** to have intense love and admiration for (a person) ▷ *n* **3** religious adoration or devotion **4** formal expression of religious adoration, for example by praying **5** intense love or devotion to a person

▶ HISTORY Old English *weorthscipe* > **worshipper** or US **-shiper** *n*

Worship *n* **Your** or **His** or **Her Worship** chiefly Brit a title for a mayor or magistrate

worshipful *adj* feeling or showing reverence or adoration

worst *adj, adv* **1** the superlative of **bad, badly** ▷ *n* **2** the least good or the most terrible person, thing, or part: *the worst is yet to come* **3 at one's worst** in the worst condition or aspect of a thing or person: *it was television at its worst* **4 at worst** in the least favourable interpretation or conditions: *all the questions should ideally be answered 'no', or at worst 'sometimes'* ▷ *vb* **5** old-fashioned to defeat or beat ▶ HISTORY Old English *wierrest*

worsted (**wooss**-tid) *n* a close-textured woollen fabric used to make jackets and trousers ▶ HISTORY after *Worstead*, a district in Norfolk

worth *prep* **1** having a value of: *the fire destroyed property worth $200 million* **2** worthy of; meriting or justifying: *if a job is worth doing, it's worth doing well* **3 worth one's weight in gold** extremely useful or helpful; very highly valued **4 worth one's while** worthy of spending one's time or effort on something: *they needed a wage of at least £140 a week to make it worth their while returning to work* ▷ *n* **5** monetary value: *the corporation's net worth* **6** high quality; value: *the submarine proved its military worth during the Second World War* **7** the amount of something that can be bought for a specified price: *$10 billion worth of property* ▶ HISTORY Old English *weorth*

worthless *adj* **1** without value or usefulness: *worthless junk bonds* **2** without merit: *he sees himself as a worthless creature* > **worthlessness** *n*

worthwhile *adj* sufficiently important, rewarding, or valuable to justify spending time or effort on it

worthy *adj* **-thier, -thiest 1** deserving of admiration or respect: *motives which were less than worthy* **2 worthy of** deserving of: *he would practise extra hard to be worthy of such an honour* ▷ *n, pl* **-thies 3** often facetious an important person > **worthily** *adv* > **worthiness** *n*

would *vb* **1** used as an auxiliary to form the past tense or subjunctive mood of **will** [1]: *he asked if she would marry him; that would be delightful* **2** used as an auxiliary to express a polite offer or request: *would you like some lunch?* **3** used as an auxiliary to describe a habitual past action: *sometimes at lunch time I would choose a painting to go and see*

would-be *adj* wanting or pretending to be: *would-be brides*

wouldn't would not

wound[1] *n* **1** an injury to the body such as a cut or a gunshot injury **2** an injury to one's feelings or reputation ▷ *vb* **3** to cause an injury to the body or feelings of ▶ HISTORY Old English *wund* > **wounding** *adj*

wound[2] *vb* the past of **wind**[2]

wove *vb* a past tense of **weave**

woven *vb* a past participle of **weave**

W

wow *interj* **1** an exclamation of admiration or amazement ▷ *n* **2** *slang* a person or thing that is amazingly successful: *he would be an absolute wow on the chat shows* ▷ *vb* **3** *slang* to be a great success with: *the new Disney film wowed festival audiences* ▶ HISTORY Scots

wowser *n* *Austral & NZ, slang* **1** a fanatically puritanical person **2** a teetotaller ▶ HISTORY dialect *wow* to complain

WPC (in Britain) woman police constable

wpm words per minute

WRAC (formerly, in Britain) Women's Royal Army Corps

wrack¹ *n* same as **rack²** ▶ HISTORY Old English *wræc* persecution

wrack² *n* seaweed that is floating in the sea or has been washed ashore ▶ HISTORY probably from Middle Dutch *wrak* wreckage

WRAF (formerly, in Britain) Women's Royal Air Force

wraith *n* *literary* a ghost ▶ HISTORY Scots
> **wraithlike** *adj*

wrangle *vb* **-gling, -gled 1** to argue noisily or angrily ▷ *n* **2** a noisy or angry argument ▶ HISTORY Low German *wrangeln*

wrap *vb* **wrapping, wrapped 1** to fold a covering round (something) and fasten it securely: *a small package wrapped in brown paper* **2** to fold or wind (something) round a person or thing: *she wrapped a handkerchief around her bleeding palm* **3** to fold, wind, or coil: *she wrapped her arms around her mother* **4** to complete the filming of (a motion picture or television programme) ▷ *n* **5** *old-fashioned* a garment worn wrapped round the shoulders **6** (in the filming of a motion picture or television programme) the end of a day's filming or the completion of filming **7** *Brit, slang* a small packet of an illegal drug in powder form: *a wrap of heroin* **8 keep something under wraps** to keep something secret ▷ See also **wrap up** ▶ HISTORY origin unknown

wraparound *adj* **1** (of a skirt) designed to be worn wrapped round the body **2** extending in a curve from the front round to the sides: *wraparound shades*

wrapper *n* a paper, foil, or plastic cover in which a product is wrapped: *a single sweet wrapper*

wrapping *n* a piece of paper, foil, or other material used to wrap something in

wrap up *vb* **1** to fold paper, cloth, or other material round (something) **2** to put warm clothes on: *remember to wrap up warmly on cold or windy days* **3** *informal* to finish or settle: *he will need 60 to 90 days to wrap up his current business dealings* **4** *slang* to stop talking **5 wrapped up in** giving all one's attention to: *wrapped up in her new baby*

wrasse *n* a brightly coloured sea fish ▶ HISTORY Cornish *wrach*

wrath (roth) *n* *old-fashioned or literary* intense anger ▶ HISTORY Old English *wræththu*
> **wrathful** *adj*

wreak *vb* **1 wreak havoc** to cause chaos or damage: *this Australian sun will wreak havoc with your complexions* **2 wreak vengeance on** to take revenge on ▶ HISTORY Old English *wrecan*

wreath *n, pl* **wreaths 1** a ring of flowers or leaves, placed on a grave as a memorial or worn on the head as a garland or a mark of honour **2** anything circular or spiral: *a wreath of smoke* ▶ HISTORY Old English *writha*

wreck *vb* **1** to break, spoil, or destroy completely **2** to cause the accidental sinking or destruction of (a ship) at sea ▷ *n* **3** something that has been destroyed or badly damaged, such as a crashed car or aircraft **4** a ship that has been sunk or destroyed at sea **5** a person in a poor mental or physical state ▶ HISTORY from Old Norse

wreckage *n* the remains of something that has been destroyed or badly damaged, such as a crashed car or aircraft

wrecker *n* **1** a person who destroys or badly damages something: *a marriage wrecker* **2** (formerly) a person who lured ships on to the rocks in order to plunder them **3** *chiefly US, Canad & NZ* a person whose job is to demolish buildings or dismantle cars **4** *US & Canad* a breakdown van

wreckers *pl n* *NZ* a business which sells material from demolished cars or buildings

wren *n* a very small brown songbird ▶ HISTORY Old English *wrenna*

Wren *n* *informal* (in Britain) a member of the former Women's Royal Naval Service ▶ HISTORY from abbreviation WRNS

wrench *vb* **1** to twist or pull (something) violently, for example to remove it from something to which it is attached: *he grabbed the cable and wrenched it out of the wall socket* **2** to move or twist away with a sudden violent effort: *she wrenched free of his embrace* **3** to injure (a limb or joint) by a sudden twist ▷ *n* **4** a violent twist or pull **5** an injury to a limb or joint, caused by twisting it **6** a feeling of sadness experienced on leaving a person or place: *it would be a wrench to leave Essex after all these years* **7** a spanner with adjustable jaws ▶ HISTORY Old English *wrencan*

wrest *vb* **1** to take (something) away from someone with a violent pull or twist **2** to seize forcibly by violent or unlawful means: *she must begin to wrest control of the army and the police* ▶ HISTORY Old English *wræstan*

wrestle *vb* **-tling, -tled 1** to fight (someone) by grappling and trying to throw or pin him or her to the ground, often as a sport **2 wrestle with** to struggle hard with (a person, problem, or thing): *I wrestled with my conscience* ▶ HISTORY Old English *wræstlian* > **wrestler** *n*

wrestling *n* a sport in which each contestant tries to overcome the other either by throwing or pinning him or her to the ground or by forcing a submission

wretch *n* *old-fashioned* **1** a despicable person **2** a person pitied for his or her misfortune ▶ HISTORY Old English *wrecca*

w

wretched (retch-id) *adj* **1** in poor or pitiful circumstances: *a vast wretched slum* **2** feeling very unhappy **3** of poor quality: *the wretched state of the cabbages* **4** *informal* undesirable or displeasing: *what a wretched muddle* > **wretchedly** *adv* > **wretchedness** *n*

wriggle *vb* **-gling, -gled** **1** to twist and turn with quick movements: *he wriggled on the hard seat* **2** to move along by twisting and turning **3 wriggle out of** to avoid (doing something that one does not want to do): *he wriggled out of donating blood* ▷ *n* **4** a wriggling movement or action ▶ HISTORY Middle Low German *wriggeln*

wring *vb* **wringing, wrung** **1** Also: **wring out** to squeeze water from (a cloth or clothing) by twisting it tightly **2** to twist (a neck) violently **3** to clasp and twist (one's hands) in anguish **4** to grip (someone's hand) vigorously in greeting **5** to obtain by forceful means: *to wring concessions from the army* **6 wring someone's heart** to make someone feel sorrow or pity ▶ HISTORY Old English *wringan*

wringer *n* same as **mangle²** (sense 1)

wrinkle *n* **1** a slight ridge in the smoothness of a surface, such as a crease in the skin as a result of age ▷ *vb* **-kling, -kled** **2** to develop or cause to develop wrinkles ▶ HISTORY Old English *wrinclian* to wind around > **wrinkled** or **wrinkly** *adj*

wrist *n* **1** the joint between the forearm and the hand **2** the part of a sleeve that covers the wrist ▶ HISTORY Old English

wristwatch *n* a watch worn strapped round the wrist

writ *n* a formal legal document ordering a person to do or not to do something ▶ HISTORY Old English

write *vb* **writing, wrote, written** **1** to draw or mark (words, letters, or numbers) on paper or a blackboard with a pen, pencil, or chalk **2** to describe or record (something) in writing: *he began to write his memoirs* **3** to be an author: *he still taught writing, but he didn't write* **4** to write a letter to or correspond regularly with someone: *don't forget to write!* **5** *informal, chiefly US & Canad* to write a letter to (someone): *I wrote him several times* **6** to say or communicate in a letter or a book: *in a recent letter a friend wrote that everything costs more in Russia now* **7** to fill in the details for (a cheque or document) **8** *computers* to record (data) in a storage device **9 write down** to record in writing: *write it down if you find it too embarrassing to talk about* ▶ HISTORY Old English *writan*

write off *vb* **1** *accounting* to cancel (a bad debt) from the accounts **2** to dismiss from consideration: *he wrote her off as a tense woman* **3** to send a written request (for something): *he wrote off for leaflets on the subject* **4** *informal* to damage (a vehicle) beyond repair ▷ *n* **write-off** **5** *informal* a vehicle that is damaged beyond repair

write out *vb* **1** to put into writing or reproduce in full form in writing **2** to remove (a character) from a television or radio series: *another actress is to be written out of the BBC soap*

writer *n* **1** a person whose job is writing; author **2** the person who has written something specified: *the writer of this letter is pretty dangerous*

write up *vb* **1** to describe fully, complete, or bring up to date in writing: *she would write up her diary in bed* ▷ *n* **write-up** **2** a published account of something, such as a review in a newspaper or magazine: *I see the Herald didn't give you a very good write-up*

writhe *vb* **writhing, writhed** to twist or squirm in pain: *writhing in agony* ▶ HISTORY Old English *writhan*

writing *n* **1** something that has been written: *the writing on the outer flap was faint* **2** written form: *permission in writing* **3** short for **handwriting** **4** a kind or style of writing: *creative writing* **5** the work of a writer: *Wilde never mentioned chess in his writing*

written *vb* **1** the past participle of **write** ▷ *adj* **2** recorded in writing: *written permission*

WRNS (formerly, in Britain) Women's Royal Naval Service

wrong *adj* **1** not correct or accurate: *the wrong answers* **2** acting or judging in error; mistaken: *do correct me if I'm wrong* **3** not in accordance with correct or conventional rules or standards; immoral: *this group argues that even gently slapping a child is wrong* **4** not intended or appropriate: *I ordered the wrong things; you've picked the wrong time to ask such questions* **5** being a problem or trouble: *come on, I know when something's wrong* **6** not functioning properly: *there's something wrong with the temperature sensor* **7** denoting the side of cloth that is worn facing inwards ▷ *adv* **8** in a wrong manner: *I guessed wrong* **9 get someone wrong** to misunderstand someone: *don't get me wrong—I'm not making threats* **10 get something wrong** to make a mistake about something: *he had got his body language wrong* **11 go wrong a** to turn out badly or not as intended **b** to make a mistake **c** (of a machine) to stop functioning properly: *pilots must be able to react instantly if the automatic equipment suddenly goes wrong* ▷ *n* **12** something bad, immoral, or unjust: *how can such a wrong be redressed?* **13 in the wrong** mistaken or guilty ▷ *vb* **14** to treat (someone) unjustly **15** to think or speak unfairly of (someone) ▶ HISTORY Old English *wrang* injustice > **wrongly** *adv*

wrongdoing *n* immoral or illegal behaviour > **wrongdoer** *n*

wrong-foot *vb* **1** *sport* to play a shot in such a way as to catch (an opponent) off-balance: *he constantly wrong-footed his opponent with fine passing* **2** to gain an advantage over (someone) by doing something unexpected: *China wrong-footed Vietnam by supporting the peace plan*

wrongful *adj* unjust or illegal: *wrongful imprisonment* > **wrongfully** *adv*

wrote *vb* the past tense of **write**

W

wrought (rawt) *vb* **1** *old-fashioned* a past of **work**
▷ *adj* **2** *metallurgy* shaped by hammering or beating: *wrought copper and brass*

wrought iron *n* a pure form of iron with a low carbon content, often used for decorative work

wrung *vb* the past of **wring**

WRVS (in Britain) Women's Royal Voluntary Service

wry *adj* **wrier, wriest** *or* **wryer, wryest 1** drily humorous; sardonic: *wry amusement* **2** (of a facial expression) produced by twisting one's features to denote amusement or displeasure: *a small wry smile twisted the corner of his mouth* ▶ HISTORY Old English *wrīgian* to turn > **wryly** *adv*

wrybill *n* a New Zealand plover whose bill is bent to one side enabling it to search for food beneath stones

wryneck *n* a woodpecker that has a habit of twisting its neck round

wt. weight

WTO World Trade Organization

WV West Virginia

WWI World War One

WWII World War Two

WWW World Wide Web

WY Wyoming

wych-elm *or* **witch-elm** *n* a Eurasian elm with long pointed leaves ▶ HISTORY Old English *wice*

WYSIWYG *n, adj* *computers* what you see is what you get: referring to what is displayed on the screen being the same as what will be printed out

W

x *maths* **1** (along with *y* and *z*) an unknown quantity **2** the multiplication symbol

X **1** indicating an error, a choice, or a kiss **2** indicating an unknown, unspecified, or variable factor, person, or thing: *Miss X* **3** the Roman numeral for ten **4** (formerly) indicating a film that may not be publicly shown to anyone under 18: since 1982 replaced by symbol 18

x-axis *n maths* a reference axis, usually horizontal, of a graph along which the *x*-coordinate is measured

X-chromosome *n* the sex chromosome that occurs in pairs in the females of many animals, including humans, and as one of a pair with the Y-chromosome in males

Xe *chem* xenon

xenon *n chem* a colourless odourless gas found in minute quantities in the air. Symbol: Xe ▶ HISTORY Greek: something strange

xenophobia (zen-oh-**fobe**-ee-a) *n* hatred or fear of foreigners or strangers > **xenophobic** *adj*
- ■ **WORD HISTORY**
- ■ 'Xenophobia' comes from the Greek words
- ■ *xenos*, meaning 'foreigner' or 'stranger', and
- ■ *phobos*, meaning 'fear'.

xerophyte *n bot* a plant such as a cactus, which is adapted for growing or living in dry surroundings

Xerox (**zeer**-ox) *n trademark* **1** a machine for copying printed material **2** a copy made by a Xerox machine ▷ *vb* **3** to produce a copy of (a document) using such a machine

Xhosa (**kawss**-a) *n* (*pl* **-sa** *or* **-sas**) a member of a Black people living in the Republic of South Africa **2** the language of this people > **Xhosan** *adj*

Xmas (**eks**-mass) *n informal* short for **Christmas** ▶ HISTORY from the Greek letter *chi* (X), first letter of *Khristos* Christ

XML *n* extensible markup language: a computer language used in text formatting

X-rated *adj* **1** (formerly, in Britain) (of a film) considered suitable for viewing by adults only **2** *informal* involving bad language, violence, or sex: *an X-rated conversation*

X-ray *or* **x-ray** *n* **1** a stream of electromagnetic radiation of short wavelength that can pass through some solid materials **2** a picture produced by exposing photographic film to X-rays: used in medicine as a diagnostic aid, since parts of the body, such as bones, absorb X-rays and so appear as opaque areas on the picture ▷ *vb* **3** to photograph, treat, or examine using X-rays

X-ray diffraction *n physics* the scattering of X-rays on contact with matter, resulting in changes in radiation intensity, which is used for studying atomic structure

xylem (**zile**-em) *n bot* a plant tissue that conducts water and mineral salts from the roots to all other parts ▶ HISTORY Greek *xulon* wood

xylene (**zile**-lean) *n chem* a hydrocarbon existing in three isomeric forms, all three being colourless flammable volatile liquids used as solvents and in the manufacture of synthetic resins, dyes, and insecticides ▶ HISTORY Greek *xulon* wood

xylophone (**zile**-oh-fone) *n music* a percussion instrument consisting of a set of wooden bars played with hammers ▶ HISTORY Greek *xulon* wood + *phōnē* sound > **xylophonist** *n*

Yy

y *maths* (along with *x* and *z*) an unknown quantity

Y **1** an unknown, unspecified, or variable factor, number, person, or thing **2** *chem* yttrium

ya *interj* *S African* yes

yabby *n, pl* **-bies** *Austral* **1** a small freshwater crayfish **2** a marine prawn used as bait ► HISTORY from a native Australian language

yacht (yott) *n* **1** a large boat with sails or an engine, used for racing or pleasure cruising ▷ *vb* **2** to sail or cruise in a yacht ► HISTORY obsolete Dutch *jaghte* > **yachting** *n, adj*

yachtsman *or fem* **yachtswoman** *n, pl* **-men** *or* **-women** a person who sails a yacht

yahoo *n, pl* **-hoos** a crude, brutish, or obscenely coarse person ► HISTORY after the brutish creatures in *Gulliver's Travels*

Yahweh *or* **Yahveh** *n* *Bible* a personal name of god ► HISTORY Hebrew YHVH, with conjectural vowels

yak¹ *n* a Tibetan ox with long shaggy hair ► HISTORY Tibetan *gyag*

yak² *slang* *n* **1** noisy, continuous, and trivial talk ▷ *vb* **yakking, yakked** **2** to talk continuously about unimportant matters ► HISTORY imitative

yakka *n* *Austral & NZ, informal* work ► HISTORY from a native Australian language

Yale lock *n* *trademark* a type of cylinder lock using a flat serrated key ► HISTORY after L. *Yale*, inventor

Yalta Conference *n* *history* a conference held in 1945, when US, Soviet, and British leaders met to plan the final defeat and occupation of Nazi Germany

yam *n* **1** a twining plant of tropical and subtropical regions, cultivated for its starchy roots which are eaten as a vegetable **2** the sweet potato ► HISTORY Portuguese *inhame*

yammer *informal* *vb* **1** to whine in a complaining manner ▷ *n* **2** a yammering sound **3** nonsense or jabber ► HISTORY Old English *geōmrian* to grumble

Yang *n* See **Yin and Yang**

yank *vb* **1** to pull (someone or something) with a sharp movement: *I yanked myself out of the water* ▷ *n* **2** a sudden pull or jerk ► HISTORY origin unknown

Yank *n* *slang* a person from the United States

Yankee *n* **1** *slang* same as **Yank 2** a person from the Northern United States ▷ *adj* **3** of or characteristic of Yankees ► HISTORY perhaps from Dutch *Jan Kees* John Cheese, nickname for English colonists

yap *vb* **yapping, yapped** **1** to bark with a high-pitched sound **2** *informal* to talk at length in an annoying or stupid way ▷ *n* **3** a high-pitched bark **4** *slang* annoying or stupid speech ► HISTORY imitative > **yappy** *adj*

yarborough *n* *Bridge, whist* a hand in which no card is higher than nine ► HISTORY supposedly after the second earl of *Yarborough*, said to have bet a thousand to one against its occurrence

yard¹ *n* **1** a unit of length equal to 3 feet (0.9144 metre) **2** *naut* a spar slung across a ship's mast to extend the sail ► HISTORY Old English *gierd* rod, twig

yard² *n* **1** a piece of enclosed ground, often adjoining or surrounded by a building or buildings **2** an enclosed or open area where a particular type of work is done: *a shipbuilding yard* **3** *US, Canad & Austral* the garden of a house **4** *US & Canad* the winter pasture of deer, moose, and similar animals ► HISTORY Old English *geard*

Yard *n* **the Yard** *Brit, informal* short for **Scotland Yard**

yardang *n* *geol* (in arid areas) a ridge formed by wind erosion, often parallel to the direction of the prevailing wind

yardarm *n* *naut* the outer end of a ship's yard

yardstick *n* **1** a measure or standard used for comparison: *there's no yardstick for judging a problem of this sort* **2** a graduated measuring stick one yard long

yarmulke (yar-mull-ka) *n* a skullcap worn by Jewish men ► HISTORY Yiddish

yarn *n* **1** a continuous twisted strand of natural or synthetic fibres, used for knitting or making cloth **2** *informal* a long involved story **3 spin a yarn** *informal* to tell such a story ► HISTORY Old English *gearn*

yarrow *n* a wild plant with flat clusters of white flowers ► HISTORY Old English *gearwe*

yashmak *n* a veil worn by a Muslim woman to cover her face in public ► HISTORY Arabic

yaw *vb* **1** (of an aircraft or ship) to turn to one side or from side to side while moving ▷ *n* **2** the act or movement of yawing ► HISTORY origin unknown

yawl *n* **1** a two-masted sailing boat **2** a ship's small boat ► HISTORY Dutch *jol* or Middle Low German *jolle*

yawn *vb* **1** to open one's mouth wide and take in air deeply, often when sleepy or bored **2** to be open wide as if threatening to engulf someone or something: *the doorway yawned blackly open at the end of the hall* ▷ *n* **3** the act or an instance of yawning ► HISTORY Old English *geonian* > **yawning** *adj*

yaws *n* an infectious disease of tropical climates characterized by red skin eruptions ► HISTORY Carib

y-axis *n* *maths* a reference axis, usually vertical, of a graph along which the *y*-coordinate is measured

Yb *chem* ytterbium

Y-chromosome *n* the sex chromosome that occurs as one of a pair with the X-chromosome in the males of many animals, including humans

yd yard (measure)

ye¹ (**yee**) *pron old-fashioned or dialect* you ▶ HISTORY Old English *gē*

ye² *adj* (definite article) *old-fashioned or jocular* the: *ye olde Rose and Crown pub* ▶ HISTORY a misinterpretation of *the*, written with the old letter thorn (Þ), representing *th*

yea *interj* **1** *archaic* yes ▷ *adv* **2** *archaic or literary* indeed or truly: *they wandered about the church, yea, even unto the altar* ▶ HISTORY Old English *gēa*

yeah *interj informal, spoken* same as **yes**

year *n* **1** the time taken for the earth to make one revolution around the sun, about 365 days **2** the twelve months from January 1 to December 31 **3** a period of twelve months from any specified date **4** a specific period of time, usually occupying a definite part or parts of a twelve-month period, used for some particular activity: *the financial year* **5** a group of people who have started an academic course at the same time **6 year in, year out** regularly or monotonously, over a long period **7 years a** a long time: *the legal case could take years to resolve* **b** age, usually old age: *a man of his years* ▶ HISTORY Old English *gēar*

yearbook *n* a reference book published once a year containing details of events of the previous year

yearling *n* an animal that is between one and two years old

yearly *adj* **1** occurring, done, or appearing once a year or every year **2** lasting or valid for a year: *the yearly cycle* ▷ *adv* **3** once a year

yearn *vb* **1** to have an intense desire or longing: *he often yearned for life in a country town* **2** to feel tenderness or affection: *I yearn for you* ▶ HISTORY Old English *giernan* > **yearning** *n, adj*

yeast *n* a yellowish fungus used in fermenting alcoholic drinks and in raising dough for bread ▶ HISTORY Old English *giest* > **yeasty** *adj*

yebo *interj* S African, informal* yes ▶ HISTORY Zulu *yebo* yes, I agree

yell *vb* **1** to shout, scream, or cheer in a loud or piercing way ▷ *n* **2** a loud piercing cry of pain, anger, or fear ▶ HISTORY Old English *giellan*

yellow *n* **1** the colour of a lemon or an egg yolk **2** anything yellow, such as yellow clothing or yellow paint: *painted in yellow* ▷ *adj* **3** of the colour yellow; of the colour of a lemon or an egg yolk **4** *informal* cowardly or afraid **5** having a yellowish complexion ▷ *vb* **6** to make or become yellow or yellower ▶ HISTORY Old English *geolu* > **yellowish** *or* **yellowy** *adj*

yellow-belly *n, pl* -**bellies** *slang* a coward > **yellow-bellied** *adj*

yellow belly *n Austral* a freshwater food fish with yellow underparts

yellow card *n soccer* a piece of yellow pasteboard raised by a referee to indicate that a player has been booked for a serious violation of the rules

yellow fever *n* an acute infectious tropical disease causing fever and jaundice, caused by certain mosquitoes

yellowhammer *n* a European songbird with a yellowish head and body ▶ HISTORY origin unknown

Yellow Pages *pl n trademark* a telephone directory that lists businesses under the headings of the type of business or service they provide

yelp *vb* **1** to utter a sharp or high-pitched cry of pain ▷ *n* **2** a sharp or high-pitched cry of pain ▶ HISTORY Old English *gielpan* to boast

yen¹ *n, pl* **yen** the standard monetary unit of Japan ▶ HISTORY Japanese *en*

yen² *informal n* **1** a longing or desire ▷ *vb* **yenning, yenned 2** to have a longing ▶ HISTORY perhaps from Chinese *yän* a craving

yeoman (**yo**-man) *n, pl* -**men** *history* a farmer owning and farming his own land ▶ HISTORY perhaps from *yongman* young man

yeoman of the guard *n* a member of the ceremonial bodyguard (**Yeomen of the Guard**) of the British monarch

yeomanry *n* **1** yeomen collectively **2** (in Britain) a former volunteer cavalry force

yes *interj* **1** used to express consent, agreement, or approval, or to answer when one is addressed **2** used to signal someone to speak or keep speaking, enter a room, or do something ▷ *n* **3** an answer or vote of yes **4** a person who answers or votes yes ▶ HISTORY Old English *gēse*

yes man *n* a person who always agrees with his or her superior in order to gain favour

yesterday *n* **1** the day before today **2** the recent past ▷ *adv* **3** on or during the day before today **4** in the recent past

yet *conj* **1** nevertheless or still: *I'm too tired to work, yet I have to go on* ▷ *adv* **2** up until then or now: *this may be her most rewarding book yet* **3** still: *yet more work to do* **4** now (as contrasted with later): *not ready for that yet* **5** eventually in spite of everything: *I'll break your spirit yet!* **6 as yet** up until then or now ▶ HISTORY Old English *gīeta*

yeti *n* same as **abominable snowman** ▶ HISTORY Tibetan

yew *n* an evergreen tree with needle-like leaves, red berries, and fine-grained elastic wood ▶ HISTORY Old English *īw*

Y-fronts *pl n trademark* men's or boys' underpants that have a front opening within an inverted Y shape

YHA (in Britain) Youth Hostels Association

Yiddish *n* **1** a language derived from High German, spoken by Jews in Europe and elsewhere by Jewish emigrants, and usually written in the Hebrew alphabet ▷ *adj* **2** of this language ▶ HISTORY German *jüdisch* Jewish

yield *vb* **1** to produce or bear **2** to give as a return: *some of his policies have yielded large savings* **3** to give up control of; surrender **4** to give way, submit, or surrender, through force or persuasion: *the players finally yielded to the weather* **5** to agree (to): *governments too weak to say no repeatedly yielded to petitions for charters* **6** to grant or allow: *to yield right* *of way* ▷ *n* **7** the amount produced ▸ HISTORY Old English *gieldan*

yielding *adj* **1** compliant or submissive **2** soft or flexible: *he landed on a yielding surface rather than rock or board*

Yin and Yang *n* two complementary principles of Chinese philosophy: Yin is negative, dark, and feminine, Yang is positive, bright, and masculine ▸ HISTORY Chinese *yin* dark + *yang* bright

yippee *interj* an exclamation of joy, pleasure, or anticipation

YMCA Young Men's Christian Association

yob or **yobbo** *n, pl* **yobs** or **yobbos** *Brit, Austral & NZ, slang* a bad-mannered aggressive youth ▸ HISTORY perhaps back slang for *boy*
> **yobbish** *adj*

yodel *vb* **-delling, -delled** or US **-deling, -deled** **1** to sing with abrupt changes back and forth between the normal voice and falsetto, as in folk songs of the Swiss Alps ▷ *n* **2** the act or sound of yodelling ▸ HISTORY German *jodeln* (imitative)
> **yodeller** or US **yodeler** *n*

yoga *n* **1** a Hindu system of philosophy aiming at spiritual, mental, and physical wellbeing by means of deep meditation, prescribed postures, and controlled breathing **2** a system of exercising involving such meditation, postures, and breathing

- ■ **WORD HISTORY**
- ■ 'Yoga' comes from Sanskrit *yoga*, meaning
- ■ 'union'. The practice of yoga was intended to
- ■ produce a mystical union between the
- ■ practitioner and the Supreme Being.

yogi *n* a person who practises or is a master of yoga

yogurt or **yoghurt** *n* a slightly sour custard-like food made from milk curdled by bacteria, often sweetened and flavoured with fruit ▸ HISTORY Turkish

yoke *n* **1** a wooden frame with a bar put across the necks of two animals to hold them together so that they can be worked as a team **2** a pair of animals joined by a yoke **3** a frame fitting over a person's shoulders for carrying buckets **4** an oppressive force or burden: *people are still suffering under the yoke of slavery* **5** a fitted part of a garment to which a fuller part is attached ▷ *vb* **yoking, yoked 6** to put a yoke on **7** to unite or link ▸ HISTORY Old English *geoc*

yokel *n disparaging* a person who lives in the country, esp. one who appears simple and old-fashioned ▸ HISTORY perhaps from dialect *yokel* green woodpecker

yolk *n* the yellow part in the middle of an egg that provides food for the developing embryo ▸ HISTORY Old English *geoloca*

Yom Kippur *n* an annual Jewish holiday celebrated as a day of fasting, with prayers of penitence ▸ HISTORY Hebrew *yōm* day + *kippūr* atonement

yon *adj* **1** *chiefly Scot & N English dialect* that: *yon dog* ▷ *adv* **2** yonder: *he flicked glances hither and yon* ▷ *pron* **3** *chiefly Scot & N English dialect* that person or

thing: *yon was a pretty sight* ▸ HISTORY Old English *geon*

yonder *adv* **1** over there ▷ *adj* **2** situated over there: *a tree at yonder waterfall* ▸ HISTORY Old English *geond*

yonks *pl n Brit, informal* a very long time: *he must have been planning this for yonks* ▸ HISTORY origin unknown

yoo-hoo *interj* a call to attract a person's attention

yore *n* **of yore** a long time ago: *in days of yore* ▸ HISTORY Old English *geāra*

yorker *n cricket* a ball bowled so as to pitch just under or just beyond the bat ▸ HISTORY probably after the *Yorkshire* County Cricket Club

Yorkist *English history n* **1** a supporter of the royal House of York, esp. during the Wars of the Roses ▷ *adj* **2** of or relating to the supporters or members of the House of York

Yorkshire pudding *n* a baked pudding made from a batter of flour, eggs, and milk, often served with roast beef ▸ HISTORY from *Yorkshire*, county in NE England

Yoruba *n* **1** a member of a people of West Africa **2** the language of this people

you *pron* **1** (refers to) the person or people addressed: *can I get you a drink?* **2** (refers to) an unspecified person or people in general: *stick to British goods and you can't go wrong* ▷ *n* **3** *informal* (refers to) the personality of the person being addressed: *that hat isn't really you* ▸ HISTORY Old English *ēow*

young *adj* **1** having lived or existed for a relatively short time **2** having qualities associated with youth: *their innovative approach and young attitude appealed to him* **3** of or relating to youth: *he'd been a terrorist himself in France in his young days* **4** of a group representing the younger members of a larger organization: *Young Conservatives* ▷ *pl n* **5** young people in general: *that never seems very important to the young* **6** offspring, esp. young animals: *a deer suckling her young* ▸ HISTORY Old English *geong* > **youngish** *adj*

youngster *n* a young person

your *adj* **1** of, belonging to, or associated with you: *ask your doctor to make the necessary calls* **2** of, belonging to, or associated with an unspecified person or people in general: *it is not right to take another baby to replace your own* **3** *informal* used to indicate all things or people of a certain type: *these characters are not your average housebreakers* ▸ HISTORY Old English *ēower*

yours *pron* **1** something belonging to you: *my reputation is better than yours* **2** your family: *a blessed Christmas to you and yours* **3** used in closing phrases at the end of a letter: *yours sincerely; yours faithfully* **4** **of yours** belonging to you: *that husband of yours*

yourself *pron, pl* **-selves** **1 a** the reflexive form of *you* **b** used for emphasis: *you've stated publicly that you yourself use drugs* **2** your normal self: *you're not yourself today*

youth *n* **1** the period between childhood and maturity **2** the quality or condition of being young, immature, or inexperienced: *his youth told against him in the contest* **3** a young man or boy **4** young people collectively: *there is still hope for today's youth* **5** the freshness, vigour, or vitality associated with being young ▶ **HISTORY** Old English *geogoth*

youth club *n* a club that provides leisure activities for young people

youthful *adj* **1** vigorous or active: *the intermediate section was won by a youthful grandmother* **2** of, relating to, possessing, or associated with youth: *youthful good looks* > **youthfully** *adv*

> **youthfulness** *n*

youth hostel *n* an inexpensive lodging place for young people travelling cheaply

YouTube *n* a website on which subscribers can post video files

yowl *vb* **1** to produce a loud mournful wail or cry ▷ *n* **2** a wail or howl ▶ **HISTORY** Old Norse *gaula*

yo-yo *n, pl* **-yos 1** a toy consisting of a spool attached to a string, the end of which is held while it is repeatedly spun out and reeled in ▷ *vb* **yo-yoing, yo-yoed 2** to change repeatedly from one position to another ▶ **HISTORY** originally a trademark for this type of toy

YT Yukon Territory

ytterbium (it-**terb**-ee-um) *n chem* a soft silvery element that is used to improve the mechanical properties of steel. Symbol: Yb ▶ **HISTORY** after *Ytterby*, Swedish quarry where discovered

yttrium (**it**-ree-um) *n chem* a silvery metallic element used in various alloys and in lasers. Symbol: Y ▶ **HISTORY** see YTTERBIUM

yuan *n, pl* **-an** the standard monetary unit of the People's Republic of China ▶ **HISTORY** Chinese *yüan* round object

yucca *n* a tropical plant with spiky leaves and white flowers ▶ **HISTORY** from a Native American language

yucky *or* **yukky** *adj* **yuckier, yuckiest** *or* **yukkier, yukkiest** *slang* disgusting or nasty ▶ **HISTORY** from *yuck*, exclamation of disgust

Yugoslav *adj* **1** of the former Yugoslavia ▷ *n* **2** a person from the former Yugoslavia

Yule *n literary or old-fashioned* Christmas or the Christmas season: *Yuletide*

- ■ **WORD HISTORY**
- ■ Although 'Yuletide' is an archaic word virtually
- ■ synonymous with 'Christmas-time', Yule (Old
- ■ English *geola*) was actually a pagan festival. It
- ■ went on for twelve days around the time of the
- ■ winter solstice.

yummy *slang adj* **-mier, -miest 1** delicious or attractive: *yummy sauces* ▷ *interj* **2** Also: **yum-yum** an exclamation indicating pleasure or delight, as in anticipation of delicious food ▶ **HISTORY** *yum-yum* (imitative)

yuppie *n* **1** a young highly-paid professional person, esp. one who has a fashionable way of life ▷ *adj* **2** typical of or reflecting the values of yuppies: *a yuppie accessory* ▶ **HISTORY** *y(oung) u(rban)* or *u(pwardly mobile) p(rofessional)*

yuppify *vb* **-fies, -fying, -fied** to make yuppie in nature: *Mount Pleasant was being yuppified*

> **yuppification** *n*

YWCA Young Women's Christian Association

Y

Zz

z¹ or **Z** *n, pl* **z's, Z's** or **Zs 1** the 26th and last letter of the English alphabet **2 from A to Z** See **a** (sense 3)

z² *maths* (along with *x* and *y*) an unknown quantity

Z *chem* atomic number

zakat *n Islam* a tax paid by all Muslims to help poor people in their community ▶ HISTORY Arabic

zany (**zane**-ee) *adj* **zanier, zaniest** comical in an endearing way

■ **WORD HISTORY**
■ 'Zany' comes from Italian *zanni*, meaning
■ 'clown'. 'Zanni' is the Venetian form of the
■ Italian name *Giovanni*, meaning 'John', and was
■ the name often given to comic characters in
■ medieval Italian plays.

zap *vb* **zapping, zapped** *slang* **1** to kill, esp. by shooting **2** to change television channels rapidly by remote control **3** to move quickly ▶ HISTORY imitative

zeal *n* great enthusiasm or eagerness, esp. for a religious movement ▶ HISTORY Greek *zēlos*

zealot (**zel**-lot) *n* a fanatic or an extreme enthusiast > **zealotry** *n*

zealous (**zel**-luss) *adj* extremely eager or enthusiastic > **zealously** *adv*

zebra *n, pl* **-ras** or **-ra** a black-and-white striped African animal of the horse family ▶ HISTORY Old Spanish: wild ass

zebra crossing *n Brit* a pedestrian crossing marked by broad black and white stripes: once on the crossing the pedestrian has right of way

zebu (**zee**-boo) *n* a domesticated ox of Africa and Asia, with a humped back and long horns ▶ HISTORY French

zed *n* the British and New Zealand spoken form of the letter *z*

zee *n* the US spoken form of the letter *z*

Zeitgeist (**tsite**-guyst) *n* the spirit or general outlook of a specific time or period ▶ HISTORY German, literally: time spirit

Zen *n* a Japanese form of Buddhism that concentrates on learning through meditation and intuition

Zend-Avesta *n* the Zoroastrian scriptures (the **Avesta**), together with the traditional interpretive commentary known as the **Zend**

zenith *n* **1** the point in the sky directly above an observer **2** the highest or most successful point of anything: *he was at the zenith of his military career*

▶ HISTORY Arabic *samt arrās* path over one's head > **zenithal** *adj*

zephyr (**zef**-fer) *n* a soft gentle breeze ▶ HISTORY Greek *zephuros* the west wind

zeppelin *n* a large cylindrical rigid airship ▶ HISTORY named after Count Ferdinand von Zeppelin, German aeronautical pioneer

zero *n, pl* **-ros** or **-roes 1** the cardinal number between +1 and −1 **2** the symbol, 0, representing this number **3** the line or point on a scale of measurement from which the graduations commence **4** the lowest point or degree: *my credibility is down to zero* **5** nothing or nil **6** the temperature, pressure, etc. that registers a reading of zero on a scale ▷ *adj* **7** amounting to zero: *zero inflation* **8** *meteorol* (of visibility) limited to a very short distance ▷ *vb* **-roing, -roed 9** to adjust (an instrument or scale) so as to read zero ▷ See also **zero in on** ▶ HISTORY Arabic *sifr* empty

zero gravity *n* the state of weightlessness

zero hour *n* **1** *mil* the time set for the start of an operation **2** *informal* a critical time, usually at the beginning of an action

zero in on *vb* **1** to aim a weapon at (a target) **2** to concentrate one's attention on

zero population growth *n* the condition in which population numbers remain static since births and immigration do not exceed deaths and emigration

zero-rated *adj* denoting goods on which the buyer pays no value-added tax

zest *n* **1** invigorating or keen excitement or enjoyment: *he has a zest for life and a quick intellect* **2** added interest, flavour, or charm: *he said that she would provide a new zest for his government* **3** the peel of an orange or lemon, used as flavouring ▶ HISTORY French *zeste* > **zestful** *adj*

Zeus *n Greek myth* the ruler of the gods

ziggurat *n* (in ancient Mesopotamia) a temple in the shape of a pyramid ▶ HISTORY Assyrian *ziqqurati* summit

zigzag *n* **1** a line or course having sharp turns in alternating directions ▷ *adj* **2** formed in or proceeding in a zigzag ▷ *adv* **3** in a zigzag manner ▷ *vb* **-zagging, -zagged 4** to move in a zigzag ▶ HISTORY German *zickzack*

zilch *n informal* nothing ▶ HISTORY origin unknown

Zimmer *n trademark* a tubular frame with rubber feet, used as a support to help disabled or infirm people walk

zinc *n chem* a brittle bluish-white metallic element that is used in alloys such as brass to form a protective coating on metals, and in battery electrodes. Symbol: Zn ▶ HISTORY German *Zink*

zinc chloride *n chem* an odourless soluble poison used in manufacturing parchment paper, preserving wood, for embalming and as a medical astringent and antiseptic

zinc ointment *n* a medicinal ointment consisting of zinc oxide, petroleum jelly, and paraffin

zinc oxide *n chem, pharmacol* a white insoluble powder used as a pigment and in making zinc ointment

zing *n* **1** *informal* the quality in something that makes it lively or interesting **2** a short high-pitched buzzing sound, like the sound of a bullet or vibrating string ▸ HISTORY imitative

zinnia *n* a plant of tropical and subtropical America, with solitary heads of brightly coloured flowers ▸ HISTORY after J. G. Zinn, botanist

Zion *n* **1** the hill on which the city of Jerusalem stands **2 a** the modern Jewish nation **b** Israel as the national home of the Jewish people **3** *Christianity* heaven

Zionism *n* a political movement for the establishment and support of a national homeland for Jews in what is now Israel > **Zionist** *n, adj*

zip *n* **1** *Brit* Also called: **zip fastener** a fastener with two parallel rows of metal or plastic teeth, one on either side of a closure, which are interlocked by a sliding tab **2** *informal* energy or vigour **3** a short sharp whizzing sound, like the sound of a passing bullet ▸ *vb* **zipping, zipped 4** (often foll. by *up*) to fasten with a zip **5** to move with a sharp whizzing sound: *bullets zipped and ricocheted all around us* **6** to hurry or rush ▸ HISTORY imitative

zircon *n mineral* a hard mineral consisting of zirconium silicate, used as a gemstone and in industry ▸ HISTORY German *Zirkon*

zirconium *n chem* a greyish-white metallic element, occurring chiefly in zircon, that is exceptionally corrosion-resistant. Symbol: Zr

zit *n slang* a spot or pimple

zither *n* a musical instrument consisting of numerous strings stretched over a flat box and plucked to produce notes ▸ HISTORY Greek *kithara* > **zitherist** *n*

zloty *n, pl* **-tys** or **-ty** the standard monetary unit of Poland ▸ HISTORY Polish: golden

Zn *chem* zinc

zodiac *n* **1** an imaginary belt in the sky within which the sun, moon, and planets appear to move, and which is divided into 12 equal areas called **signs of the zodiac,** each named after the constellation which once lay in it **2** *astrol* a diagram, usually circular, representing this belt ▸ HISTORY Greek *zōidion* animal sign, from *zōion* animal > **zodiacal** *adj*

zombie or **zombi** *n, pl* **-bies** or **-bis 1** a person who appears to be lifeless, apathetic, or totally lacking in independent judgment **2** a corpse brought to life by witchcraft

■ **WORD HISTORY**

■ 'Zombie' comes from an African word *zumbi*, ■ meaning a 'fetish' or 'good-luck charm'.

zone *n* **1** a region, area, or section characterized by some distinctive feature or quality: *a demilitarized zone* **2** *geog* one of the divisions of the earth's surface according to temperature **3** a section on a transport route **4** *maths* a portion of a sphere between two parallel lines intersecting the sphere **5** *NZ* a catchment area for a specific school ▸ *vb* **zoning, zoned 6** to divide (a place) into zones for different uses or activities ▸ HISTORY Greek *zōnē* girdle > **zonal** *adj* > **zoning** *n*

zonked *adj Brit, Austral & NZ, slang* **1** highly intoxicated with drugs or alcohol **2** exhausted ▸ HISTORY imitative

zoo *n, pl* **zoos** a place where live animals are kept, studied, bred, and exhibited to the public ▸ HISTORY from *zoological garden*

zooid (**zoh**-oid) *n* **1** any independent animal body, such as an individual of a coral colony **2** a cell or body produced by an organism and capable of independent motion, such as a gamete ▸ HISTORY Greek *zōion* animal

zool. 1 zoological **2** zoology

zoological garden *n* the formal term for **zoo**

zoology *n* the study of animals, including their classification, structure, physiology, and history ▸ HISTORY Greek *zōion* animal + -LOGY > **zoological** *adj* > **zoologist** *n*

zoom *vb* **1** to move very rapidly: *the first rocket zoomed into the sky* **2** to increase or rise rapidly: *stocks zoomed on the American exchange* **3** to move with or make a continuous buzzing or humming sound ▸ *vb* **4** the sound or act of zooming **5** a zoom lens ▸ HISTORY imitative

zoom in or **out** *vb photog, films, television* to increase or decrease rapidly the magnification of the image of a distant object by means of a zoom lens

zoom lens *n* a lens system that can make the details of a picture larger or smaller while keeping the picture in focus

zoophyte (**zoh**-a-fite) *n* any animal resembling a plant, such as a sea anemone ▸ HISTORY Greek *zōion* animal + *phuton* plant

Zoroastrianism (zorr-oh-**ass**-tree-an-iz-zum) or **Zoroastrism** *n* the religion founded by the ancient Persian prophet Zoroaster, based on the concept of a continuous struggle between good and evil > **Zoroastrian** *adj*

Zr *chem* zirconium

zucchetto (tsoo-**ket**-toe) *n, pl* **-tos** *RC Church* a small round skullcap worn by clergymen and varying in colour according to the rank of the wearer ▸ HISTORY Italian

zucchini (zoo-**keen**-ee) *n, pl* **-ni** or **-nis** *chiefly US, Canad & Austral* a courgette ▸ HISTORY Italian

Zulu *n* **1** (*pl* **-lus** or **-lu**) a member of a tall Black people of Southern Africa **2** the language of this people

zygote *n* the cell resulting from the union of an ovum and a spermatozoon ▸ HISTORY Greek *zugōtos* yoked

Z

Unique Survival Guide

Contents

UNIQUE SURVIVAL GUIDE

Introduction

The ability to write and communicate well is one of the keys to success at school and beyond.

In this supplement, you will find practical guidance on writing for different purposes, making presentations, punctuation, spelling and grammar, with tips to help you do your best in the CXC exam.

In addition to this, you will find a guide to writing CVs and help with writing for business, so you can use this supplement whenever and whatever you are writing. You should soon see an improvement in your writing skills.

Improving your writing style

- The more you read, the better your writing will become, since you will find it easier to recognize what works and what does not.
- Use a thesaurus to expand your vocabulary and look up words you don't know; precise and thoughtful word choices from a wide-ranging vocabulary make for more stimulating reading.
- Think about the tone of what you are writing. Avoid using informal and slang terms in a formal piece; by the same token, if you are writing a personal letter or an e-mail, a more informal tone may be appropriate.
- Try varying the length of your sentences to make your writing read more interestingly.
- You may find it useful to read your work aloud to check that you have expressed yourself clearly.
- If a sentence does not read well as it is, try rearranging it. Just moving the end of a sentence to the beginning can work wonders.

Finding the right reference materials

Before starting on a piece, you will probably already have material from your lessons, reading list and notes. You may want to supplement this, however, with information from:

- a library or family reference books;
- the Internet;
- TV and radio programmes;
- people with first-hand experience of your chosen topic.

If you are new to using the Internet, make sure you know the best ways to refine your searches. Try looking at the search tips provided by the search engines or asking a teacher or an experienced Internet surfer for advice. This will help you avoid wasting time wading through screenfuls of irrelevant hits.

Remember that not all websites are equally reliable; concentrate on academic and other authoritative sites, such as government ones or those of well-known institutions.

Writing a bibliography

It is important to acknowledge the information that you use. There are different styles that are recommended by different subjects, like APA or MLA. They require you to include the name of the author, the name of the text, the publishing information and the page number. As you do your research you should write down this information.

Planning

If you are writing an essay or report, plan it before you start. This means:

- thinking through your ideas to make sure you have a clear picture of the subject and of how you are going to tackle it;
- thinking about the person or group for whom you are writing, what they need to know and how it should be presented;
- deciding what you are going to include in the introduction, development and conclusion as well as in each paragraph.

Your written plan may consist of just a few key words per heading, or else contain quotations, ideas and sentences to help you stay on track. Include all the ideas you have under each heading at the planning stage even if you reject some afterwards. This will make it less likely that you will forget something vital when you write your piece.

REMEMBER
The more you practise your essay-planning skills, the faster you will become, and the more successful your essays will be.

Some golden rules

General

- <u>Keep checking the title or the question you are answering to ensure that you are keeping to the point.</u>
- Don't lose sight of the person or group for whom you are writing.
- Avoid irrelevant detail.
- Make sure that what you write makes sense and that your argument follows logically.
- Watch that you are not endlessly repeating a particular word or expression.
- Don't try to write in an overcomplicated style.
- Always check what you write in terms of sense, spelling and punctuation (including apostrophes).

Structure and paragraphing

- Don't clutter paragraphs with too many ideas. Aim for one unifying idea per paragraph.
- Sketch out what point each paragraph is covering at or near the start of it.
- Develop the idea logically.
- Try to organize your paragraphs so that they lead on naturally from one another.
- Use signposting words to show the progress of an argument, e.g.:
  firstly, *finally* to show progress;
  moreover, *what is more*, *in addition* to provide support for a case;
  however, *nevertheless*, *on the other hand* to introduce a counter-argument;
  in conclusion, *to summarize* to round up.

You may find it useful to make a list of these and other expressions that are used in a similar way for future reference.

Sentences

- Link sentences together logically.
- Avoid sentences that are longer than three lines. If it looks too long, break it up.
- Use short sentences for impact, followed by longer sentences to explore an idea.
- Avoid saying the same thing twice in a sentence. Make every word count.

Writing for different purposes

Giving information

As with any writing, think about the person or group for whom you are writing and what and how much they need to be told. Summarize the facts briefly, clearly, objectively and in a logical order using simple language. If working on a computer, try experimenting with different page layouts and type sizes to help divide up the information and draw the reader's attention to the most important facts.

Explaining

Think about your audience and how much or how little you need to explain. Plan your explanation so that it follows a sensible order and is easy to understand.

Describing

When writing descriptively, your aim is to show the reader how interesting aspects look, taste, sound or feel through the use of carefully chosen words and contrasts. Avoid using too many adjectives at once. It is generally better to pick a strong adjective that captures a feeling or impression rather than using three less punchy ones. It is often useful to use comparison, metaphor and simile.

Persuading

When writing to persuade, you need to sound reasonable and trustworthy. Avoid ranting as it is likely to distance your readers. Think about who you are writing for and get them on your side by appealing to their aspirations and interests. Alternatively, you may be able to shame them into supporting a worthwhile cause by highlighting the differences between their circumstances and those of the less fortunate group for whom you are seeking support.

Advising

Tailor the style of your advice to the person or group for whom it is meant. If it is personal advice, a more informal style may be appropriate. Give the advantages and disadvantages of any options you propose. To make your advice sound well thought out, back it up with facts or an anecdote.

UNIQUE SURVIVAL GUIDE

Arguing

When presenting an argument, you need to look at both sides of it, even if you focus more attention on the side you support. Structure your piece logically. Try to sum up the key points and draw conclusions from these.

Make sure your line of argument is reasonable and takes all the necessary facts into account. Do justice to the opposing side and never resort to abusive comments or statements you cannot back up.

Analysis, review and comment

Look at a variety of newspapers and magazines to see how journalists analyse, review and comment on current affairs. Note how their approaches and focuses vary to suit their differing readerships.

As when explaining or arguing, you should first establish the main facts and then move on to analysis, review or comment. The essential difference between the three is this:

- analysis: an objective exploration of the facts
- review: a detached presentation of the facts followed by impressions and opinions
- comment: an opinion, either personal or political, on the overall topic

An important part of text analysis is examining the language that is used. You should be able to identify various features.

- Tone: the attitude expressed by the speaker, conveying the mood or emotion in the work.
- Register: the level of formality of the work, such as slang, informal or formal.
- Code: the language used by a specific group.
- Style: the manner of statement, including form, structure and language.
- Syntax: the way in which words are ordered and connected to make phrases or sentences.
- Morphology: the way in which words can change their form, for example to show a change of tense or to become plural.

Writing essays

Before starting

- Read the question closely, look up any unfamiliar words and, if a quotation is included, make sure you know its context.
- Pay close attention to the verbs used in the title.

Analyse	Break up into parts; investigate
Compare	Look for similarities and differences between
Contrast	Bring out the differences between
Define	Give the meaning of
Describe	Give a detailed account of
Discuss	Investigate, giving reasons for and against
Distinguish	Indicate the differences between
Enumerate	List in order
Evaluate	Give a judgment based on evidence
Examine	Look closely into
Explain	Give reasons for
Explore	Consider from a variety of viewpoints
Illustrate	Make clear by using examples
Interpret	Show the meaning of
Justify	Respond to the most obvious objections concerning
Outline	Give only the main features of
Relate	Tell in order
Relate to	Show how one thing is connected to another
State	Present in a clear form
Summarize	Give a concise account of, omitting details
Trace	Show the development of a topic from a particular point

- Think about the question and note down any ideas that occur to you in rough, including any further questions you might want to raise which are triggered by the essay title.
- Write out a plan of what to include in your introduction, conclusion and development, if not in every paragraph.
- Write any quotations, data and facts that you want to include beside the relevant points in your plan.

Introduction

This should typically be a concise paragraph that includes a short, clear statement of the subject you are going to discuss, your definition of any technical terms used in the question and an indication of how you are going to tackle the question.

Remember to make it interesting to engage your readers.

Development

Keep to your plan, be aware of the question at all times and keep your writing relevant.

Conclusion

Like the introduction, this will be fairly short and should summarize the essence of the essay, bringing together all of the major points and referring back to the question to demonstrate that you have answered it. Don't be afraid to make a bold statement on the subject at this point or to include a choice quotation which supports your conclusion; similarly, if there are further questions that have occurred to you in the course of planning or writing the essay, you could include these here, provided they offer an interesting natural progression from what has gone before.

Word counts

Make sure you keep to the required number of words. Doing otherwise is likely to lose you marks.

Writing summaries

Summarizing stories, articles and reports is a skill everyone employs from time to time, whether it is explaining to a friend what happened in the latest episode of a television serial, or whether it is condensing the findings of a long report for the benefit of others.

What are the features of a good summary?

- It is concise and to the point.
- It provides an accurate overview of what was discussed in the original.
- It is objective and therefore does not reveal the views of the summarizer.
- It is written in the summarizer's own words and does not plagiarize.
- From the start, it contains phrases which clarify whose views are being presented, e.g. *Murphy argues that…*; *the writer claims that…* .

Tips for summary writing

- Read the text once or twice, mentally identifying the main points.
- Next, jot these down from memory.
- Go through the text highlighting or noting any other key points made by the writer and amending your jottings as necessary.
- Now write the summary in your own words as concisely as you can or as required.
- After you have done this, reread the text to check that you have mentioned all the essential points.
- If a word count has been given, count the words you have used and make sure your summary is the right length. If not, you will need to edit it. If it is too long you can leave out the examples that give support to the facts.
- Once the summary is the right length and contains everything it should, reread it to ensure that it follows on logically and that you have not accidentally cut something vital for it to make sense.

Timing

If you are working under exam conditions, you may need to leave enough time to make a clean copy of your summary. If time is too short, be especially careful to make all alterations neatly and clearly.

Writing reports

For some subjects, such as geography or sociology, you may need to write a report presenting the results of a field trip or project.

Points to remember

Keep all of the information you gather during the field trip in one place.

Stick to the introduction-development-conclusion model.

Avoid using *I* or *we*; adopt an objective tone instead: *The field trip was... The information gathered showed that... The aim of...*

Clear presentation

Where helpful, use simple graphs, bar and pie charts to represent data.

These provide a quick overview of the results and can aid understanding.

Organize the information into different sections, giving each one a clear heading to help the reader navigate the report.

If there are a lot of sections, it may be helpful to number them. If one section is composed of several smaller sections, number them as follows:

> 1. [*Section heading*]
> 1.1 [*Subsection heading*]
> 1.2 [*Subsection heading*]

If you need to include a large amount of data in the report but do not want to interrupt the flow of the text, put it in an appendix.

Be consistent in your presentation; pay attention to the numbering of sections and appendices.

The professional look

To achieve a really professional-looking report, try structuring as follows:

▶ **Title page**
This includes the title, author and date.
▶ **Abstract**
This is a short summary of the report, including aims, methods and conclusions.

- ▶ **Contents**
  This lists the different sections of the report along with the corresponding page numbers.

- ▶ **Introduction**
  This explains the purpose of the report and the methods used.

- ▶ **Development**
  This contains the information you have collected for the report in a number of clearly headed sections.

- ▶ **Conclusion and recommendations**
  This is a brief, easy-to-understand section saying what you have found and what you think needs to be done.

- ▶ **Appendices**
  These contain additional information that has been omitted from the main body of the text but which is relevant to the report as a whole.

- ▶ **Notes**
  These give details that would be too cumbersome to include in the main text.

- ▶ **Bibliography**
  This gives an alphabetical list of books, journals, websites, newspapers, etc. to which you have referred during your investigation or in the text itself. Included with the source is the author, title, publisher and place and date of publication.

Writing up experiments

As you will doubtless already be used to writing up experiments in chemistry, physics or biology following the *methods–results–conclusion* model, this section deals with slightly longer experiments.

Be clear, be concise

Explain why and how the experiment was performed, what results were obtained and what conclusions can be drawn.

Imagine your reader has never carried out the experiment and make no assumptions about his or her knowledge of the processes involved. Explain each step of the experiment fully, logically and concisely. Avoid using *I* or *we*; adopt an objective tone instead: *The solution was placed... The aim of...*

Clear presentation

Organize the information into different sections, giving each one a clear heading to help the reader navigate.

If there are a lot of sections, it may be helpful to number them. If one section is composed of several smaller sections, number them as follows:

  1. [*Section heading*]
  1.1 [*Subsection heading*]
  1.2 [*Subsection heading*]

Be consistent in your presentation; pay attention to the numbering of sections and figures.

Always include units with quantities, whether in the text, table column headings, graph axes or diagrams (mm, kg, cm^3).

The professional look

To achieve a really professional-looking write-up of your experiment, try structuring as follows:

▶ **Title**
   This indicates what the experiment is about.

▶ **Aims**
   A brief summary of the aims of the experiment.

▶ **Introduction**
   This details the theory behind the experiment and any equations to be used in the calculation of results, chemical reaction pathways, and principles

behind the methodology. It explains the assumption on which the experiment is based, e.g. *If A is mixed with B, it produces C.*

▶ **The Experiment**
This describes what occurred during the experiment: what you did and what happened as a result. Instead of using *I* or *we*, it adopts an objective tone: *The aim of the experiment was... The magnesium ribbon was placed in the flame...* This part of the write-up can be divided up if it helps present the information more clearly, e.g. **Description of Apparatus** (with diagrams) or **Method** (saying how you did what you did, including any special precautions or techniques used).

▶ **Results**
Where possible, these are shown in tables and graphs to aid comprehension. Also included are any external factors which may affect the results, e.g. room temperature, pressure.

▶ **Discussion**
Here, the results of the experiment are compared with the theory or expected behaviour described in the introduction. Also detailed are any calculations based on the results.

▶ **Conclusion**
This is a summary of the conclusions you draw from the experiment.

Writing in exams

If panic strikes because you cannot see any questions you know you can tackle, relax and read the questions again. Provided you have done your revision, there will be a number of questions you are equipped to answer. However, do not be tempted to bend questions to allow you to make use of essay material you have worked on previously.

Top tips

▶ **Revision time**
- Revision does not have to be dull. Help motivate yourself by watching any relevant television programmes advised by your teachers and by going on field trips designed to help your studies.
- Read round your subjects as advised by your teachers.
- Look at past papers, noting the kind of questions, the amount of detail required to answer them and so on.
- Get used to sketching out a brief plan to answer each question. You should spend no more than a couple of minutes doing this.

- Practise answering these questions under timed conditions. Be strict with yourself – practising writing against the clock outside the exam room will give you more confidence and focus inside it.
- Revise and learn any mnemonics that will help you remember facts, dates, spellings, etc.
- Don't procrastinate. Decide to do a realistic amount of revision each week and try to keep to it. On the other hand, don't be obsessive about it; allow some time for relaxation.
- Don't endlessly write out revision plans when you could be revising. Be honest with yourself; these are often a way of putting off doing that all-important revision.

REMEMBER
The best results are likely to be achieved by those who read over their work regularly. Well-planned revision is essential, however, for refreshing your memory and ensuring you do your best in your exams.

▶ **Before the exam**
- Instead of talking to the other candidates outside the exam room, take the opportunity to <u>collect your thoughts</u> and prepare.
- Have to hand a short <u>list of quotations</u> or any other brief information you need to memorize before entering the exam room. Read it on the way to the exam but do not forget to leave it outside.

▶ **During the exam**
- Make sure you <u>know how many questions you have to answer</u>, then work out how much time you need to spend on each one, giving the most time to the questions that carry the most marks.
- <u>Read each question</u> slowly and <u>carefully</u>. Make sure that you have understood it properly before you jot down your <u>plan</u>. Sketch out a brief plan for any essay, plus any quotations you wish to include.
- Refer back to the plan as you write, <u>ticking off the points</u> as you go. This way you will know you have included everything you meant to.
- At the end of each paragraph, link it back to your question. This way you know you are on the right track.

▶ **In the last few minutes**
Try to complete all your answers with a few minutes to spare at the end of the exam; this is to give you time to <u>double-check your spelling</u> and <u>punctuation</u> and to reassure yourself you have answered all the <u>questions</u> or parts of them that are required. If you discover you have missed out a vital point, you will still be able to add it at this stage.

▶ Points to watch

- <u>Read each question carefully</u>. Don't assume it is identical to one you have answered as a practice question.

- To ensure you remember to <u>answer each part of a complex question</u>, underline or highlight the elements that you need to consider.

- If there is a <u>choice of questions</u>, make sure that <u>you pick the ones you can answer best</u> and which allow you the most scope to show off with thorough, focused answers.

- If asked to comment on a piece of writing containing some unlikely views, <u>think about whether it is meant to be taken literally</u> or whether the writer is making use of irony or satire.

- <u>Plan the essay</u> before you start writing. This leads to more focused, relevant answers.

- <u>Keep to the point</u>. Avoid the temptation to go off at a tangent.

- <u>Split your time between the questions</u>. Don't fall into the trap of spending all your time on question 1.

- <u>Make use of paragraphs</u> to show each new idea. This makes it easier for the examiner to follow your argument. If your ideas are clearly presented, there is a greater chance of your gaining good marks.

- <u>Use commas</u> to indicate natural breaks in sentences; if in doubt, insert commas where you would pause for breath.

▶ Common errors

- <u>Spelling mistakes</u> are common in exam scripts. If you often misspell a word, invent a mnemonic to help you remember it correctly.

- Candidates often make silly errors such as writing *there* when they meant *their*, or *by* instead of *buy*, etc. <u>Always check your work carefully</u> to ensure you have not made careless and preventable mistakes.

- <u>Apostrophes</u> are often misused, with the most common problems being a confusion of *it's* and *its* or an inappropriate apostrophe at the end of a word that is merely plural.

- Be careful not to write *should of, could of* and *would of* instead of *should have, could have* and *would have*.

▶ Extra marks

- Use your vocabulary to its fullest extent.

- Show the examiner that you know your subject by including a range of quotations, where appropriate, and briefly mentioning any secondary texts.

- Show you have understood the question by relating points back to it.

- Clarify any potentially confusing parts of the question.

Giving a presentation

As with writing, one of the keys to giving a good presentation is organizing your material. Your topic should be clearly stated, logically thought through and explained interestingly enough to hold the interest of your audience.

Notes

- Don't learn your presentation by heart or write it down word for word. Such strategies make for very boring presentations.
- Make notes to refer to during the presentation in case you dry up. If you write these on index cards, you will be able to put each card to the back of the pile once you have used it and will therefore not lose your place.
- Try practising your presentation in front of a supportive friend or family member. Ask him or her to point out any distracting habits you may have and which you should avoid; for example, fiddling with your hair or saying "you know" too often can be very off-putting to your audience.

Content

- Try to start with something exciting but relevant to make your audience sit up and listen.
- Give an introductory outline of your talk and make sure you stick to it in what follows.
- Avoid introducing a completely new subject later or changing the tone of your presentation halfway through.
- Use linking sentences to lead from one point to the next.
- Give specific examples – this gives the audience something to discuss in a question-and-answer session.
- If you are presenting an argument, build from the weakest to the strongest point.
- Include a few light jokes or puns to entertain your audience, but remember that they should be appropriate to the overall tone.
- Try to bring your own perspective to the presentation material – there may be facts that are known to people in your audience but anything extra you can add will be of interest.
- Don't be afraid to express your opinions.
- Consider including some aspect of audience participation, provided it is not intimidating and provided you are not dependent on getting a reaction – audiences do not always cooperate. In general, some degree of interaction makes a presentation more interesting.

- Your presentation should end with a quick recap of the main points and a strong, and preferably exciting, conclusion.

Visual aids

- Use visual aids to illustrate your presentation, provided they are simple, useful and clearly visible from the back of the room.

- Do not overdo the number of visual aids; the last thing you want is to overwhelm your audience with too much visual information and to distract them from your talk.

- If you have access to a computer, you might like to use a presentation program such as PowerPoint®. Keep the number of slides to a minimum and have a maximum of four bullet points per slide. Keep each one short and to the point.

- If giving your audience hand-outs, make sure you have enough for everyone. Do not rely on being able to do photocopies at the last minute.

Timing

- Practise giving your presentation in advance, making sure that you tailor it to fit the time you have been given. Failing to complete your talk by the time the next speaker is due to come on can be a disaster. Similarly, finding that there is too much time to fill can be very stressful and look unprofessional.

- When you practise your presentation and when you give it, make sure you do not talk too quickly. Take your time. Don't speak at the same rate as you would when chatting to a friend. Slow down and pause for breath between points. This also helps the audience know when you are moving on to a different subject.

Venue

- If you are going to use a computer or interactive whiteboard in your presentation, make sure you are familiar with how it works beforehand. Fumbling for an on-switch in front of your audience will not increase your confidence.

- Make sure there are enough seats to accommodate your audience.

- Familiarize yourself with the venue and its acoustics to ensure that you feel comfortable speaking and know how to project your voice into all corners of the room.

You, your body language and your voice

- If you feel nervous before you begin speaking, practise deep breathing and rehearse your opening sentences to yourself.

- Stand up or sit straight and keep your chin up as you talk. Posture says a lot about how you feel and a positive, strong stance will both improve your confidence and convince the audience that you have something interesting to say.

- If you are nervous, standing behind a lectern or table may help you feel less vulnerable, as well as give you something to lean on and to put any notes on.

- Speak sincerely and with warmth.

- Vary your tone of voice. Slightly exaggerate the rising and falling notes to add interest.

- Vary your pace, but do not talk too fast as you will lose your audience.

- Smile from time to time. It will relax you and encourage a link with your audience.

- Look members of your audience very briefly in the eye when you can, though avoid looking at any one individual for too long. Look round the faces with a sweeping glance.

- Allow pauses for audience reaction.

- Don't be put off if you make a mistake during the presentation. Apologize quickly and move on.

Working within a group

- An important part of working in a group is effective communication. This means that everyone should get a turn to contribute and be listened to and respected. Don't let the more confident people talk over the quieter ones.

- You should assign roles within the group – the leader, the person who records the decisions, the time-keeper and the presenter.

- Keep focused on the task. It's easy to get sidetracked when you are working with other people.

Written conventions to remember

Abbreviations

There are no set rules about how to write abbreviations, but these guidelines will help:

- Use a full stop after any abbreviation that does not end with the final letter of the word.

  e.g. *Co.*, *Jan.*, *misc.*

- A full stop is unnecessary when the last letter of the abbreviation is the final letter of the word.

  e.g. *Dr*, *Mr*, *Mrs*, *Revd*, *Mgr*

- Treat as words acronyms and common abbreviations for countries, organizations and institutions formed from initial letters.

  e.g. *NATO*, *AIDS*, *UK*, *EU*, *VAT*

- Only use abbreviations in formal writing when it would look odd to write the full form of the word.

- The first time you mention an abbreviation that is uncommon in everyday speech and writing, make sure you always explain what it is by giving the full form too.

Capital letters

Use a capital letter in the following cases:

- for the first word in a sentence: *Let's go*
- for the first word in each line of most poems: *Hence, loathed Melancholy, Of Cerberus, and blackest Midnight born...*
- to begin each word in a person's name: *Seamus Heaney*
- for official, royal and courtesy titles: *Prime Minister, Prince William*
- to begin all significant words in book and film titles: *Far from the Madding Crowd, Raiders of the Lost Ark*
- for trade names: *Hoover*®
- for the names of countries: *Sri Lanka*
- for the names of peoples and languages: *Spanish, Thai*
- for religions, their gods and their holy books: *Islam, God, Koran*
- for adjectives derived from proper nouns: *Islamic, Russian*

However, use a lower-case letter when referring to points of the compass, the seasons and for the first word after a semicolon:

It was a long hot <u>s</u>ummer; <u>we</u> were heading <u>n</u>orth to escape the heat.

Numbers

- Write out numbers from one to ten, use numerals from 11–99, but use common sense to judge if the number should be written in words, e.g. two million, five thousand.

- Hyphenate numbers from 21–99 if written out; again, use common sense to decide. If it will look unwieldy, avoid writing it out in words.

- Use commas when giving figures greater than 999: 1,354; 3,078,000.

Using quotations and references

- Put " ..." or '...' around quotations if the words are not your own.

- You can include a brief quotation inside a sentence: *Macbeth says life is "a walking shadow".*

- If you are quoting a couple of lines of poetry, show where the line breaks with a slash: *Macbeth calls life "a walking shadow, a poor player, / That struts and frets his hour upon the stage".*

- When quoting a longer piece of poetry, keep the lines and indent the entire section quoted:

  As Macbeth says:
  "Life's but a walking shadow, a poor player,
  That struts and frets his hour upon the stage,
  And then is heard no more".

- Indicate missing words in a quotation with ..., and put square brackets round any words added to make sense: [*he*].

- If quoting the title of a book or film in a handwritten text, underline it. If working on a computer, use italics.

- Indicate your sources, either by using footnotes or briefly in the text immediately after the quotation. Include the title, author's name and, if quoting from a play, the act, scene and line number(s).

- If required, supply a bibliography listing all of your sources, including websites, at the end of the essay. For each source significantly referred to or quoted, you should include: author, title, publisher and place and date of publication. Arrange the sources alphabetically.

Punctuation

Punctuation marks are an essential part of good writing. They help the reader understand what is meant and how something should be read.

Apostrophe '

> **Examiner's top tip**
>
> Misusing or omitting the apostrophe is one of the commonest punctuation errors made by CXC candidates. Remember that, while many Caribbean dialects indicate ownership or possession without an apostrophe, e.g. *the boy pencil*, in Standard English an apostrophe is essential, e.g. *the boy's pencil*. Examiners are sure to notice this sort of mistake, so be careful!

▶ Possession

The apostrophe is used to show that something belongs to someone.

- **'s** is added to the end of singular words:
    e.g. *a child's cry* ◆ *Hannah's book*
- **'s** is added to the end of plural words not ending in **s**:
    e.g. *children's games* ◆ *women's clothes*
- **'** An apostrophe alone is added to plural words ending in **s**:
    e.g. *workers' rights* ◆ *ladies' fashion*
- **'s** is added to the end of names and singular words ending in **s**:
    e.g. *James's car* ◆ *the octopus's tentacles*

    But if the word is a classical Greek name, or an historical building, an apostrophe only is sometimes preferred:
    e.g. *Socrates' Athens* ◆ *St Giles' Cathedral*
- When the possessor is an inanimate object (rather than a living thing), the apostrophe is not used and the word order is changed:
    e.g. *the middle of the street* (not *the street's middle*) ◆ *the front of the house* (not *the house's front*)
- **'s** is added to the end of certain professions or occupations to indicate workplaces:
    e.g. *She's on her way to the doctor's.* ◆ *James is at the hairdresser's.*

To test whether an apostrophe is in the right place, think about who the owner is:
    e.g. *the boy's books* [= the books belonging to the boy]
        the boys' books [= the books belonging to the boys]

- Possession or ownership can also be indicated by possessive adjectives and pronouns:

    e.g. *This is **her** car.* ✦ *This car is **hers**.*

    Never add an apostrophe to a possessive pronoun:

    e.g. *This car is mine* (**not** *mine's*). ✦ *This car is yours* (**not** *your's*).
    This car is his (**not** *his's*). ✦ *This car is hers* (**not** *her's*). ✦ *This car is ours* (**not** *our's*). ✦ *This car is theirs* (**not** *their's*).

▶ **Missing letters and figures**

An apostrophe is used in shortened forms of words where letters have been missed out. Note that only one apostrophe is used in a given position even though several letters may have been missed out from there:

    e.g. *it's* [= *it is* or *it has*] ✦ *he'll* [= *he will*] ✦ *you don't* [= *you do not*]
    he'd have [= *he would have*] ✦ *she'd like* [= *she would like*]
    we'd have liked [= *we would have liked*] ✦ *rock'n'roll* [= *rock and roll*]

- Sometimes the apostrophe is dropped at the beginning of a shortened word. For example, nowadays people usually write **phone** (not *'phone*) and **flu** (not *'flu*).

- An apostrophe is used in front of two figures referring to a year or decade:

    e.g. *French students rioted in '68* [short for *'1968'*]. ✦ *He worked as a schoolteacher during the '80s and early '90s.*

- An apostrophe is **not** used to form the plurals of words:

    e.g. *2 kilos of potatoes* ✦ *The girls laughed.*

    However, an apostrophe **can** be used in plurals of letters and numbers to make them more readable:

    e.g. *p's and q's* ✦ *His 2's look a bit like 7's.* ✦ *She got straight A's in her exams.*

REMEMBER
it's = it is or **it has**   e.g. *It's a holiday today.*
its = belonging to it   e.g. *The dog was scratching its ear.*

Brackets ( )

- Brackets, also called **parentheses**, are used to enclose a word or words which can be left out and still leave a meaningful sentence:

    e.g. *The wooded area (see map below) is approximately 4,000 hectares.* ✦ *This is a process which Hayek (who came to different conclusions) also observed.*

- Brackets are also used to show alternatives or options:

    e.g. *Any student(s) interested in taking part should e-mail me.* ✦ *A goat should give from three to six pints (1.7 to 3.4 litres) of milk a day.*

Note that when the structure of the sentence as a whole demands punctuation after a bracketed section, the punctuation is given *outside* the brackets.

> e.g. *I haven't yet spoken to John (I mean John Maple, my boss), but I have a meeting with him on Friday.* ◆ *For lunch we had sandwiches (pastrami on rye and so on), salami, coleslaw, fried chicken, and potato salad.*

Punctuation is given before the closing brackets only when it applies to the bracketed section rather than to the sentence as a whole:

> e.g. *He's very handsome (positively gorgeous in fact!) and still single.*

Colon :

- Like the semicolon, the colon indicates a break between two main clauses which is stronger than a comma but weaker than a full stop.

- A colon is used in front of a list or explanation:

  > e.g. *I used three colours: green, blue and pink.* ◆ *To be authentic, these garments must be of natural materials: cotton, silk, wool and leather.* ◆ *Nevertheless, the main problem remained: what should be done with the two murderers?*

- The colon is also used after introductory headings:

  > e.g. *Cooking time: about five minutes.* ◆ *Start time: 10 o'clock.*

- The colon is also used, in more formal writing, between two main clauses that are connected:

  > e.g. *It made me feel claustrophobic: what, I wonder, would happen to someone who was really unable to tolerate being locked into such a tiny space?* ◆ *Be patient: the next book in the series has not yet been published.*

- A colon is used in front of the second part of a book title:

  > e.g. *a volume entitled Farming and Wildlife: A Study in Compromise*

- A colon can also be used to introduce direct speech, especially to indicate that what follows is important:

  > e.g. *I said: 'Perhaps your father was right.'*

Comma ,

The comma marks a short pause between elements in a sentence.

- Commas are used to separate **three or more** items in a list or series:

  > e.g. *bread, butter, and jam (but bread and butter)*

  Note that the comma is not always given before the final *and* or *or* in such cases in everyday English:

  > e.g. *dogs, cats, rabbits and hamsters* ◆ *Jim, Mark, Peter or Eddy*

- A comma is used between two long main clauses joined by a conjunction:

    e.g. *He was talking quite loudly, but I couldn't hear him.*

- A comma is often used to separate an introductory word or phrase from the main clause in a sentence, or to separate a subordinate clause or short phrase that comes after the main clause:

    e.g. *If we get another goal, we'll have won the league.* ◆ *He'll be there, come what may.* ◆ *In winter, we usually go skiing.*

- When words like *however*, *therefore* and *moreover* are included in a sentence, these words should be marked off by commas:

    e.g. *The forecasters got it wrong. There was no warning, therefore, of the heavy rain and flooding that hit the south.*

- Commas are also used to separate off a subordinate clause inserted into a main clause:

    e.g. *A new model, which will be made in Spain, is to be introduced.*

- Commas are used to separate the name of a person or group being addressed from the rest of the sentence:

    e.g. *And now, ladies and gentlemen, please raise your glasses in a toast.*

- A comma is used to separate words in direct speech from the rest of the sentence, if there is no question or exclamation mark after the quotation:

    e.g. *"I don't understand this question," said Peter.*

- Commas are also used after reporting verbs such as *say*, *ask* and *exclaim*, when they are followed by a quotation:

    e.g. *Peter said, "Dream on!"*

- Remember that you could also punctuate this last sentence using a colon instead of the comma:

    e.g. *Peter said: "Dream on!"*

- A comma must be used between the day of the month and the year when the two numbers are next to each other:

    e.g. October 29, 1989

Dash –

- The dash is used at the beginning and end of a comment that interrupts the flow of a sentence:

    e.g. *Now children – Kenneth, stop that immediately! – open your books on page 20.*

- The dash (–) also separates off extra information:

    e.g. *Boots and shoes – all shapes, sizes and colours – tumbled out.*

- The dash is also used to indicate a range:

    e.g. *pages 26–42*

Exclamation mark !

The exclamation mark is used after exclamations and emphatic expressions:

    e.g. *I can't believe it!* ✦ *Oh, no! Look at this mess!*

The exclamation mark loses its effect if overused. It is better to use a full stop after a sentence expressing mild excitement or humour:

    e.g. *It was such a beautiful day.*

Full stop .

- A full stop is used to mark the end of a sentence, when it is a statement:

    e.g. *Harry loves football.* ✦ *Norman Manley was born in 1893 and died in 1969.*

- Full stops are used after initials and abbreviations (but see **Abbreviations** under **Written conventions to remember**):

    e.g. *George W. Bush* ✦ *etc.* ✦ *Rev. Adams*

- Remember that a full stop is used after an indirect question or a polite request:

    e.g. *He asked if the bus had left.* ✦ *Will you open your books on page 14.*
      ✦ *I wonder what's happened.* ✦ *She asked him where he was going.*

In American English, the full stop is called a **period**.

> **Examiner's top tip**
>
> Students often fail to notice, and indicate, where one sentence ends and the next one begins. Missing out full stops is a common mistake, and will be marked down by examiners. Remember that a sentence is a group of words which expresses a statement, question or command. A sentence usually has a verb and a subject. Think hard about where each sentence ends, by asking yourself whether what you are looking at is a complete sense unit i.e. a complete thought, idea or piece of information. If so, you need to indicate the end of the sentence by a full stop (or a question mark if a question is being asked).

Hyphen -

The hyphen joins words or parts of words.

- Hyphens are used at the ends of lines where a word has been split, to warn the reader that the word continues on the next line. If the word you need to split is clearly made up of two or more smaller words or elements, you should put the hyphen after the first of these parts. Otherwise, you put the hyphen at the end of a syllable:

    e.g. *wheel-barrow* ✦ *inter-national* ✦ *listen-ing* ✦ *compli-mentary* ✦ *infor-mation*
      ✦ *He was just leaving the house when he remem-*
      bered that he'd left his lunch on the kitchen table.

It is best not to add a hyphen if the word is a short one, or if it would mean writing just one or two letters at the end or beginning of a line. For example, it would be better to write 'unnatural' on the line below, rather than writing 'un-' on one line and 'natural' on the next.

- Prefixes that are used in front of a word beginning with a capital letter always have a hyphen after them:

  e.g. *a wave of anti-British feeling* ◆ *on the steps of the neo-Byzantine cathedral*

- A hyphen is used between two adjectives or noun modifiers that indicate that two countries or groups are involved in something or that an individual has two roles or aspects:

  e.g. *Swedish-Norwegian relations improved* ◆ *the United States-Canada free trade pact* ◆ *mathematician-philosopher*

- A hyphen is also used to indicate that something goes between two places:

  e.g. *the Anguilla-St Kitts flight* ◆ *the New York-Montreal train*

- A hyphen is used to join two or more words that together form an adjective, where this adjective is used *before* the noun it describes:

  e.g. *an up-to-date account* ◆ *a last-minute rush* ◆ *a six-year-old boy*

- The hyphen is omitted when the adjective so formed comes after the noun or pronoun it describes:

  e.g. *The accounts are up to date.* ◆ *It was all rather last minute.* ◆ *He's six years old.*

- Some common compound nouns are usually written with hyphens:

  e.g. *mother-in-law* ◆ *great-grandmother*

- Hyphens can be used to split words that have been formed by adding a prefix to another word, especially to avoid an awkward combination of letters or confusion with another word:

  e.g. *re-elect* ◆ *re-covering furniture* ◆ *re-creation*

Question mark ?

Examiner's top tip

Remember that question marks are only used in direct questions i.e. the actual words of a speaker. If the sentence you are writing is not a direct question, then it should end with a full stop.

So, there is a question mark in *The lady said, 'Where are you going?'* but there is a full stop in *The lady asked where you were going.* This is because, in the second example, the lady's actual words, and their order, have been changed. This is also made clear through the omission of inverted commas in the second example.

The question mark marks the end of a question:

e.g. *When will we be arriving?* ◆ *Why did you do that?* ◆ *Does any of this matter?*
◆ *He's certain to be elected, isn't he?*

- Note that you put a question mark at the end of a question, even if the words in the sentence are not in the normal question order, or some words are omitted. Care is needed here as such a sentence can look, at first sight, like a statement rather than a question:

e.g. *You know he doesn't live here any longer?* (More formally, this would be: *Do you know that he doesn't live here any longer?*)

- A full stop, rather than a question mark, is used after a reported question or an indirect question:

e.g. *George asked when we would be arriving.* ◆ *He asked me where I was going.*
◆ *I wonder what's happened.*

- A full stop also replaces a question mark at the end of a sentence which looks like a question if, in fact, it is really a polite request:

e.g. *Will you please return the completed forms to me?* ◆ *Would you please call my brother and ask him to collect my car.*

Semicolon ;

- The semicolon marks a stronger break than a comma, but a weaker one than a full stop. It is used to mark a break between two main clauses when there is a balance or contrast between the clauses. A useful test to work out when to use a semicolon is to ask yourself whether the two clauses could be written instead as separate sentences, or are linked by **and**, **or**, **but** or **yet**. If the answer is 'yes', then you can use a semicolon. NB: It is quite acceptable to use a full stop in these cases, but a semicolon is preferable if you wish to convey the sense of a link or continuity between the clauses in your narrative. Compare, for example:

The engine roared into life. The propellers began to turn. The plane taxied down the runway ready for takeoff.

The engine roared into life; the propellers began to turn; the plane taxied down the runway ready for takeoff.

Although both examples are grammatically correct, the effect of dividing up the first example into three separate sentences is to focus on each individual action. In the second example, there is a sense of the link between the actions, with each flowing into the next:

e.g. *I'm not that interested in jazz; I prefer classical music.* ◆ *I can see no remedy for this; one can't order him to do it.* ◆ *He knew everything about me; I had never even heard of him.* ◆ *He cannot easily reverse direction and bring interest rates down; yet a failure to do so will almost certainly push the economy into recession.*

- A semicolon is also used to separate items in a list, especially if the listed items are phrases or clauses, which may already contain commas:

    e.g. *The holiday was a disaster: the flight was four hours late; the hotel was overbooked; and it rained for the whole fortnight* ◆ *...when working with the things he seemed to like: their horse, Bonnie; the cart he brought the empty bottles home in; bits of old harness; tools and things.*

Slash, oblique /

The slash separates letters, words or numbers. It is used to indicate alternatives, ratios and ranges, and in website addresses:

    e.g. *he/she/it* ◆ *200 km/hr* ◆ *the 2001/02 accounting year* ◆ *http://www.abcdefg.com*

Speech marks/inverted commas/quotation marks/quotes "" "

- These four terms are used interchangeably. Although these paired punctuation marks may be either single ('') or double ("") and British writers use both, American writers tend to use double speech marks.

- Speech marks mark the beginning and end of direct speech (a speaker's words written down exactly as they were said):

    e.g. *"I will," said Ian.* ◆ *Jo declared abruptly, "We're leaving."*

    Remember that, if the sentence ends with the last word of the quote, then the quote should end with a full stop, question mark or exclamation mark, as appropriate, and then a closing quotation mark (or marks):

    e.g. *"We have to go home."* ◆ *"Are we there yet?"* ◆ *"Hurry up!"*

    If information about the speaker of the quoted material is added, remember that the full stop found at the end of the quote is replaced by a comma. However, a question mark or exclamation mark in this position remains unaffected:

    i.e. *'We have to go home,' said Winston.* ◆ *'Are we there yet?' wailed the children.* ◆ *'Hurry up!' Marcia shouted.*

- Speech marks can be used to indicate the title of a book, poem, piece of music, film or work of art, although italics and underlining are probably more usual:

    e.g. *Have you read "The Lord of the Rings"?* ◆ *music from "Swan Lake"*

- Speech marks are also used to show that a word is being used in an unusual way, or that the word itself is being discussed:

    e.g. *Braille allows a blind person to "see" with the fingers.* ◆ *What is the French for "egg"?*

- Speech marks are not used for indirect or reported speech (what someone has said, but not in their exact words):

    e.g. *Ian said that he would.* ◆ *Jo declared abruptly that they were leaving.*

Spelling rules

- Most people know the rule **i before e, except after c**, when they make the *ee* sound. For example:

ach**ie**ve	br**ie**f	ch**ie**f
gr**ie**ve	n**ie**ce	rel**ie**f
s**ie**ge	th**ie**f	p**ie**ce

c**ei**ling	conc**ei**t	dec**ei**t
dec**ei**ve	rec**ei**pt	rec**ei**ve

but note some common exceptions:

s**ei**ze	prot**ei**n

- Many words can be spelled with either of the endings *-ize* or *-ise* (and *-ization* or *-isation*). Care should be taken, however, because some words can only be spelled with *-ize* and others only with *-ise*.

Verbs (and nouns) only spelled with -ize:

caps**ize**
pr**ize** [= value highly]

Verbs (and nouns) only spelled with -ise:

advert**ise**	desp**ise**	franch**ise**	surpr**ise**
adv**ise**	dev**ise**	improv**ise**	telev**ise**
chast**ise**	disgu**ise**	pr**ise** [= force]	
compr**ise**	exc**ise**	rev**ise**	
comprom**ise**	exerc**ise**	superv**ise**	

- A final silent *e* is dropped when an ending that begins with a vowel is added:

servile + ity	=	servil**ity**
response + ible	=	respons**ible**
tolerate + ing	=	tolerat**ing**
value + able	=	valu**able**
excuse + ed	=	excus**ed**

- But the *e* is kept if an ending beginning with a vowel is added to a word that ends in *-ce* or *-ge* and these letters keep a soft sound:

change + able = change**able**
notice + able = notice**able**
outrage + ous = outrage**ous**
peace + able = peace**able**

- When an ending beginning with a vowel is added to a word that ends in a single vowel + a consonant (other than *h, w, x* and *y*), the consonant is doubled if the stress is on the end of the base form:

  admit + ance = admi**tt**ance
  begin + ing = begi**nn**ing
  occur + ence = occu**rr**ence
  equip + ed = equi**pp**ed
  stop +ing = sto**pp**ing

- When an ending beginning with a vowel is added to a word that ends in a vowel + *l* or *p*, the *l* or *p* is usually doubled:

  cancel + ation = cance**ll**ation
  dial + ing = dia**ll**ing
  fulfil + ed = fulfi**ll**ed
  kidnap + er = kidna**pp**er
  slip + ing = sli**pp**ing

- When the adverb suffix *-ly* is added to an adjective that ends in a consonant followed by *-le*, the *-le* in the adjective is usually dropped:

  gentle + ly = gent**ly**
  idle + ly = id**ly**
  subtle + ly = subt**ly**

- When the adjective suffix *-ous* or *-ary* is added to a word that ends in *-our*, the *u* of the *-our* is dropped:

  glamour + ous = glam**or**ous
  honour + ary = hon**or**ary
  humour + ous = hum**or**ous

- When an ending beginning with *e, i* or *y* is added to a word that ends in *c*, a *k* is added to the *c* to keep its hard sound:

  mimic → mimic**k**ed → mimic**k**ing
  picnic → picnic**k**ing → picnic**k**ed

- When an ending other than *-ing* is added to a word that ends in a consonant + *y*, the *y* usually changes to *i*:

  beauty → beaut**i**ful
  crazy → craz**i**ly
  woolly → wooll**i**er

- But, with certain short adjectives that end in a consonant + y, the -ly ending is added after the y:

  shy → shy**ly**
  wry → wry**ly**

- The plural of a word that ends in a consonant + y is made by changing the y to i and adding -es:

  memory → memor**ies**
  whisky → whisk**ies**

- The plural of a word that ends in a vowel plus y is made by adding -s:

  donkey → donkey**s**
  buoy → buoy**s**
  whiskey → whiskey**s**

- The plural of a word that ends in s, x, z, sh or ch is made by adding -es:

  bus → bus**es**
  mass → mass**es**
  fox → fox**es**
  buzz → buzz**es**
  rash → rash**es**
  match → match**es**

- The suffix -ful is spelt with one l:

  grate**ful**   faith**ful**   cup**ful**

- But -fully is spelt with two:

  grate**fully**   faith**fully**

Words that are sometimes confused

accept – VERB – e.g. *Please accept my apologies.*
except – PREPOSITION & VERB – e.g. *every day except Friday / If we except cats, most animals only kill for food.*

advice – NOUN – e.g. *He gave me some good advice.*
advise – VERB – e.g. *You could go that way but I wouldn't advise it.*

affect – VERB – e.g. *Tiredness affects concentration.*
effect – NOUN & VERB – e.g. *the effects of global warming / prospects for effecting real change*

allude – VERB – e.g. *He never alluded to the difficulties he'd had.*
elude – VERB – e.g. *I recognized his face, but his name eluded me.*

altar – NOUN – e.g. *There were some flowers on the altar.*
alter – VERB – e.g. *His tone altered suddenly.*

ascent – NOUN – e.g. *the first ascent of Everest*
assent – NOUN & VERB – e.g. *The king gave his assent. / He assented.*

aural – ADJECTIVE – e.g. *They use music as a kind of aural wallpaper.*
oral – ADJECTIVE & NOUN – e.g. *You'll have to talk in the oral (exam).*

breath – NOUN – e.g. *There wasn't a breath of wind.*
breathe – VERB – e.g. *Breathe deeply a couple of times.*

broach – VERB – e.g. *She didn't dare broach the subject of a pay rise.*
brooch – NOUN – e.g. *a gold brooch set with emeralds and diamonds*

canvas – NOUN – e.g. *a hammock made from heavy canvas*
canvass – VERB – e.g. *pollsters canvassing opinion*

ceiling – NOUN – e.g. *a high domed ceiling*
sealing – VERB & ADJECTIVE – e.g. *sealing the edges with putty / sealing wax*

cent – NOUN – e.g. *four dollars and fifty cents*
scent – NOUN & VERB – e.g. *the scent of roses / He scented victory.*
sent – VERB – e.g. *Have you sent your Christmas cards yet?*

cereal – NOUN – e.g. *corn and other cereals*
serial – NOUN & ADJECTIVE – e.g. *a TV serial / a serial killer*

chute – NOUN – e.g. *a laundry chute to the basement*
shoot – VERB & NOUN – e.g. *Stop or I'll shoot! / a film shoot*

cite – VERB – e.g. *He could cite several examples.*
sight – NOUN & VERB – e.g. *My sight is failing. / He was sighted in a bar.*
site – NOUN & VERB – e.g. *the site of a battle / It will be sited near shops.*

coarse – ADJECTIVE – e.g. *a coarse cloth which scratched the skin*
course – NOUN & VERB – e.g. *the course of the river / Tears coursed down her cheeks.*

compliment – NOUN & VERB – e.g. *My compliments to the chef. / He complimented her on her dress.*
complement – NOUN & VERB – e.g. *a ship with its full complement of men / wine to complement your meal*

council – NOUN – e.g. *the local council / a council of war*
counsel – VERB & NOUN – e.g. *He counsels victims of crime. / give good counsel*

cue – NOUN & VERB – e.g. *the leading lady's cue / billiard cues / I'll cue you in.*
queue – NOUN & VERB – e.g. *a long queue for tickets / We queued for hours.*

curb – VERB & NOUN – e.g. *You must curb your appetite. / price curbs*
kerb – NOUN – e.g. *The taxi drew up at the kerb.*

currant – NOUN – e.g. *raisins, sultanas and currants*
current – NOUN & ADJECTIVE – e.g. *ocean currents / current affairs*

dairy – NOUN – e.g. – *milk from the local dairy*
diary – NOUN – e.g. – *I'll put the date in my diary.*

dependant – NOUN – e.g. *Do you have children or other dependants?*
dependent – ADJECTIVE – e.g. *We are dependent on aid.*

desert – NOUN & VERB – e.g. *the Gobi Desert / The sentry deserted his post.*
dessert – NOUN – e.g. *Would you like ice cream or fresh fruit for dessert?*

device – NOUN – e.g. *a device for slicing vegetables very thinly*
devise – VERB – e.g. *We've devised a cunning plan.*

draft – NOUN & VERB – *a first draft of the report / He's drafting a reply.*
draught – NOUN – e.g. *There's a draught coming under that door.*

dual – ADJECTIVE – e.g. *Their children have dual nationality.*
duel – NOUN & VERB – e.g. *They fought a duel. / an injury sustained while duelling*

Words that are sometimes confused 33

dying – VERB – e.g. *The weakest are dying first, of hunger and cold.*
dyeing – VERB – e.g. *Have you been dyeing your hair again?*

eerie – ADJECTIVE – e.g. *an eerie silence*
eyrie – NOUN – e.g. *Two unfledged chicks were in the golden eagle's eyrie.*

envelop – VERB – e.g. *A greenish haze seemed to envelop the landscape.*
envelope – NOUN – e.g. *Send a stamped addressed envelope.*

excerpt – NOUN – e.g. *He played an excerpt from a Mozart opera.*
exert – VERB – e.g. *He is keen to exert his influence.*

flair – NOUN – e.g. *a flair for design*
flare – VERB & NOUN – e.g. *His nostrils flared. / a distress flare*

flour – NOUN & VERB – e.g. *Bread is made from flour. / Lightly flour a rolling pin.*
flower – NOUN & VERB – e.g. *wild flowers / It flowers in August.*

forth – ADVERB – e.g. *He ran back and forth.*
fourth – ADJECTIVE & NOUN – e.g. *fourth gear / the fourth of July*

gamble – VERB & NOUN – e.g. *He's gambling on the lottery. / It's a gamble.*
gambol – VERB – e.g. *puppies gambolling in the sunshine*

gilt – NOUN – e.g. *a clock decorated with silver gilt*
guilt – NOUN – e.g. *The evidence proves his guilt.*

hoard – NOUN & VERB – e.g. *a hoard of treasure / He's been hoarding food.*
horde – NOUN – e.g. hordes of noisy football supporters

its – ADJECTIVE & PRONOUN – e.g. *The cat had hurt its paw. / Jo's dog hasn't got brown eyes; its are blue.*
it's – short form – e.g. *It's a lovely day. / It's been fun.*

lead – VERB & NOUN – e.g. *You lead the way. / pipes made of lead*
led – VERB – e.g. *I led the way.*

leant – VERB – e.g. *He leant against the tree.*
lent – VERB – e.g. *She lent me her bike.*

licence – NOUN – e.g. *a driver's licence*
license – VERB – e.g. *licensed to drive heavy goods vehicles*

loath – ADJECTIVE – e.g. *I'm loath to ask him for money.*
loathe – VERB – e.g. *We loathe each other.*

loose – ADJECTIVE & VERB – e.g. *a loose tooth / He loosed the dogs.*
lose – VERB – e.g. *Be careful not to lose your pocket money.*

medal – NOUN – e.g. *a gold medal*
meddle – VERB – e.g. *Don't meddle in other people's affairs.*

miner – NOUN – e.g. *a coal miner*
minor – ADJECTIVE & NOUN – e.g. *a minor problem / a 14-year-old minor*

practice – NOUN – e.g. *a common practice / a dental practice*
practise – VERB – e.g. *He has a law degree but has never practised.*

principal – ADJECTIVE & NOUN – e.g. *the principal reason / the school principal*
principle – NOUN – e.g. *Telling fibs is against my principles.*

precede – VERB – e.g. *summer precedes autumn*
proceed – VERB – e.g. *Let's proceed with the meeting.*

rain – NOUN & VERB – e.g. *We need some rain. / It rained on Friday.*
rein – NOUN & VERB – e.g. *the horse's reins / You must rein in your spending.*
reign – NOUN & VERB – e.g. *the Queen's reign / She has reigned for 50 years.*

stationary – ADJECTIVE – e.g. *The bus skidded and hit a stationary vehicle.*
stationery – NOUN – e.g. *paper, envelopes and other office stationery*

their – ADJECTIVE – e.g. *It's not their fault.*
they're – short form – e.g. *They're not to blame.*
there – ADVERB – e.g. *There is no reason to punish them.*

vain – ADJECTIVE & NOUN – e.g. *He's vain and self-opinionated. / It was all in vain.*
vein – NOUN – e.g. *Veins carry blood back to the heart.*

Grammar

This grammar guide has been written specifically for CXC candidates. It is not a comprehensive grammar; instead we have concentrated on highlighting and explaining the grammatical points that we know cause problems to students. We have identified these areas of difficulty by consulting CXC examiners and teachers.

> **Examiner's top tip**
>
> Get into the habit of pausing briefly after completing your work, and then re-reading it. This will help you to spot, and correct, errors.

The sentence and its structure

▶ **Simple sentences and complex sentences**

- A sentence usually has a **verb** and a **subject**. A **simple sentence** is the most basic type of sentence and has one clause:

    e.g. *She is sitting.* ◆ *Clarence is hungry.* ◆ *Marcie cradled the baby.*

    By adding words or phrases to a simple sentence, we can provide more information:

    e.g. *She is sitting **patiently in the kitchen**.* ◆ *Clarence is **extremely** hungry.*
    ◆ *Marcie **gently** cradled the tiny baby.*

    Sometimes we want to make a statement which is too complex or detailed to be expressed in a single clause. We make statements of this kind by putting two or more clauses together in one sentence.

    A **complex sentence** or **compound sentence** consists of two or more clauses. Remember that a **clause** is a group of words containing a verb; although a clause may be a sentence, more often it forms only part of a sentence.

    In a **complex sentence**, there is at least one **main clause** and a **subordinate clause**. A subordinate clause gives more information about a main clause, and is introduced by a **subordinating conjunction** (such as *because*, *if*, *whereas* or a *wh-* word). Subordinate clauses can come in front of, after, or inside the main clause:

    e.g. *She is sitting down **because she is feeling faint**.* ◆ ***If Clarence is hungry**, he gets really grumpy.* ◆ ***When she had gone**, Desmond sighed.*

    In the examples above, the subordinate clauses are highlighted in bold. In a **compound sentence**, two or more **main clauses** (clauses which refer to two separate actions or situations and which are equally important) are simply linked together with a **coordinating conjunction** (such as):

    e.g. *Abdul packed his gear and walked outside.* ◆ *I like films but I hardly ever go to the cinema.*

Note that the subject of the second clause can be omitted if it is the same as that of the first clause:

> e.g. *I wrote to him but received no reply.*

Questions and orders can also consist of more than one clause:

> e.g. *What will they do if he doesn't come?* ◆ *If he is rude, just leave.*

Examiner's top tip

Remember that a sentence has a capital letter at the beginning and a full stop, question mark or exclamation mark at the end. Students frequently forget this basic rule, and are always marked down in their exams for this.

Agreement

▶ **Singular and plural**

The **singular** is the form of a **count noun** or a verb which you use when referring to one person or thing. The **plural** is the form which you use when referring to more than one person or thing. So, it is very important to make sure that subject and verb are in **agreement**.

▶ **Agreement within a noun group**

A **possessive determiner** (such as **my**, **your**, **his**, **her**, **its**, **our**, **their**) or an adjective in a noun group has the same form whether the noun is singular or plural e.g. **my** hat, **my** hats. However, the determiner **this** has the plural form **these**, and the determiner **that** has the plural form **those**:

> e.g. *Deonath is well on his way to solving **this problem**.* ◆ *He worried about **these problems** all the time.* ◆ ***That person** has been following us all day.* ◆ *For **those people**, however, there was no happy ending.*

Remember that some general determiners, such as **each**, are only used with singular **count nouns**; some, such as **all**, are only used with **uncount nouns** or plural forms of nouns; and some, such as **several** and **many**, are only used with plural forms of nouns:

> e.g. ***Each child** received an apple.* ◆ ***All jewellery** should be removed before the gym lesson.* ◆ ***Several politicians** objected to this new law.*

▶ **Agreement of the verb with a noun group**

When you use a verb in a statement or question, you must choose a singular verb form or a plural verb form to agree with the **subject**:

> e.g. ***My mother loves** her.* ◆ ***They love** each other.* ◆ ***Hilton likes** football but **I prefer** cricket.* ◆ ***The man** who delivered the flowers **has** left behind his cap.*

Examiner's top tip

Pay particular attention to the last example, in which the subject and the verb are separated by a **subordinate clause** containing a noun (*flowers*) which is different in **number** to the **subject** of the main clause (*The man*).

Many students make the mistake of thinking that, because the noun in the subordinate clause and the verb are next to one another, the verb should agree in number with this noun, rather than the subject. As a result, they write: *The man who delivered the flowers **have** left behind his cap.*

The same problem occurs where a noun group consists of a singular noun followed by a plural noun, or vice versa:

e.g. *A battalion of soldiers **is** coming to the rescue. ◆ The harvesting of coffee beans **has** been halted.*

These rules also apply to the use of the **gerund**:

e.g. ***Carrying** heavy bags is very tiring.*

This error in agreement is probably the most common mistake made by CXC students because, in everyday speech, this form of the verb is not used in the Caribbean.

With all verbs except **be**, only one form is used for the **simple past tense**, and modals only have one form, so in these cases no choice regarding agreement needs to be made:

e.g. ***Tracey walked** slowly back toward the store. ◆ They walked towards the gate. ◆ Power must be shared.*

You also have to choose an appropriate verb form when using **there** followed by **be**. The verb form agrees with the noun group after **be**:

e.g. ***There was a car** parked there. ◆ There were no cars outside.*

However, when you are talking about two people or things joined by **and**, you use the singular form of be:

e.g. ***There was a computer and a printer** on the desk.*

▶ **Use of the singular verb form**

The singular form of a verb is used with:

• the singular form of count nouns, uncount nouns, **he**, **she** and **it**

• **this** and **that**

• indefinite pronouns such as **anybody**, **no-one** and **something**

• noun groups referring to a single quantity of something, such as **a lump of sugar** or **a kilo of coffee**.

Note that when you are referring to a period of time or an amount of something, you use a singular verb, even though you are using the plural form of a noun:

e.g. *Twenty years **is** a long time.* • *Three hundred dollars **is** missing.*

▶ **Use of the plural verb form**

The plural form of a verb is used with:

- the plural form of count nouns
- plural nouns such as **clothes** and **goods**:

  e.g. *Cool clothes **are** essential in this climate.*
- **we** and **they**
- **you**, even when referring to just one person:

  e.g. *Thank you, Vera: you **are** always so kind to me.*
- **these** and **those**
- pronouns such as **several** and **many**
- quantifiers such as a **couple of** and **few of**:

  e.g. *A couple of the teachers **are** leaving now.*

Some plural forms of count nouns do not look plural because they do not end in '**s**'. However, they are still used with a plural verb form:

e.g. *All **men are** equal.*

On the other hand, some nouns that end in '**s**' and look plural are uncount nouns and are used with a singular verb form:

e.g. ***Physics** is difficult for me.*

A small group of plural nouns refer to single items that have two linked parts, such as **jeans**, **trousers**, **tights**, and **scissors**. They are used with the plural form of a verb:

e.g. *These **scissors** are sharp.* • *Her **tights** are laddered.*

However, if you refer to one of these items using **a pair of**, you can use a singular or plural verb form:

e.g. *The pair of jeans **was/were** lying on the bedroom floor.*

In the case of **collective nouns**, such as **family** and **government**, you can use a singular or a plural verb form after the singular form of the noun:

e.g. *The family **was/were** gathered in the kitchen.*

Auxiliary verbs

An **auxiliary** or **auxiliary verb** is a verb that is used with a main verb to form a verb group. The auxiliaries **be** and **have** are used to form tenses: **be** is used for continuous tenses, and **have** for perfect tenses. The auxiliary **do** is most often used in questions and negative clauses:

> e.g. I *am* feeling reckless tonight. ✦ *Have* you finished your homework yet?
> ✦ They *have been* looking for you. ✦ *Did* you see him? ✦ I *do* not remember.

The auxiliary **be** is also used to form **passive** verb groups:

> e.g. Thirteen people were injured. ✦ Ten flights from Kingston *have been* cancelled today. ✦ Three broad strategies *are being* adopted.

Auxiliaries are often used without a main verb when the verb has already been used:

> e.g. I didn't want to go but Carlton *did*. ✦ 'Have you been there before?' – 'Yes, I *have*.'

Modal auxiliaries

> **Examiner's top tip**
>
> The use of modal auxiliaries (or **modals**) in Caribbean English is quite different to that of Standard English. Remember to employ Standard English usage, as described below, in the CXC examination.

Modals (can, could, dare, may, might, must, need, shall, should, will and **would)** are also a type of auxiliary verb. They are used, for example, to indicate ability and the possibility or necessity of an event, and to make requests, offers and suggestions. They can also be used to make what you are saying more tactful or polite. A modal is always the first word in a verb group. All modals are followed by the base form of a verb (the infinitive without 'to'), unless the verb has already been mentioned:

> e.g. I *must leave* soon. ✦ The law *will* be changed. ✦ Things *might have been* so different. ✦ She *must have been* dozing.

▶ **Can and could**

Can and **could** are particularly versatile modals. The negative form of **can** is **cannot** or **can't**. **Cannot** is never written 'can not'.

The negative form of **could** is **could not** or **couldn't**. A synonym for these words is **be able to**, and its negative is formed by putting **not**, or another negative word, in front of **able**, or by using the expression **be unable to**. So:

> Many elderly people *cannot* afford computers. ✦ My wife *can't* sew. ✦ It was so dark you *could not* see a thing. ✦ We *were not able* to give any answers.

Ability: the present

Can, **could** and **be able to** are all used to talk about a person's physical, intellectual or learned ability to do something. You use **can** or **be able to** to talk about the ability in the present. **Be able to** is more formal than **can**:

> e.g. *You can all read and write.* ◆ *The sheep are able to move around and they can all lie down.*

Could is also used to talk about ability in the present, but it has a special meaning. If you say that someone **could** do something, you mean that they have the ability to do it, but they haven't yet done so:

> e.g. *We could do a great deal more in this country to educate people.*

Ability: the past

You use **could** or a past form of **be able to** to talk about ability in the past:

> e.g. *He could run faster than anyone else.* ◆ *Many of them couldn't read or write.* ◆ *She wasn't able to complete the crossword.*

If you say that someone **was able to** do something, that usually means that they had the ability to do it and they did it (while **could** does not have this meaning):

> e.g. *After treatment he was able to return to work.* ◆ *The farmers were able to pay the new wages.*

If you want to say that someone had the ability to do something but did not in fact do it, you say that they **could have done** it:

> e.g. *You could have given me some warning!* ◆ *He could have been a little bit tidier.*

If you want to say that someone did not do something because they did not have the ability to do it, you say that they **could not have done it**:

> e.g. *I couldn't have gone with you, because I was in Kingston at that time.*

If you want to say that someone had the ability to do something in the past, although they do not now have this ability, you say that they used to be able to do it:

> e.g. *I used to be able to speak fluent Russian.* ◆ *You used to be able to see the house from here but now it's hidden by new buildings.*

Ability: the future

You use a future form of **be able to** to talk about ability in the future:

> e.g. *I shall be able to answer that question tomorrow.*

Ability: reported speech

Could is often used in reported speech. For example, if a man says 'I can speak Arabic', this would be reported as 'He said he **could** speak Arabic':

> e.g. *Ferguson said that I could ask for a transfer if, after six months, I still don't like the job.*

Possibility: the present and the future

Could and **can** are used to talk about possibility in the present or future. You use **could** to say that there is a possibility that something is or will be the case:

    e.g. *Don't eat it: it **could** be a toadstool.* ♦ *Some people say that there **could** be life on Mars.* ♦ *He was jailed in 1992 and **could** be released next year.*

Might and **may** can be used in a similar way:

    e.g. *It **might** be a trap.* ♦ *Hilton's career **may** be ruined.*

When **might** and **may** are used in this way, **may** is more formal than **might**. If you want to say that it is impossible that something is the case, you use **cannot** or **could not**:

    e.g. *You **cannot** possibly know what he is planning to do.* ♦ *You **can't** get blood from a stone.*

You use **can** to indicate that something is sometimes possible:

    e.g. *Shifts in public opinion **can**, on occasion, have dramatic consequences.*

Possibility: the past

You use **could have** to say that there is a possibility that something was the case in the past:

    e.g. *He **could have** been doing his homework in his room.*

Might have and **may have** can be used in a similar way:

    e.g. *The teacher **might have** recognized the thief.* ♦ *That **may have** been a lucky escape.*

You also use could have to say that there was a possibility of something being the case in the past, although it was not in fact the case:

    e.g. *It **could have** been so much worse.* ♦ *Malik **could have** made a fortune as a lawyer.*

If you want to say that it is impossible that something was the case, you use **could not have**:

    e.g. *She **couldn't have** been drunk because she had been drinking nothing but orange juice all evening.*

▶ **Might and may**

Possibility: the present and the future

You can use **might** or **may** to say that it is possible that something is true or that something will happen in the future:

    e.g. *His political views **might** be the same as yours.* ♦ *This **may** be why women enjoy going back to work.* ♦ *They **might** be able to remember what he said.*

You can use **could** in a similar way, but only in positive sentences:

    e.g. *Don't eat it: it **could** be a toadstool.*

You can use **might well** or **may well** to indicate that it is fairly likely that something is the case:

> e.g. *You **might well** be right.* ✦ *I think that **may well** have been his intention.*

You use **might not** or **may not** to say that it is possible that something is not the case:

> e.g. *He **might not** be in Jamaica at all.* ✦ *That **mightn't** be true.* ✦ *That **may not** seem like a lot of money to you but it's a lot to me.*

You do not use **might not** or **may not** to say that it is impossible that something is the case. Instead you use **could not**, **cannot** or **can't**:

> e.g. *This knowledge **could not** have been gained in any other way.* ✦ *I **cannot** help you unless you tell me the truth.*

Remember that you never use **may** when you are asking if something is possible. So, instead of saying 'May he be right?', you would say 'Might he be right?' or, more usually, 'Could he be right?':

> e.g. ***Might** the film start even earlier?* ✦ ***Could** this be true?* ✦ ***Could** he remember having met her before?*

Possibility: the past

You use **might** or **may** with **have** to say that it is possible that something happened in the past, although you do not know whether it actually happened:

> e.g. *Desmond **might have** secretly married Eugenia.* ✦ *I **may have** seemed to be overreacting.*

Could have can be used in a similar way:

> e.g. *It is just possible that a child **could have** crawled in through this gap in the fence.*

However, if something did not happen and you want to say that there was a possibility of it happening, you can only use **might have** or **could have**; you do not use 'may have'. For example, you say 'If he hadn't hurt his ankle, he **might have** won the race.' You do not say 'If he hadn't hurt his ankle, he may have won the race':

> e.g. *A lot of men, who **might have** died otherwise, were saved because of the policeman's bravery.*

You use **might not** or **may not** with **have** to say that it is possible that something did not happen or was not the case:

> e.g. *They **might not have** considered their behaviour risky.* ✦ *She **mightn't have** been to blame.* ✦ *She **may not have** been ready for motherhood.*

You do not use 'might not' or 'may not' with 'have' to say that it is impossible that something happened or was the case. Instead you use **could not have** or (in British English) **cannot have**:

> e.g. *The sales figures **couldn't have** been wrong: I checked them myself.*
> ◆ *He **cannot have** been serious about leaving Barbados forever.*
> ◆ *A campaign like this **cannot have** been planned in a fortnight.*

▶ **Will (and shall)**

Will and **shall** are used to make statements and ask questions about the future. **Will** and **shall** are not usually pronounced in full when they come after a pronoun. When you write down what someone says, you usually represent **will** and **shall** as 'll and add it to the end of the pronoun:

> e.g. **He'll** *come back.* ◆ **They'll** *join us for the picnic.*

Shall and **will** have the negative forms **shall not** and **will not**. In speech, these are usually shortened to **shan't** and **won't**. **Shan't** is rather old fashioned and is used far less often than **won't**:

> e.g. *I **shan't** ever do that again.* ◆ *You **won't** believe what I'm about to tell you.*

In addition to its role making basic statements about the future, **will** is also used when:

making a prediction:

> e.g. *Shontelle left St Michael at noon, so she **will** be here soon.* ◆ *It's midnight so the children **will** be tucked up in bed.*

making a decision:

> e.g. *I'll take the car so that I'm not late for work.*

stating an intention:

> e.g. *I'll phone you as soon as I get home.*

expressing willingness:

> e.g. *I'll be delighted to put you all up for the night.*

insisting on something:

> e.g. *You **will** stop fighting right now!*

describing behaviour typical of someone:

> e.g. *James **will** never leave his wife.*

It used to be considered correct to write **shall** after I or **we**, and **will** after any other pronoun or noun group. However, most people now write **will** after I and **we**, and this is no longer considered wrong, although **shall** is still sometimes used after I and **we**:

> e.g. *I hope that some day I **will** meet you.* ◆ **We will** *be able to pick you up at 3 o'clock.* ◆ *I **shall** not be able to attend the next committee meeting.*

Ability

Will is sometimes used to say that someone or something is able to do something:

> e.g. This **will cure** anything. ✦ The car **won't start**.

You do not normally use **shall** or **will** in clauses beginning with words and expressions such as **when**, **before** or **as soon as**. You do not say, for example, 'I'll ring as soon as I shall get home.' Instead, you use the simple present tense and say 'I'll ring as soon as I **get** home.'

▶ Would

This modal is used in a number of different ways.

Would is sometimes used with a similar meaning to 'should', when making requests and offers:

> e.g. *If I could help, I **would** be delighted to do anything within my power.* ✦ *I **would** like to ask you one question please.*

Again as a variant of 'should', **would** can be used when you are formally announcing that you are going to do something:

> e.g. *I **would** like to make some general observations.*

The following are some other ways in which you can use **would**.

Please note that you cannot use 'should' in any of these ways.

Talking about the past

You can use **would** to talk about something which happened regularly in the past but which no longer happens:

> e.g. *We **would** normally spend the winter in Miami.* ✦ *She **would** often hear him complaining.* ✦ *When he was a boy, he **would** spend all his pocket money on books.*

Note that **used to** can be used in a similar way:

> e.g. *She **used to** get quite cross with Percival.* ✦ *In the afternoons, I **used to** paint and draw.*

Would is also used of persistent behaviour patterns, especially where the speaker's tone is one of disapproval:

> e.g. *He **would** keep on talking about the accident, even though I told him it was upsetting me.* ✦ *She **would** keep on smoking despite her doctor's advice.*

You use **would have** to talk about actions and events that were possible in the past, although they did not in fact happen:

> e.g. *It **would have** been unfair if we had won.* ✦ *Tracey **would have** gone to the party, but she was ill.*

When **would not** is used to talk about something that happened in the past, it has a special meaning. It is used to say that someone was unwilling to do something, or refused to do something:

e.g. *They just **would not** believe what we told them*.

Would is sometimes used in stories to talk about someone's thoughts about the future:

e.g. *He thought to himself how wonderful it **would** taste.* ◆ ***Would** he always be lonely?*

Used in conditional sentences

You use **would** in a conditional sentence when you are talking about a situation which you know does not exist. You use **would** in the main clause; in the conditional clause, you use the simple past tense, the past continuous tense, or **could**:

e.g. *If I had enough money, I **would** buy a new car.* ◆ *If he **was coming**, he **would** ring.* ◆ *If I **could** afford it, I **would** buy a boat.* ◆ *If I ruled the world, I would abolish exams.*

You do not use 'would' in the conditional clause in sentences like these. You do not say, for example, 'If I would have enough money, I would buy a new car.'

When you are talking about the past, you use **would have** in a conditional sentence to mention an event that might have happened but did not in fact happen. In this kind of sentence, you use the past perfect tense in the conditional clause and 'would have' in the main clause:

e.g. *Perhaps if he **had realized**, he **would have** run away while there was still time.* ◆ *If he **had been** faster on his feet, he **would have** got away.*

Used in reported clauses

Would is also used in reported clauses:

e.g. *He asked if I **would** answer some questions.* ◆ *He made me promise that I **would** never tell anyone his secret.* ◆ *I felt confident that everything **would** be all right.*

Requests, orders and instructions

You can use **would** to make a request

e.g. ***Would** you do me a favour?*

You can also use **would** to give an order or instruction:

*Put the light on, George, **would** you.* ◆ ***Would** you ask them to leave, please.*

Offers and invitations

You can say 'Would you...?' when you are offering something to someone, or making an invitation:

> e.g. **Would** you like a drink? ◆ **Would** you care to stay with us?

Examiner's top tip

Pay particular attention when you are using the verbs **will** and **would** in your writing, as their use in Standard English is quite different to usage in Caribbean dialects. They cause many CXC students problems, and are responsible for losing them marks in their exams. So, always take your time, and re-read your work carefully.

Verbs

▶ **Tenses**

Tenses are the different verb forms and verb groups that indicate roughly what time you are referring to. **Simple tenses** are used to refer to situations, habitual actions and single completed actions:

> e.g. I **like** him very much. ◆ He always **gives** both points of view. ◆ He **walked** out of the kitchen.

Continuous tenses are used when talking about temporary situations at a particular point in time:

> e.g. Inflation **is rising**. ◆ We believed we **were fighting** for a good cause.

Perfect tenses are used when relating an action or situation to the present or to a moment in the past:

> e.g. Football **has become** international. ◆ She did not know how long she **had been lying** there.

Examiner's top tip

A mistake commonly made by CXC candidates is not to use the correct form of the past tense consistently in their work. Frequently, a student will start off well but will then slip into using the uninflected form of the verb:

> e.g. I **left** work, **went** home and **prepared** supper (not I left work, **go** home and **prepare** supper).
> ◆ Percival **asked** me for a lift so I **drove** him to the airport (not Percival asked me for a lift so I **drive** him to the airport).

This blind spot is not at all surprising, as 'pastness' is conveyed this way in Caribbean dialects. However, this is not acceptable in Standard English. So, take care and remember to re-read and check your work for this avoidable error.

► Past participles

The **past participle** of a verb is used to form perfect tenses, passives and, in some cases, adjectives. It is also called the '**-ed' form**, especially when it is used as an adjective:

> e.g. *Advances have **continued**, though actual productivity has **fallen**.* ◆ *Jobs are still being **lost**.* ◆ *We cannot refuse to teach children the **required** subjects.*

The past participle is usually the same as the past form of the verb (e.g. *I **called** Shavar to invite him to the party* and *He is **called** Shavar*) except in the case of irregular verbs (e.g. *Shavar **came** to the party* and *I saw that Shavar had **come** to the party*).

The passive

The passive (voice) is used when the subject of a clause is the person or thing affected by an action. When you use the passive, you do not have to mention the performer of the action, as in 'He was given a medal for bravery.' Compare this with the active (voice): 'The Queen gave him a medal for bravery'; here, the subject of the clause is performing the action.

Tenses in the passive voice are formed by using an appropriate tense of **be** followed by the **past participle** of the main verb. For example, if you want to use the passive of the simple past of 'eat', you use the simple past of 'be' (**was or were**) and the past participle of 'eat' (**eaten**). You can have passive infinitives, such as **to be eaten** and passive '-ing' forms, such as **being eaten**.

Nearly all transitive verbs (verbs which can have an object) can be used in the passive:

> e.g. *The room **has been cleaned**.* ◆ *Some very interesting work **is being done** on this.* ◆ *The name of the winner **will be announced** tomorrow.* ◆ *The flag **is raised** every morning and **lowered** every evening.*

A few transitive verbs are rarely or never used in the passive: elude, escape, flee, get, have, let, like, race, resemble, suit.

Many phrasal verbs which consist of an intransitive verb and a preposition can also be used in the passive:

> e.g. *In some households, the man **was referred to** as the master.* ◆ *Morgan asked if such men could **be relied on** to keep their mouths shut.*

Note that the preposition is still put after the verb, but it is not followed by a noun group because the noun group it applies to is being used as the subject.

'by' and 'with'

In a passive sentence, if you want to mention the person or thing that performs an action, you use the preposition **by**:

> e.g. *He had been poisoned **by his girlfriend**.* ◆ *He was brought up **by an aunt**.*

If you want to mention the thing that is used to perform an action, you use the preposition **with**:

> e.g. *A circle was drawn in the dirt with a stick.* ◆ *Moisture must be drawn out first with salt.*

▶ Object complements

Some verbs can have a complement after their **object**. The complement is an adjective or noun group which describes the object.

When these verbs are used in the passive, the complement is put immediately after the verb:

> e.g. *In August, he **was elected Vice President of the Senate***.

▶ 'get'

In conversation, **get** is sometimes used instead of **be** to form the passive:

> e.g. *Our windows **get cleaned** about once a month.* ◆ *Last week my uncle **got fined** for speeding.*

▶ Direct speech

One way of reporting what someone has said is to repeat their actual words. When you do this, you use a reporting verb such as **say**:

> e.g. *I said, 'Where are we?'* ◆ *'I don't know much about music,' Judy said.*

Sentences like these are called direct speech or **quote structures**. Direct speech is used mostly in storytelling. Please look at the Punctuation section for more information on how to punctuate direct speech.

In stories, you can put the reporting verb after the quote. The subject is often put after the verb:

> e.g. *'I see,' **said John***.

However, when the subject is a pronoun, it must go in front of the verb:

> e.g. *'Hi there!' **he said***.

The reporting verb you would generally use in conversation is **say**, although in very informal situations **go** or **be like** are now sometimes used. These should never be used in formal writing:

> e.g. *So he **went** 'What's the matter with you?'* ◆ *I'm **like** 'What happened?'*

In stories you can indicate what kind of statement someone made using reporting verbs such as **ask**, **explain** or **suggest**:

> e.g. *'What have you been up to?' he **asked**.* ◆ *It's a symptom of the disease,' **explained** the doctor.* ◆ *'Perhaps,' he **suggested**, 'it was just an impulse.'*

You can also use verbs such as **add**, **begin**, **continue** and **reply** to show when one statement occurred in relation to another:

> e.g. *'I want it to be a surprise,'* I **added**. ◆ *'Anyway,'* she **continued**, *'it's quite out of the question.'* ◆ She **replied**, *'My first thought was to protect him.'*

In a story, if you want to indicate the way in which something was said, you can use a reporting verb such as **shout**, **wail** or **scream**:

> e.g. *'Jump!'* **shouted** *the elderly woman.* ◆ *'Get out of there!'* I **screamed**.

▶ **Indirect speech or reported speech (or report structures)**

In conversation, you normally give an idea of what someone said using your own words, rather than quoting them directly. You also use this report structure to report people's thoughts:

> e.g. *She said it was a very expensive watch.* ◆ *They thought that he should have been found guilty of the crime.*

Report structures are also often used in writing. A report structure consists of two parts: a **reporting clause** and a **reported clause**.

Reporting verbs

The reporting clause contains the **reporting verb** and usually comes first:

> e.g. *I told him that nothing had happened.* ◆ *I asked what was going on.*

The reporting verb with the widest meaning and use is **say**. You use **say** when you are simply reporting what someone said and do not want to imply anything about their statement:

> e.g. *He said that you knew his family.* ◆ *They said the house was surrounded by police.*

You can use a reporting verb such as answer, explain and suggest to indicate what kind of statement you think the person was making:

> e.g. *She explained that a friend of her husband's had been arrested.* ◆ *I suggested that it was time to leave.*

You can also indicate your own personal opinion of what someone said by using a reporting verb such as **claim** or **admit**. For example, if you say that someone **claimed** that they did something, you are implying that you think that they may not be telling the truth. If you say that someone **admitted** something, you are implying that they are telling the truth:

> e.g. *He claims he can speak fluent Italian.* ◆ *She admitted that she is madly in love with James.*

Reporting verbs with a negative

With a small number of reporting verbs, you usually make the reporting clause, rather than the reported clause, negative. For example, you would usually say 'I don't think Mary is at home' rather than 'I think Mary is not at home':

> e.g. I **don't think** I will be able to afford it. ◆ I **don't believe** we can enforce a total ban.

The following reporting verbs are often used with a negative in this way:

> believe, expect, feel, imagine, propose, suppose, think.

The second part of a report structure is the **reported clause**:

> e.g. She said **that she had been to Kingston**. ◆ The man in the shop told me **how much it would cost**.

There are several types of reported clause. The type used depends on whether a statement, order, suggestion or question is being reported.

Clauses with 'that'

A report clause beginning with the conjunction **that** is used after a reporting verb to report a statement or someone's thoughts:

> e.g. He said **that the police had been very helpful**. ◆ She thought **that Comfort needed a holiday**.

Note that **that** is often omitted from such a clause:

> e.g. They **said** I should go home at once. ◆ I **think** there's something wrong.

However, **that** is nearly always used after some verbs, for example answer, argue, complain, explain, recommend and reply:

> e.g. He **answered that** the chief executive had already left the building.

A 'that'-clause can contain a modal, especially when someone makes a suggestion about what someone else should do:

> e.g. He proposes that the Government **should** hold an enquiry.

Writing for business

Throughout life you often need to communicate your thoughts and feelings in writing. Writing concise and effective letters, speeches and emails is easy, once you know exactly what you want to say. The following section covers the basic rules of style and form to follow.

Job applications

▶ **FAQ**

Q. *Should my letter be typed or handwritten?*

A. It should be typed on A4 paper. Only the signature should be handwritten.

Q. *To whom should I address my letter?*

A. If you do not know the name of the person who would deal with your application, call the company to find out their name.

Q. *Is it OK to send out the same letter to all those companies I'm interested in?*

A. No. Try to avoid generalisable letters. Find out as much as you can about the company, and tailor your letter accordingly.

Q. *Should I mention salary in my accompanying letter?*

A. It is usually best not to touch on the subject of salary at this stage, unless requested in the advertisement.

▶ **Useful phrases**

First of all, identify the job you are applying for:

- I would like to inquire as to whether there are any openings for junior telesales operators in your company.
- I am writing to apply for the post of senior marketing manager.
- I would like to apply for the position of online learning coordinator, as advertised on your website.
- I am writing to apply for the above post, as advertised in *The Trinidad Guardian* of 2016-5-25.

Next, give some examples of personal achievements:

- I have gained experience in several major aspects of publishing.
- I co-ordinated the change-over from one accounting system to another.
- I developed designs for a new range of knitwear.

- I have supervised a team of telesales operators on several projects.
- I contributed to the development of our new database software.

Then outline your personal qualities:

- I see myself as systematic and meticulous in my approach to work.
- I am a fair and broad-minded person, with an ability to get on well with people from all walks of life.
- I am hardworking and business-minded, and I tend to thrive under pressure.

Explain why you want this job:

- I am now keen to find a post with more responsibility.
- I now wish to find a more permanent full-time position.
- I would like to further my career in the field of production.
- I feel that your company's activities most closely match my own values and interests.

Express your willingness to attend an interview:

- I would be happy to attend an interview at any time.
- I look forward to the opportunity of an interview.

When applying for an advertised post, ensure that you head the letter with the exact name of the post, quoting any reference number given.

39 Main Street
Bagatelle Village
Scarborough
Tobago

30 June 2016

Mr D Trotman
Tobago Citrus Growers Cooperative
Orange Hill Road
Scarborough
Tobago

Dear Mr Trotman,

Application for post of Warehouse Manager, post no: 513/6

I am writing in response to your advertisement in *Newsday*, and am enclosing my CV for your review.

As you will see, I have gained valuable experience in the warehouse environment, and have a valid forklift licence. I am hardworking and reliable, and can work as an effective leader of a team.

I am currently working as a team supervisor at Crown Port International Airport, where my duties include loading supervision, vehicle operation and leading a team of six baggage handlers. My employers will be happy to supply a reference for me.

I look forward to having the opportunity to discuss this further with you.

Yours sincerely,

Carlton Spencer

Carlton Spencer

► A speculative job application

When applying for a job on a speculative basis, try to speak to the person responsible for recruitment in the appropriate department beforehand. This way, you will have a specific person to write to, as well as having established a relationship with them.

> 42 Pickford St
> Savanna-La-Mar
> Westmoreland
> Jamaica
>
> 19 July 2016

Ms Lataya Stewart
Recruitment Officer
Kingston Sugar Company Ltd
15 Hagley Park Road
Kingston 12
Jamaica

Dear Ms Stewart

Post of website developer

Thank you very much for taking the time to speak to me yesterday about the possibility of a position as website developer with your company.

Please find attached a CV which highlights my prior professional experience, and the qualities which I feel make me suited to this position. You will see that I have a strong interest in, and knowledge of, staff management, and have gained extensive experience in handling large development projects and meeting deadlines.

I see myself as being well-organized and self-motivated, and have excellent communication skills. I am keen to develop my career with the Kingston Sugar Company, and so would very much appreciate the opportunity to discuss further my suitability for the post.

Please feel free to contact me, either by email: hchambers@netserve.com, or by leaving a message on 918-2002. I look forward to speaking to you soon.

Hilton Chambers

▶ **FAQ**

Q. *How should a CV be presented?*

A. It should be constructed on a computer, well laid out and printed on a good quality printer. Do not use too many different font types and sizes. Use bullets or similar to start sub-sections or lists.

Q. *I usually send the same CV out to all potential employers. But should I be tailoring it to different jobs?*

A. Yes, you should. Consider carefully how your skills, education and experience compare with the skills that the job requires. Ask for more detail if needed. Spend time researching the employer - their structure, products and approach.

Q. *What details do I need to include in my CV?*

A. You should include the following:

personal details: name, home address, phone number, email address, URL of your own web page if you have one, date of birth.

education: Give places of education where you have studied, with most recent first.

work experience: List your most recent experience first. Give the name of your employer, job title and what you actually did and achieved in that job. Make sure all time periods are accounted for.

interests: If you have little employment experience, an employer will be particularly interested in activities where you have responsibility, or which involve you in relating to others in a team.

skills: Ability in other languages, computing experience or possession of a driving licence should be included.

references: Usually give two names. Make sure that referees are willing to give you a reference. If you do not wish to name them on your CV, it is perfectly acceptable to write 'on request'.

Q. *How long should my CV be?*

A. Keep it as short and relevant as possible. One page is ideal.

Q. *I've heard people talk about writing a 'personal objective statement' at the top of a CV. Is this expected/appropriate?*

A. It can be a good idea to start with a personal objective statement. This is a short overview of your skills, qualities, hopes and plans. If you are replying to a specific job advertisement, review what key words and tasks were used. Which of these words apply to you? Use these words in your statement. But if you do not feel confident about doing this, there is no obligation to include one.

CV
Cynthia Ramlogan

Date of birth	29.02.95
Address	1291 Donald Street
	Belmont
	Port of Spain
	Trinidad
Telephone	625 5431
Email	cynthiaramlogan@atlantic.net
Nationality	Trinidadian

Education

2013–2016	**BA Hons in Modern Languages, University of the West Indies** (final grade 2.1)
2011–2013	**South College, San Fernando** *CAPE Caribbean Studies 2: CAPE Communication Studies 2: CAPE Spanish 2: CAPE History 2: CAPE Literature 1*
2006–2011	**Abercromby Secondary School, Port of Spain** CXC CSEC Examinations: Mathematics 2; English 1; History 1; French 1; Literature 1; Spanish 1; German 1

Employment history

2012–2013	**Sales Assistant, Williams Bookshop, Port of Spain** I was responsible for training and supervising weekend and holiday staff.
2013–2014	**Classroom Assistant, Eric Williams Secondary School, St Augustine** I taught conversational Spanish to pupils aged 12-18, preparing the older students for both technical and more academic qualifications.

Positions of responsibility held

2013–2014	**Entertainments Officer for University Student Social Society** I organized and budgeted for entertainment for a student society with over 1000 members.
2013–present	**Captain of the university women's netball team** I was in charge of training, organizing and motivating the women's team from 2003 to date.

Other skills
Fluent French and Spanish
Extensive knowledge of Microsoft Word, Excel and Access
I hold a clean driving licence

References
on request

Writing business letters

▶ **FAQ**

Q. *Is there a particular style I should use?*

A. Most companies have their own way of doing things. They have a 'house style' for layout and punctuation so if you are unsure or new to a company, look back in the filing to find out which style has been used as the house style.

Q. *What do I need to include in a business letter?*

A. You should include: the company letterhead; the letter reference; date; addressee's name and address; salutation (opening); subject heading; body of the letter; subscription (closing); signature or signatory.

▶ **Tips**

- Keep letters short and to the point.
- The subject heading indicates the subject of the letter for quick reference and should only be two or three words.
- Make sure you open with a statement of intent and close with a request or promise of action.
- Avoid using ambiguous words or phrases. If there is any chance of a misunderstanding, find an alternative way to say it.
- Think out your letter before you start to compose it. Make notes if it helps to organize the information in a logical order.
- Remember that the standard method of closing before the signature depends on the opening at the start of the letter. If you opened with 'Dear Sir', you should close with 'Yours faithfully', if you opened with 'Dear Mr....' you should close with 'Yours sincerely'.
- All parts of a letter are designed to give important information. If your letters give accurate information, you will increase efficiency.
- If you can amend a standard or similar letter to say what you need to say, do so. It will save you time.
- If the sender is not available to sign, the letter can be signed *per procurationem* ('for and on behalf of') by another person (the signatory). This is indicated by the abbreviation 'pp' written or typed before the signatory.
- Always proofread your letters for spelling errors and other details.
- Don't rely on your computer spell-check facility.
- If the letter has been marked 'Personal', 'Private' or 'Confidential', ensure that the envelope has been marked in the same way. Private means personal, confidential means sensitive.

- Thank you for your letter/email ...
- With regard to ... I am writing to ...
- Further to our recent telephone conversation ...
- Further to your recent email ...
- If you require further information please don't hesitate to get in touch.

Ms Vera Williams
111 Windward Road
Ocho Rios
Jamaica

27th January 2016

Dear Ms Williams

I am writing to thank you for coming to the office yesterday so that we could discuss the possibility of our company taking over responsibility for publishing *The Big Book of Yo-Yos*. This is an exciting opportunity for us and I hope that we are able to reach a mutually beneficial agreement.

I will present this title to my sales and marketing team at our regular meeting midweek, and will then take the proposal to the more formal acquisitions meeting early next week.

I have sounded my marketing director out already and he is as enthusiastic as I am to publish your book, so I am not anticipating too many problems getting a positive response from the sales team.

I will also look at the financial side of the project, and you are kindly going to send me a copy of your current contract, detailing royalty rates. I have requested a copy of our standard author contract from the legal department and will forward this to you as soon as it arrives.

I enjoyed meeting you on Friday and hope that this is the start of a fruitful relationship. I will of course keep you up to date with progress.

Yours sincerely
Eugenia Macaulay
Publishing Manager

Writing memoranda

▶ **FAQ**

Q. *What is a memorandum?*

A. A memorandum (or memo) is a short letter or note sent to a particular in-house member of staff or circulated to groups of people.

Q. *Can I send a memo to someone in another company?*

A. Memos are not usually sent out of house.

Q. *What information does a memo usually contain?*

A. A memo usually contains: the sender's name and department; the addressee's name and department; date; and the subject.

Q. *Can memos be used for confidential information and do they need a signature?*

A. They are not normally used for confidential information, but if they are they should be placed in a sealed envelope marked 'Confidential'.
Memos are not usually signed, but if they contain financial information it may be usual for the sender to add initials.

Q. *Do I need to keep a copy?*

A. Always keep and file copies of all memoranda, as with other forms of correspondence.

To: Shontay Broomes   From: Jada Reid
Publishing Production   Editorial Department

23/01/16

THE BIG BOOK OF YO-YOS
TEXT PRINTING COPY

Shontay,
With regard to passing the book for press, I enclose the text printing copy:

– complete set of text pages, with book pages marked and margins ruled up for all prelims.
– pagination and margins list.
– sheet showing book pages and their content.

Please pass this and request a full set of proofs from the printer for checking.

Cover copy for this edition already passed.

Thanks,
Jada

Writing business emails

- Make sure you have the correct email address for the person you are contacting.
- Make sure you spell their name correctly.
- Put the subject of the email in the subject line so the recipient knows immediately what the email is about.
- Use the cc function if you want other people to receive the email, and the bcc function if you don't want them to see who else has been copied in. You may want to copy yourself in as well, if you want to keep a full history of the correspondence.
- Use an appropriate greeting, nothing too informal.
- As a rule, try to keep the email as short and clear as possible. People get a lot of emails at work and it helps if you keep to the point.
- Use an appropriate closing, again, nothing too informal.
- If you say you are sending an attachment to the email, remember to attach it!

Writing business reports

▶ **FAQ**

Q. *How do I start?*

A. You will find it much easier to write if you have a clear idea in your mind of the line of argument you want to take before you begin to write. Begin by making a note of all the evidence you have amassed and decide on a line of argument. Group together the evidence under various headings and gradually the argument will begin to take shape.

Q. *What should a report contain?*

A. Reports should include: a heading; a reason for the report; an argument; a conclusion or recommendation.

Q. *How do I persuade the reader to accept my proposal?*

A. The golden rule is to find out what the priorities of your reader are, and then write the report from that point of view.

▶ **Tips**

- Aim to be accurate, concise and brief.
- Never use words that you don't understand. Keep jargon to a minimum, but use technical words accurately.
- Reports on meetings should be written in the third person: 'It was decided', 'A proposal was put forward'. Individual reports can be written in the first person: 'I looked into the cost of ...'

- Think about whether or not you need to include graphics or illustrations (such as pie charts, bar graphs, line graphs or flow charts) in your report and choose the ones that are best suited to your purpose.
- Decide whether you want to use paragraph numbering or headings. Paragraph numbering is often much clearer than using headings and allows you to refer back and forward to specific paragraphs by number. It also reduces the need for page numbering. If you do decide to use headings, make sure that the hierarchy is consistent.
- Also think about the general layout. Do you want the text to be justified or unjustified? Where are you going to position the page numbers, if you use them? Are you going to include footnotes and a bibliography?
- To make sure you've included everything, ask yourself four questions:
  - Have I included all the information that may be needed for the reader to make a decision?
  - Have I covered all the possible options and made a convincing case for the alternative that I am recommending?
  - Have I explained my proposal adequately and proved that it is better than alternatives?
  - Have I successfully put myself in the reader's shoes, and presented the problem and the solutions with his or her priorities in mind?
- Always pay attention to:
  - consistency in headings or numbering.
  - accuracy of information in graphics, tables, footnotes, etc.
  - spelling, punctuation and grammar.
  - overall order of the argument

Writing a letter of resignation

▶ **Tips**

- Keep it simple.
- If giving your reason for leaving, try to avoid indirectly criticizing the company or your co-workers.
- Thank the recipient for any help or support you feel they have given you during your time at the company.
- Show that you are willing to make the transfer as easy as possible.

▶ Useful phrases

- I have decided that it is time to move on and I have accepted a position elsewhere.
- This is to inform you that an opportunity has presented itself that will enable me to work in the area of …
- Please accept this letter as my formal resignation as Systems Administrator for DAL publishing, to become effective as of …
- I am tendering my resignation from your company and wish to advise you that … will be my last day of employment.
- As required by my contract of employment, I hereby give you 4 weeks' notice of my intention to leave my position as …
- I am confident that my new role will help me to move towards some of the goals I have for my career.
- I believe this position will offer me more opportunity for advancement, and allow me to broaden my own experience.
- I want to take this opportunity to thank you for your time and efforts in my training and advancement.
- The support shown by you and the rest of the management team has been greatly appreciated.
- My experience with FTL has been very rewarding.
- Thank you for your time and consideration, and I wish you all the best in the future.
- Please be assured that I will do all I can to assist in the smooth transfer of my responsibilities before leaving.

Free Hill
Black Rock Gardens
St Michael
Barbados

15 October 2016
Mr Malik Braithwaite
Managing Director
Geode Publishing
PO Box 4287
Bridgetown BB2122
Barbados

Dear Malik

Resignation

I am writing to inform you that I have decided it is time to move on, and I have accepted a position at Topline Publishing, starting on 28 November 2016. I believe this position will offer me more opportunity for advancement, and allow me to broaden my own experience and knowledge.

I want to take this opportunity to thank you for your time and effort in my training during the past three years, and wish you all the best for continued success in the future.

Please be assured that I will do all I can to assist in the smooth transfer of my responsibilities before leaving.

Yours sincerely

James Alleyne

James Alleyne